mass/weight

imperial/metric

1 ounce (oz)	= 437.5 grains	= 28.35 g
1 pound (lb)	= 16oz	= 0.4536 kg
1 hundredweight (cwt)	= 112lb	= 50.802 kg
1 (long) ton	= 20cwt	= 1.0161 t
1 US (short) ton	= 2000lb	= 0.9072 t

metric/imperial

1 milligram (mg)		= 0.0154 grain
1 gram (g)	= 1000mg	= 0.0353 oz
1 kilogram (kg)	= 1000g	= 2.2046 lb
1 tonne (t)	= 1000kg	= 0.9842 ton

time

60 seconds (s)	=	1 minute (min)
60 min	=	1 hour (hr)
24 hr	=	1 day (d)
7 days	=	1 week
365¼ days	=	1 year
10 years	=	1 decade
100 years	=	1 century
1,000 years	=	1 millennium
1 mean solar day	=	24 hr 3 min 56.555s
1 sidereal day	=	23hr 56min 4.091s
1 solar, tropical, or equinoctial year	=	365.2422d (365d 5hr 48min 46s)
1 sidereal year	=	365.2564d (365d 6hr 9min 9.5s)
1 synodic (lunar) month	=	29.5306d (29d 12hr 44min 3s)
1 synodic year = 354d	=	12 synodic months

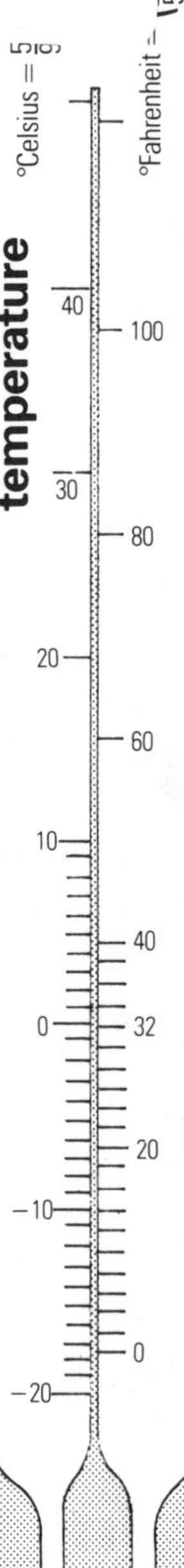

HUTCHINSON
FACTFINDER

HUTCHINSON

FACTFINDER

Concise Encyclopedia

E M Horsley

GUILD PUBLISHING LONDON

This edition published 1986 by Book Club Associates by arrangement with Century Hutchinson

Reprinted 1986, 1987 (Twice), 1988 (Twice)

Set in Times and Univers

Printed and bound in Great Britain by
Mackays of Chatham Ltd, Kent

INTRODUCTION

The *Hutchinson Factfinder* is a high-speed reference book, an encyclopedia that compresses an overview of human knowledge into 960 fact-filled pages. For the expert, it will provide a means of checking the odd name, fact, or date when memory fails. For the non-expert – the student at school or college, the man or woman at home or at work – it provides the up-to-date essentials. Its handy format means it can find a place on the bookshelf of the smallest flat, the most cramped of offices and workshops, or be popped into the bag or briefcase when working on the train or the school bus.

To cover so much, brevity has been vital, but liveliness has also been aimed at. The book is up-to-date, not only in its facts, but in its approach to them, and the past is dealt with chiefly as it obviously affects the present. Space has been found for the striking and the curious, as well as the 'standard' fact, and the occasional intriguing speculation is included. The endeavour has been not only to inform, but to stimulate thought and mental exploration. It is enlivening to know that chess is estimated to have more variations than there are atoms in the Universe, or that the visitors to the suburban bird-table may be among the nearest living relatives of the dinosaurs. And sometimes, since this is a book for humans, even a glint of humour may break in.

EMH

editor Michael Upshall

managing editor Adrian Stenton

consultants Nigel Wood BSc, AKC, BA
Dr Anne Woollins PhD
Lorna Smith BA, PDESL

editors Gillian Beaumont
Sue Engineer
Sue Lambert
Paula Parrish
Helen Stenton

update editor Jane Anson

research June Ross ALA

illustrators Rodney Paull
Taurus Design
Marlborough Design
Swanston Graphics

keyboarding Alison Kepple

typesetting Saxon Printing Ltd

Aachen or *Aix-la-Chapelle* industrial city (electronics, glass, rubber) and spa in N Rhine-Westphalia, W Germany; population 243 000. Charlemagne◊ founded the cathedral 796, and the 14th-century town hall is built on the site of his palace□

Aachen Treaty of. Ended the War of the Austrian◊ Succession 1748□

Aalto Alvar 1898–1976. Finnish architect and furniture designer, noted for his bentwood chairs□

aardvark Afrikaans name, 'earth-pig', for the nocturnal, burrowing mammal *Orycteropus afer* (only member of order Tubulidentata); with a long, sticky tongue to feed on termites□

aardwolf an mammal of the hyena◊ family□

Aaron in Old Testament, elder brother of Moses◊, leader of the tribe of Levites◊. He made an image of a golden calf in response to the request of the Israelites◊ for a god, when they despaired of Moses coming down from Mt Sinai◊. The priesthood was confined to his descendants□

Aasen Ivar Andreas 1813–96. Norwegian philologist, creator of modern literary Norwegian, *Landsmaal* 'country language', replacing formal Dano-Norwegian□

abacus method of calculating with a handful of counters on a flat surface, used by the Greeks and Romans, and possibly by the builders of Stonehenge. Later types of abacus include those with beads on wires, still used in China. The method has principles in common with the electronic calculator□

Abadan oil port in Iran; population 296 000. The nationalization in 1951 of the refineries initiated the world-wide movement by oil-producing countries to control their own resources. It was under siege 1980–1 by Iraq in the Iran–Iraq◊ War□

Abakan coalmining city in S USSR; population 123 000□

abalone snail-like edible marine mollusc, genus *Haliotis*, with a bluish mother-of-pearl shell (used in ornamental work), family Haliotidae□

Abbado Claudio 1933– . Italian conductor, long associated with La◊ Scala, Milan; principal conductor of London Symphony Orchestra from 1979; worked with European Community Youth Orchestra from 1977□

Abbas the Great c1557–1628. Shah of Persia from 1586; his empire stretched from the Tigris to the Indus□

Abbasids caliphs of the Muslim Empire 750–1258, descended from Abbas, Mohammed's uncle. Their golden age was the reign of Harun-al Rashid 786–809, of *Arabian Nights* fame. Their capital (Baghdad) was burnt by the Tatars◊ 1258, but they retained limited power as caliphs of Egypt till 1517□

Abbey Theatre theatre, opened in Dublin 1904, the focus of the Irish literary revival, with which Lady Gregory◊, Sean O'Casey◊, J M Synge◊, and Yeats◊ were associated□

Abd el-Krim el Khettabi 1881–1963. Moroccan chief, the 'Wolf of the Rif'; he defeated the Spanish in a Berber◊ revolt 1921, and surrendered only to a large French army under Pétain◊ 1926□

Abdul Hamid II 1842–1918. Last sultan of Turkey 1876–1909, when he was deposed by the revolutionary 'Young Turks'; his brutal suppression of the Armenian◊ Revolt 1894–6 earned him the titles 'Great Assassin' and 'Abdul the Damned', and still motivates Armenian terrorism against the Turks□

Abdullah Sheikh Mohammed 1905–82. Kashmiri leader, known as the 'Lion of Kashmir'; he was imprisoned for insisting that Kashmir◊'s people decide their own future in 1947, but was Prime Minister of Kashmir 1975–82, accepting Indian sovereignty□

Abdullah ibn Hussein 1882–1951. Arab leader who worked with T E Lawrence◊ in the Arab revolt of World War I; he became king of independent Transjordan◊ 1946; and following the incorporation of Arab Palestine (after 1948–9 Arab-Israeli War), he renamed the country the Hashemite Kingdom of Jordan. He was assassinated by an Arab fanatic□

Abdul Rahman Tunku 'Prince' 1903– . Malaysian negotiator of the formation of the Federation of Malaysia 1961–2; he was its first Prime Minister 1963–70□

Abel in Old Testament, second son of Adam◊ and Eve◊; as a shepherd, he made burnt offerings of meat to God which were more acceptable than the fruits offered by his brother Cain; he was killed by the jealous Cain□

Abelard Peter 1079–1142. French philosopher; see logic◊ and scholasticism◊. Canon of Notre Dame, Paris, and master of the cathedral school from 1115, he seduced and secretly married his pupil Héloise. She took the veil and he was castrated by ruffians at the instigation of Héloise's uncle, and became a monk. His autobiographical *Historia Calamitatum* drew from Héloise a series of love letters□

Aberdeen industrial city (engineering, chemicals, food processing, paper) in Scotland, seaport, holiday resort, and offshore oil 'capital' of Europe; population 208 900. There are many handsome buildings in granite, and of special interest are St Machar's Cathedral, Marischal College (part of Aberdeen University), the children's museum in James Dun's House, the maritime museum in Provost Ross's House, and the art gallery□

Aberdeen George Hamilton Gordon, 4th Earl of Aberdeen 1784–1860. British Conservative Prime Minister 1852–5, when he resigned on criticism of his mismanagement of the Crimean◊ War□

Aberfan mining village in Mid Glamorgan, Wales. Coal waste overwhelmed a school and houses in 1966; of 144 dead, 116 were children□

aberration apparent displacement of a star resulting from the combined effects of the speed of light, and the speed of earth as it moves in its orbit round the sun, about 30 km per sec/19 mi per sec□

Aberystwyth town in Wales; population 10 700. It is the unofficial capital of the Welsh-speaking area of Wales, and the University College of Wales 1872, Welsh Plant Breeding Station, and National Library of Wales are here□

Abilene town in Kansas, USA; population 6 600. A Wild West town, it was tamed by Marshal Wild Bill Hickok◊ in 1871; there is an Eisenhower Memorial Museum□

abominable snowman man-like creature, covered with reddish-grey hair, reported since 1832 as living in the Himalayan region; it is also known as the yeti□

Aborigine original inhabitant of any country, but in particular the c116 000 Aborigines of Australia, of whom 40% live in remote desert areas, especially in the Northern Territory; and 60% are casual labourers on town fringes. Some 250 000 may have been killed in the cultural clash of the white colonial period. They are noted for their legends, songs, rituals, and bark and cave paintings concerned with their 'dreamtime', a magical period when man was first on earth□

abortion medically, expulsion of the foetus from the womb before it is capable of independent life – before the sixth month. It is controversial as a means of birth control (methods include the use of drugs, vacuum aspiration, etc.), but was legalized within certain guidelines in the UK in 1967 if carried out during the first 28 weeks of pregnancy. When it happens naturally it is normally called a miscarriage□

Abraham in Old Testament, founder of the Jewish nation c2300BC. Born at Ur◊, he migrated via N Mesopotamia to Canaan, and received God's promise of the land to his descendants. Isaac◊ was his son by his wife Sarah. See Canaanite◊ Empire□

Abraham Sir Edward Penly 1913– . British biochemist, who isolated the antibiotic cephalosporin, capable of destroying penicillin-resistant bacteria□

Abraham Plains/Heights of. Plateau near Quebec, Canada, where Wolfe◊ defeated the French, under Montcalm◊, 13 Sept 1759□

Abruzzi wild region in the Apennines (including Gran Sasso d'Italia massif 2912 m/9560 ft), E central Italy; capital L'Aquila; population 1 225 827□

Absalom In Old Testament, favourite son of King David; when defeated in a revolt against his father, he fled on a mule, but was caught up by his hair in a tree branch, and killed by Joab, one of David's officers. See Tamar◊□

absinth drink containing 60–80% alcohol, which was originally flavoured with oil of wormwood; the latter attacks the nervous system, and is widely banned, so that substitutes are used□

absolute magnitude the brightness a star would have at a standard distance of 10 parsecs◊□

absolute zero the lowest possible temperature, equivalent to −273.16°C/0K when molecules would have their minimum energy. Near this temperature physical properties of materials change, for example, electrical resistance of certain metals is lost□

abstract art non-representational concept of art, found in earlier cultures, but triggered into a movement by the invention of photography which rendered unnecessary the making of representational records for their own sake. The pioneer 20th-century work was a Kandinsky◊ watercolour of 1910□

Abstract Expressionism term used in 20th-century (especially American) painting to describe non-figurative canvases painted with large brushstrokes and many colours, often forming an intricate pattern. Generally the result is not as important as the method by which it was reached. Similar to action◊ painting; see Jackson Pollock◊□

Absurd Theatre of the. Plays of the 1950s by Albee◊, Beckett◊, Ionesco◊, and N F Simpson◊, for whom, in a godless universe there can be no meaning in the absurdity of human existence. See also Jarry◊□

Abu-Bekr name meaning 'father of the virgin', used by Abd-el-Ka'aba 573–634, from about 618 when Mohammed◊ married his daughter. On Mohammed's death, he became the first caliph◊□

Abu Dhabi see United Arab Emirates◊□

Abuja newly-built and centrally placed capital of Nigeria replacing Lagos in 1986. Shaped like a crescent, it was designed by Kenzo Tange◊□

Abu Simbel site of ancient temple in Egypt. See under Rameses◊ II□

Abydos ancient city in Upper Egypt; the Great Temple of Seti I dates from c1300BC□

abyssal zone dark ocean area 2–6000 m/6500–19 500 ft deep; temperature 4°C/39°F. Some fish and crustaceans living there may be blind, or have their own light sources□

Abyssinia former name of Ethiopia◊□

acacia genus of evergreen trees and shrubs, family Leguminosae◊, including ***gum arabic tree*** *A senegal* of N Africa, used in manufacturing jellies and sweets (90% of world supplies come from Sudan); ***Australian silver wattle*** *A dealbata* (the 'mimosa' of the florist); and a number of wattle species with fluffy golden flowers, adapted to warm, dry regions, such as Australia, where the wattle is the national floral emblem□

Academy Plato's school of philosophy in the gardens of Academe, north west of Athens; it was closed by the Byzantine Emperor Justinian◊, with the other pagan schools, in 529AD□

Academy French, or **Académie Française.** Literary society founded by Richelieu◊ in 1635; it is especially concerned with the purity of the French language; membership is limited to 40 'immortals' at a time□

Academy of Arts Royal. British society founded by George◊ III in London in 1768 to encourage painting, sculpture, and architecture; it is now housed in Old Burlington House, Piccadilly. There is an annual summer exhibition for contemporary artists, and tuition is provided for students at RA schools□

Academy of Sciences Soviet. Society founded in 1725 by Catherine the Great in Leningrad; it has been responsible for such achievements as the Sputnik◊, and has branches in the Ukraine (welding, cybernetics), Armenia (astrophysics), Georgia (mechanical engineering)□

acanthus genus of Mediterranean plants, family Acanthaceae; the handsome leaves were used as a motif in classical architecture□

Acapulco port and holiday resort in Mexico; population 457 000□

Accad see Akkad◊□

acceleration the rate of increase in the velocity of a moving body, as measured in metres per second squared, m/s^2□

accelerator device to bring charged particles (e.g. protons) up to high kinetic energies◊, at which they have uses in industry, medicine and in pure physics: when high energy particles collide with other particles the products formed give insights into the fundamental forces of nature (see particle◊ physics). To give particles the energies needed requires many successive applications of a high voltage to electrodes placed in the path of the particles. To save space the particles can be confined to a circular track using a magnetic field. The first ***accelerator*** to work on this principle was the ***cyclotron*** built in the early 1930s. Whereas the first cyclotrons were some 30 cm in diameter, the Super Proton Synchrotron at CERN◊ near Geneva, which came into operation in 1976, has an unravelled

accelerator

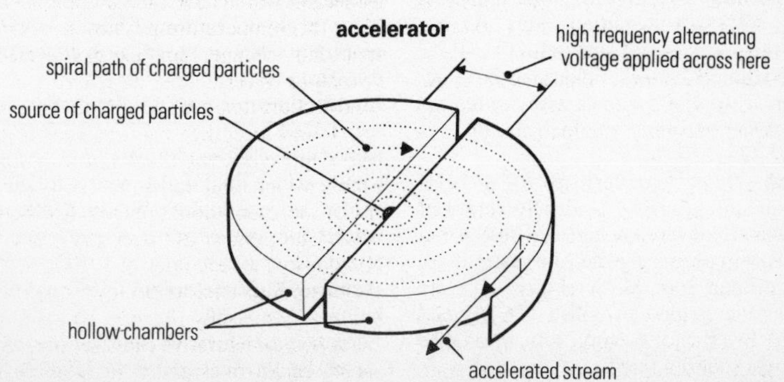

length of some 2.2 km; the Large Electron Proton Machine due to start up in 1987 will have a total length of 30 km□

accordion box-like portable instrument, with bellows and keyboard; invented by Buschmann in Berlin in 1822□

accountancy financial management of a firm, etc., from balance sheets to policy decisions. Forms of inflation accounting, CCA (current cost accounting) and CPP (current purchasing power) enable valid financial comparisons over a period in which money values change□

Accra capital and port of Ghana; population 903 500. Christiansborg Castle is the presidential residence, and the University of Ghana is at nearby Legon□

Accrington industrial town (textiles, engineering) in Lancashire, England; population 36 500□

acer genus of trees, the maples◊ and sycamores, family Aceraceae□

acetaldehyde see aldehydes◊□

acetate see under textile◊□

acetic acid (ethanoic acid, CH_3COOH) Fatty acid used to make acetate plastics. Vinegar is 3–6% acetic acid□

acetone (propan-2-one) colourless, mobile, inflammable liquid, CH_3COCH_3, used as a solvent. Used in production of rayon□

acetylcholine see under brain◊□

acetylene (ethyne). Colourless, inflammable gas C_2H_2; it burns in oxygen at 3000°C; it is used in oxyacetylene welding, and as a starting material in the manufacture of chemicals□

Achaea in ancient Greece, and also today, an area of the N Peloponnese; the ***Achaeans*** were the predominant group in the Mycenaean period, and are said by Homer to have taken part in the siege of Troy□

Achaean League union in 275BC of most of the cities of the N Peloponnese, which managed to defeat Sparta, but was itself defeated by the Romans 146BC□

Achaemenids dynasty of the Persian◊ Empire 550–530BC, named after Achaemenes, the ancestor of Cyrus◊ the Great□

Achebe Chinua 1930– . Nigerian novelist. *Things Fall Apart* 1958 deals with the impact of missionaries and colonialism on his people□

Acheson Dean Gooderham 1893–1971. American statesman; as Under-Secretary of State 1945–7, he was associated with George C Marshall in preparing the Marshall◊ Plan, and succeeded him as Secretary of State 1949–53. He helped establish NATO and criticized Britain for having 'lost an empire and not yet found a role'□

Achill largest of the Irish islands, off County Mayo; area 148 sq km/57 sq mi□

Achilles Greek hero of Homer◊'s *Iliad*, the son of the sea nymph Thetis. She rendered him invulnerable, except for the heel by which she held him, by dipping him in the River Styx◊. He killed Hector in the Trojan◊ War, and was himself killed by Paris with a poisoned arrow in the heel□

Achilles tendon tendon pinning the calf muscle to the heelbone. It is one of the largest in the body□

acid substance which in solution in an ionizing solvent (usually water) gives rise to hydrogen ions◊. Acids have a sharp taste, are often corrosive, turn litmus red, and neutralize or combine with alkalis◊ to form salts; they also act as solvents◊. The first-known acid was vinegar (acetic acid). Inorganic acids include boracic, carbonic, hydrochloric, nitric, phosphoric, and sulphuric acid; organic acids include acetic, benzoic, citric, formic, lactic, oxalic, and salicylic acid. The strength of an acid is measured by its hydrogen–ion concentration, indicated by pH value 0=extremely acid, through 7=neutral, to 14=extremely alkaline□

aclinic line the magnetic equator, an imaginary line near the Equator, where the compass has no 'dip' or magnetic inclination□

acne skin eruption caused by inflammation of the sebaceous glands which secrete an oily substance (sebum), the natural lubricant of the skin□

Aconcagua highest peak in the Americas, in the Argentine Andes; height 6960 m/22 834 ft. It was first climbed by Vines and Zeebruggen 1897□

aconite genus of plants *Aconitum*, family Ranunculaceae◊, many of which are poisonous, e.g. ***monk's hood*** or ***wolf's bane*** *A anglicum*; the roots yield aconitine, a narcotic and analgesic◊□

acorn fruit of the oak◊ tree: for the ***sea acorn*** see barnacle◊□

acoustics science of sound, founded by the German physicist Ernest Chladni 1756–1827, especially sound in space, as in concert halls, theatres, etc.□

Acquired Immunity Deficiency Syndrome see AIDS◊□

acquittal the setting free of someone charged with a crime. In English courts it follows a verdict of 'not guilty', but in Scotland the verdict may be either 'not guilty' or 'non-proven'□

acre English land measure, 4840 sq yd/0.405 ha□

Acre seaport in Israel; population 34 500. Taken by the Crusaders◊ in 1104, it fell to siege by Saladin◊ in 1187, but was retaken by Richard◊ the Lionheart in 1191. Napoleon◊ failed in a siege in 1799; Allenby◊ captured it in 1918; and Israel overran it in 1948□

acromegaly the unsightly enlargement of prominent parts of the body, e.g. hands, feet, and – more conspicuously – the eyebrow ridges and lower jaw, caused by excessive output of growth hormone in adult life by the pituitary◊ gland□

acronym word formed from the initial letters or syllables of other words, e.g. NATO, radar□

acropolis citadel of an ancient Greek town, especially Athens, but also used of analogous structures, as in Great Zimbabwe◊□

acrostic poem with initial letters of the lines forming a word or sentence□

acrylic acid ($CH_2CHCOOH$) acid obtained from the aldehyde◊ acrolein. Derivatives of the acid are polymerized to form acrylic resins, glass-like thermoplastic resins used for transparent components and lenses; adhesives; synthetic textiles such as Acrilan and Orlon; and brilliant paints, such as those used by Hockney◊ and others□

Actaeon in Greek mythology, a hunter who surprised Artemis◊ bathing; she changed him to a stag and he was torn to pieces by his own hounds□

ACTH see under hormone◊□

actinides group of radioactive elements with atomic numbers from 89 to 103, all of which beyond 92 (uranium) are man-made□

actinium element
symbol Ac
atomic number 89
physical description silvery metal
features radioactive element which gives its name to the actinide◊ series
uses a source of alpha particles (see particle◊ physics) and to produce neutrons◊□

action painting abstract◊ Expressionist style developed in New York in the 1950s, named by art critic Harold Rosenberg; the paint was often violently applied, for example by bicycling over the canvas. See Jackson Pollock◊□

Actium promontory (modern Akri) in W Greece, off which Octavian defeated the fleets of Antony◊ and Cleopatra◊ in 31BC□

Act of Congress bill or resolution (USA) passed by both Senate and House of Representatives, which has received the assent of the president□

act of God sudden and irresistible act of nature which could not reasonably have been foreseen, such as exceptional storms, snow, etc.□

Act of Indemnity in Britain, an Act◊ of Parliament relieving someone from the consequences of some act or omission which, at the time it took place, was illegal□

Act of Parliament in Britain, a change in the law originating in Parliament. Such acts may be either public (of general effect) or private (of local effect). Before an act receives the royal assent and becomes law it is a 'bill'□

Actors Studio theatre workshop in New York City, established 1947 by Cheryl Crawford, Elia Kazan, and Robert Lewis for the study of Stanislavsky◊'s method: 'method' actors include Marlon Brando and James Dean□

acupuncture system developed in ancient China of inserting needles into the body (Latin *acu* 'with a needle') at predetermined points to produce a degree of anaesthesia and assist healing. The method is thought to work partly by suggestion and partly by stimulating production of the brain's own painkillers. See Endorphin◊, Encephalin◊. It may be used in Western medicine as electroacupuncture, or (in surgery) combined with analgesia□

Adam in Old Testament, founder of the human race (Hebrew *adham* 'man'). Formed by God from the dust, and given the breath of life, Adam was placed in the Garden of Eden, where Eve◊ was given to him as a companion. With her, he tasted the forbidden fruit of the Tree of Knowledge of Good and Evil, and was expelled with her from the Garden□

Adam Adolphe Charles 1803–56. French composer of light opera, best remembered for the ballet *Giselle*□

Adam Robert 1728–92. Scottish architect and interior decorator, leader of the British neo-classical revival. In the interiors of Harewood House, Luton◊ Hoo, Syon House, Osterley Park, etc, he employed delicate stucco decoration with neo-classical motifs. With his brother ***James Adam*** 1732–94, also an architect, he speculatively developed the Adelphi near Charing Cross, London, largely rebuilt 1936□

Adam de la Halle c1240–90. French poet-composer. His *Jeu de Robin et Marion* written in Italy c1282, was the first comic opera□

Adams Henry Brooks 1838–1918. American historian, the grandson of John Quincy Adams◊; he wrote a classic autobiography *The Education of Henry Adams* 1907□

Adams John 1735–1826. President of the USA 1797–1801; vice-president 1789–97. A signatory of the Declaration of Independence◊, he went to France in 1779 to negotiate the treaties which ended the War of American◊ Independence; he was the first US ambassador in London from 1785□

Adams John Couch 1819–92. British astronomer who deduced the existence of the planet Neptune◊ from its influence on the motion of Uranus◊□

Adams John Quincy 1767–1846. President of the USA 1825–9. Eldest son of President John Adams, he became Monroe◊'s Secretary of State in 1817, and succeeded him in the presidency□

Adams Richard 1920– . British novelist. A civil servant 1948–72, he achieved fame with *Watership Down* 1972, a children's tale of a rabbit community, which has allegorical overtones for adults□

Adams Samuel 1722–1803. American statesman, second cousin of President John Adams, who was the chief prompter of the Boston Tea Party◊; was also a signatory of the Declaration of Independence◊, and anticipated Napoleon◊ in calling the British a 'nation of shopkeepers'□

Adamson Joy 1910–85. German-born author-painter, born Gessner, who with her third husband, British game warden ***George Adamson,*** was famous for work with wildlife in Kenya, especially the lioness Elsa described in *Born Free* 1960. She was murdered by an employee□

Adana major cotton-growing centre in Turkey-in-Asia; population 347 455□

adder poisonous European snake◊□

Addington Henry 1757–1844. British Tory Prime Minister 1801–4, later Viscount Sidmouth□

Addinsell Richard 1904–77. British composer; especially noted for his *Warsaw Concerto*, written for the film *Dangerous Moonlight* 1941□

Addis Ababa capital of Ethiopia; population 1 084 000. Menelik Palace, the former residence of the Emperor, is now occupied by the Chairman of the Provisional Military Council; the city is the headquarters of the Organization of African Unity□

Addison Joseph 1672–1719. British writer. In 1704 he celebrated Marlborough◊'s victory at Blenheim in a poem, 'The Campaign' and subsequently held political appointments. In 1711 he was co-founder with Richard Steele of the periodical the *Spectator* in which his essays set a new standard of easy elegance in English prose; especially notable were the Coverley papers concerning an idealized country squire, Sir Roger de Coverley. As a literary critic, he was satirized by Alexander Pope◊ as 'willing to damn with faint praise' any rival□

Addison Thomas 1793–1863. British physician; the first to recognise Addison's disease□

Addison's disease disease affecting the suprarenal capsules. See adrenal glands under hormone◊□

additive in food, a chemical substance added, under increasing legal restriction, to ensure: longer shelf life (salt, antibiotics); attractive colour or flavour; greater food value (vitamins, minerals); greater manufacturing convenience (such as, easier flow for semi-liquids).

Antibiotics may not only be added to carcases, e.g. to poultry to inhibit decay during transport, but to treat living animals and plants for disease, so that any residue, after slaughter or cropping, may be ingested by the human consumer□

Adelaide 1792–1849. Queen consort of William◊ IV from 1818□

Adelaide capital and industrial city of S Australia; population 933 300. Founded in 1834, it was named after William IV's queen, and is a fine example of town-planning□

Aden capital of S Yemen; population 264 300□

Adenauer Konrad 1876–1967. Chancellor of West Germany 1949–63, known as the 'Old Fox'; with de◊ Gaulle he achieved the post-war reconciliation of France and Germany □

adenoids in children, overgrowth of the glandular tissue on the back of the upper throat, where there is an opening to the nose; it is caused by infection, and chronic blockage may require surgical removal. The voice acquires a nasal twang□

adhesive traditionally, industrial gelatine (glue), made from bones, hide, and fish offal, or vegetable gums◊. Now, adhesives are often synthetic thermoplastic, thermosetting, and elastomeric resins. The latter are usually toluene◊-based, and by 1984 the problem of addicts 'glue-sniffing' (which can lead to brain damage) had led to the development of water-based products□

Adige after the Po, the longest river in Italy, 410 km/254 mi□

Adirondacks see under New◊ York State□

Adler Alfred 1870–1937. Austrian psychologist, who joined the Freudian circle in Vienna about 1900. He saw the 'will to power' as more influential in accounting for human behaviour than the underlying sexual drive theory of Freud◊. Adler parted company with him after a ten-year collaboration□

Adler Larry 1914– . American musician. See harmonica◊□

admiral highest ranking naval officer; in the Royal Navy (in descending order) Admiral of the Fleet, Admiral, Vice-Admiral, Rear-Admiral; in the US Navy, Fleet Admiral, Admiral, Vice-Admiral, Rear-Admiral□

Admiral's Cup sailing series first held in 1957 and since held biennially for three-boat national teams which compete in three inshore and two offshore courses; the series culminates in the Fastnet race; similar series are the Southern Cross, Rio Circuit and the Onion Patch□

Admiralty The Board of the. In Britain, the controlling department of State for the Royal Navy from the reign of Henry VIII until 1964, when most of its functions passed to the Ministry of Defence□

Admiralty Islands group of small islands in the SW Pacific, part of Papua◊ New Guinea; population 21 000□

Adonis in Greek mythology, a youth beloved by Aphrodite◊. He was killed while boar-hunting, but was allowed to return from the lower world for six months every year to rejoin her. Worshipped as a god of vegetation, he was known as ***Tammuz*** in Babylonia, Assyria, and Phoenicia (where it was his sister, Ishtar◊, who brought him from the lower world). He seems also to have been identified with Osiris◊□

adoption the legal acquisition of a child not one's own; it was first legalized in England in 1926; in 1958 an adopted child was enabled to inherit on parental intestacy; and from 1975 an adopted child was enabled to know its original name at 18. See custodianship◊□

adrenal glands see under hormone◊□

Adrian IV 1100–59. Nicholas Breakspear, Pope 1154–9, the only British Pope. He secured the execution of Arnold◊ of Brescia; crowned Frederick◊ I Barbarossa as German Emperor; refused Henry◊ II's request that Ireland should be granted to the English crown in absolute ownership; and was at the height of a quarrel with the Emperor when he died□

Adrian Edgar, 1st Baron Adrian 1889–1977. British physiologist, recipient of a Nobel prize in 1932 for his work with Sherrington◊ on nerve impulses□

Adriatic Sea see under Mediterranean◊□

adultery voluntary sexual intercourse by a married person with someone other than their legal partner. It is one factor demonstrative of 'irretrievable breakdown' of marriage in suits for judicial separation or divorce in Britain; and is almost universally recognized as grounds for divorce in the USA, and is theoretically a punishable offence in some states□

Aduwa Battle of. Defeat of the Italians by the Ethiopians in 1896. See Menelik◊ II□

Advent in the Christian calendar, the preparatory season for Christmas, including the four Sundays preceding it□

Adventists Christian sects, such as the Seventh Day Adventists, who anticipate the Second Coming of Christ□

advocaat an alcoholic drink. See liqueur◊□

advocate see under barrister◊□

Advocate Judge. Manager of the prosecution in British courts martial□

Advocate Lord. Chief law officer of the Crown in Scotland□

Aegean Sea see under Mediterranean◊□

Aegis see under Zeus◊□

Aeneas In Greek mythology, a Trojan prince, son of Aphrodite and Anchises; he escaped from the fall of Troy to found Rome; Julius Ceasar◊ and Augustus◊ claimed descent from him. See Virgil◊, and also under Athena◊□

Aeolus in Greek mythology, the god of the winds, who kept them imprisoned in a cave on the Lipari◊ Islands□

aerobics strenuous combination (Greek 'air' + 'life') of dance, stretch exercises, and running that became a health fashion in the eighties□

aeroplane see flight◊□

aerosol popularly a can in which a gas under pressure, or a liquefied gas with a pressure greater than that of the atmosphere at ordinary temperature, is used to produce a mist spray (insecticide, paint, hair lacquer)□

Aeschylus c525–456BC. Greek dramatist, who fought at Marathon◊. He wrote some 90 plays of which seven survive including *The Suppliant Women, The Persians* (dealing with Salamis◊ and Plataea◊ within a decade of the event, in the same way as modern television 'documentary drama'), *Seven Against Thebes*, and the *Oresteia* trilogy, dealing with the curse on the house of Agamemnon◊□

Aesculapius in Greek and Roman mythology, the god of medicine; his emblem was a staff with a snake coiled round it, since snakes seemed to renew life by sloughing their skin. See Epidaurus◊, hospital◊□

Aesop mid-6th century BC. Greek slave noted for his animal fables; he may have been a Negro brought from N Africa, and is represented as deformed□

Aesthetic movement artistic movement of the last quarter of the 19th century. With the motto 'Art for art's sake', it reached its apogee with Wilde◊, and the periodical *The Yellow Book* 1894–7. See also Pater◊, Beardsley◊, Whistler◊, Dowson◊, and J A Symonds◊□

aestivation see under hibernation◊□

affiliation order English magistrate's order for maintenance of an illegitimate child, made against the father at the instance of an unmarried mother. In 1969 blood tests were first used to prove 'non-paternity'; they are not equally conclusive of paternity□

affinity relationship by marriage not blood, e.g. between step-parent and step-child, which may legally preclude their marriage. A Church of England report 1984 recommended the ending of this and some other prohibitions□

Afghan hound a breed of dog◊ related to the greyhound□

Afghanistan Democratic Republic of

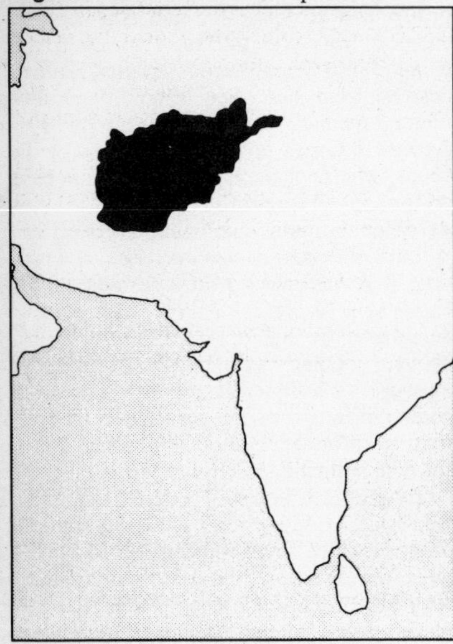

area 636 00 sq km/246 000 sq mi
capital Kabul
towns Kandahár, Herát
features Hindu Kush range (Khyber and Salang passes, and Panjshir Valley, focus of resistance to USSR); Amu Darya, Kabul, and Helmand rivers; Wakhan salient
exports dried fruit, rare minerals, natural gas (piped to USSR), karakul lamb skins, Afghan coats
currency afghâni
population 14 448 000; more than three million have become refugees since 1979
language Pushtu
religion 80% Sunni Islam, 20% Shi'ite
government there is a 'puppet regime' (backed by USSR) with Babrak Karmal of the People's Democratic (Communist) Party as Prime Minister. The Party Secretary is Major-General Najibullah (from 1986)
recent history an independent emirate from 1747, Afghanistan was seen by Britain as a threat to its interests in India in the 19th century (see Afghan◊ Wars). King Mohammed Zahir Shah was deposed in a military coup and abdicated 1973, and the new republic signed a treaty of friendship in 1978 with the USSR, which was used as a pretext for a Soviet invasion Dec 1979–Jan 1980. Guerrilla resistance continues (largest organization National Islamic Front of Afghanistan, NIFA), and the United Nations General Assembly condemned the Soviet occupation□

Afghan Wars wars waged between Britain and Afghanistan to counter the threat to British India from expanding Russian influence in Afghanistan.
First Afghan War 1838–42, when the British garrison at Kabul was wiped out.
Second Afghan War 1878–80, when General Roberts captured Kabul and relieved Kandahar.
Third Afghan War 1919, when peace followed the despatch by Britain of the first aeroplane ever seen in Kabul□

Africa second largest of the continents, and three times the area of Europe.
area 30 097 000 sq km/11 617 000 sq mi
largest cities Cairo, Algiers, Lagos, Kinshasa, Abidjan, Tunis, Cape Town, Nairobi
features dominated by a central plateau, which includes the world's largest desert (Sahara◊); Nile and Zaïre rivers, but generally there is a lack of rivers, and also of other inlets, so that Africa has proportionately the shortest coastline of all the continents; comparatively few offshore islands; 75% is within the tropics; Great Rift Valley◊; immensely rich fauna and flora
exports has 30% of the world's minerals; cash crops, e.g. coffee, cocoa
population 474 628 000
language Hamito-Semitic in the north; Bantu below the Sahara; Khoisian languages with 'clicks' in the far south
religion Islam in the north; Animism below the Sahara, with superimposed Christianity (both Catholic and Protestant) in some areas; and Protestantism among the Caucasoids of the far south□
history see Africa: history

Africa: history
BC
14 million Africa, which is considered the 'cradle-continent', probably produced the first man-like creatures
3–5 million direct line of descent of modern man was established in E Africa; see Richard Leakey◊
15 000 agriculture first practised in Egypt
10 000–2000 the originally fertile Sahara became a barrier desert between north and south

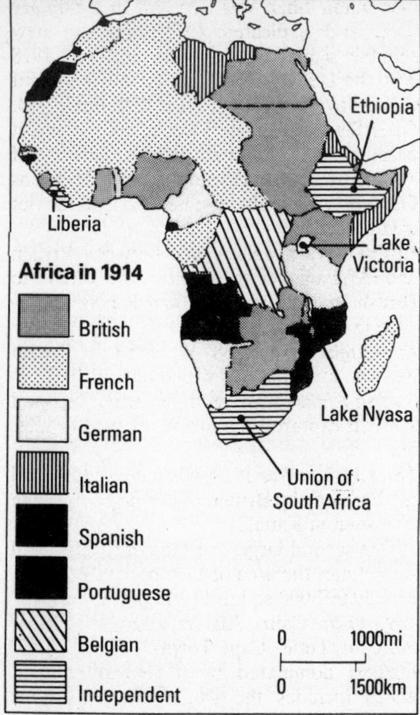

5450–2500 era of Saharan rock and cave paintings, as in the Tassili◊
7th century ***BC–6th century AD*** Assyria, Persia, Greece, Rome, and Byzantium in turn made conquests in N Africa. Meroe◊: the Egyptian and Negro tradition met in the Nubian kingdom of Kush◊
AD
320–50 the kingdom of Axum◊ flourished in Ethiopia, and gave rise to the later legend of Prester◊ John
640 Islamic expansion began in N, E and Central Africa
300–1500 period of the great medieval states: Ghana◊, Mali◊, Songhai◊, Benin◊, Ife◊, and the culture of Great Zimbabwe◊
12–15th centuries era of the Arab travellers: e.g. Ibn Batuta◊, etc.; and of trade, e.g. Kilwa◊
1488 Diaz rounded the Cape of Good Hope
15–16th centuries European sea trade in gold, ivory, timber, pepper, etc.
17–19th centuries height of the Atlantic and Indian Ocean slave trade
18–19th centuries European travellers in Africa: Park◊, Livingstone◊, Stanley◊, Speke◊, Mary Kingsley◊
19th century colonial wars against well-organized native states: Ashanti, Dahomey, Zululand
1880–90 peak of European colonization in the 'scramble for Africa'
1899–1902 South◊ African War, the first large-scale war between whites in Africa
1920 League◊ of Nations 'mandate' system introduced the idea of European 'trusteeship'
1936 Italy's conquest of Ethiopia
1942 World War II reached its turning point in the Battles of Alamein◊
1951 Libya became the first independent state to be declared by the United Nations
1954–62 civil war in Algeria precipitated the end of the French Fourth Republic◊ in 1958
1957 Ghana◊ became independent, the first of the revived black nation states
1952–60 Mau-Mau◊ movement in Kenya began the ousting of white settlers south of the Sahara
1963 Organization of African Unity◊ founded
1967–70 revolt of Biafra within the federation of Nigeria constituted the first civil war in a modern black state
1975 Mozambique's independence led to the end of dictatorship in Portugal
1979 Zimbabwe's achievement of independence left S Africa as the last white-ruled state in Africa
1980 future of the OAU doubtful due to division over Western Sahara and Libyan aggression towards Chad□

Africa Horn of. Somalia and the adjacent territories□

African National Congress (ANC) organization formed in 1912 in South Africa to oppose discrimination and extend the franchise to blacks. After the Sharpeville◊ massacre in 1960 the ANC was banned, but continues as a guerilla movement□

African violet plant *Saintpaulia ionantha*, family Gesneriaceae, native to tropical E Africa, grown for its scentless white, pink, or purple flowers□

Afrikaans an official language of the Republic of South Africa, a development of the language of the original Dutch colonists □

Afrika corps the German army in the Western Desert of N Africa in World War II 1941–3 □

Afrikaner white, Afrikaans-speaking citizen of S Africa; usually of Boer◊ descent□

Agadir seaport in Morocco; population 61 200. It was destroyed by an earthquake in 1960, but rebuilt□

Agadir Incident demand in 1911 by William II of Germany, expressed by sending the gunboat *Panther*, for territorial concessions in Morocco from France – hence 'gunboat diplomacy'□

Aga Khan see Ismaili◊ sect□

agama a type of lizard. See lizard◊□

Agamemnon in Greek mythology, a Greek hero, son of Atreus, King of Mycenae. He married Clytemnestra, and their children included Electra◊, Iphigenia◊, and Orestes◊. Setting out from Aulis to the Trojan◊ War, he would have sacrificed Iphigenia to Artemis◊ to secure fair winds (she was saved by the goddess and made a priestess). He led the capture of Troy, received Priam◊'s daughter Cassandra◊ as a prize, and was murdered by Clytemnestra and her lover, Aegisthus, on his return home. Orestes and Electra later killed the guilty couple. Aeschylus◊, Euripides◊, T S Eliot◊, O'Neill◊ and Sartre◊ all based plays on the theme□

Agana capital of Guam, island in the W Pacific; population 2200□

agar-agar substance derived from *Gelidium* species of red algae; used in bacteriology to form the jelly in which bacteria are grown□

agaricus genus of fungi◊, family Agaricaceae, class Basidiomycetes◊, characterized by radially arranged gills and a fruiting body with a central fleshy stalk, e.g. ***common mushroom***◊ *A campestris*, and ***horse mushroom*** *A arvensis*□

agate banded or cloudy kind of silica◊ used in ornamental work□

agave see amaryllidaceae◊□

ageing life's 'programme' of growth from baby to adult followed by later deterioration. According to current theories, ageing may be: ***genetic*** predetermined (like the 'clocks' which control the achievement of sexual maturity) to produce pre-programmed obsolescence; ***error-induced*** caused by an accumulation of mistakes in the replication of the series of genetic instructions contained in the DNA◊ of the body cells when they reproduce by division; ***actively induced*** by plasmids (nomadic circular pieces of DNA which resemble cancer-causing viruses) which are produced too abundantly by ageing cells□

Agincourt village south of Calais, N France; Henry◊ V of England defeated the French here on 24 Oct 1415, St Crispin's Day□

Agnew Spiro 1918– . American Republican vice-president to Nixon, who resigned 1973, pleading 'no contest' to charges of tax-evasion□

Agni Hindu god of fire□

Agnon Shmuel Yosef 1888–1970. Israeli Hebrew novelist; his most famous work is *A Guest for the Night*; he shared a Nobel prize 1966□

agnostic someone who declares it impossible to know whether God exists or not; the word was coined by T H Huxley◊ in 1869□

agouti small Central and S American rodent◊□

AGR abbreviation for **advanced gas-cooled reactor.** See electricity◊ generation□

Agra city in Uttar Pradesh, India; population 637 800. The capital of Baber◊ from 1527, it was beautified by Shah◊ Jehan with the Taj Mahal, etc.; in decline following the removal of the capital to Delhi in 1658, it is now a commercial and university centre□

Agricola Gnaeus Julius 37–93AD. Roman governor of Britain 78–85, who extended Roman rule to the Firth of Forth in Scotland, and won the battle of Mons Graupius (site uncertain, but see Grampian◊ mountains), before being recalled by Domitian◊, who had grown jealous. His fleet sailed round the north of Scotland and proved Britain an island. His daughter married Tacitus◊□

agriculture cultivation of land by man, developed in Egypt at least 17 000 years ago. Its modernization began in 18th-century Britain, and its mechanization in 19th-century USA. Following World War II, there was an explosive growth in agricultural chemicals – herbicides, insecticides, fungicides, fertilizers, etc.; in the 1960s there was development of high-yielding species for special conditions, especially in the ***green revolution*** in the Third World, and in the industrialized countries cattle and poultry production on 'production lines' and battery systems; in the 1970s there was a movement towards more sophisticated natural methods and a reversion to ***organic farming*** without chemical sprays and fertilizers whose continued use become essential as fertility declines; in the 1980s hybridization by genetic engineering methods was developed□

Agrigento town in Sicily noted for Greek temples; population 55 000□

agrimony plant *Agrimonia eupatoria,* family Rosaceae◊, with small pale yellow flowers borne on a spike; the leaves give a yellow dye□

Agrippa Marcus Vipsanius 63–12BC. He commanded the victorious fleet at Actium◊ and married Julia, daughter of Augustus◊□

Aguascalientes city in central Mexico, with hot springs; population 239 000□

Agulhas southernmost cape in Africa, S Africa□

Ahab 875–854BC in Old Testament, king of Israel; he married Jezebel◊, and died in battle at Ramoth◊ Gilead□

Ahaggar mountainous plateau in central Sahara, Algeria. The Tuareg people of the region are no longer nomads, and the men no longer wear the traditional blue veils□

Ahasuerus see The Wandering◊ Jew□

ahimsa rule of respect for all life, and consequently non-violence, in Hinduism◊,

Buddhism◊, and especially Jainism◊; it arises in part from the concept of reincarnation◊. See Ghandi◊□

Ahmadabad capital of Gujerat, India; population 2 515 195. Gandhi◊ marched to the sea from here in 1930 to protest against the government salt monopoly□

Ahriman in Zoroastrianism◊, the supreme evil spirit□

Ahura Mazda in Zoroastrianism◊, the spirit of supreme good□

Ahvenanmaa Island or ***Aland Island*** located in the Gulf of Bothnia, Finland. The population is Swedish-speaking and agitated until the island was made an autonomous province of Finland□

Ahwaz capital of the Arab province of Khuzestan, Iran; population 329 000□

Aidan St c600–51AD. Irish monk from Iona who converted Northumbria and founded Lindisfarne monastery; feast day 31 Aug. See Holy◊ Island□

AIDS (*A*quired *I*mmunity *D*eficiency *S*yndrome◊) a disease marked by weight loss, diarrhoea, swollen glands, and resulting in the destruction of the body's immune system, leaving it vulnerable to viruses and bacteria. It is as yet incurable, resulting in death within four years. Identified 1980, it may be caused by a blood-borne virus. It is transmitted by sexual contact; by shared syringes among drug addicts; and by infected blood transfusions to haemophiliacs. In the West, sufferers are predominantly homosexual men, but the disease is also transmitted by heterosexual intercourse. In the UK, patients in a condition dangerous to others, e.g. bleeding badly, may be legally detained in hospital under a Public Health Act of 1984□

Aigun Treaty of. Treaty between Russia and China signed in 1858 at the port of Aigun in China on the Amur river. It ceded the left bank to Russia, but has since been repudiated by China□

Aiken Conrad Potter 1899–1973. American poet and novelist; he was associated with the Imagist◊ movement; his novel *Great Circle* 1933 reflects his own life – when he was a boy, his father committed suicide after killing Aiken's mother□

Aiken Howard 1900– . American computer pioneer; he originated the concept of 'time-sharing'□

aikido see under martial◊ arts□

Ailsa Craig rocky islet in the Firth of Clyde, Scotland; it is a famous breeding ground for birds□

Ain river of France, a right-bank Rhône tributary□

Ainsworth William Harrison 1805–82. British historical novelist. He helped popularize the legends of Dick Turpin◊ in *Rookwood* 1834 and Herne◊ the Hunter in *Windsor Castle* 1843□

Aintree racecourse, Liverpool, Merseyside; its most famous race is the ***Grand National*** steeplechase (1839) in Mar/Apr, over 7 km 220 m/4 mi 856 yd, with 30 formidable jumps□

Ainu aboriginal race of Japan; fair-skinned, blue-eyed, and hairy. In the 4th century AD they were driven out by the modern Japanese, but c16 000 survive on the island of Hokkaido. They are noted for blue-tattooed lips in their women, and a language with few links with any other□

air see under atmosphere◊□

aircraft carrier sea-going military airport. The first to be purpose-designed was the Japanese *Hosho* 1925. The aircraft carrier replaced the battleship as the largest and most powerful fighting ship until its cost and vulnerability led to its being phased out in all but the navies of the USA and USSR. Smaller carriers with planes, helicopters and missiles aboard developed in the 1980s, e.g. HMS *Ark Royal*, laid down 1979, Invincible class, 19 500 tonnes (8 Sea Harrier aircraft, 9 Sea King helicopters)□

Airedale terrier a breed of dog◊□

air force see services◊ armed□

airglow faint glow arising in upper atmosphere, related to the Aurora Borealis◊. It interferes with astronomical observation. See Canary◊ Islands□

air raid aerial attack, usually on a civilian population. In World War II, raids were usually made by bomber aircraft, but many thousands were killed in London in 1944 by German V1 and V2 rockets. The air raids on Britain became known as 'the Blitz'. Most famous individual raids in World War II:

Hiroshima 6 Aug 1945 (the first use of the atom bomb) in an air raid by the US, 78 150 immediate deaths, 140 000 after a few weeks, 270 000 after five years

Dresden 13–14 February 1945, 135 000 dead

Tokyo 9–10 Mar 1945, 83 793 dead

Coventry 14–15 Nov 1940, 380 dead□

airship power-driven, streamlined hull balloon with rigid inner structure; the ***Zeppelin***, named after Count von Zeppelin 1838–1917, was a pioneer of the types used in raids on Britain in World War I; the ***R101*** (British 1930) and ***Hindenburg*** (German 1937) were both destroyed by fire because of the inflammable gas used (hydrogen); when supplies of helium (non-inflammable) became available in the 1970s fresh experiments were made in the USSR and elsewhere, because airships can lift heavy loads with minimum fuel□

Aisne river of N France. There was heavy fighting here in World War I◊ 1916□

Aix-en-Provence capital of Provence region, France; population 111 000. Dating to Roman times, it was the birthplace of Cézanne◊□

Aix-la-Chapelle see Aachen◊□

Aix-les-Bains spa with hot springs in Savoy, France; population 20 720□

Ajaccio capital of Corsica and birthplace of Napoleon◊, commemorated by a museum; population 42 300□

Ajanta see under Maharashtra◊□

Ajax Greek hero of Homer◊'s *Iliad*. When Agamemnon◊ awarded the armour of the dead Achilles◊ to Odysseus◊, Ajax first went mad with jealousy, and then committed suicide in shame□

Ajman see United Arab Emirates◊□

Ajmer town in Rajasthan, India; population 262 480□

Akbar Jellaladin Mohammed 1542–1605. Greatest Mogul◊ emperor of India, the 'Guardian of Mankind'; he succeeded his father in 1556 and established just rule through all India north of the Deccan□

Akhetaton capital of ancient Egypt established by the monotheistic pharaoh Ikhnaton◊ as the centre for his cult of the Aten, the sun's disc; it is the modern Tell el Amarna 300 km/190 mi south of Cairo. His palace had fine, formal enclosed gardens◊. After his death it was abandoned, and the ***Amarna tablets*** are probably the contents of the 'wastepaper' baskets of his officials, outdated 'foreign office' letters, etc.□

Akhmatova Anna. Pseudonym of Russian poet Anna Gorenko 1889–1966, noted for love lyrics□

Akhnaton see Ikhnaton◊□

Akihito 1933– . Crown Prince of Japan, the son of Hirohito◊; he married in 1959 Michiko Shoda, the first commoner to enter the Imperial family□

Akkad ancient city of central Mesopotamia, founded by Sargon◊, and an imperial centre in the 3rd millennium BC; the site is unidentified, but it was on the Euphrates□

Akola cotton and grain trade centre in Maharashtra, India; population 168 454□

Akron rubber capital of the USA in Ohio, which processes almost half the world supply; population 237 000□

Akrotiri peninsula on the S coast of Cyprus; it has a British military base□

Aksum modern town of N Ethiopia, near the site of the ruins of the ancient capital (of the same name) of the Greek-influenced Semitic kingdom of Aksum or ***Axum***, which flourished 1st–6th centuries AD□

Aktyubinsk industrial city in Republic of Kazakh, USSR; population 188 000□

Alabama SE state of the USA; Heart of Dixie/Cotton State

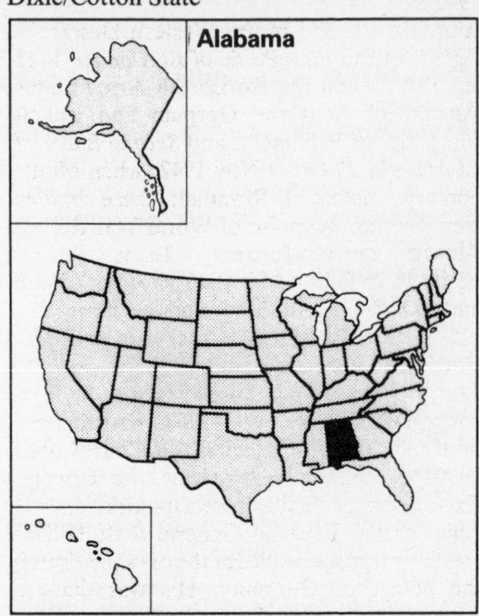

area 133 665 sq km/51 609 sq mi
capital Montgomery
towns Birmingham, Mobile
features Alabama and Tennessee rivers; Appalachian mountains; George Washington Carver◊ Museum at the Tuskegee Institute (founded for blacks by Booker T Washington◊) and Helen Keller◊'s birthplace at Tuscumbia
products cotton no longer prime crop, though still important; soybeans, peanuts; wood products; coal, iron
population 3 861 470
famous people Nat King Cole, Helen Keller, Joe Louis, Jesse Owens, Booker T Washington
history first settled by the French, it was ceded to Britain in 1763, passed to the USA in 1783, and became a state in 1819 with land added in the Louisiana◊ Purchase in 1803. See Confederate States◊□

Alabama Confederate warship in the American Civil◊ War. Built in Britain, she was allowed to leave port by the British, and sank many US merchantmen, until herself sunk by a US man-of-war; the international court later awarded damages to the USA, an important legal precedent□

alabaster see gypsum◊□

Alain-Fournier pseudonym of French novelist Henri Fournier 1886–1914. His haunting fantasy *Les Grand Meaulnes/The Lost Domain* 1913 was a cult of the 1920s and 1930s□

Alamagordo town in New Mexico, USA; population 23 000. The first atom bomb exploded at Trinity site near the town Jul 16 1945□

Alamein El. Site in the Western Desert, N Egypt, of the ***First Battle of El Alamein*** 1–27 Jul 1942, when the British 8th Army under Auchinleck held the German and Italian forces under Rommel◊; and ***Second Battle of El Alamein*** 23 Oct–4 Nov 1942, when Montgomery◊ defeated Rommel; these battles were the turning point of World War II□

Alamo mission-fortress, Texas, USA; besieged 23 Feb–6 Mar 1836 by Santa Anna◊ and 4000 Mexicans; they killed the garrison of c150, including Davy Crockett◊ and Jim Bowie◊□

Alanbrooke Alan Francis Brooke, 1st Viscount Alanbrooke 1883–1963. British field marshal. He commanded the 2nd Corps 1939–40, helping to extricate the British◊ Expeditionary Force from Dunkirk, and as Chief of the Imperial General Staff 1941–6 was largely responsible for the organization of the defeat of Germany. His war diaries, edited by Sir Arthur Bryant, were controversial in their depiction of Churchill◊□

Aland Island see Ahvenanmaa◊ Island□

Alarcón Pedro Antonio de 1833–91. Spanish novelist; his *El Sombrero de tres picos/The Three-Cornered Hat* 1874 was the basis of Manuel de Falla◊'s ballet□

Alaric 370–410. King of the Visigoths◊. He captured and sacked Rome in 410, and the River Busento was diverted by his soldiers so that he could be buried in its course with his treasures; the labourers were killed to keep the secret□

Alaska NW Pacific state of the USA, and the largest
area 1 500 000 sq km/586 400 sq mi
capital Junau (a new capital is planned at Willow South, to the north of Anchorage)
towns Anchorage, Fairbanks, Fort Yukon, Holy Cross
features Yukon river; Rocky mountains, including Mt McKinley 6194 m/20 320 ft, the highest peak in N America; Mt Katmai, volcano which erupted 1912 (one of largest ever known) and formed the Valley of Ten Thousand Smokes (the smoke and steam still escaping from fissures in the floor) now a national monument; Arctic Wild Life Range, with the only large herd of N American caribou; Little Diomede Island, which is only 3.9 km/2.4 mi from Big Diomede/Ratmanov Island in the USSR; reindeer herds on the

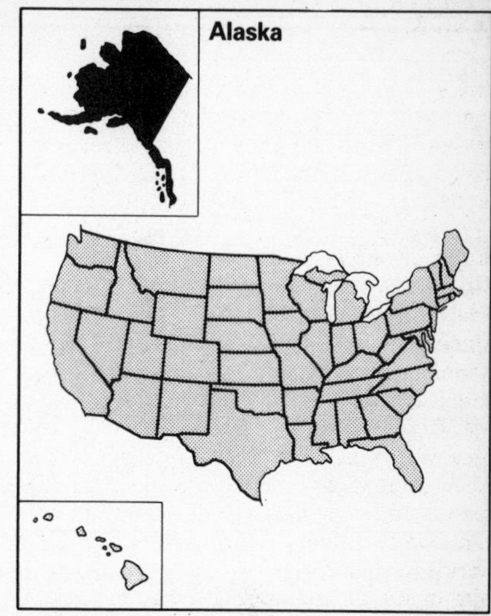

tundra; an Act of 1980 gave environmental protection to 42 million ha/104 million acres
products oil and natural gas which is piped south from Prudhoe Bay; gold (e.g. the 'rush' to the Klondike river 1896–1910), timber, furs, salmon
population 400 500, including about 50 000 American Indians, Aleuts and Inuits
history discovered in 1741 by Vitus Bering◊, Alaska was a Russian colony until purchased by the USA in 1867 for $7 200 000; it became a state in 1959□

Albacete town in Murcia, Spain; population 117 125. Famous for cutlery and flick knives□

albacore several fish, including species of tunny◊□

Alban St d. 303AD. First Christian martyr in England. Traditionally a converted Roman soldier, he was born at Verulamium (now named St Albans after him), and was beheaded for giving shelter to a Christian priest□

Albania Socialist People's Republic of
area 28 748 sq km/11 100 sq mi
capital Tirana
towns Shkodër, Vlorë, and the chief port Durrës
features Dinaric Alps, with wild boar and wolves
exports crude oil, bitumen, chrome, iron ore, nickel, coal, copper wire, tobacco, fruit; there is potential hydroelectric power
currency lek
population 2 800 000
language Albanian
religion formerly Islam, now it is the only officially atheist state in Europe

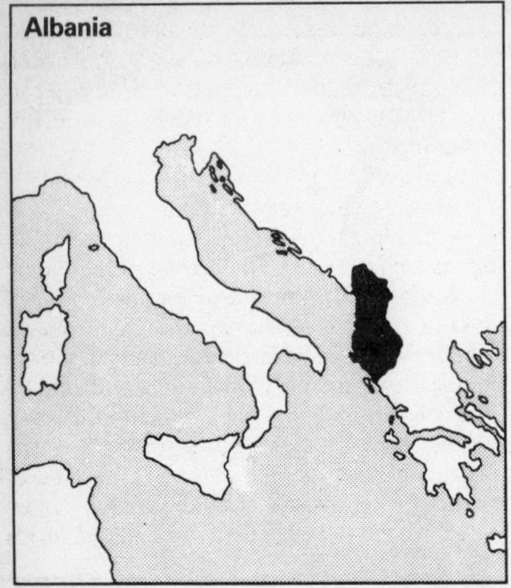
Albania

government under the 1976 constitution Albania is the 'state of the dictatorship of the proletariat'; the unicameral people's assembly is elected by universal suffrage, but real power resides with the First Secretary of the Communist Party (Ramiz Alia◊ from 1985)
recent history formerly under Turkish rule, Albania became independent in 1912, and a republic in 1925, President Ahmed Beg Zogu being proclaimed as King Zog in 1928. Overrun by the Italians and Germans from 1939, it was liberated 1944, became a Communist republic 1946, and was under a Stalinist regime (see Enver Hoxha◊) till 1985. Relations with the USSR were severed in 1961, because of Khrushchev◊'s 'revisionism', and with China in 1978 because of post-Maoist 'revisionism'; economic difficulties even prompted approaches to the West in 1982. Potentially a rich country, Albania was W Europe's poorest in 1985□

Albany capital of New York State, USA; population 102 780. It is linked by Erie canal with Lake Erie◊□

Albany port in W Australia; the 'Albany doctor' is a cooling afternoon sea breeze□

albatross world's largest seabird. See under petrel◊□

albedo in astronomy, the ratio of solar light reflected from a body to the total amount it receives□

Albee Edward 1928– . American playwright, author of *Who's Afraid of Virginia Woolf?* 1962, later filmed with Elizabeth Taylor and Richard Burton as the quarrelling, alcoholic couple□

Albéniz Isaac (Manuel) 1860–1909. Spanish composer and pianist, born in Catalonia. He composed the suite *Iberia* and other impressive piano pieces, making use of traditional Spanish tunes; he also wrote operas and orchestral works□

Albert 1818–61. Prince Consort of the UK; 2nd son of the Duke of Saxe-Coburg-Gotha, he married Queen Victoria◊, his first cousin, in 1840. He planned the Great Exhibition of 1851, the only international exhibition ever to make a handsome profit; this was used to buy the sites of all the S Kensington museums and colleges, and the Royal Albert Hall, built 1871. The Albert Memorial 1872, designed by Sir Gilbert Scott, in Kensington Gardens, typifies Victorian decorative art. Albert popularized the Christmas tree in England, but was suspect himself because of his German connections and his intelligence□

Albert Lake. See Lake Mobutu◊□

Alberta Western 'producer' province of Canada

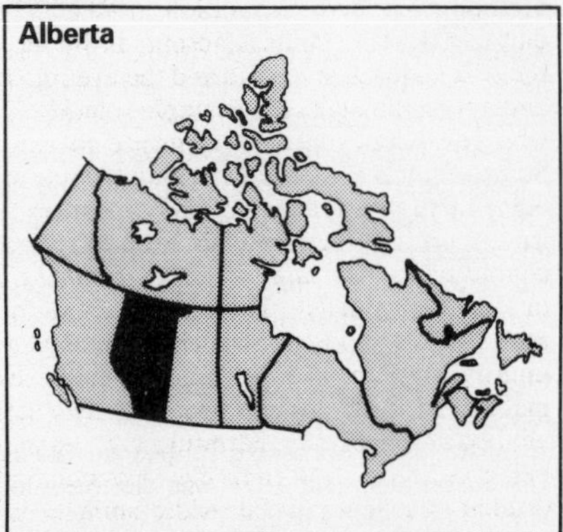
Alberta

area 661 187 sq km/255 285 sq mi
capital Edmonton
towns Calgary, Lethbridge
features Rocky◊ mountains, including some of the highest peaks; Peace River Valley, the most northerly farming land in Canada; Banff, Jasper, and Waterton Lake national parks
Products cereals are grown on a vast scale; more than a million cattle graze the foothills of the Rockies; lumber and other wood products; largest coal resources in Canada and the country's leading producer of oil and natural gas; also has bituminous sand in the McMurray district and the Athabasca tar sands; chemicals
population 2 348 800
history in the 17th century much of its area was part of a grant to the Hudson◊'s Bay Co for the fur trade. It became a province in 1905□

Alberti Leon Battista 1404–72. Italian Renaissance◊ architect and theorist, noted for his recognition of the principles of classical architecture and their modification for Renaissance practice in *On Architecture* 1452□

Albertus Magnus St 1206–80. German philosopher; known as 'doctor universalis' because of the breadth of his knowledge, he gained a reputation as a wizard; St Thomas Aquinas◊ was one of his pupils□

Albert Victor Duke of Clarence. See under George◊ V□

Albi town in S France; population 46 600. It was the centre of the Albigensian heresy (Albigenses◊) and the birthplace of Toulouse◊-Lautrec (with a museum)□

Albigenses Christian heretics (also called Cathars) in the neighbourhood of Albi◊ in the 11–12th centuries; they believed Jesus was a rebel against the cruelty of an omnipotent God; the Pope declared a crusade against them under the elder Simon de Montfort◊, and thousands were killed before the movement was crushed in 1229□

albinism hereditary condition in which the dark pigment melanin is absent; in humans the hair and skin are white and the eyes pink, and among animals, for example, blackbirds which are wholly or partly white are not rare. Some animals are bred to achieve albinism, e.g. white rabbits, and in others partial albinism occurs as a healthy adaptation to special conditions (e.g. an annual change to white fur in Arctic mammals). The reverse condition ***melanism*** also occurs, in which an animal has unusual dark colouring, e.g. a near-black mallard duck sometimes appears. Accidental albinism is generally harmful, e.g. human beings without protective eye pigment find ordinary daylight painful; white animals are generally more noticeable to predators, and hence shortlived□

Albinoni Tomaso 1671–1750. Italian composer and violinst, whose work was studied and adapted by Bach. He composed over 40 operas□

Albion name for Britain used by the Greeks and Romans□

albumin class of proteins occurring in most animal fluids and tissues, also in the seeds of plants (leucosin in wheat, rye, and barley; legumin in peas, lentils, and soybeans; egg-albumin in white of egg; serum-albumin in blood serum)□

Albuquerque city in New Mexico, USA; population 329 000. Founded in 1706, it was named after a Spanish viceroy; it specializes in electronics□

Albuquerque Alfonso de 1453–1515. Viceroy and founder of the Portuguese E Indies 1508–15, when the King of Portugal replaced him by his worst enemy and he died at sea on the way home; his ship *Flor del Mar*, was lost between Malaya and India with all his treasure□

Albury-Wodonga twin town on the New South Wales/Victoria border, Australia; population 45 000. Planned to relieve overspill from Melbourne and Sydney, it produces car components□

Alcaeus c611–c580BC. Greek lyric poet□

Alcatraz see San Francisco◊□

alcázar Moorish palace (Arabic 'fortress') in Spain; one of five in Toledo was defended by the Nationalists against the Republicans for 71 days in 1936 during the Spanish Civil◊ War□

alchemy supposed art of transmuting base metals (lead, mercury) into silver and gold by 'the philosopher's stone' which also gave eternal life. It originated in Egypt and was bound up with the medieval beginnings of chemistry; in the 20th century such transmutations have been made in small quantities in the nuclear laboratory. See atom◊□

Alcibiades 450–404BC. Athenian general. Handsome and dissolute, he became the archetype of capricious treachery for his military intrigues against his native state with the Spartans◊ and Persians◊; the Persians eventually had him assassinated. He had been brought up by Pericles◊ and was a friend of Socrates◊, whose reputation as a teacher suffered by the association□

Alcock Sir John William 1892–1919. British airman; 14 Jun 1919 he and Lieutenant Whitten-Brown made the first direct crossing of the Atlantic in an aeroplane (Vickers-Vimy)□

alcohol organic compound characterized by the presence of one or more OH-groups in the molecule; alcohols may be either liquids or solids, according to the size and complexity of the molecule.

The five best-known alcohols form a series in which the carbon and hydrogen atoms increase progressively: methanol (CH_3OH), also known as methyl alcohol or wood spirit; ethanol (C_2H_5OH), also known as ethyl alcohol or spirit of wine; propanol (C_3H_7OH), also known as propyl alcohol; butanol (C_4H_9OH), also known as butyl alcohol; and pentanal ($C_5H_{11}OH$), also known as amyl alcohol. The lower alcohols are liquids miscible with water; higher members are oily liquids not miscible with water, and the highest are waxy solids.

The main uses are in alcoholic liquors (ethanol only); lacquers and varnishes (as a solvent) and dyes; essential oils in perfumery; pharmaceuticals and the manufacture of chloroform, ether, chloral, iodoform, etc.; and as fuels□

alcoholic liquors intoxicating drinks; ethyl alcohol, a colourless liquid, C_2H_5OH, is the basis of all common intoxicants:

wines, ciders, sherry and other drinks in which alcohol is produced by direct fermentation using yeasts of the sugar content in the relevant fruit.
malt liquors beers, and stouts in which the starch of the grain is converted to sugar by malting, and the sugar is then fermented into alcohol by yeasts.
spirits distilled from malted liquors or wines.
A concentration of 0.15% alcohol in the blood causes mild intoxication; 0.3 definite drunkenness and partial loss of consciousness; 0.6 endangers life□
Alcoholics Anonymous voluntary organization established 1934 in the USA to help alcoholics to help each other to combat the condition; organizations now exist in many other countries□
Alcott Louisa May 1832–88. American author of the girls' classic *Little Women* 1869, which drew on her own home circumstances, she herself resembling the heroine Jo□
Aldabra island in the Seychelles. Rare plants and animals include the giant tortoise□
Aldebaran see star◊□
Aldeburgh town in Suffolk, England; population 2 550. It has an annual music festival founded by Benjamin Britten◊, and the Britten-Pears School for Advanced Studies. See also Crabbe◊□
aldehydes group of organic compounds prepared by the oxidization of primary alcohols; or by alcohol dehydrogenation (removal of hydrogen). They are usually liquids. Examples include: ethanal (CH_3CHO) or acetaldehyde, methanal ($HCHO$) or formaldehyde, and benzaldehyde (C_6H_5CHO)□
alder genus of northern temperate trees and shrubs *Alnus*, family Betulaceae◊; e.g. the water-loving ***common*** or ***black alder*** *A glutinosa*□
Alderman until its abolition in the 1970s, the title of the senior members of the borough or county councils in England and Wales (Old English 'older man'); it is still used in the City of London□
Aldermaston village in Berkshire, England; site of an atomic and biological weapons research establishment; in 1958 nuclear disarmament campaigners made it the goal of an Easter protest march from London; 1959–64 there were annual marches in the reverse direction□
Alderney third largest of the Channel Islands◊; area 8 sq km/3 sq mi; with its capital at St Anne's. It gives its name to a breed of cattle□
Aldershot town in Hampshire, England; population 34 540; there has been a military camp since 1854, the largest in England. A 19th-century barrack room is preserved□
Aldington Richard 1892–1962. British Imagist◊ poet, novelist, and critic, who was married to Hilda Doolittle◊ 1913–37. He wrote biographies of D H Lawrence and T E Lawrence with detailed research into aspects previously ignored or glossed over□
Aldiss Brian 1925– . British science fiction writer, noted for theoretically sound fantasies, e.g. *Non-Stop* 1958, dealing with a lost space ship, and *Helliconia Summer* 1983□
aleatoric music composition (pioneered by John Cage◊) from c1945 in which the elements are assembled by chance, e.g. by using dice (Latin *alea*) or by computer□
Aleixandre Vicente 1898–1984. Spanish lyric poet; an invalid for much of his life, he remained a spiritual rebel under Franco◊; Nobel prize 1977□
Alençon town in France; population 33 400. The former centre of the French hand-made lace industry□
Aleppo town in Syria (modern Haleb); population 700 000. Dating from 2000BC, it was the chief Europe-Asia trade centre until the Cape of Good Hope sea route opened□
Alessandria town in Italy; population 102 900. There is an annual motorcyclists' rally at the shrine of their patroness, the Madonna of the Centaurs□
Aletsch most extensive glacier in Europe, 16 km/10 mi long, beginning on the S Jungfrau in the Bernese Alps□
Aleutians strategic island chain in the N Pacific, stretching 1900 km/1200 mi SW of Alaska, of which it forms part; it is barren and actively volcanic since it runs along the Aleutian◊ Trench; population 6000 Inuits, plus a large US defence establishment□
Aleutian Trench the marine trench dividing the N American and Pacific 'plates' of Earth's lithosphere□
alewife a type of herring◊□
Alexander eight popes, including:
Alexander III Pope 1159–81; his authority was opposed by Frederick◊ Barbarossa, but Alexander eventually compelled him to render homage, and also humbled Henry◊ II of England after the murder of Thomas à Becket.
Alexander VI Pope 1492–1503, known as the 'infamous Borgia pope'. He was of Spanish origin, and bribed his way to the papacy, where he furthered the advancement of his illegitimate children, who included Cesare and Lucrezia Borgia◊. He secured the execution of Savonarola◊ when he preached against his corrupt practices, and is said to have died of poison he had prepared for his cardinals.

He was a great patron of the arts. See Raphael◊, Michelangelo◊□

Alexander three tsars of Russia:

Alexander I 1777–1825. Tsar of Russia from 1801. Defeated by Napoleon◊ at Austerlitz, he made peace at Tilsit 1807, but later broke with Napoleon's economic policy and opened Russian ports to British trade; this led to Napoleon's ill-fated invasion of Russia.

Alexander II 1818–81. Tsar of Russia from 1855. He is remembered as 'the Liberator' for his freeing of the serfs in 1861, but the revolutionary element remained unsatisfied, so that Alexander became increasingly autocratic and reactionary. He was assassinated by Nihilists.

Alexander III 1845–94. Tsar of Russia from 1881, when he succeeded his father, Alexander◊ II. He pursued a reactionary policy, persecuting the Jews and relentlessly Russifying the subject peoples□

Alexander the Great 356–323BC. King of Macedonia◊ and conqueror of the Persian Empire. Son of Philip◊ II of Macedon, he was tutored by Aristotle◊, and made his mark as a boy by taming the great horse Bucephalus. In 336 he succeeded to the throne on his father's assassination and immediately established his rule in Macedonia and Greece. In 334 he crossed the Dardanelles to what is now Asiatic Turkey, and began his assault on the Persian Empire (see Gordian Knot◊), defeating Darius◊ at Issus in 333, and treating the Persian king's wife, mother, and children humanely. Making a side-trip to Syria and Egypt, he founded Alexandria◊, and then resumed his pursuit of Darius. In 331 he defeated Darius again at Arbela on the Tigris with 47 000 men against a Persian army of half a million (which included an 'armoured division' of scythed chariots and elephants). He continued his trail of conquest in a great arc into N India as far as the Sutlej, where he was only deterred from going on to the Ganges by the revolt of his weary soldiers. Turning back, he attempted to consolidate his empire by intermarriage between his followers and his new subjects, himself marrying one of Darius' daughters in addition to his wife Roxana (daughter of a chieftain in the Hindu Kush). He died in Babylon, his intended capital. He lives in modern legend (see novels of Mary Renault◊), by his powerful personality, strategic skill, intellectual stature (he always travelled with a copy of the *Iliad*, and sponsored exploration and scientific experiment), and his vision of a humanely civilized empire□

Alexander Harold, 1st Earl Alexander of Tunis 1891–1969. British field marshal. He commanded the 1st Division from 1938, and in 1939 organized the last phases of the defence against the German advance through France, being the last man to leave Dunkirk◊. From Mar 1942 he was Commander-in-Chief Burma, and fought a delaying action against superior Japanese forces. In Aug 1942 he succeeded Auchinleck as Commander-in-Chief Middle East, and under Alexander's overall command, Montgomery◊ achieved victory at Alamein◊. The latter again served under him when he commanded the Allied armies in Italy 1944–5. He was Governor-General of Canada 1946–52; received an earldom 1952 and Order of Merit 1959□

Alexander Samuel 1859–1938. Australian philosopher. He originated the theory of Emergent Evolution: that the space-time matrix evolved matter; matter evolved life; life evolved mind; and finally God emerged from mind□

Alexander Nevski St 1220–63. Russian hero, son of the Grand Duke of Novgorod; in 1240 he defeated the Swedes on the banks of the Neva (hence Nevski), and in 1242 defeated the Teutonic◊ knights on frozen Lake Peipus□

Alexander Severus 208–35AD. Roman emperor from 222, who campaigned against the Persians with some success in 232, but was killed in a mutiny on his way to defend the Gaulish frontier□

Alexandra 1844–1925. Queen consort of Edward◊ VII of the UK, whom she married in 1863 (she was the daughter of Christian IX of Denmark). An annual Alexandra Rose Day in aid of hospitals commemorates her charitable work□

Alexandra 1872–1918. Last Tsarina of Russia◊; grand-daughter of Queen Victoria◊, she married Nicholas◊ II in 1894. From 1907 she fell under the spell of Rasputin◊, brought to the palace to try and cure her son of haemophilia, though there are no grounds for an alleged more intimate relationship between them. She was shot with the rest of her family by the Bolsheviks□

Alexandra Princess 1936– . Grand-daughter of George◊V, and sister of the Duke of Kent◊. She married businessman ***Angus Ogilvy*** 2nd son of the Earl of Airlie 1928– , in 1963□

Alexandretta see Iskenderun◊□

Alexandria chief port of Egypt; population 2 260 000. Founded by Alexander◊ the Great in 331 BC, it became the principal centre of Hellenistic culture (Callimachus◊, Claudian◊, Theocritus◊, Euclid◊, Hiero◊, Ptolemy◊), and the marble lighthouse on the island of Pharos in the harbour was one of the

Wonders of the World. Relics of the ancient period are the obelisks which now stand in London on the Thames (Cleopatra's Needle), in Paris, and in New York. Modern Alexandria is linked by canal with the Nile and is an industrial city with oil refineries□

Alexandrian Museum founded in Alexandria 330BC by Ptolemy◊ I Soter, it was the world's first state-funded scientific institution, with a library including much ancient Greek literature. It was finally destroyed in 646AD following the Arab conquest□

alfalfa plant, also known as lucerne, *Medicago sativa*, family Leguminosae◊, native to Europe and Asia, and an important fodder crop□

Alfonso XIII 1886–1941. King of Spain 1886–1931, who assumed power 1906 and married Princess Ena, grand-daughter of Queen Victoria◊ in the same year. Unpopular (a bomb was thrown at the wedding carriage), he was exiled on the declaration of a republic in 1931□

Alfred the Great 848–99. English king, born at Wantage in Berkshire, the youngest son of Ethelwulf, King of the W Saxons. He defeated the Danes at Ashdown in 871 and succeeded his brother Ethelred◊ the same year. By 878 the Danes had reasserted their power to such an extent that Alfred had to flee to Athelney◊, whence he finally emerged to win the victory of Edington, Wiltshire◊. By the Peace of Wedmore in 878, the Danish leader, Guthrum, agreed to withdraw from Wessex and from Mercia north of Watling Street. Despite some further Danish landings, Alfred was now free behind the defence of the strong navy he created, to establish a golden age of law and order. He greatly encouraged education, himself translating Bede◊'s *History* and Boethius◊' *Consolation of Philosophy* from Latin into English for popular use, and firmly establishing the *Anglo-Saxon Chronicle*, a record of happenings year-by-year (annals). He was buried at Winchester□

algae class of simple plants, *Algus*, in the division Thallophyta (see classification of plants◊). It includes single-celled forms such as the minute freshwater *Chlamydomonas* on the borderline between animal and plant, which swims freely in the water, and *Chlorella* which can increase its weight fourfold in 12 hours and has potential human food value, as has ***spirulina*** *Spirulina platensis* which is 70% protein, and rich in vitamin B12 and minerals. A simple multi-cellular form is *Spirogyra*, whose tiny filaments form part of the green scum on ponds. The class also includes the seaweeds◊. See chalk◊, diatom◊□

Algarve southernmost province of Portugal. It includes Cape St Vincent◊, and was formerly an independent kingdom. It is a tourist region; chief town Faro□

algebra solution of mathematical problems by the use of symbols (letters and signs) when figures are inadequate (the numbers involved may be very large or not exactly known). The basics of algebra were familiar in Babylon 2000BC, and were practised by the Arabs in the Middle Ages, Mohammed ibn Musa al Khwarizmi in the 9th century used the word *al-jabr* in the title of a book. More advanced algebra is used to work out general problems, e.g. the equations derived by Einstein◊ from his general theory of relativity, and the method of algebraic reasoning devised by George Boole◊ is used in working out the construction of computers□

Algeciras port in Spain; population 82 000□

Algeria Democratic and Popular Republic of

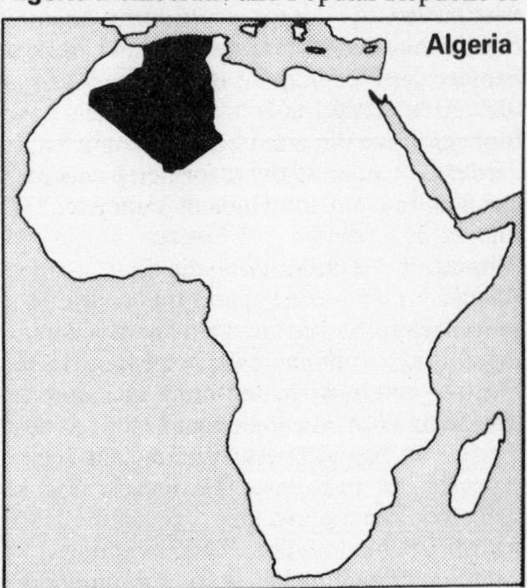

area 2 381 745 sq km/919 590sq mi
capital Algiers
towns ElDjazair, Wahran, Qacentina; ports are Oran, Annaba
features Atlas mountains, Barbary Coast
exports oil, natural gas, iron (Tindouf◊), wine, olive oil
currency dinar
population 21 351 000, Arab 75%, Berber 25%
language Arabic, official; Berber, French
religion Sunni Islam
famous people Ben Bella, Boumédienne
government one-party 'irreversible' socialism under National Liberation Front (FLN); President is Benjedid Chadli◊ and there is a National Assembly.
recent history a former French colony, Algeria became more closely integrated with France after World War II; after a bitter civil war

1954–62, de◊ Gaulle held referenda in both France and Algeria which resulted in Algerian independence under Muslim majority rule, many of the French colonists settling in France and especially in Corsica. Algeria supports an independent Western Sahara◊ against Morocco◊□

Algiers capital of Algeria; population 2 200 000. The old hill-fortress of the Turkish rulers, the Kasbah, survives□

Algiers Battle of. The bitter conflict in Algiers 1954-62 between the Algerian nationalist population and the French army and French settlers. The conflict ended with Algeriann independence in 1962□

alginate salt of alginic acid, obtained from brown seaweeds, and used in textiles, paper, food products, and pharmaceuticals□

Algonquin N American Indians of the sub-Arctic; noted for their porcupine quill ornamental work and the accurate prophecies of their shamans◊. Languages of an Algonquian type are spoken by many other American peoples on the Atlantic coast, etc. Akin to the Algonquins are the Mohicans and Mohegans (two related peoples confused by Fenimore Cooper◊) who formerly occupied Connecticut and the Hudson Valley: c 3000 survive□

Alhambra see under Granada◊□

Ali 600–61. Fourth caliph; the cousin and son-in-law of Mohammed◊, he had a claim to succeed him, but this was not conceded till 656. He was assassinated after an inept and stormy reign, but is important as the cause of the split in Islam between Sunni◊ and Shiah◊ – the former deny his right to the caliphate and the latter support it□

Ali Muhammad 1942– . Name adopted by American boxer Cassius Clay on joining the Black Muslim Movement; he was world heavyweight champion 1964–7 (losing the title for refusing military service), 1974–Feb 1978, Sept 1978–Oct 1980. He could 'dance like a butterfly and sting like a bee'□

Alia Ramiz 1925– . Albanian statesman. Once a partisan, he became chairman of the presidium (Head of State) 1982, and succeeded Hoxha 1985 as First Secretary of the Communist Party□

alibi Latin 'elsewhere': the legal defence that the accused was at some other place at the time of the commission of the crime□

Alicante seaport and resort in Valencia, Spain; population 251 390□

Alice Springs town in N Territory, Australia; population 11 000. Named after the wife of Sir Charles Todd, who directed construction of the S-N transcontinental telegraph line, it is a tourist centre. Nearby Pine Gap is a US intelligence centre□

alien someone owing allegiance to a foreign country. See citizen◊□

Aligarh city in Uttar Pradesh, India; population 254 000□

alimony money allowance given by court order to a former wife or husband after separation or divorce; the principle was extended in the USA in 1979 to live-in friends when 'palimony' was paid to Michelle Marvin, six-year companion of actor Lee Marvin, a judgment reversed 1981□

aliphatic compounds group of organic open chain compounds, either linear (lexane C_6H_{14}) or branched (propan-2-ol, $(CH_3)_2$ CHOH also known as isopropanol). See also aromatic◊ and cyclic◊ compounds□

alkali in chemistry, a base which is soluble in water; alkalis neutralize acids, turn red litmus blue, and are soapy to the touch; the hydroxides of reactive metals are alkalis□

alkaloids physiologically active and frequently poisonous substances contained in some plants, including morphine, cocaine, atropine, quinine, nicotine, strychnine, reserpine□

Alken Henry Thomas 1784–1851. Painter of British field sports□

Alkmaar town in the Netherlands; population 67 550. There is a famous cheese market□

Allah Islamic name for God, Arabic *al-Ilah* 'the God'□

Allahabad holy city in Uttar Pradesh, India; population 514 000. The first Indian National Congress, held here in 1885, made it the focus of opposition to British rule; Gandhi◊'s ashes were scattered here and it was the home of Nehru◊□

Allan David 1744–96. Scottish painter with a vein of realistic humour, as in 'Scotch Wedding'□

Allan Sir William 1782–1850. Scottish historical painter, e.g. scenes from the Waverley novels by Scott◊□

Allegheny mountains mountain range in Pennsylvania/Virginia, USA. They initially hindered western migration, the first settlement to the west being Marietta in 1788□

allegiance loyalty as pledged to the Sovereign (UK), or other symbol of the state, in an ***Oath of Allegiance*** taken by aliens on being granted citizenship□

allegory story having a meaning other than that immediately apparent, such as Spenser◊'s *Faërie Queene*, Bunyan◊'s *Pilgrim's Progress*, and (arguably) Tolkien◊'s *Lord of the Rings*□

Allegri Gregorio 1582–1652. Italian composer whose *Miserere* for the Sistine◊ chapel was reserved for performance only by the chapel choir until Mozart◊ (then only 14) defeated the ban by listening to it and writing out the music from memory□

allelopathy see under plant◊□

Allen Bog of. Morasses east of the Shannon, Republic of Ireland, the country's main source of peat fuel□

Allen Ethan 1738–89. American hero of the War of Independence◊; he led the Green Mountain Boys (irregular militia) in taking Ticonderoga◊ 1775; he was captured in an expedition against Montreal and imprisoned by the British 1775–8□

Allen Woody. Pseudonym of American comedian, film director, and jazz clarinettist Allen Stewart Konigsberg 1935– . His films include *Play It Again Sam* 1972 (writer, actor), *Annie Hall* 1977 (Academy Award) and *Zelig* 1983, all of which he also directed□

Allenby Edmund Henry Hynman; 1st Viscount Allenby 1861–1936. British Field Marshal. As commander of the British Forces in the Near East 1917–19, he captured Jerusalem, and his victory over the Turks at Megiddo in Sept 1918 was followed almost at once by Turkish capitulation. His campaign was a classic of mobility and surprise tactics, using the Bible as a handbook□

Allende Salvador 1909–73. President of Chile 1970–3, he was the first Marxist head of state to be elected by democratic vote in the Western world; he advocated a 'quiet revolution' to Socialism. The country was destabilized by anti-government forces within the country, probably aided by the American CIA; Allende died during fighting following a military coup□

allergy abnormal bodily sensitivity to certain foreign substances, such as specific proteins◊, animals, dust, etc. This results in an exaggerated response of the natural defence mechanism. Drugs may reduce sensitivity or produce tolerance to allergens□

All Fools' Day see April◊ Fools' Day□

Allied Mobile Force see North◊ Atlantic Treaty Organization◊□

Allies the. Term used for the 23 countries allied against Germany in World War I, notably Britain, France, Italy, Russia, and US; and for the 49 countries allied against the Axis◊ in World War II, notably Britain, US and USSR□

alligator an American reptile of the crocodile◊ family□

Allingham Margery 1904–66. British detective novelist, creator of detective Albert Campion, as in *More Work for the Undertaker* 1949□

allium see onion◊□

allopathy treatment of disease by exciting a disease process of another kind alien to the initial illness□

alloy a metal blended with some other metallic or non-metallic substance in order to give it special qualities, such as resistance to corrosion, greater hardness, tensile strength, etc. Among the oldest alloys is bronze◊, and among the most recent are the superplastic alloys which may stretch 100% at specific temperatures. For example, at 450°C, aluminium plus zirconium stretches so easily that it can be injected into moulds as easily as plastic. Today, complex alloys are widespread, e.g. a cheaper alternative to gold in dentistry is made of chromium, cobalt, molybdenum, and titanium□

All Saints' Day festival on 1 Nov for all Christian saints and martyrs who have no special day of their own□

All Souls' Day festival on 2 Nov observed in the Catholic Church in the conviction that the faithful, by prayer and self-denial can hasten the deliverance of souls expiating their sins in Purgatory◊□

allspice a type of spice◊□

Allston Washington 1779–1843. American artist, a Romantic◊ painter of religious subjects, known as 'the American Titian'□

Alma Ata capital of the Republic of Kazakh, USSR; population 871 000□

alma mater Latin 'bounteous mother', the title given by the Romans to Ceres◊; it is applied to universities and schools as 'foster-mothers' of their students□

Alma-Tadema Sir Laurence 1836–1912. Anglo-Dutch artist; his depictions of Greek and Roman life enjoyed a revival in the 1980s□

Almeraila town in Andalusia region, Spain; population 141 000. The area is noted for white grapes□

almond small W Asian tree *Prunus amygdalus*, family Rosaceae◊, with a green fruit and oval, edible nut-like seed□

aloe genus of African plants, family Liliaceae◊, with long fleshy leaves from which the purgative drug aloes is prepared□

Aloysius St 1568–91. Italian Jesuit who died while nursing plague victims. He is the patron saint of youth. Feast day: 21 Jun□

alpaca a species of llama. See under camel◊ family□

alpha and **omega** first (α) and last (ω) letters of the Greek alphabet, hence the beginning and end, or sum total, of anything□

alphabet written symbols denoting a given sound or sounds (*alpha* and *beta* – the first 2 letters of the Greek alphabet). The earliest known alphabet is that discovered at Ugarit◊;

of the 13th century BC, it comprises 22 letters expressing consonants only. The Latin alphabet, derived via Phoenician◊, Greek, and Etruscan◊ versions of this early prototype, has survived almost unchanged as our modern alphabet□

alpha particle see particle◊□

Alps mountain chain, the barrier between N Italy and France, Germany and Austria.
famous peaks include ***Mont Blanc*** the highest at 4807 m/15 772 ft, first climbed by Jacques Balmat and Michel Paccard 1786; ***Matterhorn*** in the Pennine Alps 4477 m/14 688 ft, first climbed by Edward Whymper 1865 (four of the party of seven were killed when the rope broke during their descent); ***Eiger*** in the Bernese Alps/Oberland, 3970 m/13 101 ft, with a near-vertical rock wall on the north face; ***Jungfrau*** 4166 m/13 668 ft, of exceptional beauty, and ***Finsteraarhorn*** 4274 m/14 014 ft.
famous passes include ***Brenner*** the lowest, Austria/Italy; ***Great St Bernard*** the highest, 2472 m/8110 ft, Italy/Switzerland (by which Napoleon◊ marched into Italy 1800); ***Little St Bernard*** Italy/France (which Hannibal◊ is thought to have used), and ***St Gotthard*** S Switzerland, which Suvorov◊ used when ordered by the Tsar to withdraw his troops from Italy. All have been superseded by all-weather road/rail tunnels. See also Thomas Cook◊ and Whymper◊. The Alps extend into Yugoslavia with the Julian and Dinaric Alps□

Alps Australian. Highest area of the E Highlands in Victoria/New South Wales, Australia, noted for winter sports. They include the ***Snowy mountains*** and ***Mt Kosciusko*** Australia's highest mountain 2229 m/7316 ft (it was first noted by Polish-born Sir Paul Strzelecki 1829, and named after the Polish hero)□

Alps Lunar. See moon under planet◊□

Alps Southern. Mountain range extending along the W central coast of South Island, New Zealand; the highest peak is Mt Cook◊□

Alsace-Lorraine area of NE France which has been disputed since the 4th century between France and Germany; conquered by the Germans in 1870–1, (chiefly for its iron ores) it was regained by France in 1919, then again annexed by Germany 1940–4 when it was liberated by the Allies◊. It now forms the modern French regions of ***Alsace*** capital Strasbourg; population 1 570 000 and ***Lorraine*** capital Nancy; population 2 320 000. The German dialect spoken does not have equal rights with French, and there is autonomist sentiment. Outdated iron and steel industries are being replaced by electronics, chemicals, and precision engineering. The ***Cross of Lorraine*** with double cross bars, emblem of Joan◊ of Arc, was adopted by the Free French forces in World War II□

alsatian a breed of dog◊□

alsike see clover◊□

Altai Mountains mountain system of W Siberia/Mongolia; the highest peak is Belukha 4540 m/15 157 ft□

Altamira see under Santander◊□

Altdorf town on Lake Lucerne, Switzerland; population 9000. It was the scene of the legendary exploits of William Tell◊□

Altdorfer Albrecht 1480–1538. German artist, whose *'Landscape with a Footbridge'* 1518/20, in the National Gallery, London, is the first known European landscape without figures□

alternating current electric current flowing first in one direction and then in the opposite one, so that the voltage can be raised or lowered economically by a transformer – high for transmission, low for utilization and safety (in railways, factories, domestic appliances)□

alternation of generations appearance of two different forms of a plant or animal in successive generations, which may reproduce in different ways, as occurs in jellyfish◊ and ferns◊□

alternator see generator◊□

Althing the parliament of Iceland, established c 930 and the oldest in the world□

Altmark German auxiliary cruiser which was intercepted and cornered in a Norwegian fjord Feb 1940 by HMS *Cossack* under Captain Vian; 299 captive British merchant sailors were released from the cruiser. This became known as the ***Altmark Incident***□

alto highest male voice, more properly counter-tenor◊, or lowest female voice, contralto◊□

alum white crystalline powder, a double sulphate of potassium and aluminium, which is used in paper-making, and to help colour 'take' in dyeing textiles□

aluminium element
symbol Al
atomic number 13
physical description silvery-white metal
features the most common metal, remarkable for lightness, easy working, and the variety of its alloys, which include; aluminium brass and aluminium bronze, as well as such light alloys as aluminium copper, aluminium sillicon, etc., and the new super plastic alloys (see zirconium◊).
uses kitchenware, aircraft, car parts, electric conductors, sheathing for nuclear reactor fuel and as a 'window' in X-ray tubes□

Alva Ferdinand Alvarez de Toledo, Duke of Alva1508–82. Spanish soldier; he exercised a reign of terror, as Governor of the Netherlands 1567–73, to suppress an economic-religious revolt by the Dutch; he was forced to admit defeat□

Alwyn William 1905–85. British composer, especially noted for film scores including *Desert Victory, The Way Ahead,* and *Odd Man Out*□

Alzheimer's Disease see dementia◊□

Amalekites in Old Testament; a Semitic◊ tribe, inveterate enemies of the Israelites whom they harried after the crossing of the Red Sea; defeated by Saul◊ and David◊, they were finally crushed by Hezekiah◊□

amanita genus of fungi◊ closely allied to *Agaricus*◊; species have a ring (volva) around the stem, warty patches on the cap, and clear white gills; many species are highly coloured and poisonous e.g. ***fly agaric*** *A muscaria*, and the ***death cap*** *A phalloides*□

Amarillo town in the Texan panhandle, USA; population 149 000. The centre of the world's largest cattle-producing area, it processes the live animal into frozen supermarket packets in a single continuous operation on an assembly line. It also assembles all the nuclear warheads for Western defence□

Amarna Tell el. See Akhetaton◊□

amaryllidaceae family of bulbous plants allied to the Liliaceae◊, and mainly tropical or subtropical, e.g. ***agave*** or ***Mexican 'century plant'*** *Agave americana* which flowers only after many years; and the ***tuberose*** a perennial Mexican agave *Polyanthes tuberosa.* See also Sisal◊, Tequila◊. Temperate members include the daffodil◊ and snowdrop◊□

Amaterasu see under Shinto◊□

Amazon a member of a group of legendary female warriors living near the Black sea, who cut off their right breasts to use the bow more easily; their queen, Penthesilea, was killed by Achilles◊ at the siege of Troy□

Amazon the world's largest river by volume, and 2nd longest 6518 km/4050 mi; main headstreams the Marañón and Ucayali, which rise in central Peru and unite to flow east across Brazil. The total network of navigable waterways drains nearly half S America; the estuary is 80 km/50 mi wide, and fresh water remains at the surface 65 km/40 mi out to sea. The name derives from American Indian 'destroyer of boats', navigation being hindered by floods, rapids, and tidal waves□

Amazonia Amazon basin which takes up half S America, 5 million sq km/2 million sq mi; its rainforest supplies 25% of the world's oxygen. It has been bulldozed for timber and agriculture, although the soil rapidly loses fertility; from 1979 there was some reconsideration of this policy. Its resources also include natural gas and oil, iron, bauxite, gold, nickel, copper, and tin. The Trans-Amazon Highway crosses it east to west□

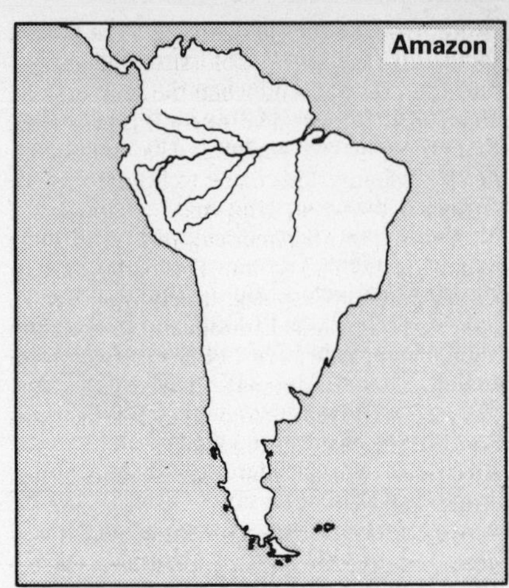

ambary see kenaf◊□

ambassador highest ranking officer in the diplomatic service□

amber fossilized gum from coniferous trees of the Middle Tertiary period, often washed ashore on the Baltic coast with plant and animal specimens preserved in it. When rubbed, it attracts light objects, such as feathers, as the ancient Greeks noticed. The effect is due to acquisition of (negative) electric charge, hence the adaptation of the Greek word for amber, *elektron*, for the negatively charged particle, the electron, and the derived term 'electricity'□

ambergris see sperm whale, under whale◊□

Ambler Eric 1909– . British thriller writer, who has made brilliant use of Balkan and Levant settings, e.g. *The Mask of Dimitrios* 1939, *Journey into Fear* 1940□

Ambrose St 340–97. Father of the Church. Roman governor of N Italy, he was spontaneously chosen bishop of Milan in 374, though not yet baptized. He wrote many hymns, introduced hymn singing to public worship, and devised the Ambrosian plain chant still used in Milan□

ambrosia Greek 'immortal', the food of the gods, supposed to confer eternal life□

amen Hebrew 'so be it', hence commonly used at the end of a prayer□

Amenhotep four Egyptian pharaohs, including:

Amenhotep III 1400BC, built great monuments at Thebes, including the temples at Luxor;

two portrait statues at his tomb were known to the Greeks as the Colossi of Memnon – one was cracked, and when the temperature changed at dawn gave out a weird sound, then thought supernatural. His son ***Amenhotep IV*** changed his name to Ikhnaton◊□

America the great land mass composed of N, Central and S America; area 42 000 000 sq km/16 000 000 sq mi. The name derives from Amerigo Vespucci, falsely supposed to have been the first Euuropean to reach the mainland in 1497: see Leif Ericsson◊, John Lloyd◊, and Columbus◊. It is usually considered as divided into the North◊ and South◊ American continents□

American Civil War see Civil◊ War, American□

American Federation of Labor and Congress of Industrial Organizations federation of US trade unions (AFL-CIO)□

American Independence War of. The revolt 1775–83 of the British N American colonies which resulted in the establishment of the USA. It was caused by colonial resentment at the contemporary attitude that commercial or industrial interests of any colony should be subordinate to those of the mother country; and the unwillingness of the colonists to pay for a standing army.

It was preceded by:

1773 a government tax on tea led citizens disguised as N American Indians to board the ships carrying the tea and throw it into the harbour, the 'Boston Tea Party'

1774–5 the ***First Continental Congress*** held in Philadelphia to call for civil disobedience in reply to British measures

The War:

1775 19 Apr hostilities began at Lexington and Concord Massachusetts, the first shots being fired when British troops, sent to seize illegal military stores, were attacked by the local militia (Paul Revere◊). The first battle was ***Bunker Hill*** Massachusetts, 17 Jun 1775, in which the colonists were defeated; George Washington◊ was appointed colonial commander soon afterwards

1775–6 the ***Second Continental Congress*** on 4 Jul 1776 issued the Declaration of Independence◊. See also Ticonderoga◊

1776 27 Aug at ***Long Island*** Washington was defeated, forced to evacuate New York and retire to Pennsylvania but re-crossed the Delaware to win successes at ***Trenton*** (26 Dec) and ***Princeton*** (3 Jan 1777)

1777 a British plan, for Sir William Howe (advancing from New York) and General Burgoyne (from Canada) to link up, miscarried. Burgoyne surrendered at ***Saratoga*** (17 October), but Howe invaded Pennsylvania, defeating Washington at ***Brandywine*** (11 Sept) and ***Germantown*** (4 Oct), and occupying Philadelphia; Washington wintered at Valley Forge 1777–8

1778 France and Spain entered the war on the American side (see John Paul Jones◊)

1780 12 May capture of ***Charleston*** the most notable of a series of British victories in the American south, but they alienated support by attempting to enforce conscription

1781 19 Oct Cornwallis, besieged in ***Yorktown*** by Washington and the French fleet, surrendered

1782 peace negotiations opened

1783 3 Sept ***Treaty of Paris*** American independence recognized□

American Indian an aboriginal of the Americas. They were called Indians by Columbus◊ because he believed he had found, not the New World, but a new route to India. They entered N America from Asia via the former land-bridge, Beringia, from 35 000BC or even 60 000BC. Their languages and cultures developed in great variety and intermingled. They were the first cultivators of maize, potatoes, sweet potatoes, manioc, peanuts, peppers, tomatoes, pumpkins, cacao, and chicle and were the first users of the drugs tobacco◊, coco (cocaine)◊, peyote (mescalin)◊, and cinchona (quinine)◊.

They number:

Canada 300 000, including the Inuits; the largest group are the Six Nations (Iroquois), with a reserve near Brantford, Ontario, for 7000. They are organized in the National Indian Brotherhood of Canada.

United States 1 000 000, more than half living on reservations, mainly in Arizona, where the Navajo have the largest of all reservations, Oklahoma, New Mexico, California, N Carolina, S Dakota. The population level is thought now to be the same as at the time of Columbus, but now includes many people who are of mixed race. There is an organized American Indian Movement (AIM).

Latin America comparatively few pure Indians, the majority being mestizo (mixed Indian-Spanish descent), e.g. half the 12 million in Bolivia and Peru. Since the 1960s there has been an increasing stress on the Indian half of their inheritance in terms of their language and culture. The few 'wild tribes' formerly beyond white contact are being transported or killed in the clearing of Amazonia◊. See also the countries of the Americas and cross-referenced items in the list below.

Peoples

North America: Arctic Inuit-Aleut◊; ***Sub-Arctic*** Algonquin◊, Cree, Ottawa; ***NE***

Woodlands Huron, Iroquois◊, Mohican◊, Shawnee (Tecumseh◊); ***Great Plains***◊ Blackfoot, Cheyenne, Comanche, Pawnee, Sioux◊; ***NW Coast*** Chinook, Tlingit◊, Tsimshian; ***Desert West*** Apache◊, Navajo◊, Pueblo◊, Hopi, Mojave, Shoshone; ***SE Woodlands*** Cherokee, Choctaw, Creek, Hopewell◊, Natchez◊, Seminole.

Central America: Maya◊, Toltec◊, Aztec◊, Mexican.

South America: Eastern Carib◊, Xingu◊; ***Central*** Guarani◊, Miskito◊; ***Western*** Araucanian◊, Aymara◊, Chimu◊, Inca◊, Jivaro◊, Quechua◊□

America's Cup international seven-race series (every three years) for yachts (12-metre sloops). First contest (round the Isle of Wight) won by US yacht *America* 1851 and trophy held by USA until 1984 (when *Australia II* was the winner) in races off Newport, Rhode Island; next series 1987 to be held in Western Australia□

americium element
symbol Am
atomic number 95
physical description metallic
features an artificial radioactive element, made by bombardment of an isotope of uranium◊ with alpha particles
uses none at present□

Amersfoort town in the Netherlands; population 87 200□

Amery Julian 1919– . British Conservative politician, the son of L S Amery◊; he was Minister for Housing 1970–2 and for Foreign and Commonwealth Affairs 1972–4□

Amery Leopold Stennett 1873–1955. British Conservative◊ politician; Secretary of State for India and Burma 1940–5; famous for his exhortation to Neville Chamberlain◊ in May 1940, in words adapted from Cromwell◊: 'In the name of God, go!'□

amethyst semi-precious stone, a kind of quartz coloured violet by a little manganese; it is traditionally used for a bishop's ring of office□

Amiens capital of Picardy, France; population 136 000. There is a fine Gothic cathedral. An RAF raid (Operation Jericho) on Amiens prison in 1944, where Resistance prisoners were held, allegedly carried out to facilitate escapes, is still controversial□

Amiens Battle of. The battle in 1918 that marked the launching of Haig◊'s victorious offensive in World War I□

Amies Hardy 1909– . British couturier. Noted from 1934 for his tailored clothes for women, he designed even more successfully for men from 1959. He is one of Elizabeth II's dressmakers□

Amin Dada Idi 1926– . President of Uganda 1971–9. He led the coup which deposed Obote◊ in 1971, expelled the Asian community in 1972, and exercised a reign of terror over his own people. He fled when 'rebel' Ugandan and Tanzanian troops invaded his country in 1979□

amine derivative of ammonia (NH_3) in which one or more of the three hydrogen atoms has been replaced by one or more hydrocarbon radicals (e.g. CH_3)□

amino acid any of a series of organic acids which have amino groups (NH_2) in place of a hydrogen atom in the hydrocarbon radical; they are found in all plant and animal tissue and link together to form proteins. The simplest is ***glycine***, which is stored in the liver of animals and 'burnt' by the muscles to produce energy. Its characteristic radio signal is a means of checking by radio telescope whether animal life of the same type as our own exists in space□

Amis Kingsley 1922– . British novelist, author of *Lucky Jim* 1954, a comic realization of life in a 'red-brick' university; and *Take a Girl Like You* 1960, set in the 'promiscuous' sixties□

Amman capital of Jordan; population 700 000. The Old Testament Rabbath-Ammon, it was the capital of Israel's enemies, the Ammonites, who made human sacrifices to their god, Moloch. There is a fine Roman amphitheatre. Many of the population are Palestinian refugees□

ammeter instrument for measuring electric current□

Ammon in Egyptian mythology, the king of the gods, the equivalent of Zeus◊/Jupiter◊; the name is also spelt Amen/Amun, as in the name of the pharaoh Tutankh*amen*; he had famous temples at Siwa oasis, Libya and Thebes◊, Greece. See Ikhnaton◊, Ra◊□

ammonia colourless, pungent-smelling gas (NH_3) of about two-thirds the density of air; so-named because ammonium chloride, used in soldering, was formerly made from camel dung in the neighbourhood of Ammon's Libyan temple. Today its compounds are made synthetically and used in many industrial processes, but overwhelmingly in nitrogenous fertilizers□

ammonite a fossil mollusc. See under cephalopod◊□

Ammonite a member of an ancient Semitic◊ people. See Amman◊□

Amnesty International organization established 1961 to mitigate and publicize the treatment of political prisoners worldwide; politically unaligned, it was awarded a Nobel prize in 1977□

amoeba one of the simplest living animals, genus *Amoeba* belonging to the Protozoa◊. A minute speck of colourless protoplasm found in fresh water, its activities are controlled by its nucleus, and it feeds by flowing round its food and engulfing it; it reproduces by 'fission' (splitting), not sexually. Some of its relatives are harmful parasites. See amoebiasis◊□

amoebiasis infection of the intestines, caused by the amoeba◊ *Endmoeba histolytica,* resulting in chronic dysentery and consequent weakness and dehydration. Endemic in the Third World, it is now occurring in Europe and N America□

amorite a member of an ancient Semitic◊ people who provided a number of Babylonian kings. See Hammurabi◊□

Amos c760BC. First of the Old Testament prophets◊□

Amoy see Xiamen◊□

ampere unit (symbol A) of electrical current producing a force between long, straight parallel conductors, one metre apart in a vacuum, of $2x10^{-7}$ newtons◊ per metre length□

Ampère André Marie 1775–1836. French physicist and mathematician. The ammeter◊ and ampere◊ are named after him□

amphetamine synthetic drug ($C_6H_5CH_2CHNH_2CH_3$, or its sulphate or phosphate), which stimulates the central nervous system. It relieves depression, increases alertness, and counteracts fatigue. After World War II it was used by teenagers for 'kicks', notably as benzedrine, or in the barbiturate◊-amphetamine combination known as 'purple hearts'□

amphibia class of vertebrates (Greek 'double life'), which generally spend their larval stage in fresh water, transferring to land at maturity. However, they generally return to water to breed. Like fish and reptiles, they continue to grow throughout life, and cannot maintain a temperature greatly differing from that of their environment. The class includes ***caecilians***, limbless members of the order Gymnophiona/Apoda, which are worm-like in appearance and are chiefly tropical; ***salamanders***◊; and ***frogs***◊ and ***toads***□

amphitheatre oval or circular building (Greek *amphi* 'around'), used by the Romans for gladiatorial contests, wild beast fights, etc. See Colosseum◊□

amphora large pottery storage jar in the Graeco-Roman world used for wine, oil, and dry goods□

ampulla narrow-necked Roman bottle, today used for holy oil in coronations, etc.□

Amritsar industrial city in the Punjab, India; population 458 000. It is the holy city of Sikhism◊, with the Golden Temple (from which armed fanatics were evicted by the Indian Army 1984, and which is still the headquarters of the Akali Dal Sikh (moderate) political party, and of the extremist All-India Sikh Students' Federation) and Guru Nanak University, named after the first Sikh guru□

amphibian: life cycle

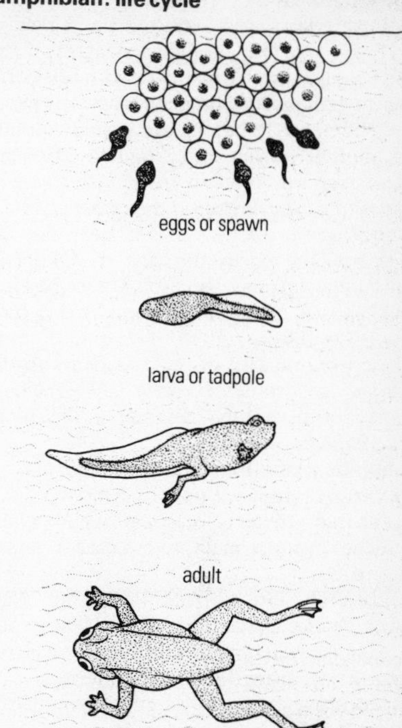

Amritsar Massacre the killing of 379 people in Amritsar in 1919, when British troops under Brigadier-General Dyer fired on 10 000 followers of Gandhi◊□

Amritsar Siege storming of the Golden Temple in Amritsar by Indian General Dayal in 1984 to flush out Sikh 'extremists' (325 killed). See Sikhism◊□

Amsterdam capital of the Netherlands; population 738 450. Canals cut through the city link it with the N Sea and the Rhine, and as a port it is second only to Rotterdam. There is shipbuilding, printing, food processing, banking, and insurance. Schipol international airport is to the south-west. Art galleries include Rijksmuseum, Stedelijk, Vincent Van Gogh Museum, and Rembrandt house. Notable also are the Royal Palace 1655, and the Anne Frank◊ house□

Amu Darya river (anciently Oxus) in Soviet central Asia, flowing 2540 km/1490 mi from the Pamirs◊ to the Aral◊ Sea□

Amundsen Roald 1872–1928. Norwegian explorer, who raced Scott◊ to the S Pole in 1911. He was also the first navigator of the NW Passage; in 1926 he joined with Ellsworth and the Italian Gen Nobile to cross the N Pole (Spitsbergen-Alaska) in an airship; Nobile led another airship expedition in 1928 and Amundsen was killed in an aircrash trying to rescue him. See Arctic◊ and Antarctic◊ lists□

Amur river in the Soviet Far East, flowing 4345 km/2700 mi to the Sea of Okhotsk, much of it forming the Sino-Soviet border. The Treaties of Aigun 1858 and Peking 1860 ceded 984 200 sq km/ 380 000 sq mi of territory north and east of the two rivers to the Tsarist government; from 1962 China demanded the return of the area, and there have been border clashes□

anableps a carp-like four-eyed fish□

anabolic steroid see under hormone◊□

anabranch stream (Greek *ana* 'again') which branches from a main river, then reunites with it□

Anabranch Great. Anabranch◊ in New South Wales, Australia which leaves the Darling near Menindee, and joins the Murray below the Darling-Murray confluence□

anaconda a species of S American constricting snake◊□

Anaconda town in Montana, USA; population 10 000. It has the world's largest copper plant□

anaemia condition of someone who has too few red blood cells or too little haemoglobin◊, so that the sufferer becomes quickly tired, faint and breathless. It may result from iron deficiency (as in pregnant women), be linked with rheumatoid◊ arthritis, be the result of nuclear radiation, or inherited. Genetic anaemic diseases include ***sickle cell anaemia,*** found in African and Asian peoples, in which sufferers have two genes producing distorted, sickle-shaped red blood cells (those with only one affected gene remain healthy and are also resistant to malarial infection) and ***thalassaemia,*** found in Mediterranean peoples, in which the red blood cells are also distorted. ***Pernicious anaemia*** is a failure of the stomach to secrete the substances necessary to produce blood from food, and is cured by doses of vitamin B12□

anaesthesia an induced state of insensibility to pain. Sir Humphry Davy◊ first suggested that nitrous oxide (laughing gas) be used to produce loss of sensation in surgery, etc., and in 1844 Horace Wells, a New England dentist, had a tooth extracted in this way. Chloroform, used by James Simpson◊ on women in childbirth, received the royal accolade when used by Queen Victoria at the birth of Prince Leopold in 1853. Varied anaesthetics are now given, both general and local, and there have been experiments with acupuncture◊ and hypnosis◊, which are less easily controlled, but have no side-effects. ***Epidural anaesthesia*** (injection into the space outside the outermost membrane covering the spinal cord) is used in childbirth, and increasingly for major abdominal operations; the patient remains conscious, and there is reduced risk of complication, with quicker recovery□

analgesic drug reducing sensitivity to pain, including aspirin, paracetamol◊; and, for deep-seated internal pain, morphine◊, pethidine◊, etc.□

Anand Marg fanatical Indian religious sect, 'the pathway to bliss'; their leader ***Prahbat Ranjan Sarkar*** 1921– claims to be god incarnate. Imprisoned for alleged murder of defectors from the sect, he was released after acquittal in 1978□

anarchism the political belief that society should have no government, laws, police, etc., but should be a free association of all its members. It is alleged to have existed in the early Christian Church, and its theorists have included Tolstoy◊, Gandhi◊, W Godwin◊, Shelley◊, P J Proudhon◊, Bakunin◊, and especially Kropotkin◊. Popularly, and often erroneously, anarchism is associated with terrorism, as with the bombing and shooting incidents attributed to the 'Angry Brigade' in Britain 1968–71. In the 1980s in the UK, the activities of anarchist groups have been directed towards peace and animal rights issues, and in demonstrating against huge financial and business corporations ('Stop the City' campaign)□

Anastasia 1901–18. Russian grand duchess, youngest daughter of Nicholas◊ II. She was killed with her parents, but was often alleged to have escaped. Most famous of the claimants was Anna Anderson 1902–84, whose claim was rejected by the German Federal Supreme Court in 1970□

Anatolia Turkey-in-Asia (Turkish Anadolu)□

ANC abbreviation for African◊ National Congress□

ancestor worship religious attitude to deceased members of a group or family prevalent in societies which have religions other than Christian, Jewish, or Muslim. Adherents believe that the souls of the dead remain involved in this world, and may influence it if appealed to□

Anchorage port of Alaska, USA; population 126 500□

anchovy a small fish of the herring◊ family□

Ancien Régime see under French◊ Revolution□

ancient lights see under prescription◊□

Ancona port and naval base, capital of Mare, Italy; population 106 500□

Andalusia fertile autonomous region (Spanish Andalucía) of S Spain (includes Almería◊, Cádiz◊, Córdoba◊, Granada◊, Málaga◊, and Seville◊); population 6 442 000. It is noted for its Moorish architecture, having been under Muslim rule 8–15th centuries□

Andamans island group in the Bay of Bengal, forming with the Nicobars a Union Territory of India; population 188 255. It was a penal settlement till 1945, and its pygmy aboriginal people have been reduced to a few hundred, but were once a race spread over E Asia□

Andean Group organization established in 1969 for tariff integration and economic cooperation among Bolivia, Chile, Colombia, Ecuador, Peru, Venezuela□

Andersen Hans Christian 1805–75. Danish writer of children's stories, born at Odense. Son of a cobbler, he was backward at school and was too clumsy to be an actor, as he had wanted. Fame came with his fairy stories, which he himself did not originally value, including 'The Ugly Duckling', 'The Emperor's New Clothes', and 'The Snow Queen'□

Anderson Carl David 1905– . American physicist, who discovered the positive electron or positron in 1932; he shared a Nobel prize 1936□

Anderson Elizabeth Garrett 1836–1917. British doctor, born Garrett. She qualified in 1865 as a medical practitioner, despite prejudiced opposition, and established a dispensary for women in 1866, which survives as the Elizabeth Garrett Anderson Hospital (diagnostic). In 1908 she became mayor of her native Aldeburgh, England's first woman mayor□

Anderson Sir John. See Lord Waverley◊□

Anderson Maxwell 1888–1959. American playwright, noted for his World War I *What Price Glory?* 1924□

Anderson Sherwood 1876–1941. American writer, noted for his short stories of a Mid-West small town – *Winesburg, Ohio* 1919□

Andes mountain system (cordillera) forming the western fringe of S America; 6500 km/4000 mi long; its peaks (mostly volcanic) exceed 3600 m/12 000 ft for half its length, and include Aconcagua, the highest mountain in the New World, Cotopaxi, Chimborazo, Cerro de Pasco, Huascaran, Illampu, and Ojos del Salado. Newcomers to the Andean plateau, which includes Lake Titicaca◊, suffer from *puna*, mountain sickness, but indigenous peoples have hearts and lungs adapted to altitude. Andean mineral wealth includes gold, silver, tin, tungsten, bismuth, vanadium, copper, lead□

Andhra Pradesh E central state of India
area 276 814 sq km/ sq mi
capital Hyderabad
towns Secunderabad
population 47 900 000
language Telugu
history formed 1953 from the Telegu-speaking areas of Madras◊, and enlarged 1956 from the former Hyderabad state□

Andorra

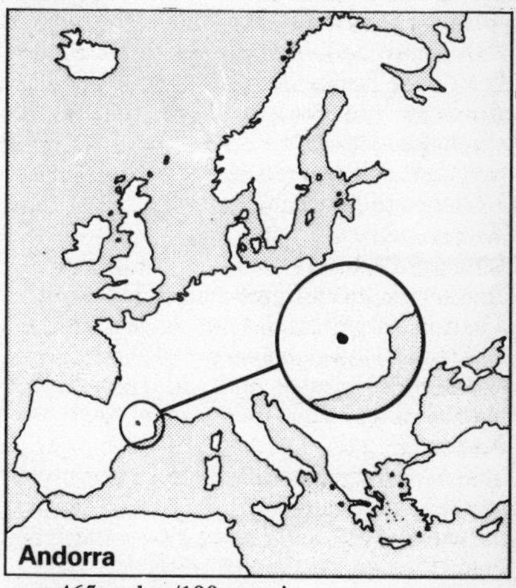

area 465 sq km/190 sq mi
capital Andorre-la-Vella
features set in narrrow valleys of the E Pyrenees
exports main industries tourism and smuggling
currency French franc and Spanish peseta
population 45 000, Andorrans 25%, immigrant Spanish workers 75%
language Catalan official; French, Spanish
religion Roman Catholicism
government executive council (head of government (Josep Pintat Soleus from 1984), and legislative general council of the valleys, which elects a 'first syndic'
recent history traditionally made independent by Charlemagne, Andorra was placed 1278 under the joint suzerainty of the Count of Foix (his rights now being vested in the President of France) and the Bishop of Urgel in Spain, but their powers are nominal□

André John 1751–80. British soldier. He served in America from 1774, and was chosen to negotiate when Benedict Arnold◊ offered to betray West◊ Point to the British during the War of American◊ Independence. Captured and hanged by the Americans, he was commemorated by a monument in Westminster Abbey□

Andrea del Sarto 1486–1531. Italian Renaissance painter, born d'Agnola, but called del Sarto because he was the son of a tailor. Born in Florence, he is noted for fresco and portrait work, and painted his wife in various roles. In 1518, he went to work for Francis◊ I in France, but returned to Italy in 1519 with funds to enlarge the royal French art collection; he spent it on a house for himself and never went back. His frescoes in Florence (especially the *Birth of the Virgin*) rank among the greatest of the Renaissance□

Andrew St d. 70AD. Apostle◊, who worked with James and John, and with his brother Peter, as a fisherman; they formed the inner group of the disciples. Traditionally, he accompanied John to Ephesus◊, preached in Scythia◊, and was crucified at Patras◊ on an X-shaped (St Andrew's) cross; his feast day is 30 Nov and he is the patron saint of Scotland□

Andrew Prince 1960– . Prince of the UK, 2nd son of Queen Elizabeth◊ II. He served as a helicopter pilot with HMS *Invincible* in the Falkland Island Conflict◊ in 1982 and married Miss Sarah Ferguson on 23 Jul 1986. He was made Duke of York on the same day□

Andrews Julie 1935– . British singer-actress. Formerly a child performer with her mother and father in a music-hall act, she was the original *My Fair Lady* 1956 on stage, and made the film *The Sound of Music* 1964□

Androcles 1st century AD. Roman slave. Traditionally, he fled from a cruel master to the African desert, where he drew a thorn from the paw of a crippled lion. Recaptured, and sentenced to combat a lion in the arena, he found his adversary was his old friend. Tiberius◊ was said to have freed them both. See G B Shaw◊□

Andromeda in Greek mythology, a princess chained to a rock as a sacrifice to a sea monster. She was rescued by Perseus◊ and gives her name to a constellation□

Andropov industrial city (until 1984 Rybinsk) on the Volga in W USSR; population 243 000. There is a large reservoir for hydroelectric power□

Andropov Yuri 1914–84. Soviet statesman. As ambassador to Hungary, he was involved in the suppression of the revolt in 1956, but is alleged to have opposed the invasion of Czechoslovakia in 1968 while head of the KGB◊ 1967–May 1982. In Nov 1982 he succeeded Brezhnev◊ as General Secretary of the Soviet Communist Party, also becoming president in Jun 1983□

Andrzejewski Jerzy 1909–83. Polish novelist; *Ashes and Diamonds* 1948, set in post-war Poland, was filmed by Wajda◊□

anemometer wind gauge (Greek *anemos* 'wind'); the simplest form has four cups rotating on arms from a common centre, at speeds recorded electrically on a chart□

anemone genus of plants, family Ranunculaceae◊, including ***wood anemone*** *A nemorosa* and ***pasque flower*** *A pulsatilla*□

aneroid see barometer◊□

aneurysm dilation of a weakened artery wall into a rounded balloon, with the danger of its bursting□

angel supernatural being (Greek *angelos* 'messenger') intermediate between God and man in Christian, Jewish, and Muslim belief. The Christian hierarchy has nine orders; Seraphim, Cherubim, Thrones (who contemplate God and reflect his glory); Dominations, Virtues, Powers (who regulate the stars and the Universe); Principalities, Archangels, and Angels (who minister to humanity). In traditional Catholic belief, every human being has a guardian angel□

angel English coin 15–17th centuries, with an angel design□

Angel Falls world's highest waterfall (more than one leap), on the Caroni river, Venezuela; 979 m/3212 ft□

angelfish marine, brilliantly coloured tropical fish of the family Chaetodontidae, up to 65 cm/2 ft long, living on coral reefs. See also cichlids under perch◊□

angelica genus of tall, perennial N hemisphere plants, family Umbelliferae◊; cultivated angelica *A archangelica* gives an oil used in liqueurs and perfumery, and the candied stems are used in confectionery□

Angelico Fra Guido di Picto, 1387-1455. Italian Renaissance artist, a Dominican Friar, whose nature was so angelic as to earn him the nickname. The monastery of San Marco, Florence, where he lived, is now a museum of his work. He produced devotional frescoes in some 50 of the cells□

Angell Sir Norman 1872–1967. British political economist; *The Great Illusion* 1919, maintained that war was as ruinous to the victors as to the vanquished. Nobel peace prize 1933□

angina or ***angina pectoris***, Latin 'tightness of the chest', a heart disease caused by restricted blood supply to the heart because a coronary artery is narrowed; the pain travels across the chest and arm, rather than appearing to come from the heart□

angiosperms see under plant◊□

Angkor ancient capital of the Khmers, Kampuchea◊; ruined palaces and temples originally dedicated to Hindu◊ gods include

Angkor Vat, a 12th-century temple to Siva. Angkor was damaged in the civil war 1970–5, and then neglected by the Communist regime□

anglerfish order of fish, Lophiiformes, including the ***angler*** or ***monkfish*** *Lophius piscatorius*, family Lophiidae; 1.5 m/5 ft long; in which the enlarged tip of the thread-like first ray of the dorsal fin dangles over its own mouth as bait for its prey. It is camouflaged by seaweed-like mouth growths and a smooth stone-like body□

Anglesey island in Gwynedd, Wales; population 60 000. It is linked to the mainland across the Menai Straits by the Britannia tubular railway bridge and Telford◊'s suspension bridge 1819–26 (later reconstructed). The chief town is Beaumaris, with a castle, and the port of Holyhead is on Holy Island to the west; the south eastern village of Llanfair PG is famous for the length of its full name Llanfairpwllgwyngyllgogerywyrndrobwllan-dysilliogogogoch (St Mary's church in the hollow of the white hazel near to the rapid whirlpool of St Tysillio's church, by the red cave). The island is rich in plant and bird life. The Romans (who called the island Mona from Welsh Ynys Môn) defeated the Druids◊, who made their last stand here, in 41AD. There is an Advanced Flying School at RAF Valley□

Anglican Communion The. Family of Protestant churches including the Church of England. It originated in the 2nd century during the Roman occupation of Britain and was established as part of the Catholic Church by the mission of St Augustine◊. At the Reformation◊, the Sovereign (Henry VIII) replaced the Pope as its head, and assumed the right to appoint bishops and archbishops. The Book of Common Prayer dates from Edward VI, the Thirty-Nine Articles of doctrine from Elizabeth I, and the Authorized Version of the Bible from James I – modernizations of all three have been controversial.

In England the two archbishops head the provinces of Canterbury◊ and York◊, which are subdivided into bishoprics, and a General Synod of three houses (bishops, miscellaneous clergy, and laity) regulates Church matters, subject to Parliament and the Royal Assent. A decennial ***Lambeth Conference*** (from 1967), suggests policies which are often put into practice. *Crockford's Clerical Directory,* established 1858, and famous for its anonymous prefaces, was taken over in 1985 by the Church of England itself

In N America the successors of the three bishops consecrated after the War of American Independence still lead the Episcopal◊ Church in the USA; an Anglican presence was also established early in Australia, New Zealand, and India; missionary work extended to Africa in the 19th century and to S America in the 20th.

The main parties have been (from the 19th century):

Evangelical (Low Church) emphasizing Protestantism

Anglo-Catholic (High Church) emphasizing continuity with the pre-Reformation Church (Keble◊, Froude◊, Newman◊, Pusey◊)

Liberal-Modernist emphasizing reconciliation with modern thought

Pentecostal Charismatic movement, emphasizing spontaneity, speaking with tongues, etc.

Controversial issues have been: reunification with the Methodist and Catholic churches; ordination of women (achieved in Hong Kong 1944, and in the American Epsicopalian Church 1976); links with 'freedom fighters' in Africa, S America, etc., via the World Council of Churches□

angling fishing with rod and line; the most popular 'sport' in the UK.

freshwater coarse fishing includes members of the carp family and pike (not usually eaten but thrown back); freshwater game fish are salmon and trout.

seafishing the catch includes flatfish, bass, mackerel; big-game fish (again usually not eaten) include shark, tuna or tunny, marlin, and swordfish, usually caught from specially equipped motor-boats□

Anglo-Saxon portmanteau word for a member of the Germanic peoples who conquered Britain in the 5–7th centuries and mixed to some extent with the Romanized Celts◊ in possession (see Heptarchy◊). Their language (the basis of modern English) cannot be read today without special study. Cultural achievements include the annals of the *Anglo-Saxon Chronicle* (see Alfred◊) and the epic *Beowulf*; illuminated books and splendid jewellery (Sutton◊ Hoo) which incorporated Celtic features; and architecture, such as the cathedral-like church at Brixworth, Northamptonshire□

Angola People's Republic of
area 1 246 700 sq km/481 350 sq mi
capital and chief port Luanda
towns Lobito and Benguela, also ports
features Kwanza river and the dependency of Cabinda◊
exports oil, coffee, diamonds, palm oil, sisal, iron ore, fish
currency kwanza

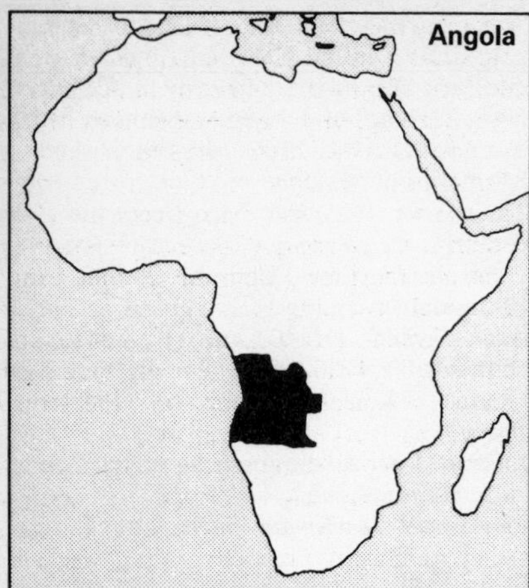

population 7 770 000, largest ethnic group Ovimbundu, to which Savimbi belongs
language Portuguese, official; Umbundu, Kimbundu
religion Roman Catholic 46%, Protestant 12%, Animist 42%
government Marxist executive president (José dos Santos from 1979) and unicameral national assembly; only one political party is permitted
recent history a Portuguese colony from 1491; in 1961 the people rose against the Portuguese and civil war ensued with Cuban troups aiding the fight against the Portuguese-led forces. Independence was achieved in 1975, after the liberization of the regine in Portugal. South African backed guerrilla warfare continued and after a military incursion in 1981, South Africa created a 100 mile buffer zone controlled by anti-government Jonas Savimbi◊, who by 1984 controlled a third of the country, capital Jamba. His Unita forces have several times taken Europeans hostage in a vain effort to persuade Western governments to recognize his party as the legal government of Angola. Cabinda◊ has agitated for separate independence□

Angora earlier form of Ankara◊, which gave its name to the angora goat (source of mohair wool), and so to other long-haired animals, such as the angora rabbit (source of angora wool)□

Angostura see Ciudad Bolivar◊□

Angoulme town in France; population 92 000□

Angry Young Men group of British writers who emerged after World War II, including Kingsley Amis◊, John Wain◊, John Osborne◊, Colin Wilson◊; Iris Murdoch◊ and Kenneth Tynan◊ were also linked with the group□

Angström Anders Jonas 1814–74. Swedish physicist. See Angström unit◊□

Angström unit unit of measurement for the wavelength of electromagnetic radiations, named after the physicist, but gradually being replaced by the SI unit, i.e. the angstrom = 0.1 of a nanometre◊□

Anguilla

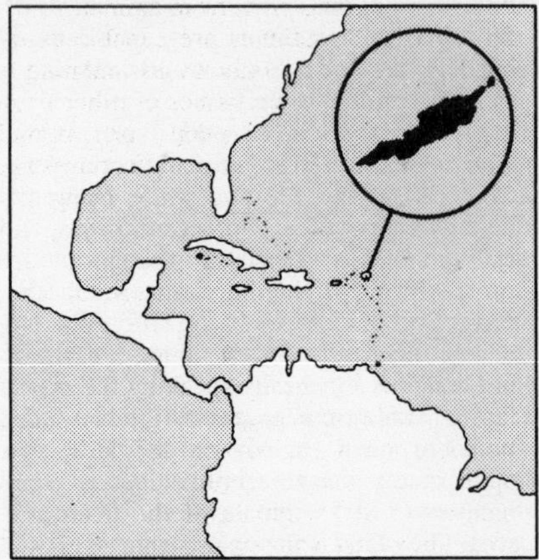

area 90 sq km/35 sq mi
capital The Valley
features white coral sand beaches
exports lobster, salt
currency Eastern Caribbean dollar
population 7000
language English and Creole
government from 1982, governor, executive council, and legislative house of assembly (chief minister Emile Gumbs from 1984)
recent history a British colony from 1650, Anguilla was long association with St Kitts◊, but revolted against alleged domination by the larger island, and in 1969 declared itself a republic. A small British force restored order, and Anguilla retained a special position at her own request, since 1980 a separate dependance of the UK□

Anhui province (formerly Anhwei) of E China
area 139 900 sq km/54 000 sq mi
capital Hefei
features Chang◊ Jiang
products cotton, rice, tea; iron and steel
population 48 030 000□

aniline simplest known aromatic base (aminobenzene $C_6H_5NH_2$), originally prepared by dry distillation of indigo (Portuguese *anil*); colourless, oily, probably carcinogenic, liquid with a characteristic odour, which occurs in coal tar, and is much used in dyeing processes□

animal an organism of the kingdom Animalia, one of the two major divisions of living things, the other being that of plants◊, but see also under life◊.

Both plants and animals are seen under the microscope to be assemblies of particles of protoplasm (called cells◊). Those of plants are characteristically equipped with cellulose walls, and, except in the simplest forms (e.g. those consisting of a single cell) there is little difficulty in telling plant from animal.

Physiologically, animals are capable of living and developing only by assimilating as food the protoplasmic tissues of other living organisms, whether plant or animal, whereas most plants can manufacture sugar from carbon dioxide and water using sunlight as energy (see photosynthesis◊). Logically, therefore, animals are thought to have succeeded plants in the evolution of living things.

Sexual differences in the animal world are not uniform. Generally speaking the male is larger (birds of prey are a notable exception; see under eagle◊) and more showy in appearance, since both features are indicators to the female of the health and strength which will ensure that their offspring will survive. The female, however, often needs to be smaller and less obtrusive to ensure she escapes predators long enough to bring up the family (frequently, but not always her prerogative)□

animal classification there are over one million species of animal in the world. Animals can be readily divided into those with a backbone, the ***vertebrates,*** and those without, the ***invertebrates.*** Invertebrates represent some 95% of all animals; they vastly outnumber vertebrates in terms of species also, and they show a greater variety of forms. Classification of the animal kingdom is into phyla (from the Greek word for 'race'). Each phylum is then subdivided into classes, orders, families, genera, and species. The class Mammalia, to which humans belong, numbers less than 5,000 species, and of these, nearly half are rodents and about a quarter are bats. An example of the class Mammalia is the tiger, which belongs to the order Carnivora◊, family Felidae◊ (see cat◊), and is grouped with the lion, leopard and jaguar in the genus *Panthera,* and is distinguished as a species by the addition of the species name, *Panthera tigris*. See also plant◊ classification□

Animism belief in spiritual unseeen agencies behind the physical world, e.g. in stones, animals, trees, clouds, winds, etc. It may be linked with fetishism◊, and ancestor worship◊□

anion an ion that will travel towards a positive electrode. See anode◊□

anise a type of spice◊□

Anjou ancient province of N France; capital Angers. Henry II of England was Count of Anjou before his accession, but the territory was one of those lost by King John□

Ankara capital (formerly Angora) of Turkey; population 1 236 000. It replaced Istanbul◊ (then in Allied occupation) as capital in 1923, and has the presidential palace and Grand National Assembly buildings; three universities, including a technical university to serve the whole Middle East; Atatürk◊'s mausoleum on a nearby hilltop, and the largest mosque in Turkey at Kocatepe□

ankh the ancient Egyptian hieroglyph 'sign of life' (a cross in which the upper part forms a loop) used as a good luck charm□

Annaba seaport (former Bône, anciently Hippo) in Algeria; population 313 200□

Annam former independent kingdom (capital Hué), now central Vietnam□

Annapolis seaport and capital of Maryland, USA; population 30 000. It was in session here Nov 1783–Jun 1784 that Congress◊ received Washington◊'s resignation as Commander-in-Chief in 1783, and ratified the peace treaty of the War of American Independence. The US Naval Academy is here, and John Paul Jones◊ is buried in the chapel crypt□

Annapurna see Himalayas◊□

Anne 1665–1714. Queen of Great Britain and Ireland, 2nd daughter of James◊ II. She married in 1683 Prince George of Denmark, by whom she had 17 children, all dead by 1700. Sarah Churchill (see Marlborough◊) was her close friend, and, under her influence, she transferred her allegiance from her father to her brother-in-law, William◊ of Orange, during the Revolution of 1688. She succeeded William on the throne in 1702, and was an able ruler, less subordinate to the Churchills than once thought. In 1710 she replaced Sarah as her confidante by the Duchess's intriguing cousin and protégée, Mrs Abigail Masham. See Augan Age◊□

Anne 1950– . Princess of the UK; 2nd child of Queen Elizabeth◊ II. She gained a European reputation as a horsewoman, and in 1973 married ***Lieutenant Mark Phillips*** 1949– , of the Queen's Dragoon Guards, himself a gold medallist in equestrian events at the 1972 Olympics. Their son Peter 1977– was the first direct descendant of the Queen not to receive a title□

Anne of Cleves 1515–57. Fourth wife of Henry◊ VIII of England, she was the daughter of the Duke of Cleves, and was recommended to Henry as a wife by Thomas Cromwell◊, who wanted an alliance with

animal classification

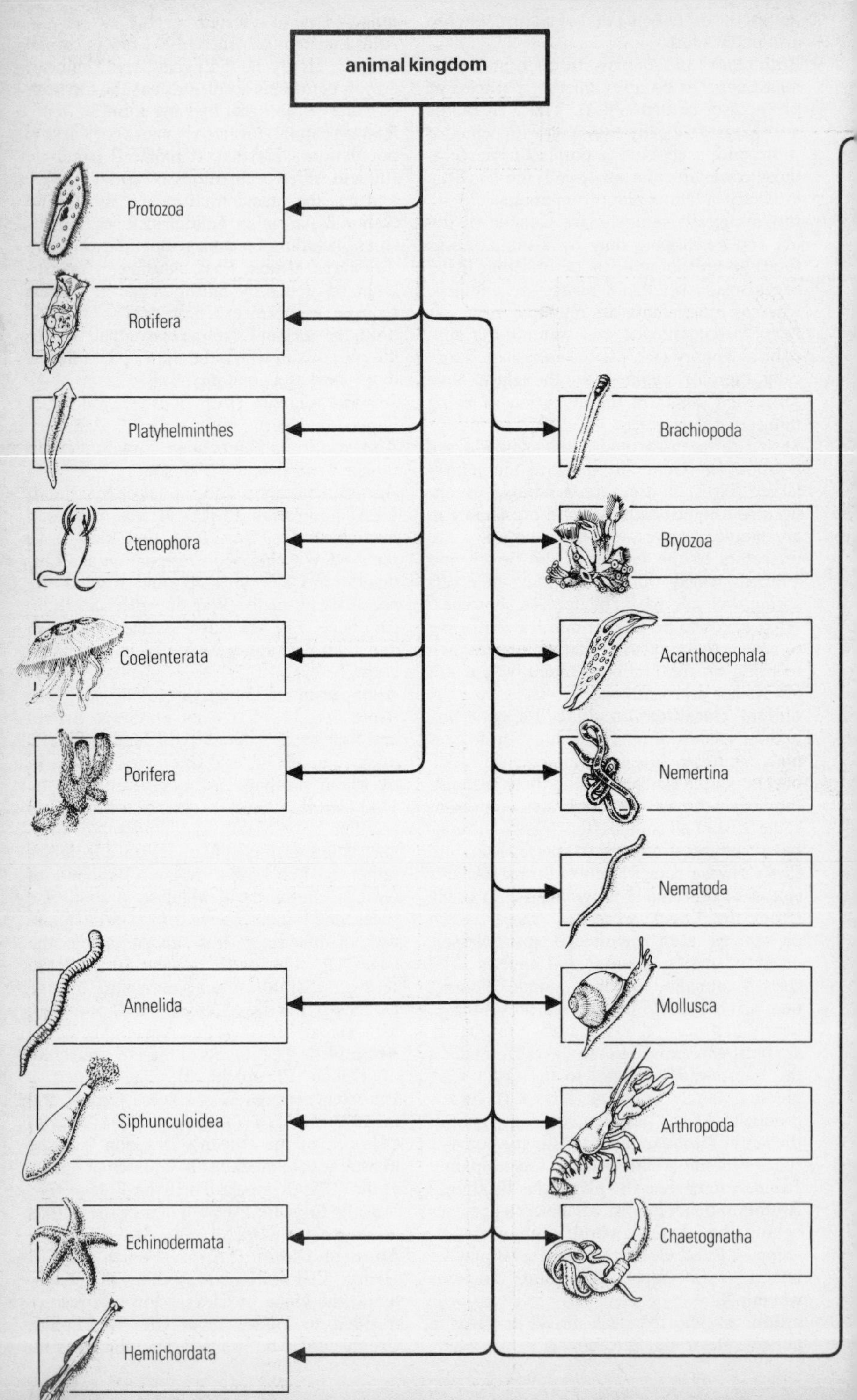

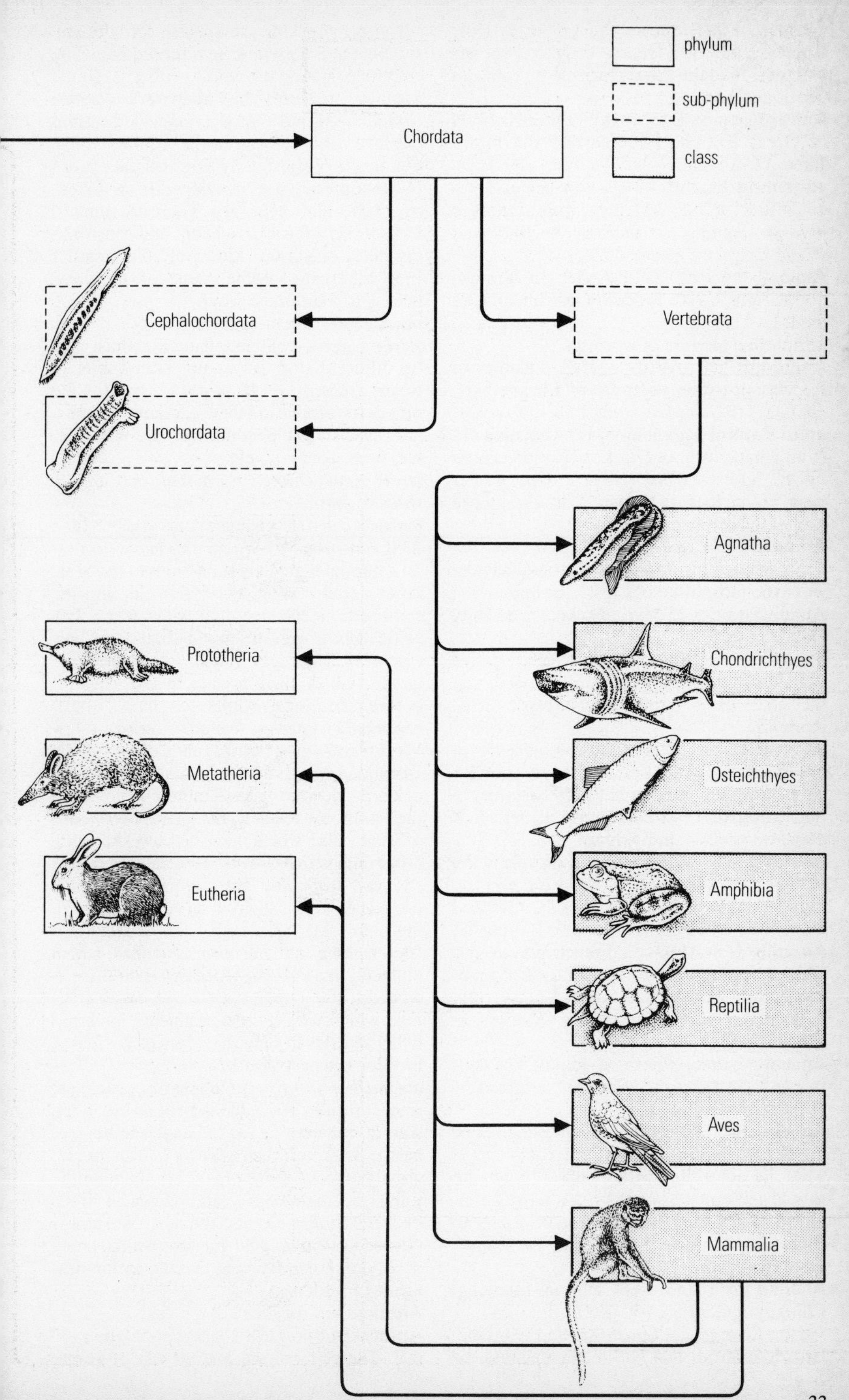
phylum
sub-phylum
class
Chordata
Cephalochordata
Urochordata
Vertebrata
Agnatha
Chondrichthyes
Osteichthyes
Amphibia
Reptilia
Aves
Mammalia
Prototheria
Metatheria
Eutheria

German Protestantism against the Holy Roman Emperor. Henry, disgusted by her plainness, had the marriage declared void and pensioned her□

Anne of Denmark 1574–1619. Queen consort of Great Britain, who married the future James◊ I in 1589□

annealing heating of glass or metal for a given time at a given temperature, followed by slow cooling, to increase ductility and strength□

Annecy town on Lake Annecy in France; population 56 700. Precision instruments are made□

annelida a phylum of worms◊□

Annigoni Pietro 1910– . Italian painter of Renaissance-style portraits of Elizabeth II, etc.□

anno domini beginning of the Christian era (Latin 'in the year of Our Lord'), represented by the letters AD used with a date; earlier years are BC (before Christ): Christ was more probably born in 5AD□

Annunciation in the New Testament, the announcement to Mary by Gabriel◊ that she was to be the mother of Christ; the feast of the Annunciation is 25 Mar, also known as Lady Day□

anode the electrode towards which negative particles (anions) move within a device, e.g. the cells of a battery, electrolytic cells, diodes□

anomie Emile Durkheim◊'s coinage for a breakdown of order and social values under conflicting pressures, as in the 20th century in both capitalist and communist societies. It may also occur in individuals□

anorexia lack of desire to eat, especially the pathological condition of ***anorexia nervosa,*** found in girls or boys who may be obsessed with a desire to slim, etc. See also Bulimia◊□

Anouilh Jean 1910– . French playwright, whose plays dramatize the contrast of innocence and experience, using fantasy, e.g. *L'Invitation au Château/Ring Round the Moon* 1947□

Anschluss union (German 'joining') of Austria and Germany 12 Mar 1938 enforced by Hitler◊□

Anselm St 1033–1109. Italian Benedictine monk. As archbishop of Canterbury 1093–1109, he quarrelled with Henry◊ I over who should appoint bishops. In theology, he inferred God's existence from our capacity to conceive of a perfect being. See Lanfranc◊, scholasticism◊□

Anshan iron and steel city in Liaoning, China; population 1 500 000□

Anson George, 1st Baron Anson 1697–1762. British admiral. In 1740 he commanded the squadron attacking the Spanish colonies and shipping in S America; he returned home, by circumnavigating the world, with £500 000 of Spanish treasure; his chaplain's *Voyage Round the World* 1748 is a classic. He carried out invaluable reforms at the Admiralty◊□

ant insect of the family Formicoidae, order Hymenoptera◊; ants developed from wasps◊ over 100 million years ago. There are some 10 000 species, all social in habit, and constructing nests of various kinds; in cold weather they hibernate. White 'ants' or termites◊ belong to a different group.

communities comprise three types:

workers sterile, wingless females, which may be differentiated, as in the honey ants of desert areas, to serve as storage jars for the others to feed from (they exist only as enormously distensible stomachs filled with nectar) or as 'soldiers', etc.;

fertile females fewer in number, and usually winged; and

males usually also winged, and smaller than their consorts, with whom they leave the nest on a nuptial flight at certain times of the year. After aerial mating, the males die, and the fertilized queens lose their wings when they settle laying eggs to found their own new colonies. The eggs hatch into worm-like larvae, which then pupate in silk cocoons before emerging as adults.

remarkable species include: ***army*** (New World) and ***driver*** (Africa) ants, of sub-family Dorylinae, which march nomadically in huge columns, devouring even tethered animals in their path; the ***bulldog*** ants, genus *Myrmecia*, of Australia, which have a powerful sting (Australia is rich in ants, especially primitive species); ***leaf-cutter*** ants, genus *Atta*, which use pieces of leaf to grow an edible fungus in underground 'gardens'; the ***robber*** or ***'slavemaking'*** ant *Formica sanguinea*, which abducts pupae of other species to rear them as workers; the ***weaver*** ant *Oecophylla smaragdina* which uses its silk-producing larvae as living shuttles to bind the edges of the leaves forming the nest together.

ant intelligence presents fascinating problems, since it resides not in the individual but in the colony functioning as a single intelligent being. Ants find their way by light patterns, gravity (special sense organs are found in the joints of their legs), and chemical trails between food areas and the nest. Warfare is advanced, formic acid jets and stings being used, and barriers being erected in the nest against invaders□

Antakya see Antioch◊□

Antalya free port in S Turkey; population 130 000. The ruins of the ancient city of Perga, visited by St Paul◊, and noted for its cult of Artemis◊ are nearby□

Antananarivo capital (formerly Tananarive) of Madagascar, on the interior plateau, with a rail link to Tamatave◊; population 400 000□

Antarctic The. All the land and ice-covered sea south of 60° S, including Antarctica◊□

Antarctica the Antarctic continent

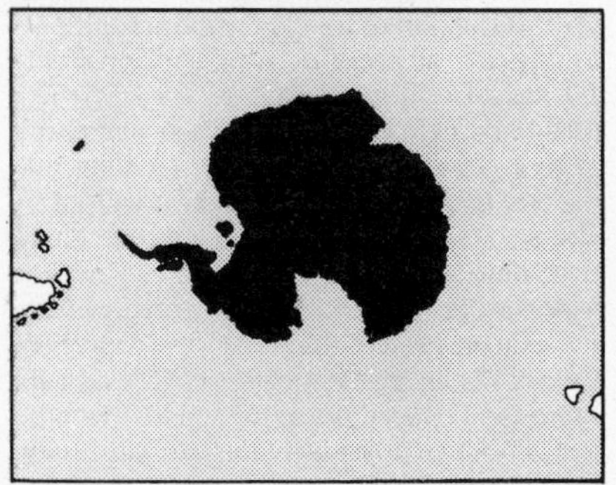

area 13 727 000 sq km/5 300 000 sq mi

features there is less than 50 mm/2 in of rainfall a year (less than the Sahara). Little more than 1% is ice-free, the temperature falling to -70°C/-100°F and below, and in places the ice is 5000 m/16 000 ft deep, comprising over two-thirds of the world's fresh water. Each annual layer of snow preserves a record of global conditions, and where no melting at the surface of the bedrock has occurred the ice can be a million years old. It covers extensive mineral resources, including iron, coal, and with indications of uranium and other strategic metals, as well as oil (see also meteorite◊). There are only two species of flowering plants, plus a number of mosses, algae, and fungi; see under lichen◊. Animal life is restricted to visiting whales, seals, penguins, and other seabirds. There is no permanent human population, only research stations.

The continent, once part of Gondwanaland◊, is a vast plateau, of which the highest point is the Vinson Massif in the Ellsworth mountains, 5139 m/16 860 ft high. The Ross Ice Shelf is formed by several glaciers coalescing in the Ross Sea, and Mt Erebus on Ross Island is the world's southernmost active volcano. Fossils of apemen have been found; see Antarctic◊ history.

The territorial claims of the nations are in cold storage, and that of Britain is overlapped by later claims of Argentina and Chile. The Soviet Union and USA have made no claim, but recognize no one else's.

population settlement limited to scientific research stations with changing personnel.

history see Antarctic◊ exploration□

Antarctic exploration

1773–4 James Cook◊ first sailed in Antarctic seas, but exploration was difficult until the development of iron ships able to withstand ice pressure

1819–21 Antarctica circumnavigated by Bellingshausen◊

1823 James Weddell◊ sailed into the sea named after him

1841–2 James Ross◊ sighted the Great Ice Barrier named after him

1895 Borchgrevink◊ was one of the first landing party on the continent

1898 Borchgrevink's British expedition first wintered in Antarctica

1901–4 Scott◊ first penetrated the interior of the continent

1907–8 Shackleton◊ came within 182 km/113 mi of the Pole

1911 Amundsen◊ reached the Pole, 14 Dec, overland with dogs

1912 Scott reached the Pole, 18 Jan, initially aided by ponies

1928–9 Byrd◊ made the first flight to the Pole

1935 Ellsworth◊ first flew across Antarctica

1957–8 Fuchs◊ made the first overland crossing

1959 Soviet expedition from the West Ice Shelf to the Pole

1959 International Antarctic Treaty suspended all territorial claims, reserving an area south of 60° S latitude for peaceful purposes

1961–2 Bentley Trench discovered, which suggested that there may be an Atlantic-Pacific link beneath the Continent

1966–7Specially Protected Areas established internationally for animals and plants

1979 fossils of apemen resembling E Africa's Proconsul found 500 km/300 mi from the Pole

1980 International Convention on the exploitation of resources – oil, gas, fish, krill

1982 first circumnavigation of earth (2 Sept 1979–29 Aug 1982) via the Poles by Sir Ranulph Fiennes and Charles Burton (UK)□

Antarctic Ocean popular name, not used by the International Hydrographic Bureau, for reaches of the Atlantic, Indian, and Pacific Oceans extending south of the Antarctic Circle, 66° 33' S. Except for a few weeks in the year, it is covered by drifting pack ice□

Antarctic Territory Australian. See under Australian◊ Antarctic Territory□

anteater a family of edentata◊□

antelope mammal (sub-family Antilopinae) in the cattle◊ family, Bovidae, with a range from S Europe through Asia and Africa, many species being distinguished for grace and speed. They include:

chamois *Rupicapra rupicapra,* of Europe and SW Asia, exceptional in being a mountain species; 75 cm/27in high – from whose hide chamois leather used to be made.
duikers of Africa, genera *Cephalopus* and *Sylvicapra*, the smallest species at 30 cm/1ft.
eland *Taurotragus oryx* of Africa, spiral-horned, with humped shoulders and dewlap, the largest species at 2 m/6 ft.
gazelles genera *Gazella* and *Procapra* of Africa and Asia, large-eyed and graceful.
gnu or ***wildebeest*** of Africa, especially the brindled *Conochaetes taurinus*, rather like a slender cow with a heavily tufted tail.
hartebeest of Africa, such as *Alcelaphus buselaphus,* with sculptured, lyre-shaped horns.
impala *Aepyceros melampus* of Africa, noted for leaping at great speed.
oryx, genus *Oryx*, of Africa and Arabia, with long straight horns, which look at a distance like a single horn – hence possibly the legend of the unicorn. The white Arabian oryx *O leucoryx* is very rare.
springbok *Antidorcas marsupialis*, which has a spirited, jumping run, and is the national emblem of South Africa.
bushbuck *Tragelaphus scriptus*, c70 cm/2 ft high, the male having a spiral turn to its horns, common south of the Sahara.
Rocky mountain 'goat' *Oreamnos americanus* has a thick white coat and back-curving horns.
bongo *Boocerus euryceros* rare central African forest antelope, with white stripes□

Antheil George 1900–59. American composer and pianist; his *Ballet Mécanique* 1923–4 is scored for anvils, aeroplane propellers, electric bells, automobile horns, and 16 player pianos□

Anthelion the antisun, a kind of solar halo, sometimes appearing at the same altitude as the sun, but opposite to it□

Anthony St 250–350. A desert hermit of Egypt, he founded Christian monasticism (as a group of hermits' huts) in 305, his disciple St Pachomius developing the concept into the first communal monastery in Egypt 346AD. St Anthony's alleged fleshly temptations in the desert were a subject relished by medieval artists; his feast day is 17 Jan□

Anthony Susan Brownell 1820–1906. American pioneer of women's suffrage; her profile is on the US dollar coin of 1979, but the coin was unpopular because easily confused with a 'quarter'□

Anthony of Padua St 1195–1231. Disciple of St Francis, who entered the Franciscan order in 1220 and became a great preacher; he is the patron saint of lost objects, and his feast day is 13 Jun□

anthozoa class of animals of phylum Coelenterata, including sea anemones, corals, etc.; they are sedentary polyps, never passing through a free-swimming medusa stage□

anthracene white glistening crystalline hydrocarbon, $C_{14}H_{10}$, with a faint blue fluorescence; it occurs in coal tar and is used in the dyeing industry□

anthracite glossy, slow-burning coal producing intense heat (found in S Wales, Pennsylvania, Donbas, Shanxi)□

anthrax cattle and sheep disease communicable to man, usually via infected hides and fleeces; a black lesion and fever is caused by *Bacillus anthracis*, and treatment is by penicillin□

anthropology science of man, Greek *anthropos+logos*, 'man'+'discourse', the coinage of Otto Casman in 1594, but only developed following 19th-century evolutionary theory to deal with man physically, socially, culturally, etc.□

anthropometry science of comparative measurement of the human body□

anthropomorphism attribution of human characteristics to gods (as in Greek and Scandinavian mythology), plants, animals, or the inanimate (the wind, stones, etc.)□

anthroposophy see Rudolf Steiner◊□

Antibes resort, which includes Juan les Pins, on the French Riviera; population 48 000. There is a Picasso collection in the 17th-century castle museum□

antibiotic chemical produced by moulds and bacteria which can destroy or prevent the growth of other micro-organisms; penicillins (see Alexander Fleming◊) have been largely replaced by the wider range of cephalosporins; they are used against bacterial diseases, including forms of pneumonia and veneral disease, TB, etc. See also additive◊, streptomycin◊□

antibody protein produced in the blood when a toxin produced by bacteria, etc., is present (an antigen); the antibody and antigen combine (like a key in a lock) and the toxin is rendered innocuous. See immunity◊. Artificial cloning of antibodies (monoclonal antibodies) which can be tailor-made for specific purposes, offers hope for the eventual treatment of cancer, etc.; the technique also has potential in medical diagnosis, as well as in industrial processes□

Antichrist in New Testament, the ultimate opponent of Christ, by whom he is finally to be conquered; candidates have included Nero, Napoleon, and Hitler. Extreme Ulster Protestants refer to the Pope in this way□

Anti-Comintern Pact pact between Germany and Japan 25 Nov 1936 against the

Communist International◊; Italy adhered 1937; Hungary, Spain, and Manchukuo 1939□

anticyclone area of high atmospheric pressure, caused by descending air which becomes warm and dry; winds radiate from a calm centre (clockwise direction in the N hemisphere and anti-clockwise in the S hemisphere). It is associated with clear weather, without rain or violent winds; in summer, it brings hot sunny days, and in winter, fine frosty spells, sometimes plus fog and low cloud. 'Blocking' anticyclones caused the summer drought in Britain 1976, and the severe winters 1947, 1963□

antietam see Civil◊ War, American□

antigen substance promoting the creation of antibodies◊□

antigone in Greek legend, the daughter of Jocasta by Oedipus◊□

Antigua and Barbuda The State of

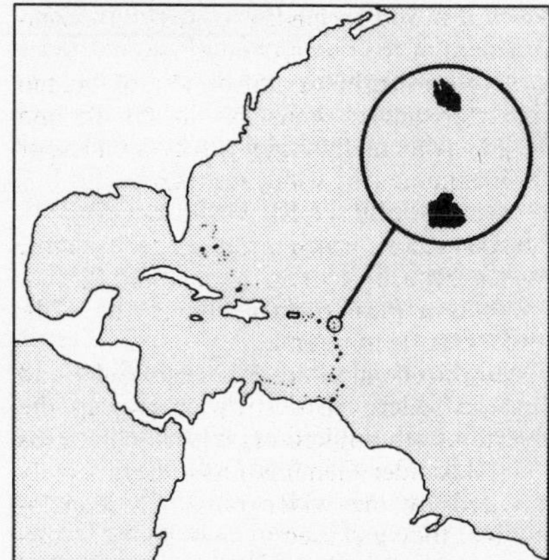

area 280 sq km/108 sq mi, plus Barbuda 50 km/30 sq mi to the N, and Redonda 1 sq km/0.6 sq mi

capital and chief port St John's

features Antigua is the largest of the Leeward Islands, Redonda is uninhabited.

exports sea island cotton, rum

currency East Caribbean dollar

population 78 000 (including Barbuda 1000)

language English

religion Christianity

famous people Viv Richards

government governor general and house of representatives (Prime Minister from 1976 Vere C Bird, Labour).

recent history first settled by the British in 1632, Antigua became an Associated◊ State in 1967 and together with Barbuda, became independent within the Commonwealth in Nov 1981□

Antilles

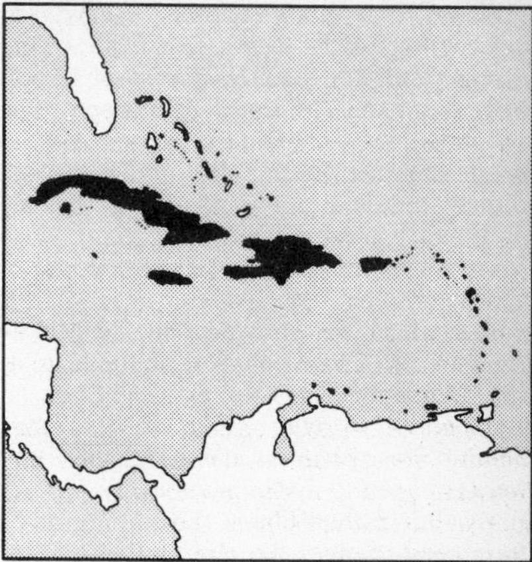

the whole group of West Indian islands, divided north-south into the Greater Antilles (Cuba◊, Jamaica◊, Haiti-Dominican Republic◊, Puerto Rico◊) and Lesser Antilles, subdivided into the Leeward Islands (Virgin Islands◊, St Kitts-Nevis◊, Antigua and Barbuda◊, Anguilla◊, Montserrat◊ and Guadeloupe◊) and the Windward Islands (Dominica◊, Martinique◊, St Lucia◊, St Vincent and the Grenadines◊, Barbados◊, Grenada◊)□

antimatter matter made up of antiparticles: Positrons instead of electrons, antiprotons instead of protons and antineutrons instead of neutrons. See particle◊ physics□

antimony element

symbol Sb

atomic number 51

physical description several forms, including a blue-white metal, and yellow and black non-metals

features its isotopes are a source of penetrating gamma radiation (higher energy than X-rays)

uses batteries and as a hardener in alloys□

Antioch capital (modern Turkish Antakyah) of the ancient Greek kingdom of Syria, founded 300BC and an early centre of Christianity□

Antiochus thirteen kings of Syria of the Seleucid dynasty including:

Antiochus IV ruled 175–164BC. He occupied Jerusalem in 170BC, seizing the temple treasure and instituting Greek-style worship; this resulted in the revolt of the Maccabees◊, Antiochus dying before he could suppress it□

Antipodes places exactly opposite on the globe (Greek 'opposite feet'); in Britain, Australia and New Zealand are the Antipodes□

Antipodes Islands islands lying off SE New Zealand, they are therefore the Antipodes of London□

antirrhinum see snapdragon◊□

antisemitism discrimination against, or persecution of the Jews. The further Diaspora◊ prompted 70AD by the fall of Jerusalem, led many to settle in Europe. The adoption of Christianity as the official religion of the Roman Empire in the 4th century then led to a reinforcing of existing prejudice against a distinctive group, since Jews were considered the murderers of Christ.

Antisemitism was increased in the Middle Ages by the Crusades◊, and by the legislation forbidding Jews to own land or be members of a craft guild, so that they became money lenders and middlemen, and were confined to live in ghettoes.

Early 19th-century liberal thought improved their position until the rise of the unscientific theory of a pure Aryan race. Antisemitism became strong in Austria, France (see Dreyfus◊), and Germany, and from 1881 pogroms◊ in Poland and Russia led to the flight of refugees to Britain and the USA.

World War I was ascribed to the supposed machinations of 'International Jewry', and, in combination with Hitler's extension of the racial theory, this led to the Holocaust◊ of 1933–45, when about six million Jews died in concentration camps (Auschwitz, Belsen, Buchenwald, Dachau, Maidanek). See Anne Frank◊.

Many early political theorists of the Left were Jewish, including Marx, so that anti-Communist fervour was directed against them, but Communists were also opposed to them because they were unamenable to the idea of an all-powerful state (see Jewish◊ Autonomous Region).

A lull in antisemitism after World War II occurred in W Europe, but in 1948 the creation of Israel led to Palestinian anti-Zionism◊, backed by the Arab world, and antisemitism has also revived in the USSR and the Eastern bloc□

antiseptic substance killing or hindering the growth of germs. See Joseph Lister◊□

anti-theatre see Peter Handke◊□

antivivisection movement for the abolition of experiments on live animals, or at least its minimization under strict control, especially as animal tests may not duplicate human response and alternative approaches may be more fruitful. Especially under attack are tests of inessentials (cosmetics, shampoos, etc.) and student duplication of already ascertained fact□

ant lion tropical family of winged insects, Myrmeleonidae, with formidable larval forms which dig pits to trap insects□

Antofagasta port in N Chile; population 150 000. Nitrates from Atacama◊ are exported□

Antonine's Wall Roman line of fortification 142–200AD, the Roman Empire's north west frontier, between the Clyde and Forth, Scotland. See Antoninus◊ Pius□

Antoninus Pius 86–167AD. Roman emperor, who had been adopted in 138 as Hadrian's heir, and succeeded him later that year; he enjoyed a prosperous reign. His daughter married Marcus◊ Aurelius, and the *Age of the Antonines* (especially the reigns of himself and his son-in-law) became a focus of nostalgic regret. See Antonine◊'s Wall□

Antonioni Michelangelo 1912– . Italian film director; his work includes *L'Avventura* 1960, *Blow Up* 1967, and *The Passenger* 1974, dealing with the neuroses and relationships of the leisured classes□

Antony Mark. See Mark◊ Antony□

Antrim county of Northern Ireland
area 2906 sq km/1122 sq mi
towns Belfast (county town), port of Larne
features Giant's Causeway of natural hexagonal basalt columns which, in legend, was built to enable the giants to cross between Ireland and Scotland; Antrim borders Lough Neagh
products potatoes, oats; linen, and synthetic textiles
population 355 700
famous people James Galway□

Antwerp port (Flemish Antwerpen, French Anvers) in Belgium on the Scheldt◊; population 1 000 000. One of the world's busiest ports, it has shipbuilding, oil-refining, petrochemical, textile, diamond-cutting industries, etc. Historic treasures include the home of Rubens (many of his works are in the Gothic cathedral), and an art gallery with a collection of the Flemish school□

Anubis in Egyyptian mythology, the jackal-headed god of the dead□

Anuradhapura site of the ruins of the capital of the Sinhalese kings of Sri Lanka 5th century BC–8th century AD; rediscovered in the mid-19th century, it has a bo◊ tree descended from the original□

ANZAC *A*ustralian and *N*ew *Z*ealand *A*rmy *C*orps, but applied to all troops of both countries in World War I and to some extent in World War II□

Anzac Day public holiday in Australia and New Zealand, commemorating the Anzac landing at Gallipoli 25 Apr 1915□

Anzhero-Sudensk coal-mining town in W Siberia, USSR; population 105 000□

Anzio Battle of. The beach-head invasion of Italy 22 Jan–23 May 1944, by Allied troops; failure to use Ultra◊ intelligence information led to Allied troops stranded for a period after German attacks□

Anzus Treaty 1951, establishing a collective security relationship among *A*ustralia, *N*ew Zealand, *US*A; it was temporarily replaced by SEATO◊ 1954–77, and in 1985 was rendered partly inoperative by New Zealand's refusal to accept US warships which might be nuclear-armed□

Aosta capital of Valle◊ d'Aosta, Italy; population 37 000□

Apaches group of N American Indian peoples, related to the Navajo, who number 10 000. They have reservations in Arizona (the Apache state), SW Oklahoma, and New Mexico. Formerly great warriors (the name means 'enemy'), they were considered particularly treacherous by the white settlers taking their land; their greatest leader was Geronimo◊□

apartheid the policy of racial segregation of the government of S Africa. The word was coined by the S African Bureau for Racial Affairs (Sabra) in the late 1930s. Apartheid was legally first formulated in 1948 under Afrikaner control (see also Verwoerd◊). It means 'apartness' and is now known there as 'plural democracy'. It comprises 'petty apartheid', which covers separate facilities, racial laws and regulations, and which has been modified under Botha from 1979, e.g. the prohibition of marriage or sex between whites and any other race was scrapped in 1985; and 'grand apartheid', the long-term plan for 'Black◊ National States'. Racial classification is on an 11-point scale, e.g. 00=white, 01=Cape Coloured, 05=Indian, etc., with a special sub-classification for blacks. ***Neo-apartheid*** is the retention of class divisions economically, which leave the colour power structure unchanged.

Black opposition to appartheid is becoming more and more intensified. See Sasolburg◊, Soweto◊□

ape strictly the four anthropoid apes◊, but popularly includes a few monkeys◊, e.g. the Barbary ape of Gibraltar◊□

apes anthropoid. A species of primate◊ able to walk upright on two legs, Greek *anthropos+eidos* 'manlike'. Studies, including that of mitochondrial DNA◊, suggest that gibbons were the first to break from the main ancestral stock, that orang-utans were the next, that man diverged from the gorilla-chimpanzee line about 5 million years ago (the pygmy chimpanzee possibly being his closest living relative), and that gorillas diverged from the chimpanzees about 3 million years ago.

gibbon, genus *Hylobates*, N India to Borneo; agile tree-dwellers, living in troops, they are noted for their howling evening chorus, the black Sumatran ***siamang*** *H syndactylus* being the largest at 1 m/3 ft.

orang-utan *Pongo pygmaeus*, of Borneo and Sumatra; covered in long, reddish hair, they are lethargic and, though of amiable temperament, lead a solitary arboreal life. They reach 1.65 m/5.5 ft.

gorilla *Gorilla gorilla* of W and central Africa; they have blackish fur and live in family parties of a male and several females, constructing tree nests for overnight use; breast-beating indicates nervous excitement rather than rage, and they are of gentle disposition. In contrast with orang-utans, they do not seem to recognize themselves in a mirror, i.e. they are not self-conscious. Only about 240 survive in the Virunga mountains in Zaïre/Rwanda/Uganda, and a studbook is kept for those in captivity to try to ensure advantageous breeding.

chimpanzee *Pan troglodytes*, of W and Central Africa ; they are distinguished by bare buttocks, and thinnish black body hair, and have arms slightly shorter than other species; they live in large family groups, share man's aggressive behaviour, can combine to hunt, and are primitive tool users. They are about 1.35 m/4.5 ft tall, and 99% of their genes are identical with those of man.

Both gorillas and chimpanzees, who are not vocally equipped for speech, have some ability to acquire a vocabulary (using the sign language of the deaf), but not to use it grammatically as a child does. All anthropoid species are mainly vegetarian, and all are under threat of extinction□

Ape City Yerkes Regional Primate Center, Atlanta, Georgia, USA, where large numbers of primates are kept for physiological and psychological experiment□

Apennines mountain backbone of Italy, which continues over the Strait of Messina along the north Sicilian coast, and crosses the Mediterranean in a series of islands to the Atlas mountains of N Africa; highest peak Monte Corno 2912 m/9554 ft□

Apennines lunar mountain range on the moon, south-east of the Sea of Showers□

aphasia see under Pierre Broca◊□

aphid a type of insect. See under hemiptera◊□

aphrodisiac anything which increases sexual desire (see Aphrodite◊), which may be stimulated in humans or animals by drugs affecting the pituitary gland. This is sometimes done for clinical or commercial farming purposes. Preparations commonly sold for the purpose are dangerous (cantharidin) or useless (rhinoceros horn), and alcohol and cannabis, popularly thought to be effective, because they lessen inhibition, are likely to act in reverse□

Aphrodite in Greek mythology, the goddess of love (Roman Venus◊, Phoenician◊ Astarte, Babylonian Ishtar◊); said to be either a daughter of Zeus◊ or sprung from the foam of the sea. She was the unfaithful wife of Hephaestus◊, the mother of Eros◊, and was awarded the prize for beauty by Paris◊; centres of her worship were Cyprus (Paphos◊) and Cythera□

Apia capital and port of Western Samoa; population 30 000. It was the home of R L Stevenson◊ 1889–94□

Apis Egyptian god, linked with Osiris◊ and bull-headed (hence the name for the Ptolemaic god Serapis◊); his cult centres were Memphis and Heliopolis, where sacred bulls were mummified□

apocalypse prophetic writing (Greek 'revelation'), usually of disasters, but promising supernatural deliverance; specifically the New Testament *Book of Revelation*□

Apocalypse group of writers 1938, who were influenced by the 'apocalyptic' features of the work of Dylan Thomas◊□

Apollo in Greek mythology, the god of sun, music, poetry, and prophecy, the twin child (with Artemis◊), of Zeus◊ and Leto. His chief cult centres were his birthplace on the island of Delos◊, and Delphi◊. He was the type of manly beauty. See also Surya◊□

Apollo Object a type of interplanetary object (over a 1000 being larger than one km in diameter), with an orbit which carries it through the path of earth. See Impact Crater◊□

Apollo of Rhodes see Colossus of Rhodes◊□

Apollo Project US space project initiated by J F Kennedy, 1961–72, to land a man on the moon◊□

apoplexy see cerebral◊ haemorrhage◊□

apostle one of the 12 disciples sent to preach by Jesus (Greek 'messenger')□

Apostles discussion group at University of Cambridge, founded 1820; members included Tennyson◊, G E Moore◊, Bertrand Russell◊, Strachey◊, Leonard Woolf◊, Maynard Keynes◊, Guy Burgess◊ and Anthony Blunt◊□

Apostolic Age period in the Christian Church dominated by those personally known to Jesus or his disciples□

apostolic succession the passing down of spiritual power in the Christian Church from Christ, via his apostles, and from them through 'laying on of hands' from generation to generation of bishops□

Appalachians mountain sytem of eastern N America, running 2400 km/1500 mi Alabama–Quebec, and including the Allegheny◊, Blue◊ Ridge and Catskill◊ mountains. The eastern edge has a fall line to the coastal plain on which Baltimore, Philadelphia and Washington stand. There is timber and coal, and depopulation was reversed by a 'return to the wilds' from the 1970s□

Appalachia area of the Appalachian mountains (Alabama, Kentucky, North Carolina, Tennessee, Virginia, and W Virginia), isolated by migration to the far west in the 19th century, and economically backward until it achieved a boom in the 1980s (timber, coal, oil shale, uranium, etc.). Its hillbilly culture of music, poetry, dance, and a language with elements of 17th-century British usage, survives□

appeasement conciliation of the Nazi-Fascist dictators, as in Chamberlain's Munich◊ Agreement of 1938; it was ended by Hitler's occupation of Czechoslovakia in Mar 1939□

appendicitis inflammation of the small blind extension of the bowel in the lower right abdomen, the ***appendix***. This is about the size of a little finger. In ***acute appendicitis*** the infection spreads to the peritoneum (see peritonitis◊), e.g. by the bursting of the appendix. Removal of the appendix became fashionable after Edward VII had the operation. It is less common today, partly because the condition is more easily controlled by antibiotics. The appendix is not essential to healthy life□

Appert Nicolas 1750–1841. French pioneer of food canning□

apple tree (genus *Malus* family Rosaceae◊) grown for its fruit, and derived from the sour wild ***crab apple*** *Malus sylvestris*. A temperate commercial crop in USA, Canada, Australia, New Zealand, S Africa, Britain, and France, apples are specifically bred for eating (Cox's Orange pippin, Golden Delicious, Crispin), cooking (Bramley), and cider-making (a blend is used)□

Appleton Sir Edward Victor 1892–1965. British physicist, who worked at Cambridge under Rutherford◊ from 1920. He proved the existence of the Kennelly◊-Heaviside layer in the atmosphere, and the Appleton◊ layer beyond it, and was involved in the initial work on the atom bomb. Nobel prize 1947□

Appleton layer the uppermost layer of the ionosphere (F region), discovered by Appleton◊, at a height of some 150–1000 km; it varies daily and seasonally, and is affected by solar activity. Without it, short wave radio signals would disappear into space, instead of being deflected, so that they can be bounced round the world□

Appomatox village in Virginia, USA, site of the court house where on 9 Apr 1865 the Confederate◊ Army under Robert E Lee surrendered to the Federals under Grant; this ended the Civil◊ War; the restored court house is a museum□

apricot African and W Asian tree *Prunus armeniaca* family Rosaceae◊, grown for its yellow-fleshed edible fruit□

April Fool's Day 1 Apr; when, in W Europe and USA, it is the custom to expose people to ridicule by making them believe some falsehood or go on a foolish errand; in France an April fool is an 'April fish'; there is a similar Indian custom on the last day of the Huli festival in late Mar□

Apsley House home of the Duke of Wellington at Hyde Park Corner, London, from 1820, now a Wellington Museum□

Apuleius Lucius c160AD. Roman lawyer, philosopher◊ and author, whose picaresque adventure tale *Metamorphoses, or The Golden Ass*, is considered the world's first novel. See Psyche◊□

Apulia region (Puglia) of Italy, the south eastern 'heel'; capital Bari, chief industrial centre Taranto; population 3 908 485□

Aqaba only port of Jordan, on the Gulf of Aqaba; population 10 000□

Aqaba Gulf of. An extension of the Red Sea◊. The frontiers of Israel, Egypt, Jordan, and Saudi Arabia converge here□

Aquae Sulis see Bath◊□

aquamarine see beryl◊□

aquarium institution displaying and studying aquatic (salt or freshwater) life; the most famous include Monaco, Plymouth, Woods Hole, Scripps Institute. See oceanarium◊□

aquatint see print◊□

Aquaviva Claudius 1543–1615. General of the Jesuits◊ from 1581, he was an able organizer and educator□

aqueduct raised artificial water channel; famous examples are those at Nîmes in France (Roman 18AD, still standing); the Chimu system in Peru (13–15th century, of which there has been some modern restoration), their civilization being destroyed when it was cut by the Inca; the Bridgewater Canal over River Irwell (Britain's first modern aqueduct 1759–72); and the Colorado River aqueduct, 400 km/250 mi long, which supplies Los Angeles□

Aquinas St Thomas 1226–74. Italian Dominican monk and theologian, the 'Angelic Doctor'. His *Summa Contra Gentiles*, and *Summa Theologica* are designed to show that reason and faith are compatible. His works embodied the world view taught in universities up till the mid-17th century, and include scientific ideas derived from Aristotle; in 1879 they were recognized as the basis of Catholic theology. See scholasticism◊□

Aquitaine region of SW France, capital Bordeaux; population 2 584 400. Eleanor of Aquitaine married the future Henry II of England in 1152, and brought it to him as her dowry; it remained an English possession till 1452. Red wines, e.g. Margaux and St Julien, are produced in the district of Médoc, north of Bordeaux and bordering the Gironde. There are remains of early man in the Dordogne◊□

Arab Emirates United. See United◊ Arab Emirates□

Arabia SW Asian peninsula, comprising Bahrein, Kuwait, Oman, Qatar, Saudi Arabia, United Arab Emirates, N and S Yemen; area 3 000 000 sq km/1 200 000 sq mi. Although parts of Arabia reached a high degree of civilization more than a thousand years BC, a United Arab identity began with the foundation of Islam (7th century) and its militant expansion, when Arabian cities were eclipsed by Damascus, Baghdad and Cairo. Colonialism in the 19th century touched only the fringes of Arabia itself (Aden◊), but European travellers (Gertrude Bell◊, T E Lawrence◊, H St John Philby◊, Freya Stark◊, Charles Doughty◊) produced literary classics. Nationalism emerged at the end of World War I, and the major oil discoveries from 1953 brought Arabia into modern politics, with an influential economic role from the oil crisis of 1973□

Arabian Gulf see Gulf◊□

Arabian Nights oriental tales in oral circulation among Arab storytellers from the 10th century, and probably having roots in India. They include *Ali Baba, Aladdin,* and *Sindbad.* They were supposed to have been told to the sultan by his bride Scheherazade to avoid her predecessors' fate of execution following the wedding night (to prevent their infidelity). She began a new tale each evening, which she would only agree to finish on the following night. Eventually the 'sentence' was rescinded□

Arabian sea the NW branch of the Indian Ocean◊□

Arabic chief of the S branch of the Semitic languages; pure classical Arabic, the language of the Koran, survives in Saudi Arabia, but the accepted best colloquial form is that of Egypt, established by radio broadcasts from Cairo, the 'Voice of the Arabs' and the Egyptian newspaper *Al Ahram*. Other forms may not be mutually intelligible; many Arabic words (especially scientific) appear in other languages; the script requires 300–1000 characters (a factor in high illiteracy rates), and the graceful script is much used in decoration because of Islamic prohibition of the depiction of human beings and animals in art (as likely to lead to idolatry)□

Arabic numerals signs 0123456789, which actually originated in India, and were introduced to Europe by the Arabs via Spain; they replaced Roman numerals from the 10th century□

Arab-Israeli Wars wars between members of the Arab◊ League and Israel, which originated with Arab opposition to Zionist◊ aims in Palestine from 1913 (see Balfour◊ Declaration).

From 1920 there were anti-Zionist riots under Britain's League of Nations mandate in Palestine, and in 1936 an Arab revolt led to a British Royal Commission which recommended partition (approved by the United Nations in 1947, but rejected by the Arabs).

First Arab-Israeli War 14 October 1948–13 Jan/24 Mar 1949. This followed the British surrender of the mandate, when the Arabs attacked the new state, and resulted in the enlargement on all fronts of the original Israeli boundaries.

Second Arab-Israeli War 29 Oct–4 Nov 1956. Coincident with the Suez◊ crisis, it resulted in the Israelis capturing Sinai and the Gaza Strip, from which they withdrew after the entry of a UN force.

Third Arab-Israeli War 5–10 Jun 1967, the 'Six Day War'. It resulted in the Israeli capture of the Golan Heights from Syria; Old Jerusalem and the West Bank from Jordan; and, in the south, occupation of the Gaza Strip and Sinai Peninsula as far as the Suez Canal.

Fourth Arab-Israeli War 2–22/24 Oct 1973, the 'Oct War' or 'Yom Kippur War'. So-called because the Israeli forces were taken by surprise on the Day of Atonement◊. It resulted in the recrossing of the Suez Canal by Egyptian forces and initial gains, though there was some later loss of ground by the Syrians in the north.

The Arab cause was adopted by the USSR and the Israeli by the USA; terrorist outrages by Arab extremist groups (see terrorism◊) and retaliation by Israelis continued. In 1978 the Camp◊ David Agreements brought Egypt–Israeli peace, but this was denounced by other Arab countries. Israel withdrew from Sinai 1979–82, but no final agreement on Jerusalem and the establishment of a Palestinian state on the W Bank was reached.

Fifth Arab-Israeli War from 1978 the presence of Palestinian guerrillas in Lebanon led to alternate Arab raids on Israel and Israeli retaliatory incursions, but on 6 Jun 1982 Israel launched a full-scale invasion. By 14 Jun Beirut was encircled, and PLO◊ and Syrian forces were evacuated (mainly to Syria) 21–31 Aug, but in Feb 1985 there was a unilateral Israeli withdrawal from the country without any gain for losses incurred. This, however, has not prevented Israeli incursions making the withdrawal more nominal than actual□

Arabistan see Khuzestan◊□

Arab League an organisations of Arab states established in Cairo in 1945 to promote Arab unity, especially in opposition to Israel; in 1979 its headquarters was transferred to Tunis in protest against the Egypt-Israeli peace□

Arachne in Greek mythology, a girl weaver who beat Athena◊ in a contest, and was transformed by her into a spider (Greek *arachne*)□

arachnida class in the animal phylum Arthopoda which includes spiders◊, mites◊, ticks◊, harvestmen◊, and scorpions◊□

arack see under palm◊□

Arad industrial town in Romania; population 147 000□

Arafat Yassir 1929– . Palestinian politician. President of the Palestine Liberation Organization (PLO) from 1969, he was forced to evacuate Lebanon 1983, but remained leader of the majority of the PLO. In 1985 he agreed with Hussein of Jordan on *de facto* recognition of Israel if territory seized since 1967 is restored□

Arafura Sea the area of the Pacific Ocean between N Australia and Indonesia□

Aragón autonomous region of NE Spain (including Saragossa); population 1 213 000. The medieval kingdom of Aragon was united with Castile in 1469 by the marriage of Ferdinand◊ and Isabella◊□

Aragon Louis 1897–1982. French poet and novelist, a leader of the Surrealists◊ and a Communist from 1930. In World War II he was in the resistance□

Aral Sea inland 'sea', the world's 4th biggest lake; divided between Kazakhstan and Uzbekistan, USSR; former area 62 000 sq km/24 000 sq mi. Water from its feeder rivers, the Amu and Syr Darya, has been diverted for irrigation and city use, and the sea is disappearing, with long-term consequences for the climate, etc.□

Aram Eugene 1704–59. British philologist. He was arrested but released in 1745 on suspicion of murdering a friend and possible accomplice in crime, but hanged when the man's skeleton was found. See Knaresborough◊□

Aramaic semitic language allied to Hebrew, the *lingua franca* of the Near East from the 5th century BC. Hebrew having died out as a spoken tongue, Aramaic was the language of Christ, and still survives in parts of Lebanon and Syria. The modern printed Hebrew alphabet is Aramaic□

Aran Islands three islands in the mouth of Galway Bay, Republic of Ireland; population 4600. The capital is Kilronan. J M Synge◊ used the colourful language of the islands in his plays□

Aranjuez town south east of Madrid, Spain, with a former royal summer palace; population 29 000□

Ararat double-peaked mountain on the Turkish-Iranian border; the higher, Great Ararat, 5156 m/17 000 ft was the reputed resting place of the Ark after the Flood□

Ararat wheat and wool centre in NW Victoria, Australia; population 8300□

Araucanian Indians a member of a group of American Indian peoples, the aboriginals of central Chile; population 200 000; they defeated the Incas and resisted the Spaniards for 200 years□

araucaria genus of large coniferous trees, notably *A araucana*, the monkey puzzle, a native of Chile□

arbitration submission of a dispute to a third unbiased party for settlement, e.g. personal litigation, trade union issues, and international disputes (see Alabama◊). The first permanent international court was established at The Hague in 1900, and the League of Nations set up an additional Permanent Court of International Justice in 1921 to deal with frontier disputes, etc. The latter was replaced in 1946 by the United Nations International Court of Justice – neither was effective. More effective is the European Court of Justice of the Common Market, which rules on disputes arising out of the Rome◊ treaties□

Arbor Day tree planting day in USA, S Australia, New Zealand□

Arbroath fishing town in Tayside, Scotland; population 22 600. In 1320 the Scottish Parliament asserted Scotland's independence here in a letter to the Pope□

Arbuthnot John 1667–1735. Scottish physician, attendant on Queen Anne 1705–14. He created the national character of John Bull, depicted as a prosperous farmer, in his *The History of John Bull* 1712, pamphlets advocating peace with France□

arbutus genus of evergreen shrubs, family Ericaceae◊, especially the ***strawberry tree*** *A unedo*, grown for its ornamental strawberry-like fruit□

Arcadia central plateau of S Greece; later writers idealized the life of shepherds here in antiquity. See Sir Philip Sidney◊□

Arc de Triomphe triumphal arch in the Place de l'Étoile, Paris, France, built 1806–36 in imitation of those honouring ancient Roman generals. It was intended by Napoleon to commemorate his victories of 1805–6; in 1920 the 'Unknown Soldier' of France was buried beneath it□

Arc de Triomphe. Prix de l'. French equivalent of the Derby, run at Longchamp□

Arch Joseph 1826–1919. British trade unionist. A Methodist preacher, he founded the National Agricultural Union for farmworkers in 1872, the first of its kind□

archaeology the study of prehistory and ancient periods of history, based on the examination of their physical remains.

14–16th century Renaissance interest in classical art, e.g. Cellini◊

1748 Pompeii◊ rediscovered, and aroused the interest of connoisseurs, e.g. Sir William Hamilton◊

1790 John Frere◊ identified Old Stone Age tools and large extinct animals

1822 Champollion◊ deciphered Egyptian hieroglyphics

1832 Charles and John Deane◊ pioneered the recording of underwater finds, *Mary Rose*, etc.

1836 C J Thomsen◊ devised the Stone, Bronze, and Iron Age classification

1840s Layard◊ excavated the Assyrian capital, Nineveh

1868 Great Zimbabwe◊ ruins first seen by white men

1871 Schliemann◊ began work at Troy◊

1879 Stone Age paintings were first discovered at Altamira◊

1880s Pitt-Rivers◊ developed the technique of stratification

1891 Petrie◊ began excavating Tell el Amarna (Akhetaton◊)

1899–1935 A J Evans◊ excavated Minoan Knossos in Crete

1911 Hiram Bingham◊ discovered the Inca city of Machu Picchu◊

1911–12 Piltdown◊ skull 'discovered'; proved a fake in 1949

1914–18 Osbert Crawford developed the technique of aerial survey of sites

1922 Tutankhamen◊'s tomb opened by Howard Carter◊

1935 A E Douglas◊ developed dendrochronology

1939 Anglo-Saxon ship burial treasure found at Sutton Hoo◊

1947 first of the Dead Sea Scrolls◊ discovered
1948 Proconsul apeman discovered by Mary Leakey◊ in Kenya
1953 Ventris◊ deciphered Minoan 'Linear B'
1960s radiocarbon dating◊, thermoluminescence◊, etc. developed
1961 Swedish warship *Wasa* raised at Stockholm◊
1963 W B Emery pioneered 'rescue archaeology' at Abu Simbel
1974 tomb of Shi◊ Huangdi discovered in China
1978 tomb of Philip◊ of Macedon (Alexander's father) discovered
1979 Aztec capital, Tenochtitlán◊ excavated beneath Mexico city
1982 Henry VIII's warship *Mary Rose*◊ raised
1985 major work on wreck of the Dutch East Indiaman *Amsterdam* near Hastings begun□

archaeopteryx earliest known bird (160 million years ago), of which fossils have been found in Bavaria. It was the size of a pigeon, fully feathered, but with reptilian features, e.g. grasping 'hands' on the front of its wings, sharp teeth, and a long tail. It was probably warm-blooded□

Archangel port (Russian Archangelsk), blocked by ice half the year, in the N USSR; population 391 000. It was used in 1918–20 by the Allied interventionist armies in collaboration with the White◊ Army in their effort to overthrow the newly established Soviet State; in World War II it was the receiving station for Anglo-American supplies. An open city in a closed area, it can be visited by foreigners only by air, and has one of the world's largest concentrations of IBM◊ computers. Plesetsk, to the south, is a launch site for cosmonauts□

archbishop see Anglican Communion◊□

Archer Fred(erick) 1857–86. British jockey. He had 2748 wins in 8084 races, including five Derby◊ wins 1877,1880, 1881, 1885, 1886; he shot himself□

Archer Jeffrey 1940– . British author and politician. A Conservative MP 1969–74, he lost a fortune in a disastrous investment, but recouped it as a best-selling novelist, e.g. *Not a Penny More, Not a Penny Less* 1975 and *First Among Equals* 1984. In 1985 he became deputy chairman of the party□

archerfish family of fish, Toxotidae (Australia, SE Asia), of which *Toxotes chatareus* stuns insects just above the water with a jet of water from its mouth□

archery the use of a bow and arrow as a war and hunting weapon, or for sport. It was practised in prehistory in Assyria and Egypt; Crécy was a famous victory of English longbowmen; in 14–16th century warfare it was phased out as guns were introduced, but even today the Queen's bodyguard in Scotland is the Royal Company of Archers. In the 1780s it was revived as a target sport, governed by the Fédération Internationale de Tir á l'Arc (FITA); the USA has an association for hunting with the bow, but this is banned in Britain□

Archimedes 287–212BC. Greek mathematician who made discoveries in geometry, hydrostatics◊ and mechanics. He proved that the goldsmith of the King of Syracuse had adulterated a gold crown with silver by a fluid displacement method, formulated when he stepped into the public bath and saw it overflow (see Archimedes◊ principle). He was so delighted that he rushed home naked, crying 'Eureka! Eureka!' ('I've got it! I've got it!')□

Archimedes principle a law which states that the apparent loss of weight of anything immersed in a fluid is equal to the weight of the displaced fluid□

Archimedes screw. a pump consisting of a spiral screw revolving inside a close fitting cylinder; used, for example, to raise irrigation water□

Archipenko, Alexander 1887–1964. Russo-American sculptor, pioneer of Cubism and carved plastic□

architecture the style of building, especially of a particular country or period of history. Styles include:
4000–1st century BC Egyptian: stonework and stylized sculptural ornament of massive appearance and exact symmetry, numerous columns as roofing supports, decorative sculptures and wall painting, examples include the Pyramids, Karnak, Akhetaton, Abu Simbel, tombs of the Valley of the Kings, temple of Isis at Philae.
16th–2nd century BC Greek: perfection of form in temples and use of orders of columns◊, e.g. Parthenon◊; many open-air theatres. Later styles which use the forms of Greek, and also Roman, architecture are referred to as ***classical,*** e.g. Renaissance.
7th century BC–5th AD Roman: emphasis on impressive public buildings; first use of bricks and cement to produce the vault, arch and dome; Tuscan◊ and Composite◊ orders added, e.g. baths of Caracalla◊, amphitheatres (Colosseum◊), basilicas (Pantheon◊), triumphal arches, (Trajan's◊ Column), aqueducts (Nîmes◊).
4–10th century AD byzantine: originating in Byzantium; churches based on the Greek cross plan (Hagia Sophia, Istanbul◊; St Mark's, Venice◊); use of formalized, sym-

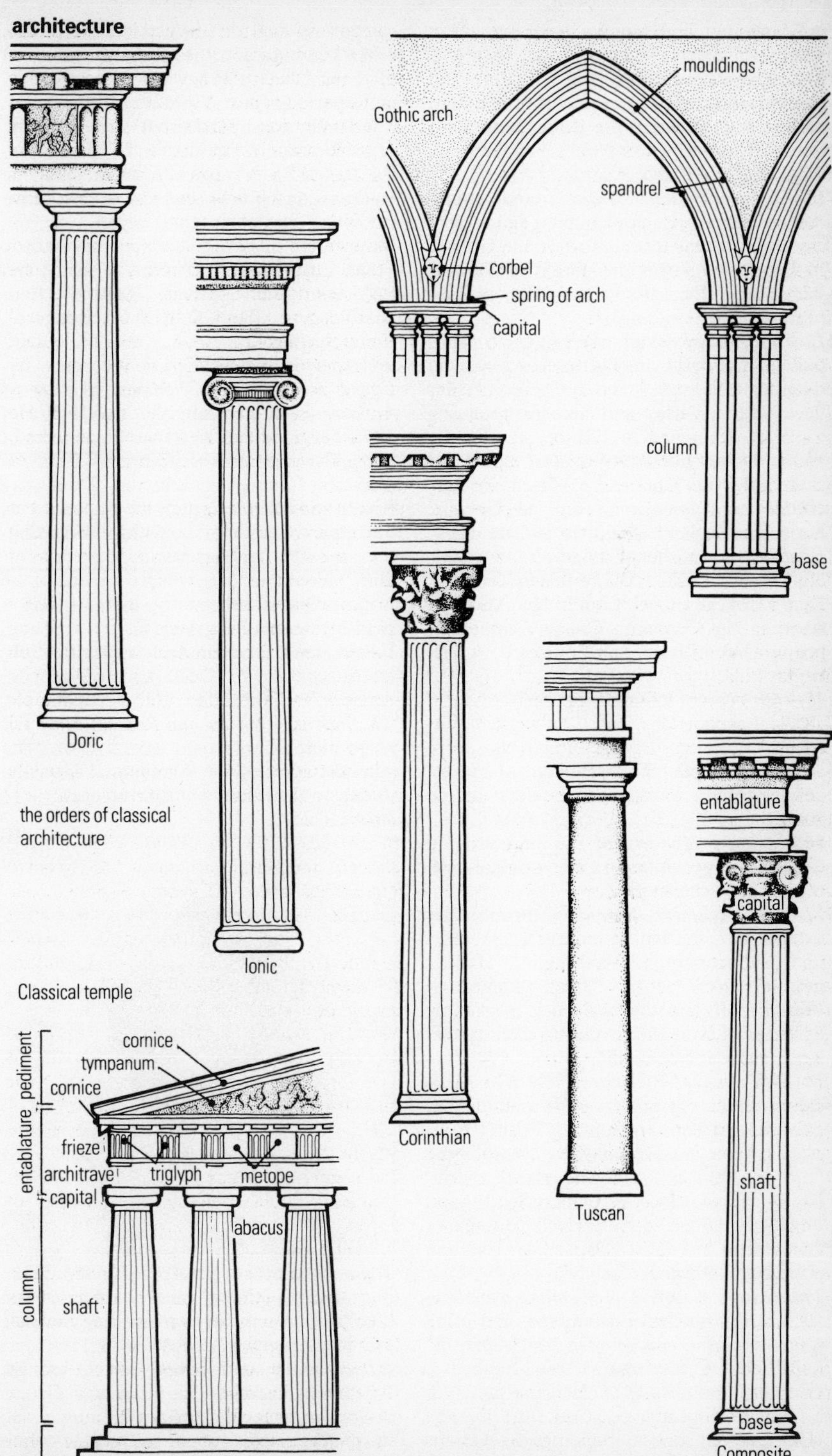
architecture
Gothic arch
mouldings
spandrel
corbel
spring of arch
capital
column
base
Doric
the orders of classical architecture
Ionic
Corinthian
Tuscan
entablature
capital
shaft
base
Composite
Classical temple
pediment
cornice
tympanum
cornice
entablature
frieze
architrave
triglyph
metope
capital
abacus
column
shaft

bolic painted and mosaic decoration (San Vitale, Ravenna◊).
7–17th century Islamic: use of dome and pointed arch, the latter incorporated into Gothic, e.g. Dome of the Rock, Jerusalem; Great Mosque, Cordova◊; Alhambra◊, Granada, Taj Mahal, Agra◊.
10–13th century Romanesque: rounded arch, marked perpendicular elements, and experiments in vaulting leading toward the Gothic. In England this was the period of ***Norman*** architecture (Durham◊ cathedral has an early example of rib vaulting).
13–16th century Gothic: use of the rib vault, pointed arch and flying buttress, especially in religious buildings; stress on perpendicular lines with galleries and arcades replacing walls. It developed in 12th-century France and is divided into *Early Gothic,* e.g. Sens◊ cathedral; *High Gothic,* e.g. Chartres◊; *Late Gothic* or *Flamboyant*◊, e.g. St Gervais, Paris. In England the divisions are *Early English,* e.g. Salisbury Cathedral; *Decorated,* e.g. Wells◊ Cathedral: *Perpendicular,* e.g. King's College chapel, Cambridge. Also outstanding, in Germany, Cologne cathedral, begun 1248; in Italy, San Francesco, Assisi, begun 1228.
15–16th century Renaissance: readoption of classical proportions, based on work of Vitruvius◊; major Italian architects were Alberti, Brunelleschi, Bramante, Michelangelo, Raphael, Palladro; in England Indigo Jones.
16th century Mannerism: use of motifs in deliberate opposition to their original concept, e.g. Michelangelo◊.
17–18th century Baroque: exuberantly extravagant, and usually large scale; see Bernini◊, Borromini◊, Vanbrugh◊, Hawksmoor◊, Wren◊, Le Vau◊, Hardouin-Mansart◊. Its last stage is ***Rococo,*** marked by lightness of style and favouring shell motifs, e.g. Balthasar Neumann◊.
18–19th century Neoclassical: return to classical principles, e.g. in large-scale rebuilding of London and Paris by Adam◊, Nash◊, Haussmann◊ (see also Regency◊); but also in the later 18–19th-century ***Gothic revival***, especially in churches (see Sir Gilbert Scott◊) and official buildings, e.g. Barry◊'s Houses of Parliament. For the 1890s, see ***Art Nouveau*** (Gaudi◊, C R Mackintosh◊)
20th century Modern Functionalism excluding all that did not serve a purpose, and using glass, steel and concrete (in which Paxton◊ had been a forerunner) see Bauhaus◊, Gropius◊, but a ***modified classicism*** survived, e.g. Sir Edwin Lutyens◊. Concentration was also less on specific buildings in various categories, than on their relationship with other buildings and the environment (town planning), and whole new cities were planned in the period of post World War II expansion. The results were particularly striking in the Third World, e.g. Brasilia◊ and Chandigarh◊. By the 1970s a reversion from synthetic materials and box-like effects to decorative detail and natural materials began.
Major architects of the 20th century include Frank Loyd Wright◊, Mies◊ van der Rohe, Le◊ Corbusier, Alvar Aalto◊, Eero Saarinen◊; in the UK Richard Rodgers◊, James Stirling◊□

archives historically valuable records.
United Kingdom: the ***National Register of Archives*** is in London; the ***Public Record Office*** (London and Kew) has documents of law and government departments from the Norman Conquest, including Domesday Book◊ and Magna Carta◊; the ***National Portrait Gallery*** has photos, paintings and sculptures; the ***BBC Archives*** has sound recordings, films, videotapes, etc., which form one of the world's largest collections; there is also a British National Film Archive.
United States: ***National Archives Hall***, Washington, contains the Declaration of Independence, US Constitution, Bill of Rights, etc; the ***National Archives and Records Service*** is responsible for preserving federal records and administration of the presidential libraries, usually in the incumbent's birthplace□

Arctic The.

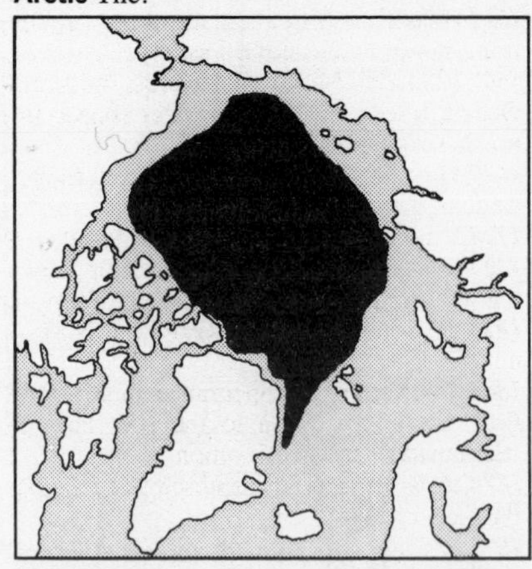

The region north of the Arctic Circle◊. There is no Arctic continent, merely pack ice (which breaks up in summer) surrounding the Pole and floating on the Arctic◊ Ocean. Pack ice is carried by the south flowing current into the Atlantic as icebergs◊. In the winter the sun disappears below the horizon for a time (and in summer remains above it), but the cold is not so severe as in parts of E Siberia or the Antarctic. Land areas in the Arctic have mainly stunted tundra vegetation, with an outburst of summer flowers; animals include reindeer, caribou, musk ox; foxes, hares, lemming, and wolves; polar bear, seal, walrus; few birds, except in summer, when there is much insect life, especially mosquitoes. The aboriginal people are the Inuit◊ of the American/Canadian Arctic and Greenland. The most valuable resource is oil□

Arctic Circle an arbitrary line drawn round the North Pole at 66°33′N□

Arctic exploration

35 000 BC ancestors of the Inuit and American Indians began migration from Siberia to N America by the 'lost' landbridge of Beringia

320BC Pytheas, Greek sailor contemporary with Alexander the Great, possibly reached Iceland

9–10th centuries AD Vikings colonized Iceland and Greenland, which then had a much warmer climate

c1000 Leif Ericsson◊ reached Baffin Island and Labrador

1497 John Cabot◊ first sought the NW Passage as a trade route round N America for Henry VII

1553 Richard Chancellor◊ tried to find the NE Passage round Siberia and first established direct English trade with Russia

1576 Martin Frobisher◊ reached Frobisher Bay, but found only 'fools' gold' (iron pyrites) for Elizabeth I

1594–7 Willem Barents made three expeditions in search of the NE Passage

1607 Henry Hudson◊ failed to cross the Arctic Ocean, but his reports of whales started the northern whaling industry

1670 Hudson's Bay Company started the fur trade in Canada

1728 Vitus Bering◊ passed Bering Strait

1773 Nelson◊, as a midshipman, accompanied the naval expedition of Constantine Phipps

1829–33 John Ross◊ discovered the N Magnetic Pole

1845 mysterious disappearance of Sir John Franklin◊'s expedition to the NW Passage stimulated further exploration

1878–9 Nils Nordenskiöld◊ discovered the NE Passage

1893–6 Fridtjof Nansen's◊ ship *Fram* drifted across the Arctic, locked in the ice, proving that no Arctic continent existed

1903–6 Roald Amundsen◊ sailed through the NW Passage

1909 Robert Peary◊, Matt Henson, and four Inuits, reached the N Pole on 2 Apr

1926 Richard Byrd◊ and Floyd Bennett flew to the Pole on 9 May

1926 Umberto Nobile and Amundsen crossed the Pole (Spitzbergen–Alaska) in the airship *Norge* on 12 May

1954 first regular commercial flights over the 'short-cut' polar route by Scandinavian Airlines

1958 submarine *Nautilus* (USA) crossed the Pole beneath the ice

1960 from this date a Soviet nuclear-powered icebreaker has kept open a 4000 km/2500 mi Asia-Europe passage along the north coast of Siberia 150 days a year

1969 first surface crossing, by dog sled, of the Arctic Ocean (Alaska–Spitzbergen) by Wally Herbert◊, British Transarctic Expedition, Feb-May

1977 icebreaker *Arktika* (USSR) made the first surface voyage to the Pole

1982 first circumnavigation of Earth (2 Sept 1979–29 Aug 1982) via the Poles by Sir Ranulph Fiennes and Charles Burton□

Arctic Ocean ocean surrounding the North Pole; area 14 090 000 sq km/5 440 000 sq mi. Because of the Siberian rivers flowing into it, it has comparatively low salinity and freezes readily. It is divided into various seas:

Beaufort off Canada/Alaska coast, named after Sir Francis Beaufort◊; oil drilling is allowed only in winter because the sea is the breeding and migration route of the bowhead whales, staple diet of the local Inuit.

Greenland between Greenland and Svalbard, and ***Norwegian*** between Greenland and Norway.

West to east along the north coast of the USSR:

Barents named after Willem Barents◊, which has oil and gas reserves and is strategically important as the meeting point of the NATO and Warsaw Pact forces.

Kara renowned for treacherous weather, and known as the 'great ice cellar'.

Laptev between Taimyr Peninsula and New Siberian Island.

East Siberian and ***Chukchi*** between USSR/USA; the semi-nomadic Chukchi people of NE Siberia finally accepted Soviet rule only in the 1930s. See also White◊ Sea□

Arden Forest of. Idyllic forest of Shakespeare's *As You Like It*, in N Warwickshire; only traces survive□

Arden John 1930– . British playwright. His *Serjeant Musgrave's Dance* 1959 is a Brechtian attack on war□

Ardennes wooded plateau in NE France, SE Belgium and N Luxembourg, cut through by the River Meuse; there was heavy fighting here in both World Wars. See Champagne◊-Ardenne□

Ardennes offensive Hitler's concept, code 'Watch on the Rhine', of a breakthrough by Rundstedt◊ aimed at the American line here 16 Dec 1944–31 Jan 1945; also known as the *Battle of the Bulge*. There were 77 000 US casualties; 130 000 German, including Hitler's last powerful reserve, his Panzer élite□

areca see betel-nut◊□

Arecibo town in NW Puerto Rico; population 70 000. There is a large radiotelescope□

Arequipa city in Peru; population 561 000. It was founded by Pizarro◊ in 1540□

Ares in Greek mythology, the god of war (Roman Mars◊)□

Arezzo town in Italy; population 81 500. Petrarch◊ was born here□

Argentina Republic of

area 2 780 000 sq km/1 073 000 sq mi

capital Buenos Aires

towns Rosario◊, Córdoba◊, Tucumán◊, Mendoza◊, Santa Fé◊; ports are La Plata◊ and Bahía Blanca◊

features Andes◊, Aconcagua◊; rivers Paraná◊ and Colorado◊; Gran Chaco◊, Pampas◊, Tierra del Fuego◊

exports beef, livestock, cereals, wool, tannin, groundnuts, linseed oil, minerals (coal, copper, molybdenum, gold, silver, lead, zinc, barium, uranium), and the country has huge resources of oil, natural gas, and hydro-electric power

currency austral

population 30 097 000, mainly of Spanish or Italian origin, only about 30 000 American Indians surviving

language Spanish

religion Roman Catholicism (state supported)

famous people Che Guevara◊, Jorge Luis Borges◊. (See also W H Hudson◊)

government senate and house of deputies, and a president (Raul Alfonsin of the Radical party from 1983) elected by popular vote, through electoral colleges

recent history originally inhabited by American Indians, who were almost wiped out by the Spaniards in the 19th century, Argentina established her independence from Spain (under the leadership of San Martín◊) 1810–16, when she became a republic. The outstanding political figure of the 20th century was Perón◊, whose Peronist following continues, sometimes in collaboration with the left-wing guerrilla Montoneros. From 1976 overall control was exercised by a military junta, and about 15 000 people 'disappeared' (*los desaparecidos*) during a campaign against socialists and trade unionists. Although a return to civilian rule had been promised, General Leopoldo Galtieri retained his post within the junta on assuming the presidency in 1981. The Falkland◊ Islands were abortively invaded in 1982, and in Jun Galtieri was replaced by Reynaldo Bignone until elections could be held in 1983.

Argentina's dispute with Chile over islands in the Beagle Channel off Tierra◊ del Fuego ended in 1985□

argon. element

symbol Ar

atomic number 18

physical description colourless gas

features an inert gas, forming 1% of the atmosphere

uses as an inert atmosphere for electric light bulbs, fluorescent tubes, radiation counters, and in argon lasers□

argonaut see nautilus◊□

Argonauts see Jason◊□

Argonne wooded plateau in NE France, scene of fierce fighting in World Wars I and II□

Argos city in ancient Greece, at the head of the Gulf of Nauplia, once a cult centre of Hera◊□

Argus in Greek mythology, a giant with a hundred eyes, which Hera◊, eventually transplanted to the tail of her favourite bird, the peacock□

Argyll line of Scottish peers, including:

Archibald Campbell, 8th Earl of Argyll 1607–61; he led the Covenanting Party during the Civil Wars; he crowned Charles II in 1651 and submitted to Cromwell in 1652; he was beheaded after the Restoration.

Archibald Campbell, 9th Earl of Argyll 1629–85; he was executed for leading a rebellion in co-operation with Monmouth's rising.

John Campbell, 2nd Duke of Argyll 1678–1743; he became a peer of the UK for helping to promote the Union of England and Scotland□

Ariadne see Theseus◊□

Ariane booster rocket (French form of Ariadne) for launching space satellites from Kourou, French Guiana; run by the European consortium Ariane-Space. First successful commercial launch 1983□

Arianism see Arius◊□

Arica port in Chile; population 40 000. It is much used by land-locked Bolivia, which is negotiating a land corridor at this point□

Ariosto Ludovico 1474–1533. Italian poet-diplomat. His romantic epic *Orlando Furioso* deals with Orlando, the follower of Charlemagne◊, who was driven mad by the flirtatious Angelica, Princess of Cathay□

Aristarchus of Samos 310–264BC. Greek astronomer. The first to argue that the earth moves round the sun, he was not believed□

Aristides 530–468BC. Athenian statesman. He was sent into political exile in 482 because the citizens tired of hearing him praised as 'Aristides the Just' (he had allocated the war taxes meticulously). He later fought at Marathon◊, Salamis◊ and Plataea◊□

Aristippus 435–356BC. Greek philosopher, a pupil of Socrates and founder of the Hedonist◊ school□

Aristophanes 448–380BC. Greek comic dramatist. His most famous plays are *The Clouds*, ridiculing Socrates; *The Birds*, in which the birds build the utopia of Cloud-cuckoo-land; and *Lysistrata,* in which the women force an end to war by refusing their husbands conjugal rights until peace is made□

Aristotle 384–322BC. Greek philosopher. He studied under Plato◊, became tutor to Alexander◊ the Great, and in 335 opened a school in the Lyceum (grove sacred to Apollo) at Athens. He walked up and down as he talked, hence 'peripatetic school', and his works are really a collection of these lecture notes: on logic, metaphysics, physics, astronomy, biology, psychology, ethics, politics, literary criticism, etc. He taught that sense experience is the only source of knowledge and stressed the value of reason, but medieval scholars tended to accept his awe-inspiring output without question; his basic ideas reappeared in both Christian and Islamic thought. See logic◊, scholasticism◊□

arithmetic counting in units or parts of units (fractions/decimals); basic operations, addition, subtraction, multiplication, division. ***Powers***, repeated multiplication of the same number, are represented by an index: $2^5 = 2$ to the 5th $= 2 \times 2 \times 2 \times 2 \times 2$. ***Roots*** are the reverse: the 5th root of 32 is 2, since $2 \times 2 \times 2 \times 2 \times 2 = 32$. See logarithms◊.

The essential feature of modern arithmetic is ***place value***: the decimal system has nine numerals plus 0, which in itself has no value, but is used to keep the other numerals in their right places. Each place has a value ten times greater than the one to its right; 3 = 3, but 3 moved one place to the left, 30 = 3 tens. Base ten has no particular virtue; base 12 would be more flexible, and earlier cultures used quite different bases, Babylonian 60 and Maya 20; modern computers use base 2, which uses only two figures 0 and 1 (see binary◊ number system). ***Modular arithmetic*** deals with events recurring in regular cycles, and is used in describing the functioning of petrol engines, electrical generators, etc. In the modulo-twelve system, the answer to a question as to what time it will be in five hours if it is now ten o'clock is expressed 10 + 5 = 3□

Arius 256–336AD. Priest of Alexandria who denied the complete divinity of Christ; excommunicated 318. His heresy ***Arianism*** became so popular that Athanasius◊ was called in to refute it; by 1979 it was again causing concern to the Vatican in the writings of Edouard Schillebeeckx□

Arizona mountain state in SW USA; Grand Canyon State

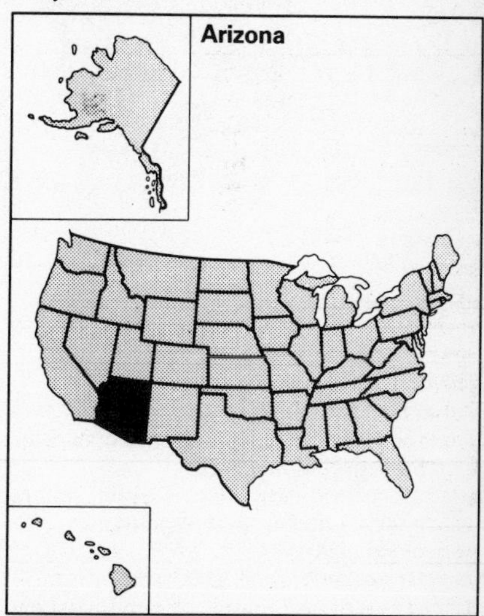

area 295 023 sq km/113 909 sq mi
capital Phoenix
towns Tucson
features Grand Canyon National Park (the multi-coloured gorge through which the Colorado flows, 6–29 km/4–18 mi wide, up to 1.5 km/1 mi deep and 350 km/217 mi

long), Painted Desert (including the Petrified Forest, of fossil trees), Organ Pipe Cactus National Monument Park, Gila Desert, and Sonoran Desert; Colorado river; Roosevelt and Hoover dams; old London Bridge was transported 1971 to the tourist resort of Lake Havasu City
products cotton under irrigation; livestock; copper, molybdenum, silver; electronics, aircraft, etc. overspilling from California
population 2 717 866, including over 100 000 American Indians (Navajo, Hopi, Apache), who still own a quarter of the state
famous people Geronimo◊, Barry Goldwater◊, Zane Grey◊, Percival Lowell◊, Frank Lloyd Wright◊
history originally colonized by Spain, Arizona was ceded to the USA in 1848 after the Mexican War, and became a state in 1912□

Arkansas border state in S central USA; Wonder State/Land of Opportunity

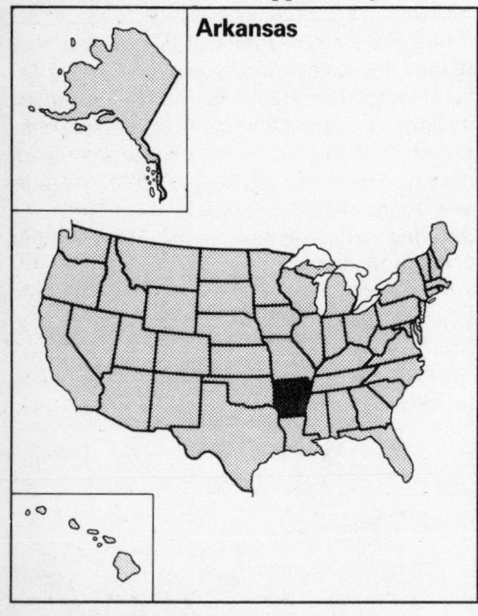

area 137 533 sq km/53 102 sq mi
capital Little Rock
towns Fort Smith
features Ozark mountains; Mississippi river; Hot Springs National Park
products cotton, soybeans, rice; oil, natural gas, bauxite; timber, processed foods
population 2 285 513
famous people Douglas MacArthur
history part of the Louisiana Purchase in 1803, it became a state in 1836. See Confederate States◊□

Arkwright Sir Richard 1732–92. British inventor of a spinning frame 1769, which could supply the strong downward (warp) thread for cotton cloth, so making mass production possible. He was execrated by hand spinners and his patents were infringed by manufacturers□

Arles town in SE France; population 47 000. Its Roman remains include an amphitheatre seating 25 000, and Van Gogh lived here at the end of his life□

Arlington suburb of Washington, USA; the National Cemetery for the dead of US wars includes the grave of the Unknown Soldier of World War I, and John and Robert Kennedy are also buried here□

Armada see Spanish◊ Armada□

armadillo a scaly mammal. See under edentata◊□

Armageddon in New Testament, the site of the final battle between the nations which will end the world; it has been identified with Megiddo◊□

Armagh county of Northern Ireland
area 1266 sq km/489 sq mi
towns county town Armagh
features smallest county of N Ireland; its border with the Republic has made it the scene of many IRA terrorist incidents
products chiefly agricultural, apples, potatoes, flax□

Armagh county town of Armagh, Northern Ireland; population 12 300. It is the seat of the Protestant Archbishop of Armagh, nominally 'Primate of All Ireland'□

Armenia constituent republic of the Soviet Union from 1936
area 29 800 sq km/11 500 sq mi
capital Yerevan
towns Leninakan
features mainly mountainous and wooded
products copper, molybdenum, etc; cereals, cotton, silk
population 3 000 000, 89% Armenian
language Armenian
religion traditionally Armenian Christian
recent history a member of the Transcaucasian Federation in 1917, Armenia became an independent republic in 1918, but was occupied by the Red Army in 1920. (See Georgia◊)□

Armenia mountainous region (see Ararat◊) on the USSR-Turkey-Iran border□

Armenian Church Church founded in the 3rd century by St Gregory the Illuminator, it is closer to Roman Catholicism than other eastern churches□

Armenian Question problem from 1878 of the Armenian Christians oppressed under Turkish Islamic rule. When promised reforms failed to be made, Armenian nationalist unrest was followed by massacres of Armenians 1895, 1909, 1915. Demands for the re-creation of Turkish Armenia by exiles have involved terrorist outrages in the 1980s□

Armentiéres town in N France; population 27 500. Held by the British in World War I, it was flattened by German bombardment in 1918 and rebuilt□

Armidale town in New South Wales, Australia; population 20 000. The University of New England is here, and mansions of the squatters◊ survive□

Arminius 17BC–21AD. German chieftain. An ex-Roman army man, he annihilated a Roman force led by Varus in 9AD, and saved Germany from becoming a Roman province. He also ensured that the Empire's frontier was withdrawn to the Rhine□

Arminius Jacobus. Latinized name of Jakob Harmensen 1560–1609, founder of ***Arminianism***; more optimistic than Calvinism◊, it claimed that forgiveness and eternal life were open to all repentant sinners; it is the basis of Wesleyan Methodist theology in England□

Armory Show art exhibition Feb 1913 in the armory of the 69th Cavalry Regiment, New York, which marked the arrival of modern non-realistic art in the USA. The rioting crowd threatened to rip to pieces the Cubist work by Marcel Duchamp *Nude Descending a Staircase*□

armour personal body protection worn in battle. The craftsmanship of the armourer reached its height in design in the 15th century, when knights were completely encased, although freedom of bodily movement was retained. Suits of armour in the Tower of London were studied by US designers of astronaut wear. Modern armour, used not only by the army, but by police and security guards and assassination-prone statesmen, uses nylon, fibre-glass, etc., and is often worn beneath other clothing□

Armstrong Edwin Howard 1890–1954. American radio engineer, inventor of superheterodyne tuning for reception over a very wide spectrum of radio frequencies; and frequency modulation for static-free listening□

Armstrong Louis 1900–71. American jazz trumpeter, nicknamed Satchmo – 'satchelmouth'. Born in New Orleans, he joined Kid Ory's band in 1917 and formed his own in 1924□

Armstrong, Neil 1930– . American astronaut. He was the first man to step on the moon in 1969, when he said: 'That's one small step for a man, one giant leap for mankind'□

Arnauld Antoine. See Jansenism◊□

Arne Thomas Augus 1710–78. British composer, whose musical drama *Alfred* includes the song 'Rule Britannia!'□

Arnhem town in the Netherlands, on the Rhine south east of Utrecht◊. Sir Philip Sidney died here in 1586□

Arnhem Battle of. Airborne operation, 17–27 Sept 1944, to secure a bridgehead over the Rhine for an Allied drive to the heart of Germany. It failed, with 7600 casualties, owing to miscalculations and the accidental presence of General Model's Panzers□

Arnhem Land plateau of the central peninsula in Northern Territory, Australia. It is the largest of the Aboriginal reserves, and a traditional way of life is maintained, now threatened by mineral exploitation□

Arno river in N Italy; 240 km/150 mi long. Florence and Pisa are on its banks□

Arnold Benedict 1741–1801. American soldier, who in 1780 plotted to betray the strategic post at West Point to the British. Major André was sent by the British to discuss terms, but was caught and hanged. Arnold himself escaped and was given a British army command□

Arnold Malcolm 1921– . British composer, popularly best known for his film music, e.g. *The Bridge on the River Kwai*□

Arnold Matthew 1822–88. British poet, son of Thomas Arnold◊. He was a school inspector 1851–86. His best-known poems are 'The Forsaken Merman', 'Thyrsis' – commemorating his friend A H Clough, 'Dover Beach', and 'The Scholar Gypsy'. His *Essays in Criticism* 1865 and 1888 demand 'high seriousness' and 'a criticism of life' in the poet; *Culture and Anarchy* 1869, attacks 19th-century Philistinism□

Arnold of Brescia 1100–55. Italian Auginian monk, who attacked the holding of property by the Church; he was hanged, burnt, and the ashes were thrown into the Tiber□

Arnold Thomas 1795–1842. British schoolmaster, father of Matthew Arnold◊. He established the best in 19th-century public school ethos by his regime at Rugby 1828–42. See Thomas Hughes◊□

Arp Hans 1887–1966. French painter and sculptor, a founder of Dadaism◊, noted for sculptures with boneless curves, and torn-paper designs□

Arran mountainous island holiday resort in the Firth of Clyde, Scotland□

Arras town in N France; population 72 100□

Arras Battles of. Five battles of World War I, the fiercest in 1917. The town was captured in 1940 by the Germans in the advance on Dunkirk□

Arromanches fishing village in Normandy. A prefabricated 'Mulberry Harbour' was used here on D-day to assist in the assault on the German 'Atlantic Wall'□

arrowroot edible starch derived from the rhizomes of *Maranta arundinacea,* a plant in the family Marantaceae□

arsenic element
symbol As
atomic number 33
physical description Widely distributed semi-metal, found in minute qantities in earth, sea water, and in the human body
features in larger amounts in the human body it is a cumulative poison, resulting in faintness, nausea and eventual death
uses metal working, and (in certain forms) in medicine to treat amoebic dysentery, sleeping sickness, pesticides etc.□

arson setting fire to property, crops, etc.; it is covered in Britain by the Criminal Damage Act 1971□

art see painting◊ and sculpture◊□

Artaud Antonin 1896–1948. French theatrical director, whose idea of a 'Theatre of Cruelty' to release repressed feelings was influential. In 1936 he became insane□

Art Deco style, in art and architecture, originating in France in 1925, and continuing through the 1930s, using rather heavy, geometric simplification of form, e.g. Radio City Music Hall, New York□

Artemis in Greek mythology, the goddess (Roman Diana◊) of chastity, childbirth, and the young; she was envisaged as a virgin huntress; her cult centre was at Ephesus◊. See Selene◊□

arteriosclerosis hardening of the arteries, the thickening and loss of elasticity of the circulatory system. It is associated with aging and the consumption of a high cholesterol (excessive hard animal fat) diet□

artesian well a boring through impermeable rock to water-containing beds, named from Artois, where it was first used in Europe□

arthritis inflammation of the joints◊, genetically based in the case of ***rheumatoid arthritis***, when it is an auto-immune disease◊, probably triggered by a virus infection. More common in women, it usually begins in the small joints of the hands and feet. ***Osteoarthritis***, more common in men, tends to attack the larger joints of the knee and hip. It may appear in later life in manual labourers, athletes, dancers, etc., in whom the joints are subject to stress and damage. However, it is generally less common in those physically active and appears to be linked with crystal deposits, in the form of calcium phosphate, in cartilage, a discovery which suggests hope of eventual prevention. Aspirin is the most commonly used drug. See cortisone◊ and mussel◊□

Arthropoda phylum of the animal kingdom including Arachnida◊, Crustacea◊, Insecta◊ – all with segmented bodies in a horny casing. Of an estimated more than 30 million species, 75% are insects□

Arthur 6th century AD. Romano-British leader against pagan Saxon invaders, who was the victor in a battle at Mt Badon (unidentified) c500. The story of the Round Table (so-shaped to avoid strife over precedence among the knights of his court at Camelot◊), and the quest for the Holy Grail◊, was developed in the 12th century by Geoffrey of Monmouth. Later writers on the theme include the anonymous author of *Sir Gawayne and the Greene Knight* 1346, Sir Thomas Malory◊, Tennyson◊, and T H White◊, J C Powys◊, John Steinbeck◊. Arthur is said to have been born at Tintagel◊ and be buried at Glastonbury◊□

Arthur 1187–1203. Duke of Brittany, grandson of Henry II of England, and nephew of King John◊, who had him murdered as a rival for the crown□

Arthur 1486–1502. Prince of Wales, the eldest son of Henry VII. He married Catherine of Aragon◊□

Arthur Chester Alan 1830–86. 21st President of America; a Republican, he was vice-president to Garfield, succeeding him (1881–5) on his assassination□

Arthur's Pass road-rail link across the Southern Alps, New Zealand, linking Christchurch with Greymouth□

Arthur's Seat hill of volcanic origin, Edinburgh, Scotland, only fancifully linked with King Arthur□

artichoke two plants, family Compositae◊, eaten as vegetables; the ***true artichoke*** *Cynara scolymus* is tall with blue flowers and the bracts of the unopened flower are eaten; the ***Jerusalem artichoke*** *Helianthus tuberosus* has edible tubers□

artificial intelligence (AI), the branch of computer science which explores how the mind works, and produces 'models' simulating the way a task is learned and how problems are solved□

artificial respiration the maintenance of breathing when the natural process is either permanently suspended, as in paralysis, when an ***iron lung*** is used, or temporarily so, as in cases of electric shock, apparent drowning, etc., when the first choice is the expired air method, the '***kiss of life***' by mouth to mouth breathing□

artillery one of the two main divisions of firearms◊. Cannon were in general use from the 14th century, but were most effective in siege warfare until, in the Napoleonic period, field artillery became smaller and more mobile. The howitzer, halfway between a gun and a mortar (muzzle-loading cannon), was used from the 16th century in sieges, and in World War I to demolish trench systems.

Giant cannon were also favourite weapons in World War I, not only in the entrenched conditions of the Western Front, but at sea against the lumbering, heavily armoured battleships. However, the fire accuracy on small or moving targets was poor, even by World War II. The breakthrough came in the 1970s (see weapons◊ list) with electronically-operated target devices and remote control firing; on modern battleships gun turrets are also unmanned. Even howitzers are today self-mobile, computer-controlled, and can fire a 43 kg/95 lb shell 32 km/20 mi in 5 seconds, or a nuclear warhead. Total withdrawal of the human element from the battlefield, however, is unlikely owing to the expense of shells. These may be made to home in automatically on an unseen target, such as a tank, but so far cannot distinguish tanks already disabled□

artiodactyla cloven-hoofed mammals with an even number of toes: camels, cattle, deer, hippopotami, sheep and goats□

Art Nouveau art style developed in France in the 1890s, marked by sinuous lines and stylized flowers and foliage. See Beardsley◊, Gaudi◊, Sir Alfred Gilbert◊, C R Mackintosh◊, René Lalique◊□

Artois former province of France, with its capital at Arras□

Arts Council of Great Britain arts organization incorporated in 1945; it aids music, drama, and visual arts from government funds□

arum family of flowering plants, Araceae, which includes the ***wild arum*** or ***cuckoopint*** *Arum maculatum* of Europe, which has large 'arrow-head' leaves, and tiny flowers which give rise to a cylindrical 'spike' of bright-red, poisonous berries; the ***arum lily*** or ***calla*** *Zantedeschia aethiopica* of southern Africa, which has a white funnel-shaped 'petal', actually a modified leaf, surrounding the central flower spike; and the ***monstera*** *Monstera deliciosa* of tropical America, also known as the ***Swiss cheese plant*** because of the holes which develop in its leaves (popular as house plant, in its native setting it produces edible fruits). The ***taro*** *Colocasia esculenta* is another member of the family, and produces rhizomes which, poisonous until boiled, are then used as a vegetable, in bread, etc., in SE Asia□

arum lily plant *Zantedeschia aethiopica*, family Araceae, with a white funnel-shaped 'petal', actually a modified leaf, surrounding the central flower spike□

Arunachal Pradesh NE Union Territory of India ('Hills of the Rising Sun'; until 1972 the NE Frontier Agency); population 628 050. Capital Ziro. The border with Tibet is disputed with China, which invaded the area in 1962□

Arundel town in Sussex, England; population 2500. The magnificent castle, much rebuilt, is associated with the Howard family. See Duke of Norfolk◊□

Aryan people supposed to have lived between Central Asia and E Europe, and to have reached India about 1500BC; they were lighter in colour than the aboriginal Dravidians◊. German theorists seized on the idea of their having been a white-skinned master-race, of which the blue-eyed, fair-haired Nordic was the finest expression; Adolf Hitler, its foremost proponent, was not himself cast in this mould. See antisemitism◊□

asbestos heat-resistant, fibrous-structured substance mostly obtained from chrysotile (see serpentine◊); used in suits for firemen and spacemen, for insulating wires in furnaces, and (blended with cement) in the construction industry. Exposure to asbestos is recognized as a cause of industrial cancer (mesothelioma) and regulation is stringent□

ascariasis infection by ***roundworm*** *Ascaris lumbricoides*, an intestinal parasite of man□

Ascension British island of volcanic origin in the S Atlantic; population 1200. A dependency of St Helena◊, it was uninhabited until occupied by Britain in 1815; the chief settlement is Georgetown. It is famous for sea turtles and sooty terns, and its role as a staging post to the Falklands□

Ascension day or ***Holy Thursday*** feast day commemorating the ascension of Christ to Heaven; the 40th day after Easter□

Asch Sholem. See Yiddish◊□

Ascham Roger 1515–68. English scholar, who became tutor to Princess Elizabeth in 1548; he retained favour under Edward VI and Queen Mary, though a Protestant, and returned to the service of Elizabeth as her secretary after she became queen. He wrote *The Scholemaster* 1570 on the art of education□

ascomycetes sac fungi◊, whose spores have a bag-like form. They include:

ergot a parasite *Claviceps purpurea* on rye; ergot alkaloids are used to induce childbirth, and in treating migraine; ***ergotism***, with hallucinations, convulsions, and gangrene, is caused by eating infected rye bread. The 'witchcraft' outbreak in Salem◊ has been attributed to ergot, from which the hallucinogen ***LSD*** (*ly*sergic acid *d*iethylamide) is derived. Colourless, odourless, and easily synthesized, it is non-addictive, but is unpredictable in effect, and sometimes disastrous.

mildew minute plants which appear like a white film in damp conditions causing plant disease, e.g. ***downy mildew*** (family Peronosporaceae) and ***powdery mildew*** (family Erysiphaceae), and also rotting leather, paper, wood, etc.
morel including the club-shaped ***common morel*** *Morchella esculenta* abundant in Europe and N America; it has a yellow/brown edible pitted cap.
blue-green moulds genus *Penicillium* including the ***common blue-green mould*** *P notatum* which forms an organic acid (***penicillin***) during its growth which prevents the development of harmful bacteria, e.g. staphylococci, streptococci, and the organisms of pneumonia, gonorrhoea, meningitis, anthrax, and tetanus. Its properties were discovered by Alexander Fleming◊, and practically developed by Florey◊ and Chain◊.
truffle genus *Tuber* which have edible subterranean fruiting bodies, usually growing under trees, e.g. the rounded, black-fleshed *T melanospermum* from Périgord, used in paté de foie gras. Dogs and pigs are used to find them by their distinctive smell (they contain a steroid like the one produced by boars during pre-mating behaviour), but a method of growing them by inoculating tree roots with spores is being developed.
yeast single-celled genus *Saccharomyces* capable of coverting sugar to alcohol; each of the mass of minute circular or oval cells is a complete plant capable of producing new cells by budding. Placed in a sugar solution *Saccharomyces cerevisiae* multiplies and converts the sugar into alcohol and carbon dioxide; it is used to leaven bread, ferment beer and wine, etc, and yeast extract is rich in vitamins of the B complex. Others may be parasitic on man causing thrush, meningitis◊ etc.□

ascorbic acid see vitamin C◊□

Ascot village in Berkshire, England. A racecourse was established by Queen Anne in 1711, and events include the Gold Cup and international King George VI and Queen Elizabeth Stakes□

ASEAN see Association◊ of South-East Asian Nations□

asexual reproduction animal and plant reproduction without a sexual process; examples are amoeba◊, the gardener's 'division' of one plant into two, and the clone◊□

ash a tree of genus *Fraxinus*, Oleaceae family; the ***common ash*** is *F excelsior*. See mountain ash◊□

Ashanti independent kingdom (more correctly Asante) of W Africa in the 17–19th centuries, which is now a region of Ghana, with its capital at Kumasi. British annexation in 1901 was only achieved after four military expeditions. The symbol of the nation, the Golden Stool (actually a chair), was returned by Britain in 1935, and is still paraded when the Asantahene (king) holds durbars, the most splendid in Africa. The rest of the Ashanti treasure is in the British Museum□

Ashby-de-la-Zouch town in Leicestershire, England; population 9000. It was named from the La Zouche family who built the castle, which was later used to imprison Mary Queen of Scots□

Ashcan school American painters of 1900–10, who included John Sloan and George Bellows, noted for their squalid cityscapes□

Ashcroft Dame Peggy 1907– . British actress. She was born in Croydon, where a theatre is named after her. Her roles include Desdemona (with Paul Robeson), and appearances in the TV series *The Jewel in the Crown* 1984 and the film *A Passage to India* 1985□

Ashdod deepwater port in Israel; population 73 000□

Ashes The. Cricket trophy theoretically held by the winning team in England-Australia Test Match series (it actually remains with the MCC at Lords). The urn contains the ashes of stumps and balls used in the match in 1883, and was presented by the Melbourne ladies to the victorious British captain, Ivo Bligh□

Asheville textile town in N Carolina, USA; population 57 700. Showplaces include the 19th-century Biltmore mansion, home of millionaire George W Vanderbilt, and the home of Thomas Wolfe◊□

Ashford town in Kent, England; population 35 000□

Ashford Daisy 1881–1972. British author of *The Young Visiters* 1919, a classic of unconscious humour written at the age of nine□

Ashkenazim see under Israel◊□

Ashkenazy Vladimir 1937– . Russian pianist and conductor, who excels in Rachmaninov, Prokofiev, and Liszt□

Ashkhabad capital of Republic of Turkmen, USSR; population 302 000. 'Bukhara' carpets are made here, and it is the hottest place in the USSR□

Ashley Laura 1925–85. Welsh designer, born Mountney. Born in Merthyr Tydfil, she established a neo-Victorian country look in clothes and furnishings from 1953 and an international chain of shops to sell them□

Ashmore and Cartier Islands uninhabited group of islands north west of Northern Territory, Australia, with which it is administered□

ashram Indian community leading a simple life of discipline and self-denial, and carrying out social service, under a guru, e.g. those at Wardha (see Gandhi◊) and Sandiniketan (see Sir Rabindranath Tagore◊)□

Ashton Sir Frederick 1904– . British dancer and choreographer, director of the Royal Ballet 1963–70. His works include *Façade* 1931, *Cinderella* 1948, *La Fille Mal Gardée* 1960, *Marguerite and Armand* – for Fonteyn and Nureyev – 1963. Order of Merit 1977□

Ashton under Lyme industrial town in Greater Manchester, England; population 48 600□

Ash Wednesday first day of Lent, the period in the Christian calendar leading up to Easter; in the Catholic Church the foreheads of the congregation are marked with a cross in ash, as a sign of penitence□

Asia largest of the continents, the area of Eurasia to the east of the Ural mountains, one third of the total land surface of the world.

area 44 000 000 sq km/17 000 000sq mi

largest cities (over 5 million) Tokyo, Peking, Seoul, Jakarta, Tehran, Bangkok

features world's highest mountains (Himalayas◊, Everest◊) and lowest point (Dead Sea◊); rivers (over 2000 miles) Ob-Irtysh◊, Yangtze◊, Huang◊, Amur◊, Lena◊, Mekong◊, Yenisei◊, Euphrates◊; lakes (over 7000 sq mi) Caspian◊ and Aral◊ seas, Baikal◊, Balkhash◊

exports range from the most sophisticated electronics to the most price-vulnerable cash crops and minerals

population 2 519 600 000, the most densely populated of the continents

language predominantly tonal languages (Chinese◊, Japanese◊) in the east, Indo-Iranian languages in central India and Pakistan (Hindi/Urdu◊), and Semitic (Arabic◊) in the south-west

religion Hinduism, Islam, Buddhism, Christianity, Confucianism, Shintoism

history See Asia◊ history

Asia: history

BC

c3000 first dynasties of Mesopotamia; king Gilgamesh◊

2800-2205 Sage Kings in China, earliest Chinese dynasty; civilization spread to all of China

2500-1500 Indus◊ Valley civilization

1950-1282 first Babylonian◊ Empire

625 Chaldeans established second Babylonian Empire

570 birth of Mohammed◊

560 birth of Buddha◊

551 birth of Confucius◊

538 Cyrus◊ the Great defeated last Babylonian ruler and founded Persion Empire

334-326 Alexander the Great conquered the Persian◊ Empire

246 Great Wall of China

166 Tartar◊ invasion of China

AD

93 Mesopotamia became part of Roman Empire

320-550 Gupta◊ dynasty in India

1192 First Muslim kingdom of India established

1280 Kublai Khan became emperor of China

1395 Tamerlane defeated the Golden Horde

1398 Tamerlane◊ captured Delhi

1526 Babur◊ established Mogul empire (which lasts until 1857)

1600 British East India Company chartered

1757 Clive◊ defeated the Nawal of Bengal at Plassey◊

1840-2 Opium◊ War between Britain and China ended with ceding of Hong Kong to Britain

1854 US Commodore Perry forced Japanese Shogun to grant commercial treaty

1857-8 Indian◊ Mutiny

1904-5 Russo-Japanese War

1931 Japan invaded China

1941 Japan attacked US Fleet at Pearl Harbor◊

1947 India and Pakistan gained independence

1949 Chiang-Kai-Shek forced by Chinese Communists to flee to Formosa

1950 Korean War

1954 End of French war in Indo-China

1965 US troops sent to support South Vietnamese in large numbers

1971 E Pakistan declared independence as Bangladesh◊

1976 death of Mao-Tse Tung◊

1980 trial of Mao's widow

Asia Soviet Central formerly Russian Turkestan, an area consisting of the Kazakh◊, Uzbek◊, Tadzhik◊, Turkmen◊ and Kirghiz◊ Republics of the USSR. These were subdued by Russia as recently as 1866–73, and even under Soviet rule nationalist sentiment persists, leading to shortfalls in agricultural production, etc., and the establishment in 1962 of a Central Asian Bureau to strengthen centralized control by the Party Praesidium. These republics are also the home of the majority of the Muslims of the USSR□

Asia Minor former name for Asiatic Turkey□

Asimov Isaac 1920– . American science-fiction author and professor of biochemistry at Boston from 1979. Born in Russia, he is best-known for his 'Foundation' trilogy 1950–3, continued in *Foundation's Edge* 1983□

Asmara capital of Eritrea, Ethiopia; population 296 000. There is a naval school. In 1974 unrest here precipitated the end of the Ethiopian Empire□

Asoka reigned 264–228BC. Indian emperor, a grandson of Chandragupta◊. A Buddhist convert, he had edicts enjoining the adoption of his new faith carved on pillars and rock faces, etc., throughout his dominions, and many survive. See also Patna◊. Gandhi was influenced by his pacifist outlook□

asp a type of snake◊□

asparagus genus of plants, Liliaceae◊ family; ***vegetable asparagus*** *A officinalis* is grown for its young shoots; ***asparagus fern*** is *A plumosus*□

Aspasia c440BC. Greek courtesan, the mistress of Pericles◊. As a 'foreigner' from Miletus, she could not be recognized as his wife, but their son was later legitimized. Socrates◊ visited her salon, and her free thinking led to a charge of impiety, from which Pericles had to defend her□

aspen see poplar◊□

Aspen winter sports resort in the Rocky mountains, Maryland, USA. It was the original headquarters of the Aspen Institute for Humanistic Studies (now in New York City), which has been influential with world governments, and whose fellows include Kissinger□

Aspen Lodge see Camp David◊□

asphalt bitumen◊, which is combined with various materials for roadmaking, roofs, insulation, dampcourses, etc.□

asphodel yellow or white-flowered plants of the genera *Asphodelus* or *Asphodeline*, family Liliaceae◊; the Greek asphodel of the Elysian fields is thought to have been the daffodil□

aspidistra genus of plants, Liliaceae◊ family; the broad-leaved ***Japanese aspidistra*** *A lurida* was popular with the Victorians as a hardy house plant□

aspirin acetylsalicylic acid, a popular pain reliever for headaches, arthritis, etc.; in the long term, even moderate use may involve side effects including kidney damage, hearing defects, etc. See Hippocrates◊□

Asquith Lady Cynthia 1887–1960. British author; born Charteris, she married Herbert, second son of H H Asquith◊, and wrote a diary of the World War I years□

Asquith Herbert Henry, 1st Earl of Oxford and Asquith 1852–1928. British Liberal statesman, who was Home Secretary 1892–5, Chancellor of the Exchequer 1905–8 (when he introduced old age pensions), and succeeded Campbell-Bannerman as Prime Minister in 1908. Forcing through the radical budget of his Chancellor (Lloyd George◊) led him into two elections in 1910, which resulted in the Parliament Act of 1911, limiting the right of the Lords to veto legislation. His endeavours to pass the Home Rule for Ireland Bill led to the Curragh◊ Incident, and incipient civil war. Unity was re-established by the outbreak of World War I, and a coalition government was formed in May 1915. However, his attitude of 'wait and see' was not adapted to all-out war, and in Dec 1916 he was replaced by Lloyd George. In 1918 the Liberal election defeat led to the eclipse of the party. His second wife, Margot 1868–1945, born Tennant, was a wit and offended many by her indiscreet memoirs□

Asquith Raymond 1878–1916. Eldest son of H H Asquith◊, a leader of his social circle, who was killed in action in World War I□

ass a member of the horse◊ family□

Assad Hafez al 1930– . Syrian statesman, Baathist and Shia (Alawite) Muslim; he became Prime Minister after the bloodless military coup in 1970, and in 1971 was the first president to be elected by popular vote; re-elected 1978□

Assam NE state of India

area 78 523 sq km/000 000 sq mi

capital Dispur

towns Shilling

features half India's tea is grown here, and half her oil produced

population 20 000 000, including 12 000 000 Assamese (Hindus), 5 million Bengalis (chiefly Muslim immigrants from Bangladesh), and Nepalis; and 2 000 000 native people (Christian and traditional religions); in 1983 there were massacres of Muslim Bengalis by Hindus

language Assamese□

assassinations, famous

BC

681	Sennacherib of Assyria
336	Philip II of Macedon
44	Julius Caesar

AD

41	Caligula, Roman emperor
1170	Thomas à Becket
1437	James I of Scotland
1488	James III of Scotland
1584	William the Silent
1610	Henry IV of France
1628	Duke of Buckingham
1634	Prince Wallenstein
1793	J.P. Marat
1801	Paul I of Russia
1812	Spencer Perceval
1865	Abraham Lincoln
1881	J.A. Garfield
1881	Alexander II of Russia

1900 Humbert I of Italy
1903 Alexander and Draga of Serbia
1908 Carlos of Portugal
1913 Geoge I of Greece
1914 Archduke Francis Ferdinand
1934 Dr. Dollfuss
1934 Alexander of Yugoslavia
1940 Leon Trotsky
1942 Reinhard Heydrich
1948 Mahatma Gandhi
1963 J.F. Kennedy
1966 H.F. Verwoerd
1968 M. Luther King
1968 R.F. Kennedy
1975 Faisal (Saudi Arabia)
1979 Lord Mountbatten
1981 Anwar Sadat
1984 Indira Gandhi

assault ship naval vessel with a platform for helicopters, a dock for large landing craft, tank decks, troop accommodation, and defended by missiles, machine guns and anti-aircraft guns. The Royal Navy's *Fearless* and *Intrepid* took part in the Falklands landings□

assaying usually the testing for purity of gold, silver and platinum for hallmarking□

assent Royal. British Sovereign's formal consent to an Act of Parliament, usually given by Letters Patent, the Lord Chancellor in the Lords and the Speaker in the House of Commons merely make an announcement that consent has been given□

Assisi town in Umbria, Italy; population 24 400. St Francis was born here, and is buried in the Franciscan monastery. See Gothic under architecture◊□

Associated State of the UK. Status with full internal government, within the Commonwealth◊, under which Britain is responsible for external relations and defence. It is designed for countries with too few resources for full independence: the first created was Antigua◊□

association football see football◊□

Association of South East Asian Nations (ASEAN) a regional alliance formed in 1967; it took over the non-military role of SEATO◊ in 1975. Its members are Indonesia, Malaysia, the Philippines, Singapore, Thailand and (from 1984) Brunei; headquarters Jakarta□

Assumption feast of the Virgin in the Catholic Church, 15 Aug, commemorating her translation to heaven□

Assy village in Savoie region, France; its church (1950) is decorated by Braque, Chagall, Matisse, Derain and Roualt□

Assyria see Iraq◊□

Astaire Fred 1899– . American singer and dancer who gave a balletic quality to tap dancing; his films include *Roberta, Top Hat,* etc., with Ginger Rogers; *You Were Never Lovelier,* with Rita Hayworth; *Easter Parade* with Judy Garland, and others□

Astarte see Ishtar◊□

astatine element
symbol At
atomic number 85
physical description less than 30 grams/1 oz in the earth's crust at any time
features a radioactive element with a very short half-life (8.3 hours); a member of the halogen* series
uses none at present□

aster genus of plants, family Compositae◊, with daisy-like flowers including the ***sea aster*** *A tripolium,* and the cultivated Michaelmas daisy◊□

asteroids known more properly as minor planets, the asteroids are small bodies (mainly of iron and silicon) circling the sun between the paths of Mars and Jupiter. They are thought to have condensed from the primordial cloud of gas and dust from which the solar system was formed. Over 2000 asteroids are now numbered and named. Since, unlike planets, asteroids are subject to severe orbital perturbations, collision is theoretically possible. Collisions between earth and an asteroid are thought to occur on average every 100 million years, and one is thought to have happened about 65 million years ago at the end of the Cretaceous◊ period. Some 75% of all animal and plant life (including the dinosaurs) may then have become extinct, for the dust created would have turned day into night for 3–5 years. Only small animals, including the squirrel-sized ancestors of man would have survived on persisting vegetation. See iridium◊
The most interesting asteroids include:
Ceres the largest asteroid, 1000 km/620 mi in diameter.
Eros one of the few which depart from the main swarm; it may approach earth fairly closely; it is elongated (19x6 km/ 12x4 mi), rotates in 5 hr 17 min, and its mean distance from earth is 217 000 000 mi.
Herculina an asteroid 220 km/137 mi in diameter, with a satellite 45 km/28 mi in diameter.
Icarus asteroid whose orbital plane intersects with that of earth; its orbital period is 409 days, and it passes through the plane twice a year; about 1.5 km/1 mi in diameter.
Vesta the brightest and the only one visible with the naked eye, 535 km/332 mi in diameter□

asthma recurrent difficulty in breathing in (inhaling) due to the contraction of muscles in the walls of the breathing passages. It is either allergic in origin or caused by a form of heart disease (cardiac asthma) and can be brought on by anxiety□

Aston Francis William 1877–1945. British physicist, the discoverer of isotopes◊; Nobel prize 1922□

Astor John Jacob 1763–1848. American millionaire, whose son ***William Backhouse Astor*** 1792–1875, continued the tradition and was known as the 'landlord of New York'; John Jacob's great-grandson ***Waldorf Astor***, 2nd Viscount Astor 1879–-1952, was chief proprietor of the British *Observer* newspaper, and married Nancy Witcher Langhorne, ***Lady Astor***, the first woman MP to take her seat in the House of Commons – she was also a temperance fanatic and great political hostess. Government policy was said to be decided at Cliveden, their country home□

Astrakhan city in the S USSR; population 466 000. It is the chief port for the Caspian fisheries□

astrology study of the relative position of the planets and stars in the belief that they influence events on earth. For individuals the time of birth or conception is considered particularly relevant in casting a ***horoscope*** which indicates the direction of their future life. It has no scientific basis. See zodiac◊□

astron large-scale cosmic impact feature on earth (possible examples are the bulge of W Africa, and the Great Australian Bight), the moon, etc.□

Astronomer Royal astronomer in charge of the UK Royal Observatory (F Graham Smith from 1982). See Herstmonceux◊□

astronometry branch of astronomy dealing with the accurate measurement of the positions of stars, so providing the means of calculating cosmic distances, and enabling scientists to gauge the age of the universe. In 1986 the European Space Agency will launch satellite Hipparcos (***H***igh ***P***recision ***Pa***rallax ***Co***llecting ***S***atellite – named after Hipparchus◊)□

astronomy the scientific study of heavenly bodies

BC

3379 Maya◊ record of a total eclipse of the Moon

2300 Chinese astronomers made their earliest observations

2000 Babylonian priests made their first observational records

1900 Stonehenge◊ constructed: first phase

365 Chinese observed the satellites of Jupiter with the naked eye

3rd century Aristarchus◊ argued that the sun is the centre of the solar system

2nd century Ptolemy◊'s complicated earth-centred system promulgated, which dominated the astronomy of the Middle Ages

AD

1543 Copernicus◊ revived the ideas of Aristarchus

1608 Lippershey◊ invented the telescope, which was first used by Galileo in 1609

1609 Kepler◊'s first two Laws of Planetary Motion published; 3rd in 1619

1632 Leiden◊ established the world's first official observatory

1633 Galileo◊ condemned by the Inquisition

1675 Royal Greenwich Observatory◊ founded

1687 Newton◊'s *Principia* published, including his 'law of universal gravitation'

1718 Halley◊ predicted the return of the comet named after him, observed in 1758: last seen in 1986

1781 Herschel discovered Uranus◊ and recognized stellar systems beyond our galaxy

1796 Laplace◊ elaborated his theory of the origin of the solar system

1801 Piazzi discovered the first asteroid: Ceres

1814 Fraunhofer◊ founded spectroscopy

1846 Neptune◊ discovered by Galle and D'Arrest

1859 first beginnings of astrophysics◊

1887 earliest photographic star charts produced

1889 E E Barnard◊ took first photos of the Milky Way

1890 first beginnings of spectrography◊

1908 Tunguska comet◊ fell in Siberia

1920 Eddington◊ began the study of interstellar matter

1923 Hubble◊ proved that the galaxies are systems independent of the Milky Way, and by 1930 had confirmed the concept of an expanding universe◊

1930 Pluto◊ was discovered by Clyde Tombaugh at Flagstaff, Arizona

1931 Jansky◊ founded radioastronomy

1945 radar◊ contact with the moon established by Z Bay of Hungary and the US Army Signal Corps Laboratory

1948 200-inch Hale reflector telescope installed at Mount Palomar, California

1955 Jodrell Bank radioastronomy 'dish' in England completed

1957 Sputnik (USSR) opened the age of space observation

1962 first X-ray source discovered in Scorpio

1963 first quasar◊ discovered by Mt Palomar observatory

1967 first pulsar◊ identified by Jocelyn Bell, Cambridge

1969 first manned moon◊ landing (USA)
1970 first confirmation of black hole◊ theory
1976 236-inch reflector telescope installed at Mt Semirodniki (USSR)
1977 Uranus◊ discovered to have rings
1977 spacecraft Voyager 1 and 2 launched, the latter passing Jupiter and Saturn 1979–81; due Uranus 1986, Neptune 1989
1978 spacecraft Pioneer Venus 1 and 2 reached Venus
1978 Pluto satellite discovered by James Christie, astronomer at Flagstaff, Arizona
1978 Herculina discovered to be the first asteroid◊ with a satellite◊
1979 infra-red◊ telescope established on Hawaii by the UK
1985 return of Halley's comet
1986 Voyager 2 discovered six new moons around Uranus□

In addition to the astronomy of visible light studied by means of optical telescopes, other regions of the electromagnetic spectrum are now explored: ***X-ray astronomy*** began in 1949 when the US Naval Research Laboratory launched a V2 rocket from the White Sands missile range in New Mexico, which detected X-rays from the sun. Many other bodies, notably neutron stars, clusters of galaxies and possibly black holes, also emit X-rays□

astrophysics the application of physical principles to problems concerning the state and evolution of the universe. Relevant data includes that obtained by spectrographic analysis of radiation received from remote systems, by radio, infra-red, ultraviolet, X-ray, and neutrino astronomy□

Asturias autonomous region of N Spain (including Oviedo); population 1 127 000. It was once a separate kingdom and the eldest son of a king of Spain is still called Prince of Asturias□

Asunción capital and port of Paraguay; population 500 000□

Aswan town in Upper Egypt, near the High Dam 1960–70, which maintains the level of the Nile constant throughout the year without flooding; see Lake Nasser◊; population 246 000□

Asyut commercial centre in Upper Egypt; population 248 000. It was an ancient Graeco-Egyptian city□

Atacama desert in N Chile; there are silver and copper mines, and nitrate deposits□

Atahualpa 1502–33. Last Inca king of Peru. Taken prisoner by the Spaniards in 1532, he agreed to pay a huge ransom and received baptism in the belief that his life would be spared. He was strangled on the orders of Pizarro◊. See Huascar◊□

Atalanta in Greek mythology, a huntress who challenged all her suitors to a foot race; if they lost they were killed. Milanion was given three golden apples to drop by Aphrodite; this ensured that when Atalanta stopped to pick them up, she lost the race□

Atatürk name assumed by Mustafa Kemal Pasha 1881–1938 in 1934; it means 'Father of the Turks'. In 1915 he was largely responsible for the defence of the Dardanelles against the British, and in 1918 established a provisional government in opposition to that in Constantinople (then under Allied control). In 1921 he expelled the Greeks occupying Asia Minor, and, by diplomacy, avoided war with Britain, and ensured that Turkey-in-Europe passed under his control. In 1923 he became the first president of the new republic of Turkey, but his westernizing reforms were not deep-rooted among the mass of the people, and from the 1970s there was widespread reversion to Islamic custom□

ataxia lack of muscular co-ordination, caused by brain disease□

Atget Eugène 1857–1927. French photographer, noted for his street scenes, especially of Paris and its environs□

Athabasca Lake. Lake in Alberta and Saskatchewan, Canada, with huge tar sand deposits (source of 'heavy oil') to the south-west□

Athanasian creed creed defining the Trinity, named after Athanasius◊, though it was not written till many years after his death□

Athanasius St 298–373. Bishop of Alexandria, chief supporter of the doctrine of the Trinity□

atheism the positive denial of the existence of a god or gods, as in Communist states, e.g. Albania, USSR; see also Agnosticism◊, Democritus◊, Lucretius◊, Hobbes◊. Modern atheists often prefer the more moderate term 'unbeliever'□

Athelney Isle of. Area of firm ground in the midst of marshland, near Taunton in Devon, England. In 878 it was the headquarters of King Alfred◊ when he was in hiding from the Danes, and it was here he was said to have burnt the cakes of the peasant woman who sheltered him□

Athena in Greek mythology, the goddess (Roman Minerva◊) of war, wisdom, and the arts and crafts, who was supposed to have sprung fully-armed from the head of Zeus◊. Her chief cult centre was Athens, where the Parthenon was dedicated to her. In Rome a statue of her (the 'Palladium'), allegedly brought by Aeneas◊ from Troy, was kept in the temple of Vesta◊□

Athens capital of Greece from 1834; population 2 540 000, including the port of Piraeus.

Dominated by the Acropolis◊, it reached its cultural and political zenith under Pericles◊, and declined after the death of Alexander◊ the Great, though it remained an intellectual centre till the schools of philosophy were closed by Justinian◊ in 529AD. ***Piraeus*** founded c493BC, was linked with the city by the 'protective' Long Walls (from c460BC); the port declined after its sack by Sulla◊ 86BC and is now an industrial suburb. There is an international airport at Hellenikon□

athletics competitive track and field events, especially forms of running, jumping, walking, throwing◊, etc. Among the Greeks, vase paintings show that competitive athletics were established at least by 1600BC (Olympic◊ Games). However, the concept of the unpaid amateur is a recent British innovation, ancient athletes having been well paid and sponsored. Aristotle◊ paid the expenses of a boxer contestant at Olympia, and chariot races were sponsored by the Greek city states.

Recent athletics has been dominated by the 'world record'; development of computer selection of the best potential competitors and analysis of motion for greatest speed, etc.; specialization of equipment for maximum performance (glass fibre vaulting poles, foam landing pads, aerodynamically designed javelins, composition running tracks, etc.), and the unlawful use of drugs, such as anabolic steroids◊ and growth hormones□

Athos Mount. Peninsula on the Macedonian coast of Greece; it is occupied by monastic communities, no woman or female animal being allowed to enter□

Atkins Tommy. Popular name for a British soldier; allegedly it was originally that of a soldier mortally wounded under Wellington◊, who later used it on an army document□

Atlanta capital of Georgia, USA; population 1 850 000. It was burned by General Sherman◊ during the Civil War in 1864 (as described in Mitchell's *Gone With the Wind*). There are Ford and Lockheed assembly plants, and it is the headquarters of Coca-Cola. Hartsfield International Airport has (in its Mid Field Airport Terminal, 1980) one of the world's largest air passenger buildings. Nearby is ***Stone Mountain Memorial***, the world's largest stone carving (58x93 m/190x350 ft), showing Jefferson Davis, Robert E Lee, and Stonewall Jackson; of several artists working on it, Gutzon Borglum was the first. The Carter presidential library is at Emory University□

Atlantic City pleasure resort in New Jersey, USA; population 48 000. Five piers jut from the 'boardwalk'; and the Miss America contest has been held here since 1921□

Atlantic Ocean the most saline of the great oceans, and the one with the largest tidal range. Its area, including the Arctic Ocean and Antarctic Seas, is 106 200 000 sq km/41 000 000 sq mi; the average depth is 3 km/2 mi; and its greatest depth is in the Puerto Rico Trench 9219 m/27 498 ft□

Atlantis legendary island continent, said to have foundered 9600BC, following submarine convulsions. Although the Atlantic Ocean is named after it, the structure of the sea bottom rules out its ever having existed there. The story told by Plato◊ (derived from an account by Egyptian priests) may refer to the volcanic eruption which destroyed an island (Santorini in the Cyclades◊ north of Crete) c1500BC. The collapse of the empire of Minoan Crete by related earthquakes followed□

Atlas in Greek mythology, a N African king, transformed for his sins to a peak of the Atlas mountains, which were envisaged by the Greeks as supporting the heavens. Mercator◊ used a picture of him on volumes of maps, hence called atlases. See Caryatid◊, Pleiades◊□

Atlas mountains mountain system of Morocco-Tunisia, 2400 km/1500 mi long; highest peak Mt Toubkal 4165 m/13 665 ft□

atman in Hinduism, the individual soul□

atmosphere the mixture of gases which surrounds the earth, prevented from escaping by the pull of the earth's gravity. As we go higher in the atmosphere, a small and smaller fraction of it is 'resting' above us, so atmospheric pressure decreases. In its lowest layer, the ***troposphere,*** the atmospheric pressure consists of nitrogen (78%) and oxygen (21%), both in molecular form (two atoms bounded together). The other 1% is largely argon, but there are very small quantities of other gases, as well as water vapour. The troposphere is heated by the earth, which is warmed by infra-red and visible radiation from the sun. Warm air rises in the troposphere, cooling as it does so. This is the primary cause of rain and most other weather phenomena.

Infra-red and visible radiations form only that part of the sun's output of electromagnetic◊ radiation. Almost all the shorter wavelength 'ultra-violet' radiation is filtered out by the upper layers of the atmosphere. The filtering process is an active one: at heights above about 50km ultra-violet photons◊ collide with atoms, knocking out electrons◊ to create a plasma◊ of electrons and positively-charged ions◊. The resulting ***ionosphere*** acts as a

The earth's atmosphere

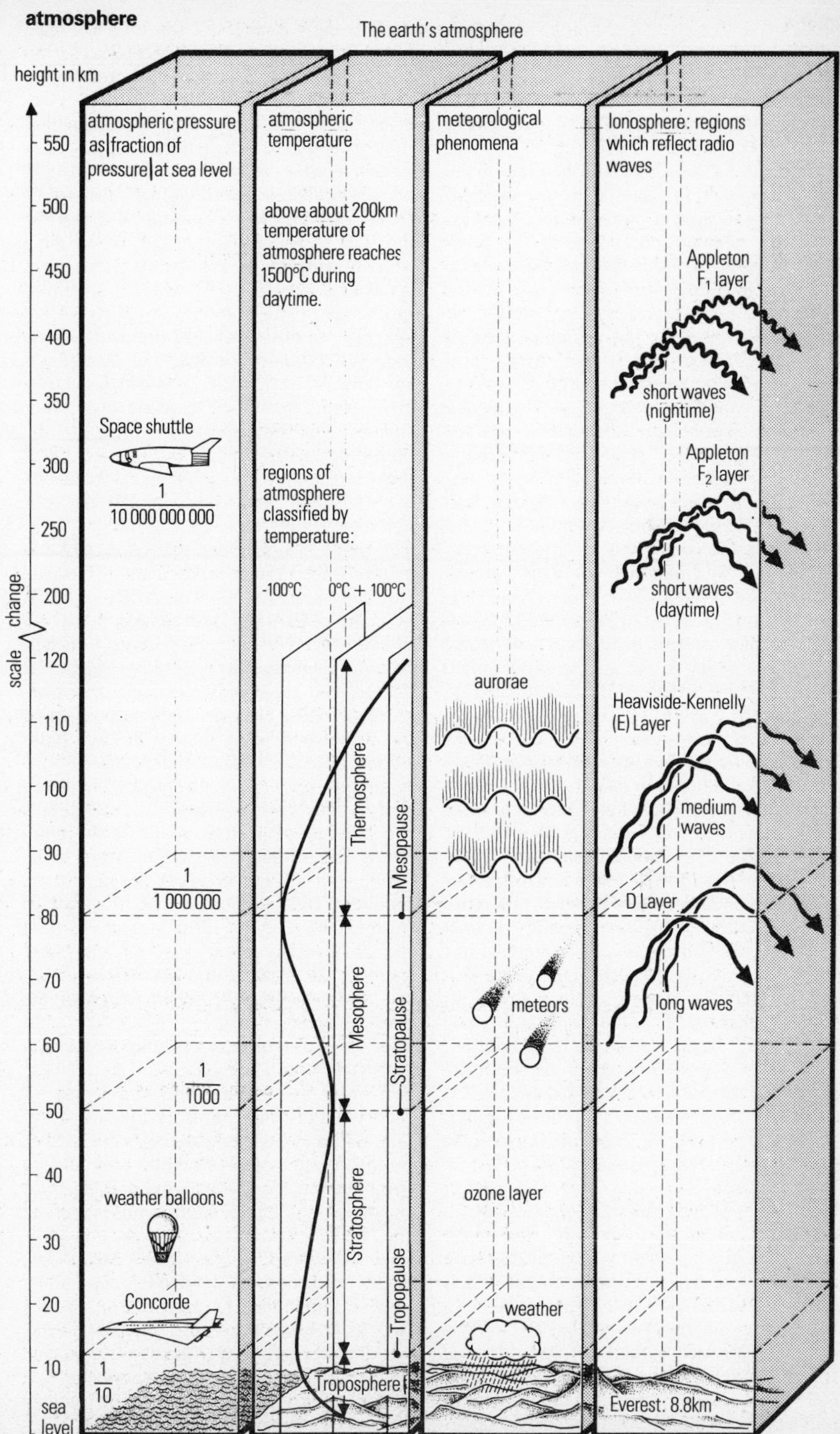

reflector of radio waves, enabling radio transmissions to 'hop' between widely-separated points on the earth's surface. As shown on the diagram, waves of different wavelengths are reflected best at different heights. The collisions between ultra-violet photons and atoms lead to a heating of the upper atmosphere, though as we descend from a great height through the ***thermosphere*** the temperature drops as the high-energy photons have progressively been absorbed in collisions.

Between the thermosphere and the tropopause (at which the warming effect of the earth starts to be felt) there is a 'warm bulge' in the temperature vs. height graph, at a level called the ***stratopause.*** This is due to longer wavelength ultra-violet photons which have survived their journey through the upper layers and which, now encountering molecules, split them apart into atoms. These atoms eventually bond together again, but often in different combinations. In particular, many *ozone* molecules (oxygen atom triplets) are formed. Ozone is a better absorber of ultra-violet than even ordinary (two-atom) oxygen, and its is the *ozone layer* which prevents lethal amounts of ultra-violet from reaching the earth's surface.

Far above the atmosphere, as so far described, lie the ***Van Allen Radiation Belts.*** These are regions in which high energy charged particles travelling outwards from the sun (as the so-called 'Solar Wind') have been 'captured' by the earth's magnetic field (see magnetism◊). The outer belt (at about 1600km) contains mainly protons, the inner belt (at about 2000km) contains mainly electrons. Sometimes electrons spiral down towards the earth, especially at polar latitudes, where the magnetic field is strongest. When such particles collide with atoms and ions in the thermosphere, light is emitted. This is the origin of the glows visible in the sky as the ***Aurora Borealis*** (Northern Lights) and the ***Aurora Australis*** (Southern Lights). A fainter, more widespread, *airglow* is caused by a similar mechanism□

atoll see coral◊□

atom the minute separate entities which make up all matter, and are the tiniest quantities of an element which still have the chemical properties of that element. Their size ranges from 10^{-10} (1/10 000 000 000 of a metre) for the smallest, to $4x10^{-10}$ for the largest. This means that they are so small that an atom of tungsten magnified 2 600 000 times (by a field ion microscope), appears as a bright spot not much larger than a pin's head. On this minute scale physicists cannot 'see' in a direct visual sense, but rely on methods, such as interpretation of the 'diffraction pattern' produced by electrons 'fired' through a thin specimen of a substance in an 'electron microscope'.

Atoms consist of a relatively very small nucleus, only one ten-thousandth the size of the atom, which in the traditional model has particles of negative electricity called electrons moving round it in orbits which form concentric 'shells'. However, quantum mechanics, which looks at particles as 'waves', supplies a newer concept of the atom. According to this, the nucleus is surrounded by 'clouds' of electrons which may assume dumb-bell, cloverleaf, or other shapes. The outermost of these clouds, according to their shape and density, allow the prediction of what chemical reactions are possible and how molecules will combine.

The simplest atom (hydrogen) has only one electron, the most complex naturally occurring (uranium) has 92. The nucleus itself is made up of particles (protons and neutrons) bound together by the strong nuclear force◊. Protons have positive electrical charges and are exactly the same in number as the orbiting electrons, which have equal but negative charges, so that the two types of particle counterbalance each other exactly in this respect. Neutrons are 'neutral', that is, they have no electrical charge. It is the number of protons which is the chief factor in deciding the kind of atom being dealt with, since it gives it its atomic number. By addition or subtraction of protons and electrons, it is possible to fulfil the alchemist's dream, e.g. to transmute mercury (80 protons) into gold (79 protons), but the cost would be far in excess of the gold produced.

Protons and neutrons are composed of yet smaller sub-particles, quarks◊; electrons are indivisible and are not covered by quark theory. Quarks have proved difficult to isolate, and may even be, by their very nature, impossible to isolate. Particles may change from one form to another, and perhaps most important of all in its implications is the fact that their behaviour is not exactly predictable. Physicists (with some exceptions, notably Einstein◊) accept that it is impossible, even in principle, to predict entirely the future behaviour of the particles (e.g. simultanous values of their position and momentum); see uncertainty◊ principle. See also antimatter◊, nuclear energy◊, particle physics◊, radioactivity◊□

atom bomb see nuclear◊ weapons□
atomic energy see nuclear◊ energy□
atomic time time derived from integrating seconds intervals as realized by caesium beam atomic clocks; it gives microsecond accuracy□
atomic weight weight of an atom of an element on a scale on which the weight of an oxygen atom is 16□
Aton in Ancient Egypt, the sun's disc as an emblem of the deity whose worship was enforced by Ikhnaton◊, who probably himself composed the great hymn to the Aton□
atonality desertion of an established key in a musical work, which developed into the ***twelve-tone system*** or ***serialism*** in which the musical scale consists of 12 semitones of equal value, used in prescribed ways. Wagner◊ and Scriabin◊ were forerunners, but the system was fully formulated by Schoenberg◊ 1911–23, and used by Berg◊, Webern◊, and Krenek◊□
Atonement The. In Christian theology, the Doctrine (a 'bringing to be at one') that Christ suffered on the Cross to effect reconciliation and forgiveness between God and man□
Atonement Day of. See Observances under Judaism◊□
atropine poisonous alkaloid obtained from deadly nightshade, so named from Atropos (see fates◊), with medicinal uses, e.g. in anaesthesia and to dilate the pupil of the eye for optical examination□
attar of roses essential oil of roses (distilled from their petals) used as a perfume base□
Attempt Criminal. Offence in the UK under the Criminal Attempts Act 1981, which repealed the 'suspected person offence', commonly known as the 'sus' law. The offence must involve 'more than a mere preparatory act' to commit a crime□
Attenborough Sir David 1926– . British traveller and zoologist; director of programmes for BBC TV 1969–72, and commentator in the television series *Life on Earth* 1979, etc. Knighted 1985□
Attenborough, Sir Richard 1923– . British actor and film director, brother of David Attenborough. His film roles include Pinkie in *Brighton Rock* 1943 and murder suspect Christie in *10 Rillington Place* 1970; films directed include *Oh! What a Lovely War!* 1968, *A Bridge Too Far* 1976, dealing with Arnhem, and *Gandhi* 1982 (8 Oscars)□
Attica Athens and the district round it, where in classical times language, art and philosophical thought reached a very high level. This is referred to as Attic purity□
Attila 406–53. King of the Huns, the 'Scourge of God'. His conquests ranged from the Rhine to Iran, but when he invaded Gaul in 451, he was defeated near Châlons-sur-Marne by the Romans and Visigoths. He invaded Italy in 452, Pope Leo personally intervening to prevent his sacking Rome. He died on the night of his wedding to Ildico, poison being suspected□
Attila Line line dividing Greek and Turkish Cyprus, so-called because of a fanciful identification of the Turks with the Huns□
Attlee Clement Richard, 1st Earl Atlee 1883–1967. British Labour statesman, whose early social work in the East End and co-operation with the Webbs◊ led him to Socialism. Leader of the Opposition from 1935, he held various posts in the World War II Coalition government, besides being Deputy Prime Minister to Churchill 1942–5. In Jul 1945, he succeeded him as Prime Minister after a Labour landslide in the general election, and introduced a programme of nationalization and social services, the Welfare State. His majority was reduced in the 1950 election; he was defeated in 1951, being awarded an Order of Merit, and on his retirement as Opposition leader in 1955, an earldom. He achieved his results by skilled committee management of his Cabinet□
attorney in the USA, a lawyer combining the functions of barrister and solicitor; the district attorney is the state prosecuting officer in a particular district□
Attorney General in England, principal law officer of the Crown and head of the English Bar; in the USA, the chief law officer of the government and head of the department of Justice□
Auber Daniel François Esprit 1782–1871. French composer of the comic opera *Fra Diavolo* 1830□
aubergine the eggplant, *Solanum melongena*, family Solanaceae◊, native to Africa and S Asia; the dark purple-skinned fruits are eaten as a vegetable□
Aubrey John 1626–97. British antiquary, who wrote gossipy anecdotes of his contemporaries in his *Brief Lives*, and first spread the misinformation that Stonehenge was a Druid◊ temple□
aubrietia genus of dwarf perennial plants, family Cruciferae◊, trailing in habit and bearing purple flowers□
Aubusson town in Limousin region, central France; population 6 800. It is famous for flat-woven carpets, and, at a factory founded by Colbert◊, tapestries (Gobelin and Beauvais types)□
Auchinleck Sir Claude 1884–1981. British soldier, nicknamed 'the Auk' because of his reticent dignity. He succeeded Wavell in the

Middle East Jul 1941, and in the summer of 1942 was forced back to the Egyptian frontier by Rommel, but his victory at the 1st Battle of El Alamein◊ is regarded by some as more the turning point of World War II than the 2nd. In 1943 he became Commander-in-Chief India, and founded the modern Indian and Pakistani armies, and gave background support to the Burma campaign□

Auckland largest city in New Zealand; population 797 000. Officially founded as the country's capital (1840–65), it is still the chief port and leading industrial centre, with iron and steel, engineering, car assembly, textile, food-processing industries, etc. The university was founded in 1882, and the international airport is at Mangere□

Auckland Islands six volcanic islands 480 km/300 mi south of South Island, New Zealand□

auction public sale to the highest bidder. Either the bid or an item may be withdrawn before the auctioneer knocks on his rostrum with a gavel; a seller may not bid without giving open notice; 'rings' of dealers agreeing to keep prices down are illegal; an owner's reserve price is kept secret, but an upset price is made public before a sale. A Dutch auction, as in street markets, has goods offered at a decreasing price until a buyer is found□

Auden Wystan Hugh 1907–73. British-American poet. Educated at Oxford, he was (with C. Day Lewis◊ and Spender◊) one of the 'committed' poets of the thirties, espousing left-wing politics and the Spanish Republican cause. By the time of the long poem *The Age of Anxiety* 1947, he had moved to a more conventional Christian viewpoint. He collaborated with Isherwood◊ in verse dramas, *The Dog Beneath the Skin* 1935 and *The Ascent of F6* 1936; collaborated in the libretti for Stravinsky's *The Rake's Progress* 1951 and Henze's *The Bassarids* 1966. A naturalized American from 1946, he became professor of poetry at Oxford 1956–61. His daring technique, influenced by Hopkins and Eliot, opened the way for younger writers□

audiometer electrical instrument testing pitch and loudness of sounds heard in cases of deafness□

auditor specialist accountant who gives annual independent checking of a company's accounts as required by law, to ensure the company balance sheet reflects the true state of its affairs□

Audubon John James 1785–1851. Originally Jean Jacques Rabin, illegitimate child of a Haitian planter, who adopted him, he settled in the USA in 1803. As naturalist and artist, his great work is *Birds of North America* 1827; the National Audubon Society, 1886, of USA and Canada, is for the study and protection of birds□

Auerbach Frank Helmuth 1931– . British artist, whose portraits and landscapes blend Representationalism and the abstract□

Augsburg industrial city in Bavaria, W Germany; population 246 200. Noted for its great medieval merchant families, the Fuggers and the Welsers; as the birthplace of Holbein◊; and as the site of the Messerschmitt works in World War II□

Augsburg Confession of. Statement of the Protestant faith as held by the German Reformers (see Melanchthon◊); it was presented to Charles V at the conference known as the Diet of Augsburg in 1530; it is the creed of the modern Lutheran Church□

augurs college of Roman priests interpreting the will of the gods from 'auspices', e.g. the flight of birds being to the right or left, the condition of the entrails of sacrificed animals, etc. This was done when a general was about to start a campaign, or at other times of crisis□

Augustan age the golden age of Augustus◊; the name was also given to later periods of classic culture and refinement, such as that of Queen Anne in England□

Augustine of Canterbury, St d. 604AD. First Archbishop of Canterbury, from 601. He had been sent on a mission to England by Pope Gregory I, and converted Ethelbert, King of Kent, in 597. He is thought to have restored a church which had existed in Roman times on the site of the present Canterbury Cathedral. In 603 he failed to unite the Roman and Celtic churches, the latter surviving beyond the area of the Anglo-Saxon invasion□

Augustine of Hippo, St 354–430AD. African Latin Church Father. Algerian-born, he studied at the university of Carthage, and had a natural son (Adeodatus) before he was twenty. Prompted by the wish of his mother (St Monica) that he marry, he despatched the mother of Adeodatus to a convent, and, since his intended bride was still too young, took a temporary concubine; his famous prayer; 'Give me chastity, but not yet!' is linked with this episode. The marriage seems not to have taken place. Both he and his son were baptised in 387, the latter dying when he was only 17, and Augustine became bishop of Hippo (modern Annaba◊) in 396. He devoted great energy to refuting heresy, but is remembered for his *Confessions,* and the 22 volumes of his *De Civitate Dei/City of God.* He died during a siege of Hippo by the Vandals□

Augustinian order order of canons (pastoral clerics, living communally under vows, but not strictly monks), who followed a 'rule' based on the writings of St Augustine◊ of Hippo, and drawn up in the 6–7th centuries; also an order of friars and hermits, etc.□

Augustus Gaius Julius Octavianus 63BC–14AD. First Roman emperor. He was the adopted son of his great-uncle, Julius Caesar◊, and, following the latter's murder, formed (with Mark Antony◊ and Lepidus◊), the triumvirate which divided the Roman world among them, and proceeded to eliminate the opposition. By his return to Rome in 29BC, he was in sole command (Antony a suicide and Lepidus in retirement); he restored the forms of the republic, but exercised a 'presidential rule' himself, backed by a 'kitchen cabinet' including Agrippa, Maecenas, and his second wife, Livia; Virgil and Horace were the 'poets laureate' and 'public relations' men of the new regime. Empire frontiers were established on defensible lines; a sound administration was created; and a professional army was formed with fixed pay and length of service, as well as a permanent fleet. Rome was given an adequate water supply, a fire brigade, a police force, and fine public buildings. The title Augustus 'venerable', was awarded to him by the populace in 27BC. Having no male heir, he married his profligate daughter Julia (see Ovid◊) to his unwilling stepson Tiberius◊, with disastrous results. In 6AD a serious revolt in Pannonia (modern Yugoslavia) took his stepsons two years to subdue, and brought the threat of invasion to Rome itself. The three finest Roman legions were annihilated by Varus◊ in 9AD, so that Augustus died a broken man, saying: 'Varus, give me back my legions!'□

Auld Lang Syne song by Robert Burns 1789, based on lines attributed to Sir Robert Ayton, and particularly associated with New Year gatherings; the title means 'old long since' or 'long ago'□

Auld Reekie 'old smoky', former nickname of Edinburgh□

Aurangzeb 1618–1707. Most brilliant of the Mogul◊ emperors of India; 3rd son of Shah Jehan, he made himself emperor by a palace revolution in 1658□

Aurelian 214–275. Roman emperor, who was chosen by his troops to succeed Claudius◊ in 270. He defeated the Goths and Vandals, defeated and captured Zenobia◊ of Palmyra, and was planning a campaign in Parthia (modern Iran) when he was murdered by some of his officers□

Aurelius Marcus. See Marcus◊ Aurelius

Auric Georges 1899–1983. French composer, one of ***Les Six,*** a group influenced by Erik Satie, he was noted for ballet and film music□

Auriol Vincent 1844–1966. French statesman, first president of the Fourth Republic 1947–54□

aurochs a type of bison. See cattle◊ family□

Aurora in Roman mythology, the goddess of dawn (Greek Eos◊)□

Aurora light, with great range of colour, in the night sky; ***Aurora borealis*** occurs in the northern hemisphere and ***Aurora australis*** in the southern. Both are caused, at a height of 100 km/60 mi, by a fast stream of charged particles, originating in the sun. These enter the upper atmosphere◊ and, by bombarding the gases in the atmosphere, cause them to emit visible light. The magnetic field of the earth divides the concentration into two zones□

Austen Jane 1775–1817. British novelist. Born at Steventon, Hampshire, where her father was rector, she moved to Bath with the family in 1801, and (after the death of her father in 1805) to Southampton. They finally settled in 1809 at Chawton, Hampshire, with her brother Edward, and the house, now a museum, still has the door which creaked to warn her of the approach of others when she was writing. Her first attempt was the burlesque *Love and Freindship* (sic) written in 1790; her mature works are: *Sense and Sensibility* 1811 (like its successors, published anonymously), *Pride and Prejudice* 1813, *Mansfield Park* 1814, *Emma* 1816, *Persuasion* 1818, which possibly contains a hint of a romance of her own that went astray, and *Northanger Abbey* 1818, a skit on the Gothic◊ novel set in Bath◊. Her work is delicately ironic, and she spoke herself of the 'little bit (two inches wide) of ivory' on which she wrote. The same spirit pervades her *Letters*, especially to her sister Cassandra. She died at Winchester and is buried in the cathedral□

Austin capital of Texas, USA; population 343 500. The Human Research Centre of Texas University has the largest collection of modern literary manuscripts and memorabilia in the world, mainly English, e.g. D H Lawrence, and Evelyn Waugh□

Australasia ill-defined geographical term, usually meaning Australia, New Zealand, and such Pacific islands as either are or were their dependencies. It is disliked by Australians and New Zealanders themselves□

Australia The Commonwealth of

area 7 704 441 sq km/2 974 693 sq mi

capital Canberra

towns Adelaide, Alice Springs, Brisbane, Darwin, Melbourne, Perth, Sydney

features the world's driest continent; Great Australian Desert, Great Barrier Reef,

Great Dividing Range, Darling river and the Murray system, Lake Eyre, Nullarbor Plain; unique animals include kangaroo, koala, numbat, platypus, wombat, Tasmanian devil and 'tiger'; budgerigar, cassowary, emu, kookaburra, lyre bird, black swan, and such deadly insects as the bulldog ant and funnel web spider

exports cereals, meat and dairy products; wool (30% of world production) fruit, wine, nuts, sugar, and honey; minerals include bauxite (world's largest producer), coal, iron, copper, lead, tin, zinc, opal, mineral sands, and uranium; machinery and transport equipment

currency Australian dollar

population 15 462 000, 95% British, 3% other Europeans, 0.5% Aborigines◊

language English

religion Anglican 36%, other Protestant 25%, Roman Catholic 33%

famous people *architecture* Roy Grounds (victoria Arts Centre, Melbourne) *art* Russell Drysdale, Sir Sidney Nolan, Tom Roberts, Sir William Dobell, Albert Namatjira, Phil May *ballet* Sir Robert Helpmann *entertainment* Rolf Harris, Barrie Humphries *music* Percy Grainger, Malcolm Williamson *performers* Peter Dawson, Dame Joan Hammond, Dame Nellie Melba, Dame Joan Sutherland *literature* A B 'Banjo' Paterson, Christopher Brennan, Judith Wright. Rolf Boldrewood, Marcus Clarke, Thomas Keneally, Henry Handel Richardon, Patrick White *science* Sir Frank Burnet, Sir John Cornforth

government Australia is a federal commonwealth (within the Commonwealth◊) with a Governor-General, representing the sovereign of the UK, senate and house of representative, all six states (New South Wales, Queensland, South Australia, Tasmania, Victoria, Western Australia) having equal representation in the former, but proportional representation in the latter; the federal prime minister (since 1983) is Bob Hawke. Each state (except Queensland) has a governor and parliament of two houses, and the Cabinet is headed by a premier.

Australia also comprises the Australian Capital Territory, and the self-governing Northern Territory. Under Australian administration are Norfolk Island, Ashmore and Cater Islands, Heard and McDonald Islands, Cocos (Keeling) Island, Christmas Island, and the Australian Antarctic Territory

recent history during World War II the USA superseded the UK as Australia's chief ally, and the entry of Britain to the Common Market reinforced Australia's realignment to other markets, especially Japan. From the 1970s Australia took up a new focal position among her Australasian◊ neighbours. See ASEAN◊, and Australia◊ history□

Australia Day public holiday, the anniversary of Captain Phillip's arrival in Sydney 26 Jan 1788 to found the first colony□

Australia: history

30 000–10 000 BC Aboriginal immigration from S India, Sri Lanka and SE Asia

1606 first European sightings of Australia include Dutch ship *Duyfken* off Cape York

1770 Captain Cook claimed New South Wales for Britain

1788 Sydney founded

19th century the great age of exploration: coastal surveys (Bass◊, Flinders◊), interior (Sturt◊, Eyre◊, Leichhardt◊, Burke and Wills◊, McDouall Stuart◊, Forrest◊)

Also the era of the bushrangers◊, overlanders◊ and squatters◊, and individuals such as William Buckley◊ and Ned Kelly◊

1804 Castle Hill Rising by Irish convicts in New South Wales

1813 the barrier of the Blue mountains crossed

1825 Tasmania separated from New South Wales

1829 Western Australia formed

1836 South Australia formed

1840–68 convict transportation ended

1851–61 gold rushes (Ballarat◊, Bendigo◊)

1851 Victoria separated from New South Wales

1855 Victoria achieved responsible government

1856 New South Wales, South Australia, Tasmania achieved responsible government

Australian Prime Ministers

Sir Edmund Barton (*Liberal*)	1901	Sir Earle Page (*Country Party*)	1939
Alfred Deakin (*Liberal*)	1903	R.G. Menzies (*United Australia Party*)	1939
John Watson (*Labour*)	1904	A.W. Fadden (*Country Party*)	1941
Sir G. Reid (*Free Trade*)	1904	John Curtin (*Labour*)	1941
Alfred Deakin (*Liberal*)	1905	F.M. Forde (*Labour*)	1945
Andrew Fisher (*Labour*)	1908	J.B. Chifley (*Labour*)	1945
Alfred Deakin (*Liberal*)	1909	R.G. Menzies (*Liberal*)	1949
Andrew Fisher (*Labour*)	1910	Harold Holt (*Liberal*)	1966
Sir J. Cook (*Free Trade*)	1913	John McEwen (*Liberal*)	1967
Andrew Fisher (*Labour*)	1914	J.G.Gorton (*Liberal*)	1968
W.M. Hughes (*Labour*)	1915	William McMahon (*Liberal*)	1971
W.M. Hughes (*National*)	1917	Gough Whitlam (*Labour*)	1972
S.M. Bruce (*National*)	1923	Malcolm Fraser (*Liberal*)	1975
J.H. Scullin (*Labour*)	1929	Robert Hawke (*Labour*)	1983
J.A. Lyons (*United Australia Party*)	1932		

1859 Queensland formed from New South Wales and achieved responsible government
1860 (National) Country Party founded
1860s Australian type football developed
1890 Western Australia achieved responsible government
1891 Depression gave rise to the Australian Labour Party
1899–1900 South African War – forces offered by the individual colonies
1901 creation of the Commonwealth of Australia
1911 site for capital at Canberra acquired
1914–18 World War I – Anzac◊ troops in Europe, but more especially at Gallipoli◊
1939–45 World War II – Anzac◊ troops in Greece, Crete, and N Africa (El Alamein◊) and the Pacific (Battle of the Coral Sea◊)
1941 Curtin's appeal to US for help in World War II marked the end of the special relationship with Britain
1944 Liberal Party founded by Menzies◊
1948–75 two million new immigrants, the majority from continental Europe
1950–3 Korean War – Australian troops formed part of the United Nations forces
1964–72 Vietnam War – Commonwealth troops in alliance with US forces
1966–74 mineral boom typified by the Poseidon nickel mine
1967 Australia became a member of ASEAN◊
1973 Britain entered the Common Market, and in the 1970s Japan became Australia's chief trading partner
1974 Whitlam◊ abolished 'white Australia' policy
1975 Constitutional crisis; Prime Minister (Whitlam◊) dismissed by the Governor-General
1975 United Nations Trust Territory of Papua-New Guinea became independent
1978 Northern Territory achieved self-government
1979 opening of uranium mines in Northern Territory
1983 Hawke◊ convened first 'national economic summit□

Australian Antarctic Territory
area 5 402 480 sq km/2 085 899 sq mi
government administered by the federal government of the Commonwealth of Australia◊
recent history In 1933 all islands and territories (other than Adèlie Land), situated south of 60° S and between 160° E and 45° E, came under Australian authority. See Antarctic◊ exploration□

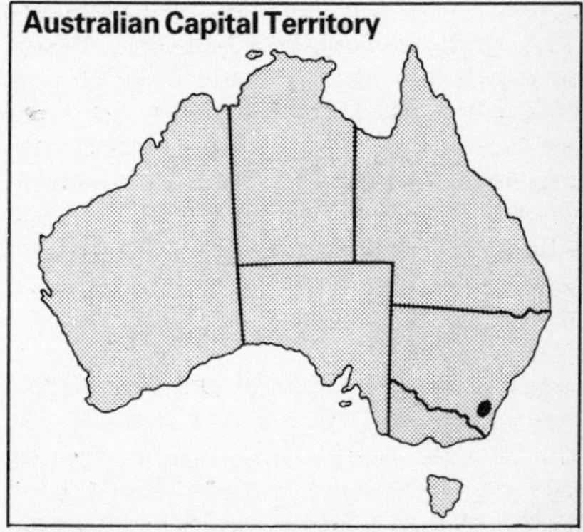

Australian Capital Territory a territory ceded to the Commonwealth of Australia by New South Wales in 1911 to provide the site of Canberra◊, with its port at Jervis Bay, which was ceded in 1915; area 2432 sq km/939 sq mi□

Austral Islands see under French◊ Polynesia□

Austria Republic of (German *Österreich*)
area 83 850 sq km/32 375 sq mi
capital Vienna
towns Graz, Linz, Salzburg, Innsbruck
features Austrian Alps (including Zugspitze and Brenner and Semmering passes), Vienna

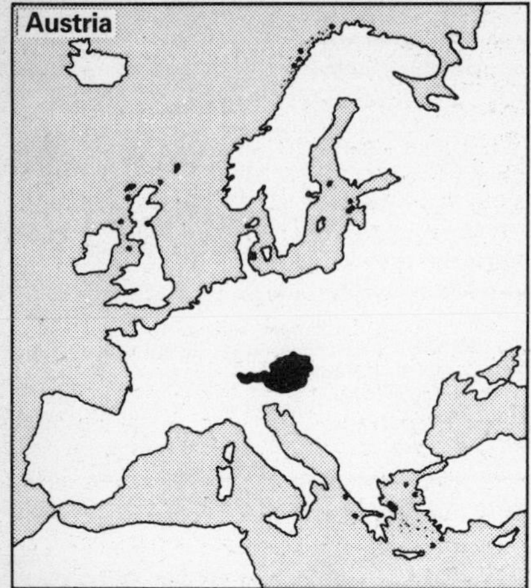

Plain, River Danube; Hainburg, the largest primeval rain forest left in Europe, now under threat from a dam
exports minerals, manufactured goods
currency Schilling
population 7 550 000
language German
religion Roman Catholicism 90%
famous people *art* Egon Schiele *history* Francis Joseph, Francis Ferdinand *music* Mozart, Schubert, Johann Strauss (father and son), Brahms, Bruckner, Mahler, Schoenberg, Webern, Berg; *literature* Schnitzler, Hofmannsthal, Rilke, Kafka, Musil, Handke *psychiatry* Sigmund Freud
government there is a popularly elected non-executive president and a National Assembly of two chambers: Nationalrat (Chancellor from 1983 Fred Sinowatz 1929– ; a Socialist) and Bundesrat. There are three political parties Socialist Party, People's Party. and Freedom Party
recent history the rule of the Hapsburgs◊ was ended in 1918, when a republic was proclaimed, which was incorporated by Hitler in the greater German 'Reich' from 1938. Austria remained in Allied occupation 1945–55. Under a Socialist government from 1970, Austria has the highest degree of public ownership in Western Europe. Austria is a member of EFTA◊, but its vulnerable borders with Czechoslovakia, Hungary, and Yugoslavia prevent membership of EEC or NATO. Kurt Waldheim was re-elected President in 1986 despite widespread allegations of his involvement in Nazi atrocities during World War II□

Austria-Hungary 'Dual Monarchy' of the Hapsburg◊ Empire, established by Francis Joseph◊ to satisfy Hungarian demands for equality with Austria, and existing 1867–1918□

Austrian Succession War of the. War 1740–8 between Austria (backed by England and Holland) and Prussia, France, and Spain; see Frederick◊ the Great. The succession of Maria Theresa, daughter of Emperor Charles VI, to her father's dominions had been disputed (because she was a woman) by the latter powers, hungry for territory. Battles include: 1743 ***Dettingen,*** a victory of the British, Austrians and Hanoverians under George II (the last action in which a British sovereign was personally engaged) over the French; 1745 ***Fontenoy*** a defeat for the Austro-English army.
Britain made gains in America and India, and British naval superiority was confirmed; the war ended with the Treaty of Aix-la-Chapelle 1748□

authoritarianism rule of a country by a 'strong' man or men, who ruthlessly repress opponents and the free press to maintain their own wealth and power. They are frequently indifferent to activities not affecting their security, as in many Latin-American countries. See totalitarianism◊□

autism condition of rigid withdrawal in children, who fail to develop normally in their intellect or emotions; it is caused by neurological defects, possibly genetic□

auto-da-fé ceremony (Portuguese 'act of faith') including a procession, solemn mass, and sermon; it accompanied the sentencing of heretics by the Spanish Inquisition before they were handed over to the secular authorities for punishment, usually burning□

auto-immune diseases those in which the body's defences are turned against itself, as in rheumatoid arthritis◊, Grave's disease◊, some types of diabetes◊, multiple sclerosis◊, AIDS◊, etc.□

automation term coined by US businessman John Diebold; it covers the addition of control devices, using electronic sensing and computing techniques (following the pattern of human nervous and brain functions) to already mechanized physical processes of production and distribution in steel processing, mining, chemical production, and road, rail, and air control□

automaton mechanical animal or human figure, entertaining rather than functional; the earliest recorded is an Egyptian wooden pigeon of 400BC. See robot◊□

autonomic nervous system nervous system which controls the involuntary activities of the heart, glands, and the smooth muscles of the alimentary canal and reproductive tract. The mechanics of facial muscle movement are closely linked with the autonomic nervous system. See also nerve◊□

auto-suggestion conscious or unconscious acceptance of an idea as true, without demanding rational proof, but with potential subsequent effect for good or ill. Pioneered by Coué◊ in healing, it is used in modern psychotherapy to conquer nervous habits, dependence on tobacco, alcohol, etc.□

autumn crocus the mauve ***meadow saffron*** *Colchicum autumnale*, family Liliaceae. It yields ***colchicine***, used in treating gout, and is used in in plant breeding (it causes plants to double the numbers of their chromosomes)□

Auvergne region of S central France, capital Clermont-Ferrand; population 1 320 000. It is in the heart of the mountainous Massif◊ Central, where hot springs occur among volcanic rocks□

Auxerre town in central France; population 40 000□

Avalon in Celtic myth, the island of the blest in the western ocean; in Arthurian legend, the location (identified with Glastonbury) to which King Arthur's body was taken□

Avar a member of a Tatar nomadic people who in the 6th century invaded the area of Russia north of the Black Sea previously held by the Huns□

avatar descent of a Hindu deity to earth in human form, as with the ten avatars of Vishnu□

Avebury Europe's largest stone circle (diameter 412 m/450 yd), Wiltshire, England; probably constructed in the Neolithic period 3500 years ago; it is linked with nearby Silbury◊ Hill□

Avebury John Lubbock, 1st Baron Avebury 1834–1913. British Liberal banker, chief originator of 'bank holidays'□

Ave Maria 'Hail Mary' a prayer to the Virgin Mary; it takes its name from the Archangel Gabriel's salutation of the Virgin Mary, when announcing that she would be the mother of the Messiah□

Avernus circular lake, near Naples, Italy. Formerly giving off bird-killing fumes, it was thought by the Romans to be the entrance to the lower world□

Aviemore winter sports centre, in the Highlands, Scotland, south east of Inverness among the Cairngorms□

Avignon town in S France on the River Rhône; population 90 900. Once a Roman city, it has a papal palace, seat of the papacy 1334–42, and the 12th-century bridge (only half still standing) of the nursery song 'Sur le pont d'Avignon'□

Avila town in central Spain; population 30 000. It was the birthplace of St Teresa◊ of Avila□

avocado dark green 'fruit' of the tree *Persea americana*, family Lauraceae◊, first cultivated by S American aboriginals, who named it from their word for 'testicle' in allusion to its shape. It is now a commercial salad crop in USA, Israel, etc.□

avocet genus of small, graceful, black-and-white wading birds, with 'upward-turned' bill, family Recurvirostridae, order Charadriiformes◊, including the ***European avocet*** ***Recurvirostra avosetta,*** especially associated with Minsmere reserve, Suffolk□

Avogadro Amedeo Conte di Quaregna 1776–1856. Italian physicist. His work on gases still has relevance for modern atomic studies□

Avogadro's Law a physical law formulated 1811: equal volumes of gases at the same pressure and temperature contain the same number of molecules□

Avon SW county of England
area 1346 sq km/520 sq mi
towns administrative headquarters Bristol; Bath, Weston-super-Mare
features River Avon
products aircraft and other engineering, tobacco, chemicals, printing; dairy products
population 922 600
famous people John Cabot, Thomas Chatterton□

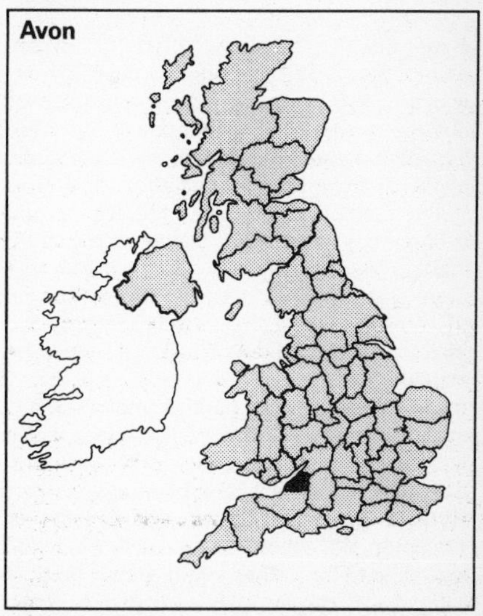

Avon several rivers of England and Scotland, including ***Upper (Warwickshire) Avon,*** joining the Severn at Tewkesbury; ***Lower (Bristol) Avon,*** flowing into the Bristol Channel at Avonmouth; and ***East (Salisbury) Avon,*** flowing into the English Channel at Christchurch□

Awe the longest Scottish freshwater loch, Strathclyde, 37 km/23 mi long; drained by the River Awe into Loch Etive, it has hydro-electric installations which are a tourist attraction□

Axholme Isle of. See Humberside◊□

Axis alliance of Nazi Germany and Fascist Italy from 1936, which was extended to include Japan Sept 1940, and collapsed with the fall of Mussolini in 1943□

Axminster town in Devon, England; population 4500. It produces cut-pile, patterned carpets which combine up to 240 colours□

axototl a Mexican amphibian. See salamander◊□

Axum see Aksum◊

ayatollah honorific, meaning 'sign of God', awarded to Shi'ite holy men in Iran by popular consent. See Khomeini◊□

Ayckbourn Alan 1939– . British dramatist and actor, director of the Theatre-in-the-Round, Scarborough, from 1959. He has a rich ear for comic dialogue, e.g. *Relatively Speaking* 1967, the trilogy *The Norman Conquests* 1974, and *Just Between Ourselves* 1977□

aye-aye primitive primate *Daubentonia madagascariensis,* only member of its family Daubentoniidae, found in Madagascar. A long-tailed tree-dweller, with a body 1 m/3 ft long, it is unique in its rodent-like teeth, and the long thin middle finger with which it probes for insects□

Ayer Sir Alfred Jules 1910– . British philosopher, who expounded in his *Language, Truth and Logic* 1936 a version of 'logical positivism', presenting a criterion by which meaningful statements (essentially truths of logic and mathematics, as well as statetements deriving from observation and experience) could be distinguished from metaphysical utterances (e.g. claims that there is a God, or that the world external to our own minds is illusory), which the logical positivists considered to be meaningless□

Ayers Rock ovate, pinkish monolith 335 m/1100 ft high, and 9 km/6 mi round, which was named after a premier of S Australia; there are Aboriginal rock paintings□

Ayesha 611–78 favourite (third) wife of Mohammed◊, whom he married when she was nine. Her father, Abu Bekr, became caliph◊ on the prophet's death, and she bitterly opposed the later succession to the caliphate of Ali◊, who had once accused her of infidelity□

Aylesbury administrative headquarters of Buckinghamshire, England; population 40 860. Waddesdon Manor, in the French Renaissance style, was bequeathed to the nation in 1957 by James de Rothschild□

Aymara a member of American Indian people of Bolivia and Peru, who were conquered first by the Incas and then by the Spaniards. Their language survives and their modern Roman Catholicism incorporates their old beliefs□

Ayot St Lawrence see Hertfordshire◊□

Ayr town in Strathclyde, Scotland; population 48 000. Burns was born at Alloway to the south, and Prestwick airport is to the north□

Ayrton Michael 1921–75. British painter, sculptor and illustrator, noted for his bronzes of Icarus◊□

ayurveda ancient Hindu system of medicine derived from the Vedas□

azalea a deciduous member of the genus *Rhododendron*◊, family Ericaceae, found in N America and S Asia□

Azerbaijan constituent republic of the Soviet Union from 1936
area 86 600 sq km/33 400 sq mi
capital Baku
towns Kirovabad
features Caspian Sea; the country ranges from semi-desert to Caucasus mountains
products oil, iron, copper, etc; fruit, vines; cotton, silk; carpets
population 6 100 000, 74% Azerbaijani, 10% Russian, 9% Armenian
language Turkic
religion traditionally Shi'ite Muslim
recent history A member of the Transcaucasian Federation in 1917, it became an independent republic in 1918, but was occupied by the Red Army in 1920. (See Georgia◊)□

Azerbaijan Iranian. Two provinces of NW Iran◊□

Azhar El. Muslim university in Cairo, founded in 970, and claimed as the oldest in the world□

Azores group of nine islands in the N Atlantic; area 2335 sq km/922 sq mi; population 336 000. They are outlying peaks of the Mid-Atlantic Ridge, and are volcanic in origin. The capital is Ponta Delgada on the main island, San Miguel. Portuguese from 1430, they were granted partial autonomy in 1976, but remain a Portuguese overseas territory. They command the Western shipping lanes, and a separatist movement is backed by USSR and Libya□

Azov inland sea of the USSR forming a gulf in the north east of the Black Sea□

Aztec one of the native people of Mexico, who migrated from further north in the 12th century AD. They built their capital, Tenochtitlan (modern Mexico◊ City), in 1325, and under Montezuma◊ I created an empire in central and southern Mexico. Their gods include Huitzilopochtli (Hummingbird Wizard) and also Quetzalcoatl◊, whom they inherited from the conquered Toltecs◊ (see Tula◊). The Aztecs, led by Montezuma◊ II, put up only slight resistance when Cortes◊ landed in 1519. They had magnificent architecture, jewellery (gold, jade, turquoise), and textiles; their writing combined the hieroglyphic and the pictograph. A complex calendar combined a sacred period of 260 days with a solar year of 365 days, with propitiatory rites performed at the dangerous period (once every 52 years) when the beginning of the two coincided, and all temples were rebuilt (a datemark for archaeologists). They practised wholesale human sacrifice, tearing the heart from the living body and flaying people alive – both war captives and their own people. They played a type of football with a solid rubber ball, propelled by legs rather than feet, in which one of the teams was killed after the game; it is not certain whether the losers were sacrificed for losing, or the winners promoted to the other world for having won□

B

Baader-Meinhof gang see terrorism◊□

Baal divine title, Hebrew 'lord', of the chief Phoenician, Canaanite, and other Semitic male gods; see Palmyra◊. Their orgiastic rites were denounced by the Hebrew prophets (see Jezebel◊)□

Baalbek originally a centre of Baal worship, its ruins (including Roman temples) survive NE of Beirut, Lebanon□

Ba'ath Party socialist party aiming at the extended union of all Arab countries; see Iraq◊, Syria◊□

Babbage Charles 1801–1871. British mathematician, who assisted John Herschel◊ in his astronomical calculations, and designed calculating machines which were the forerunners of computers◊□

Babel see Babylon◊□

Bab-el-Mandeb strait, known as the 'gate of tears' because of its currents, which joins the Red Sea and the Gulf of Aden□

Babi faith see Baha'i◊ faith□

Babington Anthony 1561–86. English traitor who hatched a plot to assassinate Elizabeth◊ I and replace her by Mary◊, Queen of Scots; its discovery led to her execution and his own□

Babi Yar site of a massacre of Jews by the Germans in 1941, near Kiev, USSR □

baboon a type of monkey◊□

Babur title, meaning 'tiger', of Zahir ud-din Mohammed, 1483–1530. The first Great Mogul of India, he was a grandson of Tamerlane◊, and inherited Turkestan from his father when he was 12. By 1526 he had taken Delhi and established a dynasty nominally enduring till 1858□

Babylon capital of Babylonia (on Euphrates S of Baghdad). The ***Tower of Babel*** was a ziggurat or staged temple seven storeys high (100 m/300 ft), with a shrine of Marduk◊ at the summit. It was built by Nabopolassar, father of Nebuchadnezzar◊, and was destroyed when Sennacherib◊ sacked the city 689BC. The ***Hanging Gardens*** (one of the Seven Wonders of the World), were erected on a vaulted stone base, the only stone construction in the mud-built city. They formed a series of terraces, irrigated by a hydraulic system. The ***Ishtar Gate*** now reconstructed in Berlin, spanned a processional way of the god Marduk, and was decorated with bulls and dragons in blue-enamelled brick. The city was captured by Alexander◊ 331BC, and in 275 its people were forcibly deported to the new capital of Seleucia; by 24BC it was a desert. Excavated cuneiform texts include observations useful to modern astronomers, especially the records of lunar and solar eclipses□

Babylonia fertile plain of the Tigris and Euphrates, now forming the major part of Iraq◊□

Babylonian captivity originally, the exile of Jewish deportees to Babylon after Nebuchadnezzar◊'s capture of Jerusalem in 586BC; traditionally, it lasted 70 years, but Cyrus◊ actually allowed them home in 536BC. By analogy, the name was also applied to the Papal exile to Avignon◊ 1309–77□

baccarat casino card game with two forms: *chemin de fer* and *banque*. The cards are dealt from a shoe-like box□

Bacchus in Greek and Roman mythology, the god of fertility (see Dionysus◊) and of wine; his rites were orgiastic□

Bach Johann Christian 1735-82. German composer. The eleventh son of J S Bach◊. Born in Leipzig, he became well known in Italy as a composer of operas. In 1762 he was invited to London, where he became music master to the royal family. He remained in England till his death□

Bach Johann Sebastian 1685–1750. German composer. Born in Eisenach, he was organist at Arnstadt at 19 and to the Duke of Weimar 1708–17; he was musical director of St Thomas' choir school in Leipzig from 1723, and in 1747 visited the court of Frederick the Great. His music is the culmination of the polyphonic style, but his greatness was not recognized by his contemporaries. His works include ***sacred music*** some 200 cantatas, the Easter and Christmas oratorios, passions according to St Matthew and St John, and the Mass in B minor; ***orchestral music*** six concertos written for the Margrave of Brandenburg, and four orchestral suites; ***keyboard music*** the collection of 48 preludes and fugues known as *The Well-tempered Clavier*, the *Goldberg Varia-*

tions, Italian Concerto, French and *English suites; **organ music*** nearly 150 choral preludes; and an unfinished last work *The Art of Fugue*, a series of exercises all based on the same theme. Many of his secular works, including both cantatas and instrumental music, have been lost. At the end of his life his sight failed; he married twice, but his 20 children mostly died in infancy□

Bach Karl Philip Emmanuel 1714–88. German composer. The most gifted of the children of J S Bach◊, he was in the service of Frederick◊ the Great 1740–67. He preferred the clavier to the old-fashioned harpsichord, was a brilliant concert performer, and developed a style of composition better suited to the modern piano□

bacillus see bacteria◊□

backgammon board game (Old English 'back game'), of which the children's version is ludo. The board is marked out in 24 triangular points of alternating colours, 12 to each side. Throwing two dice, the players move their 15 flat, circular pieces round the board to the six points which form their own 'inner table'; the first player to move all his pieces off the board is the winner. Players have included Tutankhamun, Chaucer, Henry VIII, and Pepys. In the 1920s it became a casino game when a group was allowed to play a single opponent, and the American innovation of a 'doubling cube' made it more exciting by repeatedly doubling the stakes□

Bacon Francis 1561–1626. English statesman, philosopher, and man of letters. The nephew of Queen Elizabeth's adviser, Lord Burghley◊, he was a follower of the Earl of Essex◊, but when his patron lost favour, he helped secure his conviction as a traitor. Knighted on the accession of James I, he became Lord Chancellor in 1618 and a peer, first as Baron Verulam, then in 1621 as Viscount St Albans. Later in 1621 he was accused of bribe-taking, and, having confessed, was fined and spent four days in the Tower of London. Although he had taken the money, he claimed that he didn't always give the verdict to his paymasters. His works include *Essays* 1597, thick with proverbial brevity; *The Advancement of Learning* 1605, a seminal work discussing scientific method; and *The New Atlantis* 1626, describing a Utopian state in which scientific knowledge is systematically sought and exploited□

Bacon Francis 1909– . British artist, born in Dublin. His work is characterized by lurid colour and terrifyingly blurred, featureless figures, such as *Study after Velásquez* 1953, a series of variations on that artist's portrait of Pope Innocent X□

Bacon Roger 1214–92. English Franciscan◊ friar and scientist, one of the boldest thinkers of the Middle Ages. In 1277 he was condemned and imprisoned by the Church, and not released till 1292. He followed the maxim 'Cease to be ruled by dogmas and authorities; look at the world!' He foresaw the magnifying properties of convex lenses, the extensive use of gunpowder, and the possibility of mechanical cars, boats, and flying machines□

bacteria microscopic, usually unicellular organisms. Their proteins are unlike those of supposedly more 'advanced' organisms, so that it has been suggested that they may actually themselves be a more advanced form, or even that two different types of cell originated at the period of creation: they lack a nuclear membrane. See procaryote◊.

They are now classified biochemically, but the varying shape of their transparent cells (without a nucleus) gives a rough classification: ***cocci*** – round or oval; ***bacilli*** – cylindrical; and ***spirochaetae*** – spiral or undulatory. They reproduce by fission, which may occur every 20 minutes, so that a single bacterium has the potential of becoming 16 million in one day. In the laboratory they are grown on culture media, and may mutate, a characteristic which accounts both for the emergence of strains resistant to antibiotics, and for the use of bacteria in genetic research. The common intestinal bacterium *Escherichia coli* has been genetically re-engineered to produce insulin◊ and interferon◊. Unlike viruses they do not necessarily need contact with a live cell to become active.

Bacteria cause such diseases as anthrax, cholera, diphtheria, enteric fever, pneumonia, scarlet fever, tuberculosis, and venereal infections; see also food◊ poisoning. However, the majority are beneficial. They perform useful functions in the healthy human body, in soil fertility, etc; are essential in many food processes (in making butter, cheese, yoghurt, and the new synthetic foods); and are valuable industrial aids (in curing tobacco, tanning leather, sewage disposal, extraction of minerals from mines, cleaning a ship's bottom, derusting storage tanks – the last three by virtue of bacterial ability to attack metal). Bacteria generally do not survive temperatures above 100°C (see pasteurization◊), but those in deep-sea hot vents in the E Pacific withstand temperatures of 350°C□

Bactria former region of central Asia (modern Afghanistan, Pakistan and Soviet Central Asia) which was partly conquered by Alexander◊ the Great; 3rd–6th century BC it was a great centre of E–W trade and cultural exchange□

Baden former German state, now part of Baden-Württemberg◊□

Baden-Baden Black Forest spa, Baden-Württemberg, W Germany; population 50 000. Fashionable in the 19th century, it is now a conference centre□

Baden-Powell Agnes 1854–1945. Sister of Robert Baden-Powell◊, she helped him found the Girl Guides◊□

Baden-Powell Robert Stephenson Smyth, 1st Baron Baden-Powell 1857–1941. British soldier, the defender of Mafeking◊, who retired in 1910. He had held a camp for Boy Scouts on Brownsea Island, Poole Harbour, in 1907 and devoted his retirement to developing the Scout◊ movement. He became a peer 1929, Order of Merit 1937□

Baden-Württemberg Land of W Germany
area 35 750 sq km/13 805 sq mi
capital Stuttgart
towns Karlsruhe, Mannheim, Freiburg, Heidelburg
features Black Forest; Rhine boundary S and W; source of the Danube; see also Swabia◊
products wine; jewellery, watches, clocks; musical instruments; textiles, chemicals, iron and steel, electrical equipment, surgical instruments
population 9 277 000
religion Roman Catholicism 47%, Protestantism 44%□

Bader Sir Douglas 1910–82. British air ace. He lost both legs in a stunt accident in 1931, but won 227 victories as a fighter pilot in World War II. Knighted 1976 for his work for the disabled□

badger a burrowing nocturnal mammal. See under weasel◊□

Bad Godesburg SE suburb of Bonn◊. A spa, it was the meeting place of Chamberlain◊ and Hitler◊ before the Munich◊ Pact; the mansion La Redoute is used by the W German government for entertaining□

badlands dry, heavily eroded areas, as in S Dakota, USA. The spectacular rock formations are familiar in numerous Westerns and form a national monument□

badminton game originating at Badminton House, Gloucestershire, seat of the Duke of Beaufort, in the 1860s. It is played by 2–4 players with rackets and shuttlecocks, and has become a spectator sport since World War II. Badminton House is also noted for the ***Badminton Horse Trials***, established 1949, for international teams□

Badoglio Pietro 1871–1956. Italian general, the ruthless conqueror of Ethiopia◊, who succeeded Mussolini◊ as Prime Minister of Italy Jul 1943–Jun 1944□

Baedeker Karl 1801–59. German publisher of the famous foreign travel guides; these now based in Hamburg (before World War II Leipzig)□

Baedeker raids German air raids in World War II on British cities, accurately pinpointing architectural treasures□

Baekeland Leo Hendrik 1863–1944. American chemist, the inventor of bakelite, the first commercial plastic◊. He later made a photographic paper, Velox, which could be developed in artificial light□

Baer Karl Ernst von 1792–1876. German zoologist, the founder of comparative embryology◊□

Baez Joan 1941– . American folk singer, a pacifist and opponent of the Vietnam War□

Baffin William 1584–1622. English Arctic◊ voyager of astonishing range 1612–17; the veracity of his accounts was not confirmed for 200 years□

Baffin Bay sea area between N America and Greenland. It was discovered by Baffin, seeking the Northwest◊ Passage in 1612□

Baffin Island largest island of the Canadian Arctic, NW Territories; area 507 450 sq km/195 930 sq mi□

bagatelle a variant of billiards, a forerunner of the electric pinball machine□

Baggara Moslem Arab of the Sudan, formerly nomad warriors□

Baghdad capital of Iraq; population 3 200 000. A route centre from the earliest times, it was developed by Harun-al-Rashid◊, though little of the Arabian Nights city remains, and became the capital of modern Iraq in 1921. To the SE, on the Tigris, are the ruins of ***Ctesiphon***, capital of Parthia◊ c250BC–c226AD, and the Sassanian◊ Empire c226–c641; the remains of the Great Palace include the world's largest single-span brick arch 26 m/85 ft wide and 29 m/95 ft high□

Baghdad Pact defence treaty of 1955 concluded by Britain, Iran, Iraq, Pakistan and Turkey, with the USA co-operating; it was replaced by the Central Treaty Organization when Iraq withdrew in 1958□

Bagnold Enid 1889–1981. British author; her works include a novel and play about the Grand National, *National Velvet* 1935, and the play *The Chalk Garden* 1954□

bagpipe ancient musical instrument of many countries, which consists of a chanter (melody) pipe and drones (which emit invariable notes to supply a ground base). All are supplied from a wind-bag inflated by the performer. The most famous variety is that of the Highlands, the Scottish national instrument: others are the Irish and Greek□

Bahá'ī faith religion foreshadowed by Iranian Mirzá 'Ali Muhammad 1819–50, who was shot by the government for claiming that Islam was not God's final revelation. Husayn 'Ali 1817–92, who called himself Bahá'u'lláh ('God's glory'), claimed to be the new prophet in 1863 with a faith incorporating the best in all other religions. It stresses the oneness of mankind, regardless of race, sex, colour, class, or creed, and has a worldwide following. The headquarters is in Haifa, since the Bahá'ī were driven from Iran in the 19th century, persecution being renewed under Khomeini◊. There is a nine-member ruling council□

Bahamas Commonwealth of the

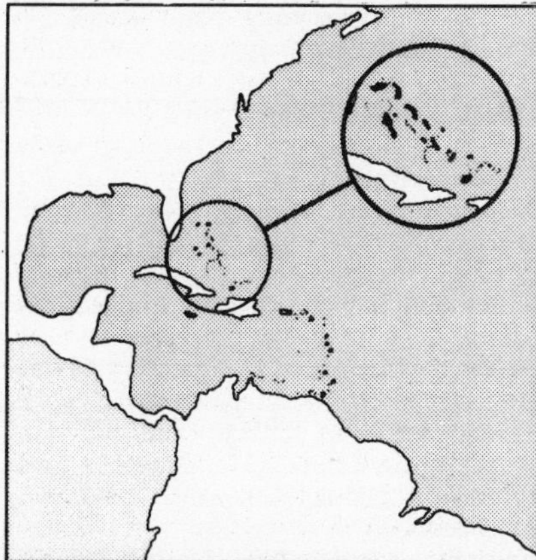

area 13 935 sq km/5380 sq mi
capital Nassau on New Providence
features comprises 700 coral islands and about 1000 cays, only 30 are inhabited; Blue Holes of Andros, the world's longest and deepest submarine caves
exports cement, pharmaceuticals, petroleum products, crawfish, rum, pulpwood; over half the islands' employment comes from tourism
currency Bahamian dollar
population 234 000
language English
religion Christianity
famous people Columbus, who made his first landing in the New World on San Salvador in 1492; Edward Teach, alias 'Blackbeard', and other pirates, who formerly made it their base; and the former Edward VIII, who was governor 1940–45
government under the constitution of 1973 there is a governor-general, senate and house of assembly (Prime Minister from 1967 Lynden O Pindling).
recent history having finally become British in 1783, following disputes with Spain, the Bahamas became independent within the British Commonwealth in 1973□

Bahawalpur industrial town in Pakistan; population 134 000□

Bahia Blanca river port in Argentina; population 182 000□

Bahrain

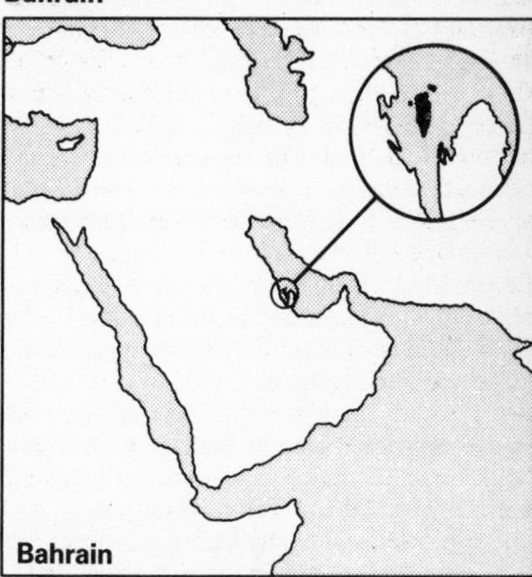

area 600 sq km/400 sq mi
capital Manama on the largest island (also called Bahrain) of the 33 in the group
towns oil port Minister a Sulman
features a causeway 25 km/15 mi long (1985) links Bahrain to the mainland of Saudi Arabia; Sitra island is a communications centre for the lower Gulf, and has a satellite tracking station; there is a wild life park featuring the oryx◊ on Bahrain, and most of the S of the island is preserved for the ruling family's falconry
exports oil and natural gas
currency Bahrain dinar
population 409 000, two thirds are nationals
language Arabic, Farsi
religion Islam (Shiah 60%, Sunni 40%)
government the Amir from 1961 is Sheikh Isa bin Sulman Al-Khalifa 1933– ; administration is by a cabinet, and revival of the National Assembly is planned.
recent history under British protection from 1816, Bahrain became independent under Sheikh Isa in 1971□

Baikal largest lake in Asia, E USSR; 31 500 sq km/12 150 sq mi; it is also the deepest in the world 1620 m/5315 ft. Pollution threatens sturgeon fisheries and the unique fauna, which includes its own breed of seal□

Baikonour Cosmodrome see under Kazakhstan◊□

bail the liberation, on security (given by the accused or some other person) of someone held in custody; if he does not attend court at the stated time, the bail is forfeit□

Baile Atha Cliath the Gaelic name of Dublin□

Bailey Sir Donald 1901–85. British inventor of the Bailey military bridge in World War II, made of interlocking, interchangeable, adjustable, and easily transportable units□

Baillie Dame Isobel 1895–1983. British soprano. Born in Hawick, Scotland, she had an ethereal purity of tone□

Bainbridge Beryl 1933– . British novelist, Liverpool-born and originally an actress, whose works have the drama and economy of a stage-play. They include *The Dressmaker* 1973 and *The Bottle Factory Outing* 1974□

Bainbridge Kenneth 1904– . American physicist, who worked at Cambridge in the 1930s and was director of the first atom bomb test at Alamagordo◊ in 1945□

Baird John Logie 1888–1946. British television pioneer. Born in Helensburgh, Scotland, he studied electrical engineering at the University of Strathclyde (Glasgow), also undertaking practical apprenticeships. He was working on television as early as 1912, and took out his first provisional patent in 1923, giving his first public demonstration at Selfridges◊ in 1925. He also pioneered fibre◊ optics 1926; radar◊ 1926, in advance of Watson-Watt; infra-red television 1926 for the long-distance detection of objects; video-recordings on wax and also on magnetic steel discs 1926–7; 3D-colour television 1925–46; transatlantic television 1928; and facsimile television 1944, forerunner of the viewdata system. In 1936 his mechanically scanned 240–line system competed with EMI-Marconi's 405–line, but the latter was preferred for the BBC from 1937, partly because it could handle live indoor scenes with smaller, more manoeuvrable cameras□

Bairnsfather Bruce 1888–1959. British cartoonist, the creator of 'Old Bill', a realistic embodiment of the serviceman in the World War I trenches, which was at first officially disapproved of□

Baja California mountainous peninsula forming the two states (N and S) of Lower (*baja*) California, Mexico: see Mexicali◊, Tijuana◊. The south is still undeveloped□

bakelite a type of plastic◊□

Baker Sir Benjamin 1840–1907. British engineer, designer (with Sir John Fowler) of London's first underground railway in 1869, and of the Forth◊ Bridge 1890□

Baker Dame Janet 1933– . British mezzo-soprano, noted as Dido in *The Trojans*, Marguerite in *Faust*, as well as for her interpretation of lieder◊; DBE 1976□

Baker Sir Samuel White 1821–93. British explorer. He was anticipated by Speke◊ and Grant in discovering the source of the Nile, but was the first European to sight Lake Albert/Mobutu, and to find that the Nile flowed through it□

Bakewell town in Derbyshire, England; population 4100. Chatsworth House and Haddon Hall are nearby□

Bakst Leon 1866–1924. Russian artist born Rosenberg, who designed scenery for Diaghilev◊'s ballets□

Baku capital and oil port, Republic of Azerbaijan, USSR; population 1 435 000□

Bakunin Mikhail 1814–76. Russian anarchist.p×aescaped from Siberian exile, joined the 'First International◊' in 1869, but quarrelled with Marx◊ and was expelled in 1872. His main following was in Latin America□

Bala Lake. Lake in Gwynedd◊, N Wales□

Balaclava town in the Ukraine, USSR. ***Balaclava helmets*** were knitted hoods worn here by soldiers in the bitter weather of the Crimean◊ War□

Balaclava Battle of. Battle in the Crimean◊ War, 25 Oct 1854, which included the charge of a Light Brigade of cavalry against Russian entrenched artillery; 700 participated, 195 returned□

Balakirev Mily Alexeievich 1837–1910. Russian composer, whose nationalistic works include folk-song settings, and the symphonic poem *Tamara*. He influenced Mussorgsky, Rimsky-Korsakov, Borodin, Tchaikovsky□

balalaika Russian stringed musical instrument, resembling a triangular guitar□

balance of payments the difference between debits and credits in the buying and selling of goods and services between one country and other countries (usually the rest of the world). A balance of payments crisis usually means that more is leaving the country (in paying for imports) than is coming in (in payments for exports)□

Balanchine Georges 1904–83. American choreographer. Ballet master to Diaghilev◊ 1925–9, he was artistic director of the New York Ballet Company from 1948. His dance number 'Slaughter on Tenth Avenue', for the musical comedy *On Your Toes* 1936, entered the classical repertory in 1968. Individual ballets created include *The Prodigal Son* and *Theme and Variations*□

Balaton Lake. Lake in W Hungary; area 600 sq km/230 sq mi□

Balboa Vasco Nunez de 1475–1517. Spanish conquistador◊. The first white man to see the Pacific Ocean on 29 Sept 1513, from Darien, he was made Admiral of the Pacific and Governor of Panama. He was removed by Spanish court intrigue, imprisoned and executed□

Balcon Sir Michael 1896–1977. British film producer, responsible for the 'Ealing comedies' *Kind Hearts and Coronets* 1949 and *The Lavender Hill Mob* 1951, etc, and *The Cruel Sea*□
baldness hair loss from the upper scalp, especially common in older Caucasian men. Its onset is affected by the genetic makeup of the individual and the male sex hormones. There is no 'cure' and 'implants' from elsewhere on the head are seldom effective. It can be caused in both sexes by poor health□
Baldur in Norse◊ legend, the wisest and most loved of the gods, son of Odin◊ and Frigga◊. He was killed at the instigation of the evil god Loki◊ by a twig of mistletoe thrown by the blind god Hoder□
Baldwin I 1058–1118. King of Jerusalem. A French nobleman, who joined the First Crusade◊ in 1096, he established the kingdom in 1100, which was destroyed by Islamic conquest in 1187□
Baldwin James 1924– . American author, born in Harlem, who joined the civil rights agitation of the 1960s. His works include the autobiographical *Notes of a Native Son* 1955, and the novel *Just Above my Head* 1979□
Baldwin Stanley, 1st Earl Baldwin of Bewdley 1867–1947. British Conservative◊ statesman. The son of an iron and steel magnate, he affected a countrified image that concealed a shrewd intelligence. He was a leader in the disruption of the Lloyd◊ George coalition of 1922, and as Chancellor under Bonar◊ Law, achieved a settlement of war debts with the USA, and succeeded him as Prime Minister in 1923. He lost his clear majority after the general election of Dec 1923,and resigned on his defeat in the Commons in Jan 1924. During his second premiership Oct 1924 to 1929, he weathered the General◊ Strike 1926, but was badly defeated in the general election of May 1929, though he joined the National government of MacDonald◊ in 1931 as Lord President of the Council. During his third premiership 1935–7, he handled the abdication crisis of Edward◊ VIII, but was later much criticized for his failure to resist popular desire for an accommodation with Hitler◊ and Mussolini◊, and failure to rearm more effectively□
Bâle see Basel◊□
Balearic Islands
Mediterranean group of islands (Spanish *Baleares*) forming an autonomous region of Spain. The largest is Majorca (*Mallorca*), on which is the capital Palma◊; products include fruit (figs, olives, oranges), wine and brandy, and minerals (coal, iron, slate). Robert Graves◊ had his home on the island. Other

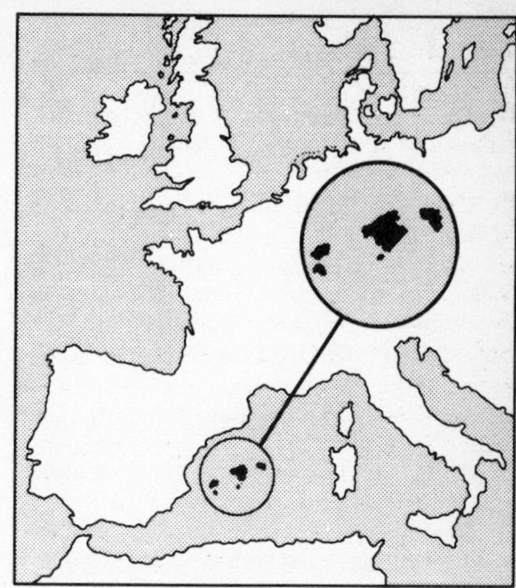

islands are Minorca (*Menorca*), chief town Mahón, with a shoe industry; Iviza (*Ibiza*), chief town also Iviza, especially popular with tourists; Cabrera, and Formentera. Total area 5014 sq km/1935 sq mi; population 685 000□
Balfour Arthur James, 1st Earl of Balfour 1848–1930. British Conservative statesman. He was nicknamed 'bloody Balfour' as Secretary for Ireland 1887, but was courtly in private life and wrote philosophical works. He succeeded Salisbury◊ as Prime Minister in 1902, but the cabinet was divided over Chamberlain◊'s Tariff Reform, and he was crushingly defeated in the 1905 election. He retired as party leader in 1911. As Foreign Secretary in the Asquith◊ coalition of 1916–19, he issued the Balfour Declaration◊, though in many ways himself prejudiced against the Jews, and signed the Versailles◊ Treaty. He received an Order of Merit 1916, and an earldom in 1922□
Balfour Declaration a letter, 2 Nov 1917, from A J Balfour to Lord Rothschild (chairman, British Zionist Federation) stating: 'HM government view with favour the establishment in Palestine of a national home for the Jewish people'; it led to the foundation of Israel□
Bali see under Sunda◊ Islands□
Balkans peninsula (Turkish 'mountains'), comprising Albania, Bulgaria, Greece, Romania, Turkey-in-Europe and Yugoslavia. Waves of invasion left a great diversity of peoples, so that it became a byword for dissension. It sparked World◊ War I, and there are still elements of instability, e.g. in Yugoslavia◊, and possibility of Russian intervention□
Balkan Wars two wars 1912–13 among Balkan countries, which resulted in the

expulsion of Turkey from Europe except for a toehold round Istanbul. See under Serbia◊ □

Balkhash shallow lake in the Republic of Kazakh, USSR; area 17 300 sq km/668 sq mi□

Ball John d. 1381. English priest, who led the Peasants◊' Revolt in 1381. He preached from the text: When Adam delved and Eve span, Who was then the gentleman? He was executed□

ballad song-poem with a story, originally for use in communal ring-dances. There are series dealing with Robin◊ Hood, Jesse James◊, etc, and literary examples were produced by Wordsworth, Coleridge, Kipling, etc.□

Ballarat industrial town in Victoria, Australia; population 60 700. It was founded in the 1851 gold rush, and the restored mining village and workings are now a tourist attraction; there is a Gold Museum. The ***Eureka Stockade*** was a revolt by aggrieved miners in which 30 miners and several soldiers were killed when the military took the stockade 3 Dec 1854. The captured rebels were all acquitted of treason□

Ballard J(ames) G(raham) 1930– . British novelist, his works include science fiction, *The Drowned World* 1963, and the partly autobiographical *Empire of the Sun* 1984, dealing with his internment in China during World War II□

ballet combination of music and dance in theatrical presentation which originated in Italy, was brought to France by Catherine de Medici◊, and was established as public entertainment by Molière◊ and Lully◊.

1661 Louis◊ XIV founded L'Académie de la Musique et de la Danse

1720s Marie Camargo◊ introduced *danse en l'air*

1778 Mozart's *Les Petits Riens* choreographed by Noverre◊

1830 romantic era of Taglioni◊, the calf-length classical white dress, and dancing *en pointe*

1862 Petipa◊ at Russian Imperial Ballet

1909 Diaghilev◊'s Ballet Russe, with Nijinsky◊; and, in opposition, Isadora Duncan◊

1931 Ninette de◊ Valois director of the Vic-Wells Ballet

1933 Balanchine◊ in the USA; New York Ballet, with choreographer Jerome Robbins◊ established American classic style

1934–59 Margot Fonteyn◊ era of perfect line; see also Nureyev◊

1956 Royal◊ Ballet incorporated; see choreographers Ashton◊, Macmillan◊

1957 Bernstein◊'s *West Side Story* combined modern ballet and opera

1986 Dowell◊ director of the Royal Ballet□

Ballinasloe town in Galway Bay, Republic of Ireland; population 6000. The Oct livestock fair is the largest in Ireland□

ballistics study of projectile motion inside a weapon and after launching. With a gun, external factors include temperature, barometric pressure, and wind strength; with nuclear missiles, they include the speed at which the earth turns, etc.□

balloon impermeable fabric bag which rises when filled with gas lighter than the surrounding air. The first successful human ascent was piloted by Pilâtre de Rozier, Paris 1783, in a hot-air balloon designed by the Montgolfier◊ brothers. Balloons were first used in war for observation during the French revolutionary period; in World War II they were used to defend London against low-flying aircraft. They are now used for sport, and as an economical means of meteorological, infrared, gamma ray, ultra-violet, etc, observation. The first transatlantic crossing was made 11–17 Aug 1978 by a US team□

balm a type of herb◊□

Balmoral Castle see under Grampian◊□

balsa tropical American tree *Ochroma lagopus*, family Bombacaceae; the very light wood is used for rafts and model-making□

Balthus pseudonym of French artist Balthazar Klossovski de Rolla 1908– . Noted especially for his street scenes and slightly erotic pictures of dreamy young women□

Baltic Battle of the. British victory, 2 Apr 1801, when Nelson◊ secured the surrender of the entire Danish fleet after putting his telescope to his blind eye when his commander, Admiral Parker, signalled 'disengage'□

Baltic Sea

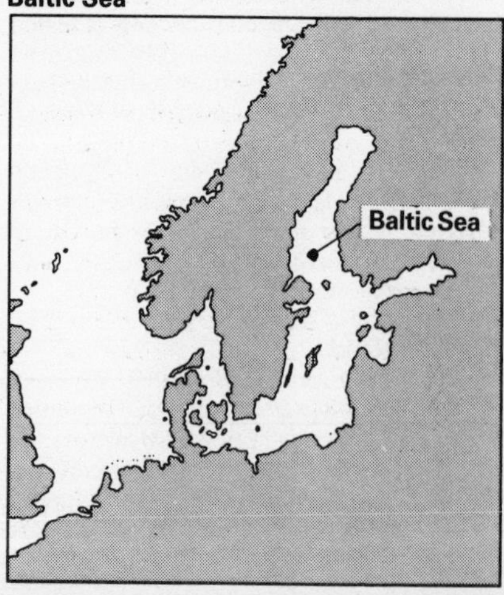

large shallow arm of the North Sea; area 422 300 sq km/163 000 sq mi. It is linked with the North Sea via the Skaggerak, Kattegat, Göta, and Kiel canals; and from 1975 with the White Sea via the Leningrad-Belomorsk seaway enabling Soviet warships to escape NATO surveillance. Its tides are hardly perceptible, its weather treacherous, and navigation is dangerous. The low salt content allows preservation of such ancient timber wrecks as the Wasa◊□

Baltic States Estonia, Latvia, Lithuania, when spoken of collectively□

Baltimore port in Maryland, USA; population 1 335 000. The homes of Edgar Allan Poe◊ and Babe Ruth◊ are preserved, as is Fort McHenry, where Francis Scott Key wrote 'The Star Spangled Banner'. It also has the Maryland Science Center and a unique aquarium of eco-systems□

Baluchistan mountainous desert area, comprising a province of Iran (capital Zahedan), population 1 000 000, a province of Pakistan (capital Quetta), population 2 500 000, and a small area of Afghanistan, population 300 000. The Moslem nomadic people have agitated for an independent 'United Baluchistan', possibly with Soviet backing, the USSR wishing to control a warm-water port (Gwadar, in Pakistan) on the Indian Ocean and the Strait of Hormuz□

Balzac Honoré de 1799–1850. French novelist, born at Tours. A disastrous printing and publishing venture enmeshed him in a lifelong web of debt, despite his large output of fiction. His first success, *Les Chouans* 1829, was inspired by Scott◊, but his major work was the series *La Comédie humaine* (planned as 143 volumes, of which only 80 were completed), which castigated vice and folly. It includes *Eugénie Grandet* 1833, dealing with avarice; *Père Goriot* 1834, doting fatherly love; *Cousine Bette* 1846, jealousy; and *Cousin Pons* 1847, greed. He had a tortured personal emotional life, notably his relationship with the Polish countess Éveline Hanska, whom he met in 1833; they corresponded constantly, but married only four months before his death□

Bamako capital and port of Mali; population 404 000□

Bamberg town in Bavaria, W Germany: population 77 000□

bamboo woody-stemmed tropical and subtropical grasses, genus *Bambusa*, family Gramineae. Some reach a remarkable size, and the hollow, jointed stems are used in furniture, house, and boat construction. The young shoots are edible (see panda◊). Simultaneous worldwide flowering of a species is followed by death of part or all of the plant. This may occur at intervals of up to 120 years, and to ensure continuation of the species huge quantities of seed are produced that can result in sudden plagues of rats□

Banaba see under Kiribati◊□

banana tree-like tropical plants 8 m/25 ft high, family Musaceae, which include the ***commercial banana***, varieties of *Musa sapientium*. The curved yellow fruits, arranged in rows of 'hands', form cylindrical masses of a hundred or more, and are exported green (often after being grown in plastic bags to avoid damage), and ripened aboard refrigerated ships. The plant is destroyed after cropping. The ***plantain,*** a larger coarser subspecies which is used green, as a cooked vegetable, is a staple of the diet in many countries□

Banbury town in Oxfordshire, England; population 30 000. The ***Banbury Cross*** of the nursery rhyme was destroyed by the Puritans◊ in 1602, but replaced in 1858; ***Banbury cakes*** are criss-cross pastry cases with a mince-pie style filling□

band music group, usually falling into a specialist category, e.g. ***military***, comprising woodwind, brass, percussion, for which the British Royal Military School of Music (Kneller Hall, Twickenham) is a famous training centre; ***brass***, solely brass and percussion, which are especially typical of the N of England, many being sponsored by collieries or industrial firms; ***marching***, a variant of the brass, which developed as an adjunct of American football, and is associated with baton-twirling showmanship, a younger mixed-sex membership, and popular repertoire, and has been introduced to Britain; ***dance***◊; ***jazz***◊; and ***steel*** popular in the West Indies, especially Trinidad, and having the percussion instruments made from oildrums□

Banda Hastings Kamuzu 1905– . Malawi statesman. Once a student and medical practitioner in Britain, he led his country's independence movement, and was Prime Minister of Nyasaland from 1963, and first president of Malawi from 1966□

Bandaranaike Sirimavo 1916– . Sri Lanka stateswoman, the widow of Solomon Bandaranaike 1899–1959, who was Prime Minister from 1956 until his assassination. She succeeded him as the world's first woman Prime Minister 1960–5, 1970–7, but was expelled from parliament in 1980 for abuse of her powers while in office□

Bandar Seri Begawan capital of Brunei; population 72 500□

bandicoot a small marsupial mammal; see under marsupialia◊□

Bandung commercial city in Java, Indonesia; population 1 200 000□

Bandung Conference the first conference (1955) of the Afro-Asian nations, proclaiming anti-colonialism and neutrality between East and West□

Banff holiday resort in Alberta, Canada; population 3500. It is a centre for Banff National Park (1885 – Canada's first) in the Rocky Mountains□

Bangalistan state advocated by Amra Bengali in 1969 to include W Bengal, Tripura, Bengali-speaking areas of Assam, Orissa and Bihar, and possibly Bangladesh□

Bangalore capital of Karnataka, Republic of India; population 2 913 537□

Bangkok capital and port of Thailand; population 4 743 000. Notable are the Temple of the Emerald Buddha and the vast Palace complex□

Bangladesh People's Republic of

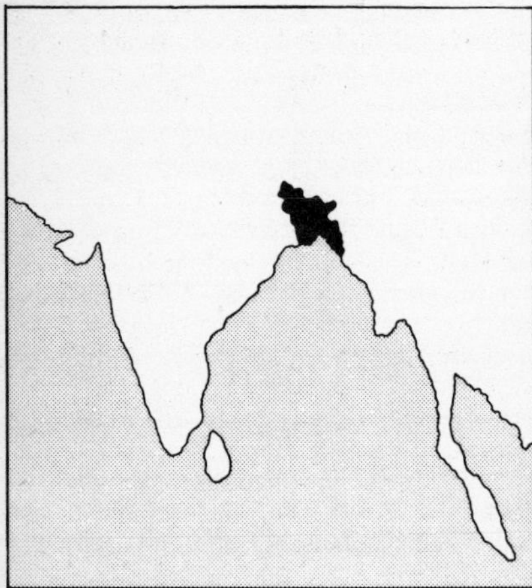

area 143 000 sq km/55 000 sq mi
capital Dhaka
towns ports Chittagong, Khulna
features Bangladesh is an alluvial plain, part of the Ganges-Brahmaputra river system; it has an annual rainfall of 2540 mm/100 in; some 75% of the land is less than 3 m/10 ft above sea level and tidal waves, triggered by the cyclones common in the area, as well as tidal surges, can cause devastation additional to river water flooding.
exports jute (50% of world production), tea
currency taka
population 99 585 000
language Bangla (Bengali)
religion Sunni Islam 85% (there is a unique system of using imams◊ as 'worker-priests'), Hinduism 14%
famous people Sheikh Mujib◊
government normally a unicameral parliamentary system, with a president (General Hossain Ershad from 1983), in preparation for a return to civilian rule after the lifting of martial law (in force under General Ershad from 1982).
recent history formerly part of British India, the area constituted E Pakistan 1947–71, when Bangladesh ('Bengal Nation') was proclaimed an independent state (within the Commonwealth◊ from 1972): in the brief civil war that ensued Bangladesh was supported by India. There was much subsequent emigration to India, especially to Assam, and in 1984 a barbed wire fence was erected by India to exclude illegal immigrants. A referendum 1985 (in which all opposition was barred) and elections of May 1986 gave Ershad an extended mandate□

Bangor cathedral city in Gwynedd, N Wales; population 16 000. University College, of the University of Wales, is here□

Bangui capital and river port of the Central African Republic; population 302 000□

Banjermasin river port in Indonesia; population 281 700□

banjo stringed musical instrument of tinny quality, with a long neck, circular drum-type sound-box; it is played with a plectrum. It originated in the USA with black slaves, and, introduced to Britain in 1846, became a popular amateur instrument□

Banjul capital and chief port of Gambia; population 54 000□

bank intermediary financing institution, which uses funds it doesn't own to lend to others. A central bank issues currency for the government, in order to control a country's money supply. Computerization renders the handling of small sums quick, easy, and secure – also profitable – hence workers' wages are increasingly paid through accounts. Customers are issued with plastic cards which include:
bank cards to facilitate withdrawal of money already in an account, from automatic machines, etc.
cheque cards guaranteeing payment by the issuing bank when presented together with a cheque, which cannot then be 'stopped'.
credit cards enabling the holder to obtain goods or services on credit.
Fraud is frequent, and various types of 'smart cards' are being developed which would be charged with so many units of account for use in terminals at shops. The card (safeguarded from fraud by the use of holograms) would incorporate a microprocessor, so that the transaction would be recorded both on the card and at the terminal, whence the debit

would be notified automatically via telephone line to the bank handling the customer's account□

Bank World. See World◊ Bank□

Banka Indonesian island, one of the world's richest sources of tin□

Bank for International Settlements a bank established 1930 to handle German reparations settlements from World War I, which today assists cooperation of central banks; its London agent is the Bank of England. Its headquarters is in Basel□

Bankhead Tallulah 1903–68. American actress, noted for her wit and flamboyant lifestyle; starred in *The Little Foxes* 1939, etc. See Beckett◊□

Bank of England English bank founded with government backing in 1694, it was entrusted with note issue in 1844, and nationalized in 1946. It is known by its London site as the 'Old Lady of Threadneedle Street'□

bankruptcy the legal division among his creditors of the assets of someone unable to pay his debts. This is done by trustees, either at the instance of creditors or of the bankrupt himself, and, until he is 'discharged', a bankrupt is severely restricted in his financial activities□

Banks Sir Joseph 1743–1820. British naturalist-explorer. He accompanied Captain Cook◊ on his voyage round the world, and was a founder of the Botanical Gardens, Kew. See banksia◊□

banksia Australian genus of shrubs and trees, family Proteaceae, including the 'honeysuckle tree'; they are named after Sir Joseph Banks◊□

Bannister Sir Roger 1929– . British doctor-athlete. He was the first man to run a mile in under four minutes: 6 May 1954, 3 min 59.4 sec□

Bannockburn town in Central region, Scotland; population 6000. Robert◊ the Bruce defeated the English under Edward◊ II here on 24 Jun 1314□

Banting Sir Frederick Grant 1891–1941. Canadian discoverer, with Macleod, Best and others, of insulin treatment for diabetes in 1922; he shared a Nobel prize in 1923□

Bantock Sir Granville 1868–1946. British composer of works with a Scottish flavour, e.g. *Hebridean Symphony*□

Bantu language group (Zulu 'people') of Africa, south of the Sahara. Till 1978 it was also the unpopular designation of the black people of S Africa, and the Black National States◊ were formerly called Bantustans□

Bantustan see Black National State◊□

Banville Theodore Faullain de 1823–91. French Romantic◊ poet, e.g. *Les Cariatides* 1841□

banyan see under fig◊□

baobab tree *Adansonia digitata*, family Bombacaceae, with root-like branches (hence its nickname 'upside-down tree'); the edible fruit are known as monkey bread. It may live 1000 years and is found in Africa and Australia, a relic of the time when both were part of Gondwanaland◊□

baptism religious initiation rite, Greek 'to dip', which has been universal in the Christian Church from its beginning. It was originally administered to adults by immersion, and infant baptism has been common only since the 6th century□

Baptist a member of a Protestant◊ Christian sect practising baptism by immersion only on profession of faith, and originating among English religious refugees in Holland in the early 17th century. The first English Baptist was the Anglican◊ cleric the Reverend John Smyth; the first US Baptist church was established by Roger Williams, Rhode Island 1639. All Baptist communities are linked by the Baptist World Alliance, 1905□

Barabbas in New Testament, the robber released at Passover◊ instead of Jesus□

Barbados

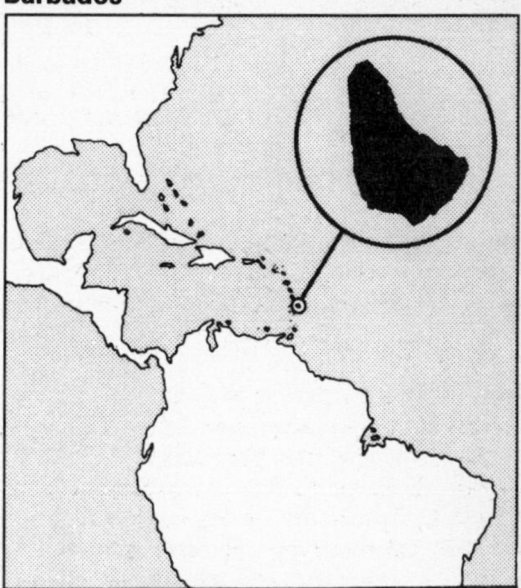

area 430 sq km/166 sq mi
capital Bridgetown
features subject to hurricanes; most easterly island of the W Indies
exports sugar and rum, oil
currency Barbados dollar
population 258 000
language English
religion Christianity
famous people Sir Garfield (Gary) Sobers
government a Governor-General, Senate and House of Assembly (Prime Minister Errol Barrow from 1986).

recent history British since 1627, Barbados became independent within the Commonwealth in 1966□

Barbarossa nickname, 'redbeard' of the German Emperor, Frederick◊ I; it was used as the code name for the German invasion plan for Russia in 1941□

Barbary old name for western N Africa, derived from its Berber◊ people; the ***Barbary Coast*** was famous for corsairs◊□

barbary ape more accurately a monkey, *Macaca sylvana*; yellowish-brown and tailless, it is found in N Africa, whence it was introduced to Gibraltar. Legend has it that Britain will lose Gibraltar if the ape colony is allowed to die out□

barbel a freshwater fish; see carp◊□

Barbellion W N P. Pseudonym under which Bruce Frederick Cummings 1889–1919, an authority on lice, who died of multiple sclerosis, published his *The Journal of a Disappointed Man* 1918□

Barber Samuel 1910– . American composer, with an increasingly dissonant style, whose works include *Adagio for Strings* 1936 and the opera *Vanessa* 1958□

barber's shop unaccompanied close-harmony singing, which originated among waiting customers in such shops in 19th century USA. Temporarily superseded by radio, it was taken up in the 1970s as a hobby, and large touring choirs were formed□

barbet a type of woodpecker◊□

Barbirolli Sir John 1899–1970. British conductor of the Hallé◊ Orchestra from 1943□

barbiturate salt or ester◊ of barbituric acid, which is derived from malic acid (found in unripe apples and urea). It is used as a sleeping aid, and as an anaesthetic in the control of epilepsy. It is addictive in indiscriminate prescription, and in the UK from 1979 there were legal penalties for misuse□

Barbizon French village near the Forest of Fontainebleau◊; the ***Barbizon School*** of artists – inspired by Constable◊ – include Corot◊, Courbet◊, Daubigny◊, Millet◊, Rousseau◊□

Barbuda see under Antigua◊ and Barbuda□

Barcelona capital, industrial city (textiles, engineering, chemicals), and port of Catalonia, second city of Spain

features the Ramblas, tree-lined promenades which lead from the Plaza de Cataluña, the largest square in Spain; Gaudí◊'s unfinished church of the Holy Family 1883; the Pueblo Espagñol 1929, with specimens of Spanish architecture of all periods; a replica of Columbus's ship, the *Santa Maria*, in the Maritime Museum; a large collection of Picasso's◊ works; the Miró◊ Foundation

population 1 755 000

recent history it was the Republican capital in the Spanish Civil War 1936–9, and was the last major city to surrender to Franco□

Bardeen John 1908– . American physicist, who won a Nobel prize, with Brattain and Shockley, in 1956, for the development of the transistor in 1948. In 1972 he was the first double winner of a Nobel prize in the same subject (with Cooper and Schrieffer) for his work on superconductivity□

Bardot Brigitte 1934– . French film actress, known as the 'sex kitten'; her films include *And God Created Woman*□

Bardsey Island see under Gwynedd◊□

Bareilly city in Uttar Pradesh, India; population 326 000□

Barenboim Daniel 1942– . Israeli pianist and conductor. He made his debut as a pianist in his native Buenos Aires at the age of seven, and as a conductor is a celebrated interpreter of Beethoven. He married Jacqueline du Pré◊□

Barents Willem 1550–97. Dutch explorer, who made three expeditions to seek the North-East◊ Passage; he died on the last. The Barents Sea is named after him□

Barents Sea see under Arctic◊ Ocean□

Barham Richard Harris 1788–1845. British writer and clergyman, author of verse tales of the supernatural, etc, and *The Ingoldsby Legends*, published under his pseudonym Thomas Ingoldsby□

Bari port in S Italy on the Adriatic; population 387 000. The part of the town known as Tecnopolis is the Italian Silicon Valley□

barium element

symbol Ba

atomic number 56

physical description silvery-white metal

features opaque to X-rays

uses barium sulphate is used as a 'barium meal' to show up abnormalities in a patient's digestive tract; it is also used in paints, glass, fireworks□

bark protective outer covering of the stems of trees and shrubs, and used in tanning, the production of cork. Cinnamon◊, angostura◊, cascara◊, and quinine◊ all come from bark□

Barker George 1913– . British poet, noted for his vivid imagery, as in *The True Confessions of George Barker* 1950□

Barker Sir Herbert 1869–1950. British manipulative surgeon, whose work established the popular standing of orthopaedics, but who was never recognized by the world of orthodox medicine□

Barking and Dagenham borough of E Greater London
features Ford motor industry at Dagenham
population 152 600□
Barkly Tableland large-scale open-range cattle raising area in Northern Territory and Queensland, Australia□
Bar Kokhbar Jewish leader of the revolt against Hadrian◊ 132–5, which led to the razing of Jerusalem□
bark paintings animal-based designs or abstracts painted on the inner side of tree bark by Australian Aborigines□
Barletta port on the Adriatic, Italy; population 80 000□
barley a type of cereal◊□
bar mitzvah initiation of a boy (Hebrew 'son of the commandment') into the adult Jewish community; less common is the bat mitzvah for girls□
barnacle sub-class (Cirripedia) of Crustacea, with free-swimming larvae which become sedentary adults (sometimes parasitic), enclosed in a shell through which only the cirri (slender tentacles) protrude to sweep food into the mouth. They include the stalked ***goose barnacle*** *Lepas anatifera* found on ships' bottoms and the ***sea acorn*** *Balanus balanoides* common on rocks□
Barnard Christiaan 1922– . South African surgeon, who carried out the first human heart transplant at Groote Schuur Hospital on 3 Dec 1967, when Louis Washkansky received the heart of a woman, but died 18 days later□
Barnardo Thomas John 1845–1905. British philanthropist of Irish-Jewish extraction, who was known as Dr Barnardo, though not medically qualified. He opened the first of a series of homes for destitute children in 1867 in Stepney, London□
Barnaul industrial city in the Republic of S Siberia, USSR; population 522 000□
Barnet borough of NW Greater London.
features site of the Battle of Barnet◊; Hadley Woods; Hampstead Garden Suburb; part of the Welsh Harp (see Brent◊); department for newspapers and periodicals of the British Library at Colindale; residential district of ***Hendon***, which includes Metropolitan Police Detective Training and Motor Driving Schools, and the RAF, Battle of Britain, and Bomber Command museums
population 296 600□
Barnet Battle of. See under Wars of the Roses◊ 1471□
Barnsley town in S Yorkshire, England; population 222 100□
Barnstaple fishing port in N Devon, England; population 1800, where 'Barum' pottery is made□
Barnum Phineas Taylor 1810–91. American creator of the 'Greatest Show on Earth' 1871, which included a circus, menagerie, and 'freaks', all transported in 100 rail cars□
Baroda see Vadodara◊□
barograph device in which a pen, governed by the movements of an aneroid barometer◊, makes a continuous line on a paper strip on a cylinder which rotates over a day or week to create a ***barogram***, a permanent record of variations in atmospheric pressure□
barometer measure of atmospheric pressure as an indication of weather.
In a ***mercury barometer*** a column of mercury in a glass tube roughly 0.75 m/2 ft high (closed at one end, curved upward at the other), is balanced by the pressure of the atmosphere on the open end; any change in the height of the column reflects a change in pressure. An ***aneroid barometer*** achieves a similar result by changes in the distance between the faces of a shallow cylindrical metal box which is partly exhausted of air□
baron lowest rank in the UK peerage; the first creation was in 1387. Life peers◊ are always barons□
baronet hereditary title in the UK below the rank of baron, but above that of knight;

barometer

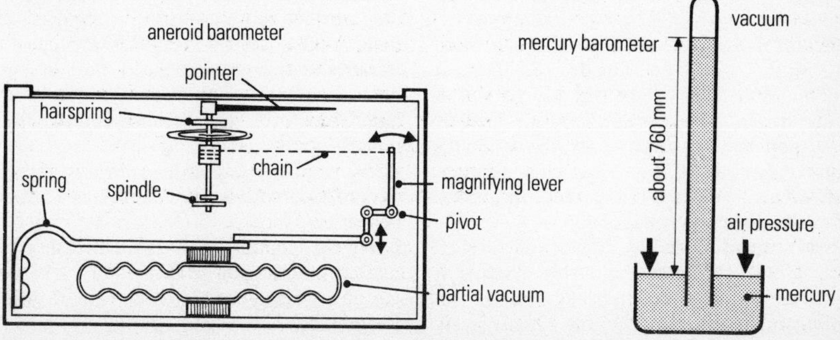

the first creations were in 1611 by James I, who needed funds from their sale to finance an army in Ulster□

Barons' Wars civil wars in England:
1215–17 between King John◊ and his barons, over his failure to honour Magna◊ Carta
1264–7 between Henry◊ III (and the future Edward I) and his barons (led by Simon de Montfort◊); ***1264*** 14 May ***Battle of Lewes*** at which Henry III was defeated and captured; ***1265*** 4 Aug Simon de Montfort was defeated by Edward at Evesham and killed□

Baroque exuberant and extravagant style developed in 17th and early 18th century Europe in art (Caravaggio◊, Rubens◊) and architecture, when it often involved large-scale building, e.g. Versailles◊ and Wren◊'s plan for London: see Bernini◊, Borromini◊, Vanbrugh◊, Hawksmoor◊, Le Vau◊, Hardouin-Mansart◊. In music the Baroque era ranges from Monteverdi◊ to Bach◊. The term was first applied to irregular pearls□

Barossa Valley wine-growing area in the Lofty mountain ranges, S Australia□

Barotseland see under Zambia◊□

Barquisimeto city in NW Venezuela; population 331 000□

barracuda pike-like fish *Sphyraena barracuda*, family Sphyraenidae, of warmer seas, which may attack man; it is a food fish□

Barragán Luis 1902– . Mexican architect, noted for his use of rough wooden beams, cobbles, lava, and adobe; his simple houses with walled gardens, and his fountains. Pritzker Award 1980□

Barranquilla sea and riverport in Colombia; population 692 000□

Barras Paul François, Comte de Barras 1755–1829. French revolutionary, who helped overthrow Robespierre◊ in 1794, and became a member of the Directory◊ in 1795. He married his former mistress, Josephine, to Napoleon◊ in 1796, and assumed dictatorial powers. After Napoleon's coup d'état on 19 Nov 1799 he was in disgrace□

Barrault Jean Louis 1910– . French actor and director of the Théâtre de France/ Odéon 1959–68. He showed his gifts as a mime in the film *Les Enfants du Paradis* 1944, and also appeared in *La Ronde* 1950□

Barre Raymond 1924– . French statesman, known as 'Monsieur Economy', who was Prime Minister 1976–81□

barrel organ portable cylindrical musical instrument. When a handle is turned, it produces tunes mechanically, since an arrangement of pins is thus successively released to open the pipe valves. Later the name was also given to a type of piano with a similar barrel mechanism, which was used by street buskers□

Barren Lands/Grounds. The tundra◊ region of Canada, W of Hudson Bay□

Barrie Sir James Matthew 1890–1937. Scottish author, born at Kirriemuir, Tayside, the 'Thrums' of his early sketches and novels of Scottish rural life. His plays include *Quality Street* 1901, *The Admirable Crichton* 1902, *What Every Woman Knows* 1908, *Dear Brutus* 1917, and *Mary Rose* 1920, which have a sinister note of realism underlying their apparent sentiment. His marriage to Mary Ansell ended in divorce, and he found consolation in his obsessive affection for four young boys, whom he virtually adopted when their mother was widowed; these children inspired the children's play *Peter Pan* 1904. Baronet 1913, Order of Merit 1922□

barrister lawyer qualified by study at the Inns◊ of Court to plead for a client at the Bar (the railed division separating off the judges and officers of the court); barristers remain outside the Bar till they become King's/ Queen's Counsel, when they 'take silk' – wear a silk instead of a stuff gown – and are called 'within the Bar'. Barristers are grouped in 'chambers' and act for clients only on the instructions of a solicitor (the actual arrangements being made by their shared 'clerk'), and in the highest courts only they can be heard on behalf of a litigant. Britain is almost alone in the English-speaking world in maintaining the distinction between barrister and solicitor◊; in Scotland a barrister is an 'advocate'□

barrow burial mound, from Old English *beorg* hill. They may be 'long' and of the New Stone◊ Age period, or 'round' and of the Bronze◊ Age. The burial itself may be in a stone or wood-built chamber, an urn or a Viking ship (Sutton Hoo◊). See also Wayland◊□

Barrow most northerly town in the USA, at Point Barrow, Alaska; population 3000. It is the world's largest Inuit settlement, and there is oil at nearby Prudhoe Bay□

Barrow-in-Furness industrial port in Cumbria, England; population 72 000. Scrap metal is exported and nuclear submarines are built□

Barry port in S Glamorgan, Wales; population 42 000. With Barry Island, it is a holiday resort□

Barry Sir Charles 1795–1860. British architect of the neo-Gothic Houses of Parliament at Westminster 1840–60. See Augus Pugin◊□

Barry Comtesse du. See Du◊ Barry□

Barrymore American acting family which included ***Lionel Barrymore*** 1878–1954; his sister ***Ethel*** 1879–1959, after whom a New York theatre was named in 1928; and his brother ***John*** 1882–1942, a flamboyant personality remembered for his film *Dr Jekyll and Mr Hyde*□

Barstow Stan 1928– . British novelist. Born in W Yorkshire, his books include *A Kind of Loving* 1960□

Bart Lionel 1930– . British composer of both words and music for *Fings Ain't Wot They Us'd t'Be* 1959 and *Oliver* 1960□

barter trade by the exchange of goods, which preceded the introduction of money; from the 1970s it revived among the Western middle classes, especially in exchange for professional services, to beat inflation and avoid taxation□

Barth Karl 1886–1968. Swiss Protestant◊ theologian; socialist in his political views, he attacked the Nazis◊. His *Church Dogmatics* 1932–62, makes the resurrection of Jesus the focal point of Christianity□

Bartholdi Auge 1834–1904. French sculptor of the Statue of Liberty◊□

Bartholomew Massacre of St. See under Huguenots◊□

Bartholomew St. Christian saint, one of the 12 Apostles◊, supposedly martyred by being flayed alive. His feast day is 24 Aug□

Bartók Béla 1881–1945. Hungarian composer, who was a child prodigy pianist. From 1905 he began the research into Hungarian folk music with Kodaly◊ which was to colour his later compositions; these include string quartets, violin and piano concertos, orchestral suites, and operas□

Bartolommeo Fra also called ***Baccio della Porta*** 1472–1517. Florentine painter, who entered a Dominican convent on Savonarola's death, but turned again to painting in 1504. His works, influenced by Leonardo◊ and Giogione◊, are the best Florentine examples of High Renaissance classicism□

Bart's St Bartholomew's Hospital, Smithfield; a London teaching hospital, it was founded by Henry◊ VIII□

baryon see particle◊ physics□

basalt the commonest volcanic rock, usually dark grey. It has a glassy or finely crystalline ground mass, sometimes with large crystals embedded. Successive eruptions may form great plateaux, as in Colorado and the Indian Deccan, and shrinkage during solidification can cause the formation of hexagonal columns, as in Fingal◊'s Cave and the Giant's◊ Causeway, Antrim□

baseball the US national summer game, which traditionally originated in New York in 1839. Two teams of nine men play on a pitch marked out in the form of a 'diamond', which has a base at each corner. The ball is struck with a cylindrical bat, and the players try to make a run by circuiting the bases round the diamond before the ball can be retrieved. See Babe Ruth◊□

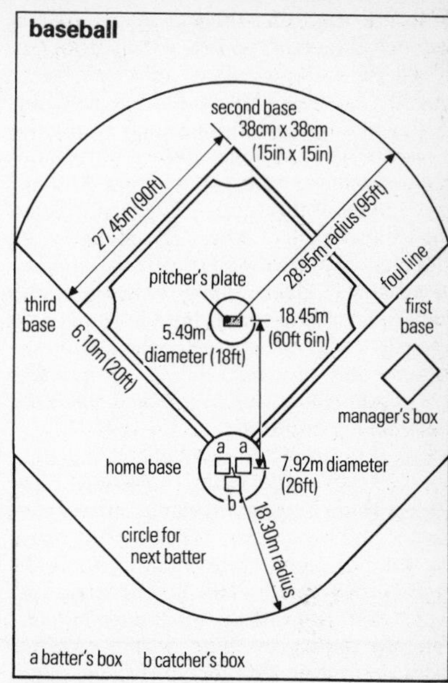

Basel Swiss financial and industrial centre (also known as ***Basle***; the French form is ***Bâle***), a key trade and transport junction for Europe; population 206 000. It has the chemical firms Hoffman-La Roche, Sandoz, Ciba-Geigy (dyes, vitamins, agro-chemicals, dietary products, genetic products). There are trade fairs, and it is the headquarters of the Bank◊ for International Settlements□

basenji a breed of dog◊□

Bashkir a Republic of the USSR, annexed in 1557; rich in minerals and oil; area 143 600 sq km/55 430 sq mi; population 3 860 000. Capital Ufa□

Basic *B*eginner's *A*ll-purpose *S*ymbolic *I*nstruction *C*ode, a computer language designed at Dartmouth, USA. Intended as a simple teaching language, it rapidly became adapted as the most common language for home computers□

Basic English *B*ritish-*A*merican-*S*cientific-*I*nternational-*C*ommercial; a simplified form of English, with a vocabulary of 850 words, devised as an international auxiliary language in 1926 by C K Ogden◊ and I A Richards□

basidiomycetes or ***basi diomycotina*** class of fungi◊ whose spores are produced on stalks. Striking examples are ***bracket fungus*** family

Polyporaceae, with a bracket-shaped fruiting body which grows out like a shelf from tree trunks, and the ***common stinkhorn*** which sends up from underground an evil-smelling, phallus-like spongy fruiting body, attractive to insects. They also include:
mushroom the word is popularly used for any edible fungi of this form, e.g. genus *Boletus*. European fungi, of which the majority are edible, include *B edulis* and genus *Cantharellus* notably *C cibaris* which forms yellowish funnels. Strictly it means those fungi of genus *Agaricus* with a characteristic umbrella-shaped spore-producing body, e.g. ***common field mushroom*** *A campestris* and ***cultivated mushroom*** *A bisprous*.
toadstool saprophytic members of the Basidiomycetes◊, some being poisonous. The latter include ***fly agaric*** *Amanita muscaria* of Europe and N America, which is often bright red with rings of white scales, and is the typical toadstool of illustrated children's books; and the ***death cap*** *Amanita phalloides* white to dark grey, with a ring of tissue hanging from under the cap, which can be fatal if only a small piece is eaten.
rusts and ***smuts*** diseases of plants caused by minute parasitic fungi, e.g. ***black rust*** order Uredineae, on wheat *Puccinia graminis;* and ***smut*** and ***bunt*** order Ustilaginales, infesting flowering plants, especially cereals□

Basie 'Count' (William) 1904–84. American pianist and big-band jazz leader, originator of the 'jump swing' sound, e.g. 'One O'Clock Jump'□

basil a type of herb◊□

Basil the Great, St 330–79. The founder of the form of monastic rule followed in the Greek◊ Orthodox Church, who was bishop of his native Caesarea (Qisarya, Israel) from 370; his feast day is 14 Jun□

Basildon 'new town' in Essex, England; population 146 000. It was made from several small towns in 1955□

Basilica type of Roman public building, consisting of a hall with side aisles divided off by rows of columns, which was adopted by Christians for early churches□

Basilicata mountainous region of S Italy (Roman Lucania); capital Potenza; population 612 785□

Basingstoke industrial town in Hampshire, England; population 125 600□

basketball ball game invented by YMCA instructor, James Naismith, Springfield, Massachusetts, USA in 1891. There are two teams of five, plus seven substitutes, and a large inflated ball is thrown through a circular net goal 3.05 m/10 ft above the ground at each end of a rectangular court□

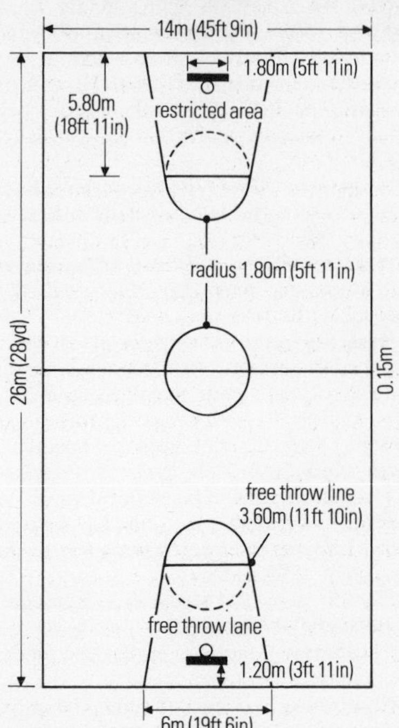

Basle See Basel◊□

Basque a member of people directly descended from the Stone Age hunters of Altamira◊, and who occupy the autonomous Basque region (created 1980) of N Spain and the French department of Pyrénées-Atlantiques (see Bayonne◊). In 778 they annihilated the rearguard of Charlemagne◊'s army at Roncesvalles◊. During the Spanish◊ Civil War of 1936–9, they were on the Republican side, and were vindictively crushed by Franco. Terrorism from 1968 by ETA (*Euskadi ta Azkatasuna* Basque Nation and Liberty), and the French organization *Enbata* (Ocean Wind), aimed at securing a united Basque state, was not ended by autonomy. Their language, Euskara, is unrelated to French and Spanish, and was officially recognized in 1980. The national game is pelota◊□

Basque Country autonomous region (Euskadi) of NW Spain (including Bilbao, San Sebastián, Vitoria); population 2 135 000. See Basque◊, Guernica◊, and Navarre◊□

Basra port in Iraq; population 450 000□

bass a freshwater fish; see under perch◊□

Bassein port in Burma; population 356 000□

basset a breed of dog◊□

Basseterre capital and port of St Kitts◊; population 16 000□

Basse-Terre capital and port of Guadeloupe◊; population 16 000□

basset horn a musical instrument, see under woodwind◊□

bassoon a musical instrument, see under woodwind◊□

Bass Rock islet in the Firth of Forth, Scotland□

Bass Strait channel between Australia and Tasmania, named after the British explorer George Bass 1760–1912, where oil was discovered in the 1960s□

Bastia commercial centre in Corsica; population 51 000□

Bastille fortress prison in Paris, taken by the mob at the start of the French◊ Revolution 14 Jul 1789; it held only seven prisoners. The governor and most of the garrison were killed, and the building razed□

Basutoland see Lesotho◊□

bat order of flying mammals, Chiroptera; next to the rodents, they are the largest, most widespread and most varied of mammal groups. They are nevertheless under threat, and in the UK their roosts have been protected by law since 1981. They are intelligent and social. A thin, hairless membrane, with its own internal musculature, extends between the much-modified 'fingers' of the forelimb, and also from the body, to take advantage of the support to be gained from the hind limbs and tail, and so forms a 'wing'. They are nocturnal, sleeping upside down during the day, suspended by the claws on their hind feet. They mostly live in caves. The majority are blind and navigate by means of emitting a high-pitched sound and listening for the echo, different distances giving different echoes. They comprise:

fruit-eaters Megachiroptera, which are mainly larger species, including the ***flying fox*** *Pteropus edulis*, of Africa, S Asia and Australia, with a wingspan of 1.5 m/4.5 ft.

insect-eaters Microchiroptera, which are mainly smaller species with particularly poor vision. The group includes the ***pipistrelle***, small brown species of the genus ***Pipistrellus***, family Vespertilionidae, which are of worldwide distribution; and the ***common vampire*** *Desmodus rotundus*, family Desmodontidae, of S America. Their sharp incisors draw blood from birds and mammals, an anti-clot substance continuing the flow; the bite is not in itself dangerous, since the bats are only 9 cm/4 in long, but it may carry the infection of rabies. See vampire◊□

Bataan peninsula in Luzon, the Philippines, which was defended against the Japanese by US and Filipino troops, under MacArthur◊, 1 Jan–9 Apr 1942. MacArthur was evacuated, but some 70 000 Allied prisoners died on the ***Bataan Death Mar*** to camps in the interior□

Batavia see Jakarta◊□

Bates H(erbert) E(rnest) 1905–74. British author of short stories, inspired by RAF experiences, under the pseudonym 'Flying Officer X' and novels; these include *Fair Stood the Wind for France* 1944 and *The Darling Buds of May* 1958□

Bates Henry Walter 1825–92. British naturalist, whose observation in S America of insect imitation of the appearance of species unpleasant to predators, gave its name to 'Batesian mimicry'□

Bath city in Avon, England; population 840 000. The city has the only natural hot springs in Britain, 37°C/93°F. The Roman city of Aquae Sulis ('Waters of Sul' – the British goddess of wisdom) was built in the first 20 years after the Roman invasion, and the ruins of the great temple and the rectangular bathing pool are the finest Roman remains in Britain. Excavations in 1979 revealed thousands of coins and 'curses', offered at a place which was thought to be the link between the upper and lower worlds. Bath Abbey is a relic of medieval times, but the city was transformed in the 18th century by the two John Woods◊ to a fashionable spa. At his home here Herschel◊ discovered Uranus◊. The Assembly Rooms (1771, which were destroyed in an air raid in 1942, but reconstructed in 1963) were presided over by 'Beau' Nash◊: visitors included Smollett◊, Fielding◊, and Jane Austen◊. The University of Technology was established 1966□

Bath Order of the. See Knighthood◊□

Bathurst town in New South Wales, Australia; population 19 600□

Bathurst a zinc-mining town in New Brunswick, Canada; population 16 300□

batik Javanese technique of hand-applied colour design for fabric; areas undyed in any colour are successively sealed with wax□

Batista Fulgencio 1901–73. Cuban dictator 1933–59; he was overthrown by Castro◊□

Baton Rouge capital and port of Louisiana, USA; population 219 000. The bronze and marble state capitol was built by the demagogic ***Huey Long*** 1893–1935, state governor 1928–31, famous for his filibusters, who was assassinated□

Batten Jean 1909– . New Zealand aviator, who made the first return solo flight by a woman Australia–Britain 1935, and established speed records□

Battenberg see Mountbatten◊□

Battersea see Wandsworth◊□

battery energy storage device allowing release of electricity on demand. A battery comprises cells, each containing two conducting 'electrodes' usually separated by a liquid 'electrolyte', in a container. When an outside connection (e.g. through a lamp-bulb) is made between the electrodes, a current flows through the circuit, and chemical reactions releasing energy take place within the cells. Primary batteries are disposable, secondaries are rechargeable. The common 'dry cell' is based on the Leclanché cell and consists of a carbon electrode with magnesium dioxide soaked in ammonium chloride solution as the electroyte□

Battle town in Sussex, England; population 5000. The Battle of Hastings◊ actually took place here (site acquired for the nation 1976)□

battle cruiser warship with the size and armament of a battleship, plus the speed and lighter armour of a cruiser, largely obsolete since World War II□

battleship warship, formerly predominating over all others in armour and firepower, but obsolete from World War II□

Batumi capital and port of the Republic of Adzhar USSR; population 111 000. There are oil refineries□

Baudelaire Charles Pierre 1821–67. French poet. Born in Paris, he was sent out to India by his guardians as a check on his dissipation, but returned still incurably extravagant, as well as addicted to opium, hashish, and oriental imagery. His *Les Fleurs du mal/Flowers of Evil* 1857 influenced Yeats◊, Eliot◊, etc, and the condemnation of the book by the censor was reversed by a quashing of the sentence in 1949. He combined concentrated rhythmic and musical perfection with a morbid romanticism and eroticism, finding beauty in decadence and evil; he was translated by Poe◊□

Baudouin 1930– . King of the Belgians from 1951 (see Leopold◊ III). He married in 1960 Spanish aristocrat Fabiola de Mora y Aragón 1928– □

Bauhaus Staatliches. A German art and architecture school, the 'State Building House' founded 1919 in Weimar by Walter Gropius◊, who attempted to fuse architecture and all other crafts. In 1925 it removed to Dessau, and was closed by the Nazis 1933. Kandinsky◊, Klee◊, and Mies van der Rohe◊ were all associated with it. The archive was installed in W Berlin 1972□

Baum Lyman Frank 1856–1919. American author of the children's fantasy *The Wonderful Wizard of Oz* 1900□

bauxite aluminium ore, reddish owing to the presence of iron compounds, and named after its first source at Les Baux, France□

Bavaria (German ***Bayern***) Land (State) of W Germany

area 70 550 sq km/27 230 sq mi

capital Munich

towns Augsburg, Nuremberg, Regensburg

features largest of the German Länder, it forms the Danube basin (see also Swabia◊); Rhine-Main-Danube canal (under construction); festivals at Bayreuth and Oberammergau

products beer; electronics, electrical engineering, optics, cars, aerospace, chemicals, plastics, oil-refining, textiles, glass, toys

population 10 940 000

religion 70% Roman Catholicism, 26% Protestantism

famous people Ludwig III; Prince Albert 1905– , claimant to the Bavarian throne, and also inheritor of the Stuart claim in Britain; Lucas Cranach, Hitler, Franz Josef Strauss, Richard Strauss□

Bax Sir Arnold 1883–1953. British composer, whose tone poem *Tintagel* 1917, shows Celtic influence□

bay see laurel◊/herbs◊□

Bayard Pierre du Terrail, Seigneur de Bayard 1475–1526. French knight, chivalrously magnanimous, known as 'without fear and without reproach'□

Bay City industrial city of Michigan, USA; population 50 000□

Bayern see Bavaria◊□

Bayeux town in N France; population 13 000. See Bayeux Tapestry◊□

Bayeux Tapestry linen hanging 70 m/231 ft long; it is an embroidery rather than a 'tapestry'; it records in 72 scenes William◊ the Conqueror's invasion of England□

Bay of Pigs inlet on the S coast of Cuba, site of an unsuccessful invasion attempt by anti-Castro◊ exiles 17–20 Apr 1961; sanctioned by Eisenhower◊, it was executed by Kennedy◊ □

Bayonne river port in SW France; population 120 400. The bayonet was invented here, and it is a centre of Basque◊ life□

bayou oxbow◊ lake or sluggish tributary as in the lower Mississippi region□

Bayreuth town in Bavaria, W Germany; population 61 000. The Wagner theatre was established 1876, and festivals are held□

Beachy Head see E Sussex◊□

Beaconsfield town in Buckinghamshire, England; population 12 000. Disraeli◊'s title was taken from it and his home, Hughenden Manor, is a museum□

Beaconsfield Earl of. See Disraeli◊□

beagle a breed of dog◊□

Beagle Channel see Tierra◊ del Fuego□

beaker people people of Iberian origin who spread out over Europe in the 2nd millenium BC, and who began Stonehenge◊. Their remains include beakers□

Beale Dorothea 1831–1906. British educationist, head of Cheltenham Ladies College from 1858, where she raised the standard of women's education□

bean family of plants, Leguminosae, of which the seeds are used as food, including:

broad bean *Vicia faba*, grown in Europe from prehistoric times.

carob or ***locust*** *Ceratonia siliqua*, a small Mediterranean tree, with long dark pods which are the traditional 'locusts' eaten by St John in the wilderness, and the 'husks' of the Prodigal◊ Son; they are the source of a chocolate substitute.

kidney or ***haricot*** *Phaseolus vulgaris*, of which the canned 'baked bean' is a special variety; ***lima*** *P lunatus* of S America; ***mung*** *P mung* of Asia, familiar as 'bean sprouts'; ***scarlet runner*** *P multiflorus,* with attractive flowers.

soya *Glycine soja*, of far-eastern origin, now a widely-distributed crop (35% of the seed weight is protein and is used as a meat substitute, etc, and 18% is oil, which is used in polyunsaturated margarine, etc).

winged *Psophocarpus tetragonolobus*, of Asia, of which the tuberous roots were recently discoverd to have a 20% protein content□

bear family of heavily-built mammals Ursidae, which are largely vegetarian, including:

common brown bear *Ursus arctos* of Europe and Asia, about 2.1 m/7 ft long; varieties are the ***grizzly*** *Ursos arctos horribilis* of N America 2.75 m/9 ft, and ***Kodiak***◊, a variant which is the largest living carnivore at 3 m/10 ft. These bears hibernate for up to five months, lowering their body temperature 3–4 degrees, and so using and re-utilizing their body resources (built up during the summer) that they neither eat nor drink, nor even need to urinate. Females also give birth to their young during this period.

Asiatic black *Selenarctos tibetanus*, with a handsome white v-mark on the chest.

polar *Thalarctos maritimus* an excellent swimmer□

Bear Great and Little. See Ursa Major and Ursa Minor under constellation◊□

bear baiting baiting by dogs of a chained bear; a 'sport' illegal in Britain from 1835□

Beardsley Aubrey Vincent 1872–98. British illustrator in black-and-white. He was associated with the *Yellow◊ Book*, for which he produced delicate unorthodox work which was attacked as decadent. A Roman Catholic from 1897, he died of tuberculosis□

bears and bulls on the Stock Exchange, bears are speculators who anticipate a fall in share prices, and bulls are those who anticipate a rise□

Beas tributary of the Sutlej, see under Indus◊□

beat generation The 'beatniks' of the 1950s, characterized by opting out of conventional life styles and opting for life on the road, drugs, etc. See Kerouac◊□

beatification see canonization◊□

Beatitudes in New Testament, the sayings of Jesus (Matthew v 1–12), which denote the characteristics of members of the Kingdom of God□

Beatles British popular music group formed in 1960: the members who reached fame, all born in Liverpool, were ***George Harrison*** 1943– ; ***John Winston Lennon*** 1940–81; ***James Paul McCartney*** 1942– ; and ***Richard Starkey*** stage-name 'Ringo Starr' 1940– . They made their name in the Cavern Club in Liverpool (later razed, but restored in 1982). Using songs written by Lennon and McCartney, they took the pop world by storm 1963–5 with the 'Liverpool Sound'; they influenced the dress, life-style and thought of young people, even beyond the break-up of the group in 1971, when they developed as individual performers, especially John Lennon (with his wife, Yoko Ono, until he was gunned down in 1981), and Paul McCartney with the group Wings. Numbers of the original 'group' period include 'She Loves You', 'Can't Buy Me Love', 'Yesterday', 'Yellow Submarine', 'A Hard Day's Night', 'Eleanor Rigby'; and also the complex electronic syntheses of their album *Sergeant Pepper's Lonely Hearts Club Band*, which took six months in the recording studio, and is a classic example of the pop product which is impossible to reproduce before a live audience□

Beaton Sir Cecil 1904–80. British photographer, noted for his celebrity portraits, e.g. the Sitwells, in the 1920s and 1930s; and his stage and film designs, e.g. *My Fair Lady* and *Gigi*□

Beaton David 1494–1546. Scottish cardinal and statesman, adviser to James◊ V. Under Mary◊ Queen of Scots, he was opposed to the alliance with England and persecuted reformers, such as George Wishart, who was condemned to the stake; he was assassinated by Wishart's friends□

Beatrix 1936– . Queen of the Netherlands. The eldest daughter of Queen Juliana◊, she succeeded to the throne on her mother's abdication in 1980. She married in 1966 W German diplomat, Claus von Amsberg 1926– , who was created Duke of the Netherlands:

her heir is Prince Alexander 1967– □

Beatty David, 1st Earl Beatty 1871–1936. British admiral, who commanded the cruiser squadron 1912–16 and bore the brunt of the Battle of Jutland◊; his strategy was later criticized, but he was created an earl 1919□

Beaufort Sir Francis 1774–1857. British admiral, who was hydrographer to the Royal Navy from 1829; the Beaufort scale◊ and the Beaufort Sea in the Arctic◊ Ocean are named after him□

Beaufort scale international scale, devised by Sir Francis Beaufort 1806 to record wind velocity, and ranging from 0 (calm) to 12 (greatest hurricane force)□

Beaufort Sea see under Arctic◊ Ocean□

Beauharnais Alexandre, Vicomte de Beauharnais 1760–94. French liberal aristocrat, who was the first husband of Josephine, consort of Napoleon◊ I. Their daughter, Hortense 1783–1837, married Louis, a younger brother of Napoleon, and their son became Napoleon◊ III. Beauharnais was guillotined for his eventual lack of zeal for the revolutionary cause□

Beaujolais red wine of the *massif central* area of France, which is drunk while young; the broaching date is the third Thursday in Nov, when the new vintage is taken to London in 'the new Beaujolais race'□

Beaulieu village in Hampshire, England; population 1200. The former abbey is the home of Lord Montagu of Beaulieu, and has the Montagu Museum of vintage cars□

Beauly Firth arm of the North Sea cutting into Scotland N of Inverness, which is linked with the Black Isle by Kessock Bridge 1982□

Beaumarchais Pierre Augin Caron de 1732–99. French dramatist. His comedies *Le Barbier de Seville* 1775 and *Le Mariage de Figaro* 1778 are best-known by the operatic versions of Rossini◊ and Mozart◊□

Beaumont Francis 1584–1616. English poet and dramatist. He collaborated from about 1608 with John Fletcher◊, with whom he shared lodgings until the latter married an heiress in 1613. Attributed to Beaumont alone are *The Woman Hater* and *The Knight of the Burning Pestle*; joint works include *The Maid's Tragedy* and *A King and No King*□

Beaune town SW of Dijon, France; population 17 500. Centre for the Burgundian wine trade□

Beauregard Pierre 1818–93. American Confederate◊ general whose opening fire on Fort Sumter started the Civil◊ War□

Beauvais town NW of Paris; population 50 000. It has a fine Gothic◊ cathedral and is famous for tapestries (Gobelin◊), now made in Paris□

Beauvoir Simone de 1908–1986. French feminist and author. Her book *The Second Sex* 1949 is an attack on the man-made world women must inhabit; her novel of post-war Paris, *Les Mandarins* 1954, has characters resembling Camus◊, Koestler◊ and Sartre◊ (she was long associated with the last-named); and she also published autobiographical volumes□

beaver a N American rodent◊□

Beaverbrook William Maxwell Aitken, 1st Baron Beaverbrook 1879–1964. Canadian newspaper proprietor. Having made a fortune in cement in Canada, he entered British politics, first in support of Bonar◊ Law, then of Lloyd◊ George, becoming Minister of Information 1918–19. In the inter-war years, he used his newspapers, especially the *Daily Express,* to campaign for Empire Free Trade and against Baldwin◊; in World War II, he was a successful Minister of Aircraft Production 1940–1□

Bebington town in Merseyside, England; population 63 000. Soap, margarine, and oil are manufactured, and there is a model housing estate originally built for Unilever workers, Port Sunlight□

Beccaria Cesare, Marese di Beccaria 1738–94. Italian philanthropist, who opposed capital punishment and torture; advocated education as a crime preventative; influenced Bentham◊; and coined the phrase 'the greatest happiness of the greatest number', the watchword of Utilitarianism◊□

Bechuanaland see Botswana◊□

Becket St Thomas 1118–70. English churchman. A personal friend of Henry◊ II, he was his Chancellor 1155–62, but on becoming Archbishop of Canterbury transferred his allegiance to the Church. In 1164 he opposed Henry's attempt to regulate the relations between Church and State, and had to flee the country, returning in 1170, but the reconciliation soon broke down. Encouraged by a hasty outburst of the King's, four knights murdered Becket before the altar of Canterbury cathedral. He was canonized 1172, and his shrine became the most revered centre of pilgrimage in England (see Chaucer◊) until the Reformation. See T S Eliot◊□

Beckett Samuel 1906– . Irish dramatist. Settling in Paris, and writing originally in French, he made a reputation with spare, symbolic plays, notably *Waiting for Godot* 1952, of which Tallulah Bankhead◊ said 'there is less in this than meets the eye', and *End Game* 1957; he gained a Nobel prize in 1969□

Beckford William 1760–1844. British eccentric and author. Forced out of England by scandals about his private life, he published *Vathek* 1787 in Paris, a fantastic Arabian Nights' Tale, and on returning to England in 1796, rebuilt his home, Fonthill Abbey in Wiltshire, as a Gothic◊ fantasy□

Beckmann Max 1884–1950. German Expressionist◊ painter. Born in Leipzig, he fought in World War I, and was discharged following a breakdown, reflected in the agony of his work; pictures include *Carnival,* and *The Titanic*□

Becquerel Antoine Henri 1852–1908. French physicist, who discovered penetrating, invisible radiation coming from uranium salts, the first indication of radioactivity◊, and shared a Nobel prize with the Curies◊ in 1903□

bedbug a parasitic insect; see under Hemiptera◊□

Bede 673–735. English historian and theologian, given the title of 'Venerable' in the 9th century. He entered the monastery at Jarrow at seven, and remains of the 'cell' in which he worked have been excavated. His *Ecclesiastical History of the English People* is an important source for early English history, and he wrote many scientific works□

Bedford town and administrative headquarters of Bedfordshire, England; population 73 000. Bunyan◊ began writing *The Pilgrim's Progress* in Bedford gaol, and the Bunyan Meeting House stands on the site of the barn where he preached□

Bedford John Robert Russell, 13th Duke of Bedford 1917– . English peer. Succeeding to the title 1953, he restored the family seat Woburn Abbey, Bedfordshire, now visited by thousands annually□

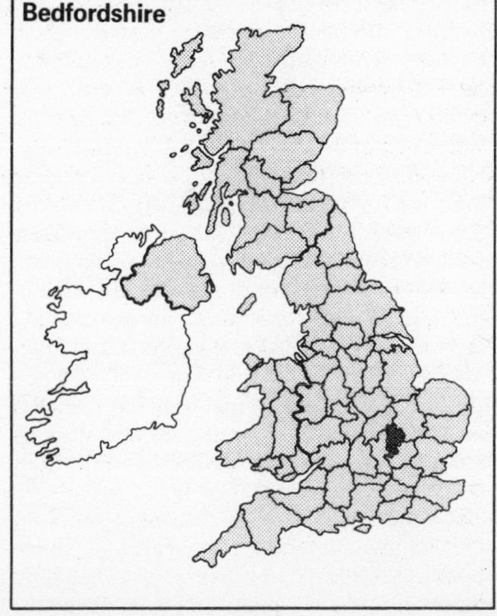

Bedfordshire South Midland county of England

area 1235 sq km/477 sq mi

towns administrative headquarters Bedford; Luton (with additional facilities for London Airport), Dunstable

features Whipsnade Zoo 1931, near Dunstable, a zoological park belonging to the London Zoological Society (2 sq km/ 500 acres); Woburn Abbey, seat of the Duke of Bedford

products cereals, vegetables; agricultural machinery, electrical goods

population 508 300

famous people John Bunyan□

Bedlam popular abbreviation of the name, Bethlehem, of the earliest mental hospital in Europe; it was opened in the 14th century in a former priory in Bishopsgate, London, and the hospital is now near Croydon□

Bedouin nomadic people, Arabic 'desert-dweller' of Arabia and N Africa, now becoming increasingly settled□

bee four-winged insect of the super-family Apoidea in the order Hymenoptera, usually with a sting. There are over 12 000 species, of which less than 1 in 20 are social in habit.

solitary bees include species useful in pollinating orchards in spring, and may make their nests in tunnels under the ground, in hollow plant stems, etc; the 'cuckoo' bees lay their eggs in the nests of bumblebees, which they closely resemble.

social bees include the stingless S American ***vulture bee*** *Trigona hypogea*, discovered in 1982, which is solely carnivorous. More familiar is the ***bumblebee*** genus *Bombus*, which is larger and stronger than the hive bee and so is adapted to fertilize plants in which the pollen and nectar lie deep, as in red clover; species of the genus are so unaerodynamic that they should not be able to fly, but produce power more efficiently than aero-engines; they also produce their own central heating and can work in colder weather than the hive bee. The ***hive*** or ***honey bee*** *Apis mellifera* establishes perennial colonies of about 80 000, the majority being infertile females or workers, with a few larger fertile males or drones, and a single very large fertile female or queen. In commercial beekeeping the natural aerial mating of an emergent daughter queen with the most powerful of the drones has been replaced by artificial insemination; swarming, the exit from the hive of the old queen, with her attendants, leaving the new queen in possession, is not allowed to happen. The wax 'comb' (made from a secretion exuded by the workers) of hexagonal cells is used to rear new members of the colony and store honey◊, but to concentrate energy on honey production, partly artificial combs are commercially used. Bees transmit information to each other about food sources by a 'dance', each movement giving rise to sound impulses which are picked up by tiny hairs on the back of the bee's head, the orientation of the dance also having significance. They use the sun in navigation (see also under migration◊). Besides their use in crop pollination and production of honey and wax, these bees (by a measure of contaminants brought back to their hives) provide an inexpensive and effective monitor of industrial and other pollution of the atmosphere and soil.

Most bees are pacific unless disturbed, but some species of S America are aggressive. In those who are allergic, bee stings may be fatal, and a vaccine treatment with concentrated venom has been developed; see melitin◊□

beech genus of trees *Fagus*, family Fagaceae◊. ***common beech*** *Fagus sylvaticus* is one of the handsomest of European forest trees, with a smooth grey trunk and edible nuts or 'mast' – the timber is used in furniture□

Beecham Sir Thomas 1879–1961. English conductor, the grandson of the founder of the Beecham pharmaceutical firm. He established the Royal Philharmonic Orchestra in 1947, and made unrivalled recordings of Haydn, Mozart, and Delius. He established the musical reputation of the last-named. He was renowned for his wit, as in the autobiographical *A Mingled Chime*□

Beecher Henry Ward 1813–87. American Congregational minister and opponent of slavery, son of pulpit orator ***Lyman Beecher*** 1775–1863 and brother of Harriet Beecher Stowe◊□

beer alcoholic drink made from malt (fermented barley, etc.), flavoured with hops; stronger types are often referred to as ale. Like beer ***stout*** is top fermented, but is sweet and strongly flavoured with roasted grain; ***lager*** is a light beer bottom fermented and matured over a longer period (German *Lager* 'store')□

Beerbohm Sir Max 1872–1956. British caricaturist and author. A perfectionist in style, he contributed to the *Yellow Book*◊; wrote the novel of Oxford undergraduate life *Zuleika Dobson* 1911; and published volumes of caricature, e.g. *Rossetti and his Circle* 1922. He was knighted 1939□

Beersheba industrial town in Israel; population 81 000. It is the chief centre of the Negev◊, and Nafha maximum security prison is to the south□

beet genus *Beta* family Chenapodiaceae, of plants including ***common beet*** *B vulgaris*, of which one variety is used to produce sugar, and another, the mangelwurzel, grown as cattle fodder; the ***beetroot*** or ***red beet*** *B rubra* is a salad plant. The family also includes the Asian ***spinach*** *Spinacia oleracea* of which the leaves are used as a vegetable, especially in USA, though its nutritional value (as claimed by Popeye◊) has been much exaggerated; ***spinach beet*** used as a spinach substitute is *Beta vulgaris cicle;* (see Goosefoot◊)□

Beethoven Ludwig van 1770–1827. German composer. Born in Bonn, the son and grandson of musicians, he became deputy organist at the court of the Elector of Cologne at Bonn before he was 12; later he had lessons from Mozart◊ and Haydn◊, whose influence dominated his early work. From 1801 deafness overtook him, becoming total by 1824, but he continued composition, and from 1809 had a small allowance from aristocratic patrons. Often in love, frequently with his noble pupils, he never married. A shiftless nephew, whose guardian he was, caused him great grief. He was influential in the development of all musical forms, but especially the symphony. His works include the *Egmont* overture; the opera *Fidelio*; 5 piano concertos and one for violin; 32 piano sonatas, including the *Apassionata;* 16 string quartets; the *Mass in D* (*Missa Solemnis*); nine symphonies, notably the Third (*Eroica,* originally intended to be dedicated to Napoleon, with whom Beethoven became disillusioned), the Fifth (*Victory,* because the rhythm of the opening corresponds to the 'V' in Morse code and was used in Allied radio broadcasts to the Nazi-occupied Continent in World War II), the Sixth (*Pastoral*) and Ninth (*Choral*), which includes the passage chosen as the national anthem of Europe□

beetle an insect in the order Coleoptera (Greek 'sheath-winged'), with leathery fore-wings folding down in a protective sheath over the membraneous hindwings which are those used for flight. They pass through a complete metamorphosis, the young larval forms being very varied, and include some of the largest and smallest of all insects; the largest is the American ***Hercules beetle*** *Dunastes hercules* 15 cm/6 in long. The largest single order in the animal kingdom, beetles number some 250 000 species, and though many are useful to man, others are extremely destructive.

click beetle or ***skipjack*** species are members of the family Elateridae, and are so called because, if they fall on their backs, they right themselves with a jump and loud click; the

larvae, known as ***wireworms***, feed on the roots of crops. In some tropical species of Elateridae, the beetles have luminous organs between the head and abdomen, and are known as ***fireflies***, e.g. genus *Photinus*, which have a combined communication code of flight path and time between flashes used in courtship. See also glow worm below.
colorado beetle *Leptinotarsa decemlineata*, family Chrysomelidae; it is striped in black and yellow, and is a notifiable imported pest (among potato crops) in the UK.
cotton boll weevil *Anthonomus grandis*, family Curculionidae, of which the larvae destroy cotton bolls in N America; and the ***granary weevil*** *Calandra granaria*, of which the larvae attack stored grain.
death watch beetle *Xestobium rufovillosum*, family Anobiidae, of which the larvae bore tunnels in old timber; to attract the female, the male beetle produces a ticking sound by striking its head upon wood, and this was formerly superstitiously regarded as a death omen; and ***woodworm*** *Anobium punctatum*, of which the larvae are a common pest, producing smaller holes by their tunnelling through old household furniture.
devil's coach horse *Staphylinus olens,* family Staphylinidae, the largest British beetle. It is black, pugnacious, a carrion feeder, and when alarmed turns up its rear end and emits an evil-smelling fluid.
glow worm species of luminous beetle in the family Lampyridae, of which *Lampyris noctiluca* is European, but the majority are tropical. The light has sexual significance and is stronger in the female; it is a 'cold' light using little energy and has been studied with a view to commercial production of the method; a handful of glow worms provides enough light to read by.
scarab or ***dung beetle*** *Scarabeus sacer*, family Scarabeidae, which feeds on dung, and lays its eggs in balls of it; it was revered by the ancient Egyptians as an emblem of resurrection and used on seals.
Spanish fly or ***blister beetle*** *Cantharis vesicatoria*, family Cantharidae, which is bright golden-green, and from the dried body of which the dangerous aphrodisiac cantharides is prepared.
ladybird small, round-backed, and red or yellow with black spots, family Coccinellidae. With their larvae, they feed on aphides, scale insects, etc, and attempts are being made to breed 'domesticated' species which can be released in specific areas to assist the gardener□

Beeton Isabella 1836–65. British housewifery expert. She wrote *Beeton's Household Management* 1859, the first really comprehensive work on the subject□

Begin Menachem 1913– . Israeli statesman, born in Poland. He was a leader of the extremist Irgun Zvai Leumi organization in Palestine from 1942; he was Prime Minister of Israel 1977–83, as head of the right-wing Likud, and in 1978 shared a Nobel peace prize with Sadat◊ for work on the Camp◊ David peace agreement□

begonia genus of the tropical and subtropical plant family Begoniaceae, with fleshy and succulent leaves, and often large, brilliant flowers□

Behan Brendan 1923–64. Irish playwright. Born in Dublin, he was a member of the IRA at 16, and in 1939 was sent to Borstal on explosives charges immediately on his arrival in England. He was imprisoned 1942–6 when involved in an Easter Day parade incident in Dublin which resulted in the shooting of a policeman. His works include the autobiographical *Borstal Boy* 1958, and the plays *The Quare Fellow* 1956 and *The Hostage* 1958□

behaviourism school of psychology, originated in America by John Broadus Watson 1878–1958, which seeks to explain all human behaviour by conditioned reactions or 'reflexes', and the habits formed in consequence (see Pavlov◊). It was opposed to the approach of Freud◊□

Behrens Peter 1868–1940. German architect of the AEG turbine factory in Berlin 1909, a landmark in industrial design□

Behring Emil von 1854–1917. German bacteriologist, founder of immunology. Nobel prize 1901□

Behring Vitus. See Bering◊□

Beiderbecke Bix (Leon Bismarcke) 1903–31. American jazz composer, a virtuoso of the piano and cornet□

Beijing Pinyin form of Peking◊□

Beira Port in E Mozambique; population 114 000□

Beirut capital and port of Lebanon; population 702 000. Destroyed as an international financial and educational centre by the civil war 1975–6, it also formerly had a reputation as a centre of espionage (see Philby◊)□

Beirut Battle of. Siege and virtual destruction of the city by the Israeli army Jul–Sept 1982 to enforce the withdrawal of the forces of the Palestinian Liberation Organization. After the ceasefire, there was a massacre of 500 Palestinians in the Sabra-Chatila camps 16–18 Sept by dissident Phalangists◊ and Maronite◊ troops, with alleged Israeli complicity□

Bejaia seaport (formerly Bougie) in Algeria; population 104 000□

Belau Republic of. Island of the Carolines◊, formerly known as Palau, which became internally self-governing in 1980; a free association agreement with the USA signed 1982 has not yet been ratified□

Belém port and naval base in N Brazil; population 772 000. The chief trade centre of the Amazon Basin, it is also known as Pará, the name of the branch of the Amazon on which it stands□

Belfast capital and chief port of N Ireland; population 362 000. The former parliament buildings are to the S at Stormont; from 1968 there was heavy damage from the activities of political extremists. Industries include shipbuilding, engineering, electronics, textiles (mainly synthetic), and tobacco. There is an international airport at Aldergrove (see Freeport◊). The Ulster Museum and open-air Ulster Folk Museum are nearby in county Down; also of interest are Queen's University, St Anne's Protestant cathedral 1899, and the City Hall 1906□

Belfort capital of the department of Territoire de Belfort, France, strategic Belfort Gap between the Vosges and Jura mountains□

Belgium Kingdom of

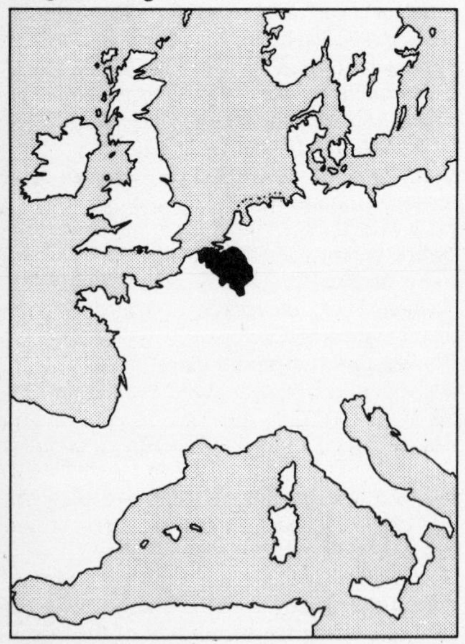

area 30 513 sq km/11 779 sq mi
capital Brussels
towns Ghent, Liège, Charleroi, Bruges, Mons, Blankenburghe, Knokke; ports are Antwerp, Ostend, Zeebrugge
features Ardennes; rivers Scheldt and Meuse
exports iron and steel, textiles, manufactured goods, petrochemicals
currency Belgian franc
population 9 855 000 comprising Flemings (of Germanic origin) and Walloons (a Celtic people who came under Roman rule), the latter were formerly predominant, but are now outnumbered by the former.
language in the north (Flanders) Flemish (a Dutch dialect, known as Vlaams) 57%, in the south (Wallonia) Walloon (a French dialect which is almost a separate language) 30%, with 11% bilingual, and German (eastern border); all are official.
religion Roman Catholicism
famous people art Jan van Eyck, Hieronymus Bosch, Pieter Brueghel, Peter Paul Rubens, Van Dyck, James Ensor, René Magritte; *literature* Verhaeren, Georges Simenon; *music* César Franck
government Belgium is a constitutional monarchy (see Baudouin◊), and the Senate and Chamber of Representatives is elected by proportional representation.
recent history formerly part of the Netherlands, Belgium became an independent kingdom in 1830, under Leopold◊ I (see also Leopold◊ II). She was invaded by Germany both in 1914 and 1940, and the circumstances of her surrender under Leopold◊ III led to his supersession. Since World War II the wealth of French-speaking Wallonia, dependent on the declined coal and steel industry of Mons, Charleroi and Liège, has been overtaken by the oil refining, pharmaceuticals, fertilisers, plastics, and textile industries of Flemish-speaking Flanders. The language question is a perennial source of controversy. Because of its central position in the Common Market, Belgium has become a major distribution centre□

Belgrade capital (*Beograd*) of Yugoslavia and Serbia; population 1 204 000. It is a Danube river port and is linked with the newly-developed port of Bar on the Adriatic. Tito◊'s former home, where he is buried, is a museum□

Belgravia district of London, laid out in solidly magnificent squares by Thomas Cubitt◊ in 1825–30; it is bounded to the N by Knightsbridge□

Belisarius 505–65. General under the Emperor Justinian◊□

Belitung see under Sunda◊ Islands□

Belize
area 22 965 sq km/8867sq mi
capital Belmopan
towns port Belize City
features half the country is forested, much of it high rain forest
exports sugar, citrus, rice, lobster tails
currency Belize dollar

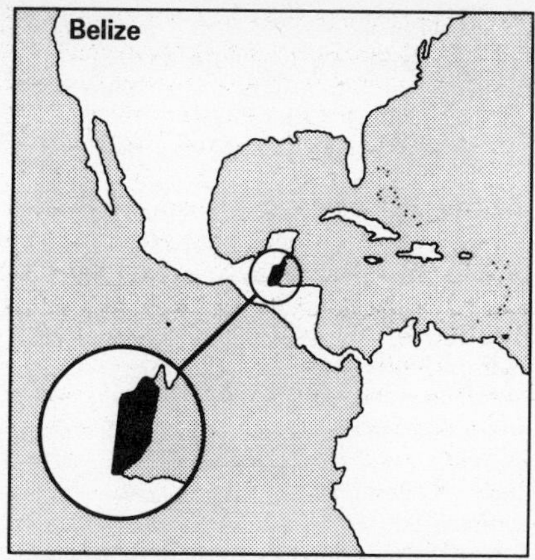

population 158 000, including Maya minority in the interior
language English official, but Spanish is widely spoken
religion 60% Roman Catholic, 35% Protestant, Hindu and Muslim minorities
government there is a governor-general, senate and house of representatives (Prime Minister from 1984 Manuel Esquivel, United Democratic Party).
recent history occupied by British woodcutters in 1638, Belize was known as British Honduras until 1973, and became independent in 1981, although British troops remained at the request of Belize, pending withdrawal of claims by Guatemala to all Belize□

Belize City chief port of Belize; because of its liability to hurricanes, it was replaced as capital by Belmopan◊ 1970; population 40 000□

bell instrument of hollowed metal (usually four parts bronze to one of tin) struck to produce a musical sound. The world's largest is the ***Tsar Kolokol*** or ***King of Bells***, 220 tonnes, cast 1734, which still stands on the ground in the Kremlin, Moscow, where it fell when being hung. The ***Peace Bell*** at the United Nations headquarters, NY, was cast in 1952 from coins presented by 64 countries. See Big◊ Ben□

Bell Alexander Graham 1847–1922. British inventor. Born in Edinburgh, he moved to Brantford, Canada, and then to Boston, USA, opening a school for teachers of the deaf in 1872; in 1876 he patented his invention of the telephone□

Bell Vanessa 1879–1961. British artist, sister of Virginia Woolf◊, she married critic Clive Bell 1881–1964, and was the mistress of Roger Fry◊. She also loved the homosexual Duncan Grant◊, who shared the Bell farmhouse, Charleston in E Sussex□

belladonna an alkaloid drug obtained from the leaves and root of the plant deadly nightshade◊□

Bellarmino St Roberto 1542–1621. Italian theologian; stoneware drinking jugs bearing raised bearded faces were called by his name because of a fancied resemblance□

Bellingshausen Fabian Gottlieb von 1779–1852. Russian explorer, first to sight Antarctica, but without realizing what it was□

Bellingshausen Sea section of the S Pacific off the Antarctic coast□

Bellini Gentile 1429–1507. Italian artist of the Venetian school, founded by his father Jacopo Bellini 1400–70. He worked at the court of Mohammed◊ II at Constantinople, but hurriedly returned home when the Sultan demonstrated an inaccuracy in his depiction of the severed head of John the Baptist by cutting off the head of one of his slaves. He excelled in portraits and processional groups□

Bellini Giovanni 1430–1516. Italian artist, the younger brother of Gentile Bellini◊; he was one of the first painters to work in oils□

Bellini Vincenzo 1801–35. Italian composer, noted for his opera *Norma* 1831□

Belloc (Joseph) Hilaire Pierre 1870–1953. British Roman Catholic author, son of a French father and an English mother, he was naturalized in 1902. With G K Chesterton◊, he advocated a return to the Distributist◊ theories of the late Middle Ages in place of modern Capitalism or Socialism. He is best remembered by his *The Path to Rome*, a walker's classic, and nonsense verse for children, *The Bad Child's Book of Beasts* 1896 and *Cautionary Tales* 1907□

Bellow Saul 1915– . American novelist. Canadian-born of Russo-Jewish extraction, he settled in Chicago with his family at the age of nine, assisting his father in bootlegging; his works include the picaresque *The Adventures of Augie March* 1953, the philosophically speculative *Herzog* 1964, *Humboldt's Gift 1975*, and *The Dean's Dec* 1982, all displaying subtle humour. Nobel prize 1975□

bell ringing the art of ringing church bells. ***Change ringing*** by hand (by means of a rope fastened to the wheel of the bell mechanism) is an English art perfected by Fabian Stedman, a Cambridge printer, in the 17th century. Mathematical permutations are rung on 5–12 bells, and ringers are organized in guilds. The ***carillon*** method, popular on the Continent and in USA, involves a single executant using a 'keyboard' linked only to the clapper of the bells□

Bell's theorem hypothesis of Swiss physicist John S Bell, that an unknown force, of which space, time and motion are all aspects, continues to link separate parts of the universe which were once united, and that this force travels faster than the speed of light□

Belmopan capital of Belize, SW of Belize City◊; population 4000□

Belo Horizonte industrial city in Brazil; population 1 558 000□

Belorussia 'White Russia', a constituent republic of the USSR from 1922.
area 207 600 sq km/80 150 sq mi
capital Minsk
features Pripet Marshes◊ in the east
products cereals, flax, meat and dairy produce; peat; transport vehicles
population 9 600 000, 81% Belorussian, 10% Polish
language White Russian, a dialect allied to Great Russian
religion traditionally Russian Orthodox
recent history in 1918 there was an attempt to establish an independent joint republic with Lithuania, but by 1921 the western area had passed to Polish occupation, although reunited with Byelorussia in 1939 by Soviet conquest□

Belsen site of a Nazi concentration camp in Lower Saxony W Germany□

Beltane Celtic◊ Mayday festival, marked by fires lit on hilltops□

Benares see Varanasi◊□

Ben Barka Mehdi 1920–65. Moroccan leftist politician. Lured to Paris, he was shot by Moroccan agents with the aid of the French secret service, but his body was never found. The case led to de Gaulle◊'s reorganization of the secret service□

Ben Bella Ahmed 1916– . Algerian leader of the National Liberation Front (FLN) from 1952; he was Prime Minister of independent Algeria 1962–5, when he was overthrown by Boumédienne◊ and detained till 1980. He founded a new party, Mouvement pour la Démocratie en Algerie 1985□

Benbow John 1653–1702. English admiral, who died of wounds received in a great fight with the French off Jamaica, and became a popular hero□

Benchley Robert 1889–1945. American humorous essayist, and maker of minifilms e.g. *How to Sleep*□

Benda Julien 1867–1956. French author, who attacked Bergson◊, and, in *Le Trahison des Clercs/The Treason of the Intellectuals* 1927, the failure of his contemporaries to adhere to the ideal of absolute truth□

Bendigo industrial town in Victoria, Australia; population 50 200. It was the scene of a gold rush in the 1850s□

bends see decompression◊ sickness□

Benedict St 480–547AD. Italian founder of the Benedictine◊ order. Of a wealthy family, he became a solitary anchorite, then in 529 founded the monastery of Monte Cassino◊, where he formulated a 'rule' stressing physical work combined with scholarship□

Benedictine order monastic order founded by St Benedict◊, which became the chief guardian of medieval scholarship and agricultural development. Members included Augine◊ and Bede◊, and were called 'black monks' because of the colour of their habits. A number of Oxford and Cambridge colleges have a Benedictine origin, and famous modern houses include Ampleforth, Buckfast, Downside and Prinknash in Britain, and Latrobe, Pennsylvania and St Meinrad, Indiana, USA□

Benelux customs union of ***Be***lgium, ***Ne***therlands and ***Lux***embourg (agreed 1944, fully effective 1960); precursor of the Common Market◊□

Beneš Eduard 1884–1948. Czech statesman. President of the republic from 1935 until forced to resign by the Germans, he headed a government in exile in London during World War II. Returning home as President in 1945, he was again forced to resign when the Communists gained control in 1948□

Benét Stephen Vincent 1898–1943. American poet, noted for his narrative poem of the Civil◊ War *John Brown's Body* 1928□

Benevento town in Campania, Italy; population 590 000□

Bengal East. See Bangladesh◊□

Bengal West NE state of India
area 87 853 sq km/000 000 sq mi
capital Calcutta
features on the alluvial plain of the Ganges (shares delta with Bangladesh) and Brahmaputra, it has an annual rainfall of over 25 cm/100 in; heavily industrialized. The ***Battle of Plassey*** 1757, a victory by Clive◊ over Suraj-ud-Dowlah, was fought near the village of that name, but the battle site has been eroded by the river Bhagirathi.
population 49 800 000
language Bengali□

Bengali language of Bangladesh and W Bengal. See Bangalistan◊□

Benghazi second city of Libya; population 282 000. It changed hands several times between Allied and Axis◊ forces 1941–2, and after World War II developed under the stimulus of oil discoveries in the interior and offshore in the Gulf of Syrte□

Benguela port in Angola; population 43 000. There are rail links with central Africa, but these were inoperative from 1979 owing to attack from anti-Soviet guerrillas□

Ben Gurion David 1886–1973. Israeli statesman, the country's first Prime Minister 1948–53, 1955–63□

Benin former black African kingdom 1200–1897, now part of Nigeria; its capital was Benin◊ City□

Benin People's Republic of

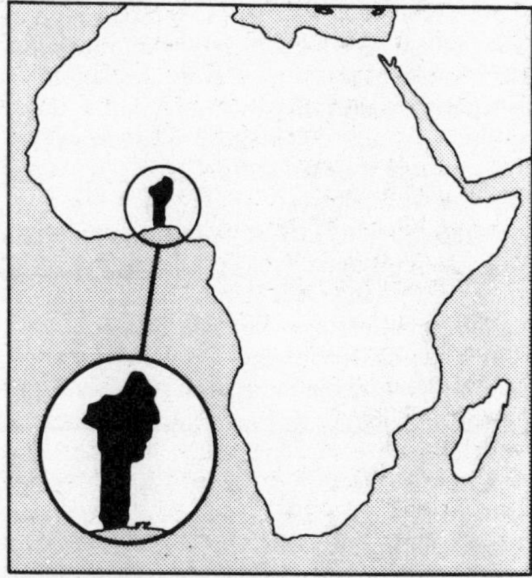

area 112 600 sq km/43 480sq mi
capital Porto Novo
towns Abomey, Natitingou; chief port Cotonou
features coastal fishing villages on stilts
exports cocoa, groundnuts, cotton, oil palm
currency CFA franc
population 3 910 000
language French official; 47% Fan
religion Animism 65%, Christianity 17%, Islam 13%
government unicameral National Revolutionary Assembly of 336 People's Commissioners established under the Marxist-Leninist constitution of 1977; President Ahmed Kerekou came to power by a coup in 1972.
recent history formerly the African kingdom of Dahomey, it came under French control from 1851, and achieved independence in 1960. A series of military coups followed. In 1975 the name of the country was changed to Benin, but it has no historical connection with the former kingdom of Benin□

Benin City city in S Nigeria; population 136 000. Former capital of the kingdom of Benin◊, it was captured by a British expedition in 1897, following the murder of some Europeans. It was famous for ivory work and for brasses, which include portrait heads used on ancestral altars in the royal palace and plaques on its wooden pillars (1000 are known, bearing scenes from Benin history and legend); some of these are now in the British Museum, and their return has been requested□

Benn Anthony Wedgwood 1925– . British Labour◊ politician. Son of Lord Stansgate, a Labour peer, he succeeded his father in 1960, though never using his title, and in 1963 was the first person to disclaim his title under the Peerage Act. He was Minister of Technology 1966–70 and of Industry 1974–5, but his campaign against entry to the Common Market led to his transfer to Energy 1975–9. In 1981 he challenged Healey◊ unsuccessfully for the deputy leadership of the party, but was so narrowly defeated that he established himself as the acknowledged leader of the Left□

Bennett Alan 1934– . British playwright, whose settings are usually his native North country, and subjects senility, illness and death, treated with macabre comedy. His work includes TV films e.g. *An Englishman Abroad* 1982, the cinema film, *A Private Function* 1984, and plays *Forty Years On* 1968 and *Getting On* 1971□

Bennett (Enoch) Arnold 1867–1931. British novelist. Born in Hanley, Staffordshire, one of the 'five towns' of the Potteries which formed the setting of his major books, he became a London journalist in 1893, and editor of *Woman* in 1896. His books include *Anna of the Five Towns* 1904, *Sacred and Profane Love* 1905, *The Old Wives' Tale* 1908, and the trilogy *Clayhanger*, *Hilda Lessways* and *These Twain* 1910–15□

Bennett Richard Rodney 1936– . British composer of jazz, film music, *Far From the Madding Crowd, Nicholas and Alexandra* and – for TV – *Tender is the Night* 1985, symphonies, and operas e.g. *Victory* 1970□

Ben Nevis see under Grampian◊ mountains□

Benoni industrial town in the Transvaal, S Africa; population 150 000□

Benson E(dward) F(rederic) 1867–1940. British novelist, son of ***Edward White Benson*** 1829–96, archbishop of Canterbury from 1883. His work was lightly satirical, e.g. *Dodo* 1893 and its sequels, and a series, concerning two ladies of a fictionalized Rye◊ ('Tilling'), which includes *Mapp and Lucia* 1931□

Bentham Jeremy 1748–1832. British philosopher and legal reformer. His *Fragments on Government* 1776 and *Principles of Morals and Legislation* 1789 outline his Utilitarian◊ philosophy that laws should be 'for the greatest happiness of the greatest number', and he later contended that 'utility' was best served by allowing every man to pursue his own interests unhindered by restrictive legislation. He left his body for dissection to University College, London, and the preserved and clothed remains can still be seen there□

Bentinck Lord William Cavendish 1774–1839. British soldier. First Governor-General of India 1828–35, he acted against thuggee and suttee◊, and to simplify further education established English as the medium of instruction□

Bentley Edmund Clerihew 1875–1956. British author. He invented the four-line doggerel verse, the 'clerihew', and wrote the classic detective story *Trent's Last Case* 1912□

Benue river in Nigeria, largest affluent of the Niger; it is navigable for most of its length 1400 km/870 m□

Benz Karl 1844–1929. German engineer, who in 1885 produced the world's first petrol-driven motor car□

benzaldehyde clear liquid C_6H_5CHO, also known as oil of bitter almonds, although now made synthetically from toluene; it is used in making perfumes, dyes, and as a solvent□

benzedrine trade name for a type of pep pill or amphetamine◊□

benzene clear liquid aromatic hydrocarbon, C_6H_6, with a characteristic smell; it is used as a solvent and in the synthesis of many important chemicals□

benzodiazepine mood-altering drug (tranquillizer), e.g. Librium and Valium. It interferes with the process by which information is transmitted from one brain cell to another, and various ill effects arise from continued use□

Beograd see Belgrade◊□

Beowulf hero of the Old English epic poem of the same name; he killed the water-monster Grendel, and then ruled his country for 50 years before being himself killed by a dragon. Composed about 700AD, it is the only survivor of many such tales□

Berber people and language of Barbary◊; their culture survives in the mountain communities of the Kabyles in Algeria (see Zouaves◊) and the Rifs◊ of the Atlas range in Morocco□

Berbera seaport in Somalia, with the only sheltered harbour on the S side of the Gulf of Aden, and in a strategic position on the oil route□

Berchtesgaden village in SE Bavaria, site of Hitler◊'s country residence, the Berghof; it was captured by US troops 4 May 1945 and destroyed□

Berdyaev Nikolai Alexandrovich 1874–1948. Russian philosopher whose religious interpretation of Marxist theory led to his exile in 1922; his ideas have influenced modern Soviet dissidents□

Berdyansk port in the Ukraine, USSR; population 110 000□

Berezniki town in W USSR; population 176 000. There are chemical industries based on local salt and potash□

Berg Alban 1885–1935. Austrian composer, a pupil of Schoenberg, who composed twelve-tone music (see atonality◊); his opera *Wozzeck* 1925 is a grim story of working class life□

Bergamo industrial town in Lombardy, Italy; population 126 500. There is a major art collection in the Academia Carrara□

bergamot see citrus◊□

Bergen port and city in Norway; population 212 000. Fine merchant houses survive from the Hanseatic period; Ibsen◊ was once manager of the theatre and Grieg◊ lived at nearby Troldhaugen. There are shipbuilding, engineering and fishing industries□

Bergman Ingmar 1918– . Swedish theatre and film director; his films include *The Seventh Seal* 1956 and *Face to Face* 1976□

Bergman Ingrid 1917–82. Swedish actress, whose films include *Casablanca* 1943, *For Whom the Bell Tolls* 1943, *Anastasia* 1956, and *Murder on the Orient Express* 1974. By leaving her husband for film producer Roberto Rossellini, whom she married in 1950, she was the first openly to break the unofficial moral code of Hollywood 'star' behaviour and was ostrasized for many years□

Bergson Henri 1859–1941. French philosopher of Anglo-Jewish extraction, who became a naturalized Frenchman. In *Creative Evolution* 1907, he attempted to prove that all evolution and progress are due to the working of an *élan vital* or life-force□

Beria Lavrenti 1899–1953. Soviet head of the secret police under Stalin◊, who was responsible for the deportation and death of hundreds of thousands. On Stalin's death, he formed a brief 'triumvirate' with Malenkov◊ and Molotov◊, but was shot after a secret trial□

beri-beri endemic polyneuritis, an inflammation of the nerve endings, occurring mainly in the tropics and resulting from vitamin B1 deficiency□

Bering Vitus 1680–1741. Danish explorer, the first European to sight Alaska. He died on Bering Island in Bering◊ Sea, both named after him, as are Bering◊ Strait and Beringia◊□

Beringia land bridge 1600 km/1000 m wide between Asia and America before c35 000BC and between 24 000–9000BC; now covered by Bering◊ Strait and Chukchi◊ Sea□

Bering Sea section of the Pacific between Asia and the Americas to the N of the Aleutians. The four ***Pribilof Islands*** are part of Alaska, with which they were sold to USA by Russia 1867; area 168 sq km/65 sq mi□
Bering Strait the strait linking the Pacific and Arctic oceans□
Berkeley town on San Francisco Bay, seat of the University of California, which is noted for its atomic research; population 103 000□
Berkeley Busby 1895–1976. American film director, who used female dancers to create large-scale pattern effects in ingeniously extravagant sets, e.g. *Gold Diggers of 1933*□
Berkeley George 1685–1753. Irish philosopher, a bishop in the Anglican Church. One of the school of 'British Empiricists', but an opponent of Locke◊'s empiricist philosophy, he put forward his alternative of 'subjective idealism', according to which all objects exist simply in the mind of the beholder, and 'to be' means merely (but for Berkeley, amply) 'to be perceived', in *Principles of Human Knowledge* 1710, etc. See Scholasticism◊□
Berkelium element
symbol Bk
atomic number 97
features produced by bombarding americium◊, it is available only in minute quantities
uses none at present□
Berkshire southern county of England

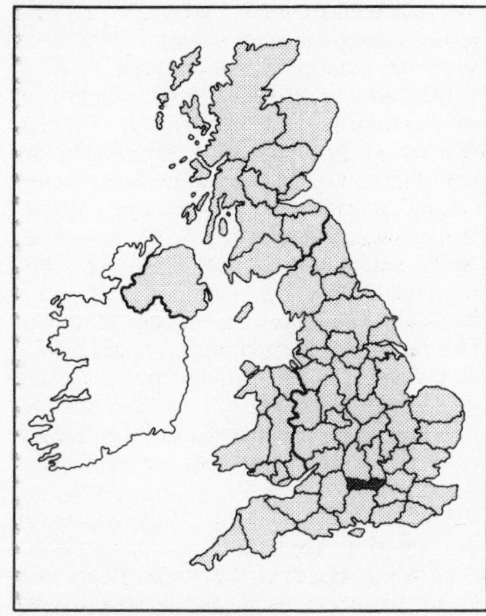

area 1259 sq km/486 sq mi
towns administrative headquarters Reading; Eton, Slough, Maidenhead, Ascot, Bracknell, Newbury, Windsor
features rivers Thames and Kennet; Inkpen Beacon 297 m/975 ft; Bagshot Heath; Vale of the White Horse (the latter is a Hill◊ figure); Ridgeway Path, walkers' path (partly prehistoric) running from Wiltshire across the Berkshire Downs into Hertfordshire; Windsor Forest and Windsor Castle (a home of the Sovereign); village of Stoke Poges, Thomas Gray◊ is buried in the churchyard; Eton College; Royal Military Academy at Sandhurst (for both men and women since 1985); atomic weapons research establishment at Aldermaston◊, and the main UK base for US cruise missiles at RAF Greenham Common, Newbury
products general agricultural and horticultural, electronics
population 698 700
famous people King Alfred, Stanley Spencer□
Berlin city which was the capital of a united Germany 1871–1945, when it was captured in World War II by the Allies◊ and divided into four sectors (British, French, US, and Russian). From 1949, following Soviet withdrawal from the combined board, the first three became W Berlin◊, and the Russian sector became E Berlin◊□
Berlin Congress of. Congress held by the European powers under Bismarck◊'s presidency in 1878 to determine the boundaries of the Balkan states after the Russo◊-Turkish War; Disraeli◊ was Britain's chief envoy□
Berlin East. Capital of E Germany and E Berlin district
area 403 sq Km/155 sq mi
features the fine (restored) thoroughfare of Unter den Linden; Staats Oper and Komische Oper (opera houses); Berliner Ensemble Theatre founded by Brecht◊; developments such as the Alexander Platz complex, with its television tower; white marble Palace of the Republic (the E German parliament house) on Marx-Engels Platz; the Sports and Recreation centre; the Lenin and Karl Marx Allees.
population 1 116 641
religion none official□
Berlin Irving 1888– . Adopted name of Israel Baline, Russian-born American composer, whose hits include 'Alexander's Ragtime Band,' 'Always,' 'White Christmas,' and the musicals *Top Hat, Annie Get Your Gun* 1950, and *Call Me Madam* 1953□
Berlin Sir Isaiah 1909– . British philosopher, given the Order of Merit in 1971 for his contributions to social and political theory, as in *Historical Inevitability* 1954 and *Four Essays on Liberty* 1969□
Berlin West. Land (State) of W Germany
area 480 sq km/185 sq mi
features divided from E Berlin by the Berlin◊ Wall; the Kurfürstendamm (fashionable shopping street), Europa-Center, Funkturm

(equivalent of the Eiffel Tower) beneath which trade fairs are held; the modern residential Hansa quarter; Kaiser-Wilhelm Gedachtniskirche (memorial church, rebuilt 1959–61, but with a 19th century tower); Reichstag (former parliament building); Schloss Bellevue (Berlin residence of the president); Schloss Charlottenburg (now museums); Schöneberg (Town Hall, seat of the Land government); Brandenburg Gate, the modern Congress Hall, State Opera (restored), Komische Oper (opera), Philharmonic Hall (home of the Berlin Philharmonic and von Karajan◊), 20th Century Art Gallery, Dahlem picture gallery, Tiergarten (zoo), Spandau military prison, and the Grünewald Forest and lakes (Wannsee and Tegelersee), etc. There are airports at Tegel (international) and Tempelhof (military)
products electronics, electrical goods, machine tools, chemicals, clothing, paper, and books
population 1 927 000, including 250 000 foreign workers, of whom 120 000 are Turks
religion Protestantism 70%, Roman Catholicism 13%, Islam 6%
famous people Willy Brandt□

Berlinguer Enrico 1922–84. Italian Communist, who freed the party from Soviet influence, and by 1976 was near to the premiership, but the Red Brigade murder of Aldo Moro◊ revived the Socialist vote□

Berlin Wall the dividing line between E and W Berlin which, from 13 Aug 1961, was reinforced by the Russians with armed guards and barbed wire to prevent the escape of unwilling workers of E Berlin to the greater freedom of W Berlin. The interconnecting link between E and W Berlin is Checkpoint Charlie, where both sides also exchange captured spies. Escapers from east to west are shot on sight□

Berlioz Hector 1803–69. French composer, founder of modern orchestration. He defied his parents in abandoning medicine for the study of music. His life was as noted for romantic excess as his music, especially in his infatuation for the English Shakespearean actress, Harriet Smithson, whom he married in 1833. She inspired his *Symphonie Fantastique* 1830. His other works include operas (*Les Troyens* 1863); the dramatic cantata *La Damnation de Faust* 1846; sacred music (*Requiem* 1837 and oratorio *The Childhood of Christ* 1854), and the dramatic symphony *Roméo et Juliette* 1839□

Bermuda
area 54 sq km/21 sq mi
capital and chief port Hamilton

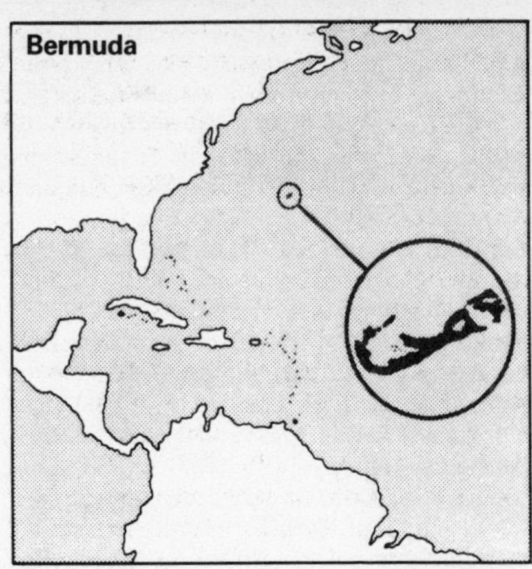

features consists of about 150 (20 inhabited) small coral islands, linked by bridges and causeways; Britain's oldest colony; the USA has a naval air base and there is a NASA tracking station
exports Easter lilies, pharmaceuticals
currency Bermuda dollar
population 55 000
language English
religion Christianity
government under the constitution of 1968, Bermuda is a fully self-governing British colony, with a Governor, Senate and elected House of Assembly (premier from 1982 John Swan, United Bermuda Party).
recent history the islands were named after Juan de Bermudez, who visited them in 1515, and were settled by British colonists in 1609. Racial violence in 1977 led to intervention, at the request of the government, by British troops, but there is no pressure for full independence. The economy is strong, tourism flourishing and banking, insurance, and international business interests expanding

Bermuda Triangle sea area in the Bermuda-Florida-Puerto Rico triangle, which gained its nickname in 1964 when it was suggested that ships and aircraft disappeared particularly frequently here; analysis of the data did not confirm the theory, but see Tall◊ Ships Race□

Bernadette St 1844–79. Marie Bernarde Soubirous, a peasant girl born at Lourdes◊, who saw a vision of the Virgin Mary in a grotto there Feb 1858, and became a nun. She died of tuberculosis, and was canonized 1933; feast day 18 Feb. The grotto shrine has a reputation for miraculous cures□

Bernadotte Count Folke 1895–1948. Nephew of the King of Sweden, he was assassinated by Stern◊ Gang terrorists while

United Nations mediator in Palestine□

Bernadotte Jean Baptiste Jules 1764–1844. Marshal in Napoleon◊'s army, who became Charles◊ XIV of Sweden 1818, and founder of the present royal house□

Bernard of Clairvaux, St 1090–1153. Founder in 1115 of Clairvaux monastery in Champagne, France, he reinvigorated the Cistercian◊ order; he preached the Second Crusade◊ in 1146, and had Abelard◊ condemned for heresy□

Bernard of Menthon, St 923–1008. Founder of the hospices for travellers on the Alpine passes that bear his name; the large, heavily-built St Bernard dogs formerly used to find travellers lost in the snow were also called after him. See Alps◊□

Berne capital of the Swiss Confederation from 1848; population 2893 600. Named after the bear on its coat of arms, it has had a bear pit since the 16th century□

Bernese Oberland see under Alps◊□

Bernhard Prince. See Juliana◊□

Bernhardt Sarah 1845–1923. Stage-name of French actress Rosine Bernard, of Jewish extraction. She dominated the stage of her day, as the heroine of Racine◊'s *Phèdre,* Dona Sol in Hugo◊'s *Hernani*, and in the male roles of Hamlet, and of Napoleon's son in Rostand◊'s *L'Aiglon*. She lost a leg in an accident in 1915, but continued her career□

Bernini Giovanni Lorenzo 1598–1680. Italian architect, sculptor, and painter in the Baroque◊ style; he created the piazza colonnade outside St Peter's, Rome□

Bernoulli Swiss family of mathematicians: ***Jacques Bernoulli*** 1654–1705, discovered Bernoullian numbers, a complex series of fractions used in higher mathematics; his brother ***Jean Bernoulli*** 1667–1748, discovered the exponential calculus; Jean's son ***Daniel Bernoulli*** 1700–82, made discoveries in hydrodynamics□

Bernstein Leonard 1918– . American conductor and composer. His works include symphonies and scores for musicals, especially *West Side Story* 1957, which established a vogue for realistic, contemporary themes□

Berrigan Daniel 1921– and Philip 1924– . American Catholic priests, who were imprisoned for opposition to the Vietnam◊ War. In 1972 Father Philip was tried with others for allegedly conspiring to kidnap Kissinger◊ and blow up offices in Washington, and sentenced to two years□

Berry Chuck (Charles Edward) 1931– . American popularizer of rock-and-roll, and composer of such songs as 'Roll over Beethoven' 1956□

berserker member of a legendary Scandinavian warrior cult, who went into battle in a frenzy of destructive energy – hence to go 'berserk' – and who were rendered immune to sword and flame□

Bertolucci Bernardo 1940– . Italian film director, e.g. *The Spider's Stratagem* 1969□

Berwick-upon-Tweed fishing port in Northumberland, England; population 11 800. Alternately held by English and Scots for centuries, Berwick became a neutral town in 1551, and then in 1885 was attached to Northumberland. It has some fine old houses□

beryl a mineral, beryllium aluminium silicate, $Be_3Al_2Si_6O_{18}$, which forms crystals chiefly in granite: it is the chief ore or beryllium◊. Two of its forms are aquamarine (light blue crystals) and emerald (dark green crystals)□

beryllium element

symbol Be

atomic number 4

physical description silvery-white metal

features resists corrosion; found naturally in beryl◊

uses used in 'windows' of X-ray tubes, in nuclear reactors, and in alloys□

Berzelius Jöns Jakob 1779–1848. Swedish chemist. Specializing in the determination of atomic and molecular weights, he invented the system of chemical symbols now in use and did valuable work in the use of catalysts□

Bes in Egyptian mythology, the god of music and dance, usually shown as a grotesque dwarf□

Besançon industrial town, capital of Franche-Comté, France; population 126 200. It has fortifications by Vauban◊, and Victor Hugo◊ was born here□

Besant Annie 1847–1933. British Socialist, feminist, and activist. Separated from her clerical husband in 1873 because of her free-thinking views, she was associated with the radical atheist Charles Bradlaugh and the Fabians◊, and became a disciple of Mme Blavatsky◊ in 1889. She thereafter preached theosophy and, as a supporter of Indian independence, became president of the Hindu National Congress in 1917□

Besier Rudolf 1878–1942. British playwright, whose *The Barretts of Wimpole Street* 1930, about the Brownings◊, blackens the character of Mr Barrett□

Bessarabia territory, annexed by Russia in 1812, which broke away at the Russian◊ Revolution to join Romania. The cession was confirmed by the Allies◊, but not by Russia, in a Paris treaty of 1920; Russia re-occupied it in 1940 and divided it between the Moldavian and Ukrainian Republics. Romania recognized the position in the 1947 peace treaty, but the question re-emerges from time to time□

Bessel Friedrich Wilhelm 1784–1846. German astronomer, the first man to measure the distance from earth to a star in 1838, and founder of modern precision astronomy□

Best Charles Herbert 1899–1978. Canadian physiologist, the discoverer with Banting and Macleod of insulin◊□

Best George 1946– . British footballer, who played for Manchester United when they won the FA (twice) and European Cups, but was too temperamental to continue□

beta blockers drugs used from the 1970s to block nerve impulses to special sites (beta receptors) in body tissues; they reduce the rate of heartbeat and the force of its contractions, and are used (e.g. propranolol) in post-heart attack treatment. See Sir James Black◊□

beta particle an electron or positron emitted from a radioactive substance whilst undergoing spontaneous disintegration. They do not exist in the nucleus, but are created on disintegration when a neutron converts to a proton to emit an electron, or a proton converts to a neutron to emit a positron. See particle◊ physics, radioactivity◊□

betel or ***betel nut*** the seed of the palm *Areca catechu,* which is chewed, with the leaves of the betel pepper◊ and lime, by Eastern peoples as a narcotic. There is a possible link with oral cancer□

Betelgeuse see star◊□

Bethe Hans Albrecht 1906– . German-American physicist, who received a Nobel prize in 1967 for his work on energy production (nuclear fusion) in the stars□

Bethlehem town to the S of Jerusalem (modern Beit-Lahm in Jordan), which was occupied by Israel in 1967; population 60 000. In the New Testament, the birthplace of Jesus Christ, it was also associated with David◊□

Bethlehem steel city in Pennsylvania, USA; population 70 420□

Bethmann Hollweg Theobald von 1856–1921. German chancellor 1909–17, when Ludendorff◊ forced his resignation□

Betjeman Sir John 1906–84. English poet. His peculiarly English light verse is nostalgic and delights in Victorian bric-à-brac, Neo-Gothic◊ architecture, etc. *Summoned by Bells* 1960 is a verse autobiography. Knighted 1969; Poet Laureate from 1972; see also under Cornwall◊□

betting wagering money on the outcome of a game, race, or other event. In the UK on-course betting on ***horses*** and ***dogs*** may be through individual bookmakers at given odds, or on the tote (totalizator), when the total amount (with fixed deductions) staked is divided among those making the correct forecast. Off-course betting is mainly through betting 'shops' (legalized 1960) which, like bookmakers, must have a licence. ***Football*** betting is in the hands of 'pools' promoters who must be registered with a local authority to which annual accounts are submitted. The size of the money prizes is determined by the number of successful forecasts of the results of matches received; if only one 'punter' gives a correct forecast, the win may be above the £ million mark, except in fixed odds betting□

Betws-y-coed village tourist centre, noted for its waterfalls, in Gwynned, Wales□

BeV American symbol for one billion electron volts or 10^9 electron volts□

Bevan Aneurin 1897–1960. British Labour◊ politician. Son of a Welsh miner, and himself a miner at 13, he became MP for Ebbw Vale (1929–60). As Minister of Health 1945–51, he inaugurated the Health Service, and was Minister of Labour Jan–Apr 1951, when he resigned (with Harold Wilson◊) on the introduction of Health Service charges, and led a Bevanite faction against the government. He was a superb orator□

Beveridge William Henry, 1st Baron Beveridge 1879–1963. British economist. A civil servant, he acted as Lloyd◊ George's lieutenant in the social legislation of the Liberal◊ government before World War I, and his 'Beveridge Report' 1942, formed the basis of the Welfare State in Britain□

Beverly Hills residential city adjoining Los Angeles, California, USA, famous as the home of Hollywood stars□

Bevin Ernest 1881–1951. British Labour◊ statesman. Chief creator of the Transport and General Workers' Union, he was its General Secretary 1921–40, when he entered the War Cabinet as Minister of Labour and National Service. He organized the 'Bevin boys', chosen by ballot to work in the coal mines as war service, and was Foreign Secretary in the Labour government 1945–51□

Bewick Thomas 1753–1828. British wood engraver, excelling in animal subjects, e.g. *British Birds* 1797–1804. His birthplace, Cherryburn, Mickley, Northumberland, is a museum of wood engraving, with many of his original blocks□

Bexhill seaside resort in E Sussex, England, SW of Hastings; population 33 000□

Bexley borough of Greater London.
features river Thames in N; Thamesmead, a model community on reclaimed marshland
population 217 000□

Bèziers industrial town in France; population 82 000. It is a centre of the wine and spirit trade□

bèzique card game resembling whist◊□

Bhagalpur city in E Bihar, India; population 172 700□

Bhagavad-gita religious and philosophical poem (The Song of the Blessed) forming an episode in the sixth book of the *Mahabharata*◊; it is the supreme religious work of Hinduism□

bhang see cannabis◊□

Bharat Hindi name for India□

Bhatpara city in W Bengal, India; population 205 000. It has jute industries□

Bhavnagar port in Gujerat, India; population 226 000. There are textile industries□

Bhopal industrial city, capital of Madhya Pradesh, India; population 392 000. Nearby Bhimbetka Caves, discovered 1973, have the world's largest collection of prehistoric paintings which are about 10 000 years old. In 1984 poisonous vapours from a Union Carbide pesticide plant killed at least 2000, and injured 200 000□

Bhubaneswar capital of Orissa, India; population 105 000. It has many temples and is a noted centre of Siva◊ worship□

Bhumibol Adulyadej 1927– . King of Thailand. He succeeded on the assassination of his brother in 1946, and in 1973 ended a long sequence of army-dominated regimes by overthrowing Field Marshal Kittachorn.□

Bhutan Kingdom of

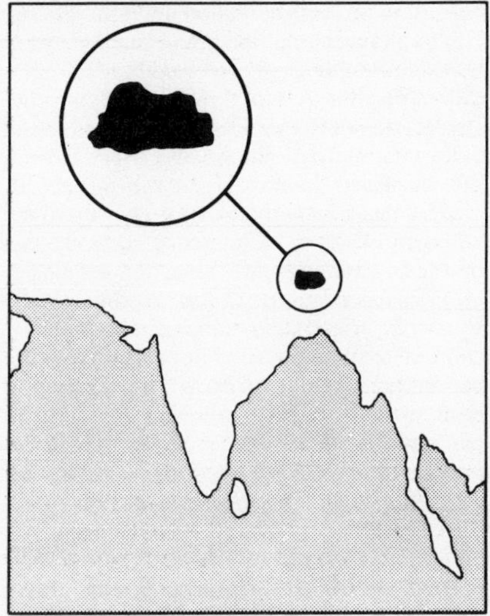

area 46 600 sq km/18 000 sq mi
capital Thimphu
features occupies southern slopes of the Himalayas, and is cut by valleys of tributaries of the Brahmaputra
exports timber, minerals
currency ngultrum; also Indian currency
population 1 400 000
language Dzongkha (a Tibetan dialect), Nepali and English, all official
religion Mahayana Buddhism
government democratic monarchy (King Jigme Singye Wangchuck 1955– , succeeded 1972), with a National Assembly, two-thirds elected.
recent history Treaties of 1865 and 1910 with the British government were replaced on independence in 1949 by one with India, under which Bhutan receives a subsidy and is guided in external relations by the Indian government□

Bhutto Zulficar Ali 1928–79. Pakistani statesman, who was president 1971–3, and then Prime Minister until the 1977 military coup. In 1978 he was sentenced to death for conspiracy to murder a political opponent, and was hanged. His followers, led by his daughter ***Benzair Bhutto,*** continue in opposition to the new regime□

Biafra republic proclaimed by Colonel Odunmegwu Ojukwu in the predominantly Ibo eastern region of Nigeria in 1967. It ceased to exist in 1970 at the end of a bitter civil war□

Biafra Bight of. See Bonny◊□

Bialystok industrial city in Poland, NE of Warsaw; population 626 000□

Biarritz seaside resort in SW France; population 2700. It was popularized by Queen Victoria and Edward VII□

Biber Heinrich von 1644–1704. Bohemian composer, conductor at the archbishop of Salzburg's court. A virtuoso violinist, he composed sonatas, and his church music includes a requiem□

Bible the authorized documentation (Greek *ta biblia* 'the books') of the Christian and Jewish religions. It comprises the ***Old Testament*** books recognized by both Jews and Christians (the first five are traditionally ascribed to Moses and known as the Pentateuch); ***Apocryrypha*** books not included in the final Hebrew canon, but recognized by Roman Catholics, though segregated or omitted in Protestant bibles, and the ***New Testament*** books recognized by the Christian Church from the 4th century as canonical. See Dead◊ Sea Scrolls, Gospel◊□

bicarbonate of soda sodium hydrogen carbonate, $NaHCO_3$, a weak base, used in indigestion tablets, baking powder, and fizzy drinks□

bicycle a two-wheeled vehicle with pedals. The first pedal-bicycle was invented by the Scotsman Kirkpatrick Macmillan c1840, pneumatic tyres being added from 1846, and by 1888 these had been improved by J B Dunlop to boost the cycling craze of the turn of the century. Design changes were then minor until the small-wheeled Moulton after World War II.

Racing is on tracks; or cyclocross across country; or along strenuous road routes, e.g. the annual ***Tour de France*** established 1903 for professional cyclists (variable route of c4000 km/2400 mi, covered in three weeks, and always ending in Paris), and in which the rider with the shortest overall time at the close of each day's stage wears a yellow jersey. Britain's ***Milk Race*** is a less prestigious version□

Bideford port in N Devon, England; population 11 000. It was the home of Sir Richard Grenville◊□

Biedermeier German style of art (naturalistic) and furniture (conventional) in the first half of the 19th century, so named from Gottlieb Biedermeier, a fictional character embodying bourgeois taste□

Biel industrial town (French *Bienne*) in Switzerland; population 90 000□

Bielefeld industrial town in N Rhine-Westphalia, W Germany; population 313 000□

Bierce Ambrose 1842–1914. American writer and newspaperman. He served with the Union army in the Civil◊ War; showed his mastery of supernatural and psychological horror in *Tales of Soldiers and Civilians* 1891 and *Can Such Things Be?* 1893; and disappeared during the Mexican Civil War when he was attached to Villa◊'s force□

bigamy offence, punishable with seven years imprisonment, of marrying another person when one's husband or wife is still alive, and the marriage has been neither annulled nor dissolved□

big bang See universe◊□

Big Ben the bell, not as in popular usage the clock to which it belongs, in the clock tower of the Houses of Parliament, Westminster. Cast in 1858, it was named after Sir Benjamin Hall, First Commissioner of Works at the time, and weighs 13 700 kg/13.5 tons□

Bight a coastal indentation, such as the Bight of Bonny◊ and Great Australian Bight◊□

Bihar N state of India.
area 173 876 sq km/67 132 sq mi
capital Patna
features India's richest iron producing area; the ancient kingdom of Magadha roughly corresponded to central and southern Bihar (see Maurya◊ dynasty, and Patna◊), and many incidents in Buddha◊'s life took place here
population 61 800 000
language Hindi
famous people Chandragupta, Asoka□

Bikaner industrial city in Rajasthan, India; population 189 000□

Bikini see Marshall Islands◊□

Biko Steve 1946–79. S African 'black consciousness' leader. He founded the South African Students' Organization (SASO) 1968, was arrested 1977, and died of injuries received in detention□

Bilbao industrial (iron and steel) port in the Basque Country; population 433 000. Iron ore is exported□

bilberry see Vaccinium◊□

bile brownish fluid secreted by the liver of vertebrates and stored in the gall bladder, a small pear-shaped bag on its under-surface; it plays an important role in the digestive processes of the intestines□

bilharzia see schistosomiasis◊□

billiards game played with cues and composition balls (one red, two white) on a rectangular table covered with a green cloth, and with six pockets, one at each corner and in each of the long sides. The world's greatest player was Walter Lindrum, whose phenomenal skill helped to kill the game in favour of pool, in which there is a greater element of chance; the most popular form of the latter is snooker◊□

Billingham see Stockton-on-Tees◊□

Billingsgate fish market in the Isle of Dogs, London. Near London Bridge 9th century–1981, its building (designed by Sir Horace Jones 1875) was preserved□

billion in Britain a million million; in the USA a thousand million (the equivalent of a British billion being called a milliard)□

Bill of Rights Act of 1689 embodying the Declaration of Rights presented by the House of Commons to William◊ and Mary before they replaced James◊ II on the throne. It made illegal the suspension of laws by royal authority without Parliament's consent; the power to dispense with laws; the establishment of special courts of law; levying money by royal prerogative without Parliament's consent; a standing army in peacetime without Parliament's consent. It also asserted a right to petition the sovereign, freedom of parliamentary elections, freedom of speech in parliamentary debates, and the necessity of frequent parliaments. See constitution◊□

Bill of Rights American. The first ten amendments (1791) to the American constitution:
1 freedom of worship, speech, the press, assembly and to petition the government;
2 the right to keep and bear arms (which has hindered modern attempts to control illicit use of arms);
3 covers the conditions for billeting soldiers in private homes;

4 regulations for the rights of search and seizure;
5 none to be 'deprived of life, liberty or property without due process of law' or be compelled in any criminal case to be a witness against himself (frequently quoted in the McCarthy◊ era);
6 the right to speedy trial, call witnesses, and have defence counsel, etc;
7 the right to trial by jury;
8 excessive bail or fines or 'cruel and unusual punishment' not to be inflicted (used in recent times to oppose the death penalty);
9 and *10* safeguard to the states and people all rights not specifically delegated to the central government□

Billy the Kid nickname of American Wild West 'hero', William H Bonney 1859–81. A leader in the Lincoln County cattle war in New Mexico, he was sentenced to death for murdering a sheriff. He escaped, killing two guards, but was later shot□

Biloxi fishing port with a large canning industry (shrimps, oysters, etc.), Mississippi, USA; population 48 500□

binary number system system in which numbers are represented by the digits 0 and 1 by using combinations of successive powers of 2 (1,2,4,8,16, etc.), as against the decimal system in which successive powers of 10 (1,10,100,1000,etc) are used. Thus the decimal number 5 would be written as 101, meaning $(1 \times 4) + (0 \times 2) + (1 \times 1)$. It is widely used in computers, because electrically 0 can be read as 'off' and 1 as 'on'□

binary star see under star◊□

bindweed see convolvulus◊□

bingo game played with cards divided into randomly numbered squares. As numbers are called, the players mark off the appropriate squares until one has a complete line or 'full house' (hence the alternative name 'housey-housey'), and receives a prize□

binturong a mammal related to the Civet◊ family□

Binyon Laurence 1869–1943. British poet, best remembered for his ode 'For the Fallen' 1914□

Bio-bio longest river in Chile; 370 km/ 230 m. The name is a native language term 'much water'□

biochemistry science concerned with the chemistry of living materials and processes□

bioeconomics theory of Chicago economist Gary Becker 1979 that the concepts of sociobiology◊ also apply in economics. The competitiveness and self-interest built into human genes make capitalism an effective economic system, whereas the selflessness and collectivism proclaimed as the socialist ideal are contrary to human genetic make-up and so produce an ineffective system□

biological warfare use of living organisms, or of infectious material derived from them, to bring about death or disease in man, animals, or plants. It was condemned by the Geneva Convention 1925, to which the United Nations has urged all states to adhere. See also chemical◊ warfare□

biology the scientific study of living things. There are two main components: zoology◊, the study of animals; and botany◊, the study of plants□

bioluminescence see chemiluminescence◊ □

biopsy removal of tissue from a living body for the purpose of diagnostic examination□

bio-rhythms three rhythmical cycles which some theorists claim remain unchanged throughout human life: the ***intellectual*** (33 days), the ***emotional*** (28 days), and the ***physical*** (23 days). The day when any of these passes from its positive to its regenerative stage is regarded as critical, especially if one coincides with that of another cycle. In USA and Japan commercial firms are claimed to have used the theory successfully in reducing accident rates by special precautions on critical days□

biosphere or ***ecosphere*** region of earth's surface (land and water) and the atmosphere above it, which can be occupied by living organisms. Each planet and star may have a biosphere□

biotechnology industrial processing of materials by biological agents, such as microorganisms, to create various products and services, e.g. a biofuel (such as methane◊), can be made from biodegradable waste, and a food product, such as single cell protein◊, can be made from methanol (made from methane). A service, such as the more effective displacement of oil from deep wells, may be secured by the use of microbial polysaccharides◊□

birch genus of trees *Betula*, family Betulaceae, native to cool N temperate areas and valued for their quick-growing, durable timber; the bark is used for tanning and dyeing leather; e.g. ***silver birch*** *B pendulata*, and the N American ***paper birch*** *B papyrifera*□

Birch John M 1918–45. American Baptist missionary, commissioned by the USAF to carry out intelligence work behind the Chinese lines, where he was killed by the Communists; the US ultra-nationalist John Birch Society 1958 is named after him□

bird
crown
beak
nape
throat
back
rump
breast
wing
feet
tail
Struthioniformes
ostrich
Rheiformes
rhea
Casuariformes
cassowary
emu
Apterygiformes
kiwi
Tinamiformes
tinamidae
Podicipediformes
grebe
Procellariformes
petrel
Sphenisciforme
penguin
Pelicaniformes
pelican
Anseriformes
goose
Falconiformes
falcon
Ciconiiformes
stork
Galliformes
pheasant
Gruiformes
crane
Charadriformes
plover
Gaviformes
diver
Columbiformes
pigeon
Psittaciformes
parrot
Cuciliformes
cuckoo
Strigiformes
owl
Caprimulgiformes
nightjar
Apodiformes
swift
Coliformes
mousebird
Trogoniformes
trogon
Coraciiformes
kingfisher
Piciformes
woodpecker
Passeriformes
apapane
thrush

bird class, Aves, of warm-blooded, feather-bearing, egg-laying vertebrates, adapted for flight by having wings and feathers, identified by the vast range of colours (female usually more dull e.g. brown) for the breast, crown, wings etc. The shape of the beak reveals if the bird digs for grubs in the sand and mud of a river bed or catches flies etc. Birds of prey hover and then swoop, whereas a heron flies straight with its long legs trailing out behind. These long legs are for wading; other birds have webbed feet or claws. Each bird is adapted to its own environment. They have the same arrangement of reproductive and excretory organs, and pattern of embryonic growth as reptiles, and may have evolved from them, or via the dinosaurs◊. See Archaeopteryx◊, Teratorn◊.

The body temperature is higher than that of mammals at 41°C/105.8°F. Their life-span is shorter, averaging two to six years.

Birds generally moult twice yearly; have elaborate courtship displays, and establish a nesting territory. Many are migratory (see migration◊). Most British birds lay two to five eggs but only one or two young survive to adulthood due to predators, migration problems, or winter hardship.

The following simple classification of orders ranges approximately from the most 'primitive' to the most 'advanced', with the 'type' bird in bold letters

Struthioniformes ***ostrich***
Rheiformes ***rhea***
Casuariformes ***cassowary*** emu
Apterygiformes ***kiwi*** moa (extinct)
Tinamiformes ***tinamou***
The above five orders are the flightless 'running birds'
Podicipediformes ***grebe***
Procellariformes ***petrel*** albatross, shear-water
Sphenisciformes ***penguin***
Pelecaniformes ***pelican*** booby, cormorant
Anseriformes ***goose*** duck, swan
Falconiformes ***falcon*** eagle, hawk, vulture
Ciconiiformes ***stork*** heron, ibis, spoonbill
Galliformes ***pheasant*** grouse, ptarmigan, turkey, hoatzin
Gruiformes ***crane*** bustard, coot, rail
Charadriformes ***plover*** auk, avocet, gull, puffin
Gaviformes ***diver***
Columbiformes ***pigeon*** dodo (extinct), dove
Psittaciformes ***parrot*** cockatoo
Cuculiformes ***cuckoo*** roadrunner
Strigiformes ***owl***
Caprimulgiformes ***nightjar*** frogmouth
Apodiformes ***swift*** hummingbird
Coliformes ***mousebird***
Trogoniformes ***trogon***
Coraciiformes ***roller*** kingfisher, hoopoe, hornbill
Piciformes ***woodpecker*** honey guide, toucan
Passeriformes ***sparrow*** bird of paradise, crow, honey eater, jay, lark, lyrebird, shrike, starling, swallow, thrush, tit, warbler, wren
The passerines or perching birds form the largest and most varied of all the orders□

bird-eating spider see spider◊□

bird of paradise various species of bird in the family Paradiseidae, order Passeriformes, native to New Guinea and neighbouring islands. The drab females show the family's close relationship with the crows, but the males have beautifully coloured fountain-like plumes, used in courtship display. Hunted almost to extinction for their plumage, they are now being actively conserved□

Birkenhead Frederick Edwin Smith, 1st Earl of Birkenhead 1872–1930. British Conservative politician. A flamboyant character, known as 'FE', he joined with Carson◊ in organizing armed resistance in Ulster to Irish Home Rule; was Lord Chancellor 1919–22, and a much-criticized Secretary for India 1924–8□

Birkenhead seaport in Merseyside, England; population 137 000. It specializes in bulk cargoes, and is linked by road and rail tunnels with Liverpool across the Mersey estuary□

Birmingham second largest city of the UK, in the West Midlands; population 1 062 000. Noted for its National Exhibition Centre at Bickenhill 1976 and the Bull Ring shopping centre. There are two universities (Birmingham and Aston), the latter linked with a successful science◊ park; a school of music and symphony orchestra; and the refurbished Hippodrome, with a growing ballet tradition. The art gallery and museum has a Pre-Raphaelite collection; and at the Midlands Art Centre the public practise arts and crafts. The repertory theatre was founded 1913 by Sir Barry Jackson 1897–1961 (rehoused 1971). There is a plaque on the house where Lawn Tennis was invented. Sutton Park, in the residential suburb of Sutton Coldfield, has been a public country recreational area since the 16th century. Industries include cars, passenger and commercial vehicles (British Leyland is at Longbridge), machine tools, aerospace control systems, plastics, chemicals, food products, and jewellery. The international airport at Elmdon to the south is linked with a freeport◊□

Birmingham largest city in Alabama, USA; population 282 000. It is the industrial heart of the southern USA, with iron, steel, chemical, building material and textile industries but the biggest money-spinner is the Universities of Alabama's Medical Center□

Biro Lazlo 1900–85. Hungarian-born Argentinian inventor of a ballpoint pen in 1944. His name became generic for ballpoint pens□

Birobijan capital of the Jewish Autonomous Region (sometimes also called Birobijan), E USSR; population 67 000□

birth control see contraception◊□

birthmark mark, consisting of an abnormal layer of fine blood vessels lying within the deeper skin layers. Smooth marks respond well to argon laser beam treatment in which the beam is absorbed only by the red blood cells in the vessels of the mark; this causes the blood to clot, so that the blood vessels then seal up and disappear□

Birtwhistle Harrison 1934– . British composer and clarinetist. He has specialized in chamber music (opera *Punch and Judy* 1967), and experimented in electronic music□

Biscay Bay of. Bay of the Atlantic between N Spain and W France, famous for rough seas and exceptionally high tides□

bise see under wind◊□

bisexuality in general terms the co-existence of male and female attitudes in all human beings, and in particular the practice of both homosexual and heterosexual relationships□

bishop clergyman (Greek 'overseer') next in rank to an archbishop◊ in the Roman Catholic, Greek Orthodox and Anglican Churches. Originally, they were chosen by the congregation, but in the Roman Catholic Church are appointed by the Pope, although in some countries, such as Spain, the political authority nominates appointees. In the Greek Orthodox Church bishops must be unmarried, and so are always monks. In the Church of England the Prime Minister selects bishops on the advice of the Archbishop of Canterbury; when a diocese is very large, assistant (suffragan) bishops are appointed□

Bishop Sir Henry Rowley 1786–1855. British composer of the song 'Home Sweet Home'□

Bishop William Avery 1894–1956. Canadian air ace, who won the VC in 1917.

Biskra oasis town in Algeria on the edge of the Sahara; population 60 000□

Bisley village in Surrey, England, site of National Rifle Association events and forces competitions since 1890□

Bismarck Otto Eduard Leopold, Prince von Bismarck 1815–98. German statesman. Ambitious to establish Prussia's hegemony inside Germany and eliminate the influence of Austria, he became Foreign Minister in 1862. He secured Austria's support for his successful war of 1863–4 against Denmark, then in 1866 went to war against Austria and her allies, his victory forcing Austria out of the German Bund, and unifying the N German states in the N German Confederation under his own chancellorship in 1867. He then defeated France, under Napoleon III, in the Franco-Prussian War of 1870, proclaimed the German Empire in 1871, and annexed Alsace◊-Lorraine. He tried to secure his work by a Triple Alliance (1881) with Austria and Italy, but ran into difficulties at home with the Roman Catholic Church and the Socialist movement, and was dismissed by William II in 1890. See Congress of Berlin◊□

Bismarck Archipelago

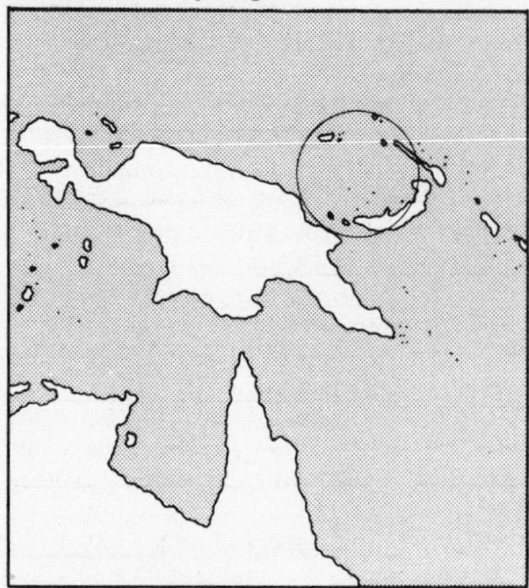

group of over 200 islands in SW Pacific, part of Papua◊ New Guinea; area 49 660 sq km/19 200 sq mi. Largest island New Britain, chief town Rabaul□

bismuth element

symbol Bi

atomic number 83

features poor conductor of heat and electricity

uses used in alloys of low melting point, and in medical compounds to soothe gastric ulcers, etc.□

bison genus of cattle◊, formerly wild, but now existing only in protected herds. The ***European wisent*** *Bison bonasus* is about 2 m/6 ft high, and weighs a tonne. The ***American 'buffalo'*** *Bison bison* is slightly smaller, but with heavier mane, and of the same brown colour. Crossed with domestic cattle, the latter has produced a hardy modern hybrid, the ***beefalo***, producing a lean carcass on an economical grass diet□

Bissau capital and chief port of Guinea-Bissau; population 65 000□

Bitolj town (formerly Monastir) in Macedonia, S Yugoslavia; population 65 850□

bittern genus of birds *Botaurus* in the heron family Ardeidae. The typical ***European bittern*** *B stellaris* has a curious 'booming' call□

bittersweet see nightshade◊□

bitumen impure mixture of naturally occurring hydrocarbons (including petroleum, asphalt and natural gas), though the word is often restricted to a soft pitch◊ used in road surfacing□

bivalve marine or freshwater mollusc◊ of class Bivalvia. The body is enclosed between two hinged shells. They include:

Clam includes the marine edible English ***gaper*** *Mya truncata* and the N American ***hard shell clam*** *Venus mercenaria* used in clam chowder and formerly as money (*wampum*) by the Indians. The tropical ***giant clam*** *Tridacna gigas* may weigh 225 kg/500 lb, and is c1.5 m/4.5 ft across; if the valves close on a diver's foot, he may not be able to free himself.

Cockle family Cardiidae, with ribbed, heart-shaped shells, e.g. European ***common cockle*** *Cardium edule*, gathered from the sands for food

Mussel family Mytilidae, includes the blue-black ***edible mussel*** *Mytilus edulis* found in clusters attached to rocks in the N Atlantic and Mediterranean. The freshwater ***pearl mussel*** family Unionidae, includes *Unio margaritiferus* found in N American and European rivers. The ***green-lipped mussel*** found only off New Zealand, supplies an extract useful in treating arthritis.

Oyster marine species with a concave lower valve and flat upper one, joined by a ligament. Oysters are remarkable for their changes of sex, which may alternate annually or more frequently, and by the number of their eggs, sometimes a million at one spawning. Commercially exploited food species, family Ostreidae, includes the ***European oyster*** *Ostrea edulis* farmed at Whitstable, Kent, Colchester, etc. and the ***American oyster*** *O virginica* of the Atlantic coast. The pearl◊ oyster belongs to family Aviculidae.

Teredo the ***shipworm*** eg *Teredo navalis* family Teredinidae, which is wormlike, and has teeth on the two valves of its shell to rasp tunnels through timber; it was a menace in the days of wooden sailing ships□

Bizerta port in Tunisia, with metal and oil industries□

Bizet Georges 1838–75. French composer. His operatic masterpiece *Carmen*, on a libretto based on Prosper Mérimée's story, was produced a few months before his death in 1875, and was initially a failure□

black term used in UK and US to describe non-white ethnic minorities; a socio-political category□

Black Sir James 1924– . British physiologist, director of therapeutic research at Wellcome Laboratories from 1978. He was active in the development of beta-blockers◊, and the anti-ulcer drug Tagamet. Knighted 1981□

Black-and-Tans nickname (from the colours of their uniforms) of the specially raised military police force used by the British 1920–1 to combat Sinn Fein in Ireland□

blackberry edible fruit of the N temperate prickly ***bramble*** *Rubus fruticosus*, family Rosaceae. In fact the fruit is not a berry but a group of succulent drupels◊□

blackbird British resident bird *Turdus merula* in the thrush family Turdidae; the male is coal-black with yellow bill and eyelids, and the female dark brown. Its magnificent song is perfected over several years□

blackbirding the slave trade in South Sea Islanders (Kanakas – Hawaian 'man') for plantation labour in Queensland and Fiji 1860–1900□

black box popular name for the robust box, usually orange-painted for easy recovery, containing an aeroplane's flight and voice recorders, monitoring the plane's behaviour and the crew's conversation, thus providing valuable clues as to the cause of a disaster□

Blackburn town in Lancashire, England; population 142 900. Noted for mechanical and electrical engineering□

blackcap see warbler◊□

blackcock see under fowl◊□

Black Country central area of England, focused on Birmingham, which became the county of W Midlands 1974; so known from its chimneys formerly belching black smoke□

Black Death epidemic of bubonic plague◊ (or possibly anthrax◊) which spread from China to devastate Europe, up to half England's population dying 1348–9; the last outbreak in London was the Great Plague of 1665, when 100 000 of the 400 000 population died□

black earth fertile soil belt stretching from Czechoslovakia to NE China□

black economy the hidden economy of a country, which includes undeclared earnings from a second job ('moonlighting'), enjoyment of undervalued goods and services (company 'perks'), etc, designed for tax evasion purposes□

Blackett Patrick Maynard Stuart, Baron Blackett 1897–1974. British physicist, awarded a Nobel prize 1948 for his work on cosmic radiation□

Blackfoot group of Plains Indians◊, so-called because of their black mocassins: they now live in Saskatchewan□

Black Forest (German) mountainous tourist region of coniferous forest in Baden-Württemberg, W Germany, now greatly affected by virus disease□

Blackheath English common which gives its name to a residential suburb of London, partly in Greenwich, partly in Lewisham; Wat Tyler◊ encamped here 1381□

black hole a concentration of matter in space whose particles are so densely packed that nothing, including light, can escape from it, owing to the strength of its gravitational pull. It is estimated that a spoonful of such matter would weigh millions of tonnes. Any matter in the vicinity of a black hole is sucked into it and never seen again; for such a victim time is distorted by being stretched out, so that a second lasts a billion years.

General Relativity◊ theory predicts that black holes should form by spontaneous contraction of stars of mass above about 1.5 times that of the sun, when their thermonuclear fires have burnt out. However, by applying quantum mechanics◊, Stephen Hawking◊ has predicted that there may also exist huge numbers of microscopic black holes, which would glow brillantly, radiating energy and shrinking still further until they exploded in sub-atomic debris□

blackmail the criminal offence of demanding money, etc, with menaces of violence and other injury, or of exposure of some misconduct on the part of the victim (from French *maille* rent, paid in labour or base coin); punishable with 14 years imprisonment□

black market illegal trade in food or other rationed goods, e.g. petrol, clothing, during World War II and after□

Blackmore Richard Doddridge 1825–1900. British novelist, e.g. *Lorna Doone* 1869, set on 17th century Exmoor: see Doone◊□

Black Mountains group of hills in S Powys, Wales, overlooking the Wye Valley and honeycombed with caves discovered in 1966□

Black Muslim a black adherent of a variant of Islam practised in the USA from the 1930s; the movement first advocated creation of a separate black state in the USA. The movement grew rapidly from 1946, when it was joined by the charismatic Malcolm◊ X□

Black National State an area set aside in the Republic of S Africa for development to full self-government by black Africans in accordance with the theory of plural democracy (see Apartheid◊): before 1980 these states were known as Black Homelands or Bantustans. They comprise less than 14% of the country; tend to be in arid areas, though some have mineral wealth; and may be in scattered 'blocks'. Those which have so far reached nominal independence are Transkei 1976, Bophuthatswana 1977, Venda 1979, Ciskei 1981. They are not recognized outside S Africa because of their racial basis, and 11 million blacks live permanently in white-designated areas of South Africa□

Blackpool seaside resort in Lancashire, England; population 147 300. There are 11 km/7 mi of promenade, with celebrated 'illuminations' of coloured lights, funfairs, and a tower 152 m/500 ft high□

Black Power concept developed by blacks in the USA in the 1960s that equal rights with whites should be fought for by the use of all political and economic means, the abandonment of non-violence when under attack, and the demand for the creation of a separate black state by plebiscite under United Nations auspices. It was rejected by Martin Luther King◊, but adopted by the ***Black Panther Party*** founded 1966 by Huey Newton and Bobby Seale. See Black Muslim◊□

Black Prince see Edward◊ the Black Prince, eldest son of Edward III of England□

Black Sea

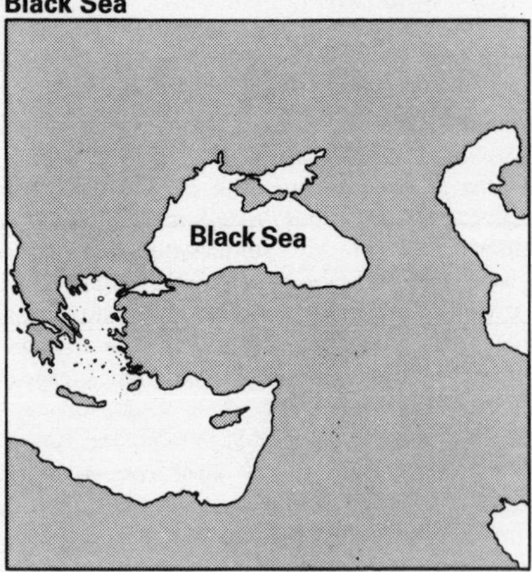

inland sea in SE Europe, linked with the seas of Azov◊ and Marmara◊, and via the Dardanelles◊ with the Mediterranean. Uranium deposits beneath it are among the world's largest□

Blackshirts see Nazi◊ Party, Fascism◊□

Blackstone Sir William 1723–80. British jurist, author of *Commentaries on the Laws of England* 1765–9□

blackthorn densely branched spiny bush, *Prunus spinosa*, family Rosaceae, with white blossom on black and as yet leafless branches. The sour blue-black fruit sloe is used to flavour sloe gin□

Black Thursday the day of the Wall Street stock market crash 29 Oct 1929, which was followed by the worst depression in American history□

blackwater fever form of malaria in which the urine is a reddish brown because of blood content□

Blackwell Elizabeth 1821–1910. First British woman doctor; taken to the USA when 11, she qualified there in 1849, and was admitted to the English register in 1859□

black widow a type of spider◊□

Blake Robert 1599–1657. British admiral. Appointed 'general at sea' for the Parliamentary◊ forces in 1649, he destroyed Prince Rupert◊'s fleet off Cartagena in 1650. In 1652 he won several engagements against the Dutch before being defeated by Tromp◊ off Dungeness, and revenged himself in 1653 by defeating the Dutchman off Portsmouth and the N Foreland. In 1654 he bombarded Tunis, the stronghold of the Barbary corsairs◊ and in 1657 captured the Spanish treasure-fleet in Santa Cruz□

Blake William 1757–1827. British poet-artist. Born in Soho, London, he was apprenticed to an engraver 1771–8, and studied at the Royal Academy under Reynolds◊, of whom he formed a very low opinion. His works, for which he engraved both text and illustrations himself, embody his own mystic mythology, and include *Songs of Innocence* 1789, *The Marriage of Heaven and Hell* 1793, *Songs of Experience* 1794, and *Milton* 1804 (his most famous lines 'And did those feet in ancient time', set to music by Parry◊, are taken from the preface). He also produced illustrations for *Paradise Lost*, *The Book of Job*, and Dante◊'s *Divina Comedia*□

Blamey Sir Thomas Albert 1884–1951. First Australian field marshal 1950; he was Commander-in-Chief of the Allied Land Forces in the SW Pacific 1942–5□

Blanc Louis 1811–82. French socialist. In 1839 he founded the *Revue du Progrès,* advocating co-operative workshops, etc□

Blanqui Louis Auge 1805–81. French revolutionary politician who formulated the theory of the 'dictatorship of the proletariat', used by Marx◊□

Blantyre parish on the Lanarkshire coalfield, Strathclyde, Scotland; the birthplace of David Livingstone◊ is preserved□

Blantyre-Limbe chief industrial-commercial centre of Malawi, formed by the union 1959 of Blantyre (named after Livingstone's birthplace) and Limbe (site of the University of Malawi); population 228 500□

Blarney town in Cork, Republic of Ireland; population 1130. The ***Blarney Stone***, reputed to give those kissing it persuasive speech, is inset in the castle wall□

Blashford-Snell John 1936– . British soldier-explorer, who made the first descent of the Blue Nile 1968; crossed the Americas, Alaska–Cape Horn 1971–2; and first navigated the entire Zaire river 1974–5□

blasphemy written or spoken insult, (Greek 'evil-speaking'), directed against God, religious beliefs or sacred things, with deliberate intent to outrage belief. In the UK it has been recommended by the Law Commission that it should cease to be a crime, though the law as regards abusive and insulting behaviour in places of worship should be strengthened□

Blaue Reiter Der. German art movement 1911–14, named from *Der blaue Reiter/The Blue Rider* by Kandinsky◊, averse to academic rule and proclaiming the artist's 'inner necessity' for expression. See also die Brücke◊□

Blavatsky Helena Petrovna 1831–91. Russian mystic, founder of the Theosophical Society (see Theosophy◊) 1875, which has its headquarters near Madras. Her books include *Isis Unveiled* 1877 and *The Secret Doctrine* 1888□

bleaching decolorization of coloured materials by the use of hydrogen peroxide, calcium oxychloride (bleaching powder) which liberates sulphur dioxide, or the ultra-violet rays in sunshine. Bleaching agents attack only a small part of the highly complex molecule of natural or chemical colouring matter which produces the actual colour, resulting in a colourless substance similar in chemical structure□

bleak a type of freshwater fish; see under carp◊□

Blenheim German village in Bavaria, near which Marlborough defeated the French and Bavarians on 13 Aug 1704. See Nicholas Hawksmoor◊, Duke of Marlborough◊, Sir John Vanbrugh◊, and Woodstock◊□

Blenheim centre of a sheep-grazing area in the NE of South Island, New Zealand; population 15 000□

blenny a type of small coastal fish; see under perch◊□

Blériot Louis 1872–1936. French aviator, who constructed a monoplane and made the first flight across the English Channel 25 Jul 1909□

Bligh William 1754–1817. British admiral, who accompanied Captain Cook in his second voyage 1772–4, and in 1787 commanded HMS *Bounty* on an expedition to the Pacific. On the return voyage in 1789 the crew mutinied and cast Bligh adrift, with 18 men, in a boat. The mutineers settled in Tahiti and on Pitcairn◊. He was appointed Governor of New South Wales in 1805, where his excessive discipline again led to mutiny in 1808, but he was promoted to admiral on returning to England in 1811□

blight number of plant diseases caused mainly by parasitic species of fungi◊, mainly Erysipaceae, which produce a whitish appearance on leaf and stem surfaces e.g. ***potato blight*** *Phytophthora infestans.* General damage caused by aphids, pollution, etc. to plants is sometimes called blight□

Blighty popular name for England among British troops in World War I, Hindi *bitayati* 'foreign' land□

blimp term for a barrage balloon. British lighter than air aircraft were divided in World War I into A-rigid, and B-limp (i.e. without rigid internal framework), a barrage balloon therefore becoming known as a blimp. Low◊, the cartoonist, adopted the name for his stuffy character Colonel Blimp□

blind cave fish Mexican freshwater fish *Anoptichthys jordani*, family Characidae (see Characin◊) which has its eyes overgrown by its own flesh soon after hatching□

blindness complete absence of sight. Also used to describe impairment of sight to a degree that precludes normal education or normal employment; in effect, someone who may see clearly at 3 m/10 ft in comparison to 60 m/200 ft for a normal-sighted person.It may be caused by heredity, accident, disease, deterioration with age, etc. Aids to the blind include the use of the Braille◊ or Moon◊ alphabet in reading, or of electronic devices which convert print to recognizable mechanical speech; guide dogs and sonic torches which warn of objects in the way more adequately than a white stick□

blindworm a type of lizard◊□

Bliss Sir Arthur 1891–1975. British composer, Master of the Queen's Musick from 1953. His works include music for the ballet *Checkmate* 1937 and for the film *The Shape of Things to Come* 1935□

blister beetle a type of beetle◊□

blitzkrieg (German 'lightning') military campaigns, as in 1939–41, when Hitler's Germany conquered Poland, France, Yugoslavia, and Greece, and advanced to Moscow□

Bloch Felix 1905–83. American physicist, winner in 1952 of a joint Nobel prize with E M Purcell for work on nuclear magnetic resonance (NMR). As a medical diagnostic method, it was revolutionary in avoiding dangerous radiation and painful injections□

Bloemfontein capital of the Orange Free State, S Africa; population 180 200. Founded in 1846, it was taken by Lord Roberts in 1900 during the South African War, and has been the seat of the S African Supreme Court since 1910□

Blois town in central France; population 45 000. The chateau was a royal residence in the 15–17th centuries, and the 3rd Duke of Guise◊ was assassinated there□

Blok Alexander Alexandrovich 1880–1921. Chief poet of the Russian Symbolist◊ school, who backed the 1917 Revolution, as in his most famous poems *The Twelve* 1918, and *The Scythians* 1918, the latter appealing to the West to join in the revolutionary process□

Blondin Charles. Assumed name of the French tightrope-walker Jean François Gravelet 1824–97. He crossed Niagara Falls in 1859□

blood circulation

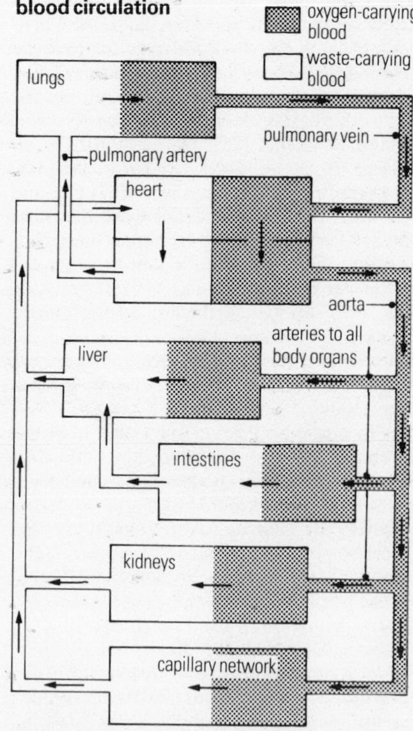

blood fluid circulating through the heart and blood vessels of humans and higher animals. It consists of a colourless plasma, red and white blood cells, hormones, proteins, etc. Its purpose is to carry oxygen from the lungs to all parts of the body and to remove waste material. It is the red cells, rich in haemoglobin, which act as the oxygen carriers. The white cells are part of the defence system, attacking bacteria. Another important constituent is fibrinogen, which causes clotting. Blood in humans is maintained at 37 C/98.4 F, and the human body contains approximately 5.5 litres/10pints□

blood circulation blood is pumped round the body by the heart. After taking up oxygen in the lungs, the blood is pumped into the right side of the heart via the pulmonary vein. It then leaves through the aorta (the main artery) and is distributed throughout the body using a network of arteries and capillaries (see blood vessel◊). Oxygen is absorbed by the organs (e.g. liver, stomach, etc.) which in turn release their waste matter (e.g. carbon dioxide) into the veins. The carbon dioxide laden blood is pumped back into the left side of the heart (via the vena cava), out again (via the pulmonary artery) to the lungs in order to lose the carbon dioxide and absorb oxygen again. A one-way system is maintained by a series of non-return valves; two in the heart, one each in the pulmonary artery and the aorta, plus several in all the body's veins□

blood groups genetically determined types of human blood labelled according to the factors which will cause the red blood cells to cohere to each other: there are four main types A, B, AB, and O. The distinction is vital in transfusions and transplants to avoid this cohesion, and ensure that patient and donor are compatible. The most usual types are A and O. See antibody◊, rhesus factor◊□

bloodhound a breed of dog◊□

blood poisoning infection caused by bacteria or bacterial toxins present in the blood (septicaemia); treatment is by large doses of antibiotics□

blood pressure the pressure in the blood vessels. Measured by a sphygmomanometer, which records the pressure needed to stop the flow of blood in an artery. High blood pressure is sometimes caused by arteriosclerosis◊, and brings with it the danger of cerebral haemorrhage◊, etc. Persistently low blood pressure is also indicative of ill-health□

blood vessel a muscular tube in the body containing blood. Arteries carry the oxygen - rich blood from the lungs via the heart to all parts of the body. Veins complete the circuit, carrying the waste, e.g. carbon dioxide, back to the lungs. The arteries are bright red in colour whilst the veins are a darker red. Capillaries are the smaller tubes found at the junction of an artery vein and any organ.□

Bloomer Amelia Jenks 1818–94. American advocate of women's rights, who introduced c1849 a knee-length skirt combined with loose trousers gathered at the ankles□

Bloomsbury see Camden◊□

Blow John 1648–1708. English composer, who influenced his pupil, Purcell◊, and wrote the anthem 'I was glad when they said unto me' and the masque *Venus and Adonis*□

blowfly a type of fly◊□

Blücher Gebhard Leberecht von 1742–1819. Prussian field marshal who shared with Wellington the triumph over Napoleon at Waterloo◊□

Bluebeard folktale hero (historically identified with Gilles de Rais◊), who murdered six wives for disobediently entering a locked room, but was himself killed before murdering the seventh□

bluebell plant *Endymion nonscriptus* (Scottish 'wild hyacinth'), family Liliaceae◊; the ***Scottish bluebell*** *Campanula rotundifolia*, is the English harebell◊□

blueberry see Vaccinium◊□

bluebird N American bird, genus *Sialia*, (see thrush◊), especially the ***eastern bluebird*** *Sialia sialia* which heralds spring□

bluebottle a type of fly◊□

bluegrass species of grass, genus *Poa*, of Europe, Asia and N America with blue/green leaves, grown for pasture and lawns; the ***Kentucky bluegrass*** is *P pratensis*□

blue gum see eucalyptus◊□

Blue Mountains see Great Dividing Range◊□

blue riband the highest distinction in any sphere, e.g. the blue riband of the Turf is the Derby; it derives from the blue riband of the Order of the Garter (see under Knighthood◊). The ***Blue Riband of the Atlantic*** is held by the vessel making the fastest crossing in both E and W directions. Holders have included the *Great Western* 1838, *Queen Mary 1938–52,* and *United States* from 1952 (3 days, 10 hr, 40 min). An actual trophy, originally presented 1935 by Harold K Hales 1868–1942, was in abeyance until accepted by the United States Lines 1952. The *Virgin Atlantic Challenger* a British twin-hulled speedboat challenged the record 1985, but sank; it succeeded at the second attempt in 1986□

Blue Ridge mountains range extending from W Virginia to Georgia, USA, and including Mount Mitchell 2045 m/6684 ft. See Appalachians◊□

blues popular jazz or ragtime music, in which the second line of the three-line verse is a repetition of the first, with variations, so giving the singer time to improvise the third line. It is melancholy and originated among American blacks. Composers include J A Carpenter, George Gershwin, Milhaud,

Duke Ellington, and W C Handy. Primarily secular, e.g. singer ***Bessie Smith*** 1894–1937, it has its religious counterpart in 'gospel', e.g. ***Mahalia Jackson*** 1911–72; the two were blended by ***Ray Charles*** 1930– after World War II, and from this 'soul' developed in the 1960s, e.g. ***Aretha Franklin*** 1942– □

blue stocking disparagingly, a learned woman, from the literary London gatherings c1750 at the house of Mrs Montagu, which were attended by poet Benjamin Stillingfleet in unfashionable blue worsted stockings□

Blum Léon 1872–1950. French Jewish statesman, first Socialist premier of France in 1936, and again premier for a few weeks in 1938. He was imprisoned in 1942 for his supposed responsibility for the fall of France, but released by the Allies◊ in 1945, and was again briefly premier in 1946: see Riom◊□

Blunden Edmund 1896–1974. British poet, who wrote innocuous verse about the countryside; influenced by Clare◊□

Blunt Anthony 1907–83. British art historian. As a Cambridge don, he recruited for the Soviet Secret Service, and, as a member of the British Secret Service 1940–5, passed information to the Russians. In 1951 he assisted the defection of Burgess and Maclean. Unmasked in 1964, he was given immunity after his confession, but was stripped of his knighthood in 1979 when the affair became public□

Blunt Wilfrid Scawen 1840–1922. British poet. He married Lady Anne Noel, and travelled with her in the Middle East, becoming a supporter of Arab aspirations. He also supported Irish Home Rule (imprisoned 1887–8), and wrote anti-imperialist books, and individualist poetry and diaries□

Blyton Enid 1897–1968. British children's writer. Originally a teacher, she created the litle boy Noddy with his gnome-like hat, and the adventures of the 'Famous Five' and 'Secret Seven', but is disapproved of by educationists□

Boa a genus of snakes◊□

Boadicea see Boudicca◊□

boar wild. A type of pig◊□

Boat Race rowing race between Oxford and Cambridge University crews, first held at Henley 1829, and since 1845 usually on the Thames (Putney–Mortlake, 6.8 km/ 4.25 mi)□

bobcat a N American lynx; see under cat◊□

bobolink a N American bird; see under oriole◊□

Bobruisk town in Byelorussia, USSR; population 151 000□

bobsledding the racing of steel-bodied, steerable toboggans down a mountain ice-chute, manned by 2–4 people at speeds up to 130 kmph/80 mph□

Boccaccio Giovanni 1313–75. Italian poet. Son of a Florentine merchant, he lived in Naples 1328–41, where he fell in love with the unfaithful 'Fiametta', inspiration of his early poetry. His great work is the *Decameron*, a hundred stories told by ten young people seeking refuge in the country from the plague: they are remarkable for licentiousness and narrative skill and inspired Chaucer, Shakespeare, Dryden, and Keats. Boccaccio was a friend of Petrarch◊□

Boccherini Luigi 1743–1805. Italian cellist and composer of much chamber music for strings□

Bochum industrial town in the Ruhr, N Rhine-Westphalia, W Germany; population 344 000□

Bode Johann Elert 1747–1826. German astronomer, who published the law, originated by Johann Titius in 1772, and known as the ***Titius-Bode Law***, which states that the proportionate distances of the planets from the sun out to Uranus are found by adding 4 to each term of the series 0,3,6,12,24, etc, if the asteroids are included between Mars and Jupiter; it fails for Neptune and Pluto□

Bodensee German name for Lake Constance◊□

Bodhidharma 6th century BC. Indian Buddhist◊ who entered China c520, and founded the school of Mahayana Buddhism in which intuitive meditation leads to enlightenment; and from which the better-known Zen◊ is derived□

Bodin Jean 1530–96. French economist, whose six-volume *De la République* 1576 tackled the problem of inflation due to the influx of precious metals from the New World, and originated political economy□

Bodleian Library see Oxford◊□

Boehme Jakob 1575–1624. German mystic. A shoemaker, author of the treatise *Aurora* 1612. He claimed divine revelation of the unity of everything and nothing, and found in God's eternal nature a principle to reconcile good and evil□

Boeotia ancient district of central Greece, of which Thebes◊ was the chief city; the ***Boetian League*** (formed by ten city states, 6th century BC) superseded Sparta◊ in the leadership of Greece in the 4th century. See Epaminondas◊, Orion◊□

Boer name formerly applied to the Dutch settlers (Dutch 'farmer') in S Africa◊, see Afrikaner◊□

Boer Wars see South◊ African Wars□

Boethius Anicius Manilus Severinus 480–524. Roman statesman-philosopher. While imprisoned on suspicion of treason by Theodoric◊, he wrote *De Consolatione Philosophiae*. A favourite book of the Middle Ages, it was translated by Alfred the Great◊□

Bogarde Dirk 1921– . Stage-name of British actor and writer Derek van den Bogaerde, whose films include *Death in Venice* 1970 and *A Bridge Too Far*; and who has written volumes of autobiography and novels, e.g. *Gentle Occupation* 1980□

Bogart Humphrey 1899–1957. American film actor, a cult figure from the 1970s as the tough 'loner'; his films include *The Petrified Forest* 1936; *The Maltese Falcon* 1941; *Casablanca* 1942, with Ingrid Bergman; *To Have and Have Not*, with Lauren Bacall, who became his fourth wife in 1945; and *The Caine Mutiny* 1954. See also Katherine Hepburn◊□

Boğazköy see under Hittites◊□

Bognor Regis seaside resort in W Sussex, England, so named because of a convalescent visit by King George V in 1929□

Bogotá capital of Colombia; population 2 885 000. Founded in 1538, it is 2640 m/8660 ft above sea level on the edge of the plateau of the E Cordillera◊; there is a rail link with the port of Buenaventura□

Bohemia kingdom of central Europe from the 9th century; it was under Hapsburg rule 1526–1918, when it was included in Czechoslovakia◊□

Bohm Karl 1894–1981. Austrian conductor, noted for his interpretation of Beethoven, and of the Strauss and Mozart operas□

Bohr Niels 1885–1962. Danish physicist. He helped to originate the quantum◊ theory of the atom in 1913. Developing Rutherford◊'s model, he claimed that electrons could only move around the nucleus in certain orbits with specific energies. He assisted in the development of the atom (nuclear fission) bomb. Nobel prize 1922. His son ***Aage Bohr*** 1922– , also a physicist, shared a Nobel prize in 1975 for work on atomic theory□

boil abscess originating at a hair root or in a sweat gland, usually caused by a staphylococcus◊□

Boileau Nicolas 1636–1711. French poet and critic, a friend of Racine◊, Molière◊ and La Fontaine◊, whose *L'Art Poétique* established 'correct' standards in the 18th century□

boiling point the temperature at which the vapour pressure◊ of a liquid equals atmospheric pressure, i.e. a liquid and its vapour are in equilibrium. For water, at sea level, this occurs at 100°C or 212°F□

Bois-le-Duc French form of 's Hertogenbosch◊□

Boldrewood Rolf. Pseudonym of Australian novelist Thomas Alexander Browne 1826–1915. Born in London, he was taken to Australia in 1830; became a pioneer squatter, and a police magistrate in the goldfields. His best known book is *Robbery Under Arms* 1888□

boletus see under Basidiomycetes◊□

Boleyn Anne c1507–36. Second queen of Henry◊ VIII, who married him and gave birth to the future Queen Elizabeth◊ I in 1533; accused of adultery and incest with her half-brother, she was beheaded□

Bolingbroke Henry St John, Viscount Bolingbroke 1678–1751. British Tory◊ statesman-philosopher. He was Secretary of War 1704–8, became Foreign Secretary in Harley◊'s ministry in 1710, and in 1713 negotiated the Treaty of Utrecht◊. His plans to restore the 'Old Pretender◊' were ruined by Queen Anne◊'s death only five days after he had secured the dismissal of Harley in 1714, and he fled abroad, returning in 1723, when he worked to overthrow Walpole◊. His books, such as *Idea of a Patriot King* 1738, influenced Disraeli◊□

Bolivar Simón 1783–1830. S American soldier-statesman, known as the Liberator for his ceaseless struggle (1813-22) to free his native Venezuela, Colombia, Ecuador, Peru, and Bolivia from Spanish rule. He succeeded in liberating these countries, but failed to join them in one confederation□

Bolivia Republic of

area 1 098 000 sq km/424 000 sq mi
capital La Paz (seat of government), Sucre (legal capital and seat of judiciary)

towns Santa Cruz, Cochabamba
features Andes, and Lakes Titicaca and Poopó
exports tin (second largest world producer), other non-ferrous metals, oil, gas (piped to Argentina), agricultural products
currency peso boliviano
population 5 950 000; Quechua 30%, Aymara 25%, Mestizo 25–30%, European 10%
language Spanish, official; Aymara, Quechua
religion Roman Catholicism, state recognized
government executive president Víctor Paz Estenssoro 1907– of the National Revolutionary Movement from 1985; senate and chamber of deputies.
recent history once part of the Inca◊ Empire, Bolivia was conquered by Spain, but achieved independence in 1825, being named in honour of Bolívar, whose lieutenant Sucre became the first president. Bolivia lost a narrow coastal strip to Chile in a war with Chile in 1883; see also Chaco◊. After a history of some 200 coups since independence, Bolivia returned to civilian government Oct 1982. In the elections of 1985 General Hugo Bánzer of the Nationalist Democratic Action Party was ahead of Paz Estenssoro, but without an overall majority; the final vote was left to Congress. Inflation in 1984 at 2000% and in 1985 at 1500% was the highest in the world□

Böll Heinrich 1917–85. German novelist. A radical Catholic and anti-Nazi, he attacked the materialism of contemporary German society. His books include *Billiards at Half-Past Nine* 1959 and *Group Portrait with Lady* 1971; Nobel prize 1972□

boll-weevil a type of small beetle◊□

Bologna industrial city, capital of Emilia-Romagna, Italy; population 490 250. The university laid the foundations of the study of anatomy and was attended by Dante◊, Petrarch◊, Tasso◊, and Copernicus◊. See under terrorism◊□

Bolshevism the doctrine of the destruction of capitalist political and economic institutions and the setting up of a socialist state with power in the hands of the workers, held by the Bolsheviks, members of the Russian Communist Party (formed 1903). Their social-democratic opponents were the Memsheviks (Russian *bolshinstvo* 'majority', *menshinstvo* 'minority')□

Bolt Robert (Oxton) 1924– . British dramatist, noted for *A Man for All Seasons* 1960, filmed 1967, and for his screenplays including *Lawrence of Arabia* 1962, *Dr Zhivago* 1965□

Bolton town in Greater Manchester, England; population 261 000. Textile machinery, chemicals, etc. are made□

Boltzmann Ludwig 1844–1906. Austrian physicist, noted for his work on the kinetic theory of gases, e.g. the Boltzmann constant; and the principle of the equipartition of energy, worked out with his teacher Josel Stefan and known as the Stefan-Boltzmann law. He committed suicide owing to the poor reception of his work by many continental physicists. See also under James Clerk Maxwell◊□

Bolzano capital of northern Trentino-Alto Adige, Italy; population 105 180□

Boma river port in Zaïre; population 62 000□

Bombay capital and chief port of Maharashtra, India; population 8 202 759. It originally passed to Britain as part of Catherine of Braganza◊'s dowry. A major financial and industrial centre, it is India's 'Hollywood' and has the National Centre for Performing Arts□

Bombay duck Indian food fish *Harpodon nehereus*, family Harpodontidae, about 40 cm/15 in long□

Bonaparte Corsican family of Italian origin, which gave rise to the Napoleonic dynasty: see Napoleon I◊, Napoleon II◊, and Napoleon III◊.
Other well-known members were the brothers and sister of Napoleon:
Joseph 1768–1844, whom Napoleon made King of Naples 1806 and Spain 1808.
Lucien 1775–1840, whose handling of the Council of Five Hundred on 10 Nov 1799 ensured Napoleon's future.
Louis 1778–1846, made King of Holland 1806–10, and who was the father of Napoleon III.
Caroline 1782–1839, who married Joachim Murat◊ in 1800.
Jerome 1784–1860, made King of Westphalia in 1807. A descendant of the last-named, ***Louis Jerome*** 1914– , is the present Bonaparte 'pretender'□

Bond Edward 1935– . British dramatist, noted for the savagery of his themes, e.g. the brutal killing of a baby in *Saved* 1965□

Bône see Annaba◊□

bone hard animal tissue consisting of a network of collagen (insoluble fibrous protein) impregnated with calcium phosphate; human beings have about 200 distinct bones, which preserve the shape of the body and provide fixed points from which the muscles can work, and to which ligaments are anchored. Within each bone is a cavity filled with marrow. From 1981 bone paste, made of ground human bone, was being used to promote growth where a patient had bone missing, as in cleft palate, and where broken bones failed to heal□

bongo a type of antelope◊□

Bonham-Carter Lady Violet. See Asquith◊ of Yarnbury, Lady□

Bonhoeffer Dietrich 1906–45. German Lutheran theologian. Involved in an anti-Hitler plot, he was executed, but his *Letters and Papers from Prison* became the textbook of modern radical theology, anticipating the prospect of a secular 'religionless' Christianity□

Boniface St 680–754. English Benedictine◊ who became the evangelizing 'Apostle of Germany' at the behest of Gregory◊ II, but was martyred. His feast day is 5 Jun□

Boniface VIII c1228–1303. Pope from 1294, he tried to exempt the clergy from taxation by the secular government, but was forced to give way by Philippe IV of France and Henry III of England. He also tried to assert papal supremacy over the temporal power□

Bonin Islands small Japanese group of islands in the Pacific, which were under US control 1952–68□

Bonington Chris(tian) 1934– . British mountaineer, who took part in the first British ascent of the N face of the Eiger 1962 and climbed Everest 1985; see also Kongur Shan◊□

Bonington Richard Parkes 1801–28. British artist, noted for seascapes and landscapes in oil and watercolour□

Bonn capital of the W German Federal Republic from 1949; population 286 000. It is an industrial city making chemicals, textiles, etc. Beethoven's birthplace is a museum□

Bonnard Pierre 1867–1947. French painter, influenced by the Impressionists◊, whose subjects include Paris street scenes, landscapes, and interiors with figures, noted for their light and colour□

Bonneville Salt Flats bed of a prehistoric lake, Utah, USA, of which the Great Salt Lake is the surviving remnant. It has been used for motor speed records□

Bonny Bight of. Name since 1975 of the former ***Bight of Biafra***, an area of sea off the coasts of Nigera and Cameroon□

bonsai art of growing dwarf trees in pots by selective pruning, first practised in China and, later, Japan. The oldest specimen in the Japanese Royal collection is 800 years old□

booby a type of pelican◊□

Booker prize prize of £15 000 awarded annually (from 1969) by the conglomerate Booker McConnell to a novel published in the UK during the previous years. Winners include William Golding◊□

booklouse wingless insect *Trogium pulsatorium* order Psocoptera, which feeds on starch in bookbindings□

Book of the Dead book known to the ancient Egyptians as the *Book of Coming Forth by Dayä*, it was buried with the dead as a guidebook to reach the kingdom of Osiris◊□

Boole George 1814–64. British mathematician, whose *The Mathematical Analysis of Logic* 1847, established the basis of modern mathematical logic, and whose ***Boolean algebra*** can be used in designing computers□

boomerang hand-thrown wooden missile which returns to the thrower if it does not hit its target, developed to its greatest perfection by the Australian Aborigines□

Boone Daniel 1734–1820. American frontiersman, who blazed the Wilderness Road (E Virginia/Kentucky) in 1775 for the first westward migration□

Booth Charles 1840–1916. British sociologist, author of the pioneer *Life and Labour of the People in London* 1891–1903, and of an old-age pension scheme□

Booth John Wilkes 1839–65. American actor who shot President Lincoln◊ 14 Apr 1865; he escaped with a broken leg and was later shot when he refused to surrender□

Booth William 1829–1912. British founder of the Salvation◊ Army in 1878, and its first 'General'□

Boothe Clare 1903– . American journalist-playwright, noted for her mordant play *The Women* 1936; she married Henry Luce, founder of *Time* and *Life* magazines□

Bootle port in Merseyside, England, adjoining Liverpool; population 73 000. The National Girobank headquarters is here□

bootlegging the illegal selling or smuggling of alcoholic liquor. In the USA, when the sale of alcohol to American Indians was illegal, bottles were hidden for sale in the legs of the jackboots of unscrupulous traders, and the term was then used for all illegal liquor sales in the period of Prohibition◊□

Bophuthatswana Republic of
area 40 330 sq km/15 571 sq mi
capital Mmbatho or Sun City, a casino resort frequented by many white South Africans
features divided into six 'blocks'
exports platinum, chrome, vanadium, asbestos, manganese
currency S African rand
population 1 417 000
language Setswana, English
religion Christianity
government executive president elected by the Assembly: Chief Lucas Mangope.
recent history first 'independent' Black National State from 1977, but not recognized by any other country□

borage a type of herb◊□

Boras textile town in SW Sweden; population 103 500□

borax hydrated sodium borate ($Na_2B_4O_7$), naturally occurring white crystals. A major industrial source is Borax Lake, California. It provides a starting material for perborates◊ (used in bleaches and washing powders), and is also used in glazing pottery, soldering, and as a mild antiseptic□

Bordeaux port on the Garonne, capital of Aquitaine, France; population 226 280. The medieval and 18th century areas of the city have been preserved, and it is a centre for transatlantic traffic, aeronautics and space industries, and the wine trade. Mauriac◊ was born here□

Borders region of Scotland

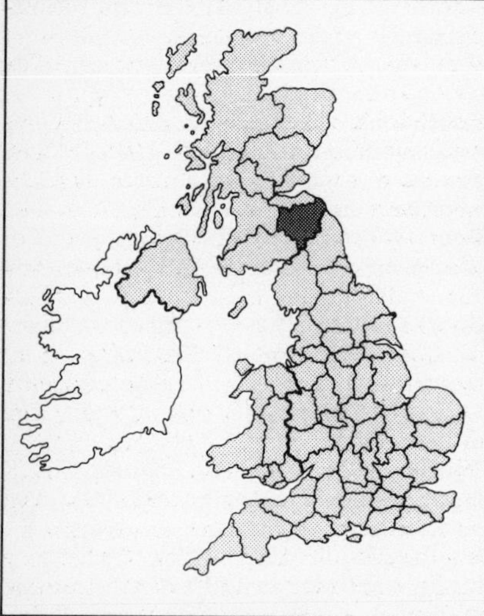

area 4670 sq km/1803 sq mi
towns administrative headquarters Newtown St Boswells; Hawick, Jedburgh
features river Tweed; Lammermuir, Moorfoot and Pentland Hills; birthplace of Mary◊ Queen of Scots at Newtown St Boswells; home of Sir Walter Scott◊ at Abbotsford; Dryburgh Abbey, burial place of Haig◊ and Sir Walter Scott; ruins of 12th century Melrose Abbey.
products knitted goods, tweed
population 100 470
famous people Duns Scotus, Mungo Park□

bore tidal wave which occurs in rivers with funnel-shaped estuaries, e.g. Severn, Amazon, Yangtze-Kiang□

Borg Björn 1956– . Swedish lawn-tennis player, winner of the Wimbledon singles championship 1976–80□

Borges Jorge Luis 1899–1986. Argentinian poet and short-story writer, e.g. *Ficciones/ Fictions* 1944. He was almost blind□

Borgia Cesare 1476–1507. Italian soldier, illegitimate son of Pope Alexander◊ VI. Made a cardinal at 17 by his father, he resigned the honour to become captain-general of the Papacy, campaigning successfully against the city republics of Italy. Ruthless and treacherous in war, he was an able ruler (the model of Machiavelli◊'s *The Prince*) of conquered territory, but his power crumbled on the death of his father. He was a patron of artists, including Leonardo da Vinci□

Borgia Lucrezia 1480–1519. Illegitimate daughter of Pope Alexander◊ VI, and sister of Cesare Borgia◊, she was married at 12 and again at 13 to further her father's ambitions, both marriages being annulled by him. At 18 she was again married, her husband being murdered in 1500 on the order of her brother, with whom (as well as with her father) she was said to have committed incest. Her final marriage in 1501 was to the son and heir of the Duke of Ferrara, and she made the court a centre of culture□

Borglum Gutzon 1871–1941. American sculptor who worked on the Mount Rushmore monument; see under South◊ Dakota□

Boris III 1894–1943. Tsar of Bulgaria from 1918. He backed Hitler to win World War II, hoping to regain Macedonia◊ and Thrace◊, and died suddenly after being summoned to meet him. There seems no foundation to the theory that he was poisoned because he wished to change sides□

Borlaug Norman 1914– . American scientist, breeder of high-yielding wheat, etc, for Third World countries ('the green revolution'); Nobel peace prize 1970□

Bormann Martin 1900–45. German Nazi, 'party chancellor' from May 1941 after Hess◊'s flight to England. Sentenced to death in his absence at Nuremberg, he was long rumoured to be alive, but his skeleton was identified in Berlin in 1973□

Born Max 1882–1970. British physicist, of German origin, who received a Nobel prize in 1954 for fundamental work on quantum◊ mechanics□

Borneo see under Sunda◊ Islands□

Bornholm Danish island in the Baltic Sea□

Bornu black African kingdom of the 9–19th centuries, of which the greater part is now the state of Bornu in Nigeria (capital Maiduguri); converted to Islam in the 11th century, it reached its greatest strength in the 15–18th century□

Borobudur see under Yogyakarta◊□

Borodin Alexander Porfirievich 1834–87. Russian composer. A professor of chemistry, who composed in his spare time, he is best-remembered for his unfinished opera *Prince Igor*, completed by Rimsky◊-Korsakov and Glazunov◊, which includes the Polovtsian Dances□

Borodino village NW of Moscow where Napoleon◊ defeated the Russians under Kutusov 7 Sept 1812□

boron element
symbol B
atomic number 5
physical description yellow crystals
features there is a trace in the human body
uses used in hardening steel, nuclear engineering (an alloy with steel for control rods since boron absorbs slow neutrons), making heat proof glass, etc.□

borough unit of local government in the UK from the 8th century until 1974, when it continued as an honorary status granted by royal charter to a district council, thus enabling its chairperson to have the title of mayor□

Borromeo St Carlo 1538–84. Cardinal arch–bishop of Milan, he largely drew up the catechism that contained the findings of the Council of Trent◊, and was an important figure of the Counter-Reformation◊. His feast day is 4 Nov□

Borromini Francesco 1599–1667. Italian Baroque◊ architect. He worked under Bernini◊, later his rival, on St Peter's, Rome and created the oval-shaped San Carlo alle Quattro Fontane, Rome□

Borrow George Henry 1803–81. British writer and traveller, with a wide knowledge of languages and gypsy culture. He published *Zincali* 1840 and *The Bible in Spain* 1843, both dealing with Spain; *Lavengro* 1851 and *The Romany Rye* 1857, mingling autobiography and fiction; and *Wild Wales* 1862□

Borrowdale beautiful valley in the Lake District, Cumbria, from Derwentwater to Scafell Pike□

Borstal prison near Rochester, Kent, England, where the Borstal system of reformatories (from 1983 known as Youth Custody Centres) was first introduced in 1908 for young offenders□

Borzoi a breed of dog◊□

Bosch Hieronymus c1460–1516 or ***Jerom van Aeken***. Dutch artist, noted for his fantastic, allegorical paintings, as in *The Garden of Earthly Delights* in the Prado◊. He was neglected until Freud◊ and Jung◊ analysed his imagery□

Bose Sir Jagadis Chandra 1858–1937. Indian naturalist and physicist, who studied the reaction of plants to electrical stimuli, etc, and founded the Bose Research Institute, Calcutta□

Bose Satyendranath 1894–1974. Indian physicist who formulated with Einstein◊ the statistics of quantum◊ mechanical systems of particles of integral spin (called Bosans)□

Bosnia and Herzegovina constituent republic of Yugoslavia
area 51 129 sq km/19 745 sq mi
capital Sarajevo
features barren, mountainous country
population 4 124 000, including 1 630 000 Muslims, 1 321 000 Serbs, 758 000 Croats
language Serbian variant of Serbo-Croat
religion Sunni Islam, Serbian Orthodox and Roman Catholicism
history once the Roman province of Illyria◊, it enjoyed brief periods of independence in medieval times, then was under Turkish rule 1463–1878 and Austrian 1878–1918, when it was incorporated in the future Yugoslavia. It was a Bosnian student who murdered the Austrian Archduke Ferdinand at Sarajevo◊ in 1914. Muslim extremists have campaigned to make it the first Muslim state of Europe□

Bosporus strait linking the Black Sea and Sea of Marmara, and crossed by a bridge linking Istanbul and Turkey-in-Asia;□

Bossuet Jacques Bénigne 1627–1704. French bishop, noted for funeral sermons and brilliant essays□

Boston industrial and commercial centre, capital of Massachusetts, USA; population 3 700 000. It is a publishing centre, has high-technology (Route 128), and Harvard University and Massachusetts Institute of Technology are nearby. Notable are Paul Revere◊ House; the mother church of Christian Science; and the John F Kennedy Library. Residents have included Franklin, Poe, Emerson, Hawthorne, Thoreau, and Longfellow□

Boston seaport in Lincolnshire, England; population 27 000. St Botolph's parish church, claimed as England's largest, has a tower known as 'Boston Stump'□

Boswell James 1740–95. Scottish biographer (1791) of Samuel Johnson◊, whom he first met in 1763. He was admitted to the Scottish Bar in 1766, but habitually visited London from 1772 as an intimate member of the Johnsonian circle, and made the journey with Johnson recorded in *Journal of a Tour to the Hebrides* 1785. His own frank *Journals* are of exceptional interest□

Bosworth final battle of the Wars of the Roses◊ 1485□

botany see plant◊□

Botany Bay inlet S of Sydney, Australia, where Captain Cook landed in 1770, and which was so-named because of its many varied plants. Chosen as the site of a penal settlement in 1787, which was established instead at Sydney, its name nevertheless continued to be used generically for Australian convict settlements□

botfly horse. a type of fly◊□

Botha Louis 1862–1919. S African general. In the South African War, he besieged Ladysmith◊, and in 1900 became commander of the Transvaal forces. As Prime Minister of the Union of S Africa 1910–19, he suppressed a pro-German revolt by Christian de Wet in World War I, and went on to conquer German SW Africa□

Botha Pieter Willem 1916– . S African statesman. Prime Minister from 1978, he initiated a modification of apartheid which later slowed owing to the force of Afrikaner◊ opposition. In 1984 he became first executive state president□

Bothwell James Hepburn, 4th Earl of Bothwell c1536–78. Scottish nobleman alleged to have engineered the explosion which killed Darnley◊. Acquitted, he abducted Mary◊, Queen of Scots and, having divorced his wife, married her on 15 May 1567. He fled the country when a revolt ensued; Mary obtained a divorce in 1570 on the ground of having been ravished before marriage, and Bothwell died insane in a castle in Zeeland□

bo tree see under fig◊□

Botswana Republic of

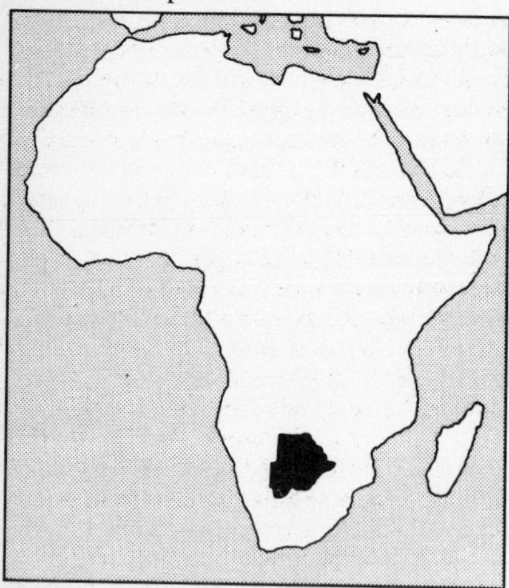

area 575 000 sq km/222 000 sq mi
capital Gaborone
features larger part of Kalahari◊ Desert, including Okovango Swamp, remarkable for its wildlife
exports diamonds, copper-nickel and meat
currency pula
population 1 060 000, 80% Bamangwato, 20% Bangwaketse
language English, official; Setswana, national
religion Christianity (majority)
government executive president (Quett Masire from 1980), National Assembly and advisory House of Chiefs
recent history Bechuanaland, a British Protectorate since 1884, became an independent member of the the Commonwealth◊ in 1966, named Botswana. Sir Seretse Khama 1921–80, whose marriage to an Englishwoman (opposed by the people) had led to his renunciation of the chieftaincy 1956, was Prime Minister 1965 and first president of Botswana until his death in 1980□

Botticelli Sandro. Nickname 'little barrel', passed on to him from his elder brother, of the Florentine painter Alessandro di Mariano Filipepi 1444–1510. He was patronized by the Medici◊, with whom he broke after their execution of Savonarola◊, and became more sombre and religious in his later style. His best-known works are *Primavera* and *The Birth of Venus,* both in the Uffizi◊□

bottlebrush either of two types of Australian tree or shrub, *Callistemon* and *Melalevca,* both family Myrtaceae, with long-stamened flower heads like bottle brushes□

botulism often fatal type of food poisoning, caused by the bacterium *Clostridium botulinum,* sometimes found in canned meat.□

Boucher François 1703–70. French Rococo artist, court painter to Louis XV from 1764, famous for pastoral scenes and cupids□

Boucher De Perthes Jacques 1788–1868. French geologist who, in 1837, recognized Palaeolithic◊ handaxes as confirming that human history extended beyond the accepted 'creation date' of 4000BC□

Boudicca or ***Boadicea*** d. AD62. Queen of the Iceni◊. On the death of her husband, King Prasutagus, in 61, his territory was annexed by Rome, and Boudicca was flogged and her daughters raped. SE England rose in revolt, and Boudicca burnt London and Colchester, but she was defeated by Paulinus◊ somewhere between London and Chester and poisoned herself□

Boudin Eugène Louis 1824–98. French marine painter, noted for his skies□

Bougainville largest of the Solomon◊ Islands□

Bougainville Louis Antoine de 1729–1811. French navigator, who sailed round the world 1766–9□

bougainvillea genus of S American climbing plants, family Nyctaginaceae, cultivated for the red and purple bracts, which cover the flowers. They are named after Bougainville◊□

Bougie see Bejaia◊□

Boulanger Nadia 1887–1979. French music teacher, whose pupils include Leonard Bernstein, Virgil Thomson, Aaron Copland, Roy Harris, Walter Piston, and Lennox Berkeley□

Boulder high-tech industrial town in Colorado, USA□

boules French form of bowls, in which two teams or players try to place their boules (11 cm/4.5 in diameter) nearer the target jack than their opponent□

Boulez Pierre 1926– . French composer and conductor, whose work was influenced by Messiaen◊ and Webern◊, and includes *Le Marteau sans Maître* 1955, and *Poésie pour Pouvoir* (for orchestra and eight-track tape recorder) 1958□

Boulogne-sur-Mer port and resort of N France; population 50 000. There are cross-Channel services, fishing, food, oil and metallurgical industries□

Boult Sir Adrian 1889–1983. British conductor, founder of the BBC Symphony Orchestra 1930, noted for his interpretation of Elgar, Holst, and Vaughan Williams. Knighted 1937□

Boulting John 1913–85 and Roy 1913– . British twin film producers, e.g. *Brighton Rock* 1947, *Lucky Jim* 1957, and *I'm All Right Jack* 1959□

Boulton Matthew 1728–1809. British engineer, the partner of Watt◊ in developing the steam engine□

Boumédienne Houari. Adopted name of Algerian statesman Mohammed Boukharouba 1925–78, who brought Ben◊ Bella to power by a revolt in 1962, and superseded him as president 1965–78 by a further coup□

Bounty Mutiny on the. See Bligh◊□

Bourassa Robert 1933– . Canadian Liberal statesman. Premier of Quebec◊ 1970–76, he lost office to the French separatists on accusations of authoritarianism and over-spending□

Bourbon French royal house (succeeding that of Valois◊) beginning with Henry◊ IV, and ending with Louis◊ XVI, with a brief revival under Louis◊ Philippe; the present pretender is ***Henri d'Orléans*** Count of Paris 1908– , who served in the French Foreign Legion 1939–40. They also ruled Spain almost uninterruptedly from Philip◊ V to Alfonso◊ XIII, and were restored in 1975 (Juan◊ Carlos); as well as Naples and several Italian duchies□

bourgeoisie French term for the class between the nobility and the workers and peasants, but in Marxist terms, the whole propertied class as against the proletariat□

Bourges town in central France; population 80 000. It has one of Europe's finest Gothic◊ cathedrals, and is an industrial centre□

Bourguiba Habib ben Ali 1903– . Tunisian statesman, who became the first president of independent Tunisia from 1957□

Bournemouth seaside resort in Dorset, England; population 148 000. Noted for its sands, double tides, and its symphony orchestra□

Bouts Dierick c1400–75. Dutch painter, known for his portraits, and his feeling for landscape□

Bouvet Island uninhabited Norwegian dependency in the S Atlantic□

Bovet Daniel 1907– . Swiss physiologist who pioneered the use of antihistamine drugs in treating nettle rash and hay fever, and received a Nobel prize in 1957 for his development of synthetic curare as a muscle relaxant in anaesthesia□

Bow Clara 1905–65. American silent film actress, known as the 'it' girl from the sex appeal of her appearance in *It* 1927□

Bow bells bells of Bow Church, Cheapside, London; those born within their sound are considered true Cockneys◊□

Bowdler Thomas 1754–1825. British editor who made censored 'family' versions of Shakespeare, etc.□

Bowen Elizabeth 1899–1973. Anglo-Irish novelist, best-known for *Death of the Heart* 1938□

bowerbird family of birds Ptilonorhynchidae of Australia and New Guinea, order Passeriformes. The male constructs a tunnel-like bower of twigs decorated with petals, bright pebbles, bottle-tops, etc, in which he displays and courts his mate□

Bowie David 1947– . Stage-name of British pop star David Jones 1947– . Born in Brixton, London, and inspiration in the 1970s of 'glitter rock' and 'European' electronic music; his albums include *Ziggy Stardust* 1972□

Bowie 'Jim' 1796–1836. American folk-hero, a colonel in the Texan forces in the Mexican◊ War, said to have developed the single-edged, guarded Bowie knife for throwing and hunting. He died at the Alamo◊□

bowls English outdoor game played on flat or 'crown' greens with biased wooden balls (13 cm/5 in in diameter), bowled as near the small white jack as possible: teams number 1–4 players□

box genus *Buxus* of small evergreen trees and shrubs, family Buxaceae; ***common box, B sempervirens***, is slow growing, and ideal for hedging□

boxer a breed of dog◊□

Boxers see China◊ list under 1900□

boxfish see under tetraodon◊□

boxing fighting with the fists. The modern sport dates from the 18th century when fights were bare-knuckle and without rounds; Jack Broughton 1705–89, who was champion 1729–50, laid down the first 'rules' in 1743, and introduced gloves for his pupils; Queensberry Rules (drawn up by the 8th Marquess in 1866) still prevail in modified form; the ring is 6.10 m/20 ft by 4.3 m/14 ft square. Boxers are classified from flyweight 51 kg/112 lb through bantamweight, featherweight, lightweight, welterweight, middleweight, light-heavyweight, to heavyweight 80 kg/175 lb, with no upward limit.
great heavyweights include: John L Sullivan (bare-knuckle champion) 1882–92; Jim Corbett (first Marquess of Queensberry champion) 1892–7; Jack Dempsey 1919–26; Joe Louis 1937–49; Floyd Patterson 1956–9, 1960–2, and Muhammad Ali◊□
Boycott Charles Cunningham 1832–97. Land agent of Lord Erne, county Mayo, Ireland; he opposed the Land◊ League and peasants refused to work for him, i.e. 'boycotted' him□
Boyer Charles 1899–1977. French film actor, celebrated as the 'great lover' in *Mayerling* 1937, etc.□
Boyle Robert 1627–91. British scientist. He published the seminal *The Skeptical Chymist* 1661; enunciated Boyle's◊ law in 1662; was one of the founders of the Royal◊ Society; and endowed the Boyle Lectures for the defence of Christianity□
Boyle's law law of the compressibility of gases, i.e. that the volume of a fixed mass of gas varies inversely with its pressure if the temperature stays the same□
Boyne river of the Republic of Ireland□
Boyne Battle of. Battle in which William◊ III defeated James◊ II north of Dublin 11 Jul 1690□
boy scouts see scouts◊□
Bozen German form of Bolzano◊□
Bo Zhu Yi 772–846. Chinese poet (formerly Po Chü-i). President from 841 of the imperial war department, he criticized government policy, and checked his work for clarity of expression with an old peasant woman□
Brabant former duchy, capital Louvain, now divided between Belgium and the Netherlands□
Bracegirdle Anne c1663–1748. British actress, the mistress of Congreve◊, and possibly his wife; she excelled as Millamant in his *The Way of the World*□
brachiopoda phylum of invertebrate marine animals, known as lamp shells because their bivalved shells look like ancient Roman lamps. They are among the oldest fossils known, and are useful for dating purposes□
bracken see under fern◊□
bracket fungi fungi◊, class Basidiomycetes◊, with bracket-shaped fruiting body□
Bracknell town in Berkshire, England; population 50 000. The headquarters of the Meterological Office is here, and (with Washington DC) is one of the only two global area forecasting centres (of upper-level winds and temperatures) for the world's airlines. The Wilde◊ Theatre opened 1984□
Bracton Henry de d. 1268. English judge, who wrote the first comprehensive account of English law□
Bradbury Malcolm 1932– . British satirical novelist, born in Sheffield, professor of American Studies at University of E Anglia from 1970. His books include *The History Man* 1975 and *Rates of Exchange* 1983□
Bradbury Ray 1920– . American fiction and science fiction writer, basing his work on the development of existing inventions and mental attitudes, e.g. *The Martian Chronicles* 1950 and *Something Wicked This Way Comes* 1962□
Bradford city in W Yorkshire, England; population 480 000;. Its dominance of the wool industry from the 13th century was undermined in the 1970s by Third World and Common Market competition. Notable are Cartwright Hall (including a museum and art gallery); the National Museum of Photography, Film and Television 1983 (with Britain's largest cinema screen 14 × 20 m); the restored Alhambra Music Hall and the mid-19th century warehouses of 'Little Germany'. Ethnic communities have included Irish, Poles and Ukrainians, and most recently W Indians and Asians□
Bradley Francis Herbert 1846–1924. British Idealist◊ philosopher who attacked utilitarianism◊, and in *Appearance and Reality* 1895 outlined his doctrine of the universe as a single ultimate reality□
Bradley Omar Nelson 1893–1981. American general, who in 1944 led the US troops in the invasion of Normandy, making a spectacular breakthrough at St Lô□
Bradman Sir Donald 1908– . Australian cricketer who captained Australia 1936–48, and achieved the highest aggregate score and greatest number of centuries in England v Australia Test Matches□
Braemar see under Grampian◊□
Braga town in N Portugal; population 41 000□

Bragança town in NE Portugal, which gave its name to the ruling house of Portugal 1640–1853, and Brazil 1822–89□

Bragg Sir William Henry 1862–1942. British physicist, who in 1915 shared with his son Sir (William) ***Lawrence Bragg*** 1890–1971 a Nobel prize for work on X-ray diffraction and crystal structure□

Brahé Tycho 1546–1601. Danish astronomer, whose accurate observations laid the foundations of modern astronomy; Kepler◊ was his assistant□

Brahma the Supreme Spirit of Hinduism◊□

Brahmanism earliest stage in the development of Hinduism◊□

Brahmaputra river flowing through Tibet and India to join the Ganges◊ in Bangladesh; length 2900 km/1800 mi□

Brahms Johannes 1833–97. German composer. Born in Hamburg, he was aided by Schumann, and eventually became very attached to his widow Clara, who helped popularize his piano pieces. He settled in Vienna in 1862. Though his music has romantic qualities, he preferred the classical tradition rather than the new Liszt-Wagner romanticism. His works include four symphonies, *Liede*, concertos for piano and for violin, and the choral *A German Requiem* 1868□

Braille a system of writing for the blind. Letters are represented by a combination of raised dots on paper, etc, which are then read by touch. It was invented by ***Louis Braille*** in 1829, who was blind from the age of three□

brain in higher animals, the anterior part of the central nervous system which is enlarged and elaborated to coordinate and control the activities of the whole nervous system.

Structure in vertebrates: an enlarged portion of the upper spinal cord is called the medulla oblongata which contains centres for the control of respiration and cardiovascular reflexes. Overlying the medulla is the cerebellum which is concerned with coordinating complex muscular processes such as maintaining posture and moving limbs. The cerebral hemipheres (cerebrum) are paired outpushings of the front end of the forebrain, in early vertebrates mainly concerned with sense of smell but in higher vertebrates greatly developed. In mammals the cerebrum is the largest part of the brain, forming the cerebral cortex. This consists of a thick surface layer of cell bodies (grey matter) below which fibre tracts (white matter) connect various parts of the cortex to each other and to other points in the central nervous system. As cerebral complexity grows the surface of the brain becomes convoluted into deep folds. Areas of this surface can be assigned some sensory or motor function but in higher mammals there come to be large unassigned areas of the brain which seem to be connected with intelligence, personality and other complex functions. Certain functions are localized to one side of the brain e.g. language which is controlled in two special regions usually in the left side of the brain; Broca's area which governs the ability to talk (although comprehension may be normal) and Wernicke's area which is responsible for the comprehension of spoken and written words. It has been suggested that the left side of the brain is specialized for verbal and analytical tasks and the right is more important for musical abilities and other artistic or intuitive skills□

Braine John 1922– . British novelist, whose *Room at the Top* 1957, featured the 'angry young man'◊ and go-getter Joe Lampton□

Braithwaite Eustace Adolph 1912– Guyanese author whose experiences teaching in London inspired the film *To Sir With Love* 1959□

Bramante Donato c1444–1514. Italian Renaissance architect and artist. Inspired by classical designs, he was employed by Pope Julius II in rebuilding part of the Vatican and

brain

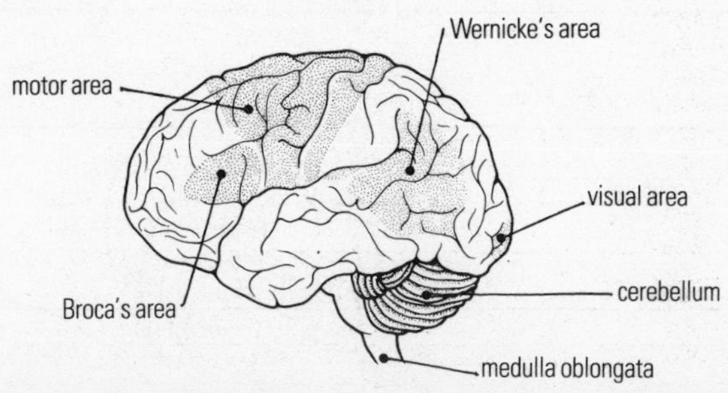

St Peter's□

bramble bush that produces the blackberry◊□

brambling a Eurasian finch◊□

Brancusi Constantin 1876–1957. Romanian sculptor, celebrated for his abstract forms, e.g. *Bird in Space* 1919□

Brandenburg former German electorate which enlarged to become the kingdom of Prussia in 1701. It became a province of united Germany in 1871, and in 1945 part passed under Polish administration, and the rest is now the Neubrandenburg, Potsdam, Frankfurt-an-der-Oder, and Kottbus administrative districts of E Germany□

Brandenburg industrial town of E Germany; population 95 000□

Brando Marlon 1924– . American film actor, the best-known exponent of method◊ acting, as in *A Streetcar Named Desire* 1952, *On the Waterfront* 1954, *The Godfather* 1972, *Last Tango in Paris* 1973, and *Apocalypse Now* 1979□

Brandt 'Bill' (William) 1904–84. British-born photographer of Russian descent, noted for his portraits and atmospheric landscapes□

Brandt Willy 1913– . German statesman, an anti-Nazi active in the resistance movement, he became mayor of W Berlin, and was Federal Chancellor 1969–74, when one of his aides was found to be an E German spy. His Ostpolitik◊ led to treaties with the USSR and Poland and a 'Basic Treaty' between E and W Germany, and he won a Nobel peace prize in 1971. He became chairman of the 'Brandt Commission' on international development in 1977, publishing reports on relations between the rich North hemisphere and the poor South in 1980 and 1983, calling for urgent action□

brandy spirit distilled from fermented grape juice (notably that of France, e.g. Armagnac and Cognac), or that of other fruits□

Brandywine Battle of the. See American Independence◊, War of□

Brangwyn Sir Frank 1867–1956. British artist. He worked for William Morris as a textile designer, but developed as a large-scale decorative artist, completing panels for the House of Lords 1925 (rejected; they now hang in Brangwyn Hall, Swansea) and Radio City, New York 1932. There are Brangwyn museums at Bruges (his birthplace) 1936 and Orange in Vaucluse 1947□

Braque Georges 1882–1963. French artist, associated with Picasso in introducing the Cubist◊ movement in 1908, and the main initiator of *papiers collés,* paper and wood, etc, being glued to his canvases□

Brasilia capital of Brazil from 1960; popula-

brass instruments

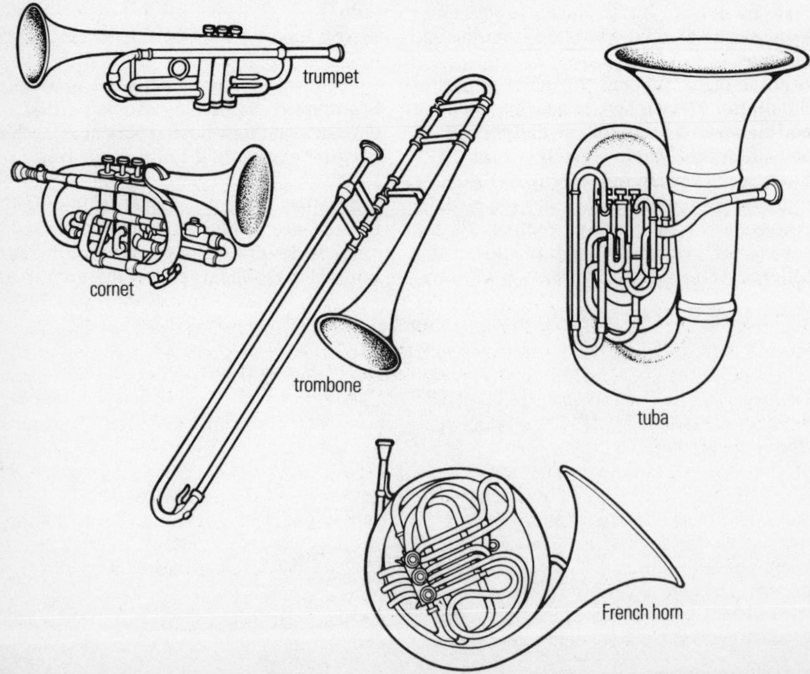

tion 763 255. Some 1000 m/3000 ft above sea level, it was designed by Lucio Costa, with Oscar Niemeyer as chief architect□

brass alloy of copper◊ and zinc◊, of varying composition. Produced in the form of sheets, tubes, and wire□

brass musical instruments formerly made of brass, but now also of other metals, directly blown through a 'cup' or 'funnel' mouthpiece. Brass instruments include:

symphony orchestra: french horn a descendant of the natural hunting horn, valved and curved into a circular loop, with a wide bell; ***trumpet*** a cylindrical tube curved into an oblong, with a narrow bell and three valves (the state ***fanfare trumpet*** has no valves); ***trombone*** instrument with a 'slide' to vary the effective length of the tube (the ***sackbut*** common from the 14th century, was its forerunner); ***tuba*** normally the lowest toned instrument of the orchestra; valved and with a very wide bore to give sonority, its bell points upward

brass band: cornet three-valved instrument, looking like a shorter, broader trumpet, and with a wider bore; and then in descending order of tone: ***flugelhorn*** valved instrument, rather similar in range to the cornet; ***saxhorn; euphonium; trombone, 'bombardon'*** type of bass tuba□

Bratislava city (German *Pressburg*) and chief port of Czechoslovakia, on the Danube; population 368 000. It was the capital of Hungary 1526–1784. There are engineering, chemical, and oil industries□

Brattain Walter Houser 1902– . American physicist, who shared a Nobel prize in 1956 with William Shockley and John Bardeen for the development of the transistor◊ in 1948□

Brauchitsch Walther von 1881–1948. German field marshal, who was Commander-in-Chief of the Army from 1938 until his dismissal after the failure before Moscow. Captured in 1945, he died before trial□

Braudel Fernand 1902–85. French historian of the Annales school (so-named from the periodical founded by Lucien Febvre◊ and Marc Bloc in 1929). He deals with the mass of the people within their environment, e.g. *The Mediterranean and the Mediterranean World in the Age of Philip II* 1949–73, not with great historical figures□

Braun Eva 1910–45. German mistress of Hitler from about 1933; they were married in the Chancellery air raid shelter, Berlin, 29 Apr 1945, and then committed suicide together□

Braun Werner von 1912–77. German director of the liquid-fuel rocket and guided-missile centre at Peenemünde 1937–45, where the V1 and V2 were developed (see Missile◊); after the war he worked in the USA on guided missiles, and from 1960 for NASA, see Apollo◊ project□

Brazil Federal Republic of

area 8 512 000 sq km/3 286 000 sq mi
capital Brasilia
towns Sao Paulo; ports are Rio de Janeiro, Belo Horizonte, Recife, Porto Alegre, Salvador
features Amazon Basin, Mount Roraima, and enormous energy resources, both hydroelectric (Itaipú dam on the Paraná, and Tucurui, on the Tocantins) and nuclear (uranium ores); Xingu National Park including Indian reserves
exports coffee, sugar, cotton; textiles and motor vehicles; iron, chrome, manganese, tungsten and other ores, as well as quartz crystals, industrial diamonds, etc.
currency cruzado (introduced 1986; value = 100 cruzeiros, the former unit)
population 123 000 000, including 200 000 Indians, survivors of 5 000 000 (see Xingu◊), especially in Rondonia and Mato Grosso, mostly living on reserves
language Portuguese; there are 120 Indian languages
religion Roman Catholicism majority; Indian faiths
famous people Oscar Niemeyer, Heitor Villa-Lobos, Paulo Freire
government under the 1969 constitution a president, enabled to legislate by decree on economic or national security questions (José Sarney, who as vice-president succeeded Neves 1985), indirectly elected by an electoral college.

recent history in 1822, Brazil became an independent empire ruled by Dom Pedro, the son of the refugee King Jao◊ VI of Portugal; in 1889 Pedro◊ II was deposed and Brazil proclaimed a republic; a military revolution in 1964 led to a less democratic regime and the development of an urban guerrilla movement. A more liberal trend was started by President João Figueiredo 1979–85, and in 1985 Tancredo Neves became the first civilian president since 1964, but died before inauguration. Since 1983 the country has been in financial crisis with enormous foreign debts (the highest in the world)□

brazil nut edible, oil-rich seed of the S American tree *Bertholletia excelsa,* family Lecythidaceae; the fruit contains 10-20 nuts arranged like the segments of an orange□

Brazzaville capital and river port of the People's Republic of Congo; population 310 500. Founded in the 1800s, it was the headquarters of the Free French forces in World War II□

bread food made with ground cereals, usually wheat, and water, though with many other variants of the contents. The dough may be unleavened, or raised (usually with yeast) and then baked□

breadfruit round edible fruit of the tree *Artocarpus communis*, family Moraceae, a staple food in the S Sea Islands□

Breakspear Nicholas. See Adrian◊ IV□

Bream Julian 1933– . British guitar virtuoso, reviver of much Elizabethan lute music; Britten and Henze have written for him□

bream a type of carp◊□

bream sea. A type of perch◊□

Breasted James Henry 1865–1935. American archaeologist, noted for his work on the linguistic aspects of Egyptology□

breathalyzer instrument for on-the-spot checking by the police of the amount of alcohol drunk by a suspect driver, who breathes into a plastic bag connected to a tube containing a chemical (such as a diluted solution of potassium dichromate in 50% sulphuric acid) which changes colour□

Brecht Bertolt 1898–1955. German writer, who wished to destroy the 'suspension of disbelief' usual in the theatre, and express Marxist ideas. He first made a name with his adaptation of John Gay's *Beggar's Opera* as *The Threepenny Opera* 1928, set to music by Kurt Weill. As an anti-Nazi, he left Germany in 1933. Later plays are *Galileo* 1938, *Mother Courage* 1941, set in the Thirty◊ Years' War, which attacks all war, and *The Caucasian Chalk Circle* 1949. He became an Austrian citizen after World War II, and from 1949 established in E Germany the theatre group, the Berliner Ensemble□

Breda town in S Netherlands; population 118 000. Charles II lived in exile here, and made the ***Declaration of Breda*** which paved the way for the Restoration◊ in 1660□

Bréitigny Treaty of. Treaty of 1360, ending the first phase of the Hundred◊ Years' War, by which Edward III received Aquitaine in return for renouncing his claim to the French throne□

Bremen capital of the Administrative Region of Bremen◊, W Germany; population 555 700. Once a leading city of the Hanseatic◊ League, in World War II it was the headquarters of U-boat construction, and of final SS resistance under Himmler□

Bremen Administrative Region of W Germany
area 404 sq km/156 sq mi
features consists of the city of Bremen◊, the capital, and its outport Bremerhaven
products iron and steel, refined oil, chemicals, aircraft, ships, cars
population 693 850
religion Protestantism 83%, Roman Catholicism 10%□

Bremerhaven see Bremen◊, Administrative Region of□

Brendan St 484–c578AD. Irish abbot of Clonfert. In the 11th century *Navigation of St Brendan*, he is reputed to have sailed across the Atlantic to St Brendan's isle in a leather boat, but the tale may refer to the Orkneys or Hebrides. His feast day is 16 May□

Brenner Pass see under Alps◊□

Brent borough of NW Greater London
features part of Brent Reservoir ('The Welsh Harp': see Barnet◊); Wembley sports stadium; population 253 275□

Brentano Klemens 1778–1842. German writer, leader of the Young◊ Romantics, he published a seminal collection of folktale and song with Ludwig von Arnim (*Des Knaben Wunderhorn*) 1805–8, and popularized the legend of the Lorelei (see under Rhine◊). He also wrote mystic religious verse *Romanzen vom Rosenkranz* 1852, eventually suffering from religious melancholia□

Brenton Howard 1942– . British dramatist, noted for *The Romans in Britain* 1980, and a translation of Brecht's *The Life of Galileo*□

Brescia industrial city in N Italy; population 213 000□

Breslau see Wroclaw◊□

Brest commercial port and naval base in NW France; population 172 000. In World War II it was a German U-boat base□

Brest town in Byelorussia, western USSR; population 186 000. Before 1921 it was known as Brest-Litovsk, and as Brzesc nad Bugiem was in Poland 1929–39□

Brest-Litovsk Treaty of. Treaty between Russia and the Central Powers 3 Mar 1918, by which Russia agreed to recognize the independence of the Baltic states, Georgia, the Ukraine and Poland and pay heavy 'compensation'; it was annulled under the Nov 1918 Armistice between the Central Powers and the Allies◊□

Breton Celtic language of Brittany, with links to Cornish and Welsh. It is a recognized language of France; the Breton Liberation Movement claims equal status for it with French, and in 1985 the government agreed that it should be promoted□

Bretton Woods township in New Hampshire, USA, site of a conference 1–22 Jul 1944 resulting in the setting up of the International Monetary Fund◊ and International Bank for Reconstruction and Development◊□

Breuer Josef 1842–1925. Austrian physician, collaborator with Freud in *Studies in Hysteria* 1895, and the originator of psychoanalysis◊□

Breuer Marcel Lajos 1902–81. American architect and furniture designer, born in Hungary. He taught at the Bauhaus◊, originated the tubular steel chair, and designed the Whitney Museum of American Art, New York, and the UNESCO offices in Paris□

Breuil Henri 1877–1961. French prehistorian, who established the genuine antiquity of Palaeolithic cave art□

brewing the preparation beer◊□

Brewster Sir David 1781–1868. Scottish physicist who made discoveries regarding the diffraction and polarization of light, and invented the kaleidoscope□

Brezhnev Leonid Ilyich 1906–82. Russian statesman. President of the USSR 1960–4, he ousted Khrushchev, succeeding him as secretary of the Soviet Communist Party, in Oct 1964, and from 1977 was the first to combine both offices□

Brezhnev doctrine laid down in 1968 as a duty for the USSR to maintain 'correct' socialism within the Soviet sphere (to justify the invasion of Czechoslovakia); it was extended outside that sphere in 1979 by the invasion of Afghanistan□

Briand Aristide 1862–1932. French socialist statesman, Prime Minister of France 1909–11, 1913, 1915–17, 1921–2, 1925–6 and 1929, and was subsequently often Foreign Minister. He concluded the Locarno◊, and Kellogg◊ pacts, and advocated a united Europe; Nobel peace prize 1926□

bridge a structure built to cross a gap.

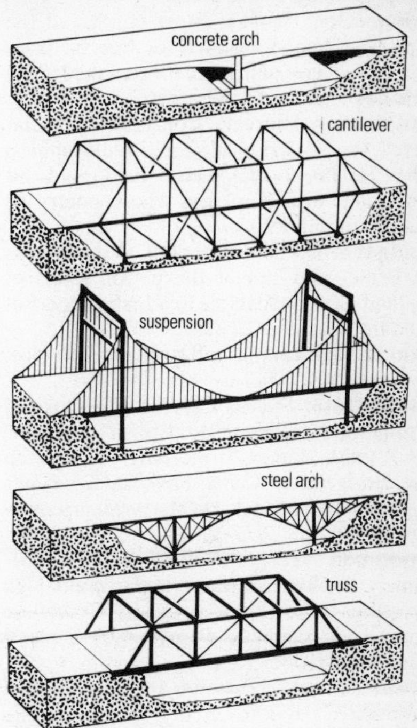

Famous bridges of various types include:
arch Sydney Harbour Bridge; Waterloo Bridge, London
girder Rio-Niteroi at Guanabara Bay, Brazil (world's longest continuous box and plate girder bridge), with centre span 300 m/984 ft, length 13 900 m/8 mi 3363 ft)
cantilever Forth Bridge (1658 m/5440 ft long, with two main spans, each consisting of two cantilevers, one from each tower)
suspension Verrazano Narrows Bridge, New York City (1964) (world's longest, total length 4174 m/13 700 ft); Humber Bridge (1980) (world's longest single main span 1410 m/4628 ft)□

bridge card game, derived from whist◊ and introduced to Britain c1880, of which the most popular form is ***contract bridge*** developed in USA from 1925 and made popular by American expert Ely Culbertson 1891–1955. Played by two teams of two, who 'contract' to win a stated number of 'tricks' and who can name their own trumps. One partner's cards are exposed (the 'dummy') and played by the other partner□

Bridge Frank 1879–1941. British composer, the teacher of Benjamin Britten. His works include the orchestral *The Sea* 1910–11, and *Oration* 1930 for cello and orchestra□

Bridgeport industrial city in Connecticut, USA; population 142 500□
Bridger Jim 1804–81. Most famous of the American 'mountain men' or free fur trappers; discoverer of the Great Salt Lake 1824□
Bridges Robert Seymour 1844–1930. British Poet Laureate from 1913, remembered for his lyrics, his tepid philosophical *The Testament of Beauty* 1929, and his friendship with Hopkins◊ whose poetry he published in 1918□
Bridget St 453–523. Irish saint, also known as St Bride, and one of the patron saints of Ireland. She founded the first Irish nunnery at Kildare; feast day 1 Feb□
Bridgetown capital and port of Barbados; population 88 000□
Bridgewater Francis Egerton, 3rd Duke of Bridgewater 1736–1803. British engineer, who (with James Brindley◊) constructed the Bridgewater Canal 1760–72, England's first modern canal, Worsley-Manchester-Liverpool□
Bridgman Percy Williams 1882–1961. American physicist, whose research into high pressures led to a Nobel prize in 1946, and the creation of synthetic diamonds by General Electric in 1955□
Bridie James. Pseudonym of Scottish dramatist Osborne Henry Mavor 1888–1951, professor of medicine, and a founder of Glasgow Citizens' Theatre. Plays include *Tobias and the Angel* 1930, and *The Anatomist* 1931□
Brie district of N France between the Seine and Marne, noted for its soft cheese□
Briggs Henry 1561–1630. British mathematician, who constructed the modern system of logarithms (to base ten, rather than the system of Napier◊)□
Bright John 1811–89. British Liberal statesman and orator. A founder of the Anti-Corn Law League, he joined with Cobden◊ to lead the struggle in Parliament for free trade, achieved 1846. He opposed the Crimean War, supported the North in the American Civil War, and helped secure the passage of the 1867 Reform Act□
Brightlingsea fishing and sailing centre in Essex, England; population 6500. From 1983 its port facilities were redeveloped for European trade□
Brighton seaside resort in E Sussex, England; population 152 700. It was made fashionable by the Prince Regent (later George IV) who built the oriental Royal Pavilion, and has Regency terraces and squares, picturesque Lanes, the University of Sussex 1963, a boating marina, conference centre, and Roedean school for girls is nearby□
Brillat-Savarin Anthelme 1755–1826. French gastronomist, author of *Physiologie du Goût*□
Brindisi passenger port and naval base in SE Italy; population 82 000□
Brindley James 1716–72. British engineer, builder of the Bridgewater◊ and other canals□
Brinell Johann Auge 1849–1925. Swedish engineer, deviser of the ***Brinell Hardness Test*** for metals and alloys in 1900□
Brisbane capital and chief port of Queensland, Australia; population 1 015 000. It was named after Governor Sir Thomas Brisbane, who took over the site as a penal colony 1824–39, opened to free settlers in 1842. There are two universities, and the Parliament House 1869□
brisling a type of fish. See under herring◊□
Brissot Jacques Pierre 1754–93. French revolutionary, leader of the moderate Girondins◊/Brissotins, who fell foul of Robespierre and was guillotined□
bristlecone pine see pine◊□
bristletail primitive wingless insect. The 3-pronged Thysanura include the silverfish *Lepisma* which feeds on bookbindings and other organic material, and the firebrat *Thermobia domestica* a kitchen pest; the 2-pronged Diplura live under stones and fallen branches□
Bristol city (administrative headquarters) and port (including Avonmouth, Portishead, and Portbury docks) in Avon, England; industries include aircraft engines, nuclear and general engineering, microelectronics, tobacco, chemicals, paper, printing; chocolate, and wines and spirits are imported; population 408 000. John Cabot◊ sailed from here to discover Newfoundland, and there was a great trade with the American colonies and the West Indies in the 17–18th centuries, including slaves. Notable are the 12th century cathedral; 14th century St Mary Redcliffe (see Chatterton◊); 16th century Acton Court, built by Sir Nicholas Poynz, a courtier of Henry VIII; the Georgian residential area of Clifton; the university 1909; and the Council House 1956. Other features include Clifton Suspension Bridge (see Brunel◊) and Brunel's *S.S. Great Britain*□
Bristol Channel the seaward extension of the Severn estuary, with very high tides□
Britain the larger of the two British Isles, comprising England, Scotland and Wales. See Great◊ Britain□
Britain Battle of. Air battle over Britain 10 Jul–31 Oct 1940. The main conflict was between some 600 Hurricanes and Spitfires and the Luftwaffe's 800 Messerschmitt 109s

and 1000 bombers (Dornier 17s, Heinkel 111s and Junkers 88s). Losses Aug–Sept: RAF 832 fighters; Luftwaffe 668 fighters and some 700 bombers and other aircraft. It resulted in the indefinite postponement of Hitler's invasion plan *Seeloewe* (Sealion) 17 Sept, and its abandonment 10 Oct. See Lord Dowding◊□

British Antarctic Territory British colony established 1962, includes the British sector of Antarctica, and the South◊ Orkney Islands and South◊ Shetlands□

British Broadcasting Corporation (BBC) converted from a private company (established 1922) to a public body under royal charter (1927), it operates television, and national and local radio stations, financed solely by the sale of television viewing licences, and not allowed to carry advertisements, but overseas radio broadcasts (World Service) have a government subsidy. See also Independent◊ Broadcasting Authority□

British Columbia western 'producer' province of Canada on the Pacific

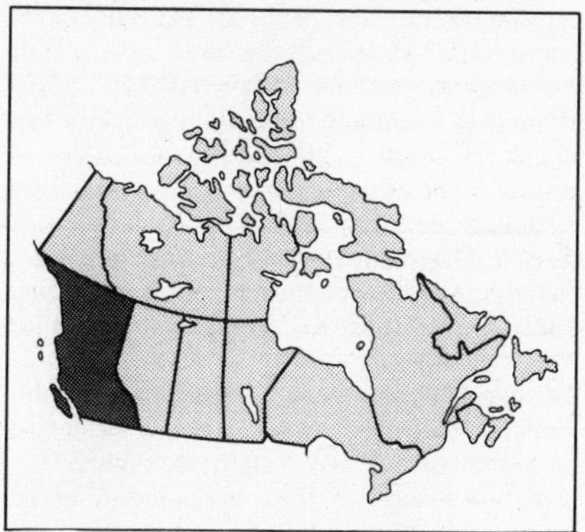

area 948 599 sq km/366 255 sq mi
capital Victoria
towns Vancouver, Prince George, Kamloops, Kelowna
features Rocky Mountains and Coast Range; the coast is deeply indented, rivers include the Fraser and Columbia, there are more than 80 lakes, and more than half the land is forested, all attractive to tourists
products fruit and vegetables; timber and wood products; fish; coal, copper, iron, lead, etc; oil and natural gas, and hydroelectricity.
population 2 870 800
history Captain Cook◊ explored the coast in 1778; a British colony was founded on Vancouver Island in 1849, and the gold rush of 1858 extended settlement to the mainland; it became a province in 1871□

(British) Commonwealth (of Nations) see Commonwealth◊□

British Council semi-official body established 1935 (royal charter 1940) for promoting overseas knowledge of the UK and the teaching of English (excluding politics and commerce)□

British Empire see Orders of Knighthood◊□

British Expeditionary Force the army (BEF) which served in France in World War I 1914–18 (see Earl of Ypres◊ and Haig◊); also the army of World War II 1939–40, which was evacuated from Dunkirk◊; commander General Gort◊□

British Honduras see Belize◊□

British Indian Ocean Territory British colony (BIOT) established 1965 to provide UK/USA defence facilities, and now comprising only the Chagos Archipelago◊. The Islands of Aldabra◊, Farquhar and Desroches were returned to the Seychelles 1976□

British Isles the island group of Great Britain (England, Wales, Scotland), Ireland, the Channel Islands, Orkney and Shetlands, Isle of Man, etc.□

British Legion Royal. Non-political organization to help war veterans and their dependents established by Haig◊ 1921. Flanders poppies made by disabled members raise much of its funds (Remembrance Sunday◊)□

British Library created 1973, it comprises
reference division (the former library departments of the British Museum, being rehoused at the Euston Road, London site);
lending division at Boston Spa, Yorkshire; from 1986 full text documents and graphics will be sent, using a satellite link (launched by Ariane) to western Europe; and
bibliographic services division (incorporating the British National Bibliography)□

British Museum London museum, founded 1753, with the purchase of Sir Hans Sloane's library and art collection, its present buildings were designed by Sir Robert Smirke 1852; the circular British◊ Library reading room (where Marx◊ studied) was added in 1857, and the Edward VII galleries (north wing) 1914. The National History Museum was transferred to S Kensington in 1881□

British Standards Institution (BSI) institution established 1901 to approve standards in clothes' sizes, engineering and building work, etc, and to award approved products a kite mark symbol of quality□

British Telecom separated from the Post Office in 1980, and privatized in 1984, it is responsible for telecommunications, including the telephone network, and radio and television broadcasting. Previously a monopoly, it now faces commercial competition for some of its services. The Telecom tower (189 m/620 ft), London, is the highest inhabited building in Britain, with equipment able to handle more than 150 000 simultaneous telephone conversations and 40 television channels◊□

British Volunteer Programme the various schemes for volunteer aid to developing countries, e.g. Voluntary Service Overseas 1958, which inspired the American Peace Corps◊□

Briton Celtic inhabitant of southern Britain: under Roman rule in the 1st century they continued to some extent organized in small kingdoms (see Boudicca◊), but were largely driven out by the Anglo-Saxon invasions (see Brittany◊). Their priests were the Druids◊□

Brittain Vera 1894–1970. British socialist writer, a nurse to the troops overseas 1915–19, as told in her reminiscent *Testament of Youth* 1933; *Testament of Friendship* 1950 commemorated Winifred Holtby◊. She married political scientist Sir George Catlin 1896–1979; their daughter is Shirley Williams◊□

Brittan Leon 1939– . British Conservative politician, and lawyer. Chief Secretary to the Treasury 1981–3, he was Home Secretary 1983–5, and Minister for Trade and Industry 1985–6 when he resigned over his part in the Westland◊ affair□

Brittany region (*Bretagne*) of NW France; capital Rennes; population 2 707 900. It occupies the Breton peninsula between the Bay of Biscay and the English Channel. As Armorica, it was conquered by Julius Caesar in 56BC, and was devastated by the Northmen after the Roman withdrawal. During the Anglo-Saxon invasion of Britain so many Celts migrated across the Channel that it gained the name of Brittany. By 1547 it had been formally annexed by France, and the Breton◊ language was banned in education. A separatist movement developed after World War II, and there have been terrorist outrages. A dam on the river Rance 1960–7 uses the 13 m/44 ft tides to feed the world's first successful tidal power station. The military college founded by Napoleon at St Cyr, near Versailles, was destroyed in an air raid in World War II and transferred to Coëtquidan, SE of Rennes□

Britten Benjamin, Baron Britten 1913–76. British composer, founder of the Aldeburgh Festival◊ in 1948. He wrote much for the individual voice, e.g. Peter Pears and Janet Baker; his operas include *Peter Grimes* 1945, *Billy Budd* 1951, *Gloriana* 1953, *A Midsummer Night's Dream* 1960, and *Death in Venice* 1973. Notable are the orchestral *Variations on a theme by Frank Bridge* (under whom he studied) 1937, and the choral *A War Requiem* 1962. Order of Merit 1965, peerage 1976□

brittle star see Echinoderm◊□

Brixham fishing port in S Devon, England, part of the composite holiday resort of Torbay◊. William of Orange landed here in 1688□

Brno industrial city in Czechoslovakia, where the Bren gun was first manufactured; population 369 000;.Gregor Mendel◊ devised the theory of inheritance here□

broad bean see bean◊□

Broadmoor site of special hospital (established 1863) at Crowthorne, Berkshire, England, for those formerly described as 'criminally insane'□

Broads The Norfolk. Area of some 12 interlinked fresh-water lakes created about 600 years ago by the digging out of peat deposits; they are noted for wildlife and boating facilities□

Broadway major street of Manhattan◊, New York, famous for its theatres◊□

Broca Pierre Paul 1824–80. French neurologist who identified the area of the left hemisphere of the brain which, when damaged, caused ***aphasia,*** difficulty in speaking, reading, and writing; the area was named Broca's area□

broccoli see cabbage◊□

Broch, Hermann 1880–1951. Austrian novelist, later an American citizen, best-known for his *Der Tod des Vergil/The Death of Virgil* 1945□

Brocken highest peak of the Harz◊ mountains, E Germany, where witches were said to gather on 1 May (Walpurgis◊ night). The ***Brocken Spectre*** is the phenomenon of an enlarged shadow of an observer, accompanied by coloured rings, being cast by the low sun on a cloud bank, first scientifically observed here□

Broglie Louis, 7th Duc de. See de◊ Broglie□

Broken Hill mining town (zinc, lead, tin, silver) in New South Wales, Australia; population 28 600□

Bromberg German name of Bydgoszcz◊□

bromine element
symbol B
atomic number 35
physical description red evil-smelling liquid
features poisonous, a member of the halogen◊ series, found in small quantities in sea water
uses used as an anti-knock petrol additive; compounds are used in photography, medicine, and in the chemical and pharmaceutical industries□

Bromley borough of SE Greater London
features largest borough in area, including Biggin Hill airport, most famous of the RAF stations in the Battle of Britain◊
population 295 400□

bronchitis inflammation of the bronchi (the tubes admitting air to the lungs), usually caused initially by a viral infection (a cold or flu); chronic bronchitis may develop in those exposed to pollutants (e.g. sulphur dioxide SO_2) or cigarette smoke□

Brontë gifted family, of which the three sisters ***Charlotte*** 1816–55, ***Emily Jane*** 1818–48 and ***Anne*** 1820–49, and their brother ***Patrick Branwell*** 1817–48, were brought up by an aunt at Haworth rectory (now a museum) in Yorkshire. In 1846 the sisters published a volume of poems under the pseudonyms Currer (Charlotte), Ellis (Emily) and Acton (Anne) Bell. In 1847 (using the same names), they published the novels *Jane Eyre* (in which Charlotte reflected her experiences at boarding school), *Wuthering Heights* (in which a share with Emily, has been claimed for Branwell on insufficient evidence), and *Agnes Grey*, Anne's much weaker work. During 1848–9 Branwell, Emily, and Anne all died of tuberculosis, aided in Branwell's case by alcohol and opium addiction: he is remembered for his portrait of the sisters. Charlotte subsequently published *Shirley* 1849, in which the heroine resembles Emily, and *Villette* 1853 which recalls her years teaching in Brussels. Charlotte married her father's curate, A B Nicholls, in 1854, and died during pregnancy□

brontosaurus see under dinosaur◊□

Bronx northernmost borough of New York City, including Yankee Stadium, one of America's largest zoos, and the cottage where Poe◊ wrote 'The Bells,' 'Annabel Lee,' etc.□

bronze an alloy of copper with tin, or, under various modifying names, with other metals□

Bronze Age see under prehistory◊□

Bronzino Il pseudonym of Florentine Mannerist artist Agnolo di Cosimo 1503–72, who was influenced by Michelangelo and was noted for his cold, elegant portraits, including many of the Medici□

Brook Peter 1925– . British director, noted for his work with the Royal Shakespeare Company, and the Paris-based Le Centre International de Créations Théatrâles; his films include *Lord of the Flies* 1962 and *Meetings with Remarkable Men* 1979□

Brooke Sir James. See under Sarawak◊, history□

Brooke Rupert Chawner 1887–1915. British poet, remembered for 'Grantchester,' 'The Great Lover,' and the war sonnets published immediately after his death (from blood poisoning) on the Greek island of Skyros on the way to fight in the Dardanelles; he symbolized the 'lost generation' of the war□

Brooklyn borough of New York City, with a botanic garden, and Coney Island◊. Brooklyn Heights has fine Victorian houses. It is linked to Manhattan (Brooklyn Bridge 1883) and Staten Islands (Verrazano Narrows Bridge 1964), and has the Brooklyn US Navy Yard□

Brookner Anita 1938– . British novelist and art historian, whose novels include *Hotel du Lac* 1984, winner of the Booker◊ McConnell prize□

Brooks Mel 1926– . American film director, whose films include *Blazing Saddles* 1974, *Elephant Man* 1979, and *History of the World Pt I* 1981□

broom a shrub of the family Leguminosae, especially species of *Cytisus*, e.g. the ***common broom*** *C scoparius*, with yellow flowers, of Britain□

Brougham Henry Peter, 1st Baron Brougham and Vaux 1778–1868. British Whig◊ politician who defeated the attempt of George IV to divorce Queen Caroline in 1820; he was Lord Chancellor 1831–5, and designed the light carriage known by his name□

Brouwer Adriaen c1605–38. Flemish artist, influenced by Hals◊, who excelled in scenes of peasant revelry□

Brown Ford Madox 1821–93. British artist, linked with the Pre-Raphaelite◊ Brotherhood; his works include *Christ Washing St Peter's Feet,* and *The Last of England*□

Brown George, Baron George-Brown 1914–85. British Labour statesman, a flamboyant Foreign Secretary 1966–8. He was defeated by Harold Wilson◊ in the contest for the party leadership□

Brown John 1800–59. American anti-slavery activist, who seized the government arsenal at Harper's Ferry, W Virginia, on the night of 16 Oct 1859, for weapons. On 18 Oct the arsenal was stormed by the future general Robert E Lee◊, and Brown was tried and hanged on 2 Dec, becoming a martyr, and the hero of the song 'John Brown's Body'□

Brown John c1825–83. Scottish servant and confidant of Queen Victoria from 1858□

Brown Lancelot 1716–83. English gardener and architect, known as 'Capability Brown' because he said sites had 'capability'; his works include Blenheim, with mounds, curved paths, and lakes; Highclere (Hampshire◊); and Bowood (Wiltshire◊). See ha-ha◊□

Brown Robert 1773–1858. British botanist, noted for his observation of the Brownian◊ movement, and his work on cell structure□

Browne Hablot Knight 1815–82. English illustrator, pseudonym 'Phiz', of Dickens' novels□

Browne Robert 1550–1633. English Puritan◊ leader, founder of the Brownist communities which gave rise to modern Congregationalism□

Browne Sir Thomas 1605–82. English author and physician, noted for his personal richness of style in *Religio Medici/The Religion of a Doctor* 1642 and *Urne Buriall* 1658□

Brownian movement continuous random motion of particles in a fluid medium (gas or liquid) as they are subject to impact from the molecules of the medium, observed by Robert Brown◊ in 1827 but not convincingly explained until Einstein◊ in 1905□

Browning Elizabeth Barrett 1806–61. British poet, whose fall from a pony when a child led to her being treated by her father as a confirmed invalid. Her *Poems* 1844 including 'The Cry of the Children', initiated a friendship and secret marriage with Robert Browning◊ in 1846, and her *Sonnets from the Portuguese* 1847 reflect their courtship. The poetic novel *Aurora Leigh* 1857 belongs to their years in Italy□

Browning Robert 1812–89. British poet. Early works such as *Sordello* 1840 show the obscurity, use of psychological analysis and interest in little-known historical characters which also marked his maturity. The pamphlet series *Bells and Pomegranates* 1841–6 includes the popular 'Pippa Passes' and 'The Pied Piper of Hamelin'; *Men and Women* 1855 contains some of his finest love poems and dramatic monologues; and 'The Ring and the Book' 1868–9, is a poem based on an old Italian murder case. Following his wife's death, Browning settled in England□

Brownshirts see Nazi◊ Party□

Brubeck Dave 1920– . American jazz 'intellectual', a student of Milhaud◊, whose quartet (formed 1951) combines improvization with modern classical discipline□

Bruce James 1730–94. Scottish explorer, the first European to reach the source of the Blue Nile in 1770, and to follow the river downstream to Cairo□

Bruce Robert 1274–1329. Scottish hero, who shared in Wallace◊'s rising, and soon after the latter's execution in 1305 rose again against Edward I of England and was crowned King of Scotland in 1306. He defeated Edward II at Bannockburn◊, and in 1328 the Treaty of Northampton recognized Scottish independence□

Bruce Stanley Melbourne, 1st Viscount Bruce of Melbourne 1883–1967. Australian statesman. As Prime Minister and Minister for External Affairs in a National-Country Party coalition 1923–9, he was noted for his unemployment insurance scheme, and other social and welfare measures; he was a member of the British war cabinet 1942–5□

brucellosis disease of cattle, known when transmitted to man as ***undulant fever*** since it recurs in the same way as malaria. It was named after Scottish doctor Sir David Bruce 1855 – 1931, and is caused by bacteria present in the milk of infected cattle. Eradication has been achieved in most of Britain□

Bruch Max 1838–1920. German composer and conductor best known for his G minor violin concerto□

Brücke Die. Expressionist◊ art movement (German 'the bridge') 1905–13; Kirchner◊ was a founder. see also der Blaue◊ Reiter□

Bruckner Anton 1824–96. Austrian composer, cathedral organist at Linz 1856–68, much influenced by Wagner◊. His works include nine symphonies and many choral works□

Bruderhof see under Mennonites◊□

Brueghel Pieter c1525–69. Flemish artist, nicknamed 'Peasant' Brueghel, noted for humorous pictures of peasant life. His son ***Pieter Brueghel the Younger*** 1564–1637, called 'Hell' Brueghel, specialized in religious subjects, and another son ***Jan Brueghel*** 1568–1625, called 'Velvet' Brueghel, painted flowers and land and seascapes, and collaborated with Rubens◊□

Bruges industrial city (Flemish *Brugge*) in NW Belgium; population 118 250. Named from its many bridges, it was the capital of medieval Flanders◊, and was the chief European wool manufacturing town as well as its chief market. Notable are the 14th century cathedral, the church of Notre Dame with a Michelangelo statue of the Virgin and Child, and the Market Hall with outstanding chimes. The College of Europe is the oldest centre of European studies□

Brugge Flemish form of Bruges◊□

Brummell George Bryan 1778–1840. British man of fashion, known as 'Beau Brummell'. A friend of the future George IV, he later quarrelled with him, and was driven by gambling losses to exile in France□

Brunei

area 5800 sq km/2226 sq mi

capital (and chief port) Bandar Seri Begawan

features 75% of the area is forested; the Limbang valley splits Brunei in two, and its cession to Sarawak◊ in 1890 is disputed by Brunei

exports liquefied natural gas (world's largest producer) and oil, but both expected to be exausted by 2000AD

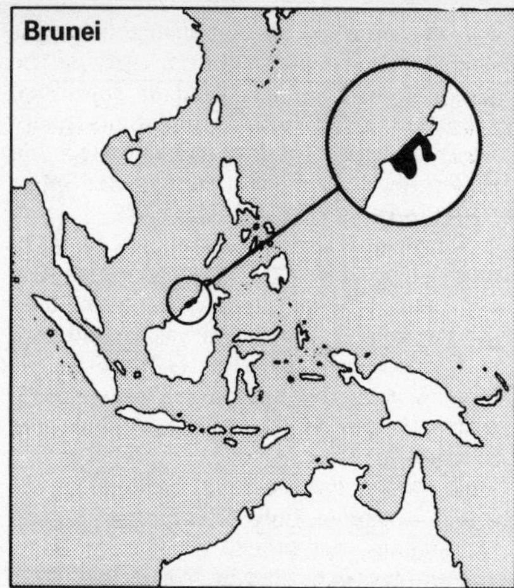

currency Brunei dollar
population 220 000; 120 000 of Malay stock; 50 000 Chinese (few granted citizenship)
language Malay, official; English
religion Islam
government the Sultan, Sir Hassanal Bolkiah 1922– , who succeeded in 1967, is also Prime Minister, and there is a cabinet.
recent history British protectorate from 1888, Brunei was occupied by the Japanese 1941–in 1963. Brunei became independent within the Commonwealth in 1984, but the sultan warned that there would be no initiation of democracy (an internal rebellion had been quelled in 1962). The British-led army is modern and well-equipped, and includes Gurkha troops□

Brunel Isambard Kingdom 1806–59. British engineer, son of Sir Marc Brunel◊, who worked with his father on the Thames (Rotherhithe) tunnel. His own works include the Great Western Railway from 1833; Clifton Suspension Bridge; and the ships *Great Britain* (1843, first large screw-driven ship, see under Bristol◊), *Great Western* 1837, and *Great Eastern* 1858□

Brunel Sir Marc Isambard 1769–1849. French engineer, who devised the tunnelling shield which allowed the construction of the Wapping to Rotherhithe tunnel under the Thames 1825–43, on which he worked with his son Isambard Kingdom Brunel◊□

Brunelleschi Filippo 1377–1446. Italian Renaissance architect. One of the earliest and greatest Renaissance architects, he was responsible for the construction of the dome of Florence Cathedral (completed 1438), a feat deemed impossible by many of his comtemporaries□

Brüning Heinrich 1885–1970. German statesman, Reich Chancellor 1930–2, when he resigned on failing to defeat economic crisis with deflation□

Bruno Giordano c1548–1600. Italian Dominican◊ who was arrested by the Inquisition◊ in 1593 and burned at the stake for his adoption of Copernican◊ astronomy and his pantheistic theology□

Bruno St c1030–1101. The founder of the Carthusian◊ order; feast day 6 Oct□

Brunswick former independent duchy, a republic from 1918, which is now part of Lower Saxony◊, W Germany□

Brunswick city (German *Braunschweig*) in Lower Saxony, W Germany; population 261 670□

Brussels capital (Flemish Brussel/French Bruxelles) of Belgium from 1839; population 1 009 000, 80% French-speaking, the suburbs Flemish. Notable are the 13th century church of Sainte Gudule; the Grande Place, on which stand the Hôtel du Ville and Maison du Roi; the Royal Palace, and Houses of Parliament. Lace, textiles, machinery, and chemicals are made. It is the headquarters of the European Economic Community and since 1967 of the international secretariat of NATO◊□

Brussels Treaty of. Pact of economic, political, cultural, and military alliance established 17 Mar 1948 for 50 years by Britain, France, and the Benelux◊ countries, joined by W Germany and Italy in 1954. It was the forerunner of NATO◊ and the Common◊ Market□

brussels sprout see cabbage◊□

Brutus Marcus Junius c78–42BC. Roman soldier, a supporter of Pompey◊ in the Civil War. Pardoned by Caesar◊, he nevertheless plotted his assassination to restore the purity of the republic. When he was defeated (with Cassius◊) by Mark◊ Antony at Philippi, he committed suicide□

Bruxelles French form of Brussels□

Bryansk industrial town in the W USSR; population 401 000□

Bryant William Cullen 1794–1878. American poet, editor-in-chief of the New York *Evening Post* from 1829. He combined puritan idealism with love of nature, e.g. *Thanatopsis*□

bryony either of two hedgerow climbing plants found in Britain; ***white bryony*** *Bryonia dioica* belonging to the gourd family Cucurbitaceae, and ***black bryony*** *Tamus communis* of the yam family Dioscoreaceae□

bryophyta see classification of plants◊□

Bryusov Valery 1873–1924. Russian Symbolist◊ poet and critic□

Brzezinski Zbigniev 1928– . American Democrat politician. National Security Adviser to President Carter from 1977. He was the chief architect of Carter's human rights policy□

bubble chamber vessel filled with a transparent liquid, usually hydrogen or helium, super-heated above its normal boiling point. Ionising particles make tracks of bubbles through it which are photographed to study particle behaviour. See also Donald Glaser◊, and Spark chamber◊□

Buber Martin 1878–1965. Israeli philosopher, a Zionist◊ and advocate of the reappraisal of ancient Jewish thought in modern terms□

Bucaramanga industrial and commercial city in N Central Colombia; population 387 900□

buccaneers pirates off the American coast in the 17th century who plundered Spanish ships and colonies, e.g. Henry Morgan; the growth of naval power in the 18th century ended their activities□

Bucer Martin 1491–1551. German Protestant◊ reformer, professor at Cambridge from 1549, who tried to reconcile the views of Luther◊ and Zwingli◊□

Buchan John, (Baron Tweedsmuir) 1875–1940. British author of historical biographies, and of thrilling adventure stories including *Prester John* 1910, *The Thirty-Nine Steps* 1915, *Greenmantle* 1916, *Huntingtower* 1922, *The Three Hostages* 1924, and *The House of the Four Winds* 1935. He was Governor General of Canada 1934–40□

Buchanan George 1506–82. Scottish humanist, author of a *History of Scotland* biased against Mary◊ Queen of Scots, to whom he was tutor□

Bucharest capital of Romania; population 1 832 000. Once a citadel built by Vlad the Impaler (see Dracula◊) to stop the advance of the Ottoman◊ invasion in the 14th century, it became the capital in 1861. It includes several museums, including the 18th century Mogosoaia Palace, and there is an international airport at Otopeni□

Buchenwald village NE of Weimar, E Germany, site of a Nazi concentration camp 1937–45□

Buchman Frank 1878–1961. American originator of the Oxford◊ Group (noted for its group confessionals), and of the anti-Communist campaign for Moral Rearmament 1938□

Buck Pearl S 1892–1973. American novelist, Nobel prizewinner 1938 for *The Good Earth* 1933, set in China□

Buckingham George Villiers, 1st Duke of Buckingham 1592–1628. English courtier, favourite of James I, who failed to arrange a marriage of the future Charles I with the Spanish Infanta in 1623, but negotiated his alliance with Henrietta Maria, sister of the French king. He also failed in a planned expedition to Cádiz in 1625, and in an attempt in 1627 to relieve the Protestants besieged in La Rochelle, and was assassinated after attacks in Parliament on his policy□

Buckingham George Villiers, 2nd Duke of Buckingham 1628–87. English politician, dissolute son of the 1st duke, he was brought up with the royal children, and was a member of the Cabal◊ under Charles II. His play *The Rehearsal* satirized the style of Dryden◊, who portrayed him as Zimri in *Absalom and Achitophel*□

Buckingham Palace London home of the British Sovereign, built 1705 for the Duke of Buckingham, but bought by George III in 1762 and reconstructed by Nash◊ 1825-36; a new front was added in 1913□

Buckinghamshire south Midland county of England

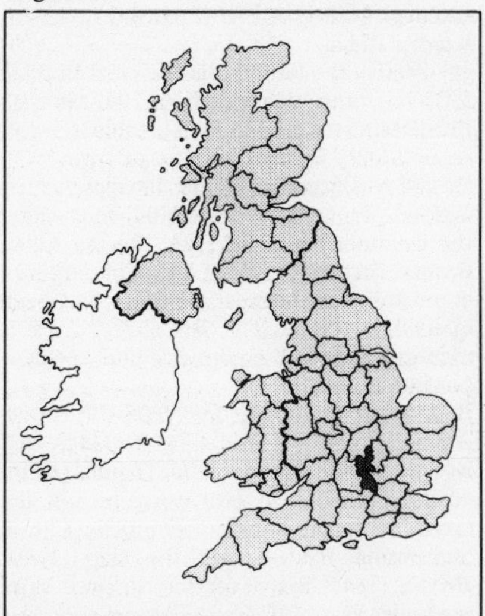

area 1883 sq km/727 sq mi

towns administrative headquarters Aylesbury; Buckingham, High Wycombe, Beaconsfield, Olney◊

features Chequers◊; Burnham Beeches and the church of Gray's 'Elegy' at Stoke Poges; National Spinal Injuries Centre at Stoke Mandeville; Cliveden, designed by Barry◊ (now a hotel, it was used by the Astors◊ for house parties); Bletchley Park (see Ultra◊), now used as a training centre for GCHQ (Britain's communications 'Spy centre'); Chenies Manor, where there has been a medical herb garden since 1979; homes of William Cowper at Olney, Disraeli at Hughenden, and John Milton at Chalfont St Giles.

products furniture, especially beech; agricultural
population 550 100
famous people John Hampden, Ben Nicholson□

Buckley William 1780–1856. Australian convict, who escaped and lived 1803–35 among the Aborigines before giving himself up, hence ***Buckley's chance*** is an 'outside chance'□

Buckley William Frank 1925– . American author, founder-editor of the *National Review* 1955, and, by such books as *Up from Liberalism* 1959, and a weekly TV debate 'Firing Line', responsible for the left-to-right shift in US intellectual fashion which assisted Reagan to power□

buckwheat high nutritive value grain plant *Fagopyrum esculentum*, family Polygonaceae. It can grow on poor soil in a short summer□

Budapest capital and chief industrial city (chemicals, textiles, etc) of Hungary; population 2 060 000. Buda, on the right bank of the Danube, includes the former royal palace, and Pest, on the left, includes the houses of Parliament, etc. Buda became the Hungarian capital in 1867, and was joined with Pest in 1872. It saw fighting between German and Russian troops in World War II 1944–5, and between the Hungarians and Russian troops in the rising of 1956□

Buddha title of prince Gautama Siddhartha c563–483BC born at Lumbini◊ in Nepal. At the age of 29, he left his wife and son to seek a way of escape from the burdens of existence, and after six years of austerity became enlightened (Buddha means 'enlightened one') under a banyan or bo tree near Buddh◊ Gaya. He acquired the Four Truths: the fact of pain or ill; that pain has a cause; that pain can be ended; and that it can be ended by following the Eightfold Way of right views, right intention, right speech, right action, right livelihood, right effort, right mindfulness, and right concentration, and so arriving at Nirvana, the extinction of all craving for things of the senses. He began teaching at Varanasi, and founded the Sangha, or order of monks, eventually dying at Kusinagara in Uttar Pradesh. See also Kandy◊□

Buddh Gaya village in Bihar, India, where Gautama became Buddha◊; a descendant of the original banyan tree is preserved□

Buddhism religion derived from the teaching of Buddha◊, who is regarded as one of a series of such beings, the next incarnation being due c3000AD.
scriptures known as Pitakas or 'baskets' they form three divisions: ***Vinaya*** or Discipline, listing offences and rules of life; ***Dhamma*** or Doctrine, the exposition of Buddhism by Buddha and his disciples; ***Abhidhamma*** or Further Doctrine, later discussions on doctrine. The fundamental doctrine is that of ***karma***, good or evil deeds meeting an appropriate reward or punishment either in this life or (through transmigration or rebirth) in a long succession of lives. The self is not regarded as permanent, and the aim of the Noble Eightfold Way is to break the chain of karma, and achieve dissociation from the body by attaining ***Nirvana*** ('blowing out', the eradication of all desires, either in annihilation, or by absorption of the self in the infinite). There are no gods, but great reverence is accorded to Buddha, and other such advanced incarnations; see also Kuanyin◊, Mantra◊.
divisions: Theraveda Buddhism, the School of the Elders, which is also known as ***Hinayana*** or Base Career, prevails in southern Asia (Sri Lanka, Thailand, and Burma), and its scriptures are written in ***Pali*** an Indo-Aryan language with its roots in N India; ***Mahayana*** or Great Career, which arose at the beginning of the Christian era, exhorts the individual not merely to attain Nirvana as an individual, but to become a trainee Buddha (or Boddhisattva), and so save others. This prevails in northern Asia (China, Korea, Japan, and Tibet). The form established in Tibet◊, ***Lamaism,*** dates from 750AD when the Dalai◊ Lama became both spiritual and temporal ruler; its outward forms include prayer wheels and it had strong magical elements. In India itself Buddhism was replaced by Hinduism◊, but still has five million devotees, and is growing by adherence of the Harijans◊. ***Zen*** originated with a Mahayana monk, Bodhidharma, c520AD, in China, and from the 12th century was adopted in Japan; it is characterized by anecdotes giving rise to exchanges between master and pupil which result in sudden enlightenment. Japan is also noted for such lay organizations as ***Soka Gakkai*** (Value Creation Society), founded 1937, which equates absolute faith with immediate material benefit, and by 1980 was followed by more than seven million households□

buddleia genus of shrubs and trees, family Buddleiaceae, of which the best-known is the ***butterfly bush*** *B davidii*, of which the purple or white flower heads attract the insects□

budgerigar Australian parakeet; see parrot◊□

Buenos Aires capital and industrial city of Argentina, largest city in S America; population 9 667 200. Founded in 1536, it became the capital in 1853, and was developed on a modern 'gridiron' plan; notable are the Palace of Congress, and, on the Plaza de Mayo, the cathedral and presidential palace (known as the 'Pink House'), as well as its luxurious shopping precincts. The birthplace of W H Hudson◊ at nearby Florencio has been a museum since 1956□

buffalo wild cattle◊, notably the ***African buffalo*** *Syncerus caffer* of the bush S of the Sahara, and the ***Asiatic water buffalo*** *Bubalus bubalis* of India, with long, widely separated horns. They are easily domesticated. The so-called buffalo of N America is the bison◊□

Buffalo port in New York state, USA, linked with New York City by the New York State Barge Canal; population 357 000□

Buffon Georges Louis Leclerc, Comte de Buffon 1707–88. French naturalist, a popularizer of the subject, who anticipated aspects of evolutionary theory□

bug specifically, the insect sub-order Heteroptera of the order Hemiptera. Parasitic; thousands of species include the ***bed-bug*** *Cimex lectularis*, a brownish, flattened, wingless insect, with an unpleasant smell, which sucks the blood of human beings; the ***squash bug*** *Anasa tristis*, which sucks the juice of squashes and pumpkins; and the various families of ***water boatmen*** and ***pondskaters***□

Bug two rivers of E Europe; the West Bug rises in the SW Ukraine and flows to the Vistula, and the South Bug rises in the W Ukraine and flows to the Black Sea□

Buganda former kingdom of the Baganda within Uganda of which it now forms two provinces; the Kabaka or king, Sir Edward Mutesa II 1924–69, was the first president of independent Uganda 1962–6□

bugle wind instrument of the brass family, with a shorter tube and less expanded bell than the trumpet□

building society institution originating in Britain in Birmingham in 1781, which attracts investment in order to make home loans on the security of first mortgage on the property. Its 'shares' are attractive to small investors because both savers and borrowers gain tax concessions□

Bujumbura capital of Burundi; population 157 100. Steamers cross Lake Tanganyika to Kigoma, and there is an international airport□

Bukavu port in E Zaîre, on Lake Kivu; population 209 050□

Bukhara city in the Republic of Uzbek USSR; population 188 000. It is an Islamic centre; Bukhara carpets (made in Ashkhabad) used to be marketed here□

Bukhovina region of SE Europe ceded by Turkey to Austria in 1777, and included in Romania in 1918. North Bukhovina was incorporated in the Ukraine Republic by the Soviet Union in 1940, and the cession was confirmed in the peace treaty of 1947, but the question of its return has been mooted by Romania□

Bulawayo city in Zimbabwe; 363 000. Built on the site of the fired kraal of Matebele◊ chief, Lobengula, in 1893, its buildings include Government House (the former home of Rhodes◊, who is buried in the Matopo hills above the city)□

bulb instrument of vegetative reproduction consisting of a modified leaf bud with fleshy leaves containing a reserve food supply; roots form from its base. Characteristic of many monocotyledenous plants e.g. daffodil, snowdrop, onion. Bulbs are grown on a commercial scale in temperate countries, especially England and Holland□

Bulganin Nikolai 1895–1975. Marshal of the Soviet Union, organizer of Moscow's defences in World War II; Prime Minister 1955–8 until ousted by Khrushchev◊□

Bulgaria People's Republic of

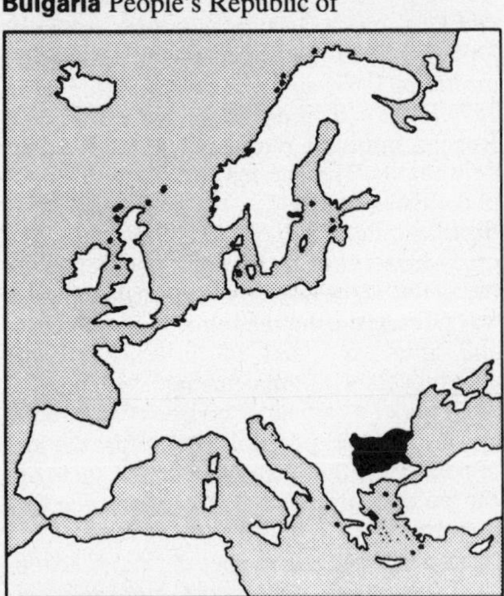

area 110 840 sq km/42796 sq mi
capital Sofia
towns Plovdiv, Rusé; Burgas and Varna are Black Sea ports
features Balkan mountains, Black Sea coast
exports textiles, chemicals, non-ferrous metals, timber, minerals, machinery
currency lev
population 8 880 000, including 900 000 ethnic Turks now subjected to compulsory assimilation (change to Bulgarian name, etc.)
language Bulgarian, Turkish
religion Eastern Orthodox Christianity 90%, Sunni Islam 10%, but the latter faith is discouraged

famous people Ferdinand I and Georgi Dimitrov
government under the 1971 constitution the council of state (chairman Todor Zhivkov) is elected by the unicameral national assembly, itself popularly elected. Real power lies with the Politburo, also headed by Zhivkov.
recent history in 1908 Bulgaria became a kingdom independent of Turkish suzerainty. An ally of the Axis◊ powers in World War II, it came under Soviet occupation 1944–47, becoming a Communist republic in 1946. Having achieved independence while under Soviet rule, it remains the most loyal of all the satellites□

bulimia counteraction of stress or depression by uncontrollable overeating (Greek 'ox hunger'), compensated for by forced vomiting or an overdose of laxatives□

Bull John. Typical Englishman, as originated by Dr John Arbuthnot in his *History of John Bull* 1712, advocating the Tory◊ policy of peace with France□

Bull Olav 1883–1933. Norwegian lyric poet□

Bull Papal. Papal document (from the circular seals *bullae* attached to them), e.g. those condemning Luther◊ in 1520, and proclaiming papal infallibility in 1870□

bull-baiting 'sport', illegal in UK from 1835, of setting dogs to attack a chained bull□

bulldog a breed of dog◊□

Buller Sir Redvers Henry 1839–1908. British commander against the Boers◊ in the South African War, who was defeated at Colenso and Spion Kop, but relieved Ladysmith◊; he was superseded by Lord Roberts◊□

bullfighting 'sport' of Spain (introduced by the Moors in the 11th century), Spanish America, etc. ***Picadores*** on horseback first wound the bull with lances; ***banderillos*** then plunge darts into its neck; and finally a ***matador*** with sword and ***muleta*** (a red cloth attached to a stick) attempts to deal a death blow by plunging his sword between the bull's left shoulder and the shoulder blade□

bullfinch a type of European finch◊□

bullhead a small fish; see under perch◊□

bullroarer aboriginal magical musical instrument; a piece of wood fastened by one of its pointed ends to a cord, by which it is whirled round the head to make a whirring noise□

Bull Run Battle of. see Civil◊ War, American□

bull terrier a breed of dog◊□

Bülow Prince Bernhard von 1849–1929. German statesman, Chancellor 1900–9, who precipitated Europe into the opposing power groups of the Triple Entente (Britain, France, Russia) and Triple Alliance (Germany, Austria-Hungary, Italy)□

Bülow Hans von 1830–94. German pianist-conductor. He studied with Wagner◊ and Liszt◊, and in 1857 married Cosima, daughter of the latter. From 1864 he served Ludwig◊ II of Bavaria, conducting first performances of *Tristan* and *Meistersinger*. His wife left him to live with Wagner, whom she married in 1870□

Bulwer-Lytton see Lytton◊□

bumble-bee a type of bee◊□

Bunche Ralph 1904–71. American United Nations under-secretary, who acted as mediator in Palestine 1948–9, and as special representative in the Congo 1960; Nobel peace prize 1950□

Bunin Ivan Alexeyevich 1870–1953. Russian writer of realistic stories of peasant life, who received a Nobel prize in 1933, his short story 'The Gentleman from San Francisco' being specially cited□

Bunker Hill Battle of. See American◊ Independence, War of□

Bunsen Robert Wilhelm von 1811–99. German chemist, who invented and popularized the bunsen burner, developed spectrum analysis (see Kirchhoff◊), and used it to discover caesium◊ and rubidium◊□

bunting stoutly built sub-family (Emberizinae) of the finches◊, mainly New World, but including the Old World ***yellowhammer*** *Emberiza citrinella* and ***snow bunting*** *Plectrophenax nivalis*. The ***ortolan*** *Emberiza hortulana*, with yellow throat and fawn and pink body, stores up fat ahead of autumn migration from Eurasia southward. The ortolan is eaten in France□

Buñuel Luis 1900– . Spanish Surrealist◊ film director, e.g. *The Discreet Charm of the Bourgeoisie* 1972□

Bunyan John 1628–88. English author. Born near Bedford, son of a tinker, he joined the Baptists◊ in 1650 and was gaoled for preaching 1660–72, and in 1675. In confinement, he wrote the autobiographical *Grace Abounding* 1666, and began *The Pilgrim's Progress* 1678□

bunyip Australian Aborigine mythical version of the hippopotamus; in 'Strine' (Australian dialect slang) it means 'a fake'□

Burbage Richard c1567–1619. English actor, thought to have been the original Hamlet, Othello, and Lear, who built the Globe Theatre c1599; see also under Theatre◊□

burbot freshwater fish related to the cod◊□

burdock plant *Arctium lappa*, family Compositae◊, with hairy leaves and ripe fruit protected by hooked burs□

Burgas Black Sea port in Bulgaria; population 163 650□

Bürger Gottfried 1747–94. German Romantic◊ poet, remembered for his ballad 'Lenore' 1773□

Burgess Anthony 1917– . British novelist. A teacher, he was invalided home from Borneo because of a suspected brain tumour in 1959, and concentrated on writing in his 'one year to live'. His works include *A Clockwork Orange* 1962 and *Earthly Powers* 1980□

Burgess Guy. See under Kim Philby◊□

burgh former unit of Scottish local government, abolished in 1975, headed by provost, magistrates and councillors; the terms burgh and royal burgh are now only an honorary distinction□

Burgh Hubert de d. 1243. English justiciar (chief political and legal official) 1215–32. He was a supporter of King John◊ against the barons; ended French intervention in England by his defeat of the French fleet in the Strait of Dover in 1217, but was dismissed under Henry III□

Burghley William Cecil, Baron Burghley 1520–98. English statesman. One of Edward VI's secretaries, he lost office under Queen Mary, but on Queen Elizabeth's succession became one of her most trusted ministers. He was largely responsible for the religious settlement of 1559, and took a leading role in the events preceding the execution of Mary◊, Queen of Scots, in 1587. He carefully avoided a premature breach with Spain, and was created Baron Burghley 1571, and Lord High Treasurer 1572□

burglary entering a building, etc, with the intent to commit theft or other serious crime; the maximum sentence is 14 years, though aggravated burglary (involving the use of firearms, etc.) can mean life imprisonment□

Burgos city in Castilla-León, Spain; population 156 500. El Cid◊ is buried in the cathedral□

Burgoyne John 1722–92. British general and dramatist. On the outbreak of the War of American Independence, he was given command of a force intended to invade the colonies from Canada, but surrendered at Saratoga in 1777. His comedies include *The Heiress* 1786□

Burgundy modern region (Bourgogne) of France, capital Dijon; population 1 595 100. A former independent kingdom and duchy, it was incorporated in France in 1477. It is famous for its wines, e.g. Chablis, and Nuits-Saints-Georges, and for its cattle (the Charolais herdbook is maintained at Nevers). The village of *Taizé* has a Protestant monastic community founded 1940 by Swiss theologian Roger Schutz 1915– ; it became in the 1960s an ecumenical centre for young people interested in the 'struggle and contemplation' combined in communal Christianity□

Burke Edmund 1729–97. British Whig◊ statesman and political theorist. Born in Dublin, he achieved literary fame with his aesthetic *Essay on the Sublime and Beautiful* 1756; opposed the government's attempts to coerce the American colonists, e.g. *Thoughts on the Present Discontents* 1770; attacked Hastings◊' misgovernment in India and promoted his impeachment; and, as a resolute opponent of direct democracy, denounced the French Revolution in *Reflections on the Revolution in France* 1790. By modern Conservatives◊ he is regarded as the greatest of their political theorists□

Burke John 1787–1848. First publisher in 1826 of 'Burke's Peerage', the register of the British ancestory□

Burke Robert O'Hara 1820–61. Australian explorer, who in 1860–1 made the S–N crossing of Australia (Victoria–Gulf of Carpentaria), with William Wills 1834–61. Both died on the return journey, only one man of their party surviving□

Burke and **Hare** two Irishmen, William Burke and William Hare, living in Edinburgh, who dug up the dead to sell for dissection. They increased their supplies by murdering at least 15 people. Burke was hanged in 1829 on the evidence of Hare□

Burkina Faso 'Republic of Honest Men', formerly Republic of Upper Volta

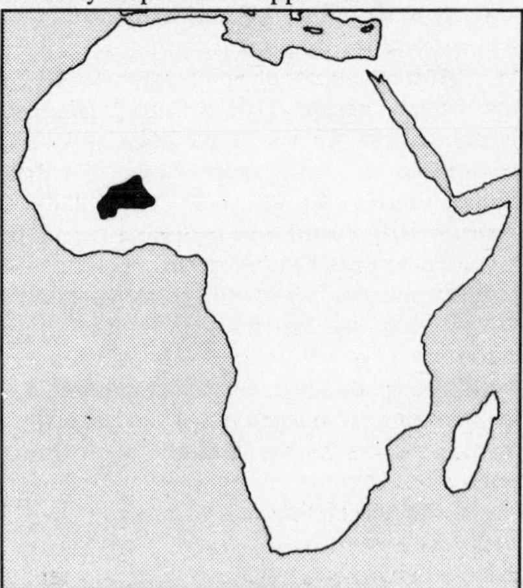

area 274 000 sq km/106 000sq mi
capital Ouagadougou
towns Bobo-Doiulasso
features landlocked plateau savannah country; headwaters of the river Volta
exports cotton, groundnuts, livestock, hides and skins

currency CFA franc
population 7 090 000, 48% Mossi
language French, official; there are about 50 native languages
religion Animism 53%, Sunni Islam 36%, Roman Catholicism 11%
government a mainly civilian government was overthrown by a military coup in 1983 led by Captain Thomas Sankara, the then Prime Minister, who became President, with a council of ministers.
recent history under French rule from 1896, Upper Volta became independent in 1960, but the government proved unstable and subject to military intervention. In 1983 Sankara agreed to submit a border dispute with Mali to the International Court of Justice. The name of the country was changed 1984, as part of the break with a colonial past□
Burma Socialist Republic of the Union of

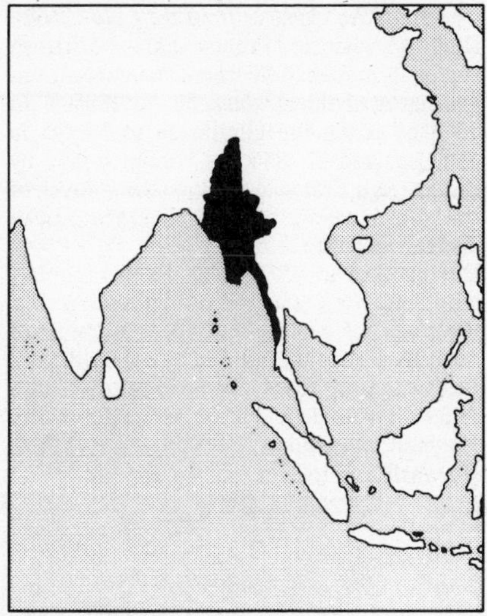

area 678 000 km/261 789 sq mi
capital (and chief port) Rangoon
towns Mandalay, Karbe
features over half is forested; rivers Irrawaddy and Chindwin
exports rice, rubber, jute, teak; varied minerals; jade, rubies, sapphires
currency kyat
population 33 000 000
language Burmese
religion Hinayana Buddhism; religious centre Pagan
government under the constitution of 1973, it is a one-party socialist republic, with a president (General San Yu◊) and council of state, elected by the people's assembly.
recent history Burma came gradually under British rule following the three Burmese Wars (1824–6, 1852, 1885–6), when it was united as a province of India until made a separate country with its own constitution in 1937. It was invaded and occupied by Japan 1941–5, and in 1948 achieved independence outside the Commonwealth. Following a military coup in 1962, General Ne Win◊ was effective head of state 1962–81, when he was succeeded by General San Yu. Various ethnic groups, include the Karens◊, conduct a guerrilla struggle for autonomy□

burn tissue damage (first degree turning the skin red, as in sunburn; second degree causing blistering; and third degree resulting in damage to deeper tissue) caused by heat, light, other radiation, or corrosive substances; similar damage by hot liquid or vapour is a scald. Treatment is directed against shock and infection (by use of antibiotics); wet 'soaks' to cover the wound; air cushion 'hoverbeds' to support the badly burned; and artificial skin grafts (animal cartilage + silicon + a derivative of cowhide) to avoid problems of 'rejection'□

Burne-Jones Sir Edward Coley 1833–98. British Pre-Raphaelite◊, who devoted himself to art rather than the Church under Rossetti◊'s influence, drawing inspiration from medieval legend, as in *King Cophetua and the Beggar Maid.* He also designed tapestries and stained glass for William Morris◊□

burnet a type of herb◊□

Burnet Sir Frank McFarlane 1899–85. Australian immunologist, who shared a Nobel prize with Sir Peter Medawar in 1960 for his work on acquired tolerance to donor transplants□

Burnet Gilbert 1643–1715. British historian: *History of His Own Time* 1723–4. Adviser to William◊ of Orange, with whom he sailed to England in 1688, he was appointed Bishop of Salisbury in 1689□

Burnett Frances Eliza Hodgson 1849–1924. British writer, living in USA from 1865, who wrote the children's stories *Little Lord Fauntleroy* 1886, and *The Secret Garden* 1909□

Burney Frances (Fanny) 1752–1840. British novelist, daughter of the musician Charles Burney 1726–1814, she achieved fame with *Evelina* 1778, became a member of Dr Johnson◊'s circle, received a post at court from Queen Charlotte, and in 1793 married the émigré General D'Arblay□

Burnham Forbes 1923–85. Guyanese statesman. A Marxist-Leninist, he was Prime Minister 1964–80, leading the country to independence 1966, and declaring it the world's first cooperative republic 1970. He was executive president 1980–5. Resistance to the US landing in Grenada◊ in 1983 was said to be due to his forewarning the revolutionaries of the attack□

Burnley industrial town in Lancashire, England; population 90 700□

Burns John 1858–1943. British labour leader, sentenced to six weeks' imprisonment for his part in the Trafalgar Square demonstration on 'Bloody Sunday' (13 Nov 1887), and leader of the strike in 1889 securing the dockers' tanner (wage of 2½p per hour). An Independent Labour MP 1892–1918, he was the first working man to be a member of the Cabinet, as President of the Local Government Board 1906–14□

Burns Robert 1759–96. Scottish poet. Born at Alloway near Ayr, he became joint tenant with his brother of his late father's farm at Mossgiel in 1784, but was unsuccessful, as well as being crossed in his love for Jean Armour, among others. His emigration to Jamaica was only prevented by the success of his *Poems, chiefly in the Scottish dialect* 1786, which enabled him to marry Jean Armour in 1788 and settle to farming at Ellisland, near Dumfries. From 1789 he was a part-time district excise-officer, becoming full-time on the failure of his farm in 1791. His fame rests equally on his poems (eg 'Holy Willie's Prayer', 'Tam o'Shanter', 'The Jolly Beggars', and 'To a Mouse') and his songs, of which he contributed some 300 to Johnson's *Scots Musical Museum 1787–1803*, and Thomson's *Scottish Airs with Poetry* 1793–1811, sometimes wholly original, sometimes adaptations□

Burns Sir Terence 1944– . British economist. A monetarist◊, he was director of the London Business School for Economic Forecasting 1976–9, and became chief economic adviser to the Thatcher◊ government 1980. Knighted 1983□

Burr Aaron 1756–1836. American politician. He tied with Jefferson◊ in the presidential election of 1800, but Alexander Hamilton◊ influenced the House of Representatives to vote Jefferson in, Burr becoming vice-president. Burr killed Hamilton in a duel in 1804, became a social outcast, and had to leave the USA for some years following his attempt to raise a force to invade Mexico□

Burra Edward 1905–76. British genre watercolourist with a Surrealist◊ touch. His work includes street scenes in Harlem and Islington, and landscapes□

Burroughs Edgar Rice 1875–1950. American author of *Tarzan of the Apes* 1914, dealing with a lost aristocratic child reared in the African jungle by chimpanzees□

Burroughs William 1914– . American novelist, member of a big-business family who 'dropped out', and produced the 'beat' novels *Junkie* 1953 and *The Naked Lunch* 1959□

Bursa town in NW Turkey, with a port at Mudania; population 276 000. It was the capital of the Ottoman◊ Empire 1326–1423□

Burt Sir Cyril 1883–1971. British psychologist. He was a pioneer in intelligence tests, but in 1976 his data were found to have been altered to fit his prejudices in favour of hereditary rather than environmental influences□

Burton Richard 1925–84. Welsh actor, born Jenkins. He was remarkable for his voice, as in the radio adaptation of Dylan Thomas◊'s *Under Milk Wood*; his marital and acting partnership with Elizabeth Taylor◊ (*Who's Afraid of Virginia Woolf?* 1966); and the film *The Spy Who Came in from the Cold* 1966□

Burton Sir Richard Francis 1821—90. British traveller, master of 35 oriental languages, and translator of the *Arabian Nights* 1885–8. In 1853 he made the pilgrimage to Mecca in disguise, and in 1856 was commissioned by the Foreign Office to explore the sources of the Nile, and (with J H Speke◊) reached Lake Tanganyika 1858□

Burton Robert 1577–1640. British scholar, who wrote an analysis of depression *The Anatomy of Melancholy* 1621, a mine of miscellaneous material used by later authors□

Burton upon Trent engineering town, also famous for its ale and bitter, in Staffordshire, England; population 50 000□

Burundi Republic of

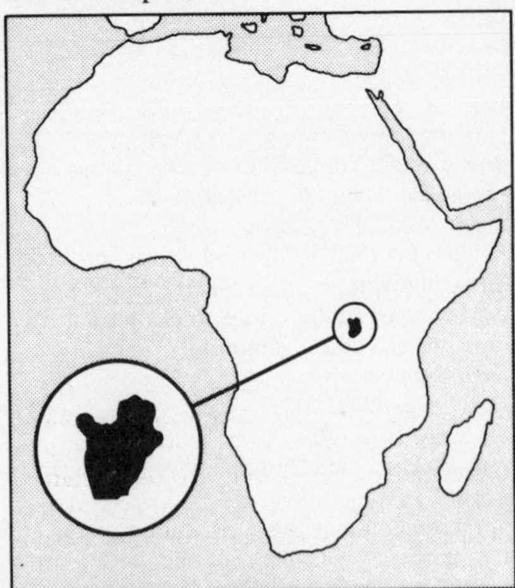

area 27 834 sq km/10 747 sq mi
capital Bujumbura
towns Kitega

features Lake Tanganyika, Great Rift Valley
exports coffee, cotton, tea; nickel; hides, livestock; there are also 500 million tonnes of peat reserves in the basin of the Akanyaru river
currency Burundi franc
population 4 280 000, of whom 15% are the Nilotic Tutsi, still holding most of the land and political power, and the remainder the Bantu Hutu. An unsuccessful Hutu rebellion in the early 1970s led to 150 000 Hutu deaths
language Kirundi (a Bantu language) and French, official; Kiswahili
religion Roman Catholicism over 50%; minority Sunni Islam
government president (Colonel John Baptiste Bagaza) appointed by the supreme military council
recent history formerly part of Ruanda-Urundi, Burundi became an independent kingdom in 1962, and a republic was established following a political coup in 1966. A military coup ensued in 1976, and the regime has become increasingly dictatorial□

Bury textile town in Greater Manchester, England; population 182 400. Sir Robert Peel◊ was born here□

Buryat Republic of the USSR, in Soviet Central Asia on Lake Baikal, annexed from China 1689–1727; area 351 300 sq km/135 650 sq mi; population 917 500. Capital Ulan-Udé□

Bury St Edmunds town in Suffolk, England; population 29 500. Named after St Edmund◊□

Bush Alan Dudley 1900– . British composer. A student of Ireland◊, he later adopted a didactic simplicity in his compositions which include the operas *Wat Tyler* 1953 and *Men of Blackmoor* 1956□

Bush George 1924– . American Republican politician, director of the CIA 1975–6, and from 1981 vice-president to Reagan◊□

bushbuck a species of antelope◊□

bushido chivalric code of honour of the Japanese military caste, the Samurai□

bushmaster a type of large poisonous snake◊□

Bushmen the aboriginal people of southern Africa, still living to some extent nomadically, especially in the Kalahari Desert, and calling themselves Kung. Of small stature and with dark yellow skins, they are traditionally hunters and gatherers, and have a language marked by the same 'clicks' as that of the Hottentots◊. Their early art, surviving in cave paintings, is remarkable□

bushrangers Australian armed robbers of the 19th century, originating with escaped convicts; the last gang was that of the Kelly brothers 1878–80□

business school institution for training in management and marketing, e.g. London Business School (LBS) 1965; Harvard in USA, Insead in France□

Busoni Ferruccio Benvenuto 1866–1924. Italian composer, who first appeared as a pianist at the age of seven, and composed for the instrument, e.g. his piano concerto opus 39. His operas include Doktor Faust (unfinished; first performed in England in 1986)□

bustard family of game birds, Otididae, including the ***great bustard*** *Otis tarda*, one of the world's heaviest flying land birds at 18 kg/40 lb; its re-naturalization is being attempted in Britain. See crane◊□

butadiene an inflammable gas, CH_2:CHCH:CH_2, derived from petroleum, used in making synthetic rubber□

butane alkane (paraffin hydrocarbon) gas, C_4H_{10}, by-product of petroleum manufacture or from natural gas. Liquefied under pressure, it is used as a fuel for industrial and domestic purposes, e.g. in portable cookers□

Bute island and holiday resort in the Firth of Clyde, Strathclyde, Scotland; area 122 sq km/47 sq mi. The chief town is Rothesay□

Bute John Stuart, 3rd Earl of Bute 1713–92. British Tory◊ statesman, confidant of George III until 1765, and Prime Minister 1762–3. He was influential in breaking the power of the Whigs◊, and, as the supplanter of the popular Pitt◊, was widely hated□

Buthelezi Chief Gatsha 1929– . Zulu statesman, Prime Minister of KwaZulu from 1970. Great-grandson of Cetewayo◊, he is strongly opposed to KwaZulu becoming a Black◊ National State, but envisages a confederation of the black areas, with eventual black majority rule over all S Africa under a one-party socialist system. He is founder-president of ***Inkatha*** (from the grass coil worn by Zulu women for carrying head loads; its many strands give it strength) 1975, a non-violent organization for attaining a non-racial democratic political system□

Butler Joseph 1692–1752. British churchman, who became Dean of St Paul's in 1740 and Bishop of Durham in 1750; his *Analogy of Religion* 1736 argued that it is no more rational to accept Deism◊ than revealed religion□

Butler Josephine Elizabeth 1828–1906. British social reformer, born Grey. She promoted women's education and the Married Women's Property Act, and campaigned against the compulsory examination of women prostitutes for VD as degrading to women□

Butler Reg 1913– . British sculptor, using distortion of the human figure to gain striking effects, as in *Unknown Political Prisoner* 1953□

Butler Richard Austen, Baron 1902–82. British Conservative◊ politician, known from his initials as Rab. As Minister of Education 1941–45, he was responsible for the Education Act 1944; was Chancellor of the Exchequer 1951–5 and Lord Privy Seal 1955–9. As a candidate for the premiership, he was defeated by Macmillan◊ in 1957 (under whom he was Home Secretary 1957–62), and by Douglas-Home◊ in 1963, but was Foreign Minister 1963–4. He was Master of Trinity College, Cambridge 1965–78. His attitude to politics was summed up in his autobiographical *The Art of the Possible* 1971□

Butler Samuel 1612–80. English satirist, whose poem *Hudibras* 1663–78, ridiculed the Puritans□

Butler Samuel 1835–1902. British author, who resisted his clerical father's pressure to enter the Church, and tried sheep-farming in New Zealand 1859–64. In 1872 he made his name with his satiric attack on contemporary utopianism, *Erewhon* ('nowhere' reversed), but is now remembered for his autobiographical *The Way of All Flesh* 1903□

Butlin Sir William 'Billy' 1899–1980. British pioneer of holiday camps, chalet complexes with amusements and meals 'all-in'. See Jersey◊□

Butor Michel 1926– . French 'anti-novelist', writing according to the theories of Robbe-Grillet◊, e.g. *Passage de Milan* 1954 and *L'Emploi du temps* 1963□

buttercup species of *Ranunculus* with divided leaves and yellow flowers, family Ranunculaceae◊, e.g. ***common buttercup*** *R acris* and ***creeping buttercup*** *R repens*. Britain's rarest plant is the ***Badgeworth buttercup*** *Ranunculus ophioglossifolius* in the Cotswolds. See celandine◊□

butterfly insect (200 000 species) belonging (like the moth◊) to the order Lepidoptera, but distinguished from the moth by being active during the day; having the antennae clubbed, rather than plumed or feathery; having no 'lock' between the fore and hindwing; and resting with wings in the vertical position, rather than flat or sloping. Like the moth, the butterfly has wings covered in microscopic scales, and usually feeds on nectar, etc, through a tubular proboscis, although some species are carnivorous. Metamorphosis is complete, the caterpillars being very varied, and the pupa or chrysalid usually being without the protection of a cocoon. Adult lifespan may be only a few weeks, but some species hibernate and lay eggs in the early spring or summer.

The largest family, Nymphalidae, has some 6000 species: it includes the Peacock, Tortoiseshells, and Fritillaries. The family Pieridae includes the ***cabbage white***, one of the few butterflies injurious to crops. The Lycaenidae are chiefly small, often with metallic coloration, e.g. the Blues, Coppers and Hairstreaks. The ***large blue*** *Lycaena arion,* extinct in Britain from 1979, but being re-established 1984, has a complex life history, in that it lays its eggs on wild thyme, and the caterpillars are then taken by Myrmica ants to their nests, where they milk their honey glands, while the caterpillars feed on the ant larvae; in the spring the caterpillars finally pupate and emerge as butterflies. The mainly tropical Papilionidae, or Swallowtails, are large and very beautiful, especially the S American species. The world's largest butterfly is ***Queen Alexandra's birdwing*** *Ornithoptera alexandrae* of Papua New Guinea, with a body 7.5 cm/3 in long and a wingspan of 25 cm/10 in. The most spectacular migrant is the orange and black ***monarch butterfly*** *Danaus plexippus* which flies in tens of thousands from western USA and Canada to California to over-winter□

butterfly fish fish of tropical W Africa *Pantodon buchholzi*, 10 cm/4 in long, which can glide short distances with very large wing-like pectoral fins. See also under perch◊□

butterwort see insectivorous plants◊□

Buxtehude Diderik 1637–1707. Danish composer and organist at Lübeck, who influenced Bach◊ and Handel◊, remembered for his cantatas written for his evening concerts or *Abendmusiken*□

Buxton spa in Derbyshire, England; population 20 000. Famous from Roman times, it has a restored Edwardian opera house, and the former Pump Room houses a Micrarium (collection of projection microscopes: images are projected on screens, instead of viewed through an eyepiece)□

buzzard a type of hawk; see under eagle◊□

Byblos town (modern Jebeil) N of Beirut in Lebanon. A Phoenician◊ city state, it was noted for its celebration of the resurrection of Adonis◊□

Bydgoszcz river port in N Poland, which as Bromberg, was Prussian 1772–1919; population 344 000□

Byelorussia see Belorussia◊□

Byng George, (viscount Torrington) 1663–1733. British admiral. He captured Gibraltar in 1704; commanded the fleet which prevented an invasion of England by the Old

Pretender◊ in 1708; and destroyed the Spanish fleet at Messina in 1718. John Byng◊ was his fourth son□

Byng John 1704–57. British admiral, son of George Byng◊. He failed to relieve Fort St Philip when Minorca was invaded by the French in 1756, and was court-martialled and shot. As Voltaire◊ said, it was done 'to encourage the others'□

Byng of Vimy Julian Byng, 1st viscount Byng of Vimy 1862–1935. British field marshal. He commanded the IXth Army Corps at the Dardanelles◊, and the Canadian Army Corps in 1916–17 in France, taking over the 3rd Army after his victory at Vimy◊ Ridge, and in Nov 1917 making the brilliant tank attack on Cambrai◊□

Byrd Richard Evelyn 1888–1957. American explorer. Born in Virginia, he flew to the North (1926) and South Pole (1929), and led five overland expeditions in Antarctica. See Arctic and Antarctic tables◊□

Byrd William 1543–1623. English composer, who shared with Tallis◊ the honorary post of organist to Queen Elizabeth's Chapel Royal. He founded the English school of madrigalists, and composed for the virginals, but his church music is his most important achievement□

Byron Auga Ada 1815–51. British mathematician, daughter of Lord Byron◊. She was the world's first computer programmer, working with Babbage◊'s mechanical invention, and in 1983 America named its new common high-level computer language ADA after her□

Byron George Gordon, 6th Baron Byron 1788–1824. British poet. Born in London, he succeeded his great-uncle in the title in 1798. Educated at Harrow and Cambridge, he published his first volume *Hours of Idleness* 1807, and attacked its harsh critics in *English Bards and Scotch Reviewers* 1809. Overnight fame came with the first two cantos of *Childe Harold* 1812, romantically describing his tours in Portugal, Spain and the Balkans (third canto 1816, fourth 1818). In 1815 he married the mathematician Anne Milbanke (see Auga Byron◊), separating from her a year later. During his resultant 'exile' he produced *The Prisoner of Chillon 1816,* under the influence of Shelley◊; *Beppo* 1818, *Mazeppa* 1819, and his masterpiece *Don Juan* 1819–24. He dabbled in Italian revolutionary politics, and sailed for Greece in 1823 to further the Greek struggle for independence, but died of fever at Missolonghi. He is remembered for his lyrics, his colloquially easy *Letters*, and, on the Continent, as the patron saint of romantic liberalism. See Moore◊, Thomas□

Byron Robert 1904–41. British writer on travel and architecture, including *The Byzantine Achievement* 1929 and *The Road to Oxiana* 1937, an account of a journey Iran–Afghanistan in 1933–4□

Byzantine Empire the Eastern Roman Empire. Following Constantine◊'s removal of his capital to Constantinople (Byzantium◊) in 330AD, the Roman Empire was in 364 divided into eastern and western halves. When the Western Empire was overrun by barbarian invaders, the Eastern or Byzantine Empire stood firm, and Justinian◊ temporarily recovered Italy, N Africa and parts of Spain in the 6th century. In the 7th century Syria, Egypt, and N Africa were lost to the Arabs, who twice besieged Constantinople 673–7, 718, but Asia Minor was retained. In 867 the Greek Church broke with the Roman, but under the Macedonian◊ Dynasty 867–1056 the Byzantine Empire reached its greatest prosperity. The Seljuk◊ Turks conquered most of Asia Minor 1071–3, and in 1204 the Crusaders◊ sacked Constantinople and set Baldwin◊ of Flanders on the throne. The Latin Empire was overthrown 1261, and in 1453 the Turks captured Constantinople□

Byzantine Style see architecture◊□

Byzantium Greek city founded c660BC, and (as Constantinople◊) capital of the Byzantine◊ Empire; it is the modern Istanbul◊□

C

cabal clique of scheming politicians, especially Charles II's ministry of 1667–73, whose initials by coincidence made up the word: *C*lifford, *A*shley, *B*uckingham, *A*rlington, and *L*auderdale□

cabbage plant, *Brassica oleracea capitata,* a variety of the wild cabbage or seakale, family Cruciferae◊; it is grown in Britain almost throughout the year as a green vegetable. Varieties of cabbage include ***kale*** (variety *acephala*), grown as a winter crop and also used for animal fodder; ***brussels sprouts*** (variety *gemmifera*), in which small edible buds develop along the stem; crinkled-leaf ***savoy*** (variety *bullata*); ***cauliflower*** (variety *cauliflora*) and hardy ***broccoli***, both grown for the immature flower heads which in the former are grouped in a single head, and in the latter form several small heads; ***sprouting broccoli*** (variety *botrytis*) has branching stems and small clusters of flowers; ***kohl-rabi*** (variety *gongyloides*) produces a swollen turnip-like upper stem, and is mainly used for animal fodder. More exotic is ***Chinese cabbage*** or ***Chinese leaves, Brassica pekinsensis*** or *chinensis,* a salad plant□

cabbala see kabbala◊□

caber tossing the. Scottish sport of hurling a tapering tree trunk 6.1 m/20 ft long some 12 m/40 ft□

Cabinda or ***Kabinda*** African coastal enclave, a province of Angola◊. Capital also Cabinda. There are oil reserves. Cabinda has made claims to separate independence□

Cabinet in Britain the committee of most important ministers, which had its beginnings under the Stuarts (see Privy◊ Council). When George I ceased to attend Cabinet meetings, the office of Prime Minister, not officially recognized until 1905, came into existence to provide a chairman (see Walpole◊). Cabinet policy is collective and the meetings are secret, minutes being taken by the secretary of the Cabinet, a high civil servant; secrecy has been infringed in recent years by the memoirs of Crossman◊, Castle◊, etc., and by contemporary 'leaks'. Members are chosen by the Prime Minister, but the Labour Party has plans for selection by the party, as is already the case with their 'Shadow Cabinet' in opposition.

The ***joint intelligence committee*** (JIC) is a weekly British Cabinet committee at which, under a secret intelligence concordat of 1946, USA, Canada, Australia, and New Zealand representatives are present for the initial period when international intelligence is discussed.

In the USA, where the term was used from 1793, the Cabinet does not initiate legislation (as happens in Britain). Members are selected by the president, and are responsible to him alone, neither being members of Congress nor able to speak there□

Cabot John 1450–98. Italian navigator. Commissioned by Henry VII to discover unknown lands, he arrived at Cape Breton Island on 24 Jun 1497, thus, according to tradition, the first modern European to reach the N American mainland (he thought he was in NE Asia). In 1498 he sailed again and probably died on the voyage□

Cabot Sebastian 1474–1557. English navigator and cartographer, the son of John Cabot. He explored the Brazilian coast for Charles V and was employed by both Henry VIII and Edward VI. He opened up British trade with Russia□

Cabral Pedro Alvarez c1460–1526. Portuguese explorer, who claimed Brazil for Portugal in 1500□

Cabrini Frances 1850–1917. First Catholic saint in the USA; born in Lombardy, she founded the Missionary Sisters of the Sacred Heart in America□

cachalot a genus of whales◊□

cactus popular name for more than 2000 species in the succulent family Cactaceae, in which the leaves are generally reduced to spines or even absent. The stems are swollen for water storage. The flowers are often large and brightly coloured, not necessarily appearing each year. Chiefly native to the Americas, they have been naturalized in other hot and dry regions. See Arizona◊, peyote◊, prickly pear◊□

caddis fly common name for moth-like insects of the order Trichoptera, which feed on the juices of plants and have aquatic larvae□

Cade Jack d. 1450. English rebel landowner. He led an initially successful revolt in Kent against misgovernment by Henry VI in 1450, and was promised pardon and reforms, but was hunted down and killed□

Cádiz port and naval base in Andalusia, Spain, on a peninsula linked by a bridge (completed in 1969) with the shore; population 157 800. Founded by the Phoenicians c1100BC, it traded (in tin) with Cornwall, and from 1492 with the Americas. Drake burnt a Spanish fleet here in 1587 to prevent the sailing of the Armada◊. ***Rota*** across Cádiz Bay to the NW is also a naval base□

cadmium element
symbol Cd
atomic number 48
physical description white metal, occuring naturally with zinc
features one of the most toxic metals
uses in steel alloy, electroplating and (because of its high absorbtion of neutrons) for nuclear reactor control rods, being essential in emergency shut down; cadmium sulphide is used in photovoltaic cells□

caecilian amphibian of the order Gymniphiona/Apoda (Greek 'without limbs'), and of worm-like appearance; they are chiefly tropical□

Caedmon 7th century AD. First known English Christian poet. A cowherd at the monastery of Whitby, he was commanded to sing by a stranger in a dream, and on waking produced a hymn on the Creation. He became a monk□

Caen capital of Lower Normandy◊, France; population 122 800. The church of St Étienne was founded by William the Conqueror and the university by Henry VI of England in 1432. Caen was captured by the British in World War II, after five weeks' fighting, on 9 Jul 1944□

Caerleon town in Gwent, Wales; population 5000. It is on the site of the Roman fortress of Isca, and there is a Legionary Museum and remains of an amphitheatre□

Caernarfon town, administrative headquarters of Gwynedd, Wales; population 9000. The first Prince of Wales (Edward II) was born in the castle, and Prince Charles was invested here in 1969□

Caerphilly town in Mid Glamorgan, Wales; population 42 000. Noted for mild Caerphilly cheese□

Caesar powerful family of ancient Rome which included Gaius Julius Caesar◊, whose grand-nephew and adopted son Augustus◊ assumed the name of Caesar, and in turn passed it on to his adopted son Tiberius◊. Henceforth, it was borne by the successive emperors, becoming a title of the Roman rulers. The title Tsar in Russia and Kaiser in Germany are both derived from Caesar□

Caesar Gaius Julius c102–44BC. Roman statesman and general. A patrician, he allied himself with the popular party, and when elected Aedile in 65BC nearly ruined himself with lavish amusements for the Roman populace. Although a free thinker, he was elected chief pontiff in 63BC, and in 61 was appointed governor of Spain. Returning to Rome in 60BC, he formed with Pompey◊ and Crassus◊ the first triumvirate, but as governor of Gaul was engaged in its subjugation 58–50, defeating the Germans under Ariovistus, and selling thousands of the Belgic tribes into slavery. In 55BC he crossed into Britain, with a further campaigning visit in 54. A revolt by the Gauls in 52, under Vercingetorix◊, was crushed in 51. His own Commentaries on the campaigns have a mastery worthy of fiction, as does his account of the ensuing Civil War.

His governorship of Spain was to end in 49, and, Crassus being dead, Pompey was now a rival. Declaring 'the die is cast', Caesar crossed the Rubicon (the small river separating Gaul from Italy) to meet the army raised against him. In the ensuing Civil War, he followed Pompey to Epirus in 48, defeated him at Pharsalus, and chased him to Egypt, where he was murdered. Caesar stayed some months in Egypt, where he had a son (Caesarion) by Cleopatra◊, then executed a lightning campaign in 47 against King Pharnaces in Asia Minor, which he summarized: *Veni vidi vici* 'I came, I saw, I conquered'. By his final victory in Spain at Munda in 45, over the sons of Pompey, he established his position, having been awarded a ten-year dictatorship in 46. On 15 Mar 44, however, he was stabbed to death at the foot of Pompey's statue (see Brutus◊, Cassius◊) in the Senate house.

As statesman, general, author, Caesar was unparalleled but fell victim to the weakness of those whom he ruled and for whom he came to have contempt□

Caesarea see Qisaraya◊□

caesarean section birth of a child through an incision in the abdominal wall, as was believed to be the case with Julius Caesar□

caesium element
symbol Cs
atomic number 55
physial description silvery-white metal
features the most reactive metal
uses in photoelectric cells for burglar alarms, etc., and as the basis of atomic clocks□

Caetano Marcello 1906–80. Portuguese statesman, the liberal successor to Salazar◊, who was overthrown by a military coup in 1974 and exiled□

caffeine an alkaloid◊ found in coffee, tea, etc., and partly responsible for its stimulant effect□

Cage John 1912– . American composer. A pupil of Schoenberg◊, he defined the role of music as 'purposeless play', and composed using all sounds, e.g. electrical buzzers and tin cans in 'Imaginary Landscape'. See also aleatoric◊ music□

Cagliostro Alessandro di, Count. Assumed name of Giuseppe Balsamo 1743–95, Italian specialist in the occult. He was involved in 1785 in the affair of the 'diamond necklace' – supposed to have been ordered by Marie Antoinette, but in fact by a band of swindlers – and was imprisoned in the Bastille. Later arrested by the Inquisition in Rome, he died in prison□

Cagnes-sur-mer town SW of Nice, France; population 23 000. Renoir lived and died here 1900–19, and is commemorated in the château□

Cain in Old Testament, the first-born son of Adam and Eve. He murdered his brother Abel□

Cain James Mallahan 1892–1977. American novelist, author of thrillers: *The Postman Always Rings Twice* 1934; *Double Indemnity* and *Mildred Pierce* 1941□

Caine Michael. Stage name of Maurice Micklewhite 1933– . British actor. Born in S London, his films include *The Ipcress File* 1965 (and other thrillers from Len Deighton novels); and *The Eagle has Landed* 1976□

Cairngorms see Grampians◊□

cairn terrier a breed of dog◊□

Cairo capital (Arabic *El Qahira*) of the Arab Republic of Egypt, and largest city in Africa; population 8 143 000. Some 32 km/20 m N of the site of the first capital, the ancient Egyptian centre of Memphis◊, Cairo has the Great Pyramids and Sphinx at nearby Giza. The Arab city was founded c641AD: notable are the Mosque of 'Amr 643AD; the mosque housing El Azhar University (founded 970); and the 12th-century Citadel built by Saladin. It is the administrative, commercial, and industrial centre of the country. Its power is drawn from the Aswan High Dam□

Cajun French-speaking population of Louisiana◊□

Calabar port in SE Nigeria; population 103 000. It was a centre of the 18th–19th-century slave trade□

calabash evergreen tree, *Crescentia cujete*, family Bignoniaceae, found in S America, India, and Africa, producing gourds 50 cm/1.5 ft, used as pots, etc.□

Calabria mountainous earthquake region of southern Italy; capital Catanzaro, industrial centre Reggio; population 2 078 400□

Calais port in N France; population 79 500. Taken by Edward III in 1347, it was saved from destruction by the personal surrender of the Burghers of Calais commemorated in Rodin's sculpture; the French retook it in the reign of Mary in 1558. In German occupation May 1940–Oct 1944, it surrendered to the Canadians□

Calais Pas de. French name for the Strait of Dover□

calamine a zinc mineral. In Britain it refers to zinc carbonate ($ZnCO_3$), in USA it refers to zinc silicate ($Zn_4Si_2O_7(OH)_2$). When referring to skin-soothing lotions and ointments calamine means a pink powder of zinc oxide and 0.5% iron (II) oxide□

Calamity Jane American heroine, Martha Jane Burke c1852–1903, of Deadwood, S Dakota, mining camps. She adopted male dress and, as a dead shot, promised 'calamity' to any aggressor□

Calas Jean 1698–1762. French Protestant, executed in 1762 for allegedly murdering his son to prevent his conversion to Rome; his widow, aided by Voltaire, succeeded in proving his innocence□

calceolaria genus of plants, family Scrophulariaceae, with brilliantly coloured slipper-shaped flowers, native to S America. Introduced to Europe in the 1830s, they are now common house plants□

calcite natural, crystallized form of calcium carbonate, $CaCO_3$, the constituent of chalk, limestone and marble; Iceland spar, in which the crystals have the property of double refractions, is used in optical instruments□

calcium element
symbol Ca
atomic number 20
physical description silvery-white metal
features very widespread, occurring mainly in calcium carbonate (the chief constituent of chalk, limestone, shells); forms 1.5% of the human body (bones and teeth)
uses in steel making; valuable compounds include lime, plaster of Paris, and calcium cyanamide, the basis of pharmaceuticals, fertilizers, and plastics□

calculator pocket calculating device performing (electronically from 1971) a minimum of addition, subtraction, multiplication, and division. Square root, logarithm, sine, cosine, etc., may also be included, and many may be programmed and retain data and programs (continuous memory) when switched off. By the mid-1980s their capacity was within sight of that originally achieved by the early computers which occupied a room to themselves□

calculus methods of calculating continuously varying quantities, as developed by Archimedes◊, Descartes◊, Fermat◊, Newton◊, Leibniz◊.

integral calculus deals with the adding together of the effects of continuously varying quantities; ***differential calculus*** deals similarly with rates of change, many applications arising from the study of speeds, e.g. aircraft in flight. Both deal with small quantities which, during the process, are made smaller and smaller, hence both comprise the infinitesimal calculus.

differential equations involve rates of change and integrals are the empirical solutions; if no standard solutions are available, the integrations are made graphically, etc.□

Calcutta industrial port, capital of W Bengal, India; population 9 165 650. Founded 1686–90 as an East India Company post, it was captured by Suraj-ud-Dowlah in 1756 during the Anglo-French wars in India (see Calcutta Black Hole of◊), and retaken by Clive in 1757. It was the seat of government of British India 1771–1912□

Calcutta Black Hole of. According to tradition Suraj-ud-Dowlah confined 146 British prisoners on the night of 20 Jun 1756 in one small room, of whom only 23 survived; later research reduced the deaths to 43, the result of negligence rather than intention□

Calder Alexander 1898–1976. American artist, who invented 'mobiles', suspended sculptures, with their parts moved by air currents, in 1932□

Calderón de la Barca Pedro 1600–81. Spanish poet-dramatist. First a law student, then a soldier, he became a Franciscan in 1650, after the death of his mistress. He was master of the revels at the court of Philip IV from 1636, when his first volume of plays was published, and as chaplain to the king from 1663 produced a number of outdoor religious dramas for the church festival of Corpus Christi. Best known of some 118 plays are: *La Vida es sueno/Life is a Dream* 1635, and *El Alcalde de Zalamea/The Mayor of Zalamea* 1642□

Caldwell Erskine Preston 1903– . American novelist, born in Georgia, and noted for *Tobacco Road* 1932 and *God's Little Acre* 1933, earthy and vivid presentations of the poverty-stricken southern sharecroppers□

Caldey Island see Dyfed◊□

Caledonia Roman name for N Scotland. The ***Caledonian Forest*** once covered the whole of the central Highlands□

Caledonian Canal waterway in NW Scotland, 98 km/61 mi long (37 km/23 mi artificial, constructed by Telford◊ 1803–23, the rest comprising lochs Lochy, Oich, and Ness)□

calendar the divisions of the year◊, and the method of ordering the years. The original ***lunar month*** (period between one new moon and the next) averages naturally 29.5 days, but the Western calendar (see also below) uses for convenience a ***calendar month*** with a complete number of days, 30/31, except that Feb has 28. Since there are still slightly fewer than six extra hours a year left over, they are added to Feb as a 29th day every 4th (or 'leap') year. The English month names have the probable derivation: Jan from Janus◊, Feb from *februar,* Roman festival of purification, Mar from Mars◊, Apr from Latin *aperire* to open, May from Maia, a Roman goddess, Jun perhaps from Juno◊, Jul from Julius Caesar◊, Aug from Augustus◊, Sept, Oct, Nov, Dec (originally the 7th–10th months, named from the Latin words meaning 7th, 8th, 9th, and 10th respectively. The days of the weeks are Monday (which in Britain replaced Sunday as the first day of the week 1971) named after the moon, Tuesday from Tiu/Tyr, Anglo-Saxon and Norse god of war, Wednesday from Woden◊, Thursday from Thor◊, Friday from Freya◊, Saturday from Saturn◊, and Sunday named after the sun.

The ***Western*** calendar derives from that of Rome, as revised by Julius Caesar in 46BC and adjusted in 1582 by Gregory XIII, who eliminated the accumulated error, and avoided its recurrence by restricting century leap years (those with an extra day) to those divisible by 400. Other states only gradually changed from 'Old Style' to 'New Style'; Britain adopted it in 1751, when the error amounted to 11 days and 3 Sept 1752 became 14 Sept (at the same time the beginning of the year was put back from 25 Mar to 1 Jan). Russia did not adopt it till the Oct Revolution of 1917, so that the event (25 Oct) is currently celebrated on 7 Nov. The assumed date of the birth of Christ is taken as a mark; events before that date being reckoned backwards from it (BC), and subsequent events forward from it (AD, Latin *anno domini,* in the year of the Lord).

The ***Jewish*** calendar is a complex combination of lunar and solar cycles, varied by considerations of religious observance. A year may have 12 or 13 months, which normally alternate between 30 and 29 days; New Year (Rosh Hashanah) falls between 5 Sept and 5 Oct. Its beginning is dated from the Creation (taken as 7 Oct 3761BC).

In ***China*** both the Western (from 1911) and the local calendar are in use; the latter is lunar, with a cycle of 60 years.

The ***Muslim*** calendar is purely lunar, with 12 months of alternately 30 and 29 days, and a year of 354 days. This results in the calendar rotating round the seasons in a 30-year cycle, so that when the 9th month of Ramadan (when Muslims fast without eating or drinking in the day) occurs in summer, hardship is incurred. The era is counted as beginning on the day Mohammed fled from Mecca in 622AD□

Calgary city in Alberta, Canada; population 470 000. Founded in 1875 by the NW Mounted Police as Fort Calgary, it is now the oil and financial centre of W Canada. The commercial heart of the city bounded on the N by the river Bow is known as the 'Golden Crescent'. The annual Calgary Exhibition and Stampede is held in Jul□

Calhoun John Caldwell 1782–1850. American statesman, vice-president 1825–32, a defender of 'States Rights' and of the institution of slavery□

Cali industrial city in SW Colombia; population 1 255 200□

calico plain (in the USA printed) cotton material, the name deriving from Calicut, India□

California Pacific state of the USA; the Golden State

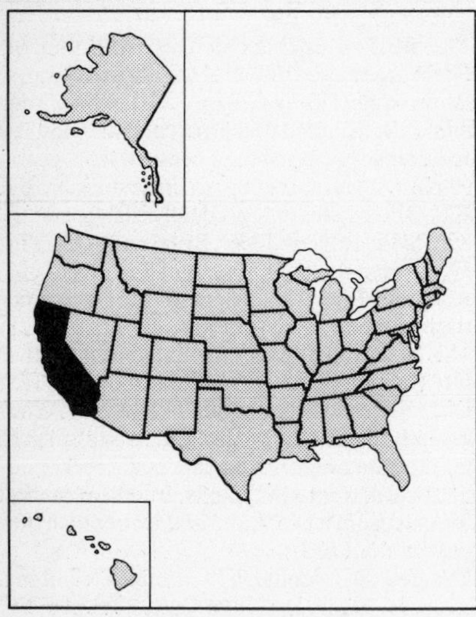

area 411 013 sq km/158 693 sq mi
capital Sacramento
towns Los Angeles, San Diego, San Francisco
features Sierra Nevada (including Yosemite and Sequoia National Parks, Lake Tahoe and Mount Whitney); and the Coast Range (including Reagan's Rancho del Cielo in the Santa Ynez mountains); Death Valley 86 m/282 ft below sea level; Colorado and Mojave deserts (Edwards Air Force base is in the latter); Monterey Peninsula; Salton Sea; offshore in the Pacific there are huge underwater volcanoes with tops 8 km/5 mi across; California Institute of Technology (Caltech); Lawrence Livermore Laboratory (named after Ernest Lawrence◊), which shares nuclear weapons research with Los Alamos; Stanford University, which has the Hoover Institute, and is the centre of Silicon◊ Valley; Paul Getty art museum at Malibu
products leading agricultural state with fruit (peaches, citrus, grapes), nuts (pistachios, almonds), vegetables, cotton, rice, all mostly grown by irrigation, the water being carried by immense concrete-lined canals to the Central Valley (valley of the San Joaquin and Sacramento rivers) and Imperial Valley; beef cattle; timber; fish; oil and natural gas; aerospace, electronics (see Silicon◊ Valley), food-processing; films and television programmes.
population 23 668 560, largest of the USA, 66% non-Hispanic white; 20% Hispanic; 7.5% Black; Asian (including many Vietnamese) 7%
famous people Bret Harte, W R Hearst, Jack London, Marilyn Monroe, Richard Nixon, William Saroyan, John Steinbeck
history colonized by Spain, it was ceded to the USA after the Mexican War of 1848, and became a state in 1850. Gold had been discovered in the Sierra Nevada in Jan 1848, and was followed by the gold rush 1849–56 (the 'Forty-niners'), using the California Trail overland and the California clippers (e.g. *Flying Cloud*) by sea□

California lower. See Baja◊ California□

californium element
symbol Cf
atomic number 98
features artificial radioactive metal made in very small quantities
uses in reactors as a neutron source□

Caligula Gaius Caesar 12–41AD. Roman emperor, son of Germanicus, and successor to Tiberius in 37; a tyrant and alleged to be mad, he was assassinated by an officer of his guard□

calima dust cloud (Spanish 'haze') from the Sahara Desert which sometimes causes heat-wave and eye irritation in Europe□

caliph title (Arabic *khalifah* 'successor') adopted by Mohammed's successors as civic and religious heads of Islam: the first was Abu Bekr◊. Nominally elective, the office became hereditary and was held by the Ummayads◊ and then by the Abbasids◊. After the death of the last Abbasid in 1258, the title was held by a number of Egyptian, Turkish, and Indian claimants, of whom the most powerful were the Turkish sultans of the Ottoman Empire (the last was deposed by Atatürk in 1924)□

calla genus of aquatic plants. See also arum◊□

Callaghan (Leonard) James 1912– . British Labour statesman. As Chancellor of the

Exchequer 1964–7, he introduced corporation and capital gains tax, and resigned in 1967 following devaluation. He was Home Secretary 1967–70, and as Foreign Secretary 1974–6 renegotiated Britain's entry to the Common Market. Succeeding as Prime Minister on Wilson's resignation in 1976, he entered into a pact with the Liberals in 1977 to maintain his government in office, but strikes in the 'winter of discontent' 1978–9 forced him into a lost election in May 1979, and in 1980 he resigned the party leadership under left-wing pressure□

Callao main naval base, commercial (see Lima◊) and fishing port of Peru; population 296 200□

Callas Maria. Stage name of lyric soprano Maria Calogeropoulos 1923–77, born in New York of Greek parents. A fine actress, she excelled in *Norma*, *Madame Butterfly*, *Aïda*, *Lucia,* and *Medea*□

calligraphy the art of handwriting, regarded in China and Japan as the greatest of the visual arts, and playing a large part in Islamic art because the depiction of the human and animal form is forbidden owing to the risk of idolatry. Printing and the typewriter destroyed the art in the West until the 20th-century revival by Edward Johnston 1872–1944□

Callimachus 310–240BC. Greek poet, noted for his epigrams; he was head of the Alexandrian library□

Calliope in Greek mythology, the Muse of epic poetry, and chief of the Muses◊□

Callisto in Greek mythology, the nymph◊ beloved by Zeus□

Callisto one of the moons of Jupiter◊, rather larger than the planet Mercury, and with icy patches and brown blotches on its surface□

Callot Jacques 1592–1635. French engraver, best known for his *Miseries of War* 1632–3, prompted by the Thirty Years' War□

Calmette Albert 1863–1933. French bacteriologist, a student of Pasteur, who developed in 1921 (with Camille Guérin 1872–1961) the BCG vaccine against tuberculosis□

calomel mercurous chloride, Hg_2Cl_2, a white, heavy powder formerly used as a laxative, now used as a pesticide and fungicide□

calorie a unit of heat (i.e. the quantity of heat required to raise the temperature of 1 gram of water by 1°C), which has now been replaced by the joule◊, equivalent to 0.24 calories. In dietetics, a calorie is 1000 of the units defined above. It measures the energy value of food in terms of its heat output□

Caltanissetta town in Sicily; population 65 000. It is a centre for the sulphur industry□

Calvados apple brandy distilled from cider in Normandy□

Calvary in New Testament, the site (Aramaic *Golgotha* 'skull'), of Christ's crucifixion at Jerusalem, thought to have been where the Church of the Sepulchre now stands□

Calvin John 1509–64. French theologian. Invited to Geneva in 1536 to assist in the Reformation, he was at first found too drastic and expelled in 1538, but returned in 1541 to establish a strict theocracy. In 1553 he had Servetus burnt for heresy. He was a supporter of the Huguenots and of the English Protestants persecuted by Mary. He originated Calvinism◊ and the Presbyterian◊ system of church government□

Calvinism Christian doctrine as interpreted by John Calvin◊ and adopted in Scotland, parts of Switzerland, and Holland. Its central doctrine is predestination, under which the elect are predestined by God to salvation, and the rest to damnation. Although Calvinism is rarely accepted today in its strictest interpretation, the 20th century has seen a Neo-Calvinist revival via Karl Barth◊□

Calypso in Greek mythology, a sea nymph◊ who waylaid the homeward-bound Odysseus for seven years□

calypso the wittily scurrilous ballads of local life sung in Trinidad□

Camagüey town in Cuba; population 197 000□

Camargo Marie-Anne de Cupis de 1710–70. French ballet dancer, whose shortening of her skirt above the ankles first allowed *danse en l'air*□

Camargue see under Rhône◊□

Cambodia see Kampuchea◊□

Camborne town in Cornwall, England; population 14 000. It has a School of Metalliferous Mining□

Cambrai town in NE France; population 41 100□

Cambrai Battles of. In the ***First Battle*** Nov–Dec 1917 the town was almost captured by the British when large numbers of tanks were used for the first time; in the ***Second*** 26 Aug–5 Oct 1918 the town was taken during the final Allied offensive□

Cambridge city in Cambridgeshire (administrative headquarters), England, on the river Cam (a river sometimes called by its earlier name, Granta); population 103 000. A Roman settlement grew up on a site occupied as early as 100BC.

University of Cambridge oldest of the colleges is Peterhouse, founded in 1284; many back onto gardens and lawns through which the Cam flows (known as the Backs). Among the most beautiful buildings is King's College Chapel, noted for its choir. Famous students of the university include: Rupert Brooke, S T

Coleridge, Thomas Gray, Christopher Marlowe, John Milton, Samuel Pepys, William Wordsworth. The Cambridge science◊ park, started by Trinity College 1973, is the most successful in Europe. Industries include scientific instruments, radio and electronics, paper, flour milling, and fertilizers□

Cambridge city in Massachusetts, USA; population 95 350. Harvard University 1636 (oldest educational institution in the USA, named after John Harvard 1607–38, who bequeathed it his library and half his estate), Massachusetts Institute of Technology 1861, and the John F Kennedy School of Government and Memorial Library are here, as well as a park named after him□

Cambridgeshire eastern Fenland county of England

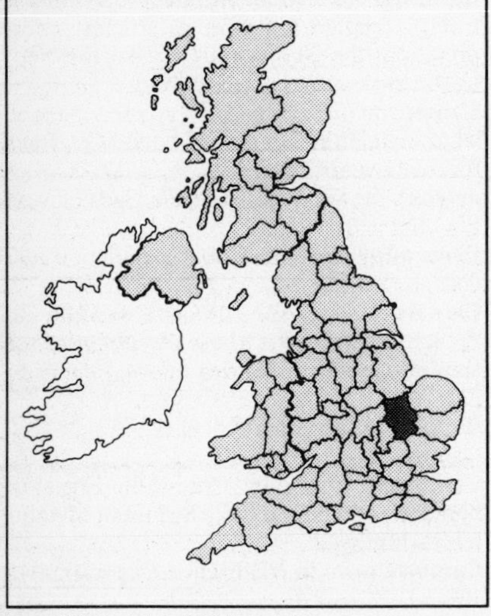

area 3409 sq km/1316 sq mi
towns administrative headquarters Cambridge; Ely, Huntingdon, Peterborough
features rivers Ouse and Nene, Isle of Ely; RAF Molesworth, near Huntingdon, Britain's 2nd cruise◊ missile base
products mainly agricultural
population 606 760
famous people see Cambridge◊□

Cambyses reigned 529–522BC. Emperor of Persia. He succeeded his father Cyrus the Great, assassinated his brother Smerdis and conquered Egypt in 525, outraging its religious customs, but failed to win Carthage and Ethiopia. He died on his homeward journey in Syria, by suicide or accident□

Camden William 1551–1623. English antiquary, author of the topographical survey *Britannia* 1586, and headmaster of Westminster School from 1593. The ***Camden Society,*** 1838, commemorates his work□

Camden inner borough of NW Greater London
features highest ratable value; the Camden Town Group◊ of artists; includes the districts of ***Bloomsbury*** including London University, Royal Academy of Dramatic Art (RADA), and the British Museum; and home between World War I and II of 'intellectual' writers and artists including Leonard and Virginia Woolf, and Lytton Strachey; ***Fitzrovia*** west of Tottenham Court Road with the Post Office Tower and Fitzroy Square as its focus, and including Pollock's Toy Museum and many ethnic restaurants; ***Hampstead,*** with Primrose Hill, Hampstead Heath, and nearby Kenwood House; Keats's home, now a museum; Constable is buried in the churchyard; and Hampstead Garden Suburb; ***Highgate***, with a cemetery which has the graves of George Eliot, Michael Faraday, and Karl Marx; ***Holborn***, with the Inns of Court (Lincoln's Inn and Gray's Inn); Hatton Garden (diamond mart), the London Silver Vaults; ***Somers Town*** between Euston and King's Cross rail stations.
population 186 000□

Camden industrial city in New Jersey, USA; population 84 910. Linked with Philadelphia by bridge across the Delaware. Walt Whitman House, where the poet lived 1884–92, is a museum□

Camden Town Group British art group 1911–13; based in Camden Town, London, it included Sickert◊, Duncan Grant◊, Spencer Gore 1878–1914 and Harold Gilman 1876–1919□

camel family (Camelidae) of cud-chewing mammals, order Artiodactyla, which includes:
camel of which there are two species: ***Arabian camel*** or ***dromedary,*** *Camelus dromedarius,* with one hump, and ***Central Asiatic*** or ***Bactrian camel,*** *C bactrianus,* with two. They range in colour from dark brown to cream. The hump contains a fatty tissue, a food reserve, and an extra large membrane in the nostrils extracts moisture from the air, enabling the animal to go without food or drink for a fortnight. Used as a beast of burden mainly in deserts, it has the useful capability of closing its eyes, ears, and nostrils during sand storms. A working camel can maintain a pace of 5 kmph/3 mph for 50 km/30 mi, carrying 270 kg/600 lb; racing dromedaries reach 100 kmph/60 mph. In Saudi Arabia they are also being bred for milk (half the output of a dairy cow) and meat.

llama *Lama glama* with no hump, and slighter than a camel, rather resembling a large, long-necked sheep. They were formerly used by the American Indians of Peru for carrying loads, and are still bred for their meat and long, fine, silky wool (white/brown/black or spotted). When annoyed they spit profusely. ***alpaca*** *Lama pacos*; a smaller animal than the llama, it is similarly bred for meat and wool. Both llama and alpaca are thought to have developed from the wild brown ***guanaco,*** *Lama guanacoe,* a smaller species than either. ***vicuna*** *Vicugna vicugna* smallest of the S American group at 30 cm/1 ft high, it is brown above and white below, with especially soft wool, which is taken from the wild herds. It is in danger of extinction, and all the S American species are to some extent under threat□

camellia genus of oriental evergreen shrubs, family Theaceae, introduced to Europe and cultivated for their dark glossy leaves and large, showy flowers; *C sinensis* is the tea◊ plant□

Camelot legendary capital of King Arthur◊, possibly the Iron Age hill fort of South Cadbury Castle, near Yeovil, Somerset□

Camembert village in Normandy, France, where creamy Camembert cheese originated□

cameo small relief carving, usually on a semi-precious stone, popular in Rome, Greece, at the Renaissance, and in the Victorian era□

camera apparatus used in photography◊ or moving pictures□

Cameron, Julia Margaret 1815–79. British portrait photographer, whose sitters included Darwin and Tennyson□

Cameroon United Republic of

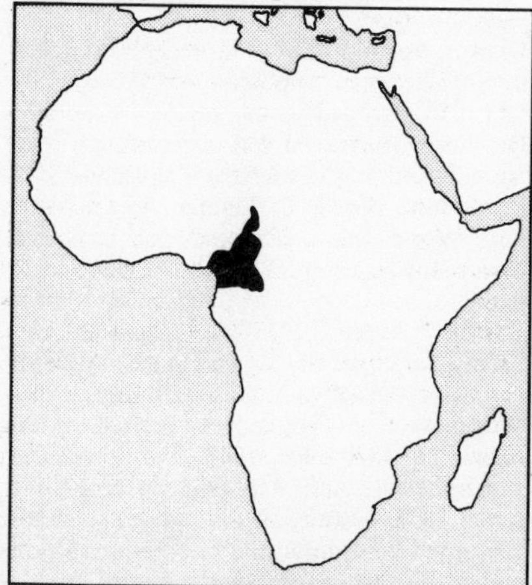

area 474 000 sq km/183 580 sq mi
capital Yaoundé
towns chief port Douala
features Mount Cameroon 4070 m/13 352 ft, an active volcano on the coast
exports cocoa, coffee, bananas, cotton, timber
currency CFA franc
population 9 506 000
language French and English (in pidgin variations) (official), but there has been some discontent with the emphasis on French; there are 163 indigenous peoples with many African languages
religion Roman Catholic 35%, Animism 25%, Islam 22%, Protestant 18%
famous people Ahmadou Ahidjo, president 1960–82
government there is an executive president, (Paul Biya from 1982) and national assembly, both elected for five years; only one political party is allowed.
recent history a German possession 1884–1916, it was captured in World War I by Allied forces and divided between England and France as a League of Nations mandate. French Cameroons became independent in 1960; British Cameroons, after plebiscites in both its sections in 1961, was divided: the N chose to remain with Nigeria (with which it had been administered), and the S chose to join French Cameroons in what is now the United Republic of Cameroon. A border dispute continues with Nigeria□

Camoens or ***Camões,*** Luís Vaz de 1524–80. Portuguese soldier-poet. He lost an eye fighting in N Africa, and, having wounded an equerry of the king in 1552, was banished to India. He went on various military expeditions, and was shipwrecked in 1558, but the manuscript of his poem, the *Lusiads*, was saved with him. It was published in 1572, telling the story of da Gama, and incorporating much Portuguese history, so that it is the country's national epic. He received a small pension, but died in poverty of plague. His posthumously published lyric poetry is also now valued□

camomile or ***chamomile*** aromatic perennial herb *Anthemis nobilis*, family Compositae◊. The flowers are used for camomile tea, and the plant makes excellent lawns which do not have to be mown□

Camorra secret society formed about 1820 by criminals in the dungeons of Naples, and continued once they were 'outside'. It dominated politics from 1848, was suppressed in 1911, but many members eventually surfaced in the US Mafia◊. It still flourishes in the Naples area□

Campania region of S Italy, including Vesuvius◊; capital Naples, industrial centres Benevento, Caserta and Salerno; population 5 513 500□

Campanulaceae family of flowering plants of the temperate N hemisphere, with bell-shaped flowers e.g. British ***harebell,*** *C rotundifolia*; ***Canterbury bell,*** *C medium* and the ***N American bellflower,*** *C americana*□

Campbell Sir Colin. See Clyde◊, Colin Campbell, lst Baron Clyde□

Campbell Donald Malcolm 1921–67. Car and speedboat enthusiast, son of Sir Malcolm. He established a water record of 444.57 kmph/276.3 mph on Lake Dumbleyung, Australia in 1959 (turbo-jet hydroplane); and a land record of 648.7 kmph/403.1 mph at Lake Eyre salt flats, Australia in 1964; and died in attempting to raise the former record (reaching 527.9 kmph/328 mph) at Coniston Water, England – all in vehicles called *Bluebird*□

Campbell Sir Malcolm 1885–1949. British speed record holder, including the world land speed record in 1935 with his *Bluebird* at 484.5 kmph/301.1 mph and the water record with his boat of the same name in 1939 at 228.1 kmph/141.74 mph□

Campbell Gordon 1886–1953. British admiral. He commanded Q ships, which masqueraded as unarmed merchantmen to decoy German U-boats for destruction in World War I, and won the VC□

Campbell Mrs Patrick 1865–1940. British actress, born Beatrice Stella Tanner, whose great roles included Paula in Pinero's *The Second Mrs Tanqueray* 1893, and Eliza in *Pygmalion*, specially written for her by Shaw, with whom she had a witty correspondence□

Campbell Roy 1901–57. S African poet, who became a professional bullfighter in Spain, and fought for Franco in the Civil War; he established his individualist reputation with *The Flaming Terrapin* 1924□

Campbell-Bannerman Sir Henry 1836–1908. British Liberal statesman. Becoming Prime Minister in 1905, he led the Liberals to a landslide victory in 1906. He granted self-government to the S African colonies, and passed the Trades Disputes Act 1906 (widening the scope for strikes). He resigned in 1908 and died shortly after□

Camp David official country home of US presidents in the Appalachians, Maryland, USA; it was originally named Shangri-la by F D Roosevelt; was renamed Camp David by Eisenhower (after his grandson), and was briefly known (for security reasons) as Camp Number Four after the Kennedy assassination. It is guarded by Marines, and consists of a series of lodges, Aspen Lodge being the presidential residence□

Camp David Agreements two framework agreements signed at Camp David in 1978 by Begin and Sadat at the instance of Carter, covering: 1 Egypt–Israel peace treaty and phased withdrawal of Egypt from Sinai, which was completed in 1982; 2 overall Middle East settlement including the election by the Palestinians of the West Bank and Gaza Strip of a 'self-governing authority'. The latter remained unsettled in 1985□

Campeche Bay of. SW area of the Gulf of Mexico, site of the world's worst oil pollution disaster from the field off Yucatan peninsula in 1979□

Camperdown village in NW Netherlands, off which a British fleet defeated the Dutch 11 Oct 1797□

camphor volatile aromatic ketone $C_{10}H_{1}6O$ obtained from the wood of the camphor tree *Cinnamomum camphora*, family Lauraceae, of China and Japan. It is used in insect repellents, and in the manufacture of celluloid□

Campinas coffee-trading centre in Brazil; population 468 000□

Campion Edmund 1540–81. English Jesuit. A deacon of the Anglican church, he recanted in 1571, became a Jesuit in 1573, and returned to England as a missionary in 1580. He was hanged, drawn, and quartered as a traitor spy, and canonized in 1970□

Campion Thomas 1567–1620. English poet, author of the critical *Art of English Poesie* 1602, and four *Bookes of Ayres*, for which he composed both words and music□

campion flowering plants of genera *Lychnis* and *Silene*, family Caryophyllaceae, with white or reddish flowers, e.g. ***bladder campion***, *S vulgaris*□

Campo-Formio Treaty of. Peace settlement in 1797 between Napoleon and Austria, by which France gained the region of modern Belgium and Austria was compensated with Venice, and part of modern Yugoslavia□

Cam Ranh port in S Vietnam. In the Vietnam War it was a US base, and is now a major staging complex for the Soviet Pacific fleet□

Camus Albert 1913–60. Algerian-born French writer, of Breton and Spanish parentage, who was active in the Resistance during World War II. His novels include *L'Étranger/The Outsider* 1942, *La Peste/The Plague* 1948, and *L'Homme Révolté/The Rebel* 1952, a study of revolutionary ideals corrupted by murder and oppression, which ended his association with Sartre. Nobel prize 1957□

Canaanite Empire at its height c2400BC, it included Syria, Palestine, and part of Mesopotamia, and had its capital at Ebla, excavated 1976–7 in Syria, where an archive of inscribed tablets includes place-names such as Gaza and Jerusalem, and personal names such as Abraham, David, and Saul, though the latter cannot be identified individually with the heroes of the Old Testament. Canaan or the 'Promised Land' of the Israelites was the coastal area on the Mediterranean, which they occupied c1200BC. The Canaanites were a mixed-race, Semitic-speaking people, known to the Greeks of the 1st millennium BC as Phoenicians. See Phoenicia◊□

Canada Dominion of

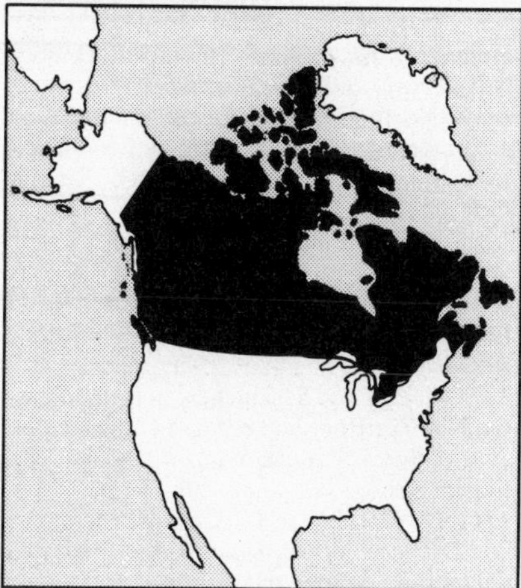

area 9 975 223 sq km/3 851 809 sq mi, including freshwater lakes
capital Ottawa
towns Toronto, Montreal, Vancouver, Winnipeg, Edmonton, Quebec, Hamilton, Calgary
features St Lawrence Seaway, Mackenzie river; Great Lakes; Arctic Archipelago; Rocky Mountains; Great Plains or Prairies; Canadian Shield
exports wheat; timber, pulp and newsprint; fish, especially salmon; furs (ranched fox and mink exceeds the value of wild furs); oil and natural gas; aluminium, asbestos, coal, copper, iron, nickel; motor vehicles and parts, industrial and agricultural machinery, fertilizers
currency Canadian dollar
population 23 900 000, including 300 000 American Indians, of whom 75% live on over 2000 reserves in Ontario and the four Western Provinces; some 300 000 Métis (people of mixed race) and 19 000 Inuit (or Eskimo), of whom 75% live in the NW Territories. Over half Canada's population lives in Ontario and Quebec.
language English, French, (both official) (about 70% speak English, 20% French, and the rest are bilingual); there are also N American Indian languages and the Inuit Inuktitut
religion 40% Roman Catholic, 35% Protestant
famous people literature (novelists) Mazo de la Roche, Stephen Leacock, Brian Moore, Mordecai Richler, Lucy Montgomery, Saul Bellow, Margaret Laurence (poets) Robert W Service *sociology* Marshall McLuhan
government Canada is a federal union (within the Commonwealth) of 10 provinces (Alberta, British Columbia, Manitoba, New Brunswick, Newfoundland, Nova Scotia, Ontario, Prince Edward Island, Quebec, and Saskatchewan◊) and two territories (the Yukon Territory and Northwest Territories◊), the latter comprising more than one third of Canada with an average population density of 0.1 per sq mi.
federal government the Queen is represented by a Governor-General, who acts as Chief of State, and there is a Senate of 104 members (appointed until age 75) and House of Commons of 264 members elected by universal suffrage for five years (Prime Minister Brian Mulroney◊ from 1984). The chief parties are the Progressive Conservative, Liberal, and New Democratic.
provincial government the Queen is represented by a Lieutenant-Governor in each province, appointed by the Governor-General; and there is an Executive Council and a Legislative Assembly (Quebec having an additional Legislative Council). The provinces enjoy sovereign authority in all local matters.
territories each has a resident commissioner appointed by the federal government, the latter retaining control over all natural resources, and is represented by a single member in the Senate and House of Commons. There is support for increased autonomy or adoption of provincial status, and claims by the native peoples for control of land were under negotiation in 1983.
recent history see Canada◊ history□

Canada: history
1497 John Cabot landed on Cape Breton Island
1534 Jacques Cartier discovered the Gulf of St Lawrence
1603 Champlain began his exploration of Canada
1608 Champlain founded Quebec

Provinces	area in sq km	population (1981)	capital	English-speaking	French-speaking
Alberta	661,187	2,237,724	Edmonton	2,175,579	62,145
British Columbia	948,599	2,744,467	Victoria	2,698,852	45,615
Manitoba	650,088	1,026,241	Winnipeg	973,681	52,560
New Brunswick	73,437	696,403	Fredericton	462,373	234,030
Newfoundland	404,517	567,681	St John's	565,026	2,655
Nova Scotia	54,558	847,442	Halifax	811,412	36,030
Ontario	1,068,587	8,625,107	Toronto	8,149,502	475,605
Prince Edward Island	5,657	122,506	Charlottetown	116,426	6,080
Québec	1,540,676	6,438,403	Québec	706,115	5,732,288
Saskatchewan	651,901	968,313	Regina	942,778	25,535
Territories					
Northwest Territories	3,379,689	45,471	Yellowknife	44,231	1,240
Yukon Territory	536,327	22,135	Whitehorse	21,555	580
	9,975,223	24,341,893		17,667,530	6,674,363

1759 Wolfe captured Quebec
1763 France ceded Canada to Britain under the Treaty of Paris
1775–83 War of American Independence involved Loyalist influx to New Brunswick and Ontario
1791 Canada divided into English-speaking Upper Canada (Ontario) and French-Speaking Lower Canada (Quebec)
1793 Sir William Mackenzie reached Pacific by land
1812–14 War of 1812 between Britain and US fought mainly in Upper Canada; American invasions repelled by both provinces
1840 Responsible government granted, and Upper and Lower Canada united
1866 British Columbia created, entered confederation 1871
1867 British North America Act created the Dominion of Canada (Ontario, Quebec, Nova Scotia and New Brunswick)
1869 Northwest Territories created and entered confederation; rising by Louis Riel◊
1870 Manitoba created (from NW Territories) and joined confederation
1873 Prince Edward Island entered confederation
1885 Northwest Rebellion crushed and leader Louis Riel hanged
1885 Canadian Pacific Railway completed
1905 Alberta and Saskatchewan formed from the NW Territory and entered confederation
1901–2 South African War – Canadian contingent sent
1914–18 World War I – Canadian troops at 2nd Battle of Ypres, Vimy Ridge, Passchendaele, the Somme, and Cambrai
1931 Canada became a self-governing Dominion
1931 Norway renounced her claim to the Sverdrup Islands, confirming Canadian sovereignty in the entire Arctic Archipelago N of the Canadian mainland
1939–45 World War II – Canadian participation in all theatres; see also Dieppe◊
1949 Newfoundland joined the confederation
1950–53 Korean War – Canada participated in United Nations force, and subsequently participated in almost all United Nations peacekeeping operations
1972 adoption of 'Third Option' policy to reduce US influence by economic links with Europe and Japan
1980 Quebec referendum rejected demand for independence
1982 British North America Act amended to patriate the Canadian constitution
1984 John Turner◊ succeeded Trudeau◊ in leadership of Liberal Party
1984 Sept Brian Mulroney (PCP) returned to power in general election□

Canadian Prime Ministers

Sir John A. Macdonald (*Conservative*)	1867
Alexander Mackenzie (*Liberal*)	1873
Sir John A. Macdonald (*Conservative*)	1878
Sir John J. Abbott (*Conservative*)	1891
Sir John S.D. Thompson (*Conservative*)	1892
Sir Mackenzie Bowell (*Conservative*)	1894
Sir Charles Tupper (*Conservative*)	1896
Sir Wilfrid Laurier (*Liberal*)	1896
Sir Robert L. Borden (*Conservative*)	1911
Arthur Meighen (*Conservative*)	1920
William Lyon Mackenzie King (*Liberal*)	1921
Arthur Meighen (*Conservative*)	1926
William Lyon Mackenzie King (*Liberal*)	1926
Richard Bedford Bennett (*Conservative*)	1930
William Lyon Mackenzie King (*Liberal*)	1935
Louis Stephen St. Laurent (*Liberal*)	1948
John G. Diefenbaker (*Conservative*)	1957
Lester Bowles Pearson (*Liberal*)	1963
Pierre Elliot Trudeau (*Liberal*)	1968
Joseph Clark (*Progressive Conservative*)	1979
Pierre Elliot Trudeau (*Liberal*)	1980
John Turner (*Liberal*)	1984
Brian Mulroney (*Progressive Conservative*)	1984

canal man-made waterway for irrigation or inland navigation.
irrigation the systems of the Nile (Aswan Dam), Upper Indus (India and Pakistan), Murray Basin (Victoria, Australia), Great Valley (California, USA).
ship canals and waterways:
Baltic-Volga (USSR 1964–) 2430 km/1510 mi
Baltic-White Sea (USSR 1933) 235 km/146 mi
Corinth Canal (Greece 1893) 6.4 km/4 mi
Grand Canal (China 485BC–AD1972) 1050 km/650 mi
Kiel (W Germany 1895) 98 km/61 mi
Manchester (England 1894) 57 km/35.5 mi
Rhine-Rhône Waterway (Rotterdam-Marseilles) and Rhine-Main-Danube Waterway (Rotterdam-Costanza, on the Black Sea), both under construction in the 1980s
St Lawrence Seaway (Canada/USA combined St Lawrence river, three canals, and the Great Lakes in 1959, so linking the Atlantic with Duluth, Minnesota at the W end of Lake Superior) 3770 km/2342 mi
Suez (Egypt 1869) 166 km/103 mi□

Canaletto Antonio. Nickname of Giovanni Canale 1697–1768. Venetian artist, whose views of the city have remarkable handling of perspective and control of colour□

canary olive-green bird *Serinus canarius*, family Fringillidae (see finch◊), found wild in Madeira and the Canary Islands. It has been bred as a cagebird (in yellow and other colours) in Europe since the 15th century; the most valued singers are 'rollers' which are taught to sing by being placed in the same room as a 'master' bird□

Canary Islands group of volcanic islands, which forms an autonomous region of Spain.

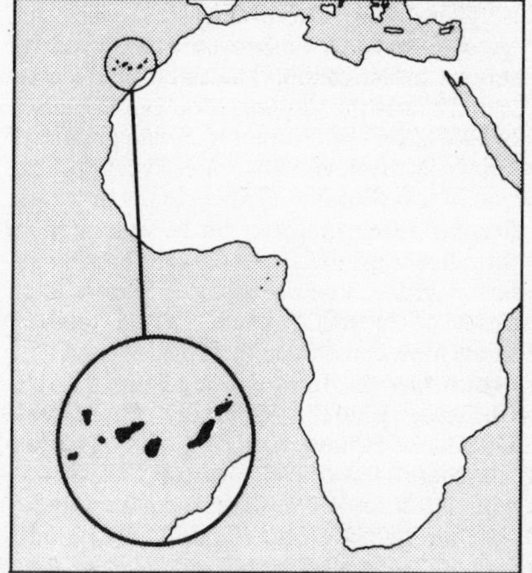

area 7273 sq km/2808 sq mi
population 1 440 600
features The chief centres are Santa Cruz on Tenerife (which also has the highest peak in extra-continental Spain, Pico de Teyde 3713 m/12 182 ft), and Las Palmas on Gran Canaria. The Northern Hemisphere Observatory 1981 is on the island of La Palma, the first in the world to be remotely controlled: see Herstmonceux◊. Observation conditions are among the best in the world: no moisture, no artificial light pollution, and little natural airglow◊. The Organization of African Unity supports an independent Guanch Republic (so-called from the indigenous islanders, a branch of the N African Berbers) and revival of the Guanch language□

Canberra federal capital of the Commonwealth of Australia from 1908; area of the Capital territory (enclosed in New South Wales, and including the port of Jervis Bay to the south-west acquired by the government in 1915) 2432 sq km/939 sq mi; population 222 300. Planned by US architect Walter Burley Griffin, it contains the Parliament House 1927, Australian National University 1946, Canberra School of music 1965, and the National War memorial□

cancan high-kicking stage dance for women (solo or line of dancers) originating in Paris about 1830, and later associated with the *galop* from Offenbach's *Orpheus in the Underworld*□

cancer group of diseases resulting in malignant tumours classified as carcinomas, growing from the skin or mucous membrane, and sarcomas, which affect bone, cartilage, and muscle (connective tissue), but including leukaemia and cancer of the blood.
Production of cancer cells seems to be triggered by the activation of genes which are present in normal cells, but which are either dormant or expressed at very low levels. Such cells then grow and divide without restriction, forming 'lumps' and sometimes spreading to other parts of the body. Triggering agents include chemical carcinogens, e.g. asbestos dust, benzpyrene, household chemicals, cigarette-smoking, excess alcohol, food additives, hormones, parasites, viruses; radiation, e.g. X-rays; psychological stress, e.g. bereavement. Avoiding such factors would avert some 70% of cancers. Treatment of cancer includes surgery, radiotherapy, and cystostatic (cell-stopping) drugs which prevent cell division. Cancer cells are immortal, so that tumour cells can be grown for ever in culture□

Cancún Caribbean resort, Mexico, site in 1981 of a North-South summit to discuss the widening gap between the developed countries and the Third World□

Candela Felix 1910– . Spanish-born Mexican architect, originator of the hypar (hyperbolic paraboloid) from 1951, in which doubly curved surfaces are built up on a framework of planks sprayed with cement□

Candia see Iráklion◊□

Candlemas feast of the Purification of the Virgin Mary, and presentation of the Infant Christ in the Temple, celebrated 2 Feb□

Canea capital (Greek Khaniá) and chief port of Crete; population 40 565□

Canetti Elias 1905– . Writer, a Sephardic Jew, born in Bulgaria, he was exiled from Austria in 1938 and writes in German. In 1939 he settled in England. His books include the novel *Auto da Fé/Die Blendung*; and an autobiography. Concerned with crowd behaviour and the psychology of power, he received a Nobel prize in 1981□

Canidae family of carnivorous mammals who walk on their toes, have non-retractile claws, and an elongated muzzle, e.g. the dog, fox, jackal, wolf□

cannabis tall annual herb, *C sativa*, family Urticaceae, originally Asian. Some strains are cultivated for fibre, birdseed, and oil; others for the dried leaf, female flowers, and resin, known as bhang (India), dagga (S Africa), hashish (Arabia), kif (N Africa), and pot or marijuana, which are hallucinogens when smoked or eaten and have an intoxicating and stimulating effect. Cannabis is a 'soft' drug in that it creates psychological rather than physical dependence. It has medicinal use in countering depression and the side effects of cancer therapy (pain and nausea). Its cultivation is illegal in the UK and USA□

Cannae village in Apulia, Italy, site of Hannibal's defeat of the Romans in 216BC□

Cannes resort in S France; population 70 225. The world's most important film festival is held here annually□

Canning Charles John, 1st Earl 1812–62. British administrator, son of George Canning. As Governor-General of India from 1856, he suppressed the Indian Mutiny with an unvindictive firmness which earned him the nickname 'Clemency Canning', and was the first Viceroy of India from 1858□

Canning George 1770–1827. British Tory statesman. His verse, satires, and parodies for the *Anti-Jacobin* 1797–8 led to his advancement by Pitt. As Foreign Secretary 1807–10, he was largely responsible during the Napoleonic Wars for the seizure of the Danish fleet and British intervention in the Spanish peninsula, but his disapproval of the Walcheren expedition involved him in a duel with Castlereagh◊ and led to his resignation. On Castlereagh's death in 1822, he again became Foreign Secretary, supported the national movements in Greece and S America, and was briefly Prime Minister in 1827□

canning food preservation in hermetically sealed containers by the application of heat. Originated by Frenchman Nicolas Appert in 1809 with glass containers, it was developed by Englishman Peter Durand in 1810 with tin cans, which are actually made of sheet steel with a thin coating of tin to postpone corrosion□

canoe lightweight craft pointed at both ends, and usually propelled by paddles. The modern sporting canoe may be a kayak, derived from the skin-covered Inuit model, which has a keel and in which the canoeist sits; or the Canadian style, derived from the birch-bark American-Indian model, which has no keel and in which the canoeist kneels. The modern versions are made of plastic, fibre-glass, etc. Englishman Michael Jones 1952–78, killed canoeing in the Himalayas, had made it a prestige sport, straightforward racing being varied by slalom courses with artificial rapids and rocks to provide 'wild-water' conditions□

canonical hours set periods of devotion in the Catholic Church: matins, prime, terce, sext, nones, vespers, compline. In the Anglican Church, the period 8 am–6 pm within which marriage can be legally performed□

canonization in the Catholic Church the admission of one of her members to the calendar of saints◊. Since 1969 the gathering of the proof of the candidate's virtues has been left to the bishop of the birthplace, and, miracles being difficult to substantiate, stress is placed on extraordinary 'favours' or 'graces' that can be proved or attested by serious investigation. The findings are contested before the Congregation for the Causes of Saints by the Promotor Fidei, popularly known as the devil's advocate. Papal ratification of a favourable verdict results in 'beatification' (the candidate can be venerated in the neighbourhood), and full sainthood (conferred in the Vatican basilica) follows after proof of further 'favours'. Many modern saints have come from the Third World□

canon law the rules and regulations of the Christian Church, especially the Greek Orthodox, Roman Catholic, and Anglican churches. That of the Anglican Church was completely revised in 1969, and is kept under constant review by the Canon Law Commission of the General Synod. In 1983 Pope John Paul II issued a new canon law code reducing offences carrying automatic excommunication, extending the grounds for annulment of marriage, removing the ban on marriage with non-Catholics, and banning trade union and political activity by priests□

Canossa ruined castle near Reggio, Italy. It was here that Emperor Henry IV◊ did penance before Pope Gregory VII in 1077 for having opposed him in the question of investitures□

Canova Antonio 1757–1822. Italian Neoclassical◊ sculptor of sentimental delicacy who executed the tombs of Popes Clement XIII, Pius VII, and Clement XIV, but is best remembered for his marbles *Cupid and Psyche* and *The Three Graces*□

Cantabria autonomous region of N Spain (including Santander◊ and Altamira◊); population 511 000□

Cantabrian Mountains mountains running along the N coast of Spain, ranging in height to 2400 m/8000 ft, and containing coal and iron□

Cantal volcanic mountain range in central France□

cantaloup a type of melon◊□

cantata a musical work for voices. See under sonata◊□

Canterbury city in Kent, England; population 118 600. The Roman Durovernum, it was the capital of the Saxon kings of Kent. In 597 King Ethelbert◊ welcomed Augustine's mission to England here, and the city has since been the metropolis of the Anglican Communion and seat of the Archbishop of Canterbury. The foundations of the present cathedral were laid by Lanfranc◊, Archbishop 1070–89, but subsequent additions range from Norman to Perpendicular. In the Middle Ages it was a centre of pilgrimage to the tomb of Thomas Becket, murdered in the cathedral in 1170, but the shrine was destroyed by Henry VIII. The Black Prince and Henry IV are buried there. The city has links with Chaucer, Christopher Marlowe, and Somerset Maugham◊, and the first college of the University of Kent established in 1965 was named after T S Eliot□

Canterbury Archbishop of. Primate of All England, metropolitan of the Church of England, and first peer of the realm, ranking next to royalty. He crowns the sovereign, has a seat in the House of Lords, and is a member of the Privy Council. His seat is Lambeth Palace, with a second residence at the Old Palace, Canterbury. He is appointed by the Prime Minister on the recommendation of the Crown Appointments Commission, a church group. The first holder of the office was Augine◊; his 20th-century successors have been: Randal T Davidson 1903, C G Lang 1928, William Temple 1942, G F Fisher 1945, A M Ramsey 1961, D Coggan 1974, and R A A Runcie 1980□

Canterbury Plains grassland on the E coast of South Island, New Zealand, source of Canterbury lamb□

cantharides an aphrodisiac made from the dried bodies of the Spanish fly beetle◊□

Canton see Guangzhou◊□

canton one of the subdivisions of the Swiss confederation□

Canton and Enderbury two atolls of the Phoenix Group: see Kiribati◊□

Canute c995–1035. King of England, Denmark, and Norway. Accompanying his father on his invasion of England (see Vikings◊), Canute was acclaimed king by the army on his father's death in 1014. In 1016 he defeated Edmund◊ Ironside at Assandun in Essex, and ruled Mercia and Northumbria until he inherited the whole kingdom on Edmund's death. He compelled King Malcolm to pay homage by invading Scotland in c1027; succeeded his brother Harald as king of Denmark in 1018; and conquered Norway in 1028. His empire collapsed on his death. He was buried at Winchester. He deflated his flattering courtiers by showing that the sea would not retreat at his command□

canyon deep, narrow hollow running through mountains, usually cut by a river, e.g. Grand Canyon, Colorado□

Cao Chan 1719–63. Chinese novelist (formerly Ts'ao Chan) whose tragic love story *The Dream of the Red Chamber*, which involves the downfall of a Manchu family, is semi-autobiographical□

capacitance see capacitor◊□

capacitor device for storing electric charge, used in electronic circuits; it consists of two metal plates separated by an insulating 'dielectric'. Its capacitance is the ratio of the charge stored on either plate to the potential difference between plates. 1 farad is a capacitance of 1 coulomb stored per volt, but most capacitors have much smaller capacitances, and the microfarad (a millionth of a farad) is more commonly used□

Cape Breton island forming the N part of the province of Nova Scotia, Canada□

Cape Byron most easterly extremity of Australia, in New South Wales□

Cape Canaveral see under Florida◊□

Cape Coast port in Ghana; population 71 600□

Cape Cod peninsula in Massachusetts, USA, where the Pilgrim Fathers landed in 1620□

Cape Coloured people of mixed African and European blood in S Africa, mainly living in Cape Province□

Cape gooseberry a type of gooseberry◊□

Cape Horn southernmost point of S America where frequent gale-force winds endanger shipping□

Čapek Karel Matelj 1890–1938. Czech playwright, best-remembered for *R.U.R.* (Rossum's Universal Robots) 1921, in which robots rebel against their masters. See Robot◊□

Cape of Good Hope headland of S Africa; the first European to see it was Bartholomew Diaz◊□

Cape Province (Afrikaans *Kaapprovinsie*) largest province of the Republic of S Africa.
area 721 00 sq km/278 400 sq mi, excluding Walvis Bay
capital Capetown
towns Port Elizabeth, East London, Kimberley, Grahamstown, Stellenbosch
features Orange river, Drakensberg, Table Mountain (highest point Maclear's Beacon 1087 m/3567 ft); Great Karoo Plateau, Walvis Bay◊
products fruit (citrus, peaches, etc.), vegetables, wine; meat, ostrich feathers; diamonds, copper, asbestos, manganese
population 5 091 400, including 2 226 200 Coloured; 1 569 000 Black; 1 264 000 White; 32 120 Asian
history the Dutch occupied the Cape in 1652, but it was taken by the British in 1795 after the French Revolutionary armies had occupied the Netherlands, and was sold to Britain for £6 million in 1814. It was an original province of the Union in 1910□

caper shrub *Capparis spinosa*, family Capparidaceae, native to the Mediterranean; the flower buds are preserved in vinegar as a condiment□

capercaillie or ***capercailzi*** wood-grouse of the Scottish Highlands. See fowl◊□

Capet Hugh c938–96. King of France. Claiming the throne on the death of Louis◊ V, he founded the Capetian dynasty, of which various branches continued to reign until the French Revolution. See under Valois◊ and Bourbon◊□

Cape Town (Afrikaans *Kaapstad*) port and oldest town of S Africa; population 1 096 597. It is the legislative capital of the Republic of S Africa, and capital of Cape Province, and was founded in 1652 by Johan van Riebeeck of the Dutch East India Company. It includes the Houses of Parliament, City Hall, Cape Town Castle (1666), and Groote Schuur, 'great barn', the estate of Cecil Rhodes (he designated the house as the home of the premier, and a university and the National Botanical Gardens occupy part of the grounds). The naval base of ***Simonstown*** is to the SE; in 1975 Britain's use of its facilities was ended by the Labour government in disapproval of S African racial policy□

Cape Verde Republic of

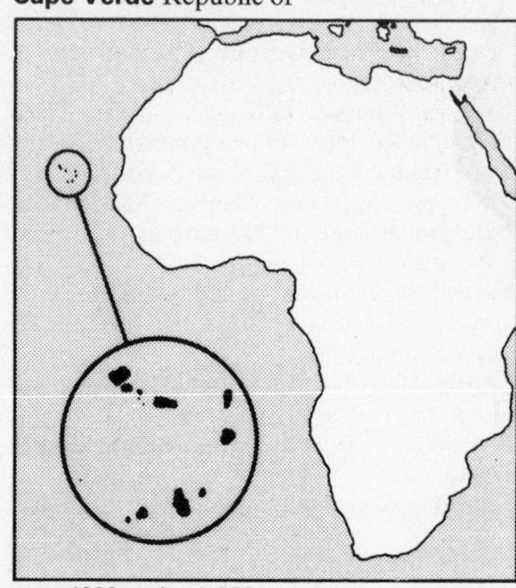

area 4033 sq km/1557 sq mi
capital Praia
features archipelago of 10 islands 565 km/350 mi W of Senegal, strategically important because it dominates the western shipping lanes
exports bananas, coffee
currency Cape Verde escudo
population 360 000, including some 100 000 Angolan refugees
language Creole dialect of Portuguese
religion Roman Catholicism 80%
government executive president Aristide Maria Pereira◊) and one-party National Assembly.
recent history formerly Portuguese, Cape Verde became independent in 1975, and initially there were plans for eventual union with Guinea-Bissau, with which it was administered in colonial times□

Cape Wrath headland at the NW extremity of Scotland□

Cape York peninsula, the most northerly point of the Australian mainland. There are large aboriginal reservations, with fine rock paintings. Its isolation is threatened by exploitation of bauxite deposits□

capillary any fine, smallbore tubing, especially one of the minute blood vessels (about 8/1000th of a millimetre in diameter) forming part of a network between the small arteries and the small veins□

capitalism economic system in which the principal means of production, distribution, and exchange are in private (individual or corporate) hands. A 'mixed economy', as in Britain, combines the private enterprise of capitalism and a degree of state monopoly, as in the nationalized industries. See also privatization◊□

capital punishment punishment by death. At the end of the 18th century in England, it was the penalty for more than 200 offences, though not always inflicted, and was carried out by hanging in public until 1866. The number of offences was gradually reduced, and from 1838 capital punishment was in practice almost invariably imposed only for murder; and from 1965 was in effect abolished. In the USA it is in use in some states and not in others, and methods vary through electrocution, injection, lethal gas, hanging, and shooting□

Capo-di-Monte village N of Naples, where soft-paste porcelain (especially figures of tramps, urchins, etc.) has been produced from 1736□

Capone Al(phonse) 1898–1947. American gangster with a criminal organization in the Chicago of the Prohibition◊ period. He was imprisoned 1931–9, for income tax evasion□

Caporetto village (now Kobarid, Yugoslavia) where the Italians were defeated by the Austro-Germans in 1917□

Capote Truman 1924–84. American novelist. Born in New Orleans, he used a Southern setting in *The Grass Harp* 1951; set a trend in 'faction' novels with *In Cold Blood* 1966, reconstructing a Kansas killing; and mingled recollection and fiction in *Music for Chameleons* 1980□

Capp Al. Pseudonym of American cartoonist Alfred Caplin 1909–79, creator of the *Li'l Abner* 'strip', featuring the hillbillies of Dogpatch, Kentucky□

Cappadocia high volcanic plateau in central Anatolia, Turkey. Rock villages have been carved from the soft tufa◊ rock, and natural erosion has created spectacular scenery□

Capra Frank 1897– . American film director with a sentimental streak, e.g. *Mr Deeds Goes to Town* 1936 and *You Can't Take It With You* 1938□

Capri island in the Bay of Naples. It is famous for its Blue Grotto, reached by sea□

Caprivi Strip north-east access strip for Namibia to the Zambezi river□

capsicum genus of plants, family Solanaceae◊, native to S America, cultivated for their fruit. The ***chilli**, C frutescens,* is used in cooking for a 'hot' flavour, or ground to give ***cayenne pepper***; the large, fleshy mild ***green*** and ***red peppers*** are used in salads and as a cooked vegetable, and the latter are the source of the spice ***paprika***□

Capua town in S Italy; population 17 600□

Capuchin a Franciscan◊ friar□

capuchin An American monkey◊□

capybara largest of the rodents◊ (1.5 m/ 4.5 ft), *Hydrochoerus hydrochoerus*, family Caviidae, of S and Central America□

caracal a kind of lynx. See cat◊□

Caracalla Marcus Aurelius Antoninus 186–217AD. Roman emperor. He succeeded his father Septimius Severus in 211, ruled with cruelty and extravagance, and was assassinated□

Caracas capital and industrial city (cement, textiles, tobacco, paper, etc.) of Venezuela; population 3 507 800. Its port is La Guaira on the Caribbean coast. Simon Bolivar was born here□

Caractacus d. c54AD. British chieftain, who headed resistance to the Romans in the SE 43–51AD, but was defeated on the Welsh border. Shown in Claudius's triumphal procession, he was released in tribute to his courage and died in Rome□

Caradon Baron. See Hugh Foot◊□

carat (US karat) unit of purity in gold. Pure gold is 24-carat; 22-carat (the purest used in jewellery) is 22 parts gold and two parts alloy (to give greater strength). The metric carat of 0.200 grams is the unit of weight for diamonds and other precious stones□

Caravaggio Michelangelo Merisi da 1573–1610. Italian Baroque◊ painter named after his birthplace near Milan. He killed a man in a brawl in 1606, and had to flee Rome for Naples, where he influenced Neapolitan painting profoundly with his controversial realism, such as depicting peasant characters, then considered unsuitable for religious paintings. Works include *The Supper at Emmaus* (National Gallery, London)□

caraway genus of plants, family Umbelliferae◊, grown for their aromatic fruit, known as caraway 'seed', used in cookery, medicine, and perfumery□

carbides compounds of carbon and usually one other chemical element, the 2nd element being a metal, silicon, or boron. They are important in engineering, e.g. in high-speed tools□

carbohydrates large group of compounds of carbon, hydrogen, and oxygen. They include sugars◊, starches◊, and cellulose◊. Essential to life; energy being stored in the form of starch, whilst cellulose is the principle component of plants□

carbolic acid see phenol◊□

carbon element
symbol C

atomic number 6
physical description non-metallic element occurring in three pure forms: diamond (crystalline), graphite (loosely connected layers) and as amorphous (powder) carbon (e.g. candle dust)
features carbon compounds are extensive in the earth as carbonates (chalk, limestone etc.), in the air as carbon dioxide, and in all living matter (cellulose in plants, starch and sugar in animals). The science of organic chemistry deals purely with carbon compounds (see organic◊ chemistry).
uses Carbon-12 is used as the standard for atomic weights; carbon-14 in radio carbon-dating◊□

Carbonari revolutionary secret society in S Italy, originally rebels against Murat, the Bonapartist king of Naples, and later part of Mazzini's 'Young Italy' movement□

carbon dioxide colourless gas, CO_2, formed when carbon is burnt in an adequate supply of air. When solid, 'dry ice', it is used as a refrigerant. The gas is absorbed (during photosynthesis◊) from the atmosphere by plants, which in the process give out oxygen. See under carbon◊ and greenhouse◊ effect□

carbon fibres fine, black silky filaments of pure carbon produced by heat treatment from a special grade of Courtelle and bonded by resin, etc. Eight times stronger and a quarter the weight of high-tensile steel, the resultant product is a strong, flexible, and non-combustible material used in aerospace, cars, electrical equipment, sports gear, etc.□

carbon monoxide gas (CO) formed when carbon is oxidized in a limited supply of air. It is a short-term poisonous constituent of car exhaust fumes which forms a stable compound with haemoglobin in the blood totally prohibiting the haemoglobin from transporting oxygen□

carborundum silicon carbide, a black artificial compound of carbon and silicon, used as an abrasive, etc.□

carbuncle a multiple boil□

carbuncle a garnet cut to resemble a rounded knob□

carburation regulated combustion in an enclosed space, e.g. car engines, of carbon compounds: petrol, paraffin, fuel oil, etc. A *carburettor* prepares the liquid, by atomizing it (forming a very fine spray) and mixing it with air□

Carcassonne city in SW France; population 46 500. It has the finest medieval (restored) fortifications in France□

Carchemish centre (modern Karkamis, Turkey), on the Euphrates, of the New Hittite◊ empire, and taken by Sargon II of Assyria 717BC. Also site of a battle in which Nebuchadnezzar defeated the Egyptians 605BC□

Cardano Girolamo 1501–74. Italian physician, mathematician, and gambler, remembered for his theory of chance, his use of algebra, and many medical publications, notably the first clinical description of typhus fever□

Cárdenas Lázaro 1895–1970. Mexican general, president 1934–40. Freely elected, he was the first president to retire voluntarily, having completed a programme of socialist measures, including oil nationalization□

Cardiff capital of Wales (from 1955) in S Glamorgan; population 280 000. It is mainly administrative, but industries include engineering, telephone equipment, and radioactive isotopes; the now derelict docks are being redeveloped for industry, and Cardiff is a free port◊. Notable are the castle, the public buildings in Cathays Park (Law Courts, City Hall, National Museum of Wales, Welsh Office, the Institute of Science and Technology, National School of Medicine, College of Music and Drama, and University College of S Wales), Llandaff cathedral (12th century, restored after German air raid damage in 1941, has Epstein's sculpture *Christ in Majesty*), the New and Sherman theatres, Cardiff College of Music and Drama, Cardiff Arms Park (home of Welsh rugby), Welsh National Folk Museum at St Fagan's, Welsh Industrial and Maritime Museum, and the Royal Mint at Llantrisant. It is the headquarters of the Welsh National Opera□

Cardin Pierre 1922– . French fashion designer, the first to show a collection for men, in 1960□

Cardinal in the Roman Catholic Church, the highest rank next to that of Pope. Cardinals form a Sacred College, of whom 120 (below the age of 80) elect the Pope, and are themselves nominated by him. They act as an advisory body to the Papacy□

Carew Thomas c1595–1640. English poet, probably the best lyricist of the 'Cavalier Poets' of Charles I's court□

cargo cult Melanesian native belief, from the 19th century, in the arrival of the trappings of Western life (the cargo) through the agency of some messianic spirit figure. Rituals are performed and 'warehouses' built for the expected goods. It was reinforced by the supplies delivered by air to US troops evicting Japanese troops from the islands□

Carib American Indian people of the West Indies and S America□

Caribbean part of the Atlantic Ocean in which the West Indies◊ lie. It is here that the Gulf Stream turns in the direction of Europe□

Caribbean Community organization (CARICOM) for economic and foreign policy co-ordination in the Caribbean region from 1973. The leading member is Trinidad and Tobago; headquarters Georgetown, Guyana. From 1979 a left-wing Grenadan coup led to a progressive regional sub-group including St Lucia and Dominica□

caribou a type of N American reindeer. See deer◊□

caricature exaggerated artistic representation, for the purpose of ridicule. Caricaturists include Gillray, Hogarth, Rowlandson, Cruikshank, Lear, Doyle, Du Maurier, Beerbohm, Low, 'Vicky', 'Giles', Cummings, Ronald Searle, Lancaster, Calman, Herb Block, Gerald Scarfe, Ralph Steadman (the last two producing grotesque, distorted figures), and Peter Fluck and Roger Law (three-dimensional puppets for television series *Spitting Image*)□

CARICOM see Caribbean◊ Community□

caries disease or deterioration of teeth or bones. Dental caries is erosion of the teeth by bacterial decay, stimulated especially by a high sugar diet, and failure to clean the teeth. See fluorine◊□

Carinthia former independent duchy, now a province of SE Austria, capital Klagenfurt. See Slovenes◊□

Carisbrooke village near Newport, Isle of Wight. Charles I was imprisoned in its castle 1647–8□

Carissimi Giacomo 1605–74. Italian composer, a pioneer of the oratorio and cantata□

Carl XVI Gustaf 1946– . King of Sweden from 1973; the monarchy was effectively stripped of all power at his accession□

Carlisle city and administrative headquarters of Cumbria, England; population 98 300. Situated at the W end of Hadrian's Wall, it has a troubled history due to its proximity to the Scottish border. There is a Norman castle and cathedral, and it is still an important rail junction□

Carlists supporters of the claims of Don Carlos de Bourbon 1788–1855, and his descendants, to the Spanish crown. He had been excluded by an abrogation of the Salic Law◊ (see Isabella◊ II). The latest claimant, Carlos Hugo de Bourbon Parma, renounced his claim in 1977 following the accession of King Juan Carlos□

Carlow county (county town Carlow) of the Republic of Ireland, province of Leinster◊□

Carlyle Thomas 1795–1881. Scottish author. A teacher of mathematics, he married Jane Baillie Welsh (1801–66) in 1826 and from 1834 lived with her at Cheyne Row Chelsea (the house is now a museum). After his wife's death he devoted himself to editing her letters and to his reminiscences, which shed an unfavourable light on his character and the neglect of her, for which he could not forgive himself. His best-known works are *Sartor Resartus* 1836, a partly fictional account of spiritual crisis, and his *French Revolution* 1837□

Carmelites mendicant order of friars in the Roman Catholic Church, historically originating with the foundation of the first house on Mount Carmel in Palestine by the crusader Berthold in 1155. They were known from their white overmantle (over a brown habit) as White Friars. St Teresa◊ of Avila founded a stricter Carmelite order of barefoot friars and nuns□

Carmichael Hoagy 1899–1981. American pianist, composer of the romantic song, 'Stardust' 1928□

Carmina Burana medieval lyric miscellany compiled from the work of wandering 13th-century scholars, and including secular (love songs and drinking songs) as well as religious verse. They have been set to music by Carl Orff◊ and others□

Carnac village in Brittany with megalithic remains of tombs and stone alignments of the period 2000–1500BC. The largest of the latter has some 1000 stones up to 4 m/13 ft high arranged in 11 rows, with a circle at the W end. They suggest an astronomical link□

Carnap Rudolf 1891–1970. German-American philosopher, the chief exponent of logical empiricism. Influenced by Mach◊, he produced *Meaning and Necessity* 1956□

Carnarvon Range see Great Divide◊□

carnation the numerous double-flowered cultivated varieties of the fragrant clove-pink *Dianthus caryophyllus,* family Caryophyllaceae□

carnauba a type of palm◊□

Carné Marcel 1903– . French film director, noted for his atmosphere and subtle characterization, e.g. *Le Jour se lève* 1939 and *Les Enfants du Paradis* 1944□

Carnegie Andrew 1835–1919. Scottish-American industrialist, who made a fortune in railways, oil, and steel, and from 1901 devoted his wealth to endowing libraries, universities, etc., in the UK and USA.

Carnegie Hall, New York, was so named because of his contributions to it□

Carnegie Dale 1888–1955. American YMCA instructor in public speaking who made his name with *How to Win Friends and Influence People* 1938□

Carnera Primo 1906–67. Italian world heavyweight champion boxer 1933–4, known as the man-mountain (he was 1.98 m/6 ft 6in tall)□

Carnivora order of mammals whose teeth are specially adapted for tearing and shearing flesh (e.g. big pointed canine teeth), but may be to varying extents also herbivorous. It includes bears (Ursidae); dogs (Canidae); pandas and raccoons (Procyonidae); weasels, badgers, etc. (Mustelidae); mongooses, etc. (Viverridae); and cats (Felidae)□

Carnot Lazare 1796–1832. French general, whose transformation of French military technique in the Revolutionary period earned him the title of 'Organizer of Victory'. His work on fortification, *De la défense de places fortes* 1810, is a classic□

Carnot Sadi 1837–94. French soldier-scientist, son of Lazare Carnot, who founded thermodynamics. See Carnot◊ cycle□

Carnot cycle idealized reversible cycle of physical changes in a substance in a heat engine: 1 isothermal expansion (i.e. without change of temperature); 2 adiabatic expansion (i.e. without heat flow); 3 isothermal compression; and 4 adiabatic compression. See Sadi Carnot◊□

Caro Anthony 1924– . British sculptor, noted for his bold simplicity of form, use of paint, and for free-standing pieces without formal bases□

carob a type of bean◊ pod□

Carol two kings of Romania:

Carol I 1839–1914, first King of Romania 1881–1914, after its freeing from Turkish rule under the Treaty of Berlin.

Carol II 1893–1953. He renounced the succession in 1925, to settle with his mistress Madame Lupescu in Paris, but replaced his son Michael as king 1930–8, when he was forced to abdicate by the pro-German Iron Guard. He went to Mexico and married his mistress in 1947□

carol song, in medieval times associated with a round dance, and then with May Day, New Year, and often the more secular aspects of Easter and Christmas□

Carolina see North◊ and South◊ Carolina□

Caroline of Anspach 1683–1737. Queen of George II of Great Britain, whom she married in 1705, following him to England on his father's accession in 1714. As Princess of Wales, she held court at Leicester House, and was a supporter of Walpole□

Caroline of Brunswick 1768–1821. Queen of George IV of Great Britain, whom she married in 1795, separating from him in 1796 following the birth of the Princess Charlotte◊. In 1820, on her husband's accession, she resisted attempts to make her renounce the title of queen and live abroad, returning to London to live in royal state. A government bill in Jul 1820 to dissolve the marriage was abandoned, but a royal order forbade her presence at the coronation, and she died on 7 Aug. Her funeral was the occasion of popular riots□

Carolines Micronesian archipelago of some 500 coral islets (the chief being Kosrae, Ponape, Truk, Yap, and Palau), formerly part of the US Trust Territory of the Pacific Islands, and now constituting the Federated States of Micronesia◊, and Republic of Belau◊□

Carolingians Frankish dynasty descending from Pepin◊ the Short and named after his son Charles the Great (Charlemagne◊), and ending with Louis V of France 966–87, who was followed by Hugh Capet◊□

carp family of freshwater fish, Cyprinidae. The Asian ***common carp***, *Cyprinus carpio,* has been been bred for centuries in European fish ponds to provide fish on Fridays. Also familiar are the ***goldfish,*** *Carassius auratus,* of China and Japan, bred into fantastic forms (the chief breeding centre is the Pei-Hai Kung-Yuan garden in Peking), e.g. the white veil-tail which has fins and tail extended into flowing 'white chiffon' veils; and the Chinese grass carp *Ctenopharyngodon idella*, introduced (one sex only) to European rivers for weed control.

coarse fish members of the family, caught for sport not eating, include ***barbel*** *Barbus barbus*; ***bleak*** *Alburnus lucidus*; ***bream*** *Abramis brama*; ***chubb*** *Leuciscus cephalus*; ***dace*** *Leuciscus leuciscus*; ***gudgeon*** *Gobio gobio*; ***minnow*** *Phoxinus phoxinus*, 12 cm/4.5 in, which is not generally caught, but is valued as food for trout; ***orfe*** *Leuciscus idus*; ***roach*** *Rutilus rutilus*; ***rudd*** *Scardinius erythrophthalmus*; ***tench*** *Tinca tinca.*

The family Cyprinodontidae resemble carp, but have toothed jaws. They include the South American genus *Anableps*, notably the four-eyed fish, which has eyes horizontally divided, so that it sees equally well above and below water□

Carpaccio Vittorio c1465–1522. Venetian artist, painter of his native city and of religious works, famous for the cycle of paintings on *The Legend of Saint Ursula*□

Carpathians Central European mountain system, forming a semi-circle through Czechoslovakia-Poland-USSR-Romania, 1450 km/900 mi. The central ***Tatra mountains*** on the Czech-Polish frontier include the highest peak, Gerlachovka, 2663 m/8737 ft□

Carpentaria Gulf of. Shallow gulf on the N of Australia, named after a 17th-century governor of the Dutch East Indies□

carpet heavy woven or knotted material for covering floors or stairs. Countries with a long tradition in hand-knotted carpets in silk, wool, cotton, etc., include Afghanistan, China, India, Iran, Pakistan, Turkey. Most famous of antique carpets is the Ardabil Carpet 1539–40, made at Kashan (340 knots per in and 11.6 m/c38 ft x 5.4 m/c18 ft) for the mosque at Ardabil, Iran, now in the Victoria and Albert Museum, London. Modern machine-made carpets include 1 ***Wilton***, with a fine close texture lending itself to design effects; 2 ***Axminster***, including many colours and economical in material because the tuft is on the surface with none hidden in the fabric, as with Wilton; and 3 ***tufted***, as at Kidderminster, a process which often uses modern synthetic fibres. In the first two processes the wools are pre-dyed, but in the third the already tufted plain carpet may be patterned in sharp detail by dyes applied by high-pressure jets; or different types of fibre (sometimes the same fibre treated with different chemicals) may be used which each absorb a different colour from the dye bath□

carpet-bagger in US history, Northerners who went South after the Civil War of 1861–5, with nothing but what they carried in their carpet-bags, and exploited the new black voters to establish corrupt governments and make fast profits□

Carpini Johannes de Plano c1182–1252. Franciscan friar, sent by the Pope on a fact-finding mission to Mongolia 1245–7, who wrote a Mongol history□

Carracci three Italian painters, teachers at a famous academy of painting in Bologna 1582, which combined selected aspects of the masters of the Renaissance. ***Ludovico*** c1555–1619 was its founder, and of his two cousins ***Agostino*** c1557–1602 and ***Annibale*** c1560–1609, the latter became the most famous, decorating the ceiling of the Farnese Gallery, Rome□

carragheen or ***carrageen*** a kind of seaweed◊□

Carrara town in Tuscany, Italy with quarries of the world's finest white marble, worked from Roman times, and used by Michelangelo□

Carrel Alexis 1873–1944. French surgeon, whose method of suturing blood vessels prepared the way for organ transplants; Nobel prize 1912□

Carrhae ancient town near modern Haran, Turkey, where Crassus◊ was defeated by the Parthians in 53BC□

carriage driving sport in which the events include dressage and obstacle driving, and the marathon, in which less elegant carriages are used. It was popularized by Prince Philip□

Carrickfergus seaport on Belfast Lough, County Antrim, N Ireland; population 10 000□

Carrington Peter Alexander Rupert, 6th Baron Carrington 1919– . British Conservative statesman. Defence Secretary 1970–4, and while Foreign Secretary 1979–82, he negotiated independence for Zimbabwe, but resigned after failing to anticipate the Falklands crisis. He became Secretary-General of NATO in 1984□

Carroll Lewis. Pseudonym of Charles Lutwidge Dodgson 1832–98, children's writer. Born at Daresbury, Cheshire, he lectured in mathematics at Oxford, and wrote *Alice's Adventures in Wonderland* 1865 for Alice Liddell, the young daughter of Dean Liddell, head of his college. *Through the Looking Glass* 1872 was a sequel, and he also wrote the nonsense poem *The Hunting of the Snark* 1876. A shy man, with a stammer, he never married. He was among the pioneers of portrait photography□

carrot hardy European biennial *Daucus carota*, family Umbelliferae◊, grown since the 16th century for its edible root which has a high sugar content and also contains carotene, which can be converted by the human liver to vitamin A□

Carse of Gowrie fertile lowland plain, Tayside region, Scotland□

Carson Christopher 'Kit' 1809–68. American frontiersman, guide, and Indian agent, who later fought for the Federal side in the Civil War. See Carson City◊, and Frémont◊□

Carson Edward Henry, Baron Carson 1854–1935. Irish lawyer-politician. He played a decisive role in the prosecution of Oscar Wilde, and was a leader of Ulster's resistance to Irish Home Rule. He was Attorney-General under Asquith in 1915, and First Lord of the Admiralty under Lloyd George in 1916□

Carson Rachel 1907–64. American biologist, author of *The Sea Around Us* 1951 and *Silent Spring* 1962, both of which were pioneer pleas for environmental protection□

Carson City capital of Nevada, USA; population 30 810. Smallest of the state capitals, it is named after Kit Carson◊□

Cartagena port and industrial city in N Colombia; population 419 000. It was taken by Drake in 1586□

Cartagena port and industrial city in Murcia, Spain, the country's largest naval base; population 147 000. It was founded by Hasdrubal◊□

cartel an amalgamation of industrial firms which retain their identities (and therefore do not form a trust), but which are pledged to regulate output and prices; both EFTA◊ and the EEC◊ have provisions to control such arrangements□

Carter Angela 1940– . British novelist, author of the Gothic fantasy *Nights at the Circus* 1984□

Carter 'Jimmy' (James Earl) 1924– . 39th president of the USA 1977–81. Born in Plains, Georgia, he served in the Navy, studied nuclear physics, and after a spell as a peanut farmer entered politics as a Democrat in 1953. In 1976 he narrowly wrested the presidency from Ford◊. Features of his presidency were the Panama Treaty◊, the Camp David Agreements◊, and the Iranian seizure of American Embassy hostages. He was defeated by Reagan in 1980□

Carter Doctrine assertion in 1980 of a vital US interest in the Gulf region (prompted by Soviet invasion of Afghanistan): any outside attempt at control would be met by force if necessary□

Carthage Phoenician city on the Gulf of Tunis, now a suburb of Tunis◊, Founded, according to tradition, in 814BC by emigrants from Tyre led by Dido◊, it was the leader of the Phoenician colonies in N Africa and Spain, first in conflict with Greece, and then Rome:

First Punic War 264–241BC the Carthaginians were defeated at sea and expelled from their strongholds in E Sicily, but, under Hamilcar◊ Barca they built up their empire and army in Spain. From here Hamilcar Barca's son, Hannibal◊, launched the

Second Punic War 218–201BC, crossing the Pyrenees and Alps to defeat the Romans crushingly in Italy before they managed to force him back to Africa and defeat him at Zama 202BC. There followed the

Third Punic War 149–146BC, Carthage was finally defeated and the city destroyed in 146BC. Julius◊ Caesar settled colonists there in 45BC and it became the capital of the Roman province of Africa, but it declined, after its capture by the Vandals◊ in 439AD, into a nest of pirates. It was part of the Byzantine Empire 533–698, when it was finally destroyed by the Arabs. In the 2nd century BC it had a population of 700 000, and excavations reveal that human sacrifice was carried out. Its real strength lay in its commerce and its navy; the Carthaginian armies were mercenaries. In 1985 the mayor of Rome finally signed a peace treaty with a representative of Carthage□

Carthusians Roman Catholic order of monks and later nuns, founded by St Bruno in 1084 at Chartreuse◊, near Grenoble. Living chiefly in unbroken silence, they ate one vegetarian meal a day and supported themselves by their own labours□

Cartier Sir Georges Étienne 1814–73. French-Canadian statesman. He fought against the British in the rebellion of 1837, but was joint Prime Minister with Sir John Macdonald 1858–62, and brought Quebec into the federation in 1867□

Cartier Jacques 1491–1557. French navigator, who sailed up the St Lawrence river in 1534, and named the site of Montreal, later further exploring Canada□

cartomancy the practice of telling fortunes by cards: see tarot◊□

cartoon a preliminary design for a painting, tapestry, etc., but often applied to caricatures◊□

Caruso Enrico 1873–1921. Italian tenor, born in Naples, and remembered for operatic roles such as Canio in *Pagliacci*, and the Duke in *Rigoletto*□

Carver George Washington c1864–1943. American agricultural chemist. Born in Missouri, he promoted peanut production in the South, developing some 300 products, and was a pioneer in the work on plastics□

Cary (Arthur) Joyce (Lunel) 1888–1957. Irish novelist, born in Londonderry, who became a member of the British colonial service. His books include *Mister Johnson* 1939, *A House of Children* 1941, and *The Horse's Mouth* 1944, dealing with a Bohemian artist, Gulley Jimson□

caryatid building support or pillar, in the shape of a woman; a male figure is a telamon or atlas□

Casablanca (Arabic *Dar el-Beida*), port, commercial and industrial centre on the Atlantic coast of Morocco; population 2 175 000□

Casablanca Conference meeting of Churchill and Roosevelt, 14–24 Jan 1943, at which the Allied demand for the unconditional surrender of Germany, Italy, and Japan was issued□

Casals Pablo 1876–1973. Widely acclaimed Spanish cellist, who was noted for his free technique. He was exiled by Franco in 1936. He married the Portuguese cellist Suggia□

Casanova de Seingalt Giovanni 1725–98. Italian adventurer, spy, violinist, librarian, and – according to his *Memoirs*, published unexpurgated only in 1960 – one of the world's great lovers□

Cascade Range volcanic mountains in Washington, USA. They include Mount St Helens and Mount Rainier (the highest peak 4392 m/14 408 ft) noted for its glaciers□

casein the protein of milk (familiar as cheese) coagulated using rennet or acid. Its commercial applications include glues, paints, distempers, artificial silk, and plastics□

Casement Roger David 1864–1916. Irish nationalist. In 1914 he went to Germany to attempt to induce Irish prisoners-of-war to form an Irish brigade to take part in a republican rising. He returned to Ireland by submarine in 1916, actually to postpone, not start the Easter rising, and was arrested, tried, and hanged for treason. His controversial diaries, revealing his homosexuality, were made available by the British government in 1959□

Caserta town in S Italy; population 63 000. The base for Garibaldi's campaigns in the 19th century, it was the Allied headquarters in Italy 1943–5, and the German forces surrendered to Field Marshal Alexander here in 1945□

cashew tree of tropical America *Ana cardium occidentale,* family Anacardiaceae, with an edible kidney-shaped nut in a hard shell□

cashmere expensive, very soft wool fabric made from the underfleece of a Kashmir goat, used in shawls, coats, etc.□

Caspian Sea world's largest inland sea, divided between Iran and USSR

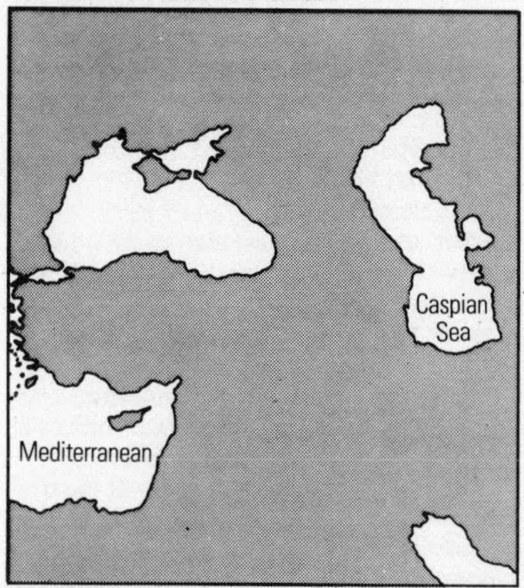

area c400 000 sq km/155 000 sq mi, approx 28 m/90 ft below normal sea level. Shrinkage and pollution, caused by industrial use, have damaged the caviar industry□

Cassandra in Greek mythology, the daughter of Priam◊, whose prophecies (e.g. of the fall of Troy) were never believed, because she had rejected the love of Apollo. She was murdered with Agamemnon◊□

Cassatt Mary 1855–1926. American artist, noted for Impressionistic renderings of mothers and children□

cassava genus *Manihot* of S American plants, family Euphorbiaceae◊, with starch-filled tubers, 'manioc'; ***sweet cassava M dulcis*** is used as a vegetable; ***bitter cassava M utilissima***, poisonous before treatment, yields tapioca. About half the population of Africa, 200 million, depend on it as a staple□

Cassavetes John 1929– . American actor and film director, who appeared in *The Dirty Dozen*, etc., and has made experimental apparently improvised films, e.g. *Shadows* 1960, *The Killing of a Chinese Bookie* 1980□

Cassel see Kassel◊□

cassia aromatic bark of *Cinnamonum cassia*, family Lauraceae, used as a substitute for cinnamon◊. See also senna◊□

Cassino town in S Italy; population 25 000. The Abbey of Monte Cassino, founded by St Benedict in 529, was destroyed by Allied bombardment in Feb 1944; it was rebuilt in 1956□

Cassiopeia in Greek mythology, the mother of Andromeda◊□

Cassiopeia brilliant W-shaped constellation near the Pole star, which includes Cassiopeia A (a powerful radio source) and Tycho's star, both remnants of supernovae□

Cassius Gaius d. 42BC. Roman soldier. Pardoned for fighting with Pompey against Caesar at Pharsalus, he yet became a leader in the murder conspiracy of 44, and committed suicide after his defeat at Philippi◊□

Cassivelaunus chieftain of the British tribe, the Catuvellauni, who led the British resistance to Caesar in 54BC□

Casson Sir Hugh 1910– . British architect, director of architecture for the Festival of Britain 1948–51□

cassowary a kind of running◊ bird□

castanets Spanish percussion instrument made of two hollowed wooden shells, held in the hand to produce a rhythmic accompaniment to dance, etc.□

caste grouping of Hindu society (Portuguese *casta* 'race') from ancient times into four main classes from which some 3000 subsequent divisions derive: Brahmans (priests), Kshatriyas (nobles and warriors), Vaisyas (traders and farmers), and Sudras (servants); plus a fifth class (probably the aboriginal inhabitants of the country), known variously as Scheduled Castes, Depressed Classes, Untouchables, Harijan (name coined by Gandhi, 'children of God'), whose way of life (as sanitary workers, slaughtermen, etc.) makes them polluting by touch, or even by sight, to others. Discrimination against the last-named was made illegal in 1947, but persists□

Castel Gandolfo castle SE of Rome built by Pope Urban VIII in the 17th century, and still the summer residence of the Pope; there is an observatory, built in 1936□

Castellón de la Plana city in Valencia, Spain; population 126 465. It is an orange-growing area□

Castelo Branco Camilo 1825–90. Portuguese novelist, best remembered for *Amor de perdičao/Love of Perdition* 1862, written during his imprisonment for adultery, and showing his obsession with love as a motive force. He committed suicide when overtaken by blindness□

Castiglione Baldassare, Count 1478–1529. Italian author and diplomat, remembered for his picture of the perfect Renaissance gentleman *Il Cortegiano/The Courtier* 1528□

Castile historic kingdom (founded in the 10th century), occupying the central plateau of Spain. Its union with Aragon in 1479 was the foundation of the Spanish state. It corresponded very approximately to the modern autonomous regions of:

Castilla-Léon (including Burgos, León, Salamanca, and Valladolid); population 2 577 000

Castilla-La Mancha (including Albacete and Toledo); population 1 628 000

La Rioja (including Logroño); population 253 300, famous for its rich red wines; and Madrid◊□

Castilla-La Mancha region of central Spain. See under Castile◊□

Castilla-León region of central Spain. See under Castile◊□

Castle Barbara, Baroness Castle 1911– . British Labour politician, born Betts. She was Minister of Overseas Development 1964–5, Transport 1965–8, Employment 1968–70 (when her White Paper 'In Place of Strife', on trade union reform, was abandoned as too controversial), and Social Services 1974–6, when she was dropped from the Cabinet by Callaghan (an opponent of her White Paper, who was criticized in her controversial *Diaries* 1980). She led the Labour group in the European Parliament from 1979□

castle fortified medieval stronghold, probably influenced in its earliest development by ancient Egyptian practice, e.g. the complex structures of the Nubian defences excavated by W B Emery◊. The main elements of the Norman castle were the keep (a rectangular tower); an inner bailey or courtyard surrounding the keep, and separated from an outer courtyard by a defensive wall; crenellated battlements, through which missiles were discharged; and a drawbridge over a water-filled surrounding moat. Cannon ended the usefulness of castles□

Castleford town in W Yorkshire, England; population 56 000□

Castle Hill Rising Irish convict revolt in New South Wales, Australia, 4 Mar 1804; a number were killed while parleying with the military under a flag of truce□

Castlemaine Lady 1641–1709. Mistress of Charles II of England. Born Barbara Villiers, she was the wife from 1659 of Roger Palmer, created Earl of Castlemaine in 1661. She was the chief mistress of Charles 1660–70, when she was created Duchess of Cleveland. Among her descendants, through her son the Duke of Grafton, is the Princess of Wales: see Diana◊□

Castlemaine town in Victoria, Australia; population 7000. Site of one of the earliest gold strikes in 1851, it then had a population of 30 000□

Castlereagh Robert Stewart, Viscount Castlereagh 1769–1822. British Tory statesman. As Chief Secretary in Ireland 1797–1801, he suppressed the rebellion of 1798, and helped (the younger) Pitt secure the union of England, Scotland, and Ireland in 1801. He was War Secretary 1805–6 and 1807–9, when he had to resign following his duel with Canning◊, and Foreign Secretary from 1812, when he devoted himself to the overthrow of Napoleon and represented Britain at the Congress of Vienna◊. At home he repressed the Reform movement, and popular opinion held him responsible for the Peterloo Massacre◊. His mind unhinged, he committed suicide and his burial in Westminster Abbey saw rejoicing crowds□

Castor second brightest star in the constellation Gemini, the 'twins'; see Castor and Pollux◊□

Castor and Pollux/Polydeuces in Greek mythology, twin sons of Leda (by Zeus◊), brothers of Helen◊ and Clytemnestra◊. Protectors of seamen, they were transformed at death to the constellation Gemini□

castoreum the preputial follicles of the beaver, abbreviated as 'castor', and used in perfumery□

castor oil plant tropical and subtropical tall shrub ***Palma Christi Ricinus communis,*** family Euphorbiaceae; the seeds yield the purgative castor oil, and also ricin, one of the most powerful poisons known, which is 'targeted' to destroy cancer cells, while leaving normal cells untouched□

Castro Ruz Fidel 1927– . Cuban statesman. In 1959 he overthrew the Batista regime, becoming Prime Minister a few months later. He was a Marxist-Leninist until 1974. He rejected the formula 'from each according to his ability and to each according to his need' for each 'receiving according to his work'. He became president in 1976, and from 1979 was also president of the Non-Aligned Movement, although promoting the line of the Soviet Union, which subsidized his regime. Closely associated with him, as Minister of Armed Forces from 1959, was his brother Raúl□

casuarina genus of Australian and East Indian feathery evergreen trees, valuable for timber□

cat family, Felidae◊, of carnivorous mammals, mostly nocturnal. Their beautiful pelts have led to the near extinction of many species. They include:

lion of Afro-Asia *Panthera leo* which has a tawny coat (the young have stripe and spot markings which later disappear), tufted tail, and (in the male) a heavy mane and a large tuft at the end of the tail; body-length c2 m/6 ft. They live in a 'pride' consisting of a dominant male, several younger males, and lionesses with their cubs; if the leadership changes, the new dominant male will kill all the cubs of his predecessor. The lionesses then come into heat again, and the cubs of the interloper are born earlier than they otherwise would be. Most of the hunting is done by the lionesses in groups; man-eating is the resort of the old and weakened beast. In zoos a *liger* is the offspring of a male lion and female tiger, and a *tigon* that of a male tiger and female lion.

tiger of central Asia, largest of the great cats *Panthera tigris* which has a reddish fawn coat with handsome stripe markings; rare black or cream specimens have been known. The largest are the ***Siberian tigers,*** of whom only c200 survive; body-length c2.6 m/7 ft. Living either solitarily or in family parties, tigers are good swimmers, and are voracious feeders, mainly on deer and cattle.

leopard or ***panther*** (name especially for the black variety) *Panthera pardus* of Afro-Asian jungles, c2 m/6 ft long, with a yellowish coat and black rosette-like spots. The smaller ***ounce*** or ***snow-leopard*** *Panthera uncia* of central Asia, c1 m/3 ft, with a tail the same length, is long-haired with similar markings. The ***clouded leopard*** *Neofelis nebulosa* of SE Asia has blotchy markings. Allied to the leopard is the ***jaguar*** *Panthera onca* of the Americas, c1.2 m/4 ft long, with larger spots and a shorter tail, and credited with even greater ferocity. Both have black forms, and even occasional albinos, in which the rosettes appear like markings in watered silk.

cheetah or ***hunting leopard*** *Acinonyx jubatus* with an Afro-Asian range; yellowish, with black spots, it has a more 'doglike' appearance, and blunt, only partially retractile claws. Standing 45 cm/1.5 ft high, it is higher at the rear than at the shoulder, the powerful legs making it an extremely speedy (110 kmph/70 mph) daylight hunter. It has for centuries been domesticated for chasing game.

puma or ***cougar*** or ***mountain lion*** *Felis concolor* of the Americas; reddish-brown, it is c2.5 m/5 ft long, including a long tail, and will often 'shadow', but not attack, human beings.

lynx of Canada and N Europe *Felis lynx* which has a very thick grey-brown mottled pelt, ear tufts, and a short tail; body-length over 1 m/3 ft. Closely allied are the ***bay lynx*** or ***bobcat*** *Lynx rufus* of USA, with a more reddish fur, striped or spotted in a darker colour; and the ***desert lynx*** or ***caracal*** *Lynx caracal* of N Africa and S Asia, also reddish, with dark ear tufts.

ocelot of S and Central America *Felis pardalis* with dark splotches and bars on a light brownish coat, much in demand as a luxury fur; body-length c1 m/3 ft.

serval of Africa *Felis serval* slender, long-limbed cat with a rich brown, black-spotted coat; body-length just under 1 m/3 ft.

domestic cat *Felis catus*, whose ancestors probably included the ***African***, *F libyca,* and the ***European wild cat*** *F silvestris*. On Iriomote Island, S Japan, there is a very fine wild cat long thought extinct. Show cat species are subdivided into Persian or 'long-haired' varieties; short-hairs, and Siamese□

catacomb underground cemetery, especially those of the early Christians beneath the basilica of St Sebastian in Rome, where bodies were buried in niches in the walls of the tunnels□

Catalan language related to Provençal◊ and spoken in Catalonia (see Spain◊) Balearic Isles, SE France, Andorra, etc.□

Catalaunian Fields defeat of Attila◊ by the Roman general Aëtius near Troyes, France, in 451AD: it freed Europe from imminent Asiatic domination□

catalepsy an extreme form of resistive stupor, sometimes resembling death, of uncertain duration, and possibly the result of emotional conflict. It may occur in association with schizophrenia, hysteria, or without other symptoms□

Çatal Hüyük Neolithic site of 6000BC discovered by James Mellaart in 1961 in Turkey, which showed a much earlier development of urban life in the ancient world than had previously been imagined□

Catalonia autonomous region (*Cataluña*) of NE Spain, which includes Barcelona, Lérida, and Tarragona; population 5 958 000. It is Spain's leading industrial area. With a long tradition of independence, it was autonomous 1932–9, but lost the privilege until 1980 (when official use of the Catalan language was also restored) for supporting the Republican cause in the Civil War.

French Catalonia is the adjacent department of Pyrénées-Orientales□

catalpa genus of trees, family Bignoniaceae, with heart-shaped leaves and trumpet-like flowers; *C bignoides* is found in Asia and N America and in Britain as an ornamental□

catalyst substance which alters the speed (faster or slower) of reaction in a chemical process, itself remaining unchanged at the end of the reaction. Industrially often metal gauze□

catamaran fast, twin-hulled sailing vessel, based on the aboriginal craft of S America and the Indies, made of logs lashed together, with an outrigger□

Catania industrial port in Sicily; population 398 500. It exports local sulphur, etc.□

cataract opacity of the lens of the eye, most commonly occurring in those over 50, when the usual treatment is extraction of the lens. This enables the patient to see, but not to alter focus, but a plastic lens may be implanted with which a change of spectacles will change focus□

catarrh the excessive secretion of mucous fluid, sometimes mixed with pus, from the nose, etc., as the result of a cold, hay fever, etc.□

Catastrophe Theory mathematical theory developed by René Thom in 1972, in which he showed that the growth of an organism proceeds by a series of gradual changes, which are triggered by, and in turn trigger, large-scale changes or 'catastrophic' jumps. It also has applications in engineering, e.g. the gradual strain on the structure of a bridge which eventually results in a sudden collapse, and has been extended to economic and psychological events, e.g. a quarrel between husband and wife, which reaches a point where it suddenly escalates to a crisis – perhaps of physical violence□

catchment area area from which water is collected by a river, hence area from which a school draws pupils, etc.□

catechism teaching by question and answer on the Socratic method, but especially as a means of instructing children in the basics of the Christian creed□

caterpillar the larvae of butterflies◊ and moths◊□

catfish smooth-skinned freshwater fish of worldwide distribution, with barbels at the mouth, family Siluriformes. The species *Silurus glanis* reaches 5 m/16 ft and 300 kg/660 lb. In Britain the name is applied to the wolf-fish *Anarrhichas lupus*, an unrelated sea species□

Cathars or *Cathari* heretic Christian sect, originating in the Balkans in the 10th century (Bogomils), and destroyed or suppressed in W Europe in the 14th century by the Inquisition◊: they were often identified with the Albigenses◊. They identified humankind with the rebellious legions of Satan, who could escape reincarnation only by union with Christ, achieved by baptism with the spirit (the Paraclete or Comforter). The Perfect, or ordained priesthood practised strict self-denial and chastity, and the Believers could approach God only through them□

cathedral church containing the throne of a bishop or archbishop, which is governed by a dean and chapter□

Cather Willa Sibert 1876–1947. American novelist. Born in Virginia, she wrote about Western pioneer life, e.g. *Death Comes for the Archbishop* 1927, set in New Mexico□

Catherine two empresses of Russia:

Catherine I 1683–1727. Of humble origin, she became the mistress of Peter the Great, who divorced his wife in 1711 to marry her. In 1725, she succeeded him as empress, and allied herself with Austria and Spain against England. She founded the Academy◊ of Sciences.

Catherine II the Great 1729–96. Of Prussian origin, she married the unbalanced future Peter III in 1745. Six months after his accession in 1762, she took over power, and extended Russia's territory by additions from Turkey in 1774, Sweden in 1790, and the partitions of Poland. She had a notorious private life (see Potemkin◊), but aided the Encyclopedists and corresponded with Voltaire◊ and D'Alembert◊□

Catherine de' Medici 1519–89. French queen consort of Henry II, whom she married in 1533, and mother of Francis II, Charles IX, and Henry III. At first outshone by Diane de Poitiers◊, she became regent 1560–3 for Charles IX, and was politically powerful until his death in 1574. At first scheming with the Huguenots, she later opposed them (see Massacre of St Bartholomew◊). She patronized the arts□

Catherine of Aragon 1485–1536. First queen of Henry VIII of England. She married Henry's elder brother, Prince Arthur, in 1501 (the marriage allegedly being unconsummated), and on his death in 1502 was betrothed to Henry, marrying him on his accession in 1509. Of their six children, only a daughter (later Mary◊ I) lived. Desirous of a male heir, Henry sought an annulment in 1526 on the grounds that the union with his brother's widow was invalid despite a Papal dispensation. When the Pope demanded that the case be referred to him, Henry married Anne Boleyn, afterwards receiving the desired decree of nullity from Cranmer◊ in 1533. The Reformation in England followed, and Catherine went into retirement till her death□

Catherine of Braganza 1638–1705. Queen of Charles II of England, whom she married in 1662, bringing the Portuguese possessions of Bombay and Tangier as her dowry. Her childlessness and practice of her Catholic faith were unpopular, but Charles resisted pressure for divorce□

Catherine of Genoa St 1447–1510. Italian mystic, who devoted herself to the sick and to meditation. Her feast day is 15 Sept□

Catherine of Siena St 1347–80. A Dominican Tertiary from the age of 16, she is said to have received the stigmata in 1375, and in 1376 persuaded Pope Gregory XI to return from Avignon to Rome. She wrote the mystical *Dialogue*. Feast day 30 Apr□

Catherine of Valois 1401–37. Queen of Henry V of England, whom she married in 1420, becoming the mother of Henry VI. After the death of Henry V, she secretly married Owen Tudor c1425, and their son became the father of Henry VII□

cathode the electrode towards which positive particles (cations) move within a device, e.g. the cells of a battery, electrolytic cells, diodes□

cathode ray tube A vacuum tube in which a beam of electrons is produced and focused on a fluorescent screen, as in television receivers, oscilloscopes, etc.□

Catholic Church the whole body of the Christian Church, though by those who accept Papal supremacy usually applied only to themselves. Members of other churches add the qualifying term 'Roman' when speaking of them. See Roman-Catholicism◊, Old Catholics◊□

Catholic Emancipation acts passed in Britain 1780–1829 to relieve Catholics of restrictions imposed from the time of Henry VIII□

Catiline (Lucius Sergius Catilina) c108–62BC. Roman politician. Twice failing to be elected to the consulship in 64/63, he planned a military coup, but Cicero◊ laid bare his conspiracy. He died at the head of the insurgents□

Catlin George 1796–1872. American ethnologist and artist, who recorded American Indian life□

Cato Marcus Porcius 234–149BC. Roman statesman. Appointed censor (senior magistrate) in 184, he excluded from the senate those who did not meet his high standards, and was so impressed by the power of Carthage◊, on a visit in 157, that he ended every speech by saying 'Carthage must be destroyed.' His farming manual is the earliest surviving work in Latin prose□

Cato Street Conspiracy unsuccessful plot hatched in Cato Street, Edgware Road, London, to murder Castlereagh◊ and his ministers on 20 Feb 1820. The leader, radical Arthur Thistlewood 1770–1820, who intended to set up a provisional government, was hanged with four others□

cats' cradles worldwide game played on the fingers with looped string, and linked with magic and folk-tale□

Catskills mountain range in SE New York state, USA, which includes Slide Mountain 1261 m/4204 ft. See Appalachians◊□

Catterick village near Richmond in N Yorkshire, England, where there is an important military camp□

cattle group of large ruminant mammals in the family Bovidae, order Artiodactyla. It includes the buffalo, bison, gaur, musk ox, and yak◊, as well as the European breeds, which are variants of *Bos taurus* descended from the extinct ***wild ox*** or ***aurochs*** *Bos primigenius*; and the ***zebu*** *Bos indicus,* the sacred humped cattle of India. See also prongbuck◊. The word ox is also generally used for castrated male domesticated cattle, still used for ploughing, etc., in the Third World, as they formerly were in Europe.

Modern breeds include: Charolais, much used for crossing with other breeds (see under Burgundy◊); Jersey, Aberdeen Angus, Guernsey, Friesian. They are bred for meat or milk□

Catullus Gaius Valerius c84–54BC. Roman poet, noted for lyrics describing his unhappy love affair with Clodia, the wife of the consul Metellus, and his short verses to his friends□

Caucasoid or ***Caucasion*** a member of the light-skinned race of mankind; so-named because J F Blumenbach in c1800 theorized that it originated in Caucasus. The theory of race is disputed□

Caucasus series of mountain ranges between the Caspian and the Black Sea, USSR; 1200 km/750 mi. Highest peak Elbruz 5633 m/18 480 ft. Arabian thoroughbreds are raised at Tersk farm in the N foothills. See also telescope◊□

caucus in the USA a closed meeting of regular party members, e.g. (in smaller states without primaries◊) to choose a presidential candidate□

cauliflower a variety of cabbage◊□

Causley Charles Stanley 1917– . British poet, born at Launceston, Cornwall. He published his first volume *Hands to Dance* in 1951; noteworthy is his ballad 'Samuel Sweet'□

Cavafy Constantinos 1863–1933. Greek poet. A civil servant and homosexual of Alexandria, he re-created the ancient world; translated by E M Forster◊, he also influenced Lawrence Durrell◊□

Cavaliers supporters of Charles I in the Civil War, typically horsemen with courtly dress and long hair (see Roundhead◊); also supporters of Charles II after the Restoration□

Cavalier poets poets of Charles II's court: Thomas Carew, Robert Herrick, Richard Lovelace, Sir John Suckling◊□

Cavalli Francesco 1602–76. Italian composer, organist at St Mark's Venice, and the first to make opera a popular entertainment, e.g. *Xerxes* 1654, for Louis XIV's wedding□

Cavan (county town Cavan) county of the Republic of Ireland, province of Ulster◊. It is drained by the river Erne□

cave hollow in earth's crust usually produced by water action; vertical shafts are known as potholes. Famous caves include: ***Ajanta***◊ cave temples ***Altamira***◊, near Santander, Spain; cave art ***Blue Grotto***, Malta; basalt ***Blue Holes of Andros***, Bahamas; longest, deepest submarine caves on earth ***Carlsbad Caverns***, New Mexico, USA – largest in USA, including world's largest single cave 457 m × 91 m × 91 m/1500 ft × 300 ft × 300 ft high; ***Cheddar Caves, Somerset***□

cave fish members of the family Amblyopsidae (Latin 'dim-eyed'), e.g. *Amblyopsis spelaeus* of Mammoth Cave, Kentucky, which have adapted to life in the darkness of caves by dispensing with sight□

Cavell Edith Louisa 1865–1915. British matron of a Red Cross hospital in Brussels in World War I, who helped Allied soldiers escape to the Dutch frontier. She was court-martialled by the Germans and condemned to death. Her last words were: 'Patriotism is not enough. I must have no hatred or bitterness towards anyone'□

Cavendish Lord Frederick Charles 1836–82. Chief secretary to the Lord Lieutenant of Ireland, he was murdered in Phoenix Park, Dublin, with Burke, the Under-Secretary, by 'Irish Invincibles'□

Cavendish Henry 1731–1810. Eccentric British physicist, discoverer of the composition of water, and first to recognize the properties of hydrogen. See Cavendish◊ Experiment□

Cavendish Experiment a measurement of the gravitational attraction between lead and gold spheres, which enabled Henry Cavendish◊ to calculate a mean value for the density of earth, using Newton◊'s Law of Universal Gravitation□

cave temples see cave◊□

caviar the beaten, salted roe of sturgeon◊, eaten as an hors d'oeuvre□

Cavite port on Luzon, the Philippines; population 76 000. The US Seventh Fleet continues to use the naval base□

Cavour Camillo Benso, Count 1810–61. Italian statesman. Prime Minister of Piedmont 1852–9 and 1860–1, he enlisted the support of Britain and France for the concept of a united Italy, achieved in 1861□

cavy a large rodent◊ of S America□

Cawdor village in Highland region, Scotland; King Duncan was, according to tradition, murdered in the castle by Macbeth in 1040□

Cawnpore see Kanpur◊□

Caxton William c1422–91. English printer, who learnt the technique in Cologne, and set up his own press in Bruges with Colard Mansion. The first book from this press, and the first book printed in English, was his own version of a French romance, *Recuyell of the Historyes of Troye* 1474. Returning to England, he established himself in Westminster in 1476, and produced the first book printed in England, *Dictes and Sayenges of the Phylosophers* 1477, followed by editions of Chaucer, Gower, Lydgate, Malory◊, etc.□

Cayenne capital, port, and international airport of French Guiana; population 30 500. It was used as a penal settlement 1854–1946□

cayenne pepper see capsicum◊□

Cayley Arthur 1821–95. British mathematician, who worked in non-Euclidean geometry, and developed matrix algebra, used by Heisenberg in his elucidation of quantum mechanics□

Cayley Sir George 1773–1857. British aviation pioneer, both using models and producing the first manned glider in 1853. He also invented the caterpillar tractor. See also polytechnic◊□

Cayman Islands British island group in the West Indies

area 260 sq km/100 sq mi

capital George Town

features comprises three low-lying islands, Grand Cayman, Cayman Brac and Little Cayman

exports farmed green turtle; seawhip coral, a source of prostaglandins

currency CI dollar

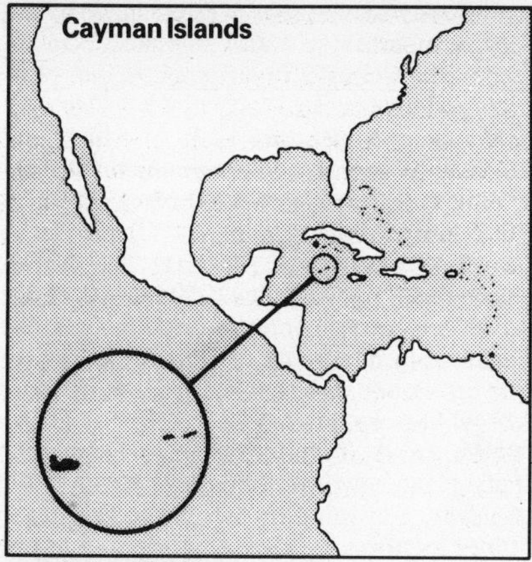

population 17 050
language English
government Governor, Executive Council and Legislative Assembly
recent history They were settled by military deserters in the 17th century and became a pirate lair in the 18th. Administered with Jamaica until 1962, when they became a separate colony, they are now a tourist resort, international financial centre, and tax haven□

Ceauşescu Nicolae 1918– . Romanian statesman. Secretary-General of the Communist Party from 1965, he became in 1974 the first president of the republic, and was re-elected in 1980□

Cebu chief town of the island of the same name in the Philippines; population 490 000□

Cecil Robert, 1st Earl of Salisbury c1563–1612. Son of Lord Burghley◊ by his 2nd wife, he succeeded him as Secretary of State to Elizabeth, and was afterwards chief minister to James I, who created him Earl of Salisbury in 1605□

Cecilia St 2nd or 3rd century. Martyred in Rome, her patronage of music arises from her having sung hymns under torture. Her feast day is 22 Nov□

cedar genus *Cedrus* of coniferous trees, family Pinaceae◊, forming a broad flattened shape at maturity, e.g. ***cedar of Lebanon*** *C Libani* originally from the Lebanon; the wood is red and fragrant. Perfume for the soap industry is extracted from woodchips of the ***Himalayan cedar*** *Cedrus deodara* which is also used to repel clothes moths, mosquitoes, cockroaches, and houseflies□

Cedar Rapids town in E Iowa, USA; population 110 125□

Ceefax one of the UK's two teletext systems. See videotext◊□

celandine two plants, dissimilar but for bright yellow flowers:

greater celandine *Chelidonium majus*, family Papaveraceae◊; and

lesser celandine *Ranunculus ficaria*, family Ranunculaceae◊□

Celebes see Sulawesi under Sunda◊ Islands□

celery salad plant *Apium graveolens dulce*, family Umbelliferae, a form of wild celery; ***celeriac*** is a turnip-rooted type□

celestial sphere an imaginary sphere, with the observer at its centre, on the surface of which can be projected the position of the stars and other objects in space□

Céline Louis Ferdinand. Pseudonym of Louis Destouches 1884–1961. French novelist, whose writings (the first of which was *Journey to the End of the Night* 1932) were controversial for their cynicism and misanthropy□

cell .

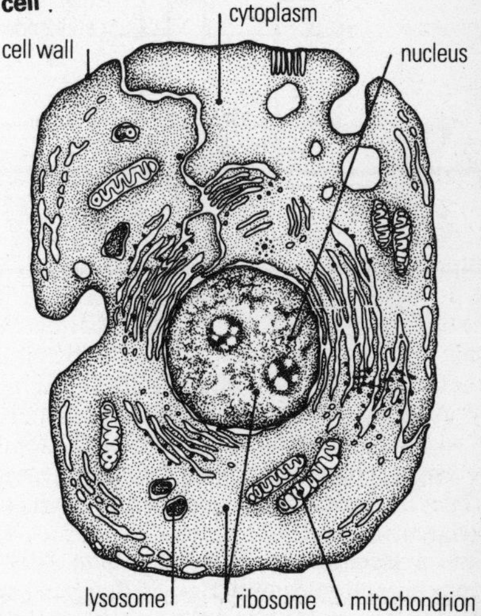

cell the unit of physical life, the simplest organisms consisting of a single cell (bacteria, amoebae, etc.). Even human beings originate from a single cell – an ovum or egg-cell generated by the female and fertilized by fusion with a spermatozoon or seed-cell generated by the male. The fertilized ovum (embryo) is a microscopic body. Under a light microscope it appears, within its membraneous wall, to consist for the most part merely of protoplasm or translucent jelly, but new microscopic techniques show it to have close-packed filament networks made of protein which maintain its three-dimensional form through all its activities. It also contains structural and functional units (organelles), e.g. the minute bodies (mitochondria) which include enzymes producing energy, and a small spherical body, the nucleus, which is an essential part of most cells, without which they cannot reproduce. See DNA◊.

A fertilized cell contains chromosomes from both parents, and the sex of the new individual is determined by the distribution of the special sex chromosomes. An ovum contains one X chromosome, and a spermatozoon either an X or a Y chromosome: the combination XX results in a girl, and XY in a boy. See genetic◊ code□

cell, electric

a lead-acid cell

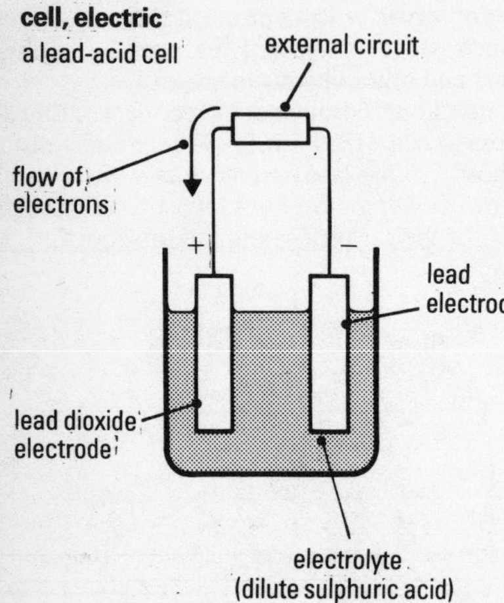

cell electric. Apparatus in which chemical energy is converted into electrical energy (popularly a 'battery' though strictly a battery is an assembly of interconnected cells), comprising a container with two conducting electrodes immersed in a substance that conducts electricity□

Cellini Benevenuto 1500–71. Italian artist, sculptor, and goldsmith. Born in Florence, he went to Rome in 1519, and eventually worked for the Papal mint, once being imprisoned on a charge of embezzling the pontifical jewels. As a sculptor, his best-known work is the bronze group of Perseus holding the head of Medusa, and as a goldsmith, the saltcellar he made for Francis I. His autobiography is famous for its anecdotes□

cellular radio see radio◊ cellular□

cellulite fatty compound alleged by some dieticians to be produced in the body by liver disorder and to cause lumpy obesity□

cellulitis inflammation of body tissue, accompanied by swelling, redness, and pain□

celluloid inflammable plastic material (cellulose nitrate), now largely replaced by non-inflammable cellulose acetate□

cellulose complex carbohydrate, the chief structural material of the plant kingdom, forming the cell walls, fibres, etc., and familiar (in various states of combination) as cotton, paper, wood, etc.□

cellulose nitrate series of esters made by the action of nitric acid and sulphuric acid on cellulose, and used in lacquers, rayon, plastics, and explosives□

Celsius a temperature scale in which one division or degree is taken as one hundredth part of the interval between the freezing point (0°C) and the boiling point (100°C) of water at standard atmospheric pressure. The degree centigrade (°C) was officially renamed Celsius in 1948 to avoid confusion with the angular measure (a hundredth of a grade) known as the centigrade, but remains in use in meteorology. See centigrade◊□

Celtic group of Indo-European languages, falling into two well-marked groups: the ***Goidelic***, consisting of the Gaelic language, under its forms of Irish, Scottish, and Manx Gaelic, each with several sub-dialects, and the ***Brythonic***, which includes Welsh, Cornish, Breton, and Gallic, the language of Gaul before the introduction of Latin. Celtic languages were formerly much more widespread, as can be seen from place-names in N Spain, Switzerland, S Germany, and N Italy□

Celtic League Irish-based nationalist organization (1975), aiming at an independent Celtic federation, with representatives from Alba (Scotland), Breizh (Brittany), Eire, Kernow (Cornwall), Cymru (Wales), and Elan Vannin (Isle of Man)□

Celtic Sea name coined by oilmen in the 1970s for the sea between Wales, Ireland, and SW England, to avoid nationalist significance□

Celts people whose first known territory was in central Europe c1200BC. They developed a transitional civilization between the Bronze and Iron Ages, 9th–5th century BC (the Hallstatt Culture, from its site SW of Salzburg). Pioneers of iron working, they reached their peak in the period from the 5th century to the Roman conquest (the La Tène culture, from the site at Lake Neuchâtel, Switzerland), when they produced magnificent swords, goods with intricate linear designs, and bronzes decorated with coral and enamel. They overran France, Spain, Portugal, N Italy (sacking Rome in 390BC), the British Isles and Greece, though never established a united empire. Their language survives in the Goidelic branch: Manx, and Scottish (Erse) and Irish Gaelic; and Brythonic: Welsh, Cornish, and Breton. Their priesthood were the druids◊□

cement various bonding agents, but particularly Portland cement (invented by Joseph Aspdin 1824; so-called because resembling Portland stone). Made by burning together a mixture of lime or chalk, and clay, it is the universal 'glue' for building in brick or stone, or for the production of concrete. By 1981 a form ten times stronger, to replace more expensive wood and plaster in stress conditions, had been developed□

cenotaph Greek 'empty tomb', a commemoration of those not actually buried at the site, as in the Whitehall Cenotaph (Sir Edwin Lutyens◊), London, to commemorate the dead of both World Wars□

censors in ancient Rome the two officials elected every five years for 18 months to be responsible for public morality, a census of the citizens, revising the senatorial list, etc.□

censorship the suppression by authority of the immoral, heretical, subversive, libellous, information damaging to state security, etc. Most stringent under Communist or strongly religious regimes, it survives in democratic countries, e.g. in the British defence regulations of both World Wars, and the modern D-Notice◊; in the libel laws in Britain which are more rigid than in France or the USA, etc. Books, plays, films, television, etc. are not subject to official censorship, but a degree of self-censorship is exercised, e.g. the British Board of Film Censors is a body set up by the film industry in the UK and there is a similar body in the USA□

census official numeration (originally for military call-up) of the population of a country, later incorporating other varied information. The first American census was taken in 1790 and in Britain in 1801, but it is now used also to assess social trends and forecast calls on social services. They will become unnecessary as databanks are built up, and ceased in Denmark in 1982□

centaur in Greek mythology, a creature half human and half horse. They were supposed to live in Thessaly, and be wild and lawless: the mentor of Hercules, Chiron, was an exception□

centigrade a scale in 100 parts. Formerly a temperature scale, now replaced by Celsius◊. Also an angular measure□

centipede class of animals Chilopoda, in the phylum Arthropoda, distinguished from insects by their bodies being composed of segments (which may number nearly 200), each of similar form and bearing a single pair of legs. Nocturnal, frequently blind, and all carnivorous, they have long antennae, and a pair of poison claws, some tropical species being dangerous to man. Most are small, but the tropical *Scolopendra gigantea* may reach 30 cm/1 ft in length. The related ***millipedes***, class Diplopoda, have a lesser number of segments (up to 100), but have two pairs on each. They eat either plant or animal food, usually when rotten, and live in moist, dark places. They protect themselves by a poisonous secretion□

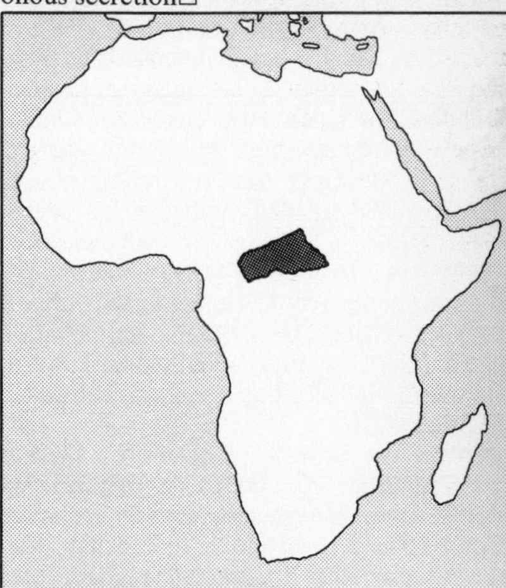

Central African Republic
area 625 000 sq km/240 000 sq mi
capital Bangui
features mainly a plateau, with tropical rain forest in SW
exports diamonds, uranium, coffee, cotton, and timber
currency CFA franc
population 2 610 000
language Sangho, French (both official)
religion Animism over 50%; Christianity 35% Islam 10%
government from 1981 a Military Committee for National Recovery, headed by General André Kolingba; all political parties were suspended, but a new constitution was in preparation in 1985.
recent history formerly the French territory of Ubangi-Shari, it became independent in 1960 under President David Dacko. Jean Bokassa◊ seized power in a coup in 1966, renaming the country the Central African Empire, with himself as Emperor. He in turn was overthrown in 1979, David Dacko returning as president, with the aid of French troops, until he was replaced in a peaceful coup by General André Kolingba in 1981□

Central America the part of the Americas which links Mexico with the Isthmus of Panama, comprising Belize, Costa Rica, El Salvador, Guatemala, Honduras, Nicaragua, and Panama.

Much of Central America formed part of the Mayan◊ civilization, which was in decline centuries before the arrival of the Spaniards in the 1500s. There was little gold or silver, and Spanish settlers married indigenous women, the area remaining out of the mainstream of Spanish Empire history. When the

Spanish Empire broke down, in the early 1800s, all Central America was briefly one country, with a constitution based on that of the USA, but this broke down in fratricidal warfare in little more than a decade. Demand for cash crops (bananas, coffee, cotton), especially from the USA, created a strong landowning class controlling a serf-like peasantry by military means. There was also US military intervention, as in the case of Nicaragua, where the dynasty of Somoza was founded. President Carter reversed support for such regimes; the Reagan administration again favours military and financial aid to selected political groups, e.g. the contras in Nicaragua◊□

Central American Common Market established in 1960, ODECA (***Organización de Estados Centro-americanos***) including Costa Rica, El Salvador, Guatemala, Honduras (seceded 1970), and Nicaragua□

Central Criminal Court Crown Court in the City of London, able to try all offences committed in the City or Greater London. It was first established 1834, and is popularly known as the Old Bailey from the part of the medieval defences of London once here□

Central Intelligence Agency intelligence organization established in the USA by Truman, and developed from the wartime Office of Strategic Services. Its active interventions overseas include the restoration of the Shah of Iran 1953; S Vietnam; Zaïre (when it was still the Congo); Chile (against Allende); Cuba (see Bay of Pigs◊). For its alleged illegal domestic espionage, it was marginally involved in Watergate◊, and in the 1970s lost public confidence when US overseas influence collapsed in Iran, Afghanistan, Nicaragua, Yemen, etc.□

Central Lancashire New Town see under Lancashire◊□

Central Mount Stuart mountain, height 844 m/2770 ft, the approximate central point of Australia; named after J McDougall Stuart◊□

Central Scotland region of Scotland, formed 1975 from the counties of Stirling, S Perth, and W Lothian

area 2518 sq km/971 sq mi

towns administrative headquarters Clackmannan; Falkirk, Stirling

features Stirling Castle; field of Bannockburn◊; Loch Lomond (east side); Doune Castle; Wallace Monument

products agriculture; industries include brewing and distilling, engineering, electronics, petrochemicals, dyes, glass, and paper

population 272 662

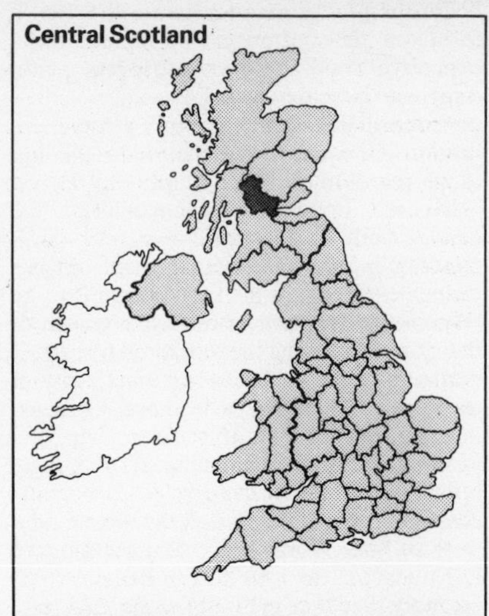

famous people George Buchanan (1506–82); Rob Roy McGregor (1671–1734); Sir George Harvey (1806–76)□

Central Treaty Organization defence organization (CENTO) which replaced the Baghdad Pact◊ in 1959; it collapsed when the withdrawal of Iran, Pakistan, and Turkey left the UK as the only member in 1979□

Centre The Central Australia, including the tourist area between the Musgrave and MacDonnell ranges which contains Ayers Rock, Lake Amadeus, etc.□

Centre region of N central France; capital Orléans; population 2 264 000. George Sand◊'s home is preserved at Nohant□

centrifuge apparatus used to separate substances of differing densities by rotating them at high speeds, e.g. the separation of cream from milk. Very high-speed centrifuges are used in colloid- and bio-chemistry. Large-scale centrifuges are used in physiological research, e.g. in testing astronaut response to many times the normal acceleration due to gravity (g)□

Cephelonia see Keffallinia◊□

cephalopod class Cephalopoda (Greek 'head-footed') of predatory marine molluscs◊, which have the mouth and head in the foot, and (except for the nautilus and cuttles) have only vestigial shells. They include the most intelligent, the fastest-moving, and the largest of all invertebrates, and there are remarkable luminescent forms which float at abyssal depths. Typically (squid, octopus, cuttle) they move by swimming with the mantle, aided by the arms, but enjoy spurts of speed, using their funnel or siphon to squirt out water and propel themselves backward by jet propulsion. They grow very rapidly, reach adult weight within a year, reproduce once and die. They have the most highly developed nervous and sensory systems of all invertebrates, but are deaf, possibly a protection against loud sounds emitted by whales to stun their prey. See also convergent evolution◊. They include:

nautilus the species of ***pearly nautilus*** genus *Nautilus* of the Indo-Pacific Ocean have a spiral mother-of-pearl shell used in inlay, etc. They are the only surviving relatives of the Ammonites◊ of Mesozoic times, which had shells curved round in a flat spiral like the ram's horns symbolic of Ammon◊, hence the name. Some were 2 m/6 ft across.

cuttle-fish family Sepiidae, have 10 suckered arms (two very long for seizing prey), an internal calcareous shell (the cuttle-bone given to cage birds), and live mostly concealed on the sea bottom. The ***common European cuttle-fish*** *Sepia officinalis* is up to 250 mm/10 in long, and covers its retreat by discharging a blackish fluid (the pigment sepia).

octopus genus of family Octopodidae, order Octopoda ('eight-limbed'), living among rocks in all temperate and tropical waters, and having a round or oval body, and eight arms with two rows of suckers on each. Themselves colour-blind, they have two layers of special skin cells which enable them to change colour and pattern, either to mesmerize prey or escape a predator. The ***common octopus*** *O vulgaris* reaches 2 m/6 ft, and is edible; the ***Pacific giant octopus*** *O apollyon* may be over 8 m/26 ft, but is less dangerous than its legend. The blue-ringed octopus has poison glands that make its bite fatal to man.

squid genera of the order Decapoda ('ten-limbed'). They have 10 arms, including two specially extended for seizing prey, live socially in shoals. In squids change of pattern and colour intensity in their skins acts as a method of black-and-white signalling to each other. The ***giant squid*** *Architeuthis princeps* is 15 m/45 ft long, and its eyeballs are 38 cm/15 in in diameter□

cephalosporin antibiotic extracted from a mould, used to deal with penicillin-resistant bacteria; see E P Abraham◊ and Dorothy Hodgkin◊□

ceramics non-metallic minerals used in articles, created from a powder and sintered at high temperatures, e.g. heavy clay products (bricks, roof-tiles, drainpipes, sanitary ware); refractories or high-temperature materials (furnace linings and fuel elements in nuclear reactors); pottery◊ (from opaque and porous earthenware to translucent white bone china and porcelain); ***super-ceramics***, e.g. silicon carbide, are lighter, stronger, and more heat-resistant than steel for use in motor and aircraft engines, and have to be cast to shape since they are too hard to machine□

ceramics articles produced by shaping clay and baking till hard. BC ***10 000*** earliest known pottery in Japan. AD ***7th–10th century Tang, Song,*** and ***Ming*** porcelain (China); ***16th century Maiolica*** Italian tin-glazed earthenware with painted decoration, especially large dishes with figures; ***Faience*** (from Faenza◊) name applied both to this and delftware (see below); ***17th century Delftware*** tin-glazed earthenware brought to perfection in Delft, especially the white with blue decoration, also copied in England; ***18th–19th century Wedgwood*** unglazed pottery, especially with white decoration in classical designs on a blue ground (see also Josiah Wedgwood◊); ***18th century*** English porcelain ***Worcester***◊ from 1751; ***Minton***◊ from 1798; ***19th century Coalport*** bone china made near Shrewsbury□

Cerberus in Greek mythology, the three-headed dog guarding the entrance to Hades◊□

cereals grain-bearing grasses grown for food and including: ***barley*** *Hordeum vulgare* variety *distichum*, one of the earliest to be grown, now mainly used for fodder and brewing◊; ***maize*** *Zea mays*, originally grown by American Indians, introduced to Europe by Columbus, and used for food, animal fodder, industrial alcohol, and corn oil (***sweetcorn*** is a variety in which sugar is not converted to starch, so that the 'nibs' remain soft and sweet to eat); ***millet*** *Panicum miliaceum*, grown in Europe for grain and fodder; ***oats*** *Avena sativa*, used for food and fodder; ***rice*** *Oryza* species, grown in the East from prehistoric times, and requiring flooding during the growing period (unhusked paddy rice includes valuable vitamins and new varieties with increased protein are being developed); ***rye*** *Secale cereale*, used in N Europe for black bread and in Britain for fodder (see ergot◊); tropical ***sorghum/durra*** *Sorghum* species grown for grain, hay, and as a source of syrup (also called Indian millet, guinea corn, and in E Asia *kaoliang*); ***triticale*** is a hardy, high-producing, high food value hybrid between wheat and rye; ***wheat*** *Triticum vulgare*, derived from a wild Middle Eastern grass and grown from Neolithic times for bread, pasta, semolina, etc.□

cerebral haemorrhage the bursting of a blood vessel in the brain, caused by a blood clot, high blood pressure combined with hardening of the arteries, chronic poisoning with lead or alcohol, etc.; it is popularly known as a 'stroke' or apoplectic fit□

cerebral palsy caused in children (known as *spastic*) by interference with the brain while it is actively growing before birth, at birth, or in the first year of life. It may cause difficulty in movement or speech, and affect intelligence□

Ceres in Roman mythology, the corn goddess identified with the Greek goddess Demeter◊□

cerium element
symbol Ce
atomic number 58
physical description steel-grey solid
features metal in the lanthanide◊ series
uses a sparking component in lighter flints□

CERN familiar name, from its initials, of the *Organisation* (formerly ***C****onseil*) ***E****uropéenne pour la* ***R****echerche* ***N****ucléaire*, near Geneva. Research is carried on into the structure of matter by teams from 12 participating states. In 1983 CERN scientists announced that they had found the W particle◊ – of crucial importance in confirming theories unifying the fundamental physical forces. The world's largest LEP (***l****arge* ***e****lectron-****p****ositron* (accelerator)) is planned to start operating in 1987; new particles should be discovered after the collision of accelerated electrons and positrons. See particle physics◊□

Cernauti see Chernovtsy◊□

Cervantes Saavedra Miguel de 1547–1616. Spanish writer. Born at Alcalaal de Henares, he was wounded in the Battle of Lepanto, and was captured and enslaved by Barbary corsairs on his way back to Spain in 1575. Among varied posts, he helped to collect stores for the Armada, and acted as a very inefficient tax collector, being imprisoned for deficiencies in the accounts. His masterpiece *Don Quixote* 1605, telling of a knight errant out of his time, and of his servant (Sancho Panza), was followed by a sequel in 1615□

cervical cancer cancer◊ of the cervix (the neck of the womb)□

cestoda see tapeworm◊□

Cetacea specialized order of fish-like mammals, including whales, dolphins and porpoises, but distinguished in appearance from fish by their tail-fins (flukes) being horizontal rather than vertical□

Cetewayo c1836–84. King of Zululand 1873–83, who defeated the British at Isandhlwana 1879, but was himself defeated at Ulundi. Restored to his throne in 1883, he was ousted by an enemy□

Ceuta Spanish seaport and military base in Morocco, captured 1580; population 71 000□

Ceylon see Sri Lanka◊□

Cézanne Paul 1839–1906. French artist, leader of the Post-Impressionist◊ school. Born at Aix◊-en-Provence, he studied in Paris, was a friend of Zola, and was at first in sympathy with Pissarro and other Impressionists. He broke away to develop a style giving a greater sense of solidity, and by his grasp of the geometrical structure of a subject greatly influenced later artists; see Cubism◊□

Chablis village in central France, famous for white burgundy□

Chabrier Emmanuel 1841–94. French composer, best-known for his orchestral rhapsody *España*, whose handling of the orchestra influenced Debussy and Ravel□

Chaco see Gran Chaco◊□

Chaco War war over boundaries in the N Gran Chaco between Bolivia and Paraguay 1932–5, settled by arbitration in 1938□

Chad Lake. Lake in W Africa
area according to season 50 000 sq km/20 000 sq mi to 20 000 sq km/7000 sq mi. The basin is being developed by the riparian states Chad, Niger and Nigeria, and Cameroon□

Chad Republic of

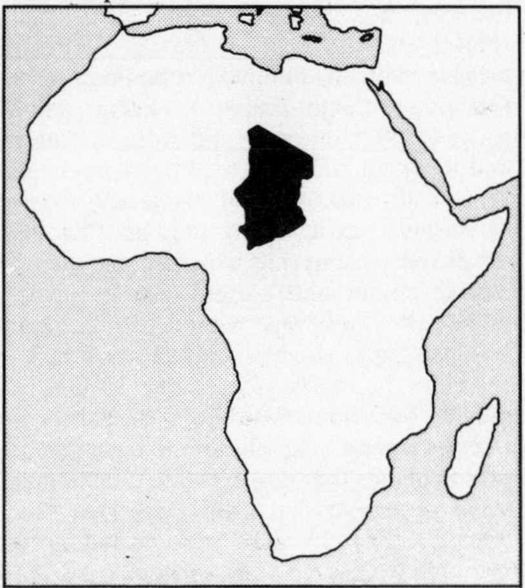

area 1 284 000 sq km/495 753 sq mi
capital N'djamaelna
features Lake Chad, Sahara Desert
exports cotton; meat, livestock, hides and skins; there are resources of bauxite, uranium, gold, oil
currency CFA franc
population 5 000 000
language French (official) Arabic
religion Islam (north); Christianity, Animism (south)
government in 1982 Hissène Habré (1942–) became president, first head of a united country since 1965, and backed by Egypt, Sudan, and USA.
recent history formerly one of the four territories of French Equatorial Africa, Chad became independent in 1960. There was civil

war 1965–80, first between the Muslim north and Christian south and then between the victorious Muslim factions. The party backed by Libya achieved supremacy, and Libyan troops occupied the country 1980–1, then withdrawing in face of an OAU peacekeeping force, and the troops of Hissène Habré, who ousted the Libyan-backed government of Goukouni Oueddi. Libya retained the uranium-rich Aouzou strip on the Libyan border annexed in 1973, and continued to support the Goukouni faction in the north. France and Zaïre aided Habré□

Chadli Benjedid 1929– . Algerian statesman. An army colonel, he supported Boumédienne in the overthrow of Ben Bella, and succeeded the former in 1979 (re-elected 1984) pursuing less extremist socialist policies□

chador black mantle for women, originating in the period of Cyrus◊ the Great in Persia, and adopted by the Arab conquerors of the Byzantines in response to the Koran request for 'modesty' in dress□

Chadwick Sir James 1891–1974. British physicist. He studied under Rutherford at Cambridge, and in 1932 was the discoverer of the neutron; Nobel prize 1935□

chafer beetle of the family Scarabeidae, which damages foliage of plants and whose larvae eat the roots; chafers include the ***cockchafer*** *Melolontha vulgaris*, ***rose chafer*** *Cetonia aurata*, etc.□

chaffinch a type of British finch◊□

Chagall Marc 1887–1985. Russian artist, of Jewish origin, who studied under Bakst◊. A precursor of Surrealism, he lived mainly in France from 1922 (citizen 1947); he decorated a chapel at Vence◊, and there is a Chagall National Museum at Nice. His art broke through the bounds of natural law to a dream world of floating animals and figures, and strange colours and juxtapositions of objects□

Chagas' Disease named from Brazilian doctor Carlos Chagas 1879–1934, it is caused by a trypanosome parasite transmitted by insects, and results in incurable damage to the heart and brain□

Chagos Archipelago group in the Indian Ocean; area 197 sq km/76 sq mi. Formerly a dependency of Mauritius◊, it now forms the British Indian Ocean Territory◊. The chief island is Diego Garcia, now a UK/USA strategic base□

Chain Sir Ernst Boris 1906–79. German-born biochemist, who emigrated to England in 1933, and worked under F Gowland Hopkins◊ at Cambridge. With Florey◊, he initiated the work on penicillin which led to the discovery of its curative properties, and shared a Nobel prize with Fleming◊ and Florey in 1945□

Chaka c1783–1828. Zulu chief who built up an empire from the border of Cape Colony to the Zambezi; he was murdered□

chalcedony a precious or semi-precious stone. See under silica◊□

Chaldaea see Babylonia◊□

chalice cup, usually of precious metal, used in celebrating the Eucharist◊□

chalk soft, fine-grained white rock chiefly formed from the remains of coccoliths, unicellular lime-secreting algae, and consisting mainly of calcium carbonate. Laid down in the later Cretaceous period (see geology◊), it covers a wide area of Europe, and forms the white cliffs of SE England□

chalk figures see hill figures◊□

Chalmers Thomas 1780–1847. Scottish theologian. A leader of the 'Disruption' of the Church of Scotland in 1843, he withdrew from the church along with a large body of other divines, with the consequent foundation of the Free Church of Scotland□

Châlons Battle of. Defeat of Attila◊ at Châlons-sur-Marne in 451, during his attempt to invade Gaul, by the Roman general Aëtius and the Visigoth Theodoric◊□

Chamberlain (Arthur) Neville 1869–1940. British Conservative statesman. Younger son of Joseph Chamberlain, he succeeded Baldwin in the premiership in 1937, and attempted to 'appease' the demands of the dictators in Europe. When in 1938 he returned from Munich, having negotiated with Hitler the settlement of the Czechoslovak question, he claimed to have brought 'Peace with Honour'. Soon, however, he agreed that he had been tricked, and when Britain declared war on 3 Sept 1939, he summoned the people to fight the 'evil things' that Hitler stood for. He resigned 10 May 1940, and died later that year□

Chamberlain Joseph 1836–1914. British Liberal politician. Three times mayor of Birmingham, he entered parliament in 1876 as a member of the left wing of the Liberal Party led by Dilke◊, and was President of the Board of Trade under Gladstone 1880–5. In 1885 he put forward his Unauthorized Programme (free education, graduated taxation, smallholdings of 'three acres and a cow', etc.), and finally broke with Gladstone in 1886 over the introduction of the Irish Home Rule Bill, sacrificing possible future leadership of the party. As leader of the Liberal-Unionists, he was Colonial Secretary 1895–1903, when he resigned to campaign for Imperial Preference or 'Tariff Reform' as a means of consolidating the empire. From 1906 he was incapacitated by a stroke□

Chamberlain Sir (Joseph) Austen 1863–1937. British Conservative politician, half-brother of Neville Chamberlain. A Liberal-Unionist MP from 1892, he was Chancellor of the Exchequer 1919–21, and as Foreign Secretary 1924–9 negotiated the Locarno◊ Pact (Nobel peace prize 1925)□

Chamberlain Lord. Chief officer of the royal household, who engages staff and appoints tradesmen; until 1968 he licensed and censored plays before their public performance□

Chamberlain Lord. The only Officer of State whose position survives from Norman times; responsible for the arrangements for the opening of parliament, assisting with the regalia at coronations, etc.□

chamber music music originally intended for performance privately, rather than in a concert hall. Important forms include the *string quartet* (two violins, viola, cello) and *string trio* (violin, viola, cello)□

Chambers Sir William 1726–96. British architect, popularizer of Chinese influence (Kew Gardens pagoda) and designer of Somerset House, London□

Chambéry old capital of Savoy◊, now an industrial town as well as a holiday and health resort; population 57 000□

chameleon variety of reptile able to change colour to suit surroundings. See under lizard◊□

chamois a goat-like antelope◊ found in mountain ranges of Europe and Asia□

chamomile see camomile◊□

champagne French wine, for which the grapes are grown in a strictly defined area about Reims and Épernay in Champagne. Its effervescence is caused by fermentation after the bottle has been sealed□

Champagne-Ardenne region of NE France; capital Reims; population 1 346 000. It is formed by the plains of the Paris basin, and is famed for its vineyards. See also Ardennes◊□

Champaigne Philippe de 1602–74. French painter, born in Brussels, noted for poised, elegant portraits, including Richelieu◊, and religious works□

champignon edible fungus *Marasmius oreades*, very popular in France□

Champlain Samuel de 1567–1635. French soldier-explorer, who in 1608 founded and named Quebec□

Champlain Lake. Lake in NE USA. Discovered in 1609 by Champlain◊□

Champollion Jean François, le Jeune 1790-1832. French Egyptologist, who in 1822 deciphered Egyptian hieroglyphics with the aid of the Rosetta Stone◊□

chance theory of probability, devised by Blaise Pascal◊ (with Pierre de Fermat◊) after a friend asked him how to reduce his gambling losses. It underlies the science of statistics, as used in life assurance and atomic physics□

Chancellor Lord High. State official, originally the royal secretary, today a member of the Cabinet, whose office ends with a change of government. He acts as Speaker of the House of Lords, may preside over the Court of Appeal, and appoints the judges and justices of the peace□

Chancellor of the Duchy of Lancaster honorary post held by a Cabinet minister who has other non-departmental responsibilities□

Chancellor of the Exchequer Cabinet minister responsible for the national economy, usually regarded as ranking next to the Prime Minister□

Chancery division of the High Court of Justice limited to such matters as the administration of the estates of deceased persons, the execution of trusts, foreclosure of mortgages, partnerships, and the estates of minors□

Chan Chan capital of the Chimu◊ kingdom□

Chandigarh city and Union Territory of NW India; population 300 000. The city, planned by Le◊ Corbusier, is the capital of both Punjab and Haryana◊, until a new capital is built for the latter□

Chandler Raymond 1888–1959. American crime writer, born in Chicago, but educated at Dulwich College, London. He was the creator of 'private eye' Philip Marlowe, a hard-boiled knight errant, in *The Big Sleep* 1939, *Farewell, My Lovely* 1940, and *The Long Goodbye* 1954□

Chandragupta Maurya ruler of N India c321–c296BC, founder of Maurya◊ dynasty. See Asoka◊□

Chanel Coco (Gabrielle) 1883–1970. French fashion designer, creator of the 'little black dress', informal cardigan suit, and perfumes□

Changchiakow see Zhangjiakou◊□

Changchun industrial city, capital of Jilin province, China; population 1 400 000. It was the capital of Manchukuo◊ 1932–45□

Chang Jiang greatest river (formerly Yangtze Kiang) of China, flowing c5470 km/3400 mi from Tibet to the Yellow Sea. It has 204 km/127 mi of scenic gorges, below which is Gezhou Ba, the first dam to harness the river□

Channel English stretch of sea between England and France (French *la Manche* 'sleeve', because of its shape); 450 km/290 mi long and 27 km/17 mi wide at its narrowest point, from Gris Nez to Dover◊□

Channel Country SW Queensland, Australia, where channels are cut by intermittent rivers (e.g. Cooper's Creek, where Burke and Wills◊ died in 1861), and grass from summer rains supports cattle herds□

Channel Islands

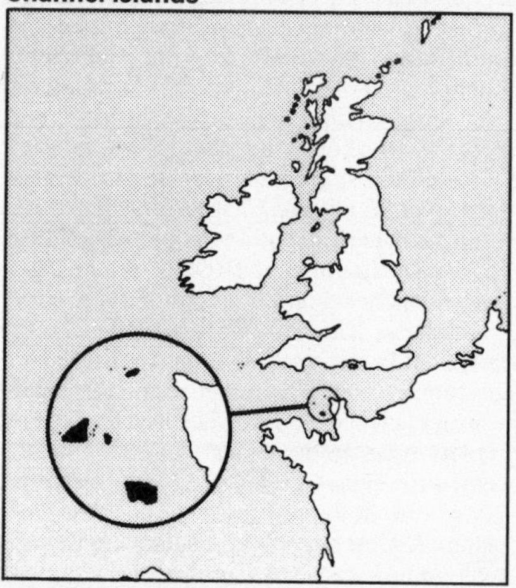

area 194 sq km/75 sq mi
features comprise Jersey, Guernsey, Alderney, Great and Little Sark, with the lesser Herm, Brechou, Jethou, and Lihou
exports flowers, vegetables
currency English pound, plus local coinage
population 130 000
language English and French (a form of Norman-French◊) (official)
religion chiefly Anglican
famous people Lily Langtry
government the main islands have their own parliaments.
history originally part of the Duchy of Normandy, the islands came under English rule in 1066, and are dependent territories of the English Crown, owing allegiance to the monarch, but with no direct link with parliament, though the British government is responsible for defence and external relations□

Channel swimming unbroken swim across the English Channel. The first to succeed was Captain Webb on 25 Aug 1875; Dover–Calais in 21 hr 42 min; fastest crossing (England–France) Penny Dean (USA) 7 hr 42 min in 1978□

Channel Tunnel projected tunnel under the English Channel◊□

chant simple melody used in services of the Christian Church, for singing the psalms, canticles, etc. The Ambrosian and Gregorian chants are forms of plainsong◊ melody□

chanterelle bright yellow edible fungus *Cantharellus cibarius* growing in woodlands□

Chantrey Sir Francis Legatt 1781–1841. British sculptor of portrait busts and child studies (*Sleeping Children* in Lichfield cathedral). The ***Chantrey Bequest*** provides for the Royal Academy to buy works of art, which are housed in the Tate Gallery□

Chao Phraya chief river (formerly Menam) of Thailand; length 1200 km/750 mi□

chaos theory branch of mathematics used to deal with chaotic systems, e.g. an engineered structure, such as an oil platform, which is subjected to irregular, unpredictable wave stress□

chaparral the thick scrub country of SW USA, mainly evergreen oaks□

Chapel Royal the royal retinue of priests, singers, and musicians of the English court from 1135. There are Chapels Royal, in the sense of buildings, at the former royal palaces of St James's, Hampton Court, and the Tower of London, besides private chapels in today's royal residences□

Chaplin Sir Charles Spencer ('Charlie') 1889–1977. British actor-director. Born in S London, he made silent films as the little tramp with smudge moustache, bowler hat, and cane, e.g. *The Gold Rush* 1925. Later came *City Lights* 1931, *Modern Times* 1938, *The Great Dictator* (guying Hitler) 1940, *Monsieur Verdoux* (in which he spoke for the first time) 1947, and *Limelight* 1952. He left the USA when accused of Communist sympathies. Knighted 1975□

Chapman George 1559–1634. English poet-dramatist. His translations of Homer (completed 1616) are celebrated, and his plays include the comedy *Eastward Ho!* (with Jonson and Marston), and the tragedy *Bussy d'Amboise*□

char genus of fish *Salvelinus* in family Salmonidae, related to the trout; the typical *S alpinus* is found in England□

characin small, colourful, carnivorous freshwater fish of Africa and N America, family Characidae (order Cypriniformes). Popular in aquaria are the ***tetras***, e.g. the ***neon tetra*** *Cheirodon innesi*, with a glowing band of neon orange at the tail end□

Charadriiformes order of birds, with two sub-divisions: 1 ***Charadrii,*** waders with long legs and short sensitive bills, and including many long-distance migrants (Plover◊, Jacana◊, Killdeer Snipe◊), and 2 ***Lari*** marine birds, magnificent fliers with characteristic loud cries (gull◊, kittiwake◊, tern◊)□

charcoal form of carbon◊, produced by heating wood in the absence of air, which is used as a fuel, and in making black-and-white drawings□

Chardin Jean Baptiste Siméon 1699–1779. French artist, noted for his kitchen still-lifes□

Chardonnet Hilaire Bernigaud, Comte de Chardonnet 1839–1924. French chemist, who developed artificial silk in 1883, the first artificial fibre. See under textile◊□

Charged Particle Beam beam (CPB) of electrons or protons, which does not burn through the surface of its target like a laser, but cuts through it. Such beams are being developed as weapons. See laser◊□

Charge of the Light Brigade see Balaclava◊□

Charing Cross district in Westminster, London, deriving its name from one of the stone crosses erected by Edward I at the resting-places of the coffin of his queen, Eleanor□

Charlemagne or ***Charles the Great*** 742–814. King of the Franks 768–814 and Holy Roman Emperor 800–814, son of Pepin the Short. He campaigned against the Saxon tribes and the Lombards, and in N Spain, where the great warrior Roland◊ was killed by the Basques◊ at Roncesvalles. As ruler of Western Christendom, he introduced legal reforms; standardized coinage and weights and measures; organized and reformed the Church, and initiated the Carolingian Renaissance by attracting Alcuin◊ to his court at Aachen in 781. He had himself collected the old heroic lays, and on his death became the hero of a cycle of Romance which survives in the work of Ariosto◊, Boiardo◊, and Tasso◊□

Charleroi coal and steel town in S Belgium, on the Sambre; population 222 000□

Charles two kings of Great Britain and Ireland:

Charles I 1600–49. King from 1625. Born in Dunfermline, son of James I, he married Henrietta Maria◊. Friction with parliament on taxation, religion, and foreign policy (see Buckingham◊, Laud◊, Strafford◊) began from his accession, and he ruled without summoning parliament 1629–40. The ***Short Parliament*** Apr–May 1640 refused to grant money to enable him to suppress Scottish opposition to an English-style prayer-book, without redress of grievances. The ***Long Parliament*** 3 Nov 1640–60 forbade extra-parliamentary taxation, use of Star Chamber◊ and other prerogative courts, and dissolution of parliament without its own consent. On 4 Jan 1642 Charles left London, after failing to arrest the parliamentary leaders, and on 22 Aug declared war on parliament – see Civil War◊. In May 1646 he surrendered at Newark to the Scots, who handed him over to parliament in Jan 1947. Removed by the army to Hampton Court, he intrigued with the Scots to invade England, and in Nov escaped to Carisbrooke◊, but was held there. Cromwell defeated the Scottish invasion of 1648, and in Jan 1649 a court established by the House of Commons condemned Charles to death. He was beheaded on 30 Jan.

Charles II 1630–85. King from 1660. Born at St James's Palace, he married Catherine of Braganza◊. Following his father's defeat by parliament, he withdrew to the Continent, but accepted the Covenanters' offer to make him king, landing in Scotland in 1650, and being crowned at Scone 1 Jan 1651. Cromwell defeated the attempted invasion of England; (see Civil War◊) and Charles returned to the Continent until negotiations by Monck◊ led to the Declaration of Breda◊, promising a general amnesty and freedom of conscience. Proclaimed King on 8 May 1660, Charles landed at Dover on 26 May, and entrusted his government to Clarendon◊ until the disastrous Dutch War of 1665–7 caused the latter's replacement by the cabal◊. In 1670 Charles signed the secret Treaty of Dover, by which he would declare himself a Catholic, re-establish Catholicism in England, and support Louis's intended war against the Dutch, in return for aid against any British resistance. War with Holland followed in 1672 and Charles issued a Declaration of Indulgence suspending all penal laws against both Dissenters and Catholics, but parliament enforced withdrawal of the Indulgence, acceptance of a Test Act◊, and termination of the war with Holland in 1674. Danby◊ built up a Court Party by bribery, but the Popish Plot◊ of 1678 gave Shaftesbury the chance to introduce an Exclusion Bill to exclude the future James II from the succession, with the hope of replacing him by Monmouth◊. Charles defeated it by delaying tactics, and called his last parliament at Oxford in 1681. The Whigs attended armed, but when Shaftesbury rejected a last compromise, they fled in terror. Charles henceforth ruled without parliament, relying on French subsidy. A patron of arts and science, Charles enjoyed a lively personal life: see Lady Castlemaine◊, Nell Gwyn◊, Lady Portsmouth◊, Lucy Walter◊□

Charles (Philip Arthur George) 1948– . Prince of the United Kingdom, heir apparent to the British throne, and Prince of Wales from 1958. Born at Buckingham Palace 14 Nov, he is the first-born child of Elizabeth II and the Duke of Edinburgh, and was educated at Gordonstoun, and Trinity College, Cambridge. He served in the RAF and Royal Navy, and in 1981 married Lady Diana◊ Spencer. They have two sons: Prince William◊ and Prince Harry (Henry Charles Albert David, born 15 Sept 1984)□

Charles seven rulers of the Holy Roman Empire:

Charles I see Charlemagne◊.
Charles II the Bald 823–77. Holy Roman Emperor 875–77, and (as Charles II) King of France 843–77.
Charles III, the Fat 832–88. Holy Roman Emperor 881–7, he united for the last time the whole of Charlemagne's dominions.
Charles IV 1316–78. Holy Roman Emperor 1355–78 and King of Bohemia 1346–78.
Charles V 1500–58. Holy Roman Emperor 1519–56. Son of Philip of Burgundy and Joanna of Castile, he inherited the Netherlands from his father in 1506, Spain, Naples, Sicily, Sardinia, and the Spanish dominions from his maternal grandfather (Ferdinand V) in 1516, and from his paternal grandfather (Maximilian) the Hapsburg dominions in 1519, when he was elected emperor.
Such vast possessions led to rivalry from Francis I◊, whose alliance with the Turks brought Vienna under siege in 1529 and 1532. From 1517 the Empire was split by the rise of Lutheranism◊, Charles making unsuccessful attempts to reach a settlement at Augsburg◊ in 1530, and being forced by the Treaty of Passau◊ to yield most of the Protestant demands. Worn out, he abdicated in favour of his son, Philip II in the Netherlands 1555 and Spain 1556; yielded the imperial crown to his brother Ferdinand.
Charles VI 1685–1740. Holy Roman Emperor 1711–40, father of Maria Theresa, whose succession to his Austrian dominions he tried to ensure, and himself claimant in 1700 to the Spanish throne: see Spanish Succession◊.
Charles VII 1697–1745. Holy Roman Emperor 1742–5, opponent of Maria Theresa's claim to the Austrian dominions of Charles VI□

Charles or ***Karl*** 1887–1922. Emperor of Austria and King of Hungary, the last of the Hapsburg◊ emperors. Succeeding his great-uncle, Francis Joseph, in 1916, he was deposed in 1919, but refused to abdicate. Trying to regain the Hungarian crown in 1921, he was deported to Madeira□

Charles ten kings of France:
Charles I see Charlemagne◊.
Charles II see under Holy Roman Empire◊.
Charles III the Simple 879–929, ruled from 893, and in 911 ceded Normandy to Rollo◊.
Charles IV the Fair 1294–1328, succeeded Philip V in 1322, as the last of the direct Capetian line.
Charles V the Wise 1337–80, was regent during the captivity of his father (John II) in England 1356–60, and became king 1364; he reconquered nearly all France from England 1369–80.
Charles VI 1368–1422, succeeded in 1380, and was under the regency of his uncles until 1388. He went mad in 1392, civil war broke out, and Henry V of England invaded France in 1415, conquering Normandy, and in 1420 forcing Charles to sign the Treaty of Troyes, recognizing Henry as his successor.
Charles VII 1403–61, excluded from the succession by the Treaty of Troyes, was yet recognized by the S of France, and in 1429 Joan of Arc had him crowned at Reims. By 1453 he had expelled the English from all of France except Calais.
Charles VIII 1470–98, succeeded Louis XI in 1483. He claimed the crown of Naples without success, and when he entered it in 1495 was forced to withdraw by a coalition of Milan, Venice, Spain, and the Emperor.
Charles IX 1550–74, succeeded his brother Francis II in 1560, but remained under the domination of his mother, Catherine de' Medici◊, who instigated his order for the Massacre of St Bartholomew◊.
Charles X 1757–1836, grandson of Louis XV and brother of Louis XVI and XVII. When he succeeded in 1824, he attempted to reverse their achievements; a revolt ensued in 1830, and he fled the country□

Charles fifteen kings of Sweden, of whom the best-known are:
Charles X 1622–60, who succeeded his cousin Christina in 1654, and waged war with Poland and Denmark. In 1657 he invaded Denmark from the S, leading his army over the frozen sea.
Charles XII 1682–1718, who succeeded Charles XI in 1697, and successfully waged war against Denmark, Poland, and Russia until defeated at Poltava◊ in 1709. He fled to Turkey, and was eventually killed invading Norway.
Charles XIV 1763–1844, born Jean Baptiste Jules Bernadotte. One of Napoleon's marshals, he was elected crown prince in 1810, and succeeded to the throne in 1818, founding the present dynasty□

Charles (Spanish *Carlos*) four kings of Spain, including:
Charles I was also Charles V◊, Holy Roman Emperor.
Charles II 1661–1700, was the last of the Spanish Hapsburg kings, and succeeded in 1665. Imbecilic from birth, he bequeathed his dominions to Philip of Anjou, grandson of Louis XIV, which led to the War of the Spanish Succession◊.
Charles III 1716–88, succeeded 1759, was twice at war with Britain – during the Seven Years' War, when he sided with France and lost Florida, and when he backed the

Americans in the War of Independence and regained it□

Charles the Bold 1433–77. Duke of Burgundy. Son of Philip the Good, he succeeded in 1465. In 1471 he revolted against Louis XI of France in an attempt to create a Burgundian kingdom, which united much of Europe against him, and was killed in battle□

Charles Ray 1930– . American jazz pianist-songwriter, e.g. 'Georgia on my mind'□

Charles Edward Stuart 1720–88, 'The Young Pretender'. Son of James◊, the Old Pretender, he landed in Inverness in Jul 1745 with seven companions, raised his father's standard and entered Edinburgh with 2000 Highlanders. Easily defeating General Cope at Prestonpans◊, he reached Derby on 4 Dec, but withdrew for lack of English support. At Culloden◊ he was routed by Cumberland, and for five months wandered the Highlands with a price on his head before escaping to France□

Charles Martel 'the Hammer' c688–741. Frankish ruler, grandfather of Charlemagne◊. His defeat of the Moors between Poiters and Toulouse in 732 earned him his nickname and halted the Islamic invasion of Europe□

Charles's Law law stated (by French physicist Jacques Charles 1746–1823) in 1787, and independently by Gay-Lussac in 1802: the volume of a given mass of gas at constant pressure increases by 1/273 of its volume at 0° C for each degree C rise of temperature□

Charleston chief port of S Carolina, USA; population 67 000. The Civil War began when Fort Sumter at Charleston was bombarded by Confederate batteries 12-13 Apr 1861□

Charleston the back-kicking dance of the 1920s which originated in Charleston, S Carolina□

Charleston capital of W Virginia, USA; population 72 000. Daniel Boone◊ lived here□

Charlotte commercial and industrial city in N Carolina, USA□

Charlotte Auga Princess 1796–1817. Only child of George◊ IV and Caroline of Brunswick, she married Prince Leopold◊ of Saxe-Coburg in 1816, but died in childbirth□

Charlotte Sophia 1744–1818. Queen consort of George III, whom she married in 1761, bearing him nine sons and six daughters□

charm a property of some elementary particles (see particle◊ physics), proposed to account for their unexpectedly long lifetimes compared to the other elementary particles with which they are otherwise identical. See also strangeness◊□

Charon in Greek mythology, the boatman who ferried the dead over the river Styx. See Pluto◊□

Charpentier Gustave 1860–1956. French composer of the opera of Paris working-class life *Louise* 1900□

Charpentier Marc-Antoine 1634–1704. French composer of the operas *Médée* and *La Descente d'Orphée aux enfers*, church music, etc.□

Charteris Leslie 1907– . British-American novelist, born at Singapore, creator of Simon Templar, 'The Saint', gentleman-adventurer on the wrong side of the law, in 1928□

Chartism British working-class Radical movement 1838–50. The 'People's Charter' proposed: universal manhood suffrage; equal electoral districts; vote by ballot; annual parliaments; abolition of the property qualification for MPs; and paid MPs. See Feargus O'Connor◊□

Chartres town in N central France with superb 13th-century Gothic cathedral; population 41 250□

chartreuse green liqueur distilled by the Carthusian◊ monks at La Grande Chartreuse monastery□

Charybdis in Greek mythology, a dangerous whirlpool in The Strait of Messina◊□

Chase James Hadley. Pseudonym of novelist René Raymond 1906–85, author of 'tough' novels, e.g. *No Orchids for Miss Blandish* 1939□

Chasidim an 18th-century sect of Judaism◊□

château French medieval castle, but later used to describe any fine country house□

Chateaubriand Franois René, Vicomte de Chateaubriand 1768–1848. French author, a precursor of Romanticism◊, with *Atala* 1801 (written after his encounters with American Indians); *Le Génie de Christianisme* 1802; and *Mémoires d'outre tombe* 1849–50. Having fought on the royalist side during the Revolution, he held diplomatic appointments under Louis XVIII□

Château-Thierry town in N France; population 14 000. Site of the 2nd Battle of the Marne◊□

Chatham town in Kent, England; population 59 000. The Royal Dockyard 1588–1984 was from 1985 converted to a 'new town' including an industrial area, marina, and museum as a focus of revival for the whole Medway area□

Chatham Islands two Pacific islands, forming a county of South Island, New Zealand; area 963 sq km/372 sq mi; population 700. Chief settlement Waitangi◊□

Chatterton Thomas 1752–70. British poet. Born in Bristol, he composed poems he ascribed to a 15th-century monk, 'Thomas

Rowley', which were accepted as genuine. Going to London in 1770, Chatterton failed to gain patronage as a writer and poisoned himself with arsenic. His medieval poems influenced the Romantics, especially Coleridge◊□

Chaucer Geoffrey c1340–1400. English poet, born in London. He was taken prisoner in the French wars and had to be ransomed by Edward III in 1360. He married Philippa Roet in 1366, becoming in later life the brother-in-law of John of Gaunt◊. He gained various appointments, e.g. controller of London customs, and was sent on missions to Italy (where he may have met Boccaccio◊ and Petrarch◊), France, and Flanders. At first under more formal French influence, as in his translation of the *Romaunt of the Rose*, he achieved maturity with his absorption of Italian realism, as in his long narrative poem *Troilus and Criseyde*, adapted from Boccaccio, while in his masterpiece, *The Canterbury Tales*, a collection of tales told by pilgrims on their way to Becket's shrine, he developed his English genius for metre and characterization. The popularity of his work assured the dominance of southern English in literature□

chauvinism warlike patriotism, as exhibited by Nicholas Chauvin, one of Napoleon's veterans; and more recently 'male chauvinism', an inveterate conviction of the superiority of the male sex□

Chavez Carlos 1899–1978. Mexican composer, who used the complex rhythms of his country's folk music□

Cheapside City of London street, from St Paul's to Poultry, once the chief market or 'cheap'□

Checheno-Ingush republic of the W USSR, conquered in the 1850s and rich in oil; area 19 300 sq km/7350 sq mi; population 1 170 000. Capital Grozny□

Cheddar village in Somerset, England; population 3000. It is famous for cheese, and for its limestone gorge□

cheese the curd of milk (from cows, goats, sheep, etc.), separated from the whey, and variously treated to produce three main types:

hard-pressed: Cheddar, Cheshire, Cantal, Parmesan, Gruyère.

semi-hard: Stilton, Gorgonzola, Wensleydale, Roquefort, Pont l'Evêque, Gouda, Lymeswold.

soft: Camembert, Brie, Quark/Fromou.

In France (from 1980) cheese has the same *appellation controlée* status as wine if made only in a special defined area, e.g. Cantal and Roquefort, but not Camembert and Brie, which are also made elsewhere□

cheesecloth muslin used to press curds, but also from 1967 a handwoven cotton crepe, developed in India for export, which stretches to fit the body□

cheetah a type of large cat◊□

Cheever John 1912–82. American writer, born in Quincy, Massachusetts. His books include *The Wapshot Chronicle* 1937, *Bullet Park* 1969, and *Falconer* 1977□

Chefoo see Yantai◊□

Cheka Russian secret service. See under KGB◊□

Chekhov Anton Pavlovich 1860–1904. Russian writer. Born at Taganrog, he preferred writing short stories to medical practice, e.g. *The Lady with the Dog* 1898. His play *The Seagull* 1896 was at first a failure, but succeeded when revived by Stanislavsky◊ for the Moscow Arts Theatre in 1898, for which Chekhov wrote *Uncle Vanya* 1899, *The Three Sisters* 1901, and *The Cherry Orchard* 1904. His sense of atmosphere and internal development of character is less valued in Russia than abroad, where the plays are often over-solemnified□

Chekiang see Zhejiang◊□

Chelmsford town (administrative headquarters) in Essex, England; population 58 500. Its industries include electrical, engineering, and agricultural machinery□

Chelonia order of reptiles including tortoises◊, turtles◊ and terrapins◊□

Chelsea historic area of the borough of Kensington and Chelsea, London, which includes the Royal Hospital, founded in 1682 by Charles II for old soldiers, 'Chelsea pensioners'; National Army Museum 1960 (covering campaigns 1485–1914); Physic Garden (botanical research from the 17th century); Carlyle's home in Cheyne Row. There is a famous annual Flower Show□

Cheltenham spa in the Cotswolds, Gloucestershire, England; population 78 000. There are annual literary and music festivals, a racecourse (Cheltenham Gold Cup), Cheltenham College 1854, the home of Holst◊ is a museum, and to the SW is Prinknash Abbey, a Benedictine house famous for its pottery. The ***Government Communications headquarters*** (GCHQ◊ for electronic eavesdropping) is here□

Chelyabinsk major iron and steel town of the S USSR; population 1 042 000□

chemical element see element◊ and under individual elements□

chemical warfare use of gaseous, liquid, or solid substances with toxic effect to man, animals, or plants; with Biological Warfare◊, it was banned in 1925, and from 1980 the subject has been under review.

Chemical weapons are of five types:
irritant gases which may cause permanent injury or death, such as chlorine, phosgene (Cl_2CO) and mustard gas ($C_4H_8Cl_2S$) used in World War I; and tear gases, e.g. CS gas used in riot control, which are intended to have less permanent effect.
nerve gases organophosphorus compounds allied to insecticides, which are taken into the body through the skin and lungs and break down the action of the nervous system. Developed by the Germans for World War II, they were not used.
incapacitants drugs designed to put an enemy temporarily out of action by impairing vision, inducing hallucinations, etc. Not so far used.
toxins eaten, drunk, or injected, e.g. ricin (see castor oil◊) or the botulism◊ toxin. Ricin has been used in individual cases.
herbicides defoliants used to destroy vegetation sheltering guerrillas and crops of hostile populations. Used in the Malayan Emergency by Britain and by the USA in Vietnam. Agent Orange (see dioxin◊) became notorious because of later allegations that it had caused cancer and birth abnormalities among Vietnam war veterans and US factory staff.
Some stocks are held by a number of countries for retaliation or the development of preventative measures. ***Binary weapons*** are those in which the two chemical components become toxic only when mixed, which happens on the battlefield, when the shell is fired. See also biological◊ warfare□

chemiluminescence 'cold light' emitted without heat during some chemical reactions, and by some animals, e.g. fireflies and some deepsea fish (bioluminescence). Synthetic fluorescent molecules are being used instead of radioactive tracers◊, as more stable and offering no problems in disposal□

chemisorption chemical binding of a clean solid surface, usually metallic, and a foreign substance, usually a gas, as in corrosion. The basis of many industrial processes, in particular, catalysis□

chemistry study of the composition of matter, and the changes which take place in it under varying conditions. Major names in the development of chemistry include: Boyle, Joseph Black, Lavoisier, Priestley, Cavendish, Davy, Berzelius, Dalton, Newlands, Mendeleyev, Kekulé, Werner, Wöhler, Pauling, Taube.
The chief subdivisions are: ***inorganic*** the description, properties, reactions, and preparation of the elements and their compounds, with the exception of carbon compounds; ***organic*** dealing with carbon compounds; and ***physical*** dealing with particular changes which materials may undergo in special circumstances, e.g. the movement of molecules, the effects of temperature and pressure, which leave the composition of the material unaltered□

Chemnitz see Karl-Marx-Stadt◊□

Chemulpo former name of Inchon◊□

Chenab a tributary of the River Indus◊□

Chengchow see Zhengzhou◊□

Chengdu (formerly Chengtu) capital and industrial city, Sichuan province, China; population 3 700 000□

Chengtu see Chengdu◊□

Chénier André Marie de 1762–94. French poet. Associated from 1790 with a constitutional royalist group, he went into hiding in 1793, though continuing to write. He was finally imprisoned and guillotined, but while in prison wrote some of his most famous poems, including 'La jeune Tarantiae' and the political 'Iambes'□

Chepstow town on the river Wye in Gwent, Wales; population 6500. The tides on the Wye are the highest in Britain, up to 15 m/50 ft above low level. Tintern Abbey is nearby□

Chequers country seat of the Prime Minister of the day in the UK. It is an Elizabethan mansion in the Chilterns near Princes Risborough, Bucks, and was bequeathed to the nation by Lord Lee of Fareham 1917□

Cher river in central France, joining the Loire below Tours; 355 km/220 mi long□

Cherbourg port and naval base in NW France; population 79 000. There is an institute for studies in nuclear warfare, and a nuclear processing plant at Cap la Hague. In World War II it was captured by the Allies in Jun 1944, as their first large port of entry into France□

Cherenkov Paul 1904– . Russian physicist. He discovered ***Cherenkov Radiation*** which occurs, as a bluish light, when charged atomic particles pass through water or other media at the speed of light in that medium. He shared a Nobel prize in 1958□

Cherepovets iron and steel city in W USSR, on the Volga-Baltic waterway; population 279 000□

Chéret Jules. See under poster◊□

Chernenko Konstantin 1911–85. Soviet statesman, a specialist in political propaganda, and protégé of Brezhnev. Defeated in the immediate power struggle after Brezhnev's death, he succeeded Andropov as party leader Feb 1984–Mar 1985, the briefest ever tenure of the leadership□

Chernigov industrial river port (cotton, chemicals, timber) on the Desna,

Ukraine, USSR; population 252 000□

Chernobyl town in the Ukraine, and site of Europe's worst nuclear power station accident 1986. See nuclear◊ accident□

Chernovtsy industrial city (as Cernauti, part of Romania 1918–40) in the Ukraine, USSR; population 224 000□

Cherokee American Indian tribe of Iroquois stock which sided with the British against the French, and fought against the rebel colonists in the American War of Independence. They now live mainly in N Carolina and Oklahoma, with their capital at Tahlequah. One of them, Sequoyah c1770–1843, devised the syllabary used for writing down the Indian languages□

cherry tree with spherical smooth-skinned red, purple, or yellow fruit, family Rosaceae; the ***sweet cherry*** derives from *Prunus avium*, the ***sour cherry*** from *Prunus cerasus*□

Cherubini Maria Luigi Carlo Zenobio Salvatore 1760–1842. Italian composer of operas (*Medée* 1797), and church music□

chervil one of several types of herbs◊□

Cherwell Frederick Alexander Lindemann, Viscount Cherwell 1886–1957. British physicist, personal adviser to Churchill on scientific and statistical matters during World War II□

Chesapeake Bay largest of the inlets on the Atlantic coast of the USA. Known as the 'queen of the nation's estuaries' because of its beauty and wildlife, but now under threat□

Cheshire Geoffrey Leonard 1917– . British airman, a World War II VC, who was an observer at the dropping of the atom bomb on Nagasaki. A Roman Catholic, he was moved to found the first Cheshire Foundation Home for the Incurably Sick in 1948: Order of Merit 1981. He married in 1959 ***Susan Ryder*** (1923– ; created Baroness Ryder 1978), who established a foundation for the sick and disabled of all ages in 1978□

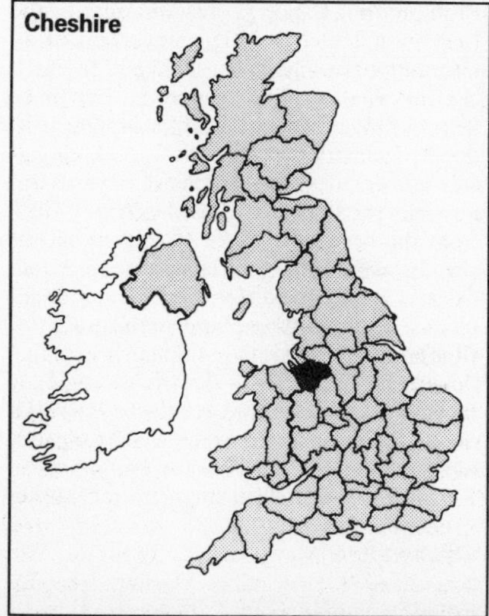

Cheshire

Cheshire NW county of England
area 2328 sq km/899 sq mi
towns administrative headquarters Chester; Macclesfield, Warrington. It is chiefly a fertile plain with dairy-farming.
features salt mines and geologically rich former copper workings at Alderley Edge, both tourist attractions; Little Moreton Hall; mainland Britain's first bogman (see under Peat◊)
products textiles and chemicals
population 939 100
famous people Mrs Gaskell lived at Knutsford (the locale of *Cranford*)□

Chesil Bank shingle bank extending 19 km/11 mi along the Dorset coast□

chess notation

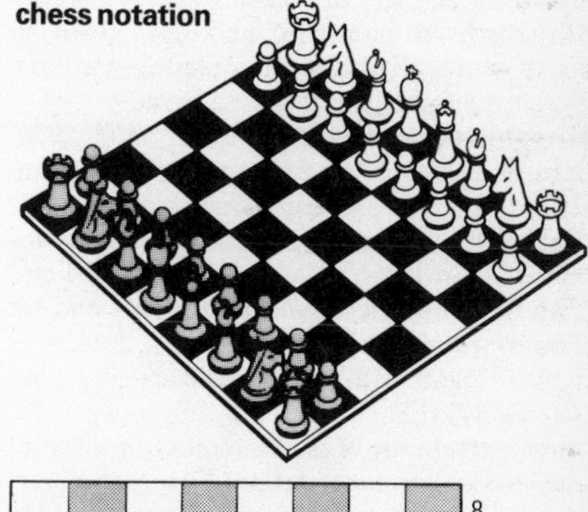

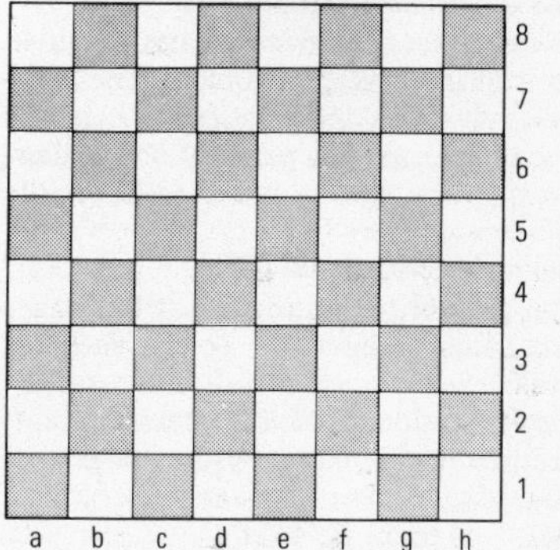

chess board game originating at least as early as the 2nd century AD. Two players use 16 pieces each, on a board of 64 squares of alternating colour, to try and force their opponent into a position where the chief piece cannot be moved or allowed to remain in the same position without its being taken. There are said to be more variations than there are atoms in the universe. A world championship was established in 1866: post-war champions have been Boris Spassky 1969–72, Bobby

Fischer 1972–5, Anatoly Karpov 1975–85, and Gary Kasparov 1985– . Players of the rank of grand master can now be defeated by a computer. There is a World Chess Federation (FIDE)□

Chester city (administrative headquarters) and seaport of Cheshire; population 62 500. It is the only English city to retain its two miles of medieval walls intact; the Rows are covered medieval arcades of shops, and the cathedral is 11th-century. There are metallurgical industries, car components, etc.□

Chesterfield Philip Dormer Stanhope, 4th Earl of Chesterfield 1694–1773. English politician, an opponent of Walpole. A member of the literary circle of Swift, Pope, and Bolingbroke, he wrote a worldly-wise series of letters to guide his illegitimate son, and incurred the wrath of Johnson for failing to carry out an offer of patronage□

Chesterfield industrial and coal town in Derbyshire, England; population 68 000. George Stephenson is buried here□

Chesterton Gilbert Keith 1874–1936. British author. A Roman Catholic from 1922, he advocated Distributism (see Belloc◊), but is now best remembered for his verse, as in *Wine, Water and Song* 1915 and *The Ballad of the White Horse* 1911, and his fantasy stories of a naive priest-detective, which began with *The Innocence of Father Brown* 1911□

chestnut genus of north temperate deciduous trees *Castanea*, family Fagaceae◊, e.g. ***Spanish chestnut*** *C sativa* which has an edible brown fruit in a prickly involucre. The ***horse chestnut*** *Aesculus hippocastanum,* family Hippocastanaceae, has panicles or 'candles' of pink or white flowers and its fruits are the schoolboy's 'conkers'□

Chevalier Maurice 1888–1972. French actor, dancing partner to Mistinguett at the Folies Bergère, and singer of songs such as 'Louise'□

Chevening residence near Sevenoaks, Kent, bequeathed to the nation by the 7th Earl of Stanhope for royal or ministerial use; Prince Charles lived there 1974–80□

Cheviots range of hills forming the border between England and Scotland, and long a battleground. Mainly in Northumberland, they reach 816 m/2676 ft in The Cheviot□

chewing gum confectionery patented in USA in 1871, and made from sweetened chicle◊□

Chiang Ching see Jian Qing◊□

Chiang Ching-Kuo 1910– . Taiwanese statesman, son of Chiang Kai-shek. Prime Minister from 1971, he became president in 1978□

Chiang Kai-shek 1887–1975. Chinese statesman (Pinyin: *Jiang Jie Shi*). He took part in the Revolution of 1911, and after the death of Sun Yat-sen was made Commander-in-Chief of the Guomindang armies in S China in 1925. The initial collaboration with the Communists, broken in 1927, was resumed following the Xi An incident (see Chinese history◊), and he nominally headed the struggle against the Japanese invaders, receiving the Japanese surrender in 1945. Civil War then resumed between Communists and Nationalists, and ended in the defeat of Chiang in 1949, and the limitation of his rule to Taiwan. His son is Chiang Ching-Kuo◊□

Chibchas S American Indians of Colombia, whose civilization was overthrown by the Spaniards 1538. They used to powder their chief with gold dust, a rite which fostered the legend of El Dorado◊□

Chicago second city of the USA, in Illinois; population 2 969 570, including the world's largest Polish population outside Poland. Situated on the Chicago river, which cuts the city into three 'sides', it was first visited by Jesuit missionaries in 1673, and Fort Dearborn was established in 1803. The old town was destroyed by fire in 1871, but the world's first skyscraper was built here in 1887–8, and the Sears Tower, 443 m/1454 ft, is the world's highest building. The Museum of Science and Industry, opened in 1893, has 'hands on' exhibits including a coal-mine, World War II U-boat, Apollo spacecraft and lunar module; and exhibits by industrial firms, and 50 km/30 mi to the W is the Fermilab, the US centre for particle physics. Chicago was notorious for its gangsters (e.g. Al Capone◊) in the years of Prohibition◊; Capone's headquarters in the Lexington Hotel is under conversion to an international women's museum and research centre. The opening of the St Lawrence Seaway in 1959 brought Atlantic shipping to its docks. Industries include iron, steel, chemicals and textiles; the famous stockyards are now closed. It is known as the Windy City, from the breezes of Lake Michigan, and its citizens' voluble talk; the lake shore (the Gold Coast) is occupied by luxury apartment blocks. There is a symphony orchestra□

Chicanos Mexican Spanish-speaking Americans in the SW of the USA. Originally those Mexicans acquired as citizens as a result of the Spanish–American War 1846–8, they have been reinforced from the 1910 Mexican Revolution, and illicit immigration subsequently□

Chichen-Itza Maya city of the 11th–13th centuries in Yucatán, Mexico; remains include a temple mound, observatory, and a

well into which human sacrifices were cast□
Chichester Sir Francis 1901–72. British yachtsman, knighted for his circumnavigation of the world in *Gipsy Moth IV* 1966–7□
Chichester city (administrative headquarters) in W Sussex; population 21 100. There is a 12th-century cathedral; Chichester Festival Theatre 1962; and a Roman palace at nearby Fishbourne□
chicken a young bird, especially of domestic hens. See poultry◊□
chickenpox a mild disease, caught especially by children. See herpes◊□
chickpea seed of the annual *Cicer arietinum*, family Leguminosae◊, grown for food in Asia, Africa, etc.□
chickweed weed *Stellaria media* family Caryophyllaceae, with small white star-like flowers□
chicle juice of the sapodilla tree *Achras zapota* of Central America, which is the basis of chewing gum◊□
chicory hardy perennial *Cichorium intybus*, family Compositae◊; the blanched leaves are used in salads, and the root is used as a coffee substitute or diluent. See endive◊□
Chiengmai chief centre (tea, lac, handicrafts) of N Thailand; population 70 000□
chiff chaff small bird of the warbler◊ family□
Chifley Joseph Benedict 1885–1951. Australian Labour statesman. As Prime Minister 1945–9, he carried out a welfare and nationalization programme, and the Snow mountains hydroelectric scheme□
Chihuahua industrial city in Mexico; population 386 645□
chihuahua a breed of dog◊□
chilblain inflammation of the feet or hands, caused by cold, which can lead to ulceration. Dilation of the blood vessels by drugs may be attempted in some cases□
childbirth expulsion of a child from the womb, after an average of 40 weeks from conception; if it occurs before the end of the 7th month, the child usually requires medical assistance to survive□
Childe V. Gordon 1892–1957. Australian archaeologist, discoverer of prehistoric Skara Brae◊ in the Orkneys□
Childers Robert Erskine 1870–1922. Irish Sinn Féin politician. A supporter of de Valera, he took up arms against the Irish Free State in 1922, and was captured, court-martialled, and shot by the Irish Free State government of W T Cosgrave. He is remembered for his 'German spy' novel, *The Riddle of the Sands* 1903. His son, ***Erskine Childers*** 1904–74, was President of Ireland 1973–4□
Chile Republic of
area 741 765 sq km/286 400 sq mi

capital Santiago
towns Concepción, Vina del Mar, Temuco; ports are Valparaiso, Antofagasta, Arica, Iquique
features Andes mountains, Lake Titicaca, Atacama desert; includes Easter Island, Juan Fernandez Island, and half of Tierra del Fuego
exports copper, iron, nitrate (Chile is the chief mining country of S America); paper and pulp
currency peso
population 11 655 000, the majority *mestizo*, of mixed American Indian and Spanish blood
language Spanish
religion Roman Catholicism
government under the 1980 constitution, Pinochet was to remain president for 10 years, the National Congress was dissolved, and all political parties were banned.
recent history following a rising in 1810, Chile was proclaimed a republic and Spanish rule ended in 1818. Boundary disputes led to war with Bolivia◊ and Peru◊ 1879–1883, Arica being ceded by Peru and Antofagasta by Bolivia. The first elected Marxist government was established by Allende 1970–3, but US intervention by the CIA◊ led to a coup by General Pinochet◊ Ugarte, who became Supreme Head of State in 1974. There were some admitted 600 *desaparecidos* ('missing persons') after the coup, but the regime later became more liberal, and the economy stabilized. A 10-year state of emergency was lifted in 1983. A boundary dispute with Argentina over islands in the Beagle◊ Channel was resolved in Chile's favour in 1984□

chilli the pod, or powder made from this, of the capsicum◊□

Chillon see under Montreux◊□

Chiltern Hundreds British MPs may not resign; they therefore apply for the nominal office of steward of the Chiltern Hundreds, which, being an office of profit under the Crown, disqualifies them from being an MP□

Chilterns range of chalk hills in Oxfordshire, Buckinghamshire, and Hertfordshire. See Chequers◊□

chimaera genus of fish, allied to the sharks and rays, class Selachia, and with similar cartilaginous skeleton, e.g. ***rabbit fish*** *C monstrosa,* c1 m/3 ft long, caught off Britain□

Chimkent industrial city (chemicals and textiles) in Kazakhstan, USSR; population 327 000□

chimpanzee a large Africa ape. See anthropoid apes◊□

Chimu pre-Inca civilization in Peru 1200–c1470AD, characterized by *huacas* (adobe brick platforms surmounted by temples and palaces); realistic portrait pottery; 'writing' by painting on beans; and the maze city for royal burials (accompanied by human sacrifice), ***Chan Chan***, near Trujillo. The Incas conquered its people finally by cutting the aqueducts of their complex irrigation system□

China people's Republic of. In Chinese: *Zhonghua Renmin Gonghe Guo*

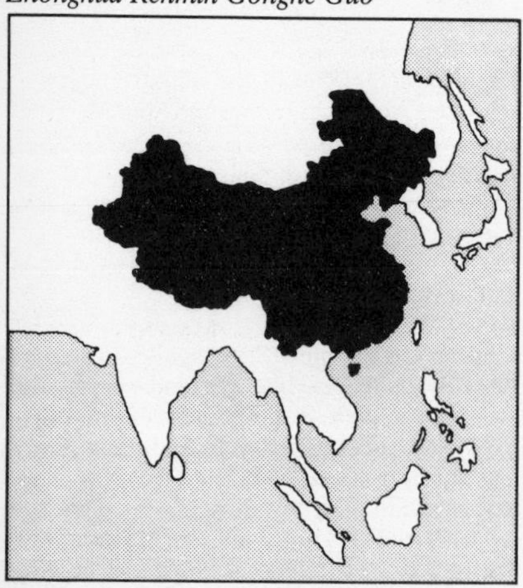

area 9 569 700 sq km/3 694 000 sq mi
capital Beijing (Peking◊)
towns Chongqing (Chungking), Shenyang (Mukden), Wuhan, Nanjing (Nanking), Harbin; ports Tianjin (Tientsin), Shanghai, Qingdao (Tsingtao), Lüda (Lü-ta), Guangzhou (Canton)
features rivers Huang He (Yellow River), Chang Jiang (Yangtze-Kiang), Xi Jiang (Si Kiang); Great Wall of China; Kongur Shan
exports tea; livestock and animal products; textiles (silk and cotton); oil, minerals (China is the world's largest producer of tungsten), chemicals; light industrial goods
currency yuane
population 1 008 175 000, of whom the majority are Han (ethnic Chinese); the 67 million of other races (including Tibetan, Uigur, and Zhuang) live in border areas. By 2000AD the population is estimated to be 2000 million, hence the encouragement of late marriage and restriction of births (preferably to a single child) by penalties such as deduction of 'workpoints' (which affects the income of the couple's commune). There is also an Overseas Chinese community of some 24 million.
language Chinese◊
religion officially atheist, but traditional religions are Taoism◊, Confucianism◊, and Buddhism◊; Islam 13 000 000; Catholicism 3–6 000 000 (divided between the 'patriotic' church established 1958, and the 'loyal' church subject to Rome); Protestantism 3 000 000
famous people literature (poets) Li Bo, Du Fu, Bo Zhu Yi; (prose-writers) Luo Guan-zhong, Cao Chan, Lu Xun; (philosophers) Lao Tzu, Confucius, Mencius
government under the 1982 constitution there is a president (from 1983 Li Xiannian 1905–), and a National People's Congress, both elected for five years. The latter chooses the Prime Minister (Zhao◊ Zi-yang), who heads a State Council of ministers, appointed on his recommendation. Since 1980 there have been elected people's governments in the 29 provinces, autonomous regions, and special municipalities. Both central and local government is now freer from Communist Party control, though the Party (General Secretary Hu◊ Yaobang) remains powerful. Deng◊ Xioaping continues to be influential in promoting a mixed economy: state, collective, and individual enterprise now being allowed. In 1984 an identity card system, for all over 16, was introduced, issued by the Minister of Public Security.
history Chinese civilization is the oldest in existence: for events and dynasties see China history◊□

China: history

BC c1 000 000 Yuanmou Man
c500 000 Peking Man◊
2205 Xia Dynasty, the first of the traditional dynasties
1700–1030 Shang Dynasty, capital Xibo (see under Henan◊), noted for its striking bronzes.
1028–221 Zhou Dynasty established; began to disintegrate in the Spring and Autumn Period 770–745, followed in the Warring

States Period 475–221 by the transition to feudalism; noted for Confucianism◊ and Taoism◊, spade-shaped coinage, and the study of astronomy, magnetism, and medicine
221–206 Qin◊ Dynasty, Shi Huangdi unified all China and built the Great Wall
206BC–220AD Han Dynasty, noted for their burial suits of small jade plaques, their introduction of the exam system for public servants; Buddhism◊ was introduced in the 1st century AD, and acupuncture, calligraphy, paper, silk weaving, the seismograph, and wind and water mills were developed
221–580 period of division
581–618 Sui Dynasty, under which the Grand Canal◊ was built
618–907 Tang Dynasty, under which porcelain, poetry, and wood-block printing flourished, and trade along the Silk Road reached its height; Islam◊ was introduced◊
907–960 period of decline and disorder
960–1279 Song Dynasty, noted for porcelain, lacquer work, and use of movable type, the compass, gunpowder, rocket propulsion for spears, and paper money
1271–1368 Yüan, or Mongol Dynasty, which finally subdued the Song in 1279; see Genghis Khan◊. The dynasty ruled not only China, but Moscow, Kiev, Damascus, Baghdad, and Kabul
1368–1644 Ming Dynasty, widespread foreign trade, including Europe; fine porcelain produced; opium introduced as a narcotic; in 1582 the first Christian missionary (the Jesuit Matteo Ricci) arrived
1644–1911 Qin, or Manchu Dynasty, who introduced the 'pigtail'; in 1793 Lord Macartney headed the first British political mission
1840–2 Opium War with Britain, following Chinese attempts to stop the opium trade by destroying British merchants' stocks; ended with the opening of five 'treaty ports' (under foreign control) for trade, and the cession of Hong Kong to Britain
1851–64 Taiping Heavenly Kingdom, a peasant revolt against the Manchus, led by a man believing himself to be the younger brother of Jesus Christ; it was in part defeated by General Gordon◊
1858 and *1860* successive Aigun and Peking treaties with Russia, under which 984 200 sq km/380 000 sq mi, N and E of the Amur and Ussuri rivers, were ceded by China
1860 Peking sacked by the French and British and the Summer Palace burnt down
1895 war with Japan
1900 Boxer Rebellion, a revolt by the Society of the Righteous and Harmonious Fists, encouraged by the Dowager Empress Zi Xi◊ (Tzu Hsi) against foreign domination; Peking again sacked by the foreign powers, including USA
1908 Empress Dowager Zi Xi succeeded by Pu Yi◊
1912 Republic declared 1 Jan by Sun Zhong Shan (Sun Yat-sen)
1919 demonstration against the Versailles Treaty under which Japan kept her gains in China and the Western powers their pre-war concessions
1926 Jiang Jie Shi (Chiang Kai-shek◊), with initial Communist co-operation, attempted to defeat the warlords and unite China
1931–3 Japanese occupied Manchuria
1934–5 Long March, the Communists under Mao Ze Dong (Mao Tse-tung◊) retreated from Jinggan Shan to Yan'an in order to re-group after Nationalist onslaughts
1936 Xi'an Incident; Jiang Jie Shi kidnapped and forced into coalition with the Communists against the Japanese
1937–45 Sino–Japanese War, precipitated by the China Incident, in which Japanese soldiers were killed at the Marco Polo Bridge near Peking
1946 Truman ended aid to the Nationalists
1949 People's Republic of China proclaimed by Mao Ze Dong
1950 diplomatic relations resumed with Britain
1956–7 Hundred Flowers Movement, when free expression of opinion was briefly encouraged
1958–60 Great Leap Forward, when the masses were organized in communes with 'backyard' industrial production, the result being economic disaster; 27 million are thought to have died
1960 rift with Russia over Russian 'revisionism'
1962 punitive invasion of India over disputed border issue
1963 first official claim on the USSR for the return of territories ceded to Tsarist Russia in 1858 and 1860
1966–8 Great Proletarian Cultural Revolution; started by Mao with the Red Guards in order to regain power from Liu Shaoqi◊; idea of perpetual revolution promulgated
1967 British Embassy sacked
1969 border clashes with the USSR
1972 Nixon visited Peking
1974 Deng Xiao-ping announced his Three Worlds◊ policy to the United Nations
1976 Zhou En Lai◊ (Chou En-Lai) succeeded by Deng as Prime Minister; and Hua Guofeng◊ succeeded Mao

1979 punitive invasion of Vietnam 17 Feb–16 Mar because of border incursions; Democracy Wall (for free expression posters) removed after a year
1980 Hua Guofeng replaced by Zhao Ziyang◊, protégé of Deng
1980–81 trial and imprisonment of Mao's wife, Jiang Qing
1982 Deng went into semi-retirement owing to ill-health
1982 sixth Five-Year Plan adopted to increase agricultural and industrial production by 20%□

China clay see kaolin◊□

China Sea area of the Pacific Ocean to the E of China; area 3 568 225 sq km/1 377 335 sq mi. See Paracels◊□

chincherinchee S African plant *Ornitho galum thyrsoides,* family Liliaceae, with spikes of white or yellow wax-like flowers which are long-lasting□

chinchilla a small S American rodent◊□

Chindwin river of N Burma, which joins the Irrawaddy; length c1000 km/600 mi□

Ch'in dynasty see Qin◊□

Chinese language◊ of the Sino-Tibetan family. It is written in ideographs (symbols directly representing an object or idea), so that the written language has always been understood throughout the country, but the spoken language has differed widely according to region, e.g. Cantonese is spoken by most overseas Chinese in Hongkong, California, and London. Today ***putonghua*** ('common speech') based on the Peking dialect (Mandarin) is promoted for both speaking and writing as the 'national language' *kuo-yu* of China. The language is becoming less monosyllabic (relying on pitch and inflection to convey differences of meaning) and more polysyllabic (extra syllables carrying the meaning). The characters, formerly vertical and read right–left, are now placed horizontally and read left–right, and 2000 simplified characters have been introduced. A 25-letter Roman alphabet (excluding 'v') is used in schools to help with pronunciation, and this *Pinyin* ('transcription') is prescribed for foreigners to bring place-names, etc., closer to their Chinese sound, e.g. Beijing rather than Peking. The Pinyin forms are requested in postal use, and are used generally in this volume, but Pinyin is not accepted on Taiwan□

Chinese cabbage/leaves a type of cabbage◊□

Chinghai see Qinghai◊□

Chioggia port on an island in the Venetian lagoon; population 50 000□

chip popular name for the single piece of silicon, typically 2.5 x 2.5 mm square by 0.1 mm thick, which constitutes an electronic integrated circuit◊. See also wafer◊□

chipmunk rodent of the squirrel◊ family, found in N America and Europe. The ***Siberian chipmunk*** *Tamias sibiricus* has five dark stripes along the back, and all chipmunks have cheek pouches for carrying food□

Chippendale Thomas c1718–79. English furniture designer, whose *The Gentleman and Cabinet Maker's Director* 1754 was the first book of its kind. He favoured Louis XIV, Chinese, Gothic, and neo-Classic styles, and dark mahogany□

Chirac Jacques 1932– . French statesman. Prime Minister under Giscard◊ D'Estaing 1974–6, he resigned after differences with him, and was a presidential candidate himself in 1981. He again became Prime Minister in 1986 under Mitterrand◊□

Chirico Giorgio de 1888–1978. Artist of Italian parentage born in Greece, a Surrealist precursor, e.g. *The Uncertainty of the Poet* (Tate Gallery, London)□

Chiron in Greek mythology, the son of Cronos by a sea nymph. A centaur◊, he was the wise tutor of Jason, Achilles, etc.□

Chiron 'mini-planet' discovered in 1977, orbiting between Saturn and Venus. It appears to have a dark surface resembling that of asteroids in the outer solar system, and probably consists of a mixture of ice and dark stony material□

chiropody the care and treatment of the feet□

chiropractic manipulation of the spine, etc., to relieve apparently non-related conditions, claimed to be caused by pressure on the nerves. It is not fully recognized by orthodox medicine□

Chiroptera the order of mammals which includes the bat◊□

Chita industrial town (engineering, coal) in the E USSR; population 308 000□

Chittagong industrial port in Bangladesh; population 890 000. See Dacca◊□

chivalry the medieval knightly class, and hence the code of honour they were supposed to observe□

chives purple-flowered hardy perennial *Allium schoenoprasum,* family Liliaceae; the slender hollow leaves are used in salads etc. See herbs◊, onion◊□

chloracne cutaneous eruption symptomatic of contact with chlorinated organic chemicals and a contaminated environment□

chloral or ***trichloroethanal*** oily, colourless liquid, CCl_3CHO; its compound chloral hydrate is a powerful hypnotic. It is also used in the manufacture of DDT□

chlorates the salts of chloric acid, containing various proportions of chlorine and oxygen□

chlorella single-cell, freshwater alga, 3–10 micrometres in diameter, which obtains its growth energy from light and can increase its weight by four times in 12 hours. Nutritive content: 50% protein, 20% fat, 20% carbohydrate, 10% phosphate, calcium, etc. Unappetizing *au naturel*, it can be flavoured, and may be a food for space travellers, etc.□

chlorides salts of hydrochloric acid commonly formed by its action on various metals, or by the direct combination of metal and chlorine□

chlorine element
symbol Cl
atomic number 71
physical description colourless gas
features member of the halogen◊ group, highly reactive, and poisonous in concentrated form; it forms 0.2% of the human body. Common salt is sodium chloride (NaCl)
uses compounds are used in bleaches, disinfectants, and water purification, as well as in chemical manufacturing, e.g. PVC plastics□

chloroform colourless liquid with a pungent smell, $CHCl_3$, used in making fluorocarbon◊, in cleansing agents and refrigerants, and formerly as an anaesthetic□

chlorophyll the green colouring of plants. It is made by plants in a way very similar to that in which animals make haem (the red blood pigment). It is used to synthesize sugar from carbon dioxide and water in the presence of light. See photosynthesis◊□

chocolate a drink or confectionery. See cocoa◊□

Choiseul Étienne François, Duc de Choiseul 1719–85. French statesman. A protégé of Mme de Pompadour, he was Foreign Minister, 1758–70, banished the Jesuits and supported Voltaire, Diderot, etc.□

cholera intestinal infection by a bacterium (*Vibrio cholerae*), formerly with a high death rate, reduced to 1% by Leonard Roger◊'s treatment with copious injections of saline fluid to prevent dehydration□

cholesterol fatty alcohol found in bile, blood, animal fat, etc. It forms gallstones, and an excess may cause atherosclerosis (see under arteriosclerosis◊), etc.□

Chomsky Noam 1928– . American professor of linguistics, who became very influential with his theory of transformational generative grammar. This work attracted widespread interest outside linguistics because of the claims it made about the relationship between language and the mind, and the universality of an underlying language structure. Chomsky was also an active opponent of the American involvement in the Vietnam◊ War□

Chongqing industrial centre (formerly Chungking) of Sichuan province, China; population 6 000 000. For 4000 years a commercial and route centre in one of the country's most remote and economically backward regions, it is now one of China's most dynamic free-enterprise markets. During the war with Japan it was the capital of China 1938–46□

Chopin Frédéric François 1810–49. Polish composer. Born near Warsaw, he made his debut as a pianist at nine, and from 1831 lived in Paris, performing in the intimate atmosphere of its fashionable salons. In 1836 he was introduced by Liszt to George Sand◊, with whom he had a liaison 1838–47; at Majorca she nursed him (he had tuberculosis), and for a time he regained his health. He died in Paris in 1849. A passionate nationalist, he produced solo piano pieces – preludes, nocturnes, polonaises◊, etc. – of lyric and individual quality□

chordates phylum of animals which have some sort of supporting rod (e.g. backbone) at some time of their life□

chorea a disease of the nervous system marked by involuntary movements of the face muscles and limbs, formerly called St Vitus◊'s dance□

Chou En-lai see Zhou En lai◊□

chough large black bird of the crow family, Corvidae; the ***common chough*** *Pyrrhocorax pyrrhocorax* has a red bill and legs□

chow chow a breed of dog◊□

Chrétien de Troyes 12th century AD. French poet, born in Champagne, who produced courtly Arthurian romances, which first introduced the concept of the Holy Grail, for Philip, Count of Flanders□

Christ see Jesus Christ◊□

Christchurch town in Dorset, England; population 36 700. It has a fine Norman priory church□

Christchurch city and port on South Island, New Zealand; population 327 300. The Anglican cathedral was designed by Sir Gilbert Scott, and the University of Canterbury was founded in 1873. Chief centre of the Canterbury Plains, it has canning, meat-processing, fertilizer, and chemical plants□

Christian eight kings of Denmark and Norway, including:
Christian IV 1577–1648, reigned from 1588, sided with the Protestants in the Thirty Years' War, and was the founder of Christiania (see Oslo◊).

Christian IX 1819–1906, reigned from 1863; his daughter Alexandra married Edward VII of the UK, and his son George became king of Greece. In 1864 he lost Schleswig-Holstein following a war with Austria and Prussia.
Christian X 1870–1947, reigned from 1912, and was a prisoner of the Germans in Copenhagen 1943–5□

Christiania see Oslo◊□

Christianity religion derived from the teaching of Jesus◊ Christ; overall membership c1024 million.
scriptures the Bible, especially the four gospels (Matthew◊, Mark◊, Luke◊, and John◊) of the New Testament, of which Mark is thought to have been produced nearest to the events. The chief commandment was love of God, and of one's neighbour as of oneself. See also Trinity◊, Apostles◊, creed◊, original◊ sin.
divisions
Roman Catholicism which acknowledges the supreme jurisdiction of the Pope◊, infallible when he speaks *ex cathedra* 'from the throne', a tenet which remains the chief stumbling block in attempted reunion with other churches; the doctrine of the Immaculate◊ Conception, and an allotment of a special place to the Virgin Mary is also at issue (see also Eucharist◊, sacraments◊). The final split with the Eastern Orthodox Church was in 1054, and a further schism came with the Reformation◊, to which the Counter-Reformation provided only a partial answer. An attempt to update its doctrines in the late 19th century, was condemned by Pius X in 1907, and more recent moves have been stifled by John◊ Paul II. See monasticism◊, prayer◊, purgatory◊. Membership 585 million.
Eastern Orthodox a federation of self-governing churches (some founded by the Apostles◊ and their disciples), whose only confession of faith is the Nicene◊ Creed. There is elaborate ritual and singing (no instrumental music) in services, and in the marriage service the bride and groom are crowned. There is a married clergy, except for bishops; the Immaculate Conception is not accepted; only icons◊, not images, are allowed in churches. See monasticism◊.
Protestantism originating with the Reformation◊, and named from the protest of Luther and his supporters at the Diet of Spires 1529 against the decision to reaffirm the Edict of the Diet of Worms◊ against the Reformation. The chief sects are the Anglican Communion, Baptists, Christian Scientists, Lutherans, Methodists, Mormons, Pentecostal Movement, Presbyterians, Unitarians. See Ecumenical◊ Movement, Liberation Theology◊, Mission◊□

Christian Science interpretation of the Christian faith originating with Mary Baker Eddy◊, and claiming that in those properly attuned to the Divine Spirit there can be no place for evil, sin, and disease□

Christie Dame Agatha 1890–1976. British crime writer, born Miller. Her first book, *The Mysterious Affair at Styles* 1920, introduced Hercule Poirot, a Belgian detective, and a later creation was Miss Jane Marple, an elderly spinster detective. She had married in 1914 Colonel Archibald Christie, and in 1926 caused a nationwide sensation by disappearing for 10 days (possibly as a result of amnesia) when her husband fell in love with another woman. After a divorce in 1928, she married in 1930 Sir Max Mallowan 1904–78, an archaeologist. Her books, many filmed, include *The Murder of Roger Ackroyd* 1926, *Murder on the Orient Express* 1934, and *Death on the Nile* 1937, and her play *The Mousetrap* 1952 is still running□

Christina 1626–89. Queen of Sweden. Succeeding her father Gustavus Adolphus in 1632, she assumed power in 1644, but disagreed with the former regent Oxenstjerna◊. Refusing to marry, she eventually nominated her cousin Charles Gustavus as her successor. As a secret convert to Rome, she had to abdicate in 1654, and ended her life as a pensioner of the Pope after a succession of scandals□

Christmas day on which the birth of Christ is celebrated by Christians. Although the actual birth date is unknown, the choice of a date near the winter solstice owed much to missionary desire to facilitate conversion of pagans, e.g. in Britain 25 Dec had been kept as a festival long before the introduction of Christianity. Many of its customs also have a heathen origin. See Christmas card◊, Santa Claus◊, Christmas tree◊□

Christmas Island island in the Indian Ocean; area 135 sq km/52 sq mi; population 3000. Discovered on Christmas Day 1643; annexed by Britain 1888; occupied by Japan 1942–5, and transferred to Australia 1958. After a referendum in 1984, it was included in Northern◊ Territory. There are phosphate deposits□

Christmas Island see Kiritimati◊□

Christmas rose see hellebore◊□

Christmas tree see spruce◊□

Christoff Boris 1919– . Bulgarian bass singer, whose roles include Boris Godunov and Ivan the Terrible□

Christophe Henri 1767–1820. King of Haiti from 1812. A Negro slave, he was a leader of the revolt against the French in 1790. Though capable, he was cruel. He shot himself when his troops deserted him□

Christopher St 3rd century. Traditionally martyred in Syria, he became the patron saint of travellers, being said to have carried the Christ child over a stream, and found the burden heavy, since Christ himself bore all the sins of the world. See canonization◊. His feast day is 25 Jul□

chromatography a technique for separating mixtures into pure compounds for analysis and quantification. ***Gas chromatography*** separates gases and volatile liquids. ***Liquid chromatography*** separates liquids and solutions. ***Thin layer*** and ***paper chromatography*** is used for small amounts of solid in solution for analysis only (detection of trace quantities, e.g. in forensic science◊□

chromium element
symbol Cr
atomic number 24
physical description grey metal
features there is a trace in the human body and its presence gives the green colour to emerald
uses to prevent corrosion of steel and to increase the hardness and heat resistance of steel alloys□

chromosome a structure in a cell nucleus responsible for the transmission of hereditary characteristics. See genetic◊ code□

chromosphere the red gaseous envelope around the sun◊□

chronometer instrument measuring equal intervals of time accurately, used in navigation□

chrysanthemum genus of plants, family Compositae, native to all countries except Australia. British species include ***ox-eye daisy*** *C leucanthemum,* and ***corn marigold*** *C segetum.* Garden hybrids have been developed from oriental and other species, e.g. ***marguerite*** with white ray-florets round a yellow centre, originally from the Canaries. The dried flowers of Eurasian *C pyrethrum* yield an insecticide without the dangers of DDT□

chrysolite see olivine◊□

chub a river fish of the carp◊ family□

Chubb Crater prehistoric meteor-made crater discovered in 1950 in Quebec by F W Chubb; 411 m/1350 ft deep, it has a raised rim 168 m/550 ft, and contains a lake□

Chufu see Qufu◊□

Chukchi Sea see under Arctic◊ Ocean□

Chukovsky Kornel Ivanovitch 1882–1969. Russian linguist, also beloved as Grandpa Kornel Chukovsky for his nonsense poems for children on Lewis Carroll lines□

Chungking see Chongqing◊□

Church Frederick Edwin 1826–1900. American landscape artist of the Hudson River School□

Churchill Charles 1731–64. British political satirist, whose verse was coarse and personal□

Churchill Lord Randolph Henry Spencer 1849–95. British Conservative statesman. Son of the 7th Duke of Marlborough, he formed in 1880 a so-called 4th Party (with Drummond Wolff, Gorst, and Arthur Balfour). Chancellor of the Exchequer in 1886, he resigned when he disagreed with the demands on the Treasury made by the armed forces. He married the American Jenny Jerome in 1874, and their elder son was Sir Winston Churchill◊. He died insane□

Churchill Sir Winston Leonard Spencer 1874–1965. British Conservative statesman. Son of Lord Randolph Churchill, he was educated at Harrow, and as war correspondent in the S African War, made a dramatic escape from a prisoner-of-war camp. Entering parliament in 1900, he was President of the Board of Trade 1908–10, Home Secretary 1910–11, and First Lord of the Admiralty 1911–15. His sponsorship of the Gallipoli◊ operation led to his exclusion from the first coalition government of 1915, but he was Minister of Munitions under Lloyd George in 1917, when he was concerned with the development of the tank. As Secretary for War 1918–21 he was active in support of White◊ opposition to the Bolsheviks in Russia, then as Chancellor under Baldwin 1924, he returned Britain to the gold◊ standard and was prominent in the defeat of the General Strike of 1926. He was out of office from 1929 until he returned to the Admiralty on the outbreak of World War II, and on 10 May 1940 succeeded Chamberlain in the premiership, making his historic 'blood and tears, toil and sweat' speech to the Commons on 13 May. His coalition government conducted the war in alliance with the USSR and USA, but was defeated in the general election of 1945. He returned to power 1951–55. He received the Nobel prize for literature 1953; his books include a life of Marlborough and *The Second World War* 1948–54. He was buried near Blenheim Palace, where he was born, and his home at Chartwell, Kent, is a museum□

Churchill town in Manitoba◊, Canada□

Church of England see Anglican Communion◊□

Church of Scotland see Scotland◊, Church of□

Chu Teh see Zhu De◊□

Chuvash a republic of W USSR, annexed in the 16th century; area 18 300 sq km/7100 sq mi; population 1 301 000. Capital Cheboksary□

CIA see Central◊ Intelligence Agency□

Ciano Galeazzo 1903–44. Italian politician, Foreign Minister 1936–43. For voting against Mussolini, his father-in-law, at the Grand Council meeting which overthrew the dictator, he was shot□

cicada a type of tropical insect. See under Hemiptera◊□

Cicero Marcus Tullius 106–43BC. Roman statesman. As consul in 63BC, he saved the republic when it was threatened by Catiline◊'s conspiracy, but when the first Triumvirate◊ was formed he was exiled, and devoted himself to literature. On the outbreak of the Civil War in 49, he followed Pompey to Greece, but was treated well by Caesar on his return to Italy. After Caesar's assassination he supported Octavian (the future Augustus◊) against Mark Antony, but pleaded in passionate speeches for the restoration of republicanism. When Antony and Octavian came to terms in 43, he was killed while trying to escape to the East. His speeches and essays survive and had immense influence on later literature, and his letters have great personal interest, referring to his wives, both of whom he divorced, and his daughter, Tullia, who died young□

cichlid a fish of the family of freshwater perch◊□

Cid Rodrigo Diaz de Bivar c1040–99. Legendary Spanish hero, nicknamed *El Cid* ('the lord') by the Moors. Essentially a mercenary, fighting with or against the Moors, he died while defending Valencia against them, and in subsequent romances became Spain's national hero□

cider fermented apple juice, made chiefly in Normandy, Brittany, and the West of England□

Cienfuegos port and naval base in Cuba; population 296 000. There is a tobacco trade□

cigar originally a sheath of palm leaves filled with tobacco, smoked by the Indians of Central and N America. The most expensive, e.g. those from Cuba, are still hand-rolled. Small machine-made versions have been in some demand in recent years□

cigarette literally 'a little cigar'. First smoked in S America c1750, they became so popular that tax on them now provides a large slice of national revenue in many Western countries. When their link with the incidence of lung cancer became inescapable in the 1960s, various substitutes were developed by the manufacturing companies, but failed to satisfy the consumer□

cigarette cards originating in the USA in the 1870s, they were included in packs of cigarettes until by World War II they became uneconomic; they are collectible□

Cimabue Giovanni. Pseudonym of Italian painter Cenni de Peppi 1240–c1302. The master of Giotto, he was one of the first to paint from a living model□

Cimarosa Domenico 1749–1801. Italian opera composer, especially *The Secret Marriage* 1792□

Cimino Michael 1943– . Film director: *The Deer Hunter* 1978, *Heaven's Gate* 1981□

cinchona genus of shrubs and trees, family Rubiaceae, native to Amazonia. Quinine is extracted from cinchona bark□

Cincinnatti industrial city (machine tools) and inland port on the Ohio river, Ohio, USA; population 383 000□

Cincinnatus Lucius Quinctius 5th century BC. Roman general. As dictator, he defeated the Aequi in 458BC, then insisted on returning to life as a farmer□

cinnabar see mercury◊□

cinnamon aromatic bark of the tree *Cinnamonum zeylanicum* of Sri Lanka, family Lauraceae, used as a flavouring and in medicine□

cinquefoil genus of plants *Potentilla,* family Rosaceae; their leaves have five (*cinque*) divisions□

Cinque Ports association of ports which during 11th–15th century were bound to supply ships and men against the invasion of England. Originally five (*cinque*), Sandwich, Dover, Hythe, Romney, Hastings (later including Rye, Winchelsea, etc.). The honorary office of Lord Warden, official residence Walmer Castle, survives□

circadian rhythm human metabolic rhythm, usually coincident with the 24-hour day, but which may shift out of phase□

Circassia part of the N Caucasus ceded to Russia by Turkey in 1829, now included in the Karachayevo-Cherkess◊ Region□

Circe in Greek mythology, an enchantress. In the *Odyssey* of Homer◊ she turned the followers of Odysseus into pigs when she held their leader captive□

circle the path followed by a point which moves so as to keep a constant distance, the ***radius***, from a fixed point, the ***centre***. The distance from one side to the other of a circle, called the ***diameter***, is thus twice the radius. The ration of the distance all the way round the circle – the ***circumference*** – to the diameter is an irrational◊ number called π (***pi***), roughly equal to 3.14159. A circle of radius r has a diameter of 2r and a circumference of $2\pi r$.

A ***chord*** is a straight line cutting a circle at two points; it divides the area of the circle into

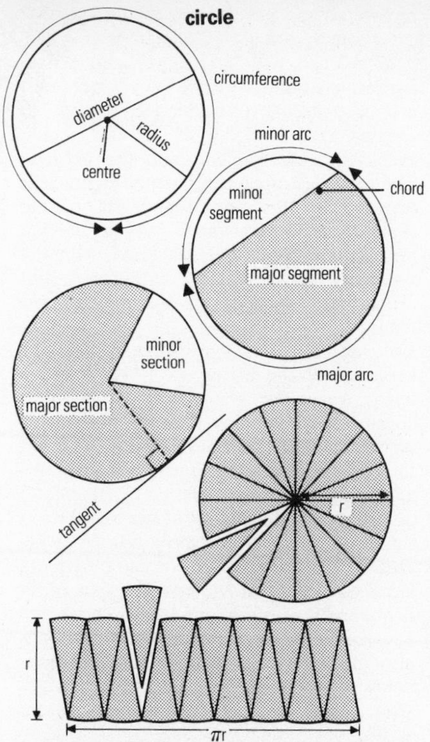

major and minor ***segments***, and the circumference into major and minor ***arcs***. If a circle is divided up by two radii, then the resulting divisions are termed major and minor ***sectors***. A line which touches a circle at only one point is called a ***tangent***. It is at right angles to the radius which goes through that point.

The area of a circle of radius r is equal to πr^2. This can be shown by dividing a circle into thin sectors and reassembling them to make an approximate rectangle. The approximation gets better the thinner the sectors□

circumcision removal of a part of the foreskin of the penis◊ in males. Performed originally for sanitary reasons especially by Jews and Muslims, it is now a religious ritual. Female circumcision, removal of the clitoris (see under penis◊), is performed among some peoples. Together with other measures, it forms part of a mutilatory method of ensuring the virginity of girls before marriage; and has been illegal in the UK since 1985□

circumnavigation see Magellan◊, Cabot◊, Drake◊□

Cirencester town in Gloucestershire, England, the 'capital' of the Cotswolds◊; population 14 500. The Royal Agricultural College is here, and the Corinium Museum (the town was second largest in Roman Britain, and has an amphitheatre which seated 8000)□

Ciskei Republic of. Independent Black◊ National State 1981
area 19 943 sq km/7700 sq mi
capital Bisho
features one of the two homelands of the Xhosa people created by South Africa (the other is Transkei◊). It was declared independent in 1981, but this is not recognized by any other country
products pineapples, timber, metal products, etc.
population 660 000
language Xhosa
government president (Lennox Sebe from 1981), with legislative and executive councils□

Cistercians Roman Catholic monastic order established at Cîteaux in 1098 by St Robert de Champagne, as a stricter form of the Benedictine◊; it advanced farming methods. The ***Trappists,*** so-called from the original house at La Trappe in Normandy (founded by Dominique de Rancé in 1664), follow an even stricter version of the Cistercian rule (including the maintenance of silence, manual labour, and a vegetarian diet); their order has now been absorbed again in the former□

citizenship status as a member of a state. Under the British Nationality Act 1981, only a British citizen has a right of abode in the UK, i.e., basically anyone born in the UK to a parent who is a British citizen, or who is lawfully settled in the UK. Other categories are: Citizen of British Dependent Territories, e.g. Hong Kong; and British Overseas Citizen, i.e. the remainder of existing 'citizens of the UK and Colonies'□

citizens' band or ***CB*** short-range radio waveband used by members of the public and legalized in the UK in 1981□

citric acid organic acid, $C_6H_8O_7$ found especially in citrus fruits, a white crystalline powder. It is commercially obtained by fermenting sugar with various moulds, and is used in food processing, etc.□

citronella the lemon-scented oil obtained from *Cymbopogon cardus*, used in cosmetics and insect-repellents□

citrus genus of over 16 species of evergreen, aromatic trees, and shrubs, family Rutaceae◊, grown for their edible fruit including the ***lemon*** *C limonia*, a pale yellow oval fruit with a sharp taste introduced to Europe by the Moors in the 12th–13th centuries, of which the juice is used in cooking and perfumery; ***pomelo*** *C decumana*, possibly the oldest citrus fruit, with a very large acid fruit, of which the ***grapefruit***, *C paradisei*, is a variety; ***lime*** *C aurantifolia*, a green oval

Indian fruit, the first scurvy preventative, grown in the West Indies for its juice; ***citron*** *C medica*, a small yellow fruit with a thick aromatic rind used for candied peel; ***orange***, of which varieties include ***bitter*** or ***Seville*** *C aurantium*, used in marmalade, the rind yielding an essential oil and the petals the perfume Oil of Neroli; ***bergamot*** *C bergamia,* producing an essential oil used in eau de Cologne and flavouring Earl Grey tea; ***tangerine*** *C nobilis* (very similar are the ***clementine***, ***mandarin***, ***satsuma***, and ***wilking***); and ***sweet/dessert orange*** *C sinensis*. Hybrids are cultivated to produce more juice, less pith, peel, and pips, e.g. ***kara*** satsuma x wilking, ***minneola*** grapefruit x tangerine; ***ortanique*** orange x tangerine, developed in Jamaica; ***temple*** orange x tangerine; ***ugli fruit*** orange x grapefruit□

city large and important town; in Britain one awarded the title by the Crown, and traditionally a cathedral town□

City The. See London◊□

Ciudad Bolívar city (formerly Angostura) in Venezuela, linked with Soledad across the Orinoco; population 110 000□

Ciudad Guayana river port on the Orinoco in Venezuela; population 143 540□

Ciudad Juárez city in N Mexico; population 597 100. El Paso◊ is across the US border□

Ciudad Real city in central Spain; population 42 000. There is a 13th-century cathedral□

civet typical member of the cat-like, carnivorous family of mammals, Viverridae, which includes:

civet of which the ***African civet*** *Viverra civetta* yields an extract from a gland near the sexual organs which is commercially used to give longer life to perfume. It is greyish, with dark spots, 1.2 m/3.5 ft long, including a tail 30 cm/1 ft long.

binturong blackish-grey, with a rough coat, *Arctictis binturong* is the largest of the family, 1.5 m/4.5 ft including its prehensile tail. It is a tree-dwelling vegetarian of SE Asia.

genet of Europe and Africa, with light-coloured, spotted or striped fur; the largest is the ***African genet*** *Genetta victoriae*, 1 m/3 ft long with a 50 cm/1.5 ft tail.

mongoose of which the most familiar is the grey-brown ***Indian mongoose*** *Herpestes mungo* 50 cm/1.5 ft long, with a tail almost as long again, which is easily tamed and kept for its ability to kill snakes□

Civil Defence The protection of the population by civilians against military attack. For World War II the Minister of Home Security was created in 1939 to direct ***Air Raid Precautions (ARP)***. The country was divided into 12 regions, each under a commissioner to replace central government in the event of cut communications. Volunteer air raid wardens worked with ambulance and rescue parties, gas officers, breakdown gangs, etc., and a National Fire Service (based on existing local services), c5 000 000 people enrolling as firewatchers and fire fighters. The total destruction threatened by nuclear war led in 1968 to disbandment of the skeleton services retained, but in 1980 a restructured ***Home Defence*** force, with the voluntary services, local authorities, and Territorial Army co-operating, was planned□

civil list annual sum provided to meet the expenses of the Sovereign (three-quarters being wages for the Royal Household); consort of a Sovereign; children of a Sovereign (except the Prince of Wales, who has the revenues from the Duchy of Cornwall); and widows of those children. Payments to other individual members of the Royal Family are covered by a contribution from the Queen. See Privy Purse◊. In the USA there is no equivalent of the civil list, but presidents and vice-presidents have salaries and allowances for entertaining, etc. Provision is also made for their widows, and ex-presidents are pensioned and have free office space, with free post and allowances for staff□

civil list pensions pensions, no longer paid from the Sovereign's civil list, which are awarded to distinguished people on the nomination of the Prime Minister□

civil service the civilian staff working in the departments of state. The two main divisions of the British civil service are the Home and Diplomatic services. As Minister for the Civil Service, the Prime Minister is responsible for the Management and Personnel Office (MPO), but manpower numbers and remuneration are controlled by the Treasury. Most civil servants are professional specialists, and the Civil Service College (Sunningdale Park, Ascot) was established in 1970 to develop training. They may not take an active part in politics, and do not change with the government. Their permanence gives those in the upper echelons an advantage over ministers, who are birds of passage, and they have been alleged to block policies opposed to their views.

In the USA there are competitive examinations and permanency of appointment for certain posts, but others are still given as a reward for political services, and their holders change with the party in power□

Civil War English. Struggle between Charles◊ I and his Royalist supporters, and

the Parliamentarians or Roundheads.
First Civil War Charles I raised his standard at Nottingham 22 Aug 1642; the chief battles were: Edgehill on 23 Oct 1642, which was indecisive; Marston Moor W of York on 2 Jul 1644, in which Prince Rupert◊ and the Duke of Newcastle were defeated by the Parliamentarians (with notable cavalry charges by Cromwell◊) and the Scots (under Leven◊); Naseby in Northamptonshire 14 Jun 1645, the decisive defeat by Cromwell and Fairfax◊ of the Royalists. Charles surrendered to the Scottish army at Newark on 5 May 1646.
Second Civil War Royalist and Presbyterian rising Mar–Aug 1648, which was soon crushed by Cromwell and his New Model Army.
extensions of the Civil War were Cromwell's invasion of Ireland 1649–50 (see Drogheda◊), and the campaign in which he defeated the Royalists under Prince Charles (Charles II) at Dunbar on 3 Sept 1650 and Worcester on 3 Sept 1651□

Civil War American. War 1861–5 between the Southern or Confederate States (South Carolina, Mississippi, Florida, Alabama, Georgia, Louisiana, and Texas; joined later by Virginia, Arkansas, Tennessee, and North Carolina), and the northern or Federal States. The former wished to maintain their 'state rights', in particular the institution of Negro slavery, and claimed the right to secede from the Union; the latter fought to maintain the Union.
1861 seven southern states set up the Confederate States of America (president Jefferson Davis) on 8 Feb; Fort Sumter, Charleston (see Beauregard◊), captured 12–14 Apr; Lee (Confederate) was victorious at the first Battle of Bull Run 21 Jul
1862 Battle of Shiloh 6–7 Apr was indecisive. Grant captured New Orleans in May, but the Confederates were again victorious at the second Battle of Bull Run 29–30 Aug. Lee's advance was then checked by McClellan◊ at Antietam on 17 Sept
1863 the emancipation proclamation was issued by Lincoln on 1 Jan, freeing the slaves; Battle of Gettysburg (Union victory) on 1–4 Jul marked the turning point of the war; Lincoln delivered the ***Gettysburg Address*** at the dedication of the national cemetery on 19 Nov; Grant overran the Mississippi states, capturing Vicksburg on 4 Jul
1864 Battles of Cold Harbor near Richmond, Virginia; in the first, on 27 Jun 1862, Lee defeated McClellan, and by the second Grant was delayed in his advance on Richmond. Sherman marched through Georgia to the sea, taking Atlanta on 1 Sept and Savannah on 22 Dec
1865 Lee surrendered to Grant at Appomattox Court House on 9 Apr; Lincoln was assassinated on 14 Apr; last Confederate troops surrendered on 26 May
There were 359 528 Union dead and 258 000 Confederate□

Civil War Spanish. Followed in 1936–39 the successful military revolt of Franco◊. His insurgents (Nationalists, who were supported by Fascist Italy and Nazi Germany) seized power in the S and NW, but were suppressed in Madrid, Barcelona, etc. by the workers' militia. The loyalists (Republicans) were aided by the USSR, and the volunteers of the International Brigade, e.g. George Orwell (see also Hemingway◊). ***1937*** Bilbao and the Basque country were bombed into submission; ***1938*** Catalonia was cut off from the main republican territory; ***1939*** Barcelona fell in Jan and Madrid in Apr, and Franco established a dictatorship□

Civitavecchia seaport in central Italy; population 48 500□

Clacton-on-Sea resort in Essex, England; population 40 000. St Osyth's priory is nearby□

cladistics method (Greek 'branch') of defining relationships in biological classification by means of a branching diagram or ***cladogram*** which summarizes the pattern of 'character' (an attribute, function, or structure which is determined by a gene or group of genes), distribution in a group of animals, plants, and so forth. It is based on the theory of German scientist Willi Hennig in 1950□

Clair René. Pseudonym of French film director René Lucien Chomette 1898–1981. His *Sous les Toits de Paris* 1930 was one of the first French sound films□

clam a type of shellfish. See bivalve◊□

clan social grouping most familiar in the Highland clans of Scotland, theoretically each descended from a single ancestor from whom the name is derived, e.g. clan MacGregor ('son of Gregor') from one of the sons of King Alpin. Rivalry between them was often bitter (see Glencoe◊), and they played a large role in the Jacobite revolts of 1715 and 1745, after which their individual tartan highland dress was banned 1746–82□

Clare St. Italian follower of St Francis, born like him at Assisi, and founder of the feminine equivalent of the Franciscans, the ***Order of Poor Clares***. She is the patron saint of television, because in 1252 she saw from her convent sickbed the Christmas services in a church at Assisi. Feast day 12 Aug□

Clare John 1793–1864. British poet, son of a farm labourer, remembered for his *Poems of Rural Life* 1820 and *The Shepherd's Calendar*

1827; he spent his last years in Northampton asylum□

Clare county (county town Ennis) in the Republic of Ireland, province of Munster◊; Shannon (Irish *Rineanna*) Airport, on the river Shannon, is here□

Clarence ducal title, of which the last holder was Albert Victor 1864–92, eldest son of Edward VII. See Jack the Ripper◊□

Clarendon Edward Hyde, 1st Earl of Clarendon 1609–74. English statesman. Although he opposed Charles I's unconstitutional actions, and supported the impeachment of Stafford, he broke with the revolutionary party in 1641, remaining loyal to the Crown. From 1651 he was chief adviser to the exiled Charles II, and at the Restoration was created Earl of Clarendon, further increasing his influence by the marriage of his daughter Anne to the future James II. The ***Clarendon Code*** (directed against Dissenters) was designed to secure the supremacy of the Church of England, but his comparative moderation was unpopular, and when the Dutch sailed up the Thames in 1667, he fell from power. In exile he wrote his *History of the Rebellion* 1702–4□

Clarendon Constitutions of. Code of laws 1164 intended to regulate relations between Church and State, which Becket◊ refused to accept. His ensuing quarrel with Henry II led to his murder□

claret since the 17th century the English term for the light red wines of Bordeaux□

clarinet a type of musical instrument. See under woodwind◊□

Clark Joe (Joseph) Charles 1939– . Canadian Progressive Conservative party leader 1979–83, Prime Minister May 1979–Feb 1980, when his budget was rejected□

Clark Kenneth, Baron Clark 1903–83. British art historian, director of the National Gallery 1934–45, presenter of TV series *Civilization* 1969, and author of *The Nude* 1955, etc.□

Clark Mark Wayne 1896–84. American general. He led a secret submarine mission in 1942 to N Africa to prepare for the Allied landing; commanded the 5th Army invading Italy and, by his obsession with being first to reach and capture Rome, allegedly caused unnecessary casualties. He was Commander-in-Chief of the United Nations armies in Korea 1952–3□

Clarke Arthur Charles 1917– . British scientist, originator of the plan for the modern system of communications satellites in 1945, and collaborator with the astronauts in their book *First on the Moon* 1970. He also wrote the sci-fi classic *2001: A Space Odyssey* 1968□

Clarke Jeremiah c1659–1707. Engish organist, composer of the 'Trumpet Voluntary' long attributed to Purcell; he shot himself when disappointed in love□

Clarke Marcus Andrew Hislop 1846–81. Australian novelist, author of *For the Term of His Natural Life* 1874, dealing with the prison settlements□

Clarkson Thomas 1760–1846. British philanthropist, campaigner against slavery; the trade in slaves ended in 1807, and slavery in British colonies in 1833□

Classicism in the arts, the style considered characteristic of Greece and Rome, and marked by reason, objectivity, restraint, clear definition, strictness and simplicity of form: see Romanticism◊□

classification of plants and animals: the biological science of taxonomy, a method of identifying individual members of the plant and animal kingdoms. Species are differentiated by certain characteristics; their evolutionary history, including fossil evidence; form and structure (morphology); physiology; behaviour; and their sexual characteristics. The principles of classification and nomenclature are based on those introduced by Linnaeus◊ in the 18th century. A ***species***, the only natural classification, comprises (very generally) those plants or animals which interbreed to produce offspring like themselves. Nevertheless, especially in cultivated plants, breeding and hybridization lead to the production of subspecies and varieties. Each species is identified by two Latin names, the second individual to itself, and the first held in common with others of its ***genus***, i.e. those animals or plants which appear very closely related to it. For example, the lesser celandine is *Ranunculus ficaria* and the creeping buttercup is *Ranunculus repens*. The lion is *Panthera leo*, and the leopard is *Panthera pardus*. The various genera are grouped in families, themselves grouped in orders, which are again grouped in classes, classes are grouped in phyla e.g. Chordata (which are the vertebrates). There is an international standard of classification in an attempt to ensure uniformity. See animal◊ classification, plant◊ classification□

clathrates compounds formed by small molecules filling in the holes in the structural lattice of another compound. Cathrates are thus intermediate between mixtures and compounds. One example is methane trapped in ice formed as sea sediment under the low temperature and pressure conditions at depths of c1000 m/c3000 ft, that is, over 90% of the world's seafloor. The gas is released when the sediment is heated, and is a great potential source of world energy□

Claudel Paul 1868–1955. French poet-dramatist, a fervent Catholic influenced by the Symbolists, e.g. *Soulier de satin/The Satin Slipper* 1924□

Claude Lorrain Pseudonym of Claude Gellée 1600–82, French artist, born in Lorraine, the first to devote himself entirely to landscape. He excelled in rendering light at particular times of day; his *Liber Veritatis* includes some 200 drawings after his finished works□

Claudian c370–404. Last of the great Latin poets, born in Alexandria. He wrote the epic *The Rape of Proserpine*, official panegyrics, epigrams, etc.□

Claudius 10BC–54AD. Nephew of Tiberius◊, made Roman emperor by his troops in 41, after the murder of Caligula, though more inclined to scholarly pursuits. In 43 he took part in the invasion of Britain. He was long dominated by his 3rd wife, Messalina◊, and is thought to have been poisoned by his 4th (Agrippina the Younger). He wrote histories: see Robert Graves◊□

Clausewitz Karl von 1780–1831. Prussian soldier, author of *Vom Kriege/On War* 1873, putting forward a concept of strategy valid till World War I□

Clausius Rudolf Julius Emanuel 1822–88. German physicist, a founder of thermodynamics◊, and enunciator in 1850 of its second law: heat of itself cannot pass from a colder to a hotter body□

clavichord an early keyboard instrument. See under piano◊□

Clay Cassius. See Muhammad Ali◊□

Clay Henry 1777–1852. American politician, a founder of the Republican party. He supported the war of 1812 against Britain, tried to hold the Union together on the slavery issue by the Missouri Compromise of 1820, and was Secretary of State 1825–9□

Clay Lucius DuBignon 1897–1978. American Commander-in-Chief of the US occupation forces in Germany 1947–9, he broke the Berlin blockade of 1948 (a 'siege' by the Russians lasting 327 days) with an 'airlift'□

clay consolidated mud, composed of fine rock particles (grain size, less than 0.002 mm). Essentially hydrated silicate of alumina, plus sand, lime, iron, oxides, magnesium, potassium, soda, organic substances, etc. Plastic when moistened, it hardens when heated, and is used in bricks, cement, and pottery□

Cleave Peter 1907– . British naval surgeon, nicknamed the Bran Man. He fed World War II sailors with bran to compensate for the lack of natural roughage in modern processed foods, which he recognized as responsible for many common diseases□

Cleethorpes seaside resort in Humberside, on the Humber estuary; population 36 500□

cleft palate fissure of the roof of the mouth, often accompanied by hare lip, the result of genetic defect□

Cleland John 1709–89. British author of the pornographic *Fanny Hill – Memoirs of a Woman of Pleasure* 1748–9□

clematis genus of temperate woody climbers with showy flowers, family Ranunculaceae◊; ***traveller's joy*** or ***old man's beard***, *C vitalba*, is the only British species, although many have been introduced□

Clemenceau Georges 1841–1929. French statesman, known as 'The Tiger' from his ferocious attacks on political opponents. He was Prime Minister 1906–9, and 1917–20 was again called to the premiership. He appointed Foch generalissimo, and presided over the Versailles peace conference, where he failed to secure the Rhine frontier for France□

Clemens Samuel Langhorne. See Mark Twain◊□

Clement VII 1478–1534. Illegitimate son of a brother of Lorenzo the Magnificent (see under Medici◊), he was Pope 1523–34. He refused to allow the divorce of Henry◊ VIII and Catherine◊ of Aragon. He and Leo X commissioned monuments for the Medici chapel from Michelangelo◊□

Clement of Alexandria c150–c215AD. Greek theologian who applied Greek philosophical ideas to Christian doctrine, and was the teacher of Origen◊□

Clementi Muzio 1752–1832. Italian pianist, whose *Gradus ad Parnassum* 1817 is still in use today□

Cleon d. 422BC. Athenian military leader in the Peloponnesian War, an opponent of Pericles and of peace with Sparta; he was killed fighting against them at Amphipolis□

Cleopatra c68–30BC; Queen of Egypt 51–48 and 47–30. She succeeded her father jointly with her younger brother Ptolemy◊ XIII, whom she married according to Pharaonic custom. When Julius Caesar arrived in Egypt in 49BC, he restored her to the throne from which she had been ousted in favour of her brother. She became his mistress, returning with him to Rome until his assassination, and bore him a son, Caesarion. In 41BC she met Mark◊ Antony who, after returning to Rome in 40 to marry Octavia (sister of the future Augustus◊), settled with Cleopatra in Egypt, where she bore him three sons. In 32BC open war broke out with Augustus, and after Actium◊

in 31BC, Antony and Cleopatra were besieged in Alexandria. Cleopatra killed herself with an asp after Antony's suicide. By descent she was Macedonian, not Egyptian. Caesarion was put to death by Augustus□

Cleopatra's Needle name for two obelisks, actually much older than Cleopatra's time, erected at Heliopolis in the 15th century BC by Thothmes III, and taken to Alexandria by Augustus c14BC. One has been in London, on the Victoria embankment, since 1878; the other in Central Park NY since 1881□

Clerk Maxwell James. See Maxwell◊□

Clermont-Ferrand industrial city (rubber, textiles), capital of the Auvergne, France; population 153 400. At a council here Urban II ordered the First Crusade 1095□

Cleveland Stephen Grover 1837–1908. 22nd and 24th President of the USA. The first Democratic president to be elected after the Civil War, he was the only president to hold office for two non-consecutive terms, 1885–9 and 1893–7□

Cleveland NE county of England.

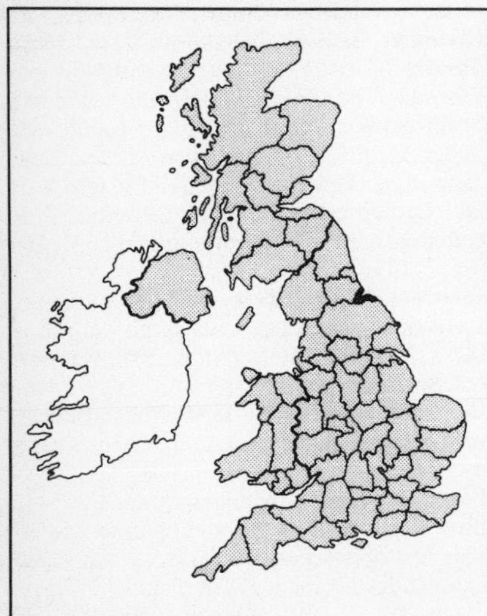

area 583 sq km/225 sq mi
towns administrative headquarters Middlesbrough; Stockton on Tees, Billingham, Hartlepool
features river Tees, with Seal Sands wildfowl refuge at its mouth; North Yorkshire Moors National Park
products Teesside, the industrial area at the mouth of the Tees, has Europe's largest steel complex (at Redcar) and chemical site (ICI, using gas and local potash), as well as an oil fuel terminal at Seal Sands and natural gas terminal at St Fergus
population 568 700□

Cleveland largest city in Ohio, USA; population 2 050 000. Industries include iron and steel, and oil refining□

click-beetle a type of beetle◊□

climate the average weather conditions of a place. Primary factors determining the variations of climate over the surface of earth are: 1 the effect of latitude and the tilt of earth's axis to the plane of the orbit about the sun; 2 the difference between land and sea; 3 contours of the ground. There may also be variations in the amount of heat given out by the sun over an extended period; and catastrophic variations may be caused by the impact of another planetary body, or clouds resulting from volcanic activity□

Clio in Greek mythology, the inventor of epic poetry and history. See Muses◊□

Clive of Plassey. Robert, Baron Clive of Plassey 1725–74. British soldier-administrator, known as Clive of India, who established British rule in India, as against the French. In 1751 he captured and held Arcot (SW of Madras) against the French for 53 days and in 1757 recaptured Calcutta from the Nawab of Bengal, Suraj-ud-Dowlah (of Black Hole of Calcutta◊ notoriety), who favoured the French, and defeated him at Plassey, securing control of Bengal. As Governor of Bengal 1757–60 and 1765–6, he carried out many great and necessary reforms, but his enemies secured a parliamentary inquiry into his conduct 1772–3. He was virtually acquitted, but the charges preyed on his mind, and he committed suicide□

Cliveden country house of Lord Astor, near Maidenhead on the Thames, a hotel from 1985. Lady Astor used it for politically influential house-parties. A cottage in the grounds, let to Stephen Ward, became notorious for events connected with the Profumo◊ Affair 1961–3□

clock any device for measuring time. Sundials, water clocks, and sand glasses (in use in the Royal Navy until 1820) were early means of measurement. The Chinese developed an astronomical clock in the 11th century, but the first public clock in Europe was set up in Milan in 1353, and the first watches were made in Nuremberg shortly after 1500. The most accurate method of timekeeping (to one millionth of a second per day) is the atomic clock, in which electronic circuits link with the atomic resonance of caesium atoms to control the frequency of a quartz crystal oscillator□

clock biological. An inherent rhythm in the physiology of living organisms. Such clocks (possibly a function of enzyme systems and membrane activity) are common to all animals (except organisms without a discrete nucleus), and in higher organisms there may be a series, e.g. human body temperature and activity cycles are normally set to 24 hours, but these may vary independently, showing two clocks are involved. See circadian rhythm◊□

cloisonné ornamental technique in which strips of metal follow a pattern on a metal surface, and the interstices are filled with coloured enamels□

clone a sexual reproduction of a genetic 'carbon copy' of an animal or plant (from the Greek for 'twig'), e.g. orchids and commercial oil palms are produced by test-tube culture of an almost invisible segment of tissue. With animals, it has been achieved with mice – in Switzerland in 1981, by Karl Ilmensee (Swiss) and Peter Hoppe (USA) – and is potentially possible with human beings, i.e. the nucleus of an unfertilized human egg cell would be replaced by the nucleus of a cell from the person to be cloned□

closed shop any body which requires its employees to be a member of a designated union; the practice became legally enforceable in the UK in 1976, but was rendered largely inoperable by the Employment Acts of 1980 and 1982. Usually demanded by unions, it may be preferred by employers as simplifying negotiation, but it was condemned by the European Court of Human Rights in 1981□

clothes moth a type of moth◊□

cloud a mass of water particles visible in the sky. Clouds are formed by the cooling of air containing water vapour which condenses generally on tiny dust particles: fog◊ (including smog) and mist are 'clouds' at ground level. Clouds in the sky are classified by their height and form:

high 10 000 m/30 000 ft approx: ***cirrus*** feathery wisps; ***cirro-stratus*** thin white sheet.

medium 3–7500 m/10–24 000 ft: ***cirro-cumulus*** overall tufts; ***altocumulus*** larger tufts, also arranged in lines; ***altostratus*** grey sheet

low up to 2000 m/7000 ft: ***stratocumulus*** dull grey leaden sky; ***nimbus*** dark grey, shapeless rain clouds; ***stratus*** sheets parallel to the horizon, high 'fogs'

vertically extending 1500–2000 m/4500–6000 ft ***cumulus*** flat-based cotton wool clouds; 6000 m/20 000 ft ***cumulonimbus*** tall, domed 'cauliflowers'

Otherwise ordinary-looking clouds may be associated with strong erratic winds (microbursts), lasting only a few minutes, which move downward and outward with sufficient power to bring down an airliner□

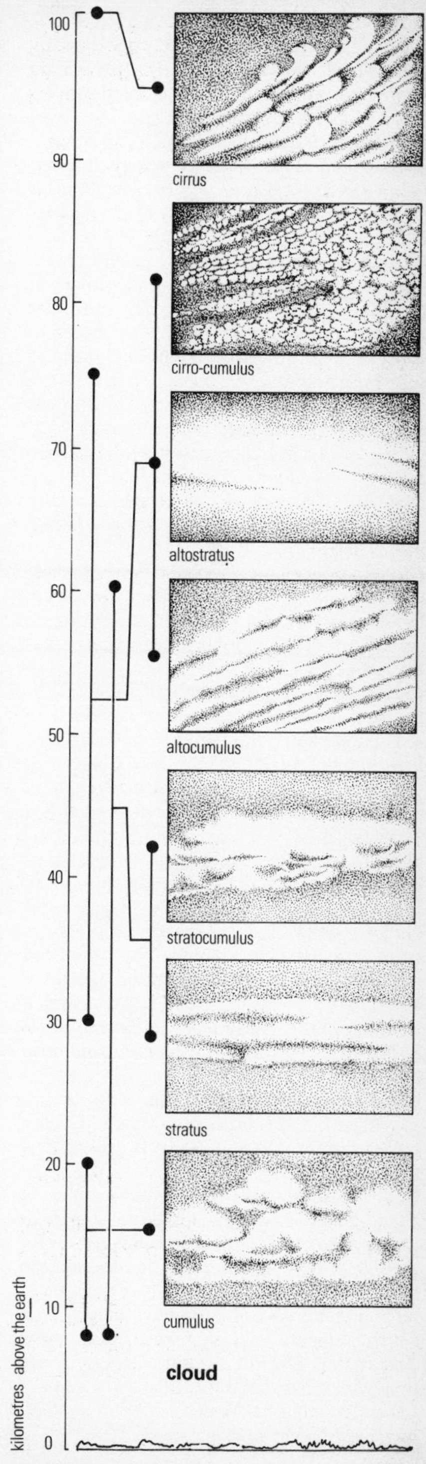

cloud

cloud chamber apparatus devised by C T R Wilson◊ to track electrically charged particles, which leave a condensation trail behind them if passed through a vessel filled with air or gas, supersaturated with vapour. See bubble chamber◊□

Clouet Jean c1846–1541. French artist, court painter to Francis I, as was his son ***François Clouet,*** who also served Henry II and Charles IX□

Clough Arthur Hugh 1819–61. English poet, friend of Matthew Arnold◊, and subject of the latter's elegy 'Thyrsis'. His verse has regained popularity in the 20th century as expressive of religious doubt and lack of self-commitment□

clover herbaceous plants, *Trifolium* species, with trifoliate leaves, family Leguminosae, e.g. the perennial Eurasian ***alsike*** *T hybridum*, introduced to England from the Netherlands as a pasture crop with soil-enriching (nitrogen-fixing) properties□

cloves the aromatic unopened flower buds of the tropical ***clove tree***, *Eugenia aromatica*, family Myrtaceae◊; used for flavouring in cookery; oil of cloves has tonic and carminative properties□

Clovis 465–511. Merovingian king of the Franks, succeeding his father Childeric in 481. He defeated the Gallo-Romans at Soissons in 486, the Alemanni near Cologne in 496, and the Arian Visigoths at Poitiers in 507. He made Paris his capital, and was a Christian□

clubfoot congenital deformity of the forepart of the foot, which does not allow the foot to rest flat on the ground□

club mosses class Lycopodiales of plants belonging to the Pteridophyta. Important and numerous in Palaeozoic◊ times, often as large trees, they are now mostly widely distributed small species, e.g. ***common club moss*** or ***stag's horn moss*** *Lycopodium clavatum*, found on upland heaths□

clubroot disease attacking the roots of cabbages and other brassicas, which develop knotty outgrowths and die; it is caused by a slime-mould◊□

Cluj industrial city, the former capital of Transylvania, Romania; population 274 000□

Cluny town in E France; population 3570. Its abbey, now in ruins, was the foundation house of the Cluniac order, originally a reformed branch of the Benedictines□

Clutha longest river in South Island, New Zealand; 338 km/210 mi; there are hydroelectric installations□

Clwyd county of N Wales

area 2427 sq km/937 sq mi

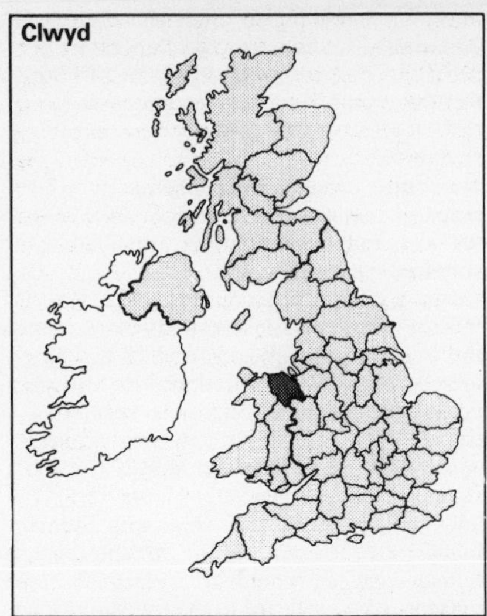

towns administrative headquarters Mold; Flint, Denbigh, Wrexham; seaside resorts Colwyn Bay, Rhyl, Prestatyn

features rivers Dee and Clwyd; Clwydian Range with Offa's Dyke along the main ridge; Chirk, Denbigh, Flint, and Rhuddlan castles; Blaenau Ffestiniog Railway (steam) and the nearby Llechwedd slate 'caverns'; Greenfield Valley, NW of Flint, was one of the generators of the industrial revolution before steam, and is now a country park and museum of industrial archaeology, from 1984

products dairy and meat products; optical glass, chemicals, limestone

population 383 680

language 19% Welsh-speaking□

Clyde Colin Campbell, 1st Baron Clyde 1792–1863. British field marshal. He commanded the Highland Brigade at Balaclava◊, and as Commander-in-Chief during the Indian Mutiny raised the siege of Lucknow and captured Cawnpore□

Clyde river in Strathclyde, W Scotland; 170 km/106 mi long. The Firth of Clyde and Firth of Forth are linked by the Forth and Clyde canal, 56 km/35 mi long. The shipbuilding yards have declined, but are still important, and there are the nuclear submarine bases of Faslane (Polaris) and Holy Loch (USA Poseidon)□

Clydebank town on the Clyde, in Strathclyde, Scotland; population 51 656. John Brown's shipyard produced the transatlantic liners e.g. *Queen Elizabeth II*□

Clytemnestra In Greek Mythology, the wife of Agamemnon◊□

coal fossil fuel formed by the heating and compression of plant remains in prehistoric times: the stages in its creation being represented by the increasingly harder and darker peat, lignite or brown coal, bituminous coal, and anthracite. Extraction is now mechanical, with underground gasification being preferred where the coal is of a suitable type, as in USA. Synthetic petrol can be made from it, as in S Africa, but its chief importance is as a cheaper fuel for industry, etc., than oil□

coastguard organization to prevent smuggling, formed in Britain after the Napoleonic Wars, and which (administered by the Department of Trade) also assists distressed ships, watches for oil slicks, etc. The ***US Coast Guard***, established in 1915, has wider duties, including the enforcement of law and order on the high seas, maintaining lighthouses, etc. The ***Australian Coastwatchers***, established in 1919, civilians organized for home defence, won distinction in World War II in an active role in New Guinea and the Pacific Islands against the Japanese□

Coatbridge industrial town in Strathclyde, Scotland; population 50 866□

coati climbing mammal, with a long flexible nose, a larger relative of the raccoon, genus *Nasua*, of S and Central America, family Procyonidae□

cobalt element
symbol Co
atomic number 27
physical description silvery-white metal
features there is a trace in the human body. It remains hard during intense heat
uses in steel alloys; radioactive cobalt-60, produced by neutron radiation in heavy water reactors (see nuclear◊ energy) is used in cancer therapy and as a tracer element□

Cobbett William 1763–1835. British journalist. Son of a farmer, he was initially Tory, but from 1802 published the weekly *Political Register,* advocating social reform. His *Rural Rides* 1830 give an excellent account of life in early-19th-century England□

Cobden Richard 1804–65. British Liberal politician and economist, who devoted himself (with John Bright◊) to the repeal of the Corn Laws◊□

Cóbh port and yachting centre in Cork, Republic of Ireland; population 6700□

Coblenz see Koblenz◊□

cob nut a type of large nut. See hazel◊□

cobra a type of poisonous snake◊□

coca S American shrub *Erythroxylon coca*, family Erythroxylaceae, grown in Bolivia for the dried leaves, the source of cocaine◊□

cocaine derivative of the leaves of the coca◊ plant, which gives a stimulus similar to amphetamine – a feeling of drive, sparkle, energy – without hangover or initial physical addiction. However, continued use leads to hallucinations, insomnia, paranoia, weight loss, and such psychological dependence that it is eventually addictive□

Cochabamba city in Bolivia; population 204 400□

Cochin port in Kerala state, India; population 438 400. Founded by Vasco da Gama in 1502, it was the first European trading post in India, and from 1530 St Francis Xavier made it a missionary centre□

Cochin former princely state of India, now included in Kerala□

Cochin-China former French colony, part of Vietnam◊ from 1949□

cochineal red dye obtained from the Mexican scale-insect *Dactylopius coccus*, order Hemiptera. Used in food and fabrics□

cockatoo a type of parrot◊□

cockchafer see chafer◊□

Cockcroft Sir John Douglas 1897–67. British physicist. He worked with Rutherford◊ at Cambridge, and in 1932 (with E T S Walton) (joint Nobel prize 1951). He later worked on the atom bomb, and was knighted in 1948 (Order of Merit 1957)□

cock-fighting the pitting of gamecocks, often armed with steel spurs, in battles on which bets are made. Banned in Britain since 1849, it continues to some extent illicitly, and is legal in some countries□

cockle a type of shellfish. See bivalve◊□

cockney a native of the City of London, traditionally born within sound of Bow Bells, Cheapside; the Cockney dialect includes a rhyming slang□

cockroach insect of the mainly tropical family Blattidae, which survive as imported pests in Europe, e.g. ***common cockroach*** *Blatta orientalis*, found in dirty houses, etc. Nocturnal and omnivorous, it leaves a disgusting smell, caused by its saliva, on whatever it touches. Australia has the world's largest, *Macropanesthinia rhinoceros*, 8 cm/3 in long□

cocoa and **chocolate** food products made from cacao 'beans' (contained in the fruit pods of the tropical American tree *Theobroma cacao*, family Sterculiaceae) which are roasted and ground. For chocolate all the cocoa butter is retained, but for drinking cocoa a proportion is removed□

coconut the hard-shelled fruit of the coconut palm. See under palm◊□

Cocos (Keeling) Islands coral atolls (27) in the Indian Ocean
area 14 sq km/5.5 sq mi
features owned by the Clunies-Ross family 1827–1978
exports copra

population 625
history discovered by William Keeling 1609, they were annexed by Britain 1857, and transferred to Australia 1955. After a referendum 1984, they were integrated within Northern Territory□

Cocteau Jean 1891–1963. French writer, who produced Dadaist verse, ballets (e.g. *Le Boeuf sur le toit,* or *The Nothing doing Bar* 1920), plays (e.g. *Orphée*), and the novel *Les Enfants terribles* 1929, which he filmed in 1950□

cod typical fish of the family Gadidae, *Gadus morhua*, brown to grey with spots. It is an important food fish found especially off Newfoundland and Iceland, and is the source of cod liver oil (rich in vitamins A and D). In the same family are the ***haddock*** *Melanogrammus aeglefinus*, usually sold split and sometimes smoked (most famous are those from Finnan, near Aberdeen); ling, pollack, whiting, and the only freshwater member, ***burbot*** *Lota lota*, of Europe and N America, 1 m/3 ft, also a food fish. Closely allied is the ***hake*** *Merluccius merluccius*, another food fish, abundant off S Britain□

codeine a drug made from opium◊□

Cod Wars the extension of Iceland's fishing limits to waters traditionally used by other nations (especially Britain) led to disputes known as Cod Wars 1952–6, 1971–3, and 1975–6□

Cody William Frederick 1846–1917. American scout and showman, known as Buffalo Bill from his contract to supply carcasses to railway labourers (over 4000 in 18 months). From 1883 he toured with a Wild West show□

Coelacanth fish, *Latimeria chalumnae,* order Crossopterygii. Found off SE Africa, it has flipper-like fins and was thought until 1938 to be extinct. It can be traced back 300 million years by fossil remains□

Coelenterata phylum of the animal kingdom distinguished from higher forms by having only one opening, the mouth, through which food is taken into the body and waste subsequently ejected. They include coral◊, jellyfish◊, sea anemones◊, and hydrozoa (which include the freshwater hydra◊). Many, such as corals and hydras, have green algae living inside them in symbiosis◊, some of the sugars photosynthesized by the algae going to the animal, and nitrogenous material from the animal going to the algae. Most spectacular of the hydrozoa is the marine ***Portuguese man-of-war*** in which the chief member of the colony develops a blue or reddish semi-transparent 'frill' which serves as a sail, and the rest are polyps with stinging tentacles dangerous to swimmers□

Coetzee J(ohn) M 1940– . South African author. In 1983 he won the Booker◊ Prize with *Life and Times of Michael K*□

coffee the 'beans', actually seeds, of cultivated forms of the tropical shrub *Coffea arabica*, family Rubiaceae; *C robusta* is used for 'instant coffee'. In plantations, it is pruned to c2 m/7 ft, and yields for 30 years; Brazil is the greatest producer□

Cognac town in SW France near which cognac brandy is produced; population 22 600□

Coimbatore industrial city in Tamil Nadu, India; population 393 100□

Coimbra former capital of Portugal 1139–1385; population 56 600□

coins pieces of metal of definite weight and value, officially stamped and used as money. See numismatics◊□

Coke Edward 1552–1634. Lord Chief Justice of England. As Attorney-General from 1594, he conducted the prosecution of Essex, Raleigh, and the Gunpowder◊ Plot conspirators, and from 1606, as Chief Justice of the Common Pleas, championed the common law against James I's attempts to exalt royal prerogative. He drew up the Petition of Right of 1628, and his *Institutes* are a legal classic□

Coke Thomas William, Earl of Leicester and Holkham 1752–1842. Known as 'Coke of Norfolk', he pioneered agricultural improvement, especially sheep breeding□

coke light industrial and domestic smokeless fuel produced by the carbonization of coal, a by-product of the manufacture of coal gas□

cola genus of tropical trees, family Sterculiaceae. Their nuts are chewed in W Africa for their high caffeine content, and in the West are used with coca leaves to flavour soft drinks□

Colbert Jean Baptiste 1619–83. French statesman. Succeeding Mazarin as chief adviser to Louis XIV, he reorganized the economy, encouraged the foundation of colonies, and tried to equal English and Dutch naval power. He was supplanted in Louis's favour eventually by Louvois, who advocated foreign conquest□

Colchester town in Essex, England; population 80 000. Founded c10AD by Cunebolinus (Cymbeline), King of the British tribe, the Catuvellauni, it was a colony of Roman veterans from 50AD (*Camulodunum*). Light industries include engineering and printing□

cold common, minor disease caused by approximately 150 different types of rhinovirus, so that a vaccine is impossible, although drugs are under development to stop the viruses multiplying□

Cold Harbor see under Civil War (1864)◊, American□

Colditz town in E Germany, near Leipzig, site of a castle used as a high-security prisoner-of-war camp (Oflag IVC) in World War II. Among daring escapes was that of Captain Patrick Reid and others in Oct 1942□

cold war term coined by Truman's adviser Bernard Baruch 1870–1965 for the economic and political hostility between the West and the East 1947–75 which resulted from reluctance to resort to nuclear war. It supposedly ended with the Helsinki Conference◊□

Coleoptera a order of beetle◊□

Coleridge Samuel Taylor 1772–1834. British poet. While at Cambridge, he was driven by debt to enlist in the Dragoons, and then in 1795, as part of an abortive plan to found a communist colony in America with Robert Southey◊ (see Susquehanna◊), married Sarah Fricker, from whom he afterwards separated. In 1798 he collaborated with Wordsworth in *Lyrical Ballads*, which include 'The Ancient Mariner', and broke with the Classical tradition of English poetry: 'Kubla Khan' and 'Christabel' were also written at this time. He became enslaved by opium and from 1816 lived at Highgate under medical care. As a philosopher, he argued inferentially that even in registering sense-perceptions the mind was performing acts of creative imagination, rather than being a passive arena in which ideas interacted mechanistically. As a critic, he brought the psychological method to bear, as in *Biographia Literaria* 1817□

Coleridge-Taylor Samuel 1875–1912. British composer, with an English mother and a father from Sierra Leone. He is remembered for his choral work *Hiawatha* 1898–1900□

Colet John c1467–1519. English humanist, influenced by Savonarola◊ and Erasmus◊. He reacted against the scholastic tradition in his interpretation of the Bible, and founded modern biblical exegesis. In 1505 he became Dean of St Paul's□

Colette Sidonie-Gabrielle 1873–1954. French writer. At twenty she married Henri Gauthier-Villars, a journalist known as 'Willy', and under this name her four 'Claudine' novels, based on her own early life, were published. Divorced in 1906, she was a striptease artist and mime for a while, but continued to write, e.g. *Chéri* 1920, *La Fin de Chéri* 1926, and *Gigi* 1944. Her work is rich with her native Burgundian countryside, and a sensitive treatment of animals□

coleus genus of perennial shrubs, family Labiatae◊, grown as house plants for their brightly coloured foliage□

Coligny Gaspard de 1519–72. French Huguenot leader, a favourite of Charles IX◊, who was killed on the eve of the St Bartholomew◊'s Day Massacre□

colitis inflammation of the walls of the colon (the large intestine). See digestion◊□

collage Dada technique of gluing (French *coller*) or sewing materials onto canvas as part of a painting. See Schwitters◊□

collagen the fibrous constituent of connective tissue, bone, and cartilage. It is used to make artificial skin for burn victims, etc.□

collective unconscious the idea of shared human ancestral memories. See Jung◊□

College of Arms see Heralds'◊ College□

collie a breed of dog◊□

Collier Jeremy 1650–1726. Anglican cleric, a Non-juror◊, who was outlawed in 1696 for granting absolution on the scaffold to two men who had tried to assassinate William III. His *Short View of the Immorality and Profaneness of the English Stage* 1698 was aimed at Congreve and Vanbrugh□

Collier Lesley 1947– . British ballerina, a principal dancer of the Royal Ballet from 1972, notably successful in *Sleeping Beauty*□

collimator in physics, a device for producing parallel rays of light, a defined beam of radiation, particles, etc.□

Collingwood Cuthbert, Baron Collingwood 1750–1810. British admiral, a friend of Nelson. He distinguished himself at the Battles of the 'Glorious First of June' in 1794 and St Vincent in 1797, and at Trafalgar◊ succeeded to the command on Nelson's death. He was buried beside Nelson in St Paul's□

Collins Michael 1890–1922. Irish Sinn Féin leader who was mainly responsible with Arthur Griffith for the treaty establishing the Irish Free State in 1921. Despite opposition from de Valera and the Republicans, he persuaded the Dáil to accept the Treaty, and during the ensuing civil war commanded the Free State forces. When Griffith died on 12 Aug, Collins became head of the State and the army, but was ambushed 10 days later and killed□

Collins William 1721–59. British pre-Romantic poet, remembered for his series of Odes, especially that 'To Evening'. After 1750 he became insane□

Collins (William) Wilkie 1824–89. British novelist, author of the dramatic, though involved narratives of *The Woman in White* 1860 (with its fat villain Count Fosco), and *The Moonstone* 1868 (with Sergeant Cuff, one of the first detectives in English literature)□

Collodi Carlo. Pseudonym of Italian writer Carlo Lorenzini 1826–90. His *The Adventure of Pinocchio* 1881–3 tells of a wooden puppet who became a boy□

colloid substance in which minute particles of one substance are finely dispersed in another, and which tend to flocculate, i.e. the particles gather together and sometimes form silt. These properties are used in casting ceramics; coating papers and photographic film; purifying water, etc. Familiar colloids include milk, ink, soap, cosmetics, fog, and opal◊. Colloids are further differentiated as ***emulsions*** when both substances are liquid (an 'emulsion paint' is one in which the particles of paint are suspended, commonly in a synthetic resin, before being dispersed in water); ***sols*** when one substance is solid and the other liquid (e.g. a solution of gelatine in water), and ***gels*** (e.g. a solution of gelatine and water which has set□

Colman Ronald 1891–1958. British actor, noted for romantic roles in *Lost Horizon* 1937 and *The Prisoner of Zenda*□

Colmar city in NE France; population 62 400. The Unterlinden Museum, a former Dominican monastery, has a famed Grünewald altarpiece□

Cologne river port (German *Köln*) and industrial city on the Rhine, N Rhine-Westphalia, W Germany; population 976 150. Some 85% of the city was destroyed in World War II, but the 13th-century cathedral survived; the university was founded 1388□

Colombes industrialized suburb of Paris, France; population 83 500□

Colombey-les-Deux-Églises village in E central France, where de Gaulle lived and was buried□

Colombia Republic of

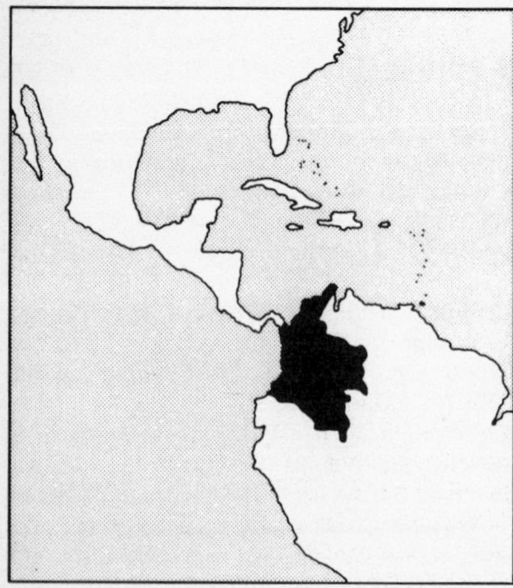

area 1 139 000 sq km/456 500 sq mi
capital Bogotá
towns Medelln, Cali, Bucaramanga; ports are Barranquilla, Cartagena
features Andes mountains
exports emeralds (world's largest producer), coffee (2nd largest world producer), bananas, cotton, meat, sugar, oil, skins and hides
currency peso
population 26 500 000, mainly of mixed Spanish-American Indian descent
language Spanish
religion Roman Catholicism
government executive president (Belisario Betancur Cuartas from 1982) and senate and house of representatives, directly elected for four years; conflict between the Liberal and Conservative parties was ended in 1957 by the formation of a National Front sharing power which successfully blocked the National Popular Alliance opposition. Colombia remains a democracy, though guerrilla activity and terrorism continue.
recent history the republic of Greater Colombia, comprising modern Colombia, Panama, Venezuela, and Ecuador, was established by Bolívar◊ in 1819, but by 1866 Colombia was within its present boundaries, except for Panama, which became a separate republic in 1903□

Colombo capital and sea port (with a fine artificial harbour) of Sri Lanka; population 562 700□

Colombo Plan Commonwealth plan for cooperative economic development in S and SE Asia which came into operation in 1951. It has 21 local members, plus Australia, Canada, Japan, New Zealand, the UK and the USA□

Colón port at the Caribbean entrance to the Panama Canal, Panama; population 1 400 000□

Colón *Archipiélago de* official name of the Galápagos Islands□

Colorado mountain state of the central USA; Centennial State
area 270 240 sq km /104 247 sq mi
capital Denver
towns Colorado Springs
features Rocky Mountain National Park; Pike's Peak; prehistoric cliff dwellings of the Mesa Verde National Park; Garden of the Gods (natural sandstone sculptures); Dinosaur and Great Sand Dunes national monuments; 'ghost' mining towns
products cereals, meat and dairy products; oil, coal, molybdenum, uranium; iron, steel, machinery
population 2 888 834
famous people Jack Dempsey, Douglas Fairbanks
history acquired partly from the Louisiana Purchase in 1803, and partly from Mexico in 1848, it became a state in 1876□

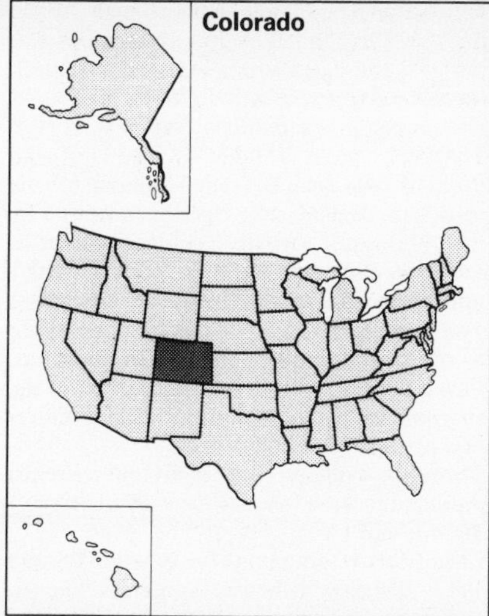

Colorado river flowing 2300 km/1450 mi from the Rocky Mountains to the Gulf of California. Hoover, Glen Canyon, and other dams for power and irrigation have destroyed its ecology, and very little water reaches the sea. The ***Colorado Desert*** to the W is an arid area 5000 sq km/2000 sq mi. See also Grand Canyon under Arizona◊□

Colorado beetle a type of beetle ◊□

Colorado Springs scenic health resort at 1800 m/6000 ft, Colorado, USA; population 207 000. Home of the US Air Force Academy and US Air Defence Command□

Colosseum ruined amphitheatre◊ in Rome built by Vespasian◊ 75–80AD; 187 m/615 ft long and 49 m/160 ft high, it seated 50–70 000. Christians were martyred here by wild beasts and gladiators. It could be flooded for mimic sea battles□

Colossus of Rhodes bronze statue (30 m/100 ft high) of Apollo erected at the island's harbour entrance 292–80 BC. One of the Seven◊ Wonders of the World, it was destroyed by an earthquake□

colour quality or wavelength of light emitted or reflected from an object. Visible white light consists of electromagnetic◊ radiation of various wavelengths, and if a beam is refracted through a prism, it can be spread out into a spectrum◊, in which the various colours correspond to the different wavelengths. From high to low wavelengths the colours are red, orange, yellow, green, blue, indigo, violet. When a surface is illuminated, some parts of the white light are absorbed, depending on the molecular structure of the material and the dyes applied to it. A surface that looks red will have absorbed the light from the blue end of the spectrum, but have a high reflection of light from the red, long-wave end□

colour blindness inability to discriminate colours, of which the most common type is an inability to distinguish red and green. It is usually hereditary and sex-linked, being more common in men than women□

colugo order of arboreal mammals (also known as flying lemurs) Dermoptera, which contains only two species. Resembling flying squirrels, they have a membrane extending round the body from head to tail, enabling them to glide□

Colum Padraic 1881–1972. Irish poet, a member of the Irish Renaissance, author of plays and homely lyrics□

Columba St 521–97. Irish saint, the apostle of Scotland, who founded the monastery of Iona◊ as his base, and whose cell there was discovered in 1958. His feast day is 9 Jun□

Columbia river flowing 1930 km/1200 mi through W Canada and USA□

Columbia capital of S Carolina, USA; population 114 000. Fort Jackson is nearby□

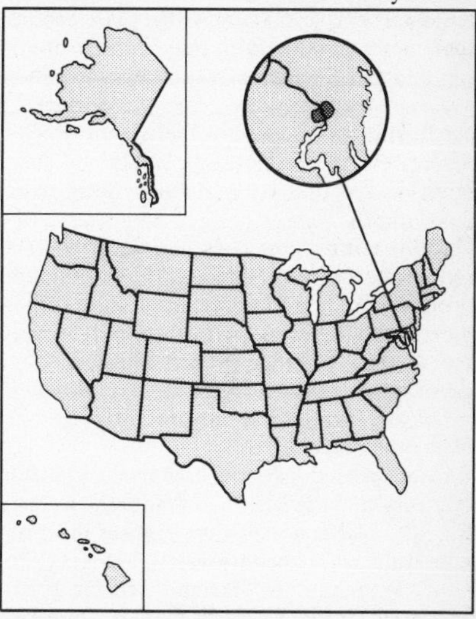

Columbia District of. Seat of the federal government of the USA, coterminous with the capital, Washington◊. Situated on the Potomac river, it was ceded by Maryland as the national capital site in 1790.

area 178 sq km/69 sq mi□

population 638 000

history the District of Columbia, comprising land ceded from Maryland and Virginia, was established by Act of Congress in 1790–1, and became the seat of Congress in 1800□

Columbine a plant of the family Ranunculaceae◊□

columbium see niobium◊□

Columbus Christopher 1451–1506. Italian navigator. Sponsored by Ferdinand◊ and Isabella◊ of Spain to find a new route to the East, he set sail on 3 Aug 1492, and on 12 Oct sighted Watling Island (now San Salvador: see Bahamas◊), later sighting Cuba and Haiti (site of his wrecked flagship, *Santa Maria*, off Hispaniola, located in 1968). He made a 2nd voyage 1493–6, discovering more West Indian islands; and a 3rd in 1498, in which he discovered S America and the Orinoco. However, his colonists complained about him, and he was sent home in chains. Recovering favour, he made a 4th voyage 1502–4, still trying to find a passage to India. He died in poverty, and is buried in Seville Cathedral. The cost of his initial voyage was queried, until it was pointed out that it cost the same as one banquet for Isabella□

Columbus industrial city (cars, planes, missiles, etc.), capital of Ohio, USA; population 561 950□

column round or polygonal vertical support for a building, of which the classical Greek types (orders) are: ***Doric*** with a plain capital; ***Ionic*** more slender, with large volutes on the capital; and ***Corinthian*** which has acanthus◊ leaves instead of volutes. See architecture◊□

coma state of unconsciousness from which a person cannot be roused, caused by head injuries, cerebral haemorrhage, drug overdose, etc.□

Combination Acts laws passed 1799–1800 rendering trade unions illegal in Britain, and prompted by fear of political agitation such as had caused the French Revolution; they were repealed in 1824. See Francis Place◊□

combined operations war operations in which air, land, and sea forces work together. See commandos◊□

Comecon established in 1949 by the USSR in opposition to the Marshall Plan◊, the ***Co***uncil for ***M***utual ***E***conomic ***Co***operatio***n*** links her with Bulgaria, Czechoslovakia, Hungary, Poland, Romania, E Germany (from 1950), Mongolia (from 1962), Vietnam (from 1978), and Albania (1949–61). The Soviet Union makes large-scale deals with the West, though discouraging them in other members, and so controls the dissemination of Western-derived science and expertise, so that Comecon differs from the Common Market in having no real central organization, and no free trade□

Comédie Française French national theatre (for both comedy and tragedy) in Paris, founded by Louis XIV in 1680. Its base is the Salle Richelieu on the right bank, and the Théâtre de l'Odéon on the left tries out avant-garde ideas□

comet celestial body with a small frozen nucleus, surrounded by an envelope of tenuous gas, and often with a long luminous tail: the solar system has a 'halo' of them thought to number many millions (see Jan Oort◊). The most famous is Halley's◊. The Tunguska event of 1908, which levelled Siberian forests near Lake Baikal, may have been caused by the collision of a comet nucleus with earth; they may also cause Ice Ages, cooling earth's upper atmosphere with their dust particles; or even have carried the 'building blocks' of life to our own and other planets. In the future they may be exploited for mineral resources, and used as space bases, especially for undertaking journeys to the stars□

Comines Philippe de c1445–1509. French diplomat in the service of Louis XI, author of *Mémoires*□

Cominform Communist Information Bureau 1947–1956, established by Andrei Zhdanov to exchange information between European Communist parties. Yugoslavia was expelled in 1948□

Comintern abbreviation of ***Com***munist ***Inter******n***ational◊□

commandos originally Boer military raiders against native African peoples or the British in the S African War. In World War II, the 'amphibious guerrillas' used by the British after Dunkirk in raids on German-occupied territory, etc., as at St Nazaire◊, Dieppe◊, Rommel's headquarters in the Western Desert in Nov 1941, in Normandy on D-Day, and the later crossing of the Rhine. After the war they were disbanded, but the organization was carried on by the Royal Marines□

Commissioners for Oaths those appointed by the Lord Chancellor, usually practising solicitors, to administer oaths or take affidavits□

committal proceedings a hearing before a UK magistrate to decide whether there is a case to answer before a higher court. It is unreported to safeguard the defendant, unless he wishes the restrictions lifted□

Commodoro Rivadavia port in SE Argentina; population 70 000. Argentina's main oilfields are nearby□

Commodus Lucius Aelius Aurelius 161–92AD. Roman emperor from 180. Son of Marcus◊ Aurelius, he was a tyrant, and was strangled by his household□

common an unfenced area of grassland which all people are free to use. See under manor◊□

common law English law not embodied in legislation, but in judicial decisions□

Common Market another name for the European◊ Economic Community□

Common Prayer Book of. Church of England service book, based on the Roman breviary, and first published in 1549 (subsequently revised); the *Church's Alternative Service Book* 1980, in modern language, coexists with it□

Commons House of, the lower but more powerful, of the two parts of the British and Canadian Parliament◊□

Commonwealth of Nations The (British) name from 1931 (suggested by Smuts◊ in 1917) of the British Empire; the adjective 'British' ceased to be used after World War II. Its 48 members (one third of the world's independent sovereign states, and c1 150 000 000 people) are as follows, with dates of independence (those in *italics* are not independent):

Africa Botswana 1966, *British Indian Ocean Territory*, Gambia 1965, Ghana 1957, Kenya 1963, Lesotho 1966, Malawi 1964, Mauritius 1968, Nigeria 1960, *St Helena*, Seychelles 1976, Sierra Leone 1961, Swaziland 1968, Tanzania 1961–3, Uganda 1962, Zambia 1964, Zimbabwe 1980.

The Americas *Anguilla*, Antigua 1981, Bahamas 1973, Barbados 1966, Belize 1981, *Bermuda, British Virgin Islands*, Canada 1867, *Cayman Islands*, Dominica 1978, Grenada 1974, Guyana 1966, Jamaica 1962, *Montserrat*, St Kitts-Nevis 1983, St Lucia 1979, St Vincent and the Grenadines 1979, Trinidad and Tobago 1962, *Turks and Caicos Islands*.

Asia Bangladesh 1972, *Brunei*, Cyprus 1961, *Hong Kong*, India 1947, Federation of Malaysia 1957–63, Singapore 1965, Sri Lanka 1948, Maldives 1982.

Australia and the Pacific Australia 1901, Fiji 1970, Kiribati 1979, Nauru 1968, New Zealand 1907, Papua New Guinea 1975, *Pitcairn*, Solomon Islands 1978, Tonga 1970, Tuvalu 1978, Vanuatu 1980, Western Samoa 1970.

Europe United Kingdom, *Gibraltar*, Malta 1964.

Other countries formerly linked with Britain, but not now members of the Commonwealth, are:

Burma, part of Cameroon, Egypt, Iraq, the areas which now form Israel and Jordan, Maldive Islands, Pakistan, part of Somalia, South Africa, Sudan, South Yemen.

Bodies dealing with Commonwealth affairs include the Foreign and Commonwealth Office, headed by the Foreign Secrtary; Commonwealth Development Corporation 1948; Royal Commonwealth Society 1868; Commonwealth Institute 1887, with permanent galleries in Kensington High Street, London, and Commonwealth Foundation 1965, for contacts between professional people. See also Commonwealth Conference◊ and Commonwealth Day◊□

Commonwealth Conference top-level consultations originating in the Colonial Conferences held at intervals from 1887, but now more informal and convened anywhere in the Commonwealth. Since 1965 there has been a permanent organization headed by a Secretary-General; Canadian diplomat Arnold Smith 1965–75, Shridath Ramphal 1975– □

Commonwealth Day celebrated on the official birthday of Elizabeth II in Jun□

Commune the two periods of government in France:

The Paris municipal government 1789–94 established after the storming of the Bastille, and powerful in the French Revolution until after the fall of Robespierre.

The provisional national government 18 Mar–May 1871 often considered the first socialist government in history. Elected after the right-wing National Assembly at Versailles tried to disarm the National Guard, it fell when the Versailles troops captured Paris and massacred c20 000 people 21–8 May□

Communism revolutionary socialism◊ based on the idea, expressed by Marx◊ and Engels◊ in the *Communist Manifesto* 1848, that human society, having passed through successive stages of slavery, feudalism, and capitalism (the last being now also outmoded), must advance to a communist society based on common ownership of the means of production and a planned economy.

Only in 1917 in Russia, where the underlying communal basis of feudalism was still strong, was such a system imposed (see Lenin◊ and Stalin◊) in Europe. After World War II Communism was enforced in those countries which came under Soviet occupation, and in China, which until 1961 was under Soviet tutelage, as the fount of doctrine and source of technological aid. Communism was also influential in Third World countries which identified colonialism with capitalism, although Russia, in terms of areas occupied and held from the colonialist period, still remains the world's largest colonial power. The denunciation of Stalinism by Khrushchev◊ in 1956 was the first crack in the Soviet Communist ideal, and was followed by the Hungarian revolt: see also Czechoslovakia◊, Poland◊, Romania◊, Yugoslavia◊. Many Communist parties inside Europe (e.g. the Eurocommunism of France, Italy, and the major part of the British Communist Party) and outside (e.g. Japan) have rejected since the 1960s or later any suggestion of automatic Soviet dominance. In the 1980s there was an expansion of economic freedom in E Europe: USSR, E Germany, Czechoslovakia, and Romania remaining strongly socialist, and stressing modernization and technical efficiency; whereas Hungary, Bulgaria, Poland, and Yugoslavia moved towards decentralization, competition, and the market place. See also Chile◊, Cuba◊, Kampuchea◊, North Korea◊, Libya◊, Nicaragua◊, Vietnam◊□

Communism Peak highest mountain (*Pik Kommunizma*) in the USSR; 7495 m/24 589 ft□

community service work for the elderly, handicapped, etc., introduced in the UK in 1972 as an alternative to prison for minor offenders□

commutator electromechanical device transforming alternating current produced by a dynamo into direct current□

Como city on Lake Como, Italy; population 95 600. The lake shores are very beautiful□

Comorin the most southerly cape of the Indian sub-continent□

Comoro Islands archipelago in the Mozambique Channel, NW of Madagascar□

Comoros Federal Islamic Republic of

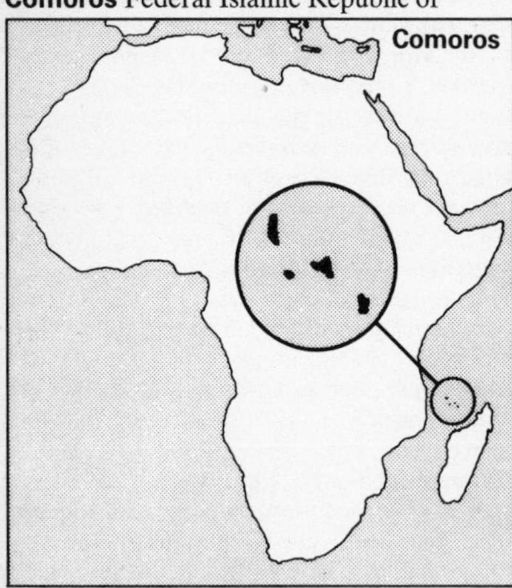

area 2170 sq km/838sq mi
capital Moroni
features comprises islands of Grand Comore, Anjouan, Maheli
exports copra, vanilla, cacao, sisal, coffee, cloves, essential oils
currency CFA franc
population 300 200
language French, Arabic (official); Comorian (Swahili dialect)
religion Islam (official)
government under the 1978 constitution an executive president (Ahmed Abdallah Abderemane), and a unicameral federal assembly.
recent history formerly French, the islands became independent in 1975 (except for the island of Mayotte◊). They have a reputation as a mercenary hideaway and French secret service gathering point□

Companions of Honour British order of chivalry 1917: members (65 men or women) add the letters CH to their names□

company a group of people combined together for business or trade. Public companies must have at least seven members, and their shares are offered to the public; whereas those of a private company, minimum membership two, are not. The word 'Limited', as in Public Limited Company (plc), indicates that the liability of the members is limited, i.e. usually to the amount of their shares if the firm becomes insolvent.

Common in Europe is a supervisory board representing shareholders, workers, and, where necessary, the public. This two-tier system may become mandatory throughout the Common Market, and would act as a check on the operations of companies which are active in more than one country□

compass

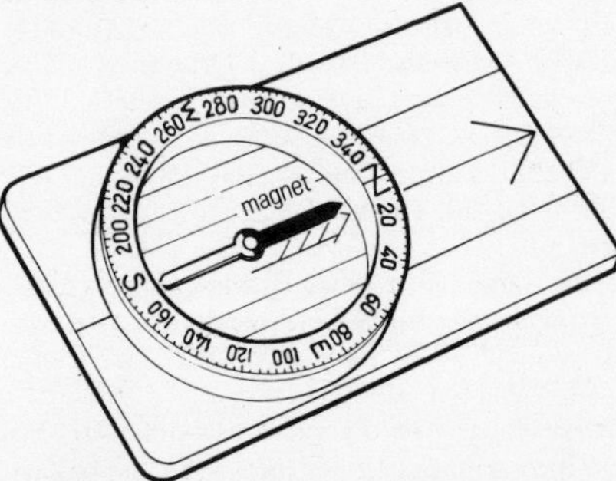

compass an instrument for showing direction. A ***magnetic compass*** comprises a freely pivoted magnetic needle which turns to the magnetic north, from which the true north can then be found by correction. In a ***gyrocompass,*** a gyroscope◊ has its axis kept horizontal, pointing always to the true north. See also magnetism◊□

Compiègne town in N France; population 40 720. The château was built by Louis XV, and the armistices of 1918 and 1940 were signed (the latter by Hitler–Pétain) in a railway coach in the Forest of Compiègne□

complex (psychology) a group of ideas, repressed as unpleasant, but still active in the unconscious mind and continuing to affect a person's actions, e.g. the Oedipus◊ and inferiority complexes□

complex number ordered pair of real numbers obeying certain defined rules of combination. For historical reasons, in the complex number (a, b), (often written a + ib), a is called 'the real part' and b 'the imaginary part'. Thus i would be the complex number (0, 1). By the rules of complex algebra (0, 1) x (0, 1) = (-1, 0) i.e. $i^2 = -1$. Thus i can be regarded as the square root of −1□

Compositae the daisy family; dicotyledenous flowering plants characterized by flowers borne in composite heads. It is the largest family of flowering plants, the majority being herbaceous. Birds seem to favour the family for use in nest 'decoration', possibly because many species either repel or kill insects (see pyrethrum◊). Species include the daisy and dandelion; food plants artichoke, lettuce, safflower; and the garden chrysanthemum, dahlia, daisybush, and zinnia□

composite engineering material combining complementary constituents, e.g. fibres of asbestos, glass, or carbon steel, or 'whiskers' of silicon carbide, which are dispersed in a continuous matrix of plastic, concrete, steel, etc.□

Compton-Burnett Dame Ivy 1892–1969. British novelist, who used dialogue to convey the tyranny of family relationships e.g. *Pastors and Masters* 1925 and *The Mighty and Their Fall* 1961□

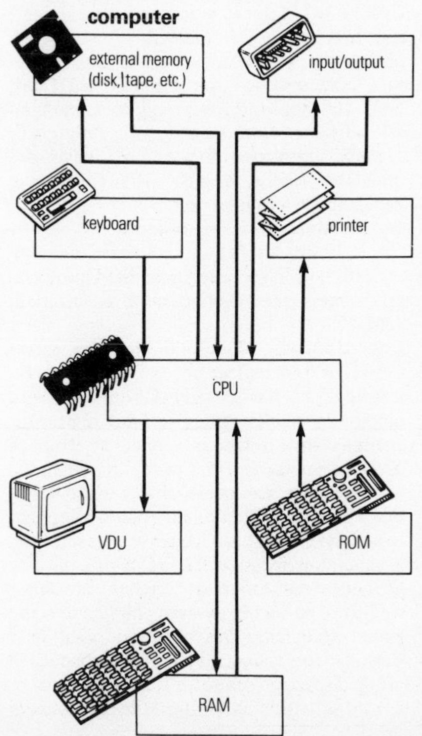

computer a programmable electronic device that can store, retrieve, and process data (words and numbers). A typical ***microcomputer*** consists of several pieces of ***hardware***: a ***system unit***, which contains the processor; a ***keyboard***, which is used to input data and instructions; a screen or ***visual display unit*** (VDU), which is used to display data; and some form of memory storage, usually in the forma of ***floppy*** or ***hard disks***. Computer memory is of two kinds: ***read-only memory*** (ROM) which cannot be erased by the user, and ***random-access memory*** (RAM), which holds whatever information the user requires. To make the computer operate, some form of ***software*** is required: an ***operating system***, which enables the user to carry out certain functions on the machine; and a ***program***, usually designed to do one particular function, e.g. financial analysis (a spreadsheet), word processing, or data manipulation (a database). In the 1980s microcomputers established themselves in both the home and business, one particular microcomputer, the IBM PC, dominating the business market to such an extent that it set a standard which other manufacturers were obliged to follow.

Minicomputers are essentially similar machines, physically larger and free-standing, which enable more than one user access at the same time.

Mainframe computers are larger still and more powerful, and are used in large businesses and government departments where there is a need to process huge amounts of data□

computer games are generally of three types:

arcade games e.g. *Space Invaders* which depend chiefly on quickness of reaction and motor control;

puzzle games which involve strategic decisions and exercise the memory;

adventure games which may follow a prescribed plot, as in educational ones based on Shakespeare's plays, or may incorporate an element of chance, so that the player creates his own story of how he defeats the evil opponent confronting him. More recently games combining all three of these principles have been developed□

computer graphics method of creating pictures and patterns by a computer program (see also fractal◊). It is used for scientific purposes, flight simulators (for training pilots to fly), film cartoon animation, and computer games. The range of colour and speed of animation has been rapidly increased, but, to rival first-rate colour photography, an 18 000-line video display is required, as against the 625 lines of a domestic television screen□

Comte Auguste 1798–1857. French mathematician-philosopher. He founded Positivism◊ or the Religion of Humanity, in the belief that man has no knowledge of anything but phenomena, and such knowledge is relative not absolute. Instead of God, adoration is directed to the Great Being or personification of humanity as a whole. J S Mill◊ financially assisted his work□

Conakry capital and chief port of the Repubic of Guinea on the island of Tombo, linked with the mainland by a causeway; population 525 750□

concentration camp a large enclosed area where political prisoners etc. are imprisoned. In World War II, Nazi detention and mass extermination camps for Jews, political opponents, etc.: Belsen, Buchenwald, Dachau, Ebensee, Mauthausen, and (in Poland) Maidanek and Oswiecim (Auschwitz). Some six million are estimated to have been sent to the gas chambers in these camps, and medical experiments on the living were carried out. See Eichmann◊□

Concepción coal and steel city in Chile; population 170 000□

concertina wind musical instrument with free reeds, consisting of two keyboards of buttons connected by expansible and folding bellows. The English concertina, was invented by Wheatstone◊ in 1829□

concerto composition, usually in three movements, for solo instrument or instruments and orchestra□

conch a type of shellfish. See under gastropod◊□

Conchobar king of Ulster, whose intended bride, Deirdre, eloped with Noïse. She died of sorrow when her jilted lover killed her husband and his brothers□

conclave Papal. The gathering of cardinals at Rome to elect a new Pope, when they are accommodated in individual wooden cells, and locked in secret conclave ('with a key') until they reach a decision by vote. Results are given by smoke signal: black for an indecisive vote, white for an agreed choice□

Concord town in Massachusetts, USA; population 16 200. Site of the first battle of the War of American Independence, 19 Apr 1775. Emerson, Thoreau, Hawthorne, and Louisa Alcott lived here□

concordat agreement regulating relations between the Papacy and a secular government, e.g. that for France between Pius VII and Napoleon, which lasted 1801–1905; and in Italy Mussolini's Concordat, which lasted 1929–78, and which safeguarded the position of the Church, until replaced by that of 1984 in which Roman Catholicism was no longer the 'state religion'□

concrete mixture of cement, sand, and crushed stone or gravel, which when dry has stone-like qualities. First used by the Romans before 500BC, but the type known as Portland cement was not invented till 1824 by Joseph Aspdin□

Condé French family founded by ***Louis de Bourbon*** 1530–69, an uncle of Henry IV of France, who was prominent as a Huguenot leader in the Wars of Religion. ***Louis II***, called the Great Condé 1621–86, won brilliant victories during the Thirty Years' War at Rocroi in 1643 and Lens in 1648, but rebelled in 1651 and entered the Spanish service. Pardoned in 1660, he commanded Louis XIV's armies against the Spaniards and the Dutch□

conditioned reflex response to an associated stimulus, e.g. a dog's mouth watering not only on seeing food, but when the meal bell rings, and considered not consciously learnt, but the result of nerve processes in the brain. See Behaviourism◊, Pavlov◊□

condominium joint rule by two or more states, e.g. Canton and Enderbury Islands◊□

condor a type of vulture◊□

Condorcet Marie Jean Antoine Nicolas Caritat, Marquis de Condorcet 1743–94. French philosopher-politician. One of the Girondins◊, he opposed the execution of Louis XVI, and was imprisoned and poisoned himself. His *Historical Survey of the Progress of Human Understanding* 1795 envisaged inevitable future progress, though not the perfectibility of human nature□

Coney Island see Long Island◊□

Confederate States the Southern states of the USA, which seceded from the Union and established the Confederacy government 1861–5□

Confederation of British Industry established 1965 to replace several earlier organizations, it voices general policies of employers on all economy related matters□

confession a religious service at which a person tells his sins to a priest. It originated with the Jews, and passed into Christian use. For a Roman Catholic, auricular confession, to a priest empowered to give him absolution, is an annual obligation; it is also practised by Orthodox and Oriental churches, as well as spilling over into Protestant practice to some extent from the 19th century. Since 1977 Catholic confession may be made openly in group discussion or face-to-face with a priest, as well as in the anonymity of the confessional 'box'□

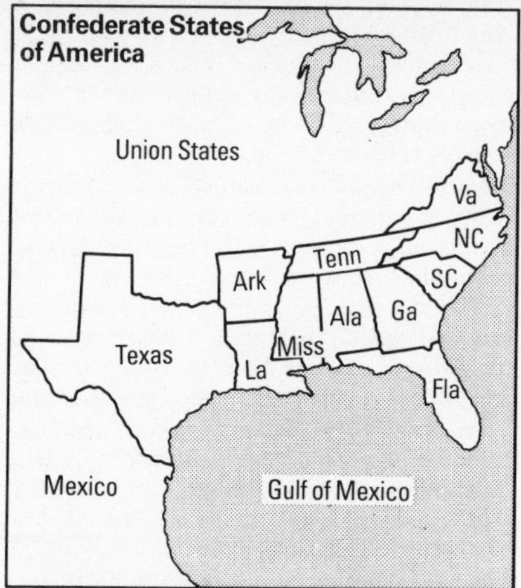

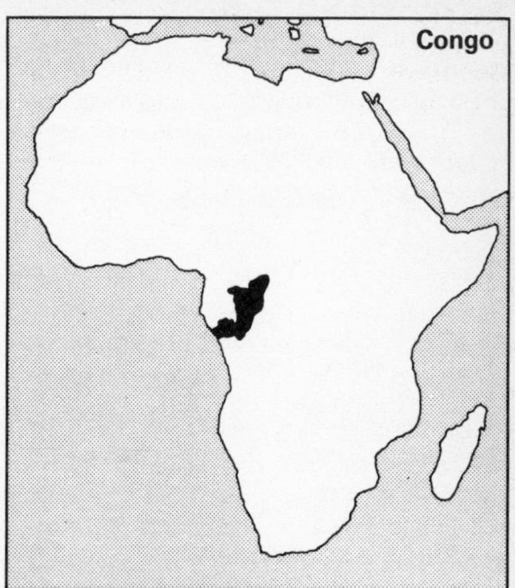

confirmation rite admitting the baptized to full Christian Church membership through the laying on of hands by a bishop, so that the gift of the Holy Spirit may be received□

Confucianism code of living derived from the canonical books, known as the *Five Ching*, 'edited' rather than originated by Kong Zi◊; they include historical material, philosophy (see Yin and Yang◊), poetry, rites, and ceremonies, and the ***I Ching,*** a method of divination. The writer advocated humane order in family life as in society as a whole, in fact a Golden Rule of temperate behaviour in all circumstances, without venturing into religious speculation. His teachings were adopted as the Chinese 'national religion', continuing even under Communism from 1912 until the anti-Confucius campaign 1974–6, but in 1982 Kong Zi was rehabilitated by the Communist Party□

Confucius see Kong Zi◊□

conga a Latin American dance, originally from Cuba, in which the participants, usually in a line, take three steps forwards or backwards and then kick□

congé d'élire (French 'permission to elect') a writ from the King or Queen to a cathedral chapter stating the name of a person who is to be invited to become bishop of that diocese. Introduced in England in 1533□

conger a type of large eel◊□

conglomerate a coarse-grained sedimentary rock, consisting of small pieces of former rocks joined together; used in roadmaking□

Congo see Zaïre◊□

Congo People's Republic of the
area 342 000 sq km/132 000 sq mi
captial Brazzaville
towns chief port Pointe Noire
features Zaïre (Congo) river on the border; half the country is rainforest.
exports timber, potash, petroleum
currency CFA franc
population 1 580 000, chiefly Bantu
language French (official)
religion Animism 50%, Christianity 48%
government under the 1979 constitution there is an executive president (Denis Sassou-Nguesso from 1979) and people's national assembly; since 1969 the Parti Congolais de Travail (PCT) has been the sole political party.
recent history a French colony from 1882, it became independent in 1960. Periodic fighting and military interventions occurred until Sassou-Nguesso took office. Links with the Soviet Union have been strengthened (treaty of cooperation 1981)□

Congregationalism form of Protestant church organization in which each congregation manages its own affairs, though there may be a consultative body, e.g. the United Reformed Church (England and Wales) 1972, and its Scottish counterpart the Congregational Union of Scotland. See Robert Browne◊□

Congress national legislature of USA: House of Representatives (435 members, apportioned to the States on the basis of population, serving two-year terms) and Senate (100 senators, two for each State, elected for six years, one third elected every two years). The Senate and the House of Representatives have equal legislative responsibility□

Congress of Industrial Organizations see American Federation of Labor and Congress of Industrial Organizations◊□

Congress Party the Indian National Congress was founded by Englishman A O Hume in 1885. Later leaders include Gandhi◊, Nehru◊, and Indira Gandhi◊, and it remained almost continuously in power from independence in 1947□

Congreve William 1670–1729. English dramatist, most brilliant of Restoration comic writers, e.g. *Love for Love* 1695 and *The Way of the World* 1700□

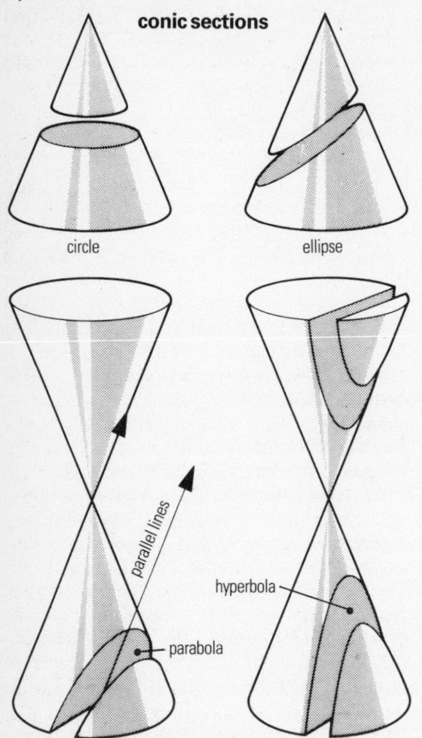

conic sections the curves (circle, ellipse, parabola, hyperbola) obtained when a cone is intersected by a plane□

conifers largest class, Coniferales, of the Gymnosperms◊. Mainly conebearing, temperate evergreen trees of pyramidal form, they have small-scale or needle-like leaves. The chief of five families are:

Pinaceae which include the ***pines*** genus *Pinus*, valuable timber trees of high altitudes (see pest◊ control) whose resin is the source of turpentine and rosin; notably the ***Scot's pine*** *P sylvestris*, the only conifer native to Britain; ***N American pitch pine*** *P ponderosa*; and ***bristlecone pine*** *P aristata* which is long-lived, some specimens being c5000 years old. The family also includes the genera *Picea* and *Tsuga*, notably the ***Christmas tree/Norway spruce*** *P abies* and the ***hemlock spruce*** *T canadensis*, both important sources of timber; and genus *Larix*, remarkable for its light green foliage, e.g. the ***common larch*** *L decidua* (unusual in that it is a deciduous conifer) and the ***N American tamarack*** *L Americana*.

Cupressaceae which includes genus *Cupressus*, notably the Mediterranean ***common cypress*** *C sempervirens* and ***garden hedging cypress*** *C leylandii*.

Taxodiaceae an unusual species is the N American timber tree, the ***swamp cypress*** *Taxodium distichum*, with red/brown fibrous bark, whose roots grow above the water to get air□

conjunctivitis inflammation (formerly ophthalmia) of the conjunctiva or membrane which covers the front of the eye. A severe form of it, ***trachoma***, is caused by the bacterium *Chlamydia trachomatis* which flourishes in poor living conditions in tropical and semi-tropical countries. It is the greatest single world cause of blindness□

Connacht NW province of Republic of Ireland, comprising the counties of Mayo, Galway, Roscommon, Sligo, and Leitrim; area 17 122 sq km/6611 sq mi; population 424 410. It is the stronghold of the Irish language, and the Connacht dialect is the national standard□

Connecticut New England state of the USA; Constitution/Nutmeg state

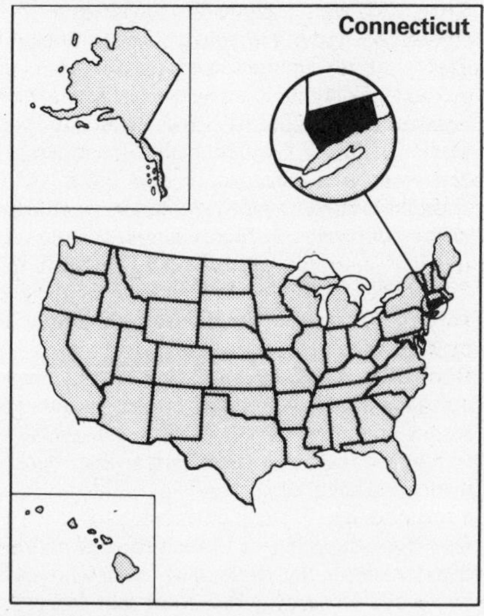

area 12 973 sq km/5 009 sq mi
capital Hartford
towns Bridgeport, New Haven
features Yale University; Mystic Seaport (reconstruction of 19th-century village, with restored ships); Shakespeare Festival at Stratford
products market garden, dairy, and poultry products; tobacco; watches, clocks, silverware; helicopters, jet engines, nuclear submarines

population 3 107 576
famous people Phineas T Barnum, Katharine Hepburn, Harriet Beecher Stowe, Mark Twain
history settled by Puritan colonists from Massachusetts in 1635, it was one of the Thirteen Colonies, and became a state in 1788□

Connell James d. 1929. Irish socialist who wrote 'The Red◊ Flag' during the 1889 London strike□

Connemara see Galway◊□

Connolly Cyril 1903–74. English essayist and novelist, founder-editor of the literary magazine *Horizon* 1930–50□

conquistador any early explorer-adventurer in the Americas, e.g. Cortés◊, Pizarro◊□

Conrad several kings of the Germans including:
Conrad II d. 1039, who reigned from 1024 and ceded the march Sleswick to Canute.
Conrad III 1093–1152, first king of the Hohenstaufen◊ dynasty from 1138; throughout his reign a fierce struggle between his followers, the Ghibellines, and the Guelphs, the folowers of Henry the Proud, Duke of Saxony and Bavaria, and his son Henry the Lion, continued. Conrad took part in the 2nd Crusade□

Conrad Joseph 1857–1924. British novelist. Of Polish parentage, he was born Teodor Jozef Konrad Korzeniowski in the Ukraine. A merchant seaman, he landed at Lowestoft with no knowledge of English in 1878, but in 1886 gained his master mariner's certificate and became a naturalized British subject. He retired in 1894 to write. His novels include *Almayer's Folly* 1895, *Lord Jim* 1900, *Nostromo* 1904, *The Secret Agent* 1907, and *Under Western Eyes* 1911. He plumbed the psychological isolation of the 'outsider'□

consanguinity relationship by blood, by virtue of a common ancestor. It has legal consequences, e.g. in inheritance of property, and in marriage, the latter being forbidden between parties closely related by blood□

conscientious objectors originally parents who objected to compulsory vaccination; later those refusing compulsory service, usually military, on moral, religious, or political grounds□

conscription system making citizens legally liable to serve with the armed forces, originating in France in 1792, and used in the American Civil War 1861–5. Introduced in Britain in World War I in 1916, it was used again in World War II (from 1939; extended to women in 1941)□

conservation the careful preservation and protection of the environment in order to prevent its exploitation or neglect. Many conservationists feel that the inter-reacting whole of the environment is under threat unless positive corrective measures are taken by government and private agencies like the World Wildlife Fund◊□

Conservation Laws laws of nature identifying quantities which do not change, even during interactions. The laws of conservation of electric charge, linear momentum, angular momentum, and mass-energy are perhaps the most fundamental of all physical principles. Some quantities (such as parity and 'strangeness') are conserved only in certain circumstances, so the associated laws are less fundamental. They are philosophically appealing, as they reveal constancy amidst apparent change and decay. Physicists have become increasingly aware of the profound mathematical connection between conservation laws and symmetries□

Conservative Party one of the two historic British parties, known as 'Tory'◊ till c1830 (and still pejoratively by opponents), and originally representing landed interests as against the *laissez-faire* of the Liberal manufacturers, but see Peel◊ and Disraeli◊. By 1983 it tended to include many technocrats with a grammar school education: see Thatcher◊. In the European Parliament◊, where 'Conservative' has a more extreme connotation, members belong to the ***European Democratic Group***. See list of Prime Ministers◊□

Constable John 1776–1837. English landscape painter. Born at E Bergholt, Suffolk, the son of a miller, he studied art in London from 1795. His most famous picture, *The Haywain*, created a sensation when exhibited at the Royal Academy in 1821 (it was subsequently awarded a Gold Medal at a Paris Salon); others include *Flatford Mill* 1825, *The Cornfield* 1826, and *Salisbury Cathedral* 1831. His work is noted for its weather effects, and sense of calm□

Constance town in Baden-Württemberg, W Germany; population 65 000□

Constance Lake lake (German *Bodensee*) between Germany, Austria, and Switzerland, through which the Rhine flows. Area 540 sq km/200 sq mi□

Constance Council of. See Great◊ Schism□

Constanta chief seaport of Romania on the Black Sea; population 280 000. Oil from Ploiesti is refined and exported□

constantan alloy, about 40% nickel and 60% copper, in which electrical resistance changes little with temparature; designed for use in high-quality resistors◊□

Constant de Rebecque Henri Benjamin 1767–1830. French liberal writer, an advocate of the Revolution, who opposed Napoleon, and proposed a constitutional monarchy after his fall in 1814. He published the autobiographical novel *Adolphe* 1816, which reflects his affair with Mme de Stael◊□

Constantine II 1940– . King of the Hellenes. Succeeding his father Paul I◊ in 1964, he went into exile in 1967 (formally deposed in 1973); his heir is Prince Paul 1967– □

Constantine the Great c274–337AD. First Christian emperor of Rome, and founder of Constantinople◊. Son of Emperor Constantius (ruler of the Western Empire 305–6), who died at York in 306, he was acclaimed by the troops there as his successor. He defeated his rival Maxentius in 312, and then, by his defeat of Licinius in 324, established his rule over the Eastern Empire also. In 313 he recognized Christianity as one of the legal religions of the Empire by the Edict of Milan, summoned and presided over the first general council of the Church at Nicaea◊ in 325, and with the aid of the Church established a close-knit network of autocratic authority. He died on an expedition to defend the Euphrates frontier against the Persians□

Constantine city in Algeria; population 350 200. Named after Constantine the Great, who rebuilt it in 313AD; noted for carpets and leather goods□

Constantinople capital of the Eastern Roman and Turkish Empires, now Istanbul◊. Founded by Constantine the Great by the enlargement of the Greek city of Byzantium in 328, it was the seat of the imperial government from 330. It was captured by crusaders in 1204, and was the seat of a Latin kingdom until recaptured by the Greeks in 1261. It was taken by the Turks, after nearly a year's siege, on 29 May 1453□

constellation a group of stars. Many have been named after mythological figures in antiquity. The best-known are:

northern Andromeda, Aquila, Auriga, Boötes, Cassiopeia, Cepheus, Corona Borealis, Cygnus, Draco, Hercules, Lyra, Ophiuchus, Pegasus, Perseus, Sagitta, Ursa Major, Ursa Minor.

Zodiacal Aquarius, Aries, Cancer, Capricornus, Gemini, Leo, Libra, Pisces, Sagittarius, Scorpius, Taurus, Virgo.

southern Canis Major, Centaurus, Cetus, Corona Austrina, Corvus, Crater, Crux Australis (Southern Cross, the four main stars forming a cross which appears on the flags of Australia and New Zealand), Eridanus, Hydra, Lepus, Lupus, Orion□

constitution the fundamental laws of a state, laying down the system of government, and defining the relations of the legislative, executive, and judiciary to each other and to the citizens□

constitution the body of laws and principles according to which the country is governed.

British Britain is a parliamentary monarchy, sovereignty being vested in the Sovereign and parliament◊. Judges are appointed by the Crown, on ministerial advice, for life; they can be removed only on petition of both Houses of Parliament. No single document defines the system of government, which depends on:

statute law laid down by parliament and enforced by the courts (including Magna Carta◊, Habeas Corpus Act◊, Bill of Rights◊, Act of Settlement◊, Act of Union◊), and ***subsidiary legislation*** through statutory instruments and other regulations (covering such matters as social security benefit rates, emergency powers, immigration, and so on), and local authority by-laws.

common law arising from precedent – what happened in previous cases – and enforced by the courts; closely allied to this are the constitutional ***conventions*** enforced by custom (such as the individual and collective responsibility of ministers to parliament; the origination of money bills solely in the Commons; and the duty of the Sovereign to act on ministerial advice and give assent to any bill passed by parliament).

law arising from Britain's membership of the EEC, and which is enforced both by the European Court of Justice and British courts; and ***law arising from British membership of other bodies***, such as NATO, the United Nations, International Monetary Fund, and European Commission of Human Rights, which is enforced only by moral pressure.

Proliferation of law under both aspects of 1 has led to demands, especially on the grounds of the rights and duties of citizens, for a single document such as that comprising the constitutions of most other countries.

American adopted in 1787, that of the USA is the oldest written constitution. Noted amendments include: 1791 the '5th amendment' with the provision that none should be compelled 'to be a witness against himself'; 1865, slavery abolished; 1870, equal voting rights without regard to race; 1951, limitation of presidential terms to two (prompted by Roosevelt◊'s 4th term); and the proposed 'equal rights for women' under discussion in 1983. Most judges are elected by popular vote. See also United States◊□

Constructivism abstract◊ art movement arising in the 1930s from Cubism◊, notable especially in the sculpture of N Gabo◊, B Nicholson◊, B Hepworth◊, and Mondrian◊□

consuls the two chief magistrates of ancient Rome, following the expulsion of the last king in 510BC; they were elected annually, and of equal power, both civil and military. Under the Empire the office became honorary. See also foreign relations◊□

consumer protection laws and measures designed to ensure fair trading for customers. An early organization attempting consumer protection was the British Standards Institution, established in 1901, which lays down specifications of quality, performance, and safety: goods reaching these standards may carry a certification, known from its shape as the 'kitemark'. Legal protection is given by the Trade Descriptions Act of 1968, rendering it a criminal offence to describe goods or provisions falsely; Fair Trading Act of 1973; Sale of Goods Act of 1979, under which goods must be of 'merchantable quality'; and Supply of Goods and Services Act of 1982 to control standards, time taken and prices charged for services.
In the USA, where there are both federal and state regulations, J F Kennedy set down four basic consumer rights: to safety, to be informed, to choose, and to be heard□

contact lenses lenses in contact with the eye, used as a substitute for spectacles, to cope with defects incapable of correction by other means, or for cosmetic purposes. They may be either 'soft' or 'hard', and can be designed for 'extended wear' without frequent removal, since they 'breathe' like the wearer□

Contadora Group established in 1983 at a meeting on Contadora, one of the islands of the Pearl Group in the Gulf of Panama, by Colombia, Mexico, Panama, and Venezuela to promote economic, social, and political advance and cooperation in the area□

continent one of the seven land-surface divisions of earth: Africa, N America (including Central America), S America, Antarctica, Asia, Europe, and Oceania◊. Possibly land once covered the whole globe, and there was a later expansion of the planet; the continental area is now 5/16ths of the surface. Each continent continues under the sea in a continental shelf (depth 200 m/600 ft), then dropping sharply by the continental slope to the ocean deeps. ***Continental drift*** following the break-up of the original single continent Pangaea into two super-continents Laurasia (N) and Gondwanaland (S) gradually brought the continents to their present position: see Wegener◊ They 'float' on the rocks of the mantle of the earth, and are still in motion: the comparatively recent drifting together of Asia and India means that Mount Everest is getting higher, Africa is moving closer to Europe, and the Americas are moving further away: see Mid-Atlantic◊ Rift◊□

Continental Congress see American◊ Independence War of□

Continental Divide or ***Great Divide*** the great watershed of N America as formed by the Rocky Mountains□

continental drift

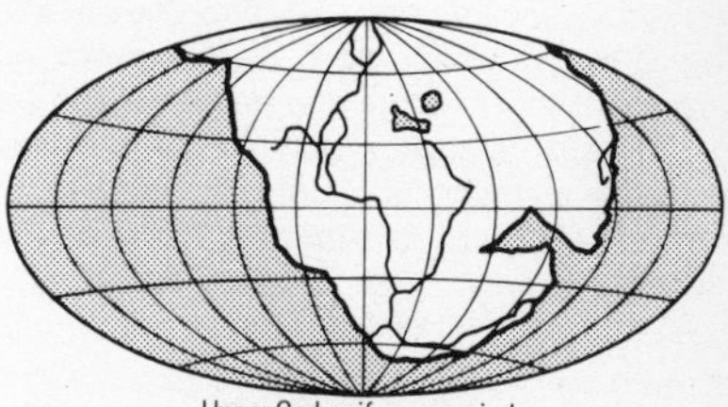

Upper Carboniferous period

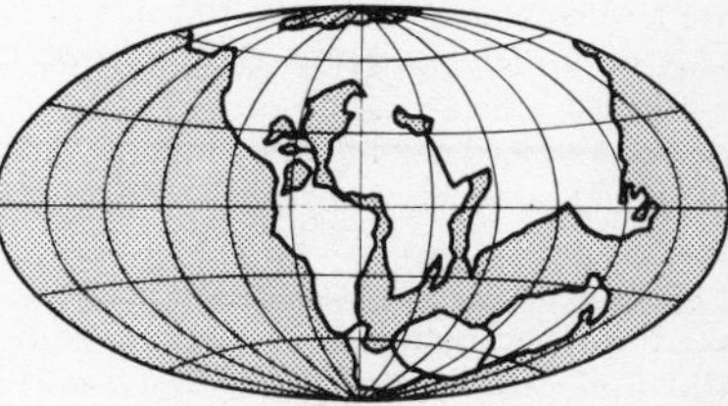

Eocene

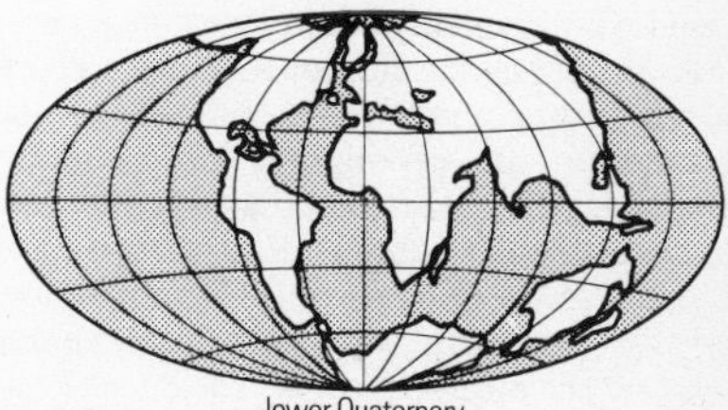

lower Quaternary

theory in geology first proposed by Alfred Wegener (German meteorologist and geophysicist 1880–1930) that the earth consisted some 200 million years ago of a single large continent, which he called ***Pangaea,*** and which subsequently broke apart to form the continents as we know them today. The theory of plate◊ tectonics has provided a convincing explanation of how such vast movement may have occurred□

Continental System Napoleon's attempted economic blockade of Britain 1806–12□

contraception prevention of conception. For humans, methods of contraception include: 1 non-invasive methods such as the 'rhythm method' approved by the Catholic Church (avoidance of intercourse at certain stages of the menstrual cycle); 2 chemical methods including the use of spermicides and the pill◊; 3 mechanical methods such as the sheath◊, cap◊, and IUD◊ (Intra-Uterine Device)□

contract an agreement (offering a 'consideration' which is accepted) between two or more parties which will be enforced by law□

convolvulus genus of plants, e.g. ***common bindweed** C arvensis*, family Convolvulaceae, with pinkish-white flowers (the petals united in a tube) and twining stems.

In the same family are the tropical American ***morning glory** Ipomoea purpurea* with rich blue flowers, which close in the afternoon (one variety has a trace of a substance similar to LSD◊ in its seeds), and the ***sweet potato** Ipomoea batatas*, a perennial native to tropical America; its tuberous roots have a white to orange flesh, and are used as a vegetable, as well as a source of starch and alcohol□

Conwy Welsh port (formerly Conway) on the river Conway; population 12 160. It still has its medieval walls, and ruins of the castle built by Edward I in 1284□

Coober Pedy opal-mining town in the Great Central Desert, Australia; population 100. Temperatures reach 60°C/140°F□

Cook James 1728–79. British explorer. Yorkshire born, he commanded a naval expedition in the *Endeavour* to the S Pacific in 1768–71 to witness the transit of Venus, then sailed round New Zealand and surveyed the E coast of Australia, giving European names to New South Wales and Botany Bay. With the *Resolution* and *Adventure* 1772–75, he circumnavigated the Antarctic Continent, determined the location of Easter Island, and sighted New Caledonia and Norfolk Island. On his 3rd voyage 1776–9, after attempting the NW Passage from the Pacific end, he returned to Hawaii, where he was killed by the natives in a scuffle to recover a stolen boat. See Joseph Banks◊□

Cook Peter 1937– .British writer and comedian, who appeared in revue (*Beyond the Fringe* 1959–64), and opened London's first satirical nightclub *The Establishment* in 1960 with ***Dudley Moore*** 1935– , his partner in comic dialogues□

Cook Thomas 1808–92. Pioneer British travel agent, founder of Thomas Cook & Son. He organized his first tour, to Switzerland, in 1863, and introduced travellers' cheques ('circular notes'), in the early 1870s□

Cook Mount see Alps◊, Southern□

Cooke Alistair 1908– . Anglo-American journalist. Born in Lancashire, he later worked in USA, and was *Guardian* correspondent 1948–72, also broadcasting a weekly 'Letter from America': KBE in 1973□

Cookham-on-Thames village in Berkshire, where Stanley Spencer◊ is commemorated by a gallery□

Cook Islands self-governing territory of New Zealand (with which there is common citizenship) from 1964; area 230 sq km/90 sq mi; population 18 100. The capital is Avarua on the chief island of Rarotonga; see also Niue◊. They were discovered by Cook◊ in 1773, annexed by Britain in 1888, and transferred to New Zealand in 1901□

Cook Strait divides N and S Island, New Zealand□

coolabah Australian riverside tree *Eucalyptus microtheca*□

Coolidge John Calvin 1872–1933. 30th president of the USA. A Republican, he became vice-president in 1921 and President, on the death of Harding, in 1923; re-elected on a wave of prosperity in 1924□

Cooney Ray (Raymond) 1932– . British actor, director, and playwright, best known for his farces *Two into One* 1981 and *Run for your Wife* 1983□

Cooper Alfred Duff see Norwich◊, Lord□

Cooper Gary 1901–62. American film actor, born in Montana, epitome of the Yankee in *The Virginian* 1929, *Sergeant York* (Academy Award 1941), and *High Noon* 1952□

Cooper Henry 1934– . British heavyweight boxer; British and Empire titles 1959–71; European 1964 and 1968–71; in 1967 he was the first to win three Lonsdale belts outright□

Cooper James Fenimore 1789–1851. American writer, born in New Jersey, remembered for *The Last of the Mohicans* 1826, and other stories of settlers and American Indians in the mid-18th century□

Cooper Samuel 1609–72. English miniaturist, who painted Milton, Cromwell, Charles II's Court, and Pepys's wife□

cooperative organization of individual traders, farmers, manufacturers, or consumers for mutual assistance, e.g. the Cooperative Wholesale Society (CWS) in the UK, which shares profit in its stores with members by dividend stamps. Workers' cooperatives increased in the UK when factories were otherwise threatened with closure in the depression of the late 1970s and 1980s. See Robert Owen◊□

Cooperative Commonwealth Federation (CCF). see New Democratic Party◊□

Cooperative Party founded in Britain in 1918 by the Cooperative movement, it contests seats by agreement with the Labour Party□

Cooperative Wholesale Society see Cooperative◊□

Cooper's Creek see Channel Country◊□

coot a type of water bird. See rail◊□

Coote Sir Eyre 1726–83. Irish soldier. His victory at Wandiwash, followed by the capture of Pondicherry in 1760, ended French hopes of supremacy in India; as Commander-in-Chief from 1779, he defeated Hyder Ali◊ several times□

Copán town in W Honduras. The nearby site of a Maya city, including temple, pyramids, etc., was bought by American John Stephens in the 1830s for $50□

cope sleeveless semi-circular cape, worn by priests of the Western Church on formal occasions, though not at Mass□

Copenhagen capital of Denmark: population 1 382 000. To the NE is the royal palace at Amalienborg; the 17th-century Charlottenburg Palace houses the Academy of Arts, and parliament meets in the Christiansborg Palace. The statue of Hans Andersen's 'Little Mermaid' (by Edvard Eriksen) is at the harbour entrance. It has the world's first centre for the treatment of torture victims□

Copenhagen Battle of. Naval victory on 2 Apr 1801 by a British fleet under Sir Hyde Parker and Nelson over the Danish fleet. Nelson put his telescope to his blind eye and refused to see Parker's signal for withdrawal□

Copepoda sub-class of Crustacea◊, freshwater and marine, mainly microscopic, and found in plankton, etc.□

Coper Hans 1920–81. German potter, originally an engineer. A refugee from Hitler, he became a pupil of Lucy Rie◊. His work resembles Greek (Cycladic) archaic pots in its monumental quality□

Copernicus Nicolaus 1473–1543. Polish astronomer, whose *De revolutionibus orbium coelestium/Concerning the Movement of the Heavenly Bodies* 1543, argued that the sun is the centre of the solar system and that the earth rotates about its own axis and orbits the sun□

Copland Aaron 1900– . US composer, whose works include the ballet *Billy the Kid* 1939 (with a variant of the cowboy song 'Bury Me Not on the Lone Prairie'); *Rodeo* 1942; *Appalachian Spring* 1944, based on a poem by Hart Crane; and his popular *Fanfare for the Common Man*□

Copley John Singleton 1737–1815. Leading American portraitist of the colonial period, who from 1774 lived mainly in England, e.g. *The Death of Chatham*□

copper element

symbol Cu

atomic number 29

physical description reddish-bronze metal

features there is a trace in the human body; it is easily worked, yet tough, and has high conductivity of electricity and heat, and is fairly resistant to corrosion

uses for electricity conduction, and a component of brass◊ and bronze◊□

Coppola Francis Ford 1939– . American film director, born in Detroit. His films include *The Godfather* 1972, *The Great Gatsby* 1974, *Apocalypse Now* 1979□

copra the dried flesh of the coconut, from which oil is pressed to make soap□

Coptic see under Egypt◊ language□

Copts descendants of the ancient Egyptians who accepted Christianity in the 1st century and refused to adopt Islam after the Arab conquest. The Coptic Church is headed by Shenouda III (b. 1923), 117th Pope of Alexandria. He was imprisoned by Sadat 1981–5, and is opposed by Muslim fundamentalists□

copyright the right in law to be the only producer, seller, or broadcaster of literary, musical, or artistic works, including plays, recordings, films, and radio and television broadcasts. It prevents reproduction of the work without consent of the author, and under English law, subsists for 50 years from the year of the author's death, or from date of publication, where posthumous. See Public Lending Right◊□

coral marine organism, class Anthozoa, phylum Coelenterata, with a skeleton (calcium carbonate and calcium oxide) of lime extracted from the surrounding water. Corals live in a symbiotic relationship with microscopic algae (zooxanthelae) which are incorporated into the structure. The algae receive carbon dioxide from the polyps, and the polyps receive nutrients from the algae. They are also in relationship with the fish which rest or take refuge within their branches, and which excrete nutrients which make them grow faster. Sedentary, the majority of corals are omnivorous, and form large colonies (up to 20 000 000 polyps), and their accumulated skeletons form coral reefs and atolls (see Great Barrier Reef◊). Some are valued in jewellery e.g. Mediterranean ***red coral*** *Corallium rubrum*□

Coralli Jean 1779–1854. French choreographer, e.g. *Giselle* 1841 for Grisi□

Coral Sea part of the Pacific Ocean off NE Australia□

Coral Sea Battle of the. Victory of the Americans over the Japanese 4–8 May 1942; the first Allied success in the Pacific, it saved Australia from invasion□

coral snake various species of snake◊□

coral tree tropical species of *Erythrina*, family Papilionaceae, with bright red/orange flowers, and very lightweight wood□

cor anglais a type of musical instrument. See under woodwind◊□

Corby town in Northamptonshire, England; population 55 000. A former major steel centre, it now makes plastics, etc.□

Corday Charlotte 1768–93. French Girondist◊ who stabbed to death the Jacobin leader, Marat◊, with a bread-knife as he sat in his bath. She was guillotined□

Córdoba industrial city in Argentina, with an air force college; population 800 000□

Córdoba city in Andalusia, Spain; population 284 850. The former mosque (founded in 785), now a cathedral, is the largest Christian church in the world except St Peter's, Rome□

Corelli Arcangelo 1653–1713. Italian composer. He was one of the first great violinists, and his works include a set of *concerti grossi* and five sets of chamber sonatas□

Corelli Marie. Pseudonym of British romance writer Mary Mackay 1855–1924, e.g. *The Romance of Two Worlds* 1886□

Corfu see Ionian Islands◊□

coriander annual plant *Coriandrum sativum*, family Umbelliferae◊, of Asia, America, and S Europe. The seeds and leaves are used in cookery, etc.□

Corinth port (Greek Kórinthos) on the Isthmus of Corinth, Greece; population 23 000. An ancient city-state, involved in the Peloponnesian War◊, it was conquered by Rome in 146BC. St Paul visited it and addressed epistles to the Church there. There is a ruined temple of Apollo, 6th century BC□

Coriolis effect named after its discoverer, French mathematician Gaspard Coriolis 1792–1843, it results from the deflective force of the earth's W-to-E rotation. Winds and ocean currents are deflected to the right in the N and to the left in the S hemisphere. It has to be allowed for in launching guided missiles, but has negligible effect on the clockwise or anti-clockwise direction of water running out of a bath□

Cork largest county (county town Cork) of the Republic of Ireland, province of Munster◊. It includes Bantry Bay and the village of Blarney◊. Natural gas from off Kinsale is supplied to N Ireland□

Cork industrial port in County Cork, Republic of Ireland; population 136 269

Spike Island, in the harbour, was formerly a naval training base, re-opened in 1985 as a prison, 'Ireland's Alcatraz'□

cork the light waterproof cellular outer layers of the bark of trees and shrubs, especially the ***cork-oak*** *Quercus suber*, of S Europe and N Africa, used for engine gaskets, isolation of vibration, and heat insulation□

cormorant a type of seabird. See under pelican◊□

corncrake a type of water bird. See rail◊□

Corneille Pierre 1606–84. French dramatist. As one of the five poets appointed in 1634 to mould Richelieu's dramatic ideas for the stage, he proved intractable and was soon dismissed. In 1636 he achieved sensational success with *Le Cid*, although it was fiercely attacked by Academicians under the influence of Richelieu, but reconciliation followed, and *Horace* 1639, like all his later plays (e.g. *Cinna* 1640 and *Polyeucte* 1643) observed Aristotle's◊ unities. He glorified strength of will governed by reason, and established the French classical drama of the next two centuries□

cornet a type of musical instrument. See under brass◊□

cornflower a plant of the Compositae◊ family□

Cornforth Sir John 1917– . Australian chemist, completely deaf since boyhood. In 1975 he shared a Nobel prize with Vladimir Prelog for utilizing radio-isotopes as 'markers' in work on enzymes. Knighted in 1977□

Corniche La Grande Corniche is the road, Nice–Menton, built by Napoleon and rising to 520 m/1700 ft; La Moyenne and Petite Corniche are parallel supplementaries□

Cornish branch of the Brythonic group of the Celtic◊ languages. The last Cornish speaker, Dolly Pentreath, died in 1777, but there is a modern revival begun by Henry Jenner *Gwas Myhal* 1849–1934, who published a handbook□

Corn Laws laws regulating the import/export of cereals to stabilize supply and price, but tending to drive up price. They were repealed by Peel◊ in 1846□

Cornwall SW county of England

area (excluding Scillies) 3548 sq km/1370 sq mi

towns administrative headquarters Truro; Camborne, Launceston; resorts of Bude, Falmouth, Newquay, Penzance

features Bodmin Moor (including Brown Willy 419 m/1375 ft), Land's End peninsula, St Michael's Mount, rivers Tamar and Fowey; Poldhu◊; Stannary or Tinners' Parliament, established 11th century and revived in 1974 as a separatist demonstration; Cornish◊ language

products growing electronics industry; spring flowers; tin, kaolin; fish

population 354 792

famous people John Betjeman (buried at Trebetherick on the N coast), Sir Humphry Davy, Daphne du Maurier, William Golding□

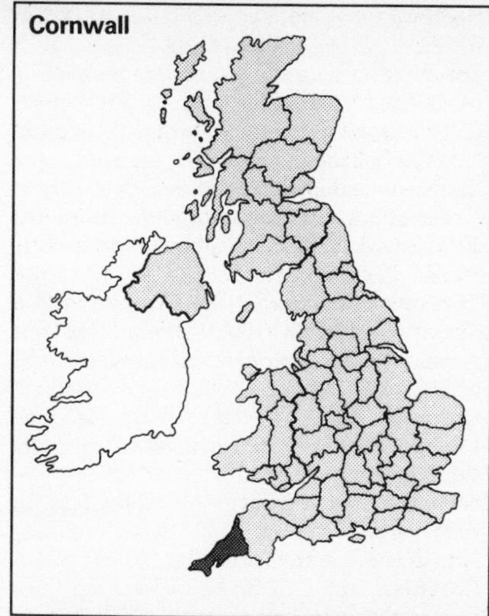

Cornwallis Charles, 1st Marquess Cornwallis 1738–1805. British soldier, whose surrender at Yorktown ended the War of American Independence. He was later twice Governor-General of India (annexing half Tippoo◊ Sahib's sultanate in 1792) and Viceroy of Ireland□

Coromandel the east coast of Tamil Nadu, India; also ***Coromandel Peninsula***, North Island, New Zealand, E of Auckland□

coronary heart disease disease of the coronary arteries (Latin *corona* 'crown', from their encircling of the heart). Blockage by thickening of the artery walls (atherosclerosis), trapping a blood clot (thrombus), is thought to cause a heart attack. Infarct is death of part of the walls of the heart (myocardium); arrhythmia is irregular heart beat; fibrillation is extreme irregularity preventing the heart from pumping blood effectively; angina is the chest pain associated with heart disease□

coronation the ceremony at which a sovereign is crowned. The main features of the British ceremony (in Westminster Abbey since that of Harold in 1066) are: presentation to the people; administration of the oath; presentation of the Bible; anointing of the sovereign; presentation of the spurs and sword of state, emblems of knighthood; presentation of the armilla, the royal robe, the orb, the ring, the sceptre with the cross, and the rod with the dove; coronation with St Edward's Crown; benediction; enthroning; and the homage of the princes of the blood and the peerage□

Coronel port in Chile, off which on 1 Nov 1914 Admiral von Spee defeated Admiral Cradock, who went down with his ship□

coroner officer, with medical/legal qualifications, appointed by an English county council to inquire (with a jury of 7–11 people) into the deaths of persons who have died suddenly by acts of violence, under suspicious circumstances; and also into treasure trove. See also procurator-fiscal◊□

coronet small crown worn by a peer at a coronation and the state opening of parliament, and varying in design according to rank□

Corot Jean Baptiste Camille 1796–1875. French landscape painter of the 'Barbizon school', excelling in early morning or twilit scenes□

corporative state state in which not individual citizens, but particular trades, industries, and professions are represented. The concept was developed by the Syndicalist◊ movement, and partly adopted by the dictatorial regimes of Franco◊, Mussolini, and Salazar◊□

Corpus Christi port, industrial city, and resort in Texas, Southern USA; population 230 700□

Corpus Christi Feast of. Celebration, Latin 'body of Christ', of the institution of the Eucharist◊; on the 2nd Thursday after Whit Sunday□

Correggio Antonio Allegri da c1494–1534. Italian Renaissance painter, named after his birthplace near Modena. Several examples of his tender, rather sickly, yet dramatic style are in Parma, including the frescoed dome of Parma Cathedral. He was very popular in the 19th century□

Corregidor island at the mouth of Manila Bay, Luzon, Philippine Republic, defended by survivors of the Bataan campaign under General Wainwright against the Japanese, 9 Apr–6 May 1942; US troops recaptured it on 15 Feb 1945□

Corrientes river port in Argentina, on the Parana; it exports cotton, rice, and tobacco; population 137 000□

corroboree dance of the Australian aborigines, with historical, religious, or simply theatrical significance□

corsairs Barbary◊ pirates who plundered Mediterranean and Atlantic shipping from the 16th century till the French occupied their stronghold in Algiers in 1830. Some were English, e.g. the half-brother of Sir Edmund Verney◊, Sir Francis Verney□

Corse French name of Corsica◊□

Corsica island region (French *Corse*) of France
area 8680 sq km/3367sq mi
capital and port Ajaccio

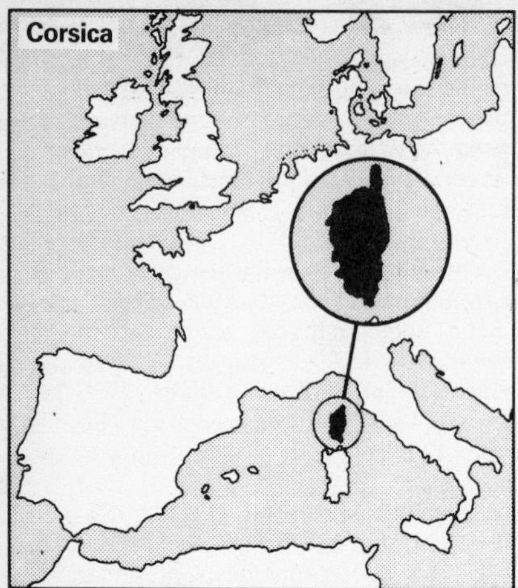

features maquis◊ vegetation; its mountain bandits were wiped out in 1931, but the tradition of the vendetta or blood feud lingers; it is the main base of the Foreign Legion◊.
exports wine, olive oil
population 240 180, of whom just under 50% are native Corsicans; there are c400 000 émigrés, mostly to Mexico and Central America, who return to retire.
language French, (official); the majority speak Corsican, an Italian dialect
religion Roman Catholicism
famous people Napoleon
government its special status involves a regional assembly from 1982 with uncertain powers.
recent history under Italian rule 1077–1768, when it was sold to France, it was also occupied by Italy 1942–3. From 1962 French *pieds noirs* (refugees from Algeria) were settled here, and this fuelled a 'national liberation front' (FNLC), banned in 1983, aiming at independence□

Corsican (language) see under Corsica◊□

Cort Henry 1740–1800. British iron-master, whose improvement of the processing of wrought iron, etc., furthered the Industrial Revolution□

Cortés Hernán 1485–1547. Spanish commander of an expedition to Mexico in 1518. Landing with only 600 men, he was at first received by Montezuma◊ as a god and, when expelled from Tenochtitlán (Mexico City) by a revolt, recaptured it in 1521, with the aid of native allies, and conquered the whole country□

cortisone steroid hormone, a product of the adrenal glands, which (with related products) is now produced synthetically. It is used for treating rheumatoid arthritis, allergies, certain cancers, etc.□

Cortona town in Italy; population 22 000. It still has its Etruscan city walls□

corundum naturally occurring aluminium oxide, Al_2O_3; the colour of its crystals varies (ruby◊, sapphire, etc.) according to additional minerals present. It is next on the scale of hardness to diamond, and ***emery***, a variety including haematite and magnetite, is used as an abrasive. Synthetic sapphires are used in record player styluses□

Corunna port (Spanish *La Coruña*) in NW Spain; population 190 000. In 1588 the Armada sailed from here, and it was sacked by Drake in 1589□

Corunna Battle of. Victory by Sir John Moore◊ over the French in the Peninsular War 1809□

corvette term revived from sailing days for small armed vessels, e.g. those escorting British convoys in World War II□

Corvidae family of birds, order Passeriformes, which are omnivorous. They have a fondness for other birds' eggs and sometimes for other birds. All extremely intelligent, they will mimic other bird calls and any other noise, including machinery, and are longer-lived than most birds, up to 20 years in the wild. They include:
crow genus *Corvus* including the Eurasian ***carrion crow*** *C corone* of Eurasia, glossy black and not limited to feeding on dead flesh; ***raven*** *C corax* purplish-black and largest (60 cm/2 ft, with a 1 m/3 ft wingspan) of the 'songbirds' (actually, like the other Corvidae, it has a harsh, croaking call); ***rook*** *C frugilegus* which nests in large colonies in treetops, and is blue-black, with areas of bare skin at the base of the grey bill, and ***jackdaw*** *C monedula*, black, with a grey cap, and pale yellow-grey eyes, and having a highly organized social life. Interesting members of other genera include the ***chough*** *Pyrrhocorax pyrrhocorax*, black, with a red bill and legs, now limited in its British range by its love of nesting on lonely cliffs, but with a stronghold on the Lleyn peninsula (see Gwynedd◊), and having great skill in aerobatics; ***magpie*** *Pica pica*, strikingly black-and-white, 'weighed down' in flight by its long, spreading tail, and even more attracted than most of the family to bright, glittering objects, which it will collect; and the woodland ***jay*** *Garrulus glandarius*, handsome in fawn, black, and white, with blue-barred wing patches□

Corvo Baron. See Rolfe◊, F R□

coryphaena a type of game fish. See dolphin◊□

Cos a Greek island. See Dodecanese◊□

Cosenza town in Italy, burial place of Alaric◊; population 103 000□

Cosgrave William Thomas 1880–1965. Irish statesman, he was Prime Minister 1922–32, and leader of the Fine Gael◊ opposition 1933–44. His son ***Liam Cosgrave*** 1920– was Prime Minister of a Fine Gael–Labour coalition 1973–7□

cosmic radiation high-speed particles (atomic nuclei), some of which originate in the sun, but most coming from beyond the solar system. Those of low energy seem to be galactic in origin, and detectors (the water-Cherenkov detector near Leeds has an area of 12 sq km/4.5 sq mi) are in use to detect extra-galactic sources (possibly the rotating discs of infalling matter round black holes) of high-energy rays□

cosmonaut Russian term for an astronaut□

Cossacks in Russia before the Revolution of 1917, when their resistance was brutally suppressed, men holding more land than the ordinary peasant in return for military service for 20 years. Some fought for the Germans in World War II. They were fine horsemen□

Costa Rica Republic of

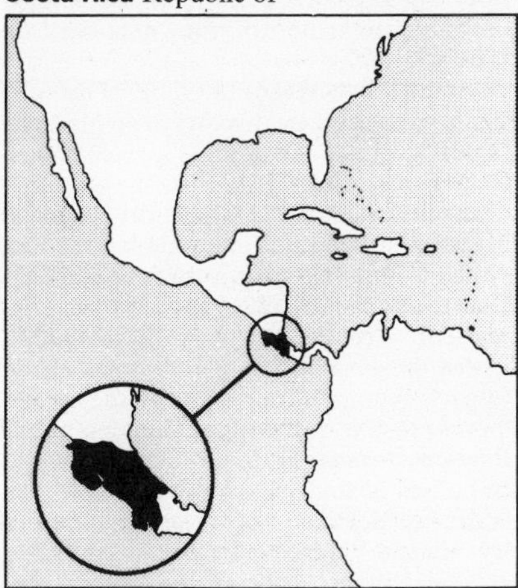

area 50 997 sq km/19 690 sq mi
capital San José
towns ports Limón, Puntarenas
features highest literacy rate in Latin America; there has been no standing army since the civil war of 1948–9
exports coffee, bananas, cocoa, sugar
currency colone
population 2 700 000, including 1200 Guaymi Indians (declining)
language Spanish
religion Roman Catholicism
government executive president (Luis Monge Alvarez from 1982) elected for four years, and a Legislative Assembly.
recent history independent from Spain from 1821, Costa Rica had boundary disputes with her neighbours in the 19th and early 20th centuries; there is currently tension with Nicaragua because of anti-government guerrillas on Costa Rican territory. Recession brought political terrorism from 1981□

Coster Laurens Janszoon 1370–1440. Dutch printer, said to have invented movable type. An apprentice ran off to Mainz with the blocks after his death to begin a printing business with Gutenberg◊□

cost of living the cost of goods and services needed for an average standard of living. In Britain the first cost of living index was introduced in 1914 and based on the expenditure of a working-class family of man, woman, and three children; the standard is 100. Known from 1947 as the Retail Price Index (RPI), it is revised to allow for inflation, etc. Supplementary are the Consumers' Expenditure Deflator (formerly Consumer Price Index) and the Tax and Price Index (TPI)□

cot death death of an apparently healthy baby during sleep, also called Sudden Infant Death Syndrome (SIDS); possible causes include poor heart rhythm and irregular breathing□

Côte d'Azur see Provence-Côte d'Azur◊□

Cotman John Sell 1782–1842. British landscape painter, born at Norwich, famous for his stark monumental watercolour studies of natural features, bridges, etc.□

cotoneaster genus of trees and shrubs, family Rosaceae; the leaves have woolly undersides and the black and red fruits persist through winter□

Cotonou chief port of Benin; population 178 000□

Cotopaxi formerly the world's highest active volcano◊, Ecuador; 5897 m/19 347 ft□

Cotswolds range of hills in Avon–Gloucestershire, England, 80 km/50 mi long□

Cottbus capital of Cottbus district and industrial city (textiles, carpets) in E Germany; population 111 500□

cotton tropical and sub-tropical herbaceous plant, genus *Gossypium* family Malvaceae, producing fibres round the seeds in the ripened fruit or 'boll', which are spun into yarn for cloth. Cotton disease (byssinosis), caused by cotton dust, affects the lungs of those working in the industry. The seeds are used to produce cooking oil and livestock feed, and the pigment gossypol has potential as a safe male contraceptive in a modified form□

cotton stainer a type of insect. See under hemiptera◊□

cottonwood several species of N American poplar, especially *Populus angulata* which has recently been widely planted in Australia. It has its name because the seeds are clothed in a white cottony down; also the tree *Hibiscus tiliaceus*, family Malvaceae, of Australia and the SW Pacific□

couch grass several types of coarse grass. See grasses◊□

Coué Emile 1857–1926. French psychological healer, with the slogan, 'Every day, and in every way, I am becoming better and better'□

cougar a large wild cat◊□

Coulomb Charles Auge de 1736–1806. French physicist, who, using a torsion balance, discovered the inverse square law of forces between electrical charges and between magnetic poles. See coulomb◊□

coulomb the practical unit of electrical charge – the quantity of electricity conveyed by a current of one ampere in one second□

council see Local Government◊□

Council for Mutual Economic Assistance see Comecon◊□

Council of Europe established in 1949, headquarters Strasbourg, members being: Great Britain, France, Italy, Belgium, the Netherlands, Sweden, Denmark, Norway, Republic of Ireland, Luxembourg, Greece, and Turkey; Iceland, W Germany, Austria, Cyprus, Switzerland, Malta, Portugal, Spain, and Liechtenstein joined subsequently. The widest association of European states, it has a Committee of Foreign Ministers, Parliamentary Assembly (members from national parliaments), and a European Commission investigates violations of Human Rights□

counter-espionage see Secret◊ Service□

counterfeiting fraudulent imitation, especially of banknotes, which is countered by special papers, elaborate watermarks, and skilled printing, sometimes also insertion of a metallic strip□

counterpoint originating in plainsong, with two independent vocal lines sung simultaneously (Latin *punctus contra punctum* 'note against note'), it combines melodies to form a special texture. It reached its height in the 16th century□

Counter-Reformation see under Reformation◊□

countertenor 'male alto' or highest natural male voice, favoured by the Elizabethans, Purcell◊ himself singing in this range; revived in the UK by Alfred Deller 1912–79□

country and western popular derivation from Anglo-American folk song, 'hillbilly'; the centre, from 1925, is Nashville, Tennessee. Singers have included Hank Williams, Jerry Bradley, Elvis Presley, Charlie Pride, Johnny Cash, Gene Autry, and Merle Haggard□

country dancing see folk dancing□

Country Party see National Country Party◊□

Countryside Commission estabished in 1968 to replace in England and Wales the National Parks Commission, it controls over 160 country parks, and has a Demonstration Farms Project. Scotland has its own commission□

county unit of local government◊ in England, Wales, and N Ireland, and in some other countries□

county council see Local Government□

county court see Law◊ Courts□

Couperin Franois 1668–1733. French court composer for the harpsichord, called *le Grand*, as the most famous of a musical family□

Courbet Gustave 1819–77. French landscape and genre painter, associated with the Barbizon◊ school. He spent six months in prison for being a member of the Paris Commune in 1871□

Courrèges André 1923– . French dress designer, originator of the 'mini-skirt' in 1964□

coursing the chasing (and killing) of hares by greyhounds, as a field sport, Sept–Mar: the Waterloo Cup (Courser's Derby) is competed for in Feb at Altcar□

Courtauld Samuel 1793–1881. British textile industrialist, whose firm developed the first synthetic fibre (viscose rayon) from 1904□

Courtauld Samuel 1876–1947. British connoisseur. The great-nephew of the industrialist, he gave his house and art collection (especially Impressionists and Post-Impressionists) to the University of London as the *Courtauld Institute* in 1931: the collection is to be housed in Somerset House in 1988□

court-martial a court of officers appointed to try military offences. In Britain they are governed by the code of the service concerned, with, from 1951, an appeal court for all three services□

Courtneidge Dame Cicely 1893–1980. British actress. Born in Sydney, she was a stage and film comedienne and singer, e.g. 'Vitality'. She married comedian Jack Hulbert 1892 –1978□

Court of Session see Law◊ Courts□

Court of the Lord Lyon Scottish heraldic body□

Courtrai industrial town (damask, linen, lace, etc.) (Flemish *Kourtrijk*) in Belgium; population 76 000□

Courtrai Battle of, also 'Battle of the Spurs' because so many were collected from the field after the defeat of French knights by the Flemings of Ghent and Bruges□

Courts Law. See Law◊ Courts□

Cousteau Jacques-Yves 1910– . French oceanographer, commander of *Calypso* from 1951. He shared in the invention of the aqualung in 1943 and pioneered in marine archaeology and using television cameras under water; his books include *The Silent World* 1953□

couvade custom of a man behaving as if he were about to give birth when his child is being born, observed among primitive peoples, presumably to reinforce his link with the baby□

Covenanters the Presbyterians who swore to uphold their forms of worship in a National Covenant, signed on 28 Feb 1638, when Charles I attempted to introduce a liturgy on the English model into Scotland. A general assembly abolished episcopacy, and in 1643 the Covenanters signed with the English parliament the Solemn League and Covenant, promising military aid in return for the establishment of Presbyterianism in England. A Scottish army entered England and fought at Marston Moor.

At the Restoration Charles II revived episcopacy in Scotland, evicting resisting ministers, etc., so that revolts followed in 1666, 1679, and 1685. However, Presbyterianism was again restored in 1688□

Covent Garden London square (named from the convent garden once on the site) laid out by Inigo Jones in 1631; the Royal Opera House, also housing the Royal Ballet, is here, and a Transport Museum. The former fruit and vegetable market (at Nine Elms, Wandsworth, from 1973) buildings were adapted for shops and leisure, e.g. the Theatre Museum, planned to open in 1987, is in the Old Flower Market□

Coventry industrial city in West Midlands, England; population 310 200. It originated when Leofric, Earl of Mercia and husband of Lady Godiva◊, founded a priory in 1043. Its modern industry began with bicycles in 1870, and today includes cars, electronic equipment, machine tools, agricultural machinery. Notable are the cathedral designed by Sir Basil Spence, and incorporating the steeple of the building of 1373–95 destroyed in the German air raid of 14 Nov 1940; St Mary's Hall, built 1394–1414 as a guild centre; two gates of the old city walls 1356; Belgrade Theatre 1958; Art Gallery and Museum, Museum of British Road Transport, and Lanchester Polytechnic□

Coverdale Miles 1488–1569. First translator of the Bible into English, born in Yorkshire. A Protestant convert, he fled abroad from persecution, published his translation in 1535 (dedicated to Henry VIII), and returned in 1548, to become bishop of Exeter in 1551. He fled again under Mary, but was again in England under Elizabeth□

Coward Sir Noël 1899–1973. British man-of-the-theatre. From his first success with *The Young Idea* 1923, he wrote and appeared in sophisticated plays and comedies: *The Vortex* 1924; *Hay Fever* 1925; *Private Lives* 1930, with Gertrude Lawrence; *Cavalcade* 1931; *Design for Living* 1933; *Blithe Spirit* 1941. There was also the script for the film *In Which We Serve* 1942, the subtle *Brief Encounter* 1945, and revue appearances singing 'Mad Dogs and Englishmen', etc.□

Cowes seaport and resort on the Isle of Wight; population 19 000. It is the headquarters of the Royal Yacht Squadron which holds the annual Cowes Regatta; Osborne House is a museum□

cowfish a type of fish. See under tetraodon◊□

Cowley Abraham 1618–67. British poet. Joining King Charles at Oxford in 1644, he went to Paris with the queen, becoming a royalist secret agent. He introduced the Pindaric ode to English poetry, and published metaphysical verse with elaborate 'conceits', as well as attractive essays□

Cowper William 1731–1800. British poet. Born in Hertfordshire, he developed suicidal depression, underwent an evangelical conversion in the asylum he entered in 1763, and on recovery lived with a Mr and Mrs Unwin in Huntingdon. She continued to look after him in widowhood, but their friendship eventually ended, probably because of Mrs Unwin's jealousy of the influence on him of Lady Austen, who turned him from hymns ('God moves in a mysterious way') to secular verse, notably *Table Talk* 1782, the six books of *The Task* 1785, and the comic poem 'John Gilpin'. He wrote excellent letters, and was devoted to his pet hares□

cowry gasteropod, mainly-tropical molluscs, family Cypraeidae, in which the interior spiral form is concealed by a double outer 'lip'. Hard, shiny, and often coloured, they may be used by women as fertility charms, because of their shape, and the ***money cowry*** *Cypraea moneta* is used as currency□

cowslip a plant of the primrose◊ family□

Cox David 1783–1859. British watercolour artist, noted for the cloud effects of his landscapes□

coyote the small, yellowish ***prairie wolf*** *Canis latrans* of North America□

coypu S American rodent *Myocastor coypus*, introduced to Europe; it has big orange front teeth, webbed hind feet, and rat-like tail, and is 50 cm/2 ft long. It is bred for its fur (nutria), but it is a pest when it escapes in the wild, damaging crops and waterways□

Cozens Alexander c1717–86. British artist born in Russia, where his father was shipbuilder to Peter the Great. In 1742 he settled in England, where he taught at Eton and George III's sons were his pupils. He sometimes used blots as inspiration for his watercolour landscapes in brown, grey, or black washes□

Cozens John Robert 1752–97. British watercolour landscapist, the son of Alexander Cozens◊. He produced Alpine and Italian studies on visits to Italy, e.g. with William Beckford◊, and his work influenced Turner◊ and Girtin◊. He became mentally unstable after 1793□

crab Crustacea included in the suborder Reptantia 'walking' (with the lobsters◊ and crayfish◊) of the Decapoda◊. Though mainly marine, they may also live in fresh water or on land. They are intelligent carnivores, who act as scavengers. They have a typical 'sideways' walk and strong pincers. Distinguishable from lobsters by a broad shell (carapace) protecting the upper part of the body, and by their tucking their small abdomens◊ under the body. Periodically the outer shell is cast to allow for growth. There are two subdivisions:

1 ***Brachyura*** or ***true crabs*** including the European ***shore*** or ***green crab*** *Carcinus maenas* and ***edible crab*** *Cancer pagurus*; ***S European river crab*** *Thelphusa fluviatilis*; N American ***fiddler crab***, genus *Uca*, with one enlarged claw, waved to attract females; ***spider crabs*** genus *Macropodia*, etc., with small bodies and very long legs; ***land crabs*** a family, Gecarcinidae, which may visit the sea or fresh water only occasionally, and are found in the tropical Americas.

2 ***Anomura*** which includes the small, soft-bodied ***hermit crabs***, genus *Pagurus*, etc., which use whelk shells as protective homes; and the edible ***king crab*** *Paralithodes camtschatica* of Japan and Alaska□

crab apple a small sour apple◊□

Crabbe George 1754–1832. British poet, born in Aldeburgh◊. Originally a doctor, he became a clergyman in 1781, and wrote grimly realistic verse of the poor of his own time: *The Village* 1783, *The Parish Register* 1807, *The Borough* 1810 (which includes the story of the Britten◊ opera *Peter Grimes*), and *Tales of the Hall* 1819□

Cracow see Kraków◊□

Craig Edward Gordon 1872–1966. British stage designer, and innovator in the non-realistic use of light and colour. He was the son of Ellen Terry◊ by the architect E W Godwin□

Craik Dinah Maria 1826–87. British novelist, born Mulock, author of *John Halifax, Gentleman* 1857□

Craiova industrial town in Romania; population 221 000□

crake a type of weland bird. See rail◊□

Cranach Lucas 1472–1553. German artist, born at Kronach, Bavaria, who worked at the Wittenberg court from 1504. A friend of Luther, whom he painted several times. He used classical themes with gay inventiveness, and produced numerous woodcuts and copperplates□

cranberry a type of berry. See bilberry◊□

Crane (Harold) Hart 1899–1932. US poet, born in Ohio, whose *The Bridge* 1930 deals mystically with American history. See Aaron Copland◊□

Crane Stephen 1871–1900. American journalist and novelist, whose *Red Badge of Courage* 1895 deals with the American Civil War□

Crane Walter 1845–1915. British watercolourist and wood engraver for book illustration, e.g. Spenser's *Faerie Queene* 1894–6□

crane family of birds, Gruidae, wading birds with long legs, neck, and bill. Includes ***common crane*** *Grus grus* of N Europe, noted for its social dance (not limited to breeding pairs) and trumpeting cry; and ***whooping crane*** *Grus americana* of Canada and USA. The rails◊ and bustards◊ belong in the same order, Gruiformes, as do the ***trumpeters***, family Psophiidae, of the S American forest floor, which form flocks and have a powerful trumpeting cry. Many species of the order are close to extinction□

crane for lifting goods, etc., they include overhead ***gantries*** travelling on rails; revolving ***jib*** cranes, as used on trucks or on docks for loading/unloading; and ***tower*** cranes used on large-scale building sites□

crane-fly or ***daddy-long-legs***, family Tipulidae, in insect order Diptera◊, the larvae of the typical genus being 'leather-jackets' which attack plant roots, especially grasses□

crane's bill any species of geranium◊□

Cranko John 1927–73. British choreographer, born in S Africa, whose ballets include *Pineapple Poll* 1951 and *Onegin* 1965, and the revue *Cranks* 1952□

Cranmer Thomas 1489–1556. Archbishop of Canterbury from 1533. He had suggested in 1529 that the question of Henry VIII's marriage to Catherine of Aragon should be referred to the universities of Europe rather than the Pope, and now declared it null and void. A Protestant convert, under Edward VI he was responsible for the issue of the Prayer Books of 1549 and 1552, and supported the succession of Lady Jane Grey. Condemned for heresy under Mary, he at first recanted, but when his life was not spared, resumed his position and was burnt, first holding to the fire the hand which had signed his recantation□

craps casino game with two dice, originating in the USA in the 19th century; winning throws are 7 or 11 and losers 2, 3, and 12□

Crashaw Richard 1613–49. English Metaphysical poet. A Catholic convert, he settled in France, and published religious verse, e.g. *Steps to the Temple* 1646□

Crassus Marcus Licinius c108–53 BC. Roman general who crushed the Spartacus◊ rising in 71. In 60 he joined with Caesar and Pompey in the first Triumvirate and in 55 obtained command in the East. Invading Mesopotamia, he was defeated by the Parthians, captured, and put to death□

crater impact, crater formed by the collision of meteorites (or Apollo◊ objects), with earth, the moon, or other planetary bodies. They may be small, but about 100 craters over 1 km/1100 yds across are known, and some are so huge that they may have modified earth's geographical features (see astron◊), or its climate and the course of evolution. One pointer to the fact that these craters were formed by meteors is the concentration of iridium◊ and other heavy metals, which are typical of meteorites, in two of their sedimentary layers: 65 million years ago (between the Cretaceous and Tertiary periods), and 38 million years ago (between the Oligocene and Eocene periods)□

Crater Lake see Chubb Crater◊□

Crawley 'new town' (plastics, engineeering, printing) in W Sussex, England; population 72 500□

crayfish a type of small lobster◊□

creationism a theory concerned with the origins of matter, life, etc. Creation science claims, as does the Bible in Genesis, that the world and humanity (with no link with the great apes) was created, by a supernatural Creator, only some 6000 years ago. It is not recognized by scientists as having a scientific basis□

Crécy-en-Ponthieu village NE of Abbeville, N France, where Philip VI was defeated by Edward III in 1346□

credit card card issued by a bank, etc. (the first was Diner's Club in the USA in 1950), enabling a holder to obtain goods or services on credit; ***bank cards*** facilitate withdrawal of money already in an account□

creed verbal confession of faith (Latin *credo* 'I believe') in the accepted doctrines of the Christian Church, e.g. the 2nd-century ***Apostles' Creed***; ***Nicene Creed*** 381 (see Nicaea◊); ***Athanasian Creed***, probably 5th century. Only the Nicene is recognized by the Eastern Orthodox Church□

cremation disposal of the dead by burning (as among Greeks, Romans, Teutons, etc.), but discouraged by Christianity because of belief in the bodily resurrection of the dead. It was revived in Europe in the 1870s, and shortage of ground space makes it increasingly used. It requires two medical certificates□

Creole in the West Indies and Spanish America, people of European descent born in the New World; in the Louisiana region, either someone of French or Spanish descent, or (popularly) of mixed European and African descent□

Creole (language) in the Caribbean, the language of the blacks□

creosote wood preservative distilled from coal tar, or a pharmaceutical distilled from wood tar□

crescent moon in its first or last quarter, used as the emblem of the Turks on their taking of Constantinople in 1453, and to denote Islam in flags, and in the Red Crescent (equivalent of the Red Cross)□

cress or ***watercress*** a plant of the genus nasturtium◊□

cress several pungent-tasting plants, mostly family Cruciferae, but especially ***common cress** Lepidium sativum*, eaten at the cotyledon (seed leaf) stage, together with mustard◊, in salad, 'mustard and cress'□

Crete Mediterranean island (Greek *Kríti*)

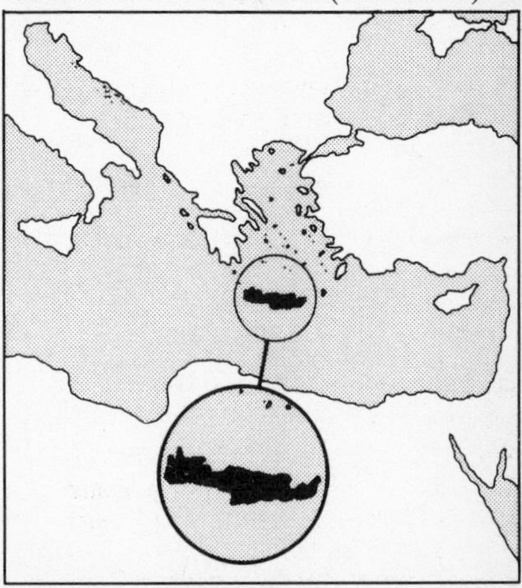

area 8378 sq km/3235 sq mi
capital Khana (Canea)
towns largest town Iráklion (Candia)

features largest of the Greek islands; remains of the Minoan◊ civilization 3000–1400BC (see Knossos◊)
products citrus, fruit, olives, wine
population 456 640
language Cretan dialect of Greek
famous people Mountbatten
history coming successively under Roman, Byzantine, Venetian, and Turkish rule, the island was annexed by Greece in 1913. In 1941, it was captured by German airborne forces from Allied troops (who had retreated from the mainland) and recaptured in 1944□

cretinism disease caused by thyroid deficiency (see under hormone◊), resulting in mental retardation, dwarfism, and facial distortion□

cribbage card game for two or four players in which they try to win a set number of points before their opponents□

Crichton James c1560–82. Scottish scholar, 'the Admirable Crichton' because of his gifts as poet, linguist, athlete, and swordsman□

Crick Francis 1916– . British molecular biologist, who shared a Nobel prize in 1962 (with Maurice Wilkins and James D Watson) for discoveries on the structure of DNA◊, and the means whereby characteristics are transmitted from one generation to another□

cricket insect of the order Orthoptera◊, looking like a grasshopper, but with longer antennae: they stridulate (rub their front wings together to produce a chirping noise). They include the ***house cricket*** *Acheta domesticus*, family Gryllidae; and the ***mole cricket***, family Gryllotalpidae, that digs burrows which amplify its stridulation to 90 decibels□

cricket game played on grass between two teams of 11 players, the two wickets being 20.12 m/22 yds apart. The batsmen try to score 'runs' by hitting a hard leather-covered ball with a willow bat. The rules were first codified in 1774. Test matches (taking several days, rather than the usual three) are played among England, Australia (from 1877), West Indies, New Zealand, India, and Pakistan (see also Ashes◊). The headquarters is Marylebone Cricket Club (MCC), St John's Wood (see Lord's◊), London. Great cricketers have included W G Grace, Sir Jack Hobbs, W R Hammond, and Sir Len Hutton; the Australian Sir Don Bradman; the Indian K S Ranjitsinhji; the South African A D Nourse; and the West Indians Sir Leary Constantine, Sir Frank Worrell, Sir Gary Sobers, and Viv Richards□

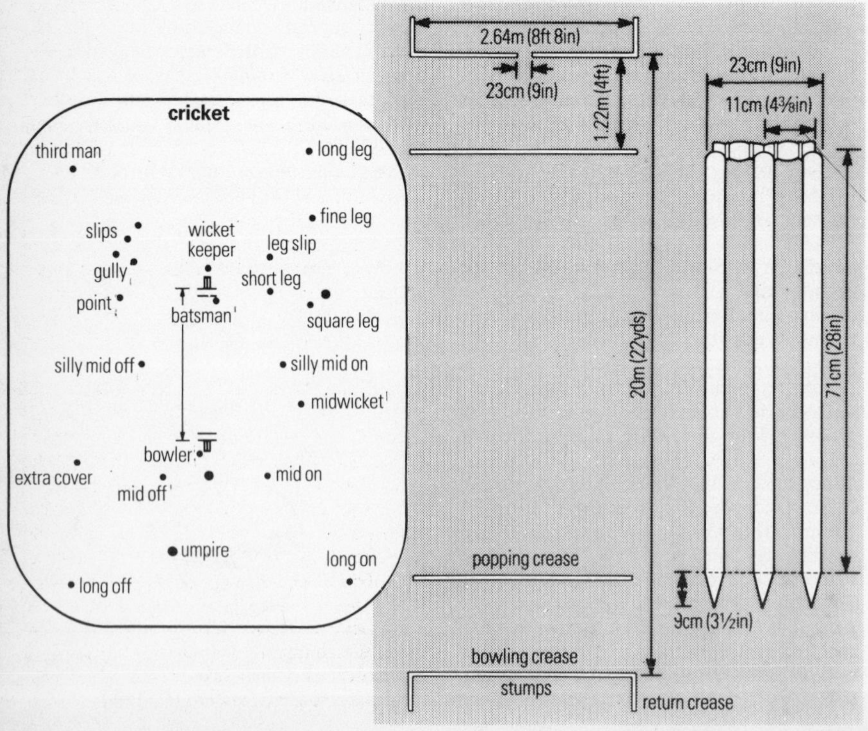

Crimea N peninsula on the Black Sea, a region of Ukraine◊ Republic, USSR from 1954.
area 27 000 sq km/10 400 sq mi
capital Simferopol
towns Sevastopol, Yalta
features mainly steppe, but the S coast is a holiday resort
products iron, oil
population 2 000 000
recent history Turkish 1475–1774, a subsequent brief independence was ended by Russian annexation in 1783. It was the republic of Taurida 1917–20, and the Crimean Autonomous Soviet Republic from 1920 until it was occupied by Germany, Jul 1942–May 1944. It was then reduced to a region, its Tatar people being deported for collaboration to Uzbekistan; even though they were exonerated in 1967, and some were allowed to return, others were forcibly re-exiled in 1979□

Crimean War 1853–6 nominally fought over Russian claims to protect all Orthodox Christians, but actually over Russian expansionism in the Balkans.
1853 Russia invaded the Turkish-ruled Balkans (occupying Moldavia and Wallachia) in Jul, but was forced to withdraw by Austrian pressure. Turkey declared war on Russia on 4 Oct, but in Nov the Turkish fleet was destroyed at *Sinop*
1854 Mar Britain and France declared war on Russia; 20 Sept, Allied victory at Alma, and again on 25 Oct at Balaclava◊ (the Charge of the Light Brigade) and on 5 Nov at Inkerman (Russian attack on the British army besieging Sevastopol repulsed)
1855 Sept, Russians surrendered Sevastopol
1856 Feb, Treaty of Paris. See Florence Nightingale◊, Lord Raglan◊, and Sir William Russell◊□

Criminal Injuries Compensation Board board established in 1964 in UK to administer the scheme for government compensation for victims of crimes of violence□

Criminal Investigation Department see under police◊ and Scotland Yard◊□

criminology the study of crime, its causes (physical, psychological, environmental, etc.), and prevention. See Cesare Lombroso◊□

Crinoidea class of echinoderms◊, the feather-stars and sea-lilies, which are distinguished by being fixed by a stalk for at least part of their life□

Crippen Henry Hawley 1861–1910. American murderer of his wife, variety artist Belle Elmore, who buried her remains in the cellar of his London home and tried to escape to the USA with his mistress Ethel le Neve (dressed as a boy). He was arrested on shipboard following a radio message, the first criminal captured 'by radio', and was hanged□

Cripps Sir (Richard) Stafford 1889–1952. British Labour statesman, nephew of Beatrice Webb◊. A founder of the Socialist League, he was expelled from the party 1939–45 for supporting a 'Popular Front' of all opposed to Chamberlain's appeasement policy. He was ambassador to Moscow 1940–2, Minister of Aircraft Production 1942–5, and Chancellor of the Exchequer 1947–50□

Crivelli Carlo c1430–c1493. Venetian painter of religious subjects, rich in detail and colour□

Croatia constituent republic of Yugoslavia;
area 56 538 sq km/21 824 sq mi
capital Zagreb
features Adriatic coastline with large islands; very mountainous, with part of the Karst region and the Julian and Styrian Alps; some marshland
population 4 601 500, including 3 455 000 Croats, 531 500 Serbs, 25 500 Hungarians
language the Croatian variant of Serbo-Croat
religion Roman Catholicism□

Croce Benedetto 1866–1952. Italian philosopher, an opponent of Fascism. Like Hegel, he held that ideas do not *represent* reality but *are* reality; but unlike his master he rejected every kind of transcendence□

crochet see knitting◊□

Crockett Davy 1786–1836. American Tennessee-born frontier-hero, who became a Democrat Congressman, and died defending the Alamo□

crocodile typical reptile of the order Crocodylia, a survivor of the line which includes the dinosaurs◊. They have a long narrow snout and a very powerful tail. Crocodiles are equally adapted to living on land and in water, ballast themselves with stones in their stomachs to keep submerged in fast-flowing rivers, and swim chiefly with their tails. Special flaps cover their nostrils and allow them to stay under water for up to an hour; this means that they need only hang on to their prey under water and it will drown. They gain some control over their temperature by lying with their jaws open for ventilation, which also enables scavenging birds to pick their teeth. Mainly carnivorous, they have good eyesight to locate prey, and unlike most reptiles have a kind of outer ear. Mating takes place at night, when the males call to the females; the hard-shelled eggs are laid in holes or nest-mounds of vegetation, with the female remaining nearby to answer the call of the young for help in hatching. She then takes

them to the water in her mouth (which has led to unfounded accusations of cannibalism) and spends several weeks teaching them to feed, etc. The order comprises:
crocodiles, family Crocodylidae, which are the largest forms, with broad heads; they are found in Africa, Asia, and S America. Among the largest is the ***Orinoco crocodile*** *Crocodylus intermedius* at 7 m/21 ft, but specimens of the ***saltwater crocodile*** *Crocodylus porosus* of Australia, India, and Fiji, now being farmed in Papua New Guinea, may be even larger.
alligators, family Alligatoridae, with narrower heads, of which some American species are known as caimans.
gavials or ***gharials***, family Gavialidae, long-snouted Indian fish-eating species, harmless to man□

crocus widespread genus of plants, family Iridaceae (see iris◊), with white, yellow, or purple flowers followed by long slender leaves. The Asian ***saffron crocus*** *C sativus*, with purple flowers and long drooping stigmas, is the source of an orange extract used for colouring and flavouring□

Croesus d. c546BC. Last king of Lydia, famed for his wealth. His court included Solon◊, who warned him that no man could be called happy till his life had ended happily. When Croesus was overthrown by Cyrus the Persian in 546 and condemned to be burnt to death, he called out Solon's name. Cyrus, having learnt the reason, spared his life. See numismatics◊□

Croker Richard 1841–1922. American politician,'Boss' of Tammany Hall◊, 1886–1902□

Cromagnon see under Dordogne◊□

Crome John 1768–1821. British artist, 'Old Crome', as distinguished from his artist son ***John Berney Crome*** 1794–1842. Born at Norwich, he was apprenticed to a signpainter, and developed a rich Dutch-influenced landscape style□

Cromer Evelyn Baring, 1st Earl of Cromer 1841–1917. British statesman, member of the Baring banking family, who went out to order Egyptian finances in 1877, and as agent and consul-general 1883–1907 was virtual ruler of the now solvent country□

Crompton Richmal. Pseudonym of R C Lamburn 1890–1969. A teacher, she wrote stories about the dishevelled schoolboy 'William'□

Crompton Samuel 1753–1827. British inventor. Born in Lancashire, he invented in 1779 the 'spinning mule', combining the ideas of Arkwright◊ and Hargreave◊, widely adopted but bringing him little return□

Cromwell Oliver 1599–1658. English general and statesman. Born at Huntingdon, son of a small landowner, he entered parliament and was active in events leading to the Civil War. He raised cavalry forces (later called Ironsides) which aided the victories at Edgehill and Marston Moor, and organized the New Model Army, which he led (with Fairfax) to victory at Naseby. Failing to secure a constitutional settlement with Charles I 1646–8, he defeated the 1648 Scottish invasion at Preston. A special commission, of which Cromwell was a member, tried the king and condemned him to death, and a republic was set up. The Levellers◊ wished to go further, but he executed their leaders in 1649; used terror to crush Irish clan resistance 1649–50 (see Drogheda◊); and defeated the Scots (who had acknowledged Charles II) at Dunbar and Worcester. Having forcibly expelled the corrupt 'Rump' Parliament, he summoned a convention ('Barebone's Parliament'), soon dissolved as too radical, and under a constitution (Instrument of Government) drawn up by the army leaders, became Protector (king in all but name). The Parliament of 1654–5 was dissolved as uncooperative, and after a period of military dictatorship, his last parliament offered him the crown: he refused because he feared the army's republicanism. He established religious toleration, and Britain's prestige in Europe on the basis of an anachronistic alliance with France against Spain. At the Restoration his body was removed from Westminster Abbey□

Cromwell Richard 1626–1712. Son of Oliver Cromwell◊. He succeeded his father as Protector, but resigned in May 1659, living in exile after the Restoration until 1680, when he returned to England□

Cromwell Thomas, Earl of Essex c1485–1540. English statesman. Originally in Wolsey's service, he became secretary to Henry VIII in 1534 and the real director of government policy. He had Henry proclaimed head of the Church, suppressed the monasteries, ruthlessly crushed all opposition, and favoured Protestantism, which upheld the divine right of kings against the divine right of the Pope. His mistake in arranging Henry's marriage to Anne of Cleves◊ (to cement an alliance with the German Protestant princes against France and the Empire) led to his being accused of treason and beheaded□

Cronin A(rchibald) J(oseph) 1896–81. Scottish novelist. He was a doctor, until enabled by the success of *Hatter's Castle* 1931 to devote himself to writing, e.g. *The Citadel*

1937 and the stories which became the basis of *Dr Finlay's Casebook* (TV and radio series)□

Cronos see under Saturn◊□

Cronos in Greek mythology, one of the Titans◊, and father of Zeus□

Crookes Sir William 1832–1919. British physicist and chemist. By his work on electrical discharges in gases, he paved the way for the discovery of the electron and X-rays, and Edison's development of light bulbs. He also discovered thallium◊□

croquet open-air game played with mallets and balls on a level grass lawn 27 m/90 ft by 18 m/60 ft. Two or more players drive the balls through a series of hoops set to a pattern on the ground, and a player may have his ball advanced by his partner or retarded by his opponent. Played in France 16th–17th centuries, it was popular in England in the 1850s, and revived from the 1950s. The headquarters is the Croquet Association, established in 1897, at the Hurlingham Club, London□

Crosby 'Bing' (Harry Lillis) 1904–77. American dance-band singer from 1925, e.g. 'Pennies from Heaven', 'Blue Skies', 'White Christmas', 'The Bells of St Mary's' (featured in films with those titles). He also made a series of 'road' film comedies, with Dorothy Lamour and Bob Hope, e.g. *Road to Singapore*□

cross originally a simple stake used to execute low-class criminals, as the Western emblem of Christianity (the Roman cross), it has a crossbar near the top of the stake. Other forms include: St Anthony's (crossbar right at the top); St Andrew's (two diagonals); Greek (square cross with equal arms); Maltese (tapered, and often indented, triangular, equal arms); Celtic (Latin type with a superimposed circle); Cross of Lorraine (double crossbar: the emblem of the French Resistance in World War II); Papal (triple crossbar); and, oldest of all, the *ankh*, or ancient Egyptian *crux ansata*, the emblem of life – a cross with a loop top. See St Helena◊□

crossbill a type of finch◊□

Crossman Richard 1907–74. British Labour politician. A 'Bevanite' (see Aneurin Bevan◊), he was Minister of Housing and Local Government 1964–6, Health and Social Security 1968–70. His posthumous *Crossman Papers* 1975 revealed confidential Cabinet discussion□

crossword puzzle diagram divided into squares, in which those which are numbered with 'clues' must be filled in with words, which read 'down' and 'across': popular from 1923□

croup inflammation (usually viral) of a child's larynx and trachea, with croaking breathing and a cough□

crow a bird of the family Corvidae◊□

crowfoot a plant of the family Ranunculaceae◊□

Crowley Aleister (Edward Alexander) 1875–1947. British dabbler in drugs, sex, and magic, self-styled the 'Great Beast', who established a 'lay community' at Cefalu, Sicily□

crown the most famous crowns are: ***Britain*** St Edward's and Imperial State (see regalia◊); ***Hungary*** St Stephen's◊; ***Papal*** (tiara) a tall, rounded diadem with three encircling coronets; ***Charlemagne's,*** eight gold plates (preserved at Vienna)□

Crown Agents for Overseas Governments and Administrations, public corporation acting as business and financial agent for governments inside and outside the Commonwealth, public authorities, etc.□

Crown Colonies British colonies not yet having a fully responsible or representative government, and administered either by a Crown-appointed governor or by elected or nominated legislative and executive councils with an official majority□

Crown Courts see Law◊ Courts□

Crown Proceedings Act an Act of Parliament which provided that the Crown (i.e. government departments, etc.) could from 1948 be sued like a private person□

Croydon borough of S London

features 11th-century Lanfranc's palace, former residence of Archbishops of Canterbury; Ashcroft Theatre, founded 1962; overspill office development from central London

population 319 100□

Cruciferae family of N temperate flowering plants with a cruciform petal arrangement; many of over 200 genera are food plants, e.g. cabbage◊, radish◊, watercress◊□

crucifixion ancient method of execution by nailing or binding a criminal to a cross; see Jesus◊□

Cruden Alexander 1701–70. Scottish compiler of a Biblical *Concordance* 1737□

Cruelty Theatre of. See Antonin Artaud◊□

Cruft Charles 1852–1938. British organizer of the first annual dog show – Cruft's – in 1886□

Cruikshank George 1792–1878. British artist, remembered especially for his illustrations to Dickens's *Oliver Twist*, Ainsworth's *Tower of London*, etc.□

cruiser medium-sized warship, designed for high speed and long 'cruising' range (especially when nuclear-powered), and capable of anti-aircraft, submarine, or guided missile work, e.g. *Ticonderoga* USA, 9600 tons, gas-turbine powered. Larger is the ***battle cruiser*** e.g. the nuclear-powered, 28 000 tonne *Kirov* USSR□

crustacean: the crayfish

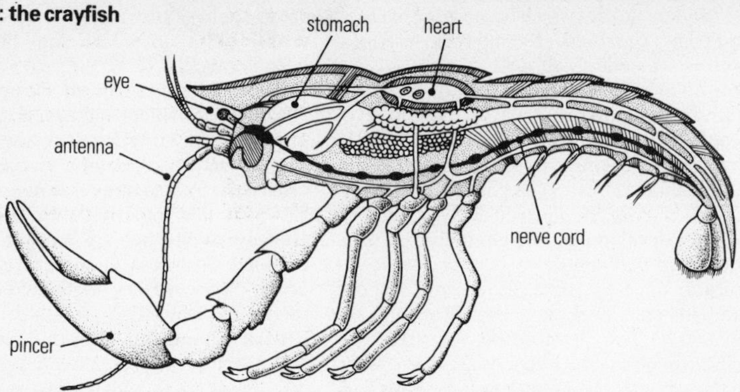

Crusades military ventures 1096–1291, especially to recover the Holy Land◊ from Islam, including: ***First Crusade*** 1095–9 resulting in the recovery of Jerusalem and the establishment of a chain of Latin kingdoms along the Syrian coast; ***Second Crusade*** 1147–9, led by Louis VII of France and Emperor Conrad III of Germany; they failed in a siege of Damascus; ***Third Crusade*** 1189–92, led by Philip II Augus of France and Richard I of England, failed to recapture Jerusalem (it had fallen to Saladin◊ in 1187); ***Fourth Crusade*** 1202–4, ended in the brutal sack of Christian Constantinople and division of its empire among the crusaders; ***Children's Crusade*** 1212, abortive attempt by 50 000 children from France and Germany to go and recapture Jerusalem, which ended in most of them being sold into slavery; ***Sixth Crusade*** 1228–9, led by the Emperor Frederick II, who recovered Jerusalem (finally lost in 1244) from the Egyptian sultan by negotiation; ***Seventh Crusade*** 1249–54 and ***Eighth Crusade*** 1270–2, both led by Louis◊ IX of France (in the latter associated with Edward◊ I of England); Acre, the last Christian fortress in Syria, was lost in 1291□

Crustacea class of mainly marine animals in phylum Arthropoda, including barnacles, crabs, lobsters, crayfish, prawns, shrimps, woodlice◊, etc. Nearly all breathe by using gills and have a segmented abdomen. The number of legs, pincers, and antennae varies. The subclass ***Ostracoda*** are minute bivalves, with completely enclosed body and working limbs, whose presence is useful in working out the relationship of geological strata when prospecting for oil□

cryogenics science of very low temperatures (approaching absolute zero), including the liquefaction of gases such as nitrogen, helium, hydrogen; and exploitation of special properties produced at these low temperatures, e.g. the disappearance of electrical resistance (superconductivity◊)□

cryolite rare crystalline mineral (Na_3AlF_6) found in Greenland, comprising fluoride of sodium and aluminium, used in refining aluminium□

cryonics process of freezing at the moment of clinical death to enable eventual resuscitation. The first human treated was James H Bedford, a lung cancer patient of 74, in USA in 1967. The body, drained of blood, is indefinitely preserved in a thermos-type container filled with liquid nitrogen at −196°C□

cryptography science of codes, e.g. that produced by the Enigma coding machine used by the Germans in World War II (see Ultra◊), and those used in commerce by banks encoding electronic fund transfer messages, business firms sending computer-conveyed memos between headquarters, and in the growing field of electronic mail. No method of encrypting is completely unbreakable, but decoding can be made so complex that the time and equipment needed is difficult to arrange□

crystal a substance with an internal orderly three-dimensional arrangement of its atoms or molecules, thereby creating an external surface of clearly defined smooth faces having characteristic angles between them. Examples are common salt and quartz□

crystallography study of crystals, and the determination of the atomic patterns within them by X-ray diffraction. These patterns may be complex when the crystals are of living matter or metal alloys, etc.□

Crystal Palace glass and iron building (see Paxton◊) housing the Great Exhibition of 1851 in Hyde Park, London; later rebuilt in modified form at Sydenham Hill in 1854 (burnt down in 1936). The site is partly filled by the National Sports Centre□

Ctesiphon see Baghdad◊□

Cuba Republic of

area 114 524 sq km/44 200 sq mi

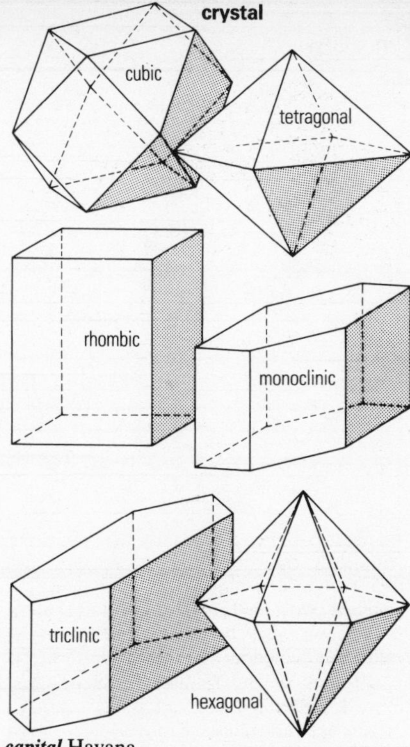

capital Havana
features largest of the West Indian islands; US base (on perpetual lease since 1934) at Guantánamo Bay (Gitmo), and Soviet base at Cienfuegos
exports sugar (largest producer after USSR), tobacco, coffee; iron, copper, nickel
currency Cuban peso
population 9 710 000, of which 66% are of Spanish descent, but with a large black and Mulatto element

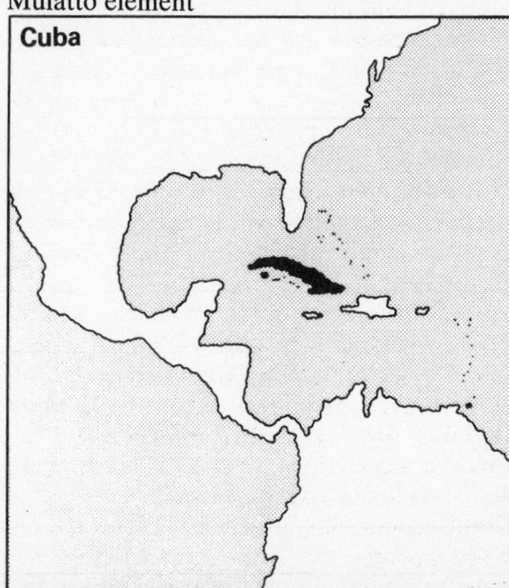

language Spanish
religion Roman Catholicism 45%
government under the constitution of 1976 there is a an executive president (Fidel Castro◊) and council of ministers, and the Communist Party prevails
recent history sighted by Columbus in 1492, followed by Spanish conquest and the importation of African slaves. Corrupt Spanish rule was thrown off in 1895, and Spain recognized Cuban independence in 1898 (after defeat by the USA who herself did not finally withdraw troops until 1902). A dictatorship by Batista, from 1952, was ended by Castros'◊ revolution in 1959. His anti-US policies resulted in US backing for an attempt by exiled Cubans to overthrow him 17–20 Apr 1961, known from their landing site as the ***Bay of Pigs*** incident. The economy is heavily subsidized by the USSR, and Soviet missiles installed in 1962 were withdrawn only under pressure from J F Kennedy. Cuban troops have been used in Africa and Central America to advance the Soviet communist cause□

Cubism art movement arising out of Post-Impressionism; in 1908 Matisse◊ used the word derogatively of a painting by Braque◊. It expresses reality through abstract forms, e.g. Picasso◊ cuts up human features into a number of geometrical forms. Other exponents: André Derain, Albert Gleizes, Fernand Léger, Jacques Lipchitz, and Francis Picabia. Suprematism◊ is a simplified form□

Cuchulain chief hero of a cycle of Irish legends, in which he is associated with his uncle Conchobar, king of Ulster; he is the Irish 'Achilles'◊□

cuckoo family of birds Cuculidae, order Cuculiformes, including the ***European cuckoo*** *Cuculus canorus*, which has a persistent two-note call. Arriving from the south in spring, it lays a series of single eggs (not always hatched and reared) in the nests of smaller birds; the large 'changeling' then ejects the other 'competing' eggs. The habit is not universal among cuckoos; the ***yellow-billed cuckoo*** *Coccyzus americanus* rears its own broods. A species of N and Central America is the ***roadrunner*** or ***chaparral cock*** *Geococcyx californianus*, accident-prone from its habit of running on roads□

cuckoo-pint a plant, the wild arum◊□

cuckoo spit the frothy fluid surrounding and exuded by the larvae of the frog-hopper◊□

cucumber plant *Cucumis sativa*, family Cucurbitaceae◊, producing long, green-skinned fruit with crisp translucent flesh; small cucumbers, especially the fruit of *Cucumis anguria*, are pickled as 'gherkins'□

Cucurbitaceae family of tropical and subtropical plants, which include the cucumber, gourd, marrow, pumpkin, squash, etc.□

Cuenca city in SW Ecuador; population 104 500□

Cuenca city in central Spain, once famed for silverware, and now for its Museum of Abstract Art; population 35 400□

Cuiabá town (with nearby gold and diamond mines) in Brazil; population 100 000□

Culbertson Ely. See bridge◊□

Culdees Celtic Christian monks in Ireland and Scotland 9th–12th centuries; few survived the adherence to Roman usage then imposed□

Culham see Oxfordshire◊□

Culicidae insect family, order Diptera, including gnats, mosquitoes, and midges□

Culloden Moor site near Inverness, Highland Region, Scotland, of the defeat of the Young Pretender by the Duke of Cumberland in 1746□

Cumae first Greek colony near Naples, Italy, founded c740BC. See Sibyl◊□

Cuman ancestors of the Turkic-speaking peoples of the USSR, who established an empire from the Volga to the Danube 11th–12th centuries, but were defeated by the Mongols in 1238, and took refuge in Hungary□

Cumberland Ernest Augus, Duke of Cumberland 1771–1851. Fifth son of George III, an unpopular high Tory who opposed all reform. He succeeded William IV as King of Hanover 1837–51 (Victoria being excluded by the Salic Law, see Salian◊): his reign was stormy□

Cumberland William Augus, Duke of Cumberland 1721–65. British general, 3rd son of George II. In 1746 he ended the Jacobite rising in Scotland at Culloden◊, and his brutal repression of the Highlands earned him the nickname of 'Butcher'□

Cumbernauld 'new town' in Strathclyde, Scotland; population 61 680. Founded in 1956 to take Glasgow's overspill□

Cumbria NW county of England

area 6810 sq km/2629 sq mi

towns administrative headquarters Carlisle; Barrow, Kendal, Whitehaven, Workington

features Lake District National Park (including Scafell Pike 978 m/3210 ft, highest mountain in England; Helvellyn 950 m/3118 ft; Lake Windermere, the largest lake in England, 17 km/10.5 mi long, 1.6 km/1 mi wide (the Grizedale Forest sculpture project is nearby); lakes Derwentwater, Ullswater, etc.; Yorkshire Dales National Park; Furness peninsula; atomic stations at Calder Hall and Sellafield (reprocessing plant), formerly

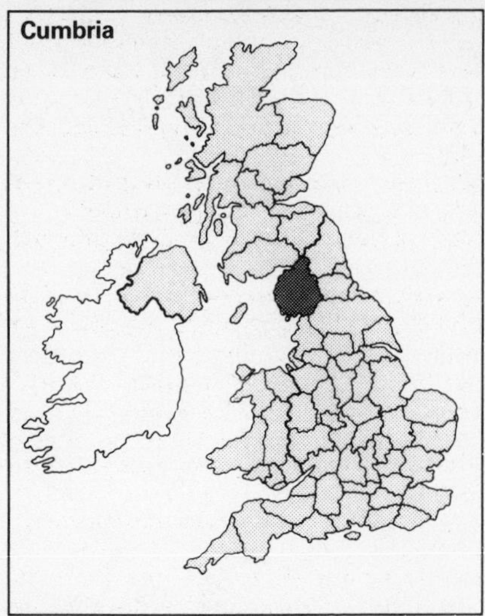

Windscale (site of a nuclear accident Oct 1957).

products traditional coal, iron, and steel of the coast towns has been replaced by newer industries including chemicals, plastics, and electronics; N and E there is dairying and West Cumberland Farmers is the country's largest agricultural cooperative.

population 468 500

famous people birthplace of Wordsworth at Cockermouth, and home at Grasmere; homes of Coleridge and Southey at Keswick; Ruskin's home, Brantwood on Coniston Water; de Quincey□

cumin aromatic seed of the Mediterranean herb *Cuminum cyminum*, family Umbelliferae□

Cumming Sir Mansfield 1859–1923. British naval officer, first head of the British Secret Intelligence Service: the head of the service has always since been known by the initial letter 'C'□

Cummings Bruce. See W P N Barbellion◊□

Cummings E(dward) E(stlin) 1894–1962. American poet whose verse was marked by peculiar punctuation and typographical devices; also author of the novel *The Enormous Room* 1922□

cuneiform system of wedge-shaped writing on clay invented by the Sumerians in the mid-4th millennium BC, and modified by the Assyrians, Babylonians, Elamites, Hittites, Persians, etc. until the 5th century BC. Modern decipherers were G F Grotefend◊ 1802 and H C Rawlinson 1846□

Cunningham Andrew Browne, 1st Viscount Cunningham of Hyndhope 1883–1963. British admiral, Commander-in-Chief in the

Mediterranean 1939–42 maintaining British control: see Taranto◊ and Matapan◊; and as Commander-in-Chief of the Allied Naval Forces in the Mediterranean Feb–Oct 1943 received in Sept the surrender of the Italian fleet□

Cupid in Roman mythology, the god of love, identified with the Greek god, Eros◊□

cuprite red oxide of copper, Cu_2O, in crystalline form□

cupro-nickel copper alloy (75% copper, 25% nickel) used for 'silver' coins in the UK from 1946□

Curaçao island in the Netherlands Antilles◊
area 338 sq km/210sq mi
capital Willemstad
features Curaçao, orange-flavoured liqueur originated here
exports refined oil (imported from Venezuela)
currency guilder
population 160 625
language Dutch (official); Spanish and English
religion Roman Catholicism (majority)
government internal autonomy (from 1951), with Lieutenant-Governor, Executive Council, elected Island Council
history sighted by Europeans in 1499, it was formerly a Spanish colony, becoming Dutch in 1634□

curare resin of the S American tree *Strychnos toxifera*, family Loganiaceae, used as an arrow poison (causing muscle paralysis) by Indians, and in surgery as a muscle relaxant. It is related to strychnine◊. Curarine is an alkaloid extracted from curare for medical purposes□

curate in England, a clergyman assisting a parish priest□

Curia Romana the judicial and administrative bodies through which the Pope carries on the government of the Catholic Church□

Curie Marie 1867–1934. Polish chemist, born in Warsaw (Marya Sklodovska), and wife of physicist ***Pierre Curie*** 1859–1906, from 1895. They were awarded the Nobel prize for physics (with Becquerel) in 1903 for their work on radioactivity, and in 1911 Marie received the Nobel prize for chemistry for her discovery of polonium and radium. She died a victim of the radiation emitted by the chemicals with which she worked. Her daughter and son-in-law, ***Irene Joliot-Curie*** 1896–1956, and ***Frédéric Joliot*** 1900–59, received a Nobel prize for chemistry in 1935 for their creation of artificial radioactivity□

curie unit of radioactivity equal to 37 thousand million disintegrations per second□

Curitiba industrial city in Brazil; population 843 745□

curium element
symbol Cm
atomic number 96
physicl description silvery-white metal
features one of the actinide◊ series; it is produced artificially from americium◊ and was named after the Curies◊. It has several long-life isotopes which emit alpha particles
uses none at present□

curlew wading bird, especially the ***Eurasian curlew*** *Numenius arquata*, family Scolopacidae (see snipe◊), with a long curved bill and haunting flute-like call□

curling a national game of Scotland, in which two teams of four players deliver handled stones as near as possible to the tee (rather as in bowls◊), and which is played either on ice or an artificial surface□

Curragh see Kildare◊□

Curragh Mutiny demand in Mar 1914 by General Hubert Gough and his officers that they should not be asked to force Protestant Ulster to participate in Home Rule. Partition was eventually adopted□

currant dried berry of a variety of grape, first grown near Corinth, hence the name, and now grown in Greece, California, etc. and used in cakes, etc.□

currant species of shrubs, genus *Ribes*, family Grossulariaceae: ***red currant*** *R rubrum*, ***white currant*** *R sativum*, and ***blackcurrant*** *R nigrum*□

currency the particular type of money◊ in use in a country□

current the flow of a body of water moving in a definite direction. Oceanic currents may be: ***drift currents***, broad and slow-moving; ***stream currents***, narrow and swift-moving, e.g. Gulf Stream◊ and Kuroshio/Japan Current; ***upwelling currents*** which bring cold, nutrient-rich water from the ocean bottom to provide food for plankton, which in turn supports fish and sea birds, e.g. Gulf of Guinea Current and the ***Peru (Humboldt) Current***. Once in 10 years or so, the latter, which runs from the Antarctic up the W coast of S America, turns warm, with heavy rain and rough seas, and disastrous results (as in 1982–3) for the Peruvian anchovy industry and wildlife. The phenomenon is called *el Niño* ('the Child') because it occurs towards Christmas□

Curtin John 1885–1945. Australian Labour statesman. As Prime Minister from 1941, he organized the mobilization of Australia's resources to meet the danger of Japanese invasion□

Curwen John 1816–80. British musician, who perfected c1840 the ***tonic sol-fa*** system of music notation (originated in the 11th century by Guido d'Arezzo) in which the notes of a scale are named by syllables (doh, ray, me, fah, soh, lah, te, with the key indicated) to simplify singing by sight□

Curzon George Nathaniel, 1st Marquess Curzon of Kedleston 1859–1925. British Conservative statesman. Viceroy of India from 1899, he resigned in 1905 following a controversy with Kitchener, and was Foreign Secretary 1919–22. On Bonar Law's resignation in 1923 he was bitterly disappointed when passed over for the premiership in favour of Baldwin. He was the lover of Elinor Glyn◊□

Curzon Line Polish-Russian frontier first proposed by the Versailles conference of 1919 (named after Curzon◊ because of his advocacy of it in 1920), but not implemented until 1945□

custard apple tropical fruit, the 'bullock's heart', of several species of *Annona*, family Annonaceae, with thick custard-like pulp especially *A reticulata*, of tropical America, whose large dark-brown fruit contains a sweet reddish-yellow pulp□

Custer George Armstrong 1839–76. American Civil War general, who later died fighting the Sioux. See American Indians◊□

custodianship the right of caring for someone. In 1984 in the UK effect was given to the provision under the Children Act of 1975 for 'custodianship' by step-parents, foster-parents, etc. It transfers many parental rights needed by a permanent guardian without affecting the legal status of the real parents□

Customs and Excise Board of. British government department with responsibility for the collection of all indirect taxes. ***Customs duties*** are taxes levied on imports, e.g. tobacco, wines and spirits, perfumery, and jewellery; ***excise duties*** are levied on goods produced, e.g. beer, and include VAT; or on licences to sell wines and spirits, etc., or on activities e.g. theatrical productions, betting□

Cuthbert St d. c635–87. Northumbrian shepherd who, after a vision, entered the monastery of Melrose, and because of his miracles on his missionary journeys was called the 'wonderworker of Britain'. A chapel marks the site of his hermitage on the Farne Islands◊, and in 685 he became Bishop of Lindisfarne; his body was removed to Durham 995□

cuttle-fish a type of sea animal. See cephalopod◊□

Cutty Sark tea◊ clipper (Scottish 'short chemise' built in 1869, and preserved at Greenwich from 1957), one of those which used to race to be first home with their cargo from China: she was named from the witch in Burns's poem 'Tam O'Shanter'□

Cuvier Georges, Baron Cuvier 1769–1832. French comparative anatomist, the first to relate the structure of fossil animals to that of their living allies□

Cuxhaven port on the Elbe, W Germany, an outport for Hamburg; population 48 000□

Cuyp Albert 1620–91. Dutch landscape artist, son of ***Jacob Gerritsz Cuyp*** 1594–1652, also a landscape and portrait painter. Famous for his depiction of light□

Cuzco city in S Peru 3350 m/11 000 ft above sea level; population 120 900. Founded in the 11th century by the first of the Incas, it was captured by Pizarro in 1533; nearby Inca irrigation works are being restored, and the Inca mountain sanctuary of Machu Picchu built c1500, and first seen by a European (Bingham) in 1911, lies NW. There is a fine Renaissance cathedral□

Cwmbran 'new town' and administrative headquarters of Gwent, Wales, founded in 1949: population 45 700. Its industries include car components and nylon, and the Llantarnoun Hightech Park (floppy disks, etc.)□

Cybele in Phrygian mythology, an earth goddess, identified by the Greeks with Rhea◊ and honoured in Rome. The Corybantes (eunuch priests) celebrated her worship with orgiastic dances□

cybernetics science of the organization, communication, regulation, and reproduction of living systems, and their mode of evolution and learning: founded by US mathematician Norbert Wiener 1894–1964. The processes are replicated in the laboratory to make electronic limbs, robots, and automated factories in which management decisions are also made by machines□

cycad class of plants belonging to the Gymnosperms◊, including c80 species of the most primitive flowering plants. They resemble tree ferns, were once widespread, but are now confined to tropical America, Africa, and Australia□

Cyclades group of c200 Greek islands (Greek *Kikládhes*) in the Aegean Sea; area 2579 sq km/996 sq mi; population 121 000. They include Andros, Delos (the smallest, which has a temple of Apollo, 4th century BC), Melos (where the *Venus de Milo*, now in the Louvre, was discovered in 1820), Paros, Naxos, and Siros, on which is the capital Hermoupolis. The most southerly, ***Thera*** (formerly Santorini) has been linked with the legend of Atlantis◊□

cyclamates derivatives of cyclohexysulphamic acid, banned as sweeteners in the UK and USA from 1970 because of harmful side effects□

cyclamen genus of Mediterranean perennial plants, family Primulaceae◊, with corms, heart-shaped leaves, and white or pink butterfly-like flowers□

cyclic compounds organic ring species. They may be alicyclic, aromatic, or heterocylic. Alicyclic compounds have localized bonding i.e. all the electrons are confined to their own particular bond; in contrast to aromatic compounds, where certain electrons have free movement throughout the ring. Alicyclic compounds include cyclopentane (C_5H_{10}) and cyclohexanol ($C_6H_{11}OH$). Their chemical properties are similar to their straight-chain (aliphatic) counterparts. Aromatic compounds undergo entirely different chemical reactions.

Heterocyclic means a ring of carbon atoms with one or more carbon replaced by another element, usually nitrogen, oxygen, or sulphur. For instance pyridine is a six-membered ring with five carbons and one nitrogen (C_5H_5N). Furan is a five-membered ring containing one oxygen (C_4H_4O). Uracil contains two nitrogens in a six-membered ring ($C_4H_4N_2O_2$). These compounds may be aliphatic or aromatic in nature□

cyclone violent storm characterized by strong rotating winds formed by the mixture of cold, dry polar air with warm, moist equatorial air, as the two meet in temperate latitudes. Warm air rises over the cold, resulting in rain, snow, etc. Winds blow in towards the centre in an anticlockwise direction in the N hemisphere, clockwise in the S hemisphere. A fast-moving cyclone is a tornado◊□

cyclopes in Greek mythology, giants who lived in Sicily, had a single eye, and lived as shepherds; Odysseus encountered them. *Cyclopean walls* are those made of large blocks of undressed stone□

cyclotron a form of particle accelerator◊□

cymbal musical percussion instrument; two round metal plates which are struck together□

Cymru Celtic name for Wales◊□

Cynewulf c750AD. Anglo-Saxon religious poet, author of *Juliana, The Fates of the Apostles*, etc., in which he inserted his name in runic◊ acrostics◊□

Cynic school of philosophy founded at Athens c400BC by Antisthenes, a disciple of Socrates, advocating stern morality and disregard of comfort. His followers, led by Diogenes◊, also regarded human affection as weakness, a 'snarling' sort of attitude which led them to be called cynics, from the Greek word for 'dog-like'□

cypress a genus of conifers◊□

Cyprian St c210–258. Bishop of Carthage c249, he was martyred under Valerian, and wrote on the unity of the church. His feast day is 16 Sept□

Cyprus

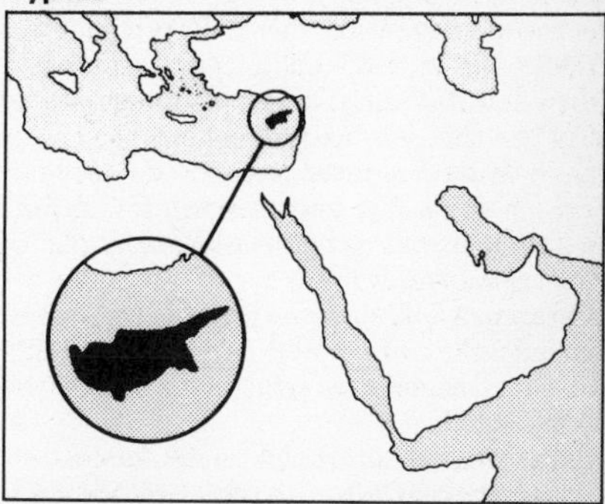

Mediterranean island, divided between the southern Republic of Cyprus (Greek *Kypros*), and the Turkish Republic of Northern Cyprus (Turkish *Kibris*)

area 9251 sq km/3572 sq mi, 40% in Turkish hands

capital Nicosia (divided between the Greeks and Turks)

towns ports of Paphos, Limassol, and Larnaca (Greek); and Morphou, and ports Kyrenia and Famagusta (Turkish)

features Attila Line◊; two British military enclaves on the S coast; there is also an outpost of the Government Communications Headquarters in the mountains

exports citrus, grapes, Cyprus sherry, potatoes; copper, pyrites

currency Cyprus pound

population 624 600, 80% Greek Cypriot, 20% Turkish Cypriot

language Greek and Turkish (official); English

religion Greek Orthodox, Sunni Islam

government Greek president (Spyros Kyprianou from 1977; re-elected 1983) and house of representatives ***Turkish*** president (Rauf Denktash from 1976) and legislative assembly

history colonized by Greeks from the mainland from the 15th century BC, Cyprus formed part of all the ancient empires in turn. Taken by Turkey in 1571, it was surrendered to British administration in 1878, and annexed by Britain in 1914. Terrorism, by Greek Cypriots who aimed at *enosis* (union with Greece) from 1954, was countered by the Turkish minority demand for partition. After independence in 1960 (within the Commonwealth from 1961), terrorism continued and the first president, Makarios◊, was overthrown in 1974 by a Greek-supported military coup. The Turks then invaded and occupied the northern part of the island, and in 1975 proclaimed a Turkish Cypriot federated state (unilaterally proclaimed a republic in 1983), and 200 000 Greek Cypriots fled to the south as refugees. From 1964 there has been a United Nations peacekeeping force there. Kyprianou was re-elected in 1985 on a campaign not to negotiate with the Turkish Cypriots until all Turkish troops evacuate the north□

Cyrano de Bergerac Savinien de 1619–55. French writer and soldier, noted for his long nose, immortalized by Rostand◊ in his play of the same name□

Cyrenaica former province of Libya, which includes the cities of Benghazi◊ and Tobruk◊, and the magnificent ruins of Cyrene, Apollonia, etc.□

Cyrenaics school of philosophy founded by Aritippus of Cyrene, a pupil of Socrates, maintaining that pleasure was the only good in life□

Cyril of Alexandria St 376–444AD. Archbishop of Alexandria from 412, persecutor of Jews and heathens, and hated for his suspected share in the death of Hypatia◊□

Cyril and **Methodius** Saints. Greek brothers, sent to Moravia to Christianize the Slavs in 863, who devised for their scripture translations the ***Cyrillic◊ alphabet*** which is still used in Bulgaria and the USSR□

Cyrus the Great d. 529BC. Founder of the Persian Empire. King of Persia, originally as vassal to the Medes◊, whose empire he overthrew in 550, he captured Croesus◊ in 546, and conquered all Asia Minor, adding Babylonia (including Syria and Palestine) to his empire in 539. The exiled Jews were allowed to return to Jersualem. He died fighting in Afghanistan□

cystic fibrosis genetic disorder causing thickening of the mucus throughout the body, and resultant blockage, e.g. in the lungs, and in the pancreatic duct, where it prevents enzymes for digestion being formed. Life is prolonged by antibiotics, and in 1985 the small region of the chromosomes in which a defect occurs brought the prospect of a cure nearer□

cystitis inflammation of the bladder caused by bacterial infection, and resulting in frequent and painful urination□

Czechoslovakia Social Republic of
area 127 895 sq km/ 49 381 sq mi
capital Prague
towns Brno, Bratislava, Ostrava
features Carpathian Mountains, rivers Morava, Labe (Elbe), Vltava (Moldau); divided by valley of the Morava into the western densely populated area with good communications, and the eastern sparsely populated, comparatively little-developed Slovak area
exports machinery, timber, ceramics, glass, textiles
currency koruna
population 15 466 000, 60% Czech, 30% Slovaks, with Hungarian, Polish, German, Russian, and other minorities
language Czech and Slovak (official)
religion Roman Catholicism, with Protestant minority
famous people literature Capek, Kafka, Vaclav Havel, Jaroslav Seifert *music* Biber, Zelenka, Janáček, Dvořák, Smetana *politics* Jan and Thomas Masaryk
government president (from 1975 Gustav Husak) and a federal assembly comprising a chamber of the people (two to one Czech majority) and chamber of the nations (half Czech, half Slovak)
history an independent republic from 1918 (by the combination of Bohemia, Moravia, and Slovakia, after the break-up of the Austro-Hungarian Empire), it was annexed by Hitler in 1938–9 (see Munich◊ Agreement). It was liberated in 1945 by the USSR and the USA, the Sudeten Germans were expelled, and Czech Ruthenia was returned to the USSR. By 1948 the Communists were in control, Beneš having resigned, and the liberal programme introduced in 1965 by Dubček◊ led to a Warsaw Pact invasion in 1968 to restore the orthodox Communist line. By 1984 the dissident civil rights movement, Charter 77, had been largely suppressed□

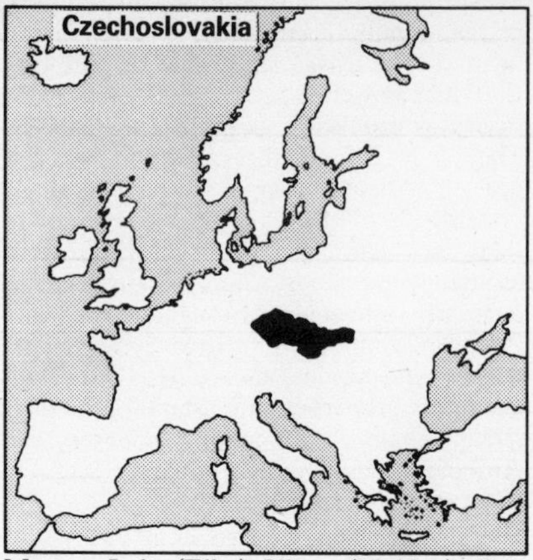

D

dab a type of flatfish◊□

dabchick a type of water-bird. See grebe◊□

Dacca see Dhaka◊□

dace a small fresh-water fish. See under carp◊□

Dachau see concentration◊ camps□

dachshund a breed of dog◊□

Dadaism movement in the arts 1915–22. Short-lived and nihilistic, but its cultivation of irrationality, incongruity, and irreverance helped to prepare the way for Surrealism◊. Associated artists include Marcel Duchamp and Max Ernst□

Dadd Richard 1817–1886. British artist, confined as insane for murdering his father. His work has a mad intensity, vivid colour and fantastical detail□

daddy-long-legs informal name for a crane-fly◊ or Harvestman◊□

Dadra and Naga Haveli formerly part of Daman◊, they became in 1961 a Union Territory of W India; population 103 700. Capital Silvassa□

Daedalus in Greek mythology, an Athenian craftsman supposed to have constructed for King Minos the labyrinth in which the Minotaur◊ was imprisoned. He fled from Crete with his son Icarus◊ using wings made from feathers fastened with wax; Icarus flew too near the sun, and fell to his death◊□

daffodil bulbous plant, genus *Narcissus* family Amaryllidaceae◊, having yellow and white flowers with trumpet-shaped corollas and long narrow leaves, e.g. ***wild daffodil*** *N pseudonarcissus*. Numerous cultivated species include ***pheasant's eye narcissus*** *N majalis*, and the ***jonquil*** *N jonquilla*□

Dagestan mountainous republic of the W USSR, annexed from Iran in 1723, which strongly resisted Russian conquest (see Shamyl◊). It became an autonomous republic in 1921; capital Makhachkala; area 50 300 sq km/14 700 sq mi; population 1 700 000□

Daguerre Jacques. See under photography◊□

Dahl Roald 1916– . British writer, celebrated for short stories with a twist, e.g. *Tales of the Unexpected* 1979, and for children's book's including *Charlie and the Chocolate Factory* 1964□

dahlia genus of brilliantly showy flowering Mexican plants, family Compositae◊, introduced to England in 1789□

Dahomey the former name (until 1975) of the People's Republic of Benin◊□

Dahrendorf Ralph 1929– . German sociologist, director of the London School of Economics 1974–84, who sees management as 'a permanent process of persuasion'. Honourable Knight of the British Empire in 1982□

Dáil Éirann the representative assembly of the Republic of Ireland◊□

Daimler Gottlieb. See under motor◊ car□

daisy genus *Bellis* of hardy perennials, family Compositae◊, e.g. ***common daisy B perennis***, an abundant wildflower with single white or pink flower head rising from a rosette of leaves□

Dakar capital and chief port (with man-made harbour) of Senegal; population 978 560. In World War II (Jul 1940) British and Free French forces failed to take it as an Allied base□

Dakota see North◊ Dakota and South◊ Dakota□

Daladier Édouard 1884–1970. French Radical statesman. As Prime Minister Apr 1938–Mar 1940, he was largely responsible both for the Munich Agreement and France's declaration of war on Germany. Arrested on the fall of France (see Riom◊), he was a prisoner in Germany 1943–5□

Dalai Lama 14th Incarnation 1935– . Spiritual and temporal head of the Tibetan State until 1959, when he fled to India after the Chinese invasion. See Panchen◊ Lama□

Dale Sir Henry Hallett 1875–1968. British physiologist, who in 1936 shared a Nobel prize with Otto Loewi for work on the chemical transmission of nervous effects. Order of Merit in 1944□

D'Alembert see Alembert◊□

Dalgarno George 1626–87. Scottish schoolmaster and inventor of the first deaf-and-dumb alphabet in 1680□

Dalhousie James Andrew Broun Ramsay, 1st Marquess and 10th Earl of Dalhousie 1812–60. Governor-General of India 1848–56, who annexed the Punjab and Lower

Burma, and carried out social and economic reforms□

Dali Salvador 1904– . Spanish Cubist and Surrealist artist and designer, born near Barcelona. Inspired by Freud's theory of the unconscious, he painted with photographic realism startling images from dreams and hallucinations□

Dalian one of the two cities comprising the Chinese port of Lüda◊□

Dallas commercial city in Texas, USA. Its industries include banking, insurance, oil, aviation, aerospace, electronics, machinery, clothing, food, printing, publishing; population 901 450. It is a cultural centre (symphony orchestra, opera, ballet, theatre). Dallas–Fort Worth Regional Airport (opened 1973) is one of the world's largest, and there is an annual Texas State Fair. There is a Kennedy Memorial: see J F Kennedy◊□

Dalmatia coastal region of Croatia, Yugoslavia; capital Split□

Dalmatian a breed of dog◊□

Dalton Hugh, Baron Dalton 1887–1962. British Labour Chancellor of the Exchequer from 1945, he resigned in 1947 following an innocently indiscreet disclosure to a Lobby correspondent before a Budget speech□

Dalton John 1776–1844. British chemist. First to propose the existence of atoms which he considered to be the smallest part of matter. From experiments with gases he noted that the proportions of two components combining to form another were always consistent. From this he suggested that if substances combine in simple numerical ratios then the macroscopic weight proportions represent the relative atomic masses of those substances. Extending the range of compounds, he produced the first list of relative atomic masses, *Absorption of Gases* 1805□

Dalziel family British wood-engravers, the brothers *George* 1815–1902, *Edward* 1817–1905, *John* 1822–60, and *Thomas* 1823–1906, who illustrated the classics, etc.□

dam engineering structure damming water for flood control, irrigation◊, hydroelectric power◊, etc. Major dams include: ***Rogun*** (USSR), the world's highest at 325 m/1067 ft; ***New Cornelia Tailings*** (USA), the world's biggest in volume, 209 million cu m; ***Owen Falls*** (Uganda), the world's largest reservoir capacity, 204.8 billion cu m; and ***Itaipu*** (Brazil/Paraguay), the world's most powerful, 12 700 megawatts. A valuable development in arid areas, as in parts of Brazil, is the underground dam where water is stored among sand and stones on a solid rock base with a wall to ground level, so avoiding rapid evaporation□

Daman or *Damão* see Goa◊□

Damaraland central region of Namibia, home of nomadic Bantu-speaking Hereros□

Damascus capital of Syria from 1941; population 1 042 000. Probably the oldest city still inhabited, it was captured by all the great ancient empires, and in World War I was taken from the Turks by the British (Allenby◊) with Arab aid in 1918, becoming in 1920 the capital of French mandated Syria. Noted are the 'street which is called straight' (associated with St Paul who was converted while on the road to Damascus); the tomb of Saladin◊; and the 5th century Great Mosque (once a Christian church)□

damask reversible textile, usually silk or linen, with a figured pattern, first made in Damascus□

Dame title of a woman who has been awarded the Order of the British Empire. Legal title of the wife (or widow) of a knight◊ or baronet◊□

Damien Father 1840–89. Belgian missionary (Joseph de Veuster), resident priest from 1873 at the leper settlement at Molokai, Hawaii; he became infected□

Damietta English name for the Egyptian port of Dumyat◊□

Damocles in classical legend a courtier of the elder Dionysius◊, ruler of Syracuse in the 9th century BC, who extolled his happy state. Dionysius invited him to a feast at which a sword was suspended above his head by a single hair – a parable of royal insecurity. The phrase ***the sword of Damocles*** is now used to refer to an impending disaster□

Damōdar river in NE India; length 560 km/350 mi before it joins the Hooghly◊; its valley is a centre of Indian heavy industry□

Dampier William 1652–1715. English buccaneer-explorer, born in Somerset, who circumnavigated the world three times. His last voyage (as a pilot) in 1708–11 rescued Alexander Selkirk◊□

Dampier salt-exporting port in Western Australia, facing the ***Dampier Archipelago*** both named after the explorer□

damson a blue-black edible fruit. See under plum◊□

Dana Richard Henry 1815–82. American author of *Two Years before the Mast* 1840□

Danae in Greek mythology, imprisoned maiden visited by Zeus in a shower of gold; she became the mother of Perseus◊□

Da Nang port (formerly Tourane) in S Vietnam; population 500 000. An American base in the Vietnam War, it is now used by the USSR□

Danby Thomas Osborne, Earl of Danby 1631–1712. British Tory statesman. Chief minister to Charles II 1673–8 (created Earl of

Danby 1674), he was impeached 1678 because of a secret treaty with France. A signatory in 1688 of the invitation to William◊ of Orange, he was again chief minister 1690–5. In 1694 he was created Duke of Leeds□

dandelion N temperate wildflower *Taraxacum officinale* family Compositae◊, with bright yellow flower heads; its milky juice has laxative properties, the leaves can be eaten in salads and the root roasted as a coffee substitute□

Dandie Dinmont a breed of small terrier. See under dog◊□

Dandolo Enrico c1120–1205. Doge of Venice from 1193, who extended the republic's dominions and went on the Fourth Crusade◊□

Daniel Samuel 1562–1619. English sonneteer, master of the revels at court from 1603, for which he wrote masques□

Dankworth John 1927– . British jazz musician, composer of film scores e.g. *Saturday Night and Sunday Morning* and television music e.g. *The Avengers* series, etc. In 1960 he married singer Cleo Laine□

D'Annunzio Gabriele 1863–1938. Italian poet, novelist and playwright. For the actress Duse◊ he wrote *La Gioconda* 1898. He helped to prepare the way for Fascism by his mystic nationalism□

Dante Alighieri 1265–1321. Italian poet, soldier and politician. A Florentine, he fell in love with Beatrice (Portinari) in 1274, a love which survived her marriage to another and her death in 1290, as described in *La Vita Nuova* c1295. His later years were spent in exile. His *Divina Commedia* c1300–21, an imaginary journey through Hell, Purgatory, and Paradise, under the guidance of Virgil◊ and Beatrice is the greatest poem of the Middle Ages□

Danton Georges Jacques 1759–94. French organizer of the rising of 10 Aug 1792 which overthrew the monarchy, and secured the formation in Apr 1793 of the Committee of Public Safety. From Jul he lost power, and when he attempted to recover it was guillotined□

Danube second longest European river; 2820 km/1750 mi. It rises in West Germany and enters the Black Sea in Romania. Formerly it was interrupted by rapids, now ironed out by an artificial lake. Underneath the latter is the site of Europe's oldest urban settlement, Lepenski Vir (6th millenium BC). The Danube's tributaries include the ***Tisza*** rising in the USSR and joining the mainstream just above Belgrade; length 1300 km/800 mi□

Danzig German name for the Polish port of Gdansk◊□

Daphne genus of Eurasian shrubs, family Thymeleaceae, e.g. ***spurge laurel*** *D laureola* with evergreen leaves, green flowers, and black, poisonous berries□

Daphne in Greek mythology, a nymph, changed into a laurel tree to escape from Apollo's amorous pursuit□

Daqing see Harbin◊□

D'Arblay Madame. See Fanny Burney◊□

Dardanelles

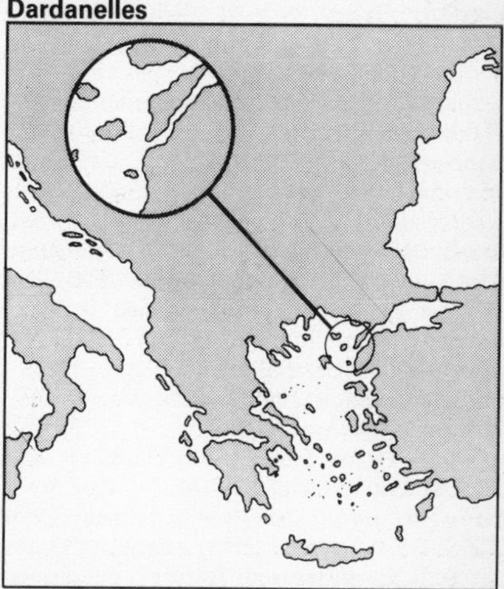

Turkish strait (ancient name Hellespont, Turkish name Çanakkale Boğazi) linking the Sea of Marmara and the Aegean, c6 km/4 mi wide. See Gallipoli◊□

Dar El-Beida Arabic name for the port of Casablanca◊□

Dar es Salaam seaport (Arabic 'haven of peace') in Tanzania, and its former capital; population 870 000. It is the Indian Ocean terminus of the TanZam◊ railway□

Darién former name for the whole Panama isthmus. The ***Great Atrato Swamp*** 60 km/

35 mi across, is over 300 m/1000 ft deep. The Scots made an ill-fated attempt to colonize the isthmus 1698–9□

Darío Rubén. Pseudonym of the Nicaraguan poet, Félix Rubén Sarmiento 1867–1916, founder of the Modernist movement, and remembered for *Songs of Life and Hope* 1905□

Darius I the Great c558–486BC. King of Persia from 512, he inscribed his conquests on a mountain rock-face at Behistun, but is chiefly remembered for his defeat by the Greeks at Marathon◊ (see also Scythians◊)□

Darjeeling tea-producing centre in W Bengal, India, 2150 m/7000 ft above sea level; population 40 700□

Darkhan industrial town in Outer Mongolia; population 47 000. Its Copper Mountain is also being exploited for molybdenum□

Darlan Jean François 1881–1942. French admiral, commander of the French navy 1939–40, who served in the Vichy government until 1942, when he was sent to North Africa. Recognized as Chief of State by the Americans when they landed, he was assassinated by a young Frenchman□

Darling Grace 1815–42. British heroine, daughter of a lighthouse keeper on the Farne Islands, who rowed out with her father to a wreck, and so saved nine lives□

Darling Australian river, a tributary of the Murray, 3075 km/1910 mi long. Its waters are conserved in Menindee Lake 155 sq km/60 sq mi, and others nearby□

Darlington engineering town in County Durham, England; population 85 890. The world's first railway was opened between Darlington and Stockton 27 Sept 1825□

Darmstadt industrial town (chemicals, electrical engineering, etc.) in Hessen, W Germany; population 138 300□

Darnley Henry Stuart, Lord Darnley 1545–67. Second husband of Mary, Queen of Scots, his first cousin, whom he married in 1565. On the advice of her secretary, David Rizzio, Mary refused Darnley the crown matrimonial; in revenge he had Rizzio murdered in Mary's presence. Mary and Darnley were reconciled, but Bothwell plotted against him, and Darnley was found strangled after the house (Kirk o'Field) in which he had been lying ill was blown up. James◊ I was his son□

Darrow Clarence Seward 1857–1938. American lawyer, he defended trade union leaders on many occasions and was counsel for the defence in the Dayton 'monkey' trial of 1925 in which a teacher was tried for teaching Darwin◊'s theory of evolution□

Dart Raymond 1893–1985. Australian anthropologist, discoverer in 1924 of *Australopithecus africanus* (southern African ape). See primate◊□

Dartford industrial town (chemicals, engineering, paper) in Kent, England; population 45 250□

Dartmoor moorland plateau (a National Park) in SW Devon, England; area over 1000 sq km/400 sq mi, with granite 'tors'(the highest Yes Tor 618 m/2028 ft). ***Dartmoor Prison*** 1809 is in the centre of the moor, near Tavistock◊□

Dartmouth yachting centre and seaport in Devon, England; population 5480. Britannia Royal Naval College was established 1905□

Dartmouth port in Nova Scotia, Canada; population 65 341. There is a naval research station and engineering industries□

darts English game possibly first played with broken arrow-shafts, and reaching approximately its present form with a segmented round target by the 17th century. Some seven million players take part in the World Cup□

Darwin Charles Robert 1809–82. British naturalist. Joining the surveying voyage in the southern hemisphere of HMS *Beagle* (see Robert Fitzroy◊) 1831–6, he developed the theory that living things evolve through a process of natural selection, embodied in *On the Origin of Species by Means of Natural Selection* 1859, which placed the whole world of living things in an intelligible pattern, linking man and animals together. This theory caused bitter controversy because it did not agree with the account of the Creation in the Book of Genesis: see evolution◊, Galapagos◊ Islands. He was buried in Westminster Abbey□

Darwin capital and port of Northern Territory, Australia; population 50 600. There is uranium mining nearby, and it is a telecommunications, tourist and wildlife centre□

Dasht-e-Kavir Desert Great Salt Desert near Tehran, Iran; USA landed forces in 1980 in an abortive mission to rescue the American Embassy hostages□

Dassault Marcel 1892–1986. French aircraft designer of the Mystère and Mirage jets. In World War II, he was sent to Buchenwald for refusing to work for the Nazis□

dasyure catlike Australasian marsupial, a nocturnal carnivorous climber, family Dasyuridae□

data any form of information, often in tabular or graphical form. See also computer◊□

data protection the safeguarding of information about individuals stored on computers: in the UK the Data Protection Act,

1986, requires computer databases containing personal information to be registered; that users process only accurate information; and retain the information only for a necessary period and for specified purposes. Individuals have a right of access, and sometimes of correction or erasure. See also under privacy◊□

date the edible fruit of the date palm◊□

datura genus of plants, family Solanaceae, with handsome trumpet-shaped blooms, which have narcotic properties□

Daudet Alphonse 1840–97. French writer, born at Nîmes, which inspired his sketches *Lettres de mon moulin* 1866 and the autobiographical *Le Petit Chose* 1868; he also wrote the play *L'Arlésienne* 1872, for which Bizet composed the music□

Daugavpils town (Russian *Dvinsk*) in Latvia, USSR; population 117 000□

Daulaghiri a mountain in the Himalayas◊□

Daumier Honoré 1808–79. French artist, born in Marseilles. His caricatures for the journals *La Caricature*, *Charivari*, etc. were not valued in his lifetime, but his paintings are now recognised as anticipating Impressionism□

dauphin title of the eldest sons of the kings of France, derived from the personal name of a count, whose lands, the ***Dauphiné*** (capital Grenoble), traditionally passed to the heir to the throne from 1349 to 1830□

Dávao port in the Philippine Republic; population 611 310□

Davenant Sir William 1606–68. English poet laureate (from 1638) and dramatist, whose *Siege of Rhodes* 1656, is considered the first English opera. He was rumoured to be a son of Shakespeare□

Daventry town with light industries in Northamptonshire, England; population 13 400□

David c1060–970BC. Second king of Israel, anointed by Samuel◊ to succeed Saul◊, for whom he played the harp (he may also have written some of the psalms), and slew Goliath◊. Saul's son, Jonathan, became his friend, but Saul, jealous of his prowess, schemed to murder him and he was forced into exile. On the death of Saul and Jonathan in battle, David succeeded and made Jerusalem◊ his capital. In order to marry Bathsheba, he sent her husband, Uriah, to death in battle. See Absalom◊ and Solomon◊□

David St lived 5–6th century. Patron saint of Wales, traditionally an uncle of King Arthur◊. He founded a monastery at Menevia (now St◊ David's) and is said to have adopted the leek as the national emblem of Wales□

David two kings of Scotland:

David I 1084–1153. King from 1124. He invaded England in 1138, in support of Queen Matilda◊, but was defeated at Northallerton in the Battle of the Standard.

David II 1324–71. King from 1329. Son of Robert the Bruce. In 1346 he invaded England, but was captured at the battle of Neville's Cross and imprisoned for eleven years by Edward III□

David Félicien César 1810–76. French composer, one of the first in the West to introduce oriental scales and melodies into his music□

David Gerard c1450–1523. Flemish painter, famous for his altar-pieces□

David Jacques Louis 1748–1825. French painter. An ardent republican, he was a member of the Committee of Public Safety, but later narrowly escaped the guillotine. His paintings, e.g. *The Sabine Women* and *Mme Récamier*, are the perfection of Neoclassicism. As court painter to Napoleon, he was banished by the restored Bourbons□

Davidson John 1857–1909. Scottish poet whose modern, realistic idiom e.g. 'Thirty bob a week' influenced T S Eliot□

Davies Sir Henry Walford 1869–1941. English composer (e.g. *Solemn Melody* and the cantata *Everyman*) and organist, Master of the King's Music from 1934□

Davies Peter Maxwell 1934– . British composer, especially of chamber music and opera, e.g. *Taverner* (based on the life of John Taverner◊) 1972 and *The Lighthouse* 1979. His music reflects the sounds of his island home in Orkney◊□

Davies Robertson 1913– . Canadian novelist, including *A Mixture of Frailties* 1958 and *The Rebel Angels* 1981□

Davies W(illiam) H(enry) 1871–1940. British poet, born in Monmouthshire. While in USA, living as a hobo, he lost his right foot jumping onto a moving train. In 1908 he published his *Autobiography of a Super-Tramp*□

Da Vinci see Leonardo da Vinci□

Davis Bette 1908– . American film actress, born in Massachusetts; films include *Dangerous* 1935 and *Jezebel* 1938 (both academy awards), and *Of Human Bondage*, *The Petrified Forest*, *Private Lives of Elizabeth and Essex*, and *The Little Foxes*□

Davis Sir Colin 1927– . British conductor, musical director of the Royal Opera 1971–86. Knighted 1980□

Davis Dwight Filley 1879–1945. American tennis player, donor in 1900 of the Davis Cup, an international competition□

Davis Jefferson 1808–89. American statesman. Leader of the Southern Democrats, and a defender of 'humane' slavery, he issued in 1860 a declaration in favour of secession, and early in 1861 he was elected President of the Confederate States, but had no grasp of strategy. Captured in 1865, he spent two years in prison□

Davis Joe 1901–78. British billiard and snooker player, and creator of the modern snooker game, world champion 1927–46□

Davis John c1550–1605. English explorer, born near Dartmouth. He three times sailed in search of the Northwest Passage 1585–7 (Davis Strait is named after him); fought against the Spanish Armada in 1588, and was eventually killed by Japanese pirates□

Davisson Clinton 1881–1958. American physicist. He shared a Nobel prize with G P Thompson 1937 for his confirmation of de Broglie's theory that electrons, and therefore all matter, have wave structure□

Davos winter sports centre at 1559 m/5115 ft above sea level, Switzerland; population 11 500□

Davy Sir Humphry 1778–1829. British chemist, born at Penzance. While a laboratory superintendent at Bristol, he discovered the respiratory effects of 'laughing gas' (nitrous oxide) in 1799, and in 1802 became professor at the Royal Institution, London. There he discovered, by electrolysis, the metals sodium, potassium, calcium, magnesium, strontium, and barium. He invented the 'safety lamp' for use in mines where methane was present, in effect enabling the men to work in previously unsafe conditions. He was elected President of the Royal Society in 1820□

Dawes Charles Gates 1865–1951. American politician, originator of the 'Dawes Plan' 1924, aimed at reconstructing the German economy after World War I and enabling Germany to pay reparations to the Allies. He received a Nobel peace prize in 1925, but the plan had to be superseded as unworkable in 1929□

Dawson Canadian town, now a 'ghost town', founded in the 1896 gold rush, and capital till 1953 of the Yukon Territory□

Dawson Creek town in British Columbia, SE terminus of the Alaska Highway; population 10 500□

Dayak or ***Dyak*** an indigenous people of Borneo◊□

Dayan Moshe 1915–81. Israeli general. Army Chief of Staff 1953–8, he was Minister of Defence 1967–74, being largely responsible for victory in the Six Day War, but criticized for his conduct of the Oct War. He was Foreign Minister 1977–9□

Day Lewis Cecil 1904–72. British poet, born in Ireland. With Auden◊ and Spender◊, he was an influential left-wing poet of the 1930s, and poet laureate from 1968. His volumes include *Overtures to Death* 1938, and the more lyrical *The Whispering Roots* 1970, and a translation of the *Aeneid*. As 'Nicholas Blake', he wrote detective fiction□

Dayton industrial city (precision machinery, electrical goods, etc.) in Ohio, USA; population 842 150. There is an aeronautical research centre, and it was the birthplace of the aviator Orville Wright◊□

Dayton small town in Tennessee, USA, where John T Scopes was tried in 1925 for teaching Darwin◊'s theory of evolution; his fine was waived. See also Little◊ Rock□

Daytona Beach seaside resort and motor-racing centre in Florida, USA; population 45 327□

Dazai Osamu. Pseudonym of Shuji Tsushima 1909–48. Japanese novelist, of radical political beliefs. The title of his *The Setting Sun* 1947, is synonymous in Japanese with the dead of World War II. He committed suicide□

D-Day day of the Allied invasion of Europe in World War II, 6 Jun 1944□

DDT Insecticide (***D***ichloro-***D***iphenyl-***T***richloroethane, discovered in 1939 by Swiss chemist Paul Müller 1899–1965. It is useful in control of insects that spread malaria◊, etc., but resistant strains develop, and DDT persists in the environment so that its use is banned in many countries□

deacon third order of the Christian ministry; in the Anglican Communion a candidate for holy orders is ordained deacon, proceeding to the priesthood after a year. The lay order of women deaconesses was revived in 1962 (legally recognized 1968): they may not administer the sacraments, but may conduct public worship and preach. In 1985 the General Synod voted to allow ordination of women as deacons, enabling them to perform marriages and baptisms, but not to take communion, or give absolution and the blessing. In the Presbyterian and Free Churches a deacon is a lay assistant□

Dead Sea large, very salt lake (394 m/1292 ft below sea level) divided between Israel and Jordan, and now dried up in the centre by over-use. Israel plans a canal link to the Mediterranean. The ***Dead Sea Rift*** is part of the fault between the African and Arab plates□

Dead Sea Scrolls a group of Hebrew and Aramaic scrolls found 1947–56 in caves in Jordan, S of Jericho◊. They are thought to date from 250BC to 70AD, and include scripts of Old Testament books a thousand years earlier than those previously known. See Qumran◊□

deafness lack or deficiency in the sense of hearing, either because of an inborn deficiency, or caused by injury or disease of the inner ear. It is often accompanied by an inability to speak if deafness was present at, or soon after, birth. Of assistance are hearing aids, lip-reading, a cochlear implant in the ear in combination with a special electronic processor, sign language (signs for concepts), and 'cued speech' (phonetic)□

Deakin Alfred 1856–1919. Australian Liberal statesman, Prime Minister 1903–4, 1905–8 (when he introduced state pensions), and 1909–10□

Deal port and resort in Kent, England; population 26 120. Julius Caesar landed here in 55BC; the castle (built by Henry VIII) is a museum□

dean Anglican Communion head of the chapter of a cathedral or collegiate church; ***Rural Dean*** presides over a division of an archdeaconry; ***Roman Catholic*** senior cardinal bishop, head of the college of cardinals□

Dean Basil 1888–1978. British founder and director-general of ENSA◊ (providing entertainment for the Allied forces in World War II)□

Dean Forest of. Wooded area in W Gloucestershire, England, much of it Crown property. Iron and coal are mined.

Dean James. Professional name of James Byron 1931–55, American film actor, the 'first American teenager', killed in a road crash after the showing of his first film, *East of Eden* (1955); most famous was *Rebel Without a Cause* (1955) released after his death□

Dearborn industrial city (cars, aircraft parts, etc) in Michigan, USA; population 184 000; Henry Ford was born here, and it is the headquarters of the Ford Motor Company□

death a permanent ending of all the functions needed to keep an organism alive. Death used to be pronounced when a person's breathing and heartbeat stopped. The advent of mechanical aids have made this point difficult to determine, and a person is now pronounced dead when the brain ceases to control the vital functions. For a donor in transplant surgery the World Health Organization definition 1968 is that there should be no brain–body connection, muscular activity, blood pressure, or ability to breathe unaided by machine.

In religious belief it may be seen as the prelude to rebirth (see Hinduism◊, Buddhism◊); under Islam◊ and Christianity◊, there is the concept of a Day of Judgment, and consignment to Heaven or Hell; Judaism◊ tends to concentrate more on survival through descendants□

death cap a poisonous fungus. See Amanita◊□

Death Valley depression 85 m/280 ft below sea level in SE California, USA, the lowest point in N America, and one of the world's hottest places□

death watch a type of beetle◊□

Deauville seaside resort in Normandy, France; population 5200. Noted for its casinos and horse racing at Le Touquet□

De Bono Edward 1933– . British doctor, originator of 'Lateral Thinking' 1967. See under psychology◊□

Debray Régis 1941– . French Marxist theorist, e.g. *Strategy for Revolution* 1970, who was imprisoned in Bolivia 1967–70 for association with Che Guevara◊□

Debrecen commercial centre in E Hungary; population 196 000. Kossuth◊ declared Hungary independent of the Hapsburgs here in 1849□

Debrett John 1753–1822. London publisher of a directory of the Peerage 1802, still called by his name□

de Broglie Louis, 7th Duc 1892– . French physicist, who established that all particles can be described either by particle equations or by wave equations, so laying the foundation of wave mechanics. Nobel prize 1929□

de Broglie Maurice, 6th Duc 1875–1960. French physicist, brother of the 7th Duc de Broglie. He worked on X-rays and gamma rays, and helped to establish the Einsteinian description of light in terms of photons□

de Broglie Louis Victor, 7th Duc 1892– . French physicist, awarded a Nobel prize in 1929 for his work in nuclear physics, when he established the basis of wave mechanics□

Debs Eugene V(ictor) 1855–1926. American labour organizer and founder of the US Socialist party, and five times unsuccessful presidential candidate□

Debussy Claude Achille 1862–1918. French composer, who won fame with his *L'après-midi d'un faune* 1894, and the opera *Pelléas et Mélisande* 1902. His rejection of classical diatonic harmony makes him the first of the modern composers□

Debye Peter 1884–1966. Dutch-American physicist, who worked on X-ray powder photography and molecular physics including electric dipole moments and specific heat capacities of solids. Nobel prize 1936. He extended the Arrhenius theory of iron interaction in solution to the crystalline state□

Decalogue in the Old Testament the ten commandments delivered by Jehovah to

Moses◊ and recognized by Jews and Christians□

Decapoda order of crustacea◊ with ten 'feet', and including crabs◊, lobsters◊, prawns◊□

decathlon an athletics competition for men, which consists of ten different events: 100m, 400m and 1,500m running races, 110m hurdles, javelin, discus, shot put, pole vault, high jump and long jump. The competition takes place over two days□

Decatur Stephen 1779–1820. American naval hero, born in Maryland. He distinguished himself against the Tripoli pirates 1801–5, and during the war with England he surrendered in 1814 only after a desperate resistance. Killed in a duel, he was famed for the toast 'our country, right or wrong'□

Decatur industrial city (engineering, food processing, plastics) in central Illinois, USA; population 90 400□

Deccan the Indian peninsular south of the River Narmada□

decibel a logarithmic unit, symbol dB, used to express ratios of power, voltage current or sound intensity. See noise◊□

decimal fraction system of fractions◊ expressed by the use of the decimal point, which have a denominator of 10, 100, 1000, etc., e.g. 3/10 = 0.3□

decimal system system of weights and measures, or coinage based on one standard unit (e.g. metre, dollar), divided into or multiplied by multiples of 10. Revolutionary France was the first to decimalize her currency; the UK did so in 1971. See also metric system◊□

Decius Gaius Messius Quintus Traianus 201–51AD. Roman emperor from 249, he was a persecutor of the Christians, and was killed campaigning against the Goths□

Declaration of Independence statement issued by the American Continental Congress on 4 Jul 1776, it ended the political connection with Britain. It was drafted chiefly by Jefferson◊□

Declaration of Rights conditional offer of the British crown to William◊ and Mary◊ by the Convention◊ Parliament Feb 1689; its conditions were embodied in the Bill of Rights◊□

decompression sickness an illness, brought about by a sudden and substantial change in atmospheric pressure. It is caused by a too rapid release of nitrogen which has been absorbed into the bloodstream under pressure. It causes breathing difficulties, joint and muscle pain, and cramp, and is experienced mostly by deep-sea divers who surface too quickly. It is popularly known as 'the bends'□

Dee John 1527–1608. English alchemist and mathematician, a favourite of Elizabeth I, who was employed as a secret agent. He claimed to have turned base metal to gold, but died in poverty□

Deed legal document passing an interest in property or binding someone to perform or abstain from an action. An ***indenture*** binds two parties, but a ***deed poll***, e.g. where someone changes a name, applies only to one□

deer ruminant hoofed mammal, family Cervidae akin to antelope◊ and cattle◊, but usually distinguished by antlers in the male. They do not occur in Australia or most of Africa. Native to Britain are the European ***red deer*** *Cervus elaphus*, increasingly farmed for meat (the N American ***wapiti*** *Cervus canadensis* is closely related); ***fallow deer*** *Dama dama*, fawn with white spots in summer; and ***roe deer*** *Capreolus capreolus:* all are hunted, stalked, etc. Largest of the deer is the ***elk*** *Alces alces*, of N Eurasia, 2 m/6 ft, and closely related to the N American ***moose*** *Alces americana*. Other species include the subarctic ***reindeer*** *Rangifer tarandus*, in which both sexes are antlered (known in America as caribou; see Alaska◊); ***muntjac*** (genus *Muntiacus*), of which the Chinese species, known from its call as the 'barking deer', is naturalized in Britain (it is solitary and nocturnal); and small central Asian ***musk deer*** *Moschus moschiferus*, which yields musk and has no antlers. See also prongbuck◊□

deerhound a breed of dog◊, like a greyhound□

de Falla Manuel. See Falla◊, Manuel de□

defamation attack on a person's reputation by libel◊ or slander◊□

Defence Ministry of. British government department which from 1964 absorbed the former Admiralty◊, Air Ministry and War Office, following the example of the USA, where a single department of Defense had been created from 1947. Defence commands of both countries interlock with those of Europe in the North Atlantic Treaty Organisation (NATO)□

Defender of the Faith title (Latin *Fidei Defensor)* conferred on Henry VIII by Pope Leo X in 1521: it appears on British coins as F.D.□

deflation a decrease in the supply of money leading to a reduction in the level of economic activity in an economy. See under inflation◊□

Defoe Daniel c1660–1731. English novelist and journalist. Born in Stoke Newington, London, son of a butcher, he was fined, pilloried and imprisoned in Newgate for one of his political pamphlets, the ironic *The*

Shortest Way with Dissenters 1702. His novel *Robinson Crusoe* 1719 was followed by others including *Moll Flanders* and *Colonel Jack,* both in 1722□

Degas Hilaire Germain Edgar 1834–1917. French Impressionist painter and sculptor, who worked almost entirely in pastel, e.g. studies of ballet, horses and jockeys, and representations of contemporary life. Later he became blind□

de Gaulle Charles 1890–1970. French statesman. In 1940 he refused to accept Pétain◊'s truce with the Germans, and became leader of the Free French◊ in England. In 1944 he entered Paris in triumph and was briefly head of the provisional government before resigning in protest at the defects of the new constitution of the Fourth Republic in 1946. When bankruptcy and civil war loomed in 1958 he was called to form a government, promulgated a constitution subordinating the legislature to the presidency and in 1959 became President (re-elected 1965). He quelled the student-worker unrest of 1968, but in 1969 resigned after the defeat of the government in a referendum on constitutional reform. See Colombey◊□

degree the 360th part of the circumference of a circle, which is subdivided into 60 minutes: i.e. one degree 60 minutes is expressed 1 ° 60′. See circle◊□

degree a unit of temperature on a stated scale, symbol °. See centigrade◊□

De Havilland Sir Geoffrey 1882–1965. British aircraft designer, founder of his own company in 1920. His planes include the civilian *Moth*, the *Mosquito* (World War II fighter-bomber), and post-war *Comet* (world's first jet-driven airliner). Knighted 1944, Order of Merit 1962□

Dehra Dun town in Uttar Pradesh, India; population 199 450. The Indian Military Academy is here□

dehydration reduction of food to powder form for preserving by removal of its water content. To retain flavour food is first quick-frozen by accelerated freeze drying (AFD), then dehydrated in vacuo. Partial dehydration, which leave the food intact, is called drying, i.e. dried fruit□

Deighton Len 1929– . British author of spy fiction, including *The Ipcress File* 1963 and the trilogy *Berlin Game, Mexico Set, London Match* 1983–5, featuring the endearing spy Bernard Samson□

Deirdre in Celtic mythology, intended bride of Conchobar◊□

deism a belief in God (usually as a creator, not as an intervenor in earthly affairs), held on grounds of its reasonableness rather than by appeal to scripture, religious traditions, etc. It gained favour in England in the late 17th and early 18th centuries□

Dekker Thomas c1572–c1632. English pamphleteer and realistic dramatist, e.g. *The Shoemaker's Holiday* 1600, and many in collaboration, e.g. *The Honest Whore* (with Middleton◊) and *Sir Thomas Wyat* (with Webster◊); see also William Rowley◊□

Delacroix Ferdinand Victor Eugène 1798–1863. French artist, possibly a son of Talleyrand◊. Leader of the Romantic movement in France, he excelled in religious and historical subjects, e.g. *Liberty Leading the People* 1831, and visits to Spain and Morocco introduced an exotic element. His portraits, e.g. of Paganini and Chopin, and his lithographs and murals are notable. He kept a remarkable *Journal*□

Delafield E M. Pseudonym of Edmée Elizabeth Monica de la Pasture 1890–1943, British author of a comic *Diary of a Provincial Lady* 1931□

de la Mare Walter 1873–1956. English poet, born in Kent. His *Songs of Childhood* 1902, for children, was published under the pseudonym Walter Ramal; later volumes, with an element of the weirdly mysterious, include *The Listeners* 1912. Order of Merit 1953□

de la Ramée Louise. British novelist who wrote under the name of Ouida◊□

Delaroche Hippolyte, called Paul 1797–1856. French historical artist, a friend of Géricault and Delacroix, with whom he was in revolt against the classicism of David◊□

de la Roche Mazo 1885–1961. Canadian novelist, author of the 'Whiteoaks' family saga□

Delaunay Robert 1855–1941. French artist, whose *Windows* 1912, is believed to be the first Cubist painting in colour□

Delaware mid Atlantic state of the USA; First State/Diamond State
area 5 328 sq km/2 057 sq mi
capital Dover
towns Wilmington
features one of the most industrialized states; headquarters of the Dupont chemical firm (see nylon◊)
products dairy, poultry and market garden produce; chemicals, motor vehicles, textiles
history One of the Thirteen Colonies, it became in 1787 the first state of the USA.
population 595 225
famous people J P Marquand□

De La Warr Thomas West, Baron 1577–1618. Known as Lord Delaware. American colonial governor of Virginia 1610–18, who arrived just in time to prevent the desertion of the

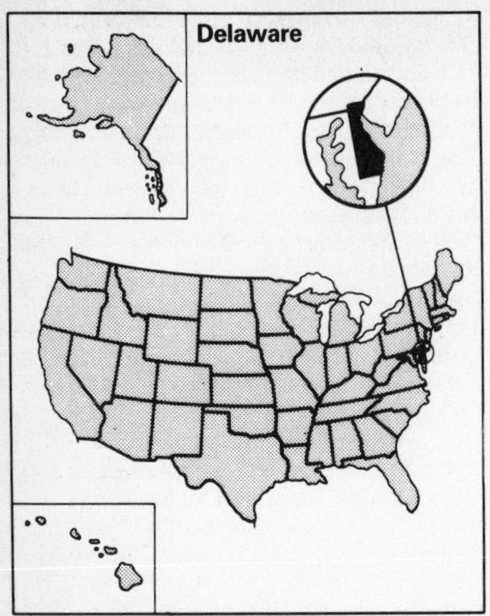

Jamestown colonists: Delaware state is named after him□

Delcassé Théophile 1852–1923. French Foreign Minister 1898–1905 and 1914–15, largely responsible for the *Entente Cordiale*◊ with Britain□

Delft town in W Netherlands; population 87 000. William the Silent◊ was murdered here, and it is famous for blue-and-white china□

Delhi Union Territory of India; population 6 196 414. The chief town is Delhi◊□

Delhi capital of the Republic of India; population 4 000 000. Old Delhi, reconstructed by Shah◊ Jehan, was the capital of the Mogul Empire until the establishment of British rule in 1857; notable are the wall with seven gates, the Red Fort (formerly the Imperial Palace), and the Great Mosque, both 17th century. New Delhi, to the SW, with magnificent government buildings, was created by Sir Edwin Lutyens◊ and Sir Herbert Baker◊ 1912–31, following the removal of the capital of British India from Calcutta. The National Defence College is here□

Delilah in Old Testament Philistine mistress of Samson◊□

Delius Frederick 1862–1934. British composer. Born in Bradford, he tried orange-growing in Florida before studying music at Leipzig. Eventually he settled at Grez-sur-Loing, near Paris, and from 1925 was blind and paralyzed. He wrote choral works (*Appalachia, Sea Drift, A Mass of Life, A Song of the High Hills*); the opera *A Village Romeo and Juliet* 1906; music for the play *Hassan* 1923; orchestral works such as *Brigg Fair* and *In a Summer Garden*; chamber music and songs. His reputation was established by Beecham◊□

Dell Ethel M 1881–1939. British romance writer, e.g. *Way of an Eagle* 1912; she invented the 'ugly hero'□

Deller Alfred 1912–79. British counter-tenor◊□

Delos Greek island, smallest in the Cyclades◊. The 4th century temple of Apollo is here□

Delphi former city on the S slopes of mountain Parnassus, Greece, site of the oracle of Apollo, uttered through the Pythian priestess until it was closed down by Emperor Theodosius◊ 390AD□

delphinium genus of plants, also known as ***larkspur***, family Ranunculaceae, with spikes of blue, white or pink flowers□

Del Sarto Andrea 1486–1531. See Sarto◊□

delta a triangular tract of land at a river's mouth, formed by deposited silt or sediment, e.g. Mississippi, Ganges and Brahmaputra, Rhône, Po, Danube, and Nile□

Delta Force US anti-terrorist force, based on Fort Bragg, N Carolina, and modelled on the British SAS◊

dementia a state of mental deterioration accompanied by emotional disturbance. It may be caused by faulty blood supply to the brain, but 80% of those over 55 who die from dementia suffer from ***Alzheimer's disease*** (loss of brain cells, tangling and distortion of those remaining, and biochemical imbalance). In 1983 evidence was found that it was linked with enzyme deficiency in the area of the brain controlling memory and learning ability□

Demerara river in Guyana; 174 km/180 m. Demerara sugar is named after it□

Demeter in Greek mythology, goddess of agriculture (see Ceres◊), daughter of Cronus and Rhea, and mother of Persephone◊. See Isis◊ and mystery◊ religions□

Demetrius Donskoi 1350–89. Grand Prince of Moscow from 1363. He achieved the first Russian victory over the Tatars on the plain of Kulikovo, next to the Don (hence his nickname) in 1380□

De Mille Cecil B(lount) 1881–1959. American film director, specializing in biblical epics, e.g. *The Sign of the Cross* and *The Ten Commandments*□

democracy government by the people; in ***direct democracy*** the whole people meet for the making of laws or the direction of executive officers (ancient Athens, and, allegedly, modern Libya); ***indirect democracy*** entrusts such power to elected representatives. The use of the referendum is a version of direct democracy□

Democratic Party one of the two main political parties (see Republican◊ Party) of the USA, founded by Jefferson◊ 1792. It has traditionally been stronger in the South, but is today associated with more liberal policies than its rival. ***Tammany Hall*** was the Democratic organisation dominant in New York from its foundation in 1789 as the Society of St Tammany (an American Indian chief) until its power was broken, because of its reputation for gangsterism, by La◊ Guardia□

Democritus c460–361BC. Greek philosopher, early proponent of an atomic view of the universe□

Demosthenes c384–322BC. Athenian statesman. Leader from 351BC of the party opposed to Philip◊ of Macedon he incited the Athenians to war by the oratory of his 'Philippics', with resultant defeat at Chaeronea in 338. After Alexander's death, he led an abortive revolt, and took poison to avoid capture by the Macedonians□

demotic a form of writing derived from Egyptian hieratic. See hieroglyphic◊□

Dempsey 'Jack'. Professional name of William Harrison Dempsey 1895–1983. American boxer, known from his birthplace in Colorado as the Manassa Mauler, world heavyweight champion 1919–26□

dendrochronology study of annual tree growth rings in relation to archaeology and climatology□

dengue viral fever transmitted by mosquitoes; ***dengue haemorrhagic fever***, probably caused by a secondary infection, also causes internal bleeding□

Deng Xiaoping 1904– . Chinese statesman. He held various prominent Party posts after the establishment of the People's Republic of China in 1949 but was dismissed during the Cultural Revolution. He was acting Prime Minister following Chou En-lai's heart attack in 1974, but again disgraced 1976–7. As Vice-Premier 1973–76 and 1977–80, he was in charge of the modernization programme, and helped oust Hua Guofeng◊ in favour of Zhao Ziyang◊. His policy, misinterpreted in the West as a drift to capitalism, was 'Socialism with Chinese characteristics'□

Den Haag Dutch form of The Hague◊□

Den Helder fishing port and naval base in the Netherlands; population 63 000□

denier measure of fine yarns; 9000 m of 15 denier nylon (as used in tights) weighs 15 g, the thickness of thread then being 0.00425-mm/0.0017in□

Denikin Anton Ivanovich 1872–1946. Russian general. After the Bolshevik Revolution of 1917 he organized an army of 60,000 Whites◊, but in 1919 was routed and escaped to France□

Denis St martyred by the Romans 275AD. Patron saint of France, the first Bishop of Paris□

Denmark Kingdom of

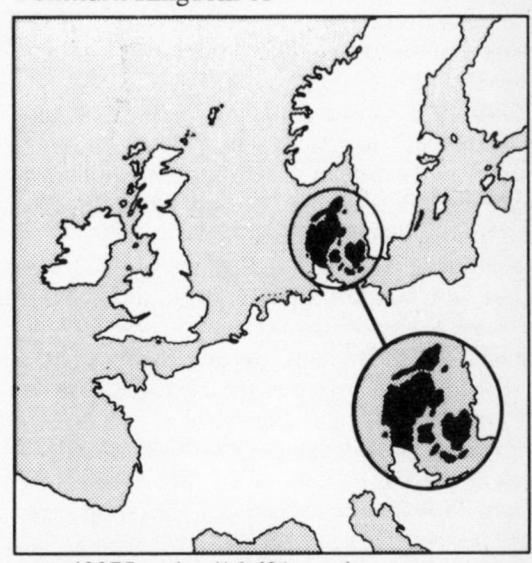

area 43075 sq km/16 631sq mi
capital Copenhagen
towns Aarhus, Odense, Aalborg, Esbjerg, all ports
features comprises the peninsula of Jylland/Jutland, plus the islands of Sjaelland, Fünen, Lolland, Bornholm, etc.; there are sand dunes and lagoons on the W coast and long inlets on the E; see also Faeroe◊ Islands and Greenland◊
exports bacon, dairy produce, eggs, fish, mink pelts; car and aircraft parts, electrical equipment, textiles
currency krone
population 5 120 000
language Danish (official)
religion Lutheran (official)
government constitutional monarchy (Queen Margrethe II from 1972), with a unicameral Folketing (parliament) elected by proportional representation. The Social Democrats are the largest party: Prime Minister Poul Schlüter, coalition, from 1982.
recent history First unified by Harald Bluetooth c940–85, Denmark formed part of Canute's◊ empire with England and Norway 1014–35: see also Vikings◊. Later centuries were dominated by attempts to rule Norway and Sweden. In the Napoleonic period Denmark adhered to armed neutrality, which resulted in her naval defeat by Britain at Copenhagen◊ in 1801, and the bombardment of Copenhagen and seizure of the Danish fleet to keep it from Napoleon in 1807. In 1815 Denmark was reduced to her approximate present boundaries. Despite strong resistance, she was occupied by Germany in World War II 1940–45□

Denning Alfred Thompson, Baron Denning 1899– . British judge, Master of the Rolls 1962–82. In 1963 he conducted the inquiry into the Profumo◊ scandal, and was controversial in his defence of the rights of the individual against the state, the unions, etc.□

density a measure of the compactness of a substance; its mass per unit volume, measured in kg per cubic metre. ***Relative density*** is the ratio of the density of a substance to that of water at 4°C□

dentistry care and treatment of the teeth and their supporting tissues. Decay is caused by micro-organisms (strains of oral streptococci) which are harmless until sucrose (from refined sugar) is present. Fluoride◊ in the water supply reduces this effect, and in 1979 a vaccine was developed. ***Orthodontics*** deals with the straightening of the teeth, and ***periodontology*** with care of the supporting tissue□

Denver industrial city (coal, rubber, mining machinery, canning, meat packing, etc.) in the USA; population 1 574 000. Site of the US mint; rivals Houston as an oil and gas centre; and has a mining school, and Performing Arts Centre 1979□

deodar a Himalayan cedar◊ tree□

depilatory instrument (e.g. electrolytic needle) or substance used to eradicate growing hair from the body, usually for cosmetic reasons□

depression state of mental misery which may be brought on by events (and so normal) or not (when it becomes a psychiatric illness). ***Manic depression*** is a psychiatric illness which is marked by an alternation of elation and overactivity (e.g. the sufferer talks non-stop, has unrealistically optimistic ideas, and may be aggressive and quarrelsome) with periods of deep depression, in which some become suicidal□

de Quincey Thomas 1785–1859. British author, born in Manchester. He ran away from school to a poverty-stricken London life with a young orphan Ann, but in 1803 he was reconciled to his guardians, and went to Oxford, where he became addicted to opium. In 1809 he settled with the Wordsworths and Coleridge in the Lake District, but in 1820 moved to London where he published his *Confessions of an English Opium Eater* 1821. He also wrote the fine critical piece 'On the Knocking at the Gate in Macbeth' 1823, and the essay 'Murder Considered as One of the Fine Arts' 1827□

Derain André 1880–1954. French Post-Impressionist artist, originally a leader of Fauvism◊, with landscapes and Paris scenes, who had a gift for fantasy, as in costumes and scenery for Diaghilev's ballet *La Boutique Fantasque*□

Derby Edward Geoffrey Smith Stanley, 14th Earl of Derby 1799–1869. British statesman. Originally a Whig, he became Secretary for the Colonies in 1830, and introduced the bill for the abolition of slavery. He joined the Tories in 1834, and the split in the Tory Party over Peel's free-trade policy gave him the leadership for twenty years. He was Prime Minister 1852, 1858–9, and 1866–8, with Disraeli◊ as his lieutenant in the Commons□

Derby Edward George Villiers Stanley, 17th Earl of Derby 1865–1948. British Conservative statesman. In the Lloyd George coalition of 1916–18 he was Secretary for War, and again 1922–4□

Derby industrial city (rail locomotives, Rolls-Royce cars and aero-engines, chemicals, paper, electrical, mining and engineering equipment) in Derbyshire, England; population 218 000. Noted are the museum collections of Crown Derby china (still made); the Rolls-Royce collection of aero engines; the Derby Playhouse, and the Eagle Centre shopping precinct. British Rail has research laboratories, and training and technical centres□

Derby chief English horse race, established by the 12th Earl of Derby 1780, over 2.4 km/1.5 mi at Epsom. The American equivalent is the ***Kentucky Derby*** 1875, at Churchill Downs, Louisville over 2 km/1.25 mi

Recent Derby Winners
(Year, horse, owner, jockey)
1970 *Nijinksy* Charles Engelhard (L Piggott)
1971 *Mill Reef* P Mellon (G Lewis)
1972 *Roberto* John Galbreath (L Piggott)
1973 *Morston* Arthur Budgett (E Hide)
1974 *Snow Knight* Sharon Phillips (B Taylor)
1975 *Grundy* Carlo Vittadini (P Eddery)
1976 *Empery* Nelson Bunker Hunt (L Piggott)
1977 *The Minstrel* R Sangster (L Piggott)
1978 *Shirley Heights* Earl of Halifax (G Starkey)
1979 *Troy* Sobell/Weinstock (W Carson)
1980 *Henbit* Arpad Plesch (W Carson)
1981 *Shergar* Aga Khan (W R Swinburn)
1982 *Golden Fleece* R Sangster (P Eddery)
1983 *Teenoso* E Moller (L Piggott)
1984 *Secreto* Luigi Miglitti (Christy Roche)
1985 *Slip Anchor* Lord Howard de Waldon (S Cauthen)
1986 *Shahrastani* The Aga Khan (Walter Swinburn)□

Derbyshire Midland county of England
area 2631 sq km/1016sq mi
towns administrative headquarters Matlock; Derby, Chesterfield, Ilkeston

Derbyshire

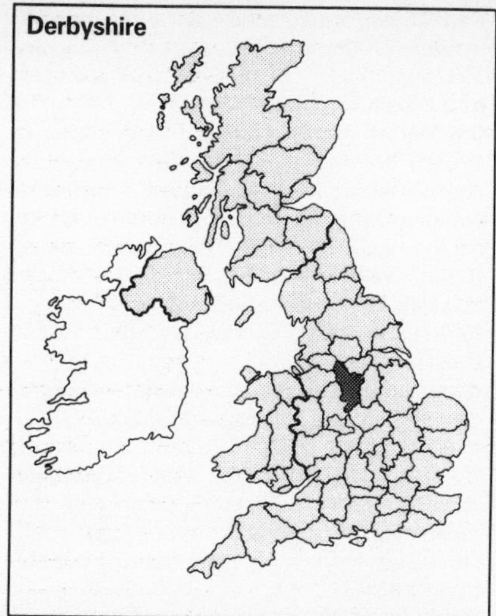

features Peak District National Park (including Kinder Scout 636 m/2088 ft); rivers Derwent, Dove, Rother, Trent; Chatsworth House, Bakewell (seat of Duke of Devonshire), Haddon Hall.
products cereals are grown in the S and E, and there is dairy farming, and sheep on the hills. There have been pit and factory closures, but the area is being redeveloped, and there are large reserves of fluorspar
population 910 000□

dermatitis inflammation of the skin, caused by allergy, industrial processes, disease, etc.□

derris climbing plant of SE Asia *Derris elliptica* family Leguminose, its roots contain rotenone, a strong insecticide□

Derry city (known as Londonderry 1609–1984, following its being granted to the City of London for development) in N Ireland; population 52 200. It was unsuccessfully besieged 1688–89 by James II for 105 days. In 1968–9 there were 'civil rights' disturbances which led to local government reform□

dervish member of an Islamic brotherhood, sometimes single mendicants, who claim close communion with the deity through ecstatic dancing (whirling dervishes), gashing themselves with knives (howling dervishes), etc. See Hafiz◊, Konya◊□

Desai Morarji 1896– . Indian statesman, leader of the Janata Party and Prime Minister 1977–9□

desalination removal of salt, especially from seawater, for irrigation, etc., usually by evaporation, distillation or use of polymer material which acts as a filter by reverse osmosis□

Descartes René 1596–1650. French philosopher who exposed the doubtful nature of commonly accepted 'knowledge' (e.g. that acquired through the senses). He then attempted to rebuild human knowledge using a foundation 'Cogito ergo sum' (I think, therefore I am), i.e. a thinking thing. The latter, Descartes identified with the human soul or consciousness; the body, though somehow interacting with the soul, was a physical machine, secondary to, and in principle separable from the soul. This is called Cartesian Dualism. This dualism, and his acceptance that the initial impulse that sets all matter in motion comes from God, preserved him from Church condemnation. Descartes' scientific speculations, e.g. in biology, optics, and astronomy, were influential. In mathematics he pioneered an algebraic approach to geometry□

desert barren area, not necessarily infertile, but with almost no rainfall. Almost 33% of the earth's surface is desert, and this could increase to 35%, either because of the extension of existing desert, or erosion of marginal farmland. Some 135 million people are affected, chiefly in Africa, the Indian subcontinent, and S America. The process can be reversed by special planting, by the use of water-absorbent plastic grains with the sand, etc. See Gobi, Great Sandy Desert, Kalahari, Rub' al Khali, Sahara, etc.□

Desert Rats nickname of the British 8th Army, in North Africa in World War II, originating in a military shoulder-flash of a jerboa◊ (capable of great leaps forward)□

De Sica Vittorio 1901–74. Italian actor-director, whose most famous film was *Bicycle Thieves* 1946□

Design Council for Industrial. British official body set up in 1944 to improve design standards; annual awards are made, and there are Centres for display in Haymarket, London and in Glasgow□

Des Moines capital and industrial city of Iowa, USA; population 286 100□

Desmoulins Camille 1790–94. French revolutionary, who gave the call to arms on 12 Jul 1789, which led to the attack on the Bastille. A Jacobin, he was elected to the National Convention 1792, and his *Histoire des Brissotins* prompted the overthrow of the Girondins◊, but then seeming too moderate he was guillotined□

Dessalines Jean Jacques 1758–1806. Emperor of Haiti 1804–6. He succeeded Toussaint-L'Ouverture◊ in leadership of the slave revolt against the French, and proclaimed himself Emperor. He was killed in a rising provoked by his cruelty□

Dessau industrial town (chemicals, machinery, chocolate, etc.) in Halle district, E Germany; population 101 970. The Junker aircraft works was here□

destroyer fast, lightly armoured warship, usually 3500 to 6000 tonnes. Heavily armed, they also carry guided missiles□

detergent mixture of water-softening and bleaching agents, and the surfactants (surface-acting) chemicals which do the actual cleaning. The latter have long-chain molecules. A salt group at one end of these is insoluble in grease, but soluble in water, and becomes ionized; and a long hydrocarbon 'tail' at the other end is soluble in the oil or grease which usually attaches dirt to clothes. Thus the oil-bound dirt is 'pulled' from the clothing water and since it remains in suspension in the water is washed away. ***Cold water detergents*** are a mixture of various alcohols, with an added ingredient to break down the surface tension of the water, so that it can penetrate clothes fibres, but are said to be less effective against stains□

determinism theory that everything that happens is predetermined by what has happened in the past; it is the opposite of the doctrine of Free Will and rules out moral choice or responsibility. Stoicism◊ and Calvinism◊ adopt this view, and support has been drawn from psychoanalysis. In the physical sciences, quantum mechanics◊ (see uncertainty◊ principle) implies that small-scale events are non-deterministic□

Detroit industrial city (site of Ford, Chrysler, and General Motors) in Michigan, USA; population 4 161 660. Once famous for jazz, it became noted in the 1960s and 1970s for the rock and soul music of Diana Ross, Stevie Wonder, Aretha Franklin and Alice Cooper; and it has a symphony orchestra□

Dettingen Battle of. Last battle in which a British sovereign took part: George II led British, Hanoverian and Austrian troops to victory over the French in Bavaria on 27 Jun 1743 in the War of the Austrian Succession□

deuterium a form of hydrogen◊□

De Valera Éamon 1882–1975. Irish statesman, born in New York. In 1917 he was released from a commuted death sentence (for his part in the Easter◊ Rebellion), and became a British MP and president of Sinn◊ Féin. Re-arrested in 1918, he escaped in 1919 to the USA, returning in 1920 to direct the struggle against the British government from a hiding-place in Dublin. He authorized the negotiations of 1921, but refused to accept the treaty which ensued. Civil war followed, and in 1923 De Valera was arrested by the Free State government, and spent a year in prison. In 1926 he formed a new party, *Fianna Fáil* 'soldiers of destiny', and was Prime Minister 1932–48, 1951–4 and 1957–9, and president of the Irish Republic 1959–73□

De Valois Dame Ninette. Stage-name of Edriss Stannus 1898– , British dancer-choreographer. A member of Diaghilev's company, she was founder–director 1931–63 of the Sadler's Wells Ballet (later Royal Ballet), and founded the Royal Ballet School. Her ballets include *Job* and *The Rake's Progress*. Dame of the British Empire 1951□

devaluation the lowering of the value of a currency in the international market, which makes exports cheaper and imports dearer. It is usually intended that devaluation should improve a country's balance of payments. Revaluation is the opposite process□

Deventer town in E Netherlands; population 64 824□

Devil in Christian theology, the supreme spirit of Evil (Beelzebub, Lucifer, etc.), or an evil spirit generally. Liberal Protestant theology in the 19th century tended to explain away a personal devil as mere personification, but the traditional concept was retained by Roman Catholics□

devil wind minor form of tornado, occurring usually in fine weather, and formed from rising thermals of warm air (see also cyclone under meteorology◊). A fire creates a similar updraught, and a *fire devil* or *firestorm* may occur in oil refinery fires, or in the firebombings of cities, e.g. Dresden◊ in World War II□

devil ray a type of ray◊ fish□

devil's coach-horse a type of beetle◊□

Devil's Island smallest (Île du Diable) of the Îles du Salut, off French Guiana: they were all collectively popularly known by the name Devil's Island, and formed a penal colony until 1938. Political prisoners were on Devil's Island, and dangerous criminals on St Joseph, where they were subdued by solitary confinement in tiny cells or subterranean cages. The largest island, Royale, now has a tracking station for the French rocket site at Kourou□

Devil's Marbles granite boulders in Northern Territory, Australia□

Devis Arthur 1711–87. English portrait artist, noted for his conversation pieces□

Devizes market town in Wiltshire, England; population 10 150□

devolution in the later 20th century, the movement to decentralize governmental power: see Scotland◊ and Wales◊□

Devolution War of. Waged 1667–8 by Louis XIV to gain Spanish territory in the

Netherlands, which had allegedly 'devolved' on his wife Maria Theresa: it ended in the Treaty of Aix-la-Chapelle□

Devon SW county of England

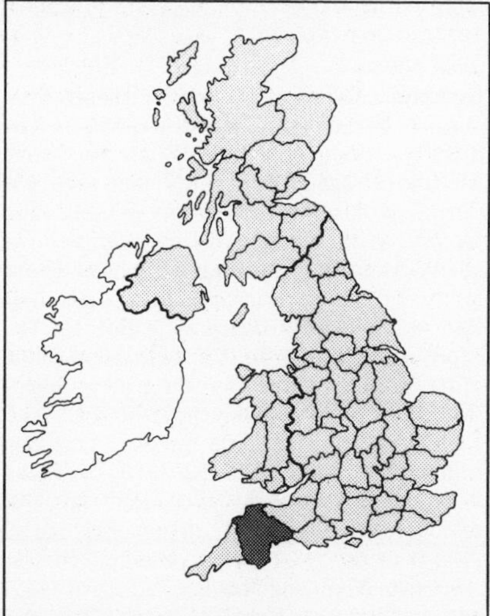

area 6711 sq km/2590 sq mi

towns administrative headquarters Exeter; Plymouth, and the resorts Paignton, Torquay, Sidmouth, Exmouth, Teignmouth in the S, and Lynton, Ilfracombe, Barnstaple, and Bideford in the N.

features rivers Dart, Exe, Tamar; Dartmoor and Exmoor National Parks; villages e.g. Clovelly, and Princetown, site of Dartmoor Prison, opened 1809; wild rocky coast to N and S; rich, red soil.

products mainly agricultural, with sheep and dairy farming; Devon cider and clotted cream; kaolin in the S; Honiton lace; Dartington glass.

population 962 700

famous people Sir Francis Drake, Sir John Hawkins, Charles Kingsley, Robert F Scott□

Devonport town adjacent to Plymouth◊□

Devonshire William Cavendish, 7th Duke of Devonshire 1808–91. Developer of Eastbourne, an early example of town planning□

Devonshire Spencer Compton Cavendish, 8th Duke of Devonshire 1833–1908. Liberal statesman, known as Lord Hartington 1858–91, and leader of the Liberal Party 1874–1880. He broke with Gladstone over Irish Home Rule 1885, and was President of the Council 1895–1903 under Salisbury and Balfour□

dew ground moisture formed by condensation of water vapour in the air as the temperature falls at night. If the 'dewpoint' is below freezing, it condenses directly to hoar frost□

Dewey John 1859–1952. American philosopher. A pragmatist, influenced by William James, he maintained that there is only the reality of experience, and made 'inquiry' the essence of logic, as in *Reconstruction in Philosophy* 1920□

Dewey Melvil 1851–1931. American librarian, deviser of the widely-used Dewey Decimal Classification for books in 1876□

De Wint Peter 1784–1849. English landscape water-colourist of Dutch descent, born in Staffordshire□

Dhaka (until 1984 Dacca) capital and industrial city (jute goods, chemicals, muslin) of Bangladesh; population 3 000 000. Its ports are Chittagong◊ and Chalna□

Dhofar a region of Oman◊□

dhole untameable wild dog of Asia *Cuon alpinus*, which hunts in packs□

diabetes disease (*diabetes mellitus*) in which a deficiency in the islets of the pancreas prevents the body reducing sugars properly. In adults, when it is often inherited, it may be controlled by diet and/or insulin◊; in children it is possibly viral (with the hope of a vaccine) and needs daily insulin injection. Untreated it causes death in coma□

Diaghilev Sergei Pavlovich 1872–1929. Russian ballet impresario, who produced Chaliapin in *Boris Godunov* in 1908 in Paris, and in 1909 founded the Ballet Russe (headquarters Monte Carlo), which he directed for twenty years, and which went to London in 1911. Artists included Pavlova and Nijinsky, and composers Falla, Ravel, and Stravinsky□

dialectical materialism the political, philosophical, and economic theory of Marx and Engels. See Marxism◊□

dialysis process of separating colloids and substances in solution by diffusion through a semipermeable membrane (as in kidney machines, and ambulatory systems, to remove impurities from the blood)□

diamond precious gem stone, the hardest natural substance known (10 on Mohs' scale◊). Composed of carbon, it crystallizes in the cubic system. Gems are valued by weight (see carat◊), cut (which highlights the stone's optical properties), colour, and clarity (which is on a 6-point scale from P ('pique', showing a flaw visible to the naked eye) to FL ('flawless')). Only 20% of rough diamonds are gem quality, the rest being used industrially for cutting (e.g. the tungsten carbide tools used in steel mills are themselves cut with diamond tools), grinding, polishing. Industrial diamonds (20 tonnes per annum) are also produced synthetically from graphite. See P W Bridgman◊. Diamonds act as perfectly transparent windows, and do not absorb infra-red

radiation, hence their use aboard NASA space-probes to Venus in 1978. Chief sources include S and W Africa; Yakutia (USSR); and for industrial diamonds W Australia, Zaïre and Brazil.
Famous Diamonds: Cullinan world's largest rough diamond (1905, S Africa) 3106 carats/ over 20 oz (see also under Regalia◊), ***Koh-i-noor*** 'mountain of light', central stone of the British queen consort's crown (presented to Queen Victoria 1849 after the annexation of the Punjab; its return has been suggested)□

Diana in Roman mythology, goddess of hunting and the moon (see Artemis◊), daughter of Jupiter and twin sister of Apollo□

Diana 1961– . Princess of Wales, popularly known as Princess Di. The daughter of the 8th Earl Spencer, she married Prince Charles at St Paul's cathedral in 1981, the first English bride of a royal heir since 1659. She is descended from the only sovereigns from whom Prince Charles is not descended, Charles II and James II□

DIANE the collection of information suppliers or 'hosts' for the European computer network, ***D***irect ***I***nformation ***A***ccess ***N***etwork for ***E***urope□

diarrhoea excessive action of the bowels so that the stools are fluid, due to food poisoning, disease (dysentery, cholera), etc.□

diary daily record of personal events, the first in English being that of Edward VI◊ ***17–18th century:*** Pepys, Evelyn, Boswell, Fanny Burney, Jules and Edmond Goncourt, duc de Saint-Simon, Swift, John Wesley, James Woodforde ***19th century:*** Thomas Creevey, Emerson, Gladstone, Charles Greville, Francis Kilvert, Queen Victoria ***20th century:*** Lady Cynthia Asquith, Gide, Katherine Mansfield, Sir Harold Nicolson ***fictitious:*** see E M Delafield, G Grossmith, A Loos, S Townsend□

Diaspora the dispersal of the Jews from Palestine from the time of the Babylonian Captivity in 586BC. See under Israel◊□

diathermy generation of heat in body tissues by the passage of high-frequency electric currents between two electrodes placed on the body. It is used to relieve arthritic pain, etc., and in surgery a cutting electrode reduces bleeding□

diatom class of microscopic unicellular algae◊ (marine or freshwater), class Bacillariophyceae, which as fossils constitute diatomaceous earth (diatomite) used in the rubber and plastics industries, and as living creatures are a constituent of plankton◊□

Diaz Bartolomeu c1450–1500. Portuguese explorer. First European to reach the Cape of Good Hope 1488 and to establish a route round the S extremity of Africa□

Diaz Porfirio 1830–1915. Mexican President 1877–80 and 1884–1911, when he was driven from power□

Dickens Charles 1812–70. British novelist. Born in Portsmouth◊, son of a clerk, he had little systematic education. While his father was imprisoned for debt in Marshalsea prison during 1824, he worked briefly in a blacking factory, as did the hero of *David Copperfield* 1849, which is largely autobiographical. From lawyer's clerk, he progressed to reporter, and then author, with *Sketches by Boz* for the *Morning Chronicle*. In 1836 he married Katherine Hogarth, three days after the publication of the first number of the *Pickwick Papers*, which made him famous. This was followed by: *Oliver Twist* 1838, *Nicholas Nickleby* 1839; *Barnaby Rudge* 1840; and *The Old Curiosity Shop* 1841, all in weekly parts. A visit to the USA in 1842 was reflected in *American Notes* and *Martin Chuzzlewit* 1843, and *A Christmas Carol*, also 1843, was the first of his Christmas books. Later novels were *Dombey and Son* 1848; *Bleak House* 1853; *Hard Times* 1854; *Little Dorrit* 1857, in which he evoked his memories of the Marshalsea; *A Tale of Two Cities* 1859, indebted to Carlyle's *French Revolution*; *Great Expectations* 1861; *Our Mutual Friend* 1864; and the unfinished *Edwin Drood*, influenced by Wilkie Collins's mystery stories. In 1856, he separated from his wife, his sister-in-law caring for his children, and formed an association with actress Ellen Ternan. His public readings, begun in 1858, were enormously successful, but drained his energy. He died at his home, Gadshill, near Rochester□

Dickens Monica Enid 1915– . British novelist, great-granddaughter of Charles Dickens, author of *One Pair of Hands*, etc.□

Dickinson Emily 1830–86. American poet. Born in Amherst, Massachusetts, she lived there in almost complete seclusion from about 1862, although an alleged unhappy love affair seems disproved by her letters. Of her many short poems, of an increasingly mystical character, very few were published during her lifetime□

dicotyledons a plant◊ with two seed-leaves□

dictator originally a Roman magistrate invested with extraordinary emergency powers, but in modern usage any absolute ruler□

dictatorship of the proletariat Marxist term for the transition period from capitalism to complete communism after a socialist revolution□

Diderot Denis 1713–84. French philosopher, who embodied the spirit of the Enlightenment in his vast *Encyclopedia* 1751–80, in which Voltaire, D'Alembert, Rousseau, Montesquieu, etc., collaborated□

didjeridu musical wind instrument, made from a hollow bamboo section 1.5 m/4 ft long, played by Australian Aborigines□

Dido Phoenician princess, legendary founder of Carthage; she killed herself to avoid marriage with a local prince, but Virgil records her as doing so because she was deserted by Aeneas◊□

Diefenbaker John George 1895–1979. Canadian Progressive Conservative statesman, born in Ontario. As Prime Minister from 1957, he achieved the greatest landslide in Canadian election history in 1958, but was defeated in 1963, and resigned the party leadership in 1967□

Diego Garcia island in the Chagos Archipelago◊□

dielectric a non-conducting substance, or insulator, such as ceramics, glass, etc. See capacitor◊□

Diels Otto 1876–1954. German organic chemist, awarded a Nobel prize with his former assistant, Kurt Alder, in 1950 for research into the chemistry of 'dienes' (organic compounds containing two double-bonded carbon atoms)□

Diemen Anthony van 1593–1645. Dutch admiral, who as Governor-General of the Dutch E Indies, wrested Ceylon and Malacca from Portugal, and supervized Tasman's expeditions in which he reached Van Diemen's Land (now Tasmania◊)□

Dien Bien Phu Battle of. The decisive battle of the Indochina war in which Vietnamese forces defeated the French. 13 Mar–7 May 1954. It resulted in the end of French control of Indochina and the fall of the French 4th Republic□

Dieppe seaport in N France with ferry services to Newhaven; population 35 000. It was held by England 1066–87 and 1135–1204□

Dieppe raid. In World War II the first Allied combined-operations raid was carried out here 19 Aug 1942; out of a mainly Canadian force of 7000, there were 3500 casualties□

diesel engine a type of internal◊ combustion engine◊□

diet meeting of the princes, etc., of the Holy Roman (German) Empire◊□

diet a particular selection of food◊, usually recommended for medical reasons□

dietetics a specialized branch of human nutrition, dealing with the promotion of health through good nutrition. See food◊□

Dietrich Marlene. Stage-name of Berlin-born Maria Magdalene von Losch 1904– ; US citizen 1937, film actress-singer. She made her name with Emil Jannings in *The Blue Angel* 1930□

differential calculus method of calculating continuously varying quantities. See calculus◊□

diffraction when light is passed through an aperture (such that the hole is smaller than the wavelength of the light) the resultant beam 'appears' larger than the hole. The light has been spread out, and has in effect travelled round corners. This spreading out process is called diffraction. It occurs with all waves, e.g. light, sound, and X-rays.

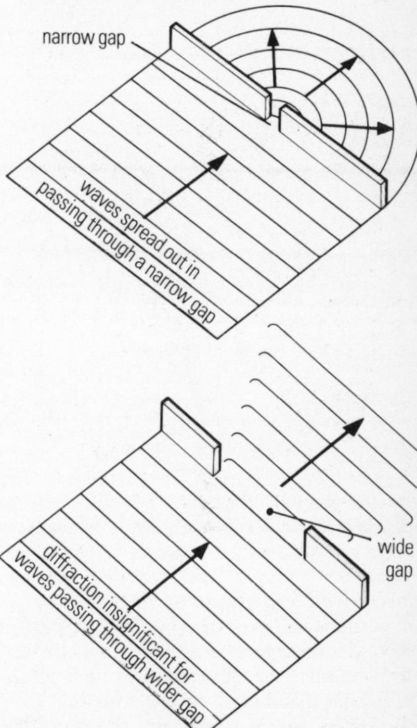

At close inspection the new beam is seen to have a bright centre surrounded by light and dark bands or interference fringes. A certain series of holes or slits (e.g. a diffraction grating) will give a distinct pattern; a certain series of objects in space (e.g. atoms in a crystal) will also give a distinctive pattern. This diffraction pattern is used to reveal the atomic structure of the crystal□

diffusion the mixing of gases or liquids into another gas or liquid. There are many physical laws governing this phenomenon. It can also mean their passage through a membrane or porous plate, etc. Enforced diffusion through a porous plate is used in the separation of uranium isotopes to obtain enriched fuel for nuclear reactors□

digestive system the internal organs which absorb food into the bloodstream.

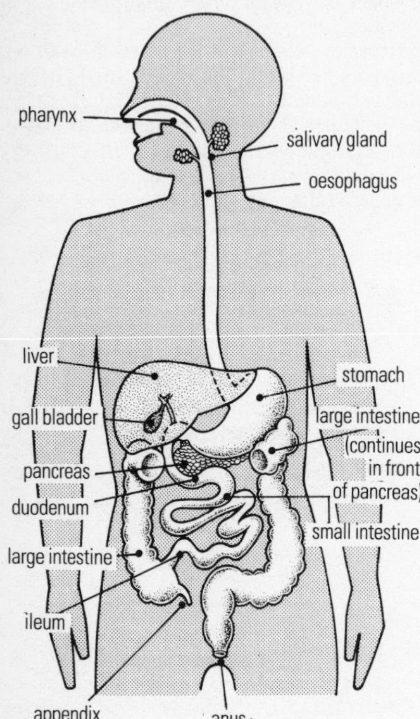

In the human digestive system, food is mixed with saliva in the mouth by chewing and is swallowed. It enters the stomach, where it is gently churned for some time and mixed with acid gastric juice. It then passes into the small intestine. In the first part of this, the ***duodenum,*** it is more finely divided by the juice of the pancreas and of the duodenal glands and mixed with bile from the liver, which splits up the fat. The ***jejunum*** and ***ileum*** continue the work of digestion and absorb most of the nutritive substances from the food. The large bowel (***colon***) completes the process and ejects the useless residue□

Diggers or ***True Levellers*** socialist sect headed by Gerrard Winstanley who set up communal colonies in 1649, and whose ideas influenced the early Quakers◊□

digitalis a drug derived from the foxglove◊□

Dijon industrial city (metallurgical, chemicals, etc.), capital of Burgundy, France; population 156 800. It has a wine trade and is famed for mustard□

Dilke Sir Charles Wentworth 1843–1911. British Liberal politician. His career was ended in 1885 by a divorce case□

dill a type of herb◊□

diminishing returns Law of. In economics, the law that additional application of money, labour, etc., which at first results in rapidly increasing output, eventually yields declining returns unless other factors are modified to sustain the increase, e.g. additional employees may increase output, but eventually the increase will become less for each employee added, unless a new machine, etc. is also installed□

Dimitrov Georgi 1882–1949. Bulgarian Communist, tried in 1933 for setting fire to the Reichstag◊. He forced an acquittal by his spirited defence, was General Secretary of the Comintern◊ until 1943, and Prime Minister of Bulgaria from 1946□

Dinan town in N France, on the River Rance, which is harnessed for tidal hydroelectric power; population 32 600□

Dinant town in S Belgium; population 6500. Almost destroyed by the Germans, Aug 1914, it is a tourist centre for the Ardennes□

Dinaric Alps see Alps◊□

Dingaan d. 1840. Zulu king 1828–40, noted for cruelty. Defeated in Natal by the Boers (16 Dec 1838 – 'Dingaan's Day'), he was subsequently killed□

dingo Australian wild dog *Canis familiaris*, brought by the Aborigines from Asia□

dinosaur extinct creature living 225–155 thousand million years ago (Mesozoic◊ era). The name means 'terrible lizard', but they were possibly all warm-blooded, and so would be in a class of their own, neither lizards, nor mammals, though one theory is that birds are the descendants of the little, fast-moving species. Some certainly nested in colonies, and many eggs have been found. They were the dominant class of life on earth for 100 million years, and the reason for their extinction is not known, but may have resulted from a sudden change of climate which allowed the survival only of small creatures (see impact crater◊). There were two distinct orders:

Saurischia which included the huge land types, e.g. ***Tyrannosaurus*** (15 m/45 ft long) of N America, which was bi-pedal (two-footed) and carnivorous; and the four-footed vegetarian amphibians, e.g. ***Diplodocus***, largest-ever land animal (27 m/90 ft long, and weighing some 35 tonnes) and ***Apatosaurus*** (formerly ***Brontosaurus***)

Ornithischia all vegetarians, included the four-footed ***Stegosaurus*** which had a spiked tail, and spinal plates (probably adjusted for temperature control), and ***Triceratops*** (8 m/25 ft) with three horns, and a neck frill; the bi-pedal ***Iguanodon***; and such small bi-pedal species as the S African ***Heterodontosaurus tucki*** (90 cm/3 ft)□

Diocletian (Gaius Valerius Diocletianus) 245–313AD. Roman emperor 284–305, when he abdicated in favour of Galerius. He reorganized and sub-divided the Empire, with two joint and two subordinate emperors, and in 303 initiated severe persecution of the Christians□

Diogenes c412–323BC. Greek philosopher of the Cynic◊ school, advocating self-discipline and disregard for conventional morality. The legend of his living in a tub like a dog arose only from Seneca having said that it was where a man so crabbed ought to live□

Diomede two islands off Alaska. ***Little Diomede*** belongs to USA, and ***Big Diomede*** to the USSR; the channel between is only 3.9 km/2.4 mi wide□

Dion Cassius surnamed ***Cocceianus***. c150–235AD. Roman historian, who gives the only surviving account of Claudius's invasion of Britain□

Dionysia festivals of Dionysus◊ (Bacchus◊) celebrated in ancient Greece, especially in Athens□

Dionysius either of two tyrants of Syracuse. ***Dionysius the Elder*** c432–367BC seized power in 405 and extended the power of Syracuse in two wars with Carthage before being defeated c375 in a third. He was a patron of Plato◊; see also Damocles◊. He was succeeded by his son ***Dionysius the Younger*** tyrant 367–356 and 353–343□

Dionysus in Greek mythology, god of wine (son of Semele and Zeus◊), and also of orgiastic excess (an animal, or on occasion a child, being torn to pieces alive and eaten); he was identified with Bacchus◊, whose rites were less savage. His festivals, the ***Dionysia***, were particularly associated with Athens; see theatre◊. Attendant on him were wild women (***maenads***) and goat-like men (***satyrs***) with pointed ears, horns and a tail (see Silenus◊). See also Thrace◊□

Diophantus c250AD. Greek mathematician at Alexandria, whose *Arithmetica,* is one of the first known works on problem-solving by algebra, in which both words and symbols were used□

dioptre optical unit in which the power of a lens is expressed as the reciprocal of its focal length in metres□

Dior Christian 1905–57. French couturier, who established his name with the 'New Look' in 1947 – long and full after war-time austerity□

dioxin toxic chemical (tetrachlorodibenzo-dioxin), produced as a by-product of a defoliant in the Vietnam War, and of the weedkiller 245-T. It causes chloracne, cancer, deformed births, and miscarriages. Disaster involving dioxin have occurred at Seveso◊ and Times◊ Beach□

diphtheria infectious disease in which a false membrane forms in the throat, causing death by asphyxia. It is preventible by immunization. See also Schick◊ test□

diplodocus a type of dinosaur◊□

diplomatic service see foreign relations◊□

dipnoi an order of lungfish◊□

dipper the, also ***water ouzel Cinclus cinclus*** family Cinclidae, order Passeriformes. A brownish, white-breasted freshwater diving bird, it can also walk under water□

diptera order of insects which includes the fly◊□

Dirac Paul Adrien Maurice 1902–84. British physicist who worked out a version of quantum mechanics◊ consistent with Special Relativity◊. The existence of the positron◊ was one of its predictions. He shared a Nobel prize 1933□

Dis in Roman mythology, god of the underworld (Greek Pluto). See under Hades◊□

disarmament the reduction of a country's weapons of war. League◊ of Nations attempts to achieve disarmament failed in the 1930s. After World War II President Johnson's proposals 1967 for ***Strategic Arms Limitation*** (SALT) were delayed by the Soviet invasion of Czechoslovakia, but Salt I was operative 1972–7; Salt II, signed by Brezhnev and Carter to operate 1979–85, was never ratified, but both the US and the USSR abided by it. In 1986 he revoked this pledge, against the advice of his European NATO partners. See nuclear◊ arms verification. Biological and chemical weapons, as well as conventional weapons, have also come under discussion at the United Nations. In Mar 1985 US/USSR negotiations reopened on intermediate range nuclear weapons, strategic arms, and weapons in outer space.

In Britain the ***Campaign for Nuclear Disarmament*** (CND, see Aldermaston◊), with which Lord Brockway, Canon Collins, Michael Foot, and Tony Benn were associated, enjoyed a spectacular revival in the 1980s□

'Discovery' ship used by Rober F Scott◊ on his Antarctic expedition□

discrimination unequal distinction between individuals or groups where one such has the power to effect unfavourable treatment of the other. Discrimination may be on grounds of difference of race, nationality, religion, politics, culture, class, sex, age, or a combination of such factors. Legislation has been to some degree effective in the case of ***racial discrimination*** against which there is a United Nations convention 1969 and national legislation in the UK and USA. See also anti-semitism◊, apartheid◊, caste◊, slavery◊□

discus circular object thrown by athletes. See throwing◊ events□

disinfectant agent killing or preventing the growth of micro-organisms, either chemically (formaldehyde, chlorine, iodine, etc.) or by physical means (boiling water or steam, heat, detergents, sound waves, ultra-violet light, etc.). See Joseph Lister◊□

Disney Walt (Walter Elias) 1901–66. American film-maker. Born in Chicago, he produced his first Mickey Mouse cartoon, *Plane Crazy*, in 1928: later were the feature-length *Snow White and the Seven Dwarfs* 1938, *Pinocchio* 1939, *Bambi* 1943 etc.; the music-based *Fantasia* 1940; nature study films, e.g. *The Living Desert* 1953, and films with human casts, e.g. *The Swiss Family Robinson* 1960. He also originated the idea of pleasure parks, of which Disneyland, California, 1955 was the first. Walt Disney World, Florida, 1972, includes the Epcot (Experimental Prototype Community of Tomorrow) Centre, a cross between a science museum and a theme park, opened 1982□

Disraeli Benjamin (Earl of Beaconsfield) 1804–81. British Conservative◊ statesman, son of Isaac d'Israeli◊. Born a Jew, he was baptized a Christian at 13. Entering Parliament in 1837, he was laughed at as a dandy, but when his maiden speech was shouted down, he said: 'The time will come when you will hear me.' He opposed Peel's decision to repeal the Corn◊ Laws in 1846, and as leader of the Young◊ England group moved towards leadership of the party. He was Chancellor of the Exchequer, under Derby◊ as Prime Minister, in a series of minority governments 1852, 1858–9. 1866–8, taking over as Prime Minister just before the Conservative electoral defeat of 1868. In Opposition, he established the Conservative Central Office, the prototype of the modern party organization. In 1874 he became Prime Minister with a landslide majority, bought a controlling interest in the Suez◊ Canal in 1875, made Queen Victoria Empress of India in 1876, brought home 'peace with honour' from the Congress of Berlin in 1878 (see Neville Chamberlain◊), and 'duelled' with Gladstone◊ on foreign policy: he retired on his electoral defeat in 1880. He established the Conservative Party as one for which the working man, whom he enfranchised in 1867, might vote. Best known of his political novels were *Coningsby* 1844 and *Sybil* 1845. Peerage 1876□

D'Israeli Isaac 1766–1848. British Jewish scholar, father of Lord Beaconsfield◊ and author of *Curiosities of Literature*□

Dissenters historically, those Protestants dissenting from the Established Church, e.g. Baptists, Presbyterians, and Independents (now known as Congregationalists)□

dissident dissenter, especially from the official Communist line, especially in the USSR from 1968. They may advocate (see samizdat◊) a more democratic Communism; emphasise the role of religion (Islam or Christianity); or be nationalist Armenians, Lithuanians, Ukrainians, Tartars, etc., or Jews wishing to emigrate. They are penalized by exile, prison, labour camps, mental institutions, or job discrimination, e.g. Sakharov◊ and Solzhenitsyn◊□

distemper virus disease in young dogs, foxes, etc., preventible by vaccination□

district council see local government◊□

District of Columbia see Columbia◊□

Diu island off the coast of Gujurat. See Goa◊□

diver or ***loon*** straight-billed, long-bodied diving birds of the northern N hemisphere, family Gaviidae, order Gaviiformes, found in lakes and estuaries. Scarcely able to stand on land, they fly, swim and dive powerfully, the largest is the ***white-billed diver*** *Gavia adamsii* of the Arctic□

diverticulitis inflammation of hernias of the large intestine, may be caused by lack of bulk in the diet□

divination attempted reading of the future by supernatural or non-rational means, such as interpreting the flight of birds, or the condition of the entrails of sacrificed animals, as in ancient Rome, or studying dreams, palms, crystals, cards, sacred texts such as the Bible, etc. See astrology◊, sibyl◊, Tarot◊□

divine right of kings doctrine that monarchy is divinely appointed as in the Bible, and that rebellion is therefore a sin against God. It was a useful weapon against the Papacy in 16th century Europe, and was supported in England in the 17th by the Royalist followers of Charles I□

diving sport of entering the water from various starting positions, and with mid-air variations, practised from a low ***springboard*** or ***highboard*** 10 m/30 ft□

diving apparatus any apparatus used to enable a person to spend time underwater. Diving bells were in use in the 18th century, but the first ***diving suit***, with large metal helmet and supplied with air by pipeline, was invented by the brothers John and Charles Deane in 1828. Complete freedom of movement came with the ***aqualung,*** see Cousteau◊. For great depths ***saturation diving*** was developed in the 1970s: divers live in a special chamber on the sea floor for weeks at a time, breathing a mixture of oxygen and helium, and take four days to readjust on surfacing. See submarine◊□

divorce legal dissolution of a marriage. This was possible in England only by private Act of Parliament until 1857. Since 1971 the sole ground for divorce is the irretrievable break-down of the marriage. Emphasis is on provision for the children, and in 1984 further legislation put a time limit on maintenance payments. Divorce may be applied for after one year from the date of marriage.

In the USA the law differs from state to state, and divorce tends to be frequent and rapid. The costliness of getting rid of unwanted partners, however, has led to the cohabitation of unmarried couples under 'pre-cohabitation agreements', which stipulate financial arrangements in the event of a break-up.

The Roman Catholic Church does not permit divorce, and under John Paul II has tightened conditions for 'annulment'. Among Muslims a wife cannot divorce her husband, but he may divorce her by repeating the formula 'I divorce you' three times□

Diwali festival of Lakshmi◊, Hindu goddess of light

Dixie the southern states of the USA□

Diyarbakir industrial city (textiles, gold and silver filigree work, etc.) in Asiatic Turkey; population 235 600□

Djakarta variant spelling of Jakarta◊□

Djibouti, Republic of

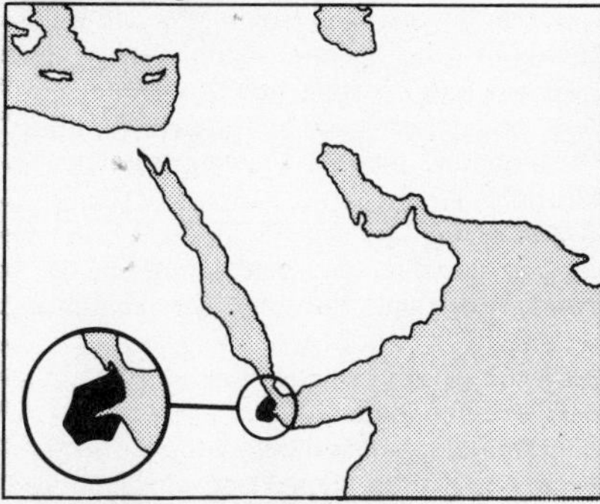

area 23 000 sq km/8880 sq mi

capital and chief port Djibouti; population 150 000

exports acts mainly as a transit port for Ethiopia

currency Djibouti franc

population 350 000, 40% Issa, 35% Afar, 25% Arab

language Somali, Afar, French, Arabic

religion Sunni Islam

government President (Hassan Gouled Aptidon from 1977) plus a chamber of deputies

recent history formerly known as French Somaliland 1892–1967, and French Territory of the Afars and Issas 1976–77, it became independent in 1977. There is tension between the two main ethnic groups, and formal declaration of a one-party state was justified in 1981 on this ground□

DNA (*d*eoxyribo*n*ucleic *a*cid) a molecule found within every cell, coded with complete instructions to build and run the body. DNA usually exists as a double strand (called the 'double helix' by Francis Crick◊ and his fellow-workers), the two halves being 'zipped' together chemically down their length. Extended to its full length, the DNA in each cell stretches to 2 m/6 ft. Instructions are written on it in an alphabet of four 'letters' (the chemical 'bases' of nucleic acids). The individual pieces of coding along its length are genes◊, and number about 100 000; genes are activated (only 10–20% may be operating at any one time) by a complex control system.

In more complex animals and plants, genes are 'packaged' into chromosomes, and many have a particular function, e.g. the production of proteins such as insulin, or the transmission of hereditary characteristics. Others have no apparent function, containing no recipes for making a protein, and are known as 'nonsense' or 'parasitic' DNA. However, sequences of DNA have been found to move about, even from one chromosome to another, and such movements (especially in the 'nonsense' DNA) and the changes they bring about may be of vital importance in the differentiation of new species, and may explain the origin of sex. In 1985 it was also found that the DNA genetic code is not universal, but that the rules are broken by certain minute creatures, bacteria and protozoans. The DNA of each individual is unique in the same way as a fingerprint◊, and blood or semen samples from incidents of murder or rape can be accurately identified; the procedure is also useful in paternity cases. See mitochondrion◊□

Dneprodzerzhinsk industrial port (chemicals, iron and steel, etc.) on the Dnieper in Ukraine, USSR; population 257 000□

Dnepropetrovsk industrial city (iron and steel, chemicals, engineering) in Ukraine,

USSR, powered by the Dnieper Dam; population 1 100 000. It was founded 1786 as Ekaterinoslav (named after Catherine the Great)□

Dnieper Russian river, Europe's third longest; length 2250 km/1400 mi.

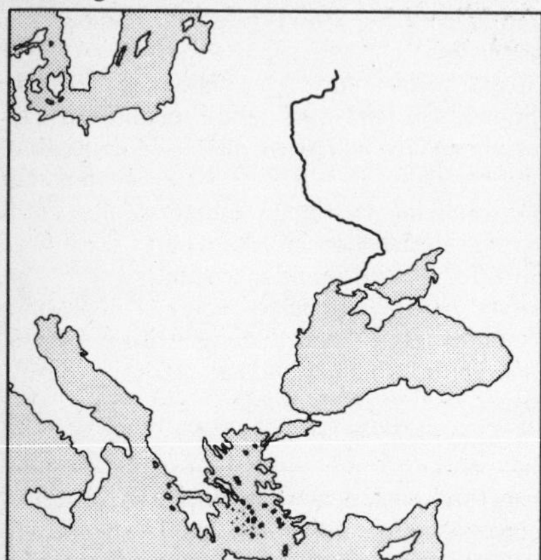

Its tributaries include the Pripet, the *Pripet marshes* being the largest in Europe and of strategic importance in both World Wars□

Dobell Sir William 1899–1970. Australian artist and portraitist. Born in New South Wales, he was originally an architect. Knighted 1966□

dobermann a breed of large dog◊□

Dobruja alluvial plain on the Black Sea divided between Bulgaria and Romania□

dock various temperate plants of the species of *Rumex,* family Polygonaceae; the large leaves are used to soothe nettle stings□

dock port accommodation for commercial and naval vessels, usually simple linear quayage adaptable to ships of any size, but with specialized equipment for handling bulk cargoes, refrigerated goods, container traffic, oil tankers, etc. Flexible 'floating' docks are used for repairs□

dodder genus of parasitic plants, *Cuscuta,* family Convolvulaceae◊, without leaves or root. The thin stem twines round the host, and penetrating suckers withdraw nourishment□

Dodds Sir Edward Charles 1899–1973. British biochemist, largely responsible for the discovery of stilboestrol, the powerful synthetic hormone used in treating prostate conditions and also for fattening cattle□

Dodecanese group of some 20 Greek islands (Dhodhekánisos) in the Aegean.

Once Turkish, the islands were Italian 1912–47, when they were ceded to Greece. They include Rhodes◊ (the largest, 1412 sq km/545 sq mi, which was held by the Knights

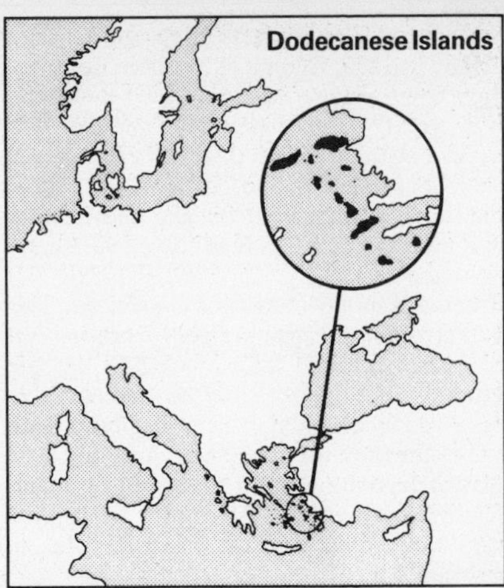

Hospitallers of St John 1306–1522, taken from Turkish rule by the Italian occupation in 1912, and ceded to Greece 1947); Cos, after which the lettuce is named, and Pátmos, where the exiled St John◊ is said to have written *Revelation*□

Dodge City City in SW Kansas, USA; population 14 000. On the Santa Fé Trail, it was famous in the days of the Wild West□

Dodgson C L. Writer whose pen name was Lewis Carroll◊

dodo extinct flightless bird, of the pigeon◊ order□

Dodoma Capital of Tanzania from 1975, replacing Dar-es-Salaam; population 45 700. Chosen because in the centre of the country, it is 1132 m/3713 ft above sea level□

dog species *Canis familiaris.* Animal descended from an ancestor resembling the dingo◊ and dhole◊, and like the jackal, fox and wolf, belonging to the family Canidae; see also raccoon dog. There are some 400 modern breeds, and some 150 are registered by the Kennel Club (1873) and grouped into sporting breeds (hound, gundog, and terrier) and non-sporting (utility, working, and toy) for showing (see Charles Cruft◊).

Breeds of dog

Afghan hound see under greyhound below

basenji small smooth-coated African hunting dog which does not bark

basset hound see hound below

beagle see hound below

bloodhound see hound below

boxer large, short-coated dog with a docked tail and a set-back nose to enable it to breathe when holding on to bear, boar, etc.

bull terrier originally a cross between the bulldog and the terrier, formerly used in bullbaiting

cavalier King Charles spaniel see under spaniel below
chihuahua the smallest dog, sometimes only 0.900 kg/ under 2 lb; with a round head and full eyes; it originated in N Africa, and was taken to Mexico by the Spaniards
chow chow breed originating in China where it is eaten (the name is pidgin-English for 'food'); it has a thick coat in one colour and black tongue
cocker spaniel see under spaniel below
collie large dog with a tapered muzzle, long coat and swirling tail, originally used in herding sheep
dachshund see under hound below
dalmatian see under hound below
Dandie Dinmont see under terrier below
deerhound see under greyhound below
dobermann large powerful guard dog, dark in colour, with tan markings, high-set ears and a docked tail. It derives from the smaller German breed, the Pinscher
fox terrier see under terrier below
great dane very large dog, 1 m/3 ft at the shoulder, used in boarhunting, with a short coat and proud carriage
greyhound type of a group of dogs used for their speed in hunting, and which includes: the *Irish wolfhound*, the largest, which is rough-haired, as is the more slimly built *deerhound*; the slimly-built, profusely-haired and ringtailed *Afghan Hound* introduced to Britain by army officers serving on the NW frontier; and the short-coated *Saluki* used for hunting gazelle; the smooth-coated *greyhound*, used both in hare coursing (when two dogs compete to kill a live hare, as at the Waterloo Cup meeting), and in greyhound racing (when the dogs chase a mechanical hare); the small *whippet*, and the similar but more delicate *Italian greyhound*
harrier see under hound below
hound dog hunting by scent, includes the *basset hound*, a long-bodied, low dog, with wrinkled forehead and pendulous ears, formerly used to flush game from the undergrowth; *beagle*, short-haired, with pendant ears, sickle tail, and bell-like voice used for hunting hares on foot ('beagling'); *bloodhound* massive hound with tracking powers, and sad, 'bloodshot' eyes; *foxhound*, small, and bred in England for 300 years for speed and stamina in foxhunting (the *harrier*, smaller and slower, resembles it); *dachshund* (German 'badger-dog'), short-legged and long-bodied, which may be smooth, long-haired or wirehaired; *dalmatian*, white with dark spots
husky Inuit sledge dog, with pricked ears, thick fur and bushy tail; the Siberian *Samoyed* resembles it, and is used by the Samoyed people
Irish wolfhound see under greyhound above
Italian greyhound see under greyhound above
laika Russian sporting dog, of which a specimen was the first animal sent into space;
mastiff large sporting dog with a short coat and broad muzzle, once used in bull and bear-baiting; the *St Bernard* is a large, long-haired version with square build, pendulous ears and lips, and large feet; the monks of St Bernard's Pass once kept them for finding lost travellers
Mexican hairless medium-sized dog, also known at the Xoloizcuintli, alleged to be the original edible breed of the Mayas, Toltecs and Aztecs; it is the only breed to be hairless
Pekingese small toy with shortened muzzle, long coat and feathered ears and tail, favoured at the Chinese Imperial Court, where tiny specimens were known as 'sleeve-dogs'. They became popular in Europe when several were looted from the Summer Palace in 1860
pointer and setter group of large gundogs hunting by air scent includes the *English setter*, a large white dog with coloured markings, and *Irish Setter*, all-red in colour, which 'set' or crouch in the presence of game, and the *pointer*, which 'points' to game
pomeranian toy dog first bred in Pomerania, a small version of the German spitz, or husky (see above)
poodle intelligent dog with pendant ears, and unmarked felting coat in varied colours, which is recognised in three sizes: standard, miniature and toy – the only dog permitted to be clipped (in various styles) for showing
pug small dog of Chinese origin, with wrinkles on the forehead that form the Chinese character for 'prince', and a tightly curled tail
retriever gundog used for retrieving game, includes: the *Labrador retriever*, large, smooth-coated, and usually either black or yellow; and *Golden retriever* – always golden – which is either flat or wavy-coated, and has *water-spaniel* blood
St Bernard see under mastiff above
saluki see under greyhound above
schipperke Belgian tailless watchdog; black, with erect ears
setter see pointer and setter above
sheepdog, Old English. Large, 'square', heavily coated dog, usually greyish and often with white markings. Originally used with sheep
shih tzu small short-legged, long-bodied Tibetan breed with long hair and white blaze and tail tip

spaniel gundog which works partly like a hound and partly like a pointer, includes the *springer spaniel* medium-sized, with medium pendant ears, and close straight coat, and so-named because originally used for 'springing' game; *cocker spaniel* small, lively and silky-coated, with long ears; *Irish water spaniel* with a curly coat; *cavalier King Charles spaniel* mainly a pet
springer spaniel see under spaniel above
terrier varied group which includes the large, rough-haired, black-and-tan *Airedale terrier*; *bull terrier* a cross between the terrier and bulldog, formerly used in bullbaiting; *fox terrier* bred to be small enough to get into a fox's earth, and white with coloured patches (either smooth or rough-haired), and *Irish terrier* wiry-haired and brown. Also group of small ***thick-set terriers***, probably all derived from the same original source, which includes the *Scottish terrier*, usually with a brindled coat; *Skye*, longer-coated and longer-bodied; *cairn*, often with dark 'points' on the ears and muzzle; *Dandie Dinmont* with drooping ears, a favourite of Sir Walter Scott; *West Highland white*, and the *Sealyham* (named after the place in Dyfed where it is said to have originated as a cross between the Welsh and Jack Russell terriers) and *Yorkshire*, a toy dog with long straight hair reaching to the ground and a tied-back topknot
Welsh corgi low-set, working dog, used in driving cattle. The *Pembroke* has prick ears, short tail, and a dense, usually reddish coat with a white chest; the *Cardigan* has a long tail
whippet see under greyhound above□
doge chief magistrate of Venice◊□
dogfish small member of various families of shark, of which the most familiar species are *Scyliorhinus caniculus* and *S maculatus*, sold for eating as 'rockfish'□
Dogger Bank shoal in the North Sea. A rich fishing ground□
Dogger Bank Battle of the. Indecisive naval battle between British and Germans 24 Jan 1915□
Doggett Thomas died 1721. British actor, commemorated by the prize of 'Doggett's Coat and Badge', for the winner of a sculling race on the Thames on 1 Aug□
Dogs Isle of. See under Tower◊ Hamlets□
Doha capital and chief port of Qatar; population 190 000. The Doha regional training centre provides vocational training for all the Gulf states; the Gulf (football) tournament is played in Kahlifa Stadium□
dolerite dark, heavy, igneous, coarsely crystalline rock, resembling basalt□
Dolgellau tourist centre and market town (formerly Dolgelley) in Gwynedd, Wales; population 2400. Nearby are the Gwynffynydd, 'White mountain' and Clogau goldmines; a nugget from the latter has supplied gold for the wedding rings of royal brides since 1923□
dollar monetary unit of 100 cents, adopted in the USA in 1785, and subsequently by countries such as Australia, Canada, Hong Kong, etc.□
Dollfuss Engelbert 1892–1934. Austrian chancellor 1932–34. In an attempted Nazi coup 25 Jul 1934, the Chancellery was seized and Dollfuss murdered□
dolmen neolithic monument of stone uprights plus roofing slab, usually a grave chamber; in Wales it is a ***cromlech***□
dolphin marine mammal, cetacean◊, family Delphinidae: typical species the ***common dolphin*** *Delphinus delphis*, dark grey above and whitish beneath; over 2 m/6 ft long; and with a 150 mm/6 in 'beak'. They are thought to have once been land animals (the flippers have the structure of five-toed limbs; there are vestigial hind-limbs, and they seem to have been covered with hair). By specialized modifications of the skin, they reach 56 kph/35mph in the water. Very intelligent, they use sound for echolocation, for communication, and (by emitting a beam of sound about 9° wide, with a power of about 100 decibels, a metre from their heads) can disable and possibly kill their prey. The ***bottle-nose dolphin*** *Tursiops truncatus*, popular in oceanariums, solves the problem of remaining alert while asleep by having a brain of which only half sleeps at any one time. The ***killer whale*** *Orcinus orca* is the only one of the family to feed on other dolphins, seals, etc.; it is noted for its leaps in oceanariums.
The name dolphin is used also for the gamefish *Coryphaena hippurus* (1.5 m/5 ft), and (in USA) for the porpoise◊□
Domagk Gerhard 1895–1964. German biochemist, awarded a Nobel prize 1939 for his research on sulphonamide◊ drugs□
Domenichino title of ***Domenico Zampieri*** (1581-1641), Italian Baroque painter. Born in Bologna, he trained under the Carracci◊, and worked in Rome and Naples. He is one of the founders of landscape painting□
Domesday Book record of the survey of England carried out in 1086 for William the Conqueror, and used for assessing taxation, etc. It is preserved in two volumes. at the Public Record Office, London, and was so-called because thought as final a judgment as that of Doomsday□
Domingo Placido 1941– . Spanish tenor, who emigrated with his family to Mexico as a

boy; his opera roles include Othello and Hoffmann□

Dominic St 1170–1221. Founder of the Catholic order of Dominicans◊. Sent on a mission to the Provençal Albigenses by Innocent III 1205–15, he supported the Papal decision to suppress their heresy by force in 1208. Feast day 4 Aug□

Dominica Commonwealth of

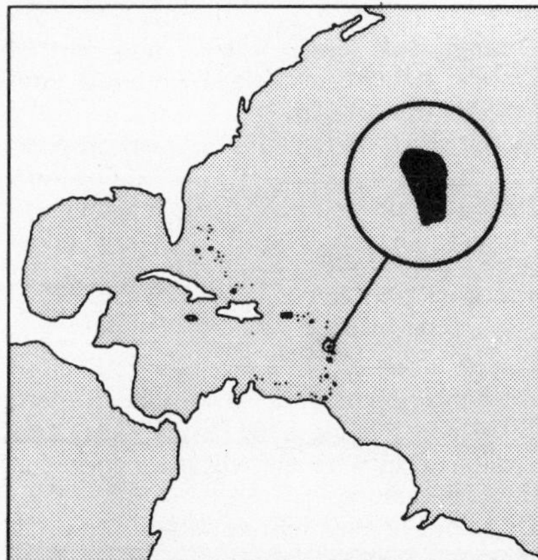

area 750 sq km/290sq mi
capital Roseau, with a deepwater port
features largest of the Windward Islands◊; of great beauty, it has mountains of volcanic origin rising to 1620 m/5315 ft; Boiling Lake, an effect produced by escaping subterranean gas
exports bananas, coconuts, citrus, lime and bay oil
currency E Caribbean dollar, pound sterling, French franc
population 74 069, mainly black African in origin, but with a small Carib◊ reserve of c500
language English (official), but the Dominican *patois* still reflects earlier periods of French rule
religion Roman Catholicism 80%
government non-executive president, with a part-elected, part-nominated house of assembly (Prime Minister from 1980 Eugenia Charles, Freedom Party, re-elected 1985)
recent history First reached by Europeans (Columbus) in 1493, it was disputed between Britain and France, but ceded to Britain in 1783. In 1878 it achieved independence within the Commonwealth. There has been a state of emergency since 1981, owing to threatened coups against the conservative government of the Dominican Freedom Party (DFP)□

Dominican Republic
area 48 430 sq km/18 700sq mi
capital Santo Domingo

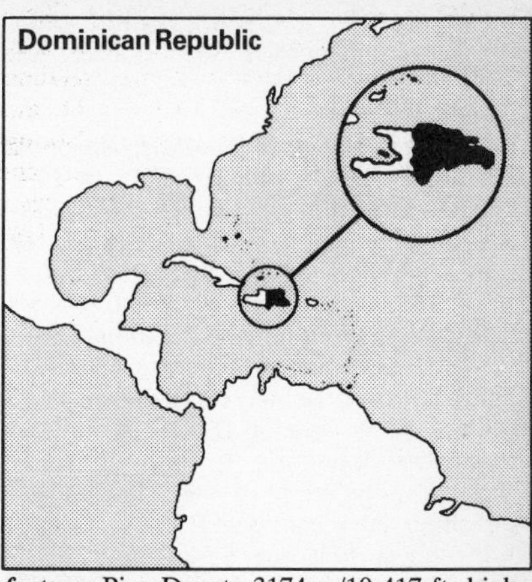

features Pico Duarte 3174 m/10 417 ft, highest point in the Caribbean islands
exports sugar, gold, coffee, ferro-nickel
currency peso
population 6 416 000
language Spanish (official)
religion Roman Catholic
famous people Toussaint L'Ouverture
government under the constitution of 1966, there is an executive president (Salvador Jorge Blanco from 1982), Senate and House of Representatives
recent history First reached by Europeans (Columbus) in 1492 and named Hispaniola, it is the oldest settlement of European founding in America. Independent from Spain in 1821, it threw off attempted rule by Haiti 1822–44. Occupied by the USA 1916-24, it was stabilized under the dictatorship of Trujillo◊ 1930–61. US troops intervened in 1965 when there was civil war. Free elections were held in 1966, and US backing was given against later takeover attempts by the military□

Dominicans Catholic order of friar-preachers founded by St Dominic◊ in 1215; there is also an order of contemplative nuns; the habit is black and white. They have included Thomas Aquinas◊, Savonarola◊, Las Casas◊□

Dominions see Commonwealth◊□

Domitian (Titus Flavius Domitianus) 51–96AD. Roman emperor from 81. He finalized the conquest of Britain (see Agricola◊), strengthened the Rhine–Danube frontier, and suppressed immorality as well as freedom of thought in philosophy (see Epictetus◊), and religion (Christians were persecuted). His fears of assassination were justified in 96 when the plotters included his wife□

Don Russian river, linked by canal with the Volga; length 1900 km/1200 mi□

Donat Robert 1905–58. British actor, especially remembered for the films *The Thirty-Nine Steps* 1935 and *Goodbye Mr Chips* 1939□

Donatello or ***Donato di Niccolo di Betto Bardi*** 1386–1466. Italian sculptor, born in Florence. As Brunelleschi◊ revived the classical style in architecture, so Donatello did for sculpture. His works include the bronze *David* (Florence), one of the first free-standing nude sculptures of the Renaissance, and the equestrian statue of *Gattamelata* (Padua), setting the style for this genre also□

Donbas abbreviation of Donets Basin◊□

Doncaster coalmining town in S Yorks, England; population 85 000. The railway workshops have contracted. Horse races at Doncaster include the St Leger (1776) in Sept. The ruined Norman castle features in Scott's *Ivanhoe* as Athelstan's stronghold□

Donegal county (county town Lifford) of the Republic of Ireland, province of Ulster◊. It is famous for tweed, and in 1981 uranium was discovered□

Donets river of the USSR flowing into the Don; length 1080 km/670 mi□

Donets Basin industrial region, (chemicals, iron, steel, etc.) abbreviated as Donbas, which produces about 40% of Soviet coal, plus salt, mercury, lead, etc.□

Donetsk industrial city (iron and steel, chemicals, coal-mining) in Ukraine USSR; population 1 040 000. It was known as Stalino 1924–61□

Dongola town in N Sudan; population 6000. It was the capital of the Christian kingdom of Dongola 6–15th centuries□

Dongting lake in Hunan province, China; area 10 000 sq km/4000 sq mi□

Dönitz Karl 1891–1980. German admiral, originator of the wolf-pack submarine technique which sank 15 million tonnes of Allied shipping in World War II. He succeeded Hitler in 1945, capitulated and was imprisoned 1946–56□

Donizetti Gaetano 1797–1848. Italian composer of over 60 melodiously flowing operas including *Lucia di Lammermoor* 1835 and *Don Pasquale* 1843□

Don Juan legendary 14th century Spaniard, notorious for debauchery, featured by Tirso de Molina, Molière, Mozart, Byron and G B Shaw□

donkey a member of the horse◊ family□

Donne John 1571–1631. British metaphysical poet. As a law student, notorious for his wit and reckless living, he sailed as a volunteer with Essex and Raleigh in 1596, and on his return became private secretary to Sir Thomas Egerton, the Lord Keeper. This appointment was ended by his secret marriage to Ann More (died 1617), niece of Egerton's wife, and they endured many years of poverty: she was the subject of many of his love poems. Originally Roman Catholic, he took orders in the Anglican Church in 1615, and as Dean of St Paul's 1621–31, preached famous sermons. His verse was not collected for publication till after his death□

Donnybrook former village, now part of Dublin, Republic of Ireland, notorious until 1855 for riotous fairs□

Doolittle Hilda 1886–1961. American poet, who signed her work HD, associated with Ezra Pound◊ and Richard Aldington◊ (to whom she was married 1913–37) in founding the Imagist◊ school of poetry□

Doomsday Book a variant spelling of Domesday Book◊□

Doone family of legendary Exmoor freebooters portrayed by novelist Richard Blackmore◊; living in the Doone Valley near Lynton. They were allegedly exterminated in the 17th century□

Doppler Christian Johann 1803–53. Austrian physicist. See Doppler effect□

Doppler effect change in observed frequency of waves due to relative motion between wave source and observer. Responsible for the perceived change in pitch of an ambulance siren as it approaches and then recedes, and, on a somewhat grander scale, for the shift, towards the red end of the spectrum, of light from distant stars. See Hubble's Law◊. Named after the Austrian physicist Christian Doppler (1803–53)□

Dorati Antal 1906– . American conductor, born in Budapest, Conductor Laureate of the Royal Philharmonic Orchestra□

Dorchester town (administrative headquarters) in Dorset, England; population 14 000. There are Roman remains (amphitheatre, etc.), and Thomas Hardy◊ was born nearby (it is the 'Casterbridge' of the novels). ***Maiden Castle*** to the SW, occupied as a settlement from c2000BC became an Iron Age hillfort◊ with a rampart 18 m/60 ft high enclosing an area of 18 ha/45 acres, which was stormed by the Romans 43AD□

Dordogne river in SW France; length 490 km/300 mi. The valley of the Dordogne is a popular tourist area. The Lascaux cave system, discovered 1940, has the earliest known examples of cave art (bulls, bison and deer). They were painted by the Cro-Magnon people (named from skeletons found 1868 in Cro-Magnon Cave, near Les Eyzies). The opening of the caves to tourists led to deterioration of the paintings; the caves were closed 1963 and a facsimile opened 1983. See Gironde◊□

Dordrecht industrial river port (shipbuilding yards, plastics and heavy machinery) in SW Netherlands; population 108,040□

Doré Gustave 1832–83. French artist, best-known for his book illustrations (Rabelais, Dante, Cervantes, the Bible, Milton and Poe), which are often grotesque or sardonic□

Dorians Hellenic people (chief cities: Sparta, Argos, Corinth), who conquered most of the Peloponnese from the Achaeans by 1100–1000BC and destroyed the Mycenean◊ civilization□

Doric a style of column◊□

dormouse arboreal, nocturnal, hibernating rodent◊ distinguished from rats and mice by its bushy tail, family Gliridae. The ***common European dormouse*** *Muscardinus avellanarius* is reddish fawn and 15 cm/6 in long. The ***fat*** or ***edible dormouse*** *Glis glis*, is twice the size□

Dorneywood country house in Buckinghamshire, England, given by Lord Courtauld-Thomson to the nation, and used by the Foreign Secretary□

Dornier Claude 1884–1969. German aircraft designer, inventor of the seaplane and maker in World War II of the Luftwaffe's 'flying pencil' bomber□

Dorpat German name of the Estonian city of Tartu◊□

Dorset Earl of. See Sackville◊□

Dorset SW county of England

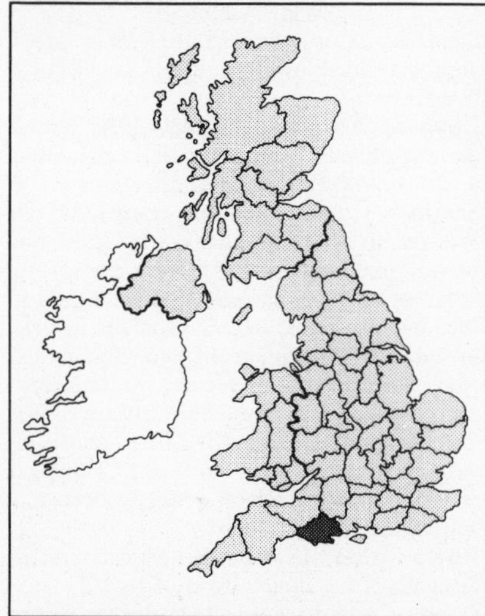

area 2654 sq km/1024 sq mi

towns administrative headquarters Dorchester; Poole, Shaftesbury, Sherborne; resorts Bournemouth, Lyme Regis, Weymouth

features Chesil Bank (shingle bank along the coast 19 km/11 mi); Isle of Purbeck, a peninsula where china clay and Purbeck 'marble◊' is quarried, and which includes Corfe Castle and the holiday resort of Swanage; Dorset Downs; Cranborne Chase; rivers Frome and Stour; Maiden Castle (see Dorchester◊, Iron◊ Age); Tank Museum at Royal Armoured Corps Centre, Bovington, where the cottage of T E Lawrence is a museum

products Wytch Farm is the largest onshore oilfield in the UK

population 604 500

famous people Thomas Hardy, the novelist, born at Higher Bockhampton (Dorchester is 'Casterbridge', the heart of Hardy's Wessex)□

Dort another name for Dordrecht◊□

Dortmund major industrial centre of the Ruhr◊, W Germany; population 609 400. It is the southern terminus of the Dortmund-Ems canal□

dory a type of fish; John◊ Dory□

Dos Passos John 1896–1970. American novelist, born in Chicago. His masterpiece is the *USA* trilogy 1930–6, in which the fiction is backed by newspaper headlines and contemporary events□

Dostoevsky Fyodor Mihailovich 1821–81. Russian novelist. Born in Moscow, he was for a short time an army officer, and in 1849 was reprieved only at the last moment from execution as a Socialist revolutionary. This, and four years at Omsk penal settlement, increased his epileptic tendency. The psychological insight of such books as *Crime and Punishment* 1866, an analysis of a murderer's reactions, *The Idiot* 1868–9, *The Possessed* 1871–2, and *The Brothers Karamazov* 1880, was influential beyond Russia□

dotterel a Eurasian plover◊□

Dou Gerard 1613–75. Dutch painter of interiors, born at Leyden, a student of Rembrandt□

Douai coal and steel town of N France; population 47 570. The ***Douai Bible*** 1582–1610, was prepared at the English Catholic college, and influenced the King James Version□

double coconut a tree-like palm◊ plant□

Doughty Charles Montagu 1843–1926. Suffolk-born traveller in Arabia 1876–8, who recorded his experiences in antique prose in *Travels in Arabia Deserta* 1888□

Douglas Lord Alfred 1870–1945. British poet, son of the 8th Marquess of Queensbury. His association with Oscar Wilde◊ led to the latter's action for libel against Queensbury, which ultimately resulted in Wilde's own imprisonment□

Douglas Gavin 1475–1522. Scottish poet, whose translation of the Aeneid is the first in English□
Douglas Norman 1868–1952. British diplomat and travel writer (*Siren Land* 1911 and *Old Calabria* 1915), dealing with Italy; his novel *South Wind* 1917 is set in his adopted island of Capri□
Douglas capital of the Isle of Man; population 19 900. It has the Manx Museum and the House of Keys (Parliament)□
Douglas-Home William 1912– . British playwright, younger brother of Lord Home◊ of the Hirsel. His plays include *The Chiltern Hundreds* 1947 and *Lloyd George Knew My Father* 1972□
Doukhobors Russian religious sect, with teachings resembling Quakerism, whose refusal of military service provoked persecution. In 1898 members were allowed to emigrate to Canada, where they number c13 000, of whom c100 were imprisoned for terrorist activities in the 1960s□
Doulton Sir Henry 1820–97. British ceramist, who developed both industrial ware, e.g. stoneware drainpipes in 1846, and from 1870 at Lambeth and Burslem, art pottery and domestic tableware□
Doumer Paul 1857–1932. President of France from 1931, who was assassinated by Gorgulov, a mad White Russian émigré□
Douro river of N Spain and Portugal, length 800 km/500 mi□
dove a type of pigeon◊□
Dover Cinque port in Kent, nearest point of Britain to the Continent (34 km/21 mi) and the main ferry and hovercraft terminal; population 34 000. Watling Street◊ ended here, and the Roman lighthouse 50AD within the Norman castle grounds is one of the oldest buildings in Britain□
Dover Strait of. Sea link (French: Pas-de-Calais◊) between the English Channel and the North Sea; length 35 km/22 mi. It is one of the world's busiest sea lanes, and traffic routeing was enforced from 1972□
Dowding Hugh Caswall Tremenheere, 1st Baron Dowding 1882–1970. British air chief marshal, who headed Fighter Command in the Battle of Britain◊. He wrote works on spiritualism□
Dowell Anthony 1943– . Senior principal dancer (e.g. the prince in *Sleeping Beauty*) Royal Ballet, 1967–86, and director from 1986□
Dowland John 1563–1626. English composer of songs to lute accompaniment, who was patronised by the Stuarts◊ from 1612□
Down county of Northern Ireland
area 2465 sq km/952 sq mi
towns Downpatrick (county town); the small town of Hillsborough was the site of signature of the ***Hillsborough Agreement*** (see Northern Ireland◊)
features Mourne mountains; Strangford Lough
products dairying area
population 312 000□
Downing Street street in Westminster, London, named after 17th century diplomat Sir George Downing; No 10 is the Prime Minister's residence and No 11 that of the Chancellor of the Exchequer□
Downs chalk hills of S England which run from Salisbury Plain to S Foreland ***(North Downs)*** and through Sussex to Beachy Head ***(South Downs;*** see also E Sussex◊)□
Down's syndrome chromosomal abnormality (the presence of an additional chromosome in all the sufferer's cells) which produces a rather flattened face and fold of skin at the inner edge of the eye (hence the former name 'mongolism'), as well as mental retardation in children□
dowsing location of water, minerals, etc., by use of a forked twig, pendulum, etc., possibly in response to a local change in the pattern of electrical forces. Though not recognized by science, it is a commercially valuable talent□
Dowson Ernest 1867–1900. British 'decadent' poet remembered for the refrain of his lyric 'Cynara': 'I have been faithful to thee, Cynara! in my fashion'□
Doxiadis ***Constantinos*** 1913–75. Greek architect and town planner. See Islamabad◊□
Doyle Sir Arthur Conan 1859–1930. British author, born in Edinburgh, and originally a doctor until the creation of private detective Sherlock Holmes, and his companion Dr Watson, in *A Study in Scarlet* 1887, led him to full-time authorship: there were several volumes of short stories (first published in the *Strand Magazine*), as well as novels, including *The Hound of the Baskervilles* 1902. See Meiringen◊. He also wrote historical romances, e.g. *The White Company* 1891, and the science fiction *The Lost World* 1912, with an irascible hero, Professor Challenger (see Roraima◊). In later years he became a spiritualist□
Doyle Richard 1824–83. British caricaturist, designer of the *Punch* cover of 1849□
D'oyly Carte Richard (1844–1901). British producer of the Gilbert and Sullivan operas at the Savoy Theatre, London, which he built□
Drabble, Margaret 1939– . British novelist, whose books e.g. *The Millstone* 1966 and *The*

Middle Ground 1980, deal with the frustrations of suburban life, and its moments of illumination. Edited the 1985 edition of the *Oxford Companion to Literature*□

draco a flying lizard◊

Draco 7th century BC. Athenian statesman, who first codified the laws of the city-state, and with such severity that 'draconian' means 'harsh'□

Dracula historically a 15th century prince of Romania, known as 'the Impaler', because he slowly impaled a Turkish invading army 20 000 at a time, though the actual name derives from his father Vlad Drakul ('the Devil'). In Bram Stoker◊'s novel *Dracula* 1897, he became a caped count who, as a vampire◊, drank the blood of beautiful women. Dracula's castle, N of Bucharest, is a tourist attraction□

draft to select for compulsory military service; conscription◊□

dragon a mythical monster, with a huge scaly body and long tail, and which breathes fire□

dragonfly large, brilliantly coloured insect of the order Odonata, remarkable for their large compound eyes (30 000 facets), strong-toothed mouthparts, and darting flight with membraneous, glassy wings (living species span 180 mm, but a prehistoric dragonfly spanning 70 cm/2 ft is the largest insect ever known). Both adults and the underwater immature nymphs are predatory on other insects□

dragoon originally a French mounted soldier carrying a 'dragon' or short musket; only the name is retained by some regiments□

Drake Sir Francis c1545–96. English sailor, born near Tavistock. He accompanied Sir John Hawkins◊ in a disastrous voyage to the Guinea Coast in 1567, and made voyages to plunder the Spanish Main, the most famous being in the *Pelican* (renamed *Golden Hind*) Dec 1577–Sept 1580, in which he made the second circumnavigation of the world, and the first by an Englishman. He was knighted on her deck at Deptford by Elizabeth I when the Spaniards demanded his punishment. In 1587 he 'singed the King of Spain's beard' by destroying 10 000 tons of shipping at Cadiz, and served as a Vice-Admiral in the *Revenge* in the battle against the Armada in 1588. He sailed with Hawkins to the West Indies in 1595, and died on his ship off Nombre de Dios. A national park in California marks the site where Drake anchored the *Golden Hind* in 1579□

Drakensberg mountain range (Sesuto name Quathlamba) in S Africa, highest point Mont aux Sources 3482 m/10 822 ft, near Natal National Park□

drama any work performed by actors.

2700BC world's earliest known play *The Triumph of Horus* drafted, and in 88BC inscribed on wall of Temple of Edfu

6th century Thespis originated Greek tragedy

5th–4th century flowering of Greek drama: Aeschylus, Sophocles, Euripides, Menander, Aristophanes

3rd century BC–1st century AD Roman drama follows in the Greek tradition: Terence, Plautus, Seneca◊

12–16th century AD mystery and miracle plays from Bible stories.

14–16th century aristocratic *No* plays developed in Japan

15th century re-discovery of classical drama in Italy, and development of popular improvisatory *commedia del arte*

16th–17th century flowering of European drama: *England* Lyly, Green, Peele, Kyd, Marlowe, Shakespeare, and then the Jacobean Webster, Massinger, Middleton, Ford, Jonson, Beaumont and Fletcher and Shirley, followed by the Restoration comedy of Etherege, Wycherley and Congreve; *France* Corneille, Racine and Molière; *Spain* Lope de Vega and Calderón de la Barca; and in the Orient there was a development of popular theatre in India, China and Japan (Kabuki◊).

18th century tended either to the mannered or the sentimental; *England* Sheridan, Goldsmith; *the Continent* Beaumarchais, Goldoni, Lessing, Schiller

19th century Romanticism embodied by Victor Hugo, but the beginnings of Realism in Dumas *fils*, led on to Ibsen and Strindberg, less forcefully expressed in England by Robertson, Pinero, and H A Jones

20th century before World War I: Chekhov, Wilde, Shaw, Pirandello; between the wars: Coward, Rattigan, Cocteau, Mayakovsky, O'Neill, Capek, Brecht, Toller, Elmer Rice, Odets; during and after World War II: Sartre, Anouilh and Salacrou.

1950s Theatre of the Absurd: Ionesco, Simpson, Beckett, and Albee; more realistic drama of Osborne, Wesker, Pinter and John Arden in England, Brendan Behan in Ireland, Genet, Dürrenmatt and Ugo Betti on the Continent, and Miller, Jack Gelber and Tennessee Williams in America.

The re-association, begun by Claudel, of the poet and the playhouse in the 20th century led to the rise of the Irish Abbey Theatre, with plays by J. M. Synge and W. B. Yeats, and to the poetic drama of Lorca in Spain, and of T. S. Eliot, Spender, Auden, Isherwood and Fry, in England and America.

1960s Peter Brook revives ideas of Artaud's Theatre of Cruelty with Weiss's *Marat/Sade,* and besides more traditional plays, such as those of Peter Schaffer and Tom Stoppard, there was the more radical output of Joe Orton.

1970s Alan Ayckbourn, Athol Fugard

1980s Howard Brenton, David Hare, Christopher Hampton, David Mamet, Sam Shepard□

draughts game also known as ***checkers*** because of the 'checkered' board of 64 squares, which has elements of a simplified form of chess. Each of the two players has 12 men (discs), and attempts either to capture all of the opponent's men or to block their moving□

Dravidian group of people of the Deccan and northern Sri Lanka, shorter and darker than the more recently invading peoples of north India. Their languages include Tamil, Telugu, Malayalam, and Kannada□

Drayton Michael 1563–1631. English poet, author of a topographical survey of England, *Polyolbion* 1613–22, in 30 books□

dream series of events, pictures, etc. which occurs during sleep. For the purposes of (allegedly) foretelling the future, dreams fell into disrepute in the scientific atmosphere of the 18th century, but were given importance by Freud◊ who saw them as wish fulfilment (nightmares being failed dreams prompted by fears of 'repressed' impulses). Dreams occur in periods of rapid eye movement (REM) by the sleeper, when the cortex of the brain is approximately as active as in waking hours, and they occupy a fifth of sleeping time. They could be a means of forgetting, so as to clear an 'overloaded network', a nightmare being brought to conscious attention so that the anxiety causing it can be dealt with. If a high level of acetylcholine is present (see under brain◊) dreams occur too early in sleep, causing wakefulness, confusion and depression◊, which suggests that a form of memory search is involved. Prevention of dreaming, e.g. by taking sleeping tablets, has similar unpleasant results. The surrealist progression of some dreams could be because the brain desperately tries to make sensible links between fragments of what is passing before it as waking consciousness gradually returns. Some people achieve a degree of control of their dreams□

Dreiser Theodore 1871–1945. American realistic novelist, best-remembered for *An American Tragedy* (1925), based on the real life crime of a man who in 'making good' becomes a murderer□

Dresden capital of Dresden district and industrial city in E Germany; population 516 284. Dresden china initially made here in 1709, has been made at Meissen since 1710. The city was bombed by the Allies 13–14 Feb 1945, casualty estimates ranging 35 000–135 000□

Dreyfus Alfred 1859–1935. French soldier. Of Jewish origin, he worked in the War Ministry and in 1894 was accused of betraying military secrets to Germany, court-martialled, and sent to Devil's◊ Island. Although the real culprit, Major Esterhazy, was discovered in 1896, it was not until 1906 that Dreyfus was finally declared innocent, although he had been 'pardoned' after a retrial in 1899: he was championed by Clemenceau◊ and Zola◊□

drill a large arboreal baboon (*Mandrillus leucophaeus*) of W Africa, with a very short tail and a long prehensile great toe. The face is black, not coloured as in the mandrill◊□

Drogheda seaport in county Louth, Republic of Ireland; population 19 800. The inhabitants were massacred when it was stormed by Cromwell in 1649, and in 1690 it surrendered to William III after the Battle of the Boyne□

Droitwich see under Hereford◊ and Worcester□

dromedary a type of camel◊ with a single hump□

dropsy popular name for oedema◊□

drosera an insectivorous◊ plant◊□

drosophila a small fruit fly◊□

drought prolonged absence of rain due either to natural weather conditions, or to alteration of the environment (destruction of trees, etc.). In the UK 15 days with less than 0.2 mm of rain constitutes an 'absolute drought'□

drowning death by immersion in liquid. Unless spasm of the muscles of the larynx prevents the entry of water to the lungs, death is caused by hindrance of the passage of oxygen to the bloodstream, as well as direct effects on the blood itself. The latter occur more rapidly in the case of fresh water (3 min) than sea water (8 min). See artificial respiration◊□

drug delivery system any means of administering a drug. In order to administer a drug over a long period or in minute amounts highly sophisticated methods may be employed. The drug may be dispersed into a medium which in tablet form is hard to digest in the stomach. Alternatively the tablet or capsule may be implanted just beneath the skin. In hospitals a syringe pump may be used whereby a small volume (e.g. 10ml) can be injected over a 40hr period yet at a constant rate□

drug misuse the abuse of medicinal drugs. Under the UK Misuse of Drugs Acts they comprise: 1 ***most harmful*** heroin, morphine, opium, and other narcotics; hallucinogens,

e.g. mescalin and LSD, and injectable amphetamines, e.g. methedrine 2 ***less harmful*** narcotics such as codeine and cannabis; stimulants of the amphetamine type, e.g. Benzedrine and barbiturates 3 ***least harmful*** milder drugs of the amphetamine type. ***Designer drugs*** are variants of illegal narcotics made by criminal chemists to evade the law, and may be many times more powerful and dangerous.
Sources of traditional drugs include the 'Golden Triangle' (where Burma, Laos and Thailand meet), Mexico, China and the Middle East□

druidism religion of the Celtic peoples of pre-Christian Britain and Gaul. Doctrines include reincarnation, and allegedly human sacrifice, and its priests (druids) were expert in astronomy. The oak was a sacred tree, and an important rite involved cutting mistletoe from it with a golden sickle. A last stand against the Romans in S Britain was made in Anglesey◊, but they survived in Scotland and Ireland, and are thought to have re-emerged in Christian times as the Culdees◊□

drum percussion instrument, essentially a piece of skin (parchment, plastic or nylon) stretched over a resonator and struck with a stick, the hands, etc.□

Drummond William 1585–1649. Scottish poet, Laird of his native Hawthornden, hence known as Drummond of Hawthornden. He was the first Scots poet of note to use southern English□

drupe a 'stone fruit' such as plum, cherry or peach. See fruit◊□

Drury Lane Theatre theatre first opened 1663 on the site of earlier London playhouses, rebuilt 1812, and in continuous use since□

Druze a member of Islamic sect founded in the 11th century, and incorporating some Christian doctrines, as well as transmigration through various lives to Paradise. They number c500 000, half in Lebanon and half in Syria, with a small number in Israel. In 1983 they agitated for their own state in the Chouf mountains of Lebanon□

Dr Who hero of science-fiction TV series, created in 1962 by Sidney Newman and Donald Wilson; his space vehicle is the *Tardis* (***T***ime and ***R***elative ***D***imensions in ***S***pace)□

dryad in Greek mythology, a forest nymph or tree spirit□

dry cleaning method of cleaning textiles based on the use of volatile solvents, e.g. trichloroethylene, first developed in France 1849□

Dryden John 1631–1700. British poet, born at Aldwinkle, Northamptonshire◊. His plays include *The Conquest of Granada* 1669–70, the bombastic height of 'heroic tragedy'; the comedy *Marriage à la Mode* 1671; and *All for Love* 1678, a reworking of Shakespeare's *Antony and Cleopatra*. Their prefaces, and his *Essay of Dramatic Poesy* 1668, contain sound criticism. As a verse satirist, he is best remembered for *Absalom and Achitophel* 1681; other poems include 'Annus Mirabilis', and his odes on 'St Cecilia's Day' 1687 and to the 'Memory of Mrs Anne Killigrew'. On occasion, he trimmed his politics and his religion to the prevailing wind, and, as a Roman Catholic convert under James II, lost the laureateship (to which he had been appointed in 1688) at the Revolution of 1688. Later ventures to support himself include a translation of Virgil in 1697. He was a master of all verse forms, but especially of the heroic couplet□

dry-point a means of engraving a print◊□

dry rot fungal infection of timber in damp conditions by *Merulius lachrymans*, etc., which gives the wood a dry cracked appearance. Spores rapidly spread through a building□

Drysdale Sir George Russell 1912–69. Sussex-born Australian artist, known for his pictures of the Outback. Knighted 1969□

dualism philosophical theory that ultimate reality comprises two elements, e.g. mind and matter, usually regarded theologically as good and evil. ***Monism*** regards ultimate reality as indivisible, and pluralism as having many elements. See Descartes◊□

Dubai one of the United◊ Arab Emirates□

Du Barry Marie Jeanne Bécu, Comtesse 1743–93. Mistress of Louis XV◊ of France from 1768. At his death in 1774 she was banished to a convent, and at the Revolution fled to London. Returning to Paris in 1793, she was guillotined□

Dubček Alexander 1921– . Czech statesman. As First Secretary of the Communist Party 1967–9, he launched a liberalization campaign. He was arrested by invading Soviet troops, and expelled from the party in 1970□

Dublin capital and greatest port of Republic of Ireland (Gaelic *Baile Atha Cliath*); population 544 586. Guinness have one of the world's largest breweries, and there are textile, biscuit, pharmaceutical, electrical and machine tool industries. Dublin Castle (1220) was the seat of English rule until 1922. There is some fine 18th century architecture, including the restored Custom House (burned in the 1921 rising). It also has the University of Dublin (Trinity College library contains the Book of Kells, a splendidly illuminated 8th century gospelbook produced at the monastery of Kells in county Meath, founded by St Columba) and National University of Ireland; the National Art Gallery and Municipal Gallery of Modern Art; the Catholic pro-Cathedral of St Mary (1816) and two Protestant cathedrals; Leinster House in which the Dáil Eireann sits, and the Abbey and Gate theatres□

Dublin county (county town Dublin) of the Republic of Ireland, province of Leinster; population 384 583. It includes the port of Dun Laoghaire□

Dubrovnik Yugoslav port and Adriatic tourist resort; population 31 000□

Dubuffet Jean 1901–85. French artist and sculptor, admirer of the work of children and psychotic mental patients. He originated in the 1940s *l'art brut* or 'raw art', using materials such as coal or steel wool, advocating the naively primitive, and being inspired by graffiti□

Duccio di Buoninsegna c1255–1319. Earliest painter of the Sienese school, influenced by the Byzantine tradition and noted for his altar-piece in the cathedral 1308–11□

Duce title adopted by Mussolini◊; it is Italian for 'leader'□

Duchamp Marcel 1887–1968. French artist, founder with Picabia◊ of Dadaism◊, and associated with Surrealism◊. See Armory Show◊□

duck a small aquatic bird. See waterfowl◊□

duckbilled platypus see platypus◊□

ductless glands glands which produce hormones◊ in the higher animals□

Dudley industrial city (light engineering, clothing) in W Midlands, England; population 296 400□

Dufay Guillaume c1400–74. French composer of masses, magnificats, etc. Regarded as one of the most outstanding composers of the Middle Ages, he travelled widely in France and Italy, and was a member of the Papal choir for many years□

Du Fu 712–70AD. Chinese poet (formerly Tu Fu). Having failed in the public examinations, he became a wandering poet, recording the famines and civil wars of his times□

Dufy Raoul 1877–1953. French artist, especially noted for pictures of sport and recreation□

Duisburg industrial city of W Germany, and largest inland European port (at confluence of Rhine and Ruhr). In World War II it was bombed 1940–45, when it was captured by US troops 30 Mar□

Dukas Paul 1865–1935. French composer, best-known for his orchestral scherzo *The Sorcerer's Apprentice* 1897□

duke highest title in the English peerage, introduced from France when Edward III created his son Edward Duke of Cornwall□

Dukeries see Nottinghamshire◊□

dulcimer musical instrument; wire strings across a box resonator are struck with hammers□

Dulles Alan 1893–1969. American lawyer, brother of John Dulles, and director of the Central◊ Intelligence Agency (CIA) 1953–61□

Dulles John Foster 1888–1959. American statesman. Senior US adviser at the founding of the United Nations, he largely drafted the Japanese peace treaty of 1951, and as Secretary of State 1952–9 was critical of Britain in the Suez crisis. He was the architect of US Cold◊ War foreign policy□

Duluth port on Lake Superior, Minnesota, USA; population 92 800□

Dulwich a residential district of Southwark◊□

Dumas Alexandre 1802–70. French author, known as Dumas *père*. He was the grandson of a Norman landowner and one of his Santo Domingo Negro slaves. His play *Henri III et sa Cour* 1829 established French romantic historical drama, but today he is read for his romances, the re-worked output of a 'fiction-factory' of collaborators. They include *The Three Musketeers* 1844 and its sequels; *The Count of Monte Cristo* 1844, and *The Corsican Brothers* 1845. Dumas *fils* was his natural son□

Dumas Alexandre 1824–95. French author, Dumas the Younger, son of Dumas *père* and remembered for the play *La Dame aux Camélias* 1852, based on his own novel, and source of Verdi's opera *La Traviata*□

Du Maurier Dame Daphne 1907– . British novelist, daughter of actor-manager Sir Gerald du Maurier, and grand-daughter of George du Maurier◊. Best-known of her romantic works are *Jamaica Inn* 1936, *Rebecca* 1938, and *My Cousin Rachel* 1951□

Du Maurier George 1834–96. British *Punch* cartoonist, and book illustrator, e.g. his own *Trilby*, 1894 – in which a girl model becomes a famous singer under the hypnotic influence of Svengali□

Dumbarton industrial town (marine engineering, whisky distilling) in Strathclyde, Scotland; population 25 500□

Dumfries administrative headquarters of Dumfries and Galloway region, Scotland; population 29 300. It has knitwear, plastics and other industries□

Dumfries and Galloway region of Scotland
area 6369 sq km/2458 sq mi
towns administrative headquarters Dumfries
features Solway Firth; Galloway Hills, setting of John Buchan's *The Thirty-Nine Steps*; Glen Trool National Park; Ruthwell Cross, a

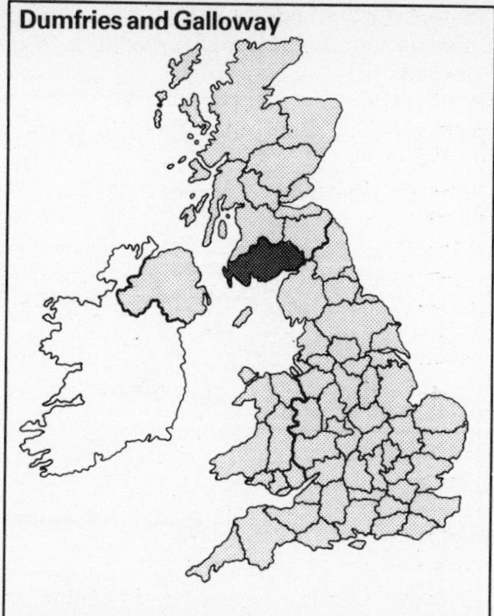

Dumfries and Galloway

runic cross of c800 at the village of Ruthwell; Stranraer provides the shortest sea route to Ireland

products horses and cattle, for which the Galloway area was especially famous; sheep; timber

population 144 220

famous people home of Robert Burns at Dumfries; birthplace of Carlyle at Ecclefechan☐

Dumouriez Charles Francois 1739–1823. French general. Minister of Foreign Affairs in 1792, he resigned to command the army in the victories of Valmy and Jemappes in 1792, but became disillusioned, surrendered to the Austrians and settled in England☐

Dumyat port (formerly Damietta) on the Nile delta, Egypt☐

Dunant Jean Henri 1828–1910. Swiss originator of the Red Cross◊. As a doctor, he witnessed the suffering at the battle of Solferino (1859), and proposed the establishment of an international body☐

Dunbar William c1460–c1520. Scottish poet at the court of James IV☐

Dunbar port and resort in Lothian region, Scotland; population 4000. Cromwell defeated the Scots here in 1650☐

Duncan Isadora 1878–1927. American dancer, opposed to the classical style, who recreated ancient Greek dances from vase paintings, etc. She died when her scarf caught in the wheel of her sports car☐

Duncan-Sandys Duncan Edwin Sandys, Baron 1908– . British Conservative politician. As Minister for Commonwealth Relations 1960–4, he negotiated the independence of Malaysia 1963☐

Dundalk county town and seaport in Louth, Republic of Ireland; population 25 610☐

Dundee seaport, administrative headquarters of Tayside, Scotland; population 174 746. Industries include jute, shipbuilding, engineering, watches and clocks, fruit canning, preserves such as marmalade, and confectionery. Servicing North Sea oil extraction has brought added prosperity. There is a university (1967: derived from Queen's College, founded 1881) and an institute of art and technology☐

Dundee John Graham of Claverhouse, Viscount Dundee c1649–89. Scottish soldier, known as 'Bonny Dundee', who defeated the Covenanters◊ at Bothwell Bridge 1679, and continued the persecution of the peasantry till 1688. He took up arms in support of James II in 1688, but was mortally wounded when he defeated Macky at Killiecrankie in 1689☐

Dunedin port in South Island, New Zealand; population 118 700. Otago University (1869) is the oldest in New Zealand☐

Dunfermline industrial (engineering and textiles) town in Fife region, Scotland, which incl the naval base of Rosyth; population 54 600. Robert the Bruce is buried in Dunfermline Abbey☐

Dungeness shingle headland on the S coast of Kent, England. It has nuclear power stations, a lighthouse and bird sanctuary☐

Dunham Katherine 1910– . American dancer, born in Chicago. Using a free, strongly emotional method, she founded her own school and company in 1945☐

Dunhuang site (formerly Tunhuang) in Gansu, China, of the Thousand Buddha Caves (about 500 rock-cut caves full of Buddhist carvings); the Diamond Sutra 868AD (the world's oldest printed book) was found in the library here in 1900 and is now in the British Library, London☐

Dunkirk industrial seaport (oil refining, textiles, machinery) (French *Dunkerque*) in N France; population 83 760. It was almost in the front line during much of World War I, and in World War II, 337 131 Allied troops (including c110 000 French) were evacuated from the beaches☐

Dun Laoghaire port of Dublin, Republic of Ireland, with sea services to Holyhead and Liverpool; population 54 405☐

dunlin species of sandpiper◊☐

Dunlop John Boyd 1840–1921. Scottish inventor, who developed the first commercial pneumatic rubber tyre for bicycles from 1887, replacing the then current solid tyres. Later adapted to cars☐

Dunmow Flitch an Essex custom. See under Essex◊☐

Duns Scotus John c1265–c1308. Scottish philosopher; see Scholasticism◊. A Franciscan monk of great learning who attacked the Aristotelianism of the Dominican, St Thomas Aquinas◊ on certain points. He was on the 'losing' side, hence the word 'dunce'□

Dunstable John died 1453. English composer, mathematician and astrologer, remembered for his songs and anthems□

Dunstan St c924–88AD. Archbishop of Canterbury from 960. As Abbot of Glastonbury from 945, he made it an educational centre and was chief minister under Edred and Edgar. Feast day 19 May□

duodecimal system system of arithmetic using 12 as a base instead of 10□

Duparc Henri 1848–1933. French composer. A student of Franck, he wrote 15 songs 1868–84, which have a unique place in French song-writing□

du Pré Jacqueline 1945– . British cellist, who married Daniel Barenboim◊ in 1967, but whose professional partnership with him was ended by her multiple sclerosis□

duralumin a group of aluminium based alloys containing various amounts of copper, manganese, magnesium, silicon and iron. Heat treatment of the alloy produces its great strength□

Duras Marguerite 1914– . French author of novels (*Le Vice-Consul* 1966, the semi-autobiographical *L'Amant* 1984), plays (*La Musica*) and film scripts (*Hiroshima Mon Amour* 1960)□

Durazzo Italian form for the Albanian town of Durrës◊□

Durban industrial port (sugar refining, car assembly) and holiday resort in Natal, S Africa; population 506 000□

Dürer Albrecht 1471–1528. German Renaissance artist, born at Nuremberg◊. At 13 he drew the first self-portrait in European art, and after travelling widely returned to Nuremberg to execute a number of copperplate engravings, and also his famous series of woodcuts of the 'Apocalypse' 1498. His first important painting, *The Adoration of the Magi*, is dated 1504. He worked for the Emperor Maximilian I 1512–19, and was court painter to Charles V from 1520. A friend of Luther, he was greatly influenced by the Reformation◊□

Durga consort of the Hindu god Siva. See Hinduism◊□

Durham John George Lambton, 1st Earl of Durham 1792–1840. British statesman. Appointed Lord Privy Seal in 1830, he drew up the first Reform Bill of 1832, and as Governor-General of Canada briefly in 1837 drafted the Durham Report which led to the union of Upper and Lower Canada□

Durham NE county of England

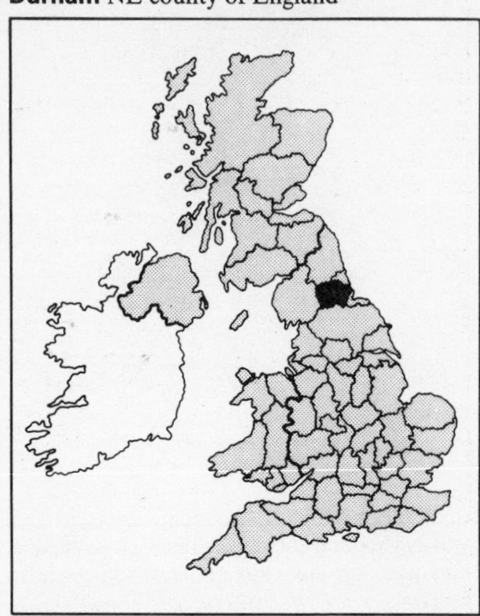

area 2436 sq km/6309 sq mi

towns administrative headquarters Durham; Darlington, and new towns of Peterlee and Newton Aycliffe

features Beamish open-air industrial museum

products sheep and dairy farming are carried on, and the county lies on one of Britain's richest coalfields.

population 606 600□

Durham city (administrative headquarters) of the county of Durham, England; population 27 550. Founded in 995, it has a superb Norman cathedral 1093, where the remains of Bede◊ were transferred in 1370; the castle was built by William I in 1072, and the university was founded in 1832. Summer events include a rowing regatta on the River Wear, and the Miners' Gala□

Durkheim Emile 1858–1917. French sociologist, who stressed scientific method and the mechanical determination of human society. His *Suicide* 1897 was a pioneering study in social statistics□

durra a variety of sorghum grass◊□

Durrell Lawrence George 1912– . British novelist and poet. Born in India, he joined the Foreign Service, and has lived mainly in the E Mediterranean setting of his novels, e.g. the Alexandrian Quartet: *Justine, Balthazar, Mountolive* and *Clea* 1957–60; in turn interlinked with the Avignon Quintet (in progress); he has also written travel books□

Durrell Gerald Malcolm 1925– . British author, brother of Lawrence Durrell◊, director of Jersey Zoological Park, and author of travel books, e.g. *My Family and Other Animals* 1956□

Dürrenmatt Friedrich 1921– . Swiss dramatist, author of grotesquely farcical tragedies, e.g. *The Physicists* 1962, in which three sane nuclear physicists flee to a Swiss asylum□

Dürres chief port (Italian *Durazzo*) and commercial centre of Albania; population 61 000. There is flour milling, distilling and an electronics plant□

Duse Eleonora 1859–1924. Italian actress. She was the mistress of D'Annunzio from 1897, as recorded in his novel *The Flame of Life*, and he wrote *La Gioconda* for her□

Dushanbe capital (Stalinabad 1929–61) of Tadzhik, USSR: population 510 000□

Düsseldorf industrial (food processing, brewing, agricultural machinery, textiles and chemicals) Rhine river port, and commercial and financial centre of the Ruhr◊, W Germany; population 592 200. It has large exhibition facilities, and is a university city□

Dustbowl area of USA including parts of Kansas, Oklahoma and Texas, ruined by erosion in the droughts of 1934–7 following the adoption of large-scale wheat-farming (see Steinbeck◊). It has been partly rehabilitated□

Dutch East Indies former name (until 1945) of Indonesia◊□

Dutch elm disease a fungus disease of elm◊ trees□

Dutch Guiana former name (until 1948) of Surinam◊□

Duval Claude 1643–70. French-born highwayman, and former valet. Famed for his gallantries, he operated in England from the Restoration and was hanged at Tyburn□

Duvalier François 1907–71. President of Haiti from 1957. Known as 'Papa Doc', he ruled through his terror organization the Tontons Macoute, 'bogeymen'. See Jean Duvalier□

Duvalier Jean Claude 1951– . Haitian statesman, 'Baby Doc,' son of Francois Duvalier◊, he was President from 1971 until forced to flee in 1986. His rule was marginally less oppressive than his father's□

Duve Christian de (1917–). French scientist, who shared a Nobel prize for medicine in 1974 for his work on the functioning of cells□

Duvivier Julien 1896– . French film director, whose work included *Un Carnet de Bal, La Fin du Jour* 1938□

Duwez Pol 1907– . American scientist, born in Belgium, who in 1959 developed with his team metallic glass◊ at the California Institute of Technology□

Dvinsk Russian name of Daugavpils◊□

Dvořák Antonin 1841–1904. Czech composer. Born near Prague, the son of a butcher, he played the viola in cafés before joining the orchestra of the Prague National Theatre in 1862, and later became a church organist. He achieved international success with his series of Slavonic dances 1877–86, and was Director of the National Conservatory, New York, 1892–5, his *New World Symphony* (1893) and such works as the *American Quartet* showing his interest in black music. His works include nine operas, including *Rusalka*; large-scale choral works, the *Carnival* and other overtures, violin and cello concertos, chamber music, piano pieces, songs, etc.□

dwarfism restricted growth, which is treated by human growth hormone (HGH) (extracted from the pituitary glands of the dead) or, more commonly, a synthetic product□

dye colouring agent. Dyes may be ***direct*** combining with the fabric to yield a coloured compound, or ***indirect*** in that they require a mordant to be present to enable the dye to 'take'. Vat dyes, e.g. indigo◊ and many synthetics, are usually colourless soluble substances which on oxidation by exposure to air yield an insoluble coloured compound. See Perkin◊□

Dyfed SW county of Wales

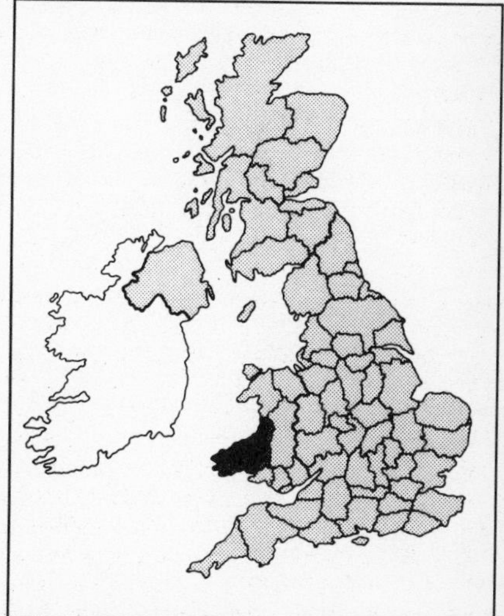

area 5766 sq km/2226 sq mi

towns administrative headquarters Carmarthen; Aberystwyth, Cardigan, Lampeter

features Pembrokeshire Coast National Park, part of the Brecon Beacons National Park, including the Black Mountain, and part of the Cambrian Mountains, including Plynlimon

Fawr 752 m/2468 ft; the village of Laugharne, at the mouth of the Towey, was the home of Dylan Thomas, and features in his work as 'Milk Wood'; Caldey Island, where the Cistercian community produces perfume; Museum of the Woollen Industry at Dre-fach Felindre, and of Welsh religious life at Tre'r-ddôl
products dairy produce; small-scale woollen mills; oil refining at Milford Haven
population 326 600
language English, Welsh (46% Welsh-speaking)
famous people Taliesin, Dylan Thomas□

Dylan Bob. Stage-name of American folk-singer Robert Zimmerman 1941– , whose songs of the 1960s spoke for the protest movement; they include 'The Times They Are A-Changin' and 'A Hard Rain's A-Gonna Fall'; he became a Christian convert, e.g. the album 'Slow Train Coming' 1979□

dynamics branch of mechanics that deals with the forces that effect motion in bodies. See under mechanics◊, and Isaac Newton◊□

dynamite explosive mixture of nitro-glycerine and kieselguhr (a white rock made up of diatom◊ skeletons, which is included to make it safer to handle). Gelignite is a type of dynamite. See Alfred Nobel◊□

dynamo generator of direct electrical current□

dysentery infective ulceration of the large bowel, causing diarrhoea containing blood and mucus, and caused usually by either amoebae or bacillae. Treatment is by drugs, and in the more serious amoebic dysentery the amoebae must be killed□

dyslexia popularly 'word-blindness', an inability to read, write and spell correctly, etc., although the person is of normal intelligence. Treatment is at present educational□

dyspepsia disturbance of digestion, which may be caused by faulty diet, nervous tension, or disease, e.g. cancer of the stomach□

dysprosium element
symbol Dy
atomic number 66
physical description silvery metal
features one of the lanthanide◊ series
uses with argon in mercury vapour lamps to increase brightness□

E

eagle bird of prey, family Accipitridae, order Falconiformes. Eagles include the typical ***golden eagle*** *Aquila chrysaetos*, with a wingspan of 2 m/6 ft, the national emblem of Mexico; the sea eagles, among which are the ***bald eagle*** *Haliaeetus leucocephalus*, national emblem of the USA, and the ***white-tailed sea-eagle*** *Haliaeetus albicilla* extinct in Scotland in 1916, but reintroduced from Norway and breeding in the 1980s, and ***harpy eagle*** *Harpia harpyga*, largest of the eagles and immensely strong, which terrifies the monkeys and sloths of the Central and S American rain forest.

The eagle was sacred to Zeus◊, and, as the standard of the Roman legions, became the imperial symbol of the Russian, German, Austrian and Napoleonic empires.

In the same family are:

hawks small, with an untoothed bill and short wings, which include the woodland ***sparrowhawk*** *Accipiter nisus* and ***goshawk*** *A gentilis* resembling the peregrine falcon◊, and used in falconry.

harriers includes the slim-built ***marsh harrier*** *Circus aeruginosus* and ***Montagu's harrier*** *C pygargus* both sometimes seen in Britain.

buzzards larger and heavier-built hawks, e.g. the Eurasian ***common buzzard*** *Buteo buteo* now fairly rare in Britain.

vultures have bare head and neck, shaggy feathers, and hooked beak and claws. True vultures occur only in the Old World and include the Eurasian ***black vulture*** *Aegypius monachus*; the Mediterranean and African ***lammergeier*** *Gypaetus barbatus* which breaks up large bones and live turtles by dropping them from a height. New World vultures, family Cathartidae, include ***Andean condor*** *Vultur gryphus*, largest bird of the order Falconiformes, with a wingspan of 3 m/9 ft, weighing 11 kg/21 lb; it has a special place in Inca◊ ritual, the men still dressing up in striking condor costume. The ***Californian condor*** *Gymnogyps californianus* is on the verge of extinction.

kites have forked tails, capable of a spread which aids their speedy, stylish flight; they include the ***red kite*** *Milvus milvus* c60 cm/2 ft long, formerly an abundant scavenger on London streets, now rare; and ***black kite*** *M migrans* which ranges throughout the Old World.

Like other birds of prey, the entire family is under threat, especially through infertility from ingestion of agricultural chemicals□

Eagling Wayne 1950– . Canadian dancer, born of an English father and Canadian mother, he grew up in California. He joined the Royal Ballet, appearing in *Gloria* 1980, etc □

Ealing borough of W Greater London

features first British sound-film studio built here 1931 ('Ealing comedies' a noted genre); large Indian community at Southall

population 277 000□

Eanes Antonio dos Santos Ramalho 1935– . Portuguese statesman. He helped plan the 1974 coup, put down the left-wing revolt of 1975, and was president 1976–86□

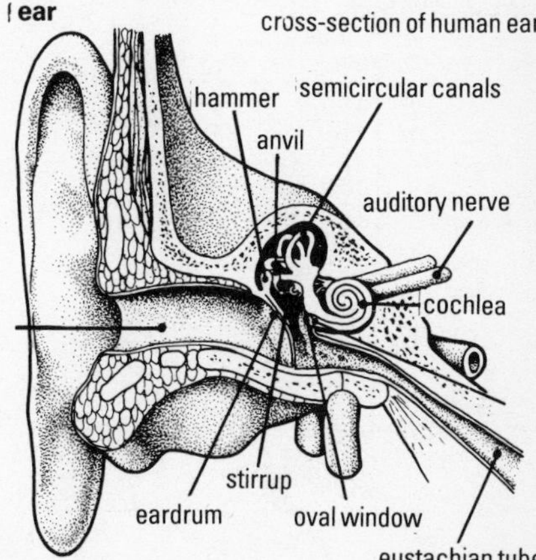

ear organ of hearing, comprised of three sections, the outer, middle and inner ear. The outer ear is the cartilage part we see. Sound waves enter the outer ear causing the skin of the ear drum (the tympanic membrane) to vibrate. This vibration is transmitted via three small bones (the ossicles) in the middle ear to the membranous canal of the inner ear and on to the auditory nerve which carries the sound impulses to the brain. The ***Eustachian tube***, linking the middle ear to the back of the nose, keeps pressure there equal to that of the outside world so that the tympanum remains free to vibrate. The liquid-filled canals of the inner ear are partly responsible for our sense of balance□

Earhart Amelia 1898–1937. American airwoman, born in Kansas. In 1932 she was the first woman to fly the Atlantic alone, and in 1937 disappeared without trace while making a Pacific flight□

Earl oldest title in the British peerage (of Scandinavian origin), and third in rank (between Marquis and Viscount); an Earl's wife is a Countess. The premier Earldom is Arundel, now united with the Dukedom of Norfolk◊□

Earl Marshal English office of state, hereditary in the family of Howard, dukes of Norfolk since 1672. The Earl Marshal heads the College of Arms and arranges coronations, etc□

Early English one of the three periods of the English Gothic style first suggested by Thomas Rickman (1776–1841). See Gothic under architecture◊□

earth the third planet from the sun
mean distance from the sun 149 500 000 km/93 000 000 mi
diameter 12 756 km
rotation period 23 hr 56 min 4.1 sec
year (sidereal period) 365 days 5 hr 48 min 46 sec
atmosphere nitrogen 78.09%, oxygen 20.95%, argon 0.93%, carbon dioxide 0.03%, and less than 0.0001% neon, helium, krypton, hydrogen, xenon, ozone, radon
surface temperature range −58°C/−72°F to 34°C/94°F
surface land surface 150 000 000 sq km/57 500 000 sq mi (greatest height Mount Everest◊); water surface 361 000 000 sq km/139 400 000 sq mi (greatest depth Mariana◊ Trench in Pacific). Interior thought to be an inner core c1300 km/800 mi from the centre of solid iron and nickel; outer core c2250 km/1400 mi molten iron and nickel; and mantle of solid rock c2900 km/1800 mi thick, separated by the Mohorovičić◊ Discontinuity from the outer crust which is 5 km/3 mi thick at its thinnest beneath certain points in the oceans, and 32 km/20 mi thick beneath the continents; the outer crust forms about half a dozen plates (on top of which the continents◊ slowly drift) and stretches and contracts; age 4 600 000 000 years, possibly formed when a swarm of meteorites was drawn from the sun by the attraction of a passing star; life began c4 000 000 000 years ago; average speed round the sun 30 km/18.5 mi a second; the plane of its

earthquake belts

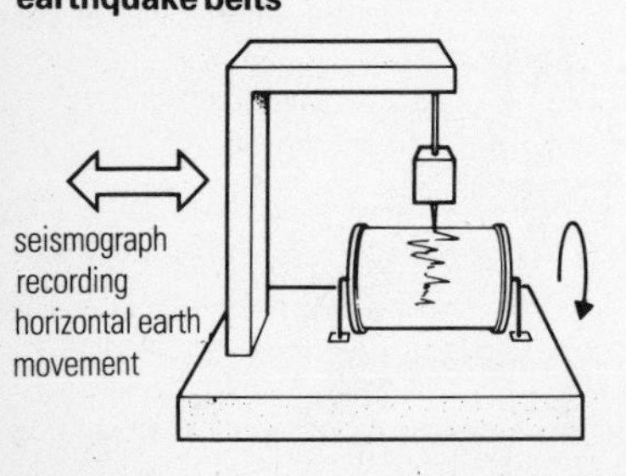

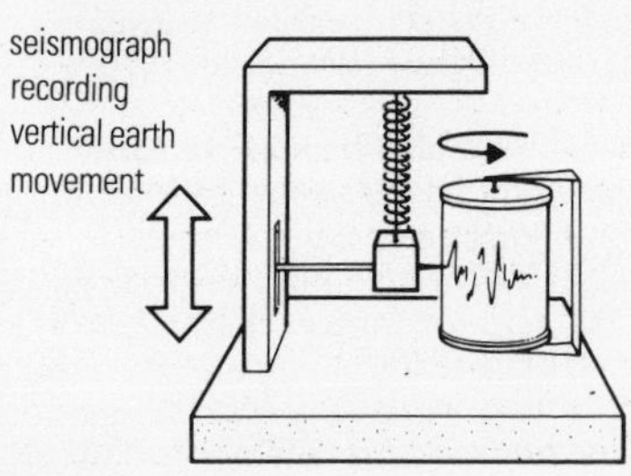

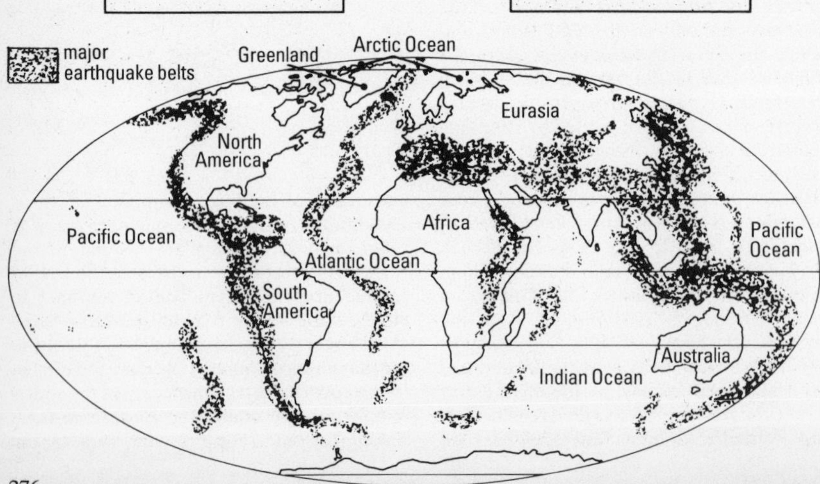

orbit is inclined to its equatorial plane at an angle of 23.5°, which is the reason for changing seasons; it is 'pear-shaped', with a small rise at the N Pole and small depression at the S Pole. ***satellites*** see moon◊□

earthquake vibration of the earth's surface, usually caused by sudden movements along fault lines in earth's crust. Underground pressure waves, changes in the gases in earth's crust, and the behaviour of animals who may hear either high or low frequency sound waves, aid prediction. Major earthquake belts lie along the Mediterranean, down the W coast of the Americas, and E of the Asiatic coast, running S round Australia. The largest earthquake in Britain for a century occurred 1984, measuring 5.5 on the Richter◊ scale. Earth tremors are recorded by a ***seismograph***; ***seismology*** is the study of earthquake phenomena□

earthworm a type of worm◊□

earwig nocturnal, mainly tropical insect, order Dermaptera. The ***common European earwig*** *Forficula auricularia* has the typical short, leathery forewings which close over the large rear ones, but the insects seldom fly. They damage plants, but also feed on other insects, dead or alive□

easement legal right over another's land, e.g. a right of way, or over prevention of building which would exclude light from existing windows□

east one of the four cardinal points of the compass. As the point where the sun rises, the east has significance both in pagan and Christian faith. Pagan altars were at the east end of temples, and in the 2nd century it became usual for Christians to worship facing east, and to bury their dead with their feet to the east so as to face the direction whence Christ would come on Resurrection morning□

East Anglia area of E England, formerly a Saxon kingdom, and including Norfolk, Suffolk, and part of Essex and Cambridgeshire. Its ports have greatly developed as trade with the Continent increases. See Norwich◊□

Eastbourne seaside resort in E Sussex, England; population 71 850. The old town lies a mile inland, and the 'new' was developed in the early 19th century as a model of town planning, largely due to the 7th Duke of Devonshire. See Beachy◊ Head□

Easter feast of the Christian Church, commemorating the Resurrection of Christ. It developed from the Jewish Passover, but the English name derives from Eostre, Anglo-Saxon goddess of spring, who was honoured in Apr. In the UK it may fall at any time 22 Mar–25 Apr, being a moveable feast calculated according to the incidence of a hypothetical full moon, for which tables are given in the Book of Common Prayer□

Easter Island the Chilean *Isla de Pascua/Rapa Nui*, in the S Pacific; population 1000, chiefly Polynesian. Chief centre Hanga-Roa. First reached by Europeans on Easter Sunday, 1722, it has huge stone statues up to 12 m/40 ft high, carved by neolithic peoples possibly of S American origin□

Eastern Orthodox Church see Christianity◊□

East India Company trading company chartered by Elizabeth I of England in 1600 and given a monopoly of eastern trade. In the 18th century it was the effective ruler of much of India, but was abolished in 1858, following the Indian Mutiny◊□

East Kilbride 'new' town (jet engines, printing, etc) in Strathclyde, Scotland; population 71 300. It was designed to take overspill from Glasgow to the SE, and the National Engineering Laboratory is here□

East London port and resort in Cape Province, S Africa; population 160 582□

East River tidal strait between Manhattan and the Bronx, and Long Island, New York, USA; most famous of many bridges is Brooklyn Bridge□

East Siberian Sea see under Arctic◊ Ocean□

East Sussex southern county of England

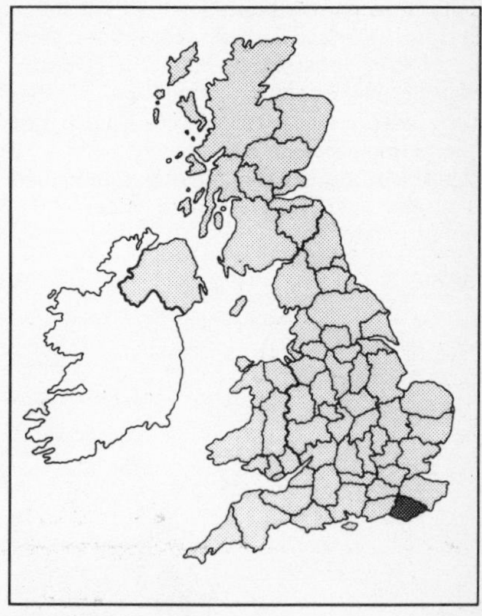

area 1795 sqkm/693 sq mi

towns administrative headquarters Lewes; cross-channel port of Newhaven; Brighton, Eastbourne, Hastings, Bexhill, Winchelsea, Rye

features Beachy Head, highest headland on the S Coast at 180 m/590 ft, the southern end

of the S Downs◊; the Weald (including Ashdown Forest), the modern Friston Forest; rivers Ouse, Cuckmere, E Rother; Romney Marsh; the 'Long Man' hill figure at Wilmington, near Eastbourne; village of Herstmonceux, with a 15th century castle (conference and exhibition centre) and adjacent modern buildings housing from 1958 Greenwich Royal Observatory; other castles at Hastings, Lewes, Pevensey and Bodiam; Battle Abbey and the site of the Battle of Hastings
products 663 200
famous people Vanessa Bell, Henry James (see Rye◊), Virginia Woolf□

Eastwood Clint 1930– . American film actor, who started the vogue for 'spaghetti westerns'□

eau de Cologne perfume invented by Giovanni Farina, who settled in Cologne to manufacture it in 1709□

Ebbw Vale industrial town in Gwent, Wales; population 25 710◊□

ebony tropical tree, genus *Diospyros* family Ebenaceae; the black timber is used for cabinet-making, inlay, etc.□

Eboracum see York◊□

Eccles Sir John Carew 1903– . Australian physiologist, who in 1963 shared a Nobel prize (with Hodgkin◊ and Huxley) for work on conduction in the central nervous system. He argues that the mind has an existence independent of the brain□

Eccles industrial town (cotton textiles, machinery, pharmaceuticals) in Greater Manchester, England; population 37 400. ***Eccles cakes*** (rounded pastries with a rich fruit filling) originated here□

echidna a toothless egg-laying mammal of Australia and New Guinea. See under monotremata◊□

echinoderm marine invertebrate, phylum Echinodermata, which has a basic body structure divided into five sectors (giving greater strength, since by this arrangement the sutures between the body plates do not form a line of weakness across the body). The phylum includes:
sea lilies and ***feather stars*** class Crinoidea. The former are rare, deep water creatures with a rooted 'stem', a cup-like body and ten radiating feathery arms. The latter dispense with a stem, and are free-swimming, but spend most of their time clinging to rocks or weed, and collecting food via their very long, gracefully curling feathered arms.
starfish class Asteroidea, have bodies extended (most commonly) into five 'arms', and are covered with spines. They are carnivorous, some species using their suckered feet to force open the shells of bivalve molluscs, then straddling their prey and feeding by extruding their stomach through their mouth. When they multiply too fast they may create havoc in fisheries, or, as in the case of the poisonous 'crown of thorns', which has a population explosion about every 70 years, cause great destruction to the coral of the Australian Barrier Reef.
brittle stars class Ophiuroidea, have a small central rounded body, and long serpentine spiny arms, which they use to walk with.
sea cucumbers class Holothuroidea, have cylindrical bodies, tough-skinned, knobbed or spiny. They are sometimes several feet long, and, when dried, those from tropical waters, e.g. N Australia and the American Pacific seaboard, are relished as a delicacy (***trepang***) by the Chinese. They defend themselves by ejecting sticky filaments from the anus to ensnare attackers.

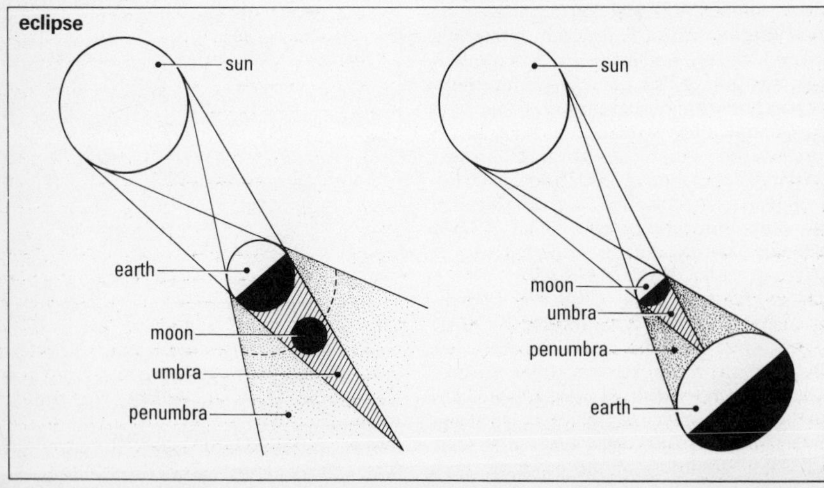

sea urchins Echinoidea, are usually spherical or disc-shaped, and are covered in spines. They steadily eat their way through seaweed with five sets of teeth, and some are venomous as a means of defence□

Eckhart Johannes Meister c1260–1327. German Dominican mystic, whose doctrines were condemned as heretical□

eclipse the obscuring of one heavenly body by another, as in a ***solar eclipse,*** when the moon passes in front of the sun, or a ***lunar eclipse,*** when the moon passes into the shadow of earth□

Eco Umberto 1932– . Italian semiologist and literary critic (*The Role of the Reader* 1979), and author of the 'philosophical thriller' *The Name of the Rose* 1983□

École Nationale d'Administration French government school (ENA) established in Paris in 1945 to turn out apolitical top administrators. Giscard◊ d'Estaing and Chirac◊ were students□

ecology term used by Ernst Haeckel in 1866 to denote the study of living organisms in their natural habitat; an ***ecosystem*** is the live interaction between the two. See Charles Elton◊□

econometrics see economics◊□

economic community or ***Common Market*** an organization of autonomous countries formed to promote trade, etc. Examples include: Caribbean◊ Community (Caricom) 1973, Central African Economic Community 1985, European◊ Economic Community (EEC) 1957, Latin◊ American communities□

economics was defined by Paul Samuelson as "the study of how people end up choosing, with or without the use of money, to employ scarce productive resources that could have alternative uses – to produce various commodities and distribute them for consumption". Economics came of age as a separate area of study with the publication of Adam Smith◊'s *The Wealth of Nations* in 1776; the economist Alfred Marshall (1842–1924) established the orthodox position of "neo-classical" economics, which, as modified by J M Keynes◊ (1883–1946) remains the standard today. Major divisions of economics are:

microeconomics the study of the behaviour of individuals and firms

macroeconomics concerned with the behaviour and policies of countries, especially in such areas as public spending and taxation

econometrics is the application of statistical methods to the study of economic relationships; pioneers in this field include Ragnar Frisch◊ and Leonid Kantorovich◊.

Major economic thinkers include Adam Smith, Ricardo, Malthus, J S Mill, Marx, Alfred Marshall, J M Keynes, and Milton Friedman□

Ecuador Republic of

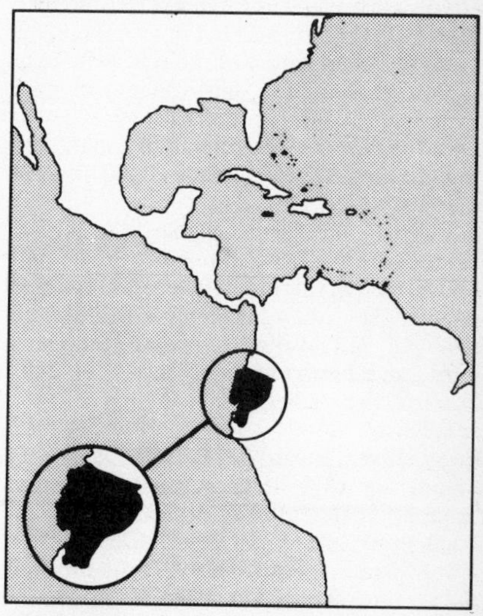

area 301 150 sq km/116 270 sq mi

capital Quito

towns Cuenca; chief port Guayaquil

features Andes mountains, which are divided by a central plateau, or Valley of the Volcanoes, including Chimborazo, and Cotopaxi◊, which has a large share of the cultivable land and is the site of the capital; untouched rainforest of the Amazon basin with a wealth of wild life; Ecuador is crossed by the Equator, from which it derives its name; Galapagos◊ Island

exports bananas, cocoa, coffee, sugar, rice, balsa wood, fish

currency sucre

population 9 091 000

language Spanish (official); Quechuan, Jivaroan

religion Roman Catholicism

government under the 1979 constitution, there is a president (Léon Febres Cordero from 1984; right-wing Social Christian Party (PSC)), and single-chamber elected congress.

recent history formerly part of Greater Colombia, Ecuador became an independent republic in 1830. In 1942, Ecuador ceded half her Amazonian territory, which had been occupied by Peru in 1941 and in 1981 there was renewed fighting in this oil-rich area□

ecumenical movement movement for reunification of the various branches of the Christian church. It began in the 19th century with the extension of missionary work to the

Third World, where the divisions created in Europe were incomprehensible; gathered momentum from the need for unity in the face of growing secularism in Christian countries and of the challenge of such faiths as Islam. The ***World Council of Churches*** was founded 1948□

eczema inflammation of the skin, with itching, vesicle formation, and exudation of fluid: sometimes of allergic origin□

Edam town in the Netherlands; population 14 200. Famous for round, red-skinned cheeses□

Eddington Sir Arthur Stanley 1882–1944. British astrophysicist, director of the Cambridge observatories from 1914, and popularizer of Einstein◊'s theories of relativity. In 1919 his observation of the stars during an eclipse confirmed Einstein's prediction that light is bent when passing near the sun□

Eddy Mary Baker 1821–1910. American founder in 1879 of the Church of Christ, Scientist, a system of faith healing she outlined in *Science and Health* 1875. Though living in retirement from 1892, she directed the movement until her death□

Eddystone Rocks rocks marked by a lighthouse in the English Channel, S of Plymouth□

edelweiss perennial alpine *Leontopodium alpinum* family Compositae◊, with a white woolly flower, found in Eurasia and the Andes□

Eden Anthony, 1st Earl of Avon 1897–1977. British Conservative statesman. In 1935 he became Foreign Secretary, resigning Feb 1938 in protest against Chamberlain's decision to open conversations with Mussolini, and again Dec 1940–45 and 1951–Apr 1955, when he succeeded Churchill as Prime Minister. He negotiated an interim peace in Vietnam 1954. His military intervention in Suez◊, when already a very sick man, led to his resignation in Jan 1957, but he continued to maintain that his action was justified, as having prevented World War III. In 1952, he married as his second wife, Clarissa, niece of Winston Churchill, and received an earldom 1960□

Eden in Old Testament, the 'garden' from which Adam◊ and Eve were expelled following their disobedience□

edentata ('without teeth') order of Central and S American mammals which includes:

anteater family Myrmecophagidae. They have long snouts and extensile tongues to pick up ants as food, and include the ***great anteater*** *Myrmecophaga tridactyla*, over 1 m/3 ft long, with a bushy tail.

For the ***spiny anteater*** see under monotremata◊.

armadillo family Dasypodidae. They have horny armour plates and roll into a ball when threatened. The ***giant armadillo*** *Priodontes giganteus* is 1.5 m/4.5 ft long.

sloth family Bradypodidae. They are slow-moving, nocturnal tree-dwellers, with shaggy brown hair camouflaged by greenish algae◊, and include the three-toed ***ai*** *Bradypus tridactylus* and two-toed ***unau*** *Choloepus didactylus* 75 cm/2 ft long. The extinct genus *Megatherium* comprised herbiverous, sloth-like beasts 6 m/18 ft long, which lived in America in the Pliocene/Pleistocene period□

Edgar the Atheling ('of royal blood') c1050–c1130. English prince, grandson of Edmund II, who was supplanted as Edward◊ the Confessor's heir by William◊ the Conqueror. After revolts against William in 1068 and 1069, he made peace with him□

Edgehill see Civil◊ War, English□

Edgeworth Maria 1767–1849. Irish novelist of Anglo-Irish country society, e.g. *Castle Rackrent* 1800, and *The Absentee* 1812□

Edinburgh capital of Scotland and administrative headquarters of Lothian◊; population 419 187. Named from Edwin of Northumbria, who took the town c617, it grew up round the fortress of Castle Rock, and was finally united in 1856 with the township of Canongate which had developed round the abbey of Holyrood (founded 1128 by David I). The royal residence, Holyrood House, was built on the site of the abbey by James IV; Rizzio◊ was murdered here in the apartments of Mary Queen of Scots. Edinburgh's port was established at Leith by Robert◊ the Bruce, but the city lost political importance after Scotland's union with England in 1707, though remaining a cultural centre, e.g. Edinburgh University 1583 (with a medical school, and the Koestler chair of parapsychology 1985; one of its buildings formerly housed St Trinnean's girls' school, which inspired Ronald Searle◊) and Heriot-Watt University (for technical subjects). The Royal Observatory (1776) has been at Blackford Hill from 1896. Noted buildings include St Margaret's chapel, in Edinburgh castle; Parliament House 1632 (seat of the supreme courts); St Giles parish church 15th century, and the episcopal cathedral of St Mary 1879. Princes Street and the Royal Mile are the chief thoroughfares□

Edirne town (formerly Adrianople) in European Turkey; population 54 000□

Edison Thomas Alva 1847–1931. American inventor, born in Ohio. He invented the phonograph (ancestor of the gramophone), the alkaline storage battery and (in 1879) the electric filament lamp. He patented numerous inventions in telegraphy, cinematography, etc. However, he favoured the use of DC (direct current) for electrical transmission rather than the more efficient AC system□

Edmonton capital of Alberta province, Canada; population 521 205. Centre of an oil and mining area, it is linked by pipeline with USA□

Edmund St c840–70. King of East Anglia from 855. He was canonized for preferring martyrdom to renunciation of Christianity, when he was defeated and captured by the Danes in 870. See Bury St Edmunds◊□

Edmund Ironside c989–1016. King of England, son of Ethelred◊ the Unready, whom he succeeded in 1016. Defeated by Canute◊ at Assandun (Ashington) in Essex, he divided his kingdom with his conqueror□

Edom in Old Testament, a mountainous area of S Palestine (Dead Sea–Gulf of Aqaba) inhabited by enemies of the Israelites□

Edward eleven kings of England or the UK:

Edward (the Elder) d. 924. King of England from 901, son of King Alfred. He crushed Danish risings and extended his kingdom to the Humber.

Edward St (the Martyr) c963–78. King of England from 975. Son of King Edgar, he was murdered at Corfe Castle, probably at his stepmother Aelfthryth's instigation (she wished to secure the crown for her son). He was canonized 1001.

Edward St (the Confessor) c1003–1066. King of England from 1042, son of Ethelred II. Power was held by Earl Godwin◊ and his son Harold◊ while the king devoted himself to religion. He was buried in Westminster Abbey, which he had rebuilt; canonized 1161.

Edward I 1239–1307. King of England from 1272. Son of Henry III, he led the royal forces in the Barons'◊ War 1264–7, and was on a crusade when he succeeded to the throne. He established English rule over all Wales 1282–4, and secured recognition of his overlordship from the Scottish king, though the Scots (under Wallace and Bruce◊) fiercely resisted actual conquest. In his reign Parliament took its approximate modern form with the Model Parliament of 1295.

Edward II 1284–1327. King of England from 1307. Son of Edward I, he was created the first prince of Wales in 1301 (see Caernarfon◊). Incompetent and frivolous, he invaded Scotland in 1314, and was defeated at Bannockburn◊. He was deposed in 1327 by his wife Isabella and her lover Mortimer◊, and murdered in Berkeley Castle.

Edward III 1312–77. King of England from 1327. Son of Edward II, he assumed the government from his mother in 1330, and achieved a victory over the Scots at Halidon Hill 1333. In 1337 he started the Hundred◊ Years War. Temporary peace came with the Treaty of Brétigny, under which he gave up his claim to the French throne in return for Calais, Aquitaine, and Gascony, but hostilities were renewed in 1369.

Edward IV 1442–83. King of England from 1461. Son of Richard, Duke of York, he was known as Earl of March until his proclamation as king to replace Henry◊ VI. He consolidated his position by defeating the Lancastrians at Towton 1461, and capturing Henry, but the latter was temporarily restored by Warwick◊ (previously Edward's supporter) 1470–1. Edward recovered the throne by victories at Barnet and Tewkesbury.

Edward V 1470–83. King of England from 1483. Son of Edward IV, he was deposed three months after his accession in favour of his uncle (Richard◊ III), and is traditionally believed to have been murdered (with his brother) in the Tower of London on Richard's orders. Richard's innocence is maintained by the Richard III Society.

Edward VI 1537–53. King of England from 1547, son of Henry◊ VIII and Jane Seymour. The regency was held first by his uncle the Duke of Somerset◊, and then from 1549 by the Earl of Warwick (later Duke of Northumberland◊). Edward strongly supported the Reformation◊, though still a child. He died of tuberculosis.

Edward VII 1841–1910. King of Great Britain and Ireland from 1901. Eldest son of Queen Victoria◊, who considered him too frivolous to be allowed to take part in political life, he yet took a close interest, and after his accession promoted the *Entente◊ Cordiale* 1904, and Anglo-Russian agreement of 1907. He married in 1863 Princess Alexandra of Denmark, by whom he had six children. He was a leading figure in society, keen yachtsman and follower of field sports, gambled at cards, and had a bevy of mistresses.

Edward VIII 1894–1972. King of Great Britain and Northern Ireland 20 Jan–11 Dec 1936. Eldest son of George◊ V, he was created Prince of Wales in 1910. His wish to marry ***Mrs Simpson*** born (Bessie) Wallis Warfield 1896–1986, a twice-divorced American, caused a constitutional crisis, and he abdicated. They married in 1937 and lived in France, as Duke and Duchess of Windsor□

Edward the Black Prince 1330–76. Prince of Wales, eldest son of Edward III, his later nickname supposedly deriving from his black armour. During the Hundred◊ Years' War he served at Crécy◊; defeated and captured the French king at Poitiers◊, and in 1367 invaded Castile and restored to the throne the deposed king, Pedro the Cruel. Ill-health kept him from public life after 1371□

Edward Prince 1964– . Prince of the UK, third son of Queen Elizabeth II□

Edward Lake. Lake (known as Idi Amin Dada 1973–9) in Uganda/Zaïre□

Edwards Sir George 1908– . British civil and military aircraft designer, chairman of the British Aircraft Corporation 1963–75. He was associated with the *Viking, Viscount, Valiant V-bomber, VC-10* and *Concorde;* Order of Merit 1971□

Edwards Jonathan 1703–58. American theologian, who took a Calvinist◊ view of predestination, and initiated a religious revival, the 'Great Awakening'. His *The Freedom of the Will* (defending Determinism) 1754 received renewed attention in the 20th century□

Edwin c585–633. King of Northumbria from 617; he fortified Edinburgh◊, and was killed in battle with Penda of Mercia□

eel order of fish Anguilliformes including:
European eel *Anguilla anguilla*, freshwater family Anguillidae; its snakelike body has some 260 vertebrae, weighs 75 kg/15 lb, and is valued as food. Capable of travelling long distances overland, eels die after spawning in special grounds at a depth of 7000 m/23 000 ft in the Sargasso◊ Sea; the fry return after a period of years to European rivers, helped by the N Atlantic Drift.
common Moray *Muraena helena,* of the Mediterranean, etc, family Muraenidae, is brightly coloured and aggressive, reaching 2.5 m/8 ft. The flesh, poisonous till cooked, was thought a delicacy by the Romans.
conger eel family Congridae, of the Mediterranean and Atlantic, is also aggressive, and reaches 3 m/9 ft, 65 kg/140 lb□

eel-grass flowering plant of tidal mud flats, *Zoster marina*, family Zosteraceae, one of the few flowering plants to adapt to marine conditions□

eelworm a tiny parasitic worm◊□

EFTA see European◊ Free Trade Association□

Egbert d. 839. King of the W Saxons from 802, he united England for the first time under one king by 829□

egg in animals, the ovum, or female reproductive cell. When fertilized by a male sperm cell, it develops by division into further cells to form the embryo□

eggplant see aubergine◊□

Egmont Lamoral, Count of Egmont 1522–68. Flemish patriot, who was a leader of the revolt against Spanish misrule until in 1567 the Duke of Alva was sent to crush the resistance, and Egmont was beheaded□

Egmont Mount. Symmetrical extinct volcano in North Island, New Zealand; 2517 m/8260 ft□

egret tall white bird, related to the heron◊□

Egypt Arab Republic of

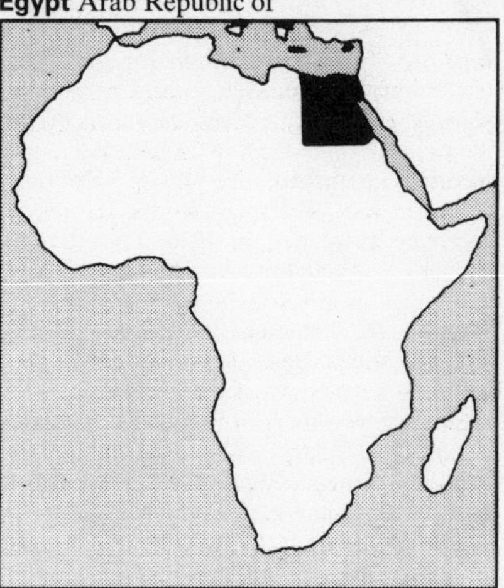

area 1 000 000 sq km /386 198 sq mi
capital Cairo
towns Gīza; ports Alexandria, Port Said
features River Nile; Aswan High Dam and Lake Nasser; Sinai◊; remains of Ancient Egypt (Pyramids, Sphinx, Luxor, Karnak, Abu Simbel, El Faiyum◊)
exports cotton and textiles
currency Egyptian pound
population 47 000 000
language *ancient* survives to some extent in Coptic, used in the ritual of the Coptic Church (see Copts◊), and written in a modified Greek alphabet; *modern* Arabic
religion *ancient* owing to development from local deities, a consistent theology was never developed, but beliefs were less primitive than animal-headed gods suggest (they were often emblematic, in the same way that Christ is represented as a lamb), and there was also the concept of a single deity, see Aton◊; Osiris◊, Isis◊, Horus◊, Set◊; Ra◊, Ammon◊; Anubis◊, Thoth◊, Bast◊, Aten◊; *modern* Sunni Islam 95%; Coptic Christianity 5%
famous people Fuad, Farouk I and II, Nasser, Sadat
government under the constitution of 1971, Egypt is a 'democratic socialist state', with an executive president (Hosni Mubarak◊

from 1981), nominated by a popularly elected People's Assembly and confirmed by plebiscite for a six-year term.
recent history for early history see Egypt: history. A British protectorate 1914–22, when it became an independent kingdom under Fuad. It became a republic in 1953, following the military coup of 1952, the last British troops having left the Suez Canal Zone in Jun 1956. The Canal was nationalized by Nasser (see also Suez◊). Egypt's involvement in the Arab◊-Israeli Wars was ended by the Camp◊ David Agreements in 1978. From 1981 increasing reversion to fundamentalist Islam led to attacks on the Coptic minority. In 1982 a trial ten-year Charter of Integration was signed with Sudan◊, with a Nile Valley Parliament. The chief party is the National Democratic Party established by Sadat 1978□

Egypt: history

BC

5000 Egyptian culture already well-established in the Nile Valley
3200 Menes◊ united Lower Egypt (the Delta) with his own kingdom of Upper Egypt to form the Egyptian state
2800 Imhotep◊ built step pyramid at Sakkara◊
c2600 Old Kingdom reached the height of its power and the kings of the 4th Dynasty built the pyramids◊ at Gîza
c2200–1800 Middle Kingdom, under which the unity lost towards the end of the Old Kingdom was restored
1730 invading Asiatic Hyksos◊ established their kingdom in the Delta
c1580 New Kingdom established by the 18th Dynasty, following the eviction of the Hyksos, with its capital at Thebes◊. High point of Egyptian civilization: see Thothemes◊, Hatshepsut◊, Amenhotep◊, Ikhnaton◊, Nefertiti◊, Tutankhamen◊, and Tell el-Amarna◊
c1321 19th Dynasty: see Rameses◊, Karnak◊ and Abu Simbel◊
1191 Rameses III defeated the Indo-European 'Sea Peoples', but after him there was decline and eventual anarchy
8–7th centuries brief interlude of rule by kings from Nubia◊
666 the Assyrians under Ashurbanipal occupied Thebes
525 after a brief resurgence of independence, Egypt became a Persian province following conquest by Cambyses◊
332 conquest by Alexander◊; on the division of his empire, Egypt went to Ptolemy◊, whose descendants ruled until Cleopatra's◊ death in 30BC
30 conquest by Augustus◊; Egypt a province of the Roman and Byzantine empires

AD

641 conquest by the Arabs, so that the Christianity of later Roman rule was replaced by Islam; see Copts◊. See also Saladin◊ and Mamelukes◊
1517 Egypt became a Turkish province
1798–1801 Napoleon's invasion and the French occupation; see Battle of the Nile◊
1805 Mehemet Ali◊ established the modern royal house which ended with Farouk◊II. Under his successors there was increasing financial and political control of the country by France and Britain
1869 opening of the Suez◊ Canal, a vital Empire link for Britain
1922 Egypt an independent kingdom. For recent history see under Egypt◊□

Ehrenburg Ilya Grigorievich 1891–1967. Russian writer, born in Kiev. He is best-known in the West for *The Thaw* (1954), depicting artistic circles in the USSR, and marking the slackening of censorship in the 1950s□

Ehrlich Paul 1854–1915. German bacteriologist, concerned mostly with immunology. He developed the arsenic compounds used in the treatment of syphilis before the discovery of antibiotics. He shared a Nobel prize 1908□

Eichendorff Joseph, Freiherr von 1788–1857. German poet, whose superb lyrics were set to music by Schuman, Mendelssohn and Wolf□

Eichmann Karl Adolf 1906–62. Austrian SS official in Hitler's reich. Located in Argentina in 1960, he was abducted by agents from Israel, and, after trial, executed there for his part in the extermination of six million Jews□

eider duck a type of waterfowl◊□

Eiffel Tower iron tower (320 m/1050 ft) designed by Gustave Eiffel for the Exhibition of 1889, now in the Champ de Mars, Paris□

Eiger see Alps◊□

Eijkman Christiaan 1858–1930. Dutch bacteriologist, who isolated vitamin B_1 as a cure for beri-beri, and pioneered the recognition of vitamins as essential to health. Nobel prize 1929□

Eilat see Elat◊□

Eindhoven industrial town (electrical and electronic goods) in S Netherlands; population 195 670□

Einstein Albert 1879–1955. German-Swiss-US physicist. Born at Ulm of Jewish stock, he was later a Swiss, and from 1940 an American citizen. While director of the Kaiser Wilhelm Institute for Physics, Berlin, 1913–33, he received a Nobel prize 1921, but was later deprived of his post by the Nazis. His chief contributions to physical theory were in statistical mechanics, quantum theory and above all his Special (1905) and General (1915)

Theories of Relativity◊. His final concept of the basic laws governing the universe was outlined in his unified◊ field theory (1953)□

einsteinium element
symbol Es
atomic number 99
physical description metal
features one of the lanthanide◊ series, created by irradiation of uranium-238 with neutrons in the first thermonuclear explosion
uses no present use□

Einthoven William 1860–1927. Dutch physiologist, inventor of the electrocardiograph, used in detecting coronary disease, etc□

Eire Gaelic name for the Republic of Ireland◊□

Eisenach industrial town (pottery, vehicles, machinery), Erfurt district, E Germany; population 51 000. Martin Luther made the first translation of the Bible into German in Wartburg Castle and J S Bach was born here□

Eisenhower Dwight David ('Ike') 1890-1969. 34th President of the USA, born at Denison, Texas. In World War II he was sent to England in Jun 1942 as US Commander, European theatre; became Commander-in-Chief of the American and British forces for the invasion of N Africa Nov 1942; commanded the Allied invasion of Sicily Jul 1943, and announced the surrender of Italy on 8 Sept 1943. In Dec he became Commander of the Allied invasion of Europe, and from Oct 1944 commanded all the Allied armies in the West. He resigned from the army in 1952 to campaign for the presidency as a Republican; he was elected, and re-elected in 1956□

Eisenstein Sergei Mikhailovich 1898–1948. Soviet film director. He pioneered the use of montage as a means of propaganda, as in *The Battleship Potemkin* 1925. His *Alexander Nevsky* 1938, was the first part of an uncompleted trilogy, the second part, *Ivan the Terrible* 1944, being banned in Russia□

Eisteddfod annual gathering in Wales (Welsh 'sitting'), traditionally originating in pre-Christian times, for the bardic arts of music, poetry, literature, etc. The chief ceremony is the 'chairing' of the bard (the best contestant in verse)□

Ekaterinburg see Sverdlovsk◊□

Ekaterinodar see Krasnodar◊□

Ekaterinoslav see Dnepropetrovsk◊□

El Aaiún see Layoun◊□

eland a large African antelope◊□

elasticity ability of a solid to recover its shape automatically once deforming forces (stresses modifying its length or shape) are removed. Metals are elastic up to a certain stress (the 'elastic limit'), beyond which greater stress gives them a permanent deformation. See Hooke◊'s Law□

Elba Italian island; area 223 sq km/86 sq mi; population 29 000. Capital Portoferraio. Napoleon was exiled here 1814–15, and the small, uninhabited island of ***Monte Cristo*** 40 km/25 mi to the south supplied a title for Dumas' hero in *The Count of Monte Cristo*□

Elbe river of E and W Germany; length 1166 km/725 mi□

Elbing see Elblag◊□

Elblag port (German *Elbing*) and industrial town (shipbuilding, engineering, vehicles) in Poland; population 93 000□

Elbruz highest mountain in Europe, 5642 m/18 510 ft, in the Caucasus◊, Georgian Republic, USSR□

Elburz volcanic mountain range in NW Iran, including Mount Demavend 5770 m/18934 ft□

elder genus, *Sambucus*, of deciduous trees and shrubs, family Caprifoliaceae. The Eurasian ***common elder*** ***S nigra*** has a smooth bark and heads of small sweet-scented white flowers followed by clusters of black berries; both are used in wine-making□

Eldon John Scott, 1st Earl of Eldon 1751–1838. British lawyer, Lord Chancellor 1801–6 and 1807–27, who established the principles of equity (see under law◊)□

El Dorado fabled city of gold believed by 16th century Spaniards to exist in the Americas. See Chibchas◊□

Eleanor of Aquitaine c1122–1204. Queen of Henry◊ II of England from 1154; she was married 1137–51 to Louis◊ VII of France, but the marriage was annulled on grounds of consanguinity. Henry imprisoned her 1174–89 for supporting their sons, the future Richard I and King John, in revolt against him□

Eleanor of Castile d. 1290. Queen of Edward◊ I of England from 1254, she accompanied him on crusade 1270–3, and he erected crosses, e.g. Charing Cross, London, at points where her body rested on her funeral journey□

Elector one of the German princes who elected the Holy Roman Emperors from the 13th century until the dissolution of the Holy Roman Empire in 1806. There were originally six Electors, then seven, and finally ten□

electoral college indirect system of presidential voting in the USA. Each state has as many electors, chosen by popular vote, as it has senators and representatives in Congress, and the whole electoral college vote of each state goes to the winning party (and its candidate)□

electoral system the method of election to a parliamentary body. The three main types are:
first-past-the-post, with single-member constituencies in which the candidate with most votes wins (UK, USA).
proportional representation (PR), in which seats are shared by parties according to their share of the vote, e.g. ***single transferable vote*** (STV), in which the voter numbers candidates according to preference, and 'surplus' votes beyond a required quota are transferred to runners-up (Republic of Ireland); or the ***list system*** in which the voter indicates his preference for his party's list and seats for each constituency are distributed according to the parties' share of the total vote in that constituency (general in the EEC).
preferential vote, in which the voter indicates his second choice either by ***alternative vote*** (AV), in which if no candidate achieves over 50% of the votes, the voters' second choices in the case of the most hopeless candidates are successively transferred until one candidate does achieve 50% (Australia); or by ***second ballot***, when no candidate has an absolute majority on the first count (France).
When only one party is allowed (as under Communist rule and in some African countries, etc.), some degree of choice may be enjoyed by voting for particular candidates within the party list□

Electra see under Agamemnon◊□

electrical relay see relay◊ electrical□

electric charge property of some bodies which causes them to exert forces on each other, such that two bodies both with positive or negative charges repel each other, while oppositely or 'unlike' charged bodies attract each other, since each is in the ***electric field*** of the other. Electrons◊ possess a negative charge, and protons◊ an equal positive charge, the unit of charge being the ***coulomb*** (C). Atoms◊ have no charge but can sometimes gain electrons to become negative ***ions*** or lose them to become positive ions. So-called ***static electricity***, seen in such phenomena as the charging of nylon shirts when they are pulled on or off, is in fact the rubbing-on or rubbing-off of electrons from the surface atoms.
A flow of charge (such as electrons through a copper wire) constitutes an ***electric current***; the rate of flow of current is measured in ***ampères***. See energy◊□

electric current see under electric◊ charge□

electric eel actually a fish, *Electrophorus electricus*, family Electrophoridae, of the Orinoco and Amazon; its modified muscle fibres generate 650 volts, sufficient to stun a horse□

electric energy see electric◊ charge and energy◊□

electric field see under electric◊ charge□

electric fish various fish which use an electric current to stun their prey, e.g. the electric◊ eel. All fish generate a weak electrical field, and may use it for electrolocation and communication (as in courtship), or have it used against them (sharks use it as a beacon to home in on their prey)□

electricity properly the name of the subject dealing with electric◊ charge and its behaviour; but loosely used to mean electric charge itself, or, sometimes, electrical energy. For ***static electricity***, see electric◊ charge□

electricity generation the conversion of other forms of energy into electrical energy. Electrical energy◊ can easily and safely be converted into heat, light, or mechanical forms. Equally conveniently, it can be conveyed efficiently from place to place by means of metal wires, so its generation can be carried out on a large scale at a small number of power stations. Two commonly used methods are the coal-fired and the nuclear power station.
In a ***coal-fired*** station, water is converted into steam in the tubes of a boiler heated by the burning of coal dust carried into its furnace in a blast of pre-heated air. The steam is saturated by exposure to water in the boiler drum and then superheated to a temperature of about 550°C. Under a pressure of about 160 atmospheres it is made to turn the blades of a high pressure turbine◊ from which, after reheating, it is fed to intermediate and low pressure turbines. After leaving the last of these it is condensed to lower its pressure and increase turbine efficiency. The water so formed is recycled. All three turbines drive a generator which is essentially an electromagnet rotating inside coils of wire, so as to induce alternating voltages in them. Three voltages of 22 000 volts having the same frequency◊ as each other, but alternating out of phase with each other are produced. This three phase system has advantages for power transmission. Each voltage is stepped up by transformers◊ to 400 000 volts, for feeding into the main arteries of the national grid. By using such a large scale voltage, the power transmission wires, usually taken across country on pylons, carry relatively small currents and do not waste much energy by themselves becoming hot. The voltages are transformed down in successive stages (typically 132 000 volt and 11 000 volts) to 240V. Industrial and other users are often supplied at higher voltages and are able to make use of all three voltages or phases.

electricity generation

coal-fired power station (highly simplified)

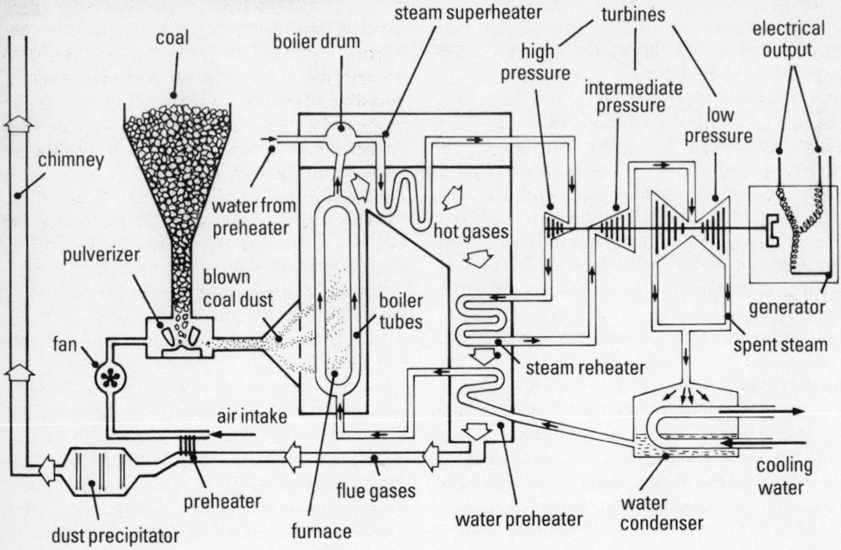

steam superheater
turbines
high pressure
intermediate pressure
low pressure
electrical output
coal
boiler drum
chimney
water from preheater
hot gases
pulverizer
blown coal dust
boiler tubes
generator
fan
spent steam
steam reheater
air intake
cooling water
preheater
flue gases
water condenser
water preheater
dust precipitator
furnace

advanced gas-cooled (AGR) reactor (highly simplified)

loader
reactor core
hot carbon dioxide
concrete biological shield
turbines
electrical output
high pressure steam
reheater
electrical generator
water
boiler
condenser
heat shield
fuel rod
boron steel control rod

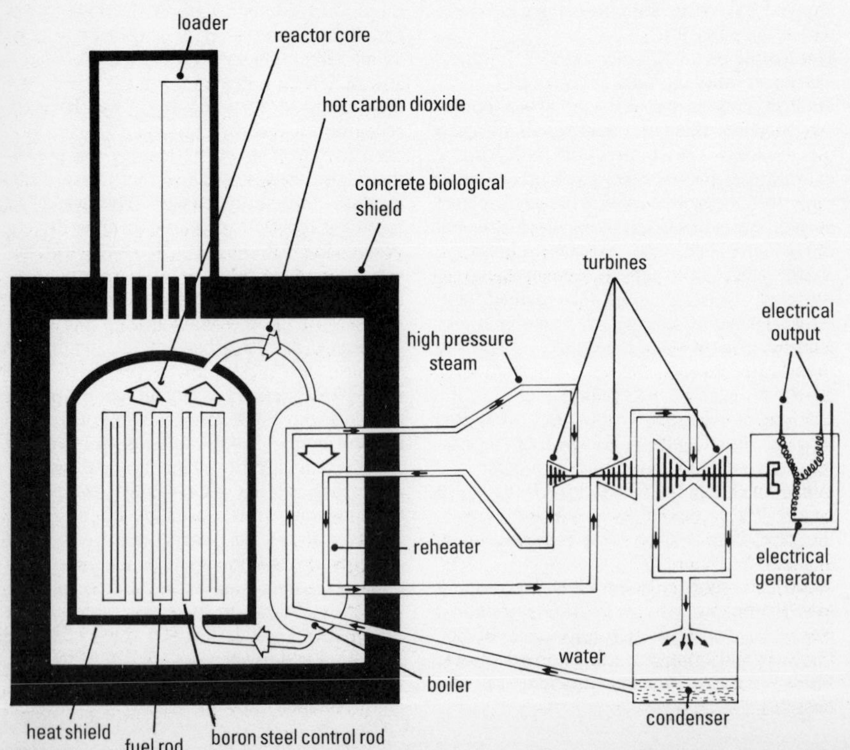

In a nuclear power station of the ***advanced gas-cooled reactor*** (AGR) type, nuclear fission (see nuclear◊ energy) takes place inside the uranium contained in bars within the fuel rods. Neutrons released by the fission are slowed down by graphite sheets which encase the uranium. Central rods of boron steel are automatically raised or lowered between the fuel rods to absorb neutrons to prevent the fission reaction from proceeding too fast or too slowly. The heat liberated by the fission is carried away by carbon dioxide gas circulated rapidly through the reactor core. The carbon dioxide is used to heat water and produce steam to drive turbines, as in a coal-fired station□

electric ray a flat electric◊ fish. See under ray◊□

electrocardiography the recording of electrical impulses generated by the heart muscle (shown as an ***electrocardiogram***), as a guide to heart malfunction□

electroconvulsive therapy or ***ECT*** a treatment for schizophrenia, depression, etc, given under anaesthesia and with a muscle relaxant. An electric current is passed through the brain to induce alterations in the brain's electrical activity□

electrocution execution (in many states of USA) by administering an electric shock (1800–2000 v) while the recipient is strapped in a special chair□

electrode conductor by which an electric current passes in or out of a substance, e.g. in an electric furnace or neon tube□

electrodynamics study of the interaction between charged particles and their emission and absorption of electromagnetic radiation◊. ***Quantum electrodynamics*** (QED) applies quantum mechanics◊ and relativity◊ theory, making exceedingly accurate predictions about subatomic processes involving charged particles, e.g. electrons and protons□

electro-encephalography study of the electrical discharges of the brain, used in diagnosis of epilepsy, brain tumours, etc.□

electrolysis passage of an electrical current through an electrolyte◊ to produce chemical changes in it. See electroplating◊□

electrolyte conducting solution, or other medium in which an electric current flows as a result of chemical changes resulting in the movement of ions◊□

electromagnetic field region of space in which a particle with an electric◊ charge experiences a force. If it does so only when moving, it is in a pure ***magnetic field***, if it does so when stationary, it is in an ***electric field***. Both can be present simultaneously□

electromagnetic spectrum see electromagnetic◊ waves□

electromagnetic waves oscillating electric and magnetic fields travelling together through space at a speed of nearly 300 million metres per second. The (limitless) range of possible frequencies◊ of electromagnetic waves which can be thought of as making up a 'spectrum', (***electromagnetic spectrum***) are radio waves, infra-red, ultra-violet, X-rays and gamma radiation. Dividing 300 million by the frequency in Hz (see Hertz◊) gives the wavelength of the waves in metres. See Maxwell◊, Hertz◊□

electromotive force or ***emf*** agency causing the movement of charge in a circuit, measured by the work done per unit charge flowing. The unit is the volt□

electron stable, negatively charged elementary particle◊, a constituent of all atoms◊, and the basic particle of electricity. Diffraction (passing a beam of electrons through a special lattice, in a similar way to that in which light is diffracted) demonstrates the wave aspect of these particles. See Sir Joseph Thomson◊□

electronics the design and application of devices which amplify and switch electrically, without moving parts. The first device was the thermionic valve (using electrons moving in a vacuum) on the basis of which electronics developed during the first half of the twentieth century to the stage of producing radio, radar, black and white television and the earliest true computers. Solid-state technology, that of the transistor◊ (invented 1949) and multi-transistor circuits in the form of silicon chips, has almost entirely superseded the valve, for reasons of cheapness, compactness, reliability, and low power consumption. Using solid-state devices, circuits can be constructed of a complexity previously only dreamed of, and there has been an accelerating trend from the simple but distortion-prone ***analogue*** signal-processing techniques to the superior ***digital*** ones; for example, from the representation of a sound wave by a voltage varying instant-by-instant in step with the air-pressure variation, to a representation in terms of binary◊ numbers giving values obtained only at frequently-spaced sampling times. Digital techniques have more obvious uses, in calculators, computers◊, digital clocks and watches□

electron microscope see microscope◊□

electron volt in atomic physics, the energy (1.602×10^{-9} J) acquired by an electron in passing through a potential difference of 1 volt□

electrophoresis motion of charged particles in a colloid◊ produced when electrodes are

electromagnetic waves

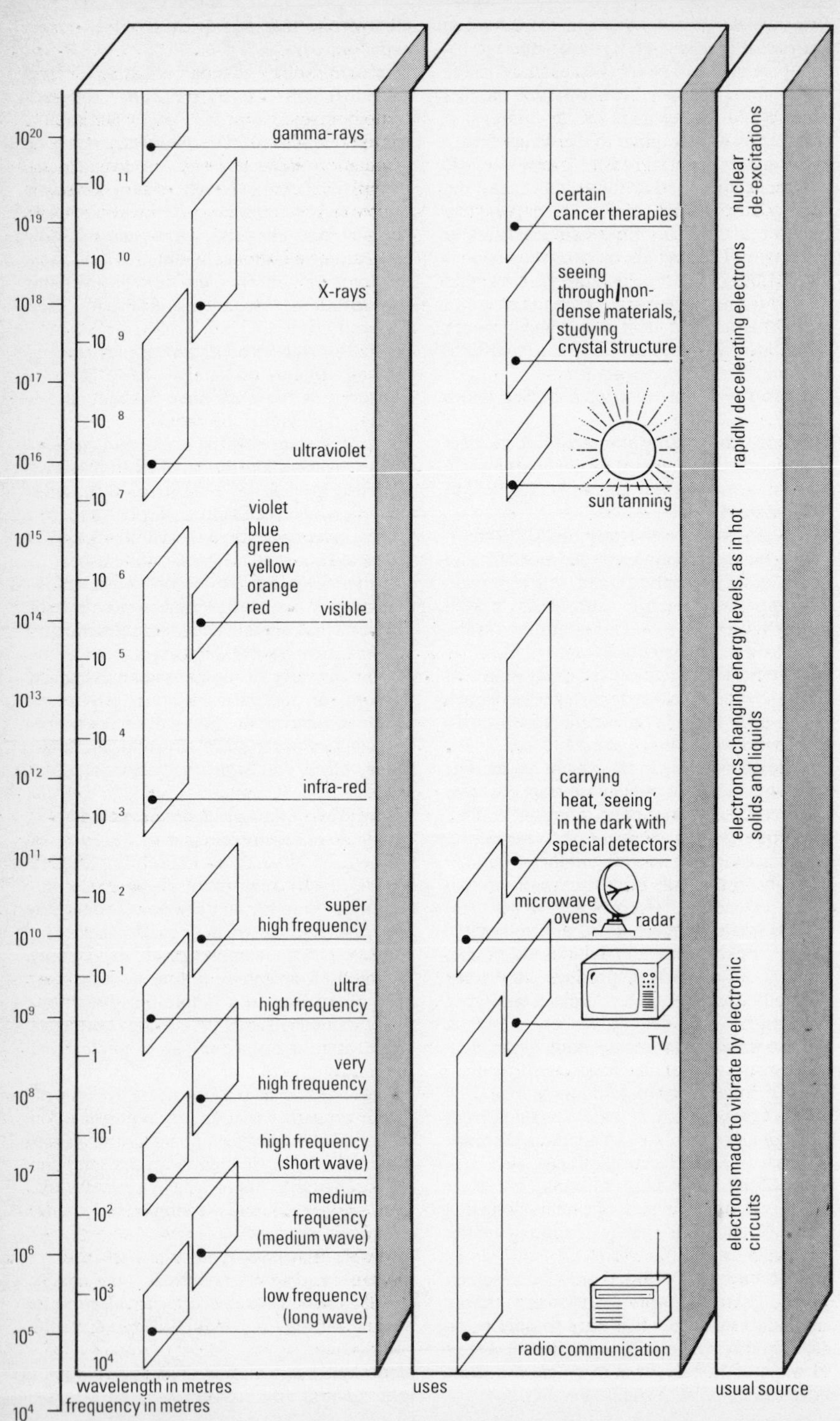

introduced. The process is affected by gravity, hence scientific experiments involving it are ideally carried out in space□

electroplating electro-deposition (using electrolysis◊) of a coat of one metal on another for decorative or protective purposes, e.g. chrome on steel, gold or silver on copper, etc.□

electrostatics study of electric charges from stationary sources (not currents), e.g. amber◊ and lightning◊□

electrum alloy of gold and silver used by ancient smiths, e.g. Scythians◊□

element one of the 105 known substances, of which 92 occur naturally, which consist of atoms having the same number of protons in their nuclei. Hydrogen and helium were produced in the 'Big Bang' (see universe◊); of the rest, those up to number 56 (iron) are produced by nuclear fusion within the stars, but the more massive, such as lead, uranium, etc, are produced when an old star explodes (see Supernova under star◊) and its gravitational energy as it collapses squashes nuclei together. The transuranium elements are those synthetic elements produced by bombarding uranium with various atomic particles. See chemistry◊, and table of elements on pages 290-291□

elephant mammal of family Elephantidae. The only surviving members of the order Proboscidea are the ***Asiatic elephant*** *Elephas maximus* (smaller, more easily tamed) and ***African elephant*** *Loxodonta africanus* (with huge ears). The trunk is used to obtain food and water, and the tusks are made of the finest ivory. Herds are led by an elderly female, and social organization is strong. They have the longest mammalian gestation period (19–22 months), and lowest metabolic rate, hence they supposedly forget slowly, and remember kindness or injury. Hannibal's elephants were N African, smaller than the other species, and a few still survive in Mauretania◊.

The extinct ***mammoths*** (*Mammuthus*) of the Pleistocene period were larger, with inward-curving tusks. The ***imperial mammoth*** *M imperator* reached 4.5 m/15 ft, as against the 3 m/10 ft of modern elephants, and the ***woolly mammoth*** *M primigenius* had thick fur. Perfectly preserved specimens have been found in Arctic ice.

The ***mastodons*** (*Mammuth*) of the Pliocene period have been found in all continents except Australia; some early species were double-tusked, but they were generally less tall, though longer than the modern elephant. In N America they survived until c6000 BC□

elephantiasis painful enlargement of part of the human body, e.g. leg, breast, caused by the tropical disease filariasis. The larval form of the roundworm *Filaria* is carried by mosquito bite, and blocks lymphatic glands, etc□

Eleusis small town near Athens, Greece; population 2500. There are remains of the Temple of Demeter◊ where the ***Eleusinian mysteries*** were celebrated. Visions linked with the underworld, to which Persephone◊ had been abducted, were seen in a darkened room by worshippers, who may have eaten fungi containing LSD□

Elgar Sir Edward 1857–1934. British composer. B. in Broadheath, Worcestershire, he became an organist, and was associated as conductor with the Three Choirs Festival. He gained recognition with the *Enigma Variations* 1899; other works include the oratorio setting of Newman◊'s *The Dream of Gerontius* 1900; the series of *Pomp and Circumstance* marches; two symphonies, a violin and a cello concerto. Knighted 1904, Order of Merit 1911□

Elgin town (whisky distilling, etc.) in Grampian region, Scotland; population 18 800. ***Gordonstoun*** public school, attended by many male members of the British Royal family, is nearby. This house, when owned by Sir William Gordon Cumming, was the scandalous scene of a card game in which Gordon Cumming was accused of cheating; the future Edward VII was an innocent participant, and gave evidence in the subsequent court case□

Elgin Marbles collection of ancient Greek sculptures, mainly from the Parthenon at Athens, bought by the 7th Earl of Elgin to avoid their destruction by the Turks. They are now in the British Museum, but Greece demands their return□

Elijah mid-9th century BC. In Old Testament, the Hebrew prophet◊ in the reigns of Ahab and Ahaziah who defeated the prophets of Baal◊, and was carried to heaven in a whirlwind□

Eliot George. Pseudonym of British novelist Mary Ann Evans 1819–80. Born at Chilvers Coton, Warwickshire, she was converted in 1841 from evangelicalism to freethinking, and from 1851 worked in London on the *Westminster Review*. From 1854 she lived with philosopher and critic George Henry Lewes (1817–78, who was separated from his wife), and with his encouragement published *Amos Barton*, the first of the *Scenes of Clerical Life,* in 1857 under the name of George Eliot. Her major works are *The Mill on the Floss* 1860, *Silas Marner* 1861, and *Middlemarch* 1872, her masterpiece. In 1880 she married her old friend John Cross 1840–1924□

Periodic table of the elements

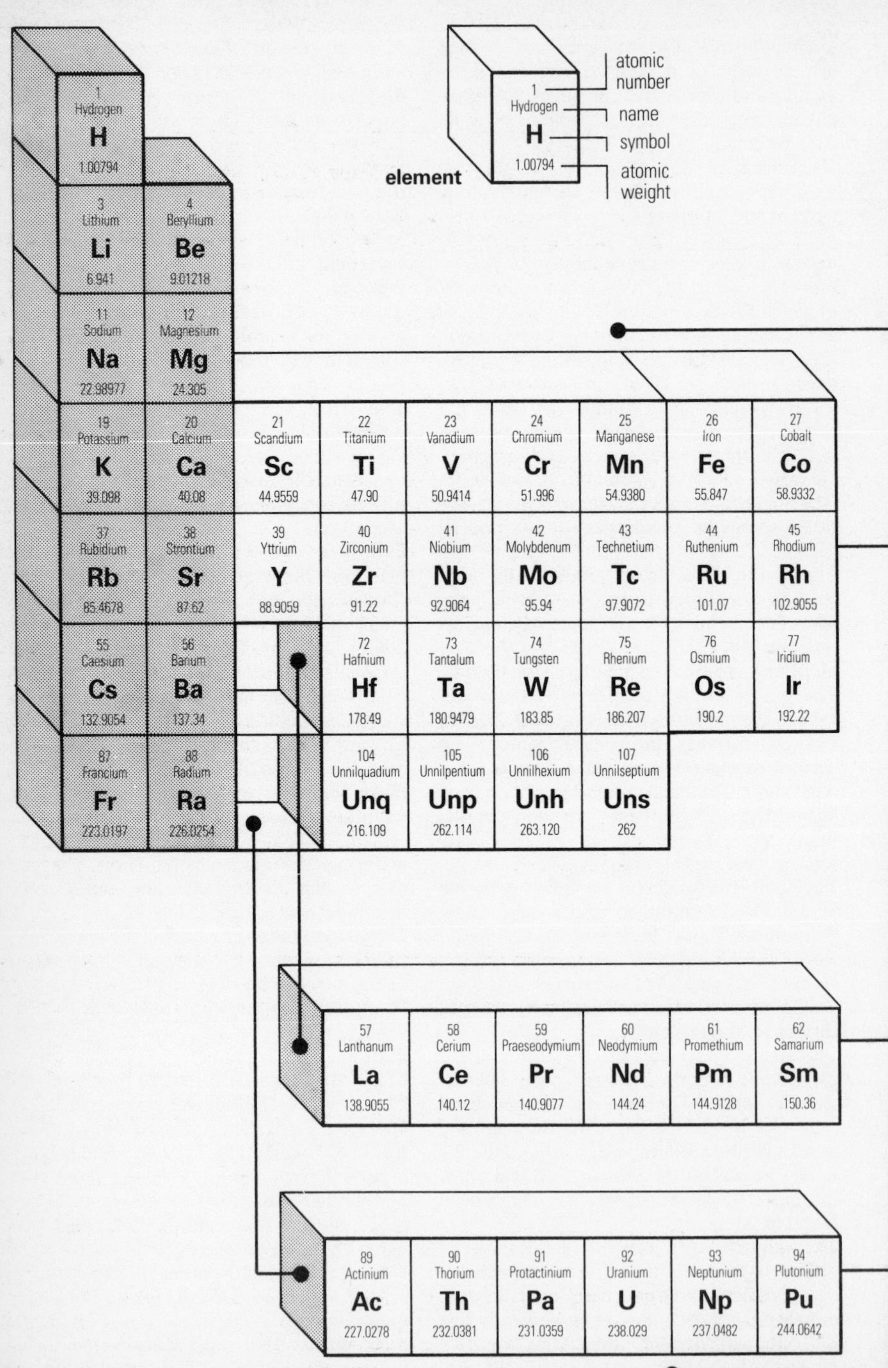

								2 Helium **He** 4.00260
			5 Boron **B** 10.81	6 Carbon **C** 12.011	7 Nitrogen **N** 14.0067	8 Oxygen **O** 15.9994	9 Fluorine **F** 18.99840	10 Neon **Ne** 20.179
			13 Aluminium **Al** 26.98154	14 Silicon **Si** 28.086	15 Phosphorus **P** 30.97376P	16 Sulphur **S** 32.06	17 Chlorine **Cl** 35.453	18 Argon **Ar** 39.948
28 Nickel **Ni** 58.70	29 Copper **Cu** 63.546	30 Zinc **Zn** 65.38	31 Gallium **Ga** 69.72	32 Germanium **Ge** 672.59	33 Arsenic **As** 74.9216	34 Selenium **Se** 78.96	35 Bromine **Br** 79.904	36 Krypton **Kr** 83.80
46 Palladium **Pd** 106.4	47 Silver **Ag** 107.868	48 Cadmium **Cd** 112.40	49 Indium **In** 114.82	50 Tin **Sn** 118.69	51 Antimony **Sb** 121.75	52 Tellurium **Te** 127.75	53 Iodine **I** 126.9045	54 Xenon **Xe** 131.30
78 Platinum **Pt** 195.09	79 Gold **Au** 196.9665	80 Mercury **Hg** 200.59	81 Thallium **Tl** 204.37	82 Lead **Pb** 207.2	83 Bismuth **Bi** 208.9804	84 Polonium **Po** 209.9871	85 Astatine **At** 209.9871	86 Radon **Rn** 222.0176

63 Europium **Eu** 151.96	64 Gadolinium **Gd** 157.25	65 Terbium **Tb** 158.9254	66 Dysprosium **Dy** 162.50	67 Holmium **Ho** 164.9304	68 Erbium **Er** 167.26	69 Thulium **Tm** 168.9342	70 Ytterbium **Yb** 173.04	71 Lutetium **Lu** 174.97
95 Americium **Am** 243.0614	96 Curium **Cm** 247.0703	97 Berkelium **Bk** 247.0703	98 Californium **Cf** 251.0786	99 Einsteinium **Es** 252.0828	100 Fermium **Fm** 257.0951	101 Mendelvium **Md** 258.0986	102 Nobelium **No** 259.1009	103 Lawrencium **Lr** 260.1054

Eliot Sir John 1592–1632. English statesman. A Cornish MP, he was primarily responsible in 1628 for the Petition of Right◊ opposing Charles II. Imprisoned in the Tower of London in 1629, he died there, refusing to submit□

Eliot T(homas) S(tearns) 1888–1965. American-born poet and critic; British subject 1927. Born at St Louis, Missouri, he was educated at Harvard, Paris, and Oxford. Settling in London in 1915, he became a bank clerk, and later a publisher. His first volume, *Prufrock and other Observations* 1917, showed his great talent and he established his reputation with *The Waste Land* 1922. *Ash Wednesday* 1930 reflected his emergence in 1927 as an Anglo-Catholic, as did the poetic drama *Murder in the Cathedral* 1935, dealing with Becket◊. *The Cocktail Party* 1949 attempted a revival of contemporary verse drama. An influential critic, he edited *The Criterion* 1922–39. Order of Merit and Nobel prize 1948□

Elisabethville see Lubumbashi◊□

Elisha mid-9th century BC. In Old Testament, a Hebrew prophet, successor of Elijah◊□

Elizabeth two queens of England or the UK: ***Elizabeth I*** 1533–1603. Queen of England. Daughter of Henry◊ VIII and Anne Boleyn◊, she was born at Greenwich. Under Queen Mary◊ her Protestant sympathies required that she live in retirement at Hatfield until she became queen in Nov 1558. Securing her throne by making a broad religious settlement, she refused to endanger her position by marriage or naming a successor, but she flirted with favourites (Leicester◊, Raleigh◊, Essex◊) and royal suitors. Mary◊ Queen of Scots, who arrived in England in 1568 and whom Elizabeth imprisoned, was a focus of revolt and foreign intrigue, especially by Spain, until her execution in 1587. Open war with Spain and the despatch of the Armada◊ followed, but neither this, nor growing Puritan discontent (see Reformation◊), nor growing assertiveness by Parliament, endangered Elizabeth's hold on the country. The rebellion by Essex in 1601 failed hopelessly. In literature and the arts, the reign of the 'Virgin Queen' was outstanding.

Elizabeth II 1926– . Queen of Great Britain and Northern Ireland. The elder daughter of King George VI, Princess Elizabeth was born at 17 Bruton Street, London, home of her maternal grandparents, on 21 Apr 1926. Privately educated, she served in the ATS (Auxiliary Territorial Service) in World War II, and married her third cousin, the Duke of Edinburgh (see Philip◊), in Westminster Abbey on 20 Nov 1947. They have four children: see Charles◊, Anne◊, Andrew◊, Edward◊. In 1952 she succeeded to the throne while in Kenya with her husband, and in 1977 celebrated her Silver Jubilee as queen□

Elizabeth 1900– . Consort and queen of George◊ VI. The daughter of the 14th Earl of Strathmore and Kinghorne (see Glamis◊) she married Albert, Duke of York, the future George VI, in 1923, and had two children: Elizabeth II◊ and Princess Margaret◊. She adopted the style Queen Mother after her husband's death□

Elizabeth 1709–62. Empress of Russia. Daughter of Peter◊ the Great, she carried through a palace revolution in 1741 and supplanted her cousin, the infant Ivan VI, on the throne. She continued Peter's westernizing policy, and allied herself with Austria against Prussia□

Elizabeth industrial city (automobiles, tools, oil refining) in New Jersey, USA; population 106 200□

elk the largest member of the deer◊ family□

Ellesmere second largest island of the Canadian Arctic archipelago, Northwest Territories; area 212 687 sq km/82 119 sq mi□

Ellesmere Port oil port and industrial town in Cheshire, England, on the River Mersey and the Manchester Ship Canal; population 85 500. Formerly the biggest trans-shipment canal port in the NW, it now has the National Waterways Museum 1976, with old 'narrow boats', blacksmith's forge, etc.□

Ellice Islands see Tuvalu◊□

Ellington Edward ('Duke') 1899–1974. American composer and jazz pianist who played in New York's Cotton Club, then formed his own band. Numbers include *Mood Indigo, Sophisticated Lady, In My Solitude,* and *Black and Tan Fantasy*□

Ellis Henry Havelock 1859–1939. British author of the pioneer *Studies in the Psychology of Sex* (seven volumes 1898–1928)□

Ellis Island an island off New Jersey, USA; former reception centre (1892-1943) for immigrants, e.g. Sam Goldwyn, Irving Berlin. It is no longer used for this purpose and was declared a National Historic site in 1965□

Ellora see under Maharashtra◊□

elm genus of northern temperate trees *Ulmus*, family Ulmaceae, including ***common/English elm*** *U procera*; ***N American white elm*** *U americana*; ***red*** or ***slippery elm*** *U fulva*, of which the bark is used to treat dysentery, etc. ***Dutch elm disease*** is a fungoid disease carried by beetles which kills the trees; a similar decline in elms appears to have occurred in neolithic times, aided by climatic change and extension of agriculture. See fungi◊□

El Niño warm ocean surge (called 'the child' because first apparent at Christmas), recurrent every 7–14 years in the E Pacific off S America. It disrupts the climate of the area disastrously, causing in 1983 famine in Indonesia and bush-fires in Australia because of drought, rainstorms in California and S America, and destruction of Peru's anchovy harvest from the Humboldt◊ Current□

El Obeid market town in Sudan; population 91 000□

El Paso city on the Rio Grande, Texas, USA; population 425 260. Across the border is the Mexican city Ciudad Juarez◊; population 597 000□

El Salvador Republic of

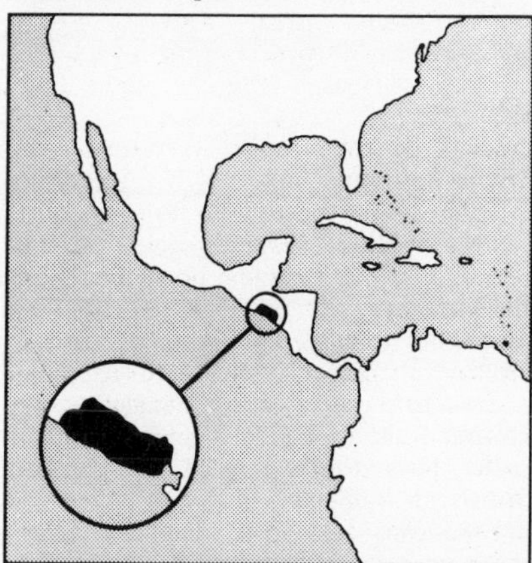

area 21 393 sq km/8 236 sq mi
capital San Salvador
features smallest and most thickly populated Central American country
exports coffee, cotton
currency cólon
population 5 100 000, mainly of Spanish-Indian extraction (including some 500 000 illegally in the USA)
language Spanish
religion Roman Catholicism
government executive president (José Napoleón Duarte 1980–82, and from 1984; Christian Democrat) and legislative assembly.
recent history until 1821 under Spanish rule, it was part of the Federation of Central America until independence in 1839. Tension between El Salvador and Honduras, because of emigration from the former to the latter, led to the 'Football War' lasting several weeks in 1969 (following the defeat of Honduras by El Salvador in a football match); there was a peace treaty 1980. There is long continuing conflict between government (backed by USA) and left-wing guerrilla forces, e.g. the assassination of Archbishop Romero and leaders of the Revolutionary Front in 1980. Land reform has been blocked by large landowners, and political assassination by 'death squads' is widespread. In 1985 the kidnapping of the president's daughter by the guerrillas, and his handling of the affair, weakened the government position□

Elsinore see Helsingör◊□

Elton Charles 1900– . British pioneer ecologist; director of the Bureau of Animal Population at Oxford 1932–67, and author of *The Pattern of Animal Communities* 1966. He originated the 'pyramid of number', i.e. that in an ecosystem a large number of minute animals at the bottom are eaten by a smaller number of bigger ones; the pyramid of 'food chains' successively continues until it ends in a small number of large animals. See food◊ chain□

Éluard Paul. Pseudonym of French Surrealist poet Eugène Grindel 1895–1952. A Communist, he was a member of the Resistance in World War II□

Ely cathedral city in Cambridgeshire, England; population 10 200. Hereward◊ the Wake had his stronghold on the Isle of Ely, so-called because the area was once cut off from the surrounding countryside by the Fens◊□

Élysée Palace of the. Paris home of Mme de Pompadour and Napoleon I, and from 1870 official residence of French presidents□

Elysium in Greek mythology, the Elysian Fields, or Islands of the Blessed, the equivalent of paradise◊□

Elytis Odysseus. Pseudonym of Greek lyric poet Odysseus Alepoudelis 1911– . Parts of his cycle *Worthy it is* ... 1959 were set to music by Theodorakis◊. Nobel prize 1979□

embroidery the art of decoration by needlework. Ancient Egypt, Greece, Phrygia, Babylon, and China were renowned for their embroidery, as were the Anglo-Saxons (earliest surviving work the stole and maniple recovered from the tomb of St Cuthbert at Durham, England 905AD). After World War II there was a revival of creative embroidery, after the depression caused by the advent of the sewing machine□

embryo early developmental stage of animals and plants. In animals the embryo exists within an egg (where it is nourished by food contained in the yolk), or in the ***uterus*** of the mother. In mammals (except marsupials) the embryo is fed through the ***placenta***. In humans the term embryo is used to describe the fertilized egg during its first seven weeks of existence; from the eighth week onwards it

embryo
foetal development (not to scale)

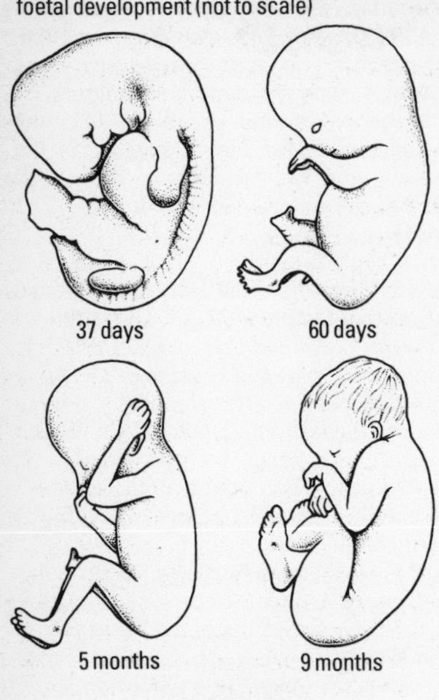

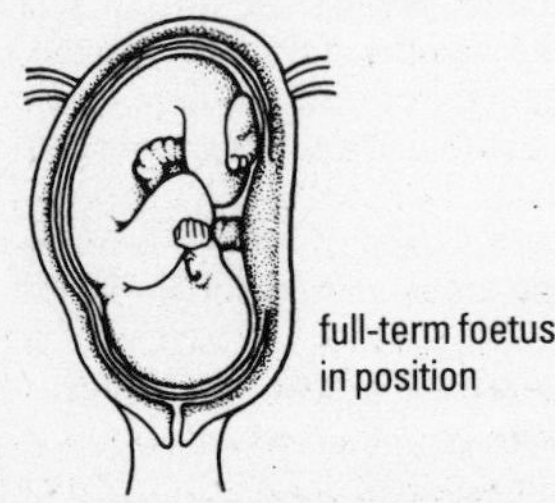
full-term foetus in position

is referred to as the foetus. The plant embryo sometimes consists of only a few cells, but usually includes root, shoot (or primary bud) and cotyledons which nourish the seedling□
embryology study of the changes undergone by living matter in its early life-history from fertilization to birth or hatching□
embryo research the study of human embryos at an early stage, in order to detect hereditary disease, genetic defects, etc., and to investigate the problems of infertility. The UK Medical Research Council laid down 1982 that experiments on human embryos were acceptable for approved research purposes, provided that both donors agreed. There must also be no intent to transfer the embryo to the uterus, or to culture it beyond the stage when implantation was possible. The Warnock Report 1984 proposed to limit experiment to up to 14 days after fertilization. It also recommended strict controls on AID (artificial insemination by donor); IVF (*in vitro* fertilization), fertilization outside the body ('test-tube baby') when either the sperm or the egg (or both) do not necessarily come from the couple involved as eventual parents; and condemned surrogate motherhood, or 'womb leasing', in which a woman is artificially inseminated and bears a child for another couple□
Emden port in W Germany; population 65 000. It is linked with the Ruhr by the Dortmund-Ems canal□
emerald green precious stone. See beryllium◊□
Emerson Ralph Waldo 1803–82. American poet-essayist. Born in Boston, he was originally a Unitarian◊ minister, but from 1833 settled at Concord as leader of the Transcendentalists◊□
Emery Walter Bryan 1903–71. British archaeologist, discoverer of the royal tombs of the mysterious X-group people in Nubia 1929–34□
emery see corundum◊□
Emilia-Romagna region of N central Italy including much of the Po valley; capital Bologna; other towns Reggio, Rimini, Parma, Ferrara, Ravenna; population 3 957 400□
Éminence grise see Père Joseph◊□
Emmental district in Berne, Switzerland, where a hard rennet cheese is made□
Emmet Robert 1778–1803. Irish nationalist leader, hanged after a failed revolt against British rule in Dublin□
Empedocles c490–430BC. Greek (Sicilian) philosopher, who thought the universe consisted of four elements (air, earth, fire, and water) which are forever destroyed and reconstructed by the counteraction of love and discord. He is said to have committed suicide by jumping into the crater of Etna□
emphysema lung disease (often caused by smoking) in which the air spaces lose their elasticity, and are unable to expel air sufficiently. The result is progressive shortness of breath□
empiricism philosophical theory that all human knowledge is based ultimately on sense experience. See Locke◊, Berkeley◊, Hume◊□
Empson Sir William 1906–84. English poet-critic, noted for his examination of the potential variety of meaning in poetry in *Seven Types of Ambiguity* 1930□
emu a large flightless Australian bird; see running◊ birds□
enamel vitreous glaze fused to a metal base for decorative purposes, often either in compartments formed by metal strips (cloisonné) or in holes in the metal (champlevé)□

encaustic obsolete method of painting with a wax medium fixed by heat, e.g. on Egyptian mummy cases□

encephalin or ***endorphin*** hormone in the brain which has the effect of morphine, acting as a natural painkiller, and which can be carried round the body in the blood. See pain◊□

encephalitis inflammation of the brain, such as may occur with malaria, rabies, etc. ***Japanese encephalitis*** is a virus disease found in migrating birds, and transmitted by mosquitoes who first bite the birds and then humans, causing death in 30% of cases. ***Sleeping sickness*** or ***encephalitis lethargica***, which results in coma, was epidemic in the 1920s□

enclosure appropriation of common lands as private property, or the changing of open-field systems to enclosed fields (often used for sheep), as happened in England from the 14th century. It resulted in revolts (1536, 1569, 1607) and depopulation until the mid-19th century□

encyclical letter addressed by the Pope to his bishops. See Pope Paul◊ VI□

encyclopedia book containing articles on many subjects or on aspects of a specific subject. The earliest known was compiled by Pliny◊ the Elder□

Encyclopédistes a group of French scholars who, inspired by the English encyclopedia produced by Ephraim Chambers 1728, wrote (1751-65) their own (see Diderot◊). Religious scepticism and enlightened social and political views were a feature of the work□

endive hardy annual *Cichorium endivia*, family Compositae, grown in England since the 16th century for its leaves, used in salads. See chicory◊□

endocrine gland or ***ductless gland*** organ of body which secretes hormones◊ directly into the bloodstream, in order to regulate many of the metabolic functions. The chief endocrine glands include:

pituitary sometimes called the 'leader of the orchestra' in keeping the body working harmoniously. It lies beneath the floor of the brain within the skull, and secretes: ***adrenocorticotrophic*** (ACTH) ***hormone***, produced under physical stress, which stimulates the adrenal gland (see below), and is used in treating skin diseases, rheumatoid arthritis, etc; ***thyroid stimulating hormone*** (TSH), ***growth hormone*** (GH), see dwarfism◊; ***gonadotrophic hormones*** which stimulate the ovary and testis (see gonadotrophin under fertility◊ drugs), etc. See hypothalamus◊.

thyroid which lies at the front of the throat. Its chief product is ***thyroxine*** (containing iodine), released under the 'command' of the pituitary gland. This controls the body metabolism, stimulates growth, etc; either deficiency or excess causes problems. See goitre◊, hypothyroidism◊, cretinism◊.

endocrine glands

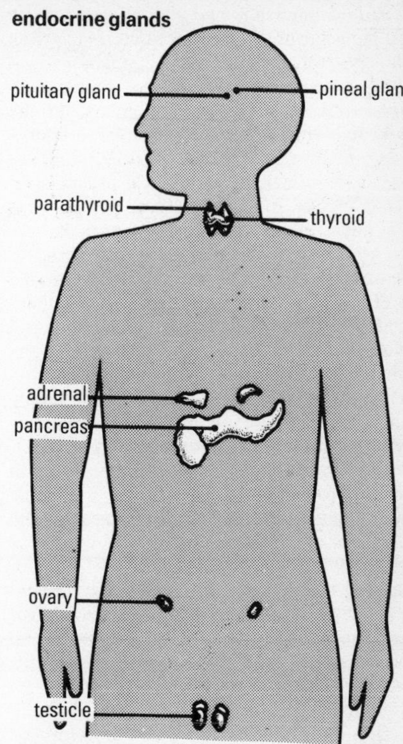

parathyroid closely associated with the thyroid, which secretes ***parathyroid hormone*** (PTH), which controls the distribution of calcium and phosphate in the body.

adrenal pair of glands above the kidneys. The outer section secretes hormones (steroids) related to sexual development, including male muscular strength; the inner section secretes ***adrenaline***, which by constricting blood vessels elsewhere allows more blood to be available for the heart, lungs, and voluntary muscles in 'flight or fight' situations.

pancreas secretes, via the cells called the Islets of Langerhans, the hormone ***insulin***; a deficiency causes diabetes◊, and either pig, cow, or synthetic insulin may be used in treatment (see bacteria◊). The digestive juices also secreted by the pancreas are themselves stimulated by the hormone ***secretin*** (released by the small intestine as food enters from the stomach), the first hormone to be discovered.

sex glands in women the ***ovary*** produces ***oestrogens***, a group of hormones stimulating the menstrual cycle (and oestrus in other female mammals), and ***progesterone*** which prepares the uterus for pregnancy; and in men the ***testes*** produce ***testosterone***, the chief androgen, responsible for producing male characteristics, e.g. facial hair in humans, and the coxcomb in chickens. The synthetic androgens, known as ***anabolic steroids,*** similarly stimulate constructive chemical processes in living creatures, i.e. to produce phenomenal size and strength (as is illegally done in the case of athletes); in women their use tends to develop masculine characteristics. ***Oestradiol*** secreted by the ovary, but also present in men, and at increased level in post-menopausal women, may be linked (at a high level in the blood) with increased risk of heart attack.

Plant hormones or ***phytohormones*** are simple chemical compounds produced by plants (though not in special organs such as glands), which control every aspect of plant growth and reproduction, e.g. even the way most plants reach towards light is the result of the presence of a hormone□

endorphin see encephalin◊□

energy the capacity for doing work◊. ***Potential energy*** (PE) is energy deriving from position: thus a stretched spring ***elastic*** PE; an object raised to a height above the earth's surface, or the water in an elevated reservoir, has a ***gravitational*** PE; a lump of coal and a tank of petrol, together with the oxygen needed for their combustion, have ***chemical*** PE (due to relative positions of atoms). Other sorts of PE include ***electrical*** and ***nuclear***. Moving bodies possess ***kinetic energy*** (KE).

Energy can be converted from one form to another, but the total quantity stays the same (see Conservation◊ Laws). For example, as an apple falls it loses gravitational PE but gains KE. Einstein◊'s Special Theory of Relativity (1905) correlates any gain, E, in KE with a loss, m, in 'rest-mass', by the equation $E=mc^2$, in which c is the speed of light. The equation applies universally, not just to nuclear reactions, though it is only for these that the percentage change in rest-mass is large enough to detect.

Although energy is never lost, after a number of conversions it tends to finish up as KE of random motion of molecules (e.g. of the air) at lowish temperatures. This is 'degraded' energy in that it is difficult to convert back to other forms, whereas so-called ***energy resources*** are stores of convertible energy. ***Non-renewable resources*** include the fossil fuels (coal, air, and gas) and nuclear fission 'fuels' e.g. uranium-235. Burning fossil fuel causes acid rain and is gradually increasing the carbon dioxide content in the atmosphere, with unknown consequences for future generations. Coal-fired power stations also release significant amounts of radioactive materials. Nuclear power stations are not without their hazards. For these reasons ***renewable resources***, depending ultimately on the sun's energy, are receiving increasing attention: hydro-electric schemes are well established, and wind-turbines and tidal systems are being developed. The ultimate non-renewable but almost inexhaustible energy source would be nuclear fusion, but controlled fusion is a long way off. Harnessing resources generally implies converting their energy into electrical form, because electrical energy is easy to convert to other forms, and to transmit from place to place, though not, alas, to store□

Enesco Georges 1881–1955. Romanian violinist composer, the teacher of Menuhin◊. His works include *Romanian Rhapsodies* for orchestra; the opera *Oedipus* 1936 and three symphonies□

Enfield borough of NE Greater London
features includes district of Edmonton, where Keats and Charles Lamb once lived (Lamb and his sister are buried there) and the Bell Inn, referred to in Cowper's 'John Gilpin'; the Royal Small Arms factory (famous for its production of the Enfield rifle); and the Lea Valley, London's first regional park.
population 257 200□

Engadine see under Switzerland◊□

Engels Friedrich 1820–95. German socialist, manager of a Manchester cotton factory. He befriended Marx◊ from 1844, supporting both him and his family, and working out with him the materialist interpretation of history. His books include the *Condition of the Working Class in England in 1844* 1845□

engineering design, construction and maintenance of works, machinery, and installations (civil or military); divisions include space and aeronautical, chemical, civil, electrical, gas, marine, mechanical, mining, metallurgical, municipal, production, radio and structural□

England largest division of the United Kingdom◊.
area 130 763 sq km/50 487 sq mi
capital London
towns Birmingham, Cambridge, Coventry, Leeds, Leicester, Manchester, Newcastle-upon-Tyne, Nottingham, Oxford, Sheffield, York; ports Bristol, Dover, Felixstowe, Harwich, Liverpool, Portsmouth and Southampton
features variability of climate and diversity of scenery; among European countries, only the Netherlands is more densely populated

England: counties

	area in sq km	population (1982)	density (per sq km)	administrative headquarters
Avon	1,338	930,900	696	Bristol
Bedfordshire	1,235	511,900	414	Bedford
Berkshire	1,256	699,500	557	Reading
Buckinghamshire	1,883	580,800	300	Aylesbury
Cambridgeshire	3,409	596,600	175	Cambridge
Cheshire	2,332	931,900	400	Chester
Cleveland	583	566,900	972	Middlesborough
Cornwall	3,546	429,600	121	Truro
Cumbria	6,809	482,500	71	Carlisle
Derbyshire	2,631	910,900	346	Matlock
Devon	6,715	966,200	144	Exeter
Dorset	2,654	604,600	228	Dorchester
Durham	2,436	608,100	250	Durham
East Sussex	1,795	670,600	374	Lewes
Essex	3,674	1,484,100	404	Chelmsford
Gloucestershire	3,117	495,300	159	Gloucester
Hampshire	3,772	1,453,400	393	Winchester
Hereford & Worcester	3,925	636,400	162	Worcester
Hertfordshire	1,634	960,500	588	Hertford
Humberside	3,512	851,000	242	Kingston upon Hull
Kent	3,730	469,700	126	Maidstone
Lancashire	3,005	1,374,100	457	Preston
Leicestershire	2,553	845,600	331	Leicester
Lincolnshire	5,885	550,900	99	Lincoln
London, Greater	1,580	6,745,891	4269	
Manchester, Greater	1,284	2,595,000	2021	
Merseyside	648	1,509,000	2328	Liverpool
Norfolk	5,515	699,200	126	Norwich
Northamptonshire	2,367	543,700	230	Northampton
Northumberland	5,034	296,000	58	Newcastle upon Tyne
North Yorkshire	8,316	661,300	79	Northallerton
Nottinghamshire	2,108	977,000	463	Nottingham
Oxfordshire	2,612	554,700	212	Oxford
Shropshire	3,490	381,000	109	Shrewsbury
Somerset	3,458	427,200	123	Taunton
South Yorkshire	1,562	1,304,100	835	Barnsley
Staffordshire	2,660	1,019,700	383	Stafford
Suffolk	3,807	608,400	160	Ipswich
Surrey	1,655	1,008,500	609	Kingston upon Thames
Tyne & Wear	567	1,130,432	1994	Newcastle
Warwickshire	1,980	480,100	242	Warwick
West Midlands	958	2,686,700	2804	Birmingham
West Sussex	2,017	633,600	314	Chichester
West Yorkshire	2,039	2,018,000	990	Wakefield
Wiltshire	3,481	527,700	151	Trowbridge

exports agricultural (cereals, rape, sugar beet, potatoes); meat and meat products; electronic (especially software), and telecommunications equipment (main centres Berkshire and Cambridge); scientific instruments; carpets, textiles and fashion goods; North Sea◊ oil and gas, petrochemicals, pharmaceuticals, fertilizers; beer; china clay, pottery and porcelain, as well as glass; film and television programmes, and sound recordings. Tourism is important. There are world-wide banking and insurance interests.
currency pound sterling
population 46 221 000
language English, with more than 100 minority languages
religion Christianity, with the Anglican Communion◊ as the established church, plus various Protestant sects, of which the largest is the Methodist◊; Roman Catholicism about 4 000 000; Judaism 410 000; and Islam, a growing minority
government there is no written constitution◊. The Queen (Elizabeth◊ II from 1952) is a constitutional monarch, and is also Head of the Commonwealth◊. There is a Parliament◊ of two Houses: see also local◊ government.
history see England◊: history□

England: history

BC

Old Stone Age remains at Cheddar Caves, Somerset; Kent's Cavern, Torquay, etc.
New Stone Age long barrows◊
Bronze Age round barrows◊
c1800 invasion of the Beaker people who began Stonehenge◊; see also Avebury◊
c450 Iron Age begins
400 Celtic invasion; see hillfort◊; chariot◊ burial; Garton◊ Slack; Yorkshire◊
55 and 54 Julius Caesar's raiding visits

AD

43 Roman conquest begins; see Claudius◊, Agricola◊, Tacitus◊; surviving remains at Bath, Fishbourne (Chichester◊), Hadrian's Wall, Dover, St Alban's (open-air theatre)
407 Roman withdrawal, but partial reoccupations c417–27 and c450
5–7th centuries Anglo-Saxons overran all England except Cornwall and Cumberland, forming independent kingdoms, e.g. Northumbria◊, Mercia◊, Kent◊, Wessex◊
c597 St Augustine◊ converted England to Christianity
829 Egbert◊ of Wessex accepted as overlord of all England
878 Alfred◊ ceded N and E England to the Danish invaders though keeping them out of Wessex
1066 Norman Conquest: see Harold◊, William◊ the Conqueror
1171 Henry◊ II established a colony in Ireland
1215 King John◊ forced to sign Magna◊ Carta
1284 Edward◊ I completed conquest of Wales begun by the Normans
1295 Model◊ Parliament set up
1338–1453 Hundred◊ Years' War with France enabled parliament to secure control of taxation, and, by impeachment, of the king's choice of ministers
1348–9 Black◊ Death rages
1381 social upheaval led to Peasants'◊ Revolt, brutally repressed
1399 Richard◊ II deposed by parliament for absolutism
1414 Lollard◊ revolt repressed
1455–85 Wars of the Roses◊
1497 Henry◊ VII ended the power of the feudal nobility with the suppression of the Yorkist revolts (see Warbeck◊)
1529 Henry◊ VIII became head of the English church
1536–43 Acts of Union united England and Wales after conquest
1547 Edward◊ VI adopted Protestant doctrines
1553 reversion to Roman Catholicism under Mary◊ I
1558 Elizabeth◊ I adopted religious compromise
1588 Spanish◊ Armada attempted to invade England
1603 James◊ I united the English and Scottish crowns; parliamentary dissidence increased
1642-52 Civil◊ War between royalists and parliamentarians
1649 Charles◊ I executed and the Commonwealth set up
1653 Cromwell◊ appointed Lord Protector
1660 restoration of Charles◊ II
1685 Monmouth◊ rebellion
1688 William◊ of Orange invited to take the throne; flight of James◊ II
1707 Act of Union between England and Scotland under Queen Anne◊
For subsequent history see Great◊ Britain: history□

England: sovereigns see table on page 299□

English Channel see Channel◊□

English Civil War see Civil◊ War□

English language one of the western division of Germanic languages, introduced to Britain by the Teutonic invaders of 5–7th centuries (see Anglo◊-Saxons). In the 7th century Old English was still inflectional (see Latin◊) and had a complex Germanic grammar. There were four main dialects, but King Alfred◊'s active interest was to make West Saxon the dominant literary language. Old English was not initially greatly influenced by the 'French' of the Norman conquerors of

England: sovereigns from 900

dynasty	name	date	title
West Saxon Kings	Edward the Elder	901	son of Alfred the Great
	Athelstan	925	son of Edward I
	Edmund	940	half-brother of Athelstan
	Edred	946	brother of Edmund
	Edwy	955	son of Edmund
	Edgar	959	brother of Edwy
	Edward the Martyr	975	son of Edgar
	Ethelred II	978	son of Edgar
	Edmund Ironside	1016	son of Ethelred
Danish Kings	Canute	1016	son of Swelyn
	Hardicanute	1040	son of Canute
	Harold I	1035	son of Canute
West Saxon Kings (restored)	Edward the Confessor	1042	son of Ethelred II
	Harold II	1066	son of Godwin
Norman Kings	William I	1066	
	William II	1087	son of William I
	Henry I	1100	son of William I
	Stephen	1135	son of Adela (daughter of William I)
House of Plantagenet	Henry II	1154	son of Matilda
	Richard I	1189	son of Henry II
	John	1199	son of Henry II
	Henry III	1216	son of John
	Edward I	1272	son of Henry III
	Edward II	1307	son of Edward I
	Edward III	1327	son of Edward II
	Richard II	1377	son of the Black Prince (son of Edward III)
House of Lancaster	Henry IV	1399	son of John of Gaunt
	Henry V	1413	son of Henry IV
	Henry VI	1422	son of Henry V
House of York	Edward IV	1461	son of Edward III
	Richard III	1483	brother of Edward IV
	Edward V	1483	son of Edward IV
House of Tudor	Henry VII	1485	son of Edward III
	Henry VIII	1509	son of Henry VII
	Edward VI	1547	son of Henry VIII
	Mary I	1553	daughter of Henry VIII
	Elizabeth I	1558	daughter of Henry VIII
House of Stuart	James I	1603	Great-grandson of Margaret
The Commonwealth	Charles I	1625	son of James I
House of Stuart (restored)	Charles II	1660	son of Charles I
	James II	1685	son of Charles I
	William III and Mary	1689	son of Mary (daughter of Charles I)/ daughter of James II
	Anne	1702	daughter of James II
House of Hanover	George I	1714	son of Sophia (granddaughter of James I)
	George II	1727	son of George I
	George III	1760	son of Frederick (son of George II)
	George IV	1820	son of George III
	William IV	1830	son of George III
	Victoria	1837	daughter of Edward (son of George III)
House of Saxe-Coburg	Edward VII	1901	son of Victoria
House of Windsor	George V	1910	son of Edward VII
	Edward VIII	1936	son of George V
	George VI	1936	son of George V
	Elizabeth II	1952	daughter of George VI

1066, but interaction with the closely related language of the Danes (see under Vikings◊ and Denmark◊) who first raided, then settled about the country, was probably the factor which led to the wholesale dropping of gender and case endings, etc. (which survive today in German, and other Germanic languages). Old English emerged in the 12th century as a simplified, streamlined language. Under the influence of Chaucer◊, the dialect of London established a lead (reinforced by the setting up of the first printing press in London by Caxton◊ 1477), as an essential 'standard' for easy communication, though local dialects survived. However, Norman French did in time greatly influence the vocabulary of the church, government, and the law, and made easier the incorporation of Latin and Greek forms when new words for the various sciences were needed from the 17th century. Subsequent borrowings have been world-wide, and the influence of the USA in the 20th century has been very strong. English has also in the past two centuries developed new forms (not only vocabulary) where it has become the first language of other countries, as in the USA, and in forms such as pidgin◊, and has established a lead as the world's 'second language'. See also language◊□

engraving see print◊□

Eniwetok see Marshalls◊□

Ennis county town of County Clare, Republic of Ireland; population 6000□

Enniskillen county town of County Fermanagh, N Ireland; population 7000□

Ennius Quintus 239–169BC earliest Latin epic poet, author of *Annales* on the history of Rome□

Enosis see Cyprus◊□

Enschede textile town in the Netherlands; population 144 350□

Ensor James 1860–1949. Belgian artist, noted for macabre satire and dissonant colour, e.g. *Entrance of Christ into Brussels* 1888□

entail largely obsolete settlement of land on a successive line of inheritors, either 'general' (to the eldest child of either sex), or 'special' (according to some specific arrangement)□

Entebbe former administrative headquarters of Uganda 1894–1962; population 22 000□

Entebbe Incident hijacking in 1976 of a French aircraft to Entebbe by a Palestinian liberation group; Israeli hostages were rescued by Israeli aircraft□

Entente Cordiale 'friendly understanding' between Britain and France 1904 recognizing Britain's interest in Egypt and that of France in Morocco□

enterprise zone zone in the UK from 1980, exempt from rates, development tax, etc, to encourage regional investment□

entomology see insect◊□

Enugu coal and steel town in S Nigeria; population 187 000□

Enver Pasha 1881–1922. Turkish soldier, who led the Young Turk revolution of 1908□

enzyme biological catalyst able to convert one chemical to another quickly, and without itself being destroyed, e.g. those in yeast, used in making bread and alcohol, and those within the human body which digest food, e.g. pepsin in the stomach. Bulk production of enzymes from bacteria, and increasingly the re-use of pure enzymes bonded to glass, etc, underpins the manufacture of detergents, low-cost processed cheese, etc. In medicine enzymes may be used to correct disorders of the body's metabolism, etc.□

Eos see Aurora◊□

Epaminondas c420–362BC. Theban general. He twice defeated the Spartans, at Leuctra 371 and Mantinea, when he fell at the moment of victory□

Épernay town in NE France, centre of the champagne industry; population 31 000□

ephedrine drug allied to adrenalin and benzedrine, derived from the *Ephedra* genus of shrubs; used for asthma, hay fever□

Ephesus ancient Greek seaport in Asia Minor, with a temple of Artemis◊ destroyed by the Goths 262AD. St Paul visited the city. It is one of the world's largest archaeological sites, and in the 2nd century AD had a population of 300 000□

epic long narrative poem of great events. See Gilgamesh◊, Homer◊, Mahabharata◊, Beowulf◊, Virgil◊, Milton◊, Tasso◊□

Epictetus c60–110AD. Greek Stoic philosopher. Banished by Domitian◊ from Rome in 89AD, he was an advocate of the brotherhood of man and abandonment of self-interest□

Epicureanism system advocated by Epicurus◊: soundly based human happiness is the highest good, so that its rational pursuit is to be adopted. See Lucretius◊□

Epicurus 341–270BC. Greek philosopher, advocate of Epicureanism◊ at Athens from 306BC□

Epidaurus ancient Greek port in the NE Peloponnese, with a temple of Aesculapius◊. The buildings included a theatre (4th century BC)□

epilepsy disorder of nervous system involving attacks of loss or alteration of consciousness, usually with convulsions. It is controlled by drugs. Sufferers included Julius Caesar, Byron, Dostoevsky□

Epinal textile town in E France; population 42 000□

Epiphany feast (6 Jan) of the Christian Church, celebrating the coming of the Magi, and the manifestation of Christ to the world. It marks the end of the Christmas festivities, and many ceremonies were linked with the 'Twelfth Night' after Christmas□

epiphyte plant which grows on another for support, but derives no nourishment from it, e.g. lichens, mosses, ferns, orchids□

Epirus district of ancient Greece, now divided between Albania and NW Greece□

epistle formal letter, as in the New Testament (St Paul◊), and in literature (Horace◊, Boileau◊, Dryden◊, and Pope◊)□

epoxy resin see plastic◊□

Epping Forest see Essex◊□

Epsilon Aurigae see under star◊□

Epsom town in Surrey, England; population 70 000. In the 17th century it was a spa producing Epsom◊ salts; there is a racecourse, and the site of Henry VIII's palace of Nonsuch was excavated 1959□

Epsom salts hydrated magnesium sulphate, $MgSO_4.7H_2O$, a saline purgative; originally produced at Epsom◊□

Epstein Sir Jacob 1880–1959. American-born British sculptor. His work expressed human emotion without regard to conventions of form, and aroused fierce controversy, e.g. the tomb of Oscar Wilde in Paris 1901, the *Rima* memorial to W H Hudson in Hyde Park 1925; *Genesis* 1931; the aluminium *Christ in Majesty* for Llandaff Cathedral, 1957; and *St Michael and the Devil* for Coventry Cathedral 1959. His portrait busts, e.g. Vaughan Williams and Einstein, were more romantic in style□

equator the ***terrestrial equator*** is the great circle whose plane is perpendicular to earth's axis, i.e. to the line joining the poles; length 40 076 km/24901.8 mi. The ***celestial equator*** or equinoctial is the circle in which the plane of the terrestrial equator intersects the celestial sphere□

Equatorial Guinea Republic of
area 28 100 sq km/10 852 sq mi
capital Malabo
features comprises mainland Rio Muni, plus the small islands of Corisco, Elobey Grande and Elobey Chico, and Bioko Island (formerly Fernando Po) together with Pagalu Island (formerly Annobon).
exports cocoa, coffee, bananas, timber
currency ekpwele
population 275 000
language Spanish, (official); pidgin English is widely spoken, and on Pagalu (whose people were formerly slaves of the Portuguese), a Portuguese dialect.

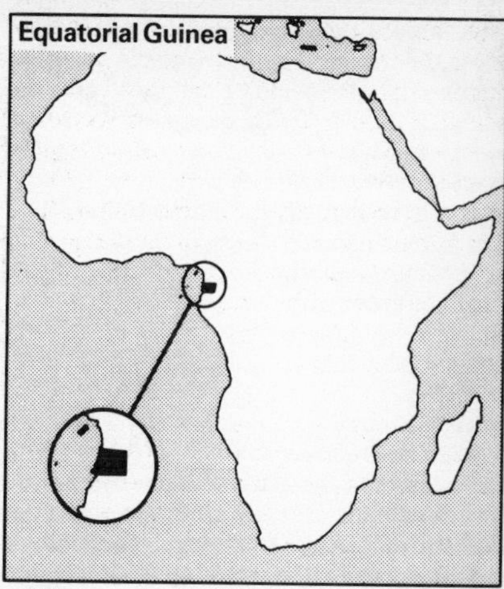

religion nominally Christian, mainly Catholic, but in 1978 Roman Catholicism was banned.
government executive president (Lietenant Colonel Teodoro Obiang Nguema Mbasogo from 1979, confirmed in office for seven years from 1982) with cabinet and national assembly.
recent history formerly two overseas provinces of Spanish Guinea, the country achieved independence in 1968 as Equatorial Guinea. The first president, Francisco Macias Nguema, was appointed for life. He was deposed and executed in 1979□

equestrianism horsemanship, especially as practised under International Equestrian Federation rules when it is an Olympic sport. It comprises: ***dressage*** or ***haute école*** (high school), exercises in which the horse is guided with minimum use of reins; ***cross-country***, done at speed; ***show-jumping***◊. The Royal International Horse Show, Wembley, is a major annual event□

equinox the point in spring (vernal) and autumn at which the sun crosses the celestial equator◊, so that the day and night are of approximately equal length□

equities stocks and shares◊, which do not (like debentures and preference shares) pay interest at fixed rates□

equity see under law◊□

Erasmus Desiderius c1469–1536. Dutch humanist. Illegitimate son of Rogerius Gerardus (whose story is told in Charles Reade◊'s novel, *The Cloister and the Hearth*), he himself adopted the Latin-Greek name which means 'beloved'. In 1499 he first visited England, meeting Linacre, More, and Colet, and for a time taught at Cambridge. His pioneer edition of the original Greek New Testament was published in 1516. More than 3000 of his letters have survived□

Erastianism theory, named from German-Swiss theologian Thomas Erastus 1534–83, that the Church should be subordinate to the State□
Erato see Muses◊□
Eratosthenes c276–c194BC. Greek geographer whose map of the ancient world was the first to contain lines of latitude◊ and longitude◊; and who calculated the earth's circumference with an error of less than 200 m□
Erbium element
symbol Er
atomic number 68
physical description metal
features one of the lanthanide◊ series
uses an erbium laser is used in eye surgery□
Erebus in Greek mythology, the god of darkness and the intermediate region between upper earth and Hades◊□
Erebus Mount. See under Ross Sea◊□
Erfurt industrial city (textiles, typewriters, electrical goods) in E Germany; population 210 687. Luther was a monk here□
ergonomics use of engineering skills to improve human performance at work and play by removing sources of muscular stress and general fatigue, presenting data and control panels in easy-to-view form, making office furniture comfortable, etc.□
ergosterol plant sterol which gives rise to vitamin D under the action of ultra-violet rays; the chief commercial source is yeast. It is present in fats of animals, sunlight (ultra-violet rays) converting it to vitamin D. A deficiency of vitamin D affects bone formation and causes rickets◊□
ergot see under Ascomycetes□
Erhard Ludwig 1897–1977. German statesman, whose policy of 'social free enterprise' (*Marktwirtschaft*) during his chancellorship 1963–6 resulted in the West German 'economic miracle' after World War II□
Eric 'the Red' c940–1010AD. Son of a Norwegian chieftain, banished from Iceland for homicide c982, who allegedly discovered Greenland□
erica see heather◊□
ericaceae family of dicotyledenous flowering plants; they are widely distributed in the cool and temperate parts of the world and include heather◊, rhododendron◊, bilberry◊, azalea◊□
Ericsson Leif. Norse explorer, son of Eric◊ 'the Red', who traditionally sailed W from Greenland c1000AD to 'Vinland' (N America). Remains of a Viking settlement were found near the fishing village of L'Anse-aux-Meadows, Newfoundland, in 1963□
Eridu see Sumerian civilization under Iraq◊□
Erie industrial city and port on Lake Erie, Pennsylvania, USA; population 119 125□
Erie Lake. See Great◊ Lakes□
Erigena Johannes Scotus c815–77. Medieval philosopher who tried to combine Christianity and Neoplatonism◊ as head of the school at Charles◊ the Bald's court in France from c847□
Erin poetic name for Ireland, derived from the Gaelic□
Eritrea province of N Ethiopia.
area 118 500 sq km/45 745 sq mi
capital Asmara
towns ports Assab and Massawa are Ethiopia's outlet to the sea
features coastline on the Red Sea 1000 km/670 mi
exports coffee, salt
currency birr
population 2 295 800
language Amharic (official)
religion Islam
recent history an Italian colony 1889–1941, when it came under British military administration until 1952. Eritrea was then federated with Ethiopia by United Nations decision. It enjoyed autonomy 1952–62, but its reduction to a region prompted a demand for independence, and the various Eritrean Liberation fronts continued resistance in 1986 (aided by the conservative Gulf states), and in some cooperation with guerrillas in Tigré province□
Erivan alternative transliteration of Yerevan◊□
Erlangen industrial town (textiles, electrical goods), in Bavaria, W Germany; population 100 900□
ermine small European mammal similar to the weasel◊; its white winter coat is used in ceremonial robes□
Ernie see saving◊□
Ernst Max 1891–1976. German Surrealist painter. An active Dadaist◊, he went to Paris in 1922, where he helped found the Surrealist◊ movement in 1924□
Eros in Greek mythology, boy-god of love (Roman ***Cupid***), son of Aphrodite◊, and armed with bow and arrows; he fell in love with Psyche◊□
Eros see asteroids◊□
Erse alternative word for Gaelic◊□
Erskine Thomas, 1st Baron Erskine 1750–1832. British barrister, noted for his defence of Lord George Gordon◊, Thomas Paine◊, and Queen Caroline◊; Lord Chancellor 1806–7□
erysipelas skin disease caused by streptococcal infection, and producing a swollen, blistered red patch and general fever□

ESA abbreviation for European◊ Space Agency□

Esarhaddon d. 669BC. King of Assyria from 680, when he succeeded his father Sennacherib◊. He conquered Egypt 671–4□

Esau in Old Testament, the son of Isaac◊, and elder twin of Jacob◊, to whom he sold his birth-right for a 'mess of red pottage'□

escalator a moving staircase which carries passengers between floors/levels. The first escalator was exhibited in Paris in 1900□

escape velocity the velocity an object (e.g. a space vehicle) requires to 'escape' from a planet against its gravitational pull without further power: for earth 11.3 km/7 mi per second; moon 2.5 km/1.5 mi per second; Mars 5 km/3.1 mi per second; Jupiter 60 km/37 mi per second□

Escaut French form of Scheldt◊□

Escher M(aurits) C(ornelis) 1902–72. Dutch graphic artist, specializing in effects of paradox and illusion□

Escoffier Auge 1846–1935. French chef of Savoy Hotel, London; deviser of *peach Melba*□

Escorial El. See Madrid◊□

Eskimo see Inuit◊□

Eskisehir industrial town in Turkey, noted for meerschaum pipes; population 309 450□

esparto see grasses◊□

Esperanto international artificial language invented in 1887 by Dr L L Zamenhof of Warsaw 1859–1917□

Esquimalt see Vancouver◊ Island□

essay short literary piece of prose. The first essayist was Montaigne◊. Famous essayists include Bacon, Addison, Steele, Hazlitt, De Quincey, Macaulay, George Orwell, F R Leavis, T S Eliot□

Essen industrial city (textiles, chemicals, electrical goods) in North Rhine-Westphalia, W Germany; population 650 200. It was the former home of the Krupp armament works, and the Krupp home (Villa Hugel) is preserved□

Essene a member of a sect of pre-Christian Jewish monastic ascetics in Palestine; St John the Baptist and Christ himself may have lived among them for a time at Khirbet Qumran◊, a site (excavated 1951) in the hills to the NW of the Dead◊ Sea occupied from the late 2nd century BC until the buildings were burnt down in 68AD. The Dead◊ Sea Scrolls comprise their library, hidden for safe-keeping and never reclaimed□

Essequibo chief river of Guyana◊, where the Kaietur Fall is the chief feature of the Kaietur National Park; length 960 km/600 mi□

Essex county in SE England
area 3672 sq km/1417 sq mi

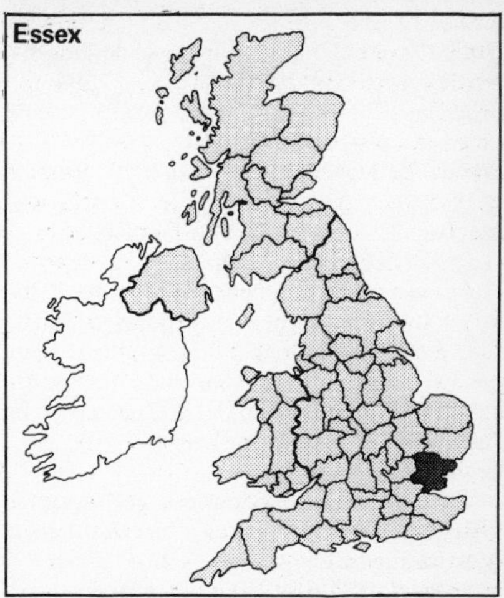

towns administrative headquarters Chelmsford; Colchester; ports Harwich, Tilbury; resorts Southend, Clacton
features former royal hunting ground of Epping Forest (controlled from 1882 by the City of London); the marshy coastal headland of The Naze; birdlife at Maplin Sands
products dairying, cereals, fruit
population 1 482 600□

Essex Robert Devereux, 2nd Earl of Essex 1566–1601. English soldier-politician. He served in the Netherlands with distinction and became a favourite of Elizabeth I from 1587. In 1599 he became Lieutenant of Ireland but signed a truce with Tyrone in Ulster and returned without permission to England. He was forbidden to return to court, and when he marched into London at the head of his supporters, was arrested and beheaded for treason□

Essex Robert Devereux, 3rd Earl of Essex 1591–1646. English soldier, eldest son of the 2nd Earl. He commanded the Parliamentary army at the battle of Edgehill in 1642 (see Civil◊ War), and resigned in 1645 after a disastrous campaign in Cornwall□

ester organic compound formed by the reaction between an alcohol and an acid, with the elimination of water. Esters occur in explosives, plastics, photographic films, vegetable and animal fats and oils, soaps, paints and varnishes, flavourings, and perfume□

Esther in Old Testament, the wife of the Persian king Ahasuerus◊, who prevented the extermination of her people by the vizier Haman, as celebrated in the Jewish festival of Purim□

Estonia constituent republic of the Soviet Union from 1940.
area 45 100 sq km/17 400 sq mi

capital Tallinn
features mild climate, lakes and marshes in a partly forested plain.
products oil from shale, wood products, flax, dairy and pig products.
population 1 507 000, Estonian 65%, Russian 28%
language Estonian, allied to Finnish
religion traditionally Lutheran
recent history an independent republic 1920–40, Estonia was then incorporated in the USSR. As in the other Baltic republics, there has been nationalist dissent since 1980, influenced by Poland's example, and prompted by the influx of Russian workers and officials□

etching see print◊□

ethane colourless, odourless gas, formula C_2H_6, chiefly important as a fuel in the form of natural gas□

Ethelbert c552–616. King of Kent, England. Succeeding his father Eormenric in 560, he extended his rule over all England S of the Humber. Married to a Christian (Bertha), he received St Augustine in 597, and was later baptized□

Ethelred I d. 871. King of Wessex, England, elder brother of Alfred◊ the Great. He succeeded his brother Ethelbert in 866, and warred against the Danes□

Ethelred II 968–1016. King of England, nicknamed the 'Unready', i.e. 'lacking in foresight'. Son of King Edgar◊, he succeeded his murdered half-brother, Edward◊ the Martyr, in 978. He tried to buy off the Danish raiders by paying 'Danegeld', and precipitated war with Sweyn◊ of Denmark by his massacre of Danish settlers□

ether medium formerly thought to occupy all space, and to enable electromagnetic waves to be propagated; see under Albert Michelson◊□

ether (chemistry) ($C_2H_5OC_2H_5$, strictly called diethyl ether) colourless, volatile, inflammable liquid, prepared by treating ethanol with concentrated sulphuric acid. It is used as an anaesthetic, and as a solvent in the extraction of oils, resins, alkaloids, etc.□

Etherege Sir George c1635–c1691. British Restoration dramatist, known for his comedy *The Man of Mode* 1676□

Ethical Movement movement claiming morality as the essence of religion, founded by Felix Adler, who established an Ethical Society in New York in 1876; in 1888 the first English branch was formed, later the South Place Ethical Society□

ethics philosophical assessment of the right and wrong of human conduct. The problems were discussed by Plato, Aristotle, Epicurus, Stoics◊, and the 'Christian ethic' is chiefly a combination of the two first-named with the New Testament. Great modern ethical philosophers include Hobbes, Hume, Bentham (see utilitarianism◊), Kant, G E Moore, John Dewey, R M Hare□

Ethiopia Republic of (formerly also known as *Abyssinia*)

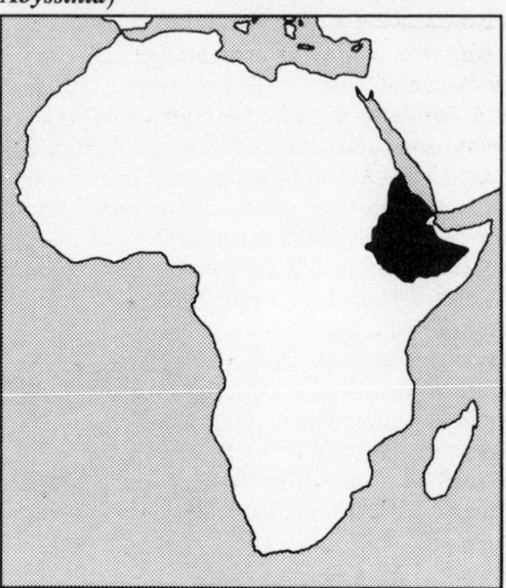

area 1 000 000 sq km/395 000 sq mi
capital Addis Ababa
towns Asmara (capital of Eritrea◊), Dire Dawa; ports are Massawa, Assab
features Danakil and Ogaden deserts, Blue Nile; ancient remains at Aksum, Gondar, Lalibela, etc; only African country to retain its independence during the colonial period.
exports coffee, pulses, oilseeds, hides and skins
currency birr
population 30 400 000, dominant Amhara and Tigréans 30%, Gallas 40%
language Amharic (official); Tigre, Galla, Arabic
religion Christianity (Ethiopian Orthodox Church, which has had its own patriarch since 1976) 50%, Sunni Islam 50%
famous people Queen of Sheba, Prester John, Menelik II
government Unitary Socialist one-party state, with a Provisional Military Administrative Council (The Derg) established 1974 (chairman Lieutenant Colonel Mengistu Haile Mariam).
recent history independent from the 11th century, Ethiopia was safeguarded by Menelik◊ II's defeat of the Italians in 1896 from the 'scramble for Africa' in the 19th century, but Mussolini conquered the country 1935–6. The Emperor, Haile Selassie◊, was enabled to return by the Allied defeat of the Italians in 1941, but was deposed in a military coup in 1974. Eritrea◊'s struggle for independence

from Ethiopia is supported by Saudi Arabia and Sudan, and there has been almost continuous fighting since 1977 against Somalia, which seeks the return of the Ogaden◊. Famine is widespread, and during 1985-6 there was a world-wide campaign led by Bob Geldof◊ to raise money for relief□

ethnology branch of anthropology dealing with the social, economic and cultural aspects of mankind□

ethology the comparative study of animal behaviour, in the natural environment, founded by K Lorenz and K von Frisch◊.

In recent years ethology has thrown light on the development of human behaviour, intelligence and consciousness. Animals attempt to maximize the number of young which will enable their own genes to survive in a new generation. A male will mate with as many females as possible where food supplies are abundant enough for all his young to survive, and a female may mate with more than one male to have extra food providers for her young. The same motive leads to collaboration and self-sacrifice to protect young of sisters, brothers, etc., who share the same genes. Higher intelligence seems to arise more among animals that are hunters, and who need to collaborate and adjust constantly to changing situations, rather than among herbivores, whose patterns of feeding, etc., are static. Its spectacular advance among primates◊ seems due to their complex social relationships which depend on acute observation, and self-consciousness, i.e. an ape (but not a monkey) may recognize itself in a mirror. See also formative◊ causation□

ethyl alcohol (ethanol, C_2H_5OH) colourless liquid with a pleasant odour (see alcoholic◊ liquor). The vapour forms an explosive mixture with air and may be used as an additive in high-compression internal combustion engines (gasahol). Used chiefly as a beverage (alcohol) and an industrial solvent□

Etna see under Sicily◊□

Eton town in Berkshire, England; population 5000. ***Eton College*** most famous of England's public◊ schools, was founded 1440 by Henry VI. Old Etonians include Chatham, Wellington, Gladstone, Eden, Macmillan, and Lord Home□

Etruscan member of an ancient people of N Italy whose cities in Etruria (modern Tuscany) reached the height of their power c500BC. They were defeated by the Carthaginians 474BC in a naval battle off Cumae, their northern conquests were lost to the Celts c400BC, and they were gradually superseded by Rome. They produced remarkable sculpture, pottery, bronzes, and mural painting, but their Indo-European language, despite a number of inscriptions, is very imperfectly known□

Etty William 1787–1849. British artist, a student of Sir Thomas Lawrence◊. He is celebrated for his nudes□

etymology branch of linguistics dealing with the origin and development of words, both sound and meaning□

Euboea largest of the Greek Aegean islands; 3755 sq km/1480 sq mi; population 165 400. Capital Chalcis, linked by bridge with the mainland□

eucalyptus genus of tall Australian evergreens ('gum trees'), family Myrtaceae. They include timber trees, e.g. ***jarrah*** *E marginata*, which is dark, close-grained and durable and c16 m/50 ft high; ***karri*** *E diversicolor,* which reaches 35 m/100 ft, and the ***ironbarks,*** e.g. ***redgum*** *E resinifera*, noted for their rough hard bark. They have blue/green aromatic glabrous leaves and trunks which exude gum. Oil of eucalyptus comes from the ***blue gum*** *E globulus*; and methanol obtained from eucalyptus wood is a potential petrol substitute□

eucaryote class of living cell in which there is a defined nucleus. See Procaryote◊, bacteria◊□

Eucharist chief Christian sacrament (Greek 'thanksgiving'), also known as the Lord's Supper, Holy Communion, and (amongst Roman Catholics, who believe that the bread and wine are transubstantiated, i.e. converted to the body and blood of Christ) the Mass. The doctrine of ***transubstantiation*** was rejected by Protestant Churches at the Reformation□

Euclid c300BC. Greek mathematician, who systematized previous work in geometry, his texts remaining in school use for 2000 years□

Eugène of Savoy, Prince 1663–1736. Austrian general. Refused a commission by Louis XIV, he joined the Austrian army, defended Vienna against the Turks in 1683, and expelled them from Hungary by the Battle of Zenta 1697. He aided Marlborough's victories against the French in the War of the Spanish◊ Succession (Blenheim, Oudenarde, and Malplaquet). He again defeated the Turks in 1716–18□

eugenics science founded by Sir Francis Galton◊ (Greek 'well-born') and aiming at the improvement of the physical and mental quality of a people by agencies under social control□

Eugénie 1826–1920. Empress of the French. Of Spanish birth, she married the future Napoleon◊ III in 1853, encouraged his intervention in Mexico, and after Sedan◊ settled with him in England□

Euler Leonhard 1707–83. Swiss mathematician who studied under Bernoulli◊. He developed the theory of differential equations, the calculus of variations, etc.□

Eumenides see Furies◊□

eunuch castrated male employed in a harem in the East, often being promoted to high offices of state in China, India, Persia, etc. The Italian ***castrati*** were boy singers castrated to preserve their singing voices; Pope Leo XIII ended the practice in 1878□

Eupen-et-Malmédy region of Belgium round these two towns, Prussian from 1814 until it became Belgian in 1920 after a plebiscite; there was fierce fighting here in the German Ardennes offensive Dec 1944□

euphonium see under brass◊ instruments□

Euphrates river rising in E Turkey, and, after flowing through Syria and Iraq, linking with the Tigris to form the Shatt-el-Arab◊; length 3600 km/2235mi. Babylon◊, Eridu◊ and Ur◊ were on its course□

Euratom see under European◊ Community□

Eureka plan for European Technological Cooperation, 1985. See under Archimedes◊□

Eureka Stockade see Ballarat◊□

eurhythmics see Jaques◊-Dalcroze, Émile□

Euripides c484–407BC. Greek dramatist. A realist, he was bitterly attacked for his unorthodox 'impiety' and sympathy for the despised: slaves, beggars and women. He went into voluntary exile from Athens to Macedonia at the end of his life. He wrote more than 80 plays, of which 19 survive, the most famous being: *Alcestis* 438, *Medea* 431, *Andromache* 420, *Trojan Women* 415, *Electra* 413, *Iphigenia in Tauris* 413, *Iphigenia in Aulis* 405, *Bacchae* 405□

Europa in Greek mythology, princess of Tyre, carried off by Zeus◊ (in the form of a bull); she personifies the continent of Europe□

Europa (astronomy) a satellite of Jupiter◊□

Europe second smallest continent, formed of the land W of the line of the Ural mountains; 8% of earth's surface, 14.5% of world population

area 10 400 000 sq km/4 000 000 sq mi

largest cities (over 2 million) Moscow, London, Istanbul, Leningrad, Madrid, Rome, Athens, Kiev, Budapest, Paris

features North European Plain on which London, Paris, Berlin, and Moscow stand; Central European Highlands (Sierra Nevada, Pyrenees, Alps, Apennines, Carpathians, Balkans) and Scandinavian highland, which takes in the Scottish Highlands, etc; highest point Mount Elbruz in Caucasus mountains. Rivers (over 1000 miles) Volga, Don, Dnieper, Danube; lakes (over 2000 sq mi) Ladoga, Onega, Vanern. Climate ranges from the variable NW, modified by the Gulf Stream, through the Central Zone with warm summers and cold winters, which become bitterly cold in Eastern Europe, to the Mediterranean zone with comparatively mild winters and hot summers. The last is the richest zone for plant life, but animal species have long been reduced everywhere by the predominance of man.

exports mainly items of high technology, engineering skill, etc.

population 702 300 000,

languages Indo-European

religion Christianity (Protestantism, Roman Catholicism, Greek Orthodox), Islam

history see Europe◊: history□

European Community an organization which comprises the European Coal and Steel Community 1952; European Atomic Energy Community/Euratom 1957; and European Economic Community/EEC/ popularly 'Common Market', both the last-named created under the two ***Treaties of Rome*** signed there Mar 1957. Since 1967 they have shared the institutions of ***The Commission***, which initiates action (president Jacques Delors from 1986); ***The Council of Ministers***, which decides on the Commission's proposals (both with headquarters in Brussels); ***European Parliament◊;*** and ***European Court of Justice*** (headquarters Luxembourg), which interprets the Rome Treaties. Original members were Belgium, France, W Germany, Italy, Luxembourg, Netherlands; subsequently Denmark, Republic of Ireland, UK 1973 (Norway withdrew her application 1972); Greece 1981; Spain and Portugal 1986□

European Democratic Group see Conservative◊ Party□

European Free Trade Association (EFTA) an organisation established 1959 and now consisting of Austria, Finland, Iceland, Norway, Sweden, and Switzerland. There are no import duties between members□

European Monetary System established 1979, the EMS is a voluntary system of semi-fixed exchange rates based on the ecu (***European currency unit***), which is a weighted average of all the currencies in the system. Most EEC countries (except the UK and Greece) are members□

European Space Agency (ESA) organization established 1975 which encourages weather, telecommunications and other space programmes including the launching of geostationary satellites by the consortium Ariane-Space◊ 1980□

Europe: history
BC
3000 Bronze Age civilizations: Minoan◊, Mycenaean◊
6–4th centuries Greek civilization at its height; Alexander◊
3rd century Rome in control of the Italian peninsula
146 Greece a Roman province, and Carthage◊ destroyed
1st century Augustus made the Rhine and Danube the Roman Empire's northern frontiers; see Celts◊
AD
1st century Britain brought within the Roman Empire
2nd century Roman Empire ceased to expand
4th century Christianity the established religion of the Roman Empire
4–6th centuries W Europe overrun by Anglo-Saxons, Franks, Goths, Lombards
7–8th centuries Christendom threatened by the Moors◊ (Arabs)
800 Charlemagne◊ given title of Emperor by the Pope; (see Holy Roman Empire◊)
1073 Gregory◊ VII begins 200 years of conflict between Empire and Papacy
1096–1272 Crusades◊
12th century setting up of German, Flemish and Italian city states, which in the 14–15th centuries fostered the Renaissance◊, which flowered in these new nation states
1453 Constantinople◊ captured by the Turks
16–17th centuries dominated by rivalry of France and the Hapsburgs◊, the Protestant Reformation◊, and the Catholic Counter-Reformation◊
17th century absolute monarchy came to prevail (Louis◊ XIV) in Europe, although in England supremacy of Parliament established by Civil◊ War
18th century War of the Austrian◊ Succession and Seven◊ Years War ended in the loss of the French colonial empire to Britain, and the establishment of Prussia as Europe's emergent power
1789–95 French Revolution led to the united opposition of the rest of Europe in the Revolutionary◊ and Napoleonic◊ Wars
1821–9 Greek War of Independence marked the end of Turkish control of the Balkans◊
1848 year of revolutions (see Louis◊ Philippe, Metternich◊, Risorgimento◊)
1914–1918 World◊ War I arose from the Balkan Question, Franco-German rivalry, and colonial differences; it destroyed the Austrian and Turkish empires and initiated that of the Soviet Union
1933 Hitler◊ came to power
1939–45 World◊ War II resulted in decline of European colonial rule in Africa, Asia, etc.; full emergence of Soviet power, and the marshalling of post-war resistance under the aegis of the USA (NATO◊), the Cold War
1956 Khrushchev◊'s denunciation of Stalin◊ ended unquestioned Soviet political leadership
1957 establishment of the European Economic Community, the 'Common Market', marked the beginning of European independence of the USA
1973 enlargement of the European Community to include Britain, etc.
1979 first direct elections to the European Parliament
1985 accession to power in the Soviet Union of Mikhail Gorbachev marked an apparent relaxation of political and economic bureaucracy□

europium element
symbol 63
physical description metal
features one of the lanthanide◊ series; it is extremely rare
uses in lasers and colour television tubes□

Euskadi see Basque◊ Country□

Eustachio Bartolommeo c1520–74. Italian anatomist whose name was given to the *Eustachian tubes* leading from the middle ear on either side to the pharynx◊□

Euterpe see Muses◊□

euthanasia painless killing of the incurably ill, usually with their consent (Greek 'to die well'). Voluntary euthanasia bills were defeated in the UK 1969 and 1976□

eutrophication over-enrichment of lake waters by chemicals from sewage, industrial waste, fertilizers, etc. Plant life overgrows and extinguishes animal life□

evangelicalism the beliefs of some Protestant Sects which stress 'fundamental' Biblical authority, 'faith', and the personal commitment of the 'born-again' experience. See Billy Graham◊, Jimmy Carter◊, Bob Dylan◊□

evangelist a person travelling among the heathen to spread the Christian gospel, and especially the authors of the four Gospels□

Evans Sir Arthur John 1851–1941. British archaeologist, whose excavation of Knossos◊ in Crete, resulted in the discovery of the Minoan◊ civilization□

Evans Dame Edith 1888–1976. British actress, best-remembered as Lady Bracknell in *The Importance of Being Earnest* 1939□

Evansville industrial city (pharmaceuticals, plastics) in Indiana, USA; population 287 600. Abraham Lincoln◊ spent his boyhood in nearby Spencer County□

Eve wife of Adam◊; see also Lilith◊□

Evelyn John 1620–1706. English diarist 1640–1706, who was much in favour under Charles II. He was a friend of Pepys◊, and a founder of the Royal◊ Society□

evening primrose American plant in the family Onagraceae, especially *Oenothera biennis* of which the bright yellow flowers die the next day. It is grown as a field crop for the oil it produces, which is used in treating eczema and pre-menstrual tension□

eventing sport (horse trials) giving an all-round test of a horse in a three-day event: dressage, testing a horse's response to control; speed and endurance across country; and finally a modified showjumping contest□

Everest Mount. See under Himalayas◊□

Everglades see Florida◊□

everlasting flower flower head with coloured bracts which retains its colour when cut and dried, e.g. *Ammobium, Helichrysum, Xeranthemum* species□

Evesham town in Hereford and Worcester, England; population 14 150. Fruit and vegetables from the fertile ***Vale of Evesham*** are canned□

Evesham Battle of 1265. See Barons'◊ Wars□

evolution the slow process of change by which all living things have come to be as we know them. That there has been such a process, rather than an arbitrary 'moment' of creation by a deity, is an idea which can be traced to Lucretius◊, but it was not seriously reconsidered until the 18–19th centuries (see Erasmus Darwin◊, Sir Charles Lyell◊, J B Lamarck◊, Charles Darwin◊). Charles Darwin assigned the major role in evolution to natural selection ('the survival of the fittest'), but although the general concept of evolution is not disputed by scientists, the precise method is uncertain. Darwin envisaged minute changes over millennia producing new species ('gradualism'). One of the factors in this would be mixing of genes during sexual reproduction. However, the fossil record is very incomplete, and it now seems (e.g. by the study of fossil snails at Lake Turkana◊) that long periods of stability may have been interspersed by comparatively short periods of rapid change ('punctuated equilibrium'), a suggestion that tends to be supported by molecular biology in its study of genetic material (see DNA◊, and Barbara McClintock◊). To adaptive 'selection', it seems necessary to add chance increase of particular genes in a population (known as 'drift') and also the complex process by which change of genetic make-up in a population can occur in unison ('molecular drive'). Motoo Kimura of Japan has suggested in his 'neutral theory of evolution' that most evolutionary changes at the molecular level are achieved less by selection of advantageous mutation than by random fixation of mutations neither advantageous nor disadvantageous, but which may gain importance if the environment changes, and so become subject to Darwinian selection. Another line of thought suggests that viruses might pick up genetic material from one species, and later deposit it in the chromosomes of cells of hosts of another species. See also ethology◊□

evolution convergent. The development by widely separated life forms, e.g. fish and cephalopods◊, of remarkably similar solutions to the physiological problems of existence. The eye structure and double circulatory system of the octopus are closer to those of human beings than they are to those of fish□

Évreux industrial town (pharmaceuticals, rubber) in NW France; population 50 400□

Evzones Greek infantry regiment with white spreading short skirts□

excavator motorized soil stripper, earth mover, ore extractor, etc, either a track-mounted crawler, or with rubber wheels□

excise see Customs◊ and Excise□

exclusion principle see Pauli◊□

excommunication exclusion of an offender from the rights and privileges of the Roman Catholic Church; famous offenders included King John, Henry VIII and Elizabeth I□

executor person appointed in a will to carry out the instructions of the deceased. The executor, who may refuse to act, also has a duty to bury the deceased, prove the will and obtain a grant of probate (i.e. establish that the will is genuine and obtain official approval of his acting)□

Exeter city, administrative headquarters of Devon, England; population 96 000. With medieval, Georgian and Regency architecture, it remains a modern market centre, and university (1955) town. It manufactures agricultural machinery, etc. There is a cathedral 1280–1369 and Maritime Museum□

Existentialism philosophical viewpoint based on ideas of Kierkegaard◊ and Heidegger◊ and popularized c1943 by J P Sartre◊, maintaining that 'Existence precedes Essence', i.e. 'Facts come before Ideas'. It is the facts of human evolution that determine human qualities, human purpose and the 'essence' of human existence□

Exmoor moorland in Devon and Somerset, England, forming (with the coast Minehead to Combe Martin) a National Park 1954. High point Dunkery Beacon 520 m/1707 ft. It includes the Doone◊ Valley□

exobiology study of life-forms such as may exist elsewhere in the universe□

Exodus in Old Testament, the departure of the Israelites from slavery in Egypt, under the leadership of Moses◊, for the Promised Land (see Israel◊). The journey included the miraculous parting of the Red Sea, Pharaoh's pursuing forces being drowned as the waters returned. Modern research questions the historical basis for the biblical account□

exorcism rite, as in the Catholic and Pentecostal churches, for the expulsion of so-called 'evil spirits'□

explosive material capable of a sudden release of energy and rapid formation of a large volume of gas, leading, when compressed, to the development of a high-pressure wave (blast), e.g. dynamite, TNT, nitroglycerine◊. Nuclear weapons produce a similar effect by the conversion of mass into energy◊□

Expressionism style in painting, sculpture, or literature concerned with the inner world of feeling rather than the outer world of fact, often depicted in a deliberately distorted way. The term is applied particularly to the art of the first thirty years of this century in Germany, Austria, and N Europe. See Blaue◊ Reiter, Brücke◊, Fauvism◊□

Extremadura autonomous region of W Spain (including Badajoz); population 1 050 000□

extrovert and **introvert** psychological types (defined by Jung◊ c1916), the ***extrovert*** having his energies directed to the outward objective world, and the ***introvert*** being the contemplative dreamer□

Eyck Van. See Van◊ Eyck□

eye

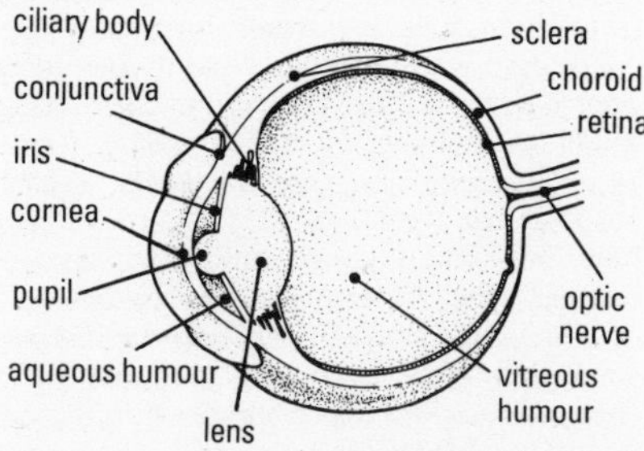

eye organ of vision. The ***human eye*** is a roughly spherical structure contained in a bony socket. It has six muscles to give it rotatory movement, and is moistened by the secretion of the tear glands. Light enters it through the transparent cornea, and passes through the circular opening (pupil) in the ***iris*** (the coloured part of the eye). The pupil has radiating muscles to dilate, and circular ones to contract it in response to the stimulus of decreasing or increasing light. The light is focused by the combined action of the curved cornea, the internal fluids or 'humours', and the lens (the rounded transparent structure behind the iris). The ciliary muscles act on the lens to change its shape, so that images of objects at different distances away can be focused on the retina, a region packed with light-sensitive cells (rods and cones) connected to the brain by the optic nerve.

In contrast, the ***insect eye*** is compound, and of two main types: those of bees have facets which each collect light and direct it separately to a receptor to build up an image; those of moths have facets which 'collaborate', light being refracted through adjacent facets before reaching the receptor□

eyebright semiparasitic annual, genus *Euphrasia*, family Scrophulariaceae, with purple-streaked white flowers. It was formerly used to treat eye disorders□

Eyre Edward John 1815–1901. Yorkshire-born British explorer (*Expeditions into Central Australia* 1845), and Governor of Jamaica 1864, where he was suspended in 1865 for harshly suppressing a Negro riot□

Eyre Lake. A lake (a salt marsh in dry seasons) in S Australia, discovered by Eyre◊ 1840; area c7770 sq km/3000 sq mi□

Eyre Peninsula peninsula in S Australia; iron ore is mined□

Eysenck H(ans) J(urgen) 1916– . British psychologist. He is controversial for preferring the treatment of symptoms to Freudian psychoanalysis; stressing the role of heredity rather than environment in intelligence□

Ezekiel born c622BC. In Old Testament, a Hebrew prophet. Carried into captivity in Babylon by Nebuchadnezzar◊ in 597BC, he preached that Jerusalem's fall was due to the sins of Israel□

Ezra in Old Testament, a Jewish scribe who was allowed by Artaxerxes to lead his people back to Jerusalem from Babylon in 458BC, and re-established the Mosaic Law, eradicating intermarriage, etc.□

F

Fabergé Peter Carl 1846–1920. Russian goldsmith, noted for his series of jewelled Easter eggs for the Imperial Court□

Fabian Society socialist propagandist organization 1884, which proposed to achieve the transition to socialism by gradual means (see Fabius◊ Maximus). Early members were George Bernard Shaw◊ and the Webbs◊□

Fabius Laurent 1946– . French Socialist statesman. Protégé of Mitterand◊, he became minister for the budget 1981, for research and industry 1983, and Prime Minister 1984-6□

Fabius Maximus Quintus. Roman general, known as Cunctator or 'Delayer' because of his tactics against Hannibal◊ 217–214BC, when he continually harassed his armies, but never risked a set battle□

fable story in which animals or inanimate objects point the moral: see Aesop◊, La Fontaine◊, Gay◊□

Factory Acts acts of parliament from 1802 governing working conditions in British factories; similar legislation was extended to offices, shops and railway premises from 1963. Inspectors were appointed from 1883. See Lord Shaftesbury◊□

Fadden Sir Arthur 'Artie' 1895–1973. Australian statesman, leader of the Country Party 1941–58, and Prime Minister Aug–Oct 1941□

Faeroe Islands, Faeroes see Faroe◊ Islands□

Fahd 1921– . King of Saudi Arabia. He succeeded his half-brother Khaled in 1982, also becoming Prime Minister, and is a modernizer□

Fahrenheit Gabriel Daniel 1686–1736. German physicist, inventor of the Fahrenheit thermometric scale; freezing point of water 32° and boiling point 212°□

Fairbanks Douglas 1883–1939. American actor, famous for swashbuckling style, whose silent films include *The Three Musketeers* 1915. He married Mary Pickford in 1920□

Fairbanks Douglas, Jnr 1909– . American actor, son of Douglas Fairbanks, and excelling in similar roles, e.g. *The Prisoner of Zenda*◊ 1937□

Fairfax Thomas, 3rd Baron Fairfax 1612–71. English general, Commander-in-Chief of the parliamentary army in the Civil◊ War. With Cromwell he formed the New Model Army and defeated Charles I at Naseby□

Faisal Ibn Abdul Aziz 1905–75. King of Saudi Arabia. Prime Minister 1953–60 and from 1962, he superseded his elder brother, the reactionary King Saud, on the throne from 1964. He was assassinated by his nephew□

Faiyûm El. City in N Egypt; population 167 000. Centre of prehistoric culture; crocodile god Sobek used to be worshipped nearby, and famous realistic mummy portraits of 1–4th centuries AD were found in the area□

fakir originally a Muslim mendicant of some religious order, etc., but in India a general term for an ascetic□

Falange Española Spanish Fascist Party, founded 1933, led from 1937 by Franco◊, when it was the country's only legal party□

Falasha a member of a small community (about 25 000) of black Jews in Ethiopia. They suffered discrimination, but, after being accorded Jewish status by Israel, about 15 000 were settled in Israel in the early 1980s□

falcon genus of birds of prey *Falco*, family Falconidae, order Falconiformes. The ***peregrine falcon*** *Falco peregrinus* up to about 50 cm/18 in long, has been re-established in N America and Britain, after near extinction by pesticides, and human predation by falconers (for whom it is the prime bird) and egg collectors. When 'stooping' on its intended prey it is the fastest creature in the world, timed at 240 kph/150 mph. About 30 cm/14 in maximum long are the ***hobby*** *F subbuteo*; ***merlin*** *F columbarius* (10–13 in) steel-blue above and reddish below, which nests in heather (the N American ***pigeon-hawk*** *F columbanus* is similar); and ***kestrel*** *F tinnunculus* with grey head and tail, and light chestnut back with black spots, which has an unmistakeable quivering hover□

Falconet Étienne Maurice 1716–91. French sculptor, who also modelled figures for the Sèvres porcelain factory. His equestrian statue of Peter the Great in Leningrad is one of the world's masterpieces□

falconry the training of falcons or hawks to catch small game, practised from ancient times in the Near East, and common in medieval times in the West□

Falkender Marcia, Baroness Falkender 1932– . British political secretary to Harold Wilson◊ from 1956, she was influential in the 'kitchen cabinet' of 1964–70, as described in her book *Inside No 10* 1972. Life peer 1974□

Falkland Lucius Cary, second Viscount Falkland c1610–43. English soldier-politician. Opposed to absolute monarchy, he was yet alienated by Puritan extremism, and when he failed to secure a compromise peace between royalists and parliamentarians, he flung away his life at the battle of Newbury in the Civil◊ War. The Falkland◊ Islands are named after him□

Falkland Islands British Crown Colony in the S Atlantic

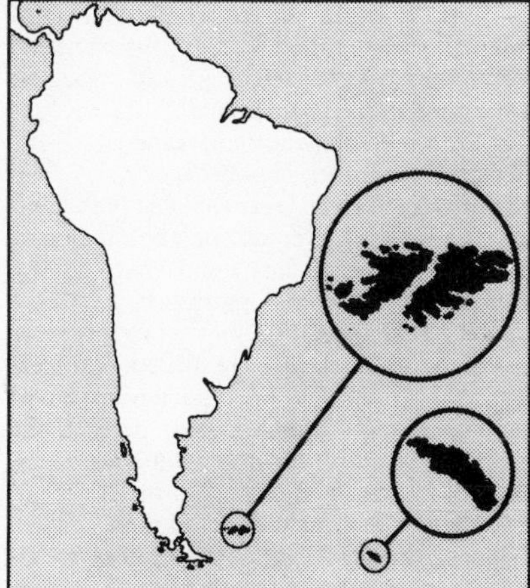

area 12 173 sq km/4700 sq mi (E Falkland 6760 sq km/2610 sq mi, W Falkland 5413 sq km/2090 sq mi, including some 200 adjacent small islands)
capital Port Stanley, on E Falkland; new port facilities were opened 1984, and Mount Pleasant airport 1985
features in addition to the two main islands, there are about 200 small islands, all with wild scenery and rich bird life
exports wool, alginates from seaweed beds
currency pound sterling
population 1800
government there is a Governor (Gordon Jewkes from Oct 85) advised by an executive council, and a mainly elected legislative council. Administered with the Falklands, but separate dependencies of the UK, are South Georgia and the South Sandwich Islands◊; see also British Antarctic Territory◊.
history discovered by Englishman John Davis in 1592, and later named after Lord Falkland◊, the Falklands were settled by Britain 1765. Spain bought out a French settlement in 1766, and ejected the British 1770–1, but British sovereignty was never ceded, and from 1833, when a few Argentines were expelled, British settlement was continuous. Argentina asserts its succession to the Spanish claim to the 'Islas Malvinas', but the population opposes cession. The islands were invaded and occupied by Argentina 2 Apr 1982, and recaptured by British military forces in May–Jun of the same year□

Falkland Islands Battle of the. British naval victory (under Admiral Sturdee) 8 Dec 1914 over German Admiral von Spee□

Falla Manuel de 1876–1946. Spanish composer, born at Cadiz. His works, with strong folk idiom, include the ballet *The Three-Cornered Hat* 1919; *Nights in the Gardens of Spain;* songs, etc.□

Fallopio Gabrielle 1523–62. Italian anatomist, after whom the Fallopian tubes (linking ovaries and uterus) are named□

fall-out radioactive material released into the atmosphere in the debris of a nuclear explosion□

fallow deer a type of deer◊□

family planning see contraception◊□

Fantin-Latour Henri 1836–1904. French artist, noted for flower studies and portraiture (*Homage to Delacroix* includes Baudelaire, Whistler, and himself)□

farad see capacitor◊□

Faraday Michael 1791–1867. British scientist. Son of a London blacksmith, he became assistant to Humphry Davy◊ in 1813, and succeeded him as Professor of Chemistry at the Royal Institution in 1827. He began experimenting in electro-magnetism in 1821, and ten years later discovered how to use a magnetic field to induce electric currents, making in effect the first dynamo and transformer. In 1833–4 he published his laws of electrolysis, (see Faraday's◊ Laws) describing quantitatively the chemical effect of passing electric currents through electrolytes◊. His discovery that inserting a solid 'dielectric' into the air-space between the plates of a capacitor◊ increased its capacitance was made in 1835. At the end of this productive decade his health failed, but he recovered to do more original work, e.g. finding (in 1845) that a magnetic field could rotate the plane of polarization of light. Faraday's many discoveries were not chance events; he was led to them through his own nascent theory of electric and magnetic fields; his development of the concept of 'lines of force' led Maxwell◊ to the equations which predicted electromagnetic waves□

Faraday's Laws of electrolysis. Two physical laws laid down by Faraday◊ 1833–44, the first stating that the chemical effect resulting from electrolysis is directly proportional to the quantity of electricity which has passed through the electrolyte; and the second that the quantity of each substance chemically changed, or liberated, at an electrode by the passage of a definite quantity of electricity is directly proportionate to the equivalent weight of the substance□

Far East all Asia east of the Indian subcontinent. See also Soviet◊ Far East□

Fargo William George 1818–81. American pioneer expressman, a founder of the American Express Company 1850 and Wells Fargo & Company 1851□

Farnborough town in Hampshire, England; population 43 500. Napoleon III and the Empress Eugénie lived in exile, and are buried, at Farnborough Hill, and the experimental Royal Aircraft Establishment is here□

Farne rocky island group off Northumberland, England. St Cuthbert◊ had his hermitage on Inner Farne; Longstone lighthouse is associated with Grace Darling◊, and the islands are a sanctuary for birds and grey seals□

Farnham town in Surrey, England; population 33 000. The parish church was once part of Waverley Abbey, after which Scott◊ named his Waverley novels; and Swift◊ met Stella at Moor Park□

Faroe Islands, Faroes or ***Faeroe Islands, Faeroes*** island group (18 out of 21 inhabited) in the N Atlantic, forming an outlying part of Denmark

area 1399 sq km/540 sq mi

capital Thorshavn on Stromo

features name means 'Sheep Islands'; they do not belong to the EEC

exports fish, crafted goods

currency Danish krone

population 13 760

government since 1948 they have had full self-government.

history first settled by Norsemen in the 9th century, they were a Norwegian province 1380–1709□

Farouk 1920–65. Last king of Egypt, son of Fuad◊; compelled to abdicate by a military coup in 1952, his little son Fuad was briefly proclaimed in his stead□

Farquhar George 1677–1707. Irish dramatist, remembered for *The Recruiting Officer* 1706, and *The Beaux Stratagem* 1707□

Farragut David Glasgow 1801–70. The first American admiral, he took New Orleans in 1862 and Mobile in 1864, during the American◊ Civil War□

Farrell J(ames) G(ordon) 1935–79. British historical novelist, born in Liverpool, author of *Troubles* 1970, set in Ireland; and *The Siege of Krishnapur* 1973□

Farrell James T(homas) 1904–79. American novelist. His trilogy, *Studs Lonigan* 1932–5, describes growing up in his native Chicago□

farthing formerly the smallest English coin, a quarter of an old penny, obsolete from 1 Jan 1961□

fasces bundle of wooden rods, the symbol of power over the people in Ancient Rome, and revived as the symbol of Fascism◊□

Fasching period preceding Lent in German-speaking towns, especially Cologne, Munich and Vienna; marked by masquerades, formal balls, and street parades□

Fascism in Italy, Mussolini◊'s totalitarian nationalist movement from 1919, the units originally being called *fasci di combattimento* 'combat groups' (see fasces◊). Nazism◊ developed in the same mould□

Fashoda see Kitchener◊, Marand◊□

Faslane see under Clyde◊□

Fassbinder Rainer Werner 1946–1982. German film director, noted for enormous productivity (over 30 films) and stylized films about love, hate, and prejudice, e.g. *Fear Eats the Soul* 1974□

Fates in Greek mythology, the three female figures, Atropos, Clotho and Lachesis, envisaged as elderly spinners, who decided the length of human life, and analogous to the Roman Parcae◊ and Norse Norns◊□

Father of the Church one of the Christian sages of the lst–7th centuries whose works were regarded as authoritative. They included Ignatius, Polycarp, Clement of Alexandria, Origen, Tertullian, Cyril of Alexandria, Athanasius, John Chrystostom, Basil the Great, Ambrose, Augustine, Boethius, Jerome, Gregory the Great, Bede□

fathom unit of depth measurement (6 ft/ 1.829 m) used especially in marine soundings until metrication□

Fatimite a member of the Muslim Shi'ite dynasty, founded by Obaidallah (alleged descendant of Mohammed◊'s daughter Fatima) in 909AD, which ruled Egypt 1169–1171, when it was overthrown by Saladin◊□

fats esters of glycerol (glycerides) with fatty◊ acids of general formula C_nH_{2n+1} COOH, the first member of which is acetic◊ acid (CH_3 COOH). The most common fatty acids in fats are oleic, palmitic and stearic. Oils are glycerides that are liquid at room temperature, whilst fats are solid at this temperature. Boiling fats in alkali forms soaps (saponification). Fats are essential constituents of food in animals□

fatty acids group of organic compounds,the higher members of which are found combined with glycerol in fats◊. Saturated fatty acids include acetic, butyric, palmitic and stearic acid; and unsaturated include oleic and linoleic□

Faulkner William 1897–1962. American novelist. Born of a declined Mississippi aristocratic family, he made a popular reputation with *Sanctuary* 1931, a deliberately horrific moneyspinner, but his literary reputation rests on his novels of 'Jefferson in Yoknapatawpha County', beginning with *Sartoris* 1929, and including *The Sound and the Fury* 1929, which initiated his stream of consciousness technique. His style is involved and a single sentence may be longer than a page. Nobel prize 1949□

faun in Roman mythology, a rural deity with goat's ears, horns, tail and hind legs□

Faunus in Roman mythology, god of fertility and prophecy, identified with the Greek Pan; in 1979 archaeological evidence showed that he was worshipped in Britain□

Fauré Gabriel Urbain 1845–1924. French composer. A pupil of Saint-Saëns, he is remembered for his songs, chamber music, and a *Requiem* 1887□

Faust legendary magician. The historical Faust, on whom the legend was built, was a 16th century German conjurer Georg Faust. Writers who have used the legend include Marlowe, Lessing, Goethe, Heine, Thomas Mann; and composers Busoni, Schumann, Berlioz, Gounod□

Fauvism art movement originating in 1903 with Matisse, and including Roualt, Derain, Vlaminck and Marquet; so-named because in 1905 art critic L Vauxcelles called their exhibition gallery *une cage aux fauves* (cage of wild beasts). The movement was characterized by strong pure colours and natural subjects□

Fawcett Percy Harrison 1867–1925. British explorer. In 1925 he set out, with his son John and a friend, into the Mato Grosso to find the legendary 'lost cities' of the ancient Indian civilization. They were never seen again□

Fawkes Guy 1570–1606. English conspirator and Catholic convert, born in York. In 1604 he joined in the Gunpowder Plot to blow up the king (James I) and both Houses of Parliament. Arrested in the cellar underneath on 4 Nov 1605, he was tortured and executed. The event is still commemorated with bonfires and fireworks on 5th Nov.□

FBI see Federal◊ Bureau of Investigation□

feather star see echinoderm◊□

Fechner Gustav Theodor 1801–87. German physicist, who studied the measurement of sensation, and in the Weber-Fechner Law restated the work of Ernst Weber◊ 1795–1878□

Federal Bureau of Investigation agency (FBI) of the US department of Justice especially concerned with internal security, and whose agents are known as G-men from the department's code letter. The Bureau was under the directorship (from 1924) of J Edgar Hoover 1895–1972. In 1973 L Patrick Gray, the acting director, resigned when it was revealed that he had destroyed relevant material in the Watergate◊ investigation□

federation system under which two or more separate states unite under a common central government, retaining some degree of autonomy (a confederation being a looser association), e.g. Switzerland, USSR, USA, Canada, Australia, Malaysia and, potentially, the Common Market□

Feisal two kings of Iraq:

Feisal I 1885–1933. King from 1921

Feisal II 1935–58. King from 1954 after a regency 1939–53. He was assassinated, and a republic followed□

feldspar or **felspar** type of rock-forming mineral, the chief constituent of igneous rock◊. Feldspars contain aluminium silicate with varying proportions of silicates of sodium, potassium, calcium, and barium; are white, grey, or pink; and may form striking crystals. The type known as ***moonstone*** has a pearl-like effect, and is used in necklaces, etc. They are used in ceramics industry (approximately 4000 tonnes annually)□

felidae see under cat◊□

Felixstowe resort and major port opposite Harwich in Suffolk, England; population 19 500. Britain's busiest container port; there are also ferries to Rotterdam and Zeebrugge□

Fellini Federico 1920– . Italian film director, most famous for *La Dolce Vita* 1960, *8½* 1963 (i.e. he had by this time made 8½ films), and *City of Women* 1981□

fencing sport using the ***foil,*** derived from the light weapon used in practice duels; ***epée,*** a heavier weapon derived from the duelling sword proper; and ***sabre,*** in which cuts (it has two cutting edges) count as well as thrusts. Masks and protective jackets are worn, and hits are registered electronically in competitions□

Fénélon François de Salignac de la Mothe 1651–1715. French philosopher and archbishop of Cambrai from 1695. Tutor from 1869 to a grandson of Louis XIV, he wrote for him *Télémaque* 1699, envisaging an ideal commonwealth at odds with the rule of Louis, who banished him from court. His defence of Quietism◊ in his mystic *Maximes des Saints* 1697 had already earned him papal condemnation□

Fenian a member of an Irish-American republican secret society, 1858, named after the ancient legendary warrior band of the Fianna. It failed to achieve its aim of an independent Irish republic by an invasion of Canada from the USA 1866, and a rising in Ireland 1867, but continued to exist till 1922□

fennec small desert fox◊□

fennel perennial plant with feathery green leaves, family Umbelliferae. Fennels have an aniseed flavour and the thickened leafstalks of ***sweet fennel*** *Foeniculum dulce* are eaten, while the leaves and seeds of *F vulgare* are used in seasoning□

Fens low-lying area of England in Lincolnshire, Cambridgeshire and Norfolk, drained in the 17th century (from a bay of the North Sea) and agriculturally productive. Burwell Fen and Wicken Fen remain as nature reserves□

Ferber Edna 1887–1968. American writer. Her novel *Show Boat* 1926 was adapted as an operetta by Jerome Kern and Oscar Hammerstein II□

Ferdinand five kings of Castile, including:
Ferdinand I the Great c1016–65. King from 1035, he began the reconquest of Spain from the Moors.
Ferdinand V 1452–1516. King from 1474 and from 1497 also ***Ferdinand II*** of Aragon. Married in 1469 to his cousin Isabella, the heiress of Castile, he became in 1497 the first king of all Spain. He introduced the Inquisition◊ 1480, expelled the Jews and received the surrender of the Moors at Granada in 1492, financed Columbus's discovery of America, and conquered Naples 1500–3, becoming ***Ferdinand III*** of Naples in 1504□

Ferdinand three Holy Roman Emperors:
Ferdinand I 1503–64, who succeeded Charles V in 1556.
Ferdinand II 1578–1637, emperor from 1619, and a fanatical Catholic who provoked the Bohemian revolt which led to the Thirty◊ Years' War. He was King of Bohemia 1617–19, 1620–37, and of Hungary 1621–37.
Ferdinand III 1608–57, in whose reign, from 1637, the war ended in 1648. He was King of Hungary 1625–57□

Ferdinand 1861–1948. Tsar of independent Bulgaria from 1908, he allied with Germany in 1915, and abdicated in 1918□

Ferdinand 1865–1927. King of Romania from 1914, he sided with the Allies in 1916, and made large territorial gains in 1918□

Fermanagh county of Northern Ireland
area 1701 sq km/657 sq mi
towns Enniskillen (county town)
features Upper and Lower Lough Erne
products mainly agricultural; tweeds, clothing
population 50 300□

Fermat Pierre de 1601–65. French mathematician, founder of the theory of numbers (his ***last theorem***, believed to be true, may have been proved by him, but no one else since has succeeded in doing so) and (with Pascal◊) the theory of probability□

Fermat's Principle the principle which states that light travelling between two points takes the route involving least time□

Fermi Enrico 1901–54. Italo-American physicist. Awarded a Nobel prize 1938 for his work on radioactivity, he worked out the theory of nuclear chain reactions, relevant both to the nuclear power station and the 'atom' (fission) bomb. See also Fermilab under Chicago◊□

Fermilab see under Chicago◊□

fermium element
symbol Fm
atomic number 100
physical description metal
features one of the actinide◊ series, named after Fermi◊; it has been produced only in minute quantities□

fern class of plants, Filicales, division Pteridophyta◊; non-flowering perennial herbs with a low-growing rootstock, the leaves being fronds. New Zealand, whose emblem is a fern, is specially rich in them. There are over 7000 species, including ***bracken*** *Pteridium aquilinum* family Dennstadtiaceae, common in most parts of Europe, and having a perennial root stock which throws up large fronds; ***Hart's tongue fern*** *Phyllitis scolopendrium*, and the delicately fronded ***maidenhair*** *Adiantum capillis-veneris*. ***Tropical tree ferns,*** family Cyatheaceae, have thick stems up to 25 m/80 ft tall. Allied to the ferns are the horsetails◊ and club mosses◊. Ferns reproduce asexually by producing spores which develop into tiny plants unrecognizable as 'children' of their 'parents', but which in turn produce male and female organs so that new ferns develop from fertilized ova and complete the cycle (alternation of generations). Ferns produce toxins which discourage browsing animals and insects and research is being undertaken into transferring this toxin-producing ability to crop plants□

Fernández Juan. 16th century Spanish explorer, discoverer in 1563 of the islands that bear his name; in 1576 he possibly sighted Easter Island, Australia and New Zealand□

Fernando Po see Bioko Island under Equitorial Fuinea◊□

Ferrara industrial city in N Italy; population 151 640. It has the castle of its medieval rulers, the House of Este, and palaces and museums. Savonarola◊ was born here, and Tasso◊ was confined in the asylum 1579–86□

ferret a small mammal related to the weasel◊□

Ferrier Kathleen 1912–53. British contralto. Born in Lancashire, she was the first to play the title role in Britten's *Rape of Lucretia* 1946. She died of cancer□

Ferrier Susan Edmundstone 1782–1854. Scottish novelist, born in Edinburgh, a friend of Scott. Her acutely observed and anonymously published books are *Marriage* 1818, *The Inheritance* 1824 and *Destiny* 1831□

fertility drug drug taken to increase a female's fertility. For humans, the best-known is gonadotrophin (from hormones extracted from the pituitary gland), which stimulates ovulation and, unless carefully controlled, produces multiple births□

fertilizer substance containing some of the twenty-odd chemical elements essential to plant growth. It may be ***organic*** manure, compost, bonemeal, blood, fishmeal, or ***inorganic*** usually compounds of nitrogen (e.g. ammonium nitrate), phosphate and potash (source of potassium), applied in solid or liquid form. The latter have disadvantages in that they may result in trace element deficiency, poor soil structure, loss of taste in the crop, etc.□

Fès religious centre (formerly ***Fez***), former capital of Morocco 808–1062, 1296–1548 and 1662–1912; population 800 000. Kairwan Islamic University dates from 859□

fescue see grasses◊□

feudalism tiered hierarchical system in Europe during the Middle Ages, under which the monarch owned all land, which was held by his great vassals in return for military service, who in turn 'sub-let' such rights. At the bottom of the pile was the serf, who worked on his lord's manor in return for being allowed to cultivate some land for himself, and so underpinned the system. He could not be sold as if he were a slave, but also could not leave the estate. The system declined from the 13th century, partly owing to the growth of a money economy and partly owing to revolt by the peasants. Serfdom ended in England in the 16th century, lingered in France till 1789, and in the rest of W Europe until the early 19th century. In Russia it continued till 1861□

fever rise in body temperature from the normal 36.9°C/98.4°F; if over 41°C/106°F it sometimes leads to death□

Fez see Fès◊□

Fianna Fáil (Gaelic 'Soldiers of destiny') Irish republican party founded by De Valera in 1926 to achieve a united independent Ireland□

Fibonacci Leonardo. 13th century Italian mathematician, whose *Liber Abaci* 1202 helped to popularize Arabic notation in Europe□

fibonacci numbers sequence discovered by Fibonacci◊ in which each member is the sum of its two predecessors, e.g. 1,1,2,3,5,8,13, etc.□

fibre optics transmission of light through glass fibres; reflection from the inside wall enables light to follow the fibres around corners. Bundles of very fine, optically-insulated fibres can be used to inspect the inside of a machine or the human body. Fibres are superseding copper wires for data transmission; telephone conversations, television pictures etc., are made to 'modulate' a light beam sent through the fibre□

fibres man-made: see textile◊□

Fichte Johann Gottlieb 1762–1814. German philosopher. A disciple of Kant, he had to resign his chair at Jena when inaccurately charged with atheism. His ***subjective idealism*** in *Foundations of the Laws of Nature* 1796, envisages the world as the creation of the human spirit as divinely inspired: he influenced Hegel, Schopenhauer, and Emerson◊. He also advocated a socialist Utopia of a rather dictatorial kind□

Fichtelgebirge mineral-rich mountain chain in Bavaria, West Germany; highest peak Schneeberg 1051 m/3448 ft□

Fidei Defensor title of 'defender of the faith' (still retained by British sovereigns) conferred by Pope Leo X on Henry VIII to reward his writing of a treatise against Martin Luther◊□

fieldfare see under thrush◊□

Fielding Henry 1707–54. English novelist. Born in Somerset, he was educated at Eton with Fox and the elder Pitt. A man-about-town, he attempted to abduct an heiress in 1725, wrote a number of comedies, and in 1740 was called to the Bar. In 1742 he parodied Richardson's *Pamela* in *Joseph Andrews* then took seriously to the craft with *Jonathan Wild the Great* 1743; his masterpiece *Tom Jones* 1749; and *Amelia* 1751. As a writer, and, as Justice of the Peace for Middlesex and Westminster (see police◊), he exercised the same compassion as appears in his novels. In failing health, he went to recuperate in Lisbon in 1754 and died there□

field marshal highest ranking officer in the British Army, and some others; see general◊

field mouse see rodent◊□

Field of the Cloth of Gold site near Calais of a meeting between Henry VIII and Francis I of France Jun 1520, remarkable for lavish clothes and tent pavilions□

Fields Dame Gracie. Stage-name of British comedienne and singer Grace Stansfield 1898–1979. Born in Rochdale, she was originally a mill-girl. Her films include *Sally in our Alley* and *Sing as We Go* 1934. DBE 1979□
Fields W C. Adopted name of American juggler-comedian William Claude Dukenfield 1880–1946. Averse to children and dogs, he had a ripe turn of phrase, and a rasping delivery. His films include *The Bank Dick* 1940 and *My Little Chickadee* 1940□
Fife region of Scotland

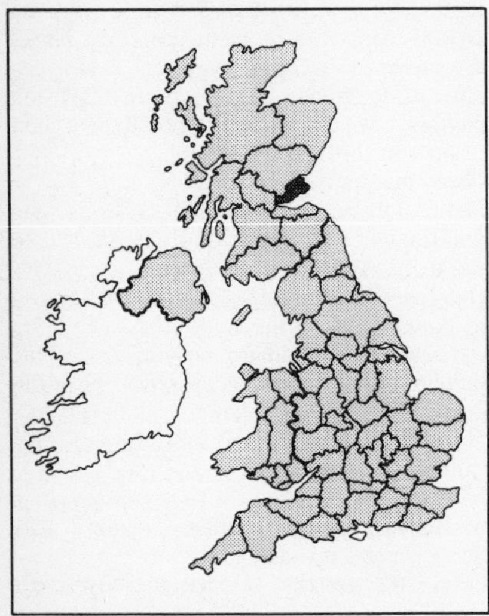

area 1305 sq km/504 sq mi
towns administrative headquarters Glenrothes; Dunfermline, St Andrews, Kirkcaldy, Cupar
features rivers Eden and Leven; Lomond Hills; Rosyth naval base and dockyard (used for nuclear submarine refits) on N shore of the Firth of Forth; Tentsmuir, possibly the earliest settled site in Scotland
products potatoes, cereals, sugar beet; electronics, petrochemicals (Mossmorran), light engineering
population 340 200□
fife see flute under woodwind◊
Fifteen The. Jacobite rebellion 1715, led by the 'Old Pretender' (James Edward◊ Stuart) and the Earl of March, in order to place the former on the throne. March was checked at Sheriffmuir, and the revolt collapsed□
Fifth Column those aiding the enemy from within. When Madrid was under siege by four columns of Franco's troops in the Civil War in 1936, General Mol boasted of a fifth column of Franco supporters inside the town□
fig fruit of the W Asian tree *Ficus caria*, family Moraceae, produced in two or three crops a year, and eaten fresh or dried; they have a high sugar content and laxative properties. In the wild they are totally dependent on the fig wasp for pollination, and the wasp is completely parasitic on the flowers. The tropical ***banyan*** *Ficus benghalensis* has less attractive edible fruit, and roots which grow down from its branches, looking like separate 'trunks'. The ***bo tree*** under which Buddha became 'enlightened' is the Indian peepul or wild fig *Ficus religiosa*□
fighting fish Siamese. See under perch◊□
Fiji

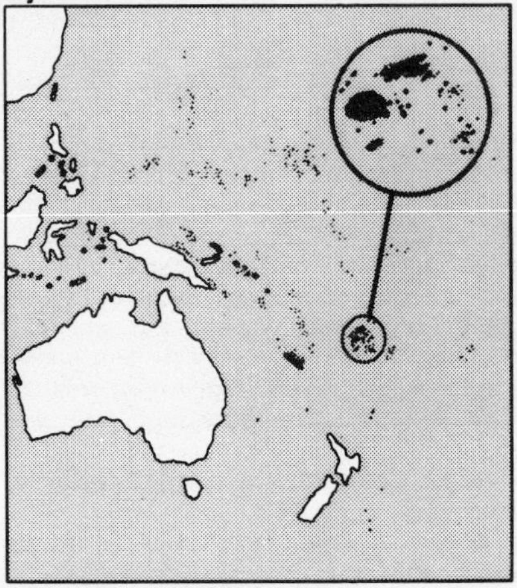

area 18 272 sq km/7055 sq mi
capital Suva on Viti Levu
features comprises some 800 islands (about 100 inhabited), the largest being Viti Levu (10 386 sq km/400 sq mi) and Vanua Levu (5535 sq km/2137 sq mi); Nadi airport is an international Pacific staging post
exports sugar, coconut oil, ginger, timber, canned fish; tourism is important
currency Fiji dollar
population 686 000, 44% Fijian (holding 80% of the land communally), and 50% Indians introduced in the 19th century to work the sugar crop
language English, official; Fijian, Hindi
religion Hinduism (50%); Methodism (44%)
government there is a senate and house of representatives, headed by a Prime Minister (Kamisese Mara from 1970), and a Governor-General who represents the Queen. See also Pitcairn◊.
recent history reached by Tasman in 1643 and visited by Cook 1773, the islands came under British sovereignty in 1874; independent 1970 within the Commonwealth□
filariasis see elephantiasis◊□
Fillmore Millard 1800–74. 13th President of the USA. As Vice-President to Zachary

Taylor from 1848, he succeeded on Taylor's death. A Whig, he advocated a compromise on slavery to reconcile North and South, and failed to be renominated□

film a series of photographs on a thin transparent material, which, when projected onto a screen gives the impression of 'moving pictures' due to the eye's persistence of vision
19th century various machines invented to show moving images: the stroboscope, zootrope, and thaumatrope
1872 Eadweard Muybridge (1830–1904) demonstrated movement of horses' legs using a series of 24 cameras
1887 the first series of images on a perforated film (Augustin le Prince 1842–90)
1888 William Friese-Green (1885–1921) showed the first celluloid film and patented a movie camera
1889 Edison◊ invented 35mm film
1894 Edison's Kitetoscope (for a single viewer)
1895 the Lumière brothers, Auguste (1862–1954) and Louis (1864–1948) projected, to a paying audience, a film of a train arriving at a station. Some of the audience fled in terror
1902 George Méliès (1861–1938) made *A Trip to the Moon*
1903 *The Great Train Robbery* by Edwin S Porter
1906 earliest colour film
1915 D W Griffith◊ (1875–1948): *The Birth of a Nation*
1923 first sound film demonstrated
1927 *The Jazz Singer*: the first major sound film; the first Oscar◊ award
1932 Technicolor (three-colour) process used for a Walt Disney cartoon film
1952 Cinerama
1953 Cinemascope□

film and television awards earliest and still the most famous are those of the ***American Academy of Motion Pictures*** which were established 1927, and became known as ***Oscars*** when a secretary said of the ten bronze-gilt statuettes awarded: 'That's like my uncle Oscar!'. In Britain the ***BAFTA*** (British Academy of Film and Television Arts) awards cover all aspects from drama to documentary□

Financial Times Index average of 30 main industrial share prices used by the *Financial Times* as an indicator of movement on the Stock Exchange. A better indicator is the ***Top 100 Share Index***, which monitors the movement of the 100 best-performing companies. Its US equivalent is the ***Dow Jones Index***.
None of these indicators, however, is adjusted for inflation, thus limiting its usefulness□

finch family of birds, Fringillidae, in the order Passeriformes, which are seed-eaters with stout conical beaks. They include the ***canary finch*** *Serinus canarius* of the Canary Islands, greenish when wild, but varied to yellow, etc. in domestication; ***gold-finch*** *Carduelis carduelis* a songbird of Europe, North Africa, etc, which is brilliantly coloured (black, white, and red about the head, with gold and black wings), and usually leaves Britain in the autumn; ***greenfinch*** or ***green linnet*** *Carduelis chloris* of Eurasia; ***siskin*** *Carduelis spinus* greenish yellow, with an attractive song, and found from Britain to Japan; ***linnet*** *Acanthis cannabina* of Eurasia and North Africa, with pinkish breast, grey head and brownish back; ***chaffinch*** *Fringilla coelebs* of Europe, chestnut brown, with two white bands on the upper wing, and a good songster; ***bullfinch*** *Pyrrhula pyrrhula*, with a roseate breast, and which damages orchards in bloom; ***crossbill*** *Loxia curvirostra*, in which the two parts of the bill cross over to enable it to extract spruce seeds; and the ***woodpecker finch*** *Cactospiza pallida*, a remarkable 'tool user', which holds a thorn in its beak to poke insects from holes.
The family is very variable, and it was the differences between finches on the individual islands of the Galapagos◊ which helped to alert Darwin◊ to the possibility of the development of new species by evolution. There, the ***sharp-beaked ground finch*** not only cleanses boobies of their insect parasites, but has developed 'vampyrism,' piercing the birds' wings to drink their blood. See also bunting◊□

Fine Gael Irish political party, *United Ireland*, founded by W J Cosgrave◊, and led by Garret FitzGerald◊ from 1977□

Fingal see Finn◊ Mac Cumhaill□

fingerprints identification system based on the ridge pattern of the skin on a person's finger tips, which is constant through life and with no two being exactly alike. First used as a means of identifying suspects in India, it was adopted by the English police in 1901□

Finisterre Cape. Promontory in NW Spain□

Finland Gulf of. Eastern arm of the Baltic◊□

Finland Republic of
area 337 050 sq km/130 125 sq mi
capital Helsinki
towns Tampere, and the port of Turku
features one third is within the Arctic Circle; Saimaa Canal; it includes the Åland Islands
exports metal, chemical and engineering products (icebreakers and oil rigs); paper, timber, and textiles; fine ceramics, glass, and furniture
currency Finnish mark

population 4 873 000
language Finnish, Swedish, official; Lapp
religion 90% Lutheran
famous people architecture Alvar Alto, *literature* (poetry) Elias Lönnrot, compiler of the Kalevala◊, *music* Sibelius
government executive elected president (Mauno Koivisto from 1982) and unicameral parliament (Prime Minister Kalevi Sorsa from 1982, Social Democratic Party, SDP)
recent history long subject to rule by Sweden and Russia, Finland became independent in 1917, but in 1939 was invaded by the USSR to compel the cession of territory. During World War II Finland attempted to regain possession, but by 1944 was compelled to make further concessions, among them the Petsamo area on the Arctic coast which gave the USSR a frontier with Norway. ***Finlandization*** (a term rejected by the Finns) signifies the state of docility induced by such great power pressure, and a treaty of cooperation was signed in 1948 (renewed 1983)□

Finn Mac Cumhaill legendary Irish hero, identified with a general who organized an Irish regular army in the mid 3rd century AD. James Macpherson (1736–96), featured him (as 'Fingal') and his followers in the verse of his popular, but largely forged epics 1762–3, which were supposedly by a 3rd century bard, Ossian. Although challenged by Dr Johnson, the poems were influential in the Romantic◊ movement. Fingal's Cave (see Hebrides◊) was fancifully linked with him□

Finsen Niels Ryberg 1860–1904. Danish physician, the first to use ultra-violet light treatment for skin diseases; Nobel prize 1903□

Finsteraarhorn see under Alps◊□

fir general term applied to conifers◊, but correctly applied only to a few species, e.g. ***silver fir*** *A alba*, which may produce dense growths of small branches, 'witches' brooms', after attack by rust◊ fungi; ***Douglas fir*** *Pseudotsuga menziesii*; and the ***Christmas tree*** or ***spruce fir*** *Picea abies*. ***Canada Balsam*** is the resin obtained from certain N American species□

Firbank Ronald 1886–1926. British novelist, whose books included *Caprice* 1916, and *Valmouth* 1918. They have a malicious humour□

Firdausi (Abdul Qasim Mansur) 940–1020. Iranian poet, whose epic *Shahnama,* the Book of Kings, including the legend of Sohrab and Rustum (the father unknowingly kills his son in battle), was used by Matthew Arnold◊□

firearms see weapons◊□

firebrat see bristletail◊□

fireclay clay resistant to high temperatures because of a high silica and alumina content, and used to line furnaces□

firedamp see under methane◊□

firefly winged nocturnal insect which emits light. See under beetle◊□

Firenze see Florence◊□

fire protection methods available for fighting fires. In Britain, from 1707, horse-drawn fire engines were provided by the parish, but insurance companies soon established more efficient private services to buildings bearing their own firemark, and in the 19th century the two amalgamated. Large buildings today depend on ceiling fire sprinklers, which are automatically activated by abnormally high temperature, presence of smoke, etc. For oil and petrol fires, chemical foam rather than water must be used; where electricity is involved, vaporizing liquids create a non-inflammable barrier; inflammable vapours require carbon dioxide; and for some chemicals only various dry powders can be used□

firework a container or 'case' enclosing one chemical, e.g. potassium nitrate, which enables others (capable of producing a 'bang', coloured lights, sparks, etc.) to burn without oxygen from the air. Firework displays are a form of entertainment worldwide. The same principle is used for practical purposes, as in aircraft ejector seats, and the separation of the various stages of a space rocket□

First World War see World◊ War I□

Fischer Emil 1852–1919. German biochemist. Nobel prizewinner 1902 for his work with Julius Tufel on the production of synthetic sugars; he also worked on the synthesis of proteins□

Fischer Hans 1881–1945. Nobel prizewinner in 1930 for his work on the colouring matter of the blood□

Fischer-Dieskau Dietrich 1925– . German baritone, especially famous for his interpretation of Schubert's songs□

fish water-living animals with backbones which use gills to breathe. The ***skeleton*** is usually composed of bone, but in the lamprey, shark, and skate families it is of cartillage. Movement is controlled by ***fins***. The body is usually covered with ***scales*** of varying size and thickness. The ***lateral line***, along the side of the body, enables the fish to feel movement in the water. The ***gills***, layers of tissue supported on bony arches, are situated in the head. Water is taken in through the mouth and passes over the gills, where oxygen is absorbed by the blood vessels; the water then leaves via the gill slits. Many fish have an ***air bladder***, which alters the specific gravity of the fish in accordance with water pressure. Fish ***coloration*** is usually such that will conceal the animal in its surroundings, and in many varieties the colour changes with the background. At the spawning season, however, they display their colours, which often become much brighter. Reproduction is by means of eggs, which are frequently very small and numerous: some, e.g. guppies, are live-bearers, with eggs hatching inside the body□

fish classification fish can be divided into two superclasses and five classes, which are in turn divided into sub-classes and orders (fish listed here have individual entries):
superclass ***Agnatha*** 'jawless fish':
class ***Cyclostomata*** 'circular-mouthed': ***Petromyzoniformes*** lamprey
Myxiniformes hagfish
superclass ***Gsnathostomata*** 'jawed fish':
class ***Elasmobranchii*** with gills like 'metal grills':
Selachii shark
Batoidei ray
class ***Holocephali*** with 'undivided skull':
Chimaeriformes rabbit fish
class ***Dipnoi*** lungfish
class ***Ichthyes*** 'bony fish':
Sub-class ***Crossopterygii*** 'lobe-finned':
Coelacanthiformes coelacanth
Sub-class ***Chondrostei*** 'cartilaginous':
Acipenseriformes sturgeon
Sub-class ***Teleosti*** 'recent bony fish'
Elopiformes tarpon
Clupeiformes herring
Salmoniformes salmon and trout, pike, butterfly fish
Cypriniformes carp
Siluriformes catfish
Anguilliformes eel
Beloniformes garfish
Gadiformes cod
Zeiformes John Dory
Gasterosteriformes stickleback
Syngnathiformes pipefish
Mugiliformes grey mullet
Perciformes perch, bullhead, goby, mackerel, mudskipper, pilotfish, swordfish
Dactylopteriformes flying gurnard
Thunniformes tunny
Pleuronectiformes flatfish
Echeneiformes sucking fish
Tetraodontiformes tetraodons, puffer fish, sunfish
Lophiiformes anglerfish□

Fisher Andrew 1862–1928. Australian Labour statesman, Prime Minister 1908, 1910–13, and 1914–15□

Fisher Geoffrey, Baron Fisher of Lambeth 1887–1972. British churchman. He succeeded Temple as archbishop of Canterbury 1945–61, and was the first holder of this office to visit the Pope for 600 years□

Fisher John, St c1469–1535. British churchman, bishop of Rochester from 1504, and a friend of More◊ and Erasmus◊. Tried in 1535 on a charge of denying the royal supremacy, he was beheaded. Canonized 1935□

fish

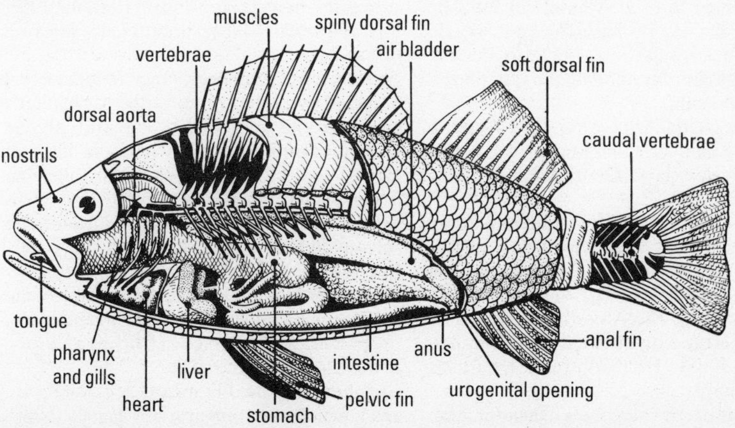

Fisher John Arbuthnot, 1st Baron Fisher 1841–1920. British admiral. As First Sea Lord 1904–10, he introduced the Dreadnought battleship. He was re-appointed in 1914, but resigned in 1915, having disagreed with Churchill over the Dardanelles◊ venture□

fish farming breeding fish in a controlled environment. In the 1980s one tenth of the world's fish requirements (either for the table or restocking) were farmed, notably trout and Atlantic salmon, turbot, eel; and the shellfish, mussels and oysters□

fishing the catching of fish. In the 20th century, industrialization, with the creation of factory ships which process the catch on board ready for market, has depleted stocks. There has been some success in artificial breeding and the release of small fry into the sea. See also krill◊.

There is international competition (see Cod◊ Wars), and, in the EEC, division of fishing areas provides for exclusive access zones, generally of 12 miles, for individual maritime states□

fission nuclear. See nuclear◊ energy□

Fittipaldi Emerson 1946– . Brazilian motor racing driver. He was world champion twice, in 1972 and 1974□

Fitzgerald Edward 1809–83. British poet and translator, born in Suffolk. His version of Omar Khayyam's *Rubaiyat* 1959 is more an original creation□

Fitzgerald F(rancis) Scott (Key) 1896–1940. American novelist, born in Minnesota. His *The Great Gatsby* 1925 epitomized the Jazz Age. His wife Zelda Sayre 1900–47, a schizophrenic, was in an asylum from 1930. Her descent into madness forms the subject of *Tender is the Night*, 1934□

Fitzgerald Garret 1926– . Irish Fine Gael statesman. Leader of the party from 1977, he was Prime Minister 1981–March 1982, and from November 1982. He was instrumental in setting up the Anglo-Irish Accord, which provides for consultations between Britain and the Republic of Ireland on the situation in Northern Ireland□

Fitzherbert Maria Anne 1756–1837. Widow who became the secret morganatic wife to the Prince of Wales (later George IV) in 1785; they parted in 1803□

fives game of handball for two or four players in an enclosed court, chiefly played in public schools; Eton, Rugby and Winchester each have their own rules□

Fixx James 1932–84. American founder of the jogging craze with his book *The Complete Book of Running*. He died of a heart attack while jogging□

fjord or ***fiord*** narrow sea inlets in a mountainous area, named after those of Norway□

flag a piece of cloth displaying the emblem of a country or organization. The British national flag, the ***Union Flag,*** popularly the 'Union Jack', unites the crosses of St George, St Andrew, and St Patrick◊; the ***Red Ensign*** or 'red duster', flag of the British mercantile marine, has the national flag in the canton of a red flag (first used 1674, and shared with the Royal Navy till 1864); the flag of the Navy now has the national flag in the canton of a large St George's Cross.

Australia and New Zealand retain the 'Union Jack' as part of their national flags, in both of which the stars of the Southern◊ Cross are the chief element, but Canada omitted it when changing to a maple leaf design. South Africa, though no longer a Commonwealth member, still includes it to represent the British element of the population.

The ***Stars and Stripes*** of the USA, 'Old Glory', has 50 stars (one for each state) and 13 stripes to denote the 13 original states.

The ***Soviet flag*** has a crossed hammer and sickle (representing the workers of town and country) on a red ground (red being the colour of revolution) and a five-pointed star bordered in gold to symbolize peace among the continents. The oldest national flag is the Danish ***Dannebrog*** 'strength of Denmark', used for 700 years.

special uses the ***Red Cross*** originated in Switzerland, and its emblem is the Swiss national flag with reversed colours; Islamic countries use a flag with a Red Crescent. Flown upside-down, a flag is a signal of distress, for a salute, it is 'dipped'; and when flown a little below the masthead it denotes mourning. The ***Blue Peter,*** blue with a white centre, announces that a vessel is about to sail; and a half red and half white flag shows that a pilot is on board. A white flag signifies surrender, or a plea for truce; yellow indicates quarantine; and black traditionally marks a pirate.

Among personal flags, the ***British Royal Standard*** (more correctly 'armorial banner') combines the lions of England (twice), the lion rampant of Scotland and the harp of Wales, and is flown only when the Sovereign is personally present; in the USA the ***Presidential Standard*** displays the American eagle surrounded by 50 stars□

flag (botany) a type of iris◊□

flagellant a religious fanatic who uses the scourge as a means of discipline and penance; the practice was common in Christian Europe in the 11–16th centuries□

flagellata microscopic members of the Protozoa◊, which have one or more flagella (whiplike extensions), used mainly to move forward, but also for food collection□

Flaherty Robert 1884–1951. American pioneer documentary film director, e.g. *Nanook of the North* 1920 and *Man of Aran* 1934□

Flamboyant Gothic architectural style with flame-like decorative work in windows, balustrades, etc. See architecture◊□

flamen sacrificial priest in ancient Rome, whose tenure was only ended by the death of his wife (who assisted the ceremonies) or misdemeanour□

flame tree smooth-stemmed semi-deciduous tree (*Sterculia acerifolia*) with red/orange flowers, native to tropical Asia, S America and Africa□

flamingo long-legged and long-necked wading bird, family Phoenicopteridae, order Ciconiiformes (see stork◊), but also closely allied to the spoonbill◊, and having some features in common with the waterfowl. Largest of the family is the ***greater*** or ***roseate flamingo*** *Phoenicopterus ruber*, of both Africa and S America, with delicate pink plumage, and 1.25 m/4 ft high. They probe the mud for food with their downbent bills, and build colonies of high, conelike mud nests, with a little hollow for the eggs at the top□

Flaminius Gaius d. 217 BC. Roman general. He constructed the Flaminian (Rome to Rimini) Way 220BC, and was killed fighting Hannibal◊□

Flamsteed John 1646–1719. First astronomer-royal, appointed by Charles II in 1675. His observatory, Flamsteed House (designed by Wren◊) is part of the National Maritime Museum at Greenwich□

Flanagan Bud. Stage-name of Robert Winthrop 1896–1968, leader of the 'Crazy Gang' 1931–62, who popularized, with his partner Chesney Allen, songs such as 'Underneath the Arches'□

Flanders former name of the area of the Low Countries now mainly comprising the Belgian provinces of E and W Flanders. There was fierce fighting here in World War I□

flash point temperature at which a liquid gives off an ignitable vapour□

flatfish bony fish of order Pleuronectiformes having a characteristically flat, asymmetrical body with both eyes (in adults) on the upper side, although in practice they tend to lie upside-down in shallow water. Species include turbot, halibut, plaice, sole, and flounder□

flat racing see under horse◊ racing□

Flaubert Gustave 1821–80. French novelist, one of the greatest 19th century writers, born at Rouen. His masterpiece is *Madame Bovary* 1857, story of a country doctor's wife who commits suicide after a series of unhappy love affairs. Other works include *Sentimental Education* 1869, *Three Tales* 1877, and *Dictionary of Trite Ideas*, a collection of clichés and stock phrases amassed throughout his life□

flax plant, family Linaceae, of almost world-wide distribution, 1.25 m/4 ft high, with small leaves and bright blue flowers. The seeds yield ***linseed oil*** used in paints and varnishes, the residue being fed to cattle; the stems are steeped in water to separate out the long fibres, which are then spun into ***linen*** thread, twice as strong, yet more delicate than cotton, and especially suitable for lace; shorter ones make twine or paper. Russia, Belgium, Netherlands, and N Ireland, where cultivation has recently been revived, are producers□

Flaxman John 1755–1826. British sculptor. Originally a designer for Wedgwood◊, he was the first professor of sculpture at the Royal Academy◊. His works include portrait sculptures of Reynolds (St Paul's) and Burns and Kemble (Westminster Abbey)□

flea wingless insect, order Siphonaptera, with blood-sucking mouthpart. Fleas are parasitic on warm blooded animals, and leave when the host dies. Species include *Pulex irritans*, which lives on man; the ***rat flea*** *Xenopsylla cheopis*, the transmitter of plague and typhus; and (fostered by central heating) the ***cat*** and ***dog fleas*** *Ctenocephalides felis* and *canis*. Some fleas can jump 130 times their own height. The world's largest flea *Histricopsylla talpe* is about 8 mm/0.25 in long□

Flecker James Elroy 1884–1915. British poet, born at Lewisham. He worked in the Orient in the consular service, and died of tuberculosis. His verse includes 'The Golden Journey to Samarkand'□

Fleet Street see Westminster◊□

Fleming Sir Alexander 1881–1955. British bacteriologist, discoverer in 1928 of penicillin. He shared a Nobel prize 1945 with E B Chain and Sir Howard Florey, who developed it for practical use. Knighted 1944□

Fleming Ian 1908–64. British author, educated at Eton, Sandhurst and Munich and Geneva Universities. A banker and stockbroker, he was personal assistant to the Director of Naval Intelligence in World War II, and in 1953 created 'James Bond', Secret Service agent No 007 (the prefix '00' indicating 'licensed to kill')□

Fleming Sir John Ambrose 1849–1945. British electrical physicist, inventor in 1904 of the thermionic valve□

Flemish see under Belgium◊□

Flemish art style of painting, marked by detailed realism and exquisite technique, practised in Flanders◊ (now part of Belgium) in the 14-17th centuries. The early masters include Hubert and Jan Van Eyck, Rogier van der Weyden, Dierick Bouts, Hugo van der Goes, Hans Memling, and Gheerardt David. Bosch and Brueghel were the chief names of the 16th century, and Rubens, Van Dyck, Jordaens, Brouwer and Teniers of the 17th□

Fletcher John 1579–1625. English dramatist. He collaborated with Beaumont◊ in *Philaster* 1610, *The Maid's Tragedy* 1611, etc., and allegedly with Shakespeare in *The Two Noble Kinsmen* and *Henry VIII* in 1612. Alone he wrote *The Faithful Shepherdess* 1610 and *Rule a Wife and Have a Wife* 1624□

fleur-de-lis heraldic device, French 'flower of the lily', adopted by the Bourbons◊□

flight the act of flying by a machine

1804 model glider flown by Sir George Cayley

1853 first piloted glider

1903 Wright brothers made first powered flight

1909 Blériot◊ crossed the Channel

1917 first big twin-engined plane, the Handley Page bomber

World War II supremacy of internally braced monoplane structures, e.g. Hawker Hurricane and Supermarine Spitfire fighters, and the Avro Lancaster and Boeing Flying Fortress bombers. In 1939 the Heinkel 178 was the first turbo-jet to fly, followed by the British Gloster E 28/39 in May 1941 (see Whittle◊). After the war the jet ousted the piston engine on almost all military and civil types, either as a turbo-prop or as a pure jet, since they were more powerful as well as more economical in flight over 15 500 m/50 000 ft

1948 John Derry (UK) first reached supersonic speed 1085 kph/675 mph, and broke the sound barrier; see Mach◊ Number. Supersonic airliner projects were the Anglo-French Concorde and the Soviet Tu-144

For speed, combined with flexibility in operation of flights below 800kph/500mph, V/STOL (vertical and/or short take-off) aircraft provided a solution, e.g. the Hawker P–1127, which is also capable of supersonic level flight. Development of swing-wing or variable geometry aircraft, capable of much higher speed, encountered setbacks in both Europe and the USA in the 1960s, but by 1974 problems had been solved. See aeroplane◊, balloon◊□

Flinders Matthew 1774–1814. British explorer, born in Lincolnshire. He explored the Australian coasts, 1795–9 and 1801–3. ***Flinders Island*** in Bass Strait, Tasmania; ***Flinders Range*** in S Australia; and ***Flinders River*** in Queensland, are all named after him□

flint hard, brittle silicate rock; grey, brown or black; found in nodules in chalk deposits. It fractures with a cutting edge, and was used by ancient peoples for weapons and implements (see Stone◊ Age), and also to strike sparks for a fire, or firing early guns. ***Lighter flints*** are made of cerium◊ alloy□

Flodden site in Northumberland of the defeat of the Scots under James IV by the English under the Earl of Surrey 9 Sept 1513; Scots casualties were heavy□

flood in Old Testament, disaster alleged in Genesis to have obliterated all humanity except a chosen few (see Noah◊). It may represent memories of a major local flood, e.g. excavations by Woolley◊ at Ur◊ revealed 2.5 m/8 ft of water-laid clay dating before 4000BC□

Flora in Roman mythology, goddess of flowers, youth, and of spring□

Florence industrial city (*Firenze*), capital of Tuscany◊, Italy; population 448 330. It has printing, engineering, and optical industries, and many crafts, leather, gold and silver, and embroidery. In 1250–1532 it was an independent republic, was immensely prosperous despite conflict between the Guelph◊ and Ghibelline families and reached its apogee of culture in the 15th century: see also Dante◊, Boccaccio◊, and Savonarola◊.

Its architectural treasures include the Ponte Vecchio 1345 over the Arno; the Pitti and Vecchio palaces; cathedral of Santa Maria del Fiore 1314; and the Uffizi Gallery has one of Europe's finest art collections, based on that of the Medici◊□

Florey Howard Walter, Baron 1898–L68. British pathologist, born in Australia. For his work on making penicillin available for use, he shared a Nobel prize with Sir Alexander Fleming◊ 1945. Life peer and Order of Merit 1965□

Florida most southerly state of the USA; Sunshine State

area 151 700 sq km/58 560 sq mi

capital Tallahassee

towns Miami, Tampa

features 50% forested; lakes (including Okeechobee 1 800 sq km/700 sq mi); Everglades National Park (rich birdlife, cypresses, alligators); Palm Beach, an island resort between the lagoon of Lake Worth and the Atlantic; Florida Keys; John F Kennedy Space Center at Cape Canaveral; Disney World theme park

products citrus fruit, melons, vegetables; fish and shellfish; phosphates (one third of world supply), chemicals (fertilizers, etc.), largest US producer of uranium; space research

population 9 739 992, including 500 000 Cubans, and many Haitian refugees

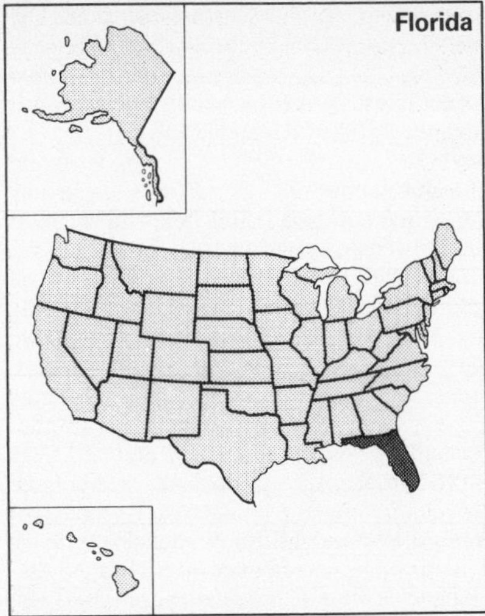

history under Spanish rule from 1513 until its cession to England in 1763, it was returned to Spain in 1783, and purchased by the USA in 1819, becoming a state in 1845□

Florida Keys chain of bridge-linked coral islands extending from the Florida 'panhandle'. The most important are Key Largo and Key West (with a US nàval and air station); there is fishing and tourism□

flotsam, jetsam and **lagan**
flotsam goods found floating at sea after a shipwreck; *jetsam* those thrown overboard to lighten a sinking vessel; *lagan* those on the sea bottom, or secured to a buoy; all belong under British law to the Crown unless the owner is known□

flounder small edible flatfish◊□

flower the blossom characteristic of the Phanerogams (flowering plants), whose function is the creation of reproductive organs and the formation of seed. A typical flower consists of a ring or spiral of petals (the corolla) in which the male organs (stamen) containing the pollen are held high up on filaments for easy access to bees etc., for fertilization purposes. In the centre or lower part of the flower lies the carpels (female nuclei, ovules) which when fertilized form the fruit and seeds of the plant.
The world's oldest flowers, 80 million-year-old fossils found in Norway, are only 1 mm across, and are related to the hydrangea□

flugelhorn see under brass◊□

fluids supercritical. Fluids brought by a combination of heat and pressure to the point when, as a near vapour, they combine the properties of gases and fluids. Used as solvents in chemical processes, such as the

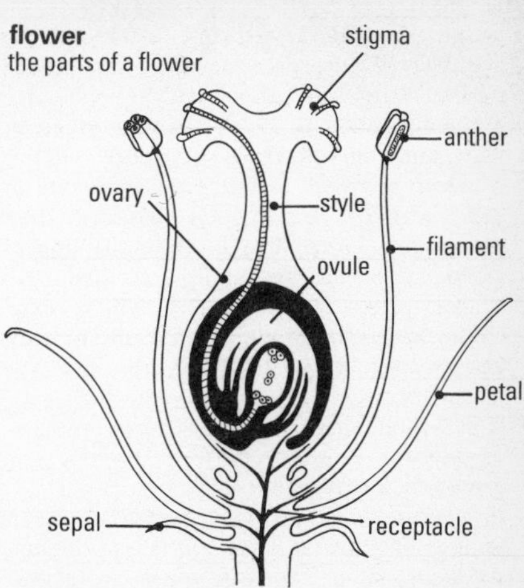

extraction of lubricating oil from refinery residues or the decaffeination of coffee, they avoid the energy-expensive need for phase changes – from liquid to gas and back again – which are required in conventional distillation processes□

fluke a type of worm◊□

fluorescence see luminescence◊□

fluorine element
symbol F
atomic number 9
physical description highly poisonous and reactive gas
features very corrosive and never found free (by itself); there is a trace in the human body; it is the first of the halogen◊ series; it unites directly with nearly all elements and occurs as fluorspar and cryolite
uses sodium fluoride is added to the water supply to retard dental decay in children – one part per million□

fluorspar cubic mineral (calcium fluoride CaF_2), in a range of colours. Derbyshire ***Blue-john*** is a fibrous variety used to make vases, etc. Colourless fluorspar is used for lenses, pottery glazing, etc.□

flute a musical instrument. See under woodwind◊□

fly two-winged insect of the order Diptera, which includes some 90 000 species; the hindwings are represented only by a pair of knob-like organs on slender stalks (halteres) which balance the fly in flight. The mouthparts project from the head as a proboscis used for sucking fluids, and in some species are modified to pierce a victim's skin and enable blood to be withdrawn. They are enabled to walk up a window by discs at the ends of the hairs on their feet, which secrete a fluid enabling them to adhere to the glass. Flies undergo complete metamorphosis; their

larvae are without true legs, and the pupae are rarely enclosed in a cocoon. The sexes are similar, coloration rarely vivid, though some are remarkable for being metallic green or blue. They fall into three suborders:
Nematocera which includes the ***craneflies*** or ***daddy-long-legs,*** e.g. *Tipula paludosa* (their grey-brown larvae live in the soil), family Tipulidae; ***mosquitoes*** family Culicidae, such as the genus *Anopheles*, of which some species transmit the malaria parasite to man; ***midges*** delicate insects of the mosquito type which form dancing clouds, and may 'bite' (Ceratopogonidae) or not (Chironomidae), or may produce galls◊, the Cecidmyiidae, and ***gnats*** which may bite.
Brachycera which includes the ***horse/gad flies*** family Tabanidae, of which *Tabanus sudeticus* has a 5 cm/2 in wingspan, a loud hum, and painful bite (the females suck blood); and ***robberflies*** family Asilidae, which suck other insects dry.
Cyclorhapha which includes the ***blow-fly*** or ***bluebottle*** *Calliphora erythrocephala*, which lays its eggs on carrion, family Calliphoridae; ***flesh-fly*** family Sarcophagidae; ***small fruit fly*** family Drosophilidae, of which *Drosophila melanogaster* is famous for its use in genetic studies (it has only eight chromosomes and reproduces rapidly); ***true fruit fly*** family Trypetidae, especially the ***Mediterranean fruit fly*** *Ceratitis capitata* which ravages Californian orchards; and the the hairy, bee-like ***horse botfly*** *Gasterophilus intestinalis* which has parasitic larvae. Bacterial disease (e.g. typhoid and dysentery) is spread by the ***house-fly*** *musca domestica* family Muscidae, which breeds in rubbish dumps, producing 1000 eggs in its life cycle; and its relative the ***tsetse fly*** genus *Glossina* which transmits trypanosomiasis◊ to cattle, and sleeping sickness◊ to man. Many flies have become immune or resistant to normal pesticides□

fly agaric see amanita◊□

flying dragon a type of lizard◊□

flying fish Atlantic fish *Exocoetus volitans*, family Exocoetidae, of order Beloniformes, which can glide 100 m/325 ft, with expanded pectoral fins, over the wave tops□

flying fox several species of bat◊□

flying lemur two species of small mammal; see colugo◊□

flying lizard a type of lizard◊□

flying squirrel several species of squirrel◊□

Flynn Errol 1909–59. Australian film actor, noted for dashing films e.g. *Captain Blood* 1935 and *The Master of Ballantrae* 1953□

Foch Ferdinand 1851–1929. Marshal of France. In World War I, he was largely responsible for the victory of the Marne◊, commanded on the North-West front Oct 1914–Sept 1916, and became chief of general staff in 1917. Generalissimo of the Allied armies from Apr 1918, he launched the Allied advance in Jul which ended the war□

fog cloud at earth's surface, the condensation of water vapour on dust particles, caused by the air temperature falling below dew◊ point where two currents of air (one cooler than the other) meet, or where warm air flows over a cold surface. Officially fog reduces visibility to 1 km/1100 yds, or less; mist gives a visibility of 1–2 km/1100–2200 yds. In drought areas, e.g. Baja California, Canary Islands, Cape Verde, Namib Desert, Peru/Chile, coastal fogs enable plant and animal life to survive without rain, and are a potential source of water for human use by means of water collectors utilizing condensation. ***Smog*** is natural fog plus impurities (unburned carbon and sulphur dioxide) from domestic fires, industrial furnaces and internal combustion engines (petrol or diesel). The use of smokeless fuels, the treatment of effluent and penalties for excessive smoke from poorly maintained and operated vehicles can be effective, but many cities still suffer□

föhn see under wind◊□

Fokine Michel 1880–1942. Russian dancer-choreographer who worked with Diaghilev◊□

Folies-Bergère Paris music-hall named after its original proprietor□

folk traditional culture common to the people of a country. Folk art is expressed in the decoration and hand-fashioning of articles for use in the home; dance and music express the spirit of a people in a way which is later taken up at a more formal level, e.g. the minuet, waltz and polka were originally peasant dances and, for music, see Cecil Sharp◊, Grieg◊, Dvořák◊, Vaughan Williams◊, Bartók◊, Bob Dylan◊, etc. Folklore includes traditional customs, stories, games, etc. See the brothers Grimm◊, J G Frazer◊, B Malinowski◊□

Folsom site in New Mexico, USA, where a flint weapon point was found in 1926. It proved that man had existed in America in the Pleistocene period□

Fonda Henry 1905–82. American actor, born in Omaha, whose films included *Grapes of Wrath* 1940, *My Darling Clementine* 1946, *12 Angry Men* 1957, and *On Golden Pond* 1982□

Fonda Jane 1937– . American actress, daughter of Henry Fonda◊, active in left-wing politics; academy awards for *Klute* 1971 and *Coming Home* 1979□

Fontainebleau town SE of Paris (see also Barbizon◊), with a royal palace built by Francis I, associated with Mme de Montespan

food chain

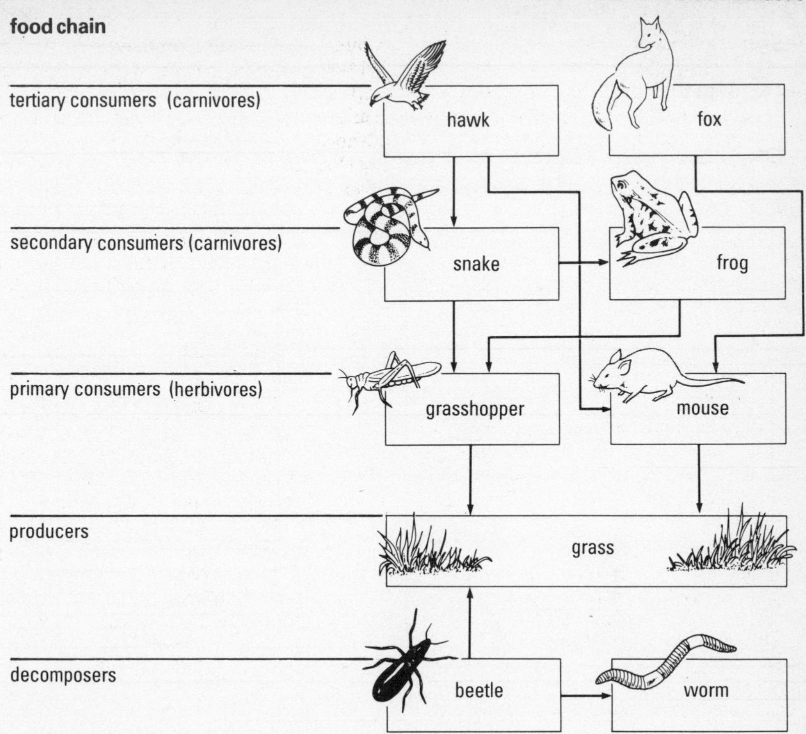

and Mme du Barry, and where Napoleon I signed his abdication; population 19 600□

Fontanne Lynn. See Alfred Lunt◊□

Fontenoy see Austrian◊ Succession□

Fonteyn Dame Margot 1919– . British dancer, born Margaret Hookham. With the Royal Ballet 1934–59, she had faultless technique and beauty of line (*Giselle, Swan Lake, Sleeping Beauty*), and had a celebrated partnership with Nureyev◊. Dame of the British Empire 1956□

Foochow see Fuzhou◊□

food the means of sustaining life. Essential for human beings are: ***protein*** for body building and repair (sources – meat, milk, fish, eggs, and some vegetables); ***fats***◊ to provide energy; ***carbohydrates*** also provide energy and are found in bread, potatoes, cereals and sugar, which form the bulk of the diet; ***vitamins***◊ required only in small quantities to assist the body to make full use of its food; ***minerals*** which are also required in small quantities. Essential foods also include water and roughage (e.g. bran, green leaves for digestion) although these give little nourishment. The energy value of food is expressed in joules or calories□

Food and Agriculture Organization see under United◊ Nations□

food chain the transferring of energy by one organism feeding on another, which in turn is eaten by a third, and so on. A sequence of animals and plants can therefore be established to illustrate their interdependence□

food-poisoning acute illness caused by harmful bacteria; poisonous food (some mushrooms, puffer fish, etc.); poisoned food (lead, arsenic introduced during manufacture, etc.). The most frequent cause of food poisoning is ***salmonella***. This comes in many forms, and strains are found in a high percentage of cattle, pigs, and poultry. There they develop resistance to the antibiotics◊ which are used not merely to treat sick animals but as growth promoters to produce more meat more quickly. Consequently food poisoning is becoming more common and more lethal, and spreads quickly from human to human by contact with faeces or unwashed hands□

Foot Michael 1913– . British Labour politician. Associated with the left-wing weekly *Tribune*, he was Secretary of State for Employment 1974–6, Lord President. of the Council and Leader of the House 1976–9, and succeeded Callaghan as Labour Party leader 1980–3□

foot and mouth disease contagious eruptive viral fever which causes deterioration of milk yield and abortions in cattle, etc. In the UK affected herds are destroyed; inoculation

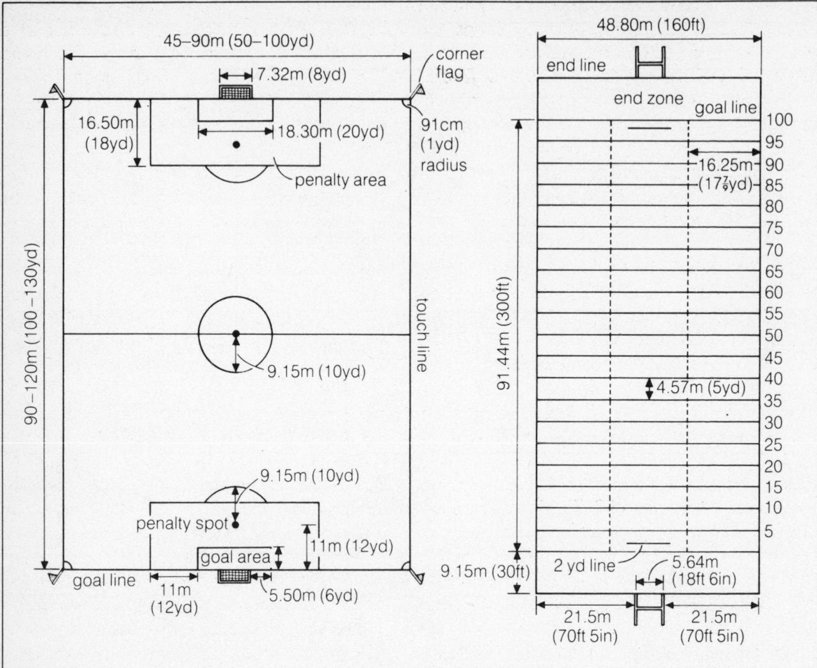

is practised in Europe, and in the US a vaccine has recently been developed□

football a team game.

The earliest form of the game is ***Association football*** or ***'soccer'*** originating in rural football in the UK. It is now played worldwide, under rules of the Football Association 1863. There are two teams of 11, with a large round ball and a low netted goal; only the goal-keeper may touch the ball with his hands. Major events are the World Cup 1930 (every four years), the European Cup 1958 (annually) and the F(ootball) A(ssociation) Cup 1872 (annually in the UK).

Rugby football originated at Rugby 'public school' in 1823, when a boy ran with the ball for the first time. There are 15 players a side, an oval ball, and the goal is high (above a crossbar). 'Tries' may also be scored, by 'touching down' the ball beyond the goal-line. Its most characteristic feature is the 'scrum(mage)', a kind of heads-down free-for-all which restarts the game after some infringements of the rules. The Rugby Union was founded in 1871.

American football formally originated in a Princetown University/Rutgers University game in 1869. The goals and ball are those of English rugby, but the players are kitted out in protective suits against rough tackling, and the two teams of 11 men play on a field marked out in 'gridiron intervals', much closer together than those of the rugby pitch. Only the man with the ball may be tackled, his team-mates running with him to prevent this, and the scoring rules are complex. It is strenuous and games are divided into four 15-minute periods.

Australian football originated in the goldfields of the 1850s, and has teams of 18 men, who use a ball slightly heavier than that of rugby. The pitch is laid out with an oval marking, and the goal has secondary side posts, a ball passing between these and the main posts gaining a lesser score. While running, the player must kick, punch, or bounce the ball every few steps; tackling is not allowed□

foraminifera single-celled marine animals, an order of Protozoa◊. They are enclosed by a thin shell. Some form part of plankton◊, e.g. the many-chambered *Globigerina* whose shells eventually form the chalky ooze of the ocean floor, others live on the sea bottom□

Forbidden City see Peking◊□

force that which tends to change the state of rest or the uniform motion of a body in a straight line. It is measured by the rate of change of momentum of the body on which it acts, that is, the mass of the body multiplied by its acceleration. See Newton◊□

forces fundamental. These are believed to be four fundamental interactions at work in the physical universe. ***Gravity***, which keeps the planets in orbit around the sun, acts between all particles with mass. ***Electromagnetic forces***, which stop solids from falling apart, act between all particles with electric charge. In addition to those long-range forces, there are two very short-range forces: the ***weak***, responsible for the reactions which fuel the sun, and for the emission of beta◊ particles from certain nuclei; and the ***strong***, which binds together the protons and neutrons in nuclei. By 1971 a theory developed by Steven Weinberg, Sheldon Glashow (in USA), Abdus Salam (in England) and others, suggested that the weak and electromagnetic forces were linked; experimental support came from observation at CERN◊ in 1982-3. Physicists are working on theories to unify all four forces□

Ford Ford Madox 1873–1939. English writer (originally Ford Madox Hueffer), a grandson of Ford Madox Brown◊. He is best-remembered as editor of the *English Review* 1908 to which Hardy◊, D H Lawrence◊ and Conrad◊ contributed, and for his novel *The Good Soldier* 1915□

Ford Gerald R(udolph) 1913– . 38th President of the USA, born Leslie King (he took the name of his stepfather). Born in Omaha, Nebraska, he was exceptional as a college footballer, but refused to turn professional and went into law. A Republican, he was nominated by Nixon◊ to succeed Vice-President Spiro Agnew on the latter's resignation in 1973. In 1974 he succeeded Nixon himself in the presidency, and controversially gave his predecessor a free pardon after he was forced to resign over Watergate◊, and amnestied Vietnam draft-dodgers. In 1976 he was narrowly defeated by Carter◊□

Ford Henry 1863–1947. American motor-car manufacturer. He built his first car in 1893 and ten years later founded the Ford Motor Company. His model T 1908–27 was the first car made purely by mass-production methods; 15 million were sold. In 1936 he founded with his son Edsel 1893–1943 the philanthropic Ford Foundation□

Ford John 1586–1640. English dramatist. His most famous play is the study of incest between a brother and sister *'Tis Pity She's a Whore* 1633□

Ford John. Assumed name of Sean O'Fearn 1895–1973, Irish-American film director. One of the greatest directors of the 'western', e.g. *Stagecoach* 1939, and *My Darling Clementine* 1946, he also produced the socially aware *The Informer* 1935, and *Grapes of Wrath* 1940□

Foreign Legion a volunteer Corps of foreigners within a country's army. The French Légion Étrangère, formed 1831, is the most famous of a number of similar forces. Enlisted men are of any nationality, but the officers usually French. Headquarters till 1962 Sidi Bel Abbés, Algeria; its main base is now Corsica□

foreign relations a country's dealings with other countries. In the UK these are handled by the Foreign and Commonwealth Office, an amalgamation of the former separate Foreign and Commonwealth offices in 1968, with a single Diplomatic Service. In the USA they are the responsibility of the State Department (from 1789), and in the USSR of a Foreign Ministry, headed since 1985 by Shevardnadze.

Reasons of national pride dictate that most countries are today represented by ambassadors, the top diplomatic rank, rather than by a minister, envoy or chargé d'affaires, as formerly for minor countries. Consuls combine political and commercial responsibilities in looking after their country's citizens in major foreign cities. Professionally trained spies often inflate the numbers of 'diplomats' accredited to foreign countries□

forest land area covered, either naturally or by design, with trees. Every year some 245 000 sq km, approximately the size of Britain, are cleared and it is estimated that two million of earth's five million plant and animal species will disappear with the remaining area in the next half century. The chief types are: ***coniferous*** (see conifers◊), as in N Europe; ***hardwood*** (temperate), as in old-established forests in southern Britain, oak, beech, elm; ***evergreen*** (subtropical), as in the Mediterranean, southern America and New Zealand; ***savannah*** (tropical) scattered trees in grassland, including ebony; ***high forest*** (tropical), includes both the evergreen forest of S America, SE Asia and Africa, and the areas of deciduous trees where there is a dry season, and where the trees include teak and mahogany.

The understanding of the potential of forests for ameliorating harsh climatic effects, controlling erosion, maintaining soil fertility, and controlling pests, is comparatively recent, and there is as yet little research into the value of food forestry, by which there is cropping at three to five levels from trees or treelike plants (e.g. bananas and plantains, mangoes, citrus, avocadoes, cocoa, coffee), in combination with plants on the ground, without damage to the land. A tropical forest may then yield medicinal plants, oils, spices, gums, resins, tanning and dyeing materials, animal forage, beverages, insect and rodent poisons, green manure, rubber, and animal products□

Forester C(ecil) S(cott) 1899–1966. British novelist, who established his name with *The African Queen* 1938. His reputation rests on his series dealing with the career of Horatio Hornblower in the Napoleonic Wars, beginning with *The Happy Return* 1937□

Forest Hills residential district on Long Island, New York City, USA, noted for tournaments at its West Side Tennis Club□

forget-me-not several plants of genus *Myosotis*, family Boraginaceae◊; the annual ***common forget-me-not*** has bright blue flowers. There are many others of the genus, also known as scorpion-grass□

formaldehyde or ***methanal*** at ordinary temperatures a strong-smelling gas (HCHO) , which condenses at 221°C. When dissolved in water it is known as formalin and is used as a biological preservative. It is used in manufacture of plastics, dyes, foam (e.g. urea-formaldehyde foam, used in insulation), and in medicine as a disinfectant□

Formby George 1904–61. British comedian, son of the music-hall star of the same name, who achieved a stage and screen reputation as the not-so-gormless Lancashire lad. His songs to ukulele accompaniment include 'Mr Wu' and 'Cleaning Windows'□

formic acid or ***methanoic acid*** organic acid (HCOOH), a colourless, slightly fuming liquid. It is secreted by ants and stinging nettles, and blisters the skin. Used in dyeing, tanning and electroplating□

Formosa see Taiwan◊□

Forrest John, 1st Baron Forrest 1847–1918. Australian explorer, who made a dual crossing of his native state of Western Australia (1870/1874), and was its first premier 1890–1901□

Forrestal James Vincent 1892–1949. American Democratic statesman. Secretary of the Navy from 1944, he organized its war effort, and was the first Secretary of Defense 1947–9□

Forssmann Werner 1904–79. W German heart specialist, who originated cardiac catheterization (the passing of a tube into the heart from an arm artery for diagnostic purposes); shared Nobel prize 1956□

Forster E(dward) M(organ) 1879–1970. British novelist, born in London. He is best-known for *A Passage to India* 1924, a sensitive study of the inter-relationship of British and Indians in India. Order of Merit 1969□

Forster William Edward 1818–86. British Liberal reformer. A Bradford woollen manufacturer, he was Gladstone's Vice-President of the Council 1868–74 (securing the passage of the Education Act in 1870 and the Ballot Act 1872), and was Chief Secretary for Ireland 1880–2□

Forsyth Frederick 1938– . British thriller writer, author of *The Day of the Jackal* 1970, *The Fourth Protocol* 1984. Born at Ashford, Kent, he was formerly a foreign correspondent□

forsythia species of temperate E Asian shrub which in spring bears yellow flowers before the leaves appear; Oleaceae◊ family□

Fortaleza industrial port (also called ***Ceará***) in NE Brazil; population 648 815□

Fort-de-France capital and port of Martinique; population 99 000□

Forth river in SE Scotland, which flows 72 km/45 mi from Ben Lomond to the ***Firth of Forth***, reaching the North Sea after a further 80 km/50 mi. It is crossed near Edinburgh by the Forth road (1964) and rail (1890) bridges, and is linked with the Clyde by the ***Forth and Clyde Canal*** 1768–90□

Fort Knox US army post and gold depository in Kentucky, established 1917 as a training camp□

Fort Lamy see N'djamena◊□

Fort Sumter see Charleston◊, South Carolina□

Fortuna in Roman mythology, goddess of chance and good fortune. (Greek *Tyche*)□

Fort Wayne industrial town (electrical goods and electronics, farm machinery) in Indiana, USA; population 377 900. A fort was built on the site against the North American Indians in 1794 by General Anthony Wayne (1745–96), hero of a surprise attack on a British force at Stony Point, New York, in 1779, which earned him the nickname 'Mad Anthony'□

Fort Worth city in Texas, USA; population 385 140. It is a grain, oil and rail centre□

Forty-five The. Jacobite◊ rebellion of 1745, led by Prince Charles◊ Edward. He and his Highlanders occupied Edinburgh and advanced as far as Derby, but then turned back. See Culloden◊□

fossil remains of an animal or plant from an earlier geological period (Latin *fossilis* dug up) preserved in rocks, etc. They may be formed by refrigeration (Siberian mammoths◊), preservation of the skeleton only, carbonization (leaves, etc., in coal), formation of a cast (dinosaur or human footprints in mud), etc. They are tantalizingly incomplete for the study of evolution□

Foster Norman 1935– . British architect, whose works include Sainsbury Centre for Visual Arts at University of East Anglia 1979; headquarters Hongkong and Shanghai Bank; and BBC Radio Centre, Portland Place, London (commissioned 1983)□

Foucault Jean Bernard Léon 1819–68.

French physicist who demonstrated the differing speeds of light in different media in 1850; the rotation of earth by means of a pendulum 1851. He invented the gyroscope 1852□

Fouché Joseph, Duc d'Otrante 1759–1820. French politician, who organized the conspiracy which overthrew Robespierre◊, and was Napoleon's efficient minister of police□

Fou-Liang see Jingdezhen◊□

Fountains Abbey see N Yorkshire◊□

Four Freedoms The. Four kinds of liberty essential to human dignity defined in address to the American Congress by F D Roosevelt 6 Jan 1941: freedom of speech and expression, freedom of worship, freedom from want, freedom from fear□

Fourier François Charles Marie 1772–1837. French Socialist who advocated in his *Le nouveau monde industriel* 1829–30, that society should be organized in cooperative units of about 1800 people□

Fourteen Points the terms proposed by President Wilson of the USA in 1918 as a basis for the post-war world. They included: open diplomacy; freedom of the seas; removal of economic barriers; international disarmament; adjustment of colonial claims; German evacuation of Russian, Belgian, French, and Balkan territories; the restoration of Alsace-Lorraine to France; autonomy for the Austro-Hungarian peoples and those under Turkish rule; an independent Poland; and a general association of nations. Many were embodied in the peace treaties□

fourth estate the Press: name coined by Burke◊□

Fourth of July in the USA, the anniversary of the Declaration of Independence 1776□

Fourth Republic the French regime of 3 Jun 1944–4 Oct 1958□

fowl order of land birds, Galliformes, of worldwide distribution, including many beautifully plumaged species, and many that are edible:

Grouse game birds, family Tetraonidae, including the ***black grouse*** or ***blackcock*** *Lyrurus tetrix*; ***red grouse*** *Lagopus scoticus*; and also the ***willow ptarmigan*** *Lagopus lagopus* of the subarctic, which is always white beneath, and entirely white in winter; and the flightless ***capercailzie*** or 'old man of the woods' *Tetrao urogallus*, which is the size of a turkey, grey, brown and black, glossed with green, and has a remarkable courtship display. In Britain Grouse are shot over dogs or by driving 12 Aug–10 Dec.

Pheasant long-tailed birds, family Phasianidae, of which the ***common pheasant*** *Phasianus colchicus* was traditionally brought from Asia to Europe by the Argonauts (shot as a game bird in Britain 1 Oct–1 Febuary). Most popular of ornamental pheasants is the ***golden pheasant*** *Chrysolophus pictus* of China. The family also includes the ***grey partridge*** *Perdix perdix* shot as a game bird in Britain 1 Sept–1 Feb; ***common peafowl*** or ***peacock*** *Pavo cristatus,* 2 m/6 ft long, counting the magnificent eye-spotted 'tail' of the male (it sometimes occurs as an albino with watered-silk effect patterning); and ***red jungle fowl*** *Gallus gallus* of India and Malaya, ancestor of all domestic chickens. Smallest of the family are the quails, including the ***common quail*** *Coturnix coturnix* squat-bodied, short-tailed, and reddish brown, found in Eurasia and Africa, and netted as a luxury food during migration.

Guinea Fowl game birds of Africa, family Numididae, especially the ***helmet guinea fowl*** *Numida meleagris* which has a horny growth on the head, white-spotted feathers, and fleshy cheek wattles, and is the ancestor of the domesticated guinea hen.

Turkey largest of the game birds, family Meleagrididae of N and Central America, which includes the ***wild turkey*** *Meleagris gallopavo* 11 kg/24 lb, of North America, which was domesticated by the North American Indians and introduced to Europe by the Spaniards.

Hoatzin pheasant-like bird of S America *Opisthocomus hoazin* only member of family Opisthocomidae, also known as the 'stink-bird' because of its musky smell; the young are unusual in that they have 'claws' on their wings which enable them to climb trees□

Fowler William 1911– . American astrophysicist. In 1983 he was awarded a Nobel prize, with Subrahmanyan Chandrasekhar for their independent work on the life-cycle of stars, and the origin of chemical elements□

Fowles John 1926– . English novelist, whose complex novels have a cult following, e.g. *The Collector* 1963, *The French Lieutenant's Woman* 1969, and *Mantissa* 1983□

Fox George 1624–91. Founder of the Society of Friends. Born in Leicestershire, England, he became a travelling preacher in 1647, and in 1650 was imprisoned for blasphemy at Derby, where the name Quakers◊ was first applied to him and his followers. He suffered further imprisonments, made missionary journeys, and wrote a *Journal,* published 1694□

fox doglike carnivorous mammal, family Canidae, which includes the European ***red fox*** *Vulpes vulpes*, with white-tipped tail; ***Arctic fox*** *Alopex lagopus,* valued for its fur; and ***desert fox*** or ***fennec*** *Fennecus zerda*, smallest of the foxes and a nocturnal insect-eater, with very large ears to hear its prey□

Foxe John 1516–87. English Protestant, a canon of Salisbury from 1563. His *Book of Martyrs* 1563, luridly described persecutions under Queen Mary◊, reinforcing popular hatred of Catholicism□

foxglove several Eurasian herbaceous plants, family Scrophulariaceae. The ***common foxglove Digitalis purpurea***, has purple or white flowers; the leaves yield digitalis, used to treat heart complaints□

foxhound a breed of dog◊□

fox-terrier a breed of dog◊□

fox-trot ballroom dance originating in the USA about 1914, which has the alternate rapid and slow movements of the fox□

fractal term invented by French mathematician Benoit Mandelbrod (Latin *fractus* irregular) for irregular shapes outside the rules of conventional geometry. Generated on a computer screen on a mathematical base, they are used in creating 'models' for geographical or biological processes (e.g. formation of a coastline, growth of trees), and for computer art, e.g. their use by George Lucas◊ to create scenes in his science fiction films□

Fra Diavolo assumed name of Italian brigand-leader ***Michele Pezza*** 1771–1806. A renegade monk, he was eventually executed at Naples, and has no link with Auber◊'s opera□

Fragonard Jean Honoré 1732–1806. French painter of Rococo love-scenes, e.g. *The Swing*□

Frame Janet. Pseudonym adopted by New Zealand novelist Janet Paterson Frame Clutha 1924– . Her experiences after being wrongly diagnosed as schizophrenic 1945–54 are reflected in her work, e.g. the novel *Faces in the Water* 1961, and the autobiographical *An Angel at My Table* 1984□

franc French coin, so-called from 1360 when it was a gold coin inscribed *Francorum Rex*, 'King of the Franks'. The ***franc CFA*** is the currency of the French Community in Africa (in the Pacific, ***CFP***). The currency unit of Belgium, Luxembourg, and Switzerland is also called a franc□

France Anatole. Pseudonym of the French writer Jacques Anatole Thibault 1844–1924. His books include the novel *Le Crime de Sylvestre Bonnard* 1881, the satiric *L'Île des Pingouins* 1908. He was a socialist and a supporter of Dreyfus◊; Nobel prize 1921□

France Republic of

area (including Corsica) 551 553 sq km/212 960 sq mi

capital Paris

towns Lyon, Lille, Bordeaux, Toulouse, Nantes, Strasbourg; ports are Marseille and Nice

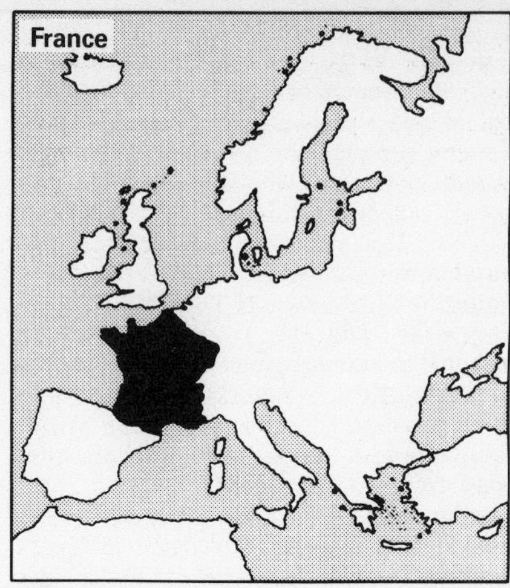

features rivers Seine, Loire, Garonne, Rhône, Rhine; mountain ranges Alps, Massif Central, Pyrenees, Jura, Vosges, Cévennes Vosges; Ardennes, Auvergne, Dordogne, Riviera

exports fruit (especially apples), wine, cheese; cars, aircraft, chemicals, jewellery, silk, lace; tourism is very important

currency franc

population 54 872 000, including 4 500 000 immigrants, chiefly from Portugal and N Africa (Algeria, Morocco and Tunisia); immigration policy was tightened from 1974

language French (regional languages include Breton◊)

religion mainly Roman Catholicism (not recognized by State); Islam 2 000 000; Protestantism 750 000

government under the fifth Republic there is an executive president (François Mitterand◊ from 1981) elected for seven years, who presides over the Council of Ministers and appoints the Prime Minister (from 1986 Jacques Chirac 1932–). There is also a senate (indirectly elected) and a directly elected national assembly (five-year term). The chief parties are: Socialist (Mitterand); Rassemblement pour la République (RPR neo-Gaullist, Chirac); Union pour la Démocratie Française (UDF Giscardian); National Front (rightist, Jean-Marie Le Pen 1930–); Communist (Marais◊). The right-wing victory in the general election of 1986 led for the first time to a combination of Socialist president and neo-Gaullist◊ prime minister.

In local government there has been devolution under Mitterand, and the 22 *régions* have from 1984 directly elected councils headed by a president (with the powers of a former regional prefect◊); each of the 96 *départements* in turn has an elected general council

France: Rulers

Kings:	
Pepin III/Childerich III	751
Pepin III	752
Charlemagne (Charles I)	768
Charlemagne (Charles I)	771
Louis I	814
Lothair I	840
Charles II	843
Louis II	877
Louis III	879
Charles III (the Fat)	882
Odo	888
Charles III (the Simple)	898
Robert I	922
Rudolf	923
Louis IV	936
Lothair II	954
Louis V	986
Hugues Capet	987
Robert II	996
Henri I	1031
Philippe I	1060
Louis VI	1108
Louis VII	1137
Philippe II	1180
Louis VIII	1223
Louis IX	1226
Philippe III	1270
Philippe IV	1285
Louis X	1314
Jean I	1316
Philippe V	1328
Charles IV	1322
Philippe VI	1328
Jean II	1350
Charles V	1356
Charles VI	1380
Charles VII	1422
Louis XI	1461
Charles VIII	1483
Louis XII	1498
François I	1515
Henri II	1547
François II	1559
Charles IX	1560
Henri III	1574
Henri IV	1574
Louis XIII	1610
Louis XIV	1643
Louis XV	1715
Louis XVI	1774
National Convention	1792
Directory (five members)	1795
First Consul:	
Napoléon Bonaparte	1799
Emperor:	
Napoléon I	1804
King:	
Louis XVIII	1814
Emperor:	
Napoléon I	1815
Kings:	
Louis XVIII	1815
Charles X	1824
Louis XIX	1830
Henri V	1830
Louis-Philippe	1830
Heads of State:	
Philippe Buchez	1848
Louis Cavaignac	1848
President:	
Louis Napoléon Bonaparte	1848
Emperor:	
Napoléon III	1852
Presidents:	
Adolphe Thiers	1871
M. Patrice MacMahon	1873
Jules Grevy	1879
François Sadi-Carnot	1887
Jean Casimir-Périer	1894
François Faure	1895
Émile Loubet	1899
Armand Falliéres	1913
Raymond Poincaré	1913
Paul Deschanel	1920
Alexandre Millerand	1920
Gaston Doumergue	1924
Paul Doumer	1931
Albert Le Brun	1932
H. Philippe Pétain (Vichy Government)	1940
Provisional Government	1944
Vincent Auriol	1947
René Coty	1954
Charles de Gaulle	1959
Alain Poher	1969
Georges Pompidou	1969
Alain Poher	1974
Valéry Giscard d'Estaing	1974
François Mitterand	1981

with a president who has taken over most of the powers of the former prefect, the latter (renamed 'commissioner of the republic') now deals only with public order; the departments are subdivided into *communes* with a municipal elected council headed by a mayor. French overseas possessions are 'overseas territories' or 'departments', the latter sometimes having additional status as 'overseas regions': Guadeloupe◊, French Guiana◊, Martinique◊, Mayotte◊, Réunion◊, St Pierre◊ and Miquelon◊; Southern and Antartic Territories (French◊ Antarctica), New◊ Caledonia, French◊ Polynesia, Wallis◊ and Futuna. See also Andorra◊, and Monaco◊. Countries having former colonial links with France, many of which retain commercial or cultural links with her, include: Algeria◊, Benin◊, Cameroon◊, Canada◊, Central◊ African Republic, Chad◊, Comoros◊, Congo◊, Djibouti◊, Dominica◊, Egypt◊, Gabon◊, Guinea◊, Haiti◊, India◊, Kampuchea◊, Laos◊, Lebanon◊, Madagascar◊, Mali◊, Mauretania◊, Morocco◊, Niger◊, Senegal◊, Syria◊, Togo◊, Tunisia◊, Upper Volta◊, Vanuatu◊, Vietnam◊.

history see France◊: history□

France: history

BC

57–51 Julius Caesar◊ conquered the Celtic tribes (Gauls◊)

AD

3–5th century decline of the Roman Empire; country overrun by Germanic tribes

481–511 Clovis◊ established rule over whole country (see Merovingians◊)

8th century Charlemagne◊ made France the centre of his empire; see Carolingians◊

9th century Norsemen invaded France and settled in Normandy (William◊ the Conqueror was of this descent)

987 House of Capet◊ established rule over Paris district, gradually extending its power

1337–1453 Hundred◊ Years' War; Charles◊ VII expelled the English from France (see Joan◊ of Arc)

1483 Louis◊ XI reunited France

16–17th centuries struggle with Spain for supremacy in Europe: see Charles◊ VIII, Henry◊ IV, Richelieu◊, Mazarin◊, Louis◊ XIV

1701–14 War of the Spanish◊ Succession

1740–8 War of the Austrian◊ Succession

1756–63 Seven◊ Years' War

1789 French◊ Revolution: see Louis◊ XVI, Commune◊, Napoleon◊

1814 return of the Bourbons: see Louis◊ XVIII, Charles◊ X

1852 restoration of the Empire by Napoleon◊ III

1870–1 Franco◊-Prussian War, followed by Third Republic; see also Commune◊

1914–18 World◊ War I

1939–45 World◊ War II: see Pétain◊, de Gaulle◊

1944 (3 Jun)–1958 (4 Oct) Fourth Republic

1946–54 war in Indochina (see Vietnam◊)

1954–62 war in Algeria (see Algiers◊, Battle of)

1958 crisis in Algeria led to recall of de Gaulle from private life; inauguration of the Fifth Republic, with greatly increased power for the president

1962 independence granted to Algeria

1968 student and worker unrest

1969 Pompidou◊ replaced de Gaulle, and was succeeded in 1974 by Giscard◊ d'Estaing

1981 Socialist victory achieved by Mitterand◊□

Francesca Piero della c1418–92. Italian Renaissance artist, born San Sepolcro, Tuscany. He is noted for the monumental poise and balance of his figures. There is a fresco series, *Legend of the True Cross*, in the church of St Francis at Arezzo□

Franche-Comté region of E France; capital Besançon; population 1 084 000; Once a 'countship', it was fought over by France, Burgundy, Austria and Spain from the 9th century until it became a French province under the Treaty of Nijmegen 1678□

Francis or ***François*** two kings of France:

Francis I 1494–1547. King from 1515. Succeeding his cousin Louis XII, he warred against his rival, Charles V, 1521–9 (when he was captured at Pavia, and only released on signing a humiliating treaty), 1536–8, and 1542–4. At home he became absolute monarch. See Field◊ of the Cloth of Gold, Marguerite◊ d'Angoulême.

Francis II 1544–60. He married Mary, Queen of Scots, in 1558, and succeeded his father, Henry II, in 1559. He was dominated by his mother, Catherine de' Medici◊□

Francis of Assisi, St 1182–1226. Italian founder of the Franciscan◊ order 1209. The son of a wealthy merchant, his life was changed by two dreams during an illness in his early twenties. Determined to follow literally the commands of the New Testament, he preached to all, including animals and birds□

Francis of Sales, St 1567–1622. French saint, a leader of the Counter-Reformation and founder in 1610 of the Order of the Visitation for nuns□

Francis II 1768–1835. Last Holy Roman Emperor 1792–1806 (succeeding his father,

Leopold◊ II) and (as ***Francis I***) Emperor of Austria from 1804. He was at war with France 1792–7, 1798–1801, 1805, 1809, and 1813–14□

Franciscans Catholic order of friars (***Friars Minor*** or ***Grey Friars***), founded 1209 by Francis◊ of Assisi, and noted for their preaching and ministry among the poor. Most famous of their sub-divisions are the ***Capuchins***, founded in 1520 to return to the original simple rule, and noted for missionary activity, and their habit with pointed hood (French *capuche*). A second (female) order the ***Poor Clares*** was founded by St Clare◊, and lay people, who adopt a Franciscan regime without abandoning the world, form a third (***Tertiaries***). See also Roger Bacon◊□

Francis Ferdinand or ***Franz Ferdinand*** 1863–1914. Archduke of Austria from 1889, when he became heir apparent to his uncle Francis◊ Joseph. He was assassinated on a visit to Sarajevo 28 Jun 1914. Austria made this the pretext for attacking Serbia, and World War I began□

Francis Joseph or ***Franz Joseph*** 1830–1916. Emperor of Austria-Hungary from 1848, succeeding on the abdication of his uncle Ferdinand I. He suppressed the revolts of 1848, but his defeats in the Italian War of 1859 and Prussian War of 1866 forced him to grant Austria a parliamentary constitution in 1861, and Hungary equality with Austria in 1867. His wife was assassinated in 1897. In 1914 he made the assassination of Francis◊ Ferdinand the excuse for attacking Serbia, precipitating World War I□

francium element
symbol Fr
atomic number 87
physical description heaviest alkali metal
features radioactive, very rare metal; it is naturally present in earth's crust at any moment in a quantity of about 30 grm/1 oz, and is usually made in the laboratory
uses none, due its exceptionally short half-life□

Franck César Auguste 1822–90. Belgian Composer, organist at St Clotilde, Paris, from 1858. His music is mainly religious, and includes *Symphonic Variations* for piano and orchestra, the violin sonata, and the oratorios *Redemption,* and *Les Béatitudes,* a choral masterpiece□

Franco Bahamonde Francisco 1892–1975. Spanish dictator. Born in Galicia, he became Chief of Staff in 1935, but in 1936 was demoted to Governor of the Canary Islands, and so plotted an uprising (with German and Italian assistance) against the Republican government. As leader of the insurgents (Nationalists) during the Spanish◊ Civil War, he proclaimed himself *Caudillo* (leader) of Spain, and the defeat of the Republic in 1939 brought all Spain under his rule. During World War II he observed a cautious general neutrality, and as head of state for life from 1947, slightly liberalized his regime. In 1969, he nominated as his successor and future king of Spain, Juan◊ Carlos; he relinquished the premiership in 1973, and by his death had presided over considerable economic growth. See Falange◊ Española□

François see Francis◊□

Franco-Prussian War 1870–1. War provoked by Franco-Prussian rivalry. Bismarck used the candidature of a German for the Spanish throne to needle Napoleon III into a declaration of war, and, after trouncing him at Sedan◊, successfully besieged Paris. The Treaty of Frankfurt in May 1871 brought Prussia Alsace and Lorraine, plus a large French indemnity, and established Prussia as Europe's leading power. See also Commune◊ of Paris□

frangipani tropical American tree *Plumeria rubra*, family Apocynaceae; perfume is made from its strongly scented flowers□

Frank a member of the Germanic people who over-ran Belgium and N France in the 4–5th centuries. Their king, Clovis◊, became Christian, founded the French monarchy, and all France and W Germany was temporarily united under his descendants. One branch of the Franks gave its name to France, and were fused by the 9th century into a single people with the Gallo-Romans, speaking the modified form of Latin which became modern French. See Salic◊ Law□

Frank Anne 1929–45. German diarist. Born at Frankfurt-am-Main, she fled to Holland with her family in 1933 to escape Nazi anti-Semitism. The house in which they took final refuge 1942–4 is preserved as a museum. After their betrayal, Anne died in Belsen concentration camp. Her moving diary was published in 1947□

Frankenstein Law US Supreme Court ruling in 1980 that laboratory-created forms of life may be patented: see Mary Shelley◊□

Frankfurt-am-Main industrial, banking and commercial city and inland port in Hesse, W Germany; population 629 200. A free city until incorporated in Prussia 1886, it has an annual international book fair□

frankincense resin of trees of the Old World genus *Boswellia*, family Burseraceae, used in incense□

Franklin Benjamin 1706–90. American statesman and scientist. Born in Boston, he combined a successful printing business with scientific experiment. He proved that lightning is a form of electricity by the very dangerous experiment of flying a kite in a storm, distinguished between positive and negative electricity, and invented the lightning-conductor. A member of the Pennsylvania Assembly 1751–64, he was sent to England to lobby Parliament about tax grievances, and later helped to draft the Declaration of Independence. As ambassador to France, 1776–85, he negotiated an alliance with France and the peace settlement with Britain. He was president of Pennsylvania 1785–8, and helped draw up the American constitution. His autobiography appeared in 1781□

Franklin Sir John 1786–1847. British naval explorer. Born in Spilsby, Lincolnshire, he fought at Trafalgar and in 1845 commanded an expedition to look for the North◊ West Passage. Its fate remained a mystery until 1859, when records were discovered by a search party. In 1984 two of its members buried on King Edward Island were found to be perfectly preserved in the frozen ground of their graves□

Franklin a district of the Canadian Northwest◊ Territories□

Franz Ferdinand see Francis◊ Ferdinand□

Franz Josef Land archipelago of about 85 islands in the Arctic Ocean; area 20 720 sq km/8000 sq mi. There are scientific stations□

Franz Joseph see Francis◊ Joseph□

Fraser Lady Antonia 1932– . British author of biographies, e.g. *Mary Queen of Scots* 1969, and a series of detective novels featuring investigator 'Jemima Shore'. The daughter of Lord Longford, she married first Sir Hugh Fraser, and secondly, in 1980, playwright Harold Pinter◊□

Fraser Malcolm 1930– . Australian Liberal statesman. A millionaire sheep farmer, he replaced Snedden in the party leadership 1975. In Nov, following the Whitlam government's loan difficulties, he blocked finance bills in the Senate, became Prime Minister of a 'caretaker' government and won the Dec election, but lost to Hawke 1983□

Fraser Peter 1884–1950. New Zealand Labour statesman, Prime Minister 1940–9□

fraternity and **sorority** a student society for men or women respectively in US universities and colleges, usually named with Greek letters, e.g. the earliest, Phi Beta Kappa, at William and Mary College, Virginia, 1776□

fraud a false representation, e.g. by a factually untrue statement, which is known to be untrue, and which is intended to be acted upon, so that the person to whom the statement is made suffers by doing so□

Fraunhofer Joseph von 1787–1826. German physicist, who in 1814 first identified chemical elements known on earth in the sun's atmosphere, by the dark lines, ***Fraunhofer lines***, crossing the solar spectrum□

Fray Bentos river port in Uruguay; population 20 000. Linked by bridge over the Uruguay with Puerto Unzue in Argentina, it is famous for corned beef□

Frazer Sir James George 1854–1941. Scottish anthropologist, remembered for his romanticized pioneer work on primitive religion and sociology *The Golden Bough* 1890□

Frederick two Holy Roman Emperors:

Frederick I c1123–90. Emperor from 1152, known as ***Barbarossa***◊ 'red-beard'. He failed in a struggle with the papacy (Alexander◊ III) 1159–77, the Lombard cities, headed by Milan, taking the opportunity to become independent of imperial control. He joined the Third Crusade, and was drowned in Asia Minor.

Frederick II 1194–1250. Emperor from 1212. He led the 5th Crusade, which recovered Jerusalem by treaty without battle, but at the same time quarrelled with the Pope, who thrice excommunicated him. A complete sceptic in religion, he was probably the most cultured man of his age□

Frederick three kings of Prussia:

Frederick I 1657–1713. He became Elector of Brandenburg in 1688, and assumed the title of King of Prussia in 1701.

Frederick II, called ***the Great*** 1712–86. King from 1740, he was given a Spartan education by his father, Frederick◊ William I. He started the War of the Austrian◊ Succession by his attack on Austria in 1740 to gain Silesia, and displayed consummate generalship in the Seven◊ Years' War. At home he embarked on thoroughgoing reforms, acquired W Prussia in the first partition of Poland 1772, and left Prussia as Germany's foremost state.

Frederick III 1831–88. King and German Emperor in 1888. The son of William◊ I, he married Queen Victoria of England's eldest daughter (Victoria), and, as a liberal, frequently opposed Bismarck◊□

Frederick William 1620–88. Elector of Brandenburg from 1640, 'the Great Elector'. By successful wars with Sweden and Poland, he prepared the way for Prussian power in the 18th century□

Frederick William four kings of Prussia:

Frederick William I 1688–1740. King from 1713, he developed Prussia's military might and commerce.

Frederick William II 1744–97. Nephew of Frederick◊ II and king from 1786, he was unsuccessful in waging war on the French

1792–5, and lost all Prussia west of the Rhine.
Frederick William III 1770–1840. King from 1797, he was defeated by Napoleon 1806, but joined in his final defeat and profited in territory allotted at the Congress of Vienna◊.
Frederick William IV 1795–1861. King from 1840, he was a believer in divine◊ right of kings, but had to grant a constitution in 1850 after the Prussian revolution of 1848. He became insane in 1857□

Free Church protestant denomination in England and Wales which is not established by the State, e.g. the Methodist Church, Baptist Union, and United Reformed Church (Congregational and Presbyterian). These churches joined for common action in the Free Church Federal Council in 1940□

Free Church of Scotland the Church of those who seceded from the Presbyterian Church of Scotland 1843. They were reunited 1929□

Freedom of a city, etc. In Britain, and some other countries, an honour, of which the privileges are today nominal, granted to distinguished people□

Freedom Presidential Medal of. Highest peacetime civilian honour in the USA, established by Kennedy in 1963, and conferred each Independence Day□

freefalling see skydiving◊□

Free French French forces in World War II who continued to fight under de Gaulle◊ after the Franco-German armistice in Jun 1940. Their emblem was Joan of Arc's Cross of Lorraine, with two 'bars'□

Freemasonry linked national organizations for men, originating in a 14th century English masonic guild, the stone masons. The first modern Grand Lodge (governing body) was established in 1717, and the movement spread from Britain throughout the world. In many countries it became political and often anticlerical, resulting in Papal condemnation and state suppression; in Italy in the 1980s, widespread corruption has been linked to a freemason organization ('P2')□

free port in the UK, a port (Cardiff, Liverpool, Southampton; and, linked to airports, Belfast, Birmingham, Prestwick) allowed to operate without normal Customs duties and VAT being applied, e.g. if foreign firms land goods for assembly, which are then exported. Duties and tax become payable only if the products are then imported into the UK□

freesia genus of S African plants, family Iridaceae; commercially grown for their scented funnel-shaped flowers□

free thought post-Reformation movement opposed to Christian dogma, represented in Britain by the 17–18th century Deists◊, and in the 19th century by the radical thinker Richard Carlile 1790–1843, a pioneer of a free press, and in the 20th by Bertrand Russell◊. The tradition is upheld by the Rationalist Press Association and Secular Society□

Freetown capital and port of Sierra Leone; population 274 000□

free trade international trade free of duties, which was secured in Britain by the repeal of the Corn◊ Laws 1846. According to traditional economic theory, free trade allows nations to specialize in those commodities which can be produced most efficiently. In the 20th century the idea of free trade was revived in 1947 with the General Agreement on Tariffs and Trade (GATT). In the 1980s long-continued recession swung the pendulum back towards ***protectionism*** which discourages by heavy duties foreign imports likely to compete with home products□

free will the doctrine that human beings are free to control their own actions and that these actions are not fixed in advance by God or fate. This doctrine is hard to reconcile convincingly with the view that people are part of a world governed by either physical laws (see determinism◊) or God's will. Some Christian theologians assert that God gave humanity free will to choose between good and evil; others that God has decided in advance the outcome of all human choices (predestination, as in Calvinism◊)□

freezing the change from a liquid to a solid state at a particular temperature (freezing point). Most liquids contract on freezing, but water expands (hence burst pipes), so that ice is less dense than water. Dissolved substances lower the freezing point, e.g. salty sea water freezes at a lower point than fresh.
Animals in arctic conditions, e.g. insects or fish, cope either by manufacturing natural 'antifreeze' and staying active, or by allowing themselves to freeze in a controlled fashion, i.e. they manufacture proteins to act as nuclei for the formation of ice crystals in areas which will not produce cellular damage, and so enable themselves to thaw back to life again (see also under frog◊)□

Frege Gottlob 1848–1925. German philosopher, founder of modern mathematical logic with *The Foundations of Arithmetic* 1884, which influenced Russell◊ and Wittgenstein◊□

Freiburg-im-Breisgau industrial city (pharmaceuticals, precision instruments) in

Baden-Württemberg, Germany; population 175 800. There is a fine 12th century cathedral□

Fremantle chief port of Western Australia, SW of Perth◊; population 23 780□

French Sir John Denton Pinkstone, 1st Earl of Ypres 1852–1925. British field marshal. In the South◊ African War, he relieved Kimberley and took Bloemfontein, and in World War I was Commander-in-Chief of the British Expeditionary Force in France 1914–15; he resigned after being criticized as indecisive□

French Antarctica territory, in full ***French Southern and Antarctic Territories,*** created 1955; area 10 100 sq km/3900 sq mi; population about 200 research scientists. It includes Adélie Land, on the continent, and the Kerguelen (where Port-aux-Français is the chief centre) and Crozet archipelagos and Saint Paul and Nouvelle Amsterdam islands in the southern seas□

French Community France and those overseas territories joined with it by the constitution of the Fifth Republic, following the referendum of 1958. In that form, it no longer exists, but in practice all former French colonies have close economic and cultural as well as language links with France□

French Guiana overseas region of France from 1976

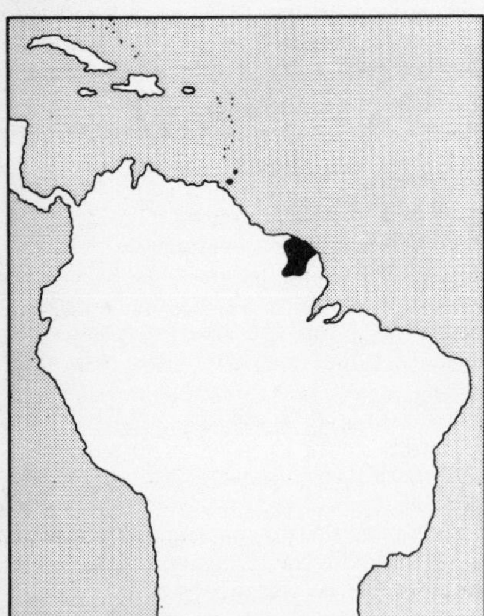

area 91 000 sq km/34 740 sq mi
capital Cayenne
towns St Laurent
features Eurospace rocket launch pad at Kourou; Îles du Salut, which include Devil's Island◊
exports timber, shrimps
currency franc
population 73 000
language French
religion Roman Catholicism
famous people Captain Dreyfus◊
history first settled by France in 1604, the territory became a French possession in 1817□

french horn see under brass◊□

French India former French possessions in India (Pondichéry, Chandernagore, Karikal, Mahé, and Yanaon (Yanam)), all transferred to India by 1954□

French language romance language developed from the everyday (Vulgar) Latin used in Roman Gaul◊, and which had become a separate language from the 9th century. North of the Loire dialects formed the *langue d'oui*, and to the south, the *langue d'oc* (distinguished by their differing words for 'yes'). By the 13th century the dialect of the Ile de France was supreme, and was enforced by the Decree of Villers-Cotterêts in 1539 as the language of administration and the courts. From 1635 the French Academy◊ became its guardian, e.g. the use of *franglais*, the use of Anglo-American terms in broadcasting, etc., was made illegal in 1976. French is also one of the languages of Luxembourg, Belgium and Switzerland. See also language◊□

French Polynesia French overseas territory (from 1961) in the S Pacific
total area 3940 sq km/1520 sq mi
capital Papeete on Tahiti
features comprises five archipelagos (see below)
exports cultivated pearls, coconut oil, vanilla; tourism is important
total population 149 000
languages French, Tahitan (official)
government a High Commissioner (Alain Ohrel) and Council of Government; two deputies are returned to the National Assembly in France
recent history first visited by Europeans in 1595,the Polynesian islands became famous as living 'proof' of Rousseau◊'s theory of the noble savage when visited by Bougainville in 1768. Became French Protectorate 1843, self-governing 1977. Following demands for independence in New◊ Calendonia 1984–5, agitation increased also in Polynesia.
major divisions
Society Islands, divided into Leeward and Windward groups; area 1685 sq km/650 sq mi; population 165 000. Administrative headquarters Papeete on Tahiti, the largest island, area 1040 sq km/402 sq mi, population 96 000. Tahiti was visited by Cook◊ 1769 and by Bligh◊ of the *Bounty* 1788, and its striking people and beautiful scenery have attracted

artists, e.g. Gauguin◊, and modern tourists. Claimed by the French 1768, the group became a French protectorate 1843.

Marquesas Islands, area 1270 sq km/490 sq mi; population 5420. Administrative headquarters Atuona on Hiva Oa. Annexed by France 1842.

Tuamotu Islands, area 1064 sq km/411 sq mi; population 8540. Administrative headquarters Apataki. Mururoa Atoll has been a controversial French nuclear test site since 1966. The ***Gambier Islands*** are grouped with them.

Tubuai/Austral Islands, area 163 sq km/63 sq mi. To preserve the nature culture, no outside visitors are allowed□

French Revolution the forcible abolition of the *Ancien Régime* 'old order of things' (feudalism and absolute monarchy) 1789–99.

1789 5 May the States General (an assembly of the three 'estates', nobles, clergy, and commons) met at Versailles, bent on establishing a new constitution; 17 Jun National Assembly formed by the Third Estate (commons); 14 Jul Bastille◊ was taken by the mob when Louis◊ XVI attempted repressive moves; see also first Paris Commune◊

1791 20 Jun flight of the royal family to Varennes; 14 Sept Louis, brought back as a prisoner, accepted the new constitution

1792 20 Apr war declared on Austria, which threatened to suppress the revolution; 10 Aug royal palace stormed by the French mob; 21 Sept First Republic proclaimed

1793 21 Jan Louis XVI executed; 2 Jun overthrow of the moderate Girondists◊ by the Jacobins◊; rule of the dictatorial Committee of Public Safety (see Carnot◊, Danton◊, Robespierre◊); 5 Sept the mass executions of the Terror◊ began

1794 27 Jul (9 Thermidor under the Revolutionary calendar) fall of Robespierre and end of the Terror; the Directory (a body of five directors) established to hold a middle course between Royalism and Jacobinism. It ruled until Napoleon◊ seized power in 1799□

French Somaliland see Djibouti◊□

French Sudan see Mali◊□

French West Africa group of French colonies administered from Dakar 1895–1958, the modern Senegal, Mauretania, Sudan, Burkina Faso, Guinea, Niger, Ivory Coast, and Benin□

Freneau Philip Morin 1752–1832. American poet, whose *A Political Litany* 1775, was a mock prayer for deliverance from British tyranny□

frequency number of cycles of a vibration occurring per unit of time. The unit of frequency is the ***hertz*** (Hz); 1 Hz = 1 cycle per second, 1 KHz (1 kilohertz) = 1 000 Hz, 1 MHz (1 megahertz) = 1 000 000 hz. Human beings can hear sounds from objects vibrating from about 20 Hz to 15 000 Hz. ***Ultrasonic frequencies*** are above that range. For use in radio see electromagnetic◊ waves□

Frere John 1740–1807. British archaeologist. In 1790 he recognized that palaeolithic tools found in Suffolk must be older than the conventional biblical time scale of his era□

fresco see painting◊□

Freud Anna 1895–82. British psychiatrist, daughter of Sigmund Freud, and the founder of child analysis□

Freud Clement 1924– . British Liberal MP and television personality, grandson of Sigmund Freud□

Freud Lucian 1922– . British portrait artist, grandson of Sigmund Freud□

Freud Sigmund 1865–1939. Austrian psychiatrist, an originator of psychoanalysis◊. Influenced by Charcot◊ and Breuer◊, he developed the method of free association and interpretation of dreams which is still the basic technique of psychoanalysis. His theory of the repression of infantile sexuality as the root of neuroses in the adult (see Oedipus◊) was controversial, and his associates Adler◊ and Jung◊ parted company with him. In 1938, following the Nazi occupation, he left Vienna for London. His books include *The Interpretation of Dreams* 1900, *The Psychopathology of Everyday Life* 1901, *Totem and Taboo* 1913, and *The Ego and the Id* 1923. His work, long accepted as definitive by many, has been increasingly questioned in recent years□

friar originally brother (Latin *frater*) of the mendicant monastic orders, i.e. the Franciscans, Dominicans, Carmelites, and Austin Friars, but now of any order□

friction force tending to prevent one body sliding over another, which occurs in solids, liquids and gases, and may be either reduced by lubricants or enhanced, as in brake linings, etc.□

Friedman Milton 1912– . American economist, Nobel prizewinner 1976, who argues that a country's economy, and hence inflation, can be controlled through its money supply□

friendly society or in US ***benefit society*** association designed to meet the needs of sickness and old age. They developed especially in the late 18th and early 19th centuries, and were the forerunners in the UK of National Insurance, e.g. National Deposit, Odd Fellows, Foresters and Hearts of Oak□

Friends Society of. Christian sect (popularly known as Quakers, because they quaked, that is trembled, before the Lord) founded by

George Fox◊ in the 17th century. Originally marked out by their sober dress, use of 'thee' and 'thou' to all as a sign of equality, etc, they incurred penalties by their pacifism, and refusal to take oaths or pay tithes and many emigrated to form communities abroad, e.g. in Pennsylvania and New England, USA. In the 19th century many Friends were prominent in social reform, e.g. Elizabeth Fry◊. They now form a world-wide movement of about 200 000, and their worship is marked by its stress on meditation, and by the freedom of all to take an active part in the service. They have no priests or ministers□

Friesland northern maritime province (capital Leeuwarden) of the Netherlands, in which land is still being reclaimed from the sea. Friesian (black and white) cattle originated here. The ***Eleven Cities Tour*** 1909, is a 210 km/124 mi skating marathon on the canals of the province held only in the rare years when the ice is hard enough. See Frisians◊□

frigate general purpose anti-aircraft and anti-submarine escort vessel of up to 3000 tonnes. Britain's type-23 (1988) is armoured, heavily armed (4.5 inch naval gun, 32 Sea Wolf anti-missile and anti-aircraft missiles and a surface-to-surface missile), and, for locating submarines, a large helicopter and a hydrophone array towed astern. Engines are diesel-electric up to 17 knots, with gas turbines for spurts of speed to 28 knots□

frigate bird a type of pelican◊□

frilled lizard a type of lizard◊□

Frink Dame Elisabeth 1930– . British sculptor. Among her works are the *Horseman* (opposite the Ritz in London), *In Memoriam* (heads), and *Running Man* 1980. DBE 1982□

Frisch Karl von 1886–82. German zoologist, co-founder of ethology, who discovered how bees communicate with each other, and shared a Nobel prize in 1973 with Lorenz◊ and Tinbergen◊□

Frisch Max 1911– . Swiss writer, formerly a journalist and architect. His novels include the satirical *Stiller* 1954, and his plays the dark comedy *The Fire Raisers* 1958 and *Andorra* 1961□

Frisch Otto 1904–79. Austrian physicist. A refugee from Hitler, he coined the term 'nuclear fission', and worked from 1943 at Los Alamos◊, then at Cambridge. He is the nephew of Lise Meitner◊□

Frisch Ragnar 1895–1973. Norwegian economist, the inventor of econometrics; he shared a Nobel prize in 1969 with Tinbergen◊□

Frisian a member of a Germanic people with a language closely related to English, which survives in Friesland◊. They may have accompanied Anglo-Saxons in their invasion of Britain□

Frisian Islands chain of low-lying islands off the Netherlands, Germany and Denmark, formed by the sinking of the intervening land; ***Texel*** is the largest and most westerly□

fritillary (botany) plant, genus *Fritillaria* in the family Liliaceae, which has bell-shaped flowers marked in a similar pattern to that of the fritillary butterfly□

fritillary (zoology) butterfly with black markings on an orange ground, family Nymphalidae, found in British woods□

Friuli-Venezia Julia special autonomous region of NE Italy; capital Trieste; population 1 231 170. Formed in 1947, with the addition of Trieste in 1954, it has strong Slav minority agitation for complete independence□

Frobisher Sir Martin c1535–94. English explorer, born in Yorkshire. He sought the North◊West Passage in 1576 (when he visited Labrador and Frobisher Bay in Baffin Land), 1577 and 1578. He served as vice-admiral in Drake's West Indian expedition of 1585, and was knighted 1588 for helping to defeat the Armada□

Froebel Friedrich Aug Wilhelm 1782–1852. German educationist, influenced by Pestalozzi◊, who founded the first kindergarten ('garden for children') in Blankenburg in 1836, using instructive play□

frog amphibian of the order Anura (Greek 'without a tail' – because the adult forms are tail-less). Squat-bodied, they have hind legs which may be specialized for jumping or by webbed feet for swimming. The ***flying frogs*** of Malaysia, using webbed fore and hind feet, can achieve a 12 m/36 ft glide. Many frogs and toads use their long extensible tongues to capture insect prey and are useful to farmers, gardeners, etc.

The males attract the females in great gatherings, usually by croaking. In some tropical species the inflated vocal sac may exceed the rest of the body in size. Other courtship 'lures' include thumping on the ground and 'dances'. Eggs (spawn, laid in large masses) may be left to float in water to hatch into tadpoles, which then develop gradually to frogs; or nests may be constructed, some S American frogs build little mud pool 'nests' and African ***tree frogs*** make foam nests from secreted mucus. In other species the eggs may be carried in 'pockets' on the mother's back, or brooded by the male in his vocal sac, or, as with the ***midwife toad*** *Alytes obstetricans*, carried by the male wrapped round his hind legs until hatching.

Certain species of frog have powerful skin poisons (alkaloids). They vary in size from the smallest *Smin hillus limbatus*, 12 mm/under 0.5 in long, to the giant frog *Telmatobius culeus* of Lake Titicaca 50 cm/20 in, which is edible.

true frogs family Ranidae, includes the ***common frog*** *Rana temporaria*, becoming rare in Britain as small ponds disappear; the ***edible frog*** *Rana esculenta* (only the legs are eaten); and ***bullfrog*** *Rana catesbeiana*, with a croak that carries for miles, and able to jump nine times its own length (annual jumping races are held at Calaveras, California). Some frogs, e.g. the ***wood frog*** *Rana sylvatica* of N America, are the only vertebrates known to survive freezing of their bodies in nature.

true toads family Bufonidae, differ from frogs in their usually rougher skins, short hind legs (which limit them to clumsy hops), nocturnal habits, and absence of teeth. They gain some protection from predators by having an unpleasant skin secretion. They include the ***common toad*** *Bufo bufo* of Britain□

frog-hopper family of brown leaping insects, Cercopidae, order Hemiptera, which suck the juice from plants. Their larvae, 'froth-flies', are pale green and protect themselves (from drying out and from predators) by secreting froth ('cuckoo-spit') from their anus□

frogmouth Australian bird; see under nightjar◊□

Froissart Jean 1338–1410. French chronicler, secretary to Queen Philippa, wife of Edward III of England. He travelled in Scotland and Brittany, went with the Black◊ Prince to Aquitaine, and in 1368 was in Milan with Chaucer◊ and Petrarch◊. He recorded in his *Chronicles* events of 1326–1400, often at first hand□

Fromm Erich 1900–80. German-American psychoanalyst, driven from Germany in 1933. His *The Fear of Freedom* 1941 and *The Sane Society* 1955, were source books for modern alternative life-styles□

Fronde French revolts 1648–53 against the administration of Mazarin◊ during Louis XIV's minority. In 1648–9 the Paris *parlement* attempted to limit the royal power, its leaders were arrested, Paris revolted, and the rising was surpressed by the royal army under Condé◊. Condé then (1650) led a new revolt of the nobility, but this was surpressed by 1653□

Frontenac et Palluau Louis de Buade, Comte de 1620–98. Governor of French Canada from 1672 till recalled for his expansionist aims in 1682. A disastrous war with the Iroquois◊ followed, and Frontenac was reinstated in 1689□

Frost Robert Lee 1874–1963. American poet. Born in San Francisco, he became an unsuccessful farmer in New Hampshire◊. In 1912–15 he was in England, where he published *A Boy's Will* 1913, and *North of Boston* 1914, which established his reputation. His traditional verse is written with an individual voice and penetrating vision, his best-known poems include 'Mending Wall' ('something there is that does not love a wall'), 'The Road Not Taken', and 'Stopping by Woods on a Snowy Evening'□

frost the freezing and crystallization of water in the atmosphere on exposed objects when air temperature is below 0°C/32°F. As cold air is heavier than warm, ***ground frost*** is the most common; ***hoar frost*** forms in the same way as dew◊□

frostbite the cut-off of blood supply, especially to bodily extremities (feet, hands, nose, ears), so that the part starts to die (gangrene, necrosis). The treatment is massage with snow or cold water□

Froude James Anthony 1818–94. British historian, whose *History of England from the Fall of Wolsey to the Defeat of the Spanish Armada* 1856–70, has a dramatic realization of events. He was influenced by the Oxford◊ Movement, in which his brother, ***Richard Hurrell Froude*** 1803–36, collaborated with Newman◊□

fructose fruit sugar, $C_6H_{12}O_6$, which occurs in honey, cane sugar, nectar of flowers, and many sweet fruits. Sweeter than cane sugar, it is prepared from the latter on a large scale□

fruit the ripe ovary of a flower, containing the seeds of a new plant. The fruit assists the dispersal of the seeds and helps to protect them. Fruits can be divided into simple, multiple, aggregate, and accessory, depending on the number and arrangement of seeds contained. Fruits vary widely in the manner in which they are dispersed; the most important to humans is the edible fruit, such fruits are commercially very important and are cultivated throughout the world□

fruit fly a type of small fly◊□

Frunze capital (formerly ***Pishpek***) and industrial city (textiles, farm machinery, metal goods) of Kirgiz Republic, USSR; population 552 000□

Fry Christopher 1907– . British dramatist, leader of the revival of verse drama after World War II, e.g. *The Lady's Not for Burning* 1948□

Fry Elizabeth 1780–1845. British Quaker, wife of the London merchant Joseph Fry, who formed an association for the improvement of female prisoners in 1817, and worked with her brother, Joseph Gurney, on an influential report (1819) on prison reform□

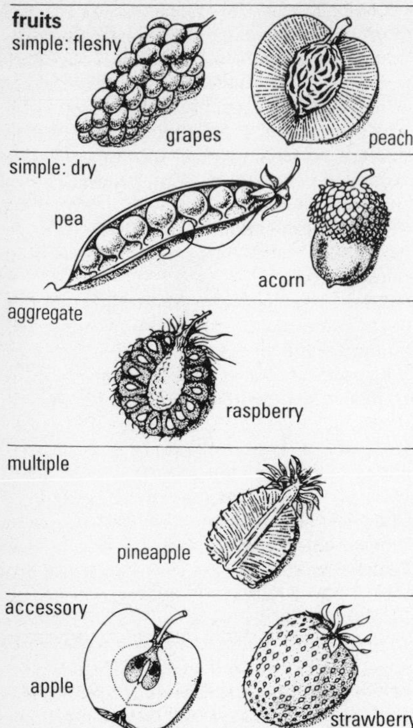

Fry Roger Elliott 1866–1934. British artist and art critic, who introduced Post-Impressionism◊ to England; see also Vanessa Bell◊□

FT Index see Financial◊ Times Index□

Fuad I 1868–1936. Sultan of Egypt from 1917, becoming king on Egyptian independence in 1922□

Fuad II 1952– . See under Farouk◊□

Fuchs Klaus 1911– . German spy, who worked on atom bomb research in Britain in World War II, and was imprisoned 1950–9 for passing information to the USSR. He resettled in E Germany□

Fuchs Sir Vivian 1908– . British explorer, who led the Commonwealth Trans-Antarctic Expedition 1957–8, and was knighted 1955□

fuchsia genus of small shrubby S American plants, family Onagraceae, with ballerina-like downward-hanging flowers in white to pink and purple. It was named after German botanist Leonhard Fuchs 1501–66, and is related to the willowherbs, and evening primroses. Commonly grown in Europe today□

fuel cell cell, working to convert chemical energy directly to electrical energy on the same principle as a battery, but continually fed with the fuel, usually hydrogen. Hydrogen is passed over an electrode containing a catalyst, which strips electrons of the atoms. These pass through the external circuit while hydrogen ions◊ pass through the electrolyte to the other electrode, over which oxygen is passed. Water is formed at this electrode in a chemical reaction involving electrons, hydrogen ions, and oxygen atoms. If the spare heat also produced is used for hot water and space heating, some 80% efficiency in fuel is achieved. Cells are silent, reliable (no moving parts), but expensive to produce□

Fujairah see United Arab Emirates◊□

Fujian Province (formerly ***Fukien***) of SE China

area 123 100 sq km/47 516 sq mi

capital Fuzhou

features dramatic coastline being developed for tourists; also designated 1980 as pace-setting province for modernization

products sugar, rice, special aromatic teas, tobacco; timber

population 24 800 000□

Fujiyama volcano on Honshu Island, Japan; height 3778 m/12 390 ft. Extinct since 1707, it has a Shinto◊ shrine and a weather station, and features in Japanese art□

Fukien see Fujian◊□

Fulbright William 1905– . American politician, a Rhodes◊ Scholar. The Fulbright Act 1946 established grants for thousands of Americans to study overseas and overseas students to enter the US□

Fuller Richard Buckminster 1895–1983. American architect, inventor in 1947 of the lightweight geodesic dome, a half-sphere of triangular components independent of buttress or vault□

Fuller Roy 1912– . British poet and London solicitor, whose volumes include *In the Middle of a War* 1942 and *Epitaphs and Occasions* 1949□

Fuller Thomas 1608–61. English cleric, who served with the Royalist army during the English Civil◊ War, and at the Restoration◊ became the royal chaplain. He is remembered for his biographical *Worthies of England* 1662□

fulmar a seabird of the petrel◊ family□

Fulton Robert 1765–1815. American engineer-inventor, who put the first commercial steam vessel, the *Clermont* on the Hudson in 1807, and designed the first steam warship, the *Fulton* 1814–15□

Funafuti see Tuvalu◊□

Funchal Portuguese name for the island of Madeira, and also for its capital and chief port; population 54 000□

Functionalism see modern under architecture◊□

fundamentalism religious movement in the USA just after World War I which insisted on belief in the literal veracity of everything in the Bible. It confronted evolutionary theory in 1925 (see Dayton◊, Tennessee), and underlies modern Creationism◊□

Fundy Bay of. Canadian Atlantic inlet, with a rapid tidal rise and fall of 18 m/60 ft (being harnessed for electricity 1984), and fog in summer□

Fünen see Fyn◊□

Fünfkirchen see Pécs◊□

fungi sub-group of plants in group Thallophyta, which lack chlorophyll◊ and therefore cannot make their food by photosynthesis◊, so that they are mainly either parasites◊ or saprophytes◊, though some are even predatory, e.g. ***oyster mushroom*** which produces a substance which anaesthetizes certain types of worm, which are then gradually enveloped. Fungi reproduce by means of spores. Some are edible, e.g. mushroom, truffle, etc; and some are important in medicine, either as the cause of disease (thrush, meningitis, athlete's foot) or in curing it, e.g. in making penicillin◊; and in food and industrial processes, e.g. yeasts. Among the most familiar of destructive fungi is the ***bread mould*** *Mucor mucedo* which forms on stale bread. See also Ascomycetes◊, Basidiomycetes◊□

funnel-web spider a type of spider◊□

fur pelts of animals used as clothing, mainly as a luxury trade, which had its modern origin in the furs of N America, exploited by the Hudson's Bay Company from the late 17th century. The chief centres of the fur trade are London, New York, Leningrad, and Kastoria. Mink, chinchilla and sable are among the most valuable, the wild furs being finer than the farmed; it is illegal to import furs or skins of endangered species such as leopard. Since World War II synthetic fibres have been widely used as substitutes□

Furies in Greek mythology, the Erinyes, winged women with snake-like hair, spirits of vengeance, sometimes referred to appeasingly as the 'Kindly ones' (Eumenides)□

furlong traditional measure, an eighth of a mile◊□

Furness Peninsula see under Cumbria◊□

furniture beetle a type of beetle◊□

Furtwängler Wilhelm 1886–1954. German conductor of the Berlin Philharmonic Orchestra 1922–54, noted for his interpretation of Tchaikovsky and Wagner. A tribunal cleared him of Nazism□

Fuseli Henry Johann Heinrich 1741–1825. Swiss-born British artist, influenced by Blake◊. Fancifully macabre, his work was admired by the Surrealists◊□

fusel oil evil-smelling liquid, also called potato spirit, obtained by distilling the product of any alcoholic fermentation; used in paints, varnishes, essential oils, and plastics□

Futurism literary and artistic movement 1909–14, originating in Paris; see Marinetti◊. Modern machines and war were glorified, and light and colour were used to give dynamic effects in painting□

Fuzhou industrial port (formerly ***Foochow***), capital of Fujian province in SE China; population 1 000 000. There are joint foreign and Chinese factories. Mazu (Matsu) Island, occupied by the Nationalist Chinese is offshore□

Fyffe Will 1885–1947. Scots music-hall comedian, remembered for his song 'I Belong to Glasgow'□

Fylingdales see under Yorkshire◊, North□

Fyn Island (German *Fünen*) between the mainland and Zealland, Denmark; area 2976 sq km/1149 sq mi; capital Odense□

G

Gabès port in Tunisia; population 256 000. Fertilizers and dates are exported□

Gable Clark 1901–60. American actor, nicknamed the 'King of Hollywood'. His most famous role was Rhett Butler in *Gone with the Wind* 1939. His third wife, actress Carole Lombard, was killed in an air crash 1942□

Gabo Naum 1890–1977. Russian Constructivist◊ sculptor, who later lived in England and USA. He used modern synthetic materials□

Gabon Republic of

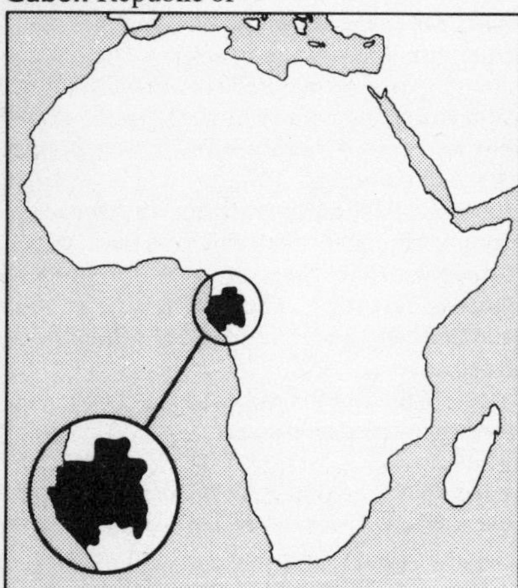

area 266 700 sq km/103 000 sq mi
capital Libreville
features Gabon river; Schweitzer hospital at Lambaréné
exports petroleum; manganese, iron, uranium; timber
currency CFA franc
population 958 000
language French, official; Bantu
religion Animist 60%; Catholic Christianity 35%; small Islamic minority
government executive president (Omar Bongo from 1967), and unicameral national assembly; the Democratic Party is the only party allowed
recent history annexed by France in 1888, Gabon became independent in 1960□

Gabor Dennis 1900–79. Hungarian-British physicist, awarded a Nobel prize in 1971 for his invention (theoretically advanced in 1947) of holography◊□

Gaborone capital of Botswana from 1964, mainly an administrative centre; population 59 700□

Gabriel in the New Testament, the archangel who, announced the birth of John the Baptist to Zacharias and of Christ to the Virgin Mary□

Gaddi surname of three Florentine religious painters:
Gaddo c1260–1333; his son ***Taddeo*** 1300–66; and grandson ***Agnolo*** c1333–96□

gadfly a type of fly◊ which bites cattle□

gadolinium element
symbol Gd
atomic number 64
physical description silvery-white metal
features one of the lanthanide◊ series; found in the products of nuclear fission
uses in electronic components, alloys, and products needing to withstand high temperatures□

Gaelic see Celts◊□

Gagarin Yuri 1934–68. Russian cosmonaut, who completed the first manned space flight on 12 Apr 1961, orbiting earth at c30 000 kph/18 650 mph. He was killed on a routine training flight. An asteroid in constellation Leo is named after him□

Gaia in Greek mythology, the goddess (also Ge) of the earth, sprung from primordial Chaos, she herself produced Uranus◊, by whom she was the mother of the Cyclopes and Titans◊□

Gainsborough Thomas 1727–88. British artist. Born at Sudbury, Suffolk, he was largely self-taught, and in 1759 became a fashionable portrait-painter in Bath (including portraits of Garrick, and the *Blue Boy*), and from 1774 in London (the Royal Family, Mrs Siddons, Johnson, Burke and Sheridan). His work is clear-toned, graceful, and naturalistic, and in his preferred subject, landscapes, he was one of the first English artists to follow the Dutch in using real scenery rather than imaginary Italian□

Gainsborough market town in Lincolnshire, England; population 18 000. The river Trent periodically rises in a tidal wave, the 'eagre'□

Gaitskell Hugh Todd Naylor 1906–63. British Labour statesman. In 1950 he succeeded Cripps◊ first as Minister of Economic Affairs and then as Chancellor of the Exchequer until Oct 1951. In 1955 he defeated Bevan◊ for the succession to Attlee as party leader, and tried to reconcile internal differences on nationalization and disarmament. He was re-elected in 1960□

Galápagos Islands island group in the Pacific, belonging to Ecuador (Archipiélago de Colón); area 7800 sq km/3000 sq mi. Capital San Cristobal on the island of the same name. The unique fauna (giant tortoise, iguana, penguin, flightless cormorant, Darwin finches◊) are under threat from introduced species□

Galatea in Greek mythology, a Nereid◊. See Pygmalion◊□

Galati industrial Danubian port in Romania; population 261 000□

Galatia part of the inland plateau of modern Asiatic Turkey, occupied in the 3rd century AD by the Gauls◊, and a Roman province from 25BC□

galaxy any of the large group of star◊s which make up the universe□

Galbraith John Kenneth 1908– . Canadian political economist, author of *The Affluent Society* 1958 and *Economics and the Public Purpose* 1974□

Galen c130–c200AD. Graeco-Roman physician, personally attending Marcus◊ Aurelius. His treatises remained the encyclopedic authority until the Renaissance□

Galicia mountainous, but fertile region of NW Spain, formerly an independent kingdom, which includes La Coruña, El Ferrol, Santiago de Compostela, and Cape Finisterre. The language is close to Portuguese. See also Franco◊□

Galicia former province of central Europe, occupying the N slopes of the Carpathians to the Czech-Romanian border. Once part of Austria, it was included in Poland after World War I, and divided in 1945 between Poland and Russia□

Galilee region of N Israel (once a Roman province), which includes Nazareth and Tiberias. See Jesus◊ Christ□

Galilee Sea of. See Lake Tiberias◊□

Galileo Galilei 1564–1642. Italian mathematician, astronomer, and physicist, born at Pisa. He developed the telescope and was the first to see the four main satellites of Jupiter, mountains and craters on the moon, and Venus's appearance going through 'phases' as would be expected if it were orbiting the Sun. In mechanics, Galileo argued convincingly that freely-falling bodies, great or small, had the same, constant acceleration (though the story of his dropping cannon balls from the Leaning Tower is probably apocryphal), and that a body moving on a perfectly smooth horizontal surface would neither speed up nor slow down. Galileo's observations and arguments were an unwelcome refutation of the ideas of Aristotle◊ currently taught at the (church-run) universities, especially because they made plausible for the first time the sun-centred theory of Copernicus◊. Galileo's persuasive *Dialogues on the Two Chief Systems of the World* (1632) was banned by the church authorities at Rome, while its author was made to recant by the Inquisition◊ and put under house arrest for his last years□

Gall Franz Joseph. See phrenology◊□

gall swelling produced on any part of a plant by insects (see midges under Fly◊ and gall wasp under Hymenoptera◊), bacteria, fungi, etc. The most familiar include 'oak apples'□

Galla people of E Africa, especially Ethiopia, who speak a Hamito-Semitic language◊□

gall bladder small sac attached to the liver which stores bile, a yellow-brown liquid. Its salts, released into the intestine, assist the digestion of fat, but if some of the contents crystallize, they form ***gallstones***. These may be surgically removed, or even broken down by minute induced explosions□

Gallico Paul 1897–1976. American author of *The Snow Goose* 1941, illustrated by Sir Peter Scott◊□

Gallipoli port in European Turkey, giving its name to the peninsula on which it stands. In World War I under Sir Ian Hamilton◊ there was a naval and military attempt Feb 1915–Jan 1916 (with British Empire and French troops) to force the narrows and link up with Russia. See Australian history□

gallium element

symbol Ga

atomic number 31

physical description a blue-grey metal which becomes liquid at just above room temperature

features it is a semiconductor; chemically similar to aluminium◊

uses the pure metal is used in high-temperature thermometers; gallium arsenide crystals are used in microelectronics because electrons travel through them a thousand times faster than through silicon□

Gällivare iron-mining town in Sweden; population 27 500□

gallon former imperial liquid or dry measure, equal to 4.546 litres, and subdivided into 4 quarts and 8 pints□

Galloway see Dumfries◊ and Galloway□

Gallup George Horace 1901–84. American journalist and statistician, founder in 1935 of the American Institute of Public Opinion and deviser of *Gallup Polls*□

Galsworthy John 1867–1933. British writer, born in Kingston, Surrey. His novel sequence *The Forsyte Saga* 1906–30 centred in Soames Forsyte the 'man of property' and embodiment of Victorian values. His plays deal with social issues, e.g. *The Silver Box* 1906 and *Loyalties* 1922. Order of Merit in 1929□

Galt John 1779–1839. Scottish novelist of rural life, e.g. *Annals of the Parish* 1821□

Galtieri Leopoldo Fortunato 1926– . Argentinian general, leading member of the military junta 1979–82, who seized the Falkland Islands 1982. He and his fellow junta members were tried for abuse of human rights, and also court-martialled for their conduct of the war; he was sentenced to 12 years in prison in 1986□

Galton Sir Francis 1822–1911. British anthropologist, cousin of Charles Darwin. He advocated the use of fingerprints for identification, and selective breeding to improve the human stock (see eugenics◊)□

Galvani Luigi 1737–98. Italian physiologist. His observation of frog legs twitching when touched with pairs of different metals led quickly to Volta◊'s invention of the electric battery, and eventually to an understanding of how nerves control muscles□

galvanizing method of protecting iron from rust by coating it with zinc, either by dipping or electro-deposition□

galvanometer instrument for measuring small electric currents by their magnetic effect□

Galway James 1939– . British flautist, born in Belfast; Richard Rodney Bennett and Thea Musgrave have written works for him□

Galway fishing port in county Galway, Republic of Ireland; population 27 000. University College is part of the national university, and Galway Theatre stages Irish Gaelic plays□

Galway county (county town Galway) of the Republic of Ireland, province of Connacht◊□

Gama Vasco da c1460–1524. Portuguese navigator, who discovered the Cape route to India in 1498, and founded Mozambique in 1502□

Gambetta Léon Michel 1838–82. French statesman, organizer of resistance in the Franco–Prussian◊ War, and founder in 1871 of the Third Republic□

Gambia river in W Africa, which gives its name to Gambia◊; 1000 km/620 mi long□

Gambia Republic of the

area 11 000 sq km/4000sq mi

capital Banjul

features Gambia river; the republic is surrounded on three sides by Senegal, and is the smallest state in Black Africa

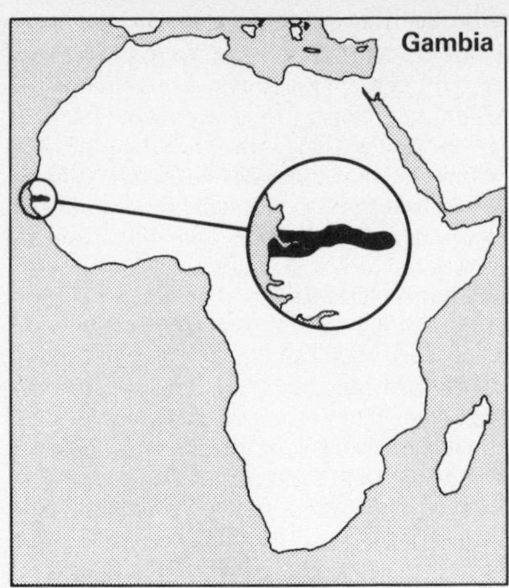

exports groundnuts, palm oil, fish

currency dalasi

population 695 886

language English, official

religion 70% Islam, with Animist and Christian minorities

government executive president (Sir Dawda Jawara from 1970) elected for five years, and house of representatives

recent history site of a British trading post from the 17th century, the Gambia became a colony in 1843, attained independence in 1965, and became a republic in 1970 within the Commonwealth. A state of emergency has existed since 1981. A confederal Senegambia◊ was achieved in 1982□

Gambier Islands see under French◊ Polynesia 3□

gamelan orchestra a percussion orchestra◊ in Indonesia□

Gamelin Maurice Gustave 1872–1958. French Commander-in-Chief of the Allied armies in France in 1939. Replaced by Weygand on the German breakthrough at Sedan in 1940, he was tried as a scapegoat before the Riom◊ 'War Guilt' court in 1942. He refused to defend himself, and was detained in Germany 1942–5□

gamma radiation very high-frequency electromagnetic radiation emitted by the nuclei of radioactive substances during decay, similar in nature to X-rays, but of shorter wavelength. It is used to kill bacteria and other micro-organisms, sterilize medical devices, change the molecular structure of plastics to modify their properties (e.g. improve heat and abrasion resistance for insulation purposes) Most cosmic gamma rays cannot pass through earth's atmosphere and telescopes to detect them must be placed above Earth's atmosphere. Only a few of the many sources have been identified, including pulsars, radio galaxies, and quasars. See electromagnetic waves◊□

Gandhi Indira 1917–84. Indian stateswoman, daughter of Nehru◊. She married in 1942 Feroze Gandhi (d. 1960), not related to the Mahatma, and had two sons. ***Sanjay Gandhi*** 1946–80, who died in an air crash, and Rajiv Gandhi◊. She became leader of the Congress Party and Prime Minister in 1966, but Sanjay's social and economic programme (including a ruthless family planning policy) led to her defeat in 1977, though he masterminded her return to power in 1980. She was assassinated by members of her Sikh bodyguard, resentful of her use of troops to clear malcontents from the temple at Amritsar◊□

Gandhi Mohandas Karamchand 1869–1948. Indian leader, called Mahatma ('Great Soul'). Born in Porbandar, he studied in London, and then led the Indian community in S Africa in opposition to racial discrimination. Returning to India in 1915, he led the struggle for Indian independence by *satyagraha* ('defence of and by truth' = non-violent non-cooperation), including several 'fasts unto death': see Leo Tolstoy◊. He was several times imprisoned by the British authorities, was influential in the Congress (nationalist) Party, and in the independence negotiations in 1947. His fasts, etc., were less effective against his fellow-countrymen, and he was assassinated by a Hindu nationalist in the violence which followed Partition□

Gandhi Rajiv 1945– . Indian statesman. Son of Indira Gandhi◊. He was an airline pilot, and became political adviser to his mother on the death of his brother Sanjay. He entered the Lok Sabha in 1981, and in 1984 succeeded his mother as Prime Minister. In 1985 he reached a political settlement with the moderate Sikhs□

Ganesa Hindu god, represented as elephant-headed, and worshipped as a remover of obstacles□

Ganges great river of India and Bangladesh, most sacred river of the Hindus; length 2506 km/1557 mi. Its chief tributary is the ***Yamuna*** (Jumna); length 1385 km/860 sq mi, which joins the Ganges near Allahabad, where there is a sacred bathing place. Nehru, his daughter Indira Gandhi, grandson Sanjay Gandhi, as well as the Mahatma were all cremated on the banks of the Yamuna at Delhi. The Ganges is joined in its delta in Bangladesh by the Brahmaputra◊, and its most commercially important and westernmost channel to the Bay of Bengal is the ***Hooghly***□

gangrene local tissue death, caused by wounds, burning, freezing, etc.; poisoning; failure of the blood supply, e.g. too tight bandaging or thrombosis◊□

gannet a type of sea-bird of the pelican◊ family□

Gansu province (formerly Kansu) of NW China

area 530 000 sq km/204 633 sq mi

capital Lanzhou

features subject to earthquakes; the 'Silk Road' (now a motor road) passed through it in the Middle Ages carrying trade to central Asia

products coal, oil, hydroelectric power from the Yellow River

population 19 000 000, including many Muslims□

Ganymede in Greek mythology, a youth so beautiful he was chosen as cupbearer to Zeus□

Ganymede see Jupiter◊□

Gaoxiong mainland Chinese form of Kaohsiung◊□

Garbo Greta. Assumed name of Swedish actress Greta Lovisa Gustafsson 1905– . One of the first silent Hollywood stars, e.g. *Anna Christie* 1930; her 'talkies' include *Queen Christina* 1933, *Anna Karenina* 1935, *Camille* 1936, and *Ninotchka* 1939□

Garching see under Munich◊□

García Lorca Federico 1899–1936. Spanish poet and dramatist, born in Granada. His works include *Gipsy Ballad-book* 1928; the 'Lament for the Death of a Bullfighter' 1935; *The Poet in New York* 1940; and the play *Blood Wedding* 1933□

García Márquez Gabriel 1928– . Colombian novelist, whose *One Hundred Years of Solitude* 1967, the story of six generations of a family, initiated a renaissance of Latin American literature. Nobel prize in 1982□

Garda Lake. Largest lake in Italy; 370 sq km/143 sq mi□

garden city self-sufficient community, combining the advantages of town and country living, proposed in 1899 by Sir Ebenezer Howard 1850–1928, founder of the association which established Letchworth (see under Hertfordshire◊)□

gardenia genus of subtropical and tropical trees and shrubs of Africa and Asia, family Rubiaceae with evergreen foliage and flattened rosettes of fragrant waxen-looking blooms, often white□

Garden of the Gods see under Colorado◊□

Gardiner Stephen c1493–1555. English churchman, bishop of Winchester from 1531. An opponent of Protestantism, he was imprisoned under Edward VI, and as Lord Chancellor 1553–5 under Mary tried to restore Roman Catholicism□

Garfield James Abram 1831–81. 20th president of the USA. A Republican, he was inaugurated in 1881, but was shot by a madman□

garfish type of fish with a long spear-like snout, including ***common garfish*** *Belone belone* order Beloniformes, family Belonidae, which has an elongated body, and, despite its green bones, is edible□

gargoyle projecting roof water-spout, given ornamental form in Gothic architecture as fantastic animals, angels, or human heads□

Garibaldi Giuseppe 1807–82. Italian soldier. A follower of Mazzini◊, he fled abroad after condemnation to death for treason. Returning during the revolution of 1848, he served with the Sardinians against the Austrians, and led the army of the Roman Republic in defending the city against the French. In 1860, at the head of his 1,000 Redshirts, he conquered Sicily and Naples for the new kingdom of Italy□

Garland Judy 1922–69. American singer and actress, *née* Frances Gumm, in Grand Rapids, Michigan, USA. Her films include *The Wizard of Oz* 1939 (including the song 'Over the Rainbow'), *Meet Me in St Louis* 1944, and *A Star is Born* in 1954. Her daughter ***Liza Minelli*** 1946– , also a singer and actress, won an academy award for her performance in the film *Cabaret* in 1972□

garlic perennial plant *Allium sativum*, family Liliaceae, with white flowers. The bulb, made of small segments, 'cloves', is used in cookery, and its pungent essence has an active medical ingredient (allyl methyl trisulphide) which prevents blood clotting□

garnet group of minerals used as semi-precious gems (usually pink to deep red) and abrasives. They occur in crystallized limestones, gneiss, and schist, etc.□

Garonne see under Gironde◊□

Garrick David 1717–79. British actor-manager. Born in Hereford, he was a pupil of Samuel Johnson at Lichfield, and both set out for London together in 1737. His naturalistic acting style and brilliant mimicry soon made him famous. He was noted for his performance as Richard III, Lear, Hamlet, and Benedick in Shakespeare's plays, and Abel Drugger in Ben Johnson's *The Alchemist*□

Garter, Order of the. The senior British order of knighthood, founded by Edward III c1347; motto *Honi soit qui mal y pense* ('Shame be to him who thinks evil of it'). Besides royalty, there are only 25 members. St George's Chapel, Windsor, is the chapel of the order□

Garvey Marcus 1887–1940. Jamaican black founder of the 'Back to Africa' movement in 1911; he was in the USA from 1916. See Rastafarianism◊□

gas form of matter in which the molecules (single atoms or small groups of atoms) move randomly in otherwise empty space, colliding with each other and filling any size or shape of container into which the gas is put. A sugar-lump sized cube of air at room temperature contains 30 million million million molecules moving at an average speed of 500 m/s (about 1200 m.p.h). Gases can be liquefied by cooling, which lowers the speed of the molecules and enables attractive forces between them to bind them together. Argon, helium, krypton, neon, radon, and xenon are known as 'noble' or 'inert' gases owing to their reluctance to react chemically. See Boyle◊'s Law, Charles's◊ Law□

Gascony ancient province of SW France; it was acquired by Henry II through his marriage to Eleanor of Aquitaine, and was often in English hands until 1451□

Gaskell Elizabeth Cleghorn 1810–65. British novelist; *née* Stevenson, she married a Unitarian minister. Her books include *Mary Barton* (set in industrial Manchester) 1848, *Cranford* (set in the village in which she was brought up, Knutsford, Cheshire◊) 1853, *North and South* 1855, *Wives and Daughters* 1866, and a life of her friend Charlotte Brontë◊□

gastritis inflammation of the stomach lining, e.g. by corrosive poisons, too much alcohol, or infection□

gastroenteritis inflammation of the stomach and intestines, with vomiting and diarrhoea, usually caused by 'food poisoning'□

gastropod very large class (Gastropoda) of molluscs; single-shelled (in a spiral or modified spiral form), in some cases with eyes on stalks, and moving with a flattened, muscular foot. Some are marine, some freshwater, and others land creatures, but all tend to damp places. They include:

Limpet of which the ***common limpet*** *Patella vulgata* is found in Britain. Its cone-shaped shell is resistant to wave shock, and, after grazing under water, it always returns at low tide to its original position on the rocks. It has 200 rows of teeth to scrape algae from rocks, and these have been studied to improve the 'teeth' of dredgers.

Whelk of which the edible common whelk *Buccinum undatum* found off Britain reaches 12 cm/4 in long.

Periwinkle or ***winkle*** found in brown seaweed between tidemarks; the edible ***common winkle*** *Littorina littorea,* found in Britain, has blackish rings on a greyish shell, and is naturalized in N America.

Conch of which the ***giant conch*** *Strombus gigas* has a coloured spiral shell, and is so

large that, when pierced, it is used as a primitive trumpet.
Snail of which the ***common garden snail*** *Helix aspersa* is very destructive to plants; and the edible ***Roman snail*** *Helix pomatia* is 'rounded up' from the wild population for gourmet consumption, since it cannot be bred, and is hence endangered. Snails are hermaphroditic.
Slug which has little if any shell remaining. The commonest British species is the ***grey field slug*** *Agriolimax agrestis,* a crop and garden pest□

gas warfare see Chemical◊ warfare□

Gateshead industrial port (engineering, chemicals, glass) in Tyne and Wear, England; population 211 700□

Gatwick see under London◊□

gaucho part Indian, part Spanish 'cowboys', formerly working on the Argentine and Uruguayan pampas□

Gaudi Antonio 1852–1926. Spanish architect, influenced by Moorish and medieval styles. His Church of the Holy Family, Barcelona, begun 1883, was still under construction when he died□

Gaudier-Brzeska Henri 1891–1915. French Vorticist sculptor, e.g. *The Dancer* and *The Embracers*□

Gauguin Paul 1848–1903. French artist. He threw up his job as a banker in 1881 in order to paint (e.g. *The Yellow Christ* 1889). In 1891 he went to Tahiti (where he died) finding inspiration in the people and rich colours of the islands (e.g. *Nevermore*). He was a friend of Van◊ Gogh□

Gauls Celtic-speaking people (see Celts◊) who lived in France and Belgium in Roman times. The Romans conquered Cisalpine Gaul (between the Alps and the Apennines) c225BC; Southern Gaul (between the Mediterranean and the Cevennes) c125BC; and the remaining Gauls up to the Rhine were conquered by Caesar◊ 58–51BC□

gaur Asiatic wild ox *Bos gaurus* which is dark grey and nearly 2 m/6 ft tall at the shoulders but much lower at the horns□

Gauss Karl Friedrich 1777–1855. German mathematician who worked on the theory of numbers, non-Euclidian geometry, and on the mathematical development of electric and magnetic theory; in World War II the method of countering German magnetic mines was called 'degaussing'. The old measure of magnetic flux density was named after him; it has now been replaced by the SI unit, the tesla◊□

Gautier Théophile 1811–72. French Romantic poet, whose later work emphasized form perfection and polished beauty (e.g. *Émaux et Camées* 1852) He was also a novelist (*Mlle de Maupin* 1835)□

Gay John 1685–1732. British poet, a friend of Pope◊, best remembered for *The Beggar's Opera* 1728, the first opera in English and which used English folk-tunes. Its political touches led to the banning of *Polly*, a sequel□

Gay-Lussac Joseph Louis 1778–1850. French physicist, who investigated the physical properties of gases. See Charles's◊ Law□

Gaza capital of the Gaza◊ Strip, once a Philistine city, and scene of three World War I battles; population c120 000 Palestinian refugees□

Gaza Strip strip of Palestine under Israeli administration; capital Gaza; area 260 sq km/100 sq mi; population 365 000. It was invaded by Israel in 1956; reoccupied in 1967, and retained in 1973. See Arab–Israeli◊ Wars□

gazelle a type of Antelope◊□

GCHQ Government Communications Headquarters. The centre of the British government's electronic surveillance operations. It monitors broadcasts of various kinds from all over the world. In addition there are six listening stations at Bude, Cornwall; Culm Head, Somerset; Brora and Hawklaw, Scotland; Irton Moor, N Yorks; and Cheadle, Greater Manchester. There is an outpost in Cyprus. It was established in World War I, and was successful in breaking the German 'Enigma' code in 1940. In 1982 Geoffrey Prime (1939–) a linguist there, was convicted of handing the secrets of US spy satellites to the USSR□

Gdańsk port (German *Danzig*) in Poland; population 448 000. Formerly a member of the Hanseatic League, it was in almost continuous Prussian possession 1793–1919, when it again became a free city. Annexed by Germany in 1939 (the beginning of World War II), it reverted to Poland in 1945, when the churches and old merchant houses were restored. The shipyard strikes of 1980 were symptomatic of resistance to Communist rule□

GDP abbreviation for ***Gross Domestic Product***□

Gdynia industrial port (shipbuilding) and naval base in Poland; population 231 000. It was established in 1920 to give newly constituted Poland a sea outlet to replace lost Gdańsk◊□

Ge see Gaia◊□

gecko a type of Lizard◊□

Geelong industrial port (textiles, glass, fertilizers) in Victoria, Australia; population 125 300. Prince Charles was a student at the Church of England Grammar School in 1966□

Geiger counter device for measuring high-energy radiation (especially beta◊ particles), invented in 1913 by Hans Geiger (1882–1945, German-born physicist)□

geisha female entertainer (music, singing, dancing, etc.), in Japanese teahouses and private parties□

gelatine water-soluble protein prepared from boiled hide and bone, used in cookery for jellies, and in glues◊ and photographic emulsions□

Gelderland also *Guelders* E province (capital Arnhem) of the Netherlands. In the NW is the Valuwe, a favourite holiday district□

Geldof Bob 1954– . Irish rock musician with the Boomtown Rats. He was the inspiration behind Band◊ Aid and Live◊ Aid 1984–86. Band Aid produced a record, and Live Aid was a combination of two concerts, one in London and one in New York, broadcast live to the world's largest ever TV audience. Both were charity events raising large sums of money for famine relief, especially in Ethiopia◊. Knight Commander of the British Empire 1986□

gelignite a type of dynamite◊□

Gell-Mann Murray 1929– . American physicist, awarded a Nobel prize 1969 for his work on elementary particles and their interaction. He formulated in 1964 the theory of the quark◊. See particle physics□

Gelsenkirchen industrial (iron and steel, chemicals, glass) city in the Ruhr◊, W Germany; population 303 000□

gem mineral valued for its beauty and rarity; approximately 25 are in common use in jewellery. They include the ***precious*** diamond, emerald, ruby, and sapphire; ***semi-precious*** topaz, amethyst, opal, aqua marine, etc. Some have been made synthetically, e.g. diamonds in 1955. Pearls are not technically gems, though sometimes referred to as such□

Gemara part of the Talmud, the compilation of ancient Jewish law. See under Judaism◊□

Gemayel Amin 1942– . Lebanese (Maronite Christian) president from 1982. He succeeded his brother, president-elect ***Bechir Gemayel***, on his assassination on 14 Sept 1982□

gene see genetic◊ code□

Genée Adeline. Stage-name of British dancer Dame Adeline Genée-Isitt 1878–1970, whose work is commemorated by the ***Adeline Genée Theatre*** established 1967), E Grinstead, Sussex□

general senior military officer, the ascending grades being in Britain (and USA) lieutenant general, major general, and general; in the USA the rank of general of the army is equivalent to a British field marshal◊□

General Agreement on Tariffs and Trade an organization withing the United Nations◊ which aims to encourage trade between nations through low tariffs, abolitions of quotes, etc.□

General Assembly see Church of Scotland◊□

general paralysis of the insane see Syphilis◊□

gene-splicing technique invented in 1973 by Stanley Cohen and Herbert Boyer (Stanford University/University of California) for inserting a foreign gene into bacteria in order to generate commercial biological products, e.g. synthetic insulin, hepatitis-B vaccine, interferon. It was patented in the USA in 1984□

genet a type of civet◊□

genetic code All organisms, both animal and plants, are composed of cells, each containing a nucleus which contains chromosomes. Each species has a constant number and pattern of chromosomes (e.g. a mouse has 40 and humans have 46. In humans they exist as 22 identical pairs plus two sex chromosomes, XX for females and XY for males. A chromosome consists of a DNA (DeoxyriboNucleic Acid) backbone surrounded and intertwined with protein. The DNA double helix is like a spiral ladder, two rods held together by rungs. The rods are made up of sugars (s) and phosphates (p) whilst the rungs are base pairs – cytosine (C) and guanine (G) or adenine (A) and thymine (T). The ordering of the four bases is called the ***genetic code,*** and this determines the characteristic of the species.

A sequence of three bases is *one* unit of genetic code, called a gene, and is responsible for the production of *one* amino acid. (Amino acids are the most fundamental part of proteins which make up cells. There are twenty amino acids in nature.) When a cell divides, the two strands of DNA become separated (the chromosomes bisect) and the original cell manufactures more nucleotides (phosphate, sugar, base units) to exactly match the separated halves. Each chromosome in the nucleus simultaneously separates and is built upon, thereby producing two new cells identical to the original one. Thus the genetic code is passed on.

Occasionally the code is not passed on correctly, and a change occurs, usually only in one gene of the entire chromosome. This is called mutation and will affect the characteristics of the organism. A change can be induced by using radiation, chemicals or more sophisticated techniques such as gene splicing (inserting a foreign gene into a DNA molecule), or the complete introduction of new DNA. Artificial changes made in this

genetic code
How a cell divides

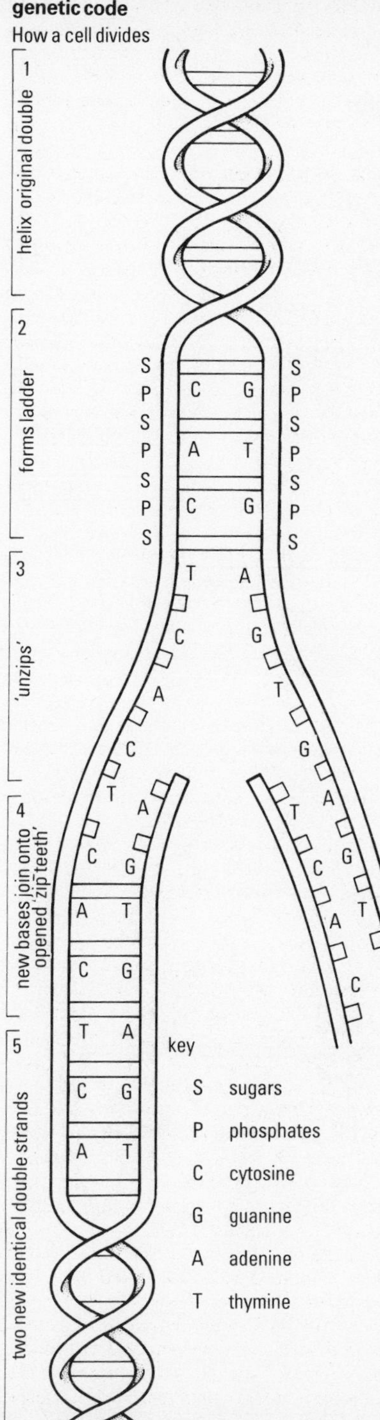

way is called ***genetic engineering***. It has frightening moral consequences, but can be advantageous in, for example, the modification of bacteria to produce drugs such as insulin and interferon commercially□

genetic diseases disorders caused by defective genes or chromosomes, of which there are some 3000, including Arthritis, Autism, Cleft palate, Cystic fibrosis, Down's syndrome, Haemophilia, Huntington's chorea, some forms of Anaemia, Spina bifida, Tay-Sachs disease□

genetics study of heredity and variation in living things. see genetic◊ code□

Geneva industrial city (watches, scientific and optical instruments, jewellery) in SW Switzerland, on Lake Geneva◊; population 335 400. Under Calvin◊ it became a centre of the Reformation 1536–64; in 1864 the International Red Cross Society was founded here. Formerly the headquarters of the League◊ of Nations, it is now the headquarters of many United Nations◊ agencies□

Geneva Lake. largest of the central European lakes (French *Lac Léman*), between Switzerland and France; area 580 sq km/225 sq mi□

Geneva Convention international agreement of 1864 on the treatment of those wounded in war, later also the sick, prisoners, and civilians□

Genf German form of Geneva◊□

Genghis Khan 1162–1227. Mongol conqueror (original name Temujin), who established his supremacy over all Mongol tribes by 1206, and assumed the name Genghis ('perfect warrior'). At his death he ruled an empire reaching from the Yellow Sea to the Black Sea. His alleged remains are at Ejin Horo, Inner Mongolia, and the spring ceremonies celebrating this achievement were revived in 1980 by China, but he is disapproved of by the USSR. See also Golden◊ Horde; Karakorum◊□

Gennesaret Lake of. See Lake Tiberias◊□

Genoa industrial city (oil-refining, chemicals, engineering, and textiles) (Italian *Genova*) Italy's largest port and capital of Liguria; population 762 895. Mazzini◊ was born here□

Genova Italian form of Genoa◊□

genre pictures depicting everyday life. See Pieter Brueghel◊, Adriaen Brouwer◊; Teniers◊, Frans Hals◊; Hogarth◊, and Sir David Wilkie◊□

Genscher Hans-Dietrich 1927– . W German statesman, leader of the Free Democratic Party 1974–85, and Foreign Minister from 1974. He supports greater W European unity, and east-west détente□

geology

geological era

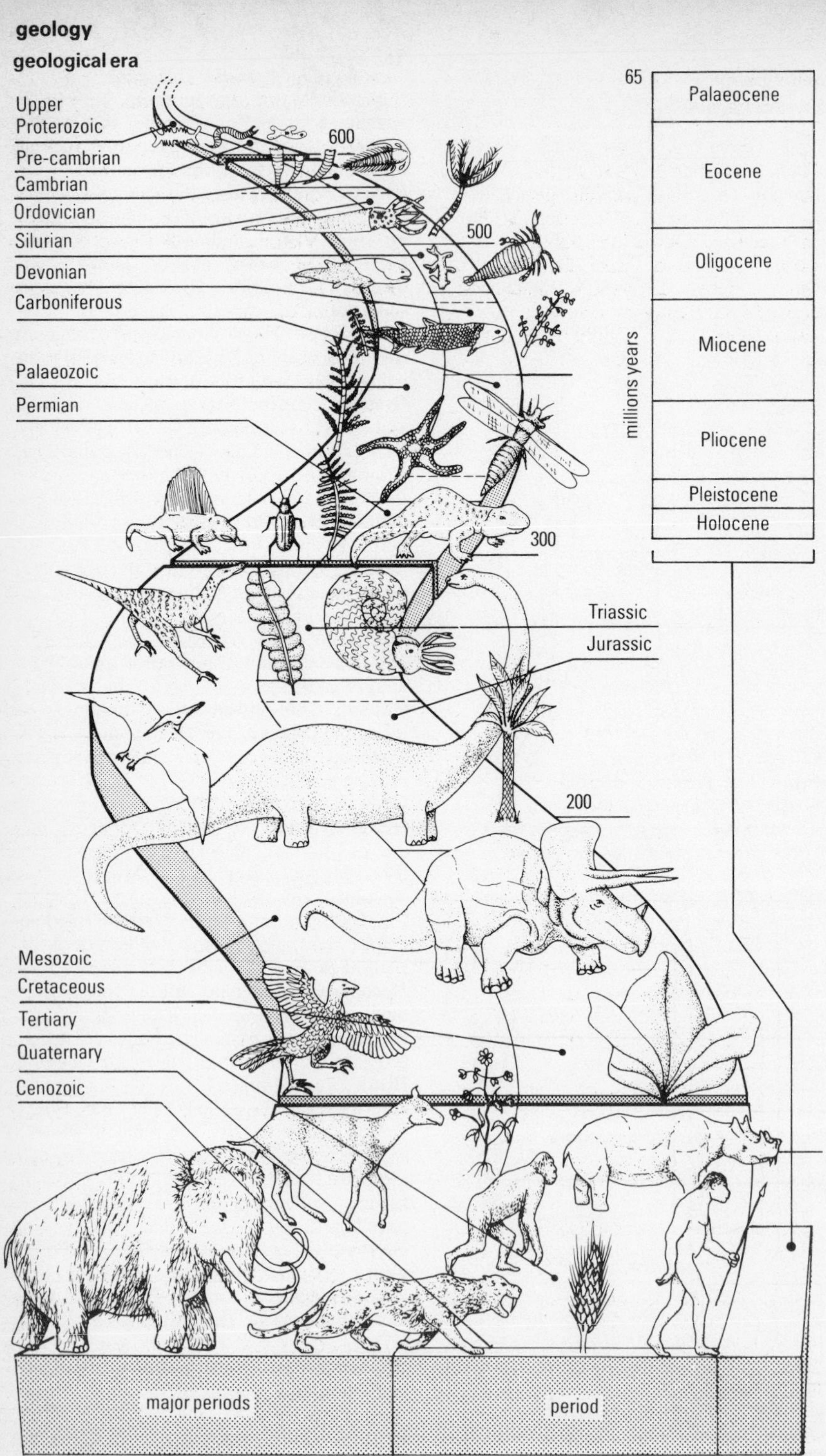

gentian two genera of flowering plants, *Gentiana* and *Gentianella*, Gentianaceae family, with bright blue trumpet-shaped flowers, and including many alpines□

Gentili Alberico 1552–1608. Italian Protestant jurist who fled religious persecution to lecture at Oxford. His *De Jure Belli libri tres* 1598 founded international law□

genus group of species of plants or animals with common structural characteristics derived from a common ancestor□

geography the study of the distribution and interrelation of phenomena connected with the Earth's surface□

geology study of rocks, the earth's origin, structure and history, including remains of extinct life. See table of geological eras□

geometry branch of mathematics concerned with investigating the properties of space: see Thales◊, Pythagoras◊, Euclid◊. ***Non-Euclidean geometry*** dispenses with Euclidean assumptions about plane and solid 'elements' (see Gauss◊, Lobachevski◊, Riemann◊), and has applications in the study of General Relativity◊. ***Analytical*** or ***co-ordinate geometry*** applies the analytic method by means of co-ordinates (numbers) determining positions in space relative to lines or 'axes'. (Descartes◊)□

George six kings of Great Britain:

George I 1660–1727 king from 1714. The son of the elector of Hanover (see Sophia◊), whom he succeeded in 1698, he spent most of his reign there. He married Sophia of Zell 1682.

George II 1683–1760 king from 1727, when he succeeded his father, George◊ I. His victory at Dettingen in 1743 was the last battle commanded by a British king. He married Caroline of Anspach 1705.

George III 1738–1820 king from 1760, when he succeeded his grandfather George II. Although bent on strengthening royal influence, his alleged domination of Parliament by corrupt 'King's friends' is a discredited Whig invention. He supported his ministers in a hard line towards the American colonies, and opposed Catholic emancipation, and other reforms. Possibly suffering from porphyria◊, he had repeated attacks of insanity, permanent from 1811. He married Princess Charlotte of Mecklenburg-Strelitz.

George IV 1762–1830 king from 1820, when he succeeded his father George III, for whom he had been regent during his insanity 1811–20. Strictly educated, he reacted by entering into a life of debauchery, and in 1785 married a Catholic widow, Mrs Fitzherbert◊, but in 1795 also married Princess Caroline of Brunswick, in return for payment of his debts. Attempting to divorce Caroline after his accession in 1820, he had to desist for fear of revolution.

George V 1865–1936 king from 1910, when he succeeded his father Edward◊ VII. He was the 2nd son, and became heir only in 1892 on the death of his elder brother Albert◊ Victor, Duke of Clarence, 1864–92. He married in 1893, Princess May of Teck (Queen Mary◊), formerly betrothed to his brother.

George VI 1895–1952 king from 1936, when he succeeded his brother Edward◊ VIII. Created Duke of York in 1920, he married in 1923 the Lady Elizabeth Bowes-Lyon, and their children are Elizabeth II and Princess Margaret◊□

George two kings of Greece:

George I 1845–1913, king from 1863, who was assassinated at Salonika.

George II 1890–1947, king from the expulsion of his father Constantine in 1922, and himself overthrown in 1923. Restored by the military in 1935, he set up a dictatorship under Metaxas, and went into exile during the German occupation 1941–6□

George St. Patron saint of England, allegedly martyred in Palestine in the reign of Diocletian, and whose cult was brought home by the Crusaders. He came to the aid of a girl by slaying a dragon (cf Perseus◊). Feast day, 23 Apr□

George Stefan 1868–1933. German poet who conceived of himself as regenerating the German spirit, as in *Der Siebente Ring/The Seventh Ring* 1907. Realizing that World War I had not had the right purifying effect, he rejected Nazi overtures and emigrated in 1933 to Switzerland□

George Cross/Medal see under Medals◊□

Georgetown capital and port of Guyana; population 183 000□

Georgetown Declaration of. Call in 1972, at a conference of non-aligned countries in Guyana, for a multi-polar system to replace the two world power blocks□

Georgetown chief port of the Federation of Malaysia, and capital of Penang, on the Island of Penang; population 250 600□

Georgia Southern state of the USA; Empire State of the South/Peach State

area 152 500 sq km/58 880 sq mi

capital Atlanta

towns Columbus, Savannah

features Okefenokee National Wildlife Refuge (1700 sq km/60 sq mi of swamp, with alligators, bears, rich birdlife)

products poultry, livestock; tobacco, maize, peanuts, cotton; china clay, crushed granite; textiles, carpets, aircraft

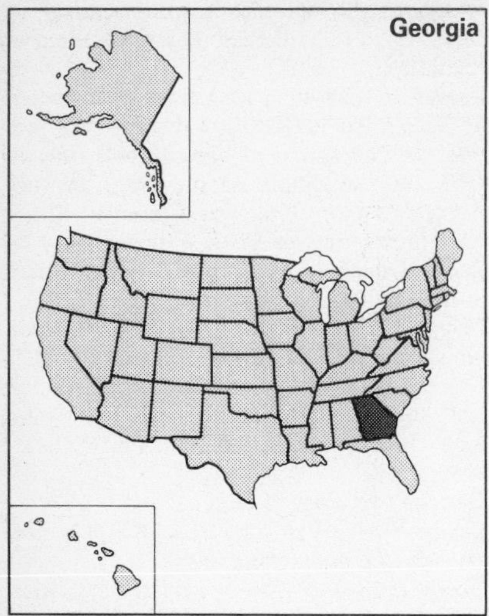

population 5 464 000
famous people James Bowie, Erskine Caldwell, Jimmy Carter, Martin Luther King, Margaret Mitchell
history named after George II, Georgia was founded in 1733 and was one of the Thirteen◊ Colonies, becoming a state in 1788□

Georgia constituent republic of the SW Soviet Union, from 1936
area 69 700 sq km/26 900 sq mi
capital Tbilisi
features holiday resorts and spas on the Black Sea; good climate
products subtropical, such as tea, citrus, orchard fruits, tung oil, tobacco, vines, silk
population 5 000 000, 67% Georgian, 10% Armenian, 9% Russian
language Georgian
religion Georgian Church, independent of the Russian Orthodox since 1917
famous people Stalin
recent history an independent republic 1918–21, it was invaded by the USSR in 1921, and was linked with Armenia and Azerbaijan as the Transcaucasian Republic within SW USSR 1922–36□

geostationary orbit circular path 36 000 km (22 000 mi) above the equator in which gravity will maintain a satellite which is moving at the speed just to keep pace with the earth spinning 'beneath' it. Thus, seen from the earth, the satellite is stationary. See Telecommunications◊□

geothermal energy either subterranean ***hot water*** pumped to the surface and converted to steam or run through a heat exchanger, or dry steam, directed through turbines to produce electricity□

Gera capital of Gera district and industrial city in the S of E Germany; population 127 400□

geranium genus of wildflowers, the ***crane's bills,*** family Geraniaceae, with showy red or pink flowers. Cultivated geraniums chiefly belong to the genus *Pelargonium*□

gerbil a type of small rodent◊□

Géricault (Jean Louis André) Théodore 1791–1824. French artist, noted for pictures including horses, e.g. *The Derby at Epsom,* and for his *Raft of the Medusa* 1819, showing an incident in which shipwrecked seamen had deliberately been set adrift□

German Sir Edward. Name used by British composer Edward German Jones 1862–1936, remembered for his operetta *Merrie England* 1902□

Germanic languages branch of the Indo-European family which includes 1 ***East Germanic*** Gothic, now extinct; 2 ***N Germanic*** or ***Scandinavian*** Icelandic, Norwegian, Danish, Swedish; and 3 ***W Germanic*** German, Dutch, Frisian, and English, the last two being more closely inter-related. See Language◊□

Germanicus Caesar 15BC–19AD. Roman general. Adopted son of Tiberius◊, he married Augustus's granddaughter Agrippina. Though he refused the suggestion of his troops that he claim the throne on the death of Augustus◊, his military successes in Germany made Tiberius jealous. Sent to the east, he died near Antioch, possibly murdered at the instigation of Tiberius. He was the father of Caligula◊, and of Agrippina, mother of Nero◊□

germanium element
symbol Ge
atomic number 32
physical description greyish semi-metal
features like silicon◊, it can act as a semiconductor
uses it is used in electronics for transistors and integrated circuits. The oxide is transparent to infra red radiation, and is used in defence□

German measles virus disease (rubella), usually of children, marked by sore throat, pinkish rash, and slight fever. If contracted in the first three months of pregnancy, it may affect a woman's unborn child, and immunization in girlhood is advised□

German Ocean German name for the North◊ Sea□

Germany single state of central Europe, which was divided after World War II into: E and W Germany, and land to the E of the Oder and western Neisse rivers which was split between Russia and Poland. Restoration of these 'lost territories' (Silesia◊, Pomerania◊, the Sudetenland◊ and E

Prussia◊), a third of the former area, remains a political issue, as does the reunion of the two Germanies□

Germany (East) German Democratic Republic

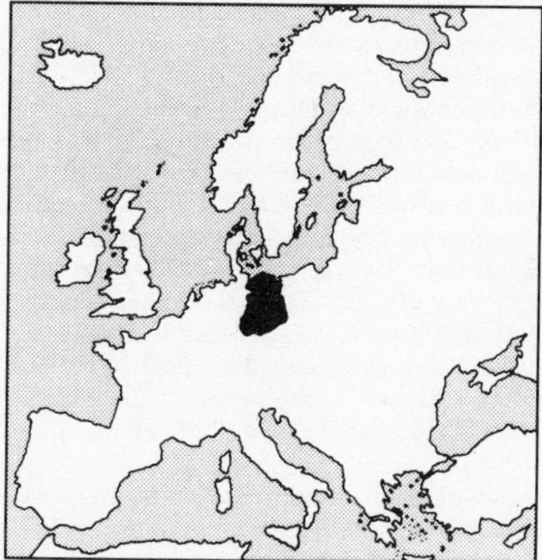

area 108 180 sq km/41 768 sq mi
capital East Berlin
towns Leipzig, Dresden, Karl-Marx-Stadt, Magdeburg; chief port Rostock
features Harz mountains, Erzgebirge, Fichtelgebirge, Thüringer Wald; rivers Elbe, Oder and Neisse; many lakes, including Müritz
exports lignite; rare minerals (uranium, cobalt, etc); coal, iron, and steel; fertilizers; plastics
currency GDR Mark
population 16 700 000
language German
religion Protestant 80%, Catholic 11%
famous people Walter Ulbricht *literature* Christa Wolf, Siegfried Lenz *theatre* Bertolt Brecht *music* Karl Müchinger
government under the 1968 constitution there is a chairman (Erich Honecker from 1976) of the council of state, the latter being elected by the elected people's chamber of 500 deputies. The Socialist Unity Party (SUP) or Communist Party is the only party permitted. For local government, to obliterate old associations, the country is divided into 14 *Bezirke* (districts), named after their chief towns.
recent history established in 1949 (see Germany◊) from the Russian zone of occupation, it became a sovereign state in 1954, but remained integrated with the economy of Communist E Europe and politically under Soviet influence. By the 1970s it was a world industrial power; emigration to W Germany was virtually impossible through a militarily guarded frontier□

Germany (West) Federal Republic of

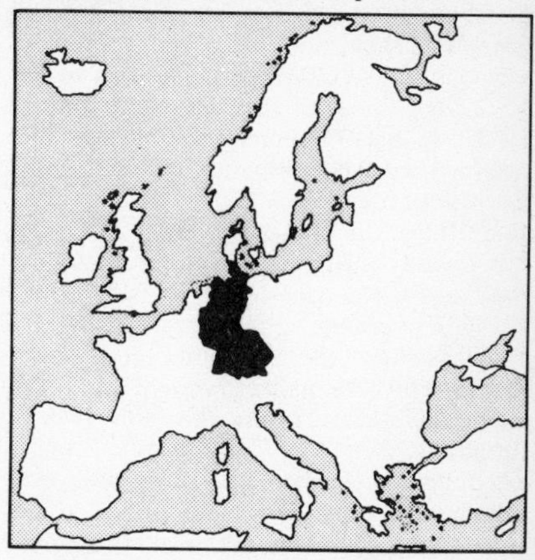

area 248 651 sq km/95 984 sq mi
capital Bonn
towns W Berlin, Cologne, Munich, Essen, Frankfurt-am-Main, Dortmund, Düsseldorf; ports Hamburg, Kiel, Cuxhaven, Bremerhaven
features rivers Rhine, Weser, Elbe, Danube; Black Forest, Alps
exports machine tools (world's leading exporter); cars and commercial vehicles, electronics, industrial goods, textiles, chemicals, iron and steel; wine
currency Deutsche Mark (DM)
population 61 600 000, including 4 400 000 'guest workers' (*Gastarbeiter*), of whom 1 600 000 are Turks; the rest are Yugoslavs, Italians, Greeks, Spanish, and Portuguese
language German
religion Protestantism 49%, Roman Catholicism 47%
famous people Konrad Adenauer *literature* Heinrich Böll, Gunther Grass *painting* Joseph Benys *sport* Boris Becker *cinema* Wim Wenders, Volker Schlöndorff *music* Karlheinz Stockhausen, Hans-Werner Henze
government under the constitution of 1949, there is a non-executive federal president (Richard von Weizscher from 1984), and a parliament of two houses, the upper (*Bundesrat*) consists of delegates from the states (*L̈nder*) into which W Germany is subdivided, and the lower (*Bundestag*), the cabinet being headed by the Federal Chancellor (Helmut Kohl from 1982).
recent history established in 1949 by the fusion of the British, US, and French zones of occupation, W Germany (under Adenauer◊) received recognition as a sovereign state in 1955. The 'economic miracle' of the 1960s (under Erhard◊) made her the leading industrial power of Europe and the dominant

member of the European Economic Community. Under chancellors Brandt◊ and Schmidt◊, there was some rapprochement with the East (*Ostpolitik*), but this halted before the threat of Russian expansionism. By 1984, 300 000 immigrant workers had returned home under an incentive scheme□

Germany: history

BC *51* Julius Caesar (as Governor of Gaul◊) established the Rhine as a frontier against the warlike German tribes

AD *4–5th century* Franks◊ (a Germanic people) overran 'Belgium and France'

8th century Charlemagne◊ brought the area of modern Germany within the Holy Roman Empire◊

870 Louis 'the German' 804–876, grandson of Charlemagne, became the founder of the German kingdom on the final division of Charlemagne's lands

962 Otto◊ I received the Imperial Crown from the Pope, establishing the (German) Holy Roman Empire (notable emperors being Otto the Great, Henry III, Henry IV (see Canossa◊), Frederick I Barbarossa, Henry VI, Frederick II, Rudolf of Hapsburg, Maximilian I, Charles V)

mid-14–15th century Hanseatic League◊

1517 Luther's Wittenberg theses opened the period of religious strife

1618–48 Thirty Years War◊

1756–63 Seven Years War◊ (under Frederick◊ the Great) marked the emergence of Prussia rather than Austria as the dominant German state

1806 Napoleon defeated Prussia

1866 Austro–Prussian War, by which Bismarck◊ re-consolidated Prussia's position in Germany

1870 Franco–Prussian War made Germany leading power in Europe

1914–18 World◊ War I (under William◊ II), in which Germany lost territory (see Silesia◊ and all her colonies

1918 Weimar Republic (see Hindenburg◊)

1929 economic crisis

1933 Nazis attain power under Hitler◊

1936 occupation of the Rhineland, and alliance with Italy and Japan (see Axis◊)

1936–9 intervention on the side of Franco in the Spanish Civil War◊

1938 annexation of Austria and the Sudetenland◊

1939 invasion of Poland precipitates World War II

1945 surrender to the Allies at Lüneburg◊

1949 division into E and W Germany◊□

Germiston industrial town (gold refining, chemicals, steel, textiles) in the Transvaal, Republic of S Africa; population 117 500□

Gerona industrial town (textiles, chemicals) in NE Spain; population 87 700□

Geronimo 1829–1909. Apache Indian warrior chief. Captured in 1886, he escaped, only to surrender later on condition his men were returned to their Florida home. Instead they were imprisoned, and later settled elsewhere□

Gerry Elbridge 1744–1814. American governor of Massachusetts, who in 1812 had his men redraw the state's electoral map to his party's advantage. The shape resembled a salamander, hence 'to gerrymander'□

Gershwin George 1898–1937. American composer of popular songs ('The Man I Love, Lady Be Good', etc.), to many of which his brother ***Ira Gershwin*** 1896–1983 wrote the lyrics, and also of jazz classics 'Rhapsody in Blue' 1924 and the opera *Porgy and Bess* 1935□

Gestapo abbreviated form of *Geheime Staatspolizei,* the Nazi secret political police, formed in 1933 and condemned at the Nuremberg◊ trials□

gestation the pregnancy◊ of mammals, which may range from 18 months in elephants to three weeks in the large kangaroos, in which the young are still very immature at birth. See Marsupial◊□

Gethsemane site on the Mount of Olives, just E of Jerusalem, of the garden where Judas, according to New Testament, betrayed Jesus□

Getty John Paul 1892–1976. American oil millionaire, founder of the Getty Museum (the world's richest) at Malibu, California. In 1985 ***John Paul Getty jnr*** established an endowment fund of £50 million for the National Gallery, London. He recieved an honorary knighthood in 1986□

Gettysburg borough of S Pennsylvania, USA, site of the Battle of Gettysburg (see Civil War◊, American), now a national cemetery at the dedication of which President Lincoln delivered the Gettysburg Address on 19 Nov 1863□

geyser natural spring which explosively discharges into the air a column of steam and hot water, e.g. Old Faithful (because of its regularity), Yellowstone National Park, Wyoming, USA; and those in New Zealand and Iceland□

Gezira El, fertile (by irrigation) plain in the Republic of Sudan, between the Blue and White Niles□

Ghana Sudanese empire of 4th–10th centuries AD with its capital at Timbuktoo, after which modern Ghana is named□

Ghana Republic of

area 238 537 sq km/92 100 sq mi

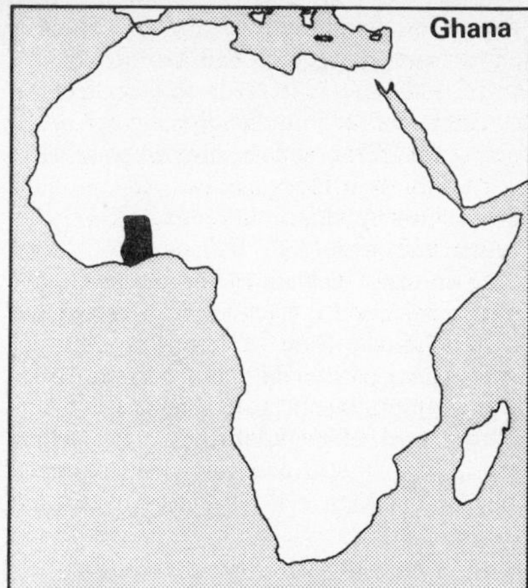

capital Accra
towns Kumasi, and ports Sekondi-Takoradi, Tema
features river Volta; traditional kingdom of Ashanti◊
exports cocoa, coffee, timber; gold, diamonds, manganese and bauxite
currency cedi
population 13 804 000
language English, official
religion Christianity 43%, Animism 38%, Islam 12%
government under the constitution of 1979 a president elected for a four-year term, a council of state, and a parliament forbidden to introduce a one-party regime, but see under history below
recent history Ghana was created in 1956 by the union of the British colony of the Gold Coast, and the trusteeship territory of Togoland, achieved independence 1957, and became a republic in 1960. The first president, the flamboyant Nkrumah◊ was overthrown by a military coup in 1966, and the government remained unstable. Flight Lieutenant Jerry Rawlings took over by a coup on 4 Jun 1979 from a military government, and again from an ineffectual elected government on 31 Dec 1981; he has been subject to repeated attempted coups□

Ghats Eastern and Western. twin mountain ranges in S India, to the E and W of the central plateau; a few peaks reach c3000 m/9000 ft□

Ghent industrial city (textiles, chemicals, metallurgy) and port in E Belgium; population 237 700. The cathedral of St Bavon (12–14th centuries), has paintings by van Eyck and Rubens□

gherkin a young or small green cucumber◊□

ghetto area of a town where Jews were by law compelled to live from 16th century until they were swept away, except in E Europe, in the 19th century. The concept was revived by the Germans and Italians 1940–5, and it is now used generally for any minority slum quarter□

Ghiberti Lorenzo 1378–1455. Italian sculptor, whose bronze doors (with Pollaiuolo◊) for the baptistery of his native Florence are one of the finest works of the Renaissance□

Ghirlandaio Domenico. Name by which the Florentine fresco painter, Domenico Bigordi, c1449–94, is known□

Giant's Causeway stretch of hexagonal columnal basalt on the N coast of Antrim, N Ireland, forming a promontory□

Gibberd Sir Frederick 1908–84. British architect, designer of the Catholic Cathedral, Liverpool, and the Central London mosque at Regent's Park. Knighted in 1967□

Gibbon Edward 1737–94. British historian. He set out on a tour of Europe in 1763, and while in Rome planned *The History of the Decline and Fall of the Roman Empire* 1766–88□

Gibbon Lewis Grassic. Pseudonym of Anglo-Scottish novelist James Leslie Mitchell 1901–35, author of the trilogy *A Scots Quair* 1932–4, set in the area S of Aberdeen, the Mearns, where he was born and bred□

gibbon a type of ape◊□

Gibbons Grinling 1648–1721. English woodcarver, born in Rotterdam. Recommended to royal patronage by Evelyn◊, he produced delicate work (especially birds, flowers, and fruit) for St Paul's cathedral, Petworth, etc□

Gibbons Orlando 1583–1625. English composer, especially of madrigals and motets□

Gibbs James 1682–1754. English Neo-classical architect whose works include St Martin's-in-the-Fields 1722–6, Radcliffe Camera, Oxford 1737–49, and Bank Hall, Warrington 1750□

Gibraltar City of
area 6.5 sq km/2.5 sq mi
features strategic naval and air base, with NATO underground headquarters and communications centre; colony of Barbary apes◊; the frontier zone is adjoined by the Spanish port of La Línea
exports mainly a trading centre for the import and re-export of goods. There is a commercial dockyard, and tourism is important
currency Gibraltar government notes and UK coinage
population 29 787
language English
religion mainly Roman Catholicism

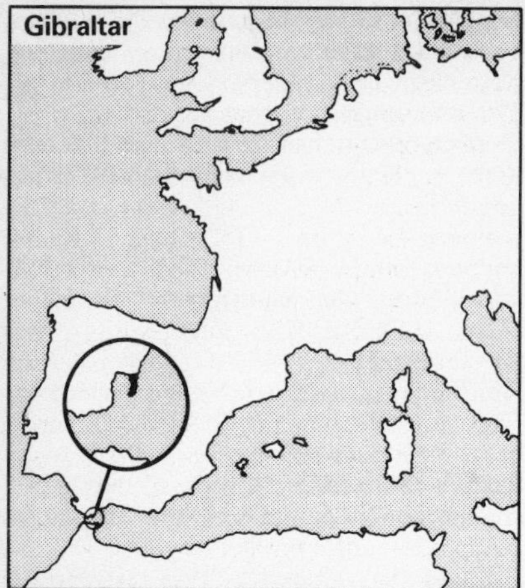

government the Governor has executive authority, with the advice of the Gibraltar council, and there is an elected house of assembly (chief minister Sir Joshua Hassan 1964–9 and from 1972)

recent history captured from Spain by Sir George Rooke in 1704, it was ceded to Britain in 1713 under the Treaty of Utrecht. A referendum in 1967 confirmed the wish of the people to remain in association with Britain, but Spain continues to claim sovereignty, and closed the border 1969–85□

Gibraltar Strait of. Strait between N Africa and Spain, with Gibraltar on the N side and Ceuta◊ on the South, the so-called Pillars of Hercules◊□

Gibson Desert desert in central Western Australia; area 220 000 sq km/85 000 sq mi□

Gide André 1869–1951. French novelist, born in Paris. His work is largely autobiographical and concerned with the themes of self-fulfilment and renunciation between which he swung. It includes *L'Immoraliste* 1902, *La Symphonie Pastorale* 1919, *Les Caves du Vatican* 1914, and *Les Faux-Monnayeurs* 1926; and an almost lifelong *Journal*. Nobel prize in 1947□

Gielgud Sir John 1904– . British actor and producer. He is noted for his 'golden voice' and his greatest stage role was in Shakespeare's *Hamlet* 1929; film roles include Clarence in Shakespeare's *Richard III* 1955 and the butler in *Arthur* 1981 (for which he won an Oscar)□

Gigli Beniamino 1890–1957. Italian lyric tenor, especially successful in roles from Puccini, Gounod and Massenet□

gila monster a type of lizard◊□

Gilbert Sir Alfred 1854–1934. British sculptor, remembered for his *Eros* in Piccadilly Circus, London□

Gilbert Sir Humphrey c1539–83. English soldier and navigator, half-brother of Sir Walter Raleigh◊, born at Dartmouth. In 1583 he claimed Newfoundland (landing at St John's) for Elizabeth I; he died when his ship sank on the return voyage□

Gilbert Sir William Schwenk 1836–1911. British humorist (*Bab Ballads* 1869, 'Bab' being an early nickname) and dramatist (14 light opera libretti) in collaboration with Sir Arthur Sullivan from 1871. It was a perfect professional partnership, but personal relations were often cool. Knighted in 1907□

Gilbert and Ellice Islands former British colony, a protectorate 1892–1915. Known since independence in 1978 as Tuvalu and Kiribati◊□

Giles (Carl Ronald) 1916– . British *Daily Express* cartoonist, creator of a family with a formidable 'Grandma'□

Gilgamesh hero of Sumerian, Hittite, Akkadian and Assyrian legend, originating some 2000 years BC. One-third mortal, two-thirds divine, he is Lord of Uruk, and his friend Enkidu, who is half-beast, half-man, dies for him. The incident of the Flood inspired Old Testament writers□

Gilgit town and region on the NW frontier of Kashmir under the rule of Pakistan (see Northern Territories◊)□

Gill Eric 1882–1940. British sculptor (façade of Broadcasting House, London) and engraver, deviser of the type Gill Sans (i.e. *sans serif*, 'without serifs')□

Gillray James 1757–1815. British caricaturist, especially of George III□

gillyflower common name for the piquantly scented carnation group (as in Chaucer, Shakespeare, and Spenser)□

Gilpin William 1724–1804. British artist and cleric, the inventor of the 'picturesque' according to specific rules□

gin alcoholic drink made by distilling a mash of maize, malt, and rye, with juniper flavouring□

ginger SE Asian reed-like perennial *Zingiber officinale*, family Zingiberaceae; the underground root is used as a 'hot' condiment and in preserves□

ginger ale and **beer** sweetened, carbonated drinks containing ginger flavouring, sugar, syrup, etc.; ginger beer also contains bitters□

ginkgo the ***maidenhair tree*** *Ginkgo bilboa* only living representative of the class Ginkgoales of the Gymnosperms◊. A 'living fossil', it was characteristic of the Mesozoic landscape (see geology◊), still grows wild in Zhejiang, China, and is a sacred tree in the East. It reaches 30 m/100 ft, and the fruit has edible seeds with a poisonous pulp□

Ginsberg Allen 1926– . American poet of the Beat◊ generation, e.g. *Howl* 1956□

ginseng medicinal plants *Panax quinquefolium* of N America and *P schinseng* of Korea and Japan, family Araliaceae. The roots have been used in China for over 3000 years, and by Russian cosmonauts, to increase resistance to fatigue and stress, but the effects are controversial□

Giolitti Giovanni 1842–1928. Italian Liberal Prime Minister 1892–3, 1903–5, 1906–9, 1911–14, and 1920–1. His policy of broad coalitions was ineffective against rising Fascism□

Giorgione name by which Giorgio of Castelfranco 1478–1511, Venetian artist, is known, although few details of his life are certain. He created the Renaissance poetic landscape, with rich colours and sense of intimacy. His most famous work is the *Tempest* (Venice). He influenced Titian◊□

Giotto di Bondone c1266–1337. Italian artist and architect, who introduced a naturalistic style, painting saints, etc, as real people. In one of the series of frescoes he painted for the Cappella dell' Arena, Padua, he made the Star of Bethlehem appear as a comet (Halley◊'s comet had appeared in 1303, just two years before). From 1334 he was official architect to Florence, and designed the cathedral *campanile* (bell-tower)□

giraffe tallest (over 5.5 m/15 ft) of the mammals, *Giraffa camelopardalis,* family Giraffidae. It has two skin-covered horns; skin mottled red-brown and fawn in a distinctive pattern (according to the region of southern Africa from which it comes), and a long neck and tufted tail.

Belonging to the same family is the smaller, nocturnal ***okapi*** *Okapia johnstoni* which has a short neck, barely discernible horns, and is a rich brown, which shades through irregular dark stripes on the rear and legs to cream. They were not seen by Europeans until 1900, and are now limited to a few hundred in the forests of Zaïre□

Giraldus Cambrensis ('Gerald the Welshman') c1146–c1223. He wrote accounts of Ireland and Wales and an autobiography□

Giraudoux (Hippolyte) Jean 1882–1944. French diplomat and playwright, e.g. *Tiger at the Gates* 1935 and *The Madwoman of Chaillot* 1945□

Girl Guides organization founded in 1910 by Baden-Powell◊ and his sister Agnes. There are three branches: Brownie Guides, 7–11 year-olds; Guides, 10–16 year-olds; Ranger Guides, 14–20 year-olds, and adult leaders – Guiders. In the USA five-year olds can enter Daisy Troops. The World Association of Girl Guides and Girl Scouts (as they are known in USA) has over 6 500 000 members□

giro system of direct transfer of payments between one bank or post office account and another. The British National Girobank, established in 1968, run via the Post Office, has its headquarters at Bootle, Merseyside□

Gironde navigable estuary (80 km/50 mi long) formed by the mouths of the Garonne, length 580 km/360 mi, and Dordogne◊ rivers, SW France. The Lot, length 480 km/300 mi, is a tributary of the Garonne□

Girondins right-wing republicans of the French Revolution whose leaders came from the Gironde department; driven from power by the Jacobins in 1793□

Girtin Thomas 1775–1802. English painter of watercolour landscapes, a friend of Turner□

Giscard d'Estaing Valéry 1926– . French Independent Republican statesman, Minister of Finance under de Gaulle 1962–6 and Pompidou from 1969, succeeding the latter as president 1974–81, when he was defeated by Mitterrand◊□

Gissing George Robert 1857–1903. British novelist. He lived for many years in near destitution, after having stolen money to assist a prostitute, and was politically a pessimistic socialist. His best-known book is *New Grub Street* 1891□

Giza see under Cairo◊□

glacier compacted ice mass formed where annual snowfall exceeds annual melting and drainage, so that as it moves downwards from the mountains it is constantly replenished. If it passes over an uneven surface, dangerous crevasses are created in it, and when it reaches the sea it breaks up into icebergs◊. In earth's ice◊ ages, glaciers played a large part in forming the landscape, one glaciation feature being U-shaped valleys□

gladiators professional fighters 3–5th century AD, recruited mainly from slaves, criminals, and prisoners of war, who fought to the death to entertain the ancient Romans□

gladiolus genus of S European and African cultivated perennials, family Iridaceae◊, with brightly-coloured funnel-shaped flowers, borne in a spike; the sword-like leaves spring from a corm□

Gladstone William Ewart 1809–98. British Liberal statesman, born in Liverpool. He left the Tory Party with the Peelite group in 1846, and became a Liberal in 1859. He was Chancellor of the Exchequer 1852–5 and 1859–66. As Prime Minister 1868–74 he carried through the disestablishment of the Church of Ireland, the Irish Land Act, the

abolition of the purchase of army commissions and of religious tests in the universities, the introduction of elementary education and of vote by ballot.
During Disraeli's government of 1874–80, Gladstone strongly resisted his imperialist and pro-Turkish policy, and by his Midlothian campaign of 1879 helped to overthrow him. Gladsone's 2nd government of 1880–5 faced problems in Ireland, Egypt, and S Africa, and lost prestige through its failure to relieve General Gordon◊. Returning to office in 1886, Gladstone introduced his Irish Home Rule Bill, which was defeated by the secession of the Liberal Unionists, and he thereupon resigned. He formed his last government in 1892, resigning after the Lords' rejection of his second Home Rule Bill. His work for the reclamation of prostitutes caused great controversy□

glandular fever viral disease (also known as infectious mononucleosis: see Herpes◊), causing fever, painfully swollen lymph nodes (in the neck), and changes in the blood cells (lymphocytes) which produce antibodies□

Glaser Donald Arthur 1926– . American physicist, awarded a Nobel prize in 1960 for his invention of the 'bubble chamber◊' for observing high-energy nuclear phenomena□

Glasgow city and administrative headquarters of Strathclyde, Scotland; population 762 288. Industries include engineering, chemicals, printing, distilling. Buildings include the cathedral of St Mungo (12th century), and the Cross Steeple (part of the historic Tolbooth); universities of Glasgow established in 1450 (modern buildings by Sir Gilbert Scott◊) and Strathclyde established in 1963; Royal Exchange, Stock Exchange, Kelvingrove Art Gallery (Impressionist◊ collection); the Burrell Collection at Pollok Park (bequeathed by shipping magnate Sir William Burrell 1861–1958); Mitchell Library. The Gorbals slum district has largely been cleared. Prestwick international airport is to the SW□

glass brittle, usually transparent or translucent substance, made by fusing various types of sand (silica). This fusion occurs naturally in the case of volcanic glass (see Obsidian◊). In industrial production of glass, the type of sand used and the particular chemicals added to it (e.g. lead, potassium, barium), as well as refinements of technique, make the difference between the cheap product (soda glass) and flint glass (used in cut-crystal ware), optical glass, stained glass◊, heat resistant glass, glasses that exclude certain ranges of the light spectrum, etc. Common commercial types of glass include:
blown glass which is either blown individually from molten glass, using a tube 1.5 m/4.5 ft long for expensive, crafted glass, or automatically blown into a mould e.g. light bulbs, bottles, etc.
pressed glass which is simply pressed into moulds, for jam jars, cheap vases, light fittings, etc.
sheet glass for windows is made by putting the molten glass through rollers to form a 'ribbon' which is cut to size.
fibreglass fine glass fibres, which in bulk can be used as insulation material in construction work; woven into curtain material; made into glass-reinforced plastic (GRP). It has good electrical, chemical, and weathering properties. Used for boat hulls, motor bodies, aircraft components, etc.
See also Metallic◊ glass◊, Laurence Whistler◊, and Corning Museum under New◊ York State□

glass snake a type of legless lizard◊□

Glastonbury market town in Somerset, England; population 6600. According to tradition, Joseph◊ of Arimathaea founded a church here in the 1st century, and King Arthur and Guinevere are said to have been buried in the area□

Glauber's salt crystalline sodium sulphate decahydrate, which melts at 31°C; the latent heat stored as it solidifies makes it a convenient thermal energy store. Used in medicine□

Glencoe see Strathclyde◊□

Glendower Owen c1359–1415. Welsh leader of a revolt against the English in N Wales, who defeated Henry IV in three campaigns 1400–2, though Wales was reconquered 1405–13□

Gleneagles glen in Tayside, Scotland, famous for golf and the ***Gleneagles Agreement*** formulated 1977 at the Gleneagles Hotel by Commonwealth heads of government, that 'every practical step (should be taken) to discourage contact or competition by their nationals' with S Africa□

gliding use of air currents to fly unpowered craft. Pioneers included Sir George Cayley, Lilienthal, and the Wright◊ brothers. Troop-carrying gliders were used in World War II by the Germans in Crete, and by the Allies at Arnhem◊. In the 1970s ***hang-gliding*** in which the aeronaut is strapped into a carrier, attached to a sail-wing of nylon, was developed in the USA by engineer Rogallo◊□

Glinka Michael 1803–57. Russian composer of the orchestral *Kamarinskaya* and two folk-inspired operas, *A Life for the Tsar (Ivan Susanin)* 1836 and *Russlan and Ludmilla*

1842, which broke with foreign tradition□

globefish a type of tropical fish. See under Tetraodon◊ 1□

Globe Theatre see under Southwark◊□

globigerina a type of simple marine animal. see under Foraminifera◊□

Gloucester Richard, Duke of 1944– . Prince of the UK, grandson of George◊ V. In 1972 he married Birgitte von Deurs. His heir is Alexander, Earl of Ulster 1914– □

Gloucester city, port, and administrative headquarters of Gloucestershire, England; population 92 135. Its 11–14th century cathedral has a Norman nucleus and additions in every style of Gothic. Aircraft and agricultural machinery are made in the city□

Gloucestershire W Midland county of England

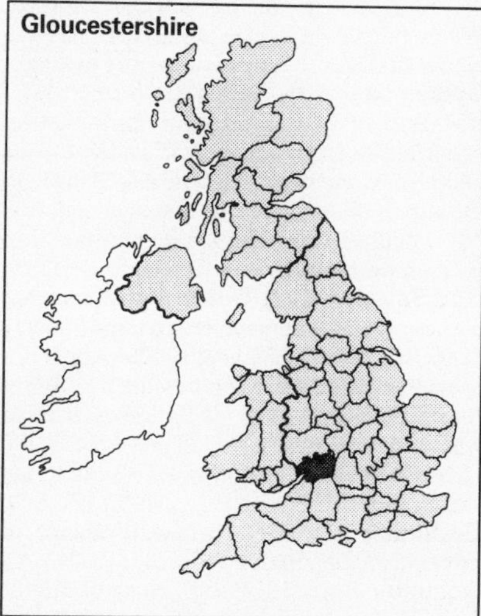

area 2643 sq km/1020 sq mi

towns administrative headquarters Gloucester; Stroud, Cheltenham, Tewkesbury, Cirencester

features Cotswold Hills; river Severn and tributaries; Berkeley Castle (see Edward◊ II); Prinknash Abbey, famous for pottery; Cotswold Farm Park, near Stow-on-the Wold, for rare and ancient breeds of farm animals

products cereals, dairy products; engineering, coal in the Forest of Dean

population 503 500□

glow-worm a type of Beetle◊ (6)□

Glubb Sir John Bagot 1897–1986. British soldier, founder of the modern Arab Legion, Jordan, which he commanded 1939–56□

Gluck Christoph Willibald 1714–87. Austrian opera composer. His *Orfeo ed Euridice* 1762 revolutionized opera by giving free scope to dramatic effect. His style was supported by Marie Antoinette and that of his rival Piccini by Mme du Barry, but with *Armide* 1777 and *Iphigénie* 1779, Gluck established his supremacy in Paris□

glucose yellowish syrup containing dextrose which purifies to a white crystalline powder, $C_6H_{12}O_6$, and is found in fruit and honey, and in the blood. It is a source of energy for the body, being produced from other sugars and starches. Commercially prepared from starch and other carbohydrates, it is used in brewing, jam and confectionery□

glue see adhesive◊□

glycerine (technical term ***glycerol***) colourless, viscous, sweetish liquid, $CH_2OH.CHOH.CH_2OH$, obtained from vegetable and animal oils and fats, and used to make high explosives; antifreeze and plastics; in cosmetics, and in pharmacy□

glycine an Amino-acid◊□

Glyndebourne estate in E Sussex, England, site of an opera house established in 1934 by John Christie 1882–1962□

gnat a small fly◊□

gneiss rock which has been affected by pressure and heat, so that the minerals in it are arranged in leaflike crystalline layers. Mica is a good example. Garnets◊ often occur in gneiss□

Gnetals order of gymnosperm plants◊ which include the welwitschia◊□

gnome in fables, a small, mischievous spirit of the earth. The males are bearded, wear tunics and hoods, and often guard an underground treasure. The ***garden gnome,*** an ornamental representation of these spirits, was first was brought from Germany to England in 1850 by Sir Charles Isham for his mansion, Lamport Hall, Northants□

Gnosticism esoteric cult of Divine Knowledge (a synthesis of Christianity, Greek philosophy, Hinduism, Buddhism, and the mystery cults of the Mediterranean), which was a rival to early Christianity, as shown by the 4th century codices discovered in Egypt in the 1940s. They include the ***Gospel of St Thomas*** (unconnected with the disciple), a Gnostic collection of 114 of Christ's sayings, discovered in Egypt 1945, and probably originating c35AD. Gnosticism envisaged the world as a series of emanations from the highest of several gods, emphasized the distinction between spirit (good) and matter (evil), gave women cult-equality with men, and opposed private property. It influenced the development of Christianity; and the French Cathars◊ and the modern ***Mandeans*** in S Iraq (whose sacred book is the *Ginza*) descends from it□

GNP abbreviation for ***Gross◊ National Product***□

gnu or ***wildebeest*** a type of antelope◊□

go Japanese national game, more subtle than chess, and originating in China 3000 years ago. The board is squared by 19 lines horizontally and vertically, and the pieces move along the lines, the board starting empty and being filled with black and white round, flattened stones as territory is won from the 'enemy'□

Goa, Daman, and Diu Union Territory of India comprising the former Portuguese coastal possessions of Goa and Daman, and the island of Diu, forcibly seized by India in 1961; population 1 082 000. Capital Panaji□

goat ruminant mammal, genus *Capra*, family Bovidae, closely related to the sheep. Domestic varieties are kept for milk, or for mohair (the angora◊ and cashmere◊); males are usually bearded and smell strongly. Noted wild species are the ***ibex*** *C ibex*, of the Alps, and ***markhor*** *C falconeri* of the Himalayas, 1 m/3 ft high and with handsome twisted horns. For the ***Rocky mountain goat,*** see under antelope◊□

Gobbi Tito 1915–84. Italian baritone, noted for his opera characterizations, especially Figaro, Scarpia, and Iago□

Gobelin French tapestry manufacturers from the 16th century, bought out by Louis XIV in 1662, and still state-supported□

Gobi Asian desert divided between the Mongolian People's Republic and Inner Mongolia, China; 800 km/500 mi N–S, and 1600 km/1000 mi E–W. The Mongol and Kalmuck people are nomadic. It is rich in fossil remains of extinct species, such as the dinosaur and mastodon□

goby small coastal fish, in the family Gobiidae, order Perciformes, with a big head and ventral fins modified to form a single sucker, e.g. the British ***goby*** *Gobio capito,* 25 cm/10 in long. In the same family are the tropical ***mudskippers*** genus *Periophthalmus,* which walk over mudflats, and even climb on land, using their strong pectoral fins as 'legs', and have 'pop' eyes close together on top of their heads□

God in its most highly evolved form (***monotheism***) the concept of a supreme being, a unique personal creative entity, assumed to be completely good, as opposed to belief in many gods (***polytheism***); see also animal worship, animism◊, fetishism◊. The rise of science since the 17th century has had a complex influence on man's belief in God. See deism◊, theism◊, and pantheism◊; religion◊ and theology◊□

Godalming town in Surrey, England; population 19 200. Site of Charterhouse School, Institute for Marine Environmental Research, and headquarters of the World Wildlife Fund□

Godard Jean-Luc 1930– French film director, e.g. *À Bout de souffle* 1959 *Masculin-Féminin,* etc., with a sharply casual approach to cutting and journalistic visual juxtapositions□

Godavari sacred river of the Republic of India; length 1450 km/900 mi□

Gödel Kurt 1906–78. American mathematician, whose ***Gödel's proof*** states that a mathematical system will always contain statements which can be neither proved nor disproved within the system□

Godfrey de Bouillon c1060–1100. Crusader. 2nd son of Count Eustace II of Boulogne, he and his brothers (Baldwin and Eustace) led 40 000 Germans in the 1st Crusade in 1096. When Jerusalem was taken in 1099, he was elected its ruler, but refused the title of king□

Godiva Lady 11th century AD. Wife of Leofric, Earl of Mercia. Legend has it that he promised to remit a heavy tax on the townspeople of Coventry if she rode naked through the streets at noonday. All remained indoors, but 'Peeping Tom' bored a hole in his shutters, and was struck blind□

God Save the King/Queen British national anthem. The tune resembles a composition by John Bull 1563–1628, and similar words are found from the 16th century. In its present form it dates from the 1745 Rebellion, when it was used as an anti-Jacobite Party song. In the USA 'My country, 'tis of thee' is sung to the same tune□

Godthaab capital (Greenlandic *Nuuk*) of Greenland; population 9850□

Godunuv Boris 1552–1605. Tsar of Russia from 1598, who died during a revolt led by Dmitri, brother and rightful heir of the previous tsar Fyodor◊ I, whom Boris was said to have murdered. See Mussorgski◊□

Godwin d. 1053. Earl of Wessex from 1020, he secured Edward◊ the Confessor's succession in 1042; King Harold◊ was his son□

Godwin William 1756–1836. British atheist philosopher and novelist. His *Enquiry concerning Political Justice* advocated an anarchic society based on a faith in man's essential rationality. His novel *Caleb Williams* 1794 promoted his views. His first wife was Mary Wollstonecraft◊□

Goebbels Paul Josef 1897–1945. German Nazi leader, in charge of the party's propaganda from 1929. On the capture of Berlin by the Allies he poisoned himself□

Goering Hermann Wilhelm 1893–1946. German field marshal from 1938 and Nazi leader. A renowned fighter pilot in World War I, he became commander of the SA (Storm◊ Troops), and in 1933, as Minister of the Interior, allegedly arranged the Reichstag◊ fire, directing the reign of terror which followed. As Commissioner for Aviation he built up the Luftwaffe◊. Appointed successor to Hitler 1939, he later lost favour, and was expelled from the party in 1945. Tried at Nuremberg, he poisoned himself before he could be executed□

Goes Hugo van der c1440–82. Flemish artist, whose work has an emotional intensity owing something to the fits of insanity of his later years, e.g. the *Portinari altarpiece* (Uffizi) and the *Death of the Virgin* (Bruges)□

Goethe Johann Wolfgang von 1749–1832. German poet, novelist, and dramatist, born at Frankfurt-am-Main. At first a law student, he was inspired by Shakespeare, to whom he was introduced by Herder◊, to write the play *Götz von Berlichingen* 1773, and became the leader of the romantic *Sturm◊ und Drang* movement, e.g. the autobiographical *The Sorrows of the Young Werther* 1774, which made him a European figure, and his masterpiece the poetic play *Faust* 1808, completed in a second part in 1831. He was Prime Minister at the court of Weimar 1775–85. A visit to Italy 1786–8 inspired the classical dramas *Iphigenie auf Tauris* 1787 and *Tasso* 1790. Also memorable are the *Wilhelm Meister* novels 1796–1829. He was a friend of Schiller◊. A series of love affairs inspired his lyrics□

Gogh Vincent Van 1853–90. Dutch Post-Impressionist painter. In 1886 he went to Paris where he became a friend of Gauguin◊, working with him for a time in Arles◊. His works include *Sunflowers*, *The Yellow Chair*; *A Cornfield with Cypresses*, and striking self-portraits, e.g. when he cut off part of his right earlobe following a quarrel with Gauguin. He spent the last years of his life in asylums, and committed suicide□

Gogol Nicolai Vasilyevich 1809–52. Russian author of short stories, e.g. *The Overcoat* 1842; the comedy *The Inspector General* 1836, an attack on bureaucracy; and the picaresque novel *Dead Souls* 1842□

goitre swelling on the front of the neck caused by an enlargement of the thyroid gland due to iodine deficiency. It may arise from lack of iodine in the water in certain areas, e.g. Derbyshire (potassium iodide is now added to salt sold for use in the home) or by under– or over–activity of the gland□

Golan Heights plateau on the Syrian border with Israel, bitterly contested in the Arab-Israeli Wars, and annexed by Israel on 14 Dec 1981□

gold element
symbol Au
atomic number 79
physical description shiny metal, easily worked
features highly resistant to corrosion, and temperature changes
uses it is used as a store of wealth and in jewellery. Gold compounds are used in photography and medicine; dentistry, and industrially; world supplies are jointly controlled by South Africa and the USSR□

Gold Coast historically, the W coast of Africa (Cape Three Points to the Volta river) where alluvial gold is washed down. A British trading settlement of 1618 developed into the colony of the Gold Coast, with its dependencies of Ashanti, and Northern Territories: see Ghana◊□

gold standard system under which gold coins were the monetary unit. The system broke down in World War I, and attempted revivals were undermined by the Great Depression. After World War II the par values of the currency units of the International◊ Monetary Fund (which includes nearly all members of the United Nations not in the immediate Soviet Communist bloc) were fixed in terms of gold and the US dollar, but by 1976 floating exchange rates (already unofficially operating from 1971) were legalized. Holdings of gold are still retained because it is an internationally recognized commodity money, which cannot be legislated upon or manipulated by interested countries□

goldcrest a small bird, a type of warbler◊□

golden calf in the Old Testament, an image of worship devised by Aaron◊□

golden eagle a type of Eagle◊□

Golden Fleece in Greek mythology, fleece of the winged ram Chrysomallus, which hung on an oak tree at Colchis guarded by a dragon. It was stolen by Jason◊ and the Argonauts; the story may have had its origin in the ancient use of greasy sheep fleeces to recover alluvial gold□

Golden Fleece formerly an order of knighthood in Spain and Austria□

Golden Gate see under San◊ Francisco□

Golden Horde the invading Mongol-Tatar army which first terrorized Europe from 1237 under the leadership of Batu, a grandson of Genghis◊ Khan. Tamerlane◊ broke their power in 1395, and Ivan◊ III ended Russia's payment of tribute to them in 1480□

goldenrod tall, leafy N American perennial, *Solidago virgaurea*, family Compositae, with heads of many small yellow flowers□

goldfish a type of carp◊□

Golding William 1911– . British novelist. Born in Cornwall, he has lived most of his life in Wiltshire, served in the RN in World War II, and afterwards became a schoolmaster. His first and most famous book is *Lord of the Flies* 1954; later volumes include *The Paper Men* 1984. Nobel prize in 1983□

Goldoni Carlo 1707–93. Italian dramatist, who excelled in realistic comedy, e.g. *La Locandiera* 1753□

Goldsmith Oliver 1728–74. British author. Irish-born, he studied medicine in Edinburgh, but took up a wandering life on the continent before returning to England as a hack writer. In 1761 he met Johnson◊ and became a member of his 'club', and in 1764 established his reputation with his poem *The Traveller,* followed by *The Deserted Village* 1770. His novel, *The Vicar of Wakefield* 1766, was sold to keep him from imprisonment for debt. His masterpiece is the comedy *She Stoops to Conquer* 1773□

Goldwyn Samuel 1882–1974. American film producer, famed for Goldwynisms, e.g. 'Anyone who visits a psychiatrist should have his head examined'□

golf game in which a small rubber-cored ball is hit with any of 14 clubs (woods or irons, according to the clubhead) from a platform tee into a series of 18 holes, usually c275 m/250 yd distant, round a landscaped course. In ***medalplay*** the object is to take fewer strokes than an opponent, but in ***matchplay*** the result depends on the winner of individual holes. The main fairway has short grass, and the green surrounding the hole is almost manicured, but sand bunkers or water at strategic points provide obstacles to progress, and the ball is also more difficult to extricate from the long bordering grass and shrubs, the 'rough.' A course measures c5500 m/6000 yd, for which a good player will have a score of under 70 strokes (par for the course); handicaps match unequal opponents. Golf originated in the 15th century in Scotland, where the Royal and Ancient Club at St Andrews dates from 1754. Major events include the British and US Open, Masters Tournament, and US Professional Golfers Association. Famous winners of the Open include J Nicklaus, L Trevino, and T Watson (all USA) and Gary Player (S Africa)□

Goliath in the Old Testament, champion of the Philistines◊, who was said (I *Samuel*) to have been slain with a stone from a sling by David◊ in single combat in front of their two armies□

gonadotrophin see fertility◊ drug□

Goncharov Ivan Alexandrovitch 1812–91. Russian novelist, whose masterpiece *Oblomov* 1858 satirized the indolent Russian landed gentry□

Goncourt Edmond de 1822–96 and his brother ***Jules*** 1830–70, were French novelists and critics, who wrote in collaboration, even their *Journal* 1887–96. Edmond founded under his will the Académie Goncourt, which awards the prestige equivalent of the Booker◊ for the best French novel; it is now worth 50 francs□

Gondwanaland Mesozoic southern continent of the ancient (Mesozoic) landmass which included modern South America, Africa, Australia, and Antarctica. See Baobab◊, Wegener◊□

gonorrhoea venereal disease caused by a bacterium, usually transmitted by intercourse. Certain strains are now resistant to antibiotics, but a vaccine is being developed□

Goodman Benny 1909– . American clarinetist, the 'king of swing', leader of his own band from 1934, known for e.g. 'Blue Skies' and 'King Porter Stomp'. Bartók's *Rhapsody* for clarinet and violin was written for him□

Goodwin Sands shoals off the Kent coast, England, exposed at low tide, and famous for wrecks. According to legend, they are the remains of the island of Lomea, owned by Earl Godwin in the 11th century□

Goodwood see under West◊ Sussex□

Goodyear Charles 1800–60. American inventor of vulcanized rubber 1839□

Goonhilly see under Cornwall◊□

goose a type of waterfowl◊□

gooseberry edible fruit (usually green, globular, and hairy) of *Ribes grossularia,* family Grossulariaceae, closely allied to the currant◊. The ***Cape gooseberry*** is the edible purple or yellow fruit of *Physallis peruviana,* family Solanaceae□

goosefoot plants of the family Chenopodiaceae, including ***fat-hen*** or ***white goosefoot*** *Chenopodium album* of which the seeds were used as food in Europe from Neolithic times, and also from early times in the Americas. The green part is a spinach◊ substitute□

gopher a small rodent◊□

Gorakhpur town in Uttar Pradesh, N India; population 306 000□

Gorbachev Mikhail Sergeievich 1931– . Soviet statesman, born in the N Caucasus. A Moscow law graduate, he became a Komsomol◊ official, and was in charge of agriculture 1978–84. A Politburo member from 1980, he was groomed for power by Andropov◊, became Chairman of the Foreign Affairs Committee in 1984. He succeeded Chernenko◊ as party leader in 1985□

Gordian knot in Greek myth, the knot tied by King Gordius of Phrygia, only to be unravelled by the future conqueror of Asia. According to tradition, Alexander cut it with his sword in 334BC☐

Gordimer Nadine 1923– . S African novelist, an opponent of apartheid, her works include *The Conservationist* 1974, and *Jul's People* 1981☐

Gordon Adam Lindsay 1833–70. Australian poet, who worked as a mounted policeman, sheep farmer, politician, etc. *Sea Spray and Smoke Drift* 1867 contains some of his best verse☐

Gordon Charles George 1833–85. British general, known as 'Chinese Gordon' from his part (while there in 1859–65) in suppressing the Taiping Rebellion. He was governor of the Sudan 1877–9, returning in 1884 to rescue Egyptian garrisons under attack by the Mahdi◊, but was himself besieged by the Mahdi's army in Khartoum. He was killed two days before Wolseley◊ arrived to relieve him, and Gladstone's government was toppled largely as a result☐

Gordon Lord George 1751–93. British organizer of the 'Gordon Riots' of 1778 in protest against removal of penalties imposed on Roman Catholics; he was acquitted on a treason charge. He figures in Dickens's novel *Barnaby Rudge*☐

Gordon Richard O 1921– . British novelist. His series, beginning with *Doctor in the House* 1952, was also a film success☐

Gordonstoun see under Elgin◊☐

Gorgas William Crawford 1854–1920. American military doctor, who cleared the Panama Canal Zone of malaria and yellow fever, and discovered that the latter is also transmitted by the mosquito☐

Gorgons in Greek mythology, three sisters with wings, claws, enormous teeth, and snakes for hair. Medusa, the only one who was mortal, was killed by Perseus, but her head was still so frightful, it turned the onlooker to stone. See Pegasus◊☐

Gorgonzola small town NE of Milan, Italy, famous for cheese☐

gorilla the largest of anthropoid Apes◊☐

Gorky industrial city (cars, locomotives, aircraft, etc.) in central USSR; population 1 358 000. Formerly Nijni-Novgorod, it was renamed in honour of Maxim Gorky in 1932; in 1980 Sakharov◊ was sentenced to 'internal exile' here☐

Gorky Arshile 1904–48. Armenian-born American artist, a founder of Abstract Impressionism☐

Gorky Maxim. Pseudonym of Russian writer Alexei Peshkov 1868–1936. Born at Nizhri Norgoros (renamed Gorky in 1932 in his honour), he was exiled 1906–13 for his revolutionary principles. His works include the play *The Lower Depths* 1902, and the recollections *My Childhood* 1913, and combine realism and faith in the potential of the industrial proletariat, which explains his official popularity☐

Gorlovka industrial town on the Donbas coalfield, Ukraine, USSR; population 338 000☐

gorse or ***furze*** or ***whin, genus*** *Ulex* family Leguminosae◊, common on heaths and sandy areas. It blooms throughout the year☐

Gorshkov Sergei 1910– . Russian admiral, Commander-in-Chief of the Soviet Navy from 1956, and responsible for its major development since the period of Khrushchev☐

Gort John Vereker, 1st Viscount Gort 1886–1946. British general, a VC of World War I, who commanded the British Expeditionary Force 1939–40, conducting a fighting retreat to Dunkirk◊☐

Gorton Sir John Grey 1911– . Australian Liberal statesman. Prime Minister from the death of Holt◊ in 1967 till 1971☐

gospel the message of Christian salvation; and later the four written accounts of Christ◊'s life by Matthew, Mark, Luke, and John in the New Testament. The first three (the Synoptic Gospels) give approximately the same account, but their differences from John have raised many problems. See also St Thomas's Gospel under Gnosticism◊☐

Gosport see under Portsmouth◊☐

Gosse Sir Edmund William 1849–1928. British critic, author of the autobiographical masterpiece *Father and Son* 1907☐

Göteborg port (German *Gothenburg*) in Sweden on the Göta Canal (built in 1832), which links it with Stockholm; population 428 200☐

Gotha town in E Germany, former capital of the duchy of Saxe-Coberg-Gotha; population 57 000☐

Gotha Almanach de. Annual survey of the European 'upper crust' published in Gotha 1763–1944; a shrunken successor, *Le Petit Gotha,* was revived in Paris from 1968☐

Gothenburg German form of Goteborg◊☐

Gothic architecture see under architecture◊☐

gothic novel genre established by Horace Walpole's *The Castle of Otranto* 1765, and marked by mystery, violence, and horror. See also Mrs Radcliffe◊, Jane Austen◊, Bram Stoker◊, E A Poe◊☐

Goths E Germanic people who settled near the Black Sea c2nd century AD. The eastern branch, the ***Ostrogoths***, were conquered by the Huns◊ c370, while the western, the ***Visigoths***, migrated to Thrace. Under Alaric◊ the latter raided Greece and Italy 395–410, sacked Rome, and established a kingdom in S France. Expelled thence by the Franks, they established a Spanish kingdom which lasted until the Moorish conquest of 711. The Ostrogoths regained their independence in 454, and under Theodoric◊ conquered Italy in 488–93; they disappeared as a nation after Justinian◊ reconquered Italy 535–55□

Gotland Swedish island in the Baltic Sea; area 3160 sq km/1220 sq mi. Capital Visby□

Gottfried von Strassburg c1210. German poet, author of the unfinished epic *Tristan und Isolde* which inspired Wagner◊□

Gottingen industrial town (printing, publishing, precision instruments, chemicals) in Lower Saxony, W Germany; population 130 200. Its university was founded by George II of England in 1734, and a Handel festival is held here□

Gouda town in W Netherlands; population 59 000. It produces round flat cheeses□

Gough Sir Hubert 1870–1963. British general. Initially blamed, as commander of the 5th Army 1916–18, for the German breakthrough on the Somme, he was superseded, but his force was later admitted to have been too small for the length of the front□

Goulburn town in New South Wales, Australia; population 22 400□

Gounod Charles François 1818–93. French opera composer, e.g. *Faust* 1859 and *Romeo and Juliet* 1867□

gourd the various members of the family Cucurbitaceae whose dried fruit is ornamental in flower arrangements, etc., e.g. ***bottle gourd*** *Lagenaria vulgaris*□

gout disease marked by an excess of uric acid in the blood and inflammation of the joints (especially the big toe), and largely confined to older men. If it becomes chronic, it affects the kidneys: diet and drugs are used to prevent the deposit of urate of soda in the system□

Government Communications headquarters see GCHQ◊□

Gower John c1330–1408. English poet, a friend of Chaucer, remembered for his tales of love *Confessio Amantis* 1390□

Gower Peninsula see under West◊ Glamorgan□

Gowon Yakubu 1934– . Nigerian head of state, by a military coup, 1966–75. After the Biafran Civil War 1967–70, he reunited the country with a policy of 'no victor, no vanquished'□

Goya y Lucientes Francisco José de 1746–1828. Spanish artist, born in Aragon, who was for a time a bullfighter, the subject of some of his etchings. From 1786 he was court painter to Charles IV. Later etchings include *The Disasters of War,* depicting the French invasion of Spain 1808–14□

GPU the Russian secret police. See KGB◊□

Graaf Regnier de 1641–73. Dutch physician who in 1672 discovered the ***Graafian follicles*** of the female ovary which contain the developing egg□

Gracchus the brothers ***Tiberius Sempronius*** 163–133BC and ***Gaius Sempronius*** 153–121BC. Roman agrarian reformers. As tribune in 133, Tiberius tried to prevent the ruin of small farmers by making large slave-labour farms illegal, but was murdered. Gaius, tribune in 123 and 122, revived his brother's legislation, and introduced other reforms, but was outlawed by the Senate and committed suicide□

Grace W(illiam) G(ilbert) 1848–1915. British cricketer, who scored over 54 000 runs, and helped establish cricket as the national game□

Graces in Greek mythology, three goddesses (Aglaia, Euphrosyne, and Thalia), daughters of Zeus and Hera, the personification of grace and beauty□

Grafton town of New South Wales, Australia; population 17 250□

Graham Billy 1918– . American evangelist, whose Evangelistic Association conducts worldwide 'crusades'□

Graham Martha 1894– . American choreographer and dancer, who broke with the traditional approach, e.g. *Appalachian Spring* (score by Aaron Copland) and *Clytemnestra* 1958□

Grahame Kenneth 1859–1932. British author of the animal fantasy *The Wind in the Willows* 1908, originally created for his little son, which was dramatized by A A Milne as *Toad of Toad Hall*□

Graham Land peninsula of Antarctica, formerly a dependency of the Falkland Islands and from 1962 part of the British◊Antarctic Territory; discovered by John Biscoe in 1832□

Grail Holy, cup used by Christ at the Last Supper, which was an object of quest by King Arthur's knights: see Parsival◊. According to legend the Blood of Christ was collected in it by Joseph◊ of Arimathea at the Crucifixion, and he brought it to Britain□

gram metric unit of weight; one thousandth of a kilogram◊□

Grampian region of Scotland
area 8702 sq km/3359 sq mi
towns administrative headquarters Aberdeen

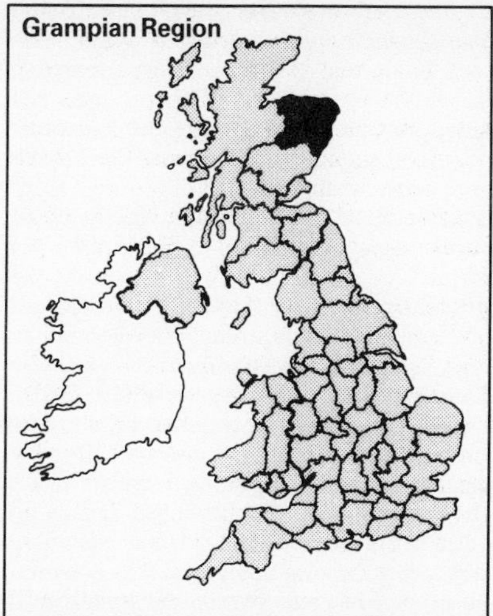
Grampian Region

features part of the Grampian Mountains (the Cairngorms); valley of the river Spey, with its whisky distilleries; Balmoral Castle (royal residence on the river Dee near Braemar, bought by Prince Albert in 1852, and rebuilt in Scottish baronial style); Braemar Highland Games in Aug
products beef cattle (Aberdeen Angus and Beef Shorthorn); fishing, including salmon; North Sea oil service industries; tourism is important, with winter skiing
population 483 000□

Grampian Mountains a range which separates the Highlands from the Lowlands of Scotland, running NE from Strathclyde, the S Highland region (which includes Ben Nevis, the highest mountain in the British Isles at 1340 m/4406 ft), the northern Tayside, and the S border of Grampian region itself (the Cairngorms, which includes Ben Macdhui, 1309 m/4296 ft). They include Aviemore, Britain's first complete winter holiday and sports centre, and the Highland Wildlife Park at Kincraig□

Grampians west end of Australia's eastern highlands, in Victoria; highest peak Mount William, 1167 m/3829 ft□

Gramsci Antonio 1891–1937. Italian Marxist, one of the founders of the Italian Communist Party in 1921□

Granada city in Andalucia, Spain; population 262 200. Founded by the Moors high in the Sierra Nevada in the 8th century, it was the capital of an independent kingdom 1236–1492, when it was the last Moorish stronghold to surrender to the Spaniards. Ferdinand and Isabella are buried in the cathedral (built 1529–1703). The ***Alhambra***, a fortified hilltop palace was built by the Moorish kings□

Granada industrial city in Nicaragua; population 99 600□

Granados Enrique 1867–1916. Spanish composer-pianist. His piano-work *Goyescas* 1911 was converted to an opera in 1916. He died when the Atlantic liner *Sussex* was torpedoed□

Granby John Manners, Marquess of Granby 1721–70. A popular cavalry officer in the Seven◊ Years' War, his head appears on many English inn signs□

Gran Chaco great level zone in Argentina, Paraguay, and Bolivia, which includes many lakes and swamps, and forests, a source of quebracho◊□

Grand Banks continental shelf of the N Atlantic off SE Newfoundland, where the shallow waters are rich fisheries, especially for cod□

Grand Canal world's longest canal◊ (Chinese *Da Yunhe*); see also Venice◊□

Grand Canyon see under Arizona◊□

Grand Guignol genre of horror play produced at the theatre of that name in (called after the bloodthirsty character 'Guignol' in 18th-century marionette plays) in Montmartre, Paris□

Grand National an annual race for horses held at Aintree◊□

Grand Rapids industrial city (furniture, motor bodies, plumbing fixtures, electrical goods) in Michigan, USA; population 181 840□

granite very hard volcanic rock formed at great depth and pressure beneath the earth (see Obsidian◊). It consists largely of silica, with substantial potash and soda content, and quartz, feldspar, etc. are present. Typical granite areas are the Scottish Highlands, Dartmoor, and Vermont□

Gran Patajen 'lost city' of a 5th-century civilization which came under Inca domination in the 15th century; in the Peruvian Andes, 485 km/300 mi N of Lima, 2620 m/8600 ft asl. Built of wood and slate, with striking wooden carvings, it was being excavated in 1985□

Grant Cary. Stage-name of Anglo-American actor Archibald Leach 1904– , born in Bristol (US citizen in 1942). Films include *The Philadelphia Story* 1940, and *Notorious* 1946□

Grant Duncan 1885–1978. Scottish artist, member of the Bloomsbury Group (see Vanessa Bell◊), influenced by Post-Impressionism◊□

Grant Ulysses Simpson 1822–85. American general, 18th President of the USA 1869–77. Commanding on the Mississippi front from

1862, he captured Vicksberg in 1863, and as Commander-in-Chief of the Federal Armies 1864–5, wore down Lee's resistance, receiving his surrender at Appomattox□

Grantham market town in SE Lincolnshire, England; population 29 000. Margaret Thatcher was born here□

Granville-Barker Harley 1877–1946. British theatre director of provocative productions (Shaw, Galsworthy, etc.), dramatist (*The Voysey Inheritance* 1905 and *The Madras House* 1907), and critic (*Prefaces to Shakespeare* 1927–47)□

grape fruit of the vine◊□

grapefruit a citrus◊ fruit□

graphite blackish-grey crystalline form of carbon◊, also known as ***plumbago*** or ***black lead***. It is widely used as a lubricant and as the active component of pencil lead, because it flakes easily. In its very pure form it is used as a moderator in nuclear reactors□

Grasmere English lake and village in the Lake District, Cumbria; Dove Cottage was the home of Wordsworth 1799–1808 (now a museum) and later of De Quincey; both Coleridge and Wordsworth are buried in St Oswald's churchyard□

Grass Günter 1927– . German novelist (e.g. the grotesquely humorous *Die Blechtrommel/The Tin Dumm* 1963), and playwright (*Onkel, Onkel* 1958)□

Grasse town in S France, near Cannes, where orange blossom and roses are grown for perfumes; population 35 500□

grasses important family, Gramineae, of Monocotyledons◊ with about 9000 species distributed worldwide except in the Arctic regions. The majority are perennial, with long and narrow leaves, hollow stems, and hermaphroditic flowers borne in spikelets. Usually the growing point remains close to the ground, growth continuing when the grass is grazed. They are well represented in Britain, many being economically important, and include:

Cereals◊

Meadow and ***Ornamental Grasses*** which include ***common meadow Grass*** *Poa pratensis*; ***couch grass*** *Agropyron repens*; ***fescue*** *Festuca pratensis*; ***marram grass*** *Ammophila arenaria*, a coarse perennial grass which flourishes on sandy patches; its tough creeping rootstocks are important in dune formation; ***rice grass*** *Spartina townsendii*, hybrid grass with deeply penetrating roots and abundant branching rhizomes which consolidate mud, much used in land reclamation schemes; ***pampas grass*** *Cortaderia argentea*, ornamental grass with tall leaves and large panicles of white flowers

Commercially important Grasses include ***bamboo◊; esparto*** *Stipa tenacissima*, grass native to S Spain and N Africa whose grey/green leaves are used to make paper, ropes, baskets, mats etc.; ***reed*** *Phragmites communis*, perennial aquatic grass with stiff erect leaves and straight stems which produces tough durable grass of great value for thatching; ***sugar cane*** *Saccharum officinarum*, see Sugar◊□

grasshopper insect of the order Orthoptera, able to leap with its strongly-developed hind legs. There are two families:

Short-horned Acridiidae, voracious feeders on vegetation, which stridulate or 'chirp' by rubbing the protruding joints of the legs against the hard wing veins. Eggs are laid in the ground, and the unwinged larvae are adult in six months. They include the ***migratory locust*** *Locusta migratoria* which used to be carried in great swarms for hundreds of miles by the wind, and destroy all crops over wide areas. Satellites now monitor the danger, and sudden infestations are eradicated by insecticide spray from the air. There are several small, harmless British species.

Long-horned Tettigoniidae, which have long antennae, and chirp by passing the two wing covers over one another. They include the ***large green grasshopper*** *Phasgonura viridissima* a British species 38 mm/1.5 in long, and the N American ***katydids*** (so-called from their chirp), the Phanopterinae□

grass snake a type of snake◊□

grass-tree plant of the lily family *Xanthorrhoea* of Australia, the tall, thick stems have a grass-like tuft at the top, and are surmounted by a flower-spike resembling a spear□

Grattan Henry 1746–1820. Irish Leader of the Opposition who in 1782 secured the abolition of all claims by the British Parliament to legislate for Ireland, but failed to prevent the passage of the Act of Union 1800□

Graves Robert Ranke 1895–1985. English author. He was wounded on the Somme◊ in World War I (see the autobiographical *Goodbye to All That* 1929), published many volumes of lyric verse (first volume *Over the Brazier* 1916); novels of Imperial Rome *I Claudius* 1934 and *Claudius the God* 1934; and books on myth and literary criticism. He married 'Nancy', a daughter of Sir William Nicholson, and for 10 years from 1926 lived with Laura Riding◊□

Gravesend town on the Thames, Kent, England, linked by ferry with Tilbury opposite; population 53 000. Pocahontas◊ is buried here□

gravitation the force of attraction that bodies exert on each other. The force of ***gravity*** that acts between all celestial bodies holds the planets in their course round the Sun, and the moon round Earth, is now thought of as conveyed by ***gravitons,*** hypothetical particles of the gravitational field. See Newton◊, relativity◊□

Gray Thomas 1716–61. English poet. A close friend at Eton of Horace Walpole◊, he made a continental tour with him 1739–41, which he cut short when they quarrelled; an account of the tour is given in his vivid letters. His 'Elegy Written in a Country Churchyard' (written, according to tradition, at Stoke Poges) 1750 is one of the most quoted poems in the language. Others include the 'Ode on a Distant Prospect of Eton College', 'The Progress of Poesy', and 'The Bard'. Found by critics, such as Johnson, to be obscure, these poems were precursors of Romanticism◊□

grayling freshwater edible game fish genus *Thymallus,* family Thymallidae, related to salmon□

Graz industrial city (chemicals, iron and steel), capital of Styria province, Austria: population 243 400□

Great Australian Bight broad bay in S Australia. See Astron◊□

Great Barrier Reef see under Queensland◊□

Great Britain official name from 1603 for England◊, Scotland◊, and Wales◊, and the adjacent islands, when the English and Scottish crowns were united (see James◊ I). With Northern◊ Ireland it forms the United Kingdom□

Great Britain: history

For history of individual kingdoms to 1707 see individual country entries

1707 Act of Union between England and Scotland

1721 Walpole◊ unofficially the first Prime Minister under George◊ I

1783 loss of the N American colonies (see USA, Lord North◊)

1800 Act of Ireland united Britain and Ireland

1819 Peterloo◊ massacre: cavalry charge on meeting of supporters of parliamentary reform

1832 Great Reform◊ Bill became law

1846 repeal of Corn Laws (see Robert Peel◊)

1848 Chartists◊ movement formed

1851 Great Exhibition in London

1867 Second Reform Bill introduced by Disraeli◊ and passed

1906 Liberal victory: programme of social reform

1911 Powers of House of Lords curbed

1914 Irish Home Rule Bill introduced

1916 Lloyd◊ George became Prime Minister

1920 Home Rule Act incorporates the north-east of Ireland (Ulster) into the United Kingdom of Great Britain and Northern Ireland

1921 Ireland, except for Ulster, became a dominion (Irish free State, later Eire (1937))

1924 first Labour government (see Ramsay Macdonald◊)

1926 General◊ Strike

1931 National government; unemployment reaches 3,000,000

1940 Churchill◊ became head of coalition government

1945 Labour government under Attlee◊; birth of Welfare State

1951 Conservatives defeated Labour

1961 Britain applied unsuccessfully to join EEC

1964 Labour victory under Wilson◊

1967 Second unsuccessful application to join EEC

1970 Conservatives under Heath◊ defeated Labour

1972 parliament prorogued in Northern Ireland, direct rule from Westminster began

1973 Britain joined EEC

1974 Three day week; coal strike; Wilson replaces Heath

1975 peak of IRA terror campaign

1976 defeat of Devolution◊ Bills

1977 Liberal-Labour pact

1979 victory for Conservatives under Thatcher◊

1981 formation of Social Democrat◊ Party; riots in inner cities

1982 unemployment over 3,000,000

1984-5 coal strike, the longest in British history

1986 abolition of metropolitan counties□

great circle a plane cutting through the centre point of a sphere passes through the surface along a 'great circle', so that all meridians of longitude and the Equatorial parallel of latitude are approximately half great circles. Since the path along a great circle is the shortest distance between two points, on earth many air routes pass over the N Pole□

Great Dane a breed of dog◊□

Great Divide or ***Great Dividing Range*** Mountain range extending from Cape York Peninsula, Queensland to Victoria (3700 km/2300 mi). It includes the Carnarvon Range, Queensland, which has many Aboriginal cave paintings; the Blue Mountains in New South Wales, and the Australian Alps◊□

Great Grimsby see Grimsby◊□

Great Lake Australia's largest freshwater lake, Tasmania; area 114 sq km/44 sq mi, 1025 m/3380 ft above sea level□

Great Lakes series of five freshwater lakes along the USA–Canada border, comprising Lakes Superior. Michigan, Huron, Erie, and Ontario. By means of inter-connecting canals they are navigable by large ships. The Lakes are drained by the Saint Lawrence◊ River. Area 245 000 sq km/94 600 sq mi□

Great Rift Valley longest 'split' in Earth's surface, 8000 km/5000 mi, running from the Dead Sea (Israel/Jordan) to Mozambique□

Great Sandy Desert desert in northern Western Australia; area 415 000 sq km/ 160 000 sq mi□

Great Schism period 1378–1417 in which there were rival popes at Rome and Avignon; it was ended by the Council of Constance 1414–17. See Martin◊ V□

Great Wall of China continuous defensive wall stretching from W Gansu to the Gulf of Liaodong (2250 km/1450 mi), though surveys in remote areas show it once to have been even longer. It was built from 214BC against the Turkish and Mongol tribesmen. Some 8 m/25 ft high, it has a series of square watch towers, and has been carefully restored□

Great Yarmouth see Yarmouth□

grebe flighted freshwater diving birds of the worldwide order Podicipediformes, which build floating nests, e.g. ***dabchick*** or ***little grebe*** *Podiceps ruficollis;* and ***great crested grebe*** *Podiceps cristatus* with a complex courting display□

Greco El. Spanish artist, Doménico Theotocopuli 1541–1614, called 'the Greek' because he was born in Crete. He studied under Titian◊, and finally settled in Toledo c1575, which he found congenial to his fanatically religious temperament, e.g. *The Burial of Count Orgaz* and *The Agony in the Garden.* His sense of colour is almost lurid, and his forms exaggeratedly elongated□

Greece (Hellenic Republic)
area 131 944 sq km/50 944 sq mi
capital Athens
towns Thessaloniki, Patras, Larisa, Heraklion – all are ports
features include a large number of islands, notably Crete, Corfu, and Rhodes; Corinth canal; Mount Olympus; archaeological sites (see Athens◊, Crete◊, Olympia◊, etc.); there are US bases at Hellenikon, Nea Makri (both near Athens), and (on Crete) at Souda Bay and Iraklion
exports tobacco, fruit (including currants) and vegetables, olives and oil, textiles
currency drachma
population 9 700 000

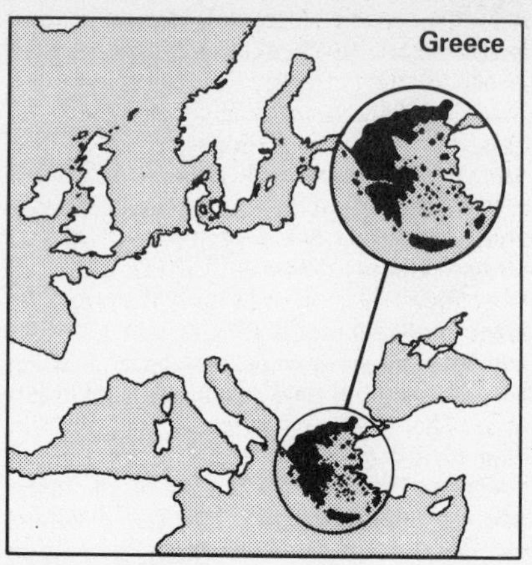

language Greek
religion Greek Orthodox 97%
famous people *architecture* Doxiadis *literature (poetry)* Homer, Hesiod, Pindar, Sappho, George Seferis *(prose)* Herodotus, Thucydides, Xenophon; Demosthenes, Isocrates; Aristotle *(drama)* Aeschylus, Euripides, Sophocles, Aristophanes, *sculpture* Phidias, Praxiteles *music* Theodorakis *(Zorba the Greek)* Nikos Kazantzakis *philosophy* Aristotle, Socrates, Plato, Epicurus, Zeno
government under the constitution of 1975 there is a president (Christos Sartzetakis from 1985), elected by a unicameral parliament (Prime Minister from 1981 Andreas Papandreou, Pan-Hellenic Socialist Movement/Pasok); opposition leader Constantine Mitsotakis, New Democracy Party. Under Papandreou a programme of devolution from the ministries to the nomarchs (equivalent of the French prefects) and local councils of the nomoi (regions) was begun, and he planned removal of presidential checks on the government's executive power
history see Greece: history□

Greece: history
BC ***c1600–1200*** Mycenean◊ civilization
c1180 Siege of Troy◊
c1100 Dorian invasion, and the rise of the Greek city states, of which the greatest were Athens◊ and Sparta◊ (see Solon◊)
750–550 trading colonies founded round the Mediterranean, Black Sea, etc.
5th century Persian Empire sought to establish its rule over the Greeks
490 Persians defeated at Marathon◊
480 Thermopylae◊, the Spartans fought a delaying action against a fresh invasion by Xerxes◊, and the Persians were defeated at sea (Salamis◊ in 480) and on land (Plataea◊ 479)

461–429 Pericles◊ attempted to convert the alliance against the Persians into the basis of a Greek empire
431–404 Peloponnesian War◊ prompted by Sparta's suspicion of Pericles's ambitions, with the resultant destruction of Athens's political power
378–371 Sparta, successor to Athens in the leadership, overthrown by Thebes
358–336 Philip◊ II of Macedon seized his opportunity to establish supremacy over Greece
334–331 Philip's son Alexander the Great◊ defeated the decadent Persian Empire, and went on to found his own
3rd century Greek cities formed the Achaean and Aetolian Leagues to try and maintain their independence against Macedon, Egypt, and Rome
146 Greece annexed by Rome
AD ***529*** closure of the University of Athens by Justinian ended Greek cultural predominance
330 capital of Roman Empire◊ transferred to Constantinople
1453–60 Constantinople captured, then rest of Greece taken by the Turks
1821 Greek War of Independence ended successfully in 1829 after intervention by Britain, France, and Russia secured the destruction of the Turkish fleet at Navarino◊
1912–13 Balkan Wars◊ secured for Greece most of the territory still claimed from Turkey
1940 Italian invasion resisted, but the German *blitzkrieg* of 1941 overwhelmed the Greeks, despite British assistance; on the German withdrawal in 1944 British troops occupied the country and assisted the royalists against the leftwing in a civil war
1973 bloodless military coup inaugurated a republic (see Constantine◊), with Colonel George Papadopoulos as president, but the regime of 'the colonels' became increasingly oppressive, the composer Theodorakis◊ being among those imprisoned
1974 military coup in Cyprus supported by Greece, and precipitated Turkish invasion of the island; recall of Karamanlis◊
1981 Greece joined the Common Market
1981 Socialist Movement ousted the New Democracy Party of George Rallis
1985 Karamanlis◊ denied a second presidential term, and Pasok (headed by Papandreou◊, again returned in the general elections

Greek an Indo-European language descended from the Attic form (see Attica◊) of the Ionic (see Ionians◊) dialect which was supreme in Greece by the 4th century BC. ***Modern Greek*** developed among the common people under the Turkish occupation, and though it still uses the ancient alphabet, is greatly changed in phonetics and grammar. Purist attempts at a return to the classical standard have failed and the everyday speech was officially adopted from 1976 in schools□

Green Henry 1905–74. British novelist, an expert in social comedy, e.g. *Loving* 1945□

Greenaway Kate 1846–1901. British illustrator of children's books, e.g. *Mother Goose*□

Greene (Henry) Graham 1904– . British novelist. Born at Berkhamsted, son of a headmaster, he became a literary journalist, and in World War II served in the Foreign Office. A Catholic convert from 1926, he is deeply concerned with religious issues. His books include *The Man Within* 1929, *Brighton Rock* 1938, *The Power and the Glory* 1940, *The Heart of the Matter* 1948, *The Third Man* 1950, *Our Man in Havana* 1958, *The Honorary Consul* 1973, and *Monsignor Quixote* 1982□

greenfinch a type of finch◊□

greenfly an aphid. See under Hemiptera◊ 1□

greenhouse effect the atmosphere, like the glass of a greenhouse, lets much of the sun's visible and near ultraviolet radiation through it to warm the earth's surface. The warm earth re-radiates electromagnetic◊ radiation but of a far lower frequency (for infrared) to which the atmosphere, like glass, is not as transparent. This 'trapping' or 'greenhouse' effect contributes to raising the earth's temperature. Activities of man, such as burning fossil◊ fuels, which increase the carbon◊ dioxide (a good infrared absorber) in the atmosphere are tending to promote the greenhouse effect; conceivably the earth's temperature could rise enough for polar ice to melt, raising the sea level dangerously□

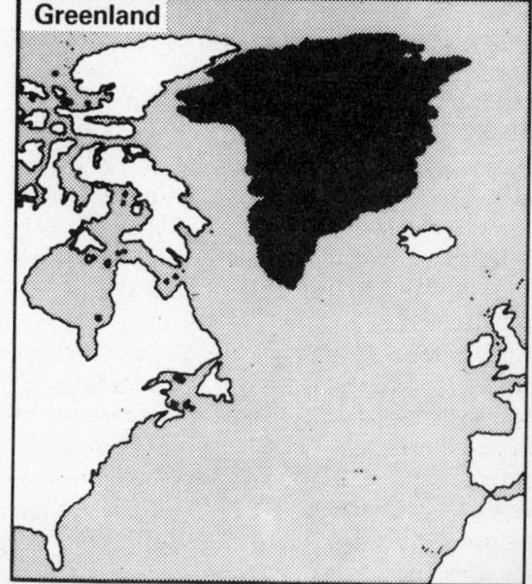

Greenland (Greenlandic *Kalaallit Nunaat*)
area 2 175 600 sq km/840 000 sq mi
capital Godthaab (Greenlandic *Nuuk*)
features the world's largest island; the interior is covered by an ice sheet averaging 300 m/1000 ft deep
exports fish, furs, cryolite◊
currency krone
population 50 650; Inuit 75%; Danish 25%
language Greenlandic
religion Lutheran Christianity
government an integral part of Denmark, Greenland has had internal autonomy from 1979, with a parliament (*Landsting*), Prime Minister from 1979 Jonathan Motzfeldt, heading a coalition
history it was reached by Eric the Red◊ c982, but the early Norse colonies died out, and after its rediscovery in the 16th century, it became a Danish colony in the 18th century. It has great strategic importance, and defence is shared with the USA. Greenland left the EEC 1985□

Greenland Sea see under Arctic◊ Ocean□

green monkey disease see Marburg◊ disease under haemorrhagic◊ fever□

Green Mountain Boys see Vermont◊□

Greenock industrial seaport (shipbuilding, engineering, electronics, etc.) in Strathclyde, Scotland; population 57 324□

Green Party (German *die Grünen*) environmentalist party, which first achieved entry to the W German Parliament in 1983. There is a similar Ecology Party in Britain, which in 1985 changed its name to the Green Party. There are links with the activist organization ***Greenpeace*** whose vessel *Rainbow Warrior*, on its way to protest against French atmospheric nuclear testing in the S Pacific, was sunk by French agents in 1985, killing a crew member□

greenshank a large sandpiper◊□

Greenwich inner borough of E Greater London;
features Queen's House (see Inigo Jones◊); Royal Naval College (designed by Wren◊); National Maritime Museum; historic Royal Greenwich Observatory (see under Herstmonceux◊); *Cutty Sark* and *Gipsy Moth IV* (Francis Chichester◊); also includes ***Woolwich*** with the Royal Arsenal; Eltham Palace 1300
population 213 500□

Greenwood Walter 1903–74. British novelist of the Depression, born in Salford. His own lack of a job gave authenticity to *Love on the Dole* 1933, later dramatized and filmed□

Gregg Sir Norman 1892–1966. Australian surgeon, who discovered in 1941 that German measles in a pregnant woman could cause physical defects in her child; knighted in 1953□

Gregory 16 popes, including:
Gregory I St, the Great c540–604, pope from 590, who asserted Rome's supremacy, and exercised almost imperial powers. In 596 he sent St Augustine◊ to England. He introduced Gregorian chant (see under music◊) into the liturgy. Feast day, 12 Mar.
Gregory VII St (original name Hildebrand) c1023–85, pope from 1073. He claimed power to depose kings, denied lay rights to make clerical appointments, and attempted to suppress simony and enforce clerical celibacy, making enemies on all sides, so that he was driven from Rome and died in exile. Feast day, 25 May. See Henry◊ IV (Holy Roman Emperor).
Gregory XIII 1502–85, pope from 1572, who introduced the Gregorian calendar◊□

Gregory Isabella Auga, Lady 1852–1932. Irish playwright, associated with W B Yeats in creating the Abbey◊ Theatre in 1904□

Gregory of Tours St 538–94. French bishop of Tours from 573, author of a *History of the Franks*□

Grenada southernmost of the Windward Islands◊

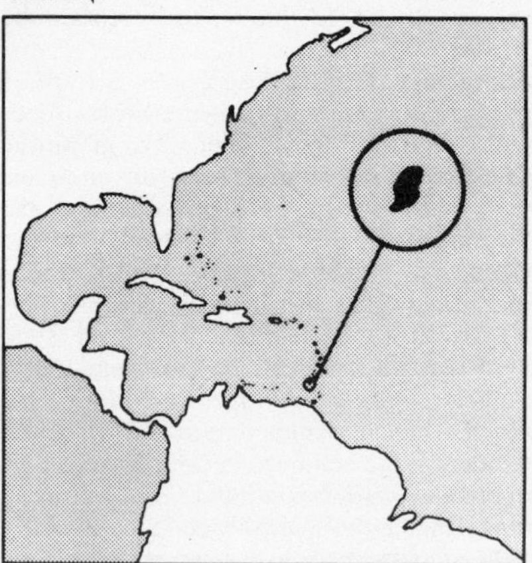

area (including the Grenadines◊, notably Carriacou) 344 sq km/133 sq mi
capital St George's
features smallest independent nation in the western hemisphere
exports cocoa, nutmeg, bananas, mace
currency Eastern Caribbean dollar
population 113 000
language English
religion Roman Catholicism
government governor-general and 15-member parliament (Prime Minister from 1984 Herbert Blaize 1918– of the New National Party).

recent history discovered by Columbus, Grenada was ceded to Britain by France in 1783, became an Associated State in 1967 and independent within the Commonwealth in 1974. The People's Revolutionary government (PRG) of Maurice Bishop, which ousted autocratic premier Eric Gairy by a coup in 1979, did not introduce a new constitution, held many political prisoners, muzzled the press, and had close relations with Cuba. Overthrown and replaced by a military council in Oct 1983, Bishop and three of his ministers were murdered. Military intervention by the USA followed (see Forbes Burnham◊), but combatant troops were withdrawn by Dec 1983, and elections held in Dec 1984□

Grenadines chain of small islands in the Caribbean divided between St Vincent◊ and the Grenadines and Grenada◊□

Grenfell Julian 1888–1915. British poet killed in World War I, author of 'Into Battle'□

Grenoble industrial town (computers, 'new-wave' technology) in SE France; population 450 000. It was the birthplace of Stendhal, commemorated by a museum, and the Beaux Arts gallery has a modern collection. The Institut Laue-Langevin is for nuclear research, and an advanced physics centre was planned in 1985□

Grenville George 1712–70. British Whig statesman, Prime Minister 1763–5. His government prosecuted Wilkes◊ in 1763, and passed the Stamp Act 1765 which precipitated the American War of Independence□

Grenville Sir Richard c1541–91. English sailor. He commanded the fleet sent by his cousin, Sir Walter Raleigh, to colonize Virginia in 1585, and in 1591, in an attempt to capture a Spanish treasure fleet, was cut off from the main English fleet. Aboard *Revenge*, he fought for 15 hours against 15 Spanish ships, and was fatally wounded□

Grenville William Wyndham, Baron Grenville 1759–1834. British Whig statesman, son of George Grenville◊, he headed the 'All the Talents' coalition of 1806–7□

Gresham Sir Thomas c1519–79. English economist, who paid for the building of the first Royal Exchange, founded Gresham College, and propounded ***Gresham's Law*** that 'bad money tends to drive out good money from circulation'□

Gretna Green border village in Dumfries and Galloway, Scotland; famous for runaway marriages (after they were banned in England in 1754) until in 1856 a Scottish residential qualification was introduced□

Greuze Jean Baptiste 1725–1805. French genre painter, whose sentimental paintings include *A Father explaining the Bible to his Children* 1755□

Greville Charles Cavendish Fulke 1794–1865. British diarist of the Court and politics, who was Clerk of the Council in Ordinary 1821–59□

Grey Charles, 2nd Earl 1764–1845. British Whig statesman. As Prime Minister 1830–4, he carried the Great Reform Bill in 1832□

Grey Henry, 3rd Earl 1802–94. British Whig statesman, son of the 2nd earl. As Colonial Secretary 1846–52, he was noted for maintaining that the colonies should be governed for their own benefit, not that of the mother country□

Grey Sir George 1812–98. British governor of S Australia 1841– 5, and New Zealand 1845–53, later returning to New Zealand after service in Cape Colony, again being governor 1854–61 and then Prime Minister 1877–79. He attempted good relations with the Maoris□

Grey Lady Jane 1537–54. Queen of England 9–19 Jul 1553. She was the great granddaughter of Henry VII, and since she was a Protestant, Edward VI was persuaded by Northumberland◊ to alter the succession in her favour. The people, however supported, the succession of Mary◊, and Lady Jane was executed□

Grey Zane 1875–1939. American Ohio-born dentist, author of 'Westerns', e.g. *Riders of the Purple Sage* 1912□

Grey Edward, 1st Viscount Grey of Fallondon 1862–1933. British Liberal statesman, nephew of 2nd Earl Grey. As Foreign Secretary 1905–16 he negotiated an entente with Russia in 1907, and backed France against Germany in the Morocco crises of 1905–6 and 1911 (see Agadir Incident◊). In 1914 he said: 'The lamps are going out all over Europe; we shall not see them lit again in our life-time'□

greyhound a breed of dog◊□

greyhound racing sport of watching a mechanically propelled dummy hare pursued by greyhounds round a circular track. Invented in the USA in 1919, it is popular in Britain and Australia□

Grieg Edvard Hagerup 1843–1907. Norwegian composer, born at Bergen◊. Greatly influenced by the folk tunes of his country, he is best remembered for his only *Piano Concerto* 1868, incidental music for *Peer Gynt* 1876, songs, and the Holberg Suite for strings□

Grierson John 1898–1972. British documentary film pioneer: e.g. *Drifters* 1929, *Song of Ceylon* 1934□

griffin mythical guardian of treasure, with the body, tail, and hind legs of a lion, and the head, forelegs, and wings of an eagle, as in the armorial crest of the City of London□

Griffith David Wark 1875–1948. American pioneer of the film flashback, cross-cut, close-up and longshot. His masterpiece as director was *Birth of a Nation* 1915□

Grillparzer Franz 1791–1872. Austrian poet-dramatist. His works include adaptations of Greek myth (the trilogy *The Golden Fleece* 1821), and *A Dream is Life* 1834□

Grimaldi Joseph 1779–1837. British clown, son of an Italian actor, who gave his name 'Joey' to all later clowns, and excelled as 'Mother Goose'□

Grimm Jacob 1785–1863. Pioneer philologist (see Grimm◊'s Law) and collaborator with his brother ***Wilhelm*** 1786–1859 in the *Fairy Tales* 1812–14. Their informants were less 'folk' than middle-class, and they greatly reworked the material□

Grimm's Law the rule by which certain historical sound changes have occurred in some 'related' European languages: compare e.g. Latin 'p' with English and German 'f' sound, as in *pater/father, vater*□

Grimmelshausen Hans Jacob c1625–76. German picaresque novelist whose *The Adventurous Simplicissimus* 1669 reflects his own Thirty◊ Years' War experiences□

Grimond Joseph, Baron Grimond 1913– . British Liberal politician, leader of the party 1956–67; life peer in 1983□

Grimsby fishing port in Humberside, England; population 91 800. It declined in the 1970s when Icelandic waters were closed to Britain□

Grodno industrial town in Byelorussian republic, USSR; population 212 000. Long disputed, it was ceded to Poland in 1923, and ceded back to Russia in 1945□

Gromyko Andrei 1909– . President of the USSR from 1985. Ambassador to the USA from 1943, he took part in the Tehran, Yalta, and Potsdam conferences; as United Nations representative 1946–9, he exercised the Soviet veto 26 times, and as Foreign Minister 1957–85 returned from the 'thaw' to the Stalinist line□

Groningen industrial town (textiles, sugar refining) in NE Netherlands; population 165 145□

Gropius Walter Adolf 1883–1969. American architect, founder-director of the Bauhaus◊ school in Weimar 1919–28, advocate of team architecture, and artistic standards in industrial production. From 1937 he lived in USA, designing the Harvard Graduate Centre 1949–50, etc□

Gross Domestic Product (GDP) a measure of the total domestic output of a country; including exports, but not imports. See Gross◊ National Product□

Grossmith George 1847–1912. British actor and singer, especially in Gilbert and Sullivan opera roles, and author with his brother ***Weedon*** 1853–1919 of the fictitious *Diary of a Nobody* 1894□

Gross National Product (GNP) the most commonly used measurement of the wealth of a country. GNP is the Gross◊ Domestic Product plus income from abroad, minus income earned during the same period by foreign investors within the country. The national◊ income of a country is the GNP minus whatever sum of money needs to be set aside to replace ageing capital stock□

Grotefend George Frederick 1775–1853. German language scholar, decipherer of ancient Persian cuneiform◊□

Grotius Hugo 1583–1645. Dutch jurist and politician, whose *De Jure Belli et Pacis* 1625 founded International◊ Law□

ground-nut S American annual, the ***peanut, earthnut*** or ***monkey nut*** *Arachis hypogaea,* family Leguminosae. After flowering, the flowerstalks bend and force the pods into the earth so that they can ripen without desiccation ('drying out') in near desert conditions. The nuts are now a staple food in many tropical countries and also yield a valuable edible oil; the processed shells have potential as cattle food□

ground squirrel a type of burrowing squirrel◊□

grouper a type of large sea perch◊□

grouse a game bird. see under fowl◊□

Grozny industrial oil town, capital of the republic of Chechen-Ingush, USSR; population 379 000□

Grundy Mrs. Character referred to in T Morton's play *Speed the Plough* 1798 as one who knows the proprieties□

Grünewald chief and last of the German Gothic◊ artists, ***Mathis Gothardt Neithardt*** c1460–1528. His work has great religious intensity, e.g. the Isenheim altarpiece now at Colmar□

Gruyère district in W Switzerland, famous for pale yellow cheese with large holes□

Guadalajara industrial city in W Mexico; population 2 343 000. A key communications centre, it has a fine cathedral dating from the 16–17th century, Governor's Palace, and an orphanage with murals by Orozco◊□

Guadalcanal see Solomon◊ Islands□

Guadeloupe French West Indian island group in the Lesser Antilles, forming an overseas region; area 1702 sq km/657 sq mi; population 328 400. The main islands are

Basse-Terre, on which is the chief town of the same name, and Grande-Terre□

Guam see under Marianas◊□

guanaco an animal of the camel◊ family□

Guanch Republic see Canaries◊□

Guangdong province (formerly Kwantung) of S China
area 231 400 sq km/90 246 sq mi
capital Guangzhou
features Hainan, Leizhou peninsula, and Hongkong and Macao in the Xi Jiang delta
products rice, sugar, tobacco; minerals; fish
population 56 810 000□

Guangxi Zhuang autonomous region (formerly Kwangsi Chuang) in S China
area 220 400 sq km/85 074 sq mi
capital Nanning
features Zhuang people are allied to the Thai, and form China's largest ethnic minority
products rice, sugar, fruit
population 34 700 000□

Guangzhou trading city (formerly Kwangchow/Canton), capital of Guangdong province, China; population 3 000 000. Sun Yat-sen Memorial Hall, a theatre, commemorates the statesman, who was born nearby. There is a permanent exhibition at the Foreign Trade Centre□

guarana Brazilian woody climbing plant *Paullinia cupana,* family Sapindaceae; a drink made from it contains caffeine, and it is the source of the drug known as zoom in the USA. Its more commercial uses include the extraction of starch, gum, and several oils□

Guarani South American Indian people; mingled with their Spanish conquerors they form the modern mestizo population of Paraguay, S Brazil, and Bolivia□

Guardi Francesco 1712–93. Italian artist, noted for almost Impressionist pictures of his native Venice□

Guareschi Giovanni 1909–68. Italian author of short stories of the friendly feud between parish priest Don Camillo and the Communist village mayor□

Guarnieri family of violin-makers at Cremona, especially of whom ***Giuseppe Antonio Guarnieri*** 1687–1745 produced the finest models□

Guatemala Republic of
area 108 889 sq km /42 042 sq mi
capital Guatemala City
towns Quezaltenango, Puerto Barrios (naval base)
features earthquakes are frequent
exports coffee, bananas, cotton
currency quetzal
population 7 956 000, American Indians 54%, Mestizos 42%, Caucasian 4%
language Spanish

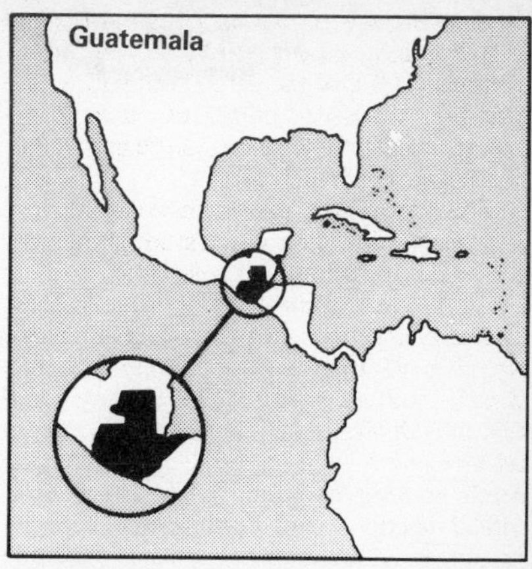

religion Roman Catholicism
famous people poet-novelist ***Miguel Angel Asturias*** 1899–1974, Nobel prize in 1967
government elections for a constituent assembly were held in 1984, and a presidential election was held in 1985.
recent history previously a member of the Federation of Central America, Guatemala became independent in 1839. Her boundaries were not fixed until 1936, and her claims on Belize delayed the latter's independence until 1981, British troops remaining in Belize to prevent subsequent Guatemalan action. In 1982 a military coup unseated the ruling junta, and General Ríos Montt became president. He proved a religious fanatic, and was overthrown by right-wing troops in Aug 1983, General Oscar Mejía becoming head of state: the USA was allegedly involved in the coup. Guerrilla activity continued especially in the highly militarized Peten zone by the Indians, and political killings, especially of Indians, also continued. the first civilian elections were held in 1985, after more than 30 years of almost uninterrupted military rule. President from Jan 1986 is Mario Unicio Cerezo□

Guatemala City capital of Guatemala, founded in 1776 when its predecessor (Antigua) was destroyed in an earthquake; population 1 500 000□

guava tropical American tree *Psidium guajava,* family Myrtaceae; the astringent yellow pear-shaped fruit is used to make guava jelly□

Guayaquil city and chief port of Ecuador; population 823 200□

guayule greyish shrub *Parthenium argentatum,* family Compositae, of SW North America; the sap is a source of rubber. The USA is developing it commercially□

Guderian Heinz 1888–1954. German general, creator of the Panzer armoured divisions which achieved the breakthrough at Sedan◊ in 1940 and the advance to Moscow in 1941□

gudgeon a fish of the carp◊ family□

guelder rose a plant of the genus Viburnum◊□

Guelders see Gelderland◊□

Guelph industrial town (food processing, electricals, pharmaceuticals) in Ontario, Canada; population 67 000□

Guelphs and Ghibellines rival partisans, originally in 12th century Germany (see Lothair◊ II), of the house of Welph (Italian *Guelph*) and the lords of Hohenstaufen and Waiblingen (Italian Ghibelline) especially in the struggle for the imperial crown after the death of Henry◊ VI in 1197. The conflict spread to Italy, and became one between supporters of the imperial power (Ghibelline e.g. Dante◊) and Papal power (Guelph e.g. Petrarch◊)□

Guernica town in the Basque◊ country, where the Castilian kings formerly swore to respect the rights of the Basques. It was destroyed in 1937 by German bombers aiding Franco, and rebuilt in 1946. The bombing inspired a painting by Picasso◊□

Guernsey second largest of the Channel◊ Islands; area 63 sq km/24.5 sq mi; with its capital at St Peter Port. Products include tomatoes, flowers, and more recently butterflies; electronics; and from 1975 it has been a major international financial centre. Guernsey cattle are a pale fawn, with rich cream milk□

Guevara Ernesto 'Che' 1928–67. Argentine revolutionary, an opponent of Perón. He aided Castro's struggle for power in Cuba, and then in turn moved on to the Congo in 1965, and Bolivia, where he was killed in leading an abortive peasant rising. He was an orthodox Marxist, and his guerrilla techniques were influential□

Guiana see French Guiana◊, Guyana◊, and Surinam◊□

Guido see Reni◊□

Guienne former province of SW France, which in the 12th century formed with Gascony the duchy of Aquitaine◊□

guild in ecology 'a group of species that exploit the same class of environmental resources in a similar way' (as defined by Richard Root in 1967). The group most frequently numbers about seven, and it applies also to human beings, e.g. the small fighting units of the Roman, and modern US and British armies, reach top efficiency at this number. See also guilds◊□

Guildford city, administrative headquarters of Surrey, England; population 124 200. It has ruins of a Norman castle; a cathedral (Sir Edward Maufe◊) 1936–61; University of Surrey 1966, and a theatre (1964) named after the comedy actress Yvonne Arnaud 1895–1958□

guilds associations of merchants, craftsmen, etc. to maintain standards and further common interests, which in Europe became politically powerful. In England they flourished from the 9th century until their suppression in 1547. The craft guilds which later took over much of local government (maintenance of roads, bridges, schools, religious charities, and so on), included employers as well as all grades of workers; looked after distressed members; regulated prices, wages, working conditions, standards of craftsmanship, etc. The beginning of trade unionism is sometimes traced back to them□

Guillan-Barre syndrome virus infection of the spinal cord and nervous system which affects the use of the limbs□

guillemot a diving bird of the auk◊ family□

guillotine beheading machine commonly in use in the Middle Ages, but introduced in an improved design (by physician Joseph Ignace Guillotin 1738–1814, after whom it was named) in France in 1792 during the Revolution□

guinea English gold coin, not minted since 1817, but used in billing professional fees, etc. as 21 shillings (equivalent to £1.05)□

Guinea Republic of

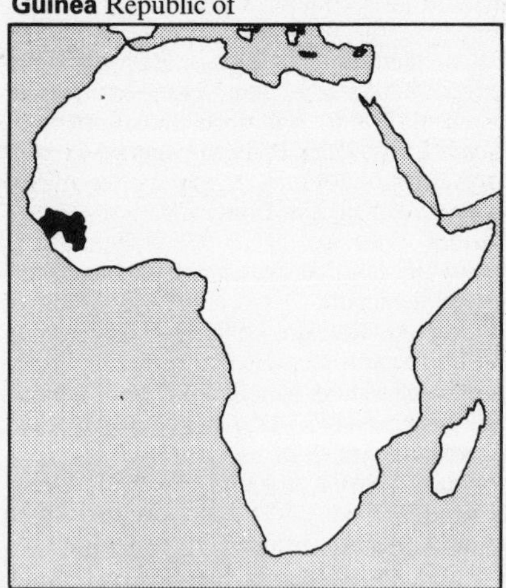

area 245 860 sq km/95 000 sq mi
capital Conakry
towns Labe, N'Zerekore, KanKan
features Fouta Djallon, area of sandstone plateaux, cut by deep valleys
exports coffee, rice, palm kernels; alumina, bauxite, diamonds
currency sily
population 5 579 000, chief peoples being Fulani 40%, Mandingo 25%

language French, official
religion Islam 62%; Christianity 15%; tribal 35%
government president (Colonel Lansana Conté from 1984) heading a collectively responsible committee of the armed forces
recent history French colony from 1888, Guinea became independent in 1958, with Ahmed Sékou Touré 1922–84 as absolute president 1958–84. On his death, the armed forces denounced his 'bloody and ruthless dictatorship', and themselves assumed control. The national assembly and the one permitted political party were dissolved□

Guinea-Bissau

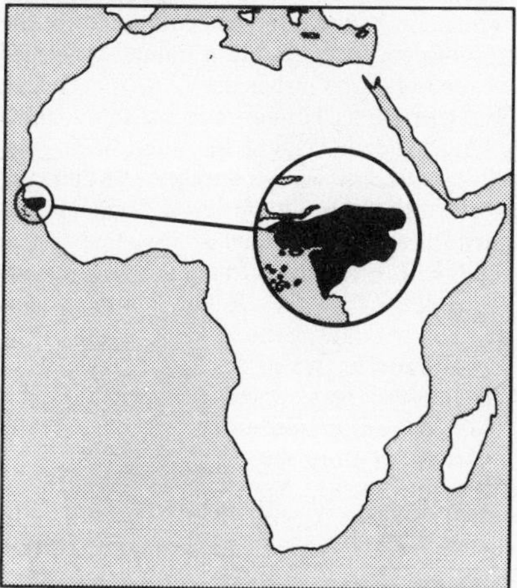

area 36 125 sq km/14 000 sq mi
capital and chief port Bissau
features include the archipelago of Bijagos
exports rice, coconuts, peanuts; fish; salt
currency peso
population 842 000
language Crioulo, Cape Verdean dialect of Portuguese
religion 40% Islam, 4% Christian
government executive head of state (Major João Vieira from 1980) with a council of state, national people's assembly and eight regional councils. The African Party for the Independence of Guinea and Cape Verde (PAIGC) is the only political party.
recent history formerly Portuguese Guinea, it was ruled together with Cape Verde until armed struggle brought independence from Portugal in 1974. The constitution provides for eventual union with Cape Verde, but resentment of dominance by Cape Verde mestizos within the Guinea-Bissau government led to the coup in 1980 by Vieira. There was a return to constitutional rule in 1984, and the union remains a long-term aim□

Guinea Coast the W Africa coast between Gambia and Cape Lopez□

guinea fowl an African game bird. see under fowl◊□

guinea pig a type of small rodent□

Guinness Sir Alec 1914– . British actor. His stage appearances include Shakespeare's Hamlet in modern dress in 1938 and Lawrence of Arabia (in *Ross* in 1960); and in 1980 he gained a 'lifetime achievement' Oscar (films include *Kind Hearts and Coronets* 1949 and *The Bridge on the River Kwai* 1957). Knighted in 1959□

Guise French noble family active in the 16th-century religious wars:
Francis, 2nd Duke of Guise 1519–63, combatted the Huguenots and was assassinated; his son ***Henri*** 3rd Duke of Guise 1550–88, also assassinated, was largely responsible for the Massacre of St Bartholomew (see under Huguenot)□

guitar six-stringed, flat-backed musical instrument plucked with the fingers, and derived from a Moorish orginal. Popular 17–mid-19th century, it was revived for concert purposes by Andrés Segovia◊ and Julian Bream◊; see also John Williams◊. From 1890 it was an instrument of American mountain folk musicians; from 1930 electrically amplified versions were used in jazz and dance bands; and from the 1950s the solid-bodied ***electric guitar*** became the dominant instrument of 'pop' music, e.g. the Beatles◊. The ***Hawaiian guitar*** or ***ukelele*** ('jumping flea') has a 'singing tone' achieved by sliding ***up and down*** the metal bar across the strings, which is used (instead of the fingers) to 'stop' them□

Guiyang capital (formerly Kweiyang) and industrial city of Guizhou province, China; population 670 000□

Guizhou province (formerly Kweichow) of S China
area 174 000 sq km/67 164 sq mi
capital Guiyang
features includes many minority groups which have often been in revolt
products rice, maize; non-ferrous minerals
population 27 310 000□

Guizot François Pierre Guillaume 1787–1874. French statesman, Prime Minister from 1847, whose resistance to all reforms precipitated the Revolution of 1848□

Gujarat W state of India
area 195 984 sq km/75 668 sq mi
capital Gandhinagar
features heavily industrialized; includes most of the Rann of Kutch; the Gir Forest is the last home of the wild Asian lion
population 33 961 000
languages Gujarati, Hindi□

Gulf States oil-rich countries sharing the coastline of the Arabian/Persian Gulf (Iran, Iraq, Bahrein, Kuwait, Oman, Qatar, Saudi Arabia, and the United Arab Emirates). The last six formed a Gulf Co-operation Council (GCC) in 1981. In the USA, those states bordering the Mexican Gulf (Alabama, Florida, Louisiana, Mississippi, Texas)□

Gulf Stream ocean current◊ arising from the warm waters of the equatorial current, which flows N from the Gulf of Mexico. It slows to a broadening 'drift' off Newfoundland, splitting as it flows E across the Atlantic, and tempering the harshness of the climate of the British Isles and W Europe□

Gulf War see Iran–Iraq War◊□

gull seabird of the order Charadriiformes◊, sub-division Lari, which includes:

Gulls family Laridae, e.g. ***black-headed gull*** *Larus ridibundus* with a dark patch on the head only in the breeding season; ***herring gull*** much larger, with a wingspan of 1.5 m/4.5 ft; ***great black-backed gull*** *Larus marinus* the largest gull, wingspan 1.75 m/ almost 6 ft; and black-legged ***kittiwake*** *Rissa tridactyla* of the Atlantic and Pacific, always at sea, except when breeding. The terns, e.g. the far-ranging ***common tern*** *Sterna hirundo* belong to the sub-family Sterninae.

Skuas family Stercorariidae, e.g. ***great skua*** *Catharacta skua* of the N Atlantic, largest of the group 60 cm/2 ft long, and dark brown on the upper side. Skuas seldom fish for themselves, but divebomb the gulls to force them to disgorge their catch□

gum arabic substance obtained from certain species of acacia◊□

Gummer John Selwyn 1939– . British Conservative politician. Minister of State for Employment and Chairman of the Party from 1983, he became Paymaster General in 1984□

gums complex hydrocarbons, usually soluble in water, they form five groups: exudates from plants and trees, mainly in dry regions; marine plant extracts; seed extracts; fruit and vegetable extracts; and synthetics. They are used in adhesives◊, confectionery, medicine, textile finishes, etc.□

gum tree see eucalyptus◊□

gun see artillery◊, small◊ arms, weapons◊□

gunmetal tough alloy of copper (88%) and tin (10%), sometimes with a little zinc or lead, used in castings, etc□

gunpowder explosive mixture of sulphur, saltpetre, and charcoal. Superseded as a propellant, it is still used for blasting and fireworks□

Gunpowder Plot Catholic conspiracy to blow up James I and his parliament on 5 Nov 1605. Guy Fawkes was caught in the act in the cellar beneath the House, and he and seven of his co-conspirators were executed. It is commemorated by fireworks and burning 'guys' on bonfires□

Guomindang Chinese National People's Party, founded 1894 by Sun Yat-sen◊, which overthrew the Manchu Empire in 1912. By 1927 the right wing, led by Chiang Kai-shek, was in conflict with the left, (see Mao Tse-tung◊) until the Communist victory in 1949 (except for the period of the Japanese invasion 1937–45). It survives in Taiwan◊, where it is still spelt Kuomintang◊□

Gurdjieff George Ivanovitch 1877–1949. Russian occultist. He used stylized dance to 'free' people to develop their full capabilities, and influenced the modern human-potential movement. See Ouspensky◊□

Gurkhas ruling Hindu caste in Nepal. Fine soldiers, they have been recruited since 1815 for the British army, and the Brigade of Gurkhas has its headquarters in Hong Kong□

gurnard a type of perch◊□

Gush Emunim Israeli fundamentalist group ('Bloc of the Faithful'), founded in 1973, who claim divine right to the W Bank, Gaza Strip, and Golan Heights as part of Yeretz Israel through settlement, sometimes extending the claim to the Euphrates□

Gustavus Adolphus 1594–1632. King of Sweden from 1611, he waged successful wars with Denmark, Russia, and Poland, and in the Thirty Years War championed the Protestant cause. He was mortally wounded in the Battle of Lützen in 1632, at which he defeated Wallenstein□

Gustavus Vasa 1496–1560. Leader of the Swedish revolt against Danish rule, he was elected king of Sweden in 1523, and established Lutheranism as the State religion□

Gutenberg Johann Gensfleisch c1397–1468. German printer, credited with the invention of movable type (see Coster◊); see also Mainz◊. He produced a number of Bibles, but was not financially successful□

Guthrie Sir Tyrone 1900–71. British theatrical director, long associated with the Old Vic◊; a founder of the Ontario (Stratford) Shakespeare Festival in 1953; and of the Minneapolis theatre now named after him□

gutta percha juice of tropical trees, family Sapotaceae, which is hardened to form a flexible, rubbery substance used for insulating cables, etc., but largely replaced by synthetics□

Guyana Co-operative Republic of
area 210 000 sq km/83 000 sq mi
capital and port Georgetown
features Mount Roraima◊; Kaietur National Park including Kaietur Fall on the Potaro

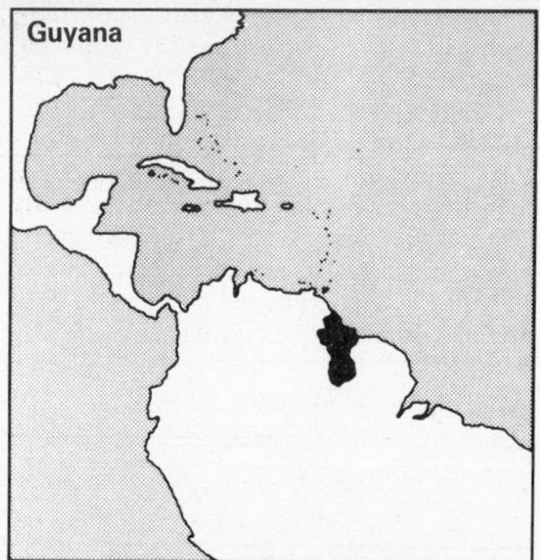

(tributary of Essequibo) 250 m/822 ft (five times height of Niagara)
exports sugar, rice, rum, timber, diamonds
currency Guyana dollar
population 775 000, 50% E Indian (introduced to work the sugar plantations after the abolition of slavery), 30% Negro; 5% Amerindian
language English, official; Hindi
religion Christianity 57%, Hinduism 33%, Sunni Islam 9%
famous people Eustace Braithwaite
government executive president Desmond Hoyte from 1985, and National Assembly elected for five years by proportional representation. Divisions are racial; the People's National Congress (PNC) Negro; People's Progressive Party (PPP), led by Cheddi Jagan◊, E Indian.
recent history captured by Britain from the Dutch in 1796 (formally ceded in 1814), British Guiana became independent as Guyana in 1966 (see Forbes Burnham◊), and became a republic within the Commonwealth in 1970. In 1979 about 900 US People's Temple sect members committed suicide under the dominance of their leader, the 'Rev' Jim Jones, at an agricultural commune they had established in the country. Guyana is in dispute with Venezuela over territory in the Essequibo region; Surinam also maintains a claim on Guyanese territory□

Guys Constantin 1805–92. French artist, with Byron◊ at Missolonghi, and noted for sketches of the Crimean War for the *Illustrated London News* and realistic drawings of Parisian life□

Gwalior city in Madhya Pradesh, India; population 560 000. Formerly a small princely state□

Gwent county of S Wales
area 1376 sq km/531 sq mi

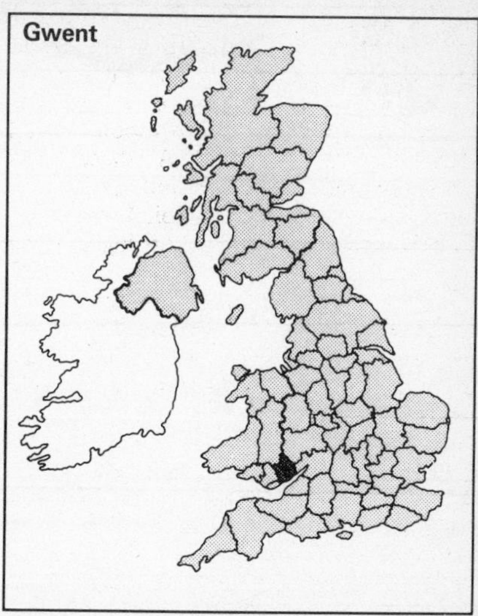

towns administrative headquarters Cwmbran; Abergavenny, Newport, Tredegar
features Wye Valley; Tintern Abbey; Legionary Museum of Caerleon, and Roman amphitheatre; Chepstow and Raglan castles
products salmon and trout on the Wye and Usk; iron and steel at Llanwern, tinplate Ebbw Vale
population 435 500
language 2.5% Welsh-speaking
famous people Aneurin Bevan and Neil Kinnock, both born in Tredegar; Alfred Russel Wallace□

Gwyn Nell (Eleanor) 1651–87. English comedy actress from 1665, formerly an orange-seller at Drury Lane Theatre. Dryden◊ wrote parts for her, and from 1669 she was the mistress of Charles II (the elder of her two sons by him was created Duke of St Albans in 1684), almost his last wish being 'Let not poor Nellie starve.' Largely instrumental in the establishment of the Royal Hospital for old soldiers at Chelsea◊, she was buried at St Martin-in-the-Fields□

Gwynedd NW county of Wales
area 3867 sq km/1493 sq mi
towns administrative headquarters Caernarfon; resorts Pwllheli, Criccieth, Barmouth
features Snowdonia National Park including Snowdon (Welsh *Eryri*; the highest mountain in Wales, with a rack railway to the top from Llanberis) 1085 m/3559 ft, Cadr Idris 892 m/2928 ft, and the largest Welsh lake, Llyn Tegid (Bala) 6 km/4 mi long, 1.6 km/1 mi wide; Caernarfon Castle; Anglesey◊ is across the Menai Straits; Lleyn Peninsula and to the SW Bardsey Island, with a 6th-century ruined abbey, once a centre for pilgrimage;

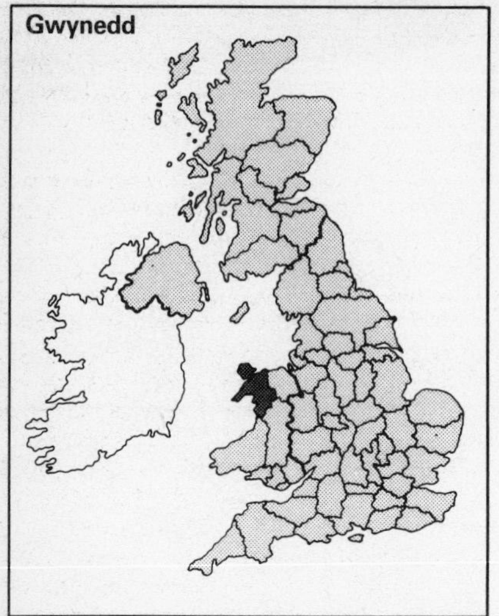

Welsh Slate Museum at Llanberis; Segontium Roman Fort Museum, Caernarfon; Criccieth and Harlech castles; Bodnant Garden; and the fantasy resort of Portmeirion (see Williams-Ellis◊), setting of the cult television film series *The Prisoner*
products cattle and sheep, gold (see Dolgellau◊)
population 228 600
language 61% Welsh-speaking□

gymnastics physical exercises, originally merely for health and training (so-named from the way in which men of ancient Greece trained *gymnos* 'naked'), and first revived in 19th century Germany as an aid to military strength. Today an increasingly popular spectator sport.
Men's gymnastics includes floor, horizontal bar and ring exercises, many difficult and dangerous; ***women's gymnastics*** has followed the same course, so that the best executants are the young and immature in physique, e.g. Olga Korbut and Nadia Comaneci. Also popular are ***sports acrobatics*** performed by gymnasts in pairs, trios, or fours to music, where the emphasis is on dance, balance, and timing, and ***rhythmic gymnastics*** choreographed to music and performed by individuals of six-girl teams, with small hand apparatus including ribbons and hoops□

gymnosperms a division of plants◊□

gypsies wandering people, the name being a corruption of 'Egyptian', but they call themselves Rom (language Romany) and they probably originated in India. See also under Hungary□

gypsum form of calcium sulphate ($CaSO_4 . 2H_2O$), which when heated to 120°C loses most of its water to make ***plaster of paris*** (which is used in making casts and moulds). In orthopaedic surgery, for setting fractured bones, it is being replaced by synthetics ***alabaster*** is a fine-grained form used in its original state for ornamental vases and statues□

gyroscope

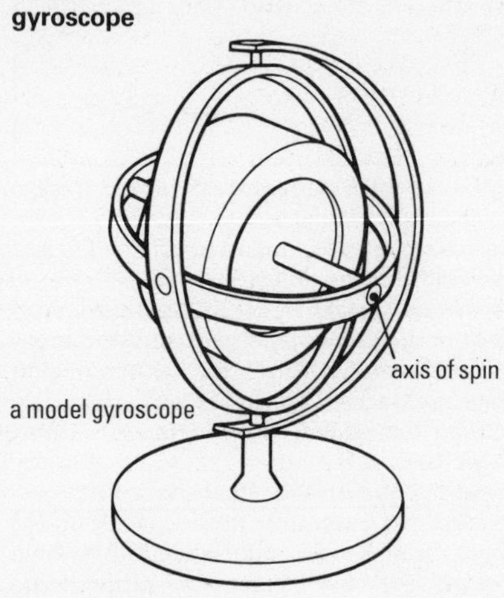

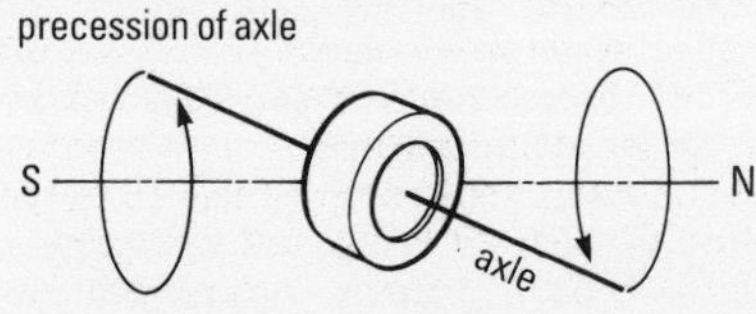

gyroscope a wheel which is mounted on a system of pivoted frames so that it can be set spinning with its axis in any direction, not necessarily horizontal. Even when the outer frame is moved or turned, the wheel's axle keeps pointing in the same direction relative to the stars, and undisturbed by the earth's motion, hence the use of gyroscopes in guidance systems (e.g. in rockets). If the wheel's axle is weighted off-centre, the axle 'precesses (sweeps out a cone). If the precession is damped out by frictional forces, the axle settles in a true North-South direction – the principle of the gyro-compass (see compass◊)□

Haakon VII 1872–1957. Elected King of Norway from 1905, on its separation from Sweden. He married in 1896 Maud 1869–1938, youngest daughter of Edward VII of the UK. He refused to surrender on the German invasion, and carried on resistance from Britain 1940–5□

Haarlem industrial town (textiles, printing) in the W Netherlands; population 156 000. It is famous for bulbs, and has a 15–16th-century cathedral and a Frans Hals◊ Museum□

habeas corpus in England since 1679, a writ (Latin 'have the body') ordering that a prisoner be produced before the court to explain why he is detained in custody□

Haber Fritz 1868–1934. German chemist, whose fixation of atmospheric nitrogen by producing synthetic ammonia founded the synthetic fertilizer industry. His study in the combustion of hydrocarbons led to the commercial 'cracking' or fractionating of natural oil into its components e.g. diesel, petrol, paraffin, etc. In electrochemistry he was first to demonstrate that oxidation and reduction takes place at the electrodes; from this he developed a general electrochemical theory. In World War I he worked on poison gas and devised gas masks, hence there were protests against his Nobel prize in 1918□

Habsburg see Hapsburg□

Hackney inner borough of N central Greater London

features Hackney Downs and Hackney Marsh, formerly infested with highwaymen, now a leisure area; includes ***Shoreditch***, site of England's first theatre (The Theatre) in 1576; ***Hoxton***, with the Geffrye Museum of the domestic arts; ***Stoke Newington***, where Defoe once lived

population 177 800□

Haddington agricultural market town in Lothian, Scotland; population 6 700. The birthplace of John Knox□

haddock a fish of the cod◊ family□

Hades in Greek mythology, the underworld, presided over by the god Hades or Pluto (Roman Dis). He was the brother of Zeus, and married Persephone, daughter of Demeter and Zeus◊. She was allowed to return to the upperworld for part of the year, bringing spring with her. The entrance to Hades was guarded by the three-headed dog Cerberus◊. ***Tartarus*** was the section where the wicked were punished, e.g. Tantalus◊□

Hadhramaut district of the People's Democratic Republic. of Yemen (South Yemen). A remote plateau 1400 m/4500 ft high, it attracted travellers such as H St John Philby◊ and Dame Freya Stark□

Hadrian 76–138AD. Roman emperor, adopted by his kinsman, the emperor Trajan, whom he succeeded in 117. He abandoned Trajan's conquests in Mesopotamia, and adopted a defensive policy; see Hadrian's Wall◊. Part of his Roman villa is now a museum□

Hadrian's Wall Roman fortification built AD122–6 to mark Britain's N boundary; it runs c185 km/115 mi from Wallsend on the Tyne to Maryport, W Cumbria, and possibly then goes further south. The fort at South Shields, Arbeia, built to defend the eastern end, is being reconstructed as a unique experiment. At least in part, the wall was covered with a glistening, white coat of mortar. In 1985 Roman letters (on paper-thin sheets of wood), the earliest and largest collection of Latin writing, were discovered at Vindolanda Fort□

Haeckel Ernst Heinrich 1834–1919. German scientist, a supporter of Darwin, whose own 'recapitulation theory'(that embryonic stages recapitulate past stages of the organism) has been superseded, but which stimulated research□

haematite or ***hematite*** a red or red-black mineral. The principal ore of iron◊□

haemoglobin the red colouring matter in the blood◊□

haemophilia hereditary disease, uncontrollable bleeding through deficiency in the blood of the normal clotting substances; it occurs only in males, and is transmitted through the mother. It can be alleviated by drugs, but haemophiliacs suffer the pain of bleeding into the joints, crippling, etc. Testing is now possible before birth□

haemorrhage loss of blood externally or internally, from a wound or disease, e.g. an ulcer or cancer of the stomach. Severe haemorrhage causes shock, with eventual death, and must be remedied by blood transfusion□

haemorrhagic fever any of several virus diseases of the tropics, in which high temperatures over several days end in haemorrhage from nose, throat, and intestines, with up to 90% mortality. The causative organism lives in rats in the case of West African Lassa fever, but in Marburg disease and Ebola fever, the host animal, which betrays no symptoms, is unknown. Cases are beginning to occur in temperate areas□

haemorrhoids see piles◊□

Hafiz c1300–88. Persian poet, a dervish◊ teacher in his native Shiraz, whose odes extol the pleasures of life□

hafnium element
symbol Hf
atomic number 72
physical description silvery metal
features closely associated with zirconium: it is highly absorbent of neutrons
uses in control rods in nuclear reactors□

Haganah Zionist military organization established in Palestine under Turkish rule, the basis of the modern Israeli army; many members served in the British forces in both World Wars, and after World War II it condemned terrorism□

Hagen industrial city (iron and steel, textiles) in the Ruhr, W Germany; population 218 000□

hagfish eel-like parasitic marine fish, family Myxinidae, order Petromyzoniformes. They live mainly on dead and dying fish, boring into them with a rounded mouth equipped with a toothed tongue and surrounded by barbels□

Haggadah see under Judaism◊□

Haggai minor Old Testament prophet c520BC, who promoted the rebuilding of the temple in Jerusalem□

Haggard Sir H(enry) Rider 1856–1925. British novelist, born in Norfolk, who used his experience in colonial service posts in S Africa to write the adventure stories *King Solomon's Mines* 1885, *She* 1887, etc.□

haggis Scottish dish comprising a sheep's or calf's heart, liver, and lungs, etc., minced up with onion, oatmeal, suet, spice, pepper and salt, and boiled in the animal's stomach□

Hague The (Dutch *s'Gravenhage*) seat of the Netherlands government, linked by canal with Rotterdam and Amsterdam; population 454 300. It is also the seat of the United Nations International Court of Justice, and the seaside resort of Scheveningen (patronized by Wilhelm II and Churchill), with its Kurhaus, is virtually incorporated□

ha-ha sunken boundary wall permitting an unobstructed view beyond a garden; a device much used by Capability Brown◊□

Hahn Kurt 1886–1974. German educationist, founder-headmaster of Gordonstoun School (see under Elgin◊); founder of the Outward Bound Trust and inspirer of United◊ World Colleges□

Hahn Otto 1879–1968. German physicist-chemist, discoverer of nuclear fission; but ardently against its use (i.e. in the atom-bomb) for the military, (see also Lise Meitner◊). Nobel prize in 1944□

hahnium former name for unnilpentium◊□

Haifa industrial port (oil refining, chemicals) in NE Israel; population 230 000□

Haig Alexander Meigs 1924– . American general. A former Kissinger aide, he became Nixon's White House Chief of Staff at the height of Watergate◊, was NATO commander 1974–9, and was Secretary of State to President Reagan 1981–2□

Haig Douglas, 1st Earl 1861–1928. British field marshal from 1917. He succeeded French as Commander-in-Chief Dec 1915–18, and was responsible for the Somme (summer 1916), and Passchendaele (Jul–Nov 1917) offensives, achieving little for huge losses. When Foch took over supreme command of the allied forces, Haig extended the new offensive in Sept 1918 to the N, so breaking the Hindenburg Line. He was first president of the British◊ Legion□

haiku 71-syllable Japanese verse form. See Matsuyama◊□

Haile Selassie 1891–1975. Emperor of Ethiopia 1930–74. He appealed in vain to the League of Nations, when Italy invaded Ethiopia 1935–6, but was restored in 1941, until his deposition in a military coup□

Hailsham Quintin Hogg, Baron Hailsham of St Marylebone 1907– . British Conservative politician, grandson of Quintin Hogg 1845–1903 (see under polytechnic◊). He was the first Minister for Science and Technology 1959–64, and is remembered for his rallying of the party conference at Brighton in 1957 by ringing a handbell. He was Lord Chancellor 1970–4, and from 1979□

Hainan Chinese island, part of Guangdong province, in the S China Sea; area 34 000 sq km/13 000 sq mi. Capital Haikou. It is farmed by Chinese settlers and aboriginals survive in the mountains□

Hainaut industrial province (coal, iron, and steel) of SW Belgium; population 1 305 165. Capital Mons□

Haiphong naval and industrial port (shipyards, cement, textiles) in N Vietnam; population 1 500 000□

hair outgrowth of mammalian skin, ornamental to humans, but an insulation for most other mammals, and sometimes 'moulted' to give a lesser thickness in summer, and extra warmth in winter. The growing 'root' is embedded in the follicle, a cavity in the second layer (true skin), but the shaft is of dead horny material, which includes keratin◊. The cross-section of hair varies from round (straight hair) through oval (curling) to flat (woolly) □

hairstreaks a type of butterfly◊□

Haiti Republic of (French *Haïti*)

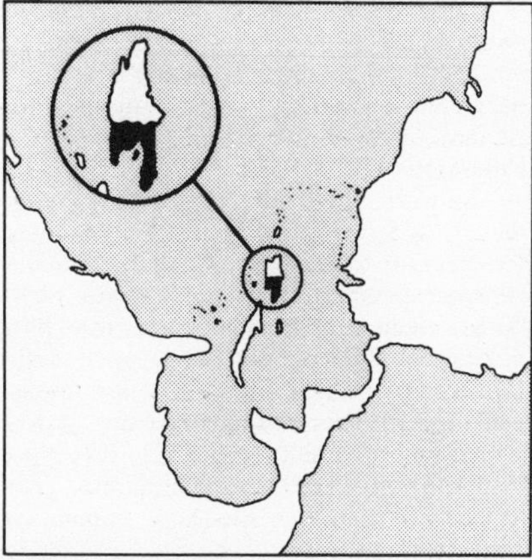

area 27 740 sq km/10 710 sq mi

capital Port-au-Prince

features only French-speaking republic in the Americas; voodoo◊ ceremonies; the island of La Tortuga off the N coast was formerly a pirate lair; US military base at Môle St Nicolas, the nearest point to Cuba

exports coffee, sugar, sisal, cotton, cocoa, rice

currency lempira

population 6 000 000

language French, official (spoken by the mulatto bourgeoisie); Créole, spoken by 90% Negro majority

religion Roman Catholicism, official, but opposed to the government

famous people Toussaint L'Ouverture

government following the departure in Feb 1986 of Jean-Claude Duvalier, power is now in the hands of a joint military and civil council, headed by General Henry Namphy.

recent history discovered by Columbus in 1492, the island had its Indian people exterminated by Spain, and was repopulated with African slaves. Ceded to France in 1697, it became independent in 1804 under Dessalines◊ (successor to Toussaint◊ L'Ouverture). It has since had a troubled history, and was occupied by the USA 1915–34. In 1957 François Duvalier◊ established a virtual dictatorship, and was succeeded by his son, Jean-Claude. Under reforms of 1985 political parties were to be re-established in 1987, but under strict conditions and requiring government approval. Duvalier, however, fled the country aboard a US plane after a popular uprising inspired by student rebellion and the Catholic Church's concern for human rights□

Haitink Bernard 1929– . Dutch conductor. Associated with the Concertgebouw Orchestra, Amsterdam, from 1964, and with Glyndebourne Festival from 1978□

hake a fish of the cod◊ family□

Hakluyt Richard c1553–1616. English geographer, whose great work was *The Principal Navigations, Voyages and Discoveries of the English Nation* 1589–1600, in which he was assisted by Raleigh◊; see also Samuel Purchas◊. The ***Hakluyt Society*** established in 1846 publishes similar later accounts of exploration, etc.□

Hakodate port in Hokkaido, Japan; population 300 000. The earliest port opened to the West, in 1854, it has well-preserved 19th-century European-style buildings□

Haldane Richard Burdon, Viscount Haldane 1856–1928. British Liberal statesman. As Secretary for War 1905–12, he established an expeditionary force, backed by a territorial army, and under the unified control of an imperial general staff□

Halévy Ludovic 1834–1908. French librettist, collaborator with Hector Crémieux for Offenbach's *Orpheus in the Underworld*; and with Henri Meilhac for Bizet's *Carmen*□

Haley Bill 1927–81. American pioneer of rock and roll. 'Rock Around the Clock' was first heard in Britain in 1955, recorded by his group The Comets in the film *Blackboard Jungle*□

half-life time in which the strength of a radioactive source decays to half its original value. It may vary from millionths of a second to thousands of millions of years□

halibut a type of flatfish◊□

Halicarnassus ancient city of Asia Minor (now Bodrum in Turkey), where the tomb of Mausolus, built c350BC by widowed Queen Artemisia, was one of the seven wonders of the world. Herodotus◊ was born here□

Halifax capital and naval station of Nova Scotia, Canada's chief winter port; population 277 725. Founded in 1749, its industries include lumber, steel, sugar refining, etc.□

Halifax woollen textile town in W Yorkshire, England; population 89 000. St John's parish church is Perpendicular Gothic, All Souls' is by Sir Gilbert Scott◊ (built for a millowner named Ackroyd, whose home, Bankfield, is now a museum); the Town Hall is by Sir

Charles Barry◊; and the Piece Hall of 1779 (former cloth market) has been adapted to modern use; the surviving gibbet (predecessor of the guillotine) was used to behead cloth stealers 1541–1650□

Halifax Charles Montagu, Earl of Halifax 1661–1715. British financier. As Commissioner of the Treasury 1692, he raised money for the French war by instituting the National Debt, and in 1694 established the Bank of England□

Halifax Edward Frederick Lindley Wood, 1st Earl of Halifax 1881–1959. British Conservative statesman. As Viceroy of India 1926–31, he worked with Gandhi◊; as Foreign Secretary 1938–40 was associated with Chamberlain's 'appeasement' policy, and was in line to succeed him as Prime Minister in 1940, but stood aside in favour of Churchill. He was ambassador to the USA 1941–6□

Halifax George Savile, 1st Marquess of Halifax 1633–95. English statesman. Known as 'the trimmer' from his middle course between extremes, he was at first favoured, then dismissed, by Charles II. He was prominent in achieving the revolution of 1688□

halitosis offensive breath, caused by dirty teeth, disease of the mouth, throat, nose, or lungs, or disturbance of the digestion□

Hall Sir Peter (Reginald Frederick) 1930– . British theatre director (Royal Shakespeare Theatre, Stratford 1960–68, National Theatre from 1973), and also artistic director at Glyndebourne from 1984□

Halle capital of Halle district and industrial city (salt from brine springs, lignite mining) in E Germany; population 232 220. Handel◊'s birthplace survives□

Halley Edmund 1656–1742. English Astronomer Royal from 1720, a friend of Newton◊ whose *Principia* he financed. In 1682 he observed Halley's comet◊, predicting its return in 1759. In 1986 the spacecraft Giotto◊ was sent to probe its heart□

hallmark official marks (on gold, silver, and platinum) instituted in 1300 in the UK for the prevention of fraud. Tests of the metal content are carried out at authorized Assay Offices at Goldsmiths' Hall, London, Birmingham, Sheffield, and Edinburgh, each of which has its distinguishing mark, to which is added a maker's mark, date letter, and mark guaranteeing the standard. Since 1975 there has been an international alternative. Standards of quality are expressed in parts per thousand of pure (fine) gold, silver, or platinum in a thousand parts of alloy. See also carat◊□

Hallowe'en evening of 31 Oct, immediately preceding Hallowmas or All Saints' Day. Many of its traditional customs pre-date Christianity□

Hallstatt village in Upper Austria, SW of Salzburg. In 1846 over 3000 graves of a 9–5th-century BC Celtic civilization transitional between Bronze and Iron ages were discovered□

halogen group of five elements with similar chemical bonding properties and showing a gradation of physical properties. In order of reactivity, the elements are halogen◊, flourine◊, chlorine◊, bromine◊, iodine◊, and astatine◊. Together, they form a linked group of the periodic table of elements◊□

hallucinogen a drug◊ which induces hallucinations□

Hals Frans 1580/81–1666. Dutch artist born at Antwerp, best known for his tavern scenes, and such portraits as the *Laughing Cavalier*□

Halsey William Frederick 1882–1959. American admiral. In command of the Third Fleet in the S Pacific 1942, he compelled the Japanese to withdraw 1943–4, and they signed the surrender document ending World War II on his flagship *Missouri*□

Hamadán city in NW Iran (on the site of the ancient Ecbatan, see Medes◊); population 156 000□

Hambledon see under Hampshire◊□

Hamburg largest port of W Germany and capital of the Land of Hamburg◊; population 1 648 800. In alliance with Lübeck it founded the Hanseatic League◊; headquarters of Axel Springer's newspapers (*Die Welt*, *Die Zeit*). It is the site of DESY (*D*eutsches *E*lektron-*Sy*nchroton), the German accelerator laboratory□

Hamburg Land of W Germany
area 756 sq km/292 sq mi
capital Hamburg
features consists of the city and surrounding districts; the ***hamburger*** (a fried and seasoned round of chopped beef) invented by medieval Tatar invaders of this Baltic area, was taken to the USA in the 19th century, whence it was reintroduced to Europe in the 1960s (see under Illinois◊)
products refined oil, chemicals, electrical goods, ships, processed food
population 1 645 000
religion Protestantism 74%, Roman Catholicism 8%□

hamburger see under Land of Hamburg◊□

Hameln town in W Germany; population 65 000. Old buildings include the rat-catcher's house, and the town is famous for the Pied Piper legend□

Hamersley Range range of hills above the Hamersley Plateau, Western Australia, with coloured rocks and fine river gorges, as well as iron reserves□

Hamilcar Barca c270–228BC. Carthaginian general, father of Hannibal◊, who harassed the Romans in Italy 247–241, and died heading a battle expedition to Spain□

Hamilton capital of Bermuda, on Bermuda Island; population 3000□

Hamilton industrial town (textiles, engineering) in Strathclyde, Scotland; population 51 530□

Hamilton industrial port, nicknamed Steel City (half Canada's steel), in Ontario, Canada; population 542 000. Linked with Lake Ontario by the Burlington Canal, it has a large hydro-electric plant, heavy machinery, electrical, chemical, and textile industries. McMaster University has an outstanding medical centre, and there is a Philharmonic Orchestra and art gallery□

Hamilton industrial and university town in North Island, New Zealand; population 160 200□

Hamilton Alexander 1757–1804. American statesman, who influenced the adoption of a constitution with a strong central government, and was the first Secretary of the Treasury 1789–95. He cast the deciding vote against Aaron Burr◊ and in favour of Jefferson◊ for the presidency in 1801, and was eventually mortally wounded in a duel with Burr□

Hamilton Lady (Emma) c1765–1815. British courtesan, born Amy Lyon, daughter of a Cheshire blacksmith. In 1782 she became the mistress of Charles Greville, and in 1786 of his uncle Sir William Hamilton◊, who married her in 1791. After Nelson's return from the Nile in 1798 she became well known as his mistress; and her daughter by him, Horatia, was born in 1801. She died in poverty in Calais□

Hamilton Iain Ellis 1922– . Scottish composer, whose works include viola and 'cello sonatas, a ballet (*Clerk Saunders*), the *Pharsalia* cantata, the opera *The Royal Hunt of the Sun* 1977, and symphonies□

Hamilton Sir Ian 1853–1947. Scottish general, deputy to Kitchener◊ in the S African War, and director of land operations at Gallipoli◊ in 1915□

Hamilton James 1st Duke of Hamilton, 1606–49. Scottish adviser to Charles I, he led an army against the Covenanters◊ 1639, and in the 2nd Civil◊ War led the Scottish invasion of England, but was captured at Preston and executed□

Hamilton Sir William 1730–1803. British diplomat, envoy to the court of Naples 1764–1800, whose collection of Greek vases was bought by the British Museum. Fragments of his second collection, wrecked off the Scillies, were recovered by Roland Morris in 1974□

Hamilton Sir William Rowan 1805–65. Irish mathematician, whose formulation of Newton's◊ mechanics proved adaptable to quantum◊ mechanics, and whose 'quarternion' theory was a forerunner of vector◊ analysis□

Hamite African peoples, decended, according to tradition, from Ham, son of Noah◊: they include the ancient Egyptians, and modern Berbers◊ of N Africa and Tuareg of Sudan. Hamitic languages are related to the Semitic◊. See also language◊□

Hamm industrial town in N Rhine-Westphalia, W Germany; population 85 000□

Hammarskjold Dag 1905–61. Swedish Secretary-General of United Nations 1953–8; he was opposed to Britain in the Suez◊ Crisis, and was killed in an aircrash while trying to solve the problems of the Congo (now Zaïre)□

hammer in athletics, one of the throwing◊ events□

Hammerfest fishing port in NW Norway, northernmost town of Europe; population 7500□

hammerhead a species of shark◊□

Hammersmith and Fulham inner borough of W Greater London

features White City stadium; Olympia exhibition centre; BBC television centre; Fulham Palace, residence of the Bishop of London; Hurlingham Park (polo); part of Kensal Green cemetery (where Wilkie Collins, Cruickshank, Thackeray, Trollope are buried); Wormwood Scrubs prison

population 141 750□

Hammerstein Oscar. See under Richard Rodgers◊□

Hammett Dashiell 1894–1961. American crime novelist, a former Pinkerton◊ agent. *The Maltese Falcon* 1930, *The Glass Key* 1931, and *The Thin Man* 1932 pioneered the hard-bitten 'private eye'. In 1951 he was imprisoned for contempt of court during the McCarthy◊ era□

Hammond Dame Joan 1912– . Australian soprano, known in oratorio and opera (*Madame Butterfly, Tosca, Martha*)□

Hammurabi c1792–50BC. King of Babylon, who united his country and took it to the peak of civilization, although his consolidation of the legal code was bloodthirsty in its punishments□

Hampden John c1594–1643. English statesman, born at Great Hampden, Buckinghamshire. In 1636 he refused to pay Ship◊

Money, and when Charles I attempted to arrest him and four other leading MPs, the outbreak of civil war was inevitable. He was mortally wounded in the skirmish of Chalgrove Field□

Hampshire county of southern England

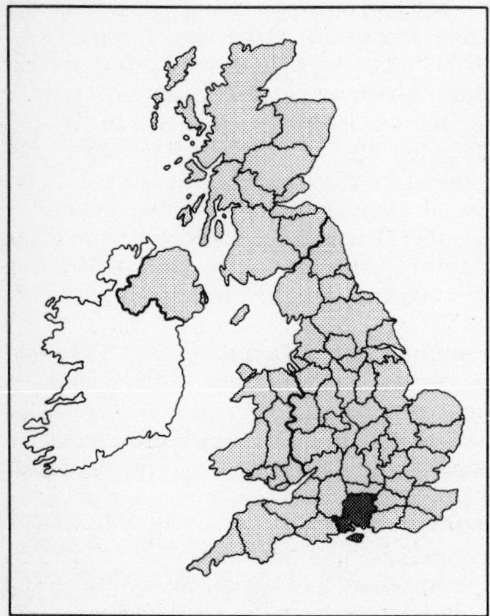

area 3777 sq km/1458 sq mi
towns administrative headquarters Winchester; Southampton, Portsmouth, Gosport
features New Forest, area 373 sq km/144 sq mi, a Saxon royal hunting ground which was enlarged by William◊ I (see also William◊ II); Hampshire Basin, where Britain has onshore and offshore oil; Danebury, 2500-year-old Celtic hillfort; Beaulieu (including National Motor Museum); Broadlands (home of Lord Mountbatten◊); Highclere (home of the Earl of Carnarvon, and gardens by Capability Brown); Hambledon, home of the village cricket team which in the 18th century could beat any other in England; Jane Austen's home at Chawton; birthplace of Charles Dickens at Portsmouth; The Wakes, home of Gilbert White at Selborne; site of the Roman town of Silchester, the only one in Britain known in such detail
products agricultural; oil from refineries at Fawley
population 1 481 000□

Hampstead see under Camden◊□

Hampton Christopher 1946– . British dramatist, resident at the Royal Court Theatre 1968–70. His plays include the comedy *The Philanthropist* 1970 and *Savages* 1973□

Hampton Court Palace see under Richmond◊ upon Thames□

hamster a type of small rodent◊□

Hamsun Knut 1859–1952. Norwegian novelist, son of a poor farmer, whose *Sult/Hunger* 1890 made him famous; Nobel prize in 1920. Some of his ideas made him sympathetic to Nazism, and he was fined in 1946 for collaboration□

Hancock John 1737–93. First American politician to sign the Declaration of Independence, so that his name is often used as the equivalent of 'a signature'□

Hancock Tony (Anthony John) 1924–68. British radio and television comedian. 'Hancock's Half Hour' from 1954 showed him always at odds with everyday life□

handball game in which the ball is hit with the gloved hand, as in ***English fives*** (chiefly a public school game), on an enclosed court, with 2–4 players; or, in a team (7 or 11 players) version popular on the Continent, is thrown or punched from one player to another until a goal is scored□

Handel George Frideric 1685–17 59. German composer, British subject from 1726. Born at Halle, he became Kapellmeister to the elector of Hanover 1709, taking leave without permission in 1712 to settle in England, and was for a time in disgrace when the elector succeeded as George I in 1714. However, he wrote for him in 1715 the *Water Music* and from 1720 directed the opera at the King's Theatre, Haymarket. Rivalry with his operas (of which he wrote 41, including *Rinaldo* 1711 and *Julius Caesar* 1724), from the fashionable Italian composer Bononcini, and Gay◊'s ridicule of Italianate opera in *The Beggar's Opera*, made him turn to oratorio (*Saul* 1739, *Messiah* 1742 (first performed in Dublin), *Belshazzar* 1745). Other works include the pastoral *Acis and Galatea* 1721 and the set of variations, in his 1720 suite for harpsichord, which were later nicknamed 'The Harmonious Blacksmith'. From 1751 he became totally blind, and was always in financial difficulty□

Handke Peter 1942– . Austrian writer, whose first novel *Die Hornissen* and first play *Insulting the Audience* both appeared in 1966. The latter caused the greatest discussion since Brecht – the idea of anti-theatre. He directed and scripted the film *The Left-handed Woman* 1979□

Handley Tommy 1896–1949. British radio comedian, born in Liverpool. His 'ITMA' (It's That Man Again) with its catch-phrases, e.g. 'After you, Claud', and characters, e.g. 'Mrs Mop' and 'Mona Lot,' ran from 1939□

Hangchow see Hangzhou◊□

hanging execution by suspension, usually with a drop of 2–6 ft, so that the powerful jerk of the tightened rope breaks the neck, instead of forcing the base of the tongue to block the air passages, a much slower death□

Hangzhou industrial port (formerly Hangchow), capital of Zhejiang province, China; population 1 100 000. Capital of China under the Sung dynasty 1127–1278, it has jute, chemical, tea, and silk industries, and fine landscape gardens□

Hankow see Wuhan◊□

Hanley see Stoke-on-Trent◊□

Hannibal 247–182 BC. Carthaginian general from 221, son of Hamilcar◊ Barca. His siege of Saguntum (modern Sagunto, near Valencia) precipitated the 2nd Punic◊ War. Following a brilliant campaign in Italy (after crossing the Alps in 218 with 57 elephants◊), Hannibal was the victor at Trasimene in 217 and Cannae in 216, but failed to take Rome. In 203 he returned to Carthage◊ to meet a Roman invasion, but was defeated at Zama in 202, and was exiled in 196 at Rome's insistence. He fled first to Syria, then to Bythinia (on the Black Sea), Rome always seeking his extradition, and poisoned himself rather than fall into their hands□

Hannibal town in Missouri, USA, where Mark Twain lived as a boy, the setting of the events of *Huckleberry Finn*; population 20 000□

Hanoi capital of Vietnam, and of French Indo-China 1902–40; population 2 000 000□

Hanover (German ***Hannover***) industrial city (machinery, vehicles, electrical goods, rubber, textiles, oil refining), capital of Lower Saxony◊, W Germany; population 531 100. From 1386 it was a member of the Hanseatic◊ League, and from 1692 capital of the electorate of Hanover (created a kingdom in 1815). George◊ I of England was also Elector of Hanover, and the ruler of the two countries was the same person until the accession of Victoria in 1837. Since no woman could rule in Hanover, the throne passed to her uncle Ernest, Duke of Cumberland. His son was forced by Bismarck to abdicate in 1866, Hanover becoming a Prussian province□

Hansard official report, issued by the Stationery Office, of the proceedings of the British Parliament; named from Luke Hansard 1752–1828, printer of the House of Commons *Journal* from 1774□

Hanseatic League federation of N German trading cities from the 13th century to 1669, when nationalism and new trade routes took over. Of the 70 cities, the chief include Lübeck, Hamburg, Cologne, Bremen, Breslau, and Cracow□

Hansom Joseph Aloysius 1803–82. British architect (Birmingham Town Hall 1831), and introducer of the Hansom cab in 1834□

Hanuman in the Ramayana◊, the monkey ally of Rama, worshipped as a deity in parts of India□

Hanway Jonas 1712–86. British traveller in Russia and Persia, an advocate of prison reform, and pioneer of the use of an umbrella□

Hanyang see Wuhan◊□

Hapsburg (German ***Habsburg***) former imperial house of Austria-Hungary. The Hapsburgs held the title Holy◊ Roman Emperor 1273–91, 1298–1308, 1438–1740, and 1745–1806. They ruled Austria from 1278, under the title emperor 1806–1918. The Archduke Otto Hapsburg-Lothringen, son of the last emperor, became a Euro MP in 1979□

hara-kiri Japanese mode of ritual suicide (more correctly *seppuku*) by disembowelment (women cut their own throats), used to avoid ignominy or, as in World War II, capture□

Harappa see Indus◊ Valley Civilization□

Harar ancient walled city and Islamic centre in E Ethiopia; population 59 000□

Harare capital (formerly Salisbury) of Zimbabwe, c1525 m/5000 ft above sea level; population 686 000. It was renamed in 1982 after a former chief. There are tobacco, metallurgical, and food processing industries□

Harbin industrial city, capital of Heilongjiang province, China; population 2 100 000. Daqing oilfield is nearby□

Harcourt Sir William Vernon 1827–1904. British Liberal statesman. Home Secretary 1880–85, and Chancellor of the Exchequer 1886 and 1892–5, remembered for his remark in 1892: 'We are all Socialists now'□

Hardicanute c1019–42. King of England from 1042. Son of Canute, he was a harsh ruler□

Hardie James Keir 1856–1915. Scottish socialist and pacifist, a founder first of the Independent◊ Labour Party, and then of the Labour◊ Party; MP for West Ham 1892–5, and Merthyr Tydfil from 1900□

Harding John, 1st Baron Harding of Petherton 1896– . British field marshal, Chief of Staff to Alexander in Italy in World War II. As governor of Cyprus 1955–7, he attempted to crush Eoka terrorism, and deported Makarios◊□

Harding Warren Gamaliel 1865–1923. 29th President of the USA 1921–3. A Republican, he concluded the peace treaties of 1921 with Germany, Austria, and Hungary□

Hardy Sir Alistair 1896–1985. British marine biologist, who was also founder-director from 1969 of the Religious Experience Research

Unit (based in Manchester College, Oxford), and winner of the Templeton prize in 1985□

Hardy Thomas 1840–1928. British poet and novelist. Born near Dorchester in the heart of 'Wessex◊', the setting of his novels, he was originally an architect. In his books human loves and hates are played out in the path of a harshly indifferent force he believed to govern the world: *Far From the Madding Crowd* 1874, *The Return of the Native* 1878, *The Mayor of Casterbridge* 1886, *The Woodlanders* 1887, and *Tess of the D'Urbervilles* 1891, which caused an outcry because the heroine was a woman seduced. Even greater antagonism was roused by *Jude the Obscure* 1895, which reinforced his decision to confine himself to verse. He produced remarkable love lyrics, especially those linked with his dead first wife Emma Gifford, and a blank-verse panorama of the Napoleonic wars, *The Dynasts* 1904–8. Order of Merit in 1910□

Hardy Sir Thomas Masterman 1769–1839. British admiral, Nelson's flag-captain in the *Victory* at Trafalgar, who was with him in his dying moments□

hare rodent lagomorph◊ *Lepus capensis*, family Leporidae, larger than the rabbit◊, and with very long black-tipped ears. Throughout the long breeding season Jan–Aug, there are chases and 'boxing-matches' among males; the saying 'mad as a March hare' arises from their behaviour when lack of cover makes them more visible then. They do not burrow□

Hare David 1947– . British dramatist, whose plays include *Slag* 1970, *Teeth 'n' Smiles* 1975, and *Pravda* 1985 (with Howard Brenton◊)□

harebell the ***bluebell of Scotland*** *Campanula rotundifolia*, family Campanulaceae□

hare-lip facial deformity, a cleft in the upper lip and jaw, which may extend back into the palate, and is remedied by surgery□

Harewood George Henry Hubert Lascelles, 7th Earl of Harewood 1923– . Elder son of the 6th earl, and Princess Mary, daughter of George V, he was artistic director of the Edinburgh Festival 1961–5, director of the English National Opera 1972–85, and has been a governor of the BBC since 1985□

Harfleur leading medieval port of NW France, it was superseded by Le◊ Havre; population 11 000□

Hargeisa trading centre in NW Somalia; population 70 000□

Hargraves Edmund Hammond 1815–91. British discoverer of gold in the Blue◊ Mountains, New South Wales, in 1851□

Hargreaves James d. 1778. British inventor in 1764 of a 'spinning-jenny,' enabling a number of threads to be spun simultaneously by one operator□

Harijan see under caste◊□

Haringey borough of N Greater London
features Alexandra Palace, with a park and race-course; Finsbury Park (once part of Hornsey Wood); Shopping City at Wood Green; includes ***Tottenham*** with Bruce Castle, originally built in the 16th century on a site belonging to Robert Bruce◊'s father (Rowland Hill◊ once ran a school here)
population 212 000□

Harlech town in Gwynedd, Wales; population 1250. The song 'March of the Men of Harlech' originated in the siege when it was captured in 1468 by the Yorkists in the Wars of the Roses□

Harlem district of Manhattan, New York City, with a large Black population□

Harley Robert, 1st Earl of Oxford 1661–1724. British Tory statesman, chief minister to Queen Anne 1711–14, when he negotiated the Treaty of Utrecht in 1713. Accused of treason as a Jacobite after the accession of George I, he was imprisoned 1714–17□

Harlow 'new' town in Essex, England; population 79 200□

Harlow Jean 1911–37. American film actress, *née* Harlean Carpentier, the first 'platinum blonde'. Her films include *Hell's Angels* 1930 and *Saratoga* 1937□

harmattan dust-laden NE wind from the Sahara, in the dry season, e.g. in Nigeria□

harmonica either ***musical glasses*** graded and filled with water, playable with small hammers, for which Mozart and Beethoven composed, or ***mouth organ*** invented by Wheatstone◊ in 1829, in which small metal reeds of varied size, affixed to small slots in a narrow box, produce the notes when blown upon; chiefly amateur, but see Larry Adler◊□

harmonium pipeless, reed-vibrated organ, worked by air compression with a five-octave keyboard and an air chamber filled by the action of foot-worked pedals□

harmony art of combining musical sounds into chords, and moving from one chord to another, as developed in Europe from c1650; major pioneers were J S Bach, Beethoven, Wagner, Stravinsky, Bartók, and Holst□

Harmsworth Alfred. See Lord Northcliffe◊□

harness racing a form of horse◊ racing□

Harold two kings of England:
Harold I died 1040. elected in 1037. Known as 'Harefoot', he was the illegitimate son of Canute◊, whom he succeeded, and claimed the throne in 1035.
Harold II c1022–66. elected in Jan 1066. Son of Earl Godwin◊, he succeeded his father in

1053 as Earl of Wessex. In 1063 William of Normandy tricked him into swearing to support his own claim to the English throne, and when the Witan elected Harold to succeed Edward◊ the Confessor, William prepared to invade. Meanwhile, Harold's treacherous brother Tostig joined the king of Norway, Harald III (Hardrada) in invading Northumbria: Harold routed and killed them at Stamford Bridge on 25 Sept. Three days later William landed at Pevensey◊; Harold was killed by an arrow in the eye at the Battle of Hastings◊□

harp largest musical instrument to be plucked by hand, the concert harp having 48 strings on an upright triangular frame, with several pedals (to alter pitch) at the base, and a long soundbox□

Harper's Ferry see John Brown◊□

Harpies in early Greek mythology, wind spirits; in later legend they have horrific women's faces and the bodies of vultures□

harpsichord an early type of piano◊□

harrier a bird of the eagle◊ family□

harrier a breed of dog◊□

Harriman (William) Averell 1891– . American administrator of Lease-Lend in World War II; negotiatior of the nuclear test ban treaty with the USSR in 1963, and governor of New York 1955–8□

Harris S part of Lewis-with-Harris in the Hebrides◊□

Harris Sir Arthur Travers 1892–1984. British Marshal of the RAF, 'Bomber Harris', Commander-in-Chief Bomber Command 1942–5. See Dresden◊□

Harris Frank 1856–1931. Irish journalist, who wrote highly coloured biographies of Wilde and Shaw, and an autobiography, *My Life and Loves* 1926, banned in the UK and US□

Harris Joel Chandler 1848–1908. Georgian-born, American author of the folk-tales of 'Uncle Remus', based on black folklore, about Br'er Rabbit, the Tar-Baby, etc., from 1879□

Harris Roy 1898–1979. American composer, born in Oklahoma, who used American folk tunes. Notable are the 'Lincoln' symphony (6th), his cantata *Abraham Lincoln Walks at Midnight,* and the orchestral *When Johnny Comes Marching Home*□

Harrisburg industrial city (food processing, machinery) capital of Pennsylvania, USA; population 446 580. A nuclear reactor breakdown at Three Mile Island plant in 1979 focused anti-nuclear agitation. See nuclear◊ accidents□

Harrison Benjamin 1833–1901. 23rd president of the USA 1889–93. A Republican, he called the first Pan-American Conference. See William Harrison◊□

Harrison Rex Carey 1908– . British comedy actor. Lancashire-born, his most famous role was as Professor Higgins in the musical *My Fair Lady* 1956, also filmed□

Harrison William 1773–1841. 9th president of the USA, elected 1840, but died a month after taking office; Benjamin Harrison◊ was his grandson□

Harrisson Tom 1911–76. British anthropologist. After studying Borneo headhunters, he applied the same techniques to Bolton cotton mill operators, and established in 1973 with Charles Madge the Mass Observation, first organization to analyse public opinions and attitudes□

Harrogate resort and spa in N Yorkshire, England; population 65 000. There is an American communications station at Menwith Hill nearby□

Harrow borough of NW Greater London
features parish church consecrated by St Anselm in 1094; Harrow public school, established in 1571 (pupils include Byron, Churchill, Trollope)
population 198 000□

Hart Sir Basil Liddell. See Liddell◊ Hart□

Harte Francis Bret 1839–1902. American author. He was a goldminer at 18, and wrote short stories of the pioneer West, e.g. 'The Luck of Roaring Camp', and verse, e.g. 'The Heathen Chinee'□

hartebeest a type of antelope◊□

Hartford industrial city (aircraft engines, typewriters, tools) and capital of Connecticut, USA; population 726 115□

Hartlepool industrial port (engineering, paper, brewing, clothing) in Cleveland, England; population 94 500□

Hartley L(eslie) P(oles) 1895– 1972. British novelist, who established his name with the trilogy *The Shrimp and the Anemone* 1944, *The Sixth Heaven* 1946, and *Eustace and Hilda* 1947, on the intertwined lives of a brother and sister. Later books include *The Go-Between* 1953 (also filmed). All show the influence of Jane Austen and Henry James□

Hartley Marsden 1877–1943. American artist. Born in Maine, and best known for the brooding landscape series of the state, *Dark Landscapes*□

Hartmann Eduard von 1842–1906. German philosopher, whose *Philosophy of the Unconscious* 1869, maintained that the unconscious was the absolute of existence□

Hartmann Nicolai 1882–1950. German philosopher, noted for his *Ethics* 1925, and his exposition of essentially insoluble metaphysical problems, e.g. free will, regarded as implied in any system of morality□

Hartz Mountains range, part forming a national park, running N–S in Tasmania, and including Hartz Mountain 1254 m/4113 ft and Adamson's Peak 1224 m/4017 ft□

Harun al-Rashid 763–809. Caliph of Baghdad from 786, a lavish patron of music, poetry, and letters□

Harvard see under Cambridge◊, Massachusetts□

harvestman arachnid◊ with roundish body and long slender legs, sometimes called in USA ***daddy-long-legs,*** found in both tropical and temperate zones□

harvest-mite a type of mite◊□

Harvey William 1578–1657. English physician to James I and Charles I, discoverer in 1628 of the circulation of the blood□

Harwell see under Oxfordshire◊□

Harwich seaport in Essex, England; with ferry services to Scandinavia and the North Continent; population 15 000. Reclamation of Bathside Bay mudflats is making it a rival to Felixstowe□

Haryana NW state of India
area 44 222 sq km/000 000 sq mi
capital Chandigarh
features part of the Ganges plain, and a centre of Hinduism
population 12 850 900
language Hindi□

Harz Mountains range mainly in Lower◊ Saxony, but the highest point, the Brocken◊, is in E Germany□

Hasdrubal d. 207BC. Carthaginian general, brother of Hannibal◊, who left him in command in Spain in 218, to fight against the Scipios. In 208 he marched to Italy to relieve Hannibal, and was defeated and killed NW of Ancona□

Hašek Jaroslav 1883–1923. Czech writer, who in 1915 deserted to the Russians, and eventually joined the Bolsheviks. His comic masterpiece is the unfinished *The Good Soldier Schweik* 1920–3□

hashish a form of cannabis◊□

Hasidim the beliefs of an 18th-century Jewish sect. See Judaism◊□

Haslemere town in Surrey, England; population 14 000. The Dolmetsch family workshops re-create instruments of the 16–18th centuries, and have held an annual music festival since 1925□

Hassall John 1868–1948. British 'king of poster artists', e.g. 'Skegness is so bracing'□

Hassan II 1930– . King of Morocco from 1961; from 1976 he undertook the occupation of Western Sahara□

Hastings resort in E Sussex, England; population 76 100. The chief of the Cinque◊ Ports, it has ruins of a Norman castle, and the wreck of the Dutch East Indiaman, *Amsterdam* 1749, is under excavation. It is adjoined by St Leonard's, developed in the 19th century□

Hastings Battle of, between William the Conqueror and Harold◊ on 14 Oct 1066 at Senlac Hill (see Battle◊)□

Hastings Warren 1732–1818. British administrator. A protégé of Clive◊, he carried out major reforms, and became governor of Bengal in 1772, and governor-general of India in 1774. In 1780, when British India was under threat from the French and Hyder◊ Ali, he acted promptly to save the situation. Impeached for corruption on his return to England in 1785, he was acquitted in 1795□

Hatfield town in Hertfordshire, England; population 49 000. The magnificent Hatfield House (1611), home of the Salisburys, replaced the 12th-century palace of the bishops of Ely seized by Henry VIII. Elizabeth I was being held here when she succeeded to the throne□

Hathaway Anne 1556–1623. Wife of Shakespeare◊ from 1582; her cottage at Shottery, near Stratford-upon-Avon, survives□

Hathor in ancient Egyptian mythology, the sky-goddess, identified with Isis◊□

Hatshepsut c1510–c1469. Queen of Egypt, half-sister and widow of Thothmes II, she made her regency for her stepson a stepping stone to her own rule (from c1489). She built a magnificent mortuary temple at Deir el-Bahri, near Thebes□

Hatteras cape on the N Carolina coast, USA, noted for shipwrecks□

Hattersley Roy 1932– . Labour politician. On the right wing, he was Prices Secretary 1976–9, and in 1983 became deputy leader of the party□

Haughey Charles 1925– . Irish Fianna Fail statesman of Ulster descent. Dismissed in 1970 from Jack Lynch's Cabinet for alleged complicity in IRA gun-running, he was afterwards acquitted. Prime Minister 1979–81, and Mar–Nov 1982□

Hausa Muslim Negro people of N Nigeria, whose Hamitic◊ language is a lingua franca of W Africa□

Haussmann Georges Eugène, Baron Haussmann 1809–91. French administrator, who replanned medieval Paris 1853–70, with wide boulevards and parks□

Havana capital and port of Cuba; population 2 000 000. The palace of the Spanish governors, and the stronghold of La Fuerza

(1583), survive. In 1898 the blowing up of the US battleship *Maine* in the harbour began the Spanish–American war◊. Cigars and tobacco are made here□

Havel Vaclav 1936– . Czech satiric playwright, e.g. *The Garden Party* 1963, and *Largo Desolato* 1985, about a dissident intellectual. He was imprisoned 1979–83 for support of Charter 77 (see Czechoslovakia◊)□

Havelock Sir Henry 1795–1857. British general who retook Cawnpore (now Kanpur◊) and relieved Lucknow in the Indian Mutiny of 1857□

Havering borough of NE Greater London
features Romford and Hornchurch were united to form the borough in 1965; both were previously part of Essex
population 239 800□

Havre Le. See Le◊ Havre□

Hawaii Pacific island state of the USA; Aloha State

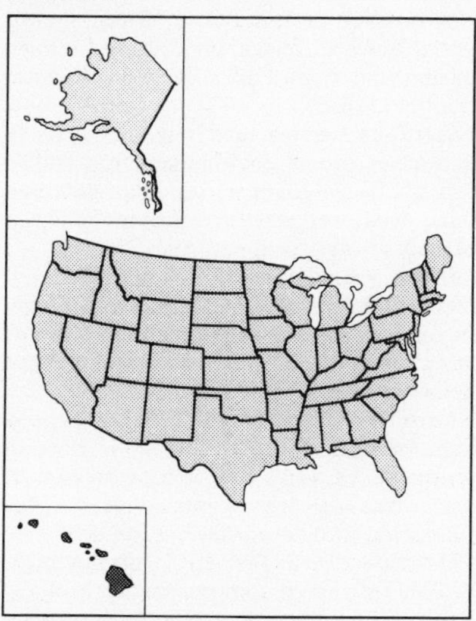

area 16 705 sq km/6450 sq mi
capital Honolulu on Oahu
towns Hilo
features Hawaii consists of a chain of some 20 volcanic islands, of which the chief are: ***Hawaii*** itself, noted for *Mauna Kea* 4201 m/13 784 ft, the world's highest island mountain (site of a UK infrared telescope◊) and Mauna Loa, 4170 m/13 680 ft, the world's largest active volcanic crater; ***Maui*** second largest island; ***Oahu*** third largest, with the greatest concentration of population and tourist attractions, e.g. Waikiki beach, and site of Pearl◊ Harbor; ***Kauai*** and ***Molokai,*** see Father Damien◊; see also Hawaiian guitar, under guitar◊
products sugar, coffee, pineapples, bananas and flowers; there are offshore cobalt, nickel and manganese deposits
population 963 620, of whom about 30% are European, 30% Japanese, 15% Filipino, and 5% Chinese
language English
religion Christianity; minority Buddhism
famous people Father Joseph Damien
history Captain Cook, who called them the Sandwich Islands, was the first known European visitor in 1778. A kingdom until 1893, Hawaii became a republic in 1894, ceded itself to the USA in 1898, and became a state in 1959□

Hawaiian guitar a type of guitar◊□

Hawarden town in Clwyd, N Wales; population 8500. W E Gladstone lived at Hawarden Castle for many years, and founded St Deiniol's theological library in Hawarden□

Haw-Haw Lord. See William Joyce◊□

Hawick town in Borders, Scotland; population 16 500□

hawk a small bird of the eagle◊ family□

Hawke Bob (Robert) 1929– . Australian Labor statesman. A Rhodes scholar at Oxford, he was president of the Australian Council of Trade Unions 1970–80, entered parliament in 1980, and in 1983 defeated Malcolm Fraser in a general election to become Prime Minister; re-elected in 1984 with a reduced majority. Rather 'left of centre' than 'left', he tended to pursue a consensus, but was committed to an eventual Australian republic□

Hawke Edward, 1st Baron Hawke 1705–81. British admiral, who destroyed in 1759 in Quiberon Bay a French fleet intended to cover an invasion of Britain□

Hawke Bay bay in North Island, New Zealand, on which Napier stands□

Hawker Robert Stephen 1803–75. British poet ('Song of the Western Men'), vicar of Morwenstow, Cornwall, from 1834, and originator of the harvest festival□

Hawkes Jacquetta 1910– . British anthropologist and archaeologist, who collaborated with her first husband, Christopher Hawkes, in *Prehistoric Britain* 1944, and married J B Priestley◊ in 1953□

Hawkesbury river in New South Wales; length 480 km/300 mi; a major source of Sydney's water□

Hawking Stephen 1942– . British physicist, professor of gravitational physics at Cambridge from 1977. His discoveries include the radiation of particles of matter by the strong gravitational field around a black hole. Commenting on Einstein's remark: 'God does not play dice with the

Universe,' he said: 'God not only plays dice, he throws them where they can't be seen'□

Hawkins Sir Anthony Hope. See Anthony Hope◊□

Hawkins Sir John 1532–95. English navigator, born in Plymouth. Treasurer to the navy 1573–89, he was knighted for his services as a commander against the Armada□

Hawkins Sir Richard c1562–1622. English navigator, son of Sir John Hawkins. He held a command against the Armada in 1588; was captured in an expedition against Spanish possessions 1593–4, and not released till 1602; knighted in 1603□

hawk moth see under moth◊□

Hawks Howard 1896–1977. American film producer, e.g. *Scarface* 1930, *To Have and Have Not* 1944, and *The Big Sleep* 1946, with Humphrey Bogart and Lauren Bacall in the main roles□

Hawksmoor Nicholas 1661–1736. English architect, assistant to Wren◊ in city churches and St Paul's; joint architect with Vanbrugh◊ of Castle Howard and Blenheim Palace. The original west towers of Westminster Abbey, long attributed to Wren, are his□

Haworth see under Keighley◊□

Haworth Sir Norman 1883–1950. British organic chemist, first to synthesize a vitamin (C) in 1933, he shared a Nobel prize in 1937□

hawthorn genus of small deciduous trees and shrubs *Crataegus*, of the N temperate zone, family Rosaceae. The ***common hawthorn, may,*** or ***whitethorn*** *C monogyna* has clusters of white flowers followed by red berries (haws)□

Hawthorne Nathaniel 1804–64. American author, born at Salem◊. He became a customs official, but won fame with *The Scarlet Letter* 1850 and *The House of the Seven Gables* 1851, and classic legends retold for children, *Tanglewood Tales* 1853. He was a friend of Melville◊□

Haydn Franz Joseph 1732–1809. Austrian composer. Kapellmeister 1761–90 to Prince Esterházy, and on visits to London 1791–2 and again 1794–5, wrote the 'Surprise', 'Military', 'Clock', 'Drum-roll', 'London', and 'Oxford' symphonies; the oratorios *The Creation* and *The Seasons* were also written for English audiences. He established the regular symphonic form and composition of the orchestra which were to be used by Mozart and Beethoven, and was the first great master of the quartet. His work also includes operas, church music, songs, etc., and he composed the 'Emperor's Hymn', later adopted as the German national anthem□

Haydon Benjamin Robert 1786–1846. British artist, who attempted 'high art' on gigantic canvases, e.g. *Christ's Entry into Jerusalem* 1820, but excelled more in genre painting e.g. *The Mock Election* and *Chairing the Member*. His autobiography and journals are lively, but he shot himself because of his debts□

Hayek Friedrich Aug von 1899– . Austro-British economist, British subject from 1938, whose *The Road to Serfdom* 1944 studied socialistic trends in Britain; Nobel prize in 1974□

Hayes Rutherford Birchard 1822–93. 19th president of the USA 1877–81. A Republican, he withdrew the army of occupation from the southern states□

hay fever a common allergic reaction to pollen, causing sneezing and asthmatic symptoms. In those specially sensitive, powerful body chemicals, related to histamine◊, are produced at the site of entry, causing great irritation. This discovery in 1984 brings hope of effective treatment nearer□

Hay-on-Wye town in Powys, Wales, known as the 'town of books' because of the huge secondhand bookshop started by Richard Booth in 1961□

hazardous wastes mainly industrial waste dangerous to the environment, e.g. acidic resins, arsenic residues, residual hardening salts, lead, mercury, non-ferrous sludges, organic solvents, and pesticides□

hazel genus *Corylus* of N temperate trees, family Betulaceae◊, including ***common hazel*** or ***cobnut*** *C avellana* (of which the ***filbert*** *C maxima* is the cultivated variety), and the ***American hazel*** *C Americana*□

Hazlitt William 1778–1830. British writer, born at Maidstone. Becoming a London journalist, he was a superb controversialist, and wrote perceptive critical essays, e.g. *Characters of Shakespeare's Plays* 1817–18; *Table Talk* 1821–2; *The Spirit of the Age* 1825, dealing with his contemporaries□

Head Edith c1900–81. American costume designer for a thousand films, who won eight Oscars, including *The Heiress*, *All About Eve,* and *The Sting*□

headache pain in the head, which has causes ranging through minor eye strain, the psychological, and severe physical illness, e.g. brain tumour. See migraine◊□

Healey Denis 1917– . British Labour politician. Minister of Defence 1964–70, he was Chancellor of the Exchequer 1947–9. In 1980 he contested the party leadership with Callaghan, and was deputy to Foot 1980–3□

health service provision of medical care on a national scale. From 1948 the UK has had a National Health Service which includes hospital◊ care, but charges for ordinary doctors' prescriptions, spectacles, and dental treatment are waived only for those unable to pay. Private health schemes such as BUPA◊ have flourished. In the USA the Medicare health insurance scheme provides care (towards which patients pay a share) out of hospital for the elderly and disabled, and the Medicaid state scheme (to which the federal government contributes) for the rest of the population unable to afford private care. Many Americans have personal subscriptions to private health schemes, such as Blue Cross (established 1929) and Blue Shield (established 1917), and from 1985 fees for Medicare patients to join health maintenance organizations (HMOs, covering visits to a group of doctors and hospital fees) have been paid for them□

Heaney Seamus (Justin) 1939– . Irish poet, born in Derry, who has written powerful verse about the polical situation in Northern Ireland. Collections include *North* (1975), and *Field Work* (1979)□

Heard and McDonald Islands group of islands in the S Indian Ocean; area 412 sq km/159 sq mi; uninhabited, except for a weather station on the largest, glacier-covered Heard Island, which has a still active volcano, Big Ben 2743 m/9000 ft□

Hearst Patty 1955– . Granddaughter of William R Hearst, she was kidnapped in 1974, by the Symbionese Liberation Army, joined her captors in a bank raid, and was imprisoned 1976–9□

Hearst William Randolph 1863–1951. American newspaper proprietor, founder of sensational 'yellow journalism', and a strong isolationist, the original of 'Citizen Kane' (see Orson Welles◊); his home San Simeon (Hearst Castle) is a state museum. See under California◊□

heart muscular organ supplying blood to all parts of the body, the timing of its beat being regulated by its own local nervous system. The first human heart transplant (in Louis Washkansky) was carried out in 1967 in Cape Town by Christiaan Barnard◊; the first human to receive an artificial heart was Barney Clark in 1982, but he lived only 112 days□

heartburn irritation of the gullet by excessively acid stomach contents, as sometimes happens in the course of pregnancy, in cases of duodenal ulcer, etc.□

heat energy in transit from a high-temperature region to a low-temperature region without work◊ being done on a visible scale. It can flow by:

convection in a fluid (gas or liquid) currents of fluid can take heat with them. 'Natural' convection currents arise because hotter fluid is slightly less dense, and can float upwards through colder fluid ('hot fluids rise' not 'heat rises').

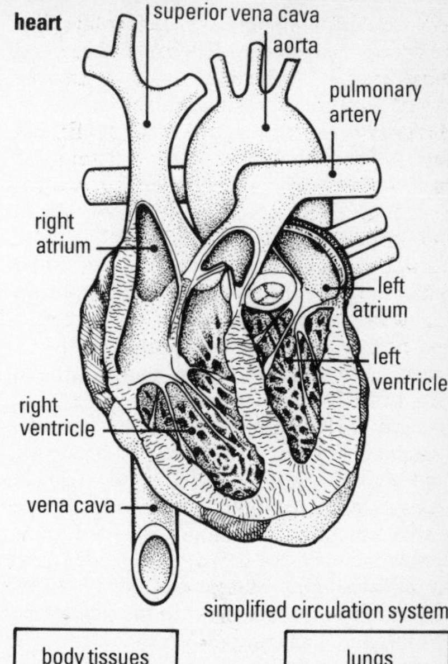

conduction heat can be passed from atom to atom in a solid in the form of energy of random vibrations, via the interatomic forces. Conduction can also take place (generally poorly) in fluids. Thermal insulators are usually effective by having many pockets of air, each too small to support much convection.

radiation there can be a net transfer of heat from a hotter to a colder body by means of electromagnetic radiation◊. The sunshine which reaches us first via empty space, then through the atmosphere, carries roughly equal energy in the visible and infra-red regions.

Absorption of heat by a body usually results in its increasing its temperature (its atoms vibrate more vigorously). However, heat supplied to make a solid melt or a liquid vaporize (so-called 'latent heat') does not induce a temperature rise□

heat capacity term in physics describing the quantity of heat required to raise the temperature of a substance by one degree. The ***specific heat capacity*** of a substance is the heat capacity per unit of mass, given in joules per kg per kelvin of temperature (British Thermal Units per lb per degree Fahrenheit)□

heath family Ericaceae of low-growing woody evergreen shrubs (also known as ***heathers***) of Europe and Africa. With bell-shaped pendant flowers, they are popular garden plants. The ***bell heather*** *E cinerea* is often found with common heather◊. Oil of wintergreen (now synthetically made), used in the treatment of rheumatism, used to be extracted from the N American *Gaultheria procumbens*□

Heath Edward Richard George 1916– . British Conservative statesman, born at Broadstairs. He succeeded Home as leader of the party in 1965 (the first elected leader), and though defeated in 1966, achieved a surprise victory in the general election of 1970. A miners' strike, resulting from his attempt to control inflation (including wages) led to his narrow inconclusive defeat in Feb 1974, and defeat by a larger margin in Oct 1974. This resulted in his replacement in the leadership by Margaret Thatcher◊□

heather low-growing evergreen shrubs, common on sandy or acid soil, especially ***common heather*** or ***Scottish ling*** *Calluna vulgaris*, with white, red, or purple flowers and small leaves on a shrubby stem. See also heath◊□

Heathrow see London◊□

heat pump machine run by electricity, etc., on a similar principle to a refrigerator, i.e. to cool the interior of a building or, conversely, by extracting energy from the atmosphere to give space heating. Some 2.5 times more energy may be transferred as heat than is used to run it□

heat storage usually achieved by using materials which undergo phase changes, e.g. Glauber◊'s salt, and sodium pyrophosphate, which melts at 70°C (used to store off-peak heat in the home, the salt being liquefied by cheap heat during the night, and then freezing – to give off heat during the day). Other developments include the use of plastic crystals, which change their structure rather than melting, and could be incorporated in curtains or clothing□

heatstroke above a body temperature of 40°C/104°F, the human brain swells, resulting in confusion of thought; the body becomes dehydrated, blood circulation slows, and organs, such as the kidneys, fail to function. Coma may ensue and end in cardiac arrest□

heaven in Christianity, and some other religions, the destination of the virtuous after death. Modern theologians avoid the concept of 'physical' joys, in favour of the beatific vision, when the soul sees God as He really is□

Heaviside Oliver 1850–1925. British physicist, a pioneer in theoretical telephony, and predictor in 1902 of the existence of an ionized layer of air in the upper atmosphere which was verified by Kennelly◊ (the Kennelly-Heaviside layer, now known as the 'E layer'). Deflection from it makes possible the transmission of radio signals round the world, which would otherwise be lost in outer space. See ionosphere◊□

heavy water deuterium oxide, D_2O, that is water containing deuterium (an isotope of hydrogen containing a neutron) instead of hydrogen. Its chemical properties are identical with ordinary water, but its physical properties differ slightly, e.g. its density and boiling point. It occurs naturally in ordinary water in the ratio of one part deuterium to 5000 parts by weight of ordinary hydrogen◊□

Hebe in Greek mythology, the goddess of youth, daughter of Zeus◊ and Hera◊, and handmaiden of the gods□

Hebei province (formerly Hopei or Hupei) of N China

area 202 700 sq km/79 053 sq mi

capital Shijiazhuang

features include special municipalities of Beijing and Tianjin

products cereals, textiles, iron and steel

population 51 046 000□

Hebrew Semitic◊ language, closely related to Aramaic◊, which had supplanted it as the popular tongue by the 1st century. In the 18–19th centuries it was revived, on the classic model of the Old Testament, and is the language of modern Israel□

Hebrides group of over 500 islands (fewer than 100 inhabited) off W Scotland. Total area 2900 sq km/1120 sq mi. The ***Inner Hebrides*** are divided between the Highland and Strathclyde regions. The largest is Skye, area 1665 sq km/643 sq mi, capital Portree, where Bonnie Prince Charlie (Charles◊ Edward Stuart) took refuge after Culloden◊. The others include Mull (chief town Tobermory), Jura, Islay (which produces the finest of malt whisky, and whose wild life includes eagles and flocks of rare wintering geese), and uninhabited Staffa, which has Fingal◊'s Cave, lined with natural basalt columns, and visited by Mendelssohn in 1829. Of special interest is Iona, where St Columba◊ founded a monastery in 563, which was a centre of Celtic Christianity until destroyed by Norse pirates in 807; a later Benedictine foundation (1203) was restored from 1938. The ***Outer Hebrides*** form the islands area of the Western◊ Isles, separated from the Inner group by the Little Minch. The largest is Lewis-with-Harris 2225 sq km/859 sq mi, capital Stornoway, others being N and S Uist, all of which are famous for tweeds. To the W of Harris is ***St Kilda,*** a small island group uninhabited since 1930; a missile tracking station linked with a rocket range on S Uist was established in 1957. It is famous for its seabirds□

Hebron (Arabic *El Khalil*) city on the West Bank of the Jordan, occupied by Israel from 1967; population 54 000, including 4000 Jews. Within the mosque is the traditional site of the tombs of Abraham, Isaac, and Jacob□

Heb-Sed royal festival in ancient Egypt, apparently commemorating Menes's union of Upper and Lower Egypt□

Hecate in Greek mythology, the goddess of witchcraft and magic, also identified with Artemis◊□

hectare unit of area in the metric system, equalling 100 ares or 10 000 sq metres or 2.471 acres. Trafalgar Square, London's only 'metric square', was laid out as one hectare□

Hector in Greek mythology, a Trojan prince, son of Priam◊, who was killed by Achilles◊ in the siege of Troy◊□

Hecuba in Greek mythology, the wife of Priam◊, and mother of Hector and Paris◊, captured by the Greeks after the fall of Troy◊□

hedgehog a spiny, nocturnal animal of the order Insectivora◊□

hedge sparrow European slender-billed songbird, the ***dunnock*** *Prunella modularis*, family Prunellidae, which resembles the sparrow only in size and colouring□

hedonism term embracing the moral philosophies of the Cyrenaics◊, and of the Epicureans◊. Later hedonists, e.g. Bentham◊ and Mill◊, see the happiness of society, rather than the individual, as the aim□

Hefei capital (formerly Hofei) of Anhui province, China; population 630 000□

Hegel Georg Wilhelm Friedrich 1770–1831. German philosopher, author of *The Phenomenology of Mind* 1807, *Encyclopaedia of the Philosophical Sciences* 1817, and *Philosophy of Right* 1821. As a 'rightist', he championed religion, the Prussian State, and the existing order, but 'leftist' followers include Marx, who used Hegel's dialectic to attempt to show the inevitability of radical change and attacked both religion and the social order. Hegel saw the world as a single organism constantly developing by its own internal necessity through a series of triadic stages: thesis, antithesis, and the emerging synthesis, and thus developing into the gradual embodiment of reason□

hegemony originally the dominance of Athens over the other Greek city states; later applied to Prussia in Germany, and by China in propaganda against Vietnam in SE Asia, and the USA and USSR throughout the world□

Hegira Arabic 'flight', applied to the Muslim era, which is dated from Mohammed's flight from Mecca to Medina on 16 Jul 622AD; Islamic dates are preceded by AH *anno hegirae* (Latin, 'in the year of the Hegira')□

Heidegger Martin 1889–1976. German philosopher, author of *Being and Time* 1927. He denied being an Existentialist◊, but is often regarded as the chief exponent of the theory□

Heidelberg town in Baden-Württemberg, W Germany; population 133 600. It has the oldest university in Germany, established in 1386, and has a picturesque ruined castle 13–17th centuries. It is the headquarters of NATO◊'s Allied Mobile Force□

Heidelberg village near Melbourne, Australia, where a group of Impressionist artists (including Roberts, Streeton, Conder◊) worked in 'teaching camps' 1888–90□

Heifetz Jascha 1901– . Russian-born violinist; Walton◊'s concerto was written for him□

Heilbronn town in Baden-Württemberg, W Germany; population 112 000□

Heilongjiang province (formerly Heilungkiang) of NE China

area 710 000 sq km/274 060 sq mi

capital Harbin

features China's largest oilfield near Anda

products cereals, gold, coal

population 32 000 000. See Manchuria◊□

Heilungkiang see Heilongjiang◊□

Heine Heinrich 1797–1856. German-Jewish revolutionary poet. Schubert and Schumann set many of his songs, as in *Buch der Lieder* 1827. From 1848 he was confined to bed by spinal paralysis□

Heinkel Ernst 1888–1958. German aircraft designer, whose first jet aircraft (1939) was developed independently of the Whittle◊ jet of 1941; in World War II he was Germany's biggest producer of warplanes□

Heisenberg Werner Carl 1901–76. German physicist, an originator of quantum mechanics◊ and the formulator of the Uncertainty (Indeterminacy) Principle, one form of which is that accurate measurement of a particle's position forces us to sacrifice accurate knowledge of its momentum and vice versa; the act of measuring disturbs the system. These irreducible uncertainties are negligible except for sub-atomic systems. Nobel prize in 1932. See particle◊ physics□

Hejaz see under Saudi◊ Arabia□

Hel or ***Hela*** in Norse mythology, the goddess of the underworld□

Helen in Greek mythology, the daughter of Zeus◊ and Leda◊, the most beautiful of women. Married to Menelaus, king of Sparta, she eloped with Paris◊ in his absence, which precipitated the Trojan War. Afterwards she returned home with her husband□

Helena St c 247–237. Mother of Constantine the Great, she was alleged to have discovered the true cross of Christ at Jerusalem□

helicopter aircraft with power-driven horizontal rotors, giving it vertical take-off and landing, movement in any direction, and stationary hover. They are increasingly used in naval and military warfare (especially heavily-armed ***helicopter gunships***), and unmanned miniatures, less easy to shoot down than a full-sized aircraft, may be used for reconnaissance□

Heligoland German island naval base in the North Sea, off the mouth of the Elbe, used in both World Wars; the fortifications were destroyed in 1947; area 0.6 sq km/150 acres; population 3000□

Heliopolis ancient Egyptian centre (biblical On) of the worship of the sun-god Ra, NE of Cairo□

Helios in Greek mythology, the sun-god, thought to make his daily journey across the sky in a chariot. See Phaethon◊□

heliotrope genus *Heliotropium* of decorative plants, family Boraginaceae, with distinctive spikes of blue, lilac, or white flowers, especially the ***Peruvian*** or ***cherry pie heliotrope*** *H peruvianum*□

helium element

symbol He

atomic number 2

physical description colourless, odourless gas, lighter than air

features one of the inert◊ gases

uses in airships, and as part of a mixture to dilute oxygen for use by divers, avoiding the problems caused by nitrogen – the 'bends'. See decompression◊ sickness□

hell in Christian doctrine (and similarly in Islam), the place in which unrepentant sinners suffer the eternal torments of the damned. Modern theologians regard it as a state rather than a place□

hellebore genus *Helleborus* of herbaceous plants, family Ranunculaceae, including the poisonous ***stinking hellebore*** *H foetidus*; and also the ***Christmas rose*** *H niger*□

helleborine temperate orchids of genera *Epipactis* and *Cephalanthera*, including the British ***marsh helleborine*** *E palustris*, with pink and white flowers□

Hellenes the Greeks, whose name for their country is *Hellas*□

Hellenic (from *Hellas,* Ancient Greek name for Greece) term describing the classical period of Ancient Greek civilization, from the first Olympic Games in 776 until the death of Alexander the Great in 323 BC□

Hellenistic (Greek *Hellenizo,* to speak Greek) term for Greek civilization following the death of Alexander in 323 BC, describing the areas in the Mediterranean which came under Greek influence□

Heller Joseph 1923– . American novelist. In World War II, he served in the USAF, and then entered advertizing. Best-known is his *Catch-22* 1961, satirizing war and bureaucratic methods□

Hellespont see Dardanelles◊□

Hellman Lilian 1907–84. American playwright, born in New Orleans, and note for her strong themes: *The Children's Hour* 1934, *The Little Foxes* 1939; *Watch on the Rhine* 1941. She lived some 31 years with Dashiell Hammett◊, and in her will founded a fund to promote Marxist doctrine□

Helmholtz Hermann Ludwig Ferdinand von 1821–94. German physicist, an early developer of the Principle of Conservation of Energy◊, who made important studies in colour vision and acoustics□

Helmont Jean Baptiste van 1577–1644. Belgian doctor. The first to realize that gases exist apart from the atmosphere, he claimed to have coined the word 'gas'□

Helms Richard 1913– . American secret agent. Originally with the OSS, he was Director of the CIA 1966–73, when he was dismissed by Nixon. In 1977 he was convicted of lying before a Congressional Committee because he refused to reveal secrets he knew his oath as chief of intelligence compelled him to keep from the public□

helot a serf of ancient Sparta◊□

Helpmann Sir Robert 1909– . Australian dancer, who partnered Margot Fonteyn◊, and choreographed (*Miracle in the Gorbals* 1944); knighted in 1968□

Helsingborg industrial port in SW Sweden, linked with Helsingör across the Sound by ferry; population 102 200□

Helsingfors Swedish name of Helsinki◊□

Helsingör port in NE Denmark, linked by a ferry with Helsingborg◊; population 56 200. Shakespeare made it the scene of *Hamlet*□

Helsinki (Swedish *Helsingfors*) capital and port (kept open by ice-breakers in winter) of Finland; population 910 500. It has the parliament house and 18th-century cathedral, and the homes of architect Eliel Saarinen and Sibelius◊ outside the town are museums□

Helsinki Conference international conference 1975, at which agreement was supposedly reached among 35 countries, including the Soviet bloc and USA, on cooperation in security, economics, science, technology, environment, and human rights□

Helvellyn see under Cumbria◊□

Helvetia Roman province including part of modern Germany and Switzerland; the name is sometimes used poetically for Switzerland□

Helvetius Claude Adrien 1715–71. French philosopher, who maintained that self-interest was the mainspring of human action; there is no absolute good or evil; and intellectual differences are only a matter of education□

Hemans Felicia Dorothea 1793–1835. British poet, remembered for 'Casabianca'('The boy stood on the burning deck ...')□

Hemel Hempstead 'new' town (paper, electrical goods, office equipment) in Hertfordshire, England; population 77 600□

Hemingway Ernest 1898–1961. American novelist, born in Illinois. He became a reporter, and in World War I he was wounded as a volunteer ambulance man in Italy (see *A Farewell to Arms* 1929). Settling in Paris, he was much influenced by Gertrude Stein◊, who interested him in bullfighting (see his first novel *The Sun also Rises* 1926, and *Death in the Afternoon* 1932). He was a war correspondent in the Spanish Civil War (see *For Whom the Bell Tolls* 1940), and World War II. His passion for big-game hunting emerges in short stories, e.g. 'The Snows of Kilimanjaro' and 'The Short Happy Life of Francis Macomber'. His style of simple sentences attracted imitators, mostly injudicious. Awarded the Nobel prize in 1954. He committed suicide in a fit of depression□

Hemiptera order of insects, the ***bugs***, with mouthparts adapted for feeding by puncture and suction, subdivided into ***Homoptera*** and ***Heteroptera***. Homoptera, with front wings of uniform consistency, include

aphid also called ***greenfly*** or ***plant lice***, family Aphididae. Colonies live on plant stems and leaves, feeding on sap and excreting honeydew (see ant◊); they also transmit virus diseases, and may reach a density of up to 2000 million per ha/2 acres. Nevertheless, they may be beneficial by removing surplus sugar from the plants as honeydew, since this promotes fertility in the soil beneath by raising the rate of nitrogen fixation. Closely related to them is the ***vine phylloxera*** *Phylloxera vitifolia* family Phylloxeridae, which almost destroyed the French wine industry in the 19th century, and attacked US vines (which had been used to restock Europe) in 1985, which had lost their resistance with time.

cicada mainly tropical family Cicadidae, which live by sucking the juices of trees; the males 'chirp' loudly, by using a muscle to contract and relax a special plate which may make a 1000 clicks a second.

scale insect super-family Coccoidea. Females are wartlike, males are winged insects; the immature forms feed on tropical crops (citrus, coffee, rubber, sugar cane), and also attack trees, e.g. ***horse-chestnut scale*** *Pulvinaria regalis* especially those in urban conditions.

Heteroptera, with leathery tips to their membraneous forewings, include:

bedbug (common) *Cimex lectularis* family Cimicidae, a brownish, flattened, wingless insect, with an unpleasant smell, which sucks the blood of human beings.

cotton stainer family Pyrrhocoridae, which pierces and stains cotton bolls.

waterbugs including ***pond-skaters*** family Hydrometridae and ***water-boatman*** family Notonectidae□

hemlock poisonous European plant *Conium maculatum*, family Umbelliferae. An extract from it paralyses the nervous system and was used by the Greeks as a form of capital punishment. See Socrates◊□

hemp an Asian plant. Its strong fibres are used for making rope, etc. and several drugs are obtained from it. See cannabis◊□

Henan province (formerly Honan) of E central China

area 167 000 sq km/64 462 sq mi

capital Zhengzhou

features comprises river plains of the Huang Ho; in the 1980s ruins of Xibo, the 16th-century BC capital of the Shang dynasty (see China◊: history) were discovered here, and Anyang, their last capital, is also in the province

products cereals and cotton

population 71 890 000□

henbane poisonous, evil-smelling yellow-flowered plant *Hyoscyamus niger*, family Solanaceae◊, common in Britain. The drug ***hyoscine***, also called ***scopolamine***, is derived from it and used in surgery and obstetrics (with morphine) as a sedative, and to prevent travel-sickness□

Henderson Arthur 1863–1935. British Labour statesman, who as Foreign Secretary 1929–31 accorded the Soviet government full recognition; Nobel peace prize 1934□

Hendon see under Barnet◊□

Hengist d. c488AD. Leader, with his brother Horsa, of the Jutes◊ who settled in Kent c450. See Merlin◊□

Henie Sonja 1912–69. Norwegian skater, world figure champion ten times, Olympic champion three times□

Henley-on-Thames town in Oxfordshire, England; population 12 000. The annual regatta (since 1839) is in Jul; Henley Management College, established in 1946, was the first in Europe□

henna tropical tree *Lawsonia inermis,* family Lythraceae, yielding a dye which makes the hair and fingernails orange-red□

Henrietta Maria 1609–69. Queen consort of Charles I from 1625, daughter of Henry IV of France. She encouraged her husband's absolutism, and was highly unpopular□

Henry eight kings of England:

Henry I 1068–1135, king from 1100, when he succeeded his brother William II. An able administrator, he established a professional bureaucracy and a system of travelling judges. See Robert◊ II of Normandy.

Henry II 1133–89, king from 1154, when he succeeded Stephen◊, he was the son of Matilda◊ and Geoffrey of Anjou. He curbed the power of the barons, but his attempt to bring the Church courts under control had to be abandoned after the murder of Becket◊. He began the conquest of Ireland. See under Eleanor◊ of Aquitaine and Woodstock◊.

Henry III 1207–72, king from 1216, when he succeeded John◊, but did not assume royal power until 1227. Subservience to the Papacy and his foreign favourites led to de Montfort◊'s revolt in 1264. Henry was imprisoned and not restored until the royalist victory at Evesham in 1265.

Henry IV 1367–1413, king from 1399. Son of John◊ of Gaunt, he was banished by Richard◊ II for political activity, and returned in 1399 to head a revolt and be accepted as king by Parliament. He had difficulty in keeping the support of Parliament and the clergy, and had to deal with baronial unrest and Glendower◊'s rising.

Henry V 1387–1422, king from 1413, son of Henry IV. Invading Normandy in 1415, he captured Harfleur, and defeated the French at Agincourt◊. He invaded again 1417–19, and in 1420 married Catherine de Valois to gain recognition as heir to the French throne by his father-in-law Charles VI.

Henry VI 1421–71, king from 1422. Son of Henry V, he assumed royal power in 1442. Married in 1445 to the dominant Margaret of Anjou, he became unpopular as he lost England's conquests in France. Edward, Duke of York◊ claimed the throne, and though he was killed in 1460, his son Edward proclaimed himself king in 1461 (see Wars of the Roses◊). Henry was captured in 1465, temporarily restored in 1470, but again imprisoned 1471 and then murdered.

Henry VII 1457–1509, king from 1485, son of Edmund Tudor, Earl of Richmond, and a descendant of John of Gaunt◊. In 1485 he landed in Britain from France to lead the rebellion against Richard III which ended at Bosworth◊. Yorkist revolts continued till 1497, but he restored order after the Wars of the Roses◊ by the Star◊ Chamber, and achieved independence of Parliament by amassing through confiscations, etc., a private fortune.

Henry VIII 1491–1547 king from 1509, when he married Catherine◊ of Aragon. Initially he was guided in foreign policy by Wolsey◊, but when the cardinal failed to obtain a divorce for him, he proclaimed himself head of the English Church, and dissolved the monasteries (assisted by Thomas Cromwell◊). Divorcing Catherine in 1533, he married in turn Anne Boleyn, Jane Seymour, Anne of Cleves, Catherine Howard, and Catherine Parr. He never lost his popularity, but wars with France and Scotland towards the end of his reign sapped the economy, and in religion he not only executed Roman Catholics for refusing to acknowledge his supremacy in the Church (see Thomas More◊), but burnt Protestants who maintained his changes had not gone far enough□

Henry four kings of France:

Henry I 1008–60, king from 1031, who spent much of his reign in conflict with William the Conqueror, then Duke of Normandy.

Henry II 1519–59, king from 1547, whose conquests included Calais from the English, and who died in a tournament.

Henry III 1551–89, king from 1574, who fought both the Huguenots◊ (headed by his successor, Henry of Navarre), and the Catholic League (headed by the Duke of Guise). The latter expelled him from Paris in 1588, and in alliance with the Huguenots, he besieged the city, but was assassinated.

Henry IV 1533–1610, king from 1589. Son of Antoine de Bourbon and Jeanne, queen of Navarre, he was brought up as a Protestant, and from 1576 led the Huguenots◊. On his accession he accepted Catholicism, while tolerating Protestantism, and restored France to prosperity, but was assassinated by a Catholic fanatic. See Marie◊ de Médicis□

Henry seven Holy Roman Emperors:

Henry I the Fowler c876–936, king of Germany from 919, about to claim the imperial crown at his death

Henry II the Saint 973–1024, emperor from 1002, a defender of the Papacy

Henry III 1017–56, emperor from 1093, who raised the empire to its peak (including Poland, Bohemia, Hungary).

Henry IV 1050–1106, emperor from 1056, who was involved from 1075 in a struggle with the Papacy (see Gregory◊ VII).

Henry V 1081–1125, emperor from 1106. He continued the struggle until the settlement of the investitures question in 1122.

Henry VI 1165–97, emperor from 1190. He captured and imprisoned Richard I of England, and compelled him to do homage.

Henry VII c1269–1313, emperor from 1308. He failed to revive the imperial supremacy in Italy□

Henry the Navigator 1394–1460. Portuguese prince, under whose patronage Madeira, the Azores, and Cape Verde Islands, were explored and colonized; and the African coast explored as far as Sierra Leone□

Henry Joseph 1797–1878. American physicist, inventor of the electromagnetic motor 1829, and a telegraphic apparatus; also discoverer of the principle of electromagnetic induction, roughly at the same time as Faraday◊, and the phenomenon of self-induction. The unit of inductance (henry) is named after him□

Henry Patrick 1736–99. American statesman, who in 1775 supported the arming of the Virginia militia against George III by a speech ending: 'Give me liberty or give me death!' He was governor of the state 1776–9, 1784–6□

Henry William 1774–1836. British chemist, formulator of *Henry's law* in 1803: the mass of gas which dissolves in a liquid at a given temperature is proportional to the gas pressure□

Henryson Robert c1430–c1505. Scottish poet, who continued Chaucer's poem *Troilus and Griseyde* with a *Testament of Cresseid*□

Henty George Alfred 1832–1902. British war correspondent, whose books for boys, e.g. *With the Allies to Peking* 1904, became a 1980s cult□

Henze Hans Werner 1926– . German opera composer, e.g. *Boulevard Solitude* 1952, based on Prévost◊'s *Manon Lescaut,* and *The Bassarids* 1974, based on the *Bacchae* of Euripides. He was influenced by Schoenberg◊□

hepatitis inflammation of the liver. Hepatitis B is a chronic viral disease of the third world, causing jaundice, and linked with liver cancer, but treatable by vaccine from 1980. It is carried by the blood and other body fluids; a tenth of recovered patients become carriers (the virus remains in the liver)□

Hepburn Katharine 1909– . American actress, born in Connecticut, whose films include *Morning Glory* 1933, *The African Queen* 1951, and *On Golden Pond* 1981. Noted for her husky voice, and winner of four academy awards□

Hephaestus in Greek mythology, the god of fire and metalcraft (Roman Vulcan◊), son of Zeus◊ and Hera◊; he was lame, and married Aphrodite◊□

Hepplewhite George d. 1786. British furniture-maker, especially chairs with shield- or heart-shaped backs, with inlaid or painted decoration (feathers, shells, wheat-ears)□

Heptarchy later term for the seven Saxon kingdoms thought to have existed in the 7–9th centuries: Northumbria, Mercia, E Anglia, Essex, Kent, Sussex, and Wessex□

Hepworth Dame Barbara 1903–75. British sculptor, especially in stone. She lived from 1939 at St Ives, Cornwall, where her home is a museum. Her second husband was Ben Nicholson◊□

Hera in Greek mythology, a goddess, sister-consort of Zeus◊, mother of Hephaestus◊, Hebe◊, and Ares◊; protector of women and marriage, and identified with Roman Juno□

Heracles in Greek mythology, a hero (Roman Hercules), son of Zeus◊ and Alcmene◊, famed for strength. While serving Eurystheus, king of Argos, he performed 12 Labours, including the cleansing of the Augean stables□

Heraclitus c540–475BC. Greek philosopher, born at Ephesus. His *On Nature* outlined a coherent theory that the ultimate principle of the Universe is fire, and that everything is in a state of flux□

Heraklion see Iráklion◊□

Heralds' College or ***College of Arms*** founded in 1484 by Richard III, it establishes the right to bear arms, granted by letters patent□

Herát city in NW Afghanistan; population 140 350□

herb any plant (tasting sweet, bitter, aromatic, or pungent) used in cookery, medicine, or perfumery. See table of herbs◊ and spices on page 398□

Herbert Edward, 1st Baron Herbert of Cherbury 1583–1648. English philosopher, brother of George Herbert. His *De veritate* 1624, with its theory of natural religion, founded English Deism□

Herbert Frank (Patrick) 1920–86. American science fiction writer, especially the Dune saga from 1965 onwards; they are among the most successful science fiction novels ever written□

Herbert George 1593–1633. English religious poet, e.g. *The Temple* 1633. Brother of Lord Herbert◊, he was a friend of Donne, Walton, and Bacon, and was vicar of Bemerton, Wiltshire from 1630; he died of tuberculosis□

herb

herbs

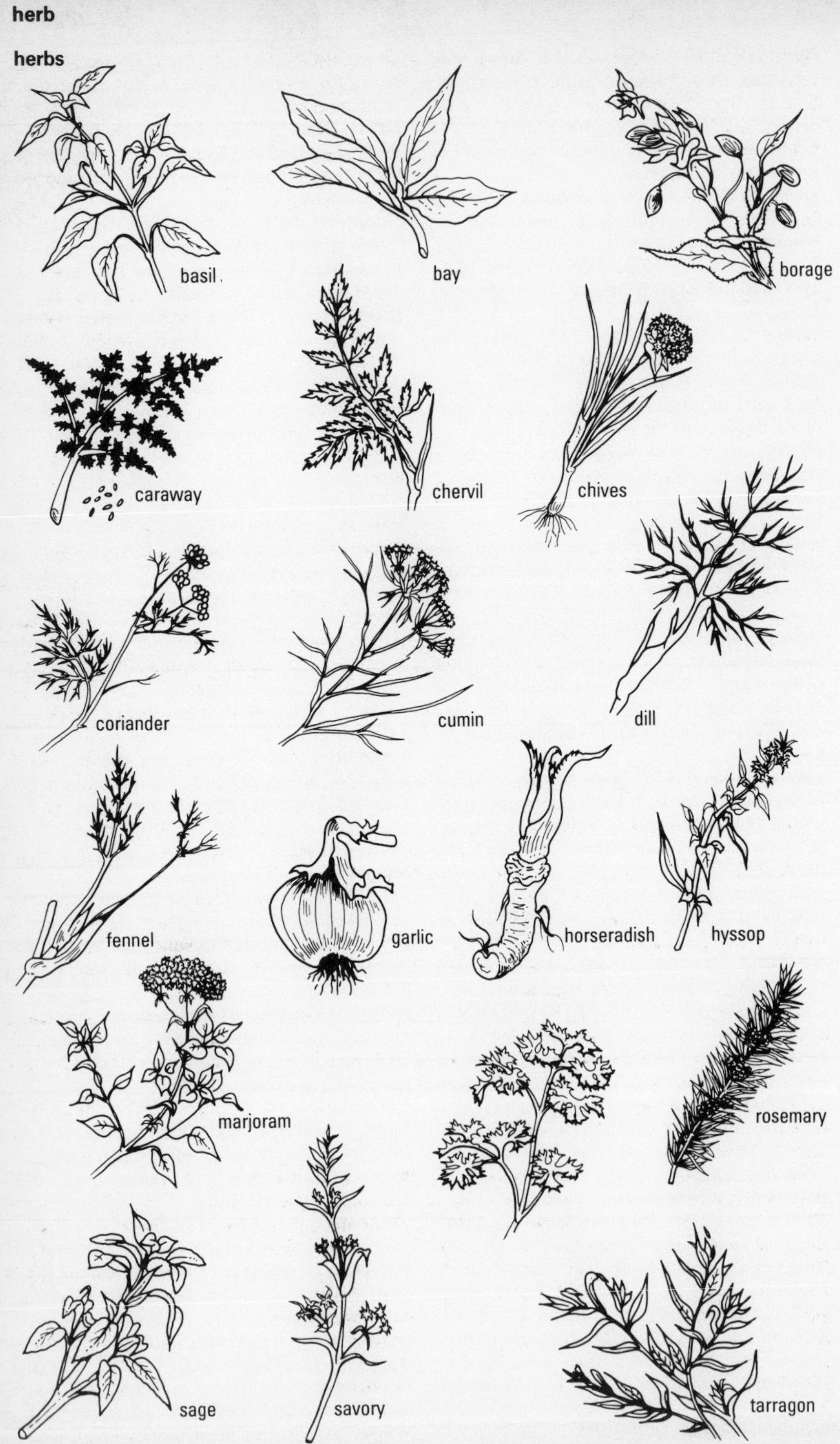
basil
bay
borage
caraway
chervil
chives
coriander
cumin
dill
fennel
garlic
horseradish
hyssop
marjoram
rosemary
sage
savory
tarragon

Herbert Wally (Walter) 1934– . British surveyor-explorer, who crossed the Arctic Ocean 1968–9 by dogsled, Alaska–Spitzbergen, 6000 km/3800 mi□

herb Robert a common species of geranium◊□

herbs and spices plant products used as flavouring in food, including:

allspice or ***pimento*** berry of tree of tropical America, *Pimenta officinalis,* family Myrtaceae (combines flavours of cinnamon, clove, and nutmeg)

aniseed liquorice-flavoured seed of Mediterranean plant *Pimpinella anisum,* family Umbelliferae

balm aromatic leaves of *Melissa officinalis,* family Labiatae

basil leaves of the Indian plant *Ocimum basilicum,* family Labiatae

bay leaves of the Mediterranean tree *Laurus nobilis,* family Lauraceae

borage leaves and flowers of the Mediterranean plant *Borago officinalis,* family Boraginaceae

burnet leaves of plants of temperate genera *Sanguisorba* and *Poterium,* family Rosaceae, used in salads

caraway seed of Eurasian plant *Carum carvi,* family Umbelliferae

cardamon seed of *Elettaria cardamomum,* family Zingiberaceae

cayenne or ***red pepper*** see chilli below

celery seeds of the celery◊ plant

chervil aniseed-flavoured leaves of Eurasian plant *Anthriscus cerefolium*

chilli fruit of species of Capsicum◊, also ground to produce ***cayenne pepper***

chives onion-flavoured leaves of *Allium schoenoprasum,* family Liliaceae

cinnamon yellowish-brown bark of the tree *Cinnamomum zeylanicum,* family Lauraceae

cloves flower buds of the east Asian tree *Eugenia aromatica* family Myrtaceae

coriander seeds of the Mediterranean plant *Coriander sativum,* family Umbelliferae

cumin seeds of the plant *Cuminum cyminum,* family Umbelliferae

curry powder mixture of cumin, coriander, ginger, turmeric, etc.

dill leaves and seeds of the Eurasian plant *Anethum graveolens,* family Umbelliferae

fennel◊ seeds and feathery leaves of *Foeniculum vulgare,* family Umbelliferae

garlic bulb of the originally Asian plant *Allium sativum,* family Liliaceae

ginger root of *Zingiber officinale,* family Zingiberaceae

horseradish◊ pungent root of *Armoracia rusticana,* family Cruciferae

hyssop leaves of the Asian plant *Hyssopus officinalis,* family Labiatae

mace fleshy covering of the nutmeg (see below)

marjoram leaves of the Mediterranean plant *Origanum hortensis,* family Labiatae, used in salads and seasoning

mint leaves of plants of genus *Mentha,* family Labiatae. Common species include peppermint and spearmint

mustard seed of plants of *Brassica*◊ genus

nutmeg seed of the Asian tree *Myristica fragrans,* family Myristicaceae; the fleshy outer covering also used as a spice is known as 'mace'

paprika obtained from the sweet red capsicum◊

parsley frilly leaves of the Mediterranean plant *Petroselinum crispum,* family Umbelliferae

pepper the fruits (peppercorns) of the Indian vine *Piper nigrum,* family Piperaceae; black pepper is ground from the whole fruit, and white pepper from the central part

pimento see allspice above

poppy seed (harmless) of the opium poppy, used for decorating bread, etc.

rosemary greyish leaves of the European shrub *Rosmarinus officinalis,* family Labiatae

sage leaves of the Mediterranean plant *Salvia officinalis,* family Labiatae

savory leaves of Mediterranean genus *Satureja,* family Labiatae

sesame seeds of *Sesame indicum,* family Pedaliaceae

sorrel leaves of genus *Rumex,* family Polygonaceae, used in salads and for seasoning

tarragon leaves of the Asian plant *Artemisia dracunculus,* family Compositae

thyme leaves and flowers of the Eurasian plant *Thymus vulgaris,* family Labiatae

turmeric gingery ground rhizomes of the tropical Asian plant *Curcuma longa,* family Zingiberaceae, which also provides a yellow dye which does not require a mordant or 'fixer'□

Hercegovina or ***Herzegovina*** see Bosnia-Hercegovina◊□

Herculaneum ancient city between Naples◊ and Pompeii◊, overwhelmed by the same eruption of Vesuvius as that which destroyed the latter; excavated from the 18th century□

Hercules Roman spelling of Heracles◊□

Hercules Pillars of. The rocks (at Gibraltar and Ceuta) which guard the entrance to the Mediterranean□

Herder Johann Gottfried von 1744–1803. German poet-critic and philosopher, a friend of Goethe◊. Court preacher at Weimar from

1776, he led the *Sturm*◊ *und Drang* movement; collected folk songs of all nations, and in *Outlines of a Philosophy of the History of Man* 1784–91, sketched human cultural development□

Hereford town in Hereford and Worcester, England; population 47 900. The cathedral was begun in 1079, and the Three Choirs Festival is held in Hereford every 3rd year (in turn with Gloucester and Worcester). Products include cider, beer, metal goods, etc. David Garrick◊ was born here□

Hereford and Worcester county of western England

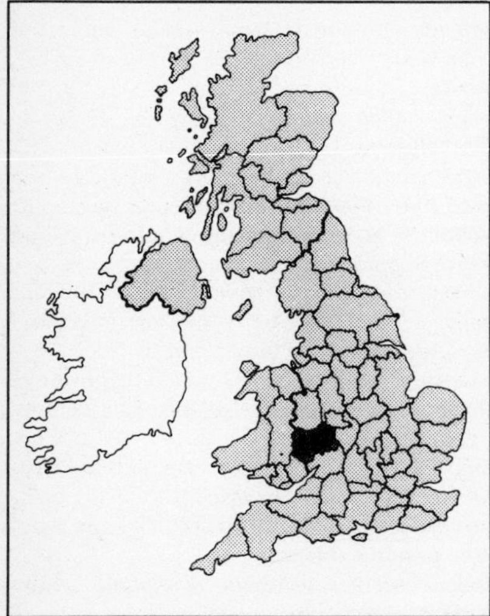

area 3927 sq km/1516 sq mi
towns administrative headquarters Worcester; Hereford, Kidderminster, Evesham, Ross-on-Wye, Ledbury
features rivers Wye and Severn; Malvern Hills (high point Worcester Beacon 425 m/1395 ft) and Black Mountains; Droitwich, once a Victorian spa, reopened its baths in 1985 (the town lies over a subterranean brine reservoir with waters buoyant enough to take a laden tea tray); fertile Vale of Evesham
products mainly agricultural, apples, pears, and cider; hops and vegetables; Hereford cattle; carpets, porcelain, some chemicals and engineering
population 636 400
famous people Samuel Butler (*Hudibras*), Sir Edward Elgar, A E Houseman, William Langland, John Masefield□

Herero nomadic Bantu-speaking people living in Namibia, SW Africa□

heresy doctrine opposed to orthodox belief, especially in religion. Those holding ideas considered heretical by the Anglican◊ Church include Gnostics, Arians, Pelagians, Montanists, Albigenses, Waldenses, Lollards, Anabaptists, and Unitarians. Among modern dissidents in the Catholic Church is Hans Kung◊□

Hereward the Wake lived c1070. English leader of a revolt against the Normans in 1070, whose stronghold in the Isle of Ely was captured by William the Conqueror in 1071. Hereward escaped, but his fate is obscure□

hermaphrodite condition in which an organism has both ovaries and sperm-producing organs; pseudo-hermaphrodites have the internal organs of one sex, but the external appearance of the other. Rare in humans, hermaphroditism can be the norm in other species, e.g. the snail and oyster, and is standard in flowering plants□

Hermaphroditus in Greek mythology, the son of Hermes and Aphrodite◊, he was loved by a nymph who prayed for eternal union with him, so that they became one body with dual sexual characteristics, hence the term hermaphrodite◊□

Hermes in Greek mythology, a god, son of Zeus◊ and Maia◊, and messenger of the gods; he has winged sandals and a staff around which serpents coil. Identified with the Roman Mercury and ancient Egyptian Thoth, he protected thieves, travellers, and merchants□

Hermes Trismegistus supposed author of the *Hermetica* 2–3rd century AD, advocating a cosmic religion in which the sun is the visible manifestation of God; they possibly contain some ancient Egyptian material□

hermit religious votary living in seclusion, often practising extremes of mortification, e.g. Simeon◊ Stylites; modern hermits, e.g. the Anglican community at Bede house, Kent, have bungalow 'cells'□

hermit crab a type of crab◊□

Hermon snow-topped mountain (Arabic *Jebel esh-Sheikh,* 2814 m/9232 ft), on the Syria/Lebanon border. According to tradition, Jesus was transfigured here□

Herne Bay seaside resort in Kent, England; population 26 000□

hernia or ***rupture*** protrusion of part of an internal organ through a weakness in the surrounding muscular wall□

Hero and **Leander** in Greek mythology, a pair of lovers. Hero was a priestess of Aphrodite at Sestos on the Hellespont◊, in love with Leander on the opposite shore at Abydos. When he was drowned while swimming across during a storm, she threw herself into the sea□

Hero of Alexandria 2nd century BC. Greek mathematician who invented a stationary steam-engine□

Herod the Great 74–4BC. King of Judaea under the Romans from 40BC, who with the aid of Mark Antony made Jerusalem his capital in 37. He rebuilt the Temple, but was suspect for his Hellenizing tendencies. He established in his last years a reign of terror which culminated in the murder of the infants of Bethlehem to ensure the death of Christ, whom he thought of as an earthly rival. He was the father of Herod◊ Antipas. See also Herod Agrippa I and II□

Herod Agrippa I d. 44AD. Grandson of Herod◊ the Great, he was made tetrarch of Palestine by Caligula◊, and king by Claudius◊. He put St James to death and imprisoned St Peter□

Herod Agrippa II d. 100AD. King of Chalcis (now S Lebanon), son of Herod Agrippa I. He helped Titus◊ take Jerusalem in 70AD, then went to Rome where he died. In 60AD he tried St Paul◊□

Herod Antipas 21BC–39AD. Governor (tetrarch) of Galilee 4BC–9AD, son of Herod the Great. He divorced his wife to marry his niece Herodias, and the latter got her daughter Salome to ask for St John◊'s head when he reproved Herod's action. Jesus Christ was sent to him (as a Galilean) by Pontius Pilate, but he returned Christ without giving any verdict. In 38AD he went to Rome to try to get Caligula to make him 'king,' but was banished for his pains. Remains of one of his royal palaces were excavated at Masada 1963–4□

Herodotus c484–c424BC. Greek historian, the first to apply a critical sense, as in his study of the Graeco–Persian wars, and the preceding history of both states. He was widely travelled□

heroin a drug derived from opium◊□

heron bird, family Ardeidae, order Ciconiiformes (see stork◊). The widely distributed ***grey heron*** *Ardea cinerea* forms colonies of nests in trees. Included in the same family are the egrets, the ***great white egret*** *Egretta alba* which has snowy-white plumes formerly used as hat decorations, and smaller ***cattle egret*** *Aroleola ibis* which rids the cattle of pests. See also bittern◊□

herpes group of viruses, including *Herpes simplex* (type 1), which causes ***fever blisters*** or ***cold sores***; the virus remains within the body (in nerve ganglia at the base of the spine) and is triggered by sunburn, stress, etc. Serious outbreaks of sores on the genitals are caused by *Herpes simplex* (type 2), and the only effective drug, acyclovir (ACV), has side-effects. Also caused by herpes viruses are ***chicken pox*** or ***varicella*** marked by fever, small blisters and a rash (there is a vaccine); ***shingles*** (caused by a reactivation of the chicken pox virus, *Herpes zoster*), and marked by blisters at nerve endings, sometimes over the ribs in a 'girdle'; and ***glandular fever*** or ***infectious mononucleosis*** (feverish sore throat, painful lymph nodes, and changes in the blood). Encephalitis◊ may also be caused by a herpes virus□

Herrera two Spanish artists:

Francisco de Herrera, the Elder 1576–1656 born in Seville. A master of chiaroscuro, he may have taught Velasquez.

Francisco de Herrera, the Younger 1622–85 son of the elder Herrera, from whose bad temper he fled. He was remarkable for still lifes□

Herrick Robert 1591–1674. English poet and cleric, the friend of Ben Jonson, and excelling in the lyric, e.g. 'Gather ye rosebuds', and 'Cherry Ripe'□

herring marine family of fish, Clupeidae, order Clupeiformes, which include the ***common herring*** *Clupea harengus*, formerly abundant, but now needing conservation due to excess fishing by man (the young are eaten as ***whitebait***); ***alewife*** *Pandopus pseudoharengus*, a small N American edible coastal species (also in the Great Lakes), 30 cm/ 10 in, of commercial value; ***shad*** a genus *Alosa* of both sides of the Atlantic; ***pilchard*** *Sardina pilchardus*, of which the young is the only legally recognized sardine, though other small herring-like fish (almost indistinguishable in taste) are sold as sild, brisling (alias the ***sprat*** *Clupea sprattus*) etc.; ***anchovy*** *Engraulis encrasicholus,* of the Mediterranean, richly flavoured. See also tarpon◊□

Herriot Édouard 1872–1957. French Radical Prime Minister 1924–5, 1926, and 1932. As an opponent of Vichy, he was imprisoned by the Germans 1943–5□

Herriot James. Pseudonym of British writer James Alfred Wright 1916– . A veterinary surgeon in Thirsk, Yorkshire from 1940, he wrote of his experiences in *If Only They Could Talk* 1970 etc.□

Herschel Sir John Frederick William 1792–1871. British astronomer, son of Sir William Herschel. He established an observatory near Capetown in 1834, where he discovered thousands of binary stars◊, and nebulae◊. He used photography in his work, inventing sensitized photographic paper, and the use of sodium hyposulphite for fixing□

Herschel Sir William 1738–1822. British astronomer, born in Hanover, who discovered Uranus in 1781, and several of its satellites; astronomer to George III from in 1782, he discovered the motion of the double stars round one another, 1783, and infra-red solar rays in 1800□

Herstmonceux see East◊ Sussex□
Hertford administrative headquarters of Hertfordshire, England; population 22 000□
Hertfordshire county of southern England

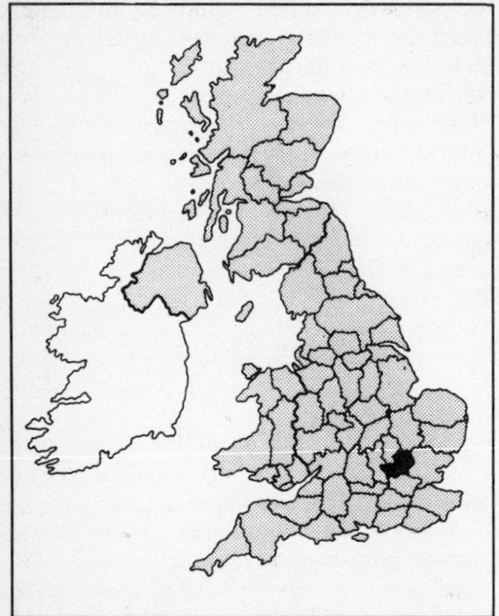

area 1634 sq km/631 sq mi
towns administrative headquarters Hertford; St Albans, Watford, Hatfield, Hemel Hempstead, Bishop's Stortford, Letchworth (the first garden city◊, followed by Welwyn in 1919, and Stevenage in 1947)
features rivers Lea, Stort, Colne; part of the Chiltern Hills; Hatfield House (see Elizabeth I◊); Knebworth House (see Lord Lytton◊); Brocket Hall (home of Palmerston and Melbourne); home of G B Shaw at Ayot St Lawrence; Berkhamsted Castle (Norman); Rothamsted agricultural experimental station
products engineering, aircraft, electrical goods, paper and printing; general agricultural
population 960 500
famous people Graham Greene born at Berkhamsted□
Hertogenbosch see 's Hertogenbosch◊□
hertz derived SI unit (Hz) of frequency (the number of repetitions of a regular occurrence in one second), named after Heinrich Hertz◊□
Hertz Heinrich 1857–94. German physicist, who confirmed the electromagnetic theory of Maxwell◊ by generating waves electrically and showing that they had the light-like properties predicted by him□
Hertzog James Barry Munnik 1866–1942. South African statesman, founder of the Nationalist party in 1913, and opponent of participation in both World Wars; he was Prime Minister from 1924 till his resignation in 1939□
Herzl Theodor 1860–1904. Austrian journalist, founder of political Zionism by his book *The Jewish State* 1896□
Heseltine Michael 1933– . British Conservative politician. Secretary of State for the Environment 1979–83, he succeeded John Nott as Minister for Defence in Jan 1983 but resigned in Jan 1986 over the Westland◊ affair□
Hesiod c700BC. Greek poet, born in Boeotia. His *Works and Days* deals with agriculture, *Theogony* with the origin of the world and the gods□
Hesperides mythical Greek maidens who guarded a tree bearing golden apples in the Islands of the Blessed□
Hess Dame Myra 1890–1965. British pianist, interpreter of Beethoven, and transcriber of the Bach chorale 'Jesu, Joy of Man's Desiring'□
Hess Victor 1883–1964. Austrian physicist, who shared a Nobel prize in 1936 for his discovery of cosmic radiation□
Hess Walter Richard Rudolf 1894– . German Nazi leader, Hitler's deputy from 1932, he headed the *Ausland* organization (fifth-column activities abroad), and on 10 May 1941 flew to Britain with compromise peace proposals. He was sentenced at Nuremberg◊ to life imprisonment (see Spandau◊)□
Hesse Hermann 1877–1962. German writer, Swiss citizen since 1923. His later works, e.g. *Das Glasperlenspiel* 1943, tend to the occult; Nobel prize in 1946□
Hessen administrative region (German *Land*) of W Germany
area 21 125 sq km/8156 sq mi
capital Wiesbaden
towns Frankfurt am Main, Darmstadt, Kassel
features valleys of the Rhine and Main; Taunus mountains, rich in mineral springs, as at Homburg and Wiesbaden; see also Swabia◊
products wine, timber; chemicals, cars, electrical engineering
population 5 602 925
religion Protestantism 61%, Roman Catholicism 33%□
Hestia in Greek mythology, the goddess (Roman Vesta) of the hearth, daughter of Chronos◊ (Roman Saturn) and Rhea◊□
Heteroptera a sub-division of the order Hemiptera◊□
Hewish Antony 1924– . British radioastronomer, awarded a Nobel physics prize (with Martin Ryle◊) in 1974, for work leading to the discovery of pulsars◊□
hexachlorophene bactericide, used in minute quantities in soaps and surgical disinfectants, and in herbicides. An error in its

preparation can lead to release of a highly toxic by-product, causing chloracne and deformed births, as at Seveso, Lombardy, Italy, in 1976□

Heydrich Reinhard 1904–42. German Nazi, deputy 'protector' of Bohemia and Moravia from 1941, whose assassination led to reprisals including the massacre of the population of Lidice□

Heyerdahl Thor 1914– . Norwegian ethnologist. In 1947 he sailed on the raft Kon-Tiki from Peru to the Tuamotu◊ Islands along the Humboldt◊ Current, proving that Polynesians could have been migrants from S America; and in 1969–70 used ancient-Egyptian-style papyrus-reed boats to cross the Atlantic, so possibly explaining the presence in the New World of a sun-orientated pyramid◊ culture□

Heywood Thomas c1570–c1650. English actor-dramatist, author or adapter of over 200 plays including the domestic tragedy *A Woman Kilde with Kindnesse* 1607□

Hezekiah in the Old Testament, king of Judah 715–687. Against the advice of Isaiah◊ he allied with Egypt in revolt against Assyria, and was defeated by Sennacherib□

Hiawatha 16th century North American Indian teacher and Onondaga chieftain, who welded the Six Nations of the Iroquois◊ into the league of the Long House. Longfellow's epic *Hiawatha* 1855 was based on the data collected by Henry R Schoolcraft 1793–1864□

hibernation storage of energy by dormancy in winter (badger, dormouse, hedgehog, etc.) when food is short and temperatures low; it is triggered by a build-up in the body of special chemicals which slow down metabolism up to 99% and body temperature from 37°C to 4.5°. Some animals, e.g. some bats and birds, temporarily 'hibernate' nightly year-round to counter low night temperatures; deciduous trees shed their leaves for similar reasons. A comparable reaction is ***aestivation*** when animals go into a dormant condition in summer under drought conditions, e.g. lungfish◊□

hibiscus genus of tropical plants with bright bell-shaped flowers, family Malvaceae, e.g. ***rose mallow or tree hollyhock*** *H syriacus* and ***okra*** or ***gumbo*** *H esculentus*, grown in Africa for its edible gummy pods, used unripe in soup, or eaten fresh, etc.□

hiccup sharp noise caused by a sudden spasm of the diaphragm with closing of the windpipe, commonly due to digestive disorder, etc. One remedy for ordinary hiccups is to cause a feeling of suffocation by breathing into a paper bag□

Hickey William 1749–1830? British lawyer of dissipated life, who eventually made good at the Indian bar, and whose *Memoirs* give a racy account of his age□

Hickok James Butler 'Wild Bill' 1837–76. American sharpshooter and scout for the Union army, and afterwards a marshal in Kansas, killing many desperadoes□

hickory genus *Carya* of N American trees, family Juglandaceae, including ***pecan*** *C illinoensis* with fruit resembling a smoothly ovate walnut; and ***shagbark*** *C ovata*□

hieroglyphic

CLEOPATRA

K L E O P A T R A **10** feminine ending
1 2 3 4 5 6 7 8 9

1 2 3 4 5 6 7 8 9 10 11

11 determinative following a name

hieroglyphic Egyptian writing system mid 4th millennium BC–3rd century AD, which combined picture signs with those indicating letters. It was deciphered (in 1922 by J F Champollion◊) with the aid of the ***Rosetta Stone*** of 197BC, which was found by one of Napoleon's officers at the Delta town of Rosetta (modern Rashid), but later fell into British hands and was placed in the British Museum in 1802. The stone has the same inscription carved in hieroglyphic, demotic, and Greek. Demotic is a cursive script (for quick writing) derived from Egyptian hieratic, which in turn is a more easily written form of hieroglyphic□

hi-fi 'high fidelity' reproduction of the complete audio range of the original signal of sounds (music, speech, etc.) via radio, disc, or tape cassette, with two speakers for stereophonic effect, and four for the full quadrophonic, all-round, in-depth effect□

Higgins Jack see Harry Patterson◊□

high commissioner representative of one independent Commonwealth country in the capital of another; they rank with ambassadors□

High Country mountainous land above c1000 m/3000 ft in South Island, New Zealand. Lakes provide hydroelectric power, and it is a paradise for the skier, mountaineer, and tourist□

Highland Region administrative region of Scotland

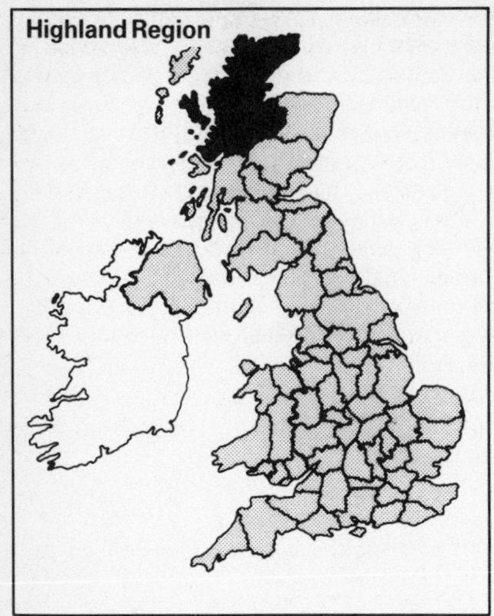

area 25 141 sq km/9704 sq mi
towns administrative headquarters Inverness; Thurso, Wick
features comprises almost half the country; Grampian Mountains◊; Loch Ness, Caledonian Canal; Inner Hebrides; Queen Mother's castle of Mey at Caithness; John O'Groats's House; Dounreay (with Atomic Energy Authority's prototype fast reactor, a nuclear processing plant, and a controversial planned larger processing plant to serve both Britain and Europe)
products provision of winter sports, grouse and deer shooting and salmon fishing
population 192 000 □

Highlands general name for the plateau of broken rock which covers almost all Scotland, and extends south of the Highland region itself□

Highsmith Patricia 1921– . American crime novelist, e.g. *Strangers on a Train* 1950, filmed by Hitchcock; and the series dealing with the amoral Tom Ripley□

highwaymen thieves on horseback, notorious in the 17–18th centuries for holding up the new regular coach services passing through Hounslow and Bagshot Heaths, Epping Forest, etc. They included Jonathan Wild◊, Claude Duval◊, Dick Turpin◊□

High Wycombe market town in Buckinghamshire, England, famous for furniture; population 60 510.
In 1982 nearby Daws Hill was named as the alternative contingency headquarters for the US European Command (Eucom). See Stuttgart◊□

hijacking a form of piracy◊□

Hildebrand former name of Gregory◊ VII□

Hildesheim industrial town in Lower Saxony, W Germany; population 102 400□

Hill Sir Rowland 1795–1879. British post office official who invented adhesive stamps, and prompted the introduction of the penny pre-paid post in 1840 (previously the recipient paid, according to distance, on receipt)□

Hillary Sir Edmund 1919– . New Zealand mountaineer, born in Auckland. In 1953, with Norgay Tenzing◊, he conquered Everest◊, and in 1958 was the first man to reach the South Pole overland since Scott, in the course of laying depots for Fuchs's continental crossing□

Hiller Dame Wendy 1912– . British actress, e.g. Sally Hardcastle in *Love on the Dole* 1935, and Eliza in the film *Pygmalion* 1938□

hill figures figures, usually of animals, cut from downland turf to show the underlying chalk, e.g. the White Horse on Bratton Hill, Wiltshire, said to commemorate Alfred the Great's victory over the Danes at Ethandun in 878; and the White Horse at Uffington, Berkshire, 110 m/360 ft long, and probably a tribal 'totem' of the Early Iron Age, 1st century BC. One of the rarer human figures is the Long Man of Wilmington, E Sussex◊□

hillfort European Iron Age site with massive banks and ditches for defence, used not only as a military camp, but as a permanent settlement. There are evidences of cannibalism◊. One of the most striking is Maiden Castle◊□

Hilliard Nicholas c1547–1619. English miniaturist, born at Exeter, and also goldsmith to Elizabeth I□

Hillingdon borough of W Greater London
features London Airport at Heathrow (built on the site of a Neolithic settlement); Jacobean mansion (Swakeleys) at Ickenham; Brunel◊ University (technical); Grand Union Canal; including ***Uxbridge***
population 288 710□

Hilton James 1900–54. British novelist, born in Lancashire. His books include *Lost Horizon* 1933, and *Goodbye, Mr Chips* 1934, the story of a schoolmaster□

Hilversum town in central Netherlands, chief centre of Dutch broadcasting; population 90 900□

Himachal Pradesh NW state of India
area 55 673 sq km/000 00 sq mi
capital Simla
features mainly agricultural state, a third forested, with softwood timber industry
population 4 237 600, chiefly Hindu
language Pahari□

Himalayas central Asian mountain system covering part of Tibet and the small states of Bhutan, Nepal, and Sikkim. The two highest peaks are:

Mount Everest (Nepalese name *Sagarmatha* 'Head of the Earth'; the English name comes from Sir George Everest 1790–1866, Surveyor-General of India), the world's highest mountain, on the China/Nepal frontier; height 8848 m/29 028 ft. First climbed by Edmund Hillary◊ and Norgay Tenzing◊ in 1953; see also Lord Hunt and Eric Shipton◊.
Kangchenjunga third highest in the world, on the Nepal/Sikkim border; height 8597 m/28 208 ft; first climbed by a British expedition in 1955.
Other major peaks include Makalu, Annapurna, and Nanga Parbat, all over 8000 m/26 000 ft□

Himmler, Heinrich 1900–45. German Nazi, reorganizer of the SS (see Nazi◊ Party) and from 1936 commanding all the German police forces, including the Gestapo◊. Captured in 1945, he committed suicide□

Hinckley market town (engineering, footwear, hosiery) in Leicestershire, England; population 49 000□

Hindemith Paul 1895–1963. German composer, banned by the Nazis for the modernity of his *Philharmonic Concerto* etc. Later works include the opera *Mathis der Maler* 1938□

Hindenburg Paul Ludwig Hans von Beneckendorf und von Hindenburgh 1847–1934. German field marshal and statesman. In command of E Prussia from Aug 1914, he was credited with the defeat of the Russians at Tannenberg, and with Ludendorff directed German policy in World War I. He was elected president of the German Republic in 1925 (re-elected in 1932), and was compelled to invite Hitler to assume the chancellorship in Jan 1933□

Hindenburg Line German western line of fortifications built 1916–17□

Hindi official language◊ of the Republic of India, ultimately derived from Sanskrit◊, and closely related to Urdu◊. ***Hindustani*** is the popular lingua franca derived from these two languages, which is spoken throughout India□

Hinduism religion of the Hindus, which has a triad of three chief gods (the Trimurti):
Brahma the Supreme Spirit, or *Atman*, who works creatively, as one of the triad, and (personified as Isvara) brought into being the cosmos which is both real and an illusion (*'maya'*), since its reality is not lasting; the cosmos is itself personified as the goddess Maya.
Vishnu the preserver, who is thought to have taken various human forms including ***Krishna*** (hero of the epic *Mahabharata*◊, the guise in which he receives most popular adoration) and ***Rama*** (see *Ramayana*◊). As ***Jagganath*** 'Lord of the World' he has a famous temple at Puri◊.
Siva/Shiva the destroyer and the generator (symbolized by the phallus or lingam◊) of new life, and often sculptured as Nataraja, Lord of the Dance, in his cosmic creative character. The female principle, Sakti (symbolized by the female genitalia or *yoni*) is important in the worship of Siva, whose consort may be known, according to aspect, as ***Durga*** (goddess of war), or ***Kali*** (goddess of death and destruction: black, with four arms, fangs, and a skull necklace); the ***Thugs,*** a sect suppressed c1830, sacrificed travellers to Kali by strangling them, also appropriating their belongings.
There are numerous lesser divinities (see Ganesa◊, Hanuman◊, Lakshmi◊, Surya◊), demons, ghosts, and spirits, etc, who are also reverenced. See also mantra◊ and Manu◊.
Important tenets are the transmigration◊ of souls and karma◊; Varanesi◊ (*Benares*) is the chief holy city; the Ganges◊ the holiest river; the priests constitute the highest (Brahmin) caste◊.
The ***Veda*** (Sanskrit 'divine knowledge') comprises four main collections of scriptures, the earliest dating from 2000 BC: Rigveda (hymns and praises); Yajurveda (prayers and sacrificial formulae); Sâmaveda (tunes and chants); and Atharvaveda, or Veda of the Atharvans, the officiating priests at sacrifices. Not counted with these are the ***Puranas,*** 8th-century AD Sanskrit poems dealing with the gods and heroes. The ***Upanishads*** c400BC are spiritual prose and verse commentaries on the Veda.
Jainism is an offshoot, its sacred books recording the teaching of Mahavira 599–527BC the latest of many seers. Its outstanding tenet is that no living being should be injured, e.g. even the mouth being veiled by extremists to prevent the accidental swallowing of a fly. There is no deity, but a belief in karma◊, and, like Buddhism◊, Jainism is a monastic religion. The two main sects are the Digambaras (originally practising complete nudity) and the Swetambaras□

Hindu Kush mountain range in central Asia; length 800 km/500 mi; greatest height Tirich Mir 7690 m/25230 ft, Pakistan. The ***Khyber Pass***, a narrow defile (53 km/33 mi long), separates Pakistan from Afghanistan, and was used by Baber and other invaders of India. The present road was built by the British in the Afghan Wars□

Hindustani see Hindi◊□

Hipparchus 2nd century BC. Greek astronomer, father of trigonometry. He calculated the length of the solar year and lunar month; discovered the precession of the equinoxes; and catalogued 800 fixed stars. See astronometry◊□

Hippocrates c460–c377BC. Greek physician, who was born and practised on the island of Cos. He published medical books and discovered aspirin◊ in willow bark. The ***Hippocratic Oath*** embodies the essence of medical ethics□

Hippolytus in Greek mythology, the son of Theseus◊, who cursed him for his supposed dishonourable advances to his stepmother Phaedra. Killed by Poseidon◊ as he rode near the sea in his chariot, he was restored to life when his innocence was proved□

hippopotamus mammal (Greek 'river horse'), family Hippopotamidae; good swimmers, they leave the water to graze at night. The ***common hippopotamus*** *Hippopotamus amphibius* of central Africa is slate-grey, with an 'armour-plated' skin; c4 m/13 ft long, 1.2 m/4 ft high, and weighs 3–4 tonnes; the ***pygmy hippopotamus*** *H liberiensis* is found in W Africa□

hire purchase system of retail trading under which the buyer makes instalment payments at fixed intervals over a certain period for a particular item. It has been largely superseded by bank credit cards, 'budget accounts' offered by shops, etc.□

Hirohito 1901– . Emperor of Japan from 1926. After Japan's defeat in 1945, he formally rejected belief in the divinity of the emperor and accepted curtailed powers under the 1946 constitution□

Hiroshige Ando 1797–1858. Japanese artist, whose landscape colour prints influenced the Impressionists, e.g. Whistler◊□

Hiroshima industrial city (Mazda cars) and port on Honshu, Japan; population 1 000 000. In World War II the first atom bomb was dropped here on 6 Aug 1945; c10 sq km/4 sq mi was obliterated, and 136 989 died out of a population of 343 000, 78 150 initially, the rest later. There is a Peace Memorial Park with tragic sculptures and a museum of atomic relics here□

Hispanics Spanish-speakers within the USA, whether native-born or immigrant from Cuba, Mexico, Puerto Rico, Spain, etc.□

Hispaniola W Indian island, first landing place of Columbus in the New World, 6 Dec 1492; now divided into Haiti◊ and the Dominican Republic◊□

Hiss Alger 1904– . US politician, controversially imprisoned in 1950 for perjury. Hiss, one of President Roosevelt's advisors at the 1945 Yalta◊ conference, was accused in 1948 by a former Soviet agent of having passed information to the Soviet Union during the period 1926–37. He was convicted of perjury for swearing before the Committee on Un-American Activities that he had not spied for the Soviet Union. Doubts about the justice of his conviction have increased since Watergate◊, for Richard Nixon◊ was a leading member of the prosecution□

histamine amine which dilates blood vessels, stimulates gastric secretions, etc., and is formed at the site of injury or allergic reaction (see hay◊ fever), travel sickness, etc. Drugs to neutralize these effects are antihistamines□

Hitachi industrial city (electrical goods) on Honshu, Japan; population 204 000□

Hitchcock Alfred 1899–1980. British-American film director, naturalized American in 1955, honorary knighthood in 1980. Noted for creating suspense in his mystery films, his camera work, and his hallmark of making 'walk-ons' in his own films: *The Thirty-Nine Steps* 1935, *The Lady Vanishes* 1939, *Rebecca* 1940, *Strangers on a Train* 1951, *Psycho* 1960, *The Birds* 1963□

Hitchens Ivon 1893–1979. British painter of abstracts, landscapes, and murals e.g. *Day's Rest, Day's Work* 1963, Sussex University□

Hitchin market town in Hertfordshire, noted for lavender products; population 30 000□

Hitler Adolf 1889–1945. German dictator, born at Braunau-am-Inn, Austria. He served in World War I, founded the Nazi◊ Party in 1921, and after a failed rising in 1923 (Munich Putsch), spent nine months in prison, writing *Mein Kampf* ('My Struggle'). Supported by the industrialists from 1930, Hitler became chancellor in 1933, and succeeded Hindenburg◊ as Head of State (with the title of *Führer*) in 1934. In 1936 he occupied the Rhineland; 1937 allied himself with Mussolini; 1938 annexed Austria and secured the Sudetenland (under the Munich Agreement); 1939 annexed the rest of Czechoslovakia in Mar, signed a non-aggression pact with Russia in Aug, and invaded Poland (with resultant declaration of war by Britain and France) in Sept. See World◊ War II. Hitler narrowly escaped assassination in 1944 in a bomb plot by high-ranking officers (see von Stauffenberg◊) and on 29 Apr 1945 married Eva Braun and committed suicide with her in a Berlin bunker as the Russians took the city. See Fascism◊, Jews◊, Nazi Party◊□

Hittites people of mixed origin who lived in the area of modern Turkey and N Syria; capital Hattusas (modern Boghazköy) in central Turkey), where tablet archives have been recovered. A great military power c1400–1200BC, they waged war against Egypt. The empire was destroyed by the Sea◊ Peoples, the chief of the surviving city states being Carchemish◊ in N Syria. Their language was Indo-European, and written in a cuneiform◊ script□

hoatzin a S American bird. See under fowl◊□

Hoban James c1762–1831. Irish-born architect of the White House, USA, who also worked on the Capitol and other public buildings□

Hobart capital and port of Tasmania, Australia; population 170 900. Founded in 1804, it was named after Lord Hobart, then Secretary of State for the Colonies, and has the University of Tasmania, established 1890□

Hobbema Meindert 1638–1709. Dutch landscape artist, e.g. *Avenue at Middelharnis*□

Hobbes Thomas 1588–1679. English political philosopher, tutor to the exiled Prince Charles 1646–8 (see Charles◊ II), and advocate of absolutist government, e.g. *Leviathan* 1651, whether by a king or Cromwellian dictator. See Scholasticism◊□

Hoboken city and port in New Jersey, USA; population 42 460□

Hochhuth Rolf 1933– . Swiss dramatist, whose controversial *Soldiers* 1968 implied that Churchill was involved in a plot to assassinate Sikorski◊□

Ho Chi Minh 1892–1969. N Vietnamese statesman. He headed the Communist Vietminh from 1941, campaigned against the French colonial rulers 1946–54, and became president of the Democratic Republic at the armistice□

Ho Chi Minh City chief port (formerly Saigon) and industrial city (shipbuilding, textiles, rubber) of southern Vietnam; population 3 500 000. Saigon was the capital of the Republic of Vietnam (S Vietnam) 1954–76, when it was renamed. It has a flourishing black capitalist economy, denounced as a bad example to the country by the government□

Ho Chi Minh Trails N Vietnamese troop and supply routes to S Vietnam via Laos, especially during the Vietnam◊ War□

hockey game played with a ball and hooked sticks in ancient Greece, and as 'hurley' and 'shinty' in Ireland and Scotland: modern hockey rules were drafted in 1886. There are two teams of eleven, and players try to send the ball into goals at either end of the ground□

Hockney David 1937– . British artist, born in Bradford. His work has a bright, childlike sense of colour, and he excels in the representation of water□

Hodgkin Sir Alan Lloyd 1914– . British physiologist who, with A F Huxley, researched the mechanism of conduction in peripheral nerves 1946–60, and in 1963 shared with Sir John Eccles◊ a Nobel prize; Order of Merit in 1973□

hockey

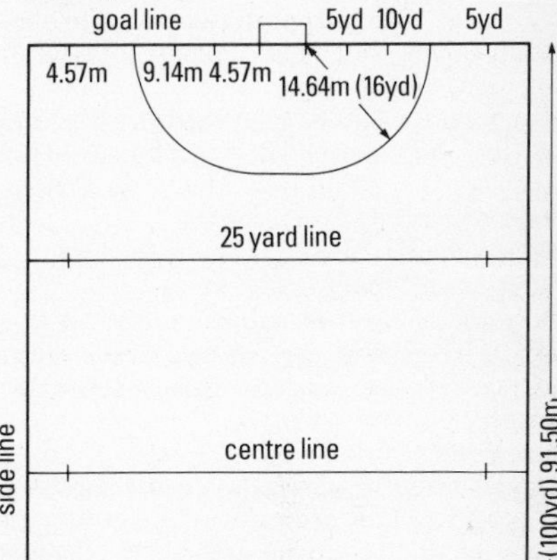

Hodgkin Dorothy Crowfoot 1910– . British chemist, Nobel prizewinner in 1964 for work on the structure of biochemical compounds such as vitamin B12, a liver extract used against pernicious anaemia, and penicillin. Order of Merit in 1965□

Hodgkin Thomas 1798–1856. British physician, who first recognized ***Hodgkin's disease*** (lymphadenoma), a cancerous enlargement of the lymphatic glands□

Hofei see Hefei◊□

Hoffa James Riddle 1913–75. American president of the International Brotherhood of Teamsters (truckdrivers), jailed 1964–71 for attempted bribery of a Federal Court Jury after he was charged with corruption. In 1975 he disappeared, believed disposed of in a paper-shredder by the Mafia◊□

Hoffman Dustin 1937– . American actor whose films include *The Graduate* 1967, *Midnight Cowboy* 1969, and *Kramer vs Kramer* 1979 (academy award)□

Hoffmann Ernst Theodor Amadeus 1776–1822. German composer (eg opera *Undine*

1816) and writer, whose *Fantastic Tales* inspired Offenbach's *Tales of Hoffman*□

Hogarth William 1697–1764. British artist and engraver. Born in London, he established his fame with series of paintings on a theme, e.g. *A Harlot's Progress* 1731, *A Rake's Progress* 1735, and his masterpiece *Marriage à la Mode* 1745. His portraits are sympathetically direct, with an informality not appealing to his time□

Hogg James 1770–1835. Scottish poet, the 'Ettrick Shepherd'. Illiterate till he was 30, he wrote verse, and the powerful novel *Confessions of a Justified Sinner* 1824□

Hogg Quintin. See Lord Hailsham◊□

Hoggar see Ahaggar◊□

Hogmanay Scottish name for the last day of the year; also the oatmeal cakes given to child carol singers going house to house□

hogweed genus of plants *Heracleum*, family Umbelliferae, of which the ***giant hogweed*** *H mantegazzianum* grows over 3 m/9 ft; skin exposed to the sap in sunlight develops a rash□

Hohenlinden Battle of, 1800. See under Revolutionary◊ Wars□

Hohenstaufen German princely family, including many Holy Roman Emperors 1138–1208, e.g. Conrad III, Frederick I, Henry VI, and Frederick II◊□

Hohenzollern German family, originating in Württemberg, which held the titles of elector of Brandenburg from 1415, king of Prussia from 1701, and German emperor from 1871. The last emperor, William◊ II, was dethroned in 1918□

Hohhot industrial city (textiles) and capital (formerly Huhehot) of Inner Mongolia (*Nei Monggol*) autonomous region, China; population 500 000. There are Lamaist monasteries and temples here□

Hokkaido most northerly of the four main islands of Japan; capital Sapporo. Snow-covered for six months of the year, it was developed only from 1868 when disbanded Samurai were settled here, and has been intensively exploited (coal, mercury, manganese, oil and natural gas, timber, and fisheries) since World War II. See Ainu◊□

Hokusai 1760–1849. Japanese print and water-colour artist, born at Yedo. His most famous work is *The Wave*, which towers over a tiny boat□

Holbein two German artists:

Hans, the Elder c1460–1524 born at Augsburg. His masterpiece is the altarpiece of St Sebastian 1515 (Munich Pinakothek).

Hans, the Younger 1497–1543 son and pupil of the Elder, and friend of Erasmus, he was born at Augsburg. In England from 1527, he was court painter to Henry VIII from 1536 till his death from plague. His works include the wood engravings *The Dance of Death*, the *Meyer Madonna* at Darmstadt, and portraits of Erasmus, Sir Thomas More, and Christina, Duchess of Milan, who escaped being one of Henry's wives. His painting of small portraits on playing cards began the English vogue for the miniature□

Holborne Anthony d. 1602. English composer. His book of *Pauans, Galliards, Almains and Other Short Aeirs* 1599, includes 'The Fairie Round', which was among the pieces on the LP record sent into space aboard *Voyagers I* and *II* in 1977. See under space◊ research□

Holden Edith 1871–1920. British artist-naturalist, born in Birmingham. Her journal, illustrated with her water colours, was published in 1977 as *The Country Diary of an Edwardian Lady*. She drowned in the Thames, near Kew Gardens, having overbalanced when reaching for a specimen□

Holford William, Baron Holford 1907–75. British architect and town planner, including St Paul's Cathedral Precinct□

Holinshed Ralph c1520–c1580. English author of *Chronicles of England, Scotland and Ireland* 1578, used by Shakespeare in his history plays□

holism philosophically, the concept that the whole is greater than the sum of its parts, but in the 1980s specifically the idea that human well-being, physical and mental, is inextricably mingled, e.g. a prescribed drug is not enough to cure an illness, etc. The British Holistic Medicine Association was established in 1983□

Holland Henry Richard Vassall Fox, 3rd Baron Holland 1773–1840. British Whig politician, whose home at Holland House, Kensington◊ was the centre of Whig political and literary society□

Holland North and South. Two provinces of the Netherlands, with their capitals at Haarlem and The Hague, respectively. As the wealthiest area of the Netherlands, the name became frequently used for the whole country – even by Dutchmen□

Hollar Wenceslaus 1607–77. Bohemian engraver, who worked for many years in England, and produced views of London before the Great Fire□

Holliday Billie. Stage-name of American jazz singer Eleanor Gough McKay 1915–59, also known as 'Lady Day'. She died as a result of drug addiction□

Hollis Sir Roger. Head of MI5 1956–65. See under Kim Philby◊□

holly trees and shrubs of genus *Ilex,* family Aquifoliaceae, including the ***English Christmas holly*** *I aquifolium,* an evergreen with spiny, glossy leaves, small white flowers, and poisonous scarlet berries on the female tree, and ***brazilian holly*** *I paraguayensis*, from the leaves of which ***yerba maté***, or ***Jesuits' tea***, is made□

Holly Buddy 1936–1959. American rock and roll singer and composer. Born in Lubbock, Texas, his hallmark was dark hornrim glasses, and his songs include 'That'll be the Day', 'Peggy Sue', and 'Maybe Baby'. He died in a plane crash□

hollyhock Asian perennial plant *Althaea rosea* with large showy flowers borne on a spike, family Malvaceae, a cottage garden plant from the 17th century□

Hollywood see under Los◊ Angeles□

Holmes Oliver Wendell 1809–94. American essayist, and professor of anatomy. With Lowell◊, he founded the *Atlantic Monthly* in which the series published as *The Autocrat of the Breakfast-Table* 1858, first appeared□

holmium element
symbol Ho
atomic number 67
physical description silvery metal
features one of the lanthanide◊ series
uses in electronic devices, but mainly in laboratory research□

holocaust wholesale destruction, literally by fire, but applied today especially to the annihilation of c6 000 000 Jews by the Hitler régime 1933–45 at the concentration camps of Auschwitz, Belsen, Buchenwald, Dachau, and Maidanek□

holography technique of reconstructing a three-dimensional image (hologram) from the reflected waves of a source of single frequency, which operates equally well in sound or light. Used to 'see', in 3D, inside awkward places e.g. human internal tubing, sewage and water pipes (for cracks), and into large manufacturing apparatus without the need to dismantle it. Special holograms, 'holographic optical elements'(HOEs), may also be used as replacements for mirrors and lenses in scientific instruments; at supermarket check-outs to read the bar codes on goods; or to provide the 'head-up' displays which enable a pilot to read his instruments without looking away from his windscreen. One potential is to make three-dimensional holograms of actors (by filming them), then use laser light to put on large-cast productions. See bat◊, Dennis Gabor◊, laser◊□

Holst Gustav Theodore 1874–1934. British composer, born at Cheltenham, of Swedish descent. His works include the opera *Sāvitri* 1908, the choral 'The Hymn of Jesus' 1917, and the orchestral 'Egdon Heath', 1927 and suite 'The Planets' 1917□

Holt Harold Edward 1908–67. Australian Liberal Prime Minister 1966–7, when he disappeared in a swimming accident□

Holtby Winifred 1898–1935. British feminist novelist, e.g. *South Riding* 1936, set in her native Yorkshire. See Vera Brittain◊□

Holyhead seaport on Holyhead Island off Anglesey, Wales; population 11 000□

Holy Island or ***Lindisfarne Island*** linked by causeway to Northumberland, England. See St Aidan◊. ***Holyhead◊ Island*** is sometimes called Holy Island□

Holy Land see Palestine◊□

Holy Loch see under Clyde◊□

Holyoake Sir Keith Jacka 1904–83. New Zealand National Party statesman, Prime Minister for two months in 1957, and then 1960–72□

Holy Office tribunal of the Roman Catholic church that deals with ecclesiastical discipline. See Inquisition◊□

holy orders Christian priesthood, as conferred by the 'laying on of hands' by a bishop. The Anglican church has three orders (bishop, priest, and deacon), but the Roman Catholic church includes also sub-deacons, acolytes, exorcists, readers, and doorkeepers. See also Tertiaries□

Holy Roman Empire the empire of Charlemagne◊ and his successors; and the German Empire 962–1806, both regarded as reviving the Roman Empire□

Holyrood House see under Edinburgh◊□

Holy Shroud ancient piece of linen bearing the imprint of a body, claimed to be that of Christ. See Turin◊□

Homburg town and spa in W Germany; population 25 000. Edward VII was a patron, hence the name of the soft felt hat he made fashionable there□

Home Alex Douglas-Home, Baron Home of the Hirsel 1903– . British Conservative statesman. Foreign Secretary 1960–3, when he succeeded Macmillan as Prime Minister, he renounced his peerage (as 14th Earl of Home) to fight (and lose) the general election of 1964; he resigned as party leader in 1965. He was again Foreign Secretary 1970–74, when he received a life peerage. See William Douglas-Home◊□

Home Daniel Dunglas 1833–86. British medium whose demonstrations of levitation were vouched for by Sir William Crookes and others. In 1864 he was expelled from Rome as a sorcerer□

home counties counties close to London: Hertfordshire, Essex, Kent, Surrey, and (formerly) Middlesex□

Home Guard unpaid force of men aged 17–65 formed in 1940 (known May–Jul as Local Defence Volunteers) to repel any German invasion; by 1944 it was two million strong; disbanded 1945. See Home Service Force◊□

Home Office government department established in 1782 to deal with England's internal affairs unless specifically assigned to other departments, and headed by the Home Secretary (who also has certain duties in respect of N Ireland, the Channel Islands, and the Isle of Man). Wales (since 1964) and Scotland have their own Secretaries of State□

homeopathy treatment of illness by the same drugs which would produce similar symptoms in a healthy person, but in small quantities. It was introduced by the German doctor Samuel Hahnemann 1755–1843. See allopathy◊□

Homer c800BC. Greek epic poet, traditionally a blind wandering minstrel. His *Iliad* tells of the siege of Troy◊, and the *Odyssey* of the adventures of Ulysses returning from it, and uses traditional material□

Homer Winslow 1836–1910. American artist, noted for the Civil War *Prisoners from the Front* 1866, and land and seascapes□

Home Rule Irish nationalist slogan 1870–1914 popularized by Isaac Butt◊ and Parnell◊, for the re-establishment of an Irish Parliament (see Act◊ of Union); Gladstone's bills of 1886 and 1893 were both defeated; Asquith's became law in 1914, but was suspended during World War I, and after 1918 the demand was for an independent Irish republic□

Home Service Force force (HSF) established in the UK in 1982, linked to the Territorial Army◊, and recruited from volunteers of ages 18–60. It was intended to guard key points and installations likely to be the target of enemy 'special forces' and saboteurs, so releasing other units for mobile defence roles□

Homoptera a sub-division of the order Hemiptera◊□

homosexuality homosexuals are males or females who are sexually attracted to persons of their own sex; in women it is usually referred to as lesbianism◊. Men or women who are both homosexual and heterosexual are referred to as bisexual□

Homs industrial city (silk textiles, oil refining, jewellery) in W Syria; population 215 425. See Zenobia◊□

Honan see Henan◊□

Hondecoeter Melchior 1636–95. Dutch artist, born at Utrecht, famous for bird paintings□

Hondo another name for Honshu◊□

Honduras Republic of

area 112 088 sq km/43 227 sq mi
capital Tegucigalpa
towns San Pedro Sula; ports Henecan (on Pacific), La Ceiba
features 45% forested, and with areas still unexplored
exports coffee, bananas, timber (including mahogany, rosewood, etc.)
currency lempira/peso
population 4 424 000, 90% mestizo, 10% Indians, Europeans
language Spanish
religion Roman Catholicism
government executive president (Roberto Suazo Córdova from 1982) elected for four-year term, and unicameral Congress of Deputies
recent history discovered by Columbus in 1502, Honduras threw off Spanish rule in 1821, and left the Federation of Central America to become independent in 1838. Military rule was almost uninterrupted 1963–82, when Suazo became civilian president. There is tension with El Salvador◊, and with Nicaragua◊, where there is valuable timber in the Caribbean border region, Gracias a Dios (formerly La Mosquitia), in which guerrillas opposing the Sandinistas have taken refuge□

Honecker Erich 1912– . East German statesman, a security specialist, who became first secretary of the East German Communist Party in 1971, and chairman of the Council of State (i.e. head of state) in 1976□

Honegger Arthur 1892–1955. Swiss composer, whose works include the ballet *Skating Rink* 1921, oratorio *Le Roi David* 1922, and programme music *Pacific 231* 1923, inspired by a railway engine, and five symphonies□

honey made by honey bees◊ from nectar collected from flowers, and made in excess of their needs as food for the winter. It comprises various sugars, especially laevulose and dextrose, with enzymes, colouring matter, acids, pollen grains, etc.□

honey-eater Australasian family of long-tongued birds, Meliphagidae, order Passeriformes, which collect nectar from flowers□

honey guide Afro-Asian family of birds, Indicatoridae, order Piciformes, members of which guide animals and men to the nests of wild bees; they cannot tackle the insects themselves, but ensure (in a form of symbiosis◊) that they share in the honey and the wax (they are one of the few creatures able to digest the latter)□

honeysuckle genus of climbing plants, family Caprifoliaceae, including ***common honeysuckle*** or ***woodbine*** *Lonicera periclymenum,* with sweetly-scented yellow and white flowers□

Honfleur port in N France, on the Seine estuary opposite Le◊ Havre; population 9200□

Hong Kong British Crown Colony

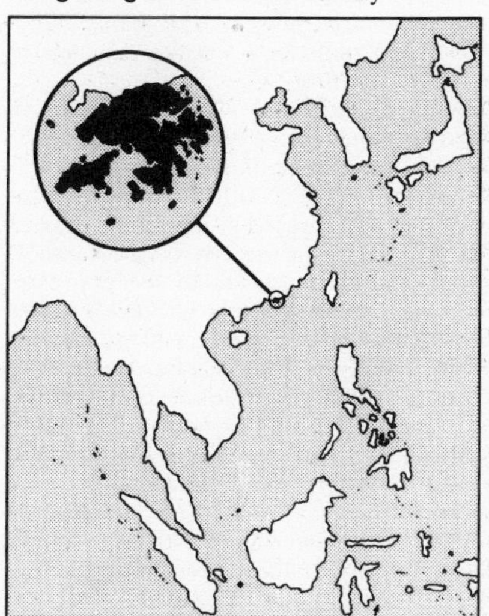

area 1243 sq km/404 sq mi
capital Victoria (popularly Hong Kong City)
towns Kowloon, Tsuen Wan (in the New Territories)
features an enclave of Kwantung province, China, it has one of world's finest natural harbours; Hong Kong Island is connected with Kowloon by undersea railway; a world financial centre, its stock market has four exchanges; across the border of the New Territories in China itself is the Shenzhen Special Economic Zone
exports textiles, clothing, electronic goods, clocks, watches, cameras, plastic products, etc; a large proportion of the exports and imports of S China are transhipped here, and China's special economic zone Shenzen is only 25 miles away; tourism is important
currency Hong Kong dollar
population 5 500 000, 57% Hong Kong Chinese, most of the rest refugees from the mainland
languages English and Chinese
religion Confucianism, Buddhism, Taoism, with Moslem and Christian minorities
government governor (Sir Edward Youde), with executive and legislative councils
recent history a British crown colony, it comprises Hong Kong Island, ceded to Britain in 1841; Kowloon peninsula, added in 1860, and the New Territories on the mainland, acquired on a 99-year lease in 1898. It was occupied by the Japanese 1941–45. Under the 1984 agreement on the reversion of all Hong Kong to China in 1997, it will become a special administrative region (with its own currency, budget, and tax system), the economy remaining capitalist till 2047. It will also remain a free port, international financial centre, and member of international trade agreements in its own right□

Honiton market town in Devon, England; population 5600. Its hand-made pillow-lace industry is undergoing a revival□

Honolulu capital, port, and holiday resort in Hawaii (on Oahu), USA; population 365 115. There are naval and military installations at Pearl Harbor to the SW, which were attacked by Japan on 7 Dec 1941, so bringing the USA into World War II. Waikiki Beach and the extinct volcano Diamond Head are tourist attractions□

Honours List military and civil awards approved by the Sovereign of the UK at New Year, on her official birthday, etc. Many Commonwealth countries, e.g. Australia and Canada, have their own□

Honshu chief island, 'mainland', of Japan, linked by bridges and tunnels◊ with the islands of Hokkaido, Kyushu, and Shikoku. It includes Tokyo, and most of the main cities of Japan□

Honthorst Gerard van 1590–1656. Dutch portrait artist□

Hooch Pieter de 1629–c1683. Dutch painter of interiors, and courtyard and garden scenes□

Hood Samuel, 1st Viscount Hood 1724–1816. British admiral, born in Dorset. A masterly tactician, he defeated the French at Dominica in 1783, and in command in the Mediterranean 1793–4, captured Toulon and Corsica□

Hood Thomas 1799–1845. British comic verse writer, e.g. *Miss Kilmansegg,* who also wrote the serious 'Bridge of Sighs' and 'The Song of the Shirt', a protest against poorly paid labour□

Hooghly see under Ganges◊□

Hooke Robert 1635–1703. British physicist, who discovered that the tension in a lightly-stretched spring is proportional to its extension from its natural length (Hooke's Law) and who helped perfect such scientific instruments as the microscope, telescope, and barometer, and designed the London Monument□

Hooker Richard 1554–1600. Anglican theologian, whose *The Laws of Ecclesiastical Polity* 1593–7 established the basis of the Church of England□

Hook of Holland cape (Dutch *Hoek van Holland*) and ferry port to Harwich in the SW Netherlands□

hookworm a worm◊ which lives in the intestines of man□

hoopoe Eurasian bird *Upupa epops,* the, only member of its family Upupidae, order Coraciiformes. The wings are banded in black and white, and it has a bright buff-coloured crest which expands into a fan shape as the bird alights. It sometimes visits Britain□

Hoover Herbert Clark 1874–1964. 31st president of the USA 1929–33, a Republican. He lost public confidence after the stock-market crash of 1929, when he opposed direct government aid for the unemployed in the Depression, and was succeeded by Roosevelt◊. See Hoover Dam◊□

Hoover John Edgar 1895–1972. See under Federal◊ Bureau of Investigation□

Hoover William Henry 1849–1932. American manufacturer who perfected the Hoover vacuum cleaner, so that it became a generic name for the type□

Hoover Dam highest concrete dam in the USA, 221 m/726 ft, on the Colorado river; known as Boulder Dam 1933–47, its name was restored by Truman as Herbert Hoover's reputation revived□

Hope Anthony. Pseudonym of British novelist Sir Anthony Hope Hawkins 1863–1933, whose romance *The Prisoner of Zenda* 1894, and its sequel *Rupert of Hentzau* 1898, established the imaginary Balkan state of Ruritania on the map□

Hope Bob. Stage-name of 'the deadpan wisecrack' comedian Leslie Townes Hope 1904– , born in Britain, but taken to the US in 1907. With Bing Crosby and Dorothy Lamour, he made a series of 'Road' films, e.g. *The Road to Rio*□

Hopei see Hebei◊□

Hopewell N American Indian culture about AD200, noted for burial mounds up to 12 m/40 ft high, and also for Serpent Mound, Ohio◊. See moundbuilders □

Hopkins Sir Frederick Gowland 1861–1947. British biochemist, born at Eastbourne. He shared a Nobel prize in 1929 for his investigation of the sources of muscular energy, and demonstration that vitamins were essential to healthy life; Order of Merit in 1935. Jacquetta Hawkes◊ is his daughter□

Hopkins Gerard Manley 1844–89. British poet, born at Stratford, Essex. A Roman Catholic convert (under Newman◊'s influence), he trained as a Jesuit◊. His verse is concerned with directness of experience, achieved by an individualized vocabulary, manipulated word order, and the use of stress as the basis of versification, 'sprung rhythm'. His work, including 'The Wreck of the Deutschland', and 'The Windhover', was not published until edited by Bridges◊ in 1918□

Hopkins Harry L(loyd) 1890–1946. American politician, associated with F D Roosevelt in Depression relief work, who supervised the Lend-Lease programme from 1941, and undertook wartime missions to London and Moscow□

Hopper Edward 1882–1967. American artist who portrayed the modern face of the USA, e.g. the street scene *Early Sunday Morning*□

Hoppner John 1758–1810. British portraitist, especially George III's daughters, William Pitt and Nelson; he was a rival of Lawrence◊□

hops female fruit-heads of the hop plant *Humulus lupulus,* family Urticaceae; these are dried and used as a tonic and in flavouring beer. In designated areas in Europe, no male hops may be grown, since seedless hops (produced by the unpollinated female plant) contain a greater proportion of alpha acid which gives beer its bitter taste□

Horace (*Quintus Horatius Flaccus*) 65–8BC. Roman poet. Son of a freedman, he fought under Brutus◊ at Philippi◊ and lost his estate, but was introduced by Virgil◊ to Maecenas in c38, who gave him a small property in the Sabine hills, and recommended him to the patronage of Augustus◊. He published, in 35–30, *Satires* on contemporary society, and in his *Odes* and *Epistles* dealt with both political and personal themes with unrivalled economy and grace of language. He also wrote a critical *On the Art of Poetry,* long influential□

Hordern Sir Michael 1911– . British actor, noted for such roles as Shakespeare's Lear and Prospero, and Gandalf in the radio dramatization of Tolkien's *The Lord of the Rings*□

Hore-Belisha Leslie, Baron Hore-Belisha 1895–1957. British National Liberal politician. As Minister of Transport 1934–7, he introduced Belisha beacons to mark pedestrian crossings, and as Secretary for War 1937–40 introduced peace-time conscription□

horizon the limit of one's view across the earth's surface, at which earth and sky appear to meet; i.e. across the surface of the sea or a level plain, c5 km/3 mi at 1.5 m/5 ft above sea level, and c65 km/40 mi at 300 m/1000 ft□

hormone complex chemical substance. Hormones are the products of the ***endocrine*◊** or ***ductless glands*** of higher animals, and are secreted directly into the bloodstream. They help to regulate many metabolic functions of the animal. Sometimes the hormone acts indirectly, by stimulating in its turn another endocrine gland. Hormones are either proteins (e.g. insulin), steroids (e.g. cortisone), or other simple organic compounds (e.g. adrenaline). A number of hormones have been synthesized. See under endocrine◊ glands□

Hormuz small Iranian island in the ***Strait of Hormuz***, strategically important because oil tankers leaving the Gulf must pass through it□

horn family of musical instruments originating in animal horns. The orchestral ***French horn*** is a valved brass instrument in a spiral coil, with a funnel-shaped mouthpiece, and developed from the ***hunting horn,*** a straight metal tube with a flared end used to give signals in hunting□

Horn Cape, most southerly point of S America, in the Chilean part of the archipelago of Tierra◊ del Fuego□

Horn Philip de Montmorency, Count of Horn 1518–68. Flemish statesman, a leader of opposition to Spanish rule and the introduction of the Inquisition, he was arrested in 1567 with Egmont◊, and both were beheaded□

hornbeam genus of deciduous trees of the N hemisphere, family Betulaceae◊, which bear unisexual flowers in catkins, and ribbed nuts in which the seed is exposed when ripe. They include ***common hornbeam*** *Carpinus betulus*□

hornbill genus of tropical birds of the Old World, family Bucerotidae, order Coraciiformes. The powerful bill is surmounted by a horn-shaped bony growth or casque. The female voluntarily immures herself in the tree-hole nest, the entrance being almost wholly plastered over, and is fed by her mate until the end of incubation□

hornet an insect of the wasp◊ family□

Horniman Annie 1860–1937. British pioneer of repertory theatre, who subsidized the Abbey Theatre, Dublin, and founded the Manchester company; she was the daughter of Frederick Horniman 1835–1906, founder of the Horniman Museum (see under Southwark◊), and sister of Roy Horniman◊□

Horniman Roy 1872–1909. British actor and novelist (*Israel Rank* 1907, better known under its film title as a vehicle for Alec Guinness◊, *Kind Hearts and Coronets*)□

Hornung Ernest William 1866–1921. British novelist, who at the prompting of Conan Doyle◊ created A J Raffles, the gentleman-burglar, and his assistant Bunny Manders in *The Amateur Cracksman* 1899□

horoscope in astrology◊, a set of ideas about a person's character, life, and future□

Horowitz Vladimir 1904– . Russian-born American (from 1944) pianist, interpreter of Liszt, Schumann, and Rachmaninov□

horse family of hoofed, odd-toed grass-eating mammals, Equidae, which includes:

horse of Euro-Asian derivation *Equus caballus* ranging in colour through white, brown, and black. A few hundred of the red-brown ***Mongolian wild horse*** *Equus przewalski* (named after its Polish 'discoverer' in c1880), survive. Notable breeds are the ***Arab*** small and agile; ***thoroughbred*** derived from the Arab via English mares, used in horse-racing◊ for its speed (the present stock is descended from three Arab horses introduced to Britain in the 18th century, especially the Darley Arabian); ***quarter horse*** used by cowboys for herding; ***hackney*** high-stepping harness horse; ***Lippizaner*** pure white horses, named after their place of origin in Yugoslavia, as used in the Spanish Riding School in Vienna◊; ***shire*** largest draught horse in the world at 17 hands (descended from the medieval war horses which carried knights in armour), marked by long hair or 'feathering', round its 'ankles'; ***Suffolk punch*** sturdy all-round working horse. ***Pony*** combines the qualities of various types of horse with a smaller build (under 14.2 hands, i.e. 1.47 m/58 in). Breeds include the large ***Welsh cob***, the rather smaller ***New Forest***, and, smaller again, the ***Exmoor*** and ***Dartmoor***. The smallest is the hardy ***Shetland*** c 70 cm/2 ft 3 in high, popular with children.

ass for example ***African wild ass*** *Equus asinus* and its domestic descendant the ***donkey*** which are distinguished from the horse by their smaller size, larger ears, tufted tail, stripe markings, and characteristic bray.

mule the usually sterile offspring of a female horse and male ass, and a hardy pack-animal; the *hinny* is a similarly sterile offspring of a male horse and female ass, but less useful as a beast of burden.
See also zebra◊, rhinoceros◊, and tapir◊□

Horse Master of the. Head of the department of the royal household responsible for the royal stables□

horse chestnut a type of flowering chestnut◊ tree□

horse fly a type of fly◊□

horse racing the sport of racing mounted or driven horses:
flat racing for thoroughbreds (see under horse◊) only. It was first popularized by the Stuarts; the Classic races are the Derby 1780, Oaks 1779 (both at Epsom), St Leger 1776 (at Doncaster), 2000 Guineas 1809, and 1000 Guineas 1814 (both at Newmarket). The Jockey Club (established in 1751) is the governing body. Major races abroad are the French Prix de l'Arc◊ de Triomphe, Melbourne Cup 1861, and the US Triple Crown Kentucky Derby 1875 (at Churchill Downs, Louisville), Preakness Stakes 1773 (at Pimlico, Baltimore), and Belmont Stakes 1867 (at New York).
steeplechasing a development of foxhunting, of which the *point-to-point* is the amateur version, and *hurdling* a version with only modest obstacles. The outstanding race is the Grand National 1839 (at Aintree, Liverpool) with 30 formidable jumps. The governing body is the National Hunt Committee.
harness racing for standard-bred horses pulling a two-wheeled 'sulky' on which the driver sits. They either 'trot' (diagonally opposite legs move forward simultaneously) or 'pace' (two right and two left legs alternately moved forward). Popular in the USA, Canada, Australia, and France. The most famous race is the Hambletonian at Goshen, New York, named after the progenitor of 90% of modern harness racers□

horseradish hardy perennial of SE Europe *Armoracia rusticana,* family Cruciferae◊; the thick, cream-coloured root is used in pharmacy and cookery□

horsetails plants (class Equisetales) of the phyium Pteridophyta, which dominated earth's flora in the Carboniferous period (see geology◊), when they grew to the size of trees. The ***common horsetail*** *Equisetum arvensa,* a rush-like plant 1 m/3 ft high, is a common British weed; tropical species still reach 6 m/18 ft high□

horse trials see eventing◊□

Horsham town in W Sussex, England; population 27 000. Christ's Hospital removed here

horse

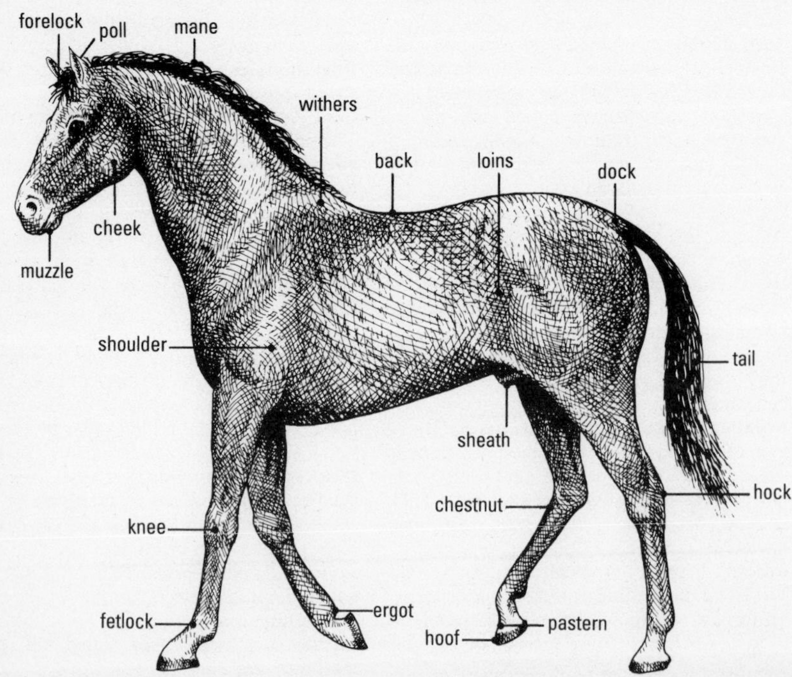

from London in 1902. Shelley was born here□

Horsley John Calcott 1817–1903. English painter of domestic scenes, and of the frescoes of the Houses of Parliament; he designed the first Christmas card□

Horthy de Nagybánya Miklós 1868–1957. Hungarian leader of the counter-revolutionary 'White' government, he became regent in 1920 when the Communist Béla Kun was overthrown. In 1944, on the German invasion, he was deported to Germany□

horticulture cultivation of vegetables, fruit, and hothouse plants. The Royal Horticultural Society, established in 1804, an advisory body, maintains a garden at Wisley, Surrey and organizes the annual Chelsea Flower Show□

Horus in ancient Egyptian mythology, the hawkheaded sun god, son of Isis◊ and Osiris◊, of whom the pharaohs were thought the incarnation□

hospice in modern terminology, a hospital catering for those who are incurable, and usually comparatively near death. See Mother Theresa◊ and Cicely Saunders◊□

hospital a place for the provision of medical, surgical, and in recent times, psychiatric care. In ancient times temples (those of Aesculapius◊) and in the Middle Ages the Church assumed this responsibility (e.g. Europe's oldest, the 7th-century Hôtel Dieu, Paris). There has always been a combination of charitable/free and fee-paid care. From 1948 most hospitals in Britain have formed part of the National Health Service, but (as in other Western countries) increasing specialization in care, an aging population, etc., have strained the resources of the service, and waiting lists for certain operations are long. Those who can afford to do so often belong to private schemes (see health◊ service), and are treated either in private sections of health service hospitals or in separate private hospitals. In the USA hospital bills for Medicare and Medicaid patients may be paid by the state up to a certain level. See health◊ service□

Hottentot aboriginal people of southern Africa, of whom the Nama of Namaqualand◊ are the chief survivors. Their language resembles that of the Bushmen, with explosive 'clicking' consonants□

Houdin Robert. See son◊ et lumière□

Houdini Harry 1874–1926. American conjurer, specializing in escaping from containers under water, etc., who also reproduced 'spiritualist phenomena' by mechanical means□

Houdon Jean Antoine 1741–1828. French realist sculptor, e.g. busts of Voltaire, Rousseau, and Napoleon□

Hounsfield Sir Godfrey 1919– . British pioneer of tomography◊, who shared a Nobel prize in 1979 with independent researcher Allan Cormack, a S African-born American. Knighted in 1981□

Hounslow borough of W Greater London
features London Airport (established 1946 at Heathrow), the world's busiest international airport, with additional facilities at Gatwick, Stansted, and Luton; Hounslow Heath, formerly famous for highwaymen; includes ***Chiswick***, with the Palladian villa of Burlington◊, and Hogarth◊'s home (now a museum); ***Heston*** site of London's first civil airport established in 1919; ***Brentford,*** reputed site of Caesar's crossing of the Thames in 54BC, and the Duke of Northumberland's seat at Syon House, and ***Isleworth***, Osterley, home of Sir Thomas Gresham◊ (both with work by Adam◊)
population 201 000□

Houphouet-Boigny Felix 1905– . Ivory Coast statesman, president since indepence in 1960□

housefly the most common type of fly◊□

Household Royal. See Royal◊ Household□

housemaid's knee inflammation and enlargement of the prepatellar bursa, a small fluid cushion in front of the kneecap□

Housman A(lfred) E(dward) 1859–1936. British poet, born in Worcestershire. Originally a Patent Office clerk, he studied the Latin 'silver poets' and became a professor at Cambridge. His best work is in *A Shropshire Lad* 1896 and *Last Poems* 1922, prompted by his friendship with Moses Jackson□

Houston industrial port (petrochemicals, chemicals, plastics, synthetic rubber, electronics) in Texas, USA; population 2 400 000. Linked by canal to the Gulf of Mexico, it is an agricultural centre, and has the Lyndon Johnson Space Centre nearby, hence 'Space City'. See Sam Houston◊□

Houston Sam 1793–1863. American general who won Texan independence from Mexico; Houston, Texas, is named after him□

Hove sedate seaside resort in E Sussex, England, adjoining Brighton; population 90 000□

hovercraft amphibious ***air cushion vehicle*** (ACV), freed from contact with the surface beneath by downward-directed blowers which create a 'cushion of air' inside a rubber 'skirt'. It was invented by (Sir) Christopher Cockerell in 1953. It copes best with comparatively level land and water surfaces. The first experimental passenger ferry service (Rhyl–Wallasey) has operated from 1962□

Howard Catherine c1520–1542. Queen consort of Henry VIII from 1540. In 1541

Cranmer◊ accused her to Henry of unchastity before marriage, and she was beheaded when Cranmer made further charges of adultery□

Howard Charles, 2nd Baron Howard of Effingham and 1st Earl of Nottingham 1536–1624. English admiral, a cousin of Queen Elizabeth, he commanded the fleet against the Armada while Lord High Admiral 1585–1618; and co-operated with the Earl of Essex in the attack on Cádiz in 1596□

Howard Constance 1919– . British embroidress, born in Northampton. She was influential in the revival of creative work that followed World War II. Her work included framed pictures with fabrics outlined in bold black threads, wall hangings, and geometric studies in strong colour□

Howard Sir Ebenezer. See garden◊ city□

Howard John 1726–90. British prison◊ reformer, high sheriff of Bedfordshire, whose work led to two Acts making gaolers salaried officials (not dependent on prisoners' contributions) and setting standards of cleanliness. His work is continued by the ***Howard League for Penal Reform,*** established in 1866□

Howard Leslie. Stage-name of British film actor Leslie Stainer 1893–1943, star of *The Scarlet Pimpernel* 1935, *Pygmalion* 1938, and *Gone with the Wind* 1939. His plane was shot down by the Germans as he was returning from a Spanish lecture, allegedly because Churchill was thought to be aboard□

Howard Trevor Wallace 1916– . British film actor, whose work ranged from the quiet impact of *Brief Encounter* 1945, to the bravura of *Conduct Unbecoming* 1975□

Howe Elias. See sewing◊ machine□

Howe Sir Geoffrey 1926– . British Conservative statesman. Under Heath◊ he was Solicitor-General 1970–2 and Minister for Trade 1972–4; and as Chancellor of the Exchequer 1979–83 under Thatcher, put into practice the monetarist policy which reduced inflation at the cost of massive unemployment. In 1983 he became Foreign Secretary□

Howe Julia Ward 1819–1910. American feminist and anti-slavery campaigner, who in 1862 wrote the 'Battle Hymn of the Republic', sung to the tune of 'John Brown's Body'□

Howe Richard, Earl 1726–99. British admiral. He co-operated with his brother William against the Americans in the War of Independence, and was in command 1792–6 against the French, winning the victory of the Glorious First of Jun 1794 off Ushant□

Howe William, 5th Viscount Howe 1729–1814. British general, brother of Richard. He won the Battle of Bunker Hill in 1775, and as Commander-in-Chief in America 1776–8, captured New York, and defeated Washington at Brandywine and Germantown. He resigned in protest at lack of home government support□

howitzer see artillery◊□

Howrah see under Calcutta◊□

Hoxha Enver 1908–85. Albanian statesman, founder in 1941 of the Albanian Communist Party. He headed the resistance 1939–44, and then ruled the country as a dedicated Stalinist until his death□

Hoyle Sir Fred (Frederick) 1915– . British astronomer and science-fiction writer, remarkable for his work on the origin of the elements. He supported 'continuous creation' and the 'steady state' theory, as opposed to the 'big bang.' His science fiction includes *The Black Cloud* 1957 and *Ossian's Ride* 1959. With mathematician-astronomer Nalin Chandra Wickramansinghe 1939– , he has propounded the theory that life on earth originated from space□

Hua Guofeng Chinese statesman (formerly Hua Kuo-feng). An orthodox party man, he was Prime Minister 1976–80, and chairman of the Communist Party Central Committee 1976–81, when Deng Xiaoping's influence ensured his removal□

Hua Kuo-feng see Hua Guofeng◊□

Huambo town (Nova Lisboa 1928–73) in central Angola; population 62 000□

Huang He river in China (formerly Hwang-ho), which gained the name (meaning 'yellow river') from its muddy waters; length 4410 km/2740 mi. Formerly known as 'China's sorrow' because of disastrous floods, it is now largely controlled through hydro-electric works and flood barriers□

Huangshan Mountains scenic mountains in S Anhui; the highest peak is Lotus Flower 1873 m/5106 ft□

Huascar c1495–1532. King of the Incas◊, he shared the throne with his half brother Atahualpa◊ from 1525, but the latter overthrew and murdered him□

Huascaran extinct Andean volcano, the highest mountain in Peru; 6768 m/22 205 ft□

Hubbard L(afayette) Ron(ald) 1911–86. American science fiction writer of the 1930s–1940s, founder in 1954 of Scientology◊□

Hubble Edwin Powell 1889–1953. American astronomer, whose research with the Mt Palomar◊ telescope confirmed de Sitter's theory of c1917 that the Universe◊ is expanding. His observations of the 'red shift' from spectral lines from distant stars he interpreted as a Doppler◊ effect, concluding that stars are receding from us at a speed proportional to their distance from us (Hubble's law – 1929). A star a million parsecs away would be receding at some 60 miles per second (Hubble's constant). Up to 1979 its value was thought to be only half as much and its re-evaluation has led to a halving (to about 9000 million years) of the estimated age of the universe□

huckleberry a berry-bearing bush. See Vaccinium◊□

Huddersfield industrial town (woollens, dyestuffs, chemicals, electrical and mechanical engineering) in W Yorkshire, England; population 130 200□

Hudson Henry d. 1611. English explorer who unsuccessfully attempted the NE Passage 1607–08. In 1610, in *Discovery*, he entered ***Hudson Strait*** in NE Canada, where his ship was icebound over the winter in ***Hudson Bay*** (both being named after him). In the spring of 1611 there was a mutiny, and Hudson and eight others were set adrift□

Hudson William Henry 1841–1922. Anglo-American author (naturalized British in 1900), born near Buenos◊ Aires. Early days in Argentina inspired his romances, e.g. *Green Mansions* 1904, with its bird-like heroine, Rima; and the autobiographical *Far Away and Long Ago* 1918. To his years in England belong *Nature in Down-Land* 1900 and *A Shepherd's Life* 1910□

Hudson river of the USA; length 485 km/300 mi. Discovered in 1524, it was explored in 1609 by Henry Hudson◊, and named after him; New York stands at its mouth□

Hudson Bay inland sea of NE Canada, linked by ***Hudson Strait*** with the Atlantic, and the Arctic by Foxe Channel; area 1 233 sq km/476 000 sq mi. Both are named after Henry Hudson◊□

Hudson's Bay Company founded by Prince Rupert◊ in 1670 to trade in furs with the N American Indians, and still Canada's biggest fur company, though its modern general department stores, oil and natural gas interests, etc. are more important□

Hué town (former capital of Annam) in S Vietnam; population 156 300. The former imperial palace is in the old city on the N bank of the Huong, the new city is on the S bank□

Huelva industrial port (chemicals and oil refining) in Andalusia, Spain; population 127 800. At nearby Palos de la Frontera, Columbus began and ended his voyage to America□

Huesca town in Aragon, Spain, with the former palace of the kings of Aragon; population 33 500□

Huggins Sir William 1824–1910. British astronomer, whose analysis of stellar spectra revealed the same elements as those found on earth, and who was a pioneer of photographic astronomy. Knighted in 1897, Order of Merit in 1902□

Hughes Howard 1905–76. American oil millionaire. A skilled pilot, he manufactured and designed aircraft, made the classic film *Hell's Angels* about airmen of World War I, *Scarface*, and *The Outlaw*, and created a legendary financial empire, but in middle age became a recluse□

Hughes Richard Arthur Warren 1900–1976. British author of e.g. the study of childhood *High Wind in Jamaica* 1929□

Hughes Ted 1930– . British poet, born in Mytholmroyd, W Yorkshire. His harsh nature poetry includes *The Hawk in the Rain* 1957 and *Remains of Elmet* 1979. In 1984 he became Poet Laureate. His first wife was Sylvia Plath◊□

Hughes Thomas 1822–96. British county court judge, author of *Tom Brown's School Days* 1857, a story of Rugby School under Arnold◊□

Hughes William Morris 1864–1952. Australian statesman, Labor Prime Minister 1915–16, and then leader of a National Cabinet till 1923□

Hugo Victor Marie 1802–85. French poet, novelist, and dramatist, born at Besançon, son of one of Napoleon's generals. His *Odes et Poésies diverses* appeared in 1822, and his verse play *Hernani* 1830 established him as the leader of French Romanticism. More volumes of grandiloquent verse followed between his series of dramatic novels which included *Notre Dame de Paris* 1831 and *Les Misérables* 1862, and another play *Ruy Blas* 1838. Banished in 1851 for opposing Louis Napoleon's coup d'état, he lived in Guernsey until the fall of the empire in 1870, later becoming a senator. He was buried in the Panthéon◊. See Verdi◊□

Huguenots French Protestants (mainly Calvinist) in the 16th century. Severely persecuted under Francis I and Henry II, they survived both the Massacre of St Bartholomew◊ on 24 Aug 1572 (when numbers were killed by the order of Catherine de' Médicis◊) and the religious wars of the next 30 years. In 1598 Henry IV (himself formerly one of them), granted them toleration under the Edict of Nantes. They lost military power after the revolt at La Rochelle 1627–9, but were still tolerated by Richelieu and Mazarin◊. Louis XIV, however, revoked the Edict, attempted their forcible conversion, and 400 000 emigrated (taking their industrial skills with them), 40 000 settling in England, where their descendants include David Garrick and Samuel Courtauld□

Huhehot see Hohhot◊□

Hull Cordell 1871–1955. American Democrat politician, Roosevelt's Secretary of State 1933–44. He was identified with the 'good neighbour' policy towards Latin America, opposed German and Japanese aggression, and was instrumental in the establishment of the United Nations, for which he won the Nobel peace prize in 1945□

Hull city and port (officially ***Kingston upon Hull***), administrative headquarters of Humberside, England; population 271 100. It is linked with the S bank of the estuary by the Humber Bridge (see bridge◊). Industries include fish processing (fishmeal and fish fingers, with imported fish), vegetable oils, flour milling, electricals, textiles, paint, chemicals, pharmaceuticals, caravans and aircraft. There are ferries to Rotterdam and Zeebrugge. Buildings include Holy Trinity Church (13th century), Guildhall, Ferens Art Gallery 1927, and university 1954□

Hulme Keri 1947– . New Zealand novelist, of Maori, Scots, and English descent. She won the Booker prize with her first novel *The Bone People* 1985□

Hulme Thomas Edward 1881–1917. British poet-critic, killed in World War I, whose *Speculations* (published in 1924) influenced T S Eliot, and whose few poems originated the Imagist◊ movement□

Hulme-Beaman Sydney George 1887–1932. British creator of Toytown (inhabited by his own hand-carved puppets, including Larry the Lamb and Ernest the Policeman), popular on radio and television□

hum environmental. A disturbing sound of frequency c40 Hz, heard by individuals sensitive to this range, but inaudible to the rest of the population. It may be caused by industrial noise pollution, or have a more exotic origin, such as the jet stream, a fast-flowing high altitude (about 15 000 metres/50 000 ft) mass of air□

human body the physical structure of a human being. It consists of a bony skeleton◊, a torso containing internal organs for respiration◊ and digestion (see digestive◊ system), limbs for movement and manipulation of objects, and a head containing the brain◊. Other organs contained in the head include the eyes◊, the ears◊, and teeth (see tooth◊). Respiration occurs by oxygen being transferred to the blood in the lungs◊ and carried around the body by the blood stream (see blood circulation◊). After digesting food, waste matter is excreted at the end of the digestive passage via the urinary◊ system. Several functions of the body are controlled by hormones secreted by the endocrine◊ glands. The body organs and skeleton are protected by layers of skin◊. Sexual reproduction takes place (see reproductive◊ system), with the resulting embryo◊ growing inside the womb of the female. See diagram on page 419□

Human Rights Universal Declaration of (by the United Nations in 1948). They include the right to life, liberty, education, and equality before the law; to freedom of movement, religion, association, and information; and to a nationality.

Under the European Convention of Human Rights of 1950, the Council of Europe established the ***European Commission of Human Rights*** (headquarters in Strasbourg), which investigates complaints by states or individuals, and whose findings are examined by the ***European Court of Human Rights*** (established 1959), whose compulsory jurisdiction has been recognized by a number of states including the UK. See also Helsinki◊ Conference□

Humberside NE county of England

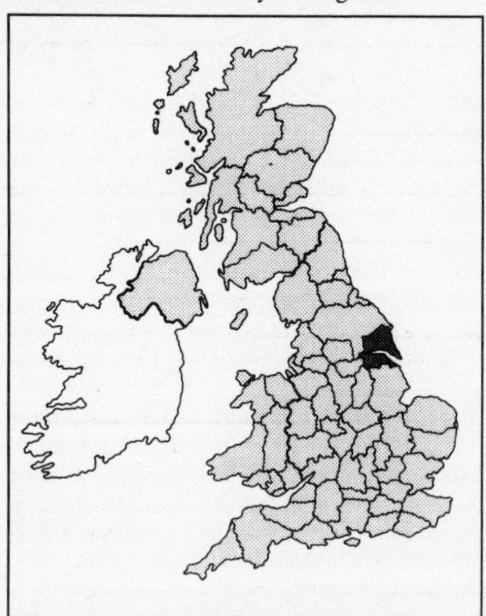

area 3512 sq km/1356 sq mi

towns administrative headquarters Beverley; Hull, Grimsby, Scunthorpe, Goole, Cleethorpes

features Humber Bridge 1980 (its main span 1410 m/4626 ft is the longest of any single-span suspension bridge); fertile Holderness peninsula; Isle of Axholme, bounded by rivers Trent, Don, Idle, and Torne, where medieval open field strip farming is still practised.

products petrochemicals and refined oil; processed fish; cereals, root crops, cattle

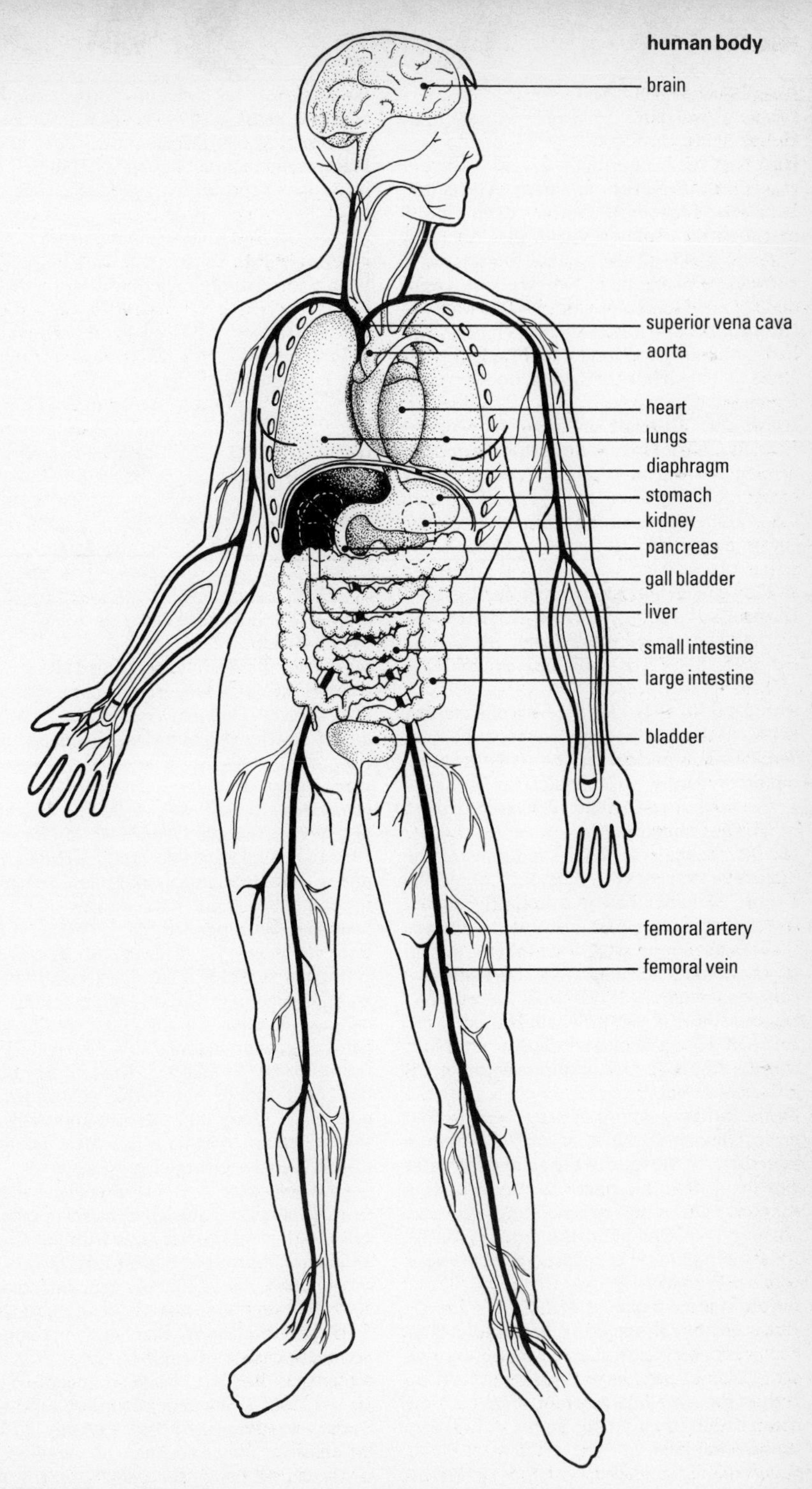
human body
brain
superior vena cava
aorta
heart
lungs
diaphragm
stomach
kidney
pancreas
gall bladder
liver
small intestine
large intestine
bladder
femoral artery
femoral vein

population 851 000
famous people Amy Johnson, Andrew Marvell, John Wesley□

Humbert see Umberto◊□

Humboldt Friedrich Heinrich Alexander, Baron von 1769–1859. German explorer of S and Central America, and in Asia. His *Cosmos* 1845–62 embodied the scientific knowledge of his time. See Wilhelm Humboldt◊, and Humboldt Current◊□

Humboldt Wilhelm 1767–1835. German diplomat-philologist, brother of Friedrich. His stress on the identity of thought and language influenced Chomsky◊□

Humboldt Current cold ocean current (named after F Humboldt◊, who charted it), flowing N from the Antarctic along the W coast of S America to S Ecuador, then westwards. It reduces the temperature of the coasts past which it flows, making the W slopes of the Andes arid because winds are already chilled when they cross the coast□

Hume Basil 1923– . British Roman Catholic Archbishop of Westminster from 1976, the first monk (Benedictine) to hold the office□

Hume David 1711–76. Scottish philosopher whose *History of England* was very popular within his own lifetime but whose indifferently-received philosophical work e.g. *A Treatise of Human Nature* 1740 has proved to be a lasting stimulus.

He shared many of the assumptions of the 'British Empiricist' School, especially Locke◊. ***Humes's Law*** in moral philosophy, states that it is never possible to deduce statements about what one *ought* to do, purely from those about what *is* the case□

Hume Hamilton 1797–1873. Australian explorer. In 1824, with William Hilton Hovell 1786–1875, he discovered the Murray river. ***Hume Highway*** (Melbourne–Sydney) is named after him□

humidity the quantity of water vapour in a given volume of the atmosphere (absolute humidity), or the ratio of the amount of water vapour in the atmosphere to the saturation value at the same temperature (relative humidity); at dew-point the latter is 100%. Relative humidity is measured by various types of ***hygrometer***□

hummingbird a type of swift◊□

Humperdinck Engelbert 1854–1921. German composer, remembered for his fairy-tale opera *Hansel and Gretel* 1893□

Hunan province of S central China
area 210 500 sq km/81 253 sq mi
capital Changsha
features Dongting Lake; farmhouse in Shaoshan village, where Mao Zedong was born
products rice, tea, tobacco, cotton; non-ferrous minerals
population 51 000 000□

Hungary Hungarian People's Republic

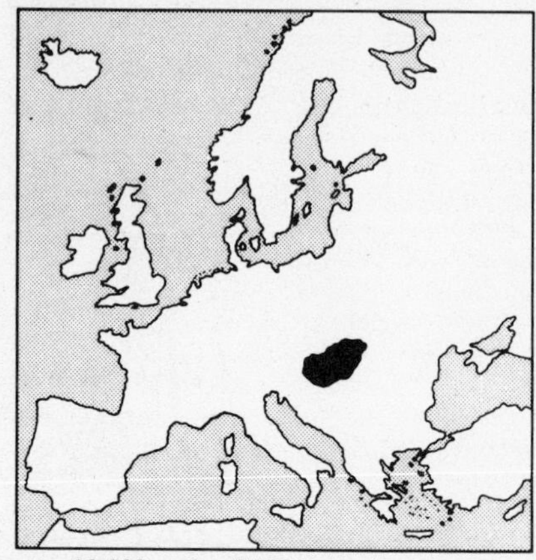

area 93 000 sq km/35 920 sq mi
capital Budapest
towns Miskolc, Debrecen, Szeged, Pécs
features Great Hungarian Plain; Bakony Forest; rivers Danube, Tisza; Lake Balaton
exports machinery, vehicles, chemicals, textiles
currency forint
population 10 710 000; including 320 000 Gypsies (a National Council was established 1985 to defend their interests). A Hungarian minority in Romania is the cause of some friction between the two countries
language Hungarian (or Magyar), one of the few languages of Europe of non-Indo-European stock. It is grouped with Finnish and Estonian in the Finno-Ugrian family
religion Roman Catholicism 50%; other Christian denominations 50%
famous people St Stephen, Kossuth *literature* lyric poet Sandór Petöfi 1823–49, and epic poet János Arany 1817–82; best-known in the West, Ferenc Molnár, *music* Béla Bartók, Zoltán Kodály, Gyorgy Ligeti, Liszt
government there is a parliament and presidential council, of which the chairman is head of state, but real power rests with the Communist politburo (see János Kádár◊).
recent history first an independent kingdom in 1001, Hungary was under Turkish rule 1526–1699 (see Mohács◊), then under Austrian domination (see Kossuth◊) until 1918. A republic 1919–20, it became a 'regency' (for an unnamed king) under Horthy◊ until the country was overrun by the Red Army in 1944 (after having joined Germany in the invasion of Russia in 1941). By 1946 Hungary was under Soviet Communist domination, and a

popular rising in 1956 was harshly suppressed by Russian forces (see Imre Nagy◊). By 1980, however, economic reform meant that Hungary had the elements of a free market economy, and by 1985 this was causing concern by its success in attracting workers from the low-standard state sector. In 1985 alternative (though still Communist only) candidates were allowed in elections□

Huns nomad Mongol peoples who in the 2nd century BC raided across the Great Wall into China. The best-known tribe later entered Europe cAD372, settled in Hungary, and subdued the Ostrogoths and other Germanic peoples. Under Attila◊ they attacked the Eastern Roman Empire, invaded Gaul, and threatened Rome. After Attila's death in 453, their power was broken by a revolt of their subject peoples. Another branch, the ***White Huns***, conquered N India in the 5th century□

Hunt James Henry Leigh 1784–1859. British poet and essayist. For attacks on the Prince Regent in his newspaper *The Examiner*, he was imprisoned in 1813. The friend, and later enemy of Byron, he also knew Moore, Keats, and Shelley. His verse is forgotten, but his book on London *The Town* 1848, and his *Autobiography* 1850, survive, and the character of Harold Skimpole in Dickens's *Bleak House* was based on him□

Hunt John, Baron Hunt 1910– . British army officer and mountaineer, leader of the successful Everest◊ expedition of 1953□

Hunt William Holman 1827–1910. British artist, one of the founders of the Pre-Raphaelite Brotherhood in 1848. He painted biblical subjects including *The Light of the World* 1854□

Hunter river in New South Wales, Australia; length 465 km/290 mi. Hunter Valley wines are famous, and is a centre for dairying and market gardening□

Hunter John 1728–93. British surgeon and physiologist, who established surgery as a science; surgeon at St George's Hospital from 1768□

Huntingdon market town in Cambridgeshire, England; population 17 500. The grammar school, established in 1565 in a 12th-century building, had Pepys and Cromwell as pupils and is now a Cromwell Museum□

Huntingdon's chorea genetic neurological disease causing paralysis and mental deterioration in middle life□

Huntsville town (aerospace research centre) in Alabama, USA; population 142 500□

Hunyadi János Corvinus 1387–1456. Hungarian soldier-statesman, who prevented Turkish conquest by defeating them before Belgrade in 1456, then died of plague□

Hunza small state on the NW frontier of Kashmir under the rule of Pakistan (see Northern◊ Territories)□

Hupei see Hebei◊□

Hurd Douglas 1930– . British diplomat and spy-story writer, who was political secretary to Edward Heath◊ 1968–74, and succeeded James Prior◊ as Ulster Secretary 1984–5, when he became Home Secretary□

Huron see under Iroquois◊□

Huron Lake. See Great Lakes◊□

hurricane a violent wind-storm or cyclone. See under meteorology◊□

Hurstmonceux alternative spelling of Herstmonceux◊. See East◊ Sussex□

husky a breed of dog◊□

Huss John c1373–1415. Bohemian reformer, rector of Prague University from 1402, who was excommunicated for attacks on ecclesiastical abuses. He defended Wycliffe when summoned before the Council of Constance in 1413, rejected the Pope's authority, and was burnt at the stake□

Hussein Ibn Ali c1854–1931. Arab leader (advised by T E Lawrence◊) of the Arab revolt 1916–18, who became King of the Hejaz in 1916, but was deposed in 1924 by Ibn◊ Saud□

Hussein ibn Talal 1935– . Great-grandson of Hussein Ibn Ali, he was king of Jordan from 1952 (after the mental incapacity of his father Talal). By 1967 he had lost all his kingdom W of the Jordan in the Arab–Israeli◊ Wars, and in 1970 suppressed the PLO◊ guerrillas acting as a terrorist force against his rule on the remaining E bank territories (see Black Sept under terrorism◊). By 1984 there was some rapprochement with Yasser Arafat◊, and Hussein proposed peace with Israel on condition of return of all territories occupied since 1967, including E Jerusalem□

Husserl Edmund Gustav Albrecht 1859–1938. Austrian philosopher, founder of phenomenology, which concentrated on what is consciously experienced rather than speculation; he influenced Heidegger◊□

Hussites followers of Huss opposed both to German and Papal influence in Bohemia. They waged successful war for some years from 1419, but in 1620 Roman Catholicism was re-established□

Hutterian Brethren a Christian sect. See under Mennonites◊□

Hutton Barbara. See under Woolworth◊□

Hutton James 1726–97. Scottish founder of scientific geology, whose elucidation of the real age of the earth incensed supporters of the theological time scale□

Huxley Aldous 1894–1963. British novelist, grandson of Thomas Huxley, and brother of

Julian Huxley. His work includes the witty *Chrome Yellow* 1921, *Point Counter Point* 1928 (including an impression of D H Lawrence, whose letters he edited); the science fantasy *Brave New World* 1932; and the short story 'The Gioconda Smile'. He emigrated to California in 1938, recording mystic experiments with mescalin◊ in *The Doors of Perception* 1954□

Huxley Sir Andrew 1917– . British physiologist, half-brother of Sir Julian and of Aldous Huxley. Awarded a Nobel prize in 1963 for his work on nerve impulses; knighted in 1974, Order of Merit in 1983□

Huxley Sir Julian 1887–1975. British biologist, grandson of Thomas Huxley and first director-general of UNESCO. One of the founders of the World Wild Life Fund□

Huxley Thomas Henry 1825–95. British biologist, known as 'Darwin's bulldog' because of his ardent defence of the theory of evolution◊. He was a humanist, opposed to theological orthodoxy, and coined the word agnosticism◊ to express his own viewpoint□

Hu Yaobang 1915– . Chinese statesman. Joining the Communists at 14, he went on the Long March◊, serving against both the Japanese and Nationalists. In disgrace during the Cultural Revolution, he became chairman of the Communist Party in 1981□

Huygens Christiaan 1629–95. Dutch astronomer-physicist, the first to formulate the wave theory of light. He discovered the 'rings' of the planet Saturn and invented the pendulum clock□

Huysmans Joris Karl 1848–1907. French Decadent novelist, author of *À rebours* 1884□

Hwange coalmining town (formerly Wankie) in Zimbabwe; population 33 000. Hwange National Park is nearby□

Hwang-Ho see Huang◊ He□

hyacinth bulb producing plant of genus *Hyacinthus,* family Liliaceae, with large, scented cylindrical heads of pink, white, or blue flowers. The British wild hyacinth is the bluebell◊; see also water hyacinth◊□

hyaline membrane disease (HMD) disorder of prematurely born children, who are unable to produce enough pulmonary surfactant (lung *surf*ace-*act*ive-*agent*) to enable them to breathe properly; the lungs become hard and glassy (Latin *hyalinus* 'glassy'). J F Kennedy's son Patrick died of HMD in 1963; a synthetic replacement has been developed□

Hydaspes see Jhelum◊□

Hyde Douglas 1860–1949. Irish poet and statesman, first president of Eire 1938–45□

Hyde Park see under Westminster◊□

Hyderabad capital and industrial city (railway rolling stock, road vehicles, textiles, pharmaceuticals) of Andhra◊ Pradesh, India, and former capital of Hyderabad, the largest of the princely states; population 2 565 540. It includes the Jama Masjid mosque, and it was in the suburb of Secunderabad that Ronald Ross discovered the cause of malaria□

Hyderabad industrial and university city in SW Pakistan; population 628 310□

Hyder Ali c1722–82. Indian Muslim general, ruler of Mysore state from 1749, who rivalled British power until three times defeated by Sir Eyre Coote in 1781. He was the father of Tippoo◊□

Hydra in Greek mythology, a monster with nine heads. Whenever a head was cut off, two new ones grew in its place. It was finally killed by Heracles◊□

hydra genus of tiny freshwater polyps, members of the phylum Coelenterata◊, with 6–10 stinging tentacles round their mouths. They reproduce by dividing into two, forming buds, or sexually□

hydrangea genus of shrubs originally from Asia and the Americas, with handsome flower heads, varying through white to pink or blue according to the alkaline or acid content of the soil, family Hydrangeaceae. See also under flower◊□

hydraulics practical study of the fluid mechanics of liquids for engineering purposes□

hydrocarbon any compound containing only hydrogen and carbon, e.g. paraffin□

hydrocephalus blockage of the flow of cerebrospinal fluid, with various consequent dangers to the brain, and with young children causing the enlargement of the head. It may resolve itself or need surgery□

hydrochloric acid highly corrosive aqueous solution (popularly 'spirits of salts') of hydrogen chloride (a colourless, corrosive gas HCl). It has many industrial uses, e.g. recovery of zinc from galvanized scrap iron, and the production of chlorides◊ and chlorine◊□

hydrocyanic acid popularly 'prussic acid', a solution of hydrogen cyanide gas (HCN) in water. It is a colourless, highly poisonous, volatile liquid, smelling of bitter almonds. ***Hydrogen cyanide,*** formed by the reaction of sodium cyanide with dilute sulphuric acid, is used for fumigation. The salts formed from it are ***cyanides*** eg sodium cyanide, used in hardening steel and extracting gold and silver from their ores□

hydrodynamics science of non-viscous fluids (water, alcohol, ether, etc.) in motion□

hydro-electric power electricity generated by water passing from a higher to a lower level through a turbine, e.g. as from Niagara Falls, or from a reservoir behind a dam. Itaipu dam on the Paraná (Brazil/Paraguay◊) has a capacity of 12 600 megawatts□

hydrofoil small ship rising at speed on struts fitted with horizontal foils which lift the hull out of the water. See Jetfoil◊□

hydrogen element
symbol H
atomic number 1
physical description lightest element known, forming 9.5% of the human body; it occurs chiefly in combination with oxygen as water
features the most common element in the universe, it is the fuel of fusion reactions which take place in the sun and stars.
uses its isotopes◊, deuterium and tritium, have been used to produce the hydrogen (H) bomb (see nuclear◊ weapons). It has many commercial and industrial uses, from the hardening by hydrogenation (addition of hydrogen) of fats and oils in producing margarine, to creating high-temperature flames for welding, and use as a component in rocket fuel. If subjected to a pressure 500 000 times greater than that of earth's atmosphere, it becomes a solid metal□

hydrogen bomb a type of atomic bomb. See nuclear◊ weapons□

hydrography study and charting of earth's surface waters in seas, lakes, and rivers□

hydrolysis a chemical reaction of a substance with water in which the water is broken down (as against hydration, in which the water is taken up by the substance as a complete module)□

hydrometer instrument used to measure the density of liquids compared with that of water, consisting of a special calibrated glass float which sinks more deeply in lighter than in heavier liquids□

hydrophobia see rabies◊□

hydrophone underwater microphone and ancillary equipment which convert water-borne sound waves into electrical signals, and is used in sonar◊□

hydroponics soil-less cultivation of plants using solutions of mineral salts, used commercially in dry areas, e.g. California and Israel□

hydrostatics science dealing with fluids in static conditions, e.g. the problems arising in the design of dams□

Hydrozoa a class of animal of the phylum Coelenterata◊□

hyena Afro-Asian family of mammals Hyaenidae, mainly scavenging carnivores, comprising the ***striped hyena*** *Hyaena hyaena*, ***spotted hyena*** *Crocuta crocuta* and the ***aardwolf*** *Proteles cristatus*, all of southern Africa. They have bone-cracking jaws, curiously shortened hind legs, and the females of the spotted hyena have mimic male external genitalia, making it difficult to distinguish the sexes□

Hyères spa in S France; population 40 000□

Hygieia in Greek mythology, the goddess of health (Roman Salus), daughter of Aesculapius□

hygrometer an instrument for measuring humidity◊□

Hyksos Semitic migrants from Syria who established their rule in Egypt c1730 BC until driven out by local princes c1580BC□

Hymen in Greek mythology, the god of marriage, shown as a youth with a bridal torch□

Hymenoptera order of insects, which includes bees, wasps, ants, which have two pairs of membranous wings, and an egg-laying organ (ovipositor) which can sting, pierce, or saw (the sawflies, Tenthredinidae, etc)□

hymn song in praise of a deity, notably Ikhnaton◊'s to the Aton◊; the ancient Greek Orphic hymns; Old Testament psalms, and extracts from the New Testament (Ave Maria, etc); later Christian hymn-writers have included John Bunyan◊ ('Who would true valour see ...'); William Blake◊ ('And did those feet in ancient time ...'), Charles Wesley◊ ('Hark the herald-angels sing ...'), Reginald Heber 1783–1826 ('From Greenland's icy mountains ...') Henry Francis Lyte 1793–1847 ('Abide with me ...'), John S B Monsell 1811–75 ('Fight the good fight ...'), Sabine Baring-Gould 1834–1924 ('Onward Christian soldiers...'). See also St Ambrose◊, Gregory◊ the Great, J M Neale◊, Henry Newman◊□

hyoscine alkaloid extracted from plants of the Solanaceae family, and used in surgery and obstetrics (with morphine) as a sedative, and to prevent travel-sickness□

Hypatia 370–415AD. Greek Neo-Platonist◊ philosopher, who succeeded her father as professor at Alexandria◊. St Cyril◊, jealous of her influence, denounced her as an enchantress, and she was murdered by a mob of monks□

hyperactivity excessive activity in children, plus inability to concentrate, with consequent learning difficulties; the cause is not exactly known, but modified diet may help, and many improve at puberty□

hypertension abnormally high blood pressure◊, the smooth muscle cells making up the arteries being constantly contracted. It involves the risk of stroke and heart attacks□

hypnosis altered state of human consciousness in which the subject becomes susceptible to suggestion, and may be made insensible to pain. Its precise nature is still unestablished, and its use in police investigation to assist the memory of witnesses is unreliable. See Anton Mesmer◊□

hypnotic drug inducing sleep, e.g. alcohol, barbiturates, thalidomide, and the benzodiazepines◊□

hypothalamus control centre for the autonomic◊ nervous system, situated below the brain, and above the pituitary gland, which it controls□

hypothermia cooling anaesthesia ('hibernation') to lower the temperature of the body for heart surgery and to tide over a dangerous phase of illness; its slows the metabolism and lessens strain on the brain and heart. In old people a temperature fall below 35.5°C (95°F), may directly cause death, or give rise to broncho-pneumonia, etc.□

hypothyroidism poor functioning of the thyroid gland, which results in slowed mental and physical performance, sensitivity to cold and infection, etc. This may be due to lack of iodine or a defect of the thyroid gland, both being productive of goitre◊; or to the pituitary gland providing insufficient stimulus to the thyroid gland. Treatment of thyroid deficiency (also called ***myxoedema***) is by thyroxine (either synthetic or from animal thyroid glands). See also under hormone◊□

hyrax catlike small mammals, often called coneys; order Hyracoidea, with toes more like hooves; they are the nearest living relative of the elephant. They include the so-called ***'coney'*** *Procavia syriaca,* of the Bible, and the ***rock rabbit*** *P capensis* of Africa□

hyssop see herbs◊ and spices; the biblical hyssop is the caper◊□

hysterectomy surgical removal of the womb, usually because of fibroid or malignant tumours□

hysteria reaction (which is involuntary and largely unrealized) to a situation that the patient is otherwise unable to face. Symptoms are produced which are normally associated with physical illness, e.g. paralysis, blindness. It is a psychoneurosis treated by psychotherapy□

Hythe seaside resort (former Cinque◊ port) in Kent, England; population 12 800. A miniature railway runs to Dymchurch and Romney□

I

Iasi also ***Jassy*** industrial city (chemicals, machinery, textiles) in NE Romania, capital of Moldavia; population 755 000□

Ibadan industrial city (plastics, vehicles) in SW Nigeria; population 1 500 000. Its ancient protective walls still stand□

Ibáñez Vincente Blasco 1867–1928. Spanish revolutionary novelist, e.g. *Blood and Sand* 1913, and *The Four Horsemen of the Apocalypse* 1918. See Valentino◊□

Iberia ancient name for the Spanish peninsula□

ibex a type of wild goat◊□

ibis bird, family Threskiornithidae, order Ciconiiformes (see stork◊), which includes ***sacred ibis*** *Threskiornis aethiopica* symbol of the Egyptian god Thoth◊□

Ibiza see under Balearic◊ Islands□

Ibn Saud 1880–1953. King of Saudi Arabia from 1932. Son of the Sultan of Nejd, who had been driven out by a rival tribe, Ibn Saud recovered his inheritance in 1902, and gradually brought the rest of modern Saudi Arabia under his rule□

Ibsen Henrik Johan 1828–1906. Norwegian poet-dramatist. Driven into exile by the opposition roused by his satirical *Love's Comedy* 1862, he wrote the verse dramas *Brand* 1866 and *Peer Gynt* 1867, and then the series of realistic social plays which revolutionized European drama: *Pillars of Society* 1877, *A Doll's House* 1879, *Ghosts* 1881, *An Enemy of the People* 1882, *The Wild Duck* 1884, *Rosmersholm* 1886, *The Lady from the Sea* 1888 and *Hedda Gabler* 1890. His later plays are more symbolic: *The Master Builder* 1892, *Little Eyolf* 1894, *John Gabriel Borkman* 1896 and *When We Dead Awaken* 1899□

Icarus see under asteroid◊□

ice colourless solid, composed of hexagonal crystals, formed by water on freezing at 0° Celsius and 32° Fahrenheit. Water expands as it freezes hence burst pipes□

ice age period when much of the earth's surface was covered by ice. Some 20 major glaciation periods occurred in the Pleistocene period (see geology◊). They are caused by solar system's passage through interstellar clouds, or (according to the Milankovitch hypothesis) by variations in Earth's orbit round the sun (the angle at which it tilts, etc.). A minor ice age occurred 1550–1850, peaking in the 17th century ('frost fairs' were held in winter on the ice of the Thames)□

ice hockey game on ice between two teams of six players, developed from hockey in Canada (where it is the national sport) in 1867. Protective clothing is worn, and the puck (a flattened rubber disc) is kept in continual motion□

Ice hockey

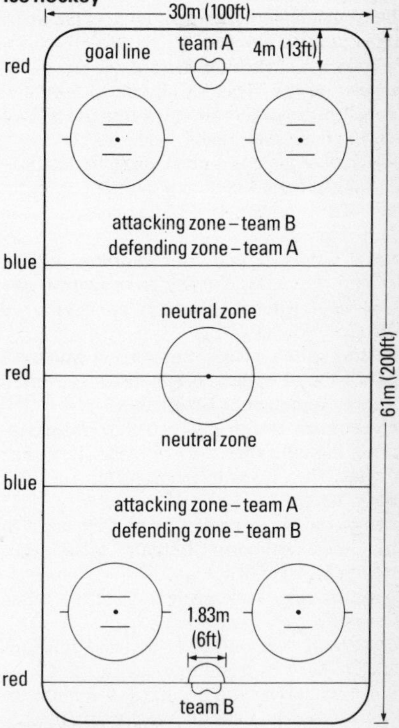

Iceland Republic of
area 103 000 sq km/ 39 758 sq mi
capital Reykjavik
features active volcanoes (Hekla was once thought the gateway to Hell), geysers, hot springs, lava fields, and new islands being created offshore (Surtsey in 1963); subterranean hot water heats Iceland's homes
exports cod and other fish products

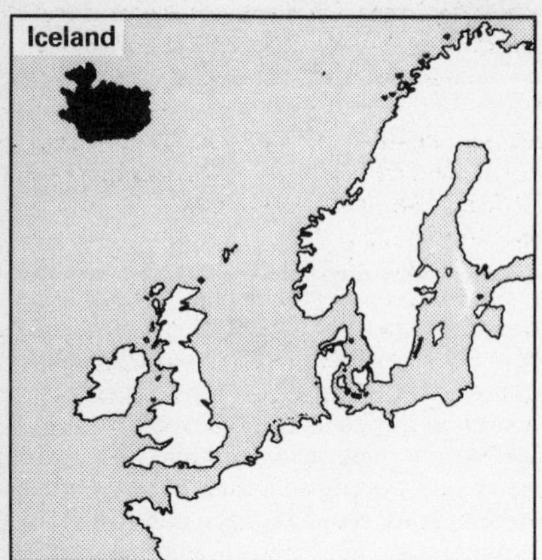

currency krona
population 239 000
language Icelandic, the most archaic Scandinavian language, in which some of the finest sagas◊ were written
religion Evangelical Lutheran
famous people Halldór Laxness 1902– , Nobel prize 1955 for saga-like novels of Icelandic life. See also Edda◊
government there is a president (Vigdís Finnbogadóttir from 1980), and parliament (Althing) of two houses, the oldest parliament in the world
recent history settled from Norway in 874, Iceland was under Norwegian or Danish rule 1264–1944, when it became independent. See also Cod Wars◊□

Iceland spar a transparent form of calcite◊□

Iceni tribe of eastern England who revolted against Rome under Boudicca◊□

ichneumon insect of the order Hymenoptera◊, though called a fly or wasp. Its larvae are parasitic on caterpillars, etc. See also mongoose◊□

icon painting, low relief or mosaic, used in the Greek Orthodox Church to assist devotion. See Virgin of Kazan◊□

Iconium city of ancient Turkey. See Konya◊□

Iconoclast person who attacks religious images; derived from member of the Christian party in Byzantium in the 8–9th centuries who refused to tolerate images in churches (Greek image-breaker)□

Idaho mountain state of the NW USA; Gem State
area 216 412 sq km/ 83 557 sq mi
capital Boise
towns Pocatello
features Rocky mountains; Snake river, which runs through Hell's Canyon (at 2330 m/7000 ft, the deepest in N America), and has the National Reactor Testing Station on the plains of its upper reaches; Sun Valley, ski and summer resort

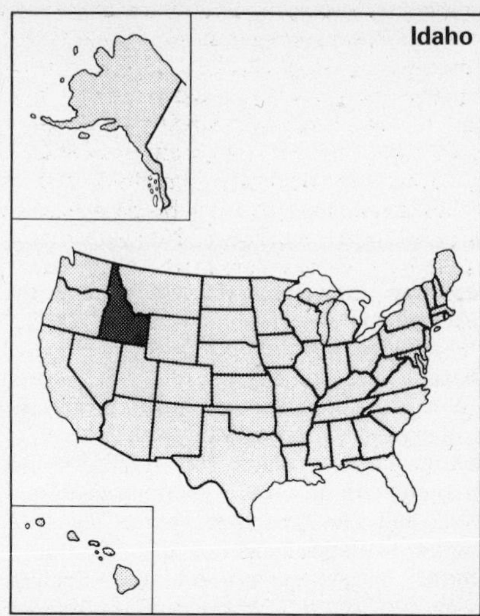

products potatoes, wheat; livestock; timber; silver, lead, zinc, antimony
population 943 935
religion Mormon Church is the largest sect
history first permanently settled in 1860, Idaho became a state in 1890□

identikit a set of drawings used to compose a likeness of a person, typically used by the police. See photofit◊□

Ides in the Roman calendar, the 15th day of Mar, May, Jul and Oct, and 13th day of all other months (originally indicating the full moon); Julius Caesar was assassinated on the Ides of Mar 44BC□

Ifni Spanish territory in NW Africa 1860–1969, when it was transferred to Morocco□

Ignatius of Antioch St d. c115AD. Traditionally a disciple of St John, he was Bishop of Antioch, and was thrown to the wild beasts at Rome. He wrote seven Epistles, important documents of early Church. Feast day 1 Feb□

Ignatius Loyola St 1491–1556. Spanish soldier converted 1521 to the religious life after being wounded at Pampeluna, and founder of the Jesuits◊ in 1540. Feast day 31 Jul□

igneous rock rock◊ formed from cooling magma or larva◊□

ignis fatuus light sometimes seen over marshy ground, thought to be burning methane◊ from decomposing organic material□

iguana a type of large American lizard◊□

iguanadon a type of dinosaur◊□

Ijsselmeer lake in Netherlands, formed 1932 after the Zuider Zee was cut off by a dyke from the North Sea; freshwater since 1944. Area 1217 sq km/470 sq mi□

Ikhnaton d. c1358BC King of Egypt (18th dynasty), who may have ruled jointly for a time with Amenhotep◊ III. His favourite wife was Nefertiti, whose portrait head (now in the Berlin Museum) is the most beautiful known from ancient times, and two of his six daughters by her were married to his successors Smenkhare and Tutankaton (later known as Tutankhamen◊). He developed the cult of the Aton◊ rather than the rival cult of Ammon◊□

Île de France region of N France; capital Paris; population 10 073 000. From here the early kings extended their authority over the whole country. It includes Sèvres and St Cloud◊□

Ilfracombe resort and touring centre, N Devon; population 9000□

Ilkeston town in Derbyshire, England; population 34 000. Mining has been largely superseded by varied industries□

Ilkley spa in W Yorkshire, noted for nearby *Ilkley Moor*; population 22 000□

illegitimacy birth outside a legal marriage; a child may be legitimated by a subsequent marriage. Otherwise, the mother has custody and may apply for maintenance from the father through the courts. Nationality of child is usually that of the mother□

Illinois midwest state of the USA; Inland Empire

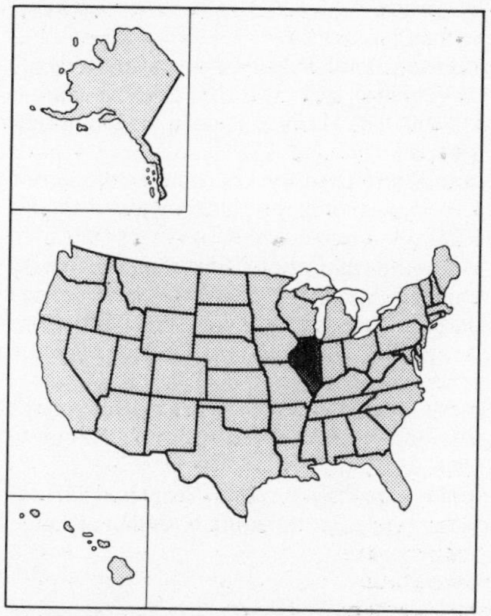

area 146 075 sq km/54 600 sq m
capital Springfield, which has a Lincoln shrine
towns Chicago, Rockford, Peoria, Decatur
features Lake Michigan, the Mississippi, Illinois, Ohio and Rock rivers; Cahokia Mounds, the largest group of prehistoric earthworks in the USA; in Des Plaines, the restaurant where the first McDonald's hamburger was served 1955, became a museum 1985.
products mainly agricultural, soybeans, cereals, meat and dairy products; machinery, electric and electronic equipment
population 11 238 000
famous people Walt Disney, James T Farrell, Ernest Hemingway, Edgar Lee Masters, Ronald Reagan, Frank Lloyd Wright
history originally explored by the French, it was ceded to Britain in 1763, passed to American control in 1783, and became a state in 1818□

Illyria eastern coastal region on the Adriatic, north of the Gulf of Corinth, conquered by Philip of Macedon and a Roman province from 9AD. The Albanians are survivors of its ancient peoples□

ilmenite iron ore, the source of titanium◊□

Imagist Anglo-American school of poets 1909–17, including T E Hulme, T S Eliot, Ezra Pound and Amy Lowell, who advocated clear-cut images, brief poems and free rhythms□

imam in a mosque, the leader of congregational prayer, but generally any notable Islamic leader□

Imhotep c2800BC. Egyptian physician and architect, adviser to King Zoser (3rd dynasty). He designed the step-pyramid at Sakkara, and his tomb (believed to be in the N Sakkara cemetery) became a centre of healing. He was deified as the son of Ptah◊, and was identified with Aesculapius◊□

Immaculate Conception Catholic dogma 1854 that the Virgin Mary was conceived without original◊ sin□

Immingham bulk cargo handling port, with petrochemical works on the River Humber, Humberside, England; population 12 000□

immunity resistance to infection, either natural (through the body's natural production of antibodies◊), or acquired artificially by inoculation. See antibody◊, auto-immune◊ diseases, and interferon◊□

impeachment means by which the House of Commons from 1376 brought ministers and officers of state to trial before the House of Lords, e.g. Bacon 1621, Strafford 1641, and Warren Hastings 1788. In the USA the House of Representatives similarly may arraign offenders before the Senate, e.g. Andrew Johnson 1868. See also Richard Nixon◊□

Imperial College of Science and Technology see under Kensington◊□

imperialism extension of political, military or economic authority of one state over. The British Empire was at its height c1880–1900;

since 1945, the two largest imperial powers have been the United states in Vietnam◊ and now in Central America, and the USSR in Afghanistan◊□

Imperial War Museum see under Southwark◊□

impetigo contagious bacterial (*Staphylococcus aureus*) infection of the skin which forms yellowish crusts□

Impressionism movement in late 19th century painting. The term was first used abusively of Monet◊'s *Impression, Sunrise* 1872; the rendition of things not as they are intellectually analysed to be, but as they are in special conditions of light and atmosphere. Other exponents: Sisley, Dégas, Renoir, Pisarro. See also Manet◊ □

Inca ruling caste of medieval Peru, immigrants from the south east c1100, who established the only empire of the Old World type ever to have existed in the Americas (estimated population 8 million at its zenith). See Quechua◊. The first emperor or 'Inca' (believed to be a descendant of the sun) was Manco Capac c1200AD. Inca rule eventually extended from Quito in Ecuador to beyond Santiago in S Chile (4000 km/2500 mi). Their creator god was Viracocha (identified with Kon-Tiki◊). Their priesthood ran a uniquely efficient socialist state, allotting labour for irrigation, building temples and fortresses (made of stone blocks, fitted together without mortar), etc., according to family groups. Produce was collected and similarly distributed (numerical records of stores being kept by means of knotted cords, 'quipus', writing being unknown). Excellent roads maintained communication and foot soldiers were easily sent to ensure order. Medicine and advanced surgery were practised and the dead were mummified. The civilization was destroyed by the Spanish conquest in the 1530s□

incandescence light emission from a substance at high temperature; the higher the temperature the whiter the light, e.g. the filament of a light bulb, which becomes white-hot as the current is switched on□

incarnation assumption of living form (plant, animal, human) by a deity, e.g. the gods of Greece and Rome, Hinduism, Christianity (Jesus Christ as the 2nd person of the Trinity), etc. ***Reincarnation*** is the assumption by the 'spirit' of a plant, animal or human of a new form as one of these after death; the belief appears in varying form in Egyptian religion, Buddhism, Hinduism, Jainism, Pythagoras, Plato, some Christian heresies, e.g. Cathars◊, etc., and is also referred to as transmigration or metempsychosis□

incest among humans, sexual intercourse between persons so related that their marriage would be illegal. Inbreeding is biologically undesirable because it reduces the range of genetic variability and increases the chances of hereditary weaknesses being emphasized; extreme outbreeding also has penalties in that useful adaptations may be broken down. Experiments seem to show that animals avoid such extremes, when given a choice, by mating with those showing a slight difference, i.e. their 'cousins'□

inch former British imperial measure of length, a twelfth of a foot◊□

Inchon (formerly Chemulpo) industrial port (steel, textiles) in S Korea, chief port of Seoul; population 1 085 000□

income tax a direct tax levied on income. See taxation◊□

incubus male spirit supposed to have intercourse with women in their sleep, the resultant progeny being witches and demons. ***succubus*** is the female equivalent□

incunabula books printed before 1500 in the infancy of Gutenberg◊s invention□

indemnity in everyday law compensation under contract for loss, damage, etc., e.g. under fire insurance agreements. An ***act of indemnity*** is passed by the UK Parliament to relieve offenders of penalties innocently incurred, as by ministers in the course of their duties□

indenture a deed◊ between two or more people□

Independence industrial city (steel, cement, oil refining) in Missouri, USA; population 112 000. The Harry S Truman federal library is here□

Independence Day US commemoration of the Declaration of Independence 4 Jul 1776□

Independent Labour Party socialist party founded 1893, largely by Keir Hardie◊. It was the precursor of the Labour Party, with which it severed all links in 1932, eventually becoming extinct□

Index Librorum Prohibitorum list of books forbidden to Roman Catholics 16th century–1966□

India subcontinent comprising Bangladesh, India (including Sikkim), Pakistan, Bhutan and Nepal

history

c2500–1600BC Indus◊ Valley Civilization

c1500BC waves of Aryan◊ invasion from the north, over-running the Deccan◊, and intermarrying with the Dravidians

321–184BC all except the far south united under the Mauryan emperors, including Chandragupta, and Asoka◊

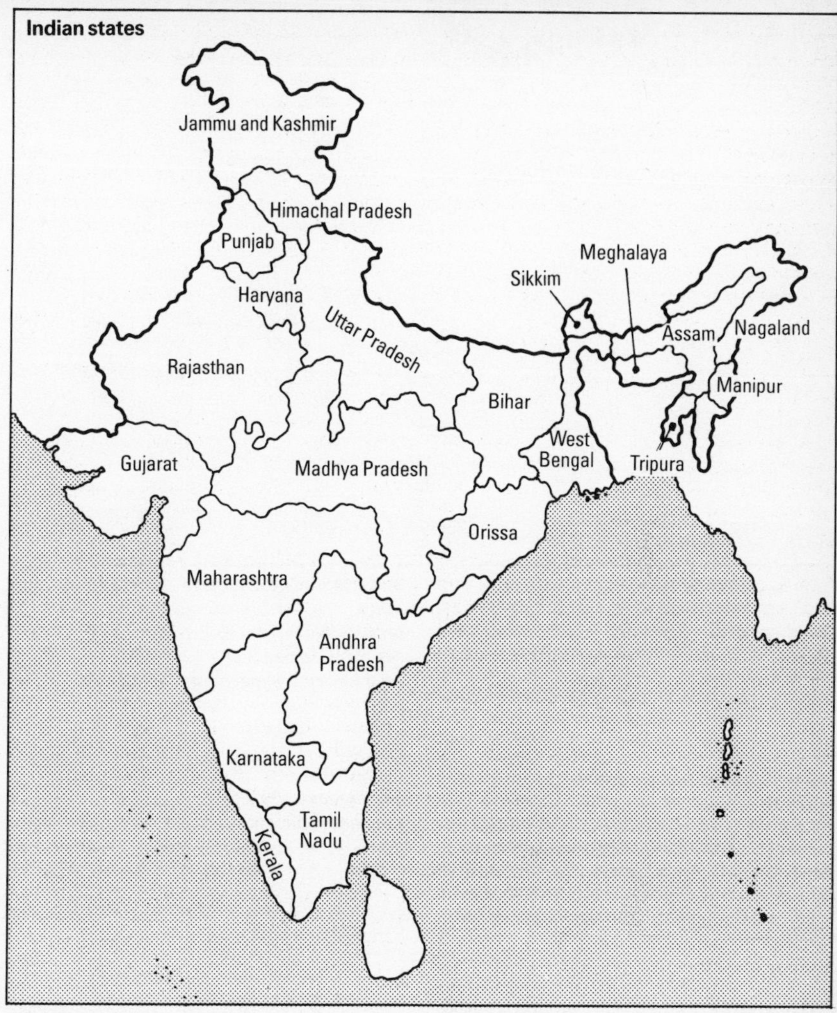

AD

c300–500 golden age of Hinduism under the Gupta dynasty, including its founder Chandra Gupta I 320–c330, and his grandson Chandra Gupta II c380–c415

5th century White Huns◊ plunged India into anarchy

1206 first Muslim dynasty established at Delhi, though the South maintained its independence

1527 Mogul Empire founded by Baber◊ and consolidated by his grandson Akbar◊

16th century coastal bases began to be established by Portuguese, Dutch, French, and English traders

1756–63 British East India Company eliminated their surviving rivals, the French, and rapidly established rule (direct or indirect, through the native princes) over all India. See Robert Clive◊, Warren Hastings◊, Tippoo Sahib◊

1857–8 Indian Mutiny◊, rule of the company replaced by the British Crown

1885 National Congress founded. See Congress◊ Party

1906 nationalist agitation, under Gandhi◊ after World War I, began. See also Nehru◊

1947 self-government achieved in the partition of British India into India and Pakistan◊□

India Republic of (Hindi name *Bharat*)
area 3 208 274 sq km/1 175 410 sq mi
capital New Delhi
towns Bangalore, Hyderabad, Ahmedabad; ports Calcutta, Bombay, Madras, Kanpur, Pune, Nagpur

India: States

States	land area in sq km	population	capital
Andhra Pradesh	276,814	53,403,619	Hyderabad
Assam	78,523	19,902,826	Dispur
Bihar	173,876	69,823,154	Patna
Gujarat	195,984	33,960,905	Ahmedabad
Haryana	44,222	12,850,902	Chandigarh
Himachal Pradesh	55,673	4,237,569	Simla
Jammu and Kashmir	101,283	5,981,600	Srinagar
Karnataka	191,773	37,043,451	Bangalore
Kerala	38,864	25,403,217	Trivandrum
Madhya Pradesh	442,841	52,131,717	Bhopal
Maharashtra	307,762	62,693,898	Bombay
Manipur	22,356	1,433,691	Imphal
Meghalya	22,489	1,327,824	Shillong
Mizoram	21,087	487,774	Aizawl
Nagaland	16,527	773,281	Kohima
Orissa	155,782	26,272,054	Bhubaneswar
Punjab	50,362	16,669,755	Chandigarth
Rajasthan	342,214	34,102,912	Jaipur
Sikkim	7,299	315,682	Gangtok
Tamil Nadu	130,069	48,297,456	Madras
Tripura	10,477	2,060,189	Agartala
Uttar Pradesh	294,413	110,858,019	Lucknow
West Bengal	87,853	54,485,560	Calcutta

features comprises 23 states (see table) and eight union territories; rivers Ganges, Indus, Brahmaputra; Deccan, Himalayas; Taj Mahal; cave paintings (Ajanta); advanced communications network via satellite TV
exports tea, coffee, fish; iron ore; leather, textiles, polished diamonds
currency rupee
population 746 388 000
language Hindi, Indira and Rajiv (official), English and 14 other recognized languages: Assamese, Bengali, Gujarati, Kannada, Kashmiri, Malayalam, Marathi, Oriya, Punjabi, Sanskrit◊, Sindhi, Tamil Telugu, Urdu
religion Hinduism 80%, Sunni Islam 10%, Christianity 2.5%, Sikhism 2%
government executive president elected for five years by members of parliament and the state assemblies (Rajiv Gandhi◊ from 1984), council of states (Rajya Sabha) and house of the people (Lok Sabha).
history formed 1947 on the division of British India into the Dominion of India and Pakistan◊ (with whom there have been disputes over Kashmir and Kutch◊, and war 3–17 Dec 1971 over alleged Indian encouragement of the secession of E Pakistan as Bangladesh). There is also border tension with China. India became a republic within the Commonwealth 1950. The Congress◊ Party has continuously retained power (except 1977–80) under Nehru◊, Shastri◊, and Gandhi◊. Sikh◊ demands for autonomy have intensified in the 1980s into violent attacks on Hindus. The Golden Temple at Amritsar◊ has become the focus of Sikh demands for an autonomous state of 'Khalistan'

Indiana midwest state of the USA; Hoosier State
area 93 994 sq km/36 291 sq mi
capital Indianapolis
towns Fort Wayne, Gary, Evansville
features Wabash river; Wyandotte Cave; undulating prairies
products cereals, building stone, machinery, electrical goods
population 4 490 200
famous people Theodore Dreiser, Cole Porter

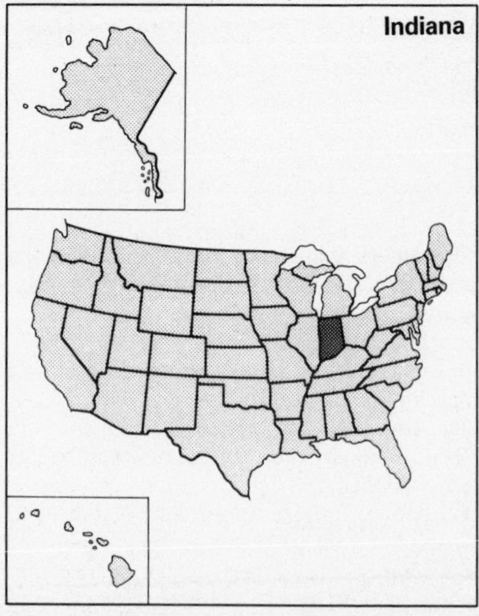

history French traders reached Indiana, and the first settlements were established 1731–5. It was ceded to Britain in 1763, passed under American control in 1783, and became a state in 1816□

Indianapolis capital and industrial city (meat packing, chemicals, vehicles) of Indiana, USA; population 711 540. Home of famous 500 mile car race□

Indian Mutiny revolt 1857–8 by the Bengal army in N India against British rule, in which Delhi was seized, then besieged and recaptured by the British, and Lucknow◊ was under siege. It resulted in the substitution of direct Crown administration for rule by the British East India Company□

Indian Ocean ocean between Africa and Australia, with India to the north, and the southern boundary being an arbitrary line Cape Agulhas/S Tasmania; area 73 500 000 sq km/28 350 500 sq mi; greatest depth Java Trench 7725 m/25 344 ft. Since the 1970s Soviet-American military competition has enhanced the value of island bases□

Indians American. See American◊ Indians□

indigenous native to a country, but especially describing its people and those peoples whose territory has been colonised by whites, e.g. Australian Aboriginals, the Maori, and American Indians. A World Council of Indigenous Peoples is based in Canada□

indigestion pain or discomfit in the digestive system. See dyspepsia◊□

indigo violet-blue vegetable dye obtained from genus *Indigofera*, family Leguminosae, but now replaced by a synthetic product. Once a chief export crop of India□

indium element
symbol In
atomic number 49
physical description metal
features metal softer than lead
uses in monitoring the neutron emission from reactors, in low-melting alloys, in electronics, and in corrosion-resistant coatings for aircraft bearings□

Indo-China French. Former name for Kampuchea◊, Laos◊, and Vietnam◊□

Indo-European a group of languages. See under language◊□

Indonesia Republic of
area 1 925 000 sq km/741 000 sq mi
capital Jakarta
towns ports Surabaya, Semarang
features world's largest Islamic state; comprises 1400 islands, including the greater part of the Sunda Islands to the west of the Moluccas, both the ***Greater Sundas***◊ (including Java and Madura, part of Kalimantan/Borneo, Sumatra, Sulawesi and Belitung) and the ***Lesser Sundas***◊/***Nusa Tenggara*** (including Bali, Lombok, Sumba, Timor), as well as Malaku/Moluccas and part of New◊ Guinea (Irian Jaya)

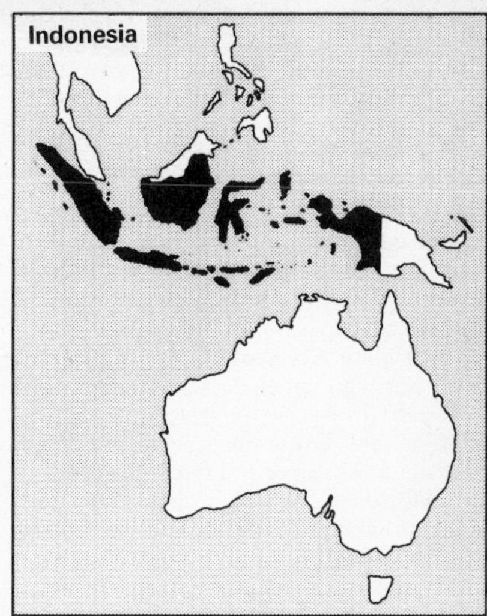

exports coffee, rubber, palm oil and coconuts, tin, tea, tobacco; oil and liquid natural gas
currency rupiah
population 169 422 000, including 300 ethnic groups
language Indonesian, closely allied to Malay
religion Islam 90%; Buddhism, Hinduism and Pancasila (a secular cult official ideology)
government there is an executive president (General Suharto◊ from 1967), and house of representatives; the people's consultative assembly (theoretically with supreme power) meets about every five years.
recent history from the 16th century until the Japanese occupation 1942–5, the area was under Dutch rule. A brief struggle for independence then ended in a republic recognized by the Dutch in 1949. Dutch New Guinea (West Irian/Irian Jaya) passed to Indonesia in 1963, but confrontation with Malaysia over claims to Sabah and Sarawak ended in 1966 with détente. E Timor◊ was incorporated in 1976, but separatist movements remain, as in Irian Jaya□

Indore city in Madhya Pradesh, India; population 827 000□

Indra Hindu god of the sky, shown as a four-armed man on a white elephant, carrying a thunderbolt. See Soma◊□

indulgence in the Catholic church the remission of temporal punishment for sin after forgiveness has been obtained. It was the sale of such indulgences by Archbishop Albert of Mainz and Magdeburg through the agency of the Dominican monk Tetzel which roused Luther to draw up his 95 'Theses' and initiate the Reformation. Indulgences still continue, especially in 'Holy Years'□

Indus Asian river rising in Tibet; length 2900 km/1800 mi. The use of its waters, including those of its five tributaries, were divided 1960 between India (Ravi, Beas, Sutlej) and Pakistan (Indus, Jhelum, Chenab). See Indus◊ Valley Civilization□

Industrial Revolution acceleration of technical development in Europe and N America from the late 18th century through the 19th century□

Indus Valley Civilization prehistoric culture existing in the NW Indian subcontinent from c2500–1600BC of which the most famous city ruins are those of the latter date: Harappa (Punjab) excavated by Sir Mortimer Wheeler in 1946, and Mohenjo Daro (Sind) in Pakistan, which had advanced sanitary facilities. Most striking artistic remains are their soapstone seals (elephants, snakes, etc.). Mystery surrounds their disposal of their dead◊□

inert gases or ***noble gases*** group of six gaseous elements, so-named because of their unreactivity: argon◊, helium◊, krypton◊, neon◊, radon◊, and xenon◊□

infante/infanta in Spain a son/daughter of the sovereign, except for the heir apparent. See Asturias◊□

infanticide killing of offspring, among human beings usually as a method of population control, and most frequently of girls (India and China), though boys will be killed in countries where bride-prices are high. Among animals infanticide is usually less for population control than a means to a fresh opportunity of mating and producing more offspring than are killed□

infantile paralysis another term for poliomyelitis◊□

inferiority complex Adler◊'s term for a patient's reaction to his or her own real or imagined inferiority which may be compensated for by an exaggerated attempt to socialize□

inflammation reaction of living tissue (heat, swelling, redness, pain, and loss of function) to injury. White blood cells and lymph pour into the affected region to combat the injurious agent and repair damage; white cells killed in the battle form yellow pus□

inflation a rise in the general level of prices, caused by an excess of demand over supply (***cost-push inflation*** e.g. the world price rise of oil in 1974), and related to an increase in the supply of money (***demand-pull inflation***). See also deflation◊□

influenza acute viral respiratory infection, which sets in sharply with fever, shivering and aching. The 'Spanish flu' epidemic of 1918 killed approximately twice as many as were killed in World War I□

infra-red radiation invisible electromagnetic radiation between the limit of the red end of the visible spectrum, and shortest microwaves. It is absorbed and radiated by all bodies above absolute zero◊ temperature. It is used in chemical analysis; in devices making it possible to 'see in the dark'; in medical photography; in astronomy (see under telescope◊), and in self-service restaurants to keep food hot. See electromagnetic◊ wave□

Ingres Jean Auge Dominique 1780–1867. French painter, a student of David◊ and like him a painter of classical style in opposition to the romanticism of Delacroix◊. Famous for his female nudes *Odalisque* 1814 and *La Source* 1856□

ink coloured liquid used for writing, drawing and printing. Traditional ink, blue when used, but later a permanent black, was produced from gallic acid, tannic acid, etc., but modern inks are based on synthetic dyes□

Inkerman Battle of 1854. See Crimean◊ War□

Innocent III 1161–1216. Pope from 1198, he asserted Papal power over secular princes, especially over the succession of Holy Roman◊ Emperors, and who made King John◊ of England his vassal. He promoted the 4th Crusade, and crusades against the pagan Livonians and Letts, and Albigensian heretics□

Innsbruck capital of the Austrian Tirol, a tourist and winter-sports centre and route junction for the Brenner Pass; population 116 100□

Inns of Court the four private societies which have power to call law students to the English Bar: Lincoln's Inn, Gray's Inn, Inner Temple, and Middle Temple□

inoculation injection into the body of dead organisms, toxins, antitoxins, etc., to produce immunity by inducing a mild form of a disease□

inorganic chemistry the branch of chemistry◊ that deals with substances that do not contain carbon□

Inquisition tribunal of the Catholic Church established 1229 to suppress heresy, which operated in France, Italy, Spain and the Empire, especially active following the Reformation◊: it was later extended to the Americas. Its trials were conducted in secret, under torture, and penalties ranged from fines, through flogging and imprisonment, to death by burning. The Inquisition or Holy

Office (re-named Sacred Congregation for the Doctrine of the Faith 1965) still deals with ecclesiastical discipline. See liberation◊ theology, Torquemada◊□

insect invertebrate animal in the phylum Arthropoda◊, having a body in three parts: head (bearing a pair of antennae, for smell and touch, and compound eyes (with many lenses); thorax (with three pairs of legs, and usually two pairs of wings) and abdomen (metabolic and reproductive centre).

Estimated total of 22 500 000 species, of which less than 5% have been properly identified, and of which 50% are to be found in tropical rainforests. They range in size from 0.02 cm/0.007 in to 35 cm/13.5 in.

In most insects mating occurs only once, and death may soon follow. On emerging from the egg, the young grow in cycles interrupted by successive moults. In less complex species, the young (***nymphs***) closely resemble their parents, and undergo a gradual transformation to adulthood (incomplete metamorphosis), continuing to feed throughout life.

In the complex species, the young undergo a complete metamorphosis. They are known as ***larvae*** when they emerge from the egg (at an earlier stage than those insects which undergo incomplete metamorphosis), and after a period of intense eating, go into a resting pupal stage when do not eat. The larval organs and tissues are transformed into those of the adult (***imago***), which (as with butterflies and moths) bears little resemblance to the larval stage, and undergoes no further growth□

insect classification insects are classed in two subclasses (one with two divisions), and 29 orders. There are separate entries for all species in bold letters:

sub-class Apterygota

Thysanura, three-pronged ***bristletails***

Diplura, two-pronged ***bristletails***

Protura, small wingless insects found in damp soil

Collembola ***springtails***

sub-class Pterygota

division 1 *Exopterygota*

Orthoptera ***grasshopper*** (locust), ***cricket***

Dictyoptera ***cockroach, mantis***

Phasmida ***stick and leaf insects***

Grylloblattodea, nocturnal insects living under stones at high altitudes

Plecoptera ***stonefly***

Isoptera ***termite***

Embioptera, webspinners, dun-coloured tropical insects which live in silk tunnels under bark, etc.

Dermaptera ***earwig***

Ephemeroptera ***mayfly***

insect

a bluebottle fly (order Diptera)

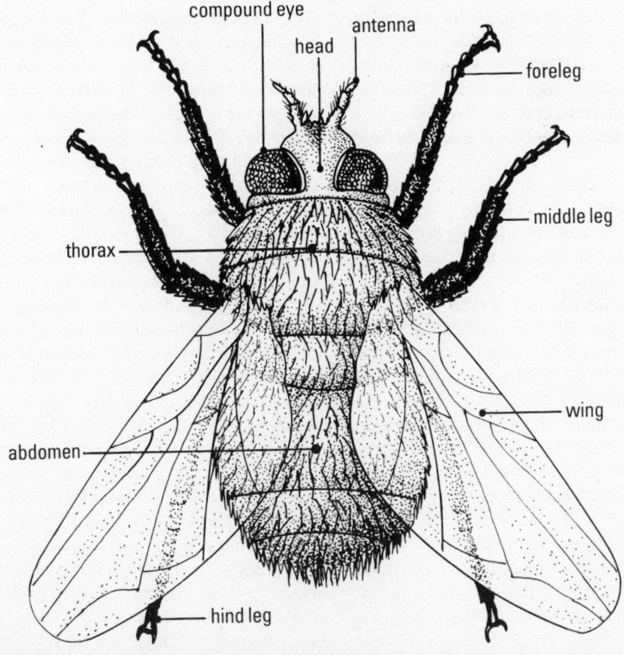

note: members of the order Diptera have only one pair of wings

Odonata ***dragonfly***
Psocoptera ***booklouse***
Anoplura ***lice*** (bloodsucking)
Mallophaga ***lice*** (biting)
Thysanoptera ***thrips***
Hemiptera◊, the bugs
Zoraptera, minute insects found in rotten wood
division 2 *Endopterygota*
Neuroptera ***lacewing, alderfly***
Mecoptera, scorpion fly, harmless though apparently armed with a sting
Tricoptera ***caddis fly***
Lepidoptera ***butterfly, moth***
Coleoptera ***beetle***
Strepsiptera, stylops (parasitic on bees and wasps)
Hymenoptera ***bee, wasp, ant, sawfly, ichneumon***
Diptera, two-winged or true species of ***fly***
Aphaniptera ***flea***□

insectivora order of primitive placental mammals. Insect-eaters, producing large litters, they include:
hedgehog family Erinaceidae, covered in spines, which rolls into a ball when alarmed; the ***common hedgehog*** *Erinaceus europaeus* is speckled-brown, with a pig-like snout, and 30 cm/1 ft long. They are notorious for the quantity of fleas and ticks, with which they swarm.
mole family Talpidae. The ***common mole*** of Europe *Talpa europaea* has a thick-set body, 18 cm/7 in long, covered in grey dense fur; tiny eyes, and limbs specialized for tunnelling for earthworms etc. They are immobilized by predators, to keep them fresh, by biting them in the head. Small mole-hills are thrown up at intervals.
shrew family Soricidae, mouselike and with a voracious appetite. The ***common shrew*** *Sorex araneus* is 7.5 cm/3 in long; the ***pygmy shrew*** *S minutus*, 4.5 cm/1.8 in long, is Britain's smallest mammal□

insectivorous plant carnivorous plant able to digest animal tissues to obtain easily assimilable nitrogen, which is lacking in its usual marshy habitat. Some are passive traps, e.g. ***pitcher plants*** *Nepenthes*, of which one species has container-traps holding two litres of the liquid which 'digests' its insect food, and may even trap rats: see kinibalu◊. Others, e.g. ***sundews*** *Drosera*; ***butterworts*** *Pinguicula* and ***Venus fly trap*** *Dionaea muscipula*, have an active mechanism. See leaf◊□

insemination artificial. Artificial introduction of semen to the female reproductive tract, either in animals or human beings; in the former to improve cattle stock by outstanding sires, in the latter to aid the infertile. The sperm may come from the husband (AIH) or a donor (AID); an AID child is illegitimate under British law. An extension of the technique was the birth in the UK in 1978 of Louise Brown, created by the external fertilization of an egg from her mother by sperm from her father, the egg then being reimplanted in the womb□

insider trading illegal use of privileged information in dealing in securities on the stock exchanges□

insulin a hormone◊ used in the treatment of diabetes◊

insurance contract indemnifying the payer of a premium against loss by fire, death, accident, etc., which is known as assurance in the case of a fixed sum (in Britain especially when the event is inevitable, e.g. payment of a fixed sum on death), and insurance where the indemnity is proportionate to the loss□

integrated circuit tiny electronic circuit on a single sliver of silicon. Compactness is achieved by including not only the circuit components (transistors◊, etc.) on the chip, but also the conducting pathways between them (formerly requiring copper wires or tracks on a printed circuit board)□

intelligence ability to perceive and understand, influenced both by heredity and environment. Advancing age, if the person remains mentally active, seems to produce not so much a fall as a change in the areas in which performance is good, e.g. skills requiring routine memorization of new material may be less, but problem-solving may even improve. ***Intelligence quotient*** or ***IQ*** is a measure of intelligence obtained from a series of standard tests; however, there are many elements in mental activity, such as creativity, which intelligence tests cannot easily monitor. See artificial◊ intelligence, psychology◊□

intelligence gathering of information on the activities of hostile countries, e.g. the British secret intelligence service M(ilitary) I(ntelligence) 6. ***Counter-intelligence*** is the gathering of information on the activities of hostile agents, e.g. the British MI5, which has as its executive arm Scotland Yard's Special◊ Branch. For the USA, see FBI◊ and CIA◊; USSR, see KGB◊. 'Double agents' increase their income, but may decrease their lifespan, by working for both sides (Mata◊ Hari); 'moles' are those within the service who betray their own side, usually 'defecting' (fleeing to the other side) when in danger of discovery (see Kim Philby◊); a 'sleeper' is a spy who is innocuous, sometimes for many years, until needed. The motive for work in intelligence may be service to country (see

T E Lawrence◊, John Buchan◊, Graham Greene◊, Ian Fleming◊, John Le Carré◊, who afterwards used their experiences in their books), money, or idealism, e.g. Fuchs◊. Much intelligence is gained by technical means, as at GCHQ◊ Cheltenham. See also Ultra◊□

intelligence test procedure for measuring of intellectual ability, temperament, aptitude, etc. Workers in this field have included Galton◊, the Frenchman Alfred Binet◊ 1857–1911, Sir Cyril Burt◊, and Hans Eysenck◊. Intelligence tests were first used large-scale in World War I in 1917 for two million drafted men in the USA. 'Sight and sound' intelligence tests, developed by Christopher Brand 1981, avoid the pitfalls of improvement by practice, and cultural bias. Subjects are shown two lines flashed on a screen, and are asked to identify the shorter of the two; and are asked to identify the higher of two musical notes□

interest payment for the use of borrowed money, calculated as so much per cent per annum. ***Simple interest*** is paid only on the original sum borrowed; ***compound interest*** on that amount plus the interest accruing each year□

interferon proteins whose manufacture is triggered by virus attacks, which act as a protection against the invading virus. When synthetically produced they have the potential of curing viral diseases and some cancers. Human interferon is made by two types of cells, the white blood cells (leucocytes) and the cells of the muscles, skin and other connective tissues. There is evidence that plants also manufacture their own interferons, and that these might be used not only to fight plant diseases, but also those of animals□

internal combustion engine engine in which fuel is burned under controlled conditions and transformed to mechanical energy by pushing pistons in combustion cylinders

The ***four-stroke petrol engine*** has four stages; valves are opened and closed as required by a mechanism driven from the crankshaft. Fuel and air enter the cylinder during the ***induction stroke*** (1). Traditionally, air is premixed with petrol vapour in a carburettor, but fuel injection eliminates the carburettor – petrol is squirted straight into the cylinders. The mixture is compressed in the cylinder by the ***compression stroke*** (2), and a distributor applies a high voltage across the sparking plugs. On the ***power stroke*** (3) the piston is pushed down by the expansion of hot gases burning in the cylinder, and made to turn a crankshaft on which a flywheel is mounted to maintain momentum during the other strokes. Burnt gases are expelled from the cylinder by the ***exhaust stroke*** (4). Most car engines have more than one cylinder; evenness of speed is promoted by staggering the power strokes of the different cylinders.

In a ***diesel engine*** no spark is needed; the compression stroke causes a great enough temperature rise for ignition to spontaneous□

International co-ordinating body established by labour and socialist organizations, including:

International Working Men's Association 1864–72 formed in London under Karl Marx.

(Socialist) International 1889–39 loose federation of Socialist parties.

(Communist) International or ***Comintern*** 1919–43 formed in Moscow (see Lenin◊),

internal combustion engine: the four-stroke cycle

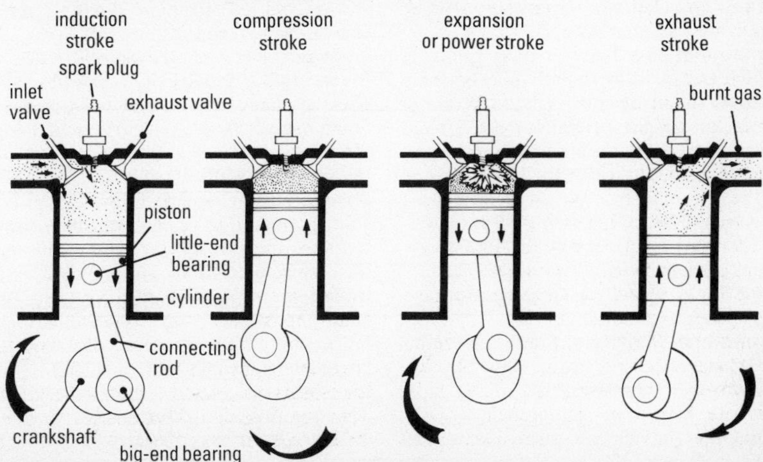

advocating from 1933 a 'popular front' (Communist, Socialist, Liberal) against Hitler.
Trotskyist International 1936, somewhat indeterminate, and anti-Stalinist.
revived ***Socialist International*** 1951 Frankfurt, largely anti-Communist association of social democrats□
International Atomic Energy Agency see under United◊ Nations□
International Bank for Reconstruction and Development the formal title of the World◊ Bank□
International Brigade international volunteer force on the republican side in the Spanish◊ Civil War 1936–39□
International Civil Aviation Organization see under United◊ Nations□
International Court of Justice the main judicial organ of the United Nations, at The Hague□
International Date Line marks the difference in date between places to the E and W, and is a modification of the 180th meridian; the date is put forward a day when going west, and back a day when going east□
International Development Association see under United◊ Nations□
Internationale international Communist anthem (words Eugène Pottier 1871/music Pierre Degeyter c1891), used as the Soviet National Anthem 1917–1943□
International Finance Corporation see under United◊ Nations□
International Fund for Agricultural Development see under United◊ Nations□
International Gothic style of art in 14th and 15th centuries characterized by intricate patterning and decoration, found especially in illuminated manuscripts. See Gentile◊ da Fabriano, Pisanello◊□
International Labour Organization see under United◊ Nations□
International Law body of rules generally accepted as governing the relations between countries, pioneered by Hugo Grotius◊. Neither the League of Nations nor United Nations proved able to enforce it, successes being achieved only when the law coincided with the aims of a predominant major power, e.g. Korean◊ War. The scope of the law is now extended to space, e.g. the 1967 treaty banning nuclear weapons from space□
International Maritime Organization see under United◊ Nations□
International Monetary Fund see under United◊ Nations□
International Settlements Bank for. Forum for European central bank, established 1930. Acts as a bank to the central banks, to prevent currency speculation□
International Telecommunication Union see under United◊ Nations□
International Trade Unionism modern organizations are the International Confederation of Free Trade Unions (ICFTU 1949, including the American Federation of Labor and Congress of Industrial organizations and the Trades Union Congress and the World Federation of Trade Unions (WFTU 1945)□
Interpol ***Inter***national Criminal ***Pol***ice Commission 1923; headquarters Paris. It has an international criminal register, fingerprint file and methods index□
intestines the digestive◊ tract beginning at the stomach outlet and ending at the anus. In humans it comprises ***small intestine*** (6 m/20 ft, divided into duodenum, jejunum, and ileum), and ***large intestine*** (150 cm/5 ft, divided into caecum, colon and rectum). These muscular tubes secrete alkaline digestive juice, and contract in a series of wave motions (peristalsis) to pass the contents slowly along. They are kept in place by a sling of connective tissue (peritoneum) which carries the blood and lymph◊ vessels and nerves□
Inuit (Inupiaq 'the people') people of Arctic N America and Greenland, also known as ***Eskimo***. They refer to themselves as Inuit; they were first called Eskimo ('eaters of raw meat') by N American Indians. Snow igloos were temporary shelters for winter travel, and traditional methods of housing using skins, etc., have given way to modern construction. Skin-covered canoes or ***kayaks*** are still made, as are ***totem poles*** which display the mythological origins of a clan chief or his family. Canadian Inuit in 1975 called for the creation of an autonomous state, Nunavat ('Our Land'). Population 73 000; language Inupiaq, now reviving□
Invalides Hôtel des. See under Paris◊□
Invercargill industrial city (saw-mills, meat-packing plants and aluminium-smelting) on South Island, New Zealand; population 54 000□
Invergordon Mutiny incident in the British Atlantic Fleet, Cromarty Firth, 15 Sept 1931. Ratings refused to prepare the ships for sea following the government's cuts in their pay; the cuts were consequently modified□
Inverness town in Highland region, Scotland; population 45 000. Tourism is important, and tweed is made; there is also engineering, distilling and tanning□
invertebrates animals without backbones. They comprise c1 500 000 species, as against c50 000 species of vertebrates◊□

investment trust a public company which invests on behalf of its shareholders. See trust◊□

Io in Greek mythology a princess loved by Zeus◊, who transformed her to a heifer to hide her from the jealousy of Hera◊□

Io moon of planet Jupiter◊□

iodine element
symbol I
atomic number 53
physical description volatile solid
features non-metal in the halogen group; it is found in crude Chile saltpetre, and is taken up from sea water by seaweeds, being commercially extracted from both; there is a trace in the human body, essential for the thyroid glands (a deficiency of iodine in the diet causes goitre).
uses poisonous in its concentrated form, it has medical uses, as an antiseptic and (in the form of a radioactive isotope) as a tracer□

ion atom, or group of atoms, which are either positively charged (***cation***) or negatively charged (***anion***), as a result of the loss or gain of electrons□

Iona see Inner Hebrides◊□

Ionesco Eugène 1912– . Romanian-born French allegorical dramatist, e.g. *Rhinoceros* 1959, attacking totalitarianism, in which every character except one turns into a rhinoceros□

Ionia in classical times the W coast of Asia Minor, settled c1000BC by the Ionians◊; it included the cities of Ephesus, Miletus, and later Smyrna□

Ionian Islands group off the W coast of Greece; area 332 sq km/860 sq mi. A British protectorate from 1815 till their cession to Greece 1864, they include Cephalonia (Kefallínia); ***Corfu*** (Kérkyra, a Venetian possession 1386–1797); ***Cythera; Ithaca*** (Itháki), the traditional home of Odysseus◊; ***Leukas*** (Levkás); ***Paxos*** (Paxoí), and ***Zante*** (Zákynthos)□

Ionians Hellenic people from beyond the Black Sea who crossed the Balkans c1980BC and invaded Asia Minor. Driven back by the Hittites, they spread over mainland Greece, later being supplanted by the Achaeans□

ionosphere ionized layer of earth's outer atmosphere◊ (60–1000 km) in which there are sufficient free electrons to modify the way in which radio waves are propagated, e.g. by reflecting them back to earth□

ion plating method of applying corrosion-resistant metal coatings in the aerospace industry which is non-polluting. The article is placed in argon gas, plus some coating metal, and when the latter vaporizes on heating, it becomes ionized as it diffuses through the gas, and forms a coating□

Iowa midwest state of the USA; Hawkeye State

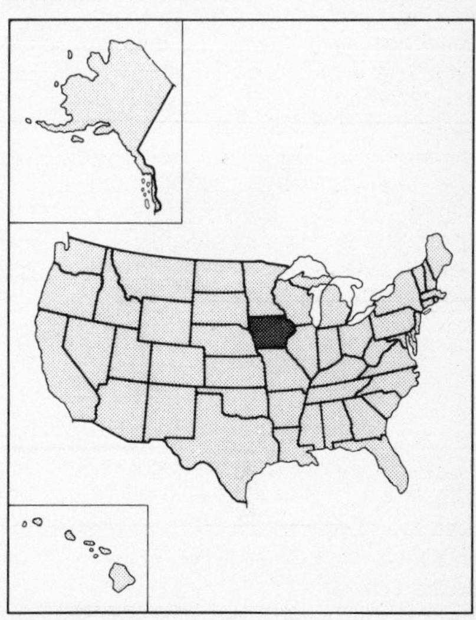

area 145 790 sq km/56 290 sq mi
capital Des Moines
towns Cedar Rapids, Davenport, Sioux City
features Grant Wood◊ Gallery in Davenport and Herbert Hoover◊ birthplace and library in West Branch
products cereals, soybeans; meat and wool; industrial products
population 2 908 800
famous people Buffalo Bill Cody
history part of the Louisiana Purchase◊ in 1803, it remains an area of smaller farms; it became a state in 1846□

ipecacuanha S American plant *Psychotria ipecacuanha,* family Rubiaceae, is used as an emetic and in treating amoebic dysentery□

Iphigenia in Greek mythology, the daughter of Agamemnon◊□

Ipswich industrial river port (engineering, agricultural machinery, electrical goods, fertilizers) on the Orwell estuary, administrative headquarters of Suffolk, England; population 120 500. The Post Office research establishment is at nearby Martlesham□

Iqbal Muhammad 1875–1938. Pakistani poet-philosopher. The concept of separate Hindu and Muslim states in the Indian subcontinent is considered to have originated with him□

Iquitos river port on the Amazon, Peru, also a tourist centre for the rainforest; population 111 350□

Iráklion chief port (Heraklion, Italian name Candia) of Crete; population 101 700. Founded c824 by the Arabs, near the site of Knossos◊; fortifications of the period of Venetian rule 1207–1669 remain□

Iran Islamic Republic of (until 1935 ***Persia***)

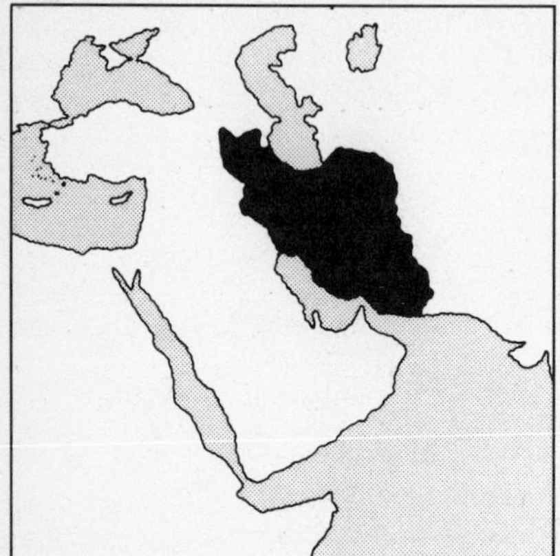

area 1 648 000 sq km/636 000 sq mi
capital Tehrán
towns Esfahán, Meshed, Tabriz, Shiraaz, Ahwaz; chief port Abadan
features Elburz and Zagros mountains; Lake Rezayeh; Dasht-Ekavir Desert; ruins of Persepolis
exports carpets, cotton textiles, metalwork, leather goods; oil and petrochemicals
currency rial
population 43 280 000, including minorities in Azerbaijan, Baluchistan, Khuzestan (Arabistan) and Kurdistan◊
language Farsi, Kurdish, Turk, Arabic, English, French
religion Shi'ite Islam, official
famous people Omar Khayyam, S'adi, Hafiz, Firdausi
government under the 1979 constitution there is an executive president (Muslim and eligible for re-election once) and a one-chamber legislative assembly, both elected for four years, but a Council of Guardians ensures that all laws conform to Islam, and power is ultimately in the hands of the religious leader, the Ayatollah Ruhollah Khomeini
history see Iran◊: history□

Iran: history

BC

c1600 overrun by Aryan tribes (including the Medes◊ and Persians◊), hence the modern name Iran
550 foundation of the Persian empire by Cyrus◊ II; it was to include Babylonia, Assyria, Asia Minor, Egypt, Thrace and Macedonia. See Achaemenids◊ (Cambyses, Darius I, Xerxes◊)
499–449 Persian Wars against Greece◊
331 conquest by Alexander◊

AD

224–636 Sassanian◊ Empire
c641 Arab conquest replaced Zorastrianism◊ with Islam◊
10–16th centuries Seljuk Turks, Mongols, etc. rule
1502–1736 native Safavid dynasty. See Abbas◊ I
19th century rivalry between Britain, France and Russia in the area (territory in the Caucasus ceded to Russia in 1828, and Persia compelled to withdraw from Afghanistan by Britain in 1857)
1901 oil discovered
1907 Persia divided into British and Russian zones of influence
1921 Reza Khan coup followed by establishment of Pahlavi◊ dynasty
1941–6 country occupied by Britain and Russia
1951 nationalization of oil by Mossadeq◊
1979 exile of the Shah, and Islamic republic established under Khomeini◊
1979 4 Nov–Jan 1981 US embassy staff held hostage in Tehran
1980 Gulf War with Iraq began; see below□

Iran-Iraq War or ***Gulf War*** between Iran and Iraq, claimed by the former to have begun with the Iraq offensive of 21 Sept 1980, and by the latter with the Iranian shelling of border posts 4 Sept 1980. Occasioned by dispute over the Shatt◊ al'Arab, it fundamentally arose because of Iran's encouragement of the Shi'ite majority in Iraq to rise against their Sunni government. Among Arab states, Iran was supported by Syria and Libya, the remainder supporting Iraq. By 1985 stalemate had led to a willingness to compromise, notably in Iran's abandonment of a demand for the resignation of President Saddam Hussein of Iraq; but sporadic fighting continues□

Iraq Republic of
area 444 000 sq km/172 000 sq mi
capital Baghdad
towns Mosul and port of Basra
features rivers Tigris and Euphrates; reed architecture of the marsh Arabs; sites of Eridu, Babylon, Nineveh, Ur, Ctesiphon
exports dates (80% of world supply); wool; oil
currency Iraqi dinar
population 15 000 000
language Arabic, official
religion Shi'ite Islam 60%, Sunni Islam 30%, Christianity 3%
government under the 1970 constitution there is a Revolutionary Command Council, which

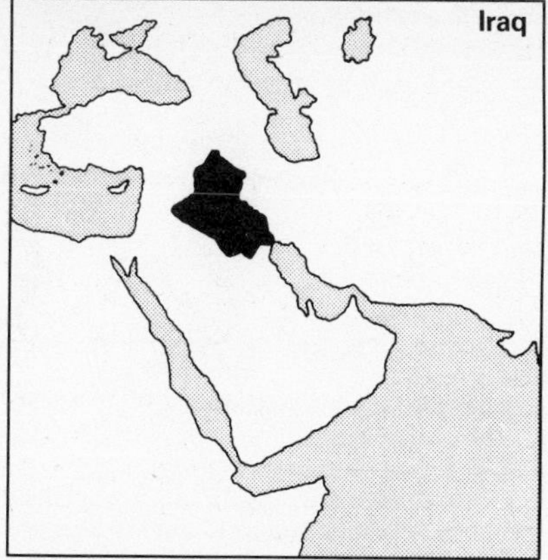

elects the president (Saddam Hussein from 1979); the only legal political party is the National Progressive Front (alliance of the socialist Ba'ath Party and Kurdish parties)
history see Iraq: history□

Iraq: history

BC

c5000–2000 Sumerian Civilization began with the foundation of Eridu (on Euphrates NW of Basra), the world's oldest city
c4000 the Great Flood; marked by an 8 ft layer of mud at Ur (near Eridu)
c3100 Uruk (higher up Euphrates, on opposite bank), the world's first writing (pictograms scratched on clay tablets, which later developed into cuneiform◊) found in excavating this city. Gilgamesh◊ was possibly a historical character of this period
2900–2370 first dynasty established at Ur; rich gold jewellery excavated by Woolley◊
2370–2230 Akkad (site unidentified) founded by Sargon◊, who united the whole of Sumer and established an empire that stretched to the Mediterranean
2230–2100 dark age in which only cities such as Lagash◊ (NE of Uruk) remained independent of invading tribes; 30 000 clay tablets give details of its temple administration
2100–2000 3rd dynasty at Ur controlled all Sumer and Akkad, and built the great Ziggurat◊ at Ur; when Ur fell to the tribes Sumeria's power was finally broken; the language was no longer spoken after 1500, but remained a literary language
c1950–612 Assyrian Civilization (capital Nineveh◊ opposite Mosul on the Tigris)
8–7th century its period of greatest influence, when it reached from Armenia to Egypt. See Sargon◊ II, Sennacherib◊, Esarhaddon◊ and Asshurbanipal◊
612 Nineveh sacked by the Medes and Babylonians
Assyrians excelled in agriculture, engineering and science; their complex mythology is symbolised in the winged bulls and eagle-masked priests of their sculptures; in warfare they skinned their enemies alive (seen in their bas-reliefs), and their thousands of clay cuneiform tablets record their commercial, legal, and literary skill
1792–539 Babylonian Civilization (capital Babylon◊) reached its first peak under Hammurabi◊
1595 Babylon sacked by the Hittites◊, and Babylonia eventually became a vassal state of Assyria, but with periods of revolt
612 Babylonians joined with Medes to sack Nineveh
605 second peak of influence reached under Nebuchadnezzar◊ II
539 conquered by Cyrus II◊ of Persia
332 conquered by Alexander the Great◊, and subsequently under Seleucid, Parthian and Sassanian◊ rule
Babylonians were great traders, lawyers, and administrators; they achieved much in astronomy, mathematics, medicine and music

AD

633–9 Arab Conquest
750–1258 Baghdad the capital of the Abbasid◊ caliphate until it fell to the Mongols
1639–1918 part of the Ottoman Empire◊
1920–32 under British mandate
1921 a kingdom under Feisal◊ I
1941–5 occupied by Britain after a pro-Nazi coup
1958 Feisal II assassinated and a republic proclaimed
1975 treaty with Shah of Iran, making territorial concessions to end Iranian support for Kurdish dissidents in Iraq
1980 treaty abrogated by Saddam Hussein, and Iran invaded, since Iran (under Khomeini◊) had incited the Shi'ite minority in Iraq to overthrow their government. See Iran-Iraq◊ War□

Ireland John 1879–1962. British composer, born at Bowden, Cheshire. Works include mystic orchestral prelude *The Forgotten Rite* 1915 and the piano solo *Sarnia* (both inspired by the years he lived in the Channel Islands) and song settings. Britten◊ was his pupil□

Ireland one of the British Isles; area 83 040 sq km/32 050 sq mi. See Republic of Ireland◊ and Northern Ireland◊□

Ireland: history

BC

5th century invasion by Celtic tribes, and division into warring kingdoms (the modern provinces), nominally under a High King

AD

Irish settlements in Wales and W England

432 St Patrick introduced Christianity
5–6th centuries height of early Irish civilization
800 period of Norse raids, ending in defeat of the Norsemen in 1014 by Brian Boru at Clontarf
12th century wars between rival kings led to the Anglo-Norman Conquest. Henry II was accepted as overlord in 1172, but English authority gradually reduced to the area of the 'Pale' round Dublin
1534 Henry VIII began reconquest and then attempted to enforce the Reformation; Roman Catholicism restored by Mary
1595 Elizabeth I sent Essex◊ to quell rebellion by O'Neill, Earl of Tyrone
1603 English reconquest complete
1610 most important of the 'plantations' of Ulster with Scottish and English settlers reinforcing existing differences between Ulster and the rest of Ireland
1641 revolt by Ireland during English Civil War; suppressed by Cromwell◊ in 1649. See Drogheda◊
1689 Irish Catholics rose in favour of James◊ II; northern Protestants besieged at Londonderry
1690 Battle of the Boyne◊: William◊ of Orange landed and defeated James II
1739–40 first Irish famine: 400 000 died
1798 French invasion of Ireland and national rising suppressed (Wolfe Tone◊)
1801 Act of Union with England enforced; end of Irish Parliament
1829 Catholic Emancipation. See Daniel O'Connell◊
1845–9 great famine, caused by potato blight: 700 000 died, over 1 000 000 emigrated (mainly to USA)
1879 Home Rule movement established. See Gladstone◊, Parnell◊; bills in 1886 and 1893 fail
1914 Asquith's successful Home Rule bill suspended during World War I; Curragh◊ Mutiny
1916 Easter Rising
1921 Anglo-Irish Treaty, which resulted in creation of the Irish Free State and secession from it of Northern Ireland◊□

Ireland Northern
area 14 147 sq km/5462 sq mi
capital Belfast
towns Derry, Enniskillen, Omagh, Newry, Armagh, Coleraine
features Mourne mountains, Belfast Lough and Lough Neagh; Giant's Causeway; comprises the six counties (Antrim, Armagh, Down, Fermanagh, Londonderry and Tyrone). See also Ulster◊
exports engineering, especially shipbuilding

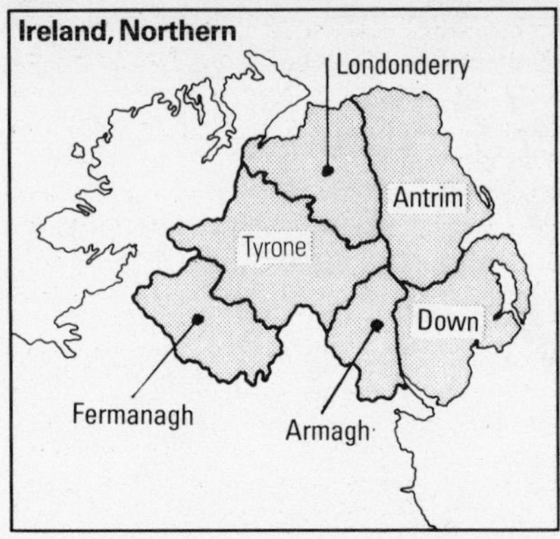

including textile machinery, aircraft components; linen and synthetic textiles; processed foods, especially dairy and poultry products – all affected by the 1980s depression and political terrorism
currency as for the rest of the UK
population 1 547 300
language English
religion 54% Protestant, 31% Roman Catholic
famous people Montgomery, Alanbrooke
government since 1972 there has been direct rule from Westminster, because of the outbreak of violence, with terrorist outrages from both Republicans (see IRA◊) and Protestant Ulster Unionists. Northern Ireland is entitled to send 12 members to the Westminster Parliament. Attempts to solve the problem repeatedly failed. Under the Anglo-Irish Agreement 1985, the Republic of Ireland was given a consultative role (via an Anglo-Irish conference) in the government of the province, but agreed that there should be no change in its status except by majority consent, and that there should be greater cooperation against terrorism. The agreement was approved by Parliament, but all 12 Ulster members gave up their seats, so that by-elections could be fought as a form of 'referendum' on the views of the province itself. A similar boycotting of the Northern Ireland Assembly since the Anglo-Irish agreement led to its dissolution in 1986 by the UK government.
recent history the creation of Northern Ireland dates from 1921 when the mainly Protestant counties of Ulster (the result of the Plantation of Ulster◊) withdrew from the newly-established Irish Free State. Spasmodic outbreaks by the IRA continued, but only in 1968–9 were there serious Civil Rights disturbances arising from Protestant political dominance and discrimination against the Roman Catholic minority in employment and housing. British

troops were sent to restore peace and protect Catholics, but disturbances continued and in 1972 the parliament at Stormont was prorogued, and superseded by direct rule from Westminster□

Ireland Republic of (Irish *Éire*)

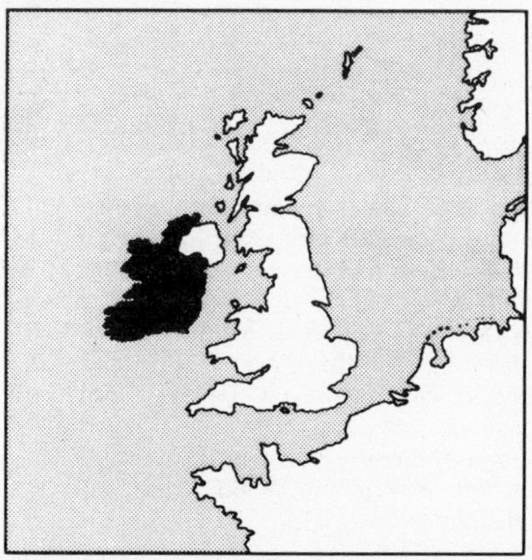

area 68 892 sq km/26 601 sq mi
capital Dublin
towns Cork, Dun Laoghaire, Limerick, Waterford, all ports
features Bog of Allen, source of domestic and national power; rivers Shannon, Liffey, Boyne; Magillicuddy's Reeks, Wicklow Mountains; Lough Corrib, lakes of Killarney; Galway Bay and Aran Islands; heavy rainfall. Tourism is important.
exports livestock, dairy products; Irish whiskey; micro-electronic components and assemblies; mining and engineering products, chemicals, tobacco, clothing
currency punt
population 3 368 000
language Irish and English, both official
religion Roman Catholicism
famous people Éamon de Valéra, *literature* James Joyce, Sean O'Casey, Brendan Behan, Samuel Beckett
government under the constitution of 1937, nominal president, with a senate (Seanad Éireann), and house of representatives (Dáil Éireann) elected by proportional representation (Prime Minister/Taoiseach Garret FitzGerald with a Fine-Gael◊/Labour coalition). The opposition party is Fianna Fáil◊.
recent history the Irish Free State came into existence in 1922, following the treaty of 1921. See Ireland◊. It was neutral in World War II, and in 1949 left the Commonwealth as the Republic of Ireland, although the British government maintained for Irish citizens in the UK most of the advantages of British subjects. Ireland entered the Common Market in 1973. The desire for a united Ireland, including Northern Ireland, remains a matter for contention between the British and Irish governments (but see Anglo-Irish Agreement under Northern Ireland◊)□

Irene in Greek mythology, goddess of peace (Roman Pax)□

Irene St c752–803AD. Byzantine empress regent 780–790, widow of Leo IV, who ruled with their son Constantine till banished for her cruelty. Returning 797, she blinded and imprisoned her son, but was deposed 802. She was canonized by the Orthodox Church□

Ireton Henry 1611–51. English civil war general, son-in-law of Cromwell◊. After the Battle of Naseby◊ he strove for a compromise with Charles I, but then played a leading role in his trial and execution. Lord Deputy in Ireland from 1650, he died of fever besieging Limerick□

Irian Indonesian name for New◊ Guinea□

iridium element
symbol Ir
atomic number 77
physical description yellow-white metal
features highly resistant to corrosion; the international prototype standard kilogram is composed of 90% platinum 10% iridium
iridium anomalies iridium enriched layers in earth's rock strata are thought to result from meteoritic impact
uses it has varied uses in electrical work and engineering□

iris perennial northern temperate flowering plants of marshes, etc., family Iridaceae, which include the wild British ***yellow iris*** or ***flag*** *Iris pseudo-corus*. Many cultivated varieties derive from *Iris germanica*. ***Orris root,*** used in perfumery, is the violet scented underground stem of the S European iris *Iris florentina*. The crocus◊ also belongs to this family□

iris the coloured muscular diaphragm that controls size of the pupil in the eye◊□

Irish Gaelic first official language of the Irish Republic, though the number of speakers (*Gaeltacht*) is small. See Connacht◊. The heroes of ancient Irish literature are Conchobar◊ and Finn◊ Mac Cumhaill□

Irish Republican Army group of militant Irish nationalists with aim of uniting Ireland by terrorism□

Irish Sweepstake Irish government run lottery◊, run on behalf of nursing services□

Irish terrier type of terrier. See under dog◊□

Irkutsk industrial city (coal, iron and steel, machine tools, gold dredging) in the southern USSR; population 568 000. See Novosibirsk◊□

iron element
symbol Fe

atomic number 26
physical description silvery-white metal
features an essential component of haemoglobin (in red blood cells) of all animals (a deficiency causes a form of anaemia, but excess is also harmful). Earth's core is made of iron. It is extracted mainly from haematite (ferric oxide $Fe_2 0_3$) and magnetite ores. Fundamental to all manufacturing industry since steel is iron with approximately 1% carbon added
uses important chemically in industry, and as the basis of permanent and electro- magnets□
Iron Age period marked by the introduction of iron tools and weapons. See under prehistory◊□
ironbark a type of eucalyptus◊ tree□
Iron Cross medal◊ awarded for valor in the German armed forces□
Iron Curtain after World War II the dividing line between Soviet-dominated Eastern Europe and Western Europe (phrase used by Churchill, 1946)□
Iron Gate see under Danube◊□
Iron Guard see under Romania◊□
iron pyrites a common iron ore FeS_2; brassy yellow, and occurring in cubic crystals; it resembles gold nuggets, hence 'fools' gold'□
Iroquois confederation of N American Indians, the Six Nations (Cayuga, Mohawk, Oneida, Onondaga and Seneca, with the Tuscorora from 1715), traditionally formed by Hiawatha (actually a priestly title) in 1570. Allies of the English and Dutch, in the Anglo-French Wars. They almost wiped out the related Wyandot (nicknamed by the French 'Huron'), after whom Lake Huron is named, in the 16–17th centuries□
irradiation exposure to radiation, used to speed up a chemical process, including ***ultraviolet*** to make vitamin products in the food and the pharmaceutical industries; ***X-radiation*** and radiation from radium and radioactive isotopes for diagnostic photography in industry and medicine, and treatment of some malignant conditions; ***particle accelerator*** and ***nuclear reactor radiation*** used in industry, agriculture and medicine, e.g. making radioactive isotopes; preservation and sterilization of foods, drugs and prepacked surgical requirements, together with control of infestation in stored grain and other foodstuffs is achieved by use of gamma rays; ***electron, gamma-ray*** or ***neutron radiation*** to produce desired properties in plastics□
Irrawaddy chief river of Burma: length 2090 km/1300 mi. Chief tributaries Chindwin and Shweli□
irrigation artificial water supply for dry agricultural areas, as in the channelling of the annual Nile◊ flood from the earliest times, and its modern control by the Aswan◊ High Dam. Its drawbacks are that continuous controlled irrigation tends to concentrate salts causing infertility, and rich river silt is retained at the dam, to the impoverishment of the land and fisheries in the estuary area. The Colorado, USA, now barely reaches the sea through over-exploitation□
Irvine new town in Strathclyde, Scotland; population 58 000. Overlooking the Isle of Arran, it is also a holiday resort□
Irving Sir Henry. Stage name of British actor John Brodribb 1838–1905. From 1871 he established his reputation at the Lyceum in partnership with Ellen Terry◊. His Shakespearean roles include Hamlet and Shylock. In 1895 he was the first actor to be knighted□
Irving Washington 1783–1859. American essayist and short-story writer. His *Sketch Book of Geoffrey Crayon* 1820, included the stories of 'Rip Van Winkle' and 'Legend of Sleepy Hollow'.□
Isaac in Old Testament, Hebrew patriarch, son of Abraham and Sarah, and father of Esau and Jacob◊□
Isabella 1451–1504. Queen of Castile from 1474, after the death of her brother Henry IV. By her marriage with Ferdinand of Aragon 1469, the crowns of the two Christian states in the Spanish peninsula were united. She introduced the Inquisition into Castile, and the persecution of the Jews, and gave financial encouragement to Columbus◊□
Isabella II 1830–1904. Queen of Spain from 1822, when she succeeded her father Ferdinand◊ VII. The Salic Law banning a female sovereign had been abrogated by the Cortes, but her succession was disputed by her uncle Don Carlos. The Carlists were defeated after seven years of civil war, but she abdicated in favour of her son Alfonso XII 1870□
Isaiah 8th century BC. In Old Testament, first major Hebrew prophet□
Isère river of SE France, a tributary of the Rhône□
Isfahan industrial city in central Iran; population 671 825. The ancient capital of Abbas◊ the Great, its features include the Great Square, Grand Mosque, and Hall of Forty Pillars□
Isherwood Christopher 1904– . British novelist, e.g. *Goodbye to Berlin* 1939, and playwright (three verse plays in collaboration with Auden◊)□
Ishmael in Old Testament, son of Abraham◊ and his wife Sarah's Egyptian maid; traditional ancestor of Mohammed and the Arab people. He and his mother were driven out by Sarah's jealousy□

Ishtar goddess of love and war worshipped by the Babylonians and Assyrians. See Semiramis and Tammuz◊□

isinglass gelatin obtained from the swim-bladders of fish, especially sturgeon, and used in clarifying wine and beer, and in cookery, e.g. jellies and confections□

Isis ancient Egyptian goddess (identified with Greek Demeter), daughter of Geb and Nut (earth and sky), and wife of Osiris◊□

Isis see Thames◊□

Iskenderun port, naval base and steel town in Turkey; population 125 000□

Islam religion (Arabic 'submission' to the will of Allah) of which the creed declares: there is no God but Allah, and Mohammed◊ is the Prophet or Messenger of Allah. Beliefs include Creation, Fall of Adam, Angels and the Jinn◊, Heaven and Hell, Day of Judgment, God's predestination of good and evil, and the succession of scriptures revealed to the prophets, including Moses and Jesus, but of which the perfect, final form is the *Koran* or ***Quran*** divided into 114 *suras* or chapters, said to have been divinely revealed to Mohammed, the original being preserved beside the throne of Allah in heaven.
sects there are two main Muslim sects:
Sunni whose members hold that the first three caliphs were all Mohammed's legitimate successors, and are in the majority. The name derives from the *Sunna* Arabic 'rule', the body of traditional law evolved from the teaching and acts of Mohammed.
Shi'ite or ***Shia*** whose members believe that Ali◊ was Mohammed's first true successor; they number c85 million, and are found in Iran, Iraq◊, Lebanon, and Bahrain. Holy men have greater authority in the Shi'ite sect, which has been called the 'Roman Catholic' division of Islam. Breakaway sub-sects include the ***Alawite*** sect to which the ruling party in Syria belongs; and the ***Ismaili*** sect with the ***Aga Khan*** IV 1936– as its spiritual head; he was the nominated successor of his grandfather, Aga Khan III 1877–1955, a noted racehorse-owner. There is an Ismaili Centre (1985) in Kensington, London. See also Samarra◊.
Later schools include ***Sufism*** a mystical pantheistic movement in 17th century Iran, influenced by Neoplatonism. Generally speaking, Islam has not been a missionary religion, but ***Tabligh*** developed after World War II as a missionary ('Revival') movement, backing the militant organizations for the 'true Islamic state'; annual gatherings are held at Tongi, near Dacca. See also Jihad◊.
Islamic law Islam differs from Christianity in embodying a secular Islamic Law (the Shari'a or 'Highway'), which is clarified for Shi'ites by reference to their own version of the ***sunna***, 'practice' of the Prophet as transmitted by his companions; the Sunni sect also take into account ***ijma'***, the endorsement by universal consent of practices and beliefs among the faithful. A ***mufti*** is a legal expert who guides the courts in their interpretation, and in Turkey (until the establishment of the republic in 1924) had supreme spiritual authority.
organization there is no organized church or priesthood, though Mohammed's descendants (the Hashim family) and popularly recognized holy men, mullahs and ayatollahs (see Khomeini◊), are accorded respect.
observances the 'Five Pillars of the Faith' are: recitation of the creed, worship five times a day (facing Mecca◊; the call to prayer is given by a muezzin, usually from the minaret of a mosque◊), almsgiving, fasting sunrise to sunset through Ramadan (9th month of the year, which varies with the calendar), and the pilgrimage to Mecca at least once in a lifetime□

Islamabad capital of Pakistan (designed by Doxiadis◊) from 1967; population 201,000□

Islay see under Inner Hebrides◊□

Isle of Man see Man◊, Isle of□

Isle of Wight see Wight◊, Isle of□

Islington borough of N Greater London
features 19th century squares and terraces at Highbury, Barnsbury, Canonbury; Wesley Museum in City Road. Mineral springs in Clerkenwell were exploited in conjunction with a music-hall in the 17th century, and Lilian Baylis◊ developed a later theatre as an 'Old Vic' annexe; the Sadler's Wells Opera Company moved from there to the Coliseum in 1969 as (from 1974) the English National Opera Company, but the Sadler's Wells Royal Ballet continues (see Royal Ballet◊)
population 169 700□

Ismail I 1487–1542. Shah of Persia 1499–1524, founder of the Safavi dynasty, who established the first national govt since the Arab conquest, and Shi'ite Islam as the national religion□

Ismail 1830–95. Khedive (viceroy) of Egypt 1866–79, who sold his Suez Canal shares to Disraeli◊ 1875, and whose bankruptcy led to Anglo-French financial control of Egypt. He was compelled to abdicate□

Ismaili a set of Shi'ite Muslims. See under Islam◊□

Ismailia city in NE Egypt; population 146 000. It was founded 1863 as the headquarters for construction of the Suez Canal and named after the Khedive Ismail◊□

isobar line drawn on weather charts to show points of equal atmospheric pressure; lines close together indicate large variations in pressure over a small distance, associated with strong winds or a depression□

Isocrates 436–338BC. Athenian orator, a pupil of Socrates. He was a professional speechwriter and teacher of rhetoric□

isolationism concentration on internal rather than foreign affairs. In the USA, usually associated with the Republican party, especially politicians of the midwest. Intervention in both World Wars was initially resisted, and after Korea◊, Vietnam◊, and the Lebanon◊ fiasco, there was resistance to further involvement in Europe, the Pacific, or the Middle East. See Monroe◊□

isomer compound having the same molecular composition and mass as another, but with different properties, owing to the changed structural arrangement of the atoms in the molecules. See Wöhler◊□

isomorphism existence of substances of different chemical composition which have similar crystalline form□

Isopoda order of Crustaceans◊ which include the woodlice◊□

isoprene CH_2:CH.C(CH_3):CH_2 volatile fluid made from petroleum, coal, etc., which is used to make synthetic rubber□

isotherm line linking on a map all places having the same temperature at a given time□

isotope one of two or more atoms which have the same atomic number, but which contain a different number of neutrons. They may be stable or radioactive, natural or synthetic. See atom, radioisotope◊ □

Israel northern kingdom of Palestine◊, formed after the death of Solomon◊ by Jewish peoples seceding from the rule of his son Rehoboam, and electing instead Jeroboam◊□

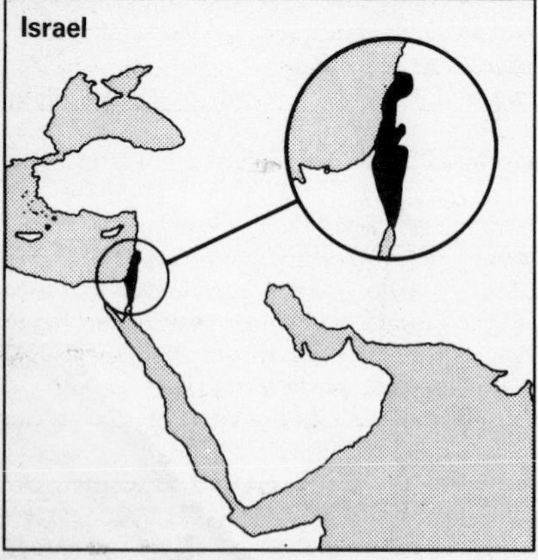

Israel State of

area 20 770 sq km/8017 sq mi (as at 1949 armistice)

capital Jerusalem (not recognized by the United Nations)

towns ports Tel Aviv/Jaffa, Haifa, Eilat; Bat-Yam, Holon, Ramat Gan, Petach Tikva, Beersheba

features coastal plain of Sharon between Haifa and Tel Aviv noted since ancient times for fertility, River Jordan, Dead Sea, Lake Tiberias, Negev Desert, Golan Heights; historic sites, Jerusalem, Bethlehem, Nazareth; Masada, Megiddo, Jericho; caves of the Dead Sea scrolls

exports citrus and other fruit, avocados, chinese leaves; fertilizers, plastics, petrochemicals, textiles; electronics (military, medical, scientific, industrial), electro-optics, precision instruments and aircraft and missiles

currency shekel

population 4 024 000 (including c750 000 Arabs as Israeli citizens and over 1 million Arabs in the occupied territories); under the Law of Return 1950, 'every Jew◊ shall be entitled to come to Israel as an immigrant', those from the East and E Europe are *Ashkenazim*, and from Spain, Portugal, Arab, N Africa, etc., are *Sephardim* (over 50% of the population is now of Sephardic descent). See also Falashas◊. An Israeli-born Jew is a *Sabra*; c500 000 Israeli Jews are resident in the USA

language Hebrew◊, Arabic, both official

religion Israel is a secular state, but the predominant faith is Jewish; the Arabs practise Sunni Islam

famous people Chaim Weizmann, David Ben Gurion, Golda Meir, Moshe Dayan, Menachem Begin. See also Theodor Herzl◊

government president, single chamber parliament (Knesset), elected for four years (Prime Minister Shimon Peres◊ of the Labour party from 1984)

recent history (for ancient history, see list below) the modern state was established 1948 on the ending of the British mandate under the League of Nations (see Palestine◊). Israel was recognized by the UN in 1949, but had been immediately attacked by her Arab neighbours (see under Arab-Israeli◊ Wars and Gush◊ Emunim). The chief issues in the election of 1984 were the establishment of settlements on the West Bank (actively supported by Likud) and the occupation of S Lebanon, initiated and maintained by Likud. Following a virtual dead heat, Shimon Peres agreed to take the premiership for two years, when he would be succeeded by Shamir of the right-wing Likud party. Extremely high inflation, and insecurity following the debacle of the invasion of Lebanon, led to large-scale emigration, more than 30 000 in 1985□

Israel: history

BC

c2000 migration of the Jews under Abraham◊ from Mesopotamia◊ to Palestine (Canaan: see Canaanite◊ Empire)

c1300–1200 migration to Egypt◊, in Hyksos period, and rescue by Moses◊ from slavery in the Exodus◊

c1274 Joshua◊ led main invasion in return to the Promised Land of Canaan◊

c1000 David◊ achieved a united kingdom, with Jerusalem◊ its capital

c923 after the death of Solomon◊, tribes seceding from the rule of his son Rehoboam formed the first kingdom of Israel, in the north under Jeroboam◊

c722 Israel conquered by Sargon◊ II

586 southern kingdom of Judah◊ conquered by Nebuchadnezzar◊ II, who held its people captive in Babylonia◊ (the beginning of the Diaspora◊)

539 Cyrus◊ the Great allowed the people to return, and the Temple at Jerusalem was rebuilt

Under subsequent conquests (see Palestine◊), the Jews retained varying degrees of autonomy, with interspersed revolts:

165 revolt of the Maccabees◊

AD

66–70 revolt against Rome which led to the destruction of the Temple at Jerusalem by Titus◊

72 Roman siege of isolated Masada◊

132–135 renewed revolt by Bar◊ Kokhbar defeated, Jerusalem rebuilt as the Roman colony of Aelia Capitolina

Israeli history became that of the scattered communities until the establishment of the modern Israeli state. See above□

Issigonis Sir Alec 1906– . British designer of the Morris Minor 1948, and Mini-Minor 1959, which added the word 'mini' to the language□

Istanbul city and chief seaport of Turkey; population 4 871 000. Founded as ***Byzantium*** c660BC it was renamed ***Constantinople*** by Constantine in 330AD, and was the capital of the Byzantine Empire◊ until captured by the Turks 1453. As ***Istamboul*** it was the capital of the Ottoman Empire until 1922. Notable are the harbour of the Golden Horn; Hagia Sophia (Justinian's church of the Holy Wisdom 537, now a mosque); Sultan Ahmet Mosque, known as the Blue, from its tiles; Topkapi Palace of the Sultans (with a harem of 400 rooms), now a museum. The Selimye Barracks in the suburb of ***Usküdar*** (Scutari) was used as a hospital in the Crimean War. The rooms used by Florence Nightingale, with her personal possessions, are preserved as a museum□

italic style of printing in which the letters slope to the right, introduced by Aldus Manutius of Venice from 1501. Very similar is the handwriting style developed in 1522 by Vatican chancery scribe Ludovico degli Arrighi for popular use (the basis for modern italic script)□

Italy Republic of

area 301 245 sq km/116 300 sq mi

capital Rome

towns Milan, Turin; ports Naples, Genoa, Palermo, Bari, Catania

features Maritime Alps, Dolomites, Apennines; rivers Po, Adige, Arno, Tiber, Rubicon; lakes Como, Maggiore, Garda; Europe's only active volcanoes, Vesuvius, Etna, Stromboli; islands of Sicily, Sardinia, Elba, Capri, Ischia; enclave of the Vatican◊

exports wine, fruit and vegetables; textiles (Europe's largest silk producer), leather goods, motor vehicles, electrical goods, chemicals, marble (Carrara), sulphur and mercury, iron and steel

currency lira

population 57 000 000

language Italian, derived from Latin◊

religion 90% Roman Catholicism

famous people *art* Duccio, Giotto, Botticelli, Leonardo, Michelangelo, Raphael, Titian, Tintoretto, Veronese, Tiepolo *architecture* Bernini, Palladio *music* Albinoni, Corelli, Vivaldi *literature* (drama) Pirandello; (prose) Boccaccio, Manzoni, Verga, (poetry) Dante, Petrarch, Ariosto, Tasso, Leopardi, Montale, Quasimodo *philosophy* Croce *politics* Borgia and Medici families, Machiavelli, Garibaldi, Cavour, Gramsci, Mussolini, Berlinguer *science* Galileo, Marconi

government under the constitution of 1947 there is a non-executive president, and a senate (elected for six years) and chamber of deputies elected for five years (Prime Minister Bettino Craxi, Socialist, from 1983, heading a left-of-centre coalition). There are 20 regions, all with their own parliaments, but five have special autonomous status: Friuli- Venezia Giulia, Sardinia, Sicily, Trentino-Alto-Adige and Valle d'Aosta
history see Italy: history◊□

Italy: history

BC

4th/3rd centuries Gauls (in the N), Etruscans (Tuscany), Latins and Sabines (central), Greek colonies (S and Sicily) united under Roman rule

AD

476 end of the Roman Empire (see Roman◊ history), Italy in turn under the Ostrogoths◊ and Lombards◊
8th century rise of the Papacy as a territorial power, annexation of the Lombard kingdom by Charlemagne, and his coronation as emperor of the west in 800
800–1250 relations between the Papacy and the Holy Roman Empire gradually soured, and in the struggle between them the self-governing city republics emerged
1300 five major powers in Italy: the Papal states, the kingdom of Naples, and the city states of Milan, Florence and Venice◊
1494–1559 their wars and rivalries allowed invasions by France and Spain; Naples and Milan came under Spanish rule
1700 Austria secured Milan and became the dominating power; Naples passed to a Spanish Bourbon dynasty, and Sardinia to the dukes of Savoy
1797–1814 Italy united under French rule, but on Napoleon◊'s fall again split among Austria, the Pope, the kingdoms of Sardinia and Naples, and four smaller duchies
1820, 1831, 1848–9 abortive nationalist revolts
1861 Victor Emmanuel◊ of Sardinia proclaimed king of Italy. See Garibaldi◊
1911–12 war with Turkey, resulted in aquisition of Tripoli and Cyrenaica
1914–18 intervention in World War I on the Allied side resulting in gain of Trieste, the Trentino, and S Tirol
1922 Mussolini◊ established a dictatorship
1929 Pope once more a temporal ruler. See Vatican City◊
1935–6 conquest of Ethiopia
1939 conquest of Albania
1940 entry into World War II as an ally of Germany
1943 Allied conquest of Sicily and fall of Mussolini; new government declared war on Germany
1943–5 Italy a battlefield between Germany and the Allies
1946 abdication of Victor◊ Emmanuel III
1947 peace treaty with the Allies
1954 Trieste returned to Italy by the Allies
1957 rapid expansion within the Common Market began
1960 monarchy rejected in a referendum. See Umberto II◊
1976 Communists reached their high point (Italy has Europe's largest Communist party, see Gramsci, Berlinguer◊, but it declined after 'historic compromise' coalition with the Christian Democrats 1973–9)
1978 kidnap and murder by leftist terrorists of former Prime Minister Aldo Moro
1980 bomb outrage killing 81 at Bologna railway station by right-wing terrorists, but thereafter decline of terrorism
1983 Bettino Craxi first Socialist Prime Minister□

Ivan six rulers of Russia, including:
Ivan III the Great 1440–1505. Grand Duke of Moscovy from 1462, who revolted against Tatar overlordship by refusing tribute to the Grand Khan Ahmed in 1480. He claimed the title of tsar, and used the double-headed eagle as the Russian state emblem.
Ivan IV called 'the Terrible', 1530–84. Grand Duke of Moscovy from 1533, he assumed power 1544, and was crowned as first tsar of Russia 1547. He conquered Kazan 1552, Astrakhan 1556, and Siberia 1581. His last years alternated between debauchery and religious austerities□

Ivanovo industrial city (textiles, chemicals, engineering) in central USSR; population 470 000□

Ives Charles Edward 1874–1954. American businessman and experimental composer, who used smaller intervals than the semi-tone in his songs and five symphonies□

Ives Frederic Eugene 1856–1937. American inventor of the halftone and three-colour printing processes for illustrations□

ivory hard white/cream dentine (calcified tissue) of which most animal teeth consist, especially the tusks of elephant, mammoth, walrus, etc. It is used for decorative carving.
Vegetable ivory is the hard albumen of seeds of the tropical palm *Phytelephas macrocarpa* from Colombia, a cheap substitute□

Ivory Coast Republic of
area 322 463 sq km/127 000 sq mi
capital Abidjan
towns Bouakeé

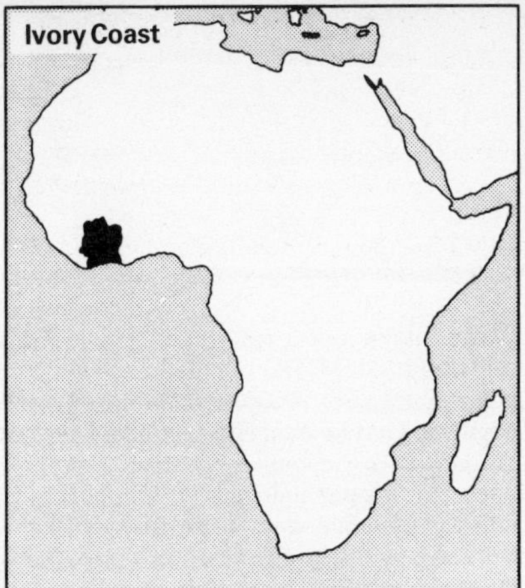

features combination of tropical rain forest (diminishing as it is exploited) in the south and savannah in the north
exports coffee, cocoa, timber, petroleum
currency CFA franc
population 9 178 000
language French, official
religion Animism 65%, Islam 24%, Christianity 11%
government executive president (Houphouët◊-Boigny from 1960), single chamber national assembly; there is only one legal party.
recent history taken over by France from 1842, it achieved independence 1960□

ivy mainly tropical climbing plants, genus *Hedera* family Araliaceae.
European ivy *H helix* has shiny evergreen leaves, clusters of small yellowish flowers, poisonous berries, and climbs by root-like suckers. N American ***poison ivy*** *Rhus toxicodendron*, which causes severe inflammation on skin contact, belongs to another family, Anacardiaceae□

Ivy League eight US universities with status similar to that of Oxford and Cambridge in the UK (including Harvard, Yale and Princeton)□

Ixion in Greek mythology, a king whom Zeus punished for his crimes by binding him to a fiery wheel rolling endlessly through the underworld□

Izhevsk industrial city (steel, agricultural machinery, machine tools), in the eastern USSR; population 574 000□

Izmir port and naval base (formerly Smyrna) in W Turkey; population 190 425. Originally Greek (founded c1000BC, it was destroyed by Tamerlane◊ 1402, and became Turkish 1424. It is the headquarters of NATO SE Command□

J

Jabalpur industrial (textile, oil and flour mills; armaments) city in Madhya Pradesh, India; population 758 000□

jábiru a large white tropical stork◊□

jaborandi S American plant *pilocarpus microphyllus,* family Rutaceae, source of pilocarpine, used to contract the pupil of the eye□

jacana wading birds, family Jacanidae, order Charadriiformes◊, with the longest toes and claws in the bird world enabling it to walk on the flat leaves of river plants, thus the name 'lily hopper'. Found in S America and Asia. It includes ***pheasant-tailed jacana*** *Hydrophasianus chirurgus*, of which the female has a 'harem' of two to four 'husbands'□

jacaranda genus of tropical American ornamental trees with fragrant wood and showy blue/violet flowers, family Bignoniaceae□

jackal Afro-Asian grey-yellow, nocturnal mammal *Canis aureus* of the dog family Canidae, 45 cm/1.5 ft high. They have a reputation as scavengers, but, when in packs, attack quite large animals□

jackdaw a bird of the crow family. See Corvidae◊□

Jackson Andrew 1767–1845. General, 7th president of the USA 1828–36. He defeated a British attack on New Orleans 1815, and as a Democrat fought against the corrupt power of US finance□

Jackson Glenda 1936– . British actress, born at Birkenhead. Her films include Oscar-winning *Women in Love* 1971 and *A Touch of Class* 1973; on television *Elizabeth R* 1971□

Jackson Thomas Jonathan, known as 'Stonewall' Jackson 1824–63. American Confederate general. He acquired his nickname and reputation at Bull◊ Run, from the firmness with which his brigade resisted the Northern attack. In 1862 he organized the Shenandoah valley campaign. He was accidentally shot by his own troops□

Jackson industrial city (furniture, cottonseed oil, iron and steel castings) and capital of Mississippi, USA; population 202 900. It was almost destroyed by Sherman◊ 1863; modern prosperity dates from gasfields discovered to the south□

Jacksonville port, resort and commercial centre, Florida, USA; population 540 900. It was named after Andrew Jackson◊. To the north the Cross-Florida Barge Canal links the Atlantic with the Gulf of Mexico□

Jack the Ripper unidentified mutilator and murderer of five women prostitutes in the Whitechapel area of London in 1888: speculative identifications include the Duke of Clarence (died 1892), elder brother of George V□

Jacob in Old Testament, Hebrew patriarch, son of Isaac◊ and Rebecca, who obtained the rights of seniority from his twin brother Esau by trickery. He married his two cousins Leah and Rachel, serving their father Laban seven years for each, and at the time of famine in Canaan joined his son Joseph◊ in Egypt. His 12 sons were the traditional ancestors of the 12 tribes of Israel□

Jacobins extremist republican club founded at Versailles 1789, which later used a former Jacobin (Dominican) friary as its headquarters in Paris. It was led by Robespierre◊, and closed after his execution 1794□

Jacobites supporters of the Stuarts◊ after the deposition of James II in 1688 (Latin *Jacobus* James). They included the Scottish Highlanders, who rose unsuccessfully under Claverhouse◊ in 1689; and those who rose in Scotland and N England under the leadership of James◊ Edward, the 'Old Pretender', in 1715, and followed his son Charles◊ Edward 1745–6 in an invasion of England which reached Derby. After the defeat of Culloden◊, Jacobitism was a spent force□

Jacquard Joseph Marie 1752–1834. French inventor of the ***Jacquard loom*** for producing complex designs by means of punched cards; the principle is still in use□

Jacquerie French peasant rising 1358, from the nickname for French peasants, Jacques Bonhomme□

Jacques-Dalcroze Émile 1865–1950. Swiss musician, developer of ***eurythmics***, a system of graceful movement to music□

jade glassy silicate of e.g. aluminium and sodium, ranging from white to green according to impurities, and used for carvings, e.g.

the 2nd century BC royal Chinese burial suits made of hundreds of small polished plaques□

Jaffa port (formerly Joppa), part of Tel◊-Aviv-Jaffa from 1949. It was captured by the Crusaders in the 12th century, by Napoleon 1799, and by Allenby◊ 1917□

Jagan Cheddi 1918– . Guianese statesman, leader of the People's Progressive Party from 1950, and first Prime Minister of British Guiana 1961–64□

jaguar a type of wild cat◊□

Jahangir 'Conqueror of the World'. Name adopted by the tyrannical Salim 1569–1627, son of Akbar◊ the Great, and 3rd Mogul emperor of Delhi from 1605. In 1622 he lost Kandahar to Persia, and his addiction to alcohol and opium gave power to his wife Nur Jahan, but he cared for literature and the arts, designing the Shalimar Gardens and buildings in Lahore□

Jahweh variant spelling of Jehovah◊□

jai alai another name for pelota◊□

Jainism a religion, regarded as an offshoot of Hinduism◊□

Jaipur capital of Rajasthan, India; population 1 005 000. It was founded by Jai Singh II 1728, who established an open-air observatory, and its fine stone buildings are coloured pink for Siva◊, with touches of yellow for Kali◊□

Jakarta (formerly Batavia 1616–1949) capital and industrial city (textiles, chemicals, plastics) of Indonesia on Java; population 6 504 000. Founded by the Dutch in 1619, it now has the president's palace and government offices, and is a tourist centre. A canal links it with its port at Tanjung Priok□

Jamaica

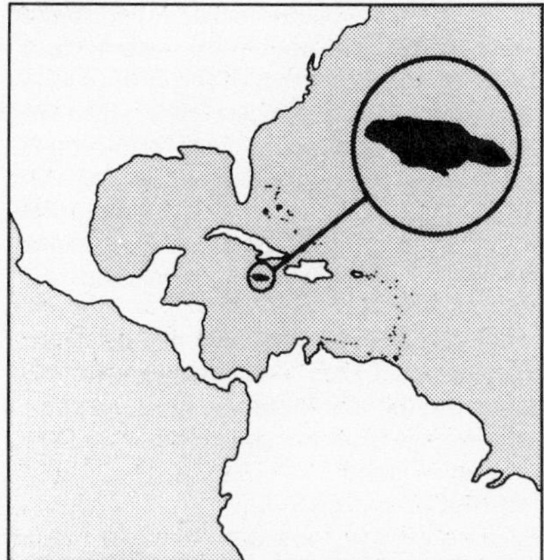

area 11 525 sq km/4411 sq mi
capital Kingston
towns Montego Bay, Spanish Town, St Andrews
features Blue mountains (so-called because of the haze over them, and famous for their coffee); partly undersea remains of the pirate city of Port Royal, destroyed by an earthquake in 1692
exports sugar, bananas, bauxite, rum, coffee, coconuts, liqueurs, cigars
currency Jamaican dollar
population 2 388 000, mixture of several ethnic groups
language English, Jamaican creole
religion all varieties of Christianity; others include Rastafarianism◊
famous people Marcus Garvey
government under the 1962 constitution a governor-general, elected house of representatives and a nominated senate. The Prime Minister (Edward Seaga from 1980; re-elected 1983) heads the Labour Party, the left-wing People's National Party (Michael Manley) is in Opposition.
history first reached by Europeans (Columbus) in 1494, Jamaica became British 1655, and independent within the Commonwealth in 1962□

James name of several saints, including:
James the Great. In New Testament, apostle, the son of Zebedee and brother of John◊. A Galilean fisherman, he was put to death by Herod◊ Agrippa
James the Little. In new Testament, disciple of Christ, son of Alphaeus
James the Just. In New Testament, brother of Jesus, to whom the latter appeared after the Resurrection; leader of the Church in Jerusalem, and author of the biblical *Epistle of James*□

James seven kings of Scotland:
James I 1394–1437, king from 1406, was captured by the English on the way to France in 1406, and although he became king the same year was held a prisoner until 1424, and was eventually murdered by his own nobles. He was also a poet.
James II 1430–60, king from 1437, assuming power 1449. He was accidentally killed while besieging Roxburgh Castle.
James III 1451–88, king from 1460, he assumed power 1469, and was murdered during a rebellion.
James IV 1473–1513, king from 1488, married Margaret (daughter of Henry VII) in 1503. He invaded England 1513, but was defeated and killed at Flodden.
James V 1512–42, king from 1513, he assumed power 1528. He was defeated by the English at Solway Moss 1542.
For James VI and VII, see James◊ I and II of Britain□

James two kings of Britain:

James I 1566–1625. King of England from 1603 and Scotland (*James VI*) from 1567. The son of Mary◊ Queen of Scots and Darnley◊, he succeeded on his mother's abdication from the Scottish throne, assumed power 1583, established a strong centralized authority, and married Anne of Denmark 1589. As successor to Elizabeth in England, he alienated the Puritans by High Church views and Parliament by his assertion of Divine Right, and was generally unpopular because of his favourites, especially Buckingham◊□

James II 1633–1701. King of England and Scotland (*James VII*) from 1685, second son of Charles I. He married Anne Hyde 1659 (mother of Mary and Anne) and Mary of Modena 1673 (mother of James Edward, the 'Old Pretender'). His conversion to Roman Catholicism led to attempts to exclude him from the succession, and though after his accession the failure of Monmouth's and Argyll's rebellions strengthened his position, his attempted arbitrary rule and favour to Catholics led Whig and Tory leaders to invite in 1688 William of Orange to take the throne. James fled to France, led a rising in Ireland 1689, but after defeat at the battle of the Boyne 1690 remained in exile in France□

James Edward 1688–1766, the 'Old Pretender' or (for Jacobites◊) James III. Son of James II, he landed in Scotland in 1715 to head a Jacobite rebellion, but withdrew owing to lack of support. In his later years he settled in Rome□

James Henry 1843–1916. Anglo-American novelist. Born in New York, he was the brother of William James◊. The chief theme of his novels is the impact of European culture upon the American soul. They include *Roderick Hudson* 1876, *The American* 1877, *The Portrait of a Lady* 1881, *Washington Square* 1881, *The Bostonians* 1886, *The Wings of a Dove* 1902, *The Ambassadors* 1903, and *The Golden Bowl* 1904. The supernatural tale 'The Turn of the Screw' 1898, was the basis of an opera by Britten◊. After 1875 he lived in Europe, becoming a naturalized British subject 1915. His style, always subtle, became increasingly complex□

James Jesse 1847–82. American bank and rail-road robber, born in Missouri and a leader (with his brother Frank 1843–1915) of the Quantrill◊ gang. Jesse was killed by an accomplice; Frank remained unconvicted□

James P(hyllis) D(orothy) 1920– . British detective novelist famous for characters (Superintendent Adam Dalgliesh and private investigator Cordelia Gray). She was in turn tax official, hospital administrator and civil servant, and her books include *Death of an Expert Witness* 1977, and *The Skull Beneath the Skin* 1982□

James William 1842–1910. American psychologist and philosopher, brother of Henry James◊. His books include *Varieties of Religious Experience* 1902; his 'pragmatic' approach to metaphysics concentrated on common sense ideas□

Jameson Sir Leander Starr 1853–1917. British colonial statesman. In 1896 he led the ***Jameson Raid*** into the Transvaal in support of the non-Boer colonists there, in an attempt to overthrow the government; he was Prime Minister Cape Colony 1904–8□

Jamestown first permanent British settlement in N America, established by Captain John Smith 1607, capital of Virginia◊ 1624–99□

Jamnagar industrial port (textiles, matches) in Gujarat, India; population 317 000□

Jamshedpur industrial city (Tata iron and steel works, coalmining) in Bihar, India; population 670 000□

Janáček Leoš 1854–1928. Czech composer and organist. His music, influenced by Moravian folk music, includes arrangements of folk songs, operas (*Jenufa* 1904, *The Cunning Little Vixen* 1924), and the choral *Glagolithic Mass* 1927)□

Janissary bodyguard of the Sultan, the Turkish standing army 1330–1826. Until the 16th century Janissaries were Christian boys forcibly converted to Islam; the bodyguard ceased to exist when it revolted at the decision of the Sultan in 1826 to raise a regular force□

Jansen Cornelius 1585–1638. Dutch Roman Catholic theologian, founder of Jansenism◊ with Auginus 1640, in which he supported the saint's more predestinatory approach to theology, as against that of the Jesuits□

Jansenism teaching of Jansen◊, which split the church in France in the mid-17th century, and was supported by Pascal◊ and Antoine Arnauld (a theologian linked with the Abbey of Port Royal, south west of Paris). Condemned by the Papacy, it died out in the early 18th century□

Jansky Karl Guthe 1905–49. American radio engineer of Czech descent, who in 1932 founded radio-astronomy by his detection of radio signals from the constellation of Sagittarius at Holmdel, New Jersey□

Janus in Roman mythology, god of doorways and passageways, the patron of the beginning of the day, month, and year, after whom Jan is named; he is represented as two-faced, looking in opposite directions□

Japan (Japanese *Nippon*)
area 370 000 sq km/142 680 sq mi

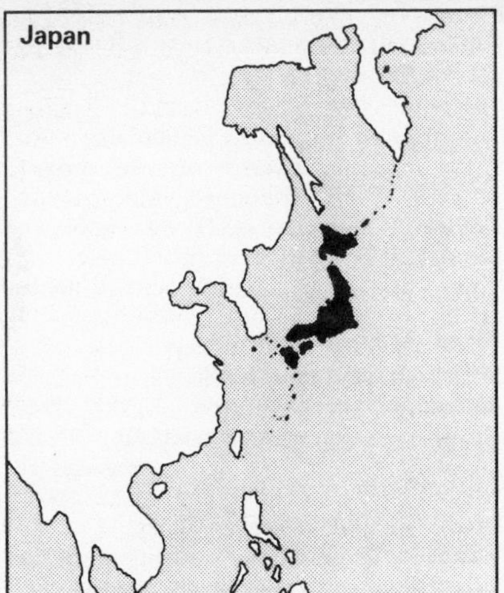

capital Tokyo
towns Fukuoka, Kitakyushu, Kyoto, Sapporo; ports Osaka, Nagoya, Yokohama, Kobe, Kawasaki
features comprises over 1000 islands, of which the chief are Hokkaido, Honshu, Shikoku, Kyushu◊
exports televisions, cassette and video recorders, radios, cameras, computers, robots, and other electronic and electrical equipment; cars and other vehicles, ships; iron and steel; chemicals, textiles
currency yen
population 119 896 000
language Japanese, official; English widely spoken. Japanese is related to Korean, is tonal and builds up words by adding simple words together to form compounds; it is written in a modified system of ideographs borrowed from the Chinese in the 3rd century, and a later simplified system (kana) has never replaced it; it has many borrowings from other languages, especially Western ones. Japanese put their family names first, e.g. Nakasone Yasuhiro
religion Shinto, Buddhism, Christianity (minority)
arts and crafts bonsai, ikebana, origami
famous people architecture Kenzo Tange *art* Hokusai, Utamaro *literature* (drama) see Bunraku, No◊ and kabuki◊; (novel) Murasaki◊ Shikibu, Yasunari Kawabata◊, Yukio Mishima◊ *poetry* see haiku◊ and Matsuyama◊ *science* Hideyo, Noguchi, Yukawa□
government headed by the Emperor (Hirohito◊ since 1926), a constitutional monarch since 1947, and the parliament has a house of councillors and house of representatives (Prime Minister from 1982 Nakasone◊, re-elected 1986), both popularly elected. The chief parties are the Liberal Democrats (LDP), in power almost continuously since World War II, and the Democratic Socialists (DSP).
history see Japan◊: history
Japan is in dispute with the USSR over the return of the Northern Territories (the island of Shikotan and the Habomai group, and the southern Kurils, Kunashiri and Etorofu).

Japan: history
400 imperial dynasty (see Amaterasu◊) began to establish control over Japan
5th century writing introduced from Korea
538 Buddhism introduced via Korea
710–94 Nara period
794–1185 Heian period
11th century ascendancy of the Samurai◊ began, which lasted until 19th century.
1185–1333 Kamakura period
1192 Yoritomo, a ruling noble assumed the title *shogun* commander-in-chief, the Emperor became only the nominal ruler.
14th century No◊ plays originated
1333–1573 Muromachi period
1542 first European traders arrived
1549 Francis Xavier introduced Christianity
1573–1603 Momoyama period
17th century Kabuki originated
1603–1868 Edo (Tokugawa) period
1853 USA (see Matthew Perry◊) insisted on opening trading relations
1867 the last shogun abdicated, and power returned to the Emperor
1868–1912 Meiji era
1894 war with China, conquest of Formosa and S Manchuria
1904–5 Russo-Japanese◊ War
1914 23 Aug Japan declared war on Germany
1919 Treaty of Versailles awarded former German colonies to Japan, e.g. Carolines, Marshall, Mariana and Pelew islands
1931–3 war with China
1937 war with China renewed; foundation of Soka Gakkai. See under Buddhism◊
1941 7 Dec attack on Pearl Harbor◊ brought Japan into World◊ War II until surrender Aug 1945, following the first use, by the US, of atomic bombs. See Horoshima◊ and Nagasaki◊
1952 Apr, end of Allied occupation of Japan (mainly US)
1955 foundation of the Liberal Democrat Party (LDP) by the merger of existing 'conservative' parties.
1972 Okinawa◊ returned to Japan
1980s pressure on Japan from EEC and USA to reduce its trade surplus□

Japan Current see Kuroshio◊□

jarrah a type of eucalyptus◊ tree◊□

Jarrow March the closure of Palmer's shipbuilding yard in Jarrow, NE England, in 1933 prompted a march of unemployed to London, a landmark of the Great Depression. A similar People's March for Jobs, Liverpool-London, was staged in 1981□

Jarry Alfred 1873–1907. French satiric dramatist, whose *Ubu Roi* 1896, foreshadowed the Theatre of the Absurd◊□

jasmine genus of plants *Jasminium*, family Oleaceae, with fragrant white/yellow flowers, and yielding jasmine oil, used in perfumes. ***Common jasmine*** is *J officinale*, and the Chinese ***winter jasmine*** *J nudiflorum*, flowers before the leaves appear□

Jason in Greek mythology, leader of the ***Argonauts*** who sailed in the Argo to Colchis (in modern Georgia, USSR) in search of the Golden◊ Fleece□

jasper a type of quartz. See under silica◊□

Jaspers Karl 1883–1969. German philosopher, who anticipated existentialism◊ in *Philosophy* 1932□

Jassy another form of Iaşi◊□

jaundice disease marked by yellowing of the skin and whites of the eyes by the presence of bile in the deeper layers, as a result of hepatitis◊, or obstruction of the bile duct by gallstones, etc. Mild cases can be cured by phototherapy□

Jaurès Jean Léon 1859–1914. French politician, founder of a united French socialist party, and of the journal *L'Humanité* 1904; he was assassinated by a half-witted youth□

Java see under Sunda◊ Islands□

javelin a type of spear used in sports events. See throwing◊ events□

jaw two bony structures which hold the teeth and frame the mouth. The upper ***maxilla*** consists of two bones centrally united early in fetal life, which join the bones of the forehead and cheek and each contains a hollow space, the maxillary sinus. The lower ***mandible*** is hinged at each side to the bone of the temple by ligaments□

jay a bird of the crow family. See corvidae◊□

Jayawardene Junius Richard 1906– . Sri Lankan statesman, leader of the United National Party from 1973, who became the country's first president in 1977, and reshaped the regime after years of instability□

jazz polyphonic, syncopated music characterized by improvization, which developed in the USA at the turn of this century out of Black American popular music.

1880–1900 originated in New Orleans

1917 centre of jazz moved to Chicago (Louis Armstrong◊) and St Louis

1920s growth of 'swing' music

1930s New York jazz orchestras: Paul Whiteman (1891–1967), Fletcher Henderson (1898–1952), Glenn Miller◊

1940s the 'big bands': Duke◊ Ellington, Woody Herman◊, Benny Goodman◊

1950s increasing diversity of styles: Charlie Parker◊, Dizzy Gillespie◊, Miles Davies (1926–), Stan Getz (1927–), Theolonius Monk (1917–82), Modern Jazz Quartet

1960s 'free form' Jazz: Ornette Coleman (1930–), John Coltrane (1926–)

1970s jazz rock: Weather Report

See also blues◊, pop◊ music□

Jeans Sir James Hopwood 1877–1946. British applied-mathematician and popularizer of science and astronomy. He worked on the kinetic theory of gases, problems of stability in astronomy, etc.□

jeans blue denim trousers, originating in jean (from 'jene fustian', a heavy canvas cloth made in Genoa), which was used in both England and America for work clothes, waggon covers, etc. Later a French fabric *serge de Nîmes* (corrupted to 'denim') was used, and in the 1960–70s, jeans became a unisex fashion cult□

Jedda see Jidda◊□

jeep (from 'GP', for general purpose) open vehicle of the American Army, adapted to driving over rough ground□

Jefferson Thomas 1743–1826. Third president of the USA 1801–9, born in Virginia, founder of the Democratic party. He was largely responsible for the drafting of the Declaration of Independence, and was governor of Virginia 1779–81, ambassador to Paris 1785–9, Secretary of State 1789–93, and vice-president 1796–1801□

Jeffrey Francis, Lord Jeffrey 1773–1850. Scottish judge and founder of the *Edinburgh Review* 1802–29. He was hostile to the Romantic poets, especially Wordsworth: 'This will never do' he wrote of *The Excursion*□

Jeffreys George, 1st Baron 1648–89. British judge noted for brutality, especially the ***Bloody Assizes*** 1685, following the Monmouth◊ Rebellion, when 320 rebels were executed. Lord Chancellor from 1685, he was captured when attempting to flee the country after the 1688 revolution, and died in the Tower□

Jehol see Chengdu◊□

Jehovah also ***Jahweh*** name of God in the biblical Old Testament; in Hebrew YHWH, to which the vowels 'a o a' were later added□

Jehovah's Witnesses Christian sect founded in the USA 1872 by Charles Taze Russell 1852–1916. They stress Christ's second coming (supposed to have invisibly taken place either in 1874 or 1914). Ensuing Armageddon and Last Judgment is to destroy all but the faithful, who will live in a Theocratic Kingdom. Their tenets, including rejection of military service, have led to conflict with authority□

Jekyll Gertrude 1843–1932. British landscape gardener, who collaborated with Edwin Lutyens◊. She used natural construction materials, was sensitive to colour, e.g. her 'grey garden' of silver-leaved plants, and abandoned Victorian 'bedding-out' to draw on the tradition of the cottage garden□

Jellicoe John Rushworth 1st Earl 1859–1935. British admiral, commander of the Grand Fleet 1914–16 (see Jutland◊), and 1st Sea Lord 1916–17, when he failed to push the introduction of the convoy system to combat U-boat attack□

jellyfish class Scyphozoa of the Coelenterata◊. When young they are *polyps* attached to rocks, etc. Adults have umbrella-shaped bodies of semi-transparent gelatinous texture (the *medusa* stage), and a fringe of stinging tentacles to paralyse their prey. Some reach over 2 m/6 ft across, and they move through the water by contraction of the muscles of the umbrella. The ***sea wasp*** of tropical waters grows to the size of a man's head and trails filaments 10 m/30 ft long; the latter eject thousands of poisonous stinging capsules on contact□

Jena industrial city (chemicals, engineering, Zeiss optical instruments) in E Germany; population 103 300; Schiller and Hegel◊ taught at the university□

Jena Battle of. Defeat of the Prussians by Napoleon 1806□

Jenkins Roy Harris 1920– . British politician. Labour Home Secretary 1965–7, and Chancellor of the Exchequer 1967–70, he became deputy leader in 1970, but resigned when he disagreed with Wilson◊ on the Common Market issue. Again Home Secretary 1974–6, he was president of the Common Market Commission 1977–80, but in 1981 became founder-leader of the Social Democratic Party until 1983□

Jenner Edward 1749–1823. British doctor who discovered the principle of the vaccine◊□

jerboa rodents of the Afro-Asian deserts, family Dipodidae (also called desert rat). Some 5–15 cm/6 in long, they have strongly developed hind legs, which enable them to make long hops□

Jeremiah 7th century BC. In Old Testament, Hebrew prophet who was imprisoned during Nebuchadnezzar◊'s siege of Jerusalem on suspicion of intending to desert to the enemy. On the city's fall, he retired to Egypt. His prophecies of disaster made him a byword□

Jerez de la Frontera city in Andalusia, Spain; population 176 250. It is famed for sherry, the fortified wine to which it gave its name□

Jericho Israeli-administered town in Jordan; population 5000;. It was settled by 8000BC, and a walled city, population 2000, by 6000BC. In the Old Testament it was the first Canaanite stronghold captured by the Israelites, its walls allegedly falling to the blast of Joshua◊'s trumpets□

Jerome St c340–420. Christian scholar, whose Latin versions of the scriptures are the basis of the Roman Catholic Vulgate. Feast day 30 Sept□

Jerome Jerome K(lapka) 1859–1927. British humorous author, e.g. the essays *Idle Thoughts of an Idle Fellow* 1889, and his *Three Men in a Boat* 1889□

Jersey largest of the Channel◊ Islands; area 117 sq km/45 sq mi; with its capital at St Helier. Like Guernsey, it is famous for cattle. The grave of Sir Billy Butlin◊ is the jolliest known, with carvings of a holiday camp, amusement park, etc.□

Jersey City industrial city (electricals, chemicals, cigarettes) of New Jersey, USA; population 223 530. It is linked by tunnel with Manhattan Island, and the former docks area has been converted to Liberty Park 1976□

Jerusalem ancient city of Palestine, divided in 1948 between the new republic of Israel and Jordan. In 1950 the western New City was proclaimed as the Israeli capital, and, following the Israeli capture of the eastern Old City in 1967 from the Jordanians, it was affirmed in 1980 by Israel that the united city was the country's capital, but the UN does not recognize the claim; population 290 000 Jews, 100 000 Arabs.

history by 1400BC Jerusalem was ruled by a king subject to Egypt, but c1000 David◊ made it the capital of a united Jewish kingdom. It was captured by Nebuchadnezzar◊ 586BC, who deported its population. Later conquerors include Alexander the Great and Pompey◊(63BC), and it was under Roman rule (see Pontius◊ Pilate) that Jesus◊ Christ was executed. In 70AD a Jewish revolt led to its complete destruction by Titus◊. It was first conquered by Islam in 637AD; was captured by the Crusaders◊ 1099, and recaptured by Saladin◊ 1187, to remain under almost unbroken Islamic rule until the British occupation of Palestine in 1917.

Notable buildings include the Church of the Holy Sepulchre (built by Constantine◊ 335), and the mosque of the Dome of the Rock.

The latter was built on the site of Solomon's Temple, and the Western ('wailing') Wall, held sacred by Jews, is part of the walled platform on which the Temple once stood□

Jerusalem artichoke a type of artichoke◊□

Jervis Bay see under Canberra◊□

Jesuits or **Society of Jesus** largest and most influential Roman Catholic religious order (26 000 members), founded by Loyola◊ in 1534, and noted for educational and missionary work, and the suppression of heresy. Their head (general) is known as the 'Black Pope' from the colour of his cassock (see Pieter-Hans Kolvenbach◊). Their political influence led to Papal suppression of the order in 1773 (revived 1814), and John Paul II attacked them in 1981 for support of revolution in S America□

Jesus Christ c4BC–29 or 30AD in the New Testament, Jesus (Hebrew *Messiah*, Greek *the Christ*) was the founder of Christianity◊, based on the account of his life in the four Gospels◊. Born in Bethlehem◊, son of the Virgin Mary◊ of the peoples of Judah and the family of David◊, he was brought up as a carpenter by Joseph◊ at Nazareth◊. In 26/27AD his cousin John◊ the Baptist began a preparatory mission, and baptized Jesus, whose Galilean ministry included two missionary journeys through the district, and the calling of the 12 apostles◊. His teaching, summarized in the Sermon on the Mount, aroused both religious opposition from the Pharisees◊ and secular opposition from the Herodian (see Herod◊ Antipas) party. When he returned to Jerusalem a week before the Passover◊, he was greeted by the people as the Messiah◊, and the Jewish authorities (aided by Judas◊) had him arrested and condemned to death (after a hurried trial) by the Sanhedrin◊. The sentence was confirmed by the Roman procurator, Pontius◊ Pilate, but three days after the Crucifixion◊, came reports of his resurrection, and later ascension to heaven□

jet black mineral related to lignite and anthracite◊, found in fine quality near Whitby, and used by the Victorians in mourning jewellery□

jetfoil type of boat with its foils set below the water surface (see hydrofoil◊), with a speed of 43 knots (80 kph/50 mph)□

jetlag effect of a sudden switch of time-zones in jet air travel, resulting in tiredness and feeling 'out of step' with day and night. See circadian◊ rhythm□

jet propulsion propulsion by a jet of water, as found in many sea creatures, e.g. the octopus, scallop, etc. The same principle is involved in the aircraft jet engine, though here it is done by the expulsion of gases through a rear-facing jet pipe which act on the engine-mountings to produce forward 'thrust'□

jetsam goods deliberately sunk in the sea to lighten a vessel in a storm, wreck, etc. See under flotsam◊□

Jew a member of the semitic people who claim descent from Abraham◊. See semite◊, antisemitism◊, Israel◊□

Jewish Autonomous Region part of the Khabarovsk Territory, USSR it was established 1934, but became only nominally Jewish after the Stalinist purges of 1936–7 and 1948–9. Cap Birobijan□

Jew's harp musical instrument, an iron frame held in the teeth, which has a steel strip twanged with the fingers to produce a single note. This is varied by changing the shape of the mouth□

Jezebel in Old Testament, daughter of the King of Sidon, she married King Ahab◊, and upset Elijah◊ by her introduction of the worship of Baal◊□

Jhansi city in Uttar Pradesh, India; population 281 000□

Jhelum see under Indus◊□

Jiang Qing 1913– . Chinese actress (formerly Chiang Ching), third wife of Mao◊ Zedong, whose exercise of power after his stroke in 1974 earned her a death sentence in 1981, commuted to life imprisonment 1983□

Jiangsu province (formerly Kiangsu) of E China

area 102 200 sq km/39 450 sq mi

capital Nanjing

features comprises swampy mouth of the Chang Jiang, and includes the special municipality of Shanghai, one of the most heavily populated areas

products cereals, rice, tea, cotton, soya; silk; ceramics, textiles; coal, iron and copper

population 59 000 000□

Jiangxi province (formerly Kiangsi) of SE China

area 164 800 sq km/63 600 sq mi

capital Nanchang

features the province was Mao◊ Zedong's original base in the first phase of the Communist struggle against the Nationalists

products rice, tea, cotton, tobacco; porcelain; coal, tungsten, uranium

population 32 000 000□

Jidda also ***Jedda*** industrial port (cement, steel, oil refining) in Saudi Arabia, which also handles pilgrim traffic to Mecca; population 561 100□

jihad Arabic 'struggle', used in the Koran for the Muslim duty of opposition to those who reject Islam. In the ***Mecca Declaration*** 1981, the Islamic powers pledged a jihad against Israel, though not necessarily military attack□

Jilin province (formerly Kirin) of NE China
area 290 000 sq km/111 940 sq mi
capital Changchun
population 24 000 000. See Manchuria◊□

Jilin city (formerly Kirin), in Jilin province, China; population 1 200 000□

Jiménez Juan Ramón 1881–1958. Spanish lyric poet whose work includes his popular odes to his donkey 'Platero': Nobel prize 1956□

jimsonweed another name for thorn◊ apple□

Jinan industrial city (formerly Tsinan) and capital of Shandong province, China; population 1 250 000□

Jingdezen town (formerly Chingtechen) in Jiangxi province; population 350 000. Ming blue-and-white ware was produced here, the name of the clay 'kaolin' being that of the hills from which it came, and some of the best Chinese porcelain is still made here□

jinn spirit in Muslim mythology able to assume human or animal shape□

Jinnah Mohammed Ali 1876–1948. Indian statesman, president of the Muslim League from 1916, who insisted in 1946 on the partition of British India into Indian and Muslim states. He became first Governor-General of Pakistan 1947–8□

Jivaro Indian peoples of Ecuador and Peru, formerly famous for keeping the shrunken heads of enemies as battle trophies□

Joachim Joseph 1831–1907. Hungarian violinist, founder of a celebrated quartet 1869–1907□

Joan mythical Englishwoman supposed to have become Pope in 855, as John VIII, and to have given birth to a child during a Papal procession□

Joan of Arc St 1412–31. French heroine, born at Domrémy, daughter of a well-to-do farmer. In 1429 she persuaded Charles VII she had a divine mission to expel the English from France, and secure his coronation. She raised the siege of Orléans, defeated the English at Patay, and Charles was crowned at Reims. However, she failed to capture Paris, was captured by the Burgundians, who sold her to the English, and having been found guilty of witchcraft and heresy, was burned at Rouen. In 1920 she was canonised□

Job in the Old Testament, chieftain who is shown in the ***Book of Job*** c5th century BC as questioning God's infliction of suffering on the righteous and endured great sufferings himself. He comes to no very exact conclusion, but does so with dramatic poetic power□

Jockey Club see horse◊ racing 1□

Jodhpur city in Rajasthan, India, formerly capital of the princely state of Jodhpur; population 494 000. It gave its name to a type of riding breeches and boots□

Jodrell Bank astronomical observatory in Cheshire, England, now the Nuffield Radio-astronomy Laboratories, part of Manchester University. See Sir Bernard Lovell◊□

Joffre Joseph Jacques Césaire 1852–1931. Marshal of France. As chief of general staff from 1911, he was surprised by the German invasion of Belgium 1914, but his stand on the Marne resulted in appointment as supreme commander of all the French armies 1915. His failure to make adequate preparations at Verdun in 1916, and the disasters on the Somme, led to his replacement by Nivelle Dec 1916□

Johannesburg largest city in S Africa, on the Witwatersrand in Transvaal, centre of the world's largest gold-mining industry; population 1 536 500. Founded after the discovery of gold in 1886, it also has engineering works, meat-chilling plants, clothing factories, etc. Notable buildings include the law courts, city hall, chamber of mines, stock exchange and Union Observatory; there are two universities. Jan Smuts international airport is to the north west□

John Augus Edwin 1878–1961. British artist. Born in Tenby, the son of a solicitor, he was famous for his portraits, including *The Smiling Woman* (his second wife, Dorelia), Order of Merit 1942. Gwen John◊ was his sister□

John Gwen 1876–1939. British artist, sister of Augustus John◊. A Catholic convert, she was for many years the mistress of Rodin◊, and in the 1980s was increasingly recognized for her figure studies. She died penniless in a Dieppe hospice□

John St New Testament apostle, identified with the unnamed 'disciple whom Jesus loved'. He and his brother James◊ were Galilean fishermen. Jesus entrusted his mother to John at the Crucifixion. Traditionally, he wrote the 4th Gospel and the Johannine Epistles, when Bishop of Ephesus, and the Apocalypse while imprisoned on Patmos◊□

John the Baptist St. Son of Zacharias and Elizabeth (a cousin of Christ's mother), he was a Nazarite from birth. After preparation in the wilderness, he proclaimed the coming of Christ, baptized him in the Jordan, and was executed by Herod◊ Antipas at the instigation of Salome◊□

John of the Cross St 1542–91. Spanish Carmelite friar from 1564, who was imprisoned for attempting to impose the reforms laid down by St Teresa. His verse is full of spiritual ecstacy. Feast day 24 Nov□

John of Damascus St c676–c754. Eastern Orthodox defender of image-worship against the Iconoclasts◊□

John name of 23 Popes including:

John XXII 1249–1334, Pope 1316–34. He spent his Papacy at Avignon, engaged in a long conflict with the emperor, Louis of Bavaria, and the Spiritual Franciscans, who preached the absolute poverty of the clergy.

John XXIII d. 1419, Pope 1410–15, attempted to end the Great◊ Schism, but was ended by it, being deposed together with the popes of Avignon and Rome. His Papacy is not recognized by the church, hence:

John XXIII (Angelo Giuseppe Roncalli) 1881–1963, Pope from 1958. One of a peasant family of 13, he improved relations with the USSR in line with his encyclical *Pacem in Terris/Peace on earth* 1963; established Roman Catholic hierarchies in newly emergent states, and summoned the Second Vatican Council, which reformed church liturgy, backed the ecumenical movement, and made the Pope more 'one among equals'□

John 1167–1216, king of England from 1199, when he succeeded Richard I, after having already tried to supplant him during his absence on Crusade. He murdered Arthur◊, whose claim to the throne (as son of his elder brother Geoffrey) was the stronger, and consequently lost all his French possessions. He was also forced by Innocent◊ III to accept Langton◊ as Archbishop of Canterbury, and in 1213 to accept that he held England only as the Pope's vassal. His tyranny then led the barons to force him to sign Magna◊ Carta 1215, and he died at Newark during the civil war which ensued when he repudiated the charter□

John several kings of France, including:

John II 1319–64, king from 1350. He was defeated and captured by the Black◊ Prince at Poitiers 1356. Released 1360, he failed to raise the money for his ransom and returned in 1364 to England, where he died□

John several kings of Poland, including:

John III 1642–96, called ***Sobieski.*** Elected King of Poland from 1674, he saved Vienna from the besieging Turks 1683□

John six kings of Portugal including:

John I 1357–1433, elected king of Portugal from 1385 by the Cortes, although a natural son of Pedro I. His claim was supported by an English army against the rival king of Castile, thus establishing the Anglo-Portuguese Alliance 1386. He married Phillippa of Lancaster, daughter of John◊ of Gaunt.

John IV 1603–56, elected king 1640 when the Portuguese rebelled against Spanish rule.

John VI 1769–1826. Regent for his insane mother Maria I 1792–1816, he fled to Brazil when the French invaded Portugal in 1807, and did not return until 1822. On his return Brazil declared its independence, with John's elder son Pedro as emperor□

John of Austria Don 1545–78. Spanish soldier, the natural son of Charles◊ V, who defeated the Turks at Lepanto◊□

John of Gaunt 1340–99. English nobleman, 4th son of Edward III, Duke of Lancaster from 1362. During Edward's last years and the minority of Richard II, he acted as head of govt, and parliament protested against his corrupt rule. He supported Wycliffe◊. Henry◊ VII's mother, Margaret Beaufort, was a descendant of John of Gaunt through his marriage with his mistress Catherine Swynford. See John◊ I of Portugal□

John Bull see under Arbuthnot◊□

John Chrysostom St 345–407. Eastern Orthodox bishop of Constantinople 398–404, an eloquent preacher□

John Dory edible sea fish *Zeus faber*, order Zeiformes, of the Atlantic and Mediterranean. It is greyish-brown with a blotch on either side of the vertically compressed body, and has spiny dorsal fins□

John o' Groats site in NE Highland region, Scotland, proverbially Britain's most northerly point; Dutchman John de Groot built a house there in the 16th century□

John Paul name of two Popes, including:

John Paul II (Karol Wojtyla) 1920– , Pope 1978– . The first non-Italian Pope since 1522, he was born near Cracow, Poland, where he became archbishop 1964. Despite personal charisma, he has been criticized for his traditionalist maintenance of papal infallibility, and condemnation of artificial contraception, women priests, married priests, and modern dress for monks and nuns. See also Liberation◊ theology. He was shot and wounded by a Turk in 1981□

Johns William Earl 'Captain' 1893–1968. British author, from 1932, of popular novels of World War I flying ace Captain James Bigglesworth ('Biggles'), now criticized for chauvinism, racism, and sexism. He retired from the RAF in 1930□

Johnson Amy 1904–41. British airwoman, born at Hull. She made solo flights to Australia 1930, and the Cape (and back) 1936. She died when her plane (Air Transport Auxiliary) was lost over the Thames Estuary□

Johnson Andrew 1808–75. 17th President of the USA 1864–9; born in N Carolina. His conciliatory policy to the defeated South culminated in his attempted impeachment (failed by one vote) before the Senate in 1868□

Johnson Dame Celia 1908–82. British actress, best-remembered for the film *Brief Encounter* 1946. She married in 1935 writer-traveller Peter Fleming□

Johnson Lyndon Baines 1908–73. 36th President of the USA 1963–9; born in Texas. He agreed to stand only as vice-president in 1960, so bringing crucial Southern votes to Kennedy, then succeeded him. After the Tonkin◊ Gulf incident, he made the first escalation of the Vietnam◊ War, which eventually dissipated the support won by his Great Society legislation (civil rights, education, alleviation of poverty), so that he declined the presidential nomination in 1968 after failing to end the war□

Johnson Pamela Hansford 1912–81. British novelist, who in 1950 married Lord Snow◊; her books include *Too Dear for my Possessing* 1940, and *The Honours Board* 1970□

Johnson Pierre-Marc 1946– . Canadian lawyer and politician. In 1985 he became leader of the Parti Québecois and Prime Minister of Quebec, fighting not for independence, but greater control of provincial affairs□

Johnson Samuel 1709–84. English lexicographer, author, and critic; born in Lichfield. The private school he opened failed, and he went to London with his pupil David Garrick◊. In 1755 he published his *Dictionary,* still interesting for the vigour of its definitions; other works include a satire (imitating Juvenal◊) *The Vanity of Human Wishes* 1749, the philosophical romance *Rasselas* 1759, an edition of Shakespeare 1765, and his *Lives of the Poets* 1779–81. He first met Boswell◊ in 1763, and in 1764 the 'Literary Club' was formed which included Reynolds, Burke, Goldsmith, and Garrick. His house in Gough Square, London, is a museum□

Johnson Uwe 1934– . German novelist, who left E Germany for W Berlin in 1959, and writes of the division of Germany, e.g. *Anniversaries* 1977□

Johore state of Malaysia, joined to Singapore by a causeway; population 1 601 500. Capital Johore Bharu□

joint place of union: in geology, it refers to a fracture or fault in the rock; in woodwork a prepared connection of two or more pieces; in an animal, a place where two bones meet. The last can be *motionless* (sutures of the skull); *slightly moveable* (sacro-iliac joints in lower back); *free-moving* (gliding, the vertebrae of the spine; hinged, as the elbow and knee; or ball-and-socket, hip and shoulder joints). At moveable joints, the bone ends are covered with cartilege for elasticity, and enclosed in an envelope of tough white fibrous tissue lined with a membrane secreting a lubricating fluid. Fibrous ligaments increase a joint's stability. See arthritis◊□

joint intelligence committee a weekly British Cabinet◊ meeting held to discuss international intelligence□

Joinville Jean, Sire de 1224–1317. French chronicler, who accompanied Louis IX on the crusade of 1248–54, which he described in his *History of St Louis*□

jojoba long-lived, grey-green evergreen shrub c2 m/6 ft high, *Simmondsia chinensis,* family Simmonsiaceae, native to the south-west USA and Mexico. It is of two sexes, and is wind-pollinated; the edible fruit resembles a hazelnut, but has a thin skin not a hard shell, and it is this which contains the liquid wax used as an industrial lubricant: a high density oil which does not disintegrate under pressure. It is also used for cooking, in cosmetics, and in medicine□

Jolson Al. Stage name of Russian-born American singer Asa Yoelson 1886–1950, star of early sound-films, e.g. *The Jazz Singer* 1927□

Jonah Hebrew Old Testament prophet, who fled by ship to evade his mission to prophesy the destruction of Nineveh. The crew threw him overboard in a storm, as a bringer of ill fortune, and he spent three days and nights in the belly of a whale before coming to land□

Jones Bobby 1902–71. American golfer who crowned his career by achieving the 'grand slam' 1930: winning the US and British amateur and open championships. He originated the Masters Tournament□

Jones Inigo 1573–c1652. The first true English Renaissance◊ architect, influenced by Palladio◊. His two visits to Italy gave him an unrivalled knowledge of Renaissance architecture in Italy. He designed scenery for Jonson's masques, the Queen's House, Greenwich 1616, and the banqueting hall, Whitehall 1619□

Jones John Paul 1747–92. American naval officer, born in Kirkcudbright, Scotland. Originally a trader and slaver, he became an American privateer 1775 in the War of Independence. Heading a small French-sponsored squadron in the *Bonhomme Richard* he captured the British warship *Serapis* 23 Sept 1799 in a bloody battle off Scarborough□

Jonestown commune of the San Francisco People's Temple Sect, established in Guyana◊ 1974 by Jim Jones 1933–78. His oppression of his black subjects brought a visit by a US congressman; the latter and his companions were shot, and Jones enforced a mass suicide (by drinking cyanide) of his followers. The 914 dead included over 240 children□

jonquil a plant of the daffodil◊ family□

Jonson Ben 1572–1637. English poet and dramatist. In 1598 he narrowly escaped the gallows for killing a fellow-player in a duel, but in the same year his *Everyman in His Humour* established the English 'comedy of humours', based on the theory that character depended on the admixture of four body fluids in varying proportions. His first extant tragedy is *Sejanus* 1603, with Burbage and Shakespeare in the original cast. The great plays of his middle years include *Volpone, or the Fox* 1606, *Epicoene, or The Silent Woman* 1609, *The Alchemist* 1610, and *Bartholomew Fair* 1614. He also produced some 30 masques before a quarrel with his associate Inigo Jones◊ 1630 lost him court favour□

Joplin Scott 1868–1917. American ragtime king pianist and composer in Chicago. His 'Maple Leaf Rag' 1899 was the first instrumental sheet music to sell a million, and 'The Entertainer' was the theme tune of the film *The Sting* 1973, and revived his popularity□

Joppa see Jaffa◊□

Jordaens Jakob 1593–1678. Flemish Baroque◊ painter, born in Antwerp, and assistant to Rubens◊. He was noted for exuberant, large-scale works, including scenes of peasant life□

Jordan Dorothea 1762–1816. British actress, mistress of the Duke of Clarence (later William IV) by whom she had ten children, given the surname FitzClarence□

Jordan river in the north of the Great Rift Valley rising on Mt Hermon in Syria; length 320 km/200 mi, flowing the via the Sea of Galilee to the Dead Sea□

Jordan The Hashemite Kingdom of

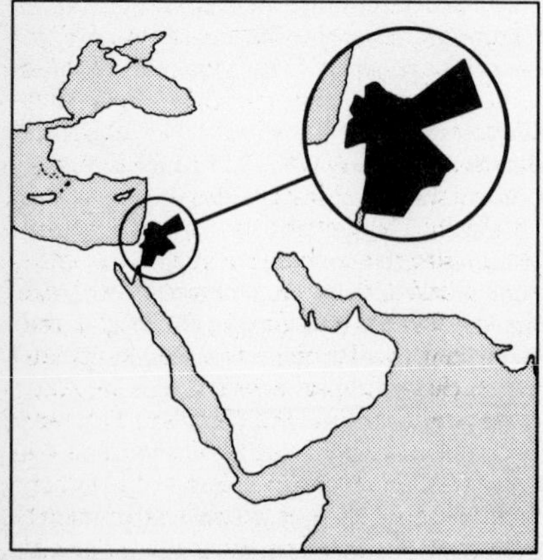

area 98 000 sq km/38 000 sq mi
capital Amman
towns Aqaba, the only port
features Dead Sea, River Jordan, archaeological sites, e.g. Jerash, Roman forum
exports potash, phosphates, citrus
currency Jordanian dinar
population 2 750 000, including Palestinian refugees
language Arabic
religion Sunni Islam
government constitutional monarchy (King Hussein◊ since 1952); the lower house of parliament is elected by universal suffrage (Prime Minister Zaid Rifai from 1985), the upper is nominated by the king, who can also dissolve parliament.
history once a Roman province, and included in the Crusaders' kingdom of Jerusalem 1099–1187, it was ruled by the Turks from the 16th century till after World War I. Placed under British mandate by the League of Nations in 1920, as part of Palestine, it became independent as The Hashemite Kingdom of Jordan under King Abdullah◊ in 1946. From 1948 Jordan was involved in the Arab-Israeli Wars◊, in 1967 losing all territory west of the Jordan (the 'West Bank') and E Jerusalem, and opposed the Camp David◊ Agreements. Jordan supported Iraq in the Iran-Iraq◊ War. In 1985 the formation of political parties was allowed to progress□

Joseph in Old Testament, eleventh and favourite son of Jacob◊, sold into Egypt by his jealous half-brothers. After he had risen to power there, they and his father joined him to escape from famine□

Joseph in New Testament, descendant of David◊, he was a carpenter, and the husband of the Virgin◊ Mary□

Joseph of Arimathaea. In New Testament, wealthy secret supporter of Jesus, who begged Jesus' body from Pilate and buried it in his own tomb□

Joseph II 1741–90. Holy Roman Emperor from 1765, son of Francis◊ I. The reforms he carried out after the death of his mother, Maria Theresa◊, in 1780, brought revolts from those who lost privileges□

Joseph Sir Keith Sinjohn 1918– . British Conservative politician. He was Minister of Local Government 1962–4, Social Services 1970–4, Industry 1979–81, and Education and Science 1981–86. He was regarded as one of Margaret Thatcher's chief influences□

Joseph Père. Religious name of Capuchin friar Francis Le Clerc du Tremblay 1577–1638, influential secretary-agent to Richelieu◊, hence nicknamed 'Grey Eminence' in reference to his grey habit□

Josephine 1763–1814. Empress of France. Born on Martinique◊, she married in 1779 the Vicomte de Beauharnais◊, and in 1796 Napoleon◊, who divorced her in 1809 because she bore him no child. Her chateau at Malmaison in a north west suburb of Paris, is a museum□

Josephs Wilfred 1927– . British composer, born in Newcastle upon Tyne. Originally a dentist, he made a popular reputation with television music, but has also written symphonies (*Pastoral Symphony*), and an opera *Rebecca* 1983□

Josephson Brian 1940– . British physicist, sharer of a Nobel prize in 1973 for his discovery of the phenomenon in superconductors◊ known as the Josephson effect□

Josephus Flavius 37–c100. Jewish historian. A Pharisee, he commanded the Jewish forces in Galilee in the revolt again Rome from 66 (which ended with the mass suicide at Masada◊). When captured, he gained the favour of Vespasian◊ and settled in Rome as a citizen. He wrote a history of the war, and of his people□

Joshua in Old Testament, successor of Moses◊, who led the Jews in their conquest of the Land of Canaan◊. See Jericho◊□

Josiah b. 647 King of Judah. The Old Testament book of *Deuteronomy* was found during his repairs of the Temple. He died in battle at Megiddo against the Egyptians□

Josquin des Près c1445–1521. Flemish composer of masses and songs, a pupil of Okeghem◊□

Jotunheim in Norse myth the home of the giants, the region of S Norway with the highest peaks (Glittertind 2470 m/8095 ft)□

Joubert Petrus Jacobus 1831–1900. Boer general who defeated Jameson◊ 1896, and achieved the early successes against the British in the S African War□

Joule James Prescott 1818–89. British physicist who gathered experimental evidence for the first law of thermodynamics◊, and determined the mechanical equivalent of heat (***Joule's equivalent***)□

joule derived SI unit of energy: the work done (energy transferred) when the point of application of a force of 1 newton◊ is displaced a distance of 1 metre in the direction of the force□

Jovian 331–64. Roman emperor from 363. Captain of the imperial bodyguard, he was chosen emperor by the troops after Julian◊'s death in battle. He concluded a humiliating peace, and restored Christianity as the state religion□

Joyce James Augin Aloysius 1882–1941. Irish writer, born in Dublin, whose works include *Dubliners* 1914 (short stories), *Portrait of the Artist as a Young Man* 1916 (semi-autobiographical), and *Ulysses* 1922 (events of a single Dublin day in direct narrative, unspoken and unconscious reactions of the characters). His *Finnegan's Wake* 1939 uses a polyglot language with impressionistic compounds, e.g. 'polyfizzy-boisterous'□

Joyce William 1906–46. Born in New York, son of a naturalized American of Irish birth, he carried on Fascist activity in Britain as a 'British subject'. During World War II he made broadcasts from Germany to Britain, his upper class accent earning him the nickname 'Lord Haw-Haw'. He was hanged for treachery□

Juan Carlos 1938– . King of Spain from 1975, following his nomination by Franco 1969; see Bourbon◊ family tree. He married 1962 Princess Sophia, daughter of King Paul of the Hellenes□

Juan Fernandez Islands three small volcanic Pacific islands belonging to Chile; almost uninhabited. The largest is named after Robinson Crusoe, and another after Alexander Selkirk◊□

Juárez Benito Pablo 1806–72. Mexican politician, first Indian president of the republic from 1858. He declared war on France in 1862 when Napoleon III militarily supported Maximilian◊ as Mexican emperor, on the pretext that the country could not meet its foreign debts. Juárez was re-elected president 1867 and 1871□

Judaea see Judah◊□

Judah district of S Palestine which, in the Old Testament, after Solomon's death, adhered to his son Rehoboam and the Davidic line. See Israel◊. In New Testament times, Judah was the Roman province of Judaea, and in modern Israeli usage refers to the southern area of the West Bank□

Judaism the religion of the Jews, founded on the Torah ('direction for living'), combining the Mosaic code and its oral interpretation. It was retained in the Babylonian exile of 586BC, and was reconstituted by Ezra on the return to Jerusalem. The ultimate destruction of the Temple at Jerusalem was countered by greater stress on the synagogue (in continental and US usage 'temple'), the local building for worship (originally simply the place where the Torah was read and expounded; its characteristic feature is still the Ark, or cupboard, where the Torah scrolls are kept) and home observance. The work of lay rabbis, skilled in the Jewish law and ritual, also grew in importance, and in modern times they either act as spiritual leaders and pastors of their communities, or devote themselves to study. The ***Talmud*** compiled c200AD combines the *Mishnah,* rabbinical commentary on the law handed down orally from 70AD, and the *Gemara* legal discussions in the schools of Palestine and Babylon. The ***Haggadah*** is that part of the Talmud which deals with stories of heroes, etc. The ***Midrash*** is the collection of commentaries on the scriptures written 400–1200AD, mainly in Palestine.

The ***creed*** rests on the concept of one God, whose will is revealed in the Torah, and who has a special relationship with the Jewish people. The orthodox formulation is that of Moses Maimonides 1135–1204.

Observances include: circumcision, daily services in Hebrew, and observance of the ***Sabbath*** (sunset on Friday to sunset Saturday), as a day of rest; the three principal festivals are ***Passover*** in spring, commemorating the Exodus from Egypt, ***Pentecost◊,*** and ***Tabernacles*** commemorating the time spent by the Israelites in the wilderness (for eight days meals are eaten in a 'summer house' roofed with branches). Observed with more solemnity are ***Rosh Hashanah*** Jewish New Year (first new moon after the autumn equinox, announced by blowing a ram's horn) and, a week later, the religious fast ***Yom Kippur*** (see also Arab-Israeli◊ Wars).

Sects include: ***Pharisees*** 2nd-century sect rejecting compromise with Hellenic culture, and emphasising strict observance of the law; after the fall of Jideas (including belief in a coming Messiah, and the immortality of the soul) formed the basis of orthodox Judaism; ***Sadducees*** opposed to the Pharisees, they rejected immortality of the soul and, as the priestly caste, emphasized ritual; ***Karaites*** 8th-century sect which rejected the Talmud, and concentrated on literal interpretation of the Old Testament; ***Hasidim/Chasidism*** 18th-century sect devoted to mysticism; ***Reform movement*** began in Germany 1810 (reached England 1842, moved on to USA from 1848); ***Liberal Judaism*** more radical than the Reform, which developed in USA (first London synagogue 1911); ***Fundamentalism*** most extreme in the claims of *Gush Emunim;* see under Israel; ***Kabbalism*** an ancient esoteric teaching (*kabbala* 'tradition') with elements of Pantheism, and akin to Neoplatonism, existing at least from the 2nd century AD in which there has been a recent revival of interest. Its most famous expression is in the 13th-century Aramaic text, the Zohar (Book of Light). See also Messiah◊□

Judas Iscariot in the New Testament, treasurer of the 12 apostles◊, who betrayed Jesus, arranging with the chief priests at the last Passover to do so in return for 30 pieces of silver. He hanged himself in remorse□

Judas tree deciduous tree *Cercis siliquastrum,* family Leguminosae, bearing purple flowers before its leaves, and said to be the tree on which Judas hanged himself□

judge person with public authority to judge civic and criminal law cases in the UK. Judges are nominated by the Lord Chancellor from among barristers◊ and solicitors◊ of long standing, except that the Lord Chief Justice is a political appointee. A ***recorder*** is a part-time judge. In the United States the Federal judiciary are executive appointments, but judges in most states are elected by popular vote□

judicial separation a suit before a magistrate's court by either husband or wife, in which it is not necessary to prove an irreconcilable breakdown of a marriage, but in which the grounds are otherwise the same as for divorce. It does not end a marriage, but a declaration may be obtained that the complainant need no longer cohabit with the defendant, is entitled to maintenance, etc. A similar procedure exists in the USA□

Judith in the Apocrypha◊, a widow who assassinated the invading Assyrian general Holofernes□

judo a form of martial◊ art□

Juggernaut or ***Jagganath*** the name for Vishnu, the Hindue god. See under Hinduism◊

Jugoslavia see Yugoslavia◊□

Jugurtha d. 104BC. King of Numidia from 113, who waged war against Rome from 111. Betrayed to them in 105, he was displayed in triumph by Marius◊, then either starved or strangled in the prison beneath the Capitol□

jujitsu a form of martial◊ art□

jujube Chinese tree *Zizyphus jujuba* producing fruit the size of small plums, preserved as 'Chinese dates'; *Z vulgaris* is the Mediterranean species. See lotus◊□

Julian c331–63. Roman emperor from 361, called the 'Apostate'. Nephew of Constantine◊ the Great, he early became a convert to paganism. Sent by Constantius II to govern Gaul in 355, he was proclaimed emperor by his troops 360, and was marching on Constantinople when Constantius's death allowed him to succeed peacefully. He revived pagan worship, and infuriated the Christians by refusing to persecute heretics. He was killed fighting the Persians□

Juliana 1909– . Queen of the Netherlands 1948–80, when she abdicated in favour of Beatrix◊□

Julius name of three popes, including:

Julius II 1443–1513, Pope from 1503. He made the Papal states the leading power in

Italy by forming alliances, first against Venice, then against France. Patron of Michelangelo and Raphael, he began the building of St Peter's 1506□

July Revolution Parisian revolution of 27–29 Jul 1830 which replaced the restored Bourbon monarchy of Charles◊ X by the constitutional monarchy of Louis◊ Philippe□

Jumna see under Ganges◊□

jumping bean seeds of the Mexican shrub *Sebastiana pringlei* which contain the caterpillars of a species of moth; when the insects move, the bean 'jumps'□

jumping mouse any of the small rodents◊, family Zapodidae, with hind legs enlarged for jumping□

Juncaceae a family of grass-like plants. See rush◊□

Junau ice-free port, capital of Alaska, USA; population 19 530. Gold and furs are exported, and there is salmon-fishing□

Jung Carl Gustav 1875–1961. Swiss psychologist, who split with Freud◊ in the matter of the latter's excessive emphasis on sexual instinct. His books include *The Psychology of the Unconscious* 1916 and *Modern Man in Search of a Soul* 1933, and are valued in the development of modern religious thought. He suggested the existence of shared human ancestral memories, the ***collective unconscious,*** which might have an adverse effect in precipitating mental disturbance, but which may also prompt achievement in the arts, etc.□

Jungfrau see under Alps◊□

jungle fowl a small bird. See under fowl◊□

juniper genus of temperate conifers *Juniperus,* family Cupressaceae, with red fragrant resinous wood. The ***common juniper*** *J communis* has berries used to flavour gin□

Junius pseudonym adopted by the writer (thought to be the War Office clerk Sir Philip Francis 1740–1818) of a series of letters to the press 1769–72 discrediting George III's government□

Junkers Hugo 1859–1935. German designer of dive bombers, night fighters, and troop carriers in World War II□

Junkers the reactionary Prussian landed class, backbone of Prussia's army□

Juno in Roman mythology, queen of the gods. Greek equivalent: Hera◊□

junta Spanish 'council', applied to military rulers of a country after a coup, e.g. the regime of Galtieri◊ in Argentina□

Jupiter in Roman mythology, king of the gods (Greek Zeus), son of Saturn. A sky god, he was associated with lightning and thunder bolts, and victory in war; he married his sister Juno◊□

Jupiter the largest planet, fifth in order from the sun

mean distance from the sun 778 000 000 km/483 300 000 mi

diameter 142 800 km/88 680 mi (11 times that of the Earth)

rotation period 9 hr 55 min

year (sidereal period) 11 years 315 days

atmosphere hydrogen 82%, helium 17% with smaller amounts of methane, ethane and ammonia 1000 km/600 mi thick

surface temperature (at cloud level) 130°C

surface no solid surface; the light and dark banded markings are fast moving cloud belts, with spots (anti-cyclones) of different colours, shapes, and sizes. Interior liquid hydrogen 70 000 km/45 000 mi deep, though a rock core may exist

features the Great Red Spot is a permanent hurricane the size of earth (24 000 km, 100 years ago twice that length) which has five streams of frozen ammonia circling round it; near the Equator giant storms occur, marked by plume-like formations in the bands; Jupiter gives out nearly twice as much energy as it receives from the sun; lightning occurs (Venus and earth are the only other two planets with lightning)

ring system thin ring c30 km/18 mi thick, 8000/5000 mi wide, 55 000 km/34 000 mi above the clouds; consists of billions of particles rather than lumps of rock.

satellites: ***Callisto*** mean distance from its planets 1 884 000 km ***diameter*** 4840 km

Europa mean distance from its planets 671 400 km ***diameter*** 3130 km

Ganymede mean distance from its planets 1 071 000 km ***diameter*** 5280 km

Io mean distance from its planets 422 000 km/260 000 mi ***diameter*** 3640 km

Small satellites Amalthea, Ananke, Carme, Elara, Himalia, Leda, Lysithea, Pasiphae, Sinope, ranging from 7-240 km in diameter□

Jura see under Hebrides◊□

Jura series of parallel mountain ranges on the French-Swiss frontier including Crête de la Neige 1723 m/5650 ft□

jurisprudence study of the principles on which legal systems are founded□

jury group of citizens sworn to reach a verdict in a court of law. In England jurors are selected from men and women 18–65 on the electoral roll (peers, doctors, MPs, ministers of religion, etc. are exempt and those with criminal convictions are disqualified from serving). They may be challenged (without explanation) by either the prosecution or defence. Their verdict is by majority to lessen the chance of corruption or intimidation (10 out of 12 secures a decision). Certain expenses are payable to them. There have been recent unsuccessful attempts to restrict jury trial to increasingly serious criminal cases, because of its high cost, and because of the technical complexity of some crimes, e.g. fraud□

jury grand. System retained in USA, though abolished in England, whereby at both federal and state level, a jury of 23 hears evidence from the prosecution to decide whether there is a case for trial. Hearings are in secret, with the jury's findings presented subsequently to a judge□

Justice of the Peace in England an unpaid magistrate appointed to deal (with one or more colleagues) with minor charges, and commit more serious ones for trial to a higher court, as well as to grant licences, e.g. for the sale of intoxicating liquor. In the USA they are usually elected, and are in receipt of fees, but deal only with very minor offences, e.g. traffic violations; they may also conduct marriages□

Justinian I 483–562. Byzantine emperor from 527. He married the actress Theodora. His general, Belisarius, recovered N Africa from the Vandals, SE Spain from the Visigoths, and Italy from the Ostrogoths, though campaigns against the Persians were indecisive. He codified Roman law (later widely used in mainland Europe), and built St Sophia at Constantinople◊□

Justin Martyr St c100–c163. Itinerant Christian missionary philosopher, martyred in Rome; feast day 14 Apr□

jute fibre obtained from plants of genus *Corchorus*, family Tiliaceae, and used for sacking, upholstery, webbing, twine, etc., now often combined with synthetics. Bangladesh is the largest producer□

Jutes Germanic people from Jutland who occupied Kent c450 (under Hengist◊ and Horsa) and conquered the Isle of Wight and the Hampshire coast in 6th cent□

Jutland also ***Jylland*** peninsula between the North Sea and the Kattegat, the south being part of Germany and the north (Jylland) part of Denmark◊□

Jutland Battle of. Off W coast of Jutland, 31 May 1916, between the British (Admiral Jellicoe◊) and German (Admiral Scheer◊) fleets in World War I. Its outcome was indecisive, but the German fleet remained in port for the rest of the war□

Juvenal c60–140AD. Roman satiric poet, who gives a brutal and often disgusting picture of Roman society□

juvenile delinquency offences committed by young people under 17, which Juvenile Courts deal with, making parents legally responsible or making supervision or care orders□

Jylland see Jutland◊□

K

Kaaba see under Mecca◊□
Kabardino-Balkar autonomous republic of the Soviet Union, annexed in 1557; area 12 500 sq km/4825 sq mi; population 688 000. Capital Nalchik□
kabbala an ancient sect of Judaism◊□
Kabinda see Cabinda◊□
kabuki Japanese 'music-dance-play', popular drama on legendary themes, first developed c1603 by the shrine maiden Okuni who gave performances with a chiefly female troupe: from 1629 only men were allowed to act, in the interests of 'propriety'. It was influenced by No◊, but in kabuki, though the scripts are ancient, they are of less importance than the staging and the virtuoso ability of the actors. The art has been modernized and its following revived in the 1980s by Ennosuke III (1940–)□
Kabul capital of Afghanistan, 2100 m/6900 ft asl, on the river Kabul; population 913 200. It commands the strategic routes to Pakistan (Khyber◊ Pass)□
Kabyles a group of Berber◊ peoples□
Kádár János 1912– . Hungarian politician. On the outbreak of the revolt in 1956, he headed a government under Soviet supervision 1956–8 and 1961–5, remaining first secretary of the Communist Party from 1956□
Kadhafi Moamer al 1942– . Libyan revolutionary leader. Overthrowing King Idris 1969, he became virtual president of a republic, although nominally giving up all except an ideological role in 1974. He supports much terrorist activity against Israel and the West and favours territorial expansion in N Africa (see Chad◊) reaching as far as Zaïre. His theories, based on those of Chairman Mao◊, are contained in a *Green Book*□
Kaduna industrial (car assembly, textiles, timber, pottery) and market town in Nigeria, on the Kaduna river; population 202 000□
Kaffir originally the Bantu-speaking peoples, including the Xhosa, of SE Africa, including Cape Province. It came to be used indiscriminately of black Africans, and is now regarded as offensive□
Kafka Franz 1883–1924. Czech novelist. Born in Prague, he worked for a time in an insurance office. He wrote in German and is chiefly remembered for his three unfinished, allegorical novels *The Trial* 1925, *The Castle* 1926 and *America* 1927, posthumously published despite his instructions that they should be destroyed. He died of tuberculosis□
Kagoshima industrial city (Satsumyaki porcelain) on Kyushu, Japan; population 505 000□
Kahlo Frida 1907–54. Mexican artist, who mingled Mexican folk art with classical and modern style; she was the wife of Diego Rivera◊□
Kahn Louis 1901–74. American architect, noted for 'service' towers surrounding the main working spaces, e.g. Salk Laboratories, La Jolla, California, and Palace of Congresses, Venice□
Kaifeng former capital of China 907–1127 in N Henan; population 470 000□
Kaingaroa see under New◊ Zealand□
Kaiser title (like Tsar◊ derived from Latin *Caesar*) formerly borne by the Holy Roman Emperors, Austrian Emperors 1806–1918, and German Emperors 1871–1918□
Kaiserslautern industrial town (textiles, cars) in Rhineland Palatinate, W Germany; population 100 500□
kakapo a flightless parrot◊□
Kalahari Desert semi-desert area forming most of Botswana, but extending into Namibia, Zimbabwe and S Africa (which has a nuclear site there); area c900 000 sq km/ 347400 sq mi. The only permanent river, the Okovango, flows into marshes rich in wild life and under threat from drainage□
kalanchoe genus of small tropical shrubs, most frequently with coral flowers; family Crassulaceae□
kale a type of cabbage◊□
Kalevala Finnish national epic poem compiled from legends and ballads by Elias Lönnrot 1835; its hero is Väinamöinen, god of music and poetry□
Kalgan see Zhangjiakou◊□
Kalgoorlie goldmining town in Western Australia; population (with Boulder) 22 000. In 1984 it was booming with fresh discoveries□
Kali in Hinduism◊, one name of Siva◊'s consort□

Kâlidâsa lived c5th century AD. Sanskrit epic poet and dramatist, e.g. the play *Sakuntala*, the love story of a king and nymph□

Kalimantan see Borneo, under Sunda◊ Islands□

Kalinin city (Tver till 1933, when renamed in honour of the president) in central USSR; population 422 000□

Kalinin Mikhail Ivanovich 1875–1946. Soviet statesman, a founder of the newspaper *Pravda* 1912, and head of state 1919–46□

Kaliningrad Soviet Baltic naval base (formerly Königsberg) in USSR. It was the capital of E Prussia until the latter was divided between Russia and Poland 1945 (Potsdam◊ Agreement), when it was renamed in honour of Kalinin◊□

Kalmuck see Kalmyk◊□

Kalmyk steppe area of the southern USSR, on the Caspian, settled by migrants from China in the 17th century; area 75 900 sq km/29 300 sq mi; population 301 000. Capital Elista. It was abolished 1943–57 because of alleged collaboration of the people with the Germans during the siege of Stalingrad□

Kamakura city on Honshu, Japan; population 175 000. It was the seat of the first Shogunate 1192–1333, which established the rule of the Samurai class, and the Hachimangu Shrine is dedicated to the gods of war; the 13th century statue of Buddha (Daibutsu) is 13 m/43 ft high. From the 19th century artists and writers, e.g. Kawabata, settled here□

Kamchatka mountainous peninsula separating the Bering Sea and Sea of Okhotsk, forming (together with the Chukchi and Koryak national districts) a region of the USSR. Capital Petropavlovsk□

kamikaze Japanese 'god wind', applied to air force pilots of World War II who deliberately crash-dived their bomb-loaded planes, usually on US warships□

Kampala capital of Uganda; population 332 000. Linked by rail with Mombasa, it trades in cotton, coffee, livestock, etc., and cigarettes are made. Notable are the Parliament buildings 1960, and Makerere University to the north west□

Kamperduin see Camperdown◊□

Kampuchea People's Republic of
area 181 000 sq km/71 000 sq mi
capital Phnom Penh
towns Battambang, and the seaport Kompong Som
features Mekong river; ruins of Angkor◊
exports rubber, rice
currency Kampuchean riel
population 6 700 000 (c7 500 000 in 1975)
language Khmer, official; French

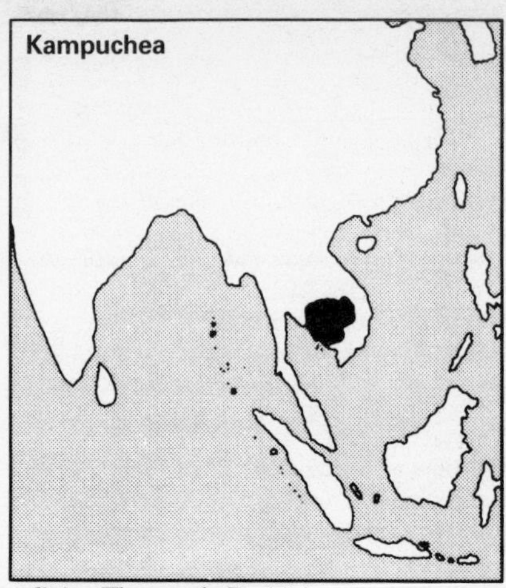

religion Theravada Buddhism
government under the 1981 constitution there is an executive president (Heng Samrin), with a council of state, council of ministers, and national assembly. World governments are divided on the question of recognition, and the United Nations still recognizes the Sihanouk regime. See under history below
history the French protectorate of Cambodia, established 1863, was occupied by the Japanese 1941–45, but in 1955 was recognised as independent by France. Prince Norodom Sihanouk, who had been elected king in 1941, then abdicated to become prime minister, and was head of state 1960–70. In 1969 Nixon had bombed the N Vietnamese bases (being used against the S Vietnamese and US troops in Vietnam◊) in the country, and in 1970 General Lon Nol (1913–85) backed by the USA, deposed the neutralist Sihanouk, himself becoming prime minister 1971–2 and then president of the re-named Khmer Republic 1972–5. Sihanouk then joined uneasily with the Communist Khmer Rouge (supported by N Vietnam and China), who regained control by 1975. The country, devastated by the disastrous civil war, was renamed Kampuchea, and Sihanouk remained head of state until 1976. Pol Pot now took power, and attempted to established a pure Communist state (estimates of those dying in the process are 2–7 million). By 1978 Pol Pot had quarrelled with his Vietnamese sponsors, and Vietnam (backed by USSR) then invaded the country and established an alternative regime under Heng Samrin. The defeated regime continued guerrilla resistance under the military leadership of Pol Pot, and in 1982 an anti-Vietnamese coalition (backed by China) was formed under Prince Sihanouk (president), Khieu Samphan (vice-president) and

Son Sann (prime minister), which includes the Khmer Rouge (which has disavowed its Communist affiliation). By 1985 Vietnam had eradicated the Chinese-supported bases of the resistance, and when Pol Pot was retired Sept 1985, hopes for a settlement revived□

Kanazawa industrial city (textiles, porcelain) on Honshu, Japan; population 418 000□

Kanchenjunga a variant spelling of Kangchenjunga◊. See under Himalayas◊□

Kandahar trading town (silk, cotton, wool, fruit) in S Afghanistan; population 178 500. General Roberts◊ relieved the besieged British garrison here in 1880. See Afghan◊ Wars□

Kandinsky Vasily 1866–1944. Russian Expressionist artist, producing completely non-representational work (e.g. ordered arrangements of squares and rectangles) by 1910, and a founder of the *Blaue Reiter*◊ movement 1911–12. After the closure of the Bauhaus◊ by the Nazis, he settled in Paris□

Kandy town in Sri Lanka; population 101 280. Capital of the Kingdom of Kandy 1480–1815, it has a temple containing an alleged tooth of Buddha (one of the most sacred Buddhist shrines). The chief campus of the University of Sri Lanka is nearby and there is a botanical garden□

kangaroo family of marsupials. See under marsupialia◊□

kangaroo paw bulbous plant *Anigozanthos manglesii* family Hameodoraceae, with a row of small white flowers emerging from velvety green tubes with red bases; floral emblem of Western Australia□

Kangchenjunga see under Himalayas◊□

Kano trading centre and industrial city (bicycles, glass, furniture, textiles, chemicals) in N Nigeria; population 399 000. The old walled city still has a market place with camel trains arriving from Sudan, etc.□

Kanpur formerly ***Cawnpore***. Commercial and industrial city (cotton, woollen, and jute mills, chemicals, plastics, iron and steel) in India; population 1 685 300. In the Indian Mutiny of 1857 British civilians who had surrendered to Nana◊ Sahib were massacred here□

Kansas prairie state of the USA; Sunflower State

area 213 063 sq km/82 264 sq mi

capital Topeka

towns Wichita, Kansas City

features Eisenhower◊ Center in Abilene

products wheat and livestock; coal, oil, natural gas, lead, zinc; aerospace, transport vehicles, oil refining

population 2 363 200

history part of the Louisiana Purchase in 1803, it became a state in 1861□

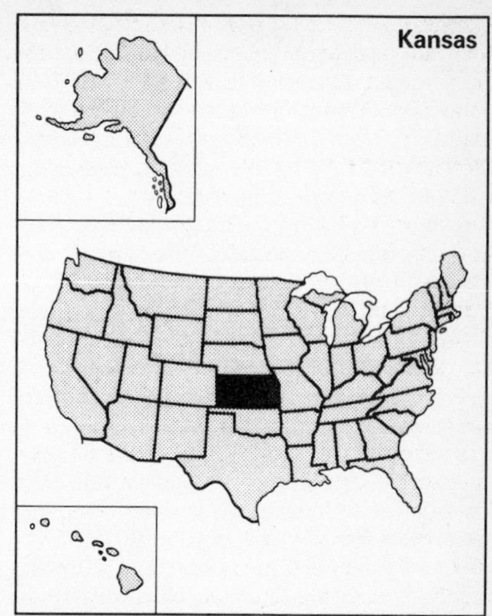

Kansas City twin city at the confluence of the Missouri and Kansas rivers, and divided between both states; population 1 350 000. Kansas City, Missouri, has car assembly plants and Kansas City, Kansas, has the majority of offices. Boss Tom Pendergast ran the city in the 1920s–1930s, and 'protected' the Twelfth Street nightclubs where jazzmen Count Basie and Charlie Parker performed□

Kansu see Gansu◊□

Kant Immanuel 1724–1804. German philosopher. In his *Critique of Pure Reason* (1781) he argued that our knowledge of the world cannot be the mere aggregate of impressions impinging on our consciousness from our senses (roughly the view of Locke◊), but that it is dependent upon the conceptual apparatus of the human understanding - which is not itself derived from experience. In ethics, Kant stressed that the right action is objectively determinable and must conform to a moral law he called 'the Categorical Imperative'; feelings and inclinations are not a basis for moral decisions□

Kantorovich Leonid 1912– . Russian mathematical economist whose theory that decentralization of decisions in a planned economy could only be made with a rational price system, challenged Soviet theory; Nobel prize 1975□

Kaohsiung commercial and industrial port (fertilizers, cement, oil refining, iron and steel, food processing) in W Taiwan; population 1 200 000□

kaoliang variety of sorghum. See under cereals◊□

kaolin China clay (see Jindezhen◊), used in porcelain, paper, paint, and cosmetics□

Kapitza Peter 1894– . Russian physicist, assistant director of magnetic research at the Cavendish Laboratory, Cambridge, 1924–32 (under Rutherford◊) before recalled to work at the Russian Academy of Science. Shared Nobel prize 1978 for his work on magnetism and low temperature physics□

kapok silky hairs produced round the seeds of certain trees, especially the ***kapok tree*** *Eriodendron anfractuosum* of India, Java, and Malaya, and the ***silk- cotton tree*** *Ceiba pentandra* of tropical America. Kapok is used for stuffing cushions, mattresses, and life belts. Oil obtained from the seeds is used in food and soap preparation□

Kara Bogaz Gol shallow gulf of the Caspian Sea; area 20 000 sq km/8000 sq mi. Rich deposits of sodium chloride, sulphates, and other salts form by evaporation□

Karachi chief port, naval base and industrial city (engineering, textiles, chemicals, plastics) of Pakistan, in Sind; population 5 103 000. Capital of Pakistan 1947–59□

Karafuto Japanese name for Sakhalin◊□

Karaganda industrial town (coal, copper, tungsten, manganese, etc.) in Kazakh Republic of USSR; population 583 000□

Karaites 8th-century sect of Judaism◊□

Karajan Herbert von 1908– . Austrian conductor. Director of the Vienna State Opera from 1976, and of the Salzburg Festival from 1964□

Kara-Kalpak a division of the S USSR, on the Aral Sea, called after the Kara-Kalpak ('black-bonnet') people, conquered by Russia 1867; area 158 000 sq km/61 000 sq mi; population c700 000, 40% Kara-Kalpaks. Capital Nukus□

Karakoram mountain range in central Asia, divided among China, Pakistan, and India. ***K2*** at 8611 m/28 250 ft is the world's second highest peak. ***Ladakh*** subsidiary range is in NE Kashmir on the Tibetan border□

Karakoram Highway constructed by China and Pakistan and completed 1978; runs 800 km/500 mi from Havelian (north west of Rawalpindi), via Gilgit◊ in Azad Kashmir and the Khunjerab Pass 4800/16 000 ft, to Kashi◊ in China□

Karakorum ruined capital of Genghis◊ Khan, south west of Ulan Bator□

Kara-Kum see under Turkmenistan◊□

Karamanlis Constantinos 1907– . Greek statesman. Prime Minister 1955–8, 1958–61, and 1961–3, he was recalled to office 1974–80 on the fall of the regime of the 'colonels', and was president 1980–5□

karate a form of martial◊ art□

Karbala holy city of the Shi'ite Muslims, Iraq; population 107 500. It is on the site where Husein, son of Ali and Fatima, was killed in battle 680AD, while defending his succession to the Khalifate. Pilgrims visit his tomb□

Karelia autonomous republic of the USSR, formed in 1956 from the Karelo-Finnish SSR set up in 1940; area 172 400 sq km/66 500 sq mi; population 746 000. Capital Petrozavodsk. Under the Tsars, political exiles were sent here□

Karelian Isthmus strip of land between Lake Ladoga and the Gulf of Finland, with Leningrad at the southern extremity. Finland ceded it to the USSR 1940–1 and from 1947□

Karens people mainly in E Burma, near the Thai border, who resisted integration into independent Burma in 1948, and from 1954 received a measure of autonomy with the formation of the Kayah and Karen states□

Kariba Dam see under Zambezi◊□

Karl-Marx-Stadt capital of Karl-Marx-Stadt district and industrial city (engineering, chemicals, textiles) (formerly Chemnitz) in E Germany, population 317 000□

Karlsbad German name of Karlovy◊ Vary□

Karlsruhe industrial town (nuclear research, oil refining) in Baden-Württemberg, W Germany; population 271 000□

karma (Sanskrit 'fate'). In Hinduism the sum of a human being's actions, carried forward from one life to the next to result in an improved or worsened fate. Buddhism has a similar belief, except that no permanent personality is envisaged, the karma relating only to the physical and mental elements carried on from birth to birth, until the power holding them together disperses in the attainment of Nirvana□

Karmal Babrak 1930– . Afghani statesman. He returned from exile with Soviet support to overthrow President Hafizullah Amin, and became president 1979– , and prime minister 1979–81□

Karnak see under Thebes◊□

Karnataka SW state of India (formerly Mysore)

area 191 773 sq km/740 024 sq mi

capital Bangalore

features mainly agricultural, but its minerals include India's only sources of gold and silver

population 37 000 000

language Kannada

famous people Hyder Ali, Tippoo Sahib□

karri a type of giant eucalyptus◊ tree□

karst originally the barren limestone shore of the NE Adriatic, characterized by caves, now applied to similar areas throughout the world□

karting miniature motor racing with low-framed, light chassis cars, originating in the

USA c1955. With standard production 2-stroke engines, karts reach speeds of 160 km/100mph□

Kasai see under river Zaïre□

Kashgar see Kashi◊□

Kashi oasis trading city (formerly Kashgar) in Xinjiang Uyghur autonomous region, China; population 180 000. It is the Chinese terminus of the Karakoram◊ Highway, and a centre of Muslim culture□

Kashmir former Muslim state of N British India, ruled by a Hindu maharajah, the latter acceding to the Republic of India in 1947. There was fighting between pro-India and pro-Pakistan factions, and open war between the two countries 1965–66, and 1971. A plebiscite decreed by the United Nations in 1949 for the state has never been held, and it remains divided: the NW is occupied by Pakistan, and the rest by India□

Kashmir Azad ('Free'). Pakistan-occupied area in the NW of the former state of Kashmir◊
population 1 500 000
administrative headquarters Muzaffarabad
features W Himalayan peak Nanga Parbat 8126 m/26 660 ft. See also Northern◊ Areas□

Kassel industrial town (engineering, chemicals, electronics) in Hessen, W Germany; population 195 500. There is the spectacular Wilhelmshöhe mountain park, and the Grimm◊ Museum commemorates the authors of fairy tales who lived here□

Katanga former name of Shaba◊□

Kathmandu capital of Nepal; population 195 260. Founded in the 8th century, it has the restored palace of Hanumandockh, Buddhist shrines, and many monasteries□

Katmai see under Alaska◊□

Kattegat North Sea channel between Jutland and Sweden; c240 km/150 mi long, 135 km/85 mi wide at broadest□

katydid a type of N American grasshopper◊□

Katyn Forest forest near Smolensk◊, USSR, where 4500 Polish officer prisoners of war (captured in the German-Soviet partition of Poland in 1940) were shot; 10 000 others were killed elsewhere. The crime was disclosed by the Germans 1943, and attributed to the Soviet secret police; the Russians attribute it to the Germans□

Katz Sir Bernard 1911– . British biophysicist, who shared a Nobel prize 1970 for elucidation of the transmission and control of signals in the nervous system□

Kaunas industrial river port (Russian *Kovno*) (textiles, chemicals, agricultural machinery) in the Lithuanian division of the Soviet Union, on the Niemen; population 383 000. Capital of independent Lithuania 1918–40□

Kaunda Kenneth David 1924– . Zambian statesman. Imprisoned in 1958 as founder of the Zambia African National Congress (released 1960), he became in 1964 first prime minister of N Rhodesia, then first president of Zambia. From 1973 he introduced one-party rule□

kauri pine New Zealand timber conifer *Agathis australis* family Araucariaceae, whose fossilised gum deposits are especially valued in varnishes; the wood is used for carving and handicrafts□

kava drink prepared from the roots of a pepper◊ plant□

Kawabata Yasunari 1899–1972. Japanese novelist, translator of Lady Murasaki◊, and author of *Snow Country* 1947 and *A Thousand Cranes* 1952. Nobel prize 1968□

Kawasaki industrial city (iron and steel, chemicals, textiles) on Honshu; population 1 041 000□

Kay John 1704–after 1764. British inventor of the flying-shuttle to speed hand-loom weaving 1733. He was financially ruined defending his patent, his home at Bury was wrecked by weavers fearing unemployment, and he died in poverty in France□

Kayah State see Karens◊□

kayak a type of canoe used especially by the Inuit◊□

Kaye Danny. Stage-name of American film and stage comedian Daniel Kominski 1913– , most famous for his films, e.g. *The Secret Life of Walter Mitty* 1946□

Kazakhstan constituent republic of the Soviet Union from 1936, part of Soviet Central Asia
area 2 717 300 sq km/1 049 150 sq mi
capital Alma-Ata
towns Karaganda, Semipalatinsk, Petropavlovsk
features largest republic in the USSR; Caspian and Aral Seas, Lake Balkhash; Steppe region; it includes the Baikonour Cosmodrome (official name for the Soviet space launch site at Tyuratam, near the coalmining town of Baikonour), and a weapons-testing area near the Chinese border
products second only to Ukraine as a grain producer; copper, lead, zinc, manganese, coal and oil
population 14 900 000, Russian 42%, Kazakh 33% (see Kirghizia◊), Ukrainian 7%
language Russian, Kazakh, related to Turkish
religion Sunni Islam□

Kazan industrial city (engineering, oil refining, petrochemicals, textiles) and capital of the Tatar republic, USSR; population 1 011 000. It was capital of a Tatar Khanate till

1552, when it was conquered by Ivan IV□

Kazan Elia 1909– . Greco-American stage director, e.g. *Skin of Our Teeth* 1942, and film director e.g. *Gentlemen's Agreement* 1948, *On the Waterfront* 1954, *East of Eden* 1954, and *The Visitors* 1972□

Kazantzakis Nikos 1885–1957. Greek poet, e.g. *I Odysseia* 1938, which continues Homer's *Odyssey*, and novelist e.g. *Zorba the Greek* 1946□

kea a type of parrot◊□

Kean Edmund 1787–1833. British actor, noted in Shakespearean roles of Shylock, Richard III, and Othello□

Keaton Buster. Stage-name of American comedian Joseph Frank Keaton 1896–1966. A sophisticated, deadpan actor, his films include *The General* 1926 and *The Cameraman* 1928□

Keats John 1795–1821. British poet. Born in London, he became a student at Guy's Hospital 1815–17, but turned to poetry, publishing *Poems* 1817, and *Endymion* 1818, the latter harshly reviewed, largely owing to his friendship with the Radical, Leigh Hunt◊. To 1819 belong the richly imaginative 'The Eve of St Agnes,' the 'Odes' (including those 'To Autumn,' 'On a Grecian Urn,' and 'To a Nightingale'), and his hopeless infatuation with Fanny Brawne. His brother Tom had died of tuberculosis in 1818, and, stricken himself, he went to Italy hoping for a cure, but died in Rome. He wrote *Letters* 1848□

Keble John 1792–1866. Anglican poet-cleric, professor of poetry at Oxford 1831–41, whose sermon on national apostasy 1833 began the Oxford◊ Movement□

Kedah state of Malaysia; population 1 102 000. Capital Alor Star□

Keeling see Cocos◊ Islands□

Keewatin a district of the Canadian Northwest◊ Territories□

Kefallinia see under Ionian◊ Islands□

Keflavik fishing port in Iceland, a NATO base from 1951; population 6700. The large international airport was built by US forces in World War II (Meeks Field)□

Keighley woollen and engineering town in W Yorkshire, England; population 57 800. Haworth, home of the Brontës, is now part of Keighley□

Keitel Wilhelm 1882–1946. German field marshal, chief of the supreme command from 1938, who signed the unconditional surrender at Berlin 8 May 1945. Tried at Nuremberg◊, he was hanged□

Kekule Friedrich Aug 1829–96. German chemist, whose theory (1858) of molecular structure revolutionized organic chemistry. He is most famous for his two resonant forms of the benzene ring□

Kelantan state of Malaysia; population 877 575. Capital Kota Bharu□

Keller Gottfried 1819–90. Swiss poet, novelist (*Der Grüne Heinrich* 1854–55) and short story writer *Die Leute von Seldwyla 1856–74*□

Keller Helen Adams 1880–1968. American author, who lost the senses of sight and hearing through an illness when 19 months old, and who remained dumb. Under the tuition of Anne Sullivan Macy, she became able to speak, took a university degree, and published *The Story of My Life* 1902□

Kells Book of. An 8th-century illuminated manuscript of the gospels. See under Dublin◊□

Kelly Edward 'Ned' 1854–80. Australian bushranger, who wounded a constable in 1878 while resisting his brother's arrest. The brothers then carried out bank robberies with their gang on the New South Wales/Victoria border. Ned Kelly wore home-made armour. He was captured in 1880 and hanged□

Kelly Grace Patricia 1928–82. American film actress, starring in *High Noon* 1952, *The Country Girl* (Academy Award) 1954, and *High Society* 1955. She married Prince Rainier◊ in 1956, and died in a road crash□

kelp a type of seaweed◊□

kelvin SI basic unit of thermodynamic temperature; symbol K; named after Lord Kelvin◊□

Kelvin William Thomson, 1st Baron Kelvin 1824–1907. British physicist, professor at Glasgow University 1846–99. He helped to establish the Second Law of Thermodynamics and showed how an absolute scale of temperature could be derived from it. In telegraphy he greatly improved transatlantic communications□

Kelvin scale of temperature (used by scientists) begins at absolute zero (−273°C) but increases in the same way as the Celsius scale, i.e. 0°C becomes 273K and 100°C becomes 373K□

Kemble Charles 1775–1854. British actor-manager, younger brother of Philip Kemble◊, whose greatest successes were in romantic roles with his daughter Fanny Kemble◊□

Kemble 'Fanny' (Frances Anne) 1809–93. British actress, daughter of Charles Kemble◊, who first appeared as Shakespeare's Juliet in 1829□

Kemble John Philip 1757–1823. British actor-manager, one of the 12 children of strolling player Roger Kemble, who also included Charles Kemble◊ and Mrs Siddons◊. He was famous for tragic roles, especially Shakespeare, including Hamlet and Coriolanus□

Kemerovo coal-mining town in southern USSR; population 486 000. It has chemical and metallurgical industries□

Kempis see Thomas◊ à Kempis□

kenaf annual plant (also known as ambary) *Hibiscus cannabinus*, related to the hollyhock, grown for a fibre similar to jute in China, India etc.□

kendo a form of martial◊ art, a type of fencing with wooden sticks□

Keneally Thomas Michael 1935– . Australian novelist, Booker◊ prizewinner with *Schindler's Ark*, whose novel was based on the true-life account of Polish Jews saved from the gas chamber by a German industrialist, 1982□

Kenilworth town in Warwickshire, England; population 20 000. Elizabeth I was lavishly entertained in the Norman castle by the Earl of Leicester 1575 (see under Sir Walter Scott◊); it was dismantled after the Civil War□

Kennedy Edward Moore 1932– . American Democrat politician. He aided his brothers John and Robert Kennedy◊ in the campaign of 1960, and entered politics as a senator, but failed to gain the presidential nomination in 1980, largely because of his delay in reporting a car crash at Chappaquiddick Island, near Cape Cod, in which his girl companion, Mary Jo Kopechne, was drowned□

Kennedy John Fitzgerald 1917–63. 35th president of the USA. Son of Joseph Kennedy◊, he was born at Brookline, Massachusetts, and served in the navy in the Pacific during World War II. In 1960 he defeated Nixon◊ for the presidency, the first Roman Catholic and the youngest man to be elected, and surrounded himself with the academics and intellectuals of the New◊ Frontier. In foreign policy he carried through the unsuccessful Bay of Pigs◊ invasion of Cuba, and in 1963 secured the withdrawal of Soviet missiles from the island. His programme for reforms at home was posthumously executed by Lyndon Johnson◊. He married Jaqueline Lee Bouvier 1929– in 1953, who later married the Greek shipping magnate Aristotle Onassis 1906–75. Kennedy was assassinated 22 Nov on a visit to Dallas by Lee Harvey Oswald, who was in turn shot dead by Jack Ruby. Kennedy's sensational death when still young helped to accord him legendary status□

Kennedy Robert Francis 1925–68. American Democrat politician. Campaign manager for his elder brother John Kennedy◊, he pursued a racket-busting policy as Attorney-General 1961–4, and in 1968 was assassinated while campaigning for the presidential nomination by a Jordanian Arab, Sirhan Sirhan□

Kennedy Space Center John F. Space-flight experimental centre on Cape Canaveral, Florida. The first manned flight to the moon was made here 1969□

Kennelly Arthur Edwin 1861–1939. American engineer, who independently predicted the existence in the upper atmosphere of the 'E layer'. See Oliver Heaviside◊□

Kensington and Chelsea Borough of Greater London

features Kensington Gardens (see Westminster◊); museums – Victoria and Albert, Natural History, Science; Imperial College of Science and Technology 1907, which has produced several Nobel prizewinners; Commonwealth Institute; Kensington Palace; Hol land House (damaged in World War II, and partly rebuilt as a youth hostel)

population 125 892□

Kent Alexander. See Douglas Reeman◊□

Kent Edward, Duke of Kent 1935– . Prince of the UK, grandson of George◊ V. He married in 1961 Katharine Worsley 1933– □

Kent William 1685–1748. British architect, e.g. the Horse Guards, London, and gardener who followed the landscapes of Claude◊ and Poussin◊, with classic temples□

Kent county of southeast England, the 'garden of England'

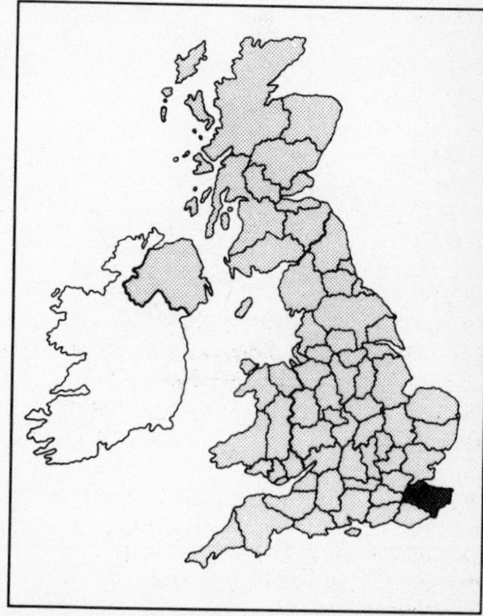

area 3731 sq km/1440 sq mi

towns admin headquarters Maidstone; Canterbury, Chatham, Rochester, Tunbridge

Wells; resorts Folkestone, Margate, Ramsgate
features a 'man of Kent' comes from east of the Medway and a 'Kentish man' from W Kent; New Ash Green, a new town; Romney Marsh; the Isles of Grain, Sheppey (on which is the resort of Sheerness, formerly a royal dockyard) and Thanet; Weald (agricultural area); rivers Darent, Medway, Stour; Leeds Castle (converted to a palace by Henry VIII), Down House (Darwin's home); Hever Castle (where Henry VIII courted Anne Boleyn); Chartwell (Churchill's country home); Knole; Sissinghurst Castle and gardens
products hops, apples, soft fruit (on the weald); sheep (on Romney Marsh); coal, cement, paper
population 469 700
famous people Charles Dickens; Christopher Marlowe□

Kent and Strathearn Edward Augustus, Duke of Kent and Strathearn 1767–1820. Fourth son of George III, whose only child was the future Queen Victoria□

Kenton Stan 1912–79. American exponent of progressive jazz, who broke into West Coast jazz in 1941 with his 'walls of brass' sound; helped introduce Afro-Cuban rhythms to US jazz; and combined jazz and classical music in his compositions, e.g. *Artistry in Rhythm*□

Kentucky border state of the USA; Blue Grass State

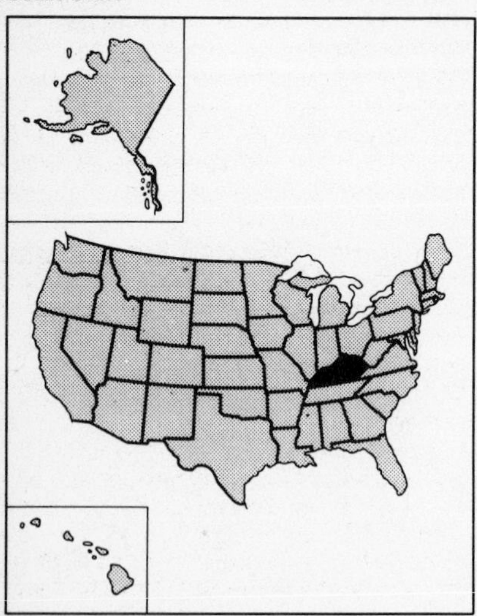

area 104 623 sq km/40 395 sq mi
capital Frankfort
towns Louisville, Lexington-Fayette
features horse racing at Louisville (Kentucky Derby); Mammoth Cave National Park (main cave 6.5 km long/4 mi long, up to 38 m/125 ft high, where Indian councils once held; Lincoln's birthplace at Hodgenville; Fort Knox, US Gold Bullion Depository
products tobacco, cereals, steel goods, textiles, transport vehicles
population 3 661 435
famous people Kit Carson, Henry Clay, Jefferson Davis
history originally part of Virginia, Kentucky was first permanently settled after Daniel Boone had blazed his Wilderness Trail, and became a state in 1792□

Kenya Republic of

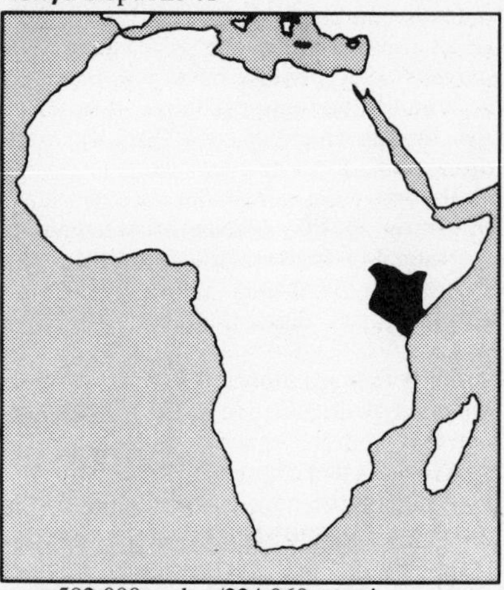

area 583 000 sq km/224 960 sq mi
capital Nairobi
towns Kisumu and the port of Mombasa
features Great Rift Valley, Mt Kenya, Lake Nakuru (flamingos), Aberdare National Park (includes Treetops Hotel, where Elizabeth II heard the she had succeeded to the throne), the Masai Mara National Park (which forms part of the same ecosystem as Tanzania's Serengeti); Tsavo National Park, Nairobi National Park, Malindini Marine Reserve, Lake Turkana (Rudolf), Olduvai Gorge
exports coffee, tea, sisal, pineapples
currency Kenya shilling
population 15 320 000, with one of the world's fastest growth rates; the dominant ethnic group is the Kikuyu, but see also Masai◊
language Swahili, but English is in general use
religion indigenous religions with Christian and Islamic minorities
famous people Jomo Kenyatta, Richard Leakey
government president (Daniel Arap Moi◊; re-elected 1983) and unicameral national assembly; it is a one-party state of the Kenya African National Union (KANU), but competition for seats allows a democratic element

recent history taken under British protection in 1895, Kenya achieved independence in 1963, and became a republic within the Commonwealth 1964. Mau-Mau, a terrorist Kikuyu secret society, was active 1952–60, and influenced later black African inde-dependence movements. Africanization 1967–8 led many Asians to leave, many entering Britain. President Moi was re-elected unopposed 1983□

Kenya Mt. extinct volcano from which Kenya is named; 5200 m/17 058 ft□

Kenyatta Jomo. Name assumed by Kenya politician Kamau Ngengi c1889–1978, *Kenyatta* meaning 'beaded belt'. A Kikuyu, he spent some years in Britain, and in 1946 returned to Kenya as president of the Kenya African Union, agitating for independence. In 1953 he was sentenced to seven years imprisonment for his management of Mau-Mau◊, though some doubt remains on his complicity. In 1963 he became prime minister (president 1964–78) of independent Kenya□

Kenyon Dame Kathleen 1906–78. British archaeologist, whose work at Jericho◊ showed that the double walls associated with Joshua◊ belonged to an earlier period, and that a Neolithic settlement had existed c6800BC□

Kepler Johann 1571–1630. German astronomer, assistant then successor to Tycho Brahe◊ as imperial mathematician 1601. In establishing that planets move in ellipses, rather than in circles or circles-upon-circles, he was one of the founders of modern astronomy. See Kepler's Laws◊□

Kepler's Laws of planetary motion: *1* the orbit of each planet is an ellipse with the sun at one of the foci; *2* the line joining each planet to the sun sweeps out equal areas in equal times; *3* the squares of the periods of the planets are proportional to the cubes of their mean distances from the sun□

Kerala state of southwest India
area 38 864 sq km/15 002 sq mi
capital Trivandrum
features most densely populated, and most literate (60%) state of India; strong religious and caste divisions make it politically unstable.
population 25 403 225
language Kannada, Malayalam, Tamil□

Kerensky Alexander Feodorovich 1881–1970. Russian politician, premier of the second provisional government, before its collapse in Nov 1917, during the Bolshevik◊ revolution led by Lenin. He lived in the USA from 1918□

Kerguelen Islands volcanic archipelago in the Indian Ocean, part of the French

Kepler's second law: area SPQ = area SXY

Kepler's law

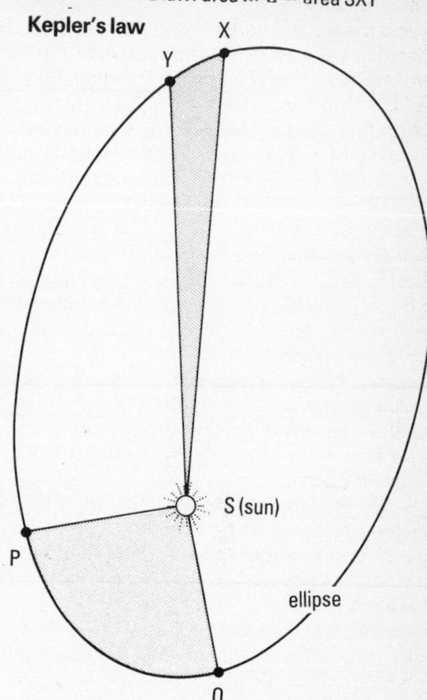

Southern and Antarctic Territories. Uninhabited except for scientists (centre for joint study of geomagnetism with USSR), they are rich in birdlife and support a unique wild cabbage containing a pungent oil□

Kerkyra see Ionian◊ Islands□

Kermadec Islands volcanic group, a dependency of New Zealand; area 34 sq km/13 sq mi. Uninhabited except for a meteorological station on the largest, Raoul□

Kern Jerome 1885–1945. American songwriter, popular operetta composer of *Show Boat* 1927□

Kernow Celtic name for Cornwall◊□

kerosene petroleum distillate known in the UK as ***paraffin***; a more highly refined form is used in jet aircraft fuel□

Kerouac Jack 1923–69. American novelist. Of French-Canadian extraction, he was born in Lowell, Massachusetts, and by his football prowess was set for a university career, but drifted into odd jobs. Jack Duluoz, king of the beatniks, is the hero of his series of books, including *On the Road* 1958, and *Big Sur* 1963□

Kerry county of the Republic of Ireland, province of Munster◊. County town: Tralee. It includes Macgillycuddy's Reeks, a group of mountains including Carrantuohill, the highest peak in Ireland at 1041 m/3414 ft, and the Lakes of Killarney□

Kesselring Albert 1885–1960. German field marshal, commander of the Luftwaffe 1939–40. He later served under Rommel in N Africa, took command in Italy in 1943, and was Commander-in-Chief on the western front in Mar 1945. His death sentence for war crimes (1947) at the Nuremberg◊ trials was commuted to imprisonment (released 1952)□

kestrel a type of small falcon◊□

Ketch Jack d. 1686. English executioner, who includes Monmouth◊ in 1685 among his victims; his name became a common nickname for an executioner□

ketone organic compound containing the carbonyl group (formula R'COR, where R and R' are alkyl or aryl groups) differentiated from an aldehyde by uniting to two atoms of carbon instead of one of carbon and one of hydrogen. Ketones are liquids or low-melting-point solids, slightly soluble in water, and form derivatives in acid solutions. ***Acetone*** (formula CH_3COCH_3) is an example□

Kew see under Richmond◊ upon Thames□

Key Francis Scott 1779–1843. American lawyer who wrote the song 'The Star-Spangled Banner' while Fort McHenry was besieged by the British 1814; from 1931 it has been the national anthem of the USA□

Keynes John Maynard, 1st Baron Keynes 1883–1946. British economist, whose *The General Theory of Employment, Interest, and Money* 1936, proposed the prevention of financial crises and unemployment by adjusting demand through government control of credit and currency. Keynes is regarded as the most important economist of the twentieth century, responsible for that part of economics now known as ***macroeconomics***; his ideas are today often contrasted with those of monetarism◊□

Key West tourist resort at the tip of the Florida peninsula, USA; population 30 000;. It is the setting of Hemingway's◊ *To Have and Have Not*□

KGB Russian secret police (***K***omitet ***G***osudarstvennoye ***B***ezhopaznosti Committee of State Security), in control of frontier and general security, and the forced labour system. Under the Tsars it was known as the ***Okhrana***; 1918–23 ***Cheka***; 1923–34 ***GPU*** or ***OGPU***; 1934–46 ***NKVD;*** and 1946–53 ***MVD.*** The counter-intelligence sub-section named ***Smersh*** familiar from the James Bond novels, was said to be an acronym coined by Stalin for 'death to spies'; its functions were later taken over by other groups. KGB officers hold key appointments in all fields of daily life, reporting to administration offices in every major town; the headquarters is in Moscow; Lubyanka Prison is behind it. Many KGB officers also hold diplomatic posts in embassies abroad□

Khabarovsk industrial city (oil refining, saw milling, meat packing) in E USSR; population 545 000□

Khachaturian Aram Ilyich 1903–78. Russian composer, noted for folk themes, e.g. in the ballets *Gayaneh* 1942, which includes the 'Sabre Dance', and *Spartacus*□

khaki the dust-coloured uniform of British and native troops in India from c1850, adopted as camouflage in the S African War, and later standard worldwide□

Khalifa The. Sudanese dervish leader ***Abdullah el Taaisha*** 1846–99, successor to the Mahdi as Sudanese ruler from 1885, he was defeated by Kitchener◊ at Omdurman 1898, and later killed at Kordofan□

Khalistan projected independent Sikh state. See Sikhism◊□

Khama Sir Seretse. See Botswana◊□

khamsin a hot wind◊ that blows in Egypt□

Khan Liaquat Ali 1895–1951. Indian statesman, who in 1947 became first prime minister of Pakistan, and was assassinated by a Muslim opponent□

Kharga oasis in the Western Desert of Egypt, headquarters of the New Valley irrigation scheme, using water from natural underground reservoirs□

Kharkov industrial city (tractors, locomotives, aircraft, etc.) in the Ukraine, USSR; population 1 485 000□

Khartoum capital of the Republic of Sudan; population 1 000 000. General Gordon◊ was killed here in 1885, but the site was recaptured by Kitchener◊ 1898. The site of ***Meroe*** the capital of Nubia◊ c600BC–350AD, is nearby. From its iron smelting slagheaps, it has been called 'the Birmingham of ancient Africa'□

Khatyn village north east of Minsk, USSR, with a memorial to the many Byelorussian villages destroyed by the Germans in World War II, of which Khatyn was one. See also Katyn◊ Forest□

Khazars people of Tatar origin from central Asia who established an empire in SE Russia 7–11th century. They were converted to Judaism c1245, and have been suggested as the ancestors of E European Jews, who would hence be of Aryan, not Semitic, descent. See Judaism◊□

khedive title granted by the Turkish sultan to his Egyptian viceroy 1867, retained by succeeding rulers till 1914□

Khmer Republic see Kampuchea◊□

Khomeini Ayatollah Ruhollah 1900– . Iranian◊ Shi'ite Muslim leader, born in Khomein. Exiled for opposition to the Shah from 1964, he returned in 1979 to established a fundamentalist Islamic republic□

Khorana Har Gobind 1922– . Indo-American biochemist, who shared a Nobel prize 1968 for interpretation of the genetic code and in 1976 led the team which first synthesized a biologically active gene□

Khorramshahr see Khuninshahr◊□

Khrushchev Nikita Sergeyevich 1894–1971. Soviet statesman. As Secretary-General of the official party 1953–64, he denounced Stalinism in a secret session of the Soviet Communist Party in Feb 1956, initiating the 'thaw' in attitudes; many 1930s purge victims were released or posthumously rehabilitated. However, the Hungarian revolt of Oct 1956 was ruthlessly suppressed. Having ousted Bulganin◊, he also took over as Prime Minister 1958, and pursued a policy of peaceful co-existence and competition with capitalism. However, he developed a feud with Mao◊ Zhedong of China. In 1963 he despatched nuclear missiles to Cuba which had to be withdrawn under US pressure. He was consequently compelled to resign in 1964□

Khufu c3000BC. Egyptian king (Greek Cheops) who built the largest of the Pyramids□

Khuninshahr port and oil-refining centre in Iran (formerly Khorramshahr, but renamed Khuninshahr 'city of blood' when it was retaken by the Iranians after capture by the Iraquis 1980); population 146 700□

Khuzestan SW province of Iran, which includes the chief Iranian oil resources. Towns include Ahwaz (capital), and the ports of Abadan and Khuninshahr. See Arabistan◊□

Khyber Pass see under Hindu◊ Kush□

Kiangsi see Jiangxi□

Kiangsu see Jiangsu□

kibbutz Israeli communal collective settlement, with shared property, earnings, work, and food; children are communally housed□

kidnapping the abduction of a person in order to gain money for their safe release. The practice arose in the 17th century with the abduction of young people to become indentured labourers in colonial plantations, from which they could be rescued by a ransom□

kidneys pair of reddish-brown organs (c11cm/4.5in by 4cm/1.5in on the rear wall of the abdomen) which excrete waste in the form of urine. They are essential to life, and if both are defective, a kidney machine, or continuous ambulatory peritoneal dialysis◊ (in which the peritoneal membrane takes over kidney function with the aid of a plastic bag of dialysis solution), or a transplant, is necessary.

kidney stones crystallized mineral deposits formed as a result of infection, etc., which may now be dispersed by ultrasonics without surgery□

Kiel Baltic port (fishing, shipbuilding, engineering), in W Germany, capital of Schleswig-Holstein; population 249 800. ***Kiel Week*** in Jun is a renowned sporting event for yachtsmen□

Kiel Canal opened 1895, links the North Sea with the Baltic, length 97 km/60 mi□

Kierkegaard Saøren 1831–55. Danish philosopher and theologian, the first existentialist, maintaining that God is known only through an encounter in the personal decision of faith; *Either-Or* 1843, *Concept of Dread* 1844□

Kiev capital of the Ukrainian republic, industrial centre and third largest city of the USSR, on the River Dnieper; population 2 248 000. The Slav domination of Russia began with the rise of Kiev (see also under Vikings◊) the 'mother of Russian cities,' founded in the 5th century. It replaced Novgorod◊ as the capital in 882, and was the original centre of the Orthodox faith in 988. St Sophia cathedral (11th century) and Kiev-Pechersky Monastery (both now museums) survive, and also remains of the Golden Gate. The Kiev opera and ballet are renowned. It was occupied by Germany 1941□

Kigali capital of Rwanda; population 117 750□

Kildare county of the Republic of Ireland, province of Leinster◊; county town: Naas. It includes part of the Bog of Allen; the village of Maynooth, with a training college for Roman Catholic priests; and the Curragh, a plain which is the site of the national stud and headquarters of Irish racing□

Kilimanjaro see under Tanzania◊□

Kilkenny county of the Republic of Ireland, province of Leinster◊ county town: Kilkenny□

Killarney market town in county Kerry, Republic of Ireland; population 7200. Most famous beauty spot in Ireland, it has Macgillycuddy's Reeks (a range of mountains) and the Lakes of Killarney to the south-west□

killer whale a mammal of the dolphin◊ family□

kilo prefix denoting in the metric system 1000 units, hence ***kilogram*** unit of mass equal to 1000 grams/2.2 lb ***kilometre*** unit of length equal to 1000 metres/3280.89 ft (approx ⅝ of a mile) ***kiloton*** unit of explosive force equivalent to 1000 tons of TNT, used in describing nuclear bombs ***kilowatt*** unit of power equal to about 1000 watts/1.34 horsepower□

kilobyte measure of a computer's memory space for data◊, abbreviation K. Eight ***bits*** (abbreviation for 'binary digit', i.e. either the digit 0 or 1) make one ***byte***, and 1024 (not 1000) bytes constitute one kilobyte. There are 1000 kilobytes in one ***megabyte***(Mb)□

Kilvert Francis 1840–79. British clergyman, whose entertaining diary of life on the Welsh border 1870–9 was not published till 1938–9□

Kimberley diamond town in Cape Province, S Africa; population 104 000□

Kimberley diamond site in Western Australia, found in 1978–9, said to have 5% of world's known gem-quality stones and 50% of its industrial diamonds□

Kim Il Sung 1912– . North Korean prime minister from 1948, and president from 1972. He has campaigned constantly for Korean reunification, and his son ***Kim Chong Il*** 1941– has been named his successor□

kimono traditional Japanese costume, still retained by women for formal wear, and fastened at the waist with the ***obi*** or sash. Men tend to wear it when relaxing at home□

kinematics the study of the movement of bodies. See under mechanics◊□

kinetics the study of bodies in motion. See under mechanics◊□

King Martin Luther 1929–68. American black Baptist pastor, who campaigned for racial desegregation: Nobel peace prize 1964. He was shot by James Earl Ray in 1969. From 1986 the 3rd Monday in Jan is a US public holiday in his honour□

King William Mackenzie 1874–1950. Canadian Liberal statesman, Prime Minister 1921–Jun 1926, Sept 1926–1930, 1935–1948□

king crab or ***horseshoe crab*** marine arthropod, subclass Xiphosura, class Arachnida. The upper side of the body is entirely covered with a rounded shell, and it has a long spine-like tail; up to 60 cm/2 ft long, it burrows in the sand. See also under crab◊□

kingcup common name for some species of Ranunculaceae◊, especially marsh marigold◊□

kingfisher bird of family Alcedinidae, order Coraciiformes, which includes the hornbills◊. The ***Eurasian kingfisher*** *Alcedo atthis* has a brilliant blue-green back and is chestnut beneath, feeds on fish and water insects, and makes a nest of fish bones in a hole in a river bank. Australian species include the largest of the family, the ***kookaburra*** or ***laughing jackass*** *Dacelo novaeguineae* sombrely grey-brown, and a broad-billed insect-eater of the eastern forests, with a cackling call□

Kinglake Alexander William 1809–91. British historian of the Crimean War, better remembered for his brilliant Near East travel narrative *Eothen* 1844□

King's Counsel in England, a barrister of senior rank. See Queen's Counsel□

king's evil popular name for scrofula◊. See under tuberculosis◊□

Kingsley Charles 1819–75. British author, born in Devon, brother of Mary Henrietta Kingsley◊. Rector of Eversley, Hampshire 1842–75, he was known as the 'Chartist clergyman' because of such campaigning novels as *Alton Locke* 1850. He was professor of modern history at Cambridge 1860–9, and wrote historical novels e.g. *Westward Ho!* 1855. His *The Water-Babies* 1863 is a children's classic. His controversy with J H Newman◊ prompted the latter's *Apologia*□

Kingsley Mary Henrietta 1862–1900. British traveller, author of *Travels in West Africa* 1897. Sister of Charles Kingsley◊. She died while nursing Boer prisoners in the S African War□

King's Lynn port (boatbuilding, brewing, agricultural machinery) at the mouth of the Great Ouse, Norfolk, England; population 31 000. Fanny Burney was born here□

King's Medal medal◊ awarded to foreign civilians who aided Britain in the Second World War□

King's proctor in England, the official representing the Crown in matrimonial cases. See under Queen's proctor◊

Kingston capital and port of Jamaica; population 643 800. Founded in the 17th century, it became the capital in 1872, and was rebuilt after the earthquake of 1907□

Kingston city and lake port in Ontario, Canada; population 60 000. Developed round the French Fort Frontenac from 1782, it was captured by England in 1748, and renamed for George III□

Kingston-upon-Hull official name of Hull◊□

Kingston upon Thames Borough of Greater London

features administrative headquarters of Surrey; Guildhall and coronation stone of the Saxon kings

population 132 300□

Kingstown see Dun◊ Laoghaire□

King-Te-Chen see Jingdezhen◊□

Kinnock Neil 1942– . Labour politician. Born at Tredegar, S Wales, and educated at Cardiff University, he took a strong stance against the traditional 'moderate' Labour (Wilson/Callaghan) position, but as leader

THE WORLD : Physical

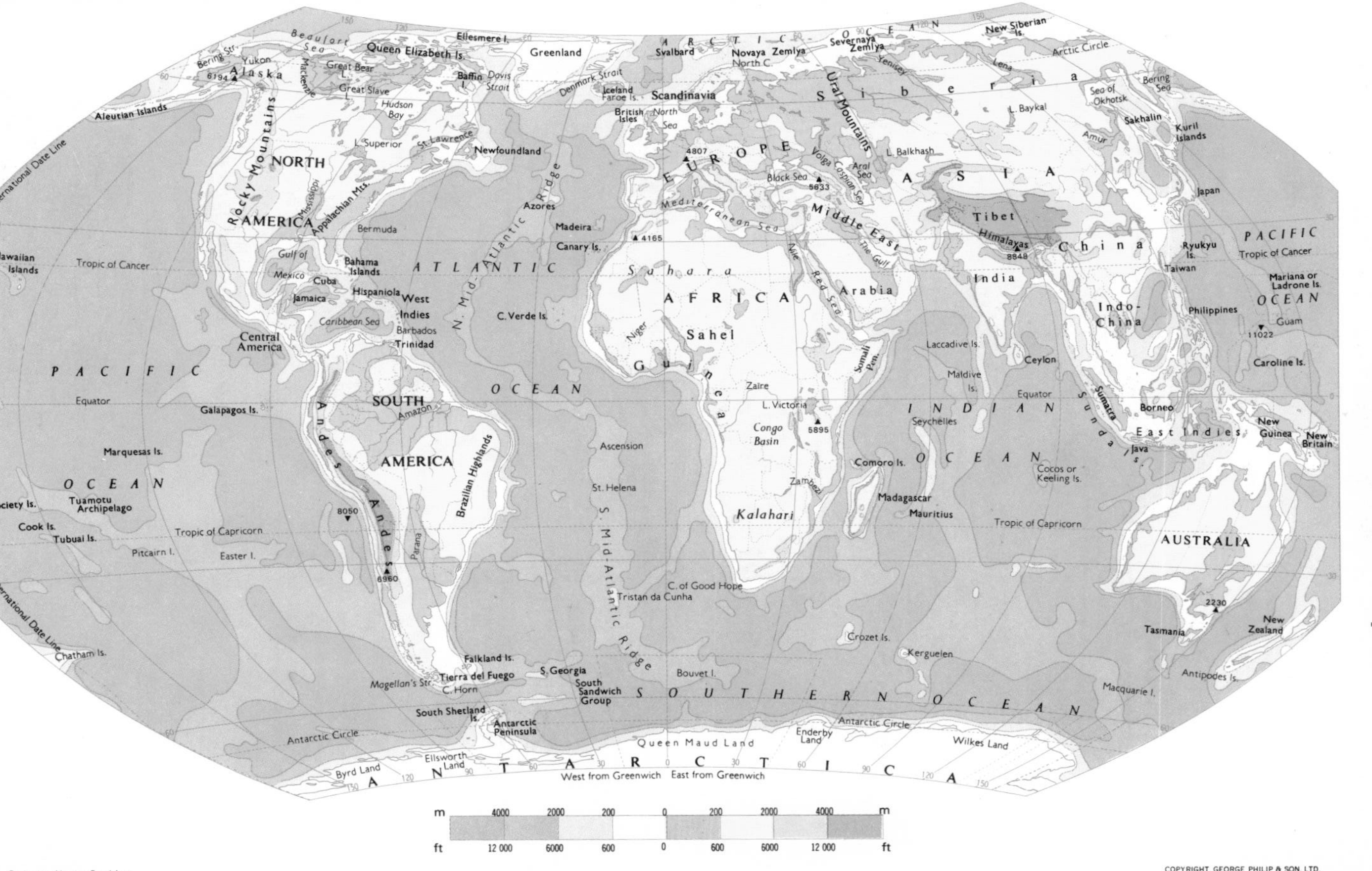

Projection: *Hammer Equal Area*

Projection: *Hammer Equal Area*

ARCTIC OCEAN
New Siberian Is.
Severnaya Zemlya
Novaya Zemlya
Svalbard (Norway)
North C.
Murmansk
Arkhangelsk
UNION OF SOVIET SOCIALIST REPUBLICS
Arctic Circle
Lena
Yenisey
Ob
Bering Sea
Sea of Okhotsk
Stockholm
Leningrad
Oslo
Copenhagen
Moscow
Gorki
Sverdlovsk
Novosibirsk
L. Baykal
Chita
Sakhalin
Kuril Islands
Berlin
Warsaw
Kiev
Omsk
Irkutsk
Ulan Bator
Amur
Harbin
Vienna
Kharkov
Budapest
Odessa
Volga
L. Balkhash
MONGOLIA
Shenyang (Mukden)
Vladivostok
EUROPE
Aral Sea
Caspian Sea
Urumchi
ASIA
Black Sea
Istanbul
Baku
Tashkent
CHINESE REPUBLIC
Peking
Lü-ta
Seoul
KOREA
JAPAN
Tokyo
Yokohama
Osaka
Rome
GREECE
TURKEY
Athens
Tehran
Tientsin
Mediterranean Sea
MALTA
CYPRUS
SYRIA
ISRAEL
IRAQ
Baghdad
Jerusalem
IRAN (PERSIA)
AFGHANISTAN
Kabul
Lahore
Nanking
Wuhan
Shanghai
Tripoli
Alexandria
Cairo
Suez
Delhi
Chungking
PACIFIC OCEAN
LIBYA
EGYPT
Nile
The Gulf
PAKISTAN
Karachi
NEPAL
Ryukyu Is.
Tropic of Cancer
Medina
SAUDI ARABIA
Mecca
Red Sea
INDIA
BANGLA-DESH
BURMA
Kwangchow
TAIWAN (FORMOSA)
Hong Kong
Calcutta
Mariana or Ladrone Is.
AFRICA
OMAN
Bombay
Hyderabad
Rangoon
THAI (SIAM)
VIET-NAM
NIGER
CHAD
Khartoum
SUDAN
SOUTH YEMEN
Aden
Madras
Bangkok
Manila
PHILIPPINES
Guam (U.S.)
Kano
NIGERIA
Lagos
Addis Ababa
ETHIOPIA
SOMALI REP.
Lakshadweep Is. (Laccadive Is.) (India)
SRI LANKA
Colombo
Phnom Penh
Ho Chi Minh City
Caroline Is. (U.S. Trust Territory)
CENTRAL AFRICAN REP.
CAMEROON
Port Harcourt
Zaire
UGANDA
KENYA
Mogadishu
Maldive Is.
MALAYSIA
EQUATORIAL GUINEA
GABON
(Congo)
L. Victoria
Equator
Sumatra
Singapore
Borneo
CONGO
ZAIRE
Kinshasa
Nairobi
Mombasa
INDIAN OCEAN
Seychelles
INDONESIA
New Guinea
PAPUA NEW GUINEA
New Britain
Zanzibar
TANZANIA
Dar-es-Salaam
Chagos Arch.
Jakarta
Surabaya
Java
Benguela
ANGOLA
Comoro Is.
Cocos or Keeling Is. (Australia)
Darwin
ZAMBIA
MALAWI
Lusaka
Harare
ZIMB.
MOZAMBIQUE
MADAGASCAR
Cairns
NAMIBIA
BOTSWANA
Beira
Mauritius
Tropic of Capricorn
Johannesburg
Maputo
AUSTRALIA
SOUTH AFRICA
Durban
Brisbane
Cape Town
C. of Good Hope
Port Elizabeth
Perth
Fremantle
Tristan da Cunha
Adelaide
Sydney
Canberra
Melbourne
Auckland
NEW ZEALAND
Tasmania
Hobart
Wellington
Christchurch
Crozet Is. (Fr.)
Kerguelen (Fr.)
Bouvet I. (Norway)
Antipodes Is. (N.Z.)
Macquarie I. (Australia)
SOUTHERN OCEAN
Antarctic Circle
Enderby Land
Queen Maud Land
Wilkes Land
NORWEGIAN DEPENDENCY
AUSTRALIAN DEPENDENCY
ROSS DEPENDENCY
ANTARCTICA
East from Greenwich

EUROPE

Projection: *Bonne* West from Greenwich 0 East from Greenwich

ROCKALL Sea areas named in weather forecasts

100 0 100 200 300 400 500 miles
100 0 200 400 600 800 km

35 40 45 50 55 60 65 70

North Cape
Lapland
Pechenga
Murmansk
FINLAND
Kola Peninsula
White Sea
Mezen
Arkhangelsk
Pechora
Narodnaya 1894
Ural Mountains
Ob
Gallivare
Luleå
G. of Bothnia
Vaasa
Kuopio
N. Dvina
Kotlas
L. Onega
Nizhny Tagil
Perm
Sverdlovsk
Kirov
Tampere
Vyborg
L. Ladoga
Helsinki
Kronshtadt
Leningrad
Vologda
UNION OF SOVIET SOCIALIST REPUBLICS
R. S. F. S. R.
RUSSIAN
Ustinov
Zlatoust
Chelyabinsk
G. of Finland
Tallinn
ESTONIA
L. Chudskoye
Novgorod
Rybinsk Res
Kostroma
Yaroslavl
Volga
Ivanovo
Gorki
Kazan
Ufa
Magnitogorsk
Pskov
LATVIA
Ulyanovsk
Kuybyshev
Orenburg
Liepaja
Riga
MOSCOW
Syzran
Daugavpils
Klaipeda
LITHUANIA
Kaunas
W. Dvina
Vitebsk
Central Russian Uplands
Tula
Penza
Uralsk
Smolensk
Kaliningrad
Vilnius
Mogilev
Orel
Tambov
Saratov
WHITE RUSSIA
Minsk
Ural
Białystok
Gomel
Voronezh
Kursk
Don
KAZAKHSTAN
WARSAW
Brest
Pripyat (Pripet)
Chernigov
Volgograd
Guryev
POLAND
Lublin
Bug
Kiev
Kharkov
Częstochowa
Kraków
Zhitomir
Dnepr (Dnieper)
UKRAINE
Voroshilovgrad (Lugansk)
Berdichev
Donetsk
Astrakhan
CASPIAN SEA
Lvov
Kirovograd
Dnepropetrovsk
Zaporozhye
Taganrog
Rostov
Carpathians
Dnestr (Dniester)
Krivoy Rog
Chernovtsy
MOLDAVIA
Nikolayev
Kishinev
Debrecen
Odessa
Kherson
S. of Azov
Stavropol
HUNGARY
Cluj
Makhachkala
ROMANIA
Galați
Crimea
Kerch
Krasnodar
Derbent
Timișoara
Brașov
Novorossiysk
Elbrus 5633
Caucasus
Novi Sad
Sevastopol
Ploesti
GEORGIA
Tbilisi
Baku
BUCHAREST
Constanța
BLACK SEA
AZERBAIJAN
Danube
Batumi
Orekhovo
Pleven
Varna
ARMENIA
Araks
Niš
Sinop
Samsun
Trabzon
Yerevan
Sofia
BULGARIA
Burgas
Bosporus
Ararat 5165
Skopje
Sliven
Kastamonu
Erzurum
Tabriz
Plovdiv
Edirne
Istanbul
Üsküdar
TURKEY
Urmia
YUGOSLAVIA
ALBANIA
Balkans
Thessaloniki
Dardanelles
Ankara
L. Van
Bursa
Malatya
Diyarbakir
Kurdistan
Balikesir
Kayseri
IRAN (PERSIA)
GREECE
Aegean Sea
Anatolia
Mosul
Izmir
Konya
Adana
Taurus
İskenderun
Patrai
Piraievs
ATHENS
Aydin
Aleppo (Halab)
IRAQ
Antalya
Tigris
SYRIA
Baghdad
Rhodes
CYPRUS
Nicosia
Homs
Euphrates
Crete
Iraklion
Limassol
30 35 40
45 40 35 50 60

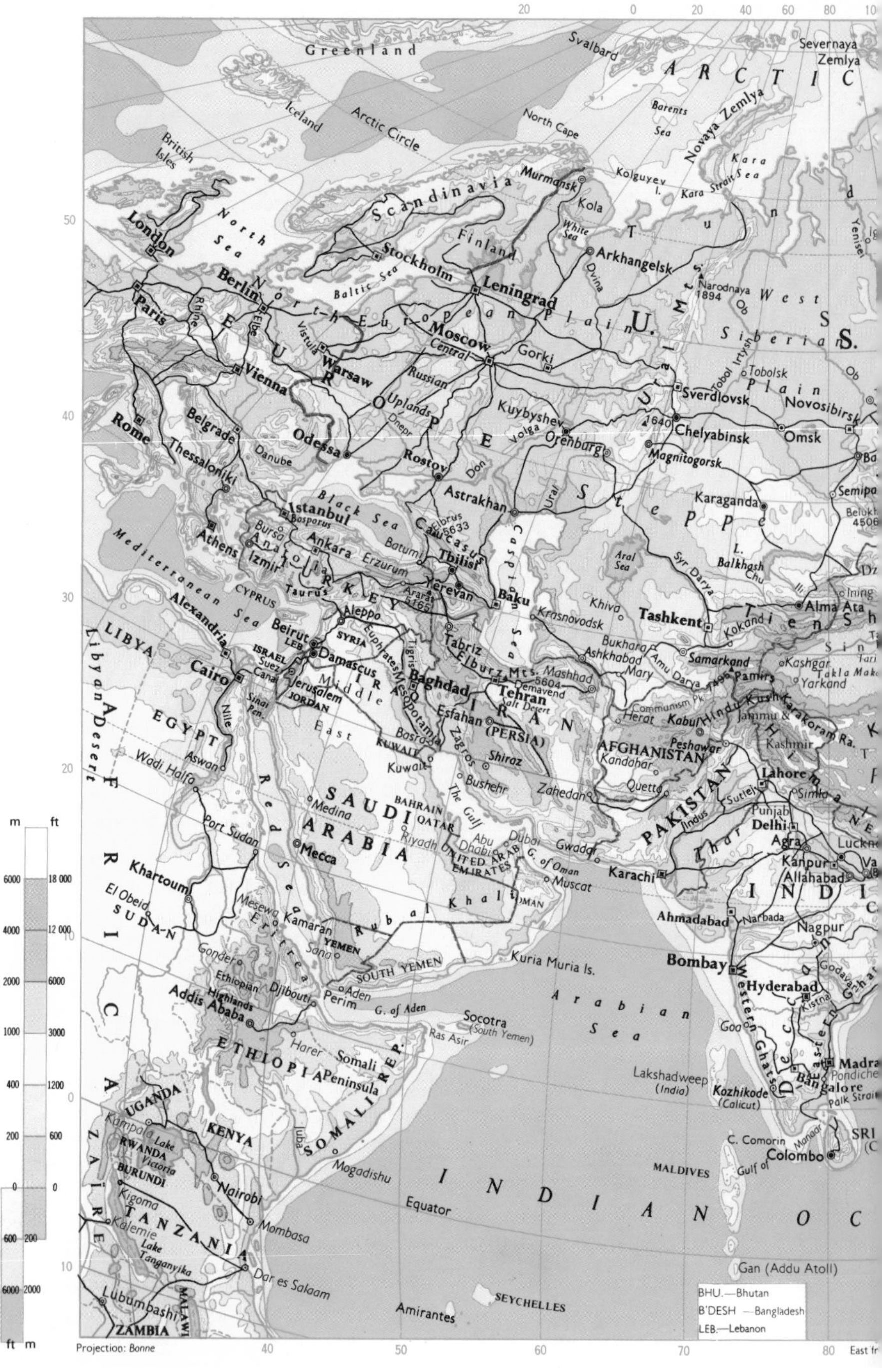
Greenland
Svalbard
ARCTIC
Severnaya Zemlya
Barents Sea
Novaya Zemlya
Kara Sea
Iceland
Arctic Circle
North Cape
British Isles
Scandinavia
Murmansk
Kola
Kolguyev I.
Kara Strait
White Sea
North Sea
London
Stockholm
Finland
Arkhangelsk
Baltic Sea
Leningrad
Narodnaya 1894
Ural Mts.
West Siberian Plain
Berlin
Paris
Rhine
Elbe
Vistula
North European Plain
Moscow
Central Russian Uplands
Gorki
U.S.S.R.
Warsaw
Vienna
EUROPE
Tobol
Irtysh
Tobolsk
Ob
Sverdlovsk
Novosibirsk
Kuybyshev
Volga
Orenburg
1640
Chelyabinsk
Omsk
Magnitogorsk
Rome
Belgrade
Danube
Dnepr
Odessa
Rostov
Don
Thessaloniki
Astrakhan
Ural
Steppe
Karaganda
Semipa
Istanbul
Bosporus
Black Sea
Elbrus 5633
Caucasus
Caspian Sea
Athens
Bursa
Izmir
Anatolia
Ankara
Batumi
Erzurum
Tbilisi
Aral Sea
L. Balkhash
Chu
Syr Darya
Mediterranean Sea
TURKEY
Taurus
Ararat 5165
Yerevan
Baku
Ili
Alma Ata
CYPRUS
Alexandria
Khiva
Krasnovodsk
Tashkent
Kokand
Tien Shan
LIBYA
Beirut
LEB.
Aleppo
SYRIA
Euphrates
Tigris
Tabriz
Bukhara
Samarkand
Kashgar
ISRAEL
Damascus
IRAQ
Elburz Mts.
Ashkhabad
Amu Darya
Mary
Mashhad
Pamirs
Yarkand
Libyan Desert
Cairo
Suez Canal
Jerusalem
JORDAN
Middle East
Mesopotamia
Baghdad
Tehran
Demavend 5604
Salt Desert
Communism Pk.
Herat
Kabul
Hindu Kush
Jammu & Kashmir
Karakoram Ra.
Sinai Pen.
Nile
EGYPT
Basra
Esfahan
IRAN (PERSIA)
Peshawar
AFGHANISTAN
Kandahar
KUWAIT
Kuwait
Zagros
Shiraz
Wadi Halfa
Aswan
Bushehr
The Gulf
Zahedan
Quetta
Lahore
Simla
Sutlej
Indus
PAKISTAN
SAUDI ARABIA
Medina
BAHRAIN
QATAR
Punjab
Delhi
Red Sea
Port Sudan
Riyadh
UNITED ARAB EMIRATES
Abu Dhabi
Dubai
G. of Oman
Gwadar
Agra
Thar
Mecca
Muscat
Karachi
Kanpur
Allahabad
Khartoum
Rub al Khali
OMAN
INDIA
El Obeid
SUDAN
Mesewa
Eritrea
Kamaran
Ahmadabad
Narbada
Nagpur
YEMEN
Sana
SOUTH YEMEN
Kuria Muria Is.
Bombay
Hyderabad
Godavari
Gonder
Ethiopian Highlands
Djibouti
Aden
Perim
G. of Aden
Arabian Sea
Kistna
Addis Ababa
Socotra (South Yemen)
Ras Asir
Goa
Western Ghats
Deccan
Eastern Ghats
ETHIOPIA
Harer
Somali Peninsula
SOMALI REP.
Madras
Pondicherry
Bangalore
Palk Strait
Lakshadweep (India)
Kozhikode (Calicut)
AFRICA
UGANDA
Kampala
KENYA
Lake Victoria
RWANDA
BURUNDI
Juba
C. Comorin
Gulf of Mannar
Colombo
Mogadishu
MALDIVES
Nairobi
ZAIRE
Kigoma
TANZANIA
Kalemie
Lake Tanganyika
Mombasa
Equator
INDIAN OCEAN
Dar es Salaam
Gan (Addu Atoll)
SEYCHELLES
Amirantes
Lubumbashi
MALAWI
ZAMBIA
BHU.—Bhutan
B'DESH —Bangladesh
LEB.—Lebanon
m ft
6000 18 000
4000 12 000
2000 6000
1000 3000
400 1200
200 600
0 0
600 200
6000 2000
ft m
Projection: Bonne
East fr

Sea of Okhotsk
Bering Sea
Sea of Japan
Yellow Sea
East China Sea
South China Sea
Celebes Sea
Banda Sea
Arafura Sea
Java Sea
Bay of Bengal
PACIFIC OCEAN
MONGOLIA
CHINA
KOREA
TAIWAN
PHILIPPINES
BURMA
THAILAND (SIAM)
VIETNAM
MALAYSIA
SINGAPORE
BRUNEI
INDONESIA
AUSTRALIA
Peking
Shanghai
Tokyo
Hong Kong (Br.)
Manila
Jakarta
Ho Chi Minh City
Tropic of Cancer
Greenwich

ATLANTIC OCEAN
British Isles
London
Paris
Bay of Biscay
Madrid
SPAIN
Lisbon
Gibraltar (Br.)
Tangier
Tetuan
Rabat
Fes
Casablanca
Marrakech
MOROCCO
Toubkal 4165
Madeira (Port.)
Canary Is. (Sp.)
Tenerife
Ifni
El Aaiun
WESTERN SAHARA
Dakhla
Ras Nouadhibou (Cap Blanc)
MAURITANIA
Nouakchott
F'Derik (Ft. Gouraud)
El Djouf
Tombouctou (Timbuktu)
MALI
Bamako
Kayes
Kankan
Senegal
SENEGAL
St. Louis
C. Vert
Dakar
GAMBIA
Banjul
GUINEA-BISSAU
Bissau
GUINEA
Conakry
SIERRA LEONE
BURKINA FASO (UPPER VOLTA)
Ouagadougou
Tamale
BENIN
Niger
Niamey
NIGER
Agades
NIGERIA
Sokoto
Kano
Kaduna
Maiduguri
Bauchi
Nguru
L. Chad
Ndjamena (Ft. Lamy)
Chari
CHAD
Abéché
3415
ALGERIA
Algiers
Oran
Constantine
Annaba (Bône)
Ghadames
Ain Salah
Tuat
2918
TUNISIA
Tunis
Bizerta
Sfax
Chott Djerid
Sahara
Mediterranean Sea
Corsica
Sardinia
Sicily
ITALY
Rome
Adriatic Sea
ALPS
Vienna
Prague
Warsaw
EUROPE
Kiev
Odessa
Black Sea
Istanbul
Ankara
TURKEY
GREECE
Athens
Crete
Cyprus
LIBYA
Tripoli
Tripolitania
Benghazi
Cyrenaica
Fezzan
Marzuq
Ghat
Al Jawf
Libyan Desert
Siwa
Alexandria
Port Said
CAIRO
El Faiyum
Suez
Sinai Pen.
EGYPT
Asyut
Nile
El Kharga
Aswan
Wadi-Halfa
Nubian Desert
Dongola
SUDAN
Omdurman
Khartoum
Atbara
Pt. Sudan
Kassala
Kordofan
El Obeid
El Fasher
Darfur
Blue Nile
White Nile
Ethiopian
Addis Ababa
Asmera
Mesewa
Tana
4620
Red Sea
Tel Aviv-Jaffa
Jerusalem
Damascus
Aleppo
Middle East
Syrian Desert
Mosul
Baghdad
Euphrates
Tigris
Basra
Caucasus
Baku
Caspian Sea
Tehran
Esfahan
IRAN
The Gulf
Bahrain I.
Riyadh
Tropic of Cancer
SAUDI ARABIA
Arabia
Medina
Mecca
Volgograd
U. S. S. R.
Aral Sea
Aden
Gulf of Aden
Perim I.
DJIBOUTI
Djibouti
Berbera
Socotra (South Yemen)
Ras Asir (C. Guardafui)

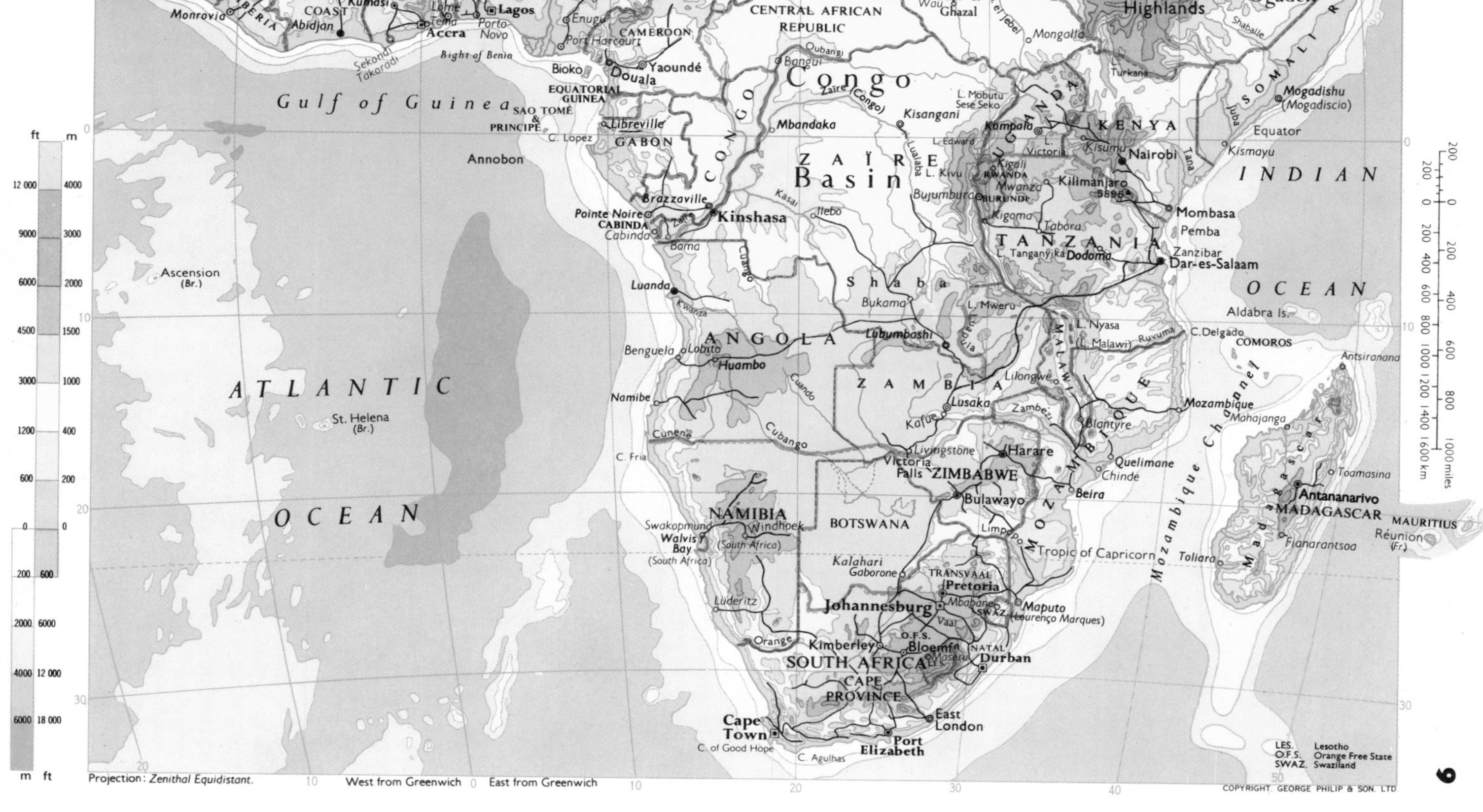

Gulf of Guinea
ATLANTIC OCEAN
INDIAN OCEAN
Congo
ZAÏRE Basin
Shaba
ETHIOPIA Highlands
Ogaden
SOMALI REP.
KENYA
UGANDA
TANZANIA
ZAMBIA
ANGOLA
NAMIBIA
BOTSWANA
ZIMBABWE
MOZAMBIQUE
MALAWI
SOUTH AFRICA
CAPE PROVINCE
TRANSVAAL
O.F.S.
NATAL
MADAGASCAR
Mozambique Channel
CENTRAL AFRICAN REPUBLIC
CAMEROON
GABON
CONGO
CABINDA
EQUATORIAL GUINEA
SAO TOMÉ & PRINCIPE
LIBERIA
IVORY COAST
GHANA
RWANDA
BURUNDI
COMOROS
MAURITIUS
Monrovia
Abidjan
Kumasi
Sekondi Takoradi
Accra
Lomé
Tema
Porto Novo
Lagos
Ibadan
Bight of Benin
Enugu
Benue
Port Harcourt
Bioko
Douala
Yaoundé
Libreville
C. Lopez
Annobon
Pointe Noire
Cabinda
Boma
Brazzaville
Kinshasa
Zaïre
Cuango
Kasai
Ilebo
Mbandaka
Bangui
Oubangi
Zaïre (Congo)
Kisangani
Lualaba
Wau
Bahr el Ghazal
B. el Jebel
Mongalla
Turkana
Shaballe
Juba
Mogadishu (Mogadiscio)
Kismayu
Equator
Tana
Nairobi
Kisumu
L. Victoria
Kampala
L. Mobutu Sese Seko
L. Edward
L. Kivu
Kigali
Bujumbura
Mwanza
Kilimanjaro 5895
Mombasa
Pemba
Zanzibar
Dar-es-Salaam
Kigoma
Tabora
L. Tanganyika
Dodoma
Aldabra Is.
C. Delgado
Ruvuma
L. Nyasa (L. Malawi)
L. Mweru
Luapula
Bukama
Lubumbashi
Lilongwe
Lusaka
Kafue
Zambezi
Blantyre
Mozambique
Quelimane
Chinde
Beira
Harare
Livingstone
Victoria Falls
Bulawayo
Limpopo
Tropic of Capricorn
Luanda
Kwanza
Benguela
Lobito
Huambo
Cuando
Cubango
Namibe
Cunene
C. Fria
Swakopmund
Walvis Bay (South Africa)
Windhoek
(South Africa)
Lüderitz
Orange
Kalahari
Gaborone
Pretoria
Johannesburg
Mbabane
SWAZ.
Maputo (Lourenço Marques)
Vaal
Kimberley
Bloemfontein
Maseru
LES.
Durban
East London
Port Elizabeth
Cape Town
C. of Good Hope
C. Agulhas
Ascension (Br.)
St. Helena (Br.)
Antsiranana
Mahajanga
Toamasina
Antananarivo
Fianarantsoa
Toliara
Réunion (Fr.)
ft m
12 000 4000
9000 3000
6000 2000
4500 1500
3000 1000
1200 400
600 200
0 0
200 600
2000 6000
4000 12 000
6000 18 000
m ft
200 0 200 400 600 800 1000 miles
200 0 200 400 600 800 1000 1200 1400 1600 km
LES. Lesotho
O.F.S. Orange Free State
SWAZ. Swaziland
Projection: Zenithal Equidistant.
West from Greenwich 0 East from Greenwich
COPYRIGHT. GEORGE PHILIP & SON. LTD.

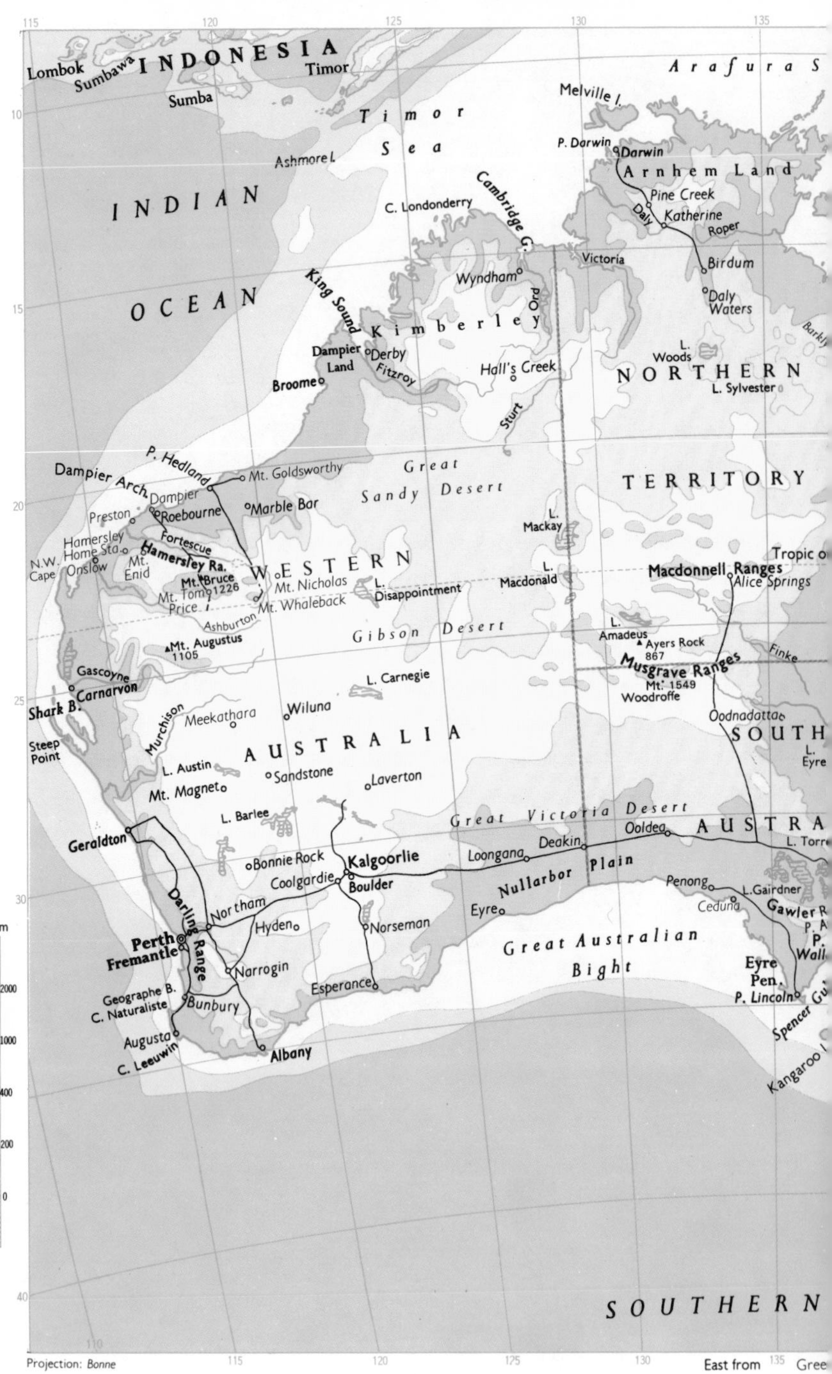
INDONESIA
Lombok
Sumbawa
Sumba
Timor
Timor Sea
Arafura S
Melville I.
P. Darwin
Darwin
Arnhem Land
Pine Creek
Daly
Katherine
Roper
Birdum
Daly Waters
Ashmore I.
INDIAN OCEAN
C. Londonderry
Cambridge G.
Victoria
Wyndham
Ord
King Sound
Kimberley
Dampier Land
Derby
Fitzroy
Broome
Hall's Creek
Sturt
L. Woods
NORTHERN TERRITORY
L. Sylvester
Barkly
P. Hedland
Dampier Arch.
Mt. Goldsworthy
Great Sandy Desert
Dampier
Roebourne
Marble Bar
Preston
L. Mackay
Hamersley Home Sta.
Fortescue
N.W. Cape
Onslow
Mt. Enid
Hamersley Ra.
Mt. Bruce 1226
Mt. Tom Price
WESTERN AUSTRALIA
Mt. Nicholas
Mt. Whaleback
L. Disappointment
L. Macdonald
Macdonnell Ranges
Alice Springs
Tropic o
Ashburton
Mt. Augustus 1105
Gibson Desert
L. Amadeus
Ayers Rock 867
Finke
Musgrave Ranges
Mt. Woodroffe 1549
Gascoyne
Carnarvon
Shark B.
L. Carnegie
Oodnadatta
SOUTH
L. Eyre
Steep Point
Murchison
Meekathara
Wiluna
L. Austin
Sandstone
Laverton
Mt. Magnet
L. Barlee
Great Victoria Desert
Ooldea
AUSTRA
L. Torr
Geraldton
Deakin
Loongana
Bonnie Rock
Kalgoorlie
Coolgardie
Boulder
Nullarbor Plain
Penong
L. Gairdner
Ceduna
Gawler R
Eyre
Darling Range
Northam
Hyden
Norseman
Perth
Fremantle
Narrogin
Great Australian Bight
P. A
P. Wall
Eyre Pen.
P. Lincoln
Esperance
Geographe B.
C. Naturaliste
Bunbury
Augusta
C. Leeuwin
Albany
Spencer G
Kangaroo I
SOUTHERN
ft m
6000 2000
3000 1000
1200 400
600 200
0
200 600
2000 6000
m ft
Projection: Bonne
East from Gree

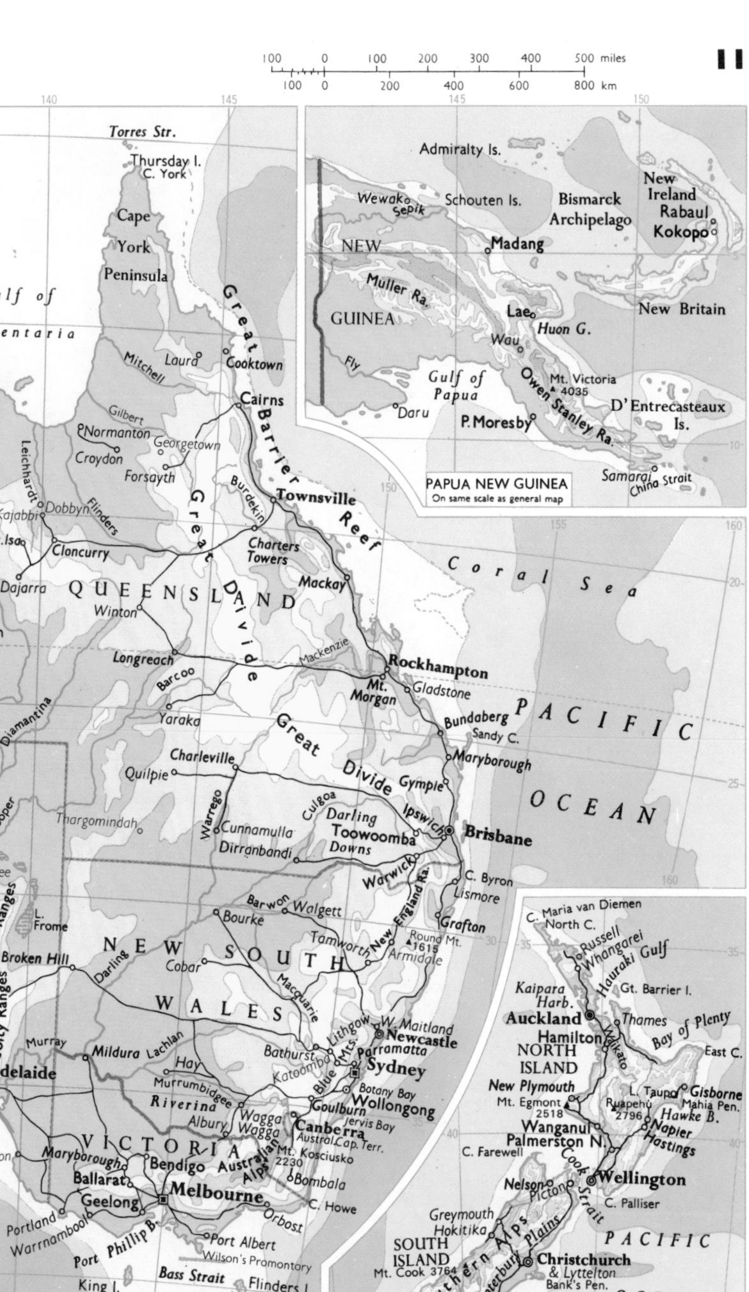
100 0 100 200 300 400 500 miles
100 0 200 400 600 800 km
Torres Str.
Thursday I.
C. York
Cape
York
Peninsula
Arnhem
Gulf of
Carpentaria
Great
Barrier
Reef
Laura
Cooktown
Mitchell
Cairns
Gilbert
Normanton
Georgetown
Croydon
Forsayth
Leichhardt
Dobbyn
Kajabbi
Flinders
Burdekin
Townsville
Mt. Isa
Cloncurry
Charters
Towers
Great Dividing
Dajarra
QUEENSLAND
Mackay
Winton
Coral Sea
apricorn
Longreach
Mackenzie
Rockhampton
Mt.
Morgan
Gladstone
Barcoo
Yaraka
Diamantina
Great
Divide
Bundaberg
Sandy C.
PACIFIC
Charleville
Maryborough
Quilpie
Warrego
Gympie
Cooper
Thargomindah
Cunnamulla
Culgoa
Darling
Downs
Toowoomba
Ipswich
Brisbane
OCEAN
Dirranbandi
Warwick
New England Ra.
C. Byron
Lismore
Marree
Flinders Ranges
L.
Frome
Barwon
Walgett
Bourke
Grafton
Round Mt.
1615
Tamworth
Armidale
NEW SOUTH WALES
Broken Hill
Darling
Cobar
Macquarie
Lofty Ranges
Lithgow
W. Maitland
Newcastle
Murray
Mildura
Lachlan
Bathurst
Blue Mts.
Parramatta
Sydney
Katoomba
Adelaide
Hay
Murrumbidgee
Botany Bay
Wollongong
Riverina
Goulburn
Wagga
Wagga
Albury
Canberra
Jervis Bay
Austral. Cap. Terr.
Kingston
S.E.
VICTORIA
Australian Alps
Mt. Kosciusko
2230
Maryborough
Bendigo
Ballarat
Bombala
Geelong
Melbourne
C. Howe
Orbost
Portland
Warrnambool
Port Phillip B.
Port Albert
Wilson's Promontory
Bass Strait
Flinders I.
King I.
TASMANIA
Mt. Ossa
1617
Launceston
Queenstown
Hobart
OCEAN
Admiralty Is.
Wewak
Sepik
Schouten Is.
Bismarck
Archipelago
New
Ireland
Rabaul
Kokopo
NEW
Madang
Muller Ra.
GUINEA
Lae
Huon G.
New Britain
Wau
Fly
Gulf of
Papua
Mt. Victoria
4035
Daru
Owen Stanley Ra.
P. Moresby
D'Entrecasteaux
Is.
Samarai
China Strait
PAPUA NEW GUINEA
On same scale as general map
C. Maria van Diemen
North C.
Russell
Whangarei
Hauraki Gulf
Kaipara
Harb.
Gt. Barrier I.
Auckland
Thames
Bay of Plenty
Hamilton
Waikato
NORTH
ISLAND
East C.
New Plymouth
L. Taupo
Gisborne
Mt. Egmont
2518
Ruapehu
2796
Mahia Pen.
Hawke B.
Wanganui
Napier
Hastings
Palmerston N.
C. Farewell
Cook Strait
Nelson
Picton
Wellington
C. Palliser
Greymouth
Hokitika
Southern Alps
Canterbury Plains
SOUTH
ISLAND
Christchurch
& Lyttelton
Bank's Pen.
Mt. Cook 3764
Timaru
Waitaki
Oamaru
Doubtful
Sd.
L. Te Anau
Dunedin
& P. Chalmers
West C.
Foveaux Strait
Invercargill
Stewart I.
Bluff Hr.
Southwest C.
NEW ZEALAND
On same scale as main map

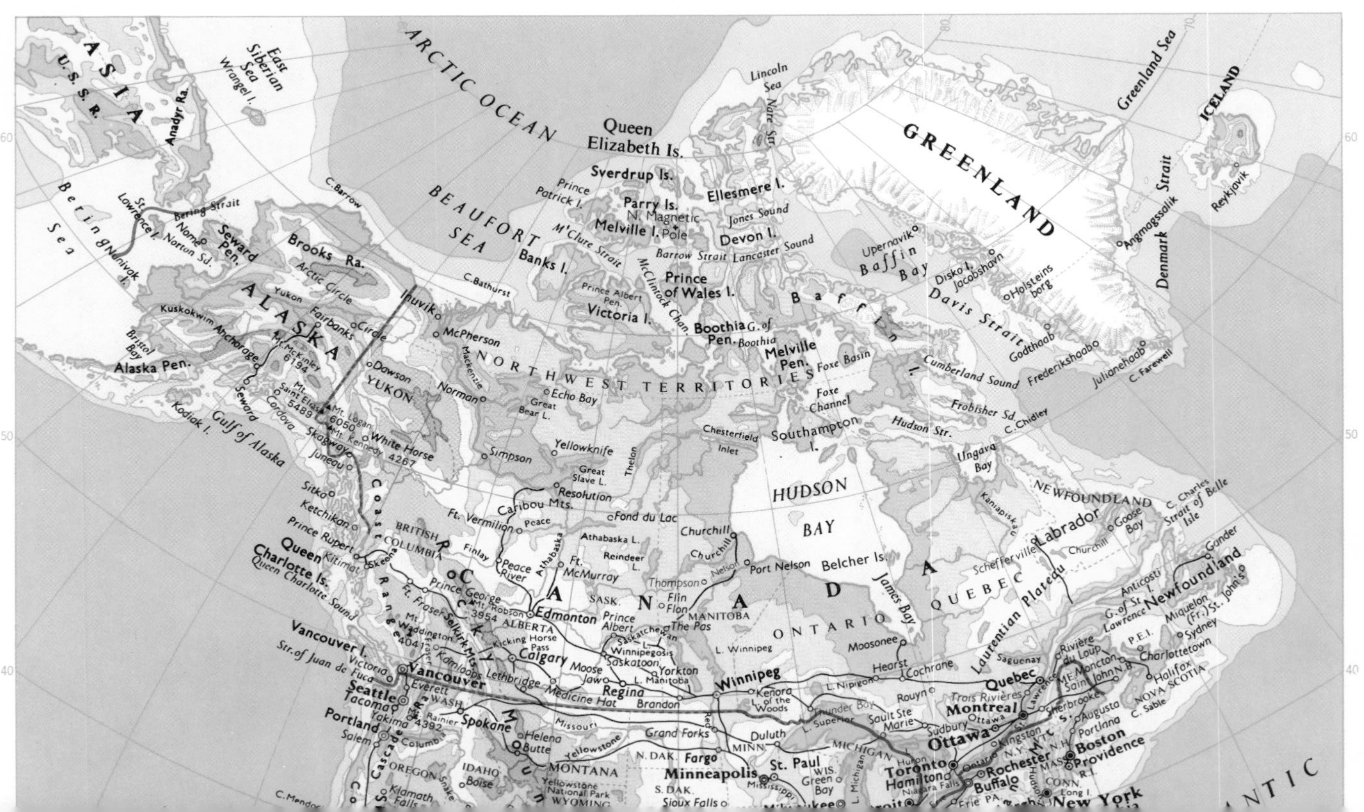

ASIA
U.S.S.R.
East Siberian Sea
Wrangel I.
Anadyr Ra.
ARCTIC OCEAN
Queen Elizabeth Is.
Lincoln Sea
Nare Str.
GREENLAND
Greenland Sea
ICELAND
Reykjavik
Denmark Strait
Angmagssalik
C. Farewell
Julianehaab
Frederikshaab
Godthaab
Holsteinsborg
Jakobshavn
Disko I.
Davis Strait
Upernavik
Baffin Bay
Baffin I.
Sverdrup Is.
Ellesmere I.
Jones Sound
Devon I.
Lancaster Sound
Parry Is.
N. Magnetic Pole
Melville I.
Barrow Strait
Prince Patrick I.
M'Clure Strait
Prince of Wales I.
McClintock Chan.
Boothia Pen.
G. of Boothia
Melville Pen.
Foxe Basin
Foxe Channel
Southampton I.
Prince Albert Pen.
Victoria I.
Banks I.
BEAUFORT SEA
C. Barrow
C. Bathurst
NORTHWEST TERRITORIES
Cumberland Sound
Frobisher Sd.
C. Chidley
Hudson Str.
Ungava Bay
HUDSON BAY
Belcher Is.
James Bay
Chesterfield Inlet
Churchill
Port Nelson
Nelson
Thompson
Flin Flon
The Pas
MANITOBA
L. Winnipeg
Winnipeg
Kenora
L. of the Woods
Thelon
Fond du Lac
Athabaska L.
Reindeer L.
Resolution
Great Slave L.
Yellowknife
Echo Bay
Great Bear L.
Simpson
Norman
Mackenzie
McPherson
Inuvik
Caribou Mts.
Peace
Ft. Vermilion
Peace River
Ft. McMurray
Athabaska
SASK.
Prince Albert
Saskatchewan
Saskatoon
L. Winnipegosis
L. Manitoba
Yorkton
Regina
Moose Jaw
Brandon
Medicine Hat
Edmonton
ALBERTA
Calgary
Lethbridge
Kicking Horse Pass
Mt. Robson 3954
Prince George
Finlay
BRITISH COLUMBIA
Selkirk Mts.
Kamloops
Ft. Fraser
Fraser
Mt. Waddington 4041
Coast Range
Skeena
Vancouver
Vancouver I.
Victoria
Str. of Juan de Fuca
Queen Charlotte Is.
Queen Charlotte Sound
Prince Rupert
Kitimat
Ketchikan
Sitka
Juneau
Skagway
White Horse
YUKON
Dawson
Circle
Fairbanks
Mt. Logan 6050
Mt. Kennedy 4267
Mt. Saint Elias 5489
Cordova
Mt. McKinley 6194
ALASKA
Anchorage
Seward
Gulf of Alaska
Kodiak I.
Alaska Pen.
Bristol Bay
Kuskokwim
Yukon
Arctic Circle
Brooks Ra.
Seward Pen.
Nome
Norton Sd.
Bering Strait
St. Lawrence I.
Nunivak I.
Bering Sea
CANADA
ONTARIO
QUEBEC
Moosonee
Hearst
Cochrane
L. Nipigon
Thunder Bay
L. Superior
Sault Ste Marie
Sudbury
Rouyn
Trois Rivières
Montreal
Ottawa
Quebec
Saguenay
Schefferville
Kaniapiskau
Laurentian Plateau
Labrador
Goose Bay
NEWFOUNDLAND
Strait of Belle Isle
C. Charles
Gander
Newfoundland
St. John's
Miquelon (Fr.)
Anticosti I.
G. of St. Lawrence
Sydney
Charlottetown
P.E.I.
Halifax
NOVA SCOTIA
C. Sable
Moncton
Saint John
N.B.
Rivière du Loup
Sherbrooke
Augusta
Portland
Boston
Providence
New York
Rochester
Buffalo
Toronto
Hamilton
Kingston
L. Huron
L. Michigan
MICHIGAN
Duluth
MINN.
St. Paul
Minneapolis
WIS.
Green Bay
Fargo
Grand Forks
N. DAK.
S. DAK.
Sioux Falls
MONTANA
Missouri
Yellowstone
Helena
Butte
Yellowstone National Park
WYOMING
IDAHO
Boise
Snake
Spokane
WASH.
Everett
Seattle
Tacoma
Mt. Rainier 4392
Yakima
Columbia
Portland
Salem
OREGON
Cascade Ra.
Klamath Falls

PACIFIC OCEAN
ATLANTIC OCEAN
WEST INDIES
UNITED STATES
MEXICO
CENTRAL AMERICA
SOUTH AMERICA
GULF OF MEXICO
CARIBBEAN SEA
BAHAMAS
CUBA
HAITI
DOM. REP.
PUERTO RICO (U.S.)
GUATEMALA
HONDURAS
NICARAGUA
COSTA RICA
PANAMA
BELIZE
EL SALVADOR
VENEZUELA
COLOMBIA
ECUADOR
PERU
BRAZIL
San Francisco
Los Angeles
San Diego
Sacramento
Oakland
Salt Lake City
Denver
Santa Fe
Albuquerque
El Paso
Phoenix
Tucson
Dallas
Fort Worth
Houston
San Antonio
Oklahoma City
Wichita
Kansas City
Omaha
Chicago
St. Louis
Memphis
New Orleans
Birmingham
Atlanta
Nashville
Louisville
Cincinnati
Indianapolis
Cleveland
Washington
Baltimore
Richmond
Norfolk
Charlotte
Jacksonville
Tampa
Miami
Havana
Kingston
Port au Prince
S. Juan
Caracas
Maracaibo
Barquisimeto
Barranquilla
Cartagena
Medellín
Bogotá
Cali
Quito
Guayaquil
Mexico
Guadalajara
Monterrey
Puebla
Veracruz
Acapulco
Guatemala
Tegucigalpa
Managua
Panama
Sierra Madre
Lower California
G. of California
Tropic of Cancer
Equator
Bermuda
Galapagos Is. (Ecuador)
Revilla Gigedo Is. (Mexico)
Yucatan
Florida Strait
West from Greenwich
Projection: Bonne
Permanent Ice
ft m
9000 3000
6000 2000
3000 1000
1200 400
600 200
0 0
200 600
2000 6000
m ft
200 0 200 400 600 800 1000 miles
200 0 200 400 600 800 1000 1200 1400 1600 km

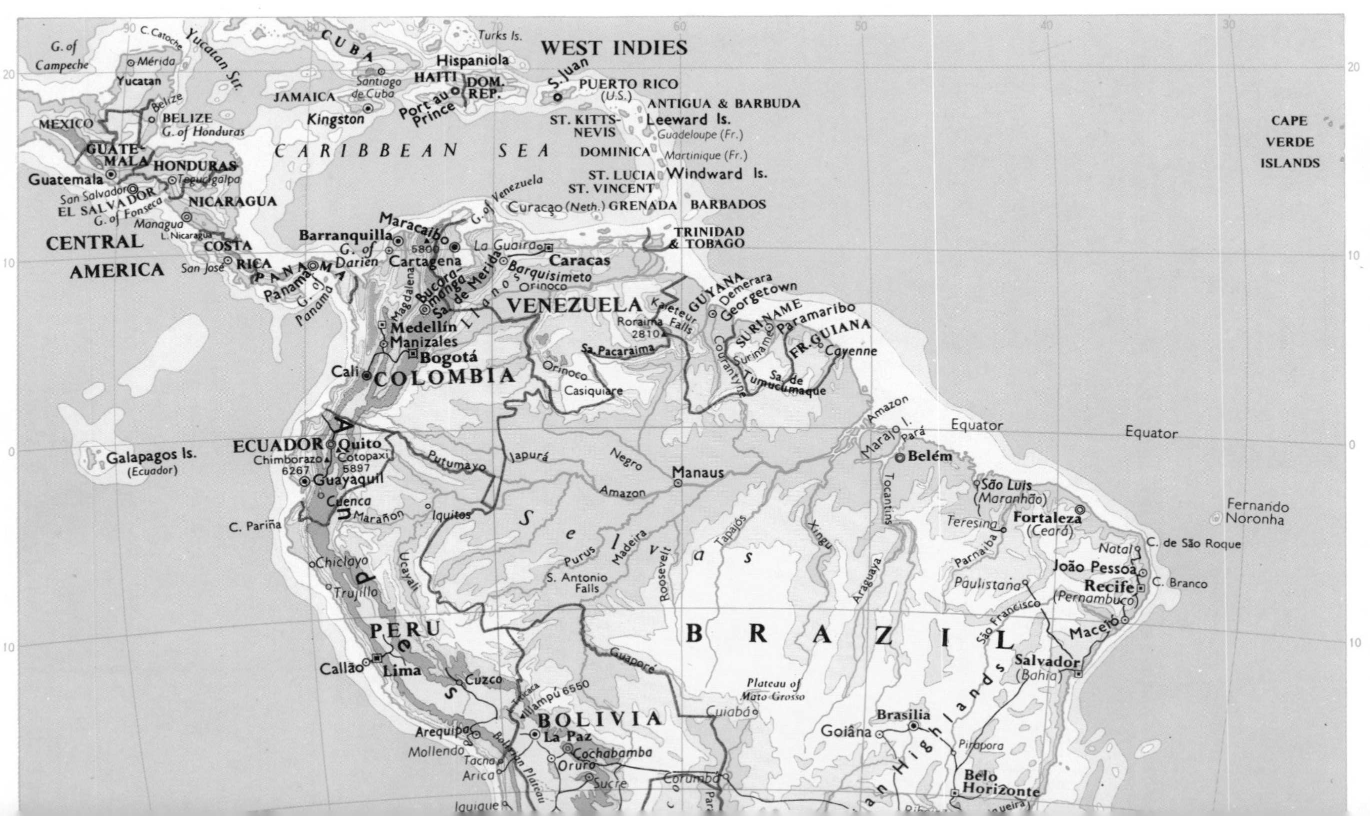

WEST INDIES
CUBA
Turks Is.
Hispaniola
HAITI
DOM. REP.
Port au Prince
Santiago de Cuba
JAMAICA
Kingston
S. Juan
PUERTO RICO (U.S.)
ANTIGUA & BARBUDA
ST. KITTS-NEVIS
Leeward Is.
Guadeloupe (Fr.)
DOMINICA
Martinique (Fr.)
ST. LUCIA
Windward Is.
ST. VINCENT
Curaçao (Neth.)
GRENADA
BARBADOS
TRINIDAD & TOBAGO
CARIBBEAN SEA
CAPE VERDE ISLANDS
G. of Campeche
C. Catoche
Mérida
Yucatan
Yucatan Str.
MEXICO
Belize
BELIZE
G. of Honduras
GUATEMALA
Guatemala
HONDURAS
Tegucigalpa
San Salvador
EL SALVADOR
G. of Fonseca
NICARAGUA
Managua
L. Nicaragua
CENTRAL AMERICA
COSTA RICA
San José
PANAMA
Panama
G. of Panama
Barranquilla
G. of Darien
Cartagena
Maracaibo
5800
G. of Venezuela
La Guaira
Caracas
Barquisimeto
Orinoco
Llanos
Bucaramanga
Sa. de Merida
Magdalena
Medellín
Manizales
Bogotá
Cali
COLOMBIA
VENEZUELA
Roraima 2810
Kaieteur Falls
GUYANA
Demerara
Georgetown
SURINAME
Suriname
Paramaribo
FR. GUIANA
Cayenne
Sa. Pacaraima
Orinoco
Casiquiare
Courantyne
Sa. de Tumucumaque
Amazon
Marajó I.
Pará
Belém
Equator
Galapagos Is. (Ecuador)
ECUADOR
Quito
Cotopaxi 5897
Chimborazo 6267
Guayaquil
Cuenca
Andes
C. Pariña
Marañon
Iquitos
Putumayo
Japurá
Negro
Amazon
Manaus
Selvas
Purus
Madeira
Roosevelt
S. Antonio Falls
Tapajós
Xingu
Tocantins
Araguaya
Ucayali
Chiclayo
Trujillo
PERU
Callão
Lima
Cuzco
Titicaca
Illampú 6550
BOLIVIA
La Paz
Cochabamba
Oruro
Sucre
Arequipa
Mollendo
Tacna
Arica
Iquique
Bolivian Plateau
Guaporé
Cuiabá
Corumbá
Plateau of Mato Grosso
BRAZIL
Brasília
Goiâna
Brazilian Highlands
Pirapora
Belo Horizonte
São Luís (Maranhão)
Teresina
Parnaíba
Fortaleza (Ceará)
Paulistana
São Francisco
Natal
João Pessoa
Recife (Pernambuco)
Maceió
Salvador (Bahia)
C. de São Roque
C. Branco
Fernando Noronha

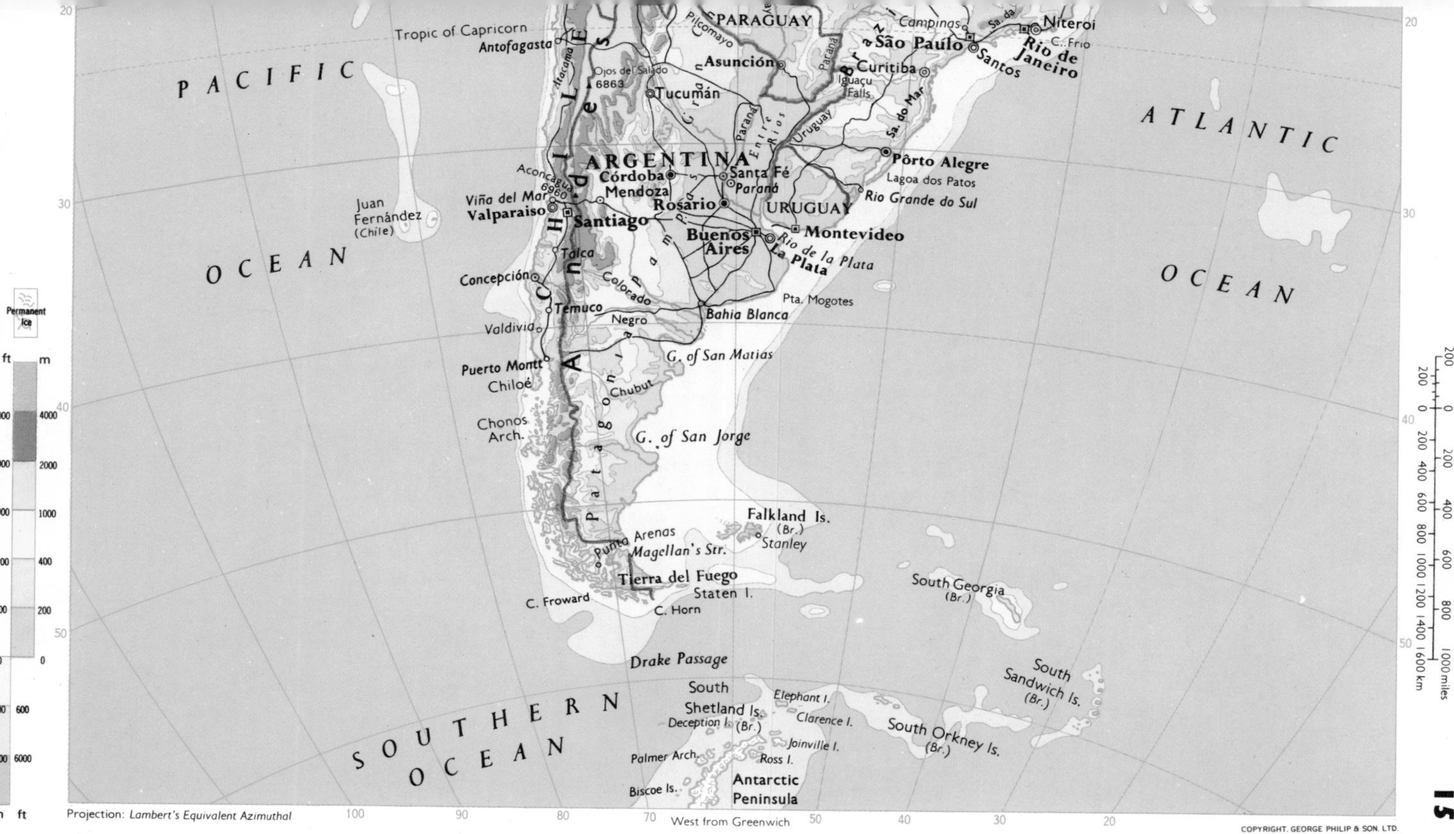
PACIFIC OCEAN
ATLANTIC OCEAN
SOUTHERN OCEAN
Tropic of Capricorn
Antofagasta
Atacama
Ojos del Salado
6863
Tucumán
PARAGUAY
Pilcomayo
Asunción
Paraná
Campinas
São Paulo
Santos
Niteroi
Rio de Janeiro
C. Frio
Curitiba
Iguaçu Falls
Sa. do Mar
Uruguay
Entre Rios
ARGENTINA
Córdoba
Santa Fé
Paraná
Aconcagua 6960
Viña del Mar
Valparaiso
Mendoza
Rosário
Santiago
Pôrto Alegre
Lagoa dos Patos
Rio Grande do Sul
URUGUAY
Montevideo
Buenos Aires
La Plata
Rio de la Plata
Juan Fernández (Chile)
Talca
Concepción
Colorado
Temuco
Negro
Bahia Blanca
Pta. Mogotes
Valdivia
Puerto Montt
Chiloé
G. of San Matias
Chubut
Chonos Arch.
G. of San Jorge
Patagonia
Pampas
Gran Chaco
Andes
CHILE
Brazil
Falkland Is. (Br.)
Stanley
Punta Arenas
Magellan's Str.
Tierra del Fuego
Staten I.
C. Froward
C. Horn
South Georgia (Br.)
Drake Passage
South Shetland Is. (Br.)
Deception I.
Elephant I.
Clarence I.
Joinville I.
Ross I.
Palmer Arch.
Biscoe Is.
Antarctic Peninsula
South Orkney Is. (Br.)
South Sandwich Is. (Br.)
Permanent Ice
ft m
12 000 4000
6000 2000
3000 1000
1200 400
600 200
0 0
200 600
2000 6000
m ft
200 0 200 400 600 800 1000 miles
200 0 200 400 600 800 1000 1200 1400 1600 km
Projection: Lambert's Equivalent Azimuthal
West from Greenwich
100 90 80 70 50 40 30 20
20 30 40 50

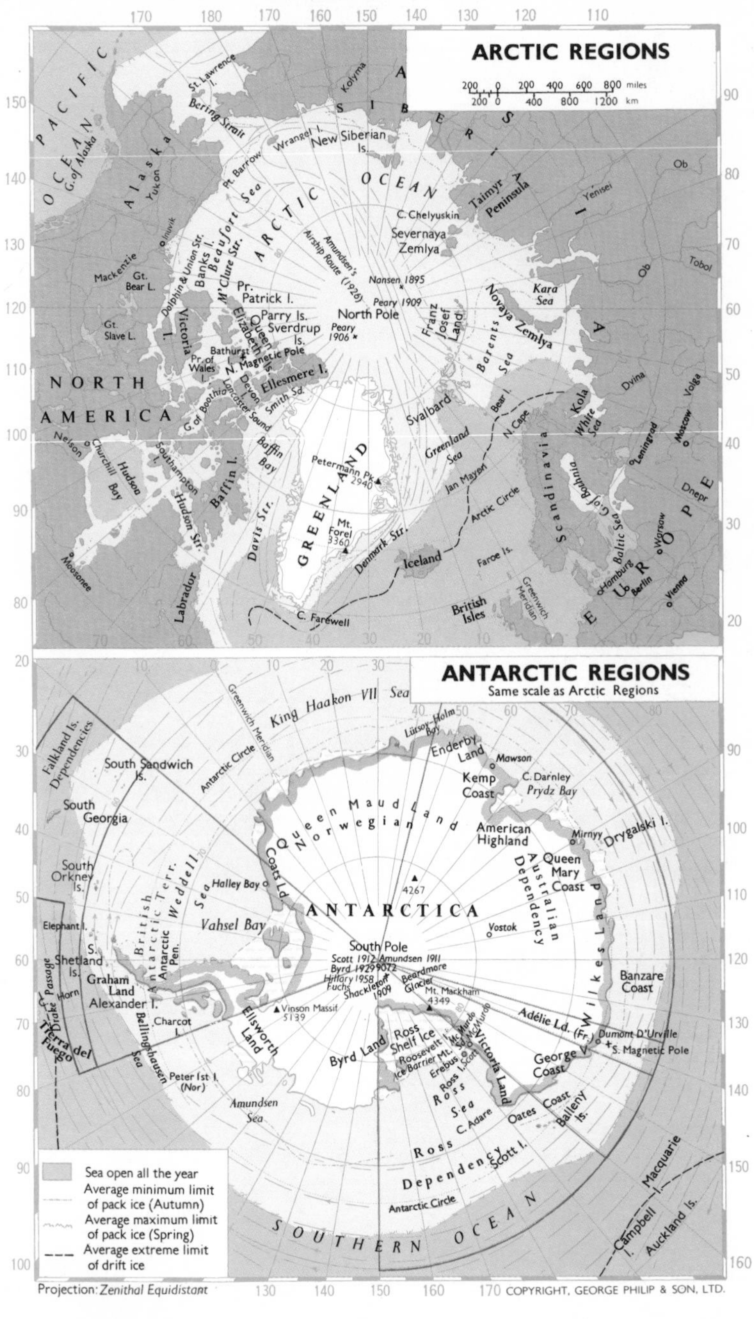

Projection: *Zenithal Equidistant*

from 1983 (in succession to Foot◊) himself adopted a more moderate position. He initiated the expulsion of Militant Tendency members from the Labour Party in 1986. He is a noted orator□

Kinsey Alfred 1894–1956. American researcher, whose studies of male and female sexual behaviour 1948–53, was the first serious published study□

Kinshasa capital (formerly Léopoldville) of Zaïre; population 3 500 000. Founded by Stanley◊ in 1887, it has chemical, textile, engineering, food processing, and furniture industries, and the National University□

Kipling (Joseph) Rudyard 1865–1936. British poet, writer, and novelist. Born in Bombay, India, he was educated at the United Services College in England (the background of his novel *Stalky and Co* 1899), and returned to India as a journalist 1882–9. His *Departmental Ditties* 1886 and short stories *Plain Tales from the Hills* 1888 prepared the way for his return to England and the height of his fame with *Barrack Room Ballads* 1892 (including 'If', 'Gunga Din' and 'The Road to Mandalay'). In 1892 he married an American, Caroline Balestier, and lived in the USA 1892–6, where he wrote *The Jungle Books* 1894–5 and *Captains Courageous* 1897, dealing with Atlantic fishermen. Finest of his later books are the Indian novel *Kim* 1901, and the children's books, *The Just So Stories* 1902 and *Puck of Pook's Hill* 1906. His 'jingoist imperialism' had a counterbalancing sensitivity and appreciation of Indian life, and he is unrivalled as a story-teller and coiner of the quotable line. He later lived in E Sussex, at Rottingdean, then Burwash. Nobel prize 1907□

Kirchhoff Gustav Robert 1824–87. German physicist, who with Bunsen◊, used the spectroscope to show that all elements, heated to incandescence, have their individual spectra□

Kirchner Ernst Ludwig 1880–1938. German Expressionist artist, a founder of Die Brücke◊. Many of his paintings were destroyed by the Nazis. He lived in Switzerland from 1917, and committed suicide in 1938□

Kirgizia republic of the Soviet Union from 1936, part of Soviet Central Asia
area 198 500 sq km/76 100 sq mi
capital Frunze
features mountainous, an extension of the Tyan Shan range
products cereals, sugar, cotton, especially by irrigation; coal and other minerals: sheep, yaks and hardy horses
history annexed by Russia in 1864, it was part of an independent Turkestan republic 1917–24, when it was reincoroporated in the Soviet Union
population 3 600 000, Kirghiz 44% (related to the Kazakhs, they are of Mongol-Tatar origin), Russian 29%, Uzbek 11%
language Kirghiz
religion Sunni Islam□

Kiribati Republic of

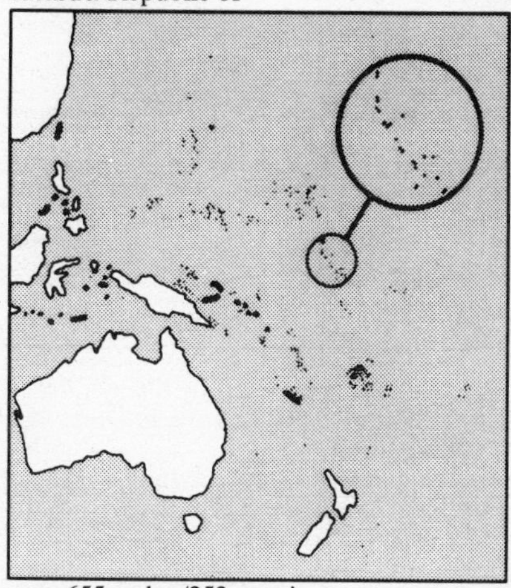

area 655 sq km/253 sq mi
capital and port Tarawa
features comprises 33 Pacific islands: the Gilbert, Phoenix◊ and Line Islands, and Banaba (Ocean Island)
exports copra
currency Australian dollar
population 61 000 Micronesian
language English and Gilbertese, official
religion Christianity, both Roman Catholic and Protestant
government there is an executive president or Beretitenti (Ieremia Tabai from 1979), with a unicameral legislature.
history proclaimed a British protectorate in 1892, the islands became independent within the Commonwealth in 1979 (Kiribati is a modified form of Gilberts). In World War II the people of ***Banaba*** were driven out by the Japanese: in 1945 Britain resettled them on Rabi in Fiji while phosphate deposits were exploited. In 1981 compensation was agreed with the UK for making good mining damage and redevelopment of the island. In 1985 Kiribati reached a fishing agreement with the USSR allowing her use of the country's strategically important waters. See Tuvalu◊□

Kirin see Jilin◊□

Kirk Norman 1924–74. New Zealand Labour statesman, known as 'Big Norm'; Prime Minister 1972–4□

Kirkcaldy port (floor coverings, paper-making) on the Firth of Forth, Fife region, Scotland; population 50 400□

Kirkpatrick Jeane 1926– . American politician and professor of political science. She was an outspoken anti-Marxist permanent representative to the United Nations (as a Democrat) 1981–5, then registered as a Republican 1985, with potential for the vice-presidential candidacy 1988□

Kirkwall administrative headquarters and port of the Orkneys, Scotland, on the north coast of Mainland; population 4700. The Norse cathedral of St Magnus dates in part from 1137□

Kirov industrial city (railway rolling stock, machine tools, etc.) in the western USSR; population 396 000□

Kirov Sergei Mironovich 1886–1934. Russian Bolshevik leader whose assassination 1934, possibly engineered by Stalin◊, led to the political trials held during the next four years□

Kirovabad industrial city (cottons, woollens, processed foods) in Azerbaijan Republic USSR; population 243 000□

Kirovograd industrial city (agricultural machinery, food processing) on a lignite field in Ukrainian Republic USSR; population 246 000□

Kisangani city (formerly Stanleyville) and communications centre in NE Zaïre; population 339 200□

Kishinev industrial city (cement and food processing) capital of the Moldavian Republic USSR; population 539 000. Founded 1436, it became Russian in 1812; was taken by Romania in 1918; re-taken by the Russians in 1940, and totally destroyed by the Germans 1941. Captured by the Russians 1944, it was rebuilt□

Kissinger Henry 1923– . American politician. He was Nixon's assistant for National Security Affairs from 1969 (Secretary of State 1973–77). His secret missions to Peking and Moscow led to détente and Nixon's visits to both countries; and he shared a Nobel prize with Le Duc Tho◊ for his Vietnam peace negotiations. He also actively pursued solutions to the Arab-Israeli, Angola, and Rhodesia crises, and in 1983 Reagan appointed him to head a bipartisan commission on Central America□

Kitakyushu coal port and industrial city (steel, chemicals, thread, plate glass, alcohol) on N Kyushu, Japan; population 1 065 000□

Kitchener industrial city (foundries, furniture) in Ontario, Canada; population 287 800□

Kitchener Horatio Herbert, Earl Kitchener of Khartoum 1850–1916. British field marshal. Commander-in-Chief from 1892, he defeated the dervishes◊ at Omdurman◊ 1898 and reoccupied Khartoum; forced the French to withdraw from Fashoda◊, and in the S African War was Commander-in-Chief 1900–2. War minister from the outbreak of World War I, he was drowned when his ship was sunk on a mission to Russia□

kite a bird of the hawk family. See under eagle◊□

kite a piece of light material stretched on a frame, and flown at the end of a string, first perfected in China and Japan. Kites have practical use in meteorology and aerial survey□

Kitson Sir Frank 1926– . British general, an expert on counter-terrorism and urban guerrilla warfare. He published *Low Intensity Operations* 1971, and became commandant of the Staff College, Camberley 1978□

kittiwake a type of gull◊□

Kitwe commercial centre for the Zambian copperbelt; population 314 800. To the south are Zambia's emerald mines□

Kitzbühel winter sports resort in the Austrian Tirol, north east of Innsbruck; population 8000□

Kivu lake in the Great Rift Valley between Zaïre and Rwanda, c105 km/65 mi long□

kiwi a flightless New Zealand bird. See under running◊ birds□

kiwi fruit or ***Chinese gooseberry*** *Actinidia chinensis* family Actinidiaceae, with cylindrical fruit flavoured similarly to a gooseberry, and with a fuzzy brown skin. They are commercially grown on a large scale in New Zealand□

Klaipeda industrial port (formerly Memel) in Lithuanian Republic USSR; population 181 000. Much disputed among neighbouring states, it was annexed by Lithuania 1923, was German-occupied 1939–45, and then returned to Lithuania□

Klaproth Martin Heinrich 1743–1817. German chemist, discoverer of uranium, zirconium, cerium, and titanium□

Klebs Edwin 1834–1913. German bacteriologist, discoverer with Friedrich Löffler 1852–1915, of the diphtheria bacterium□

Klee Paul 1879–1940. Swiss painter, who adapted infant formulas to create paintings of free-form fantasy. He was associated with Der Blaue◊ Reiter, and taught at the Bauhaus◊ 1920–6□

Klein Felix 1849–1925. German mathematician, founder of much of 'modern maths', including dynamic geometry (transformations); and originator of the ***Klein bottle***, a solid with no edges and only one side, made by running the smaller end of a tapering glass tube through the side of the tube, and then joining it to the larger end. It is the three-dimensional equivalent of the Möbius◊ strip□

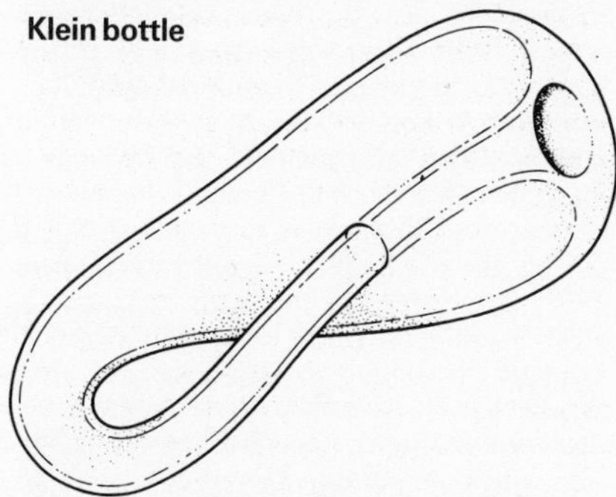
Klein bottle

Kleist (Bernd) Heinrich (Wilhelm) von 1777–1811. German dramatist, who achieved a posthumous reputation with, e.g. the comic *The Broken Pitcher* 1811, and dramatic *The Prince of Homburg* 1821. In a suicide pact, he killed first a girl-friend, and then himself□

Klemperer Otto 1885–1973. German-born American conductor, noted for interpretation of Beethoven and Bruckner□

Kliegl John 1869–1959 and Anton 1872–1927. German-born American brothers, inventors of the brilliant carbon-arc (klieg) lights used in television and films□

Klondike see under Yukon◊□

Klopstock Friedrich Gottlieb 1724–1803. German poet whose religious epic *The Messiah* 1745–73 and lyric odes prepared the way for the great age of 18th-century German literature□

Klug Aaron 1926– . British molecular biologist, born in S. Africa. Working at Cambridge, he won a Nobel prize for chemistry 1982, for elucidating the structure of chromosomes□

knapweed N temperate wildflower ***hardhead*** *Centaurea nigra* family Compositae. The hard, bract-covered buds break into purple composite heads□

knee hinge joint, with some rotary movement, between the thigh (femur) and shin bones (tibia and fibula); in front, is the protective kneecap or patella□

Kneller Sir Godfrey 1646–1723. British court portrait painter (of German descent) to Charles II, William III and George I. Famous series are the Hampton Court Beauties and 42 portraits of the members of the Whig 'Kit Cat Club'□

Knight Dame Laura 1877–1970. British artist noted for gypsy, circus, and ballet studies and as a World War II official artist□

knighthood orders of. Among the most famous medieval orders were: ***Knights Hospitallers*** which included the Knights of the Hospital of St John of Jerusalem (also known as Knights of Malta, Rhodes, etc.), founded 1070, and giving rise in the UK to the modern St John Ambulance Brigade. Their rivals were the ***Templars*** (Knights of the Temple of Solomon), a military order founded 1119 for the recovery of Palestine from the Saracens, which was suppressed 1307.

United Kingdom orders (in which the feminine rank eqivalent to Knight is Dame) include those of the: ***Bath*** (KCB) founded 1725, but traditionally going back to 1399 and Henry IV: the initiation originally involved a ritual bath; ***British Empire*** (KBE) founded 1917; ***Garter*** (KG) founded 1348 by Edward III, the oldest order, with the greatest prestige; ***Merit*** (Order of Merit) founded 1902 by Edward VII; membership limited to 24; although not conferring a knighthood, its award marks a degree of achievement which in public esteem tends to outrank the other orders; ***Royal Victorian*** (KCVO) founded 1896, and awarded for personal service to the Sovereign; ***Thistle*** (KT), Most Ancient and Most Noble Order of the. Scottish order founded 1687; its motto appears on some pound◊ coins: *Nemo me impune lacessit;* ***Knights Bachelor*** (carries no letters after the name), the lowest rank of knighthood, does not constitute a royal order, but is a survival of the tradition of a knight as someone who held his land on condition of military service for his sovereign.

continental orders include: ***Legion of Honour*** France, established by Napoleon 1802, on the plan of a knightly order; both civil and military, with five classes, it has more members than any other; decoration is a star; ***Iron Cross*** Prussia/Germany, established by Frederick William III 1813; decoration, silver-edged Maltese cross of iron worn round neck.

See also under Golden◊ Fleece□

knitting method of making fabric by twining wool, etc., with needles. Knitting may have developed from ***crochet*** which uses a single hooked needle, or from ***netting*** with a shuttle. A mechanized process for stockings was developed in the 16th century, but it was not until after World War II that machine knits with synthetic yarns took over 50% of the clothing industry for both men and women□

Knock see county Mayo◊□

Knossos site near Iráklion of the chief city of Minoan◊ Crete. Excavation of the palace of the legendary King Minos by Sir Arthur

Evans◊ showed that the story of Theseus' encounter with the Minotaur in a labyrinth possibly derived from the ritual 'bull-leaping' by youths and girls shown in the frescoes and the maze-like layout of the palace□

knot migrant wading bird *Calidris canutus* of snipe◊ family Scolopacidae. Brick-red in summer, when it breeds in the Arctic, and drab in winter when it may move as far south as Australia□

knot unit of speed for ships, 1 nautical mph; a nautical mile is the distance on the earth's surface corresponding to 1 minute of latitude (which varies over the earth's surface, but is practically taken as 1853 m/6080 ft), that is 1knot = 1.15mph. It is also used in aviation and has not yet been replaced by the SI unit (metres per second)□

knot intertwinement of ropes, etc., to fasten them together or to other objects ('bends' or temporary 'hitches'); when two ropes are joined end to end, they are 'spliced.' See also macramé◊□

Knox John c1505–72. Scottish Protestant reformer, originally a Roman Catholic priest. After the death of Wishart◊, he went into hiding, but later preached the reformed doctrines and when taken by French troops in Scotland in 1547 was first imprisoned in France, then sentenced to the galleys, being released only by intercession of the British government 1549. In England he assisted in compiling the Prayer Book, as a royal chaplain from 1551. On Mary's accession he fled abroad, but in 1559 returned to Scotland where he was the chief founder of the Church of Scotland, and published a *History of the Reformation in Scotland* 1586. He was inveterately opposed to compromise with Mary◊ Queen of Scots on religious matters□

koala a small Australian mammal. See under marsupialia◊□

Kobe port in S Honshu, Japan; population 1 343 000. ***Port Island*** created from the rock of nearby mountains 1960–8l, area 5 sq km/2 sq mi, is one of the world's largest construction projects□

Kobke Christen 1810–48. Danish portrait and landscape artist, remarkable for his rendering of light□

Koch Robert 1843–1910. German bacteriologist who isolated the tubercle bacillus in 1882, and devised the tuberculin test for cattle; he also worked on the bubonic plague and malaria; Nobel medicine prize 1905□

Kodály Zoltán 1882–1967. Hungarian composer, born at Kecskemet. With Bartok he collected Magyar folk music, and wrote much chamber and instrumental music, the comic opera, *Háry János* 1926, 'Dances of Galanta,' etc.□

Kodiak island off the south coast of Alaska, site of a US naval base; area 9505 sq km/3670 sq mi. It is also the home of the world's largest bear◊. The town of ***Kodiak*** is the largest US fishing port (mainly salmon)□

Koestler Arthur 1905–83. British-Hungarian author. Born in Budapest, he became a journalist. A convert to Communism, he was sentenced to death as a spy while in Spain during the Civil War (*Spanish Testament* 1938). Imprisoned by the Nazis in France in 1940 (*Scum of the Earth* 1941), he escaped to England, becoming a British subject after World War II. Already by 1941 (in the novel *Darkness at Noon*), he had shown his disillusion with Communism. Later books were attempted syntheses of all aspects of knowledge, e.g. *The Roots of Coincidence* 1972. He endowed Britain's first chair of parapsychology at Edinburgh, established 1984. He was joined in suicide by his wife□

Koh-i-noor a very large diamond◊□

Kohl Helmut 1930– . W German statesman. Leader of the CDU (Christian Democratic Union)/CSU (Christian Social Union) from 1976, he succeeded Schmidt◊ as chancellor in 1982, and was confirmed in office in the 1983 election. In 1986 he became W Germany's first chancellor to be under investigation while in office, for allegedly accepting bribes; the charges were later dropped□

kohl-rabi a type of cabbage◊□

Kokand industrial oasis town (fertilizers, cotton, silk) in Uzbek Republic USSR; population 155 000. It was the capital of Kokand Khanate when annexed by Russia 1876□

Koko Nor Mongolian form of Qinghai◊□

Kokoschka Oskar 1886–1980. Austro-British expressionist artist who was already startling Vienna in his late teens. He fled from the Nazis to England in 1938, becoming British 1947. He was noted for brilliantly coloured townscapes (including the Thames) and psychological portraits□

kola nut another name for cola◊ nut□

Kola Peninsula promontory in NW Soviet Union, which includes Murmansk. It is one of the most highly militarized areas in the world, with the Soviet main naval base (submarine and surface ships); bombers, fighters; two artillery divisions (one airborne) and a brigade of naval infantry. The Russians have also made here the deepest borehole in the world (12 km by 1984)□

Kolchak Alexander Vasilievich 1875–1920. Russian admiral, commander of the White forces in Siberia, who proclaimed himself Supreme Ruler of Russia 1918, but was shot by the Bolsheviks□

Kolchugino see Leninsk◊-Kuznetsky□

Kolhapur industrial city in Maharashtra, India, noted as a film production centre; population 351 000□

Köln German form of Cologne◊□

Kolvenbach Pieter-Hans 1929– . Dutch orientalist, who became general of the Jesuits◊ in 1983□

Kolwezi copper and cobalt mining town, Shabah province, Zaïre; scene of a massacre of 500 Zaïreans and 139 whites by former police of the province (invading from Angola) in 1978□

Komi autonomous republic of the USSR, annexed in the 14th century; area 415 900 sq km/160 540 sq mi; population 1 147 000. Capital Syktyvkar. It was occupied by British and American troops 1918–19□

Kommunizma Pik see Pamirs◊□

Kompong Som industrial port (formerly Sihanoukville) in Kampuchea, used by the USSR as a submarine base; population 9000□

Komsomol Soviet 'All-Union Leninist Communist Youth League' of which most young people 14–26 are members. Founded 1918, it acts as the youth section of the Communist Party, and its projects have included the rebuilding of Stalingrad 1942□

Kongur Shan see under Tyan-Shan◊□

Kong Zi 550–478BC. Chinese sage, whose Latinized name is Confucius (meaning 'Kong the Master': see Confucianism◊). Born in Lu, a small state in what is now the province of Shandong, at Qufu, he became a minor official. Taking to teaching, he gathered disciples, and was for a time so excellent a governor of a small town that he became prime minister of Lu. However, he went into exile when his advice was ignored, returning only in the last years of his life under a new ruler. He was buried at Qufu□

Koniev Ivan Stepanovich 1898–1973. Soviet marshal who liberated the Ukraine 1943, and advanced from the south on Berlin to link with the Anglo-US forces□

Königsberg see Kaliningrad◊□

Konstanz German form of Constance◊□

Kon-Tiki legendary sun king who ruled the country later occupied by the Incas◊, and was supposed to have migrated, with certain white-skinned and bearded followers, out into the Pacific. See also Heyerdahl◊□

Konya city (Roman Iconium) in SW central Turkey; population 329 200. Carpets and silks are made here, and the city contains the monastery of the dancing Dervishes◊□

kookaburra a type of large Australian kingfisher◊□

Kooning Willem de 1904– . American painter and sculptor, born in the Netherlands. He established a reputation in the early fifties with abstracts in black and white expressing the aggressivenes of women□

Koran the sacred book of Islam◊□

Korda Sir Alexander 1893–1956. Hungarian-born British film producer and director (naturalized 1936), whose films include *The Private Life of Henry VIII* 1933, *The Third Man* 1950, and *Richard III* 1955□

Korea peninsula of NE Asia. The foundation of the Korean state goes back more than 2000 years. First invaded by Japan in the 10th century, it was annexed in 1910, and after the surrender of the Japanese in 1945 remained divided. The area north of the 38th parallel, which had been administered by the USSR, became North Korea◊ and the area administered by the USA became South Korea◊. The Korean language is related to Japanese, but was given a phonetic alphabet by King Sejong in 1443. Today 95% of modern Koreans are literate. Cultural achievements include the sculptures, delicate but powerful, of the Silla kingdom (established 57BC, capital Kyongju), which unified the country in 668AD; and the ceramics of the Koryo dynasty 935–1392th century (celadon – grey-green porcelain), and Yi dynasty 1392–1910, the latter also having fine 18th century genre painters, e.g. Kim Hong-do and Sin Yun-bok□

Korea Democratic People's Republic of (***North Korea***)

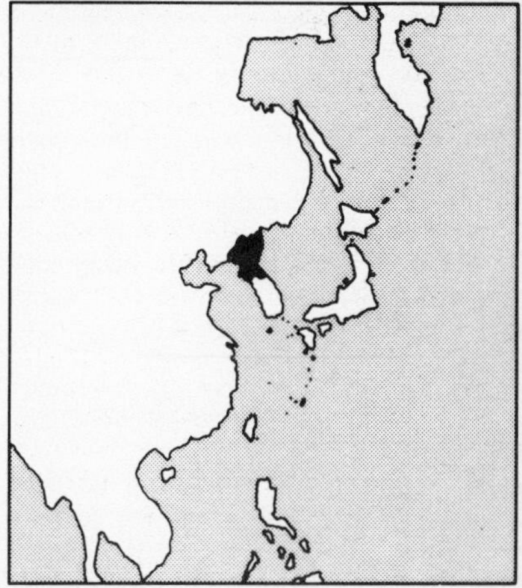

area 121 250 sq km/46 815 sq mi
capital Pyongyang
features the richest of the two Koreas in mineral resources

exports coal, iron, copper, textiles, chemicals
currency won
population 19 630 000
language Korean
religion traditionally Buddhism and Confucianism
government under the constitution of 1972 , there is an executive president (Kim Il Sung◊, who also heads the all-powerful Communist Party Central Committee) and Supreme People's Assembly.
history the republic was proclaimed in 1948 following the Russian withdrawal, and a strict Communist regime is maintained. Although he failed in the Korean War◊, Kim Il Sung presses constantly for reunification; talks again failed in 1984. It is planned that Kim Il Sung's son Kim Chong Il should succeed him in the presidency□

Korea Republic of (***South Korea***)

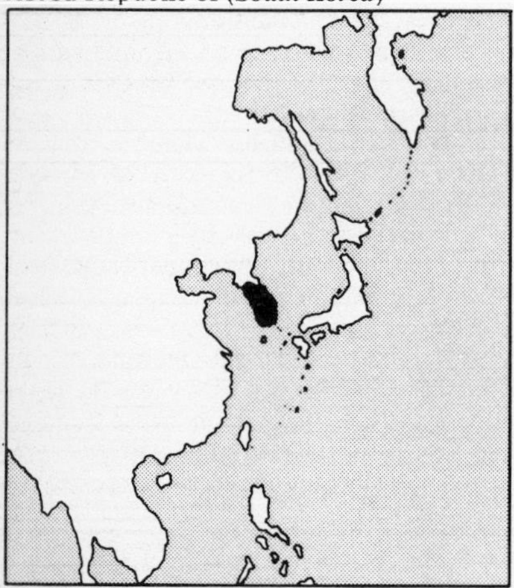

area 99 999 sq km/38 450 sq mi
capital Seoul
towns Taegu, and the ports of Pusan and Inchon
features before 1945 mainly agricultural, but with US aid became a 'workshop of Asia'.
exports steel, ships, chemicals, electronics, textiles, plastics
currency won
population 41 999 000
language Korean
religion traditionally Buddhism and Confucianism
government executive president (General Chun Doo-Hwan from 1979), and national assembly
history proclaimed in 1948 when US military government ended, the republic was under the repressive rule of Presidents Synghman Rhee 1948–60 and Park Chung Hee 1963–79, and suffered invasion by North Korea 1950–53 (see Korean◊ War). Since the war some 30–40 000 US troops have been stationed here. The regime of Chun Doo Hwan remains autocratic, and opposition leader Kim Dae Jung was imprisoned 1980–2 for alleged conspiracy to obtain power□

Korean War 1950–3, between North Korea (supported by China) and South Korea, aided by the United Nations (including the UK, though the troops were mainly US). North Korean forces invaded the South 25 Jun 1950, and the Security Council of the United Nations, owing to a walk-out by the USSR, voted to oppose them. After a 'concertina' campaign up and down the peninsula, which ended in the restoration of the original boundary on the 38th parallel, an armistice was signed with the North, although S Korea did not participate□

Kórinthos see Corinth◊□

Korolev Sergei 1906–66. Russian designer of the first sputnik, moon-rockets, and manned space-ships. His name was unknown in his lifetime. See Khrushchev◊ □

Kortrijk Flemish form of Courtrai◊□

Kos see under Dodecanese◊□

Kosciuszko Tadeusz 1746–1817. Polish revolutionary leader, defeated by combined Russian and Prussian forces in 1794, and imprisoned till 1796□

kosher Hebrew 'fit', applied by Jews to meat slaughtered according to Mosaic law□

Kosinski Jerzy 1933– . Polish-American novelist, who lost most of his family in the mass killings of the Jews by the Nazis, but escaped via Russia to the USA 1957. His novels include *The Painted Bird*, *Cockpit*, and *Being There* 1972, in which a gardener becomes presidential adviser and which he adapted for the screen□

Kosovo see under Serbia◊□

Kossuth Lajos 1802–94. Hungarian patriot. He proclaimed Hungarian independence of Habsburg rule in 1849, and when the Hungarians were later defeated, fled first to Turkey, then England□

Kosygin Alexei Nikolaievich 1904–80. Soviet statesman, prime minister 1964–80□

koto Japanese rectangular stringed (modern version 20 strings) musical instrument, plucked with the fingers as it rests horizontally on the floor□

Kottbus see Cottbus◊□

Koussevitsky Sergei 1874–1951. Russo-American conductor, founder of the ***Koussevitsky Foundation*** to encourage new composers□

Kovno Russian form of Kaunas◊□

Kowloon see under Hong◊ Kong□

Kra Isthmus of. Narrow 'waist' of Thailand proposed for the ***Kra Canal*** to link the Gulf of Thailand and Indian Ocean, avoiding the expensive detour via Singapore□

Krafft-Ebing Baron Richard von 1840–1902. German pioneer psychiatrist, author of *Psychopathia Sexualis* 1886□

Krakatoa island volcano in Sunda Strait, Indonesia, between Java and Sumatra; its eruption 1883 caused great destruction, a consequent tidal wave drowned 36 000 people in the adjacent islands, and there were long-lasting worldwide atmospheric phenomena□

Krakow industrial city (railway wagons, paper, chemicals, tobacco) in Poland (capital c1300–1595) on the Vistula; population 1 154 000□

Kramatorsk industrial town (coalmining machinery, steel, ceramics) in Ukraine Republic, USSR, in the Donbas◊; population 183 000□

Krasnodar industrial town at the head of navigation of the Kuban river, in SW USSR; population 581 000. It is linked by pipeline with the Caspian oilfields□

Krasnoyarsk industrial city (locomotive works, paper, timber, cement, gold refining) with large hydroelectric works, in central USSR; population 820 000. There is a large early warning and space-tracking radar phased array device at nearby Abalakova. See also Novosibirsk◊□

Krebs Sir Hans 1900–81. British biochemist, who shared a Nobel prize in medicine 1953 for discovering the citric acid (or 'K') cycle – the route by which food is converted into energy by living tissues□

Kreisler Fritz 1875–1962. Austrian violinist, an interpreter of Brahms and Beethoven; Elgar dedicated his violin concerto to him□

Kremenchug industrial town (road-building machinery, rail wagons, processed food) on the River Dnieper, in Ukraine Republic USSR; population 215 000□

kremlin the citadel of Russian cities, but especially that of Moscow◊ where it houses the Soviet government□

krill shrimplike Antarctic crustacean, especially *Euphausia superba Dana*, order Euphausiacea. Orange above and green beneath, it has seven pairs of light-sensitive organs along the body, and is 6 cm/2.5 in long. The enormous swarms form the food of whales, and a protein concentrate is made for human and animal consumption□

Krishna incarnation of the Hindu god Vishnu◊□

Krishna Consciousness Movement established in USA 1966 by A C Bhaktivendanta Swami Prabhupada 1896–1977. Members shave their heads, wear orange robes, chant 'Hare Krishna,' and their bible is the Bhagavad◊ Gita□

Kristallnacht the plundering of Jewish property in Germany 7 Nov 1938 (with much breaking of glass, hence the name 'glass night'), following the murder of a German embassy official in Paris, by a Polish-Jewish youth. It was followed by legislation against Jews owning businesses, etc.□

Krivoi Rog industrial city (metallurgy, based on rich iron ore) in Ukraine Republic, USSR; population 663 000□

Kronstadt Russian naval base, founded by Peter the Great 1703, on Kotlin island, Gulf of Finland, opposite Leningrad, whose defence under siege was aided by its guns 1941–43□

Kronstadt uprising a revolt in Mar 1921 by Russian sailors at Kronstadt naval base near Petrograd (now Leningrad), in sympathy with striking Petrograd workers. The sailors' demands for free elections and affirmation of the rights in theory obtained by the Revolution of 1917 were seen as a threat to Bolshevik control of power, and on Trotsky's orders the naval base was stormed and the leaders executed by Red Army soldiers. See Union◊ of Soviet Socialist Republics: history□

Kropotkin Peter Alexeivich, Prince Kropotkin 1842–1921. Russian anarchist. Imprisoned 1874, he escaped abroad 1876, and later lived some time in England. He returned to Moscow in 1917. His books include *Mutual Aid* 1902 and *Modern Science and Anarchism* 1903□

Kruger Stephanus Johannes Paulus 1825–1904. President of the Transvaal 1883–1900, he refused to remedy the grievances of the Uitlanders (English and other non-Boer white residents), and so precipitated the S African War◊□

Kruger National Park see under South◊ Africa□

Krupp German armaments firm, which developed the long distance artillery used in World War I, and supported Hitler's regime in preparation for World War II, after which the head of the firm was imprisoned. See Essen◊□

krypton element
symbol Kr
atomic number 36
physical description gas
features one of the inert◊ gases; occurs in the atmosphere in about 1 part in 1 000 000 (Greek *kryptos* secret)
uses in lasers, fluorescent lighting, and in highspeed photography flashlights□

Kryukov Fyodor see Mikhail Sholokhov◊□

Kuala Lumpur capital of Malaysia, created a federal territory 1974; population 937 875. It has a large trade in tin and rubber, exported via its port at Kelang to the north east, and the University of Malaya□

Kuanyin originally an Indian male god of mercy, but reverenced by Chinese Buddhists in female form, as she is in Japan (Kwannon)□

Kuban river of the USSR, rising in Georgia (see Krasnodar◊); length 906 km/563 mi to the Sea of Azov□

Kubelik Rafael 1914– . Czech conductor-composer (symphonies, operas, e.g. *Veronika*), musical director Royal Opera House, London 1955–8□

Kublai Khan 1216–94. Mongol emperor of China from 1259, grandson of Ghengis◊ Khan. In 1281 he attempted to invade Japan, but his 4400 ships were dispersed in battle; remains of them were thought to have been found on the sea floor in 1981□

Kubrick Stanley 1928– . British film director, whose films include *Lolita* 1962, *Dr Strangelove* 1964, *2001: A Space Odyssey* 1968, *A Clockwork Orange* 1971□

kudzu Japanese creeper *Pueraria lobata* family Leguminosae, which holds nitrogen (see nitrogen◊ cycle) and can be used as fodder, but became a pest in USA when introduced to check soil erosion□

Kuhn Thomas 1922– . American science historian, whose *The Structure of Scientific Revolutions* 1962, stresses the dominance of social and cultural factors in scientific activity□

Kuibyshev industrial river port (formerly Samara) on the Volga plain, central USSR; population 1 238 000. Aircraft, locomotives, cables, synthetic rubber, textiles, oil refining, quarrying, fertilizers, etc. in a complex built with US cooperation 1973. It was the provisional capital of the USSR 1941–3. Hydro-electric works formed the *Kuibyshev Sea* an artificial lake (480 km/300 mi long) by damming the Volga□

ku-kabul Indian name of a tree native to El Salvador *Leucaena leucocaphala*. It thrives in dry conditions, fixes its own nitrogen (see nitrogen◊ cycle), and provides excellent fodder; it is the basis of a new dairy industry in India□

Ku Klux Klan American Secret Society, founded 1865, which adopted white robes with disguising conical hats, and fiery crosses. Its aim is to ensure white supremacy by intimidation of the blacks in the Southern American states. It declined after the withdrawal of occupation forces in 1877, but revived in 1915 on an anti-Jewish-Catholic-Negro basis, and flourished in the 1950s and 1960s. In the 1980s, prompted by economic depression, it broadened its scope to include activities against Hispanics and Asians□

kulak literally 'fist'; Russian for a rich peasant who used hired labour and might act as village usurer. Opponents of collectivization, they were 'liquidated as a class', about a million families being banished to E Russia□

Kumasi capital of Ashanti◊ region, Ghana, with a trade in cocoa, rubber and cattle; population 351 700□

kumquat Chinese tree, genus *Fortunella* family Rutaceae, with fruits like miniature oranges, used in confectionery, etc.□

Küng Hans 1928– . Swiss Roman Catholic theologian, debarred by the Vatican from teaching 1979 because he queried Papal infallibility and whether Christ was the son of God. In *Does God Exist* 1980, he bases an affirmative case on universal signs of conscience among mankind, and the individual sense of inability to obey it satisfactorily□

kung fu a form of martial◊ art□

Kunlun Shan Chinese mountain range on the edge of the Tibetan plateau, 4000 km/2500 mi E–W, including Ulugh Muztag 7723 m/25 378 ft□

Kunming industrial city (chemicals, textiles) and capital of Yunnan province, China; population 1 800 000. Chinese terminus of the Burma◊ road, it is 2000 m/6300 ft asl. Remarkable limestone formations constitute the Stone Forest of Lunan nearby□

Kuomintang see Guomindang◊□

kurchatovium alternative name for element unnilquadium◊□

kurdaitcha shoes shoes made of emu feathers which leave no tracks: worn by Australian Aborigines when escaping their enemies and by sorcerers□

Kurdistan mountainous region where the borders of Iran, Iraq, Syria, Turkey, and the USSR meet. The seven million ***Kurds*** (Sunni Muslims) of all five countries have nationalist aspirations and are in frequent revolt. Saladin◊ was a Kurd□

Kure port and naval base on Honshu, Japan; population 237 000. The Japanese fleet surrendered to the Allies here 14 Aug 1945□

Kurils strategically important chain of c50 small islands in the N Pacific. Once Russian, they passed to Japan in 1875, and back to Russia 1945. Japan still claims the southernmost (Etorofu and Kunashiri) and the dispute prevents the signature of a Japan-Soviet Peace Treaty□

Kuropatkin Alexei Nikolaievich 1848–1921. Russian general who was commander-in-chief in Manchuria, but resigned after his defeat by Japan at Shenyang (Mukden) in 1903. See Russo-Japanese◊ War□

Kurosawa Akira 1910– . Japanese film director, famous for use of several cameras at once to capture immediacy of feeling and movement, e.g. *Rashomon* 1950, *Seven Samurai* 1954, and *Ran* (a version of Shakespeare's *King Lear*) 1985□

Kuroshio warm Pacific current◊ flowing in an arc from Japan towards the American west coast□

Kursk industrial city in central USSR; population 383 000□

Kutch Rann of. Salt marsh area, 90% in Gujerat, India, and 10% in Pakistan□

Kutuzov Mikhail Larionovich, Prince of Smolensk 1745–1813. Russian field marshal, who commanded the retreating Russian army in 1812, and then (after the burning of Moscow) harried the retreating French, and later commanded the united Prussian and Russian forces□

Kuwait the State of

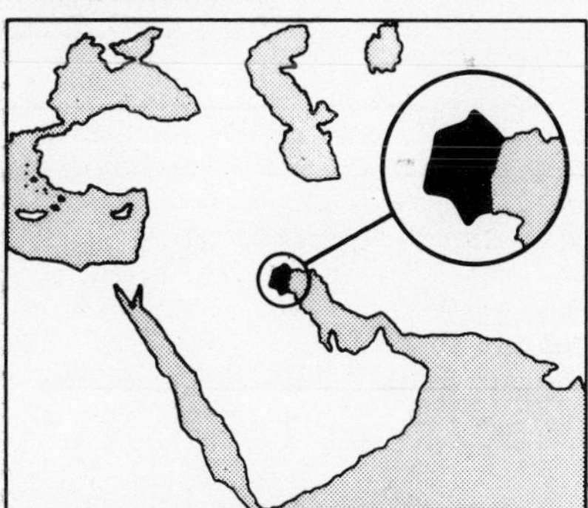

area 19 000 sq km/7400 sq mi
capital Kuwait (also chief port)
features oil revenues make it one of the world's best equipped states in public works, medical and educational services
exports oil
currency Kuwait dinar
population 1 758 000, 40% Kuwaitis; some 30% are Palestinians
language Arabic
religion Sunni Islam, with Shiah minority
government ruler HH Shaikh Jaber Al Ahmad Al Sabah 1928– , who acceded in 1978, with an elected National Assembly
history under British protection at her own request from 1897, Kuwait became fully independent in 1961: Iraq claims Kuwait's territory□

Kuwait capital and port of Kuwait; population 375 000. It has the world's largest seawater distillation plant□

Kuzbas abbrev of Kuznetsk Basin, S Siberia, USSR. It is an industrial area with coal and iron□

Kuznetsk Basin see Kuzbas◊□

Kuznetsov Anatoli 1930–79. Russian novelist, e.g. *Babi Yar* 1966, describing the wartime execution of Jews near Kiev, and regarded as anti-Soviet□

KwaNdebele Black National State◊ of South Africa
area 3318 sq km/1320 sq mi
capital Syabuswa
government chief minister since 1981: Simon Skosana□

Kwangchow see Guangzhou□

Kwangsi-Chuang see Guangxi Zhuang□

Kwangtung see Guangdong◊□

kwashiorkor Ghanaian name for child malnutrition, resulting in retarded growth, etc.; identified as a clinical condition by Cicely Williams◊ in the 1930s□

KwaZulu ('Zulu Country')
area 31 000 sq km/12 000 sq mi
capital Ulundi
features comprises one central block and ten separate areas which occupy much of Natal◊
exports sugar
population 3 000 000 in Natal (57% of the population); some 3 000 000 Zulus live elsewhere in South Africa
religion mainly Christian
government constitutional monarch (Goodwill Zwelethini), and a legislative assembly (Prime Minister Chief Buthelezi◊)
history probably based in Natal from the early 17th century, the Zulus became a formidable military power in the 19th century (see Dingaan◊). King Cetewayo◊, their last effective ruler 1873–83, was defeated by the British in the Zulu War of 1879 at Ulundi. Their lands, annexed in 1887, were incorporated in Natal 1897. The Zulu Black Homeland (KwaZulu) was established in 1970, but under Chief Buthelezi there has been refusal to accept independence as a Black National State under the aegis of South Africa. Transfer by South Africa of N KwaZulu to Swaziland, to give the latter sea access, is opposed. In 1985 there were negotiations with anti-apartheid whites on a multi-racial legislature for Natal at Ulundi□

Kweichow see Guizhou□

Kweiyang see Guiyang◊□

Kyd Thomas c1557–95. English dramatist, author of revenge play *The Spanish Tragedy* c1588, one of the most popular Elizabethan plays, and several times referred to in Shakespeare's *Hamlet*□

Kyoto industrial city (silks, embroidery, porcelain, bronze, lacquer; chemicals, electrical engineering) in S Honshu, Japan; population 1 473 000. It was the capital of Japan 794–1868, and has famous temples; to the south east is ***Ise*** site of the most sacred Shinto shrine, rebuilt every 20 years in the form of a thatched 7th-century house, and containing the octagonal mirror of the sun-goddess Amaterasu◊□

Kyrenia port in Cyprus; population 33 000. It is in the Turkish Cypriot area, and the Greek population left in 1974□

Kyushu most southerly of Japan's main islands, but linked to Honshu by bridge and road/rail tunnel; area 42 079 sq km/16 170 sq mi, including c370 small islands. The capital is Nagasaki□

Kyzyl-Kum desert in Kazakhstan and Uzbekistan, USSR; area 300 000 sq km/116 000 sq mi. Artesian water is being used for irrigation, and there is natural gas□

L

Labanotation see ballet◊□
labelled compound see radioactive◊ tracer□
Labiatae family of fragrant plants with over 3500 species; they have square stems, hairy leaves, flowers arranged in small groups on the stem, and include lavender◊, rosemary◊, thyme◊, sage◊, and mint◊□
Labour Day annual festival of the Labour movement, often linked with 1 May (the beginning of summer), e.g. in England first Monday in May, and a 'bank◊ holiday' since 1976□
Labour Party in the UK, the political party taking inspiration from socialist principles (see socialism◊), as for example in obtaining social improvement for the less wealthy. It had its forerunners in the independents Keir Hardie◊ and John Burns◊, but officially came into existence in 1906 (the chief sponsor being the trade unions, but see also Fabian◊ Society). A socialist programme was adopted in 1918, and the party was recognized as the official Opposition in 1922. It first achieved office in 1924 (see J R MacDonald◊). After World War II the party won the 1945 general election with a huge majority, and was able to implement its policies of industrial nationalization, and the introduction of a comprehensive social security system. More recently it has been criticized from within, both as being insufficiently radical, and for being excessively so. The socialist anthem, the 'Red Flag' (sometimes confused with the Internationale◊) has words by Jim Connell◊, and is now sung to the German tune of 'Der Tannenbaum' ('The Fir Tree')□
Labrador peninsula in NE Canada, divided between Quebec and the province of Newfoundland and Labrador◊. ***Labradorite*** a mineral first found here, has rainbow coloration□
Labrador retriever a type of retriever. See dog◊□
La Bruyère Jean de 1645–96. French essayist whose satirical portraits of his contemporaries in *Caractères* 1688 earned him many enemies□
Labuan see under Sabah◊□
laburnum genus of central European flowering trees, family Leguminosae◊, with pendulous racemes of yellow or purple flowers; eating the black poisonous seeds causes convulsions□
lac substance used to form shellac◊□
Laccadive, Minicoy and Amindivi Islands see Lakshadweep◊□
lace decorative openwork fabric, of which the chief types are ***needlepoint*** or ***point laces*** a development of embroidery, for which Venice, Alençon, and Argentan are famous; ***bobbin*** or ***pillow lace*** in which threads on bobbins follow a pattern pricked out with pins on paper, for which Mechlin, Valenciennes, and Honiton have a name (both types were made in Brussels); and ***machine-made*** the first true lace machine being that developed by John Leavers in 1813. See Nottingham◊□
La Ceiba chief Atlantic port of Honduras; population 64 000□
lacewing insect, green or brown, with veined semi-transparent wings, order Neuroptera; they live on greenfly, etc.□
Lachish biblical city south west of Jerusalem, where inscribed potsherds have thrown light on the early development of the alphabet. Lachish was destroyed by the Babylonians in 589BC□
Lachlan see under Murray◊□
Laclos Pierre Choderlos de 1741–1803. French army officer, whose single novel (in letter form) *Les Liaisons dangereuses* 1782 analyzed social moral corruption□
lacquer poisonous exudate of the ***lacquer tree*** *Toxicodendron verniciflua*, tapped as is a rubber tree□
lacquer the craft of painting wooden pots, furniture, etc, often in successive coloured layers, of lacquer developed in China c1700 under the Shang dynasty, and reaching its zenith under the Han dynasty□
lacrosse Canadian ball game, adopted from the American Indians, and named from a fancied resemblance of the lacrosse stick to a bishop's crozier. Thongs across its curved end form a pocket to carry the small rubber ball, and the pitch is c100 m/110 yd long and a minimum 55 m/60 yd wide in the men's game, which is played ten a side; the women's pitch is larger, and they play 12 a side. The goals are just under 2 m/6 ft square, with loose nets□

lactation secretion of milk in female mammals, which is triggered by hormones towards the end of pregnancy. Its production is preceded by a clear fluid (colostrum) containing serum and white blood cells. In addition to major nutrients (carbohydrates, protein, and fat), human milk contains minerals, vitamins, hormones, immuno-globulins (antibody proteins used in warding off diseases), and epidermal growth factor (EGF), a substance found in the body fluids□

lactic acid organic acid $C_3H_6O_3$, a colourless, almost odourless syrup, which occurs in sour milk, wine, and certain plant extracts, and is always present in the stomach. It is commercially used in food preservation, preparation of pharmaceuticals, etc.□

lactose white, crystalline disaccharide found in milk, e.g. 5% of cow's milk; it is commercially prepared from the whey obtained in cheese-making□

Ladakh see under Karakoram◊□

Ladins ethic community (c16 000) in the Dolomites whose language (Ladin) derives directly from Latin; they descend from the Etruscans and other early Italian tribes, and have links with the speakers of Romansch◊□

Ladoga largest lake (Russian *Ladozhskoye Ozero*) in Europe, NW USSR; area 18 400 sq km/7100 sq mi. Fed by the Onega, etc., it drains to the Gulf of Finland, via the Neva, and forms a link in the White Sea–Baltic Canal□

lady in the UK the correct title of the daughter of an earl, marquis, or duke; and of any woman whose husband is above the rank of baronet or knight, as well as (by courtesy only) the wives of these latter ranks□

ladybird a type of beetle◊□

Lady Day festival (25 Mar) of the Annunciation of the Virgin Mary; until 1752 it was the beginning of the legal year in England, and it is still a quarter◊ day□

Ladysmith town in Natal, S Africa; population 37 800. Named after the wife of Sir Harry Smith (governor of Cape Colony 1847–52), it was besieged by the Boers between 2 Nov 1889 and 28 Feb 1900□

laetrile patent name for an extract from the seeds of apricots, etc., which was claimed as a 'cancer cure' on no accepted evidence, and was banned in the USA□

La Fayette Marie Joseph Gilbert du Motier, Marquis de la Fayette 1757–1834. French soldier-statesman who fought against Britain in the American War of Independence. As commander of the National Guard from 1789, he fled the country in 1792 after attempting to restore the monarchy, and was imprisoned by the Austrians until 1797. He supported Napoleon during the Hundred Days, sat in the Chamber of Deputies as a Liberal from 1818, and assisted the revolution of 1830□

La Fayette Marie-Madeleine, Comtesse de la Fayette 1634–93. French author of *Mémoires* of the French court, and of *La Princesse de Clèves* 1678, the first French psychological novel and *roman à clef* ('novel with a key') in that real-life characters were presented under fictitious names, including La◊ Rochefoucauld (for many years her lover)□

La Fontaine Jean de 1621–95. French poet, friend of Molière, Racine, and Boileau, remembered for his *Fables* 1668–94□

Laforgue Jules 1860–87. French poet, whose technical innovations influenced T S Eliot and later French writers□

lagan the legal term for wreckage lying on the sea-bed See also flotsam◊□

Lagash city in ancient Sumeria (Iraq), north of Ur, which flourished under largely independent rulers c3000–2700BC. Besides valuable art objects, c30 000 clay tablets remain, which give detailed information on temple administration, etc.□

lager a type of beer◊□

Lagerkvist Pär 1891–1974. Swedish lyric poet, dramatist (*The Hangman* 1935), and novelist (*Barabbas* 1950); 1951 Nobel prize□

Lagerlöf Selma 1858–1940. Swedish writer, e.g. traditionally inspired stories of peasant life, *Gösta Berling's Saga* 1891, and (for children) *The Wonderful Adventures of Nils* 1907; Nobel prize in 1909□

lagomorph mammal of the order Lagomorpha, with two pairs of gnawing incisor teeth, e.g. rabbits, hares□

Lagos port (capital until 1982) and commercial centre of Nigeria, on an island in a lagoon linked by bridges to the mainland; population 1 060 850. Onikan Museum has one of the world's richest collections of African art. The climate is unhealthy□

Lagrange Joseph Louis 1736–1813. French mathematician, who presided over the commission which introduced the metric system in 1793. His *Mécanique analytique* 1788 applied mathematical analysis, using principles established by Newton, to such problems as the movement of the planets when affected by each other's gravitational force□

La Guardia Fiorello Henrico 1882–1947. Republican mayor of New York from 1933, who freed it from the domination of Tammany Hall◊, generally clearing up the administration, busting racketeers, clearing up slums, etc. La Guardia airport, New York, is named after him□

La Hogue naval battle off Normandy in 1692 in which the English and Dutch defeated the French□

Lahore industrial city (engineering, textiles, carpets) and capital of the Punjab, Pakistan; population 2 992 000. It is associated with the Mogul rulers Akbar◊, Jahangir◊, and Aurangzeb◊□

Laibach see Ljubljana◊□

Laing R(onald) D(avid) 1927– . Scottish psychoanalyst, originator of the 'social theory' of mental illness, i.e. schizophrenia is promoted by family pressure for its members to conform to standards alien to themselves. His books include *The Divided Self* 1960 and *The Politics of the Family* 1971□

laissez-faire theory that the state should refrain from all intervention in economic affairs, originating with the motto of the 18th-century French Physiocrats: *laissez-faire et laissez-passer* ie 'leave the individual alone, and let commodities circulate freely'. The degree to which intervention should take place is still one of the chief problems of modern economics, both in capitalist and in communist regimes. See also Adam Smith◊□

lake expanse of water unlinked to the sea, but which may be either fresh (the Great Lakes) or salt, owing to evaporation, (Aral, Caspian, and Dead Seas). The largest are Caspian Sea, Lake Superior, Lake Victoria, Aral Sea; both Aral and Caspian are drying up. Of interest are Crater Lake, Oregon◊; Lake Turkana◊; man-made Lake Nasser◊; and Kielder Water, Northumberland◊. See also Italy◊□

Lake District see under Cumbria◊□

lake dwellings Stone Age villages found throughout Europe, e.g. near Glastonbury, dating from the 1st century BC and the 1st century AD. Similar villages built on platforms over the water exist today in W Africa, S America, Borneo, and New Guinea□

Lakes Gippsland. See Victoria◊□

Lakshadweep coral island group (comprising the Laccadives and Amandivis) off Kerala◊, a Union Territory of India; population 40 250; capital Kavaratti Island□

Lakshmi Hindu goddess of wealth and prosperity, consort of Vishnu, whose festival (Diwali) in Oct/Nov is marked by the lighting of lamps and candles, feasting, and exchange of gifts□

Lalande Michel 1657–1726. French organist and composer of much fine church music for the court at Versailles□

La Linea see Gibraltar◊□

Lalique René 1860–1945. French designer of Art Nouveau◊ jewellery, glass, and house interiors□

Lallans lowland Scots dialect as used by Hugh MacDiarmid◊, etc.□

Lamaism see Buddhism◊, Tibet◊□

Lamarck Jean Baptiste 1744–1829. French naturalist. His outline of organic evolution *Philosophie Zoologique* 1809, proposed that an organism can adapt itself to suit a new environment, and that these new characteristics can be inherited. Long discredited, the theory was revived in the later 20th century. See evolution◊□

Lamartine Alphonse de 1790–1869. French poet-politician, a royalist aristocrat turned republican. His poetry, e.g. *Méditations* 1820 is musically romantic. His political career ended when he was blamed for encouraging the Paris worker revolt of Jun 1848□

Lamb Charles 1775–1834. British essayist-critic. Born in London, he was educated at Christ's Hospital (a contemporary of Coleridge◊, with whom he published some poetry in 1796), and was a clerk at India House 1792–1825, when he retired to Enfield◊. His sister ***Mary*** 1764–1847, stabbed their mother to death in a fit of insanity in 1796, and Charles cared for her between her periodic returns to an asylum. He and Mary collaborated in *Tales from Shakespeare* 1807, and his *Specimens of English Dramatic Poets* 1808 helped revive interest in Elizabethan plays. From 1820 he contributed attractive essays under the pseudonym 'Elia' to the *London Magazine* which were collected in 1823 and 1833□

Lambert John 1619–83. English general, a cavalry commander under Cromwell (at Marston Moor, Preston, Dunbar, and Worcester). He broke with him over the proposal to award Cromwell the royal title. After the Restoration he was imprisoned for life□

Lambeth borough of S central Greater London

features County Hall; Lambeth Palace (chief residence of the Archbishop of Canterbury since 1197) and the adjacent Tradescant Centre at St Mary-at-Lambeth, a museum of gardening history (see Tradescant◊); Royal Festival Hall, National Theatre, and London Weekend Television Centre; The Oval (headquarters of Surrey County Cricket Club from 1846) at Kennington, where the first England-Australia Test Match was played in 1880; Brixton Prison; there is a large black community in ***Brixton,*** and there were serious riots in 1981 and 1985

population 243 400□

Lambeth Conference see under Anglican◊ Communion□

Lamburn Richmal Crompton. See Crompton◊□

Lammas medieval festival, 'loaf-mass', on 1 Aug, still a Scottish quarter◊ day□

lammergeier a large vulture. See under eagle◊□

Lammermuir Hills range dividing Lothian◊ and Borders◊ regions, Scotland□

Lampedusa Giuseppe Tomasi di 1896–1957. Italian aristocrat, author of *The Leopard* 1958, an historical novel set in his native Sicily□

lamprey eel-like fish, order Petromyzoniformes. The Atlantic ***sea lamprey*** *Petromyzon marinus* c1 m/3 ft long, is a food fish; it fixes itself by its round mouth to other fish, and feeds by boring into the flesh with its toothed tongue. Henry◊ I is said to have died because he ate too many of them – his favourite dish□

Lamu island off the east coast of Kenya, with an Afro-Arab-Indian Ocean culture, and Islamic in religion□

Lanark town in Strathclyde region, Scotland; population 9000. William Wallace once lived here, and later returned to burn the town and kill the English sheriff. ***New Lanark*** to the south, founded in 1785 by Robert Owen, was a socialist 'ideal village' experiment□

Lancashire NW county of England

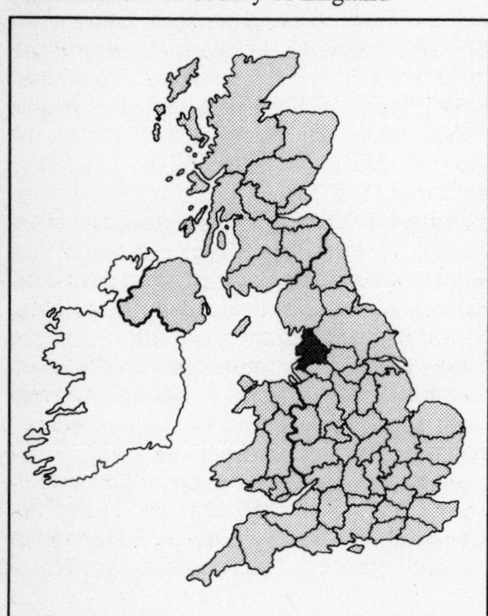

area 3063 sq km/ sq mi
towns administrative headquarters Preston, which forms part of Central Lancashire New Town (together with Fulwood, Bamber Bridge, Leyland, and Chorley, total population 250 000), Lancaster, Accrington, Blackburn, Burnley; ports Fleetwood and Heysham; resorts Blackpool, Morecambe, and Southport
features River Ribble; Pennines; Forest of Bowland (moors and farming valleys); Lancashire hotpot, a dish of stewed meat and potatoes
products 'King Cotton' has been replaced by newer varied industries
population 1 374 100
famous people Alistair Cooke, Les Dawson, Kathleen Ferrier, Gracie Fields, George Formby, Rex Harrison□

Lancaster industrial town (cotton and synthetic textiles, plastic floor coverings) in Lancashire, England; population 50 000. The castle was built on the site of a Roman fort, and was captured in the Civil War by Cromwell. The university was established in 1964□

Lancaster industrial city (tobacco, silk and cotton textiles, electrical goods) in Pennsylvania, USA; population 54 725□

Lancaster Duchy and County Palatine of. Created in 1351, and attached to the crown since 1399 (see under House of Lancaster◊). The office of Chancellor of the Duchy is actually a 'sinecure', usually held by a member of the Cabinet with a special role outside that of the regular ministries□

Lancaster House of. Family descended from Henry III's son, Edmund, Earl of Lancaster, which ruled England 1399–1461. The family estates (see Duchy of Lancaster◊) passed by marriage to John◊ of Gaunt (Duke of Lancaster from 1362), whose son Henry◊ IV obtained the throne in 1399, and was succeeded in turn by Henry◊ V and Henry◊ VI (deposed in 1461, murdered in 1471), the Lancastrian claim passing to Henry of Richmond (descendant of John of Gaunt), who became king as Henry◊ VII in 1485, first of the Tudors◊□

Lancaster Sir Osbert 1908– . British artist, known for imaginative stage designs; architectural books (he coined the phrase 'stockbroker's Tudor'); and his origination of the 'pocket-cartoon' in the *Daily Express* peopled with Establishment characters: Maudie Littlehampton, Canon Fontwater, etc.□

lancelet marine animal, genus *Amphioxus* included in the chordates◊. It has no skull, vertebral column, centralized brain, nor paired limbs, but there is a notochord (a supportive rod) which runs from end to end of the body, a tail, and a number of gillslits. Found in all seas, it burrows in the sand but when disturbed swims freely□

Lancelot of the Lake. In British legend, the most celebrated of Arthur's knights, the lover of Queen Guinevere◊. Originally a folk-hero, he was introduced into the Arthurian cycle in the 12th century□

Lanchow see Lanzhou◊□

Lancret Nicolas 1690–1743. French artist, a follower of Watteau, who painted graceful *fêtes galantes*□

Land federal unit (plural *Länder*) of W Germany□

Land Edwin. See under photography◊□

Landes The. Sandy low-lying area in SW France, largely reclaimed from heathland by planting pine and oak forests; area c12 950 sq km/5000 sq mi. Arcachon is a seaside resort; there is a rocket and missile range at Biscarosse, and oil is drilled at Parentis□

Land League Irish peasant organization, formed by Michael Davitt in 1879. By 'boycotting' (see Boycott◊) any man who took a farm from which another had been evicted, it forced Gladstone to introduce an act in 1881 giving security of tenure□

Landor Walter Savage 1775–1864. British poet and author of prose *Imaginary Conversations of Literary Men and Statesmen* 1824–9. His temper was so uncertain that he was expelled from Rugby School and rusticated from Oxford University, and incurred a libel action which sent him into final exile in Italy□

Land Registry HM state register of titles to land, established in 1862, and compulsory from 1897, which simplified subsequent buying and selling□

landscape style see garden◊□

Landseer Sir Edwin Henry 1802–73. British painter and sculptor. His sentimental studies of animals, e.g. the dogs in *Dignity and Impudence,* have a counterbalance in studies of extreme cruelty or suffering. His best-known sculptures are the lions in Trafalgar Square. Knighted in 1850□

Land's End promontory in W Cornwall, most westerly point in England, which extends into a group of dangerous rocks, guarded by the Longships lighthouse 2 km/1 mi out□

Landskrona industrial port (machinery, chemicals) in SW Sweden; population 40 000□

Lanfranc c1005–89. Archbishop of Canterbury from 1070. Born at Pavia, he became prior of the Norman monastery of Bec, where Anselm◊ was his pupil, and as archbishop rebuilt Canterbury cathedral, enforced clerical celibacy, separated the ecclesiastical from the secular courts, and replaced English clerics by Normans□

Lang Andrew 1844–1912. British historian and folklore scholar, best remembered for his series of children's *Fairy Tale Books* from 1889□

Lang Fritz 1890–1976. Austrian film producer, e.g. *Metropolis* 1926, *M* 1931, *Fury* 1936, and *The Big Heat* 1953□

Lange David Russell 1942– . New Zealand Labour statesman. Leader of the party from 1983, he narrowly defeated Muldoon in the general election of 1984□

Langevin Paul 1872–1946. French physicist, contributor to the studies of magnetism, X-ray emission, and during World War I inventor of an apparatus for locating submarines. The nuclear institute at Grenoble◊ is named after him□

Langland William c1332–c1400. British poet, probably born near Malvern◊. He took minor orders and later settled in London. His alliterative *The Vision of William Concerning Piers Plowman* c1362 develops the typical poor peasant into a symbol of Christ and condemns the social and moral evils of the time□

Langley Samuel Pierpont 1834–1906. American physicist, developer of a sensitive electrical infra-red detector and founder of the Smithsonian Astrophysical Observatory. His steam-driven unmanned aeroplane flew for 90 seconds in 1896, making the first 'flight' by an engine-equipped aircraft□

Langmuir Irving 1881–1957. American physicist. Working for the General Electric Company 1909–50, he invented the mercury vapour pump for producing high vacua; nitrogen gas-filled filament lamps; the atomic hydrogen welding process; and developed the thermionic valve. In 1932 he was awarded a Nobel prize for his work on surface chemistry□

Langobards see Lombards◊□

Langton Stephen d. 1228. English churchman, appointed archbishop of Canterbury in 1207 by Innocent III. King John refused to recognize him, and he was not allowed to enter England until 1213. He supported the barons in their struggle against John, and was mainly responsible for the Magna◊ Carta□

Langtry Lillie 1853–1929. British actress, known as the Jersey lily from her birthplace, and an intimate friend of Edward VII□

language the system of human expression by means of words. Human language, as expressed by the voice, depends for its production on certain physical characteristics, which are not possessed by the apes◊. Comprehension and expression of written and spoken language is dominated by the left hemisphere of the human brain◊. There are more than 5000 languages, or dialects, which are classified in families, though the relationships are not all well-established. For example, with a few exceptions, e.g. Basque, Finnish, and Tamil, all the languages of Europe and India belong to a single much-diversified Indo-European family.

Numerically, the most important languages (in millions of native speakers) are: Chinese 941; English 397; Hindi/Urdu 326; Russian 274; Spanish 258; Arabic 155; Bengali 151;

Portuguese 151; German 119; Japanese 119; Malay/Indonesian 115; French 107. See under language in individual country entries.

Computers (using rules of language structure devised by e.g. Noam Chomsky◊) can now translate technical documents with 80% accuracy. See also pidgin◊.

The bases of human communication have been explored by experimenters such as Beatrice and Allan Gardner at the University of Nevada in 1966 with the chimpanzee Washoe. The physical inability of apes to produce human sounds was overcome by substitution of the sign language of the deaf. There has also been much work on the means of communication in animals, which has proved much more complex than was once thought, e.g. in the vervet monkey◊, lobster◊, etc.□

Languedoc-Roussillon region of S France; capital Montpellier; population 1 926 500. In the Middle Ages dialects were spoken in the Languedoc area in which *oc* meant 'yes', as distinguished from northern France where *oui* meant 'yes', i.e. the *langue d'oui* as opposed to the *langue d'oc*; it was also known as Provençal: see Provence◊. Resembling the Spanish Catalan dialect, the forms of modern *Occitanie* are closer to Latin than northern French. This language of the troubadours◊ was revived by Frédéric Mistral◊ among others, and is spoken today in the regions Languedoc-Roussillon and Provence-Côte d'Azur, where – in conjunction with Corsica – separatist aims are popular□

Lanier Sidney 1842–81. American flautist, poet, and metrical experimenter. In the Civil War he was a Confederate blockade runner, and was captured and imprisoned□

lanolin a sticky, purified wax obtained from sheep's wool, and used in cosmetics, soap, preparing leather, etc.□

Lansbury George 1859–1940. British Labour leader in the Commons 1931–5, who resigned (as a pacifist) in opposition to the party's policy in the Ethiopian◊ War□

Lansdowne Henry Charles Keith Petty Fitzmaurice, 5th Marquis of Lansdowne 1845–1927. British Conservative statesman. As Foreign Secretary 1900–6, he abandoned Britain's isolationist policy, forming alliances with Japan and France. His proposals in 1917 for a compromise peace led to a violent controversy□

Lansing industrial city, (motor vehicles, diesel engines, pumps) capital of Michigan, USA; population 130 400□

lanthanides the 15 chemically related elements, also known as rare earths, of the lanthanide series, from lanthanum (57) to lutecium (71)□

lanthanum element
symbol La
atomic number 57
physical description silvery metal in the lanthanide◊ series, to which it gives its name
uses the making of glass, in alloys and in electronics□

Lanzhou (formerly Lanchow) industrial city (fertilizers, synthetic rubber) and capital of Gansu province, China; population 1 750 000□

Laoighis county (county town Portlaoise) of the Republic of Ireland, province of Leinster◊□

Laon town in N France; population 30 200. It has a magnificent 12th-century cathedral□

Laos People's Democratic Republic of

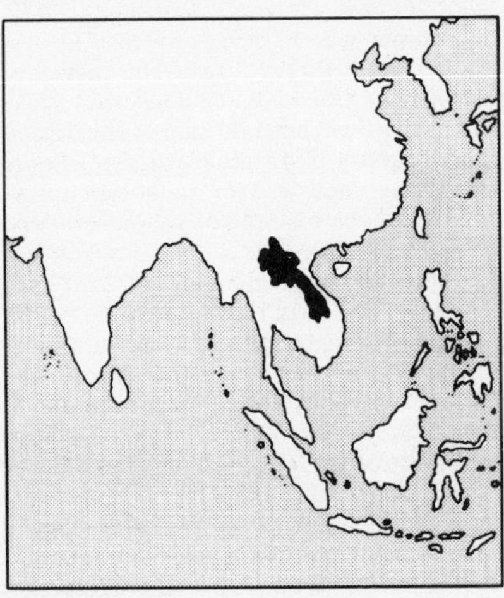

area 235 700 sq km/91 000 sq mi
capital Vientiane
towns Luang Prabang, the former capital
features Mekong river, hydroelectric power being exported to Thailand; Plain of Jars, where a prehistoric people carved stone jars large enough to hold a man; used to be known as the Land of a Million Elephants
exports tin, teak (worked by elephants)
currency kip
population 3 372 000
language Lao
religion traditionally Theravada Buddhism
government president (Prince Souphanouvong from 1975) and national assembly
history Laos, a kingdom from the 14th century, became a French protectorate in 1893, and was occupied by the Japanese 1941–5. Following the Geneva Conference of 1954, it became fully independent, but the civil war, begun in 1953, continued until the Vientiane Agreement of 1973 divided the country between the government (which had been

supported by the USA) and the Communist insurgents. By 1975 the latter were predominant in the joint governmentt, and Laos became a republic under Souphanouvong. It leans to the Vietnam-Soviet axis, with 50 000 Vietnamese soldiers and advisers in the country□

Lao Zi possibly 604–531BC. Chinese philosopher, founder of Taoism◊. Nothing is known of his life□

La Pampa see under Pampas□

La Paz city in Bolivia, the seat of government since c1900, although Sucre is the official capital; population 654 700. Founded in 1548, it is 3800 m/12 400 ft above sea level, the world's highest capital□

lapis lazuli also called ***lazurite*** and ***ultramarine***; deep blue mineral used in inlaying and ornamental work; it consists of a sodium aluminium silicate with sodium sulphide, and occurs in metamorphic limestones□

Laplace Pierre Simon, Marquis de Laplace 1749–1827. French mathematician-astronomer, who worked with Lagrange◊ on the effects of inter-planetary gravitational forces. He contributed also to the theory of surface tension, probability, and sound propagation□

Lapland region of N Europe within the Arctic circle, without political definition, divided among Norway, Sweden, Finland, and USSR. Resources include timber, minerals, hydroelectric power, and tourism. The ***Lapps*** are of Mongolian stock, and many are no longer nomadic reindeer herders. In the USSR (see Murmansk◊) they number c1750, and are mainly employees of state collective reindeer-breeding farms□

La Plata industrial city (meat packing, oil refining), E Argentina, with its port at Ensenada; population 455 000□

La Plata Rio de. See River Plate◊□

Laptev Sea part of the Arctic Ocean◊ off the north coast of the USSR between Taymur Peninsula and New Siberian Island□

lapwing a bird of the plover◊ family□

Laramie town in Wyoming, USA, bounded East and West by the Laramie mountains; population 24 400. On the Overland Trail and Pony Express route, it features in 'Western' legend□

larceny in the UK a former name for theft◊, which survives in US usage□

larch a tree of the pine family. See under conifers◊□

lard edible fat high in saturated fatty acids prepared from pigs, used in margarine, soap, and ointment□

Larderello see under Tuscany◊□

Lardner Ring 1885–1933. US sporting correspondent (especially baseball) in Chicago and New York whose short stories used the characters and argot encountered in his work, e.g. *You Know Me, Al* 1916, and *Round Up* 1929□

Laredo industrial city (oil-refining, meat-processing) on the Rio Grande, Texas, USA; population 91 300. ***Nuevo Laredo*** Mexico, on the opposite bank, is a textile centre; population 214 160. There is much cross-border trade□

Lares and Penates in Roman mythology, spirits of the farm and of the store cupboard, often identified with the family ancestors, whose shrine was the centre of family worship in Roman homes□

La Rioja region of N Spain. See under Castile◊□

Larisa textile town in Thessaly, E Greece; population 103 265□

lark songbird of the order Passeriformes◊, mainly of the Old World. The northern ***skylark*** *Alauda arvensis* breeds in Britain and migrates south in winter. Light-brown, 18 cm/7 in long, it nests on the ground, and sings as it rises almost vertically in the air□

Larkin Philip 1922–85. British poet. Born in Coventry, he was educated at Oxford, and from 1955 was librarian at Hull University. His perfectionist, pessimistic verse includes *The North Ship* 1945 and *High Windows* 1974, and he also wrote two novels. His recommendation brought Barbara Pym◊'s work back into favour□

larkspur a plant of genus delphinium◊□

Larne port in Antrim, N Ireland; population 17 000. It is the terminus of sea routes to Stranraer, Scotland□

La Rochefoucauld François, Duc de la Rochefoucauld 1613–80. French epigrammatist, a soldier in the *Fronde*◊, he later divided his time between the court and literary salons. His acute *Maximes* (published anonymously) 1665 and *Mémoires* 1664 are unrivalled. See also Mme de la Fayette◊□

La Rochelle port in W France; population 77 500. A Huguenot stronghold, it was taken by Richelieu◊ in the siege of 1627–8□

Larousse Pierre 1817–75. French author of an encyclopedic dictionary 1865–76, forerunner of many under the same name□

larva immature animal form which differs greatly from the mature one, e.g. tadpole/frog, caterpillar/butterfly□

laryngitis inflammation of the membraneous lining of the larynx◊, as often happens with a cold, when the voice may be lost for a few days□

larynx cavity at the upper end of the windpipe containing the vocal cords; it is stiffened with cartilage and lined with mucous membrane□

La Salle René Robert Cavelier, Sieur de la Salle 1643–87. French explorer, who made an epic voyage exploring the Mississippi down to its mouth, and in 1682 founded Louisiana. Returning with colonists, he failed to refind the river mouth, and was eventually murdered by his mutinous men□

lascar an E Indian seaman□

Las Casas Bartolomé de 1474–1566. Spanish priest, the 'apostle of the Indians', who in 1530 persuaded his government to forbid slavery in Peru. He also laboured as a missionary, and wrote a *Historia de las Indias* 1875–6□

Lascaux see under Dordogne◊□

Lasdun Sir Denys 1914– . British architect, whose works include the National Theatre on the South Bank; knighted in 1976□

laser (*l*ight *a*mplification by *s*timulated *e*mission of *r*adiation) a device which produces an intense narrow beam of coherent light◊ of virtually a single wavelength◊ (light from an ordinary source contains a much wider spread of wavelengths).

In an ordinary light source, excited atoms emit photons◊ (pockets of light) spontaneously and independently of each other, but in a laser the photon emission from one atom is triggered or 'stimulated' by photons arriving from other atoms, so the photons, as it were, join forces. The principle was used in the laser (1951) to amplify microwaves◊; lasers are sometimes called 'optical masers'

To respond to stimulation large numbers of atoms in the laser have to be waiting in an excited state. This was achieved in the first laser (1958), which was a small cylinder of ruby, by exposure to an intense flash of light. In gas lasers, developed later, the excitation is (indirectly) by an electrical discharge through a tube containing a mixture of gases (e.g. nitrogen and carbon dioxide). Gallium arsenide semi-conductor◊ lasers have also been developed.

High intensity lasers are used for cutting and welding; even hardened steel can be penetrated. Since the light beam is so narrow it can travel vast distances and still be detectable; laser light has been bounced back from the moon, enabling the earth–moon distance (a quarter of a million miles) to be measured very accurately. Lasers are also used in satellite tracking□

Lashio town in NE Burma, linked via the Burma Road, constructed in 1938, with Kunming, China□

Laski Harold 1893–1950. British political theorist, who taught a modified Marxism (e.g. *A Grammar of Politics* 1925) at the London School of Economics from 1926, and chaired the Labour Party 1945–6□

laser

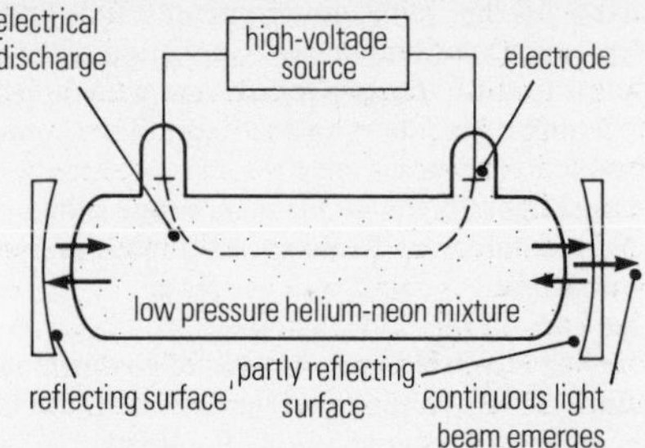

Laski Marghanita 1915– . British author, niece of Harold Laski, whose books include the novel *The Victorian Chaise Longue* 1953, and studies of Jane Austen and George Eliot□

Las Palmas tourist resort on Gran Canaria, Canary◊ Islands, adjoined by the port of La Luz; population 366 455□

La Spezia industrial port (shipbuilding, engineering, electrical goods, textiles) in NW Italy, chief Italian naval base; population 115 000. Shelley◊ drowned in the Gulf of Spezia□

lassa fever an often fatal viral disease. See haemorrhagic◊ fevers□

Lassalle Ferdinand 1825–64. German Socialist, founder in 1863 of the General Association of German Workers (later the Social-Democratic Party)□

Lasseter's Reef legendary location of a rich gold-bearing area in Rawlinson Range, Western Australia, discovered by H B Lasseter 1897, but which he could never relocate□

Lassus Roland de (Italian *Orlando di Lasso*) c1530–94. Flemish composer of many songs and madrigals, including settings of poems by his friend Ronsard◊□

Las Vegas city in Nevada, USA; population 164 675. Best known for its nightclubs and gambling casinos□

Latakia port with tobacco industries in NW Syria; population 125 715□

La Tène an Iron Age settlement. See under Iron◊ Age□

latent heat heat◊ which changes the state of a substance without changing the temperature◊□

laterite soft, friable, clay-like rock, produced by the weathering down of basalts, granites, and shales, and occurring in the tropics□

latex milky fluid exuded by certain plants, e.g. the rubber tree, and opium poppy, which include alkaloids, protein, starch, etc.□

Latimer Hugh c1490–1555. English Protestant reformer. He supported Henry VIII's case against Catherine of Aragon, but was imprisoned when he disagreed with the king's failure to drop all Roman Catholic doctrine. Under Queen Mary he was arrested for heresy in 1553, and burned at Oxford□

Latin language spoken by the Romans, from which the Romance languages (Italian, French, Spanish, Portuguese, etc.) developed. Even beyond the Middle Ages it remained the language of the learned (More, Bacon, Milton), and, had the Renaissance scholars not insisted on classical purity, might have become Europe's common second language. Latin was universally used in the Roman Catholic Church until after the reforms of the Second Vatican Council 1962–5. Like Greek, it is highly inflected, i.e. the meaning of a sentence depends less on the order of the words than on variations in the word-endings.

Latin literature *drama* Plautus and Terence; *prose* Cato, Cicero, Julius, Tacitus, Pliny the Elder and Pliny the Younger, Quintilian, Suetonius, Apuleius; *verse* Ovid, Virgil, Catullus; *writers of the Christian Church* Tertullian, Cyprian, St Ambrose; and in the medieval era St Jerome and St Augustine□

Latin America countries of S and Central America (also including Mexico) in which Spanish, Portuguese, and French are spoken. There are three economic organizations: Central American Common Market (1960); Andean Group (1969); and Latin America Integration Association (1980). The ***Latin American Economic System*** (SELA from its Spanish initial letters) established in 1975, also includes Caribbean members; headquarters Caracas. It aims at integration and industrial cooperation, and coordination of existing organizations□

latitude and **longitude** ***latitude*** is the angular distance of any point from the equator, measured north or south along earth's curved surface, and is measured in degrees, minutes, and seconds, each minute equalling one sea-mile in length. ***Longitude*** is the angular distance between the terrestial meridian drawn from the poles through a place, and a standard meridian now taken at Greenwich□

Latitudinarians from the 17th century those Anglicans willing to accept modifications of forms of church government and worship to accommodate dissenters□

Latium see Lazio◊□

La Tour Georges de 1593–1652. French artist, whose candle-lit scenes have achieved full recognition only in the 20th century□

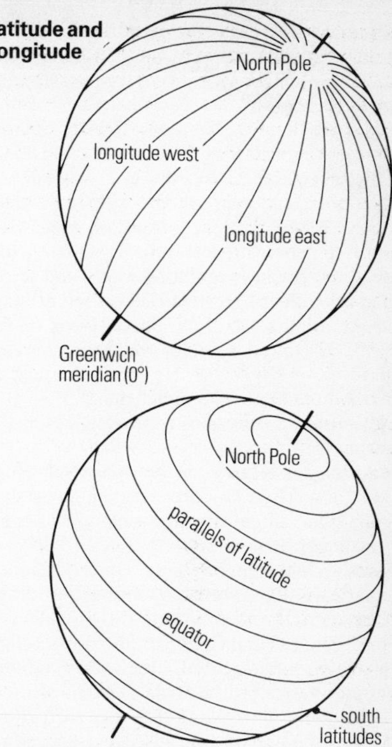

La Trobe Charles Joseph 1801–75. Australian administrator, first Lieutenant-Governor of Victoria 1851–4, after whom ***Latrobe River*** was named; it flows through one of the world's largest deposits of brown coal□

Lattakia see Latakia◊□

Latter-day Saints see Mormons◊□

Latvia constituent republic of the western Soviet Union from 1940
area 63 700 sq km/24 600 sq mi
capital Riga
towns Daugavpils, Liepaja, Jelgava, Ventspils
features lakes, marshes and wooded lowland
products meat and dairy products; communications equipment; most of Soviet consumer durables, plus large share of motorcycles and locomotives
population 2 568 000; Letts 54%, Russian 33%
language Latvian
religion mostly Lutheran Protestant with a Roman Catholic minority
recent history formerly part of the Russian empire, Latvia became an independent republic in 1918 (recognized by Russia in 1920). In 1939 the USSR demanded military bases and in 1940 incorporated Latvia as a constituent republic. As in the other Baltic

republics, there has been nationalist dissent since 1980, influenced by the Polish example, and prompted by an influx of Russian workers and officials□

Laud William 1573–1645. British churchman, Archbishop of Canterbury from 1633. His persecution of the Puritans, censorship of the press, and support for Charles I's autocracy aroused general opposition, while strict enforcement of the statutes against enclosures and of laws regulating wages and prices alienated the propertied classes. His attempt to impose the use of the Prayer Book on the Scots provoked a revolt which precipitated the English Civil War. He was impeached by parliament in 1640, and beheaded□

laudanum a substance containing opium◊ in alcohol□

Lauder Sir Harry. Stage name of Hugh MacLennan 1870-1950. Scottish music-hall comedian, singer of songs such as 'I Love a Lassie'□

Lauderdale John Maitland, Duke of Lauderdale 1616–82. Scottish statesman, a former Covenanter◊, who joined the Royalists in 1647, and as High Commissioner for Scotland 1667–79, persecuted the Covenanters; created Duke of Lauderdale in 1672□

Laue Max Theodor Felix von 1879–1960. German physicist who discovered the wave nature of X-rays and pioneered the measurement of their wavelength through their diffraction through the closely spaced atoms in a crystal; Nobel prize in 1914. See Grenoble◊□

Laugharne see under Dyfed◊□

laughing jackass a type of kingfisher◊□

Laughton Charles 1899–1962. Anglo-American character actor, born in Scarborough. His larger-than-life film roles include the king in *The Private Life of Henry VIII* 1933 and Captain Bligh in *Mutiny on the Bounty* 1935□

Launceston town in Cornwall, England; population 5000□

Launceston industrial port (engineering, sawmilling, furniture, pottery, blankets, railway workshops) in NE Tasmania, Australia; population 64 555□

Laurasia see continent◊□

laurel the true laurel tree ***sweet bay*** is *Laurus nobilis*, family Lauraceae, of which the aromatic leaves are used in cookery, and in classical times formed wreaths for athletes, etc. The ornamental shrub laurels, e.g. ***cherry laurel*** *Prunus laurocerasus*, family Rosaceae, are poisonous□

Laurel Stan 1890–1965 and **Hardy** Oliver 1892–1957. American film comedians. Laurel born Arthur Stanley Jefferson, was thin and tearful, and always provoking the temper of the fat and dominant Hardy. With a minimum of dialogue, and an underlying criticism of society from the position of the underdog, their films, e.g. *Leave 'em Laughing* 1928, were revived as a world-wide cult in the 1970s□

Laurence Margaret 1926– . Canadian writer, born in Manitoba. *The Prophet's Camel Bell* 1963 records her experiences in the Somali desert, *A Jest of God* (1966; filmed as *Rachel, Rachel*) is a novel set in Canada□

Laurier Sir Wilfrid 1841–1919. Canadian Liberal statesman. As first French-Canadian Prime Minister 1896–1911, he promoted Canadian and imperial unity□

laurustinus a shrub of genus *Viburnum*◊□

Lausanne industrial city (chocolate, scientific instruments, publishing) in W Switzerland; population 222 145□

Lausanne Treaty of. The treaty of concluding peace in 1923 between Turkey and the Allies after World War I□

lava molten substance emitted from a volcanic crater; ***basic lava*** containing less silica than ***acid lava*** flows greater distances, since it takes longer to solidify□

Laval Pierre 1883–1945. French politician, prime minister and Foreign Secretary 1931–2 and 1935–6, he was created head of the Vichy government by Hitler 1942–4. Universally hated for his share in the deportation of French labour to Germany, he was tried for treason and shot□

La Vallière Louise de la Baume le Blanc, Duchesse de la Vallière 1644–1710. Mistress of Louis XIV (by whom she had four children) 1661–74, when she retired to a convent on her supersession by Mme de Montespan. She was slightly lame and of a sweet disposition□

La Vendée see Vendée◊ La□

lavender genus of sweet-smelling Mediterranean herbs *Lavendula,* family Labiatae◊, used in perfumes and pot pourri□

Lavery Sir John 1856–1941. British portrait-painter of Edwardian society, reassessed in the 1980s□

Lavoisier Antoine Laurent 1743–94. French chemist; some say the founder of modern chemistry. He proved that combustion needed only a part of 'air' which he called oxygen. He thereby destroyed the theory of phlogiston (an imaginary 'fire element' released during combustion). Then with Laplace he showed that water was a compound of oxygen and hydrogen. In this way he established the modern basic rules of chemical combination□

Lavrentiev Mikhail 1900– . Soviet scientist. As director of the Institute for

Precision Mechanics and Computer Engineering from 1950, he developed from 1957 Akademgorodok. See Novosibirsk◊□

law rules and principles under which justice is administered in a state. In western Europe there are two main systems:

Roman law first codified in 450BC and finalized under Justinian 528–34AD, advanced to a system of international law (*jus gentium*), applied in disputes between Romans and foreigners or provincials, or between provincials of different states. Church influence led to the adoption of Roman law all over western continental Europe, and it was spread to E Europe and parts of Asia by the French *Code Napoléon* in the 19th century. Scotland and Quebec (because of their French links) and S Africa (because of its link with Holland) also have it as the base of their systems.

English law derives from Anglo-Saxon customs, which were too entrenched to be broken by the Norman Conquest, and still form the basis of the Common Law (i.e. common to the whole country) which by 1250 had been systematized by the royal judges. Alongside it there grew up a system of ***equity*** developed in the Court of Chancery, where the Lord Chancellor considered petitions, and the ordinary rules were mitigated where their application would operate harshly in particular cases. In the 19th century there was major reform of the law (e.g. the abolition of many capital offences, in which juries would not in any case convict) and of the complex system of courts (see Law◊ courts). Unique to English law are the ***judicial precedents*** whereby the reported decisions of the courts form a binding source of law for future decisions. In modified form English law was adopted by countries throughout the world which came under English influence, including the USA□

Law Andrew Bonar 1858–1923. British Conservative statesman, born in New Brunswick. Chancellor of the Exchequer 1916–19, and Lord Privy Seal 1919–21 in Lloyd George's coalition, he formed a Conservative Cabinet in 1922, but resigned on health grounds□

Law William 1686–1761. English churchman, whose *A Serious Call to a Devout and Holy Life* 1728, influenced the Wesleys◊□

law courts the legal system of England and Wales, headed by the House of Lords as a final authority, above even the Court of Appeal. At the lowest level is the Small Claims Court (for less than £500 and outside the judicial system) which attempts to settle claims (inferior goods bought in a shop, for example) with minimum expense and formality; next on the Civil Law side is the County Court (up to £5000) and the High Court of Justice (Chancery, Queen's Bench, and Family divisions) for very important cases. On the Criminal Law side, the least important cases are dealt with by Magistrate's Courts, the more important are referred to the Crown Court (presided over by a High Court Judge, Circuit Judge or Recorder according to seriousness), which in London sits at the Central Criminal Court/'Old Bailey'◊. Appeals (on points of law) may also be made from Magistrates' and Crown Courts to a Divisional Court (constituted by two or more High Court judges). There are also special courts, such as the Restrictive Trade Practices Court, or the Employment Appeal Tribunal. In Scotland the supreme civil court is the Court of Session, with appeal to the House of Lords; the highest criminal court is High Court of Justiciary, with no appeal to the House of Lords□

Lawes Henry 1596–1662. British composer, whose works include music for Milton's masque *Comus* 1634. His brother ***William*** 1602–45 was also a composer□

Lawes Sir John Bennet 1814–1900. British agriculturist, who in 1843 established the Rothamsted Experimental Station (Hertfordshire) at his birthplace; he patented the first artificial manure 'super-phosphate'□

Lawler Ray 1911– . Australian playwright, author of *The Summer of the 17th Doll* 1957, dealing with sugarcane-cutters□

lawn tennis a form of tennis◊□

Lawrence industrial town (woollen textiles, clothing, paper, radio equipment) in Massachusetts, USA; population 63 175□

Lawrence D(avid) H(erbert) 1885–1930. British novelist and poet. Son of a Nottinghamshire miner, he studied at Nottingham University, and became a teacher. He achieved fame with the semi-autobiographical *Sons and Lovers* 1913, which includes a portrayal of his mother (d. 1911). In 1914 he married Frieda von Richthofen, ex-wife of his university professor, with whom he had run away in 1912, and who was the model for Ursula Brangwen in *The Rainbow* 1915, suppressed for obscenity, and its sequel *Women in Love* 1921. His travels in search of health (he suffered from tuberculosis, from which he eventually died near Nice) prompted books such as *Mornings in Mexico* 1927. Most famous of his novels is *Lady Chatterley's Lover* 1928, banned as obscene in the UK until 1960 for its crude emphasis on emotion and the sexual impulse as creatively true to human nature. He also excelled in the short story, e.g. 'The Woman Who Rode Away', and his poems have sensitive observation of nature. See also Nottingham◊□

Lawrence Ernest O(rlando) 1901–58. American physicist, inventor of the cyclotron particle accelerator◊; Nobel prize in 1939. Lawrencium was named after him□

Lawrence Gertrude 1898–1952. English actress, whose greatest success was in Noel Coward's *Private Lives* 1930–1, in which he starred with her□

Lawrence John Laird Mair, 1st Baron Lawrence 1811–79. Viceroy of India 1864–9. Chief Commissioner for the Punjab from 1853, he disarmed troops in his area during the 1857 Mutiny, and was largely responsible for the recapture of Delhi□

Lawrence St d. 258. Christian martyr, whose answer when called on to deliver the treasures of his church, was to display the beggars on whom he had spent them. He was broiled on a gridiron. Feast day, 10 Aug□

Lawrence Sir Thomas 1769–1830. British portrait artist. Born at Bristol, son of an innkeeper, he succeeded Reynolds as painter to George III in 1792, e.g. the series of Allied sovereigns and statesmen in Windsor Castle□

Lawrence T(homas) E(dward) 1888–1935. British soldier, 'Lawrence of Arabia'. Born in Wales, he studied at Oxford University, worked on archaeological 'digs' at Carchemish, etc. 1910–14. In World War I, he was appointed to military intelligence, Cairo, and negotiated for an Arab revolt against the Turks, in which he himself took part. Disappointed that Arab independence did not ensue during the 1918 peace conference, Lawrence pseudonymously joined the RAF in 1922 (as John Hume Ross) and in 1923 transferred to the tank corps (as T E Ross), re-entering the RAF in 1925. The chief evidence for his legendary exploits in the Arab revolt is his own book *The Seven Pillars of Wisdom* 1926, and its authenticity is doubtful (see Aldington◊); *The Mint* 1936, deals with life in the RAF. He was killed in a motorcycle accident in Dorset◊□

lawrencium element
symbol Lr
atomic number 103
physical description radioactive metal
features named after Ernest Lawrence◊
uses no present use□

Lawson Nigel 1932– . British Conservative politician. A former financial journalist, he was Financial Secretary to the Treasury 1979–81, Secretary of State for Energy 1981–3, and has been Chancellor of the Exchequer from 1983□

Laxness Halldor. See under Iceland◊□

Layamon lived c1200. English poet and priest, author of an alliterative verse chronicle *Brut* giving a history of Britain, which includes the earliest English version of the Arthurian legend□

Layard Sir Austen Henry 1817–94. British diplomat and archaeologist, who excavated at Nineveh and Babylon 1845–51, and supplied the major part of the Assyrian collection in the British Museum□

La'youn capital (formerly El Aaiún) of Western Sahara; population 24 050□

Lazarus Emma 1849–87. American poet, author of the poem on the base of the Statue of Liberty which includes the words: 'Give me your tired, your poor, /Your huddled masses yearning to breathe free'□

Lazio region (Roman *Latium*) of W central Italy; capital Rome; population 5 025 160. Home of the Latins from the 10th century BC, it was dominated by the Romans from the 4th century BC. It includes the low-lying Campagna, and the unhealthy Pontine Marshes, which the Romans tried to drain, but which remained until Mussolini succeeded in 1926□

Lea river rising in Bedfordshire, England, which joins the Thames at Blackwall. The ***Lea Valley*** has been developed as a 'playground' for London□

Leach Bernard 1887–1979. British potter, established at St Ives from 1920, whose work was greatly influenced by his studies in Japan□

Leacock Stephen Butler 1869–1944. British humorist, who settled in Canada in 1876, and taught economics at McGill University, Montreal 1908–36. His books include *Literary Lapses* 1910 and *Nonsense Novels* 1911□

lead element
symbol Pb
atomic number 82
physical description dark grey-blue metal; the heaviest, softest, and weakest of the common metals
features it is a cumulative poison, and its use in plumbing, as an anti-knock additive to petrol, and in paints is potentially harmful
uses resistant to corrosion and acids, and used as a shield against radioactivity; it is used in solder and in making bronze and pewter; industrial uses include glass, ceramics, and storage batteries□

leaf lateral outgrowth on a plant stem, especially foliage leaves, typically comprising a leaf stalk (petiole) and a blade (lamina), and which may be simple (e.g. birch, lime) or compound (e.g. the leaflets of ash, blackberry, etc.). The leaves may fall in autumn (deciduous) or be evergreen (persistent). A major function of leaves is in photosynthesis◊, but leaves may be modified into bulbs, tendrils, spines, etc. All the traps of insectivorous plants are modified leaves.

A single leaf blade consists of a hard, outer layer of ***cuticle*** at top and bottom, covering the upper and lower ***epidermis***. The underside contains small pores (***stomata***) which allow gases to pass in and out (which occurs during the process of transpiration). Between the upper and lower epidermis is the ***palisade layer*** containing chlorophyll, used by the plant in photosynthesis□

cross-section of a leaf

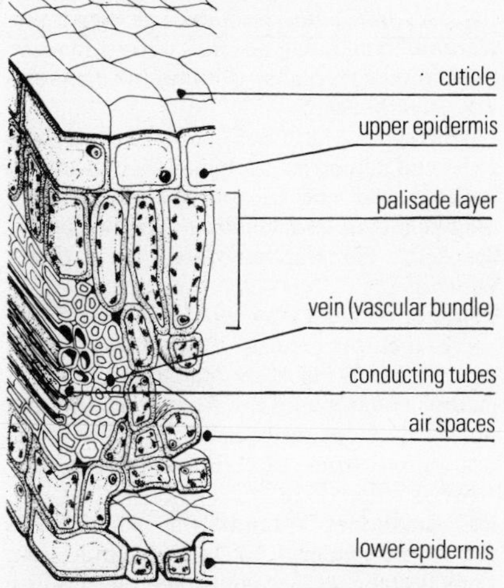

leaf insects insects, family Phyllidae, order Phasmida, mainly of SE Asia, related to the stick◊ insects, but whose bodies are flattened, veined, etc., so that they perfectly mimic living leaves□

League of Nations international organization for the prevention of war established in 1920 after World War I; headquarters Geneva. It was superseded in 1945 by the United Nations□

Leakey Louis Seymour Bazett 1903–72. British archaeologist, curator of Coryndon Museum, Nairobi, 1945–61. He discovered gigantic animal fossils at Olduvai◊ Gorge, Tanzania in 1958□

Leakey Mary 1913– . British archaeologist, wife of Louis Leakey. She discovered in 1948, on Rusinga Island, Lake Victoria, E Africa, the ape-man skull known as Proconsul, c 25 000 000 years old; and human remains at Laetolil, to the south, c3 750 000 years old□

Leakey Richard 1944– . British archaeologist, son of Louis and Mary Leakey. In 1972 he discovered at Lake Turkana, Kenya, ape forms with some human characteristics□

Leamington officially ***Royal Leamington Spa***, in Warwickshire, England; the Royal Pump Room offers modern spa treatment; population 46 000□

Lean Sir David 1908– . British film director; *Blithe Spirit* 1945, *Brief Encounter* 1946, *The Bridge on the River Kwai* 1957 (Academy Award), *Lawrence of Arabia* 1962 (Academy Award), *A Passage to India* 1985; knighted in 1984□

Lear Edward 1812–88. British artist and humorist, who published travel books on Italy, Greece, Egypt, and India with his own illustrations, and popularized the limerick in his *Book of Nonsense* 1846□

leasehold land or property held for a specified period, usually at a rent. Houses and flats in the UK are often held on a 99-year lease, for which a lump sum is paid, plus an annual 'ground rent': the entire property reverts to the original owner at the end of the period. Under the Leasehold Reform Act of 1967, tenants were in many instances given the right to purchase the freehold or extend the lease of houses; and in the 1980s extension of the right to flats was under consideration, possibly in the form of ***strata title*** a method used in Australia, where a building is subdivided (usually by voluntary agreement between landlord and tenants on payment of a capital sum) into 'strata', each comprising a standardized freehold (with specified rights, obligations, and rules of management)□

leather material prepared, mainly from the hides and skins of domesticated animals, by tanning with vegetable tannins (from tree bark, etc.), chromium salts, etc. Plastic substitutes have made leather a 'luxury' item□

Leatherhead town in Surrey, England; population 15 600. The Royal School for the Blind (established in 1799) is here□

leatherjacket the larva of the crane-fly. See fly◊□

leaven substance, e.g. yeast, causing fermentation in dough, so that it 'rises' and makes lighter bread, etc.□

Leavis F(rank) R(aymond) 1895–1978. British critic, champion of D H Lawrence and James Joyce, and opponent of C P Snow◊'s theory of 'Two Cultures'□

Lebanon Republic of

area 10 400 sq km/3400 sq mi

capital Beirut, also a port

towns Tripoli, Tyre, (all ports) and Sidon

features few of the celebrated cedars of Lebanon remain; Mt Hermon; Chouf mountains; archaeological sites at Baalbeck, Byblos, Tyre; until the civil war, the financial centre of the Middle East

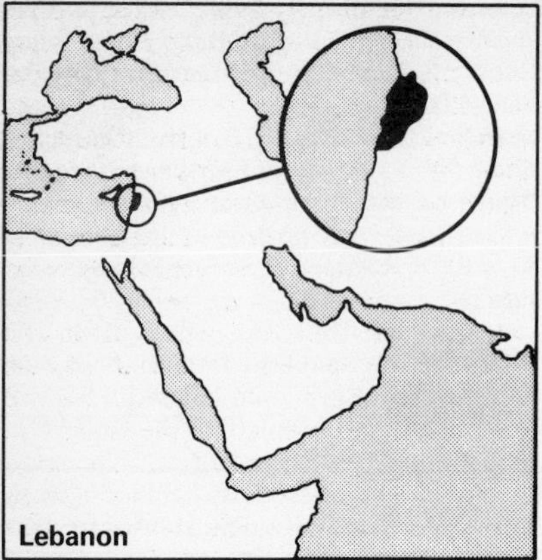

exports citrus and other fruit, and industrial products to Arab neighbours
currency Lebanese pound
population 3 060 000, including 350 000 Palestinian refugees (many driven out, killed in fighting, or massacred 1982–5)
language Arabic official, French and English
religion Christianity (Maronite and Orthodox) 40%; Islam 57% (Shi'ite 33%, Sunni 24%); Druze 3%
government president (always a Maronite Christian: Amin Gemayel from 1982), who appoints the prime minister (always a Sunni Muslim), and an elected national assembly, always presided over by a Shi'ite Muslim
recent history formerly part of the Turkish Empire, it came under French League of Nations mandate in 1922, and became independent in 1944. From the late 1960s the presence of Palestinian guerrillas in south Lebanon led to civil war between Christians and Muslims 1975–6, and Syrian intervention in an attempt to keep order. Israeli aid to the Christians was followed by armed incursions, as in 1978, and a full-scale invasion in 1982 to eliminate the PLO◊ in south Lebanon (and, further, to expel the Syrians and establish a Maronite Christian government with whom to negotiate). By Aug 1982 Israel had expelled the PLO from Beirut, but then antagonized the Shi'ite Muslims (and their *Amal*, 'Hope', militia), not to speak of their extremist wing (the pro-Khomeini *Hezbollah*, 'Party of God', backed by Syria and Iran) by their attempt to establish a pro-Israeli Christian regime. In 1985 the Israelis withdrew. National reconciliation talks 1983–4 proposed revision of the constitution to equalize power between Muslim and Christian groups. See also Arab-Israeli Wars◊□

Le Brun Charles 1619–90. French artist who decorated Versailles, and helped to found the French Academy□

Le Carré John. Pseudonym of British author David John Cornwell 1931– . After teaching at Eton, he joined the Foreign Service 1960–4. His books include *The Spy Who Came in from the Cold* 1963, *Tinker, Tailor, Soldier, Spy* 1974, and *Smiley's People* 1979. He coined the word 'mole' for a political traitor within a country□

lecithin organic substances very similar to fats but also containing nitrogen and phosphorus, found in animal and vegetable cell tissues; ***ovolecithin*** is found in eggs; ***vegelecithin*** (containing no cholesterol and much used in diet products) is found in vegetables e.g. soya beans□

Leclair Jean Marie 1697–1764. French violinist and composer. Originally a dancer and ballet-master, he composed ballet music, operas (*Scilla and Glaucus*), violin concertos, etc. He was murdered in a street crime□

Leconte de Lisle Charles Marie René 1818–94. French poet, head of ***Les Parnassiens*** a group of poets including Mallarmé◊ and Verlaine◊, who opposed the Romantics and supported 'art for art's sake'. He drew his inspiration from the ancient world, e.g. *Poémes antiques* 1852□

Le Corbusier pseudonym of Charles Edouard Jeanneret 1887–1965. Swiss-born French architect, for whom the house was a habitable machine to be designed to functional criteria. His works include the Palace of the Nations, Geneva; Cité Radieuse, Marseille, and the town-plan for Chandigarh◊, India□

Lecouvreur Adrienne 1692–1730. French actress, whose intimate admirers included Voltaire, and Maurice de Saxe; she is thought to have been poisoned by a jealous rival for the love of the latter□

Leda in Greek mythology, wife of Tyndareus, by whom she was the mother of Clytemnestra◊. By Zeus◊, who came to her as a swan, she was the mother of Helen◊ of Troy, Castor◊ and Pollux◊□

Le Duc Tho 1911– . N Vietnamese diplomat, who was awarded (with Kissinger◊) a Nobel peace prize in 1973, but indefinitely postponed receiving it□

Lee Bruce. Stage-name of American 'Chinese Western' film-actor Lee Yuen Kam 1941–73, an expert in kung◊ fu□

Lee Laurie 1914– . British poet and author, born in Slad, near Stroud, Gloucestershire, where he now lives. He published the autobiography *Cider with Rosie* in 1959□

Lee Nathaniel c1653–92. English dramatist, whose bombastic tragedies include *The Rival Queens* 1677, and who died in a fit of intoxication□

Lee Robert E(dward) 1807–70. American Confederate general, a supreme strategist. He suppressed John Brown◊'s raid on Harper's Ferry in 1859, and in command of the army of N Virginia (his native state) from 1862, he won the Seven Days' Battle against McClellan; raided Northern territory, and won battles at Fredericksburg and Chancellorsville 1862–3. Put on the defensive after Gettysburg, he surrendered in 1865 at Appomattox◊ Court House□

leech worm◊ in the class Hirudinea, and external parasite. They attach themselves to men, cattle, sharks, etc. by their strong suctorial mouth, through which they withdraw blood. The medicinal leech *Hirudo medicinalis* was extensively used by doctors when 'bleeding' was the cure for all ills, especially fever. It is still occasionally used in some parts of the world, and is the source of the anticoagulant hirudin□

Leech John 1817–464. British caricaturist, contributor to *Punch* 1841–64, and book illustrator, e.g. Dickens' *Christmas Carol*□

Leeds industrial city in W Yorkshire, England; population 704 885. Famous for woollens from the 14th century, it also has clothing, leather, engineering, printing, chemical, and glass industries, and at Killingbeck there is a Science Park for high-tech industries. Notable buildings include the Town Hall, university and art gallery; Temple Newsam, the birthplace of Darnley◊, and the well-preserved 12th-century Cistercian abbey of Kirkstall□

leek hardy Eurasian biennial *Allium porrum* family Liliaceae, of which the blanched lower leaves are edible; it is the national emblem of Wales□

Lee Kuan Yew 1923– . Singapore statesman. A third generation Straits Chinese, he studied law at Cambridge, became a founder-member of the left-wing People's Action Party (PAP), and Prime Minister of Singapore from 1959, which he led out of the Malaysian Federation in 1965□

Leeuwarden city in N Netherlands; population 84 700. Noted for gold- and silverware, it has the Friesian museum. See Friesland◊□

Leeuwenhoek Anthony van 1632–1723. Dutch anatomist, pioneer of microscopic research, e.g. the structure of red blood corpuscles, spermatozoa in animals, yeast, etc.□

Leeward Islands northern members of the Lesser Antilles◊ in the West Indies. See also French◊ Polynesia□

Le Fanu Joseph (Sheridan) 1814–73. Irish novelist (*Uncle Silas* 1864) and short story writer (*In a Glass Darkly* 1872), who specialized in the mysterious□

left-handedness use of the left hand for most actions. It occurs in about 16% of the population, predominantly males, and is associated with a higher frequency of auto-immune diseases, and conditions such as epilepsy, learning disorders (dyslexia, stuttering, etc.) and both mental retardation and genius. Right-handedness seems to have had an evolutionary advantage in that left-handed people are more sensitive to substances which act on the brain. Left-handedness may be caused by an excess of the male hormone, testosterone, while the child is still in the womb; this slows down development of the left-hand lobe of the brain, so that the right-hand lobe (which governs the left of the body) becomes dominant□

Léger Fernand 1881–1955. French artist, whose Cubist works from 1911 especially favoured cylindrical and machine forms, reducing his human beings to puppets. His works also include ballet settings, and murals□

Leghorn see Livorno◊□

legionnaire's disease pneumonia-like disease, so called because it attacked a convention of American legionnaires (ex-servicemen) in 1976. It is caused by the bacterium *Legionella pneumophila* which breeds in warm water (e.g. in the cooling towers of air-conditioning systems). It is carried out on minute water droplets, which are inhaled into the lung to spread the disease□

Legion of Honour see under knighthood□

legitimacy any child born in lawful wedlock is legitimate. A child can also be legitimized (in England and Wales) by a later marriage of its parents, even (since an Act of 1959) if they were married to others at the time of the birth. Disadvantages of the illegitimate have been much reduced by legislation, but succession to any dignity or title is still excluded. In the USA the law varies from state to state, but is generally the same as in England□

Leguminosae dicotyledonous worldwide plant family with 600 genera and 12 000 species, many of economic importance. Most have butterfly-like flowers and may have leaves modified to tendrils; the seeds are carried in a pod and the roots bear nitrogenous nodules which restore nitrates to the soil. Native to Britain are clover, derris, gorse, and vetch. See also bean◊, lentil◊, and pea◊□

Léhar Franz 1870–1948. Hungarian operetta composer; his works include *The Merry Widow* 1905 and *The Land of Smiles* 1923□

Le Havre industrial port (engineering, chemicals, oil refining) in NW France, on the Seine, which superseded Harfleur◊; population 264 400□

Lehmann Lotte 1888–1976. German-born American soprano, who excelled in Wagnerian operas and was the original Marschallin in Richard Strauss's *Rosenkavalier*□

Lehmann Rosamond Nina c1904– . British novelist, (*Dusty Answer* 1927, *Invitation to the Waltz* 1932, *The Weather in the Streets* 1936, *The Ballad and the Source* 1944), whose work enjoyed a revival in the 1980s□

Leibniz Gottfried Wilhelm 1646–1716. German philosopher and mathematician. Independently of Newton◊ he advanced and consolidated the infinitesimal calculus◊, devising symbols for differentiation and integration which are still used today. In his metaphysical works (e.g. *Monadology*, 1714) he argued that the world (i.e. the totality of everything there is) consists of innumerable units – 'monads'. Each monad's properties determine its past, present, and future, and are selected by God so that monads, though independent of each other, seem to interact predictably, and so that 'this is the best of all possible worlds' – a phrase misunderstood and ridiculed by Voltaire in his *Candide* 1759□

Leicester industrial city in Leicestershire, England; population 280 325. At the geographical centre of England, and site of a settlement in pre-Roman times, it is one of the country's oldest towns. The Battle of Bosworth◊ was fought nearby, and is frequently re-enacted on its almost unchanged site. Industries include hosiery, knitwear, and shoes; processed food, especially cheese and pork pies; light and precision engineering, electronics, printing, and plastics. There is a 14th-century Guildhall, a university and polytechnic, De Montfort Concert Hall, and Haymarket Theatre□

Leicester Robert Dudley, Earl of Leicester c1532–88. English soldier, son of the Duke of Northumberland◊, created Earl of Leicester in 1564. Queen Elizabeth I favoured him, and in 1560 the death of his wife (Amy Robsart), by a fall downstairs, led to gossip that he had murdered her to enable him to marry the Queen. In 1579, when she found he had secretly remarried the widow of the Earl of Essex three years previously, she almost sent him to the Tower. He commanded the army sent to the Netherlands 1585–7, and that raised to resist the Armada in 1588□

Leicester and Holkham, Earl of. See Coke◊□

Leicestershire Midland county of England

area 2553 sq km/986 sq mi

towns administrative headquarters Leicester; Loughborough, Melton Mowbray, Market Harborough

features include Rutland district (formerly England's smallest county, with Oakham as its county town), and Rutland Water, one of Europe's largest reservoirs, being developed as a leisure area; Charnwood Forest; Vale of Belvoir (under which are large coal deposits); famous for foxhunting

products horses, cattle, sheep, dairy products; coal

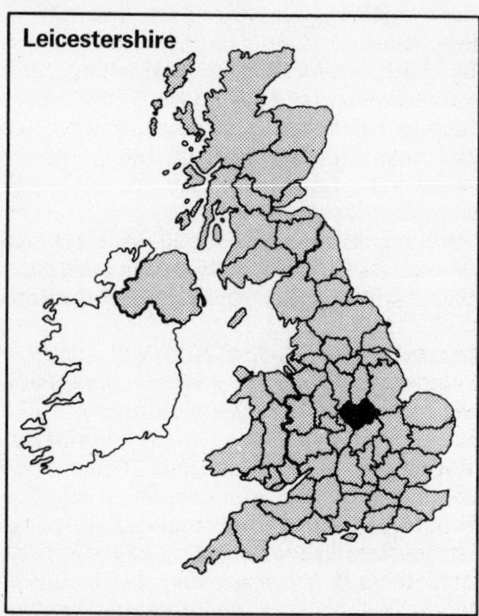

population 845 600

famous people C P Snow□

Leichhardt Friedrich 1813–48. Australian explorer; Sydney–Moreton Bay, Queensland in 1843 and Brisbane–Arnhem Land in 1844. He disappeared without trace on a further Queensland expedition in 1848. Patrick White◊ used the character of Leichhardt in *Voss*□

Leiden industrial city (woollen textiles, cigars, printing – Elzevier works, established 1580) in W Netherlands; population 103 460. Rembrandt and Jan Steen◊ were born here□

Leif Ericsson lived c1000. Viking explorer, the son of Eric◊ the Red; he is said to have discovered 'Vinland', generally identified with Nova◊ Scotia□

Leigh Vivien 1913–67. British actress of fragile beauty and vivacious fire, married to Lord Olivier◊ 1940–61. Films include *Lady Hamilton, Gone With the Wind* 1939 (Academy Award), *A Streetcar named Desire* 1951 (Academy Award)□

Leigh-Mallory Sir Trafford 1892–1944. British air chief marshal. As Air Officer

Commanding No 12 Fighter Group 1937–40, he took part in the Battle of Britain, and was Commander-in-Chief of Allied air forces during the invasion of France. He was killed in an air crash□

Leighton Frederick, Baron Leighton 1830–96. British artist and sculptor, born at Scarborough. His works are mainly historical and classical, e.g. *Cimabue's Madonna Carried in Procession,* 1855 and *The Garden of the Hesperides*, 1892□

Leinster SE province of the Republic of Ireland, comprising the counties of Carlow, Dublin, Kildare, Kilkenny, Laoighis, Longford, Louth, Meath, Offaly, Westmeath, Wexford, Wicklow; area 19 635 sq km/7581 sq mi; population 1 790 521□

Leipzig capital of Leipzig district and industrial city (motor vehicles, musical instruments, furs, leather goods, cloth, glass), E Germany; population 563 400. A famous east/west trading centre (Leipzig fairs), it has musical associations with J S Bach and Mendelssohn, and the Gewandhaus Concert Hall□

Leipzig Battle of. 'Battle of the Nations' in 1813, in which Napoleon was defeated□

leishmaniasis tropical disease caused by a parasite transmitted by the sandfly, resulting in ulcers in the liver, spleen, etc.□

Leith port on the Firth of Forth. Granted to Edinburgh◊ by Robert Bruce in 1329, it was incorporated in the city in 1920□

Leitrim county (county town Carrick-on-Shannon) of the Republic of Ireland, province of Connacht◊. It includes Lough Allen□

Leland John c1506–52. English antiquary, chaplain and librarian to Henry VIII. He toured England 1534–43, collecting manuscripts and antiquities, and his *Itinerary* was published in 1710□

Lely Sir Peter. Adopted name of Pieter van der Faes 1618–80. Anglo-German portrait artist, who worked for Charles I, Cromwell, and Charles II, who knighted him in 1679 and whose court beauties he immortalized in a series at Hampton Court□

Le Mans industrial town in NW France; population 155 245. It has held an annual Grand Prix 24-hour endurance motor race since 1923□

Lemberg see Lvov◊□

lemming a small rodent◊□

Lemnos volcanic Greek island in the N Aegean; area 466 sq km/180 sq mi. Towns Kastro and Mudros□

lemon a type of citrus◊□

lemur nocturnal family of primates, Lemuridae, found only in Madagascar, of which all species are threatened with extinction. Already extinct species were in some cases as large as today's great apes; existing species including the ***ring-tailed*** *Lemur catta*, and the ***dwarf lemurs***, only 25 cm/10 in long, including the tail□

Lena longest river in Asiatic Russia, 4800 km/3000 mi. Ice-covered for half the year, it has innumerable tributaries before flowing into the Arctic Ocean□

Le Nain family of French artists: the brothers ***Antoine*** 1588–1648, ***Louis*** 1593–1648, and ***Mathieu*** 1607–77 who mainly painted peasant life, but also portraits□

Lenclos Ninon de 1615–1705. Parisian courtesan, whose lovers included Condé◊ and La Rochefoucauld◊□

Lenglen Suzanne 1899–1938. French tennis player, Wimbledon champion 1919–25, and introducer of modern sports clothes. See Patou◊□

Lenin Vladimir Ilyich. Pseudonym of Russian statesman Vladimir Ilyich Ulyanov 1870–1924. Born at Simbirsk (now renamed Ulyanovsk), he became a lawyer in St Petersburg (now Leningrad). Sent to Siberia for revolutionary Marxist propaganda 1895–1900, he then edited the Social Democratic paper *Iskra* ('The Spark') from abroad, and visited London several times (see Tower◊ Hamlets). In *What is to be done?* 1902, he advocated a professional core of party activists to spearhead the revolution in Russia, a suggestion accepted by the majority (*bolsheviki)* at the London party congress in 1903. Active in the 1905 Revolution, Lenin had again to leave Russia on its failure, settling in Switzerland in 1914, whence he attacked Socialist support for World War I as for an 'imperialist' struggle, and wrote *Imperialism* 1917. On the renewed outbreak of revolution in Mar 1917, he returned to Russia. With the overthrow of the provisional government, he became president of a Soviet government, concluded peace with Germany, and organized a successful resistance to 'White' (pro-Tsarist) uprisings and foreign intervention. Communism proving inadequate to put the country on its feet, he introduced a private enterprise New Economic Policy (NEP) from 1921 (reversed by Stalin in 1929). He had founded the 3rd (Communist) International in 1919, but his health declined following injuries in an assassination attempt in 1918. His embalmed body is a tourist attraction in a mausoleum in Red Square, Moscow. He married in 1898 ***Nadezhda Konstantinova Krupskaya*** 1869–1939, who shared his work, and wrote *Memories of Lenin*□

Leninakan industrial city (textiles, engineering) in the Republic of Armenia USSR; population 213 000□

Leningrad second city of the USSR, capital of the Russian Empire 1709–1918 (founded by Peter the Great in 1703 as St Petersburg, it was called Petrograd 1914–24); population 4 676 000. It is linked with the Baltic by canal 1875–93; by canal and river with the Caspian and Black Seas, and a seaway connection was completed in 1975, via Lakes Onega and Ladoga, with the White Sea, so that naval ships can reach the Barents Sea free of NATO◊ surveillance. Industries include ship-building, machinery and machine tools, diesel motors, chemicals, textiles. It has splendid boulevards and beautiful 18–19th-century buildings which survived the heroically resisted German siege in World War II, Sept 1941–Jan 1943. Museums, with superb works of art, include the Winter Palace (home of the Tsars till 1917), the Hermitage, the Russian Museum (formerly Michael Palace), and St Isaac's Cathedral; the island fortress of St Peter and St Paul was a Tsarist political prison. Falconet◊'s fine statue of Peter the Great is also here. The city was the centre of all the main revolutionary movements from the Decembrist revolt of 1825 till the 1917 Revolution. See also Kronstadt◊□

Leninsk-Kuznetsky coalmining town (formerly Kolchugino) in the Kuzbas◊, central USSR; population 131 000□

Leno Dan 1861–1904. British comedian-acrobat, the greatest of pantomime dames□

Lenôtre André 1613–1700. French landscape gardener, whose masterpiece was Versailles for Louis XIV□

lens piece of glass or transparent plastic with curved surfaces, so that light passing through it is refracted (see refraction◊) to form an image of the object from which it came.

A ***converging lens*** brings the diverging rays from the points on the object to another set of points, constituting the image, which will be magnified or diminished according to how far the object is from the lens. Converging lenses rely on the angle between their faces increasing at greater distances from the centre. This is generally achieved by making the lens thicker in the middle than at the edges, though ***fresnel lenses*** (as used in some 'whole page' magnifying glasses) consist of a series of differently angled rings moulded into a piece of thin plastic. The same principle is used in lighthouses. Converging lenses are used in projectors, cameras, microscopes, telescopes, as magnifying glasses, and for correcting long-sight. ***Diverging lenses***, used for correcting short-sight, are less versatile□

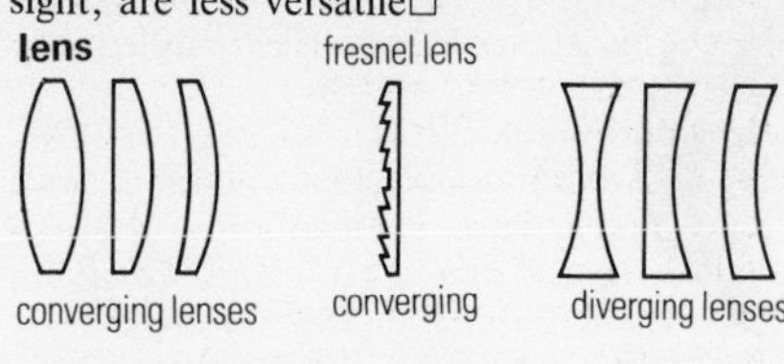

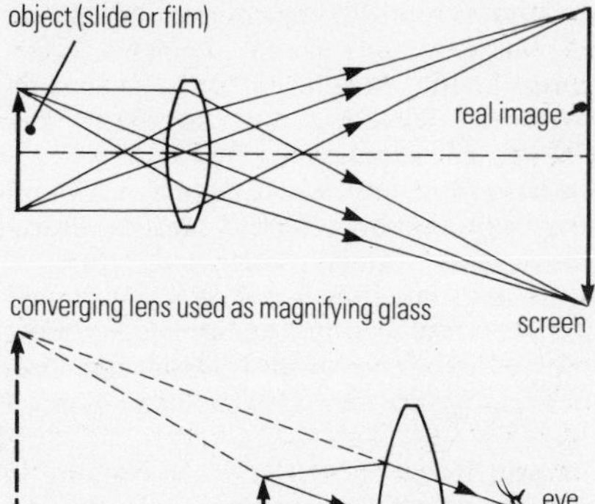

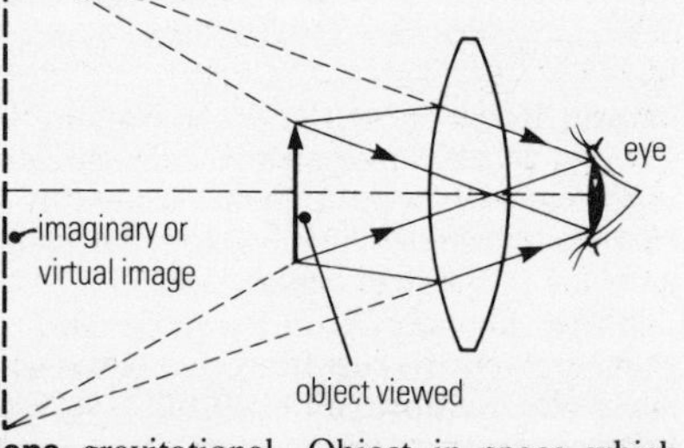

lens gravitational. Object in space which bends light by its gravitational field, so that it produces a double image of a body behind it, e.g. a quasar, and appears as if between two quasars. It also produces a magnifying effect□

Lent the 40 days of fasting preceding Easter in the Christian Church (see Ash Wednesday◊)□

lentil Mediterranean annual *Lens esculenta* family Leguminosae◊, with white or bluish flowers, and pods with edible seeds; the red pottage for which, in the Old Testament, Esau◊ sold his birthright, was made of lentils□

Lenya Lotte. Stage-name of Austrian singer Karoline Blamauer 1905–81, wife of Kurt Weill◊ from 1925, who appeared in his *The Threepenny Opera*, etc.□

Leo III the Isaurian c675-741. Byzantine soldier-emperor, who seized the throne in 717 and successfully defended Constantinople against the Saracens 717–18. He tried to suppress image-worship□

León city in Castilla-León, Spain; population 131 135. It was the capital of the kingdom of León 10th century–1230, when it was merged with Castile□

León industrial city in central Mexico; population 589 950□

León industrial city in W Nicaragua; population 220 900. Founded in 1532, it is a cultural centre and university city□

Leonardo da Vinci 1452–1519. Italian painter, sculptor, architect, musician, engineer, and scientist. Born at Vinci in Tuscany, the illegitimate son of a lawyer, he studied under Verrochio◊. From c1477 he worked under the patronage of Lorenzo◊ the Magnificent, then in 1482 became state engineer, court painter, and director of court festivities to Lodovico Sforza◊ in Milan. From 1500 he moved from place to place in Italy, including a spell in 1502 as architect and engineer to Cesare Borgia◊, then in 1516 settled in France at the invitation of Francis◊ I (at the Château Cloux, near Amboise, now a museum of his varied genius, with many models made from his technical drawings) where he died. His chief works include *The Adoration of the Magi* 1481, in the Uffizi, *The Last Supper* (badly deteriorated, but under restoration in the 1980s) 1495–8, on the wall of the refectory of Santa Maria Delle Grazie, Milan; the *Mona Lisa* (wife of Zanoki del Giocondo, hence also known as *La Gioconda*) 1503, Louvre; *Battle of Anghiari* 1504–5, formerly in the Palazzo Vecchio, Florence; and *The Virgin and Child with St John the Baptist and St Anne* (*The Virgin of the Rocks*) 1506, in the National Gallery, London. His drawings are of superb draughtsmanship, and his scientific sketches include designs for flying machines, a parachute, and a submarine□

Leoncavallo Ruggiero 1858–1919. Italian opera composer, best remembered for *I Pagliacci* 1892□

Leonidas d. 480BC. King of Sparta◊, killed in defending the pass of Thermopylae (with 300 Spartans, 700 Thespians, and 400 Thebans) against a huge Persian army□

leopard a type of large cat◊□

Leopardi Giacomo, Count Leopardi 1798–1837. Italian lyric poet, whose first collection of *Versi* appeared in 1824, and was followed by the philosophical *Operette Morali* 1827 and *Canti* 1831□

Leopold two Holy Roman Emperors: ***Leopold I*** 1640–1705, emperor from 1657, in succession to his father Ferdinand◊ III. He warred against Louis XIV and the Turks. ***Leopold II*** 1747–92, emperor in succession to his brother Joseph◊ II, was the son of Maria◊ Theresa. His hostility to the French Revolution led to the outbreak of war a few weeks after his death□

Leopold three kings of the Belgians: ***Leopold I*** 1790–1865, king from 1831, having been elected to the throne on the creation of an independent Belgium. Through his marriage to Princess Charlotte◊, he was the uncle of Queen Victoria◊, and exercised considerable influence over her.

Leopold II 1835–1909, king from 1865, son of Leopold I. He financed Stanley◊'s explorations in Africa, which resulted in the foundation of the Congo Free State (now Zaïre◊), from which he extracted a huge fortune by ruthless exploitation.

Leopold III 1901–83, king from 1934, he surrendered to the Germans in 1940. Postwar charges against his conduct led to a regency by his brother Charles, and his eventual abdication in 1951 in favour of his son Baudouin◊□

Léopoldville see Kinshasa◊□

Lepanto Italian name for the Greek port of Naupaktos on the north of the Gulf of Corinth. On 7 Oct 1571 Don John◊ of Austria (commanding Christian League forces of Spain, Venice, Genoa, and the Papal States; see Pius◊ V) won the naval ***Battle of Lepanto*** over the Turks off the city (then a Turkish possession). Cervantes◊ was wounded in the battle□

Lepenski Vir see under Danube◊□

Lepidoptera order of insects including the butterflies◊ and moths◊□

leprosy mainly tropical infectious disease caused by the bacillus *Mycobacterium leprae* which results in ulcerating nodules, skin discoloration, paralysis, shedding of fingers and toes, etc. It is curable by drugs, and in 1983 a vaccine was under trial□

Leptis Magna city founded by the Phoenicians east of Tripoli in Libya, with magnificent remains of its period of Roman rule from 47BC□

leptospirosis infectious disease of domestic animals, especially cattle, causing abortion, etc.; transmitted to humans, it causes meningitis, jaundice, etc.□

Lérida industrial city (leather, paper, glass, silk textiles) in Catalonia, Spain; population 110 000. It was captured by Caesar◊ in 49BC, and has a Moorish castle□

Lermontov Mikhail Yurevich 1814–41. Russian poet of the Byronic school, and novelist. A guards officer, he was sent to serve in the Caucasus in 1837 for a revolutionary poem on Pushkin's death. Returning to Moscow in 1838, he published his psychological novel *A Hero of Our Time* 1840. He was killed in a duel□

Lerner Alan Jay 1918–86. American lyricist, collaborator with F Loewe◊□

Lerwick fishing and oil port, administrative headquarters of Shetland, Scotland; population 6500. Hand-knitted shawls are a speciality. A Viking tradition survives in the Jan festival of Up-Helly-Aa when a copy of a longship is burnt□
Le Sage Alain René 1668–1747. French writer best remembered for his picaresque novel *Gil Blas* 1715–35, much indebted to Spanish originals□
lesbianism homosexual◊ love between women (from Lesbos◊, birthplace of Sappho◊)□
Lesbos Greek island (Greek *Lésvos*) in E Aegean Sea; area 1748 sq mi/675 sq mi; population 114 800. Capital Mytilene. Alcaeus◊ and Sappho◊ lived here□
Lesotho Kingdom of

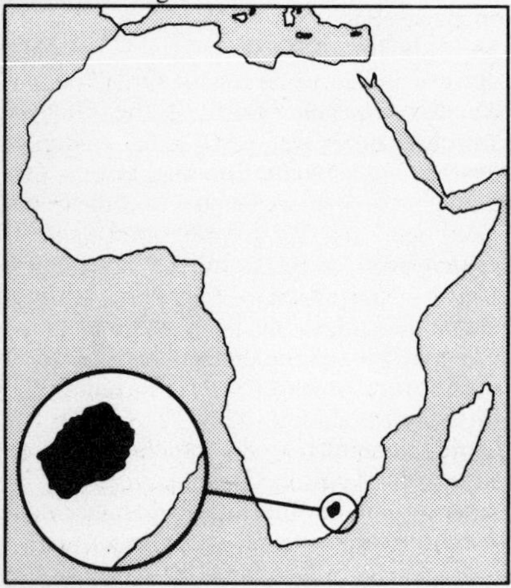

area 30 346 sq km/11 716 sq mi
capital Maseru
features Lesotho is an enclave within S Africa
exports wool, mohair; diamonds
currency loti
population 1 474 000
language Sesotho and English, official
religion Christianity 70% (Roman Catholic 40%)
government constitutional monarchy (Moshoeshoe II from 1960), with a senate (comprising chiefs and members nominated by the king) and elected national assembly (prime minister, Chief Leabua Jonathan from 1966).
recent history under British protection from 1868, Basutoland became independent within the Commonwealth as Lesotho in 1966. On the defeat of the government at the 1970 elections, Chief Jonathan suspended the constitution, ruling by a Council of Ministers, but in 1974 a National Assembly with nominated members was reintroduced. Lesotho claims land from S Africa which was 'illegally ceded' during the colonial period□
Less Developed Countries (LDCs) countries late in developing an industrial base, and dependent on cash crops and unprocessed minerals. The 'Group of 77' was established in 1964 to pressurize developed countries into giving greater aid□
Lesseps Ferdinand, Vicomte de Lesseps 1805–94. French engineer, constructor of the Suez Canal◊ 1859–69; he began the Panama Canal◊ in 1879, but failed when he tried to construct it without locks□
Lessing Doris (May) 1919– . Rhodesian-born British novelist, born Tayler, whose books include *The Grass is Singing* 1950 and *The Good Terrorist* 1985, and the autobiographical series *Children of Violence* 1952–69, from a Communist political viewpoint; science fiction, and, under the experimental pseudonym of 'Jane Somers', *The Diary of a Good Neighbour* 1981□
Lessing Gotthold Ephraim 1729–81. German dramatist (*Miss Sara Sampson* 1755, the first tragedy of ordinary German life and the comedy *Minna von Barnhelm* 1767). In his critical essays he was a champion of Shakespeare, and *Laocoon* 1766, analysed the function of poetry and the plastic arts□
Lésvos see Lesbos◊□
Letchworth industrial town (clothing, furniture, scientific instruments, light metal goods) in Hertfordshire, England; population 33 500. It was founded in 1903 as the first garden◊ city□
Lethe in Greek mythology, a river of the underworld. To drink its waters was to forget the past□
Le Touquet-Paris Plage resort in N France, fashionable in the 1920s–30s; population 4500□
letters a written or printed message which, especially as personal communications, are valuable as reflections of social conditions, literary and political life, etc. Ownership of a letter (as document) passes to the recipient, but the copyright remains with the writer. Outstanding examples include:
ancient Cicero and Pliny the Younger, and St Paul ***medieval*** Héloise and Abelard (12th-century France), the Paston letters (15th-century England) ***16th-century*** Erasmus, Luther, Melanchthon, Spenser, Sidney ***17th century*** Donne, Milton, Cromwell, Dorothy Osborne, Wotton; (France) Pascal, Mme de Sévigné ***18th century*** Pope, Walpole, Swift, Mary Wortley Montagu, Chesterfield, Cowper, Gray (see also Junius◊ and Samuel Richardson◊); (France) Bossuet, Voltaire, Rousseau ***19th century*** Byron, Lamb, Keats, Fitzgerald, Stevenson; (USA) Emerson, J R

Lowell; (France) George Sand, Sainte Beuve, Goncourt brothers; (Germany) Schiller, Goethe; (Switzerland) Gottfried Keller ***20th century*** T E Lawrence, G B Shaw and Ellen Terry, Katherine Mansfield; (Germany) Rilke□

lettres de cachet under the French monarchy letters closed by the king's 'seal' (*cachet*), used particularly to banish or imprison without trial opponents of the regime□

lettuce annual salad plant *Lactuca sativa* family Compositae◊, grown in Britain since the 16th century. Types include ***cabbage lettuce*** with round loose heads; ***cos*** with crisp upright leaves; ***iceberg*** round and crunchy□

leucite crystalline mineral often occurring in recent volcanic rocks. Silicate of potassium and aluminium, it can be a useful source of potassium□

leucocyte white blood cells, present in the proportion of 1 to 500 red. They fight infection by devouring invading bacteria, etc., and are of various kinds. See lymphocyte◊□

leukaemia form of cancer of the blood, marked by an increase in the white blood cells. Cure or control is by radiotherapy or drugs, especially successful in younger patients. See under periwinkle◊□

Levant the E Mediterranean region, or more specifically, the coastal regions of Turkey-in-Asia, Syria, Lebanon, and Israel□

Le Vau Louis 1612–70. French architect, who drafted the plan of Versailles, and built the Louvre and Tuileries□

Levellers mid-17th-century political movement (led by John Lilburne◊) widely supported 1647–9 by soldiers of Cromwell's army, yeoman farmers, artisans, and tradesmen. Their aims included establishment of a republic ruled by a unicameral parliament elected by manhood suffrage, religious toleration, and sweeping social reform. Mutinies by the army members were crushed by Cromwell in 1649□

Leven Alexander Leslie, 1st Earl of Leven c1580–1661. Scottish general who led the Covenanters'◊ army which invaded England in 1640, and the Scottish army sent to aid the English Puritans 1643–6, and shared in the victory of Marston Moor. Created Earl of Leven in 1641□

Leven Loch lake in Tayside region, Scotland; area 16 sq km/6 sq m. Drained by the River Leven, it has seven islands; Mary Queen of Scots was imprisoned 1567–8 on Castle Island□

Lever Charles James 1806–72. Irish novelist, whose rollicking tales of country and army life, e.g. *Harry Lorrequer* 1837, *Charles O'Malley* 1840, and *Tom Burke of Ours* 1844, were widely popular□

Leverkusen industrial port (chemicals) Rhine river in North Rhine-Westphalia, W Germany; population 159 500□

Leverrier Urbain Jean Joseph 1811–77. French astronomer, who predicted the existence and position of Neptune◊□

Lévesque René 1922– . Premier of Quebec 1976–85, founder of the Parti Québecois in 1968. It aimed at an independent Quebec (rejected in a referendum in 1980), and he resigned the party leadership in 1985□

leviathan in Old Testament, a mythical evil sea monster identified by later commentators with the whale□

Levin (Henry) Bernard 1928– . British journalist and broadcaster, noted for the witty elegance of his 'essays'□

Lévi-Strauss Claude 1908– . French anthropologist, who seeks the universal 'structure' governing man's social life, and myth-making, e.g. *The Savage Mind* 1966□

levitation counteraction of gravitational forces on a body. As claimed by medieval mystics, and spiritualist mediums, it is unproven. In the laboratory it can be produced scientifically, e.g. electrostatic force and acoustical waves have been used to suspend water drops, etc., for microscopic study. It is also used in technology, e.g. in magnetic levitation as in 'maglev' trains (parts of the train and the track are made like the poles of a magnet, so that the carriage is suspended slightly above the track surface)□

Levites one of the 12 peoples of Israel. Descended from Levi, a son of Jacob◊, they performed the lesser services of the Temple; the priesthood was confined to the descendants of Aaron◊□

Lewes market town (administrative headquarters) in E Sussex, England; population 81 400. Barbican House near the Castle is a museum. See also Glyndebourne◊. Simon de Montfort◊ defeated Henry III here in 1264; there is a house once belonging to Anne of Cleves; and Evelyn, the diarist, spent his boyhood at Southover. The town is famous for its 5th Nov celebrations□

Lewes George Henry 1817–78. British philosopher and critic. He left his wife in 1854 to form a lifelong union with George Eliot◊□

Lewis see Hebrides◊□

Lewis Cecil Day. See Day◊ Lewis□

Lewis C(live) S(taples) 1898–1963. British professor of medieval and Renaissance English at Cambridge 1954–63. His books include the medieval study *The Allegory of Love* 1936, *Out of the Silent Planet* (science fiction) 1938, *The Screwtape Letters* (popular theology) 1942, and children's stories□

Lewis (Harry) Sinclair 1885–1951. American novelist, born in Minnesota, who made his reputation with *Main Street* 1920, and in *Babbitt* 1922 gave a word to the American language (the hero was a conventional midwest business executive). Nobel prize in 1930□

Lewis Matthew Gregory 1775–1818. British writer known as 'Monk' Lewis from his popular terror romance *The Monk* 1795□

Lewis Meriwether 1774–1809. American explorer who, with ***William Clark*** 1770–1838, was commissioned by Jefferson◊ to find a land route to the Pacific. His route of 1804–6 was: via the Missouri river, across the Rockies, and down the Columbia river. He returned overland (via Yellowstone river) to St Louis, and was made governor of Louisiana Territory□

Lewis (Percy) Wyndham 1884–1957. British writer and artist, founder of Vorticism◊ (so christened by his friend Ezra Pound◊, with whom he founded the magazine *Blast* in 1914). His books include the novels *Tarr* 1918 and *The Childermass* 1928, and theoretical books, e.g. *Time and Western Man* 1927, which foreshadowed his link with Fascist ideas. His prose and painting style was stylized, hard, and aggressive, e.g. his portraits of Edith Sitwell and T S Eliot□

Lewisham borough of SE Greater London
features at Deptford shipbuilding yard (1512–1869), Drake was knighted and Peter the Great worked here; Crystal◊ Palace (re-erected at Sydenham in 1854) site now partly occupied by the National Sports Centre; James Elroy Flecker◊ born here
population 235 200□

Lexington town in Massachusetts, USA; population 32 000. There are printing and publishing industries. The ***Battle of Lexington and Concord*** (1775) opened the American◊ War of Independence. See also Paul Revere◊□

Lexington-Fayette town in Kentucky, USA; population 204 165. Centre of the Bluegrass Country, where horses are bred, shown, and raced. It is also a tobacco market□

Leyland industrial town (paint, vehicles, etc.) in Lancashire, England. The Rover Group (previously British Leyland) largest of British firms producing cars, buses, and lorries, has its headquarters here□

Leyte island in the E Philippines; in the ***Battle of Leyte Gulf*** 22–27 Oct 1944 the American fleet returned to the Philippines to initiate the reconquest of the area, and defeated the Japanese in the world's largest naval battle□

Lhasa (the 'Forbidden City') capital of the autonomous region of Tibet, China; population 80 000. Visitors need a fortnight to acclimatize to the altitude 5000 m/16 400 ft. Potala, former home of the Dalai◊ Lama and now a museum, has 200 000 statues, 1000 rooms, and 10 000 chapels□

Lhote Henri. See under Sahara◊□

Liao river in NE China, frozen Dec–Mar; length 1450 km/900 mi□

Liaoning province of NE China
area 230 000 sq km/88 780 sq mi
capital Shenyang
towns Anshan
features it was developed by the Japanese 1905–45, including the ***Liaodong Peninsula*** whose ports had been conquered from the Russians (see Lüda◊), and the province is one of China's most heavily industrialized areas
products cereals; coal and iron
population 34 426 000. See Manchuria◊□

Liaoyang industrial city (engineering, textiles) in Liaoning province; population 175 000□

Libau see Liepaja◊□

Libby Willard Frank 1908–80. American chemist, who originated radiocarbon◊ dating in 1947; Nobel prize in 1960□

libel defamation in permanent form, e.g. newspaper, book, or broadcast. In civil proceedings truth is usually a valid defence; in criminal libel (where the statement is so extreme as to tend to provoke the libelled person to a breach of the peace in retaliation), the statement needs also to be in the public interest. The latter became obsolete, but in the 1980s it was proposed to introduce a new offence of criminal libel to deal with 'character assassination' – the making of a statement which the maker knew and believed to be untrue, the prosecution having to prove both the untruth and the maker's knowledge and belief that it was a lie. See slander◊. Certain statements, e.g. in the courts or parliament, are 'privileged' and not counted as libellous□

Liberalism political opinions favouring changes and reforms in the direction of democracy, which developed in the 17–19th centuries during the struggle against royal, ecclesiastical, and feudal landowning power. It was equated with parliamentary government, freedom of the press, speech, and worship, and the abolition of class privileges; and, economically, with laissez-faire◊ and international free trade. It was later modified by the acceptance of universal suffrage, and a degree of state intervention to remove extremes of poverty and wealth. J S Mill◊ is the classic exponent of the Liberal principle□

Liberal Party one of Britain's two historic parties, successor to the Whig Party◊, it first achieved power 1830–41, passing the 1832 Reform Bill, abolition of slavery, etc., and was again almost continuously in power 1846–66. Under Gladstone◊ it renewed its dominance until the split over Home Rule in 1886, when many members joined the Conservatives, but in 1906 the party achieved a landslide. Another split came with Lloyd◊ George's alliance with the Conservatives 1916–22 in opposition to Asquith◊, and the party went into steady decline, reduced to a handful of MPs after World War II. Jo Grimond◊, Jeremy Thorpe◊, and David Steel◊ attempted revival, and in the 1983 general election, joined with the Social◊ Democratic Party as the ***Liberal/SDP Alliance*** and achieved 25% of the vote, but only 4% of seats: proportional representation is advocated by the Liberal Party□

Liberal Party Australian. Established in 1944 by Menzies◊ following a Labour landslide, it derived from the former United Australia Party; leader from 1983, Andrew Peacock◊□

liberation theology western intellectual theory of Christ's primary importance as the 'Liberator', himself personifying the poor and devoted to freeing them from oppression (Matthew xix 21, xxv 35, 40). Enthusiastically adopted in S America, it embodies a Marxist interpretation of the class struggle, and inevitably results in violence. One of its leaders is Leonardo Boff 1939– , a Brazilian Franciscan priest. Pope John◊ Paul II warned against involvement of priests in political activity, e.g. the holding of government posts in Nicaragua, explicitly condemned in 1984, though also warning the rich against the inevitable consequences of their position□

Liberia Republic of
area 112 820 sq km/43 548 sq mi
capital Monrovia
features nominally the world's largest merchant navy because minimal controls make Liberia's a 'flag of convenience'
exports iron ore, rubber, diamonds; coffee, cocoa, palm oil
currency Liberian dollar
population 2 180 000, 95% belonging to the indigenous peoples
language English, official
religion Moslem 20%, Christian 15%, traditional 65%

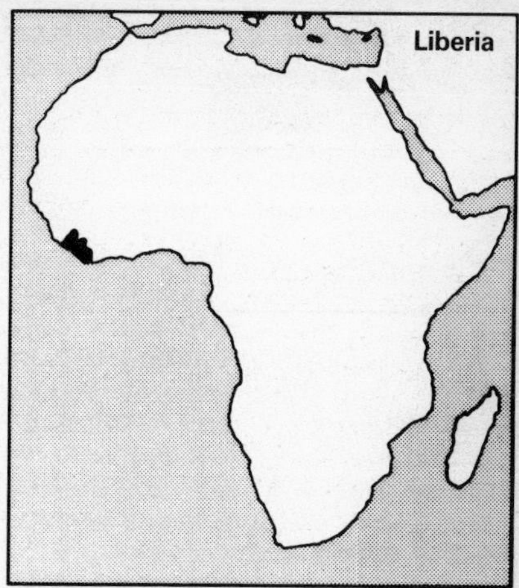

government military head of state (Samuel K Doe from 1980), pending return to civilian rule under the 1984 constitution (executive president, senate, and house of representatives) by elections in Oct 1985. These elections were won by Samuel Doe, though opposition critics claim this was fraudulently done;
recent history founded in 1822 for freed American slaves, it achieved statehood against bitter indigenous opposition in 1847. Its economy was developed largely under US control. William V S Tubman 1895–1971, president from 1944, tried to unite the country (indigenous peoples at last received the vote in 1944), but there were frequent attempts on his life, and his successor, William Tolbert, was assassinated in 1980 in a coup by Master Sergeant Doe, who became head of state and Commander-in-Chief of the army□

liberty, equality, fraternity motto of the French republic from 1793; changed 1940–44 under the Vichy regime to 'work, family, fatherland'□

Li Bo 705–62. Most famous of Chinese poets (formerly Li Po). A romantic, he sang of wine and women, and is said to have drowned when he tried to embrace the moon from a boat□

Libreville capital of Gabon; population 251 400□

Libya (Socialist People's Libyan Arab *Jamahiriyah* – or 'state of the masses')
area 1 780 000 sq km/680 000 sq mi
capital Tripoli
towns the ports of Benghazi and Misurata
features Gulf of Sirte◊, Libyan Desert; rock paintings of c3000BC in the Fezzan; Roman city sites of Leptis Magna◊, Sabratha, etc.; the plan to pump water from below the

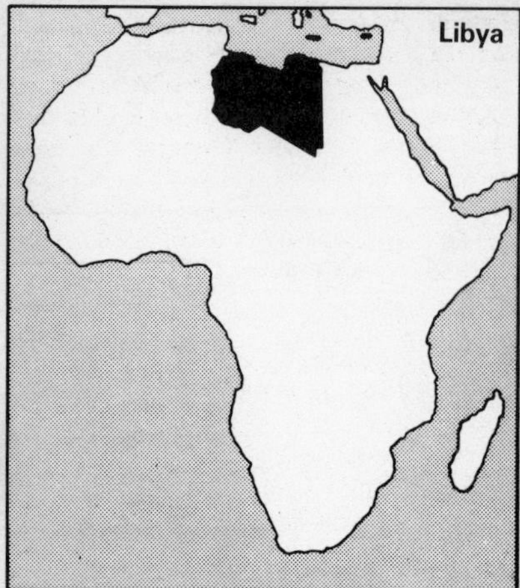

Sahara to the coast risks rapid exhaustion of a largely non-renewable supply
exports oil, natural gas
currency Libyan dinar
population 3 500 000, including 500 000 foreign workers
language Arabic
religion Sunni Islam
government local People's Congresses send officials to a General People's Congress (1000 members), which meets bi-annually for a week; this appoints the General People's Committee, of which the Secretary is prime minister, but Kadhafi◊, the 'leader of the Revolution' is effective ruler.
recent history an Italian colony 1911–43, Libya became the first independent state created by the United Nations in 1951, and a republic from 1969 following an army officer revolt (including Kadhafi). It is noted for its revolutionary expansionism (see Chad◊), opposition to Israel, support for terrorist bodies including the IRA◊, and executionary zeal in pursuing refugees from the regime abroad, e.g. the incident in which a London policewoman was shot in 1984. In 1982 a Libyan National Salvation Front was formed in Sudan (there are c100 000 Libyan exiles). There are 'boundary' disputes with Malta and Tunisia in the Mediterranean. In 1984 Libya and Morocco concluded a treaty of union, to be presided over jointly by the King of Morocco and President of Libya, and Libya and France both agreed to withdraw troops from Chad. In Apr 1986, US bombers from British bases attacked Tripoli and Benghazi, as retaliation for a terrorist attack in Berlin in which two people were killed, and for which the US claimed Libya was responsible□

lice parasitic wingless insects, with flat segmented bodies, divided into:
bloodsucking lice order Anoplura, including those occurring on man, e.g. ***head louse*** *Pediculis capitis* whose white eggs, 'nits', are laid on hair or body; the insect, white when hatched, changes colour to match the hair (they prefer clean hair, but are injured and may be eradicated by frequent combing); and ***body louse*** *P corporis* the carrier of typhus◊.
biting lice order Mallophaga, which infest many mammals and birds, and feed on skin, hair, and feathers□

lice plant. A type of aphid. See under hemiptera◊□

lichen class of plants, Lichenes, of dual composition consisting of a fungus which lives symbiotically with one or more algae. The fungus obtains the products of photosynthesis, or nitrogen fixation, from the alga, and the latter obtains water, mineral salts, and perhaps some protein from the fungus. Lichens can withstand considerable drought, becoming pliable again when damp, e.g. ***orange wall lichen*** *Xanthoria parietina.* Some have food value, e.g. ***reindeer moss*** *Cladonia rangiferina* and ***Iceland moss*** *Cetraria islandica;* others are used for dyes, such as litmus◊, or in medicine. The oldest living thing may be a lichen growing within the rocks of Antarctica, which is estimated at 10 000 years old□

Lichfield city in Staffordshire, England; population 30 000. The cathedral, 13–14th century, has three spires. Dr Johnson was born here□

Lichfield Patrick Anson, 5th Earl of Lichfield 1939– . British photographer, especially portraits□

Lichtenstein Roy 1923– . American Pop artist, noted for his use of the comic strip in 1962, and other commercial techniques□

Liddell Hart Sir Basil 1895–1970. British military correspondent, whose exposition of mechanized warfare led to the German creation of the First Panzer Division (combining motorized infantry and tanks). He was adviser to the War Office on British army reorganization in 1937□

Lidice Czech mining village, replacing one destroyed by the Nazis on 10 Jun 1942 as a reprisal for the assassination of Heydrich◊. The men were shot, the women sent to concentration camps, and the children taken to Germany. The Sudeten German responsible was hanged at Prague in 1946□

Lie Trygve Halvdan 1896–1968. Norwegian statesman, first Secretary-General of the UN◊ 1946–53. He resigned following Soviet opposition to his handling of the Korean War□

Liebig Justus, Baron von Liebig 1803–73. German chemist, a major contributor to agricultural chemistry. He introduced the theory of radicals, and was the discoverer of chloroform and chloral□

Liebknecht Karl 1871–1919. German Socialist, son of Wilhelm Liebknecht. A founder of the German Communist Party, originally known as the Spartacus League, he led an unsuccessful revolt in Berlin in 1919, and was murdered by army officers□

Liebknecht Wilhelm 1826–1900. German Socialist. A friend of Marx◊, with whom he took part in the Revolution of 1848, he was imprisoned for opposition to the Franco-Prussian War. See Karl Liebknecht◊□

Liechtenstein Principality of

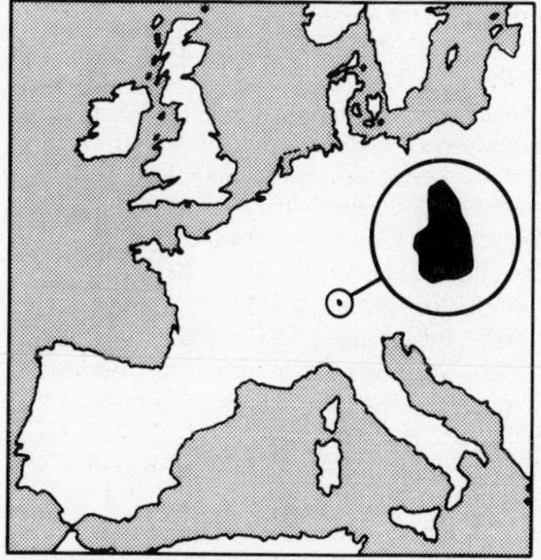

area 160 sq km/62 sq mi
capital Vaduz
features only country in the world to take its name from its reigning family; most highly industrialized country in Europe
exports microchips, precision engineering, processed foods, postage stamps; easy tax laws make it an international haven for foreign companies and banks
currency Swiss franc
population 27 000, 33% foreign
language German
religion Roman Catholicism
government constitutional monarchy (from 1984, Prince Hans Adam 1945–), which can call and dismiss parliament, and appoints the prime minister on the advice of the unicameral parliament of 15 members. Women achieved the vote only in 1984.
recent history originating in 1342, Liechtenstein was confirmed in its present boundaries in 1719 by the Austro-Hungarian monarchy, with which it broke in 1919□

lie detector see polygraph◊□

Liège (Flemish *Luik*) industrial city (specialized military weapons, textiles, paper, chemicals) and river port on the Meuse in E Belgium; population 207 500. St Martin's church dates from 692. Georges Simenon◊ was born here□

Liepaja (German *Libau)* naval and industrial port (steel, engineering, textiles, chemicals) in the Republic of Latvia, USSR; population 109 000.

Lifar Serge 1905– . Russian dancer, who joined the Diaghilev company 1923, and as choreographer at the Paris Opéra 1929–69 developed the importance of the male dancer, e.g. *Romeo et Juliette* (Prokofiev) 1955□

life classification the classification of all living things. See classification◊, animal◊ classification, plant◊ classification◊□

life criteria of. Ability 1 to respond to external stimuli, 2 to grow, 3 to reproduce. These are not absolute, since crystals (non-living) may form more organized structures and reproduce, while viruses (living) cannot themselves reproduce, but rely on their hosts to do it for them□

life extra-terrestrial. It is most likely to exist on other planets, where it could have a different base (e.g. silicon◊) from that of earth, where it is carbon◊-based. Speculation favours:
solar system possible locations are Mars, Jupiter, Titan◊.
Milky Way of the 100 billion suns, it has been estimated that hundreds of millions may have planets, a proportion of which should be able to support life.
Programmes to search for signals transmitted by space aliens include that at the NASA-Ames Research Centre, California (to monitor a huge range of frequencies from 1988); Harvard University's Oak Ridge Observatory, Tennessee (concentrating on simultaneous monitoring of 8 400 000 radio channels in the 1420 MHz frequency emitted by the hydrogen clouds of the Milky Way); and others, at Ohio State University, Jodrell Bank, and in the USSR. One of the greatest problems is the man-made signals which block out signals from space□

life origin of. It is thought to have originated on earth about 4 000 000 000 years ago. One theory supposes that the atmosphere then was probably carbon dioxide, nitrogen, and water. The passage of electric sparks or ultra-violet radiation through flasks of this mixture ('primordial soup') today results in the creation of amino acids, which are the 'building blocks' of life. More complex molecules could then develop. An alternative theory suggests that clay and other minerals, by storing the sun's energy and then slowly releasing it, provided the means by which complex proteins were formed from amino acids. Yet another theory (see Fred Hoyle◊) is that the molecules which acted as the seeds of life on earth originated in space.

The earliest fossil evidence of life is of advanced thread-like chains of cells discovered in 1980 in the north of W Australia which date back 3 500 000 000 years□

lifeboat small landbased vessel specially built for saving life at sea, or a boat carried aboard a larger ship in case of shipwreck. In Britain the Royal National Lifeboat Institution (RNLI), founded in 1824 at the instance of Sir William Hillary, provides a voluntarily manned and supported service. The US Coast Guard is part of the government service. A modern RNLI boat is c16 m/52 ft long and self-righting, so that it is virtually unsinkable. Inflatables are used for inshore work, and helicopters play an increasing role□

life insurance an insurance policy that matures on the death of the holder. See insurance and saving◊□

Liffey river in E Ireland, flowing from the Wicklow mountains to Dublin Bay; length 80 km/50 mi□

ligament short bands of tough fibrous tissue connecting two bones at a joint, enclosing a joint, supporting one of the body's organs, etc.□

ligature 'thread' (nylon, gut, wire, etc.) tying a blood vessel, limb, base of a tumour, etc., chiefly to stop the flow through it of blood, or other fluid□

Ligeti György 1923– . Hungarian composer of electronic and other experimental music, including *Requiem Mass* 1965 and the orchestral *Melodien* 1971□

light electromagnetic radiation in the visible range, i.e. from about 770 nanometres in the extreme red to 400 in the extreme violet: see under electromagnetic waves◊. Light is considered to have both wave and particle properties. The fundamental particle or quantum of light is the photon◊. The speed of light in free space is approximately 299 793 km/186 000 mi per second (a universal constant denoted by *c*), and is allegedly the fastest speed in nature, but see Bell◊'s theorem□

light-emitting diode see semi-conductor◊ diode□

lighthouse structure carrying a powerful light to aid marine navigation. The Pharos of Alexandria (c280BC) was one of the Seven Wonders of the World; the earliest in Britain was probably the Pharos at Dover built by the Romans. For easy recognition, lights are usually individually varied, being either flashing (the dark period exceeding the light) or occulting (the dark being less). Horns, sirens, and explosives take over in fog conditions. Many modern lighthouses are remotely controlled. Among famous traditional cylindrical towers is the Eddystone◊, but the light tower which replaced the Royal Sovereign off Eastbourne has a slender pillar surmounted by a helicopter pad with a small corner tower. Trinity House (chartered by Henry VIII in 1514), and the Commissioners for Northern Lighthouses, are the chief British authorities□

lightning a flow of electric charge, accompanied by a visible flash, between two clouds or a cloud and the earth, caused by a difference in potential. In dry weather the atmosphere has a positive potential with respect to the earth, increasing with distance. When the usual balance cannot be maintained, water particles coalesce to form drops, concentrating their charge, which under stress results in a flash of lightning. Lightning 'forks' as it 'looks' for a path of low resistance (such as is provided by a 'conductor' on a tall building, which safely earths the charge). So-called 'sheet' lightning is due only to the effect of intervening cloud and distance. Thunder occurs as the gases in the atmosphere suddenly expand as the lightning heats them, the sound being intensified by echoing.

ball lightning consists of a luminous sphere, apparently less dangerous the larger it is, which may hover inside a room and emit a rattling sound. If it explodes, it burns anything with which it comes in contact. It has been suggested that it is caused by a vortex ring of plasma◊□

light year measure in astronomy: the distance travelled by light in one year, a distance of 9.461×10^{12} km/nearly 6 million million miles□

lignite a type of coal◊□

Liguria region of NW Italy; capital Genoa; population 1 796 380. It includes the Italian Riviera (San Remo), and La Spezia□

lilac genus of Eurasian shrubs *Syringa* with scented clusters of white to purple flowers, family Oleaceae□

Lilburne John c1614–57. English politician, a soldier in the parliamentary army, whose advocacy of a democratic republic brought him leadership of the Levellers◊. He was imprisoned for his activities both under Charles I and Cromwell□

Liliaceae monocotyledonous family of flowering plants, most of which form bulbs or rhizomes, and have bell-shaped flowers at the top of an erect stem. It includes bluebell, lily of the valley, and lilies, as well as onion, leek, and garlic□

Lilienthal Otto 1848–96. German glider pioneer who influenced the Wrights◊ and was killed in a glider crash□

Lilith in Old Testament, Assyrian female demon of the night. According to the Talmud◊ she was the wife of Adam before Eve's creation□

Lille industrial city (textiles, chemicals, engineering, distilling), capital of Nord-Pas-de-Calais◊, France; population of urban area, with Roubaix and Tourcoing, 1 000 000. In the Middle Ages it was the capital of Flanders; there is a fortress built by Vauban, a Pasteur Institute and university (1887); and the world's first entirely automatic underground system was opened in 1982□

Lilongwe capital of Malawi; population 103 750. It has light industries, e.g. tobacco□

lily of the valley woodland plant *Convallaria majalis,* family Liliaceae◊; the flowers form small, white, hanging bells and are very fragrant□

Lima capital of Peru, and industrial city (textiles, chemicals, glass, and cement), with its port at Callao◊; population 4 164 600. Founded by Pizarro◊ in 1535, it was rebuilt after destruction by an earthquake in 1746. Survivals of the colonial period are the university (1551), cathedral (1746), government palace (the rebuilt palace of the viceroys), and the senate house (once the Inquisition)□

Limassol port in Cyprus; population 107 200. Cigarettes are made and wine traded. Richard◊ I married Berengaria of Navarre here in 1191□

limbo (theology) word (Latin 'edge') used by Thomas Aquinas◊ to denote the place, neither Heaven nor Hell, where an inferior blessedness could be enjoyed by unbaptized infants, virtuous heathens, and the prophets and fathers of the Old Testament□

limbo (dance) a West Indian dance in which the performer, his body being bent over backwards, passes under a pole, which is lowered closer to the ground at successive attempts□

Limburg duchy of Lower Lorraine until 1839, which now forms ***Limbourg*** a NE province of Belgium, capital Hasselt and ***Limburg*** a SE province of the Netherlands, capital Maastricht□

lime a type of citrus◊□

lime or genus ***linden*** of northern temperate deciduous trees *Tilia* family Tiliaceae. The ***common lime*** is *T vulgaris* which has greenish yellow fragrant flowers, succeeded by small bobbly fruits, spread by an oval modified leaf or 'wing' on the base of the flower stalk□

lime calcium oxide CaO, commercially made by heating limestone or chalk. A white powdery substance it is used to reduce soil acidity. ***Quicklime*** is calcium oxide which readily absorbs water to become *slaked lime* calcium hydroxide□

Limehouse see Tower◊ Hamlets□

Limerick city and county borough in Limerick, Republic of Ireland, on the Shannon estuary and chief port of W Ireland; population 60 736. It was unsuccessfully besieged by William III in 1691□

Limerick county (county town Limerick◊) of the Republic of Ireland, province of Munster◊. It includes part of the Golden Vale, noted for dairy farms, the Galty mountains, and the River Shannon, noted for salmon fisheries□

limestone sedimentary rock chiefly composed of calcium carbonate, $CaCO_3$, in the form of the calcareous remains of freshwater or marine organisms, e.g. crustacea, mollusca, foraminifera. Corals◊ build up solid masses of limestone. ***Marble*** is limestone which has undergone natural recrystallization at high temperature and pressure. It takes a high polish, and may be either beautifully coloured and patterned, or pure white, e.g. Carrara◊ marble. Purbeck 'marble' has not been recrystallized, but is a clayey limestone rich in the remains of freshwater gastropoda Paludina□

Limitation Statutes of. Acts limiting the time within which a remedy may be sought at law, e.g. in England, for recovery of debt, six years□

Limits Territorial and Fishing. See under Law of the Sea◊□

Limoges industrial city, (textiles, electrical equipment, metal goods) capital of Limousin◊, France; population 147 500. Fine enamels were made here in the medieval period, and it is the centre of the modern French porcelain industry. The city was sacked by the Black◊ Prince in 1370□

Limousin region of W central France; capital Limoges; population 737 150□

limpet a small marine animal. See under gastropod◊□

Limpopo river in SE Africa, rising in the Transvaal and reaching the Indian Ocean in Mozambique; length 1600 km/1000 mi□

Linacre Thomas c1460–1524. English humanist, physician to Henry VIII from 1509, from whom he obtained a charter in 1518 to found the Royal College of Physicians, of which he was first president□

Lin Biao 1908–71. Chinese soldier-politician (formerly Lin Piao), named as Mao's successor in 1969. He allegedly planned a military coup in 1971, to have been supported by Moscow in return for territorial concessions, but fled on its failure. He died when his aircraft crashed, possibly shot down in Russian Mongolia□

Lincoln industrial city (excavators, cranes, gas turbines, power units for oil platforms, cosmetics) in Lincolnshire; population 76 200. It was the flourishing Roman colony of Lindum, and had a big medieval wool trade. Paulinus◊ built a church here, and the 11–15th-century cathedral has the earliest Gothic work in Britain. The 12th-century High Bridge is the oldest in Britain still to have buildings on it□

Lincoln industrial city (engineering, oil refining, food processing) capital of Nebraska, USA; population 172 000□

Lincoln Abraham 1809–65. 16th president of the USA from 1861, born in Kentucky. Self-educated, he became a practising lawyer from 1837 at Springfield◊, Illinois, joined the new Republican Party and was elected in 1860 on a minority vote. His refusal to evacuate Fort Sumter, Charleston◊, precipitated the war, in which his chief concern was the preservation of the Union from which the slave states had seceded. In 1863 he proclaimed the freedom of the slaves in Confederate territory, and made the Gettysburg◊ Address, declaring the war aims of preserving a 'nation conceived in liberty, and dedicated to the proposition that all men are created equal' and ensuring that 'government of the people, by the people, for the people, shall not perish from the earth', Re-elected 1864, he advocated a reconciliatory policy towards the south 'with malice towards none, with charity for all', Five days after Lee'◊s surrender, he was assassinated by a Confederate fanatic, John Wilkes Booth□

Lincolnshire county of eastern England
area 5915 sq km/2283 sq mi
towns administrative headquarters Lincoln; resort Skegness
features Lincoln Wolds; marshy coastline; the Fens in the south east; rivers Witham and Welland; Burghley House (home of Lord Burghley◊, near Stamford); Belton House, a Restoration mansion
products cattle, sheep, horses; cereals; flower bulbs; oil at Nettleham
population 550 900
famous people Sir Isaac Newton, Alfred Tennyson, Margaret Thatcher□

Lind Jenny 1820–87. Swedish singer of remarkable range, the 'Swedish nightingale'□

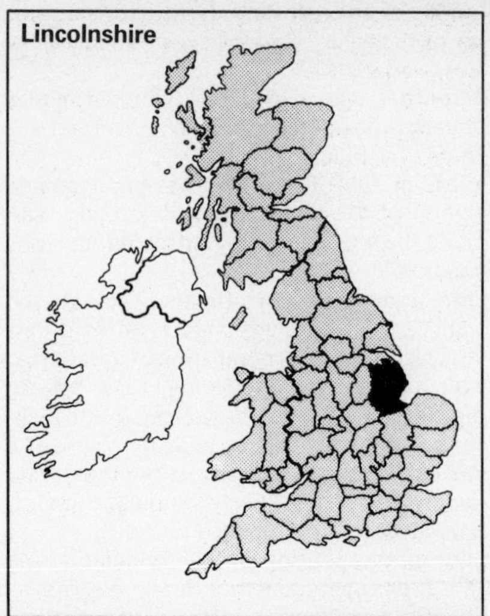

Lindbergh Charles Augustus 1902–74. American aviator who made the first solo non-stop flight across the Atlantic (New York–Paris) in 1927 in *The Spirit of St Louis.* His baby son was kidnapped in 1932, and the kidnapper (B R Hauptmann) was executed for murder in 1936□

linden another name for lime◊□

Lindisfarne see under Holy◊ Island□

Lindsay (Nicholas) Vachel 1879–1931. American poet, born at Springfield. He wandered the country, living by reciting his ballad-like verse, *General William Booth enters into Heaven* 1913, *Johnny Appleseed* 1928, etc.□

linear accelerator machine in which charged particles are accelerated to high speed (by electric fields or electro-magnetic waves) in a straight evacuated tube or waveguide□

Line Islands see Gilbert◊ Islands□

linen yarn obtain from flax◊ which has twice the strength of cotton, and is of superior delicacy, for lace, etc.□

ling a fish of the cod◊ family□

lingam in Hinduism, phallic emblem of Siva◊, the *yoni* being the female equivalent□

lingua franca simplified hybrid language used for trading, etc., between peoples of different languages. Originally the hybrid Italian used in the E Mediterranean from the Renaissance onward, See also Pidgin◊, Swahili◊□

linguistics scientific study of language from its origins (see Chomsky◊), to the changing way it is pronounced (phonetics), derivation of words through various languages (etymology), development of meanings (semantics), and the arrangement and modifications of words to convey a message (grammar)□

Linköping industrial town (engineering) in S Sweden; population 113 400□

Linlithgow tourist centre in Lothian region, Scotland; population 6000. Linlithgow Palace, now in ruins, was once a royal residence, and Mary Queen of Scots was born there□

Linnaeus Carolus. Latinized name of Carl von Linné 1707–78. Swedish botanist. From 1735 he outlined his system for naming plants and animals, based on their structure, according to species, genus, family, class, etc. See taxonomy◊□

linnet a songbird of the finch◊ family□

Lin Piao see Lin◊ Biao□

linseed the seed of flax◊□

Linz industrial port (iron and steel, metal working) on the Danube in N Austria; population 198 000□

lion a type of large cat◊□

Lipari or ***Aeolian Islands*** volcanic group of seven islands off NE Sicily, including Lipari (on which is the capital of the same name), Stromboli (active volcano 926 m/3038 ft high) and Vulcano (also with an active volcano); area 114 sq km/44 sq mi. See Aeolus◊□

Lipchitz Jacques 1891–1973. Lithuanian sculptor, a US citizen from 1941. Outstanding in his Cubist phase is *Femme assise* 1916. He excelled in bronze□

lipid group of organic compounds soluble in alcohol, but not in water. They include oils◊, fats◊, and wax◊□

Li Po see Li◊ Bo□

Lippe river of N West Germany flowing into the Rhine; also a former German state, now part of N Rhine-Westphalia□

Lippershey Hans d. c1619. Dutch spectacle-maker who invented the first telescope◊□

Lippi two Italian Renaissance artists:

Fra Filippo 1406–69 born at Florence and patronized by the Medici. His works include frescoes at Prato 1452–64, and *The Vision of St Bernard*, National Gallery, London.

Filippino 1457–1504 son of Filippo, who studied with Botticelli◊. He produced frescoes and altarpieces□

Lippizaner a breed of grey horses◊□

Lippmann Gabriel. See under photography◊□

lipreading a way of interpreting a speaker's words by watching the movement of the lips. See under deafness◊□

liqueur strongly flavoured sweetened spirits drunk after a meal, e.g. advocaat (of Dutch origin, containing brandy, egg yolk, and vanilla); curaçao◊ and cointreau (orange-flavoured); kirsch and maraschino (made from cherries)□

liquid crystal display (LCD) display of numbers (in a calculator) or picture (on pocket TV screen) produced by molecules of an organic substance in a semi-liquid state. The display is a blank until the application of an electric field which 'twists' the molecules so that they reflect or transmit light falling on them (rather than emitting their own). Thus LCD's power-consumption is comparatively minute. See semi-conductor◊ diode□

liquorice perennial European herb *Glycyrrhiza glabra,* family Leguminosae◊; the long sweet root yields an extract made into a hard black paste, used in confectionery, etc.□

lira standard Italian currency unit□

Lisbon (Portuguese *Lisboa)* capital of Portugual from 1260, with steel, textiles, chemicals, pottery, shipbuilding, etc.; population 812 835. The Castelo de São Jorge was taken from the Moors by Alfonso I in 1147, and the city reached its peak of prosperity in the period of Portugal's overseas empire in the 16th century. In 1755 it was almost completely destroyed by an earthquake. It lies on the tidal lake and estuary formed by the Tagus◊, is linked by bridge with Almada, and has a major fishing industry; wine, oil, and cork are exported. To the north east is the seaside resort of ***Estoril*** favoured by exiled royalty. Vasco da Gama◊ and Camões◊ are buried here, and Henry Fielding◊ lies in the English cemetery. Near the town of ***Torres Vedras*** to the north, Wellington built his defensive position 1809–10 during the Peninsular◊ War□

Lisburn market town in Antrim, N Ireland, famous for linen; population 30 000□

Lisieux town in NW France, with a shrine to Ste Thérèse◊; population 26 700□

Lister Joseph, 1st Baron Lister 1827–1912. British surgeon, who introduced antiseptic surgery and the prevention of infection by the utmost cleanliness in the operating-room. Created a peer in 1897; Order of Merit in 1902□

Liszt Franz 1811–86. Hungarian composer, also probably the greatest virtuoso pianist ever known: he first appeared in concert at the age of nine. By the Comtesse d'Agoult 1805–76, his mistress 1835–40, he was the father of Cosima (the wife of Wagner◊). Musical director at the court of Weimar 1849–59, he lived there with Princess Caroline Sayn-Wittgenstein, and rallied support for the music of Berlioz and Wagner. Retiring to Rome in 1861, probably to escape being pressured into marriage, he became a secular priest of the Franciscan order (hence his adoption of the title Abbé), but continued to teach, give concert tours, and indulge in several love-affairs. He died at Bayreuth. His lyrical, but technically difficult, piano works, include the popular *Liebesträume* and *Hungarian Rhapsodies,* based on gypsy music, and the Sonata in B Minor. He also composed the *Faust* and *Dante* symphonies; masses and oratorios□

litchi or ***lychee*** white fruit (enclosed in a red and green scaly skin) of the Chinese tree *Litchi chinensis,* family Sapindaceae□

literary criticism application of analytical criteria to help the appreciation of literature. Critics have included: ***classical*** Aristotle, Longinus, Horace, Quintilian; ***medieval and Renaissance*** Dante, Boccaccio, du Bellay, Sidney; ***neo-classic*** Boileau, Rapin; Pope, Addison, Johnson; la Harpe, Marmontel, and Voltaire; ***Romantic*** Diderot, Lessing, Wordsworth, Coleridge, Shelley, Hazlitt, Lamb, de Quincey; ***scientific*** Sainte-Beuve, Brunetière, Taine; ***late-Victorian*** Carlyle, Arnold, Pater; Poe, Lowell; Tolstoy; Georg Brandes, Benedetto Croce; ***20th century*** A C Bradley, Saintsbury, C S Lewis, T S Eliot, I A Richards, William Empson, F R Leavis, Edmund Wilson, Cleanth Brooks, Lionel Trilling□

lithium element
symbol Li
atomic number 3
physical description a soft silvery-white metal
features it tarnishes rapidly in air unless kept under a hydrocarbon oil; though widely distributed, it is never found free in nature
uses in alloys, in making hydrogen bombs (in the production of tritium), and lithium compounds are used in the treatment of depression□

lithography graphic reproduction by a process originated by Aloys Senefelder◊, in which a drawing is made with greasy ink on an absorbent stone, which is then washed with water. The water then repels any ink applied to the surface, and the grease attracts it, so that the drawing can be printed, and each print is an 'artist's original'. Modern lithographic printing used in book production, etc., has developed this basic principle into complex processes□

Lithuania constituent republic of the western Soviet Union from 1940
area 65 200 sq km/25 300 sq mi
capital Vilnius
towns Kaunas, Klaipeda
features River Niemen; 25% forested; lakes, marshes, and complex sandy coastline
products bacon, dairy products; cereals, potatoes; heavy engineering and electrical goods, cement, etc.
population 3 400 000, 80% Lithuanian
language Lithuanian, an Indo-European tongue which has retained many ancient features, and is related to Latvian; it is written in a Latin not Cyrillic◊ alphabet
religion only Soviet republic which is predominantly Roman Catholic
famous people Jacques Lipchitz
recent history formerly part of the Russian Empire, Lithuania became an independent republic in 1918, recognized by the Soviet Union in 1920. In 1939 the USSR demanded military bases and in 1940 incorporated it as a constituent republic. As in the other Baltic republics, there has been nationalist dissent since 1980, influenced by the Polish example, and prompted by the influx of Russian workers and officials□

litmus dye obtained from lichens, and used as an indicator to test the acidic or alkaline nature of aqueous solutions; it turns red in the presence of acid, and blue with alkali□

Little Bighorn see under Plains◊ Indians□

Littlehampton seaside resort in W Sussex, England; population 20 000□

Little Rock industrial city and capital of Arkansas, USA; population 153 500. Racial integration of the schools caused riots here in 1957. In 1981–2 (in the Scropes II trial: see Dayton◊), a federal judge ruled that a law requiring schools to teach 'Creation Science'◊ as well as evolution was merely an introduction of 'the Biblical version of creation into the public school curricula', and hence a violation of the constitutional separation of Church and State□

Littlewood Joan 1914– . British theatrical director, noted for productions at the Theatre Royal, Stratford (London), e.g. *A Taste of Honey* 1959, *The Hostage* 1959–60, and *Oh What a Lovely War!* 1963□

Liu Shaoqi 1898–1974. Chinese statesman (formerly Liu Shao-chi), president of the republic in 1959 and nominated as Mao's successor, until his opposition to 'continuous revolution' as economically disruptive led to his death in prison□

liver largest human gland (c2 kg/4 lb), in the upper right abdomen, which makes plasma proteins, stores glucose as glycogen, supplies bile (which acts as an emulsifying agent in breaking down fat into minute droplets to aid its digestion), disposes of excess amino acids which are broken down into urea and passed into the gut, etc.□

Livermore Valley see under California◊□

Liverpool city and seaport (a freeport◊), administrative headquarters of Merseyside, England; population 503 700. Developing under Charles II as American and W Indian trade grew, it was the chief centre of the slave trade. In the 19th and early 20th century, it exported the textiles of Lancashire and Yorkshire, and is still Europe's chief Atlantic port with miles of specialized, mechanized quays on the Mersey. The Maritime Museum is devoted to this aspect of its history. However, such traditional industries as ship-repairing and engineering have declined. There are industrial estates at Aintree, Kirkby and Speke, and there is also an airport at Speke. The Mersey Tunnel (1934) links Liverpool and Birkenhead, and a tunnel to Wallasey was opened in 1971. Outstanding are the classical St George's Hall (1854), the university, the Dock Offices, Liver Building and Cunard Building on Pier Head, Walker Art Gallery (1877); and a 'Tate in the North', a modern art gallery in restored dockland buildings, was planned in 1985. The Anglican Cathedral (1904–79), by Sir Giles Gilbert Scott◊, is the largest church in England; the Roman Catholic Metropolitan Cathedral of Christ the King, 1967, is by Gibberd, with glass panels by John Piper◊. The International Garden Festival Hall of 1984, was adapted as a sports complex. The Beatles◊ were born here, and appeared at the Cavern Club, recreated in a leisure complex, and a Beatles Museum was opened in 1984□

Liverpool Robert Banks Jenkinson, 2nd Earl of Liverpool 1770–1828. British Tory statesman. He was Foreign Secretary 1801–3, Home Secretary 1804–6 and 1807–9, War Minister 1809–12, and Prime Minister 1812–27. He brought the Napoleonic Wars to a successful conclusion, but repressed freedom of speech and the press to the point of revolt□

liverworts worldwide class of plants, Hepaticae, belonging to the Bryophyta◊, resembling mosses, and growing in moist freshwater sites□

livery companies the guilds◊ of the City of London. Their role is now social, many administering valuable charities, especially educational□

Livia Drusilla 58BC–29AD. Wife of Augustus◊ from 39BC, she was the mother by her first husband of Tiberius◊, and intrigued to secure his succession to the imperial crown. To the end of her life, she was politically influential□

Livingston 'new' town (electronics, forged products, etc.) in W Lothian, Scotland; population 38 700□

Livingstone town in Zambia; population 72 000. Founded in 1905, it was named after the explorer, and was capital of N Rhodesia 1907–35 There is a Rhodes-Livingstone Museum, and Victoria Falls is nearby□

Livingstone David 1813–73. Scottish missionary explorer. Born in Blantyre, Strathclyde, he took his medical degree at Glasgow University in 1840, and in 1844 went out to Africa. He reached Lake Ngami (1849); followed the Zambezi to its mouth and saw the Victoria Falls (1855); went to E and Central Africa 1858–64, reaching Lakes Shirwa and Malawi; and from 1866 disappeared to try to trace the source of the Nile, reaching Ujiji in Oct 1871, where Stanley◊ caught up with him. He died in Old Chitambo, Zambia, but was buried in Westminster Abbey□

Livorno (English Leghorn) industrial port (distilling, motor vehicles, etc.) in W Italy; population 175 370. A fortress town since the 12th century, it was developed by the Medici◊, has a naval academy, and is also a resort□

Livy (*Titus Livius*) 59BC–17AD. Latin historian, author of a *History of Rome* in 142 books. Skilled in narrative, he had a weakness for legend□

lizard reptile of the suborder Sauria in the order Squamata (which also includes the snakes◊). Like the snakes, lizards have horny scales on the body which are frequently sloughed. They have short legs enabling rapid movement and possess movable eyelids. Some store food in their tails, and may – as with geckos – 'amputate' their tails to distract a pursuer, and grow a new one. They mostly lay tough eggs, from which the young release themselves with a special egg tooth. They include:

true lizards family Lacertidae, including the ***common lizard*** *Lacerta vivipara* and ***sand lizard*** *L agilis*, both found in Britain.

skink family Scincidae, of tropical Africa and Asia, which have reduced limbs, and a smooth-scaled, lengthened body.

gecko family Gekkonidae, agile insect-hunting creatures, widely distributed, and with adhesive pads on their feet to aid in climbing; their eggs harden when laid and become fragile like those of birds.

monitor family Varanidae, of which the East Indian ***komodo dragon*** *Varanus komodensis* is the largest lizard species at 3 m/9 ft, and kills small mammals; Australia has many species including the ***lace monitor*** *V varius*, with a lace-patterned skin.

gila monster *Heloderma suspectum*. family Helodermatidae, of south-west USA and Mexico, belonging to the only poisonous genus – it has poison glands in the lower jaw,

but the bite is not usually fatal to man.
legless lizards including the ***slow-*** or ***blindworm*** *Anguis fragilis,* family Varanidae, found in Britain, which has no external limbs; and the widespread so-called ***glass snake*** *Ophisaurus* which makes its escape by letting its tail break in pieces like glass.
iguana New World family Iguanidae, of which the ***common iguana*** *Iguana iguana* is used as food.
agama Old World equivalent of the iguana, family Agamidae. Striking species include the ***Australian frilled lizard*** *Chlamydosaurus kingi*, which has an erectile collar to frighten its enemies, and ***thorny devil*** or ***moloch*** whose thorny spines give it a horrific appearance (see Moloch◊). The ***flying lizards*** genus *Draco* of SE Asia, up to 40 cm/16 in long, have folds of skin along their sides, supported by their extended ribs, which allow them to glide – many are brightly coloured.
chameleon African family Chamaeleontidae, of which the commonest is *Chamaelon chamaelon* 30 cm/l ft long; it has a prehensile tail, opposable 'fingers', eyes that rotate independently, and a tongue capable of extending 1.5 times its body length to capture insects with its sticky tip. As a defence measure it varies its colour to match its background□

Lizard Point most southerly point of England in Cornwall□

Ljubljana (German *Laibach*) capital and industrial city (textiles, chemicals, paper, leather goods) of Slovenia, Yugoslavia; population 305 220. It still has a medieval castle, but nuclear research is carried on, and it is a modern communications centre linked with S Austria by the Karawanken road tunnel under the Alps (1979–83)□

llama an animal of the camel family◊□

Llanberis see under Gwynedd◊□

Llandaff see under Cardiff◊□

Llandrindod Wells spa in Powys, Wales, administrative headquarters of the county; population 3500□

Llandudno resort and touring centre for N Wales, in Gwynedd; population 18 000. Great Orme's Head is a spectacular limestone headland□

Llanelli industrial port (formerly Llanelly) in Dyfed, Wales, with tinplate and copper smelting industries; population 26 000□

Llanfair P G village in Anglesey◊, Wales; full name Llanfairpwllgwyngyllgogerychwyrndrobwllllandysilliogogogoch (St Mary's church in the hollow of the white hazel near to the rapid whirlpool of St Tysillio's church, by the red cave)□

llanos the tropical and sub-tropical grasslands of America□

Llewellyn Richard. Pseudonym of Welsh writer Richard Llewellyn Lloyd 1907–83, most famous for his novel of a young S Wales miner *How Green Was My Valley* 1939□

Llewylyn two kings of Wales:
Llewelyn I d. 1240, king from 1194, who extended his rule to all Wales not in Norman hands.
Llewelyn II c1225–1282, king from 1246, grandson of Llewelyn I, who was compelled by Edward I in 1277 to acknowledge him as overlord and to surrender S Wales. His death, while leading a national uprising, ended Welsh independence□

Llewelyn-Davies Richard, Baron Llewelyn-Davis 1912– . British architect, consultant for the rebuilding of the London Stock Exchange and the new town Milton◊ Keynes; life peer in 1964□

Lleyn Peninsula see under Gwynedd◊□

Llosa Mario Vargas 1937– . Peruvian novelist (*The Time of the Hero* 1962, and *The War of the End of the World* 1981), who attacks both right and left in politics. *Aunt Julie and the Scriptwriter* 1982 is autobiographical□

Lloyd Harold 1893–1971. American film comedian (*Safety Last* 1923), who wore spectacles with thick horn rims□

Lloyd John 15th century. Welsh seaman, known as John Scolvus, 'the skilful', who carried on an illegal trade with Greenland and is claimed to have reached N America, sailing as far south as Maryland, in 1477 (15 years before the voyage of Columbus)□

Lloyd Marie. Stage-name of British music-hall artist Matilda Alice Victoria Wood 1870–1922, whose Cockney songs included 'Oh! Mr Porter'□

Lloyd Selwyn. See Selwyn◊ Lloyd□

Lloyd George David, 1st Earl Lloyd-George 1863–1945. Welsh Liberal statesman. Born in Manchester, he became a solicitor, and was MP for Caernarvon Boroughs from 1890. During the S African War, he was prominent as a pro-Boer, was president of the Board of Trade 1905–8, and, as Chancellor of the Exchequer 1908–15, introduced old-age pensions in 1908 and health and employment insurance in 1911. His 1909 budget (with graduated direct taxes and taxing land values) provoked the Lords to reject it, and resulted in the Act of 1911 limiting their powers. He was Minister of Munitions 1915–16, and, succeeding Kitchener◊ as War Minister in Jun 1916, advocated diversion of manpower to the eastern front (see Salonika◊). In Dec there was an open breach between him and Asquith◊, and he became prime minister of a coalition government. Securing a unified

Allied command, he enabled the Allies to withstand the last German offensive and achieve victory, and as one of the 'Big Three', with Wilson◊ and Clemenceau◊, he had a major role in the Versailles◊ peace treaty. In the 1918 elections, he achieved a huge majority over Labour and Asquith's followers, but high unemployment, intervention in the Russian Civil War, and use of the 'black and tans' in Ireland, eroded his support. Creation of the Irish Free State in 1921, and his dangerous pro-Greek policy against the Turks, led to withdrawal of the Conservatives and collapse of the coalition in 1922. He had become largely distrusted within his own party, and never regained power. He married in 1888 ***Margaret Lloyd George*** 1864–1941, born Owen, who was created Dame of the British Empire for her social work in 1919; and in 1943 ***Frances Stevenson*** 1888–1972, his secretary, and long his mistress, who published her diaries of his years in office in 1971□

Lloyds incorporated society, forming an insurance market and centre of the world's shipping intelligence in Lime Street London, England. See Richard Rogers◊. Specialist underwriters, responsible to the Council of Lloyd's, issue policies (usually on behalf of a number of fellow members or 'names', grouped in a syndicate) for their own account and risk through authorized brokers. Lloyd's originated in 1688 in the coffee house kept by Edward Lloyd, frequented by businessmen willing to insure against sea-risks, though now almost any form of insurance may be effected, and the non-specialist members are very often merely people with money to invest, willing to take a high risk for potential high returns.

The ***Lutine Bell*** from a British bullion vessel lost off Holland in 1799, and salvaged in 1859, is rung once when a ship is lost, and twice for good news.

The American equivalent of Lloyd's, the ***New York Reinsurance Exchange*** (REX), was established in 1978□

loach carp-like freshwater fish, family Bobitidae, e.g. ***stone loach*** *Noemacheilus barbatulus*, with tiny scales and six barbels at the mouth□

Lobachevski Nikolai Ivanovich 1793–1856. Russian mathematician, the founder in 1829 of non-Euclidean geometry◊. His work was unrecognized until Riemann◊'s system was published□

lobelia temperate and tropical genus of plants, family Lobeliaceae, named after French botanist Matthias de l'Obel. With flowers in white to mauve, they may, as with some African species, grow to small trees□

Lobengula c1833–94. King of Matabeleland◊ 1870–1893, when he rebelled, after accepting British protection in 1888. He was defeated near Bulawayo□

Lobito port in Angola, linked by rail with Beira, via the Zaïre and Zambia copperbelt; population 60 000□

lobster marine member of the order Decapoda◊. Lobsters are grouped with the freshwater crayfish in the suborder Reptantia ('walking'), though both lobsters and crayfish can also swim, using their fanlike tails. All have eyes on stalks and long antennae, and are mainly nocturnal. See also under crab◊ and prawn◊

true lobsters family Homaridae, are distinguished by having very large 'claws' or pincers on their first pair of legs, and smaller ones on their second and third pairs. They include the edible ***common lobster*** *Homarus vulgaris,* found off Britain, which is dark greenish before cooking; the closely related ***American lobster*** *H americanus;* and the ***Norwegian lobster*** *Nephrops norvegicus* a small orange species, taken by trawling and sold as 'scampi'.

spiny lobsters family Palinuridae, including the ***spiny lobster*** *Palinurus elephas* found off Britain, of which only the 'tail' or small abdomen is eaten; it has no claws. They communicate by means of a serrated pad at the base of their antennae, the 'sound' being picked up by tufts of hair (not ears) on their fellow lobsters up to 60 m/180 ft away: it is 'conversational', i.e. when it ceases, the rest look for shelter, and there is a warning call for overt danger.

crayfish family Astacidae, including the ***common crayfish*** *Astacus pallipes*, common in British rivers in chalky areas, where they burrow in the mud. Crayfish are increasingly farmed for food, their size increasing more rapidly in warmer water□

local government under the Local Government Act of 1972, the upper range of local government for ***England and Wales*** was established on a two-tier basis with 46 counties in the former and eight in the latter, each with its popularly elected council (local assembly). London and six other English cities were created metropolitan areas with metropolitan county councils (the latter councils were abolished in 1986, and their already limited functions redistributed to the metropolitan district councils), and the non-metropolitan 'shire' counties had county councils. The counties were subdivided into districts (each with a district council) and then, in rural areas, into parishes and in

Wales into 'communities' across the country, each again with its own council dealing with local matters. ***Scotland*** has regions and islands areas, rather than counties; these are subdivided into districts, which may in turn have subsidiary community councils, but the latter are not statutory bodies with claims on public funds as of right. ***Northern Ireland*** has a single-tier system of 26 district councils□

Locarno resort on Lake Maggiore, Switzerland; population 15 000□

Locarno Pact of. Series of diplomatic agreements (initiated by Austen Chamberlain◊) in 1925 under which Britain, France, Belgium, Italy, and Germany guaranteed the existing frontiers between Germany and France, and Germany and Belgium. The German region through which the Rhine runs was to be demilitarized. The pact was denounced by Hitler in 1936, and troops sent into the Rhineland□

Lochner Stephan c1400–51. German Gothic artist, whose idealistic works are concentrated in the cathedral and museums of Cologne, including *Madonna in the Rose Garden*□

Locke John 1632–1704. English philosopher, born in Wrington, Somerset. Originally a doctor, he became a political protégé of Shaftesbury◊, and on the latter's fall, came under suspicion, and later went into exile in Holland 1683–8. His great works are his two *Treatises on Government* (from a Whig viewpoint) and *Essay Concerning Human Understanding* both 1690. The former, influential also in America and France, supposed governments to derive authority from popular consent (regarded as a 'contract'), so that a government may be rightly overthrown if it infringes such fundamental rights of the people as religious freedom. The latter maintained that experience was the only source of knowledge (empiricism), and that 'we can have knowledge no farther than we have ideas' prompted by such experience. His journals and shorthand notebooks (the latter deciphered only this century) throw further light on his thought. See social◊ contract□

lockjaw see tetanus◊□

locomotor ataxia see syphilis◊□

locust a type of migratory grasshopper◊□

locust tree see carob◊□

Lodge Henry Cabot 1850–1924. American historian, Republican senator from 1893, who influenced the USA to stay out of the League of Nations 1920□

Lodge Henry Cabot, Junior 1902–85. Grandson of the elder Henry Cabot Lodge, he was Eisenhower's campaign manager, and US representative at the United Nations 1953–60. Ambassador to S Vietnam 1963–4, and 1965–7, he took over from Harriman as Nixon's negotiator in the Vietnam peace talks in 1969□

Lodge Sir Oliver Joseph 1851–1940. British physicist. He developed a system of wireless communication in 1894, and his work was influential in the development of radio receivers. He was also greatly interested in psychic research, his son having been killed in 1915□

Lodge Thomas c1558–1625. English author, whose romance *Rosalynde* 1590 was the basis of Shakespeare's *As You Like It*□

Lodi town in N Italy; population 45 000. Napoleon defeated the Austrians here in 1796□

Lodz industrial city (textiles) in central Poland; population 1 038 000□

loess deep and fertile yellow loam, accumulated by the wind-blown deposit of clay particles at the edge of glaciers in the ice ages. Large deposits occur in central Europe, China, and N America□

Loewe Frederick 1901– . American composer, collaborator from 1942 with Alan Jay Lerner◊ on *Brigadoon* 1947, *Paint Your Wagon* 1951, *My Fair Lady* 1956, *Gigi* 1958, and *Camelot* 1960□

Lofoten and Vesteraalen island group off NW Norway; area 4530 sq km/1750 sq mi. The surrounding waters are rich in cod and herring. The ***Maelström*** a large whirlpool hazardous to ships, which gives its name to similar features elsewhere, occurs in one of the island channels. In World War II commando raids against the Germans were made on the Lofotens□

Lofting Hugh 1886–1947. Anglo-American writer and illustrator of children's books, especially the 'Dr Doolittle' series, in which the hero can talk to animals. Originally a civil engineer, he was born in Maidenhead, and went to the USA in 1912□

log an apparatus which measures the speed of a ship, originally a piece of weighted wood (log-chip) attached to a line with knots at equal intervals. This was cast from the rear of a ship, and the vessel's speed was estimated by timing the passage of the knots with a sand glass (like an egg-timer). Modern logs use electro-magnetism, sonar, etc.□

log the daily record of events on board a ship or aircraft□

loganberry hybrid between blackberry◊ and raspberry◊ with large dull, but sweet, red fruit. It was first developed by US judge James H Logan in 1881□

logarithm a mathematical function which makes the calculation of the multiplication and division of large numbers simpler by substituting the simpler operation of addition or subtraction of numbers for multiplication and division respectively. These numbers are found by consulting a book of logarithmic tables. The principle of logarithms was also the basis of the slide◊ rule. With the general availability of the electronic pocket calculator, the need for logarithms has reduced. More formally, a logarithm is the exponent of a number to a specified base. For example, the log of 10 to the base 10 is 1. The log of 100 to the base is 2, because $10^2=10\times10=100$. To multiply 100 by 100, i.e. $10^2\times10^2$, the exponents are added together: 2+2=4. This result, 4, is then converted using table of *antilogarithms* to give the answer of 10 000, i.e. 10^4 or $10\times10\times10\times10$□

logic study of the structure of sound arguments. Deductive logic deals with 'watertight' arguments relating a conclusion to its premises or starting assumptions. Aristotle◊'s *Organon* is the founding work on logic, and Aristotelian methods as revived in the medieval church by Abelard◊ in the 12th century were used in the synthesis of ideas aimed at in scholasticism◊. As befitted the spirit of the Renaissance, Bacon considered many of the general principles used as premisses by the scholastics to be groundless; he envisaged that in natural philosophy principles worthy of investigation would emerge by 'inductive' logic through a study of many relevant particular cases. The modern contribution to logic has been its mathematical expression as by Boole◊, Frege◊, and Russell◊□

logos Greek for 'word' as the embodiment of 'reason' in the Universe; New Testament writers identified it with Christ, and hence the second person of the Trinity□

Logroño town in La Rioja, Spain; population 110 980□

Lohengrin son of Parsival◊, hero of a late 13th-century legend, on which Wagner◊ based his German opera *Lohengrin* 1847. He married Princess Elsa, who broke his condition that she never ask his origin, and he returned to the temple of the Grail◊□

Loire longest river in France, 1012 km/629 mi, flowing from the Massif Central to the Bay of Biscay, with many chateaux and vineyards along its banks□

Loki in Norse mythology, the god of evil, the slayer of Baldur◊, whose children were the Midgard serpent Jörmungander which girdles the Earth, the wolf Fenris, and Hela, goddess of death□

Lollards followers ('mutterers') of Wycliffe◊ who rejected transubstantiation, wanted church property to be put to charitable uses, and denounced war and capital punishment. Many were burned, and in 1414 they raised an unsuccessful revolt in London. Lollardy lingered in London and East Anglia, and was absorbed in Protestantism in the 16th century□

Lombards or ***Langobards.*** Germanic people who invaded Italy in 568, and occupied Lombardy (named after them; see also Monza◊) and central Italy. They were conquered by Charlemagne in 774□

Lombardy region of N Italy (Italian *Lombardia*), including Lake Como, and the country's chief industrial area; capital Milan; population 8 894 240□

lombardy poplar a type of poplar◊□

Lombok see under Sunda◊ Islands□

Lombok Strait lies between Lombok and Bali. The ***Wallace Line,*** the demarcation between Asian and Australian-type animals and plants, runs through it: discovered by A R Wallace◊□

Lombroso Cesare 1836–1909. Italian criminologist. He held the now discredited idea that there was a physically distinguishable criminal 'type'□

Lomé capital and port of Togo; population 247 000. The ***Lomé Convention*** 1975 (renewed 1979, 1985) established economic cooperation between the EEC◊ and African, Caribbean, and Pacific countries□

Lomond Loch. Largest freshwater Scottish lake, 37 km/23 mi long, area 70 sq km/25 sq mi, divided between Strathclyde and Central regions. It is overlooked by the mountain ***Ben Lomond*** 296.5m/973 ft□

London capital of the United Kingdom
area 157 946 ha/390 285 acres
population 6 745 891
It comprises:
City of London original nucleus of Greater London (see below)
area 274 ha/677 acres, known as the 'square mile'
population (resident) 5300, daytime workers more than 500 000
features; financial and commercial centre of the UK, providing the major share of the country's 'invisible earnings'; includes the Tower of London, built by William the Conqueror on a Roman site, which houses the Crown Jewels and the Royal Armouries (founded by Henry VIII); 15th-century Guildhall; Mansion House (residence of the Lord Mayor); the Monument (a column designed by Wren◊) marking the site in Pudding Lane where the Great Fire of 1666

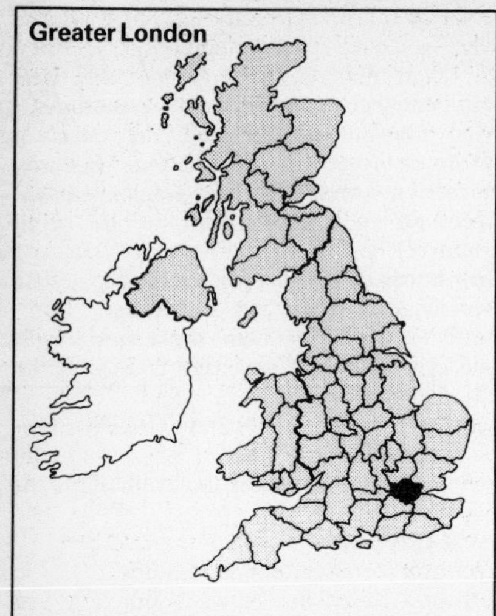

began, St◊ Paul's Cathedral; Inner and Middle Temples and the Central Criminal Court ('Old Bailey'); the Bank of England, the Stock Exchange, and Lloyd's; Barbican Arts and Conference Centre; Museum of London; and markets including Smithfield and Spitalfields (fruit and vegetables). See also Covent◊ Garden.

government by a corporation from the 12th century. Its structure and the electoral procedures for its common councillors and aldermen are medievally complex, and it is headed by the Lord Mayor (who is, broadly speaking, nominated by the former and elected annually by the latter). After being sworn in at the Guildhall, he or she is presented the next day to the Lord Chief Justice at the Royal Courts of Justice in Westminster, and the ***Lord Mayor's Show*** is a ceremonial procession there in Nov.

history Roman Londinium was established soon after the Roman invasion in 43AD on a site probably not previously settled; this was the town burnt by Boadicea in 61AD; in the 2nd century London became a walled city, part of the wall surviving (at Cripplegate, etc.); timbers of the Roman London Bridge have also been found, and remains of a Roman palace underlay Cannon Street station. See also Mithras◊. Chief city of England by the time of William the Conqueror, it gradually extended beyond the walls, and linked with the originally separate City of Westminster. Proliferating suburbs steadily took in surrounding villages, which still often give an individual character to various areas of modern Greater London.

Greater London comprises the City of London, which forms a self-governing enclave, and 32 boroughs (Inner London Boroughs): Barking and Dagenham, Barnet, Bexley, Brent, Bromley, Camden, Croydon, Ealing, Enfield, Greenwich, Hackney, Hammersmith and Fulham, Haringey, Harrow, Havering, Hillingdon, Hounslow, Islington, Kensington and Chelsea, Kingston upon Thames, Lambeth, Lewisham, Merton, Newham, Redbridge, Richmond upon Thames, Southwark, Sutton, Tower Hamlets, Waltham Forest, Wandsworth. Certain powers were exercised over this whole area by the Greater London Council (GLC) until its abolition in 1986□

London industrial city (motor vehicles, agricultural machinery, food processing) in Ontario, Canada, which is also a financial and educational centre; population 254 280□

London Jack. Pseudonym of John Griffith London 1876–1916, American novelist, born in San Francisco. Some of his books have strong socialist elements, but he is best known for adventure stories, e.g. *The Call of the Wild* 1903, *The Sea Wolf* 1904, and *White Fang* 1906, the story of a dog□

London Airport see under Hounslow◊□

Londonderry see Derry◊□

Londonderry county of N Ireland

area 2082 sq km/804 sq mi

towns Derry (county town, formerly Londonderry), Coleraine

features rivers Foyle, Bann, and Roe; borders Lough Neagh

products mainly agricultural, but farming is hindered by the very heavy rainfall; flax, dairy products; food processing, textiles, light engineering

population 131 000

famous people Joyce Cary□

Long Huey. See under Baton◊ Rouge□

Long Beach industrial city (oil refineries, aircraft), naval base and pleasure resort in California, USA; population 361 334. See also Los Angeles□

Longfellow Henry Wadsworth 1807–82. American poet, born in Portland, Maine. He was professor of modern languages at Harvard 1836–54. He is remembered for ballads ('Excelsior' and 'The Wreck of the Hesperus'), the narrative *Evangeline* 1847, and his metrically haunting *The Song of Hiawatha* 1855. See Hiawatha◊ and Coleridge-Taylor◊. He is commemorated in Poets' Corner, Westminster Abbey□

Longford county (county town Longford) of the Republic of Ireland, province of Leinster◊. It includes part of Lough Ree□

Longford Frank (Francis) Aungier Pakenham, 7th Earl of Longford 1905– . Anglo-Irish Labour politician, and leading Roman Catholic layman, an ardent advocate of penal reform. His wife, born Elizabeth Harman, 1906– , is a historian (as 'Elizabeth Longford'), e.g. *Victoria RI* 1964. See also Antonia Fraser◊□

Longinus Cassius c213–73AD. Greek philosopher. Adviser to Zenobia◊ of Palmyra, he instigated her revolt against Rome, and was put to death when she was captured. He was formerly thought to be the author of *On the Sublime*□

Longinus Dionysius lived 1st century AD. Greek critic, author of a treatise *On the Sublime* in literature which was influential until the 18th century (e.g. Dryden and Pope)□

Long Island island off the coast of Connecticut and New York, separated from the mainland by Long Island Sound. It includes two boroughs of New York City (Queens and Brooklyn) and John F Kennedy airport. Traditionally the playground of the wealthy (J P Morgan, Marshall Field, and F W Woolworth), it also has Brookhaven National Laboratory for atomic research; the world's largest automotive museum, and a whaling museum. Nazi saboteurs, landed at Amagansett in World War II, were caught before doing damage. The popular pleasure resort of Coney Island is actually a peninsula in the SW with a board-walk 3 km/2 mi long, and the New York Aquarium□

longitude see latitude◊□

Long March see under Mao◊ Zedong□

Long Parliament the period of English Parliament 1640–60, which carried through the English Civil War. After the Royalists withdrew in 1642, and the 'Presbyterian' right were excluded in 1648, the remaining 'Rump' ruled England until expelled by Cromwell in 1653. Reassembled 1659–60, the Long Parliament initiated the negotiations for the Restoration◊□

Long Range Desert Group one of the most famous 'private armies' of World War II, created by British army men stationed in Egypt in the 1930s. It was used in scouting and sabotage, often deep behind enemy 'lines', and later operated in Greece, Albania, and Yugoslavia□

loofah fruit of *Luffa cylindrica,* family Cucurbitaceae, of which the woody 'sponge skeleton' is used for washing□

Loos Anita 1893–1981. American author of the humorous fictitious diary *Gentlemen Prefer Blondes* 1925□

loosestrife perennial Eurasian riverside plants: the yellow-flowered *Lysimachia vulgaris,* family Primulaceae; and purple *Lythrum salicaria,* family Lythraceae□

Lope de Vega see Vega◊, Lope de□

López Carlos Antonio 1790–1862. Paraguayan dictator (in succession to his uncle José Francia) from 1840, who achieved some economic improvement, and was succeeded by his son Francisco López◊□

López Francisco Solano 1827–70. Paraguayan statesman, son of Carlos, who succeeded him 1862. He involved the country in a war with Brazil, Uruguay, and Argentina during which five-sixths of the people died, and was himself killed in battle□

Lop Nur see under Xinjiang◊ Uyghur□

loquat yellow pear-shaped edible fruit of the E Asian evergreen tree *Eriobotyra japonica*, family Rosaceae, the 'Japanese plum'□

Lorca Federico. See García◊ Lorca, Federico□

Lord prefix used informally as alternative to the full title of a marquess, earl, or viscount; normally also in speaking of a baron, and as a courtesy title before the forename and surname of younger sons of dukes and marquesses. Bishops are formally addressed as the Lord Bishop of –□

Lord Howe Island dependency of New South Wales, 700 km/435 mi north east of Sydney; area 15 sq km/6 sq mi; population 260□

lord-lieutenant the Sovereign's representative in a county, who recommends magistrates for appointment, etc.□

lord mayor see mayor◊□

Lord's headquarters of the Marylebone Cricket Club, regulating body of English cricket since 1788, and also the county ground of Middlesex. Thomas Lord 1757–1832 first opened a ground in Dorset Square in 1787, removing to the present site in 1814□

Lords House of. See parliament◊□

Lorelei see under Rhine◊□

Lorenz Konrad 1903– . Austrian ethologist. For his studies in animal behaviour, e.g. *King Solomon's Ring* 1952, he shared a Nobel prize in 1973 with N Tinbergen◊ and Karl von Frisch◊□

Loreto town in central Italy, where the Virgin Mary's house, said to have been carried by angels from Nazareth is preserved. Hence Our Lady of Loreto is the patron saint of aviators□

Lorient commercial and naval port in NW France; population 72 000□

Lorrain Claude. See Claude◊□

Lorraine see under Alsace-Lorraine□

Lorraine Cross of. See under Alsace-Lorraine◊□

lory a type of small parrot◊□

Los Alamos centre for atomic and space research from 1942, New Mexico, USA; population 12 000. In World War II the atom (nuclear fission) bomb (working on data from other research stations) was designed here (see Oppenheimer◊); and the H-bomb◊ developed□

Los Angeles city and port (commercial, fishing, and naval) in S California, USA; population of urban area, includes that of Long Beach 9 447 926. It has aerospace, electronic, film, chemical, clothing, printing, and food-processing industries. It includes the suburb of Hollywood, centre of the US film industry from 1911, and Beverly Hills with the homes of the film stars; the Hollywood Bowl concert arena; observatories at Mt Wilson and Mt Palomar; Disneyland and Epcot (Experimental Prototype Community of Tomorrow), a Walt Disney theme park; the Huntingdon Art Gallery and Library; and the Getty◊ Museum, the richest in the world (Greek and Roman antiquities are housed in a replica of a Pompeian villa at Malibu, and European decorative art, antiquarian books, and Renaissance paintings will be at a new extension at Brentwood). A computerized J Paul Getty Centre for the History of Art and the Humanities is also planned at Brentwood. The Olympic Games in Los Angeles in 1984 were the first to be financed by a private business consortium□

Los Angeles Victoria de 1923– . Spanish soprano, interpreter especially of Spanish songs, and the roles of Manon and Madame Butterfly in Puccini's operas□

Losey Joseph 1909–84. American film director. Black-listed as a former Communist in the McCarthy◊ era, he settled in England, where his films included *The Servant* 1963 and *The Go-Between* 1971□

Lossiemouth fishing port and resort in Grampian, Scotland; population 5900. Ramsay MacDonald◊ was born and buried here□

Lot see under Gironde◊□

Lothair two Holy Roman Emperors:

Lothair I 795–855, emperor from 817 in association with his father Louis◊ I. On the latter's death the Empire was divided between Lothair and his brothers; Lothair took N Italy and the valleys of the Rhône and Rhine

Lothair II c1070–1137, emperor 1133–7 and German king 1125–37. His election as Emperor, opposed by the Hohenstaufens◊, was the start of the Guelph/Ghibelline◊ feud□

Lothair 825–69. Son of Lothair I, King of Lotharingia (so-called after him, and later corrupted to Lorraine◊) from 855, when he inherited from his father a district west of the Rhine, between the Jura mountains and the North Sea□

Lothian region of Scotland

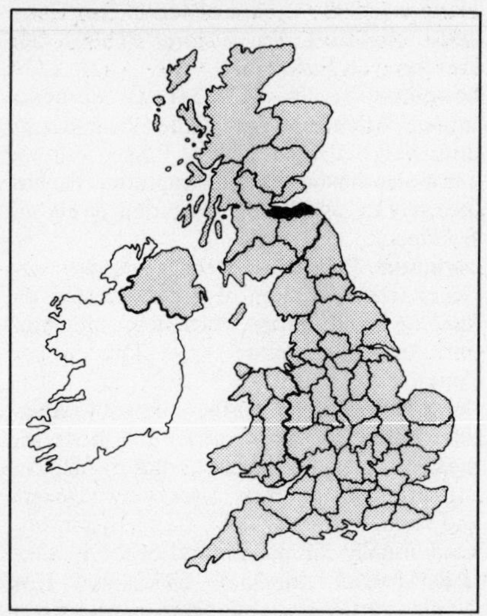

area 1753 sq km/677 sq mi

towns administrative headquarters Edinburgh; Livingston

features Lammermuir, Moorfoot, and Pentland Hills; Bass Rock in the Firth of Forth, noted for sea birds

products bacon, vegetables, coal, whisky, engineering, electronics

population 735 900

famous people birthplace of R L Stevenson in Howard Place, Edinburgh□

lottery game of chance in which tickets sold may win a prize. In the UK lotteries are subject to close restriction, the largest being in effect the government-issued ***Premium Savings Bonds*** (from 1956), repayable at par without interest, but eligible for monthly prize-winning draws. In the USA state lotteries may bring a winner many millions, e.g. in Illinois in 1984 one ticket brought a prize of $40 million□

lotus genus of plants, family Leguminosae, which includes ***bird's foot trefoil*** *Lotus corniculatis*; also two water plants, the sacred water lily of Ancient Egypt *Nymphaea lotus* and the sacred lotus of the Hindus *Nelumbo nucifera*. The ***lotus tree*** of Homer's legendary lotus-eaters may have been a type of jujube *Zizyphus lotus*: it lulled them to oblivion□

loudspeaker an electromechanical apparatus that converts electrical energy into sound waves, typically used in pairs in hi-fi equipment. See radio◊□

Loughborough industrial town (engineering, bell-founding, electrical goods, knitwear), with a university of technology from 1966, in Leicestershire, England; population 50 000□

Louis I 788–840. Holy Roman Emperor, called 'the Pious', who succeeded his father Charlemagne◊ in 814, and counts as Louis I of France□

Louis eighteen kings of France, including:

Louis V 967–87, king from 986, last of the Carolingians◊.

Louis VII c1111–80, king from 1137, who led the Second Crusade◊.

Louis VIII 1187–1226, king from 1223, who was invited to become King of England in place of John◊ by the English barons, and unsuccessfully invaded England 1215–17.

Louis IX St 1214–70, king from 1226. Leader of the Seventh and Eighth Crusades◊. He was defeated in the former by the Saracens, spending four years in captivity, and died at Tunis as he set out on the latter. Feast day, 25 Aug.

Louis XI 1423–83, king from 1461. He broke the power of the nobility (headed by Charles◊ the Bold) by intrigue and military power.

Louis XII 1462–1515, Duke of Orléans until he succeeded his cousin Charles◊ VIII in 1499. His reign was devoted to Italian wars.

Louis XIII 1601–43, king from 1610 (in succession to his father Henry IV), assuming royal power in 1617; he was under the political control of Richelieu◊ 1614–42.

Louis XIV 1638–1715, king (the 'Sun King') from 1643, though until 1661 France was ruled by Mazarin◊. The policy of Louis as ruler was summed up in his saying *L'État c'est moi* ('I am the State'). Greatest of his ministers was Colbert◊, whose work was undone by Louis's military adventures. Louis attempted 1667–8 to annex the Spanish Netherlands, but was frustrated by an alliance of Holland, England, and Sweden. Having detached England from the alliance, he invaded Holland in 1672, but the Dutch stood firm (led by William◊ of Orange) and despite the European alliance formed against France, achieved territorial gains at the Peace of Nijmegen in 1678. When war was renewed 1688–97 between Louis and the Grand Alliance (including England), formed by William of Orange, the French were everywhere victorious on land, but the French fleet was almost destroyed at La Hogue◊ in 1692. The acceptance by Louis of the Spanish throne in 1700 (for his grandson) precipitated the War of the Spanish◊ Succession, however, and the Peace of Utrecht◊ (1713) ended French supremacy in Europe. In 1660 Louis married the Infanta Maria Theresa of Spain, but he was greatly influenced by his mistresses, including Louise de La◊ Vallière, Mme de Montespan◊, and Mme de Maintenon◊

Louis XV 1710–74, great-grandson of Louis XIV; king from 1715, with the Duke of Orléans as regent until 1723. Indolent and frivolous, Louis left government in the hands of his ministers, the Duke of Bourbon and Cardinal Fleury. On the latter's death in 1743, he attempted to rule alone, but became entirely dominated by his mistresses, Mme de Pompadour◊ and Mme du Barry◊. His foreign policy led to Canada and India being lost to France

Louis XVI 1754–93, grandson of Louis XV; king from 1774. He was dominated by his queen, Marie◊ Antoinette, and the finances fell into such confusion that in 1789 the States General had to be summoned, and revolution began. Louis lost his personal popularity in Jun 1791, when he attempted to flee the country (the Flight to Varennes) and in Aug 1792 the Parisians stormed the Tuileries◊ and took the royal family prisoner. Deposed in Sept, he was tried in Dec, sentenced for treason in Jan 1793, and guillotined

Louis XVII 1785–95, nominal king, the son of Louis XVI. He was imprisoned with his parents in 1792, and probably died there.

Louis XVIII 1755–1824, younger brother of Louis XVI; he assumed the royal title in 1795, having fled into exile in 1791, but became king only on the fall of Napoleon in Apr 1814. Expelled during Napoleon's brief return (the '100 Days') in 1815 he returned after Waterloo◊, pursuing a policy of calculated liberalism until ultra-royalist pressure became dominant after 1820□

Louis Prince of Battenberg 1854–1921. British (from 1868) Admiral of the Fleet (1921). He forced to resign as First Sea Lord (1912–14) because of anti-German sentiment. In 1917 he changed his name to Mountbatten◊. He was made 1st Marquess of Milford Haven in 1917□

Louis Joe. Professional name of Joe Louis Barrow 1914–81, the American boxer nicknamed 'the brown bomber'. Born in Alabama, he was world heavyweight champion 1937–49□

Louisiana southern state of the USA; Pelican State

area 125 675 sq km/48 523 sq mi

capital Baton Rouge

towns New Orleans, Shreveport

features Mississippi delta. See New Orleans◊

products rice, cotton, sugar, maize; oil, natural gas, sulphur, salt; processed foods; petroleum products, lumber, paper

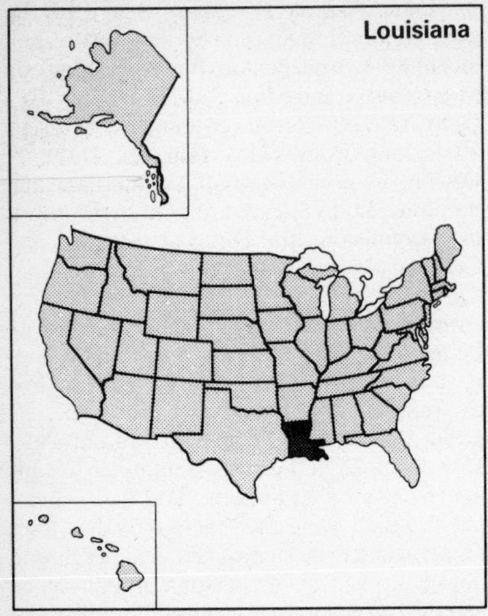

population 4 204 000, which includes the Cajuns, descendants of 18th-century religious exiles from Canada, who speak a French dialect

famous people Louis Armstrong, Pierre Beauregard, Huey Long

history explored by La Salle◊, it was named after Louis XIV and claimed for France in 1682; was Spanish 1762–1800, and passed to the USA under the Louisiana◊ Purchase in 1803□

Louisiana Purchase the acquisition by the USA of the French province of Louisiana (see Louisiana◊ history). The area east of the Mississippi was lost to Britain in 1763, so that it passed under American control in 1783. The remainder was sold to the USA by Napoleon in 1803 for $27 267 622; the state of Louisiana was formed from it in 1812, and the rest eventually formed Arkansas, Missouri, Nebraska, Iowa, and S Dakota, and part of N Dakota, Minnesota, Kansas, Oklahoma, Colorado, and Wyoming□

Louis Philippe 1773–1850. King of France 1830–48. Son of the Duke of Orleans (he was known, like him, as Philippe Egalité, from his early support of the 1792 Revolution). He fled into exile 1793–1814, but became king after the 1830 Revolution with the backing of the rich bourgeoisie. Corruption discredited his regime, and after his overthrow, he escaped to England and died there□

Louisville industrial city (electrical goods, agricultural machinery, motor vehicles, tobacco, baseball bats), and river port on the Ohio, Kentucky, USA; population 655 000. It is noted for its Kentucky Fair and Exposition Center, and the Kentucky Derby. See horseracing◊□

Lourdes town in SW France; population 18 100. See Bernadette◊□

Lourenço Marques see Maputo◊□

Louth smallest county (county town Dundalk) of the Republic of Ireland, province of Leinster◊□

Louvain (Flemish *Leuven*) industrial town in central Belgium; population 85 000□

Louvre former palace of the French kings, in Paris, converted by Napoleon to an art gallery in 1793. It contains the *Venus de Milo*, *Mona Lisa* (see Leonardo◊), and (in the Jeu de Paumes in the gardens of the Tuileries) an Impressionist collection□

love-bird a small bird of the parrot◊ family□

Lovecraft H(oward) P(hillips) 1890–1937. American recluse, author of horror stories (*The Shuttered Room*), and science fiction, a cult of the 1970s□

love-in-a-mist perennial plant of S Europe *Nigella damascena*, family Ranunculaceae, with specialized fern-like leaves, and delicate blue or white flowers□

Lovelace Richard 1618–58. English poet. Imprisoned in 1642 for petitioning for the restoration of royal rule, he wrote 'To Althea from Prison', etc., and in a second spell of jail in 1648 revised his collection *Lucasta* 1649□

Lovell Sir Bernard 1913– . British pioneer radioastronomer, director of Jodrell◊ Bank 1951–81□

Low Sir David 1891–1963. New Zealand-born cartoonist, radical creator (in *Evening Standard, Guardian,* etc.) of Colonel Blimp, the TUC carthorse, etc.□

Low Countries the region of Europe which consists of Belgium, Netherlands, and usually includes Luxembourg□

Lowell city in Massachusetts, USA; population 92 500. Once a textile centre, it became a 'national park' in 1978 as a birthplace of the US industrial revolution. New boom industries include electronics, and the old mills have found new uses□

Lowell Amy (Lawrence) 1874–1925. American free verse poet who succeeded Pound◊ as leader of the Imagists◊. Her works include *Sword-Blades and Poppy Seed* 1916□

Lowell James Russell 1819–91. American poet ('The Vision of Sir Launfal' 1848, and satirical, dialect poems *The Biglow Papers 1848*), critic and diplomat (ambassador in London 1880–85). He encouraged the growth of an American literary tradition□

Lowell Percival 1855–1916. American astronomer, founder of Lowell Observatory at Flagstaff, Arizona, who predicted the existence of Pluto◊□

Lowell Robert (Traill) (Spence) 1917–77. American left-wing poet (*Lord Weary's Castle* 1946, *For the Union Dead* 1964). A Roman Catholic convert from 1940, he was subject to bouts of mania, and was imprisoned in 1943 as a conscientious objector□

Lower California see Baja◊ California□

Lower Saxony (German *Niedersachsen*) Land of northern W Germany
area 47 475 sq km/18 300 sq mi
capital Hanover
towns Brunswick, Göttingen, Oldenburg
features formed 1946 from Hanover, Oldenburg, Brunswick, and Schaumburg-Lippe; Lüneburg Heath, where more than a million men of the German army surrendered to Montgomery on 4 May 1945; Harz◊ mountains
products cereals; cars, machinery, electrical engineering
population 7 260 700
religion Christianity: 75% Protestant, 20% Roman Catholic□

Lowestoft most easterly port in Britain, in Suffolk; population 52 300. There has been major expansion in recent years. Benjamin Britten was born here□

Lowndes Alan 1921–78. British artist, whose works include studies of the back-streets of his native Stockport□

Lowry Laurence Stephen 1887–1976. British artist. Born in Manchester, he painted the industrial landscape of the 1930s, peopled with spindly human figures, e.g. *The Pond* 1950□

Lowry (Clarence) Malcolm 1909–57. British novelist, who became a seaman, and died of alcoholism. *Under the Volcano* 1947, largely autobiographical, tells of the last day of the British consul in a Mexican city□

Loyalists the third of the population remaining loyal to Britain in the American War of Independence. Many went to Canada after 1783□

Loyalists Ulster◊ protestants who oppose any kind of united Irish state□

Loyola see Ignatius Loyola□

LP gas Liquified Petroleum◊ gas□

LSD a hallucinogenic drug. See under ascomycetes◊□

Luanda capital and industrial port (cotton, sugar, tobacco, timber, paper) of Angola; population 700 000.

Luang Prabang Buddhist religious centre and trading town at the head of navigation of the Upper Mekong; population 45 000. It was the royal capital of Laos 1946–75□

Lübeck chief Baltic port of W Germany, in Schleswig-Holstein, once head of the Hanseatic◊ League and now a major industrial city (engineering, medical instruments, ceramics, food processing); population 218 500. Founded in 1143, it has medieval buildings which survived World War II, e.g. the 13th-century Marienkirche, and some of the old merchant houses. Thomas Mann◊ was born here. See also Buxtehude◊□

Lubitsch Ernst 1892–1947. German-American film director, e.g. the stylish comedy *Ninotchka* 1939 starring Garbo◊□

Lublin industrial city (textiles, engineering, electrical goods) in Poland; population 314 000. Poland's independence was proclaimed here in 1918, and in 1944 a Russian-sponsored provisional government of Poland was established here after the German occupation□

Lubumbashi chief commercial centre (formerly Elisabethville) of the Shaba (formerly Katanga) copper and zinc mining region, Zaïre; population 452 000□

Lucan (*Marcus Annaeus Lucanus*) 39–65AD. Latin poet, born in Cordova, a nephew of Seneca◊ and favourite of Nero◊ until the emperor became jealous of his verse. He then joined a republican conspiracy and committed suicide on its failure. His epic *Pharsalia* deals with the civil wars of Caesar◊ and Pompey◊□

Lucas George 1944– . American film producer, whose imagination was fired by the comic books in his father's shop. His science-fiction films include *Star Wars* 1977, *The Empire Strikes Back* 1980, and *Return of the Jedi* 1983, dealing with the adventures of Luke Skywalker and his robot companion Artoo Detoo□

Lucas van Leyden c1494–1533. Dutch artist, influenced by Dürer, and in turn influencing Rembrandt. Born at Leiden, he is chiefly famed for his engravings□

Lucca city in NW Italy, an independent republic from 1160 until its absorption into Tuscany in 1847; population 90 000. Puccini was born here□

Luce Henry Robinson 1898–1967. American publisher, founder of the magazine *Time* in 1923, and of the pictorial weekly *Life* in 1936□

Lucerne another name for alfalfa◊□

Lucerne (German *Luzern*) tourist city in central Switzerland on Lake Lucerne; population 63 300□

Lucerne (German *Luzern*) Lake. Scenic lake in central Switzerland; area 114 sq km/44 sq mi□

Lucian c125–c190. Greek satirist, whose *Dialogues* pour scorn on all religions□

Lucknow capital and industrial city (engineering, chemicals, textiles, many handicrafts) of the province of Uttar Pradesh, India; population 1 006 943. During the Indian Mutiny, it was besieged (see Sir Henry Lawrence◊) 2 Jul–16 Nov 1857, when it was relieved by Sir Colin Campbell◊□

Lucretia in Roman legend, the matron whose rape by Sextus, son of Tarquinius◊ Superbus led to the establishment of the Roman Republic□

Lucretius *(Titus Lucretius Carus)* 99–55BC. Roman poet and Epicurean◊ philosopher, whose *De Rerum Natura/On the Nature of Things* envisaged the whole universe as a combination of atoms, and had some concept of evolutionary theory: animals were complex but initially quite fortuitous clusters of atoms, only certain combinations surviving to reproduce□

Lucullus Lucius Licinius c110–56BC. Roman general, who commanded ably against Mithridates◊ the Great 74–66, when he was superseded by Pompey and retired. His enormous wealth made 'Lucullan' feasts a by-word□

Lüda (formerly Hüta) industrial port (engineering, chemicals, textiles, oil refining, shipbuilding, food processing) in Liaoning, China, on Liaodong Peninsula, facing the Yellow Sea; population 4 200 000. It comprises the naval base of Lüshun (known under 19th-century Russian occupation as Port Arthur) and the commercial port of Dalien (formerly Talien/Dairen). Both were leased to Russia (who needed an ice-free naval base) in 1898, but were ceded to Japan after the Russo-Japanese◊ War; Lüshun was under Japanese siege Jun 1904–Jan 1905. After World War II Lüshun was occupied by Russian airborne troops (returned to China in 1955) and Russia was granted shared facilities at Dalien (ended on the deterioration of Sino-Russian relations in 1955)□

Luddites machine-wrecking rioters (because of unemployment caused by the introduction of machinery) in England 1811–16. Beginning in Nottinghamshire, they spread to Lancashire, Cheshire, and Yorkshire, and were supposedly organized by a mythical 'General Ludd'. Many Luddites were hanged or transported□

Ludendorff Erich von 1865–1937. German general, Chief of Staff to Hindenburg◊ in World War I, and responsible for the eastern front victory at Tannenberg◊ in 1914. After Hindenburg's appointment as Chief of General Staff and that of himself as Quartermaster-General in 1916, he was also politically influential (see Bethmann-Hollweg◊). Later he took part in the Nazi rising at Munich 1923, and sat in the Reichstag as a Nazi□

Lüderitz port (centre for diamond-mining) on Lüderitz Bay, SW Africa; population 4000□

Ludlow market town in Shropshire, England; population 7000. Milton's masque *Comus* was presented in the Norman castle here in 1634□

Ludwig three kings of Bavaria:

Ludwig I 1786–1868 succeeded his father Maximilian Joseph I in 1825. He made Munich an international cultural centre, but his association with the dancer Lola Montez◊ led to his abdication in 1848.

Ludwig II 1845–86 succeeded his father Maximilian II in 1864. He supported Austria during the Austro-Prussian War of 1866, but brought Bavaria into the Franco-Prussian War as Prussia's ally, and in 1871 offered the German crown to the king of Prussia. He was Wagner◊'s patron, and built the Bayreuth theatre for him. Declared insane in 1886, he drowned himself soon after.

Ludwig III 1845–1921, reigned from 1913 and abdicated in 1918□

Ludwigshafen industrial city (chemicals, dyes, fertilizers, plastics, textiles) and Rhine river port, Rhineland Palatinate, W Germany; population 158 700□

Luftwaffe German air force in World War I and also, as reorganized by Goering◊ in 1933, in World War II, when it also covered anti-aircraft defence and launching of the V1◊ and V2◊□

Lugano town on Lake Lugano◊, Switzerland; population 23 000□

Lugano Lake. Between lakes Maggiore and Como, it is partly in Italy and partly in Switzerland; area 49 sq km/19 sq mi□

Lugansk see Voroshilovgrad□

Lugard Frederick John Dealtry, 1st Baron Lugard 1858–1945. British colonial administrator, originally an army officer. He took possession of Uganda in 1890 (for the British East Africa Company), and was High Commissioner for N Nigeria 1900–7, and Governor-General of all Nigeria 1914–19. Peace and order were achieved by his concept of 'indirect rule' through native chiefs and officials, rather than western democracy□

lugworm a type of small worm◊□

Lu Hsün see Lu◊ Xun□

Luik see Liège□

Luke St. In the New Testament, compiler of the third Gospel, and of the *Acts of the Apostles* in the New Testament. Said to have been born in Antioch, and to have been a

Gentile physician (hence patron saint of doctors), he accompanied Paul◊ after the ascension of Christ. Feast day, 18 Oct□

Lulea port (exporting iron ore, and timber in ice-free months) in N Sweden; population 66 500□

Lully Jean Baptiste. Adopted name of Giovanni Battista Lulli 1639–87. Italo-French composer, a French citizen from 1661. Court composer to Louis XIV, he composed music for Molière's plays, established French opera, e.g. *Alceste* 1674, and *Armide et Renaud* 1686, and (himself a dancer) ballet. He died from blood poisoning, after hitting his foot with his long baton□

lumbago pain in the lower region of the back, due to a variety of causes, including 'slipped disc' (displacement of one of the spinal vertebrae). Usually it arises suddenly, and treatment includes rest, application of heat, and skilled manipulation. If it is allowed to become chronic, surgery may be needed□

Lumbini birthplace of Buddha◊ on the Nepalese-Indian frontier, with a sacred garden and shrine□

Lumière Auguste 1862–1954 and Louis 1864–1948. French brothers, pioneers of colour photography, and (building on the work of Edison◊) of the commercial cinema with their cinematograph (which combined camera, printer, and projector)□

luminescence emission of light from a body when its atoms are excited by means other than raising its temperature (e.g. light radiation). If emission ceases within a split second of the exciting agency being turned off (e.g. the electrons bombarding the central screen in a television set, or ultra-violet◊ hitting the inner casting of a strip-light) we have ***fluorescence***. In ***phosphorescence*** the emission persists for some time afterwards, as in the light from fireflies, glow-worms, deep sea fish, decayed fish, fungi, etc. Synthetic molecules emitting light are being used instead of radioactive tracers◊, as more stable and offering no problems in disposal□

Lumumba Patrice 1926–61. Congolese statesman, active in the independence movement, and first prime minister of independent Congo (now Zaïre) in 1960. He was deposed in a coup, and murdered. In the USSR there is a Patrice Lumumba Friendship University (for nationalist 'freedom fighters')□

Lund industrial town (printing, publishing) in SE Sweden; population 80 000□

Lundy rocky island at the entrance to the Bristol Channel; area 419 ha/1047 acres; population 40. Now a National Trust bird sanctuary, it was formerly a stronghold of privateers and pirates□

Lüneburg industrial town (chemicals, paper) in Lower Saxony, W Germany; population 60 000□

Lüneburg Heath see under Lower◊ Saxony□

lung organ of respiration, of which higher vertebrates have a pair within the chest. They are very light and spongy, consisting of multitudes of air cells and blood vessels. With every heartbeat, blood is pumped into the lungs through the pulmonary vein where it is brought into contact at the ends of the smallest divisions of the air tubes (the two bronchi which branch from the windpipe), the carbon dioxide removed and replaced with oxygen, it then returns to the heart via the pulmonary artery. Lung diseases include tuberculosis, pneumonia, bronchitis, and cancer□

lung

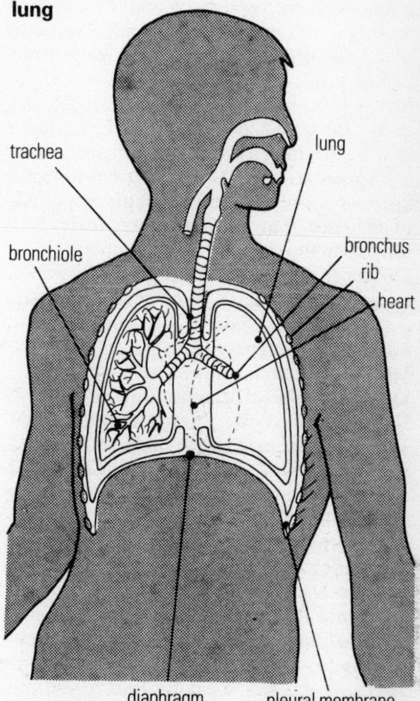

lungfish living 'fossils', three genera of the order Dipnoi (related to the coelacanth◊) found in Africa, S America, and Australia. They grow to about 2 m/6tft, are eel shaped, long-lived, and (in addition to gills) have 'lungs' (modified swim bladders) with which they can breathe air in drought conditions. See also mudfish◊□

Lunt Alfred 1893–1977. American actor, who married English-born ***Lynn Fontanne*** 1887–1983. Known as 'the Lunts', they formed a sophisticated comedy duo, and the New York Lunt-Fontanne theatre was named after them□

Luo Guan-zhong 14th century. Chinese novelist (formerly Luo Kuan-chung), who reworked popular tales into *The Romance of the Three Kingdoms* and *The Water Margin*, the latter a favourite of Mao◊ Zedong□

Luo Kuan-chung see Luo◊ Guan-zhong□

Luoyang industrial city (formerly Loyand) (machinery, tractors, etc.) and former capital of China in Henan province; population 1 114 000□

Lupercalia Roman fertility festival on 15 Feb, in which priests ran round the city with goatskin thongs; a blow from them supposedly cured infertility in women□

lupin genus of plants *Lupinus,* of the Mediterranean and America, family Leguminosae◊, with spikes of brightly coloured flowers. They produce a chemical used to ease childbirth and to improve some heart conditions□

lupus tubercular skin disease which 'eats away' the affected area (from Latin *lupus* 'wolf'). Another type of inflammation ***lupus erythematosus*** or ***LE*** is more serious in that it affects not only the surface tissue, especially of the face, but penetrates the body. It is caused by the sufferer's own antibodies□

Lurçat Jean 1892–1966. French artist influenced by the Cubists, who revived tapestry design, as in *Le Chant du Monde*□

Lurgan see Craigavon◊□

Luristan see under Iran◊□

Lusaka capital of Zambia from 1964 (of N Rhodesia 1935–64); population 538 500. Industries include flour milling, tobacco, vehicle assembly, plastics, printing. The University of Zambia dates from 1966. To the south is the Kafue hydroelectric and irrigation project, with textile, fertilizer, and steel industries□

Lüshun-Dalien see Lüda◊□

Lusitania Roman province corresponding to modern Portugal, hence the term ***lusophone nations*** for the countries formerly ruled by Portugal and still speaking Portuguese, i.e. Brazil and the African countries Angola, Guinea-Bissau, Cape Verde, São Tomé et Principé, Mozambique□

Lusitania Cunard◊ liner sunk by German submarine on 7 May 1915 with the loss of c1200 lives, including some Americans; its destruction helped bring the USA into World War I□

lusophone see under Lusitania◊□

Lü-ta see Lüda◊□

lute family of stringed musical instruments of the 14–18th centuries, which include the mandore, theorbo, and chittarone. Pear-shaped, they were plucked with the fingers, and have been revived in the 20th century. The Indian ***sitar*** with seven metal strings, a gourd body, and long neck with raised frets, is a member of this group; its characteristic 'singing' notes are produced by manipulation of the strings□

lutetium element
symbol Lu
atomic number 71
physical description silvery-white metal
features last of the lanthanide◊ series
uses in the 'cracking' or breakdown of petroleum and in other chemical processes; a radioactive isotope is used to test the age of meteorites compared to the earth□

Luther Martin 1483–1546. German Protestant reformer. Originally a monk, he became convinced of the primacy of grace over merit, 'justification by faith'. In 1517 he nailed on the church door at Wittenberg◊ his 'Ninety-five Theses against Indulgences'◊, following this in 1519 with opposition to the infallibility and primacy of the Pope, and becoming an outlaw before the Empire and an apostate before the Church (see under Worms◊). In 1525 he married an ex-nun, and in 1530 formulated the Augsburg◊ Confession, the basis of Lutheranism. His translation of the scriptures marks the emergence of modern German. Formerly condemned by Communism, he had by the 1980s been rehabilitated as a revolutionary socialist hero, and was claimed as patron saint by both E and W Germany□

Lutheranism form of Protestantism◊ derived from Luther's teaching, and the largest of the Protestant churches (headquarters in Geneva), with its main membership in Germany, Scandinavia, the American midwest, and Canada. Organization may be either under bishops or synods, and its beliefs are summarized in the Augsburg◊ Confession of 1530, and Luther's own Shorter Catechism. ***Pietism*** was a movement in Germany, headed by Philip Jaco Spener 1635–1705, to revive practical Christianity in the Lutheran Church as against increasing theological dogmatism□

Luthuli Albert 1899–1967. S African Zulu chief, president of the African National Congress from 1952. While under suspended sentence for burning his 'pass' (an identity document not required of Europeans), he was awarded the 1960 Nobel peace prize□

Lutine Bell see under Lloyd's◊□

Luton industrial town (cars, chemicals, electrical goods, ball-bearings, and straw hats) in Bedfordshire, England; population 165 000. There is a secondary airport for London, and

Luton Hoo is a fine house by Robert Adam◊□

Lutoslawski Witold 1913– . Polish composer, whose works are in part allowed to develop by chance, and include the orchestral piece *Venetian Games* 1961 and a cello concerto 1970□

Lutyens Sir Edwin Landseer 1869–1944. British architect, whose works include the government buildings in New Delhi, Hampstead Garden Suburb, the Whitehall Cenotaph, London YWCA, and the British embassy in Washington. See Gertrude Jekyll◊□

Lutyens Elisabeth 1906–83. British composer, daughter of Sir Edwin. Her works, using the 12-tone system, include a setting of Wittgenstein◊'s *Tractatus* and a cantata *The Tears of Night*□

Lützen town in E Germany, south west of Leipzig, where Gustavus◊ Adolphus defeated Wallenstein in 1632, and was himself killed in the battle, and where Napoleon defeated the Russians and Prussians in 1813□

Luxembourg Grand-Duchy of

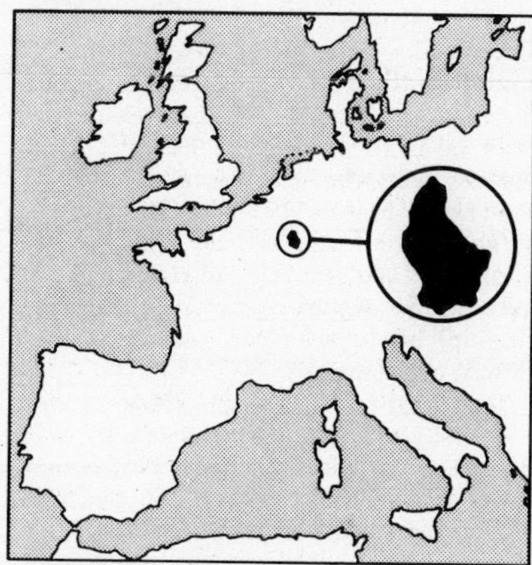

area 2586 sq km/999 sq mi
capital Luxembourg
features River Moselle; part of the Ardennes (Oesling)
exports iron and steel, chemicals, synthetic textiles; banking is very important; Luxembourg is economically linked with Belgium
currency Luxembourg franc
population 366 100
language French, official; local Letzeburgesch; German is also spoken
religion Roman Catholicism
government executive power is held by Grand Duke Jean 1921– (from 1964), who also shares legislative power with the chamber of deputies
recent history created as an independent duchy in 1815, it was occupied by Germany in both World Wars. See Benelux◊□

Luxembourg capital of Luxembourg; population 79 600. It has the 16th-century Grand Ducal Palace; European Court of Justice; and European Parliament secretariat, but plenary sessions of the parliament are now held only in Strasbourg◊□

Luxembourg Accord French-initiated agreement in 1966 that a decision of the Council of Ministers of the European Community may be vetoed by a member whose national interests are at stake□

Luxemburg Rosa 1870–1919. Polish-born German Communist, collaborator with Liebknecht◊ in founding the Spartacus◊ League, and in the 1919 Berlin Revolt, being murdered with him. She wrote famous letters while in prison in World War I□

Luxor see under Thebes◊□

Lu Xun 1881–1936. Chinese writer (formerly Lu Hsün) of satirically realistic short stories compared with those of Gorky, e.g. *The True Story of Ah Q* 1921□

Luzern see Lucerne◊□

Luzon see under Philippines◊□

Lvov (German *Lemberg*, Polish *Lwow*) industrial city (textiles, engineering, and metallurgical) in the Republic of Ukraine, USSR; population 711 000. It was Polish 1340–1772, Austrian 1772–1919, Polish 1919–39, annexed by USSR in 1945□

Lwow see Lvov◊□

lycanthropy folk belief in human transformation to a werewolf◊; or a form of insanity involving this belief□

Lyceum see under Aristotle◊□

lychee see litchi◊□

Lycurgus 9th century BC. Spartan who according to tradition, while acting as regent, gave the Spartans their constitution and educational system□

Lydgate John c1373–c1450. English poet, probably born at Lydgate, Suffolk, who spent much of his life at the Benedictine monastery of Bury St Edmund's, and was an admirer of Chaucer◊. His numerous works include adaptations e.g. his *Troy Book* (from Guido delle Colonne's *Historia Troiana*) and (from Boccaccio◊) *The Fall of Princes* 1430–38□

Lydia 7–6th century BC kingdom of Asia Minor, capital Sardis. The Lydians were the first western people to use standard coinage. See Croesus◊□

Lyell Sir Charles 1797–1875. Scottish geologist, whose *The Principles of Geology* 1830–3 established the concept of earth's crust being weathered over millennia, not the result of sudden 'catastrophes'□

Lyly John c1553–1606. English playwright and author of the romance *Euphues, or the Anatomy of Wit* 1578. Its elaborate stylistic devices gave rise to the word 'euphuism'□

Lyme Regis resort in Dorset; population 3500. The Duke of Monmouth◊ landed here in 1685; and the Cobb (a massive stone pier) features in Jane Austen's *Persuasion,* and John Fowles' *The French Lieutenant's Woman*□

Lymington port and yachting centre in Hampshire, England; population 36 000□

lymph clear saline fluid exuding from the finest blood vessels into tissue spaces between cells all over the body, carrying oxygen and nutrients and removing waste matter. Bacteria, and even cancer cells, may be safely filtered out by the ***lymph nodes***, rounded bodies of tissue at intervals along the 'return road' of the lymphatic system to the heart. However, sometimes the cells are retained, and the nodes have to be surgically removed to prevent their serving as further infection centres□

lymphocyte type of white blood cell also found in lymph, some large, but the great majority small. The latter play a vital role in developing the immune response, by helping to produce antibodies□

Lynch 'Jack' (John) 1917– . Irish Fianna Fáil statesman, prime minister 1966–73 and 1977–9□

lynching execution of an alleged offender by a summary court with no legal authority. In the USA it originated in the frontier country, though after the Civil War it was used in the South against supposed Negro offenders□

Lynn industrial city (footwear, engineering) in Massachusetts, USA; population 78 500. Mary Baker Eddy◊ lived here□

Lynn Dame Vera 1917– . British singer, the 'Forces' Sweetheart' of World War II with 'Auf Wiedersehen' and 'White Cliffs of Dover'; Dame of the British Empire 1975□

lynx a type of wild cat◊□

Lyon river port and industrial city (data processing, electronics, energy research, synthetic and silk textiles, chemicals and pharmaceuticals), capital of Rhône-Alpes, France; population 1 171 000. Captured by the Romans in 43BC, it was long an important French fortress and is the second city of France. It is a banking and communications centre – road, rail, and canal (it is at the confluence of the Rhône and Saône)□

Lyons Joseph Aloysius 1879–1939. Australian statesman, founder of the United Australia Party in 1931. He headed a coalition (with the Country Party) 1931–9□

lyre stringed instrument played (with a plectrum) in ancient Asia, Egypt, and Greece, and comprising a soundbox with two curved arms, joined by a crosspiece carrying the strings down to the bridge near the bottom of the soundbox□

lyre-bird two species of Australian bird, family Menuridae. They are brownish, but the male has a long tail, with a silvery sheen, which forms a lyre-shape in display. They are fine songsters, and make nest mounds□

Lysander d. 395BC. Spartan general who ended the Peloponnesian◊ War by capturing the Athenian fleet at Aegospotami in 405, and starving Athens into surrender in 404. Setting up puppet governments in Athens and her former allies, he intrigued to gain the Spartan crown, but was killed in battle with the Thebans□

Lysippus 4th century BC. Greek sculptor at the court of Alexander. His naturalistic work included an athlete (copy in the Vatican) and portrait busts, then a new form of art□

Lyte Henry Francis 1793–1847. British cleric, author of the hymns 'Abide With Me' and 'Praise, my soul, the King of Heaven'□

Lytham St Annes resort in Lancashire, England, headquarters for Premium Savings◊ Bonds; population 41 000□

Lytton Edward George Earle Lytton Bulwer-Lytton, 1st Baron Lytton 1803–73. British playwright and author, best remembered for his historical novel *The Last Days of Pompeii* 1834, which uses real features of the city□

Lytton, Edward Robert Bulwer-Lytton, 1st Earl of Lytton 1831–91. British statesman, viceroy of India 1876–80, where he pursued a controversial 'Forward' policy. Only son of the novelist, he was himself a poet under the pseudonym Owen Meredith, e.g. *King Poppy* 1892□

M

Maas Dutch or Flemish name for the river Meuse◊□

Maastricht industrial town in SE Netherlands; population 111 500□

Maazel Lorin 1930– . American conductor, specializing in Mozart□

Mabuse Jan. Adopted name of Flemish artist Jan Gossaert c1472–c1534, noted for portraits, his brilliant colouring, and graceful religious themes, e.g. *The Adoration of the Magi* (London)□

McAdam John Loudon 1756–1836. Scottish road engineer who used the 'macadamizing' process for roads (crushed granite, plus tar, etc.)□

macadamia nut of the Queensland tree genus *Macadamia*, family Protaceae; delicious and expensive□

Macao Portuguese possession since 1557 in S China; area 15.5 sq km/6 sq mi and separated from Hong Kong by the estuary of the Canton river; population 260 250. In 1974 China turned down a Portuguese offer to return the territory (which has practical autonomy), but in 1986, following the return of Hong Kong to China, negotiations were to begin. It has a considerable transit trade, but is economically dependent on its casinos□

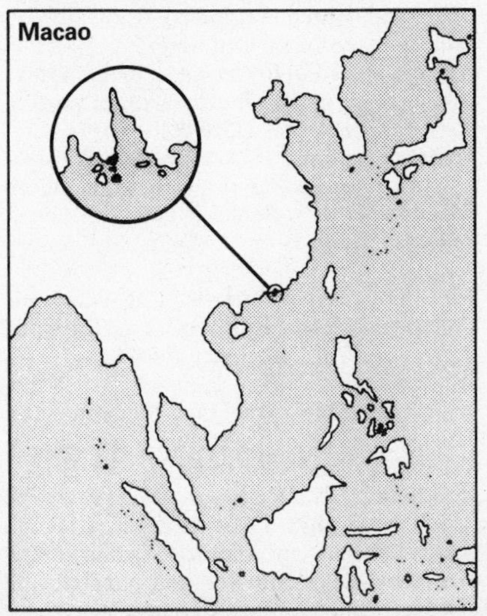

MacArthur Douglas 1880–1964. American General of the Army from 1944. As commander of US forces in the Far East, he fought the Japanese in the Philippines 1941–2, before escaping to Australia, and assuming command of Allied forces in the SW Pacific. He reconquered New Guinea 1942–5, and the Philippines 1944–5, and commanded Allied occupation forces in Japan after the surrender. In 1950 he commanded United Nations forces in Korea, but in Apr 1951 (his openly expressed views clashing with United Nations and US policy) was relieved of his commands by President Truman□

Macarthur John 1767–1834. British New South Wales colonist, who founded the sheep industry by importation of merinos from S Africa and planted the first commercial vineyard. Very quarrelsome, he was arrested by Governor Bligh◊, and then stirred up the Rum Rebellion◊ which led to Bligh's arrest and deposition□

Macassar another name for Ujung◊ Padang□

Macaulay Dame Rose 1881–1958. British novelist, with a light satiric touch in *Potterism* 1920 and *Keeping up Appearances* 1928, and a more serious note in *The Towers of Trebizond* 1956; Dame of the British Empire 1958□

Macaulay Thomas Babington, Baron Macaulay 1800–59. British critic (in the *Edinburgh Review*), poet (*Lays of Ancient Rome* 1842), and historian (a masterly *History of England* 1848–61, from the Whig viewpoint), and politician (MP 1830–4, 1839–47, 1852–6, an advocate of parliamentary reform and abolition of slavery). He also served in India 1834–8, as a member of the Supreme Council, and was mainly responsible for the Indian penal code. Peerage 1857□

macaw large tropical American parrot◊□

Macbeth d. 1057. King of Scotland from 1040, following his killing of Duncan, whose general he had been, in battle. Duncan's son Malcolm headed an invasion, and killed Macbeth at Lumphanan. Shakespeare's tragedy was based on Holinshed◊'s *Chronicle*□

McCabe John 1939– . British pianist and composer (three symphonies; orchestral works, including *The Chagall Windows*; and songs)□

Maccabees or ***Hasmonaeans***. The Jewish priest ***Mattathias*** (d. 166BC) and his sons who led a revolt against the Syrians in the 2nd century BC. ***Judas*** (d. 161) reconquered Jerusalem 165BC, and ***Simon*** (d. 135) established Jewish independence in 142BC□

McCarthy Joseph 1908–57. American Republican senator from Wisconsin, who in 1950 launched a Communist witch-hunt ('McCarthyism'), especially against the State Department, until censured by the senate in 1954□

McClellan George Brinton 1826–85. American Civil War general, Commander-in-Chief of the Union forces 1861–2. He was dismissed by Lincoln when he delayed five weeks in following up his victory over Lee at Antietam (see under Civil◊ War, American). He was the unsuccessful Democrat presidential candidate against Lincoln in 1864□

Macclesfield industrial town (silk and synthetic textiles, light engineering) in Cheshire, England; population 45 500□

McClintock Barbara 1902– . American geneticist. Working at the Carnegie Institute, Cold Spring Harbor, New York, she concluded that genes changed their position on the chromosome from generation to generation in a random way. The existence of such transposable elements (TEs) would explain how originally identical cells are enabled to take on specialized functions as skin, muscle, bone, nerve, etc., and also how evolution could give rise to the multiplicity of species□

McClure Sir Robert John 1807–73. British explorer. While on an expedition 1850–4 searching for Franklin◊, he was the first to pass through the North-West Passage□

MacCready Paul. American designer of the Gossamer Condor aircraft which made the first controlled flight by human power alone in 1977. His Solar Challenger flew Paris–London under solar power; and in 1985 he reconstructed a powered pterodactyl◊□

MacDermot Galt 1928– . American composer of the 'tribal rock-love musical' *Hair* 1966, with lyrics by Gerome Ragni and James Rado. It opened in London in 1968, the day stage censorship ended, and challenged conventional attitudes to sex, drugs, and call-up for Vietnam□

McDiarmid Hugh. Pseudonym of the Scottish nationalist and Marxist poet Christopher Murray Grieve 1892–1978, born in Langholm, Dumfries and Galloway. His works include *A Drunk Man looks at the Thistle* and two *Hymns to Lenin*□

Macdonald Flora 1722–90. Scottish heroine who assisted Prince Charles Edward, the Young Pretender, to escape to the Continent after the Battle of Culloden◊ in 1746. He travelled with her as her maid. She was arrested, but released in 1747□

MacDonald James Ramsay 1866–1937. British Labour statesman, son of a labourer. He helped to found the Labour Party, and was Prime Minister Jan–Oct 1924, when he was forced to resign on withdrawal of Liberal support. He again headed a minority government 1929–31, and, when this collapsed under the impact of the economic crisis, left the Labour Party, to lead a National government with Conservative and Liberal backing. He resigned in 1935□

Macdonnell Ranges see under Northern◊ Territory□

MacDowell Edward Alexander 1861–1908. American Romantic composer, influenced by Liszt. His works include the *Indian Suite* 1896, and piano concertos and sonatas□

mace a spice made from nutmeg◊□

Macedonia former country of SE Europe, now split into a federal republic of Yugoslavia (capital Skopje), a province of Greece (capital Thessaloniki) and SW Bulgaria. There are nationalistic demands for renewed independence□

Macedonia constituent republic of Yugoslavia.
area 25 713 sq km/9925 sq mi
capital Skopje
population 1 912 250, including 1 282 000 Macedonians, 378 000 Albanians, 87 000 Turks
language Macedonian, closely allied to Bulgarian, and written in Cyrillic◊
religion Macedonian Orthodox□

Maceió industrial town (sugar, tobacco, textile, timber) in NE Brazil, with its port at Jaraguá; population 375 800□

McEvoy Ambrose 1878–1927. British watercolourist, and painter of society women□

Macgillycuddy's Reeks a range of mountains in south west Ireland. See under Kerry◊□

McGinley Phyllis 1905–78. Canadian-born American writer of light verse, e.g. *The Love Letters of Phyllis McGinley* 1954□

McGonagall William 1830–1902. Scottish poet, remarkable for the unintentionally humorous effect of his extremely bad serious verse, e.g. his poem on the Tay Bridge disaster of 1879□

Mach Ernst 1838–1916. Austrian physicist-mathematician, and empirical scientist, founder of logical◊ positivism, and originator of the Mach◊ number. See Carnap◊□

Machado Antonio 1875–1939. Spanish poet, born in Seville, but inspired by the Castilian countryside, e.g. *Campos de Castilla* 1912□

Machel Samora 1933– . Mozambique leader from 1966 of the Frente de Libertação de Moçambique (Frelimo) against Portuguese rule, and president of Mozambique from 1975□

Machiavelli Niccolò 1469–1527. Florentine politician, who was imprisoned and then exiled in 1513 by the Medici. His *Il Principe* 1513, a guide to the ruthless exercise of power by the future prince of a unified Italian state, was execrated as 'Machiavellian', but reflects the actualities of statecraft□

machine gun a rapid-firing automatic gun. See under small◊ arms□

Mach number ratio of the speed of a body to that of sound in the undisturbed medium through which the body travels. Mach 1 is reached when an aircraft has a velocity greater than that of sound ('passes the sound barrier'). See Ernst Mach◊□

Machu Picchu a ruined Incan city in Peru. See under Cuzco◊□

McIndoe Sir Archibald 1900–60. New Zealand plastic surgeon, famed especially for his remodelling the faces of badly burned pilots in World War II, who formed the Guinea Pig Club□

Macintosh Charles 1766–1843. Scottish inventor of a now obsolete method of waterproofing fabric with rubber solution, hence 'mackintosh'□

McKellen Ian 1940– . British actor whose roles include Richard II, Edward II, Mozart in the stage version of *Amadeus*, and D H Lawrence in the film *Priest of Love* 1982□

Mackensen August von 1849–1946, German field marshal whose exploits against Serbia and Romania in World War I made him a folk hero□

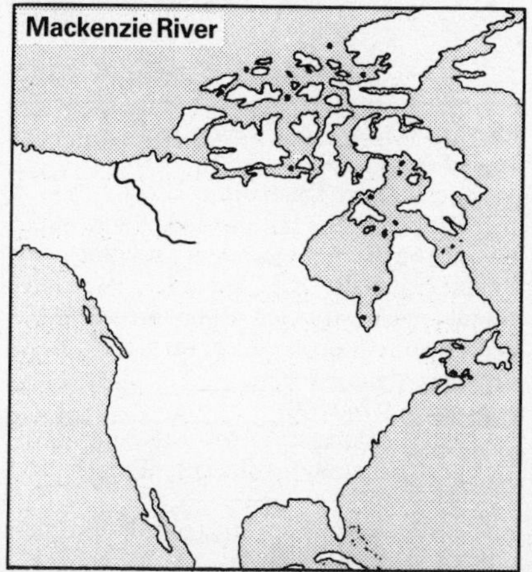

Mackenzie a district of the Canadian Northwest◊ Territories. A feature is the *Mackenzie River*; length 1600 km/1000 mi. See Sir Alexander Mackenzie◊□

Mackenzie Sir Alexander c1755–1820. British explorer, discoverer of the Mackenzie◊ river in 1789□

Mackenzie Sir Compton 1883–1972. Scottish novelist, author of *Sinister Street* 1913–14, and the comic *Whisky Galore* 1947. He was an intelligence officer in World War I, and published a multi-volume autobiography□

Mackenzie William Lyon 1795–1861. Grandfather of W L Mackenzie King◊, he led the revolt in Upper Canada in 1837 against the oligarchic rule of 'establishment' families, the Family Compact□

mackerel a spiny-finned fish. See under perch◊□

Mackerras, Sir Charles 1925– . Australian conductor, who has helped popularize Janáček◊; see also under Sir Arthur Sullivan◊. Knighted 1979□

McKinley Mount. Peak in Alaska, USA, the highest in N America, 6194 m/20 320 ft; named after William McKinley◊. See Rocky◊ Mountains□

McKinley William 1843–1901. Twenty-fifth president of the USA, born in Ohio. A Republican and imperialist (Spanish War of 1898, annexation of the Philippines, etc.), he held office 1897–1901, and was assassinated by an anarchist in Buffalo□

Mackintosh Charles Rennie 1868–1928. Scottish Art Nouveau◊ architect, designer and painter, e.g. Glasgow School of Art 1896□

Maclean Donald. British civil servant who spied for the Russians. See under Kim Philby◊□

Macleish Archibald 1892–1982. American poet. Born in Illinois, he later taught at Harvard, and was Assistant Secretary of State 1944–5. His works include the narrative *Conquistador* 1932, dealing with Cortés, and the drama *Job* 1958□

Macleod Iain Norman 1913–70. British Conservative politician. As Colonial Secretary 1959–61, he forwarded African independence, and died in office as Chancellor of the Exchequer□

Maclise, Daniel 1806–70. Irish painter, whose *The Meeting of Wellington and Blücher after Waterloo*, and *Death of Nelson* were painted for Westminster Palace□

McLuhan Marshall 1911–80. Canadian sociologist, who saw electronics as an extension of the human brain making individualism obsolete. His best-known works were *The Gutenberg Galaxy* 1962 (coining 'the global village' for the modern electronic society); and *The Medium is the Message* 1967□

MacMahon Marie Edmé Patrice, Comte de MacMahon 1808–93. Marshal of France. Captured at Sedan in 1870 during the Franco◊-Prussian War, he suppressed the Paris Commune◊ after his release, and as president of the Republic 1873–9 worked for a royalist restoration until forced to resign□

Macmillan (Maurice) Harold (Earl of Stockton) 1894– . British Conservative statesman. A member of the Macmillan publishing family, he served with distinction in the Grenadier Guards in World War I. He was Minister of Housing 1951–54, Defence 1954, Foreign Secretary 1955, and as Chancellor 1955–7 introduced Premium Bonds. He took over as Prime Minister on Eden's resignation after Suez, and by his realization of the 'wind of change' advanced the independence of former colonies in Africa. In 1959 he led the party to electoral victory with the slogan 'You have never had it so good' (in context a warning rather than a congratulation) but in 1962 dismissed seven cabinet colleagues in a re-shuffle, and was blocked by de Gaulle in an attempt to enter the Common Market in Jan 1963. In June the government was rocked by the Profumo affair, but a Nuclear Test Ban treaty was achieved in Aug before the Prime Minister's resignation in Nov owing to ill-health. His nickname 'Supermac' was the invention of cartoonist Vicky; he received the Order of Merit in 1976, and an earldom in 1984□

MacMillan Sir Kenneth 1929– . British dancer, principal choreographer of the Royal Ballet from 1977. His ballets include *Romeo and Juliet* (1965), *Song of the Earth, Anastasia* (1967); and *Isadora* (1981). Knighted 1983□

MacNeice Louis 1907–63. Anglo-Irish poet, born in N Ireland, who translated the Greek classics, and whose radio plays were collected as *The Dark Tower* 1947□

Mâcon town in E France, famous for Burgundian wine, and as the birthplace of Lamartine◊; population 40 500□

Macpherson James 1736–96. Scottish 'compiler' of verse, especially the epic *Fingal* 1761, alleged to be by the 3rd-century bard Ossian◊. He failed to produce his originals when challenged by Dr Johnson, but probably combined fragments with oral tradition, and his work influenced the Romantic movement on the Continent and in Britain□

Macquarie Lachlan 1761–1834. Successor to Bligh◊ as governor of New South Wales 1809–21, he did much to rehabilitate ex-convicts. The Lachlan and Macquarie rivers are named after him□

Macquarie Island Tasmanian dependency (named after Lachlan Macquarie), uninhabited except for a research station□

macramé knotted thread fringes and lacework; from Arabic 'striped cloth', often ornamented in this way□

Macready William Charles 1793–1873. British actor, a rival of Kean, who excelled in the roles of Macbeth, Lear, etc., and whose *Journal* was published in 1970□

macrobiotics Zen Buddhist diet system using organically-grown wholefoods, and attempting to balance the female *yin* (vegetable) and male *yang* (meat) principles□

MacWhirter John 1839–1911. British landscape painter, e.g. *June in the Austrian Tyrol, Spindrift,* and watercolours attributed to him in the 1980s□

McWhirter Norris 1925– . British compiler of the *Guinness Book of Records* from 1955, originally with his twin brother ***Ross*** 1925–75, shot by terrorists for raising funds to aid the arrest of IRA bombers in Britain□

Madagascar Democratic Republic of

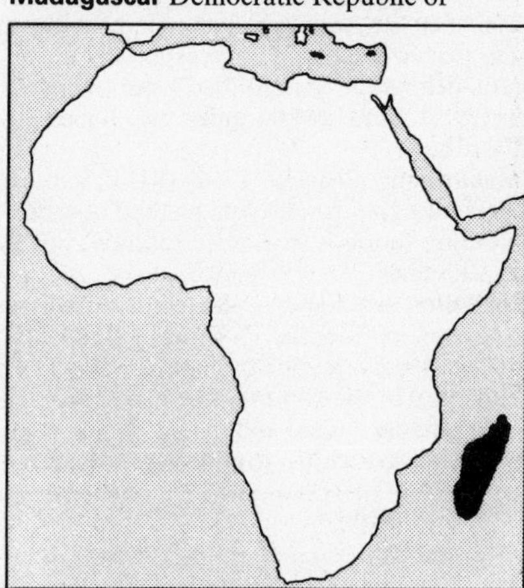

area 594 000 sq km/228 500 sq mi
capital Antananarivo
towns chief port Toamasina
features one of the last places in the world to be inhabited, it evolved in isolation with unique animals, e.g. lemur◊, now under threat from destruction of the forests
exports coffee, sugar, spice, textiles
currency Malagasy franc
population 8 740 000
language Malagasy (of the Malayo-Polynesian family) (official); French and English
religion Animist 50%, Christian 40%; Muslim 10%

government under the constitution of 1975 there is an executive president (Lieutenant Commander Didier Ratsiraka from 1975; re-elected in 1982), and senate and house of assembly.
recent history Madagascar became a French colony in 1896, and independent as the Malagasy Republic in 1960. A referendum in favour of direct democracy led to a military takeover in 1972, but in 1975 the Democratic Republic of Madagascar was proclaimed. Claims are maintained on the Indian Ocean islands of Glorieuses, Juan de Nova, Europa, and Bassas da India, currently administered by France□

Madeira group of five islands off NW Africa (Portuguese *Funchal*)

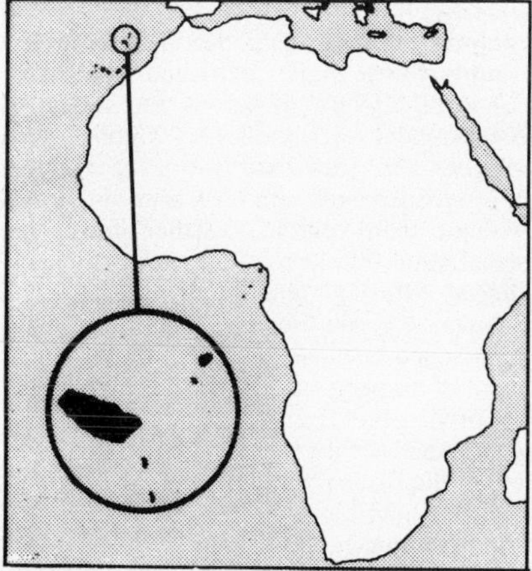

area 790 sq km/308 sq mi; population 265 100. The capital is Funchal. Their mild climate makes them a winter resort, and Madeira wine, sugar cane, fruit, fish; wickerwork and embroidered handicrafts are exported. A degree of autonomy was granted in 1980, but Madeira remains a Portuguese Overseas Territory□

Madhya Pradesh central state of India
area 442 841 sq km/170 936 sq mi
capital Bhopal
features largest of the states
population 52 131 720
language Hindi□

Madison James 1751–1836. Fourth president of the USA 1809–17. As Jefferson's Secretary of State 1801–9, he carried through the Louisiana◊ Purchase, and embarked on the war of 1812 with Britain□

Madison capital of Wisconsin, USA; population 213 700□

Madoc Prince d. 1169. Legendary Prince of Gwynned, supposed to have discovered America, and been an ancestor of a group of light-skinned, Welsh-speaking Indians in the American West□

Madonna Italian 'my lady', the Virgin Mary◊□

Madras capital, industrial city (cotton, cement, chemicals, steel) and port of Tamil Nadu, India; population 4 277 000. Fort St George, founded by the East India Company 1639, was the nucleus of the city, and Lord Clive's house is a protected monument□

Madrid capital and industrial city of Spain
population 3 188 300 (also an autonomous region, population 4 146 000)
features the highest of European capitals, it has two royal palaces, one built 1738–64 by Philip◊ V and Charles III in the tradition of Versailles, and the other, El Escorial, commissioned by Philip II◊, 44 km/28 mi to the NW, who dispatched the Armada from here (it contains a royal mausoleum and paintings by El Greco, Titian, and Velasquez); the parliament buildings, and university.
history in the Civil War Madrid fell to the Nationalists after a siege 7 Nov 1936–28 Mar 1939□

madrigal unaccompanied composition for three or more voices, originating in the Netherlands, but popular in Elizabethan England. See William Byrd◊, Orlando Gibbons◊□

Madura an island in Indonesia. See Java under Sunda◊ Islands□

Madurai city in Tamil Nadu, India; population 904 000. There is an elaborately carved 16–17th-century Hindu temple□

Maeander river now in Asiatic Turkey (Turkish *Büyük* 'great' *Menderes*) but anciently in Greek territory; length 400 km/250 mi; famous for its winding course, hence 'meander'□

Maecenas Gaius Clinius c69–8BC. Friend and adviser of Augustus◊, he was the patron of Horace◊ and Virgil◊□

maelstrom a large powerful whirlpool. See also under Lofoten◊□

maenad in Greek mythology, a woman participant in the orgiastic rites of Dionysus◊□

Maestricht see Maastricht◊□

Maeterlinck Maurice, Count Maeterlinck 1862–1949. Belgian poet-dramatist, e.g. *Pelléas and Mélisande* 1892, which inspired Debussy and Sibelius, and *The Blue Bird* 1908. Nobel prize 1911□

Mafeking see Mafikeng◊□

Mafia secret society (Italian 'swagger') of 15th-century Sicily, avenging its 'wrongs' by terror and vendetta. Spread by immigrants to the USA as *Cosa Nostra* ('Our Thing'), it is organized in 'families', each with its own boss, subordinate to the big boss of the leading cities, each of whom is a member of the national committee. Activities include gambling, loansharking, drug peddling, murder, prostitution, protection, etc. See Camorra◊, James Hoffa◊□

Mafikeng town (formerly Mafeking) in Bophuthatswana, S Africa; population 7000. Baden-Powell◊ successfully held it under Boer siege 12 Oct 1899–17 May 1900□

Magadan port for the gold mines in E Siberia, USSR; population 103 000□

Magadha kingdom of ancient India. See under Bihar◊□

Magdeburg capital of Magdeburg district and industrial city (vehicles, paper, textiles, machinery) in E Germany; population 287 600. Its 13th-century Gothic cathedral survives□

Magellan Ferdinand c1480–1521. Portuguese navigator, sponsored by Spain to sail to the E Indies by the western route. Starting from Seville, he sailed through the Strait of Magellan, crossed the Pacific, which he named, and in 1521 reached the Philippines, where he was killed in battle. Other members of the expedition completed the return voyage under Del Cano, but Magellan and his Malay slave, Enrique de Malacca, were the first circumnavigators of the globe, since they had originally sailed from the Philippines to Europe□

Magellan Strait of. Between S America and Tierra del Fuego, and named after the navigator□

Magenta town in Lombardy, Italy. The French and Sardinians defeated the Austrians here in 1859 during the struggle for Italian independence□

Maggiore Lake. Divided between Italy and Switzerland, with Locarno on its N shore; area 212 sq km/82 sq mi□

maggot legless insect larvae, especially of flies□

Maghreb NW Africa (Arabic 'west', 'sunset'): the ***Maghreb powers*** are Algeria, Libya, Morocco, Tunisia, and Western Sahara; Chad, Mali, and Mauritania are sometimes included. See also Mashraq◊□

magi priests of the Zoroastrian religion, used in the Latin Vulgate Bible where the authorized version gave 'wise men'. The three Magi were visitors to Christ with gifts of gold, frankincense, and myrrh, in later tradition referred to as 'kings'□

magic control of natural forces by supernatural means, e.g. charms and rituals (such as dances) to produce rain, success in hunting, cure illness, or cause the death of an enemy. Under Christianity existing rites of this kind were either suppressed (though they survived in modified form in folk-custom and superstition) or replaced by those of the Church itself. Modern study recognizes that some elements may have a degree of validity, e.g. in their psychological effect, or herbs included in the treatment of illness□

magic numbers in atomic physics the numbers of neutrons or protons (2, 8, 20, 28, 50, 82, 126) in the nuclei of elements of outstanding stability such as lead and helium. It is accounted for by the neutrons and protons being arranged in layers or 'shells'□

Maginot Line French semi-underground fortification system (built 1929–36 under War Minister André Maginot) on the German frontier, from Switzerland to Luxembourg. In 1940 the Germans out-flanked it via Belgium□

magma a viscous liquid. See under rock◊□

Magna Carta charter extracted from King John◊ in 1215 by his barons and sealed at Runnymede◊. It reaffirmed Church privileges, and prevented the king making excessive demands for money from his barons without their consent. Further down the social scale other provisions went to check official extortion and unfair use of legal powers, e.g. no freeman to be arrested, imprisoned or punished except by the judgment of his peers or the law of the land, and the privileges of London and other cities were guaranteed. Of the four surviving copies, two are in the British Museum, and the others in Salisbury and Lincoln cathedrals□

magnesia magnesium oxide, MgO, a white powder or colourless crystals, formed when magnesium is burnt in air or oxygen. It is used to treat acidity of the stomach, and in some industrial processes□

magnesium element
symbol Mg
atomic number 12
physical description silvery-white metal
features highly reactive when pure; burns with a brilliant flame
uses in flares and fireworks; as an alloy with aluminium in aircraft construction due to its low density, in nuclear reactors to enclose fuel elements□

magnet an object which forms a magnetic field. See magnetism□

magnetism the study of magnets and magnetic fields. Magnetic fields (see electromagnetic◊ field) are produced by moving charged particles: in electromagnets electrons flow through a coil of wire connected to a battery; in magnets spinning electrons within the atoms generate the field. Only certain ferromagnetic materials can be made into magnets; this is because forces act between adjacent atoms so that large groups, forming regions or domains, produce fields which reinforce. Magnetizing a piece of iron (e.g. by stroking it with a magnet) consists of partially aligning the various domains so that their fields reinforce.

the earth's magnetic field

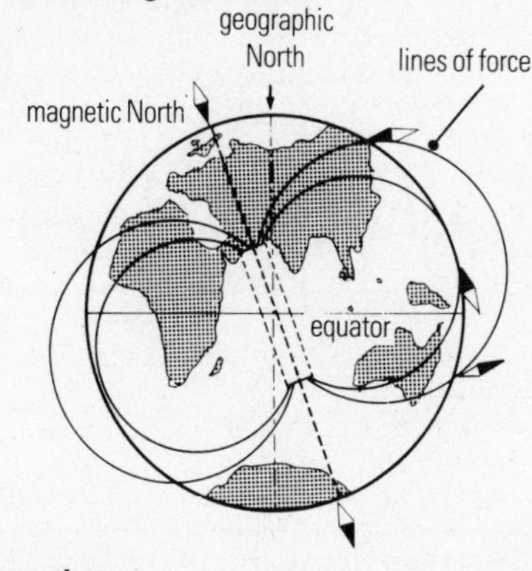

magnetism

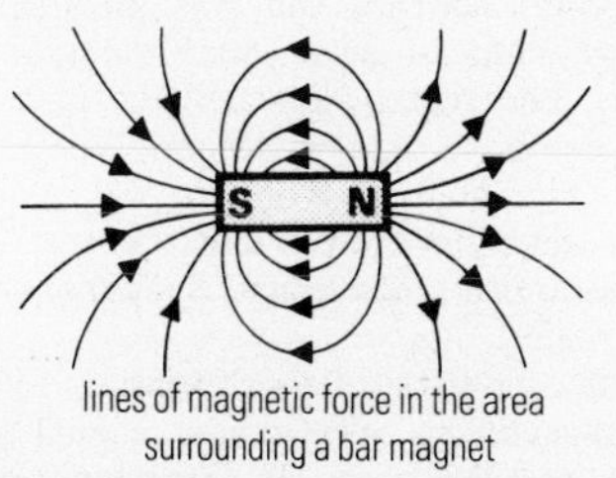

lines of magnetic force in the area surrounding a bar magnet

The forces which simple bar magnets exert on each other owing to their magnetic fields behave as if they come from two points – the north and south poles – near the end of the magnets. Like poles (e.g. two north poles) repel each other, unlike poles attract. The north pole of a magnet is the one which points roughly north (while dipping towards the earth at 67° to the horizontal in Britain, and at 90° at the earth's magnetic poles), when the magnet is freely pivoted at its centre of gravity. This compass property arises because the earth is a giant magnet, owing to conducting fluid currents in its core. The positions of the earth's magnetic poles vary somewhat from year to year, so compass readings have to be interpreted carefully. Homing pigeons rely on the earth's magnetic field for their sense of direction□

magnetite a black iron ore, magnetic iron oxide, Fe_3O_4, found in igneous rocks. It may possess polarity (a lodestone) and was used as a compass as early as the first millennium BC□

magnetosphere see atmosphere◊□

Magnitogorsk industrial city (metallurgical, steel, motor vehicles, tractors, railway rolling stock) in the Ural Mountains, central USSR; population 419 000□

magnolia genus of tropical and sub-tropical trees and shrubs, family Magnoliaceae, with glossy foliage and large simple, 'waxen' flowers, in white, pink, or purple□

magpie bird of the family Corvidae◊□

Magritte René 1898–1967. Belgian Surrealist painter e.g. *The Eye* (Museum of Modern Art, New York)□

Magyars largest ethnic group in Hungary◊□

Mahabharata Sanskrit epic 'Great poem of the Bharatas', composed c300BC. It deals with the fortunes of the rival families of the Kauravas and the Pandavas. See Krishna◊. An episode in the 6th book, the ***Bhagavad Gita*** or ***Song of the Blessed*** is the supreme religious expression of Hinduism□

Maharashtra W central state of India
area 307 762 sq km/118 796 sq mi
capital Bombay
features village of Ajanta with cave temples of 200BC–7th century AD (Buddhist murals and sculptures); also Ellora cave temples (6–9th-century Buddhist, Hindu, and Jain sculptures)
population 62 693 900
language Marathi
religion Hinduism 80%, Parsee, Jain, and Sikh minorities□

maharishi Hindu guru, or spiritual leader, especially Maharishi Mahesh Yogi, who influenced the Beatles◊ for a time□

Mahayana a school of Buddhism◊□

Mahdi title, 'he who is guided aright', of an anticipated Islamic messiah. Most famous of those assuming it was ***Mohammed Ahmed*** 1848–85 whose revolt against Egypt included the capture of Khartoum◊□

mah-jong or ***mah-jongg*** Asia's most popular game, played by four people with a pool of 144 small 'tiles', which the players build into six matched sets. It is based on a card game invented under the Chinese Sung dynasty□

Mahler Gustav 1860–1911. Austrian Romantic composer of Jewish extraction. He conducted at the Imperial Opera, Vienna 1897–1907, and in the USA at the Metropolitan Opera in 1907 and as director of the Philharmonic Orchestra, New York. His works include ten symphonies, and song cycles (*Kindertotenlieder* 1902 and *Das Lied von der Erde* 1908)□

mahogany hard, durable timber, often richly grained, derived from trees of genus *Swietenia* and *Khaya,* family Meliaceae, and grown in Spain, Africa, and S and Central

America. It is used for fine furniture◊□

Mahón port, capital of Minorca◊; population 20 000□

Mahrattas or *Marathas* people of Maharashtra◊, India, speaking the Marathi language. In the 17–18th centuries they formed a powerful military confederacy in rivalry with the Mogul emperors. The Afghan allies of the latter defeated them 1761, and, after a series of wars with the British 1779–1871, most of their territory was annexed□

Maiden Castle see under Dorchester◊□

maidenhair a class of fern◊□

maidenhair tree see gingko◊□

Maidenhead town in Berkshire, England; population 48 000□

Maidstone industrial town (agricultural machinery, paper and printing, brewing) in Kent, England, centre of a hop and fruitgrowing area; population 73 000. The Elizabethan Chillington Manor is an art gallery and museum, and there is the Tyrwhitt-Drake Carriage Museum□

Maiduguri city in NE Nigeria; population 189 000□

Maikop industrial city (timber, distilling, tanning, oil refining) in SW USSR; population 128 000□

Mailer Norman 1923– . American novelist, born in New Jersey, son of a S African immigrant. His novels include *The Naked and the Dead* 1948, dealing with World War II, and *An American Dream* 1965□

Maillol Aristide Joseph Bonaventure 1861–1944. French sculptor, originally a painter. His work is bold and leads towards the abstract in its monumental simplicity, e.g. the bronze figure *Mediterranean* 1905 and *Fame* for the Cézanne monument at Aix-en-Provence□

Maimonides Moses (Moses Ben Maimon) 1135–1204. Jewish philosopher, codifier of the Jewish law in the *Mishneh Torah* 1180□

Maine north-easternmost state of the USA, largest of the New England states; Pine Tree State

area 86 027 sq km/33 215 sq mi

capital Auga

towns Portland

features Appalachian Mountains; Acadia National Park; headquarters of the 'outdoors' mail-order firm L L Bean (founded in 1912) in Freeport; 80% of the state is forested

products dairy and market garden produce; paper, pulp and timber; textiles

population 1 124 660

famous people Longfellow, Edna St Vincent Millay, Kate Douglas Wiggin

history settled from 1623, it became a state in 1820□

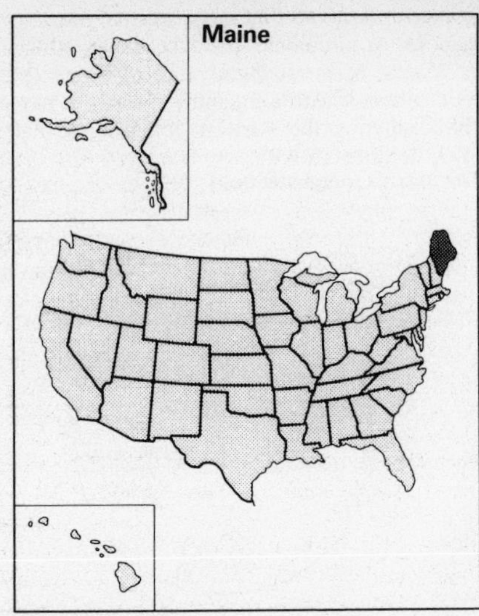

Maintenon Françoise d'Aubigné, Marquise de Maintenon 1653–1719. Second wife of Louis◊ XIV from 1684. Widow of the poet Scarron, she was governess to the children of Mme de Montespan◊ by Louis, and secretly married the king after the death of Queen Marie Thérèse in 1683. Her political influence was considerable, and, as a Catholic convert from Protestantism, her religious opinions were zealous□

Mainz industrial city (printing, paper, pharmaceuticals, electronics), capital of the Rhineland-Palatinate, W Germany; population 186 600. Birthplace of printing in Europe c1448 (see Gutenberg◊), it has a Museum of World Printing. The cathedral was founded in 975□

maiolica Italian ware. See under pottery◊, history of□

maize a type of grass◊□

Majorca largest of the Balearic◊ Islands□

Makalu see Himalayas◊□

Makarios III 1913–77. Cypriot Orthodox archbishop 1950–77. Exiled by the British to the Seychelles 1956–7 for supporting armed action to achieve union with Greece, he was president of the republic of Cyprus 1960–77 (briefly deposed by a Greek military coup Jul–Dec 1974)□

Makarova Natalia 1940– . Russian ballerina. With the Kirov Ballet 1959–70, she then sought political asylum in the West. Her great roles include Giselle, and Tatyana in *Eugene Onegin*□

Makeyevka industrial city (coal, iron and steel, chemicals) in the Donets Basin, SE Ukraine, USSR; population 446 000□

Makhachkala industrial port (oil-refining, shipbuilding, chemicals, textiles) (formerly Petrovsk) on the Caspian, capital of Daghestan, USSR; population 287 000□

Malabar Coast coastal area of Karnataka and Kerala states, India, between the Arabian Sea and the Western Ghats. Lagoons fringe the shore□

Malacca state of Malaysia; population 453 155. Capital Malacca□

Malacca Strait of. Between Sumatra and the Malay Peninsula; length 965 km/600 mi; narrows to less than 38 km/24 mi wide□

Málaga industrial seaport and holiday resort in Andalusia, Spain; population 503 250. Founded by the Phoenicians, it was taken by the Moors in 711, and was capital of an independent kingdom until captured by Ferdinand and Isabella in 1487□

Malagasy Republic former name of Madagascar◊□

Malamud Bernard 1914–86. American novelist: *The Natural* 1952, with a professional baseball player hero; *The Assistant* 1957, more typical with its Yiddish-speaking immigrant characters, *The Fixer* 1966, and *Dubin's Lives* 1979□

malaria infectious disease, marked by periodic fever and an enlarged spleen, which infects some 200 million people a year. When a mosquito of the *Anopheles* genus bites a human being with malaria, it takes in with the human blood the malaria parasite (see under life◊). This matures within the insect, and is then transferred when the mosquito bites a new victim. Inside the human body the parasite settles first in the liver, then multiplies to attack the red blood cells, when the symptoms of malaria become evident. Both mosquitoes and the malarial parasites have become 'resistant', but a vaccine is under development. See blackwater◊ fever, Sir Ronald Ross◊, and Hyderabad◊□

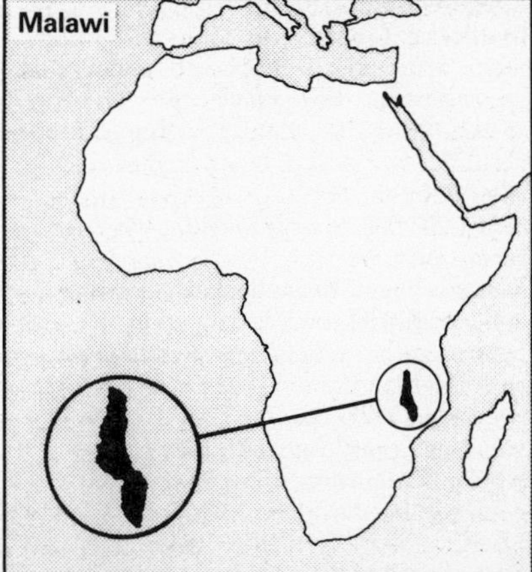

Malawi Republic of
area 117 000 sq km/47 950sq mi
capital Lilongwe
towns Blantyre-Limbe
features Lake Malawi; Livingstonia National Park on the Nyika Plateau in the N, rich in orchids, arthropods, elephants, etc.; Shiré Highlands, noted for tea and tobacco, and rising to 1750 m/5800 ft
exports tea, tobacco, cotton, groundnuts, sugar
currency kwacha
population 5 900 000
language English (official); Chichewa
religion Christianity 50%; Islam 30%
government there is an executive president (Hastings Banda from 1966) and parliament, which may include any number of nominated members in addition to those elected. The Malawi Congress Party is the only permitted political party.
recent history a British protectorate from 1891, Malawi was known from 1907 as Nyasaland, and linked with the Rhodesias 1953–63 in the Federation of Rhodesia and Nyasaland. In 1964 it became independent as Malawi, and in 1966 became a republic within the Commonwealth□

Malawi Lake. See Great Lakes◊□

Malay Peninsula southern projection of Asia; the N is divided between Burma and Thailand, and the S forms part of Malaysia◊□

Malaysia

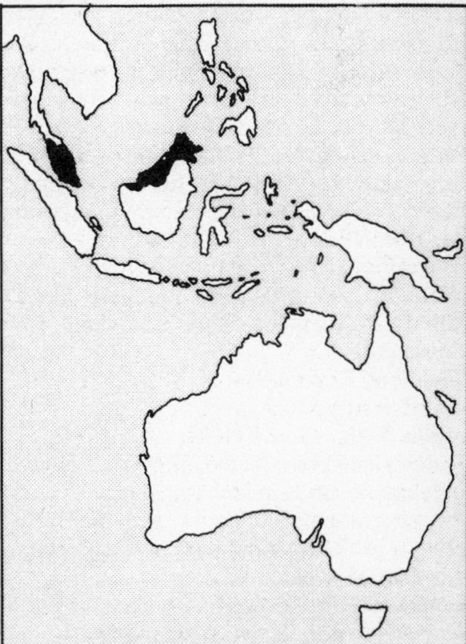

area 331 500 sq km/128 000 sq mi

capital Kuala Lumpur
towns Kuching in Sarawak and Kota Kinabalu in Sabah
features comprises W Malaysia (the nine Malay States – Perlis, Kedah, Johore, Selangor, Perak, Negri Sembilan, Kelantan, Trengganu, Pahang; plus Penang and Malacca); and E Malaysia (Sarawak and Sabah)
exports pineapples, palm oil; rubber, timber; petroleum (Sarawak), bauxite
currency ringgit
population 14 000 000; Malays (bumiputras, native-born) 47%; Chinese 34%; Indians, Pakistanis 9%, and indigenous peoples (Dayaks, Ibans) of E Malaysia 10%
language Malay (official: it is usually written in Arabic characters); in Sarawak English is also official
religion Islam (official)
government head of state (federation) (Mahmud Iskander from 1984). The head of state is elected from among their number by the nine rulers of the Malay states for five years; a senate, and an elected house of representatives (Prime Minister from 1981 Mahathir bin Mohamed).
recent history Britain extended her influence over peninsular Malaya from 1874: see also the other component areas of the modern federation. In World War II Malaya was over-run by the Japanese 1941–2, and after the war there was an 'emergency' Jun 1948–60, when the Communists attempted a takeover by guerrilla warfare (see Sir Gerald Templer◊). In 1963 the Federation of Malaysia was formed within the Commonwealth, by the linking of the former Federation of Malaya, Sarawak, N Borneo (then renamed Sabah), and Singapore (seceded in 1965). Indonesia opposed its formation, but in 1966 militant 'confrontation' ceased. There has been Communist guerrilla activity on the Thai-Malaysia border from 1969□

Malcolm III called Canmore d. 1093. King of Scotland from 1054, the son of Duncan◊; killed at Alnwick while invading Northumberland□

Maldives Republic of
area 298 sq km/115 sq mi
capital Malé
features comprises some 2000 coral islands, only about 200 being inhabited
exports coconuts and copra, and bonito (fish related to tunny), and tourism is important
currency Maldivian rupee
population 143 000
language Divehi (related to Sinhalese)
religion Sunni Islam
government executive president (Maumoon Abdul Gayoom from 1978), with a cabinet and house of representatives; no political parties are allowed
recent history under British protection from 1887, the Maldives became independent in 1965, a republic in 1968, and in 1985 became a full member of the Commonwealth□

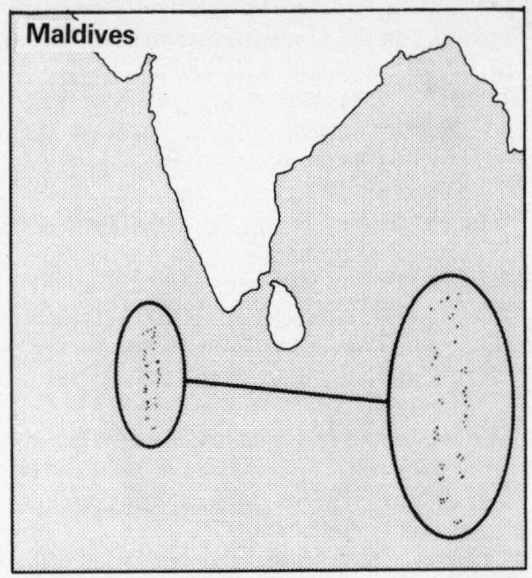

Maldon market town in Essex, England; population 15 000. The East Saxons were defeated here by the Danes in 991, as commemorated in the Anglo-Saxon poem *The Battle of Maldon*□

Malebranche Nicolas 1638–1715. French philosopher influenced by Descartes◊, who maintained that our ideas of external objects are obtainable only through God□

Malenkov Georgi 1901– . Soviet Prime Minister 1953–55, ousted by Khrushchev◊□

Malevich Kasimir 1878–1935. Russian abstract painter, born in Kiev, whose *Black Square on White Ground* 1915 launched Suprematism◊□

Malherbe François de 1555–1628. French poet, 'reformer' of the French language and versification, who made the 12-syllable Alexandrine◊ the standard form of French verse□

Mali Republic of
area 1 204 000 sq km/465 000 sq mi
capital Bamako
features Niger river; includes part of the Sahara; the old town of Timbuktu
exports cotton, groundnuts, livestock etc.
currency Mali franc
population 7 490 000
language French (official); Bambara
religion Sunni Islam 65%; Animist 35%
government executive president (General Moussa Traoré from 1969, with extensions) elected once only for six years, with a council

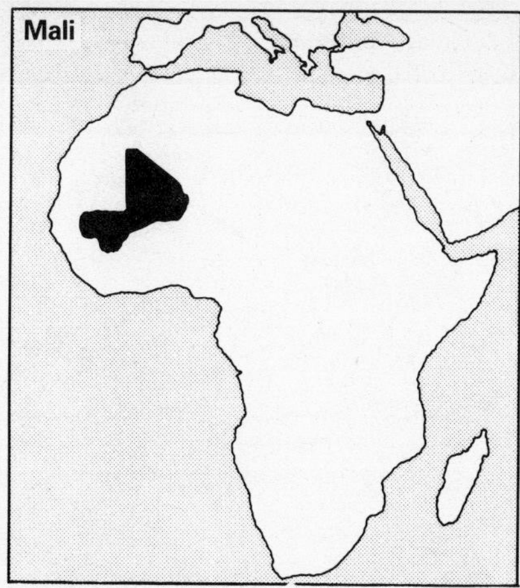

of ministers, and national assembly elected for three years. There is only one political party, the Democratic Union of the Mali People, UDPM.
recent history from 1895 annexed as French Sudan, it became an independent republic in 1960, and in 1968 there was a military coup by Traoré□

malic acid colourless acid, with needle-like crystals, obtained from fruits such as apples, plums, cherries, grapes, etc.□

Malik Yakob 1906–80. Russian diplomat, permanent representative at the United Nations 1948–53, 1968–76; his walk-out from the Security Council in Jan 1950, allowed the authorization of United Nations intervention in Korea□

Malines French form of Mechelen◊□

Malinowski Bronislaw 1884–1942. Polish anthropologist, whose study of the peoples of New Guinea led him to see every custom, etc, as 'functional'□

Malipiero Gian Francesco 1882–1973. Italian composer, editor of Monteverdi and Vivaldi. His own works include operas based on Shakespeare's *Julius Caesar* and *Antony and Cleopatra* in pre-19th-century style□

Mallarmé Stéphane 1842–98. French poet, who founded (with Verlaine◊) the Symbolist school. His *L'Après-midi d'un faune* 1876 inspired Debussy◊□

mallee mixture of dwarf eucalyptus trees (with many small stems, and thick underground stems retaining water) and more treelike forms. Before irrigation farming it characterized the mallee region of NW Victoria, Australia□

malleiodosis disease caused by a bacterium in the soil, especially in SE Asia, with 95% mortality if untreated. Local people have immunity, but foreigners and even dolphins (when soil has been washed into the sea) are vulnerable. A vaccine is being developed□

Mallorca Spanish form of Majorca◊□

mallow flowering plants of family Malvaceae, including European ***common mallow*** *Malva sylvestris*; ***tree mallow*** *Lavatera arborea*; and ***marsh mallow*** *Althaea officinalis*. See also hollyhock◊□

Malmaison see under Josephine◊□

Malmédy see Eupen◊-et-Malmédy□

Malmö port and industrial city (shipbuilding, textiles) in S Sweden; population 230 400□

Malory Sir Thomas c1400–71. English author, thought to have been a Warwickshire landowner and MP for Warwick in 1445. His prose romance *Morte d'Arthur* 1469 (printed by Caxton◊ in 1485) was compiled (from a French version and other sources) during 20 years in Newgate, following charges in 1451/2 of theft, rape, and attempted murder□

Malpighi Marcello 1628–94. Italian physiologist, who discovered the capillary system (see blood◊), a pioneer in the use of the microscope; and also worked on the kidney, spleen, etc.□

Malplaquet Battle of, 1709, in War of Spanish◊ Succession□

Malraux André 1901–76. French novelist, student of art, oriental languages, and archaeology. He became involved in the Kuomintang revolution, reflected in *La Condition humaine* (*Storm over Shanghai*) 1933; *L'Espoir* (*Days of Hope*) 1937 is set in Civil War Spain, where he was a bomber-pilot in the International Brigade. In World War II he supported the Resistance, and was Minister of Cultural Affairs 1960–9□

malt grain (usually barley) allowed to germinate and then dried, used for flavour and colour in brewing, and for malt extracts□

Malta Knights of. See St John◊ of Jerusalem□

Malta Republic of
area 316 sq km/122 sq mi
capital Valletta
features includes the island of Gozo 67 sq km/26 sq mi and Comino 2.5 sq km/1 sq mi; large commercial dock facilities
exports vegetables, knitwear, hand-made lace, plastics, electronic equipment, etc.
currency Maltese pound
population 326 200
language Maltese (related to Arabic, with Phoenician survivals and influenced by Italian)
religion Roman Catholicism
famous people St Paul was wrecked here
government president and house of representatives, elected by proportional representa-

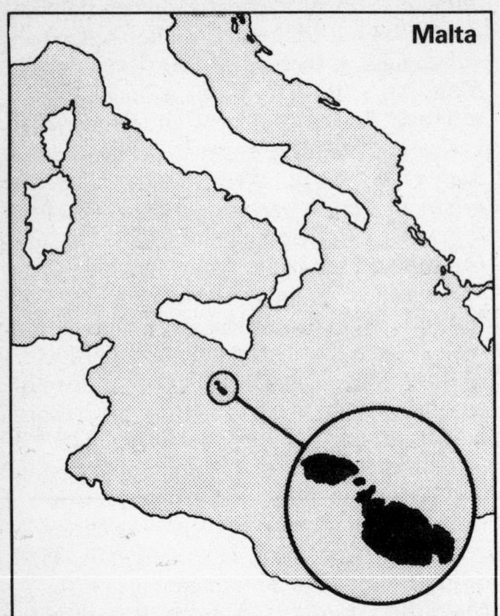

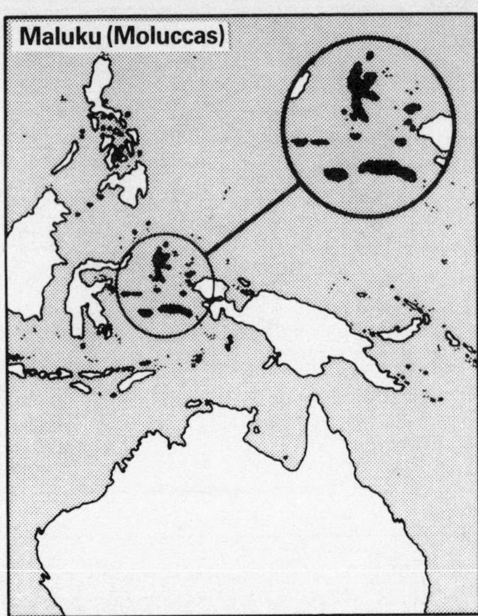

tion (Prime Minister from 1984 Carmelo Mifsud Bonnici, b. 1933)

history the island was colonized by Phoenicians, Greeks, Carthaginians, and Romans. It fell to the Arabs in 870, was the headquarters of the Knights of St John◊ from 1530, passed to France in 1798 (see Napoleonic◊ Wars), and became British in 1814. During World War II it was under siege and air attack. Independent within the Commonwealth from 1964, it became a republic in 1974, and from 1979 the British military presence and naval use of the dockyards ended. Under Labour Prime Minister Mintoff◊ the republic adopted a policy of 'positive neutralism', and opposition to the influence of the Catholic church□

Malthus Thomas Robert 1766–1834. British cleric and economist, whose *Essay on the Principle of Population* 1798 and 1803 (which influenced Darwin◊), argued for population planning by birth control since people increase in geometric ratio, and food only in arithmetical ratio□

Maluku or ***Moluccas*** group of Indonesian islands; area 83 675 sq km/32 300 sq mi. Chief town Ambon. Famous as the Spice Islands, they were formerly part of the Netherlands E Indies, and the S Moluccas attempted secession from the newly created Indonesian Republic from 1949; exiles continue agitation in the Netherlands□

Malvern spa in the Malvern Hills, Hereford◊ and Worcester, England; population 30 500. The Royal Radar Establishment is here. The ***Malvern Festival,*** associated with Shaw and Elgar, is held annually□

Malvinas Argentine name for the Falkland◊ Islands□

Mamelukes freed Turkish slaves (Arabic *mamluk* 'slave') imported by the Egyptian sultan in the 13th century as a bodyguard, but who in 1250 placed one of themselves on the throne. Mameluke rule continued till the Turkish conquest of 1517, but they remained the ruling class until massacred by Mehemet Ali in 1811□

mammal member of class Mammalia (over 4000 species) which includes all vertebrates which suckle their young and are covered with hair. Most give birth to live young (viviparous), but see under monotremata◊. The orders are:

Monotremata◊ echidna, platypus
Marsupialia◊ kangaroo, koala, opossum
Insectivora◊ shrew, hedgehog, mole
Chiroptera◊ bat
Primates lemur, monkey, ape, man
Edentata◊ anteater, armadillo, sloth
Pholidota◊ pangolin
Dermoptera◊ flying lemur
Rodentia◊ rat, mouse, squirrel, porcupine
Lagomorpha◊ rabbit, hare
Cetacea◊ whale, dolphin, porpoise
Carnivora◊ cat, dog, weasel, bear
Pinnipedia◊ seal, walrus
Artiodactyla◊ pig, deer, camel, cattle, giraffe
Perissodactyla◊ horse, rhinoceros, tapir
Sirenia◊ dugong
Tubulidentata aardvark
Hyracoidae hyrax
Proboscidae elephant□

mammoth extinct elephant◊□

Mammoth Cave see under Kentucky◊□

man the species *Homo sapiens,* a member of the primates, from whom humans have evolved. The earliest creatures resembling

Mammals: The Major Orders

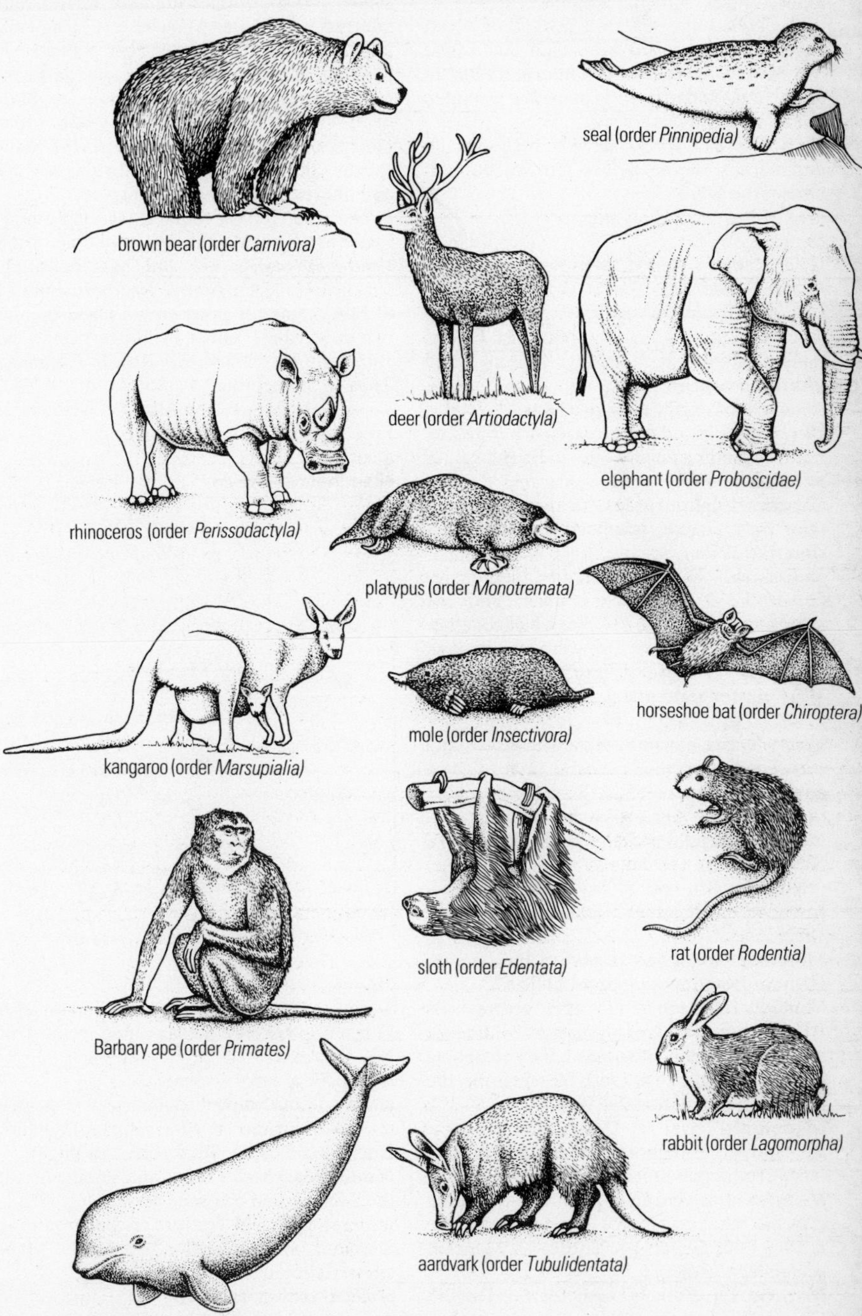

man are thought to have evolved some 14 million years ago, but it was not until 5–3 million years ago that hominids appear to have divided into several types, all of which except *Homo sapiens* have died out. Much controversy surrounds the interpretation of finds connected with early man. See primate◊ family tree and evolution◊□

Man Isle of. Island in the Irish Sea, a dependency of the British Crown, but not part of the UK
area 518 sq km/221 sq mi
capital Douglas
towns Ramsey, Peel, Castletown
features Snaefell 620 m/2034 ft; annual TT (Tourist Trophy) motorcycle races, gambling casinos, Britain's first freeport, tax haven; tailless Manx cat; tourism, banking, and insurance flourish
exports light engineering products
currency the island produces its own coins and notes (including one for 50p) in British values
population 64 700
language English (Manx, nearer to Scottish than Irish Gaelic, has been almost extinct since the 1970s)
government crown-appointed Lieutenant-Governor, a legislative council, and the representative House of Keys, which together make up the Court of Tynwald, passing laws subject to the Royal Assent. Laws passed at Westminster only affect the island if specifically so provided.
history Norwegian until 1266, when the island was ceded to Scotland, it came under Crown administration in 1765□

man primitive. See evolution◊□

Managua capital and chief industrial city of Nicaragua, on the lake of the same name; population 820 000. It has twice been destroyed by earthquake and rebuilt, in 1931 and 1972□

Manama capital and oil port of Bahrain, on Bahrain Island; population 122 000□

Manáus river port and tourist centre in N Brazil on the Rio Negro, near its confluence with the Amazon (it is reached by sea-going ships although 1600 km/1000 mi from the Atlantic); population 730 000□

Manawatu river in North Island, New Zealand; the ***Manawatu Plain*** is a dairying and lamb production area□

Mancha La. Former province of Spain (Arabic 'the dry land'), now part of the autonomous region of Castilla-La Mancha; see under Castile◊□

Manche La. French name for the English Channel◊□

Manchester industrial city (19th-century world leader in cotton textiles; modern products also including vehicles and tractors, textile machinery, chemicals, rubber, processed foods), former administrative headquarters of Greater Manchester◊, England; population 464 200. It is also a financial, banking, and insurance centre, and Manchester University was linked with a science◊ park in 1984 (including Granada Television, Ciba-Geigy, and Ferranti). Also a port: the Manchester Ship Canal links it with the Mersey and the sea, and there is an airport.
A centre of radical thought (see Peterloo◊, Pankhurst◊), it was the original home of the *Guardian* newspaper, and has the international Hallé Orchestra, Northern College of Music, fine art galleries and libraries, and two universities. Other buildings include the 15th-century cathedral, Royal Exchange Theatre, refurbished Palace Theatre, 1890, Town Hall (designed by Alfred Waterhouse), Free Trade Hall, and Cotton Exchange (now a leisure centre)□

Manchester Greater

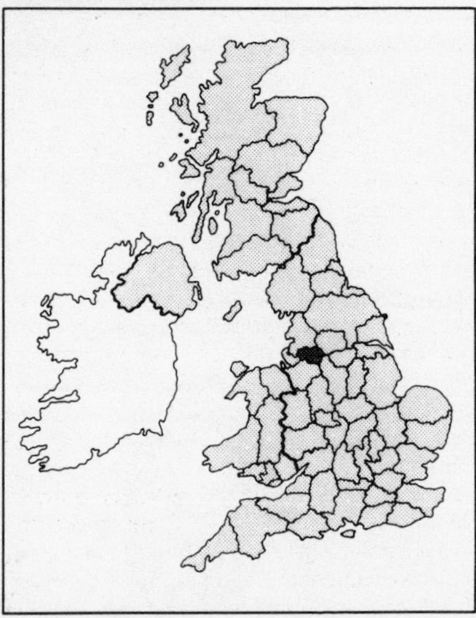

Former (1974–86) metropolitan county of NW England
area 1287 sq km/497sq mi
towns administrative headquarters Manchester; Altrincham, Bolton, Bury, Oldham, Rochdale, Salford, Stockport, and Wigan
features Manchester Ship Canal linking it with the Mersey and the sea; very little remains undeveloped; Old Trafford cricket ground at Stretford, and the football ground of Manchester United
products industrial
population 2 595 000
famous people Anthony Burgess, Gracie Fields, David Lloyd George, Emmeline Pan-

khurst, Sir William Walton□

Manchukuo see under Manchuria◊□

Manchuria European name for the NE region of China (provinces of Heilongjiang, Jilin, and Liaoning). From the 17th century it was controlled by the Manchus, and a Manchu dynasty ruled China by conquest 1644–1912. Chinese colonization of Manchuria began in the 18th century (80% of the population by 1900), but as the Chinese Empire declined Japan and Russia were rivals for its control. The Japanese gained the advantage through the Russo◊-Japanese War, although it was not until 1932 that Japan consolidated her position by creating a puppet state (Manchukuo) under Henry Pu◊ Yi (capital Hsinking, modern Chinese Changchun◊), which disintegrated on the defeat of Japan in World War II in 1945. Japanese settlers were expelled□

Mandaean or ***Mandean*** a member of a Gnostic sect. See under Gnosticism◊□

mandala circular designs in Hindu and Buddhist art which represent the Universe□

mandarin European name (from Portuguese 'counsellor') for officials of imperial China from the 7th century, chosen by examination, and speaking the dialect (of Peking) which is now standard in China. See Chinese◊□

mandarine a type of orange. See citrus◊□

mandate under the Treaty of Versailles, the system whereby the administration of former German and Turkish possessions was entrusted to Allied States by the League of Nations, the latter being replaced as the responsible authority in 1945 by the United Nations, when mandates which had not achieved independence or self-government became known as Trust Territories◊. S◊W Africa is an exception in that the Republic of S Africa does not recognize United Nations authority in this□

Mandela Nelson 1918– . South African lawyer-politician. As organizer of the banned African National Congress (ANC), he was tried for treason and acquitted 1956–61, but was jailed for life in 1964 on charges of sabotage and plotting to overthrow the government. His wife Winnie Mandela subsequently became a prominent spokesperson for the ANC and has been put under house arrest several times□

Mandelstam Osip Emilevich 1891?–1938. Russian poet, son of a Jewish merchant, first exiled, then in 1934 sent to a concentration camp, where he died. His reputation was established by the posthumous publication of his work by his widow, which has a classic brevity□

Mandeville Sir John 14th century. Supposed author of *Travels*, a manual for pilgrims to the Holy Land, which was compiled from other sources. Besides real marvels, it includes headless men with eyes in their shoulders and other wonders□

mandoline musical instrument with 8/10 strings, descended from the lute◊, and so called because it had an almond-shaped body (Italian *mandorla* = 'almond')□

mandragora genus of almost stemless plants with narcotic properties, also known as ***mandrake,*** family Solanaceae◊. They have large leaves, pale blue or violet flowers, and globose berries (devil's apples); the humanoid shape of the root started a superstition that it shrieks when pulled from the ground□

mandrake see mandragora◊□

mandrill a type of monkey□

Manes for the Romans, the spirits of the dead, revered as lesser deities, or sometimes identified with the gods of the underworld. See Hades◊□

Manet Édouard 1832–83. French painter. His *Le Déjeuner sur l'herbe* 1863, with two nude women with the dressed men of the party, and his nude *Olympia* 1863, aroused great controversy, and the former was rejected by the Salon. His freedom of treatment of the play of light brought him the support of the Impressionists◊ who were greatly influenced by him. Best known of his later works is *Un Bar aux Folies Bergère* 1882□

Mangalore industrial port (textiles, food-processing) in Karnataka, India; population 306 000□

manganese element
symbol Mn
atomic number 25
physical description silvery-white metal
features among the most common metals in the earth's crust
uses in steel alloys, as well as bronze, brass, and nickel alloys□

mangel wurzel or ***mangold wurzel*** a variety of the beet◊ plant□

mango Asian tree *Mangifera indica,* family Anacardiaceae, with large orange or red kidney-shaped fleshy edible fruit□

mangold see mangel◊ wurzel□

mangrove genus *Rhizophora* of tropical coastal and estuarine shrubs/trees, family Rhizophoraceae, which can desalinate sea water. They have roots growing from the trunk and branches, and form close-growing mangrove swamps useful for soil retention etc.; directly and indirectly they provide food for shellfish and fish, as well as shelter and nursery areas; the timber is impervious to water and resists marine worms; and they provide raw materials used in making dyes, glues, rayon, and tannin□

Manhattan an island, the business centre of New◊ York City□

Manhattan project code-name for the development of the atom bomb in the USA in World War II. See Fermi◊, Oppenheimer◊□

Manichaeism religion founded by the Persian *Mani* (Latin *Manichaeus*) c216–c276AD. He was put to death at the instigation of the Zoroastrian priesthood. He claimed the material world was an invasion of the realm of light by the powers of darkness, though the particle of god's goodness contained in man could be rescued by messengers such as Jesus, and finally himself. He continued to have followers till the 13th century, and influenced later heresies□

Manila capital and chief port of the Philippines, on Luzon; population 6 000 000. Founded by Spain in 1571, it was captured by the USA in 1898, and was largely reduced to rubble in the fighting of World War II. It was replaced as the capital 1948–76 by the suburb, Quezon City□

manioc a shrubby flowering plant. See cassava◊□

Manipur state of north eastern India
area 22 356 sq km/8629 sq mi
capital Imphal
features Loktak Lake; original Indian home of polo
population 1 433 700
language Hindi
religion Hinduism 70%□

Manitoba western prairie province of Canada

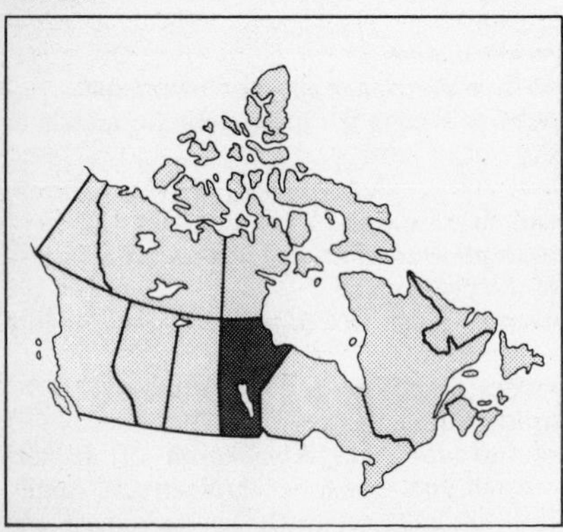

area 650 088 sq km/251 000 sq mi
capital Winnipeg
features Lakes Winnipeg, Winnipegosis, and Manitoba (area 4700 sq km/1800 sq mi); half the area is forested
exports grain, manufactured foods, and beverages; machinery; furs, fish, minerals (nickel, zinc, copper, and Manitoba has the world's largest caesium deposits)
population 1 056 500. See also Canada◊□

Manizales city in W Colombia, 2150 m/7000 ft up in the central Cordillera, so that it is linked with Mariquita by the world's longest overhead cable transport system 75 km/45 mi; population 320 000□

Mann Heinrich 1871–1950. German novelist, who fled to the USA with his brother Thomas Mann◊. He is popularly known for *Professor Unrat/The Blue Angel* 1904, basis of the Marlene Dietrich◊ film□

Mann Thomas 1875–1955. German novelist, brother of Heinrich Mann◊. His first novel *Buddenbrooks* 1900, dealt with an old Hanseatic family in his native Lübeck, and *The Magic Mountain* 1924 led to a Nobel prize in 1929. Forced abroad by the Nazi regime, he became a US citizen in 1940. Later were *Dr Faustus* 1947 and *Confessions of Felix Krull* 1954. Most famous of his short stories was 'Death in Venice' 1913□

manna sweetish exudation from trees; biblical manna was possibly that from the tamarisk, and that from the ash *Fraxinus ornus* is a laxative□

Mannerheim Carl Gustav Emil, Baron von Mannerheim 1867–1951. Finnish soldier-statesman. With German help he defeated a Russo-Finnish attempt to establish a Socialist republic; commanded the army in the Russo-Finnish wars of 1939–40 and 1941–4, and was president 1944–6□

Mannerism in painting and architecture, the term used to describe reaction away from the peak of Renaissance classicism as achieved by Raphael◊, Leonardo◊, and early Michelangelo◊. It is characterized by a conscious breaking of the 'rules' of classical composition; thus, a typical Mannerist painting displays the human body in a distorted pose, often off-centre or in the corner of the picture, using harsh, non-blending colours. The effect is one of unsettling the viewer, who is expected to understand the norms which the Mannerist picture is deliberately violating. Strictly speaking, Mannerism is used to describe painters and architects in Italy (primarily Rome and Florence) during the years 1520 to 1575 beginning with, and largely derived from, the later works of Michelangelo◊ in painting and architecture, and including the works of the painters Rosso◊ and Parmigianino◊, and the architect Giulio Romano, but the term has been extended to cover similar ideas in other arts and in other countries□

Manners Lady Diana. See Lord Norwich◊□

Mannheim industrial city (heavy machinery, glass, earthenware, chemicals) in Baden-Württemberg, W Germany; population 303

800. The modern symphony orchestra, with its balance of instruments and the important role of the conductor, originated at Mannheim in the 18th century when the elector palatine assembled the finest players of his day□

Manning Henry Edward 1808–92. British churchman, converted to Catholicism in 1851. He succeeded Wiseman as Archbishop of Westminster in 1865, and was created a cardinal in 1875, the year of his ardent dispute (*The Vatican Decrees*) with Gladstone on the question of papal infallibity□

Manning Olivia 1911–80. British novelist, author of 'The Balkan Trilogy' 1960–5 (*The Great Fortune*, *The Spoilt City*, and *Friends and Heroes*), which is based on her own experiences in World War II□

manometer instrument for measuring the pressure of liquids (including human blood pressure) or gases. In its basic form, it is a U-tube part-filled with coloured liquid; pressure of a gas entering at one side is measured by how far the liquid rises at the other□

manor basic economic unit in feudal Europe, and systematically put into effect under the Norman conquest in England. It usually comprised the lord's demesne (land round the manor house cultivated for his own use), land held by the free tenants (usually at a rent), and that held by villeins (usually in return for heavy labour on the lord's land); common land (unenclosed, on which villagers might have specific rights to pasture cattle, etc.); woodland, and waste land. Here and there traces of the system survive in England, e.g. the common land may have become an area for public recreation, but the documents sometimes sold at auction and entitling the owner to be called 'lord of the manor' seldom have any rights attached to them□

Mansart Jules-Hardouin 1646–1708. French architect of the palace of Versailles and Grand Trianon, and designer of the Place de Vendôme and the Place des Victoires, Paris□

Mansfield Katherine. Pseudonym of New Zealand writer Kathleen Mansfield Beauchamp 1888–1923. Born near Wellington, New Zealand, she settled in London, had a brief disastrous marriage with an older man (George Bowden) in 1909, and in 1918 married literary critic John Middleton Murry. She died of tuberculosis. Her volumes of short stories include *Bliss* 1920 and *The Garden Party* 1922; they have a delicate sensitivity□

Mansfield industrial town (textiles, shoes, machinery, chemicals, coal) in Nottinghamshire, England; population 58 000□

manslaughter under English law an unlawful killing of a human being in circumstances not so culpable as murder, e.g. when the killer suffers extreme provocation, or is in some way mentally sick (diminished responsibility); did not intend to kill but did so accidentally in the course of another crime or by behaving with criminal recklessness; or is the survivor of a genuine suicide pact which involved killing the other person□

Manson Sir Patrick 1844–1922. British doctor, who proved infectious diseases may have animal carriers, e.g. elephantiasis◊□

Manston see under Kent◊□

Mansûra industrial city (cotton) in N Egypt, on the Nile delta; population 258 000. In 1250 the crusading St Louis IX of France was held prisoner in the fortress for ransom□

manta large rayfish◊□

Mantegna Andrea 1431–1506. Italian artist, brother-in-law of Giovanni Bellini◊. His works include nine panels depicting *The Triumph of Caesar* at Hampton Court, and *The Madonna with John the Baptist and the Magdalen* and *The Agony in the Garden* (both London). See also Mantua◊□

mantis insect, family Mantidae, especially the ***praying mantis*** *M religiosa* of S Europe, which adapts its coloration to the background, and waits for its prey in an attitude characteristic of devotion. That the female eats the male after mating is a legend□

mantra in Hindu or Buddhist belief a word repeatedly intoned to assist concentration and develop spiritual power, e.g. *om* trisyllabic in pronunciation, and representing the names of Brahma, Vishnu, and Siva. Followers of a guru may receive their own individual mantra□

Mantua town on an island in a lagoon in Lombardy, N Italy; population 65 400. Virgil◊ was born here, and the ducal palace has frescoes by Mantegna◊□

Manu according to Hinduism, the founder of the human race. Like Noah, he was saved by a deity (Brahma) from a deluge□

Manutius Aldus 1450–1515. Italian printer, established in Venice (which he made the publishing centre of Europe) from 1490; he introduced italic type and was the first to print Greek books□

Manx Gaelic◊ language of the Isle of Man◊□

Manzoni Alessandro, Count Manzoni 1785–1873. Italian author, best-known for the historical romance *I Promessi Sposi* 1825–7; Verdi's *Requiem* commemorates him□

Maori aboriginal population of New Zealand, who traditionally migrated there from Polynesia◊ (Hawaii) c1350, overcoming and absorbing a related people already in the

North Island. Tall and muscular, they are brown-skinned, with broad noses and black hair. Numbering c150 000 at the arrival of Europeans, they had a neolithic civilization. They were skilled in working stone and wood, and brave in warfare; the women wove patterned cloth and were agriculturists. A tradition of song, dance, and story-telling was maintained, with myths of heroes and strange monsters, and a supreme god, 'Io'.

In recent years there has been increased Maori consciousness, and a demand for official status for the Maori language and review of the Waitangi Treaty of 1840 (under which the Maoris surrendered their lands to British sovereignty). The ***Maori Unity Movement/ Kotahitanga*** was founded in 1983 by Mrs Eva Rickard. See also under New◊ Zealand□

Mao Zedong or ***Mao Tse-Tung*** 1893–1976. Chinese statesman, the 'Great Helmsman'. Born in Hunan◊, he became the leader of the Communists in 1927. After the rupture with the Nationalists, led by Chiang◊ Kai-shek, Mao Zedong and his troops undertook the 'Long March' of 10 000 km/6000 mi 1934–5 from SE to NW China, the prelude to his ascent to power. Again in nominal alliance with Chiang against the Japanese 1937–45, he subsequently defeated him, and proclaimed the People's Republic of China in 1949. As Chairman of the Communist Party, he provided the pattern for the development of the country through the Great Leap Forward of 1959, and the Cultural Revolution of 1966 based on his thoughts contained in the 'Little Red Book'. His reputation plunged after his death, but was later somewhat restored. See Jiang◊ Qing□

map a diagrammatic representation, e.g. of part of the earth's surface, the distribution of the stars, etc. Modern maps are made by aerial photography, a series of overlapping stereoscopic photographs being taken which can then be used to prepare a three-dimensional image. Laser beams, microwaves, and infra-red equipment are also used for land surveying, and satellite pictures make a valuable contribution when large areas are under survey□

maple N temperate genus *Acer* of mainly deciduous trees with palmately lobed leaves, green flowers, and winged fruit; family Aceraceae. It includes the British ***field maple*** *A campestre*; N American ***sugar maple*** *A saccharatum*; and the European ***sycamore*** *A pseudoplatanus*□

Maputo capital and chief port of Mozambique (formerly Lourenço Marques), with textile and food-processing industries, etc.; population 850 000□

maquis shrubby mostly evergreen vegetation. The French underground movement that fought the German occupying forces in World War II took its popular name, the maquis, from the scrubland in which its members sometimes hid□

Maracaibo port in Venezuela; population 651 575. It exports oil from the fields of ***Lake Maracaibo,*** sugar, coffee, cocoa and hardwoods□

Marat Jean Paul 1743–93. French revolutionary leader and journalist, idol of the Paris revolutionary crowds, who was elected in 1792 to the National Convention, where he carried on a long struggle with the Girondins◊, ending in their overthrow in May 1793. In Jul he was murdered by Charlotte Corday◊□

Marathon Battle of, 490BC. Fought between the Greeks (under Miltiades) and invading Persians on the plain of Marathon, NE of Athens. The news was taken to the city by Pheidippides, who fell dead on arrival. His feat is commemorated by the ***Marathon Race*** of c42 km/26 mi 385 yds, first included in the Olympic Games at Athens in 1896, and more recently by races open to application by all comers through city streets, e.g. London Marathon from 1981□

marble a hard crystalline rock. See under limestone◊□

Marble Arch triumphal arch designed by John Nash to commemorate Nelson's victories, it was intended as a ceremonial entry to London's Buckingham Palace; in 1851 it was moved to Hyde Park at the west end of Oxford Street□

Marburg industrial town in Hessen, W Germany; population 48 500. The university was founded in 1527 as a centre of Protestant teaching, and Luther and Zwingli held a conference there in 1529□

Marburg disease see haemorrhagic◊ fevers□

Marc Franz 1880–1916. German Expressionist painter, associated with Kandinsky◊ in founding the Blaue◊ Reiter movement, he used animal symbolism, e.g. *The Tower of the Blue Horses* (1911). He was killed at Verdun in World War I□

Marceau Marcel 1923– . French mime, creator of the clown-harlequin 'Bip'□

March fenland town with engineering industries in the Isle of Ely, Cambridgeshire, England; population 14 500□

Marchais Georges 1920– . French Communist leader, who became a Euro-MP in 1979□

Marchand Jean Baptiste 1863–1934. French general whose expedition from French Congo to occupy Fashoda on the White Nile in 1898 almost led to war with France when he was confronted by British troops under Kitchener◊□

Marche Le. Region of central Italy, chiefly agricultural; capital Ancona; population 1 417 000□

Marches Anglo-Scottish and Anglo-Welsh border areas, held in the Middle Ages by lords of the Mares, later earls of March. See Marquess◊□

Marconi Guglielmo 1874–1937. Italian pioneer of radio telegraphy, successfully transmitting signals across the English Channel in 1898, and in 1901 from Poldhu, Cornwall to St John's Newfoundland; Nobel physics prize in 1909□

Marcos Ferdinand 1919– . Filipino statesman. Born on Luzon, he was convicted while a law student in 1939 of murdering a political opponent of his father, but eventually secured his own acquittal. In World War II he was a guerrilla fighter, survived Bataan◊, and became president in 1965. His regime, backed by the USA, became increasingly repressive, e.g. use of the 'secret marshals', anti-crime squads executing those only suspected of offences. Overthrown and exiled in 1986□

Marcus Aurelius Antoninus 121–180. Stoic philosopher (author of *Meditations*) and Roman Emperor from 161, when he succeeded his uncle Antoninus◊ Pius (see Verus◊). He persecuted the Christians (as politically divisive), and spent much of his reign combatting Germanic invasions. He died in Pannonia, where he had gone to fight off the Marcomanni□

Marcuse Herbert 1898–1979. American philosopher, born in Germany, whose Marxist *One-Dimensional Man* 1964, advocated the overthrow of the existing social order by non-democratic means. Students and minority groups not addicted to affluence would use the system's very tolerance to ensure its defeat. He was pained by the rise of the Red◊ Brigade and Baader◊-Meinhof gang□

Marduk in Babylonian mythology, the sun-god, creator of earth and man□

mare any of a large number of huge dry plains on the moon once thought to be seas. See under earth◊□

Marengo Battle of, 1800. See under revolutionary◊ wars□

Margaret St c1045–93. Queen consort of Malcolm III of Scotland from 1070, and sister of Edgar◊ Atheling. Through her influence the Lowlands, hitherto purely Celtic, became largely Anglicized, and the marriage of her daughter Matilda to Henry I united the Norman and English royal houses□

Margaret 1283–90. Known as the 'Maid of Norway' (whose king, Eric II, she had married), she was the granddaughter of Alexander III of Scotland. She succeeded him, but died in the Orkneys on her way to her kingdom□

Margaret of Anjou 1430–82. Queen consort of Henry VI of England from 1445. In the Wars of the Roses, she headed the Lancastrians, trying to secure the succession of her son, Edward◊. Forced to withdraw to her native France in 1463, she returned in 1471, only to be defeated and captured at Tewkesbury, where her son was killed. Allowed to return to France in 1476, she died in poverty□

Margaret (Rose) 1930– . Princess of the UK, born at Glamis Castle, younger daughter of George◊ VI. Religious and constitutional problems prevented her proposed marriage to Group Captain Peter Townsend, former court equerry, in 1955. In 1960 she married Anthony Armstrong-Jones, later created Lord Snowdon, but in 1976 they mutually agreed to live apart, and were divorced in 1978. Their children are David, Viscount Linley 1961– , and Lady Sarah Armstrong-Jones 1964– □

Margate chief seaside resort of the group including Cliftonville, Westbrook, Westgate-on-Sea, and Birchington, in Kent, England; population 50 000□

margrave German title (equivalent of marquess) for the 'counts of the March', originally guardians of the frontier of Charlemagne's empire, and later borne by such territorial princes as the Margraves of Austria and of Brandenburg□

Margrethe II 1940– . Queen of Denmark from 1972. She married in 1967 Count Henri de Laborde de Monpezat (present title HRH Prince Hendrik); heir, Crown Prince Frederik 1968– □

marguerite a cultivated garden plant. See chrysanthemum◊□

Marguerite d'Angoulême 1492–1549. Sister of Francis◊ I and, by her second marriage, queen consort of the King of Navarre from 1527. She was a skilled poet, her *Heptaméron* being an imitation of Boccaccio's *Decameron*□

Mari an area of W central Soviet Union from 1936, annexed in 1552; area 23 200 sq km/ 8955 sq mi; population 711 000, 50% of Mari stock. Capital Yoshkar Ola□

Marianas archipelago in the NW Pacific, discovered by Magellan in 1521, and comprising:

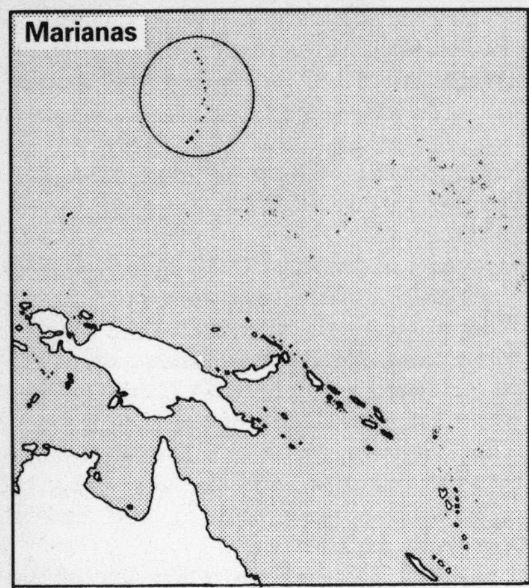

Guam Unincorporated territory of
area 535 sq km/206 sq mi
capital Agaña
towns port Apra
features largest of the Marianas; major US air and naval base, much used in the Vietnam war; tourism is important
currency US dollar
population 105 820
language English, Chamorro (basically Malay-Polynesian)
religion Roman Catholic 96%
government popularly elected Governor (Ricardo Bordallo from 1985), and unicameral legislature
recent history ceded by Spain to USA in 1898, it was occupied by the Japanese 1941–4. Granted full US citizenship and self-government from 1950
Northern Marianas Commonwealth of the
area 479 sq km/185 sq mi
capital Garapan on Saipan
features comprises 14 islands and atolls
exports sugar, coconuts, coffee
currency USA dollar
population 17 700, mainly Micronesian
language English
religion mainly Roman Catholic.
government own constitutional elected government
recent history sold to Germany by Spain in 1899, they were mandated to Japan in 1918, and taken by US Marines 1944–5 in World War II. Under US trusteeship from 1947, they voted to become a commonwealth of the US in 1978□

Mariánské Lázně spa (German Marienbad) in Czechoslovakia, with waters containing Glauber salts; population 15 000. Patrons included Edward VII□

Maria Theresa 1717–80. Austrian Empress, daughter of Emperor Charles◊ VI, whom she succeeded as Archduchess of Austria and Queen of Hungary and Bohemia in 1740. As a woman, her right to the crown was challenged by Charles of Bavaria (emperor from 1742), and Frederick of Prussia occupied Silesia. After the consequent War of the Austrian◊ Succession, she retained most of her inheritance, though not regaining Silesia, and her husband (her cousin Francis of Lorraine, whom she had married in 1736) became emperor (1745–65). Intent on recovering Silesia, she allied with France and Russia against Prussia (see Seven◊ Years' War 1756–63), which exhausted Europe and left the territorial position unchanged. Henceforward she concentrated on internal reforms. Though ruling despotically, she encouraged education, codified the law, and abolished torture. She was assisted by her son Joseph◊ II (emperor from 1765), who succeeded her in the Hapsburg domains□

Maribor industrial city (footwear, railway rolling stock) in Slovenia, Yugoslavia; population 186 000□

Marie 1875–1938. Queen consort of Ferdinand of Romania (ruled 1922–7), whom she married in 1893. Her books include an autobiography 1934–5. She was the mother of Carol◊ II□

Marie Antoinette 1755–93. Daughter of Maria◊ Theresa, and queen consort of Louis◊ XVI, whom she married in 1770. With a reputation for frivolity and extravagance, she meddled in politics in the Austrian interest, and influenced her husband to resist concessions in the revolution of 1789, e.g. Mirabeau◊'s plan for a constitutional settlement. She instigated the disastrous flight to Varennes, which discredited the monarchy, and welcomed foreign intervention against the revolution, betraying French war strategy to the Austrians in 1792. She was tried for treason in Oct 1793 and guillotined, meeting death bravely□

Marie de France c1150–1215. French poet, thought to have been the illegitimate child of Geoffrey Plantagenet (2nd husband of Matilda◊), and to have become abbess of Shaftesbury 1181–1215. She wrote *lais* (verse tales) and *Ysopet* a collection of fables□

Marie de' Medici 1573–1642. Queen consort of Henry◊ IV of France from 1600, and regent (after his murder) for their son Louis◊ XIII. She left the government to her favourites, the Concinis, until in 1617 Louis seized power and executed them. She was banished, but after she led a revolt in 1619, Richelieu◊ effected her reconciliation with her son, making it the stepping stone to his own power. When she attempted to oust him in 1630, she was again sent into exile□

Marie Louise 1791–1847. Queen consort of Napoleon I from 1810 (after his divorce from Josephine◊), she was the daughter of Francis I of Austria (see Emperor Francis◊ II). She bore him a son (see Napoleon◊ II), and on his fall returned to Austria. In 1815 she was granted the duchy of Parma□

Marienbad German name of Mariánské◊ Lázně□

Mariette Auge Ferdinand François 1821–81. French Egyptologist, whose discoveries from 1850 included the 'temple' between the paws of the Sphinx. He founded the Egyptian Museum in Cairo□

marigold several members of the plant family Compositae◊, e.g. ***pot marigold*** *Calendula officinalis,* whose orange petals flavour soups, etc.; and the tropical American ***French marigold*** *Tagetes patula*□

marijuana dried leaves and flowers of the hemp plant, used as a drug. See cannabis◊□

Marin John 1870–1953. American painter of watercolour landscapes, e.g. his studies of the Maine coast□

marines fighting men equally at home on land or sea, although the British ***Corps of Royal Marines*** established in 1664, is primarily a military force trained also for fighting at sea, and providing commando units, landing craft, crews, frogmen, etc., whereas the ***US Marine Corps,*** 1775, is primarily a naval force trained for fighting on land□

Marinetti Filippo Tommaso 1876–1944. Italian writer, author of the manifesto of Futurism◊ 1909, which called for a break with tradition in art, poetry, and the novel, and glorified the machine age□

Marini Marino 1901–80. Italian sculptor, particularly famous for bronze riders and dancers in an elongated, elegant style□

marionette an articulated doll. See puppet◊□

Maritain Jacques 1882–1973. French philosopher, at first a disciple of Bergson, who became the leading Neo-Thomist, applying the methods of Thomas Aquinas◊ to contemporary problems□

Maritime Law that part of law dealing with fishing areas, ships, and navigation. Under the UN convention of 1982 there is a 19 km/12 mi territorial limit from a country's coast; a 320 km/200 mi exclusive economic zone (EEZ increasingly adopted); and under special jurisdiction an International Seabed Authority would be established to exploit the deep seabed resources, but there was dispute as to the share allotted to developing countries of mining to be carried out by developed ones. See also oceanography◊□

Maritime Organization International. United Nations agency established in 1959, which deals with navigational safety, pollution, etc., with headquarters in London, near Lambeth Palace□

Maritime Trust equivalent of the National◊ Trust in the world of ships, established in 1970 to discover, repair, and preserve vessels of historic, scientific, or technical interest: president, the Duke of Edinburgh□

Maritsa river flowing via Bulgaria, and Greco-Turkish frontier to the Aegean; length 440 km/275 mi□

Mariupol former name (until 1948) of the port of Zhdanov◊□

Marius Gaius 155–86BC. Roman general. Consul in 107, he was appointed to defeat Jugurtha◊ (who actually surrendered to Sulla◊), was again consul 104–100, and defeated the Germanic peoples attacking Gaul and Italy in 102 and 101. Incensed at the appointment of Sulla to the command against Mithridates, he had himself substituted by 'popular demand', until Sulla reversed the situation by marching on Rome. Marius fled, returned in 88 after Sulla had gone east, attained a final consulship, and started a general massacre of his enemies, ended by his death□

Marivaux Pierre Carlet de Chamblain de 1688–1763. French comic dramatist whose polished sophistication in *Les fausses confidences* etc., led to the coining of the word *marivaudage* for the style□

marjoram aromatic perennial herb◊□

Mark St. Traditonally the compiler of the second gospel of the New Testament (actually the earliest in time) 65–70, which was used by Matthew and Luke. He accompanied Paul and Barnabas on their first missionary journey, later working with Paul in Rome, and then with Peter as his interpreter. He traditionally founded the Church in Alexandria, and was buried there. He is the patron saint of Venice; feast day, 25 Apr□

Mark Antony (*Marcus Antonius*) 83–30BC. Roman soldier-statesman, who served under Julius Caesar◊ in the later campaign in Gaul, fought with him at Pharsalus, and as consul in 44BC tried to secure for him the title of king. After Caesar's assassination, he formed a triumvirate with Octavius and Lepidus, and in 42BC helped defeat Brutus and Cassius at Philippi. Touring the eastern provinces in 41BC, Antony fell in love with Cleopatra, securing Egypt for his share when the triumvirs shared the empire among them. By 37 Antony had left his wife Octavia (sister of

Octavius) for Cleopatra, and by 33 relations between the two men had altogether broken down. The senate declared war on Cleopatra in 32BC, and when Antony was defeated by Octavius at Actium◊, he committed suicide□

markhor a large wild Himalayan goat◊□

Markievicz Constance Georgina, Countess Markievicz c1868–1927. Irish nationalist, born Gore Booth, who married the Polish Count Markievicz in 1900. Her death sentence for taking part in the Easter Rebellion of 1916 was commuted, and after her release from prison in 1917 she was elected to the Westminster parliament as a Sinn Fein candidate in 1918 (technically the first British woman MP), but did not take her seat□

Markov Andrei 1856–1922. Russian mathematician, formulator of the Markov◊ chain□

Markova Dame Alicia. Stage-name of Lillian Alicia Marks 1910– . A pupil of Pavlova, she worked with Diaghilev 1924–9, was first resident ballerina of the Vic-Wells Ballet 1933–5, and excelled as Giselle in *Giselle*. Dame of the British Empire 1963□

Markov chain chain of events governed only by established probability, uninfluenced by the past history of earlier links in the chain□

Marks Simon, 1st Baron Marks 1888–1964. British chain store magnate. Son of a Polish immigrant who had started (with Yorkshireman Tom Spencer) some 'penny bazaars' in 1887, he built up the Marks and Spencer chain from 1907□

marl soft, earthy sedimentary rocks commonly laid down in freshwater lakes, and used in cement-making and sometimes still in top-dressing agricultural land□

Marlborough John Churchill, 1st Duke of Marlborough 1650–1722. English soldier. In 1688 he deserted his patron, James II, for William of Orange, but in 1692 fell into disfavour for Jacobite intrigue. He had married Sarah Jennings 1660–1744, confidante of the future Queen Anne, who created him a duke on her accession. In the War of the Spanish◊ Succession, he saved Vienna from the French by his victory at the Battle of Blenheim, and achieved victories at Ramillies in 1706, Oudenaarde in 1708, and Malplaquet in 1709. However, the return of the Tories to power and his wife's quarrel with the Queen, led to his dismissal in 1711, and his flight to Holland to avoid charges of corruption. He returned in 1714. The Blenheim mansion in Oxfordshire◊ was granted in recognition of his services. See also Marlborough House◊□

Marlborough market town in Wiltshire, England; population 6200. Noted for its public school, Marlborough College□

Marlborough House designed by Wren, it was Marlborough◊'s London home: later users include Edward VII (as Prince of Wales), Queen Mary (consort of George V), and from 1962 gatherings of Commonwealth members□

Marley 'Bob' (Robert) Nesta 1945–1981. Jamaican folksinger, the 'King of Reggae', which he popularized throughout the world. He was a Rastafarian◊□

marlin or ***spearfish*** several genera of game fish, family Istiophoridae, order Perciformes. Some 2.5 m/7 ft long, they are found in warmer waters, and have elongated snouts, and high-standing dorsal fins□

Marlowe Christopher 1564–93. English poet-dramatist. Born in Canterbury, he was educated at Cambridge, where he is thought to have become a government agent. In London from 1587, he wrote the blank verse plays *Tamburlaine* c1587, *The Jew of Malta* c1589, *Edward II* and *Dr Faustus* both c1592. Best known of his other works are his poem *Hero and Leander* and a version of Ovid's *Amores*. His life was turbulent, with a brief imprisonment in connection with a man's death in a brawl (of which he was cleared), and a charge of atheism (following statements by Kyd◊ under torture) for which he escaped arrest only by his death in a Deptford tavern. Alleged to be in a dispute over the bill, it may have been a political killing. His magnificent verse and dramatic grandeur influenced Shakespeare and others□

Marmara inland sea linked with the Aegean by the Dardanelles◊ and by the Bosporus◊ with the Black Sea; length 275 km/170 mi, breadth up to 80 km/50 mi. See Turkey◊□

Marmes man earliest human remains (Mongol and possibly cannibal) found in the Americas (in Washington on the ranch of R J Marmes); they are 11 000 years old□

marmoset small S American monkey. See under monkey◊, New World□

marmot large ground squirrel belonging to the genus *Marmota*. See under squirrel◊□

Marne river in NE France; length 525 km/326 mi□

Marne Battles of. In World War I two unsuccessful German offensives: ***first battle*** 6–9 Sept 1914, von Moltke's advance was halted by the British◊ Expeditionary Force and the French under Foch; ***second battle*** 15 Jul–4 Aug 1918, Ludendorff's advance was defeated by British, French, and US troops under Pétain, and German morale crumbled□

Maronites Christian sect derived from Monothelite◊ refugees and now in communion with the Catholic Church; there are some 600 000 in Lebanon, and communities in Syria, S Europe, and the Americas□

maroon runaway slaves and their descendants in the W Indies and Guyana□

Marot Clément c1496–1544. French court poet, who was taken prisoner at Pavia in the service of Francis I. His Lutheran sympathies forced him into exile, where he died, but his graceful, witty style was a model for later writers□

Marprelate controversy pamphlets attacking the Church of England clergy which were published 1588–9 by a writer, or writers, using the pseudonym Martin Marprelate. John Penry, their Welsh Puritan printer, was hanged for inciting rebellion□

Marquand J(ohn) P(hillips) 1893–1960. American writer of short stories featuring the Japanese detective 'Mr Moto' and of novels gently satirizing Bostonian society (*The Late George Apley* 1937 and *H M Pulham, Esq.* 1941)□

Marquesas see French◊ Polynesia□

marquess or **marquis** rank in the British peerage between a duke and an earl, created in 1385, though lords (marchiones) of the Scottish and Welsh 'Marches◊' previously existed. The wife of a marquess is a marchioness□

Marquet Pierre Albert 1876–1947. French painter of Parisian, port, and coastal scenes, whom Matisse called the 'French Hokusai◊'; he was one of the Fauves◊□

Marquette Jacques 1637–75. French Jesuit missionary-explorer, who explored the upper lakes of the St Lawrence, and made a pioneer voyage down the Mississippi□

Márquez Gabriel García. See Garca◊ Márquez□

Marquis Donald Robert Perry 1878–1937. American humorous author, remembered for his *archy and mehitabel* 1927, the typewritten verse adventures of the cockroach, archy (he couldn't press down the capital letters)□

Marrakesh industrial city (textiles, food processing); population 439 750. Founded in 1062, and formerly capital of Morocco, it has fine palaces and mosques□

marram grass a coarse perennial grass. See grasses◊□

Marranos descendants of Spanish Jews forcibly converted to Christianity in the 14–15th centuries, but who secretly still adhered to Judaism; thousands were burnt at the stake by the Inquisition. In the 17th century Marrano refugees founded communities in Amsterdam, London, etc.□

marriage the legal union of husband and wife. In the UK no marriage is valid for either sex below the age of 16 (in the USA it varies from state to state, being as low as 13 for girls in New Hampshire). Marriage may be forbidden (or enjoined) within certain blood or other special relationships; may involve payment of a bride-price or a dowry; may be governed by rules of rank, caste, or religion; may require parental or community consent for minors, or even proof of medical fitness (e.g. the blood tests required by some US states). The chief form of marriage is ***monogamy*** one husband/one wife, although ***polyandry*** one wife with several contemporaneous husbands, and ***polygamy*** one husband with several wives, occur. The children of one-parent families are often socially and economically disadvantaged. See also morganatic◊ marriage□

marrow the soft vascular tissue (medulla) in the central cavities of bones, largely fat and white corpuscles□

marrow plant *Cucurbita pepo* family Cucurbitaceae (see cucumber◊), producing large pulpy fruits used as vegetables and in preserves; the young fruits of one variety are known as courgettes (USA zucchini)□

Marryat Frederick 1792–1848. British naval captain, author of *Mr Midshipman Easy* 1836, *The Children of the New Forest* 1847, etc.□

Mars in Roman mythology, the god of war, after whom the month of March is named□

Mars the fourth planet from the sun
mean distance from the sun 227 800 000 km/141 500 000 mi
diameter 6787 km/4200 mi
rotation period 24 hr 37 min
year (sidereal period) 687 days
atmosphere mainly carbon dioxide, with 3% nitrogen, 1.5% argon, and very slight traces of water vapour
surface temperature −89°C/−128°F to −32.2°C/−26°F
surface dusty, red eroded lava plain; dust in the atmosphere produces a pink sky; high winds recorded to 200 kph/125 mph; largest of its volcanoes is Olympus Mons 24 km/15 mi high, and all may still be active; grooves carved by glacial action radiate from the S pole; polar caps of water ice advance and retreat with the seasons, and studies in 1985 showed that enough water might exist to sustain prolonged manned missions
features may approach earth to winin 54 700 000 km/34 000 000 mi, when it is closer than any planet except Venus
satellites Phobos, Demos□

Marsala port in W Sicily, noted for export of sweet white wine of the same name; population 80 000. Garibaldi◊ landed here in 1860□

Marseillaise La. French national anthem, both words and music were composed in 1792 by army officer Rouget de Lisle□

Marseille chief seaport and 3rd largest city of France, capital of Provence-Côte d'Azur; population 1 071 000, including 150 000 N African immigrants. Founded in 600BC, it was a free city of the Roman Empire, and an independent republic from the 13th century until its inclusion in France in 1481. It is a centre for oil technology, and industries including oil refining, chemicals, and food processing. The Château d'If, constructed in 1529, on the offshore island of If, was formerly a state prison; in *The Count of Monte Cristo* Dumas made it the scene of Dantès' imprisonment□

Marsh Dame Ngaio 1899–1982. New Zealand novelist, creator of Detective Roderick Alleyn in *A Man Lay Dead* 1934, etc. Dame of the British Empire 1966□

marshal originally a servant tending horses, especially a farrier, but eventually applied to high officers of state (see Earl◊ Marshal) and the armed forces, i.e. Marshal of the RAF is a rank corresponding to that of Admiral of the Fleet in the Navy and Field◊ Marshal in the army. Marshal of France is the highest rank in the French army□

Marshall George C(atlett) 1880–1959. American soldier-statesman. While he was Secretary of State 1947–9, the ***Marshall Plan*** for US aid to Europe after World War II (European Recovery Programme) was put through by Dean Acheson◊; Marshall received a Nobel peace prize in 1953. As Secretary of Defence 1950–1, he backed Truman's recall of MacArthur from Korea□

Marshall John 1755–1835. American jurist, chief justice of the Supreme Court, who laid down a series of interpretations of the US constitution□

Marshalls the Radak (13 islands) and Ralik (11 islands) chains in the W Pacific
area 158 sq km/61 sq mi
capital Majuro
features include two atolls used for US atom bomb tests 1946–63, Bikini (hence the name given to two-piece swimsuits which had an explosive impact); radioactivity will last for 100 years, and the people have made claims for rehabilitation), and Eniwetok; and Kwajalein atoll (the largest) which has a US intercontinental missile range
products copra, phosphates, fish; tourism is important
currency US dollar
population 31 100
language English (official)
religion both Christian and native beliefs

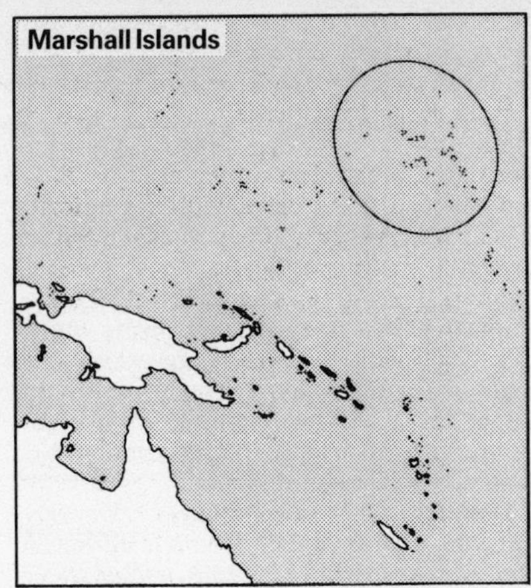

government internally self-governing, with elected governments
recent history German 1906–19, they were administered by Japan until 1946, when they passed to USA as part of the Pacific Islands Trust Territory in 1947. In 1983 an agreement for Free Association with the USA was approved by plebiscite□

marsh gas methane◊ formed by rotting vegetation□

marsh marigold a plant of the family Ranunculaceae◊□

Marsilius of Padua 1270–1342. Italian jurist who, in his *Defensor pacis* advocated the subordination of ecclesiastical to secular power□

Marston Moor Battle of. See under Civil◊ War□

marsupial mammal, order Marsupialia, in which the female has a pouch (Greek *marsupion*) to carry her young (which have a short gestation period and are very small) after birth. Now restricted to Australasia and the Americas, they formerly occurred in Africa. They have been comparatively little studied, and their alleged 'primitiveness' and 'lack of intelligence' is not established.
bandicoot family Peramelidae, which range from a rat to a rabbit in size. Especially attractive is the silky-coated ***rabbit bandicoot*** *Macrotis lagotis,* much persecuted for its fur.
kangaroo of the mainly Australian family Macropodidae. The ***great grey*** *Macropus giganticus* reaches 2.5 m/8 ft from nose to tail-tip, and the ***red kangaroo*** *Macropus rufus*, a little less. Their hindquarters are immensely powerful, and they reach speeds of 50 km/30mi per hour, with leaps (in which the tail is used as a balancer) of 9 m/30 ft. The ***wallabies*** (genus *Wallabia*) are smaller versions of the kangaroo, and the ***hare wallabies*** are under a

metre in length. Some occur in New Guinea, where there are also ***tree kangaroos*** (genus *Dendrolagus*), which have long tails, but not the enormously developed legs of other kangaroos.
koala an Australian tree-climber, *Phascolarctos cinereus* family Phalangeridae, looking like a bear and living on eucalyptus leaves (which it needs the world's largest known 'appendix', an intestinal sac c8ft long, to digest). It is tailless, has ash-grey fur, a flattened black nose, and when new-born it is barely 2 cm/0.75 in long, though growing to 60 cm/2 ft. When hand-reared they become very dependent on human company. They are subject to a disease (caused by the bacterium ***Chlamydia psittaci***) which threatens the survival of the few small, isolated populations.
opossum family of N, S, and Central America, Didelphidae, the only marsupial found outside Australasia. The ***common opossum*** *Didelphys marsupialis* is the size of a cat, and has coarse, yellowish hair. They will feign death when captured, hence 'playing possum'. They are mainly tree-dwellers, and the first brood of young migrate to the mother's back when the pouch is needed for her second.
tasmanian tiger (because of the dark stripes on its dun-coloured back) or ***wolf*** *Thylacinus cynocephalus,* family Dasyuridae, a dog-like carnivore with a kangaroo-tail. some 2 m/6 ft from toe to tail-tip, it was believed extinct until once more seen in the 1980s. To the same family belong the ***tasmanian devil*** *Sarcophilus harrisi* a compactly built bear-like animal 1 m/3 ft long; with a white-marked chest, nocturnal, carnivorous, and with a fearsome temper; and the ***numbat*** *Myrmecobius fasciatus* with a long snout for its ant and termite prey.
wombat family Phascolomidae, a small bear-like, burrowing animal; *Vombatus ursinus* being c1 m/3 ft long□

Martello towers flat-roofed round towers, sometimes moated, erected especially along the Kent and Sussex coast in 1804 against French invasion. They were named after Cape Mortella, Corsica, where British troops captured a similar tower in 1794 only with great difficulty□

marten a type of weasel◊□

Martha's Vineyard see under Massachusetts◊□

Martial (***Marcus Valerius Martialis***) c41–c104. Latin epigrammatist, born in Spain, whose works reflect the licence of Roman life□

martial arts styles of armed and unarmed combat developed in the East, including:
aikido Japanese combination of judo and karate
judo modern sport in which an opponent is compelled to submit by the use of minimum force, a development of jujitsu; loose jackets are worn, and falls are broken by a mat
jujitsu Japanese method of unarmed self-defence developed by the Samurai◊; the ancestor of judo
karate method of unarmed combat developed in 17th-century Okinawa (influenced by kung fu); it differs from judo in its emphasis on striking with the open hand or closed fist, and kicking
kendo Japanese fencing using bamboo replicas of Samurai◊ swords, and wearing masks and protective padding
kung fu Chinese unarmed combat originating in the 6th century, possibly under Indian influence in the Shaolin temple, Honan. It combines the principles of karate and judo□

martial law replacement of civilian authorities (when war, rebellion, are in progress) in the maintenance of order by the military authorities. The law on its use in England is ill-defined; in the USA it is not provided for in the constitution or by statute, but has frequently been put into effect□

Martin St c316–400. Bishop of Tours from 371, and a patron saint of France. He had been a soldier, and is usually shown dividing his military cloak with a beggar. Feast day, 11 Nov, ***Martinmas,*** when hiring fairs for farm workers used to be held; in medieval times it was also the day when cattle were slaughtered and the meat salted for the winter□

Martin V Pope 1368–1431. His election in 1417 during the Council of Constance ended the Great◊ Schism□

Martin Archer John Porter 1910– . British biochemist, Nobel prizewinner in 1952 for work with Richard Synge on paper chromatography in 1944□

Martin (Basil) Kingsley 1897–1969. British journalist who, as editor of the *New Statesman* 1931–60 made it the voice of controversy on the Left□

Martin John 1789–1854. British painter of grandiose, but impressive, landscapes and religious subjects, e.g. *Belshazzar's Feast*□

Martin Richard 1754–1834. Irish landowner, known as 'Humanity Martin'. He founded the Royal Society for Prevention of Cruelty to Animals in 1824□

Martin Violet Florence 1862–1915. Irish novelist under the pseudonym 'Martin Ross'. Born in Galway, she collaborated with her cousin, Edith Somerville, in tales of Anglo-Irish provincial life, e.g. *Some Experiences of an Irish RM* 1899□

martin a type of bird. See under swallow◊□

Martin du Gard Roger 1881–1958. French novelist, e.g. the family saga *Les Thibault* 1922–40; Nobel prize 1937□

Martineau Harriet 1802–76. British moralist, journalist, economist, and novelist. She began writing professionally to make family ends meet. Famous for popular works on political economy, she also wrote children's tales. Sister of James Martineau□

Martineau James 1805–1900. British Unitarian minister, who anticipated Anglican modernists in his theology. Brother of Harriet Martineau□

Martinet Jean d. 1762. French inspector-general of infantry under Louis XIV, remarkable for his constant drilling of the troops, hence 'to be a martinet'□

Martinez Maria Montoya c1890–1980. American Pueblo Indian potter, who revived silvery black-on-black ware (made without the wheel) at San Ildefonso Pueblo, New Mexico□

Martini Simone c1284–1344. Italian artist, a pupil of Duccio, who painted a portrait of Laura for Petrarch◊□

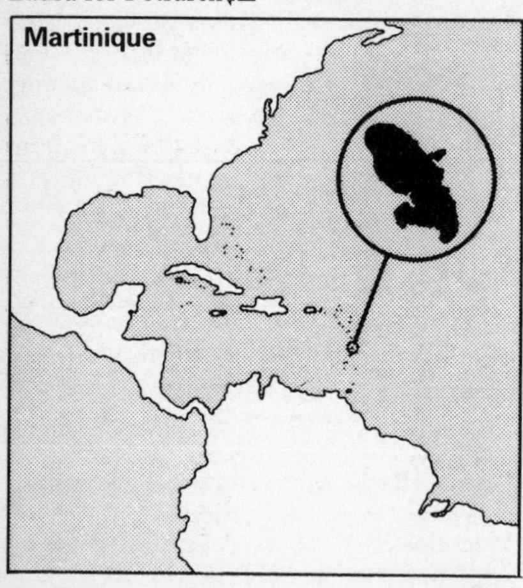

Martinique French island, and overseas region, in the Lesser Antilles, W Indies; area 1100 sq km/420 sq mi; population 326 500. The capital is Fort-de-France. Empress Josephine◊'s former home is a museum. The active volcano of Mont Pelée 1258 m/4428 ft destroyed the town of St Pierre in 1902□

Martinmas the feast of St Martin◊□

Martin's Hundred plantation town established in Virginia, USA, in 1619, and eliminated by an Indian massacre three years later. Its remains, the earliest extensive trace of British colonization in America, were discovered by archaeologist Ivor N Hume in 1970□

Martinů Bohuslav 1890–1959. Czech composer, born Polička, who studied in Paris. He left Czechoslovakia after the Nazi occupation of 1939. Works include the opera *Julietta* 1937, symphonies, and much chamber music□

martyr from Greek 'witness', a person, originally a Christian, put to death for refusing to renounce the faith. The first was St Stephen c35AD; feast day, 26 Dec□

Marvell Andrew 1621–78. English metaphysical poet, born in Winestead, Humberside. He was committed to the Parliamentary cause, being employed as tutor by Lord Fairfax◊ and Cromwell◊, and as assistant to Milton◊ when the latter was Latin Secretary to the Council of State 1657–60. He was MP for Hull from 1659. His poems include 'To His Coy Mistress' and 'Horatian Ode upon Cromwell's Return from Ireland'□

Marx Karl Heinrich 1818–83. German philosopher and socialist, born at Trier, the son of a Jewish lawyer. The radical paper he edited having been suppressed in 1843, he went first to Paris, where he met and began his collaboration with Engels◊, e.g. *The Communist Manifesto* 1848, a programme for the German refugee organization, the Communist League. His involvement in the revolutionary activities of 1848 led to his expulsion from Prussia and trouble also with the French authorities, so that he settled finally in England. In London (see Soho◊) he founded the International Working Men's Association in 1864 (collapsed in 1872), and worked at the British Museum library on *Das Kapital* volume 1 1867, volumes 2 and 3 (edited by Engels) 1885/1894. He was buried at Highgate cemetery. See Marxism◊□

Marx Brothers team of American film comedians ***Leonard 'Chico'*** (from the 'chicks' he chased) 1891–1961; ***Arthur 'Harpo'***(from the harp he played) 1893–1964; ***Julius 'Groucho'*** 1895–1977; ***Milton 'Gummo'***(from his gumshoes or galoshes) 1901–77, and ***Herbert 'Zeppo'*** (born at the time of the first zeppelins) 1900–79. Films include *Duck Soup* 1933 and *A Night at the Opera* 1935□

Marxism philosophical system, also known as 'dialectical materialism', developed by Marx◊ and Engels◊, under which matter gives rise to mind (materialism) and all is subject to change (from dialectics, see Hegel◊). As applied to history, it supposes that social and political institutions progressively change their nature as economic developments transform material conditions, so that the succession of feudalism, capitalism, socialism (called 'modes of production' the last seen as the ultimate rational system) is inevitable.

The stubborn resistance of any existing system to change necessitates its complete overthrow in the 'class struggle', in the case of capitalism by the proletariat, not an attempt at gradual modification. The belief that each successive form is 'higher' than the last provides an element of religious fervour, an 'earthly paradise' being envisaged when perfect socialism is achieved, and the state is alleged to wither away. That such perfection has never been achieved wherever the method has been tried, in the same way that the religious millennium has not yet appeared, may result only in revision of the forecast. See Communism◊, also Plekhanov◊, Lenin◊, Trotsky◊, Stalin◊, Mao Zedong◊□

Mary mother of Jesus Christ (Blessed Virgin Mary). Traditionally the child of Joachim and Anna in their old age, she married Joseph◊ and accompanied him to Bethlehem; Roman Catholic dogma assumes that the brothers of Jesus were Joseph's sons by an earlier marriage, and that she remained a virgin. The Roman Catholic Church also maintains her Immaculate Conception and bodily Assumption into Heaven, and venerates her as a mediator, Pope Paul proclaiming her 'Mother of the Church' in 1964□

Mary 1867–1953. Queen consort of George◊ V of the UK from 1893. Daughter of the Duke of Teck, she was originally engaged in 1891 to the Duke of Clarence (eldest son of Edward VII), who died in 1892□

Mary two Queens of England:

Mary I 1516–58. Queen of England and from Ireland 1553. Daughter of Henry◊ VIII and Catherine of Aragon, she succeeded Edward VI without difficulty despite the conspiracy to substitute Lady Jane Grey◊. She married Philip◊ II of Spain in 1554, restored papal supremacy, and, though instinctively humane, was known as 'Bloody Mary' because of her burning of Protestants. In 1558 she lost Calais, England's last Foothold in France. See also Sir Thomas Wyatt◊.

Mary II 1662–94. Queen of England from 1688. Elder daughter of James◊ II, she married William◊ of Orange in 1677, and accepted the throne jointly with her husband after the abdication of her father. In charge of the government during William's absences abroad, she showed resource when invasion threatened in 1690 and 1692□

Mary 1542–87. Queen of Scots from 1542. Daughter of James V, born in Linlithgow◊, she was married to Francis◊ II 1558–61. She then returned to Scotland and married in 1565 Lord Darnley◊ (see James◊ I and VI). After Darnley's assassination (possibly with Mary's connivance), Bothwell◊ carried her off and married her, but the Scots rose in revolt, and on her defeat at Carberry Hill in 1567, Mary was imprisoned at Loch Leven. Forced to abdicate in favour of her son, she escaped and fled to England, where she was imprisoned by Elizabeth I. Her implication in a plot by Anthony Babington◊ resulted in her trial and execution at Fotheringhay Castle□

Mary 1457–82. Duchess of Burgundy who married Maximilian◊ of Austria in 1477□

Mary Magdalene, St. In the New Testament, the first to see the risen Christ; she has been identified with the woman of St Luke's gospel who anointed his feet. Feast day, 22 Jul□

Mary of Modena 1658–1718. Consort of James◊ II of England from 1673. The birth of their son James◊, the 'Old Pretender', popularly thought to have fraudulently arrived in a warming pan, was the signal for the 1688 Revolution□

Mary town (ancient Merv) in Turkmenistan, S Soviet Union; population 72 000. It is at an oasis in the Kara Kum desert, where Alexander founded a city□

Maryland border state of the USA; Old Line or Free State

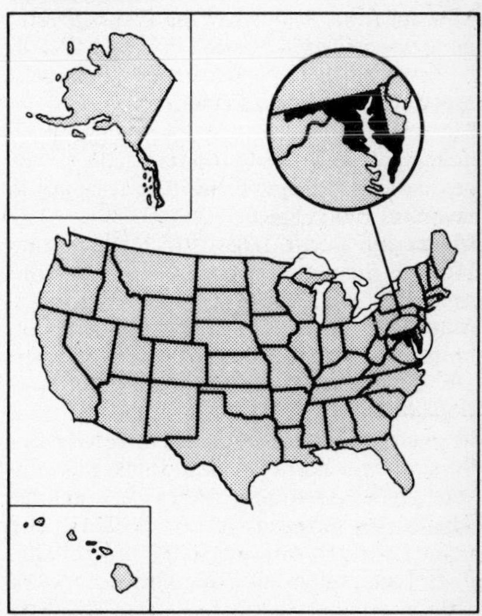

area 27 394 sq km/10 577 sq mi
capital Annapolis
towns Baltimore
features Chesapeake Bay, an inlet of the Atlantic; horse racing◊, the Preakness Stakes at Baltimore; yacht racing at Annapolis; Fort Meade, the equivalent of Britain's electronic listening centre at GCHQ◊ Cheltenham
products fruit, cereals, tobacco; fish and oysters
population 4 216 445

famous people Francis Scott Key, Stephen Decatur, H L Mencken, Upton Sinclair
history one of the Thirteen◊ Colonies, first settled in 1634, it became a state in 1788□

Mary Rose greatest warship of Henry VIII, before whose eyes she sank off Southsea on 19 Jul 1545. Located in 1971 by Alexander McKee, the wreck was raised on 11 Oct 1982 for preservation next to the Victory◊□

Masaccio Florentine painter, Tomaso di Giovanni di Simone Guidi 1401–28. With his teacher Masolino di Panicale c1384–1447, he decorated Santa Maria del Carmine, Florence. He was the first painter to apply the newly discovered laws of perspective. See Brunelleschi◊□

Masada Jewish rock fortress near the Dead◊ Sea, Israel, besieged by the Romans 72AD: sooner than surrender the population of 953 committed mass suicide□

Masai nomadic African people who speak a Hamitic language related to the Semitic, and live on the milk, meat, and blood of their humped zebu cattle. In 1963 their territory was divided between Tanzania and Kenya□

Masaryk Jan Garrigue 1886–1948. Czech diplomat, son of Thomas Masaryk◊. Foreign Minister from 1940, when the Czech government was exiled in London in World War II, he returned in 1945, but under Communist pressure committed suicide□

Masaryk Thomas Garrigue 1850–1937. Czech statesman, first president of the newly-created Czech Republic in 1918, resigning in favour of Beneš◊ in 1935□

Mascagni Pietro 1863–1945. Italian composer of the one-act opera *Cavalleria Rusticana* 1890□

Masefield John 1878–1967. British poet, born in Ledbury, Hereford and Worcester. His life as a seaman is reflected in *Salt Water Ballads* 1902 (which include 'Sea Fever'), but he made his name with the forcefully colloquial verse narrative of a drunkard's conversion *The Everlasting Mercy* 1911, and the Chaucerian *Reynard the Fox* 1919. He also wrote for children (*The Box of Delights* 1935). Poet Laureate from 1930, Order of Merit 1935□

maser acronym for ***m**icrowave **a**mplification by **s**timulated **e**mission of **r**adiation*. Device operating similarly to a laser◊, but in the microwave range between infra-red rays and radio waves. Masers are used as sensitive amplifiers in receivers for satellite communication and radioastronomy, and an ammonia maser is used as a frequency standard oscillator in clocks□

Maseru capital and trading centre of Lesotho; population 45 000. The National University is to the north□

Mashhad holy city of the Shi'ites, and industrial centre (carpets, textiles, leather goods), in NE Iran; population 670 180□

Mashonaland eastern Zimbabwe◊, the land of the Shona people; Prime Minister Mugabe◊ is a Shona. Granted to the British South Africa Company in 1889, it was included in Southern Rhodesia in 1923. The Zimbabwe◊ ruins are here□

Mashraq countries of the E Mediterranean (Arabic 'east'), i.e. Egypt and Sudan, Jordan, Syria, Lebanon. See Maghreb◊□

Masirah Island see under Oman◊□

Masoch Leopold Sacher von 1836–95. Austrian novelist, who dealt with sexual pleasure in pain inflicted on oneself – hence 'masochism'□

Mason A(lfred) E(dward) W(oodley) 1865–1948. British novelist, famed for his tale of cowardice redeemed in the Sudan, *The Four Feathers* 1902, and a series featuring the detective Hanaud of the Sûreté, including *At the Villa Rose* 1910□

Mason and Dixon Line boundary line between Maryland and Pennsylvania, named from the English astronomers who surveyed it 1763–7; it was popularly seen as dividing the North from the South (slave-owning states)□

masque lavishly staged amateur drama (performed by masqued aristocrats) on fairy or mythological themes, in which music, dancing, costume, and scenic design are more important than plot. It was introduced to England from Italy during Henry VIII's reign. Inigo Jones◊ and Ben Jonson◊ collaborated in them. See also Milton◊□

mass the quantity of matter in a body; under the SI◊ system the base unit of mass is the kilogram. Mass determines the acceleration produced in a body by a given force working upon it, the acceleration being inversely proportional to the mass of the body□

Mass the celebration of the Eucharist◊□

Massachusetts New England state of the USA; Bay State or Old Colony
area 21 385 sq km/8257 sq mi
capital Boston
towns Worcester, Springfield, Nantucket
features the two large Atlantic islands of Nantucket and Martha's Vineyard, with the summer homes of the wealthy; rivers Merrimac and Connecticut; University of Harvard, established in 1636; Massachusetts Institute of Technology (MIT), 1861; Woods Hole Oceanographic Institute; Massachusetts Biotechnology Research Park to develop new products and processes; Norman Rockwell Museum at Stockbridge

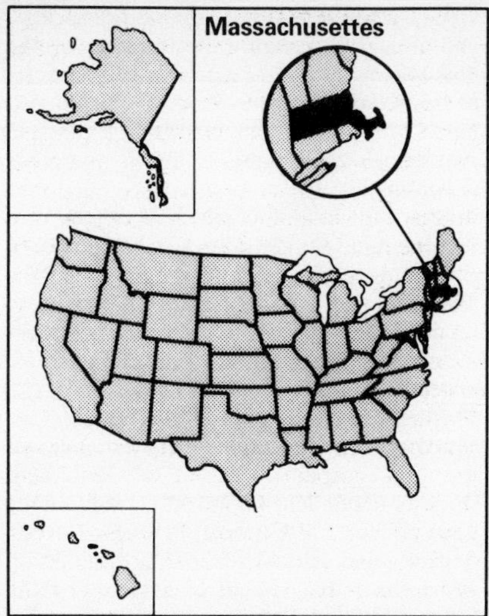

products mainly industrial, especially electronic and communications equipment, shoes, textiles, machine tools; building stone; cod
population 5 737 037
famous people Samuel Adams, Louisa May Alcott, Emily Dickinson, Emerson, Hawthorne, Oliver Wendell Holmes, Winslow Homer, Samuel F B Morse, Poe, Revere, Thoreau, Whistler
history one of the Thirteen◊ Colonies, it was first settled in 1620 by the Pilgrim Fathers at Plymouth, and became a state in 1788□

massage manipulation of the tissues and muscles of the body for therapeutic effect. The basic movements are pétrissage (moulding or kneading), friction, effleurage (stroking), tapotement (patting), and vibration. It is particularly useful in the case of sporting injuries□

Massawa chief port and naval base in Ethiopia; population 30 000. It is one of the world's hottest towns, up to 46°C/115°F. There is a Naval College. Massawa was held by the Italians 1885–1941□

Masséna André 1756–1817. Marshal of France from 1804, he commanded Napoleon's forces in Spain 1810–11, and was defeated by Wellington□

mass-energy equation ($E= mc^2$) denotes the interconversion of mass and energy (E is the energy in joules, m is the mass in kg, and c is the speed of light in metres/second). See Einstein◊'s theory of relativity□

Massenet Jules Émile Frédéric 1842–1912. French composer of operas, e.g. *Manon* 1884, *Werther* 1892; ballets, oratorios, and orchestral suites, including *scènes pittoresques*□

Massif Central mountainous plateau region of S central France; area 93 000 sq km/36 000 sq mi, highest peak Puy de Sancy 1886 m/6188 ft. It is still remote, and is a source of hydroelectricity. See Auvergne◊, Cévennes◊□

Massine Léonide 1896–1979. Russian dancer, noted for character roles with the Diaghilev Ballet, and as the choreographer of *The Three Cornered Hat* and *La Boutique Fantasque* both 1919; *Symphonie Fantastique* 1936, based on Berlioz's music; *Mam'selle Angot* 1943, etc.□

Massinger Philip 1583–1640. English dramatist, whose masterpiece is *A New Way to Pay Old Debts* c1625, noted for the usurer Sir Giles Overreach. He collaborated with Fletcher◊ and Dekker◊, and has been credited with a share in Shakespeare's *Two Noble Kinsmen* and *Henry VIII*□

Master of the Rolls English judge ranking immediately below the Lord Chief Justice; he presides over the Court of Appeal, and is Keeper of the Records and head of the Public Record Office□

Masters Edgar Lee 1869–1950. American poet, born in Kansas. In his *Spoon River Anthology* 1915, the people of a small town tell of frustrated lives□

Masters John 1914–83. British novelist, born to an army family in Calcutta, who himself served in the Indian army 1934–47. A series deals with the Savage family throughout the period of the Raj, e.g. *Nightrunners of Bengal* 1951, *The Deceivers* 1952, *Bhowani Junction* 1954□

mastiff a breed of dog◊□

mastodon extinct elephant◊-like mammal□

Matabeleland western Zimbabwe, home of the Ndebele people, e.g. Lobengula◊, and Nkomo (see under Zimbabwe◊). It was granted to the British South Africa Company in 1889, and included in Southern Rhodesia in 1923□

Matadi chief port of Zaïre on the river Zaïre, 115 km/70 mi from its mouth; population 162 500□

Mata Hari 'Eye of the Day', Dutch spy Margaretha Geertruida Zella 1876–1917. A courtesan and 'oriental dancer', she was probably a double agent for the French and Germans. She was shot by the French□

Matanzas industrial port (tanning, textiles, sugar) in Cuba; population 421 300□

Matapan southernmost cape of the mainland of Greece. A British fleet (under Admiral Cunningham◊) defeated the Italians here on 28 Mar 1941□

match small length of wood, cardboard, etc., tipped with an ignitable substance. Practical matches developed in the first decade of the 19th century, but it was 1844 before safety matches were sold, in which the oxidizing agent (e.g. potassium chlorate) is contained in the head and is struck by friction on the combustible surface (red phosphorus) incorporated on the side of the box□

materialism in philosophy, the explanation of everything that exists in terms of matter (of which mind is a product) and motion. See Democritus◊, Epicurus◊, Hobbes◊, Hume◊, Engels◊, Marx◊, Lenin◊□

mathematics science of spatial and numerical relations: ***pure mathematics*** includes algebra◊, arithmetic◊, geometry◊, the calculus◊, trigonometry◊; ***applied mathematics*** deals with the operations involved in solving problems in mechanics, astronomy, electricity, optics, thermodynamics, etc.

Great mathematicians include Thales of Miletus, Pythagoras, Euclid, Archimedes, Descartes, Newton, Leibniz, Napier, Babbage, Boole, Lobachevski, Einstein, Russell, Whitehead□

Matilda 1102–67. Queen of England, recognized during the reign of her father Henry◊ I as his heir: she married first Emperor Henry◊ V, and second Geoffrey Plantagenet, Count of Anjou. On her father's death in 1135, the barons elected her cousin Stephen king, so that Matilda invaded England in 1139, and was crowned in 1141. Civil war ensued until Stephen was finally recognized as king, with Henry II (Matilda's son) as his successor□

Matisse Henri 1869–1954. French artist-designer, one of the Fauves◊. He used pure colour, distorted and simplified forms, and subordinated subject-matter to pattern□

Matlock spa with warm springs, administrative headquarters of Derbyshire, England; population 20 320. The Peak District Mining (lead) Museum is here□

Mato Grosso (Portuguese 'dense forest') area of Brazil, now forming two states, with their capitals at Cuiaba and Campo Grande. The forests, now depleted, supplied rubber and rare timbers, and diamonds, silver, etc. are mined. See P H Fawcett◊□

matriarchy social organization in which women head the family, often associated with polyandry◊, and found in parts of India, South Sea Islands, Central Africa, and some N American Indians□

Matsue city NW of Osaka near the Sea of Japan, Honshu, Japan; population 130 000. It has remains of a magnificent castle, fine old tea houses, and the Izumo Grand Shrine (dating in its present form from 1744)□

Matsuyama largest city on Shikoku, Japan; population 390 000. There is a feudal fortress (1634), a spa at nearby Dogo has hot springs, and it is still a centre for masters of the haiku◊□

Matsys Quentin 1466–1530. Flemish artist, noted for religious pictures (Pietà triptych in Antwerp Museum) and portraits (Erasmus)□

matter the material of which all objects outside the mind are considered to be composed (the concept of its nature ranging from the hard atoms of Democritus◊ to the 'waves' of modern theory), and in most recent theory includes the mind itself as a function of matter□

Matterhorn a mountain in the Alps◊□

Matthew St. Traditionally the compiler of the first gospel of the New Testament (heavily dependent on Mark◊), traditionally a tax-collector at Capernaum under Herod◊ Antipas, and called by Christ to discipleship as he sat at the receipt of customs by the Lake of Galilee. Feast day, 21 Sept□

Matthias Corvinus 1440–90. Son of János Hunyadi◊, King of Hungary from 1458. His attempt to unite Hungary, Austria, and Bohemia involved him in long wars with the Emperor and the kings of Bohemia and Poland, during which he captured Vienna as his capital in 1485□

Maudling Reginald 1917–79. British Conservative politician, Chancellor of the Exchequer 1962–4 and Home Secretary 1970–2. He resigned when referred to during the bankruptcy proceedings of architect John Poulsen□

Maugham (William) Somerset 1874–1965. British writer. Born in Paris, he was educated at King's School, Canterbury and Heidelberg, then studied medicine at St Thomas's, London. His novel *Of Human Bondage* 1915 was largely autobiographical. Other books include *The Moon and Sixpence* 1919, based on Gauguin's life; *Cakes and Ale* 1930, satirizing Hardy and Walpole; and the volume of short stories *The Trembling of a Leaf* 1921. During World War I he was a secret agent in Russia, trying to prevent the outbreak of revolution, and his Ashenden spy stories are the first with a genuine basis. □

Maui a volcanic island in Hawaii◊□

Mau Mau Kenyan terrorist secret society with nationalist aims 1952–60, an offshoot of the Kikuyu Central Association banned in World War II. The name passed into US slang (meaning 'to terrorize')□

Maunder minimum period 1645–1715 when the sun was virtually devoid of sunspots□

Maundy Thursday precedes Easter (Latin

mandatum the first word of the service commemorating Christ's washing of the feet of the Apostles on that day). The rite of the English sovereign following this example ceased with the accession of William III, but specially coined Maundy money is still presented to poor people in Westminster Abbey (elsewhere in alternate years)□

Maupassant Guy de 1850–93. French author, born in Normandy◊. A civil servant, he was encouraged as a writer by Flaubert◊, and established a reputation with the short story *Boule de Suif* 1880; his novels include *Une Vie* 1883 and *Bel-Ami* 1885□

Mauriac François 1885–1970. French author (born in Bordeaux) whose books are usually set in his native Aquitaine. He was preoccupied with the irreconcilability of Christian practice and human nature, e.g. *Le Baiser au lépreux* 1922, *Thérèse Desqueyroux* 1927; Nobel prize 1952□

Maurice (John) Frederick Denison 1805–72. Anglican churchman, co-founder with Kingsley◊ of the Christian Socialist movement□

Mauritania Islamic Republic of
area 1 030 000 sq km/419 000 sq mi
capital Nouakchott
features mainly forms part of the Sahara Desert
exports iron ore, fish
currency ougiya
population 1 600 000, 30% Arab Berber, 30% black Africans, 30% Haratine (black or mixed race descendants of slaves, who remained slaves till 1980)
language Arabic (official); French
religion Sunni Islam

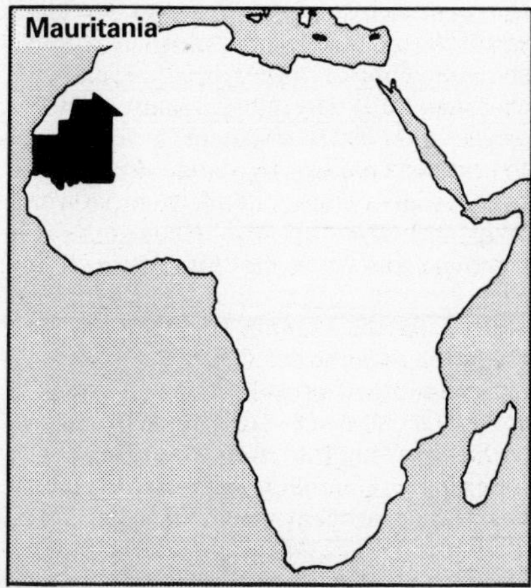

government president-prime minister (Colonel Moaouia Ould Sidi Mohamed Taya from 1981) and national assembly
recent history under French rule from 1903, Mauritania became independent in 1960. Moktar Ould Daddah was president 1961–78, when his Arabization policy resulted in a military coup; a succeeding regime was accused of corruption, and a further coup took place in 1984. See Western◊ Sahara□

Mauritius State of

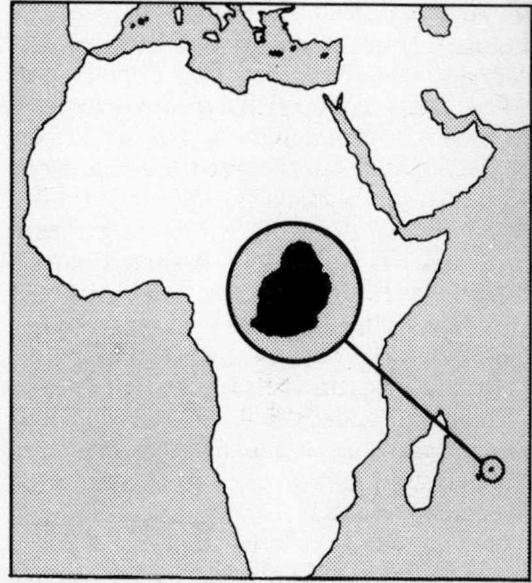

area 1865 sq km/720 sq mi; the island of Rodrigues is part of Mauritius and there are several small island dependencies
capital Port Louis
features geologically part of Gondwanaland◊, it has unusual wild life (see dodo◊, flying fox◊, lemur◊, ostrich◊), and no poisonous snakes
exports sugar, knitted goods; tourism is increasingly important
currency Mauritius rupee
population 925 000
language English (official); Creole French
religion Hinduism 45%, Christianity 30%, Islam 15%
government governor-general and legislative assembly
recent history occupied by Britain in 1810 and ceded by France in 1814, Mauritius became an independent monarchy within the Commonwealth in 1968, and declaration of a republic is under discussion. In 1965 the Chagos Archipelago◊ was transferred to the British Indian Ocean Territory, and there is now a demand (referred to the Court of International Justice in 1980) that Diego García be returned to Mauritius. There is also a claim to Tromelin island (under French sovereignty) to the north□

Maurois André. Pseudonym of Anglophile French writer Émile Herzog 1885–1967, known for his biographies of Shelley, Proust,

Byron, etc.□

Maurya a dynasty culturally magnificent in its influence, it was founded by Chandragupta◊, and ruled most of India c321–c185BC□

Mavor O H. See James Bridie◊□

Maxim Sir Hiram Stevens 1840–1916. American-born (naturalized British) inventor of the first automatic machine gun in 1884□

Maximilian 1832–67. Brother of Emperor Francis Joseph of Austria, and Emperor of Mexico 1864–7. He accepted the throne when Napoleon◊ III's troops occupied Mexico, encountered resistance from Juárez◊, and when the French withdrew on US insistence, was shot by the republicans□

Maximilian I 1459–1519. Son of Emperor Frederick III, and Holy Roman Emperor from 1493. He had acquired the Low Countries through his marriage with Mary of Burgundy in 1477; married his son Philip◊ the Handsome to the heiress to the Spanish throne, and undertook long wars with Italy and Hungary in attempts further to extend the Hapsburg power. He was the patron of the artist Dürer◊□

Maxwell James Clerk 1831–79. Scottish physicist, born in Edinburgh. He was the first professor of experimental physics at Cambridge in 1871, where he planned the Cavendish laboratory. Perhaps the greatest of 19th-century physicists, he united optics with electromagnetism by predicting the existence of electromagnetic waves travelling at the (known) speed of light; investigated the way we sense colour, and the nature of colour blindness; and was a founder of the kinetic theory of gases. See Maxwell◊-Boltzmann statistics□

Maxwell-Boltzmann statistics the basic equation covering the distribution of velocities of the molecules of a gas. See Boltzmann◊□

Maya American Indian civilization originating in the Yucatan Peninsula c2600BC, with later sites in Mexico, Guatemala, and Belize, and enjoying a classic period 325–925, when it declined. The Maya constructed stone buildings and 'stepped pyramids' without metal tools; used hieroglyphic writing in manuscripts of which only three survive; were skilled potters, weavers, and agriculturalists; and regulated their rituals and warfare by observations of the planet Venus. Their human sacrifices were on a smaller scale than those of the Aztecs◊□

Maya/maya see under Hinduism◊ 1□

Mayakovsky Vladimir 1893–1930. Russian futurist poet, who combined revolution in versification and politics in his poems *150 000 000* 1920 and *V I Lenin* 1924. However, his satiric play *The Bedbug* 1928, was taken in the West as an attack on philistinism in the USSR. He committed suicide□

May Day 1 May, the beginning of summer, still marked in England by pre-Christian magical rites, e.g. the dance round the maypole (an ancient fertility symbol). In Communist countries there are often political/military parades, and the British Labour Party made the first Monday in May a public holiday. See Labour◊ Day□

Mayence French name for the city of Mainz◊□

Mayer Julius Robert von 1814–78. German physicist who in 1842 anticipated Joule in deriving the mechanical equivalent of heat, and Helmholtz in the principle of conservation of energy□

Mayerling see Crown Prince Rudolph◊□

Mayfair a fashionable district of Westminster, London◊□

Mayflower the ship in which the Pilgrim◊ Fathers sailed from Plymouth to Massachusetts in 1620□

mayfly type of insect in the order Ephemeroptera, which in adult form cease to feed, and die after breeding; in the feeding larval stage they may live more than a year. They are food for trout in both stages□

Maynooth see under Kildare◊□

Mayo western county (county town Castlebar) of the Republic of Ireland, province of Connacht◊. It is noted for its lakes (Lough Conn) and wild Atlantic coast scenery, and includes Achill Island. At the village of Knock, two women claimed a vision of the Virgin with two saints in 1897, and John Paul II visited the shrine in 1979□

mayor principal officer of a district council which has been granted district borough status under royal charter; in certain cases the chairman of a city council may (under a similar grant by letters patent) have the right to be called ***Lord Mayor*** (a usage also followed by Australian cities). Parish councils which adopt the style of town councils have a chairman known as the 'town mayor'. See also Provost◊. The office of mayor was revived (for the first time since 1871) in Paris for Jacques Chirac in 1977□

Mayotte island of the Comoro◊ group, a *collectivité particulière* of France by its own wish: see Comoros◊ Republic. Eventually, following a referendum, it could become an overseas department. Area 374 sq km/144 sq mi; population 52 000. Capital Dzaoudzi□

Mazarin Jules 1602–61. Italian-born French statesman, who passed from the Papal diplomatic service to that of Richelieu◊ in 1639, was created cardinal in 1641, and succeeded Richelieu as chief minister in 1642. His attack on the power of the nobility led to the Fronde◊ and his temporary exile, but by his cunning diplomacy he achieved a successful conclusion to the Thirty◊ Years' War, and, in alliance with Cromwell, he gained victory over Spain. See Anne◊ of Austria□

Mazzini Giuseppe 1805–72. Italian nationalist, born in Genoa and founder of the 'Young Italy' movement. Returning to Italy (after having been condemned to death in his absence by the Sardinian government) on the outbreak of the 1848 Revolution, he headed a republican government established in Rome, but was forced into exile again on its overthrow. He acted as a focus for the concept of Italian unity□

Mbabane capital of Swaziland; population 22 300□

Mboya Tom 1930–69. Kenyan politician, a founder of the Kenya African National Union (KANU), and was Minister of Economic Planning (opposed to nationalization) from 1964 until his assassination□

mead drink made from honey and water fermented with yeast, and used by the ancient Greeks, Britons, etc.□

Mead Margaret 1901–78. American anthropologist, who questioned the conventions of Western society with *Coming of Age in Samoa* 1928, but whose field work has since been questioned□

mean ***arithmetical*** an average value of the quantities given; ***geometric*** the corresponding root of the product of the quantities□

mean free path the average distance travelled by a particle, atom, or molecule between successive collisions□

measles infectious virus disease (rubeola), especially in children, usually transmitted by coughing, sneezing, etc. Symptoms are severe catarrh, small spots inside the mouth, and a raised, blotchy red rash appearing after about a week's incubation. In the West it is not a serious disease, though serious complications may develop, but Third World children may suffer a high mortality. Prevention is by vaccination. See also German◊ measles□

meat flesh of animals taken as food, in Western countries, chiefly from cattle, sheep and pigs, and poultry: major exporters include Argentina, Australia, New Zealand, Canada, USA, and Denmark (chiefly bacon). Meat is wasteful in production (the same area of grazing land would produce much greater food value in terms of cereal crops), and modern research suggests that, in a healthy diet, meat (especially with a high fat content) should play a smaller part. ***Meat substitutes*** are textured vegetable protein (TVP), usually soya◊-based, extruded in fibres in the same way as plastics□

Meath county (county town Trim) of the Republic of Ireland, province of Leinster◊. Tara Hill, 155 m/507 ft high, was the site of a palace and coronation place of many kings of Ireland (abandoned in the 6th century) and St Patrick preached here□

Mecca city in Saudi Arabia as birthplace of Mohammed, holiest city of the Islamic world; population 366 800. Most pilgrims come via the port of Jidda◊. In the centre of the city is the ***Great Mosque*** in whose courtyard is the ***Kaaba*** an oblong building which has the black stone declared by Mohammed to have been given to the prophet Abraham by the angel Gabriel built into its NE corner□

mechanics branch of applied mathematics dealing with the motions of bodies (***kinematics***; or if the mass of the body and the force of its motion are brought into consideration ***kinetics***), and the forces causing or changing them (***dynamics***); and also the forces acting on bodies in equilibrium (***statics***)□

mechanics quantum. System based on quantum◊ theory, which has superseded the mechanics of Newton in the interpretation of physical phenomena on the atomic scale□

Mechelen industrial city (furniture, carpets, textiles) in N Belgium, formerly famous for its lace; population 77 000□

Mecklenburg area of the Baltic coast of Germany, formerly the two grand duchies of Mecklenburg-Schwerin and Mecklenburg-Strelitz, which became free states of the Weimar Republic 1918–34, and were joined in 1946 (with part of Pomerania) to form a region of E Germany. In 1952 it was split into the districts of Rostock, Schwerin, and Neubrandenburg□

medals and decorations usually coin-like metal pieces, struck or cast to commemorate historic events; mark distinguished service, whether civil or military (in the latter case in connection with a particular battle, or for individual feats of courage, or for service over the period of a campaign); or as a badge of membership of an order of knighthood, society, or other special group. Famous medallists include Pisanello, Dürer, Cellini.

Armada medal issued by Elizabeth I following the defeat of the Armada; the first English commemorative medal

George Cross 1940 highest British civilian award for bravery, the medallion in the centre of the cross depicting St George◊ and the Dragon; the ***George Medal*** 1940 is the second highest

Iron Cross German, see under knighthood◊
King's Medal established in 1945; 1 KM for courage in the cause of freedom, and 2 KM for service in the cause of freedom designed for Allied or other foreign civilians who assisted Britain in World War II
Légion d'honneur French, see under knighthood◊
Medal of Honor US highest award for the navy (1861) and army (1862) for gallantry in action; of differing design, both are bronze stars with the goddess Minerva encircled in their centres, equivalent of British Victoria Cross
Medal for Merit US civilian, 1942
Ordre National du Mérite French, civil and military, 1963, replacing earlier merit awards
Order of Merit British, see Merit◊ Order of, knighthood◊
Order of the Purple Heart US military, established by Washington in 1782, when it was of purple cloth (modern ones are of bronze and enamel); revived by Hoover in 1932, when it was issued to those wounded in action from World War I onward.
Pour le Mérite German, instituted by Frederick the Great, military in 1740, and since 1842 for science and art
Presidential Medal of Freedom USA, highest peacetime civilian award from 1963
USSR Gold Star Medal Soviet Union, civilian and military
Victoria Cross British military, 1856□

Medawar Sir Peter 1915– . British scientist, awarded a Nobel prize for medicine in 1960 (with Sir Macfarlane Burnet◊) for work in immunology. They discovered that the body's resistance to grafted tissue, etc., is undeveloped in the new-born child, and studied the way it is acquired. Order of Merit 1981□

Medea in Greek mythology, the sorceress daughter of the king of Colchis. When Jason◊ reached the court, she fell in love with him, helped him achieve his aim, and fled with him. When Jason married Creusa in her place, she killed his bride with the gift of a poisoned garment, and also killed her own two children by Jason□

Medellin industrial city (textiles, steel) and coffee-growing centre in W Colombia, 1538 m/5046 ft asl; population 1 500 000□

Medes Aryan people of NW Iran who first appear in the 9th century BC as tributaries to Assyria◊, with their capital at Ecbatana (Hamadán◊). Allying themselves with Babylon, they destroyed the Assyrian capital of Nineveh◊ in 612, and extended their conquests into central Asia Minor. In 550BC the Persians, till then subject to them under their own King Cyrus◊, successfully revolted; Cyrus ruled both peoples, who rapidly merged□

Medici family founded in Florence by ***Giovanni*** 1360–1429, businessman and banker, politically influential as a supporter of the popular party. His eldest son ***Cosimo*** 1389–1464, regarded as the embodiment of Macchiavelli◊'s *Prince,* dominated the government from 1434, and was succeeded by his inept son ***Piero*** 1416–69, and grandson ***Lorenzo the Magnificent*** 1449–92, who was also a poet and, like his grandfather, a munificent patron of the arts. Lorenzo's son ***Giovanni*** 1475–1521, became Pope in 1513 as Leo X. See Clement◊ VII□

medicine the science of preventing, diagnosing, alleviating, or curing disease

History of medicine

BC

c460 Hippocrates◊ recognized disease had natural causes

AD

2nd century Galen◊, the authority of the Middle Ages, consolidated the work of the Alexandrian doctors

1543 Andreas Vesalius◊ gave the first accurate account of the human body

1628 William Harvey◊ discovered circulation of the blood

18th century 1768 John Hunter◊ began the foundation of experimental and surgical pathology; 1785 digitalis◊ used for heart disease; the active ingredient was not isolated until 1904; 1798 Edward Jenner◊ discovered vaccination

19th century 1877 Sir Patrick Manson's◊ work on animal carriers of infectious diseases (see also Sir Ronald Ross◊); 1882 Robert Koch◊ isolated the tuberculosis bacillus; 1884 Edwin Klebs isolated the diphtheria bacillus; 1885 Louis Pasteur◊ produced the rabies vaccine; 1890 Joseph Lister◊ demonstrated antiseptic surgery; 1897 Martinus Beijerinck discovered viruses; 1899 Felix Hoffmann developed aspirin◊; Sigmund Freud◊ founded psychiatry

1900–50 1909 Paul Ehrlich◊ discovered the first specific bacterial agent, salvarsan◊ (cure for syphilis); 1923 insulin was first used to treat diabetes; 1928 Sir Alexander Fleming◊ discovered the antibiotic penicillin; 1930s development of electro-convulsive therapy (ECT); 1932 Gerhard Domagk◊ began work on the sulphonamide drugs; 1940s development of lithium treatment for depression

1950–75 manipulation of the molecules of synthetic chemicals the main sources of new drugs; 1950s major development of neuroleptic and anti-depressant drugs; 1953 vaccine for polio developed by Jonas Salk◊; late in the decade, beta-blockers for heart disease; work

on the immune system (Sir Peter Medawar◊); 1960s transplant surgery began, Christian Barnard◊; tranquillizers Librium and Valium were developed; 1971 viroid◊ was isolated
from 1975 1980s Barbara McClintock◊'s discovery of the transposable gene; 1980 smallpox eradicated; 1982 prion/virino◊ was identified; 1984 vaccine for leprosy◊ developed□

medicine alternative. Forms of medical treatment which stress use of more natural herbal drugs, and unorthodox techniques (acupuncture◊, homeopathy◊, osteopathy◊)□

Medina 'city of the Prophet', in Saudi Arabia; with the tomb of Mohammed◊, the second most holy Muslim city after Mecca; population 200 000□

meditation act of spiritual comtemplation, formerly practised only by religious and members of cults, in wider modern usage it denotes ***transcendental meditation*** (TM), the cultivation of a relaxed though wakeful condition, during which metabolic changes occur (consistent with the release of anxiety). Benefits claimed include improved resistance to stress, learning ability, creativity, and efficiency□

Mediterranean inland sea separating Europe from N Africa, with Asia to the east; extreme length 3700 km/2300 mi, and area 2 966 000 sq km/1 145 000 sq mi. It is linked to

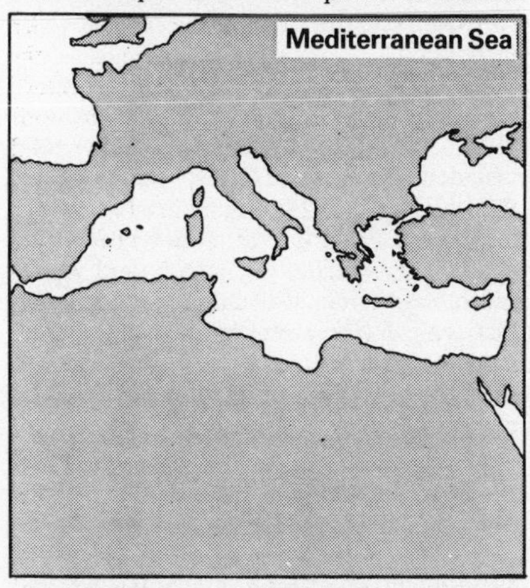

the Atlantic (at the Strait of Gibraltar), Red Sea, and Indian Ocean (by the Suez Canal), Black Sea (at the Dardanelles and Sea of Marmara); and is subdivided into the Adriatic, Aegean, Ionian, and Tyrrhenian seas. Saltier and warmer than the Atlantic, it is almost tideless, and shallows from Sicily to Cape Bon (Africa) divide it into an E and W basin. It is endangered by human and industrial waste pollution□

medlar small European fruit tree *Mespilus germanica,* family Rosaceae; the small acid brown-green 'apples' are eaten when decay has set in□

Médoc a district of SW France. See under Aquitaine◊□

Medusa in Greek mythology, a mortal woman who was transformed into a Gorgon◊□

medusa another name for jellyfish◊□

Medway river in SE England, rising in Sussex and flowing through Kent◊ to Sheerness and the Thames; length 96 km/60 mi□

meerschaum German 'sea froth', a soft white mineral (hydrated magnesium silicate) which floats on water and is used for making pipe bowls□

Meerut industrial city in Uttar Pradesh, India; population 538 000. The Indian◊ Mutiny began here in 1857□

megalith Greek 'great stone': prehistoric stone monuments, of the late Neolithic or early Bronze Age, and often of unknown purpose. They include single, large uprights (menhirs, e.g. the Five Kings, Northumberland); rows (alignments, e.g. Carnac◊); circles, generally with a central 'altar stone'(e.g. Stonehenge◊), and the remains of burial chambers with the covering earth removed, looking like a 'hut' (dolmen, e.g. Kits Coty House, Kent)□

megamouth see under shark◊□

Megatherium extinct giant ground sloths. See under Edentata◊□

Meghalaya NE state of India
area 22 489 sq km/8680 sq mi
capital Shillong
features mainly agricultural and comprises hill districts
population 1 327 825, mainly of the Khasi, Jaintia, and Garo people
language various
religion Hinduism 70%□

Megiddo site of a fortress town in N Israel, where Thothmes III defeated the Canaanites in c1469BC; the Old Testament figure Josiah◊ was killed in battle in c609BC; and Allenby◊ broke the Turkish front in 1918□

Mehemet Ali 1769–1849. Pasha◊ of Egypt from 1805, and founder of the dynasty that ruled till 1953. An Albanian in the Turkish service, he had originally been sent to Egypt to fight the French. As pasha, he established a European-style army and navy, fought his Turkish overlord in 1831 and 1839, and conquered the Sudan□

Meiji Tenno Japanese emperor. See Mutsuhito◊□

meiosis type of sexual reproduction in which a cell◊ nucleus divides into parts, each containing half of the total number of chromosomes of the original. Two of the these unite to form a new and different cell. See mitosis◊□

Meir Golda 1898–1978. Israeli Labour (*Mapai*) stateswoman. Foreign Minister 1956–66, and Prime Minister 1969–74, she resigned following criticism of Israeli unpreparedness in the 1973 Arab-Israeli War□

Meissen city in E Germany; population 45 000. It is famous for porcelain, known as 'Dresden', though the factory was removed to Meissen in 1710□

Meistersingers German lyric poets, singers, and musicians of the 14–16th centuries, who formed guilds for the revival of minstrelsy at Nuremberg◊ and elsewhere. See Hans Sachs◊, Wagner◊□

Meitner Lise 1878–1968. Austrian Jewish physicist, who fled from Hitler to Sweden. With Otto Hahn◊, she caused the first fission of a uranium atom. She refused to work on the atom bomb. See Otto Frisch◊□

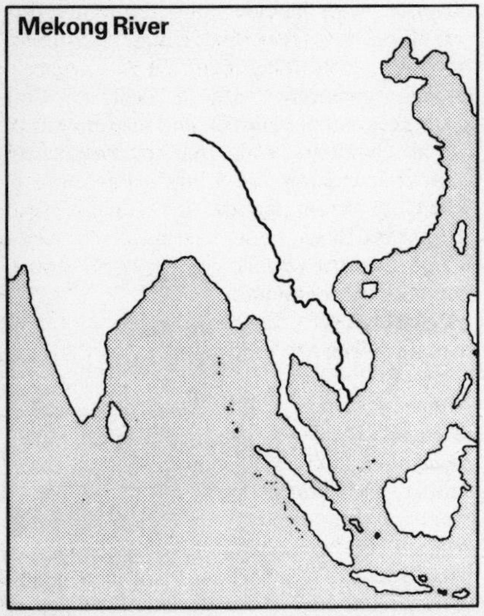

Mekong river rising in Tibet and flowing to the S China Sea; length 4500 km/2800 mi. It is being developed for irrigation and hydroelectricity by the riparian powers: Kampuchea, Laos, Thailand, and Vietnam. See Tonle◊ Sap□

Melanchthon Philip 1497–1560. German Protestant theologian (real name Schwarzerd), who helped Luther in preparing his German translation of the New Testament, and in 1521 issued the first systematic formulation of Protestant theology. He composed the Augsburg◊ Confession in 1530□

Melanesia those islands of Oceania◊, inhabited mainly by Papuans, in the central and western Pacific between Micronesia◊ to the north and Polynesia◊ to the east: from

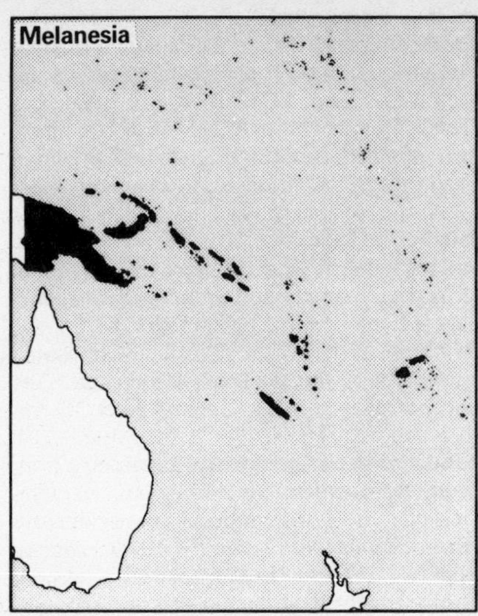

the Bismarck◊ Archipelago to Fiji◊□

melanism see under albinism◊□

melanoma skin cancer formed of dark-coloured cells (commoner among light-skinned women who sunbathe). Sunspot activity appears to increase the ultraviolet quality of sunlight, making it brighter and two years later the skin cancer rate shows an increase□

Melba Dame Nellie. Professional name of Australian soprano Helen Mitchell 1861–1931, born in Melbourne. Her roles included Donizetti's *Lucia;* Dame of the British Empire 1918, Dame Grand Cross of the British Empire 1927. ***Peach melba*** (half peach plus vanilla ice cream and melba sauce, made from sweetened, fresh raspberries) and ***Melba toast*** (crisp and thin) are named after her□

Melbourne capital of Victoria, and second city of Australia, on the river Yarra, near its mouth; population 2 836 800. Founded in 1835, it was named after Lord Melbourne in 1837, grew in the wake of the gold rushes, and was the seat of the Commonwealth government 1901–27. Features include botanic gardens, Victorian Arts Centre, the Law Courts, Houses of Parliament, two cathedrals, and three universities. Industries include engineering, food processing, clothing and textiles□

Melbourne William Lamb, 2nd Viscount Melbourne 1779–1848. British Whig statesman. He married in 1805 Lady Caroline Ponsonby (a novelist as 'Lady Caroline Lamb'), who in 1812 became infatuated with Byron◊; in 1824 she went mad, and in 1825 he won his long fight for a separation.

Home Secretary 1830–4, he was briefly Prime Minister in 1834, and then again 1835–41. Falsely accused in 1836 of seducing Caroline Norton◊, he lost the favour of William IV, but was a fatherly adviser to the young Queen Victoria in statecraft□

Melilla port and military base in Morocco, captured by Spain in 1496; population 58 500. Also administered from Melilla are three other Spanish possessions: Peñón ('rock') de Velez de la Gomera, Peñón d'Alhucemas, and the Chaffarine Islands□

melitin extract (Greek 'bee') of honey-bee poison, a powerful antibiotic□

melon two genera of vines producing oval or spherical fruit with a hard rind, family Cucurbitaceae, including the ***musk-melon*** *Cucumis melo* (varieties include the canteloupe and honeydew), all with yellowish/greenish flesh and ***water melon*** *Citrullus vulgaris*, with green rind and red, watery flesh, which may reach a weight of 90 kg/200 lb□

Melos a Greek island; one of the Cyclades◊□

Melpomene in Greek mythology, the Muse◊ of tragedy□

Melrose market town in Borders◊ region, Scotland□

meltdown term used to decribe the most serious type of nuclear accident (see nuclear◊ energy). Possible, when the core of a commercial reactor is exposed by displacement of the coolant material and a substantial part of the core reaches its melting point of c5200°F. The core would then melt the metal reactor vessel, burn through the concrete floor beneath (unless it were on a rock formation), and emit uncontrolled radiation into the earth and atmosphere□

Melton Mowbray market town in Leicestershire, England; population 21 000. A hunting and horse-breeding centre, it is also famed for Stilton cheese (named after the village in Cambridgeshire where it used to be taken to be sold) and pork pies□

Melville Herman 1819–91. American author of *Moby Dick* 1851, story of the symbolic conflict between Captain Ahab and the great white whale, which was inspired by his own whaling experiences in the South Seas. The posthumous *Billy Budd* 1924 was the basis of Britten◊'s opera□

Memel German name for Klaipeda◊□

Memling Hans c1430–94. Flemish artist, town painter in Bruges 1475–87, where some of his best work is in the Hospital of St John (*Adoration of the Magi* altar 1479, *Deposition* triptych 1480, and shrine of St Ursula 1489)□

Memorial Day remembrance day (usually 30 May) from 1863 for the dead of the American Civil War; but now also for all Americans killed in active service in later wars□

Memphis industrial port (pharmaceuticals, food processing, tobacco) and largest city in Tennessee, USA; population 810 000. There is an Elvis◊ Presley Plaza, with a statue by Eric Parks□

Memphis earliest capital of united Egypt, SW of Cairo (see Menes◊), superseded by Thebes◊ in 1570BC. It was later used as a stone quarry, but the 'cemetery city' of Sakkara survives, which has the step-pyramid built for Zoser by Imhotep◊, probably the world's oldest stone building; tombs of 'prime ministers', etc.□

Menai Strait channel of the Irish Sea, dividing Anglesey from the Welsh mainland; c22 km/14 mi long, up to 3 km/2 mi wide. It is crossed by Telford's suspension bridge, 1826 (reconstructed 1940), and Stephenson's tubular rail bridge, 1850□

Menam another name for Chao◊ Phraya□

Menander c342–291BC. Greek comic dramatist, born in Athens, who influenced Shakespeare. Of his 105 plays only fragments (many used as papier-mâché for Egyptian mummy cases) and Latin adaptations were known till the discovery in 1957 of the *Dyscholos/Bad-tempered man*□

Mencius Latinized name of Chinese philosopher Mengzi c372–289BC, founder of a school in the tradition of Confucius. After 20 years unsuccessful search for a ruler to put into practice his enlightened political programme, based on the innate goodness of man, he retired. His teachings are preserved as the *Book of Mengzi*□

Mendel Gregor Johann 1822–84. Austrian biologist, abbot of the Augustinian abbey at Brünn from 1868, where his garden experiments with successive generations of peas gave the basis for his theory of organic inheritance, governed by dominant and recessive characters (genes). His results, published 1865–9, remained unrecognized until early this century□

mendelevium element

symbol Md

atomic number 101

features one of the actinide◊ series; a radioactive element artificially produced by bombardment of einsteinium–253

uses none at present□

Mendeleyev Dmitri Ivanovich 1834–1907. Russian chemist, framer of the Periodic Law, that the chemical properties of the elements are periodic functions of their atomic weights, 1869□

Mendelism see Mendel◊□

Mendelssohn-Bartholdy Jakob Ludwig Felix 1809–47. German composer, of Jewish descent, but Christian faith, born in Hamburg. Precocious in development, he was also a pianist and conductor (he founded the Leipzig conservatoire in 1843), and made several happy visits to England. His works include the *Midsummer Night's Dream* 1826 and *Fingal's Cave* 1830 overtures; fine chamber music (including string quartets); the Italian (1833) and Scottish (1842) symphonies; *Songs Without Words* 1832–45 for the piano, including the so-called 'Spring Song' and 'The Bees' Wedding'; and the oratorios *St Paul* 1836 and *Elijah* 1846□

Mendès-France Pierre 1907–82. French Prime Minister and Foreign Minister 1954–5, when he concluded the war in Indo-China, and granted Tunisian independence□

mendicant orders friars◊ dependent on alms; Hinduism has similar orders□

Menelik II 1844–1913. Negus (emperor) of Ethiopia from 1889, who defeated the Italians at Aduwa◊, enforcing recognition of the country's independence□

Menes traditionally, the first king of the first dynasty of ancient Egypt in c3400BC, alleged founder of Memphis and of organized worship of the gods□

menhir a standing stone. See under megalith◊□

Ménière's disease condition believed to be caused by the 'ballooning' of the fluid-filled labyrinth within the inner ear. Symptoms are giddiness, tinnitus, and affected hearing□

Menin see under Ypres◊□

meningitis inflammation of the membranes enclosing the brain or spinal cord, caused by various bacteria and viruses. See under Ascomycetes◊□

Mennonites Christian sect rejecting infant baptism originating in Zürich in 1523, which refuses to hold civil office or do military service, later named Mennonites after Menno Simons 1496–1559, leader of a group in Holland. When they came under persecution, some settled at Germantown, Pennsylvania. The Hutterian Brethren (named after Jacob Hutter who died in 1536) hold substantially the same beliefs, and Hutterian principles are the basis of the Bruderhof (Society of Brothers) who live in groups of families (single persons being assigned to a family), marry only within the sect (divorce being disallowed), and retain a 'modest' dress for the women (cap or head-scarf, and long skirts). Originally established in Germany, there are Bruderhof communities in the USA, and at Robertsbridge, E Sussex; they support themselves by making high-quality children's toys□

menopause period of life during which a woman's menstrual cycle ends. See under menstruation◊□

Menorca Spanish form of Minorca◊□

Menotti Gian Carlo 1911– . Italian-born American composer, whose operas include *The Medium* 1946, *Amahl and the Night Visitors* a Christmas story, 1951, *The Consul* 1950, and *The Saint of Bleeker Street* 1954. See Spoleto◊□

Mensheviks right wing of the Russian Social-Democratic Party. See under Bolshevism◊□

menstruation monthly discharge from the womb of blood and breakdown products of the lining prepared for development of an egg-cell if fertilized, which begins at about 14 years of age and ends at menopause, about 45 (see under oestrogen◊). Even in the fully healthy the process is associated with: premenstrual tension (PMT, marked by irritability, etc.); abdominal pain at the onset (dysmenorrhoea); some women suffer over-heavy discharge (menorrhagia); or absence of the period (amenorrhoea, as in cases of anaemia, etc.), etc. Ovulation occurs at mid-cycle, and, if fertilization takes place, menstruation does not occur. Hormone replacement therapy (HRT), treatment with oestrogen, etc., has been developed to ease difficulties at menopause by inducing regular bleeding, similar to that of 'periods'□

mental disorder legally recognized forms of mental ill health are: ***mental illness*** in which patients of normal intelligence become disordered; ***severe subnormality*** in which mental development is arrested to such an extent that the patient is incapable of leading an independent life; ***subnormality*** in which special care and training can to some extent overcome the incomplete development of the mind; and ***psychopathic disorder*** in which the patient may or may not be of normal intelligence, but is characterized by extreme irresponsibility or abnormal aggressiveness which makes it unsafe for others as well as the patient if not under treatment. Boundaries are difficult to draw, but commonly recognized kinds of mental illness include: dementia◊, paranoia◊, schizophrenia◊, and manic depressive insanity, an alternation between elation (mania) and depression (melancholia). See also Autism◊, Down's◊ syndrome, Antonio Moniz◊ (prefrontal leucotomy), sedatives◊□

menthol a compound found in peppermint◊ oil□

Menton resort on the French Riviera, a favourite with Queen Victoria; population 25 300□

Menuhin Sir Yehudi 1916– . American violinist of Russian-Jewish parentage, naturalized British since 1985. A child prodigy, he achieved great depth of interpretation, and was often accompanied on the piano by his sister ***Hephzibah*** 1921– . In 1963 he founded a boarding school (named after him) at Stoke D'Abernon, Surrey, for training young musicians. Knight of the British Empire 1965□

Menzies Sir Robert Gordon 1894–1978. Australian statesman, who succeeded Lyons as Prime Minister and leader of the United Australia Party 1939–41, and in 1944 formed the Australian Liberal Party. In 1949 he became Prime Minister of a Liberal-Country Party coalition government, and was re-elected 1951, 1954, 1955, 1958, 1961, 1963, retiring in 1966. Knighted 1963□

Mercator Gerardus. Latinized form of the name of Flemish map-maker Gerhard Kremer 1512–94, deviser of ***Mercator's projection*** in which the parallels and meridians on maps are drawn uniformly at 90°. The true area of countries is increasingly distorted the further they are to the N and S of the Equator. See Atlas◊□

Mercer David 1928–80. British dramatist, born in Yorkshire, who first became known for television plays. His works include *A Suitable Case for Treatment* (TV) 1962, and *After Haggerty* (stage) 1970□

merchant navy the passenger and cargo ships of a country, the majority owned by companies, but in the USSR and other Communist countries state-owned and closely associated with the navy. To avoid strict regulations on safety or union rules on crew wages, etc., many ships are today registered under 'flags of convenience', i.e. those of countries which do not have such rules. Types of ship include: ***tramps*** either in home coastal trade, or carrying bulk cargoes worldwide; ***tankers*** the largest ships afloat, up to c500 000 tonnes and 380 m/1245 ft long, and other vessels carrying specialized cargo; ***cargo liners*** combining cargo and passenger traffic on short or world voyages. Liners for passengers only enjoyed a revival in the 1980s, and the most luxurious of all will be the P & O cruise liner, operating from California, and under construction in Finland in 1985 at a cost of £80 million (she will probably be called the *Princess Diana*).

Most merchant ships are diesel-powered, but there have been attempts to revive sails (under automatic control) in combination with diesel to reduce costs, the first commercial venture being the Japanese *Aitoku Maru* 1980. Nuclear power was used in the *Savannah* 1959 (USA), but problems with host ports mean that only the USSR builds such ships for 'internal' use, i.e. Arctic icebreakers and the 26 400 tonne N Pacific/Arctic barge carrier *Sevmorput* 1985□

Mercia an Anglo-Saxon kingdom which emerged in the 6th century, and by the 8th dominated all England south of the Humber, but from c825 came under the overlordship of Wessex◊. See Midlands◊, Penda◊, Offa◊□

Mercury in Roman mythology, the messenger of the gods identified with Greek Hermes◊□

Mercury the nearest planet to the sun
mean distance from the sun 57.9 million km
diameter 4880 km
rotation period 58.6 days
year (sidereal period) 87.97 days
atmosphere traces of helium and argon
surface temperature −180°C/−292°F to 450°C/842°F
surface similar to the earth's moon; cratered with 'seas'
features a magnetic field about 1% that of the earth's; double the moon's surface gravity□

mercury element
symbol Hg
atomic number 80
physical description liquid silvery metal
features the only common metal which is liquid at room temperature
uses in barometers and thermometers; in batteries, dental fillings, and for 'silvering' mirrors□

Meredith George 1828–1909. British novelist and poet, born in Portsmouth. Intended to be a solicitor, he left the law for journalism, and published his first realistic psychological novel *The Ordeal of Richard Feverel* 1859. His condensed and difficult style denied a wide readership to this and later works which include *The Egoist* 1879, *Diana of the Crossways* 1885, and *The Amazing Marriage* 1895. His best verse is in *Modern Love* 1862. He married twice, first in 1849 to Mary Nicolls, widowed daughter of Thomas Love Peacock◊; she left him in 1858. Order of Merit 1905□

merganser a type of duck. See under waterfowl◊□

Mérida industrial city (products from the henequen◊ grown in the area) in Mexico; population 270 000□

meridian imaginary line drawn on earth's surface so as to pass through both poles, and thus through all places with the same longitude (see latitude◊). A corresponding ***celestial meridian*** passes through both celestial poles□

Mérimée Prosper 1803–70. French author, who was employed under Napoleon III on unofficial diplomatic missions. His stories include *Colomba* 1841, dealing with a Corsican feud, and *Carmen* 1846, inspiration of Bizet◊'s opera□

merino a breed of sheep◊□

Merit Order of. British order of chivalry, founded on the lines of an order of knighthood◊□

meritocracy society ruled by those of highest intellect and talent, from Michael Young *The Rise of the Meritocracy* 1958□

Merlin magician and counsellor to King Arthur◊; he was later alleged to have supported Vortigern in fighting Hengist◊ and the Saxons, and to have built Stonehenge. Welsh bardic literature has a cycle of poems attributed to him, and he may have a historic origin. He is said to have been buried in a cave in the park of Dynevor Castle, Dyfed□

merlin a small falcon◊□

mermaid mythical sea creature (the male is a ***merman***), having a human upper part, and the lower body a fishtail. The dugong◊ and seal◊ are among suggested origins for the idea□

Meroe an ancient city of N Sudan. See under Khartoum◊□

Merovingians Frankish dynasty founded in 5th century by Merovech, which ruled France from the time of Clovis◊ to 751. See under Pepin◊□

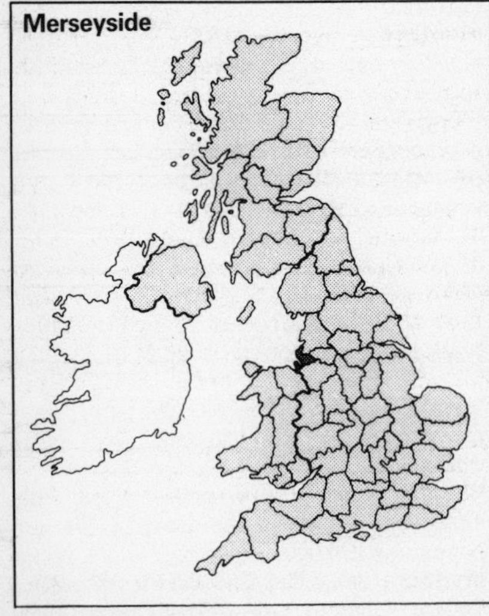

Merseyside metropolitan county of NW England 1974–86
area 652 sq km/252 sq mi
towns administrative headquarters Liverpool; Bootle, Birkenhead, St Helens, Wallasey, Southport
features river Mersey; Merseyside Innovation Centre (MIC), linked with Liverpool University and Polytechnic (see science◊ park); Prescot Museum of clock and watch making; Speke Hall (Tudor), and Croxteth Hall and Country Park (a working country estate open to the public)
products see Liverpool◊
population 1 509 000
famous people Beatles □

Mersin industrial free port (chrome, copper, and oil refining) in Turkey; population 216 300□

Merthyr Tydfil industrial town (light engineering, colour televisions, vacuum cleaners, electric tricycles) in Mid Glamorgan, Wales; population 61 500. In 1831 Richard Lewis (known as 'Dic Penderyn' from his hometown) was hanged here for stabbing a soldier during a riot, and became 'martyr of the Welsh working class'□

Merton borough of SW Greater London
features part of Wimbledon Common (includes Caesar's Camp–an Iron Age fort); All England Tennis Club, 1877
population 164 600□

Merv see Mary◊□

mesa flat-topped mountain (Spanish 'table') with steep cliff sides□

Mesa Verde high plateau in SW Colorado, inhabited by the Pueblo◊ Indians□

mescalin hallucinogenic drug. See under peyote◊□

Meshed a variant spelling of Mashhad◊□

Mesmer Franz Anton 1733–1815. Austrian physician, who claimed to reduce his subjects to trance state by consciously exerted 'animal magnetism', their willpower being entirely subordinated to his. Expelled by the police from Vienna, he created a sensation in Paris in 1778, but was denounced as a charlatan in 1785. He seems to have been an early experimenter in hypnosis◊□

Mesolithic see Stone Age under Prehistory◊□

meson unstable particle with mass intermediate between those of the electron and the proton, found in cosmic radiation and emitted by nuclei under bombardment by very high-energy particles. Its existence was predicted in 1935 by Japanese physicist Hideki Yukawa□

Mesopotamia ancient Greek name for the 'land between the rivers' (the Euphrates and Tigris), site of the civilizations of Sumer and Babylon; it is now part of Iraq. The decline of these civilizations has been attributed to salinization of irrigated areas□

Messager André Charles Prosper 1853–1929. French composer of light operas, notably *Véronique* 1898□

Messalina Valeria c22–48. Third wife of the Roman emperor Claudius◊, whom she dominated. She was a byword for her immorality, forcing a noble to marry her in 48, although still married to Claudius. The latter then had her executed□

Messerschmitt Willy 1898–1978. German plane designer, whose ME-109 was a standard Luftwaffe fighter in World War II, and whose ME-262 (1942) was the first mass-produced jet fighter (Hitler failed to appreciate its significance)□

Messiaen Olivier 1908– . French organist and composer of much church music, a pupil of Dukas◊ and teacher of Stockhausen◊. His *St François d'Assisse* was first performed in Paris in 1985□

Messiah Hebrew 'the anointed' (equivalent of the Greek 'Christ'), expected by the Jews as their deliverer from the time of the exile; Christians identify Jesus as the Messiah□

Messina city in NE Sicily; population 260 250. Originally an ancient Greek settlement, it was taken first by the Carthaginians, and then by the Romans□

Messina Strait of. A channel in the central Mediterranean Sea separating Sicily from mainland Italy; in Greek legend a monster (Charybdis), who devoured ships, lived in the whirlpool on the Sicilian side, and another (Scylla), who devoured sailors, in the rock on the Italian side. Odysseus◊ passed safely between them□

Mestrovic Ivan 1883–1962. Yugoslav-American sculptor, naturalized American in 1954, whose works include portrait busts of Rodin, Sir Thomas Beecham, and President Masaryk□

metabolism the chemical processes of living organisms, which comprise a constant alternation of building up (anabolism) and breaking down (catabolism). Among the most familiar are those by which green plants build up complex organic substances from water, carbon dioxide, and mineral salts (see photosynthesis◊), and by which animals, by taking them in as food, break them down partially by digestion and subsequently resynthesize them in their own bodies□

metal an element usually marked by its crystalline hardness; good conduction of heat and electricity; opacity, but ability to reflect light; and malleability and ductility. Some 70 are known. Recent developments in metal-working (metallurgy) include the 'ice-cream' process (rheocasting), in which the metal is rendered semi-solid, allowing working at lower temperatures and pressure, as well as development of new alloys (e.g. ***superplastic metal*** an alloy which becomes stretchable to ten times its length when heated and put under pressure, see titanium) and greater strength. See also metallic glass◊□

metallic glass substance produced from metallic materials (non-corrosive alloys rather than simple metals) in liquid state which by very rapid cooling are prevented from reverting to their regular metallic structure. Instead they take on the properties of glass, while retaining the metallic properties of malleability and relatively good electrical conductivity□

metalloid a non-metal, such as boron or silicon□

metamorphic rock rocks altered in structure and composition by pressure and heat. See under rock◊□

metaphysics the branch of philosophy that deals with first principles, especially being and knowing. See under philosophy◊□

Metastasio pseudonym of Italian poet, Pietro Trapassi 1698–1782. He was the greatest librettist of his day, creating 18th-century Italian *opera seria* (serious opera)□

Metaxas Joannis 1871–1941. Greek soldier, who restored George II, under whom he established a dictatorship as Prime Minister from 1936. He led resistance to the Italian invasion of Greece in 1941□

metempsychosis see under incarnation◊□

meteor streak of light, a 'shooting star', which appears when a meteoroid, an interplanetary rock or dust particle, enters earth's atmosphere, sets up frictional heat by its own speed and destroys itself. Generally smaller than grains of sand, meteoroids tend to travel in streams; when the earth passes through a meteor stream an often spectacular meteor shower is observed, usually at the same time each year; the most famous annual shower is that of the Perseids, in early Aug. Those too large to be destroyed, and which land on earth are meteorites◊□

meteorite natural object (originating in asteroidal collisions, disintegration of comet nuclei, etc.) landing on earth, and ranging from the minute to a record 30 tonnes. When they explode in passing through the atmosphere meteorite showers occur (a record 100 000 in Poland, 30 Jan 1868). Most are chondrites (stones with grains of metal) or achondrites (stones with no metal), but rare examples include tiny diamonds, or water and the 'building blocks' of life, amino acids and fatty acids, though of non-biological origin. Large numbers have been found in Antarctica. See astron◊, thermoluminescence◊□

meteorology the scientific observation and study of the atmosphere, to enable weather to

meteorology

stages of a depression

1

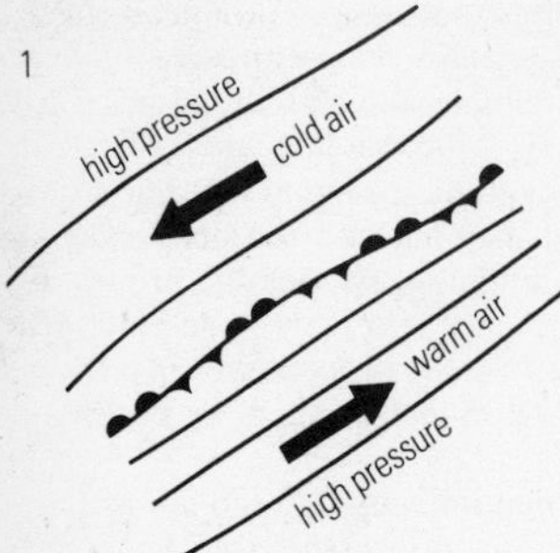

2

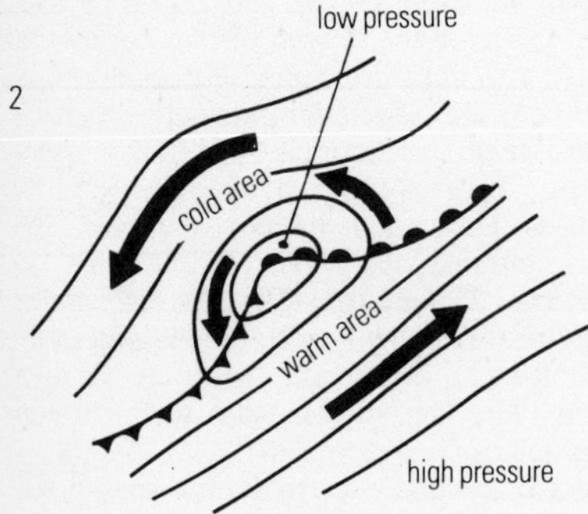

3

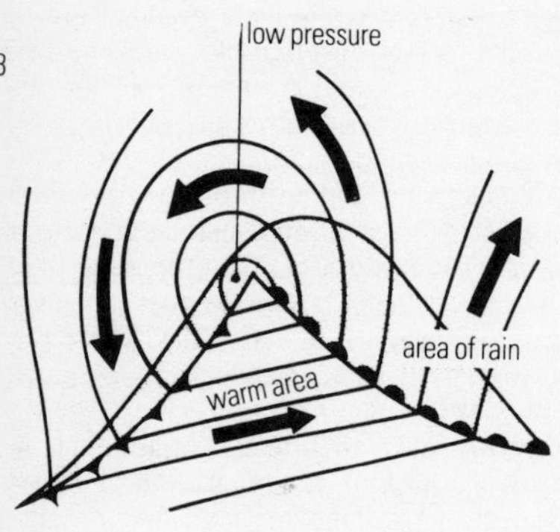

lines of equal pressure

4

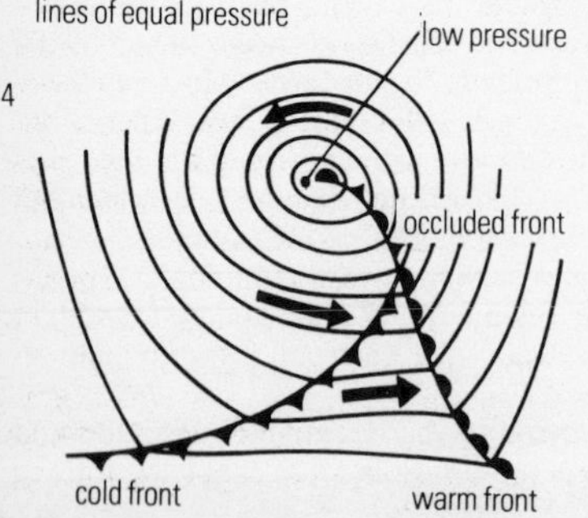

be accurately forecast. At meteorological stations readings are taken of the factors determining weather conditions: atmospheric pressure, temperature, humidity, wind (categorized by the Beaufort Scale), cloud cover (measuring both type of cloud and coverage), and rainfall (measured at 12-hourly intervals). Data from these stations and from weather satellites is collated by computer at central agencies such as the Meteorological Office in London, and a forecast based on current readings is issued at regular intervals. See also weather◊ map□

methane simplest hydrocarbon, CH_4, of the paraffin series. Colourless, odourless, and lighter than air, it burns with a bluish flame, and explodes when mixed with air or oxygen. It is the chief constituent of ***natural gas*** and also occurs in the explosive ***fire-damp*** of coal mines, and in ***marsh gas*** formed from rotting vegetation, which results by spontaneous combustion in the pale flame seen over marshland, and known as ***will-o'the-wisp*** or ***ignis fatuus***□

methanol CH_3OH, methyl alcohol◊, a poisonous, colourless liquid. It is used to produce formaldehyde, from which resins and plastics are made, and increasingly, by the MTG (methanol-to-gasoline) process, converted to petrol with the aid of zeolite◊ catalysts. See also biotechnology◊□

Methodism evangelical movement founded by John and Charles Wesley◊ in 1739, within the Church of England, which became a separate body in 1795. Its doctrines are contained in John Wesley's sermons and *Notes on the New Testament*; the church government is presbyterian in Britain (episcopal in USA), with supreme authority vested in the annual conference (50% ministers, 50% laymen); members are grouped under 'class leaders' and churches into 'circuits'□

Methodius see under Cyril◊ and Methodious□

Methuselah in the Old Testament, Hebrew patriarch who lived before the Flood; his supposed age of 969 years made him the type of longevity□

methyl alcohol another name for methanol◊. See also under alcohols◊□

methylated spirits alcohol adulterated or 'denatured' (made undrinkable) for industrial purposes, and so free of duty. Some advanced alcoholics nevertheless drink it, and death is the eventual result□

metric system system of weights and measures originating in 18th-century France, and recommended for universal adoption in a revised International System (*Système International d'Unités*, abbreviation SI) in 1960.

There are seven 'base units': metre (m) for length (redefined in 1983 as the length of the path travelled by light in vacuum during a time interval of 1/299 792 458 of a second); kilogram (kg) for mass or weight; second (s) for time; ampere (A) for electric current; kelvin (K) for thermodynamic temperature; candela (cd) for luminous intensity, and mole (mol) for quantity of matter. Two supplementary units, the radian (rad) and steradian (sr) are used to measure plane and solid angles, and various derived units, such as the watt, are in use.

prefixes and their symbols used in multiplication and division are: *era* T trillion times (10^{12}), *giga* G billion times (10^9), *mega* M million times (10^6), *kilo* k thousand times (10^3), *hecto* h hundred times (10^2), *deka* (da) ten times (10), *deci* d tenth part (10^{-1}), *centi* c hundredth part (10^{-2}), *milli* m thousandth part (10^{-3}), *micro* μ millionth part (10^{-6}), *nano* n billionth part ($10-^9$), *pico* p trillionth part (10^{-12}), *femto* f quadrillionth part (10^{-15}), *atto* a quintillionth part (10^{-18}).

SI was adopted as the primary system of weights and measures in the UK in 1965, but compulsion was abandoned in 1978. The USA passed a metric act in 1975□

Metropolitan Opera Company premier opera company of the USA (1883), established since 1966 at the Lincoln Centre, New York□

Metsu Gabriel 1630–67. Dutch painter, noted for anecdotal pictures, e.g. *The Duet* and *Music Lesson*, National Gallery, London□

Metternich-Winneburg Klemens Wenzel Lothar, Prince von Metternich-Winneburg 1773–1859. Austrian foreign minister from 1809 until the 1848 Revolution forced him to flee to England. At the Congress of Vienna of 1815 he advocated cooperation by the great powers to suppress democratic movements□

Metz industrial city (shoes, metal goods, tobacco) in NE France; population 117 200. Part of the Holy Roman Empire 870–1552, it became one of the great frontier fortresses of France, and was German 1871–1918. The Cathedral of St Étienne is largely 13th century. The poet Verlaine◊ was born here□

Meuse river (Dutch *Maas*) flowing through France, Belgium, and the Netherlands; length 900 km/560 mi. It was a line of battle in World War I (1914) and II (1940)□

Mewar another name for Udaipur◊□

Mexicali city in NW Mexico; population 361 000. There are many US companies attracted by cheap labour (Hughes Aerospace, Rockwell International, etc.)□

Mexican War war between the USA and Mexico 1846–8, begun when General Zachary Taylor invaded New Mexico. Mexico City was taken in 1847, and under the Treaty of Guadaloupe-Hidalgo, Mexico lost Texas, New Mexico, and California (half its territory) to the USA for $15 million compensation□

Mexico United States of

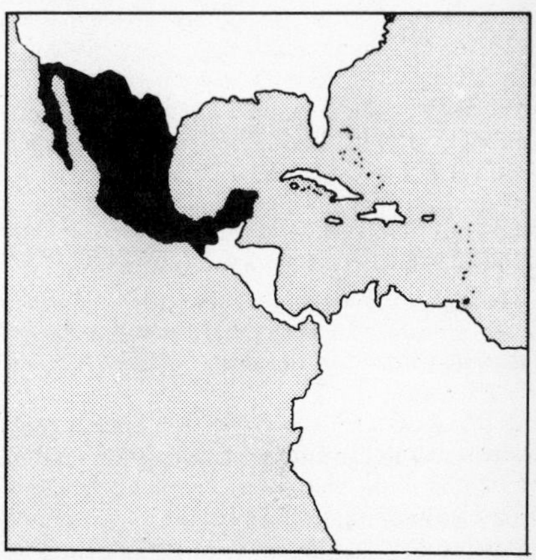

area 1 979 650 sq km/763 944 sq mi

capital Mexico City

towns Guadalajara, Monterrey; port Veracruz

features frontier of 2000 miles with USA; resorts Acapulco, Mexicali, Tijuana; the two Sierra Madres; Baja California; volcanoes, e.g. Popocatepetl; archaeological sites of pre-Spanish period

exports silver, gold, lead, uranium, etc.; oil and natural gas (to USA); traditonal handicrafts: fish and shellfish

currency peso

population 77 000 000; a minority are *criollos* of Spanish descent, but the majority are mestizo, though 12% are pure American Indian; 50% of the total are under 20 years of age

language Spanish (official); Indian languages include Nahuatl, Maya, and Mixtec

religion Roman Catholicism

famous people Luis Barragán, Frida Kahlo, Octavio Paz, Diego Rivera

government federal republic of 31 states and a federal district; executive president (Miguel de la Madrid Hurtado from 1982) elected for six years by popular vote, who cannot be re-elected; with senate and chamber of deputies. The Partido Revolucionario Institucional (Party of the Institutional Revolution) has dominated every election since 1930.

recent history for early history, see Olmecs◊, Mayas◊, Toltecs◊, Aztecs◊. Following the Spanish invasion 1519–21 (see Cortès◊),

Spanish culture and religion were substituted for that of the Aztecs, who were reduced from some 16 million to one million in the 17th century by smallpox. The struggle for independence from Spain began in 1810 and was achieved in 1821. Following a turbulent period dominated by Santa Anna◊, Mexico was at war with the USA 1846–8 (see Mexican◊ War), and suppressed a Maya Indian revolt in 1848. The country remained turbulent, and when President Benito Juarez◊ repudiated foreign debts, the French intervened and in 1863 Maximilian of Austria◊ was proclaimed emperor. Stability was only attained in the subsequently restored republic under Diaz◊; later presidents include Cárdenas◊, and Miguel Alemán 1946–52, who countered leftist pressure by declaring that wealth had to be created before it could be distributed. The 'six-year' presidential system has been compared to Aztec ritual, with the ruler granting power to his chosen successor, and then being sacrificed to allow the continuation of the system□

Mexico City capital and industrial centre of Mexico, largest city in the world; population 17 000 000 (by 2000 estimated at 35 million). It dates from c1325 when the Aztec capital of Tenochtitlán was established 2255 m/7400 ft above sea level near Lake Texcoco; the site of the city's great pyramid (on which was the temple to Huitzilopochtli, the sun god and god of war) was cleared of later building and excavated in the 1970s/80s and preserved as a museum. Notable buildings include the cathedral of St James, 16–19th centuries (on the site of the temple of Huichilobos), Palacio Nacional, 1692 (on the site of Montezuma's palace), Palacio de Bellas Artes, and the mosaic-decorated National Library at the university. To the SE is Lake Xochimilco, famous for its 'floating' gardens (actually gardens made in swamps from material excavated by making canals, as practised by the Aztecs. It was devastated by earthquake in 1985□

Meyerbeer Giacomo. Adopted name of German pianist and composer of operas Jakob Liebmann Beer 1791–1864. Most popular were *Robert le Diable* 1831 and *Les Huguenots* 1836□

mezzogiorno Italian 'mid-day'; the hot impoverished regions of S Italy□

mezzotint method of engraving a copper plate for use in printing. See print◊□

Miami city and port in Florida, USA; population 1 600 000. Following the influx of immigrants from Cuba, Haiti, Mexico, and S America, it is developing as the financial and trading capital of Latin America and the Caribbean, as well as having become in the early 1980s the 'crime capital of America'. It is also a centre for oceanographic research, and a tourist mecca for its beaches, etc.□

mica minerals with a vitreous pearly lustre, found in schists, gneisses, and granites, which have perfect basal cleavage and split into thin flakes. They are used industrially for their good thermal and electrical insulation qualities□

Micah c700BC. In the Old Testament, a Hebrew prophet whose writings denounce the oppressive ruling class of Judah, and demand justice□

Michael St, in the New Testament, an archangel, bearer of a flaming sword, and (in *Revelation*) leader of the heavenly hosts in battle against Satan□

Michael 1596–1645. Tsar of Russia from 1613, the founder of the house of Romanov◊□

Michael 1921– . King of Romania. Son of Carol◊ II, he succeeded his grandfather as king in 1927, was displaced on his father's return from exile, but was again king from his father's abdication in 1940. He overthrew the Antonescu dictatorship in 1944, so that Romania shared in the Allied victory, but abdicated in 1947□

Michaelmas daisy a type of plant. See aster◊□

Michaelmas Day festival (19 Sept) of St Michael◊ and all Angels, an English quarter day□

Michelangelo 1475–1564. Italian sculptor, painter, architect, and poet, Michelangiolo di Lodovico Buonarroti Simoni. Born near Florence, he was a student of Domenico◊ and Ghirlandaio◊, and worked for Lorenzo de' Medici◊. In Florence his works include the statue of David, the design of the Medici sepulchral chapel, and the *Pietà* in Florence Cathedral in which Nicodemus is a self-portrait. In Rome where he mainly worked 1496–1501 and 1508–64, his works include sculptures (the *Pietà,* tomb of Pope Julius II with *Moses and the Slaves*); the paintings on the ceiling and above the altar (*The Last Judgment*) of the Sistine Chapel; and the dome of St Peter's (where he was chief architect from 1547). His friendship with Vittoria Colonna◊ in his later years inspired many of his sonnets and madrigals□

Michelson Albert Abraham 1852–1931. American physicist, first US winner of a Nobel prize in 1907. The failure of the ***Michelson-Morley Experiment*** (with Edward Morley in 1887) to detect the motion of the earth through a postulated ether◊ led

Einstein◊ to the theory of relativity□

Michigan Midwest state of the USA; Great Lake State or Wolverine State

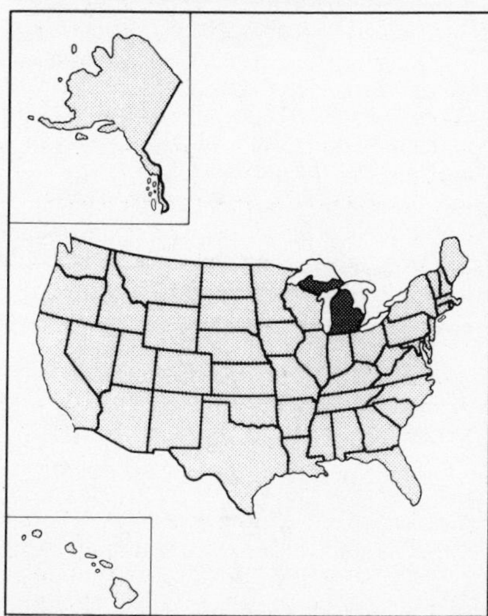

area 150 777 sq km/58 216 sq mi, including inland water
capital Lansing
towns Detroit, Grand Rapids, Flint, Lansing
features over 50% forested; Henry Ford◊ Museum at Dearborn; in 1973 97% of the population were contaminated by PBB (poly-brominated biphenyl) a flame-retardant chemical inadvertently mixed with livestock feed
products chiefly industrial; cars, iron, cement, oil
population 9 236 891
famous people General Custer, Edna Ferber, Henry Ford
history explored by the French from 1618, it became British in 1763, and a state in 1837□

Michigan Lake. See Great Lakes◊□

Mickiewicz Adam 1798–1855. Polish revolutionary poet, whose *Pan Tadeusz* 1832–4 is his country's national epic. He died at Constantinople while raising a Polish corps to fight against Russia in the Crimean War□

microbe any microscopic organism, but especially disease-causing bacteria◊□

microcomputer small computer◊ using a microprocessor◊. Microcomputers include a ***word processor,*** essentially an intelligent electric typewriter. Text is typed, appears on a screen, and can be edited (additions, deletions, changes of position, etc.), then printed out from floppy or 'hard' (much greater storage capacity) disc. A similar disc can also be used to drive a photo-setting machine to produce book-quality printing. Microcomputers may also have programs to allow them to act as a ***spread sheet*** making calculations with figures and formulae, as in business planning, and an ***accounting machine*** storing information on a firm's customers, finances, etc., so that it can be retrieved for various purposes□

microform any of the media which reduce printed text to a size unreadable by the naked eye, especially 35 mm roll film, 16 mm film and microfiche, a flat sheet of film generally 105 x 148 mm, including up to 420 pages of text□

microlight aircraft very light aircraft, including hang-gliders, which are powered by small engines, and are portable on a car roof-rack. See also Paul MacCready◊□

micrometre (previously known as ***micron***) one millionth of a metre◊□

micron obsolete name for the micrometre◊□

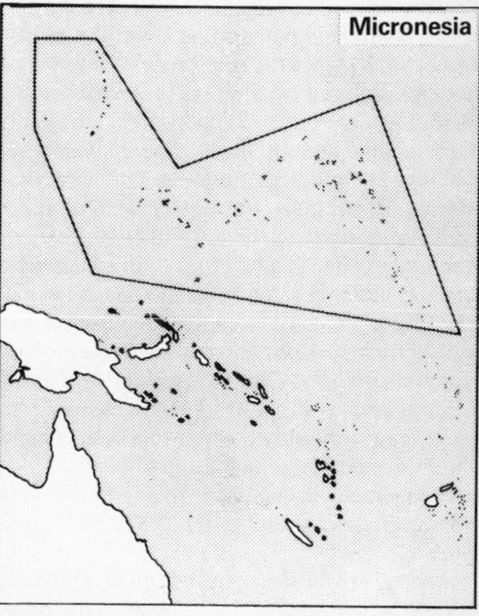

Micronesia those islands of Oceania◊ lying N of Melanesia◊, which include the Federal States of Micronesia◊, Belau◊, Kiribati◊, the Mariana◊ and Marshall◊ Islands, Nauru◊, and Tuvalu◊□

Micronesia Federated States of. Internally self-governing country from 1980, which signed a free association agreement with the USA in 1982, subject to ratification. It comprises notably Kosrae, Ponape, Truk, and Yap. See Carolines◊□

microphone device for producing an electrical voltage which varies in sympathy with sound waves. In the ***ribbon microphone***, sound waves reaching the ribbon make it vibrate. In doing so it cuts lines of magnetic flux running between the poles of the magnet, and a small voltage appears, through electromagnetic◊

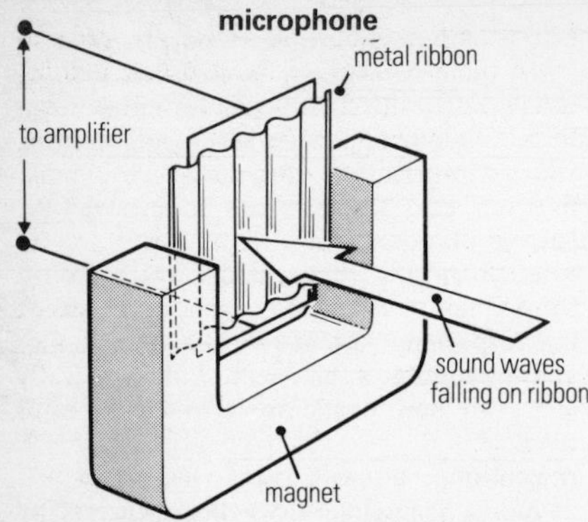

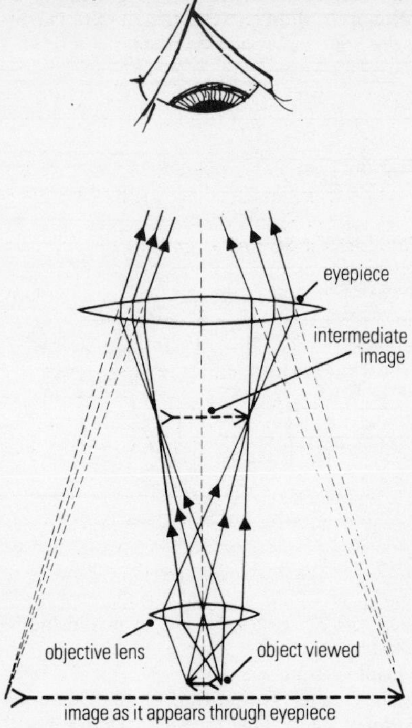

induction across its ends. Suitably amplified, the voltage can, for example, be used to drive a loudspeaker◊□

microprocessor a complex kind of integrated circuit◊ comprising 1000 to 200 000 transistors fabricated on a silicon chip◊, invented in 1972, and capable of performing complex logical operations comparable to those of the central processing unit (CPU) of a conventional digital computer. Microprocessors excel equivalent circuits made by older technologies by several hundred times in terms of size, weight, reliability, and power consumption, and their low cost means that they can be incorporated (as part of the control system) in sewing machines, motor cars, machine tool controllers, navigation equipment, word processors, electronic games, weapons guidance systems, etc. They are also widely used as the central processing unit in small general-purpose digital computers and especially the now common 'personal' computers□

microscope instrument for magnification with high resolution for detail: the chief types are:

optical usually with two sets of glass lenses and an eyepiece, invented in 1609 by Dutchman Zacharias Janssen 1580–c1638.

electron (developed from 1932) which uses a beam of electrons instead of a beam of light, and, since these are not visible, replaces the eyepiece with a fluorescent screen or photographic plate; far higher magnification and resolution is possible than with the optical microscope. A ***scanning electron microscope*** (SEM), developed in the mid-1960s, probes the surface of a specimen and represents it three-dimensionally.

acoustic which uses an acoustic wave travelling down a sapphire rod, an image being built up by scanning the specimen. This results in the object being 'seen' in a different way, which may reveal quite diffferent detail from that revealed by light or electrons, and also enables the inside of a microchip or a living cell to be made visible. The idea was suggested by D Y Sokolov (USSR) in the 1950s, and developed in the USA in 1973.

Also under development are ***X-ray*** and ***laser*** microscopes□

microwave form of radiation (see electromagnetic◊ wave and radar◊), which when used in cooking generates heat throughout the food simultaneously, instead of gradually penetrating inwards. It has industrial uses in killing insects in stored grain, destroying enzymes in processed food, sterilizing liquids, pasteurization, and the drying (seasoning) of timber and fruit□

Midas in Greek legend, a king of Phrygia whose touch converted everything to gold, and who was given ass's ears by Apollo◊ because he preferred the music of Pan◊□

MIDAS acronym for ***M***issile ***D***efence ***A***larm ***S***ystem□

Mid-Atlantic Ridge chain of mountains and valleys running N/S through both Atlantic Oceans for 65 000 km/44 000 mi, where for 225 million years lava has welled up from the earth's mantle as a result of Europe and Africa moving further apart at the rate of 25 cm/1 in each year□

Middelburg town in SW Netherlands, capital of Zeeland and former Hanseatic◊ town; population 38 620□

Middle Ages (broadly) European history from the end of the Roman Empire◊ to the Renaissance◊, 5–15th centuries; (narrowly) the period from about 1000AD to the 15th century, characterized by the rise to supremacy of the Roman Catholic Church and the rise of feudalism◊□

Middle East the Balkan states, Egypt, and SW Asia; the area known before World War II as the Near East□

Middle Kingdom a period of Egyptian history extending from the late 11th to the 13th dynasty (?2040–?1670); also a term applied to the pre-Communist Chinese Empire, so called by the Chinese because of belief in its central and superior position□

Middle Range mountain range in NE Eyre Peninsula, South Australia, rich in iron□

Middlesbrough industrial town and port on the Tees, administrative headquarters of Cleveland, England (1974–86); population 149 100. It is the commercial and cultural centre of the urban area formed by Stockton-on-Tees, Redcar, Billingham, Thornaby, and Eston. Formerly a centre of heavy industry, it diversified its products in the 1960s□

Middlesex in the 6th century the area between the kingdoms of the E and W Saxons. It remained a county until broken up in 1965, and the name is still used in cricket, etc.□

Middleton Thomas c1570–1627. English dramatist, whose tragedies include *Women Beware Women* 1621 and many works in collaboration with William Rowley◊, e.g. *The Changeling* 1622□

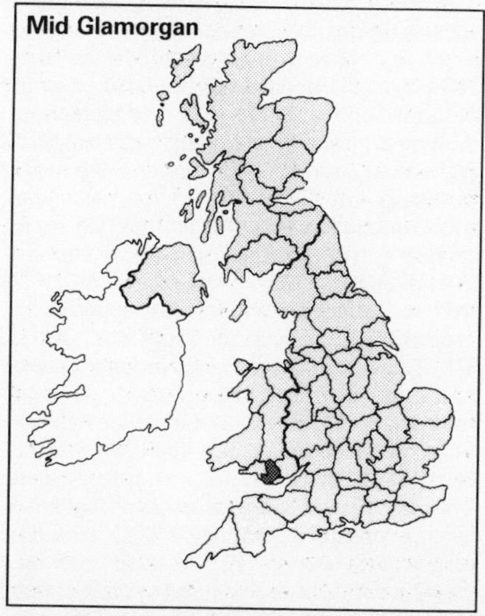

Middle West or ***Midwest***, a large area of north-central USA (Ohio, Indiana, Illinois, Michigan, Iowa, Wisconsin, and Minnesota). It is the most 'typical' area of the USA, Republican and isolationist□

midge a small fly□

Mid Glamorgan county of S Wales

area 1019 sq km/393 sq mi

towns administrative headquarters Cardiff; resort Porthcawl, Aberdare, Merthyr Tydfil, Bridgend, Pontypridd

features Caerphilly Castle, with its water defences

products formerly the N was a important coal (e.g. Rhondda) and iron and steel area; Royal Mint at Llantrisant; agriculture in the south; Caerphilly noted for creamy mild cheese

population 538 200, largest of the Welsh counties

language 8% Welsh Speaking□

Midi-Pyrénées region of SW France; capital Toulouse; population 2 323 320□

Midlands area of England corresponding roughly to the Anglo-Saxon kingdom of Mercia◊. ***E Midlands*** Derbyshire, Leicestershire, Northamptonshire, Nottinghamshire; ***W Midlands*** the former metropolitan county of West◊ Midlands created from parts of Staffordshire, Warwickshire, and Worcestershire; and (often included) ***S Midlands*** Bedfordshire, Buckinghamshire, Oxfordshire. In World War II the E Midlands was worked for oil, and substantial finds were made in the 1980s; the oilbearing E Midlands Shelf extends into Yorkshire and Lincolnshire□

midnight sun appearance of the sun (within the Arctic and Antarctic Circles) above the horizon at midnight during the summer□

midrash commentaries on the Bible composed 400–1200AD. See under Judaism◊□

midshipman trainee naval officer who has either completed his first year at the Royal Naval College, Dartmouth, or is in his first year with the fleet, after which he becomes acting sub-lieutenant□

midsummer day 24 Jun, feast of St John the Baptist. See also solstice◊□

Midway Islands two islands in the N Pacific; area 5.5 sq km/2.2 sq mi; population 455. Annexed by the USA in 1867, they are administered by the Navy. The naval ***Battle of Midway*** 3–6 Jun 1942, between the USA and Japan, was the turning point in the Pacific in World War II□

midwifery in nursing, the care of a woman before, during, and after labour, including the delivery of the child, but with the assistance of a medical practitioner when complications occur□

Mies van der Rohe Ludwig 1886–1969. German-born American architect, director of the Bauhaus◊ 1929–33. His works include the new Illinois Institute of Technology 1941, where he taught 1938–58, and the bronze and glass Seagram Building, New York□

migraine acute headaches which recur, often with advance symptoms, e.g. flashing lights, often accompanied by nausea. No cure has been discovered, but drugs may reduce pain, and changes in diet may help prevent attacks□

migration movement of animals, either seasonally, or as part of a single life cycle, or in response to special conditions, to particular feeding or breeding grounds. Some of the most remarkable migrants are birds, which, it is thought, have great visual acuity and memory of ground clues to aid them, but in long-distance flight navigate possibly by the sun and stars, perhaps in combination with an internal biological 'clock', (acting roughly in the same way as a marine chronometer) and an inbuilt 'magnetic compass', a tiny mass of tissue between the eye and brain. Homing honey-bees have similar 'compasses'□

Mihailovich Draga 1893–1946. Yugoslav soldier, leader of the guerrilla 'Chetniks' of World War II in combatting the German occupation. His feud with Tito's Communists led to the withdrawal of Allied support and that of his own exiled goverment from 1943. He turned to the Italians and Germans, and was eventually shot for treason□

mikado old title ('honorable palace gate') of the Japanese emperor, replaced in the late 19th century by *tenno* (heavenly sovereign)□

Milan financial (chief stock exchange) industrial city (aircraft, cars, locomotives) (Italian *Milano*), capital of Lombardy, Italy; population 1 604 780. In the Middle Ages Milan was an independent city-state under the Visconti and Sforza families, and became part of the kingdom of Italy in 1859. The exterior of the Gothic cathedral, begun in 1386, is a mass of pinnacles and statues, and can hold 40 000 worshippers; the convent adjoining Santa Maria dell Grazie has Leonardo da Vinci◊'s *The Last Supper* on its walls; and the church of St Ambrose is the burial place of the saint. Milan is also a cultural centre, e.g. the Scala opera house in 1778, and two universities; and is a leader in fashion design, as well as being the heart of Italy's textile industry□

Milankovitch hypothesis see under Ice◊ Age□

Mildenhall market town in Suffolk, England; population 7200. The ***Mildenhall Treasure*** of Roman silverware, now in the British Museum, was discovered in 1942–3□

mildew a type of plant disease. See under Ascomycetes◊□

Mildura town in Victoria, Australia; population 15 765. Centre of an irrigated fruit and vegetable area□

mile a measure of length used in English-speaking countries. A statute mile is equal to 1760 yds/1.60934 km, and a nautical mile (used internationally) is equal to 6076. 12 ft/1852m. It is derived from the Roman mile of 1000 paces□

Mile End a district of E London, England. See under Tower◊ Hamlets□

Miles Bernard, Baron Miles 1907– . British actor-producer, founder of the Mermaid Theatre, City of London, in 1959□

Miletus ruined site (now in W Anatolia, Turkey) of an ancient Greek port which eventually silted up□

milfoil another name for the herb yarrow◊□

Milford Haven Louis Alexander, 1st Marquess of Milford Haven. 1854–1921. See Louis◊ of Battenburg□

Milford Haven seaport (Welsh *Aberdaugleddau*) in Dyfed, Wales; population 14 000. There are oil refineries and petrochemical works□

Milhaud Darius 1892–1974. French composer, best remembered for his ballets *Le Boeuf sur le toit* 1919 and *Le Train bleu* 1924□

miliaria or ***prickly heat*** is an itching inflammation of the blocked sweat glands□

Militant Tendency a faction within the British Labour◊ Party, aligned with the newspaper *Militant.* It became active in the 1970s, with radical socialist policies based on Trotskyism (see Trotsky◊), and gained some success in local government, especially in inner city areas, e.g. Liverpool. In the mid-1980s the Labour Party considered it to be an organization within the party and banned it. A number of senior 'members' were expelled from the party in 1986, amid much legal conflict□

military law articles or regulations that apply to members of the armed services. See under martial◊ law□

militia a body of citizen (as opposed to professional) soldiers; the forerunner of the UK Territorial◊ Army, and National Guard of the states of the USA□

milk secretion of the female mammary glands of vertebrates who suckle their young (see lactation◊), for whom it is a complete food. The milk of cows, goats, and sheep (that most usually consumed by man) is c80% water, the rest includes fat, protein, milk sugar, calcium, phosphorus, a little iron, and vitamins. Pasteurization◊ eliminates the risk of disease, and further ultra-heat treatment (UHT) produces long-life milk which remains fresh for six months without refrigeration. The presence of saturated fat (a causal factor in heart attacks, etc.) has led to increased sales of fat-reduced ***skimmed milk*** left over after butter is churned; ***butter-milk*** skimmed milk soured by lactic acid produced by bacteria from milk sugar; ***yoghurt*** made from either whole or fat-reduced milk; and forms of fat-reduced dried ***milk powder***□

Milky Way central luminous band across the sky composed of stars too distant to distinguish individually with the naked eye, and which forms the main plane of our galaxy◊. At right-angles to it is a band of gas 10–20 light years thick (detected by the Very Large Array radio telescope, 1984). The presence of this band indicates that the dust clouds at the centre of the galaxy conceal some object which is spewing out a violent wind of charged particles, possibly a dense star cluster□

Mill John Stuart 1806–73. British philosopher-economist. Son of an eminent Utilitarian◊, James Mill, he published *Principles of Political Economy* 1848, but moved to a more liberal socialist individualism under the influence of Coleridge's writings, sat in Parliament as a Radical 1865–8, and was a supporter of women's rights (he introduced a motion for women's suffrage, and published *On the Subjection of Women* 1869). His masterpiece is *On Liberty* 1859□

Millais Sir John Everett 1829–96. British painter, a founder of the Pre-Raphaelite◊ Brotherhood (*Christ in the House of his Parents* 1850 and *Ophelia* 1852); later works include the sentimental *Boyhood of Raleigh* 1870 and *Bubbles,* a poster for Pears soap, 1886. In 1855 he married Effie Gray, Ruskin◊'s former wife□

Millay Edna St Vincent 1892–1950. American poet, born in Maine, author of volumes of direct emotional verse, e.g. *The Harp-Weaver* 1922□

millennium a period of 1000 years. Some Christian sects believe that Christ will return (Second Coming) to govern this earth in person for a thousand years preceding the Last Judgment. Such views become more widespread at periods of religious excitement, as at the Reformation◊. Modern millennarians include the Jehovah◊'s Witnesses□

Miller Arthur 1915– . American playwright. Deeply concerned with family relationships and contemporary American values, his plays include *All my Sons* 1947, and *Death of a Salesman* 1949; *The Crucible* 1953, an equation of the Salem witch hunt with political persecution such as 'McCarthyism' (Miller was convicted of Contempt of Congress in 1957, for refusal to name those present at a meeting of Communist writers in 1947). He was married 1956–61 to Marilyn Monroe◊, for whom he wrote the film *The Misfits* 1960, and with whom Maggie, in his play *After the Fall* 1964, has been identified□

Miller Glenn 1904–44. American trombonist, and as bandleader, creator of the 'big band sound' from 1938. He composed his signature tune 'Moonlight Serenade' and 'In the Mood'. He enlisted and disappeared without trace on a flight between England and France□

Miller Henry 1891–1980. American writer, born in New York. Years spent in the Paris underworld underpin his novels *Tropic of Cancer* 1934 and *Tropic of Capricorn* 1938. They were so outspoken that the former was banned in England till 1963, and the latter was published in the USA only in 1961□

miller's thumb a small freshwater fish. See under perch◊□

Millet Jean François 1814–75. French painter, born in Normandy, who settled at Barbizon◊ in 1848, and is best known for his peasant studies, e.g. *The Reapers* 1854 and *The Gleaners* 1857□

millet a cereal grass. See grasses◊□

Millikan Robert Andrews 1868–1953. American physicist. His isolation of the electron and determination of its charge in 1917, brought him a Nobel prize in 1923□

Millin Sarah Gertrude 1889–1968. South African novelist, an early opponent of racial discrimination, e.g. *God's Step-Children* 1924□

millipede an arthropod. See under centipede◊□

Mills Sir John 1908– . British actor-director, whose films include *Great Expectations* 1947, *Scott of the Antarctic* 1949, and *Ryan's Daughter* 1971 (Oscar as supporting actor); knighted in 1976□

Milne A(lan) A(lexander) 1882–1956. British author, best known for his children's books based on Pooh, the bear (commemorated by a statue at London zoo) and other toys of his son Christopher Robin (*Winnie the Pooh* 1926 and *The House at Pooh Corner* 1928); volumes of children's verse (*When We Were Very Young* 1924 and *Now We Are Six* 1927); and his stage adaptation of Kenneth Grahame's *The Wind in the Willows* as *Toad of Toad Hall* 1929□

Milner Alfred, Viscount Milner 1854–1925. British administrator. As Governor of Cape Colony 1897–1901, his negotiation with Kruger broke down, resulting in the South◊

African War; and as Governor of the Transvaal and Orange River Colonies 1902–5 after their annexation, he reorganized their administration. He emphasized the 'organic union' of the Empire, rather than the need for independence for its members□

Milosz Czeslaw 1911– . Polish poet, e.g. *Bells in Winter* 1980; Nobel prize 1980□

Milstein César 1927– . British molecular biologist, who in 1984 shared a Nobel medicine prize (with George Kohler◊ and Niels Jerne◊) for techniques used to produce antibodies◊ giving immunity against specific diseases□

Milton John 1608–74. English poet, who was educated at Christ's College, Cambridge (where he was known as 'the Lady of Christ's' for his fine features), and then devoted himself to study for his poetic career. His early poems include the pastoral style *L'Allegro* and *Il Penseroso* of 1632, the masque *Comus* 1633, and the elegy for a dead friend *Lycidas* 1637. His middle years were devoted to the Puritan cause and pamphleteering, including one advocating divorce, and another (*Areopagitica)* freedom of the press. From 1649 he was (Latin) secretary to the Council of State, his assistants (as his sight failed) including Marvell◊. His wives were Mary Powell, a seventeen-year-old he married in 1643, and who left him, though three daughters were born after their reconciliation in 1645 (the girls were later his somewhat unwilling amanuenses, etc.). After her death in 1652, the year of his total blindness, he married twice more, the second wife dying in childbirth, and the last surviving him for over half a century. The masterpieces of his old age in retirement are his epic poems *Paradise Lost* 1667, and *Paradise Regained* 1677, and the classic drama *Samson Agonistes*, also published in the latter year. He attained a Virgilian music and majesty of language, and his treatment of Satan inadvertently made Satan the 'hero' of *Paradise Lost*□

Milton Keynes 'new town' (see Llewelyn-Davies◊) in Buckinghamshire, England; population 150 000. It is the headquarters of the Open University, and Bletchley Park (see Ultra◊) is nearby. See under Buckinghamshire◊□

Milwaukee port (on Lake Michigan) and industrial city (meatpacking, brewing, engineering, textiles) in Wisconsin, USA; population 636 200□

mimosa genus of tropical and sub-tropical plants with pinnate leaves and yellow, fluffy flowers, family Leguminosae◊. The Brazilian ***sensitive plant*** *M sensitiva*, shrinks as if withered when touched. See also acacia◊□

minaret the slender tower of a mosque◊□

mind the entity in an individual responsible for the ability to think, feel, and will, which may be seen as synonymous with the merely random chemical reactions within the brain, or as a function of it as a whole, or (more traditionally) as existing independently of the physical brain, through which it expresses itself, or even as the only reality, matter being considered the creation of intelligence□

Mindanao second largest island of the Philippines◊□

Minden town in N Rhine-Westphalia, W Germany; population 55 000. The French were defeated here in 1759 by the Allies (Britain/Hanover/Brunswick)□

Mindoro a mountainous island in the central Philippines◊□

mine explosive charge on land or sea, or in the atmosphere, designed to be detonated by contact, vibration (e.g. from an enemy engine), by magnetic influence, or by a timing device. Counter-measures include metal detectors (useless for plastic types), specially equipped helicopters, and (at sea) ***minesweepers***: in their most modern form, small vessels c725 tonnes, built of reinforced plastic (immune to magnetic and acoustic mines), and, when they detect a mine on the sea bed by sonar, two remotely controlled miniature submarines are guided to lay destructive charges alongside□

Minehead seaside resort in Somerset, England, chief tourist centre for Exmoor◊; population 8000□

mineral true minerals are predominantly inorganic, crystalline (opal◊ is an exception), solids, of specific chemical composition, and often of great beauty and value, e.g. diamond◊, gold◊, malachite◊, pyrite◊, labradorite◊. Either in their perfect crystalline form, or otherwise, minerals are the constituents of rocks. More generally, a mineral is any substance economically valuable for mining (including coal and oil, although they have an organic origin)□

mineral water natural spring water of exceptional purity (often bottled for sale) or including salts or gases generally conducive to good health or useful for specific conditions. Famous sites include Aix-les-Bains, Evian (Lake of Geneva), Baden Baden, Bath, Buxton, Harrogate, Malvern, Mariánské Lázně, Tunbridge Wells, Vichy. Artificially made mineral waters, charged with carbon dioxide, are also sold□

Minerva in Roman mythology, the goddess of wisdom. Greek counterpart: Athena◊□

minesweeper small vessel for locating and destroying mines. See under mine◊□

miniature painting the art of painting on a very small scale, which originated in the tiny illustrations which formed part of the initials, etc. in medieval manuscripts: Latin *miniare* 'to paint with minium' (a vermilion colour). Modern miniatures, in the sense of small portraits, originated in the 16th century (see Holbein◊ the Younger). Later English artists include: Samuel Cooper, Isaac Oliver, Richard Cosway, George Engleheart; in France Jean (1486–1541) and François (c1522–72) Clouet; in Spain Goya◊, and in the USA C W Peale◊□

Minimal art in the arts in the 1960s a reduction of creative self-expression to a minimum, e.g. in painting, using simple geometrical shapes and colours; in music, not being committed to anything beyond the particular note or interval of silence being experienced at the moment□

mining extraction of minerals from under the earth or sea for industrial or domestic use. Exhaustion of easily accessible resources has led to new techniques, e.g. extraction of oil from under the North Sea and from land shale reserves, which are more difficult. Technology is also under development for the exploitation of minerals from asteroids, etc., in space, and from entirely new undersea sources:

mud deposits laid down by hot springs c350°C, i.e. sea water penetrates beneath the ocean floor, and on its return carries copper, silver, zinc, etc., with it. Such springs occur along the mid-ocean ridges of the Atlantic and Pacific, and in the geological rift between Africa and Arabia under the Red Sea.

mineral nodules which form on the ocean bed and contain manganese, cobalt, copper, molybdenum, nickel, etc.; they stand out on the surface, and 'grow' by only a few millimetres every 100 000 years.

See also bacteria◊ and law of the sea◊□

mink a small carnivorous mammal. See under weasel◊□

Minneapolis industrial city in Minnesota, USA, forming with St Paul◊ the 'Twin Cities' area; population 370 000, with a German and Scandinavian base. The world's most powerful computers (Cray 2 supercomputer, 1985) are built here: used for long-range weather forecasting, spacecraft design, codebreaking. The city centre is glass-covered against the difficult climate; there is an arts institute, symphony orchestra, university, and Tyrone Guthrie◊ theatre□

Minnesingers German minstrels of courtly love of the 12–13th centuries, of whom the most famous was Walther◊ von der Vogelweide□

Minnesota Midwest state of the USA; North Star or Gopher State

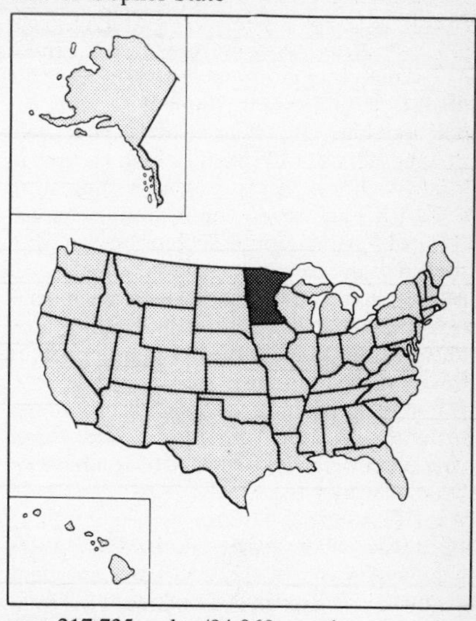

area 217 735 sq km/84 068 sq mi
capital St Paul
towns Minneapolis, Duluth
features sources of the Red, St Lawrence, and Mississippi rivers; Minnehaha Falls at Minneapolis; Mayo Clinic at Rochester
products cereals, potatoes, livestock products; pulpwood; iron ore (60% of US output); farm and other machinery
population 4 077 148
famous people F Scott Fitzgerald, Sinclair Lewis, William and Charles Mayo
history the first Europeans to explore were French fur traders in the 17th century, part was ceded to Britain in 1763, and part passed to the USA under the Louisiana Purchase in 1803; it became a state in 1858□

minnow a small slender European freshwater fish. See under carp◊□

Minoan civilization Bronze Age Cretan civilization (see Sir Arthur Evans◊), named from Minos◊, King of Crete. Originating on the island c3000BC, it was destroyed c1400BC by earthquakes related to the destruction of Santorini (see Atlantis◊). The stone-built royal palace had excellent plumbing. The Minoan language was deciphered by Michael Ventris◊ from tablets written in Linear B. See also Knossos◊, Minotaur◊□

minor the legal term for those under the age of majority (18); on reaching that age a person may make a legal marriage without parental consent, and make a valid will, but a person has only to be over the age of 16 to give valid consent to medical treatment□

Minorca second largest of the Balearic◊ Islands□

Minos in Greek mythology, a King of Crete (son of Zeus◊ and Europa◊). See under Minotaur◊□

Minotaur in Greek mythology, a monster, half man-half bull, offspring of Pasiphaë, wife of King Minos of Crete and a bull. Housed in a labyrinth (see Knossos◊), its victims were seven girls and seven youths, sent in annual tribute by Athens, until Theseus◊ slew it, with the aid of the daughter (Ariadne) of Minos□

Minsk capital and industrial city (machinery, textiles, leather) of Belorussia, USSR; population 1 333 000. It is the headquarters of the Soviet computer industry□

Minsmere see under Suffolk◊□

minster certain cathedrals and large churches originally connected to a monastery. See under monasticism◊□

mint an aromatic herb◊□

mint place where money is coined by government authority. In the UK it was for many centuries the Tower of London; in 1968 the Royal Mint was established at Llantrisant, Mid Glamorgan, where coins are made both for the UK and other countries□

Mintoff Dom (Dominic) 1916– . Labour Prime Minister of Malta 1971–84, violently intolerant of opposition. He negotiated the removal of British and other foreign military bases 1971–9, and made treaties with Libya□

Minton Thomas 1765–1836. British potter producing fine porcelain at Stoke-on-Trent from 1798□

Minuteman originally armed citizen who agreed to act 'in a minute' before the American War of Independence□

Minuteman a US three-stage intercontinental ballistic missile□

Miquelon Islands see under St Pierre◊ and Miquelon□

Mirabeau Honoré Gabriel Riqueti, Comte de Mirabeau 1749–91. French statesman. Elected as a deputy to the Third Estate in the revolutionary States General of 1789, he won the leadership of the National Assembly by his eloquence, but in reality favoured a parliamentary monarchy on English lines. From May 1790 he secretly acted as adviser to Louis◊ XVI. See also Marie◊ Antoinette□

miracle event transcending natural law as a result of divine intervention. The existence of miracles cannot be disproven, but evidence of their existence is hard to substantiate□

miracle plays medieval religious dramas (which reached their peak in the 15–16th centuries) performed at church festivals. The separate scenes were performed on mobile stages by the various town guilds; almost complete cycles of the Wakefield, York, and Chester plays survive. See morality◊ play□

Mirandola Pico della. Italian philosopher. See Pico◊□

Miró Joan 1893–1983. Spanish painter, born at Barcelona. A founder of Surrealism◊, he used primitive colour, and often favoured spindly lines and blobs, e.g. in *Still life with an Old Shoe*. He designed sets for the ballet director Diaghilev□

Mirren Helen 1946– . British actress, whose roles include Lady Macbeth, Isabella in *Measure for Measure*, and rock singer Maggie in David Hare's *Teeth 'n' Smiles*□

miscarriage spontaneous expulsion of a fetus from the womb before it is capable of independent survival. See under abortion◊□

Mishima Yukio 1925–70. Japanese novelist, using homosexual themes, e.g. *Confessions of a Mask* 1949. He founded a private army to attempt revival of the traditions of the Samurai, and committed hara-kiri◊□

Mishna part of the Talmud, the compilation of ancient Jewish law. See under Judaism◊□

Miskito American Indians. See under Nicaragua◊□

Miskolc industrial town (steel, engineering, chemicals, textiles, wine) in NE Hungary; population 210 000□

missel thrush a type of bird. See under thrush◊□

missile rocket-propelled weapon, which may be nuclear-armed (see nuclear◊ warfare). First wartime use of a long-range missile was against England in World War II, i.e. the jet-powered German V1 (*Vergeltungswaffe*, 'Revenge Weapon' 1 or Flying Bomb), a monoplane (wingspan c6 m/18 ft, length c8.5 m/25.5 ft); and the first rocket-propelled missile (with a pre-set guidance system) the German V2; see air◊ raid. A longer range version of the latter, capable of reaching New York was under preparation. After the war captured V2 material became the basis of the space race in both the USSR and USA (see von Braun◊). In the Falklands◊ conflict non-nuclear ***sea-skimming missiles*** were used (the French *Exocet*) against British ships by the Argentines; more recent types have a 95 km/60 mi range, home on target by radar (a digital computer aboard allows attack beyond the radar horizon of the launching aircraft), and can select the 'prime target' among a group of ships despite electronic decoy counter measures□

mission organized attempt to spread a faith among the unconverted. Great early Christian missionaries include the saints Paul, Patrick, Columba, and Francis Xavier. Among Protestants the Society for Promoting

Christian Knowledge, established in 1698, was a pioneer, see also John Wesley◊, David Livingstone◊, and Albert Schweitzer◊. Missionary influence has sometimes been retrograde, but has also often brought social and medical benefits. Missionary work in the West in the 20th century is often a matter of 'reconversion' of 'relapsed areas' with full use of the media, and usually of a fundamentalist character: see Billy Graham◊. Chief rival to Christianity◊ (for which work is now coordinated by the World Council of Churches) in the mission field is Islam◊, now the second religion in Europe, and making increasing numbers of converts in black Africa and the USA□

Mississippi Southern state of the USA; Magnolia State

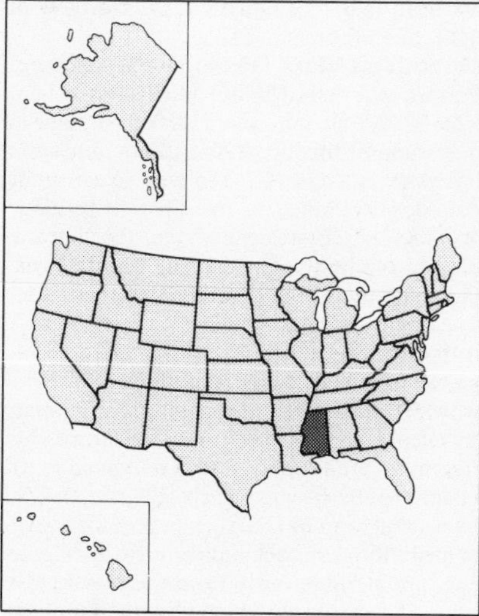

area 123 584 sq km/47 716 sq mi
capital Jackson
towns Biloxi
features Mississippi river; Vicksburg National Military Park (Civil War site)
products cotton, sweet potatoes, sugar, rice; canned sea food at Biloxi; timber and pulp; oil and natural gas, chemicals
population 2 520 640
famous people William Faulkner, Elvis Presley, Eudora Welty
history De Soto was the first European to discover the Mississippi in 1540; the area was subsequently settled in turn by French, English, and Spanish until passing under American control in 1798; it became a state in 1817, and seceded in the Civil War in 1861□

Mississippi second longest river, 3780 km/2348 mi, both of N America and of a system (world's third largest after the Amazon and

Congo) which drains 31 US states; length 19 000 km/12 000 mi, of which 14 500 km/9000 mi is navigable. Chief tributaries are the ***Missouri*** 3969 km/2466 mi, longest river in N America; ***Ohio*** (formed by the union of the Allegheny and Monongahela at Pittsburgh), 1580 km/980 mi; and ***Illinois*** 439 km/273 mi. In spring warm air from the Gulf of Mexico collides with cold fronts from the north to create tornadoes along the Red River, a western tributary□

Missolonghi the modern town of Mesolóngion in W Greece, near the Gulf of Patras◊, where Byron◊ died□

Missouri border state of the USA; Show Me State

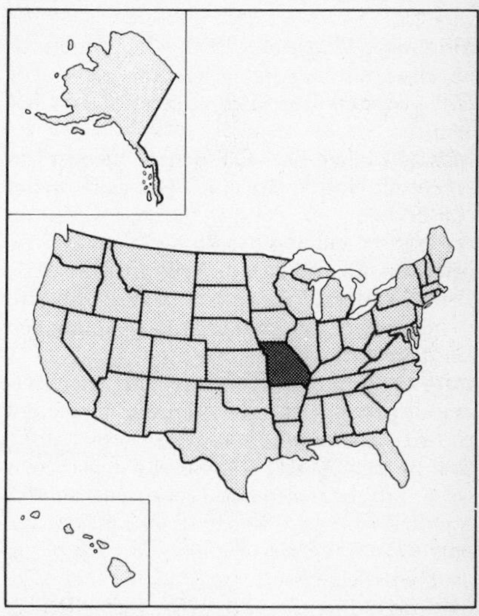

area 180 445 sq km/69 674 sq mi
capital Jefferson City
towns St Louis, Kansas City, Springfield, Independence
features Mississippi and Missouri rivers; Pony Express Museum at St Joseph; birthplace of

Jesse James; Mark Twain State Park; Harry S Truman Library at Independence; dioxin disaster town, Times◊ Beach
products meat and other processed food; aerospace, transport equipment; lead, clay, coal, etc.
population 4 906 480
famous people General Omar Bradley, George Washington Carver, T S Eliot, Joseph Pulitzer, Mark Twain
history explored by De Soto in 1541, it was acquired under the Louisiana Purchase◊, and became a state in 1821□

Missouri river see under Mississippi◊□

Mistinguett stage name of French revue artist Jeanne-Marie Bourgeois 1875–1956. She was famous for her legs, the song 'Mon homme', and her partnership with Maurice Chevalier□

mistletoe parasitic, European evergreen unisexual plant *Viscum album* which occurs on trees as a branched bush, with translucent white berries, and is used as a Christmas decoration. See druidism◊□

Mistral Frédéric 1830–1914. French poet, leader of the revival of Provençal literature; Nobel prize 1904□

Mistral Gabriela. Pseudonym of Chilean poet Lucila Godoy Alcayaga 1889–1957, famous for her *Sonnets of Death* 1915; Nobel prize 1945□

mistral cold, dry northerly wind. See under wind◊□

Mitchell Margaret 1900–49. American novelist, born in Atlanta, Georgia, setting of *Gone With the Wind* 1936, a story of the Civil War□

Mitchell Peter 1920– . British chemist; he received a Nobel prize in 1978 for work on the conservation of energy by plants during respiration and photosynthesis□

Mitchell R(eginald) J(oseph) 1895–1937. British aircraft designer, whose Spitfire fighter was a major factor in winning the Battle of Britain◊□

mite a minute creature, Arachnida◊, which is mainly parasitic on animals, including the red or rusty ***harvest-mite*** whose larvae pierce the skin of humans and animals and cause great irritation; ***red spider mite*** *Tetranychus telarius* a greenhouse pest which attacks plants; ***red mite*** *Dermanyssus gallinae* parasitic on cagebirds, etc.□

Mitford Mary Russell 1787–1855. British author of *Our Village* 1824–32, sketches of village life based on Three Mile Cross, near Reading, where she lived for many years□

Mitford sisters the six daughters of Lord Redesdale, including: ***Nancy*** 1904–73, author of the semi-autobiographical *The Pursuit of Love* 1945 and *Love in a Cold Climate* 1949, and editor and part author of *Noblesse Oblige* 1956 elucidating 'U' (upper-class) and 'Non-U' behaviour; ***Jessica*** 1917– , author of the autobiographical *Hons and Rebels* 1960 and *The American Way of Death* 1963; and ***Unity*** 1914–48, who became a fan of Hitler, and ***Diana*** who married Oswald Mosley◊□

Mithraism the ancient Persian worship of Mithras◊ popular among Roman soldiery from 68BC, and a rival to Christianity until its decline from c250. A bath in the blood of a sacrificed bull, commemorating the killing by Mithras of the sacred bull from which all life was said to spring, was part of the initiation ceremony. Mithras was worshipped in Britain, e.g. the temple remains excavated in the City of London in 1954□

Mithras in Persian mythology, the god of light, See Mithraism◊□

Mithridates VI the Great 132–63BC. King of Pontus (*NE* Asia Minor, on the Black Sea) from 120BC. He massacred 80 000 Romans in over-running the rest of Asia Minor, and went on to invade Greece. He was successively defeated by Sulla◊ in the First Mithridatic War 88–84; by Lucullus◊ in the Second 83–81; and by Pompey◊ in the Third 74–64. He committed suicide rather than surrender to captivity□

mitochondrion rodlike or spherical body within most cells, and containing enzymes by which the cells break up organic compounds to release energy. They were once possibly free-living microbes, and are valuable in genetic study because each still contains its own small loop of DNA◊ which, since sperm contribute no mitochondria in fertilizing an egg, are an inheritance from the female side only, and are always identical with that of the mother. Study of them is useful in elucidating the story both of human descent and that of animals□

mitosis type of asexual reproduction◊ in which the genetic information is reproduced exactly in the new cells, rather than by being split and recombined, as in meiosis◊□

Mitterrand François 1916– . French socialist statesman, who organized a joint left-wing front under de Gaulle and Giscard d'Estaing, defeating the latter in the presidential election of 1981. In office his policies were modified (the Communists left the government), and in 1985 his introduction of proportional representation was allegedly to weaken the growing opposition from left and right□

Mizoram former district of Assam◊, a Union Territory of India 1972, and state from 1986; population 481 775; capital Aizawl□

Mmbatho capital of Bophuthatswana◊. Its international airport completed in 1984, and TV service in English compete with those of S Africa□

moa flightless bird. See under running◊ birds□

Moab ancient country on the plateau of Jordan, East of the Dead Sea. Its Semitic people were at loggerheads with Israel, and in the time of David were under its rule. The ***Moabite Stone*** records a successful rising by their king, Mesha, against Israel c830BC□

Mobile industrial port (oil, aluminium, textiles, chemicals) in Alabama, USA; population 443 550. Founded by the French in 1702, it was British 1763–80, then Spanish until 1813□

Mobutu Sese-Seko-Kuku-Ngbeandu-Wa-Za-Banga (formerly Joseph-Désiré) 1930–. Zaïrean general who assumed the presidency by coup in 1965, and created a unitary state under his centralized government. He replaced secret voting in elections in 1976 by a system of acclamation at mass rallies□

Mobutu Lake. Formerly Lake Albert, it was renamed in 1973 by President Mobutu after himself; area 4275 sq km/1650 sq mi□

Moçambique the Portuguese name for Mozambique◊□

mocking bird American bird *Mimus polyglottus*, related to the thrushes which has remarkable powers of mimicry; it is brownish grey, with white markings on the black wings and tail□

mock orange deciduous shrub of genus *Philadelphus*, family Philadelphaceae, especially *P coronarius* which has white, strongly scented flowers, resembling those of the orange; it is sometimes referred to as syringa◊□

Modena industrial city (Ferrari and Maserati cars, textiles) in N Italy; population 180 300□

moderator a minister in the Church of Scotland◊□

moderator a substance used for slowing down the action of neutrons in a atomic reactor. See under nuclear◊ energy□

Modernism movement within Christianity□

Modigliani Amedeo 1884–1920. Italian painter of Jewish extraction, whose sculptures were influenced by Negro masks, and whose elongated portraits have a mournful attraction. Penniless, a prey to drink and drugs, he died of tuberculosis, and his pregnant mistress committed suicide the next morning□

modulation in radio◊, the intermittent change of frequency, amplitude, etc., of a carrier wave, in accordance with the speaking voice, music, or other signal transmitted□

module in construction, a part which governs the form of the rest, e.g. Japanese room sizes are traditionally governed by multiples of standard tatami floor mats; modern prefabricated buildings are mass-produced in a similar way; and in space the components of a spacecraft are designed in coordination, e.g. for the moon landings the craft comprised a command module (for working, eating, sleeping), service module (electricity generators, oxygen supplies, manoeuvring rocket), and lunar module (to land and return the astronauts)□

Mogadishu capital and port of Somalia; population 377 000□

Mogilev industrial city (engineering, chemicals, food processing) in Belorussia, USSR; population 325 000□

Moguls N Indian dynasty (named from 'Mongols', since they were descendants of Tamerlane◊) who ruled till the last Mogul emperor was dethroned and imprisoned by the British in 1857; they included Akbar◊ and Shah-Jehan◊□

Mohács river port and town on the Danube, Hungary, site of two battles: 1526, defeat of the Hungarians by Suleiman◊ the Magnificent; and 1687, victory of the Hungarians over the Turks□

mohair goat's hair. See under angora◊□

Mohammed or ***Muhammad, Mahomet, Mahound*** (Arabic 'praised') c570–632. Founder of Islam◊, born in Mecca◊. Originally a shepherd and caravan conductor, he found leisure for meditation by his marriage with a wealthy widow in 595, and received his first revelation in 610. After some years of secret teaching, he openly declared himself the prophet of God c616, the Koran (dictated by him to amanuenses while he remained in a trance) being the basis of his teaching. Persecuted as the number of his followers increased, he fled to the town now known as Medina◊ in 622 (the *Hegira* 'flight', which marks the beginning of the Islamic era). After the battle of Badr in 623, he was continuously victorious, entering Mecca as the recognized prophet of Arabia in 630. The succession was troubled. See Ayesha◊□

Mohammed six sultans of Turkey, including: ***Mohammed II*** 1430–81, who captured Constantinople in 1453 and conquered Greece; and ***Mohammed VI*** 1861–1926, the last sultan, deposed in 1922, and exiled□

Mohammedanism see Islam◊□

Mohawk N American Indian. See Iroquois◊□

Mohenjo Daro an excavated city in Pakistan. See Indus◊ Valley civilization□

Mohican N American Indian. See under Algonquin◊□

Mohorovičić Andrija 1857–1936. Yugoslav discoverer in 1909 of the ***Mohorovičić*** (***Moho***) ***Discontinuity*** which marks the transition from the earth's outer crust to the first inner layer or 'mantle': the crust varies in thickness, from 70 km/43 mi to 5 km/3 mi, being thinnest beneath the oceans□

Mohs Friedrich 1773–1839. German mineralogist, who devised in 1920 the scale (known by his name) of minerals classified in order of hardness from 1 (talc) to 15 (diamond)□

Moi Daniel Arap 1924– . Kenyan statesman, president (in succession to Kenyatta) from 1978□

Mojave Desert see California◊□

Moji one of the five cities comprising the city of Kitakyushu◊□

molasses syrup obtained from sugar◊ during refining□

Moldavia constituent republic of the Soviet Union from 1940
area 33 700 sq km/13 100 sq mi
capital Kishinev
features Black◊ Earth region
products wine, tobacco, canned goods
population 4 000 000, 65% Moldavians, a branch of the Romanian people, Ukrainian 14%, Russian 12%
language Moldavian, allied to Romanian
religion Russian Orthodox
recent history formed from part of the former Moldavian Republic of the USSR (within the Ukraine) and areas of Bessarabia ceded by Romania in 1940□

mole a small burrowing mammal. See Insectivora◊□

mole a mechanical device for boring horizontal holes underground without the need for digging trenches, etc. It is used for laying pipes and cables□

mole base unit of the SI system, symbol mol, indicating amount of substance. The mole is the amount of substance of a system which contains as many elementary entities as there are atoms in 0.012 kg of carbon 12. The entities must be specified (whether atoms, molecules, ions, electrons, etc.)□

molecule smallest portion of any substance which can exist free, yet still exhibit all the chemical properties of that substance. Molecules may consist of one atom, e.g. helium, or many thousands, e.g. complex organic substances, and their composition is governed by the forces which hold these together. See atom◊□

Molière pseudonym of French satiric dramatist Jean-Baptiste Poquelin 1622–73. Born in Paris, he became an actor, but established his reputation as a playwright with *Les Précieuses ridicules* 1659: his masterpieces are *Tartuffe* 1664, *Le Misanthrope* 1666, *Le Médecin malgré lui* 1666, *Le Bourgeois gentilhomme* 1670, and *Le Malade imaginaire* 1673□

Molinos Miguel de 1640–97. Spanish Catholic priest, whose mystic doctrine of ***quietism*** (disinterested love and attainment of spiritual repose as a means of approaching most closely to God), expressed in his *Guida spirituale* 1675 aroused Jesuit hostility. In 1687 he was sentenced to life imprisonment□

mollusc

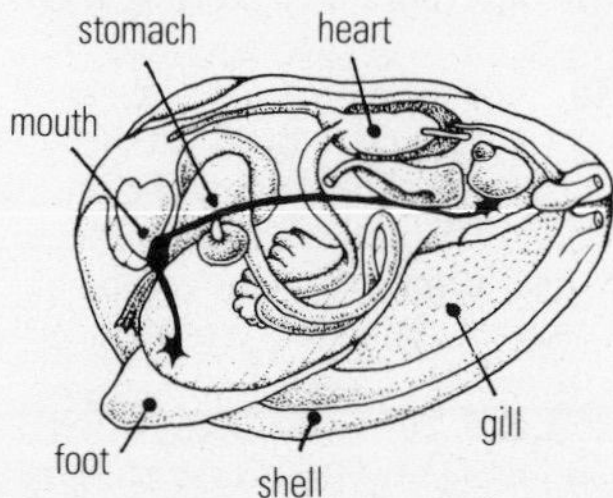

mollusc invertebrate of phylum Mollusca, which includes marine, freshwater, and land species, all with soft, limbless bodies, and having no internal skeleton, but usually a hard shell. Most breathe via a large gill but some land species have lungs. The foot is soft, flat, and broad and is used for ploughing for food and creeping along the sea bed or land. Some species are carnivorous, other vegetarian. Reproduction is by eggs, usually with the cooperation of both sexes, but some species (such as snails) are hermaphrodite. See bivalve◊, cephalopod◊, gastropod◊□

Molnár Ferenc 1878–1952. Hungarian dramatist, e.g. the circus comedy *Liliom* 1909, adapted as the musical *Carousel*□

Moloch in the Old Testament, the god associated with the Ammonites, whose worship involved the sacrifice of live children in fire□

Molokai an island in central Hawaii◊□

Molotov Vyacheslav Mikhailovich. Assumed name of V M Skryabin 1890– . Soviet Foreign Minister 1939–49, when he negotiated the nonaggression pact with Hitler, and 1953–6. In 1957 he was expelled from the government for 'Stalinist activities'□

Molotov the former name for the port of Perm◊□

molotov cocktail home-made resistance weapon of World War II (bottle of petrol fired by a wick), named after Molotov◊□

Moltke Helmuth Carl Bernhard, Count von Moltke 1800–91. Prussian field marshal. He was Chief of General Staff 1857–88, for the victorious wars with Denmark 1863–4, Austria 1866, and France 1870–1□

Moltke Helmuth Johannes Ludwig von 1848–1916. German general (nephew of Count von Moltke), chief of the German general staff 1906–14. His use of General Schlieffen's Plan for a rapid victory on two fronts failed and he was superseded□

Moluccas a group of islands in the Malay Archipelago. See Maluku◊□

molybdenum element
symbol Mo
atomic number 42
physical description silvery-white metal
features burns with a green-coloured flame
uses in steel alloys to increase hardness at high temperatures, hence in drill bits□

Mombasa industrial port (oil refining, cement) in Kenya (serving also Uganda and Tanzania) extending from Mombasa island to the mainland, most trade being through the modern harbour of Kilindini; population 341 000□

Mona Latin name for Anglesey◊□

Monaco Principality of

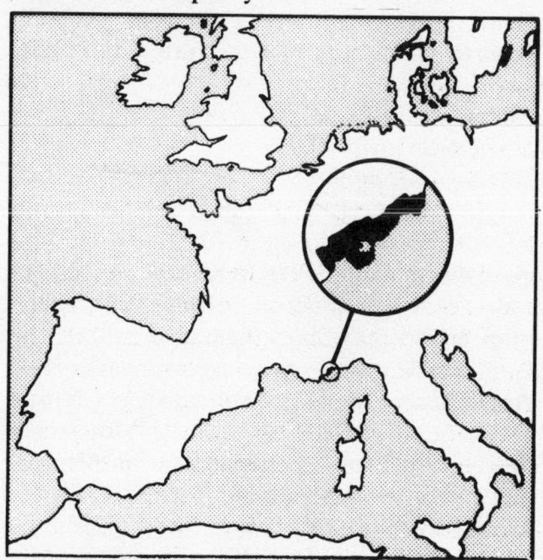

area 1.5 sq km/O.575 sq mi
capital Monaco-Ville (population 1500)
town Monte Carlo, noted for its film festival, motor races, and casino
features surrounded to landward by French territory, it is being expanded by filling in the sea; aquarium and oceanographic centre
exports some light industry, but economy depends on tourism and gambling
currency French franc
population 28 000
language French
religion Roman Catholicism
famous people Grace Kelly
government a hereditary monarchy (Prince Rainier◊ III), with elected National and Communal Councils
recent history from 1297 ruled by the house of Grimaldi, it came under French protection in 1861□

Monadnock a mountain in New◊ Hampshire□

Monaghan county (county town Monaghan) of the Republic of Ireland, province of Ulster◊□

monasticism devotion to the religious life under vows of poverty, chastity, and obedience, known to Judaism (e.g. Essenes◊), Buddhism, etc., before Christianity: see St Anthony◊ and St Pachomius◊. Possibly communities for women (nuns, from Latin *nonna* 'elderly woman') preceded those for men, and most male orders have their feminine counterpart. Full adaptation to conditions in W Europe was made by St Benedict◊ in the 6th century, his 'rule' being generally adopted, and from 910 (with the foundation of Cluny◊) a system of subordination to a 'mother house' began. The word 'minster' originally meant monastery (see such place names as Westminster), and later the word was applied to churches attached to a monastery, e.g. York minster. See also 11th-century Carthusians◊, Augustinian◊ canons; 12th-century Knights Hospitallers of St John◊, Knights Templars◊; 13th-century mendicant orders of friars, Franciscans◊, Dominicans◊, Carmelites◊, Augustinians◊. The chief post-Reformation order is that of the Society of Jesus (Jesuits◊); and the 20th-century trend in many orders is to modern dress, and involvement as 'workers' outside the monastery, despite disapproval by Pope John◊ Paul II□

Monastir Turkish name for the town of Bitolj◊□

monazite rare mineral, yellow to red, valued as a source of cerium◊ and thorium◊□

Mönchengladbach industrial town (textiles, paper) in N Rhine-Westphalia, W Germany; population 258 600. It is the NATO headquarters for northern Europe□

Mond Ludwig 1839–1909. German-born industrial chemist, naturalized British in 1867, whose firm pioneered the British chemical industry. His son ***Alfred*** 1st Baron Melchett 1868–1930, was a founder of Imperial Chemical Industries (ICI)□

Mondale Walter Frederick 1928– . American Democratic politician, Carter's Vice-President 1977–81. He was defeated by Reagan in the presidential election of 1984□

Mondrian Piet 1872–1944. Dutch abstract painter, a founder in 1917 (with ***Theo van Doesburg*** 1883–1931) of the periodical ***de Stijl*** (*The Style*). It advocated ***Neoplasticism*** a combination of abstract geometrical design and simplified colour in painting, as well as in architecture and other forms of design, and influenced the Bauhaus◊□

Monet Claude 1840–1926. French Impressionist◊ painter, noted for his atmospheric effects, and for depicting the same subject at different times of the day, e.g. his series of haystacks. In 1980 the gardens at Giverny, which he painted, were restored□

monetarism economic policy, advocated by Milton Friedman◊, which requires control of a country's money supply to keep it in step with the country's ability to produce goods, so curbing inflation. This is to be achieved by cutting government spending, both to eliminate waste and assist in the long-term aim of returning as much of the economy as possible to the private sector in the interests of efficiency. Additionally, credit is restricted by high interest rates, and industry is not cushioned against internal market forces or overseas competition (so preventing 'over-manning', 'restrictive' union practices, 'excessive' wage demands, etc.). Unemployment results, but, it is argued, less than would eventually occur if Keynesian methods were adopted. The theory was ineffectively applied by Edward Heath in the UK, and is more completely applied by Margaret Thatcher◊□

money any common medium of exchange, but today coinage (first used in the West in Lydia◊, but invented by the Chinese in the 2nd millennium BC), paper money (used in China c800AD to avoid imperial messengers being weighed down by coin when pursued by bandits), and modern developments such as the cheque and credit card. In estimating the money supply in a country, it is divided into categories: M0 (the monetary base), M1 (coins, notes, current bank accounts of companies and individuals), M2 (a rather vague concept no longer used), M3 (M1 plus term deposits, mainly deposit accounts at banks). See bank◊□

Mongolia vast plateau region of E central Asia, which includes the Gobi Desert. See Mongolian People's Republic◊ and Inner Mongolia◊; and for the medieval Mongol Empire, see Genghis Khan◊ and Kublai Khan◊□

Mongolia Inner. Autonomous region (Chinese *Nei Menggu*) of NE China from 1947
area 450 000 sq km/173 700 sq mi
capital Hohhot
features strategic frontier area with USSR ; famous for Mongol herdsmen, now becoming settled farmers
products cereals under irrigation; coal; reserves of rare earth oxides, europium, yttrium at Bayan Obo
population 18 510 000□

Mongolian People's Republic

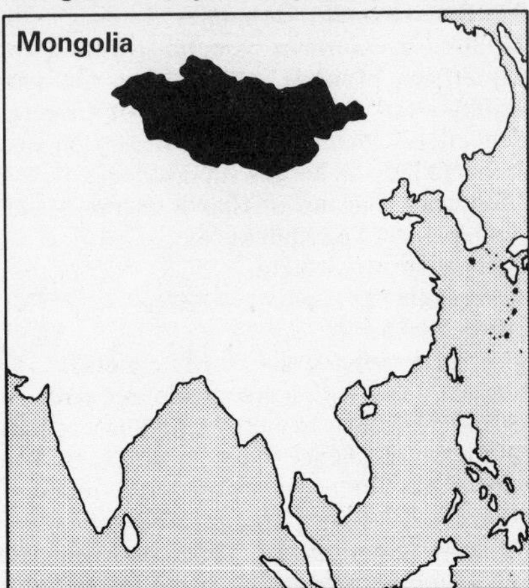

area 1 560 000 sq km/600 000 sq mi
capital Ulan Bator
towns Darkhan, Choybalsan
features Altai Mountains, part of Gobi Desert
exports meat and butter, varied minerals, furs
currency tugrik
population 1 640 000
language Mongol
religion formerly Tibetan Buddhist Lamaism; suppressed in the 1930s
government Great People Khural elected for four years by universal suffrage (the chairman of the presidium is head of state); the Communist party is the only political party.
recent history almost continuously a Chinese province from the 17th century, Mongolia's declaration of independence as the Mongolian People's Republic (formerly Outer Mongolia) in 1924 was not recognized by China until 1946. In 1966 Mongolia made a mutual assistance pact with the USSR, under whose protection it had been an autonomous state 1912–19, and many Soviet troops are permanently stationed there. In 1983 a number of resident Chinese were expelled□

mongolism see Down◊'s syndrome□

Mongoloid see under race◊□

mongoose small predatory mammal. See civet◊□

monism the doctrine that reality consists of only one basic substance or element, such as mind or matter. Compare dualism◊□

monitor a type of lizard◊□

monitor slow, shallow draught vessel designed for coastal bombardment, named from the first of its type, the Federal *Monitor* of the American Civil War. Monitors were used in World War I, e.g. off the Belgian coast, and in World War II, e.g. the Normandy invasion□

Moniz Antonio Egas 1874–1955. Portuguese neurologist, pioneer of prefrontal leucotomy (surgical separation of white fibres in the prefrontal lobe of the brain) to treat schizophrenia and paranoia, but the treatment remains controversial. Nobel prize 1949□

Monk or ***Monck*** George, 1st Duke of Albemarle 1608–69. English soldier, originally a Royalist, who served in Cromwell's Scottish campaign in 1650; at sea against the Dutch 1652–3, and under the Commonwealth (as Commander-in-Chief in Scotland) led his army into England to restore Charles II□

Monk Thelonious 1918–82. American jazz pianist. Working in Harlem during the Depression, he developed the breakaway from jazz known as bebop or bop, e.g. 'Round About Midnight', 'Blue Monk', 'Hackensack'□

monkey term for the smaller, mainly tree-dwelling primates, excluding man◊ and the anthropoid apes◊

Old World monkeys, family Cercopithecidae, of tropical Africa and Asia are distinguished by their close-set nostrils and differentiated thumbs, some also having cheek pouches and behinds with bare patches (callosities) of hardened skin. They include:

baboon of which the various species have a lengthened dog-like muzzle, cheek pouches, strikingly powerful teeth, long-haired shoulder manes, and coloured callosities on their behinds. The ***hamadryad*** or ***sacred baboon*** *Papio hamadryas* was venerated by the Egyptians, and is courageous and intelligent, living in well-organized troops. Fiercest of the baboons is the W African ***mandrill*** *Mandrillus sphinx* with red and blue ridged swellings on the muzzle and a red behind

colobus slender, long-tailed monkeys of Central and W Africa

langur slender, very long-tailed Asiatic monkeys with chin tufts

macaque including the ***Gibraltar 'ape'*** *Macaca sylvana* yellowish-brown and tail-less, of N Africa, whence it was introduced to Gibraltar (legend has it that Britain will lose the colony if the animals die out); ***rhesus*** *Macaca mulatta* of S Asia, with brown-grey hair, pinkish face, and red buttocks (widely used in medical research: see Rhesus factor◊); and Japanese ***snow monkey*** *Macaca fuscata* a hardy breed with close family ties

vervet a S African variety of grass monkey *Cercopithecus aethiops* whose varied alarm calls resemble the possible beginnings of human communication

New World monkeys of Central and S America are characterized by wide-set nostrils, and often by highly sensitive prehensile tails. They comprise:

family Cebidae which includes the larger species of the area:

saki genera *Pithecia* and *Chiropotes* thick-coated monkeys with long bushy tails

titi long-tailed monkeys *Callicebus* with richly-coloured fur

howler genus *Alouatta* which have a specially modified windpipe and a voice which carries for several miles in a dawn chorus

capuchin genus *Cebus* small monkeys with a hair 'cowl' resembling that of capuchin friars

squirrel genus *Saimiri* small, brightly coloured monkeys

spider genus *Ateles* with elongated limbs and long prehensile tail; they are easily tamed

woolly genus *Lagothrix* with a thick woolly coat beneath the longer top hairs, a long, prehensile, bare-tipped tail, and a very 'human' face

the family Callithricidae which includes the very small species, notably the marmosets and tamarins. The ***pygmy marmoset*** *Cebuella pygmaea* is the smallest of the primates (18 cm/7 in long, excluding the tail), the rarest and most spectacular of the small species; the ***golden lion tamarin***, is about the size of a guinea-pig, with a golden mane□

monkey puzzle a S American coniferous tree. See araucaria◊□

Monmouth James Scott, Duke of Monmouth 1649–85. Natural son of Charles II by Lucy Walter, he was created a peer in 1663. The Whig opposition failed to secure his succession to the throne (rather than the Catholic James◊ II) by an Exclusion Bill, and in 1684 he fled to Holland. After James's accession in 1685, he landed at Lyme Regis to claim the crown; his forces were crushed at Sedgemoor in Somerset, and Monmouth was captured and beheaded on Tower Hill. See Judge Jeffreys◊□

Monmouth market town in Gwent, Wales; population 6600. Henry◊ V was born in the now ruined castle□

Monnet Jean 1888–1979. French economist, who in 1950 produced the 'Schuman Plan' for coordinated European coal and steel production in the European Coal and Steel Community (ECSC) which developed into the Common Market (EEC)□

monocotyledon a group of flowering plants. See under plant◊ classification□

Monod Jacques 1910–76. French biochemist, who shared a Nobel prize in 1965 for the discovery of RNA. His *Chance and Necessity* 1971 asserted that 'blind chance' governed evolution□

monogamy the state or practice of having only one husband or wife over a period of time. See under marriage◊□

monophysites Christian heretics of the 5–7th centuries who maintained that Christ had 'one nature', as opposed to the Council of Chalcedon decree that he was both human and divine□

monopoly originally a royal grant of the sole right to manufacture or sell a certain article. In modern commerce the domination of a particular industry by a cartel or trust (a group of firms) which is large enough to restrict competition against itself and keep prices high. In the UK the Fair Trading Act of 1973 defines a monopoly supplier as one having 'a quarter of the market', and the Monopolies and Mergers Commission controls any attempt to reach this position; in the USA 'antitrust laws' are similarly used. In Communist countries the state itself has the overall monopoly; in capitalist ones some services such as transport or electricity supply may be state monopolies, but in the UK the Competition Act of 1980 covers both private monopolies and possible abuses in the public sector. A ***monopsony*** is a situation in which there is only one buyer, e.g. most governments are the only legal purchasers of military equipment inside their countries□

monosodium glutamate sodium salt of glutamic acid (an amino acid found in proteins which has an important role in the metabolism of plants and animals). It is used in many packaged foods because it enhances the 'flavour' of essentially flavourless concoctions, and its use is controversial□

monotheism the belief or doctrine that there is only one God□

Monotremata ('single-opening', i.e. having one opening common to both organs of generation and elimination) egg-laying mammals; only two survive:

platypus of Australia and Tasmania, a semi-aquatic mammal *Ornithorhyncus anatinus* 45 cm/1.5 ft long. It has a ducklike beak, lays leathery eggs, and builds a nest, but has a furry body, digging claws, and suckles its young, so that early specimen skins were thought to be a hoax. Males have a poison-filled ankle 'spur'.

spiny anteater or ***echidna*** of Australia and New Guinea. The Australian species *Tachyglossus aculeatus* is c45 cm/1.5 ft long. Toothless, it has a long snout, and very long sticky tongue to capture insects, and carries its egg and then its young (until the spines make the mother uncomfortable) in a pouch□

Monroe James 1758–1831. 5th president of the USA 1817–25. In 1803 he negotiated the Louisiana Purchase, was Secretary of State 1811–17, and in his 2nd presidential term laid down the ***Monroe doctrine*** of 1823 (when European intervention against rebel Spanish colonies in S America was proposed) that the American continents 'are henceforth not to be considered as subjects for colonization by any European powers'□

Monroe Marilyn. Acting name of American actress Norma Jean Mortenson 1926–62. Born illegitimate in Los Angeles, she had a wretched childhood, and became a model before making such adroit comedies as *The Seven Year Itch* 1955, *Bus Stop* 1956, and *Some Like It Hot* 1959. Her 2nd husband was baseball star Joe diMaggio, and her 3rd Arthur Miller◊. She died of a barbiturate drug overdose□

Monrovia capital and port of Liberia, founded in 1821 and named after President Monroe◊; population 306 460□

Mons coal-mining town, (Flemish *Bergen*) capital of the province of Hainaut, Belgium; population 91 900. The military headquarters of NATO is at nearby Chièvres-Casteau□

Mons Battle of, 23 Aug 1914. The first important engagement fought by the British Expeditionary Forces in World War I, it was followed by a retreat to the Marne◊, whence a counter-offensive was launched□

Monsarrat Nicholas 1910–79. British novelist, who served with the navy in the Battle of the Atlantic◊, subject of *The Cruel Sea* 1951□

monsoon a type of wind◊□

Monstera a type of plant. See under arum◊□

Montagu Edward Douglas-Scott-Montagu, 3rd Baron Montagu of Beaulieu 1926– . British car enthusiast, founder of the Montagu Motor Museum at Beaulieu, Hampshire, and chairman of English Heritage (formerly Historic Buildings and Monuments Commission) from 1983. See garden◊□

Montagu Lady Mary Wortley 1689–1762. British letter-writer and society poet, wife of the ambassador to Constantinople. She advocated inoculation against smallpox, and had a famous quarrel with Alexander Pope◊□

Montaigne Michel Eyquem de 1533–92. French creator of the essay form. A lawyer, he became mayor of Bordeaux 1581–5, publishing his essays from 1580. They deal with all aspects of life from an urbanely sceptical viewpoint, and via the translation of John Florio in 1603 influenced Shakespeare and other English writers□

Montale Eugenio 1896–1981. Italian poet, a stoic in his exploration of the themes of isolation, uncertainty, and exile, in contemporary life, e.g. *The Storm* 1956; Nobel prize 1975◻

Montana mountain state of the USA on the Canadian border; Treasure State

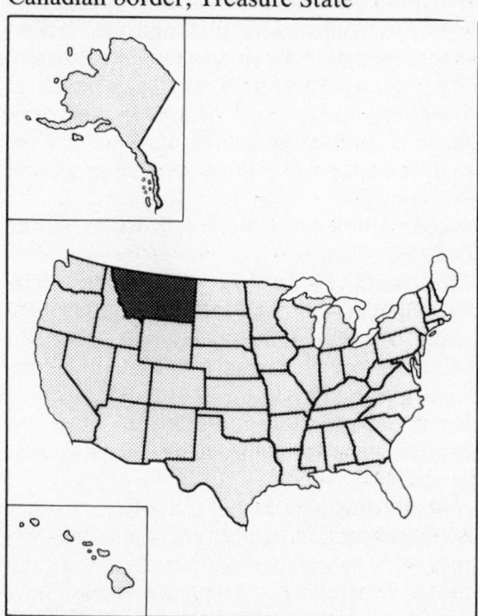

area 381 085 sqkm/147 138 sq mi
capital Helena
town Billings
features Missouri and Yellowstone rivers; Glacier National Park; Custer◊ Battlefield; Museum of the Plains Indian; seven Indian reservations, including Blackfeet, Cree, Crow, Sioux
products wheat under irrigation; cattle, wool; copper, oil, and natural gas
population 786 690
famous people Gary Cooper.
history first settled in 1809, it became a state in 1889◻

Montanism movement for a return to the simplicity of the early Christian church, originating in Phrygia c156 with the teachings of Montanus. See Tertullian◊◻

Montaubon industrial town (porcelain, textiles) in SW France; population 50 000. The painter Ingres was born here◻

Mont aux Sources see Drakensberg◊◻

Mont Blanc a mountain in the Alps◊◻

montbretia S African genus of plants, family Iridaceae, with fine yellow flowers; also the related popular garden hybrid *Crocosmia crocosmiflora* with orange flowers◻

Montcalm Louis-Joseph de Montcalm-Grozon, Marquis de Montcalm 1712–59. French general, commander in Canada from 1756, whose victories over the British ended in his defeat (by Wolfe) and death at Quebec◻

Monte Bello Islands group of uninhabited islands in the S Pacific, off Western Australia◻

Monte Carlo a town and resort in Monaco◊◻

Monte Cristo an Italian islet in the Tyrrhenian Sea. See under Elba◊◻

Montego Bay port and resort in Jamaica; population 43 000◻

Montémar town in SE France, famous for its nougat; population 30 000◻

Montenegro constituent republic of Yugoslavia
area 13 812 sq km/4226 sq mi
capital Titograd
town Cetinje
features smallest of the republics; very mountainous; Skadarsko Jezero (Lake Scutari) shared with Albania.
population 584 000 including 38 000 Albanians
language Serbian variant of Serbo-Croat
religion Serbian Orthodox
history once part of Serbia◊, it became independent in the 14th century, and never submitted to Turkish rule, being recognized as a sovereign principality under the Treaty of Berlin of 1878. Overrun by Austria in World War I, it voted in 1918 to become part of the future Yugoslavia◻

Monterey fishing port on Monterey Bay in California, USA; population 30 000. Once the state capital, it is the setting for Steinbeck◊'s *Cannery Row* 1945 and *Tortilla Flat* 1935 dealing with migrant fruit workers◻

Monterrey industrial city (iron and steel, food processing) in NE Mexico; population 2 020 000. There is a fine 18th-century cathedral, a university, and institute of technology◻

Montespan Françoise-Athénais de Rochechouart, Marquise de Montespan 1641–1707. Mistress of Louis XIV from 1667, by whom she had seven children, for whom she was unwise enough to engage the future Mme de Maintenon◊ as governess. She retired to a convent in 1691◻

Montesquieu Charles Louis de Secondat, Baron de la Brède et de Montesquieu 1689–1755. French historian. His great work *L'Esprit des lois* 1748, a 31-volume philosophical disquisition on politics and sociology, as well as legal matters, was seminal in that his approval of the British constitution influenced the initial stages of the French Revolution◻

Montessori Maria 1870–1952. Italian worker with mentally deficient children, who developed the ***Montessori method*** an educational system (less formal than then in vogue) for normal children◻

Monteux Pierre 1875–1964. French conductor, who worked with Diaghilev's ballet (first performance of Stravinsky's *The Rite of Spring* etc.), and later worked in USA□

Monteverdi Claudio 1567–1643. Italian violinist and composer, born in Cremona. He entered the service of the Duke of Mantua c1591–1612, in whose private theatre the first opera *Orfeo* 1607 was produced, and was director of music at St Mark's, Venice, from 1613. His later work included further operas, e.g. *L'Incoronazione di Poppea* 1642, many madrigals, and much church music, all noted for their innovations in harmonics, and detailed orchestration□

Montevideo capital and chief port (grain, meat products, hides) of Uruguay, on the river Plate; population 1 346 000. It is also a holiday resort□

Montez Lola. Stage-name of Irish actress Maria Gilbert 1818–61, who was the mistress of Ludwig I of Bavaria 1847–8. Jesuit opposition led to his deposition and her banishment□

Montezuma II 1466–1520. The last Aztec emperor 1502–19, when Cortés invaded Mexico and imprisoned him. He was murdered, either by the Spaniards, or by his own subjects during the Aztec attack on Cortés' force as it tried to leave Tenochtitlán□

Montfort Simon de, Earl of Leicester c1200–65. English statesman, son of the Simon de Montfort who led a crusade against the Albigensians◊. He arrived in England in 1229, and married Henry III's sister, but from 1258 led the baronial opposition to Henry III's misrule. See Barons'◊ Wars. In 1265, as head of government, he summoned the first parliament in which the towns were represented, but was killed at the Battle of Evesham□

Montgolfier Joseph Michel 1740–1810 and ***Étienne Jacques*** 1745–99. French balloonists, who made the first successful human flight on 21 Nov 1783□

Montgomery industrial city (fertilizers, machinery, cotton textiles, cigars) capital of Alabama, USA; population 272 700. It was the capital of the Confederate Government Feb–May 1861□

Montgomery market town in Powys, Wales; population 43 600□

Montgomery Bernard Law, 1st Viscount Montgomery of Alamein 1887–1976. British field marshal. An Ulsterman, he was commander of the 3rd Division in the evacuation of Dunkirk; took command of the 8th Army in Aug 1942 and in the 2nd Battle of Alamein◊ in Oct reinforced the turn in the tide of war. He was prominent in the invasion of Italy in 1944, and commanded the Allied armies during the opening phase of the invasion of France in Jun 1944, which he had planned, and from Aug commanded the British and Imperial troops which liberated the Netherlands, overran N Germany and entered Denmark. He received the German surrender at Lüneberg Heath◊ on 3 May 1945, and commanded the British occupation force in Germany till 1946. His failures were Dieppe◊ and Arnhem◊□

month one of the twelve divisions of the calendar◊ year□

Montherlant Henry de Millon 1896–1972. French novelist (*Aux Fontaines du désir* 1927 and *Le Chaos et la nuit* 1963), and playwright (*Le Mâitre de Santiago* 1947), with an obsession with the physical□

Montmartre a district of Paris◊□

Montoneros left-wing guerrillas in Argentina◊□

Montparnasse a district of Paris◊□

Montpellier industrial city (engineering, textiles, food processing, and a trade in wine and brandy), capital of Languedoc-Roussillon◊, France; population 195 600□

Montreal capital, inland port, industrial city (aircraft, chemicals, oil and petrochemicals, flour, sugar, brewing, meat packing) and commercial centre of Quebec, Canada, on Montreal island at the junction of the Ottawa and St Lawrence

population 2 828 350

features Mont Réal (Mount Royal, 230 M/ 753 ft) overlooks the city; there is a carefully preserved 'old quarter', and the Place Ville Marie is the site of a four-level underground city (shopping arcades, underground parking, and direct rail access), with a skyscraper above; a Man-made island in the St Lawrence (site of the international exhibition of 1967) now houses the world's largest permanent exhibition); three universities, Montreal (Catholic) and McGill and Sir George Williams (Protestant); headquarters of the ICAO (International Civil Aviation Organization); except for Paris, the world's largest French-speaking city

history Jacques Cartier◊ reached the site in 1535, Champlain◊ established a trading post in 1611, and the original Ville Mlrie (later renamed Montreal) was founded in 1642. It was the last town surrendered to the English in 1760. Nevertheless, when troops of the rebel Continental Congress occupied the city 1775–6, the citizens refused to be persuaded (even by a visit from Benjamin Franklin◊) to join the future USA in its revolt against the British□

Montreux winter resort in W Switzerland on Lake Geneva, in which is the island rock fortress of Chillon, where 16th-century patriot François Bonward (commemorated by the poet Byron) was imprisoned 1530–6; population 20 500. At the annual television festival (first held in 1961), the premier award is the ***Golden Rose of Montreux***□

Montreux Convention of, 1936. It allowed Turkey to remilitarize the Dardenelles□

Montrose James Graham, 1st Marquess of Montrose 1612–50. Scottish soldier, son of the Earl of Montrose. Originally a supporter of the Covenanters against Charles I, he wearied of their cause. Created a Marquess and Lietenant-General in Scotland by the king in 1641, he achieved a series of brilliant victories against the Covenanters◊ (in which he was supported by the Highlanders), but was finally defeated at Philiphaugh in 1645 and escaped to Norway. Returning in 1650 to raise a revolt, he survived shipwreck only to have his weakened forces defeated, and (having been betrayed to the Covenanters), was hanged in Edinburgh□

Mont St Michel islet in NW France converted to a peninsula by an artificial causeway. It is famed for its Benedictine monastery, founded in 708□

Montserrat British crown colony
area 101 sq km/39.5 sq mi
capital Plymouth
features hot springs; a tourist resort
exports cotton, coconuts, fruit, and vegetables
currency E Caribbean dollar
population 12 100
government governor and executive and legislative councils (chief minister John Osborne)
recent history first European discovery by Columbus in 1493, it became British in 1783. There is no pressure for complete independence□

Montserrat mountain in NE Spain, 1240 m/4070 ft. It is noted for its Benedictine monastery with a famous image of the Virgin□

Monument The. A tower commemorating the Fire of London◊□

Monza town in N Italy, once the capital of the Lombards◊; population 123 145. The 'Iron Crown of Lombardy' is preserved in the 13th-century cathedral. Umberto I was assassinated here, and there is a motor-racing circuit□

Moon Sun Myung 1920– . Korean industrialist, founder of the Unification Church in 1954 (mingling Christianity and Buddhism: claimed membership, 3 000 000). His followers (Moonies) live a communal life, giving all possessions to the church, and are allegedly subjected to 'brainwashing'. He was convicted of tax fraud in the USA in 1982□

Moon William 1818–94. British inventor of the Moon alphabet for the blind in 1847, using only nine symbols in different orientations; from 1983 written with a miniature 'typewriter'□

moon any satellite of a planet, but see especially earth◊□

Moonies a religious sect. See Sun Myung Moon◊□

moonstone a variety of gem. See under feldspars◊□

Moor person of mixed Arab and Berber descent from N Africa (named from the Roman province of Mauretania), especially modern Algeria and Morocco. Of Islamic faith, the Moors occupied Spain 711–1492□

Moore Bobby (Robert Frederick) 1941– . British footballer. Captain of West Ham United, he played for England 108 times, and headed the winning World Cup team in 1966□

Moore George 1852–1933. Irish novelist. *A Modern Lover* 1883 and *Esther Waters* 1894 were sexually frank for their time□

Moore G(eorge) E(dward) 1873–1958. British philosopher. Editor of the journal *Mind* 1921–47, he was an outstanding teacher, and in *Principia Ethica* 1903 attempted to analyse 'what is good?'. See Scholasticism◊□

Moore Gerald 1899– . British pianist, who raised the role of accompanist to singers and instrumentalists to a rare art□

Moore Henry 1898– . British sculptor, born at Castleford, Yorkshire. His work has been inspired by that of 'primitive' artists and by natural forms, and he exhibits it in open air 'sculpture parks' at his home at Perry Green, Hertfordshire. His popular reputation began with his drawings of London air-raid shelter scenes in World War II as an official artist. Order of Merit 1963□

Moore Sir (John) Jeremy 1928– . British soldier, born in Staffordshire. British Major-General Commando Forces, Royal Marines, 1979–82, he commanded the land forces in the Falklands◊ campaign; Knight Commander of the Bath 1982□

Moore Sir John 1761–1809. British general. In the Peninsular◊ War he took command in 1808 of the British army in Portugal, but, after advancing into Spain had to retreat to Corunna◊, and was killed in the battle fought to cover the embarkation□

Moore Marianne 1887–1972. American poet, whose volumes of intellectual verse of difficult form include *Observations* 1924 and *What are Years?* 1941□

Moore Thomas 1779–1852. Irish poet. He is best remembered for his *Irish Melodies* (set to music by Sir John Stevenson) 1807–35, which include 'The Minstrel Boy' and 'The Last Rose of Summer'. He was a friend of Byron◊ who gave him his manuscript *Memoirs* to assist him financially, but Moore allowed their mutual publisher, John Murray, to burn it in 1824 on grounds of propriety□

moorhen a type of bird. See under rail◊ family□

Moorhouse Geoffrey 1931– . British travel writer, born in Bolton, Lancashire. His books include *The Fearful Void* 1974, and (on cricket) *The Best-Loved Game* 1979□

moose a type of deer◊□

Moose Jaw town in Saskatchewan, Canada; population 34 000. Centre of the wheat area, it has oil refineries□

Moradabad trading city in Uttar◊ Pradesh, India; population 348 000□

morality play form of 'moralizing' medieval verse drama, developed from the miracle◊ play, and in turn influencing Elizabethan drama. Most famous was *Everyman*□

Moral Rearmament a worldwide movement for moral and spiritual renewal founded by see F N D Buchman◊ in 1938□

Morandi Giorgio 1890–1964. Italian still-life painter and etcher, noted for his subtle studies of bottles and jars□

Moravia Alberto. Pseudonym of Italian novelist Alberto Pincherle 1907– . His criticism of Mussolini, in *The Time of Indifference* 1929, led to suppression of his work; later were *The Woman of Rome* 1949 and *Two Women* 1958□

Moravia two Czech regions of Czechoslovakia, with Brno as the capital of the southern, and Ostrava of the northern. In the 9th century they were the core of the kingdom of Great Moravia, and finally became part of Czechoslovakia in 1918□

Moravian Brethren Protestant sect, an offshoot of the 15th-century Hussites (see John Huss◊), which endured much persecution. Some 50 000 live in the USA□

moray eel a type of eel◊□

Moray Firth North Sea inlet between Burghead (Grampian) and Tarbat Ness (Highland Region), Scotland□

Morazán Francisco 1792–1842. Central American statesman, born in Honduras. Elected president of the Central American Confederation in 1830, he tried to maintain it by force, and in 1842 was captured and executed in Honduras. He now symbolizes the movement for Central American unity□

Morbihan Gulf of. See under Brittany◊□

Mordovian a division of central USSR from 1934, conquered in the 13th century; area 26 200 sq km/10 110 sq mi; population 984 000. Capital Saransk□

More Sir Thomas 1478–1535. British statesman and author. From 1509 he rose rapidly in the service of Henry VIII (his *History of Richard III* c1513 has a distinct Tudor bias), becoming Lord Chancellor on the fall of Wolsey◊ in 1529. He resigned in 1532 when he failed to agree with the king's ecclesiastical policy and marriage with Anne Boleyn◊. In 1534 he refused, as a devout Catholic, to take the oath of supremacy to Henry VIII as head of the Church, was imprisoned in the Tower of London, and executed. He was also unsympathetic to the Protestants (his *English Dialogue* 1528, was directed against Tyndale◊), and wanted the harsh heresy laws maintained, contrary to the policy advocated in his own early tale of an ideal socialist commonwealth, the Latin *Utopia* 1516. He was canonized in 1935□

Moreau Jean Victor Marie 1763–1813. French general who won a brilliant victory over the Austrians at Hohenlinden; as a republican he intrigued against Napoleon, and when banished, joined the Allies and was killed at the Battle of Dresden□

Morecambe Bay inlet of the Irish Sea between the Furness Peninsula (Cumbria) and Lancashire. There are oil wells, and it has sufficient tidal rise and fall to have potential for power generation. ***Morecambe*** is a resort and adjoining ***Heysham*** a ferry port to Ireland; population 42 000□

morel a type of fungus. See under Ascomycetes◊□

Moresby John 1830–1922. British naval explorer, first European to visit New Guinea's finest harbour, now Port◊ Moresby□

Morgan Sir Henry c1635–88. Welsh buccaneer who sacked Panama in 1671, and was knighted in 1674, becoming Lieutenant-Governor of Jamaica□

Morgan John Pierpont 1837–1913. American financier-philanthropist, whose art collection was presented to the nation by his son John Pierpont Morgan 1867–1943□

Morgan Lewis Henry 1818–81. American anthropologist, who studied American Indian culture, especially the role of property, and was adopted by the Iroquois□

Morgan Thomas Hunt 1866–1945. American biologist, awarded a Nobel prize in 1933 for his theory of paired elements within the chromosomes governing heredity (based on studies of the fruit fly◊)□

morganatic marriage marriage (recognized by the Church and with legitimate issue), but in which the wife (of lower rank than the husband) is not raised to his level, and whose children do not inherit their father's rank or lands. Such an arrangement was rejected by Edward VIII◊□

Moriscos Spanish Muslims who accepted Christian baptism, and their descendants; they were expelled from the country in 1609□

Morisot Berthe 1841–95. French Impressionist◊ artist, grand-daughter of Fragonard◊, specializing in paintings of women and children□

Morland George 1763–1804. British painter, who first exhibited at the Royal Academy at the age of ten, but later combined hard work (sometimes two pictures a day) with dissipation. He excelled at painting gypsies, stable interiors, etc.□

Morley John, 1st Viscount Morley of Blackburn 1838–1923. British Liberal statesman. As Secretary for India 1905–10, he moved towards more representative government. Lord President of the Council 1910–14, he resigned in protest against the declaration of World◊ War I□

Morley Malcolm 1931– . British painter, the first photo-realist, whose works include landscapes and animals from life combined with mythological motifs, as well as abstracts□

Morley Thomas 1557–c1603. English composer, and organist at St Paul's. He had been a student of Byrd, and wrote madrigals, and songs for Shakespeare's plays, and a *Plaine and Easie Introduction to Practicall Musicke* 1597□

Mormons or ***Latter-Day Saints*** religious organization founded by Joseph Smith 1805–44. Born in Vermont, he claimed in 1827 to have received the revelation of the *Book of Mormon* (an ancient prophet), inscribed on gold plates and concealed a thousand years before in a hill near Palmyra, New York State. Christ is said to have appeared to an early American people (after his ascension) to establish his church in the New World, and the Mormon Church is a re-establishment of that by divine intervention. The book was accepted as supplementing the Bible by the 'Church of Jesus Christ of Latter-Day Saints', founded in 1830 at Fayette, New York. Brigham Young and the Twelve Apostles undertook the first foreign mission in England, and the first European converts went to the USA in 1840. Opponents of the movement killed Smith in Illinois, and Brigham Young led a migration of the majority to the Valley of the Great Salt Lake (Utah) in 1847, and Utah became a territory in 1850, with Young as Governor 1851–8. The doctrine of polygamy was proclaimed by Young in 1852 (he attributed it to Joseph Smith, but the latter is on record as condemning it); in 1890 it was repudiated by the church, and Utah became a state in 1896. The main branch of Mormons number c3 250 000□

morning glory a variety of tropical plant. See under convolvulus◊□

Moro Aldo 1916–78. Italian Christian Democrat Prime Minister 1963–8 and 1974–6, and expected to become president, when he was kidnapped and shot by Red Brigade urban guerrillas□

Morocco Kingdom of

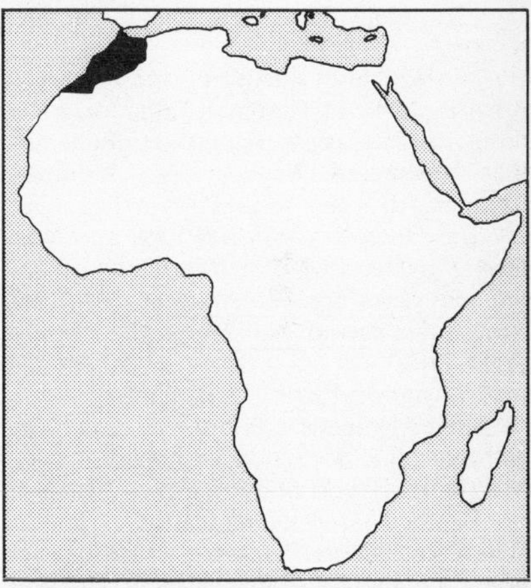

area 458 730 sq km/166 000 sq mi
capital Rabat
towns Marrakesh, Fez, Kenes; ports are Casablanca, Tangier
features Atlas Mountains; Ceuta (from 1580), Melilla (from 1492), and three small coastal settlements are held by Spain; a tunnel across the Strait of Gibraltar to Spain was planned in 1985
exports dates, figs; cork, wood pulp; canned fish; phosphates; tourism is important
currency dirham
population 19 500 000
language Arabic (official); French, Spanish
religion Sunni Islam
famous people Barbary pirates◊, Abd El-Krim◊
government constitutional monarchy (Hasan◊ II), with a unicameral legislature elected two-thirds directly and one-third indirectly through electoral colleges
recent history following the Agadir◊ incident, Morocco was divided 1912–56 between French and Spanish protectorates and the international zone of Tangier, but became independent in 1956. In 1975–9 Hassan II incorporated Western Sahara◊ into his Kingdom, and in 1984 Morocco concluded a

treaty for a Libyan-Moroccan federation, to be presided over jointly by the King and the President of Libya□

Moroni capital of the Comoros Republic on Grand Comore; population 16 000□

Morpheus in Greek mythology, the god of dreams, son of Somnus, god of sleep□

morphine an analgesic drug obtained from opium◊□

Morris William 1834–96. British poet, craftsman, and socialist. Born at Walthamstow, he was educated at Oxford, and was a friend of Burne-Jones◊, Ruskin◊, and Rossetti◊. In 1862 he founded his own firm to produce furniture, wallpaper, church decorations, etc., now highly valued; and the Kelmscott Press in 1890 (at Hammersmith, for which there are plans as a museum) to print beautifully decorated books, e.g. *Kelmscott Chaucer*. An ardent socialist (as in the romances *The Dream of John Ball* 1888 and *News from Nowhere* 1891), he translated and imitated the sages (*Sigurd the Volsung* 1876), and wrote verse narratives (*The Earthly Paradise* 1868–70)□

morris dance English folk dance (usually performed by men) with pre-Christian roots, and a costume decorated with bells□

Morrison Herbert Stanley, Baron Morrison of Lambeth 1888–1965. British Labour statesman, Home Secretary 1940–5, and Foreign Secretary Mar–Oct 1951. Gaitskell defeated him in the contest for the party leadership in 1955□

Morse Samuel 1791–1872. American inventor of the first adequate electric telegraph in 1836, and of the Morse◊ code□

Morse code international code for transmitting messages by radio using signals of short ('dots') and long ('dashes') duration, e.g. the letters SOS (3 short, 3 long, 3 short) the international distress signal because the most distinctive and easily transmitted (popularly *S*ave *O*ur *S*ouls). By radio telephone the distress code is 'Mayday', for similar reasons (popularly alleged to correspond to French *m'aider*)□

mortgage conveyance of real property (e.g. a house) as conditional security (e.g. to a bank/building society) for repayment of a loan, usually over a period of years□

Mortimer John 1923– . British barrister and playwright, e.g. *The Dock Brief* 1958, *A Voyage Round My Father* 1970, and the television series *Rumpole of the Bailey* from 1978□

Mortimer Roger de, 8th Baron of Wigmore and 1st Earl of March c1287–1330. English rebel, imprisoned by Edward◊ II for two years before escaping from the Tower to join with the English queen (Isabella), then visiting the French court. They returned to England in 1326, Edward fleeing and being deposed by Parliament. Mortimer (Earl of March from 1328) ruled England as the Queen's lover. The young Edward III had him seized (while with the Queen at Nottingham castle), and he was hanged, drawn, and quartered at Tyburn□

mosaic design, usually for a floor or wall, produced by inlay of small pieces of marble, glass, etc. Famous examples are in Hadrian's villa, Tivoli; San Vitale, Ravenna; the hall of the Houses of Parliament; Westminster Cathedral□

Moscow Russia's largest industrial city (Russian *Moskva*), capital of the Russian Soviet Federated Social Republic (RSFSR) from 1918, of the Union of Soviet Socialist Republics (USSR) from 1922, and of Imperial Russia 14th century–1709 (see Peter the Great◊)

population 8 203 000

features the 12th-century Kremlin (Citadel) lies on the N bank of the Moskva river, and includes three cathedrals, the former Imperial Palace, and the world's largest bell◊; nearby are the Kitai Gorod (government offices), and Red Square (with St Basil's Cathedral, the state department store GUM, and Lenin's tomb); the headquarters of the KGB◊, with Lubyanka Prison behind it, is in Dzerzhinsky Square; the underground railway (1935 onwards) is a showpiece. Institutions include Moscow University, 1755, and People's Friendship University (for foreign students), 1953; Academy◊ of Sciences; Tretyakov Gallery of Russian Art, 1856; Bolshoi Theatre (1780, for opera and ballet); Moscow Art Theatre, 1898; Moscow State Circus. There is a Cosmonauts' Monument, and on the city outskirts is Star City (*Zvezdnoy Gorodok*), the Soviet space centre; Zelenograd (Soviet centre for microelectronics) is 40 km/25 mi to the NW. Sheremetyevo is the international airport□

Moseley Henry Gwyn-Jeffreys 1887–1915. British physicist, originator of the series of atomic numbers in 1913. He was killed at Gallipoli◊□

Moselle a river in W Europe. See under Rhine◊□

Moses in the Old Testament, a Hebrew lawgiver. Reared in Egypt, where Pharoah's daughter found him hidden among the bulrushes of the Nile after her father had decreed all new-born Hebrew males should be killed, he led the Israelites in the Exodus◊ from Egypt. During their 40 years of wandering in the wilderness, he received the

Ten Commandments from Jehova on Mount Sinai, and died within sight of the Promised Land□

Moses Anna Mary ('Grandma') 1860–1961. American primitive painter, who began painting seriously only at the age of 67 after a life as a farmer's wife□

Mosi-oa-tunya see Victoria◊ Falls□

Moskva the Russian name for Moscow◊□

Moslem a follower of Islam◊□

Mosley Sir Oswald Ernald 1896–1980. Founder of the British Union of Fascists (BUF) in 1932, he was interned in World War II till 1943, he later revived the BUF as the Union Movement. See Mitford◊ sisters□

mosque Islamic place of worship (Arabic *mesjid*) originally based on the plan of Christian basilicas. It includes a minaret (balconied turret), from which the faithful are called to prayer; dome; prayer niche (*mihrab*) in an interior wall, indicating the direction of Mecca◊, and an open court surrounded by porticos□

mosquito a class of fly◊□

moss worldwide class (Musci) of Bryophyta◊ (see plants◊). Small and flowerless, they have a stem and leaves, but no true root and flourish best in damp conditions where other vegetation is thin. ***Peat*** or ***bog moss*** *Sphagnum* is sometimes used as surgical dressing□

Mostaganem industrial port (metalworks, cement) in NW Algeria; population 102 000. There is a gas pipeline from Hassi Messaoud□

Mostar industrial town (aluminium, tobacco) in Bosnia-Herzegovina, Yugoslavia; population 110 500. It is also famous for wines□

Mosul city in Iraq, on the right bank of the Tigris, opposite the site of ancient Nineveh◊; population 293 000. It was once famous for the light cotton fabric ***muslin*** which was named after it, and is now an oil centre□

moth insect of the order Lepidoptera◊, of which its species form the greater part: see butterfly◊. The mouthparts form a sucking proboscis for nectar, etc., but some moths have no functional mouthparts, relying for food on internal reserves built up during the caterpillar stage. They vary greatly in size, e.g. minute Nepticulidae have a wingspan under 3 mm, and the largest, e.g. the ***owlet moth*** *Erebus agrippina,* of 280 mm/11 in. The larva or caterpillar has a tube or 'spinneret' in the lower lip which emits silk to make a cocoon within which its change to pupa or chrysalis takes place. Silk glands are especially large in those of the ***silkworm moth*** *Bombyx mori* whose cocoons are plunged in boiling water to kill the pupa and enable the silk◊ to be reeled off without the threads being broken by its emergence. One cocoon has c275 m/300 yds of thread. Other moths are destructive, their caterpillars attacking fruit trees (e.g. codling moth), stored flour, and clothes (especially the ***lesser clothes moth*** *Tinea pellionella,* family Tineidae, which feeds on wool, etc.).

The mainly tropical ***hawkmoths*** family Sphingidae, includes the largest of British moths, the ***death's head hawkmoth*** *Acherontia atropos* and the ***humming bird hawkmoth*** *Macroglossa stellatarum* which reaches southern England□

mother of pearl the smooth lustrous lining in the shells of pearl-bearing molluscs. See under pearl◊□

Motherwell and **Wishaw** steel (Ravenscraig) and coal town in Strathclyde, Scotland; population 73 000□

motion picture the US term for film◊□

motor boat any boat powered by a motor. See power◊ boat□

motor car a self-propelled road vehicle designed to carry passengers

1801 Trevithick◊'s steam 'road locomotive'

1831 UK law requiring a man to precede a 'horseless carriage' with a red flag

1876 Nikolaus Otto 1832–91, German engineer, patented an effective internal combustion engine

1885 Gottlieb Daimler 1834–1900, German engineer, patented a single-cylinder high-speed engine; and the German engineer Karl Benz 1844–1929 built one of the first practical petrol-driven cars, actually a three-wheeled 'tricycle'

1895 'red flag' law, still theoretically in force, repealed

1897 Royal Automobile Club (RAC) founded

1905 Automobile Association (AA) founded

1906 beginning of Grand Prix motor-racing, in which individual events in many countries count towards the World Championship: famous circuits include (UK) Brands Hatch, Brooklands till 1939, Silverstone; (France) Montlhéry; (Germany) Nurburgring; (USA) Detroit

1912 Henry Ford◊ started mass-production of the Model T

after World War I advent of the 'baby car', cheap and light for popular motoring: (England) Austin 7, Morris Minor; (France) Citroën, Peugeot, Renault; (Italy) Fiat; (USA) Ford, Chevrolet, Dodge

1923 Le Mans 24-hour race established as the foremost proving ground for production cars

1950 first Indianapolis 500-mile race

1950s introduction of automatic transmission for small cars, rubber suspension, transverse

engine mounting, self-levelling ride, disc brakes, safer wet-weather tyres
1953 first East African Safari, the toughest of the time-checked motor rallies for production cars
1959 advent of the Mini (see Issigonis◊)
1960s agitation began against air pollution from car exhausts
1970s fuel crisis led to increased use of aluminium and plastic in the body in order to reduce weight; microprocessors were installed to measure temperature, engine speed, pressure, and oxygen content of exhaust gases, and readjust parts of the engine accordingly
1980s air pollution problems caused by chemicals in car exhaust fumes (including oxides of nitrogen, hydrocarbons, and carbon monoxide – the two former may be responsible for creating acid◊ rain) were met by increasing legal restrictions. Manufacturers met the problems by: a 'lean-burn engine' for which the ratio of air to fuel for combustion is higher (lowering the temperature, and, in consequence, the pollution level); use of a catalytic converter
1981 the UK introduced system of penalty points for motoring offences (e.g. careless driving) ending in obligatory or discretionary disqualification.
See also speed◊ records□

motorcycle a two-wheeled vehicle driven by an engine
1868 first motorcycle (steam-powered) patented by Ernest and Pierre Michaux
1885 Gottlieb Daimler (1834–1900) built a bicycle powered by an internal combustion engine
1894 Hildebrand and Wolfmüller's Pétrolette, first production motorcycle
1901 first production-line motorcycles produced with engines in modern position
1907 first Isle of Man TT (Tourist◊ Trophy) Race
1920s belt drive replaced by chain drive
1948 hydraulic front fork introduced
1970s domination of Japanese manufacturers
motorcycle racing includes a ***world championship*** based on points (gained in Grand Prix events); ***moto-cross*** or ***scrambling*** races across rough country; ***speedway*** laps round dirt tracks□

mould mainly saprophytic fungi◊ (see also Ascomycetes◊) living on food-stuffs and other organic matter, a few being parasitic on plants, animals, or each other. Many are of medical or industrial importance□

Moulmein port (especially teak exports) in S Burma; population 203 000□

Moundbuilders N American◊ Indian peoples (see Hopewell◊, Natchez◊) who built earth mounds, linear and conical in shape for tombs, and 'platforms' for chiefs' houses, and temples from c300BC. They carried out group labour projects under the rule of an elite. A major site is Monk's Mound in Mississippi. They were in decline by the time of the Spanish invasion, but traces of their culture live on in the folklore of the Choctaw and Cherokee Indians□

mountain ash or ***rowan*** flowering tree *Sorbus aucuparia*, family Rosaceae◊, with pinnate leaves, large cymes of whitish flowers, and scarlet berries. The berries yield a tasteless acid widely used in food preservation (cider, wine, soft drinks, animal feedstuffs, bread, and cheese)□

mountaineering the art and practice of mountain climbing. For major peaks of the Himalayas it was formerly thought necessary to have elaborate support from Sherpas, and fixed ropes and oxygen at high altitudes, but in the 1980s there was introduced the 'Alpine style' which dispenses with these, and relies on human ability to adapt Sherpa-style to high altitude, e.g. the assault on Kongur in 1981.
1854 ***Wetterhorn*** Switzerland, climbed by Alfred Wills, founding the sport
1865 ***Matterhorn*** Switzerland-Italy, Whymper◊
1897 ***Aconcagua*** Argentina, Zurbriggen
1938 ***Eiger*** Switzerland, (north face) Heinrich Harrer
1953 ***Everest*** Nepal/Tibet, Hilary◊/Tenzing◊
1981 ***Kongur*** China, Bonington◊

mountain lion another name for puma. See under cat◊□

Mountain States eight states (Arizona◊, Colorado◊, Idaho◊, Montana◊, Nevada◊, New Mexico◊, Utah◊, Wyoming◊) of the USA, formerly known as the Great American Desert, and still the most thinly populated. Half the land and 80% of the resources (including coal, oil, and uranium) are still owned by the government, and development in the 1970s–80s has been rapid, and includes electronics. The magnificent scenery is threatened by despoliation□

Mountbatten Louis, 1st Earl Mountbatten of Burma 1900–79. British Admiral of the Fleet, son of the Marquess of Milford◊ Haven. He served at Jutland◊, and in World War II HMS *Kelly* was sunk under him in the Battle of Crete◊ in 1941. He was Chief of Combined Operations in 1942, when he was criticized over the Dieppe◊ Raid; and was Commander-in-Chief in SE Asia from 1943 until he received the Japanese surrender at Singapore in Sept 1945. Last Viceroy of India in 1947, he became first Governor-General of independent India until 1948; Order of Merit 1965. He was killed by an IRA bomb on his yacht at Mullaghmore, County Sligo. His home at Broadlands, Hampshire, is now a museum□

Mount Erebus see under Ross◊ Sea□

Mount Isa mining town (copper, lead, silver, and zinc) in NW Queensland, Australia; population 25 570□

Mount Lofty Range see under South◊ Australia□

Mount McKinley see under McKinley◊□

Mount Rushmore see under South◊ Dakota□

Mount St Helens see under Oregon◊□

Mount Vernon see under Virginia◊□

mouse small long-tailed rodent◊□

mousebird order of birds, Coliiformes, including the single family (Culidae) of small crested birds peculiar to Africa. They have hair-like feathers, long tails and mouse-like agility; largest is the ***blue-naped mousebird*** *Colius macrocurus*, 35 cm/c1 ft long□

Moustier Le. Cave in the Dordogne◊, giving the name Mousterian to the flint tool culture of Neanderthal man; the earliest ritual burials are linked with Mousterian settlements□

mouth organ see under harmonica◊□

Moyse Marcel 1889–1984. French flautist, who made many recordings and was influential as a teacher□

Mozambique People's Republic of

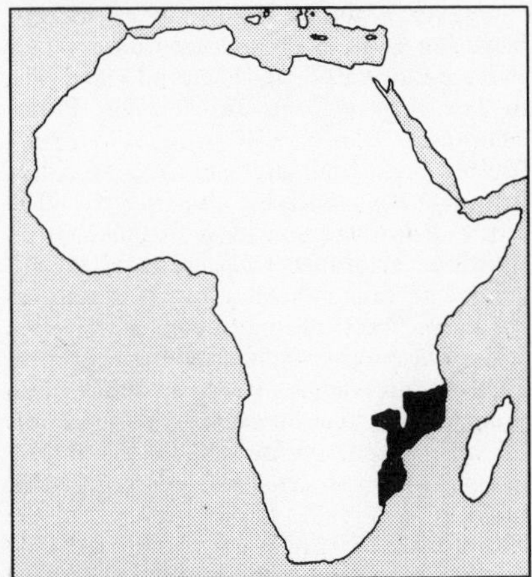

area 784960 sq km/303 070 sq mi
capital and chief port Maputo
towns other ports Beira, Nacala
features rivers Zambezi, Limpopo
exports sugar, cashews, tea; cotton, copra, sisal
currency escudo
population 12 690 000, mainly indigenous Bantu peoples; Portuguese (formerly 250 000) 50 000
language Portuguese (official)
religion Animism 69%; Roman Catholicism 21%, Islam 10%
famous people Vasco da Gama
government executive president (Samora Machel from 1975), council of ministers and elected people's assembly. Frelimo (the Marxist liberation front, Frente de Libertação de Moçambique) is the sole political party
recent history a Portuguese colony from 1505, Mozambique became independent in 1975 after a guerrilla campaign under Machel from 1964. Many Portuguese settlers left, and since the country depends on S Africa for economic survival, the regime is increasingly pragmatic owing to its need for Western aid. The Mozambique National Resistance Movement (MNRM) continues guerrilla activity backed by S Africa. The African National Congress (ANC), which aims at overthrowing the S African government, has offices in Mozambique and Angola□

Mozart Wolfgang Amadeus 1756–91. Austrian composer. Born at Salzburg, the son of a professional musician, he became a child prodigy, both as pianist and composer. Master of the court band of the Archbishop of Salzburg from 1770, he was treated like a servant and suddenly dismissed in 1781, thereafter living chiefly in Vienna. No businessman, he supported himself by recitals and teaching, but never achieved financial ease despite his wealth of compositions including: 25 piano concertos, 25 string quartets, 40 violin sonatas, and some 50 symphonies, e.g. the E flat, G minor, and C major ('Jupiter'), all composed in 1787. Of his operas the best known are *Idomeneo* 1781, *Il Seraglio* 1782, *The Marriage of Figaro* 1786, *Don Giovanni* 1787, *Cosí fan tutte* 1790, and *The Magic Flute* 1791. A *Requiem* commissioned in strange circumstances by an eccentric nobleman, remained unfinished at his death, and it has been suggested that he did not die of natural causes. See ballet◊, Salieri◊□

Mtwara port in S Tanzania; population 50 000□

Mubarak Hosni 1928– . Egyptian statesman. A technocrat, he commanded the Air Force 1972–5 (being responsible for the initial victories in the Egyptian campaign of 1973), when he became an active vice-president to Sadat, and succeeded him on his assassination in 1981□

mucous membrane thin skin found on all internal body surfaces (e.g. eyelids, breathing and digestive passages, genital tract), which secretes mucus, a moistening, lubricating, and protective fluid□

mudfish or ***lungfish*** N American fish *Amia calva* order Amiformes, with a highly developed air sac, enabling it to live some time out of water□

mudpuppy aquatic American salamanders◊, such as the axolotl, with large gills□

mudskipper a type of fish that can move on land. See under goby◊□

muezzin Muslim religious official. See Islam◊□

mufti a Muslim legal expert. See law, under Islam◊□

Mugabe Robert Gabriel 1925– . Zimbabwian statesman. Under detention in Rhodesia for nationalist activities 1964–74, he then carried on guerrilla warfare from Mozambique (in alliance with Joshua Nkomo from 1976), and in 1980 became Prime Minister of independent Zimbabwe. In 1985 he postponed the introduction of a multi-party state for five years□

Muggeridge Malcolm 1903– . British journalist, editor of *Punch* 1953–7, with controversial views on the royal family and religion (he converted to Roman Catholicism 1982)□

mugwump a neutral in politics. In US political history the Republicans who voted for Cleveland, the Democratic presidential candidate instead of for the Republican nominee□

Mühlhausen the German name for Mulhouse◊□

Mujibur Rahman, Sheikh 1921–75. Bangladesh◊i statesman, who campaigned for the autonomy of E Pakistan, and, on its independence after the 1971 civil war, became its first Prime Minister. A dictatorial president Jan–Aug 1975, he was assassinated□

Mukden a former name for Shenyang◊□

Mukden Battle of. The taking of Mukden from Russian occupation by the Japanese, 20 Feb–10 Mar 1905□

Mukden Incident surprise attack on 18 Sept 1931 by the Japanese on the Chinese garrison at Mukden which marked the beginning of the invasion of China□

mulberry genus of trees *Morus,* family Moraceae, with heart-shaped leaves; the ***black mulberry*** *M nigra* has dull red fruit and ***white mulberry*** *M alba* is used to feed silkworms□

Muldoon Robert 1921– . New Zealand statesman, leader of the National Party from 1974, and Prime Minister 1975–84□

mule see under horse◊□

Mülheim-an-der-Ruhr industrial city (electrical generators, pipes, tubes) in North Rhine-Westphalia, W Germany; population 178 800□

Mulhouse industrial city (textiles) (German *Mühlhausen*) in E France; population 120 000□

Mull island in the Inner Hebrides◊□

mullah a teacher, scholar, or religious leader of Islam◊□

mullein Eurasian plants, family Scrophulariaceae; ***common mullein*** *Verbascum thapsus* has lance-like leaves and a yellow flower spike; there are many cultivated varieties□

Muller Hermann 1890–1967. American geneticist, discoverer of the effect of radiation on genes by his work on fruit flies (see under fly◊): Nobel prize 1946□

Muller Paul. See under DDT◊□

mullet a type of fish. See under perch◊□

Mulliken Robert Sanderson 1896– . American chemist-physicist, who received a Nobel prize in 1966 for his development of the molecular orbital theory□

Mullingar county town of Westmeath, Republic of Ireland; population 7000. It is a cattle market and trout-fishing centre□

Mulock British novelist Dinah Maria Mulock Craik◊□

Mulready William 1786–1863. Irish genre painter, e.g. *Fair Time*, and book illustrator; he designed the first penny-postage envelope, known as the 'Mulready envelope'□

Mulroney Brian 1939– . Canadian statesman. A former labour lawyer, he replaced Joe Clark as Progressive Conservative Party leader in 1983, and achieved a landslide in the 1984 elections to become Prime Minister□

Multan industrial city (textiles, precision instruments, chemicals, pottery, jewellery) in central Pakistan; population 730 000□

multiple sclerosis (MS) disease of the central nervous system resulting in part of the nerve fibres turning to hard scar tissue. It may be progressively crippling, affecting all the senses, etc., or may in some cases disappear. It may be caused by the action of antibodies to viruses of childhood diseases, such as measles, entering the brain□

Mumford Lewis 1895– . American sociologist, concerned with the effect of technology on modern society, e.g. *The Culture of Cities* 1938□

mummy artificially or naturally preserved body, either animal or human, e.g. mammoths in the glacial ice of 25 000 years ago; shrunken heads preserved by the Jivaro◊; mummies of ancient Egypt; and, in modern times, the mummies of Lenin and Eva Peron. See also cryonics◊□

mumps virus infection marked by fever and swelling of the parotid salivary glands (under the ear). Usually minor in children, although meningitis is a possible complication, it may affect the fertility of adult males□

Munch Edvard 1863–1944. Norwegian artist. His severe mental illness in 1908, is reflected in the agonized tension of *The Scream* and *The Kiss*; later paintings often show agricultural scenes, e.g. *Workers in the Snow* 1910□

München German name for Munich◊□

München Gladbach see Mönchengladbach◊□

Münchhausen Karl Friedrich, Freiherr von, Baron Münchhausen 1720–97. German soldier whose 'tall' stories of his campaign adventures were worked up by Rudolph Erich Raspe 1737–94 in *The Adventures of Baron Münchhausen* 1785□

Münchhausen's syndrome production of fraudulent medical symptoms by mentally disturbed (but apparently normal) patients, to secure hospital treatment, operations, etc.□

Munich (German *München*) industrial city (brewing, printing, precision instruments, electrical goods, machinery, textiles) and capital of the state of Bavaria, W Germany; population 1 288 200. Its magnificent buildings and the art treasures of its galleries (Alte and Neue Pinakothek) owe much to Ludwig◊ I and Maximilian◊ II (see also Wittelsbach◊). There is a 15th-century cathedral, and it is the site of a university; the Bavarian National Museum, State Library, and German Museum of Science and Technology; and the European Community Patent Office. To the NE at Garching there is a nuclear research centre, and to the SW is ***Oberammergau*** a village where a passion◊ play has been performed decennially in recognition of deliverance from the plague in 1634. Its festivities include Fasching◊, and the Oktoberfest. It was the birthplace of Nazism, Hitler making his attempted *Putsch* here in 1923. See also Munich◊ Agreement□

Munich Agreement signed on 29 Sept 1938 by Chamberlain◊, Daladier◊, Hitler◊, and Mussolini◊, under which Czechoslovakia was compelled to surrender her Sudeten-German districts (the Sudetenland) to Germany. Despite signatory guarantees, Hitler seized the rest of the country in Mar 1939. After World War II the area was returned to Czechoslovakia, and over two million German-speaking people were expelled from the country□

Munnings Alfred 1878–1959. British painter, famous for his paintings of horses□

Munro Hugh Hector. See Saki◊□

Munster S province of Republic of Ireland, comprising the counties of Clare◊, Cork◊, Kerry◊, Limerick◊, N and S Tipperary◊, and Waterford◊; area 24 128 sq km/9319 sq mi; population 998 315. It was a kingdom until the 12th century□

Münster industrial city (former capital of Westphalia◊) of N Rhine-Westphalia, W Germany; population 269 900. The Treaty of Westphalia was signed here in 1648□

muntjac a kind of deer◊□

mural painting wall painting (fresco, tempera, oil, acrylic, etc.). See Cimabue◊, Giotto◊, Leonardo da Vinci◊, Diego Rivera◊□

Murasaki Shikibu 978–c1015. Pseudonym of the unknown Japanese woman writer, whose *Tale of Genji* is the world's first realistic novel□

Murat Joachim 1767–1815. One of Napoleon's cavalry commanders, whom he made King of Naples in 1808. Murat deserted him in 1813, in the vain hope of Allied recognition. In 1815 he tried to make himself king of all Italy, but was captured and shot when he landed in Calabria□

Murcia autonomous region of SE Spain (including Murcia and Cartagena); population 957 900□

Murcia industrial town (silk, glass, metal goods) in Murcia region, Spain; population 288 630□

murder unlawful killing of one person by another, who is of sound mind, has reached years of discretion, and acts with malice aforethought, express or implied□

Murdoch Iris 1919– . British novelist. Born in Dublin, she is a philosophy don at Oxford, and her novels are witty allegories, e.g. *Under the Net* 1954, *A Severed Head* 1961 (dramatized in collaboration with Priestley◊), *The Sea, The Sea* 1978, and *The Good Apprentice* 1985□

Murdock William 1754–1839. Scottish originator of gas-lighting, first using it in his home and offices in Redruth in 1792□

Murillo Bartolomé Estéban 1617–82. Spanish painter, noted for his religious pictures and studies of street urchins. Born in Seville, he was befriended in Madrid 1642–5 by Velasquez◊□

murk unit of air pollution when measured by optical absorption□

Murmansk seaport in NW USSR; population 388 000. The world's most northern metropolis, Russia's most important fishing port, and base of the icebreakers which keep open the NE Passage. The Festival of the North in Mar marks the end of the two-month Arctic night. It is the centre of Soviet Lapland◊□

Murray Gilbert 1866–1957. British scholar whose verse translations, e.g. of Euripides, made Greek plays more accessible to modern readers□

Murray Sir James 1837–1915. Scottish philologist, founder-editor of the *Oxford English Dictionary* from 1878□

Murray/Moray James Stuart, Earl of Murray/Moray c1531–70. Illegitimate son of James V of Scotland, where he was a leader of the Reformation. Becoming regent in 1657, after the deposition of his half-sister, Mary, he was assassinated by one of her supporters□

Murray chief river of Australia, length 2575 km/1600 mi. Its tributaries include the ***Lachlan*** rising in the Blue Mounains (length 1485 km/920 mi) and ***Murrumbidgee*** (length 1690 km/1050 mi). Dartmouth Dam, in the Great Dividing Range, has drought-proofed the system and provides hydroelectric power, but irrigation (for grapes, citrus and stone fruits) and navigation schemes has led to soil salinization. See Charles Sturt◊□

Murrow Ed(ward) R(oscoe) 1908–65. American broadcaster, e.g. radio reports on the London 'blitz', and television demolition of Senator McCarthy's power in 1954□

Murrumbidgee river, tributary of the Murray◊□

Murry John Middleton 1889–1957. British literary critic, husband of Katherine Mansfield◊ and friend of D H Lawrence□

Musashi Miyamato (b. 1584). Japanese exponent of the martial arts, whose manual *A Book of Five Rings* on Samurai strategy achieved immense popularity in the USA from 1974 on its appearance in translation. It was said that Japanese businessmen used it as a guide to success□

Muscat capital of the sultanate of Oman; its port is nearby Mutrah; population 25 000□

Muscat and Oman the former name of Oman◊□

muscle tissue with the special function of contraction, achieved by large numbers of long spindle-shaped elastic cells, which contract and expand in response to impulses reaching the nerves. Muscles are either voluntary, under control of the will, or involuntary, e.g. those in the walls of blood vessels, the intestines, the interior of the eye, etc. Contracting muscles create low-frequency sound. See also paralysis◊□

muscular dystrophy progressive muscular weakness of genetic origin, resulting in paralysis◊□

Muses in Greek mythology, the nine daughters of Zeus◊ and Mnemosyne (goddess of memory) and inspirers of creative arts: ***Calliope*** epic poetry; ***Clio*** history; ***Erato*** love poetry; ***Euterpe*** lyric poetry; ***Melpomene*** tragedy; ***Polyhymnia*** hymns; ***Terpsichore*** dance; ***Thalia*** comedy; ***Urania*** astronomy. See under Pegasus◊□

Musgrave Thea 1928– . Scottish composer, whose works include concertos for horn, clarinet, and viola; and operas, e.g. *Mary, Queen of Scots* 1976□

Musgrave Ranges mountain ranges on the S Australia/Northern Territory border; highest peak Mount Woodruffe 1525 m/5000 ft. The area is an Aboriginal reserve□

mushroom see Basidiomycetes◊□

music the combination of sounds in a meaningful aesthetic form. Differences between 'eastern' and 'western' music include the recognition by the former of many more subdivisions of a note than the latter, and the absence until recently of a written form for the former, which ruled out the composition of major developed works and fostered melodic and rhythmic patterns, freely interpreted (as in the Indian *raga*) by virtuoso executants. The use of synthesizers and recording has yet more recently meant that works may be composed in their 'final form' and are not meant to be replayed and interpreted by conductors and orchestras. Electronic music has also been linked to computer composition, see John Cage◊. Landmarks in the tradition of western music include:

classical Greek music which includes sung choruses in tragic drama; it is the first music for which we have notation (in letters of the alphabet), but remains are fragmentary and interpretation uncertain

6th century Gregorian chant (see Gregory◊ I) with a single part, or line of melody, not divided into regular bars; it drew on Greek and Hebrew tradition

8th century use of the organ as a church accompaniment

9th century harmonized music introduced into the church, with additional parts; notation developing towards the modern form

12th century earliest recorded secular music, that of the troubadours◊, trouvères◊, and Minnesingers◊

14–15th century development of polyphony or counterpoint, the simultaneous combination of independent melodic parts, perfected by Dunstable, Palestrina, Lassus, Byrd

16–17th century the first opera (see Peri◊), further developed by Monteverdi, Scarlatti, Lully, Purcell; development of harmony◊, the

music: notation

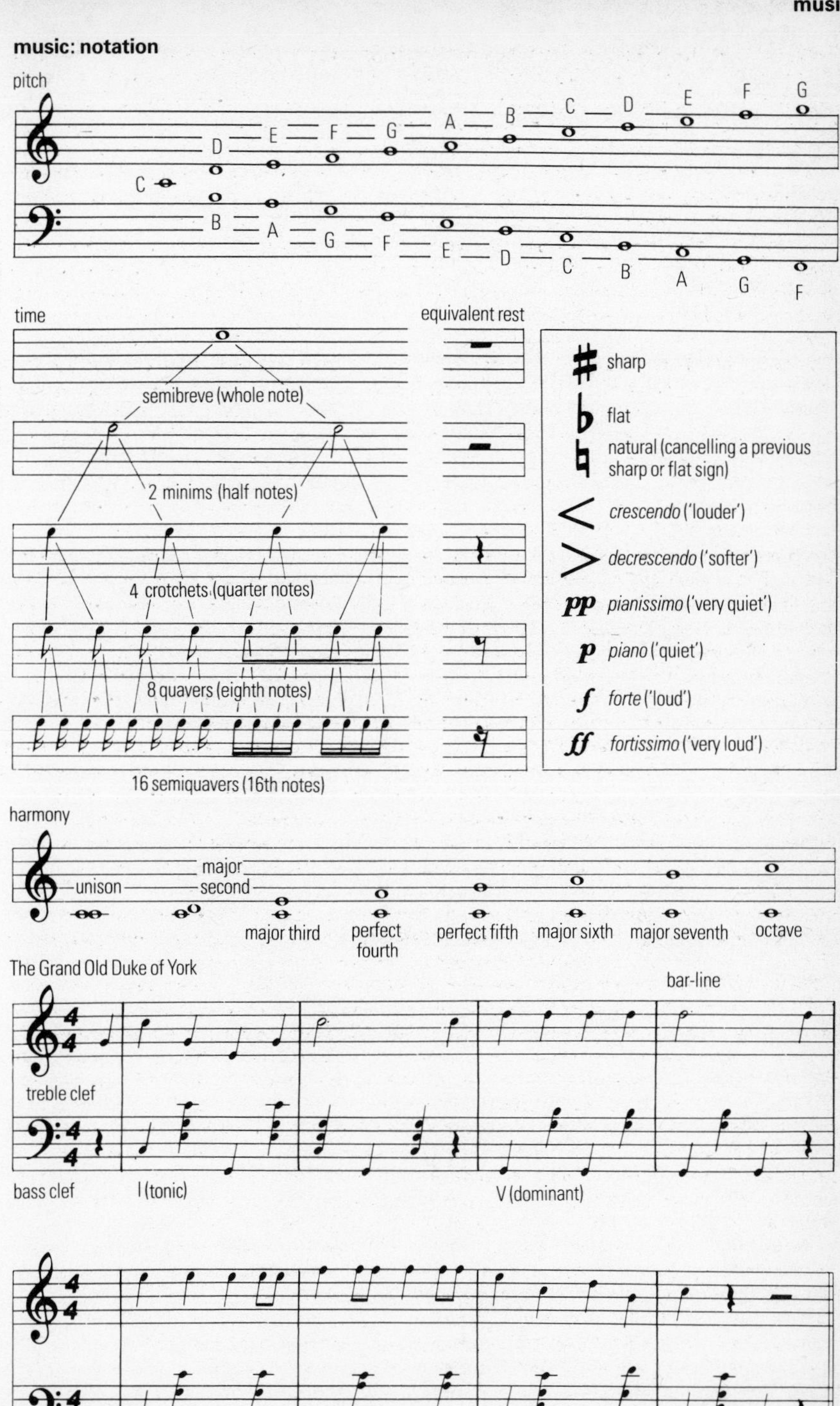

music: great composers

	dates	nationality	type of music
Okeghem, Johannes	1420-1495	Flemish	vocal music
Tallis, Thomas	1505-1585	English	vocal music
Morley, Thomas	1557-1603	English	vocal music
Monteverdi, Claudio	1567-1643	Italian	operas, vocal music
Purcell, Henry	1658-1695	English	vocal music, operas
Scarlatti, Alessandro	1660-1725	Italian	operas, keyboard music
Vivaldi, Antonio	1678-1741	Italian	concertos, chamber music
Bach, Johann Sebastian	1685-1750	German	keyboard, choral music, concertos
Handel, Georg Friedrich	1685-1759	German	oratorios, operas, orchestral music
Haydn, Franz Joseph	1732-1809	Austrian	symphonies, oratorios, chamber music
Mozart, Wolfgang Amadeus	1756-1791	Austrian	symphonies, operas, chamber music
Beethoven, Ludwig van	1770-1827	German	symphonies, chamber music, opera
Weber, Carl Maria von	1786-1826	German	operas, concertos
Rossini, Gioacchino	1792-1868	Italian	operas
Schubert, Franz	1797-1828	Austrian	songs, symphonies, chamber music
Berlioz, Hector	1803-1869	French	operas, symphonies
Mendelssohn-Bartholdy, Félix	1809-1847	German	symphonies, concertos
Schumann, Robert	1810-1856	German	piano, vocal music, concertos
Chopin, Frédéric	1810-1849	Polish	piano music
Liszt, Franz	1811-1886	French	piano, orchestral music
Verdi, Guiseppe	1813-1901	Italian	operas
Wagner, Richard	1813-1883	German	operas
Smetana, Bedrich	1824-1884	Czech	symphonies, operas
Saint-Saëns, Camille	1835-1921	French	symphonies, concertos, operas
Mussorgsky, Modest	1839-1881	Russian	operas, orchestral music
Tchaikovsky, Peter Ilyich	1840-1893	Russian	ballet music, symphonies
Dvorak, Anton	1841-1904	Czech	symphonies, operas
Grieg, Edvard	1843-1907	Norwegian	concertos, orchestra music
Rimsky-Korsakov, Nicolai	1844-1909	Russian	operas, orchestral music
Puccini, Giacomo	1858-1924	Italian	operas
Mahler, Gustav	1860-1911	Austrian	symphonies
Debussy, Claude	1862-1918	French	operas, orchestral music
Strauss, Richard	1864-1949	Austrian	operas, orchestral music
Sibelius, Jean	1865-1957	Finnish	symphonies, orchestral music
Vaughan Williams, Ralph	1872-1958	British	vocal music, symphonies
Rachmaninov, Sergei	1873-1943	Russian	symphonies, concertos
Schoenberg, Arnold	1874-1951	Austrian	operas, orchestral chamber music
Ives, Charles	1874-1951	American	orchestral music, songs
Ravel, Maurice	1875-1937	French	piano, chamber music
Stravinsky, Igor	1882-1871	Russian/US	ballets, operas
Webern, Anton	1883-1945	German	chamber, vocal music
Varèse, Edgar	1885-1965	American	orchestral, electronic music
Prokofiev, Serge	1891-1953	Russian	symphonies, ballets
Milhaud, Darius	1892-1974	French	operas, chamber music
Poulenc, Francis	1899-1963	French	operas, chamber music
Walton, William	1902-1983	British	symphonies, chamber music
Dallapiccola, Luigi	1904-1975	Italian	operas, oratorios
Tippett, Michael	1905-	British	operas, symphonies
Shostakovitch, Dimitri	1906-1965	Russian	piano
Messiaen, Olivier	1908-	French	piano, organ, orchestral music
Elliot Carter	1908-	American	chamber music
Britten, Benjamin	1913-1976	British	vocal music, opera
Boulez, Pierre	1925-	French	piano, chamber music
Henze, Hans Werner	1926-	German	operas, chamber music
Stockhausen, Karlheinz	1928-	German	electronic, vocal music

simultaneous combination of different notes (rather than melodies)
18th century the fugue, dramatic opera, oratorio, sonata, quartet, symphony developed; J S Bach, Beethoven, Handel, Gluck, Haydn, Mozart
19th century Romanticism and Nationalism; Schubert, Schumann, Brahms, Mendelssohn, Wagner, Verdi, Weber, Berlioz, Chopin, Liszt, Rimsky-Korsakov, Borodin
20th century naturalistic opera (Leoncavallo, Mascagni, Puccini; orchestral atonality◊, 12-tone music; Stravinsky, Schoenberg, Berg, Webern, Zemlinsky, Britten, Walton
1945–present musique concrète, electronic music, Serialism: Boulez, Ligeti, Penderecki, Berio, Henze, Xenakis, Messiaen, Nono, Elliot Carter, Peter Maxwell Davies□

Music Master of the King's/Queen's. Appointment to the British Royal Household, the holder composing music for state occasions. The first was Nicholas Lanier in 1625; the present holder is Malcolm Williamson◊□

musical the most recent of varied forms of dramatic musical performance, combining song, dance, and the spoken word, which merge into one another:
operetta essentially light-hearted entertainment, often of high musical content: Offenbach, Johann Strauss, Franz Lehár, and the uniquely English Gilbert and Sullivan
musical comedy an anglicization of the French *opéra bouffe* of which the first was *A Gaiety Girl* 1893 (put on by George Edwardes 1852–1915 at the Gaiety Theatre, London)
1920s typical were *Rose Marie* 1924 (Rudolf Friml 1879–1972), *The Student Prince* 1924 and *The Desert Song* 1926 (both Sigmund Romberg 1887–1951), and *No, No Nanette* 1925 (Vincent Youmans 1898–1946)
1930–40s a sophisticated era, with many filmed examples and strong US presence (see Irving Berlin, Jerome Kern, Cole Porter, and Gershwin; and in England Noel Coward and the more romantic Ivor Novello
musical no longer merely an abbreviation of 'musical comedy', but with the arrival of *Oklahoma* 1952 (see Rodgers◊ and Hammerstein◊), a much more integrated combination of plot, song, and dance, which reached a peak with Bernstein's *West Side Story* 1957 (recorded in operatic form with Kiri Te Kanawa◊ in 1985), and branched into religious and political themes with Andrew Lloyd Webber◊. See also Lionel Bart◊, Stephen Sondheim◊□

music hall light entertainment consisting of individual 'turns' which was in its heyday in the early 20th century with artists such as singer Albert Chevalier 1861–1923 ('My Old Dutch'), Marie Lloyd◊, and Vesta Tilley 1864–1952 (male impersonator, e.g. 'Burlington Bertie')□

Musil Robert 1880–1942. Austrian novelist of largely posthumous reputation, whose great work was the unfinished three-volume *The Man Without Qualities* 1930–43. It deals with the problems of the self from a mystic but agnostic viewpoint□

musk N American perennial plant *Mimulus moschatus* family Scrophulariaceae, with small oblong leaves, yellow flowers and a musky scent□

musk deer a type of deer◊□

muskeg Cree Indian name for 'swampland', of which there are some 1 300 000 sq km/500 000 sq mi in N Canada□

Muskö Swedish N Baltic naval base□

musk ox animal combining the characteristics of the sheep and ox, which at certain seasons has a musky odour. About the size of domestic cattle, it has long brown hair, and its underwool (qiviut) is almost as fine as vicuna. It is farmed in Alaska, Quebec, and Norway□

muskrat a type of rodent◊□

Muslim or *Moslem* a follower of Islam◊□

Muslim Brotherhood movement (Sunni) founded in Egypt in 1930, aimed at the establishment of a theocratic Islamic state and headed by a 'Supreme Guide'. It is also active in Jordan, Sudan, Syria, etc.□

musquash a type of rodent◊ □

mussel see Bivalve◊□

Musset Alfred de 1810–57. French author, one of Victor Hugo's circle, and the lover of George Sand◊, whom he accompanied to Italy: their relationship is reflected in *Confession d'un enfant du siècle* 1835 and the verse *Les Nuits* 1835–7. His short plays *Comèdies et proverbes* 1840 are neatly turned□

Mussolini Benito 1883–1945. Italian dictator. Son of a blacksmith in the Romagna, he founded the *fasci di combattimento* in 1919 (violently nationalist and anti-socialist; see Fascism◊) which attracted popular support, as well as that of landowners and industrialists. His Blackshirt followers were forerunners of Hitler's Brownshirts. In Oct 1922 he became Prime Minister with the backing of the king and the army, and having assumed dictatorial powers in 1925, *Il Duce* ('the leader') began a series of military ventures. In 1935–6, he successfully invaded Ethiopia; intervened in the Spanish Civil War to support Franco 1936–9; conquered Albania in 1939; and in Jun 1940 entered World War II in support of Hitler. Defeated in N Africa and Greece, and with Sicily invaded by the Allies, he was compelled to resign in Jul 1943 by his own Fascist Grand Council. German parachutists released him from prison in Sept, and set up a 'Republican Fascist' government in N Italy, but he and his mistress (Clara Petacci) were captured by partisans in Apr 1945 as they tried to flee the country. The bodies were hung upside down in Milan. See Ciano◊□

Mussorgsky Modest Petrovich 1839–81. Russian composer. Originally a guards officer, he resigned to become a government clerk and work also on his music, which includes operas *Boris Godunov* 1869, and the incomplete *Khovanshtchina* and *Sorochintsy Fair*; the orchestral *Night on the Bare Mountain;* and many songs. Rimsky-Korsakov◊ revised some of his work, which has now been restored to its harshly primitive beauty. He was a drug addict, and died in poverty□

Mustafa Kemal see Atatürk◊□

mustard table mustard is made from the seeds of ***black mustard*** *Brassica nigra* or ***white mustard*** *Sinapis alba*, both family Cruciferae; seedlings of the latter are combined with cress◊ in mustard and cress. Wild mustard is charlock◊□

Mustique see under St◊ Vincent and the Grenadines□

Mutare industrial town (vehicle assembly, engineering, textiles, paper) (formerly Umtali) in E Zimbabwe; population 70 000□

mutation in heredity, a new characteristic which appears in the offspring of a plant or animal and breeds true. This type of change is one of the bases of evolutionary theory, and may be spontaneous or induced (as by radiation). See evolution◊□

Muti Riccardo 1941– . Italian conductor, a 'purist' devoted to carrying out the composer's intentions to the last detail; music director, Philadelphia Orchestra from 1980□

Mutsuhito 1852–1912. Emperor of Japan from 1867, with the title of *Meiji Tenno* ('enlightened peace'): during his reign Japan became a world military and naval power□

mutton bird see under petrel◊□

MVD Russian Ministry of Internal Affairs. See under KGB◊□

Mwinyi Ali Hassan 1925– . President of Tanzania from 1985, when he succeeded Nyerere. A devout Muslim and socialist, he had to begin a revival of private enterprise, and control of state involvement and spending, to restore solvency□

myasthenia gravis muscular weakness caused by a defect in the body's immune system. Usually beginning in the muscles round the eye, it may spread so far as to affect breathing□

Mycenaean or ***Aegean civilization*** flourished in Crete, Cyprus, Greece, the Aegean Islands, and W Anatolia c4000–1000BC. The Mycenaeans have been identified with the Achaeans◊ of Homer, and were among the besiegers at Troy◊ (see Agamemnon◊), and may also have been the marauding sea◊ peoples of Egyptian records. They were magnificent architects, e.g. Mycenae on the plain of Argos (Lion Gate and beehive tombs) and craftsmen, and used a form of Greek written in Linear B (see Ventris◊). Their strongholds, including Tiryns on the plain of Argolis (excavated by Schliemann 1884–5), were overthrown c1200BC□

mycotoxin yellow powder extracted from the grain fungus called fusarium. Airborne, it causes blistering, nausea, bleeding, and sometimes death□

Myers F(rederic) W(illiam) H(enry) 1843–1901. British psychic investigator, coiner of the word 'telepathy'. He was a founder and first president of the Society for Psychical Research in 1882□

My Lai village in S Vietnam destroyed by US troops in 1968 in the erroneous belief that it was occupied by Viet Cong troops; the platoon commander, Lieutenant William Calley, was charged with murder and sentenced to life imprisonment, but later released□

mynah a type of starling◊□

myopia short sight, caused by a defect in the structure of the eye, causing incoming light to be focused before it reaches the retina. Concave lenses are used to correct it; surgery (a series of small slits are cut in the cornea of the eye) is controversial in its effectiveness as a cure□

Myron c500–440BC. Greek sculptor. His *Discus-Thrower* and *Marsyas*, described by ancient critics, are known through Roman copies□

myrrh Afro-Asian tree *Commifera myrrha* which produces an aromatic resin, used in perfumes, etc.□

myrtle evergreen shrubs, family Myrtaceae; ***common Mediterranean myrtle*** *M communis* has fragrant oval leaves, white flowers, and purple berries□

Mysore industrial city (engineering, silk) in Karnataka◊, India; population 476 000□

mystery religions cults open only to the initiated, e.g. those of Demeter (see Eleusis◊), Dionysus◊, Cybele, Isis◊, Mithraism◊. Underlying them is a primitive fertility ritual, in which a deity undergoes death and resurrection, and initiates feed on the flesh and blood to attain communion with the divine and ensure their own life beyond the grave. Their influence on early Christianity was considerable□

mysticism belief based on personal spiritual experience, not necessarily involving an orthodox deity, though found in all the major religions. It is more prevalent at times of crisis. Christian mystics include Julian of Norwich, Thomas à Kempis, Jacob Boehme, St Teresa, St John of the Cross, William Law, William Blake. See also Neoplatonism◊. Secular mystics include W B Yeats and Aldous Huxley□

mythology stories of gods and other supernatural beings, with whom human beings may have relationships, devised to explain the operation of the universe and human history. Great mythologies, with the names of the chief gods of each, include those of Egypt (Osiris◊), Greece (Zeus◊), Rome (Jupiter◊), India (Hinduism◊, Brahma◊), and the Teutonic peoples (Odin◊/Woden)□

myxoedema underactivity of the thyroid gland. See under hypothyroidism◊□

N

NAAFI non-profit-making association (*N*avy, *A*rmy, and *A*ir *F*orce *I*nstitutes) providing canteens for HM Forces; headquarters, Claygate, Surrey□

Nablus town on the West Bank of the River Jordan; population 50 000. As Shechem, it was the ancient capital of Samaria◊ (see also Samaritans◊), and according to tradition Joseph◊ is buried here. Allenby's defeat of the Turks here in 1918 completed the conquest of Palestine. ***Upper Nablus City*** is an Israeli settlement; population 50 000□

Nabokov Vladimir 1899–1977. Russo-American author and US citizen from 1945. He was professor of Russian literature, and a lepidopterist. His most famous book was *Lolita* 1958, which added the word 'nymphet' to the language□

Nacala seaport in Mozambique□

Nader Ralph 1934– . American lawyer. The 'scourge of corporate morality', he has led many major consumer campaigns. His book *Unsafe at Any Speed* 1965 led to car safety legislation□

nadir the point of the sky that is vertically below the observer. See under zenith◊□

naevus birthmark◊, usually a mass of small blood vessels. Smooth naevi can be successfully removed by argon laser treatment□

Nagaland state of north eastern India
area 16 527 sq km/6379 sq mi
capital Kohima
features forests with tiger and elephant
population 773 280, chiefly independent Naga peoples
language Naga dialects
religion Christianity
history occupied by British in 1826 to protect British interests in India against neighbouring Burma. Naga peoples continued to resist Indian rule until 1975□

nagana animal sleeping sickness. See tsetse◊□

Nagasaki seaport on Kyushu, Japan; population 442 000. It was destroyed by an atom bomb on 9 Aug 1945, the second Japanese city after Hiroshima to meet this fate in World War II. Of its population of 212 000, 73 884 were killed, 76 796 injured□

Nagoya industrial port, 'the Detroit of Japan', on Honshu, Japan; population 2 081 000. There is a Shogun fortress (1610) and a famous Shinto shrine, Atsuta Jingu□

Nagpur city in Maharashtra, India; population 866 150. Known for silk and cotton textiles and metallurgical industries□

Nagy Imre 1896–1958. Hungarian executed for leading a revolt against Soviet domination in 1956□

Nahum 7th century BC. An Old Testament Hebrew prophet. He forecast the destruction of Nineveh◊□

naiad water-nymph in Greek mythology□

nail horny modification of the outer layer of the skin of the fingers and toes of most primates, related to the claws and hooves of animals. They grow from a bed, or matrix, in the lower germinal layer of the skin□

Naipaul V(idiadhar) S(urajprasad) 1932– . British novelist, born in Trinidad of Hindu parents. His books include *A House for Mr Biswas* 1961 and *A Bend in the River* 1979. His brother ***Shiva(dhar) Naipaul*** 1940–85 was also a novelist (*Fireflies* 1970) and journalist□

Nairobi capital of Kenya; population 700 000. Founded in 1899, it lies at 1660 m/5450 ft. It is the headquarters of the United Nations Environment Programme (UNEP); the International Louis Leakey◊ Institute for African Prehistory was established in 1977, and the International Primate Research Institute (IPR), concerned with the breeding of laboratory animals, etc., is nearby□

Nakasone Yasuhiro 1918– . Japanese Liberal Democratic statesman, who succeeded Suzuki◊ as Prime Minister in 1982. Though embarrassed by the conviction in the Lockheed corruption scandal of 1983 of one of his supporters, former Prime Minister Tanaka, Wakasone was re-elected in 1983. He favours increasing Japan's defence capability□

Nakhodka Pacific port in USSR; US-caught pollock is processed by Soviet factory ships in a joint venture□

Namaqualand or ***Namaland*** desert area N and S of the Orange river, part in S Africa and part in Namibia, where the Hottentot Namas or Namaquas live. Copper and diamonds are mined□

Namatjira Albert 1902–59. Australian aboriginal artist. Acclaimed for his watercolour landscapes after a Melbourne exhibition in 1938□

Namib Desert see under Namibia◊□

Namibia (South West Africa)

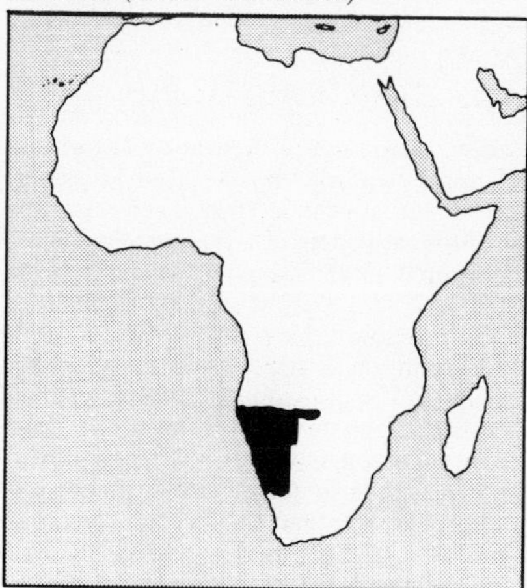

area 823 167 sq km/317 825 sq mi

capital Windhoek

towns ports Lüderitz, Walvis Bay◊

features Namib Desert c100 km/60 mi wide on the coast; mountainous central plateau; part of Kalahari Desert; economy completely interlocked with, and dependent upon S Africa

exports karakul lamb pelts; diamonds, vanadium, tin, copper

currency South African rand

population 1 040 000; 51% Ovambo; the remainder including the pastoral Hereros, the Nama, and Bushmen◊, as well as 75 600 Whites

language Afrikaans, English and indigenous languages

religion Christianity and native religions

government a 'transitional government of national unity' was introduced in 1985: S African-appointed administrator general, ministers' council and legislative assembly, but SWAPO◊ (recognized by the United Nations as the sole representative of the people) rejected the new government outright

recent history annexed by Germany in 1884, it was occupied in World War I by South African forces under L Botha◊, and was mandated to South Africa in 1920. South Africa did not accept the termination of the mandate by the United Nations in 1966, though accepting the principle of ultimate independence in 1976; in 1968 the United Nations renamed the territory Namibia. South Africa supports the Democratic Turnhalle Alliance (DTA), but there is a strong guerrilla movement, the South West Africa People's Organization (SWAPO) led by Sam Nujoma◊□

Namur (Flemish *Naeman)* industrial city in S Belgium; population 100 700. Famous for cutlery□

Nanaimo coal-mining centre of British Columbia, Canada; population 40 400□

Nana Sahib name by which Dandhu Panth 1820–c1859 was commonly known. A leader in the Indian Mutiny (see Kanpur◊), he fled to Nepál□

Nancecuke site in N Cornwall of a secret Ministry of Defence Establishment, a branch of the Chemical Defence Establishment at Porton◊ Down, until 1978. It was closed when Britain divested itself of chemical and biological weapons□

Nanchang industrial city, capital of Jiangxi◊ province, China; population 875 000. The first Communist rising 1 Aug 1927 was here□

Nancy capital of Lorraine◊, France; population 111 500. There are fine 18th-century buildings□

Nanda Devi see under Uttar◊ Pradesh□

Nanga Parbat see Azad Kashmir◊□

Nanjing capital (formerly Nanking) and industrial city of Jiangsu◊ province, China; population 3 000 000. Dating from the 2nd century, it received the name Nanjing (southern capital) under the Ming dynasty, and was the capital of China 1368–1403, 1928–37, 1946–9. Sun Yat-sen◊ is buried on Purple Mountain nearby, where there is an observatory with replicas of ancient instruments; Jiangsu Provincial Museum includes the famous royal burial suits made of linked jade plaques. The bridge (1968) over the Chang Jiang is the longest in China, 6705 m/ 22 000 ft□

Nanking see Nanjing◊□

Nanning industrial river port, capital of Guangxi Zhuang autonomous region, China; population 575 000□

nano SI unit of measurement; one thousand millionth part (10^{-9}), e.g. nanosecond□

Nansen Fridtjof 1861–1930. Norwegian explorer. In 1893 his ship the *Fram* was allowed to drift with an icefloe in the Arctic and then, continuing N on foot, he and Johansen reached 86° 14′N, the highest latitude then attained. In 1923 he received a Nobel peace prize for his work as League of Nations High Commissioner for refugees, and there is a Nansen Institute (for social research) in Oslo, 1956□

Nanshan Islands see under Spratly◊ Islands□

Nantes port in W France on the Loire, capital of Pays de la Loire; population 263 700□

Nantes Edict of. Edict by which Henry IV granted religious freedom to the Huguenots◊ in 1598□

Nantucket island and pleasure resort, formerly a whaling port, Massachusetts, USA□

napalm fuel used in flame-throwers and incendiary bombs. Produced from jellied petrol, it is named from ***nap***hthenic and ***palm***itic acids. It was first widely used in the Vietnam◊ War by the Americans□

naphtha a mixture of hydrocarbons obtained by destructive distillation of petroleum, coal-tar and shale oil, used chiefly as a solvent□

naphthalene a solid, aromatic hydrocarbon, $C_{10}H_8$, obtained from coal-tar. A white, shiny, crystalline solid with a smell of moth balls, it is used in making indigo and certain azo-dyes; also as a mild disinfectant and insecticide□

Napier Sir Charles James 1782–1853. British general. He conquered Sind◊ in India 1841–3 with a very small force and governed it till 1847. He was the first commander to mention men from the ranks in his despatches□

Napier John 1550–1617. Scottish mathematician, inventor of logarithms in 1614, and of 'N.'s Bones', an early calculating device for multiplication and division□

Napier wool port of North Island, New Zealand; population (with Hastings) 110 600□

Napier of Magdala, Robert Cornelis Napier, 1st Baron Napier 1810–90. British field marshal. Knighted for his services at Lucknow◊, and thanked by parliament for his part in the Chinese War of 1855, he stormed Magdala in the Abyssinian campaign of 1868, and was created a peer□

Naples (Italian *Napoli*) port and industrial city (cars, textiles, food processing), capital of Campania, Italy; population 1 212 400. Capital of the kingdom of Naples 1282–1860 (see Sir William Hamilton◊), it has the royal palace, San Carlo Opera House, a marine aquarium, a museum housing finds from nearby Pompeii◊, and the university (1224) is one of the world's oldest. Capri◊ is to the S□

Napoleon I Napoleon Bonaparte, 1769–1821. Emperor of the French, born at Ajaccio, Corsica. Given command against the Austrians (see Revolutionary◊ Wars) in Italy, he defeated them at Lodi, Arcole, and Rivoli in 1796–7. Egypt – seen as a halfway house to India – was overrun, and Syria invaded, but his fleet was destroyed by Nelson◊, at the Battle of the Nile. He returned to France to overthrow the government of the Directory, and establish his own dictatorship, nominally as First Consul. The Austrians were again defeated at Marengo in 1800, and the coalition against France shattered, a truce being declared in 1802. A plebiscite the same year made him consul for life.

In 1804 a plebiscite made him Emperor. War was renewed by Britain in 1803, aided by Austria and Russia from 1805, and Prussia from 1806 (see Napoleonic◊ Wars). Prevented by the Navy from invading England, he drove Austria out of the war by victories at Ulm and Austerlitz in 1805, and Prussia by the victory at Jena in 1806. Then, after the hard-fought battles of Eylau and Friedland, he formed an alliance with the tsar at Tilsit (1807).

Napoleon now forbade entry of British goods to Europe, under the 'Continental System', occupied Portugal and in 1808 placed his brother Joseph on the Spanish throne. Both countries revolted, with British aid, and Austria attempted to reenter the war, but was defeated at Wagram. In 1796 Napoleon had married Josephine◊ de Beauharnais, but now divorced her to marry the Emperor's daughter, Marie Louise◊. When Russia failed to enforce the Continental System, Napoleon occupied Moscow◊, but his retreat in the bitter winter of 1812 encouraged Prussia and Austria to declare war again in 1813, and Napoleon was defeated at Leipzig and driven from Germany. After a brilliant campaign on French soil, he abdicated in 1814, and was banished to Elba.

In Mar 1815 he reassumed power, but was defeated by the Allies at Waterloo◊. Surrendering to the British, he again abdicated, and was exiled to St Helena. His body was brought back in 1840 for interment in the Hôtel des Invalides. For his family, see Bonaparte◊□

Napoleon II 1811–32. Title given by the Bonapartists to the son of Napoleon I◊ and Marie Louise◊. Until 1814, when he was taken to the Austrian court, he was known as the king of Rome, and after 1818 as the Duke of Reichstadt. Hitler had his body removed from Vienna in 1940 and interred at the Invalides□

Napoleon III 1808–73. Emperor of the French. Son of Louis Bonaparte and Hortense de Beauharnais, brother and step-daughter respectively of Napoleon I, he led two unsuccessful revolts (Strasbourg 1836, Boulogne 1840). Imprisoned, he escaped to London in 1846, was elected president of the republic in Dec 1848, and in 1852 proclaimed emperor. To strengthen his repressive regime, he joined in the Crimean War, fought Austria 1859 (winning the battle of Solferino

near Lake Garda) and attempted to found a vassal empire in Mexico in 1863–7. In 1870 he was manoeuvred into war with Prussia, surrendered at Sedan, and went into exile in England.
He married Eugénie◊: their son ***Eugène Louis Jean Joseph Napoleon*** 1856–79, created Prince Imperial, was killed fighting with the British Army against the Zulus□

Napoleonic Wars 1803–1815 a series of wars which followed the Revolutionary◊ Wars.
1803 British renewed the war, following an appeal from the Maltese against Napoleon's seizure of the island
1805 Napoleon's planned invasion of Britain from Boulogne ended by Nelson's victory at Trafalgar; coalition formed by Britain, Austria, Russia, Sweden. Austria defeated at Ulm; Austria and Russia at Austerlitz
1806 Prussia, latest member of the coalition, defeated at Jena; Napoleon instituted an attempted blockade, the Continental System, to isolate Britain from Europe
1807 Russia defeated at Eylau and Friedland and on making peace with Napoleon under the Treaty of Tilsit changed sides, agreeing to attack Sweden, and was forced to retreat
1808 Napoleon's invasion of Portugal, and habit of installing his relatives as puppet kings, led to his defeat in the Peninsular◊ War
1809 revived Austrian opposition to Napoleon was ended by defeat at Wagram
1812 the Continental System finally collapsed on its rejection by Russia, and Napoleon made the fatal decision to invade her; he reached Moscow but was defeated by the Russian resistance, and by the bitter winter as he retreated through a countryside laid waste by the retreating Russians (380 000 French soldiers died)
1813 Britain, Prussia, Russia, Austria and Sweden formed a new coalition, defeated Napoleon at the Battle of the Nations and he abdicated and was exiled to Elba
1814 Louis XVIII became king of France, and the Congress of Vienna met to conclude peace
1815 Napoleon returned to Paris. 16 Jun Wellington defeated Ney at Quatre Bras (in Belgium, SE of Brussels), and after a Hundred Days Napoleon was finally defeated at Waterloo S of Brussels, 18 Jun. Wellington had 68 000 troops (24 000 British, the rest German, Dutch and Belgian) and Napoleon 72 000; in the last stage Wellington was supported by the Prussians under Blücher. The Congress resumed with Napoleon more securely incarcerated at St Helena□

Napoli see Naples◊□

Nara capital of Japan 710–94AD; population 191 600. Japanese art and literature originated here□

Narbonne city in S France; population 40 540. In Roman times an important port□

narcissism in psychology, an excess of conceit which amounts to insanity□

Narcissus in Greek mythology, a beautiful youth who rejected the love of the nymph Echo◊. Condemned to fall in love with his own reflection, he pined away□

narcissus a type of daffodil◊□

narcotic pain-relieving and sleep-inducing drug, e.g. opium and its derivatives, either synthetic or natural (morphine, heroin, etc.); the alcohols (ethyl alcohol, etc.); and the barbiturates (veronal, luminal, evipan, etc.) □

Narragansett Bay Atlantic inlet, Rhode Island, USA, which includes many islands□

Narvik seaport in Norway exporting Swedish iron ore; population 14 000. It was seized by the Germans in 1940, and briefly retaken by the Allies 10 May–9 Jun□

narwhal Arctic whale *Monodon monoceros* of which the male has a single spirally-fluted tusk, which grows to about 2 m/6 ft□

NASA *N*ational *A*eronautics and *S*pace *A*dministration. US government agency founded in 1958 to coordinate non-military US space flight and research□

Naseby Battle of 1645. See under Civil◊ War□

Nash John 1752–1835. British architect, who designed Regent's Park and its terraces, Regent Street (later rebuilt), and Marble Arch, intended as the entrance gate to Buckingham Palace□

Nash John Northcote 1893–1977. British landscape artist and engraver, brother of Paul Nash◊□

Nash Ogden 1902–71. American humorous poet, whose doggerel volumes include *Hard Lines* 1931 and *The Face is Familiar* 1941□

Nash Paul 1889–1946. British artist, noted for his interpretation of scenes of World Wars I and II, e.g. *Totes Meer* and *The Battle of Britain*. See John Northcote Nash◊□

Nash Richard 1674–1762. British dandy, 'Beau Nash'. As master of ceremonies at Bath from 1705, he set the tone of fashionable manners□

Nash Sir Walter 1882–1968. New Zealand Labour statesman, who was Prime Minister 1957–60□

Nashe Thomas 1567–1601. English playwright, author of pamphlets, the play *Summer's Last Will and Testament* 1592, and the first English picaresque novel *The Life of Jack Wilton* 1594□

Nashville capital and river port of Tennessee, USA (commercial and banking centre, with printing, music publishing and recording – half of all US singles are recorded here); population, with Davidson, 440 000. Cotton, tobacco, wheat and livestock are traded. The Confederate army was defeated here 1864: see Civil◊ War. It is the centre of American country and western music□

Nasmyth Alexander 1758–1840. Scottish landscape and portrait painter. He painted Robert Burns□

Nassau capital and port of the Bahamas, on New Providence Island; population 138 500□

Nasser Gamal Abdel 1918–70. Egyptian statesman. The driving power behind the Neguib coup in 1952 which ended the monarchy, he was Prime Minister in 1954–6 and president from 1956. He nationalized the Suez◊ Canal□

nasturtium genus of plants, family Cruciferae◊, including ***watercress*** *N officinale*, a perennial aquatic plant of Europe and Asia, grown as a salad crop. The garden nasturtiums, genus *Tropaeolum,* are native to S America□

Natal province of the Republic of S Africa
area 86 965 sq km/33 578 sq mi
capital Pietermaritzburg
towns chief port Durban
features Drakensberg
products sugar, fruit, vegetables, tobacco, coal
population 2 676 350, including 1 358 100 Black; 665 350 Asian; 561 860 White; 91 000 Coloured
recent history annexed to Cape Colony in 1844, it became a separate colony in 1856, and incorporated Zululand in 1897, and parts of the Transvaal in 1903. It was an original province of the Union in 1910□

Natchez North American Indians of the Mississippi region, with a complex caste system headed by a ruler priest (the 'Great Sun') unusual in N America. They were almost wiped out by the French in 1731, a few surviving in Oklahoma. See mound-builders◊□

Natchez picturesque river port in Mississippi, USA, important in steamboat days; population 20 000□

national anthem patriotic song for official occasions, such as 'God Save the King/Queen'; within the Commonwealth, some members retain this as the 'royal anthem', while normally using their own national anthem, e.g. Australia ('Advance Australia Fair' 1974–76 and from 1984), and Canada ('O Canada' 1980). The anthem of united Europe is Schiller's 'Ode to Joy', set by Beethoven in his Ninth Symphony. See also Deutschland über Alles, Internationale, Marseillaise, Star-spangled Banner□

National Army Museum museum (1960) in Chelsea, London, for the period 1485–1914 (see Imperial War Museum◊)□

National Book League British Association of all those concerned with books; originally the National Book Council (1925: renamed in 1940); headquarters Book House, Wandsworth□

National Country Party see National◊ Party□

national debt the total amount of money borrowed by the central government of a country, on which it pays interest. In Britain the national debt is managed by the Bank◊ of England, under the control of the Treasury□

National Front extreme right-wing political party in Britain, formed by a merger of existing groups in 1967. Some of its members had links with the former National Socialist Movement. Thought to influence some Conservative MPs□

National Gallery London gallery housing the British national collection (founded 1824) of pictures by artists no longer living. The present building in Trafalgar Square (1838) was designed by William Wilkins 1778–1839□

National Guard a militia force recruited by each state of the US. See militia◊□

National Heritage Memorial Fund British government fund (1980) to save the countryside, historic houses and works of art, as a memorial to those who gave their lives in World War II□

national income the total income of a state over a given period, usually a year, comprising both the wages of individuals and the profits of companies. It is equal to the value of the output of all goods and services during the same period. National income is equal to Gross◊ National Product minus an allowance for replacement of aging capital stock□

nationalism any movement aimed at strengthening national feeling, especially when aimed at unification of a nation or its liberation from foreign rule. Stimulated by the French Revolution, such movements were widespread in Europe in the 19th century, and subsequently became potent in Asia and Africa. Imperialism◊ and fascism◊ also have a nationalistic base□

nationalization policy of bringing essential services and industries under public i.e. government ownership (as pursued in the UK especially under the Labour Government 1945–51), and also taking over assets in the hands of foreign governments or companies, especially in newly emergent countries, e.g. Abadan◊, Suez◊ Canal. See also privatization◊□

National Nature Reserve area for the preservation (from 1949) of scenic formation or vegetation, and often as the habitat of rare birds or animals; Nature Conservancy Council headquarters, Belgrave Square, London□

National Park area in England and Wales conserved for public enjoyment under the National Parks Act 1949

England Dartmoor, Exmoor, Lake District, North Yorkshire Moors, Yorkshire Dales, Northumberland, Peak District ***Wales*** Brecon Beacons, Pembrokeshire coast, Snowdonia

See also National◊ Nature Reserve, wilderness◊ area□

National Party Australian political party (founded c1860), formerly known as the National Country Party; leader Ian Sinclair (1929-) from 1983□

National Physical Laboratory research establishment (founded 1900) at Teddington, England, under the Department of Industry□

National Portrait Gallery London gallery (founded 1856) of individual likenesses (paintings, busts, photographs, etc.) of distinguished Britons of the past.□

National Research Development Corporation UK corporation exploiting (from 1967) inventions derived from public or private sources, usually jointly with industrial firms□

National Security Adviser office created by Eisenhower◊ in 1953. With the appointment of Kissinger◊ 1969–75, it rivalled that of Secretary of State, an office itself taken over by Kissinger 1973–7. Brzezinski, appointed in 1977, exceeded the Secretary of State Vance in his influence on Carter◊, and Vance resigned 1980□

National Security Agency agency (NSA, the 'Puzzle Palace') handling US security communications worldwide; headquarters Fort Meade, Maryland (with a major facility at Menwith Hill, England)□

National Socialism see Germany◊, Hitler◊□

National Theatre British national theatre company established in 1963, and the theatre complex to house it on London's South Bank opened in 1975. See Sir Peter Hall◊. The ***National Theatre of Comedy*** was established in 1983 at the Shaftesbury Theatre, London (artistic director Ray Cooney). See also Comédie Française◊□

National Trust British trust founded in 1895 (in Scotland, 1931) for the preservation of land and buildings of historic interest or beauty, the largest 'landowner' in Britain. Each of the Australian states has its own National Trust organization□

nativity a Christian festival celebrating a birth: 1 ***Christmas*** celebrated 25 Dec from 336AD; 2 ***Nativity of the Virgin Mary*** celebrated by the Catholic and Greek Churches 8 Sept; 3 ***Nativity of John the Baptist*** celebrated by the Catholic, Greek and Anglican Churches 24 Jun□

NATO see North◊ Atlantic Treaty Organization□

natural gas see gas◊□

Natural History Museum natural history departments of the British Museum at S Kensington, housed in the building 1873–80 designed by Waterhouse□

Naukratis Nile delta city of Greek traders in ancient Egypt, rediscovered by Petrie◊ in 1884□

Nauru Republic of

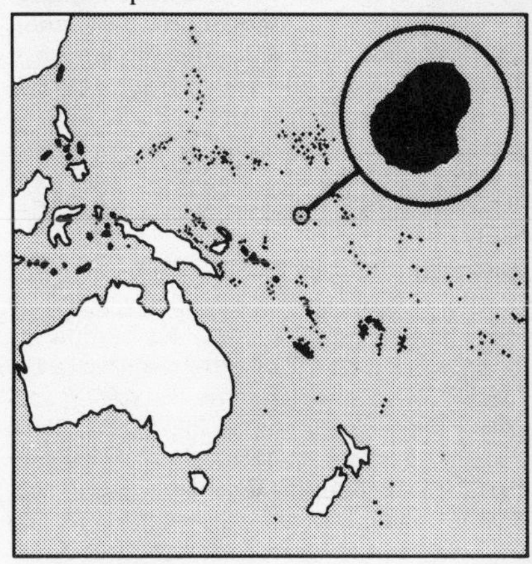

area 21 sq km/8 sq mi
products phosphates
currency pound sterling
population 7500, mainly Polynesian
language Nauruan, English
religion Protestantism 45%
government head chief and executive president (Hammer DeRoburt 1968–1976, and from 1978) and parliament of 18 members
recent history first European knowledge of island by Britain in 1798; it was annexed by Germany in 1888, and administered (by Australia, New Zealand, UK) under League of Nations Mandate from 1920, except for Japanese occupation 1942–45, until independence in 1968. On independence Nauru remained in a special relation with the Commonwealth. Approaches have been made to the Philippines for transfer of the population to an island there when the

phosphate deposits are exhausted c1990□

Nausicaa in Greek literature (the Odyssey◊) a daughter of Alcinous, king of Phaeacia, who welcomed Odysseus when he was washed up on her island□

nautilus a mollusc. See cephalopod◊□

Navajo North American Indian people, related to the Apache◊. Exiled after their defeat by Kit Carson◊ in 1864, they have the largest reservation in the USA (65 000 sq km/ 25 000 sq mi), mostly in Arizona. They have an income from uranium, tourism, and crafts; see also sand◊ painting□

Navarino Battle of. See Pylos◊□

Navarre mountainous autonomous region (*Navarra*) of N Spain (including Pamplona); population 507 400. It has the right to join the Basque◊ autonomous region if a referendum should so decide□

Navarre Kingdom of. Former kingdom comprising the Spanish province of Navarre and part of the French department of Basses–Pyrénées. It resisted the Moorish◊ conquest, and was independent until it became first French in 1284, and then was split between France and Spain in 1479□

navel round scar (umbilicus) on the human abdomen where the umbilical cord was attached during gestation until severed after birth□

navigation the means of determining the position, course and distance travelled by a ship, plane, spacecraft, etc. Navigation for ships and aircraft will be revolutionized by the US Department of Defense Navstar, space-based beacons known as the Global Positioning System (GPS), in preparation. Eighteen satellites (in six 12-hour orbits) will enable users (including motorists and walkers) of the appropriate code to triangulate their position (by signals from any three) to within 15 m/45ft□

Navigation Acts a series of acts passed from 1381 to protect English shipping from foreign competition. They were repealed in 1849□

navy a nation's ships of war. The first permanent naval organization was established by Rome in 311BC to safeguard her trade routes from pirates and eliminate the threat of rival sea power. The British navy stems from that organized by Alfred the Great to defeat the Norsemen in 878; Henry VIII built on the beginnings made by Henry VII, and raised a force with a number of true battleships (see *Mary◊ Rose*), as well as instituting the administrative machinery of the Admiralty. Later Cromwell had a very powerful fleet; in Charles II's reign Pepys was a very efficient secretary to the Admiralty; and in the 18th century Pitt◊ reorganized the navy so well that under Nelson at Trafalgar it ensured British supremacy at sea for the rest of the 19th century. Although Britain fended off the German challenge in World War I, the US navy (originating from the need to protect American harbours at the outbreak of the War of Independence) rapidly expanded in the years before World War II (to cope with the threat from both Germany and Japan), and after the war was the world's most powerful. The demonstration of Russia's impotence at sea in the Cuban missile crisis (see Cuba◊) led to a development of Soviet naval strength under Admiral Sergei Gorshkov 1910– .

In any future major war nuclear-propelled and nuclear-armed submarines are considered the prime means of combat. The UK has a force of small carriers, destroyers and frigates. This force was reprieved from defence budget cuts after its use in the Falklands◊ War. The largest surface warships of the superpowers are still aircraft carriers, e.g. the US *Carl Vinson* 1982, 81 600 tonnes, and the USSR has at least one large carrier under construction, while the *Leonid Brezhnev* and *Kirov* battle cruisers are the largest combatant warships of any other type to be built since World War II□

Naxalites Indian extremist Communist movement (founded by Charu Mazumdar 1915–72), named from Naxalbari, W Bengal site of a peasant rising 1967□

Naxos Greek Island, largest of the Cyclades. Famous for wine, it was a centre of Bacchus worship; see Ariadne◊□

Nazareth town in N Israel. In the New Testament, given as the boyhood home of Jesus; population 30 000□

Nazarite a Hebrew pledged not to infringe certain rules until a vow was fulfilled, e.g. not to cut his hair (see Samson◊)□

Nazca town S of Lima, Peru. Linear markings on the nearby plateau made by Indians in the 6th century apparently lead to sacred places, and there are also giant animal outlines. First seen by Europeans in 1927, and only properly seen from the air, they may have been viewed from hot air balloons□

Naze The. See under Essex◊□

Nazi Party German Fascists, named from the German pronunciation of the first two syllables of the full name: ***Nati**onal* Socialist German Workers' Party (see Fascism◊ and Hitler◊). Related movements were founded in Britain (see Sir Oswald Mosley◊ and National◊ Front) and elsewhere. Opponents of the Nazis were dealt with by the ***Sturmabteilung*** (SA, 'stormtroops' or Brownshirts, established in 1921): see Röhm◊. The elite

Schutz-Staffel (SS, 'protective squadron' or Blackshirts) began as a Hitlerian bodyguard in 1921 and was organized under Himmler◊ from 1928. Some 500 000 strong, it included both full-time ***Waffen-SS*** ('armed' SS) who were elite combat troops, and spare-time members: it carried out 'police' duties, the persecution of the Jews, and the brutalities of the concentration camps; it was condemned at Nuremberg in 1946□

N'djaména capital (formerly called Fort Lamy) of Chad; population 241 650□

Neagh Lough. Lake in N Ireland, largest in the British Isles; area 396 sq km/153 sq mi□

Neagle Dame Anna 1908–86. British actress, born in East London, whose films include *Nell Gwynn* 1934, *Victoria the Great* 1937, and *Odette* 1950. DBE 1969□

Neale John Mason 1818–66. Anglican cleric whose translations of ancient and medieval hymns include 'Jerusalem, the Golden'□

Neanderthal man hominid of the Palaeolithic period originating 100 000 years ago (named from a skeleton found in the Neanderthal valley in the Rhineland in 1857). Extinct from 30 000 years ago, they were replaced throughout Europe by modern *Homo sapiens*□

neap tide the small tide◊ at the first or last quarter of the moon□

Near East before World War II the Balkan states, Egypt and SW Asia, now known as the Middle East◊□

Neath town in W Glamorgan, Wales; population 28 000□

Nebraska prairie state of the USA; the Cornhusker State

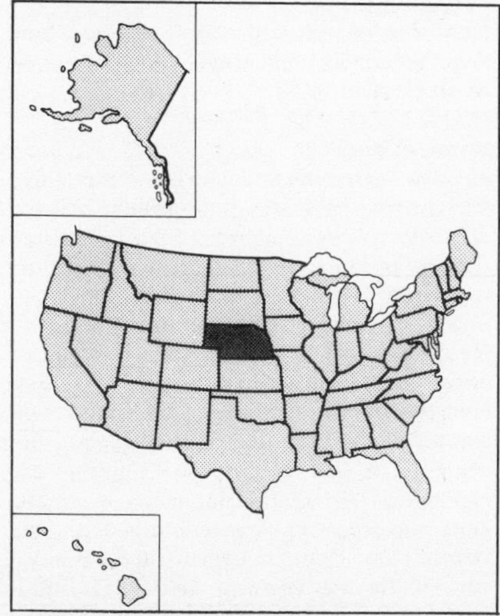

area 200 036 sq km/77 227 sq mi
capital Lincoln
towns Omaha
features Rocky Mountain foothills; tributaries of the Missouri; Boys Town, founded for the homeless by Father Flanagan, near Omaha; the ranch of Buffalo Bill, now a State Historical Park
products cereals, livestock, processed foods; fertilizers, oil, natural gas
population 1 538 788
famous people Fred Astaire, Willa Cather, Henry Fonda, Gerald Ford, Harold Lloyd, Malcolm X
recent history part of the Louisiana◊ Purchase in 1803, it became a state in 1867□

Nebuchadnezzar or ***Nebuchadrezzar*** d. 562BC. King of Babylonia◊. Shortly before his accession in 604BC he defeated the Egyptians at Carchemish and brought Palestine and Syria into his empire. Judah revolted, with Egyptian assistance, in 596 and 587–586BC; on each occasion he captured Jerusalem and carried many Jews into captivity. He largely rebuilt Babylon◊, and constructed the Hanging Gardens□

nebula a galaxy. See nebula and planetary nebula under star◊□

Necker Jacques 1732–1804. French statesman. Finance Minister 1776–81, he attempted reforms, and was dismissed through Marie◊ Antoinette's influence. Recalled in 1788, he persuaded Louis XVI to summon the States◊-General, which earned him the hatred of the court, and in Jul 1789 he was banished. The storming of the Bastille forced his reinstatement, but in Sept 1790 he resigned. See Mme de Stael◊□

nectar in Greek mythology, the drink of the gods□

nectar sugary solution produced in certain flowers to attract insect pollinators□

nectarine a type of peach◊□

needlefish long thin-bodied fish of the garfish◊ type with needle teeth□

Needles The. See under Isle of Wight◊□

Nefertiti or *Nofretète* wife of Iknaton◊, pharoah of Egypt□

Negev desert in S Israel which tapers to the port of Eilat. It is fertile under irrigation and minerals include oil and copper□

Negri Sembilan state of Malaysia; population 564 000. Capital Seremban□

Negro a member of the mainly African branch of the black race of mankind. See under race◊□

Nehemiah 5th century BC. Jewish governor of Judaea under Persian rule, who rebuilt Jerusalem's walls, and made religious and social reforms, as recorded in the Old Testament book of Nehemiah□

Nehru Jawaharlal 1889–1964. Indian statesman. Born at Allahabad, and educated at Harrow and Cambridge, he led the Socialist left wing of the Congress Party, and was second only in influence to Gandhi. Nine times imprisoned 1921–45 for his political activities. He was Prime Minister from the creation of the Dominion (later Republic) of India in Aug 1947, and originated the theory of non-alignment. See Indira Gandhi◊□

Nei Menggu see Inner Mongolia◊□

Neisse tributary of the river Oder◊ in E Europe, 225 km/140 mi long□

Neizvestny Ernst 1926– . Russian artist and sculptor, who found fame when he had an argument with Khrushchev 1962, and eventually left the country 1976. His works include a vast relief in the Moscow Institute of Electronics, and the Aswan monument, the tallest sculpture in the world□

Nejd desert region of Saudi Arabia. Inhabited by Bedouin, it includes Riyadh□

Nekrasov Nikolai Alekseevich 1821–77. Russian poet, who supported the freeing of the serfs and was politically influential□

Nelson Horatio, Viscount 1758–1805. British admiral. Born at Burnham Thorpe, Norfolk, son of the rector, he entered the navy in 1770. On service in the Mediterranean 1793–1800, he lost the sight of his right eye in 1794 and his right arm in 1797. He played a major part in the victory at Cape St Vincent in 1797, and in 1798 he almost entirely destroyed the French fleet in the Battle of the Nile. He then helped to crush a democratic uprising at Naples, where he fell in love with Lady Hamilton◊, and in 1800 separated from his wife. Although nominally second-in-command, he was responsible for the victory of Copenhagen in 1801 (the occasion on which he put his telescope to his blind eye when signalled to break off action). In 1803 he received the Mediterranean command, and for nearly two years blockaded Toulon. When in 1805 Villeneuve eluded him, Nelson pursued him to the W Indies and back, and on 21 Oct totally defeated the combined French and Spanish fleets off Cape Trafalgar, 20 of the enemy ships being captured. Nelson himself was mortally wounded; his body was brought to England, and buried in St Paul's. His signal before Trafalgar was: 'England expects that every man will do his duty'□

Nelson industrial town in Lancasire, England; population 31 400□

Nelson town in South Island, New Zealand; population 42 300. There is a farm research centre□

nematoda a phylum of worms◊□

nemertea a phylum of marine worms◊□

Nemery Jaafar Mohammed al- 1930– . Sudanese president 1971–85, after leading the military coup of 1969. He fuelled guerrilla opposition by imposing Islamic (Sharia) law on the Christians and Animists of the South, and unrest in the North when he backtracked, and was deposed□

Nemesis in Greek mythology, the goddess of retribution, especially punishing hubris (Greek *hybris*), arrogant self-confidence□

Nemi volcanic crater lake SE of Rome, with ruins of a temple of Diana. Two of Caligula◊'s pleasure barges, raised from the lake in 1930–31, were burned by the Germans in 1944□

Nemon Oscar 1906–85. Yugoslav portrait sculptor, of e.g. Churchill, Macmillan, Eisenhower, Thatcher□

Nennius c796. Welsh author of a *History of Britain* which includes the earliest reference to King Arthur◊'s wars against the Saxons◊□

Neoclassicism revival of the classical style of art c1750–1850, following the excavation of Pompeii and Herculaneum, e.g. by (sculpture) Canova, Thorvaldsen, (painting) David, Ingres, (architecture) Robert Adam, (art) Flaxman□

neodymium element
symbol Nd
atomic number 60
physical description yellowish metal
features member of the lanthanide series
uses in colouring glass□

Neo-Impressionism a late 19th-century French art movement characterized by the use of pure colours, without mixing. Artists include Seurat◊ and Pissarro◊. See Pointillism◊□

Neolithic of the last period of the Stone Age. See under prehistory◊□

neon element
symbol Ne
atomic number 10
physical description colourless, inert gas present in 18 parts per million in the atmosphere
features produces a red glow when conducting electricity in a discharge tube
uses in advertising signs, and in lasers◊□

Neoplasticism a 20th century Dutch art movement. See Mondrian◊

Neo-platonism blending of Oriental religious beliefs and the doctrines of Plato◊, developed in 3rd century Alexandria and expounded by Plotinus◊. Unity with the deity was achieved by ascetic practices. The system almost ousted Christianity when advocated by the emperor Julian◊. It influenced Augustine◊ and all Christian mysticism◊, and enjoyed a revival during the Italian Renaissance in the writings of Marsilio Ficino◊, Pico◊ della Mirandola and others□

NEP See New◊ Economic Policy□

Nepál

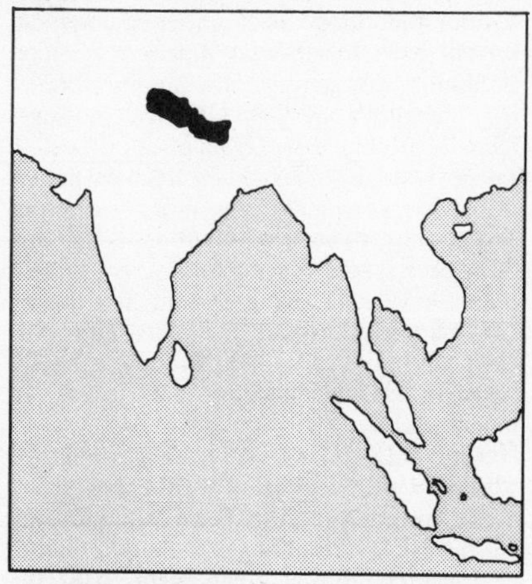

area 141 400 sq km/54 600 sq mi
capital Káthmándu
features Mt Everest, Mt Kanchenjunga
exports jute, rice, timber
currency Nepalese rupee
population 420 000, mainly known by the name of the predominant clan, the Gurkhas◊; the Sherpas, are a Buddhist minority of NE Nepál.
language Nepáli
religion Hinduism, with Buddhist minority
famous people Gautama Buddha
government constitutional monarch, King Birendra (1946–) from 1972, who still appoints a number of members to the non-party national parliament (panchayat) elected indirectly by a rising succession of village/town, district, and zone panchayats, by universal suffrage
recent history a hereditary Prime Minister of the Rana family held effective power 1846–1950, when a revolution restored power to the King, who still exercises executive power. A referendum in 1980 rejected a return to a multi-party system, but the Prime Minister is elected by the parliament rather than being chosen by the King. There is international support for Nepál being created a 'zone of peace' to ensure continued independence from both India and China. Within Nepál there is agitation against the panchayat electoral system□

nephritis inflammation of the kidneys, Bright's disease, accompanied by swelling (oedema, popularly dropsy)□

Neptune in Roman mythology god of the sea, the equivalent of the Greek Poseidon◊. *Enterprise Neptune* is the National Trust scheme from 1965 to save unspoiled coastline in the UK (720 km/450 mi by 1985)□

Neptune the eighth planet from the sun, discovered by Johann Gottfried Galle (1812–1910) in 1846.
mean distance from the sun 497 000 000 km
diameter 50 940km
rotation period 18 hr 12 min
year (sidereal period) 164 years 299 days
atmosphere turbulent, and thought to be similar in composition to that of Uranus
surface temperature 220°C
surface not known
ring system partial; it seems to consist of a series of segments or arcs, and there may be a second series closer in
satellites
Triton mean distance from its planet 355 000 km
diameter roughly same size as earth's moon
Nereid mean distance from its planet 5 562 000 km
diameter 300km□

neptunium element
symbol Np
atomic number 93
physical description silvery
features radioactive; highly reactive; a member of the actinide◊ series; produced in nuclear reactors by neutron bombardment of uranium
uses for conversion to plutonium by neutron bombardment□

Nereid in Greek mythology, a minor sea goddess who sometimes mated with mortals (see Achilles◊)□

Nereid outer satellite of Neptune◊□

Nergal Mesopotamian god of the sun, war and pestilence, ruler of the underworld, symbolized by a winged lion□

Neri St Philip 1515–95. Italian priest who organized the Congregation of the Oratory, and built the oratory over the church of St Jerome, Rome, where prayer meetings were held, and scenes from the Bible were performed with music – hence *oratorio*; canonized 1622□

Nero 37–68AD. Roman emperor, son of Domitius Ahenobarbus and Agrippina, he was adopted by his stepfather, Claudius◊, and succeeded him as emperor in 54. He is said to have murdered Claudius's son, Britannicus, his own mother, his wives, Octavia and Poppaea, and many others. He was a poet and connoisseur of art, and performed publicly as an actor and singer. After the great fire of Rome in 64, he persecuted the Christians, who were suspected of causing it, and an aristocratic conspiracy against him in 65 led to the execution or suicide of Seneca,◊ Lucan◊, and others. Military revolt followed in 68; the senate condemned Nero to death, whereupon he committed suicide□

Neruda Pablo. Pseudonym of Chilean poet Neftal Ricardo Reyes 1904–73. His work includes lyrics and the epic of the American continent *Canto General* 1950; Nobel prize 1971□

Nerva (Marcus Cocceius Nerva) c35–98AD. Roman emperor. A senator, he was proclaimed emperor on Domitian's death in 96, and introduced state loans for farmers, family allowances, and allotments of land to poor citizens□

Nerval Gérard de. Pseudonym of French Romantic poet Gérard Labrunie 1808–55, who lived a wandering life, darkened by periodic insanity, and committed suicide□

nerve cell

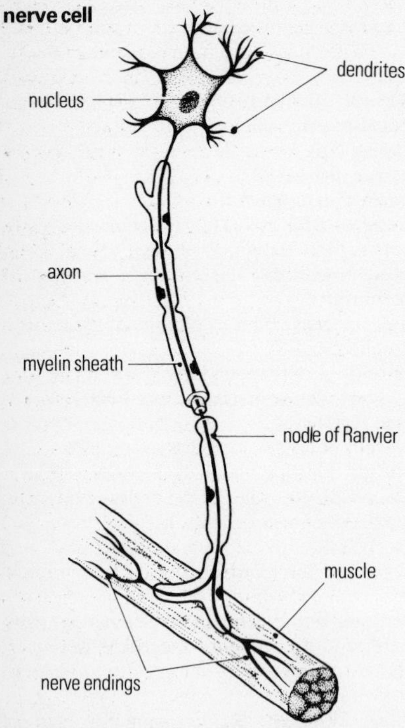

nerve cell or ***neuron*** basic cell of the nervous system of vertebrates and most invertebrates. Nerve cells transmit nerve impulses conveying messages to various parts of the body. Neurons consist of a cell body containing one nucleus and two or more long fibres (***dendrites***). Nerve impulses are received from one or more of the dendrites to the cell body (sensory nerve cells). Higher nervous systems have one long fibre (axon) which carries impulses away from the cell body, e.g. for a muscle to tense. Groups of neurons are held together by connective tissue, forming nerves. In large vertebrates neurons may be several feet long. The autonomic nervous system carries out vital functions such as breathing without any conscious control.

nerve impulses are tiny electrical messages from the brain, carried from one nerve cell to the next both by quick-acting chemical neurotransmitters and by the more numerous slower-acting chemical neuropeptides, e.g. Substance P (see under pain◊).

Plants have no nervous system, but do use electricity to transmit signals through apparently ordinary cells, notably in the touch-sensitive movements of the leaves of mimosa◊□

Nervi Pier Luigi 1891–1979. Italian architect, who used soft steel mesh within concrete to give it flowing form, e.g. Turin exhibition hall 1949, UNESCO building in Paris 1952, cathedral at New Norcia, near Perth, Australia 1960□

Neryungri coal and iron-mining town in Yakut USSR, planned as the biggest steel centre east of the Urals by the 1990s□

Nesbit E(dith) 1858–1924. British author of children's books, remarkable for their characterization, e.g. *The Treasure-Seekers* 1899, and *The Railway Children* 1906. She married the Fabian Hubert Bland (d. 1914), in 1880, her writing being the mainstay of the marriage, and had four children□

Ness Loch, very deep lake in Highland region, Scotland. There have been reports of a 'monster' since the 15th century□

Nestorius d. c451. Patriarch of Constantinople 428–431, banished for maintaining that Mary was the mother of the man Jesus only, and therefore should not be called the 'Mother of God'. His followers survived as the Assyrian Church in Syria, Iraq, Iran, etc., and as the Christians of St Thomas in S India□

Netherlands Kingdom of the (including the Netherlands◊ Antilles), popularly referred to as Holland◊

area 34 000 sq km/13 020 sq mi

capital Amsterdam

towns The Hague (seat of government); chief port Rotterdam

features almost completely flat; rivers Rhine, Schlelde (*Scheldt*), Maas; Zuider Zee; Frisian Island

exports dairy products, flower bulbs, vegetables, petro-chemicals, electronics

currency guilder

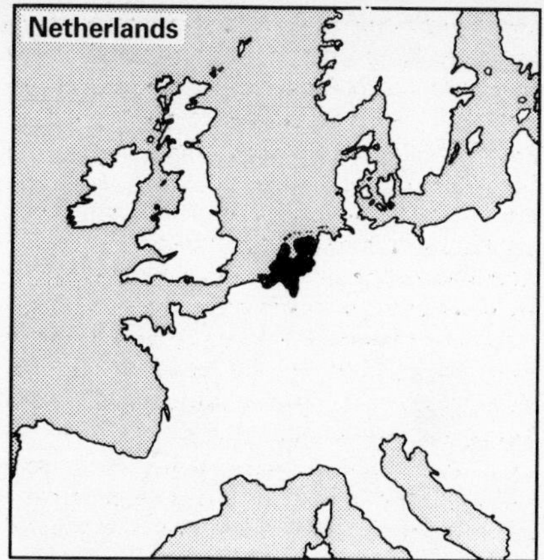

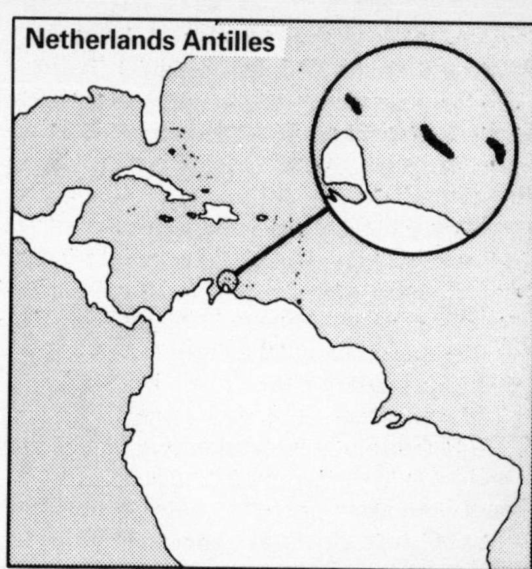

population 14 090 000, including 300 000 Eurasians of Dutch-Indonesian blood absorbed 1949–64 from the former colonial possessions (see Indonesia◊ Netherlands◊ East Indies, New◊ Guinea, Surinam◊)
language Dutch
religion Roman Catholicism 35%, Protestantism 28%
famous people Philip II of Spain, William the Silent, William III of England, Queen Juliana
government under the revised constitution of 1972, there is a constitutional monarch (Beatrix◊) of the House of Orange◊, and a parliament of two chambers, the upper elected for six years by the provincial council, and the lower elected for four years by proportional representation (Prime Minister from 1982 Ruud Lubbers(CDA), at the head of a centre-right coalition)
recent history an independent kingdom from 1839, the Netherlands was neutral in World War I, but occupied by Germany in World War II 1940–45. Joined with Belgium and Luxembourg in Benelux◊, the Netherlands was a founder member of the EEC. The chief political parties are the Labour Party (PvdA), Christian Democratic Appeal (CDA), and Party of Freedom and Democracy (VVD)□

Netherlands Antilles overseas part of the kingdom of the Netherlands comprising the islands of Curaçao◊, Aruba and Bonaire, together with St Eustatius, Saba, and the S part of St Maarten; area 990 sq km/381 sq mi; population 231 000. Capital Willemstad, on Curaçao. Oil from Venezuela is refined. There is full internal autonomy□

Netherlands East Indies former name of Indonesia◊□

netsuke toggle of ivory, wood, etc., made to secure a purse, tobacco pouch, etc., for men wearing Japanese traditional costume. Made especially in the Edo period in Japan 1601–1867, they are superb miniature sculptures□

nettle genus of plants *Urtica,* family Urticaceae. Stinging hairs on the generally ovate leaves can penetrate the skin causing inflammation. The ***common nettle U dioica*** grows on waste ground in Europe and is naturalized in N America; it yields a tough fibre which was made into cloth in Ancient Egypt□

nettle-rash an irritating skin disorder. See Urticaria◊□

Neubrandenburg capital of Neubrandenburg district and industrial (engineering, chemicals, paper) city in northern E Germany; population 50 000□

Neuchâtel city in NW Switzerland; population 40 000. It has a Horological (clock) Research Laboratory□

Neumann Balthasar 1687–1753. German military engineer and Rococo architect, e.g. the bishop's palace at Würzburg□

neuralgia a severe pain felt along the track of a nerve, especially one of the head or face□

neurasthenia unscientific term for nervous exhaustion, covering various symptoms of neurosis□

neuritis nerve inflammation caused by injury, or its degeneration as a result of alcoholic, lead, arsenical poisoning, etc.; or the toxins of diseases such as diphtheria□

neuron see nerve◊ cell□

neurosis mental disorder short of insanity, in which the patient may feel irrational anxiety, become obsessed by compulsive rituals (such as repeated washing of the hands), or be hysterical□

neuro-toxin substance, such as lead and organo-lead compounds, organo-chlorines, manganese and mercury, which poisons the nervous system□

neurotransmitter chemical substance that transmits nerve impulses between cells, etc.

See under nerve◊ cell; see also under brain◊□

Neutra Richard Joseph 1892–1970. Austro-American architect, a US citizen from 1929. His works include the Lovell Health House, Los Angeles, and Mathematics Park, Princeton□

neutrality the state of being neutral in international affairs. Under international law, neutral states may not supply troops, arms, money, or war-supplies to belligerents; or allow the passage of belligerent troops, establishment of bases on their territory, or recruiting among their subjects. Troops entering neutral territory must be interned; belligerent warships may remain in a neutral port for 24 hours, but any prisoners carried must be released. Any violation of neutrality may be resisted by force. An attitude of active sympathy towards a belligerent, known as 'benevolent neutrality', is often adopted in practice, e.g. the US attitude to Britain 1939–41, and in the Falklands dispute in 1982□

neutrino very small uncharged sub-atomic particle, very difficult to detect and of great penetrating power. All reactors emit numbers of neutrinos. See particle◊ physics□

neutron nuclear particle with no electric charge, and mass equivalent to that of a proton◊, found in the nuclei of all atoms except hydrogen, and vital to nuclear fission. See particle◊ physics□

neutron beam machine a nuclear reactor or accelerator producing a stream of neutrons, which can 'see' through metals, and is used in industry to check molecular changes in metal under stress, etc.□

neutron bomb a nuclear bomb which produces a large amount of radiation with a small blast. See under nuclear◊ warfare□

neutron gun beam of neutrons from a cyclotron◊ for treating certain cancer tumours with minimum damage to neighbouring skin and organs□

neutron star a star of very great density, resulting from the collapse of a supernova. See pulsar under star◊□

Nevada mountain state of the USA; Sagebrush or Battleborn State

area 286 300 sq km/110 540 sq mi

capital Carson City

towns Las Vegas, Reno

features Mojave Desert; Lake Tahoe; Nuclear Rocket Development Station at Jackass Flats NW of Las Vegas; fallout from nuclear tests in the 1950s were alleged to be responsible for deaths, e.g. John Wayne, who was filming there; rapid divorces

products gold, copper, oil, etc.; gaming machines

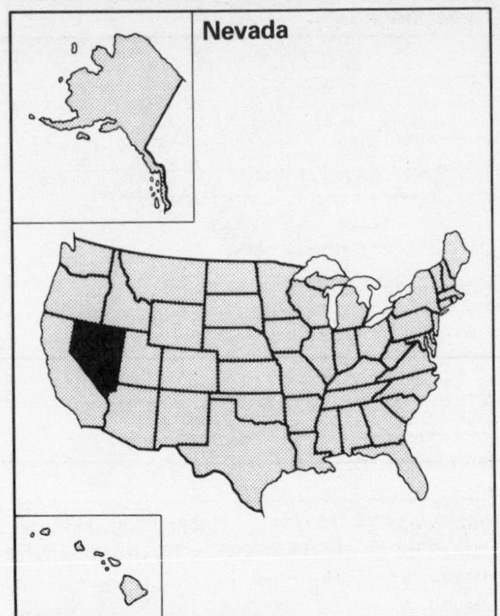

population 742 582

recent history ceded to the USA after the Mexican War in 1848, it became a state in 1864□

Nevelson Louise 1900– . Russian-born American sculptor, whose works include walls of wooden boxes filled with miscellaneous objects, and columnar shapes, e.g. the all-white *Dawn's Wedding Feast*□

Nevers industrial town in central France, capital of the former province of Nivernais; population 48 000□

Nevis see St◊ Kitts-Nevis□

New Age belief developed in the 1960s that, as the stars moved into new configurations, a 'new age' of reawakening spirit was dawning. It resulted in the spread of a number of short-lived cults, and the 'back to nature movement'□

Newark largest city (industrial and commercial) of New Jersey, USA; population 1 965 304□

Newark town in Nottinghamshire, England; population 25 000. There is engineering and brewing□

New Ash Green see under Kent◊□

Newbolt Sir Henry John 1862–1938. British poet and naval historian, remembered for his 'Songs of the Sea' 1904 and 'Songs of the Fleet' 1910, set to music by Stanford□

New Britain largest island in the Bismarck◊ Archipelago, part of Papua New Guinea; population 163 000. Capital Rabaul□

New Brunswick Eastern maritime province of Canada

area 73 437 sq km/28 340 sq mi

capital Fredericton

towns Saint John, Moncton

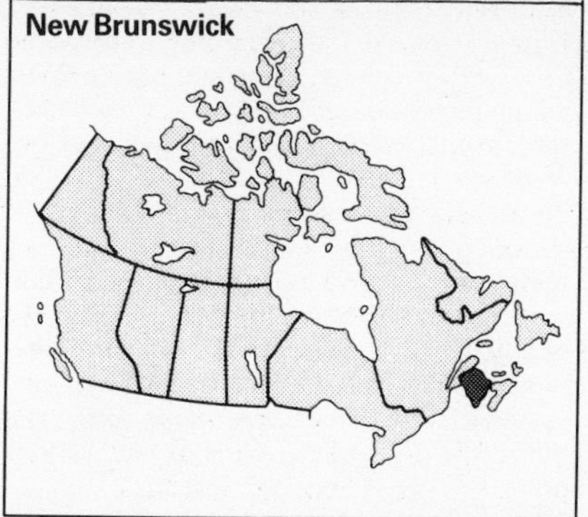

features Grand Lake, St John river; Bay of Fundy
products cereals; wood, paper; fish; lead, zinc, copper, oil and natural gas
population 713 300, one third French-speaking
history first reached by Europeans (Cartier) in 1534, it was explored by Champlain in 1604, remaining a French colony until, as part of Nova Scotia, it was ceded to England in 1713. It was separated from Nova Scotia in 1784, when many United Empire Loyalists settled there, and became a province□

Newbury market town in Berkshire, England; population 29 000. Noted for its racecourse and training stables; nearby Aldermaston◊ and Harwell◊, and electronics industries; and by 1983 the main UK base for US cruise missiles at RAF Greenham Common□

Newby (George) Eric 1919– . British sailor and explorer. His books include *A Short Walk in the Hindu Kush* 1958 and *Slowly Down the Ganges* 1966□

Newby P(ercy) H(oward) 1918– . British novelist, author of the subtle *Something to Answer For* 1968 and *Feelings have Changed* 1981, set in the BBC in the 1960s□

New Caledonia island group, a French overseas territory in the S Pacific
area 19 103 sq km/7374 sq mi
capital Nouméa on New Caledonia
exports nickel (3rd largest producer), coconut oil, pearls (cultured), citrus; tourism is important
currency franc CFP
population 146 600, Melanesian/Polynesian Kanaks 43%; European French and Caldoches 37%; Indonesian, Vietnamese, etc. 20%
language French, official
religion Roman Catholicism 60%, Protestantism 30%
government state affairs are in the hands of the high commissioner, and those of the territory are dealt with by a council of government and territorial assembly, both elected
recent history annexed by France 1853, it became an overseas territory 1958. French settlers (*Caldoches*), mainly in Nouméa, favour the continuing link with France and the Melanesians and Polynesians (Kanaks) favour independence as Kanaky; a state of emergency was declared in 1985□

Newcastle Duke of (Thomas Pelham-Holles) 1693–1768. British Whig politician, Prime Minister during the Seven Years' War, 1754–62, although Pitt◊ was mainly responsible for the conduct of the war□

Newcastle industrial city and port in New South Wales, Australia; 379 800□

Newcastle-under-Lyme industrial town (coal, bricks and tiles, clothing) in Staffordshire; England; population 116 700. Keele University is nearby□

Newcastle upon Tyne port and industrial city (administrative headquarters) in Tyne and Wear, England, also the administrative headquarters of Northumberland, and the commercial and cultural centre of the north-east; population 289 900. The 'new castle' built as a defence against the Scots in the 11th century survives in rebuilt form; other buildings include the 14th-century cathedral of St Nicholas; the Guildhall 1658, and the university. It first began to trade in coal in the 13th century; in 1826 iron works were established by George Stephenson, and the first engine used on the Stockton and Darlington railway was made here□

Newcomen Thomas 1663–1729. British inventor, whose atmospheric steam engine (or 'fire engine'), 1705, was used for pumping water from mines until Watt◊ invented one with a separate condenser□

New Deal programme introduced in USA by F D Roosevelt from 1933 to counter the depression of 1929, including employment on public works, farm loans at low rates, raising of agricultural prices by restriction of output. Combined with the programme were the introduction of old-age and unemployment insurance; prevention of sweated and child labour; protection of organization against unfair practices by employers; and loans to local authorities for slum clearance. See also the Tennessee Valley◊ scheme. Many of its provisions were declared unconstitutional by the Supreme Court in 1935–6, and full employment did not come until World War II□

New Democratic Party (NDP) Canadian political party formed in 1961 by a merger of the Labour Congress and the Cooperative Commonwealth Federation; leader Edward Broadbent 1936– , from 1975□

New Economic Policy (NEP) economic policy of the Soviet Union 1921–29 which benefitted the peasants by reinstating a limited form of free trade in agriculture. It was replaced in 1929 by the first of Stalin's Five-Year Plans◊□

New England region in NE USA, comprising the states of Maine, New Hampshire, Vermont, Massachusetts, Rhode Island, and Connecticut, originally settled by Puritan groups from England; there are now many Irish and E Europeans. It is still 80% forested□

New England district of northern New South Wales, Australia, especially the tableland area of Glen Innes and Armidale, but including Newcastle and Tamworth. Earle Page suggested in 1915 that it become a new state, but a referendum in 1967 did not give a large enough majority of votes□

New English Art Club British Society founded 1886 to secure better representation for younger painters than was given by the Royal Academy, it included Sargent, Augustus John, Paul Nash, Rothenstein, and Sickert◊□

New Forest see under Hampshire◊□

Newfoundland a breed of dog◊□

Newfoundland and Labrador eastern province of Canada

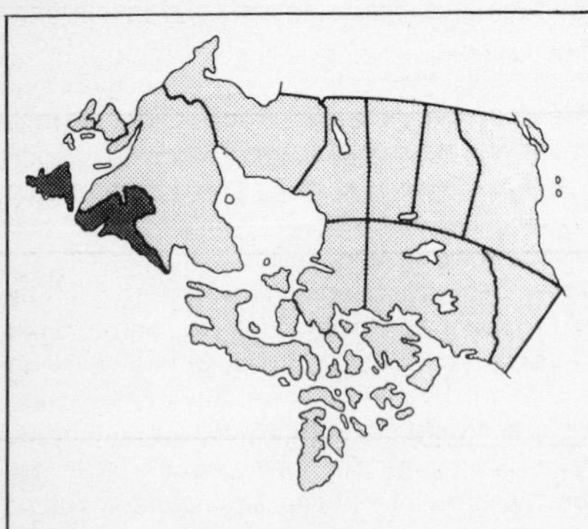

area 404 517 sq km/156 185 sq mi
capital St John's
features Grand Banks section of the continental shelf rich in cod; Gander International Airport, with an Aviation Museum
products newsprint, fish products, hydroelectric power from Churchill Falls sold to Quebec, etc.; iron, copper, zinc, uranium, and oil offshore
population 579 500
history Newfoundland was reached by Europeans (John Cabot) in 1497, and was the first English colony, Sir Humphrey Gilbert taking possession in 1583. France also made settlements and British sovereignty was not recognized until 1713, and the islands of St◊ Pierre and Miquelon are still retained. It became a province in 1949□

Newgate London prison (from the 12th century until its demolition in 1903) on the site of the Old Bailey◊. The original gatehouse was rebuilt after the Great Fire◊, and again in 1780. Public executions were held outside it 1783–1868. One of the cells is preserved in the London Museum□

New Guinea large island in the SW Pacific. The tropical rain forest harbours birds of paradise and brilliant butterflies, and various mammals, such as the small kangaroos, show the island's Australian links. The chief rivers are the Fly, Sepik, Mamberano and Digul. Its native peoples are Melanesian, some in the highlands being pygmies. The island is now divided into
West Irian (Irian Jaya), part of the Dutch East Indies from 1828, was ceded by the United Nations to Indonesia in 1963; population 1 174 000; area 420 000 sq km/162 000 sq mi. Capital Jayapura
Papua◊ New Guinea□

Newham borough of E Greater London
features Dick Turpin and Gerard Manley Hopkins once lived here; Royal Victoria and Albert and King George V docks, now only in limited operation
population 209 300□

New Hampshire New England state of the USA; Granite State

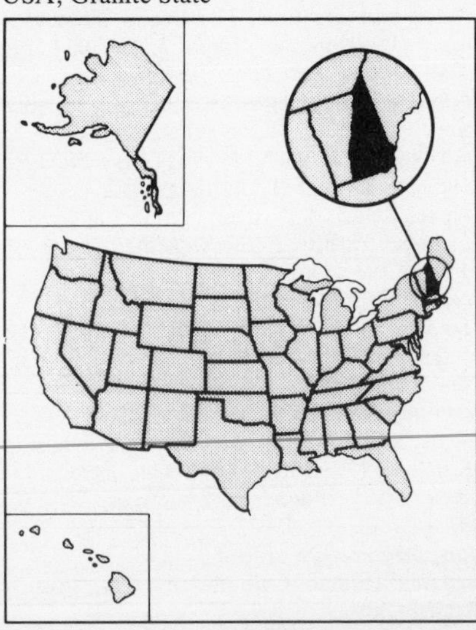

area 24 100 sq km/9304 sq mi
capital Concord
towns Manchester, Nashua
features White Mountains; Mount Monadnock 1063 m/3186 ft is an isolated mountain which has given its name to all such isolated features; the state's primary◊ elections established the order in the presidential nomination race, in that no president has ever come to office without succeeding here; fastest growing state in the northeast.
products electrical machinery, etc.; sand and gravel, etc., but no longer granite; apples and maple syrup, and livestock
population 918 830
famous people Mary Baker Eddy, Robert Frost, Augustus St Gaudens
history first settled in 1623, it was one of the Thirteen Colonies, and was the first colony to declare its independence of Britain. It became a state in 1788□

Newhaven port in E Sussex, England; population 10 000. There are cross-channel services to Dieppe, and wine is imported□

New Haven town in Connecticut, USA; population 137 700. ***Yale University,*** third oldest in the USA, was founded here in 1701 and named after Elihu Yale 1648–1721, an early benefactor; it achieved university status in 1887□

New Hebrides see Vanuatu◊□

New Jersey Mid Atlantic state of the USA; Garden State

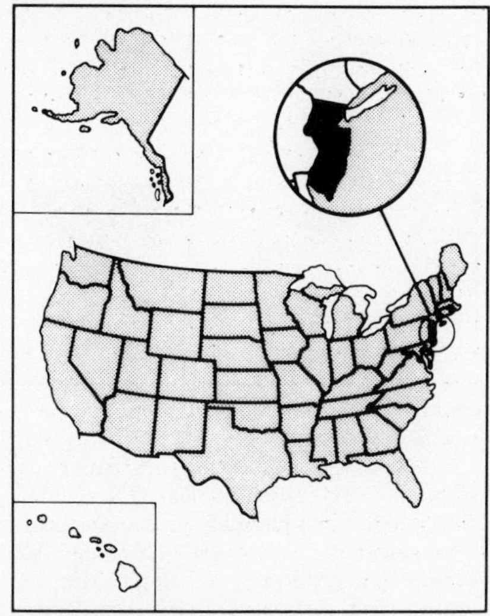

area 20 295 sq km/7836 sq mi
capital Trenton
towns Newark, Jersey City, Paterson, Elizabeth
features coastal resorts, e.g. Atlantic City; Princeton University, founded in 1746; Walt Whitman's house in Camden
products asparagus, fruit, potatoes, tomatoes, poultry; chemicals, metal goods, electrical machinery; clothing
population 7 364 160
famous people Aaron Burr, James Fenimore Cooper, Stephen Crane, Thomas Edison, Alexander Hamilton, General George McClellan, Thomas Paine, Paul Robeson, Frank Sinatra, Walt Whitman
history one of the Thirteen Colonies, it had been colonized in the 17th century by the Dutch, was ceded to England in 1664, and became a state in 1787□

New London naval base and yachting centre of SE Connecticut, USA: population 31 630□

Newlyn seaport near Penzance, Cornwall, England. The 'Newlyn School' of artists 1880–90, including Stanhope Forbes 1857–1947, is commemorated by the Newlyn Art Gallery. The Ordnance Survey relates heights in the UK to mean sea-level here□

Newman John Henry 1801–90. British cardinal. As vicar of St Mary's, Oxford, 1827–43 he published the first of the *Tracts for the Times* (which gave their name to the 'Tractarian Movement') in 1833; *Tract 90* in 1841 found the Thirty-nine Articles compatible with Roman Catholicism. He was received into the Catholic Church in 1845. Later works were *Idea of a University* 1852; his autobiography, *Apologia pro vita sua* 1864, defending himself against Kingsley's attack on the Catholic attitude to truth; the poem, 'The Dream of Gerontius' (see Elgar◊) 1866; and *The Grammar of Assent* 1870, an analysis of the nature of belief. In 1879 he was created a cardinal. His best-known hymn is 'Lead, Kindly Light'. See Oratorians◊□

Newman Paul 1925– . American Method◊ actor and director, born in Cleveland, Ohio. His films include *The Hustler* 1962, *Butch Cassidy and the Sundance Kid* 1969, *The Sting* 1973, and *Fort Apache, the Bronx* 1982. He married Joanne Woodward□

Newmarket town in Suffolk, England; population 11 350. There has been racing here since James I's reign, notably the One Thousand and Two Thousand Guineas, and Cesarewitch. It is the headquarters of the Jockey Club, and if a bookmaker is 'warned off Newmarket Heath', he is banned from all British racecourses. The National Horseracing Museum 1983 is here□

New Mexico mountain state of the USA; Land of Enchantment
area 315 113 sq km/121 666 sq mi
capital Santa Fé

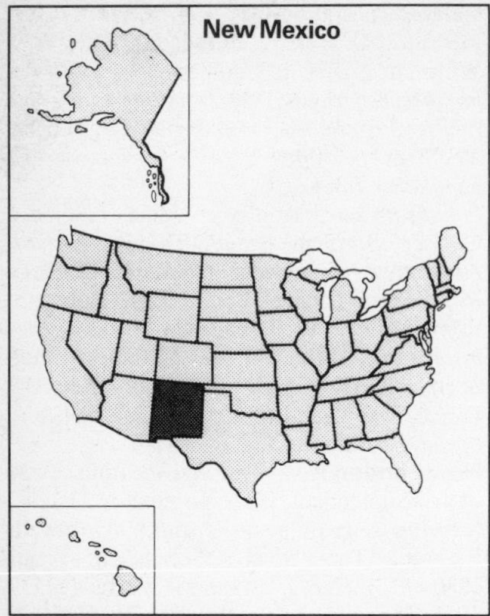

towns Albuquerque
features Great Plains and Rocky Mountains, more than three-quarters of the state being over 1200 m/4000 ft above sea level; river Rio Grande; Carlsbad Caverns, the largest known; Los Alamos atomic and space research centre; White Sands Missile Range (also used by Space Shuttle); Kiowa Ranch, site of D H Lawrence's Utopian colony in the Sangre de Christos Mountains
products uranium, oil, natural gas, cotton, cereals, vegetables
population 1 300 000
famous people Billy the Kid, Kit Carson, Lew Wallace
history explored by Spain in the 16th century, most of it was ceded to the USA by Mexico in 1848, and it became a state in 1912□

New Orleans commercial and industrial city (banking, oil refining, Saturn rockets for *Apollo* spacecraft) and Mississippi port in Louisiana, USA; population 1 183 600. Founded by the French in 1718, it still has a distinctive French Quarter, and Mardi Gras celebrations which are a tourist attraction. Jazz◊ was born here, and early exponents still play at Preservation Hall. The Superdome sports palace is among the world's largest enclosed stadiums, and is adaptable to various games, and the expected audience size□

New Plymouth town in North Island, New Zealand; population 44 600□

Newport river port, capital of the Isle of Wight, England; population 22 260. Charles I was imprisoned in nearby Carisbrooke castle□

Newport seaport in Gwent (administrative headquarters), Wales; population 111 530. There is a steelworks at nearby Llanwern, and a hightech complex at Cleppa Park□

Newport News industrial city (engineering, shipbuilding) and port of Virginia, USA; population 144 800□

Newquay seaport and resort in Cornwall, England; population 14 000□

New Right French movement, in reaction to the 1968 student revolt, which rejects Rousseauist egalitarianism, democracy, capitalism, and religion. It demands an elitist, meritocratic society, and is led by members of the Clock Club (*Club de l'Horloge*), founded 1974; its organ is *Le Figaro*□

news agency agency handling news stories and photographs, the chief being Associated Press and Reuters (see Julius Reuter◊). Once news was transmitted by pigeons, today it is 'screen-to-screen': journalists write and edit their material on a VDT (visual display terminal), then press a button to transmit it to the agency headquarters. It is coded to queue at editor's desk in order of priority (flash, urgent, etc.) for world-wide distribution. Third world countries dislike the dominance of the agencies, which are accused of 'western bias', and have attempted to start their own system□

New South Wales state of the Commonwealth of Australia

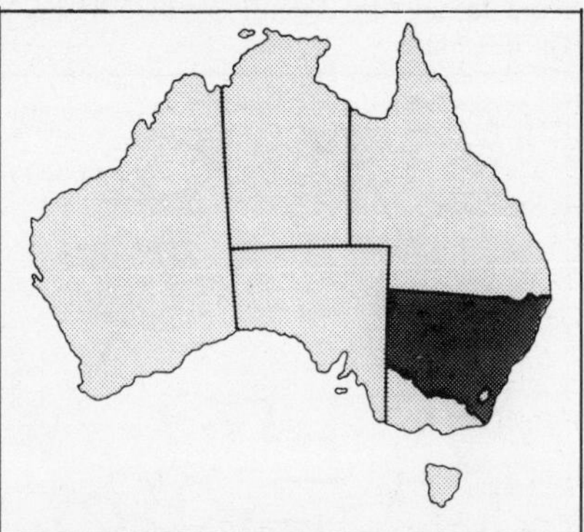

area 801 396 sq km/309 433 sq mi
capital Sydney
towns Newcastle, Wollongong, Broken Hill
features Great Dividing Range (including Blue Mountains) and part of the Australian Alps (including Snowy Mountains and Mt. Kosciusko); Murray, Darling, Murrumbidgee river system. The Riverina district between the Lachlan and Murray rivers, through which the Murrumbidgee runs, has land irrigated from the three rivers, producing wool, wheat and fruit. There is a major

radio telescope at Parkes, and Siding Spring Mountain 859 m/2817 ft, NW of Sydney, has the Anglo-Australian 3.81 m/150 in and British 1.2 m/48 in Schmidt telescopes which first enabled the central sector of our Galaxy to be adequately observed. Canberra◊ forms an enclave within the state, and New South Wales administers the dependency of Lord Howe Island◊

products cereals, fruit, sugar, tobacco; wool, meat, hides and skins; rich mineral deposits including gold, silver, copper, tin, zinc, and coal; hydroelectric power from the Snowy river

population 5 079 100, 60% living in Sydney

history it was at first called New Wales by Captain Cook, who put in at Botany Bay in 1770, and was struck by the resemblance of the coast to that of Wales. Used as a convict settlement 1788–1850, it was opened to free settlement by 1819, received self-government 1856, and in 1901 became a state of the Commonwealth of Australia. Since 1973 there has been decentralization to counteract the pull of Sydney, and the New England and Riverina districts have separatist movements□

newspaper publication giving news and comments on it. One of the earliest newspapers, the Roman *Acta Diurna*, said to have been started by Julius Caesar◊, contained announcements of marriages, deaths, military appointments, etc., and was posted up in public places. The first English newspaper, *The Weekly News,* appeared in 1622, followed by the first daily newspaper, the *Daily Courant* in 1702. The chief British daily papers are: *The Times* 1785, *Guardian* (originally *Manchester Guardian,* 1821–1959), *Daily Telegraph* 1855, *Daily Mail* 1896, *Daily Express* 1900, *Daily Mirror* 1903, *The Sun* (*Daily Herald* 1919–64) 1964, *Financial Times* 1888, *Daily Star* 1978 and *Today* 1986. Important regional dailies are the *Scotsman* 1855, *Yorkshire Post* 1866 and *Glasgow Daily Herald* 1805.

The ***Press Council*** 1953 maintains standards and considers complaints, etc.□

newt see under salamander◊□

Newton Sir Isaac 1642–1727. English mathematician and natural philosopher. When his studies at Cambridge were interrupted by the Great Plague (1666) he returned home to Woolsthorpe (Lincolnshire) for a most fruitful period of research. Independently of Leibniz◊ he developed the infinitesimal calculus◊ into a powerful system, aided by his discovery of the general binomial theorum. In optics, his prism experiments pointed to white light being a mixture of colours. Newton's most spectacular achievement was to quantify the idea of *force* and to show that Laws of Motion (see below) together with a Law of Gravitation — every particle in the universe attracts every other particle with a force proportional to the product of the particles' masses and inversely proportional to the square of their distance apart — would account not only for terrestrial phenomena such as tides and falling apples, but also for the observed elliptical parts of planets around the sun (see Kepler◊) and for the moon's 28-day revolution around the earth. Despite the daunting sweep and rigour of his *Principia Mathematica Philosophie Mathematica* (1687) Newton achieved fame in his own lifetime. He was made Master of the Royal Mint, President of the Royal Society (1703–1727), and a Whig MP (1689 and 1701–02). He was buried in Westminster Abbey□

newton derived SI unit: that force which, applied to a mass of 1 kg, gives it an acceleration of 1 metre per second□

Newton Abbot market town in Devon, England; population 18 500□

Newton's Laws of Motion 1 Unless acted upon by a net force, a body at rest stays at rest and a moving body continues moving at the same speed in the same straight line. 2 A net force applied to a body gives it a rate of change of momentum◊ proportional to the force and in the direction of the force. 3 When a body A exerts a force on a body B, B exerts an equal and opposite force on A, i.e. to every action there is an equal and opposite reaction□

Newtown town in Powys, Wales, developed as a 'new town' from 1967; population 6000. There is light industry and St Giles Science and Technology Park. Robert Owen◊ was born here□

new town a town in the UK either newly established or greatly enlarged following World War II, e.g. Cwmbran◊ and Peterlee◊, to stimulate employment locally and relieve congestion in the large towns. By the 1970s emphasis was shifting to rehabilitation of older towns□

Newtown St Boswells see under Borders◊□

New Wave French literary movement of the 1950s, a cross-fertilization of novel (Marguerite Duras, Alain Robbe-Grillet, Nathalie Sarraute) and film (directors Jean-Luc Godard, Alain Resnais and François Truffaut)□

New Westminster port on the Fraser, British Columbia, Canada; population 42 000□

New Year's Day 1 Jan, a widespread public holiday; in England until 1753, the year began for many purposes on 25 Mar□

New York E state of the USA; Empire State

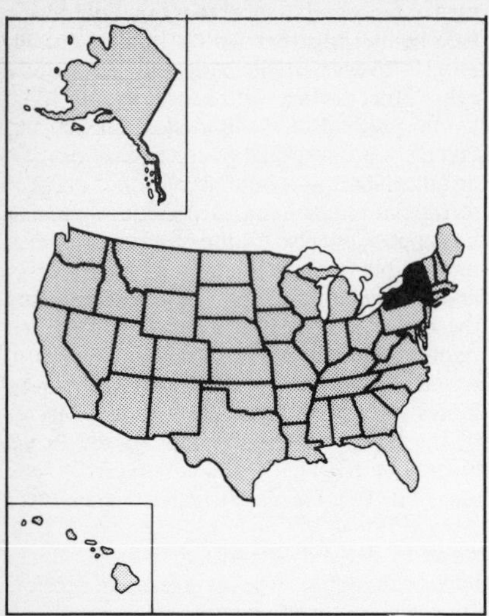

area 128 400 sq km/49 576 sq mi
capital Albany
towns New York City, Buffalo, Rochester, Yonkers, Syracuse
features Adirondack and Catskill Mountains, the former especially noted for scenery and sporting facilities and including Lake Placid; Lakes Seneca and Cayuga, and part of Erie and Ontario; Hudson river; Niagara Falls; Long◊ Island; West Point, site of the US Military Academy established in 1802; National Baseball Hall of Fame, Cooperstown; racing at Saratoga Springs; Corning Museum of Glass (1951), reputedly the world's finest collection, including the earliest glass sculpture, a portrait head of Amenhotep II of the 15th century BC; Washington Irving's home at Philipsburg Manor; Fenimore House (J F Cooper), Cooperstown; home of F D Roosevelt at Hyde Park, and the Roosevelt Library; home of Theodore Roosevelt
products clothing, printing; Steuben glass; titanium concentrate; cereals, apples, maple syrup; poultry, meat and dairy products
population 17 557 300
famous people Henry and William James, Herman Melville, Walt Whitman
history one of the Thirteen Colonies, it was settled by the Dutch in the 17th century, was ceded to England in 1664 and became a state in 1788□

New York City the commercial and financial capital, and largest city of the USA, in New York state; population 7 015 600, including large Negro (see Harlem◊) and Puerto Rican minorities, as well as large communities of European peoples (German, Greek, Hungarian, Irish, Italian, Polish and Russian); there are also about 2 000 000 Jews. The site was seen by Giovanni da Verrazano in 1524, explored by Henry Hudson in 1609, and the Dutch established a settlement in 1613. Their settlement (New Amsterdam) was captured by the English in 1664, and renamed New York; it was the first capital of the USA 1789–90□

New Zealand

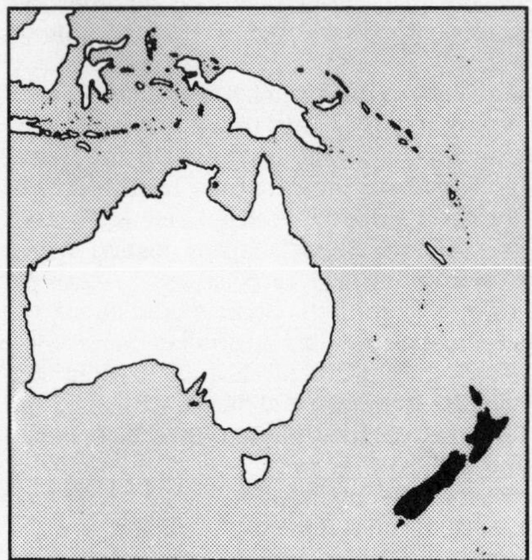

area 268 675 sq km/103 736 sq mi
capital Wellington
towns Hamilton, Palmerston North, Christchurch, Dunedin; ports Wellington, Auckland
features comprises North and South Island, Stewart and Chatham Islands. On *North Island* besides Ruapehu, at 2797 m/9175 ft, the highest of three active volcanoes, there are the geysers and hot springs of the Rotorua district, Lake Taupo (616 sq km/238 sq mi), source of Waikato river, and NE of the lake, Kaingaroa state forest, one of the world's largest planted forests. On *South Island* are the Southern Alps◊ and Canterbury Plains, famous for sheep
exports lamb and beef, wool and leather, dairy products and other processed foods; kiwi fruit became a major export crop in the 1980s; seeds and breeding stock; timber, paper, pulp; light aircraft, etc.
currency New Zealand dollar
population 3 148 900, including 270 000 Maoris and 60 000 other Polynesians; the whites are chiefly of British descent
language English, official; Maori (the Lange government pledged to give it official status)
religion Christianity, 50% Protestant, 15% Roman Catholic

famous people art Sir David Low *language* Eric Partridge *literature* (poetry) Alan Curnow; (prose) Janet Frame, Kathrine Mansfield, Ngaio Marsh, Keri Hulme *music* Kiri Te Kanawa

government under the amended constitution of 1947, there is a governor-general appointed by the Crown, aided by an executive council, and a unicameral legislature, the house of Representatives (Prime Minister David Lange◊ from 1984, Labour), elected for three years, which includes four Maori members. The Territories. Overseas comprise Tokelau Island (three atolls transferred 1926 from the former Gilbert and Ellice Islands colony) and Niue Island (one of the Cook Islands, but separately administered from 1903: chief town Alafi). The Cook◊ Islands are internally self-governing, but share common citizenship with New Zealand. The Ross◊ Dependency is in the Antarctic. See also Samoa◊

history see list below□

New Zealand: history

14th century Maoris◊ settled in New Zealand from the E Pacific

1642 coast explored by Tasman◊

1769 Cook surveyed the coast, and again in 1771 and 1777

1815 first British missionaries arrived

1840 Treaty of Waitangi, under which Maoris ceded sovereignty to Britain and British colonization began

1845–7 and 1860–72 Maori revolts against loss of their land; concessions made including representation in parliament; see Sir George Grey◊

1853 self-government achieved

1893 women achieved the vote

1898 old-age pensions introduced

1907 New Zealand granted Dominion status

1914–18 New Zealand troops served in World War I, notably at Gallipoli◊; see also Anzac◊; and Western Samoa◊ became a New Zealand League of Nations mandate

1939–45 New Zealand troops served in World War II, (Greece, N Africa and Italy)

1947 Act enabling New Zealand to amend her own constitution

1950–3 New Zealand troops formed part of the United Nations force in Korea

1973 automatic right of entry for British subjects ended

1984 nuclear vessels banned from entering New Zealand waters

1985 Greenpeace vessel sunk in Auckland harbour by French agents, killing a crew member□

Ney Michael, Duke of Elchingen, prince of the Moskowa 1769–1815. Marshal of France. He commanded the rearguard during the retreat from Moscow. When Napoleon returned from Elba, Ney was sent to arrest him, but instead deserted to him and fought at Waterloo. He was subsequently shot for treason□

New Zealand: Prime Ministers

J. Ballance (Liberal)	1891
R.J. Seddon (Liberal)	1893
W. Hall-Jones (Liberal)	1906
Sir Joseph Ward (Liberal)	1906
T. MacKenzie (Liberal)	1912
W.F. Massey (Reform)	1912
J.G. Coates (Reform)	1925
Sir Joseph Ward (United)	1928
G.W. Forbes (United)	1930
M.J. Savage (Labour)	1935
P. Fraser (Labour)	1940
S.G. Holland (National)	1949
K.J. Holyoake (National)	1957
Walter Nash (Labour)	1957
K.J. Holyoake (National)	1960
J. Marshall (National)	1972
N. Kirk (Labour)	1972
W. Rowling (Labour)	1974
R. Muldoon (National)	1975
D. Lange (Labour)	1984

Niagara Falls two waterfalls on the Niagara river, on the Canada/USA border, separated by Goat Island. The ***American Fall*** is 51 m/167 ft high, 330 m/1080 ft wide; ***Horseshoe Fall***, in Canada, is 49 m/160 ft high, 790 m/2600 ft across□

Niamey capital of Niger; population 343 600□

Nibelungenlied anonymous 12th-century German epic poem, *Song of the Nibelungs,* derived from older sources. Siegfried◊, possessor of the Nibelung treasure, marries Kriemhild (sister of Gunther of Worms) and wins Brunhild as a bride for Gunther. However, Gunther's vassal Hagen murders Siegfried, and Kriemhild achieves revenge by marrying Etzel (Attila) of the Huns, at whose court both Hagen and Gunther are killed. Wagner◊ made use of the legends in his *Ring* cycle□

Nicaea ruined city (modern Iznik) in Turkey, site in 325 of a Council of the Christian Church convened by Constantine, at which the first version of the Nicene◊ Creed was promulgated□

Nicaragua Republic of

area 148 000 sq km/57 150 sq mi

capital Managua

towns chief port Corinto

features largest state of Central America, and most thinly populated; lakes Nicaragua and Managua

exports coffee, cotton, sugar

currency cordoba

population 3 100 00, 70% Mestizo, 15%

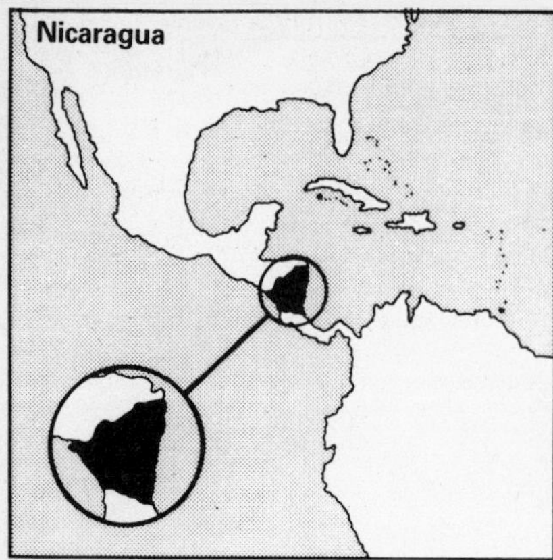

Spanish descent, 10% Indian or Negro
language Spanish, official
religion Roman Catholicism
famous people Rubén Darío, General Anastasio Somoza, William Walker
government constituent assembly elected in 1984; president from Jan 1985 Daniel Ortega (Sandinista)
recent history independent of Spain from 1821, Nicaragua was dominated from 1933 by the dictatorship of the Somoza family, under the aegis of the USA, until the Sandinista National Liberation Front (FSLN: named after General Augo Sandino, killed by a Somoza National Guard in 1934) led a revolt in 1978–9. Non-Marxist elements were soon purged, and the Sandinistas (backed by Cuba and USSR) established their own dictatorship. The elections of Nov 1984 were boycotted by the majority of the opposition. Economic sanctions by the USA (not approved by the United Nations) are in force against Nicaragua; in 1986 the US goverment procured $100 million of 'military and humanitarian aid' for the right-wing contras (Spanish 'against') guerilla movement□

Nice resort on the French Riviera; population 346 620. There is an annual 'Battle of Flowers', and chocolate and perfume are made. Chapels in the nearby village of Vence have been decorated by Chagall◊ and Matisse◊, and Nice has a Chagall National Museum□

Nicene Creed fundamental Christian creed promulgated by the Council of Nicaea◊ in 325, defining the orthodox doctrine of the Trinity□

Nicholas St 4th century. Patron saint of Russia, children, merchants and sailors, bishop of Myra (now in Turkey). His gifts of dowries to poor girls led to the custom of giving gifts to children on the eve of his feast day, 6 Dec. This was later transferred to Christmas Day – hence Santa Claus□

Nicholas two Tsars of Russia
Nicholas I 1796–1855. Tsar from 1825, whose Balkan ambitions led to war with Turkey 1827–9, and the Crimean◊ War
Nicholas II 1868–1918. Last Tsar from 1894, he was dominated by his wife, Princess Alix of Hesse, who in turn was under the influence of Rasputin◊. His mismanagement of the Russo–Japanese◊ War led to the revolution of 1905, which he ruthlessly suppressed. He took Russia into World War I 1914, was forced to abdicate in 1917, and was shot with his family by the Bolsheviks at Ekaterinburg in Jul 1918. See Anastasia◊ and Vladimir◊□

Nicholson Ben 1894– . British artist, born in Denham, Buckinghamshire, son of Sir William Nicholson◊, known for his geometrical reliefs and as an exponent of Constructivism◊; Order of Merit 1968□

Nicholson Sir William 1872–1949. British artist, noted for posters, etc., produced with his brother-in-law, James Pryde, as 'The Beggarstaff Brothers'. See Ben Nicholson◊□

nickel element
symbol Ni
atomic number 28
physical description silvery-white metal
features magnetic; resists corrosion
uses in alloys with steel, copper and chromium; it is essential to aerospace development. Also used in coinage and as an industrial catalyst□

Nicobars group of islands in the Bay of Bengal, a territory (with the Andamans◊) of the Republic of India; population 115 000□

Nicolson Sir Harold 1886–1968. British diplomat, who served on the British delegation to the Paris Peace Conference 1919. He was briefly associated with Mosley◊, but gravitated to Labour. He published historical works and biographies, but is chiefly remembered for his *Diaries and Letters 1930–1962*. He married Victoria Sackville-West◊ in 1913□

Nicosia capital of Cyprus; population 121 500. It fell to the Turks in 1571, and was again partly taken by them in the invasion of 1974. The Greek and Turkish sectors are separated by the 'Green Line'□

nicotine a poisonous chemical compound that occurs in tobacco◊ and is used as an insecticide. It causes disorders of the respiratory system, dizziness, increased blood pressure and problems with hearing and sight□

Niebuhr Barthold Georg 1776–1831. German historian, famous for his critical use of sources in his *History of Rome* 1811–32□

Niebuhr Reinhold 1892–1971. American Protestant theologian. His *Moral Man and Immoral Society* 1932, helped to turn the USA from liberalism to biblical theology, and attacked depersonalized industrial society□

Niedersachsen see Lower Saxony□

nielsbohrium former name of the element unnilpentium◊□

Nielsen Carl 1865–1931. Danish composer, once an army bugler. His works are remarkable for their progressive tonality, e.g. his opera *Saul og David* and six symphonies□

Niemeyer Oscar 1907– . Brazilian architect, joint designer of the United Nations headquarters in New York, and of many buildings in Brasilia◊□

Niemöller Martin 1892–1984. German pastor, a former U-boat commander, sent to concentration camp for campaigning against Nazification of the German Church□

Niepce Nicéphore. See under photography◊□

Nietzsche Friedrich Wilhelm 1844–1900. German philosopher, a friend and advocate of Wagner◊. He also advocated in *Thus Spake Zarathustra* 1883–5 an ideal Superman, who would reject the 'slave morality' of Christianity, and impose his will on the weak and worthless, a concept which appealed to the Nazi◊ movement□

Niger third longest river in Africa; 4185 km/2600 mi long, but its flow has been badly affected by the expansion of the Sahara Desert□

Niger Republic of

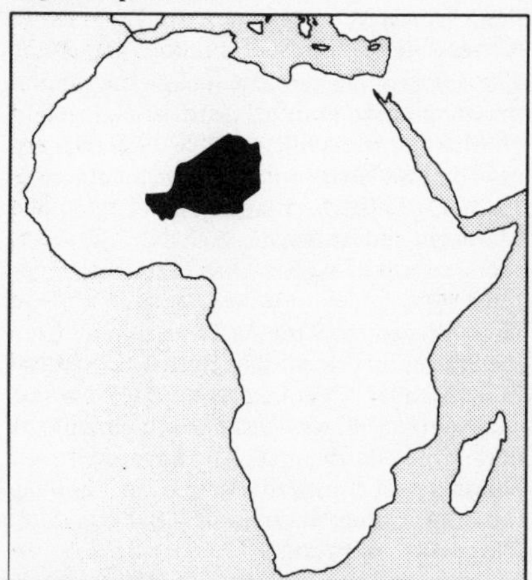

area 1 187 000 sq km/459 000 sq mi
capital Niamey
features part of the Sahara Desert and subject to Sahel◊ droughts
exports groundnuts; livestock; gum arabic; tin, uranium
currency CFA franc
population 6 284 000
language French (official), Hausa, Djerma
religion 85% Sunni Islam, 15 % animist
government a presidential system based on that of the USA, but with a single-chamber national assembly
recent history occupied by France in 1912, it became fully independent in 1960. By a military coup Colonel Seyni Kountché became president in 1974, suspending the constitution□

Nigeria Federal Republic of

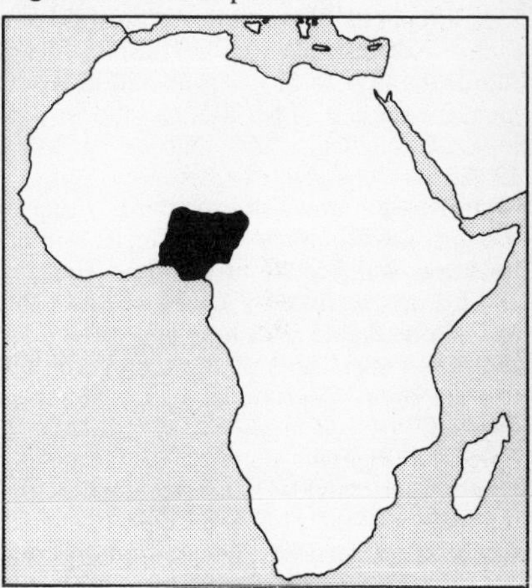

area 924 000 sq km/357 000 sq mi
capital Lagos
towns chief port Lagos; administrative headquarters Abuja; Ibadan, Ogbomosho, Kano; ports Port Harcourt, Warri, Calabar
features river Niger; harmattan◊; rich artistic heritage, e.g. Benin◊ bronzes
exports petroleum (richest African country in oil resources); cocoa, groundnuts, palm oil, cotton, rubber, tin
currency naira
population 100 000 000, of three main ethnic groups, Yoruba in the west, Ibo in the east, and Hausa-Fulani in the north
language English official; Hausa, Igbo, and Yoruba
religion Sunni Islam in the north, Christianity in the south
famous people Chinua Achebe, Wole Soyinka
government supreme military council headed by Major-General Ibrahim Babangida who became head of government in a bloodless military coup in 1985, and a federal executive council which acts as a cabinet
recent history Lagos was bought from an African chief by Britain in 1861, and the area controlled was subsequently extended. The colony and protectorate of Nigeria eventually

became independent in 1960 within the Commonwealth, and a republic from 1963. Unity was threatened by the attempted secession of Biafra◊ (see Gowon◊), and there have been later military coups, the most recent ending the civilian rule of President Alhaji Shehu Shagari 1979–83 on grounds of corruption. Economic difficulties caused by falling oil prices led in 1983 and 1985 to the expulsion of about 2 000 000 illegal immigrants (mainly Ghanaian)□

Nightingale Florence 1820–1910. British hospital reformer, born in Florence. She took a team of nurses to Scutari in 1854 and reduced the Crimean◊ War hospital death rate from 42% to 2%. An invalid in retirement for the rest of her life, she still worked to raise nursing status; Order of Merit 1907□

nightingale brownish songbird *Luscinia megarhynchos,* family Turdidae; it winters in Africa but breeds in southern England and Europe. It sings by day as well as night, and is remarkable in its tone and variety□

nightjar typical bird of the temperate and tropical order Caprimulgiformes. Members include:

European nightjar *Caprimulgus europaeus* family Caprimulgidae, an insect-feeder; and the ***whip-poor-will*** of N and Central America *Caprimulgus vociferus*, named from its cry;

tawny frogmouth *Podargus strigoides* family Podargidae, of Australia which has a startlingly big mouth, with a yellow lining, and lives on mice and insects□

nightshade plant of family Solanaceae: ***black nightshade*** *Solanum nigrum*; ***woody nightshade*** or ***bittersweet***; and ***deadly nightshade*** or ***belladonna***◊□

Nihilists Russian revolutionaries who approved of nothing (Latin *nihil*) in the existing order. Their terrorist campaign from 1878 culminated in the assassination of Alexander II in 1881□

Niigata port and industrial city in Honshu, Japan; population 439 000□

Nijinsky Vaslav 1890–1950. Russian dancer, and choreographer of *L'Après-midi d'un faune* and *Le Sacre du Printemps*. See Diaghilev◊□

Nijmegen industrial city in E Netherlands; population 147 600□

Nijmegen Treaties of. In 1678–9 signed here between Louis XIV, the Netherlands, Spain and the Holy Roman Empire, ending the Third Dutch War□

Nijni-Novgorod see Gorky◊□

Nike In Greek mythology, goddess of victory, represented as 'winged', as in the statue from Samothrace in the Louvre□

Nikolayev port and naval base on the Black Sea, in Ukraine, USSR; population 449 000□

Nile African river

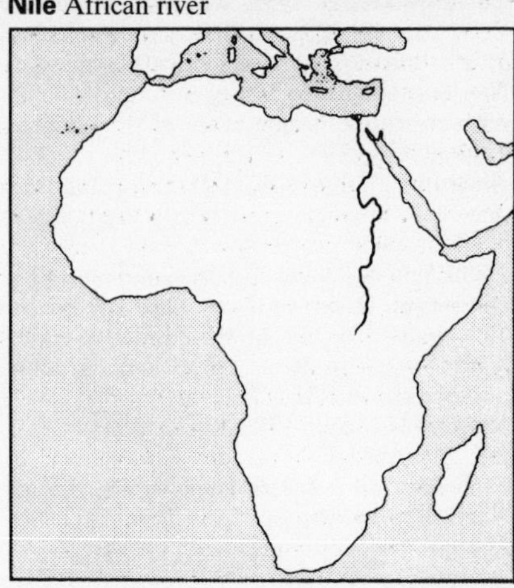

the world's longest, 6695 km/4160 mi. Its remotest headstream is the Luvironza (rising in Burundi). The Nile proper begins on leaving Lake Victoria, then flows through Lake Mobutu (Albert). From the Uganda/Sudan border to Khartoum (where it is joined by the Blue Nile, which rises in Ethiopia), it is known as the White Nile (see also Lake Nasser◊). Its delta on the Mediterranean coast of Egypt is 190 km/120 mi wide. From 1982 Nile water has been piped beneath the Suez Canal to irrigate Sinai◊□

Nile Battle of the, 1798. See under revolutionary◊ wars□

Nîmes city in the S of France; population 130 000. Roman remains include an amphitheatre and the Pont du Gard (aqueduct)□

Nimitz Chester William 1885–1966. American admiral. He reconquered the Solomons in 1942–3, Gilbert Islands in 1943, and Marianas and Marshalls in 1944, and as US representative signed the Japanese surrender□

Nineveh capital of the Assyrian Empire from the 8th century BC until its destruction by the Medes under Cyaxares 612BC (see Mosul◊ and Nahum◊). It was excavated (including the library of Ashurbanipal◊) by Layard◊□

Ningbo port (formerly Ningpo) in Zhejiang province, China; population 400 000□

Ningpo see Ningbo◊□

Ningxia Hui autonomous region (formerly Ninghsia-Hui) of NW China.

area 170 000 sq km/65 600 sq mi

capital Yinchuan

features desert plateau with nomad herdsmen

products cereals, rice, etc., under irrigation; coal

population 3 640 000, including many Muslims□

Niobe in Greek mythology, the daughter of Tantalus and wife of the king of Thebes. Contemptuous of the mere two children of the goddess Leto, Apollo and Artemis, she died of grief when her own twelve offspring were killed by them in revenge□

niobium element
symbol Nb
atomic number 41
physical description soft grey metal
features good conductor of electricity
uses in steel alloys to improve hardness and corrosion resistance, especially in aerospace□

Nippon transliteration of the Japanese name for Japan□

nirvana in Buddhism◊ final release into absolute blessedness□

Nithsdale William Maxwell, 5th Earl of Nithsdale 1676–1744. Jacobite leader captured at Preston, tried and condemned to death in 1716. His wife helped him to escape from the Tower of London in women's dress, and flee to Rome□

nitrate a salt of nitric◊ acid containing the NO_3 ion, used as a chemical fertilizer and in explosives□

nitre or *saltpetre* potassium nitrate, KNO_3, used in the making of explosives□

nitric acid mineral acid, HNO_3, also called aqua fortis, obtained by the oxidation of ammonia or the action of sulphuric acid on potassium nitrate. It is a strong oxidizing agent, dissolves most metals, and is used for nitration and esterification of organic substances; for explosives, plastics, and dyes; in making sulphuric acid and nitrates (used as fertilizers)□

nitrite any salt or ester of nitrous acid; used as a preservative, e.g. to give colour and flavour to bacon, hot dogs, etc., and to prevent the growth of botulism spores; it has been alleged to cause cancer□

nitrocellulose compound used in the manufacture of explosives, plastics, etc. See cellulose◊ nitrate□

nitrogen element
symbol N
atomic number 7
physical description colourless gas
features it forms 78% of the atmosphere and 3.3% of the human body
uses compounds are used in foods, drugs, fertilizers, dyes and explosives. As an inert gas it is used to 'blanket' computer chips during manufacture (otherwise the silicon of the chip would react with oxygen in the atmosphere and would no longer conduct electricity), and in the nuclear industry□

nitrogen cycle the continuous circle of nitrogen and nitrogen-containing compounds between the atmosphere, the soil and living organisms. Nitrifying bacteria in the roots of leguminous plants convert ammonia to nitrites and then to nitrates (*nitrification*). Some nitrates are reduced by denitrifying bacteria to nitrogen, but most are used by plants to manufacture amino acids and proteins. When animals eat plants some of this nitrogenous plant material is incorporated into animal tissues. Nitrogenous excretory products and dead organic matter decompose to produce ammonia (*denitrification*), which is fixed in the soil by certain soil bacteria (*nitrogen fixation*) so completing the cycle. Atmospheric nitrogen can also enter the cycle as a result of oxidation by lightning. The resulting nitrous and nitric acids are conveyed to the soil by rain□

nitroglycerine poisonous, explosive liquid produced by nitric and sulphuric acids acting on glycerol; used in the preparation of dynamite, cordite, etc.□

Niue one of the Cook Islands◊. It attained self-government in free association with New Zealand (with which there is common citizenship) in 1974; area 260 sq km/100 sq mi; population 4000. The port is Alofi□

Nixon Richard Milhous 1913– . American Republican president 1968–1974, born in California. In 1948, as a member of the Un-American Activities Committee, he pressed for the investigation of Alger Hiss◊. He was Vice-President to Eisenhower 1953–61, failed to defeat J F Kennedy for the presidency in 1961, but in a 'law and order' campaign defeated Vice-President Humphrey in 1968. He ended the US Vietnam commitment in 1973, and was reelected in 1972 in a landslide victory. In 1974 he was forced to resign, the first US president to do so, following the threat of impeachment on three counts: obstruction of the administration of justice in the investigation of Watergate◊; violation of constitutional rights of citizens, and failing to produce 'papers and things' as ordered by the Judiciary Committee. He was granted a controversial free pardon by President Ford◊□

Nixon Doctrine formulated in 1969 by President Nixon, it abandoned such policies of close involvement with Asian countries as would result in a Vietnam-type situation□

Nkrumah Kwame 1909–72. Ghanaian statesman. He agitated for self-government, and was imprisoned in 1950, but became Prime Minister of the Gold Coast 1952–57, of Ghana 1957–60, and first president of the republic from 1960 until his dictatorial rule led to his deposition and exile in 1966. From 1973 he was 'rehabilitated'□

NKVD see under KGB◊□

No also ***Noh*** stylized and aristocratic classical drama of Japan, developed in the 14–16th centuries, with mythical themes, and using music, chant, and dance to develop them. Costumes are elaborate, scenery limited, and all the actors are men. It influenced kabuki◊□

Noah in old Testament, father of Shem, Ham◊, and Japheth, who built an ark so that he and his family and specimens of all existing animals might survive the Flood◊; there is a Babylonian version□

Nobel Alfred Bernhard 1833–96. Swedish chemist, inventor of dynamite◊ 1867. He bequeathed the fortune gained from explosives to found the Nobel prizes◊□

nobelium element
symbol No
atomic number 102
physical description metal
features radioactive (obtained by bombarding curium); member of actinide◊ series; named after Alfred Nobel◊□

Nobel prizes annual prizes, first awarded 1901, for achievement in chemistry, physics, medicine, literature and the promotion of peace; a sixth for economics, financed by the Swedish National Bank, was first awarded 1969. Other prizes of similar rank are the *Vetlesen* for astronomy, see Oort◊; *Pritzker* for architecture, see Barragán◊; and for progress in religion, the Templeton◊□

nodule in geology a lump of mineral, etc., found within rocks or formed on the seabed surface (see mining◊)□

Nofretete see Nefertiti◊□

Noguchi Hideyo 1876–1928. Japanese bacteriologist, discoverer of the parasite of yellow fever, who died from the disease□

noise unwanted sound. Sound of any kind above 120 decibels causes incurable damage to hearing if exposure is prolonged; also below this, if the noise is in a narrow frequency band. In the UK, roadside meter tests allow a limit of 87 decibels for a saloon car and 92 for a lorry□

Nolan Sir Sidney 1917– . Australian artist, born in Melbourne, and noted for his interpretation of the outback, e.g. the 1960s series on Ned Kelly◊. Knighted 1981, Order of Merit 1983□

Nolde Emil. Name (taken from his birthplace) adopted by the German Expressionist artist Emil Hansen 1867–1956, noted for colourful seascapes and the mystic *The Last Supper* and *Joseph Tells His Dream*□

Nollekens Joseph 1737–1823. British portrait sculptor of e.g. George III, George IV, Pitt, Fox, Garrick, Sterne, etc.□

nominalism philosophical theory that classes of things have no independent reality. See scholasticism◊□

non-aligned movement theory originated by Nehru◊, adopted in 1961 by Tito◊, in general opposition to colonialism, neocolonialism and imperialism, and directed by Castro◊ from 1979 towards a 'natural' alliance with the USSR□

Nonconformists under Elizabeth I the generally Puritan section of Anglican clergy; after 1662 those who left the Church rather than conform to the Act of Uniformity requiring the use of the Prayer Book in all churches; today, the members of the Free Churches□

Nonjurors Anglican clergy who refused allegiance to William and Mary◊ in 1689, and continued as a rival Church for over a century□

Nordenskjöld Nils Adolf Erik, Baron Nordenskjöld 1832–1901. Swedish explorer who discovered the North-East Passage. See Arctic◊□

Nordic of the Germanic peoples mainly of Scandinavia. See race◊□

Nord-Pas-de-Calais region of N France; capital Lille; population 3 933 000. See also Pas-de-Calais◊□

Nore The. Sandbank at the mouth of the Thames, England; site of the first lightship 1732□

Nore Mutiny of the. Naval mutiny in 1797, caused by low pay and bad conditions□

Norfolk Miles Fitzalan-Howard, 17th duke of Norfolk 1915– . Earl Marshal of England (responsible for state ceremonial at coronations, etc.) and premier duke and earl, from 1975□

Norfolk county of eastern England
area 5368 sq km/2072sq mi
towns administrative headquarters Norwich; King's Lynn, and resorts Great Yarmouth, Cromer, and Hunstanton
features rivers Ouse, Yare, Bure, Waveney; the Broads◊; Halvergate Marshes wildlife area; traditional reed thatching; Grime's Graves (Neolithic flint mines); shrine of Our Lady of Walsingham, a medieval and modern centre of pilgrimage; Blickling Hall (Jacobean); private residence of Elizabeth II at Sandringham (built by Edward VII 1869–71)
products cereals, turnips, sugar beet; turkeys and geese; natural gas off the coast
population 699 200
famous people Fanny Burney, Cotman, 'Old Crome', Rider Haggard□

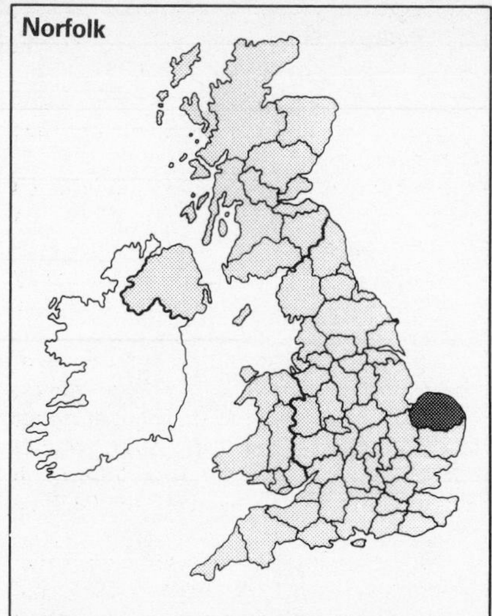

Norfolk seaport in Virginia, USA, headquarters of the American Atlantic fleet; population 262 800□

Norfolk Island Pacific island territory (from 1914) of the Australian Commonwealth; area 34 sq km/13 sq mi; population 2175. Discovered by Cook in 1774, it was settled in 1856 by descendants of the mutineers of the *Bounty* from Pitcairn Island◊. Citrus fruit and bananas are grown□

Norilsk world's most northerly industrial city, Siberia, USSR; population 250 000. It supplies most of the Soviet Union's nickel, cobalt, platinum; and also produces selenium, tellurium, gold and silver. The permafrost is 30 m/1000 ft deep, and the winter temperature may be −55°C□

Norman Montagu, 1st Baron Norman 1871–1950. As governor of the Bank of England 1920–44, his advocacy of a return to the gold standard 1925, etc., was held by many to have contributed to the Depression◊□

Norman a style of architecture, noted for semicircular arches and heavy pillars. See Romanesque under architecture◊□

Normandy two regions of N France:

Haute-Normandie

capital Rouen; other towns include Évreux, Louviers, St Etenne du Rouvray

population 1 650 300

Basse-Normandie

capital Caen; other towns include Alençon, Bayeux, Dieppe, Deauville, Lisieux, Le Havre, Cherbourg

population 1 318 200

features Monet◊'s restored home and garden at Giverny; Mont St Michel; Château Miromesnil, birthplace of de Maupassant◊; Victor Hugo◊'s house at Villequier; the invasion beaches of World War II in 1944; see also Calvados◊□

Norman-French French dialect used by the Normans in Normandy from the 10th century, and by the Norman ruling class in England after the Conquest. Although generally replaced by English in the 14th century, it remained the language of the court until the 15th century, the official language of the law courts until the 17th century, and is still used in the Channel Islands. There is a considerable literature, see Marie◊ de France□

Normans the Norsemen◊ granted Normandy by the king of France 911, and who adopted French language and culture. In the 11–12th centuries they conquered England (see William◊ the Conqueror), parts of Wales and Ireland, S Italy, Sicily, and Malta, settled in Scotland, and took a prominent part in the Crusades. They ceased to exist as a distinct people after 13th century□

Norsemen inhabitants of ancient Scandinavia. See under Vikings◊□

North Fredrick, 8th Lord North 1732–92. British statesman, Prime Minister in a government of Tories and 'king's friends' from 1770. His hard line against the American colonies was supported by George III, but in 1782 he was forced to resign by the failure of his policy. In 1783 he returned to office in a coalition with Fox◊, and after its defeat retired from politics□

North Sir Thomas c1535–1601. English translator, whose fine version of Plutarch◊'s *Lives* 1579 formed the source of Shakespeare's Roman plays□

North America third largest of the Continents (including Central America), and over twice the size of Europe

area c24 000 000 sq km/9 500 000 sq mi

largest cities (population over 1 million) Mexico City, New York, Chicago, Toronto, Montreal, Los Angeles, Guadalajara, Monterrey, Philadelphia, Detroit, Vancouver, Guatemala City, Houston

features the mountain belts to the E (Appalachians) and W (see Cordilleras◊), the latter including the Rocky Mountains and the Sierra Madre; the coastal plain on the Gulf of Mexico, into which the Mississippi river system drains from the central Great Plains; the St Lawrence and the Great Lakes, which form a rough crescent (with the Great Bear and Great Slave Lakes, and Lakes Athabasca and Winnipeg) round the exposed rock of the great Canadian/Laurentian Shield, into which Hudson Bay breaks from the north. Climatic range is wide from arctic in Alaska and N Canada (only above freezing Jun–Sept) to the

tropical in Central America, and much of the west of USA is arid. There are also great extremes within the range, owing to the vast size of the land mass
exports the immensity of the US home market makes it less dependent on exports, and its industrial and technological strength automatically tend to exert a pull on the economies north and south of it. The continent is unique in being dominated in this way by a single power, which also exerts great influence over the general world economy.
population 382 000 000; the aboriginal American Indian, Inuit and Aleut peoples are now a minority within a population predominantly of European immigrant origin, of which the fastest-growing group is the Hispanic. Many Africans were brought in as part of the slave trade.
language predominantly English
religion predominantly Christianity, Orthodox Jewish□

North America: history

BC

c60 000 American◊ Indians entered N America from Asia
9000 Marmes◊ man, earliest human remains
300 earliest Moundbuilder◊ sites

AD

c1000 Leif Ericsson◊ traditionally reached N America
12–14th centuries height of the Moundbuilder◊ and Pueblo◊ cultures
1492 12 Oct Columbus◊ first sighted land in the Caribbean
1565 first Spanish settlements in Florida
1585 first attempted English settlement in North Carolina, see Raleigh◊
1607 first permanent English settlement, Jamestown, Virginia
For subsequent history, see under individual countries, Canada, Mexico, USA□

Northampton 'new town' in Northamptonshire, England; population 162 200. Boots and shoes (of which there is a museum) are still made, but engineering has superseded them as the chief industry; there is also food processing and brewing□

Northamptonshire Midland county of England
area 2367 sq km/914sq mi
towns administrative headquarters Northampton, Kettering
features River Nene, Canon's Ashby, Tudor house, home of the Drydens for 400 years
products cereals, cattle
population 543 700
famous people John Dryden, Edmund Rubbra□

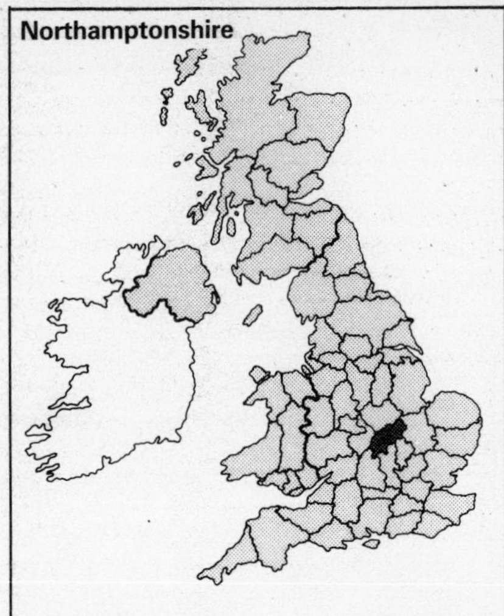

North Atlantic Treaty signed 4 Apr 1949 by Belgium, Canada, Denmark, France, Iceland, Italy, Luxembourg, Netherlands, Norway, Portugal, UK, USA; later accessions Greece, Turkey in 1952; W Germany in 1955; Spain in 1982. They agreed that 'an armed attack against one or more of them in Europe or N America shall be considered an attack against them all'. See North◊ Atlantic Treaty Organization□

North Atlantic Treaty Organization (NATO). Set up under the North◊ Atlantic Treaty, its chief body is the Council of Foreign Ministers (who have representatives functioning in permanent session), and there is an international secretariat in Brussels, where there is also a Military Committee consisting of the chiefs of staff. The military headquarters SHAPE (Supreme Headquarters Allied Powers, Europe) is at Chièvres, near Mons. Both the Supreme Allied Commanders (Europe and Atlantic) are American, but there is also an Allied Commander, Channel (a British admiral). In 1960 a permanent multi-national ***Allied Mobile Force*** (AMF) was established to move immediately to any NATO country under threat of attack; headquarters Heidelberg◊. France withdrew from the organization (not the alliance) in 1966; Greece withdrew politically, but not militarily 1974–81◊. See also Warsaw◊ Pact□

North Carolina southern state of the USA; Tar Heel or Old North State
area 136 523 sq km/52 712 sq mi
capital Raleigh
towns Charlotte, Greensboro; Winston-Salem

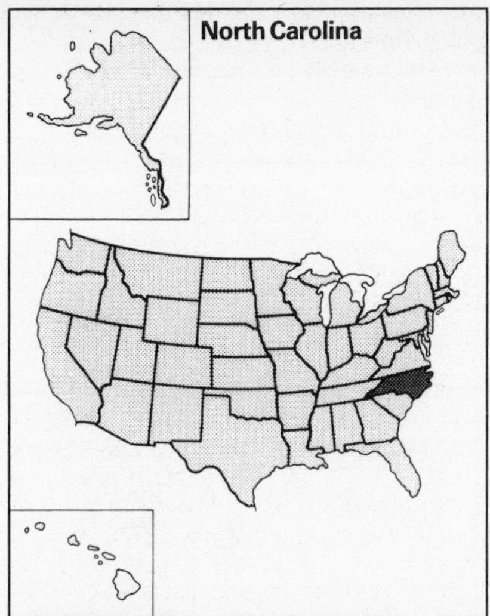

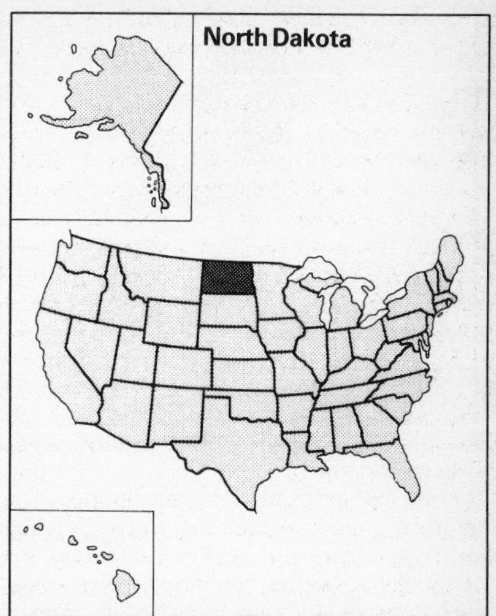

features Appalachian Mountains (including Blue Ridge and Great Smoky Mountains); site of Fort Raleigh on Roanoke Island (see under history below); Wright Brothers National Memorial at Kitty Hawk; the Research Triangle established in 1956 (Duke University, University of North Carolina and North Carolina State University) for 'high tech' industries
products tobacco, maize, soybeans; livestock, poultry and dairy products; textiles and clothing, furniture, computers; mica, feldspar, bricks
population 5 737 140
famous people Billy Graham, O Henry
history Sir Walter Raleigh◊ sent out 108 colonists from Plymouth in 1585 under his cousin Sir Richard Grenville, who established the first English settlement in the New World on Roanoke Island; the survivors were taken home by Drake in 1586. Further attempts failed there, the settlers having disappeared without trace by 1590. The first permanent settlement in the state was made in 1663. It was one of the original Thirteen Colonies, becoming a state in 1789□

Northcliffe Alfred William Harmsworth, 1st Viscount Northcliffe 1865–1922. British press baron, founder of the *Daily Mail* 1896, which inaugurated popular journalism, and the *Daily Mirror* 1903, the first picture paper. From 1908 he controlled *The Times* and was created baron in 1905, viscount in 1917□

North Dakota Prairie state of the USA; Sioux or Flickertail State
area 183 020 sq km/70 665 sq mi
capital Bismark
towns Fargo, Grand Forks
features fertile Red River Valley, Missouri Plateau; Bad Lands (including Theodore Roosevelt's Elkhorn Ranch)
products cereals, meat products; farm equipment
population 652 437
famous people Maxwell Anderson, Louis l'Amour
history acquired by the USA partly in the Louisiana◊ Purchase 1803, and partly by treaty with Britain in 1813, it became a state in 1889□

North-East Frontier Agency see Arunachal Pradesh□

North-East India area of India (Meghalaya, Assam, Mizoram, Tripura, Manipur, and Nagaland, and the Union Territory of Arunachal Pradesh) linked with the rest of India only by a narrow corridor. There is opposition to immigration from Bangladesh and the rest of India, and calls for secession□

North-East Passage sea route from the N Atlantic, round Asia, to the N Pacific, pioneered by Nordenskjöld◊ 1878–9, and developed by the USSR in settling N Siberia from 1935. The USSR owns offshore islands, and claims it as an internal waterway; the USA claims that it is international□

Northern Areas districts N of Azad Kashmir, directly administered by Pakistan but not merged with it. India and Azad Kashmir each claim them as part of disputed Kashmir. They include Baltistan, Gilgit and Skardu, and Hunza (an independent principality for 900 years until 1974)□

Northern Rhodesia see Zambia◊□

Northern Territory territory of the Commonwealth of Australia
area 1 356 165 sq km/523 620 sq mi

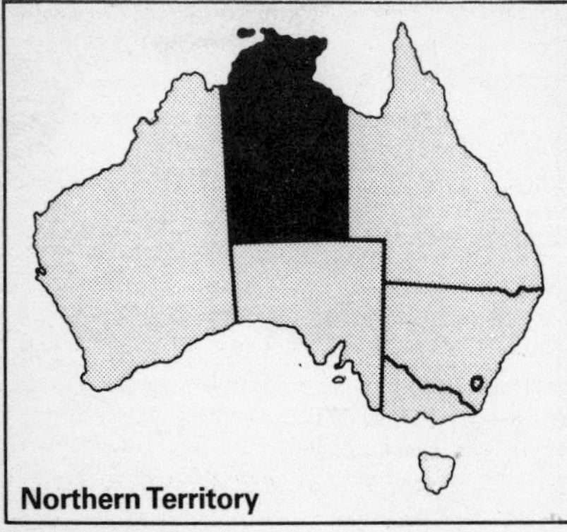
Northern Territory

capital Darwin
towns chief port Darwin; Alice Springs
features mainly within the tropics, though with wide range of temperature; very low rainfall, but artesian bores are used; Macdonnell Ranges (Mt Zeil 1510 m/4955 ft); Cocos◊ and Christmas◊ Islands were included in the Territory in 1984
exports beef cattle; prawns; bauxite (Gove), gold and copper (Tennant Creek), uranium (Ranger)
population 129 000 including Aborigines
government there is an administrator, and Legislative Assembly, and the Territory is also represented in the federal parliament.
recent history originally part of New South Wales, it was annexed in 1863 to South Australia, but 1911–78 (when self-government was granted) was under the control of the Commonwealth government□

North Ossetian see Ossetia◊□

North Pole see Poles◊□

North-Rhine-Westphalia Land of W Germany
area 34 150 sq km/13 110 sq mi
capital Düsseldorf
towns Cologne, Essen, Dortmund, Duisberg, Wuppertal
features valley of the Rhine; Ruhr industrial district
products iron and steel, coal and lignite, electrical goods, fertilizers, synthetic textiles
population 17 058 200
religion Roman Catholicism 53%, Protestantism 42%□

North Sea sea to the east of Britain; area 523 000 sq km/202 000 sq mi. There are fisheries, e.g. Dogger Bank, and oil and gas; average depth 55 m/180 ft, greatest depth 660 m/2165 ft□

Northumberland John Dudley, Duke of Northumberland c1502–53. English statesman, raised to a dukedom in 1551, and chief minister until Edward VI's death 1553. He then tried to place his daughter-in-law Lady Jane Grey◊ on the throne, and was executed on Mary◊'s accession. See Earl of Leicester◊□

Northumberland N county of England

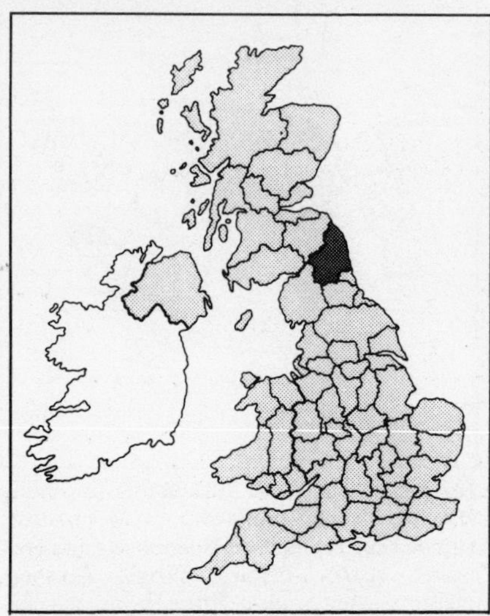

area 5032 sq km/1942 sq mi
towns administrative headquarters Morpeth; Berwick-upon-Tweed, Hexham
features Cheviot Hills, rivers Tweed and upper Tyne; Northumberland National Park in the W; Holy◊ Island; Farne◊ Islands; part of Hadrian's Wall and Housestead's Fort; Alnwick and Bamburgh castles; Thomas Bewick◊ museum; large moorland areas are used for military manoeuvres
products sheep
population 296 000□

Northumbria Anglo-Saxon kingdom which covered NE England and SE Scotland, comprising the 6th century kingdoms of Bernicia (Forth–Tees) and Deira (Tees–Humber) united in the 7th century. Influenced by Irish missionaries, it was a cultural centre until the 8th century (see Bede, Cuthbert, Wilfrid). It accepted the supremacy of Wessex◊ 827, and was conquered by the Danes in the later 9th century□

North-West Frontier Province province (capital Peshawar) of British India 1901–1947, when it became part of Pakistan. It includes the strategic Khyber Pass on the Afghanistan border. See Pathan◊□

North-West Passage Atlantic–Pacific sea route round the N of Canada; early explorers included Frobisher◊ and Franklin◊, but Amundsen◊ was the first European to sail through. Canada, which owns offshore islands, claims it as an internal waterway, the

USA insists that it is an international waterway, and sent an icebreaker through without permission 1985□

Northwest Territories territory of Canada

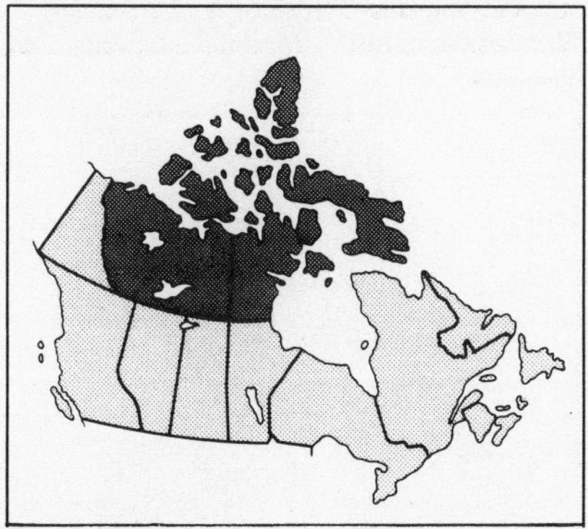

area 3 379 689 sq km/1 304 903 sq mi
capital Yellowknife
features Mackenzie river; Dawson City; Miles Canyon; the Klondike area. The area is divided into three administrative districts: Franklin area 1 422 550 sq km/549 253 sq mi, population 7747, extends to the North Pole; Keewatin area 590 930 sq km/228 160 sq mi, population 3403, extends from the district of Mackenzie to the Hudson Bay; Mackenzie area 1 336 199 sq km/527 490 sq mi, population 23 657, includes the western edge of the Canadian Shield.
products oil and natural gas, zinc, lead, gold, tungsten, silver
population 49 400□

North Yorkshire NE county of England

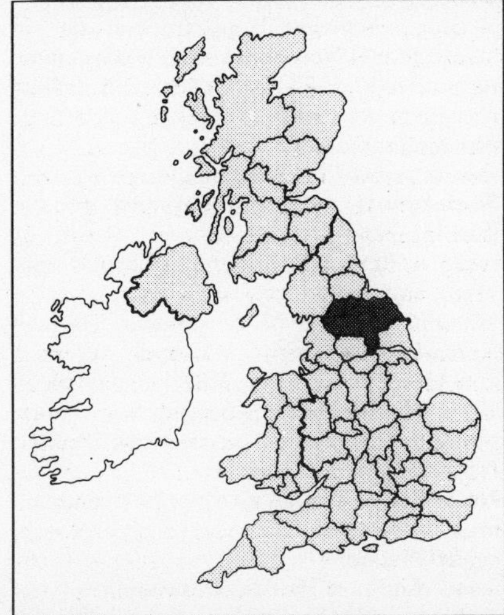

area 8309 sq km/3207 sq mi
towns administrative headquarters Northallerton; York, and the resorts of Harrogate, Scarborough, and Whitby
features England's largest county; including part of the Pennines, the Vale of York, and the Cleveland Hills and North Yorkshire Moors, which form a National Park (within the park are Fylingdales radar station to give early warning – four minutes – of nuclear attack, and Rievaulx Abbey)
products cereals; wool and meat from sheep; dairy products; coal (Selby)
population 668 800□

Norton Caroline 1808–77. British writer, granddaughter of R B Sheridan◊. Her drunkard husband falsely accused Lord Melbourne of seducing her, obtained custody of their children, and tried to obtain the profits from her books. Public reaction to this led to changes in the law of infant custody, and married women's property rights□

Norway Kingdom of

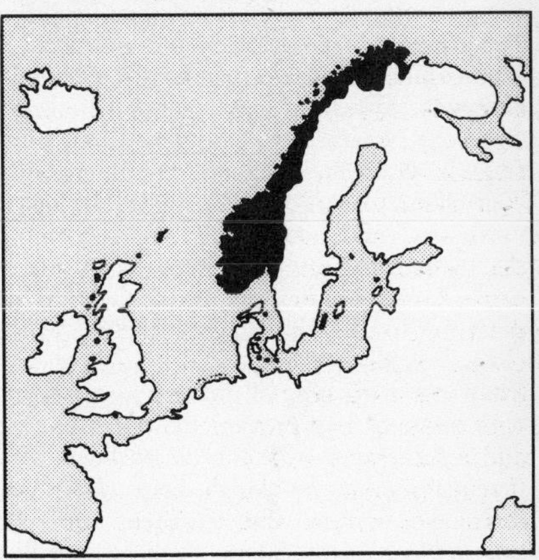

area 324 220 sq km/125 065 sq mi
capital Oslo
towns Bergen and Trondheim
features beautiful fjords, including Hardanger and Sogne, the longest 185 km/115 mi and deepest 1245 m/4080 ft; forests and glaciers cover 25%; Midnight Sun◊ and Northern Lights◊; great resources of hydroelectric power; dependencies in the Arctic (Svalbard◊ and Jan◊ Mayen) and in the Antarctic (Bouvet and Peter I Island, and Queen Maud Land)
exports petrochemicals from North Sea oil and gas; paper, wood pulp, furniture; iron ore and other minerals; hightech goods, e.g. gas turbines, TV sets; sports goods; fish, etc.
currency krone
population 4 070 000
language Riksmal (formal Dano-Norwegian) and Landsmal (based on the local dialects of Norway; see Ivar Aasen◊)

religion Evangelical Lutheran, endowed by state
famous people *exploration* Amundsen, Nansen; *literature* (poetry) poets of the Elder Edda◊, Henrik Wergeland, (novel) Knut Hamsun, Sigrid Undset; *music* Grieg, Sinding, Svendsen
government constitutional monarchy (Olav V◊), with a parliament (Storting) elected for four years (Prime Minister from 1986 Ms Harlem Brundtland)
recent history independent of Denmark from 1814, Norway finally severed links with Sweden in 1905, and became an independent kingdom. During the German occupation 1940–45, the King and government escaped to Britain; see Quisling◊. Following a referendum in 1972, Norway refused to enter the Common Market, but sought trade agreements. Since the 1930s the Labour Party has usually predominated, but there have been non-socialist coalitions since the 1960s. The Conservative coalition under Kaare Willoch 1983-6 was one such□

Norwegian Sea see under Arctic◊ Ocean□

Norwich industrial city (shoes, clothing, chemicals, confectionery, engineering, printing) in Norfolk, England; population 121 700. The 'capital' of E Anglia, it has a university, and notable buildings including the cathedral (founded 1096) and Norman castle, with a museum and collection of paintings by the Norwich school (Cotman◊, Crome◊, etc.) in the keep□

nose upper opening of the respiratory tract, with hairs to help prevent the entry of dust and insects, and with the cavity lined with mucous membrane which helps filter out dirt and warms and moistens the air breathed in. In the olfactory area, receptor cells are contained in the mucous membrane, which at least partly dissolves the molecules given off by substances that smell, so that their odour can be perceived. In some animals the sense of smell is much more highly developed□

Nostradamus (Michel de Notredame) 1503–66. French physician who served Charles IX, and was consulted by Catherine de' Medici and others for astrological predictions. More famous than accurate, they were used by Goebbels in propaganda for Hitler□

Nott Sir John 1932– . British Conservative politician, Minister for Defence 1981–3 during the Falklands◊ campaign□

Nottingham industrial city (engineering, coalmining, cycles, textiles, knitwear, pharmaceuticals, tobacco, lace, electronics) and administrative headquarters of Nottinghamshire, England; population 277 500. The castle is a museum; the Catholic cathedral is by Pugin, and there is a Playhouse and university 1881. Nearby Newstead Abbey was the home of Byron□

Nottinghamshire Midland county of England

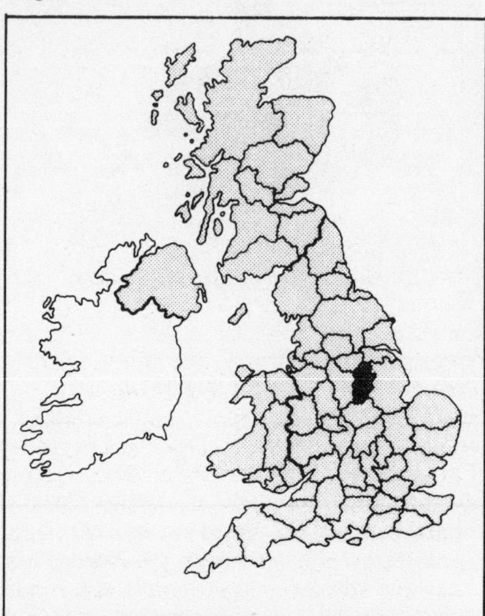

area 2164 sq km/836 sq mi
towns administrative headquarters Nottingham; Mansfield, Worksop
features river Trent; the remaining areas of Sherwood Forest (see Robin◊ Hood), formerly a royal hunting ground, are included in the 'Dukeries'; Cresswell Crags (remains of prehistoric man)
products cereals, cattle, sheep; light engineering, footwear; ironstone and oil (in World War II Nottinghamshire produced the only oil out of U-boat reach, and drilling revived in the 1980s)
population 977 000
famous people D H Lawrence, Alan Sillitoe□

Nouakchott capital of Mauritania; population 135 000□

nova a star◊ that suddenly becomes very bright and then fades again□

Novalis pseudonym of pioneer German Romantic poet Friedrich Leopold, Freiherr von Hardenburg 1772–1801. The death in 1797 of his fiancée, Sophie von Kühn, prompted his *Hymnen an die Nacht* 1800□

Nova Lisboa see Huambo◊□

Nova Scotia eastern province of Canada
area 54 558 sq km/21 065 sq mi
capital Halifax
towns chief port Halifax; Dartmouth
features Cabot Trail (Cape Breton Island), Alexander Graham Bell Museum, Fortress

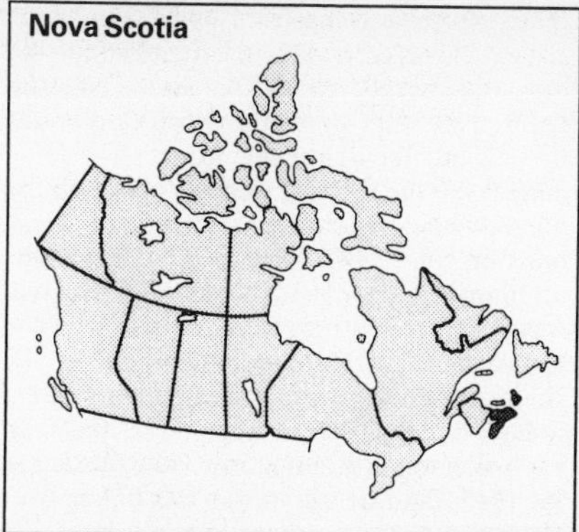

Louisbourg; Strait of Canso Superport is the largest deepwater harbour on the Atlantic coast of the continent

products coal, gypsum, etc.; dairy products, poultry, fruit; forest products; fish products, including scallop and lobster

population 869 900. See also Canada◊□

Novaya Zemlaya Arctic island group off the NE USSR; population, a few Samoyed. It is rich in birds, seals and walrus□

novel an extended work of fictitious prose. Pioneer contributors to aspects of the novel include: Petronius, Apuleius, Murasaki Shikibu, Boccaccio, Malory, Cervantes.

Major English-language novelists include:

18th century *British* Defoe, Richardson, Fielding, Sterne, Smollett

19th century *British* Sir Walter Scott, Jane Austen, Dickens, Thackeray, the Brontës, George Eliot, Trollope, Stevenson, Hardy, Henry James, Conrad *American* Cooper, Melville, Hawthorne, Twain

20th century *British* D H Lawrence, Virginia Woolf, George Orwell, William Golding *American* Theodore Dreiser, Ernest Hemingway, Sinclair Lewis, William Faulkner, Saul Bellow, Norman Mailer, Philip Roth□

Novello Ivor. Stage-name of British actor, manager, and composer I(vor) N(ovello) Davies 1893–1951. Born in Cardiff, he is remembered for the World War I song 'Keep the Home Fires Burning', and the spectacular musical plays in which he often appeared with romantically handsome charm, e.g. *Glamorous Night* 1925, *The Dancing Years* 1939, *Perchance to Dream* 1945–7, and *King's Rhapsody* 1949□

Noverre Jean-Georges 1717–1810. French dancer and choreographer, see ballet◊, who made dance tell a story□

Novgorod industrial (chemicals, engineering, clothing, brewing) city in the NW USSR; population 210 000. It was the original capital of the Russian state, founded there at the invitation of the people of the city by the Viking (Varangian) chieftain Rurik in 862□

Novi Sad industrial and commercial city, capital of the autonomous province of Vojvodina, Yugoslavia; population 257 700□

Novokuznetsk industrial city (steel, aluminium, chemicals) in the Kuzbas, S central USSR; population 564 000□

Novorossiisk USSR Black Sea port and industrial (cement, metallurgy, food processing) city; population 171 000□

Novosibirsk industrial (engineering, textiles, food processing) city in W Siberia, USSR; population 162 000. Winter lasts eight months here. At Akademgorodok 'Science City', population 25 000, advanced research is carried on into Siberia's local problems, and there are centres also at Irkutsk and Krasnoyarsk□

Noyes Alfred 1880–1958. British poet, he became a Catholic convert in 1930. He is remembered for poems about the sea, and anthology favourites 'Barrel Organ', 'Go down to Kew in lilac-time ...' and 'The Highwayman'□

Nubia African country now divided between Egypt and Sudan, which was the ancient battleground between the white and black peoples for dominance in N Africa. Ancient Egypt, which knew the N as Wawat and the S as Kush, was herself briefly ruled by Nubian kings in the 8–7th century BC. Egyptian building work in the area included Abu◊ Simbel, Philae, and a defensive chain of forts which established the lines of development of medieval fortification. Nubia's capital was ***Meroe*** c600BC–350AD, near Khartoum, now called the 'Birmingham of ancient Africa' because of its slag-heaps.

About 250–550AD most of Nubia was occupied by the mysterious ***x-group people*** whose royal mound tombs were excavated by W B Emery◊; many horses and attendants were found to have been slaughtered to accompany the richly jewelled dead□

nuclear arms verification the process of checking the number and types of nuclear weapons held by a country (see also disarmament◊), the chief means are:

reconnaissance satellites which detect submarines or weapon silos, using angled cameras to give 3-D pictures of installations; penetrating camouflage by means of scanners; and partially seeing through cloud and darkness by infra-red devices

telemetry (radio transmission of instrument readings) ***interception*** to get information on performance of weapons under test, and ***radar tracking*** of missiles in flight

seismic monitoring of underground tests, in the same way as with earthquakes; this is not accurate and on-site inspection is needed. Tests in the atmosphere, space, or the oceans are forbidden, and the ban is accepted because explosions are not only dangerous to all, but immediately detectable□

nuclear energy energy from the inner core or nucleus of atoms, as opposed to energy released in chemical processes, which is derived from the electrons surrounding the nucleus

nuclear fission as in an atom bomb, is achieved by allowing a neutron to strike the nucleus of an atom of uranium-235, which then splits apart to release perhaps two to three other neutrons. If the material is pure uranium-235, a chain reaction is set up when these neutrons in turn strike other nuclei. This happens with great rapidity, resulting in the tremendous burst of energy we associate with the atom bomb. However, the process can be controlled by absorbing excess neutrons in 'control rods' (which may be made of steel alloyed with boron), and slowing down the speed of those neutrons allowed to act. This is what is done inside a nuclear power plant.

nuclear fusion the process (release of thermonuclear energy by the condensation of hydrogen nuclei to helium nuclei) which occurred in the hydrogen bomb and, as a continuing reaction, in the sun and other stars. It avoids the loss of much of the energy produced which occurs in the original atom bomb, so that it is correspondingly more powerful. Attempts to harness it for commercial power production have so far not succeeded.

nuclear accidents the most serious have been:
Apr 1986 at Chernobyl (USSR): a leak from a non-pressurized boiling-water reactor, one of the largest in the Soviet Union, caused by overheating. The resulting clouds of radioactive isotopes were traced as far away as Sweden, and hundreds were contaminated.
1979 at Three Mile Island, Harrisburg◊, USA: a PWR (*p*ressurized *w*ater *r*eactor) leaked radioactive matter, a leak caused by a combination of mechanical and electrical failure, as well as operator error. In this type of reactor the heat formed by the fission of the uranium is carried away by a sealed and pressurized loop of irradiated water (chiefly 'heavy'◊ water) to steam generators.
1957 at Windscale (now Sellafield◊), England: fire destroyed the core of a reactor, releasing large quantities of lethal radioactive fumes into the atmosphere. See also meltdown◊, nuclear◊ waste, nuclear◊ warfare□

nuclear warfare war involving the use of nuclear weapons. Nuclear weapons derive their explosive force from nuclear energy◊. Research was carried on in Britain from 1940, but transferred to USA after America entered the war (Manhattan Project, directed by Oppenheimer◊ at Los◊ Alamos).

atom bomb the original weapon relied on use of a chemical explosion to trigger a 'chain reaction,' i.e. two pieces of the isotope uranium–235 were made to collide with great force, so that neutrons were set free, which in turn collided with atomic nuclei, and so the chain continues with accompanying great release of explosive energy. The first test explosion was at Alamogordo New Mexico 16 Jul 1945; the first use in war was 6 Aug over Hiroshima◊ and three days later at Nagasaki◊.

hydrogen bomb a much more powerful weapon, relies on the release of thermonuclear energy by the condensation of hydrogen nuclei to helium nuclei (as happens in the sun). The first detonation on earth was at Eniwetok Atoll 1952 by the USA, through the triggering of tritium (hydrogen isotope of atomic weight 3.0170) by an ordinary atom bomb.

neutron bomb or ***E**nhanced **R**adiation **W**eapon* (ERW) is a very small hydrogen bomb which has relatively high radiation, but relatively low blast, designed to kill (in up to six days) by a brief neutron radiation which leaves buildings and weaponry intact.

nuclear methods of attack now include aircraft bombs, rocket-propelled missiles◊ with nuclear warheads (long or short range, surface-to-surface, surface to air, etc.), depth charges, and high-powered landmines ('atomic demolition munitions' to blast craters in the path of an advancing enemy army). The major subjects of Soviet–US negotiation are:

intercontinental ballistic missiles (ICBMs) which have from 1968 been equipped with clusters of warheads (which can be directed to individual targets) and are known as multiple independently targetable re-entry vehicles (MIRVs). The latest US design is the MX (Peacekeeper) with up to ten warheads in each of about 100 missiles to be permanently placed in land silos. Britain retained an independent nuclear deterrent in 1980 by agreeing to buy submarine-launched Trident missiles from the USA: each warhead has eight independently targetable re-entry vehicles (each nuclear-armed); range c6400 km/4000 mi to eight separate targets within c240 km/150 mi of the central aiming point.

cruise missiles developed 1976, which are nuclear-armed pilotless planes 6 m/19 ft long, with a range of some 3000 km/2000 mi,

launched by land, sea or air, and computer-programmed to change direction to confuse defences; they have already been deployed among NATO allies in Europe (see Newbury◊). They would be launched in large numbers to assist manned strategic bombers in penetrating to targets.
methods of defence include: ***anti-ballistic missile*** (ABM) earth-based systems, with two types of missile, one short-range with high acceleration, and one comparatively long-range for interception above the atmosphere
Strategic Defence Initiative (announced by the USA 1983 to be operative from 2000, and popularly known as the 'Star Wars' programme). 'Directed energy weapons' firing laser beams would be mounted on space-based battle stations, and by burning holes in incoming missiles would either collapse them or detonate their fuel tanks□

nuclear waste is produced in three forms
gas still in small enough quantity to be released into the atmosphere
solid irradiated fuel element cans and other equipment. When of low activity, this is packaged for sea disposal (e.g. 450 km/300 mi off Land's End), but this is controversial. High activity waste may be combustible (plutonium being recovered from the incinerator), or may be buried, the latter being also controversial
liquid high activity liquid wastes pose the greatest problems of all. Storage has been proposed in salt mines, granite formations, or 'clay basins'; or on or under the seabed. Controversy is greatest on this form of waste, because no container can be guaranteed (as international authorities require) against decay, volcanic action, etc., for 100 000 years. The most hopeful proposed method is by vitrification into solid glass cylinders, which would be placed in titanium-cobalt alloy containers and deposited on dead planets in space. Beneath the sea the containers would start to corrode after 1000 years, and the cylinders themselves would dissolve within the next 1000 years. See also radioactive◊ waste□

nuclear winter apart from the destruction of life and cities, in a nuclear war, and subsequent radiation hazards, it has been calculated that the atmosphere will be so contaminated by dust, smoke, soot and ash resulting from firestorms in target areas that the sun would be blotted out for about a year, sufficient to eradicate most plant life on which other life depends, and the cold would be intense. Insects and grass have the best prospects of survival□

nucleic acid complex organic acid with long-chain spiralling molecules present in all living matter. DNA◊ (deoxyribonucleic acid) and RNA (ribonucleic acid) play an important part in protein synthesis and in the transmission of hereditary characteristics in living organisms□

nucleus (biology) the central part of an animal or plant cell which contains chromosomes determining the characteristics of the cell. See cell◊□

nucleus (physics) the positively charged central part of an atom◊□

Nuffield William Richard Morris, Viscount Nuffield 1877–1963. British car manufacturer, e.g. Morris cars, who endowed Nuffield College, Oxford, in 1937 and the Nuffield Foundation in 1943□

Nujoma Sam 1929– . Namibian politician, founder of SWAPO◊ in 1959, and controller of guerrillas from Angolan bases□

Nukua'lofa capital and port of Tonga on Tongatapu; population 18 300□

Nullabor Plain arid coastal plateau area divided between Western and S Australia; there is a network of caves beneath it. Atom bomb experiments were carried out near Maralinga in the 1950s□

Numa Pompilius legendary king of Rome c716–c679BC, who succeeded Romulus, and was credited with the introduction of religious rites□

numbat a small marsupial mammal of Australia. See under marsupialia◊□

Numidia Roman N African territory ('nomads' land'), modern E Algeria□

numismatics study of coins (see money◊) and medals◊. The earliest Chinese coins were small-scale bronze reproductions of barter objects, e.g. knives and spades. The Lydians used electrum, a natural gold/silver mixture. Most modern coinages are 'token' in that their face value is much greater than their real value. Milled edges were first introduced to avoid fraudulent 'clipping' of the edges of precious metal coins□

nun a woman belonging to a religious order. See under monasticism◊□

Nuneaton market town making industrial ceramics, tiles and bricks, in Warwickshire, England; population 69 500□

Nunn Trevor 1940– . British stage director, linked with the Royal◊ Shakespeare Company from 1968, who received a Tony award (with John Caird) for his production of *Nicholas Nickleby* 1982□

Nuremberg (German *Nürnberg*). Industrial city (electrical and other machinery, precision instruments, textiles, and toys, for which an annual fair is held) in Bavaria, W Germany; population 481 000. Created an imperial city 1219, it has an 11–16th century fortress, and many medieval buildings (restored after near destruction of 75% of the city in World War II), including the 14th-century Marthakirche, where the Meistersingers◊ met (see Hans Sachs◊). Dürer was born here, and is commemorated by a museum. From 1933 Nazi Party rallies were held here: see Nuremberg◊ Trials□

Nuremberg trials the trials of the 24 chief Nazi◊ war criminals Nov 1945–Oct 1946 by four judges (representing UK, USA, USSR and France) on charges of conspiracy to wage wars of aggression; crimes against peace; war crimes (e.g. murdering and ill-treating civilians and prisoners-of-war, and use of slave labour); and crimes against humanity (e.g. mass murder of the Jews and other peoples, and of political opponents). There were 12 death sentences (including Bormann, Goering, Ribbentrop, Kaltenbrunner, Keitel and Jodl◊); among those imprisoned, who included Raeder◊ and Doenitz◊, Hess◊ (in Spandau◊) is the only survivor in captivity. Papen was one of those acquitted. In addition the German cabinet, general staff, high command, Nazi leadership corps (SS, SA, Gestapo) were charged with criminal responsibility, and declared criminal organizations□

Nureyev Rudolf 1939– . Russian dancer of Tatar descent, who defected to England from the Kirov Ballet in 1961, and excelled in partnership with Margot Fonteyn◊□

nursery rhyme jingle current among children, often handed down orally in forms differing from those in adult collections, and some of the oldest having accompanying tunes, e.g. 'Here we go round the mulberry bush', linked with Mayday festivities and a ring game. Others contain fragments of incantations or other rites, and some commemorate actual popular figures, e.g. Jack Sprat, Jack Horner, and Mary with her little lamb□

nursing supervision of health as well as care of the sick, very young, very old and the disabled. In the pre-Christian era very limited care was associated with some temples, and in Christian times became associated with the religious orders until the Reformation brought it into secular hands in Protestant countries. Organized training first originated in 1836 in Germany, and was developed in Britain by the work of Florence Nightingale◊. Many varied qualifications are now available, standards being maintained by the National Boards (England, Scotland, Wales and N Ireland) for Nursing, Midwifery and Health Visiting, and the Royal College of Nursing (1916) is the professional body□

Nusa Tenggara see under Indonesia◊□

nut fruit consisting of a kernel with a hard outer shell which decays when ripe, releasing the seed; most nuts contain nutritive oils□

nuthatch bird, family Sittidae, order Passeriformes. Blue-grey above, and buff below, the ***European nuthatch*** *Sitta europea* feeds chiefly on nuts, climbs well, and nests in holes in trees□

nutmeg aromatic seed of the tropical evergreen tree *Myristica fragrans*; both nutmeg and its yellow-red covering (***mace***) are used in cookery□

nutrition the science of food, and its effect on the life and health of human beings (e.g. the diseases caused by lack of vitamins and protein in the Third World and those caused by high cholesterol and sugar content in the diet of wealthy countries). It also deals with animals, notably the food requirements of poultry and livestock reared for human consumption, and the formulation of animal feeds□

Nuuk Greenlandic for Godthaab◊□

Nyasa see Lake Malawi◊□

Nyasaland see Malawi◊□

Nyerere Julius Kambarage 1922– . President of Tanganyika from 1962, and of Tanzania 1962–85. A Christian and dedicated socialist, he campaigned for independence from 1954, but led his country into financial difficulties. On resigning the presidency, he remained chairman of the ruling party□

nylon a synthetic fibre◊□

nymph in Greek mythology, a guardian spirit of nature; hamadryads or dryads guarded trees; naiads, springs and pools; oreads, hills and rocks; nereids, the sea□

O

Oahu see under Hawaii◊□

oak widespread genus of trees and shrubs, family Fagaceae (see beech◊), valued for timber, and characterized by alternate lobed leaves and a fruit (acorn) borne in a cup. They include ***English oak*** *Quercus robur*; ***evergreen holm*** *Q ilex*; ***Turkey oak*** *Q cerris*; ***cork oak*** *Q suber*; and the American ***white oak*** *Q alba* and evergreen ***live oak*** *Q virginiana.* Oak wilt resembles Dutch elm disease; oak 'apples' are the rounded brown galls caused by gall wasps (see wasp◊), which lay their eggs in them□

Oakland port and industrial city (textiles, chemicals, food processing) in California, USA, linked by bridge (1936) with San Francisco; population 339 500. Jack London lived on the waterfront, and London Square commemorates him□

Oakley Annie 1860–1926. American markswoman, member of Buffalo Bill's Wild West Show, who could perforate a playing card tossed in the air□

Oak Ridge town in Tennessee, USA; population 27 700. The Oak Ridge National Laboratory for the manufacture of plutonium was established here 1943, and it has the American Museum of Atomic Energy□

Oaks see horseracing◊□

OAS see Organization◊ of American States□

Oates Laurence Edward Grace 1880–1912. British Antarctic explorer, who accompanied Scott◊ on the final dash to the Pole. On the return journey, suffering from frostbite, he went out alone into the blizzard to die rather than delay the others□

Oates Titus 1649–1705. British cleric who, after a period as a spy in Jesuit◊ colleges abroad, announced on his return to England an almost entirely ficititious 'Popish plot' to murder Charles II and establish Roman Catholicism. Many innocent Roman Catholics were executed 1678–80 on his evidence, and in 1685 he was flogged, pilloried and imprisoned for perjury. After the 1688 revolution he was pardoned and pensioned□

oats a type of grass, grown for its edible seed. See under grasses◊□

OAU see Organization◊ of African Unity□

Ob river in Asiatic Russia; length 3380 km/ 2100 mi□

Oban port in Strathclyde, Scotland, holiday capital of the W Highlands; population 7000□

OBE Order of the British Empire. See medal◊□

Oberammergau see under Munich◊□

Oberhausen inland port in N Rhine-Westphalia, W Germany; population 228 600□

Oberon king of the elves or fairies, and, according to a 13th-century French romance, an illegitimate son of Julius Caesar. Shakespeare adopted him for *A Midsummer Night's Dream,* in which his consort is Titania. See also Jonson◊, Wieland◊, and Weber◊□

obesity over-weight, which increases susceptibility to disease and strain on the body's functioning parts, and lessens life expectancy; it is remedied by healthy diet and exercise. Results differ in individuals because of variations in the natural rate of the metabolic processes, and in the structure of fatty tissue itself□

obi the witchcraft◊ of black Africa□

oboe a musical instrument of the woodwind◊ family□

Obote (Apollo) Milton 1924– . Ugandan statesman who led the independence movement from 1961. He became prime minister 1962, and was president 1966–71 and 1980–5, being overthrown successively by Amin◊ and Okello◊□

Obraztsov Sergei 1901– . Russian puppeteer. Born in Moscow, where he runs the world's largest puppet theatre (staff 300), he has a repertoire built up since 1923□

obsidian glassy volcanic rock, chemically similar to granite◊, but which cooled rapidly on the earth's surface at low pressure. Trace◊ elements unique to the site at which it is found enable archaeologists to follow trade routes, e.g.in the Middle East, N and Central America, New Zealand, since obsidian was greatly sought by early peoples for making sharp-edged tools□

O'Casey Sean 1884–1964. Irish dramatist, whose earliest plays *The Shadow of a Gunman* 1922 and *Juno and the Paycock* 1925 gave a realistic picture of Dublin slum life in the 'troubles', and whose unromantic depiction of the Easter◊ Rebellion in *The Plough and the Stars* 1926 led to riots□

Occam or **Ockham** William of c1300–49. English philosopher, born at Ockham, Surrey. A Franciscan monk, he advocated separation of Church and State, and was imprisoned at Avignon on heresy charges in 1328, but escaped. He revived Nominalism◊, and was known as the 'Invincible Doctor'. His principle, of reducing one's assumptions to the absolute minimum, was called ***Occam's razor***□

Occitanie see under Languedoc◊□

ocean great mass of salt water
area approx 70% of the total surface area of earth (363 000 000 sq km/140 000 000 sq mi)
depth (mean) 3660 m/12 000 ft, but shallow ledges (180 m/600 ft) run out from the continents, and the continental◊ slope reaches down to the abyssal◊ zone, the largest area (1800–5500 m/6000–18 000 ft), only a small area lies deeper, the deepest recorded being 11 000 m/36 198 ft (by the *Vityaz* USSR, in the Mariana Trench in the W Pacific 1957)
features deep trenches (especially off E and SE Asia, and S America), volcanic belts (especially in the mid-Pacific and Indian Ocean) and mid-ocean ridges (in the mid-Atlantic, E Pacific, and Indian Ocean) ***temperature*** varies on the surface with latitude (−2°–29°); decreases rapidly to 370 m/1200 ft, then more slowly to 2200 m/7200 ft; and hardly at all beyond that
water contents salinity averages about 3%; minerals commercially extracted include bromine, magnesium, potassium, salt; those potentially recoverable include aluminium, calcium, copper, gold, manganese, silver□

oceanarium marine aquarium in which animal and plant species are not separated into tanks, but in which there is sufficient space for them to live together as in nature; the first was Marine Studios, California 1938□

Oceania the islands of the S Pacific (Micronesia◊, Melanesia◊, Polynesia◊), and sometimes including Australasia◊ and the Malay◊ archipelago, when it is considered as one of the seven continents◊; otherwise Australia alone is the seventh continent□

Ocean Island see under Kiribati◊□

oceanography scientific study of the ocean. The International Oceanographic Commission (linked to UNESCO: see under United◊ Nations) co-ordinates marine scientific research (in the UK at Godalming, in the USA at the Naval Oceanographic Office, which cooperates with the Scripps Institute in California, and Woods Hole Institute in New England). Access by scientists is hampered by exclusive economic zones (see under Law of the Sea◊), and by the commercial value of their studies (resources such as coal, oil and gas beneath the seabed, and mineral deposits upon it, such as self-forming manganese nodules; and rich fish stocks in biologically interesting areas), and their military significance (currents are important in navigation, and acoustic signals are bent at the boundary of hot/cold water zones, so that submarines are 'invisible' in the resultant gap in a sonar scan).
Pioneers in the science were James Cook◊, Matthew Maury◊, and John and James Ross◊; research is now by manned submersibles, undersea photography, sonic soundings, etc.□

Oceanus in Greek mythology, the god (one of the Titans◊) of a river supposed to encircle the earth, and progenitor of other river gods, and the nymphs of the seas and rivers□

ocelot a large wild cat◊ of Central and South America□

O'Connell Daniel 1775–1847. Irish politician, 'the Liberator'. Ineligible as a Roman Catholic to take his seat as MP for county Clare in 1828, he forced the government to grant Catholic emancipation, and in 1841 launched a campaign for repeal of the Act of Union with Britain of 1801. A shrewd realist, he lost the backing of young extremists, who broke away to form the 'Young◊ Ireland' movement□

O'Connor Feargus 1794–1855. Irish parliamentary follower of O'Connell◊, who as editor of the *Northern Star* became the most influential figure of the Chartist movement (see Chartism◊). He died insane following its collapse in 1852□

Octavian see Augustus◊□

Oct Revolution see under calendar◊ and USSR◊□

octopus a mollusc with eight long tentacles. See Cephalopod◊□

ode lyric poem of complex form and charged emotion, originally chanted in ancient Greece to a musical accompaniment. Exponents include Sappho◊, Pindar◊, Horace◊ and Catullus◊, and among British poets: Spenser◊, Milton◊, Dryden◊, Gray◊, Collins◊, Coleridge◊, Wordsworth◊, Shelley◊, Keats◊, Tennyson◊ and Swinburne◊□

Odense industrial port (electrical goods, glass, textiles) on Fünen, Denmark; population 170 700. Hans Andersen was born here□

Oder European river flowing from Czechoslovakia to the Baltic (the Neisse◊ is a tributary); length 885 km/550 mi□

Oder-Neisse Line border between Poland and E Germany which has run along these two rivers since 1945□

Odessa seaport in the Ukraine Republic, USSR; population 1 057 000. Founded by Catherine II in 1795, Odessa still has many fine old buildings. During World War II it was occupied by the Germans 1941–44, but 10 000 partisans continued resistance from the 800 km/500 mi of 'catacombs' excavated for building stone□

Odets Clifford 1906–63. American communist playwright, most famous for his play about a strike *Waiting for Lefty* 1935□

Odin chief god of Scandinavian mythology, the Woden◊ or Wotan of the Germanic peoples. A sky god, he is resident in Asgard, at the top of the world-tree, and receives the souls of heroic slain warriors from the Valkyries, the 'divine maidens', feasting with them in his great hall, Valhalla. At Ragnarök (doomsday) the warriors were envisaged as fighting a final battle in support of Odin against the evil giants, a new order arising from the ensuing general destruction. The wife of Odin is Frigga◊ or Freyja, and Thor◊ is their son. The stories captured the imagination of Wagner◊, and attempts have been made in Scandinavia to revive the Norse◊ religion□

Odoacer c433–93. King of Italy from 476, when he deposed Romulus◊ Augustulus. He was overthrown and treacherously killed by Theodoric◊ the Great□

Odysseus Greek hero (Roman Ulysses) whose decade of adventures on his return home from the siege of Troy◊ to his home in Ithaca◊ (see Penelope◊), form the content of Homer's◊ *Odyssey*. He met the lotus◊-eaters, Circe◊, Scylla◊ and Charybdis◊, and the Sirens◊□

OECD see Organization◊ for Economic Cooperation and Development□

oedema popularly ***dropsy***. A general accumulation of lymph◊ in the body tissues or cavities, caused by failure of the heart, kidneys, liver, etc., and treated with drugs to induce greater flow of urine□

Oedipus legendary king of Thebes◊. He was exposed and left to die at birth because his father Laius had been warned by an oracle that his son would kill him. Saved and brought up by the King of Corinth, Oedipus killed Laius in a quarrel (without recognizing him) and, because he saved Thebes from the Sphinx◊, was granted the Theban kingdom and Jocasta (wife of Laius and mother of Oedipus) as his wife. Four children later, the truth was discovered; Jocasta hanged herself, Oedipus blinded himself, and as an exiled wanderer was guided by his daughter, Antigone◊. Sophocles◊ used the story in two tragedies□

Oedipus complex Freudian term for the antagonism of a son to his father, whom he sees as a rival for his mother's affection; Hamlet has been regarded as an example. For a girl antagonistic to her mother for the same reason, the term is Electra◊ complex□

Oersted Hans Christian 1777–1851. Danish physicist, the discoverer of electromagnetism□

oesophagaus a part of the alimentary canal between the pharynx and the stomach◊□

oestradiol a type of hormone◊□

oestrogen a type of hormone◊□

Offa died 796. King of Mercia◊ from 757. By his conquest of Essex, Kent, Sussex and Surrey, he brought it to the height of its power. ***Offa's Dyke*** a defensive earthwork along the Welsh border, of which there are remains from the mouth of the River Dee to that of the River Severn, is attributed to him□

Offaly county (county town Tullamore) of the Republic of Ireland, province of Leinster◊□

Offenbach Jacques 1819–80. French composer, the creator of opéra-bouffe presented at his theatre Bouffes Parisiennes, including *Orpheus in the Underworld* 1858 and *La Belle Hélène* 1864, and the full-scale opera *The Tales of Hoffman* 1881□

Official Secrets Act UK act of 1911, which superseded that of 1889, and introduced new sections making it an offence for anyone who had ever served the Crown to communicate to any person information acquired in that service, whether it is harmful to the State or not. In the 1980s there were demands that it should be replaced by a Freedom of Information Act (on US lines) which would differentiate between what was essential to be kept secret for the security of the State, and what it was merely inconvenient to the government, the civil service, etc. to have known□

O'Flaherty Liam 1897– . Irish author, born in the Aran◊ Islands, whose novels of Fenian◊ activities in county Mayo include *The Informer* 1925□

Ogaden desert plateau, rising to 1000 m/3000 ft, on which arid farming is practised by nomads. It forms a region of Harar province, SE Ethiopia, but is also claimed by Somalia□

Ogam Celtic 4–7th century script devised in Ireland, and surviving in about 400 inscriptions (mainly funerary) in the British Isles. It consists of strokes or notches suited to carving into rough-hewn stones□

Ogbomosho commercial centre in Nigeria, with textile industries; population 432 000□

Ogden C(harles) K(ay) 1889–1957. British originator, with ***I(vor) A(rmstrong) Richards*** 1893–1979, of Basic◊ English□

Ogdon John 1937– . British pianist, who shared the Tchaikovsky award in Moscow in 1962 with Ashkenazy◊, and is noted as an interpreter of Busoni◊ and Messiaen◊□

Ogilvy Angus James Bruce. See under Princess Alexandra◊□

Oglethorpe James Edward 1696–1785. English soldier, who obtained a charter 1732 for the colony of Georgia◊ (now USA) (as a refuge for persecuted Protestants from Europe and debtors), and administered it himself till 1743□

OGPU former name of the KGB◊□

O'Higgins Bernardo 1776–1842. Chilean soldier-statesman, a leader of the struggle for independence from Spanish rule 1810–17, and head of the first permanent national government 1817–23□

Ohio midwest state of the USA; Buckeye State

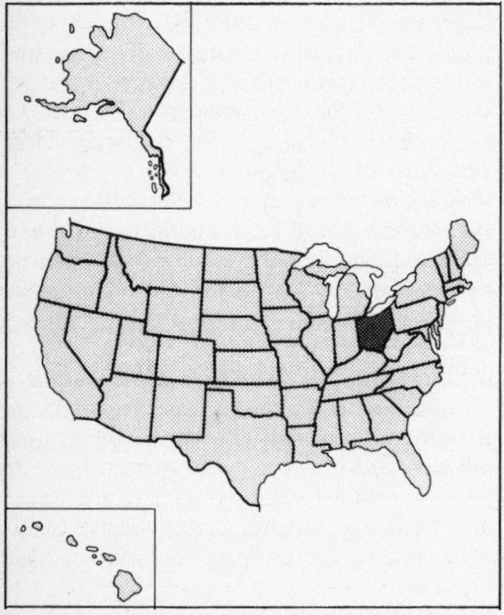

area 106 714 sq km/41 222 sq mi
capital Columbus
towns Cleveland, Cincinnati, Toledo, Akron, Dayton, Youngstown
features Ohio river; Serpent Mound, a 1.3 m/4 ft embankment, 405 m/1330 ft long, and c6m/18 ft across (built by Hopewell◊ Indians c1–2 century BC); Air Force Museum at Dayton; Pro Football Hall of Fame at Canton
products coal, cereals, livestock; machinery
population 10 797 420
famous people Sherwood Anderson◊, Ambrose Bierce◊, Thomas Edison◊, John Glenn◊, Paul Newman◊, General William Sherman◊, Orville Wright◊; six presidents (Garfield◊, Grant◊, Harding◊, Harrison◊, Hayes◊ and McKinley◊) were born in the state
history ceded to Britain by the French in 1763, it became a state in 1803□

Ohio (river) see under Mississippi◊□

Ohm Georg Simon 1787–1854. German physicist, who discovered ***Ohm's Law***: the electric current which flows through a metal wire kept at a constant temperature is proportional to the potential difference across it. See electric charge.◊□

ohm derived SI unit of electrical resistance◊; a circuit's resistance is 1 ohm when a potential difference of 1 volt is required to produce a current-flow of 1 ampere□

oil inflammable substance, usually insoluble in water, and chiefly composed of carbon and hydrogen. They may be solids (fats) at ordinary temperatures, or liquids. There are three main types:
essential oils volatile liquids which have the odour of their plant source and are used in perfumes and flavouring essences.
fixed oils mixtures of esters◊ of fatty acids, of varying consistency, found in both animals (e.g. fish oils) and plants (in nuts and seeds). They are used as food; in soaps, paints and varnishes; and for lubrication.
mineral oils which are obtained chiefly from petroleum◊□

oil palm a type of palm◊ plant□

Oise river flowing through Belgium and France; length 300 km/186 mi□

Oistrakh David Fyodorovich 1908–74. Russian violinist, for whom Shostakovich◊ wrote concertos; his son ***Igor*** 1931– , with whom he often played, is also a violinist□

okapi a mammal of the giraffe◊ family□

Okayama industrial port (textiles) in W Honshu, Japan; population 546 000□

Okeechobee see under Florida◊□

Okefenokee see under Georgia◊ (USA)□

Okeghem Jean d' c1425–c1495. Flemish composer who was a pioneer of counterpoint◊ in church music, and was court composer to Charles VII◊, Louis XI◊ and Charles VIII◊ of France. See Josquin◊ des Prés□

Okhotsk Sea of. Arm of the N Pacific, icefree only in summer, and often fogbound; area 937 000 sq km/582 000 sq mi□

Okhrana see under KGB◊□

Okinawa largest island of the Ryukyus◊, captured by the USA in the ***Battle of Okinawa*** 1 Apr–21 Jun 1945; 47 000 US casualties (12 000 dead), 60 000 Japanese (only a few hundred survived as prisoners)□

Oklahoma SW state of the USA; nicknamed Sooner State
area 181 088 sq km/69 919 sq mi

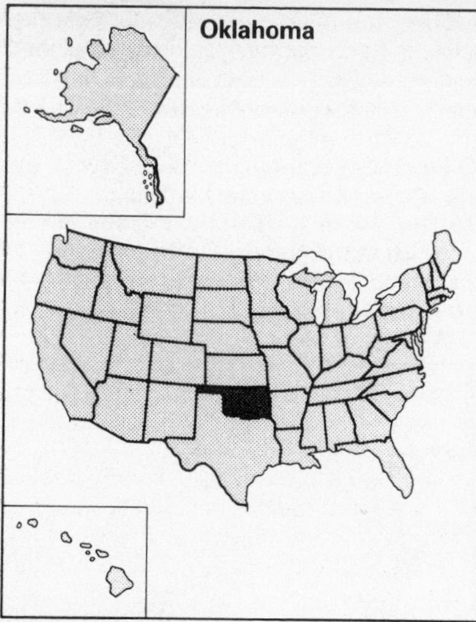

capital Oklahoma City
towns Tulsa
features Arkansas, Red, and Canadian rivers; Wichita and Ozark ranges; the Oklahoma 'panhandle' is part of the 'dust bowl'; the high plains have Indian reservations (Cherokee◊, Chickasaw◊, Choctaw◊, Creek◊ and Seminole◊)
products cereals, peanuts; livestock; oil, natural gas, helium; machinery and other metal products
population 3 025 270
famous people Woody Guthrie◊, Roy Harris◊, Karl Jansky◊, Will Rogers◊, Maria Tallchief◊
history part of the Louisiana◊ Purchase in 1803, Oklahoma became a state in 1907□

Oklahoma City capital and industrial city (oil refining, mining machinery, aircraft, communications equipment) of Oklahoma, USA; population 403 200. The National Cowboy Hall of Fame is here□

Okovango Swamp see under Botswana◊□

okra a type of hibiscus◊ plant, with edible fruit□

Olaf five kings of Norway including:
Olaf I (Tryggvesson) 969–1000, elected king 995, who began converting his people to Christianity, and was killed in a sea battle with the Danes and Swedes.
Olaf II (Haraldsson) 995–1030, king from 1015, whose centralizing policy and Christian zeal drove his chieftains to revolt (backed by Canute◊ of Denmark), but made him the patron saint of Norway from 1164.
Olaf V 1903– , who succeeded Haakon◊ VII 1957□

Old Bailey the name of the Central Criminal Court in London◊□

Old Catholics various breakaway groups from Roman Catholicism, especially those in Austria, Czechoslovakia, Germany, and Switzerland, who rejected the proclamation of Papal◊ infallibility of 1870. Their clergy are not celibate, and they have intercommunion with the Anglican church and have much in common with the Eastern Orthodox churches□

Oldenburg industrial city (electrical goods, food processing) in Lower Saxony, W Germany; population 138 000. Once the capital of Oldenburg duchy, it retains the ducal palace as a museum□

Oldham former cotton town in Greater Manchester, England, now diversified to electronics, electrical engineering, etc.; population 220 600□

Old Sarum see Salisbury◊□

Old Style a form of calendar◊ used in England before 1752□

Old Testament the first part of the Christian Bible◊□

Olduvai Gorge deep cleft in the Serengeti steppe, Tanzania◊, where the Leakeys◊ discovered 1958–9 Pleistocene◊ remains of gigantic animals. They included sheep as large as a carthorse, pigs the size of a rhinoceros, and a gorilla-sized baboon. Conditions here seem to have been so favourable that these creatures survived to a comparatively late date. The skull (*Zinjanthropus boisei*) with huge teeth, hence 'Nutcracker Man', was also found here, as well as remains of *Homo habilis* and primitive types of *Homo erectus*□

Old Vic theatre on the south bank of the Thames in Waterloo Road, built 1818, and famous under Emma Cons◊ from 1880 (as the Royal Victoria Hall, hence Old Vic) for popular opera and drama; under her niece Lilian Baylis◊, from 1914, it was famous for Shakespeare productions. It was badly damaged in 1940 air raids, but reopened 1950–81, acting as temporary home of the National Theatre 1963–76, and in 1985 was completely refurbished□

oleander or ***rose bay*** an evergreen Mediterranean shrub *Nerim oleander* family Apocynaceae, with clusters of pink flowers, and lance-like leaves secreting the poison oleandrin□

Olga St d. c969. Wife of Igor, Prince of Kiev, who (while regent for her son from 945) was baptised in 958, and tried to introduce Christianity to Russia□

Oligocene an epoch in geological history. See geology◊□

Olivares Gaspar de Guzman, Conde de Olivares 1587–1645. Spanish minister, favourite of Philip◊ IV; he ruled Spain 1621–43□

olive Mediterranean evergreen tree *Olea europaea* family Oleaceae, with spiny branches, white flowers and blue/black fruit. Olive oil for cooking, etc. is expressed from the ripe fruit; chiefly made up of glycerides◊, it is also used in soap, ointment, and as a lubricant. An olive branch is symbolic of peace and plenty□

Oliver Isaac c1556–1617. British miniaturist, originally a Huguenot◊ refugee, who studied under Hilliard◊, and portrayed John Donne◊ and members of the court of James◊ I□

Olives Mount of. Small range of hills east of Jerusalem, with the Garden of Gethsemane on the west side, the traditional site of the Ascension◊□

Olivier Laurence Kerr, Baron Olivier 1907– . British actor-director, born at Dorking, Surrey. Knighted in 1947, life peer 1970 and Order of Merit 1981, he was for many years associated with the Old Vic, was director of the National Theatre company 1962–73, and the Olivier Theatre (part of the National Theatre on the South Bank) was named after him. Famous early films include *Wuthering Heights* and *Rebecca* and his major stage roles, e.g. Henry V, Hamlet, Richard III and Archie Rice in *The Entertainer* were all transferred to film□

olivine greenish mineral, magnesium iron silicate. When transparent it is known as ***chrysolite*** when golden and ***peridot*** when pale green, and used in jewellery. The greenish rock sand is used in casting moulds and retaining heat in buildings□

Olomouc industrial city (engineering, textiles) in Czechoslovakia; population 102 000□

Olsztyn industrial town and communications centre in NE Poland; population 120 000□

Olympia sanctuary in the W Peloponnese with a temple of Zeus, and the stadium (for footraces, boxing, wrestling, etc.) and hippodrome (for chariot and horse races), where the ***Olympic games*** were held every four years during a sacred truce; records were kept from 776BC. Women were forbidden to be present, and the male contestants (originally Hellenes◊ only) were naked. The games were abolished 394AD. Money and sponsorship played a large role in them and after the revival of the games by Baron Pierre de Coubertin◊ in 1896 at Athens, it was the English who introduced the concept of amateurism. The range of sports included is much wider than in the original and winter sports are held separately. The Olympic emblem of five interlaced circles represents the linking of the five continents in fellowship, but the games, especially from that held in Berlin in 1936, have been increasingly political, e.g. the mutual boycott by the USA of those in Moscow 1980, and by the USSR of those in Los Angeles 1984□

Olympus several mountains in Greece and elsewhere, the most famous being:

Mt Olympus in N Thessaly, a group of hills in which the high point is 2918 m/9570 ft. It was identified as the abode of the gods

Mt Olympus on Mars c24 000 m/80 000 ft□

OM Order of Merit. See medal◊□

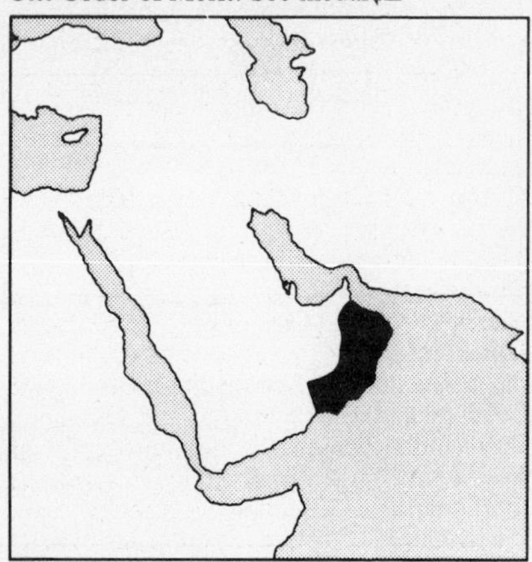

Oman Sultanate of

area 212 000 sq km/82 000 sq mi

capital Muscat

towns Salalah in Dhofar (the barren southern province)

features Jebel Akhdar highlands, plateau reaching to the edge of the 'Empty Quarter'; including Kuria Muria islands; Masirah Island is used in aerial reconnaissance of the Arabian Sea and Indian Ocean

exports oil, dates, silverware

currency Omani rial

population 1 500 000

language Arabic

religion Sunni Islam

government Sultan Qaboos bin Said is himself prime minister, legislating by decree, with the aid of a Cabinet and (from 1981) a consultative assembly

recent history the Sultan deposed his reactionary father in 1970, and with British aid suppressed left-wing guerrillas in Dhofar (who were aided across the border by S Yemen) 1965–75□

Omar c581–644. Adviser of Mohammed◊, who in 634 succeeded Abu Bekr◊ as caliph, and conquered Syria, Palestine, Egypt and Persia. He was assassinated by a slave. The Mosque of Omar in Jerusalem is attributed to him□

Omar Khayyam c1050–1123. Persian astronomer-poet, who is familiar in the West through Edward FitzGerald◊'s free version of his work, which was also translated by Robert Graves◊□

Omayyads Arab dynasty which held the caliphate 661–750. They were overthrown by the Abbasids◊, but one of the family escaped to Spain and became in 756 emir of Cordova (with the title of caliph from 929), his descendants ruling there till the early 11th century□

ombudsman official who investigates complaints of injustice which have no other means of redress, i.e. against the government and its employees. The post originated in Sweden 1809, and was adopted by other countries including the UK in 1966□

Omdurman city in Sudan, opposite Khartoum, a trading centre; population 300 000. The Mahdi◊ made it his capital 1885□

Omdurman Battle of, 1898. Victory by Kitchener◊ over the forces of the Khalifa◊□

Omsk industrial city (agricultural machinery, oil refining, food processing) in central USSR; population 1 080 000□

Onassis Jacqueline. See under John F Kennedy◊□

onchocerciasis virtually incurable disease found in tropical Africa and Latin America. It is transmitted by bloodsucking blackflies, which infect the victim with parasitic worms producing skin disorders and blindness□

Ondine water nymph of German fairy tale, whose unfaithful husband died in his sleep when she kissed him. ***Ondine's curse*** is a rare disease of babies (congenital central hypoventilation), in which the child risks death on falling asleep because the brain fails to instruct the lungs to breathe□

Onega lake (second largest in Europe) in NW USSR; area 8030 sq km/3820 sq mi. It has canal links with the White◊ Sea, and via Lake Ladoga◊ with the Baltic□

Oneida small town in New York state, USA, named after the Oneida people (a nation of the Iroquois◊ confederacy); population 12 000. It became famous for the ***Oneida Community*** a religious sect which practised a form of 'complex marriage' until its dissolution 1879. They also made fine silverware, and a commercial company took over the business 1881□

O'Neill Eugene Gladstone 1888–1953. American dramatist, born in New York City. He had varied experience as gold prospector, seaman and actor, which gave his plays a down-to-earth quality, even when he experimented with expressionism, symbolism, stream of consciousness, etc. Plays include *Beyond the Horizon* 1920, *Emperor Jones* 1921 (in which Robeson◊ later played), *Anna Christie* 1922, *Desire under the Elms* 1924 (which provoked the censor), *The Great God Brown* 1925, *Strange Interlude* 1928 (which lasted five hours), *Mourning Becomes Electra* 1931 (a trilogy on the Orestean◊ theme), and the posthumously produced autobiographical drama *Long Day's Journey into Night* (1956: written 1940). Nobel prize 1936□

O'Neill Terence, Baron O'Neill 1914– . Northern Ireland prime minister 1963–9, who resigned when opposed by his Unionist Party on the granting of universal franchise, i.e. including Roman Catholics; life peer 1970□

onion hardy biennial *Allium cepa* family Liliaceae, grown for its strong-flavoured edible bulb□

Onsager Lars 1903–76. Norwegian-American physicist, whose discovery of the 'reciprocity relations of Onsager' 1931 was vital to the production of nuclear energy; Nobel prize 1968□

Ontario central province of Canada

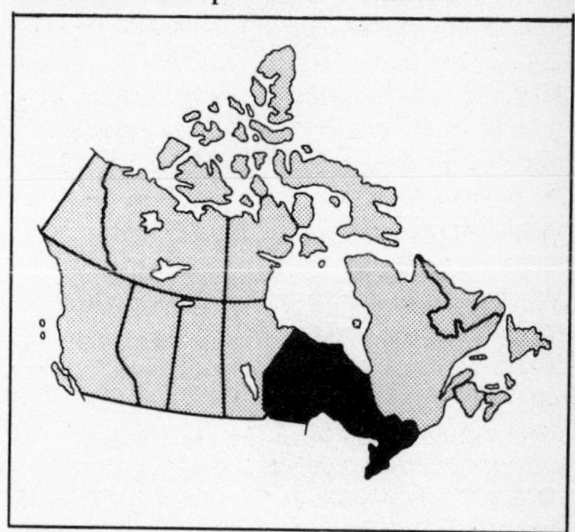

area 1 068 587 sq km/412 582 sq mi
capital Toronto
towns Hamilton, Ottawa (federal capital), London, Windsor, Kitchener, Sudbury
features Black Creek Pioneer Village, Niagara◊ Falls, Polar Bear Express; richest, chief manufacturing, most thickly populated, and leading cultural province of English-speaking Canada
products nickel, iron, gold, etc.; forest products; motor vehicles, iron and steel, paper, chemicals
population 8 937 400
history first explored by the French in the 17th century, it passed under British control in 1763 (Treaty of Paris). An attempt (1841) to form a merged province with French-speaking Quebec◊ failed, and Ontario became a separate province of Canada in 1867□

opera

first performances of selected operas

date	place	composer	libretto	title
1600	Florence	Peri	Rinuccini	Eurydice
1642	Venice	Monteverdi	Busenello	Coronation of Poppea
c1689	London	Purcell	Tate	Dido and Aeneas
1724	London	Handel	Haym	Julius Caesar
1728	London	Pepusch	Gay	The Beggar's Opera
1762	Vienna	Gluck	Calzabigi	Orpheus and Eurydice
1786	Vienna	Mozart	Da Ponte	The Marriage of Figaro
1787	Prague	Mozart	Da Ponte	Don Giovanni
1791	Vienna	Mozart	Schikaneder	The Magic Flute
1805	Vienna	Beethoven	Sonnleithner	Fidelio
1816	Rome	Rossini	Sterbini	The Barber of Seville
1826	London	Weber	Planché	Oberon
1829	Paris	Rossini	Jouy/Bis	William Tell
1842	St Petersburg	Glinka	Shirkov/Bakhturin	Russlan and Ludmilla
1845	Dresden	Wagner	Wagner	Tannhäuser
1850	Weimar	Wagner	Wagner	Lohengrin
1853	Rome	Verdi	Cammarano	Il Trovatore
1853	Venice	Verdi	Piave	La Traviata
1859	Paris	Gounod	Barbier/Carré	Faust
1865	Munich	Wagner	Wagner	Tristan and Isolde
1866	Prague	Smetana	Sabina	The Bartered Bride
1868	Munich	Wagner	Wagner	The Mastersingers of Nuremburg
1871	Cairo	Verdi	Ghislanzoni	Aida
1874	St Petersburg	Mussorgsky	Godunov	Boris Godunov
1874	Vienna	Strauss (jnr)	Haffner/Genée	Die Fledermaus
1875	Paris	Bizet	Meilhac/Halévy	Carmen
1876	Bayreuth	Wagner	Wagner	The Ring of the Nibelung
1878	London	Sullivan	Gilbert	HMS Pinafore
1880	London	Sullivan	Gilbert	The Pirates of Penzance
1881	Paris	Offenback	Barbier/Carré	The Tales of Hoffmann
1882	Bayreuth	Wagner	Wagner	Parsifal
1887	Milan	Verdi	Boito	Otello
1890	St Petersburg	Borodin	Borodin	Prince Igor
1893	Weimar	Humperdinck	Wette	Hansel and Gretel
1896	Turin	Puccini	Giacosa/Illica	La Bohème
1900	Paris	Charpentier	Charpentier	Louise
1902	Paris	Debussy	Maeterlinck	Pelléas and Mélisande
1904	Milan	Puccini	Giacosa/Illica	Madame Butterfly
1907	Berlin	Delius	Delius	A Village Romeo and Juliet
1911	Dresden	Strauss	Hofmannsthal	Der Rosenkavalier
1925	Berlin	Berg	Berg	Wozzeck
1928	Vienna	Stravinsky	Cocteau	Oedipus Rex
1933	Dresden	Strauss	Hofmannstahl	Arabella
1937	Zürich	Berg	Berg	Lulu
1945	London	Britten	Slater	Peter Grimes
1947	Paris	Poulenc	Apollinaire	The Breasts of Tirésias
1951	Venice	Stravinsky	Auden/Kallman	The Rake's Progress
1951	London	Britten	Forster/Crozier	Billy Budd
1951	Hanover	Henze	Weil	Boulevard Solitude
1954	Venice	Britten	Piper/James	Turn of the Screw
1955	London	Tippet	Mistral	Midsummer Marriage
1957	Zürich	Schoenberg	Schoenberg	Moses and Aaron
1965	Cologne	Zimmerman	Zimmerman/Lenz	The Soldiers
1978	Chicago	Penderecki	Fry	Paradise Lost
1983	Paris	Messiaen	Messiaen	St François d'Assise

Ontario Lake. See Great◊ Lakes□

o'nyong-nyong viral infection transmitted by mosquitoes, which appeared in E Africa 1961, and is marked by pains in the joints and glands, an itching rash and fever□

onyx a semi-precious mineral of silica◊□

oölite a usually calcareous (chalky) rock, most frequently formed by grains of sand or shell particles attracting a deposit of carbonate of lime in moving water, so that the resultant rock resembles the hard roe of a fish□

Oort Jan Hendrik 1900– . Dutch astronomer, who elucidated the rotation of the galaxy (1927) and its spiral structure; discovered ***Oort's Cloud*** of c1000 million comets at the edge of the solar◊ system 1950; and in 1966 was the first winner of the Vetlesen◊ Prize□

opal precious form of hydrated silicon dioxide, used as a gemstone, which owes its iridescence to the dispersion of fine silica within it (see colloid◊). Chief sources Australia (especially black opal) and Mexico (fire opal)□

op art the creative use of scientifically based optical illusions (sometimes adapted by computer), as developed in the 1960s, e.g. Bridget Riley◊□

OPEC see Organization◊ of the Petroleum Exporting Countries□

opera dramatic work in which speech is replaced by singing, and the music takes precedence over dancing and staging. See table of operas opposite.

1600 Jacopo Peri◊'s *Eurydice* originated opera in Florence

17th century composers, Monteverdi◊, Lully◊, Purcell◊

18th century height of ***opera seria*** 'serious opera' with miraculous convolutions of vocal line, formality of action, use of castrati (see castration◊); Handel, Scarlatti◊; then a move back towards drama with Gluck◊, and to a superb combination of all elements with Mozart◊

19th century a romantic, nationalistic, large-scale development into ***grand opera*** with large orchestras and choruses, as in France (Berlioz◊, Bizet, Gounod, Massenet), Germany (Wagner, Weber), Italy (Donizetti, Leoncavallo, Mascagni, Puccini, Rossini, Verdi), Russia (Borodin, Glinka, Mussorgsky, Rimsky-Korsakov)

20th century has produced experiments along divergent lines, ranging from lavishly romantic to modern in subject and technique: Austria (Berg, Schoenberg, Richard Strauss), France (Debussy), Germany (Henze, Hindemith), United Kingdom (Britten, Delius, Tippett, Vaughan Williams), United States (Gershwin, Menotti), USSR (Prokofiev, Stravinsky)□

ophthalmia neonatorum acute inflammation of the eyes of a newborn child caused by the organism of gonorrhoea◊ caught from the mother during birth. See also conjunctivitis◊□

Opie John 1761–1807. British artist, born in Cornwall. He became a London portrait-painter, and later painted historical pieces, e.g. *The Murder of Rizzio*□

opinion poll political equivalent of commercial market research, scientifically developed only in the 20th century (see George Gallup◊). After World War II they became controversial, allegedly influencing the voting by establishing a likely winner (making voters wish to join the winning side), or by suggesting a foregone conclusion (so that voters fail to turn out to the actual poll), etc. Attempts to ban them are thwarted by the poll results being published abroad, when they are then reported by the country's own media notwithstanding□

opium drug extracted from the unripe seeds of the opium poppy *Papaver somniferum* of SW Asia. An addictive narcotic, it includes the alkaloids ***morphine***, one of the most powerful natural painkillers and addictive narcotics known (***heroin***, a synthetic derivative of morphine, is even more powerful); ***codeine*** a milder painkiller; and ***thebaine*** highly poisonous. When dissolved in alcohol, opium is known as ***laudanum***□

Opole industrial town (textiles, chemicals, cement) in SW Poland; population 980 000. It was the capital of Upper Silesia◊ 1919–45□

Oporto second city of Portugal (textile, leather and pottery industries) and port 5 km/3 mi from the mouth of the River Douro, which exports port wine, especially to Britain; population 1 400 000□

opossum a small pouched mammal. See under marsupial◊□

Oppenheimer Robert 1904–67. American physicist, who worked with Rutherford◊ at Cambridge, and as director of the Los◊ Alamos laboratory 1943–5; was in charge of the development of the first atom bomb (Manhattan◊ Project). As director of the Institute of Advanced Study, Princeton, he objected to development of the H-bomb, and was declared a security risk 1953 (in the McCarthy◊ era); rehabilitated 1963 when he received a Fermi◊ award□

Opposition Leader of His/Her Majesty's. Official title (from 1937) of the leader of the largest opposition party in the Commons◊; salary £36 490□

optical contouring computerised monitoring of a light pattern projected onto a patient to detect discrepancies in movements during breathing, etc.□

optics scientific study of the phenomena of light◊ and vision□

optical fibre very fine optically insulated glass fibre through which light can be reflected to transmit an image or information from one end to the other. It can be used in inspecting parts of machines, or of the human body, otherwise inaccessible. It is increasingly used to replace copper wire in telephone cables. See fibre◊ optics□

opto-electronics the development of devices (based on gallium-arsenide) which respond not only to the electrons◊ of electronic data transmission, but also to photons◊□

opuntia a genus of prickly◊ pear□

opus dei Roman Catholic secular institution (established 1928 in Madrid, but now international) to disseminate ideals of Christian perfection, especially in intellectual and influential circles. Members are of either sex, lay or clerical□

oracle Greek sacred site where answers (also called oracles) were given by a deity to inquirers about future events; these were usually ambivalent, so that the deity was proved right whatever happened. The earliest was probably at Dodona (in Epirus◊), where priests interpreted the sounds made by the sacred oaks of Zeus◊, but the most celebrated was that of Apollo at Delphi◊ where the priestesses are thought to have inhaled volcanic vapours to induce the ecstasy productive of the best results□

Oradea industrial city (agricultural machinery, chemicals, glass, textiles) in NW Romania; population 185 000□

Oran port in Algeria; population 485 000. In World War II, on the surrender of France to Germany 1940, French warships at nearby Mers-el-Kebir naval base were put out of action by the Royal Navy to avoid their falling into German hands□

Orange House of. Netherlands royal family from 1815, originating in the small principality of Orange in S France. See also William◊ the Silent; William◊ III (of Orange); and William◊ (kings of the Netherlands)□

Orange town in New South Wales, Australia; population 31 300. Woollen textiles and fruit produced□

orange a citrus◊ tree□

Orange largest river of S Africa; length 2100 km/1300 mi. An 82 km/50 mi tunnel links the Orange with the Fish river to irrigate eastern Cape Province, and its tributaries include the Vaal length 1200 km/750 mi □

Orange Free State province of the Republic of South Africa
area 129 152 sq km/49 866 sq mi
capital Bloemfontein
features plain of the High Veld; Lesotho◊ forms an enclave on the Natal◊/Cape◊ Province border
products grain, cattle; gold and oil from coal
population 1 931 860, including 1 549 600 Black, 326 200 White, 56 000 Coloured
history original settlements from 1810 were complemented by the Great Trek, and it was recognised by Britain as independent in 1854. Following the South African or Boer War of 1899–1902, it was annexed by Britain until it entered the Union as a province in 1910□

Orangemen members of the Ulster Protestant Orange Society established 1795 to combat the United◊ Irishmen and the Roman Catholic peasant secret societies. It was a revival of the Orange Institution 1688, formed in support of William◊ (III) of Orange, the anniversary of whose victory at the Battle of the Boyne◊ 1690 is commemorated by parades on 12 Jul□

orang-utan a large ape◊□

Oratorians Roman Catholic priests living communally without taking vows, e.g. the Italian Congregation of the Oratory of St Philip Neri◊, founded 1575 at Rome, and established in England by Newman◊ 1848 (as at Brompton◊ Oratory, London, 1884). All its churches are famous for their music□

oratorio musical setting (orchestra, chorus, and solo voices), on a larger and more dramatic scale than the cantata◊, named from their 16th-century origin at St Philip Neri's◊ Oratory in Rome. Composers include Scarlatti◊, Bach◊, Handel◊, Haydn◊, Mendelssohn◊, Berlioz◊, Elgar◊, Tippett◊□

orchestra balanced grouping of musical instruments designed to play a particular type of composition. Types include:
symphony orchestra also designed for other large-scale works such as operas, has four standard sections (numbers of instruments are variable):
strings with five sub-sections: first violins (16), second violins (16), violas (12), violoncellos (12), and double basses (8). See also violin◊
woodwind◊ flutes (3), oboes (2), clarinets (2), bassoons (2), piccolo (1), cor anglais (1), bass clarinet (1), double bassoon (1)
brass◊ horns (4), trumpets (4), trombones (3), tuba (1)
percussion kettledrums (3), side drum (1), bass drum (1), triangle (1), cymbals

There is also usually a harp, the only standard plucked instrument, but in modern compositions other instruments, e.g. guitar, piano, organ, and even more exotic examples, may be incorporated for particular works.
chamber orchestra a variable smaller version of the preceding, increasingly popular for the performance of pre-19th-century music, and often made up of contemporary instruments
non-western orchestras are of very varied type, among the most colourful being the Indonesian all-percussion ***gamelan*** orchestra, mainly tuned gongs and bells□

orchid worldwide family (Orchidaceae) of monocotyledonous plants including over 15 000 species. The many tropical species are usually epiphytes◊, though some are saprophytes◊. Terrestrial orchids require a special fungus to invade their seed before it can germinate, and thereafter live with it in symbiosis◊. British species include ***early purple orchid*** *Orchis maculata* and ***bee orchid*** *Ophyris apifera;* commercially cultivated species including the showy *Cattleya*. See also vanilla◊□

Orczy baroness Emmusca 1865–1947. Hungarian-born British novelist, whose *The Scarlet Pimpernel* 1905, introduced the foppish Sir Percy Blakeney, secretly the bold rescuer of victims of the French Revolutionary 'Terror'□

ordeal medieval method of testing guilt of an accused person based on a belief in Heaven's protection of the innocent, e.g. walking barefoot over glowing ploughshares, dipping the hand into boiling water, swallowing consecrated bread. At least the last gave the innocent a chance, since fear (presumably stronger in the guilty) dries the flow of saliva, making swallowing difficult. Under Henry◊ III only trial by battle still continued□

Order in Council in the UK an order issued by the sovereign with the advice of the privy◊ council (in practice that of the Cabinet). Such orders are used to introduce emergency legislation, as in wartime, or are provided for in acts of parliament to regulate detailed administration of their provisions□

Ordnance Survey official department for the mapping of Britain established 1791; revision is continuous□

Oregon Pacific state of the USA; Beaver State
area 251 180 sq km/96 981 sq mi
capital Salem
towns Portland, Eugene
features fertile Willamette river valley; Columbia and Snake rivers; Crater Lake, deepest in the USA (589 m/1932 ft); Coast and Cascade mountain ranges, the latter

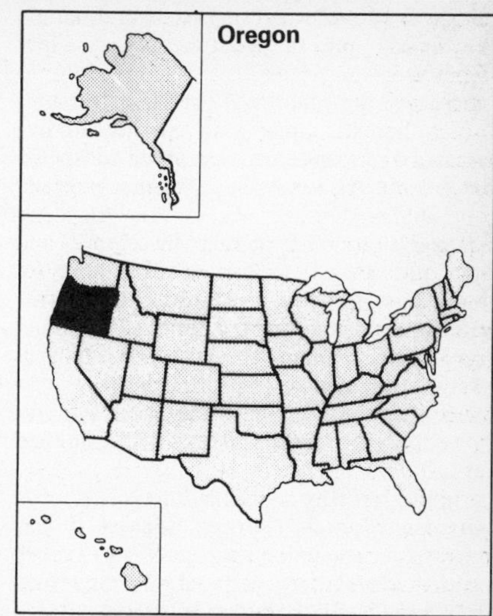

including Mt St Helens, which erupted 1980 with a force 500 times greater than the Hiroshima atom bomb (height reduced from 2945 m/9667 ft to 2560 m/8400 ft)
products wheat, livestock; timber; gold, silver, nickel
population 2 632 663
famous people Ernest Bloch◊, Chief Joseph◊, Linus Pauling◊
history the Oregon Trail (3200 km/2000 mi from Independence, Missouri to the Columbia river) was the pioneer route across the USA 1841–60. Settled from 1811, Oregon became a state in 1859 (it formerly included Washington◊)□

Orel industrial city (engineering, food processing) in the central USSR; population 322 000□

Orenburg trading and mining city in central USSR; population 500 000□

Orestes in Greek mythology, one of the children of Agamemnon◊ and Clytemnestra□

Öresund strait between Sweden and Denmark, linking the Kattegat◊ and the Baltic□

orfe a small fish. See under carp◊□

Orff Carl 1895–1982. German composer. An individual stylist, using sharp dissonances and percussion, he is best remembered for his scenic cantata *Carmina Burana* 1937, and his operas including *Antigone* 1948□

Orford Earl of. See Walpole◊□

Orford Ness see under Aldeburgh◊□

Organ (Harold) Bryan 1935– . British portraitist, born in Leicester, whose subjects include Macmillan◊, Tippett◊, Elton John◊, Prince and Princess of Wales□

organ the keyboard instrument with the greatest range, often with five (great, swell,

choir, solo and echo) or even more manual keyboards, plus a pedal keyboard. Chief types are:
pipe organ the traditional church instrument, which has its pipes (one for each note) arranged in stops (sets), prepared to 'speak' by a knob. Air is supplied by a mechanically operated bellows.
electric organ once popular in cinemas and now a museum item, had electrical impulses and relays substituted for some of the air-pressure controls, and the famous Hammond organs include many special sound effects as well as producing colour displays.
electronic organ in which the notes are produced by electronic oscillators, and amplified at will□

organic farming see agriculture◊□

Organisation de l'Armée Secrète (OAS) terrorist organization formed 1961 by French settlers devoted to perpetuating their own rule in Algeria (*Algérie Française*). It fell apart on the imprisonment 1962–68 of its leader General Raoul Salan◊□

Organization for Economic Cooperation and Development (OECD). New title of the OEEC (established 1948 for European recovery under the Marshall◊ Plan) from 1961, when the USA and Canada became full members and its original scope was extended to including development aid: headquarters Paris□

Organization of African Unity (OAU) established 1963 to eradicate colonialism, and improve economic, cultural and political cooperation; headquarters Addis Ababa. The French-speaking ***Joint African and Mauritian Organization*** *(Organisation Commune Africaine et Mauritienne: OCAM)* 1962, works within the framework of the OAU for African solidarity; headquarters Yaoundé, Cameroon□

Organization of American States (OAS) established 1890 to encourage friendly relations, and known as the International Union of American Republics 1890–1910 and Pan-American Union 1910–1948; headquarters Washington. It is now largely concerned with the social and economic development of Latin America□

Organization of Central American States (*Organizacion de Estados Centro Americanos: ODECA*), established 1951; headquarters Guatemala City. Originally a 'common market', it expanded from 1962 to political, educational, defence, and other aims□

Organization of the Petroleum Exporting Countries (OPEC) established 1960 to coordinate the interests of oil-producing states world-wide, and also to improve the position of Third World states by forcing the developed world to aid them with technology and open its own markets to the resultant products. Its concerted action in raising prices in the 1970s triggered world-wide recession, but also lessened demand. Many countries adopted fuel-saving measures and also concentrated on discovering new sources of supply□

orienteering sport of pedestrian route-finding invented in Sweden 1919. Competitors start at minute intervals, and have their control cards stamped at points (c 0.8 km/0.5 mi apart) marked on a map□

origami art of folding paper into forms such as dolls and birds, originating in Japan in 10th century□

Origen c185–c254. Christian theologian, born at Alexandria, and remembered for his fancifully allegorical interpretation of the Bible□

original sin Christian doctrine that Adam's fall rendered mankind able to achieve salvation only through divine grace□

Orinoco river of northern S America; length 2575 km/1600 mi; drainage basin 940 sq km/365 000 sq mi; rapids occur in the upper river, but it is navigable for quite large ships for 1125 km/700 mi□

oriole shy, restless bird with brilliant plumage, and flute-like call, order Passeriformes. In Africa and Eurasia, orioles belong to the family Oriolidae, e.g. ***golden oriole*** *Oriolus oriolus* an occasional visitor to Britain; in the Americas to the Icteridae, e.g. ***bobolink*** *Dolichonyx oryzivorus* so-named from its call; the male is white above and black below□

Orion in Greek mythology, a giant of Boeotia◊, famed as a hunter. See also Pleiades◊□

Orion constellation which includes Betelgeuse and Rigel (stars of the first magnitude)□

Orissa state of eastern India
area 155 782 sq km/60132 sq mi
capital Bhubaneswar
features mainly agricultural; Chilka lake with fisheries and game; temple of Jangannath or Juggernaut at Puri◊
population 26 370 270
language Oriya
religion Hinduism 90%

Orizaba industrial town (textiles, paper) and resort in SE Mexico; population 121 000. Nearby Citlaltepec (Aztec 'star mountain') erupted 1687 but is now dormant; highest mountain in Mexico at 5700 m/18 700 ft□

Orkney islands area of Scotland
area 984 sq km/380 sq mi

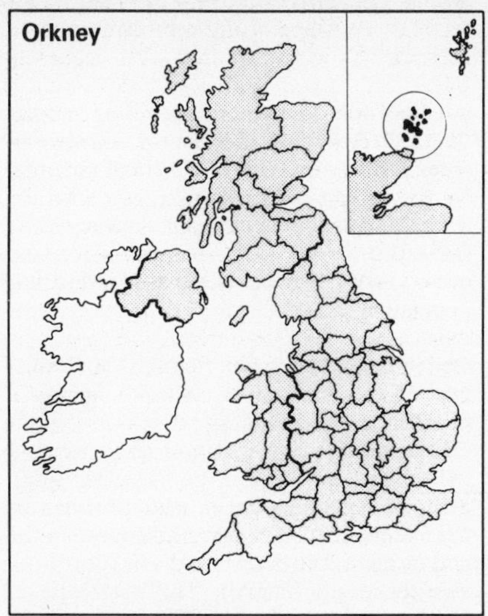

towns administrative headquarters Kirkwall, on Pomona/'Mainland'
features comprises c90 islands and islets; population , long falling, has in recent years risen as their remoteness from the modern world attracts new settlers, e.g. Peter Maxwell Davies◊ on Hoy; mild climate owing to the Gulf Stream; Skara Brae, a remarkably well preserved 'underground' Neolithic village on Pomona; Scapa Flow, between Pomona and Hoy, was a Royal Naval base in both World Wars, and the German fleet scuttled itself here 21 Jun 1919; the ***Orkney Causeway*** begun in World War I and finished 1943 in World War II (designed to protect the fleet from raiders from the east into Scapa Flow) joins four of the islands, linking them with Kirkwall by road. See also Pentland Firth◊
products fishing and farming, wind power (Burgar Hill on Mainland has the world's most productive wind generator; blades 60 m/197 ft diameter)
population 18 865
history Harold◊ I (Fairhair) of Norway conquered the islands in 876; they were pledged to James◊ III of Scotland 1468 for the dowry of Margaret of Denmark, and annexed by Scotland (the dowry unpaid) in 1472□

Orkney Islands South. See South◊ Orkney Islands□

Orlando Vittorio Emanuele 1860–1952. Italian prime minister 1917–19, when he was one of the 'big four' with Lloyd George◊, Wilson◊, and Clemenceau◊, at the Paris Peace Conference. He resigned when the Adriatic settlement he obtained for Italy was unpopular, and later supported Mussolini◊□

Orlando industrial city, centre for a citrus area, in Florida, USA; population 128 500. Kennedy◊ Space Center is to the north-west, and Disneyland◊ is also nearby□

Orléans industrial city (textiles, engineering, processed foods) capital of Centre◊ region, France; population 109 960. Joan of Arc liberated it from the English in 1429□

Ormandy Eugene 1899–1985. Hungarian-American conductor, originally a violin virtuoso. He championed Rachmaninoff◊ and Shostakovich◊, and was music director to the Philadelphia Orchestra 1936–80□

ormolu (French *or moulu* 'ground gold'), an alloy of copper, zinc, and sometimes tin, used for furniture decoration□

Ormonde James Butler, Duke of 1610–88. Irish royalist general in Ireland 1641–50 during the Irish◊ rebellion and the English◊ revolution, and lord-lieutenant 1644–7, 1661–9, and 1677–84; created marquess 1642 and duke 1661□

Ormuzd the Good God of Zoroastrianism◊□

ornithology study of birds. The British Trust for Ornithology (Beech Grove, Tring, Hertfordshire) monitors migration, age, effects of pollution, etc. by ringing (trained government-licensed operators fit numbered metal rings to captured specimens with a return address). Britain was a pioneer in protecting wild birds with the act of 1880, and the (Royal) Society for the Protection of Birds 1889, received its royal charter 1904; the Audubon◊ Society in the USA 1905 has similar aims□

Orontes river flowing through Lebanon, Syria and Turkey to the Mediterranean, and used mainly for irrigation; length 400 km/250 mi□

Orpen Sir William Newenham Montague 1878–1931. Irish portrait and genre artist, knighted 1918□

Orpheus legendary Greek poet-musician, son of Apollo◊ and a muse, author of the ***Orphic hymns***. See also Sirens◊. When his wife, Eurydice, died of snake-bite, he went down to Hades◊ to bring her back, but broke the condition on which she was allowed to return, that he should not look back to see if she were following him. In his grief at her now irretrievable loss, he rejected the blandishments of the women of Thrace◊, and was torn to pieces by them□

Orphism ancient Greek mystery cult, of which the Orphic hymns formed part of the secret rites which, accompanied by an ascetic regime, were aimed at securing eventual immortality. It became popular in

Rome, and remains of an Orphic temple were found at Hungerford, London, in 1980□

orris a plant of the iris◊ family□

Orsk industrial city (oil refining, aluminium, locomotives) in central USSR; population 259 000□

orthodontics a branch of dentistry◊□

orthopaedics correction of deformities (caused by injured or diseased bones and joints, muscle, or tissue) by surgery, drugs, physical training and therapy, and psychology: increasing use is made of electronics to stimulate residual powers of movement□

orthoptera order of terrestrial insects, including grasshoppers◊ and locusts◊, and crickets◊□

ortolan a small bird, a type of bunting◊□

Orvieto town in central Italy; population 25 500. On the site of Volsinii, an Etruscan◊ city sacked by Rome 280BC, it has many Etruscan remains□

Orwell George. Pseudonym of British writer Eric Blair 1903–50. Born in India, he won a scholarship to Eton, but developed an individual socialism which failed to survive contact with communism when he fought for the Republicans in Spain during the Spanish◊ Civil War – *Homage to Catalonia* 1938. His most famous books *Animal Farm* 1945 and *1984* 1949 reflect an equal horror for the common factors of communism and fascism□

oryx a large African antelope◊□

Osaka port and industrial city (wood pulp, paper, steel, textiles) in SW Honshu, Japan; population 8 600 000. Japan's oldest and second-largest city, it was the seat of government 4–8th centuries, and Osaka Castle (many times reconstructed) dates from 1586. It is honeycombed with waterways, and a 'technoport' on an artificial island is planned. Bunraku was invented here (see puppet◊)□

Osborne Dorothy 1627–95. Wife of Sir William Temple◊ from 1655, to whom she wrote letters of great charm□

Osborne John James 1929– . British actor-dramatist, whose greatest successes have been *Look Back in Anger* 1956, which made him the first of the 'angry young men' obsessed with the failure of the standards of all about them, and *The Entertainer* 1957, memorably acted by Olivier◊□

Osborne House see under Isle of Wight◊□

Oscar II 1829–1907. King of Sweden and Norway from 1872, who abandoned the title King of Norway 1905, on the separation of the two kingdoms□

Oscar annual cinema awards from 1927 by the American Academy of Motion Pictures, and nicknamed Oscars 1931 because a new secretary exclaimed (of the bronze statuette presented to winners) 'That's like my uncle Oscar!'□

oscillograph instrument recording oscillations, electrical or mechanical; an ***oscilloscope*** shows variations in electrical potential on the screen of a cathode◊ ray tube, by means of deflection of a beam of electrons◊□

Oshogbo market town (palm products and cocoa) in W Nigeria, with textile industries; population 282 000□

osier a type of willow◊ tree□

Osijek industrial town (textiles) and river port on the Drava in N central Yugoslavia; population 158 800□

Osiris ancient Egyptian god (who wears a tall curved hat with a plume each side), embodiment of goodness, who went to rule the underworld, after being killed by ***Set***, the god of night, the desert, and evil (portrayed as a grotesque animal). The sister-wife of Osiris was the sky and fertility goddess ***Isis***◊/***Hathor*** (who wears a cow's horns, with a sun-disc between them). Her rites were mysterious, as were those of Demeter◊, with whom she was identified by the Greeks. The son of Osiris and Isis was ***Horus*** (falcon-headed, or shown as a boy, representing the youthful sun), the pharaohs were thought to be his incarnation. Horus captured his father's murderer Set. Under Ptolemy◊ I's Graeco-Egyptian empire Osiris was developed (as a means of uniting his Greek and Egyptian subjects) into ***Serapis*** (Osiris+Apis, the latter being the bull-god of Memphis who carried the dead to the tomb), elements of the cults of Zeus and Hades being included, which did not please the Egyptians; the greatest temple of Serapis was the Serapeum at Alexandria. The cult of Osiris, and that of Isis, later spread to Rome□

Oslo capital and port of Norway, with textile and engineering industries, on Oslo fjord (kept open in winter by icebreakers). The first recorded settlement was made by Harald III (Hardrada: see under Harold◊ II), but after a fire in 1624, it was entirely replanned by Christiane IV. Notable buildings include the Viking Museum with warships such as raided Britain (Nansen◊'s *Fram* and Heyerdahl◊'s raft *Kon Tiki* are nearby); 13th-century Akershus Castle and a collection of early timber buildings in the open-air Folk Museum; the 17th-century cathedral, the Royal Palace 1848, the National Theatre (linked with Ibsen◊), and the National Gallery (with a fine collection of Munch◊'s work)□

Osman or ***Othman I*** 1259–1326. Founder of the Ottoman◊ Empire, which was named after him, and who assumed the title of sultan in 1299□

osmium element
symbol Os
atomic number 76
physical description silvery-white metal
features the heaviest known metal
uses as a catalyst and in light bulb filaments; as an alloy with platinum and iridium□

Osnabrück industrial city (engineering, textiles, paper, and processed foods) in Lower Saxony, W Germany; population 156 800. It was once a Hansa◊ town, and the Treaty of Westphalia◊ (1648) was signed here□

osprey bird of prey *Pandion haliaetus,* family Pandionidae, with spiked talons, specially adapted for hunting live fish. It has a wingspan of 2 m/6 ft. So-called 'osprey plumes' are those of the egret◊□

Ossa mountain in Thessaly, Greece; height 1978 m/6490 ft. Two of Poseidon◊'s giant sons were said to have tried to dislodge the gods from Olympus◊ by piling nearby Mt Pelion on top of Ossa to scale the great mountain□

Ossetia area of the Caucasus, home of the Ossets, who speak the Iranian language Ossetic, and who were conquered by the Russians in 1802. Some live in the ***North Ossetian*** Republic of the SW USSR; area 8000 sq km/3088 sq mi; population 601 000. Capital Ordzhonikidze. The rest live in the ***South Ossetian*** autonomous region of the Georgian Republic, capital Tshkinvali□

Ossian 3rd-century Irish bard, son of Finn◊ Mac Cumhaill. See James Macpherson◊□

Ostade Adriaen van 1610–85. Dutch painter and engraver of tavern scenes, village fairs, etc. Born at Haarlem, he was a student of Hals◊, and brother of Isaac van Ostade◊□

Ostade Isaac van 1621–49. Dutch artist, brother of Adriaen, who excelled in winter landscapes, and roadside and farmyard scenes□

Ostend seaport (headquarters of the Belgian fishing fleet) and pleasure resort, with a 5 km/3 mi promenade and casino, in NW Belgium; population 69 200□

osteoarthritis a chronic inflamation of the joints. See under arthritis◊□

osteomyelitis bacterial bone infection, often linked with a knock or fall. Symptoms are high fever and pain in the limbs; it is treated with antibiotics, but sometimes needs surgery□

osteopathy system of alternative medical practice which relies on physical manipulation to treat mechanical stress and so relieve not only postural problems and muscle pain, but asthma, autism,◊ cerebral palsy (spastics), etc.□

osteoporosis bone demineralisation, rendering fractures more likely, which occurs in women after the menopause, and also in young women runners. Suggested prevention is by increasing the daily intake of calcium, and by varying the form of physical activity□

Ostia the ancient port (naval and commercial) of Rome near the mouth of the Tiber; nearby is ***Ostia Mare*** a modern seaside resort□

ostpolitik German 'eastern policy': W German Chancellor Brandt◊'s policy of rapprochement with the communist bloc from 1971, pursued to a modified extent also by Schmidt◊□

ostracism ancient Athenian political device to preserve public order. Votes on pieces of broken pot (Greek *ostrakon*) were used to exile unpopular politicians for ten years□

Ostracoda a class of minute crustacea. See under crustacea◊□

Ostrava mining town in N Czechoslovakia; population 322 000□

ostrich a large running◊ bird□

Ostrogoths see under Goths◊□

Ostwald Wilhelm 1853–1932. German chemist, founder (by his work on catalysts◊) of the petrochemical and other industries; Nobel prize 1909□

Oswald St c605–42. King of Northumbria from 634, who had become a Christian convert during his previous exile in Iona. With the help of St Aidan◊ he furthered the spread of Christianity until he was defeated and killed by the heathen King Penda of Mercia□

Oswestry market town, also making agricultural machinery and plastics, in Shropshire, England, with a church dedicated to St Oswald◊, killed here in 642; population 12 000□

Oświęcim town in S Poland (German *Auschwitz*), site of a concentration camp□

Otaru fishing port in Hokkaido, Japan; population 187 000□

Othman c574–656. Son-in-law of Mohammed◊, caliph from 644. In his reign the Arabs became a naval power and captured Cyprus, but he was a weak ruler and was assassinated. He was responsible for the final editing of the Koran◊□

Othman I another name for Osman◊□

Otranto port in Italy on the ***Strait of Otranto*** between the Adriatic and Ionian seas□

Ottawa capital of Canada, in the province of Ontario, on the hills overlooking the River Ottawa, and divided by the Rideau Canal into the Upper (western) and Lower (eastern)

Town; it is also an industrial city (timber, pulp and paper, engineering, food processing, publishing, etc.); population 718 000. The government buildings are on Parliament Hill; there are two cathedrals: Notre Dame (Roman Catholic) and Christ Church; the National Museum, the National Art Gallery, the Observatory, Rideau Hall (the governor-general's residence), and the National Arts Centre 1969 (with an orchestra, and English/French theatre). Founded 1826–32 as Bytown (in honour of John By whose army engineers were building the Rideau Canal), it was renamed 1854 after the Outaouac Indians, and in 1858 was chosen by Queen Victoria as the country's capital□

Ottawa Agreements agreements concluded at the Imperial Economic Conference at Ottawa 1932 for preferential trade tariffs between Britain and the Dominions. They marked Britain's abandonment of her traditional free-trade policy□

otter a small freshwater mammal. See under weasel◊□

Otto four Holy Roman Emperors including:

Otto I the Great 912–73, emperor from 936, asserted his authority over the Pope, and ended the Magyar◊ menace by his victory at Lechfeld in 955.

Otto IV c1182–1218, emperor 1198–1215, came into conflict with Pope Innocent III, and was deposed after his defeat by the Pope's ally Philip of France at Bouvines in 1214□

Otto Nikolaus. See under motor◊ car□

Ottoman Empire the successor of the Seljuk◊ Empire◊ 1300–1920, founded by Osman I◊ and reaching its height with Suleiman◊. At its greatest extent its bounds were Europe as far as Hungary, part of S Russia, Iran, the Palestinian coastline, Egypt, and N Africa. In decline from the 17th century, there was an attempted revival and reform under the Young Turk party (led by Enver Pasha◊) in 1908, but the regime crumbled when Turkey took the German side in World War I. The sultanate was abolished by Atatürk◊ in 1922. See Mohamed VI◊□

Otway Thomas 1652–85. British dramatist, whose *Venice Preserved* 1682 revived blank verse Shakespearean drama; he died destitute□

Ouagadougou capital and industrial and commercial centre of Burkina Faso; population 286 450□

Oudenaarde Battle of. In 1708 during War of Spanish◊ Succession□

Oudh region of N India, now part of Uttar◊ Pradesh; as part of the British United Provinces of Agra and Oudh, its capital was Lucknow◊, heart of the Indian◊ Mutiny□

Ouessant see Ushant◊□

Ouida pseudonym of British romantic novelist Marie Louise de la Ramée 1839–1908, e.g. *Under Two Flags* 1867 and *Moths* 1880□

Oujda lead and coalmining town in N Morocco; population 175 500□

Oulu industrial port (saw mills, tanneries, shipyards) in Finland (Swedish Ulèborg); population 96 000□

ounce a snow leopard. See under cat◊□

ounce in imperial measure the equivalent of 28 grams□

Ouse several British rivers including:

Great Ouse length 250 km/160 mi; flowing to the Wash. Near King's Lynn a sluice for flood control was installed 1959

Yorkshire Ouse which joins the Trent to form the Humber

Sussex Ouse flows through the South Downs to enter the English Channel at Newhaven□

Ouspensky Peter 1878–1947. Russian mystic. Originally a scientist, he became a disciple of Gurdjieff◊, and expanded his ideas in terms of other dimensions of space and time, e.g. *Tertium Organum* 1912□

outback the inland region of Australia unsettled by Europeans except where irrigation is possible. It has a harsh beauty, and the Aboriginals◊ cope well with its droughts and dust storms□

outlawry declaration that a criminal was outside the protection of the law, with his lands and goods forfeit to the Crown, and himself liable to be killed by anyone without penalty. It was a lucrative royal 'privilege'; Magna◊ Carta restricted its use and under Edward◊ III it was further modified. Such men sometimes became popular heroes, e.g. Robin◊ Hood□

Outram Sir James 1803–63. British general. On the outbreak of the Indian◊ Mutiny in 1857, he co-operated with Havelock◊ to raise the siege of Lucknow◊, and held the city until relieved by Sir Colin Campbell◊□

ouzel or *ousel* for the *water ouzel* see under Dipper◊, and for the *ring ouzel* see under Thrush◊□

Oval The. A cricket ground in central London. See under Lambeth◊□

ovaries in human beings the paired organs in the female which generate the ova, or egg-cells, which (after fertilization) develop as a baby. They are whitish, rounded bodies about 25 mm/1 in by 35 mm/1.5 in, near the ends of the Fallopian tubes (see Fallopius◊). If an egg is unfertilized, it will pass from the body in the menstrual fluid; if fertilized, it will make its way via the Fallopian tubes to the uterus. The ovaries also secrete the hormones responsible for the secondary sexual characteristics of the female, such as smooth, hairless skin and large breasts. Other mammals share this mechanism in various forms. A ***plant ovary*** is the pocket containing one or more ovules from which the fruit containing seeds develops. See flower◊□

Overijssel NE province (capital Zwolle) of the Netherlands. Largely reclaimed land, it is mainly agricultural, but with some recent industrial development□

Overlanders 19th-century Australian drovers who opened new territory by driving their cattle to new stations or to market□

Overland Telegraph cable linking Port Augusta (S Australia) with Darwin (Northern Territory), and hence with Java, from 1872; it ended Australia's communications isolation□

overture piece of instrumental music, preceding an opera, play, etc. from the 17th century; or, later, specially written as a 'concert' overture, e.g. Elgar's *Cockaigne*□

Ovid (***Publius Ovidius Naso***) 43BC–17AD. His 'immoral' *Ars Amatoria* supposedly led Augustus◊ to exile him 8AD to Tomi on the Black Sea , where he died, having lamented his fate in *Tristia*, but exile was more probably due to some connection with the profligate Julia, daughter of Augustus. His works also include *Metamorphoses*□

Oviedo town in Asturias, Spain; population 190 125. Centre of a coal-mining area□

ovum an unfertilized female egg◊ cell□

Owen Alun (Davies) 1925– . British playwright, especially for television, e.g. *No Trams to Lime Street* 1959 and *You Can't Win 'Em All* 1962□

Owen David 1938– . British politician. Originally a doctor, he entered parliament in 1966, and was Labour Foreign and Commonwealth Secretary 1977–9. In 1981 he was associated with Shirley Williams, William Rodgers, and Roy Jenkins in the Limehouse◊ Declaration founding the Social◊ Democratic Party, and in 1983 succeeded Jenkins as its leader□

Owen Robert 1771–1858. British socialist. As joint owner of mills at New Lanark, he made them the centre of a model community, and attempted to organize a trade union take-over of industry, so that it might be run cooperatively. His ideas influenced the cooperative movement□

Owen Wilfred 1893–1918. British poet. Born at Oswestry, he enlisted in 1915, and was killed a week before the Armistice. His anti-war poetry, e.g. *Anthem for Doomed Youth*, published after his death, in 1921, owed much to the encouragement of Siegfried Sassoon◊□

Owen Falls see under Uganda◊□

Owens James ('Jesse') Cleveland 1913–80. American black athlete (a runner on the flat and over hurdles, and long jumper), who won four gold medals in the Berlin Olympics 1936, to the disgust of the Nazis□

owl order (Strigiformes) of mainly nocturnal birds of prey, with mobile heads, soundless flight, acute hearing, and forward-set eyes, set round with rayed feathers. All species lay white eggs, and begin incubation as soon as the first is laid. They disgorge indigestible remains of their prey in pellets (castings). They comprise two families:

Typical owls family Strigidae, including ***tawny owl*** *Strix aluco* a handsome species of Europe and the Middle East; ***little owl*** *Athene noctua* Greek symbol of wisdom and bird of Athena◊, found widely near human homes, and naturalized in Britain; ***snowy owl*** *Nyctea scandiaca* of the Arctic; and the largest of the owls, the ***eagle owl*** *Bubo bubo* of Eurasia, and ***powerful owl*** *Ninox strenua* of Australia, both up to 0.75 m/2.25 ft long.

Barn owls family Tytonidae, including the world-wide ***barn owl*** *Tyto alba* the world's most cosmopolitan bird, formerly common in Britain, but now diminished by pesticides and loss of habitat. In Malaysia it is used for rat control□

ox a male of the domestic cattle◊□

oxalic acid colourless, poisonous, crystalline solid $(COOH)_2$, found in rhubarb leaves. It is soluble in water, and is used in bleaches, metal polishes, etc.□

Oxbridge Oxford and Cambridge universities, referred to as the acme of academic and social prestige. See Ivy◊ League□

Oxenstjerna Axel Gustafsson, Count Oxenstjerna 1583–1654. Swedish chancellor from 1612, he supported the foreign policy of Gustavus◊ Adolphus, was regent for Queen Christina◊, and brought the Thirty◊ Years' War to a successful conclusion□

OXFAM (***Ox***ford Committee for ***Fam***ine Relief) first established 1942 to relieve poverty and famine worldwide, and fund long-term aid projects□

Oxford Edward de Vere, 17th Earl of Oxford 1550–1604. English lyric poet, once fancied as the 'author' of Shakespeare's works□

Oxford and Asquith, Earl of. See Asquith◊□

Oxford industrial (especially cars at Cowley) and university city, administrative headquarters of Oxfordshire; population 116 200. It originated in the angle of the rivers Cherwell

and Isis (as the Thames is known here). Noted buildings include 12th-century Christ Church cathedral, Carfax Tower at the intersection of the four main roads of the city, and Vanbrugh◊'s Clarendon Building (home of the Oxford University Press). During the 13th century several parliaments were held here, and during the Civil◊ War it was the headquarters of the Royalists.
University of Oxford was Britain's first, and one of the oldest in Europe, University College being established 1249; other colleges with fine buildings include Christ Church and Hawksmoor◊'s All Souls; also notable are Wren's Sheldonian Theatre, the Bodleian◊ Library (by Holt of York), and the Ashmolean◊ Museum, which has a magnificent art collection□

Oxford University of. See under Oxford◊□

Oxford Group see under Frank Buchman◊□

Oxford Movement or ***Tractarian Movement*** an attempt to revive Catholic religion in the Church of England (see Keble◊, Newman◊), which transformed the Anglican◊ Communion, and established today's Anglo-Catholicism□

Oxfordshire S Midland county of England

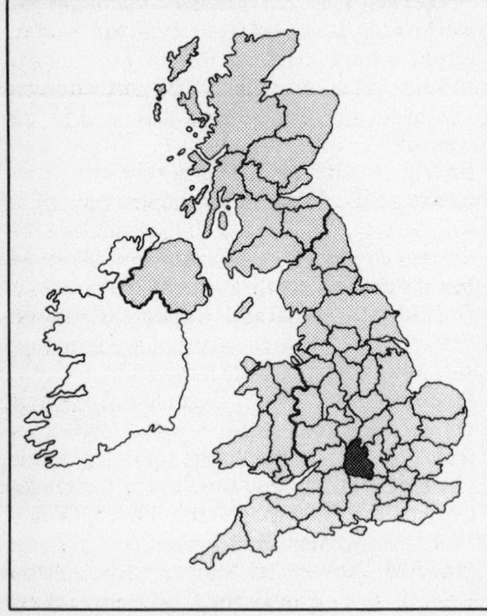

area 2608 sq km/1006 sq mi
towns administrative headquarters Oxford; Abingdon, Banbury, Henley-on-Thames, Witney, Woodstock
features River Thames and tributaries; Cotswolds and Chiltern Hills; Vale of the White Horse (chalk hill figure 114 m/374 ft long); Europe's major fusion project JET (Joint European Torus) is being built at the UK Atomic Energy Authority's fusion laboratories at Culham
products cereals; cars, paper, bricks, cement
population 554 700
famous people Flora Thompson◊□

oxide binary compound of oxygen and other elements, of which the main classes are: ***acidic oxides*** which combine with basic oxides to form salts; ***basic oxides*** which react with acids to form salts; and ***neutral oxides*** with neither acid nor basic properties□

oxlip a small woodland plant. See under primrose◊□

Oxus see Amu◊ Darya□

oxygen element
symbol O
atomic number 8
physical description colourless gas
features the most abundant element, forming 65% of the human body, and 21% by volume of the earth's atmosphere; the only gas able to support respiration
uses in welding, metal cutting, and as a rocket fuel□

oyster an edible bivalve◊ mollusc□

oyster catcher coastal bird *Haematopus ostralegus* family Haematopodidae, order Charadriiformes◊; they may live over 30 years□

Ozark Mountains varied scenic area in USA (shared by Arkansas, Illinois, Kansas, Mississippi, Oklahoma) of ridges, valleys and streams, highest point only 645 m/2300 ft; area 130 000 sq km/50 000 sq mi

ozone highly reactive blue gas O_3 comprising three atoms of oxygen, formed when the molecules of the stable form of oxygen (consisting of two atoms) is split by ultra-violet radiation. It forms a layer in the upper atmosphere, and protects life on earth from this radiation (a cause of skin cancer). Satellite studies are being carried out as to the layer's possible depletion by industrial and agricultural processes. A powerful oxidising agent, it is used in bleaching and air-conditioning□

Ozu Yasujiro 1903–1963. Japanese film director, unknown in the West until his last years. *Tokyo Story* 1953 is typical of his low camera angles, and search for the eternal in middle-class life□

P

paca a large burrowing rodent◊ of Central and South America□

Pacaraima Sierra. Mountain range along the Brazil-Venezuela frontier, and extending into Guyana; length 620 km/385 mi. Highest point ***Mt Roraima*** a plateau, c50 sq km/20 sq mi, 2629 m/8625 ft above sea level, and surrounded by 300 m/1000 ft cliffs, at the conjunction of the three countries. Formed 300 million years ago, it has a largely unique fauna and flora, owing to its isolation, but only grasses, bushes, flowers, insects and small amphibians. Conan Doyle◊'s *The Lost World* was inspired by reports of it, and he envisaged it fancifully in the palaeozoic period (see geology◊), with prehistoric monsters in primeval forest□

Pachomius St 292–346AD. Egyptian monk, founder of the first Christian monastic community living under a rule□

Pacific Islands Trust Territory of. Comprising over 2000 islands and atolls, which were under Japanese mandate 1919–47, it was administered by the USA 1947–80, when all its members, the Carolines◊, Marianas◊ (except Guam) and Marshalls◊ had achieved independence□

Pacific Ocean world's largest ocean, extending from Antarctica to the Bering Strait; area 166 242 500 sq km/64 186 300 sq mi; average depth 4188 m/13 739 ft; greatest depth of any ocean 11 000 m/36 198 ft in the Mariana◊ Trench□

Pacific War 1879–83 between an alliance of Bolivia and Peru against Chile. Chile (by seizing Antofagasta and the rest of the Bolivian Pacific coast) rendered Bolivia completely landlocked, and also annexed the Peruvian coastline (from Arica to the mouth of the Loa). Bolivia has since tried to regain Pacific access, either by a corridor across her former Antofagasta province or by a twin port with Arica at the end of the rail link from La Paz. Brazil supports the Bolivian claims which would facilitate her own transcontinental traffic. See Peru◊□

pacifism complete renunciation of violence, even in self-defence, in settling disputes, as by some Christians (e.g. Society◊ of Friends and Jehovah's◊ Witnesses), and some Hindus (e.g. Gandhi◊)□

Padang port in W Sumatra, Indonesia, founded by the Dutch in the 17th century; population 196 450□

Paderborn industrial city (precision instruments, textiles, leather goods) in N Rhine-Westphalia, W Germany; population 110 100□

Paderewski Ignacz Jean 1860–1941. Polish pianist, composer and statesman. A noted exponent of Chopin◊ and composer of many solo pieces, he became prime minister of newly-independent Poland 1919–20, having organized a Polish army in France during World War I. He resumed his musical career, but was president of the Polish National Council in Paris in 1940 in World War II□

Padua (Italian *Padova*) industrial city (engineering, textiles) in N Italy, famed for its university 1222, where Galileo◊ taught; population 234 700□

paediatrics study of diseases in children before the age of adolescence□

Paestum see under Salerno◊□

Pagalu see under Equatorial◊ Guinea□

Pagan village in Burma close to the ruins of the former capital (founded 847, taken by Kublai Khan◊ 1287). These include magnificent Buddhist temples with wall-paintings of the great period of Burmese art 11–13th centuries□

Paganini Niccolò 1782–1840. Italian violinist, a soloist from the age of nine. His satanic appearance, wild amours, and virtuosity (especially on a single string) fostered a reputation of his being in league with the Devil. His compositions exploit every potential of the instrument□

Page Sir Earle (Christmas Grafton) 1880–1961. Australian leader of the Country Party 1920–39, and briefly prime minister in Apr 1939. He represented Australia in British War Cabinet 1941–2, and as Minister of Health 1949–55 introduced Australia's health scheme 1953□

Page Sir Frederick Handley 1885–1962. British founder 1909 of the aircraft company named after him, and designer both of long-range civil aircraft and multi-engined bombers in both World Wars, e.g. the Halifax bomber in World War II□

Page Russell 1906–1985. British garden designer, e.g. Pepsi Cola offices, New York; Battersea Gardens for the Festival◊ of Britain; Pompidou Centre, Paris□

Pago Pago port on Tutuila, American Samoa; population 2450. The nearby village of Fagatogo is the administrative headquarters□

Pahang state of Malaysia; population 770 650. Capital Kuantan□

Pahlavi dynasty founded in Iran by ***Riza Khan*** 1877–1944, an army officer who took power by a coup 1921, and was proclaimed shah 1925. Britain and Russia compelled him to abdicate (because of his German sympathies) in favour of his son, and occupied the country 1941–6. His son ***Mohammed Riza Shah Pahlavi*** 1919–80, faced popular opposition, and in 1953 (having attempted to arrest the prime minister, Mossadeq◊) fled the country, but was restored with CIA aid. Helped by the USA, he tried to make the country a major military and industrial power, using Savak (contraction of the Farsi words for 'security'), the secret police he founded 1957, to suppress opponents. President Carter pressed for relaxation of his autocratic rule, and explosive unrest then forced him into exile in Egypt, where he died of cancer. His heir is ***Crown Prince Riza*** 1960– □

Pahsien see Chongqing◊□

pain sensation caused by injury, disease, etc., for which the neuropeptide ***Substance P*** (SP), which is concentrated in a certain area of the spinal cord, acts as a transmitter (see nerve impulse under nerve◊). The message may be passed on, or modified/stopped, according to the presence or absence of the body's natural chemicals, encephalins◊ and endorphins◊; the presence of counter signals (such as rubbing or pressure in the affected area), and so on. The exact processes are not as yet fully understood, but it is such factors which influence the variation in degree to which people experience pain, the initial absence of pain in some cases of serious wounds, and the feeling of pain which may seem to come from an amputated limb when the system misinterprets the signals received.

Substance P has been found in fish, and there is also evidence that the same substances that cause pain in humans, e.g. bee venom, cause a similar reaction in insects, e.g. spiders.

painkillers include aspirin◊, morphine◊, codeine◊, paracetamol, and synthetic versions of the natural pain inhibitors, the encephalins and endorphins, which avoid the side-effects of all the others□

Paine Thomas 1737–1809. British author, who went to N America 1774, where he published *Common Sense* 1776, an influential republican pamphlet, and fought for the colonists in the American◊ War of Independence. Back in England 1787, he published *The Rights of Man* 1791, and when indicted for treason escaped to France, where he represented Calais in the Convention. Narrowly escaping the guillotine, he regained his seat after the fall of Robespierre◊, and in 1793 published *The Age of Reason,* a defence of Deism◊. He died in New York□

painting the application of colour, pigment, paint, etc. to an object. The chief methods of painting are:

tempera emulsion painting, with a gelatinous (e.g. egg yolk) rather than oil base; as in ancient Egypt, and many early Italian works.

fresco watercolour painting on plaster walls before they dry, e.g. palace of Knossos◊, Crete.

oil ground pigments in linseed oil, developed by the Van◊ Eycks.

watercolour pigments combined with gum arabic and glycerine, which are diluted with water; the method was developed in 15–17th centuries from wash drawings, and reached its height with Turner◊.

acrylic developed post World War II, (see acrylic◊ acid); the colours are very hard and brilliant□

Paisley Ian 1926– . Ulster◊ Loyalist politician. Minister of the Martyrs Memorial Free Presbyterian Church from 1946, and MP in the N Ireland Parliament 1970–4, and at Westminster from 1974, he is controversial for his extreme Protestant position□

Paisley industrial town (engineering, distilling) in Strathclyde, Scotland; population 84 800. It was long famous for thread, and shawls with a curved 'fishtail' design, still used in fabrics□

Pakhtoonistan see Pathans◊□

Pakistan Islamic Republic of

area 803 900 sq km/310 400sq mi; one-third of Kashmir◊ is under Pakistani control

capital Islamabad

towns Karachi (largest city and port), Lahore

features the 'five rivers' (Indus, Jhelum, Chenab, Ravi and Sutlej), feeding one of the world's largest irrigation systems; Khyber◊ Pass; site of the Indus◊ Valley civilisation

exports cotton textiles, rice, leather, carpets

currency Pakistan rupee

population 96 628 000, 66% Punjabi, 13% Sindhi

language Urdu and English (official); Punjabi

religion Sunni Islam 75%, Shi'ite Islam 20%, Hindu 4%

famous people Jinnah◊, Abdus Salam◊□

government executive president (Zia ul-Haq

Painters

school	name	dates	representative work
Florentine	Giotto	1266-1337	*Life of St Francis*
	Fra Angelico	1417-1455	*The Annunciation*
	Uccello	1397-1475	*The Battle of San Romano*
	Botticelli	1445-1510	*The Birth of Venus*
	Michelangelo	1475-1564	*Sistine Ceiling*
	Andrea del Sarto	1488-1530	*The Madonna of the Harpies*
Umbria	Piero della Francesca	1439-1492	*Nativity*
Milan	Leonardo da Vinci	1452-1519	*Mona Lisa*
Venice	Giovanni Bellini	1459-1516	*The Coronation of the Virgin*
	Giorgione	1506-1510	*The Tempest*
	Titian	1511-1576	*Bacchus and Ariadne*
	Paolo Veronese	1528-1588	*The Marriage of Cana*
Padua	Mantegna	1430-1506	*The Triumph of Caesar*
	Raphael	1488-1520	*The Colonna Altarpiece*
Spanish	El Greco	1541-1614	*The Burial of Count Orgaz*
	Velásquez	1599-1660	*The Water Carrier*
	Murillo	1617-1682	*Virgin and Child*
	Francisco di Goya	1746-1828	*The Naked Maja*
	Pablo Picasso	1881-1973	*Guernica*
Flemish	Pieter Brueghel	1551-1569	*The Peasant Dance*
	Peter Paul Rubens	1577-1640	*Adoration of the Magi*
	van Dyck	1599-1641	*Charles I*
Dutch	Hieronymus Bosch	1450-1516	*Garden of Earthly Delights*
	Rembrandt	1606-1669	*The Night Watch*
	Franz Hals	1580-1666	*Laughing Cavalier*
	Vincent Van Gogh	1853-1890	*Old Peasant*
German	Albrecht Dürer	1471-1528	*The Four Apostles*
	Holbein the Younger	1497-1543	*Henry VIII*
	Oskar Kokoschka	1886-1980	*Portrait of Hans Tietze*
French	Nicolas Poussin	1595-1665	*Worship of the Golden Calf*
	Jean-Antoine Watteau	1684-1721	*The Embarkation for Cythera*
	François Boucher	1703-1770	*Diana Bathing*
	Jacques-Louis David	1748-1825	*The Rape of the Sabines*
	Paul Ingres	1780-1867	*Marat Assassinated*
	Edouard Manet	1832-1883	*Déjeuner sur L'Herbe*
	Claude Monet	1840-1926	*Waterlilies*
	Edgar Degas	1834-1917	*Danceuse au Bouquet*
	Jean Renoir	1841-1919	*Luncheon of the Boating Party*
	Paul Cezanne	1839-1906	*Mont Ste Victoire*
	Henri Matisse	1869-1954	*Odalisque*
English	William Hogarth	1697-1764	*Rake's Progress*
	Joshua Reynolds	1723-1792	*The Three Graces*
	Thomas Gainsborough	1727-1792	*Blue Boy*
	Joseph Turner	1775-1851	*Shipwreck*
	William Holman Hunt	1830-1896	*The Scapegoat*
	Paul Nash	1889-1946	*Dead Sea*
	Ben Nicholson	1894	*White Relief*
American	Mary Cassatt	1855-1925	*The Bath*
	John Singer Sargent	1856-1925	*Lily*
	Jackson Pollock	1912-1956	*Autumn Rhythm*

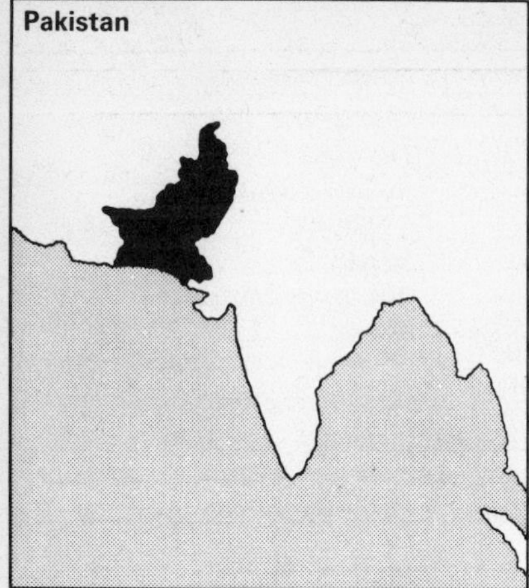

from 1977) heading a national security council, which was established 1985 to increase the presidential powers; at the same time parliament also assembled (Prime Minister Mohammad Khan Junjo)
recent history created in 1947 on the partition of British India, Pakistan originally comprised E Pakistan (from 1972 Bangladesh◊) as well as W Pakistan (provinces Baluchistan◊, Punjab◊, Sind◊, NW Frontier◊, and the federally administered Tribal Areas). Pakistan left the Commonwealth in 1972 in protest at its recognition of Bangladesh. Following a military coup in 1977 by Zia ul-Haq, his predecessor (Bhutto◊) was hanged, and martial law introduced in 1978. All political parties were banned in the elections held 1985 for a national assembly and four provincial councils. There is a programme of Islamisation□

Palaeolithic see Stone Age under prehistory◊□

palate roof of the mouth, with a bony front part, and soft at the rear, where it ends in a short appendage, the uvula. In children born with an incompletely fused or 'cleft' palate, surgery is required, otherwise speech is defective□

Palatinate historic division of W Germany, so-named because formerly ruled by a 'count palatine'. The ***Rhenish Palatinate***, capital Neustadt, now forms part of the Land of Rhineland-Palatinate; and the ***Upper Palatinate***, capital Regensburg, is part of Bavaria□

Palau see under Belau◊□

Paldiski ice-free port in Estonia, USSR, a Soviet naval base□

Palembang industrial port (oil refining and petrochemicals) on Sumatra; with a pepper and coffee trade; population 583 000□

Palermo industrial seaport (textiles, engineering), capital of Sicily, founded by the Phoenicians◊; population 702 000. It has the 12th-century Capella Palatina, built by King Roger II□

Palestine former name of the area (also called the ***Holy Land*** because of its links with Judaism◊, Christianity◊ and Islam◊) between the Mediterranean and the River Jordan, with Lebanon to the north and Sinai to the south. It was anciently dominated in turn by Egypt, Assyria◊, Babylonia◊, Persia◊, Macedonia◊, the Ptolemies◊, the Seleucids◊ and the Roman◊ and Byzantine◊ empires.
AD
636 conquest by the Muslim Arabs, which made it a target for the Crusades◊ (see also Jerusalem◊)
1516 conquest by the Turks
1917–18 Turks driven out by Allenby◊ in World War I
1922 Britain received Palestine as a League◊ of Nations mandate◊ (incorporating the Balfour◊ Declaration) to administer both historic Palestine and lands across the River Jordan which were recognized in 1923 as the Hashimite Kingdom of Jordan◊
1929 and ***1936–8*** Arab revolts fuelled by Jewish immigration (300 000 during 1920–39)
1939–45 both Arab and Jewish Palestinians served in the Allied forces in World War II
1947 following Jewish terrorist outrages, prompted by restriction of Jewish immigration, Britain put the question before the United Nations◊, which proposed partition: neither side agreed
1948 15 May (eight hours before Britain's renunciation of the mandate due) a Jewish state of Israel◊ was proclaimed. A series of Arab-Israeli◊ Wars resulted in the total loss of the Palestinian state, and Palestinian terrorism followed
1974 the Palestine Liberation Organization (headquarters Tunis; see Arafat◊) became the first non-governmental delegation to be admitted to a plenary session of the United Nations General Assembly
The name Palestine derives from the Philistines◊, but the Palestinian people (c1 500 000 in the W Bank, E Jerusalem and the Gaza Strip; 1 200 000 in Jordan; 1 200 000 in Israel; thousands in camps in Lebanon and Syria; and 100 000 in USA) are descendants of the Canaanites◊. Archaeological evidence, hotly contested, suggests that their origins and those of the Israelis are closely linked□

Palestrina Giovanni Pierluigi da 1525–94. Italian composer, choir master at St Peter's◊

and St John Lateran◊. A master of counterpoint, he composed madrigals, and much church music□

Pali the sacred language of the Buddhist canonical texts. See under Buddhism◊□

Palissy Bernard c1510–89. French potter of richly coloured rustic work, especially with realistically modelled fish and reptiles. He was favoured by Catherine de' Medici◊, but was imprisoned in the Bastille◊ as a Huguenot 1588, and died there□

Palladio Andrea 1508–80. Italian architect, who from 1540 designed country houses, e.g. the Villa Rotonda near Vicenza◊, for patrician families of the Venetian Republic. He influenced the design of Washington◊'s home at Mount Vernon, the palace of Tsarskoe◊ Selo, and in England, Holkham◊, Prior Park◊, Stowe◊, etc.□

palladium element
symbol Pd
atomic number 46
physical description silvery-white metal
features found in platinum
uses can be alloyed with gold, resulting in 'white gold'; in dentistry and jewellery; and as a catalyst□

palladium image of Pallas Athena◊, supposed to be a gift from Zeus◊ to Troy◊, which could not be captured while it remained. It was stolen by Odysseus◊ and Diomedes, and was later alleged to have been taken to Rome by Aeneas◊□

palm plant, of the mainly tropical and subtropical family Palmaceae, with a single tall stem carrying a thick cluster of large palmate or pinnate◊ leaves at the top. Some are small, but many (though not trees) are tree-like, including some of the most economically important:
coconut fruit of *Cocos nucifera* of India and SE Asia. The 'trees' mature in 7–8 years, and bear up to 100 nuts annually for some 80 years; the dried kernel ***copra*** contains 70% oil, used in margarine, cooking oil, soap, detergents, cosmetics, pharmaceutical products, and as fuel; the sap of the tree ferments into a potent spirit ***arack*** or may be boiled down to yield sugar, as in India; the leaves are woven into mats, cordage and ropes. The ***'double coconut'*** or ***coco de mer*** *Lodoicea maldivica* of the Seychelles◊ has a two-lobed edible nut, one of the largest known fruits.
date Afro-Asian 'tree' of the palm family, genus *Phoenix* especially *P dactylifera* of which the female produces bunches of 180–200 fruit (up to 11 kg/25 lb), a valuable food; the palm also supplies 'timber', rope, etc.
oil palm African palm *Elaeis guineensis* of which the fruits yield palm oil, an edible oil resembling butter, also used in soap, etc. It is a rival to rubber as a cash crop.
sago tropical Asian trees, especially *Metroxylon sagu* of which the starchy pith of the trunk is the cereal sago; the plant is also being developed for use in the bioconversion of starch into protein; and for the production of lignocellulose◊ and gasohol◊□

Palma capital and industrial port (textiles, paper, cement, pottery) of the Balearic Islands, Spain, on Majorca; population 304 425□

Palma La. See under Canary◊ Islands□

Palmas Las. See under Canary◊ Islands□

Palm Beach see under Florida◊□

Palmer Samuel 1805–81. British artist, whose landscapes show the influence of Blake◊□

Palmerston Henry John Temple, 3rd Viscount Palmerston 1784–1865. British Whig◊ statesman. Originally a Tory◊ (Secretary-at-War 1809–28), he joined the Whig cabinets of 1830–4, 1835–41, and 1846–51 as Foreign Secretary; was Home Secretary 1852 and Prime Minister 1855–8 (when he rectified Aberdeen◊'s mismanagement of the Crimean◊ War, suppressed the Indian◊ Mutiny, and carried through the Second Opium◊ War) and 1859–65. Alert to the danger of a Franco-Russian coalition, he backed the independence of Belgium and Turkey against them, and nearly involved Britain in the American Civil◊ War on the side of the South. He was adored by the populace, but his high-handed attitude annoyed Queen Victoria and Prince Albert□

Palmerston North city, centre of a timber and dairy-farming area, on N Island, New Zealand; population 92 700. Massey University 1963 has a famous agricultural college□

Palm Springs resort with hot springs, California, USA; population 21 000□

Palm Sunday the Sunday before Easter, and first day of Holy Week; so-called to commemorate Christ's entry into Jerusalem, when the crowd strewed palm leaves in his path□

Palmyra Roman name for Tadmor (the modern small town of Tadmur in Syria, north east of Damascus). It was a flourishing trading centre from c300BC until its destruction (by Aurelian◊) 272AD, after Queen Zenobia◊ led a revolt against the Romans. The ruins include a great temple of Baal◊□

Palmyra coral atoll 1600 km/1000 mi, south west of Hawaii, in the Pacific, purchased by the USA from a Hawaiian family in 1979 for the storage of highly radioactive nuclear waste from 1986□

Palomar Mt. See under telescope◊□

Pamirs central Asian plateau mainly in the USSR, but extending into China and Afghanistan, traversed by mountain ranges. Mt Communism (Kommunizma Pik 9495 m/24 590 ft) in the Akademiya Nauk range is the highest mountain in the USSR□

Pampas treeless plains in Argentina, between the Atlantic and Andes. To the east are large cattle ranches and a grain-growing area; the west is arid and unproductive. See pampas grass under grasses◊□

pampas grass genus of S American grasses◊□

Pamplona city in Navarre, Spain; population 183 220. A pre-Roman town, it was rebuilt by Pompey◊ in 68BC, sacked by Charlemagne◊ in 778, became the capital of Navarre, and was taken by Wellington◊ in 1813. There is an annual 'running of the bulls' through the streets in Jul□

Pan in Greek mythology, god (Roman Sylvanus) of flocks and herds, shown as a man with the horns, ears and hoofs of a goat, and playing a shepherd's pipe□

Panama Republic of

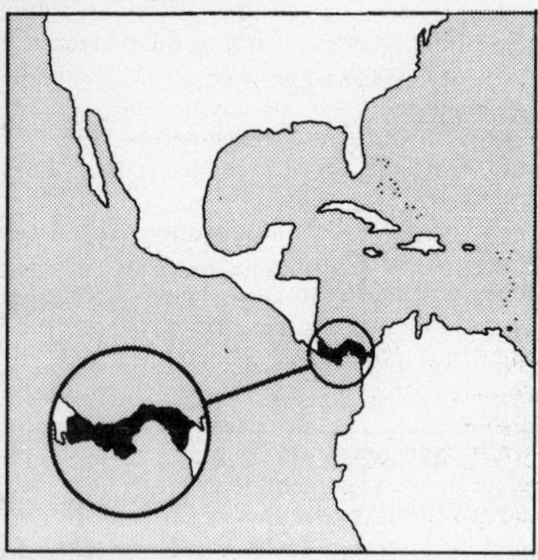

area 76 614 sq km/31 293 sq mi
capital Panama City
towns Cristóbal, Balboa, Colón
features Panama◊ Canal; Barro Colorado Island in Gatun Lake (the reservoir which supplies the canal), a tropical forest reserve since 1923; Smithsonian Tropical Research Institute
exports bananas, petroleum products; copper from one of the world's largest deposits; shrimps
currency balboa
populaton 2 000 000
language Spanish
religion Roman Catholic
famous people Balboa◊
government executive president (from 1984 Nicolás Ardito Barletta; Democratic Revolutionary Party, PRD) and legislative assembly
recent history formerly part of Colombia◊, it became independent in 1903 with the encouragement of the USA, which was interested in the Panama Canal Zone. This reverted to Panama in 1979, though USA retained management and defence of the canal till 1999, with 25% of the land of the zone. Some 10 000 US troops are stationed here, and train the Panamanian National Guard, as well as running a school for jungle warfare. The first direct presidential elections since 1968 were held 1984, but there were allegations of fraud when Arnulfo Arias Madrid (president 1941, 1951, 1969) was defeated□

Panama Canal canal in Central America linking the Atlantic and Pacific; length 80 km/50 mi. Conceived by de Lesseps◊, it was built 1879–1914, and the USA retains control of management till 1999. See Panama◊□

Panama City capital of the Republic of Panama; population 467 000. Its port is Balboa□

Pan-American Highway highway linking the USA with Central and S America; runs from Nuevo Laredo, Texas (via Mexico City, Panama City, Valparaiso) to Buenos Aires, 25 300 km/15 700 mi□

Pan-American Union see Organization◊ of American States□

Panay see under Philippines◊□

Panchen Lama 10th Incarnation 1935– . Tibetan spiritual leader, second only to the Dalai◊ Lama. A Chinese protégé since childhood, he was deputed to take over in 1959, but was in 1965 deported to China for alleged subversion□

pancreas gland in human body behind and below the stomach which secretes ferments necessary for the digestion of starch, protein and fat. See also under hormone◊□

panda herbivorous mammal, family Ailuridae, of NW China (Sichuan◊) and Tibet. The ***giant panda*** *Ailuropoda melanoleuca* 1.5 m/4.5 ft long, has black and white fur with black eye patches and feeds on bamboo shoots; on the basis of its DNA◊ it is a highly specialized bear. The ***lesser panda*** *Ailurus fulgens* 50 cm/1.5 ft long, is black and chestnut, with a long tail, and has links with the raccoons◊□

Pandora in Greek mythology, the first woman. Zeus◊ sent her to earth with a box of evils (to counteract the blessings brought to man by Prometheus◊' gift of fire); her husband opened it, and they all flew out. Only hope was left inside as a consolation□

pangolin or *scaly anteater* Afro-Asian toothless, long-tailed mammal, order Pholidota, up to 1 m/3 ft long. The upper part of the body is covered with horny plates, so that it can defend itself by curling into a ball; it also emits a powerful smell□

Pankhurst Emmeline 1858–1928. British suffragette◊, born Goulden. She launched the militant campaign votes for women in 1906, and was several times imprisoned and released after hunger-strikes; her Manchester home is a museum. She was supported by her daughters Dame Christabel 1880–1958, and Sylvia 1882–1960□

pansy a perenial garden flower. See under violet◊□

Pantelleria volcanic island south west of Sicily◊. Strongly fortified in World War II, it was the first part of metropolitan Italy to surrender to the Allies◊ 11 Jun 1944□

pantheism concept of God◊ as a pervading presence immanent in the universe□

pantheon originally a temple for worshipping all the gods, e.g. that in ancient Rome, rebuilt by Hadrian◊ and still used as a church; now as in the Panthéon, Paris, a building where famous people are buried□

panther a large wild cat◊□

pantomime among the Romans the kind of dumbshow performed by a masked actor, of which the ***mime*** performances of Marcel Marceau◊ are a modern form. The uniquely British ***pantomime*** had its origins in the 18th-century harlequin spectacles, which in the 19th century developed on fairy and folktale themes, and combined songs, dances, knockabout comedy, and increasingly magnificent 'transformation scenes', e.g. mice and pumpkin to resplendent coach and horses in *Cinderella*. See Grimaldi◊, Dan Leno◊, Vesta Tilley◊. In the 20th century pantomimes on ice became popular after World War II, and the tradition still survives on stage, television and radio□

panzer German ('armour') mechanized divisions in World War II□

Papacy the office of the Pope◊□

Papal States area of central Italy in which the Pope was temporal ruler 756–1870, when Italy became a single united state□

Papandreou Andreas George 1919– . Greek statesman, founder of the Panhellenic Socialist Movement, and prime minister from 1981, re-elected 1985. He favours a single-party quasi-Marxist◊ regime, and opposed the re-election of Karamanlis◊ as president 1985□

papaya another name for the pawpaw◊□

Papeete capital and port of French Polynesia on Tahiti; population 62 735□

Papen Franz von 1879–1969. German Chancellor in 1932, when he negotiated the Nazi-Conservative alliance which put Hitler in the chancellorship 1933. He was envoy to Austria 1934–8, and ambassador to Turkey 1939–44. Although acquitted at Nuremberg, he was imprisoned by a German denazification court for three years□

paper material made in the form of sheets, so named from the paper reed (see papyrus◊). True paper, made from broken-down plant fibres, including old cotton textiles, was the invention of a Chinese minister of agriculture 105AD. Modern paper is usually made of wood pulp, and is used for newspapers, books, etc., but also in large quantities for towels, toilet tissues, hardboard, insulation, etc. Recycling avoids some of the enormous waste of trees□

Paphos legendary birthplace of Aphrodite◊, where she rose from the seafoam, in SW Cyprus. Ruins of her temple, once a centre of pilgrimage, remain□

Papineau Louis Joseph 1786–1871. Canadian politician. He fled the country after he had organized an unsuccessful rebellion of the French against the English in lower Canada in 1837, but returned in 1847 to sit in the United Canadian legislature until 1854. See Canada◊: history□

Papua original name of the island of New Guinea, but latterly its south-eastern section, now part of Papua◊ New Guinea□

Papua New Guinea

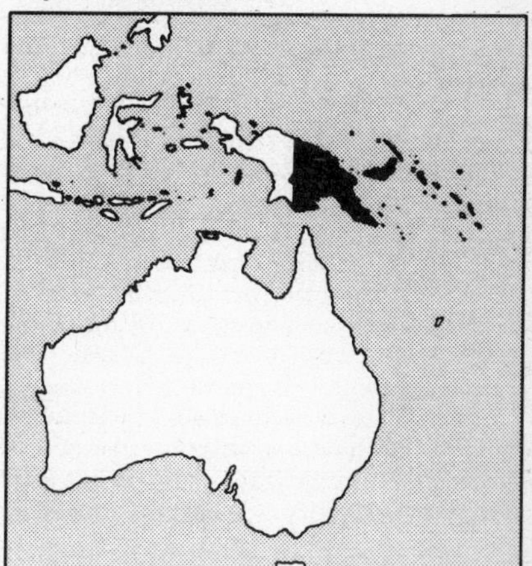

area 462 000 sq km/178 260 sq mi
capital Port Moresby
features wholly within the tropics, with a rainfall up to 200in a year; rare birds of paradise,

the world's largest butterfly◊, orchids
exports copra◊, coconut oil, palm oil, tea; copper
currency kina
population 3 140 000, including Papuans, Melanesians, Pygmies, and various minorities
language English (official); Pidgin
religion Protestantism 33%, Roman Catholicism 18%, local faiths□
government governor-general, and unicameral house of assembly; Prime Minister Michael Somare from 1982
recent history SE New Guinea was first annexed by Queensland 1883, and by 1906 was known as the Australian Territory of Papua. NE New Guinea was annexed by Germany in 1884, but was occupied by Australia in 1914, and held as a League◊ of Nations mandate 1921–1942, passing into Japanese occupation 1942–5. An Australian Trust Territory from 1946, it became independent within the Commonwealth in 1975 (with Papua and including New◊ Britain, New◊ Ireland, and – in the Solomon◊ Islands – Bougainville◊, and the Admiralty◊ Islands) as Papua New Guinea. In 1983 republican status was planned□

papyrus type of paper made by the ancient Egyptians from the stem of the ***paper reed*** *Cyperus papyrus* family Cyperaceae□

Pará see Belém◊□

Paracels group of c130 small islands (Chinese *Xisha*/Vietnamese *Hoang Sa*). In an oil-bearing area, they were occupied by the Chinese following a skirmish with the Vietnamese 1974□

Paracelsus 1493–1541. Swiss physician (original name Theophrastus Bombastus von Hohenheim), who lectured at Basle on the need for observational experience rather than traditional lore in medicine: he made a public bonfire of the works of Avicenne◊ and Galen◊□

parachute canopy device of nylon panels with shroud lines to a harness used to slow the aerial descent of human beings, stores, etc., to a safe landing speed, or to aid the landing of a plane or missile. Considerable direction control is possible for modern parachutists (see skydiving◊). In ***parascending*** the procedure is reversed, the canopy (parafoil) to which the pilot is attached being towed behind a vehicle to achieve an ascent□

Paradise Persian 'pleasure garden', e.g. the Garden of Eden◊, the Messianic kingdom, or the heaven of after life; the Islamic Paradise of the Koran◊ is a place of sensual pleasure□

paraffin a type of hydrocarbon◊ in gas, liquid or wax form. See also kerosene◊□

Paraguay Republic of

area 406 752 sq km/157 042sq mi
capital Asunción
town port Concepción
features Paraná and Paraguay rivers; Itaipú dam on border with Brazil; Chaco◊
exports cotton, soybeans, timber, tung oil, maté
currency guaraní
population 3 623 000, 95% mestizo (Guaraní Indian-Spanish)
language Spanish official, spoken by 4%; Guaraní 50%; remainder bilingual
religion Roman Catholicism
government executive president, elected for five years (Alfredo Stroessner from 1954, re-elected 1983) and parliament of two houses
recent history discovered by Cabot in 1526, the country was settled by Spain from 1537, and until 1767 (when they were expelled) ruled by the Jesuits◊ as a semi-theocratic state. It became independent of Spain in 1811, and was then at war with Brazil, Argentina, and Uruguay 1865–70, and with Bolivia 1932–5, the population being reduced by two-thirds to 200 000, mainly women and children. Stroessner achieved power by a military coup in 1954, but there has been liberalization of the regime from 1968. Rapid expansion of the economy followed installation of the Itaipú dam□

parakeet a small parrot◊□

paralysis failure of muscle◊ action, after injury (e.g. a wound) or infection (poliomyelitis◊) of the nerves supplying it. Other forms are caused by cerebral haemorrhage◊, multiple sclerosis◊, muscular dystrophy◊, myasthenia◊ gravis. Damage to one side of the brain may cause ***hemiplegia*** (paralysis of one side of the body only); damage to the spinal cord may result in paralysis of the legs only (***paraplegia***) or of both arms and legs (***quadriplegia***), according to the site of the injury□

Paramaribo capital and port of Surinam; population 151 500□

Paraná industrial river port (meat canneries, flour mills) in Argentina, on the Paraná; population 160 000□

Paraná river in S America, formed by the confluence of the Rio Grande and Paranaiba; the Paraguay joins it at Corrientes, and it flows into the Rio de la Plata with the Uruguay; length 4000 km/2500 mi. It is exploited for hydroelectric◊ power by Argentina, Brazil and Paraguay□

paranoia mental disorder marked by a single-channelled delusion, e.g. that the patient is someone of great importance, the subject of a conspiracy, etc. This dominates the whole way of life, sometimes to the danger of the patient or others□

parapsychology study of phenomena, e.g. of extra-sensory perception, which are not within (Greek *para* 'beside') the range explicable by established science (see under Koestler◊). The faculty allegedly responsible for them, and common to man and other animals, is known as ***psi*** (23rd letter of the Greek alphabet). They include:

mediumship contact with the spirits of the dead, usually via an intermediate 'guide' in the other world, a child spirit or someone of exotic antecedents.

precognition foreknowledge of events, as by Highland 'second-sight'.

telekinesis movement of objects from one position to another, as by a poltergeist◊, or by human mental concentration (as in the fall of dice). See also levitation◊.

telepathy term coined by Myers◊ for 'communication of impressions of any kind from one mind to another, independently of the recognized channels of sense'.

See also coincidence◊, dowsing◊□

paraquat non-selective contact herbicide used by farmers. Quickly degraded by soil micro-organisms, it is deadly to human beings if treatment is not given immediately after ingestion, since irreversible lung damage takes place□

parasite plant or animal living in or on another living organism, known as the host, to obtain food, e.g. fleas◊, lice◊, tapeworms◊, certain fungi◊, dodder◊, etc. Parasites weaken but rarely kill the host. See also symbiosis◊□

parathyroid one of a pair of small glands in the neck of humans. See under hormone◊□

paratyphoid fever a mild infective fever like typhoid◊□

Paris Henri, Comte de. See Bourbon◊□

Paris Matthew d. 1259. English Benedictine◊ chronicler at St Albans Abbey from 1236, whose history of England contains valuable contemporary material□

Paris capital of France and the Île-de-France◊, industrial city (chemicals, metal goods, glass, luxury goods), port on the Seine◊; population 8 600 000. Named from the Parisii, a Gaulish tribe once living in the area, it was occupied by Julius Caesar in 53BC, and became the capital of Clovis◊ c508. Most of medieval Paris disappeared in the rebuilding by Haussmann◊. The modern city includes the central Ile de la Cité (with Notre Dame); the former royal palace of the Louvre (now an art gallery); Picasso Museum 1985; the Opéra; Jardin des Plantes (botanic garden); Tuileries Gardens, Champs Elysées; Arc de Triomphe (with the tomb of the Unknown Warrior beneath); Tour Eiffel in the Champ de Mars; Bois de Boulogne, and Bois de Vincennes; Luxembourg Palace and gardens; National Centre for Art and Culture on the Beaubourg plateau; Hôtel des Invalides (founded as a home for disabled soldiers 1670, which has the tomb of Napoleon◊); the Sorbonne (the university founded in 12th century); headquarters of UNESCO; Montmartre (with the basilica of Sacré Coeur), and the more recent centre of artistic and literary activity, Montparnasse and the Latin Quarter. Orly and Charles de Gaulle are international airports□

Paris Treaties of. They include:

1763 ending the Seven◊ Years War

1783 recognizing American◊ Independence

1814 and ***1815*** following the abdication and final defeat of Napoleon◊

1856 ending the Crimean◊ War

1898 ending Spanish-American◊ War

1919–20 the conference preparing the *Treaty of Versailles* after World War I was held in Paris

1946 after World War II the peace treaties between the Allies◊ and Italy, Romania, Hungary, Bulgaria and Finland□

parish council see under local◊ goverment□

Park Mungo 1771–1806. Scottish author of *Travels in the Interior of Africa* 1799, who explored the course of the River Niger 1795–7, and died on a second expedition 1805–6□

Park Chung Hee 1917–79. President of S Korea 1963–79, who made it the world's fastest-growing economy. His authoritarianism led to his assassination□

Parker Dorothy 1893–1967. American poet with a mordant wit, whose New York salon included Lardner◊, Thurber◊ and Ogden Nash◊, and who reviewed for the magazines *Vanity Fair* and the *New Yorker*□

Parker Matthew 1504–75. English churchman, a Protestant convert, who as Archbishop of Canterbury from 1559 was largely responsible for the Elizabethan religious settlement (the formal establishment of the Church of England)□

Parkes town in New South Wales, Australia; population 10 000. It has a large radiotelescope, dish 64 m/210ft□

Parkinson Cecil Edward 1931– . British Conservative politician. As chairman of the party 1981–3, he masterminded the electoral victory of 1983, and was created Minister for Trade and Industry, but resigned in Oct 1984 following disclosure of an affair with his secretary□

Parkinson Cyril Northcote 1909– . British historian, celebrated for his study of public and business administration *Parkinson's Law* 1958, which included the dictum: 'work expands to fill the time available for its completion'□

Parkinson James 1755–1824. British neurologist, who first described Parkinson's◊ disease□

Parkinson's disease progressive deterioration of the small region of the brain that produces dopamine, a chemical used in the transmission of nerve signals. The patient's ability to walk is impaired and he suffers from tremor. It is not hereditary, and its ultimate cause is uncertain□

parliament an assembly of representatives of the people of a country□

Parliament supreme legislature of Great Britain

history it originated as a council of the chief tenants of the Norman◊ kings, but gradually included knights of the shires and burgesses from the towns (see Simon de Montfort◊). Under Edward◊ III these latter began to sit separately, forming the House of Commons. Parliament's growing power was checked under the strong rule of Yorkists◊ and Tudors◊, but the revolutions of 1640 and 1688 established parliamentary control over the executive and the judiciary, and ended any royal claim to tax or legislate without parliamentary consent. The Whig◊ and Tory◊ parties developed during these struggles; from 1688 ministers were chosen from the dominant party in the Commons.

The English Parliament was united with the Scottish 1707; with the Irish 1801–1922 (Northern Irish members still sit in the Commons); since 1911 the duration of a parliament has been fixed at five years. The middle class gained the vote under the Reform Bill of 1832; the city working class 1867; agricultural labourers 1884, and women only fully in 1928.

House of Lords presided over by the Lord Chancellor◊, comprises the lay hereditary peerage and life peers (usually superannuated members of the Commons promoted under an act of 1958, plus the Law◊ Lords, who automatically qualify by their judicial office), and the spiritual peers of the Anglican church (the two archbishops, plus 24 senior bishops). It may delay, but not reject, a Commons bill, and members receive an attendance allowance.

House of Commons presided over by the Speaker◊, its members are elected on a majority vote by constituencies kept under review by a special commission, and have been salaried since 1911. The Prime Minister must be a member of the Commons, other ministers may be members of the Lords. There is a system of ***select committees*** with an all-party membership, which deal with particular subjects; this system was enlarged by the Thatcher government 1979, and ensures control of the executive (departmental ministers attend to answer questions), and close examination of legislation, public spending and the work of government departments. The main parties are Conservative◊, Labour◊ and Liberal◊ and Social◊ Democrat, these last two forming the Alliance.

Procedure bills (put forward by the government or sometimes by private members) are given a first nominal reading, a second detailed discussion, when they may be referred to a select or standing committee, and after a third reading, sent through a similar procedure in the Lords. They then receive the royal◊ assent and become acts with legal force□

Parliament European. Governing body of the European◊ Economic Community (EEC). Originally merely consultative, it became directly elected 1979, and assumed increased powers. Though still not a true legislative body, it can dismiss the Commission en bloc, and reject the Community budget in its entirety. Full sittings are in Strasbourg; most committees meet in Brussels, and the seat of the secretariat is in Luxembourg. The socialists form the largest single group, but are outnumbered by the aggregate strength of the centre and right□

Parliament Houses of. The work of Barry◊ and Pugin◊ 1840–60, after the previous building had been burnt down 1834, it incorporates portions of the medieval Palace of Westminster◊ e.g. Westminster Hall. The Commons Chamber (destroyed in a 1941 air raid) was rebuilt by Sir Giles G Scott◊ on the same lines□

Parma industrial city (engineering, textiles, food processing) in N Italy; population 179 000. It has a Romanesque-Gothic cathedral, and is the distribution centre for Parmesan cheese□

Parnassus mountain in central Greece; height 2457 m/8062 ft, supposed abode of Apollo (see Delphi◊) and the Muses◊□

Parnell Charles Stewart 1846–91. Irish politician, an MP from 1875, and leader of the Home◊ Rule Party at Westminster from 1879, where he pursued an obstructive line, and his approval of the Land League's violent stance in gaining ownership of tenanted land led to his imprisonment in 1881. However, he welcomed Gladstone◊'s Home Rule Bill of 1886. On its defeat, he continued agitation, but in 1887 his reputation suffered from an unfounded accusation by *The Times* of his complicity in the murder of Lord Frederick Cavendish◊. He was finally ruined by Captain O'Shea's petition in 1891 for divorce on the grounds of his wife's adultery with Parnell. The 'uncrowned king of Ireland' was deposed by his party Nov 1890□

Parr Catherine 1512–48. Sixth wife of Henry◊ VIII, from 1543. Already twice widowed, she survived him, and married Lord Seymour of Sudeley 1547□

Parramatta river in New South Wales, Australia, lined by Sydney's industrial suburbs; length 24 km/15 mi□

parrot order of birds Psittaciformes, of which the single family Psittacidae belongs to the warmer parts of the world. Most familiar of the large species are the ***African grey parrot*** *Psittacus erithacus*, probably the best talker; and the S American ***blue-fronted Amazon*** *Amazona aestiva*, also a talker; and ***scarlet macaw*** *Ara macao* the traditional companion of Long John Silver, with brilliant colouring and long wedge-shaped tail, but actually less talkative.

New Zealand has two unusual species, the ***kea*** *Nestor notabilis* the only carnivorous parrot, which attacks the kidneys of live sheep (a conversion to meat-eating due to the arrival of the colonists), and ***kakapo*** *Strigops habroptilus* which is nocturnal and the only flightless parrot.

cockatoos of Australasia/Malaysia have erectile crests and include the large ***sulphur-crested cockatoo*** *Kakatoe galerita* of Australia, with large yellow crest, which is an excellent mimic.

Smaller parrot species, all brightly coloured, include:

lories sub-family Loriinae, with slender beaks adapted to taking nectar from the gum trees of Australasia.

lovebirds genus *Agapornis*, short-tailed, lively birds, with marked eye-rings, which behave affectionately to each other.

parakeets little, long-tailed birds, of which the best-known is the budgerigar *Melopsittacus undulatus* of Australia, green in its wild form, but with blue, yellow and white domesticated forms, some excellent talkers when subjected to separation from their own kind.

See psittacosis◊□

Parry Sir (Charles) Hubert Hastings 1848–1918. British composer, born in Bournemouth, whose works include songs, motets, the cantata *Blest Pair of Sirens* 1887 and a choral setting of Blake's *Jerusalem* 1915/16□

Parry Sir William Edward 1790–1855. British admiral and Arctic explorer, who made excellent charts during explorations of the North-West Passage 1819–20, 1821–3 and 1824–5, and an attempt to reach the Pole in 1827. The ***Parry Islands***, off Canada, are named after him□

Parsee a follower of Zoroastrianism◊□

Parsival one of the knights who sought the Holy Grail◊; he was the father of Lohengrin◊□

parsley a biennial herb◊□

parsnip temperate Eurasian biennial *Pastinaca sativa* family Umbelliferae, with a fleshy edible root□

Parsons Sir Charles Algernon 1854–1931. British engineer, inventor of the Parsons steam turbine 1884, a landmark in marine engineering□

Parthenon temple of Athena◊ Parthenos ('the Virgin') on the Acropolis◊ at Athens; built 447–438BC (see Phidias◊), and the most perfect example of Doric◊ architecture (by Callicrates and Ictinus). In turn a Christian church and Turkish mosque, it was then used as a gunpowder store, and reduced to ruins when the Venetians bombarded the Acropolis 1687. See Elgin◊ marbles□

Parthia ancient NE Iran. The ***Parthian Empire*** (c250BC–226AD), (capital Ctesiphon◊) dominated SW Asia, including N India. Their horsemen feigned retreat, and shot their arrows unexpectedly backwards – hence 'Parthian shot'. See Trajan◊□

particle physics in 1895 J J Thomson◊ discovered that all atoms◊ contain identical, negatively-charged particles (***electrons***◊) which could easily be freed. By 1913 Rutherford◊ had shown that electrons surround a very small, positively-charged nucleus, thus, the nucleus of a hydrogen atom consists of a single positively charged particle, a ***proton*** (identified by Chadwick◊ in 1932). The nuclei of other elements are made up of protons and uncharged particles called ***neutrons.*** Nuclei do not split apart easily; usually they need to be bombarded by particles such as protons, raised to very high kinetic energies by particle accelerators – which were first built around 1930.

1932 saw the discovery of a particle, predicted by Dirac◊, with the mass of an electron, but an equal and opposite charge – the ***positron.*** This was the first example of an ***antiparticle***; it is now believed that almost all particles have corresponding antiparticles. The following year, Pauli◊ argued that a hitherto unsuspected particle must acompany electrons in beta-emission (see radioactivity◊); this so-called ***electron-neutrino*** interacts with other particles only rarely, so neutrino radiation is extremely penetrating.

particles and fundamental forces By the mid-1930s four fundamental kinds of force◊ had emerged. The ***electromagnetic force*** acts between all particles with electric charge, and was thought to be related to the exchange between the particles of ***photons***, packets of electromagnetic radiation. In 1935, Yukawa◊ suggested that the ***strong force*** (holding neutrons and protons together in the nucleus) was caused by the exchange of particles with a mass of about a tenth that of a proton; these particles, called ***pions***, were found by Powell in 1946. Theoretical work on the ***weak force*** (responsible for beta radioactivity of the sun) began with Fermi◊ in the 1930s; current theory suggests the exchange during weak interactions of ***W*** and ***Z particles*** with masses some 100 times that of the proton. The existence of W and Z particles was confirmed in 1983 at CERN◊. The fourth fundamental force, ***gravity***, is experienced by all particles; the projected go-between particles have been dubbed ***gravitons.***

leptons, hadrons and quarks The electron and electron neutrinos are examples of ***leptons*** – particles with half-integral spin which 'feel' the weak, but not the strong force. There are known to be two more electron-like leptons plus their neutrinos: the ***muon*** (found by Anderson in cosmic radiation in 1937, and the ***Tauon*** a surprise discovery of the 1970s

hadrons (particles which 'feel' the strong force) started to turn up in bewildering profusion in experiments of the 1950s and 60s. They are classified into ***mesons***◊, with whole-number or zero spins, and ***baryons***+, with half-integral spins. It was shown in the early 1960s that if hadrons of the same spin are represented as points on suitable charts, simple patterns are formed. This symmetry enabled a hitherto unknown particle, the ***omega-minus***, to be predicted from a gap in one of the patterns; it duly turned up in experiments. In 1964 Gell-Mann and Zweig suggested that all hadrons were built from just three types or ***flavours*** of a new particle with half-integral spin and charge of magnitude either ⅓ or ⅔ that of an electron, which Gell-Mann christened the ***quark***. Mesons are quark-antiquark pairs (spins either add to 1 or cancel to zero) and baryons are quark triplets. To account for new mesons such as the ***psi*** the number of quark flavours had risen to six by 1985□

partnership in English law two or more persons carrying on a common business for shared profit (most frequently accountants, bankers, and solicitors). It differs from an ordinary company in that the individuals remain separate in identity, and are not protected by limited liability, so that absolute mutual trust is essential□

Partridge Eric 1894–1979. New Zealand compiler of dictionaries (e.g. *A Dictionary of Slang and Unconventional English* 1934/70), who settled in England□

partridge a game bird. See under fowl◊□

Pasadena city in California, USA; population 118 550. There is an annual Tournament of Roses, and on 1 Jan the East-West Football game is held in the 85 000-seat Rose Bowl. The California Institute of Technology (Caltech) owns the Hale Observatories (which include the Mt Palomar telescope), and is linked with the Jet Propulsion Laboratories (JPL)□

Pascal Blaise 1623–62. French philosopher-mathematician, born at Clermont-Ferrand. He contributed to the development of hydraulics, the calculus, and the mathematical theory of probability. After a mystical experience 1654, he took refuge in the Jansenist◊ monastery of Port Royal and defended the Jansenists against the Jesuits◊ in his *Lettres Provinciales* 1656. His influential *Pensées,* 1670, was part of an unfinished defence of the Christian religion□

Pas-de-Calais French name for the Strait of Dover◊, and also for the department bordering it (capital Arras; chief port Calais). See also Nord◊-Pas de Calais□

pasha Turkish honorary title (abolished 1934) for military commanders, and later high civil officials. It continued in use in some other Middle Eastern countries till 1952□

Pashto or ***Pushtu*** Indo-European language, officially that of Afghanistan, and also spoken in another dialect in N Pakistan□

Pasmore Victor 1908– . British artist, noted from 1947 for his geometric abstracts and reliefs; he was influenced by Constructivism◊□

Pasolini Pier Paolo 1922–75. Italian poet, novelist, and film director, e.g. *Medea* 1969, *The Gospel according to St Matthew* 1964, and *The Decameron* 1970□

Passau town in Bavaria, W Germany. The ***Treaty of Passau*** 1552 between Maurice, Elector of Saxony, and the future Emperor Ferdinand◊ I, allowed Lutherans◊ religious liberty. It led to the Peace of Augsburg. See Reformation◊□

Passchendaele village in W Flanders, Belgium, near Ypres. ***Passchendaele Ridge*** was the object of the unsuccessful British offensive Jul–Nov 1917, which cost over 400 000 casualties□

Passfield Baron title of Sidney Webb◊□

passion flower tropical American genus of climbing plants *Passiflora* family Passifloraceae. Parts of the flower resemble symbols of the crucifixion, crown of thorns, etc.□

passion play play representing the death and resurrection of a god, as of Osiris◊, Dionysus◊, and Christ (as in some medieval miracle plays, see Oberammergau◊)□

Passover An ancient Jewish spring festival which commemorates the exodus from Egypt. See under Judaism◊□

passport document issued by the foreign office of any country authorizing the bearer to go abroad and guaranteeing the bearer the state's protection. Some countries require an intending visitor to obtain a special endorsement or ***visa***. Uniform European Community Passports were introduced from 1978 as an alternative□

Pasternak Boris Leonidovich 1890–1960. Russian poet and novelist. Born in Moscow of Jewish parentage, he remained in Russia when his artist father ***Leonid Pasternak*** 1862–1945 emigrated. His volumes of lyric poems include *A Twin Cloud* 1914, and *On Early Trains* 1943, and he translated Shakespeare's tragedies. His novel *Dr Zhivago* 1958, dealing with a scientist's disillusion with the Russian revolution, was followed by a Nobel prize (which he declined), and was banned in the USSR as 'a hostile act'□

Pasteur Louis 1822–95. French chemist whose discovery that fermentation was caused by micro-organisms led to the science of bacteriology (the study of bacterial infection, prevention and immunology). He inspired his pupil Lister's work in antiseptic surgery. He later researched into silkworm disease, anthrax◊, and especially rabies◊, for which his development of a vaccine led to the foundation of the Institut Pasteur in Paris 1888. See pasteurization◊□

pasteurization heat treatment of milk by maintaining its temperature at 62.8°C–65.5°C for at least 30 minutes, followed by rapid cooling to 10°C or lower. This kills harmful bacteria (e.g. those of tuberculosis◊) and delays the development of others without affecting the milk protein□

Paston family of Norfolk, whose correspondence and documents for 1422–1509 throw invaluable light on the period□

Patagonia geographic area of S America, south of latitude 40° S. Sighted by Magellan 1520, it was claimed by both Argentina and Chile until divided between them 1881. The climate is damp and chilly, but sheep are reared, and in recent years coal and oil have been exploited□

patchouli oriental soft-wooded shrub *Pogostemon heyneanus* family Labiateae, source of the Indian perfume patchouli□

patent exclusive right to make, use, and sell an invention (ideas are not eligible, neither is anything not new) for a limited period, conferred by 'letters patent'. There is a London Patent Office, but a central office (established in Munich, with a branch at The Hague, 1977) grants patents for 20 years in 16 European countries, also covering designs and trade marks; in the USA the period of patent is only 17 years□

Pater Walter Horatio 1839–94. British critic, a noted stylist and supporter of 'art for art's sake', as in *Studies in the History of the Renaissance* 1873, and the historical novel *Marius the Epicurean* 1885□

Paterson Andrew Barton 1864–1941. Australian journalist, 'Banjo' Paterson, who adapted 'Waltzing Matilda' from a traditional song□

Pathan warrior people of NW Pakistan and Afghanistan. Formerly a constant threat to the British Raj, the Pakistani Pathans now claim independence, with the Afghani Pathans, in their own state of Pakhtoonistan□

Patinir Joachim c1485–1524. Flemish artist, noted for landscape backgrounds to his depictions of the saints□

Patmore Coventry 1823–96. British pre-Raphaelite◊ poet (*The Angel in the House* 1854–63, and the odes *The Unknown Eros* 1877) who was also a critic□

Patmos see Dodecanese◊□

Patna capital of Bihar state, India; population 916 000. Once the Maurya◊ capital, it has remains of a hall built by Asoka◊ in the 3rd century BC□

Paton Alan 1903– . S African novelist, whose *Cry, the Beloved Country* 1948 touched the heart of S Africa's racial problems□

Patou Jean 1880–1936. French designer of neat 'sporting' clothes (Suzanne Lenglen◊) from 1922 and bias-cut white satin evening dresses 1929; and creator of the perfume 'Joy' 1926□

Patras industrial port (textiles, paper) in W Greece; population 141 000□

patriarch Greek 'ruler of a family', i.e. the mythical ancestors of the human race, and especially those of the Jews from Adam to the sons of Jacob. In the Orthodox◊ Church, the term refers to the leader of a national church□

patricians in ancient Rome descendants of the original citizens, with privileges not open to plebeians◊ until the 4th century BC□

Patrick St c389–461 or 493. Patron saint of Ireland. Son of a Roman official, he was probably born in S Wales. Carried off by pirates and enslaved in Antrim in Ireland, he escaped to train as a missionary in Britain, and returned to convert the Irish. Feast day 17 Mar□

Patterson Harry 1929– . British novelist. Born in Newcastle, he has written many thrillers under his own name, including *Dillinger* 1983, as well as under the pseudonym 'Jack Higgins', e.g. *The Eagle Has Landed* 1975□

Patti Adelina 1843–1919. Italo-British soprano opera singer, noted for pure tone and superb execution, e.g. Lucia in *Lucia di Lammermoor* and Amina in *La Sonnambula*□

Patton George Smith 1885–1945. American general, who in 1942 led the Task Force which landed at Casablanca, and after commanding the 7th Army in Sicily 1943, led the 3rd Army through France (repulsing Rundstedt's Ardennes◊ offensive) and into Germany. He died after a car accident□

Pau resort and industrial city (metallurgical and electro-chemical industries) in SW France; centre of the Basque area; population 85 860□

Paul St c3–c64 or 68AD. One of the Apostles◊ (the Jewish form of his name being Saul), he was born in Tarsus, son of well-to-do Pharisees◊, and had Roman citizenship. Opposed to Christianity, he took part in the stoning of Stephen◊, but was converted by a vision on the road to Damascus. He made great missionary journeys, e.g. to Philippi◊, Ephesus◊, hence becoming known as the 'Apostle of the Gentiles◊'. See also Barnabas◊. On his return to Jerusalem, he was arrested, appealed to Caesar, and (as a citizen) was sent to Rome for trial c57 or 59. After two years in prison, he may have been released before his final arrest and execution under Nero◊. Thirteen epistles in the New Testament are attributed to him. His theology was rigorous on such questions as sin and atonement, and his views on the role of women became those of the Church generally□

Paul six Popes, of whom ***Paul VI*** (Giovanni Battista Montini) 1897–1978, succeeded Pope John 1963, and took the name of Paul as symbolic of ecumenical unity. His encyclical *Humanae Vitae* (Of Human Life) 1968, rather than following the majority view of the commission appointed by John, reaffirmed the traditional Church view on birth control□

Paul I 1754–1801. Tsar of Russia from 1796, in succession to his mother Catherine◊ II. Already mentally unstable, he pursued an erratic foreign policy, and was assassinated□

Paul 1901–64. King of the Hellenes from 1947 in succession to George◊ II. He tried to restore the popularity of the monarchy, but his wife (from 1938), ***Frederika*** 1917– , attracted attack by her political role. He was succeeded by Constantine◊ II□

Paul Elliot Harold 1891–1958. American author, born in Malden, Massachusetts. His books include the travel book *The Narrow Street/The Last Time I saw Paris* 1942□

Pauli Wolfgang 1900–58. Austrian-American physicist, a Nobel prizewinner 1945 for his work on atomic structure. He originated ***Pauli's exclusion principle*** that in a given system no two electrons◊, protons◊, neutrons◊ or other particles of half-integrated spin can be characterized by the same set of quantum◊ numbers. He also predicted the existence of neutrinos. See quantum◊ mechanics, particle◊ physics□

Pauling Linus Carl 1901– . American chemist, Nobel prizewinner 1954 for his work on the nature of chemical bonding, and also (for peace) 1962, for his opposition to nuclear testing□

Paulinus d. 644. Roman-born missionary who joined Augine◊ in Kent 601, converted the Northumbrians 625, and became first archbishop of York. Excavations 1978 revealed a church he built in Lincoln◊□

Paulus Friedrich von 1890–1957. German field marshal, who besieged Stalingrad (now Volgograd) in USSR 1942–3; he was captured and later lived in E Germany□

Pausanias see under Persian◊ Wars□

Pausanias 2nd century BC. Greek geographer, author of a valuably accurate description of Greece from his own travels□

Pavarotti Luciano 1935– . Italian operatic tenor, whose roles include Rodolfo in *La Bohème* and Cavaradossi in *Tosca*□

Pavia town in Italy, once capital of the Lombards◊; population 95 000. Buildings include the 12th-century Romanesque◊ basilica of San Michele; the law school, from which the university developed, was traditionally founded by Lanfranc◊□

Pavia Battle of, 1525. Emperor Charles◊ V defeated and captured Francis◊ I of France□

Pavlov Ivan Petrovich 1849–1936. Russian physiologist, Nobel prizewinner 1904 for research on digestion. His study of conditioned reflexes in animals influenced Behaviourism◊□

Pavlova Anna 1885–1931. Russian dancer, born at St Petersburg, who popularized Russian ballet worldwide, especially in *The Swan* music by Saint-Saëns (see Fokine◊). The ***pavlova,*** a meringue cake with fruit and whipped cream on top, was named after her□

pawnbroker someone lending money on the security of goods held; the trade sign of three gold balls was the symbol used on housefronts by medieval Lombard◊ merchants□

pawpaw S American tropical evergreen tree ***papaya*** *Carica papaya* family Caricaceae, having an edible melon-like fruit with orange flesh and black seeds. The US pawpaw is the oval berry of *Asimina triloba* family Annonaceae□

Pax see Irene◊□

Paxton Sir Joseph 1801–65. British architect, garden superintendent to the Duke of Devonshire from 1826 and designer of the Great Exhibition building of 1851 (see Crystal◊ Palace), revolutionary in its structural use of glass and iron□

PAYE (Pay As You Earn). System (in the UK from 1944) of deduction of income tax in advance by the employer on behalf of the Inland◊ Revenue. It was devised by Sir Paul Chambers◊□

Paymaster-General head of the British government department (from 1835) which acts as paying agent for most other departments□

Paysandú industrial city (meat-canning) in Uruguay, linked by bridge with Puerto Colón in Argentina from 1976; population 80 000□

Pays de la Loire region of W France; capital Nantes; population 2 930 400. See Loire◊□

Paz Octavio 1914– . Mexican poet, whose *Sun Stone* 1957 is a personal statement taking the Aztec◊ Calendar Stone as its basic symbol□

pea climbing plant *Pisum sativum* family Leguminosae, with pods of edible seeds; the ***sweet pea*** *Lathyrus odoratus* is grown for its scented flowers□

Peace river in W Canada, flowing (initially as the Finlay river) from the Rockies to the Great Slave Lake; length 1715 km/1065 mi□

Peace Corps formed in USA 1961 by President Kennedy◊ to assist developing countries through skilled volunteers. See also British◊ Volunteer Programme□

peach small tree *Prunus persica* family Rosaceae◊, producing juicy furry-skinned fruit; the ***nectarine*** is a smooth-skinned variety□

Peacock Andrew Sharp 1939– . Australian Liberal statesman. Minister for Foreign Affairs 1975–80, Industrial Relations 1980–81, and Industry and Commerce 1982–3, he became leader of the party 1983, and cut Hawke's◊ majority in the election of 1984□

Peacock Thomas Love 1785–1866. British official of the East India Company and satiric novelist (*Headlong Hall* 1816, *Nightmare Abbey* 1818, *Crotchet Castle* 1831, etc.)□

peacock a large bird. See under fowl◊□

peafowl a type of large pheasant. See under fowl◊□

Peak District see under Derbyshire◊□

Peale Charles Wilson 1741–1827. American artist, noted for portraits of Washington◊, and miniatures, e.g. Mrs Washington□

peanut another name for the groundnut◊□

pear Eurasian temperate tree *Pyrus communis* family Rosaceae◊, with a succulent edible fruit, less hardy than the apple□

pearl nacre, a calcareous secretion of many molluscs. Deposited on the inside of the shell, it forms ***mother of pearl*** used in inlay work, etc. and deposited round some irritant body, the precious ***pearl***. These are formed in various species of *Margaritifera* of the oyster family Aviculidae, and (of lesser value) in freshwater mussels. Artificial pearls were developed from 1893 in Japan: a piece of clam shell is inserted in captive oysters, and sufficient nacre forms round it to produce a marketable pearl in three years□

Pearl Harbor see under Honolulu◊□

Pears Sir Peter 1910–86. British tenor, cofounder with Britten◊ of the Aldeburgh◊ Festival and performer of many of Britten's works, as well as those of Tippett◊ and Berkeley◊. Knighted 1978□

Pearse Patrick Henry 1879–1916. Irish poet prominent in the Gaelic revival, and leader of the Easter◊ Rebellion of 1916. Proclaimed president of the provisional government, he was court-martialled and shot after its suppression□

Pearson 'Mike' Lester Bowles 1897–1972. Canadian Liberal Foreign Minister 1948–57, awarded a Nobel peace prize 1957 largely for his role in creating the United Nations Emergency Force; he was leader of the party from 1958, and prime minister 1963–8□

Peary Robert Edwin 1856–1920. American Arctic explorer, born in Pennsylvania, the first to reach the North Pole, 6 Apr 1909□

Peasants' Revolt rising of the English peasantry Jun 1381, led by Wat Tyler◊ and John Ball◊. The rebels occupied London and forced Richard◊ II to abolish serfdom, but after Tyler's murder were compelled to withdraw. The movement was then suppressed, and the king's concessions revoked□

peat deposit formed by the decomposition of aquatic plants, e.g. sphagnum◊ moss, and ranging from woody brown coal and lignite◊ to compacted fibre. Russia, Canada, Finland, Ireland, etc. have large deposits, which have been dried and used as fuel from ancient times. A number of ancient corpses, thought to have been the result of ritual murders, have been found preserved in peat bogs, and in 1984 the first 'bogman' (Lindow Man) in mainland Britain was found near Wilmslow, Cheshire, dating from about 500BC□

pecan a nut-bearing tree; a type of hickory◊□

peccary American genus of pig-like animals *Tayassu* family Tayassuidae, having a gland in the middle of the back which secretes a strong-smelling substance. Blackish in colour, they are covered with bristles, and the skins make a useful leather. Travelling in herds, they are often belligerent□

Pechora river in the NE USSR flowing to the Barents Sea; length 1800 km/1125 mi. It would be more economically useful if flowing south. See under Volga◊□

Pécs industrial town (coal-mining, metallurgy) town in SW Hungary; population 173 000□

pedometer small instrument which gives an approximate distance covered by a pedestrian; each step moves a swinging weight, which in turn causes the mechanism to rotate, so moving a pointer round the face of a dial□

Pedro two emperors of Brazil:

Pedro I 1798–1834, son of John◊ VI of Portugal, escaped to Brazil on Napoleon◊'s invasion, and was appointed regent in 1821. He proclaimed Brazil independent in 1822, and was crowned emperor, but abdicated in 1831 and returned to Portugal.

Pedro II, his son, 1825–91, who succeeded him, alienated landowners by his anti-slavery measures, and was forced to abdicate 1889□

Peel Sir Robert 1788–1850. British Conservative statesman, born at Bury. A Tory MP from 1809, he was Home Secretary 1822–7 and 1828–30, founding the modern police force (hence nicknamed 'bobbies'), and introduced catholic emancipation 1829. He resisted passage of the 1832 Reform◊ Bill, but afterwards reformed his party as the 'Conservatives', on the basis of accepting necessary reform and seeking middle-class support. He was prime minister 1834–5 and 1841–6 (when he introduced income tax in 1841), but fell when he antagonized the landowners by repealing the Corn◊ Laws in 1846. He and his followers then formed a third party between the Conservatives and Liberals◊, but the majority of the Peelites (including Gladstone◊) joined the Liberals□

Peel fishing port in the Isle of Man; population 3700□

Peele George c1558–97. English poet-dramatist, e.g. the pastoral *The Arraignment of Paris* and a satiric comedy *The Old Wives' Tale*□

Peenemünde fishing village in E Germany, used from 1937 by the Germans to develop the V1 and V2 rockets used in World War II□

peepul an Indian tree. See under fig◊□

peerage in the UK holders of the hereditary temporal dignities of Duke, Marquess, Earl, Viscount and Baron, certain of which may be held by a woman in default of a male heir. In the later 19th century they were augmented by the Lords of Appeal in Ordinary (life peers), and from 1958 by a number of specially created life peers of either sex (usually long-standing members of the Commons). Since 1963 peers have been able to disclaim their titles (e.g. Lord Home◊ and Tony Benn◊), usually to allow them to sit in the Commons□

Pegasus winged horse of Greek myth, which sprang from the blood of Medusa◊; Hippocrene, the spring of the Muses◊ on Mt Helicon was said to have sprung from a blow of his hoof, and he was transformed into a constellation□

Pegu city in S Burma, with the fine Shwemawdaw pagoda; population 254 760□

Péguy Charles 1873–1914. French Catholic socialist, author from 1900 of *Les Cahiers de la Quinzaine* on political topics, and of poetry, e.g. *Le Mystère de la Charité de Jeanne d'Arc* 1897□

Peiping name ('northern peace') of Peking◊ 1928–49□

Peipus (Russian *Chudskoye*), Lake. Alexander Nevski◊ defeated the Teutonic◊ Knights (1242) on its frozen surface□

pekan a large N American marten. See under weasel◊□

Peking capital of China (Pinyin *Beijing*) and a special municipality; population 9 230 000. Founded 3000 years ago, it was the 13th-century capital of Kublai◊ Khan (called by the Mongols Khanbaligh – Marco Polo's Cambaluc). Later replaced by Nanking, it was again capital from 1421, except 1928–49, when it was renamed Peiping, and was held by the Japanese 1937–45. Notable are: Tian Anmen Gate (Gate of Heavenly Peace) and Tian Anmen Square; the Forbidden City, built 1406–20 as Gu Gong (Imperial Palace) of the Ming◊ Emperors, when there were 9000 ladies in waiting and 10 000 eunuchs in service (it is still the seat of the modern government); the Great Hall of the People 1959 (used for banquets for foreign statesmen, etc.); the Museums of Chinese History and of the Chinese Revolution; Chairman Mao◊ Memorial Hall 1977 (shared from 1983 with Chou◊ En-lai, Chu◊ Teh, and Liu◊ Shao-chi); the Summer Palace, built by Zi◊ Xi (damaged by the European powers 1900, but restored 1903); Temple of Heaven (Tiantan); Ming tombs 50 km/30 mi to the north-west□

pekingese a type of small dog◊□

Peking Man skull found near Peking 1927, which was sent to USA for safety during the war with Japan 1941 and disappeared. Others have since been found. Dating varies from 500 000 years old to 1 500 000□

Pelagius c360–c420. British theologian, a supporter of free will against Augine◊'s doctrines of predestination and original sin. Though cleared of heresy by a Jerusalem synod 415, he was later condemned by both Pope and Emperor□

pelargonium a flowering plant. See geranium◊□

Pelé pseudonym of Brazilian footballer Edson Arantes do Nascimento 1940– , inside left and goal scorer□

Pelée Mont. See under Martinique◊□

Pelham Henry 1696–1754. British Whig◊ statesman, who served in Walpole'◊s Cabinet 1721–42, and was prime minister 1743–54□

pelican order of fishing birds, Pelecaniformes. It includes:

pelican mainly freshwater family Pelicanidae, which have a large distensible pouch beneath the long 'almond-tipped' bill for temporary storage of their fish catch. They include the ***common pelican*** *Pelecanus onocrotalus* of Eurasia and Africa; Australian ***black-backed*** *P constricillatus* largest of the family; and the marine American ***brown pelican*** *P occidentalis*.

cormorant genus of diving sea birds *Phalacrocorax* family Phalacrocoracideae. The ***common cormorant*** *P carbo* is black, glossed with bronze; it feeds voraciously, and in the East is trained to fish for its owner, a cord round the neck preventing it swallowing the catch. The very similar ***shag*** *P graculus* is glossed with green.

frigate bird various species of glossy black seabird of warm waters, family Fregatidae. They have forked tails, and a wingspan of over 2 m/6 ft, so that they fly with such ease that they settle on land only to breed.

gannet genus of seabirds *Morus* family Sulidae, especially the ***solan goose*** *Morus bassana* white, with black-tipped wings. It can dive vertically, using the same 'variable geometry' of wing employed by the Tornado◊ aircraft. To the same family belong the tropical boobies, so-called because so easily caught, e.g. ***brown booby*** *Sula leucogaster*□

pellagra disease common in countries in which the staple food is maize, which is deficient in nicotinic acid (vitamin B)□

Peloponnese peninsula forming the southern part of Greece, joined to the mainland by the Isthmus of Corinth□

Peloponnesian War 431–404BC between Athens and Sparta◊ and their allies, originating in suspicions of 'empire-building' ambitions of Pericles◊. It ended in the destruction of the political power of Athens. See Lysander◊□

pelota very fast ball-game (the name means 'ball') of Basque origin, also known as ***jai alai*** popular in Latin-America. Played in a walled court or *cancha* it resembles squash, but the players use a long, narrow, curved wickerwork basket or 'cesta' (strapped to the hand) to hurl the ball (about the size of a baseball) against the walls□

Pelsaert François c1570–1630. Dutch East India Company official aboard the ship *Batavia* wrecked off W Australia. Two of the survivors who were ringleaders in a mutiny were left behind when the rest were rescued, and became Australia's first involuntary white 'settlers'. They were never seen again, but the wreck site was rediscovered 1963□

Pemba coral island in the Indian Ocean, part of Tanzania◊□

Pembroke port in Dyfed, Wales; population 14 600. Henry◊ VII was born in the 13th-century castle□

PEN literary association (***P***oets, ***P***laywrights, ***E***ditors, ***E***ssayists, ***N***ovelists), founded 1921 by C A Dawson Scott to promote international understanding among writers□

penance in Roman Catholicism a sacrament ***rite of reconciliation*** involving confession◊ of sin, reception of absolution, and atonement (preferably by works performed rather than rote repetition of prayers)□

Penang state of Malaysia; population 911 600. Capital Georgetown□

Penates the household gods of a Roman family. See Lares◊□

Penda d. 655. King of Mercia◊ from 626, and founder of its power. He killed the Northumbrian kings Edwin and Oswald, but was eventually himself killed in battle against the Northumbrians□

Penderecki Krzystof 1933– . Polish composer of works in his own notation system, including *Threnody for the Victims of Hiroshima* 1961 and *St Luke Passion*□

Penelope wife of Odysseus◊. During his absence, she kept her suitors at bay by insisting that she must first weave a shroud for her father-in-law, but unpicked her work every night. Odysseus killed them all when he returned□

penguin order of flightless, marine diving birds found only in the Antarctic, where they fill the ecological niche held by the auks◊ in the northern hemisphere. They congregate in 'rookeries' to breed. Largest is the ***emperor penguin*** *Aptenodytes forsteri* 1.2 m/over 3ft long, whose single annual egg is brooded by the male in the warmth of a flap of his body skin, so that it rests on his feet. Among the small species is the ***jackass penguin*** *Spheniscus demersus* which lays two eggs in a scraped hollow in the ground□

penicillin an organic acid used as an antibiotic. See under ascomycetes◊□

Peninsular War 1808–14, caused by Napoleon◊'s invasion of Portugal in 1807 and creation of his brother Joseph as king of occupied Spain in 1808. See Revolutionary◊ Wars

1808 Wellington◊ sent to Portugal in response to an appeal for help, and following the victory of Vimiero, Portugal was evacuated by the French; Wellington then superseded

1809 Sir John Moore◊ killed in achieving the victory of Corunna 16 Jan; his force evacuated

1809 Wellington again in command, initially waged a defensive campaign in Spain based on the lines of Torres Vedras (constructed 1809–10)

1812 Wellington began driving the French from Spain (victories at Salamanca 1812 and Vittoria 1813), and invaded southern France

1814 10 Apr Wellington drove Soult◊ from Toulouse, compelling him to make peace 18 Apr 1814□

penis erectile, male organ of generation in mammals and reptiles. The passage through it which discharges semen (the urethra) also discharges urine from the bladder□

Penn William 1644–1718. British Quaker, who in 1681 founded Pennsylvania◊ as a refuge for the persecuted members of his sect□

Penney William, Baron Penney 1909– . British physicist, designer of the first British atom bomb, who worked at Los◊ Alamos 1944–5. He developed the advanced gas-cooled nuclear reactor used in some power stations, e.g. Dungeness◊. Life peer 1967, Order of Merit 1969□

Pennines mountain system, 'the backbone of England', broken by a gap through which the rivers Aire flows to the east and Ribble to the west; length (Scottish border to the Peak in Derbyshire) 400 km/250 mi. Britain's first long-distance footpath was the ***Pennine Way*** 1965□

Pennsylvania mid Atlantic state of the USA; Keystone State

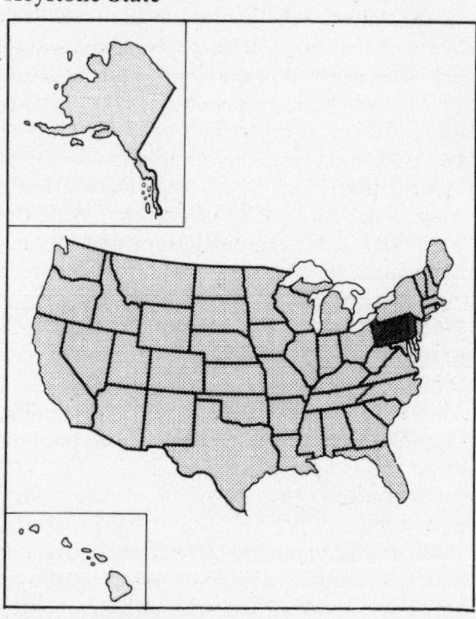

area 117 412 sq km/45 333 sq mi

capital Harrisburg

towns Philadelphia, Pittsburgh, Erie, Scranton

features Allegheny mountains; Ohio, Susquehanna and Delaware rivers; University of Pennsylvania is one of the leading research campuses in the USA; Three Mile Island nuclear plant, near Harrisburg◊

products mushrooms, fruit, flowers, cereals, tobacco; meat, poultry, dairy products; anthracite

population 11 824 560

famous people Marian Anderson◊, Maxwell Anderson◊, Andrew Carnegie◊, Stephen Foster◊, Benjamin Franklin◊, George C. Marshall◊, Robert E Peary◊, Gertrude Stein◊, John Updike◊

history founded and named by William Penn◊ in 1682, following a land grant by Charles◊ II, it was one of the Thirteen Colonies◊□

pennyroyal a moorland plant. See under herbs◊□

Pensacola port in Florida, USA, with a large naval airbase; population 57 620□

Pentagon headquarters of the American Department of Defense, Washington, constructed in five 'rings' with a pentagonal central court□

Pentateuch the first five books of the Old Testament. See under Bible◊□

Pentecost Jewish festival (50th day after the Passover◊) celebrating the end of the Palestinian grain harvest; in the Christian Church, day on which the Holy◊ Spirit descended, and commemorated on Whit◊ Sunday□

Pentecostal Movement form of Christian revivalism inspired by the baptism in the Holy◊ Spirit with 'speaking in tongues' experienced by the Apostles◊ at Pentecost◊ (hence also 'Tongues Movement', see trance◊); other claimed gifts include interpretation of the 'tongues', which appear gibberish to the uninitiated; faith healing; performance of miracles, and prophecy.

The modern movement began 4 Apr 1906 when members of the Azusa Street Mission, Los Angeles (under their minister W J Seymour) experienced 'baptism in the Spirit'. Membership of the various groupings is estimated world-wide at c10 000 000. In Britain the movement was assisted by immigrants from the Caribbean. Its theology is fundamentalist; the moral code puritanical; worship is informal and participatory; and missionary work is zealous□

Pentland Firth channel separating the Orkney Islands from N Scotland□

Penza industrial city (watches, bicycles, calculators, textiles, food processing) in USSR; population 515 000□

Penzance port (for the Scillies) and resort in Cornwall, England; population 20 000. Humphrey Davy◊ was born here. It now incorporates Newlyn◊□

peony a flowering plant. See under ranunculaceae◊□

Peoria industrial city (agricultural machinery) in Illinois, USA, a mining and agricultural centre; population 124 160. Its outlook is traditionally typical of the midwest□

Pepin d. 768. King of the Franks◊ from 751. Son of Charles◊ Martel, he was mayor of the palace to the last of the Merovingians◊ (Childeric III) until he deposed him and took the royal title himself, founding the Carolingian◊ line□

pepper genus *Piper* of Asian climbing plants, family Piperaceae. The ***common pepper*** *P nigrum* yields black pepper from the whole ripe fruit, and white pepper from the fruit less the external coat, which entails a loss of its stimulating properties. The ***betel pepper*** is *P betle* (see betel◊); ***kava*** the non-alcoholic but intoxicating beverage drunk in the S Pacific Islands is prepared from the roots or leaves of *Piper methysticum*□

peppermint herb *Mentha piperita*, family Labiatae. Peppermint oil and menthol or peppermint camphor, used commercially for toothpaste, cough drops, etc., is produced by blowing steam through the leaves; Brazil and China are the largest producers. See also herbs◊□

peptide small molecule made from the basic sub-units of protein amino◊ acids. They include encephalins◊ and endorphins◊, the 'natural' painkillers, and others are involved in breathing, digestion and reproduction. Their function was thought to be limited to carrying 'messages' to the organs via the blood, but it is now known that some are also neurotransmitters◊□

Pepusch Johann Christopher 1667–1752. German composer of the music for *The Beggar's Opera*. See Gay◊□

Pepys Samuel 1633–1703. British diarist. Born in London, he entered the navy office 1660, just after beginning his diary, written 1659–69 (when his sight failed) in shorthand. A unique record of both the period and the intimate feelings of the man, it was not deciphered till 1825. He was an excellent secretary to the Admiralty 1672–79, when he was imprisoned in the Tower on suspicion of being connected with the Popish◊ Plot; and was then reinstated in 1684 and finally deprived, after the 1688 Revolution◊, for suspected disaffection□

Perak state of Malaysia; population 1 762 300. Capital Ipoh□

Perceval Spencer 1762–1812. British Tory◊ prime minister 1809–12, when he was shot in the lobby of the House of Commons by a madman□

perch largest order of bony fish Perciformes. ***common perch*** *Perca fluviatilis* freshwater family Percidae of Eurasia and N America, is edible and greenish with dark bands on the back; the ***pikeperch*** genus *Lucioperca* of Europe and N America, is a voracious species which may be over 1 m/3 ft, of some food value.

banded sea perch of the Mediterranean, family Serranidae, is blue-striped on orange, has male/female genitals and can self-fertilise. The ***common bass*** *Dicentrarchus labrax*, of the

same family, is a voracious feeder, reaches 1 m/3 ft and is a food fish; the large game and food species (genus *Epinephelus*, etc.) of more tropical waters are known as ***groupers***, and may reach 2 m/6 ft (300 kg/700 lb).
sunfish are nestbuilding freshwater genera of the family Centrarchidae of N America.
pilotfish *Naucrates ductor* family Carangidae, accompanies large fish, such as sharks, or ships, for protective shadow.
butterfly fish family Anaetodontidae, are vertically flattened inhabitants of coral reefs, very brightly coloured.
cichlids large freshwater family (1000 species) Cichlidae, of Africa and S and Central America, are noted for the care of the young by both parents, some species feeding them on a secretion from the skin, but matrimonial squabbles are frequent. They include the Amazonian ***angelfish*** *Pterophyllum scalare* which is silvery with vertical black stripes, and wing-like fins partly extended in long 'threads', and the genus *Tilapia*, some of which are mouthbrooders, either the male or the female carrying the eggs in the mouth till hatching, and sometimes making the mouth still available to the fry for refuge.
weever fish *Trachinus vipera* family Trachinidae, has venomous dorsal spines dangerous when trodden upon by bathers (found in hot summers in southern England).
surgeon fish family Ancathuridae, have a moveable spine either side of the tail, used in fighting.
common mackerel *Scomber scombrus* family Scombridae, is a food fish, bluish with black bands above, and sheeny pink beneath, occurring off Britain in seasonal shoals, 50 cm/20 in. In the same family is the ***tunny*** *Thunnus thynnus* or ***tuna*** which reaches 5 m/14 ft, weighs c800 kg/1800 lb, and when hunting swims at c110 kph/70 mph (faster than a cheetah runs). It is a game fish, caught by rod and line from motorboats, or by commercial fishing (450 000 tonnes of tuna are annually eaten in Japan alone).
swordfish *Xiphias gladius* family Xiphiidae; its sword-shaped snout, used against other fish, can penetrate the planks of a wooden ship; it reaches 6 m/19 ft, 300 kg/660 lb.
Siamese fighting fish *Betta splendens*, family Anabantidae, are the subject of bets in Thailand, as with fighting cocks.
mud skipper *Periophthalmus barbarus* family Periophthalmidae, has swivelling eyes on top of its head like a frog, and uses fins and tail to make little leaps along the shore, and even to climb up mangrove roots, etc.
stonefish *Synanceja horrida* family Synanciidae, resembles a seaweed-covered stone, 35 cm/14 in; its poison spines may be fatal if trodden on.
gurnard *Trigla* family Triglidae, has the first 2/3 fin rays on the pectoral fin developed as feelers for sampling the bottom when feeding, but they look like little legs; 70 cm/2.5 ft. Some species are food fish off Britain.
bullhead or ***miller's thumb*** *Cottus gobio* family Cottidae, common in Europe, 15 cm/6 in long, is an important food fish for trout.
sea bream *Pagellus centrodontus* family Sparidae, a food fish.
blenny worldwide family Bleniidae, with spiny fins and a smooth body, e.g. Britain's ***smooth blenny*** *Blennius pholis*.
wrasse marine family Labridae of warmer waters, brightly coloured, with spined fins and thickened lips. They nest, have a complicated courtship, and may change their sex.
grey mullet family Mugilidae and ***red mullet*** family Mullidae, red with yellow stripes, are two food fishes of warmer estuarine waters□

percussion instruments musical instruments played by being beaten. They can be divided into those which can be tuned to produce a sound of definite pitch, and those without pitch. Examples of tuned percussion instruments include:
kettledrum a hemisperical bowl of metal with a membrane stretched across the top (developed 1837)
tubular bells suspended on a frame
glockenspiel (German *'bell play'*) using a set of steel bars
xylophone similar to a glockenspiel, but with wooden rather than metal bars.
Instruments without definite pitch include:
snare drum which has a membrane across both ends, and a 'snare' which rattles when the drum is beaten
bass drum which produces the lowest sound in the orchestra
tambourine a wooden hoop with metal plates inserted in the sides
triangle a triangular-shaped steel bar, played by striking it with a separate bar of steel. The sound produced remains distinctive even when played alongside a full orchestra
cymbals two brass plates struck together
castanets (Spanish *castanuelas*) two round-shaped pieces of wood struck together
gong a heavy circular piece of metal struck with a soft hammer.
See violin◊ family; wind◊ instruments; brass◊ instruments□

Percy Sir Henry, called ***Hotspur*** 1364–1403. English soldier, son of the 1st Earl of Northumberland. He defeated the Scots at

Homildon Hill 1402, and was killed at Shrewsbury while in revolt against Henry◊ IV□

Perelman S(idney) J(oseph) 1904–79. American humorist, born in Brooklyn, New York of Russian-Jewish descent. He wrote for the magazine the *New Yorker* and gags for the Marx◊ Brothers; shared academy award for film script *Around the World in 80 Days*□

Peres Shimon 1923– . Israeli Labour statesman, born in Poland. After a virtual dead-heat in the elections of 1984, Labour and Likud◊ formed a unity government, of which Peres was to be prime minister for two years. Peres pledged an end to the Israeli military presence in Lebanon and rapprochement with Egypt□

perfume fragrant essence in which more than 100 natural aromatic materials may be blended from a range of 60 000 flowers, leaves, fruits, seeds, woods, barks, resins, and roots, linked by natural animal fixatives

percussion instruments

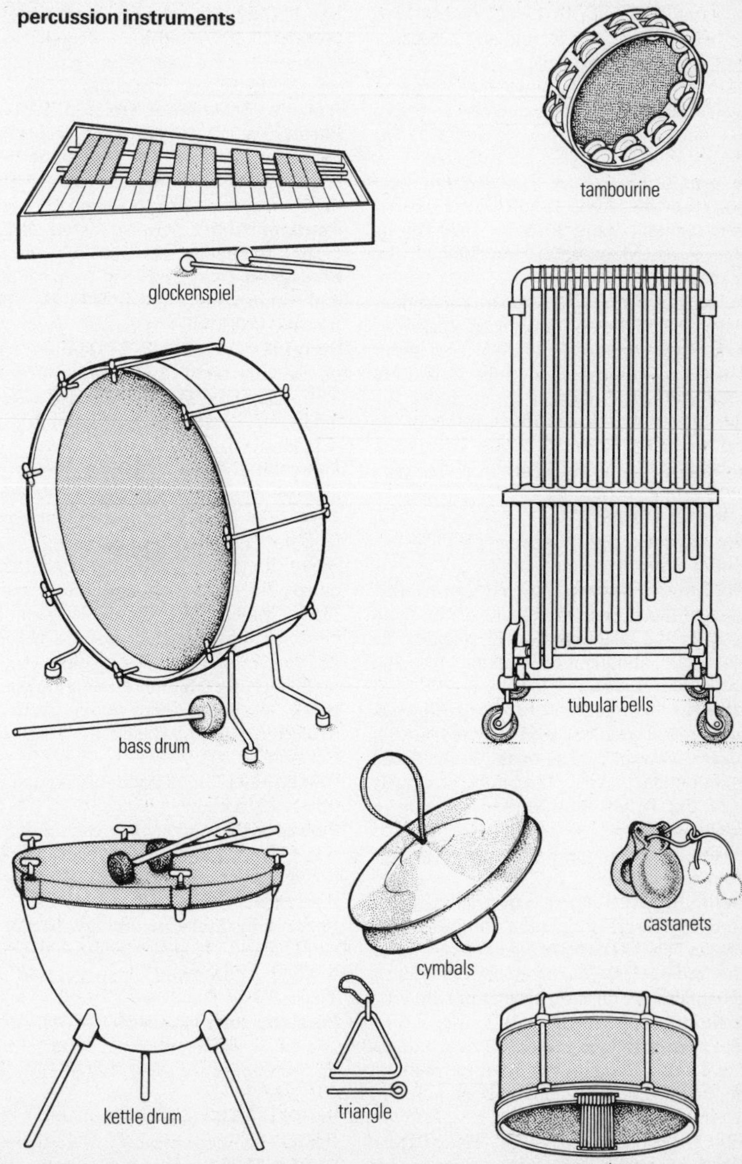

and various synthetics, the latter increasingly used even in expensive products. Favoured ingredients include balsam◊, civet◊, hyacinth◊, jasmine◊, lily of the valley◊, musk◊, orange blossom◊, rose◊ and tuberose◊□

Perga see under Antalya◊□

Pergamum capital (modern Bergama) of the ancient kingdom of Pergamum (in NW Turkey) from 283BC. Allied to Rome, it was a cultural centre with a fine library, theatre and temples, and produced sculptures, fine textiles, parchment, etc. In 133BC, its last king died, bequeathing it to Rome, and it became part of a Roman province□

peri in Persian myth, beautiful, harmless beings, ranking between angels and evil spirits, and ruled by Eblis, greatest of the latter□

Peri Jacopo 1561–1633. Italian composer, who served the Medici◊, and whose experimental melodic opera *Euridice* 1600 (by its influence on Monteverdi) established the opera form□

Pericles c490–429BC. Athenian statesman, who dominated the city's politics from 461 (as leader of the democratic party), and under whom Greek culture reached its climax. He created a confederation of cities under the leadership of Athens, but the disasters of the Peloponnesian◊ War led to his overthrow 430. Although quickly reinstated, he died soon after. See Aspasia◊□

peridot see Olivine◊□

Perim see under South Yemen◊□

periodic system see element◊□

periodontal disease (formerly ***pyorrhoea***); disease of the supporting tissues of the teeth caused by the accumulation of plaque; the gums recede, and the teeth become loose and eventually drop out□

peritonitis inflammation of the ***peritoneum*** the thin translucent bag which covers most of the large internal organs of the body within the abdominal cavity. It can be variously caused, e.g. by a wound to the abdomen, or appendicitis◊□

periwinkle the common edible winkle. See under gastropod◊□

periwinkle genus *Vinca* of trailing blue-flowered evergreen plants, family Apocynaceae. The related ***Madagascar periwinkle*** *Catharanthus roseus* produces chemicals which inhibit the division of cells and are used to treat leukaemia in children□

perjury false statement on oath by a witness in legal proceedings on a material point at issue; in Britain the penalty may be a fine or up to seven years in prison□

Perkin Sir William Henry 1838–1907. British chemist, founder of the aniline◊ dye industry□

Perlis state of Malaysia, population 148 000. Capital Kangar□

Perm industrial city (shipbuilding, aircraft, chemicals, oil refining) of USSR and river port on the Kama (known as Molotov 1940–57); population 1 037 000□

Pernambuco see Recife◊□

Perón Juan Domingo 1895–1974. Argentine leader of the Labour party and presidential dictator 1946–55, when he was deposed. See Eva Perón◊. He returned from exile to the presidency 1973, and was succeeded as president, until her overthrow in 1976, by his third wife ***Maria Estela Isabel(ita)*** 1930– . She remained under house arrest till 1981□

Perón Eva ('Evita') 1919–52. Second wife of President Perón◊ of Argentina, whose popularity with the *descamisados,* 'shirtless ones', maintained her husband in office□

Perpendicular a period or style of English Gothic architecture◊□

Perpignan industrial city (paper, textiles) and commercial centre in S France; population 108 000□

Perrault Charles 1628–1703. French author of the fairy tales *Contes de ma Mère l'Oye* 1697, including 'Sleeping Beauty', 'Red Riding Hood', 'Blue Beard', 'Puss in Boots', and 'Cinderella'□

Perry Fred 1909– . British tennis player, first to win three successive Wimbledons: 1934, 1935, 1936, where he is commemorated by a statue (David Wynne◊)□

Perry Matthew Calbraith 1794–1858. US naval officer, commander of the expedition of 1853 which reopened communication between Japan and the outside world after 250 years' isolation. He negotiated the treaty of 1854 giving America trading rights□

perry alcoholic liquor made from pears, mainly in Normandy and the English West Country□

Persephone Greek goddess (Roman Proserpina) of Hades◊□

Persepolis ruined ancient capital of the Persian Empire (north east of Shiraz◊), burned down, by accident or design, after Alexander◊ captured it in 331BC□

Perseus in Greek mythology, son of Zeus◊ and Danae◊. He slew Medusa◊, the Gorgon; rescued Andromeda◊; and became king of Tiryns◊□

Pershing John Joseph 1860–1948. American general, commander of the American Expeditionary Force sent to France 1917–18□

Persia official name of Iran◊ until 1935□

Persian see under Iran◊□

Persian Gulf see Gulf◊□

Persian Wars 499–449BC
499 Revolt of the Ionian Greeks against Persian rule
490 Darius◊ I defeated at Marathon◊
480 Xerxes◊ I victorious at Thermopylae (narrow pass from Thessaly to Locris, which Leonidas, King of Sparta◊, and 1000 men, defended to the death against the Persians); Athens captured; but Greek navy victorious at Salamis◊
479 Greeks under Spartan general Pausanias (d. c470) victorious at Plataea, driving the Persians from the country□

persimmon genus of tropical trees *Diospyros* family Ebenaceae, with a hard wood, and large reddish fruit□

perspiration the secretion of the sweat◊ glands□

Perth industrial town in Tayside, E Scotland; population (with Kinross) 119 749. Capital of Scotland from 12th century until James◊ I of Scotland was assassinated here 1437□

Perth capital of Western Australia, with its port at nearby Fremantle on the Swan river; population 918 000. It is the commercial and cultural centre of the state□

Peru Republic of

area 1 332 000 sq km/514 060 sq mi
capital Lima including port of Callao
towns Arequipa, Iquitos, Chiclayo
features Andes mountains, Lake Titicaca◊, Peru Current◊, Atacama Desert; monuments of the Chimu◊ and Inca◊ civilizations
exports coffee; alpaca, llama and vicuna wool; fishmeal; lead, copper, iron, oil, etc.
currency sol
population 19 157 000, 46% American Indian, mainly Quechua and Aymara, 43% mestizo
language Spanish, Quechua, (both official)
religion Roman Catholicism
famous people Pizarro◊, Tupac Amaru◊□
government executive president (Alan García Pérez from 1985), senate and chamber of deputies
recent history Spanish rule was established from 1541. An Indian revolt failed in 1780, and Peru was the Spanish government headquarters during the struggle for independence of other Spanish possessions, so that it was the last to achieve independence in 1824. It lost considerable territory in the Pacific War◊, and although boundary disputes were settled by arbitration with Bolivia in 1902, Colombia 1927, and Ecuador 1942, dispute was renewed with the latter in 1981. The bloodless military coup of 1968 led to the expropriation of US oil and mining interests. There is an unofficial communist terrorist movement *Sendero luminoso* 'Shining Path'; official communists participate in politics, since military dictatorship ended in 1980. Political violence led to a state of emergency from May 1983, but García's American People's Revolutionary Alliance gained absolute majorities in both the senate and chamber of deputies 1985□

Peru (***Humboldt***) **Current.** See under current◊□

Perugia industrial city (silk and wool textiles, lace, liqueurs, chocolate), capital of Umbria◊, Italy; population 142 400. There is a 14–15th-century cathedral and the Palazzo Communale has frescoes by Perugino◊□

Perugino Pietro 1446–1524. Italian artist, Pietro Vanucci, who worked chiefly in Perugia◊, but also helped to decorate the Sistine◊ Chapel. Raphael◊ was his pupil□

Pescadores group of 60 islands (Chinese P'eng-hu), a Taiwanese dependency; area 13 sq km/50 sq mi□

Peshawar capital of NW Frontier Province, Pakistan; population 268 400□

Pestalozzi Johann Heinrich 1746–1827. Swiss educationist on Rousseau◊'s 'natural' principles, as described in *How Gertrude Teaches her Children* 1801. ***International Children's Villages*** named after him have been established, e.g. Sedlescombe, Surrey□

Pétain Henri Philippe 1856–1951. French general, a national hero for his defence of Verdun◊ in 1916 ('They shall not pass'). As prime minister from Jun 1940, after the disastrous Battle of France, he immediately signed an armistice with the Germans, removed his government to Vichy◊, and established a repressive regime on the fascist model. On the Allied victory in 1945, he was sentenced to death (commuted to life imprisonment) for treason□

Peter St. Leader of the Apostles◊, named Simon, but nicknamed Cephas ('Peter', from the Greek for 'rock') by Jesus, as being the rock on which he founded his church. Originally a fisherman of Capernaum, he may have been a follower of John◊ the Baptist, and was the first to acknowledge Jesus as the Messiah◊. Traditionally, he later settled in Rome, being regarded as the first bishop of Rome, whose mantle the Pope◊ inherits. He is said to have been crucified under Nero◊ in 64AD. Bones excavated from under the Basilica of St Peter's◊ 1968 were accepted as those of the Apostle by Pope Paul. Of the Epistles◊ attributed to him, the first is probably spurious, and the second certainly is. Feast day 29 Jun□

Peter several Tsars of Russia, including:

Peter I the Great 1672–1725. Joint Tsar with half-brother Ivan from 1682, and alone from 1689. After a successful campaign against the Turks in 1696, he visited Holland and England to study western technology, himself working in the shipyards. On his return to Russia, he set out to westernize his country completely, and undertook a war with Sweden 1700–21 to obtain the Baltic lands (Estonia, and part of Latvia and Finland) which enabled him to build a new capital, St Petersburg (Leningrad◊), giving Russia direct access to the western seas. A war with Persia 1722–3 gained Baku◊ for Russia.

Peter's eldest son ***Alexius*** 1690–1718, died in prison for opposing his father's reforms, and he was succeeded by his wife, Catherine◊ I.

Peter II 1715–30. Tsar from 1727. Son of Peter◊ the Great, he had been passed over in favour of Catherine◊ I in 1725, but succeeded her in 1727. He died of smallpox.

Peter III 1728–62. Tsar 1762. Weak-minded son of Peter◊ I's eldest daughter, Anne, he was adopted 1741 by his aunt Elizabeth◊, and at her command married the future Catherine◊ II 1745. He was deposed in favour of his wife, and probably murdered by her lover Alexius Orlov□

Peter I 1844–1921. King of Serbia from 1903, and from 1918 first king of Yugoslavia□

Peter II 1923–70. King of Yugoslavia from 1934, assuming power 1941. He escaped to England after the German invasion, and was dethroned 1945□

Peterborough 'new town' with varied new-style industries in Cambridgeshire, England; population 132 380. It has a fine 12th-century cathedral and 6 mi of the River Nene running through the city as a park□

Peterhead industrial port (engineering, servicing North Sea oil rigs, whisky distilling) in Grampian, Scotland; population 15 000□

Peterlee 'new town' in Durham, England; population 26 300. It was named after Peter Lee, first Labour chairman of a county council□

Peterloo Massacre took place 16 Aug 1819 in St Peter's Fields, Manchester, when a peaceful open-air meeting in support of parliamentary reform was charged by yeomanry and hussars: 11 killed, c500 wounded□

Peter's Pence voluntary annual contribution to Papal administrative costs; formerly 10–16th century a compulsory levy of one penny per household□

Peter the Hermit c1050–1115. French priest whose eloquent preaching of the First Crusade◊ sent thousands of peasants marching against the Turks, who massacred them in Asia Minor. Peter escaped and accompanied the main body of crusaders to Jerusalem□

Petition of Right petition of parliament accepted by Charles◊ I in 1628. It made illegal: taxation without parliamentary consent, imprisonment without trial, billeting of soldiers on private persons, and use of martial law□

Petöfi Sandór 1823–49. Hungarian lyric poet the greatest writer in Hungarian literature, who died fighting in the war of independence against Russia□

Petra ruined city in S Jordan whose tombs and temples are cut out of the richly coloured sandstone cliffs. Capital of the Nabataeans, an Arab trading people, it was captured by Trajan◊ 106AD, and sacked by the Saracens◊ in the 7th century. It was not rediscovered till 1812□

Petrarch (Italian *Petrarca*), Francesco 1304–74. Italian poet, born at Arezzo, and a devotee of the classical tradition. His *Il Canzoniere* were sonnets in praise of his idealized love 'Laura' (see Martini◊), whom he first saw in 1327 (a married woman, she refused to become his mistress) and who died of plague 1348. His sonnets were influential for centuries. From 1337 he often stayed in secluded study at his home at Vaucluse, near Avignon, and, eager to restore the glories of Rome, wanted to return the Papacy there from Avignon. He was a friend of Boccaccio◊, and supported Rienzi◊'s republic in 1347□

petrel oceanic order of birds Procellariiformes, with hooked bills and tubular nostrils. They include:

wandering albatross *Diomedea exulans* family Diomedeidae, largest of all seabirds, with a wingspan 3 m/9 ft. In sailor superstition, they embodied the spirits of dead seamen, making

it unlucky to kill them (cf S T Coleridge◊ 'The Ancient Mariner').
fulmar *Fulmarus glacialis* family Procellariidae, of the N Atlantic and Pacific, and the ***giant fulmar*** *Macronectes gigantea* with over 2 m/7 ft wingspan; ***shearwater*** *Puffinus diomedea* which skims the waves as it glides, and the ***short-tailed shearwater*** or ***mutton bird*** *Puffinus tenuirostris* of Australia, of which the fat young ones are used for food (under control) by the Aborigines.
stormy petrel or ***Mother Carey's chicken*** *Hydrobates pelagicus* family Hydrobatidae, which runs over the wave surfaces, aided by its wings, coming to land only to breed□

Petrie Sir William Matthew Flinders 1853–1942. British Egyptologist, grandson of Matthew Flinders◊. A minute observer, he worked on the Pyramids, Tell◊ el Amarna, Abydos◊, etc. and taught at University College, London, where his collections are still used for teaching□

Petrograd name 1914–24 of Leningrad◊□

petroleum mineral oil, a thick greenish-brown liquid found underground in permeable rocks, formed from the remains of dead plants and animals by heat and pressure. Petroleum consists of hydrocarbons mixed with oxygen, nitrogen, sulphur, etc., in varying proportions, and is often found in association with natural gas (mainly methane). Almost useless in its natural state, by the various processes involved in refining, it is the source not only of petrol (gasoline), but of a range of products from gases through aviation spirit, kerosene, diesel fuel, lubricating oil, to bitumen. Further processes result in the manufacture of detergents, synthetic fibres, plastics, insecticides, fertilizers, pharmaceuticals, toilet requisites, synthetic rubber, etc.□

Petronius Gaius, known as Petronius Arbiter, died 66AD. Roman author of a licentious romance *Satyricon*. A companion of Nero◊, and supervisor of his pleasures, he committed suicide□

Petropavlovsk industrial city (engineering, military equipment, meat-packing) in N Kazakh Republic, USSR; population 219 000□

Petropavlovsk-Kamchatski port and naval base on the Kamchatka◊ Peninsula; population 237 000□

Petrópolis hill resort in Brazil, founded by Pedro◊ II, with the Imperial Museum; population 220 000□

Petrovsk see Makhachkala◊□

Petrozavodsk industrial city (metal goods, prefab houses, cement) and capital of Karelia Republic, USSR; population 247 000□

Petsamo see Pechenga◊□

Pevensey village in E Sussex, England; population 3000. Ruins of the Roman fort of Anderida, (which became a Norman castle after William◊ the Conqueror landed here in 1066) survive. In World War II it was prepared against a German invasion□

Pevsner Sir Nikolaus 1902–83. Leipzig-born art historian, a refugee to England from the Nazis, whose 47-volume *Buildings of England* 1951–74 covered every county□

pewter alloy of lead and tin, formerly much used for ornaments, plates, mugs, etc.□

peyote spineless cactus *Lophophora williamsii* native of Mexico and SW USA with pinkish flowers which contain the hallucinogen mescalin, and are dried and chewed□

peyote cactus *Lophopora williamsii* of Mexico and southern USA, which produces the hallucinogen ***mescalin*** used by the Indians in religious ceremonies. See Aldous Huxley◊□

Pforzheim manufacturing city (gold and silver ware, jewellery, watches, electrical goods) in Baden-Württemberg, W Germany; population 105 400□

pH scale for measuring acidity. See acid□

Phaethon son of Helios◊ who allowed him to drive the chariot of the sun one day, and almost set earth on fire when he lost control of the horses. Zeus◊ killed him with a thunderbolt□

phagocyte a white blood◊ cell□

Phalaris lived c570–554BC. Tyrant of Agrigentum, Sicily, he was said to have had a brazen bull made in which to roast his victims alive. He was killed in a revolt□

phalarope seabirds, family Phalaropodidae, order Charadriiformes, of which the two Arctic species are visitors to Britain. The male is courted by the female and hatches the eggs□

phallus in fertility rituals, a model of the male sexual organ, as in ancient Greece and Egypt, and in India (Hindu *lingam*◊)□

Pharaoh Hebrew form of the Egyptian royal title, 'Great House', from c950BC□

Pharisees Jewish sect which originated in the 2nd century BC and whose ideas became the basis of orthodox Judaism◊□

pharmacology study of drugs and the way in which they act; proven formulations are included in an official list (pharmacopoeia)□

pharynx section of the alimentary◊ canal between the mouth and the oesophagus◊ or gullet. The eustachian tubes (see under Eustachio◊), which equalise pressure in the ear with that outside, open into it, and it includes the tonsils◊□

Phasmida an order of insects◊□

pheasant a large bird. See under fowl◊□

phenacetin white crystalline solid which is metabolised in the body to paracetamol◊. It is banned in the UK as dangerous to the kidneys in long-term use as a painkiller□

phenol a derivative of benzene. See under toluene◊□

phenylketonuria condition (PKU) of genetic origin, in which a child's liver cannot control the level of phenylanine (found in protein foods) in the bloodstream by normal excretion in the urine. A special diet is prescribed□

pheromone communication chemical released by animals, e.g. some insects; a sex pheromone is a 'mating call' released by a female to attract a male; an aggregatory pheromone will attract both sexes, and can be used for pest control, e.g., in combination with a pesticide, to control Dutch◊ elm disease□

Phidias c500BC Greek sculptor, born in Athens, where Pericles◊ made him superintendent of public works. He designed the Parthenon◊, and sculpted the colossal statue of Zeus◊ that was one of the Seven Wonders◊ of the ancient world□

Philadelphia industrial city (oil refining, chemicals, textiles, food processing, printing and publishing) and river port (on the Delaware) in Pennsylvania, USA; population 3 683 000. Founded by William Penn◊ 1682 as the 'city of brotherly love', it was the first capital of the USA 1790–1800. Features include Independence Hall 1732–59 (in which the Declaration◊ of Independence was adopted and which contains the Liberty◊ Bell), City Hall 1872 (surmounted by statue of Penn), the US Mint 1792, and the grave of Benjamin Franklin◊. The Philadelphia Science Centre (see science◊ park) is linked with the University of Pennsylvania and the Franklin Institute for Applied Science 1824. The symphony orchestra is famous, and there are private and public art collections□

Philae island in the Nile with a palm-surrounded temple of Isis◊ in use c350BC–6th century AD; in 1977 it was re-erected on a nearby island to bring it above the flood level, which had been altered by the Aswan◊ Dam□

philately stamp collecting. The world's largest national collection is in the British Museum, and the world's largest private collection is that of Elizabeth◊ II. For many small countries special issues are a major source of revenue. The British National Postal Museum 1969 is at the chief Post Office in the City of London□

Philby Harold 'Kim' 1912– , son of Harry Philby◊. British intelligence officer from 1940 (already a Soviet agent from 1933), who was liaison officer in Washington 1949–51, when he was asked to resign. Named in 1963, as having warned Guy Burgess 1911–63 and Donald Maclean 1913– (similarly traitors to the service) that their activities were known, he fled to the USSR, and became a Soviet citizen and general in the KGB◊. A fourth member of the ring was Anthony Blunt◊; Sir Roger Hollis 1905–73, head of MI5◊ 1956–65, was alleged without confirmation to be a fifth□

Philby Harry St John Bridger 1885–1960. British explorer of Arabia, adviser to Ibn◊ Saud, and a Muslim from 1930. His books include *The Empty Quarter* 1933. See Harold Philby◊□

Philip St. In New Testament one of the 12 Apostles◊, he was born in Bethsaida, and is said to have been a missionary in Asia Minor; feast day 11 May□

Philip 382–336BC. King of Macedonia◊ from 359. He seized the throne from his nephew, for whom he was regent, conquered the Greek city states and formed them into a league whose forces could be united against Persia. He was assassinated just as he was planning this expedition, and was succeeded by his son Alexander◊ the Great. His tomb was discovered at Vergina, N Greece in 1978, and his skeleton having been identified by traces of an earlier eye injury from an arrow, his one-eyed head was reconstructed at Manchester University for exhibition in the city's museum in 1984□

Philip six kings of France, including:

Philip II Augus King of France from 1180. He waged war in turn against the English Kings Henry◊ II, Richard◊ I (with whom he also went on the First Crusade), and John◊ (against whom he won the final battle of Bouvines 1214) to evict them from their French possessions, and establish a strong monarchy.

Philip IV the Fair 1268–1314. King of France from 1285. Feuding with Pope Boniface◊ VIII over clerical taxation, he made him prisoner 1303, and secured the election 1305 of Clement◊ V. The latter obediently transferred the Papacy to Avignon 1309, and collaborated with Philip in suppressing the Templars◊.

Philip VI 1293–1350. King of France from 1328, first of the house of Valois◊, who was elected by the barons on the death of his cousin, Charles◊ IV. His claim was challenged by Edward◊ III of England, who in 1346 defeated him at Crécy□

Philip five kings of Spain, including:

Philip I the Handsome 1478–1506. Son of Maximilian◊ 1, and king of Castile from 1504, through his marriage 1496 to Joanna the Mad 1479–1555.

Philip II 1527–98. Son of Emperor Charles◊ V, on whose abdication 1556, he inherited Spain, the Netherlands (whose people he drove to revolt), and Spanish America; he annexed Portugal 1580. In 1554 he married Queen Mary◊ of England, would have wished to marry Elizabeth◊ I, but became involved in war with England instead (see Armada◊) and also with France from 1589. His reign marked the decline of the Spanish power.

Philip V 1683–1746. First Bourbon king of Spain from 1700, a grandson of Louis◊ XIV of France. He was not recognized by the major European powers until 1713□

Philip two dukes of Burgundy, including:

Philip the Good 1396–1467. Duke of Burgundy from 1419. An ally of England in the Hundred◊ Years' War, he made the Netherlands a centre of art and learning□

Philip 1921– . Prince of the UK. A grandson of George◊ I of Greece and a great-great-grandson of Queen Victoria◊, he was born in Corfu but raised and educated in England. In World War II he served in the Mediterranean and in the Pacific. Becoming a naturalized British subject (with the surname Mountbatten), in Mar 1947 he was created Duke of Edinburgh and married the future Elizabeth◊ II. In 1956 he established the ***Duke of Edinburgh's Award Scheme*** to encourage creative achievement among young people. He was created a prince of the UK 1957; Order of Merit 1968□

Philippeville see Skikda◊□

Philippi ancient Macedonian◊ city; Antony◊ and Octavius◊ defeated Brutus◊ and Cassius◊ here 42BC; and in c53AD it was the first European town where Paul◊ preached□

Philippines Republic of the

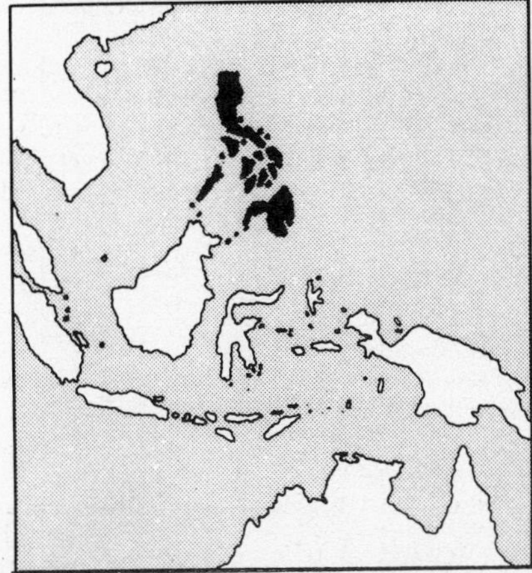

area 300 000 sq km/115 700sq mi
capital Manilla (on Luzon)
towns Quezon City
ports Cebu, Davao (on Mindanao) and Iloilu
features comprises over 7000 islands, with volcanic mountain ranges traversing the main chain north to south, and 50% of the area still forested. The largest islands are ***Luzon*** 108 172 sq km/41 765 sq mi (scene of fierce fighting in World War II, see Bataan◊ and Corregidor◊; and site of Clark Field, US air base used as a logistical base in the Vietnam War, and Subic Bay, US naval base) and ***Mindanao*** 94 227 sq km/36 381 sq mi, which has the active volcano Apo (2855 m/9369 ft) and mountainous rain forest, in which the Stone Age people of the Tasaday were discovered 1971; others include Samar, Negros, Palawan, Panay, Mindoro, Leyte◊, Cebu and the Sulu◊ group
exports sugar, copra and coconut oil; timber; iron ore and copper concentrates
currency peso
population 55 528 000, 93% of Malay stock
language Filipino (based on the Malay dialect, Tagalog), but English and Spanish are in common use
religion Roman Catholicism 84%, Protestantism 9%, Islam 5%□
government Corazón Aquino (born 1933) heads a government set up in 1986, following the deposing of President Marcos◊ after many years of increasingly despotic government
recent history conquered by Spain in 1565, after their discovery by Magellan◊, the Philippines (named after Philip◊ II) were ceded to the USA after the Spanish-American War◊, were occupied by Japan 1942–5 (see MacArthur◊), and attained complete independence in 1946. The USA retains military bases (see Luzon above). Communist insurgents, a problem since 1945, established the New People's Army (NPA) in 1969; and Islamic rebels aim at an independent state, having rejected autonomy in 1977. The Philippines renounced a claim to the Malaysian state of Sabah 1977□

Philippoplis see Plovdiv◊□

Philistines people of non-Semitic origin (possibly from Asia Minor, but see Sea◊ Peoples) who founded city states on the Palestinian coastal plain in the 12th century BC, adopting a Semitic◊ language and religion. They were at war with the Israelites◊ 11–10th centuries (hence the pejorative use of their name for anyone uncivilized in intellectual and artistic terms), were temporarily subdued by David◊, and later came under Assyrian◊ rule□

Phillip Arthur 1738–1814. British vice-admiral, founder and governor of the convict settlement at Sydney, Australia 1788–1792, and hence of New South Wales□

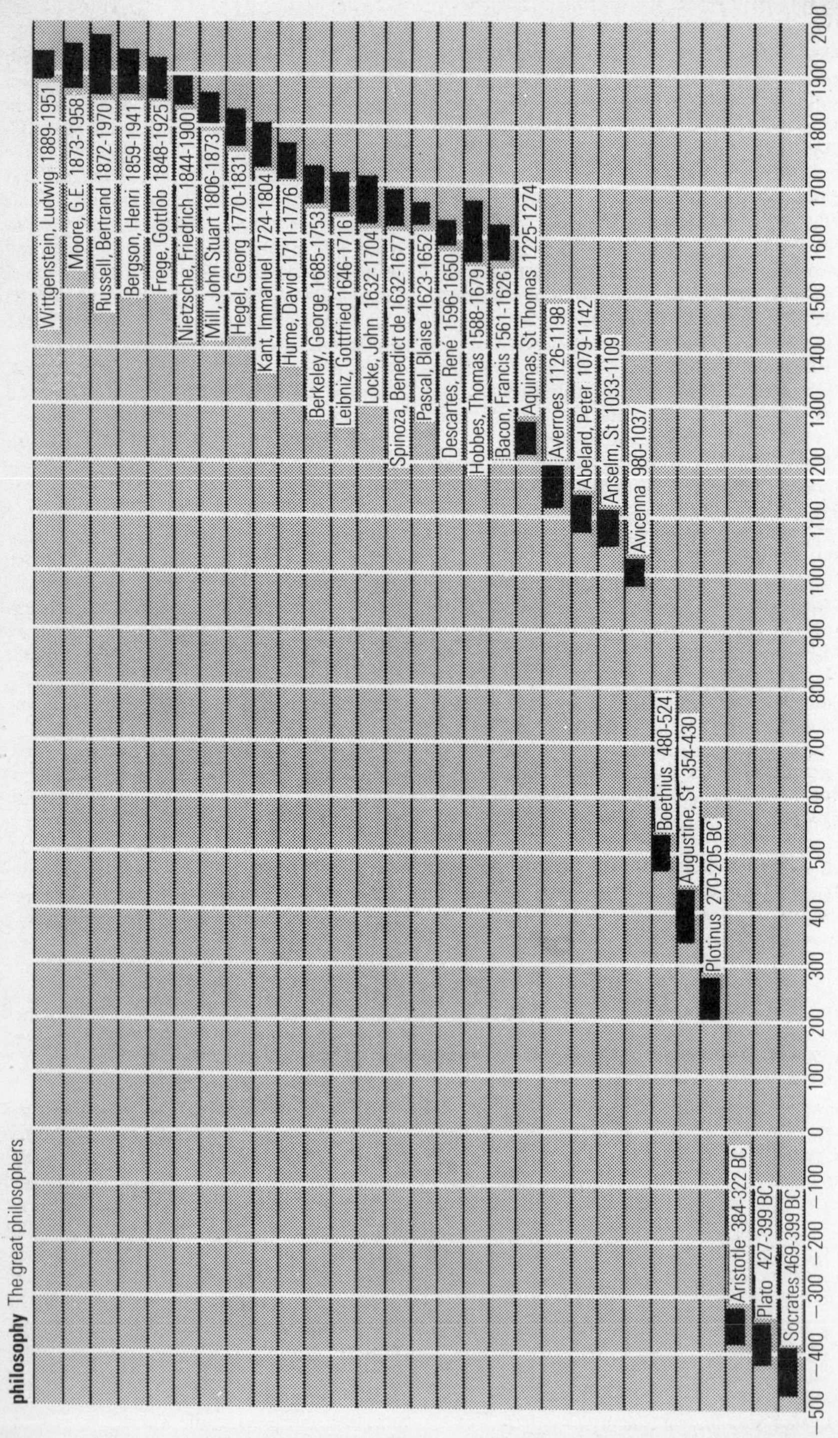

philosophy The great philosophers

Wittgenstein, Ludwig 1889-1951
Moore, G.E. 1873-1958
Russell, Bertrand 1872-1970
Bergson, Henri 1859-1941
Frege, Gottlob 1848-1925
Nietzsche, Friedrich 1844-1900
Mill, John Stuart 1806-1873
Hegel, Georg 1770-1831
Kant, Immanuel 1724-1804
Hume, David 1711-1776
Berkeley, George 1685-1753
Leibniz, Gottfried 1646-1716
Locke, John 1632-1704
Spinoza, Benedict de 1632-1677
Pascal, Blaise 1623-1652
Descartes, René 1596-1650
Hobbes, Thomas 1588-1679
Bacon, Francis 1561-1626
Aquinas, St Thomas 1225-1274
Averroes 1126-1198
Abelard, Peter 1079-1142
Anselm, St 1033-1109
Avicenna 980-1037
Boethius 480-524
Augustine, St 354-430
Plotinus 270-205 BC
Aristotle 384-322 BC
Plato 427-399 BC
Socrates 469-399 BC

−500 −400 −300 −200 −100 0 100 200 300 400 500 600 700 800 900 1000 1100 1200 1300 1400 1500 1600 1700 1800 1900 2000

Philo Judaeus lived 1st century AD. Jewish Alexandrian philosopher, who attempted to reconcile Judaism◊ with Platonic◊ and Stoic◊ ideas. In 40AD he went to Rome to petition Caligula◊ against the imperial claim to divine honours□

philology the especially historical study of language. See linguistics◊□

philosophy theoretical study (Greek 'love of knowledge') which encompasses all others until they are hived off as independent disciplines, e.g. mathematics and physics were formerly included, and logic is becoming separate. This leaves many apparently profound problems for which no systematic solving routine exists. They include the nature of mind and matter, perception, self, free will, causation, time and space, the existence of God, the subjectivenes or otherwise of moral judgements. Epistemology deals with how we can be said to 'know' anything and metaphysics with the nature of existence in general. Twentieth-century philosophers have been especially interested in the nature and limits of language and much attention has been paid to the language used to formulate philosophical problems□

Phiz pen-name of illustrator Hablot K Browne◊□

phlebitis inflammation of a vein lining, causing the blood in the area to clot (thrombosis), which may be caused by injury, infection, etc. A complication occurs if the clot is carried away in the bloodstream and lodges obstructively in a vital position□

phlox genus of N American plants, family Polemoniaceae; cultivated species derive from *P drummondi*, and have white-to-mauve, tubular scented flowers□

Phnom Penh industrial port (food processing, textiles) on the Mekong delta, capital of Kampuchea◊; population before 1975 (when it was captured by the Khmer◊ Rouge and the population dispersed) c3 000 000, now c500 000. There are many Buddhist temples□

Phoenicia Greek name in the 1st millenium BC for the seaboard of Lebanon and Syria occupied by the people who called themselves Canaanites (see Canaanite Empire◊). Craftsmen and traders, they visited the Scillies and possibly Cornwall for tin; are said to have circumnavigated Africa; and established colonies in Cyprus, N Africa (e.g. Carthage◊), Malta, Sicily and Spain. Competition from these and attacks by the Sea◊ Peoples, the Assyrians◊ and the Greeks on the original coastal cities led to their decline, which was completed by the fall of Tyre to Alexander◊ in 332BC. Their independent city states were ruled by hereditary kings and included Sidon, Tyre and Ugarit (in Syria, north of Latakia, where a 22-letter alphabet, the earliest known, was in use in the 13th century BC). The alphabet◊ was passed to Greece c0BC. Their deities include Astarte◊, Baal◊, and Moloch◊. Their exports include Tyrian purple cloth, furniture (from the timber of Lebanon), and jewellery; their workmen constructed and decorated Solomon◊'s Temple at Jerusalem. See also Etruscans◊□

Phoenix industrial city (electronics, aerospace) capital of Arizona, USA; population 790 000□

phoenix mythical Egyptian bird which burnt itself to death on a pyre every 500 years, and rose rejuvenated from the ashes□

Phoenix Islands group of eight islands included in Kiribats; area 18 sq km/11 sq mi. All have been rendered uninhabitable by drought□

phonetics the identification, description, and classification of sounds used in articulate speech, which are usually recorded in the International Phonetic Alphabet (a highly modifed version of the Roman alphabet). A ***phoneme*** is the range of sound which can be substituted without change of meaning in the words of a particular language, e.g. 'r' and 'l' form a single phoneme in Japanese, but are two phonemes in English□

phosphates salts of orthophosphoric acid H_3PO_4, used as fertilizers□

phosphoresence a form of luminescence◊□

phosphorus element

symbol P

atomic number 15

physical description found naturally in phosphates, such as the mineral apatite $Ca_5(F,Cl,OH)(PO_4)_3$

features occurs in several forms, the most important being white and red phosphorus

uses red phosphorus is used in matches; in detergents and water softeners. Phosphates are widely used as fertilizers□

photocell device for measuring or detecting light, or other electromagnetic radiation; when ***photoemissive*** the radiation causes electrons to be emitted and a current to flow; ***photovoltaic*** causes an electromotive force to be generated; and ***photoconductive*** causes resistance to vary. Usually semiconductor◊ based. they are used for burglar and fire alarms, automatic doors, and in solar arrays□

photofit originally ***identikit,*** a system (evolved by Hugh C McDonald of California 1959) of using drawings of variants of single features (eyes, nose, hairline, etc.) to help witnesses build up a likeness of a wanted criminal for the police; Jacques Penry adapted it to photographs for Scotland Yard 1970□

photography process for producing images on sensitized materials by various forms of radiant energy, e.g. visible light, ultra-violet, infra-red, x-rays; radioactive radiation; electron beam

1822 Nicéphore Niepce 1765–1833, a French doctor, produced the first photograph

1838 Niepce, in partnership with Jacques Daguerre 1787–1851, produced the first ***daguerrotype*** camera photograph

1839 Fox Talbot◊'s Calotype process, the foundation of modern photography

1891 direct colour process invented by French doctor Gabriel Lippmann 1845–1921, Nobel prizewinner 1908

1935 indirect (from three colour primaries) process developed for practical use in the Kodak laboratories

1947 Edwin Land 1909–   of USA invented the Polaroid camera, which develops the film inside the camera; and theory of 3D photography (holography◊) laid down by Dennis Gabor◊

Famous photographers include: Julia Cameron, Eugene Atget, Alfred Stieglitz, Lord Snowdon, Patrick Lichfield, Bill Brandt, Cecil Beaton□

photon the smallest 'package', 'particle' or quantum of energy in which light, or any other form of electromagnetic radiation, is emitted. See light◊, particle◊ physics□

photosynthesis two-stage plant process:

light reaction through which plants use photons◊ of sunlight to split water into oxygen (released as a by-product), protons◊ and electrons◊.

dark reaction through which they use the electrons to convert carbon dioxide (from the air) into carbohydrates e.g. glucose.

The green pigment chlorophyll◊ is usually essential to trap the light energy, but the saltwater ***purple bacterium*** *Rhodopseudomonas viridis* uses a purple pigment in the same way. The latter resembles the pigment in the retina of the human eye which converts light energy to nerve impulses.

The light reaction is a potential large-scale energy source if the electrons could be used to convert the protons to hydrogen. This is a non-polluting and easily-stored fuel usable in specially-designed aircraft or motor engines□

phrenology discredited theory (of Dr Franz Josef Gall c1796) that the skull shape revealed measurable psychological and intellectual features□

Phrygia kingdom of W Anatolia, at its zenith in the 8th century, later coming under the rule of Lydia◊. The worship of Cybele◊ passed from here to Greece and Rome, and its wealth was legendary. See Midas◊□

phylloxera genus of insects similar to aphids. See under hemiptera◊□

phylum a division of animals or plants which contains several classes□

physics study of the ultimate laws governing the structure of the universe, and of the forms of matter and energy and their interactions. More recent landmarks including:

1896 Antoine Becquerel◊ discovered radioactivity in rocks, evidence that earth was as old as Darwin◊'s theory of evolution required (4600 million, not 40 million years)

1897 J J Thomson◊'s discovery of the electron◊

1900 Max Planck◊'s quantum theory

1905 Einstein◊'s special theory of relativity

1913 Niels Bohr◊'s quantum theory of the atom

1915 Einstein◊'s general theory of relativity

1927 Heisenberg◊'s 'uncertainty principle'

1932 neutron and positron discovered

1980 David Bohm◊'s theory of 'implicate order'□

physiology biological science of how a living organism functions□

physiotherapy treatment of injury and disease, alongside surgery and drugs, by electrical stimulation, exercise, heat, manipulation, massage, etc.□

phytohormone a substance like a hormone◊, produced by a plant□

Piacenza city, an agricultural trading centre, in N Italy; population 109 000□

Piaf ('sparrow'), Edith. Stage-name of Edith Gassion 1915–63, French Parisian diseuse, whose defiant song 'Je ne regrette rien' reflected an emotionally full life that ended in drink and drugs□

Piaget Jean 1896–1980. Swiss child psychologist, who investigated the development of memory, intelligence, and identity□

piano stringed musical instrument with keyed hammers, which developed from:

clavichord (16–18th century) long, rectangular box, with the keyboard at one end; the metal blade striking the strings remained on them until released, so that it is intimately expressive.

harpsichord (16–18th century) often with two keyboards, had strings plucked by quill plectra, and looked like a miniature grand piano; the ***spinet*** 16–18th century, was a smaller version, and the ***virginal*** 16–17th century, also with plucked strings, was contained in an oblong box (keyboard along the longer side), and often placed on a table.

All these instruments have been revived in the 20th century for their own individual qualities, but were superseded by the piano because of the need for an instrument with greater volume for large concert use. The piano, with the modern hammer action, was developed by Bartolommeo Cristofori c1709 at Padua□

Picabia Francis 1879–1953. Artist of Spanish origin, who was born and died in Paris. He was associated with Impressionism◊, Dadaism◊, and Surrealism◊, and in his later years anticipated many developments of American art in the 1960s□

Picardy region of N France; capital Amiens; population 1 740 000. Low-lying, it was a major battlefield in World War I□

Picasso Pablo 1881–1973. Spanish artist, born in Málaga. He was a mature artist at ten, held his first exhibition at sixteen, and settled in Paris from 1900. In his Blue Period 1901–4, he painted mystic distorted figures in blue tones; a more supple Rose Period followed 1905–6, and in 1907 his *Les Demoiselles d'Avignon* launched Cubism◊. He subsequently ranged through many styles and media including ceramics, sculpture, stage sets for ballet (*Parade* 1917, for Diaghilev◊), book illustration, and portraiture (Stravinsky◊, Valéry◊, etc.). His masterpiece is *Guernica*◊ 1937, depicting the horrors of bombing during the Spanish◊ Civil War, sent to Spain after the death of Franco◊□

Piccard Auguste 1884–1962. Swiss physicist who, with his twin brother Jean Félix 1884–1963, made stratospheric balloon flights to study cosmic rays, etc. With his son ***Jacques Ernest*** 1922– he pioneered the bathyscaphe for deepsea scientific exploration□

piccolo a musical instrument of the woodwind◊ family□

Pickford Mary 1893–1979. American actress, born Gladys Smith in Toronto. First star of the silent screen to be known by name, she and her second husband from 1920, Douglas Fairbanks◊ senior, were known as 'the world's sweethearts'□

Pico Della Mirandola Count Giovanni 1463–94. Italian mystic philosopher whose attempt to reconcile the religious base of Christianity, Islam and the ancient world were disapproved of by the Pope□

Picts Roman term for the peoples of N Scotland, possibly meaning 'painted' (tattooed); by the time of the Roman invasion they were predominantly Celtic◊, except in the outlying regions□

pidgin originally the English business jargon used in dealing with Chinese and other Oriental traders, *pidgin* being the local form of English 'business'. It later developed a character of its own as a language between local peoples with no common means of communication, e.g. it is the popular language of Papua◊ New Guinea. Such languages (called creoles) occur elsewhere and have structures which appear universal and have been claimed as representing the innate linguistic logic in man – and so ancestral to all languages□

Pieck Wilhelm 1876–1960. German communist, a leader of the 1919 Spartacist◊ revolt, and 1949–60 president of the German Democratic Republic; the office was abolished on his death□

Piedmont region (Italian Piemonte) of NW Italy, including the upper Po valley; capital Turin; population 4 479 000. Under the House of Savoy◊ the movement for a united Italy began here, and Piedmont (with Sardinia◊) formed its nucleus 1861□

Pierné Gabriel 1863–1937. French composer, successor to Franck◊ as organist at Ste Clothilde, Paris, and conductor of the Colonne orchestra from 1903. His works include the 'Entry of the Little Fauns'□

Piero della Francesca c1420–92. Italian painter of frescoes, e.g. *Legend of the True Cross* at Arezzo. He wrote a treatise on perspective□

Piero di Cosimo 1462–1521. Italian artist, noted for mythical subjects□

Pietermaritzburg industrial city (footware, furniture, brewing) capital from 1842 of Natal, S Africa; population 2 676 340. Founded 1838 by Boer◊ trekkers from the Cape, it was named after their leaders, Piet Retief and Gert Maritz, killed by the Zulus◊□

Pietism movement within Lutheranism◊ in the 17th century which aimed to revive practical christianity□

piezoelectric effect property of some crystals, e.g. quartz, of developing an electromotive force or voltage across opposite faces when subjected to a mechanical strain, and, conversely, of altering in size when subjected to an electromotive force. Piezoelectric crystal oscillators are used as frequency standards, e.g. replacing 'balance wheels' in watches. The crystals are also used in transducers in ultrasonics◊, and in certain gas lighters□

pig mammals of family Suidae, order Ungulata, which includes the European ***wild boar*** *Sus scrofa* the ancestor of domesticated breeds; it is 1.5 m/4.5 ft long and 1 m/3 ft high, with formidable tusks, but not naturally aggressive. Other wild pigs include the hairless ***babirusa*** *Babyrousa babyrussa* of the Celebes, in which the tusks grow up through the skin of the snout and curve back to the forehead; and the African ***warthog*** *Phacochoerus aethiopicus* with a heavy mane, tusks and 'warts' on the face. Of the domestic pigs, the Tamworth is a survival from the Iron Age; modern breeders aim at a heavy carcass and lean meat, e.g. by a hybrid of the Landrace, Saddleback and Large White□

Pigalu see Pagalu under Equatorial Guinea◊□

pigeon or ***dove*** order of birds, Columbiformes, noted for the slipshod character of their nests; ***pigeons' milk*** is the lining of the crop, which breaks down as the first food of the young. Some species have a remarkable 'homing' instinct, and from early times have been used to deliver messages in peace and war (see pigeon◊ racing).

The single family Columbidae includes the ***crowned pigeon*** *Goura cristata* of New Guinea, largest of the group with a blue back and fan-shaped crest; ***wood pigeon*** *Columba palumbus* a clumsy flier, greedy feeder on grain crops, etc. and a game bird; ***rock dove*** *Columba livia* from which most domesticated pigeons (e.g. fantail, pouter and homer) descend; ***collared turtle dove*** *Streptopelia decaocto* originally of S Asia and China, which (aided by five broods a year) has overspread Europe in the 20th century; ***turtle dove*** *Streptopelia turtur* noted for its attachment to its mate; and N American ***passenger pigeon*** *Ectopistes migratoria* one of the most quickly extinct species in history, which numbered millions till 1888 (Audubon◊ observed a flock in 1813 that took three days to pass and blotted out the sun) but vanished in the wild by 1900.

Most famous of extinct species is the ***dodo*** *Raphus cucullatus* family Raphidae, of Mauritius; flightless and larger than a turkey, it was extinct by 1681□

pigeon racing transport of domesticated pigeons to a given location, whence they fly back to their home lofts, where their arrival is timed; in Britain the National Homing Union dates from 1896 and Elizabeth◊ II has a racing pigeon manager. See also magnetism◊ and migration◊□

Piggott Lester 1935– . British jockey, nine times winner of the Derby and 11 times champion jockey. He retired in 1985□

Pigs Bay of. Inlet on the south coast of Cuba where 1500 anti-Castro◊ Cuban exiles attempted an invasion 17–20 Apr 1961; 1,173 were taken prisoner. The project had been backed by the CIA◊, authorized by Eisenhower◊, and was executed under J F Kennedy◊□

pike freshwater sporting fish *Esox lucius* family Esocidae, order Clupeiformes, of Europe and N America; it is a voracious feeder and may reach 1.5 m/5 ft. Some smaller species are known in America as 'pickerel'□

pike-perch a genus of freshwater fish. See under perch◊□

Pikes Peak see under Colorado◊□

Pilate Pontius. Roman procurator of Judaea◊ 26–36AD. Unsympathetic to the Jews, his actions several times provoked riots, and in 36AD he was recalled to Rome to account for disorder in Samaria◊. He is said to have reluctantly ordered Christ's crucifixion, and to have committed suicide□

pilchard a fish of the herring◊ family□

piles varicose veins of the anus (haemorrhoids), usually caused by constipation, which may need excision, etc. if they protrude from the anus□

pilgrimage journey to sacred places. They include ***Hinduism*** Varanasi◊; ***Buddhism*** Kandy◊; ***Greeks (ancient)*** Delphi◊, Ephesus◊; ***Judaism*** Jerusalem◊; ***Islam*** Mecca◊; ***Christianity*** Jerusalem◊, Rome◊, the tomb of St James◊ of Compostella in Spain, the shrine of Becket◊ (to which a Pilgrims' Way led 195 km/120 mi from Winchester to Canterbury◊), Our Lady of Walsingham◊ in England and Lourdes◊ in France□

Pilgrimage of Grace revolt 1536, especially in Lincolnshire and Yorkshire by feudal nobility and clergy (against Henry◊ VIII's centralising policy and dissolution of the monasteries) and by the peasants (against the enclosure of common lands). The rebels were dispersed by promises, and then c230 were executed including in 1537 their leader Robert Aske□

Pilgrim Fathers English emigrants (less than a quarter Puritan refugees) who sailed from Plymouth 16 Sept 1620 in the *Mayflower* to found the first New England colony at New Plymouth, Massachusetts□

Pilgrims' Way see Becket under pilgrimage◊□

pillory wooden punishment frame, with holes for the offender's head and hands, abolished in England 1837; bystanders threw whatever was handy at the miscreant□

pilotfish a small sea fish. See under perch◊□

Pilsen German form of Plzeň□

Pilsudski Joseph 1867–1935. Polish nationalist leader, who headed the newly established republic 1918–23, and was virtually dictator from 1926□

Piltdown Man fossilized skull fragments 'discovered' by Charles Dawson (died 1916) at Piltdown, E Sussex in 1913; believed to be the earliest European human remains until proved a hoax 1953 (the jaw was that of an orang-utan). The most likely perpetrator was Samuel Woodhead, a lawyer friend of Dawson, who was an amateur palaeontologist□

pimento another name for allspice. See herbs◊□

pimpernel genus of plants *Anagallis* family Primulaceae. The ***scarlet pimpernel*** *A arvensis* has red flowers open only in fine weather□

Pincus Gregory 1903–67. American reproductive biologist, the chief originator of oral contraceptives (the 'pill')□

Pindar c552BC–442BC. Greek poet. Born near Thebes, he was famed for choral lyrics, 'Pindaric odes'□

Pindus Mountains (Pindhos Óros) mountain range in central Greece; highest point Smolikas 2637 m/8652 ft□

pine an evergreen tree. See under conifers◊□

pineal gland pea-sized gland at the base of the forebrain which secretes the hormone melatonin, which plays a role in regulating biological (circadian) rhythms, so affecting whether human beings are at their best in the day, or are 'night-owls', and the incidence of jetlag. The gland is found in all vertebrates□

pineapple tropical American plant *Ananas comosus,* family Bromeliaceae. In the second year the mauvish flowers consolidate with their bracts to form a fleshy fruit, now grown throughout the tropics□

pine-martin a type of marten. See under weasel◊□

Pinero Arthur Wing 1855–1934. British dramatist, exponent of the well-made play in his farces, e.g. *Dandy Dick* 1887, but the creator of the 'problem play' with *The Second Mrs Tanqueray* 1893□

pink a flowering plant. See carnation◊□

Pinkerton Allan 1819–84. American detective, born in Glasgow. He founded 1852 Pinkerton's National Detective Agency, and built up the federal secret service from the espionage system he developed during the Civil◊ War□

Pinkie Battle of, 1547. The Scots were defeated by the Duke of Somerset◊, near Musselburgh, Lothian□

Pinnipedia order of marine carnivores, found especially in Arctic and Antarctic waters, and hunted for their body oil and their pelts. They are divided into:

true or hair seals family Phocidae, are earless and are mainly Arctic and N Atlantic species, e.g. the intelligent ***common seal*** *Phoca vitulina* about 2 m/6 ft long, a dunnish-grey, and exploited for commercial performances and the larger, and rarer ***grey seal,*** both found off Britain. Largest of the seals is the large-nosed, Pacific ***elephant seal*** *Mirounga leonina* 6 m/18 ft long and weighing about two tonnes. The ***leopard seal*** *Hydrurga leptonyx* is the only seal which preys on other seals. Seals have their fore-limbs converted to flippers, and the hind ones are joined with the tail, so that they move by wriggling on their stomachs. See Lake Baikal◊.

fur seals or ***sea lions*** family Otariidae, found chiefly in the N Pacific and Bering Sea (genus *Callorhinus*) have sharper muzzles and vestigial hind limbs to help them move on land. They have been ruthlessly exploited for their fur which is 'plucked' to reveal the underfur, a sheeny mottled dun and grey in adults, and the pups are brutally culled for their creamy-white pelts.

walrus or ***sea cow*** *Odobenus rosmarus* family Odobeidae, found in the far north of the Atlantic and Pacific. It may reach 4 m/12 ft, has webbed flippers, and a characteristic, bristly 'walrus' moustache, and enlarged upper canine teeth. These 'tusks' are used for carvings, and it was formerly hunted for these and its oil□

pint liquid measure. See under gallon◊□

Pinter Harold 1930– . British dramatist who had a rigorous training in repertory. He specializes in the tragi-comedy of the breakdown of communication, e.g. *The Birthday Party* 1958 and *The Caretaker* 1960, and also the sophisticated nuance *The Lover* 1962□

Pinturicchio 1454–1513. Italian artist, Bernardino di Betti, who assisted Perugino◊ in decorating the Sistine◊ Chapel, Rome□

pinworm see under worm◊□

Pinyin the Chinese◊ phonetic alphabet□

Piozzi Hester Lynch 1741–1841. British writer, who published *Anecdotes of the late Samuel Johnson* 1786, and their correspondence 1788. Johnson had been a constant visitor at the home of herself and her first husband, Henry Thrale, but was alienated by her marriage to musician, Gabriel Piozzi. Her diaries and notebooks were published 1942□

pipefish fish (also called ***needlefish***) shaped like a length of pipe. The ***great pipefish*** *Synghathus acus* order Syngnathiformes, family Syngnathidae, is 30cm/12 in long, and the male has a brood pouch for eggs and developing young. Related is the ***common seahorse*** *Hippocampus guttulatus* family Hippocampidae. Ranging from a few inches to a foot long, the seahorses have a head resembling that of a horse, and swim upright. The body has bony plates raised into tubercles or spines, and ends in a prehensile tail which the fish uses to anchor itself to seaweed. The males have brood pouches and are excellent fathers□

Piper John 1903– . British artist, whose work includes landscapes, abstracts, theatre sets, and glass windows for Coventry Cathedral and panels for the lantern at Liverpool Catholic Cathedral□

pipit see under wagtails◊□

piracy seizure of a ship or its contents on the high seas, punishable under international law wherever the culprit is taken. Notable were the Corsairs◊, Buccaneers◊; Bartholomew Roberts◊, and Edward Teach◊. Piracy at sea revived in the 1980s off W Africa and in SE Asian waters where Vietnamese 'boat people', escaping with their valuables, were a particular target. ***Hijacking*** is the equivalent on land (long-distance lorries or trucks), and in the air, though in the latter case, the crime often has political motives□

Piraeus see under Athens◊□

Piran St lived c500. Missionary sent to Cornwall by St Patrick◊. There are remains of his oratory at Perranzabuloe, and he is the patron saint of Cornwall and the nationalist movement; feast day 5 Mar□

Pirandello Luigi 1867–1936. Italian writer of short stories and novels, but best-remembered for his play *Six Characters in Search of an Author* 1921; Nobel prize 1934□

Piranesei Giovanni Battista 1720–78. Italian architect, more remarkable for his powerful etchings□

piranha small freshwater S American fish *Serrasalmus niger* family Characidae (see Characin◊) which strips the flesh from its prey and will attack cattle and man□

Pisa city in Tuscany, Italy; population 104 510. A maritime republic in the 11–12th centuries, it is now famous for its cathedral (see Giovanni Pisano◊), and the Leaning Tower or campanile, though the legend that Galileo◊ made experiments in gravity from its top is unfounded. Shelley◊ was drowned to the west of Pisa 1822□

Pisanello Italian artist Antonio Pisano c1395–1455/6. A Veronese, he was noted for his medals and his frescoes, of which those in the Palazzo Ducale in Mantua were rediscovered after World War II□

Pisano Giovanni c1245–1314. Italian sculptor, son of Niccola Pisano◊. His greatest works were the pulpit in Pisa's cathedral and the original design for the facade of Siena cathedral□

Pisano Niccola c1225–c1278. Italian sculptor-architect. His pulpit in Siena cathedral initiated a revival in the art of sculpture. He worked with his son Giovanni Pisano◊□

Pisistratus c605–527BC. Athenian ruler, as dictator though under constitutional forms, who first had the Homeric poems written down and founded Greek drama by introducing the Dionysiac◊ peasant festivals to Athens□

Pissaro Camille 1830–1903. French impressionist painter, a student of Corot◊, whose chief works were landscapes. His son ***Lucien*** 1863–1944, also a landscape artist, became a naturalized Briton□

pistachio Eurasian tree *Pistacia vera* family Anacardiaceae, with edible nuts□

pistol a hand gun. See under small◊ arms□

Pitcairn Island British colony 5300 km/3300 mi north east of New Zealand
area 5 sq km/2 sq mi
capital Adamstown
features in the group are the uninhabited Henderson Island 31 sq km/12 sq mi, an unspoilt coral atoll with a rare ecology, and tiny Ducie and Oeno, annexed by Britain in 1902
exports fruit, souvenirs, etc. to passing ships
population 44
language English
government the Governor is the British High Commissioner in New Zealand
recent history discovered by British admiral, Philip Carteret, in 1767, it was first settled by nine mutineers from the *Bounty*◊ together with some Tahitians, their occupation remaining unknown until 1808□

pitch dark viscid residue of tar◊ distillation. See bitumen◊□

pitch the position of a note in the musical scale, dependent on the frequency of the predominant sound wave. In ***standard pitch*** A above middle C has a frequency of 440 H_z. To have ***perfect pitch*** means an ability to name or reproduce any note heard or asked for; it does not necessarily imply high musical ability□

pitchblende black, radioactive mineral, chief source of uranium◊□

pitcher plant an insectivorous◊ plants□

Pitman Sir Isaac 1813–97. British inventor of phonetic shorthand◊□

Pitt William, 1st Earl of Chatham 1708–78. British statesman, 'the Great Commoner'. Entering Parliament in 1735, he opposed Walpole◊, and attacked Walpole's successor, Carteret, for his conduct of the War of the Austrian Succession. As Paymanster of the Forces 1746–55, he broke with tradition by refusing to enrich himself, and was dismissed for attacking Newcastle, the Prime Minister. He was recalled by popular demand to form a goverment to mastermind the Seven Years' War in 1756, but in 1757 was forced to form a coalition with Newcastle, A 'year of victories' ensued in 1759, and the French were expelled from India and Canada. Forced to resign in 1761 by George III, he was again recalled to form an all-party government in 1768. He championed the Americans against the King, though rejecting independence, and collapsed during his last speech in the House of Lords – opposing the withdrawal of British troops – and died a month later□

Pitt William, the Younger 1759–1806. British Tory◊ statesman, son of William Pitt◊, 1st Earl of Chatham. Entering Parliament in 1781, he was Shelburne◊'s Chancellor of the Exchequer 1782–3, but with the support of the Tories and 'king's friends' became England's youngest prime minister 1783–1801. He reorganised the country's finances, and negotiated reciprocal tariff reduction with France. In 1793, however, the new republic declared war, and the dangers of the times reinforced Pitt's opposition to political reform. His policy in Ireland led to the 1798 revolt, and he tried to solve the Irish question by the Act of Union in 1800. However, he resigned in 1801 on George◊ III's rejection of Catholic emancipation. In 1793 he had organised a coalition against France, and on his return to office 1804–6, organised another (with Austria and Russia) against Napoleon◊, which was shattered at Austerlitz◊. In declining health, he died on hearing the news, saying: 'Oh, my country! How I leave my country!'□

Pittsburgh industrial city (iron and steel) and inland port, where the Allegheny and Monongahela join to form the Ohio river in Pennsylvania, USA; population 423 940. The Carnegie Institute of Technology is here, and the city markets industrial know-how as well as its basic products□

pituitary a gland attached to the base of the brain. See under hormone◊□

Pius twelve Popes, including

Pius iv 1499–1565, one of the Medici◊, Pope from 1559, he reassembled the Council of Trent (see Counter-Reformation under Reformation◊) and completed its work in 1563.

Pius V 1504–72, Pope from 1566, who excommunicated Elizabeth◊ I, and organized the expedition against the Turks which won the victory of Lepanto◊.

Pius VI 1717–99, Pope from 1775, strongly opposed the French◊ Revolution, and died a prisoner in French hands.

Pius VII 1740–1823, Pope from 1800, concluded a Concordat◊ with France in 1801, and took part in Napoleon◊'s coronation, but was a prisoner 1809–14. After his return to Rome in 1814 he revived the Jesuit◊ order.

Pius IX 1792–1878, Pope from 1846. He never accepted the incorporation of the Papal States and of Rome in the kingdom of Italy, and proclaimed the dogmas of the immaculate conception of the Virgin 1854 and Papal infallibility 1870; his pontificate was the longest in history.

Pius X 1835–1914, Pope from 1903, canonized 1954, condemned Modernism (see under Christianity◊) in a manifesto of 1907.

Pius XI 1857–1939, Pope from 1922, he signed the Concordat◊ with Mussolini◊ 1929.

Pius XII (Eugenio Pacelli) 1876–1958, Pope from 1939. He opposed anti-Semitism during World War II, though his attitude was subject to controversy. He proclaimed the dogma of the bodily assumption of the Virgin Mary 1950 and in 1951 restated the doctrine (strongly criticised by Protestants) that the life of an infant must not be sacrificed to save a mother in labour. He was subject to visions□

Pizarro Francisco c1475–1541. Spanish conquistador, who in 1532 (with only 183 followers) conquered Peru, the Inca king (Atahualpa◊) being treacherously seized and murdered, and founded Lima 1535. He was assassinated by the Spaniards□

Place Francis 1771–1854. British Radical, responsible with Hume◊ for the repeal of the Combination◊ Acts□

plague disease transmitted by fleas (carried by the black rat◊) which infect the sufferer with the bacillus *Yersinia pestis*; an early symptom is swelling of lymph nodes, usually in the armpit and groin, termed 'bubo', hence 'bubonic' plague. It causes virulent blood poisoning and the death rate is high. The term Black◊ Death is modern and has not been satisfactorily explained□

plaice a type of flatfish◊□

Plaid Cymru Welsh nationalist political party established 1925, and dedicated to an independent Wales◊□

Plains small town in Georgia◊, USA; home town of President Carter◊□

Plains Indians Indians of the High Plains of N America (Alberta–Texas), with a warrior-horseman culture 1700–1850 (skin tents or *tipis*, war paint, buffalo robes, eagle feather war bonnets, scalp-taking). Their myths include that of the ***thunderbird*** creator of the storms of the great plains. Their chief ritual was the ***sundance*** at summer solstice, when a warrior was tied to a sacred pole by ropes ending in wooden skewers thrust through the flesh, and danced until the flesh gave way, receiving in return supernatural assistance. The main tribes were Blackfoot, Cheyenne, Comanche, Pawnee, and the Dakota or Sioux (see under Montana◊). General George Custer◊ moved against a Sioux camp at Little Bighorn, Montana (under chiefs Crazy Horse◊ and Sitting Bull◊) and was killed with his troops in ***Custer's Last Stand*** 25 Jun 1876. Congress then abrogated the Fort Laramie Treaty of 1868 (granting the Indians a large area in Dakota's Black Hills, where gold had by now been found, and where today uranium, coal, oil and natural gas are worked). The last confrontation of the Sioux and US Army was at ***Wounded Knee***, S Dakota, after Chief Sitting Bull had been killed on 15 Dec 1890, allegedly resisting arrest. On 29 Dec 1890 Indians associated with him in the ***Ghost Dance Movement*** (aimed at recovering control of N America with the aid of spirits of dead braves) were surrounded and 153 killed. In 1973 the American Indian Movement held hostages in a siege of Wounded Knee 27 Feb–8 May, demanding investigation of the treaty question, and in 1980 the Sioux, who survive in S Dakota and Nebraska, received $160 million compensation□

Planck Max 1858–1947. German physicist, the framer of quantum◊ theory, for which he received a Nobel prize 1918□

plane large trees of the north temperate zone, genus *Platanus* family Platanaceae, with scaling bark and bristly spherical fruit hanging on stalks. They include the ***oriental plane*** *P orientalis;* ***American plane*** *P hispanica;* and the ***London plane***, (a hybrid of the two)□

planet a large body moving in an elliptical orbit (see Kepler◊'s Laws) around a star. The solar system containing the earth includes nine planets orbiting the sun. The orbits of the planets all lie very nearly in the same plane: if a very large, flat (heat-resistant!) piece of paper could be passed through the sun and tilted correctly all the planets (except Pluto) would lie on or close to it (in astronomical terms).

Most theorists believe that the planets were formed from a huge, rotating disc-like molecular cloud containing hydrogen, helium, and dust rich in heavier elements. Given random local dense spots in the cloud, gravitational forces would gather the dust particles together into, perhaps, bodies a few kilometers in diameter which might then have come together to form the inner planets and the cores of the outer planets. The sun may have been formed from the same molecular cloud□

planetarium optical projection device for reproducing the motions of the stars, planets, etc. on a domed ceiling, representing the sky as seen from earth□

planetary nebula see under star◊□

plankton small forms of plant and animal life that drift in fresh or salt water, and are a source of food for larger animals□

Plantaganet English royal house, reigning 1154–1399, from the nickname of Geoffrey, Count of Anjou (father of Henry◊ II) who often wore a sprig of broom 'planta genista' in his hat; Richard, Duke of York, revived it as a surname to emphasize his superior claim to the throne over Henry◊ VI□

plantain genus of plants *Plantago* family Plantaginaceae, with a rosette of leaves, common lawn weeds. See also banana◊□

plant in their simplest forms plants are difficult to distinguish exactly from animals◊ (see also life◊ classification), but are generally marked by their synthesis◊ of their food from inorganic substances. Also, their cells have cellulose walls; they are generally less responsive than animals to stimuli; have no nervous system; and are incapable of voluntary movement from place to place□

planets

planet	main constituents	atmosphere	distance from sun in millions of km	time for one orbit in earth-years	diameter in thousands of km	average density if density of water is 1 unit
Mercury	rocky, ferrous	–	5.8	0.24	4.8	5.4
Venus	rocky, ferrous	carbon dioxide	108	0.62	12.1	5.2
earth	rocky, ferrous	nitrogen, oxygen	150	1.00	12.8	5.5
Mars	rocky	carbon dioxide	228	1.88	6.8	3.9
Jupiter	liquid hydrogen, helium	–	778	11.90	142.8	1.3
Saturn	hydrogen, helium	–	1427	29.50	120.0	0.7
Uranus	icy, hydrogen, helium	hydrogen, helium	2869	84.00	51.8	1.2
Neptune	icy, hydrogen, helium	hydrogen, helium	4496	164.80	49.5	1.7
Pluto	icy, rocky	methane	5900	248.40	2.7	1.5

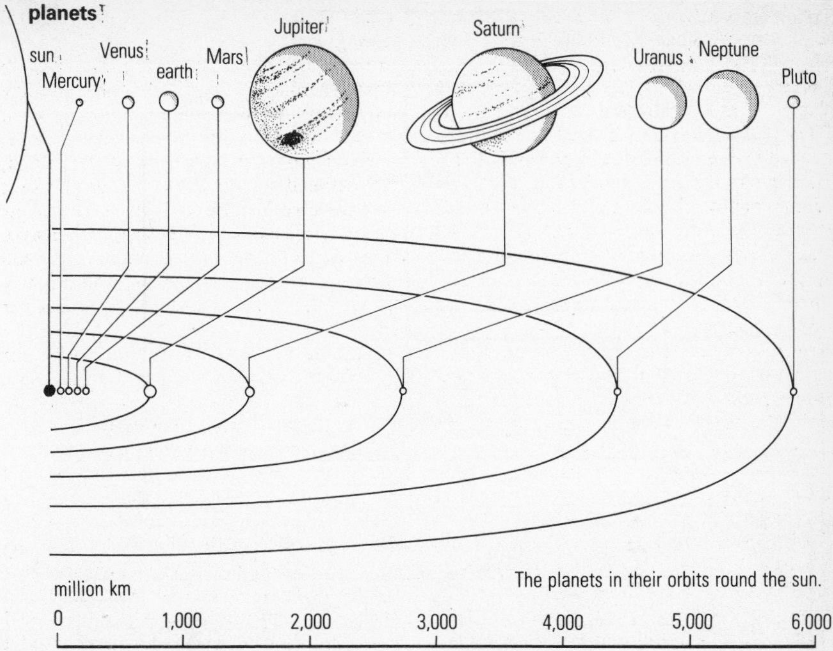

The planets in their orbits round the sun.

plant classification traditionally the plant kingdom is divided into two halves: the lower, non-flowering, spore-producing species (the ***cryptograms***), and the higher seed-bearing species (the ***Phanerograms***). However, thallophytes are often classified along with bacteria, blue-green algae, and protozoa (simple single-celled animals) as the kingdom Protista, all of which show a mixture of plant and animal characteristics. All plants except Thallophytes and Bryophytes show a differentiation of structure into roots, stems, and leaves.
The number of species is estimated at 250 000; the major divisions are shown below.
cryptogams non-seed bearing
thallophyta simplest plants possessing a thallus (plant body with no true root, stem or leaf):
algae (Algus) – simple plant e.g. algae, diatom, seaweed
fungi (Fungus) – simple non-green plant e.g. yeast, mould, mildew, mushroom
lichens (Lichenes) – algae and fungi living in symbiosis◊
bryophyta more differentiated plant bodies:
mosses (Musci) – green stem and leaf but no true root
liverworts (Hepaticae) –thalloid organism
pteridophyta green plants with definite stem, root, leaf and vascular system:
ferns (Filicales)
horsetails (Equisetales)
clubmosses (Lycopodiales)
Phanerogams seed bearing
gymnosperms flowering plants with unenclosed seeds:
conifers (Coniferales) – cone-bearing plants e.g. pine, fir, cedar
gnetals (Gnetales) – woody tropical plants
cycads (Cycadales)
ginkgos (Ginkgoales) – maidenhair tree
angiosperms flowering plants with seeds enclosed in an ovary, which ripens to a fruit
monocotyledons – plants with one cotyledon (seed-leaf) in the embryo; leaves are generally parallel-veined with smooth margins e.g. orchids, grasses, lilies
dicotyledons – plants with two cotyledons (seed-leaves); leaves are generally net-veined and serrated, lobed or compound e.g. oak, buttercup, geranium, daisy□

plasma (biology) the liquid part of blood◊□

plasma (physics) an ionized gas produced at extremely high temperatures, as in the sun and other stars, and which contains positive and negative charges in approximately equal numbers, is affected by a magnetic field and is a good electrical conductor□

Plassey see under West Bengal◊□

plaster of Paris a form of gypsum◊□

plastics normally stable synthetic materials which are fluid and can be shaped at some stage in their manufacture, and which are

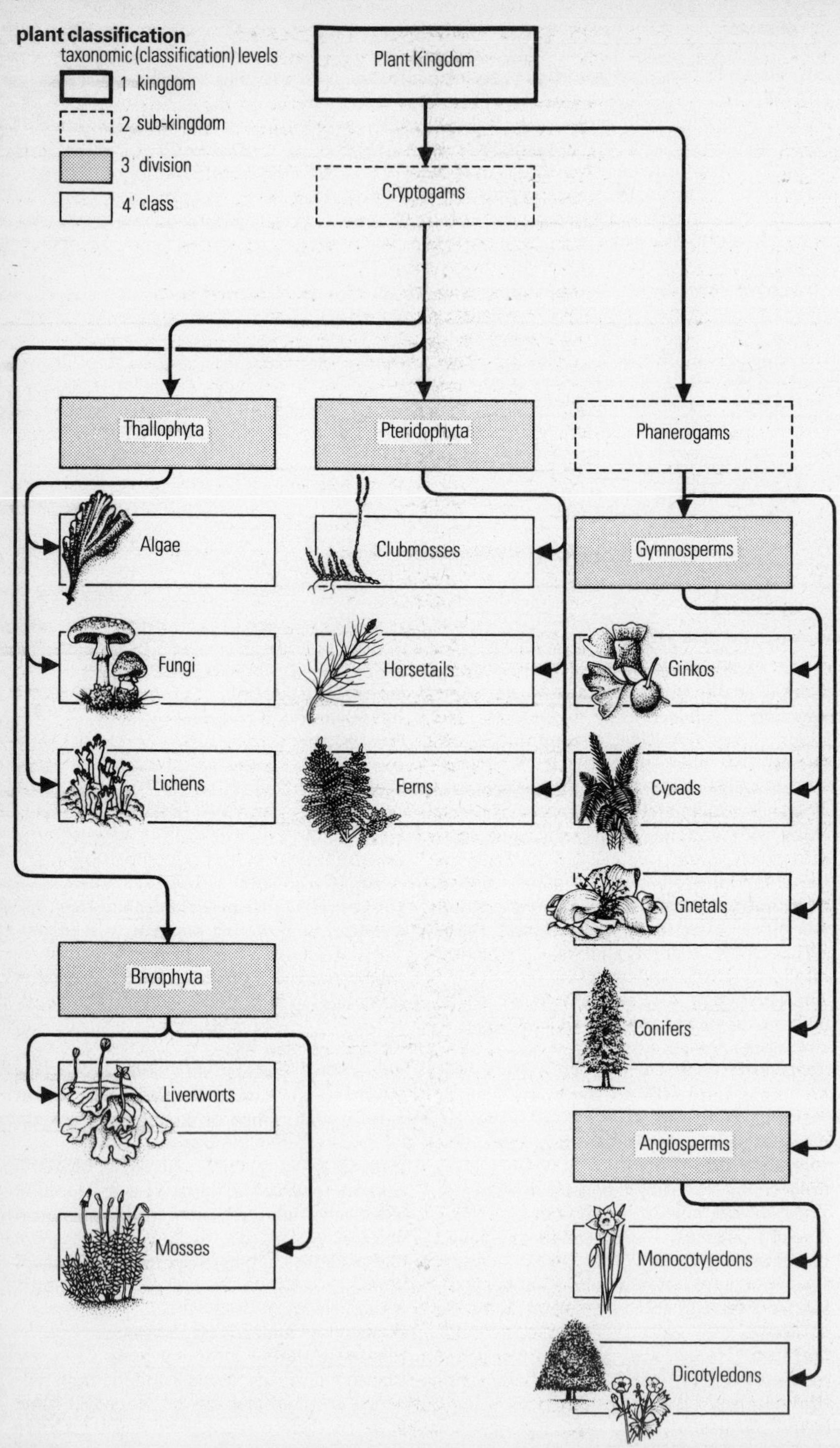
plant classification
taxonomic (classification) levels
1 kingdom
2 sub-kingdom
3 division
4 class
Plant Kingdom
Cryptogams
Thallophyta
Pteridophyta
Phanerogams
Algae
Clubmosses
Gymnosperms
Fungi
Horsetails
Ginkos
Lichens
Ferns
Cycads
Gnetals
Bryophyta
Conifers
Liverworts
Angiosperms
Mosses
Monocotyledons
Dicotyledons

today chiefly derived from petroleum. Most are polymers. Processed by extrusion, injection moulding, vacuum forming and compression, they emerge in consistencies ranging from hard and rigid to soft and rubbery. They replace an increasing number of natural substances, being lightweight, easy to clean, long or short life (as required), and capable of being rendered very strong, e.g. by the addition of carbon fibres, for building aircraft and in other engineering projects. They are divided into:
thermoplastic which soften when warmed, then re-harden as they cool, e.g. ***polystyrene*** synthetic polymer (see polymerization◊) forming a clear plastic used in kitchen utensils or (when expanded by gas injection) a stiff foam used in insulation and ceiling tiles.
polythene or ***polyethylene*** a polymer of ethylene, either rigid or highly flexible, and used for containers, wrappings, etc; ***PVC*** (*p*oly*v*inyl *c*hloride) made in varying degrees of flexibility for drainpipes, floor tiles, records, shoes and handbags.
thermosetting which remain rigid once set, e.g. ***bakelite*** forms of resin used in electrical insulation, plastic ware (e.g. telephone receivers), etc. and named after their inventor L H Baekeland 1863–1944; ***epoxy resins*** used in paints and varnishes, to laminate wood, and as adhesives (e.g. Araldite); ***polyesters*** complex compounds of hydrocarbons used in synthetic textile fibres, e.g. dacron and terylene, and, with glassfibre reinforcement, in car bodies, boat hulls, etc.; ***polyurethane*** light, synthetic polymer prepared in liquid form as a paint or varnish, which dries very hard; in foam form it is used in upholstery and in lining materials, when it may be a fire hazard; ***silicones*** based on a chain of oxygen and silicon atoms, the latter having organic groups attached to them. They are chemically inert, have good electrical properties, and repel water, e.g. silicone rubber, paints, industrial grease and domestic polishes, and water proofing for walls and stain-resistant textiles□

plastic surgery the surgical repair of seriously damaged tissues. See surgery◊□

Plata Río de la. Estuary (English River Plate) into which the Paraná and Uruguay flow; length 320 km/200 mi and width up to 240 km/145mi. The basin drains much of Argentina, Bolivia, Brazil, Uruguay and Paraguay, and all five co-operate in its development□

Plataea Battle of, 479BC. See Persian◊ Wars□

Plate River. See Río de la Plata◊. In the ***Battle of the River Plate*** Dec 1939 the German pocket battleship *Graf Spee* was scuttled here by her commander rather than engage the British cruisers *Exeter*, *Achilles*, and *Ajax*□

Plath Sylvia 1932–63. American poet (*The Colossus* 1960 and *Ariel* 1965) and novelist (*The Bell Jar* 1963); she committed suicide. She married Ted Hughes◊ in 1956□

platinum element
symbol Pt
atomic number 78
physical description silver-white malleable metal
features resists corrosion by acids
uses as a catalyst in the production of sulphuric acids; thermocouple wires; in jewellery, and in the production of laboratory apparatus□

platimum group six metallic elements which have similar properties: iridium◊, osmium◊, palladium◊, platinum◊, phodium◊, and ruthenium◊□

Plato c428–c348BC. Athenian philosopher, a follower of Socrates◊. Of noble birth, he travelled widely after the death of Socrates before returning to Athens c 387 to found his Academy, in order to train a new ruling class. Typical of his works, in a dialogue form which often makes Socrates a pariticipant, are the *Phaedo* on the immortality of the soul, and the *Republic* outlining an ideal state. He maintained that mind, not matter, is fundamental, and that material objects are merely imperfect copies of abstract and eternal 'ideas'; hence he rejected experiment as a scientific method in favour of argument□

platyhelminthes a type of flatworm. See worm◊□

platypus a small Australasian mammal. See under Monotremata◊□

Plautus Titus Maccius d. 184BC. Roman comic dramatist, who adapted Greek originals, including *Menoechmi* on which Shakespeare based *The Comedy of Errors*□

playing cards a set of small pieces of card with different markings, used in playing games. They probably originated in China or India. They first appeared in Europe in 14th-century Italy as the 78 cards (22 emblematic, including 'the hanged man', and 56 numerals) of the ***tarot pack*** used both for gaming and from the 18th century fortune-telling. However, in the 15th century they were reduced to the standard pack of 52 for most games, of which the chief now include bridge◊, whist◊, poker◊, rummy◊, cribbage◊□

Pleasence Donald 1919– . British actor, born in Yorkshire. A specialist in the sinister, his parts include the title-role in the film *Dr Crippen* 1962□

plebeians aliens and freedmen, and their descendants, in ancient Rome (as opposed to the patricians◊)□
plebiscite a direct vote by all electors on a specific issue, most usually on the status of a territory, as with the Saarland◊ in 1935 and Togo◊ at the end of the British/French United Nations trusteeship 1956□
Pléiade La. Group of seven classically-inspired poets in 16th-century France, led by Ronsard◊, and named after the star cluster□
Pleiades in Greek mythology, seven daughters of Atlas◊, who asked to be changed to a cluster of stars to escape the pursuit of Orion◊□
Pleiades or ***Seven Sisters*** a cluster of stars in the constellation Taurus, six of which (formerly seven) are visible to the naked eye□
Plenty Bay of. Inlet on the north east coast of North Island, New Zealand, where the first Maori◊ immigrants landed□
Plesetsk see under Archangel◊□
pleurisy inflammation of the secreting membrane which covers the lungs, and lines the space in which they rest. It renders breathing painful□
Pleven industrial city (textiles, machinery, ceramics) in N Bulgaria; population 131 700□
Plimsoll Samuel 1824–98. British Radical parliamentary reformer who originated the 'Plimsoll line' (Merchant Shipping Act 1876) to prevent dangerous overloading of ships□
Pliny (Gaius Plinius Secundus) the Elder c23–79AD. Roman scientist-historian; only his works on astronomony, geography and natural history survive. He was killed in the eruption of Vesuvius□
Pliny (Gaius Plinius Caecilius Secundus) the Younger c61–113. Roman administrator, nephew of Pliny◊ the Elder, whose correspondence is of great interest□
PLO abbreviation for Palestine◊ Liberation Organization. See Palestine◊, Arafat◊□
Ploesti oil city in SE Romania; population 211 500□
Plotinus c204–70AD. Greek founder of Neoplatonism◊, which deeply influenced Christian thought□
Plovdiv industrial city (chemicals, leather, textiles) in S Bulgaria; population 745 000□
plover wading birds, family Charadriidae, order Charadriiformes◊ including European ***golden plover*** *Pluviatilis apricaria* of heathland and sea coast; ***dotterel*** *Eudromias morinellus* which nests in the tundra; and ***lapwing*** *Vanellus vanellus*, noted for its courageous defence of its nest sites□
plum hardy tree *Prunus domestica* family Rosaceae◊, with edible oval red, yellow or green fruit, known when dried as prunes. Closely related is the ***damson*** ***P institita*** family Rosaceae◊, with astringent small purplish fruit□
plumbago another name for graphite◊□
pluralism the belief that reality consists of several different elements. See Dualism◊□
Plutarch c46–120AD. Greek biographer, appointed procurator (governor) of Greece by Hadrian◊, and author of *Parallel lives of Greek and Roman Statesmen,* which later inspired Shakespeare's Roman plays□
Pluto Greek god of Hades◊□
Pluto the furthest planet from the sun
mean distance from the sun 5 950 000 000 km/ 3 666 000 000 mi
diameter 2500 km/1553 mi
rotation period 6 hrs 9 minutes
year (sidereal period) 247 years 255 days
atmosphere too cold and small for an atmosphere
surface temperature 240°c
surface consists of methane ice
features its orbit is eccentric, and when closest to the sun, it may be nearer than Neptune◊, it is compact like the smaller inner planets, not gaseous like the four large outer ones
ring system none
satellites
Charon mean distance from its planet 20 000 km
diameter 1 000 km□
plutonium element
symbol Pu
atomic number 94
physical description toxic transuranic◊ element, member of the actinide◊ series
features produced from uranium–239 and hence formed in nuclear reactors
uses as a fuel in 'fast breeder' nuclear reactors and in atomic bombs e.g. that dropped on Nagasaki 1945□
Plymouth city and port in Devon, England, an amalgamation in 1914 of Plymouth, Devonport and Stonehouse; population 253 600. Sir Francis Drake◊ sailed from here when he circumnavigated the world, and traditionally played bowls on Plymouth Hoe before leaving to fight the Armada◊. It was also the last port of call for the *Mayflower*◊. Devonport has an important naval dockyard□
Plymouth Brethren fundamentalist Christian sect founded c1827 in Dublin by the Reverend John Darby 1800–82, and established by an assembly at Plymouth (hence the name) in 1831. It split between 'Open' and extremist 'Close' divisions in 1848□
Plynlimon see under Dyfed◊□
Plzeň industrial city (Skoda armament works, machinery, cars, lager) in W Czechoslovakia; population 171 000□

pneumoconiosis disease of the lungs caused by dust, especially from coal, which causes the lung to become fibrous, so that the patient has difficulty breathing; often fatal□

pneumonia inflammation of the lungs, the result of infection by bacteria (especially pneumococci) or viruses, making breathing difficult. It is treated with antibiotics□

pneumothorax presence of air in the pleural cavity between the lungs and the thorax, causing the collapse of the former□

Pnom-Penh see Phnôm-Penh◊□

Po longest river in Italy, from the Cottian Alps to the Adriatic; length 668 km/415 mi. Its valley is fertile and there is natural gas□

Pobedy Pik. See under Tyan◊-Shan□

Pocahontas c1595–1617. American Indian princess alleged to have saved the life of John Smith◊ (when he was captured by her father Powhatan). She married an Englishman, and her son has many modern American descendants. See Gravesend◊□

pochard a genus of diving duck. See under waterfowl◊□

Po Chu-i see Bo◊ Zhu Yi□

Podgorica older name of Titograd◊□

Podolsk industrial city (oil refining, machinery, cables, cement, ceramics) in W USSR; population 207 000□

Poe Edgar Allan 1809–49. American author. Born in Boston, he was orphaned 1811, and took as his middle name the surname of his adopted parents. Trying army life, he was court-martialled for neglect of duty, failed to earn a living by writing, became addicted to alcohol, and in 1847 lost his wife (commemorated in his poem *Annabel Lee*). His verse, of haunting lyric beauty, influenced the French symbolists◊ (e.g. *Ulalume* and *The Bells*). His popular reputation rests on his short stories, unrivalled in the creation of horrific atmosphere (e.g. 'The Fall of the House of Usher' 1839) and acute reasoning (e.g. 'The Gold Bug' 1843 and 'The Murders in the Rue Morgue' 1841), in which the investigators Legrand and Dupin anticipated Conan◊ Doyle's Sherlock Holmes□

Poet Laureate poet of the British royal household, so-called because of the laurel wreath awarded to eminent poets in the Graeco-Roman world. Early poets with unofficial status were Chaucer◊, Skelton◊, Spenser◊, Daniel◊, and Jonson◊; the first official title-holder was Dryden◊, whose successors have included many nonentities as well as Thomas Warton◊, Southey◊, Wordsworth◊, Tennyson◊, Alfred Austin◊, Bridges◊, Masefield◊, Cecil Day Lewis◊, Betjeman◊ and Ted Hughes◊. There is a stipend of £70 per annum, plus £27 in lieu of a traditional butt of sack□

poetry the imaginative expression of emotion or thought, its usually metrical form giving it added power, as well as aiding the memory in the days before writing. The chief forms are ***lyric*** the song, sonnet◊, ode◊, elegy◊, and pastoral◊; ***drama and narrative*** ballad◊, lay◊, and epic◊; ***moral*** satire◊ and parody◊; and ***didactic*** expositions of philosophy, religion, and practical subjects such as agriculture, which have been confined to prose since the 18th century□

pogrom Russian 'devastation', massacre, especially of Jews in Russia, often with official connivance, from 1881 until the Revolution□

Poincaré Jules Henri 1854–1912. French mathematician, who developed the theory of differential equations and was a pioneer in Relativity◊ Theory□

Poincaré Raymond Nicolas Landry 1860–1934. French statesman, a cousin of Jules Henri Poincaré◊, he was prime minister 1912–13, president 1913–20, and again prime minister 1922–4 (when he occupied the Ruhr◊) and 1926–9□

poinsettia winter flowering plant, family Euphorbiaceae, with small, greenish yellow flowers surrounded by large vermilion, pink or white bracts. The ***Mexican flame-leaf*** *Euphorbia pulcherrima* is also known as the Christmas flower and Flower of the Holy Night□

Pointe Noire chief port of the Congo; population 185 100□

pointillism style of painting (also Neo-impressionism) in dabs of pure colour, merging into harmonious tones at a distance. See Seurat◊ and Signac◊□

poisons substances applied to or introduced into the body which endanger health or life, irrespective of temperature or mechanical action. The effects may be corrosive (e.g. acids) which burn and destroy on contact; irritant (e.g. chlorine◊); narcotic◊ (e.g. opium◊ and its derivatives); destructive of the normal function of the blood (e.g. carbon monoxide) or that of the nerves (e.g. nerve gases used in warfare, such as the derivatives of phosphoric acid); or produce proliferative changes in the system (e.g. paraquat◊)□

Poitiers capital of Poitou-Charentes, France; population 85 466. Clovis◊ defeated Alaric◊ here 507; Charles Martel◊ stemmed the Saracen◊ advance 732, and Edward the Black◊ Prince defeated the French 1356□

Poitou-Charentes region of W Central France; capital Poitiers; population 1 568 230□

poker card game of US origin, in which two to eight people play (usually for stakes), and try to obtain a hand of five cards ranking higher than those of their opponents. The one with the best scoring hand wins the central pool□

Poland People's Republic of

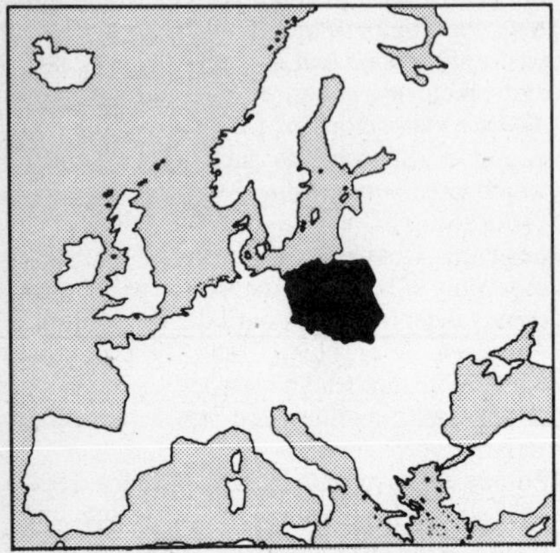

area 312 600 sq km/120 600 sq mi
capital Warsaw
towns Lódź, Kraków, Wroclaw, Poznań, Katowice, Bydgoszcz; Lublin; ports are Gdánsk, Szczecin, Gdynia
features comprises part of the great plain of Europe; Vistula, Oder and Neisse rivers; Sudeten, Tatra and Carpathian mountains; 'Black Madonna' at Czestochowa◊
exports coal, softwood timber, chemicals, machinery, ships
currency zloty
population 36 887 000
language Polish, a member of the western branch of the Slavonic family
religion Roman Catholicism 93%, actively practised
famous people Pope John Paul◊ II, Andrzej Wajda◊, Czeslaw Milosz◊, Joseph Conrad◊, Jerzy Andrzejewski◊, Chopin◊, Witold Lutoslawski◊, Krzystof Penderecki◊, Wit Stwosz (see Veit Stoss◊)□
government under the modified constitution of 1976, the nominal Head of State is the Chairman of the Council of State, elected by the Sejm (Parliament), itself elected by universal suffrage. Real power lies with the First Secretary of the Politburo (General Wojciech Jaruzelski from 1981, who is also Prime Minister and Minister of Defence)
recent history first united in the 10th century, Poland was a great power under the Jagellion◊ dynasty 1386–1572. There was then a decline under elected kings, although Stephen Bathory◊ defeated Ivan◊ the Terrible of Russia in 1581 and in 1683 John III◊ Sobieski vanquished the Turks and forced them to raise their siege of Vienna. In the 18th century the country was partitioned among Russia, Austria and Prussia 1772, 1793 and 1795, despite a patriotic rising by Tadeusz Kosciuszko◊, but in 1918 once more became an independent republic under Pilsudski◊, and the Curzon◊ Line frontier was adopted. Despite an Anglo-French pact in 1939 to assist Poland, there was an invasion by Germany on 3rd Sept which precipitated World◊ War II, and Russia then also invaded Poland from the east. Entirely occupied by Russian troops in 1945, Poland became a Soviet satellite with the restored Oder-Neisse frontier again, but unrest (1956, 1970, 1976) culminated in strikes and the foundation of the independent trade union Solidarnosc (Solidarity) in 1980, headed by Lech Walesa◊. The government ob5Yeted to its political role, and though martial law (Dec 1981–Jul 1983) ended, it was replaced by harsh legislation□

polar bear a large white bear◊ living at the North Pole□

polarized light is that in which the electric vibrations, which in ordinary unpolarized light occur in all directions at right angles to the direction of travel, are confined to just one direction, e.g. by passage through a plastic containing special long aligned molecules. This has the effect of reducing glare from horizontal surfaces, hence its use in polarizing sunglasses□

Poldhu site overlooking Mount's Bay, Cornwall, preserved by the National Trust, where the first transatlantic radio signal was sent by Marconi◊ to Newfoundland 12 Dec 1901. It became a commercial station 1905, and its programme broadcasting in 1920 led to the establishment of the British Broadcasting Corporatation 1922□

Pole Reginald 1500–58. English cardinal from 1536, who returned from Rome to England on the accession of Mary as Papal legatee to readmit England to the Catholic church, and succeeded Cranmer◊ as Archbishop of Canterbury 1556□

polecat a type of weasel◊□

poles
geographic the north and south points of penetration of the earth's surface by the axis about which it revolves. The USA maintains a high-altitude 2800 m/9200 ft geophysical research station under a geodesic dome at the South Pole.
magnetic the points where the 'dip' of a magnetic needle is 90° (at the Equator it is 0°); see magnetism◊. These points are variable (not coinciding with the geographical poles),

e.g. in 1985 the magnetic north Pole was c350 km/218 mi north west of Resolute Bay in the Northwest Territories. It moves northwards c10 km/6 mi each year, though it can vary in a day about 80 km/50 mi from its average position. It is relocated every decade in order to update navigational charts. Periodically changes within earth's core cause a reversal of the magnetic poles (the last occasion was c700 000 years ago)□

Pole Star see under stars◊□

police civil law and order force. In the UK it is under the Home Office, with 56 autonomous police forces, generally speaking organised on a 'county' basis; mutual aid is given in circumstances such as mass picketing in the 1984–5 miners' strike, but there is no 'national police force' or 'police riot unit' (such as the French CRS riot squad). The predecessors of these forces were the ineffective medieval 'watch' and London's Bow◊ Street Runners, introduced 1749 by Henry Fielding◊ (as JP for Westminster), which formed a model for the London police force established by Peel◊'s government 1829 (hence 'peelers' or 'bobbies'); the system was introduced throughout the country from 1856. Subsequent landmarks include: ***Criminal Investigation Department*** detective branch of the London Metropolitan Police (New Scotland Yard) 1878, recruited from the uniformed branch (such departments now exist in all UK forces); women police 1919; motor-cycle patrols 1921; two-way radio cars 1927; personal radio on the beat 1965; ***Special Patrol Groups*** (SPG) 1970, squads of experienced men concentrating on a specific problem (New York has a similar Tactical Patrol Force); unlike most other police forces, the British are armed only on special occasions, but arms issues grow more frequent. Foreign police forces include the Carabinieri (Italy), Civil Guards (Spain), Police Nationale under the Ministry of the Interior for the cities, and gendarmerie (part of the army) elsewhere (France)□

poliomyelitis viral inflammation of the anterior horn cells of the spinal cord (governing muscle action), causing paralysis, especially in children. It has been practically eliminated by the use of vaccines, the first developed by Salk◊□

Polish see under Poland◊□

Polish Corridor strip of land, designated under the Treaty of Versailles◊ to give Poland access to the Baltic, and which cut off E Prussia from the rest of Germany. It was absorbed when Poland took over the southern part of E Prussia in 1945□

Politburo contraction of 'political bureau', a sub-committee (known as the Praesidium 1952–66) of the Central Committee of the Communist Party in the USSR, and some other communist states, which lays down party policy□

Polk James Knox 1795–1849. Democrat president of the USA 1845–9, who admitted Texas to the Union, and forced the war on Mexico which resulted in the annexation of California and New Mexico□

polka Bohemian folk dance in lively 2/4 time originating c1830, which became fashionable in European society□

pollack see under cod◊□

Pollaiuolo Antonio 1429–98. Italian sculptor-engraver, who worked with Ghiberti◊ on the doors of the Baptistery◊, Florence, and also painted, e.g. *Martyrdom of St Sebastian,* National Gallery, London□

Pollock Jackson 1912–56. American artist, the originator of 'action painting', i.e. paint thrown or dribbled on to a surface, use of jewel colours and metal paints, and violent freedom of expression□

pollution effect on the environment of by-products of all industrial, agricultural and living processes, e.g. noise, smoke, gases, chemical effluents in seas and rivers, indestructible pesticides, sewage and household waste, and also of natural disasters, e.g. ash from volcanic activity□

Polo Marco c1254–1324. Venetian traveller. He allegedly travelled overland to China 1271–5, where he claimed to have been a favourite of Kublai◊ Khan, whom he served until he returned to Europe by sea 1292–5. He was then captured while fighting for Venice against Genoa, and in prison wrote an account of his travels. However, modern scholars suspect that he may never even have reached China, and that the reliable and valuable material in his narrative derives from conversations with merchants who had been there□

polo game played between two teams of four on horseback, which originated in Iran, spread to the East and India, and was first played in England 1869, where the rules were evolved by Hurlingham Club 1875. A game lasts about an hour, divided into 'chukkas' of 7½ minutes. The small ball is struck with the side of a mallet through goals at each end of the ground. Famous surviving clubs are Roehampton, and Cowdray Park, but the game is most popular in Argentina□

polonaise 16th-century Polish dance in stately 3/4 time, developed by Chopin◊ as a musical form□

polonium element
symbol Po
atomic number 94

physical description exists only in minute quantities
features radioactive; the largest number of isotopes of any element
uses potential use as a lightweight power source in satellites□

Poltava industrial city (food-processing and light industry) in the Ukraine, USSR; population 290 000. Peter◊ the Great defeated Charles◊ XII of Sweden here in 1709□

poltergeist German 'noisy ghost', alleged to move objects or hurl them about, start fires, etc. See parapsychology◊□

polyandry the practice of a woman having more than one husband at the same time. See under marriage◊□

polyanthus a type of primrose◊□

Polybius c201–120BC. Greek historian whose 40-volume *History of Rome* survives only in part; he was present with his friend Scipio◊ at the destruction of Carthage◊□

polyester complex compound of hydrocarbons, used in making synthetiuc fibres. See under plastics◊□

polyethylene a type of polythene. See under plastics◊□

polygamy the practice of a man having more that one wife at the same time. See under marriage◊□

polygraph instrument ('lie detector') which records on graphs thoracic and abdominal respiration, blood pressure, pulse rate and galvanic skin response. The reactions are supposed to show the degree of psychological stress prompted by a question, but much depends on the skill of the interviewer and his interpretation of the graphs□

Polyhymnia in Greek mythology, the Muse◊ of singing, mime and sacred dance□

polymerization chemical union of many (usually small) molecules, to form a new compound of larger molecular weight, either natural (e.g. cellulose) or synthetic (e.g. polythene and nylon), by:
addition simple multiples of the same compound
condensation union by the elimination of water
co-polymerization in which the polymer is built up from two or more different molecules□

Polynesia those islands of Oceania◊ east of 170° E latitude, including Hawaii◊, Kiribats◊, Tuvalu◊, Fiji◊, Tonga◊, Tokelau◊, Samoa◊, Cook◊ Islands, and French◊ Polynesia
Polynesians who including the Maori◊ of New Zealand, are probably of Asiatic origin, and are distinct from the Negroid Melanesians◊, with whom there has been a degree of mixture. Tall, brown-skinned, and with wavy hair, they are of fine physique, with great skill in carving, navigation, house and boat-building□

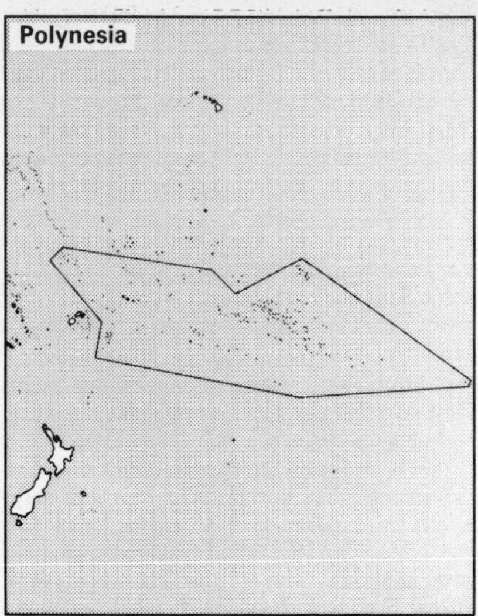

Polynesia French. See French◊ Polynesia□

polypus small 'stalked' benign tumour, most usually found on mucous membrane of the nose, bowel, etc. They are usually removed to avoid their later becoming cancerous□

polysaccharides carbohydrates (cellulose, glycogen, starch etc.) containing linked simple sugars (saccharides), which are energy-rich and 'body-building' for both animals and plants□

polystyrene a synthetic polymer. See under plastics◊□

polytechnic institution for further education up to degree level, mainly in technology. Most famous is the Regent Street Polytechnic, London, founded by Sir George Cayley◊ 1838, and reconstituted by Quintin Hogg◊ 1882□

polytheism the practise of worshipping many gods. See under God◊□

polythene a synthetic polymer. See under plastics◊□

polyurethane a synthetic polymer. See under plastics◊□

polyvinyl chloride a synthetic polymer. See under plastics◊□

pomegranate semi-tropical tree *Punica granatum* with a yellow fruit containing many seeds, each with a juicy edible outer seed-coat□

Pomerania former German province (German *Pommern*, Polish *Pomorze*) on the south shore of the Baltic, which under the Potsdam agreement 1945 was divided between E Germany and Poland. See 'lost territories' under Germany◊□

Pommern see Pomerania◊□

Pomona Roman goddess of fruit trees□

Pomorze see Pomerania◊□

Pompadour Jeanne Antoinette Poisson, Marquise de 1721–64. Mistress of Louis◊ XV from 1744, who promoted his substitution of an anti-Prussian for an anti-Austrian policy. She was patroness of Voltaire◊, Diderot◊, etc.□

Pompeii Roman port and pleasure resort south east of Naples, which was buried and largely preserved beneath lava when Vesuvius◊ erupted 79AD, 2000 people being killed. It was rediscovered 1748, and excavation continues□

Pompey the Great (Gnaeus Pompeius Magnus), 106–48BC. Roman soldier-statesman. Originally a supporter of Sulla◊ and the aristocratic party, he joined the democrats when he became consul with Crassus◊ in 70. He conquered Mithridates◊ of Pontus, and annexed Syria and Palestine. In 60 he formed the First Triumvirate with Caesar◊ (whose daughter Julia◊ he married) and Crassus◊, and when it broke down after 53, he returned to the aristocratic party. On the outbreak of civil war in 49 he withdrew to Greece, was defeated by Caesar at Pharsalia in 48, and was murdered in Egypt□

Pompidou Georges 1911–74. French statesman. A supporter of de Gaulle◊, he became premier 1962. When students and workers rioted 1968, he negotiated peace, and was forced into resignation after the Gaullist election victory of 1968. He succeeded de Gaulle as president 1969–74□

Ponce industrial port (textiles, sugar, rum) in S Puerto Rico, named after Ponce de León◊; population 189 000□

Ponce de León Juan 1460–1521. Spanish soldier-explorer, who sailed with Columbus◊ in 1493, conquered Puerto Rico 1508, and discovered Florida 1512 (believing it to be an island where the Fountain of Youth might be found). He died from an Indian arrow wound□

Pondicherry former French possession, a Union Territory of India from 1954; population 604 135. Capital Pondicherry city□

pond-skater see under hemiptera◊□

pondweed genus *Potamogeton* of aquatic plants, family Potamogetonaceae, with creeping rhizomes and small spikes of flowers□

Ponta Delgada port, resort and chief commercial centre of the Azores◊, on Sã Miguel; population 21 500□

Pontefract market town in W Yorkshire, England; population 31 500. The ruined Norman castle was built 1069, and it is here Richard◊ II was put to death. ***Pontefract*** or *Pomfret cakes* are small rounds of sweetened liquorice confectionery□

Pontiac c1720–69. American Indian Ottawa chieftain, leader of the ***Conspiracy of Pontiac*** 1763–6, when (with other groups) he rebelled against British encroachment on Indian lands□

Pontine Marshes see under Lazio◊□

Pontus kingdom of NE Asia Minor on the Black Sea from c300–65BC when its greatest ruler, Mithridates◊ VI was defeated by Pompey◊□

Pontypool industrial town (glass, synthetic textiles) in Gwent, Wales; population 36 800□

Pontypridd industrial town (chain and cable works, light industry on the Treforest trading estate) in Mid Glamorgan, Wales; population 34 500□

pony a small horse◊□

poodle a type of dog◊□

pool a form of snooker◊□

Poole industrial port (chemicals, engineering, boat-building, confectionery), yachting centre and resort, Dorset, England; population 122 700. Fine quality Poole pottery tableware is made of local clay. The first Boy Scout camp was held in 1907 on Brownsea Island in the harbour□

Poona see Pune◊□

Poor Law system in England from 1572 of raising a parish rate for the building of poorhouses, relief of the destitute and the aged, and apprenticing pauper children. From 1834 it was reorganised with boards of guardians elected by the ratepayers. Relief of the able-bodied, except within a workhouse (where conditions were deliberately made repellent) was forbidden, and the basis of administration continued until the Minister of Health, operating through county and county borough councils, took over in 1929. After World War II a series of administrative reorganisations ended in 1968 with the creation of the Department of Health and Social Security, but the system of reliefs remained so complex as to be difficult to understand, and sometimes unfair in its consequences□

pop art movement of the late 1950s, so-named by critic Lawrence Alloway because it gives a direct and representational response to items from advertising (e.g. soup tins), comics, television and films, which form popular culture. Artists associated include Andy Warhol, Richard Hamilton, and Roy Lichtenstein□

Pope the Bishop of Rome as head of the Catholic church, which claims him as the spiritual descendant of St Peter◊, who first held the office after being entrusted by Christ with the 'keys' of the Church. This primacy was never universally acknowledged, e.g. the breakaway of Constantinople◊ 1054. Through the medieval period the Papacy developed its temporal power, reaching its height in the 11–13th centuries (Gregory◊ VII and Innocent◊ III), but came under French control (headquarters Avignon rather than Rome) 1309–78, 'the Babylonian Captivity'. The 'Great Schism' followed, with rival Popes at Avignon and Rome 1378–1417; Papal political power further declined with the withdrawal of allegiance by the Protestant states at the Reformation◊, and by 1929 the Lateran Treaty recognized Papal territorial sovereignty even in Italy only within the Vatican City (see Papal◊ States). However, the 16–17th century Counter-Reformation revived Papal spiritual influence and at the Vatican Council 1870 the doctrine of Papal infallibility was proclaimed. Elected by the Sacred College of Cardinals, a Pope dates his pontificate from his coronation with the tiara, or triple crown, at St Peter's, Rome, and has (since the Second Vatican Council 1962–6) an episcopal synod of 200 bishops elected by local hierarchies to collaborate in the government of the Church. Under John◊ Paul II, however, power has been more centralized, and bishops and cardinals have been chosen from the more traditionally-minded clerics, and also often from the Third World. In 1982 a commission of both the Catholic and Anglican churches agreed that in any union between them, the Pope would be 'universal primate'□

Pope Alexander 1688–1744. British poet. As a Catholic he was subject to discrimination, and his life was embittered by the personal deformity which made him the butt of his opponents. He established his reputation with precocious *Pastorals* 1709 and *Essay on Criticism* 1711, which were followed by a superb parody of the heroic epic *The Rape of the Lock* 1712–14, and the romantically-tinged *Windsor Forest* 1713, 'Elegy to the Memory of an Unfortunate Lady' and 'Eloisa to Abelard' 1717. The success of a very 18th-century translation of Homer◊'s *Iliad* and *Odyssey* 1715–26, made it possible for him to settle on a miniature 'landscape garden' estate at Twickenham◊ from 1719, but his edition of Shakespeare attracted scholarly ridicule, for which he revenged himself by a satire on scholarly dullness, the *Dunciad* 1728. A venture into philosophy, in his *An Essay on Man* 1733–4 and *Moral Essays* 1731–5, was influenced by Bolingbroke◊. His finest mature productions are his *Imitations of the Satires of Horace* 1733–38, and his personal letters, which he judiciously 'improved' before publication. The beloved friend of Swift◊, Arbuthnot◊, and Gay◊, he is the master of 'what oft was thought, but ne'er so well expressed', and creator of the perfectly balanced heroic couplet□

Popish plot see Titus Oates◊□

poplar deciduous trees of the northern temperate hemisphere, family Salicaceae, which bear catkins followed by fruit in which the seeds are clothed in white down, hence the US name 'cottonwood'. They include ***aspen*** *Populus tremula* of which the hanging leaves tremble in the slightest wind; ***cottonwood*** *P deltoides* and ***Lombardy poplar*** *P italica*□

pop music modern popular music, a phenomenon of the boom, post-World War II, in teenage high-spenders and the electronic media, and symbolized by the new electronic instrument, the guitar:

rock and roll had its roots in the blues (see jazz◊), noted exponents being Chuck Berry◊ and Bill Haley◊ and the Comets. Elvis Presley◊ was the giant of this era. Rock has continued to splinter and variegate, e.g. the New Romanticism of Boy◊ George in female dress in the 1980s.

the Mersey Beat or ***Liverpool Sound*** partly inspired by rock and roll and partly by English and Irish folk tradition, is synonymous with the Beatles◊. It was associated with 'dropping out', seeking religion in the East rather than the West, and drug-taking.

the 'message' combined with tattered jeans or muumuus, became all important in the early 1960s with stars such as Bob Dylan◊, Joan Baez◊; talk taking over from song.

country and western grew from American 'folk', especially in Nashville◊, Tennessee since the 1940s and 50s. Famous singers include Hank Williams and Johnny Cash.

rhythm and blues brought a more earthy rebellion than the shampooed Beatles in the 1970s, with the Rolling Stones, paradoxically from the 'soft' South of England rather than the 'hard' North (see Mick Jagger◊).

soul derived even more patently from the blues, e.g. Ray Charles 1930– and Aretha Franklin 1942– .

psychedelic pop from 1967, with a flowering of advanced electronic equipment for both light and sound, leading by 1980 to the spectacular stage performance of Pink◊ Floyd in *The Wall* with a story line and modern rock.

reggae linked with black Africa (and Rastafarianism◊) in its musical themes, heavy

rhythms, and overwhelming sound; it spread with the sect, becoming a white cult in the 1970s. See Bob Marley◊.
punk American 'rotten' rock 1976/7, which returned to its unsophisticated origins, and in Britain was associated with unnaturally coloured hair in spiky styles, torn clothes and safety-pins, e.g. the Sex Pistols◊□
reggae see pop◊ music
Popocatépetl volcano (Aztec 'smoking mountain') in Mexico, south east of Mexico City; 5340 m/17 520 ft, with snow-clad summit□
Popov Alexander 1859–1905. Russian physicist, who devised the first aerial in advance of Marconi◊, but did not use it for radio communication□
Popper Sir Karl 1902–. Austrian-born British philosopher, author of *Logic of Scientific Discovery* 1934, which emphasized the conjectural nature of scientific discovery, the conjecture being then tested by attempts to prove it false ('empirical falsification' rather than 'verification')□
poppy temperate and sub-tropical plants, family Papaveraceae, with large showy flowers, including the ***corn poppy*** *Papaver rhoeas*. See opium◊□
popular front see under International◊□
porcelain see pottery◊□
porcupine a member of the rodent◊ order, with sharp quills on its body□
porcupine fish see under tetraodon◊□
Pori ice-free industrial port (nickel and copper refining, sawmills, paper, textiles) in SW Finland; population 79 000□
pornography literature, pictures, photos, films, etc., intended to arouse sexual desire, and in the case of 'hard' pornography, desire of a perverted kind. Standards are subjective as to what is offensive, hence the difficulty in agreement on lines of censorship□
porphyria rare hereditary metabolic disorder, known as the 'royal disease' because sufferers included Mary◊ Queen of Scots, James◊ I, and (controversially) George◊ III, which may cause mental confusion. Other symptoms, e.g. growth of hair, contraction of muscles to reveal the teeth, sensitivity to sunlight, and a need for sufferers to take blood from others to replace missing constituents in their own, has been suggested as the basis for vampirism and werewolf legends□
porphyry any rock composed of large crystals in a purplish matrix□
porpoise small, squat dolphin without a 'beak', the smallest of the Cetaceans◊. The ***common porpoise*** *Phocoena*, family Phocoenidae, is black above, white below and 1.8 m/5 ft long, and feeds on fish□
Porsche Ferdinand 1875–1951. German car designer, e.g. the People's Car (Volkswagen) for Hitler, actually only marketed after World War II, and Porsche sports cars□
Porson Richard 1759–1808. British classical scholar, professor of Greek at Cambridge from 1792 and editor of Aeschylus◊ and Euripides◊□
port wine sweet, fortified (with brandy) dessert wine (red, tawny, or white), from grapes grown in the Douro basin of Portugal and exported from Oporto, hence the name□
Port Adelaide chief port of S Australia, near Adelaide, with cement and chemical industries; population 40 000□
Port-au-Prince capital and industrial port (sugar, rum, textiles, plastics) of Haiti; population 458 700□
Port Elizabeth industrial port (chemicals, glass, electrical goods, car assembly) in Cape Province, S Africa; population 492 140. Founded in 1820, it was named after the wife of the Cape governor□
Porter Cole 1893–1964. American composer and lyricist of musical comedies, born in Indiana, e.g. *Gay Divorce* 1932, *Kiss Me Kate*, 1948, High Society 1956; his autobiography *Night and Day* took the title of his best-known song□
Porter Katherine Anne 1890–1980. American short-story writer, born in Texas, e.g. *Flowering Judas* 1930 and *Pale Horse, Pale Rider* 1939□
Porter Rodney Robert 1917–85. British biochemist, Nobel prizewinner (with G M Edelmann◊) 1972 for pioneering work on the chemical structure of antibodies◊□
Port Harcourt industrial port (exporting coal, tin and palm oil) in E Nigeria; population 242 000□
Port Klang rubber port in peninsular Malaysia (formerly Port Swettenham); population 114 000□
Portland William Bentinck, 1st Earl of Portland c1649–1709. Dutch statesman who accompanied William◊ of Orange to England 1688, and was created an earl 1689. He served in William's campaigns, and negotiated the Treaty of Ryswick◊ and the Partition◊ Treaties□
Portland William Henry Cavendish Bentinck, 3rd Duke of Portland 1738–1809. British statesman, originally a Whig◊, who in 1783 became nominal prime minister in the Fox◊-North◊ coalition government. During the French◊ Revolution he joined the Tories◊, and was prime minister 1807–9□
Portland industrial and timber-exporting port in Maine, USA; population 61 800. Longfellow was born here□

Portland major inland port on the Columbia, 173 km/108 mi from the sea, in Oregon, USA; population 366 500. Industries include aluminium smelting, paper, timber, lumber machinery, electronics□
Portland Isle of. Rocky 'island' off Dorset, England, joined to the mainland by the Chesil◊ Bank. Portland Castle was built by Henry◊ VIII 1520, and fine building stone is quarried□
Portmeirion see under Gwynedd◊ and Williams-Ellis◊□
Port Moresby capital and port of Papua New Guinea; population 123 625. The University of Papua New Guinea, 1965, is here□
Pôrto Alegre industrial port (chemicals, meat-packing, textiles, tanning) at the head of a tidal lake (Lago dos Patos) in SE Brazil; population 1 115 000□
Port-of-Spain port and capital of Trinidad and Tobago; population 55 800□
Porto Novo capital of Benin◊; population 132 000□
Port Phillip Bay inlet off Bass Strait, Victoria, Australia, on which Melbourne stands□
Port Pirie industrial port (smelting of ores from the Broken Hill mines, and chemicals) in S Australia; population 16 500□
Port Royal see under Jansenism◊□
Port Royal former pirate city. See Jamaica◊□
Port Said port on reclaimed land at the north end of the Suez◊ Canal; population 262 760□
Portsmouth Louise de Kéroualle, Duchess of Portsmouth 1649–1734. Mistress of Charles◊ II, a Frenchwoman who came to England as Louis◊ XIV's agent 1670, and was popularly hated□
Portsmouth industrial (high technology, etc.) and Channel ferry port and naval base on Portsea Island in Hampshire, England; population 179 500. Historic ships here include HMS *Warrior* 1861, the world's first armoured battleship; HMS *Victory* Nelson◊'s flagship at Trafalgar◊ (launched 1765, 2198 tonnes); and the *Mary Rose* warship which capsized 1545 as Henry◊ VIII watched from Southsea Castle. The D-Day invasion fleet sailed from here in 1944. The Royal Naval and Royal Marine museums are here, and the birthplace of Dickens◊ is preserved. The roadstead of Spithead is famous for naval reviews. Gosport (also a naval port) on the west of the harbour entrance, is linked with Portsmouth by ferry□
Portsmouth naval port in Virginia, USA; population 104 600. It developed from a naval yard established by the British□
Port Swettenham see Port◊ Klang□
Port Talbot port, with tinplate and steel strip mill in W Glamorgan, Wales; population 58 000□
Portugal Republic of

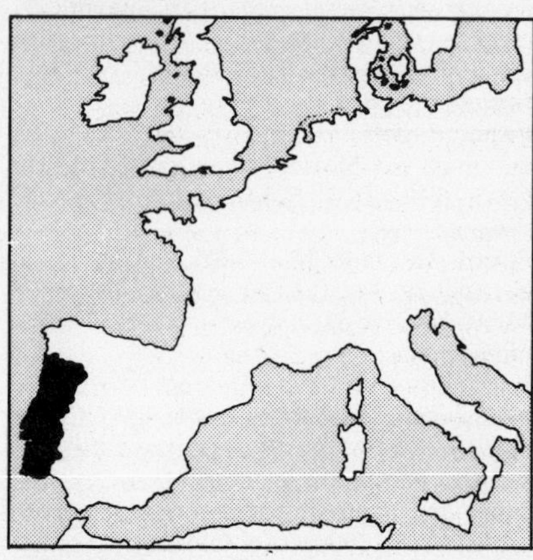

area 91 631 sq km/34 861sq mi (including Azores and Madeira◊)
capital Lisbon
towns Coimbra; and the ports Oporto, Setúbal
features rivers Minho, Douro, Tagus, Guadiana; Serra da Estrélla in the north
exports port wine, olive oil, resin, cork; sardines; textiles, pottery, pulpwood
currency escudo
population 10 045 000
language Portuguese, one of the Romance languages, ultimately derived from Latin, but considerably influenced later by Arabic. See also Lusophone◊ nations
religion Roman Catholicism
famous people Vasco da Gama◊, Pedro Cabral◊, Camöens◊, Marianna Alcoforado◊□
government president (Dr Mario Soares from 1986), a corporative chamber and national assembly (Prime Minister Aníbal Caraço e Silva, Social Democrat, from 1985)
recent history independent of León◊ from the capture of Lisbon by Alfonso◊ I in 1147. The Moors◊ were finally expelled by Alfonso◊ III in the 14th century, and in 1373 Portugal established an alliance with England that still survives. In the 15th century her seamen explored the African coast, opened the sea route to India, and discovered Brazil, establishing a great sea-borne empire. In 1580 Philip◊ II of Spain seized the crown but by 1668 Portugal had once more forced recognition of her independence. A French invasion in 1807 was followed by the Peninsular◊ War. In 1910 Portugal became a republic, and, though neutral in World War II gave Britain

air base facilities (under the 1373 treaty) in the Azores. In 1932 Salazar◊ had established a semi-Fascist dictatorship, but this was undermined by his incapacity in 1968, and peacefully overthrown in 1974. An alternation of Socialist and Centre Right (Social Democrat, Centre Democrat, Popular Monarchist) coalitions ensued. Portugal retains Macao◊, but her other imperial possessions (see Angola◊, Cape Verde◊, Brazil◊, Goa◊, Mozambique◊, Guinea-Bissau◊, São Tomé e Principe◊) have all achieved independence. Portugal entered the Common Market 1986□

Portuguese see under Portugal◊□

Portuguese East Africa see Mozambique◊□

Portuguese Guinea see Guinea-Bissau◊□

Portuguese man-of-war see under Coelenterata◊□

Portuguese West Africa see Angola◊□

Poseidon Greek god (Roman Neptune), the brother of Zeus◊ and Pluto◊. The brothers dethroned their father, Cronos◊, and divided his realm, Poseidon taking the sea, and being also worshipped as god of earthquakes (see Troy◊). See also Triton◊□

Posen see Poznan◊□

Positivism philosophical system devised by Comte◊. In the 1920s ***Logical Positivism*** developed from it, limiting knowledge to 'only empirically verifiable observations' and confining all statements to those of formal logic or mathematics. See Carnap◊, Mach◊□

postal service the system for delivering mail. In Britain regular permanent systems were not created until the modern nation state, e.g. Henry◊ VIII in 1516 appointed Sir Brian Tuke as Master of the Posts, to maintain a regular service on the main roads from London. Postmasters (usually innkeepers) passed the mail to the next post, and supplied horses for the royal couriers; private people wishing to send letters or to travel themselves 'post haste' were permitted to use the service. Private services were discouraged as losing revenue for the state service and assisting treasonable activities, the latter point being stressed by the act establishing the Post Office, passed under Cromwell◊ in 1657. Mail coaches first ran in 1784, and in 1840 Rowland Hill's prepaid penny postage stamp, for any distance within the UK, led to a massive increase in use. Services were extended to registered post 1841; post boxes 1855 (see Anthony Trollope◊); savings bank 1861; postcards 1870; postal orders 1881, parcel post 1883, air mail 1911, telephone 1912, data processing by computer 1967, and giro 1968. In 1969 the original General Post Office ceased to be a government department, and was split into two, the Post Office and British◊ Telecom. International co-operation is through the Universal Postal Union, 1875, at Berne□

poster advertising announcement for public display, often illustrated, first produced in modern form in France from the mid-19th century, when colour lithography came into its own, with the work of Jules Chéret 1836–1932 from 1858. Later artists include Millais◊, the Austrian 'Secessionist' artist Koloman Moser◊; Toulouse-Lautrec◊, Edward McKnight Kauffer◊, the Beggarstaff◊ Brothers (see Sir William Nicholson◊), Charles Dana Gibson◊□

Post-impressionism styles of painting which moved away from naturalistic impression of the fleeting moment to infuse a greater degree of subjective emotion, or distort for the sake of design effect. The term was first used by Roger Fry◊ of the work of Cézanne◊, Van Gogh◊, and Gauguin◊ 1911□

post-traumatic stress Vietnam War equivalent of World War I 'shell shock' and World War II 'combat fatigue'; its victims suffer from mental flashbacks to wartime experiences, accompanied by feelings of helplessness and guilt□

potassium element
symbol K
atomic number 19
physical description silvery-white soft metal
features reacts with water and oxidizes in air; the element is therefore stored in oil
uses mainly in fertilizers□

potato perennial *Solanum tuberosum* family Solanaceae◊, with edible tuberous roots, bred by the Andean Indians for 5000 years to eliminate bitterness and toxicity. It was introduced to Europe by the mid-16th century, and to England by Sir Walter Raleigh◊ in 1586. The roots also yield alcohol (see poteen◊). The Irish ***potato famine*** of 1845, caused by a parasitic fungus, led to large-scale emigration to the USA. See also ***sweet potato*** under convolvulus◊□

Potchefstroom oldest town in the Transvaal, S Africa, founded by Boers◊ trekking from the Cape 1838; population 60 000□

poteen Irish alcoholic liquor traditionally made from potatoes, or barley and yeast, in illicit stills. It is so potent that the drinker may remain drunk for days after a session, though drinking only water□

Potemkin Grigory Aleksandrovich 1739–91. Russian statesman, favourite of Catherine◊ II, and her lifelong friend. He was an able administrator, reforming army commander (first Turkish War 1745–7), builder of the Black Sea fleet, conqueror of the Crimea◊, and developer of S Russia□

'Potemkin' battleship of the Russian Black Sea fleet. Its crew backed the workers in the 1905 revolution. See Eisenstein◊□

Potomac river flowing through Washington, DC, USA; length 459 km/285 mi□

Potosi tin and silver-mining town in SW Bolivia, 4020 m/13 189 ft above sea level; population 77 250□

pot pourri mixture of dried flowers and leaves, e.g. rose petals, lavender, verbena, etc., used to scent the air□

Potsdam capital of Potsdam district, E Germany; population 133 225. The New Palace 1763–70 and Sans◊ Souci were both built by Frederick◊ the Great, and Hitler's Third Reich was proclaimed in the garrison church 21 Mar 1933□

Potsdam Conference conference Jul 1945 of representatives of Britain, USSR and USA. It established the political and economic principles governing the treatment of Germany in the initial period of Allied control at the end of World War II, and sent the ultimatum to Japan demanding unconditional surrender on pain of utter destruction□

Potter Beatrix 1866–1943. British author and illustrator of children's books, beginning with *Peter Rabbit* 1900; her home at Sawrey in the Lake District is a museum. Her code diaries were published 1966□

Potter Paul 1625–54. Dutch animal painter, son of the landscape painter ***Pieter Potter***□

Potter Stephen 1900–70. British author of humorous studies in *Gamesmanship* 1947, *One Upmanship* 1952, etc.□

Potteries see under Staffordshire◊□

pottery and porcelain ceramics◊ in domestic and ornamental use including:

earthenware made of porous clay and fired, whether unglazed (when it remains porous, e.g. flowerpots, winecoolers) or glazed (most tableware).

stoneware made of non-porous clay with a high silica content, fired at high temperature, which is very hard.

bone china (softpaste) semi-porcelain made of 5% bone ash and china clay (kaolin◊); first made in the West in imitation of Chinese porcelain.

porcelain (hardpaste) so-named from its hardness, ringing sound when struck, translucence, and shining finish, like that of a cowrie shell (Italian *porcellana*); made of kaolin and petuntse (fusible feldspar consisting chiefly of quartz, and reduced to a fine, white powder); first developed in China□

pottery and porcelain history of

BC

10 000 earliest known pottery in Japan

AD

6th century fine quality stoneware developed in China, as the forerunner of porcelain

7–10th century Tang porcelain in China

10–13th century Song porcelain in China

14–17th century Ming porcelain in China Hispano-Moresque ware

16th century

Maiolica Italian tin-glazed earthenware with painted decoration, especially large dishes with figures; ***faience*** (from Faenza◊) name applied both to this and delftware (see below)

17th century

Delftware tin-glazed earthenware brought to perfection in Delft◊, especially the white with blue decoration, also copied in England

18th century

Dresden in 1710 the first European hard-paste porcelain was made by Böttger 1682–1719; the factory later transferred to Meissen.

Sèvres from 1769 hard-paste porcelain as well as soft-paste made at Sèvres◊, remarkable for its ground colours.

Wedgwood c1760 cream-coloured earthenware perfected (superseding delftware) by Wedgwood◊; he also devised stoneware, especially with white decoration in classical designs on a blue ground, still among the wares made at Barlaston, Staffordshire.

English soft-paste made c1745–1810, first at Chelsea: later at Bow, Derby, and Worcester.

English hard-paste first made at Plymouth 1768–70, and Bristol 1770–81, when the stock was removed to New Hall in Staffordshire.

Bone China c1789 first produced by Josiah Spode 1754–1827; Coalport, near Shrewsbury, and Minton◊ (both 1796) similar, and from 1815 all English tableware of this type.

19th century large-scale production of fine wares, notably Royal Worcester from 1862, and Royal (Crown) Derby from 1876.

20th century there has been a revival in the craft of the individual potter, e.g. Bernard Leach, Lucy Rie, Hans Coper◊□

Poulenc Francis 1899–1963. French composer, whose works include the ballet *Les Biches* 1924; and the operas *Les Mamelles de Tirésias* 1947 and *Les Dialogues des Carmélites* 1957□

Poulsen Valdemar 1869–1942. Danish engineer who in 1900 first demonstrated (on steel tape) the magnetic recording of sound□

poultry domesticated birds kept for food and their eggs, especially chicken and turkeys (see under fowl◊), ducks and geese (see under waterfowl◊)□

Pound Sir (Alfred) Dudley Pickman Rogers 1877–1943. British admiral of the fleet, First

Sea Lord and Chief of the British Naval Staff 1939–43; Order of Merit 1943□

Pound Ezra 1885–1972. American poet, who lived in London from 1907, influencing T S Eliot◊, Yeats◊, and Joyce◊, and who, by his verse *Personae* and *Exultations* 1909, established the lines of the Imagist◊ movement. In Paris 1921–5, he was the friend of Gertrude Stein◊ and Hemingway◊, and then settled in Rapallo. His anti-Semitism and sympathy with Mussolini◊ led him to broadcast from Italy in World War II, and he was arrested by US troops 1945. Found unfit to plead, he was confined in a mental hospital until 1958. His first completely 'modern' poem was *Hugh Selwyn Mauberley* 1920, but his biggest was the series of *Cantos* 1925–1969 (intended to number 100), which gave a selective view of history. His 'versions' of Old English, Provençal, Chinese, ancient Egyptian, and other verse, are disapproved of by scholars, but have poetic value□

pound pre-metric ***standard unit of weight*** avoirdupois (UK, USA, Canada, etc.), 0.45 of a kilogram; also the ***British standard monetary unit*** issued as a gold sovereign before 1914, as a note 1914–83, and as a circular yellow metal alloy coin from 1983. (The edge inscriptions are 1983 *Decus et tutamen* An ornament and a safeguard; 1984 (Scottish) *Nemo me impune lacessit* No one injures me with impunity (see Thistle under knighthood◊); 1985 (Welsh) *Pleidiol wyf i'm gwlad* ('True am I to my country', from the national anthem). The ***green pound*** is the Common Market exchange rate for conversion of EEC farm prices to sterling□

Poussin Nicolas 1594–1665. French painter of classical landscapes, historical (*Rape of the Sabines*) and religious subjects (*The Worship of the Golden Calf* c1635), who worked mainly in Rome, except when court painter to Louis◊ XIII 1640–3□

Poverty Bay inlet on the east coast of North Island, New Zealand, on which Gisborne stands. Captain Cook◊ made his first landing here 1769□

Powell Anthony Dymoke 1905– . British novelist, whose chief work is the series of a dozen volumes *A Dance to the Music of Time* 1951–75, which portrays in infinitesimal detail the inter-relationships of Nicholas Jenkins and his circle of upper-class friends, from the 1920s onward□

Powell Cecil Frank 1903–69. British physicist, awarded a Nobel prize 1950 for his development of photographic emulsion as a method of tracking charged nuclear particles□

Powell (John) Enoch 1912– . British politician. professor of Greek at Sydney University, Australia 1937–9, he became Conservative MP for Wolverhampton 1950, was Minister of Health 1960–3, and contested the party leadership 1965. Always controversial, he made a speech on immigration at Birmingham 1968 which led to his dismissal from the shadow cabinet. Declining to stand at the Feb 1974 election, he attacked the Heath◊ government, resigned from the party, and returned to Parliament Oct 1974 as United Ulster Unionist Council member for S Down. As a speaker, he is impressive□

power rate of doing work or of converting energy. Its SI unit is the watt◊(W)□

power boat boat equipped with a hull (sometimes with hydrofoils, jetfoils, etc.) and engine designed for high speed. Race events include the ***American Gold Cup*** 1947, over a 145 km/90 mi course, and the ***Round Britain Race*** 1969□

power of attorney legal authority to act on behalf of another, for specific transactions, for a particular period, etc. It may be given by the elderly who no longer feel competent to handle their own affairs□

Powys John Cowper 1872–1963. British novelist. Born in Derbyshire, he was one of three brothers (***Theodore Francis Powys*** 1875–53 and ***Llewelyn Powys*** 1884–1939), all writers. His mystic and erotic books include *Wolf Solent* 1929 and *A Glastonbury Romance* 1933□

Powys central county of Wales

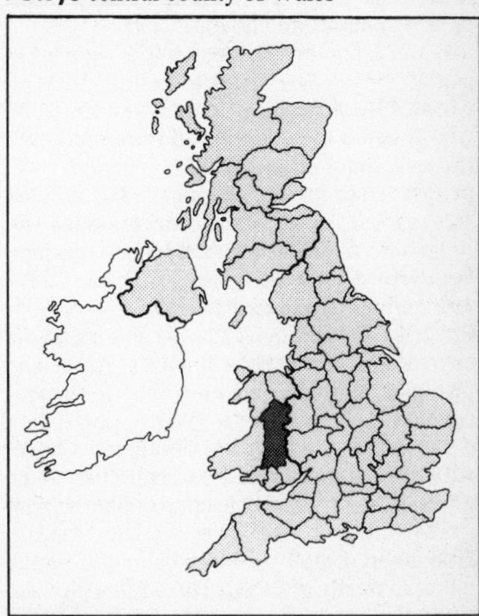

area 5077 sq km/1960 sq mi
towns administrative headquarters Llandrindod Wells

features Brecon Beacons National Park, Black mountains, rivers Wye and Severn, which both rise on Plynlimon (see Dyfed◊); Lake Vyrnwy, artificial reservoir supplying Liverpool and Birmingham, and same size as Lake Bala◊; alternative technology centre near Machynlleth
products mainly agricultural, dairy cattle, sheep
population 111 500
language 20% Welsh-speaking□

Poynter Sir Edward John 1836–1919. British artist, first head of the Slade School, London, 1871–5, and President of the Royal Academy in succession to Millais◊. He produced decorous nudes, mosaic panels for Westminster Palace 1870, etc.□

Poznań industrial city (formerly Posen) in W Poland, making locomotives, farming machinery, precision instruments, aircraft, bicycles, beer; population 866 000. Settled by German immigrants 1253, it passed to Prussia 1793, but was restored to Poland 1919. Hindenburg◊ was born here□

Pozzuoli port in S Italy; former population 60 000. Shaken by some 25 earthquakes a day, some 60% of its buildings are uninhabitable, and an eventual major eruption, as in the case of Pompeii◊, seems inevitable□

Prado see under Madrid◊□

praseodyium element
symbol Pr
atomic number 59
physical description silver-white metal
features member of the lanthanide◊ series; occurs in monazite and bastnasite
uses in carbon-arc lights and as a pigment in glass□

praetor Roman magistrate, elected annually, who assisted the consuls◊ and presided over the civil courts□

pragmatism theory advanced by William James◊ that the truth of a conception may be judged from its bearing upon human conduct. He derived the idea from C S Peirce 1839–1914, who originated it 1878□

Prague capital (Czech *Praha*) and industrial city (cars and aircraft, chemicals, paper and printing, clothing, brewing and food processing) of Czechoslovakia; population 1 182 000. It is a beautiful city on the Vltava, with fine palaces, bridges and churches, and a university founded by Emperor Charles◊ IV in 1438. Since the time of the Austro-Hungarian Empire, it has been the venue quinquennially of the Spartakadia, a physical education spectacle at the Strahov stadium in which 250,000 take part. It was occupied by Germany 1939–45, and Heydrich◊ was assassinated here□

prairie central N American Plains between the Rockies and the Great Lakes and Ohio river, and extending north into Canada. Once grass-covered, they are now a world granary□

prairie dog a burrowing rodent. See marmot◊□

Prâkrit the ancient popular Indian languages, as opposed to Sanskrit◊. In literature they were used in lyric poetry and for some characters in Sanskrit drama□

Prato industrial town (woollens) in central Italy; population 160 220. The 12th-century cathedral has masterpieces by Donatello◊, Filippo Lippi◊, and Andrea Della Robbia◊□

prawn member, together with the shrimp, of the suborder Natantia 'swimming', order Decapoda◊, as contrasted with the lobsters and crayfish, which are able to 'walk':
prawn commercially important is the edible ***common prawn*** *Leander serratus* of temperate seas, which has a long saw-edged spike or rostrum just in front of its eyes, and antennae much longer than its body-length. It is distinguished from the shrimp not only by its larger size, but by having pincers on its second pair of legs. It is a pinkish-orange when cooked. The larger ***Norwegian prawn*** *Nephrops norwegicus* are sold as 'scampi' (from the Italian for shrimp); they are so popular that demand exceeds supply, and 'manufactured scampi' are often sold
shrimp in Europe the marine ***common shrimp*** *Crangon vulgaris* is commercially valuable; it is greenish, semi-transparent, has its first pair of legs ending in pincers, possesses no rostrum, and has comparatively shorter antennae than the prawn, besides being usually much smaller. It is brownish when cooked.
Krill◊, though shrimplike in appearance is not a true shrimp□

Praxiteles 4th century BC. Greek sculptor, who lived at Athens. works includes Hermes carrying Dionysus, and relief of Aphrodite at Cnidus□

prayer address to divine power, ranging from a magical formula to attain a desired end to selfless communication in meditation. Within Christianity the Catholic and Orthodox churches sanction prayer to the Virgin, angels and saints as intercessors, whereas Protestantism limits prayer to the Godhead alone, and does not provide for prayer for the dead, which would imply the existence of Purgatory◊□

predestination the foredetermination by God of all events, including the ultimate destination of the human soul in heaven or hell. The doctrine was upheld by Augine◊ (and by Luther◊ and Calvin◊ in differing degrees), but challenged by Pelagius◊ and Arminius◊□

prefect French government official who, under the centralised Napoleonic system from 1800 to the 1980s, was responsible for enforcing government policy in each *département* and *région*. See government under France◊□

pregnancy period from conception to birth, in humans normally 40 weeks, but up to a fortnight less or more. Menstruation ceases; the breasts enlarge; and there may be 'morning sickness' after six weeks, and unusual cravings or aversions for particular foods, the result of the action of hormones released by the reproductive system. From three months enlargement of the abdomen is rapid; 'quickening', when the movements of the fetus can be felt, occurs usually in the fifth month. Prenatal care is important, and tests may be made to check for any signs of abnormality in the child which suggest the advisability of abortion. See also gestation◊□

prehistory the classification of cultures before the use of writing is still under the system devised 1816 by Christian Thomsen 1788–1865, and is based on the materials used by early man for tools and weapons

Stone age in which flint axes, etc., were predominant, divided into:

Old Stone Age (Palaeolithic), ranging generally 3 500 000BC–5000BC in which the tools were chipped into shape, and which includes Neanderthal◊ and Cromagnon (see under Dordogne◊) man; only dogs were domesticated. Outstanding cave paintings were produced 20 000–8000 years ago notably at Altamira◊ and Lascaux◊, the Central Sahara◊, Bhopal◊ and by the Aboriginals◊ of Australia

Middle Stone Age (Mesolithic) and

New Stone Age (Neolithic) when tools were ground and polished, and agriculture and domestication of cattle, sheep, etc. were practised.

A stone age culture survived in Australia until the arrival of British settlers in the 19th century; see also Irian◊ Jaya, and the Philippines◊, where isolated tribespeople at this stage were found in the 1970s and 1980s.

Bronze Age period of bronze tools and weapons beginning approx 6000BC in the Far East, and continuing in the Middle East until about 1200BC; in Britain it lasted c2000–500BC, and in Africa the transition from stone tools to iron was direct. The heroes of Homer◊ lived in the Bronze Age.

Iron Age period when ironwas hardened by the addition of carbon, so that it superseded bronze for tools and weapons; in the Old World generally, the period from c1000BC. Famous sites include:

La Tène at the east end of Lake Neuchatel, Switzerland, where magnificent swords were recovered; the culture lasted from 5th century BC to the Roman conquest

Maiden Castle Dorset, most imposing of the hilltop settlements of England, built with elaborate wooden houses; cannibalism was practised□

Preminger Otto 1906– . American producer-director, *Margin for Error* 1942, *Carmen Jones* 1954, *The Human Factor* 1979□

Premium Savings Bonds a type of lottery◊□

Pre-Raphaelite Brotherhood founded 1848 by Rossetti◊, Millais◊ and Holman Hunt◊ to abandon the rules of art developed under Raphael◊ for the naturalistic style imagined to have previously existed. It was approved by Ruskin◊, and Burne-Jones◊ and William Morris◊ were influenced by it; it broke up in 1853 when Millais abandoned the technique□

presbyterianism system of church government expounded by John Calvin◊ which gives its name to the established church of Scotland, and is also practised in England, Ireland, Switzerland, USA, etc. There is no compulsory form of worship and each congregation is governed by presbyters or elders (clerical or lay), who are of equal rank, and congregations are grouped in presbyteries, synods◊, and general assemblies□

Prescott William Hickling 1796–1859. American historian, most famous for his accounts of the Spanish conquest of Mexico (1843) and Peru (1847)□

president usual title of the head of state in a republic; powers of the office vary from that of constitutional monarch to head of government as in the USA□

Presidential Medal of Freedom see under medals◊□

Presley Elvis 1935–77. American pop singer, nicknamed 'Elvis the Pelvis' because of his gyrating hip movements. Born in Tupelo, Mississippi, he established himself with a series of rock and roll hits e.g. *Heartbreak Hotel* 1956 and *Hound Dog* and became a cult figure after his death, largely from drugs□

press the news media. See newspapers◊□

Pressburg see Bratislava◊□

Preston industrial port (textiles, chemicals, electrical goods, aircraft) on the Ribble in Lancashire, England; population 126 500□

Prestonpans town in Lothian region, Scotland; population 3100. Prince Charles◊

primate family tree

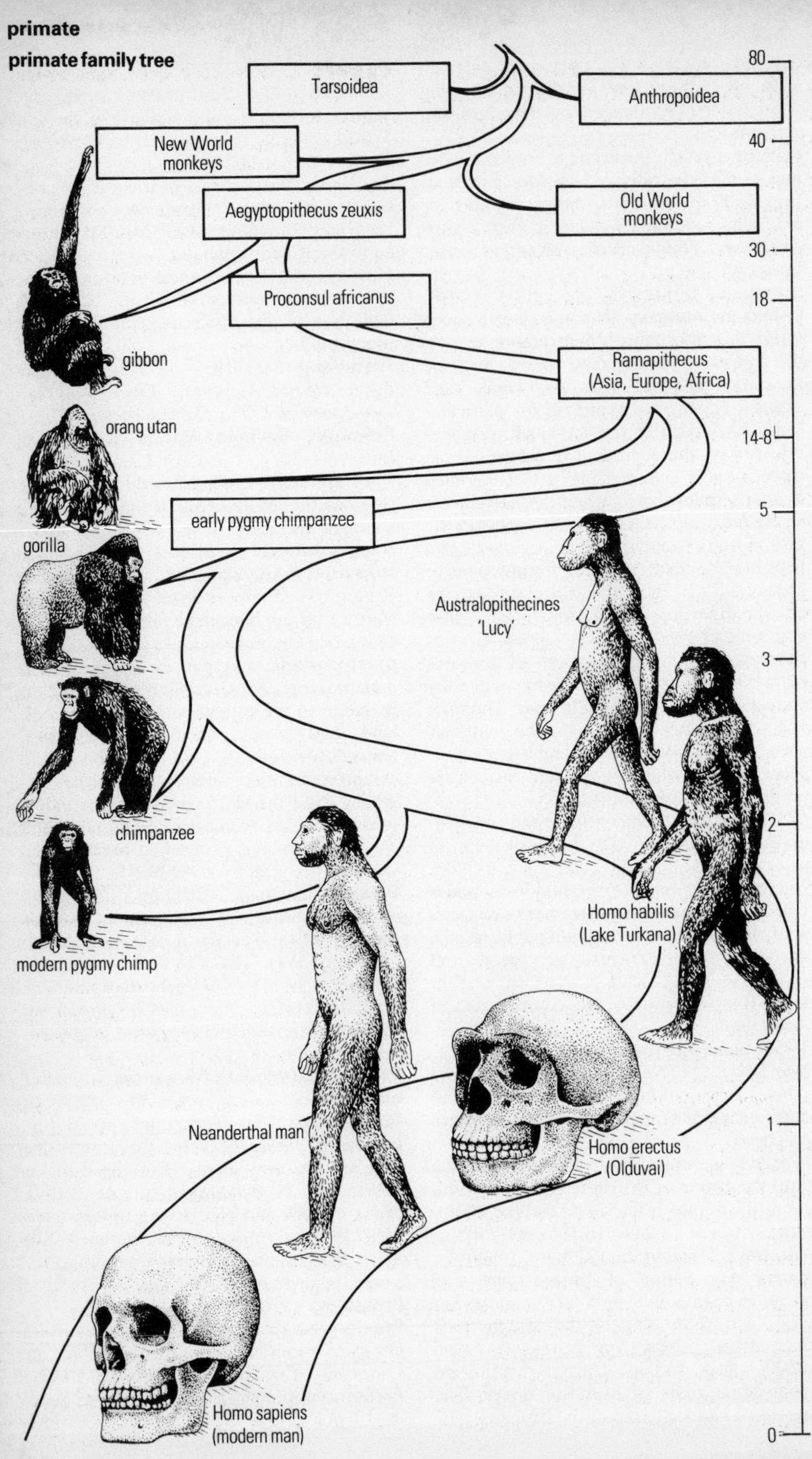

Edward defeated the English here in 1745□

Prestwick town in Strathclyde, Scotland; population 13 000. There is a famous golf course and an international airport, linked with a freeport◊□

Pretoria administrative capital of the Republic of S Africa from 1910, and capital of Transvaal province from 1860; population 528 400. Founded 1855, it was named after Boer◊ leader A Pretorius 1799–1853. Industries include engineering and iron and steel; there are two universities; Loftus Versfeld rugby stadium is the citadel of Afrikanerdom□

Previn André 1929– . German-American conductor and composer, US citizen 1943; music director of the Royal Philharmonic from 1985, and Los Angeles Philharmonic from 1986□

Prévost d'Exiles Antoine François 1697–1763. French novelist, known as Abbé Prévost, who sandwiched a military career into his life as a monk. His *Manon Lescaut* 1731 inspired operas by Massenet and Puccini□

Priapus Greek god of garden fertility, son of Dionysus◊ and Aphrodite◊, represented as grotesquely ugly, with an exaggerated phallus□

Pribilof Islands see Bering◊ Sea□

prickly heat inflammation of the sweat glands. See miliaria◊□

prickly pear American (especially Mexican) genus *Opuntia* of cactus, e.g. ***common prickly pear*** *O vulgaris* low-growing, with red and white flowers and an edible oval fruit; naturalized elsewhere, it has become a pest□

Pride Thomas d. 1658. Colonel in the Parliamentary Army in the British Civil War, who on Cromwell◊'s order excluded Presbyterian and Royalist MPs from the Commons in 'Pride's Purge' 1648□

Priestley John Boynton 1894–1984. British author. Born in Bradford, and educated at Cambridge, he achieved success in the novel (*The Good Companions* 1929 and *Angel Pavement* 1930); on the stage (with a series of plays including *Dangerous Corner* 1932 and *An Inspector Calls* 1945, and comedies, e.g. *When We Are Married* 1938); the travel book *English Journey* 1934; and wartime broadcast radio 'postscripts.' Order of Merit 1977□

Priestley Joseph 1733–1804. British chemist and Unitarian◊ minister. Born in Leeds, he was the inventor of soda water, discovered ammonia, nitrous oxide, etc., and while librarian to Lord Shelburne (see under Wiltshire◊) was the first to publish the discovery of oxygen. As a supporter of the French Revolution, he had his house in Birmingham sacked in the riots of 1791, and emigrated to America in 1794□

priest's hole hiding-place in private homes for Catholic priests in the 16–17th centuries when there were penal laws against them in Britain□

primary preliminary party political election in the majority of US states in a presidential election year. The votes received by a candidate usually govern the number of delegates who will vote for him/her at the National Conventions when the final choice is made□

primate official title for certain archbishops, e.g. the Archbishop of Canterbury is ***Primate of All England*** and of York ***Primate of England***□

primates order of mammals, including man, apes◊, monkeys◊, tarsiers◊, lemurs◊. See evolution◊, man, and table opposite□

prime minister or ***premier*** head of a parliamentary government, usually the leader of the largest party. The first in Britain is usually considered to have been Robert Walpole◊, but the office was not officially recognized until 1905. In some countries, e.g. Australia, a distinction is drawn between the prime minister of the whole country, and the premier of an individual state. In countries with an executive president, e.g. France, the prime minister is of lesser standing. See table on page 716□

primitivism influence on modern art of aboriginal cultures of Africa, Australia, the Americas, etc., and also of Western peasant art□

Primo de Rivera Miguel 1870–1930. Spanish soldier-statesman, who became effectively dictator of Spain in 1923 with the support of Alfonso◊ XIII, and was a reforming premier 1925–30□

primrose European woodland plant *Primula vulgaris* family Primulaceae, with pale yellow flowers in spring; the ***cowslip*** *P veris* and ***oxlip*** *P elatior* are in the same genus. The cultivated ***polyanthus*** is a cross between the primrose and cowslip. See also evening◊ primrose□

prince royal or noble title (derived from Roman *princeps* first, e.g. *princeps senatus* leader of the senate) from medieval times in Europe. The eldest son of the British sovereign is created Prince of Wales◊, and the eldest daughter may be created princess royal□

Prince Edward Island province of Canada
area 5657 sq km/2184 sq mi
capital Charlottetown
features named after Prince Edward of Kent, father of Queen Victoria; PEI National Park; Summerside Lobster Carnival

Prime Ministers

British Prime Ministers

Sir Robert Walpole	(Whig)	1721	B. Disraeli	(Conservative)	1868
Earl of Wilmington	(Whig)	1742	W.E. Gladstone	(Liberal)	1868
Henry Pelham	(Whig)	1743	B. Disraeli	(Conservative)	1874
Duke of Newcastle	(Whig)	1754	W.E. Gladstone	(Liberal)	1880
Duke of Devonshire	(Whig)	1756	Marquess of Salisbury	(Conservative)	1885
Duke of Newcastle	(Whig)	1757	W.E. Gladstone	(Liberal)	1886
Earl of Bute	(Tory)	1762	Marquess of Salisbury	(Conservative)	1886
George Grenville	(Whig)	1763	W.E. Gladstone	(Liberal)	1892
Marquess of Rockingham	(Whig)	1765	Earl of Rosebery	(Liberal)	1894
Duke of Grafton	(Whig)	1766	Marquess of Salisbury	(Conservative)	1895
Lord North	(Tory)	1770	A.J. Balfour	(Conservative)	1902
Marquess of Rockingham	(Whig)	1782	Sir H. Campbell-Bannerman	(Liberal)	1905
Earl of Shelburne	(Whig)	1782	H.H. Asquith	(Liberal)	1908
Duke of Portland	(Coalition)	1783	H.H. Asquith	(Coalition)	1915
William Pitt	(Tory)	1783	D. Lloyd George	(Coalition)	1916
Henry Addington	(Tory)	1801	A. Bonar Law	(Conservative)	1922
William Pitt	(Tory)	1804	Stanley Baldwin	(Conservative)	1923
Lord Grenville	(Whig)	1806	J.R. MacDonald	(Labour)	1924
Duke of Portland	(Tory)	1807	Stanley Baldwin	(Conservative)	1924
Spencer Perceval	(Tory)	1809	J.R. MacDonald	(Labour)	1929
Earl of Liverpool	(Tory)	1812	J.R. MacDonald	(National)	1931
George Canning	(Tory)	1827	Stanley Baldwin	(National)	1935
Viscount Goderich	(Tory)	1827	N. Chamberlain	(National)	1937
Duke of Wellington	(Tory)	1828	Winston Churchill	(Coalition)	1940
Earl Grey	(Whig)	1830	Clement Attlee	(Labour)	1945
Viscount Melbourne	(Whig)	1834	Sir W. Churchill	(Conservative)	1951
Sir Robert Peel	(Conservative)	1834	Sir Anthony Eden	(Conservative)	1955
Viscount Melbourne	(Whig)	1835	Harold Macmillan	(Conservative)	1957
Sir Robert Peel	(Conservative)	1841	Sir Alec Douglas-Home	(Conservative)	1963
Lord J. Russell	(Liberal)	1846	Harold Wilson	(Labour)	1964
Earl of Derby	(Conservative)	1852	Edward Heath	(Conservative)	1970
Lord Aberdeen	(Peelite)	1852	Harold Wilson	(Labour)	1974
Viscount Palmerston	(Liberal)	1855	James Callaghan	(Labour)	1976
Earl of Derby	(Conservative)	1858	Margaret Thatcher	(Conservative)	1979
Viscount Palmerston	(Liberal)	1859			
Lord J. Russell	(Liberal)	1865			
Earl of Derby	(Conservative)	1866			

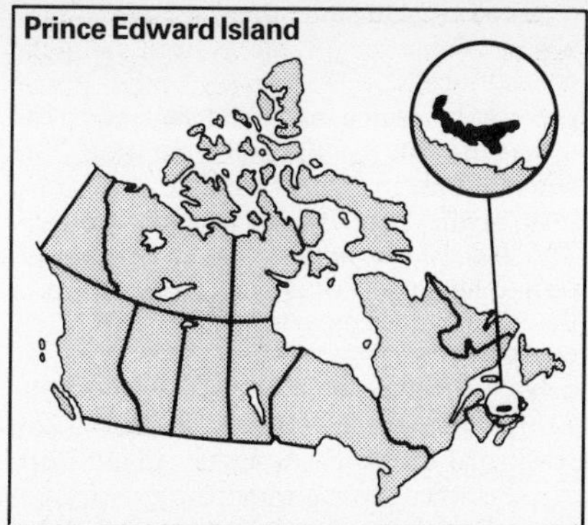

products potatoes, dairy products; lobsters and oysters; farm vehicles
population 125 300. See also Canada◊□

Prince Imperial see Napoleon◊ III□

Prince Rupert fishing port in British Columbia, Canada; population 16 200□

princess royal see under prince◊□

Princeton see New◊ Jersey□

Princetown see under Devon◊□

print a picture that is printed. In art there are three types:
wood-cuts and *wood-engraving* in which the areas and lines of the design are left in relief; Thomas Bewick◊, Eric Gill◊
Intaglio prints made by engraving (using a burin (engraver's tool) with pushing action), and etching (using corrosive acid on a design drawn through a wax coating on metal); Dürer◊, Van◊ Dyck, Hollar◊, Rembrandt◊, Whistler◊, Brangwyn◊, Sickert◊. An *aquatint* is a tone etching that gives a water-colour effect (Paul Sandby◊, Goya◊, Picasso◊, John Piper◊); *dry-point* uses no acid, but makes a burr in incising the plate which gives the lines a velvety quality (Dürer◊, Rembrandt◊, and J M Whistler◊); in *mezzotint* a copper or steel plate is roughened with a rocking tool, and the resultant burr is then scraped away where lighter tones are wanted (the process was much used to reproduce the works of Turner◊, Reynolds◊, Constable◊, Romney◊ and Lawrence◊).
surface prints, made by means of lithography (Greek *lithos* stone), are so-called because originally made with greasy ink on absorbent stone (now aluminium sheeting), which was then washed with water. The water having repelled the printing ink, the design was printed from the greasy area. Artists include Bonington◊, Delacroix◊, Daumier◊, Toulouse-Lautrec◊, Whistler◊.
Prints have gained popularity in recent times as an inexpensive means by which work from the hand of an artist may be purchased□

printing putting words or pictures onto paper using shapes covered in ink. Single wooden blocks were used in China from 6th century AD, and moveable type from 11th century, the latter being re-invented in Europe only in the 15th century (see Gutenberg◊, Caxton◊). The operation was speeded up at the end of the 19th century with the use of a keyboard to set either a line of type for newspapers, or a line of individual letters (which could be corrected) for bookwork. Electronic film-setting/photo-typesetting began 1960, when type characters were exposed onto photographic film to make a printing plate, and then in the 1970s the plate itself was dispensed with in favour of a computer-controlled laser beam, or continuous jets of ink acoustically broken up into tiny equal-sized drops which are electrostatically charged under computer control. In the 1980s word processors even allowed authors to do the preliminary setting of their own books, leaving only the more technical aspects to the printer to complete□

prion submicroscopic organism, smaller than a virus◊, claimed to have been discovered at the University of California in 1982. Composed of protein◊, and without enough nucleic◊ acid or genetic material to reproduce itself, it is thought to be the possible cause of diseases such as multiple sclerosis◊, some cancers, Parkinson's◊ disease, diabetes mellitus◊, rheumatoid arthritis◊, and scrapie◊ in sheep. See Virino◊□

Prior James 1927– . British Conservative politician. He was Minister of Agriculture 1970–2, Lord President of the Council 1972–4, Employment Secretary 1979–81 (when he curbed trade union activity with the Employment Act 1980), and Northern Ireland Secretary 1981–4□

Prior Matthew 1664–1721. British writer of light verse and diplomat, a negotiator of the treaty of Utrecht◊□

Pripet see under Dnieper◊□

prism transparent solid with a number of plane faces, e.g. used to disperse light to form the 'rainbow' effect of the spectrum◊; to change the direction of a beam of light, etc.□

prison building for the detention of criminals, etc., but originally usually only before execution, mutilation, or transportation. Not until the late 18th century was long-term detention with some idea of reformation attempted (see John Howard◊). After the colonies refused to continue to accept transported convicts, penal servitude (with hard labour) was introduced in Britain 1857, but was abolished 1948. From 1967 suspended sentences, which only come into effect if a further offence is committed, were introduced for lesser crimes. Persistent offenders may receive an extended sentence (to protect the public), but release on licence after a third (minimum a year) of a long sentence has been completed is intended to encourage reform. Community service (as a replacement for imprisonment in the case of non-violent offenders) was introduced 1972 and attempts were made to keep the merely 'inadequate' out of prison. Attempts to deal with the increasing number of young offenders include from 1982 accommodation in community homes in the case of minor offences, with (in more serious cases) 'short, sharp shock' treatment in the modern version of 'Borstal'◊□

prisoner of war under the Geneva conventions 1929 and 1949 (by which camps are inspected by the Red Cross), captured combatants are entitled to food on the same scale as the captor country's rear-line troops; clothing and footwear; medical attendance. They may also send and receive letters, and receive food parcels and reading matter. Those permanently incapacitated may be repatriated□

Pritchett Sir V(ictor) S(awdon) 1900– . British short-story writer (collections include 'You Make Your Own Life' 1938 and 'It May Never Happen' 1947) and critic, e.g. *The Living Novel* 1946. Knighted 1975□

privacy right of the individual to be free of surveillance by scientific devices, etc., and of disclosure to unauthorized persons of material in computer data banks. In the USA a Privacy Act followed on the revelations of Watergate◊, and in the UK (to enable the country to share OECD◊ computerised information) a Data Protection◊ Act was passed 1984□

private enterprise economic activity performed by individuals, or organizations under private control. See capitalism◊□

privatization reconversion of nationalized services and industries to private ownership (see nationalization◊), as under the Conservative governments in the UK from 1953, and especially the Thatcher◊ government from 1979□

privet genus *Ligustrum* of evergreen shrubs, family Oleaceae, with dark green leaves, including the wild ***common privet*** *L vulgare,* with white flowers and black berries, and ***hedge privet*** *L ovalifolium*□

Privy Council originally the chief royal officials of the Norman◊ kings in Britain, which under the Tudors◊ and early Stuarts◊ became the chief governing body. It was replaced from 1688 by the Cabinet◊, originally a committee of the council, and the council itself now retains only formal powers, in issuing royal proclamations and orders-in-council. Cabinet ministers are automatically members, and it is presided over by the Lord President of the Council. The ***Judicial Committee of the Privy Council,*** once a final court of appeal for members of the Commonwealth, is almost completely obsolete□

privy purse personal expenditure of the British sovereign (from his/her own resources, as distinct from the Civil◊ List), and the office dealing with it□

Privy Seal Lord. Until 1884, the officer of state in charge of the royal seal to prevent its misuse; the honorary title is now held by a senior Cabinet minister who has special non-departmental duties□

probability the likelihood that something will happen. See chance◊□

probate formal proof of the validity of a will, obtained by the executor. If the will is disputed, its validity is established at a Probate Court (in the Family Division of the High Court), those concerned being made parties to the action□

probation in the UK and USA, the placing of offenders under supervision in the community, as an alternative to prison. The ***probation service*** also assists the families of those imprisoned, and gives the prisoner supervisory aftercare on release, as well as assisting in preventive measures to avoid family breakdown, etc., which may lead to crime. Juveniles are no longer placed on probation, but under a 'supervision' order□

procaryote one of the two classes of living cell, that in which there is no definite nucleus, as in bacteria and blue-green algae. See eucaryote◊□

processor the central processing unit of a microcomputer□

proconsul Roman consul◊ who went on to govern a province when his term ended. Also formerly figuratively applied to great colonial administrators of the British Empire□

Proconsul the name of the ape-man skull found on Rusinga Island by Mary Leakey◊. It is believed to be 25 000 000 years old□

Procrustes in Greek mythology, a robber who tied his victims to a bed; if they were too tall for it, he cut off the end of their legs, and if they were too short stretched them□

procurator-fiscal officer of a Scottish sheriff's court who (combining the role of public prosecutor and coroner), inquires into suspicious deaths and carries out the preliminary questioning of witnesses to crime□

profit-sharing system under which workers receive a fixed share of an employer's profits. Originated in early 19th-century France□

Profumo John Dennis 1915– . Former Conservative politician, Secretary of State for War 1960–Jun 1963, when he resigned following his involvement with Christine Keeler, also mistress of a Soviet naval attaché. In 1982 he became chairman of Toynbee Hall (see Arnold Toynbee◊)□

progesterone a steroid hormone◊□

progression sequence of numbers each formed by a specific relationship to its predecessor: ***arithmetical progression*** has numbers which increase or decrease by a common sum or difference (e.g. 2, 4, 6, 8); ***geometric progression*** has numbers each bearing a fixed ratio to its predecessor (e.g. 3, 6, 12, 24), and ***harmonic progression*** is a series with numbers whose reciprocals are in arithmetical progression, e.g. 1, ½, ⅓, ¼□

prohibition law forbidding the sale of intoxicating liquor, e.g. in USA when a prohibition amendment to the US constitution (known as the Volstead Act, after the congressman who introduced it) became operative in 1920. The federal government lost revenue and it led to bootlegging (illicitly distilled liquor illegally distributed), to the financial advantage of gangsters such as Al Capone◊, and public opinion insisted on repeal 1933. It gave rise to novels, e.g. Fitzgerald◊'s *The Great Gatsby* and Hemingway's *To Have and Have Not*. Prohibition on religious grounds is enforced with varying degrees of severity in Islamic countries□

Prokofiev Sergei 1891–53. Russian composer. He lived outside the USSR 1918–33, and was condemned by the Soviet regime 1948. His works include opera *The Love for Three Oranges* 1921; ballet *Romeo and Juliet* 1935; orchestral fairy tale *Peter and the Wolf* 1936; piano and violin concertos, and seven symphonies□

Prokopyevsk chief coalmining city of the Kuzbas, Siberia, USSR; population 270 000□

proletariat in ancient Rome the propertyless class which served the state by producing children *proles*. According to Marx those in industry, agriculture, and intellectual posts, who live by the sale of their labour, as opposed to the capitalist bourgeoisie□

Promenade Concerts originally concerts in which the audience walked about, now the annual series at the Albert◊ Hall at which part of the audience stands. Their originator was Sir Henry Wood◊ in 1895□

Prometheus Titan◊ who stole fire from heaven for the human race. In revenge, Zeus◊ had him chained to a rock with an eagle preying on his liver, until he was rescued by Hercules◊□

promethium element
symbol Pm
atomic number 61
physical description silvery metal, with high boiling point (2460°C)
featurs radioactive, produced by fission of uranium
uses in nuclear power generation□

promissory note written promise to pay on demand, or at a fixed future time, a specific sum of money to a named person or bearer□

prongbuck or ***pronghorn*** *Antilocapra americana* of the N American plains, only surviving member of family Antilocapridae, between deer and cattle. It is 1 m/3 ft high, sheds its horns annually, and is a swift runner□

propane gaseous hydrocarbon, found in petroleum and used as fuel□

Propertius Sextus lived c47–15BC. Roman elegiac poet, a member of Maecenas◊' circle, who wrote of his love for his mistress 'Cynthia'□

prophets biblical succession of seers (e.g. Amos◊, Isaiah◊, and Elijah◊ who preached and prophesied in the Hebrew kingdoms in Palestine from the 8th century BC until the suppression of Jewish independence in 586 BC and possibly later. See also Mohammed◊□

proportional representation electoral system in which distribution of party seats corresponds to their proportion of the votes cast, and minority votes are not 'lost'. Forms include:
party list or additional member system (AMS). As recommended by the Hansard Society for introduction in Britain in 1976, three-quarters of the members would be elected in single-member constituencies on the traditional majority vote system, and the remaining seats be allocated according to the overall number of votes cast for each party (a variant of this is used W Germany). In France in 1985 it was proposed to introduce a system under which, after ruling out parties with less than a 5% poll in each department, the votes for the rest would be divided by the number of seats to obtain an 'electoral quotient' (e.g. if the quotient were 15 000 votes, party A with 30 000 votes would win two seats, and party B with 12 000, would win none); unallocated seats would be distributed in a second 'round' when each party's poll would be divided by the number of seats it had already won, plus one (that is, party A would now be credited with only 10 000 votes; party B, having won no seat so far, would be credited with its original 12 000, and so gain a seat

single transferable vote (STV), in which candidates are numbered in order of preference by the voter, and any votes surplus to the minimum required for a candidate to win are transferred to second preferences, as are second preference votes from the successive candidates at the bottom of the poll until the required number of elected candidates is achieved (this is in use in the Republic of Ireland). The chief argument against proportional representation is its tendency to produce unstable coalitions, and the delay in getting results. See also under vote◊□

prose the everyday expression of thought in language (see poetry◊), which can also extend to near poetic form, as well as having rhythmic and melodic qualities of its own. English prose reached a simple perfection in the reign of Alfred◊, revived in the 14th century after the eclipse of the Norman◊ Conquest, and gained precise flexibility with Dryden◊□

Prosecution Service National. Proposed under a bill of 1984, to be headed by the Director of Public Prosecutions (DPP), and so bring England and Wales in line with Scotland (see procurator◊ fiscal) in having a prosecution service independent of the police. In most cases the decision to prosecute would be made on the basis of evidence presented by the police to local Crown prosecutors in each of 43 police authority areas. The DPP had previously taken action (under the guidance of the Attorney General), only in cases of especial difficulty or importance□

Proserpina Roman equivalent of Persephone. See under Hades◊□

prostaglandin local tissue hormones which are formed by the conversion of unsaturated fatty acids, and released by stress, disease, wounds, etc. They occur in excess in arthritis, seem to be deficient in schizophrenia◊, and are used in treatment in obstetrics, gynaecology, circulatory diseases, etc.□

prostitution receipt of money by a man or woman for satisfying the sexual wishes of others. Society's attitude towards it varies according to place and period. It has formed part of religious cults, ancient and modern, and been seen as therapy by some modern psychologists; it increases the spread of venereal◊ disease. In some states, tolerance is combined with licensing of brothels and health checks on their 'staff'. In the UK a compromise system makes it legal to be a prostitute, but not to solicit for custom publicly; keeping a brothel, living on 'immoral earnings', and 'procuring' (arranging to make someone into a prostitute) are illegal□

protactinium element
symbol Pa
atomic number 91
physical description member of actinide◊ series
features present in very small quantities in pitchblende◊ as a member of the uraniun decay series
uses none at present□

protection the discouragement of free◊ trade□

protectorate in international law, an obsolete status of a small state under the direct or indirect control of a larger one. The modern equivalent is a Trust◊ Territory. In English history the rule of Oliver and Richard Cromwell◊ 1653–9 is referred to as the Protectorate□

protein organic substance containing carbon, hydrogen, oxygen and nitrogen, which constitutes an important part of living cells, and is essential to animal diet. Proteins include egg-albumen, casein in milk, haemoglobin in blood, and ossein in bone
single-cell protein (SCP) is obtained by growing algae◊, bacteria◊, fungi◊ or yeasts◊ on waste substances, e.g. animal waste and sewage sludge, waste paper and mill liquor, petroleum, natural gas, methanol◊, and ethanol◊, and also (as with algae) by exposing them to sunlight. The resultant powder, granules or pellets is then fed to cattle, poultry, etc., mixed either with conventional foods, or directly, e.g. 'yeast steak' and 'yeast milk'. The world's largest producer is the USSR, but there is danger from toxic residues (which may contaminate meat so produced), the dust and micro-organisms released (environmental pollution), and handling the raw materials (hazardous to the health of the factory workers)□

Protestantism one of the main divisions of Christianity◊□

Proteus Poseidon◊'s game warden, in charge of the sea creatures. He was gifted with prophecy, but could change himself to any form to evade questioning□

proteus amphibian *Proteus anguinus* found in the caves of Dalmatia; eyeless, white, and eel-like (though with four rudimentary legs), it develops a dark colouring and becomes fully-eyed if exposed to light. Also a genus of bacteria◊□

Protocols of Zion plans for Jewish world conquest alleged to have been submitted by Herzl◊ to the first Zionist Congress at Basle 1897, and published in Russia 1905. They were proved to be a forgery by *The Times* 1921, but were used by Hitler in his anti-Semitic campaign□

proton a positively charged elementary particle. See under particle◊ physics, atom◊□

protoplasm material within the plasma membrane of a cell◊, the basis of all living things◊□

protozoa phylum of microscopic invertebrates, including amoebae◊, flagellata◊, foraminifera◊, radiolaria◊. See protista under life◊ classification□

Proudhon Pierre Joseph 1809–65. French anarchist who, despite his dictum 'property is theft' in *What is Property?* 1840, had a plan for a highly decentralized society of small property owners. It greatly influenced French socialism□

Proust Marcel 1871–1922. French author, born at Auteuil. After the death of his father (1904) and mother (1905) he retired to the quiet of a cork-lined room in his Paris flat to write his autobiographical novel *À la Recherche de Temps Perdu* (Remembrance of Things Past) 1913–27□

Provençal see Languedoc◊□

Provence-Côte d'Azur region of SE France; capital Marseille; population 3 965 200. Provence was an independent kingdom in the 10th century, and the area still has its own language, Provencal◊; the ***Côte d'Azur*** the Mediterranean coast Menton–St Tropez, is the tourist beach paradise□

Proverbs a book of the Old Testament◊, which forms part of the wisdom literature of the ancient Hebrews, traditionally ascribed to Solomon◊. They form a series of maxims on moral and ethical matters□

Providence capital and industrial port (jewellery, silverware, watches, chemicals) of Rhode Island, USA; population 156 300. It was first settled by Roger Williams◊ 1636□

provost chief magistrate of a Scottish burgh, approximate equivalent of an English mayor□

Prudhoe Bay see under Alaska◊□

Prunus genus of trees of the northern hemisphere, family Rosaceae◊, producing fruit with a fleshy, edible pericarp; including plums, peaches, apricots, almonds and cherries□

Prussia former N German state formed 1618 by the union of Brandenburg◊ and the duchy of Prussia. Its military power was founded by Frederick◊ William, the 'Great Elector', and it became a kingdom under Frederick◊ I in 1701. Military and economic expansion, though not without setbacks, continued (see Frederick William I, Frederick◊ the Great, Frederick◊ William II, III, IV), until in 1871 William◊ I became emperor of all Germany (see Bismarck◊). Converted to a republic after World War I, Prussia lost its local independence in Hitler's Germany in 1933, and the Allies◊ abolished the state altogether

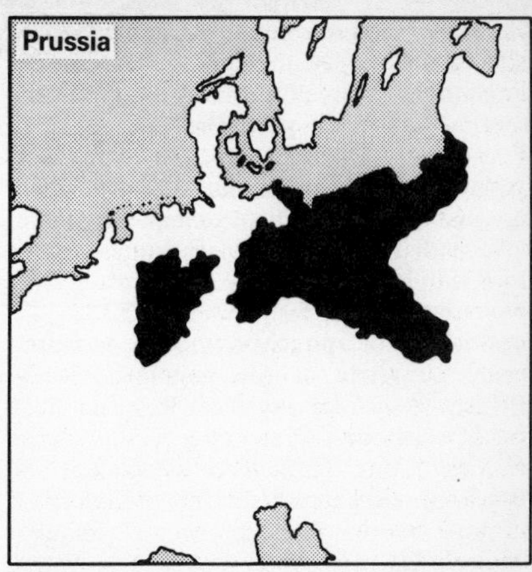

in 1946, its territories being divided among E and W Germany, Poland and the USSR□

Prussic acid see hydrocyanic◊ acid□

Prynne William 1600–69. English pamphleteer and Puritan, whose *Histriomastix* 1632, attacking stage plays, was ultimately influential in the closure of the playhouses by Parliament in 1642. Prynne was committed to the Tower, but continued to write, and in 1637 lost his ears for an attack on the bishops□

Przemyśl industrial city (timber, ceramics, flour milling, tanning, distilling, food processing) in SE Poland; population 132 000. Austrian 1722–1919, it was a frontier fortress besieged by the Russians, Sept 1914–Mar1915, and was occupied by the Germans Jun 1941–Jul 1944□

psalm song of praise with musical accompaniment, as in the Old Testament◊ Book of Psalms; there is no basis for the ascription of some of these to David◊□

PSBR see Public◊ Sector Borrowing Requirement□

PSFD Public Sector Financial Deficit. See under Public◊ Sector Borrowing Requirement□

psi in parapsychology, a hypothetical facility responsible for ESP, etc.□

psilocybe genus of fungi◊ with hallucinogenic properties, e.g. ***Mexican sacred mushroom*** *P mexicana* containing compounds which produce effects similar to LSD◊; the similarly used ***liberty cap*** *P semilanceolata* is common in England□

psittacosis virus disease, contracted from birds (especially parrots), which may result in pneumonia□

Pskov industrial city (food processing, leather) in USSR; population 185 000□

psoriasis chronic skin inflammation resulting in raised red patches, especially on the arms and legs, covered with whitish scales. Ultra-violet light and steroid creams provide some alleviation□

Psyche late Greek personification of the soul as a winged girl. The love story of Eros◊ and Psyche is told by Apuleius◊. Aphrodite◊ was so jealous of Psyche's beauty that she ordered Eros to make her fall in love with the worst of men, but he fell in love with her himself□

psychiatry see under psychology◊□

psychical or **psychophysical research** term for study of the paranormal, e.g. British Society for Psychical Research 1882 (with which Sir Oliver Lodge◊, Sir William Crookes◊, and others were associated) and Psychophysical Research Unit at Oxford. It is now more often known as parapsychology◊□

psychoanalysis the study of the unconscious mind as a means of treating mental and emotional disorders. See under Sigmund Freud◊□

psychology the behavioural study of animate beings, for which the first experimental institute was founded 1879 by Wihelm Wundt 1832–1920 at Leipzig. The subject includes the roles of instinct, heredity, environment and culture; the processes of sensation, perception, learning and memory; the bases of motivation and emotion; and the functioning of thought, intelligence and language.

Abnormal types of behaviour, diagnosed and treated by ***psychiatry*** and ***psychotherapy*** include alcohol and drug addiction, anxiety, autism (a state of withdrawal, especially in children, for which shock treatment has been used with some success), depression◊, neurosis◊, obsessions (e.g., with a job, as in the workaholic executive, or with cleanliness, as with the elderly Howard Hughes◊), psychopathy◊, schizophrenia◊, and sexual deviations and inadequacies.

Leading pioneer psychologists have include Gustav Fechner◊ (founder of psychophysics); Wolfgang Köhler 1887–1967, one of the *gestalt* or 'whole' psychologists concerned with the organizational law governing our perception of objects; Sigmund Freud◊ and his associates Jung◊, Adler◊ and Rorschach◊; and Kurt Lewin 1890–1947, developer of the less expensive 'group therapy' in which patients in effect treat each other, e.g. Alcoholics Anonymous works on these lines. Treatment may also include corrective conditioning derived from the work of Pavlov◊, and J B Watson◊ and the Behaviourist◊ school; drugs, e.g. tranquillizers and anti-confusional agents; electric shock treatment (electroconvulsive◊ therapy) for depression; psychosurgery◊; modification of home and family background (see R D Laing◊); and, in the future, genetic engineering to correct inherited mental defect. See also psychosomatic◊ medicine.

Instinct and heredity have been illuminated by the study of animals, (see ethology◊), and the comparative importance of heredity and environment, notably in discussion of any link between race and intelligence (see H J Eysenck◊) arouses unscholarly passions. Hermann Ebbinghaus 1850–1909 pioneered the study of memory (with the aid of nonsense material), and in the late 1960s Roger Brown and David McNeil explored the familiar 'tip-of-the-tongue' failure to achieve recall. The growth of human intelligence◊ was first scientifically explored by Piaget◊: see also cybernetics◊, intelligence◊, language◊, mental tests◊. Even creativity has been tackled, e.g. the 'lateral thinking' concept of Edward de◊ Bono, which involves thinking round a problem, rather than repeatedly tackling it head on.

Emotion and motivation were among aspects of psychology covered by Charles Darwin◊ and William James◊, and modern studies have been infinitely varied, e.g. the psychological causes of obesity; the nature of religious experience (see Sir Alistair Hardy◊); and the 'under-achievement of women' seen as resulting from social pressures, and previously inescapable physical conditions. Other related subjects are the nature of sleep◊ and dreams◊; possible extensions of the senses, e.g. the echo-location practised by bats and dolphins at a high level, is also used very crudely by human beings. This leads to the more controversial ground of parapsychology◊□

psychopath sufferer from a mental illness which results in an absence of a sense of social responsibility, or ability to relate to other people as individuals. Criminal acts, such as a sequence of murders, may be carried out by the psychopath to attain an end, or without any particular motive, and evoke no sense of guilt or shame. There is no particular established cause□

psychosis mental disorder in which the patient loses touch with the world as the majority perceive it, suffering from delusions, hallucinations, obsessions, depression, sleeplessness, restlessness. Most sufferers can be treated, many recovering, and their symptoms are something which most people suffer from to a mild degree in conditions of stress. See neurosis◊□

psychosomatic medicine study of the mind/body reaction, e.g. illness triggered by psychological factors, as emotional stress may be accompanied by skin disease; or cured by a ***placebo*** (Latin 'I will please'), a dummy pill given to pacify a patient, or as a 'control' to patients in a medical experiment in which other subjects are given some new drug□

psychosurgery operation to achieve some mental effect, e.g. ***leucotomy/(US) lobotomy*** the separation of the white fibres in the prefrontal lobe of the brain, as a means of relieving a deep state of anxiety. It is irreversible, the degree of personality change is not predictable, and its justification is controversial□

psychotherapy the use of psychological methods for the treatment of mental disorder. See under psychology◊□

Ptah Egyptian god, the divine potter, a personification of the creative force. He was worshipped especially at Memphis◊, and often portrayed as a mummified man. See Imhotep◊□

ptarmigan the smallest grouse◊□

pterodactyl extinct creature, a flying 'dinosaur' which existed in the Mesozoic period c210 million years ago, anticipating the birds by c75 million years. It appears not to have been a smooth-skinned flying lizard, as once thought, but a highly intelligent, furry creature, with a gliding flight on wings up to 17 m/50 ft.□

Ptolemy dynasty of Macedonian◊ kings who ruled Egypt over a period of 300 years; they included:

Ptolemy I died 283BC, King of Egypt from 304, was one of Alexander◊'s generals, and possibly his half-brother (see also Thaïs◊). He established the library at Alexandria◊.

Ptolemy XIII 63–47BC was joint ruler of Egypt with his sister-wife Cleopatra; she put him to death□

Ptolemy or ***Claudius Ptolemaeus*** 2nd century AD. Alexandrian scholar, whose *Geography* (see Ruwenzori◊) and *Ptolemaic System* which assumed earth was the centre of the universe, and that the sun, moon and stars revolved round it, were standard reference works until the 16th century□

ptomaine group of extremely toxic chemical substances produced as a result of putrefaction, but not the relevant factor in 'food poisoning', which is usually caused by bacteria of the *Salmonella* genus□

puberty stage in human development when the individual becomes capable of sexual reproduction. In boys it may occur from the age of 12 upward, and in girls from the age of 10 upward. The sexual organs take on their adult form and pubic hair grows. In girls menstruation◊ begins, and the breasts develop; in boys the voice 'breaks' (hence the short performing life of choirboys) and then becomes deeper, and a beard develops. It is also a period of mental stress□

public house in Britain a house licensed for consumption of intoxicating liquor, and either 'free' (when the landlord has free choice of suppliers), or 'tied' to a company owning the house□

Public Lending Right method (PLR) of rectifying the anomaly that, although performance of a play or piece of music involves payment of a royalty, books had been borrowed freely from libraries. Payment for such borrowings was introduced in Australia in 1974, and a form was enacted in the UK in 1979, taking effect 1984□

public order in the UK serious offences against public order e.g. riot (assembly with a common purpose, legal or illegal) and rout (attempt to execute that purpose with violence), affray (fighting and noisy disturbance) and unlawful assembly (assembly with an unlawful purpose) come under the common law, and assault, criminal damage, and threatening behaviour under the Public Order Acts of 1936 and 1963. The more widespread disorder of the 1980s led to a new Public Order Bill 1985 including a new lesser offence of 'disorderly conduct', behaving in an abusive, threatening or disorderly manner so as to cause alarm, harassment or distress; new powers were also given to the police to control marches, and the size, location and duration of demonstrations□

public schools in the UK independent schools (mainly for boys 12–18). Some (e.g. Eton◊, Harrow◊, Rugby◊, Winchester◊) are ancient foundations, usually originally intended for poor scholars; others developed in the 18–19th centuries. Among those for girls, Roedean is most popularly known, and some boys' schools take girls in the sixth form. Some discipline (less than formerly) is in the hands of senior boys/girls (prefects). The Labour Party is committed to their integration into the state system (virtual abolition), the Conservatives have encouraged state funding of selected students within them□

Public Sector Borrowing Requirement (PSBR) amount of money needed by a national economy to cover the deficit in sums needed by the central government to finance its own activities and loans to local athorities and public corporations, and the funds raised by local authorities and public corporations from other sources. The PSBR is financed chiefly by sales of debt to the public outside the banking system, (gilt-edged stocks, national savings, and local authority stocks and bonds), by external transactions with other countries, and by borrowing from the banking system. After the 1986 budget this measure was changed to the ***Public Sector Financial Deficit (PSFD),*** which is net of the asset sales which was thought to distort the PSBR□

Public Sector Financial Deficit (PSFD) see Public◊ Sector Borrowing Requirements□

Puccini Giacomo 1858–1924. Italian opera composer, whose realist works include *Manon Lescaut* 1893, *La Bohème* 1896, *Tosca* 1900, *Madame Butterfly* 1904, and the unfinished *Turandot* (finished by Franco Alfano) 1926□

Pudovkin Vsevolod Illationovich 1893–1953. Russian film director, whose greatest films were silent, e.g. *Mother* 1926 (based on Gorky◊'s novel) *The End of St Petersburg* 1927, and *Storm over Asia* 1928□

Puebla (de Zaragoza) industrial city (textiles, sugar refining, metallurgy, and hand-crafted pottery and tiles) in S Mexico; population 710 835. First founded 1535, it was later renamed after General de Zaragoza, who defeated the French here 1862□

Pueblo generic name for N American Indians of SW North America (from Spanish *pueblos* villages), of whom the best-known are the Hopi◊ (famous for their biennial Snake Dance) who build multi-story communal villages of mud-brick or stone. The ***Mesa Verde*** ('green table') cliff dwelling in Colorado, constructed c1000AD, has some 200 rooms□

Pueblo American intelligence vessel captured by the N Koreans, Jan 1968, allegedly within their territorial waters: the crew, but not the ship, were released Dec 1968□

puerperal fever infection of the genital tract after childbirth which formerly often resulted in fatal bloodpoisoning, but which is now easily dealt with by antibiotics□

Puerto Rico The Commonwealth of
area 8891 sq km/3435 sq miles
capital San Juan
towns Mayagüez and Ponce are also ports
features highest per capita income in Latin America
exports sugar, tobacco, rum and pineapples; textiles, plastics, chemicals, processed foods
currency US dollar
population 3 337 000, 62% urban
language Spanish and English (official)
religion Roman Catholicism
government under the constitution of 1952, similar to that of the USA, with a governor elected for four years, and a legislative assembly with a senate and house of representatives
history discovered in 1493 by Columbus◊, it was annexed by Spain 1509, ceded to the USA after the Spanish◊ American War in 1898, and in 1952 achieved Commonwealth status with local self-government. This was confirmed in preference to independence by a referendum 1967, but there is an independence movement, and another wishing incorporation as a state of the USA□

puff adder a type of snake◊□

puffball globulous fruiting body of certain fungi◊ which cracks with maturity, releasing the enclosed spores, e.g. ***common puffball*** *Lycoperdon perlatum*□

puffer fish a fish that can inflate its body. See under tetraodon◊□

puffin a bird of the auk◊ family□

pug a breed of small dog◊□

Pugin Augus Welby Northmore 1812–52. British architect, collaborator with Barry◊ in the detailed design of the Houses of Parliament. See Ramsgate◊□

Puglia see under Apulia◊□

Pula commercial and naval port in Croatia, Yugoslavia; population 50 000. A Roman naval base, it was seized by Venice in 1148, passed to Austria 1815, to Italy 1919, and Yugoslavia 1947□

Pulitzer Joseph 1847–1911. American newspaperman, founder 1903 of the school of journalism at Columbia University which awards the annual Pulitzer prizes in journalism and letters□

pulsar an extremely dense star◊□

pulse the impulse transmitted by the heartbeat throughout the arterial system. When the heart muscle contracts it forces blood into the aorta◊; because the arteries are elastic, the sudden rise of pressure causes a throb or sudden swelling through them all. It can be felt where the artery is near the surface, as in the wrist. The actual flow of the blood continues more or less uniformly at about 60 cm^3 a second. The pulse rate is generally about 70 per minute□

puma a large wild cat◊□

pumice light volcanic rock, with the texture of a hard sponge, used as an abrasive commercially and in the bath□

pumpkin plant *Cucurbita pepo* family Cucurbitaceae, with a large spherical fruit having a thick, orange rind, pulpy flesh and many seeds; fruits of the giant pumpkin *C maxima* reach 250 kg/550 lb. Varieties include the vegetable marrow and squash□

Punch or ***Punchinello*** hero of the puppet◊ play *Punch and Judy*. Originating in Italy, it was introduced to England at the time of the Restoration◊□

punch drink of Indian origin, made of spirits, fruit juice, sugar, spice and hot water□

Pune industrial city (chemicals; rice, sugar, cotton and paper mills; jewellery) (formerly ***Poona***) in Maharashtra, India; population 1 685 000. There is the Armed Forces Medical College, and, at nearby Khadakvasla, the National Defence Academy□

Punic Wars between Rome◊ and Carthage◊:
First 264–241BC resulted in the cession of Sicily to Rome. See Hamilcar◊ Barca
Second 218–201BC Hannibal◊ invaded Italy, defeated the Romans at Cannae◊, see Fabius◊ Maximus, but was finally defeated by Scipio◊ at Zama (now in Algeria)
Third 149–146BC ended in the destruction of Carthage, and her possessions becoming the Roman province of Africa
In 1985 Rome and modern Carthage signed a symbolic peace treaty□

Punjab name meaning 'five rivers' (the Indus tributaries: Jhelum, Chenab, Ravi, Beas and Sutlej), for a former NW state of British India. See Punjab◊ (Pakistan) and Punjab◊ (India)◊□

Punjab NW state of India
area 50 362 sq km/19440 sq miles
capital Chandigarh
towns Amritsar, Sikh holy city
features mainly agricultural, crops chiefly under irrigation; longest life expectancy rates in India (59 for women, 64 for men); Harappa, see Indus Valley◊ civilisation
population 16 669 755
language Punjabi
religion Sikhism 60%, Hinduism 30%, there is friction between the two groups□

Punjab state of Pakistan, the former W section of a state of British India
area 181 761 sq km/70 178 sq mi
capital Lahore
features wheat cultivations (by irrigation)
population 47 116 000
language Punjabi, Urdu
religion Muslem□

Punta Arenas port in S Chile; population 67 600□

puppet figure manipulated on a small stage, usually by unseen operator(s). Known from the 10th century BC in China, the types include ***finger*** or ***glove puppets*** (see Punch◊); ***string marionettes*** (which reached a high artistic level in ancient Burma and Sri Lanka and in Italian princely courts 16–18th centuries, and for which Haydn◊ wrote his operetta *Dido* for performance in the Esterhazy theatre); ***shadow silhouettes*** (operated by rods and seen on a lit screen, as in Java); and ***bunraku*** (devised in Osaka◊), in which three or four black-clad operators on stage may combine to work each puppet c1 m/3 ft high. A recent development is the use of puppets resembling famous people as television satire. See Obraztsov◊□

Puranas religious Sanskrit epics dealing with the mythology of the Hindus. See under Hinduism◊□

Purbeck Isle of. See under Dorset◊□

Purcell Henry 1659–95. English composer, a chorister and then composer to the Chapel◊ Royal, and from 1679 organist at Westminster◊ Abbey. His works include anthems, music for masques (*King Arthur* 1691 and *The Fairy Queen* 1692), and, a landmark in the history of opera, *Dido and Aeneas* 1689□

Purchas Samuel 1577–1626. English cleric and travel writer. He inherited Hakluyt◊'s papers and continued his work, e.g. the four-volume *Hakluytus Posthumus or Purchas his Pilgrimes* 1625□

purdah Persian and Hindu 'curtain', hence a symbol of the seclusion of upper-class women practised by some Islamic and Hindu peoples. It had begun to disappear with the adoption of Western culture, but the fundamentalism of the 1980s revived it, e.g. the wearing of the *chador* a black mantle, in Iran. This originated in the period of Cyrus◊ the Great in ancient Persia, and was adopted by the Arab conquerors of the Byzantines◊. The Koran◊ actually requests only 'modesty' in dress□

purgatives or ***laxatives*** drugs to ease or acclerate the emptying of the bowels, e.g. Epsom◊ salts, senna◊, castor oil◊. With a diet of proper bulk, such aids should not normally be necessary□

purgatory in Roman Catholic belief, a purificatory state for the souls of the middling-virtuous newly dead; formerly their term of penitential suffering could be lessened by the financial contributions of the faithful, but prayer only is now enjoined□

Puri town in Orissa, India, famous for the juggernaut, a statue of Krishna (see Hinduism◊) which is annually taken in procession on a large vehicle (hence the modern use of the word□

Puritans from 1564 those members of the Church of England who wished to eliminate Roman Catholic survivals in ritual or substitute a presbyterian◊ for an episcopal form of church government. They were identified with the parliamentary opposition under James◊ I and Charles◊ I, and after the Restoration◊ were driven from the Church, and more usually known as Dissenters◊ or 'Nonconformists'□

Purple Heart Order of the. See under medals◊□

purpura spontaneous bleeding beneath the skin localized in spots. It may be harmless, as sometimes with the elderly, or linked with disease□

pus yellowish liquid which forms in the body as a result of bacterial attack; it includes white blood cells (leucocytes) 'killed in battle' with the bacteria, plasma, and broken-down tissue cells□

Pusan chief port of S Korea; population 3 160 000□

Pusey Edward Bouverie 1800–82. British churchman, professor of Hebrew at Oxford University from 1828, who joined with J H Newman◊ 1835 in issuing *Tracts for the Times*. After Newman's accession to Rome, he led the High Church Party or Puseyites, trying to keep them from following Newman's example. His work continues at Pusey House, Oxford□

Pushkin Aleksandr 1799–1837. Russian national poet. Born in Moscow, he was exiled in 1820 for his political verse, and was in 1824 in trouble for his atheistic opinions. He was influenced respectively by Shakespeare and Byron◊ in his tragedy *Boris Godunov* 1825, and narrative poem *Eugene Onegin* 1832 (see under Mussorgsky◊ and Tchaikovsky◊); the philosophical poem 'The Bronze Horseman' 1833 was inspired by the statue of Peter the Great in Leningrad. His chief prose works are the short story 'The Queen of Spades' 1834 and the novel *The Captain's Daughter* 1836. He married Natalia Goncharov 1831, by whom he had four children, and was mortally wounded in a duel with his brother-in-law□

Pushkin town north west of Leningrad, USSR; population 80 000. Founded by Peter◊ the Great as Tsarskoe Selo (Tsar's Village) 1708, it has a number of imperial summer palaces, restored after the Germans devastated the town 1941–44. Since 1937 it has been known as Pushkin, the poet having been educated at the school which is now a museum commemorating him□

Pushtu see Pashto◊□

putrefaction decomposition of organic matter by micro-organisms, resulting in an offensive smell from the ammonia, hydrogen sulphide, etc., released. It is the one sure sign of death◊□

putting the shot or ***shot put.*** sport of hurling (from the shoulder) a round weight or 'shot' 7.26 kg/16lb for men, and 4kg/8.8lb for women□

Puttnam David Terence 1941– . British film producer (*Chariots of Fire* 1981, *The Killing Fields* 1984)□

Puvis de Chavannes Pierre Cécile 1824–98. French decorative artist, born in Lyons. He used oil on canvas in fresco pastel colours for murals in public buildings, e.g. the Panthéon◊. He influenced Gauguin◊□

Pu Yi Henry 1906–67. Last emperor of China (as Hsuan Tung) from 1908 until his deposition 1912; he was restored for a week in 1917. He was president (1932–34) and emperor (1934–45) of the Japanese puppet state of Manchukuo◊; captured by the Russians, he was freed by Mao◊ Zedong when the Russians handed him over in 1949, and became a deputy in the Chinese parliament 1964□

PVC polyvinylchlorides. See under plastics◊□

Pwllheli resort in Gwynedd, Wales; population 4000. The Welsh National Party, Plaid Cymru, was founded here 1925□

pyelitis inflammation of the renal pelvis, the central part of the kidney where urine accumulates before discharge□

Pygmalion legendary king of Cyprus who fell in love with an ivory statue he had carved, and when Aphrodite◊ brought it (Galatea) to life, married her. G B Shaw◊ used the idea in a play□

Pygmy small-statured peoples of equatorial Africa (Negrillos) and SE Asia and Melanesia (Negritos). They are noted for their mastery of forest lore□

Pylos port in SW Greece. The ***Battle of Navarino*** 1827, was the decisive naval action off Pylos in the Greek war of liberation which was won by the combined fleets of the English, French, and Russians under Codrington◊, over the Turkish and Egyptian fleets□

Pym Barbara 1913–80. British novelist. Born in Shropshire, she was educated at Oxford and was editorial secretary at the International African Institute 1958–74. She wrote a sextet from *Some Tame Gazelle* 1950 to *No Fond Return of Love* 1961, and was then eclipsed by fashion until praised by Philip Larkin◊ and Lord David Cecil◊. *Quartet in Autumn* appeared 1977□

Pym Francis 1922– . British Conservative politician. Defence Secretary 1979–81, he succeeded Carrington◊ as Foreign Minister in 1982, but was dismissed in the post-election reshuffle of 1983□

Pym John 1584–1643. English parliamentarian, largely responsible for the Petition◊ of Right in 1628. As leader of the Puritan◊ opposition in the Long◊ Parliament, he moved the impeachment of Strafford◊ and Laud◊, drew up the Grand◊ Remonstrance, and was the chief of the five MPs whom Charles◊ I failed to arrest in 1642. Just before his death he negotiated the alliance between parliament and the Scots□

Pynchon Thomas 1937– . American novelist, whose works include *V* 1963, *Gravity's Rainbow* 1973□

Pyongyang capital and industrial city (coal, iron and steel, textiles, chemicals) of N Korea; population 1 280 000□

pyorrhoea discharge from the gums. See periodontal◊ disease□

pyramid pyramidal building used in ancient Egypt to enclose a royal tomb, e.g. the Great Pyramid of Khufu/Cheops at Gizeh, near Cairo; 230 m/755 ft square and 147 m/481 ft high. In Babylon◊ and Assyria◊ broadly stepped pyramids (ziggurats) were used as the base for a shrine to a god: the Tower of Babel (see Babylon◊) was probably one of these. Pyramidal temple mounds were also built by the Aztecs◊ and Mayas◊, e.g. at Chichen Itza◊ and Cholula, near Mexico City, which is the world's largest in ground area (300 m/990 ft base, 60 m/195 ft high)□

Pyramus and Thisbe Babylonian lovers whose story was retold by Ovid◊. Pursued by a lioness, Thisbe lost her veil, and when Pyramus arrived at their meeting-place, he found it bloodstained. Assuming Thisbe was dead, he stabbed himself, and she, on finding his body, killed herself. Shakespeare used the story in *A Midsummer Night's Dream*□

Pyrénées; mountain range in SW Europe between France and the Iberian peninsula; length c435 km/270 miles; highest peak Aneto (French Néthon) 3404 m/11 168 ft. The Basque◊ country is on the French/Spanish frontier, and Andorra◊ is entirely within the range□

pyrethrum a type of chrysanthemum◊□

pyridine liquid heterocyclic base C_5H_5N, with a sickly smell; it occurs in coal tar and bone oil, is soluble in water, and is used as a solvent□

pyrites a common ore of iron. See iron◊ pyrites□

pyrogallol or *pyrogallic acid* $C_6H_3(OH)_3$, prepared from gallic◊ acid, and used (because its alkaline solution turns black as it rapidly absorbs oxygen) in gas analysis for the measurement of oxygen. It is also used in photograph development□

pyrometer instrument for measuring high temperatures. See under thermometer◊□

pyroxenes group of minerals, silicates of calcium, iron and magnesium, found in igneous◊ and metamorphic◊ rocks. ***Jadeite*** $NaAlSi_2O_6$, from which one of the forms of jade◊ comes, is one of the more unusual pyroxenes□

Pyrrhon c360–270BC. Greek philosopher, founder of the Sceptic◊ school, who maintained that since certainty was impossible, peace of mind lay in renouncing all claims to knowledge□

Pyrrhus c318–272BC. King of Epirus◊ from 307, who invaded Italy in 280, as an ally of the Tarentines◊ against Rome. He twice defeated the Romans, but with such heavy losses that a 'Pyrrhic victory' is a byword for one not worth winning, and he returned to Greece in 275□

Pythagoras c570–500BC. Greek philosopher who founded a politically influential religious brotherhood, suppressed in the 5th century. Its tenets included immortality of the soul and transmigration◊; mathematics was studied and much of Euclid◊ anticipated. ***Pythagoras' theorem*** states that in a right-angled triangle the square on the hypotenuse is equal to the sum of the squares on the other two sides□

Pytheas 4th century BC. Greek navigator who explored the coast of W Europe at least as far as Denmark, sailed round Britain, and reached 'Thule'◊ (probably the Shetlands)□

python a large snake◊□

pyx Latin 'box', the container used in the Catholic church for the reservation of the wafers of the sacrament. The ***Trial of the Pyx*** is the test of coinage by a goldsmith, at the hall of the Goldsmiths' Company, London, and is so-called because of the box in which specimens of coinage are stored□

Q

Qadisiyah Battle of 637AD. A battle in which a Muslim Arab force defeated a larger Zoroastrian◊ Persian army in S Iraq and ended the Sassanian◊ Empire. The defeat is still resented in modern Iran, where modern Muslim Arab nationalism threatens the break-up of the Iranian state□

qat shrub *Catha edulis* related to coffee; the leaves are chewed as a mild narcotic in some Arab countries; banned in Somalia◊ 1983□

Qatar State of

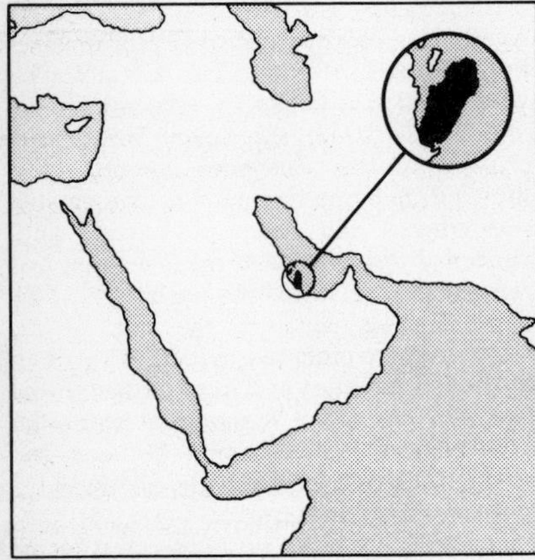

area 11 437 sq km/4250 sq mi
capital and chief port Doha
towns Dukhan, centre of oil production
features negligible rain and surface water, so that only 3% is fertile, but irrigation allows self-sufficiency in fruit and vegetables; rich oil discoveries since World War II
exports oil and natural gas, petrochemicals, fertilizers, iron and steel
currency Qatar riyal
population 276 000, mainly in Doha
language Arabic
religion Sunni Islam
government Sheikh Khalifa bin Hamad al-Thani (born 1930) from 1972, when he deposed his cousin and introduced reforms
history a British protectorate from 1916, Qatar became independent 1971, though continuing friendly relations under treaty□

Qattara Depression tract of the Western Desert, Egypt, up to 125 m/400 ft below sea level. Its very soft sand makes it virtually impassable to vehicles, and it protected the left flank of the Allied armies before and during the Battle of Alamein◊ 1942□

Qin Chinese dynasty 221–206BC. See Shi◊ Huangdi□

Qingdao industrial city (formerly Tsingtao), port and summer resort in Shandong province, China; population 1 500 000. It is famous for its beer□

Qinghai province (formerly Tsinghai) of NW China
area 721 000 sq km/278 000 sq mi
capital Xining
features mainly desert, with nomadic herdsmen
products oil
population 3 720 000, including many Tibetans and other minorities. Criminals and delinquents may be deported here as a labour force□

quadrathon a sports event in which the competitors must swim two miles, walk 30 miles, cycle 100 miles, and run 26.2 miles (a marathon) within 22 hours□

quaestor annually elected Roman financial officials, both in Rome itself, the provinces, and attached to commanding generals□

quagga extinct species of wild horse, resembling the zebra◊□

Quai d'Orsay part of the Parisian 'left bank' of the Seine, where the French Foreign Office is sited, hence synonymous with it□

quail a small bird of the partridge family. See under fowl◊□

Quakers popular name for the Religious Society of Friends◊□

quango *q*uasi-*a*utonomous *n*on-*g*overnmental *o*rganisation, e.g. the Location of Offices Bureau, established 1963 (abolished 1979, as were others by the Thatcher government). The proliferation of such bodies in the UK in the 1970s had given rise to concern because of the political patronage involved□

Quant Mary 1934– . British fashion designer. Her Chelsea boutique, Bazaar, achieved a practical off-beat revolution in women's clothing and make-up, which epitomized 'swinging London' of the 1960s□

Quantrill William Clarke 1837–65. American bandit, who became leader of a guerrilla unit on the Confederate◊ side in the Civil◊ War, which went in for robbery and murder. Jesse and Frank James◊ were among his aides, and all appear in ballad legend□

quantum theory theory in physics that many quantities such as energy◊, cannot have continuous range of values but only a smaller number of particular ones, because they are packaged in 'quanta of energy'.

The theory began with the work of Max Planck◊ in 1900 on radiated energy, and was extended by Einstein◊ to electromagnetic◊ radiation generally, including light. Niels Bohr◊ used it to explain the spectrum◊ of light emitted by excited hydrogen atoms.

Later work by Schödinger◊, Heisenberg◊, Dirac◊ and other elaborated the theory to what is called ***Quantum mechanics***. Just as the earlier theory has shown how light, generally seen as a wave motion, could also in some ways be seen as composed of discrete particles (photons◊), so quantum mechanics show how atomic particles like electrons may also be seen as having wave-like properties. Quantum mechanics is the basis of particle physics◊, modern theoretical chemistry and the 'solid state' physics which describe the behaviour of the silicon chips used in modern computers□

quarantine term (from the French *quarantaine* 40 days) applied to any period for which people, animals, a ship, and so on, may be detained in isolation when suspected of carrying disease. In the UK (to prevent the spread of rabies) immigrant dogs are kept in quarantine kennels for six months□

quarrying commercial exploitation of stone, clay, gravel, sand, chalk, slate, and other deposits, now usually on a large, mechanised scale which may devastate the countryside. Permission for such exploitation is increasingly linked either to restoring the landscape as far as possible to its previous state, or for using the excavations for improvements, e.g. filling quarries with water to provide lakes for water sports and nature reserves□

quart imperial capacity measure, equal to 2 pints or 1.2 litres□

quarter days dates on which such payments as ground-rents become due; in England 25 Mar (Lady Day), 24 Jun (Midsummer Day), 29 Sept (Michaelmas), and 25 Dec (Christmas Day)□

quartz one of the commonest rocks of earth's crust, it is hard and crystalline. In itself colourless, it is often of extraordinary beauty when impurities, such as oxides◊, occur in the hexagonal crystals, e.g. amethyst◊, tourmaline◊, agate◊, jasper◊, onyx◊, chalcedony◊, granite porphyries◊. Used in jewellery and ornamental work. Quartz is also now manufactured, e.g. natural crystals that would take 3 000 000 years to form, can now be 'grown' in pressure vessels to a standard which makes them usable in optical and scientific instruments, and in electronics, where they are used for frequency◊ standards□

quasar compact cosmic source of very intense radiation◊; PKS 2 000 minus 32, discovered in 1982, seems to emit energy at a rate 100 000 million times that of our sun. Quasars may be shells of hot gas surrounding black◊ holes of up to 500 million solar masses, and arising from the black hole's disruption of stars nearby in the nucleus◊ of a galaxy◊□

Quasimodo Salvatore 1901–68. Italian poet, whose work became increasingly preoccupied with contemporary political and social problems, e.g. *Il falso e vero verde* 1956; Nobel prize 1959□

quassia trees of S America which have a bitter bark and wood, e.g. *Quassia amara* family Simaroubaceae. An infusion was formerly used as a tonic, and quassia is now used in insecticides□

Quathlamba see under Drakensberg◊□

Quatre Bras Battle of, 16 Jun 1815. See under Napoleonic◊ Wars□

Quebec capital and industrial port (textiles and leather; timber, pulp, paper; printing and publishing) of Quebec province, Canada; population 166 475; Founded 1608 by Champlain◊, its picturesque old town survives below the citadel c110 m/360 ft above the St Lawrence river. The British, under Wolfe◊, captured Quebec 1759, after a battle on the nearby Plains of Abraham, both Wolfe and the French commander (Montcalm◊) being killed. Quebec is a centre of French culture, and there are two universities, Laval 1663 (oldest in N America) and Quebec 1969□

Quebec/Québec eastern province of Canada
area 1 540 676 sq km/594 860 sq mi
capital Québec
towns Montreal, Laval, Sherbrooke, Verdun, Hull, Trois-Riviéres
features immense water power resources, e.g. the James Bay project
products iron, copper, gold, zinc; cereals, potatoes; forest products, including paper; textiles; fish
population 6 549 000
language French is the only official language since 1974, though the legislation was modified by Quebec court rulings 1984–5. See also Canada◊

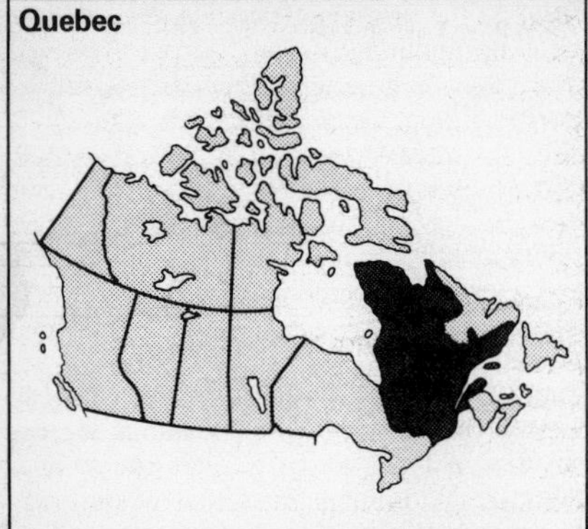
Quebec

history see under Canadian◊ history. Nationalist feeling (despite existing safeguards for Quebec's French derived civil law, customs, religion and language) led in the 1960s to the foundation of the Parti Québecois (see Lévesque◊) 1968. Premier is Pierre Marc Johnson, who suceeded Réné Lévesque in 1985□

Quebec Conference 1943, at which Roosevelt◊, Churchill◊, Mackenzie King◊ and Tseven Soong◊ approved Mountbatten◊ as supreme Allied commander SE Asia and made plans for the invasion of France, for which Eisenhower◊ was to be supreme commander□

quebracho several S American trees with very hard wood, especially the ***red quebracho*** *Schinopsis lorentzii* family Anacardiaceae used in tanning□

Quechua South American Indians of the Andes region, whose ancestors included the Inca◊; the language is the second official language of Peru, and is also spoken in Ecuador□

Queen Anne style style of furniture popular in England 1700–1720, characterized by restrained curves and the use of walnut veneer□

Queen Charlotte Islands archipelago c160 km/100 mi off British◊ Columbia, of which it forms part; area 9790 sq km/3780 sq mi; population 2500; There are timber and fishing industries□

Queen's Award in Britain, an award established 1965, and in 1976 divided into one award for Technological and the other for Export Achievement. Made to organizations, not individuals, on the real birthday of Elizabeth◊ II (21 Apr), they entitle the holder to display a special emblem for five years□

Queensberry John Douglas, 8th Marquess of Queensberry 1844–1900. British patron of boxing, who in 1867 drew up the more humane ***Queensberry rules*** which underlie modern regulations. He was the father of Lord Alfred Douglas◊□

Queen's Counsel or *QC* in England, a barrister appointed to senior rank by the Lord Chancellor◊. Known as King's Counsel when the monarch is a king□

Queensland state of the Commonwealth of Australia

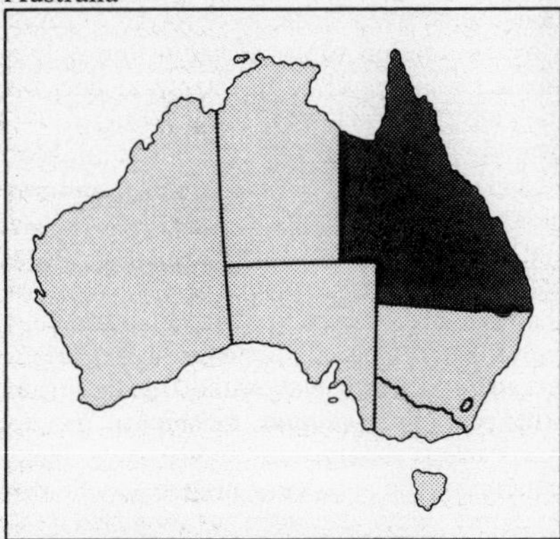

area 1 736 524 sq km/670 500 sq mi
capital Brisbane
towns Gold Coast, Townsville, Toowoomba, Rockhampton
features Great Dividing Range, include Mt Bartle Frere 1657 m/5438 ft; Great Barrier Reef (collection of coral reefs and islands c2000 km/1250 mi long off the east coast, uniquely rich in wildlife); City of Gold Coast holiday area in the south, population 120 000; Mt Isa mining area
exports sugar, pineapples; beef; cotton and wool; tobacco; copper, gold, silver, lead, zinc, coal, nickel, bauxite, uranium, natural gas
population 2 295 125
history part of New South Wales until 1859, it then became self-governing□

Queen's proctor in England, the official representing the Crown in matrimonial cases, and intervening when material facts have allegedly been suppressed. Known as King's proctor when the monarch is a king□

Queenstown former name of Cóbh◊□

Quemoy island off the south east coast of China, and administered (with Matsu◊) by Taiwan; area 130 sq km/50 sq mi; Matsu 40 sq km/17 sq mi; population c40 000. When the islands were shelled from the mainland 1960, USA declared they would be defended□

Queneau Raymond 1903–76. French surrealist poet, and humorous novelist, e.g. *Zazie dans le Métro* 1959, portraying a precocious little Parisienne□

Quesnay François 1694–1774. French physician to Louis◊ XV, and a founder c1750 of the group later known as 'physiocrats' (Greek 'nature'/'rule') because of their advocacy of political and economic rule on natural principles, with the land as the only true source of wealth□

Quetta town and summer resort in Baluchistan, Pakistan; population 285 000. There is a military staff college, and also a university□

quetzal a crested bird. See under trogon◊□

Quetzalcoatl feathered serpent god of air and water in the pre-Columbian Aztec◊ and Toltec◊ cultures. In legendary human form, he was said to have been fair-skinned and bearded, and to have reigned on earth during a golden age. He disappeared across the sea, with a promise to return; Cortes◊ exploited the coincidence of description when he invaded. Ruins of one of his temples survive at Teotihuacán in Mexico□

Quezon City capital of the Philippines 1948–76, it is a north east suburb of Manila and was named after the first president of the republic Manuel Quezon□

Qufu town (formerly Chufu) in Jinan province, China; population 27 000; It is the birth-place of Kong Fuzi (formerly Confucius◊), whose grave has not yet been excavated, and has the Great Temple of Confucius□

Quiberon peninsula and coastal town in Brittany, France; population 5000; In 1759 Hawke◊ defeated a French fleet (under Conflans◊) here□

quicksilver another name for mercury◊□

quietism Christian contemplation and meditation designed to achieve union with the deity. The founder of modern practice was Molinos◊□

Quiller-Couch Sir Arthur Thomas 1863–1944. British scholar, born in Cornwall, professor of English literature at Cambridge from 1912 and compiler of *The Oxford Book of English Verse* 1900□

Quilter Roger 1877–1953. British composer, best known for song settings from Dowson◊, Shakespeare, and others□

Quimper town in Brittany, France; population 60 500; There is a fine 15th-century Gothic◊ cathedral, and a decorative pottery industry□

quince central Asian tree *Cydonia oblonga* family Rosaceae◊; the bitter, yellow pear-shaped fruit is used in preserves□

Quincey de. See De◊ Quincey□

quinine bark extract, used to combat malaria, etc. See under cinchona◊□

quinsy old name for acute tonsillitis. See under tonsils◊□

Quintana Roo see under Yucatan◊□

Quintero Serafin Alvárez 1871–1938 and Joaquin Alvárez 1873–1945. Spanish dramatists. The brothers were born near Seville, and set most of their plays in Andalusia, producing some 200 in collaboration, e.g. *Papá Juan: Centenario* 1909 and *Los Mosquitos* 1928□

Quintilian (*Marcus Fabius Quintilianus*) c35–95AD. Roman teacher of rhetoric, who in *institutio oratorio* advocated a simple, sincere style□

quipus a device of the Incas◊ to record information, consisting of a set of knotted cords□

Quisling Vidkun 1887–1945. Leader of the Norwegian Fascist◊ party from 1933, who aided the Nazi◊ invasion in 1940 and who was made prime minister by Hitler◊ 1942. He was executed for war crimes, and his name became generic for those guilty of this form of treason□

Quito capital and industrial city (textiles, chemicals, leather, gold-, and silverware) of Ecuador, c3000 m/9350 ft above sea level in the Cordillera◊ so that it has a constant 'spring' climate; population 560 000; An ancient settlement, it was taken by the Incas◊ c1470, and by the Spanish 1534. It has a fine cathedral and two universities□

Qum holy city of the Shi'ite◊ Muslims in central Iran, 145 km/90 m south of Tehran; the Islamic academy of Madresseh Faizieh (1920) became the headquarters of Ayatollah Khomeini◊□

Qumran Khirbet. See under Essenes◊□

quoits game in which a rubber ring or quoit is thrown towards an iron hob from a point 16.5 m/18yd distant. Landing over the hob, a 'ringer' gains two points, and that landing nearest the hob, within a circle 1 m/3ft in diameter, one point□

R

Rabat capital and industrial port (cotton textiles, carpets, leather goods) of Morocco; population 518 700□

Rabaul port on New Britain, in Papua◊ New Guinea; population 15 000□

rabbi the chief religious minister of a synagogue; the spiritual leader of a Jewish congregation. See under Judaism◊□

rabbit mammal of order Lagomorpha, family Leporidae, smaller than the hare◊. Most common is the greyish-brown, long-eared ***common rabbit*** *Oryctolagus cuniculus* of Europe and N Africa (introduced to Australia and elsewhere), which reveals the white underside of its brief tail in its hopping run. It produces several large litters in a year, and is destructive to crops. Living in groups of interconnected underground burrows, 'warrens', rabbits are especially subject to the virus disease, ***myxomatosis*** which has led to some degree to an 'above-ground' lifestyle. Rabbits are bred for food; angora 'wool' made from the combed hairs of a long-haired species; and fur, the pelts usually being treated to resemble more costly furs. The N American equivalent of the species is the woodland ***cottontail*** *Silvilagus floridanus*□

Rabelais François c1495–1553. French monk, author of satirical allegories, *La Vie inestimable de Gargantua* 1535 and *Faits et dits héroiques du grand Pantagruel* 1533, the story of two giants (father and son) Gargantua and Pantagruel□

rabies or ***hydrophobia*** 'aversion to water'. Virus disease with a high mortality rate, which runs a painful course ending in spasms of the throat brought on by drinking, or by the sight of water (hence the name). It is contracted by a bite from an affected animal (usually a dog or fox). There is now an effective vaccine□

Rabin Itzhak 1922– . Israeli Prime Minister 1974–7, who resigned following involvement in a currency scandal□

raccoon or ***racoon*** carnivorous nocturnal mammal of N and Central America *Procyon lotor* family Procyonidae. About 60 cm/2 ft long, it has a grey-brown body fur, and a black and white ringed tail□

raccoon dog small wild dog *Nyctereutes procyonides* found in the Far East. Farmed in the USSR for its fawnish pelt with black markings, it has spread across Europe as a potential pest□

Rachel in Old Testament, favourite wife of Jacob◊, and mother of Joseph◊ and Benjamin□

Rachel stage-name of the French tragedienne Elizabeth Félix 1821–58. She excelled in Racine's *Phèdre*□

Rachmaninov Sergei Vassilievich 1873–1943. Russian pianist, conductor and romantic composer, who went to the USA in 1917. His works include three symphonies, four piano concertos, and the *Rhapsody on a Theme of Paganini* for piano and orchestra□

racial discrimination discrimination◊ on the basis of race□

Racine Jean 1639–99. French dramatist, the friend of Boileau◊, La Fontaine◊ and Molière◊. He is most famous for his tragedies on classical themes, e.g. *Andromaque* 1667, *Iphigénie* 1674, and *Phèdre* 1677. After the contemporary failure of the last-named he no longer wrote for the secular stage, but influenced by Mme de Maintenon◊ wrote two religious dramas *Esther* 1689 and *Athalie* 1691□

rackets or ***racquets*** game for two or four people played in an enclosed court with rackets and a small ball. It is very fast and resembles squash◊□

racoon alternative form of raccoon◊□

rad dosage unit of absorbed radiation◊, 1 rad equalling 0.01 J/kg; the average person receives a dose of 0.1 rad each year from natural sources□

radar a means of locating an object in space, direction finding, and navigation by short radio waves: ***RA***dio ***D***irection ***A***nd ***R***anging. Direction of an object is ascertained by sending a beam of small-wavelength (1cm–100cm) short-pulse radio waves, and picking up the reflected beam; and distance by timing the journey of the radio waves there and back. See Appleton◊ and Watson-Watt◊. Essential to navigation in darkness, cloud and fog, it can be thwarted in warfare by planes and missiles with a modified shape which

reduces their cross-section; radar-absorbent paints; and electronic jamming. A countermeasure in pinpointing small targets is the use of laser◊ 'radar' instead of microwaves◊.
Chains of ground radar stations are used to warn of enemy attack, e.g. North Warning System 1985, consisting of 52 stations across the Canadian Arctic and N Alaska. It is also used in meteorology◊ and astronomy◊: radar reflections from the moon were first detected during World War II, and the timed delay in receiving echoes from the sun and planets has improved the calculation of their distances from earth□

Radcliffe Anne 1764–1823. British novelist, born Ward, chief exponent of the Gothic◊ novel or 'romance of terror', e.g. *The Mysteries of Udolpho* 1794□

radiation the emission of radiant energy as particles, waves, sound, etc. See spectrum◊, electromagnetic◊ waves□

radical a group of atoms◊ forming part of a molecule◊ which takes part in reactions without disintegration, yet often cannot exist alone□

Radicals the supporters of parliamentary reform in Britain before the Reform◊ Bill of 1832, who later became the advanced wing of the Liberal◊ Party. During the 1860s (led by Cobden◊, Bright◊, and J S Mill◊) they campaigned for extension of the franchise, free trade, and laissez-faire, but after 1870, under the leadership of J Chamberlain◊ and Dilke◊, they adopted a republican and semi-Socialist programme. With the growth of Socialism◊ in the later 19th century, Radicalism ceased to exist as an organized movement. In the USA a 'radical' is anyone of left-wing opinions□

radio the transmission and reception of radio waves. The theory of electromagnetic◊ waves was first developed by James Clerk Maxwell◊ 1864, given practical confirmation in the laboratory 1888 by Heinrich Hertz◊, and put to practical use by Marconi◊, who in 1901 achieved reception of a signal in Newfoundland transmitted from Poldhu◊ in Cornwall.
radio transmission a microphone◊ converts sound◊ waves (pressure variations in the air) into an audio frequency electrical signal. The *oscillator* produces a carrier voltage of high frequency; different stations are allocated different transmitting carrier frequencies. A *modulator* superimposes the audio frequency signal on the carrier. There are two main ways of doing this: *amplitude modulation* (AM), used for long and medium wave broadcasts, in which the strength of the carrier is made to fluctuate in time with the audio signal; in *frequency modulation* (FM), as used for VHF broadcasts, the frequency of the carrier is made to fluctuate. The transmitting aerial emits the modulated electromagnetic◊ waves which travel outwards from it.
radio reception a receiving aerial produces voltages in response to the waves sent out by a transmitter. A *tuned circuit* selects a particular voltage frequency, corresponding to a particular transmitter, usually by means of a variable capacitor◊ connected across a coil of wire. (The effect is similar to altering the tension in a piano wire, making it capable of vibrating at a different frequency.) The demodulator disentangles the audio signal from the carrier, which is now discarded, having served its purpose. The amplifier boosts the audio signal for feeding to the loudspeaker which produces sound waves□

radio cellular. The use of a series of short-range transmitters at the centre of adjacent cells (each c4 km/2.5 mi in diameter), using the same frequencies over and over again throughout the area covered. It is used for personal communication among subscribers via car phones, portable units, etc.□

radioactive tracer radioactive◊ isotope◊ which replaces an ordinary atom◊ in a compound, so that its path may be followed, by geiger◊ counters, etc. The technique is used in medicine, science, and industry. See chemiluminescence◊□

radioactive waste comprises various types of nuclear waste. Tailings◊ contaminate a site where uranium◊ is mined or milled for use, and may have an active life of several thousand years. Reactor waste is of three types: ***high level*** spent fuel or the residue when nuclear fuel has been removed from a reactor and reprocessed to extract uranium and plutonium◊; ***intermediate*** which may be long- or short-lived; ***low level*** but bulky, waste from reactors, and which has only short-lived radioactivity.
Disposal by burial on land or at sea raises problems of security, either of the site or of the containers themselves, and threatens to halt development of the nuclear industry□

radioactivity spontaneous emission of radiation◊ from the nuclei of atoms of certain substances, termed ***radioactive***. The radiation is of three main types:
alpha (fast-moving helium◊ nuclei); ***beta*** (fast-moving electrons◊); and ***gamma*** (high energy highly penetrating protons◊). Beta and gamma radiation are both damaging to body tissues, but are especially dangerous if a radioactive substance is ingested or inhaled. See particle physics◊□

radioastronomy study of electromagnetic◊ radiation received from celestial objects. See

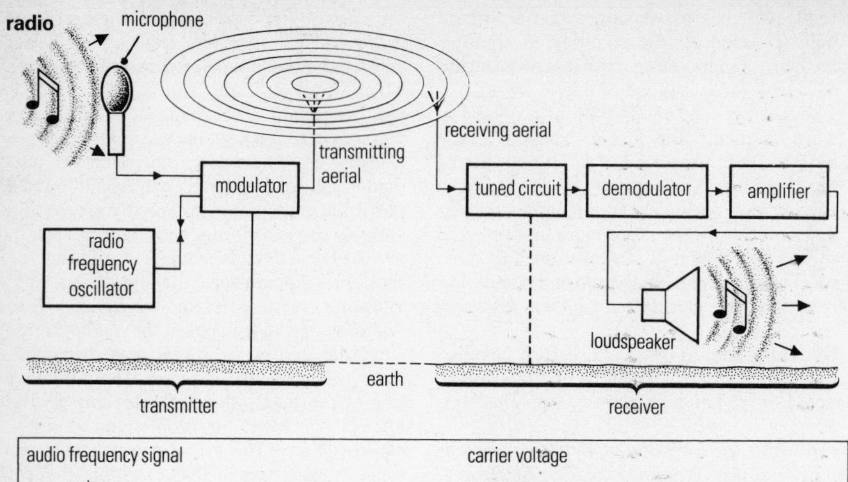
radio
microphone
receiving aerial
transmitting
aerial
modulator
tuned circuit
demodulator
amplifier
radio
frequency
oscillator
loudspeaker
earth
transmitter
receiver

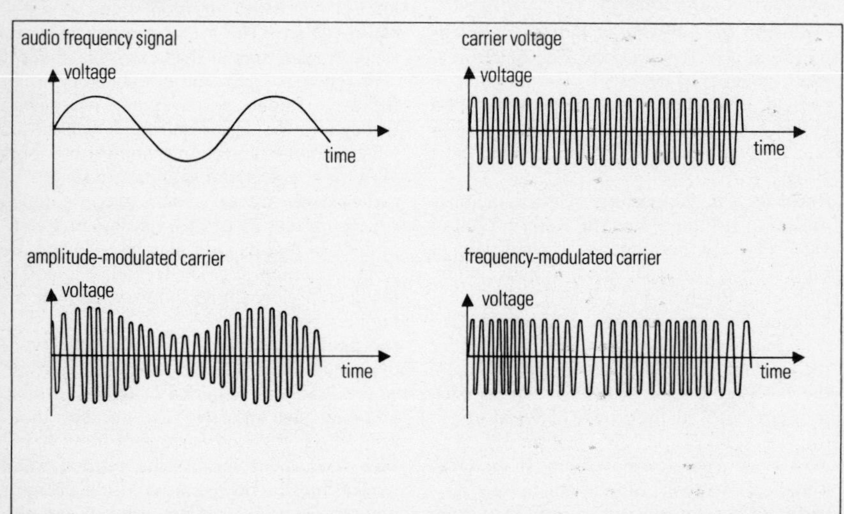
audio frequency signal
voltage
time
carrier voltage
voltage
time
amplitude-modulated carrier
voltage
time
frequency-modulated carrier
voltage
time

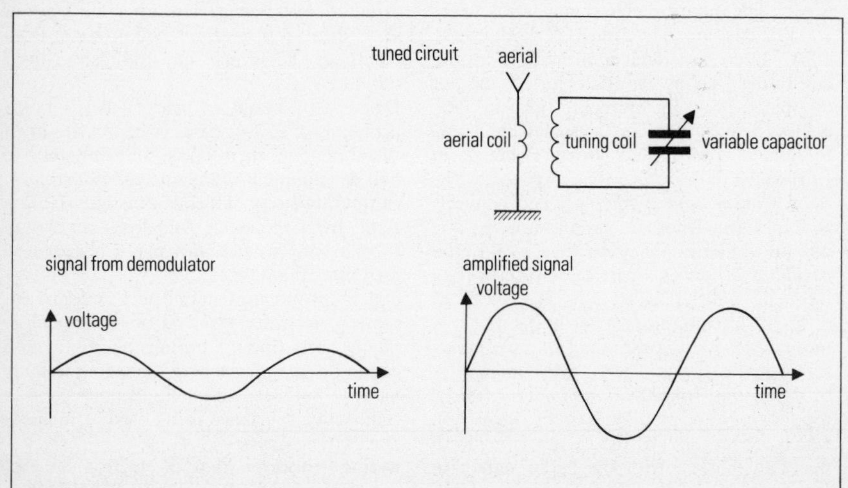
tuned circuit
aerial
aerial coil
tuning coil
variable capacitor
signal from demodulator
voltage
time
amplified signal
voltage
time

under astronomy◊, telescope◊; the pioneer was Karl Jansky◊□

radiocarbon dating method of dating organic materials used in archaeology, e.g. on death, wood ceases to take up the radioisotope◊ carbon-14 from the atmosphere and that already taken up decays at a known rate, allowing the time which has elapsed (not beyond 70 000 years) to be measured, though not with exactness. See W F Libby◊, also radiometric◊ dating□

radiochemistry the chemical study of radioactive◊ elements and their compounds, whether produced from naturally radioactive or irradiated materials, and their use in the study of other chemical processes, e.g. the biochemical functioning of the body, the testing of the action of drugs on it, medical diagnosis (cancer, foetal abnormalities, heart disease, etc.), and as an aid in reading the genetic◊ code□

radiography use of X or gamma rays to produce images on film or fluorescent screen to aid in diagnosis, both medical (cancer, tuberculosis, etc.) and industrial (faults in structures such as pipelines or 'fatigue' in metals, etc.). With a ***body scanner***, data, obtained by passing X-rays at several angles through the head, thorax, etc., is integrated digitally to produce cross-sections showing more detail than the traditional shadow photographs□

radioisotope a radioactive◊ isotope◊ of an element either occurring naturally or made by bombardment with neutrons in the core of a nuclear reactor. The radiations it then gives off can be used in radiotherapy◊, industry (as in nuclear power generation), agriculture, and various kinds of research (see radioactive◊ tracer)□

radiolaria marine and largely planktonic organisms, an order of protozoa◊, which form siliceous skeletons with radiating pseudopodia◊ for feeding; the skeletons eventually form radiolarian ooze on the sea bottom. See also under impact crater◊□

radiometric dating method of dating rock by assessing the degree of radioactive◊ decay of various elements within it. Once-living material is often dated by the radiocarbon◊ method□

radiotherapy the treatment of disease by radiation◊ from X-ray machines or radioisotopes◊. Radiation reduces the activity of dividing cells, and so is especially useful in treating cancer tissue, some non-malignant tumours and some diseases of the skin, and may be used in combination with surgery. Small sources may be implanted into the tissue being treated, in an attempt to localize the irradiation□

radish annual herb *Raphanus sativus* family Cruciferae◊, grown for its reddish, fleshy, pungent, edible root□

radium element
symbol Ra
atomic number 88
physical description white luminescent metal
features found in pitchblende◊ in small quantities and other uranium ores
uses to treat cancer in radiotherapy, and in luminous paints□

Radom industrial city (footwear, machinery, chemicals) in E Poland (Austrian 1795–1815 and Russian 1815–1918); population 198 000□

radon element
symbol Rn
atomic number 86
physical description colourless, dense, radioactive gas
features produced from the radioactive decay of radium◊, thorium◊ and actinium◊; one of the inert◊ gases
uses in radiotherapy as a source of alpha particles□

Raeburn Sir Henry 1756–1823. Scottish portraitist of Edinburgh notabilities□

Raeder Erich 1876–1960. German admiral, Commander-in-Chief of the navy 1928–43, when Hitler◊ dismissed him for failing to prevent Allied Arctic convoys reaching Russia. He was sentenced to life imprisonment at Nuremberg◊, but released in 1955□

Raffles Sir Thomas Stamford 1781–1826. British administrator. While governor of Sumatra for the East◊ India Company, he founded Singapore◊ in 1819, and was a founder of the Zoological◊ Society□

rafflesia genus of parasitic Malayan plants without stems, family Rafflesiaceae. The largest flowers in the world are produced by *R arnoldiana*. About 1 m/3 ft across, they are also contestants for the world's worst smell (that of rotting flesh) which attracts the flies which pollinate them□

raga a composition in Indian music◊□

Raglan FitzRoy James Henry Somerset, 1st Baron Raglan 1788–1855. British field marshal. He helped storm Badajoz◊, lost an arm at Waterloo◊, and commanded the British forces in the Crimean◊ War, dying of dysentery. The ***raglan sleeve*** (cut to the neck, without a shoulder seam) is named after him□

ragtime syncopated music ('ragged time'), developed among black American musicians in the late 19th century; it was influenced by folk tradition, the minstrel shows, and the marching bands, and later merged into jazz◊. See also Joplin◊□

Ragusa town in Sicily, producing oil and asphalt; population 60 000□

ragwort perennial plant *Senecio jacobaea*, family Compositae◊, prolific on waste ground; it has bright yellow flowers□

Rahman Putra Tunku ('Prince') Abdul 1903– . Malaysian statesman, who as Prime Minister 1957–70 was the prime mover in the creation of Malaysia◊ in 1963□

Raikes Robert 1735–1811. British printer, who started the first Sunday◊ school in Gloucester in 1780; the movement still continues. He also stimulated the weekday voluntary 'ragged schools' for poor children□

rail a member of the family of birds, Rallidae, which spend their lives in marginal freshwater vegetation, e.g. ***Eurasian coot*** *Fulica atra*, with a black body, greyish legs, and white 'bald patch'; ***moorhen*** *Gallinula chloropus* black-brown, with a red 'shield' above the beak; and migratory ***corncrake*** *Crex crex* a grassland bird which winters in Africa, etc., and has a harsh call. See crane◊□

railway system of parallel tracks on which vehicles can travel. Tracks to carry goods waggons were in use at collieries in the 18th century, but the first practical public passenger service was that between Stockton and Darlington in 1825, under the power of Stephenson's engine 'Locomotion': see also Trevithick◊. A railway boom ensued, and railways were the major form of land transport for passengers and goods until after World War II when the private car, coach services, internal air services, and road haulage door-to-door, destroyed their monopoly. In Britain the railways (known as British Rail from 1965) were nationalized in 1948, and the network increasingly shrank. In the USA and Canada railways made the 19th-century exploitation of the central and western territories possible, and in the USA underpinned the victory of the North in the Civil◊ War, the 'Railway War'. In countries with less developed road systems and large areas of difficult terrain, the railway is still important, as in India (where the British system survives), China, South America (system largely built by British engineers), and the USSR (see under Siberia◊). Electrification, or the use of diesel electric engines, has superseded the steam engine in Britain and other developed countries, and there has been some revival in the popularity of the train for longer distance 'inter-city' services. Interesting experiments include the Maglev train (see under levitation◊)□

rain acid. See acid◊ rain□

rainbow a colourful arch formed in the sky by the refraction of light by rain drops. See under meteorology◊□

Raine Kathleen 1908– . British poet, a schoolmaster's daughter, brought up in Northumberland (a landscape influence on her volumes *Stone and Flower* 1943 and *The Lost Country* 1971), and educated at Girton College, Cambridge. She became a Catholic convert in 1944, and was formerly married to the poet and sociologist Charles Madge◊□

Rainier III Prince. See under Monaco◊□

Rainier Mount. See Cascade◊ Range□

Rais Gilles de 1404–40. French marshal who fought alongside Joan◊ of Arc. In 1440 he was hanged for the torture and murder of 140 children, but the court proceedings were irregular. See Bluebeard◊□

raisin a dried grape. See vine◊□

Rajasthan state of NW India
area 342 214 sq km/131 995 sq mi
capital Jaipur
features the larger part of the Thar◊ Desert, where India's first nuclear test was carried out
population 34 103 000; see also under Rajput◊
language Rajasthani, Hindi
religion Hinduism 90%, Islam 3%□

Rajput high-caste Hindus◊ of India, predominantly soldiers and landowners in the north. The ***Rajput States*** of W India are now merged in Rajasthan◊□

Raleigh or ***Ralegh*** Sir Walter c1552–1618. English adventurer, born in Devon. A favourite of Elizabeth◊ I, he was knighted in 1584, and made several attempts 1584–7 to establish a colony in 'Virginia' (now North◊ Carolina). In 1595 he led an expedition to S America (described in his *Discovery of Guiana*) and distinguished himself in expeditions against the Spaniards in Cadiz◊ in 1596 and the Azores◊ in 1597. After James◊ I's accession in 1603 he was condemned to death on a charge of conspiracy, but reprieved and imprisoned in the Tower of London, where he wrote his unfinished *History of the World*. Released in 1616 to lead a gold-seeking expedition to the Orinoco◊, which failed disastrously, he was beheaded on his return under his former sentence□

Raleigh capital and industrial city (electrical machinery, food processing, and textiles) of North Carolina, USA; population 148 300□

RAM ***R***andom ***A***ccess ***M***emory. In computing, a memory device to which data can be written, and from which it can be read. RAM is volatile memory which is lost when the machine is switched off, and is used for the temporary storage of data or programs□

Rama incarnation of Vishnu◊□

Ramadan see under Observances of Islam◊□

Raman Sir Venkata 1888–1970. Indian physicist, Nobel prizewinner in 1930 for his discovery in 1928 of the ***Raman Effect***, a type of scattering of light when it is passed through a transparent substance□

Ramat Gan industrial city (textiles, food processing) in W Israel, NE of Jaffa-Tel Aviv; population 118 300□

Ramayana Sanskrit epic c300BC, in which Rama (see Vishnu◊) and his friend Hanuman (the monkey chieftain) strive to recover Rama's wife, Sita, abducted by demon king Ravana□

Rambert Dame Marie (original name Cyvia Rabbam) 1888–1982. British (from 1918) ballet dancer and teacher, born in Warsaw. She danced with the Diaghilev ballet 1912–13, and in 1926 founded the ***Ballet Rambert***; DBE 1962□

Ramblers' Association society founded in Britain in 1935 to conserve the countryside and ensure that footpaths remained open. From 1985 it also campaigned for access to areas beyond the footpath network, e.g. many moors and woods□

Rambouillet town in the south of the forest of Rambouillet, SW of Paris, France; the former royal chteau is now the presidential summer residence; population 16 500□

Rameau Jean Philippe 1683–1764. French organist and composer. He wrote an influential *Treatise on Harmony* and his varied works include many operas, e.g. *Castor and Pollux* 1737□

Ramée Louise de la. See Ouida◊□

Rameses eleven kings of ancient Egypt including:

Rameses II reigned c1300–1225BC. The son of Seti◊ I, he campaigned successfully against the Hittites◊, and built two rock temples at Abu◊ Simbel in Upper Egypt (the larger commemorates himself and the other his wife Nefertari◊). Threatened with submersion when the Aswan◊ High Dam was built in 1966, the temples were reconstructed above the water line.

Rameses III reigned c1200–1168BC. He won a naval victory over the Philistines◊ and other barbarian peoples, and asserted his suzerainty over Palestine◊□

Ramillies Battle of, 1706. See under War of Spanish◊ Succession□

Ramphal Sir Shridath Surendranath 1928– . Guyanese statesman, Minister of Foreign Affairs and Justice, Guyana, 1972–5, and Secretary-General of the Commonwealth◊ from 1975□

Ramsay Allan 1686–1758. Scottish bookseller and poet, who wrote songs and collected others in his *The Tea-Table Miscellany* 1724–7, and revived the work of such poets as Dunbar◊ and Henryson◊□

Ramsay Allan 1713–84. Scottish portraitist, son of the poet, who excelled in studies of women□

Ramsay Sir William 1852–1916. Scottish chemist. Together with Lord Rayleigh◊, he discovered argon◊ in 1894, was knighted in 1902, and received a Nobel prize in 1904 (for his continued work in discovering the inert gases)□

Ramsgate seaside resort and cross-Channel port (under major expansion in 1985) in the Isle of Thanet, Kent; population 41 000. There is a maritime museum, and Pugin◊ built a home there; the church next door (St Augustine's) is where he is buried□

Rance see under Brittany◊□

Rand abbreviation for Witwatersrand, the goldbearing ridge in Transvaal, S Africa; the name was adopted for the basic unit of the country's new decimal currency in 1961. See also under sovereign◊□

Rangoon capital of Burma on the Rangoon river, a great commercial centre, exporting rice, teak, petroleum; population 2 460 000. Its golden Shwe Dagŏn pagoda, traditionally founded in 585BC, is a centre of pilgrimage. It was occupied by the Japanese in World War II□

Ranjit Singh 1780–1839. Indian maharajah, 'the Lion of the Punjab'. He created a Sikh◊ army from 1792 which conquered Kashmir◊ and the Punjab◊□

Ransom John Crowe 1888–1974. American poet, born in Tennessee, and author of romantic verse including *Poems about God* 1919 and *Two Gentlemen in Bonds* 1926□

Ransome Arthur 1884–1967. British author. As a journalist he worked in Russia for the *Daily News* and the Foreign Office in World War I and the Russian◊ Revolution. He wrote books for children, including *Swallows and Amazons* 1930 (see under Cumbria◊) both exciting and technically instructive in sailing, etc.□

Ranunculaceae family of northern temperate herbs or shrubs with 5-petalled flowers; a number contain poisonous alkaloids. Familiar genera are:

aconite *Aconitum,* mainly poisonous, e.g. ***monk's hood*** or ***wolf's bane;*** the roots yield aconitine◊

columbine *Aquilegia,* with deeply divided leaves and spurred pinkish flowers; including ***wild columbine*** *A vulgaris,* and many cultivated species

delphinium or ***larkspur,*** with blue, pink, or white flowers borne in long terminal spikes, e.g. *D ajacis*

hellebore *Helleborus* e.g. ***green hellebore*** or ***bear's foot*** *H viridis*, and ***stinking hellebore*** *H foetidus*, both native to Britain; ***Christmas rose*** *H niger;* ***Lenten rose*** *H orientalis*

anemone notably ***wood anemone*** *A nemorosa*; ***pasque flower*** *A Pulsatilla*

buttercup or ***crowfoot*** *Ranunculus*, with divided leaves and yellow flowers, e.g. ***common buttercup*** *R acris;* ***creeping buttercup*** (see celandine◊); ***water crowfoot*** *R aquatilis*

clematis temperate woody climbers, with large showy flowers; ***traveller's joy*** or ***old man's beard*** (from its hairy seeds) is the only British species, but many varieties have been introduced for cultivation

kingcup common name for some Ranunculaceae, especially the marsh marigold

love-in-a-mist annual *Nigella damascena* with fernlike leaves and blue or white flowers

marsh marigold *Caltha palustris,* common in moist places; in USA sometimes called cowslip

peony *Paeonia,* native to Europe, temperate Asia, and NW America; cultivated for its scentless, but bright, showy flowers□

Rapallo port and winter resort in NW Italy; population 27 000. Treaties were signed here in 1920 (settling the common frontiers of Italy and Yugoslavia) and in 1922 (cancelling German and Russian counter-claims for indemnities for World War I)□

Rapa Nui see under Easter◊ Island□

rape several species of *Brassica,* family Cruciferae◊; the seeds yield oil (used in lubricants and soaps), and the plants and seed residue are used as animal feed□

rape sexual intercourse with a woman without her consent. In British courts, since 1976, the victim remains anonymous (as does her alleged attacker unless convicted); her sex history is not in question; and it is her 'absence of consent' rather than the previously required evidence of her 'resistance to violence' which is the criterion of the crime□

Raphael Sanzio 1483–1520. Italian artist, born at Urbino, he studied under his father and then under Perugino◊, and was influenced by da Vinci◊ and Michelangelo◊. Remarkable for their composition, and beauty of form and colour, his works include the *St Catherine* and the *Ansidei Madonna* in the National Gallery, London; the tapestry cartoons for the Sistine◊ Chapel on biblical subjects, some surviving in the Victoria and Albert Museum, London; his portrait of his patron Pope Julius II; and the Vatican◊ fresco cycle, including *The School of Athens* and the *Sistine Madonna*◊, now at Dresden□

Rapid Deployment Force a military strike force established by the USA in 1979 (following the Iran and Afghan crises); headquarters Fort McDill, Tampa, Florida. It was extended by Reagan◊ in 1981 and from 1983, as the US Central Command, its potential operation area covers: Afghanistan, Arabia, Egypt, Ethiopia, Iran, Iraq, Jordan, Kenya, Pakistan, Somalia, Sudan, and the Red Sea and Arabian Gulf□

rare earths oxides of metals found in certain rare minerals. See lanthanides◊□

rare gases name applied to the elements helium, neon, argon, krypton, xenon, and radon. See under gas◊□

Ras al Khaimah see under United◊ Arab Emirates□

raspberry prickly shrub *Rubus idaeus,* family Rosaceae◊. The red fruit is eaten fresh or used in preserves□

Rasputin Gregory Efimovich 1871–1916. Russian wandering 'holy man', the illiterate son of a poor peasant. He acquired great influence over the Tsarina, wife of Nicholas◊ II, because of her faith in his power to cure her son the Tsarevitch of his haemophilia◊, and hence over political matters. Notorious for debauchery (the nickname Rasputin means 'dissolute') he was murdered by a group of nobles, who (when poison had no effect) dumped him in the river Neva after shooting him□

Rastafarianism belief in Haile◊ Selassie as a deity by a black religious sect originating in Jamaica, and claiming the right to return to Africa. Its beliefs were helped to spread by Marcus Garvey◊, and by emigration from the Caribbean area after World War II. See also Reggae◊ under pop◊ music, and Bob Marley◊□

rat a small rodent◊□

rates in the UK, taxation levied on residential (subject to rebate for lower-income householders), industrial, and commercial property by local authorities to cover their expenditure. It is regarded as unfair in that a rate for a household with several wage-earners may be identical with that for a single person of retirement age, and that rebates may be so widespread that the burden of the cost of services to all may be borne by comparatively few. No agreed solution has been found, but the Thatcher◊ government curbed high-spending councils by cutting the government supplementary grant aid to them, and limiting the level of rate that could be levied ('ratecapping')□

Rathenau Walter 1867–1922. German statesman and industrialist, responsible for

German economic planning in partnership with capitalism during World War I and after. As Foreign Minister in 1922, he signed the Rapallo◊ Treaty, and was shortly afterwards assassinated by right-wing fanatics□

Rathlin island off the N Irish coast, in Antrim. St Columba◊ founded a church there in the 6th century, and in 1306 Robert Bruce◊ hid there after his defeat by the English at Methven□

rationalism belief that reason is the only means of ascertaining truth. Rationalist philosophical theories were developed by Descartes◊, Leibniz◊, Spinoza◊ and others; see also empiricism◊□

Ratisbon see Regensburg◊□

ratite bird with a breastbone without the keel to which flight muscles are attached, e.g. ostrich, rhea, emu, cassowary, kiwi. See running◊ birds□

Rattigan Sir Terence 1911–77. British naturalistic playwright of the middle classes. His work ranged from the comedy *French Without Tears* 1936, to the psychological intensity of *The Winslow Boy* 1945 (based on a real-life story of a naval cadet wrongly accused of theft), *The Browning Version* 1948 (dealing with a failed schoolmaster and a failed marriage), and *Ross* 1960, based on T E Lawrence◊. Knighted 1971□

Rattle Simon 1955– . British conductor, principal conductor of the Birmingham Symphony Orchestra from 1980, noted for interpretations of Mahler◊ and Sibelius◊□

rattlesnake a poisonous snake◊□

Ravel Maurice 1875–1937. French composer. Intensely shy, his work was both sensuous and ingenious in its construction (the latter a reflection of his interest in mechanical toys), e.g. the piano pieces *Pavane pour une infante défunte* 1899 and *Jeux d'eau* 1901 and the erotic *Boléro*□

raven a bird of the crow family. See under Corvidae◊□

Ravenna city and industrial port (oil and natural gas sustain petrochemical works, etc.) in W Italy; population 138 000. Its Byzantine◊ churches have superb mosaics, e.g. 6th-century San Vitale. Ravenna was the capital of the W Roman emperors 404–93 and of Theodoric◊ the Great 493–526. The tombs of Theodoric and Dante◊ survive□

Ravi see under Indus◊□

Rawalpindi city in Pakistan, in the foothills of the Himalayas; population 928 000. A great military, road, and rail centre, it was the capital of Pakistan 1959–67□

Rawlinson Sir Henry Creswicke 1810–95. British orientalist, political agent in Baghdad from 1844. He deciphered the Babylonian and Old Persian scripts of Darius◊'s trilingual inscription at Behistun, continued the excavation work of Layard◊, and published a *History of Assyria*□

Rawls John 1921– . American philosopher, who revived in his *A Theory of Justice* 1971 the concept of the 'social◊ contract', and its enforcement by 'civil disobedience', etc.□

Rawsthorne Alan 1905–71. British composer, born in Lancashire. His work includes *Theme and Variations for Two Violins* 1938, the tersely virile *Symphonic Studies,* and the cantata *Kubla Khan*□

Ray or ***Wray*** John 1627–1705. British botanist who, in his *Methodus plantarum* 1682, first divided flowering plants into monocotyledons◊ and dicotyledons, and made other taxonomic advances. The ***Ray Society***, 1844, commemorates him□

Ray Satyajit 1921– . Indian film director, noted for his trilogy of life in his native Bengal: *Pather Panchali, Unvanquished* and *The World of Apu* 1955–9□

ray a member of the order of fish, Batoidei, which live on the sea bottom, and have flattened heads and bodies, whiplike tails, and pectoral fins broadened into 'wings'. They include:

marbled electric ray *Torpedo marmorata*, family Torpedinidae; it produces a shock of 300 volts to stun its prey, and gives birth to live young

common skate *Raia batis*, family Rajidae; a food fish, it produces the egg cases which are thrown up on the beach as 'mermaids' purses', and may reach a weight of 34 kg/75lb

thornback ray *Raja clavata*, common in European waters

sting ray *Dasyatis pastinaca*, family Dasyatidae, which has a poisonous serrated spine on its tail

Atlantic manta or ***devil ray*** *Mantra birostris*, tropical family Mobulidae. The manta has 'horns' on its head, its winglike fins span 7 m/23 ft and it weighs 1 tonne

See also sawfish◊□

Rayleigh John W Strutt, 3rd Baron Rayleigh 1842–1919. British physicist, professor at Cambridge 1879–84 and at the Royal◊ Institute 1887–1905. He studied mostly wave theories of light and sound. With Sir William Ramsay◊, he discovered argon◊; Order of Merit 1901, Nobel prize 1904□

rayon a synthetic fibre. See under textile◊□

razor bill a sea bird of the auk◊ family□

razor shell or ***razor-fish*** genera of bivalve molluscs, with narrow elongated shells, resembling an old-fashioned razor handle and delicately coloured□

Reade Charles 1814–84. British writer of popular plays, e.g. *The Lyons Mail* 1854, but better known as a novelist, e.g. his historical masterpiece, set in the 15th century, *The Cloister and the Hearth* 1861□

Reading Rufus Daniel Isaacs, 1st Marquess of Reading 1860–1935. Liberal lawyer and statesman, Lord Chief Justice 1913–21, when he tried Roger Casement◊, Viceroy of India 1921–6, and Foreign Secretary in 1931□

Reading English town, administrative headquarters of Berkshire, an agricultural and horticultural centre (with a university founded in 1892), also noted for biscuits and electronics; population 136 300. Oscar Wilde◊ spent two years in Reading jail□

Reading industrial city (textiles, special steels) in Pennsylvania, USA; population 78 700□

Reagan Ronald 1911– . American Republican president from 1981. Born in Tampico, Illinois, he became a Hollywood◊ star in the thirties. Governor of California 1967–74, he lost to Nixon◊ in 1968 and Ford◊ in 1974 in bids for the presidential nomination, but won a landslide victory against Carter◊ in 1980, and an even greater one against Mondale◊ in 1984. He was wounded in an assassination attempt in 1981, adopted an active policy in Central America, especially Nicaragua, and intervened in Lebanon◊ and Grenada◊. In Jul 1985 he underwent surgery for a cancerous intestinal tumour. His Strategic Defence Initiative (announced in 1983, see under Weapons◊) proved increasingly controversial by 1985□

Realism the belief that physical objects, etc., exist independently of being perceived. See Scholasticism◊□

recall device whereby voters can demand the dismissal from office of elected officials, as in some states of the USA. See initiative◊, referendum◊□

Récamier Jeanne Françoise 1777–1849. French banker's wife, with a salon of literary and political celebrities. See Jacques David◊□

Recife industrial port (sugar, cotton, fruit canning) in Brazil, especially important because of its nearness to Europe; population 1 184 000□

Recklinghausen industrial river port in the Ruhr◊, N Rhine-Westphalia, W Germany; population 119 400□

recorded sound see sound◊□

recorder a part-time judge◊□

recorder a musical instrument of the woodwind◊ family□

Record Office Public. In England, the office containing the English national records since the Norman Conquest. See under archives◊□

rectifier device permitting the flow of electric current◊ in only one direction, so allowing the conversion of alternating to direct current□

rector Anglican clergyman, formerly entitled to the whole of the tithes◊ levied in his parish, as against a ***vicar*** (Latin 'deputy') who was only entitled to part□

recycling reclamation of potentially useful material from household and industrial waste. It avoids pollution, depletion of non-renewable resources, and expenditure on scarce raw materials□

Redbridge borough of NE Greater London
features part of Epping◊ Forest; Hainault◊ Forest
population 226 300□

Red Cross International. Agency founded under the Geneva Convention of 1864, which attempted to lay down rules for the treatment of the wounded and prisoners of war (see Henri Dunant◊). Through national organizations, it has since extended its range to associated problems of war, e.g. refugees and the disabled, and natural disasters, e.g. epidemics, floods, earthquakes, accidents. In Islamic countries it is known as the Red Crescent□

red deer a type of deer◊□

Redditch 'new town' (needles, fishing tackle, car components, etc.) in Worcestershire, England; population 69 250□

Red Duster popular name for the Red Ensign. See under flag◊□

Red Flag international symbol of socialism. See under flag◊□

Red Flag the Labour◊ Party anthem◊□

Redgrave Sir Michael 1908–85. British actor, whose roles included Hamlet, Lear, Uncle Vanya, and the schoolmaster in *The Browning Version*; knighted 1959□

Redgrave Vanessa 1937– . British actress, daughter of Michael Redgrave◊, whose roles include Ophelia, and the title-part in the film *Julia* 1976 (Academy◊ Award). She has also been active in left-wing politics□

Red Guards armed workers who took part in the Bolshevik◊ Revolution of 1917□

Red Guards school and college students, wearing red armbands, active in the Cultural Revolution in China◊ 1966–8□

red hot poker African plant *Kniphofia uvaria*, family Liliaceae◊ with a flame-red spike of flowers□

Red Indians see American◊ Indians□

red mite a type of mite◊□

Redmond John Edward 1856–1918. Irish statesman, Parnell◊'s successor as leader of the Nationalist Party 1890–1916. The 1910 elections saw him holding the balance of power in the House of Commons, and he secured the introduction of a Home◊ Rule bill, hotly opposed by Protestant Ulster. He supported the British cause on the outbreak of World War I, and the bill was passed, but its operation suspended till the war's end. The growth of Sinn◊ Féin and the 1916 Easter◊ Rising ended his hopes and his power□

Redouté Pierre Joseph 1759–1840. French flower painter patronized by the Empress Josephine◊, e.g. the book *Les Roses* 1817–24□

red pepper a red fruit of the capsicum◊□

Red River see under Mississippi◊□

Red Sea submerged section of the Great◊ Rift Valley (2000 km/1200 mi long by up to 320 km/200 mi wide). Egypt, Sudan, and Ethiopia (in Africa) and Arabia (Asia) are on its shores. In the Old Testament the Israelites◊ escaped from the pursuing Egyptians when its waters allegedly parted temporarily to let them pass. The sludge of its floor is mineral-rich□

redshank a type of sandpiper◊□

redshift a shift in the wavelengths of electromagnetic radiation emitted from a celestial body, as a result of the Doppler◊ effect or of the gravity of the body□

red spider mite a type of mite◊□

redstart songbird of the thrush◊ family□

redwing a type of small thrush◊□

redwood a giant coniferous tree. See sequoia◊□

Reed Sir Carol 1906–76. British film director, e.g. *Odd Man Out* 1947, and *The Fallen Idol* 1950 and *The Third Man* 1950 (both written for him by Graham Greene◊)□

reed a tall grass. See grasses◊□

Reeman Douglas 1924– . British novelist, author of sea stories, both modern and, as 'Alexander Kent', of the Napoleonic◊ period (dealing with the career of the fictional Admiral Richard Bolitho)□

Reeves William Pember 1857–1932. New Zealand politician, economist, and poet, who wrote the classic history of the country *The Long White Cloud* 1898□

referendum law passed by a legislature to come into operation if there is a popular vote in its favour. Both this and the device of an initiative◊ originated in Switzerland. Some states in the USA use them, and in 1975 there was a British referendum on entry to the Common◊ Market. See recall◊□

reflection the throwing back of waves, such as light or sound waves, when they hit a surface. The ***law of reflection*** states that the angle of incidence (the angle between the ray and a perpendicular line drawn to the surface) is equal to the angle of reflection (the angle between the reflected ray and a perpendicular to the surface). Thus, rays are reflected back at the same angle at which they strike. See also refraction◊□

reflection

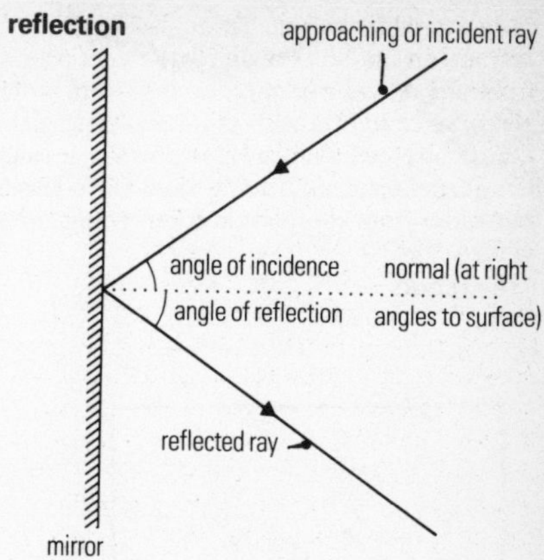

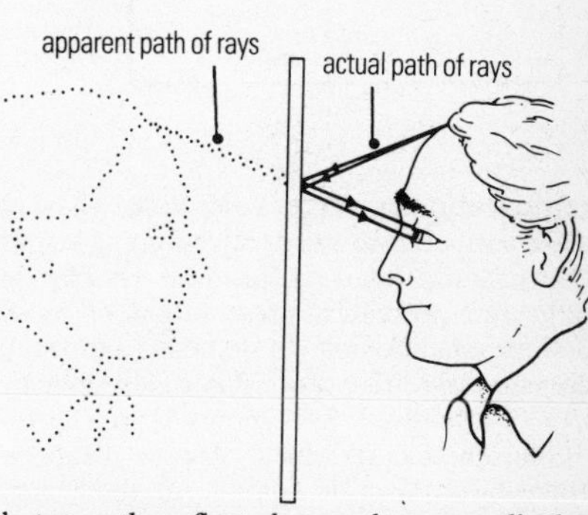

Reformation movement (anticipated from the 12th century by the Waldenses◊, Lollards◊, and Hussitees◊) to reform the Catholic church, which became effective in the 16th century when the new, centralized, absolute monarchies gave it support by challenging the political power of the Papacy◊ and confiscated church wealth. It began in Europe with Luther◊'s protest against the sale of indulgences◊ in 1517, the name 'Protestants' being in general use by 1529, and ended the religious unity of W Europe; see Zwingli◊, Calvin◊, Henry◊ VIII, and John Knox◊.

The ***Counter-Reformation*** initiated by the Catholic church at the ***Council of Trent*** 1545–1563 aimed at reforming abuses and regaining the lost ground by using moral persuasion and an extension of the Spanish Inquisition◊ to other countries. By the mid-17th century the present European alignment had been reached, but the movement in essence continues in that the modern ecumenical movement is seen by the Catholic church as a return to the true mother church by an erring flock rather than a new association of equals□

refraction the bending of light when it passes from one medium to another, e.g. from air to glass. Since light travels more slowly in glass than in air, the light bends towards the normal i.e. perpendicular, in going from air to glass, but away from the normal when going from glass to air□

refraction

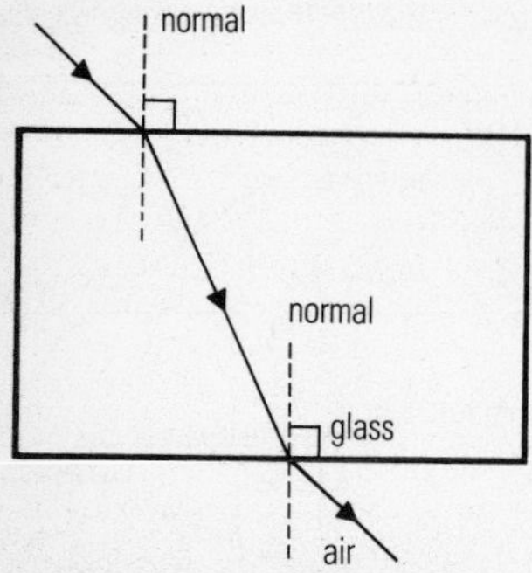

refrigeration process of absorption of heat at a low temperature and its rejection at a higher temperature, used to produce cooling in industrial processes, preservation of food, and air-conditioning. In domestic and small commercial refrigerators, it is usually done by use of the fluid Refrigerant-12 (dichlorodifluoromethane) which absorbs heat on changing from gas to liquid form; the energy to complete the evaporation/condensation cycle is supplied electrically□

regalia or ***crown jewels*** symbols of royal authority. The British set (except for the ampulla holding the holy oil and the anointing spoon) were broken up at the time of the Commonwealth◊, and now date from the Restoration◊. In 1671 Captain Blood attempted to steal them, but was pardoned and pensioned by Charles◊ II. They are kept in the Tower of London in the Crown Jewel House (1967), and major items include St Edward's Crown (a replica, worn only at the coronation); the Imperial State Crown (made for Queen Victoria); Queen Consort's Crown (see under Diamond◊), and the Orb and Sceptre (the latter including the Star of Africa cut from the Cullinan Diamond)□

Regan Donald 1918– . American Republican politician. A believer in the unfettered forces of the market-place, he was Secretary of the Treasury 1981–5, and has been Chief of Reagan◊'s White House Staff from 1985□

Regency in England the years 1811–20 during which George◊ IV, when Prince of Wales◊, acted as regent for his father George◊ III. It developed a dashing style of its own in architecture and interior decoration, based on classical ideas (see Neoclassicism, under Architecture◊), but with individual excesses, e.g. the Brighton Pavilion□

Regensburg industrial and commercial city (English Ratisbon) and Danube port in Bavaria, W Germany; population 132 300. Many medieval buildings survive□

regent person discharging the royal functions during a sovereign's minority or incapacity, or during a lengthy absence from the country. Since the time of Henry◊ VIII, the British Parliament has always appointed a regent or council of regency◊□

Reger Max 1873–1916. German pianist and composer, now chiefly remembered for his fine organ and piano music□

reggae a form of Jamaican pop◊ music□

Reggio di Calabria industrial port (farm machinery, olive oil, perfumes), capital of Calabria, Italy; population 173 500□

Regina capital and industrial city (oil refining, cement, steel, farm machinery, fertilizers) of Saskatchewan, Canada; population 162 600. Founded in 1882, and named in honour of Queen Victoria□

Regional Crime Squad see under New Scotland◊ Yard□

Reich Wilhelm 1897–1957. Austrian doctor, who combined Marxism◊ and psychoanalysis◊ to advocate sexual freedom, e.g. *The Sexual Revolution* and his controversial *The Function of the Orgasm* 1948□

Reich German 'empire'; the First Reich was identified with the Holy◊ Roman Empire; the Second Reich with the German Empire 1871–1918; and the Third Reich was Hitler◊'s Germany□

Reichstadt Duke of. See Napoleon◊ II□

Reichstag Fire burning of the Reichstag (German parliament building) on 27 Feb 1933, probably engineered by Goering◊. Van der Lubbe, a half-witted Dutchman (probably a Nazi◊ tool), Torgler, a Communist deputy, and Dimitrov◊ and two other Bulgarian Communists (Popov and Tanev) were tried by the Nazis at Leipzig. All had to be acquitted except Van der Lubbe, who was executed□

Reid Thomas 1710–96. Scottish Presbyterian minister and philosopher. His *Enquiry into the Human Mind on the Principles of Common Sense* 1764 attempted to counter the sceptical conclusions of Hume◊□

Reims capital (English spelling Rheims) of Champagne-Ardenne region, a market for champagne, France; population 183 600. From 987 all but six French kings were crowned here. Ceded to England in 1420, under the Treaty of Troyes, it was retaken by

Joan◊ of Arc, who had Charles◊ VII consecrated in the 13th-century cathedral. The German High Command formally surrendered here to Eisenhower◊ on 7 May 1945□

reincarnation the belief that the soul after death may enter another living body. See under incarnation◊□

reindeer an Arctic◊ deer◊□

Reith John Charles Walsham, 1st Baron Reith 1889–1971. British public servant, the first general manager 1922–7 and director-general 1927–38 of the BBC◊. He operated a strict, but independent, regime. The annual *Reith Lectures*, 1947, commemorate him□

relativity two theories propounded by Albert Einstein◊ concerning the nature of space and time. The ***Special Theory*** (1905) was devised to simplify the theory of electromagnetism◊, though with hindsight it can be seen as necessitated by the null result of the Michelson◊-Morley experiment. Starting with the premises that (1) the laws of nature are the same for all observers in unaccelerated motion; and (2) the speed of light is independent of the motion of its source, Einstein showed, for example, that the time interval between two events was longer for an observer in whose frame of reference the events occur in different places than for the observer for whom they occur at the same place. Such 'time dilation' has been confirmed by experiment and gives a degree of academic respectability to the notion of (forward) time-travel. Einstein's ideas were shown by Minkowski◊ to imply that time was in many respects like an extra dimension to space, so physicists now talk of four-dimensional 'space-time'. Einstein showed that for consistency with premises (1) and (2) the principles of dynamics as established by Newton◊ needed modification; the most celebrated new result being the equation $E=mc^2$ which expresses an equivalence between mass (m) and energy◊ (E), 'c' being the speed of light. The ***General Theory of Relativity*** (1915) involved a new twist to the concept of space-time; its geometrical properties were to be conceived as modified locally by the presence of a body with mass. A planet's orbit around the sun arises from its natural trajectory in modified space-time; there is no need to invoke, as Newton did, a force of gravity◊ coming from the sun and acting on the planet. Although Einstein's theory predicted almost the same orbits for the planets as Newton's theory, there were slight differences which should be observable in the case of Mercury◊; such indeed was the case. Again, according to the new theory light rays should be seen bending when they pass by a massive object, owing to its effect on local space-time. Physicists eagerly awaited the eclipse of the sun in 1919, when light from distant stars passing close to the sun would not be masked by sunlight. The predicted bending of starlight was observed. Although since modified in detail, General Relativity remains central to modern astrophysics◊ and cosmology◊□

relay electrical. A switching device operated by an electromagnet, often used as an interface between electronic control circuitry and high-current devices such as electric motors□

relic in many religions either part of some divine or saintly person, or something closely associated with them. See St Teresa◊ of Avila, St Januarius◊, St Helena◊, the shroud of Turin◊□

relief carving on a background, as against producing a free sculpture, which may be in high, medium, or low (***bas-***) relief□

religion code of belief and behaviour maintained independently of reason, though not necessarily irrational. A god◊ is not essential, but faithful adherence is usually considered to be rewarded, e.g. by escape from human existence (Buddhism◊), by a future existence (Christianity◊, Islam◊), or by worldly benefit (Soka Gakkai Buddhism). None has as yet a proved case.

Among the chief religions are:

ancient see Babylonia◊, Assyria◊, Egypt◊, Greece◊, Rome◊; *oriental* Hinduism◊, Buddhism◊, Jainism◊, Parseeism◊, Confucianism◊, Taoism◊, Shinto◊; *'religions of a book'* Judaism◊, Christianity, Islam; *combined derivation* e.g. the Bahai◊ faith, Moonies◊, Mormons◊.

Comparative religion studies the various faiths impartially, but often with the hope of finding a common denominator, to solve the practical problems of competing claims of unique truth of inspiration□

Remarque Erich Maria 1898–1970. German novelist, a soldier in World War I, whose anti-war *All Quiet on the Western Front* 1929, led to his being deprived of German nationality. He later became a US citizen□

Rembrandt Harmensz van Rijn 1606–69. Dutch painter and etcher, born in Leyden, the son of a wealthy miller. He was masterly in his use of light and shade, portraits of old people, and depiction of the ugly, e.g. *Slaughtered Ox,* as a thing of beauty. He worked mainly in Amsterdam, where he settled in 1631, and though declared bankrupt in 1656, produced some of his finest pictures in his last years. His most famous works include *The Presentation in the Temple, The Anatomy Lesson, The Night Watch, The Woman Taken in Adultery,* and his self-portraits and portrayals of his wife, Saskia□

Remembrance Sunday national day (known till 1945 as 'Armistice Day') of remembrance for both World Wars and those lost in later conflicts. In the UK it is observed by a two-minute silence at the time of the signature of the Armistice◊ with Germany on 11 Nov 1918, although since 1956 the day of commemoration has been the second Sunday of the month. Services are held and wreaths of 'Flanders poppies', symbolic of the blood shed, are laid at the Cenotaph◊ and elsewhere, and single flowers are worn by individuals; these are made by disabled members of the British◊ Legion in aid of war invalids and their dependants□

remora a type of sucking◊ fish□

Renaissance (French 'rebirth'), the intellectual movement originating in 14–16th-century Italy, and associated with the rebirth of classical studies, which spread over all Europe. It contributed to the Reformation◊, though the movements often came into conflict. Characterized by stress on the potential of the individual in this life rather than the next, it idealized the 'complete man', master not only of intellectual pursuits in philosophy and history, but of mathematics and science (including their application in war), of languages and literature, of the arts and practical crafts, and of athletics and sport.

See Dante◊, Petrarch◊, Boccaccio◊, Machiavelli◊, Ariosto◊, Leonardo da Vinci◊, Lorenzo de Medici◊, Michelangelo◊, Raphael◊, Cellini◊; Dürer◊, Erasmus◊; Henry◊ VIII, Elizabeth◊ I, Spenser◊, Milton◊, More◊, Sidney◊, Marlowe◊, Shakespeare◊, Bacon◊; Francis◊ I, Rabelais◊, Montaigne◊; Cervantes◊ and Camoens◊; Copernicus◊□

Reni Guido 1575–1642. Italian painter, influenced by Caravaggio◊, who founded a school at Bologna. His masterpiece is the fresco *Phoebus and the Hours preceded by Aurora* in Rome□

Rennes capital of Brittany◊, France, a centre of Breton◊ culture; population 205 735□

Rennie John 1761–1821. Scottish dock engineer, who built old Waterloo Bridge, and the former London Bridge, now reconstructed in Arizona◊□

Renoir Jean 1894–1979. French film director, son of Pierre Renoir◊. His films include *La Grande Illusion* 1936□

Renoir Pierre Auge 1841–1919. French artist, a leader of the Impressionists◊, whose works include scenes of contemporary life of great gaiety and colour, e.g. the blue umbrellas of *Les Parapluies* and the theatre scene *La Loge*, and also luscious female nudes□

reproduction the process by which a living

reproduction

female reproductive system

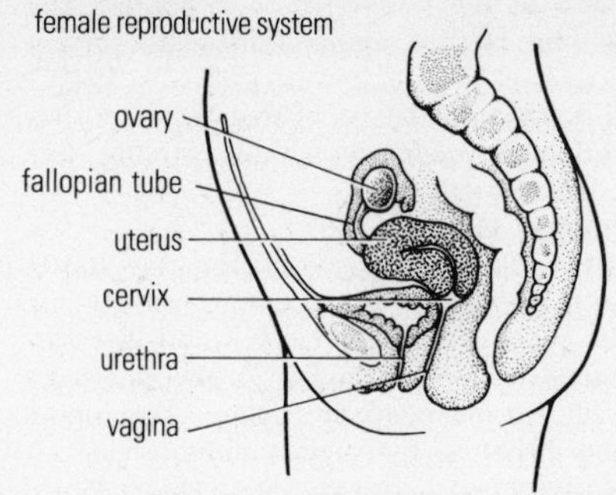

male reproductive system

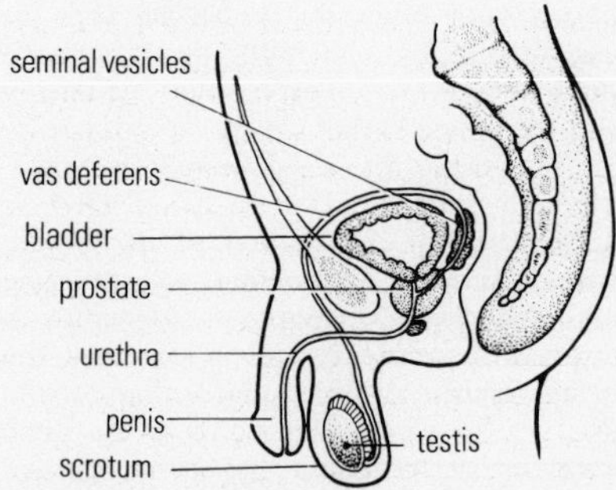

animal or plant produces other organisms similar to itself. Reproduction may be asexual or sexual.

Asexual reproduction requires only one parent organism and involves a process of growth. The resultant organism is normally an exact replica of the parent. Asexual reproduction is widespread among single-cell organisms and simple animals and plants. Normally single-cell organisms reproduce by a process called binary fission: the cell divides and produces two identical cells of the same size and genetic constitution. Some organisms reproduce by a process of multiple fission: each cell produces more than two cells by a process of repeated division. A more complex form of asexual reproduction is the process of spore formation. In plants a spore is a single cell formed by a division of the parent organism. The spores are formed and stored in a structure called the sporangium. When fully matured the sporangium ruptures, releasing the spores into the outside environment. In asexual reproduction, in general, the organisms pass all of their genetic information on to their 'offspring'. This type of cell division is known as ***mitosis*** i.e. the genetic information is not split into two halves

Sexual reproduction involves the mixing of

genetic materials of two parent organisms and is achieved by cell division (***meiosis***). In humans, the male sperm (containing half the genetic information of a man) fuses with the female egg or ovum (containing half the genetic information of a woman). Sperm cells are produced in the testicles which are contained in a bag of skin called the scrotum. The female eggs (ova) are larger than the male sperm and are stored in the ovaries. A woman has two ovaries which take turns to release one egg a month – a process called menstruation. The egg is carried along the fallopian tubes to the uterus (womb). For fertilization to occur the sperm and egg must fuse, i.e. the sperm must enter the womb. This occurs during sexual intercourse, when the blood supply to the penis is increased, causing it to become rigid, the penis is inserted into the woman's vagina and ejaculation of the semen (sperm plus secretions) sends the sperm high into the womb. Many millions of sperm are released during ejaculation. The sperm must swim to the egg by use of their long tails; if a sperm reaches the egg they stick together and fertilization takes place. The fusion of the sperm and egg produces an organism containing genetic material from both parents which is not identical to either parent (unlike asexual reproduction). The embryo (called a foetus after seven weeks) remains in the uterus of the female during pregnancy (nine months in humans)□

reptile class of vertebrates, which evolved after the amphibians◊, about 300 million years ago. Reptiles have a scaly skin, lay tough eggs, and form four orders: ***tortoises***◊ and ***turtles***; ***crocodile***◊***-like*** creatures; ***lizards***◊ and ***snakes***◊; and the ***tuatara***◊. It is through reptiles that the line of descent of both birds and mammals is thought to be traced. Like fish and amphibians, they grow throughout life, and cannot maintain a temperature greatly differing from that of their environment. They are remarkable for the slow rate of their metabolism, spending long periods inert – especially in the case of snakes – and expending energy sparingly, since a long period of rest is required for them to 'recuperate'. Intervals between meals may be long, in some instances months□

Republican Party founded in the USA in 1854 in opposition to slavery, with Abraham Lincoln◊ as the first Republican president. It became identified by the end of the century with imperialism and industrial expansion, and in the period before World War II was isolationist. See list of presidents◊□

reredos ornamental screen or wall-facing, behind a church altar□

reserpine tranquillizer, derived from the SE Asian plant ***serpent wood*** *Rauwolfia serpentina* which can lead to suicidal depression; it is also used to treat hypertension◊□

resin gummy substance exuded from pines, firs, etc., and used in varnishes and ointments; synthetic resins are used in adhesives, plastics, and modern varnishes□

resistance electrical. The degree to which opposition is offered to the flow of an electrical current through a conductor, measured by dividing the current flowing by the potential difference applied. Units: ohms (Ω)□

Resistance Movements in World War II opposition to occupation by the enemy (Axis) powers. In E Europe: Yugoslavia (Tito◊), Greece, Poland, and Russia, mainly guerrilla fighting; in W Europe, e.g. France, Belgium, Czechoslovakia (with built-up terrain), mainly sabotage of factories and railways, assassination, propaganda, and other underground activities (see maquis◊). After World War II the same methods were used, e.g. in Palestine◊, South America, and European colonial possessions in Africa and Asia, to unsettle established regimes□

Respighi Ottorino 1879–1936. Italian composer, a student of Rimsky◊-Korsakov, whose works include the symphonic poem *The Fountains of Rome* 1917, operas, and chamber music□

respiration process by which the blood gives up carbon dioxide and is charged with oxygen. Used blood is forced into the lungs by the contraction of the right ventricle of the heart◊, and on passing through fine, thin-walled capillary vessels in contact with the air cells, takes up oxygen and gives up the same quantity of carbon dioxide, together with water and small quantities of ammonia and waste matter. At rest, the adult rate of respiration is about 18 breaths a minute, but less in sleep, and much increased by exertion, emotion, or fever□

retriever a breed of large dog◊□

Retz Jean François Paul de Gondi, Cardinal de Retz 1614–79. French churchman, one of the chief leaders of the Fronde◊□

Réunion island in the Indian Ocean, a French overseas region; area 2500 sq km/970 sq mi; population 515 800; capital St Denis□

Reuter Paul Julius, Baron de Reuter 1816–99. German founder of ***Reuters*** international news agency, with a continental pigeon post in 1849. The agency became a public company in 1984□

Reval see Tallin◊□

Revere Paul 1735–1818. American patriot, a Boston silversmith, who carried the news of the approach of British troops to Lexington

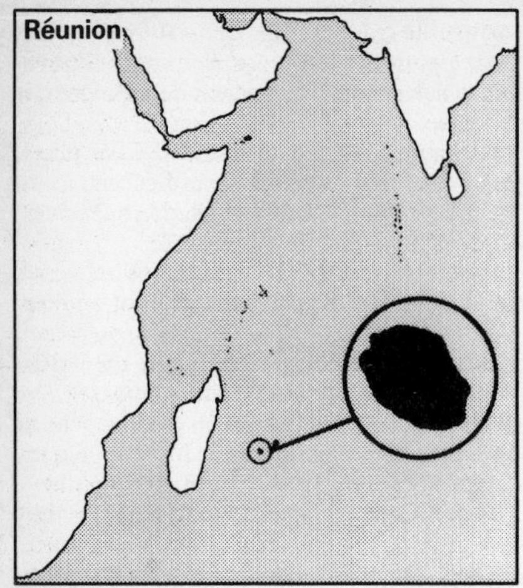
Réunion

and Concord (see American◊ War of Independence) on the night of 18 Apr 1775. Longfellow's 'Paul Revere's Ride' commemorates the event□

Revolutionary Wars 1792–1802. A series of wars between France and the combined armies of especially England, Austria, and Prussia

1791 Emperor Leopold◊ II and Frederick William◊ II of Prussia issued the ***Declaration of Pillnitz*** inviting the European powers to restore Louis◊ XVI to power

1792 France declared war on Austria, who formed a coalition with Prussia, Sardinia, and (from 1793), Britain, Spain, and the Netherlands; victories for France at Valmy and Jemappes

1793 French reverses until the reorganization by Carnot◊

1795 Prussia, the Netherlands and Spain made peace

1796 Sardinia forced to make peace by Napoleon◊'s Italian campaign

1797 Austria compelled to peace under the Treaty of Campo-Formio

1798 Napoleon's fleet, after its capture of Malta, defeated by Nelson◊ in Egypt at the Battle of the Nile (Aboukir Bay), and he had to return to France without his army; William Pitt◊ organized a new coalition with Russia, Austria, Naples, Portugal, and Turkey

1798–9 Coalition mounted its major campaign in Italy (see Suvorov◊), but dissension led to the withdrawal of Russia

1799 Napoleon, on his return from Egypt, reorganized the French army

1800 14 Jun Austrians defeated by Napoleon at Marengo in NW Italy, and again on 3 Dec (by Moreau◊) at Hohenlinden near Munich

1801 Austria made peace under the Treaty of Lunéville; Sir Ralph Abercromby defeated the French by land in Egypt at the Battle of Alexandria, but was himself killed

1802 Peace of Amiens truce between France and Britain, followed by the Napoleonic◊ Wars□

revolver a small hand gun. See pistol under small◊ arms□

revue stage presentation originating as a loosely constructed satire on current events, and including songs, dances, and sketches. Most famous are the *Ziegfeld Follies* produced by Florenz Ziegfeld 1907–31□

Reykjavik capital and chief port of Iceland; population 86 000. It is centrally heated by underground water mains linked to the volcanic springs to the east□

Reynaud Paul 1878–1966. French Prime Minister, who succeeded Daladier◊ in Mar 1940, but resigned in Jun after the German breakthrough. He was imprisoned till 1945□

Reynolds Sir Joshua 1723–92. British portraitist, born near Plymouth, who studied in Italy, then settled in London from 1752, becoming first president of the Royal Academy of Arts in 1768. He was a lifelong friend of Johnson◊, and painted him as well as Goldsmith◊, Garrick◊, and many others, in a modernized classical style. His artistic theories appear in his *Discourses*, but his practice, in experimenting with colours, led to the fading of some of his works□

Reynolds Osborne 1842–1912. British physicist and engineer best remembered for his work on fluid◊ flow□

Rhea in Greek mythology, a Titaness, wife of Cronus. See under Titans◊□

rhea a S American flightless bird. See under running◊ birds□

Rhee Syngman 1875–1965. First president of S Korea 1948–60, when his repressive rule forced his resignation and flight□

Rheims see Reims◊□

rhenium element

symbol Re

atomic number 75

physical description dense silvery-white metal with high melting point

features some rhenium alloys have superconducting◊ properties

uses in thermocouple◊ alloys and as a calalyst◊□

rhesus factor blood protein (named after the rhesus◊ monkey) present in the red blood cells of four-fifths of the population; if an Rh negative woman has an Rh positive baby, antibodies she produces may affect subsequent Rh positive pregnancies unless she receives treatment□

rhesus monkey a monkey◊ comon in N India; the rhesus◊ factor was discovered in its red blood cells in 1940□

rheumatic fever disease caused by a streptococcal throat infection which appears to trigger formation of antibodies which attack the patient's own tissues. It involves high temperature and inflammation of the joints, the chief danger being possible damage to the heart muscle□

rheumatism general term for inflammation of the joints and muscles. See arthritis◊, fibrositis◊□

Rhine European river rising in Switzerland, and reaching the North Sea via W Germany and the Netherlands; length 1320 km/820 mi.

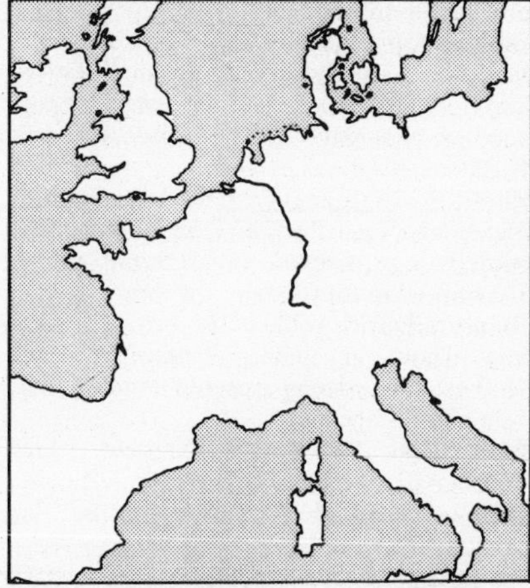

The ***Lorelei*** is a rock in the river in Rhineland-Palatinate, W Germany with a remarkable echo; Brentano◊ gave currency to the legend of a siren who lured sailors to death with her song, subject of a poem by Heine◊. Tributaries include the Moselle (length 515 km/320 mi, divided between France and Germany, and noted for its vineyards) and the German Ruhr (length 235 km/146 mi).

The ***Ruhr Valley*** with huge coal deposits was once a great iron and steel centre (now concentrated at Duisburg and Dortmund), but new industries such as petrochemicals and cars have now been introduced. The district was occupied by French and Belgian troops 1923–5 in an attempt to force Germany to pay reparations laid down by the Treaty of Versailles◊, and conquered by the Allies◊ 1–18 Apr 1945, their control ending with the creation of the European Coal and Steel Community in 1952.

The Rhine is linked with the Mediterranean by the Rhine-Rhône Waterway, and with the Black Sea by the Rhine-Main-Danube Waterway□

Rhineland-Palatinate land of W Germany
area 19 400 sq km/7500 sq mi
capital Mainz
towns Koblenz, Trier, Ludwigshafen, Worms
features river valleys of Rhine and Moselle
products wine (75% of German output), tobacco; chemicals, machinery, leather goods, pottery
population 3 642 485
religion Roman Catholicism 56%, Protestantism 41%□

rhinoceros herbivorous mammal of Africa and SE Asia, family Rhinocerotidae, related to the tapir, and also to the horse. The single-horned ***Indian rhinoceros*** *Rhinoceros unicornis* 1.50 m/5 ft at the shoulder has a tubercled skin, folded into shield-like plates. The two-horned species include the smooth-skinned African ***black rhinoceros*** *Diceros bicornis* with a prehensile◊ upper lip for feeding on shrubs and an uncertain temper, and the ***white*** (actually slate-grey) ***rhinoceros*** *Diceros simus* largest extant species at 2 m/6 ft, with a squarish mouth for grazing□

Rhode Island New England state of the USA, and the smallest, but with a very high industrial output per head; Little Rhody or the Ocean State

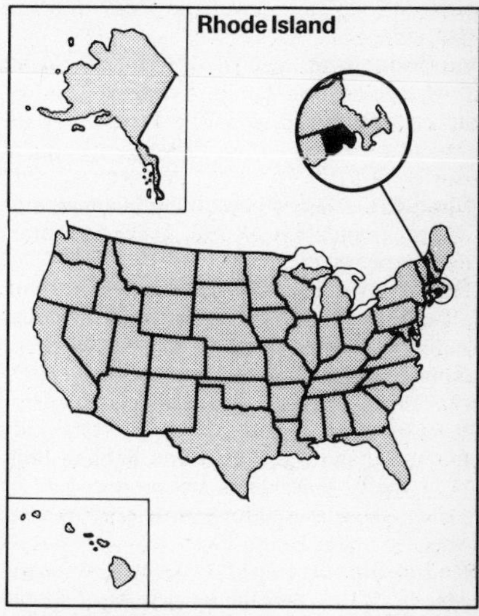

area 3144 sq km/1214 sq mi
capital Providence
features Narragansett◊ Bay
products apples, potatoes, poultry (especially Rhode Island Reds), dairy products; jewellery (30% of the workforce), textiles, silverware, machinery, rubber, and plastics
population 947 155
history founded in 1636 by Roger Williams, exiled from Massachusetts Bay colony for religious dissent, Rhode Island was one of the Thirteen Colonies□

Rhodes Cecil John 1853–1902. S African statesman. Born in Hertfordshire, he amassed a fortune in the S African goldfields, was largely responsible for the annexation of Bechuanaland (Botswana◊) in 1885, and formed the British South Africa Company which occupied Mashonaland and Matebeleland, renamed Rhodesia (see Zambia◊, Zimbabwe◊). He was Prime Minister of Cape Province 1890–6, when he was forced to resign by discovery of his complicity in the Jameson◊ Raid. He founded the ***Rhodes scholarships*** at Oxford (for Commonwealth◊, German, and US students), and in theory favoured 'Equal rights for every civilized man'□

Rhodes Zandra 1940– . British fashion designer, especially of luxury evening creations□

Rhodes see Dodecanese◊□

Rhodesia see Zambia◊, Zimbabwe◊□

rhodium element
symbol Rh
atomic number 45
physical description hard, reflective metal
features belongs to platinum◊ group of elements
uses to plate jewellery and optical instruments□

rhododendron genus of central Asian flowering shrubs, family Ericaceae◊, introduced to Britain in 1656. The ovate leaves are dark and leathery and the flowers are borne in clusters□

Rhondda industrial town in Mid Glamorgan, Wales; population 81 270. Light industries have replaced coalmining□

Rhône river in S Europe; length 812 km/505 mi. It rises in Switzerland, and divides at Arles in France into the Grand and Petit Rhône, which form a delta on the Mediterranean, W of Marseilles. This marshy area, the ***Camargue*** is noted for birds, especially flamingo, and the horses and fighting bulls bred there. Fine wines are produced in its valley, and it is used for hydroelectric power. See also under Rhine◊□

Rhône-Alpes region of E France between the Massif Central and the French Alps; capital Lyon; population 5 016 000□

rhubarb perennial plant *Rheum raponticum*, family Polygonaceae, grown for its red edible leaf stalks. The leaves are poisonous□

rhyme identity of sound, usually in the endings of lines of verse. Avoided as a blemish in Japanese, it is common in other modern Asiatic and European languages. It first appeared in W Europe in late Latin poetry, but was not used in classical Greek and Latin. In Old English poetry its place was taken by alliteration, the use within the line of words beginning with the same sound□

Rhys Jean 1894–1979. British novelist, born in Dominica, she is best known for *Wide Sargasso Sea* 1966, her recreation of the life of Rochester's mad wife in *Jane Eyre* by Charlotte Brontë◊□

rib a curved bone, one of the two sets of twelve bones (joined to the spine at the rear) which protect the lungs and heart, and allow easy expansion and contraction of the chest. The ***true ribs*** (upper seven) are joined by cartilage◊ to the breast bone (sternum); ***false ribs*** (next three) are joined by cartilage to the rib above; and ***floating ribs*** (final two) are not attached in front at all□

Ribbentrop Joachim von 1893–1946. German Nazi. Ambassador to Britain 1936–8, and Foreign Minister 1938–45, when he pursued an aggressive foreign policy. Tried at Nuremberg, he was hanged□

Ribera José (Jusepe) de 1591–1656. Spanish etcher and realist artist, fond of gruesome subjects, e.g. *Martyrdom of St Bartholomew*. He worked in Italy□

Ricardo David 1772–1823. British economist, whose *Principles of Political Economy* 1817 established long accepted 'laws' of rent, value, and wages□

Rice Tim. See under Andrew Lloyd Webber◊□

rice a cereal derived from grass. See grasses◊□

Richard three kings of England:
Richard I called Coeur-de-Lion 1157–99. King from 1189, third son of Henry◊ II, against whom he twice rebelled. He failed to recover Jerusalem in the Crusades◊, and was imprisoned by the Emperor Henry◊ VI on his overland journey home until he was ransomed. He was killed while besieging the French fortress of Châlus and, himself a poet, became a hero of later romances. See also Robin◊ Hood.
Richard II 1367–1400. King 1377–99. Born at Bordeaux, son of the Black◊ Prince, he ruled through a council of regency (see John◊ of Gaunt) until 1383, and showed courage during the Peasants'◊ Revolt. His fondness for favourites led to many of them being executed by the baronial party, headed by the Duke of Gloucester, in 1388. Recovering control in 1389, he had Gloucester murdered in 1397, and banished his cousin the Duke of Hereford (son of Gaunt) in 1398. In 1399 Hereford (see Henry◊ IV) returned to lead a revolt which resulted in Richard's deposition and imprisonment in Pontefract Castle, where he died mysteriously.
Richard III 1452–85. King from 1483. Son of Richard, Duke of York, he was created Duke

of Gloucester by his brother Edward◊ IV, and distinguished himself in the Wars of the Roses◊. On Edward's death in 1483 he became protector to his nephew Edward◊ V, and soon secured the crown for himself, alleging that Edward IV's sons were illegitimate. He ruled capably, but suspicion that he had murdered Edward V and his brother led to a revolt in 1495 led by the Earl of Richmond (see Henry VII◊), and he was defeated and killed at Bosworth◊□

Richards Frank. Pseudonym of British author Charles Hamilton 1875–1961. Writing for the boys' papers *Magnet* and *Gem,* he invented the Greyfriars public school and the fat boy, Billy Bunter□

Richards Sir Gordon 1905– . British jockey, 26 times champion 1925–53, with 4870 winners out of 21 834 mounts; knighted 1953□

Richards I(vor) A(rmstrong). See C K Ogden◊□

Richardson Henry Handel. Pseudonym of Australian novelist Ethel Henrietta Richardson 1880–1946. She was born in Melbourne, but left Australia when only 18; her best work *The Fortunes of Richard Mahony* 1917–29, reflects her father's life□

Richardson Sir Owen Williams 1879–1959. British physicist who worked on the thermionic◊ conversion of electrons. He was a colleague of J J Thomson◊ at the Cavendish laboratory, Cambridge. Nobel prize 1928□

Richardson Sir Ralph David 1902–83. British actor. Born in Cheltenham, he excelled as Falstaff, Peer Gynt, and Cyrano de Bergerac; and as Dr Sloper in *The Heiress* (stage and screen 1949), and Buckingham in Olivier◊'s film of *Richard III* 1956. Knighted 1947□

Richardson Samuel 1689–1761. British novelist and printer to the House of Commons. His *Pamela* 1740–1, written in letter form, was the 'soap-opera' of its day, and was followed by *Clarissa* 1747–8, and *Sir Charles Grandison* 1753–4. He greatly advanced the development of the novel□

Richelieu Armand Jane du Plessis de 1585–1642. French cardinal from 1622 and chief minister (through the influence of Marie◊ de' Medici) from 1624. He made the monarchy absolute by crushing the nobility and destroying Huguenot◊ power (though leaving them religious freedom), and ensured French supremacy in Europe by backing Gustavus◊ Adolphus and the German Protestant princes against Austria (and the Hapsburgs◊), and bringing France into the Thirty◊ Years' War in 1635. See Père Joseph◊□

Richler Mordecai 1931– . Canadian novelist, born in Montreal. His novels, written in a witty, acerbic style include *The Apprenticeship of Duddy Kravitz* 1959 and *St Urbain's Horseman* 1971□

Richmond capital of Virginia, USA; population 219 250. Centre of the Virginian tobacco trade, it manufactures cigarettes. It was the Confederate◊ capital 1861–5, and a museum commemorates Edgar Allan Poe◊□

Richmond town in N Yorkshire, England; population 7500. It has a theatre built in 1788□

Richmond upon Thames borough of SW Greater London

features Hampton Garrick Villa; Old Court House (Wren◊'s last home), Faraday House; Hampton◊ Court Palace and Bushy Park ***Kew*** outhoused departments of the Public Record Office; Kew Palace (former royal residence), within the ***Royal Botanic Gardens***, established in 1841. The gardens have the world's largest herbarium, and act as a plant bank, safeguarding against the extinction of species; since 1964 there have been additional grounds at Wakehurst Place, Ardingly, W Sussex (the seeds of 5000 species are preserved there in the seed physiology department, 2% of those known to exist, many of which are fast disappearing). ***Richmond*** gatehouse of former Richmond Palace (see Henry◊ VIII and Elizabeth◊ I), Richmond Hill and Richmond Park (including White Lodge, home of the Royal Ballet School); Ham House (17th century); Star and Garter Home (for disabled ex-servicemen and others). ***Teddington*** highest tidal point of the Thames; National Physical Laboratory ***Twickenham*** Kneller Hall (Royal Military School of Music); Marble Hill House (Palladian home of the Duchess of Suffolk, mistress of George◊ II); Strawberry Hill (home of Horace Walpole◊); Twickenham Rugby Ground; Alexander Pope◊ is buried in the church

population 159 800□

Richter Charles Francis 1900–85. American seismologist, deviser of the ***Richter scale*** for measuring the strength of the waves from earthquakes: 8.6 is the most severe known. Each increase of one number means a tenfold increase in magnitude□

Richter Johann Paul Friedrich 1763–1825. German author, commonly known as ***Jean Paul***. Born in Bavaria, he created a series of comic eccentrics rivalled only by those of Dickens◊. His books include the romance *Titan* 1800–3 and *Die Flegeljahre/The Awkward Age* 1804–5□

Richthofen Manfred, Freiherr von Richthofen 1892–1918. German airman, who commanded a crack fighter squadron (***Richthofen's circus***) in World War I, and shot down 80 aircraft before being killed in action□

ricin a poison obtained from the seeds of the castor◊ oil plant□

rickets a vitamin D deficiency disease of young children, marked by soft, poorly developed bones, resulting in bow legs, etc. Sunlight acts on fats to produce vitamin D necessary to enable lime to be deposited in the bones, so hardening them; lack of sunlight can therefore cause the disease□

Ridgeway The. See under Berkshire◊□

Ridley Nicholas c1500–55. English Protestant cleric, chaplain to Henry◊ VIII from 1541 and Bishop of London from 1550. A supporter of Lady Jane Grey◊, he was arrested and burned as a heretic after Queen Mary◊'s accession□

Riel Louis 1844–85. French-Canadian rebel, a champion of the Métis (people of mixed Indian-French blood), he established a provisional government in Winnipeg in an unsuccessful revolt 1869–70, and was hanged after leading a further rising in Saskatchewan 1884–5□

Riemann Georg Friedrich Bernhard 1826–66. German mathematician whose system of non-Euclidean geometry◊, thought at the time to be a mere mathematical curiosity, was used by Einstein◊ to develop his General Theory of Relativity◊□

Rienzi Cola di c1313–54. Italian political reformer, who in 1347 tried to re-establish the forms of an ancient Roman republic. He was assassinated on a second attempt□

Riff Berber◊ people of N Morocco, who under Abd◊ el-Krim long resisted the Spaniards and French□

Rift Valley Great. Formed 10–20 million years ago, it runs from the Jordan◊ valley to Mozambique, and includes the Red◊ Sea and Lake Turkana◊□

Rift Valley fever African viral disease, carried by mosquitoes, and hosted by sheep and cattle□

Riga capital and port of Latvian Republic, USSR; population 850 000. A member of the Hanseatic◊ League from 1282, Riga has belonged in turn to Poland from 1582, Sweden from 1621, Russia from 1710; it was the capital of independent Latvia 1918–40, and German-occupied 1941–4, before becoming part of the USSR□

Rigg Diana 1938– . British actress, whose television roles include Emma Peel in *The Avengers* 1965–7 and Lady Deadlock in *Bleak House* 1985; and, on stage, Heloise in *Abelard and Héloise* 1970□

Rights of Man and the Citizen Declaration of. According to the statement of the French National Assembly of 1789: representation in the legislature, equality before the law, equality of opportunity, freedom from arbitrary imprisonment, freedom of speech and religion, taxation in proportion to ability to pay, security of property. In 1946 were added: equal rights for women; right to work, join a union, and strike; leisure, social security, and support in old age; and free education□

Rigi mountain in central Switzerland, noted for its view over Lake Lucerne◊; height 1800 m/5908 ft□

Rijeka industrial port (oil refining, distilling, paper, chemicals) in NW Yugoslavia; population 129 000. It has changed hands many times, and after being seized by Gabriele d'Annunzio◊ in 1919, was annexed by Italy 1924–47; Italian name *Fiume*□

Riley Bridget 1931– . British artist, noted for her Op◊ art paintings□

Rilke Rainer Maria 1875–1926. Austrian lyric poet, for a time secretary to Rodin◊. His work has a mystic pantheism◊, and includes *Sonnets to Orpheus* and *Duino Elegies* both 1922; and the prose, semi-autobiographical *Notebook of Malte Laurids Brigge* 1910□

Rimbaud (Jean Nicolas) Arthur 1854–91. French Symbolist◊ poet, a friend of Verlaine◊, who tried to murder him when they quarrelled. He then travelled through Europe, E Indies, and Abyssinia (Ethiopia), dying at Marseilles. His work, e.g. *Les Illuminations* 1886, greatly influenced 20th century poets□

Rimet Jules 1873–1956. French football administrator, founder of FIFA, the international federation of association football, and promoter of the World Cup competition, the trophy being named after him□

Rimini industrial port (pasta, footwear, textiles, furniture) and holiday resort in Emilia-Romagna, Italy; population 127 800. It was once the terminus of the Flaminian Way from Rome. In World War II it formed the eastern strongpoint of the German 'Gothic' defence line, and was badly damaged in the severe fighting of Sept 1944 when it was taken by the Allies◊□

Rimsky-Korsakov Nikolai Andreievich 1844–1908. Russian composer, originally a naval officer. He made great use of Russian folk idiom and rhythms, and excelled in orchestration. His operas include *The Maid of Pskov* 1873, *The Snow Maiden* 1887, *Mozart and Salieri* 1898 and *The Golden Cockerel* a satirical attack on despotism, banned till 1909. Other works include the symphonic poem *Sadko* 1867 and the programme symphony *Antar* 1868. He also (rather controversially) revised or completed works by other composers, e.g. Mussorgsky◊'s *Boris Godunov*□

rinderpest viral form of cattle diarrhoea which can be fatal. Almost eliminated in the 1960s, it revived in Africa in the 1980s□

Ring of Fire the several island arcs surrounding the Pacific Ocean where regular and violent volcanic eruptions take place□

ring ouzel a bird of the thrush◊ family□

ringworm or ***tinea*** infestation by one of a group of parasitic microscopic fungi. On the scalp the fungus produces round patches of slight inflammation from which the hair falls out or breaks off. ***Athlete's foot*** is a form beginning between the toes, and spreading over the skin to produce a weeping eczema and an intolerable itch. Treatment is by antibiotics□

Río de Janeiro port (exporting coffee, sugar, hides), naval base, and resort in Brazil; the fine natural harbour has Sugar Loaf Mountain at its entrance; population 5 100 000. The name commemorates the discovery of the site by the Portuguese on 1 Jan 1502, but there is in fact no river. It was the capital of Brazil 1822–1960, when it was replaced by Brasilia◊. Exports include coffee, sugar, hides, and there are domestic consumer industries. Some colonial churches and other buildings survive, but there are fine modern boulevards, including the Avenida Rio Branco, and Copacabana is a luxurious beachside suburb□

Río de la Plata estuary into which the Parana and Uruguay rivers flow on the E coast of S America; length 320 km/200 mi, width 32–24 km/20–145 mi; it drains much of Paraguay, Argentina, Uruguay, Bolivia, and Brazil, which cooperate in developing its basin. See also under River Plate◊□

Río Grande river, length 2800 km/1800 mi, flowing from the Rockies in S Colorado to the Gulf of Mexico (where it is reduced to a trickle by irrigation demands on its upper reaches); its last 2400 km/1500 mi form the Texas-Mexico border□

Riom town in central France; population 17 000. It was the scene Feb–Apr 1942 of the 'war guilt' trials of Blum◊, Daladier◊, Gamelin◊ and others by the Vichy◊ government. The occasion turned into a wrangle over the reasons for French unpreparedness for war, and at Hitler◊'s instigation, the court was dissolved. The defendants remained in prison until released by the Allies◊ in 1945□

Río Muni see Equatorial Guinea◊□

Río Negro river, length 2250 km/1400 mi, which rises in E Colombia and joins the Amazon at Manáus□

Riot Act an act passed in 1714 to suppress the Jacobite◊ disorders. If twelve or more persons assemble unlawfully to the disturbance of the public peace, a magistrate may read a proclamation ordering them to disperse; if the rioters nevertheless continue together for an hour after the reading of the proclamation, they may be dispersed by force.
Modern methods of riot control include plastic bullets; stun bags (soft canvas pouches filled with buckshot which spread out in flight); water cannon; and CS◊ gas□

Río Tinto town in Andalusia, Spain; population 8400. Its copper mines, first exploited by the Phoenicians◊, are now almost worked out□

Ripon city and market town in N Yorkshire, England; population 12 000. There is a cathedral 1154–1520; and the nearby 12th-century ruins of Fountains Abbey are the finest monastic ruins in Europe□

Risorgimento movement (Italian 'resurrection') for Italian national unity and independence from 1815. Risings failed 1848–9, but the Austrian◊ War of 1859 was followed by the foundation of the Italian kingdom in 1861 (see Piedmont◊). Unification was finally completed with the addition of Venezia in 1866 and the Papal States in 1870. See also Mazzini◊ and Garibaldi◊□

Riva del Garda town on Lake Garda, Italy, where the Prix Italia broadcasting festival has been held since 1948□

Rivera Diego 1886–1957. Mexican mural artist, noted for his communist views. See also Frida Kahlo◊□

Rivera Primo de. See Primo◊ de Rivera□

river blindness or ***onchocerciasis*** type of blindness (caused by a parasitic worm) prevalent in Third World countries□

Riverina see under New◊ South Wales□

River Plate see Plate◊ and Río◊ de la Plata□

Riverside city in California, USA; population 170 600. Centre of a citrus-growing area, it has a research station, and the seedless orange was developed here in 1873□

Riviera the Mediterranean coast of France and Italy from Marseille to Spezia, the rest of the French Mediterranean coast being merely 'South of France'. The most exclusive section, with the finest climate is the Côte d'Azur, Menton – St Tropez, which includes Monaco. It has the highest property prices in the world□

Riyadh capital of Saudi Arabia, and of Nejd◊, in an oasis; population 667 000. It is surrounded by a high wall with six fortified gates, outside which are date gardens irrigated from deep wells. There is a large royal palace□

Rizzio David 1533–66. Italian adventurer at the court of Mary◊ Queen of Scots. After her marriage to Darnley, his influence over her incited her husband's jealousy, and he was murdered by Darnley and his noble friends□

RNA ribonucleic acid. See nucleic◊ acid□

roach a freshwater fish. See under carp◊□

roadrunner a bird of the cuckoo◊ family□

Roanoke industrial city (rail workshops, textiles, chemicals) in Virginia, USA; population 100 500□

Robbe-Grillet Alain 1922– . French novelist, leading theorist of *le nouveau◊ roman* as in his *Les Gommes/The Erasers* 1953 and *Dans le labyrinthe* 1959, which concentrates on detailed description of physical objects. Butor◊ and Sarraute◊ are other members of the school. He has also written film scripts, e.g. *L'Année dernière à Marienbad* 1961□

robbery in English law, a variety of theft: stealing from the person, with force used to intimidate the victim; maximum penalty, life imprisonment□

Robbia della. Family of Florentine architects and sculptors. ***Luca della Robbia*** 1400–82, executed a number of important works in Florence, and produced beautiful pieces in terracotta, now known as Della Robbia ware ***Andrea della Robbia*** 1435–1525, the nephew and pupil of Luca, also produced enamelled reliefs. Five of Andrea's sons carried on the family tradition; the most famous were ***Giovanni della Robbia*** 1469–1529, the equal of his father, and ***Girolamo della Robbia*** 1488–1566, also an architect and sculptor□

Robbins Jerome 1918– . American dancer and choreographer, who was ballet-master of the New York City Ballet 1969–83. His works include ballets, *Fancy Free* 1944 and *The Age of Anxiety* 1950 (based on Auden◊'s poem), both with Leonard Bernstein◊; choreography for musicals (e.g. *The King and I, West Side Story,* and *Fiddler on the Roof)*□

Robert three kings of Scotland:

Robert I see under Robert Bruce◊

Robert II 1316–90, was the son of Walter, steward of Scotland, who married Marjory, daughter of Robert I, and ruled from 1371

Robert III c1340–1406, succeeded his father in 1390□

Robert two dukes of Normandy:

Robert I, 'the Devil', d. 1035. He became duke in 1028, was the father of William◊ the Conqueror, and is the hero of several romances

Robert II c1054–1134, was the eldest son of William the Conqueror, succeeding him as Duke of Normandy (but not on the English throne) in 1087. He took part in the First Crusade◊, and was deposed by his brother, Henry◊ I in 1106, remaining a prisoner in England till his death□

Roberts Bartholomew 1682–1722. British merchant navy captain who joined his captors when taken by pirates in 1718, and became the most financially successful of all the sea rovers until surprised and killed in battle by the British navy. A teetotal Sabbatarian◊, he maintained his own wind band□

Robeson Paul 1898–1976. American bass singer, originally a law student. His successes included the film *Sanders of the River*; the musical play *Showboat* 1928 (with the song 'Ol' Man River'); and *Othello* 1930. An ardent advocate of black rights, he had his passport withdrawn for left-wing associations□

Robespierre Maximilien François Marie Isidore de 1758–94. French politician, the 'Incorruptible'. As Jacobin◊ leader in the National Convention, he supported the execution of Louis◊ XVI and the overthrow of the Girondins◊, and as dominant member of the Committee of Public Safety instituted the Reign◊ of Terror in 1793. His extremist zeal made him enemies on both left and right, and in Jul 1794 he was overthrown and guillotined□

robin small bird; the old world ***robin redbreast*** *Erithacus rubecola*, family Turdidae, has a sweet song, especially in autumn, and with its matchstick legs, brown feathers, and red, rounded breast, it is the traditional emblem of Christmas, though amongst themselves robins are aggressive, even to their partners out of the mating season. The ***American robin*** *Turdus migratorius* is larger. See also under thrush◊□

Robin Hood legendary English outlawed folk hero, who appears in ballads from the 13th century. He is said to have lived in the reign of Richard◊ I, to have feuded with the Sheriff of Nottingham, and lived in Sherwood Forest with Maid Marian and a band of followers□

Robinson Edward G(oldenberg) 1893–1973. American gangster-role film actor, e.g. *Little Caesar* 1930□

Robinson Edwin Arlington 1869–1935. American poet, fond of Browning-style psychological themes. His main volume is *The Man Against the Sky* 1916□

Robinson John Arthur Thomas 1919–83. British Anglican cleric, Bishop of Woolwich 1959–69. A left-wing Modernist◊, he wrote the controversial *Honest to God* 1963, interpreted as denying a personal God□

Robinson Sir Robert 1886–1975. British chemist, Nobel prizewinner in 1947 for his research on the structure of many natural products, e.g. alkaloids. He formulated the electronic theory now used in organic chemistry◊; Order of Merit 1949, knighted 1939□

Robinson W(illiam) Heath 1872–1944. British humorous artist. He drew fantastic machinery for simple operations, e.g. raising one's hat□

robot word coined by Karel Capek◊ for a worker automaton in human form; the majority of modern robots are pneumatically, hydraulically or electrically operated 'single-armed' systems fixed to the floor in motor vehicle factories. They can be reprogrammed to carry out different series of movements, e.g. spot welding, arc welding, paint spraying, injection moulding and placing components into machine tools, but are not intelligent, i.e. cannot react to variations in conditions.

More sophisticated robots of the 1980s have rudimentary vision (by a video camera), touch (by means of pressure sensors, some have 22 'fingers'), use laser beams to check for faults in machinery, and a microprocessor adjusts their behaviour according to information thus received. Hearing (by a microphone) and synthesized speech are less essential, and greatly increase costs.

By copying human behaviour patterns, the computer programmers are developing new robots with 'artificial intelligence'.

The science of developing more sophisticated robots is ***robotics***□

Rob Roy Scottish Highland Jacobite◊ outlaw Robert Macgregor 1671–1734. He lived by cattle theft and extortion. Pardoned in 1727□

Robsart Amy. See Leicester◊, Earl of□

Robson Dame Flora 1902–84. British actress, whose successes included Mrs Alving in *Ghosts* 1959 and Queen Elizabeth in the film *Fire Over England*□

Rochdale industrial town (textiles, machinery) in Greater Manchester, England; population 93 000. The first Cooperative◊ Society was founded here in 1844 by the 'Rochdale Pioneers'. Gracie Fields◊ was born here and a theatre is named after her□

Rochefort industrial port (metal goods, machinery) in W France; population 33 000. It was from here that Napoleon◊ embarked for Plymouth on the *Bellopheron* on his way to final exile in 1815□

Rochelle La. See La◊ Rochelle□

Rochester John Wilmot, 2nd Earl of Rochester 1647–80. British poet. He fought gallantly at sea in the Second Dutch◊ War, but chiefly led a debauched life at court. He wrote graceful lyrics, and *A Satire against Mankind* that rivals Swift◊□

Rochester upon Medway city in Kent, England; population 144 700. There is a fine 12th-century Norman castle keep, and 12th–15th-century cathedral, and many timbered buildings. A Dickens◊ Centre, established in 1982, commemorates its many links with the novelist. See also Borstal◊□

Rochester industrial city (Kodak cameras) in New York State, USA; population 241 509□

Rochester commercial centre with dairy and food processing industries in Minnesota, USA; population 57 890. The Mayo◊ Clinic is here□

rock the constitutent of the earth's crust, either in its unconsolidated form as clay, mud, or sand, or consolidated into a hard mass as:

igneous rock made from molten silica◊ or magma◊ solidifying on or beneath the earth's surface (e.g. dolerite◊, granite◊, obsidian◊). See feldspars◊

sedimentary rock formed by deposition and compression at low temperatures and pressures, e.g. sandstone from sand particles, or limestone from the remains of sea creatures or coal from those of plants

metamorphic rocks those formed by changes in existing igneous or sedimentary rocks under high pressure, heat, or chemical action, e.g. limestone to marble◊□

Rockall British islet in the Atlantic, 24 m/80 ft across and 22 m/65 ft high, part of the Hatton-Rockall bank, and 370 km/230 mi W of N Uist in the Hebrides. Part of a fragment of Greenland that broke away 60 million years ago, the bank is in a potentially rich oil/gas area. A party of Royal Marines landed in 1955 formally to annex Rockall, but Denmark, Iceland, and Ireland challenge Britain's claims for mineral, oil, and fishing rights. The ***Rockall Trough*** between Rockall and Ireland, 250 km/155 mi wide and up to 3000 m/10 000 ft deep, forms an ideal marine laboratory□

Rockefeller John (Davison) 1839–1937. American founder of Standard Oil in 1870 (which achieved control of 90% of US refineries), and of the ***Rockefeller Foundation*** in 1913. His grandson ***Nelson (Aldrich) Rockefeller*** 1908–79 was Governor of New York 1958–74 and Ford's vice-president 1974–6.

Rockefeller Centre in Manhattan, New York (which includes Radio City Music Hall) is the world's largest privately owned business and entertainment centre□

rocket device such as a firework or projectile driven through the atmosphere by a fast-burning solid, or a guided missile (e.g. the V2 of World War II, or Trident), or space craft (e.g. Apollo) or space plane (e.g. Space Shuttle), powered by the giant three-stage

Saturn 5 Rocket engine. The rocket is essential to space travel since it is the only form of propulsion available which functions in a vacuum☐

Rockhampton port in a dairying and meat-producing region, which also has coal, gold, and copper mines, in Queensland, Australia; population 55 260☐

Rockingham Charles Watson Wentworth, 2nd Marquess of Rockingham 1730–82. British Whig◊ statesman, Prime Minister 1765–6 and 1782 (when he died in office); he supported the Americans' claim to independence☐

Rockwell Norman 1894–1978. American artist, noted for his magazine covers. There is a museum of his work at Stockbridge, Massachusetts☐

Rocky Mountains chief N American mountain system, running 1950 km/1212 mi from New Mexico to Alaska; highest peak Mt McKinley◊, if the Alaska range is included (highest in the USA, Mt Elbert 4395 m/14 431 ft). Natural gas occurs in the western overthrust belt in large quantities☐

Rococo stylistic term describing the late Baroque◊ period in European art and architecture during the 18th century. The Rococo is characterized by light, deft patterns with much ornamentation; it is found especially in France, South Germany, and Austria. It was followed in the mid-18th century by Neoclassicism◊☐

rodent mammal of the worldwide order Rodentia. Besides ordinary 'cheek teeth', they have a single front pair of incisor teeth in both upper and lower jaw, which continue to grow as they are worn down. They are subdivided into three suborders, Myomorpha, Sciuromorpha, and Hystricomorpha, of which the rat, squirrel, and porcupine respectively are the typical members.

rat typical member of the rodent◊ suborder Myomorpha, which includes two main families:

rats and ***mice*** family Muridae, including the ***brown rat*** *Rattus norvegicus* 20 cm/8 in long, with a tail of equal length, and the ***black rat*** *Rattus rattus* slightly smaller, and less stocky; both occur almost worldwide, are pests of storehouses, and may carry typhus◊, salmonella◊, and the fleas which spread bubonic plague◊. They are intelligent (with a very complex system of communication with each other by ultrasound◊), courageous, and rapidly breeding 'survivors'. Equally widespread and almost as destructive is the grey-brown ***house mouse*** *Mus musculus* 7.5 cm/3 in long, with a tail of equal length, and, among crops, the more richly-coloured ***long-tailed fieldmouse*** *Apodemus sylvaticus*. The ***harvest mouse*** *Micromys minutus* 6.5 cm/2.5 in, is alone among Britain's mammals in having a prehensile◊ tail and builds a ball-like 'tree-house' nest high on the stems of corn-stalks. For the so-called 'water rat' and 'short-tailed fieldmouse', see below.

gerbils, hamsters, lemmings, muskrats, and ***voles*** family Cricetidae. Species of ***gerbil*** sub-family Gerbillinae, common in Africa, Arabia, and Asia, they range from the size of a mouse to a rat, but have extra-long hind legs, and well-haired tail. The ***hamster*** sub-family Cricetinae, has a chunky body, short tail, and cheek pouches to hold its food; the ***golden hamster*** *Mesocricetus auratus* is a popular pet. The ***lemming*** sub-family Microtinae, has a blunter muzzle than a mouse, and in the case of the ***Norway lemming*** *Lemmus lemmus* is patterned in gold and black, and tends towards population explosions which lead to mass migrations in search of food (in attempting to cross water large numbers drown in a headlong rush, but they do not 'commit suicide'). The aquatic ***muskrat*** *Ondatra zibethica* of far N America, is so-named because it gives off a musky odour. It is 30 cm/1 ft long, with webbed feet, a flattened tail and light brown fur which is sold under the American Indian name of *musquash*. The Eurasian and N American voles, sub-family Microtinae, include the ***water vole*** (wrongly referred to as the water rat) *Arvicola amphibius* which is not as big as most rats, and has small ears, short tail, and water-resistant rich-brown fur; and the ***field vole*** (wrongly referred to as the short-tailed fieldmouse) *Microtus agrestis* is more mouse-like, with a destructive appetite for field crops.

squirrel bushy-tailed tree-dwellers, family Sciuridae, including the European ***red squirrel*** *Sciurus vulgaris* which has been largely ousted in Britain by the larger ***grey squirrel*** *S carolinensis,* head-to-tail 50 cm/1.5 ft, introduced from N America. They rear their young in twig-built nests or 'dreys', and store food (nuts, etc.) in hiding places for the winter. They do not hibernate, but are less active in winter. The ***ground squirrels*** (also known as ***gopher*** and ***suslik***) of E Europe, Asia, and N America, make networks of tunnels in more open ground, and carry their food in cheek pouches, e.g. the ***European squirrel*** *Spermophilus citellus* with large eyes, short ears and tail. The nocturnal ***flying squirrel*** genus *Pteromys* of Asia and N America, glides (rather than flies), with the aid of a membrane which stretches from the 'hand' to the 'foot'.

beaver of Europe, Central Asia and N America, genus *Castor*, family Castoridae; they were formerly found in Britain and there have been controversial proposals to reintroduce them. They are adapted to living largely in water by a thick waterproof pelt (commercially exploited for fur coats), flat, broad, scaly tail and webbed hind feet for swimming. Their environment is often significantly modified by their felling of trees to feed on the bark and use of the logs to construct the 'lodges' in which they rear their young, and the dams which safeguard their underwater access to their homes and their food supplies.

porcupine rodent with sharp quills on its body, of which the ***common porcupine*** *Hystric cristata*, family Hystricidae, belongs to the Old World, and is brown with sharp black and white quills; the animal may run in reverse to drive its quills into an attacker. New World porcupines are tree dwellers, e.g. ***N American*** *Erethizion dorsatum* and have prehensile tails and much shorter spines

agorti Central and S American forest rodent, the size of a rabbit and edible. *Dasyprocta,* family Dasyproctidae. The nocturnal spotted ***paca*** in the same family, is also eaten and, since it lives in open country, is even more endangered.

chinchilla S American rodent *Chinchilla laniger*, family Chinchillidae, is the bearer of the luxury silver-grey fur, which is also farmed in N America.

guinea pig small vegetarian rodent *Cavia porcellus*, family Caviidae, descended from the wild S American ***cavy,*** and much used in laboratory experiment because it breeds rapidly□

rodeo originally a practical round-up of cattle on American ranges, it is now usually a commercial show in the USA, Australia, and Canada, in which calves are roped, near-wild horses ridden bareback, steers thrown, and so on. Considerable cruelty may be involved. One of the most famous is at Calgary◊□

Rodgers Richard 1902–80. American composer. He collaborated with librettist Lorenz Hart (1895–1943) in musicals such as *On Your Toes* 1936 and the pioneer realistic musical with a squalid hero *Pal Joey* 1940; and with Hammerstein◊ in the musicals *Oklahoma* 1943, *South Pacific* 1949, *The King and I* 1951, and *The Sound of Music* 1959□

Rodin Auguste 1840–1917. French sculptor, many of whose works are in the Rodin Museum, Paris. Influenced by Donatello◊, Michelangelo◊, and French Gothic◊ sculpture, he has realistic simplicity, e.g. *The Thinker*, *The Kiss*, and *The Burghers of Calais* (copy in Embankment Gardens, Westminster)□

Rodney George Brydges, Baron Rodney 1718–92. British admiral. In 1759–60 he destroyed ships intended for a French invasion, and safeguarded the British West Indies by defeating a French fleet under the Count de Grasse◊ off Dominica in 1782□

roe deer a small deer◊□

Roeselare textile town (French *Roulers*) in NW Belgium; population 51 650. It was a major German base in World War I□

Rogation Days three days before Ascension◊ Day in the Christian calendar, marked by processions round the parish boundaries ('beating the bounds') and blessing of crops□

Rogers Richard 1933– . British architect whose works include the Pompidou◊ Centre in Paris 1977 and the Lloyd's building in London 1986□

Roget Peter Mark 1779–1869. British physician, one of the founders of the University of London, and author of a *Thesaurus of English Words and Phrases* 1852□

Röhm Ernst 1887–1934. German Nazi◊, reorganizer of the SA◊ group in 1930. His brawling and homosexuality embarrassed Hitler, who also feared a *Putsch* from the two-million strong force. Röhm and c100 others were killed 29–30 Jun 1934, the 'Night of the Long Knives'□

Roland d. 778. French soldier, slain, with his friend Oliver and the twelve peers of France, at Roncesvalles (in the Pyrenees) by the Basques◊. He had headed the rearguard during Charlemagne◊'s retreat from his invasion of Spain. He is the hero of the 11th-century *Chanson de Roland,* Ariosto's *Orlando Furioso,* etc.□

Rolfe Frederick 1860–1913. British writer, who assumed the style Baron Corvo. A Roman Catholic convert, frustrated in his desire to enter the priesthood, he fulfilled his wish in the hero of his novel *Hadrian the Seventh* 1904, who becomes Pope□

Rolland Romain 1866–1944. French professor of the history of music at the Sorbonne, who wrote a biography of Beethoven◊, and a massive novel *Jean-Christophe* 1904–12, recording the life of an imaginary German composer, which won him a Nobel prize in 1915□

roller bird, *Coracias garrulus*, of the Old World family Coraciidae, order Coraciiformes. It is shaded blue, with a reddish brown back, and both sexes have a rolling display in flight□

roller-skating movement using special boots with wheels□

Rollo c860–932. First Duke of Normandy from 912 until his retirement to a monastery in 927, he was a Viking◊ leader who was granted the province by Charles◊ III of France□

Rolls-Royce see Royce◊□

ROM ***R**ead **O**nly **M**emory* in computing, a memory device used for the storage of data that will never require changing. Data can only be read from ROM as it is built in during manufacture□

Romains Jules. Pseudonym of French writer Louis Farigoule 1855–1972. He developed the theory of *Unanimisme*, i.e. every group has a communal existence greater than that of its individual members. He wrote plays, e.g. the farce *Dr Knock* 1923 and a cycle of novels *Men of Good Will* 1932–47□

Roman Catholicism see under Christianity◊□

romance in modern usage any prose fiction of a sentimental type remote from real life and typically addressed to women. In medieval times verse and prose narratives, originating in France c1200, which became popular throughout Europe, e.g. the adventures of Charlemagne◊ and his followers, King Arthur◊ and his knights, and of classical heroes at Troy◊, Thebes◊, etc.□

Romance languages a group of languages all of which descend directly from Latin◊□

Roman Empire see Rome◊, Ancient□

Romanesque style of W European architecture◊□

Romania or ***Rumania*** Socialist Republic of

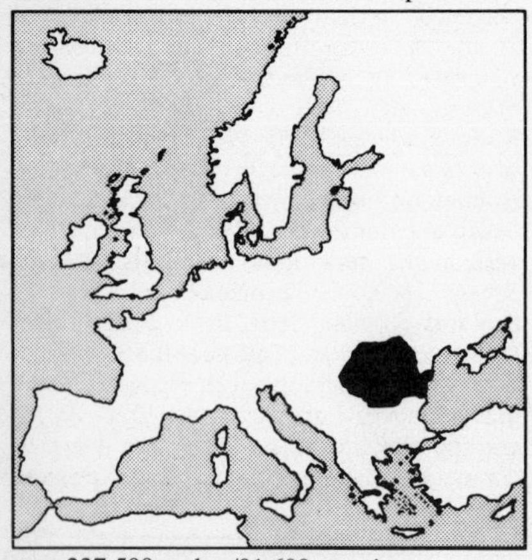

area 237 500 sq km/91 699 sq mi
capital Bucharest
towns Brasov, Timisoara, Cluj, Iasi; ports are Galati, Constanta, Sulina
features Carpathian Mountains, Transylvanian Alps, river Danube, Black Sea coast; especially rich in mineral springs; Dracula◊'s castle
exports petroleum products and oilfield equipment, electrical goods, cars, largely to Communist countries
currency leu
population 22 683 000, including 1 700 00 Hungarians, 400 000 Germans
language Romanian, a Romance language descended from that of Roman settlers, though later modified by Slav◊ influences
religion Romanian Orthodox Church (linked with the Greek Orthodox)
famous people Dracula, Georges Enesco
government grand national assembly, which sits only briefly, and a state council, headed by the president (Nicolae Ceausescu from 1967, who is also General Secretary of the Communist party, with which real power rests)
history independent under Carol◊ I from 1881, Romania was one of the Allies◊ from 1916 in World War I, but in the 1930s fell under the control of the pro-Fascist◊ Iron Guard, who compelled Carol◊ II to abdicate in favour of his son Michael◊. In 1940 Romania was occupied by Germany, and declared war first on Russia in 1941, and then when the Red Army expelled the Germans, on Germany in 1944. Under the peace treaty of 1947, Romania lost Bessarabia◊ (E Moldavia; see also under Wallachia◊) and N Bukhovina◊ to Russia and S Dobruja◊ to Bulgaria. The republic declared in 1947 rapidly came under Communist control, but after the departure of Russian occupation forces in 1958, Romania took a more independent line economically and politically. By the 1980s the country encountered serious economic difficulties□

Romanian see under Romania◊ and Latin◊□

Roman Law see under Law◊□

Romanov dynasty which ruled Russia from 1613 to the revolution of Mar 1917□

Roman religion retained early elements of reverence to stones and trees, and totemism (see Romulus◊ and Remus), and had a strong domestic base in the Lares◊ and Penates, and the cult of Janus◊ and Vesta◊. The main pantheon included Jupiter◊ and Juno◊, Mars◊ and Venus◊, Minerva◊, Diana◊, and Ceres◊, all of whom had their Greek counterparts, and many lesser deities. The deification of dead emperors served a political purpose, and also retained the idea of family, i.e. that those who had served the national family in life continued to care, as did one's ancestors, after their death. Under the empire the educated classes tended to Stoicism◊ or Scepticism◊, but there was a following for mystery cults (see Isis◊), and Mithraism◊ (especially with the army) was a strong rival to Christianity◊□

Romansh see under Latin◊ and Switzerland◊□

Romanticism imaginative expression, especially of feeling and emotion, in free form in all the arts:

literature 18th-century forerunners, e.g. Thomas Gray◊, William Collins◊; 19th century S T Coleridge◊, Wordsworth◊, Byron◊, Shelley◊, Keats◊, Mrs Radcliffe◊, Walter Scott◊, Brentano◊, Novalis◊, Eichendorff◊, Tieck◊, Chateaubriand◊, Lamartine◊, Musset◊, de Vigny◊, Hugo◊, Manzoni◊; *music* Schubert◊; Weber◊, Schumann◊, Wagner◊, Brahms◊, Mahler◊ *art* Delacroix◊, Géricault◊□

Romany (the language of the) Gypsies◊□

Rome capital (Italian *Roma*) of Italy and Lazio◊ (*Latium*), on the Tiber, 27 km/17 mi from the Tyrrhenian Sea. East of the river are the seven hills on which it was originally built (Quirinal, Aventine, Caelian, Esquiline, Viminal, Palatine, and Capitol), to the west the popular quarter of Trastevere, the more modern residential quarters of the Prati, and the Vatican◊. Remains of the ancient city include the Forum, Colosseum, Pantheon, Castel Sant' Angelo (the mausoleum of the Emperor Hadrian◊), and baths of Caracalla; Renaissance◊ palaces include the Lateran, Quirinal (with the Trevi fountain nearby), Colonna, Borghese, Barberini, and Farnese. More recent are the monument to Victor◊ Emmanuel II, University City, Policlinico, Palace of Justice, and Parliament. Churches include St Peter's (the world's largest church, with piazza by Bernini◊), San Giovanni Laterno, San Paolo (founded by Constantine◊ on St Paul◊'s grave), San Lorenzo, and Santa Maria Maggiore. Major thoroughfares include the Via dei Fori Imperiali (which traverses the Forum), Via Nazionale, Corso Vittorio Emmanuele, and Corso Umberto, and there are many fine squares. The house in which Keats◊ died is preserved near the Spanish Steps□

Rome history. See Rome ◊, Ancient: history□

Rome, Ancient civilization around the Mediterranean Sea, based at Rome, which lasted for some 800 years. Traditionally founded in 753BC, Rome became a self-ruling republic (and free of Etruscan◊ rule) only in 510BC. From then, the history of Rome is one of continual expansion, interrupted only by civil wars in the period 133–27BC, until the murder of Julius Caesar◊ and foundation of the empire under Augustus◊, and his successors. At its peak under Trajan◊, the Roman Empire stretched from Britain to Mesopotamia and the Caspian Sea. A long train of emperors ruling by virtue of military, rather than civil, power marked the beginning of Rome's long decline; under Diocletian◊, the empire was divided into two parts although temporarily reunited under Constantine◊, the first emperor formally to adopt Christianity. The end of the Roman Empire is generally dated by the sack of Rome by the Goths in 410, or by the deposition of the last Emperor in the West in 476. In the East, the Eastern Empire continued until 1453 at Constantinople◊.

The civilization of Ancient Rome had an incalculable influence on the whole of Western thought throughout the Middle Ages, the Renaissance, and beyond, but especially in the fields of art and architecture, literature, law, and engineering. See also Latin◊□

Rome, Ancient: history

BC

753 According to tradition Rome was founded

510 The Etruscan dynasty of the Tarquins was expelled, and a republic was established, governed by two ***consuls***, elected annually by the popular assembly, and a council of elders or ***Senate***. The concentration of power in the hands of the aristocracy aroused the opposition of the plebian masses

390 Rome sacked by Gauls

367 The plebians secured the right to elect tribunes, the codification of the laws, and the right to marry patricians; it was enacted that one consul must be a plebian

338 The cities of Latium formed into a league under Roman control

343–290 The Etruscans to the N were subdued during the 5–4th centuries, and the Samnites to the SE

280–272 The Greek cities of the S were conquered

264–241 First Punic War, ending in a Roman victory and the annexation of Sicily

238 Sardinia seized from Carthage and became a Roman province

226–222 Roman conquest of Cisalpine Gaul (Lombardy); conflict with Carthage, which was attempting to conquer Sicily

218 Hannibal invaded Italy and won a brilliant series of victories

202 Victory over Hannibal at Zama, followed by surrender of Carthage and relinquishing of its Spanish colonies

148 Three wars with Macedon were followed by its conversion into a province

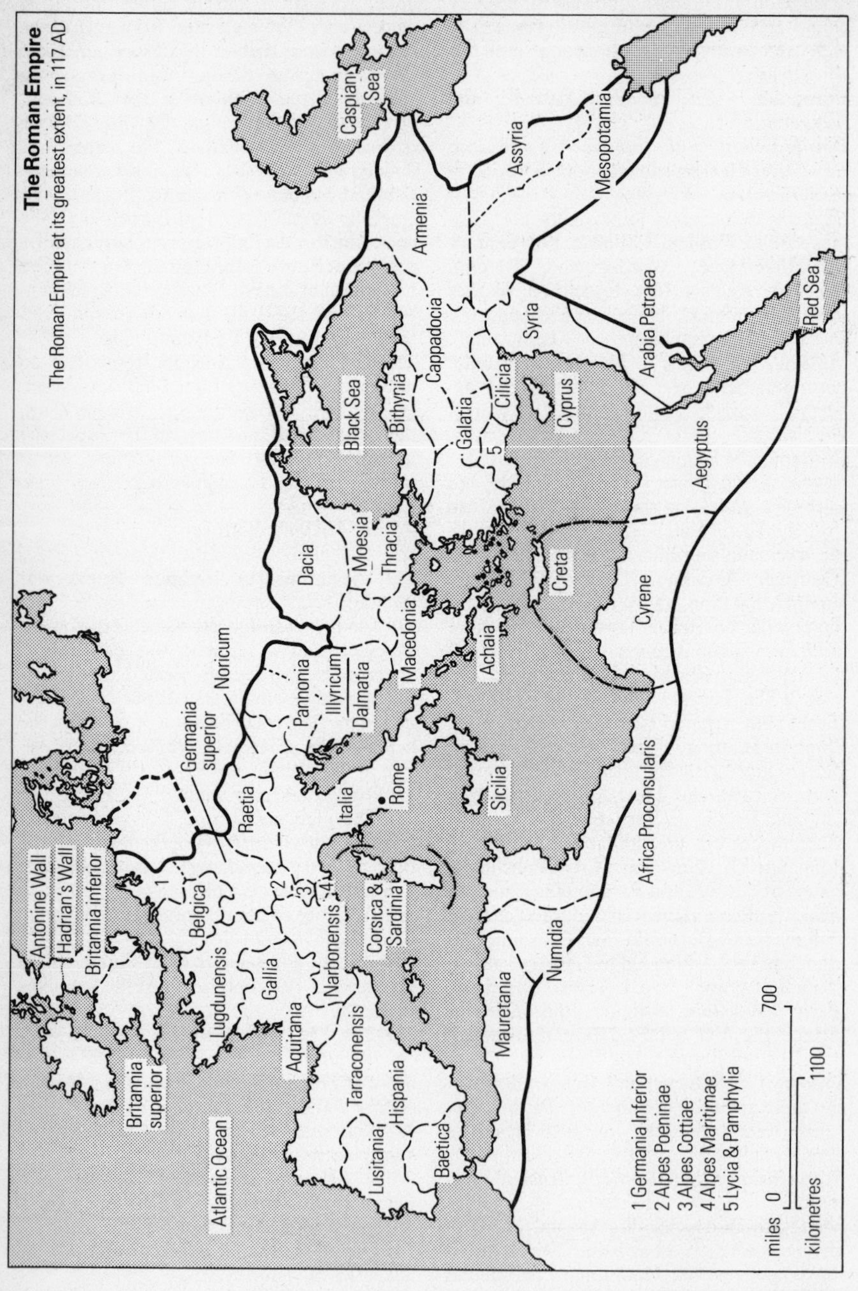

The Roman Empire
The Roman Empire at its greatest extent, in 117 AD

146 After a revolt Greece became in effect a Roman province. In the same year Carthage was annexed. On the death of the king of Pergamum, Rome succeeded to his kingdom in Asia Minor
133 Tiberius Gracchus put forward proposals for agrarian reforms and was murdered by the senatorial party
123 Tiberius's policy was taken up by his brother Gaius Gracchus, who was likewise murdered
109–106 The leadership of the democrats passed to Marius
91–88 Social War: a revolt of the Italian cities compelled Rome to grant citizenship to all Italians
87–84 While Sulla was repelling an invasion of Greece by Mithradates, Marius seized power
82 On his return Sulla established a dictatorship and ruled by terror
70 His changes were reversed by Pompey and Crassus
66–62 Defeat of Mithradates and annexation of Syria and the rest of Asia Minor
60 Pompey formed an alliance with the democratic leaders Crassus and Caesar
51 Gaul conquered by Caesar as far as the Rhine
49 Caesar's return to Italy (crossing the Rubicon◊) led to civil war between Caesar and Pompey
48 Defeat of Pompey at Pharsalus
44 Caesar's dictatorship ended by his assassination
32 The empire divided between Caesar's nephew Octavian in the West, and Antony in the East; war between them
31 Defeat of Antony at Actium◊
30 With the deaths of Antony and Cleopatra Egypt was annexed
27 Octavian took the name Augus; he was by now absolute ruler, although in title only *princeps* (first citizen)
AD
43 Augustus made the Rhine and the Danube its frontiers; Claudius added Britain
96–180 Under the Flavian emperors Nerva, Trajan, Hadrian, Antonius Pius, and Marcus Aurelius the empire enjoyed a golden age
115 Trajan conquered Macedonia; peak of Roman territorial expansion.
A century of war and disorder followed Marcus Aurelius's death, during which a succession of generals were placed on the throne by their armies
284–305 Diocletian reorganized the empire as a centralized autocracy
324–37 Constantinue I realized the political value of Christianity and became a convert
364 Constantine removed the capital to Constantinople, and the empire was divided
410 The Goths overran Greece and Italy, sacked Rome, and finally settled in Spain. The Vandals conquered Italy
451–2 The Huns raided Gaul and Italy
476 The last Western emperor was deposed□

Rome Treaties of. See European◊ Community□

Rommel Erwin 1891–1944. German field marshal, commander of the N African offensive from 1941 (when he was nicknamed 'desert fox') until defeated in the Battles of Alamein◊. He was Commander-in-Chief for a short time against the Allies◊ in Europe in 1944, but (as a sympathizer with the Stauffenberg◊ plot) was forced to commit suicide (officially said to have died of wounds received in an RAF raid)□

Romney George 1734–1802. British portraitist, born in Lancashire. He excelled in portraying women, and repeatedly painted Lady Hamilton◊□

Romney Marsh see under Kent◊□

Romsey market town in Hampshire, England; population 11 000. The fine Norman◊ church of Romsey Abbey (founded by Edward◊ the Elder) survives, as does King John◊'s Hunting Box c1206 (now a museum), and nearby Broadlands◊ was the seat of Earl Mountbatten◊ and Palmerston◊□

Romulus in Roman mythology, the legendary founder and first king of Rome, the son of Mars◊ by Rhea Silvia. He and his twin brother Remus were exposed by their great-uncle Amulius, but were suckled by a she-wolf and rescued by a shepherd. On reaching manhood they killed Amulius and founded Rome. Having murdered Remus, Romulus reigned alone until he disappeared in a storm, and thereafter was worshipped as a god under the name of Quirinus. See Roman◊ religion□

Romulus Augustulus c461AD–?. Last Roman emperor in the West from 475, who was compelled to abdicate in 476 by Odoacer◊, and died at an unknown date□

Roncesvalles see under Roland◊□

Ronsard Pierre de 1524–85. French poet, leader of the Pleiade◊. Cut off by deafness from his intended diplomatic career, he came under the patronage of Charles◊ IX, and published original verse in a lightly sensitive style, including odes and love sonnets. He was fiercely opposed by the supporters of Marot◊□

Röntgen Wilhelm Konrad 1845–1923. German physicist. While investigating the passage of electricity through gases, he discovered the emission of a sort of radiation◊ which could pass through certain substances normally opaque to light, and affect a photographic plate. The term X-rays◊ reflects early doubt as to the nature of the radiation, but its discovery revolutionized medical diagnosis. Nobel prize 1901□

rood alternative name for the cross of Christ, especially applied to the large crucifix which was placed above the rood-screen in medieval churches□

Roodepoort-Maraisburg gold-mining town in Transvaal, South Africa; population 165 300. Leander Starr Jameson◊ and his followers surrendered here in 1896◊□

rook a bird of the crow family. See under Corvidae◊□

Roon Albrecht Theodor Emil, Count von Roon 1803–79. Prussian field marshal. As War Minister from 1859, he reorganized the army and made the victories of 1866 and 1870–1 possible. See Prussia◊□

Roosevelt (Anna) Eleanor 1884–1962. Cousin and wife, from 1905, to F D Roosevelt◊, she ceaselessly supported her husband's career by social work, lectures, and a newspaper column 'My Day'. Later she worked at the UN◊, e.g. as chair of the Commission on Human Rights 1946–51□

Roosevelt Franklin D(elano) 1882–1945. 32nd president of the USA. Born at Hyde Park, New York, of a wealthy family, he entered the state senate in 1910 as a Democrat◊. He was crippled by poliomyelitis in 1921, but served as Governor of New York 1929–33, and in 1932 was elected president by a decisive margin in the midst of the Depression◊. His New◊ Deal recovery programmes did not fully extract the country from the Depression, the number of jobless remaining high until World War II, but his introduction of Social◊ Security, stock market regulation, minimum wage, insured bank deposits, etc., modified American life. He inculcated a new spirit of hope by his skilful 'Fireside Chats' on the radio to the nation, and his inaugural address statement: 'the only thing we have to fear is fear itself'. He achieved a sweeping victory in the presidential election of 1936, and broke a long-standing precedent by achieving a third term in 1940. He introduced 'lease-lend' for the supply of war materials to the Allies◊, making the USA the 'arsenal of democracy', and in 1941 drew up with Churchill◊ the Atlantic◊ Charter and defined the Four◊ Freedoms. Following the Japanese attack on Pearl◊ Harbor in Dec 1941, he devoted himself entirely to the war effort, and participated in the conferences of Casablanca◊, Quebec◊, Cairo◊, Tehran◊, and Yalta◊. He was re-elected for a fourth term in 1944, but died suddenly on 12 Apr 1945. In 1905 he married his cousin Eleanor Roosevelt◊, but fell in love with Lucy Mercer, his wife's social secretary. As a Roman Catholic, she would not have married a divorced man, but his devotion to her continued for the rest of his life□

Roosevelt Theodore 1858–1919. Republican◊ president of the USA 1901–9. Born in New York, he commanded a volunteer force of 'rough riders' in the Spanish◊ War of 1898, and served as Governor of New York 1898–1900. He was elected Vice-President to McKinley◊ in 1900, and succeeded him on his assassination in 1901. He campaigned against the great trusts◊, introduced conservation measures, and enforced US supremacy over S America. In 1912 he ran unsuccessfully for the presidency, having founded the Progressive or 'Bull Moose' movement in protest against the conservatism of Taft◊, and in World War I advocated US intervention. A big-game hunter, he refused in 1902 to shoot a bear cub, and Teddy bears are named after him□

root part of a plant, usually underground, which acts as anchor, absorber of nutrients (water and minerals) from the soil, and sometimes food store (e.g. carrot, dahlia). It may be fibrous or a single tap root, etc. See Mangrove◊□

Roquefort village in SE France, famous for cheese made from ewes' milk□

Roraima Mt. See under Pacaraima◊□

rorqual a species of whale◊□

Rorschach Hermann 1884–1922. Swiss psychiatrist, influenced by Freud◊ and Jung◊. He used ink-blot patterns, which subjects were asked to interpret, to help indicate personality type, degree of intelligence, and emotional stability□

Rosa Salvator 1615–73. Italian artist, noted for his wild and romantic landscapes□

Rosaceae widely distributed family of dicotyledonous herbs, trees, and shrubs, e.g. rose, almond, apple, cherry, peach, strawberry□

Rosario industrial river port (sugar, meat-packing, maté-processing) in Argentina; population 750 500□

rosary form of prayer used by Catholics, consisting of 150 Aves◊ and 15 Paternosters◊ and Glorias. It is linked with the cult of the Virgin◊ Mary; also a string of 165 beads for keeping count of the prayers□

Roscellinus Johannes c1050–1122. Founder of Scholasticism◊ by his defence of Nominalism◊ against Anselm◊□

Roscius Gallus Quintus c126–62BC. Roman actor, originally a slave, so gifted that his name became proverbial for a great actor□

Roscommon county (county town Roscommon) of the Republic of Ireland, province of Connacht◊□

rose genus *Rosa* of mostly Asiatic shrubs with prickly stems, family Rosaceae◊, though including the British ***dog rose*** *R canina* and ***sweet briar*** *R rubiginosa.* Roses may be bush, standard, or climbing and there are many different races, e.g. the large flowered (hybrid tea) and cluster flower (floribunda), etc. See attar◊ of roses□

Roseau capital of the Commonwealth of Dominica◊; population 16 800□

Rosebery Archibald Philip Primrose, 5th Earl of Rosebery 1847–1929. Liberal◊ statesman. Foreign Secretary 1886 and 1892–4, he succeeded Gladstone◊ as Prime Minister in 1894, but his government survived less than a year. As a racehorse-owner, he won the Derby◊ three times□

rosemary a shrub used as a herb◊□

Rosenberg Alfred 1893–1946. German Nazi◊ ideologist, minister for eastern occupied territories 1941–4; he was tried at Nuremberg and hanged□

Rosenberg Julius 1918–53 and Ethel 1915–53. American man-and-wife, accused of being leaders of a nuclear espionage ring passing information to the USSR; both were executed□

Roses Wars of the. Civil wars in England 1455–85 between the Houses of Lancaster◊ (badge, red rose) and York◊ (badge, white rose):

1455 opened with battle of St Albans on 22 May, a Yorkist victory (Henry◊ VI made prisoner)

1459–61 war renewed until Edward◊ IV, having become king, confirmed his position by a victory at Towton on 29 Mar 1461

1470 Warwick◊ (who had helped Edward to the throne), allied instead with Henry VI's widow, Queen Margaret, but was defeated by Edward at Barnet on 14 Apr and by Margaret at Tewkesbury on 4 May

1485 Yorkist regime ended with the defeat of Richard◊ III by the future Henry◊ VII at Bosworth (W of Leicester) 22 Aug□

Rosetta stone a slab of basalt with inscriptions dating from the second century BC. See under hieroglyphic◊□

rosewood aromatic timber, polishing to a rich brown, especially from the Brazilian *Dalbergia nigra*, family Leguminosae□

Rosh Hashana a two-day holiday at the start of the Jewish New Year. See under Judaism◊□

Rosicrucians early 17th-century philosophers, who used the terms of alchemy◊ to express their mystical doctrines. They were named from books published in 1614 and 1615, attributed to Christian Rosenkreutz ('rosy cross'), allegedly a real writer living c1460. Modern societies in Britain and the USA claim to be their successors□

Roskilde port and capital of Denmark from the 10th century till 1443; population 51 000. The 13th-century cathedral has the tombs of Danish kings□

Ross Sir James 1800–62. British explorer, associated with Parry◊ and his uncle Sir John Ross in Arctic exploration; he discovered the magnetic North Pole in 1831. He later went to the Antarctic; and Ross Island, Ross Sea, and Ross Dependency are named after him□

Ross Martin. Pseudonym of Violet Florence Martin◊□

Ross Sir Ronald 1857–1932. British doctor in the Indian Medical Service who, inspired by Manson◊, identified the malaria◊ parasite□

Ross Dependency Antarctic islands and territories, between 160° E longitude and 150° W longitude; area 453 000 sq km/175 000 sq mi; under New Zealand jurisdiction from 1923. See Ross Sea◊□

Rossetti Christina Georgina 1830–94. British poet, sister of Dante Rossetti◊, and a devout Anglican. Her verse includes *Goblin Market and Other Poems* 1862□

Rossetti Dante Gabriel. Abbreviated name of British poet-artist Gabriel Charles Dante Rossetti 1828–82. Son of an exiled Italian, he founded the Pre-Raphaelite◊ Brotherhood with Millais◊ and Hunt◊ in 1848. His verse includes *The Blessed Damozel* 1850, and the *Poems* 1870, recovered from the grave of his wife Elizabeth Siddal (whom he had married in 1860, and who died in 1862), which were attacked as of 'the fleshly school of poetry'. His paintings include *Beata Beatrix, Monna Vanna,* and *Dante's Dream.* See Christina Rossetti◊□

Rossini Gioachino Antonio 1792–1868. Italian composer, born in Pesaro. His works include the operas *Il Barbieri di Siviglia* 1816, the 'lost' *Il Viaggio a Reims* 1825 (reconstructed in 1984), and *Guillaume Tell* 1829; the *Stabat Mater* 1831–41; and the piano music of 1919 arranged for ballet by Respighi◊ as *La Boutique fantasque*□

Ross Island see under Ross◊ Sea□

Ross-on-Wye market town in Hereford and Worcester, England; population 6300. It is associated with John Kyrle, the philanthropist celebrated by Alexander Pope◊. Symond's Yat is a nearby beauty spot□

Ross Sea Antarctic inlet of the S Pacific. The ***Ross Ice Shelf*** is a permanent barrier midway across it (425 m/1400 ft thick). ***Ross Island*** includes the research stations Ross (New

Zealand) and McMurdo (USA), and Mt Erebus 3794 m/12 520 ft, the world's southernmost active volcano. Its lake of molten lava may provide a 'window' onto the magma◊ beneath the earth's crust which fuels volcanoes□

Rostand Edmond 1869–1918. French dramatist, remembered for *Cyrano de Bergerac* 1897, and *L'Aiglon* (i.e. Napoleon◊ II) 1900, in which Bernhardt◊ played□

Rostock capital of Rostock district and port in E Germany; population 230 280. It has restored remains of its period as a Hanseatic◊ port□

Rostov-on-Don industrial port (engineering, textiles, chemicals) in SW USSR; population 957 000□

Rostropovich Mstislav 1927– . Russian cellist-conductor, deprived of Soviet citizenship in 1978. Prokofiev◊, Shostakovich◊, Khachaturian◊ and Britten◊ wrote pieces for him□

Rosyth see under Fife◊□

Rota see under Cádiz◊□

Rotary Club society of business and professional men devoted to the ideal of service to others; founded by Paul Harris, an American lawyer (1878–1947) in 1905 and now international□

Roth Philip 1933– . American satiric Jewish novelist, author of *Portnoy's Complaint* 1969, and the Nathan Zuckerman trilogy: *The Ghost Writer, Zuckerman Unbound,* and *The Anatomy Lesson* 1984□

Rothamsted see under Hertfordshire◊□

Rothenburg ob der Tauber town in W Germany, near Nuremberg; population 1300. It is famous for its medieval buildings and walls□

Rotherham industrial town (pottery, glass, coal) in S Yorkshire, England; population 251 000□

Rothermere see Northcliffe◊□

Rothesay chief town of the Isle of Bute◊, Strathclyde region, Scotland; population 6500□

Rothko Mark 1903–70. Russian-born American artist, of Jewish extraction, founder of Abstract Expressionism◊. His large, simple canvases, in strong-toned colours, are for spiritual contemplation□

Rothschild Jewish family founded by financier Mayer Anselm 1744–1812, whose ten children founded finance houses throughout Europe. Descendants famous in other fields include the naturalist Lionel Walter, 2nd Baron Rothschild 1868–1937; the latter's nephew, Nathaniel, 3rd Baron Rothschild 1910– , scientist and head of the central policy review staff or 'think tank' established by Edward Heath◊ in 1970–4; and James de Rothschild 1878–1957, who bequeathed the nation Waddesdon Manor, Buckinghamshire□

Rotorua town with medicinal hot springs and active volcanoes in North Island, New Zealand, near Lake Rotorua; population 48 315□

Rotterdam chief port in the Netherlands; population 568 200. The rebuilt centre (destroyed by German air attack on 14 May 1940) includes the restored 15th-century Groote Kerk ('great church'). Erasmus◊ was born here, and the university, founded in 1973, was named after him□

Rouault Georges 1871–1958. French painter whose works, including *Aunt Sallies* and *The Three Judges*, reflect his original craft as stained-glass maker. See Fauvism◊□

Roubaix see under Lille◊□

Roubillac or ***Roubiliac*** Louis François 1695–1762. French sculptor who fled religious persecution to settle in England. He became the most popular sculptor of the day, e.g. statues of Handel◊, Newton◊, and George◊ I, and portrait busts of Pope◊ and Chesterfield◊□

Rouen industrial port (cotton textiles, electronics, distilling, oil refining) on the Seine, capital of Upper Normandy◊, France; population 118 335. It is a centre of the wine trade. There is a 13–16th-century cathedral, and Joan◊ of Arc was burned in the square in 1431. Flaubert◊ was born here, and the hospital where his father was chief surgeon is now a Flaubert museum□

Rouget de Lisle Claude Joseph 1760–1836. French army officer, who composed, while at Strasbourg in 1792, the 'Marseillaise', the French national anthem□

Roulers see Roeselaere◊□

roulette gambling game in which the players bet on the numbered division (0–36) of a turning wheel into which an ivory ball will fall. Players bet either on the numbers of the slots, or on 'red' or 'black', the colours of alternate slots□

Roundheads parliamentary supporters in the English◊ Civil War, so called because of their short hair styles. See Cavaliers◊□

roundworm a type of parasitic worm◊□

Rousseau Henri 1844–1910. French artist, nicknamed 'Douanier', though actually a toll collector rather than a customs inspector. An 'urban primitive', he painted poetic, sharply delineated fantasies, e.g. *The Sleeping Gypsy* and *The Snake Charmer*□

Rousseau Jean Jacques 1712–78. French philosopher, born in Geneva. He ran away from an apprenticeship to an engraver, found patrons, and published an examination of the *Origin and Foundations of Inequality Amongst Men* 1754 and *Émile* 1762, outlining a new theory of education to elicit the unspoilt nature and abilities of children, and so eliminate inequality. The charm of the idea was a little marred by the fate (as recorded by himself) of his own five children by the servant girl Thérèse le Vasseur, who were placed in a foundling hospital. These books, and the sentimental romance *The New Héloise* 1760, were immensely influential, as was his revolutionary *Social Contract* 1762, which saw governments as given authority by the people, who could also withdraw it (see also under Social◊ Contract). He suffered from paranoia◊ in his later years. His posthumously published *Confessions* 1782 set a vogue for frank revelation□

Rousseau Pierre Étienne Théodore 1812–67. French landscape painter of the Barbizon◊ school, where he settled from 1848 as a leading Romantic. He was influenced by Constable◊ and Bonington◊□

rowan a flowering tree. See mountain◊ ash□

Rowe Nicholas 1674–1718. English poet-dramatist (*The Fair Penitent* 1702 and *Jane Shore* 1714, in which Mrs Siddons◊ played), who was poet◊ laureate from 1715□

rowing propulsion of a boat by oars, e.g. by one rower with two oars (sculling) or by crews (two, four, or eight persons) with one oar each, often with a coxswain (steersman). ***Doggett's Coat and Badge*** 1715, begun for Thames watermen, and the first English race, still survives; rowing as a sport began with the English Leander Club, 1817, followed by the Detroit boat club, USA, 1839. Chief annual races in the UK are the Boat◊ Race; Thames head of the river race; and the events of Henley◊ royal regatta, also a major international event; in the USA the Harvard-Yale boat race is held on the Thames at New London, and the Poughkeepsie regatta is a premier event□

Rowlandson Thomas 1756–1827. British caricaturist of the social life of his times, e.g. *Tour of Dr Syntax in Search of the Picturesque* and its sequels 1812–21, and illustrations to Smollett◊, Goldsmith◊, and Sterne◊□

Rowley William c1585–c1642. English actor and dramatist, collaborator with Middleton◊ in *The Changeling* 1621 and with Dekker◊ and Ford◊ in *The Witch of Edmonton* 1658□

Rowse A(lfred) L(eslie) 1903– . British popular historian. He published a biography of Shakespeare 1963, and in 1973 controversially identified the 'Dark Lady' of Shakespeare's sonnets as Emilia Lanier, half-Italian daughter of a court musician□

Royal Academy of Arts society founded in London in 1768 by George◊ III to encourage painting, sculpture, and architecture; its first president was Sir Joshua Reynolds◊. Since 1867 at Burlington House, it holds an annual summer exhibition for contemporary artists, as well as loan exhibitions, and the Academy schools give instruction in painting, sculpture, etc.□

Royal Academy of Dramatic Art (RADA) school for actors founded by Herbert Beerbohm Tree◊ in 1904, its headquarters is in Gower Street, London; its Vanbrugh Theatre commemorates actress Dame Irene Vanbrugh 1872–1949□

Royal Academy of Music senior music school in the British Commonwealth, founded in 1822, which provides a full-time complete musical education□

Royal Aeronautical Society oldest British aviation body, 1866□

Royal Air Force the fighting aircraft of Britain. See armed◊ services□

Royal Ballet title under which the Sadler's◊ Wells Ballet (the senior company established at Covent Garden), Sadler's Wells Theatre Ballet (the junior company at Sadler's Wells), and the Sadler's Wells School (Richmond, Surrey) were incorporated in 1957□

Royal Botanic Gardens see under Richmond◊ upon Thames□

Royal British Legion non-political body promoting the welfare of war veterans and their dependants, established under the leadership of Earl Haig◊ in 1921□

Royal Canadian Mounted Police Canadian police force known as the 'Mounties', with uniform of red jacket and broad-brimmed hat. Their Security Service (SS), established in 1950, was disbanded in 1981 for exceeding its powers, and was replaced by an independent Security Intelligence Agency□

Royal College of Music London college, 1883, which combines with the Royal◊ Academy of Music for local examinations□

Royal Horticultural Society (RHS) society established in 1804 for the improvement of horticulture. Flower shows are held at Vincent Square, London, with an annual show at Chelsea which is also a social event. There are gardens, orchards, and trial grounds at Wisley, Surrey, and the Lindley Library has one of the world's finest horticultural collections□

Royal Household those in the personal service of the sovereign. The chief officers are the Lord Chamberlain, the Lord Steward, and the Master of the Horse. The other principal members of the Royal Family also maintain their own households□

Royal Institute of Great Britain organization for the 'promotion, diffusion, and extension of science and useful knowledge', founded in London in 1799 by Count Rumford◊. Faraday◊ and Davy◊ were its most illustrious directors□

Royal Marines British military force trained for amphibious warfare. See Marines◊□

Royal Military Academy see Sandhurst under Berkshire◊□

Royal Opera House the leading English opera house, Covent Garden, London; the original theatre opened in 1732 and the present building dates from 1858□

Royal Society The. Oldest and premier scientific society of Britain, originating in 1645 and chartered in 1660; Christopher Wren◊ and Isaac Newton◊ were prominent early members. Its headquarters is at Carlton House Terrace, London; its Scottish equivalent is the Royal Society of Edinburgh, 1783, in George Street□

Royal Society for the Prevention of Cruelty to Animals (RSPCA) formed in 1824, it promotes legislation, has an inspectorate to secure enforcement of existing laws, and runs clinics□

Royal Warrant Holders commercial firms whose products are supplied to the royal family, and who are authorized to display a royal crest□

Royce Sir Frederick Henry 1863–1933. British engineer who so impressed wealthy ***Charles Stewart Rolls*** 1877–1910 by the car he built for his own personal use in 1904 that the Rolls-Royce partnership was formed. His most famous car was the Phantom II Continental, but his greatest achievement was the Rolls-type engine which powered the Schneider Trophy-winning seaplane in 1929 and 1931, and was later developed into the Merlin engine which enabled the RAF Hurricanes◊ and Spitfires◊ to defeat the Luftwaffe◊ in World War II□

Royce Josiah 1855–1916. American idealist philosopher, who in *The Conception of God* 1895 and *The Conception of Immortality* 1900, interpreted Christianity in philosophical terms□

Ruanda see Rwanda◊□

Ruapehu see under New◊ Zealand□

Rub' al Khali see under Saudi◊ Arabia□

rubber coagulated latex obtained from plants, especially the Amazonian tree *Hevea braziliensis*, family Euphorbiaceae, now cultivated in SE Asia, e.g. in Malaysia, Indonesia, Sri Lanka, Cambodia, Thailand, Sarawak, and Brunei. It grows to 20 m/60 ft, and is then 'tapped', the sap being collected in cups attached to the tree where small incisions have been made.

synthetic rubber derived from petroleum, is made in a great variety of forms for special purposes, and is often preferable, e.g. for car tyre treads, for which it has higher abrasion resistance□

rubber plant Asiatic tree *Ficus elastica*, family Moraceae, producing latex in its stem. Young plants are grown in the West as pot plants for their shiny, leathery, oval leaves□

Rubbra Edmund Duncan 1901–86. British composer, born at Northampton. He studied with Holst◊. Works include eleven symphonies, chamber music and many vocal works□

Rubens Peter Paul 1577–1640. Flemish artist, born at Siegen, Westphalia, but taken to Antwerp in 1587, where he had a studio with many assistants, so that certain identification of his work is sometimes difficult. His masterpiece is the *Descent from the Cross* 1611–14, Antwerp Cathedral. In London, as envoy to Charles◊ I, 1629–30, he painted both the king and queen, and the *War and Peace* in the National Gallery. His work has a sensuous energy and rich fullness of colour□

Rubiaceae large family of mostly tropical flowering plants, including cinchona◊, coffee◊, and gardenia◊□

Rubicon small river entering the Adriatic NW of Rimini. See under Julius Caesar◊□

rubidium element

symbol Rb

atomic number 37

physical description soft silvery-white metal

features ignites in air and reacts violently with water

uses in ***rubidium-strontium dating***, which measures the proportion present of the naturally occurring radioisotope◊ rubidium-87, from which can be calculated the length of time that the sample (rock, fossil, etc.) has been decaying□

Rubik Erno 1944– . Hungarian architect, inventor of the ***Rubik Cube*** a plastic multicoloured puzzle which can be manipulated and rearranged in only one correct way, but c43 trillion wrong. Intended to help his students understand three-dimensional design, it became a world craze□

Rubinstein Artur 1888–1982. Polish-American pianist, specializing in Chopin◊, Debussy◊, and the Spanish composers□

ruby red, transparent form of Corundum◊, found mainly in Burma. Synthetic rubies are widely used in lasers◊□

Ruda Slaska industrial town (coal, metallurgy) in SW Poland; population 158 000□

rudd a freshwater fish. See under carp◊□

Rudolf Lake. See under Great Lakes◊□

Rudolph two Holy◊ Roman Emperors:

Rudolph I 1218–91. First Hapsburg◊ Holy Roman Emperor from 1273.

Rudolph II 1552–1612. Holy Roman Emperor from 1576, whose intolerance led to unrest that forced him to surrender Hungary to his brother Matthias in 1608 and to grant the Bohemians◊ religious freedom□

Rudolph 1858–89. Crown Prince of Austria, whose progressive views conflicted with those of his father, Emperor Francis◊ Joseph. He and his mistress, Marie Vetsera, were found shot at his hunting lodge at Mayerling, having apparently committed suicide□

rue a shrubby herb◊□

ruff a bird of the snipe family. See under sandpiper◊□

Rugby market town in Warwickshire, England; population 86 120. It is an important rail junction with engineering works. ***Rugby School*** 1567, established its reputation under Thomas Arnold◊; rugby football originated there□

Rügen island in the Baltic, part of Rostock◊ district of E Germany; it is a holiday centre, linked by causeway to the mainland; chief town Bergen□

Ruhr see under Rhine◊□

rum spirit, a by-product of the distillation of sugar cane, formerly always given colour by the addition of caramel, but more recently popular in an uncoloured milder form, known from its inventor as Bacardi□

Rumania see Romania◊□

Rumford Benjamin Thompson, Count Rumford 1753–1814. Anglo-American physicist. On the British side in the War of American Independence, he travelled in Europe, and was created a count of the Holy Roman Empire for services to the elector of Bavaria in 1791. In 1798 he published his theory that heat is a mode of motion, not a substance. He founded the Royal◊ Institute in London in 1799□

rummy card game in which the players try to obtain either cards of the same denomination, or in sequence in the same suit, to score. It probably derives from mah-jong◊□

Runcie Robert Alexander Kennedy 1921– . British cleric, Archbishop of Canterbury from 1979, the first to be appointed on the suggestion of the church Crown Appointments Commission (formed in 1977) rather than by political consultation. Opposed to the ordination of women at the present time, he favours ecclesiastical remarriage for the divorced□

Runcorn industrial town (chemicals) in Cheshire, England; population 46 000. As a 'new town' it has received Merseyside◊ overspill from 1964□

Rundstedt Karl Rudolf Gerd von 1875–1953. German field marshal. Largely responsible for the German break-through in France in 1940, he was defeated on the Ukrainian front in 1941. As Commander-in-Chief in France in 1942, he stubbornly resisted the Allied invasion of 1944, and in Dec launched the temporarily successful Ardennes◊ offensive. He was captured, but in 1949 war-crime charges were dropped owing to his ill-health□

runes the oldest Germanic script, chiefly adapted from the Latin alphabet, the earliest examples being from the 3rd century. They were scratched on wood, metal, stone, or bone, and examples in England include those on the Bewcastle and Ruthwell crosses. Several 11th-century Norse◊ runestones are claimed to have been found in the USA□

running birds flightless birds, formerly thought to have 'regressed' from fully-flighted species, but now all have been shown to be survivors of a primitive bird group which branched off early from the evolutionary tree. They include:

ostrich largest living bird *Struthio camelus*, order Struthioniformes. Found on the African savanna, it is 3 m/9 ft high; weighs 150 kg/330 lb; and has a 1.5 kg/3 lb egg. An extinct species on Mauritius was much larger (the origin of Sindbad's◊ roc), and had a 11.4 l/2.5 gallon egg. The male and female share parental duties; their kick is powerful and their running speed 50–70 kph/30–45 mph. In S Africa the ostrich is farmed for its tail plumes. Second only to it in size is the Australian ***emu*** *Dromaius novaehollandiae*, family Dromaiidae, of the same order, 2 m/6 ft high.

cassowary of the forests of N Australia and New Guinea *Casuarius casuarius*, order Casuariformes; it is 1.5 m/4.5 ft high, and able to jump its own height into the air from a standing position.

kiwi unique to New Zealand, of which it is the emblem, *Apteryx australis* belongs to the order Apterygiformes, and is very rare. Cloaks of Maori chieftains were made from its hair-like, khaki-sheen feathers. Nocturnal, it uses its long bill to forage for worms. Its egg is larger, in relation to the size of the body, than that of any other bird. The related New Zealand ***moa*** *Dinornis maximus*, extinct c1850, was 4 m/12 ft tall.

rhea family of S American birds, Rheidae, order Rheiformes, of which the largest is *Rhea americana* 1.20 m/2 ft high. Although the male has a harem, he himself cares for the young.

tinamou family of small, drab, S American birds, Tinamidae, order Tinamiformes. The ***spotted tinamou*** *Nothura maculosa*, can just about fly, but would rather not□

Runnymede see under Surrey◊□

Runyon Damon 1884–1946. American sports and crime reporter in New York, whose short stories *Guys and Dolls* 1932 deal wryly with the seamier side of the city's life in his own specially invented argot□

Rupert Prince 1619–82. English Royalist◊ general, admiral, and scientist, son of the Elector◊ Palatine and James◊ I's daughter Elizabeth. Defeated by Cromwell◊ at Marston Moor and Naseby, he commanded a privateering fleet 1649–52, until routed by Blake◊, and, returning after the Restoration◊, was a distinguished admiral in the Dutch Wars. He founded the Hudson◊'s Bay Company□

Rupert's Land area of N Canada, of which Prince Rupert◊ was the first governor. Granted to the Hudson◊'s Bay Company in 1670, it was later split among Quebec, Ontario, Manitoba, and the Northwest Territories□

rupture another term for hernia◊□

Ruse Danube port (Anglicized name Rustchuk) in Bulgaria, linked by rail and road bridge with Giurgiu in Romania; population 297 000□

rush genus of cold, temperate moisture-loving plants *Juncus*, family Juncaceae◊. They have flat, grasslike leaves, and the stems are used for matting, baskets, etc.□

Rushdie Salman 1947– . Indian novelist, who studied in Britain, and made his name with *Midnight's Children* 1981, dealing with India since independence□

Rusk Dean 1909– . American Democrat◊, Secretary of State to Kennedy◊ and Johnson◊ 1961–9, when he became unpopular through his involvement with the Vietnam◊ War□

Ruskin John 1819–1900. British art and social critic who hastened the appreciation of Turner◊ and the Pre-Raphaelites◊. His books include *Modern Painters* 1843–60, *The Stones of Venice* 1851–3, *Unto this Last* 1862, *Sesame and Lilies* 1865. He was an idealist socialist, exalting the 'craftsman', and the American Walter Vrooman founded Ruskin College, Oxford, 1899, in his honour. In 1848 he married 'Effie' (Euphemia) Gray, but in 1855 she obtained a decree of nullity, and later married Millais◊. Ruskin's later years were spent at Brantwood, Cumbria□

Russell Bertrand Arthur William, 3rd Earl Russell 1872–1970. British philosopher and mathematician, grandson of the 1st Earl Russell◊. Imprisoned as a pacifist in World War I, he advocated nuclear disarmament after World War II. His books include *Principles of Mathematics* 1903, *Principia Mathematica* 1910 (with A Whitehead◊), *History of Western Philosophy* 1946; Nobel prize for literature 1950, Order of Merit 1949□

Russell Charles Taze. See Jehovah◊'s Witnesses□

Russell George William 1867–1935. Irish nationalist writer, whose poetry was published under the pseudonym 'AE' and who helped found the Irish national theatre□

Russell John, 1st Earl Russell 1792–1878. British Liberal◊ statesman. He supported Catholic◊ Emancipation and led the movement for the Reform◊ Bill of 1832. He was Prime Minister 1846–52 and 1865–6. Pembroke Lodge in Richmond Park was granted to him as a home by Queen Victoria. See Bertrand Russell◊□

Russell John 1795–1883. British 'sporting parson', who developed the short-legged, smooth-coated ***Jack Russell terrier***: they do not breed true and so are not recognized by the Kennel◊ Club□

Russell John Peter 1858–1931. Australian artist. Having met Tom Roberts◊ while sailing to England, he became a member of the French Post-Impressionist◊ group. His portrait of Van◊ Gogh is in the Stedelijk Museum, Amsterdam□

Russell Sir William Howard 1821–1907. British correspondent for *The Times* during the Crimean◊ War, who created a sensation by his exposure of the mismanagement of the campaign□

Russia originally the name of the pre-revolutionary Russian Empire (pre-1917), and now accurately restricted to the RSFSR (Russian◊ Soviet Federal Socialist Republic) only, but because of its brevity popularly used for the whole of the present Union◊ of Soviet Socialist Republics□

Russian eastern group of the Slavonic branch of the Indo-European languages. It comprises ***Great Russian*** the language of the RSFSR (see below) and the standard means of communication throughout the USSR; ***Ukrainian*** (Ukrainians dislike its alternative name of Little Russian), and ***Byelo-Russian*** or ***White Russian*** which resembles Ukrainian, but has been affected by Polish contacts□

Russian history see under USSR◊□

Russian Soviet Federal Socialist Republic (RSFSR) constituent republic of the USSR
area 17 076 000 sq km/6 590 000 sq miles
capital Moscow
features largest of the Soviet republics, it occupies about three-quarters of the USSR, and includes the fertile Black◊ Earth district;

extensive forests; the Urals◊, with large mineral resources; the heavily industrialized area round Moscow; and Siberia; it includes 16 autonomous republics (see list below)
products three-quarters of the agricultural and industrial output of the USSR
population 138 000 000, 83% Russian
language Great Russian
religion traditionally Russian Orthodox◊, but Marxist◊-Leninism is officially approved
recent history see USSR◊
Autonomous Soviet Socialist Republics:
Bashkir ***capital*** Ufa; Buriat ***capital*** Ulan-Udé; Checheno-ingush ***capital*** Grozny; Chuvash ***capital*** Cheboksary; Dagestan ***capital*** Makhachkala; Kabardino-balkar ***capital*** Nalchik; Kalmyk ***capital*** Elista; Karelian ***capital*** Petrozavodsk; Komi ***capital*** Syktyvkar; Mari ***capital*** Yoshkar-ola Mordovian North Ossetian ***capital*** Ordzhonikidze; Tatar ***capital*** Kazan; Tuva ***capital*** Kizyl Udmurt Izhevsk Yakut ***capital*** Yakutsk□

Russo-Japanese War war, 1904–5, that arose from conflicting ambitions in Korea and Manchuria◊, especially the Russian occupation of Port Arthur (modern Lüda◊) in 1896 and of the Amur province in 1900.
1904–5 successful Japanese siege of Port Arthur May–Jan
1905 Japanese took Mukden 29 Feb–10 Mar; total defeat on 27 May of Russian Baltic fleet which had sailed half round the world to Tsushima Straits; peace signed at Portsmouth, USA, on 23 Aug. Russia surrendered her lease on Port Arthur, ceded S Sakhalin to Japan, evacuated Manchuria, and recognized Japan's interests in Korea□

rust minute parasitic plant. See under Basidiomycetes◊□

rust on iron or steel, a reddish-brown oxide (hydrated ferric oxide, Fe_2O_3 with water) formed by the action of moisture and oxygen. Paints which penetrate beneath any moisture, and plastic compounds which combine with existing rust to form a protective coating are used to avoid corrosion□

Ruth in the Old Testament, Moabite◊ ancestress of David◊ (King of Israel) by her second marriage to Boaz. When her first husband had died, she preferred to stay with her mother-in-law, Naomi, rather than return to her own people□

Ruth 'Babe' (George Herman) 1895–1948. American baseball player, one of the Boston Braves, and one of the best batters of all time□

Ruthenia region of central Europe within Austria-Hungary before World War I, which was divided among Czechoslovakia, Poland, and Romania in 1918, and from 1945–7 was all incorporated into the Ukrainian Republic□

ruthenium element
symbol Ru
atomic number 44
physical description hard blue-white metal
features member of platinum◊ group of metals
uses to harden platinum and palladium for use in electrical contacts; also a versatile catalyst□

Rutherford Ernest, 1st Baron Rutherford 1871–1937. New Zealand physicist, director of the Cavendish Laboratory, Cambridge, 1919–37. He showed (1911) that the scattering of alpha particles (see radioactivity◊) by a thin foil implied that atoms◊ of the foil – and by extension all atoms – had almost all their mass concentrated in a very small central positively charged nucleus, around which the electrons moved. Nobel prize 1908, knighted 1914, Order of Merit 1925; created a peer 1931□

rutherfordium alternative name for element unnilquadium◊□

rutiles naturally occurring crystalline form of titanium dioxide, TiO_2, from which titanium◊ is extracted; also used as pigments which give a brilliant white to paint, paper, and plastics. The coastal sands of E and W Australia are a major source□

Rutland see under Leicestershire◊□

Ruwenzori mountain mass, 'cloud king', on the Equator between Zaïre and Uganda; highest peak Margherita, 5110 m/16 763 ft. Ruwenzori is believed to be Ptolemy◊'s legendary 'Mountains of the Moon'□

Ruysdael Jacob c1628–82. Dutch landscape painter, who recorded scenes near his native Haarlem and in Germany and excelled in painting trees□

Ruyter Michael Adrianszoon de 1607–76. Dutch admiral. On 1–4 Jun 1666 he forced Rupert◊ and Albemarle to retire into the Thames, but on 25 Jul was heavily defeated off the N Foreland◊. In 1667 he sailed up the Medway to burn three men-of-war at Chatham, and captured others. He was mortally wounded in an action against the French□

Rwanda or ***Ruanda*** Republic of
area 26 338 sq km/10 169 sq miles
capital Kigali
features part of lake Kivu; volcanic mountains, highest peak Mt Karisimbi 4507 m/14 786 ft; Kagera river (whose headwaters are the source of the Nile) and National Park
exports coffee, tea, pyrethrum◊; tin and tungsten
currency Rwanda franc
population 5 580 000, including Hutu 90% (short-statured agrarians); Tutsi 9% (very

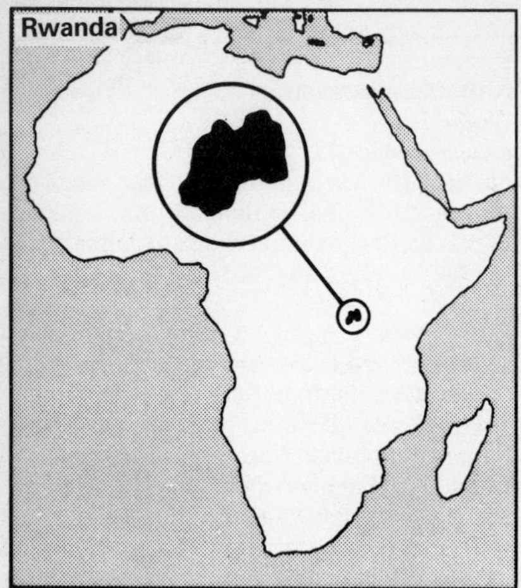

tall, pastoral people, who formed a warlike aristocracy until their dominance was broken by a Hutu revolt in 1960); and a very few Pygmies◊

language Kinyarwanda (a Bantu◊ language) and French

religion Christian (mainly Catholic) 54%; Animists◊ 45%; Muslims 1%

government executive president (Juvénal Habyarimana from 1973) and National Development Council

recent history part of German E Africa until 1918, it then passed under Belgian mandate/trusteeship (with Burundi◊) as Ruanda-Urundi, until independence in 1962□

Ryazan industrial town (engineering, agricultural machinery, footwear), near Moscow USSR; population 483 000□

Rybinsk see Andropov◊□

Ryde coast resort on the Isle of Wight, UK, linked by steamer and hovercraft with Portsmouth across the Solent; population 23 000□

rye a cereal derived from grass. See grasses◊□

Rye town (former member of the Cinque◊ Port of Hastings, but now inland) in E Sussex; population 4 500. Paul Nash◊ was a resident; Henry James◊ lived here, and E Benson◊ (who was mayor of Rye 1934–7) later lived in James's house□

Rye House Plot alleged plot by the Whigs◊ in 1683 to murder Charles◊ II, and his brother James, Duke of York, while passing the night at Rye House, Hertfordshire, and said to involve Monmouth◊. Lord Russell and Algernon Sidney were executed for complicity□

Ryle Gilbert 1900–76. British philosopher, cousin of Martin Ryle◊. His *The Concept of Mind* 1949 set out to show that the distinction between an inner and outer world in philosophy and psychology cannot be sustained. He ridiculed the mind-body dualism of Descartes◊ as the doctrine of 'The Ghost in the Machine'□

Ryle Sir Martin 1918–84. British radioastronomer, astronomer-royal 1972–82. He developed the technique of sky-mapping using 'aperture synthesis', combining smaller 'dishes' to give the characteristics of one large one, which brought confirmation of the 'big◊ bang theory'. Nobel prize with Antony Hewish◊ 1974□

Rysbrack John Michael 1694–1770. British sculptor, born in Antwerp. Settling in England in 1720, he produced portrait busts in Westminster Abbey and the equestrian statue of William◊ III, Bristol□

S

Saar river of France and Germany; length 240 km/149 mi. Its valley is noted for vineyards□

Saarbrücken capital of the Saarland, W Germany, from 1919; population 191 500□

Saarinen Eero 1910–61. American architect, son of Eliel Saarinen◊; he was born in Finland, but taken to the USA in 1923 by his father. His works include the American Embassy in London, and Dulles Airport, Washington□

Saarinen Eliel 1873–1950. Finnish-American architect, founder of the Finnish Romantic school, e.g. Helsinki railway station (his home outside the city is a museum). He contributed to US skyscraper design by his work in Chicago□

Saarland Land (state) of W Germany
area 2695 sq km/1040 sq mi
capital Saarbrücken
features after World War I, the Saar district was under French administration until a plebiscite returned it to Germany in 1935; after World War II it was occupied by France, but a referendum in 1955 returned it again to Germany; smallest and poorest of the German Länder.
products former flourishing coal and steel industries survive only by government subsidy
population 1 100 000
religion Roman Catholicism 74%, Protestantism 24%□

Sabah state of the federation of Malaysia, forming, with Sarawak, E Malaysias
area 80 500 sq km/29 400 sq mi
capital Kota Kinabalu
features chiefly mountainous (highest peak Mount Kinabalu 4098 m/3445 ft) and forested
exports hardwoods (quarter of the world's supplies), rubber, fish, cocoa, palm oil, copper
population 1 000 000, of which the largest ethnic group are the Kadazans at 30%; also included are 250 000 immigrants from Indonesia and the Philippines
language Malay (official); English is widely spoken
religion Sunni Islam 60% and Christian (the Kadazans) 30%, among whom there is unrest at increasing Islamic dominance
government constitutional head of state; chief minister, cabinet and legislative assembly
recent history in 1877–8 the Sultan made concessions to the North Borneo Company, which was eventually consolidated with Labuan as a British colony in 1946, and became the state of Sabah within Malaysia in 1963□

Sabbath see Observances under Judaism◊□

Sabine a member of a people of ancient Italy, conquered by the Romans and amalgamated with them in the 3rd century BC. The rape of the Sabine women, who eventually reconciled the two tribes, is frequently depicted in art□

sable a small carnivorous mammal related to the weasel◊□

saccharin intensely sweet, white crystalline solid, ortho-sulpho benzimide, $C_7H_5NO_3S$, which is substituted for sugar as a slimming aid. In massive quantities it causes cancer in rats, but investigations following proposals to ban it in the USA led to no conclusive findings on its effect in humans□

Sacco-Vanzetti case murder trial in Massachusetts, USA 1920–7. Italian anarchist immigrants Nicola Sacco and Bartolomeo Vanzetti were executed for murder, but in 1977 the verdict was declared unjust□

Sachs Hans 1494–1576. German master shoemaker, a prominent Meistersinger◊, and composer of 4275 *Meisterlieder*□

sackbut see under brass◊□

Sackville Thomas, 1st Earl of Dorset in 1536–1608. English poet, collaborator with Thomas Norton in *Gorboduc* 1561, the first English tragedy and the first play in blank verse. He was Lord Treasurer from 1599, and created Earl of Dorset in 1604□

Sackville-West Vita (Victoria) 1892–1962. British poet and novelist, born at Knole, Kent◊, England, and wife of Sir Harold Nicolson from 1913; *Portrait of a Marriage* 1973 by their son Nigel Nicolson described their married life. Her novels include *All Passion Spent* 1931. She created fine gardens at Sissinghurst, Kent◊□

sacrament in Christian usage, observances forming the visible sign of inward grace. In the Roman Catholic Church, sacraments are baptism, Holy Communion (Eucharist or mass), confirmation, rite of reconciliation (confession and penance), holy orders, matrimony, and the anointing of the sick; only the first two are held to be essential by the Church of England□

Sacramento capital and industrial port (detergents, jet aircraft, food processing) of California, USA; population 796 250. Founded as Fort Sutter in 1839, its old town has been restored□

Sadat Anwar 1918–81. Egyptian statesman. Succeeding Nasser as president in 1970, he restored morale by his handling of the Egyptian campaign in the 1973 war against Israel. In 1977 he visited Israel (see Camp David◊) to reconcile the countries, and shared a Nobel peace prize with Begin 1978. He was assassinated by Islamic fundamentalists□

Sadducee see under Judaism◊□

Sade Marquis de 1740–1814. French soldier and author. Imprisoned for sexual offences before finally being committed to an asylum, he wrote plays and novels dealing explicitly with a variety of sexual practices. ***Sadism***, named after him, is a form of sexual practice which delights in inflicting pain□

S'adi or ***Saadi***. Assumed name of Persian poet Sheikh Moslih Addin c1184–1291, whose chief works are *Bustan* (Tree-garden) and *Gulistan* (Flower-garden)□

Sadler's Wells see under Islington◊□

Sadowa (Czech ***Sadorá***) village in Czechoslovakia, near which the Prussians defeated the Austrians in the Battle of Sadowa or Königgrtz 2 Jul 1866, thus ending the Seven◊ Weeks' War□

safety lamp portable lamp for use where inflammable gases may be found, as in coal mines (see under Sir Humphry Davy◊). The modern electric lamp has bulb and contacts in specially protected enclosures□

safflower Eurasian plant *Carthamus tinctorius,* family Compositae, resembling a thistle. It is widely grown for the oil from its seeds (for cooking, making margarine, and also paints and varnishes); the seed residue is used as cattle feed□

saffron see under crocus◊□

Safi Atlantic port of Morocco; population 130 000. It exports phosphates and has fertilizer plants and sardine factories□

saga prose story of heroes written down 11th–13th centuries in Norway and Iceland. Sagas include the *Heimskringla* of Snorri Sturluson◊, celebrating Norwegian kings, and the anonymous legendary *Njala, Laxdaela,* and *Grettla*□

Sagamihara town on Honshu, Japan, with a large silkworm industry; population 448 000□

Sagan Carl 1934– . American physicist and astronomer, who devised the plaque, depicting a man and a woman, affixed to space probes *Pioneer* 10 and 11 in case intelligent life was encountered□

Sagan Françoise 1935– . French novelist. Her studies of love relationships include *Bonjour Tristesse* 1954 and *Aimez-vous Brahms?* 1959□

sage see herbs◊□

sago see under palm◊□

Saguenay river in Quebec, Canada, used for hydroelectric power as it flows to the St Lawrence estuary; length 765 km/474 mi□

Sahara world's largest desert, 5.5 million sq km/3.5 million sq mi. Small areas in Algeria and Tunisia are below sea level, but it is mainly a plateau with a central mountain system, including the Ahaggar Mountains in Algeria, the Aïr Massif in Niger and the Tibesti Massif in Chad. Oases punctuate the caravan routes, now modern roads. Resources include oil and gas in the north. Satellite observations have established a pattern of dried-up rivers below the surface, some as large as the Nile, which existed some two million years ago. Cave paintings confirm that even 4000 years ago there were running rivers and rich animal life (see Henri Lhote◊). The area of the Sahara has expanded by 650 000 sq km/250 965 sq mi in the last half century, and reafforestation is being attempted, e.g. in Tunisia□

Sahara Western, a region of NW Africa, formerly called ***Spanish Sahara***

area 266 000 sq km/102 000 sq mi

capital La'Youn (El Aaiún); phosphate mining town of Bou Craa

features defensive fortified ***Sahara Wall*** enclosing the phosphate area

exports phosphates

currency dirham

population 700 000

language Arabic

religion Sunni Islam

government at present in a state of war; within the Sahara Wall Morocco rules, and outside, Polisario Popular Front for the Liberation of Saguia al Hamra and Rio de Oro

recent history a Spanish possession until 1976, two thirds was taken over by Morocco, and one third by Mauritania (which withdrew in 1979 and was replaced by Morocco). Polisario proclaimed the ***Saharan Arab Democratic Republic*** in 1976, and is supported by Algeria and Libya□

Saharan Arab Democratic Republic see under Western Sahara◊□

Sahel marginal area to the south of the Sahara, Senegal to Somalia, where the desert has extended because of a population explosion, poor agricultural practice, destruction of scrub and climatic change□

Saida town in Lebanon (ancient ***Sidon***); population 24 740. Sidon was the chief city of Phoenicia◊, a bitter rival of Tyre c1400–701BC, when it was conquered by Sennacherib◊. Later a Roman city, it was taken by the Arabs 637AD, and fought over during the Crusades□

Saigon see Ho◊ Chi-minh City□

Saigon Battle of. Battle 29 Jan–23 Feb 1968 during the Vietnam War. Five thousand infiltrating VietCong were expelled by S Vietnamese and US forces, but the city finally fell to N Vietnamese forces 30 Apr 1975 following S Vietnamese withdrawal from the central highlands□

saint person eminently pious, and usually certified so by canonization◊. In 1970 Paul VI revised the calendar of saints' days: excluded were Barbara, Catherine, Christopher and Ursula (as probably non-existent); optional veneration might be given to George, Januarius, Nicholas (Santa Claus) and Vitus; insertions for obligatory veneration include St Thomas More◊ and the Uganda◊ Martyrs□

St Albans city in Hertfordshire, England; population 125 400. The cathedral was founded 793 in honour of St Alban◊; nearby are the ruins of the Roman city of Verulamium on Watling Street□

St Albans Battle of, 1455. See under Wars of the Roses◊□

St Andrews town in Fife, Scotland; population 13 400. It is the headquarters of golf and of the Royal and Ancient Club 1754, and has the oldest university in Scotland, founded in 1411□

St Augustine port and holiday resort in Florida, USA; population 12 500. Founded by the Spanish in 1565, it was burned by Drake◊ in 1586, and ceded to the USA in 1821. It includes the oldest house (late 16th century) and oldest masonry fort, Castillo de San Marcos (1672) in the USA□

St Bartholomew Massacre of. See Bartholomew◊□

St Bernard a breed of dog◊□

St Bernard Passes see under Alps◊□

St Christopher (St Kitts)-Nevis federal state comprising two islands in the Caribbean Lesser Antilles◊

area 261 sq km/100 sq mi

capital Basseterre (on St Kitts)

towns Nevis (chief town of Nevis)

features St Kitts was the first of the British W Indian islands to be colonized

exports sugar and molasses, cotton; tourism is important

currency East Caribbean dollar

population 44 000, including 9300 on Nevis

language English

religion Christianity

government governor-general appointed by the British monarch; there is a Prime Minister (Kennedy Simmonds) heading a conservative coalition from 1983 and National Assembly (nine members) for both islands on St Kitts, and a separate Assembly on Nevis

recent history both islands were reached and named by Columbus, but though settled 1623/8 were not finally recognized as British until 1713. The islands formed an 'association' with Britain in 1967 and became independent in 1983□

St Cloud town in the Île de France region, France; population 30 000. The château, linked with the names of Marie Antoinette and Napoleon, was demolished in 1781, but the park remains, see Sèvres◊□

St Cyr St Cyr see under Britanny◊□

St David's 'village' city (Welsh ***Tyddewi***) in Dyfed, Wales; population 1700. Its cathedral, founded by St David◊, was rebuilt 1180–1522□

St Denis industrial town, a suburb of Paris, France; population 97 000. Abelard was a monk at the famous 12th-century Gothic abbey, which contains many tombs of French kings□

St Dunstan's British organization for those blinded in war service, founded in 1915 by newspaper proprietor Sir Arthur Pearson 1866–1921, who had himself become blind in 1910□

Sainte-Beuve Charles Augustin 1804–69. French critic, whose articles on French literature appeared as *Causeries du Lundi* 1851–62, and whose *Port Royal* 1840–59 is a study of Jansenism◊□

Saint Elias Mountains mountain range on Alaska-Canada border, with Mt Logan 4200 m/13 780 ft, Canada's highest mountain, as its highest peak□

St Elmo's fire harmless, flamelike electrical discharge, which occurs above ships' masts or about an aircraft. St Elmo (or St Erasmus) was a patron of sailors□

St Étienne industrial city (aircraft engines, chemicals) in S central France; population 218 300. There is a school of mining (1816)□

Saint-Exupéry Antoine de 1900–44. French pioneer aviator, who disappeared on a wartime mission over occupied France. His *Le petit Prince* 1943, a children's book, is also an adult allegory□

St Gall industrial town (natural and synthetic textiles) (German ***Sankt Gallen***) in NE Switzerland; population 82 000. It was founded in the 7th century by the Irish missionary St Gall, and the Benedictine abbey library has many medieval manuscripts□

St George's port and capital of Grenada◊; population 31 000□

St George's Channel Irish Sea-Atlantic link between SW Wales and SE Ireland; length 160 km/100 mi; width 80–150 km/50–90 mi□

St Gotthard Pass see under Alps◊□

St Helena

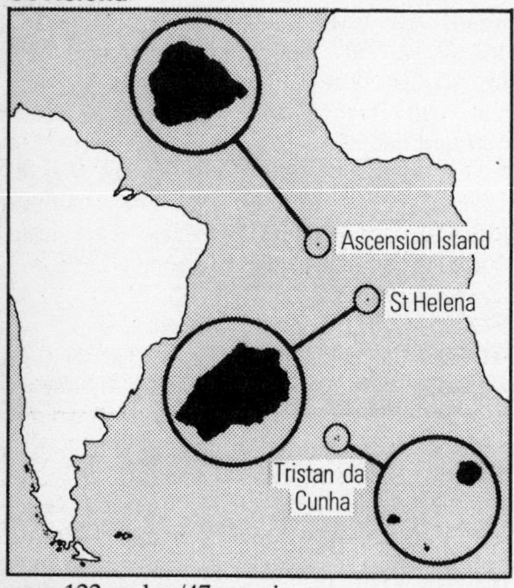

area 122 sq km/47 sq mi
capital and chief port Jamestown
features mountainous volcanic island◊; the islands of Ascension◊ and Tristan da Cunha◊ are dependencies; Napoleon lived in exile at Longwood 1815–21, and died there; it has some 40 plant species known nowhere else
currency pound sterling
population 5300
language English
religion Anglicanism
government governor, with executive and legislative councils
recent history reached by the Portuguese in 1502, it was unoccupied until taken over by the East India Company in 1659, becoming a British colony in 1834□

St Helier resort and capital of Jersey, Channel Islands; population 28 000. The 'States of Jersey', the island legislature, sits here in the *salle des états*□

St Ives fishing port and resort in Cornwall; population 10 000. Its artists' colony, founded by Sickert◊ and Whistler◊, later included Naum Gabo◊, Barbara Hepworth◊ (a museum and sculpture gardens commemorate her), and Ben Nicholson◊□

St James's Palace a palace in Pall Mall, London; it was a royal residence 1698–1837□

Saint John fishing and industrial port (shipbuilding, timber, fish processing, textiles), largest city of New Brunswick, Canada, on the St◊ John river; population 86 000□

St John river rising in Maine, USA and flowing into the Bay of Fundy◊ (the high tides there reverse its flow at Reversing Falls) at Saint John; length 673 km/418 mi□

St John of Jerusalem Knights Hospitallers of. Oldest order of Christian chivalry, named from the hospital at Jerusalem founded c1048 by merchants of Amalfi for pilgrims, whose travel routes the knights defended from the Saracens. On being forced to leave Palestine, the Knights went to Cyprus in 1291, to Rhodes in 1309, and to Malta (granted to them by Emperor Charles V) in 1530. Expelled by Napoleon (on his way to Egypt) in 1798, they established their headquarters in Rome (Palazzo di Malta). Today there are about 8000 Knights (male and female), and the Grand Master is the world's highest-ranking Roman Catholic layman.

There is a Protestant English offshoot, chartered 1888, working mainly through the St John Ambulance Association and Brigade (hospital work and first aid)□

St John's capital and chief port (cod fish processing) of Newfoundland, Canada; population 154 820. It was founded by Sir Humphrey Gilbert◊ in 1582□

Saint-Just Louis Antoine Léon Florelle de 1767–94. French revolutionary. A close associate of Robespierre◊, he became a member of the Committee of Public Safety in 1793, and was guillotined with Robespierre□

St Kilda see under Outer Hebrides◊□

St Kitts-Nevis see St◊ Christopher-Nevis□

St Laurent Louis Stephen 1882–1973. Canadian Liberal Prime Minister 1948–57, popularly known as 'Uncle Louis'. He signed the NATO pact in 1949□

Saint Laurent Yves 1936– . French couturier, partner to Dior◊, from 1954 and his successor in 1957, who opened his own house in 1962. His creations have a bold masculine look□

St Lawrence river in N America. From ports on the Great◊ Lakes, it forms, with man-made linking canals (which also give great hydro-electric capacity to the river), the ***St Lawrence Seaway*** for ocean-going ships, ending in the ***Gulf of St Lawrence***; length 1046 km/650 mi, ice-bound for four months annually (see also Montreal◊)□

St Leger see flat racing under horse◊ racing□

St Leonards see under Hastings◊□

St Lô town in Normandy, France; population 25 000. In World War II it was destroyed 10–18 Jul 1944, when US forces captured it from the Germans□

St Louis industrial river port (aerospace equipment, aircraft, vehicles, chemicals, electrical goods, steel) and chief city of Missouri, USA, on the Mississippi; population 420 000. Founded as a French trading post in 1764, it passed to the USA in 1803 under the Louisiana◊ Purchase. The Gateway Arch 1965 is a memorial by Saarinen◊ to the pioneers of the West□

St Lucia

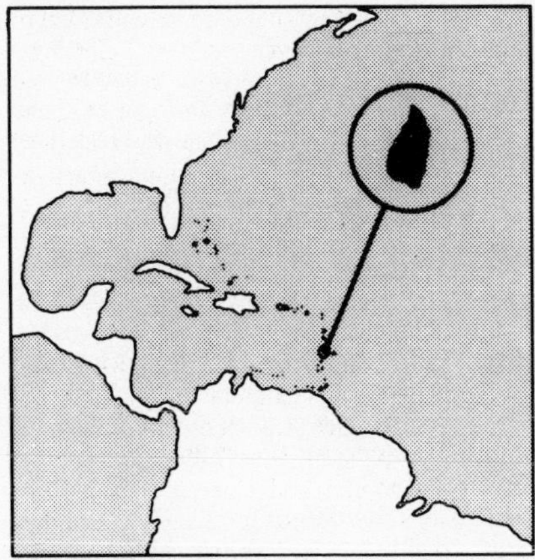

area 616 sq km/238 sq mi
capital Castries
features second largest of the Windward◊ group; mainly tropical forest
exports bananas, cocoa, copra; tourism is important
currency East Caribbean dollar
population 120 000
language English
religion 90% Roman Catholic
government governor-general, senate, house of assembly (Prime Minister since 1982 John Compton)
recent history reached by Columbus in 1500, it became French in 1635, British in 1803, and independent within the Commonwealth in 1979□

St Michael and St George see under Knighthood◊□

St Michael's Mount island in Mount's Bay, Cornwall, linked to the mainland by a causeway at low tide. See also Mont◊ St Michel□

St Moritz winter sports centre (including from 1885 the Cresta Run for toboggans) in SE Switzerland; population 6000□

St Nazaire port in Brittany, France; population 69 800. In World War II it was a German submarine base, and in a British commando raid 28 Mar 1942, 212 men of the 353 who took part were killed or missing□

St Nevis see St◊ Christopher-Nevis□

St Paul capital and industrial city (electronics, publishing and printing, petrochemicals, cosmetics, meat-packing) of Minnesota, USA; population 270 000□

St Paul's Cathedral cathedral church of the City of London, and the largest Protestant church in England. A Norman church, which had replaced the original Saxon building, was burnt down in the Great Fire of 1666; the present cathedral, built by Wren◊, was built 1675–1710. It has paintings by Thornhill and wood carvings by Grinling Gibbons, and the tombs of Wellington and Nelson□

St Peter Port only town and port of Guernsey, Channel Islands; population 16 000□

St Petersburg see Leningrad◊□

St Petersburg seaside resort and industrial city (space technology), Florida, USA; population 236 900□

Saint-Pierre Jacques Henri Bernardin de 1737–1814. French author of the sentimental romance *Paul et Virginie* 1789; the heroine refused to be saved from shipwreck at the cost of stripping off her clothes□

St Pierre and Miquelon
area St Pierre 26 sq km/10 sq mi and Miquelon-Langlade 216 sq km/83 sq mi
capital St Pierre
features comprises eight rocky islands in two small groups off S coast of Newfoundland; last surviving remnant of former French N American empire
exports fish
currency French franc
population 6100
language French
religion Roman Catholicism
government commissioner and local council; and one representative in the National Assembly in France
history settled in the 17th century, the islands were a French territory 1816–76, when they became an overseas département□

St Quentin town in N France, site of a Prussian defeat of the French in 1871, and almost obliterated in World War I; population 69 000□

Saint-Saëns Camille 1835–1921. French composer, pianist and organist, whose works include the symphonic poem *Danse macabre* 1874; opera *Samson et Dalila* 1877; and orchestral *Carnaval des Animaux* 1886□

Saint-Simon Claude Henri, Comte de Saint-Simon 1760–1825. French socialist who advocated an atheist society ruled by technicians and industrialists in *Du Système industrielle* 1821□

Saint-Simon Louis de Rouvroy, Duc de 1675–1755. French soldier, courtier, and politician, whose *Mémoires* 1691–1723 are unrivalled as a description of the French court□

St Tropez fishing port on the French Côte d'Azur, popularized as a resort in the 1960s by Brigitte Bardot◊; topless sunbathing started on Pamplona Beach 1972□

St Vincent see John Jervis◊□

St Vincent cape of the Portuguese coast off which England defeated the French and Spanish fleets 1797: see John Jervis◊, and Nelson◊□

St Vincent and the Grenadines

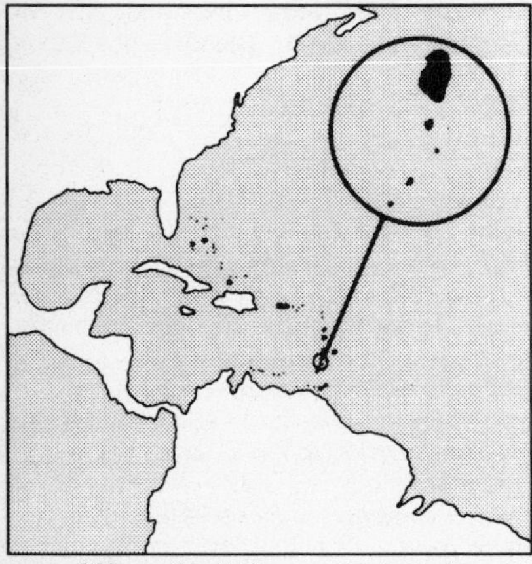

area 389 sq km/150 sq mi, including N Grenadines 44 sq km/17sq mi
capital Kingstown
features Mustique, one of the Grenadines, is an exclusive holiday resort
exports bananas, arrowroot, copra
currency Eastern Caribbean dollar
population 138 000
language English
government governor-general and house of assembly (Prime Minister James Mitchell since 1984, centrist New Democratic Party)
recent history reached by Columbus in 1498, it was an English possession, though disputed by the French, from 1627. The islands became independent in 1979, and a full member of the Commonwealth in 1985□

Saint Vincent Gulf inlet of the Southern Ocean, S Australia, on which Adelaide stands□

St Vitus's dance see chorea◊; St Vitus, traditionally martyred under Diocletian, was the patron saint of dancers, and sufferers prayed at his shrine□

Sakai industrial city (engineering, aluminium, chemicals) on Honshu, Japan; population 810 000□

sake Japanese rice-wine; it is yellowish (alcohol content 15%), and is drunk hot□

Sakhalin island in the Pacific, N of Japan, which forms with the Kurils◊ a region of the USSR.
area 76 400 sq km/29 500 sq mi
capital Yuzhno-Sakhalinsk
features militarily important, with a missile base
products agricultural in the milder south, also timber, fish, and some oil and coal
population 650 000, including aboriginal Ainu◊ and Gilyaks
history it was settled by both Russians and Japanese from the 17th century. In 1875 the south (in Japanese *Karafuto*) was ceded by Japan to Russia, but Japan regained it in 1905, only to cede it again in 1945□

Sakharov Andrei Dimitrievich 1921– . Russian physicist, who worked on the hydrogen bomb in the USSR. Founder of the Human Rights Committee (Nobel peace prize 1975), he criticized the Soviet invasion of Afghanistan and was exiled to Gorky in 1980. He is not allowed to emigrate because of his knowledge of Soviet nuclear weapons development□

Sakhti see Hinduism◊□

Saki pseudonym of British author Hugh Hector Munro 1870–1916. Foreign correspondent for the *Morning Post* 1902–8, he was killed in action on the Western Front. His short stories, and the novel *The Unbearable Bassington* 1912, are ingeniously witty□

Sakkara see Memphis◊□

Saladin or ***Sala-ud-din*** 1138–93. Sultan of Egypt from 1175, in succession to the Atabeg of Mosul on whose behalf he had conquered it 1164–74. A Kurd (see under Kurdistan◊), he conquered Syria 1174–87, and by his recovery of Jerusalem from the Christians in 1187, precipitated the 3rd Crusade◊. Saladin, who was renowned for knightly courtesy, made peace with Richard I of England in 1192□

Salado two rivers of Argentina, both rising in the Andes, and c1600 km/c1000 mi long. ***Salado del Norte*** or ***Juramento*** flows from the Andes to join the Paraná; the ***Salado del Sud*** or ***Desaguadero*** joins the Colorado to empty south of Bahía Blanca□

Salam Abdus 1926– . Pakistani theoretical physicist, his country's first Nobel prize-winner in 1979. He became director of the International Centre for Theoretical Physics, Trieste, 1964. See particle◊ physics□

Salamanca city in Castilla-León, W Spain; population 167 130. Noted for its Roman bridge, 13th-century university, and a superbly designed square, the Plaza Mayor□

Salamanca Battle of. Wellington◊'s most famous victory over the French in the Peninsular◊ War, 22 Jul 1812□

salamander amphibian of the family Salamandridae in the order Caudata ('tailed', because they have tails in both the larval and adult stage). The family includes the ***common newt*** *Triturus vulgaris* of Europe, 8 cm/3 in long; ***crested newt*** *T cristatus,* with handsome orange and black belly; ***spotted*** or ***fire salamander*** *Salamandra salamandra,* falsely believed in medieval times to be immune to fire; and the ***giant salamander*** of Japan *Andrias japonicus,* 1.60 m/5 ft. Related is the ***Mexican salamander*** *Ambystoma (Siredon) mexicanum,* family Amblystomatidae, which reaches sexual maturity in the tadpole (***axolotl***) stage, in which it is 30 cm/1ft long. It may never change to the adult form and the larval stage was long thought to be a separate species. Among Mexicans the axolotl is considered a delicacy□

Salamis island off Piraeus (see under Athens◊), Greece; the Greeks defeated the Persians in a naval battle here in 480BC and the island town of Salamis is now a naval station□

sal ammoniac or ***ammonium chloride*** a volatile salt, NH_4Cl. It forms white crystals round volcanic craters, but is prepared synthetically for use in 'dry-cell' batteries□

Salazar Antonio de Oliveira 1889–1970. Portuguese Prime Minister 1932–68, when he was disabled by a stroke. His virtual dictatorship, under a constitution introduced in 1933, allowed only his own National Union party to exist□

Sale town in Victoria, Australia, linked by canal to Bass Strait; population 13 000. It has benefited from the Strait deposits of oil and natural gas, and the brown coal to the south; and is also a marketing and processing centre for dairy produce and grain□

Salem industrial city (iron mining, textiles, etc.) in Tamil Nadu, Republic of India; population 515 000□

Salem city in Massachusetts, USA; population 48 000. In 1692 there were celebrated witch trials, ending in the execution of 19 people: see under Ergot◊□

Salerno port in SW Italy; population 157 400. The temple ruins of the ancient Greek city of ***Paestum***, with some of the earliest Greek paintings known, are nearby, and Salerno's medical school has been famous since medieval times. To the east is the ***Gulf of Salerno*** where the Allies landed 9 Sept 1943 in World War II□

Salford industrial (engineering, electrical goods, textiles, chemicals) city in Greater Manchester, England; population 245 000. It has docks, and is on the Manchester Ship Canal□

Salic Law a law (mistakenly so-called from the Salian or northern division of the Franks◊ supposed to practise it) adopted in the Middle Ages by several European royal houses; it excluded women from succession to the throne. In Sweden in 1980 such a provision was abrogated to allow Princess Victoria to become Crown Princess□

salicylic acid white solid, $C_6H_4(OH)(COOH)$, which crystallizes into prismatic needles at 159°C; used as an antiseptic, in food preparation, dyestuffs and in the preparation of aspirin□

Salieri Antonio 1750–1825. Italian composer, who taught Beethoven, Schubert and Liszt, and was the rival of Mozart, whom it has been suggested, without proof, he poisoned□

Salinger J(erome) D(avid) 1919– . American writer, born in New York. He is best-known for the novel of adolescence *The Catcher in the Rye* 1951, and his stories of the Jewish Glass family, including *Franny and Zooey* 1961□

Salisbury city in Wiltshire, England, population 36 000. The Early English cathedral 1220–66 has the highest spire in England, 123 m/404 ft. ***Old Sarum***, on a 90 m/300 ft hill to the north, originated as an Iron Age settlement, but was deserted on the foundation of the new town in 1220. It continued to send two members (elected by seven voters) to Parliament until the Reform Bill of 1832□

Salisbury see Harare◊□

Salisbury Robert Arthur James Gascoyne-Cecil, 5th Marquess of Salisbury 1893–1972. British Conservative politician. As an 'elder statesman', he was called upon by Elizabeth II when Eden◊ resigned in 1957 to assist in ascertaining party views as to a successor: Macmillan◊ was preferred to Butler◊□

Salisbury Robert Arthur Talbot Gascoyne-Cecil, 3rd Marquess of Salisbury 1830–1903. British Conservative statesman. As Foreign Secretary 1866–7, he took part in the Congress of Berlin, and as Prime Minister 1885–6, 1886–92, and 1895–1902, gave his main attention to foreign policy and for most of the time was also Foreign Secretary□

Salisbury Robert Cecil, 1st Earl of Salisbury. See Robert Cecil◊□

Salisbury Plain see under Wiltshire◊□

saliva moistening secretion of the three pairs of salivary glands in the mouth, aiding the swallowing and digestion of food□

Salk Jonas Edward 1914– . American physician. A specialist in poliomyelitis◊, he developed in 1954 the original vaccine which led to virtual eradication of the disease in developed countries□

Sallust (Gaius Sallustius Crispus) 86–34BC. Roman historian, a supporter of Caesar. He wrote accounts of Catiline's conspiracy and the Jugurthine War in a condensed and epigrammatic style□

salmon family of fish Salmonidae, order Clupeiformes, which includes ***Atlantic salmon*** *Salmo salar*, about 1.5 m/5 ft, which spends most of its life in the sea, but returns to die after spawning in the rivers where it was itself hatched. The young are successively known as ***alevins*** at hatching, ***parr*** when they start feeding, ***smolts*** at two years and ***grilse*** at three years when they are spawning. They are noted for their jumps over river obstacles on their way to the spawning grounds (guided to their home stream by its scent). They are also 'farmed' in cages, and 'ranched' (selectively bred, hatched, and fed before release to the sea). Stocking rivers indiscriminately with hatchery fish may destroy the precision of their homing instinct by interbreeding between those originating in different rivers. Closely allied to the salmon is the ***sea trout*** *Salmo trutta* (and the related variant, ***brown trout***), and the NW American ***rainbow trout*** *Salmo gairdneri*. All are edible sporting fish. In the same family are ***char*** *Salvelinus* genus, of which the typical *S alpinus* is found in England. See also grayling◊ and smelt◊□

Salome in New Testament, daughter of Herodias (see under Herod◊ Antipas) who asked for the head of St John◊ the Baptist as a reward for her dancing□

Salonika see Thessaloniki◊□

Salop see Shropshire◊□

salsify hardy biennial *Tragopogon porrifolius*, family Compositae, often called 'vegetable oyster'; its white fleshy roots and spring shoots are eaten as a vegetable□

salt (chemistry) compound comprising an acid and a base united in definite proportions, e.g. hydrochloric acid and caustic soda unite to form the salt sodium chloride, and water□

salt or ***common salt*** sodium chloride, NaCl, found in sea water, as rock salt, in brine deposits, etc. Widely used as a preservative before refrigeration became widespread. Excess salt, largely from processed food, is blamed by some medical authorities for high blood pressure, and increased risk of heart attacks□

Salt Lake City capital of Utah, USA; population 162 960. Laid out in 1847 by Brigham Young◊, it is the capital of the Mormon Church, with a great granite temple 1853–93. Mining, construction, etc., is being replaced by high technology□

Salton Sea brine lake in SE California, USA, accidentally created during irrigation works from the Colorado river. It is used to generate electricity. See solar◊ ponds□

Saluki a breed of dog◊□

Salvador industrial port (flour and sugar mills, tobacco) and naval base in Brazil; population 1 500 000. Founded in 1510, it was the capital of Brazil 1549–1763□

Salvador El. See under El◊ Salvador□

salvage compensation payable to those who by voluntary effort have saved a ship and/or its cargo and passengers from complete loss through shipwreck, fire, or enemy action□

Salvation Army Christian evangelical, social service, and social reform organization, originating 1865 with the work of William Booth◊, and known from 1878 as the Salvation Army, now a world-wide organization. It has military titles for its officials and its weekly journal is the *War Cry*; its brass bands are excellent□

sal volatile smelling salts (a mixture of ammonium carbonate, bicarbonate and carbamate)□

Salween river rising in E Tibet and reaching the Andaman Sea after flowing through Burma; length 2800 km/1750 mi, with many rapids□

Salzburg city in W Austria; population 138 200. A beautiful city, it is dominated by the Hohensalzburg fortress and has a 17th-century cathedral. Mozart's birthplace is a museum, and since 1920 an annual music festival has been held□

Samara see Kuibyshev◊□

Samaria hilly region of ancient Israel. The town of Samaria (modern Sebastiyeh on the W Bank of the Jordan) was the capital of Israel 10th–8th centuries BC□

Samaritan descendant of the colonists settled by the Assyrians in Samaria, after the destruction of the Israelite kingdom in 722BC. Samaritans adopted Judaism, but rejected all sacred books except the Pentateuch, and regarded their temple on Mount Gerizim (not that at Jerusalem) as the true sanctuary. A very small community remains at Nablus□

Samaritans the British voluntary organization aiding those tempted to suicide or despair, established in 1953 at St Stephen's Church, Walbrook, London, by the rector ***Chad Varah*** 1911– . Groups of lay people, usually under the direction of a clergyman, and consulting with psychiatrists, psychotherapists and doctors, offer friendship and counselling to those using their emergency telephone numbers day or night. They are inspired by the story of the 'good Samaritan' of the New Testament, who aided the injured traveller who had been attacked and robbed, instead of 'walking by on the other side of the road'□

samarium element
symbol Sm
atomic number 62
physical description greyish metal
features a radioactive metal in the lanthanide◊ series
uses as a neutron absorber and in carbon arc lighting, and as an organic catalyst□

Samarkand city in Uzbek Republic, USSR; population 481 000. Once an important city on the Silk◊ Road, it was occupied by the Russians in 1868. It was the capital of Tamerlane◊, who is buried here, and the splendours of his city have been restored□

Samarra ancient town in Iraq, on the Tigris, NW of Baghdad. Founded in 836 by the Abbasid Caliph Motassim, it was the Abbasid capital until 876, and is a place of pilgrimage for Shi'ites◊□

Samizdat Russian 'self-published', material circulated underground to evade censorship, e.g. reviews of Solzhenitsyn's banned novel *August, 1914* 1972□

Samoa volcanic island chain in the SW Pacific. It is divided into Western Samoa◊ and American Samoa◊□

Samoa American
area 197 sq km/76 sq mi
capital Fagatogo on Tutuila
features comprises the eastern islands, notably Tutuila
exports canned tuna, handicrafts
currency US dollar
population 33 800, mainly Polynesian
language Samoan and English
religion Christianity
government as an unorganized, unincorporated US territory, it is administered by the Department of the Interior
recent history acquired by the USA by agreement with Britain and Germany in 1899□

Samoa Western
area 2842 sq km/1097 sq mi
capital Apia on Upolu
features comprises islands of Savai'i and Upolu, with two smaller islands and islets; mountain ranges on the main islands; huge lava flows on Savai'i which cut down the area available for agriculture
exports copra, bananas, cocoa; tourism is important
currency tala
population 162 000
language English and Samoan (official)
religion Christianity
government head of state, eventually to be elected for five years (Malietoa Tanumafili II, sole head for life from 1962); legislative assembly (Prime Minister Tofilan Eti Alesana from 1982)
recent history a German protectorate from 1900 until World War I, it was under New Zealand trusteeship 1920–61, and became independent within the Commonwealth in 1962□

Samos Greek island in the Aegean. Pythagoras◊ was born here□

samoyed a breed of dog◊□

samphire perennial plant of Eurasian sea cliffs *Crithmum maritimum*, family Umbelliferae. The fleshy leaves are used in salads or pickled□

Samson in Old Testament, hero of Israel whose exploits of strength against the Philistines were ended when Delilah◊ cut off his hair□

Samuel in Old Testament, last of the 'judges' who ruled the ancient Israelites before their adoption of a monarchy, and the first of the prophets; the two books bearing his name cover the story of Samuel and the reigns of Saul◊ and David◊□

Samuel Herbert Louis, 1st Viscount Samuel 1870–1963. British Liberal statesman, High Commissioner of Palestine 1920–5, the first Jew to govern the Holy Land for c2000 years. He suggested the formation of the National Government set up in Britain in 1931, but resigned as a Free Trader in 1932, and led the Liberal Opposition until 1935□

Samuelson Paul 1915– . American economist, awarded a Nobel prize in 1970 for his application of scientific analysis to economic theory. Author of perhaps the best-selling economics text book of all time, *Economics* 1948□

Samurai feudal military caste which held power in Japan from the 12th century until the fall of the Tokugawa shogunate, in which they had assisted. They obeyed the bushido code of bravery, honour, and service. See Yukio Mishima◊□

San'a capital of N Yemen; population 278 000. A walled city, with fine mosques and traditional house architecture, it is threatened by modernization□

San Andreas Fault vertical break in earth's surface 32 km/20 m deep and 965 km/600 m long. Los Angeles rests on the western half (moving NW) and San Francisco on the eastern half (moving SE): in 50 million years the two will meet. Meanwhile built-up pressure causes earthquakes□

San Antonio industrial city (aircraft maintenance, oil refining, meat packing) in Texas, USA; population 783 300. Founded in 1718, it grew up round the site of the Alamo◊. It is a commercial and financial centre□

San Cristóbal city in Venezuela, on the Pan-American Highway; population 152 300□

sanction measure used to enforce international law, e.g. the attempted economic boycott of Italy during the Abyssinian War by the League of Nations; of Rhodesia after UDI by the United Nations; and the call for measures against South Africa on human rights grounds by the UN and other organizations in 1985–6□

Sand George. Pseudonym of French author Armandine Lucile Aurore Dupin 1804–76. After nine years of marriage, she left her husband in 1831, and, while living in Paris as a writer, had a number of liaisons, e.g. Alfred de Musset◊ and Chopin◊. She was concerned with women's rights, but from 1848 she retired to the château of Nohant. Her novels often use autobiographical material, and include *La Mare au diable* 1846 and *La Petite Fadette 1848*, and she also wrote volumes of memoirs□

sand loose grains of rock up to 0.02–2.00 mm in diameter, consisting chiefly of quartz, but owing their varying colour to admixtures of other minerals. They are used in cement-making, as abrasives, etc. Some 'light' soils contain up to 50% sand, and are subject to too rapid drainage and erosion by wind. Sands may eventually consolidate into ***sandstone***, of which the types are distinguished by the material cementing the grains together, e.g. ferruginous, siliceous, calcareous, barytic, gypseous and pyritic□

sandalwood evergreen tree of SE Asia *Santalum album*, family Santalaceae; the sweet-scented wood is used for jewel boxes, etc., and its aromatic oil in perfumery□

Sandburg Carl August 1878–1967. American poet, born in Illinois, who worked as farm labourer, bricklayer, etc., so that his poetry has an open factual content, as in *Chicago Poems* 1916. His *Always the Young Stranger* 1953 is an autobiography□

Sandhurst see under Berkshire◊□

San Diego industrial city (bio-medical technology, aircraft missiles, fish canning), and military and naval base in California, USA; population 900 000. Tijuana◊ adjoins San Diego across the Mexican border□

sand painting picture in which coloured sands are laid on an adhesive ground, produced in Japan at least from the 18th century, and also by European artists. Striking sand paintings are also used as temporary altars during Navajo Indian ceremonial□

sandpiper slender-billed wading bird, family Scolopacidae, including ***common sandpiper*** *Actitis hypleucos*, ***greenshank*** *Tringa nebularia*, with long olive-green legs, ***redshank*** *T totanus*, ***dunlin*** *Calidris alpina*, and ***ruff*** *Philomachus pugnax*, noted for the feather collar it develops in the breeding season. See snipe◊□

Sandringham see under Norfolk◊□

sandstone see under sand◊□

Sandwich resort and market town in Kent, England, with more medieval buildings than any other town in Britain. It was one of the Cinque◊ ports, but recession of the sea has left the harbour useless since the 16th century; population 4500□

Sandwich John Montagu, 4th Earl of Sandwich 1718–92. British politician. He was an inept First Lord of the Admiralty 1771–82 during the American War of Independence, and the Sandwich Islands were named after him, as are sandwiches, which he invented in order to eat without leaving the gaming-table□

Sandwich Islands a former name of Hawaii◊□

Sandys see under Duncan-Sandys◊□

San Francisco chief Pacific port of the USA, California; population 678 974. In 1578 Sir Francis Drake's flagship, the *Golden Hind*, stopped near San Francisco on its voyage round the world, and a replica is now a floating museum. San Francisco was occupied in 1846 during the war with Mexico, and in 1906 was almost destroyed by an earthquake which killed 452 people (see San◊ Andreas Fault). The UN Charter was drawn up here in 1945, and the peace treaty between the Western Allies and Japan was signed here in 1951. There is a large homosexual community, and many religious sects (see Jonestown◊).

The ***Golden Gate***, the strait giving access to ***San Francisco Bay***, is crossed by the world's 2nd longest single-span bridge, 1280 m/4200 ft, 1937. ***Alcatraz Island*** in the bay has a former military prison, used as a penitentiary 1934–63, dangerous currents preventing escapes; famous inmates included Al Capone◊ and the 'Birdman of Alcatraz', a murderer who used solitary confinement to become an authority on cagebirds. American Indian nationalists briefly occupied it in 1970 as a symbol of their lost heritage□

Sanger Frederick 1918– . British biochemist, double Nobel prizewinner for his elucidation of the structure of insulin◊ in 1958, and (shared) for his work on that of genes, and the decoding of DNA, 1980□

Sanhedrin supreme Jewish court at Jerusalem (2nd century BC–1st century AD) headed by the high priest□

San José capital of Costa Rica; population 265 445□

San José industrial city (aerospace research and development, fruit canning, wine making) in Santa Clara Valley, California, USA; population 1 243 900□

San Juan capital, port and industrial city (sugar, rum, cigars) of Puerto Rico; population 434 850□

San Luis Potosi silver-mining city in central Mexico; population 315 230□

San Marino Most Serene Republic of

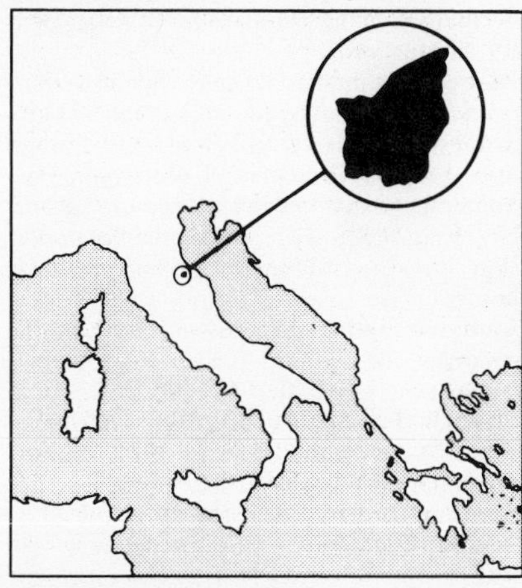

area 58 sq km/22.5 sq mi
capital San Marino
features completely surrounded by Italian territory; one of the world's smallest states
exports wine, ceramics, paint
currency Italian lira
population 23 000
language Italian
religion Roman Catholicism
government legislative great and general council, and an executive state congress, headed by two bi-annually elected regents
recent history founded in the 4th century, it was recognized in 1862 by the Kingdom of Italy□

San Martin José de 1778–1850. S American nationalist who played a large part in the liberation of Argentina, Chile, and Peru from Spanish rule□

San Salvador capital and industrial city (food processing, textiles) of El Salvador; population 500 000□

sansculotte French 'without knee breeches', a member of the trousered working classes during the French Revolution, as opposed to the nobility and bourgeoisie□

San Sebastián port and resort (formerly the summer residence of the court) in the Basque Country, Spain; population 175 580□

Sanskrit classical Indo-Iranian language of the Indo-European family, in which the Mahabharata◊, Ramayana◊, etc., were written; it is in religious use, and is still listed as one of the recognized languages of modern India. See Kâlidâsa◊, Prâkrit◊□

Santa Ana industrial city in El Salvador; population 204 570□

Santa Ana see under wind◊□

Santa Anna Antonio Lopez de 1795–1876. Mexican leader in the fight for independence from Spain, achieved in 1821. He spent the rest of his life in and out of office as president/dictator. See Alamo◊□

Santa Claus see St Nicholas◊□

Santa Cruz industrial city (oil and natural gas) in E Bolivia; population 255 600□

Santa Cruz de Tenerife capital of Tenerife and the Canary Islands, a fuelling and cable station; population 190 800□

Santa Fé capital of New Mexico, USA; population 49 000, many Spanish-speaking. Founded in 1610, it has buildings of the Spanish period, and is noted for Indian jewellery and textiles□

Santa Fé port on the Salado river, Argentina; population 287 000□

Santa Fé Trail US trade route 1821–80 from Independence, Missouri to Santa Fé, New Mexico□

Santander industrial port (vehicles, shipyards) in Cantabria, Spain; population 180 350. It was sacked by Soult◊ in 1808, and was largely rebuilt after a fire in 1941. At the nearby ***Altamira*** site, palaeolithic cave wall paintings (bison, wild boar, deer, etc.) were discovered in 1879□

Santayana George 1863–1952. American philosopher, born in Spain. A materialist, e.g. *The Life of Reason* 1905–6, he also wrote the best-selling novel *The Last Puritan* 1935□

Santiago capital and industrial city (textiles, chemicals, food processing) of Chile; population 4 085 000. Founded in 1541, it is famous for its handsome broad avenues□

Santiago de Compostela city in Galicia, Spain; population 93 695. The 11th-century cathedral was reputedly built over the grave of St James◊ the Great, one of the most popular places for medieval pilgrimage (see under scallop◊)□

Santiago de los Caballeros city in N Dominican Republic; population 242 000□

Santo Domingo capital of the Dominican Republic; population 1 103 425. Oldest city in the Americas, it was founded by Bartolomeo, brother of Christopher Columbus□

Santos port (world's greatest exporter of coffee) in Brazil; population 411 000□

San Yu 1919– . Burmese statesman. A member of the Revolutionary Council which came to power under Ne Win in 1962, he succeeded him as president in 1981□

Saône river in E France (length 480 km/300 mi); part of the canal network, it joins the Rhône at Lyon□

São Paulo city in Brazil, centre of the coffee trade and with meat-packing plants; population 7 033 530□

São Tomé et Principé Democratic Republic of

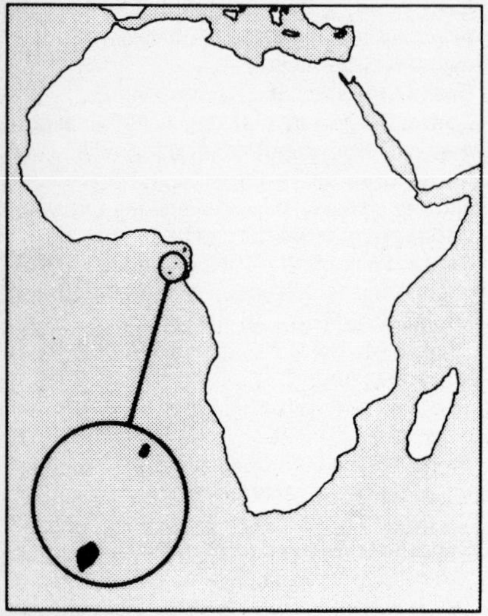

area 964 sq km/372 sq mi
capital Šo Tomé
features comprises the two main islands and several smaller ones
exports cocoa, copra
currency dobra
population 95 000
language Portuguese
religion Roman Catholicism
government executive president and people's assembly, President Manuel Pinto da Costa from 1975; only one party is allowed
recent history a former province of Portugal 1522–75, when it became independent□

Sapper pseudonym of Cyril McNeile 1888–1937, British author of *Bulldog Drummond* 1920 and its sequels; he was a lieutenant-colonel in the Royal Engineers until 1919□

sapphire see under corundum◊□

Sappho c612–c580BC. Greek lyric poet, friend of Alcaeus, and leader of a female literary coterie at Mytilene (modern Lesbos; hence lesbianism◊); legend says she committed suicide when her love for Phaon was unrequited□

Sapporo capital and industrial city (rubber, food processing) of Hokkaido◊, Japan; population 1 402 000. Giant figures are sculpted in ice at the snow festival, and there are winter sports□

saprophyte plant, usually a fungus, wholly or partly lacking in chlorophyll◊, which lives on dead plants and animals, e.g. orchids, mushrooms, mistletoe, dry rot. In sewage farms and refuse dumps they break down organic matter into nutrients easily assimilable by green plants□

Saracen Greek and Roman term for an Arab, used in the Middle Ages by Europeans for all Muslims□

Saragossa industrial city (Spanish *Zaragoza*) in Aragon, Spain; population 590 750. There are medieval city walls and bridges over the Ebro, Romanesque-Gothic and Baroque cathedrals, and a 15th-century university. In Jun 1808–Feb 1809, in the Peninsular War, it resisted a French siege with great loss before capitulation□

Sarajevo capital and industrial city (carpets, ceramics, etc.) of Bosnia-Hercegovina, Yugoslavia; population 448 500. A Bosnian, Gavrilo Princip, assassinated Archduke Francis◊ Ferdinand here in 1914, thereby precipitating World War I□

Saransk industrial city, capital of the Mordovian Republic, USSR; population 280 000□

Saratov oil and natural gas centre supplying Moscow, USSR; population 873 000. There are engineering, printing and electrical industries□

Sarawak state of Malaysia.
area 122 000 sq km/47 000 sq mi
capital Kuching
features forms, with Sabah, E Malaysia
exports oil and natural gas, rubber, timber, bauxite, and one third of the world's pepper
population 1 294 753, including 400 000 Dayaks◊, 183 000 Malays, 300 000 Chinese, and other native peoples
language Malay
state religion Sunni Islam; there is also Buddhism, Christianity, Animism
recent history in 1841 it was ceded to British explorer Sir James Brooke 1803–68, the 'White Rajah', by the Sultan of Brunei, in return for British help in a campaign against the Dayaks. Occupied by Japan 1941–5, it was a crown colony 1946–63, when it acceded to Malaysia□

sard or ***sardonyx*** see onyx◊□

sardine a small edible fish related to the herring◊□

Sardinia mountainous island (Italian *Sardegna*), special autonomous region of Italy

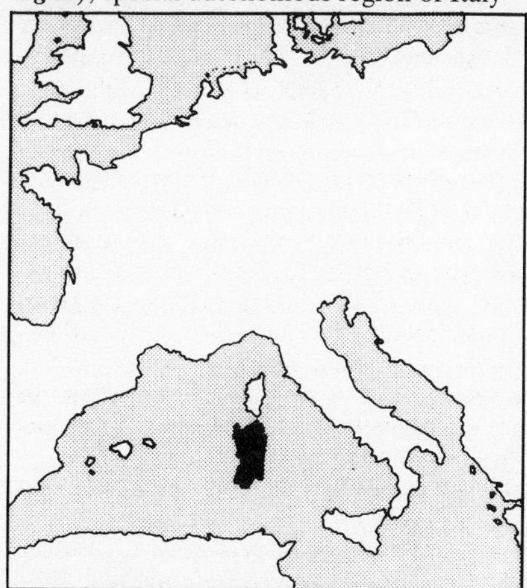

area 14 964 sq km/9298 sq mi
capital Cagliari
features second largest Mediterranean island; Costa Smeralda (Emerald Coast) tourist area in NE; *nuraghi* (fortified Bronze Age dwellings)
exports cork, petrochemicals
population 1 610 000
recent history for centuries under foreign rule, it became linked in 1720 with Piedmont, and this dual kingdom became the basis of a united Italy in 1861□

Sardou Victorien 1831–1908. French dramatist, who wrote for Bernhardt and Irving, e.g. *Fédora* 1882, *La Tosca* 1887 (the basis for the opera by Puccini◊), *Robespierre* 1902□

Sargasso Sea part of the N Atlantic left static by circling ocean currents, and covered with floating weed *Sargassum natans*□

Sargent John Singer 1856–1925. American artist, noted for portraits, e.g. Ellen Terry, T Roosevelt, R L Stevenson. His work was sometimes cruelly perceptive□

Sargeson Frank 1903– . New Zealand writer of short stories and of novels (*The Hangover* 1967 and *Man of England Now* 1972)□

Sargon name of two Mesopotamian kings:
Sargon I King of Akkad c2370–2230BC, and founder of the first Babylonian empire. His story resembles that of Moses in that he was said to have been found floating in a cradle on the Euphrates◊.
Sargon II d. 705BC. King of Assyria from 722, who assumed the name of his famous predecessor. To keep conquered peoples from rising against him, he transported them wholesale, including the Israelites from Samaria. See Carchemish◊□

Sark one of the Channel◊ Islands; area 5 sq km/2 sq mi; there is no town or even village. It is divided into Great and Little Sark, linked by an isthmus, and is of great natural beauty. The Seigneurie of Sark was established by Elizabeth I, the ruler being known as Seigneur/Dame, and has its own parliament, the Chief Pleas. There is no income tax and cars are forbidden; immigration is controlled□

Sarmatian a member of an Indo-European nomadic people who slowly ousted the Scythians◊ from the mid-3rd century BC and in turn gave way to the Goths◊ by the 3rd century AD□

Saroyan William 1908–81. American author, whose *The Bicycle Rider in Beverly Hills* 1950 told the story of his childhood in California. He is best-known for short stories, e.g. *The Daring Young Man on the Flying Trapeze* 1934, idealizing the hopes and sentiments of the 'little man'□

Sarraute Nathalie 1920– . Russian-born French novelist (*Portrait of a Man Unknown* 1948, *Do You Hear Them?* 1972), who bypasses plot, character, and style for the half-conscious interaction of minds. See Robbe-Grillet◊ □

sarsaparilla drink prepared from the long twisted roots of the Central American plant genus *Smilax,* family Smilacaceae□

Sartre Jean-Paul 1905–80. French author and philosopher. Born in Paris, he published his first novel *La Nausée/Nausea* 1937. In World War II he was a prisoner for nine months, but on his return from Germany joined the Resistance. He was a founder of Existentialism◊, edited its journal *Les Temps Modernes*, and expressed its tenets in his novels, e.g. the trilogy *Les Chemins de la Liberté/Roads to Freedom* 1944–5 and in his plays, e.g. *Huis Clos/In Camera* 1944, with two women and one man confined in the hell they make for each other. In *Crime Passionnel* 1948, he attacked aspects of Communism while retaining a general sympathy. He refused a Nobel literature prize in 1964 for 'personal reasons'□

Sarum see under Salisbury◊□

Sary-Shagan see under Kazakhstan◊□

Saskatchewan province of Canada
area 651 901 sq km/251 700 sq mi
capital Regina
towns Saskatoon
exports produces over 60% of Canada's wheat; oil, natural gas, uranium, zinc, potash (world's largest reserves), copper, and has the only Western reserves of helium outside the USA
population 1 006 200
See also Canada◊□

Saskatchewan

Saskatoon industrial city (cement, oil refining, chemicals, metal goods) with a university, in Saskatchewan, Canada; population 154 200□

Sassanian Empire empire founded 224 by Ardashir, a chieftain in the area of modern Fars in Iran, who had taken over the Parthian◊ Empire; it was so-named from his grandfather, Sasan. The capital was Ctesiphon (see Baghdad◊). After a rapid period of expansion, when it contested supremacy with Rome, it was destroyed in 637 by the Muslim Arabs at the Battle of Qadisiyah◊□

Sassoon Siegfried 1886–1967. British poet who served in France and Palestine in World War I, and whose *War Poems* 1919 expressed the disillusion of his generation. His prose includes *Memoirs of a Foxhunting Man* 1928, part of a semi-autobiographical trilogy. He encouraged Wilfred Owen◊, and subsequently published Owen's poems after the latter's death□

satellite a body which is permanently in the orbit of a planet or star. Varieties include:

artificial satellite a man-made satellite for observation and research. The first observation satellite was the Soviet Sputnik: see under space◊ research.

communications satellite satellite with one or more antennae, and devices which receive and transmit signals (transponders), so that signals weakened during transit from a ground station can be amplified before retransmission to another earth station on a different frequency (to avoid conflict with incoming signals). Solar cells provide operational energy, but the thruster rockets which shepherd it back into its correct station if it strays are powered by hydrazine (liquid fuel made from sodium hypochlorite and ammonia). The signals are transmitted in digital computer code, and then reconverted from digital data to voice (for telephone conversations), television pictures, etc., as necessary. See Arthur C Clarke◊, geostationary orbit◊.

natural satellite see under planet◊□

Satie Erik 1866–1925. French composer noted for piano pieces, e.g. *Limp preludes for a dog*, and *Pieces in the shape of a pear*□

Saturn in Roman mythology, the god of agriculture (Greek ***Cronos***) whose rule was the ancient Golden Age. He was dethroned by his sons Jupiter, Neptune, and Pluto. At his festival in Dec gifts were exchanged, and slaves were briefly treated as their masters' equals□

Saturn the sixth planet from the sun.

mean distance from the sun 11 427 000 000 km/886 100 000 mi

diameter 119 300 km/74 100 mi

rotation period 10 hr 14 min

year (sidereal period) 29 years 167 days

atmosphere resembles that of Jupiter

surface temperature −180°C/−300°F

surface like Jupiter, it is flattened at the Poles because of its rapid rotation; has belts crossing its disc (winds at the surface reach 1456 kph/900 mph), and similar 'red spots' (one being 16 000 km/10 000 mi across). The inner core is of iron and rock, and the outer of ammonia, methane, and water above the core, a region of metallic liquid hydrogen and helium.

features white when seen by telescope from earth, it is lemon-coloured close to. Its magnetic field is 1000 times stronger than earth's.

ring system brightly coloured and, though from a distance apparently divided into separate features, close up it is linked by formerly invisible rings giving it the appearance of a grooved gramophone record. The rings consist of countless boulders of ice and rock, thought to be the debris of the fragmentation by tidal forces of a former satellite or satellites. The outermost optically invisible ring may extend 480 000 km/300 00 mi into space.

satellites over 20, many discovered by Voyager 1 in 1980. The major satellites include:

Mimas: mean distance from its planet 186 000 km/115 000mi ***diameter*** 350 km/220mi

Enceladus mean distance from its planet 238 000 km/147 800 mi ***diameter*** 600 km/373 mi

Tethys: mean distance from its planet 295 000 km/183 200 mi ***diameter*** 1020 km/635 mi

Dione: mean distance from its planet 377 000 km/234 117mi ***diameter*** 1100 km/685 mi

Titan: mean distance from its planet 1222 000km/759 000 mi ***diameter*** 5150 km/3199 mi

Hyperion: mean distance from its planet 1 483 000 km/920 940 mi ***diameter*** 400 km/248 mi

Iapetus: mean distance from its planet 3 560 000 km/2 210 760 mi ***diameter*** 1500 km/930mi

Phoebe: mean distance from its planet 12 950 000 km/804 300 mi ***diameter*** 160km/100 mi□
satyagraha 'grasping truth', Gandhi◊'s term from 1918 for non-violent resistance, such as advocated by Tolstoy◊□
satyr in Greek mythology, a cross between a man and a goat; see Dionysus◊□
Saudi Arabia Kingdom of

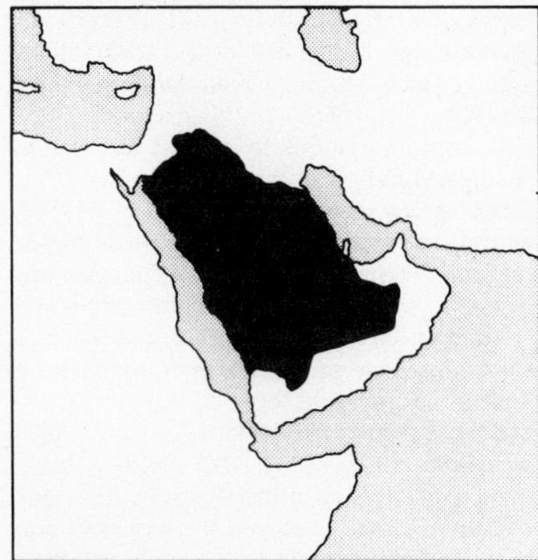

area 2 400 000 sq km/927 000 sq mi
capital Riyadh
towns Mecca, Medina, and the ports of Jidda and Dammam
features Nafud desert in the north, and the Rub' al Khali ('Empty Quarter') in the south, area 650 000 sq km/250 000 sq mi
exports oil
currency rial
population 10 794 000
language Arabic, considered the most pure form because closest to the Koran
religion Sunni Islam, with a Shi'ite minority in the east under the influence of Ayatollah Khomeini◊
famous people Mohammed, Ibn Saud, Faisal
government the king (Fahd ibn Abdul Aziz◊ from 1982) heads the council of ministers as Prime Minister; there is no formal constitution
recent history Nejd (in the interior) and the Hejaz (on the Red Sea coast) were in 1927 united under Ibn Saud as king, the country becoming known as Saudi Arabia from 1932. All subjects have access to the ruler, but the links of the regime with the West and the USA have fuelled internal opposition to Saudi rule. Sharia law is enforced (see under Islam◊); alcohol is banned, women may not drive cars, and there are no cinemas□
Saul d. c1010BC. In Old Testament, first king of Israel, who was anointed by Samuel◊ and warred successfully against the Ammonites◊ and Philistines◊. His melancholy was soothed by the playing of David◊. He turned against Samuel and committed suicide as his mind became unbalanced□
Sault Ste Marie twin industrial ports on the Canadian/US frontier, one in Ontario and one in Michigan, at the falls (*sault*) in St Mary's river joining lakes Superior and Huron, which are bypassed by canals; population 78 000 and 15 000 respectively□
sauna ancient Finnish ritual bath, in which steam at 90°C/200°F is produced by throwing cold water over heated cobble stones; beating with birch twigs stimulates circulation, and there is a final cold plunge□
Saunders Clarence 1881–1953. American retailer, who opened the first supermarket in Memphis, Tennessee, in 1919□
Sauternes village of SW France, famous for sweet white table wines□
Savannah port in Georgia, USA; population 133 700. Founded in 1733, it was the first planned 'grid-iron' city in the USA. The first Atlantic steam ship *Savannah* was built here, and in 1819 took 25 days for the voyage, mostly under sail; the first nuclear merchant ship was given the same name in 1959□
savannah originally the treeless plains of the tropical American prairies; now used elsewhere□
savings unspent income, after deduction of tax. In economics a distinction is made between investment, involving the purchase of capital goods, such as buying a house, and saving (where capital goods are not directly purchased, e.g. buying shares). In Britain, this last was a special aim of the Thatcher government from 1979 in an effort to reverse the rapid decline in individual share ownership since 1945□
Savonarola Girolamo 1452–98. Italian reformer, a Dominican friar whose eloquent preaching won him popular influence. In 1494 he led a revolt in Florence which expelled the Medicis◊ and established a democratic republic. However, his denunciations of Pope Alexander◊ VI led to his excommunication in 1497, and in 1498 he was arrested, tortured, hanged, and burned for heresy□
Savoy area, formerly a province of the kingdom of Sardinia, which was ceded to France (with Nice) in 1860 by Victor◊ Emmanuel II, in return for French help in driving the Austrians from Italy. It now forms part of the French region of Rhône-Alpes, but there is a Savoyard separatist movement□
sawfish fish of the ray◊ order. The ***common sawfish*** *Pristis pectinatus*, family Pristidae, is over 6 m/19 ft long; it resembles a shark and has some 24 teeth along an elongated snout (2

m/6 ft) which can be used as a weapon□

sawfly insect of order Hymenoptera, in which the female ovipositor (for egglaying) has a saw-like edge, which she uses to cut slits into plants to receive her eggs. Many species are plant pests, the adults feeding on them, and their larvae burrowing in their tissues□

Saxe Maurice, Comte de 1696–1750. Soldier, natural son of the Elector of Saxony, who served under Marlborough◊ and Eugène◊, and was created Marshal of France in 1743 for his exploits in the War of the Austrian◊ Succession□

Saxe French form of Saxony◊□

Saxe-Coburg-Gotha Saxon duchy. Albert, the Prince Consort of Queen Victoria◊, was a son of the first Duke (Ernest I), who was succeeded by Albert's elder brother, Ernest II□

saxhorn a musical instrument. See under brass◊□

saxifrage genus *Saxifraga* of plants of temperate mountain regions, family Saxifragaceae, including the British ***meadow saxifrage*** *S granulata* and the cultivated ***London pride*** *S umbrosa*□

Saxony former kingdom of Germany 1806–1918, capital Dresden, which forms the modern region of Leipzig, Dresden and Karl-Marx-Stadt, E Germany□

Saxony see Lower◊ Saxony□

saxophone a musical instrument. See under woodwind◊□

Sayan Mountains range in SE USSR, on the Mongolian border: highest peak Munku Sardik 3489 m/11 447 ft. Coal, gold, and lead are worked□

Sayers Dorothy L(eigh) 1893–1957. British writer of detective stories of an intellectual cast (she was educated at Somerville College, Oxford), which feature a dilettante detective, Lord Peter Wimsey□

scabies contagious infection of the skin caused by the mite *Sarcoptes scaboi* burrowing into it□

scabious Mediterranean plant, family Dipsacaceae, with many small flowers, often blue, borne in a single head; the ***small scabious*** *Scabiosa columbaria* is common in Britain□

Scafell Pike see under Cumbria◊□

scale insect a tiny plant-living insect; see under Hemiptera◊□

scallop family of marine molluscs◊, Pectinidae, with bivalve fan-shaped shells, including ***edible scallop*** *Chlamys opercularis* and ***St James's shell*** *Pecten jacobaeus* used as a badge by medieval pilgrims to Santiago◊ de Compostela. They use jet propulsion to jump up in the water to escape enemies such as starfish□

scampi a type of prawn◊□

Scandinavia peninsula in NW Europe, comprising Norway and Sweden; politically and culturally it also includes Denmark and is sometimes extended to Finland□

scandium element
symbol Sc
atomic number 21
physical description silvery-white metal
features rare metal, one of the lanthanides◊ series, which is found in abundance in the sun and stars
uses scandium sulphate is used to improve seed germination□

Scapa Flow see under Orkney◊□

scapolite name for group of white or greyish minerals, essentially silicates of aluminium, calcium, and sodium, which probably come from deep earth and may act as underground storehouses for gases such as carbon dioxide and sulphur dioxide□

scarab a type of beetle◊□

Scarlatti Alessandro 1660–1725. Italian composer, Master of the Chapel at the court of Naples, who developed the modern opera form (arias interspersed with recitative), writing more than a hundred, e.g. *Tigrane* 1715, as well as much church music, including oratorios. See Domenico Scarlatti◊□

Scarlatti Domenico 1685–1757. Italian composer, son of Alessandro. He worked mainly in Rome, and also wrote operas, including *Narciso* 1719, but is perhaps best remembered for his harpsichord sonatas, which include the so-called 'Cat's Fugue' 1738□

scarlet fever more correctly ***scarlatina***, an infectious disease caused by the bacterium *Streptococcus scarlatinae* marked by fever, and a bright red rash spreading from the upper to the lower part of the body. The rash is followed by the skin peeling in flakes. It is treated by antibiotics□

Sceptic see Pyrrhon◊□

Schaffhausen industrial town (watches, chemicals, textiles) in N Switzerland; population 37 000. The Rhine falls here in a series of cascades c60 m/180 ft high□

Scheer Reinhard 1863–1928. German admiral, commander of the High Sea Fleet in 1916 at the Battle of Jutland◊□

Scheldt river (Dutch and Flemish ***Schelde***, French ***Escaut***) rising in France and flowing to the North Sea south of Walcheren; length 400 km/250 mi. See Antwerp◊□

Scheveningen see under The Hague◊□

Schiaparelli Elsa 1896–1973. Italian dress designer, noted in the 1930s for hard-edged chic (padded shoulders), sophisticated colours ('shocking pink'), and a surrealistic tinge□

Schick test injection of small quantity of diphtheria◊ toxin to ascertain whether a person is immune to the disease or not: in the latter case a local inflammation appears□

Schiedam port in SW Netherlands, famous for its gin; population 70 000□

Schiele Egon 1890–1918. Austrian Expressionist artist. Originally a landscape painter, he later painted dynamically distorted pictures, e.g. the nudes in *Liebespaar I*□

Schillebeeckx Edouard. See under Arius◊□

Schiller Johann Christoph Friedrich von 1759–1805. German Romantic poet-playwright, born at Marbach. His historical dramas include *The Robbers* 1781, so revolutionary that it earned him 14 days' imprisonment; the trilogy *Wallenstein* 1798–9, and his masterpiece *Maria Stuart* 1800. He was a friend of Goethe◊□

schipperke a breed of dog◊□

schist foliated crystalline rock presenting layers of various minerals, e.g. mica schist, which easily split off into thin plates□

schistosomiasis or ***bilharzia*** disease contracted by bathing in water containing the snails which act as host to the first larval stage of flukes of the genus *Schistosoma* (see under worm◊); when these larvae leave the snail in their second stage of development, they are able to pass through human skin, become sexually mature, and produce quantities of eggs which pass to the intestine or bladder. The human host eventually dies, but before then numerous eggs have passed from the body in urine or faeces to continue the cycle. Some 300 million people are thought to suffer from this disease in the tropics□

schizophrenia psychological disorder characterized by delusions and withdrawal from reality. It may be caused by genetic factors□

Schlegel August Wilhelm von 1767–1845. German Romantic author, translator of Shakespeare, whose lectures on *Dramatic Art and Literature* 1809–11 broke down the old classical criteria. See Friedrich von Schlegel◊□

Schlegel Friedrich von 1772–1829. German Romantic critic, who (with his brother August) was a founder of the movement, and a pioneer in comparative philology□

Schleswig-Holstein Land (state) of W Germany
area 15 785 sq km/6095 sq mi
capital Kiel
towns Lübeck, Flensburg, Schleswig
features river Elbe, Kiel Canal, Heligoland
products shipbuilding, mechanical and electrical engineering, food processing
population 2 611 285
religion Protestantism 87%, Roman Catholicism 6%. See Seven◊ Weeks' War□

Schliemann Heinrich 1822–90. German businessman, fascinated by the legend of Troy◊, who first excavated in 1871 at Hissarlik. He was mistaken in his identification of which layer was the Homeric Troy, and also in his identification of the 'grave of Agamemnon' at Mycenae◊□

Schmidt Helmut 1918– . W German Social Democratic statesman, who succeeded Brandt◊ as Chancellor 1974–82. An 'Atlanticist', he supported NATO, but also pursued a modified Ostpolitik◊□

Schnitzler Arthur 1862–1931. Austrian Jewish novelist and dramatist, originally a doctor. He is best remembered for his play *Reigen* 1900 (filmed by Max Ophuls in 1950 as *La Ronde*)□

Schoenberg Arnold 1874–1951. Austrian composer of Jewish descent, who fled to the USA in 1933. His works (see atonality◊) include *Pierrot Lunaire* 1912, for voice and chamber orchestra and, in his mature twelve-tone◊ style, the unfinished opera *Moses and Aaron*□

Scholasticism the philosophy of the 'schools' of the medieval universities. Its literary forms were commentaries upon texts of established authorities, and attempts to reconcile their views, especially between Christian doctrine and the philosophy of Aristotle◊, the greatest synthesis being that effected by Aquinas◊. Despite the schoolmen's legendary love of wordy and sometimes fatuous disputation and their excessive respect for authority, their best work (e.g. that of Anselm◊, Abelard◊, Occam◊, and Duns◊ Scotus) contributed significantly to the philosophy of theology, language, and logic – the debate on nominalism◊ is the classic example□

Schopenhauer Arthur 1788–1860. German philosopher, whose chief work *The World as Will and Idea* 1818 expounded an atheistic, pessimistic theory akin to Buddhism. The driving force of irrational will in human beings results in an ever-frustrated cycle of desire, from which the only escape is a contemplative existence inspired by the arts, and eventual absorption into nothingness. This theory struck a responsive chord in Nietzsche◊, Wagner◊, Thomas Mann◊, and Hardy◊□

Schreiner Olive 1862–1920. South African novelist and supporter of women's rights, e.g. *The Story of an African Farm* 1883□

Schrödinger Erwin 1887–1961. Austrian physicist, who worked on atomic structure and the study of wave mechanics, sharing a

Nobel prize with Dirac◊. See quantum◊ theory□

Schubert Franz (Peter) 1797–1828. Austrian composer, born in Vienna. In 1818 and 1824 he was music teacher to the Esterházy family on their estate in W Hungary, but mainly lived a Bohemian existence in Vienna, composing prolifically. He wrote more than 600 songs, including the cycles *Die Schöne Müllerin* and *Die Winterreise*; nine symphonies; chamber and church music; and pieces for the piano□

Schuman Robert 1886–1963. French Prime Minister 1947–8, who (as Foreign Minister 1948–53) created the Coal and Steel Pool (the 'Schuman Plan' treaty of 1951) which prepared the way for the European◊ Economic Community□

Schumann Robert Alexander 1810–56. German composer and pianist, born at Zwickau. He excelled in compositions for the piano, e.g. the *Piano Concerto* of 1841 and his sonatas, and in lieder, e.g. the cycle *Dichterliebe* 1840. Having injured his hands through use of an instrument to strengthen them, he turned to music criticism. From 1854 he was confined in an asylum after a suicide attempt, and died there. His wife, pianist ***Clara Josephine Wieck*** 1819–96, whom he had married in 1841, devoted her life to popularizing his work□

Schuschnigg Kurt von 1897–1977. Austrian Chancellor 1934, in succession to Dollfuss◊. In Feb 1938 he was forced to accept a Nazi Minister of the Interior, and a month later Austria was invaded and annexed. He was imprisoned in Germany until 1945□

Schütz Heinrich 1585–1672. German composer, music director to the Elector of Saxony from 1614. He was influenced by Monteverdi; his works include *The Seven Last Words* c1645, *Musikalische Exequien* (funeral pieces), and the *German Magnificat* 1671□

Schwarzkopf Elisabeth 1915– . German soprano, noted for dramatic interpretation of operatic roles, such as Elvira in *Don Giovanni* and the Marschallin in *Der Rosenkavalier*, as well as lieder□

Schwarzwald see Black◊ Forest□

Schweitzer Albert 1875–1965. French theologian, organist, and missionary surgeon. He founded the hospital at Lambaréné in Gabon in 1913, giving organ recitals to support his work there. He wrote a life of Bach and *The Quest for the Historical Jesus* 1906, and was awarded a Nobel peace prize in 1952 for his teaching of 'reverence for life'□

Schwerin capital of Schwerin district and industrial city (machinery, chemicals) in E Germany; population 122 700. Formerly the capital of Mecklenburg◊ and earlier of Mecklenburg-Schwerin□

Schwitters Kurt 1887–1948. German portraitist who from 1918 developed collage◊, using discarded rubbish such as buttons and bus tickets. He also devised poems which consisted of sounds without words□

Schwyz capital of Schwyz canton, one of the three original cantons of the Swiss Confederation in 1291, which gave its name to the whole country from c1450□

Sciascia Leonardo 1921– . Sicilian novelist, who uses the detective novel to explore the hidden workings of Sicilian life, e.g. *The Day of the Owl* 1961 and *Equal Danger* 1974□

sciatica persistent pain along the sciatic nerve (the body's longest which runs from the hip, down the back of the thigh, and, in its branches, to the toes). Causes of such neuralgia◊ include inflammation of the nerve itself, or pressure on or inflammation of a nerve leading out of the lower spine, e.g. as a result of a slipped (intervertebral) disc□

science fiction genre of writing which varies from scientific fantasizing to use of the implications of current scientific theories. Major writers include Jonathan Swift, Mary Shelley, Jules Verne, E A Poe, H G Wells, Aldous Huxley, Brian Aldiss, George Orwell, Isaac Asimov, Ray Bradbury, J G Ballard, John Wyndham, Frank Herbert, Arthur C Clarke□

Science Museum National Museum of Science and Industry, 1853, in South Kensington, London. It includes from 1980–1 the Wellcome Museum of Medical Science; the National Railway Museum, York, 1975, is an outpost□

science park site for high-technology industries which are powered by the inventive skills of scientists from nearby universities. They originated in the USA in the 1950s (see North◊ Carolina, California◊, Boston◊, and Cambridge◊). By 1985 the UK had 13, beginning with Heriot-Watt (Edinburgh), and including Cambridge, Aston (Birmingham), Merseyside (Liverpool), Warwick, and Bradford□

Scientology the 'applied religious philosophy' of the ***Church of Scientology*** founded in 1954 by L F Hubbard◊ in California, with its headquarters from 1959 at Saint Hill Manor, East Grinstead, Sussex, England. It claims to 'increase man's spiritual awareness', but the movement has met with criticism□

scilla genus of bulbous plants with blue, pink, or white flowers, family Liliaceae◊, e.g. ***spring squill*** *S verna*□

Scilly Islands group of 140 islands and islets administered by the Duchy of Cornwall, of which county they form part; area 16 sq km/6.3 sq mi. The five inhabited islands are ***St Mary's***, the largest, on which is Hugh Town, capital of the Scillies; ***Tresco***, the most beautiful, with sub-tropical gardens; ***St Martin's***, third largest, noted for beautiful shells, ***St Agnes***, and ***Bryher***. A mild climate and rich soil enable early vegetables and flowers to be produced, and tourism is important. The islands have remains of Bronze Age settlements. The numerous wreck sites off the islands include many of Sir Cloudesley Shovel◊'s fleet in 1707. Former Prime Minister Harold Wilson has a holiday home here□

Scipio Africanus Major 236–183BC. Roman general who, having defeated the Carthaginians in Spain, invaded Africa, and defeated Hannibal at Zama in 202□

Scipio Africanus Minor c185–129BC. Roman general who destroyed Carthage in 146, and subdued Spain 210–06. He was opposed to his brothers-in-law, the Gracchi (see under Gracchus◊), and his wife is thought to have shared in his murder. See Polybius◊□

sclerosis see multiple◊ sclerosis□

scoliosis curvature of the spine◊. Correction by operations to insert bone grafts (thus creating only a rigid spine) has been replaced by insertion of an electronic stimulative device in the lower back to contract the muscles□

Scone village in Tayside, Scotland, N of Perth. Most of the Scottish kings were crowned in its former ancient palace on the Stone of Destiny (now in the Coronation Chair at Westminster)□

scopolamine see hyoscine◊□

scorpion member of the order Scorpiones, class Arachnida◊. Common in the tropics and sub-tropics, scorpions have segmented bodies, with a long tail, ending in a poisonous sting, though the venom is not usually fatal to a healthy adult. Some species reach 15 cm/6 in. They mate after a courtship dance, produce live young, and hunt chiefly by night□

Scotland

area 78 762 sq km/30 422 sq mi
capital Edinburgh
towns Glasgow, Dundee, Aberdeen
features the Highlands in the N (see Grampian◊ Mountains); central Lowlands, which include the valleys of the Clyde and Forth, with most of the country's population and industries; Southern Uplands (including the Lammermuir◊ Hills); and the islands of the Orkneys, Shetlands, and Western Isles
exports electronics, aero and marine engines, oil and natural gas, chemicals, textiles and clothing, printing and paper, food processing; tourism is very important, including fishing and hunting facilities
currency pound sterling
population 5 130 735
language English, but Scottish, a northern (lowland, hence sometimes known as *Lallans*) dialect of Anglo-Saxon existing from the 5th century (and used in verse by Burns◊ and McDiarmid◊) is enjoying a revival (after near extinction in the 18th century), as is *Erse*, the Scottish form of Gaelic spoken by 1.3%, mainly in the Highlands (see Celts◊)
religion Presbyterianism, Roman Catholicism
famous people Robert the Bruce, Scott, Burns, R L Stevenson, Adam Smith
government Scotland sends members to the UK parliament at Westminster in proportion to its population. Local government is on similar lines to that of England (see Provost◊), but there is a differing legal system, see Scots◊ Law□

Scotland: history

1st century Romans prevented by Picts from penetrating far into Scotland
5th–6th centuries Christianity introduced from Ireland (See St Columba◊)
9th century Kenneth MacAlpin united kingdoms of Scotland
946 Malcolm I conquered Strathclyde
1015 Malcolm II conquered Lothian
1263 defeat of Haakon, king of Norway at Battle of Largs
1266 Scotland gained Hebrides from Norway at Treaty of Perth
1292 Scottish throne granted by Edward I (attempting to annex Scotland) to John Baliol
1297 defeat of England at Stirling Bridge by Wallace◊
1314 Robert Bruce◊ defeated English at Bannockburn
1328 independence recognized by England
1371 first Stuart king, Robert◊ II
1513 James IV killed at Battle of Flodden◊
1540s–50s Knox introduced Calvinism to Scotland
1557 the Covenant◊
1565 Mary Queen of Scots married Darnley
1566 Rizzio murdered
1567 Darnley murdered
1568 Mary fled to England
1578 James VI took over government
1587 Mary beheaded
1592 Presbyterianism◊ established
1603 James VI became James I of England
1638 Scottish rebellion against England
1643 Solemn League and Covenant
1651–60 Cromwell conquered Scotland

1679 Covenanters defeated at Bothwell Brig
1689 Jacobites defeated at Killiecrankie
1692 Massacre of Glencoe
1707 Act of Union with England
1715, 1745 failed Jacobite risings against England
1945 first Scottish nationalist MP elected
1979 referendum on Scottish directly elected assembly fails
For other history since 1707 see Great Britain: history□

Scotland Church of. Principal Scottish Protestant Church. Established in 1560, it is Presbyterian◊ and was re-established in 1690 after attempts to impose episcopacy. Each parish has a minister (who since 1968 may be a woman) and several lay people (elders) who form the kirk session; parishes are grouped into presbyteries, and these in turn into synods, and the supreme court is the General Assembly of clerics and lay people chosen by the presbyteries, and presided over by a Moderator (who is merely first among equals)□

Scotland Yard New. Headquarters of the Criminal Investigation Department (CID) of the London Metropolitan Police, established in 1878. Originally in Scotland Yard off Whitehall, it moved to the Embankment in 1890, and in 1967 to Broadway, Westminster. It houses the ***Central Office*** dealing with international crime and serious offences throughout the country, and controlling the Flying Squad; ***Fingerprint Department*** some two million prints of convicted criminals; ***Criminal Record Office*** which also publishes the *Police Gazette*; ***Scientific Laboratory***, and ***Special Branch*** dealing with crimes against the state. There is also a national co-ordinator for the ***Regional Crime Squads*** established in London in 1954 and extended across the country in 1965. These have detectives drawn from local forces to deal with major crime□

Scots law the legal system of Scotland. Owing to modifications from the 16th century, Scotland has a system differing from the rest of the UK by incorporating elements derived from Roman law (see under law◊). In recent years there has been some adoption in England of features already existing in Scots law, e.g. majority jury verdicts, and the replacement of police prosecution by a system of public prosecution. There is no separate system of equity (see equity under law◊). The supreme civil court is the House of Lords, below which comes the Court of Session, and then the Sheriff Court (in some respects similar to the English County Court, but with criminal as well as civil jurisdiction). The supreme criminal court is the High Court of Justiciary (with no appeal to the Lords). Juries have 15 members, and a verdict of 'not proven' can be given. There is no coroner, see Procurator◊ Fiscal□

Scot's pine see under conifers◊□

Scott Sir George Gilbert 1811–78. British architect, largely responsible for the mid-19th-century Gothic revival in England; his restoration work in Ely Cathedral and Westminster Abbey had debatable results, but his Albert Memorial, Foreign Office, and St Pancras Station won contemporary and more recent praise□

Scott Sir Giles Gilbert 1880–1960. British architect, grandson of Sir George Scott, and designer of Liverpool Anglican Cathedral. Awarded Order of Merit 1944□

Scott Paul 1920–1978. British novelist, noted for *The Raj Quartet* (*Jewel in the Crown*, *Day of the Scorpion*, *Towers of Silence* and *Division of the Spoils*) 1976, dealing with the British Raj in India□

Regions of Scotland

Regions:	area in sq km	population (1982)	administrative headquarters
Borders	4,662	99,784	Newtown St Boswells
Central	2,590	273,391	Stirling
Dumfries and Galloway	6,475	145,139	Dumfries
Fife	1,308	327,362	Glenrothes
Grampian	8,550	471,942	Aberdeen
Highland	26,136	200,150	Inverness
Lothian	1,756	738,372	Edinburgh
Strathclyde	13,856	2,404,532	Glasgow
Tayside	7,668	391,846	Dundee
Island Authorities			
Orkney	974	19,056	Kirkwall
Shetland	1,427	27,277	Berwick
Western Islands	2,901	31,884	Stornoway
	78,303	5,130,735	

Scott Robert Falcon 1868–1912. British Antarctic explorer and naval officer, born in Devonport. He made his first Antarctic expedition in the *Discovery* 1900–4 and set out again in the *Terra Nova* in 1910, but reached the South Pole shortly after Amundsen◊ on 18 Jan 1912. On the return journey he and his four companions on the final stage (including Oates◊) died. His combination of exploration with wide-ranging scientific programmes set a pattern for future polar research□

Scott Sir Walter 1771–1832. Scottish poet and novelist, born in Edinburgh. He was slightly lamed in early life by infantile paralysis. He qualified as an advocate 1792, and in 1802 published the ballad collection *Minstrelsy of the Scottish Border,* following it with a series of original narrative poems, including *The Lay of the Last Minstrel* 1805 and *Marmion* 1808. With the proceeds he bought and rebuilt a farmhouse (1812) on the river Tweed as a Gothic baronial hall. When the newer style of Byron◊ captured the romance market, he created the historical novel with *Waverley* 1814, first of a series that includes *Old Mortality* 1816, *The Heart of Midlothian* 1818 and *The Bride of Lammermoor* 1819; *Kenilworth* 1821 and *Ivanhoe* 1829 had an English setting. He was created a Baronet in 1820, but was financially ruined in 1826 by the failure of publishing and printing firms with which he was associated. He drove himself to breakdown by writing non-stop to pay off his debts□

Scottish Gaelic see under Celts◊ and Scotland◊□

Scottish terrier a breed of dog◊□

Scouts non-military and non-political youth organization originating (as the ***Boy Scouts***) with an experimental camp held in 1907 by Baden◊-Powell. His book *Scouting for Boys* 1908 led to the incorporation of the Boy Scout Association by royal charter in 1912; it was renamed the Scout Association in 1966, when the rules and dress were updated. There are three branches, Cub Scouts (8–11), Scouts (11–16), and Venture Scouts (16–29). In the USA both boys and girls are known as Scouts. It is now a world-wide organization, membership 16 million□

Scrabble board game for 2–4 players, in which 'letter' counters of varying point values are used to form words. International competitions are now held□

scrapie fatal disease of sheep which attacks the central nervous system, causing deterioration of the brain cells. It is caused by a prion◊□

Scriabin Alexander Nicolas 1871–1915. Russian composer and pianist, whose tone poems, e.g. *Prometheus*, employed a revolutionary system of harmony□

Scribe member of an ancient Jewish group, both priests and laymen, who studied the law, sat in the Sanhedrin◊, and were associated with the Pharisees (see under Judaism◊)□

scrofula see under tuberculosis◊□

Scullin James Henry 1876–1953. Australian Labor Prime Minister 1929–31 in the Depression years□

sculpture the artistic shaping in relief or in the round of wood, stone, metal, and (more recently) plastic and other synthetics. Modern developments include the ***mobile*** (Calder◊); ***structure vivante*** in which a mechanism produces a pre-arranged pattern produced by magnets, lenses, bubbles, etc., accompanied by sound; and the ***sculpture garden***, including Hakone Open-Air Museum in Japan, and the Grizedale Forest sculpture project in the Lake District. World-famous sculptors and sculptures include:

Ancient World Greek Phidias, Praxiteles

Renaissance Donatello, Verrochio, Della Robbia, Michelangelo

Baroque Grinling Gibbons, Bernini, Falconet, Houdon

Neo-classic Canova, Flaxman

African Benin bronzes, Yoruba masks from Nigeria

Modern American Lipchitz, Borglum, Caro

Modern British Epstein, Henry Moore, Hepworth, Reg Butler

Modern European Arp, Gaudier-Brzeska, Rodin, Maillol, Picasso, Mestrovič, Brancusi, Marini, Neizvestny□

scurvy disease caused by lack of vitamin C; symptoms include bleeding into the skin, swelling of the gums, and drying up of the skin and hair□

Scutari see under Istanbul◊ and Shköder◊□

Scylla see under Strait of Messina◊□

scyphozoa see jellyfish◊□

Scythia region N of the Black Sea occupied by the Scythians (Indo-European nomads) 7th–1st century BC. Darius◊ I failed to conquer them in the 6th century, but from the mid-4th century BC the Sarmatians◊ superseded them. They produced gold and electrum vases with animal decoration□

sea anemone a member of an order of polyps in the class Anthozoa◊, which do not form coral. Tubelike, they attach themselves to a hard surface such as rocks and when the tide recedes fold up the tentacles about their 'mouth', expanding them again when the water covers them. Many then look like beautiful coloured flowers, hence the name.

When attached to the shell of a hermit crab, they form a mutually beneficial relationship, giving the crab camouflage in hunting, and absorbing the scraps of the meal□

Seaborg Glenn T(heodore) 1912– . American physicist, Nobel prizewinner (with E M McMillan, also of the Universities of California) in 1951 for discoveries of transuranic elements□

sea cucumber a small marine animal. See echinoderm◊□

Seaga Edward 1930– . Jamaican Labour Prime Minister from 1980, who speaks of himself as 'very much in the centre'□

seagull a type of gull◊□

sea horse small bony fish shaped like the head and neck of a horse; see under pipefish◊□

Sea Islands islands in the Atlantic off the S Carolina-Florida coast, where ***Sea Island cotton*** with a fine quality long 'staple' (fibre) was first grown□

seal a fish-eating mammal; see under pinnipedia◊□

sea law see maritime◊ law□

sea lily a small marine animal. See echinoderm◊□

sea lion a large fish-eating mammal; see pinnipedia◊; Hitler's projected invasion of Britain in 1940 was given the code name *Seelöwe*, meaning sea lion□

sealyham a breed of dog◊□

Sea Peoples unidentified seafaring warriors who may have been Achaeans◊, Etruscans◊, or Philistines◊, who ravaged and settled the Mediterranean coasts in 12th–13th centuries BC (see Hittites◊). They were defeated in 1191 by Rameses◊ III□

Searle Ronald 1920– . British artist and cartoonist, most famous for his outrageous schoolgirls of St Trinian's 1941–53□

sea sickness see travel◊ sickness□

Season London. The period May–July when the fashionable world formerly took up residence in London and young women made their social debut by being presented to their sovereign at court; it survives in various events which have a social as well as sporting significance, e.g. the horse races at Ascot□

sea squirt a small marine animal; see tunicates◊□

SEATO see South-East◊ Asia Treaty Organization□

Seattle industrial port (Boeing jet aircraft, shipbuilding, timber, paper) in Washington (state), USA; population (with Everett) 1 600 000. Founded in 1851 as the nearest port for Alaska, it developed during the Gold Rush□

sea urchin a small marine animal; see echinoderm◊□

seaweed simple green, red, or brown marine plants (see algae◊) growing respectively at increasing depths, from high water mark to 1 200 m/3600 ft; many are gathered for food, e.g. ***purple laver*** *Porphyra vulgaris* and ***carragheen moss*** *Chondrus crispus* (see also agar◊ agar).

Kelps are the large brown seaweeds; the Pacific ***giant kelp*** *Macrocystis*, reaching 100 m/320 ft, is farmed for the alginate◊ industry and is one of the fastest-growing organisms known, but is an alien pest in European waters□

Sebastian St d. c288. Roman soldier, traditionally a member of Diocletian◊'s bodyguard until his Christian faith was discovered. He was martyred by being shot with arrows; feast day 20 Jan□

Sebastopol see Sevastopol◊□

second basic SI unit of time: defined as the duration of 9 192 631 770 periods of the radiation corresponding to the transition between two hyperfine levels of the ground state of the caesium◊ 133 isotope□

secretary bird long-legged, mainly grey-plumaged bird of prey *Sagittarius secretarius*, about 1.2 m/4 ft tall. The only member of its family, Sagittaridae, order Falconiformes, it has an erectile head crest looking like a pen behind a clerk's ear. It is protected in S Africa because it eats poisonous snakes□

Secretary of State originally officials conducting the English sovereign's correspondence; now the title of some chief British ministers, e.g. the Foreign Minister is officially the Secretary of State for Foreign and Commonwealth Affairs; in the USA the Foreign Minister is officially the Secretary of State□

secretin see under hormone◊□

secret society society with membership by invitation only, often involving initiation rites, secret rituals, and dire punishments for those who break the 'code'. Originally often founded for religious reasons or mutual benefit, they can become the province of corrupt politicians or gangsters. They include the Mafia◊, Opus◊ Dei, Freemasonry◊, and the Triad◊. In the USA in the 1850s there were 'tong wars' (Cantonese *t'ang* 'office') between the societies organized among Chinese settlers in California□

Secunderabad see under Hyderabad◊□

Sedan frontier industrial town (textiles, dyes, food processing) in NE France; population 25 500. In 1870 Napoleon◊ III surrendered here to the Germans, and in 1940 Nazi Panzer divisions made their breakthrough into France□

sedan chair an enclosed chair, said to have been invented at Sedan, with a bearer in front and behind, lifting it on horizontal poles. Introduced into England by James I, it was the equivalent by the 18th century of a one-person taxi□

sedative drug or other means of calming the nerves. Drugs may have bad side effects, e.g. reserpine◊ and barbiturates◊. Most frequently used today are the benzodiazepine derivatives□

Seddon Richard John 1845–1906. New Zealand Liberal statesman, Prime Minister 1893–1906□

sedge genus *Carex* of perennial grass-like plants, family Cyperaceae, with three-cornered solid stems, common in wet ground□

Sedgemoor see under Monmouth◊ and Somerset◊□

sedimentary rock see under rock◊□

sedition in the UK an offence against the Crown and government, differing from treason◊ in that it does not carry the death penalty. It includes attempting to bring into contempt or hatred the person of the reigning monarch, the lawfully established government, or either house of parliament; inciting a change of government by other than lawful means; and raising discontent between different sections of the sovereign's subjects. Today any criticism aimed at reform is allowable□

Seeger Pete 1917– . American singer and protest song-writer, e.g. 'We shall overcome' 1960, 'Where have all the flowers gone?' 1961, and 'Little Boxes' 1962□

Seferis George. Pseudonym of Greek poet-diplomat Georgios Seferiades 1900–71, who as ambassador to the UK 1957–62 did much to solve the Cyprus crisis. His lyric poetry was influenced by Eliot◊□

Segovia town in Castilla-León, central Spain; population 40 000. It has a Roman aqueduct with 118 arches in current use, and the Moorish alcázar was the palace of the kings of Castile□

Segovia Andrés 1894– . Spanish virtuoso guitarist, for whom works were composed by De Falla, Villa-Lobos, etc.□

Seifert Jaroslav 1901– . Czech poet, who won state prizes, but became an original member of the Charter 77 human rights movement. Volumes include *Mozart in Prague* 1970 and *Umbrella from Piccadilly* 1978. Nobel prize 1984□

Seine river in N France, on which Paris and Rouen stand; length 674 km/481 mi□

seismology see earthquake◊□

Selangor state of Malaysia; population 1 467 500. Capital Shah Alam□

Selden John 1584–1654. English antiquarian and opponent of Charles I's claim to divine◊ right, for which he was twice imprisoned□

select committee see Commons under parliament◊□

Selene in Greek mythology, the goddess of the moon; in later times identified with Artemis◊□

selenium element
symbol Se
atomic number 34
physical description grey non-metallic solid
features found in association with tellurium and sulphur; there is a trace in the human body
uses used in making photovoltaic solar cells used in spacecraft□

Seleucus I (Nicator) c358–280BC. General of Alexander◊ the Great, founder of the ***Seleucid Empire*** reaching from modern Greece to India 312–64BC□

Selfridge Harry Gordon 1857–1947. American founder of the Selfridge Store, London, 1909, Britain's first mammoth department store□

Seljuk Empire empire of the Turkish people, converts to Islam from the 7th century, under the leadership of the invading Tatars or Seljuk Turks. The Seljuk Empire 1055–1243 included all Asia Minor and most of Syria. See Ottoman◊ Empire□

Selkirk Alexander 1676–1721. Scottish sailor. Serving as a privateer under Dampier◊, he was marooned 1704–9 in the Juan◊ Fernández group of islands. His story inspired Defoe◊ to write *Robinson Crusoe*□

Sellers Peter 1925–80. British comedian and film actor, specializing in impersonations and disguises, who made his name in the zany radio *Goon Show* 1949–60. His films include *I'm Alright Jack* 1960, *The Pink Panther* 1963, as the bumbling Inspector Clouseau, and *Being There* 1980□

Selwyn Lloyd (John), Baron Selwyn Lloyd 1904–78. British Conservative politician, Foreign Secretary 1955–60 during the Suez Crisis, and as Chancellor of the Exchequer 1960–2 so unpopular with his policy of wage restraint that Macmillan asked for his resignation. He was Speaker 1971–6□

Selznick David O(liver) 1902–1965. American film producer, e.g. *King Kong* 1932, *Gone With the Wind* 1939□

Semarang port in N Java, unsafe in monsoons; population 646 600□

Semele in Greek mythology, mother of Dionysus by Zeus◊. She was consumed by lightning when jealous Hera◊ suggested she ask her lover to appear in his full glory□

semiconductor crystalline material with an electrical conductivity between that of metals and insulators, and which increases with temperature, e.g. germanium◊, silicon◊, gallium arsenide◊. By introducing carefully controlled quantities of specific 'impure' atoms into adjacent regions of the same semiconductor crystal, important electronic devices can be made. The simplest is the ***diode***, which lets current pass through it in one direction only – useful for converting alternating to direct current. Light emitting diodes (***LEDs***) need less current than filament lamps; their red or green glow is often seen on instrument panels. ***Transistors*** are capable of amplifying electrical signals, and circuits containing hundreds or even thousands of transistors together with ancillary components and connections are now formed on single 'chips' of silicon (see computers◊)□

Semipalatinsk town in Kazakh Republic, USSR; population 291 000. The Kvzyl Kum atomic testing ground is nearby□

Semiramis c800BC. Assyrian queen, later identified with Ishtar◊□

Semite traditionally, a descendant of Shem, a son of Noah. Caucasians◊, Semites include such peoples of the ancient world as the Ammonites, Moabites, Babylonians, Assyrians, Chaldaeans, Carthaginians, Phoenicians, and Canaanites, and in the modern world the Jews◊, Arabs, Syrians, Ethiopians, etc.□

Semitic language language of a Semitic people, including Amharic (see Ethiopia◊), Aramaic◊, Hebrew◊, Arabic◊, Maltese◊□

semolina see wheat under cereals◊□

Senanayake Don Stephen 1884–1952. First Prime Minister of independent Sri Lanka (Ceylon)1947–52, succeeded by his son ***Dudley Senanayake*** 1911–73, who held office 1952–3, 1960, 1965–70□

senate the Roman council of patrician◊ 'elders', which advised the king, and under the republic effectively controlled finance and foreign policy, losing its powers under the Empire.

In modern times, the upper house of national legislatures in the USA (see Congress◊), Italy◊, France◊, etc., is called the senate, as are the governing bodies of the English and Welsh Inns of Court and Bar, and of some universities, e.g. Cambridge and London□

Sendai industrial city (textiles, pottery, food processing) in NE Honshu, Japan; population 665 000. There is a Metal Museum 1975, and it is a scenic centre with snow-capped volcanic mountains. See Tanabata◊□

Seneca Lucius Annaeus c4BC–65AD. Roman Stoic philosopher-playwright. Born at Cordova, he was Nero◊'s tutor, but lost favour after his accession and was ordered to commit suicide. His tragedies influenced Shakespeare□

Senefelder Alois 1771–1834. German inventor of lithography◊ 1796□

Senegal river of W Africa; length 1125 km/700 mi. The Organization of Riparian States 1968 (Guinea, Mali, Mauretania and Senegal) are developing it for power and irrigation□

Senegal Republic of

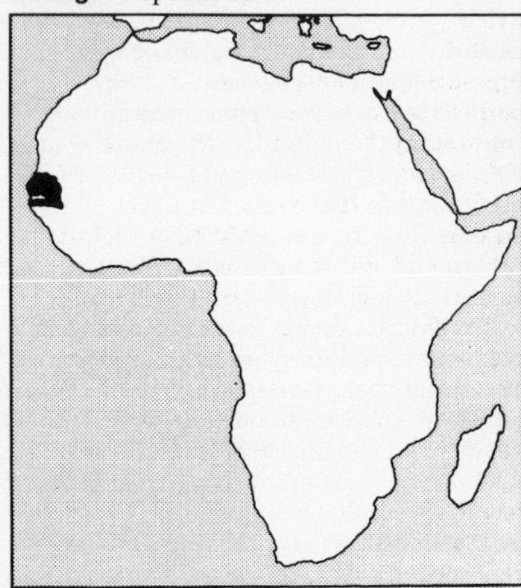

area 197 000 sq km/76 000 sq mi
capital and chief port Dakar
towns Thies, Kaolack
features river Senegal; The Gambia◊ forms an enclave within it
exports ground nuts, cotton; fish; phosphates
currency CFA franc
population 5 654 000
language French (official)
religion Islam 80%; Christianity 10% (chiefly Roman Catholic); Animist 10%
famous people Léopold Senghor
government executive president (Abdou Diouf from 1981) with a government council and national assembly. There is a multiparty system
recent history a French colony from 1659, Senegal became independent in 1960, and in 1982 (while retaining independence and sovereignty) established the Confederation of Senegambia□

Senegambia see under Senegal◊ and Gambia◊□

Senghor Léopold 1906– . President of Senegal 1960–80, also a poet and essayist□

senile dementia see dementia◊□

senna genus *Cassia* of mainly tropical trees and shrubs, family Leguminosae; the fruit pods of *C fistula* are the source of a laxative□

Sennacherib d. 681BC. King of Assyria from 704. Son of Sargon II, he rebuilt Nineveh◊, sacked Babylon in 689, and crushed Hezekiah◊, though failing to take Jerusalem. He was assassinated by his sons. See Esarhaddon◊□

Sens town in Burgundy, France; population 25 000. Its cathedral, 12th–16th centuries, has some of the earliest Gothic work in France□

Seoul capital and industrial city (engineering, textiles, food processing) of S Korea, with its chief port at Inchon◊; population 8 367 000. There is a 14th-century palace□

Sephardim see under Israel◊□

septicaemia see blood◊ poisoning□

Septuagint the oldest Greek version of the Old Testament, traditionally made by 70 scholars, hence the name□

sequoia two species of conifer native to California, family Taxodiaceae. The ***redwood*** *Sequoia sempervirens* is a valuable timber tree up to 40 m/130 ft high (the world's tallest tree) diameter 2–8 m/8–25 ft; the ***big tree*** *Sequoiadendron giganteum* grows almost as tall, and even larger in bulk, about 30 m/100 ft at the base. Some specimens are 3500 years old□

Seraphim see under angel◊□

Serapis see under Osiris◊□

Serbia constituent republic of Yugoslavia.
area 88 267 sq km/34 080 sq mi
capital Belgrade
features includes the autonomous provinces of ***Kosovo***, capital Priština, of which the predominantly Albanian population demands unification with Albania; and ***Vojvodina***, capital Novi Sad, largest town Subotica, with a predominantly Serbian population. Serbia has the fertile Danube plains in the N and is mountainous in the south
population 5 700 000, of whom about 5 million are Serbs
language the Serbian variant of Serbo-Croat, sometimes written in Cyrillic
religion Serbian Orthodox
history settled in the Balkans from the 7th century, the Serbs established an empire there in the 14th century. They were then defeated at Kossovo in 1389 by the Turks, to whom they became tributary until independence was regained in a war with Turkey 1876–8. In the two Balkan Wars of 1912–13, Serbia greatly enlarged her territory at the expense of Turkey and Bulgaria, and her designs on Bosnia and Herzegovina, backed by Russia, led to friction with Austria, culminating in the outbreak of war in 1914. Serbia was completely overrun 1915–16, but in 1918 became the nucleus of the new kingdom of the Serbs, Croats, and Slovenes (see Yugoslavia◊). Serb and Croat rivalry continues in modern Yugoslavia, the former being predominant□

serfdom see under feudalism◊□

Sergius of Radonezh, St 1314–1392. Patron saint of Russia, founder in 1334 of the monastery of the Blessed Trinity near Moscow. Mediator among Russian feudal princes, he inspired the victory of Dmitri, Grand Duke of Moscow, over the Tatar Khan Mamai at Kulikovo, on the upper Don, in 1380□

serpentine greenish to black mineral (hydrated magnesium silicate, $Mg_3Si_2O_5.2H_20$) occurring in soft rocks. Rare snake-patterned forms are used in ornamental carving, and the fibrous form ***chrysolite*** is a source of asbestos◊□

Serpent Mound see under Ohio◊□

serum the clear part of blood◊ plasma left after clotting and removal of blood corpuscles and fibrin. The term is also applied to antitoxin obtained from such serum taken from immunized animals□

serval an African wildcat; see under cat◊□

Servetus Michael 1511–53. Spanish theologian, with unitarian views, for which he was burned alive by Calvin◊ at Geneva. As a physician, he was a pioneer in the study of the circulation of the blood□

Service Robert William 1874–1938. Anglo-Canadian author, popular for his ballads of Yukon on the Gold Rush, e.g. 'The Shooting of Dan McGrew'□

service tree deciduous Eurasian tree *Sorbus domestica*, family Rosaceae◊, with alternate leaves, white flowers, and small oval fruit□

services armed. The air, sea, and land forces of a country. In the UK the history of the army and navy can be traced back to the locally raised forces which prevented Alfred's◊ Wessex◊ being overrun by the Danes◊. All three armed services are professionals, with no conscript element. The ***Royal Navy*** is known as the Senior Service, because of its formal origin under Henry VIII, whereas no permanent standing ***Army*** was raised until the time of Charles II (see also Royal◊ Marines). The Territorial◊ Army is a back-up force of volunteers. The ***Royal Air Force*** was formed in 1918 by the merger of the already existing Royal Naval Air Service and the Royal Flying Corps. ***Women's Services*** originated in World War I, and there are separate corps for all three services: Women's Royal Naval Service, Women's Royal Air Corps, and Women's Royal Army Corps (each with its own nursing service). Comparatively few states, e.g. Cuba and Israel, recruit women in a direct combatant role□

servo system an automatic control system in which the output follows the input in a predetermined way, and incorporates a feedback to the input derived from the difference between the actual and the desired result, e.g. in keeping an aircraft at the correct height and on its correct course□

sesame annual plant of tropical Asia *Sesamum indicum*, family Pedaliaceae, grown for its seeds, and their oil (gingili or til), used in cookery, etc. See under herbs◊□

Session Court of. See under Scots◊ law□

Sessions Roger 1896–1985. American composer, influenced by Stravinsky and Schoenberg, of dense and dissonant works, e.g. *The Black Maskers* 1923, *Symphony No 1* 1927, and *Concerto for Orchestra* 1981□

Set see under Osiris◊□

Seton Ernest Thompson 1860–1946. Canadian naturalist (originally named Ernest Seton Thompson), born in England. He illustrated his own books□

Setonaikai 'Inland Sea' a narrow body of water almost enclosed by the islands of Honshu, Shikoku and Kyushu, Japan. It is both a transport artery and a national park with some 3000 islands. Fish farming is practised□

setter a gundog; see pointer and setter under dog◊□

Settlement Act of. Law passed by the English Parliament in 1701 which confined the succession to the throne of England to Protestants, and (after William III and Anne) to the house of Hanover□

Seurat Georges 1859–91. French artist, founder of the technique of Pointillism◊ (with Signac◊)□

Sevastopol port and fortress in the Crimea, Ukraine Republic, USSR, base of the Russian Black Sea fleet and a seaside resort, with shipbuilding yards and a wine-making industry; population 335 000. Founded by Catherine II in 1784, it was successfully besieged by the English and French in the Crimean War Oct 1854–Sept 1855, and in World War II by the Germans Nov 1941–4 Jul 1942, but was retaken by the Russians in 1944□

Seventh Day Adventists see Adventists◊□

Seven Weeks' War war between Austria and Prussia in 1866. It was engineered by Bismarck◊, and was nominally about the possession of Schleswig-Holstein◊ (under the Treaty of Prague◊ Prussia took both Holstein, previously seized by Austria, and Schleswig), but actually to confirm Prussia's supersession of Austria as the leading German state□

Seven Wonders of the World in antiquity, the pyramids of Egypt; the hanging gardens at Babylon; the temple of Artemis at Ephesus; the statue of Zeus at Olympia; the mausoleum at Halicarnassus; the Colossus of Rhodes; and the Pharos (lighthouse) at Alexandria□

Seven Years' War war, 1756–63, between Britain and Prussia on the one hand, and France, Austria, and Russia on the other. Frederick◊ II of Prussia campaigned brilliantly against great odds, and Britain (under Chatham◊) achieved a mastery at sea, e.g. in the Battle of Quiberon◊ Bay 1759, and on land (by the victories of Wolfe◊ and Clive◊) which resulted in the conquest of Canada and the foundation of the Indian empire□

severe combined immune deficiency rare condition (SCID) of being born without the body's normal defences against infection. The child has to live within an infection-free plastic tent until a matched donor can provide a bone marrow transplant. In the USA cells from an aborted foetus are used□

Severn river rising in N Wales (NE side of Plynlimon) and flowing to the Bristol Channel, length 338 km/210 mi. The ***Severn bore*** is a 2 m/6 ft tidal wave. The Severn is crossed near Chepstow by a rail tunnel (1873–85) and road bridge (1966)□

Severus Lucius Septimus 146–211AD. Roman emperor from 193, when he was proclaimed by his troops after the murder of Pertinax. The only African to become emperor, he died at York campaigning against the Caledonians□

Seveso see under hexachlorophene◊□

Sévigné Marie de Rabutin-Chantal, Marquise de Sévigné 1626–96. French letter-writer, who gave a vivid account of social life in letters to her daughter, the Comtesse de Grignan□

Seville industrial city and river port on the Guadalquivir in Andalusia, Spain; population 653 800. It is famous for its 12th-century palace (Alcázar), Gothic 15th–16th-century cathedral, and Holy Week Festival. Murillo◊ and Velázquez◊ were born here□

Sèvres town in the Île de France region, France; population 21 000. The state porcelain factory was established in the park of St◊ Cloud in 1763, and there is a national museum of ceramics□

sewage liquid waste, both domestic and industrial, conveyed through pipes for purification (removal or breakdown of solids, and oxidization by bacterial action of the liquid). Discharge of raw sewage into the sea still continues to some extent, but is increasingly deprecated. Organic sewage sludge may be used to produce methane gas for heating, and the residue sold as a fertilizer, although processing needs to be thorough to avoid the survival of viruses, and their subsequent ingestion by human beings when the crops are eaten□

Sewell Anna 1820–78. British author of the life story of a horse, *Black Beauty* 1877□

sewing machine a machine to sew material. An early pioneer was the Englishman Thomas Saint in 1790, but the modern 'lockstitch' (which cannot accidentally be unravelled, and produces a uniform appearance on both sides of the material) was independently invented in the USA by Walter Hunt in 1834 and Elias Howe in 1846. The latter was the basis of the US patent of 1851 (by Isaac Singer 1811–75). Modern microprocessor-controlled machines produce fancy stitches, buttonholes, etc., automatically□

sex reproduction by means of the interaction of male and female. Amongst mammals, the ova, or egg-cells, are all alike in that they carry an X chromosome, but the male sperms are of two types, one carrying an X chromosome and the other a Y chromosome. If an egg is fertilized by an X sperm, the result will be female, but by a Y sperm, male, so that it is the male who determines the sex of his young. In birds, the female carries the XY chromosome pair, and the mother controls the sex of her young. The human male gamete, the ***spermatozoan***, is about 0.05 mm/0.002 in long, and comprises a rounded head linked to the tail by which it propels itself. The human female gamete, or ***ovum***, is very much larger, and is a spherical nucleated cell surrounded by a transparent capsule. Ova develop in round collections of cells (the Graafian follicles) scattered through the substance of a woman's two ovaries: at birth a female ovary contains about 30 000 rudimentary ova.

Each month (about midway between two successive menstruations) one of the follicles comes to the surface of the ovary, ruptures, and discharges the ovum into the trumpet-shaped end of the Fallopian tube. If intercourse has taken place at about this time, one of the spermatozoa released from the male penis may succeed in reaching the ovum during its passage along the tube, when it will burrow through the containing capsule, and its nucleus will unite with that of the ovum. The oosperm (the product of this union, which has half its chromosomes derived from its mother and half from its father) then begins rapidly to divide. By the end of the fifth week the rudiments of all the more important organs of the embryo will have been laid down, and after a pregnancy of about 280 days, a child is born□

sex determination in mammals sex is determined at conception, but in many other creatures, it may be governed by temperature (turtle, crocodile), food supply (some worms), day length (shrimps), etc.□

sexism discrimination◊ on the basis of sex, generally as practised by men against women. The term was first used in the 1960s by feminist writers to describe language or behaviour which implied women's inferiority. Examples include the contentious use of male pronouns to describe both men and women, and the assumption that some jobs are typically performed only by one sex, e.g. that all pilots are male, and all nurses female. There is growing public awareness□

sextant navigational instrument for determining latitude by measuring the angle between some heavenly body and the horizon; useless except in clear weather. It was invented by John Hadley in 1730.

When the horizon is viewed through the right-hand side *horizon glass*, which is partly clear and partly mirrored, the light from a star can be seen at the same time in the mirrored left-hand side by adjusting an *index mirror*. The angle of the star to the horizon can then be read on a calibrated scale□

sextant
simplified diagram of a sextant

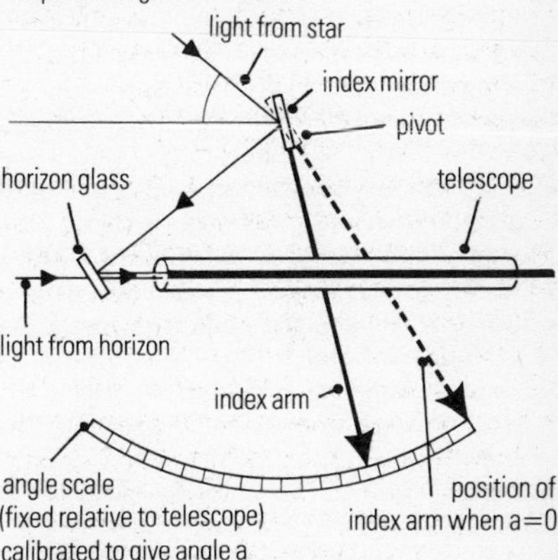

Seychelles

area 404 sq km/156 sq mi

capital Victoria on Mahé

features comprises two distinct island groups, one concentrated, the other widely scattered, totalling well over 100 islands and islets; the unique 'double coconut' (see coconut◊)

exports copra, cinnamon; tourism is important

currency Seychelles rupee

population 66 000

language Creole, spoken by 95%, English and French (all official)

religion Christianity, 90% Roman Catholic

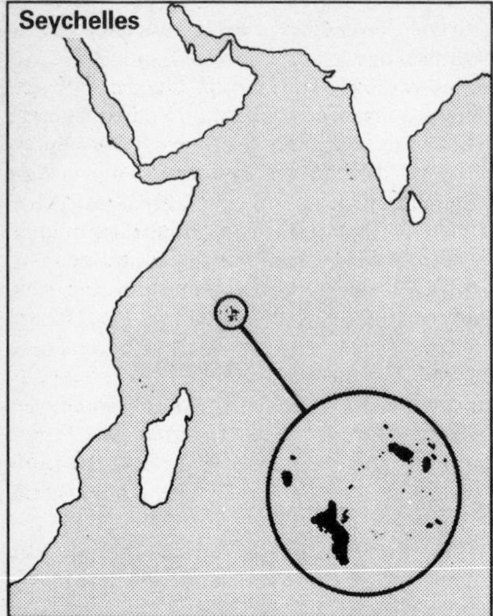

government there is an executive president (France-Albert René from 1977) with a council of ministers and people's assembly
recent history Originally French, the Seychelles became British in 1810, and in 1976 became an independent republic within the Commonwealth. Following a coup in 1977, the People's Progressive Front became the sole legal party□

Seymour Jane c1509–37. English queen consort, third wife of Henry◊ VIII, whom she married in 1536. She died soon after the birth of her son, the future Edward◊ VI□

Sforza family name of the dukes of Milan 1450–99 and 1522–35. Their court was a centre of Renaissance culture, especially under ***Ludovico Sforza*** 1451–1508, patron of Leonardo◊ da Vinci and other artists□

's Gravenhage formal Dutch name of The Hague◊□

Shaanxi province (formerly ***Shensi***) of NW China.
area 195 800 sq km/75 580 sq mi
capital Zian
features Huang He valley; one of the earliest settled areas of China
products iron and steel
population 27 000 000, including many Muslims□

Shaba see under Zaïre◊□

Shackleton Sir Ernest 1874–1922. British Antarctic explorer, commander of three expeditions: 1907–9, when latitude 88° 23′ S was reached, the S magnetic pole located, and Mount Erebus◊ climbed; 1914–16, when his ship *Endurance* had to be abandoned in the ice; and 1921–2, on which he died and was buried at his own wish in S Georgia□

shad an edible fish related to the herring◊□

Shadwell Thomas 1642–92. English poet and comic dramatist, remembered for his violent feud with Dryden◊, whom he succeeded as poet laureate□

SHAEF (*S*upreme *H*eadquarters *A*llied *E*xpeditionary *F*orce) established on 15 Feb 1944, at Norfolk House, London. It was transferred in Mar 1944 to Bushy Park, near Kingston upon Thames, where final plans for the Allied invasion of Europe (under Eisenhower◊) were worked out□

Shaffer Peter 1926– . British playwright, whose work includes *The Royal Hunt of the sun* 1964, *Equus* 1973, *Amadeus* (a play about Mozart and Salieri) 1979□

Shaftesbury Anthony Ashley Cooper, 1st Earl of Shaftesbury 1621–83. English statesman, a supporter of the Restoration◊, who became Lord Chancellor in 1672, but went into opposition in 1673 and began to organize the Whig◊ Party. He headed the demand for the exclusion of the future James II from the succession, secured the passage of the Habeas◊ Corpus Act in 1679, and when accused of treason in 1681, fled to Holland□

Shaftesbury Anthony Ashley Cooper, 7th Earl of Shaftesbury 1801–85. British Tory statesman, a strong supporter of the Ten-Hours' Act of 1847 and other factory legislation, and largely responsible for the 1842 act forbidding the employment of women and children underground in mines. He was also associated with the movement for the establishment of 'ragged' schools (providing free education) for the poor□

Shah or, more formally ***Shahanshah*** 'king of kings', traditional title of ancient Persian rulers, and also of those of the recent Pahlavi◊ dynasty□

Shah-Jehan 1592–1666. Mogul◊ emperor of India from 1627, son of Jahangir◊. He conquered the Deccan◊, but was less successful against the Persians, and from 1658 was a prisoner of his son Aurungzebe◊. He built the Taj Mahal (Agra◊), and the Red Fort (Delhi◊)□

Shahn Ben 1898–1969. Lithuanian-born American artist, concerned with social issues, e.g. Sacco◊ and Vanzetti, prohibition◊, in a photographic style; he produced murals (with Diego Rivera◊) at Radio City□

Shakers popular nickname for the United Society of Believers in Christ's Second Appearing, founded by James and Jane Wardley in England c1747, and taken to N America in 1774 by Ann Lee 1736–84. They shook ecstatically in their worship and anticipated modern spiritualist beliefs, but their doctrine of celibacy led to their extinction□

Shakespeare William 1564–1616. English dramatist and poet. Born at Stratford-on-Avon, the son of a wool-dealer, he was educated at the grammar school, and in 1582 married Anne Hathaway◊. She bore him a daughter, Susanna, in 1583, and twins Hamnet (d. 1596) and Judith in 1595. Having joined a company of players, he was by 1589 established in London as an actor and a playwright. Early plays, written c1589–93, were the tragedy *Titus Andronicus*; the comedies *The Comedy of Errors, The Taming of the Shrew,* and *Two Gentlemen of Verona*; the three parts of *Henry VI*, and *Richard III*. About 1593 he came under the patronage of the Earl of Southampton◊, to whom he dedicated his long poems *Venus and Adonis* 1593 and *Lucrece* 1594; he also wrote for him the comedy *Love's Labour's Lost*, satirizing Raleigh◊'s circle, and seems to have dedicated to him his sonnets written c1593–6, in which the mysterious 'Dark Lady' appears.

From 1594 Shakespeare was a member of the Chamberlain's (later the King's) company of players, and had no rival as a dramatist, e.g. the lyric plays *Romeo and Juliet, Midsummer Night's Dream*, and *Richard II* 1594–5, followed by *King John* and *The Merchant of Venice* in 1596. The Falstaff plays of 1597–9: *Henry IV* (parts I and II), *Henry V*, and *The Merry Wives of Windsor* (said to have been written at the request of Elizabeth I), brought his fame to its height. About the same time he wrote *Julius Caesar* 1599. The period ended with the lyrically witty *Much Ado about Nothing, As You Like It*, and *Twelfth Night* c1598–1601.

With *Hamlet* 1601, a 'darker' period seems to begin, reflected also in the comedies *Troilus and Cressida, All's Well that Ends Well*, and *Measure for Measure* c1601–4. *Othello, Macbeth*, and *King Lear* followed 1604–6, together with *Timon of Athens* in which pessimism reaches its depths. *Antony and Cleopatra* and *Coriolanus* 1607–8 have a more balanced acceptance of life.

Shakespeare was only part author of *Pericles*, but like the other plays of c1608–11, *Cymbeline, The Winter's Tale*, and *The Tempest*, it has a sunset glow about it. During 1613 Shakespeare collaborated with Fletcher in *Henry VIII* and probably in *Two Noble Kinsmen*. He had already retired to Stratford c1610, where he died on on 23 Apr 1616. His tomb there has an authentic portrait bust, and the other accepted likeness is on the collected edition of his plays (the First Folio) published in 1623 by his fellow-actors, Heminge and Condell. See Globe◊□

shallot bulbous plant *Allium ascalonicum*, family Liliaceae, used as a vegetable and in pickles□

Shalmaneser five Assyrian kings including: ***Shalmaneser III***, reigned 859–824BC, who pursued an aggressive policy, and made Babylon and Israel tributary to him□

Shamanism religion of the aboriginal tribes of N Asia, and (by extension) of the N American Indians, in which the ***shaman***, or 'medicine-man', a seer and sorcerer, plays an important role, and is believed to make contact with spirits of good and evil□

Shamir Yitzhak 1915– . Polish-born Israeli statesman. A leader of the Stern Gang terrorists under the British Mandate in Palestine, he was Foreign Minister under Begin◊ 1980–3, Prime Minister 1983–4, and again Foreign Minister in the Peres◊ unity government from 1984. In Oct 1986, he and Peres are due to exchange positions, Shamir becoming Prime Minister and Peres taking over as Foreign Minister□

shamrock several trifoliate plants, family Leguminosae◊, especially white and yellow clover, and black medick. Said to have been used by St Patrick to illustrate the Holy Trinity, the shamrock is the national emblem of Ireland□

Shamyl c1797–1871. Leader of the Dagestan◊ people in their fight for independence from Russia 1834–1859. He was taken prisoner, but his captivity was not too rigorous, and he died on pilgrimage to Mecca. Soviet attitudes to him vary according to the current party line on nationalism□

Shan a member of the people of the mountainous Thai-Burmese border area, akin to the Laos and the Thais.

Shan States, area 149 740 sq km/57 815 sq mi, were annexed by Britain in 1885, and are now part of the Burmese Union□

Shandong province (formerly ***Shantung***) of NE China

area 153 300 sq km/59 170 sq mi

capital Jinan

towns ports Yantai, Weihai, Qingdao, Shigiusuo

features crossed by the Huang He and the Grand Canal; Shandong Peninsula

products cereals, cotton; wild silk; varied minerals

population 72 310 000□

Shanghai industrial river port (steel, paper, textiles, machinery, precision instruments, oil refining) and special municipality on the Huang-pu, near its entry to the Chang Jiang estuary, in Jiangsu province, China; population 11 860 000. It handles 50% of China's imports and exports. Famous buildings include the Jade Buddha Temple 1882; the former home of Sun Yat-sen; the small house where the First National Congress of the Communist Party of China met secretly in 1921; and the house, museum, and tomb of Lu◊ Xun. In Jan 1966 there were riots during the Cultural Revolution□

Shankar Ravi 1920– . Indian composer of film music and virtuoso of the sitar, who has founded music schools in Bombay and Los Angeles□

Shannon longest river in Ireland, flowing from County Cavan to below Limerick; length 260 km/161 mi. It is famed for salmon, and there are hydroelectric installations at Ardnacrusha□

Shansi see Shanxi◊□

Shantou port and industrial city (formerly *Swatow*) in SE China, opened as a special foreign trade area in 1979; population 400 000□

Shantung see Shandong◊□

Shanxi province (formerly ***Shansi***) of NE China

area 157 100 sq km/60 640 sq mi

capital Taiyuan

features a drought-ridden plateau, partly surrounded by the Great Wall◊; the province saw the outbreak of the Boxer Rising◊

products coal and iron

population 24 472 000□

Shaoshan see under Hunan◊□

Shapiro Karl 1913– . American poet, born in Baltimore. His work includes the striking *V Letter* 1945, written after service in World War II□

sharav see under wind◊□

shares see stocks◊ and shares□

shari'a see Islamic Law under Islam◊□

Sharjah see United Arab Emirates◊□

shark marine fish (350 species) of the order Selachii, which have gill slits opening directly to the exterior in a 'grill', and a cartilaginous skeleton. They are so perfectly adapted to their way of life that they have existed, practically unmodified, for over 300 million years. One third of their brain capacity is devoted to the sense of smell, so that they pick up blood traces a quarter of a mile distant; some can hear their prey 500 m/1500 ft away; organs near the mouth also alert them to the magnetic field created by other fish or man; their sight is also good; and their teeth grow continuously in rows, moving forward to replace the worn or damaged front row. Sharks cover enormous distances, and are thought to navigate by picking up earth's electromagnetic signals. Some species lay eggs, e.g. the popular 'mermaid's purse'; others bear live young.

Species include the ***great white shark*** *Carcharodon carcharias*, the chief man-eater (the prototype of the shark in the film *Jaws*), 12 m/40 ft long, with teeth 5 cm/2 in long; ***hammerhead*** *Sphyrna makarran*, a man-eater with an eye at each end of a hammer-like extension of the head; ***tope*** or ***grey requiem shark*** *Galeorhinus galeus* of temperate and tropical seas, which reaches 2 m/6 ft, and may produce 50 live young at a time; and the ***lesser spotted dogfish*** *Scyliorhinus caniculus*, common in British waters, is eaten as 'huss' or 'rock salmon', shark flesh being protein- and vitamin-rich. A few are 'filter-feeders', which live by straining plankton from sea water, namely the temperate ***basking shark*** *Cetorhinus maximus*, second largest of living fish at 12 m/40 ft, often found off Britain; ***whale-shark*** *Rhincodon typus*, 18 m/60 ft, largest of living fish; and (found in much deeper water) the ***megamouth*** *Megachasma pelagios*, first discovered in 1976, which has a bulbous head with protruding jaws and blubbery lips, is 4.5 m/15 ft long, and weighs 750 kg/1650 lb□

Sharon see under Israel◊□

Sharp Cecil 1859–1924. British compiler of *English Folk Song* 1921, who also collected in the USA survivals of English song in the Appalachians, etc. He saved songs from extinction, but was criticized for bowdlerizing earthy originals□

Sharpeville black township, 65 km/40 mi S of Johannesburg, S Africa. During a campaign against the pass◊ laws 69 black people were killed when police fired on a crowd of demonstrators on 21 Mar 1960. On the anniversary in 1985, during funerals of black protesters against unemployment killed earlier, some 19 black people were shot at Langa near Port Elizabeth by the police□

Shastri Lal Bahadur 1904–66. Indian politician, known as 'the Sparrow' from his small stature. He succeeded Nehru as Prime Minister in 1964, but died of a heart attack in Tashkent, following signature of a peace agreement with Pakistan□

Shatt al'Arab 'river of Arabia', the joint river formed by the confluence of the Euphrates◊ and Tigris◊; length 190 km/120 mi to the Arabian Gulf. The lower reaches form a border of disputed demarcation between Iran and Iraq. See Gulf◊ War□

Shaw George Bernard 1856–1950. Irish dramatist. Born in Dublin, he settled in London in 1876, joined the Fabians◊, worked as a music (*The Perfect Wagnerite* 1898) and drama critic, and wrote several unsuccessful novels. His first play *Widowers' Houses* 1892, attacking slum landlords, showed his alliance with a new, essentially political and polemical movement in the theatre. Successors, always designed to 'shock', include *Mrs Warren's Profession* (1893, but banned till 1902 because it dealt with prostitution); *Arms and the Man* 1894 (on war); *The Devil's Disciple* 1897; *Caesar and Cleopatra* 1898 (a companion piece to the play by Shakespeare, with whom he pursued a semi-comic rivalry); *Candida* 1903; the epic *Man and Superman* 1903, expanding his theme of Creative Evolution; *Major Barbara* 1905; *Heartbreak House* 1917 (dealing with World War I); *Pygmalion* 1913, written for Mrs Patrick Campbell◊ (converted to a musical as *My Fair Lady*), and *St Joan* 1924. His theories were further elucidated in voluminous prefaces to the published plays and such books as *The Intelligent Woman's Guide to Socialism and Capitalism* 1928. His letters, e.g. to Ellen Terry◊, are always of interest; Nobel prize 1925□

shearwater several species of oceanic bird; see under petrel◊□

Sheba ancient name for modern S Yemen◊ (Sha'abijah), once famous for gold and spices; according to the Old Testament, its queen visited Solomon, and the former Ethiopian royal house traced its descent from their union□

Shechem see Nablus◊□

sheep genus *Ovis* of ruminants, family Bovidae, order Artiodactyla◊. Wild species survive in the uplands of central Asia, and their domesticated descendants are reared worldwide for meat, wool, milk, and cheese (e.g. Parmesan and Roquefort), and for rotation on arable land to maintain its fertility. Among famous breeds are the Merino (thick, soft wool), Southdown (excellent for mutton), and Welsh mountain, a very agile, hardy breed□

sheepdog a breed of dog◊□

Sheerness see under Kent◊□

Sheffield industrial city in S Yorkshire, England; population 545 000. Famous for cutlery, silverware, and plate from medieval times, it now also produces alloys and special steels, drills, precision tools, optical glass, etc. It has a cathedral, City Hall 1932, Cutlers' Hall, a university, the Graves Art Gallery, Crucible Theatre 1971, and Ruskin Museum 1877 (revived 1985). It is the headquarters of the National Union of Mineworkers□

Sheffield plate copper sheeting with a sheet of silver fused to it, sometimes on both sides, which was worked into 'silverware'. The process, invented by Thomas Boulsover of Sheffield in 1742, had a beautiful finish now valued for its own sake; it was superseded by electroplating◊□

Shelburne William Petty FitzMaurice, 2nd Earl of Shelburne 1737–1805. British Whig statesman, an opponent of George III's American policy. As Prime Minister in 1783, he concluded peace with the USA. He was created Marquess of Lansdowne in 1784□

shelduck a type of wild duck; see under waterfowl◊□

shellac resin secreted by the ***lac insect*** *Coccus lacca*, used in varnishes and polishes□

Shelley Mary Wollstonecraft 1797–1851. British author, daughter of Mary Wollstonecraft and William Godwin◊. In 1814 she eloped with P B Shelley◊, whom she married in 1816, and in 1818 published *Frankenstein*, a story of a scientist who created a man-monster and gave it life□

Shelley Percy Bysshe 1792–1822. British poet, born near Horsham. He was educated at Eton and University College, Oxford, where his collaboration in the pamphlet *The Necessity of Atheism* in 1811 caused his expulsion. In London he fell in love with 16-year-old Harriet Westbrook, whom he married in 1811, but they were soon estranged and in 1814 he left England with Mary Shelley◊ (Harriet drowned herself in 1816). He had in the meantime written pamphlets advocating vegetarianism and political freedom (also the theme of his poem *Queen Mab* 1813). By 1818 he was living in Italy, where he produced the tragedy *The Cenci* 1819, the lyric drama *Prometheus Unbound* 1820, and *Adonais* 1821, on the death of Keats, as well as his most famous short lyrics, e.g. 'Ode to the West Wind', 'The Cloud', and 'To a Skylark'. In Jul 1822 he was drowned while sailing near Spezia□

Shenandoah see under Virginia◊ and P H Sheridan◊□

Shensi see Shaanxi◊□

Shenyang industrial city (formerly ***Mukden***) and capital of Liaoning province, China; population 4 000 000. The Manchu capital 1625–44, it has the Imperial Palace Museum, and a noted acrobatic troupe□

Shenzen see under Hong◊ Kong□

shepherd's purse wild annual plant *Capsella bursapastoris*, family Cruciferae◊, so-named from the two-valved seed pouches which follow its white flowers□

Sheppard Jack 1702–24. British criminal, a popular hero for his escapes from prison. He was eventually hanged□

Sheppey see under Kent◊□

Sheraton Thomas c1751–1806. English designer of elegant inlaid furniture, as in his *Cabinet-maker's and Upholsterer's Drawing Book* 1791□

Sheridan Philip Henry 1831–88. American cavalry commander who, during the American Civil◊ War, cleared the Shenandoah Valley of Confederates, laying it waste, and forced Lee◊'s retreat to Appomattox and surrender to Grant□

Sheridan Richard Brinsley 1751–1816. Anglo-Irish dramatist, born in Dublin. His social comedies include *The Rivals* (remembered for Mrs Malaprop) 1775 and *The School for Scandal* 1777. As an MP 1780–1812, he was a noted orator, an adherent of Fox◊, and directed the impeachment of Warren Hastings◊□

sheriff in England and Wales the Crown's chief executive officer in a county for ceremonial purposes; in Scotland they are the equivalent of English county court judges; and in the USA are the popularly elected head law-enforcement officers of a county□

Sherman William Tecumseh 1820–91. American Union general, born in Ohio. During the American Civil◊ War, he collaborated with Grant◊ in the Vicksburg campaign, captured Atlanta in 1864 (whence he marched to the sea, laying Georgia waste), and then drove the Confederates northwards□

Sherpa a member of the Mongolian people of Nepal◊□

Sherriff R(obert) C(edric) 1896–1975. British dramatist, remembered for his anti-heroic war play *Journey's End* 1929□

Sherrington Sir Charles Scott 1857–1952. British physiologist, whose *The Integrative Action of the Nervous System* 1906 formulated the principles of reflex action; Order of Merit 1924; Nobel prize with Adrian◊ 1932□

sherry see under Jerez◊ de la Frontera□

's Hertogenbosch capital of N Brabant, Netherlands; population 86 775. There are shipbuilding, tobacco and electrical industries□

Sherwood Robert 1896–1955. American dramatist, whose plays include *The Petrified Forest* 1934 (see Bogart◊), *Idiot's Delight* 1936, *Abe Lincoln in Illinois* 1938 and *There Shall Be No Night* 1940□

Sherwood Forest see under Nottinghamshire◊□

Shetland islands off N coast of Scotland
area 1429 sq km/552 sq mi
towns administrative headquarters Lerwick, on Mainland, largest of 19 inhabited islands
features comprise over 100 islands; Muckle Flugga (60° 51′ 30″ N latitude) is the northernmost of the British Isles
products Europe's largest oil port is Sullom Voe, Mainland; processed fish, handknits from Fair Isle and Unst; miniature ponies

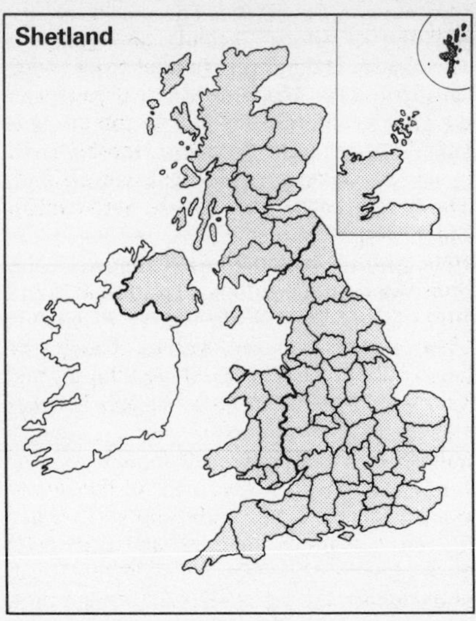

population 25 815; their dialect is derived from Norse, the islands having been under Scandinavian rule 875–1468; there is a movement for autonomy□

Shevardnadze Edvard 1928– . Russian statesman. A supporter of Gorbachev, he was First Secretary of the Georgian Communist Party from 1972, and an advocate of economic reform. In 1985 he became Foreign Minister and a member of the Politburo□

Shiah/Shi'ite see under Islam◊□

shield in physics, anything interposed between two regions hindering passage of fields or radiation. Metals shield from electric fields, soft iron from magnetic; thermal insulators with shiny surfaces block heat◊ flow; lead, concrete, etc., absorb X-rays and – at least partially – nuclear radiations (see radioactivity◊)□

Shihchiachuang see Shijiazhuang◊□

Shih Huang Ti see Shi◊ Huangdi□

Shi Huangdi c259–210BC. Emperor of China. He succeeded to the throne of the state of Qin in 246BC, and reunited the country as an empire by 228BC. He burnt almost all existing books in 213BC to destroy ties with the past; built the Great◊ Wall; created a unified writing system; and was buried in a magnificent tomb complex guarded by 10 000 individualized, life-size pottery warriors (still being excavated in the 1980s). He had so overextended his power that the dynasty and the empire collapsed at the death of his feeble successor in 207BC□

Shijiazhuang industrial city (textiles, chemicals, light engineering) (formerly ***Shihchiachuang***), Hebei province, China; population

1 000 000□

Shikoku one of the four chief islands of Japan. The climate is mild, and rainfall reaches 266 cm/105 in in the south. Rice, cereals, and fruit are grown, and salt and copper mined. It is linked by bridge and tunnel to Honshu◊, and by suspension bridge with Awajishima Island, over the Naruto whirlpool in the Setonaikai◊. Chief town Matsuyama□

shillelagh see under Wicklow◊□

Shillong capital of Meghalaya, India; population 120 000□

Shimonoseki port on Honshu, Japan; population 262 000. The peace treaty ending the first Sino◊-Japanese War was signed here in 1895□

shingles see under herpes◊□

Shinto Chinese transliteration of the Japanese indigenous faith *Kami-no-Michi* 'Way of the Gods', which mingles an empathetic oneness with natural forces and loyalty to the emperor. He is traditionally descended from the sun goddess ***Amaterasu*** whose shrine at ***Ise*** (see under Kyoto◊) is the most sacred in Japan. Shinto was disestablished as the state religion by MacArthur◊ after World War II. Its ethic is exemplary, but an aggressive, nationalistic aspect was developed by the Meiji rulers. This was symbolized by the ***Yasukuni*** shrine, near Tokyo, since 1945 a purely religious memorial to 2.5 million war dead. Nevertheless, a public visit by Premier Nakasone in 1985 aroused controversy□

shinty winter team game (12 a side) popular in Scotland and resembling hockey□

ship money medieval English tax on coastal districts to support the navy; attempts by Charles I to levy it in peacetime on the whole country, without parliament's consent, led to resistance, e.g. by John Hampden◊. It was declared illegal by Parliament 1641□

Shiráz walled city of S Iran, noted for wine, carpets, silverwork, and fine mosques; population 416 500□

Shiré Highlands see under Malawi◊□

Shizuoka industrial town (metal and food processing, especially tea) on Honshu, Japan; population 461 000□

shock circulatory failure or sudden fall of blood pressure, resulting in pallor, sweating, raised (but weak) pulse, and possibly complete collapse, caused by a heart attack, burns, loss of blood, intense fear, etc. Also the results of injury from electric shock□

Shockley William 1910– . American physicist, who worked with Bardeen◊ and Brattain◊ on the invention of the transistor◊. Nobel prize 1956□

shogi Japanese board game, probably deriving from the same Indian sources as chess, but more complex□

Shogun formerly, the hereditary Commander-in-Chief of the Japanese Army. Nominally subject to the emperor, he was the real ruler of Japan 1192–1867, when the emperor reassumed power□

Sholapur industrial town (textiles, leather goods, chemicals) in Maharashtra, India; population 514 000□

Sholokhov Mikhail Aleksandrovich 1905–84. Russian novelist. His *And Quiet Flows the Don* 1926–40, telling of the Don Cossacks, is alleged by Solzhenitsyn◊ to have been written by Fyodor Kryukov 1870–1920, whose manuscript was appropriated. Nobel prize 1965□

shop steward trade union representative in a 'shop' or department of a factory, who recruits for the union, inspects contribution cards, and reports grievances to the district committee□

shorthand any system of rapid writing, e.g. the abbreviations practised by the Greeks and Romans. Pepys (in his diary) and Dickens (as a reporter) were both shorthand users, but the first perfecter of an entirely phonetic system was Isaac Pitman◊, by which system speeds of about 300 words a minute are attainable. ***Stenotype machines***, using selective keyboards enabling several word contractions to be printed at a time, are equally speedy and accurate. The abbreviations used can be transferred by the operator to a television screen, where they enable the deaf to follow the spoken word, e.g. in the House of Commons□

Shostakovich Dmitry Dmitrievich 1906–1975. Russian composer, born in Leningrad. Of his 15 symphonies, the most famous are the 5th, sub-titled 'A Soviet Artist's Reply to Just Criticism', in 1937; the patriotic 7th or *Leningrad* 1941, which marked a temporary return to favour; and the moving 10th, 1955. He also wrote ballets and operas, the latter including *A Lady Macbeth of Mtensk* 1936, suppressed as 'too divorced from the proletariat', but revived in 1963 as *Katerina Ismailova*□

shot putting the. See throwing◊ events□

Shovell Sir Cloudesley c1650–1707. English admiral, who took part (with Rooke◊) in the capture of Gibraltar in 1704. In 1707 his flagship *Association* and four other ships of his home-bound fleet were lost off the Scillies. He was strangled for his rings as he struggled ashore□

shoveller a species of duck; see under waterfowl◊□

show jumping competitive horse jumping over a course of fences. The winner is usually the competitor with fewest 'faults' (penalty marks given for knocking down or refusing fences, etc.), but in time competitions it is the competitor completing the course most quickly, additional seconds being added for such mistakes. Famous riders include the British Pat Smythe, David Broome, Harvey Smith; the German Alwin Schockemohle; the Italian Graziano Mancinelli; and the American Bill Steinkraus□

Shrapnel Henry 1761–1842. British army officer who invented shells containing bullets, to increase the spread of casualties. Other methods are now more effective, but the word shrapnel remains in use for any shell fragments□

Shreveport industrial river port (oil and natural gas, steel, telephone equipment, glass, timber) in Louisiana, USA; population 205 800. It was named after Henry Shreeve, a riverboat captain who cleared a giant logjam□

shrew a type of small insectivorous nocturnal mammal; see under Insectivora◊□

Shrewsbury town (administrative headquarters) of Shropshire, England, on the Severn; population (with Atcham) 88 500. The Roman city of Uriconium to the east (larger than Pompeii) has been safeguarded for excavation, and it was here that Caractacus◊ fought Nero◊'s legions in 51AD. In 1403 Henry IV defeated the rebels led by Hotspur (see Sir Henry Percy◊) at Shrewsbury□

shrike the 'butcher-bird', family Laniidae, order Passeriformes, including the ***great grey shrike*** *Lanius excubitor*, which impales its prey (mainly insects, but also frogs, small mammals and reptiles) alive on thorns to form a 'larder'□

shrimp a small marine crustacean; see under prawn◊□

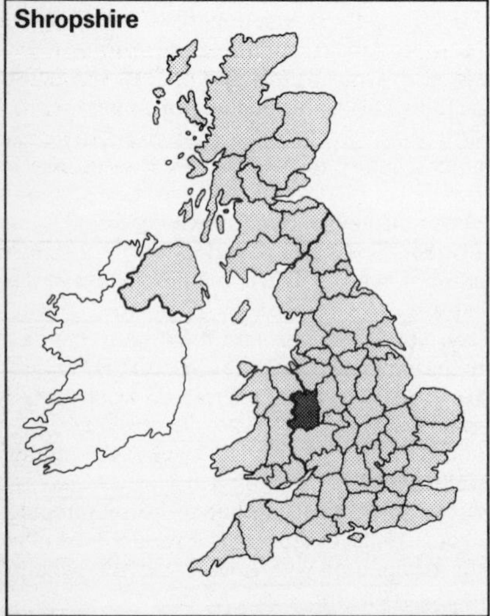

Shropshire W Midland county of England.
area 3490 sq km/1348 sq mi
towns administrative headquarters Shrewsbury
features on the Welsh border, it is bisected NW to SE by the Severn; the name is sometimes abbreviated to ***Salop***, and was officially so known from 1974 until local protest reversed the decision; Ellesmere is the largest of several lakes in the SW; and the Clee Hills rise to c610 m/1800 ft in the SW; Iron Bridge Gorge open-air museum of industrial archaeology includes the Iron Bridge 1779, which symbolized Britain's emergence as the world's first industrial nation
products chiefly agricultural, sheep and cattle being reared
population 381 000□

Shrove Tuesday the Tuesday before Ash Wednesday, the beginning of Lent in the Christian calendar, from the Old English for being shriven, i.e. the time for confession before Lent. It is also known as ***Pancake Tuesday***, recalling the eating up of rich things before the Lenten fast□

shrub perennial plant, smaller than a tree, with many woody stems at or near the base□

Shultz George 1920– . American industrial economist, Secretary of State to Reagan from 1982□

Shute Nevil. Pseudonym of British novelist N S Norway 1899–1960, who was born in Ealing, but settled in Australia in 1950. His most famous book is *A Town Like Alice* 1949□

Sialkot industrial city (surgical and sports goods, metal ware, carpets, textiles, leather goods) in Pakistan; population 296 000□

Sian see Xian◊□

Sibelius Jean Christian 1865–1957. Finnish composer, whose works include the orchestral *En Saga* 1892 and *Karelia* 1893; tone poem *Finlandia* 1900; *Valse Triste* 1904; violin concerto 1905; and seven symphonies□

Siberia Asiatic republic of the USSR from the Urals to the Pacific; area 12 050 000 sq km/4 650 000 sq mi. Overrun by Russia in the 17th century, it was used from the 18th to exile political and criminal prisoners. The first ***Trans-Siberian Railway*** 1892–1905 from Leningrad (via Omsk, Novisibirsk, Irkutsk and Khabarovsk) to Vladivostok, c8700 km/5400 mi, began to open it up, and a second branch, the ***Baikal-Amur Mainline*** (BAM) 1934–84, will tap its huge mineral resources, including gold, diamonds, oil and natural gas, iron, copper, nickel, cobalt, etc. Cities include Novosibirsk, Omsk, Krasnoyarsk, and Irkutsk. The Pacific coastline and Amur basin are often referred to as the Soviet Far East□

Sibyl in Roman mythology, priestess of Apollo, especially the Cumaean Sibyl living in a cave near Naples, Italy. She offered to sell Tarquinius◊ nine collections of prophecies, the ***Sibylline Books***, but the price was too high. When she had destroyed all but three, he bought those for the identical price, and these were kept for consultation in emergency at Rome□

Sichuan province (formerly ***Szechwan***) of China
area 569 000 sq km/219 634 sq mi
capital Chengdu
towns Chongqing
features surrounded by mountains, it was the headquarters of the Nationalist government 1937–45, and China's nuclear research centres are here; it is China's most populous administrative area, one-tenth of the total population; most of China's pandas are also here
products rice; coal, oil and natural gas
population 100 000 000
famous people Deng Xiaoping□

Sicily largest Mediterranean island (Italian ***Sicilia***)
area 25 709 sq km/9976 sq mi
capital Palermo
towns ports Catania, Messina, Syracuse, Marsala
features forms (with the islands of Lipari◊, Egadi, Ustica, and Pantelleria◊), an autonomous region of Italy; Etna, at 3323 m/10 902 ft the highest volcano in Europe, last major eruption 1971; the Mafia◊
exports Marsala wine, olives, citrus; refined oil and petrochemicals, pharmaceuticals
population 4 864 000
famous people Pirandello, Tomaso di Lampedusa, Leonardo Sciascia, Danilo Dolci
history conquered by most of the major powers of the ancient world, it flourished under the Greeks who settled there 8th–5th centuries BC. It was invaded by Carthage, and became part of the Roman empire 241BC–476AD. In the Middle Ages it was ruled successively by the Arabs; by the Normans 1059–1194, who established the ***Kingdom of the Two Sicilies*** (i.e. Sicily and the southern part of Italy), many Englishmen holding power there; by the German emperors, and then by the House of Anjou, until the popular revolt known as the ***Sicilian Vespers*** in 1282. Spanish rule was invited and continued in varying forms, with a temporary displacement of the Spanish Bourbons by Napoleon, until Garibaldi◊'s invasion in 1860 resulted in the two Sicilies being joined within a united Italy in 1861. In World War II Sicily was taken by the Allies 10 Jul–8 Aug 1943□

Sickert Walter Richard 1860–1942. British artist, son of a Danish painter, who studied under Whistler. His impressionist cityscapes of London and Venice, portraits, and domestic interiors capture subtleties of tone and light, often with a humorous touch□

sickle cell anaemia see anaemia◊□

Siddons Sarah 1755–1831. English actress, sister of Charles Kemble◊, who married William Siddons in 1773. She made an impressive debut in Otway◊'s *Venice Preserved* in 1774, and her majestic presence made her a superb Lady Macbeth. Reynolds◊ painted her as *The Tragic Muse*□

sidewinder a poisonous N American snake◊□

Sidi-Bel-Abbès trading city in Algeria; population 152 150. Until 1962 it was the headquarters of the French Foreign Legion because of its strategic position□

Siding Spring Mountain see under New◊ South Wales□

Sidney Sir Philip 1554–86. English poet, author of the sonnet sequence *Astrophel and Stella* 1591, who also wrote the earliest work of English literary criticism, *Apologie for Poetrie* 1595. His *Arcadia* is the finest of the Elizabethan romances. Appointed governor of Flushing in 1585, he died in the Battle of Zutphen□

Sidon see Saida◊□

Siegfried hero of the Nibelungenlied◊, after whom the Siegfried◊ Line was named□

Siegfried Line originally the defensive line established in 1918 by the Germans in France in World War I; in World War II the name given by the Allies to the West Wall, the German defensive line established along her western frontier, Holland to Switzerland□

Siemens four brothers, creators of an industrial empire. The eldest, ***Ernst Werner von Siemens*** 1812–92, founded the original electrical firm and made advances in telegraphy; most famous of the others was ***Sir William Siemens*** 1823–83, a naturalized Briton, who perfected the open-hearth production of steel (see steel◊)□

Siena city in Tuscany, Italy; population 70 000. Founded by the Etruscans, it has fine medieval architecture (see Pisano◊ and Donatello◊), including a 13th-century Gothic cathedral, and the Sienese school of painters including Sassetta (Stefano di Giovanni c1392–1450) who created fine altarpieces. The Palio ('banner', in reference to the prize) is an annual horse race in the main square, held since the Middle Ages□

Sienkiewicz Henryk 1846–1916. Polish author of historical novels, e.g. *Quo Vadis?* 1895, set in the Rome of Nero; Nobel prize 1905□

Sierra Leone Republic of

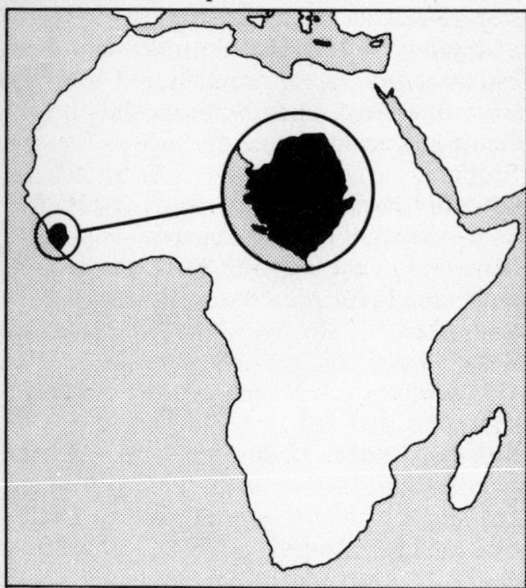

area 73 325 sq km/27 925 sq mi
capital Freetown
towns Bo, Kenema, Makeni
features coastal mangrove swamps with hot and humid climate (3500 mm/138 in rainfall annually)
exports palm kernels, cocoa, coffee, ginger; diamonds, bauxite, rutile
currency leone
population 4 000 000
language English (official), local languages
religion 60% Moslem, 30% Animist
government under the constitution of 1978, it is a one-party state (All People's Congress: APC), with an executive president (Major-General Joseph Saidu Momoh from 1985) and a House of Representatives
recent history originating in 1788 with an attempt to repatriate destitute Africans from England, it became a crown colony in 1808. Independent within the Commonwealth in 1961, it became a republic in 1971, and a one-party state in 1973□

Sierra Madre chief mountain system of Mexico, consisting of three ranges, enclosing the central plateau of the country; highest point Pico de Orizaba 5700 m/18 700 ft□

Sierra Nevada mountain range of S Spain; highest point Mulhacén 3481 m/11 421 ft□

Sierra Nevada mountain range in E California, USA; highest point Mount Whitney 4418 m/14 495 ft. It includes the King's Canyon, Sequoia, and Yosemite Valley national parks□

Signac Paul 1863–1935. French artist, associated with Seurat◊ in founding the technique of Pointillism◊ His paintings are often a mosaic of squarish blobs□

Signorelli Luca c1450–1523. Italian Renaissance artist of the Umbrian school, painter of large-scale frescoes, e.g. in Orvieto cathedral; noted for his powerful treatment of the nude, which influenced Michelangelo◊□

Sikhism monotheistic Hindu sect founded by Nanak 1469–c1539, which developed into a military confraternity. Nanak's birthday is celebrated every year at his shrine at Nankana Sahib in Pakistan. The last of the gurus died in 1708, and the Granth Sahib (the sect's holy book) has taken the place of a leader. After the partition of India, Sikhs were concentrated in E Punjab◊ and, by the efforts of Sant Fateh Singh c1911–72, this became a separate Sikh state in 1966. However, the Alkali separatist movement agitates for a completely independent Sikh state, Khalistan, and a revival of fundamentalist belief was headed from 1978 by Sant Jarnail Singh Bhindranwale 1947–84, killed in the siege of the Golden Temple, Amritsar◊. India has 10 million Sikhs□

Si-Kiang see Xi◊ Jiang□

Sikkim NE state of India: formerly a protected state, it was absorbed by India in 1975, the monarchy being abolished. China does not recognize India's sovereignty.
area 7298 sq km/2817 sq mi
capital Gangtok
features Mount Kanchenjunga; rich wildlife including birds, butterflies, and orchids
population 315 000
language English, Bhutia, Lepcha, Khaskura (Nepali) (all official)
religion Mahayana Buddhism, Hinduism□

Sikorski Wladyslaw 1881–1943. Polish general. He was Prime Minister 1922–3, and again from 1939 as the head of the exiled government in London□

silage green crops harvested for fodder, and partly fermented, usually in a cylindrical tank (silo)□

Silbury Hill steep, rounded artificial mound (40 m/130 ft high) of the Bronze Age 2660BC, in Wiltshire, near Avebury◊, England; purpose unknown, but possibly moon worship□

Silchester see under Hampshire◊□

sild a small edible fish; see under herring◊□

Silenus in Greek mythology, companion of Dionysus◊, portrayed as a jovial old man, usually drunk□

Silesia long-disputed region of Europe, Austrian 1675–1745; Prussian/German 1745–1919 (having been seized by Frederick II of Prussia); and in 1919 divided among newly-formed Czechoslovakia, revived Poland, and Germany, who still retained the major part. In 1945 all German Silesia east of the Oder-Neisse line was transferred to Polish administration: about 10 million inhabitants of German origin, both here and in Czechoslovak Silesia, were expelled. The chief towns with their German names in brackets are: Wroclaw (Breslau), Katowice (Kattowitz), Zabrze (Hindenburg), Chorzow (Königshütte), Gliwice (Gleiwitz), and Bytom (Beuthen) in Poland, and Opava (Troppau) in Czechoslovakia□

silhouette profile or shadow portrait in black on a white ground. Cheap to produce, it was named after the parsimonious French finance minister Étienne de Silhouette 1709–67□

silica silicon dioxide SiO_2, the commonest mineral, of which the most familiar form is quartz. Chalcedony is a semi-precious form, which includes the banded agate, onyx, and sardonyx (which lend themselves to the making of cameos, and are often used in other jewellery); red carnelian; brownish jasper; and flint. See also opal◊□

silicon element
symbol Si
atomic number 14
physical description grey dark crystalline solid
features very abundant, it occurs in sand, quartz, clay, etc. It resembles carbon in its ability to bond with four adjacent atoms, facilitating the construction of complex molecules
uses in glassmaking, as a hardener in steel alloys, in making silicone, grease oils and lubricants, in silicon 'chips' for microprocessors and microcomputers, and in photovoltaic cells□

silicon chip see semiconductor◊, computer◊□

silicone see plastics◊□

Silicon Valley nickname of Santa Clara county, California, USA; site of many high-technology electronic firms from the 1950s□

silicosis disease of miners and stone cutters who inhale flint dust, which makes lung tissue fibrous□

silk product of the silkworm◊□

Silk Road ancient route by which silk was brought from China to Europe in return for trade goods; it ran via Transylvania, Mount Ararat, Samarkand, and the Gobi Desert. It has been revived as a tourist rail route□

silkworm usually the larva of the ***common silkworm moth*** *Bombyx mori*, which after hatching from the egg and maturing on the leaves of white mulberry trees (or a synthetic substitute) 'spins' a protective cocoon of fine silk thread (275 m/300 yd). It is killed before emergence as a moth to keep the thread intact, and several threads are combined to form the commercial silk thread woven into textiles. Other moths produce different types, e.g. ***tussah*** from *Antheraea mylitta*. Chief textile producers are Japan, China, Italy, France, and India□

Sillitoe Alan 1928– . British novelist, famous for his first book *Saturday Night and Sunday Morning* 1958, about a frustrated factory worker in his native Nottingham; also *The Loneliness of the Long Distance Runner* 1959□

Silone Ignazio. Pseudonym of Italian novelist of peasant life Secondo Tranquilli 1900–78, e.g. the socialist *Fontamara* 1933□

silver element
symbol Ag
atomic number 47
physical description shiny metal, very easily worked
features malleable and ductile; it conducts heat and electricity better than any other metal
uses used in jewellery, tableware, electroplating; compounds used in photography□

silverfish an insect. See bristletail◊□

Simberg Hugo 1873–1917. Finnish artist, specially noted for his wistfully sympathetic etchings of devils, and for his landscapes□

Simenon Georges 1903– . Belgian crime writer, born in Liège. Initially a pulp fiction writer, he created Inspector Maigret of the Paris Sûreté in 1930. His other novels include *The Stain on the Snow* 1948□

Simeon Stylites St c390–459. Syrian Christian ascetic, who lived 37 years on a pillar□

Simla capital of Himachal Pradesh state, India, 2300 m/7500 ft above sea level, population 45 000; and the summer administrative capital of British India 1864–1947□

Simon Claude 1913– . French novelist, an exponent of the *nouveau◊ roman*. Originally an artist, he abandoned the 'time structure' in such difficult novels as *The Flanders Road* 1960. Nobel prize 1985□

Simon Herbert 1916– . American social scientist. Researching decision-making in business corporations, he discovered that maximum profit was seldom the chief motive. Nobel prize for economics 1978□

Simon John Allsebrook, Viscount Simon 1873–1954. British Liberal politician. Home Secretary 1915–16, he resigned on the issue of conscription. He was Foreign Secretary 1931–5; Home Secretary again 1935–7; Chancellor of the Exchequer 1937–40, and Lord Chancellor 1940–5□

Simon Neil 1927– . American playwright, whose wrily comic plays include *Barefoot in the Park* 1963, *The Odd Couple* 1965, and *The Sunshine Boys* 1972; and the more serious, autobiographical *Brighton Beach Memoirs* 1983. He also wrote the musicals *Sweet Charity* 1966, *Promises, Promises* 1968 and *They're Playing Our Song* 1978. The Neil Simon theatre, W 52nd Street, New York, is named after him□

Simonstown see under Cape◊ Town□

simony buying and selling church preferments, etc., from ***Simon Magus*** (Acts viii) who offered money to the Apostles for the power of the Holy Ghost□

Simplon Alpine pass Switzerland–Italy; the road was built by Napoleon 1800–5, and the Simplon Tunnel, 19.8 km/12.3 mi, is one of the world's longest□

Simpson (Cedric) Keith 1907–85. British forensic scientist, head of department at Guy's Hospital 1962–72. He sent John Haig (the acid bath murderer) and Neville Heath to the gallows, and in 1965 identified the first 'battered baby' murder in England□

Simpson N(orman) F(rederick) 1919– . British dramatist, whose comedies *A Resounding Tinkle* 1957 and *One Way Pendulum* 1959 belong to the 'Theatre of the Absurd◊'□

Simpson Desert desert area in Australia, chiefly in Northern Territory; area 145 000 sq km/56 000 sq mi□

Sinai Egyptian peninsula at the head of the Red Sea; area 65 000 sq km/25 000 sq mi. It was occupied by Israel 1967–82. Resources include oil, natural gas, manganese, and coal; irrigation water from the Nile is carried under the Suez Canal□

Sinai Mount. Mountain near tip of the Sinai Peninsula (Gebel Mûsa, 2285 m/7497 ft), alleged site at which Moses◊ received the Ten Commandments□

Sinai Battle of. Battle 14–19 Oct 1973 between Egypt and Israel; more tanks were used than at Alamein. See Arab–Israeli◊ Wars□

Sinatra Frank 1917– . American singer, born in Hoboken, New Jersey. His songs include 'Night and Day', 'You'd Be So Nice to Come Home To', and 'My Way'; as an actor, he won an Oscar for *From Here to Eternity* in 1953□

Sinclair Sir Clive 1940– . British electronics engineer, inventor of the first pocket calculator and pocket television. Knighted 1983□

Sinclair Upton 1878–1968. American left-wing novelist, born in Baltimore. He is remembered for *The Jungle* 1906, dealing with the Chicago stockyards, and his Lanny Budd series 1940–53□

Sind province of Pakistan, mainly in the Indus delta; area 122 000 sq km/47 000 sq mi; population 13 965 000. There is agitation for its creation as a separate state, Sindhudesh□

Sinding Christian 1856–1941. Norwegian composer, remembered for his *The Rustle of Spring*□

Singapore Republic of

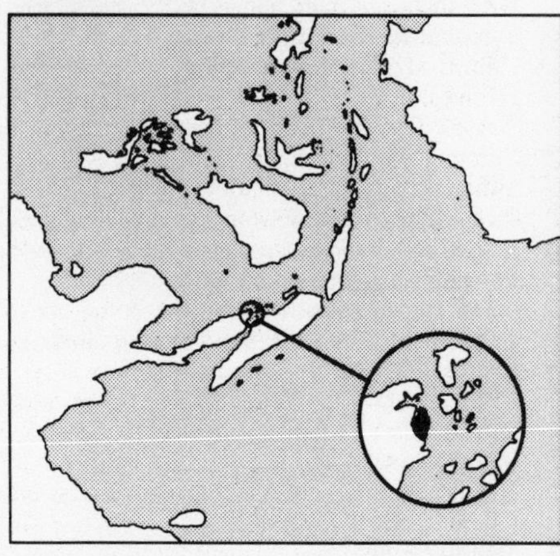

area 581.5 sq km/225.6 sq mi

capital Singapore City in the S of the island, a major world port and financial centre, founded by Stamford Raffles◊ (commemorated by a museum); its Changi Prison, where many Commonwealth and British POWs were held by the Japanese in World War II, is now open to tourists; the United◊ World College of S E Asia 1975 is here

features comprises Singapore Island (joined to the mainland by a causeway across the Strait of Johore) and 54 small islands; temperature ranges only between 24°–31°C/ 76°–87°F

exports electronics, petroleum products, rubber, machinery, vehicles, etc.

currency Singapore dollar

population 2 500 000; 75% Chinese; 14% Malay; 7% Tamil

language Malay, Chinese, Tamil and English (all official)

religion Buddhism, Taoism, Islam, Hinduism, Christianity

government there is a president (Wee Kim Wee from 1985) and unicameral parliament (Prime Minister Lee Kuan Yew◊ from 1959)

recent history leased from the Sultan of Johore in 1819 by the British East India Company on the advice of Stamford Raffles, it was in Japanese occupation 15 Feb 1942–12 Sept 1945. A separate crown colony from 1946, it became independent in 1959, was part of the Federation of Malaysia 1963–5, but then seceded as a separate republic□

single sideband transmission radio wave transmission using either the frequency band above the carrier frequency, or below, instead of both (as now)□

Sing Sing name until 1901 of the village of Ossining, New York, with a state prison from 1825□

Sining see Xining◊□

Sinkiang-Uighur see Xinjian◊ Uygur□

Sinn Féin Irish nationalist party ('We ourselves'), founded by Arthur Griffith 1905; see de◊ Valera. It is the political wing of the IRA, and is similarly split between comparative moderates and extremists□

Sino–Japanese Wars wars waged by Japan against China to secure expansion on the mainland.

First Sino–Japanese War 1894–5. Under the treaty of Shimonoseki, Japan secured the 'independence' of Korea; cession of Taiwan and the Pescadores◊, and of the Liaodong peninsula (for a naval base). France, Germany, and Russia pressurized Japan into returning the last-named, which Russia occupied in 1896 to establish Port Arthur (see Russo◊–Japanese War and Luda◊).

Second Sino–Japanese War 1931–45 was the prelude in the Pacific to World War II.

1931–2 the Japanese occupied Manchuria, which they formed into the puppet state of Manchukuo◊. They also attacked Shanghai, and moved into NE China, while Chiang◊ Kai-shek was busy attempting to suppress the Communists.

1937 Chiang Kai-shek and Mao◊ Zedong were now in alliance to fight the Japanese; full-scale war was renewed as the Japanese overran NE China and seized Shanghai and Nanjing.

1938 Japanese capture of Wuhan and Guangzhou was followed by the transfer of the Chinese capital to Chongqing◊; a period of stalemate followed.

1941 Japanese attack on Britain and the USA (see Pearl◊ Harbor) led to the extension of lease-lend aid to China, but the loss of Burma cut off a valuable source of supplies.

1944 a Japanese offensive seriously threatened Chongqing.

1945 the Chinese shared in the final offensive and received the Japanese surrender at Nanjing in Sept□

Sioux see under Plains◊ Indians□

Sioux Falls largest city in S Dakota, USA, its industry (electrical goods, agricultural machinery) powered by the Big Sioux river over the Sioux Falls 30 m/100 ft; population 81 000□

Siren in Greek mythology, a sea nymph who lured sailors on to rocks by her singing. Odysseus◊, in order to hear the Sirens safely, tied himself to the mast and stuffed his crews' ears with wax; the Argonauts (see Jason◊) escaped them because the singing of Orpheus surpassed that of the sirens□

sirenian herbivorous aquatic mammal, member of the tropical coastal order Sirenia, which allegedly gave rise to legends of mermaids, but look rather like a cross between a seal and a whale. Harmless and defenceless, they are endangered. They comprise:

dugong or ***sea-cow*** *dugong dugon* of the Indian and Pacific Oceans, 3 m/9 ft long, slow-moving and grazing on sea grass.

manatee *Trichechus* genus, of Africa and America, 4.5 m/15 ft long□

sirocco see under wind◊□

Sirte Gulf of. Gulf off the Libyan coast, on which Benghazi stands. Entry to it for manoeuvres is a bone of contention with the USA□

sisal see cannabis◊□

siskin a small finch◊□

Sisley Alfred 1840–99. French artist. Born in Paris, of English parents, he met and was influenced by Monet and Renoir. His landscapes show the effect of light at different times of day□

Sisyphus in Greek mythology, king of Corinth who, after his evil life, was condemned to roll a huge stone uphill, which always fell back before reaching the top□

sitar see under lute◊□

Sitting Bull c1834–93. American Indian chief, who led the Sioux onslaught against 'Custer's Last Stand'; see Plains◊ Indians. Amnestied, he died in later fighting□

Sitwell Dame Edith 1887–1964. British poet, sister of Osbert and Sacheverell Sitwell, with whom she enjoyed scandalizing the Establishment. She is remembered for her series of poems *Façade,* recitations to the specially written music of Walton◊ from 1923□

Sitwell Sir Osbert 1892–1969. British poet and author, elder brother of Edith and Sacheverell Sitwell, best-remembered for his series of autobiographical volumes: *Left Hand! Right Hand!, The Scarlet Tree, Great Morning, Laughter in the Next Room, Noble Essences* and *Tales My Father Taught Me* 1945–62□

Siva/Shiva see Hinduism◊□

Sixtus title of five Popes, including:

Sixtus IV 1414–84, Pope from 1471, who built the Sistine Chapel, which is named after him.

Sixtus V 1521–90, Pope from 1585, who supported the Spanish Armada against Britain and the Catholic League against Henry IV of France□

Sjaelland see under Denmark◊□

Skagerrak arm of the North Sea between

the S coast of Norway and the N coast of Denmark. See Battle of Jutland◊□

Skara Brae see under Orkney◊□

Skardu see Northern Territories◊□

skate a fish related to the ray◊□

skating self-propulsion on ice by means of bladed skates, or on other surfaces by skates with four small rollers. Ice-skating became possible as a world sport from the opening of the first artificial ice-rink in London in 1876, and the chief competitive events are figure skating, for singles or pairs, which includes both compulsory figures and freestyle combinations to music; ice-dancing, which is increasingly a choreographed combination of ballet and popular dance movements welded to an artistic whole, e.g. John Curry, and Jayne Torvill and Christopher Dean; and simple speed skating. The modern roller skate was the invention of James L Plympton, who opened the first rink at Newport, Rhode Island, USA, in 1866; events are as for ice-skating□

skeleton the hard frame which supports and protects the organs of most animals. The human skeleton consists of 200 bones, over half of which are in the hands and feet. The skull is mounted on the spinal column, a slightly curved chain of 24 vertebrae. The ribs, 12 on each side, are articulated (jointed) to the spinal column behind, and the upper seven meet the breast-bone (sternum) in front. The lower end of the spine rests on the triangular sacrum, to which are attached the two hip-bones (ilia), which are fused in front (symphysis pubis). Below the sacrum is the tail-bone (coccyx). These last four bones constitute the pelvis. The shoulder blades (scapulae) are held in place behind the upper ribs by muscles, and connected in front to the breast-bone by the two collarbones (clavicles). Each carries a cup (glenoid cavity) into which fits the upper bone of the arm (humerus). This articulates below with two bones, the radius and the ulna. The radius is articulated at the wrist to the bones of the hand. The upper end of each thigh-bone (femur) fits into a depression in the hip-bone; its lower end is articulated at the knee to both the bones of the leg (tibia and fibula), which are articulated at the angle to the bones of the foot. Bones are held together by joints (*articulations*). Some, but not all, of these allow movement of one bone on the other. At a moving joint the end of each bone is formed of tough, smooth cartilage, lubricated by synovial fluid. Points of special stress are reinforced by bands of fibrous tissue (*ligaments*)□

Skelton John c1460–1529. English poet,

skeleton

human skeleton

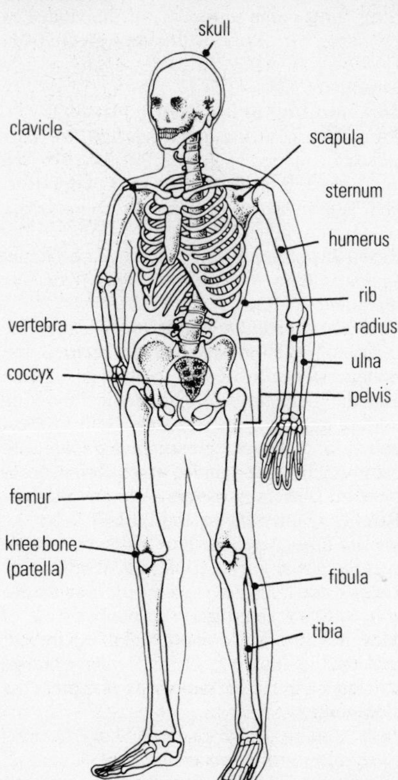

who was tutor to the future Henry VIII. His satirical poetry includes political attacks on Wolsey, e.g. *Collyn Clout* 1522 and the rumbustious *Tunning of Elynour Rumming*. He usually used short rhyming lines of irregular doggerel type□

skiing self-propulsion on snow by means of elongated runners for the feet, slightly bent upward at the tip, known from c3000BC, but developed for the modern sport only from 1896 when it became possible to manoeuvre more accurately. Events include downhill (with speeds up to 80 km/50 mi an hour); slalom, in which a series of turns between flags have to be negotiated; cross-country racing; and ski jumping, when over 150 m/400 ft is achieved from ramps up to 90 m/295 ft high. Allied to the ski is the N American Indian ***snow shoe***, a broad framework covered with a thong web, useful for travel in thick forest. In ***water skiing*** the skis are wider and shorter than those for snow, and the skier is towed by a motorboat□

skin the outer tissue covering the body. Its top layer (***epidermis***) consists of dead cells,

skin

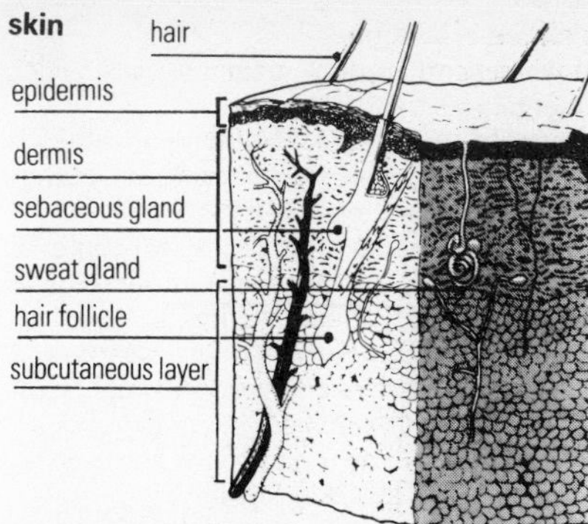

which are constantly being rubbed away and replaced from below, and the lower layer (***dermis*** or corium) of blood vessels, ***sebaceous*** (oil) ***glands***, ***sweat glands***, the endings of the sensory nerves, and hair roots, embedded in connective tissue. ***Skin diseases*** include dermatitis◊, herpes◊, impetigo◊, melanoma◊, ringworm◊. ***Skin grafts*** (following burns or other injuries) formerly needed to be taken from elsewhere on the patient's body, but artificial skin (from collagen, synthetic polymers, etc.) can now be used to aid healing□

skink a member of a family of short-limbed lizards◊□

skittles game (also known as ninepins) in which nine wooden pins, arranged with the aid of a diamond-shaped frame at one end of an alley, are knocked down by a ball thrown from the other. Either two players or two teams compete. The game resembles tenpin◊ bowling□

Skopje capital and industrial city (iron and steel, chromium mining, food processing) of Macedonia, Yugoslavia; population 506 600. It was destroyed by an earthquake in the 5th century and again in 1963, when it was rebuilt on a safer nearby site. It is an Islamic centre□

skua a large hawklike seabird. See under gull◊□

skull the assembly of 22 bones (eight flat plates, joined by sutures, forming the cranium and protecting the brain; and the irregular remainder forming the framework of the face for the eyes, nose and mouth). The mandible or lower jaw (the only movable bone) is hinged to the middle of the cranium at its lower edge. The floor of the skull is pierced by a great hole for the spinal cord and a number of other apertures through which pass other nerves and blood-vessels□

skunk a variety of N American mammal. See under weasel◊□

skydiving freefalling from an aircraft at up to 3650 m/12 000 ft, performing aerobatics, and then opening a parachute 600 m/2000 ft from the ground□

Skye see under Hebrides◊□

Skye terrier a breed of dog◊□

Skylab Mission see under Space◊ Research□

skylark a European lark◊□

Skyros see under Sporades◊□

skyscraper type of tall building first developed in 1868 in New York, USA, where land prices were high and the geology adapted to such methods of construction; today techniques have been evolved which also make them possible on London's clay and in earthquake areas. The world's highest is in Chicago◊□

Slade Felix 1790–1868. British art collector, who bequeathed his main collection to the British Museum; he endowed Slade art professorships at Oxford, Cambridge, and University College, London (where the Slade School is named after him)□

slander spoken defamatory statement (as opposed to libel◊), although if broadcast on radio or television either constitutes libel. Some slanders, such as imputing that a person is incapable in his profession, are actionable in the UK without the need to prove that pecuniary loss has been suffered□

slate fine-grained, bluish-purple rock, which readily splits into thin slabs, found in N Wales in especially high quality. Quarrying slate takes such skill and time that it is now seldom used for roofing except in restoring historic buildings; elsewhere tiles or substitutes are used□

Slav a member of an Indo-European people, speaking Slavonic languages, whose ancestors included the Sarmatians◊ and Scythians◊, and who spread outward from the Carpathians. By the 7th century they were the predominant population of east and south-east Europe, and fall into three groups: ***eastern*** includes the Russians, Belorussians, and Ukrainians; ***western*** the Poles, Czechs, and Slovaks; ***southern*** Serbs, Croats, Slovenes, Macedonians, and Bulgars□

slavery the legal and economic status of being the property of another person as in Ancient Greece and Rome; the serfdom of medieval Europe (not abolished in Russia until 1861); Negro slavery in the Americas, West Indies, etc. (see Wilberforce◊, Lincoln◊); and modern Arab states (not abolished in Saudi Arabia till 1963, and although officially abolished in Mauretania in 1980, it still survives)□

Slavkov see under Austerlitz◊□

Sleep Wayne 1948– . British dancer, who graduated from the Royal Ballet to the formation of his own company DASH in 1980; his *Hot Shoe Show* has been produced annually from 1983□

sleep unconscious state, the functions of which are obscure. Theories include:
resting the brain and ***saving energy*** (the brain uses a quarter of human energy), but the average reduction of activity, only 30%, is not highest in the areas most used in waking hours.
growth since growth hormones are released on a substantial scale in the early period of sleep, but this does not apply to all animals.
protection by keeping animals inactive and out of the way of predators.
updating, assimilating, and ***restoring the brain*** based on analogy with computers.
Length of sleep varies greatly in individual humans, and deprivation is not generally harmful, although it affects the ability to concentrate and prolonged deprivation of sleep may lead to hallucinations. In animals, a horse will sleep only two hours a day, and the giant sloth 20 hours. Sleep is divided into alternating periods of non-rapid eye movement (NREM), when the heartbeat is regular and no dreams occur, and rapid eye movement (REM) with irregular heartbeat and dreams. See also dream◊□

sleeping sickness acute disease (trypanosomiasis) caused by blood parasites (tryplariosma gambiense) carried by the tsetse fly. Symptoms are fever, rash, sensitivity of the bones, and drowsiness ending in death unless treated□

sleepy sickness epidemic form of encephalitis◊□

Sligo maritime county (county town Sligo) of the Republic of Ireland, province of Connacht◊□

Slim William Joseph, 1st Viscount Slim 1891–1970. British field marshal. A veteran of Gallipoli◊, he commanded the 14th 'forgotten' army 1943–5, stemming the Japanese invasion of India at Imphal and Kohima, and then recovered Burma. He was Governor-General of Australia 1953–60□

slime mould organism with both animal and plant characteristics, sometimes classed with fungi. It is composed of maybe 100 000 amoebae that usually feed on bacteria. When a food supply is exhausted, they form into a colony which looks like a single slug-like animal and migrates to a fresh source of bacteria. It then takes on the aspect of a plant, and fruiting bodies are formed which release spores to repeat the life cycle. One N American species is predatory on other slime moulds□

sloe see blackthorn◊□

sloth several tropical mammals; see under Edentata◊□

Slovakia area settled by Slavs in 5th–6th centuries, which in 1918 became E Czechoslovakia; former capital Bratislava□

Slovene a member of the Slav people of Slovenia◊, and parts of the Austrian Alpine provinces of Styria and Carinthia; their language resembles Serbo-Croat. Austria and Yugoslavia disagree over the rights of Slovenes in S Carinthia□

Slovenia constituent republic of Yugoslavia.
area 20 251 sq km/7819 sq mi
capital Ljubljana
features mountainous; rivers Sava and Drava
population 1 892 000, of whom over 1 700 00 are Slovene
language Slovene, resembling Serbo-Croat, written in Roman characters
religion Roman Catholicism
history until 1918 Slovenia was the Austrian province of Carniola□

slow-worm a limbless lizard◊□

small arms firearms which can be carried easily, including:
grenade container filled with explosive which is thrown by hand or fired by rifle.
pistol of which the modern forms are the ***revolver*** (invented by Samuel Colt in 1835) in which the bullet magazine chamber revolves behind the barrel to reload, and the ***automatic*** with a box magazine.
shotgun used mainly in hunting small game; it has an unrifled bore and discharges small shot at short range. A 'sawn-off' shotgun is one with the barrel shortened, usually by criminals wishing to carry it undetected.
rifle gun with spiral grooves cut inside the barrel to give the cartridge greater velocity and accuracy; the classic Lee-Enfield rifle, with bolt action, and cartridge magazine beneath the breach, remained the weapon of the British army from the late 19th century until well after World War II, and is still in use in trouble spots throughout the world, e.g. guerrilla fighting in Afghanistan. From 1985 the British army adopted the Enfield Weapon System (EWS) family, comprising the 30 round automatic SA 80 rifle and a light support weapon (light machine gun), both firing the standard Nato 5.56 mm round, and a multi-purpose bayonet.
machine gun small arm, usually mounted, which fires single shots, or bursts of ammunition, from a magazine (see Sir Hiram Maxim◊). The lighter ***sub-machine-gun*** fired from the hip, was a favourite gangster weapon in the Chicago of the 1920s, and was a widely-used weapon in World War II, e.g. the

recoil-operated Sten gun and the Thompson sub-machine gun or 'Tommy' gun. See also under rifle above□

smallpox contagious viral disease, marked by fever and skin eruptions leaving pitted scars. It was endemic in Europe until the development of vaccination, and remained so in Asia until worldwide eradication was achieved by a World Health Organization campaign 1980□

Smart Christopher 1722–71. British poet, confined to a lunatic asylum from 1756, but author of fine hymns, e.g. 'A Song to David', and 'Jubilate', the last appreciated today for its surrealism□

smelt small marine fish, family Osmeridae, related to the salmon, of which the most common European species, the ***sparling*** *Osmerus eperlanus*, has a delicate flavour□

Smersh see under KGB◊□

Smetana Bedřich 1824–84. Czech composer, conductor at the National Theatre Prague 1866–74. His music has a distinct national character, e.g. the operas *The Bartered Bride* 1866 and *Dalibor,* and the symphonic suite *My Country*. Deaf from 1874, he lost his reason in 1883, and died in an asylum□

Smiles Samuel 1812–1904. Scottish author of the extremely popular Victorian didactic work *Self Help* 1859□

Smith Adam 1723–90. Scottish economist and philosopher, whose *The Wealth of Nations* 1776 defined national wealth in terms of labour, as the only real measure of value, which is expressed in terms of wages. From this he proceeded to examine the mechanisms governing profits and rents, and advocated the free working of individual enterprise, and especially the necessity of 'free trade' rather than the protection offered by mercantile system□

Smith Bessie 1894–1937. American jazz and blues singer, born in Mississippi, known as 'Empress of the Blues' in the 1920s□

Smith (Francis) Graham 1923– . British astronomer-royal from 1982, and professor of radioastronomy at Manchester 1964–74, and from 1981□

Smith Ian Douglas 1919– . Prime Minister of Rhodesia (now Zimbabwe◊) 1964–79. He made a unilateral declaration of independence from Britain (UDI) 1965, maintaining it despite UN pressure and sanctions◊□

Smith John 1580–1631. English colonist, president of Virginia 1608–9, and explorer of New England 1614, which he named. He married Pocahontas◊, who is said to have saved his life while he was on an expedition among the American Indians□

Smith Joseph. 1805–44. US founder of the Mormons◊□

Smith Maggie (Margaret) Natalie 1934– . British actress, whose roles include the title part (winning an Oscar) in the film *The Prime of Miss Jean Brodie* 1969□

Smith Sir Ross Macpherson 1892–1922 and Sir Keith Macpherson Smith 1890–1955. Australian brothers, who made the first England to Australia flight 1919□

Smith 'Stevie' (Florence Margaret) 1902–71. British poet, for whose books include *Novel on Yellow Paper* 1936, and the verse *A Good Time Was Had By All* 1937 and *Not Waving but Drowning* 1957□

Smithfield site of a meat market (since 1868) in the City of London◊. It was formerly an open space where many Protestant martyrs were executed in the 16th century; Wat Tyler◊ was murdered 1381, and the Bartholomew◊ Fair was held 1614–1855□

Smithson James 1765–1829. British chemist and mineralogist, founder of the ***Smithsonian Institution*** Washington DC (museum, art gallery, zoo park, astrophysical observatory) by a bequest in 1846□

smog a mixture of smoke and fog◊□

Smolensk industrial city (textiles, clothing, distilleries, flour mills) in W USSR, on the river Dnieper; population 311 000. Founded 882, it was captured by Napoleon 1812, but he passed it again in his retreat from Moscow. The Germans took it 1941; it was liberated by the Russians 1943. In nearby ***Katyn Forest*** 4500 Polish officer POWs were shot in spring 1940, 10 000 others being killed elsewhere, after the German-Soviet partition of Poland; the Germans and Russians blame each other, but the balance of the evidence is against the Russians□

Smollett Tobias George 1721–71. British novelist. Born in Scotland, he became a naval surgeon, but from 1741 an author. His picaresque novels include *Roderick Random* 1748, *Peregrine Pickle* 1751, and *Humphrey Clinker* 1771, and his vivid characterization influenced Dickens◊□

smuggling illegal import or export of prohibited goods, or the evasion of customs duties on dutiable goods. In Britain in the 18-19th centuries smuggling had popular 'support' for such items as wines, brandy, tea, tobacco and lace, which were very heavily taxed. The modern large-scale international trade concentrates chiefly on illegal drug traffic□

smut and **bunt** a disease affecting flowering plants; see Basidiomycetes◊□

Smuts Jan Christian 1870–1950. S African field-marshal and statesman. In the South◊

African War he commanded the Boer forces in Cape Colony, but later worked for conciliation, and was Prime Minister of S Africa 1919–24 and 1939–48, supporting the Allied cause in both World Wars□

Smyrna former name of the Turkish port of Izmir◊□

Smyth Dame Ethel 1858–1944 . British composer. Her works include *Mass in D* 1893, and operas (*The Wreckers* 1906, *The Boatswain's Mate* 1916)□

Snaefell highest mountain in the Isle of Man◊□

snail several species of shelled mollusc; see under gastropod◊□

snake reptile of the suborder Ophidia/Serpentes, of the order Squamata, which also includes the lizards◊.

Like fish and amphibians, snakes cannot maintain a temperature differing from their environment (i.e. they are poikilotherms). Usually they have no legs but scaly skins in which the scales on the undersurface commonly assist movement. A snake is helpless on glass. The vertebrae may number 500. Hearing is chiefly limited to ground vibrations, so that it is the snake-charmer's movements rather than his music which affect a snake. Sight is poor, although movement is immediately detected, and some snakes, e.g. rattlesnakes, have a cavity between the eye and nostril sensitive to infra-red rays which assists in prey location in the dark. The sense of touch is acute, and the sense of smell is aided by the tongue, which picks up airborne particles for examination. All are carnivorous, the swallowing of large prey being assisted by their ability to open their jaws 180°.

In courtship rival males may display before the female by entwining with each other in ritual 'dances'. Some species lay eggs which are left to hatch, the young using an 'egg-tooth' to escape from the leathery capsule; others retain soft eggs until the young are ready to emerge. Snakes are seldom aggressive. Antivenins to counter their 'bites' are prepared from the snakes' own venom, which is 'milked' from them. The various venoms may act on the victim's nervous system by paralysis, or may act destructively on the blood and blood vessels. Interesting families include:

Colubridae the typical snake family, which contains three-quarters of the world's snakes, ranging from the harmless British ***grass snake*** *Natrix natrix*, to the deadly ***boomslang*** *Dispholidus typus* of S Africa.

The two families typical of snakes which kill by constriction, and are non-venomous:

Pythonidae of Africa, S Asia and Australia. Pythons may lay 100 eggs, and owing to the elasticity of their jaws can swallow large animals whole, e.g. a pig weighing 27 kg/60 lb.

Boidae of the New World, which include ***boa constrictors*** and the ***anaconda*** *Eunectes murinus* the latter being (at 11 m/36 ft) the world's largest snake.

Members of both families have rudimentary hind limbs.

Crotalidae the ***pit viper*** family, including the poisonous ***rattlesnakes*** of genera *Crotalus* and *Sistrurus* which have up to 14 horny flat rings at the end of the tail which rattle as a defensive signal when vibrated; the ***sidewinder*** *Crotalus cerastes* of N America, so-called because of its sideways forward movement (the heat-seeking air-to-air missile named after it has a similar motion); and the deadly ***bushmaster*** *Lachesis muta,* also of the New World.

Viperidae the ***viper*** family, which includes the ***adder*** *Vipera berus,* Britain's only poisonous snake (bite not usually fatal), which has a zig-zag line down the back; the very poisonous ***puff adder*** *Bitis arietans* of Africa and S Arabia, so-called because of its loud hiss; and the ***sand*** or ***horned viper*** *Cerastes cornutus,* said to be the asp of Cleopatra.

Elapidae the family to which most of the poisonous snakes belong, including the ***king cobra*** or ***hamadryad*** *Ophiophagus hannah* of S Asia, which raises a threatening 'hood' when attacked, can spit its venom 2 m/6 ft to blind an opponent, is able to kill a horse with 25 mg/.038 of a grain (a grain being 1/7000th of a pound) of venom, and reaches 5.5 m/18 ft. The Australian ***taipan*** *Oxyuranus scutellatus,* also found in New Guinea, is a small-headed cobra about 3 m/10 ft long; brown, with yellow spots beneath, it is the country's deadliest snake, the venom killing in a matter of minutes. Also highly poisonous are the arboreal ***green mamba*** *Dendroaspis angusticeps* of Africa, the ***kraits*** *Bungarus* of SE Asia and Australia, and the ***coral snakes*** *Micrurus* of America, which look like their name. ***Hydrophiidae,*** the ***sea snakes*** of Asia, E Africa and Australia, are the only snakes living in sea water□

Snake affluent of the Columbia river, USA; length 1670 km/1038 mi. It flows 65 km/40 mi through Hell's Canyon□

snapdragon perennial herbaceous plant, genus *Antirrhinum*, family Scrophulariaceae, with spikes of bright-coloured two-lipped flowers. Some garden species have been bred so large that bees have difficulty in depressing the lower lip to enter and pollinate them□

snipe characteristic marsh bird of the family Scolopacidae, order Charadriiformes; species include ***common snipe*** *Gallinago gallinago*, of Europe, and the ***great snipe*** *Gallinago media*, of which the males hold spring bachelor gatherings to show their prowess. It is closely related to the woodcock◊□

snooker game, derivative (via pool) of billiards◊, played with 22 balls: 15 reds (value 1 point); the single 'pool' balls, black (value 7 points), pink (6), blue (5), brown (4), green (3), yellow (2), and the white 'cue ball'. The object is to pocket a red ball and a 'pool' ball alternately, each time returning the 'pool' ball (but not the red) to the table until all the reds are pocketed, when the 'pool' balls are then potted in order of numerical value. The maximum possible 'break' (score at one turn) is 147, The advent of television, enabling large audiences to view the game has increased its popularity; champions include Alex Higgins, Steve Davis, Dennis Taylor, Ray Reardon□

snooker

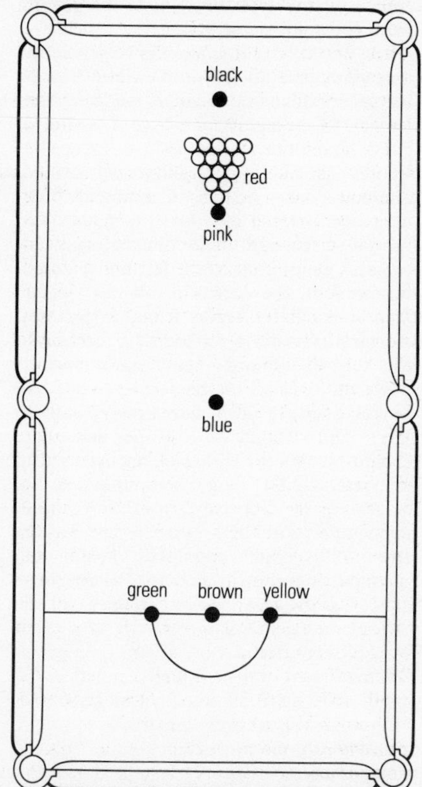

snoring noisy vibration of the soft palate during sleep when there is breathing through both mouth and nose in an attempt to increase oxygen intake. It is most liable to occur when the nose is blocked (e.g. by a cold) or among those who breathe less efficiently, especially those who are overweight and heavy smokers□

Snorri Sturluson Icelandic author of the Old Norse poems called Eddas◊□

Snow C(harles) P(ercy), Baron Snow 1905–80. English novelist and scientist, born at Leicester. His novel sequence *Strangers and Brothers* covers British society from the 1920s through the eyes of 'Lewis Eliot' (*The Masters* 1951, *The New Men* 1954, *Corridors of Power* 1964). Peerage 1964□

snow flaked particles formed by the condensation in air of excess vapour below freezing point; its whiteness comes from the reflection of light in the crystals of the flake□

Snowden Philip, 1st Viscount Snowden 1864–1937. British right-wing Labour politician, who pursued an orthodox financial policy as Chancellor of the Exchequer 1924 and 1929–31□

Snowdon the highest mountain in Wales; see Gwynedd◊□

Snowdon Anthony Armstrong-Jones, Earl of Snowdon 1930– . British photographer, who married Princess Margaret◊ 1960 (peerage 1961); divorced 1978□

snowdrop bulbous plant *Galanthus nivalis,* family Amaryllidaceae◊, with white bell-shaped flowers, touched with green, in spring□

snow leopard Asian member of the cat◊ family□

Snowy Mountains range in the Australian Alps, chiefly in New South Wales, which includes Mount Kosciusko, near which the Snowy river rises. There is a massive hydro-electric and irrigation system□

snuff finely powdered tobacco for sniffing up the nostrils; see under tobacco◊□

Soane Sir John 1753–1837. British architect, whose individual Neoclassical style resulted in works curiously presaging modern taste. Little of his major work, the Bank of England, London, remains. Other buildings include his own house in Lincoln's Inn Fields, London, now the Soane Museum□

soap chemical compound for washing, made by the action of caustic soda, or caustic potash, on animal or vegetable fats. See detergent◊□

soapstone rock from which talc is derived; see under talc◊□

Soares Mario 1924– . Portuguese Socialist statesman, who returned from exile in 1974, and as Prime Minister 1976–8, was pledged to achieve a 'socialist democracy'. In 1986 he was elected Portugal's first Socialist President□

Sobieski John. See John◊ III, king of Poland□

Sochi most popular seaside resort in the USSR, on the Black Sea; population 307 000. In 1976 it became the world's first 'no smoking' city□

social contract theory that humanity agrees to accept curbs on individual freedom to gain the greater good of a stable, civilized society. It has been used to support either absolutism (Hobbes◊) or democracy (Locke◊, Rousseau◊, Rawls◊). In the UK the term was used 1974–7 (when it broke down) to denote the unofficial Wilson government/trade union agreement that wage demands be moderated to avoid economic disruption□

Social Credit theory, of C H Douglas 1879–1952, that economic crises are caused by bank control of money, which leads to shortage of purchasing power. His remedy was payment of a 'social dividend'. There have been provincial Social Credit governments in Canada, but the central government has always vetoed the plan□

Social Democratic Party British breakaway party from Labour formed Mar 1981 by Roy Jenkins◊ (its originator and first leader), David Owen◊ (leader from 1983), Shirley Williams◊ and Bill Rodgers, hoping to gain popular support by taking a more centrist position than that of the Labour Party. The 1983 general election was fought in alliance with the Liberal◊ Party as the ***Liberal/SDP Alliance,*** the latter gaining 3 570 994 votes (Liberals 4 222 784), a quarter of the total national vote□

Socialism movement aiming to establish a classless society by substituting public for private ownership of the means of production, distribution, and exchange. The term has been used to describe positions as widely apart as anarchism and social democracy. Socialist ideas appeared in classical times, in early Christianity, among later Christian sects such as the Anabaptists◊ and Diggers◊; and in the ferment of the Revolutionary period at the end of the 18th and early 19th centuries were put forward as systematized political aims, e.g. by Rousseau◊, Saint Simon◊, Fourier◊, and Owen◊. Marx◊ (*Communist Manifesto* 1848) and Engels◊, in an age when faith in religion was being replaced among the newly literate by a faith in science, gave the movement wider appeal by promoting it on a pseudo-scientific basis as representing a stage in an inevitable historical succession (see Communism◊), the inevitability to be hastened by the 'class struggle' of the workers against the bourgeoisie (capitalists). In its perfected form, each citizen would give 'according to his abilities' and 'receive according to his need', and the state would wither away.

In the later 19th century Socialist parties arose in most European countries, e.g. in Britain the Independent◊ Labour Party, but there was a reaction against the revolutionary aspect of Marxism, e.g. in Britain the Fabian◊ Society. Divisions between 'right' and 'left' wings were accentuated by right-wing socialist support for World◊ War I, and the establishment of the first major Communist state in Russia. This lack of unity, in spite of the temporary successes of the Popular Fronts in France and Spain in 1936–8, aided the rise of Fascism◊ and National Socialism (Nazism◊) which appealed to popular nationalism and solved economic problems by similar means of state control of the economy, but in the general interests of private capital.

After World War II Communism was in the ascendant over Socialism in eastern Europe because of Soviet dominance, but in western Europe a Communist take-over of the Portuguese revolution failed 1975–6, and elsewhere, as in France under Mitterand◊, attempts at Socialist-Communist co-operation petered out. In Britain Socialism veered to the right under Wilson◊ and Callaghan◊, then again to the left under Foot◊, followed by the formation of the Social◊ Democratic Party. Under Kinnock◊ practical electoral considerations led to a reaction to the centre, although Socialism remains a powerful force within the party□

social security idea developed from the later 19th century in Europe that there should be state provision of financial aid to alleviate poverty e.g. compulsory social insurance in Germany from 1883; non-contributory old-age pensions in Britain from 1909, and compulsory health and unemployment insurance in Britain from 1911. Greatly extended in Britain under the Atlee◊ governments of 1945–51, as a result of the Beveridge Report (1942). Under the Thatcher government it was planned in the 1980s that there should be less state provision of social security benefits□

Society Islands an archipelago in French◊ Polynesia□

Socinus Latinized name of Italian Protestant theologian ***Lelio Francesco Maria Sozini*** 1525–62, whose Unitarian (see Unitarianism◊) views on the nature of Christ were developed by his nephew ***Fausto Paolo Sozzini*** 1539–1604. The latter's pacifism and anarchism constitute ***Socinianism***□

sociobiology study, originating with Edward Wilson◊, based on the assumption that social behaviour patterns in animals and man, e.g. aggression, altruism, male dominance, sexual division of labour, and xenophobia, are as much the product of evolution as are physical characteristics, and that present and future conditions may produce further change□

sociology term coined by Comte◊ 1837 for the systematic study of the development, organization, functioning and classification of human societies□

Socotra Yemeni island in the Red Sea; area 540 sq km/1400sq mi. The capital is Tamridah. Under British protection from 1886, it became part of S Yemen 1967, and is used as a military base by the USSR□

Socrates c469–399BC. Athenian philosopher, said to have been a sculptor and soldier. One of the main sources for his life is Plato◊, who may have attributed his own opinions to Socrates. He was a resolute opponent of tyranny, which may have brough about his trial. Accused in 399 on charges of impiety and corruption of youth, he was condemned to die by drinking hemlock◊□

Socratic method way of teaching used by Socrates◊, in which he aimed to guide pupils to clear thinking on ethics and politics by asking questions and then exposing their inconsistencies in cross-examination□

Soddy Frederick 1877–1956. British chemist, a pioneer of research into nuclear disintegration and radioactivity, and who coined the term isotope◊; Nobel prize 1921□

sodium element
symbol Na
atomic number 11
physical description very soft silvery-white metal
features very reactive, immediately tarnishing in air, forms compounds with most non-metals. It forms 0.2% of the human body
uses used in many chemical processes, its most common compound being common salt (sodium chloride NaC1)□

Sodom and **Gomorrah** two ancient cities in the Dead Sea area, recorded in the Old Testament as destroyed by fire and brimstone for their wickedness□

Sofia capital and industrial city (textiles, rubber, machinery, electrical equipment) of Bulgaria; population 1 082 500. The capital from 1878, it lies at the foot of the Vitosha Mountains, and is chiefly modern, with a 19th century cathedral□

software the programs written for computers. See computer◊□

Sogne the longest and deepest fjord in Norway◊□

Soho quarter of London, England between Charing Cross Road and Regent Street, with the offices of film and recording companies, boutique fashion (Carnaby Street), foreign restaurants, and many sleazy nightclubs, pornographic film shows, etc.□

Soissons industrial (metallurgy) and market town in Picardy region, N France; population 32 000. In 486 Clovis◊ defeated the Gallo-Romans here, ending their rule in France□

Sokoto trading centre in NW Nigeria; population 118 000. It was the capital of a Fula◊ sultanate from the 16th century to 1903, when it was occupied by the British□

Solanaceae temperate and tropical plant family with poisonous or narcotic constituents, and including henbane◊, mandragora◊, nightshade◊ and thorn apple◊, and the economically important potato◊, tomato◊, chilli◊, aubergine◊□

solan goose a large gannet; see under pelican◊□

solar energy energy from the sun; reaching us in the form of light and infra-red radiation. Its use for practical purposes may have been pioneered by Archimedes◊, who allegedly used mirrors to set fire to a Roman fleet attempting to conquer Syracuse. Harnessing such energy is non-polluting and cheap once the initial installation is made, whether in water heating from solar panels on a domestic roof, or in the solar furnace at Odeillo in the French Pyrenees, which uses 20 000 mirrors to generate a temperature of c3500°C/6300°F. Solar energy is also used aboard spacecraft; see under selenium◊□

solar pond natural or artificial 'pond', e.g. Dead◊ or Salton◊ Seas, in which the bottom water continually becomes saltier and hotter and so usable to generate electricity□

solar system the sun and the bodies within its gravitational field. Our solar system comprises the sun◊ and planets◊, and originated as a whole from a rotating cloud of gas and dust; similarly developing stars (such as our sun), some of which appear to have planetary systems, can be seen in other regions of space. Our solar system is part of the Milky Way (a disc-shaped galaxy◊)□

solar wind a stream of charged particles emitted by the sun; see under sun◊□

sole several varieties of flatfish◊□

Solent The. Channel between the coast of Hampshire, England and the Isle of Wight◊□

sol-fa short for tonic sol-fa, a method of teaching music, especially singing, systematized by John Curwen◊□

Solferino Battle of. See Napoleon◊ III□

solicitor in the UK; a lawyer who provides all-round legal services (making wills and winding up estates, conveyancing of property, divorce, litigation, defence of those accused of crime). In both civil and criminal cases above Crown Court level, a solicitor may not appear, but must brief a barrister◊ on behalf of his client, and in the most serious cases (e.g. murder), a Queen's◊ Council as well. Solicitors may become circuit judges and recorders□

Solicitor General in the UK; a law officer of the Crown, deputy to the Attorney◊-General, a political appointee with ministerial rank□

solid circuit see semiconductor◊□

Solingen industrial city (once famous for swords, but today producing high quality steel for razor blades, cutlery, etc.) in North Rhine-Westphalia, W Germany; population 161 100□

soliton non-linear wave, so-named from a 'solitary' wave seen on a canal by British engineer John Scott Russell in the 19th century. He raced after it on his horse for over a mile before losing it. Proceeding as a smooth, raised and rounded form, rather than widening and dispersing normally, it was characteristic in its behaviour of the waves of energy which constitute the particles of atomic physics□

Solomon King of Israel c974–c937BC. In Old Testament, the son of David◊ by Bathsheba, who built the temple at Jerusalem with the aid of heavy taxation and forced labour. Nevertheless, he was famed for his wisdom, the much later biblical *Proverbs, Ecclesiastes,* and *Song of Songs* being attributed to him. The so-called ***King Solomon's Mines*** at Aqaba (copper and iron) are of later date□

Solomon Islands archipelago in the W Pacific; c1450 km/900 mi long. The northern islands of Bougainville and Buka are part of Papua◊-New Guinea; the remainder form the independent state of the Solomon◊ Islands□

Solomon Islands

area 29 785 sq km/11 500 sq mi

capital Honiara on Guadalcanal

features comprises the southern islands of the archipelago including the largest, Guadalcanal (area 4000 sq km/2500 sq mi), Malaita, San Cristobal, New Georgia, Santa Isabel, Choiseul; mainly mountainous and forested, with rivers ideal for hydroelectric power

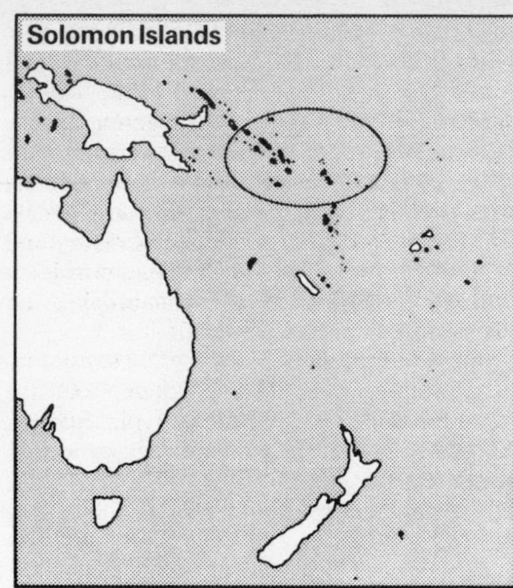

exports palm-oil, copra, rice, timber

currency Solomon Island dollar

population 263 200, the majority Melanesian

language English (official)

religion Christianity

government constitutional monarchy with Elizabeth II of Britain as head of state; governor-general and unicameral parliament (Prime Minister Sir Peter Kenilorea from 1984)

recent history the islands came under British protection 1893–9 and gained independence within the Commonwealth in 1978. During World War II the islands saw fierce fighting between Japanese and US and Australian troops, especially Guadalcanal, invaded by the Japanese Jan 1942, and retaken by US forces Aug 1942–Feb 1943□

Solomon's seal wild plant *Polygonatum multiflorum,* family Liliaceae, so-named from the 'hieroglyphic' leaf scars on its underground stem; it has bell-like flowers and blue-red berries□

Solon c638–558BC. Athenian statesman. As one of the chief magistrates c594, he carried out the revision of the constitution which laid the foundations of Athenian democracy□

solstice either of the two points reached by the sun, when its declination is greatest N or S; also the time of year at which they occur, c21 June and 21 Dec□

Solti Sir Georg 1912– . Hungarian-born British conductor, musical director at Covent Garden 1961–71□

Solway Firth inlet of the Irish Sea, formed by the estuary of the Esk, between England and Scotland at the W end of the border□

Solzhenitsyn Alexander 1918– . Russian novelist. After distinguished military service, he revolted against Stalinism and was in prison and exile 1945–57. However, Khrushchev◊ ensured publication of *One Day in the Life of Ivan Denisovich* 1962, dealing with the labour camps under Stalin. More basic criticism of the system in the novels *The First Circle* and *Cancer Ward* 1968, and the exposé of the whole Russian camp network in *The Gulag Archipelago* 1973, led to his deportation. He has adopted a Christian position, and his criticism of Western materialism is also stringent. Nobel prize 1970□

soma intoxicating drink of the gods, especially associated with Indra◊; made from an unknown plant, it was used in Vedic ritual□

Somalia Democratic Republic of

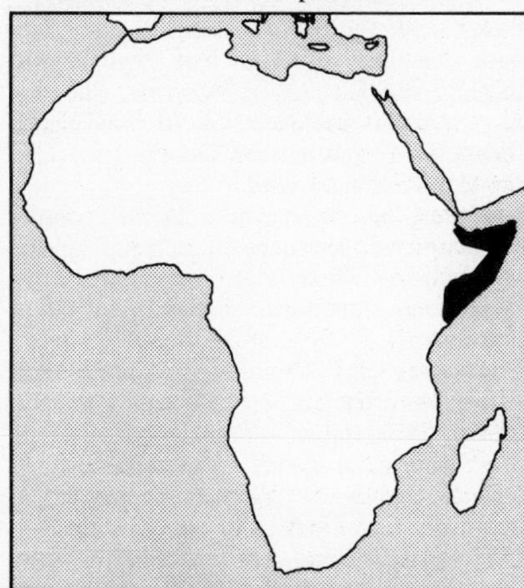

area 700 000 sq km / 270 000 sq mi
capital Mogadishu
towns Hargeisa, Kisimayu; port Berbera
features one of the world's poorest countries; many of the people are still nomadic raisers of livestock
exports livestock, skins, hides, bananas
currency Somali shilling
population 5 500 000, including 1 million refugees from W Somalia
language Somali national language; Arabic also official; Italian, English
religion Sunni Islam
government under the 1979 constitution there is an executive president (Major-General Mohammed Siyad Barre from 1969) nominated by the Revolutionary Socialist Party (the only legal party) and elected by the People's Assembly, elected by popular vote
recent history the country was formed in 1960 by the union of the British and Italian Somaliland◊, and maintains claims on Djibouti◊, Kenya's NE province, and the Ogaden◊ district of Ethiopia, all with Somali populations. Somalia invaded the last-named in 1977–8, at first aided by the USSR, but following the fall of Haile◊ Selassie the Soviet Union assisted Ethiopia instead. Somalia now has a token US presence, and guerrilla war continues□

Somaliland region of Somali-speaking peoples in E Africa including British Somaliland Protectorate (established 1887), Italian Somaliland (made a colony in 1927, conquered by Britain in 1941 and administered by her until 1950), which both became independent as the Somali◊ Democratic Republic◊ in 1960; and French Somaliland (1892–1967, when it became known as the Territory of the Afars and Issas until independence as Djibouti in 1977)□

Somerset SW county of England

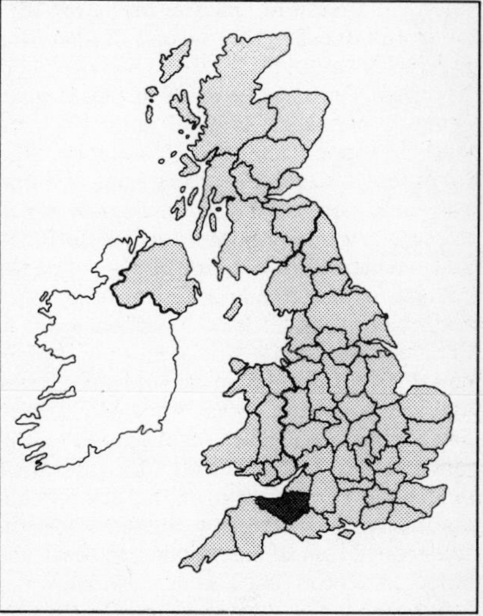

area 3451 sq km/sq mi
towns administrative headquarters Taunton; Wells, Bridgwater, Glastonbury
features rivers Avon, Parret, and Exe; marshy coastline on the Bristol Channel; Mendip Hills (including Cheddar Gorge and Wookey Hole, a series of limestone caves where Old Stone Age flint implements have been found) and the Quantock Hills; Exmoor◊
products dairy products, cider
population 427 200
famous people Henry Fielding□

Somerset Edward Seymour, 1st Duke of Somerset c1506–52. English statesman. Created Earl of Hertford, after Henry VIII's marriage to his sister Jane, he became Duke of Somerset and Protector (regent) for Edward VI in 1547. His attempt to check enclosure◊ offended landowners and his moderation in religion the Protestants, so that he was beheaded on a fake treason charge□

Somerset House building (1775) in the Strand, London, with a river facade by Sir

William Chambers◊, now used by the Principal Probate Registry (for wills), and King's College. It formerly housed the General Register Office of births, marriages, and deaths, now moved to St Catherine's House□

Somerville Edith Oenone 1861–1949. Irish novelist, collaborator with her cousin Violet Martin◊□

Somme river in N France, on which Amiens and Abbeville stand; length 240 km/150 mi□

Somme Battle of the. Allied offensive in World War I Jul–Nov 1916 Beaumont-Hamel–Chaulnes, during which tanks were first used (see Cambrai◊). The German offensive around St Quentin Mar–Apr 1918 is sometimes called the 'Second Battle of the Somme'□

Somoza Anastasio 1896–1956. Nicaraguan general, president 1937–47 and 1950–56, with US support until his assassination, who extended his power throughout Central America◊, and established a dynasty which ended when his son ***Anastasio Somoza*** 1925–80 (president 1967–72, and 1974–9) fled the country at the Sandinista (see Nicaragua) revolution, and was assassinated in Paraguay□

sonar ***so***und ***na***vigation and ***r***anging, name adopted by NATO 1963 for Asdic (***A***llied ***S***ubmarine ***D***etection ***I***nvestigation ***C***ommittee), used in World War I for submarine detection. The location of the enemy submarine is determined by the time a high-frequency beam of sound takes to reach the object and 'echo' back, hence also known as 'echo-sounder'□

sonata composition for one or two instruments (for three it is a ***trio***, for four a ***quartet***), rather than voices. There are usually three or four related movements□

sonata form musical framework of a composition, typically involving division into exposition, development, and recapitulation sections. It forms the basis for much of classical music, including sonatas◊, symphonies◊, and concertos◊□

Sondheim Stephen (Joshua) 1930– . American lyricist of *West Side Story* 1957 and of words and music of *A Little Night Music* 1974□

son et lumière French 'sound and light', the night time dramatization of the history of a famous building, town, etc. using theatrical lighting effects, sound effects, and narration; invented by Paul Robert–Houdin, curator of the Château de Chambord□

song composition for one or more singers. Great song composers include: *English* Dowland, Purcell, Arne, Parry, Delius, Warlock, Ireland, Britten *French* Gounod, Debussy, Fauré, Poulenc, Ravel *German* Mozart, Beethoven, Schubert, Schumann, Wolf, Richard Strauss, Mahler, *Hungarian* Liszt *Russian* Moussorgsky, Rachmaninov, Glinka *USA* Ives, Gershwin□

sonnet 14-line poem of Italian origin introduced to England by Sir Thomas Wyatt◊ in the form used by Petrarch (rhyming abba abba cdcdcd or cdecde), as followed by Milton and Wordsworth; Shakespeare used the form abab cdcd efef gg□

Soochow former name for the Chinese city of Suzhou◊□

Sophia 1630–1714. Electress of Hanover◊, daughter of the Elector Palatine and Elizabeth, daughter of James I of England, she married the Elector of Hanover. She was recognized as in succession to the English throne 1701, and her son George I founded the Hanoverian dynasty□

sophist Greek 'wise man', one of a group of 5th century BC lecturers on culture, rhetoric and politics, whom Plato regarded as dishonest, hence 'sophistry' meaning fallacious reasoning□

Sophocles 495–406BC. Greek dramatist, who said of Euripides◊: 'He paints men as they are, I paint men as they ought to be.' His most famous tragedies deal with Theban legend: *Antigone* 441, *Oedipus Tyrannus* date unknown, and *Oedipus at Colonus* 401. He lived at Athens under Pericles◊ and was the friend of Herodotus◊□

Sopwith Sir Thomas 1888– . British designer of the Sopwith Camel biplane used in World War I□

sorbic acid acid derived from the berries of the mountain◊ ash□

Sorbonne part of the University of Paris; see under Paris◊□

sorbus genus of deciduous trees and shrubs of the northern hemisphere, family Rosaceae◊, generally with white flowers, e.g. mountain ash, white beam, service◊ tree□

Sorel Georges 1847–1922. French philosopher, believed that socialism could only come about through a general strike; his theory of the need for a 'myth' to sway the body of the people, was used by Fascism; see also Syndicalism◊□

sorghum a genus of tropical grasses◊□

sororities a club or society for university women; see under fraternities◊□

sorrel species of plants in genus *Rumex*, family Polygonaceae, especially *R acetosa* grown for salad leaves□

SOS internationally recognized distress signal; see under Morse◊ code□

Soto Hernando de c1496–1542. Spanish

explorer. In his expedition of 1539, he explored Florida and the Mississippi□

sound vibrations of air registered by the ear in human beings, but see under lobsters◊ and spiders◊. Pitch of sound depends on the frequency◊ of vibrations, loudness, or amplitude. For humans, the lowest audible note has a frequency of about 26 Hz (26 cycles per second) and the highest, 20 000 Hz, though the upper limit falls steadily from adolescence onwards. Sound vibrations travel as waves with a speed of 340m (1120ft) per second under ordinary conditions.

Recording, in which the pioneers were Edison◊ with his phonograph and Emile Berliner, inventor of the disc record in 1896, is now done by two methods: ***analogue*** sound waves are used to make wavy undulations in the groove of a disc record, or wavy magnetic patterns in the coating of a tape; ***digital*** sound waves are electronically sliced, the measurement of each slice being rendered in binary◊ code. Each wave then emerges as if expressed in a 'Morse◊ code', not of 'dot-dash' but 'pulse-gap'. Each slice is rendered by 16 such pulses, or ***bits*** of information. Since the latter are not affected in re-recording by any background noise, any number of copies can be made without loss of quality. See radio◊□

Sound The. Strait dividing SW Sweden from Denmark and linking the Kattegat◊ and the Baltic; length 113 km/70 mi; width 5–60 mi/3–37 mi□

Souphanouvong Prince 1912– . Laotian statesman. After an abortive revolt against French rule in 1945, he led the guerrilla Pathet Lao, and in 1975 became first president of the Republic of Laos□

Sousa John Philip 1854–1932. American composer of marches, such as 'The Stars and Stripes Forever' 1897, who was bandmaster of the US Marines from 1880 and of his own band from 1892□

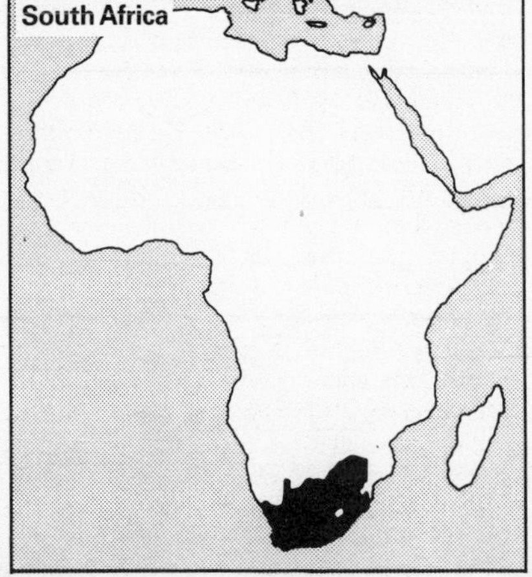

South Africa Republic of (Afrikaans ***Republiek van Suid Afrika***)

area 1 223 181 sq km/3472 294 sq mi

capital Cape Town (legislative), Pretoria (administrative)

towns Johannesburg, Bloemfontein; ports Cape Town, Durban, Port Elizabeth

features Drakensberg Mountains, Table Mountain; Limpopo and Orange rivers; the Veld and the Karroo; part of Kalahari Desert; Kruger National Park, established by Kruger 1898, largest in the world at 21 000 sq km/8000 sq mi; Johannesburg gold mines and Kimberley diamond mines; Lesotho◊ and Swaziland◊ form enclaves

exports maize, wool, fruit, gold, platinum (world's largest producer), diamonds

currency rand

population 31 700 000, 68% black (of whom the largest nations are the Zulu, Xhosa, Sotho and Tswana), 18% White, 10% Coloured, and 3% Asiatic

language Afrikaans and English, both official; there are also varied Bantu languages

religion 75% Christianity, organized on colour lines, the leading White denominations being the Nederduits Gereformeerde Kerk, Anglican, Methodist and Catholic; the three latter also have non-white congregations

famous people *dance* John Cranko *literature* Laurens van der Post, Nadine Gordimer *theatre* Athol Fugard *politics* L S Jameson, Jan Smuts, H F Verwoerd, B J Vorster, Nelson Mandela

government executive president, chosen by an electoral college drawn from the three houses of Parliament (P W Botha◊, National Party, from 1984), and a president's council (White, Coloured and Indian); black affairs are vested in the president (the Black◊ National States being held to give them self-government). Under the constitution of 1984, parliament comprises three houses: house of assembly (White), house of representatives (Coloured), and house of delegates (Indian), which legislate each for their own affairs: general legislation having to pass all three houses. Blacks are excluded from direct participation in government, and are systematically segregated from Whites under a policy of apartheid◊

recent history Dutch settlement began in 1652, but Cape Town became British in 1814 by purchase, and by 1836 the Dutch (Boers) set out on the Great Trek to found the Transvaal and Orange Free State to escape British rule (see also Natal◊). The discovery of diamonds

1867 and gold 1886 led to friction between incoming Uitlanders (foreigners) and the small number of Boers, who denied the newcomers all rights (see South◊ African Wars). A non-vindictive peace prepared the way for the formation of the independent Union of S Africa within the Commonwealth in 1910. A Boer revolt on the outbreak of World War I was crushed by Smuts◊, and German SW Africa (Namibia◊) was occupied, as was Italian E Africa (Somalia◊) in World War II. S Africa became a republic in 1960, and in 1961 left the Commonwealth, unable to accept the opposition of other members to apartheid which enforced 'separate development' for the races. Opposition to modifications of apartheid led to the establishment in 1984 of the Afrikaner Volkswag ('People's Guard') to unite various right-wing movements. There has been mounting international pressure for a general reform. Internal opposition to apartheid ranges from Buthelezi◊'s Inkatha to the African◊ National Congress (ANC) which went underground after the Sharpeville◊ massacre in 1960 and removed its base to Lusaka, Zambia; it aims at taking power by armed struggle, peaceful protest having failed (see Nelson Mandela◊). The situation worsened in 1986 with riots in the Black townships savagely repressed by the state. There are world-wide calls for stronger sanctions against S Africa□

South African Wars two wars between the Boers and the British; essentially fought for the gold and diamonds of the Transvaal:

War of 1881, was triggered by the attempt of the Boers of the Transvaal◊ to reassert the independence surrendered in return for British aid against native people. The British were defeated at Majuba, and Transvaal again became independent.

War of 1899–1902, also known as the ***Boer War***, was preceded by the armed Jameson Raid into the Boer Transvaal, inspired by Rhodes◊ to precipitate a revolt against Kruger◊, the Boer leader, which failed. The Uitlanders (non-Boer immigrants) were still not given the vote by the Boers, negotiations failed, and the Boers invaded British territory, besieging Ladysmith◊, Mafeking◊, and Kimberley◊. In 1900 Roberts succeeded Buller in command of the British, and was himself succeeded late that year by Kitchener◊. Kitchener countered Boer guerrilla warfare by putting the non-combatants who supported them into concentration camps (c26 000 women and children died of sickness). The war ended with the Peace of Vereeniging when the Boers surrendered□

South America fourth largest of the continents, nearly twice as large as Europe

area 17 854 000 sq km/6 891 644 sq mi

largest cities (over 3.5 million) Buenos Aires, São Paulo, Rio de Janeiro, Bogotá, Santiago, Lima, Caracas

features Andes in the west, Brazilian and Guiana highlands; central plains from the Orinoco basin to Patagonia; Parana-Paraguay-Uruguay system flowing to form the La Plata estuary; Amazon river basin, with its remaining great forests, with their rich fauna and flora

exports coffee, cocoa, sugar, bananas, oranges, wine; meat and fish products; cotton, wool; handicrafts; minerals incuding oil, silver, iron ore, copper

population 232 418 000, originally American◊ Indians, who survive chiefly in Bolivia, Peru, and Ecuador, and are reviving in numbers; in addition there are many mestizo (people of mixed Spanish or Portuguese and Indian ancestry) elsewhere; many people originally from Europe, largely Spanish, Italian and Portuguese; many of African descent, originally imported as slaves; and, more recently, Japanese and Vietnamese

language many American Indian languages; Spanish is the chief common language, except in Brazil (Portuguese)

religion Roman Catholicism; American Indian beliefs□

South America: history

South America
dates of independence are shown in brackets

for the archaic and later American Indian cultures, see American◊ Indians

16th century arrival of Europeans, with the Spanish (Pizarro◊) and Portuguese conquest;

the American Indians were mainly either killed, assimilated, or, where unsuitable for slave labour, replaced by imported slaves from Africa.
18th century revolt of Tupac◊ Amaru
19th century Napoleon's toppling of the Spanish throne opened the way for the independence of the Spanish colonies from the mother country; see Bolivar◊ and San Martín◊; Brazil became peacefully independent; large-scale European immigration took place (both Hispanic, and Italian and German) and interstate wars took a heavy toll, e.g. Paraguay War (see under Paraguay◊) and Pacific◊ War.
20th century rapid industrialization, and high indigenous population growth. Heavy indebtedness incurred to fund economic expansion led in the 1980s to inability to meet interest payments in the world slump□

Southampton industrial city (engineering, chemicals, plastics, flourmilling, tobacco) and port (passenger and container, a freeport◊) Hampshire, England; population 208 400□

Southampton Henry Wriothesley, 3rd Earl of Southampton 1573–1624. English courtier, patron of Shakespeare, who dedicated 'Venus and Adonis' and 'The Rape of Lucrece' to him, and may have addressed him in the sonnets□

South Asia Regional Cooperation Committee organization (SARC) established 1983 by India, Pakistan, Bangladesh, Nepal, Sri Lanka, Bhutan and the Maldives; to cover agriculture, telecommunications, health, population, sport, art, culture□

South Australia state of the Commonwealth of Australia
area 984 341 sq km/380 054 sq mi
capital and chief port Adelaide
towns Whyalla, Port Pirie
features Murray Valley irrigated area, including wine-growing Barossa Valley; Lakes Eyre◊ and Torrens◊; Mount Lofty, Musgrave and Flinders Ranges; and part of the Nullarbor◊ Plain, and Great Victoria and Simpson deserts; experimental rocket range in the arid N at Woomera; and at Maralinga British nuclear tests were made 1963 in which Aborigines were said to have died
exports meat and wool (80% of area cattle and sheep grazing); wines and spirits; dried and canned fruit; iron (Middleback Range); coal (Leigh Creek), copper, uranium (Roxby Downs); oil and natural gas in the NE; lead, zinc, iron; opals; household and electrical goods, vehicles
population 1 285 000, including 9500 Aboriginals
history possibly known to the Dutch in the 16th century, it was surveyed by Tasman◊ 1644. The first European settlement was founded in 1834, it became a province in 1836, and became a state of the Commonwealth of Australia 1901□

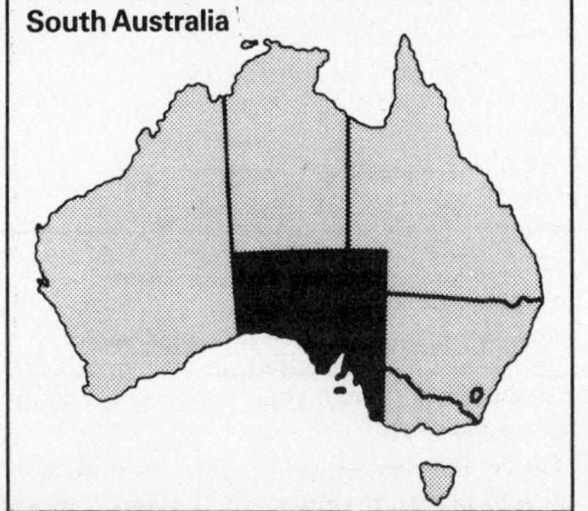

South Carolina state of the USA; Palmetto State

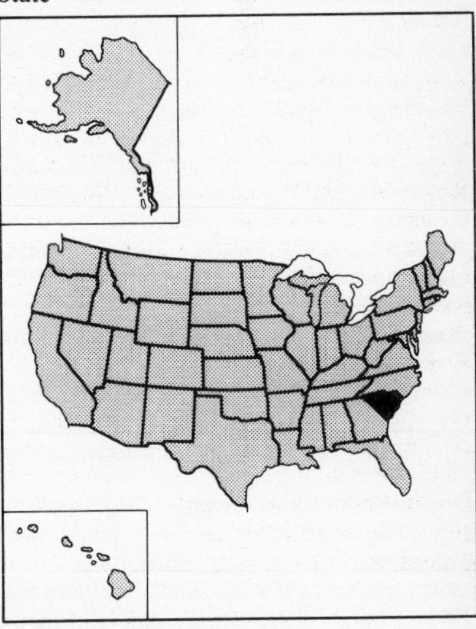

area 80 432 sq km/31 055 sq mi
capital Columbia
towns Charleston, Greenville
features large areas of woodland; subtropical climate in coastal areas
products tobacco, cotton, soybeans; meat products; textiles, clothing, paper and woodpulp, furniture, bricks
population 3 068 000
famous people John C Calhoun
history originally settled by Spain, it was one of the Thirteen◊ Colonies, and the first state to secede from the Union in 1860□

South Dakota state of the USA; Coyote or Sunshine State
area 199 550 sq km/77 047 sq mi

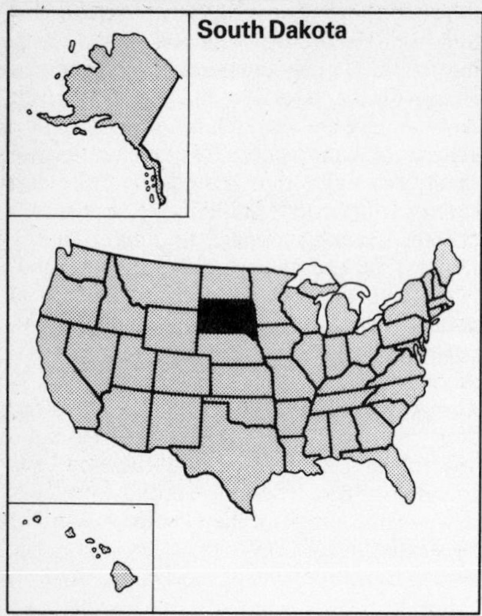

capital Pierre
towns Sioux Falls
features Great Plains; Black Hills (which include granite Mount Rushmore, on whose face giant relief portrait heads of Washington, Jefferson, Lincoln and Theodore Roosevelt are carved; see Borglum◊); Badlands
products cereals; livestock; gold (greatest USA producer)
population 690 178
famous people Crazy Horse, Sitting Bull, Ernest O Lawrence
history originally claimed by the French in the 18th century, it was settled by Americans from 1794, and became a state in 1889□

South-East Asia Treaty Organization (SEATO) collective defence system analogous to NATO established 1954 (Australia, France, New Zealand, Pakistan, the Philippines, Thailand, UK and USA, with Vietnam, Cambodia and Laos as protocol states). After the Vietnam War it was phased out by 1977, and its non-military aspects assumed by ASEAN◊. See ANZUS◊□

South-East Cape most southerly point of Australia, in Tasmania□

Southend-on-Sea resort and industrial town (light engineering, radios and boatbuilding) in Essex, England; population 157 700. The shallow water of the Thames estuary enabled the building of a famous pier 2 km/1.25 mi long□

Southern and Antarctic Territories French overseas territory created 1955. It comprises the islands of St Paul and Amsterdam (area 67 sq km/28 sq mi), the Kerguelen and Crozet Islands (7515 sq km/2902 sq mi), and Adélie Land on Antarctica itself (area 432 000 sq km/166 800 sq mi); all are uninhabited, except for research stations□

Southern Cross a small constellation of stars in the Milky Way; see under constellation◊□

Southey Robert 1774–1843. British writer, friend of Coleridge and Wordsworth. He wrote excellent letters, and a Life of Nelson; he was Poet Laureate from 1813□

South Georgia island 1300 km/800 mi SE of the Falklands◊, from which it is administered, although a dependency of the UK; area 3775 sq km/1450 sq mi; population about 20 scientists of the British Antarctic Survey at Grytviken. Cook was the first to land 1775; Argentina formally claimed it 1927, and forcibly occupied it 3–25 Apr 1982. Bird Island to the NW is one of the richest animal sanctuaries on earth□

South Glamorgan county of S Wales

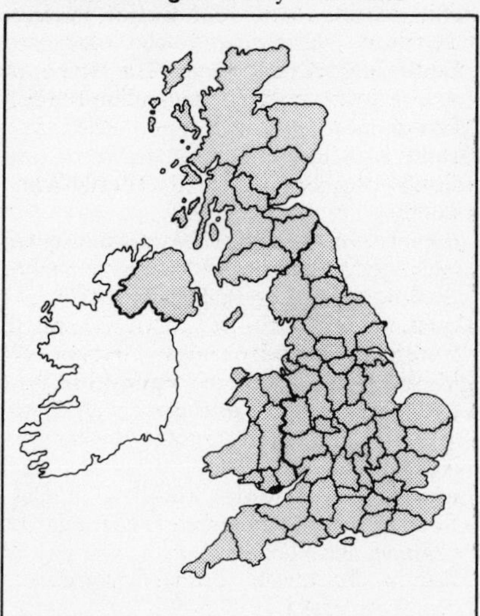

area 416 sq km/161 sq mi
towns administrative headquarters Cardiff Barry, Penarth
features fertile Vale of Glamorgan; Welsh Folk Museum, at St Fagans near Cardiff
products dairy farming, with industry round Cardiff
population 399 000
language English; 6% Welsh-speaking□

Southland Plain plain in the south of South Island, New Zealand, on which Invercargill stands□

South Orkney Islands barren, uninhabited group of islands in British◊ Antarctic Territory; area 620 sq km/240 sq mi□

South Sandwich Islands actively volcanic British group 750 km/470 mi SE of South◊ Georgia◊, administered from the Falkland Islands; area 337 sq km/130 sq mi; uninhabited; first formally claimed by Argentina in 1948; in Dec 1976 50 Argentine 'scientists' landed on Southern Thule (removed 20 June 1982). There is an ice-free port off Cumberland Bay□

Southsea English seaside resort in the district of Southsea. See under Portsmouth◊□

South Sea Bubble 1720. An 18th century British business and political scandal. In 1719 the South Sea Company, which had a monopoly of trade with S America, offered to take over the National◊ Debt in return for further concessions. Its shares soared, but when the 'bubble' burst and ministers were found to be involved, a political crisis ensued. Walpole◊ became Prime Minister and restored financial confidence□

South Shetlands archipelago of 12 uninhabited islands in the Southern Ocean; area 337 sq km/130 sq mi. See British◊ Antarctic Territory□

South Shields port in Tyne and Wear on the Tyne estuary, England; population 100 000□

South Uist an island on the Outer Hebrides◊□

Southwark borough of S central Greater London

features site of Globe Theatre (built by Burbage, Shakespeare and others in 1599 on Bankside, and burnt down 1613); 12th-century Southwark Cathedral; George Inn (last galleried inn in London); Imperial War Museum (all operations by British forces from 1914); Dulwich College and Picture Gallery, and the Horniman Museum (see Horniman◊)

population 210 000□

South West Africa former name (until 1968) of Namibia◊□

South Yorkshire former metropolitan county of England (1976–86)

area 1560 sq km/603 sq mi

towns administrative headquarters Barnsley; Sheffield, Doncaster

features River Don, part of Peak District National Park

products all the chief towns are metal-working centres; there is coal; and dairy, sheep, and arable farming is practised

population 1 300 900□

Soutine Chaim 1894–1943. Lithuanian-born Jewish artist, who lived in Paris. One of the leaders of French Expressionism, his portraits and landscapes have a distorted, frenzied form□

South Yorkshire

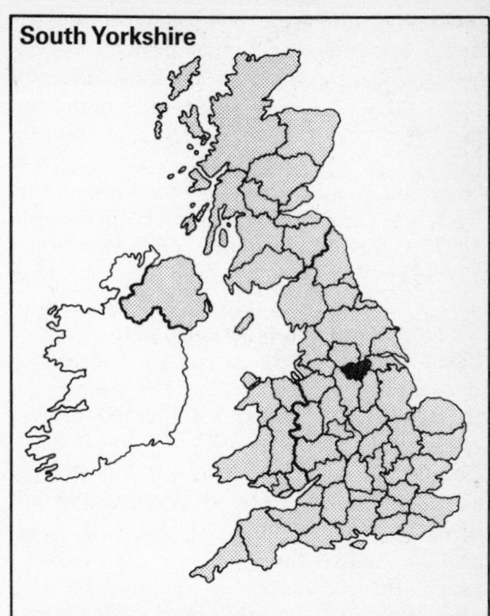

sovereign British gold coin introduced by Henry VII, and the standard British monetary unit 1817–1914. It is still struck as 'unofficial currency', notionally valued as one pound, but actually valued on the gold content. It is used abroad by those doubtful of paper currencies or bought by investors, in the same way as the Mexican 50-peso piece, S African krugerrand, and Soviet 10-rouble chervonetz□

Sovetsk city (until 1945 the Prussian ***Tilsit***) in USSR; population 50 000. In 1807 Napoleon signed peace treaties with Prussia and Russia here□

Soviet the original soviets (Russian 'council') were strike committees elected by Russian workers in the 1905 revolution, and in 1917 were set up by peasants, soldiers, and factory workers. These sent delegates to the All-Russian Congress of Soviets to represent their opinions to a future government; taken over by the Bolsheviks◊, they have ever since been mainly used to send Party instructions in the reverse direction. See USSR◊□

Soviet Far East geographical division of Asiatic USSR, on the Pacific coast, including Amur, Lower Amur, Kamchatka and Sakhalin regions, and Khabarovsk and Maritime terrs□

Soviet Union see Union◊ of Soviet Socialist Republics□

Soweto largest black city in S Africa (***So***uth ***We***st ***To***wnship) SW of Johannesburg, for which it provides a workforce. There were serious riots 1976 and 1985; population 1 000 000□

soya plant *Glycine hispida*, family Leguminosae, of E Asia. The foliage is used for forage, and the protein-rich seeds, 'soybeans', are used in cooking oils and margarine; and also made into flour and processed as textured vegetable protein (TVP)□

Soyinka Wole 1934– . Nigerian author, who was a political prisoner in Nigeria 1967–9 (prison memoirs *The Man Died* 1972). His works include the play *The Lion and the Jewel* 1963, and *Aké, The Years of Childhood,* an autobiography□

Spa town in SE Belgium; population 10 000. Famous since 14th century for its mineral springs, it gave its name to similar centres elsewhere□

Spaak Paul-Henri 1899–1972. Belgian Socialist Prime Minister 1938–9 and 1947–9, and many times Foreign Minister, he championed a united Europe□

space the continuum of the universe (see also relativity◊ theories), so-called because once thought empty. However, there is a great deal of thinly spread matter in our solar system, a vast amount of gas and dust between the stars of our galaxy, and more in inter-galactic space. The absorption of light by this tenuous material affects telescopic investigation.

Air space extends upwards from earth to 80 000 metres; ***outer space*** is the region beyond. A treaty of 1967 (UK, USA, USSR) bans the use of nuclear weapons in outer space, and the use of any celestial body for military purposes. See also space◊ research□

Space Agency European. Organization for space research established 1975 by the ten members of the European Community, superseding earlier bodies. The Ariane◊ project was taken over from it in 1980 by a consortium of banks, electronic and aerospace firms□

space research

1903 Tsiolkovsky◊ published the first practical paper on astronautics

1926 Goddard◊ launched the first liquid fuel rocket

1937–45 Von Braun◊ developed the V2 rocket

1957 Sputnik 1 ('fellow-traveller': USSR), first space satellite, orbited earth at a height of 229–898 km/142–558 mi in 96.2 min on 4 Oct

1957 Sputnik 2 (USSR), launched 3 Nov carrying a live dog 'Laika' (died on board 10 Nov)

1958 Explorer 1 (USA), the first US satellite, 31 Jan discovered Van Allen◊ radiation belts

1960 Tiros 1 (USA), the first weather satellite, launched 1 Apr

1961 Vostok 1 (USSR), first manned spaceship (Gagarin◊), recovered 12 Apr after a single orbit at a height of 175–142 km/109–88 mi in 89.1 min

1962 Friendship 7 (USA), Lieutenant Colonel John Glenn the first American in orbit round the earth on 20 Feb

1962 Telstar (USA), communications satellite, sent the first live television transmission between USA and Europe

1963 Vostok 6 (USSR), Valentina Tereshkova the first woman in space 16–19 Jun

1966 Venera 3 (USSR), space probe, launched Nov 1965, crash-landed on Venus 1 Mar, the first man-made object to reach another planet

1967 Soyuz 1 (USSR); Vladimir Komarov, the first man to be killed in space research when his ship crash-landed on earth on 24 Apr

1969 Apollo-Saturn 11 (USA), launched 16–24 Jul; Neil Armstrong◊ the first man to walk on the moon

1970 Luna 17 (USSR), 10 Nov–4 Oct; its unmanned lunar vehicle, *Lunokhod*, took photos and made soil analyses on moon

1971–2 Mariner 9 (USA), first space probe to orbit another planet, when it circled Mars

1971 Salyut 1 (USSR), the first orbital space station established 19 Apr; visited by Soyuz manned spacecraft

1972 Pioneer 10 (USA), earth's first starship (570 lb) launched 28 Feb; 1973 reached Jupiter; 1983 made first passage of the asteroid belt, reached Neptune, and passed on into the first voyage beyond our solar system

1972 Apollo 17 (USA), launched Dec; Jack Schmidt, a geologist, the first scientist in space

1973 Skylab 2 (USA), first US orbital space station established

1975 Apollo 18 (USA), 15–24 Jul, made joint flight with Soyuz 19 (USSR), in a link-up in space

1976 Viking 1 (USA), unmanned spacecraft launched 20 Aug 1975; reached Mars, the spacecraft lander touching down on 20 Jul 1976.

1976 Viking 2 (USA) launched 9 Sept 1975, lander touched down on Mars 3 Sept 1976

1977 Voyager 1 (USA), launched 5 Sept 1977 and Voyager 2 (USA), launched 20 Aug, both unmanned spacecraft, reached Jupiter Jan/Jul 1979, Uranus 1986, and expected to reach Neptune 1989

1978 Pioneer Venus 1 (USA) launched 20 May 1978 and Pioneer Venus 2 (USA)

launched 20 Aug 1978; both reached Venus Dec
1979 launched Ariane (European Space◊ Agency satellite launcher)
1981 Space Shuttle (USA), first re-usable manned spacecraft, launched 12 Apr
1982 Venera 13 and 14 (USSR) landed on Venus; soil samples indicated that the surface is similar to earth's volcanic rock
1985 two Vega probes (USSR) released balloons for the first time into the atmosphere of another planet (Venus)
1986 Space Shuttle (USA) exploded shortly after launch killing all seven crew members; space probe *Giotto* showed Halley's comet to be one of the darkest objects ever detected in the solar system, with an irregular nucleus 14.5 km/9 mi×3km/2 mi
Voyager 2 reached Uranus and found it to have six more moons than was previously thought, making 12 known moons in all; there may be more□

space sickness see travel◊ sickness□

Spain

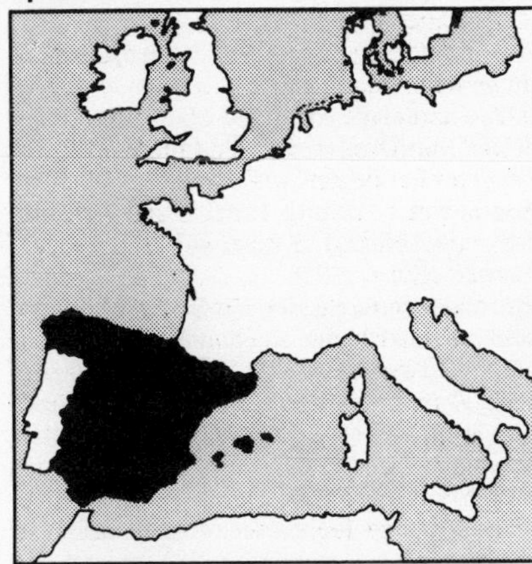

area 504 879 sq km/194 883 sq mi
capital Madrid
towns Bilbao, Valencia, Saragossa, Murcia; and the ports Barcelona, Seville, Málaga
features includes Balearic and Canary Islands, and Ceuta and Melilla; rivers Ebro, Douro, Tagus, Guadiana, Guadalquivir; Iberian Plateau (Meseta); Pyrenees, Cantabrian Mountains, Andalusian Mountains, Sierra Nevada
exports citrus, grapes, pomegranates, vegetables, wine (especially sherry), olive oil, tinned fruit and fish; iron ore, cork; cars and other vehicles; leather goods; ceramics
currency peseta
population 38 435 000, including 350 000 gypsies
language Spanish (Castilian) official, but regional languages are recognized within their own boundaries (Basque, Catalan, Galician, Valencian, and Majorcan are the chief examples)
religion Roman Catholicism; there are restrictions on the practice of Protestantism
famous people *architecture* Antonio Gaudí *art* cave paintings (Altamira◊, etc.), El Greco, Murillo, Velázquez, Goya, Picasso, Juan Gris, Salvador Dali, Joan Miró *literature: drama* Lope Félix de Vega Carpio, Pedro Calderón de la Barca, the brothers Quintero, F García Lorca *novel* Miguel de Cervantes, Saavedra, Camilo José Cela *poetry* the lays of El Cid◊; Juan Ramón Jiménez, Vincente Aleixandre *music: composers* Tomas Luis de Victoria, Enrique Granados, Manuel de Falla *performers* Segovia, Casals
government under the constitution of 1978, Spain is a parliamentary monarchy (Juan Carlos from 1975), with a Cortes Generales comprising Congress of Deputies (Prime Minister from 1982 Felipe Gonzáles, Socialist Party) elected by proportional representation, and elected Senate.
There are 17 regions which have a degree of devolved power with their own elected assemblies: Andalusia, Aragón, Asturias, Balearic Islands, Canary Islands, Cantabria, Castile-La Mancha, Castile-Léon, Catalonia, Estremadura, Euskadi (Basque Country), Galicia, La Rioja, Madrid, Murcia, Navarre, Valencia
history see Spain: history◊□

Spain: history

BC
11th century Phoenician colonies
7th century Celtic invasion
6–5th centuries Greek settlements
238 Carthaginian conquest by Hamilcar and Hasdrubal◊

AD
1st century following the Punic◊ Wars Roman rule was established; Trajan◊ and Hadrian◊ were of Spanish origin
5th century conquest of Spain by the Vandals◊ and Visigoths◊
711 conquest by the Moors◊, whose great centre was Cordova◊
1143 Portugal became independent
1478 establishment of the Inquisition◊
1479 union of Aragon◊ and Castile◊
1492 reconquest of Spain from the Moors completed by Ferdinand◊ and Isabella, with the capture of Granada◊; establishment of New World Spanish empire begun by the arrival in America of Columbus◊; Jews expelled from Spain

16th century peak of Spanish greatness under Emperor Charles◊ V, the first Hapsburg ruler.
1588 Phillip II's Armada failed to conquer Britain; beginning of Spain's decline
1713 Treaty of Utrecht (after War of Spanish◊ Succession); Spain lost Naples, Sicily, Milan, Gibraltar, and its last hold on the Netherlands
1797 French and Spanish fleets defeated by England at St◊ Vincent in Napoleonic Wars
1808–14 Peninsular◊ War followed Napoleon's creation of his brother Joseph as King of Spain
1898 Spanish◊-American War resulted in loss of Cuba, Philippines and Puerto Rico
late 19th century growth of Republicanism, Socialism, and anarchism
1923 constitutional monarchy fell after a military coup and dictatorships caused the dissolution of parliament
1925 civilian cabinet was established
1931 Republic established (see Alfonso◊ XIII)
1936 Popular Front (alliance of centre and left) introduced agrarian reforms, etc., opposed by the landlords, the Church, and General Franco◊. Spanish Civil◊ War began
1939–45 Spain nominally remained neutral in World War II
1947 Franco announced that Spain was once more a monarchy, but with himself as Regent until the succession of Juan Carlos after his death
1975 Franco's death; Juan Carlos became King; increased deamdns for decentralization
1980 Catalonia◊ and Basque◊ provinces granted elected assemblies, but some Basque groups (notably the ETA) continued terrorist activities
1981 Failure of right-wing military coup
1986 Spain joined EEC; referendum in favour of remaining in NATO; increasing terrorist attacks in Basque region□

Spalato Italian name for Yugoslav port of Split◊□

spaniel a breed of dog◊□

Spanish a Romance language, see under Latin◊, and also under Spain◊□

Spanish-American War war 1898 by Cuban revolutionaries (with US backing) against Spanish rule. The Treaty of Paris ceded Cuba, the Philippines, Guam and Porto Rico to the USA□

Spanish Armada fleet sent by Philip◊ II of Spain against England in 1588, and defeated by Howard◊ of Effingham and Drake◊ in the Channel. Many ships attempting escape round the N of Scotland were shipwrecked□

Spanish Civil War see Civil◊ War, Spanish□

Spanish fly a type of beetle◊□

Spanish Guinea former name of the Republic of Equatorial Guinea◊□

Spanish Sahara former name of Western Sahara◊□

Spanish Succession War of. War 1701–14 between Britain, Austria, the Netherlands, Portugal and Denmark (the Allies); and France, Spain and Bavaria. It was caused by Louis XIV's acceptance of the Spanish throne for his grandson, Philip, contrary to the Partition Treaty 1700, under which it would have passed to archduke Charles of Austria.
1704 French marched on Vienna to try to end the war, but were defeated at ***Blenheim*** by Marlborough◊ and Eugène◊ of Savoy
1705 Allies invaded Spain, twice occupying Madrid but failing to hold it
1706 Marlborough victorious over French (under Villeroi) at ***Ramillies*** 23 May, in Brabant, Belgium
1708 Marlborough and Eugène victorious over the French (under Duke of Burgundy and Vendôme) at ***Oudenaarde*** (near Ghent, Belgium) 30 Jun–11 Jul
1709 Marlborough victorious with Eugène◊ over the French (under Villars) at ***Malplaquet*** 11 Sept
1713 Treaties of Utrecht and ***1714 Rastatt*** under which the Allies recognized Philip as King of Spain, but Gibraltar, Minorca, and Nova Scotia were ceded to Britain, and Belgium, Milan and Naples to Austria□

Spark Muriel 1918– . Scottish novelist. Born in Edinburgh, she is a Catholic convert, and her works have an enigmatic satire: *The Ballad of Peckham Rye* 1960, *The Prime of Miss Jean Brodie* 1961, and *The Only Problem* 1984□

sparrow term for many small birds, of which the Eurasian ***house sparrow*** *Passer domesticus,* family Ploceidae, of the order Passeriformes, is common in Britain and has spread almost worldwide. With brown black-marked plumage and black chest and eye-stripe in the male, it is inconspicuous, intelligent and adaptable, with a cheery chirp and untidy nesting habits. See also hedge◊ sparrow□

sparrow-hawk hawk related to the buzzard; see under eagle◊□

Sparta ancient Greek city state (near the modern town of Sparte) in the S Peloponnese. Spartans were trained from boyhood for war, despised the arts, and reduced the people whose land they had occupied to a status (as helots) just short of slavery. Prominent in the Persian and Peloponnesian Wars, Sparta declined in the 2nd century BC□

Spartacus d. 71BC. Thracian gladiator who in 73 led a popular revolt of gladiators and slaves. He was finally defeated by Crassus◊, thousands of his followers being crucified□

Spartacus League German Socialist anti-war organization founded by K Liebknecht◊ 1916; in 1919 it became the German Communist Party. The student arm (Stalinist) of the W German Communist Party (DKP) has been known since the 1960s as ***Spartakus***□

Spartakiad quadrennial games in the USSR (so-named from ancient Sparta's stress on physical fitness for state service), in which about 10 000 Soviet athletes compete (foreigners were admitted from 1979)□

spastic a person affected by cerebral◊ palsy□

Speaker a presiding officer keeping order in a legislature. In the UK the Speaker in the House of Lords is the Lord Chancellor◊, and in the Commons the Speaker is elected for each Parliament, usually on an agreed basis among the parties, but often holds the office for many years□

Spear Ruskin 1911– . British artist, whose portraits include Laurence Olivier (as Macbeth), Francis Bacon, and satirical representations of Margaret Thatcher□

spearmint a type of herb◊□

special drawing rights the rights of member states of the International◊ Monetary Fund to apply for money to finance balance◊ of payments deficits. Since 1974 SDRs have been defined in terms of a 'basket' of the 16 currencies of countries doing 1% or more of the world's trade□

Special Air Service specialist British regiment (SAS) mainly recruited from parachute regiment volunteers; headquarters Bradbury Lines, near Hereford, England; motto 'Who dares wins' under a winged dagger. Founded originally by Colonel David Stirling in North Africa 1942; subsequent service includes Malaya, N Ireland, Falklands, and against terrorists (Iranian Embassy, London 1980)□

Special Branch section of the British police established 1883 to deal with Irish 'Fenian' terrorists. All 42 police forces in Britain now have their own Special Branches. They act as the executive arm of MI5 in its duty of preventing or investigating espionage, subversion and sabotage; carry out duties at air and sea ports in respect of naturalization and immigration, and provide armed bodyguards for public figures□

specific gravity the former name for 'relative density'; see density◊□

specific heat capacity quantity of heat required to raise unit mass of a substance by 1°C□

spectacles lenses fitted in a frame to correct defective vision, e.g. short sight (myopia◊), long sight (hypermetropia) by convex (spherical) lenses, and astigmatism (defect in curvature of the lens or cornea of the eye, causing unequal focusing) by cylindrical lenses, the direction of the axes of the cylinders being specified. Spherical and cylindrical lenses may be combined in one lens. Correction for both distance and reading is provided by ***bifocal spectacles*** two lenses of differing curvature being combined in one piece of glass. Lenses to reduce glare are made of photosensitive glass which darkens and returns to normal in average conditions. See also contact◊ lenses and eye◊□

spectroscopy a general term for the study of spectra associated with atoms or molecules in solid, liquid or gaseous phase. For example, ***emission spectroscopy*** is the study of the characteristic series of sharp lines produced when an element is heated. Thus an unknown mixture can be analysed for its component elements. Related is ***absorption spectroscopy*** dealing with atoms and molecules as they absorb energy in a characteristic way. Again, these dark lines are characteristic of the element or molecule present and can be used for analysis. More detailed structural information can be obtained using ***infra-red spectroscopy*** (dealing with molecular vibrations) or ***nuclear magnetic resonance spectroscopy*** (concerned with interactions between adjacent atomic nuclei). Using these various forms of spectroscopy it is often possible to identify an unknown compound. It is therefore an invaluable tool to scientists, industry (especially pharmaceuticals for purity checks), doctors, etc.□

spectrum the collection of frequencies of electromagnetic◊ waves from a source. The spectrum of white light, as emitted by very hot solids, and by the sun, is a continuous range of frequencies, as revealed by passing the light through a prism (see Newton◊), when a band of colours (red, orange, yellow, green, blue, indigo, violet) is produced□

Speenhamland System method of poor relief in England started by Berkshire magistrates in 1795, whereby wages were supplemented from the poor-rates. However, it encouraged the payment of low wages and was superseded by the 1834 Poor◊ Law. The concept of negative income tax is a more sophisticated equivalent□

Speke John Hanning 1827–64. British explorer, born in Somerset. He joined Burton◊ in an African expedition in which they reached Lake Tanganyika 1858, and Speke went on (after Burton was taken ill) to be the first European to see Lake Victoria◊ 1858; his claim that it was the source of the Nile was disputed by Burton, even after Speke and

spectrum

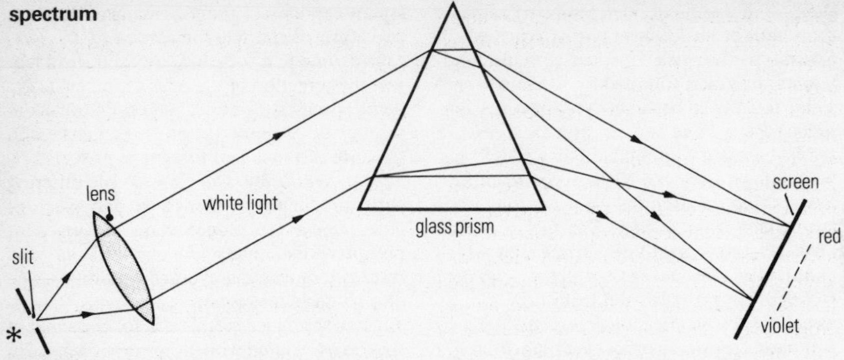

Grant made a second confirmatory expedition 1860–3. Speke accidentally shot himself out shooting in England, the day before he was due to debate the matter publicly with Burton□

speleology scientific study of caves (from the Greek for cave), including their plants and animals, the latter often blind. In the form of 'pot-holing', following the course of underground streams, it has become a popular sport□

Spence Sir Basil 1907–76. British architect, whose works include the rebuilt Coventry Cathedral, Sussex University, the British Embassy in Rome, the Home Office and Knightsbridge Barracks. Order of Merit 1962□

Spencer Herbert 1820–1903. British philosopher. An exponent of *laissez-faire* views in *Social Statics* 1851, he extended Darwin's theory of evolution to the entire field of human knowledge in his ten volume *System of Synthetic Philosophy* 1862–96□

Spencer Sir Stanley 1891–1959. British artist who was born and lived at Cookham-on-Thames, where a gallery of his work was opened 1962. He interpreted the Christian faith in terms of village life, e.g. *Christ Carrying the Cross* and *Resurrection*, both in the Tate, and murals of army life for the oratory of All Souls' at Burghclere in Berkshire□

Spencer Gulf inlet of the Indian Ocean in S Australia□

Spender Sir Stephen 1909–85. British poet, founder with Cyril Connolly of *Horizon* (co-editor 1939–41) and also co-editor of *Encounter* 1953–67□

Spengler Oswald 1880–1936. German philosopher, whose *Decline of the West* 1918 argued that civilizations go through natural cycles of growth and decay. He was admired by the Nazis□

Spenser Edmund 1552–99. English poet, the poet's poet because of his rich imagery and command of versification. In 1579 he published the pastoral *The Shepheardes Calendar,* with the Earl of Leicester◊ as his patron. Then, while secretary to the Lord Deputy in Ireland from 1580, he worked on the great moral allegory *The Faerie Queene* 1590–6 (Elizabeth I being the 'Faerie Queene'), of which the final books were probably lost when the castle was burnt down by rebels 1598□

spermaceti a wax obtained from whales; see sperm whale under whale◊□

Sperry Roger Wolcott 1913– . American neuro-biologist. Working at Caltech from 1954, he shared a Nobel prize in 1981 for his research on the 'functional specialization of the cerebral hemispheres', demonstrating that the two halves of the brain function independently with regard to learning and that various brain functions are controlled by specific areas□

Spey river in Highland region, Scotland; length 172 km/107 mi to the Moray Firth. It is famed for salmon fisheries at its mouth□

Speyer city (English ***Spires***) in Rhineland-Palatinate, W Germany; population 50 000. It was at the ***Diet of Spires*** 1529 that Protestantism (see under Christianity◊) received its name□

Spezia see La◊ Spezia□

sphagnum genus of cold, temperate bog mosses, which do not decay after death, but continue to absorb water, and form peat. Much used in packing plants and growing orchids, they also form natural surgical dressings□

Sphinx a mythological creature, represented in Egyptian, Assyrian and Greek art as a lion with a human head (e.g. the Great Sphinx at Gizeh, Egypt, 58 m/189 ft long). In Greek myth the Sphinx was female, and killed travellers who failed to answer a riddle; she killed herself when Oedipus◊ gave the right answer□

sphygmomanometer instrument for measuring blood pressure, particularly of the arteries□

spice see herbs◊ and spices□

Spice Islands another name for the Moluccas or Maluku◊□

spider animal (not an insect) of the class Arachnida◊, order Araneae; the head and breast are merged in the cephalothorax, and link with the abdomen by a characteristic narrow 'waist', and there are up to eight eyes, and eight legs. Of worldwide distribution, and forming 27 families, they are among the oldest land animals discovered. All have an exterior skeleton, and grow through a series of moults. Some, such as the wolf spiders, Lycosidae, can produce sounds by a stridulating organ on the pedipalps ('foot sensors', actually head appendages) which are also used in mating to transfer the sperm to the female. Spiders have no ears, but vibration is picked up by hairs on their legs. Courtship by the male includes long spells of dancing, but observation of spiders in the wild suggests that the females do not, as legend tells, eat their partners after mating. The hunters are swift-moving and keenly sighted, e.g. the ***zebra spider*** *Salticus scenicus* which has pads on its feet enabling it to walk even on glass. The trappers are skilled web builders, notably the Araneidae. The web of the common European ***garden spider*** *Aranea diadema* is of remarkable beauty, but is dwarfed by that of the Central American *Eriophora fuliginea* with a web 1.5 m/5 ft high and 1 m/3 ft wide, and strong enough to catch bats; and *Cyrtophora moluccensis* of New Guinea builds in colonies, covering large gaps between trees that no individual working alone could exploit. The ***water spider*** *Argyroneta aquatica* lives underwater in a diving bell home filled with air trapped on the hairs of its body. The spinnerets from which the viscid web-building fluid is exuded, hardening on exposure to air, are on the under-surface of the abdomen. All spiders have poison glands, but the result of their bite for human beings is usually exaggerated. That of ***tarantula*** *Lycosa tarantula* of S Europe, one of the wolf spiders, was supposed to cause a hysterical sickness, for which the rapid dance the 'tarantella' was the cure; the name tarantula is also given to the hairy S American ***bird-eating spider*** *Avicularia vestiaria*, whose bite causes inflammation. The bite of the N American ***black widow*** *Lathrodectus mactans* is not deadly, but that of the Australian ***funnel-web*** *Atrax robustus* can be lethal□

Spielberg Steven 1947– . American film director, whose successes include *Jaws* 1975, about a killer shark, *Close Encounters of the Third Kind* 1977, and *E.T. (The Extra Terrestrial)* 1982□

spikenard Himalayan plant *Nardostachys jatamansi,* family Valerianaceae; its underground stems give a perfume used in Eastern aromatic oils□

Spillane Mickey (Frank Morrison) 1918– . American crime novelist. Mike Hammer, his 'one-man police force' hero, appears in stories of uninhibited sex and violence, e.g. *Vengeance is Mine* and *The Long Wait*□

spin in physics, the rotation of a particle or other body. The earth possesses so-called 'angular momentum' because of both its yearly orbital motion around the sun and its daily spin about its own axis. Many particles (e.g. electrons) have an intrinsic property, rather like the earth's spin, but can only have it in certain definite amounts (see particle◊ physics)□

spina bifida a neural tube defect (NTD) in which the developing spinal canal of a baby fails to close completely; it affects the nerves controlling the legs, arms and bladder□

spinach a type of plant; see under beet◊□

spindle tree Eurasian tree *Euonymus europaeus,* family Celastraceae; the hard wood was used to make spindles. Once used (the seeds) to drive away lice from children's heads□

spine the backbone of vertebrates, in humans containing 26 bones (vertebrae) which have a semi-circular, thick rounded body at the front to take weight, a bony ring behind through which the spinal cord passes, and three projections of bone, one on each side and one to the rear. The lowest part of the spine is the sacrum, a broad triangular structure consisting of five rudimentary vertebrae fused together, jointed to the hip bones and ending in the tail bone (coccyx), which consists of four fused vertebrae. See scoliosis◊□

spinel any mineral having cubic symmetry and consisting chiefly of magnesia or alumina; the latter includes gems such as the ruby□

spinet a small type of harpsichord; see under piano◊□

spinning the drawing out of fibres into threads to make cloth, now done entirely mechanically and (in the case of synthetic fibres) by the extrusion of a liquid through the holes of a spinneret, in the same way as a spider forms the 'threads' of its web□

Spinoza Benedict or Baruch 1632–77. Dutch philosopher who abandoned Judaism for a rationalistic pantheism that owed much to Descartes◊. He taught that all that we know, mind and matter, is a manifestation of the all-embracing substance that is God, good and evil being relative. His *Ethics* 1677 is his chief work. He was persecuted by his former co-religionists□

spiny anteater Australian egg-laying mammal; see under Monotremata◊□

Spiraea genus of flowering plants and shrubs with alternate leaves and small flowers, family Rosaceae◊□

Spires English name for the German city of Speyer◊□

spirits of salt a solution of hydrochloric acid in water. See hydrochloric◊ acid□

spiritualism movement originating in the USA 1848 and based on belief in the survival of human personality and the possibility of communication between the living and the 'dead' (see also psychical◊ research) at seances. Recorded phenomena of this kind have been less frequent since the use of checks, such as infra-red radiation, on the darkness favoured by mediums for producing 'materializations' of departed spirits□

spirogyra genus of freshwater algae◊□

spirulina a genus of algae◊□

Spitalfields a district in the Greater London borough of Tower◊ Hamlets□

Spithead a roadstead between the mainland of England and the Isle of Wight◊□

Spitsbergen the main island in the Norwegian archipelago of Svalbard◊□

spitz a breed of dog◊□

spleen spongy, red organ c12.5 x 7.5 cm (5 x 3 in) under the diaphragm on the left of the human body. It forms white blood cells, destroys worn-out red ones, produces antibodies, and removes bacteria from the blood, but is not essential to healthy adult life□

Split Adriatic industrial port (engineering, textiles) (Italian ***Spalato***) in Yugoslavia; population 236 000. It was founded by Domitian◊, who retired here, It is also a tourist resort□

Spock Dr Benjamin McLane 1903– . American child-care expert. His influential *Common Sense Book of Baby and Child Care* 1946 advocated less restriction on children, but in later work discipline is more strongly stressed□

Spode Josiah 1754–1827. British potter, son of Josiah Spode the elder (an apprentice of Thomas Whieldon who started his own works at Stoke-on-Trent 1770), and his successor in the new firm in 1797. He developed beautiful tableware, and the firm survives as Copeland□

Spokane industrial city in a mining, timber and rich agricultural area, the 'inland empire', of Washington, USA; population 341 000□

Spoleto town in Umbria, central Italy, of architectural beauty; population 40 000. There is an annual opera and drama festival established by Menotti◊□

sponge mainly marine phylum (Porifera) of invertebrate animals without a nervous system, subdivided into Symplasma, containing a type of sponge, Hexactinellida, which consists of many nuclei enclosed within one cell membrane; and Cellularia, which includes all the other sponges with many cells. The more complex have specialized cells which absorb nutrients from the water, or have reproductive functions, e.g. the common toilet sponge, which is the skeleton of such a form. Sponges are classified by the nature (chalky, glassy, horny, etc.) and arrangement of the spicules which support the skeleton, and all are sessile (attached to the sea bottom, a rock, etc.)□

spoonbill bird, family Plataleidae, order Ciconiiformes (see stork◊), including the ***Eurasian spoonbill*** *Platalea leucordia* with a spoon-shaped bill flattened at the tip and used to sort through swamps for its food□

Spooner William Archibald 1844–1930. British scholar, warden of New College, Oxford, originator of 'spoonerisms', e.g. 'Kinquering congs their titles take'□

Sporades island group in the Aegean Sea. The chief island of the ***Northern Sporades*** is ***Skyros*** on which Rupert Brooke◊ is buried; area 207 sq km/79 sq mi. The ***Southern Sporades*** are more usually referred to as the Dodecanese◊□

spore one-celled reproductive body of cryptogams, the flowerless plants, and of some protozoans□

sporozoa large division of unicellular parasitic protozoa; they produce spores which are transmitted from one host to another, many causing disease, e.g. malaria and sleeping sickness□

sprain injury to the ligaments of a joint by a twist or wrench□

sprat small sea fish related to the herring◊□

Spratly Islands group of islands in a strategic position in the S China Sea, believed to have huge oil and natural gas reserves. Claims are made on them by China (who call them the Nanshan Islands), Vietnam (Truong Sa), the Philippines, Taiwan and Malaysia□

Spring Richard 1950– . Irish Labour Party leader from 1982, who entered into coalition with FitzGerald◊'s Fine Gael 1982 as deputy Prime Minister (and Minister for Energy from 1983)□

Springfield capital, and agricultural and mining centre of Illinois, USA; population 99 650. The home of Abraham Lincoln 1837–61 is preserved, and he is buried here□

Springfield industrial city (small arms, e.g. the formerly famous Springfield rifle, chemicals) in Massachusetts, USA; population 153 500□

Springfield industrial city (engineering, textiles) and agricultural centre in Missouri, USA; population 137 000□

Springs industrial and mining centre (gold, coal, uranium) in Transvaal, S Africa; population 154 000□

springtail widely-distributed order (Collembola) of wingless insects, sub-class Apterygota, which live on decaying, or sometimes living plant matter, in moist soil or in salt or fresh water. The cerci (sensory appendages) on the abdomen have been modified into a forked organ, enabling the insect to jump□

spring tide the tide◊ at or just after the new moon and full moon□

spruce a type of tree; see under conifers◊□

spurge genus of trees and shrubs in the family Euphorbiaceae, many with fleshy leaves and a milky juice; as the name suggests, they have purgative qualities□

Spurn Head see under Humberside◊□

Spurs Battle of the. A victory 1513 over the French, at Guinegate, NW France, by Henry VII of England; the name emphasizes the speed of the French retreat□

spy ship high-speed warship specializing in surveillance of enemy vessels, and monitoring their radar and sonar□

squash (botany) a marrow-like plant; see under pumpkin◊□

squash game played in an enclosed court 9.75 m/32 ft long and 6.40 m/21 ft wide, usually by two persons, with rackets and a small 'squashy' synthetic rubber ball. The ball must hit the far (front) wall of the court (away from both players) above the 1.83 m/6 ft line when served, and on rebounding may be played almost anywhere within the boundary of the court in order to prevent the other player being able to return it. Owing to the small size of the court, it did not become a spectator sport until television popularized it in the 1970s and 1980s□

squatter in modern law, illegal occupier of premises or land, but in 19th century Australia and New Zealand used of graziers (without illegal imputation) who established a politically powerful 'squattocracy', and used their wealth to build elegant mansions; see Armidale◊□

squid a type of marine mollusc; see cephalopod◊□

squire or ***esquire*** originally a trainee knight, who served as a knight's attendant;

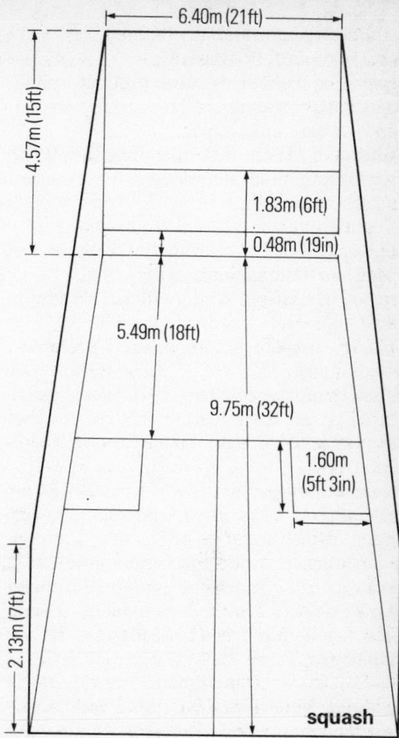

squash

from the later Middle Ages anyone ranking between a knight and a gentleman, and still used in England after the surname on letters, etc., though less than formerly□

squirrel a small tree-dwelling rodent◊□

Sri Lanka Democratic Socialist Republic of

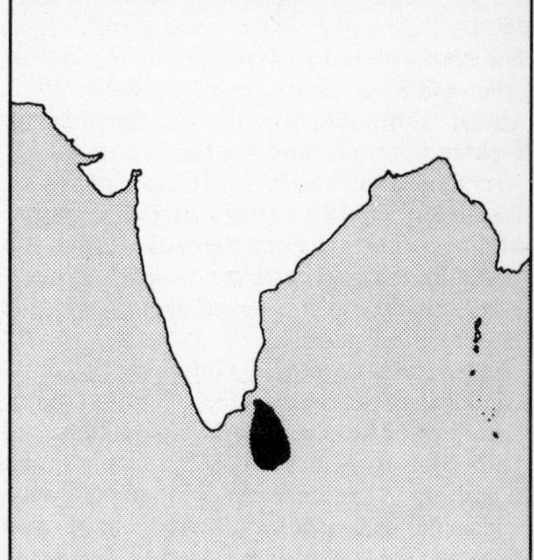

area 65 600 sq km/25 332 sq mi
capital and chief port Colombo
towns Kandy; and the ports of Jaffna, Galle, Negombo, Trincomalee

features Adam's Peak; ruined cities of Anuradhapura, Polonnaruwa
exports tea, rubber, coconut products; plumbago, sapphires, rubies, etc.
currency Sri Lanka rupee
population 15 925 000, including 2 500 000 Tamils from India, some settled for centuries, and others brought over by the British to man the tea estates
language Sinhala, official; but English and Tamil are national languages
religion Buddhism 67%, official; Hinduism 18%
famous people Solomon and Sirimavo Bandaranaike
government under the 1978 constitution there is an executive president (Junius Jayawardene◊), and House of Representatives
recent history partly ceded to the British by the Dutch in 1798, the island came entirely under British rule in 1815, and achieved independence within the Commonwealth in 1948. In 1972 it became a republic under the name Sri Lanka 'resplendent island'. The Tamil minority (headquarters Jaffna) agitate for Tamil Eelam, a separate Tamil state. A state of emergency was repeatedly renewed from 1982, but talks with separatist leaders opened 1985. The Tamils have their own administration operating in Jaffna peninsula, and have resisted attempts by the Sri Lankan army to capture the area□

Srinagar capital and resort of Jammu◊ and Kashmir; population 520 000. A beautiful city, intersected by waterways, it also has carpet, papier mǎché, and leather industries□

SS Nazi élite corps (German *Schutz-Staffel* 'protective squadron') established 1925. Under Himmler◊ its 500 000 membership included the full-time ***Waffen-SS,*** armed SS, who fought in World War II, and spare-time members. The SS performed police duties, and was brutal in its treatment of the Jews and others in the concentration camps and occupied territories; it was condemned at the Nuremberg trials◊□

Staël Anne Louise Germaine Necker, Madame de Staël 1766–1817. French author, daughter of the financier Necker◊. Banished from Paris by Napoleon 1803, because of her advocacy of political freedom, she gathered round her at Coppet, on Lake Geneva, men such as Schlegel◊ and Byron◊. She wrote semi-autobiographical novels such as *Delphine* 1802 and *Corinne* 1807 and the influential critical work *De l'Allemagne* 1810, on German literature□

Staffa an uninhibited island in the Hebrides◊□

Staffordshire Midland county of England

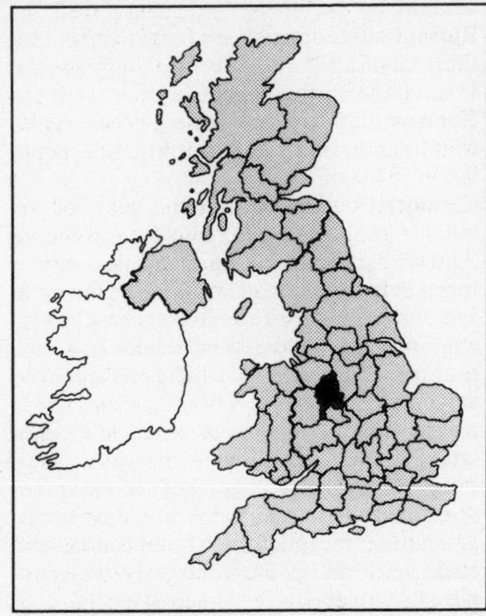

area 2716 sq km/1054 sq mi
towns administrative headquarters Stafford; Stoke-on-Trent
features largely flat, comprising the Vale of Trent and its tributaries; Cannock Chase; Keele University 1962
products coal in N; china and earthenware in the upper Trent basin, chinaware in the Potteries (see under Stoke-on-Trent◊); Staffordshire bull terriers
population 1 019 700
famous people Peter de Wint□

stained glass coloured transparent glass cut to shape, with the addition of painted detail, and joined by lead strips, or (in a technique revived more recently) facetted glass joined by cement, which is used in designs for church windows, etc. Medieval examples are in the cathedrals of Canterbury, Lincoln, Chartres, Cologne, and Rouen; modern designers include Morris, Burne-Jones, and James Hogan□

Stainer Sir John 1840–1901. British organist and composer, whose works include the oratorio *The Crucifixion* and the cantata *The Daughter of Jairus*□

Stakhanov Aleksei 1906–77. Soviet miner in the Donbas who consistently exceeded production norms, and who gave his name to the Stakhanovite movement of the 1930s, when workers were encouraged to initiate simplification and reorganization of work processes in order to increase production□

stalactite and **stalagmite** cave lime deposits formed by trickling water containing carbonate of lime; the former hang from the roof and the latter accumulate on the floor. They may take many years to form□

Stalin adopted name, meaning 'steel', of Russian statesman Joseph Vissarionovich Djugashvili 1879–1953. A Georgian, he became a Marxist and was many times exiled to Siberia under the Tsar. He became associated with Lenin◊ and in 1917, as editor of *Pravda,* joined with him in the carrying out of the 'October Revolution'. Lenin, alarmed by Stalin's rapid consolidation of a powerful following (including Molotov◊), died before being able to remove him from the General-Secretaryship of the Communist Party. Stalin, who wanted to create 'Socialism in one country', now clashed with Trotsky◊, who denied the possibility of Socialism inside Russia until revolution had occurred in western Europe. Stalin won this ideological struggle by 1927, and a series of five-year plans was launched to collectivize industry and agriculture from 1928. All opposition was eliminated by the Great Purge 1936–8, supposedly triggered by the assassination of Kirov◊, by which Stalin disposed of all real and fancied enemies. During World War II, Stalin became Chairman of the Council of People's Commissars and intervened in the military direction of the campaigns against Nazi Germany. After the war, he maintained a one-man rule of single-minded intensity. His rule was denounced after his death by Khrushchev◊□

Stalingrad name (from 1925 to 1961) of the Russian city of Volgograd◊□

Stamboul another name for the Turkish city of Istanbul◊□

stamp see philately◊, Post Office◊□

standard see special uses under flag◊□

Stanislavsky Konstantin 1863–1938. Stage-name of the Russian Konstantin Alexeev, founder of the Moscow Art Theatre, interpreter of Chekhov and Gorky, and originator of 'method' acting. See Actors◊ Studio□

Stanley see Earl of Derby◊□

Stanley Sir Henry Morton 1841–1904. British explorer-journalist, working for the *New York Herald* from 1867, who in 1871 was sent by James Gordon Bennett to find Livingstone◊. They met at Ujiji, and explored Lake Tanganyika together. He traced the course of the Zaïre (Congo) to the sea 1874–77; on a third expedition 1879–84, financed by Leopold◊ II, he established the Congo Free State (see Zaïre◊) and made a fourth 1887–89□

Stanley capital of the Falkland◊ Islands, on E Falkland; population c1000□

Stanley Falls former name of Boyoma Falls; see Zaïre◊ river□

Stanley Pool former name of Malebo Pool; see Zaïre◊ river□

Stanleyville former name of the Zaïrean port of Kisangani◊□

Stansted site of airport in Essex; England; see under Essex◊□

star globe of extremely hot gas, radiating because of nuclear processes taking place inside it, and classified according to its surface temperature, which may range from about 80 000°C to 2600°C, and its correspondent colouring from blue-white to red. Its evolution from one type into another depends on the original quantity of matter it contained when first created by condensation from a cloud of gas and dust (nebula) in space.

A ***binary star*** is a star with two (or more) separate components, moving round their common centre of gravity. The components may be virtually equal, and widely separated, or one may be much brighter than the other, e.g. ***Sirius*** and ***Sirius B***, the latter a much smaller companion star. Other binaries include ***Alpha Centauri***, the brilliant southern star, and ***Castor***, an example of the complex multiple type system.

Important individual stars include ***Barnard's star,*** a faint red dwarf only six light years away from earth, and so named because it was studied by US astronomer Edward Barnard; ***Betelgeuse,*** largest star in our galaxy, a red supergiant in the constellation of Orion.

Pole Star, star (brightest of the Ursa Minor constellation) nearest to the celestial N pole, and varying only slowly in position.

Proxima Centauri, the nearest star to earth, except the sun, it is 4.28 light years distant.

Sirius, the brightest star within 13 light years of earth, which has 26 times the luminosity of the sun.

Vega, one of the brightest stars of the night sky (twice the size of the sun and 60 times as luminous), and 26 light years from earth.

The largest known star, suspected to exist in 1981 (from its ultra-violet radiation), is in 30 Doradus nebula. Its surface temperature is 10 times higher than that of the sun; its diameter is 100 times greater; its brightness 100 times greater; and its mass 3000 times greater□

starch carbohydrate◊ produced by photosynthesis in plants, e.g. cereals, beans and root crops. Used in stiffening paper, textiles, etc.□

Star Chamber English medieval court of members of the king's council (it met in a room of Westminster Palace with a starred ceiling). The Tudors◊ used it to deal speedily with culprits too powerful for trial in ordinary courts. Its persecution of Puritans under Charles I caused its abolition 1641. Under the

Thatcher government the term was popularly revived for ministerial meetings at which ministers plead particular causes for action□

starfish a type of marine animal; see echinoderm◊□

starling bird in the family Sturnidae, order Passeriformes; the ***common starling*** *Sturnus vulgaris*, with whistling song, strutting gait and irridescent speckled feathers, is noted for its use of cities as dormitories and acrobatic flight in flocks. Related is the glossy black ***hill mynah*** *Gracula religiosa* of India, a realistic mimic of sounds and human speech□

star of Bethlehem genus of plants *Ornithogalum,* family Liliaceae◊, with white or yellow flowers; the ***spiked star of Bethlehem*** or ***Bath asparagus*** *O pyrenaicum* can be eaten like asparagus□

State Department in the USA, the government department responsible for foreign◊ relations□

Staten Island an island in the city of New◊ York, USA□

static electricity see under electric◊ charge□

statics the study of bodies in equilibrium; see under mechanics◊□

Stationery Office H M. Organization established 1786 to supply books, stationery, etc., to British government departments, and to superintend the printing of government reports, etc. It now publishes books and pamphlets on subjects ranging from national works of art to agricultural information. The US equivalent is the Government Printing Office□

Stations of the Cross series of pictures or images, usually 14, showing the final scenes of the Passion of Christ□

statistical mechanics branch of physics in which the properties of large collections of particles are predicted□

Staudinger Hermann 1881–1965. German organic chemist, founder of macro-molecular chemistry by research into the structure of albumen, cellulose, and rubber. Nobel prize 1953□

Stauffenberg Claus von 1907–44. German colonel who planted a bomb in Hitler's headquarters conference room in the Wolf's Lair at Rastenburg, E Prussia, 20 Jul 1944. Hitler was injured, and Stauffenberg and some 200 others were executed□

Stavanger oil port in SW Norway, with fish-canning and shipbuilding industries; population 93 000□

Stavropol industrial town (agricultural machinery, food processing, textiles) in S USSR; population 287 000□

steam invisible water vapour gas (used in power generation and other industrial processes); the usual visible cloud which accompanies its formation in air is caused by minute suspended water particles□

steam engine engine using steam to convert heat energy into mechanical work. As developed from more primitive forms by James Watt◊, it was one of the most important inventions of the industrial revolution, and the first practical steam-propelled vehicle was invented by Richard Trevithick 1801; see also George Stephenson◊, Robert Fulton◊□

steam engine

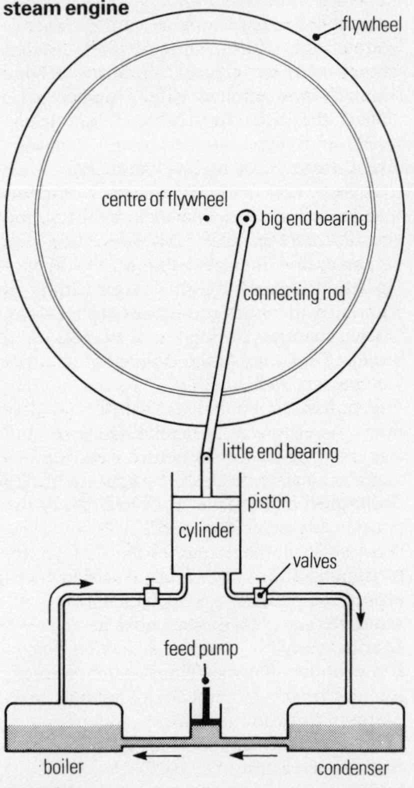

steatite a mineral of hydrated magnesium silicate; see under talc◊□

Steel David 1938– . British politician, leader of the Liberal party from 1976. He entered into a 'compact' to support the shaky Labour government 1977–8, and into an alliance with the Social Democratic Party 1983□

steel iron containing 0.05–1.5% carbon, ranging through ***mild steels*** for tinplate or structural work (reinforcing rods, etc.); ***carbon steels*** for rails, axles, etc.; ***high carbon steels*** for cutting tools, etc., to ***high-alloy steels*** for special purposes (high speed steels, which retain hardness at high temperatures and can be used in machines working very fast; corrosion resistant steels, such as stainless steel, made by adding nickel, chromium, molybdenum, manganese, tungsten, vanadium, etc.)□

steel band a type of musical group; see under band◊□

Steele Sir Richard 1672–1729. Irish essayist, a friend of Addison◊. They both contributed to *The Tatler* 1709–11, and *The Spectator* 1711–12, which were both founded by Steele□

Steen Jan 1626–79. Dutch genre painter, e.g. *Tavern Company*□

steeplechasing a form of horse◊ racing□

Steer Philip Wilson 1860–1942. British landscape and portrait artist, influenced by the French impressionists, and a founder of the New◊ English Art Club. Order of Merit 1931□

stegosaurus see under dinosaur◊□

Stein Gertrude 1874–1946. American author, born in Pennsylvania. Settling in Paris in 1904, she influenced writers such as Hemingway◊ and Scott Fitzgerald◊, by her cinematic technique, use of repetition, and absence of punctuation, devices to convey instantaneous continuity. Her books include the self-portrait *The Autobiography of Alice B Toklas* 1933□

Steinbeck John Ernst 1902–68. American novelist, born in California, the setting of a number of his books, which deal with such social problems as the plight of migrant workers. They include *Of Mice and Men* 1937, *The Grapes of Wrath* 1939, and *East of Eden* 1952. Nobel prize 1962□

Steiner Rudolf 1861–1925. Austrian philosopher, originally a theosophist◊, who developed his own mystic teaching, anthroposophy, designed to develop the whole human being. His method of teaching is followed by a number of schools named after him□

Stendhal pseudonym of French novelist Marie Henri Beyle (1783–1842). Born in Grenoble, he served in Napoleon's armies, taking part in the ill-fated Russian campaign, and then lived in Italy from 1814–1821. The reputation of his novels *Le Rouge et le noir* (1830) and *La Chartreusè de Parme* (1839), pioneering in their treatment of disguise and hypocrisy, began with a review of the latter by Balzac◊ in 1840□

stephanotis genus of Madagascan twining shrubs with leathery leaves and large white fragrant flowers, family Asclepidadaceae□

Stephen c1097–1154. King of England from 1135. A grandson of William I, he was elected to the throne although he had previously recognized Matilda◊ as Henry I's successor. Matilda landed in England 1139, and civil war reduced the country to anarchy until 1153, when Stephen acknowledged Matilda's son Henry as his own heir□

Stephen I St c975–1038. King of Hungary from 997, he was canonized 1803 for his completion of the conversion of the country to Christianity. His crown, symbol of Hungarian nationhood, was removed to the USA in 1945, but returned 1978□

Stephen Sir Leslie 1832–1904. English critic, first editor of the *Dictionary of National Biography* and father of novelist Virginia Woolf◊□

Stephen St. In the New Testament, the first Christian martyr◊; he died c35AD□

Stephens John Lloyd 1805–52. American explorer in Central America, with Frederick Catherwood◊. He recorded his findings among the ruined Maya cities in his two volumes of *Incidents of Travel* 1841–3□

Stephenson George 1781–1848. British engineer, born near Newcastle. He invented the first successful steam locomotive 1814; was engineer of the first public railway (Stockton–Darlington) 1825; and developed the more advanced 'Rocket' engine 1829□

Stephenson Robert 1803–59. British engineer, son of George. He designed railway bridges, e.g. the Menai tubular bridge□

Stepney district now part of the London borough of Tower◊ Hamlets□

stereophonic sound a system of sound reproduction; see hi-fi◊□

sterilization in medicine, the destruction of the power of reproduction. In human beings it can be done with potential reversibility in males by tying off the tubes carrying seed from the testicles to the seminal vesicles, and in females by tying the Fallopian tubes. Permanency is achieved by cutting out a portion of each tube (vasectomy) or by removing the ovaries or testicles (castration), or by giving them a sufficiently powerful dose of X-rays. The term is also used for the killing of bacteria by heat or other radiation, or by disinfectants□

Sterne Laurence 1713–68. Irish writer, vicar of Sutton-in-the-Forest, Yorkshire, from 1738. His chief works are *The Life and Opinions of Tristram Shandy, Gentleman* 1760–7, an eccentrically whimsical and bawdy novel which made him a London 'lion', and his *A Sentimental Journey through France and Italy* 1768, the result of his travels abroad in search of a cure for his tuberculosis□

sterol an organic solid alcohol, e.g. ergosterol or cholesterol◊, which is physiologically very active. A ***steroid*** is any of the large group of fat soluble organic compounds, including the sterols, various hormones and vitamin D., which occur naturally or may be synthesized. See also hormone◊□

stethoscope instrument for listening to the action of the heart and lungs, etc., invented 1819 by R T Laënnec 1781–1826, and comprising a hollow disc to be placed against the body, which is linked to the ears by flexible tubes□

Stettin German name for the Polish city of Szczecin◊□

Stevenage first place in England to be developed as a 'new town', in 1946, in Hertfordshire; population 73 000□

Stevens Wallace 1879–1955. American poet, a sensuous technician who was accused of obscurity, e.g. 'The Man with the Blue Guitar' 1937□

Stevenson Adlai 1900–65. American Democratic presidential candidate, twice defeated by Eisenhower◊ 1952 and 1956. He campaigned against corruption in public life and was chief US delegate at the founding conference of the UN□

Stevenson Robert Louis 1850–94. Scottish author and poet. Born in Edinburgh, he qualified as an advocate, but never practised. He wrote travel books, e.g. *Travels with a Donkey* 1879; essays, e.g. *Familiar Studies of Men and Books* 1882; and poetry, e.g. *A Child's Garden of Verses* 1885. However, he is best-known for his adventure novels *Treasure Island* 1883, *Kidnapped* 1886 (with its sequel *Catriona* 1893), *The Black Arrow* 1888, *The Master of Ballantrae* 1889, *Dr Jekyll and Mr Hyde,* 1886, and the incomplete *Weir of Hermiston* published in 1896 after his death. In 1890 he settled at Vailima in Samoa, where he sought a cure for the tuberculosis of which he died□

Stewart James 1908– . American actor, an air force pilot in World War II. Gangling and speaking with a soft drawl, he appeared in *Mr Smith Goes to Washington* 1939, *The Philadelphia Story* 1940 (Academy award), *The Man from Laramie* 1955□

Stewart Island volcanic island off New Zealand; area 1735 sq km/670 sq mi; population c400. Chief settlement Oban□

stick insect group of mainly tropical insects, family Phasmidae, order Phasmida, whose long bodies and legs make them resemble twigs. They are related to the leaf◊ insects□

stickleback small fish, both marine and freshwater, family Gasterosteidae, order Gasterosteiformes, so-named from the spines which take the place of a dorsal fin. The males build nests of vegetable material glued together with mucus, 'invite' any available females to deposit eggs, and guard them fiercely until the young hatch□

Stieglitz Alfred 1864–1946. American photographer who helped make photography an art form, e.g. 'Winter, Fifth Avenue' 1893 and 'Steerage' 1907□

stigmata impressions of the five wounds of Christ at the crucifixion, said to have appeared on the bodies of St Francis and other saints□

Stijl de. A group of 20th-century Dutch artists inspired by Mondrian◊□

Stilicho Flavius 359–408AD. Roman general, of Vandal◊ origin, who campaigned successfully against the Visigoths and Ostrogoths. He virtually ruled the western empire as guardian of Honorius (son of Theodosius◊ I), but was executed on the orders of Honorius when he was suspected of wanting to make his own son successor to another son of Theodosius in the eastern empire□

Stilton village in Cambridgeshire, England, once famous for the cheese named after it; see under Melton◊ Mowbray□

Stilwell Joseph Warren 1883–1946. US general, nicknamed 'Vinegar Joe'. In World War II he commanded the Chinese forces cooperating with the British (with whom he quarrelled) in Burma, and subsequently all US forces in the Chinese, Burmese and Indian theatres until recalled to the USA 1944 after differences with Chiang◊ Kai-shek. Subsequently he commanded the US 10th Army on Okinawa□

stingray a type of ray□

stinkhorn a type of fungus; see Basidiomycetes◊□

stinkwood term used for many 'smelly' trees e.g. S African tree *Ocotea bullata,* family Lauraceae, with offensive-smelling wood when newly felled, but fine, durable timber used for furniture. Another is *Gustavia augusta* from tropical America□

Stirling James 1926– . British architect, with an impressionistic style, whose works include the Florey Building at Queen's College, Oxford and Clore Gallery at the Tate 1983□

Stirling industrial town (agricultural machinery, textiles, carpets), administrative headquarters of Central region, Scotland; population 30 000. The castle predates the 12th century, and was long a Scottish royal residence. In 1314 Edward II of England (in raising a Scottish siege of the town) went into battle at Bannockburn◊. There is a university and the historic jail buildings are being developed as the centre of a Future World project□

stoat small European mammal related to the weasel◊□

stock (botany), genus of S European plants *Matthiola* family Cruciferae, grown for their bright, scented flowers, including ***night-scented stock*** *M bicornis*□

stock (financial) see stocks◊ and shares□

stock exchange institution for the buying and selling of stocks and shares (securities). The London Stock Exchange is run by a private company, has about 4500 members (who pay heavy fees and must provide sureties), with administrative units in London, Birmingham, Manchester, Glasgow, Dublin and Belfast. London's is the oldest stock exchange, opened 1801, when it replaced dealings in the coffee houses of Change Alley, in the City. The former division between brokers (who bought shares from jobbers to sell to the public) and jobbers (who sold them only to the brokers on commission, the 'jobbers' turn') is to be broken down in future legislation.

Computerization has enabled 24-hour trading, lessening the importance of actual presence on the 'trading floor', and from 1986 foreign brokers are allowed membership as Britain becomes part of the EEC Stock Exchange network. The major stock exchanges are London, New York (Wall Street) and Tokyo.

Stock exchange jargon includes: ***bear*** a speculator who has sold securities he/she does not as yet possess in the expectation of buying them more cheaply before settling day (of which there are usually two each month); ***bull*** a buyer of securities he/she does not intend to 'take up' (pay for), but hopes to sell at a higher price before settling day; and ***stag*** someone who dashes in to buy up newly-issued shares to resell them at a premium to investors as soon as possible□

Stockhausen Karlheinz 1928– . German composer. A student of Messiaen◊, he progressed from 12-note music to electronic composition, e.g. *Kontakte* 1968. Later works include a group of 12 American Indian songs, *Am Himmel wandre ich* 1972; and an operatic cycle *Licht, die sieben Tage der Woche* from 1977, for solo voices and a choir, solo instruments and an orchestra, and dancers, using both electronic and 'concrete' music□

Stockholm capital, port and industrial city (engineering, brewing, electrical goods, paper, textiles, pottery) of Sweden; population 1 527 500. It is built on a number of Islands, the 18th century royal palace being on Staden island, on the site of the 13th century fortress defending the trading settlements of Lake Mälar, round which the town first developed. Also here are the town hall (designed by Ragnar Östberg) 1923 and the Houses of Parliament. Most of Sweden's educational institutions are in Stockholm (including the Nobel Institute). The warship *Wasa* (a warship built for Gustavus◊ Adolphus) sank in the harbour 1628, but was raised and preserved in a museum 1961□

Stockholm syndrome the emotional bond which sometimes develops between hostages and their captors, first noticed in 1975 at the siege of the W German embassy, Stockholm, by the Baader◊-Meinhof gang□

Stockport industrial town (chemicals, engineering, and still some cotton textiles) in Greater Manchester, England; population 140 000□

stocks wooden structure previously used to confine the arms or legs of offenders, and expose them to ignominy and brickbats. See pillory◊□

stocks and **shares** investment in government or private companies.

In the UK, ***stocks*** represent money lent to the the government or local authorities, i.e. ***gilt-edged securities,*** so-called because the buyer is guaranteed his interest and (usually) return of his capital on a given date; however, the value of the stock goes up and down with interest rates in the intervening period, and when inflation is high the purchaser may lose heavily: or, in the case of ***debenture stock,*** money, similarly on loan at fixed interest, but to a company, and which may be secured against particular company assets, or entitle the holder to compel the company to be liquidated if the money is not repaid on time. ***Shares*** are most usually either ***ordinary shares,*** the part of the capital of a company held by its members (shareholders), and issued as units of definite face value, but which may have a much greater value when actually traded on the Stock Exchange; or ***preference shares*** which carry a fixed rate of dividend, and have first claim on the profits of a company; when profits are good this amount may be much smaller than is received by ordinary shareholders□

Stockton industrial river port (agricultural machinery, food processing) on the San Joaquin in California, USA; population 150 000□

Stockton Earl of. See Harold Macmillan◊□

Stockton-on-Tees industrial (engineering) town in Cleveland, England; population 172 470. It still has much Georgian architecture, and the oldest railway station building in the world, and nearby 18th century Preston Hall Museum□

Stoicism a school of philosophy; see under Zeno◊ of Citium□

Stoke-on-Trent city in Staffordshire, England, formed 1910 from Burslem, Hanley, Longton, Stoke-upon-Trent, Fenton and Tunstall, the heart of the Potteries; population 252 400. World's largest ceramic centre (the Gladstone Pottery Museum is the only working pottery museum; see also Minton◊, Wedgwood◊, and Arnold Bennett◊), it also produces steel, chemicals, engineering machinery, paper, rubber, and has one of Europe's richest coalfields□

Stoke Poges see under Berkshire◊□

Stoker Bram (Abraham) 1847–1912. Irish novelist, author of *Dracula*◊ 1897. A civil servant 1866–78, he then became business manager to Henry Irving◊□

Stokowski Leopold 1882–1977. US conductor, who introduced modern music, e.g. Mahler's 8th symphony, to USA, and appeared in Walt Disney's *Fantasia* 1940 etc.□

stomach pear-shaped bag of muscle in the upper abdomen for digestion of food. Food enters from the gullet (oesophagus), is digested in the stomach by its acidic juices (a mix of pepsin, rennin and hydrochloric acid) and is pushed out into the intestines (duodenum)□

Stone Sir (John) Richard 1913– . British economist, a statistics expert, whose system of 'national income accounting' has been adopted in many countries: Nobel prize 1984□

Stone Age see under prehistory◊□

stonechat European songbird; see under thrush◊□

stonefish fish related to the perch◊□

stonefly a member of Plecoptera, an order of long-tailed, winged insects, living near water, and with aquatic larvae. They are used as anglers' bait□

Stonehenge megalithic monument (c2000BC) on Salisbury Plain, Wiltshire, England, where it is one of a number of structures including about 400 round barrows◊, Durrington Walls (once an Avebury◊-style structure), Woodhenge (a 'henge' or 'enclosure' once consisting of great wooden posts), and The Cursus (a pair of banked ditches, c100 m/300 ft apart, which run straight for c3 km/2 mi; dated 4th millenium BC). The purpose of none of these is known, although it is certain that they greatly antedate the Druids◊. It seems likely they could have had a ritual purpose. Stonehenge formerly had 30 upright stones, linked to form a circle by lintels; within this was a horseshoe arrangement of five trilithons (two uprights and a lintel) which stood separately, with an 'altar-stone' or upright pillar at the open, NE end, which approximately faces the rising sun. It has been suggested that it served as an observatory□

Stopes Marie Carmichael 1880–1958. British birth-control campaigner. Founder in 1921 (with her husband A V Roe, the aircraft manufacturer) of a controversial London birth control clinic; the Well Woman Centre in Marie Stopes House, London, commemorates her work□

Stoppard Tom 1937– . British playwright, whose works include *Rosencrantz and Guildenstern are Dead* 1967, *Jumpers* 1972, *Travesties* 1974 and *The Real Thing* 1982□

Storey David Malcolm 1933– . British dramatist, son of a Yorkshire miner. His plays include *In Celebration* 1969, and *Early Days* 1980□

stork family of carnivorous wading birds, typical of the mainly tropical order Ciconiiformes, with slender bodies and long thin neck and legs. It includes the ***white stork*** *Ciconia ciconia,* which is encouraged to build on rooftops in Europe as a luck and fertility symbol; and the ***jabiru*** *Jabiru mycteria* of the Americas; up to 1.5 m/5 ft high, it is white plumaged, but with a black and red head□

stormy petrel a small sea bird; see petrel◊□

Stornoway a port on the island of Lewis in the Outer Hebrides◊□

Stoss Veit c1440–1533. German wood carver (e.g. the realistic Krakow altarpiece), also known as ***Wit Stwosz,*** because of the many years he lived in Poland□

Stourbridge market and industrial town (glass, bricks) in West Midlands, England; population 56 500□

Stowe Harriet Beecher 1811–96. US author of the anti-slavery novel *Uncle Tom's Cabin* 1851–2. The heroically loyal slave 'Uncle Tom' has become a byword for racial subservience among modern anti-racists□

Strabo c63BC–24AD. Greek geographer and historian who travelled widely to collect first hand material for his *Geography*□

Strachey (Giles) Lytton 1880–1932. British critic and biographer. His wittily mocking treatment of Arnold of Rugby, General Gordon, Florence Nightingale and Cardinal Manning in *Eminent Victorians* 1918, delighted his readers□

Stradivari Antonio 1644–1737. Italian violin-maker at Cremona in the 1660s, whose sons carried on his work. The secret of his soft varnish has never been recovered□

Strafford Thomas Wentworth, 1st Earl of Strafford 1593–1641. English statesman, originally an opponent of Charles I, but from 1628 on the Royalist side and created Viscount Wentworth. He ruled despotically as Lord Deputy of Ireland 1632–9, when he returned to England as Charles's chief adviser and received an earldom. He was impeached in 1640 by Parlaiment, abandoned by Charles as a scapegoat, and beheaded□

Straits Settlements a province of the East India Company 1826–58 and British Crown colony 1867–1946: it comprised Singapore, Malacca, Penang, Cocos Islands, Christmas Island, and Labuan◊□

Strasberg Lee 1902–82. American actor and director of Actors◊ Studio from 1948, who developed 'method' acting from Stanislavsky◊'s system; pupils include Jane Fonda, Sidney Poitier, Paul Newman□

Strasbourg industrial city (cars, tobacco, printing and publishing, preserves), capital of Alsace◊, France; population 257 300. The Council of Europe meets here, and sessions of the European Parliament alternate between Strasbourg and Luxembourg. Seized by France 1681, it was surrendered to Germany 1870–1919 and 1940–4□

Strategic Arms Limitation see Disarmament◊□

Stratford port and industrial town in Ontario, Canada; population 26 000. It has had a Shakespeare Festival from 1953□

Stratford-upon-Avon market town in Warwickshire, England; population 21 000. Shakespeare's birthplace is now a museum, his grave is in the parish church, and the Royal Shakespeare Theatre 1932 performs his works; Anne Hathaway◊'s cottage is nearby□

Strathclyde region of Scotland

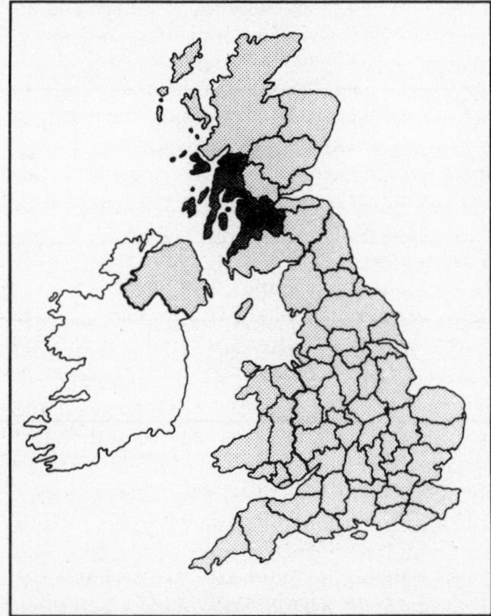

area 13 727 sq km/5300 sq mi
towns administrative headquarters Glasgow; Paisley, Greenock, Kilmarnock, Clydebank, Hamilton, Coatbridge, Prestwick
features include some of Inner Hebrides◊; river Clyde◊; part of Loch Lomond◊; Glencoe, site of the massacre of the Macdonald clan Breadalbane; the islands of Arran, Bute, Mull, etc.
products dairy, pig and poultry products; shipbuilding and engineering; coal from Ayr and Lanark; oil-related services
population 2 400 000, half the population of Scotland
famous people David Livingstone, William Burrell□

stratosphere a region of the Earth's atmosphere◊□

Straus Oscar 1870–1954. Austrian composer, best-remembered for the operetta *The Chocolate Soldier* (see G B Shaw◊)□

Strauss Franz Josef 1915– . West German politician, leader of the Bavarian Christian Social Union party, and *Land* (state) premier from 1978□

Strauss Johann 1825–99. Austrian composer, born in Vienna. Son of composer Johann Strauss 1804–49, one of the originators of the waltz, he himself became the 'waltz king' with 'The Blue Danube', 'Tales from the Vienna Woods', etc., and also wrote operettas, e.g. *Die Fledermaus*□

Strauss Richard 1864–1949. German composer, born in Munich. His works include *Four Last Songs* 1948; symphonic tone poems, e.g. *Don Juan* 1889 and *Till Eulenspiegel* 1895; and operas, e.g. *Salome* 1905, *Elektra* 1909, *Der Rosenkavalier* 1911, *Arabella* 1933□

Stravinsky Igor 1882–1971. Russian composer, an exile in Paris from 1920, and US citizen from 1945. A student of Rimsky-Korsakov, he wrote the music for the Diaghilev ballets *The Firebird* 1910, *Petrushka* 1911 and *The Rite of Spring* 1913 (controversial at the time in their unorthodox rhythms and harmony); also symphonies, concertos (for violin and piano), chamber music, and operas, e.g. *The Rake's Progress* 1951□

strawberry genus of plants *Fragaria,* family Rosaceae, producing under cultivation red fruit rich in vitamin C and multiplying by 'runners'; the ***wild strawberry*** *F vesca,* found in Britain, has tiny, delicate fruit□

strawberry tree see arbutus◊□

streptomycin antibiotic◊ discovered in 1944 and used to treat tuberculosis, influenzal meningitis, and other infections, some of which were unaffected by penicillin◊□

stress and strain in the science of materials, measures of the deforming force applied to a body and of the resulting change in its shape□

Stretford an English industrial town in Greater Manchester◊□

strike and **lockout** the former is a stoppage of work by employees to obtain or resist change in wages, hours or conditions, e.g. the lockout which began the British miners' strike of 1984–85; and the latter the weapon of the employer to enforce such change by preventing employees working, e.g. the lock out which began the British miners' strike of 1926. Strikes may be 'official' (union authorized) or 'wildcat' (undertaken spontaneously), and and may be accompanied by a 'sit-in' or 'work-in', the one being worker occupation of a factory and the other continuation of work in a plant the employer wishes to close. Another measure is the 'work to (union) rule' in which production is virtually brought to a halt, but the employer is still bound to pay wages. In a 'sympathetic' strike, action is in support of other workers on strike elsewhere, possibly in a different industry. Strikers in the UK are entitled to use 'peaceful persuasion' to bring non-striking colleagues into line, and 'pickets' (from the military term for a lookout) are posted at works entrances. 'Flying pickets' come from a distance, e.g. miners to pits in which they do not work, and 'secondary pickets' are stationed at places unconnected with the original dispute, e.g. at a steelworks using coal from a non-strike source. In the 1984–5 coal strike numbers of pickets and police were so large as to lead to disorder. Under the Thatcher government various measures to curb trade◊ union power to strike were introduced, e.g. the act of 1984 which provided for loss of immunity from legal action if a secret ballot of members is not held before a strike□

Strindberg August 1849–1912. Swedish playwright. Born in Stockholm, he lived mainly abroad after 1883, having in 1884 been unsuccessfully prosecuted for blasphemy following publication of his short stories *Marrying*. He was three times married and divorced, and regarded women with mingled adoration and hatred. His plays, influential in the development of dramatic technique, include *The Father* 1887 (in which a domineering wife drives her husband to insanity); *Miss Julie* 1887; *The Dance of Death* 1901; and *The Ghost Sonata* 1907□

stringed instrument musical instrument which produces a sound by making a stretched string vibrate. Types include:
bowed violin◊ family, viol◊ family
plucked guitar, ukelele (see guitar◊), lute◊, sitar (see lute◊), harp◊, banjo◊, lyre◊
plucked mechanically harpsichord (see piano◊)
struck mechanically piano◊, clavichord (see piano◊)
hammered dulcimer◊
See also percussion◊, brass◊, woodwind◊ instruments□

stroboscope instrument for studying periodic motion by illuminating an object with flashes at the same frequency as that of its motion. ***Strobe lighting,*** flashing in time with discotheque music at certain critical frequencies, may be conducive to hallucinatory fits (photic epilepsy)□

stroke sudden loss of consciousness with weakness or paralysis caused by interruption of blood supply to the brain; see cerebral◊ haemorrhage□

Stromboli an Italian island in the Tyrrhenian Sea; see under Lipari◊□

strontium element
symbol Sr
atomic number 38
physical description ductile silvery-white metal
features its long-lived radioactive isotope Sr–90 is produced in uranium fission; when ingested by humans it accumulates in bone and causes cancer (leukaemia)
uses in electronics; its compounds burn with a red flame and are used in fireworks□

Strophanthus genus of tropical plants of Afro-Asia, family Apocynaceae. Seeds of the handsome climber *S gratus* yield a poison, used on arrows in hunting, and in medicine as a heart stimulant□

strychnine bitter-tasting, poisonous white crystalline alkaloid obtained from the Indian plant *Strychnos nux-vomica,* family Loganiaceae. It is related to curare◊□

Stuart or ***Stewart*** House of. Royal family who inherited the Scottish throne 1371, and the English 1603. See table under House of Windsor◊□

Stuart John McDougall 1815–66. Scottish-born Australian explorer, who made the crossing of central Australia (Adelaide–Arnhem Land) 1860□

Stuart Highway first Australian all-weather route North to South across the continent (Darwin-Alice Springs 1943, extended to Adelaide 1985); it was named after the explorer John Stuart, as was Mount Stuart on the route□

Stubbs George 1724–1806. British artist, born in Liverpool, the son of a currier. His art combines portraiture, landscape and exact delineation of horses to record the turf, hunting field, and all that made the golden age of country life, e.g. *Phaeton and Pair, Gimcrack on Newmarket Heath, Haymakers*□

Stud National. British establishment founded 1915, and since 1964 located at Newmarket, where stallions are kept for visiting mares. It is now maintained by the Horserace Betting Levy Board□

sturgeon fish of sub-class Chondrostei, especially the ***beluga** Huso huso* of the Caspian, length 9 m/25 ft and weight 1500 kg/3300 lb, which lives 100 years and whose roe forms the best caviare; and ***common sturgeon** Acipenser sturio* of the Atlantic, length 4 m/14 ft, which is a 'royal fish', traditionally British Crown property, but in modern times regarded as uneatable□

Sturm Abteilung terrorist militia (SA 'storm section'), or Brownshirts, of the Nazi Party, in charge of physical training and political indoctrination□

Sturm und Drang (German 'storm and stress') German Romantic literary movement concerned with depiction of extravagant passions. Writers associated included Herder◊, Goethe◊, and Schiller◊□

Sturt Charles 1795–1869. Australian explorer, discoverer with Hume◊ in 1827 of the river Darling◊. In 1828 he explored the Murrumbidgee/Murray system□

Stuttgart industrial city (vehicles, electrical goods, publishing), capital of Baden-Württemberg, W Germany; population 582 400. headquarters of US European Command (Eucom); see also High◊ Wycombe□

Stwosz Wit. Another name for the German wood carver Veit Stoss◊□

Styria alpine province of SE Austria; once an independent state; capital Graz. See Slovenes◊□

Styx in Greek mythology, the river surrounding the underworld. See Charon◊□

Suárez Gonzalez Adolfo 1932– . Spanish prime minister 1976–81, in the transition period after the death of Franco, who helped to return the country to democratic government□

subliminal message a message delivered beneath the level of human consciousness, e.g. by words or images flashed between the frames of a cinema or TV film, or by a radio message broadcast 9000 times an hour at very low volume. It may be commercial (to sell a product, or prevent shop-lifting) or psychological (excorcise a patient's past or wean a patient from alcohol or smoking)□

submarine underwater warship designed to operate at long range and high speed. A modern nuclear-powered submarine, such as the 18 700 tonne *Ohio* (USA 1981) is 170 m/560 ft long and carries Trident missiles with a range up to 11 000 km/6750 mi; speed is approximately 30 knots/55kmph, with a usual operating depth of up to 300 m/1000 ft; see also under frequency◊ for communication. In oceanography◊, salvage, pipe-laying, and similar tasks ***submersibles*** are used. These are less speedy and wide-ranging. The Royal Navy's *Challenger* 1980 carries divers operating at 300 m/1000 ft, as well as deep-diving submersibles, and has a 'moon pool' (cylindrical, vertical, internal shaft) for lowering a three-man diving bell to reach 6000 m/20 000 ft□

Subotica largest town (with chemical, electrical machinery, and other industries) in Vojvodina, Serbia; population 154 600□

subpoena a writ (Latin 'under penalty'), requiring someone (whom it is presumed would not come forward of their own volition) to give evidence before a court or judicial official at a specific time and place□

subway American term for underground railway; see underground◊□

succubus a female demon; see incubus◊□

Suceava industrial town (textiles, lumber) in N Romania; population 80 725□

sucking fish or ***remora*** order of fish, Echeneiformes, which have an adhesive disc on the head, by which they attach themselves to sharks and turtles which (unintentionally) provide them with shelter, transport and a share of their food; a ship's bottom is often a satisfactory substitute□

Suckling Sir John 1609–42. English poet, an ardent Royalist who tried to effect Strafford◊'s escape from the Tower of London. On his failure, he fled to France and may have committed suicide. His lyrics include 'Why so pale and wan, fond lover?'□

Sucre nominal capital of Bolivia (see La◊ Paz), on the central plateau 2840 m/9330 ft; population 80 000. Founded 1538, its cathedral dates from 1553, and the university of San Francisco Xavier (1624) is probably the oldest in S America. The first revolt against Spanish rule in S America began here 25 May 1809□

Sudan The Democratic Republic of
area 2 500 000 sq km/967 500 sq mi
capital Khartoum
towns Omdurman, Juba; chief port Port Sudan
features Nile, Sudd swamp
exports cotton, gum arabic, sesame, groundnuts, durra
currency Sudanese pound
population 19 500 000; Arab and Nubian (70%) in the north, Negroid in the south
language Arabic, official; English
religion Sunni Islam 60%, mainly in the north, Animism in the south, with a Christian minority

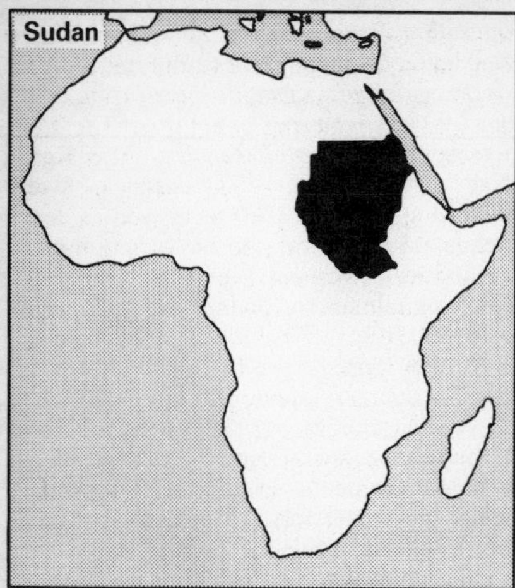

famous people Mahdi, General Gordon
government elections in April 1986 were won by Umma (a moderate Islamic Party), headed by Sadek-el-Mahdi. The new government consists of Umma merged with the Democratic Union Party, with Sadek-el-Mahdi as prime minister.
recent history subdued by an Anglo-Egyptian army under Kitchener 1896–8, Sudan was administered as an Anglo-Egyptian condominium 1899–1956, when it became a republic. Southern Sudan revolted 1956–72 against the north, but was then granted autonomy, with its own assembly at Juba. Under a charter of integration (1982), a Nile Valley parliament with equal representation of Egypt and Sudan was established 1983. In 1985 President Nemery◊ was deposed by the military, and an elected civilian government planned for 1986. In the meantime, power was taken by a transitional military council with a civilian cabinet and prime minister. The strict application of Sharia law (see under Islam◊), which had caused discontent in the south, was modified□

Sudbury nickel-mining town (90% of world production, which comes from a buried meteorite◊) in Ontario, Canada; population 160 000□

Sudbury market town in Suffolk, England; population 9000. Thomas Gainsborough was born here□

Sudetenland mountainous region of Czechoslovakia; see under Munich◊ Agreement□

Suetonius (Gaius Suetonius Tranquillius) c69–140AD. Roman historian, author of detailed *Lives of the Caesars* (Julius Caesar to Domitian)□

Suez industrial port (oil refining, fertilizers) at the Red Sea terminus of the Suez◊ Canal; population 194 000. It was reconstructed after the Arab◊-Israeli Wars□

Suez Canal artificial waterway, Port◊ Said–Suez◊, linking the Mediterranean and Red Seas from 1869 and constructed by Ferdinand de Lesseps◊. Disraeli◊ acquired a major shareholding for Britain from the Khedive of Egypt 1875, and in 1888 the Convention of Constantinople opened it to all nations. In 1956 it was forcibly nationalized by Nasser◊, and as a result of the Arab◊-Israeli Wars was blocked 1967–1975□

Suffolk eastern county of England

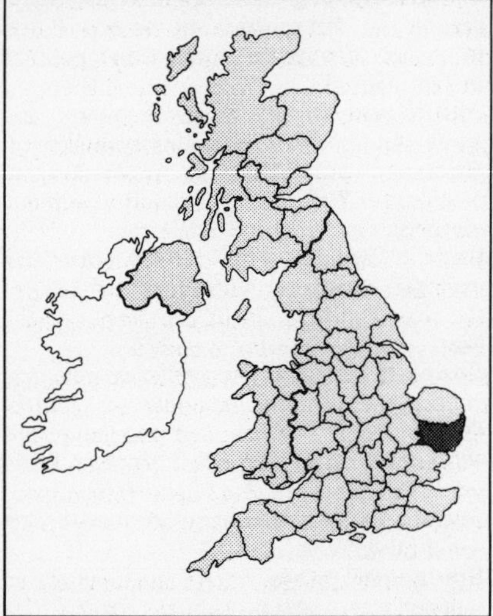

area 3797 sq km/1466 sq mi
towns administrative headquarters Ipswich; Bury St Edmunds, Lowestoft, Sudbury, Aldeburgh
features low undulating surface and flat coastline; rivers Waveney, Alde, Deben, Orwell, Stour; part of the Broads; Minsmere marshland bird reserve, near Aldeburgh; site of Sutton Hoo (7th century ship-burial of Raedwald, King of the East Angles) near Woodbridge, of which the rich jewellery, armour and weapons are in the British Museum; site of 'Sizewell B', planned as the first of Britain's controversial pressurized-water reactor (PWR) plants
products cereals, sugar beet; working horses (Suffolk punches); fertilizers, agricultural machinery
population 608 400
famous people Constable, Gainsborough, Elizabeth Garrett Anderson, Benjamin Britten, George Crabbe, Edward Fitzgerald, Ruth Rendell□

Sufism a mystical movement of Islam◊□

sugar sweet, soluble carbohydrate, either a monosaccharide or disaccharide. Monosaccharides are the simplest of sugars, examples are fructose and glucose (both from fruit and honey). Disaccharides are sugars which when hydrolysed by dilute acids give two (either the same or different) simple sugars (i.e. monosaccharides), an example is sucrose from sugar-cane. Polysaccharides (e.g. starch and cellulose) hydrolyse to many simple sugars.
Commercially, sugar (sucrose) is produced from ***sugar cane*** (one of the grasses◊), by crushing the stem. ***Molasses*** is the uncrystallized syrup drained from the sugar (fermented, it forms rum), and is then refined by stages to 'pure' whiteness (e.g. demerara, or coffee sugar, is a stage along the way); ***treacle*** and ***golden syrup*** are successive liquid stages in the refining of molasses. Bagasse, the fibrous residue, is used for paper-making, cattle feed, and fuel, and new types of cane are being bred for low sugar, and high fuel production.
Sugar is also produced from ***sugar beet***◊ when it is obtained from the roots (beet molasses, when fermented, also produces alcohol), the remaining pulp is used as cattle feed.
Highly refined forms of sugar include cube, granulated, caster, and icing; in all forms, sugar is a major source of energy (e.g. athletes suck glucose tablets) but can also cause caries or tooth decay (see teeth◊), and is credited with promoting arterial disease and heart attacks□

sugar maple a North American maple tree; see acer◊□

sugilite translucent, deep purple stone, also known as ***royal lavulite,*** classified as a rare gem in 1980 when it was first found in gem quality in S Africa□

Suharto 1921– . Indonesian general. He ousted Sukarno◊ to become president in 1966, and was re-elected for the fourth time in 1983. He ended confrontation with Malaysia, invaded E Timor in 1975, and reached a co-operation agreement with Papua New Guinea 1979□

Suhl capital of Suhl district and industrial city (cars, precision instruments, chemicals) in E Germany; population 35 000□

suicide self-murder. Until 1960 it was a criminal offence in English law, if committed while of sound mind, and was in earlier times punished by the confiscation of the suicide's possessions, and even until 1823 burial was at night, without burial service, and with a stake through the heart. Hence the frequency with which coroners' juries found that the act was committed while the person was insane□

Sukarno Achmed 1901–70. Indonesian nationalist, who cooperated during World War II in the local administration set up by the Japanese, replacing Dutch rule. In 1945 he became President of the new Indonesian Republic, assuming the presidency for life 1966; he was ousted by Suharto◊ 1967□

Sukkur river port in Pakistan, on the Indus (the Sukkur-Lloyd Barrage 1923–32 lies to the west); population 160 000□

Sulawesi an island in Indonesia; see under Sunda◊ Islands□

Suleiman I 'the Magnificent' 1494–1566. Sultan of Turkey from 1520, under whom the Ottoman Empire reached its zenith. He captured Belgrade 1521 and Rhodes in 1522; defeated the Hungarians at Mohacs 1526, and his advance into Europe was only ended by his unsuccessful siege of Vienna Sept–Oct 1529. In 1534 he conquered Iran, and then extended his rule south through almost all N Africa and even as far as Aden. He was badly mauled, however, when he tried to take Valetta from the Knights of Malta in 1565. He was a poet, and an excellent lawgiver and administrator□

Sulgrave see Northamptonshire◊□

Sulla Lucius Cornelius 138–78BC. Roman soldier-statesman, a leader of the senatorial party. Forcibly suppressing the democrats in 88, he departed for a successful campaign against Mithradates◊ of Pontus. The democrats seized power in his absence, but on his return Sulla captured Rome and massacred all opponents. As dictator, his reforms, which strengthened the senate, were backward-looking and shortlived. He retired in 79□

Sullivan Sir Arthur Seymour 1842–1900. British composer, whose light operas in collaboration with Sir William Gilbert◊ included *HMS Pinafore* 1878, *The Pirates of Penzance* 1879, *Patience* (which ridiculed the Aesthetic◊ movement) 1881, *The Mikado* 1885, *The Yeoman of the Guard* 1888, and *The Gondoliers* 1889. He also wrote the very successful ballad 'The Lost Chord', and various serious works which he valued more highly than the operettas; the music for the ballet *Pineapple Poll* 1951 was arranged from his work by Mackerras◊□

Sullivan John L(awrence) 1858–1918. American heavyweight boxer, world champion 1882–92 (defeated by Corbett). He fought the last bareknuckle fight (a victory over Jake Kilrain) in 1889□

Sully Maximilien de Béthune, Duc de Sully 1560–1641. French statesman, who served with the Huguenots in the Wars of Religion◊, and, as Henry IV's superintendent of finances 1598–1611, aided French recovery□

sulphonamide drug any of a group of compounds containing the chemical species sulphonamide $SO_2.NH_2$ (or its derivatives) which are used to treat bacterial diseases, e.g. wound infection, puerperal (childbirth) fever, pneumonia, etc. See Gerhard Domagk◊□

sulphur element
symbol S
atomic number 16
physical description yellow crystals forming 0.3% of the human body; it is present in many proteins e.g. eggs, hair
uses used in industrial processes such as the production of sulphuric acid, in fireworks, and in vulcanizing rubber□

sulphuric acid acid H_2SO_4, a dense, oily, colourless liquid which evolves much heat when added to water. It is used extensively in the chemical industry, petrol refining, and in manufacturing fertilizers, detergents, explosives, dyes, etc□

Sulu Archipelago some 870 islands off SW Mindanao in the Philippines: area 2815 sq km/1087 sq mi. The capital is Jolo, on the island (the largest) of the same name. Until 1940 the islands were an autonomous sultanate□

Sumatra second largest island in Indonesia; see under Sunda◊ Islands□

Sumer area of southern Iraq where the Sumerian civilization (see under Iraq◊'s history) was established from c5000BC. The Sumerians may possibly have been related to the Dravidians◊□

summer time practice (introduced in the UK 1916) whereby legal time from spring to autumn is an hour in advance of Greenwich mean time. Continental Europe 'puts the clock back' a month earlier than the UK in autumn□

summons citation (order) officially delivered, requiring someone (who is one of the people involved in an action) to appear in court, to answer a claim made by the plaintiff□

sun the star which is the principal light and heat source for the planets in the solar system, including the earth. It lies about 30 000 light years from its centre. Spectroscopy◊ shows that it consists mainly of hydrogen and helium, and produces its energy by nuclear fusion◊, converting the hydrogen to helium◊
diameter 1 392 000 km/865 000 mi
distance from earth 149 500 000 km/93 000 000 mi, so that it takes just over 8 minutes for its light to reach us
rotation period 25 days 9 hours
atmosphere comprises an inner layer of gas (chromosphere) between the radiating surface (photosphere) and the outer layer (corona), made up of gas at a very high temperature which extends many millions of miles; both are only visible to the naked eye during an eclipse◊. The ***heliopause*** is the boundary where the flow of charged particles from the sun ends and the interstellar medium begins
surface temperature 6000°C/10 000°F
surface features:
sunspots dark patches (cooler areas, about 4000°C) which are short-lived but may be large; they occur in an approximate cycle of 11.5 years
interior like all stars composed of intensely hot gas, chiefly hydrogen; the central temperature is 12–15 000 000°C
features: dust ring (F corona), first recorded in 1983, composed mainly of a million tonnes of silicate grains at a temperature of about 1300°C; further out, near the asteroid belt, there are apparently three more *flares,* violent outbreaks of a few hours duration associated with spot-groups; *prominences,* giant masses of glowing hydrogen which rise from the surface for some 482 700 km/300 000 mi, and may persist for weeks; *solar wind* continuous outward projection from the sun's inner corona of streams of low-density hot ionized gas or plasma which is much intensified when flares (see above) occur, and may cause radio blackouts, geomagnetic storms, and aurora displays□

Sunbelt the region of the USA south of Washington, DC, between the Californian and Atlantic coasts□

Sunbury-on-Thames market town and boating centre in Surrey, England; population 40 000. There are petroleum research laboratories and film studios□

Sunda Islands islands W of the Moluccas in the Malay Archipelago, the greater number belonging to Indonesia◊; so-called because they lie largely on the Indonesian extension of the Sunda continental shelf. They are divided into:
Greater Sundas, including:
Borneo the third largest island in the world; area 5800 sq km/2226 sq mi. It comprises *Sabah* and *Sarawak*◊ (Malaysia); *Brunei*◊; and, occupying by far the larger part, *Kalimantan* (Indonesia); area 550 200 sq km/212 380 sq mi; population 6 725 000. Chief towns, ports Banjarmasin, Pontianak, Balikpapan. In coastal areas the people of Borneo are Malays, with a mingling of Chinese, and in the interior, indigenous Dayaks.
Java chief island of Indonesia; area 132 000 sq km/51 000 sq mi; population (including the small island of *Madura*) 91 270 000. Chief town Jakarta (capital of Indonesia); ports

Surabaya, Semarang, Bandung. There is a central volcanic mountain chain including Semeru 3676 m/12 060 ft in the E; humidity is high and there is rain forest, producing teak. Other products include rice, coffee, cocoa, tea, sugar, palm oil, rubber, and petroleum; textiles, both synthetic and hand-produced batik◊. There is an ancient indigenous culture, and from the 1st century Java was colonized by Hindus, who established medieval kingdoms flourishing 8–13th centuries. As they waned, Islamic influence grew and in the later 18th century the last Hindu-Buddhist kingdom came under Islamic rule. In central Java there are magnificent Buddhist monuments, e.g. Borobudur (see Yogyakarta◊), and other remains.

Sumatra largest island of Indonesia; area 427 350 sq km/165 000 sq mi; population 28 000 000. Chief towns Palembang, Medan; port Padang. There is a volcanic mountain range to the W and a wide plain to the E, both forested. A Hindu empire was founded in the 8th century, but Islam came with Arab traders from the 13th century, and was adopted throughout in the 16th century.

Sulawesi (formerly ***Celebes***) part of Indonesia; area 190 000 sq km/73 000 sq mi; population 10 410 000. Chief town Menado; port Ujung Padang. Mountainous and forested, it produces copra and nickel.

Belitung island between Borneo and Sumatra, famous for tin.

Lesser Sundas (Indonesian name ***Nusa Tenggara***), all Indonesian, including:

Bali a volcanic island with a fine climate; area 5800 sq km/2240 sq mi; population 2 220 000. Capital Singaradja. Its Hindu culture, established in 7th century AD, survives: drama, music, dance, gold and silver work, wood carving, weaving.

Lombok comprises a fertile plain between N and S mountain ranges; area 1825 sq km/ sq mi. Capital Mataram.

Timor largest and most easterly of the group; area 33 610 sq km/12 977 sq mi. It is divided into two provinces, the western (capital Kupang) and eastern (capital Dili). The latter was an overseas province of Portugal until the civil war of 1975, when it was annexed by Indonesia. Guerilla warfare by local people seeking independence continues□

sundance a North American Indian ceremony; see Plains◊ Indians□

Sunday seventh day of the week (see Monday◊), but for Christians the first, being set aside for divine worship in commemoration of Christ's resurrection (replacing the Jewish sabbath). In the UK certain activities have been restricted since medieval times on this day, until in 1969 curbs on sports, theatres and dancing were lifted. However, a bill to enable Sunday trading was defeated in April 1986. Similar legislation in the USA has long been very laxly enforced□

Sunday School school primarily for religious instruction (see Robert Raikes◊), but also for assisting children to read and write. Universal education took over the latter function, and the modern church uses Sunday Schools to stimulate an interest in the Bible through play, stories, etc.□

Sunderland Robert Spencer, 2nd Earl of Sunderland 1640–1702. English politician, a sceptical intriguer who changed to Roman Catholicism to secure his place under James II, and then reverted with the political tide. In 1688 he fled to Holland (disguised as a woman), where he made himself invaluable to the future William III. Now a Whig, he advised the new king to adopt the system, which still prevails, of choosing the government from the dominant party in the Commons□

Sunderland industrial port (formerly only coalmining and shipbuilding, but now diversified to electronics, glass, furniture) in Tyne and Wear, England; population 298 000. There is a polytechnic and civic theatre, the Sunderland Empire□

sundew a carnivorous plant; see Insectivorous◊ plant□

sundial instrument measuring time by means of a shadow cast by the sun. Almost completely outdated by the invention of clocks, it survives ornamentally in gardens. The dial is marked with the hours at graduated distances, and a style or gnomon (parallel to earth's axis and pointing to the N) casts the shadow□

Sundsvall industrial port (timber and woodpulp) in E Sweden; population 94 000□

sunfish two types of fish; see under perch◊, and under tetraodon◊□

sunflower genus of plants *Helianthus* family Compositae◊, including the N American ***common sunflower*** *H annuus* which may reach 5 m/15 ft. It is also widely grown commercially in central Europe, Canada and the USSR for its seeds and their oil, used in cookery, margarine, etc., and (the residue) for cattle feed□

Sungari river in NE China (Manchuria◊), which joins the Amur on the Siberian frontier; length 1300 km/800 mi□

Sunni a member of the larger of the two main Muslim sects; see under Islam◊□

sunspot dark patches that appear on the sun; see sun◊□

sunstroke see heat◊ stroke□

sun Yat-sen or *sun Zhong Shan* 1867–1925. Chinese revolutionary, founder of the Guomindang◊, and moving spirit behind the revolution of 1911 which overthrew the Manchu dynasty. He was briefly president 1912, but the reactionaries gained the ascendant, and he broke away to try to establish an independent republic in S China based on Canton. He lacked organizational ability, but his three 'people's principles' of nationalism, democracy, and social reform were influential. Both the Nationalists regard him as a hero□

superconductivity property of some metals and metallic compounds (discovered by Kamerlingh Onnes 1911), whereby their resistance decreases uniformly with decreasing temperature until at a critical temperature (the superconducting point, within a few degrees of the absolute zero), the resistance suddenly falls to zero. In this superconducting state an electric current, induced (by a magnetic field) in a closed circuit or ring of the material, will continue after the magnetic field has been removed, so long as the material remains below the superconducting point. Synthetic organic conductors have also been produced which operate at much higher temperatures. Superconductivity has industrial importance, e.g. the production of powerful electromagnets□

Superior Lake. The largest of the Great◊ Lakes of North America□

supernova a star◊ which explodes, throwing most of its matter into space. It is believed that the planets of our solar system consist of matter from a supernova which was collected by the sun's gravitational field□

supersonic speed speed greater than that at which sound travels: at sea level about 1220 kmph/760 mph, but decreasing with altitude until at 12 000 m/40 000 ft it is only 1060 kmph, remaining constant above that height. Squadron Leader John Derry (UK) was the first to achieve supersonic flight, in a De Havilland 108 research aircraft, 6 Sept 1948. See Mach◊ number. When an aircraft passes the sound barrier, shock waves are built up which give rise to sonic boom, often heard at ground level□

suprarenal gland another name for the adrenal gland; see under hormone◊□

Suprematism Russian art movement initiated by Malevich◊ 1913, which exploited only purely geometrical shapes (rectangles, triangles, circles, etc.). See Cubism◊□

Supreme Court highest US judicial tribunal, composed of a chief justice (William Rehnquist from 1986), and eight associate justices. Vacancies are filled by the president, and members can be removed only by impeachment. See Law◊ Courts□

Sur Arabic name for the Lebanese port of Tyre◊□

Surabaya industrial port (oil refining, shipbuilding) in Indonesia, on Java; population 2 028 000. It is an important naval and military base□

Suraj-ud-Dowlah c1728–57. Nawab of Bengal, see Calcutta◊ and Plassey◊. He was killed at his capital, Murshidabad□

Surat industrial (textiles) city in Gujarat, India; population 913 000. The first East India Company 'factory' (trading post) in India was established here 1612□

surface tension condition which causes the surfaces of liquids to behave rather as if they were covered with weak elastic skins – this is why one can, with care, float a razor blade on water. It is caused by cohesive forces between water molecules; allied phenomena include the formation of droplets and the 'capillary action' by which water soaks into a sponge□

surfing sport of riding on the crest of large waves while standing on a narrow, keeled, plastic surfboard about 1.8 m/5 ft long, as first developed in Hawaii and Australia. In ***windsurfing*** the board has a sail attached, and can be used in any sea, with anything more than a slight breeze blowing, and has the manoeuvrability of a small yacht□

surgeon fish fish related to the perch◊□

surgery in medicine, originally the removal of diseased parts or foreign substances from the body. The surgeon now uses not only the scalpel and electric cautery, but beamed high-energy ultrasonic waves and the intense light energy of the laser. Modern extensions of the field of surgery include:

microsurgery for which the surgeon uses a binocular microscope, magnifying 25 times, e.g. in rejoining a severed limb. Sewing of the nerves and blood vessels is done with a nylon thread so fine that it is only just visible to the naked eye. Restoration of movement and sensation may be comparatively limited;

plastic surgery repair of damaged tissue (e.g. skin grafts for burns) and restructuring of damaged or deformed parts of the body; also ***cosmetic surgery*** for serious aesthetic reasons, when the patient is psychologically damaged by genuinely ugly features, and for vanity reasons, e.g. to dispose of bags under the eyes or a double chin;

psychosurgery has included leucotomy/lobotomy, the separation of the white fibres in the prefrontal lobe of the brain to relieve anxiety states, but at the price of permanent

unpredictable personality change; and burning an area of the brain thought to trigger aggression (amygdalotomy) in violent (volunteer) convicts in the USA;
transplant surgery the transfer of an embryo, genetic material, an organ, tissue, etc., from one part of the body to another, or to another body. Under the UK transplant code of 1979 covering the use of material from a donor, two doctors (being both independent of the tranplant team and clinically independent of each other) must certify the brain death of the donor. See heart◊, kidneys◊, embryology◊, genetic engineering◊. In the 1980s, experiments with rats suggested the possibility of eventual restoration of the damaged or diseased human brain by transplants of embryonic nervous tissue□

Suriname Republic of

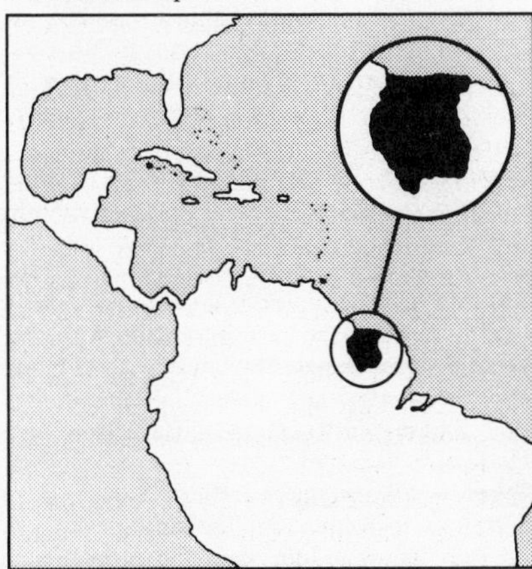

area 163 265 sq km/63 250 sq mi
capital Paramaribo
features Surinam river
exports bauxite, rice, citrus; timber
currency Surinam guilder
population 450 000, including Creole, Chinese, Hindu, and Indonesian peoples
language Dutch, English (official)
religion Christianity 35%, Hinduism 25%, Islam 17%
government National Military Council (headed by Lt-Colonel Desi Bouterse from 1982); a national assembly was appointed 1985 to draft a new constitution
recent history formerly Dutch Guiana, the country became independent in 1975 as Surinam. A left-wing pro-Cuba military coup occurred in 1980, and a right-wing attempt to return by a reverse coup to civilian government was suppressed in 1982 by Bouterse. The Netherlands had promised $1.5 billion in aid for the first decade of independence, but has suspended this since the institution of military rule□

Surrealism movement in literature, painting, commercial art, photography, film, stage design, etc., which was developed from Dadaism◊ by André Breton◊. Influenced by the Freudian theory of the unconscious it sought to embody in art and poetry the irrational forces of dreams and the subconscious mind. Those linked with it include artists Arp, Chirico, Dali, Ernst, Magritte, Miro, Picasso; poets Aragon, Éluard□

Surrey Henry Howard, Earl of Surrey c1517–47. English soldier-poet, executed on a poorly-based charge of high treason. With Wyatt◊, he introduced the sonnet to England, and was a pioneer of blank verse□

Surrey southern county of England

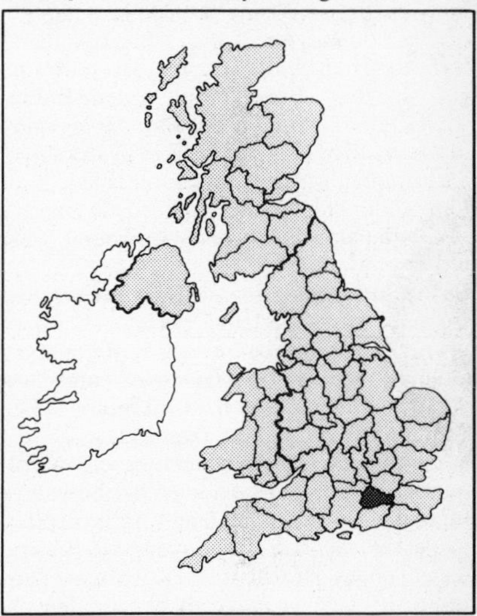

area 1679 sq km/648 sq mi
towns administrative headquarters Kingston-upon-Thames; Guildford, Woking
features rivers Thames, Mole and Wey; Box and Leith Hills; North Downs; Runnymede, Thameside site of the signing of Magna◊ Carta; Kew Palace and Royal Botanic Gardens; Yehudi Menuhin◊ School
products market garden vegetables, and general agricultural products
population 1 008 500
famous people John Galsworthy□

surrogacy the practice whereby a woman becomes pregnant with the intention of the child being handed over to a couple (of whom the man may be the natural father, even if only by artificial insemination), usually in return for payment. Such commercial surrogacy is practised in some European countries and in the USA, but is illegal (from 1985) in the UK□

survey see map◊□
Surya in Hinduism, the personification of the sun, driving a chariot and horses□
suslik a type of squirrel, see under rodent◊□
Susquehanna river rising in central New York state, USA, and flowing 715 km/444 mi to Chesapeake Bay. It is used for hydroelectric power. On the strength of its musical name, S T Coleridge◊ planned to establish a Pantisocratic (communal) settlement here with Southey□
Sutcliff Rosemary 1920– . British historical novelist for adults and children, including *The Eagle of the Ninth* 1954, *Tristan and Iseult* 1971, and *The Road to Camlann* 1981□
Sutherland Graham Vivian 1903–80. British artist, whose early work was influenced by Blake and the Surrealists. From 1936 it was individualized by using detailed presentation of some unusual insect, vegetable, or mineral form to give it symbolic force. His portraits, e.g. Maugham, Beaverbrook, Helena Rubinstein, were remarkably popular, but his study of Churchill in 1954 was disliked by its subject and eventually burnt on the instructions of Lady Churchill. He also designed the tapestry above the altar in Coventry Cathedral 1962. Order of Merit 1960□
Sutherland Dame Joan 1926– . Australian soprano of superlative richness, whose operatic roles include Lucia di Lammermoor, Donna Anna (in *Don Giovanni*), and Desdemona. Dame of the British Empire 1979□
Sutlej a tributary of the river Indus◊□
suttee Hindu custom whereby a widow voluntarily committed suicide on her husband's funeral pyre; public and family pressure often made the sacrifice 'involuntary'. It became illegal under British rule 1829. In modern India it has sporadically been illegally revived□
Sutton borough of S Greater London
features site of Nonsuch Palace built by Henry VIII, demolished in 17th century
population 167 000□
Sutton Coldfield a residential suburb in the English city of Birmingham◊□
Sutton Hoo the site of a Saxon ship burial near Woodbridge, Suffolk◊, England□
Sutton-in-Ashfield industrial town (coal, hosiery, plastics) in Nottinghamshire, England; population 44 400□
Suva capital and industrial port (soap, coconut oil) of Fiji, on Viti Levu; population 71 255□
Suvorov Aleksandr Vasilyevich 1729–1800. Russian field marshal, victorious against the Turks 1787–91, the Poles 1794 and the Directory◊'s French army in Italy 1798–99. See Revolutionary◊ Wars□
Suzhou city (formerly Soochow, and also known as Wuhsien 1912–49) in Jiangsu province, China; population 650 000. It has embroidery and jade carving traditions, and exquisite gardens (e.g. Shizilin and Zhuozheng)□
Svalbard Norwegian archipelago in the Arctic Ocean; area 62 000 sq km/24 000 sq mi; population 4000, including 2500 Russians. The chief settlement is Long Year City on the main island, Spitzbergen; other islands include NE Land, Edge Island and Barents Island. Coal is mined by Russia and Norway, and there are weather and research stations. Rich wildlife includes walrus and polar bear; fossil palms show that it was in the tropics 40 million years ago. Under the ***Svalbard Treaty*** 1925, Norway has sovereignty, but allow.2% ee scientific and economic access to others□
Sverdlovsk industrial town (mining of copper, iron and platinum; engineering, chemicals) in W USSR; population 1 286 000. Known as ***Ekaterinburg*** until 1924, it was here that Nicholas II◊ and his family were murdered in 1918□
Svevo Italo. Pseudonym of Italian novelist Ettore Schmitz 1861–1928. His books include *As a Man Grows Older* 1898 and *Confessions of Zeno* 1923□
Swabia historic region (German ***Schwaben***) of SW Germany, an independent duchy in the Middle Ages. It includes Augsburg and Ulm, and forms part of the modern *Länder* (states) of Baden-Württemberg, Bavaria, and Hessen□
Swahili a language, of Bantu origin, predominant in Kenya and Tanzania; it is an E African lingua franca, and the official language of both Kenya and Tanzania□
swallow family of birds Hirundinidae, order Passeriformes, comprising:
swallows especially the ***common swallow*** *hirundo rustica,* steel-blue above and creamy white beneath, it has a deeply forked tail and rears two broods a year in mud nests shaped like a half saucer on the sides of buildings. It is an insect-feeder and migrates from Europe to Africa and Asia in the winter
martins including the ***house martin*** *Delichon urbica,* which builds cup-shaped nests under house eaves. It is blue-black above and white below, but distinguished from the swallow by its shorter wings and less forked tail. The brownish ***sand martin*** *Riparia riparia* tunnels to make a nest in sandy banks□
swamp cypress a type of tree; see under conifer◊□
Swan Sir Joseph Wilson 1828–1914. British inventor (in the UK) of the incandescent

filament electric lamp, and of bromide paper in photography□

swan a large aquatic bird; see under waterfowl◊□

Swanage an English town on the Isle of Purbeck; see under Dorset◊□

Swansea port and administrative headquarters of W Glamorgan, Wales; population 188 100. It has an 'innovation centre', which includes a bio-technology area, with a leech◊ farm□

swastika cross in which the bars are extended, all in the same clockwise or anticlockwise direction. An Aryan and Buddhist mystic symbol, it was adopted by Hitler, first as the emblem of the Nazi Party, and then incorporated in the German national flag in 1935□

Swatow another name for the Chinese port of Shantou◊□

Swaziland Kingdom of

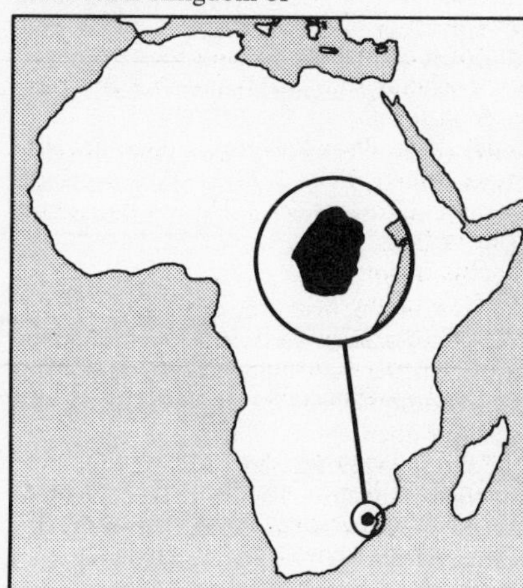

area 17 400 sq km/6704 sq mi
capital Mbabane
features landlocked enclave between S Africa and Mozambique; Mount Kilimanjaro; Serengeti National Park
exports sugar, citrus; timber, asbestos, iron ore
currency lilangeni
population 651 000
language English, Swazi (spoken by 90%), both official
religion Christianity, both Protestant and Catholic
government the King (Mswati III from 1986) nominates part of both Senate and House of Assembly, the rest being elected by an electoral college
recent history its original autonomy guaranteed by Britain and the Transvaal, Swaziland became a special High Commission Territory in 1903, and independent in 1968. On the death of King Sobhuza II 1904–82, one of his 100 wives became Queen Regent for his son, until he became king in 1986, on his 18th birthday. One month after his accession, Mswati III dissolved the supreme council of state, thus becoming absolute sovereign. Plans for the transfer by S Africa to Swaziland of the KaNgwane homeland and Ingwavuma were blocked by KwaZulu court action in 1982□

sweat salty fluid exuded by glands of the skin. In humans this 'insensible' perspiration amounts to 1.7–2.3 litres/3–4 pints a day; it becomes 'sensible' (in a hot room or as a result of exertion) as the body attempts to lower its temperature by evaporation□

swede see under Turnip◊□

Sweden Kingdom of

area 449 700 sq km/173 629 sq mi
capital Stockholm
towns Göteborg, Malmö, Uppsala, Norrköping, Vasteras
features many lakes, e.g. Väner, Vätter, Mälar, Hjälmar; islands of Öland and Gaotland; large wild herds of elk
exports aircraft, cars, domestic equipment, ballbearings, drills, missiles, electronics; petro-chemicals; textiles; furnishings, ornamental glass
currency krona
population 8 335 000, including 1 200 000 post-war immigrants (Finns, Turks, Yugoslavs, Greeks)
language Swedish, one of the Scandinavian division of Germanic languages
religion Evangelical Lutheran
famous people Swedenborg, Linnaeus, Celsius, Alfred Nobel, Strindberg, Selma Lagerlöf□
government under the 1975 constitution the powers of the monarchy (Carl XVI Gustaf

from 1973) are nominal, and the Salic◊ law was abrogated 1980, so that Crown Princess Victoria, born 1977, is first in line to succeed. The unicameral parliament (Riksdag) is elected by proportional representation (Prime Minister Olof Palme, Social Democrat, was assassinated 1986 and has been replaced by his former deputy, Ingmar Carlsson).

history united as an independent nation in the 12th century, Sweden was under Danish rule (together with Norway) 1397–1520, when revolt led to Gustavus Vasa◊ being placed on the throne. Sweden lost Finland to Russia in 1809, and seized Norway in 1814 (union dissolved 1905): see Bernadotte◊. Neutral in both wars, Sweden was almost continuously under Social Democrat governments 1932–76, so that a fully comprehensive welfare system was introduced□

Swedenborg Emanuel 1688–1772. Swedish scientist (geology, magnetic theory, brain function, etc.) and philosopher of great repute. From 1747, however, he concentrated on scriptural study, and in his *Divine Love and Wisdom* concluded that the Last Judgment had taken place in 1757, and that the ***New Church*** of which he was the prophet, had now been inaugurated. His writings are the scriptures of the sect popularly known as Swedenborgians, which still survives, and his works are kept in circulation by the Swedenborg Society, London□

Swedish one of the Scandinavian group of languages; see under Sweden◊□

sweet cicely S European plant *Myrrhis odorata,* family Umbelliferae◊; the root is eaten as a vegetable and the aniseed-flavoured leaves are used in salads□

sweet corn another term for maize; see cereals◊□

sweet pea a type of plant; see pea◊□

sweet potato tropical American plant *Ipomoea batatas,* family Convolvulaceae; the white/orange tuberous root is used as a source of starch and alcohol, and eaten as a vegetable□

sweet william perennial S European plant, the bearded pink *Dianthus barbatus,* family Caryophyllaceae, introduced to England c1575, and grown for its fragrant red/white flowers□

Sweyn I d. 1014. King of Denmark from c986, nicknamed 'Forkbeard'. He raided England, finally conquering it 1013, and being accepted as king. His early death led to the recall of Ethelred◊ II□

Swift Jonathan 1667–1745. Irish satirist and Anglican cleric. Born in Dublin, he became secretary to Sir William Temple◊ at Moor Park, Surrey, where began his friendship with the child 'Stella' (Hester Johnson 1681–1728) in 1689; his *Journal to Stella* was written to describe for her his life in London from 1710 until his appointment as Dean of St Patrick's, Dublin, in 1713. 'Stella' remained the love of his life, though not in the sense of his wishing to marry her, but 'Vanessa' (Esther Vanhomrigh 1690–1723), a Dublin girl who had fallen in love with him, jealously wrote to her rival in 1723, and so shattered his relationship with both women. His works include *The Tale of a Tub* 1704, attacking corruption in religion and learning; brilliant contributions to the Tory paper *The Examiner,* which he edited 1710–11; the scarifying *Modest Proposal for Preventing the Children of Poor People from being a Burden to their Parents or the Country* 1729 (the satiric solution being to fatten and eat them), and the masterpiece of disguised satire, *Gulliver's Travels* 1726, a fantasy book of travel to lands inhabited by giants, miniature people, intelligent horses, and so on. From c1738 his mind began to fail, and he died insane□

swift order of fast-flying birds, Apodiformes, 'footless', with extremely long primary feathers and short weak legs; it includes:

swifts family Apodidae, which include the ***common swift*** *Apus apus* a summer migrant Africa–Europe; drab-coloured, with a short, forked tail, and curved wings longer than the body. For the first three years of its life it is continuously airborne, even sleeping in flight, but will then land to nest, often in old buildings, sticking its nesting material together with saliva. The ***swiftlet*** species of SE Asia, genus *Collocalia,* make their nests in a similar way, and these are used to make soup in eastern countries.

hummingbirds American birds, family Trochilidae, which produce a humming sound by the rapid beating of their wings (up to 70 times per second), and can both hover and fly backwards. Their plumage is remarkable for its brilliant colour and metallic lustre, and they have a long tongue for taking nectar from flowers and capturing insects. The Cuban ***bee hummingbird*** *Melisuga helenae* is the world's smallest bird at 5.5 cm/2 in long, and weighs 2 g/less than 1/10 oz□

swimming self-propulsion of the body through water. The competition strokes are: breaststroke (developed from the 16th century); the front crawl (developed by the Australians from a South Sea Island method in the early 20th century, and still the fastest stroke); the backstroke (developed in the 1920s, which enables the swimmer to breathe very freely); and the butterfly (developed from the breaststroke in the USA in the 1930s, and the second fastest of the strokes). In competition the swimmer enters the water with a 'racing plunge', or dive. Diving events are divided into springboard and the higher firm-board events.

Underwater swimming, developed with the invention of frogman equipment (foot flippers, breathing apparatus, and individual motor propulsion), has techniques of its own. See also Channel◊ swimming□

Swinburne Algernon Charles 1837–1909. British poet. He attracted attention with the choruses of his Greek-style tragedy *Atalanta in Calydon* 1865, and the lyric, pagan fire of poems such as 'Laus Veneris', 'Dolores', and 'A Litany' in *Poems and Ballads* 1866. But he and Rossetti◊ were attacked in 1871 as leaders of 'the fleshly school of poetry' and the revolutionary politics of *Songs Before Sunrise* 1871 alienated yet others. In 1879 he moved to the home of Watts◊-Dunton at Putney, and lived in retirement□

Swindon industrial town (heavy engineering, electrical goods, electronics) in Wiltshire, England; population 91 000. Formerly an important railway engineering centre (1841-1985), it now has an increasing number of service and distribution industries. The birthplace of Richard Jefferies at Coate Farm has been restored□

swine fever virus disease (hog cholera) of pigs, almost eradicated in the UK from 1963 by a slaughter policy; ***swine flu*** is a virulent form of influenza, closely resembling that in humans; ***swine vesicular disease*** is a virus disease (porcine enterovirus) closely resembling foot◊ and mouth and communicable to humans□

swing music jazz◊ offshoot c1930–1940s, with a simple harmonic base (of varying tempo) from the rhythm section (percussion, guitar, piano), and superimposed solo melodic line, e.g. from trumpet, clarinet or saxophone. Exponents included Benny Goodman, Duke Ellington, Glenn Miller□

Swinton Sir Ernest 1868–1951. British soldier-historian, a major-general in World War I, who invented the tank 1916□

Swiss cheese plant see Araceae◊□

Swithun St. d. 862 English cleric, chancellor of King Ethelwolf and Bishop of Winchester◊ 852–62. He is buried in the cathedral, and, for obscure reasons, the weather on his feast day (15 Jul) is said to continue as either wet or fine for 40 days□

Switzerland (Swiss Confederation)
area 41 288 sq km/15 941 sq mi
capital Bern(e)
towns Zürich, Geneva, Lausanne; river port Basel

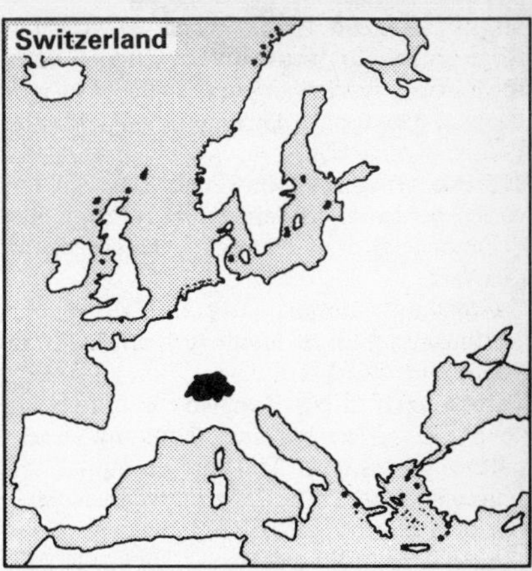

features most mountainous country in Europe (Alps◊ and Jura Mountains); winter sports area of the upper valley of the river Inn (Engadine); lakes Maggiore, Lucerne, Geneva, Constance, etc.
exports electrical goods, chemicals and pharmaceuticals, watches, precision instruments, confectionery; banking, insurance and tourism are important
currency Swiss franc
population 6 500 000
language German 69%, French 20%, Italian 10%, all official; 1% Romansch
religion Roman Catholicism 50%, Protestantism 48%
famous people William Tell ***literature*** Gottfried Keller, Herman Hesse, Friedrich Dürrenmatt, Max Frisch
government federal assembly of two houses, a directly elected National Council, and Council of States (two members chosen by each of the 26 cantons); the Assembly elects the executive federal council, and the President, who holds office for only one year
recent history the Confederation originated 1291, gradually enlarging, and in 1648 becoming independent of the Holy Roman Empire. Invaded by France in the Revolutionary Wars, it reverted to a confederation in 1815, the Congress of Vienna◊ guaranteeing its neutrality, which it maintained in both World Wars, since it was useful to the warring powers as a route of communication□

swordfish large fish related to the perch◊□

sycamore a type of tree; see maple◊□

Sydney industrial port (engineering, scientific equipment, chemicals, clothing, furniture) and capital of New South Wales, Australia; population 3 280 900. It is a financial centre, and has three universities. The main streets still follow the lines of the original waggon tracks, and the Regency Bligh House survives. Modern landmarks are the harbour bridge (single span 503.5 m/1652 ft) 1923–32, Opera House 1959–73; Centre Point Tower 1980□

syenite grey, crystalline, plutonic igneous rock, made of feldspar and hornblende, distinguished from granite by the absence of quartz□

Syktyvkar industrial city (timber, paper, tanning), capital of Komi Republic, USSR; population 209 000□

Sylhet town in NE Bangladesh; population 46 000. It is a tea-growing centre and there is natural gas nearby. The former capital of a Hindu kingdom, it was conquered by Islam in the 14th century; in the 1971 civil war, it was the scene of heavy fighting□

Sylvanus Roman equivalent of Pan◊, the Greek god of shepherds□

symbiosis closely interdependent relationship between two different species of animals or plants for their mutual benefit. For example, trichonympha live in the stomach of wood termites digesting the wood (for its food) and converting it to carbohydrate for the host. See coral◊, fig◊, lichen◊, orchid◊, termite◊□

Symbolism movement of French poetry, associated with Verlaine, Mallarmé, Rimbaud, who used words for their symbolic rather than concrete meaning. Their personal interpretation led to charges of obscurity□

Symonds John Addington 1840–93. British critic, author of *The Renaissance in Italy* 1875–86, and revealing memoirs (1984)□

Symons Arthur 1865–1945. Welsh critic, follower of Pater◊, and friend of Toulouse-Lautrec, Mallarmé, Beardsley, Yeats and Conrad. He introduced Eliot to the work of Laforgue and wrote *The Symbolist Movement in Literature* 1900□

symphony musical composition for orchestra, traditionally in four contrasted but closely related movements. Developing from the smaller sonata form, the Italian overture, and the dance suite of the 18th century, it was brought to maturity by Haydn◊ with four varying-paced movements. The form was further developed by Mozart, Beethoven, Brahms, Tchaikovsky, Brückner, and Mahler, In the ***symphonic poem,*** devised by Liszt (e.g. his *Mazeppa* from Victor Hugo), a single movement carries literary, pictorial or other overtones, and is sometimes called a ***tone poem***; other users of the form include Smetana, Sibelius, Tchaikovsky, Franck, Richard Strauss, Elgar and Honegger□

synagogue a Jewish place of worship; see under Judaism◊□

synapsida mammal-like reptiles living 315–195 million years ago, whose fossil record is largely complete, and who were for a long time earth's dominant land animals□

syncope technical word for a faint; see fainting◊□

Syndicalism movement which rejected parliamentary activity in favour of 'direct action', culminating in a revolutionary general strike to secure worker ownership and control of industry. It originated under Robert Owen◊'s influence in the 1830s, and acquired its more violent aspects in France (see Sorel◊) and also its name (from French *syndicat* 'trade union'), and also reached the USA (Industrial Workers of the World). After 1918 it was absorbed in Communism, although it continued to have an independent existence in Spain until the late 1930s□

syndrome medically, a combination of symptoms which suggest the presence of some particular disease or disorder. See AIDS◊□

synergy (medicine) the 'co-operative' action of two or more drugs, muscles or organs□

synergy (architecture) the augmented strength of systems, e.g. the strength of an Inca◊ stone wall is greater than that of its total units had they been haphazardly thrown into a pile□

Synge John Millington 1871–1909. Irish playwright. He went to the W of Ireland and the Aran Islands, where he absorbed the poetic local turns of speech, often by listening to the general conversation below, through a hole in the floor of his room. His masterpiece *The Playboy of the Western World* 1907 caused riots at the Abbey◊ Theatre, Dublin, when first presented□

synovitis inflammation of the lining of a joint, caused by injury or infection□

synthesizer device using electrical components to produce sound. ***Speech synthesizers*** can break down speech into 128 basic elements (allophones), which are then combined into words and sentences, as in the voice of electronic teaching aids. ***Music synthesizers*** may be either ***pre-set***, to produce the sound of traditional musical instruments (e.g. the typical sound wave of a violin is reproduced, and incorporates the modifications produced by the resonances of the wooden body), or ***programmable***, so that entirely new sounds may be produced at the will of the operator□

syphilis venereal disease caused by the bacterium *Treponema pallidum*. In the initial stage an ulcerated sore develops, followed some weeks afterwards by a rash, and in the final stage (after some years) by swellings under the skin and in the internal organs, and destruction of the surrounding tissues and bones. The brain may also be affected, causing ***locomotor ataxia/tabes dorsalis,*** affecting sight, co-ordination of movement, etc., and ***general paralysis of the insane,*** in which the mind deteriorates and there is progressive paralysis. Initially, the discovery of antibiotics◊ revolutionized treatment, making it quick and easy, but resistant strains of the bacterium developed□

Syracuse industrial port (chemicals, salt) in E Sicily; population 118 700. Founded 734BC, it became a centre of Greek culture, especially under the elder and younger Dionysius◊; it was taken by Rome 212BC, destroyed by the Arabs 878, and the rebuilt town came under Norman rule in the 11th century□

Syracuse industrial city (electrical and other machinery, paper, food processing) in New York state, USA; population 170 300. There are canal links with the Great Lakes, the Hudson, and the St Lawrence□

Syria (Syrian Arab Republic)

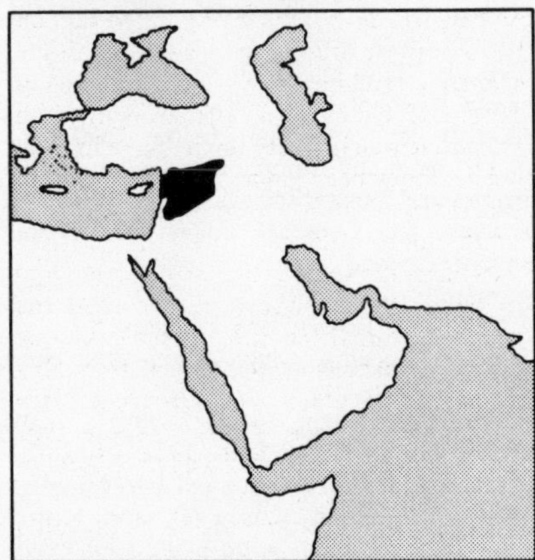

area 186 000 sq km/72 000 sq mi
capital Damascus
towns Aleppo, Homs, Hama; chief port Lattakia
features Mount Hermon, Golan Heights; river Euphrates◊; Crusader castles (Krak◊ des Chevaliers); Phoenician city sites (Ugarit◊)
exports cotton, oil, cereals, phosphates
currency Syrian pound
population 10 075 000
language Arabic (official)
religion Sunni Islam, but the ruling minority is Alawite (see Islam◊); see also Druses◊
government Executive President, who must be Muslim (General Hafez el Assad◊ from 1970) and an elected People's Council; the ruling Ba'ath party is socialist
history an ancient enemy of Israel, Syria formed part of all the great empires in turn, but also achieved independent importance (see Antioch◊ and Antiochus◊). Under Turkish rule 1516–1918, Syria was then occupied by Britain and France, being placed (with Lebanon) under French mandate in 1920, but becoming independent in 1946. In 1976 Syria became involved in the civil war in Lebanon◊, and supported Iran in the Iran/Iraq War□

syringa genus of shrubs, see Lilac◊, but the name is also popularly given to other plants, e.g. the mock◊ orange□

Szczecin port in NW Poland; population 670 000. A Hanseatic◊ port from 1278, it was Swedish 1648–1720, when it was taken by Prussia, and (as ***Stettin***) was Germany's chief Baltic port until it was captured by the Russians 1945, and passed under Polish administration. Catherine the Great was born here□

Szechwan a province in central China; see Sichuan□

Szeged industrial city (textiles) in S Hungary; population 176 000□

Szymanowski Karol 1883–1937. Ukrainian-born Polish composer of orchestral works, operas, piano music and violin concertos□

T

Tabah small area (three-quarters of a mile long) between Eilat (Israel) and the Sinai Desert (Egypt) on the Red Sea; in 1984 it was in dispute. Under an Anglo-Egyptian/ Turkish agreement in 1906, the border ran through Tabah; under a British survey of 1915 headed by T E Lawrence (who made 'adjustments' allegedly under British government orders) it runs to the east□

Table Bay inlet on the SW coast of the Cape of Good Hope, South Africa, on which Cape Town stands. It is overlooked by Table Mountain (highest point Maclear's Beacon 1087 m/3567 ft), the cloud often above it being known as the 'tablecloth'□

table tennis a development in Britain c1880 from real tennis, known until 1926 as 'ping pong'. The two or four players use solid-headed bats and plastic balls on a rectangular table 2.74 m/9 ft by 1.52 m/5 ft, over a net 15.25 cm/6 in high. Points are scored if the opponent makes a fault (fails to return a ball, strikes into the net, etc.), and 21 points make a game, a match being two out of three games□

Tabligh post-World War II missionary ('Revival') movement in Islam, which feeds the militant organizations for the 'true Islamic state'; there is an annual gathering at Tongi, near Dacca□

Tabora trading centre in W Tanzania; population 67 400. It was founded c1820 by Arab traders in slaves and ivory□

Tabriz industrial city (carpets, cotton and silk textiles, metal casting) in NW Iran; population 599 000□

tabu or *taboo.* Polynesian word 'forbidden', applied to magical and religious objects, and practices which are generally prohibited□

tachograph combined speedometer and clock which records a vehicle's speed, and the length of time it is moving or stationary; used especially to monitor a lorry-driver's working practice□

Tacitus Cornelius c55–c120AD. Roman lawyer and historian, noted for his terse style. He was consul under Nerva◊, wrote a biography of his father-in-law, Agricola◊, *Histories* covering the Empire Galba to Domitian (69–97) and *Annals* Tiberius to Nero□

Tacna city under industrial development in S Peru; population 45 000. In 1880 Chile defeated a combined Peruvian-Bolivian army nearby, and occupied Tacna until 1929□

Tacoma port in Washington state, USA, on Puget Sound; population 158 000. Founded 1868, it developed after it was chosen 1873 as the terminus of the North Pacific Railroad□

Tadema see Alma◊ Tadema□

Tadzhikistan constituent republic of the S central Soviet Union from 1929, part of Soviet Central Asia

area 143 100 sq km/55 250 sq mi

capital Dushanbe

features few areas are below 3500 m/11 000 ft; including Communism Peak◊; health resorts and mineral springs

products fruit; cereals, cotton; cattle and sheep; silks and carpets

population 4 000 000, 56% Tadzhik, 23% Uzbek, 13% Russian or Ukrainian

language Tadzhik, which differs little from Farsi (Persian)

religion Sunni Islam

recent history formed in 1924 from the Tadzhik areas of Bokhara and Turkestan□

taffeta light plainly woven silk fabric with a high lustre (Persian 'spun'), used for evening dresses and coat linings□

Taft Robert Alphonso 1889–1953. US Republican senator from 1939, and sponsor of the Taft-Hartley Labor Act 1947, restricting union power. He was the son of W H Taft◊□

Taft William Howard 1857–1930. Republican president of the USA 1909–13. He put through anti-trust legislation, but not with sufficient energy to retain the support of T Roosevelt◊, so that the Republican vote in 1912 was split. He was chief justice of the Supreme Court 1921–30. See R A Taft◊□

Taganrog industrial (iron and steel, metal goods, aircraft, machinery, shoes) port on the Sea of Azov, S USSR; population 289 000. A museum commemorates Chekhov, who was born here□

Tagore (Sir) Rabindranath 1861–1941. Indian writer in Bengali. He translated into

English his own verse *Gitanjali* ('song offerings') 1912; Nobel prize 1913□

Tagus river (Portuguese *Tejo*) rising in Spain and reaching the Atlantic at Lisbon in Portugal; length 910 km/566 mi. At Lisbon it is crossed by the Apr 25 (formerly Salazar) Bridge, so named in honour of the 1974 revolution. The ***Tagus-Segura*** irrigation scheme serves the rainless Murcia/Alicante region for early fruit and vegetable growing□

Tahiti see French Polynesia◊□

Tai Chi series of 108 complex slow-motion movements, each named (e.g. The Eye of the Tiger, The White Crane Spreads its Wings) and designed to ensure effective circulation of the 'chi' or intrinsic energy of the Universe through the mind and body. It derives partly from the Shaolin martial◊ arts of China, and partly from Taoism◊□

taiga Russian 'virgin forest', as in the permafrost zone in Siberia, with rich and varied fauna and flora; the name is applied to other similar regions□

Taine Hippolyte Adolphe 1828–93. French critic and historian, who analysed literary works as products of period and environment, e.g. *History of English Literature* 1863□

taipan a large highly venomous snake; see under snake◊□

Taipei capital (mainland spelling Taibei) and commercial centre of Taiwan; population 2 100 000. The National Palace Museum (1965) houses the world's greatest collection of Chinese art, taken there from the mainland in 1948□

Taiwan island (formerly Formosa) off the coast of the People's Republic of China. Forms (with nearby islands) the Republic of China

area 36 000 sq km/14 000 sq mi

capital Taipei

towns ports Keelung, Kaohsiung

features include Penghu Island (Pescadores), Jinmen (Quemoy) and Mazu (Matsu).

exports with US aid, Taiwan is highly industrialized: textiles, petrochemicals, steel, plastics, electronics, etc.

currency Taiwan dollar

population 19 117 000, 89% Taiwanese, 11% mainlanders whose dominance causes resentment

language Mandarin Chinese

religion officially atheist, but traditional religions are Taoism, Confucianism, and Buddhism

government there is a president (Chiang Kai-shek's son Chiang Ching-kuo from 1978; re-elected 1984) and National Assembly, elected in 1947 with indefinite life; a small number of elected native Taiwanese were admitted in 1972; ruling party Kuomintang◊

recent history Chinese 1683–1895, it was ceded to Japan 1895–1945, when it surrendered to Chiang Kai-Shek◊. From 1949 it became the last refuge of the defeated Chinese Nationalist government on its retreat from the mainland. Taiwan was expelled from the United Nations in 1971 on the admission of Communist China, but continued to be recognized as the legal Chinese government by the USA until 1978, and close relations continue□

Taiyuan industrial city (iron and steel, agricultural machinery, textiles, etc.) and capital of Shanxi province, NE China; population 1 000 000□

Taizé a Protestant religious community based in the village of that name in SE France; see under Burgundy◊□

Taj Mahal a white marble mausoleum in central India; see under Shah◊ Jehan□

Takoradi the chief port of Ghana; see Sekondi-Takoradi◊□

Talbot William Henry Fox 1800–77. British photographer, inventor of the negative/positive Calotype process 1841 which founded modern photography; he also made instantaneous photographs 1851 and photo engravings 1852□

talc hydrated magnesium silicate, which is used in talcum powder, as a lubricant, 'filler' in making paper, etc. It is also found in rock formation as ***steatite*** or ***soapstone*** which has a 'greasy' feel to it, and is used in carving ornaments, etc.□

Talcahuano industrial port (oil refining, timber) and chief naval base in Chile; population 212 865□

Talien a Chinese port; another form of Darien◊□

Taliesin c550. Legendary Welsh poet, a bard at the court of the king of Rheged in S Scotland, who allegedly died at Taliesin (named after him) in Dyfed□

Tallahassee agricultural and lumbering centre, capital of Florida, USA; population 81 550. De Soto◊ found an Indian settlement here 1539 (the name is Cree Indian 'old town')□

Talleyrand (Charles Maurice de Talleyrand-Périgord) 1754–1838. French statesman, bishop of Autun 1789–91. A supporter of moderate reform, he fled to the USA during the Terror, but became Foreign Minister under the Directory 1797–9, and under Napoleon 1799–1807. He represented France at the Congress of Vienna 1814–15, and was ambassador to London 1830–4□

Tallin (formerly Reval) industrial port (electrical and oil drilling machinery, textiles, paper) and capital of Estonian Republic, NW USSR; population 458 000. Founded 1219, it was a Hanseatic port, passed to Sweden 1561, and to Russia 1750. Vyshgorod castle (13th century) and other medieval buildings remain□

Tallis Thomas c1505–85. English composer, joint organist (with his pupil Byrd◊) of the Chapel Royal from 1572. He wrote masses, anthems, and other church music□

Tall Ships Race race for sailing ships from Bermuda to Halifax, Nova Scotia□

Talmud the main authoritative compilation of ancient Jewish law and tradition; see under Judaism◊□

Tamale industrial and commercial centre in NE Ghana; population 125 000□

Tamar in Old Testament, sister of Absalom◊. She was raped by her half-brother Amnon, who was then killed by Absalom□

Tamar river rising in N Cornwall and flowing to Plymouth Sound, for most of its length (97 km/60 mi) as the Cornish/Devonian border. Also a river in Tasmania, Australia, formed by the union of the N and S Esk; length 65 km/40 mi; it flows into Bass Strait□

tamarind African tropical tree *Tamarindus indica*, family Leguminosae◊, with pinnate leaves and red/yellow flowers followed by pods, the pulp of which is used in cooking and as a laxative□

tamarisk genus of Eurasian shrubs and trees *Tamarix*, family Tamaricaceae, resistant to drought and salt, hence the ***common tamarisk*** or ***salt cedar*** *T gallica* is used to stabilize sand dunes; sweet edible ***tamarisk manna*** is exuded by *T mannifera* from holes pierced by insects□

Tamatave the chief port of Madagascar; see Toamasina◊□

tambourine percussion instrument, a shallow drum with a single skin, and jingles set in the rim□

Tambov industrial city (chemicals, synthetic rubber, engineering) in W central USSR; population 277 000□

Tamerlane or ***Timur i Leng*** 1336–1405. Mongol ruler of Samarkand◊ from 1369, who conquered Persia, Azerbaijan, Armenia, Georgia; defeated the Golden◊ Horde 1395; sacked Delhi 1398; invaded Syria and Asia Minor, and captured the sultan at Ankara 1402; and died invading China□

Tamil language and people, see under Dravidian◊, Sri Lanka◊, Tamil Nadu◊□

Tamil Nadu state of south eastern India
area 130 069 sq km/50 207 sq mi
capital Madras
features mainly industrial; many Tamils formerly settled in Sri◊ Lanka and carried with them their literature, music and dance
population 48 297 500
language Tamil□

Tammany Hall the central organization of the Democratic◊ Party in New York county□

Tampa industrial port (cigars, fruit and vegetable canning, shipbuilding, fertilizers, clothing) and resort in Florida, USA; population 271 550□

Tampere chief industrial city (textiles, paper, footwear, turbines) in Finland; population 250 000□

Tampico port (oil refining, fishing) on the Rio Pánuco, 10 km/6 mi from the Gulf of Mexico, in Mexico; population 268 000□

Tamworth market and industrial town (engineering, paper, clothing) in Staffordshire, England; population 25 000□

Tamworth dairying centre in New South Wales, Australia; population 33 000□

Tana lake in Ethiopia, the source of the Blue Nile; 1800 m/6000 ft, area 3625 sq km/1400 sq mi□

Tanabata Japanese 'star festival' on 7 Jul, introduced from China in the 8th century and dedicated to Altair and Vega, stars in the constellation Aquila, who are united once yearly in the Milky Way. They are taken to represent two star-crossed lovers allowed by the gods to meet on that night□

tanager about 200 species of Central and S American birds, all with brilliant plumage, family Emberizidae□

Tanagra ancient Greek city in Boeotia◊. Sparta defeated Athens here 457BC, and it is also noted for characteristic terracotta statuettes excavated here in the 19th century□

Tananarive another name for Antananarivo◊□

Tanga port in NE Tanzania; population 103 500. In World War I a British force failed to take it from the Germans in 1914, but it was captured by Smuts◊ with British troops 1916□

Tanganyika former name for Tanzania◊□

Tanganyika Lake. See under Great◊ Lakes□

Tange Kenzo 1913– . Japanese architect, whose works include the National Gymnasium, Tokyo, for the 1964 Olympics, and the city-plan of Abuja◊□

tangerine a type of orange; see citrus◊□

Tangier free port (1962) and commercial city in Morocco, on the Straits of Gibraltar; population 188 000. Captured by the Portuguese in 1471, it passed to England 1662, but was abandoned 1684 and later became a lair of Barbary◊ pirates. Under a convention effective 1925, Tangier and a small surrounding enclave became an international zone, which was administered by Spain 1940–5. In 1956 it was transferred to independent Morocco□

tango slow dance in 2/4 time of partly African origin, which came to Europe via S America, where it had blended with Spanish elements (e.g. the Habanera)□

Tangshan industrial city in Tianjin province, China; population 1 000 000. Almost destroyed by an earthquake in 1976, with 200 000 killed, it was rebuilt□

Tanizaki Jun-ichirō 1886–1965. Japanese novelist, whose work matured from 1923 when he moved from Tokyo to the Kyoto-Osaka region where ancient tradition is stronger. His works include a modern version of *The Tale of Genji* 1939–41 (see Murasaki◊) and *The Makioka Sisters* 1943–8□

tank code name for the first successful tracked, armoured vehicle, typically armed with a gun; it was first used in large numbers in the Battle of the Somme 1916 (see Sir Ernest Swinton◊)□

tanker merchant ship for carrying liquid cargoes, e.g. mineral oil, liquefied gas, molasses, etc., in bulk□

Tannenberg village in N Poland, where in 1410 the Poles and Lithuanians defeated the Teutonic◊ Knights, establishing Poland as a major power; in 1914, during World War I, when it was part of E Prussia, Hindenburg◊ defeated the Russians here□

tannin class of organic compounds of vegetable origin, found in gall nuts, tree barks, roots, and fruits. A derivative of ***tannic acid***, tannin is used in dyes (as a mordant), tanning leather, ink production, and (medically) as an astringent□

Tannu-Tuva see Tuva◊□

tansy European perennial *Tanacetum vulgare*, family Compositae◊; the yellow flower heads grow in clusters and the leaves are used in cookery; see herbs◊□

Tantalus in Greek mythology a king whose crimes were punished in Tartarus◊ by food and drink he could not reach, hence the name ***tantalus*** for a lockable container for wine bottles, which leaves the liquor still visible□

tantalum element
symbol Ta
atomic number 73
physical description silvery metal
features occurs in the ore columbite together with the element niobium
uses used as a hardener in steel alloy and to give corrosion resistance, as in surgical instruments and laboratory apparatus; as a catalyst, it is used in making synthetic rubber, and tantalum carbide gives a strong cutting edge to high-speed tools□

Tanzania United Republic of

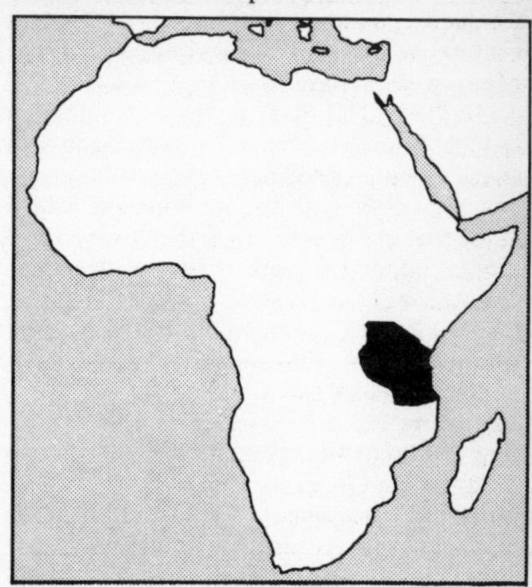

area 942 580 sq km/373 700 sq mi
capital Dodoma
towns chief port Dar es Salaam
features comprises the islands of Zanzibar, and nearby Pemba; Mount Kilimanjaro, called 'shining mountain', because of the snow and glaciers which crown it (Kibo, an extinct volcano and its highest peak, is the highest mountain in Africa 5895 m/19 340 ft); parts of Lakes Victoria and Tanganyika; Serengeti National Park, and the Olduvai◊ Gorge; Ngorongoro Crater 14.5 km/9 mi across and 762 m/2500 ft deep
exports coffee, cotton, sisal, cloves from Zanzibar, tea, tobacco
currency Tanzanian shilling
population 21 202 000
language Kiswahili, English (both official)
religion Moslem 35%, Christian 35%, tradtional 30%
government executive president and Commander-in-Chief of the armed forces (Ali Hassan Mwinyi◊ from 1985) and single-chamber national assembly. Julius Nyerere remained influential as chairman of the only permitted political party (Chama cha Mapinduzi,'Revolutionary Party'). Zanzibar has a limited degree of autonomy, but rule by decree was introduced 1964.
recent history part of German East Africa from 1884, Tanganyika was conquered by Britain in World War I, and was held as a League of Nations mandate from 1921, and United Nations trusteeship from 1946, until independence as a republic within the Commonwealth in 1961. In 1964 it joined with Zanzibar◊ and Pemba, to form Tanzania. Under Nyerere's Arusha Declaration of 1967, Tanzania was to be a socialist planned society; Nyerere stepped down 1985□

Taoism Chinese philosophical system, traditionally founded by Lao◊-zi in the 6th century BC, though the scriptures, *Tao Te Ching* were apparently compiled in the 3rd century BC. The 'tao' or 'way' denotes the hidden Principle of the Universe, and less stress is laid on good deeds than on harmonious interaction with the environment, which automatically ensures right behaviour. The second important work is that of Zhuangzi c389–286BC, *The Way of Zhuangzi*. The later magical side of Taoism is illustrated by the *I Ching* or ***Book of Changes***, a book of divination. See also Tai◊ Chi□

Taormina coastal resort in E Sicily, at the foot of Mount Etna; population 8500. There is an ancient Greek theatre□

tapestry ornamental woven wall-hanging (sometimes used also for other purposes) incorporating a design or picture. Many fragmentary ancient examples survive, and France has been famous for them since the 15th century (see Aubusson◊). Designers for tapestries include Raphael, Rubens, William Morris, Burne-Jones, Graham Sutherland. See also Bayeux◊ Tapestry□

tapeworm a class of worm; see worm◊□

tapioca a starch used in cooking; see cassava◊□

tapir ancient family (Tapiridae) of mammals, related to the rhinoceros◊, and slightly more distantly to the horse. Their black skin is thick and hairy, and they have a short tail, no horns, and a short trunk. They are vegetarian, harmless, shy inhabitants of the forests of Central and S America, and also Malaya, which has the largest species, *Tapirus indicus*, which has white hindquarters□

tar black viscid liquid obtained by destructive distillation of coal, wood, etc. See pitch◊□

Tara Hill the ancient religious and political centre of Ireland; see under Meath◊□

Taranaki peninsula in North Island, New Zealand, dominated by Mt Egmont◊; volcanic soil makes it a rich dairying area, noted for cheese□

tarantella a peasant dance from S Italy; a piece of music composed for or in the rythm of this dance in fast 6/8 time□

Taranto naval base and port, capital of Apulia, Italy, founded by Sparta in the 8th century BC; population 244 000□

tarantula a class of spider◊□

tare a type of herb; see under vetch◊□

Taree town in a dairying area of New South Wales, Australia; population 33 100□

Tarim Basin see under Xinjiang◊ Uygur□

taro a type of plant; see under arum◊□

tarot a pack of 78 cards used primarily in fortune telling; see under playing◊ cards□

tarpon marine game fish *Megalops atlanticus*, family Elopidae, order Clupeiformes, and so related to the herring◊; it reaches 2 m/6 ft, and may weigh 135 kg/300 lb□

Tarquinius Superbus legendary last king of Rome 534–510BC. He was deposed when his son Sextus violated Lucretia◊□

tarragon a type of herb◊□

Tarragona industrial port (petrochemicals, pharmaceuticals, electrical goods) in Catalonia, Spain; population 111 700.□

Tarrasa industrial town (textiles) in Catalonia, NE Spain; population 155 360□

tarsier genus *Tarsius* of small primates◊ found in Indonesia and the Philippines. Nocturnal tree-dwellers with large eyes, they have suckers for gripping at the end of their fingers. They are from 25 cm/10 in to 40 cm/16in long, of which half comprises the long hairless tail. They are intermediary between lemurs and anthropoids on the evolutionary scale□

Tarsus city in SE Turkey, formerly the capital of the Roman province of Cilicia, and the birthplace of St Paul; population 121 000□

tartan woollen cloth woven in specific chequered patterns individual to Scottish clans, with stripes of different colours and different widths criss-crossing, and used in making plaids, kilts, and trousers. Developed in the 17th century, they were proscribed after 1745 (see Jacobites◊) until 1782□

tartaric acid colourless or white crystalline acid ($COOH(CHOH)_2COOH$). Present in fruit juices in the form of salts of potassium, calcium and magnesium, it is used in effervescent drinks, baking powders, etc.□

Tartars a variant spelling of Tatars◊□

Tartarus in Greek mythology, a part of Hades◊□

Tartu industrial city (engineering, food processing) in Estonian Republic, USSR; population 109 000. Once a stronghold of the Teutonic◊ Knights, it was later held by Sweden and Poland, but has been under Russian control since 1704□

Tasaday a people of the rain forests of Mindanao in the the Philippines◊□

Tashkent capital and industrial city (mining machinery, textiles, leather goods) of Uzbek, S central USSR; population 1 986 000. Founded in the 7th century, it became Russian in 1865□

Tasman Abel Janszoon c1603–59. Dutch navigator, first European to discover Tasmania (in 1642; he called it Van Diemen's Land, but it was renamed after himself in 1856), New Zealand, Tonga, and Fiji□

Tasmania state of the Commonwealth of Australia

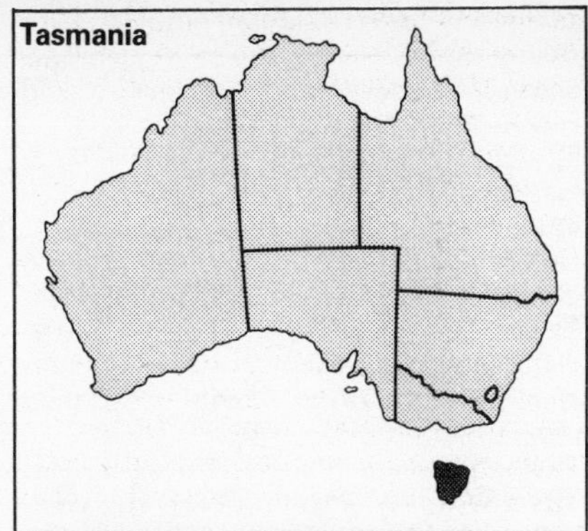

area 68 331 sq km/26 383 sq mi
capital Hobart
towns chief port Launceston
features an island state (including small islands in the Bass Strait and Macquarie Island), Franklin river, a world heritage site as a wilderness area (saved from a hydro-electric scheme 1983), which also has a rich prehistoric site; unique fauna include Tasmanian devil, 'tiger', etc.
products wool, dairy products, fruit (especially apples); timber; iron, tin, coal, copper, silver, etc.
population 422 900
recent history first reached by Europeans (Tasman◊) 1642, it joined the Australian Commonwealth as a state in 1901. The last of the Tasmanian aboriginals died 1876□

Tasmanian devil a class of marsupial; see under Marsupialia◊□

Tasmanian tiger/wolf a class of marsupial, also called thylacine; see under Marsupalia◊□

Tasman Sea the part of the Pacific Ocean between SE Australia and NW New Zealand; see under Pacific◊ Ocean□

Tass Soviet news agency: *T*elegrafnoye *A*gentstvo *S*ovyetskovo *S*oyuza□

Tasso Torquato 1544–95. Italian poet. He made his name with the romantic poem *Rinaldo* 1562, and came under the patronage of the House of Este, writing his pastoral *Aminta* 1573 for Duke Alfonso's theatre in Ferrara◊. His *La Gerusalemme Liberata* (Jersualem Delivered) 1574, a romantic epic dealing with the First Crusade, is his greatest work. From 1576 he was mentally unstable□

Tatar Republic of W central USSR, conquered by Russia in 1552; area 68 000 sq km/26 250 sq mi; population 3 453 000. Capital Kazan□

Tatars Turkic, mainly Muslim people, the descendants of the followers of Genghis◊ Khan, called the 'Golden Horde' because of the wealth they gained by plunder. They now live mainly in the USSR in the Tatar◊ Republic and the Uzbek◊ Republic (where they were deported from the Crimea◊ in 1944) and SW Siberia□

Tate Nahum 1652–1715. British poet, born in Dublin remembered for his adaptation of *King Lear* with a happy ending, and his poem 'While shepherds watched' (now a carol)□

Tate Phyllis 1911– . British composer. Her works include *Concerto for Saxophone and Strings* 1944□

Tate Gallery art gallery (British school from late 16th century, and foreign art from 1810) at Millbank, London. Endowed by sugar-merchant Sir Henry Tate 1819–99, it was opened 1897; later extensions include the Clore Gallery for Turner paintings 1983□

Tati Jacques 1908–82. French actor-film director, born Tatischeff. A brilliant comic mime, he is remembered for *Monsieur Hulot's Holiday* 1953□

Tatra Mountains the highest range of the central Carpathians◊□

Tattersall's bloodstock auctioneers established 1766, now at Knightsbridge Green, SW London; the founder was Richard Tattersall 1724–95□

tatting lace-work made from medieval times by knotting, with the aid of a small shuttle□

Taube Henry 1915– . US chemist. He established the basis of modern inorganic chemistry by his study of the loss or gain of electrons by atoms during chemical reactions. Nobel prize 1983□

Taunton market town and administrative headquarters of Somerset, England; population 38 500. The Elizabethan hall in which the Bloody Assizes were held (see Judge Jeffreys◊) survives□

Taunus Mountains see under Hessen◊□

Taupo Lake. See under New◊ Zealand□

Tauranga port (citrus, dairy produce, timber exports) in North Island, New Zealand; population 57 000□

Taurus Mountains a mountain range in S Turkey◊□

Tavener John 1944– . British composer, whose works include the dramatic cantata *The Whale* 1966; the opera *Thérèse* 1979; and much music linked with the Russian Orthodox church, to which he belongs□

Taverner John c1495–1545. English organist and composer. He was imprisoned in 1530 for heresy, and, as an agent of Thomas Cromwell◊, assisted in the dissolution of the monasteries. He wrote masses and motets, but as a Protestant renounced his art□

taxation the raising of money from individuals and organizations by the state in order to pay for the goods and services it provides. Taxation can be ***direct*** (a deduction from income), or ***indirect*** (added to the purchase price of a good or service, that is, a taxation on consumption). ***Income tax*** is the most common form of direct taxation; it was introduced in the UK by Peel◊ in 1841. The proportions of direct and indirect taxation in the total tax revenue vary widely from country to country; the USA, for example, has a high proportion of indirect taxation, while the UK has a higher proportion of direct taxation.

By varying the effect of a tax on the richer and poorer members of society, a government can attempt to redistribute wealth from the poorer to the richer, both by taxing the rich more severely, and by returning some of the collected wealth in the form of ***benefits.*** A ***progressive*** tax is one which falls proportionally more on the rich; most income taxes, for example, have higher rates for those with higher incomes. A ***regressive*** tax, on the other hand, affects the poor proportionally more than the rich. A tax of a fixed amount on bread, for example, affects more those with low incomes than those with higher. ***Wealth taxes, capital transfer tax***, and ***death duties*** are all (more or less successful) attempts at redistributing wealth.

Value-added tax (VAT) is the standard form of indirect taxation in the EEC; it is based on the French TVA (*Taxe sur la Valeur Ajoutée*), which was introduced in the UK 1973. It is paid on the value added to any goods or services at each particular stage of the process of production or distribution, and although collected from traders at each stage, it is in effect a tax on consumers' expenditure. In the USA a similar result is achieved by a ***sales tax*** deducted by the retailer at the point of sale.

In the UK, ***rates***◊ are the form of taxation which pays for local government, in other countries, including the USA, it is replaced by a local income tax.

The UK taxation system has been criticized in many respects; alternatives include an ***expenditure tax***, which would be imposed only on income spent, and the ***tax-credit system*** under which all are guaranteed an income bolstered as necessary by social security benefits, taxation beginning only above that level, hence eliminating the 'poverty trap', by which the unemployed receiving state benefits may have a net loss in income if they take employment at a low wage□

Taxodium genus of trees: see swamp cypress◊□

taxonomy the classification of things, particularly the systematic naming of plants and animals. See classification◊, animal◊ classification, and plant◊ classification□

Tay longest river of Scotland, 188 km/117 mi. See Tayside◊□

Taylor A(lan) J(ohn) P(ercivale) 1906– . British historian and TV lecturer, author of *Origins of the Second World War* 1961, etc.□

Taylor Brook 1685–1731. English mathematician who laid the foundations of differential calculus. ***Taylor's Series*** is still much used□

Taylor Elizabeth 1912–75. British novelist, Mrs J W K Taylor, born Coles. Her books include *At Mrs Lippincote's* 1946, and *Angel* 1957□

Taylor Elizabeth 1932– . British actress, whose films include *A Place in The Sun* 1950, *Butterfield 8* 1960 (Academy award), *Cleopatra* 1963, and *Who's Afraid of Virginia Woolf?* 1966. Her eight husbands have included the actors Michael Wilding and Richard Burton◊ (twice)□

Taylor Jeremy 1613–67. Anglican bishop, whose *Holy Living* 1650 and *Holy Dying* 1651 were enormously popular□

Taylor Zachary 1784–1850. Twelfth president of the USA 1849–50. Virginia-born, he commanded the invasion of Mexico 1846–7□

Tay-Sachs disease caused by a defective gene, occurring mainly in Ashkenazic (see under Israel◊) Jews and often causing death of affected children by the age of five. They become blind, deaf, mentally retarded and lack muscular control□

Tayside region of Scotland

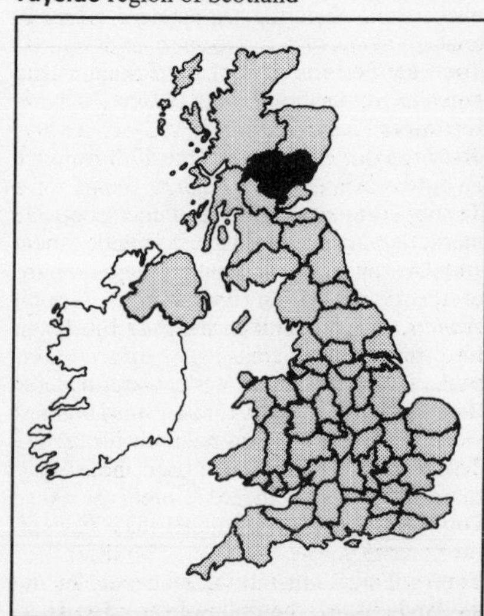

area 7511 sq km/2899 sq mi

towns administrative headquarters Dundee; Perth, Arbroath, Forfar
features river Tay; Grampian◊ Mountains; Lochs Tay and Rannoch; Ochil and Sidlaw Hills; vales of the N and S Esk
products beef and dairy products; soft fruit, etc. from the fertile Carse of Gowrie
population 391 530
famous people James Barrie□

Tbilisi capital (formerly Tiflis) and industrial city (textiles, machinery, ceramics, tobacco) of the Georgian Republic, USSR; population 1 140 000. Dating from the 4th century AD, it is a centre of Georgian culture with fine medieval churches, and the Georgian Academy of Sciences□

Tchaikovsky Peter Ilyich 1840–93. Russian composer. A friend of Balakirev◊, he was influenced by the nationalist movement. His marriage in 1877 was followed by a nervous breakdown. His works are noted for their expressive melodies. They include six symphonies; concerto in B flat minor 1875; operas (e.g. *Eugene Onegin* 1879 and *The Queen of Spades* 1890); ballets (*The Sleeping Beauty* 1890, *Swan Lake* 1895, and *The Nutcracker* 1892), and orchestral fantasies (*Romeo and Juliet, Francesca da Rimini,* and *Hamlet*)□

tea shrub or small tree *Camellia sinensis*, family Theaceae, which is restricted in cultivation to a bush 1.5 m/4 ft high, from which the young leaves are plucked by hand when it reaches about five years old. ***Black tea*** is made from dried leaves, broken up to release the essential oils and allowed to ferment until the moisture is removed in ovens from which the tea emerges blackish-brown. ***Green tea*** is steamed and quickly dried before fermentation, remaining partly green in colour.
Known in China as early as 2737BC, tea was first brought to Europe in the 17th century. Fast tea clippers (see *Cutty◊ Sark*) were developed to race to Europe and scoop the market. Modern producers include India and Sri Lanka□

teak tropical Asian timber tree *Tectona grandis*, family Verbenaceae, used in furniture, shipbuilding, etc.□

teal a type of duck; see under waterfowl◊□

teasel erect, prickly biennial Eurasian plant *Dipsacus fullonum*, family Dipsacaceae; the dry seed heads were once used industrially to 'tease' (raise the nap of) cloth□

Tebbit Norman 1931– . British Conservative politician. He was Minister for Employment 1981–83, for Trade and Industry 1983–5, and chairman of the party from 1985. He was injured in a terrorist bomb blast during the 1985 Conservative Party Conference in Brighton□

technetium element
symbol Tc
atomic number 43
physical description silvery-grey metal
features radioactive; the first element to be produced artificially, in 1937 (by the bombardment of molybdenum with deuterons)
uses as a hardener in steel alloy; among its radioactive isotopes, produced in uranium fission, technetium-99 is used in radiotherapy□

Tecumseh c1768–1813. N American Indian chief of the Shawnee, of great organizing ability and eloquence. He attempted to unite the Indian peoples against white settlers, and was killed in battle. The belief that he was backed by the British from Canada was a factor in the outbreak of the War◊ of 1812□

Tedder Arthur William, 1st Baron 1890–1967. As Deputy Supreme Commander under Eisenhower 1943–5, he was largely responsible for securing the initial success of the Normandy landings□

Tees river flowing from Pennines in Cumbria to the North Sea (see Teesside under Cleveland◊); length 130 km/80 mi□

Tegucigalpa capital and commercial and industrial (textiles, food processing) city of Honduras, population 533 600□

Tehran capital and industrial city (textile, chemical, engineering, tobacco) of Iran; population 4 496 000. The capital from 1788, it has the Gulistan Palace (the former royal residence) and several universities□

Tehran Conference 1943. During World War II the first tripartite meeting of wartime allies Stalin, Roosevelt, and Churchill was held here□

Teilhard de Chardin Pierre 1881–1955. French Jesuit mystic. Publication of his *The Phenomenon of Man* 1955 was delayed until after his death by the embargo of his superiors. He envisaged humanity as eventually in charge of its own evolution, and developed the concept of the *noosphere*, the unconscious union of thought among human beings□

Tejo Portuguese name for the river Tagus◊□

Te Kanawa Dame Kiri 1944– . New Zealand opera singer, born in Gisborne, of part-Maori descent. Dame of the British Empire 1982□

tektite small (the largest known is 5 cm/2 in across), rounded, glassy lumps (from Greek 'molten'), found especially in Australasia, and thought to be drops of molten rock thrown out by the impact of a meteorite or comet□

Tel Aviv-Jaffa industrial city (textiles, chemicals, sugar, printing and publishing) in Israel, with its port at Ashdod; population 327 300. Founded in 1909, Tel Aviv was combined with Jaffa 1949□

telecommunications the first device for communication by electromagnetic means was the ***telegraph***, the earliest practicable instrument being invented by Cooke and Wheatstone 1837 (see also Morse◊); next came the ***telephone*** in 1876 (see Alexander Graham Bell◊); then radio communication (see Marconi◊); and most recently ***international geo-stationary communications satellites*** When in orbit around the equator these remain above the same point on earth's surface; the first to be successfully launched was Syncom 2 on 26 Jul 1963 from Cape Canaveral. Telephone and television transmissions are carried simultaneously, and (as the satellite spins clockwise to maintain stability) the antenna (which enables the satellite to receive and transmit signals) spins anticlockwise at the same speed, so keeping it always in the correct position. A revolutionary development in land and under-sea communication has been the replacement of copper-core cables by beams of laser light travelling down numbers of fine glass fibres (see fibre◊ optics)□

telegraph see telecommunications◊□

Telemann Georg Philipp 1681–1767. German composer, organist and conductor at the Johanneum, Hamburg, from 1721. He was prolific in many forms: opera, cantatas, instrumental works, etc.□

telepathy 'communication of impressions of any kind from one mind to another, independently of the recognized channels of sense', as defined by Myers◊□

telephone see telecommunications◊□

telescope an optical instrument for making distant objects appear closer by use of a combination of lenses; the chief types include:

optical invented by Lippershey◊, and developed by Galileo◊ and others. It consists of lenses (see lens◊) or a combination of lenses and mirrors, which produce a magnified image of a distant object. The ***objective*** lens focuses on parallel rays coming from, say, two distant stars. These stars are imagined to be on a flat surface — the ***focal plane*** — at a distance, the ***focal length***, away from the lens. The eyepiece, whose focal length is much less than that of the objective, is used as a magnifying glass through which the observer views the objectives focal plane.

To observe faint stars a very large diameter objective is needed. It is easier to manufacture large concave mirrors than lenses of the same diameter, especially since lenses have to be corrected for their bending of different colours by different amounts, while mirrors do not. Two commonly used types of reflecting telescope are the Newtonian and Cassegrainian telescope.

The world's largest optical telescopes are the Zelenchuskaya, in the N Caucasus (USSR 1970), with a 6.0 m/236 in diameter reflector/mirror (though the mirror is defective); and the Hale Observatory, Mount Palomar, California (1948), 5.0 m/200 in.

radio telescopes pick up radio emissions from celestial bodies, and first detected pulsars◊ and quasars◊. Some take the form of a single large, steerable metal 'dish' which focuses the radio waves on an antenna linked to a receiver. Most famous of these is the pioneer instrument at Jodrell Bank (1957), in Cheshire, with a paraboloid reflecting bowl (76 m/250 ft diameter) and a range over a thousand times greater than the largest optical instruments. The world's largest single antenna dish radio telescope (unsteerable) is in a natural crater at Arecibo, New Mexico (305 m/1000 ft diameter). This is dwarfed by the Very Large Array (VLA) in New Mexico, USA, with 27 antennae, each 25 m/82 ft in diameter, which move along rail tracks arranged in the form of a Y, each branch being about 21 km/13 mi long□

telescope

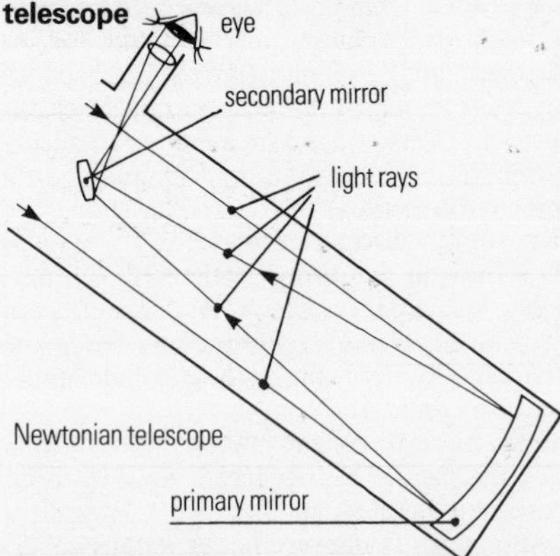

teletext an information service in which pages of text are transmitted together with normal television broadcasts; see videotext◊□

television the reproduction at a distance by radio waves of visual images. This became possible when it was realized in 1873 that, since the electrical conductivity of selenium varies according to the amount of light to which it is exposed, light could be converted

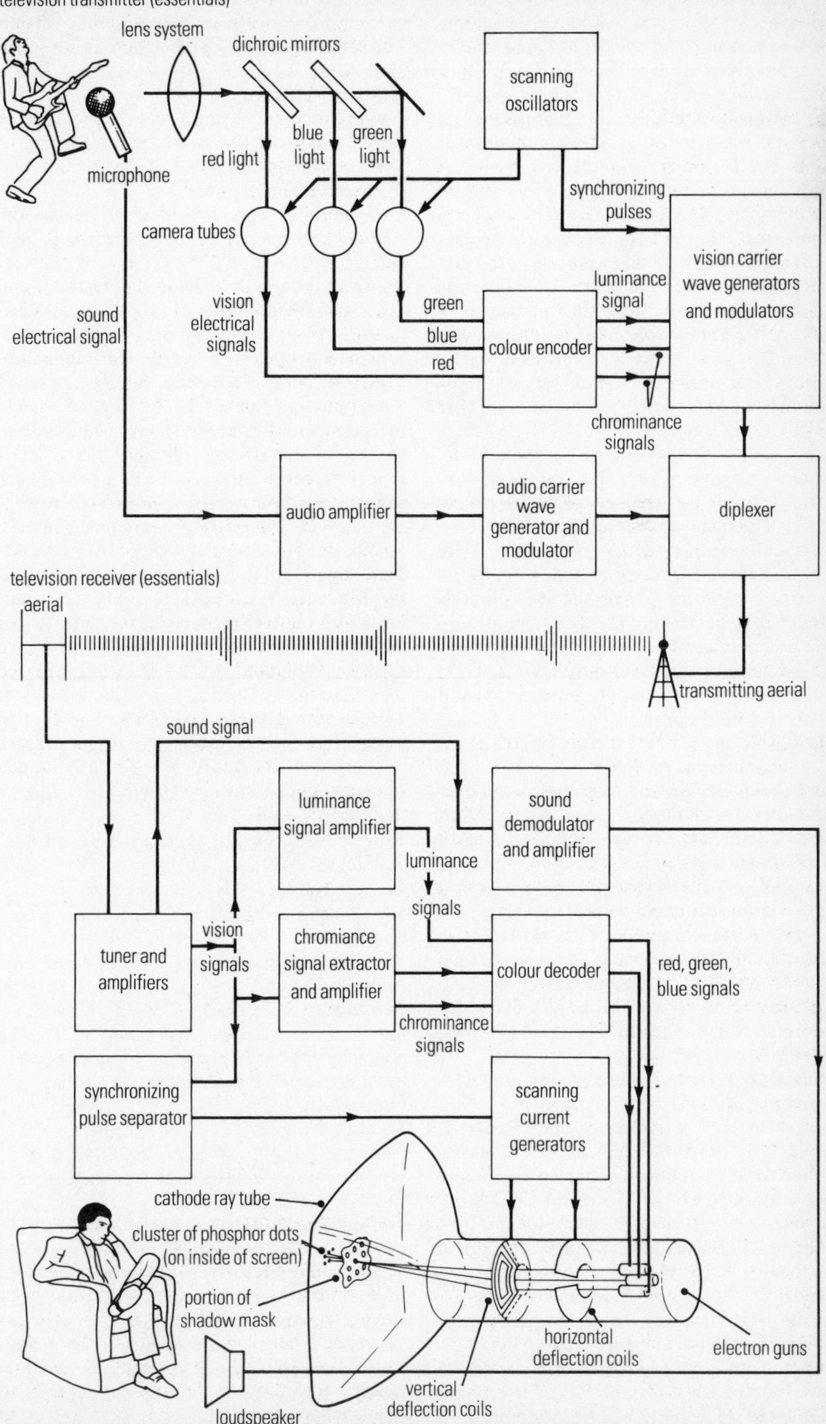
television transmitter (essentials)
lens system
dichroic mirrors
scanning oscillators
microphone
red light
blue light
green light
synchronizing pulses
camera tubes
vision carrier wave generators and modulators
luminance signal
sound electrical signal
vision electrical signals
green
blue
red
colour encoder
chrominance signals
audio amplifier
audio carrier wave generator and modulator
diplexer
television receiver (essentials)
aerial
transmitting aerial
sound signal
luminance signal amplifier
sound demodulator and amplifier
luminance signals
tuner and amplifiers
vision signals
chrominance signal extractor and amplifier
colour decoder
red, green, blue signals
chrominance signals
synchronizing pulse separator
scanning current generators
cathode ray tube
cluster of phosphor dots (on inside of screen)
portion of shadow mask
horizontal deflection coils
electron guns
vertical deflection coils
loudspeaker

into electrical impulses for transmission over a distance to a receiver, where they could be reconverted into light. The problem was to transmit information on the degree of light or shade at every point in a (changing) picture; the solution was to break the picture up into lines, scanned in rapid succession so that points are dealt with sequentially rather than simultaneously. A similar, synchronized, scanning arrangement at the receiving end reconstructs the picture. Mechanical devices were used to achieve this scanning in the first practical demonstration of television given by Baird◊ in London 27 Jan 1926, but from 1934 cathode-ray tubes were used experimentally by the BBC, and these were adopted for the world's first public television service transmitted from Alexandra Palace, London 2 Nov 1936.

Baird gave a demonstration of colour television in London in 1928, but it was not until Dec 1953 that the first service began in the USA. The receiver reproduces only three basic colours: red, green, and blue, from which all the others are blended, white being a mixture of all three. The shade required is obtained by combining the three signals into one complex signal so that it can be transmitted more or less as an ordinary black and white signal, so reducing the amount of band width it uses in transmission.

The colour screen of the receiver is composed of a fine mosaic of over one million dots, one third of which glow red when bombarded by electrons, one-third glow green and one-third blue. These dots are so small that from a normal viewing distance the colours merge into one another and a picture with a full range of apparent colours is seen.

By the 1980s the number of 'channels' in use had been greatly increased, and services such as videotext◊ were commonplace, as were videorecorders to record programmes for future viewing, and to play pre-recorded videocassettes□

television awards see under film◊ and television awards□

Telford 'new town' in E Shropshire, England; population 107 000. Named after Thomas Telford in 1963, it has engineering works, and the Ironbridge Gorge Museum of Industrial Archaeology is nearby□

Telford Thomas 1757–1834. Scottish engineer. He constructed aqueducts and canals, including the Caledonian 1803–23, and used the then little-tried suspension principle in the Menai bridge, Anglesey◊□

Tell William. Legendary Swiss archer, said to have refused at Altdorf, on Lake Lucerne, to salute the Hapsburg badge. Sentenced to shoot an apple from his son's head, he did so, then shot the tyrannical Austrian ruler□

Tell el Amarna a group of ancient rock tombs and ruins in Upper Egypt; see Akhetaton◊□

tellurium element
symbol Te
atomic number 52
physical description greyish metal
features a semiconductor
uses in steel and alloys with lead and copper, also used as a catalyst for petroleum cracking□

Tema port with oil refineries in Ghana. Opened 1962, it is Africa's largest man-made harbour□

tempera a painting medium for powdered pigments, consisting usually of egg yolk and water; see painting◊□

temperature state of hotness or coldness of a body (see Celsius◊, centigrade◊, Fahrenheit◊), which determines whether or not it will transfer heat to, or receive heat from, another body. The normal temperature of the human body is 36.8°C/98.4°F□

Templars religious order (founded 1119) of knights vowed to poverty, chastity, and obedience, and the recovery of Palestine from the Saracens in 12th–13th centuries. Envy of their wealth led Philip◊ of France to suppress the order in 1307□

Temple see under Jerusalem◊□

Temple former English headquarters (south of Fleet St, London) of the Templars◊ 1185–1313, with a round church (1185). Since the 14th century the Inner and Middle Temple (see Inns◊ of Court) have used the buildings□

Temple Shirley 1928– . American singing and dancing child prodigy, e.g. *Bright Eyes* (in which she sang 'The Good Ship Lollipop') 1934, and for which she received an Academy Award□

Temple Sir William 1628–99. English diplomat and essayist, who negotiated the Triple Alliance with Holland and Sweden 1668, and the marriage of Princess Mary to William of Orange◊ 1677◊□

Temple William 1881–1944. British churchman, archbishop of Canterbury 1942–4. He made idealist application of Christian belief to social problems□

Temple Bar former western gateway of the City of London, between Fleet Street and the Strand (site marked by griffin); the heads of traitors were formerly displayed above it on spikes. Rebuilt by Wren 1672, it was at Theobald's Park, Hertfordshire 1878–1985, when it was placed near St Paul's□

tench a European freshwater game fish; see coarse fish under carp◊□

Tenerife the largest of the Canary◊ Islands□

Teng Hsiao-ping another spelling for Deng◊ Xiaoping□

Teniers David, the Elder 1582–1649. Flemish painter, born in Antwerp and a student of Rubens, who painted scenes of everyday life□

Teniers David, the Younger 1610–90. Finest of the Flemish genre painters, and son of the elder Teniers. He was influenced by Rubens and Brouwer, and was court painter to Archduke Leopold William□

Tennessee border state of the USA; Volunteer State

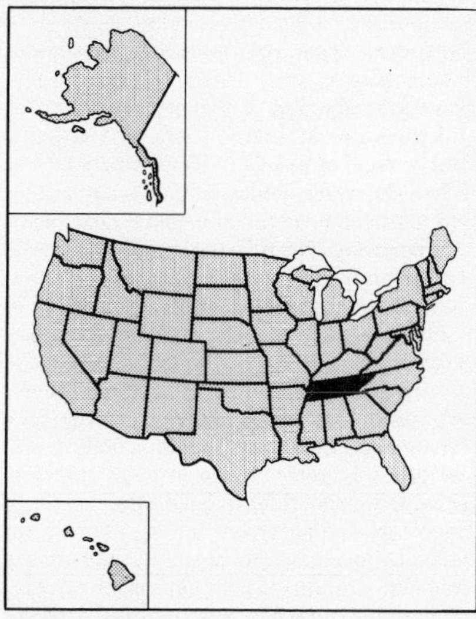

area 109 412 sq km/42 224 sq mi
capital Nashville
towns Memphis, Jackson, Knoxville, Chattanooga
features Tennessee Valley Authority; Great Smoky Mountains National Park; Grand Old Opry, Nashville
products cereals, cotton, tobacco; timber; coal, zinc, pyrites, phosphates; iron and steel and chemicals
population 4 590 750
famous people Davy Crockett, David Farragut, William C Handy, Sam Houston
recent history first settled in 1757, it became a state in 1796□

Tenniel Sir John 1820–1914. British artist, leading *Punch* cartoonist 1850–1901, and original illustrator of Carroll's 'Alice' books□

tennis a racket and ball game invented in England in 1874, and referred to as 'lawn tennis' whether played on a grass or composition court; some features (the hitting of a cloth ball over a central net) derive from real tennis◊, as does the method of scoring. The

tennis

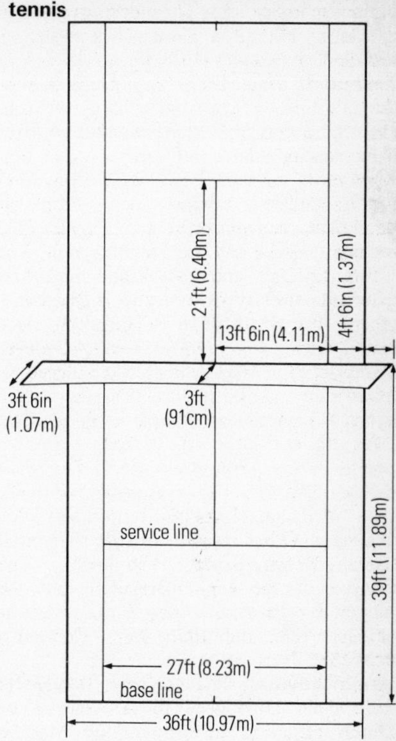

aim of the 2/4 players is to strike the ball into the prescribed area of the court, with oval-headed rackets (strung with gut or nylon), in such a way that it cannot be returned. The game is won by those first winning 4 points (called 15, 30, 40, game), unless both sides reach 40 (deuce) when 2 consecutive points are needed to win. A set is won by winning 6 games with a margin of 2 over opponents, though a tie-break system operates, i.e. at 6 games to each side. Major events include the ***Davis Cup*** 1900 for international men's competition, and ***Wightman Cup*** 1923 for US and UK women's teams, and the annual All England Tennis Club championships (originating 1877), for international professionals of both sexes at Wimbledon.

Winners of five successive titles are Martina Navratilova 1982–86, and Bjorn Borg 1976–80; youngest male winner was 17-year-old W German Boris Becker, 1985 (also 1986)□

tennis *real* racket and ball game played in France from c12th century over a central net in an indoor court, but with a sloping roof inlet into each end and one side of the court, against which the ball may be hit. Basic scoring is as for 'lawn' tennis◊, but with various modifications. The oldest court still in use is at Hampton Court, where it was installed by Henry VIII□

Tennstedt Klaus 1927– . E German conductor. With the London Philharmonic from 1983, he excels in Mozart, Beethoven, Bruckner, and Mahler□

Tennyson Alfred, Lord 1st Baron Tennyson 1809–92. British poet, born at Somersby, Lincolnshire. His *Poems* 1832 include 'The Lady of Shalott' and 'The Lotus Eaters', and established his characteristic mastery of majestic, musical language. The death of A H Hallam (a close friend during his years at Trinity College, Cambridge) in 1833 prompted the elegiac *In Memoriam* unpublished till 1850, the year in which he succeeded Wordsworth as Poet Laureate and married. A long series of poems on the Arthurian legends, *The Idylls of the King* 1857–85, was more Victorian than medieval, but has remarkably fine passages. Other poems include 'Ulysses', 'Break, Break, Break', 'The Brook', 'The Charge of the Light Brigade', and the longer narratives *Locksley Hall* 1832, *The Princess* 1847 and *Maud* 1855. Created a peer 1884□

tenpin bowling ancient game, thought to have been introduced to N America by Dutch settlers in the 17th century. Modern bowling lanes are 1.05 m/3.5 ft wide, and the pins are 38.1 cm/1.25 ft high, set in a triangle, with the nearest pin 18.30 m/60 ft from the bowler. The balls, which have three holes (for thumb and two fingers) weigh up to l7.25 kg/16 lb. Players (in teams of 3/4/5) bowl twice in each 'frame', with points for the number of pins knocked down. The USA has had a National Bowling Association since 1875, and from the 1960s the game became popular in Britain□

Tenzing Norgay popularly known as ***Sherpa Tenzing*** 1914–86. With Edmund Hillary◊, the first to reach the summit of Mount Everest in 1953. He was awarded the George Medal□

Teotihuacán ancient city in central Mexico; see under Toltecs◊□

Teplice industrial city (peat and lignite-mining, glass, porcelain, cement, paper) and spa in Czechoslovakia; population 51 500□

tequila Mexican alcoholic drink made from the agave (see Amaryllidaceae◊) and named from the place, near Guadalajara, where the Conquistadors first developed it from Aztec pulque, which would keep for only a day□

teratorn (Greek 'wonder bird') group of extinct birds including the largest known to have flown. Its fossilized bones (5–8 million years old) were found in Argentina in 1980. Length beak to tail 3.3 m/11 ft; wingspan 7.6 m/25 ft; weight 75 kg/168 lb□

terbium element
symbol Tb
atomic number 65
physical description soft silvery-grey metal
features member of the lanthanide◊ series
uses in lasers, semi-conductor devices, and colour TV tubes□

ter Borch Gerard 1617–81. Dutch artist, influenced by Hals◊, who painted studies of upper-class life, e.g. *A Lady at Her Toilet* in the Wallace Collection, London□

teredo a type of mollusc; see under bivalve◊□

Terence (***Publius Terentius Afer***) c190–159BC. Latin dramatist, born at Carthage, and brought as a slave to Rome where he was freed and came under Scipio◊'s patronage. His subtly characterized comedies are based on Greek models of New Comedy□

Teresa St 1515–82. Spanish mystic, born at Avila, who became a Carmelite nun, and in 1562 founded a new and stricter order. She wrote *The Way to Perfection* and Franco◊ ascribed the length of his rule to carrying a relic of her (one arm) wherever he went□

termite soft-bodied social insect, of the tropical order Isoptera, living in large colonies, comprising one or more queens (of relatively enormous size and producing an egg every two seconds), much smaller kings, and still smaller soldiers, workers and immature forms. Termites build galleried nests of soil particles which are centrally heated and air-conditioned, and may be 7 m/20 ft high. The Macrotermitinae construct fungus gardens from their own faeces, which are then infected with a special fungus which digests the faeces and renders them once more edible so that they can be recycled. Termites may dispose of a quarter of the vegetation litter of an area, and their fondness for wood (as in houses and other buildings) brings them into conflict with man. The wood is broken down in their stomachs by numerous species of microorganisms, living in symbiosis◊ with their hosts, and which, in the process, release gases, including carbon dioxide and methane. The world termite population may be 2400 million billion□

tern a type of seabird; see under gull◊□

Terpsichore Muse of the dance and choral song; see Muses◊□

terracotta brownish red baked clay, used in pottery, as in Greek vases; enamelled, as in Della Robbia reliefs; figurines (see Tanagra◊) and larger sculptures; and architectural features and tiles□

terrapin a small turtle; see under tortoise◊□

Terre Haute industrial city (plastics, chemicals, glass) in Indiana, USA; population 61 200□

terrier a breed of dog◊□

Territorial Army British force of volunteer soldiers, created from volunteer regiments (incorporated 1872) as the ***Territorial Force*** 1908, and renamed Territorial Army 1922. Merged with the Regular Army in World War II, it was revived 1947, and replaced by a smaller, more highly trained Territorial and Army Volunteer Reserve, again renamed Territorial Army 1979□

terrorism systematic violence, especially by small groups for political aims: ***Armed Revolutionary Nuclei*** NAR, neo-Fascist; 1980 bomb in Bologna railway station killed 76 ***Action Directe*** French group in alliance with Red Army Faction (see below) ***Black September*** from month in 1970 when PLO guerrillas active in Jordan were suppressed by Jordanian army; 1972 killed 11 Israelis at Munich Olylmpic Games ***ETA*** see under Basques◊ ***Irish Republican Army*** military wing of Sinn Féin◊, established Jan 1919 to create a united Irish Republic; its terrorist activities intensified in N Ireland◊ from 1968. The dual offshoots, Irish Republican Socialist Party (IRSP), with its paramilitary Irish National Liberation Army (INLA), were formed 1974 ***Lebanon*** various groups, see Lebanon◊ ***Palestine Liberation Organization*** see under Arafat and Palestine◊ ***Quebec Liberation Front*** 1970 kidnapped and killed minister Pierre Laporte in Canada ***Red Army Faction*** RAF, opposing 'US imperialism' formerly led by Andreas Baader and Ulrika Meinhof, active in W Germany from 1968; Meinhof committed suicide during her trial 1976 ***Red Brigades*** Italy, 1978 kidnap and murder of Prime Minister Aldo Moro; 1981 kidnap of US Brig-General James Lee Dozier ***Symbionese Liberation Army*** USA, curiously derived from symbiosis◊; 1974 kidnapped Patricia Hearst, grand-daughter of W R Hearst◊ ***Tupamaros*** founded by Raul Sendic 1960 in Montevideo, Uruguay, urban left-wing guerrillas; see Tupac◊ Amaru□

Terry Dame Ellen 1847–1928. British actress, leading lady to Irving◊ from 1878, and excelling in Shakespearean roles, e.g. Ophelia. She married G F Watts◊, but separation and divorce followed; see also Edward Gordon Craig◊. She had a delightful correspondence with G B Shaw□

tertiaries in the Roman Catholic church, members of a 'third order' (see Holy◊ Orders), i.e. laymen who, while marrying and following a normal employment, attempt to live in accordance with a modified version of the rule of one of the religious orders. The first such order was founded by St Francis◊ 1221□

Tertullian(us) Quintus Septimius Florens c155–222AD. Carthaginian Father of the Church, the first important Christian writer in Latin; he became a Montanist◊ 213□

Tesla Nikola 1856–1943. American electrical engineer, born in Croatia. He developed the AC electrical supply system, and invented fluorescent lighting□

Test Act in England 1673–1828/9, an act requiring all holders of public office to renounce the doctrine of transubstantiation and take the sacrament in an Anglican church; this effectively excluded all Roman Catholics and Nonconformists from office□

testosterone a steroid hormone; see under hormone◊□

tetanus or ***lockjaw***. Disease caused by a bacterium, *Clostridium tetani*, entering a wound; untreated, it produces muscular spasm, convulsions, and death. There is a vaccine□

Tethys in Greek mythology, one of the Titans◊, the wife of the god Oceanus◊□

Tethys Sea the sea which once separated the Indian sub-continent from the rest of Asia□

tetra a brightly coloured tropical fish; see characin◊□

tetraodon order of marine tropical fish Tetraodontiformes which includes:

puffers or ***globe-fish***, a number of species, family Triodontidae, able to fill their intestinal sac with water or air so that they resemble balloons

porcupine fish, family Diodontidae, which add poisonous spines to the 'puffer' defence mechanism

cowfish or ***boxfish***, family Ostrasionidae, with bone armour plating forming a triangular or rectangular box, with only the tail, fins, and mouth emerging

sunfish *Mola mola*, family Molidae, truncated by the reduction of its tail; 2.5 m long/2 m/6 ft deep and weighing 1000 kg/1 tonne, which is found off Britain and capable of diving to great depths□

Tétuan town in NE Morocco; population 140 000□

Teutonic Knights German religious military order, Christian, founded 1190, which crusaded against the pagan Prussians and Lithuanians from 1228. They ruled Prussia until the 15th century□

Texas South West state of the USA; Lone Star State

area 692 407 sq km/267 339 sq mi

capital Austin

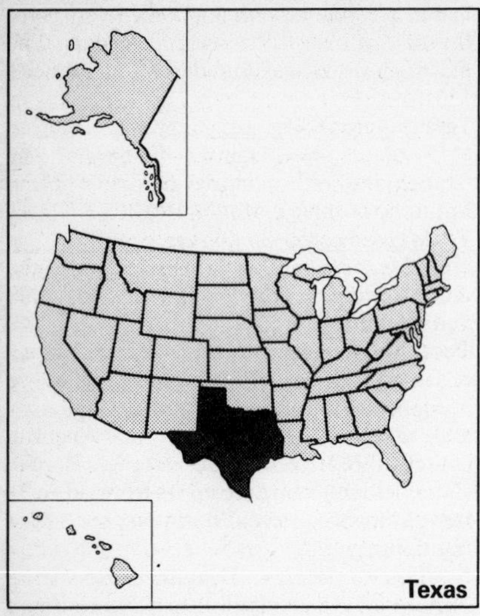

towns Houston, Dallas, San Antonio, Fort Worth, El Paso
features Rio Grande del Norte and Red rivers; arid Staked Plains, reclaimed by irrigation; the Great Plains
products rice, cotton, sorghum, peanuts, pecans, vegetables, fruit; meat products (see Amarillo◊); oil (a third of the needs of the USA), natural gas, asphalt, graphite, sulphur, salt, helium; chemicals, oil products, processed food, machinery, transport equipment
population 14 228 385
famous people James Bowie, Buddy Holly, Sam Houston, Howard Hughes, Lyndon Johnson, Katharine Ann Porter
history first settled by the Spanish in 1682, the area (then part of Mexico) won independence in 1821, and American immigration followed with resultant friction. Santa Anna◊ massacred the Alamo garrison in 1836, but was defeated by Sam Houston at San Jacinto the same year. Houston then became president of the Texas Republic 1836-45; it became a state of the USA (the only one to have previously been an independent republic) in 1845□

Texel one of the Frisian◊ Islands□

textile formerly only a material woven (Latin *texere* to weave) from natural spun thread, now loosely extended to machine-knits and spun-bonded fabrics (in which a web of fibre is created and then fuse-bonded by passing it through controlled heat) made from many other fibres and used not only for clothing and furnishings, but in industry.
natural see cotton, linen, silk, wool (including angora, llama, and many others). For particular qualities, e.g. flame resistance or water and stain repellence, these may be combined with synthetic fibres or treated with various chemicals.
synthetic the first commercial synthetic thread was 'artificial silk' or rayon (see Chardonnet◊), with filaments made from modified cellulose (wood pulp) and known according to later methods of manufacture as *viscose* (using caustic soda and carbon disulphide) or *acetate* (using acetic acid). The first fully synthetic textile fibre was *nylon*◊ (see Carothers◊) 1937; and this with the *acrylics* used in knitwear, e.g. Orlon; the *polyesters*, e.g. Terylene; and the *spandex* or *elastomeric fibres*, e.g. Lycra, form the base of most of today's industry.
geotextiles textiles made from plastic and synthetic fibres, and either felted for use as filters or stabilizing grids, or woven for strength. They form part of drainage systems, road foundations, and barriers to sea and river defences against erosion, etc.□

Thackeray William Makepeace 1811–63. British novelist, born in Calcutta, son of an E India Company official. He studied law, and then art in Paris, before settling to journalism under various pseudonyms. His first and best book was *Vanity Fair* 1847–8; later books include *Pendennis* 1848, *Esmond* 1852 and its sequel *The Virginians*, and *The Newcomes* 1857–5, all tending to sentimentality. He married in 1836, but his wife became insane in 1840□

Thailand The Kingdom of

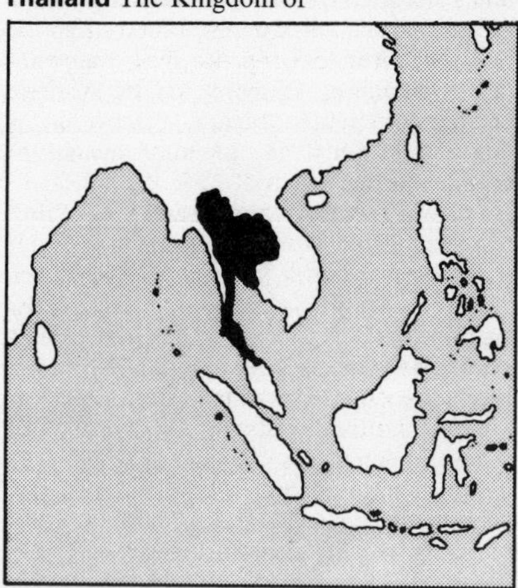

area 514 000 sq km/198 247 sq mi
capital and chief port Bangkok
towns Chiangmai
features rivers Chao Phraya, Mekong, Salween; see Bronze Age◊
exports rice, sugar; rubber, teak; tin (5th largest producer), rubies, sapphires

currency baht
population 51 725 000, Thai 75%, Chinese 14%
language Thai and Chinese, both official
religion Buddhism
government under the 1978 constitution, a constitutional monarch (Bhumibol Adulyadej◊ from 1946); and national assembly comprising senate appointed by the king on the recommendation of the prime minister (General Prem Tinsulanond from 1980; re-elected 1983), and a house of representatives elected by universal suffrage
recent history formerly Siam, the name having been changed in 1939, the country was occupied by Japan 1941–44. After World War II there was a series of military coups, but the junta was overthrown by the king in 1973. Communist guerrillas have been active since 1965, and relations with Kampuchea, Laos, and Vietnam are uneasy□

Thaïs 4th century BC. Greek courtesan, mistress of Alexander◊ the Great and later wife of Ptolemy◊ I, king of Egypt. She allegedly instigated the burning of Persepolis◊□

thalassaemia a form of anaemia◊□

Thales c624–c546BC. Greek philosopher who made advances in geometry, predicted the sun's eclipse in 585, and theorized that water was the first principle of all things□

Thalia in Greek mythology, the Muse of comedy and pastoral poetry; see Muses◊□

thalidomide tranquillizer developed in Germany 1957. When taken by pregnant women it caused malformation of the foetus (in over 5000 known cases) and the drug was withdrawn 1961□

thallium element
symbol Tl
atomic number 81
physical description white metal
features highly toxic
uses in rat and insect poison; its compounds are used in optical glassmaking, and photoelectric cells□

Thames river in SE England; its headstreams rise in the Cotswolds above Cirencester, and unite at Lechlade) length 338 km/210 mi. Above Oxford it is sometimes poetically call Isis; it is tidal as far as Teddington; and below London there is protection from flooding by means of the Woolwich barrier, completed 1984□

Thames Firth of. Inlet between Auckland and the Coromandel Peninsula, New Zealand□

Thanet Isle of. See Kent◊□

Thanksgiving (Day) national holiday (2nd Monday in Oct in Canada, and 4th Thursday of Nov in USA), first celebrated (at their first harvest) by the Pilgrim Fathers 1621□

Thant U 1909–74. Burmese diplomat, Secretary-General of the United Nations 1962–71. He helped to resolve the US-Soviet crisis over the Soviet installation of missiles in Cuba, and he made the controversial decision to withdraw the United Nations peace-keeping force from the Egypt-Israel border 1967. See Arab-Israeli◊ Wars□

Thar Desert or *Indian Desert* on the Rajasthan◊-Pakistan border; area c250 000 sq km/96 500 sq mi□

Thatcher Margaret 1925– . British Conservative stateswoman. Born Roberts, daughter of a grocer, who was later mayor of Grantham◊, she was educated at Somerville College, Oxford, qualified as a research chemist and barrister, and married in 1951 Denis Thatcher, a director of Burmah Oil. She entered Parliament in 1959, was Minister of Education 1970–4, defeated Heath for the Conservative leadership in 1975, and became Prime Minister in 1979, her government being re-elected 1983. Landmarks of the administration include the independence of Zimbabwe◊, the Falklands◊ conflict; reduction of inflation; large-scale privatization◊; the Anglo-Irish Agreement of 1985, but also a large rise in unemployment□

theatre dramatic performances formed part of ancient religious observance, e.g. at the temple of Edfu in Egypt (see drama◊), and the first European theatres were open spaces round the altar of Dionysus◊. The stone-built semicircles of seating (for up to 30 000 people) of theatres of the Graeco-Roman world survive at many sites. In medieval times there were temporary stages of wood and canvas, which were mobile in the case of the Miracle◊ plays. Permanent theatres became widespread with the Renaissance, e.g. that at Vicenza◊ and London's first theatre, the Theatre in Shoreditch in 1576, built by James Burbage◊; see also Globe Theatre under Southwark◊. Other famous theatres include Drury Lane 1663 (see Nell Gwyn◊; present building 1812); Abbey◊ Theatre; repertory theatres, e.g. Old◊ Vic and Birmingham◊; national theatres, see National◊ Theatre; and those forming part of larger cultural centres, e.g. the Lincoln Center, New York; Place des Arts, Montreal; and London's Barbican□

Theatre Museum see Covent◊ Garden□

thebaine an extract of opium◊□

Thebes Greek name of an ancient city (Niut-Ammon) in Upper Egypt, on the Nile, centre of the worship of Ammon◊, and the Egyptian capital under the New Kingdom. Magnificent temple ruins survive, near the modern villages of Karnak and Luxor, and in the nearby

Valley of the Kings the 18th–20th dynasty kings, including Tutankhamen◊, are buried. See also under Amenhotep◊□

Thebes chief city of Boeotia◊, ancient Greece. On the Persian side in the Graeco–Persian Wars, it was for a time the leading Greek city state, but was razed to the ground in 335BC, after revolting against Alexander◊ the Great. Pindar◊ was born here; see also Oedipus◊□

theft in the UK (according to the act of 1968 which placed forms of theft formerly dealt with individually, e.g. burglary and larceny, under a single head) the dishonest appropriation of another's property with the intention of depriving him/her of it permanently; maximum penalty 10 years□

theism belief in the existence of gods, but more especially in that of a single personal God◊, revealed to the world in a special revelation□

Themis in Greek mythology, the goddess of justice; see under Titans◊□

Themistocles c525–c460BC. Greek soldier-statesman. Largely responsible for the ostracizing of Aristides◊ in 483, he held almost supreme power in Athens for 10 years, created its navy, and fought with distinction in the Battle of Salamis◊ 480. Banished by Spartan influence c470, he fled to Asia□

Theocritus ?310–?250BC. Greek poet, whose *Idylls* became models for later pastoral poetry□

theodolite surveying instrument, used to measure horizontal and vertical angles, basically a specially modified telescope fitted with a spirit level□

Theodora c508–48AD. Byzantine empress, originally a courtesan, the mistress of Justinian◊, and his consort from c523. She earned a reputation for charity and courage□

Theodorakis Mikis 1925– . Greek composer of 'Zorba's dance,' etc., imprisoned 1967–70 for attempting to overthrow the military regime□

Theodoric I king of the Visigoths 418–51AD, a grandson of Alaric◊. After successful campaigns against the Romans, he united with them to fight the Huns (under Attila◊), and was killed at Châlons◊□

Theodoric the Great 455–526AD. King, in succession to his father, of the Ostrogoths from 474. He invaded Italy 488, overthrew Odoacer◊ (whom he murdered) and established his own Ostrogothic kingdom there (with its capital at Ravenna), ruling in the old tradition of the Roman emperors. He had no strong successor, and his kingdom eventually became part of the Byzantine Empire; see Justinian◊□

Theodosius I the Great c346–395AD. Roman Emperor in the East from 379; sole emperor from 394. He subdued the Goths, allowing them autonomy as allies under the peace of 382. He adopted the Nicene creed as the formulation of the state religion, but blotted his reign by massacring 7000 citizens of Thessaloniki after a riot in the circus there (St Ambrose◊ made him do penance)□

Theodosius II 401–50AD. Byzantine emperor from 408, who defeated the Persians 421 and 441, but from 441 only bought off Attila's Huns with tribute□

theology the study of God or gods, either by deductions from the natural world, or through revelation, as in the scriptures of Christianity, Islam, etc.□

theorbo an obsolete form of the lute◊□

theosophy any religious or philosophical system based on intuitive insight into the nature of the divine, but especially that of the Theosophical Society (see Blavatsky◊), based on Hindu ideas of karma◊ and reincarnation◊, with nirvana◊ as the eventual aim□

Theresa Mother. Indian Roman Catholic nun, born ***Agnes Bojaxhiu*** 1910– . Of Albanian origin, she became an Indian citizen, and founded the Missionaries of Charity, an order for men and women based in Calcutta, which especially helps abandoned children and the dying. Nobel peace prize 1979, honorary Order of Merit 1983□

Thérèse St, of Lisieux 1873–97. French Carmelite nun, who lived in the convent at Lisieux from the age of 15, and was known as 'Little Flower of Jesus'. She advocated the 'Little Way of Goodness' in small things in everyday life. She died of tuberculosis. Feast day 3 Oct□

thermic lance tube of mild steel packed with steel rods, and fed with oxygen which, on ignition, reaches temperatures above 3000°C, so that the lance becomes its own sustaining fuel. It cuts through walls or 23 cm/9 in steel doors in half a minute, and is countered (when used by criminals) by alarm systems which detect radiation emitted in action□

thermodynamics study of the relationship between the heat◊ flowing into a system (which may be as simple as a gas or as complex as a mixture of reacting chemicals), the work◊ done by the system and the system's internal energy. The Laws of Thermodynamics are: 1 The work done is equal to the heat inflow (if any) plus the fall (if any) in internal energy. See Principle of Conservation of Energy under energy◊. 2 No self-acting process can convert heat into work leaving the system with its original internal energy. 3 The absolute zero of temperature cannot be reached in a finite number of operations. The Laws are relevant to the workings of power stations and internal combustion engines, and important deductions in pure physics can be made from them□

thermography recording of heat patterns, as developed in the 1970s–80s to assist night vision by the military, e.g. by detecting the body heat of an enemy or that given off by the hot engine of a tank□

thermoluminescence light released (by most crystalline substances) which have been irradiated and are later heated. The reaction is used by geologists in dating terrestrial rocks and meteorites, and by archaeologists to date ceramics□

thermometer instrument for measuring temperature, which works by measuring some temperature-dependent property of a substance. Commonest are mercury -in-glass thermometers, using the expansion of mercury from a bulb into a narrow glass tube. The ***thermocouple thermometer*** relies on a voltage generated when the junctions between two different metals are at different temperatures. Optical ***pyrometers*** measure furnace temperatures by analysing the radiation emitted. Other types rely on the expansion of gases, or the change in electrical resistance of a metal (e.g. platinum)□

Thermopylae Battle of 480BC. See Persian◊ Wars□

thermosphere that part of the earth's atmosphere◊ that begins at about 80 km/50 mi above the earth's surface and extends to outer space. The temperature of the thermosphere increases the further away it is from earth□

Theroux Paul Edward 1941– . American novelist (*Saint Jack* 1973, *Picture Palace* 1978, and *Doctor Slaughter* 1984), and travel writer (*The Great Railway Bazaar* 1975)□

Thespis legendary 6th century BC Greek poet, said to have introduced the first actor into plays (previously presented by choruses only), hence the word 'thespian' for an actor. He was also said to have invented tragedy and to have introduced the wearing of linen masks□

Thessaly n the 4th century BC an independent state in Greece conquered by Philip of Macedon. It formed part of the Roman province of Macedonia, and was Turkish from the 14th century until incorporated in Greece in 1881 as a region which includes Larisa◊□

Thetford market town in Norfolk, England; population 17 000□

Thetford Mines town in Quebec, Canada; population 21 000. It is the site of the world's largest asbestos deposits□

Thibault J A. French writer who wrote under the pen name of Anatole France◊□

Thiers Louis Adolphe 1797–1877. French statesman and historian (*History of the French Revolution* 1823–7). He led the parliamentary opposition to Napoleon III from 1863, and as head of the provisional government in 1871 he negotiated peace with Prussia and suppressed the Paris Commune. He was first President of the 3rd Republic 1871–3□

Thimphu capital of the Himalayan state of Bhután◊; population 15 000□

Third World those countries of Africa, Asia, and Latin America (c114) which are comparatively industrially undeveloped. With about 80% of the world population, they are responsible for less than 30% of the world's industrial production.

The ***Three Worlds Theory*** was allegedly first formulated by Mao◊ Zedong: *First World* USA and USSR; *Second* Canada, Japan, Europe; *Third* Africa, Latin America, and Asia generally□

Thirteen States the thirteen states of the US who, led by George Washington, defeated the British army in the War of American Independence in 1776 to become the United States of America. See under United◊ States: history□

Thirty-nine Articles a set of formulas defining the doctrine of the Anglican church; see Anglican◊ Communion□

Thirty Years' War 1618–48. A major war in central Europe, beginning as a conflict between Protestants and Catholics, it gradually became transformed into a struggle to determine whether the Hapsburgs◊ would gain control of all Germany. After the defeat of a Bohemian revolt against Austrian rule 1618–20, some Protestant princes continued the struggle against Austria, with the aid of Denmark 1625–7. From 1630 Gustavus◊ Adolphus of Sweden intervened on the Protestant side, overrunning N Germany before his death in 1632. When the Swedes were defeated at Nördlingen 1634, Richelieu◊ brought France into the war to inflict several defeats on Austria's Spanish allies. The ***Treaty of Westphalia*** 1648 gave France S Alsace, and Sweden certain Baltic provinces, the emperor's authority in Germany becoming only nominal. The mercenary armies of Wallenstein, Tilly, and Mansfeld devastated Germany□

thistle several genera of plants, family Compositae◊, with purple, bushy flower heads and spiny, deeply-indented leaves. The thistle is the Scottish national emblem□

Thistle Order of the. A Scottish order of knighthood◊□

Thistlewood Arthur. Leader of the Cato◊ Street Conspiracy□

Thomas St. In the New Testament, one of the 12 Apostles, said to have preached in S India, hence the ancient churches there were referred to as the 'Christians of St Thomas'. See Gnosticism◊□

Thomas Dylan Marlais 1914–53. Welsh poet. Born in Swansea, he was the son of the English master at the local grammar school where he was educated. After working locally as a reporter, he went to London as a journalist, and his first verse volume *Eighteen Poems* was published 1934. Repeatedly anthologized poems include his lilting celebration of his 30th birthday 'Poem in October' and the evocation of his youth 'Fern Hill'. His radio play *Under Milk Wood* 1954, and his short stories are memorable. An alcoholic, he died on a New York lecture tour□

Thomas (Philip) Edward 1878–1917. British nature poet, As 'Edward Eastaway', he published *Six Poems* 1916, and, under his own name, *Poems* 1917 and *Last Poems* 1918. He was killed in action at Arras◊□

Thomas R(onald) S(tuart) 1913– . Welsh poet, vicar of St Hywyn, Aberdaron, 1967–78. His verse, as in *Song at the Year's Turning* 1955, contrasts traditional Welsh values with encroaching 'English' sterility□

Thomas à Kempis c1380–1471. German Augustinian monk at Zwolle◊, so-named because born at Kempen; his real surname was Hammerken. His *Imitation of Christ* is probably the best-known devotional work ever written□

Thompson Flora 1877–1948. English novelist, born at Juniper Hill, Oxfordshire, whose trilogy *Lark Rise to Candleford* 1945 deals with late Victorian rural life□

Thompson Francis 1859–1907. British Roman Catholic poet-mystic, whose poems, including 'The Hound of Heaven', were published□

Thomsen Christian. See under prehistory◊□

Thomson Sir George Paget 1892–1875. British physicist, son of Sir Joseph Thomson◊; Nobel prize 1937 (with C J Davisson) for work on interference phenomena in the scattering of electrons by crystals, which helped to confirm the wave-like nature of particles (see quantum◊ theory)□

Thomson James 1700–48. Scottish poet, whose descriptive blank verse poem *The Seasons* 1726–30 was a forerunner of the Romantic movement. He also wrote the words of 'Rule, Britannia'□

Thomson James 1834–82. English poet, who wrote as 'BV' (Bysshe Vanolis), and is remembered for his despairing poem 'The City of Dreadful Night' 1880□

Thomson Sir Joseph John 1856–1940. British physicist, who organized the Cavendish research laboratory at Cambridge, which became world-famous for nuclear research. He discovered the electron◊ 1897, and his elucidation of positive rays and their application to an analysis of neon led to Aston's discovery of isotopes◊. He was the founder of modern physics; Nobel prize 1906, Order of Merit 1913. See particle◊ physics□

Thomson Virgil 1896– . US composer, a student of Nadia Boulanger◊. His works include operas e.g. *Four Saints in Three Acts* (libretto Gertrude Stein◊) 1928, and film music□

Thor in Norse mythology, god of thunder (his hammer), and represented as a man of enormous strength defending mankind against demons. Thursday is named after him□

Thoreau Henry David 1817–62. US author and naturalist, born at Concord, Massachusetts. *Walden, or Life in the Woods* 1854 stimulated the back to nature movement□

thorium element
symbol Th
atomic number 90
physical description silvery-white metal
features radioactive; found particularly in monazite beach sands; uranium–233 is 'bred' from it for fuel in nuclear reactors
uses used in making gas mantles and electronic equipment□

thorn apple the poisonous N American jimsonweed *Datura stramonium*, family Solanaceae◊; 5 m/15 ft high, with trumpet-shaped flowers. It is a narcotic□

thornback ray a type of fish; see under ray◊□

Thorndike Russell 1885–1972. British actor-novelist, whose books feature the smuggling parson 'Dr Syn'□

Thorndike Dame Sybil 1882–1976. British actress for whom Shaw wrote *St Joan*, Dame of the British Empire 1931. The Thorndike Theatre, Leatherhead, is named after her, and the theatre workshop after her husband, actor ***Sir Lewis Casson*** 1885–1972□

Thorwaldsen Bertel 1770–1844. Danish sculptor. A friend of Canova◊, he was the epitome of Neoclassic style, e.g. 'The Triumph of Alexander'□

Thoth in Egyptian mythology, god of wisdom and learning, scribe of the gods□

Thothmes name of four Egyptian kings of the 18th dynasty: ***Thothmes I*** reigned 1540–1501BC founded the Egyptian empire in Syria. His grandson ***Thothmes III*** reigned c 1500–1446BC extended the empire to the Euphrates, and conquered Nubia□

Thousand Islands a group of about 1500 islands on the border between Canada and the USA in the upper St Lawrence river; see Lake Ontario under Great◊ Lakes□

Thrace Balkan area divided in 1923 into western Thrace (the modern Greek province of Thráki) and eastern Thrace (modern Turkey-in-Europe). However, the heart of the ancient Thracian Empire 6000BC–300AD was modern Bulgaria, where since 1945 there have been tomb finds of gold and silver dishes, drinking vessels and jewellery with animal designs, especially splendid horses. The legend of Orpheus◊ and the cult of Dionysus◊ were both derived by the Greeks from Thrace. The area was conquered by Persia, 6th–5th centuries BC and by Macedon 4th–2nd centuries BC. From 46AD it was a Roman province, then part of the Byzantine Empire, and Turkish from the 15th century until 1878; it was then subject to constant dispute until after World War I□

threadworm a class of worm; see under worm◊□

Three Rivers English name for the Canadian port of Trois◊ Rivières□

thrift tufted perennial plant, especially the ***sea pink*** *Armeria maritima*, family Plumbaginaceae, with pink flowers in dense solitary heads□

thrips tiny biting insects, irritant to humans, and a pest of crops, order Thysanoptera. They have feathery wings□

thrombosis formation of a blood clot in a blood vessel, often in the legs, where it may cause phlebitis◊, or heart, as in coronary thrombosis (see coronary◊)□

throwing events field athletic contests in which the four usual events are:

discus in which the men's discus weighs 2 kg/4.4 lb (women's 1 kg/2.2 lb), and is thrown from within a circle 2.5 m/8 ft in diameter.

hammer which has a spherical head, and may originally have been a blacksmith's hammer. It now weighs 7.26 kg/16 lb, and is thrown similarly to the discus.

javelin in which the men's javelin is 260–270 cm/c8.5 ft long (women's 220–230 cm/c7.2 ft), thrown from a line at the end of a run-up.

putting the shot a 'cannon-ball' weight, for men 7.26 kg/16 lb (women 4 kg/8.8 lb), thrown with one hand from a circle.

tossing the caber is a Highland Games event only, in which a tapered tree trunk c6 m/20 ft long and weighing c100 kg/220 lb is hurled as far as possible in a straight line from the competitor (c12.1 m/40 ft)□

thrush family of birds, Turdidae, order Passeriformes, which has many fine songsters, including the ***song thrush*** *Turdus philomelos*, brown with a lighter speckled breast; the very similar ***redwing*** *T iliacus*, with a white eye-stripe and red feathers under the wings; the larger ***missel thrush*** or ***stormcock*** *T viscivorus*; the ***fieldfare*** *T pilaris*, a winter visitor to Britain, with deeper chestnut colouring, grey head and rump, and a dark tail; and the ***ring ouzel*** *T torquatus*, a lover of rocky country, with almost black plumage and a white neck-band. Other members of the family include ***redstart*** *Phoenicurus phoenicurus*, the male having a reddish breast and tail, black face and white forehead mark; ***stonechat*** *Saxicola torquata*, of which the male has a black head and throat, tawny breast and dark back; and ***wheatear*** *Oenanthe oenanthe*, a summer visitor to Britain from India and Africa, which is grey and white, with black markings including a facepatch. See also under robin◊, mocking bird◊, and nightingale◊□

Thucydides c460–400BC. Athenian historian, who exercised command in the Peloponnesian◊ War in 424 with so little success that he was banished till 404. In his *History of the Peloponnesian War* he attempted a scientific impartiality□

Thug originally a member of a Hindu sect who strangled travellers as sacrifices to Kali◊; suppressed c1830□

Thule Greek and Roman name for the most northerly land known. It was applied to the Shetlands, the Orkneys, and Iceland, and by later writers to Scandinavia□

thulium element

symbol Tn

atomic number 69

physical description soft silvery-grey metal

features member in the lanthanide◊ series found in monazite

uses its isotope thulium-170 is used as an X-ray source, and in arc lighting□

Thunder Bay industrial city (shipbuilding, timber, paper, pulp) and lake port (wheat) on Lake Superior, Ontario, Canada, formed by the union of Port Arthur and its twin city of Fort William to the south; population 112 500□

Thunderbird a legendary bird of the N American Indians; see under Plains◊ Indians□

Thurber James Grover 1894–1961. US humorist, born in Columbus, Ohio. Contributor to the *New Yorker*, his short stories include 'The Secret Life of Walter Mitty' and his doodle drawings include preposterous impressions of dogs□

Thuringia former central state of Germany 1919–46; capital Weimar. The ***Thuringian Forest*** is of great beauty. Thuringia was enlarged as a Land until 1952, when it became the E German districts of Erfurt, Gera, and Suhl□

thylacine doglike marsupial; see Tasmanian tiger under marsupial◊□

thyme a type of herb◊□

thymus ductless gland near the root of the neck, which develops early in embryonic life, continues to grow after birth, but atrophies before adult life. It is the thymus which teaches the body's immune system the difference between 'self' and 'foreign' tissues, and it is vital to the body's resistance to infection. The food known as 'sweetbread' is an animal thymus□

thyroid see under hormone◊□

Tianjin port and industrial and commercial city (formerly Tientsin), a special municipality in Hubei province, China; population 7 760 000. Dagan oilfield is nearby, and Tianjin's handmade silk and wool carpets are famous□

Tiber river in Italy on which Rome stands; length from the Apennines to the Tyrrhenian Sea 400 km/250 mi□

Tiberias Lake. Lake in N Israel (also Sea of Galilee, Lake of Gennesaret, and Hebrew Yam Kinneret) into which the Jordan◊ flows; 210 m/686 ft below sea level; area 165 sq km/64 sq mi□

Tiberius Claudius Nero 42BC–37AD. Roman emperor, the stepson, adopted son, and successor of Augustus from 14AD. A distinguished soldier, he was a conscientious ruler under whom the empire prospered. In later life he retired to Capri□

Tibesti Mountains range in the central Saharan system, N Chad; highest peak Emi Koussi 3415 m/11 204 ft□

Tibet autonomous region of SW China (Chinese name *Xizang*)

area 1 221 600 sq km/471 540 sq mi

capital Lhasa

features Himalayas, Kunlun Mountains, Karakoram range (average elevation 4500 m/1500 ft); sources of the Sutlej, Brahmaputra and Indus rivers

products wool, furs; gold, lapis lazuli, mercury and other minerals

population 1 900 000; formerly a quarter of the population were monks and polyandry was practised; 70% illiterate

language Tibetan

religion Lamaism

recent history an independent kingdom from the 5th century AD, it passed under nominal Chinese suzerainty c1700–1912, and was ocupied by Communist China from 1951, becoming an autonomous region in 1965. Initially Communist rule was harsh, industrialization was introduced, and many Chinese settlers entered, but from 1980 traditional agriculture and livestock practices were restored. Attempts were made to persuade the Dalai Lama◊ to return, and Lamaism became tolerated. The country is of immense strategic importance to China, with c200 000 troops there, missile sites in the desert, and the chief Chinese nuclear base at Nagchuka, 265 km/165 mi N of Lhasa□

tick two families of Arachnida◊, allied to the mites◊; they are blood-sucking, disease-carrying parasites on men, animals, and birds□

tides rise and fall of sea level due to the gravitational forces of the moon and sun. High water occurs at an average interval of 12 hrs 24.5 min. The highest or spring tides are at or near new and full moon, and the lowest or neap tides when the moon is in the 1st or 3rd quarter□

Tieck Johann Ludwig 1773–1853. German Romantic poet and collector of folk-tales, e.g. 'Puss in Boots'□

Tien-Shan a mountain system of central Asia; see Tyan-Shan◊□

Tientsin industrial city in NE China; see Tianjin◊□

Tiepolo Giovanni Battista 1692–1769. Italian painter, born at Venice, and a master of decorative historical and allegorical work for churches and palaces. See Würzburg◊□

Tierra del Fuego island group divided between Chile and Argentina. They are separated from the mainland by Magellan Strait, and Cape Horn is at the southernmost point. To the south of the main island is ***Beagle Channel*** (named after the ship of Darwin◊'s voyage) with three islands at the east end, finally awarded in 1985 to Chile rather than Argentina□

Tiffany Louis Comfort 1848–1933. American stained-glass maker, and originator of iridescent Favrile glass and lampshades□

Tiflis Russian name for the city of Tbilisi□

tiger a large cat; see under cat◊□

Tigris river flowing through Turkey and Iraq (see also Mesopotamia◊), joining the Euphrates above Basra; length 1600 km/1000 mi□

Tihuanaco site of a Peruvian city, 24 km/

tides

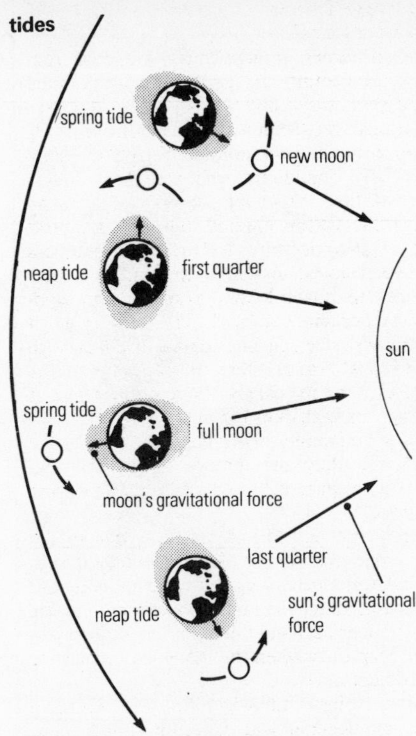

15 mi S of Lake Titicaca, which gave its name to the civilization of the 8th–14th century which preceded the Inca◊□

Tijuana city in Mexico; population 535 000. Noted for horse races and casinos. San◊ Diego adjoins it across the US border□

Tikhonov Nikolai 1905– . Russian statesman, a close associate of Brezhnev, who was Prime Minister 1980–85□

tilapia a type of fish; see under perch◊□

Tilly Jan Tserklaes, Count 1559–1632. Flemish commander of the army of the Catholic League and imperial forces in the Thirty Years' War. Notorious for his storming of Magdeburg in 1631, he was defeated by Gustavus Adolphus at Breitenfeld, and at the Lech, in which latter battle he was mortally wounded□

Tilsit the former name (until 1945) of the Russian town of Sovetsk◊□

Timaru industrial port (freezing plants, flour mills, pottery, brewing), with an artificial harbour, and resort in South Island, New Zealand; population 30 000□

timber wood for use in construction, furniture, pulp (for paper), including:

hardwoods including tropical mahogany, teak, ebony, rosewood; temperate oak, elm, beech, and (from Australia) eucalyptus◊. All are slow-growing and world supplies are near exhaustion.

softwoods (actual hardness or softness of these timbers varies) are the conifers◊, pine, fir, spruce, larch, etc, which are rapid and easy to grow, and easy to work, but inferior in quality of grain, etc.

white woods ash, birch, sycamore◊, which have light-coloured timber, are fast-growing, and can be used through modern methods as veneers on cheaper timber, are now being grown as 'crops'.

Timber is also given special treatment (moulded, hardened or proofed in various ways) and sawdust, shavings, etc. are compacted, with chemical additives, into various grades of sheet 'timber' for construction purposes□

Timbuktu town in Mali; population 20 000. A camel caravan centre from the 11th century on the fringe of the Sahara, it has since 1960 been surrounded by the southward movement of the desert, and the former canal link with the Niger is dry□

time the continuous passing of existence, recorded by division into hours, minutes, and seconds. Formerly measurement of time on earth was based on earth's rotation on its axis, but this was found to be irregular. Therefore, the second◊, the standard SI unit of time, was redefined in terms of earth's annual orbit of the sun (by the International Committee of Weights and Measures) in 1956. The difference between the new Universal Time (UT) and Coordinated Universal Time (UTC) based on earth's actual rotation is adjusted by the addition (or subtraction) of leap seconds on the last day of June or December. National observatories (in the UK the Royal Greenwich Observatory) make standard time available, and the BBC broadcasts six pips at certain hours (five short, from second 55 to second 59, and one long, the start of which indicates the precise minute). A more exact indication is broadcast from the Post Office Radio Station at Rugby. From 1986 the term Greenwich Mean Time was replaced by UTC. However, the Greenwich meridian, adopted 1884, remains that from which all longitudes are measured, and the world's standard time zones are calculated from it, each hour fast or slow corresponding to 15° longitude□

Times Beach town in Missouri, USA, which accidentally became contaminated with dioxin◊, and was bought 1983 by the Environmental Protection Agency for cleansing□

Timisoara industrial city (flour, tobacco, beer, leather, textiles, paper) in W Romania; population 287 550□

Timor an Indonesian island, largest of the Lesser Sunda Islands; see Lesser Sunda◊

time

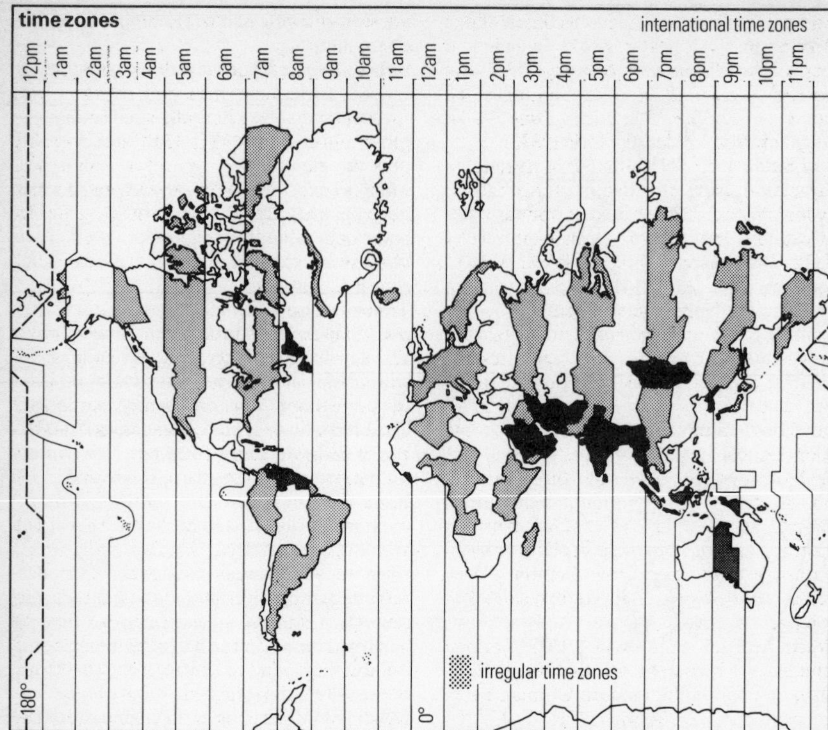

Islands□

Timoshenko Semyon 1895–70. Marshal of the USSR, the 'bald-headed eagle'. In 1940 he reorganized the Red Army to delay and then destroy the German attack in 1941□

Timothy in the New Testament, companion to St Paul◊, both on his missionary journeys and in prison. Two of the Pauline epistles are addressed to him□

tin element
symbol Sn (Latin *stannum*)
atomic number 50
physical description shiny metal, easily worked
features mainly occurs as ore cassiterite (SnO_2); the largest supplies coming from SE Asia and S America; there is a trace in the human body
uses used in giving a corrosion-resistant surface to 'tin' (composed mainly of steel) cans, and in many alloys, especially bronze and pewter□

tinamou any bird of the order Tinamiformes; see under running◊ birds□

Tinbergen Jan 1903– . Dutch economist, Nobel prizewinner 1969 (with Ragnar Frisch◊) for his work on econometrics◊. See Nikolaas Tinbergen◊□

Tinbergen Nikolaas 1907– . Dutch zoologist, brother of Jan Tinbergen◊. Specializing in the study of instinctive behaviour, he shared a Nobel prize with Konrad Lorenz and Karl von Frisch◊ 1973□

Tindouf oasis with large iron deposits in W Algeria□

tinnitus internal sounds, inaudible to others, which are heard by sufferers from malfunctions of hearing, e.g. spasm of an inner-ear muscle or infection of the middle or inner ear□

Tintagel village resort on the coast of N Cornwall, England; there are castle ruins, and legend has it that King Arthur was born and held court here□

Tintoretto Venetian painter, real name *Jacopo Robusti* 1518–94, named because his father was a dyer. A student of Titian, he painted portraits and biblical scenes. His most famous works are the enormous canvases of the life of Christ in the Scuola di San Rocco, Venice, showing Mannerist◊ features□

Tipperary county divided into N and S regions (administrative headquarters Nenagh and Clonmel respectively) in the Republic of Ireland, province of Munster◊□

Tippett Sir Michael 1905– . British composer. He first made his name in World War II with *A Child of Our Time* 1941, an oratorio, and was briefly imprisoned as a conscientious objector in 1943. Later works include the operas *The Midsummer Marriage* 1952 and *The Knot Garden* 1970; four symphonies; the choral work *The Mask of Time* 1984. Knighted 1966, Order of Merit 1983□

Tipu Sahib 1753–99. Sultan of Mysore (now Karnataka) from the death of his father, Hyder◊ Ali, in 1782. He died of wounds when his capital, Seringapatam, was captured by the British. His rocket brigade led Sir William Congreve 1772–1828 to develop the weapon for use in the Napoleonic Wars□

Tirana capital and industrial town (metallurgy, cotton textiles, soap, cigarettes) of Albania; population 198 000. Founded in the 17th century, it became the capital in 1920, and though now mainly modern has some older districts and early mosques□

Tirol former province of the Austrian Empire, famous for its mountainous forest scenery. In 1919 it was divided between Austria (now the province of Tirol, capital Innsbruck) and Italy (now Trentino-Alto◊ Adige); the cession to Italy is still resented by Austria□

Tirpitz Alfred von 1849–1930. German admiral. As Secretary for the Navy 1897–1916, he created the modern German navy; he planned the World War I U-boat campaign□

Tiruchirapalli industrial city (cotton textiles, cigars, gold and silver filigree) (formerly Trichinopoly) in Tamil Nadu, India; population 608 000. It was the capital of Tamil kingdoms 10th–17th centuries□

Tiryns ancient Greek city in the Peloponnesus on the plain of Argos; see under Mycenaean◊ civilization□

Tissot James Joseph Jacques 1836–1902. French artist. He fought in the Franco-German war, but his political leanings to the Commune being suspected, he fled to London. His eye-beguiling interpretation of Victorian high society at leisure is unrivalled□

Tisza a tributary of the river Danube◊□

tit or ***titmouse*** family of birds, Paridae, order Passeriformes, which in Britain includes the common ***bluetit*** or ***tomtit*** *Parus caeruleus* and the great tit *Parus major*, intelligent frequenter of suburban gardens, capable of great acrobatics; and the rarer crested, cole, great, marsh, and long-tailed tits□

Titan in Greek mythology, any of the giant children of Uranus and Gaia◊, who included Cronus, Rhea (see Cybele◊), Themis (mother of Prometheus and personification of law and order) and Oceanus. Cronus and Rhea were in turn the parents of Zeus◊, who ousted Cronus as the ruler of the world□

Titan the largest of the ten satellites of the planet Saturn□

Titanic British White Star liner (supposedly unsinkable), which struck an iceberg off the Grand Banks of Newfoundland on its maiden voyage 14/15 Apr 1912; 1513 lives lost. In 1985 it was located by robot submarine 4 km/2.5 mi down in an ocean canyon, perfectly preserved by the ice-cold environment□

titanium element
symbol Ti
atomic number 22
physical description whitish metal
features difficult to extract from its ores
uses in the chemical industry; its oxide producing high-grade white pigments for paint. Because of its strength, corrosion-resistance, and superplasticity (alloyed both with aluminium and vanadium) it is used in aircraft and spacecraft. ***Synroc***, a synthetic rock for retaining radioactive material for thousands of years, is made from titanium minerals to contain high-level nuclear wastes□

tithes English form of the claim under Mosaic law for a 'tenth' of a parishioner's yearly profits (in kind, later as a rent charge) for support of the local church and its incumbent. Tithes were abolished in England 1936□

Titian anglicized form of the name of Italian artist ***Tiziano (Vecellio)*** c1477–1576. He studied under the Bellinis, and was influenced by Giorgione◊. He was renowned for his colour, and his works include portraits of Charles V and Philip II of Spain, as well as religious and mythical themes, e.g. *Bacchus and Ariadne*, *Venus and Adonis*, and the *Entombment of Christ*□

Titicaca Andean lake divided between Bolivia (port at Guaqui) and Peru (ports at Puno and Huancane), 3815 m/12 500 ft above sea level (area 8300 sq km/3200 sq mi). It is noted for the reed boats of the Indians, and its huge edible frogs□

Tito assumed name of the Yugoslav soldier-statesman ***Josip Broz*** 1892–1980, born in Croatia. He organized the National Liberation Army to carry on guerrilla warfare against the German invasion of 1941, and was created marshal 1943. As Prime Minister of the Federal Republic from 1946, he settled the Yugoslav minorities question on a federal basis, and in 1953 became president (for life from 1974). He was attacked by the USSR for his successful system of decentralized profit-sharing workers' councils, and became the leader of the non-aligned◊ movement□

Titograd capital (Podgorica, until renamed 1948 in honour of Tito) of Montenegro, Yugoslavia; population 132 300□

Titus (Flavius Vespasianus) 39–81AD. Roman emperor from 79. Eldest son of Vespasian◊, he stormed Jerusalem in 70 to end the Jewish revolt; finished the Colosseum, and enjoyed a peaceful reign, except for Agricola◊'s campaigns in Britain□

Tivoli town NE of Rome, Italy; population 42 000. It has remains of Hadrian's villa, with its gardens◊; and the Villa d'Este with the finest of Renaissance gardens◊ laid out 1549 for Cardinal Ippolito d'Este□

Tlatelolco Treaty of. Signed 1967 at Tlatelolco, Mexico, it prohibited nuclear weapons in Latin America (not ratified by Argentina); it was signed also by countries responsible for territories in the area (UK, USA, France, Netherlands)□

Tlingit American Indians of the NW coast, famed for carved totem poles bearing the crests and titles of their owners; single-log canoes; and custom of the ***potlatch***, a distribution of food and gifts to guests, who had in their turn to surpass their hosts; it served as a redistribution of wealth□

TNT a yellow solid used chiefly as a high explosive; see under toluene◊□

toad an amphibian creature; see under frog◊□

toadflax species of genus *Linaria*, family Scrophulariaceae, with spurred two-lipped flowers□

toadstool a type of fungus; see under Basidiomycetes◊□

Toamasina chief port (formerly Tamatave) of Madagascar; population 60 000□

tobacco American narcotic plant *Nicotium tabacum*, family Solanaceae◊; grown in warm, dry climates for use in cigars and cigarettes◊, and (in powdered form) as ***snuff***. The leaves are cured ('dried') and matured in storage for two–three years before use. Introduced 'medicinally' to Europe in the 16th century, tobacco was recognized from the 1950s as a major health hazard: see cancer◊. The leaves also yield the alkaloid ***nicotine***, a colourless oil, one of the most powerful poisons known, used in insecticides□

Tobago an island in the West Indies; see under Trinidad◊ and Tobago□

toboggan flat-bottomed sledge, curved upward at the front, used on snow or ice slopes or banked artificial courses, e.g. the Cresta run. Olympic toboggans are either ***luge type*** seating 1/2, without brakes, or steering; or ***bobsleighs*** seating 2/4, with streamlined 'cowls' at the front, steering and brakes. A ***skibob*** is like a bicycle with skis replacing the wheels, and the rider wearing miniature foot skis□

Tobolsk river port and lumber centre at the confluence of the Tobolsk and Irtysh rivers in W Siberia, USSR; population 50 000. Founded by Cossacks in 1587, it is a centre for lumbering□

Tobruk port in Libya; population 30 000. It changed hands several times in World War II between British and Axis forces 1941–2□

Toc H army signaller's designation of the initials TH for Talbot House, founded 1915 (as an interdenominational social centre at Poperinghe, Belgium) by the Rev Neville Talbot and the Rev P T B Clayton, in memory of the former's brother, Gilbert Talbot, killed in action Jul 1915; it continues as a Christian fellowship□

Tocqueville Alexis de 1805–59. French political scientist, author of the first analytical study of the US constitution *De la Démocratie en Amérique* 1835, compared with those of the Old World□

Todd Alexander, Baron 1907– . British organic chemist, awarded a Nobel prize 1957 for work on the role of nucleic acids in genetics; Order of Merit 1977□

Todt Fritz 1891–1942. German engineer, builder of the autobahns (German motorways), and in World War II the Siegfried Line and the Atlantic Wall□

tog measure of thermal insulation used in the textile trade, e.g. a light summer suit provides 1.0 tog□

Togliatti industrial (engineering, food processing) Volga river port in W central USSR, named after the Italian Communist; population 560 000□

Togliatti Palmiro 1893–1964. Founder of the Italian Communist Party, and influential in the USSR□

Togo W African Republic of

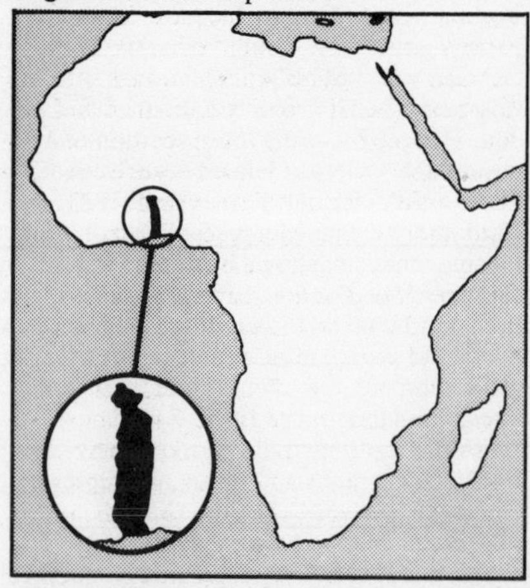

area 56 000 sq km/21 850 sq mi
capital Lomé

exports cocoa, coffee, coconuts, copra; phosphate, bauxite
currency CFA franc
population 2 960 000
language French, official; many local languages
religion traditional 60%, Moslem 20%, Christian 20%
government executive president (General Gnassingbe Eyadéma 1937–) from 1967 and unicameral national assembly; the *Rassemblement du Peuple Togolais* is the only legal political party.
recent history a German protectorate 1894–1914, it was in 1922 divided between Britain and France under mandate◊, and from 1946 under United Nations trusteeship. In 1956 British Togoland voted to integrate with Ghana◊ (Volta region), and French Togoland became independent outside the French Community□

Tojo Hideki 1884–1948. Japanese Prime Minister 1941–44, chief instigator of the attack on Pearl Harbor; tried and hanged as a war criminal□

Tokay town in NE Hungary, famous for wine□

Tokelau overseas territory of New Zealand comprising three coral atolls; area 10 sq km/ 4 sq mi; population 1575. Its resources are small and until 1975 many of its people settled in New Zealand, which has administered it since 1926□

Tokyo capital of Japan on Honshu◊; population 8 300 000. Founded in the 16th century as Yedo, it was renamed when the Emperor removed his court there from Kyoto in 1868, and was 80% destroyed from the air in World War II. Notable are the Imperial Palace, National Diet, National Theatre, Tokyo University (1877) and other educational institutions, as well as the National Athletic Stadium. The Ginza and Shinjuku are fashionable shopping centres. There are international airports at Narita and Haneda. Just outside are the world's largest Disneyland 1983, and Tsukuba 1966, a science city aimed at producing technology for the 21st century□

Toledo city in Castilla, central Spain; population 44 500. It was the capital of the Visigoths 534–712; then became an important Moorish city, famous for its sword blades (fine knives are still made); and was the Castilian capital 1085–1560. El Greco◊ worked here from c1575 (his house and garden are preserved) and the neighbouring landscape is the setting of Cervantes' novel *Don Quixote*□

Toledo industrial port (vehicles, electrical goods, glass, food processing) on Lake Erie, Ohio, USA; population 791 350□

Tolkien J(ohn) R(onald) R(euel) 1892–1973. British scholar, Merton professor of English, Oxford, 1945–59, and creator of the world of Middle Earth, portrayed in the trilogy *The Lord of the Rings* 1954–55, and peopled with hobbits, dwarfs, and strange magical creatures. His work became a cult in the 1970s□

Tolpuddle Martyrs six farm labourers of Tolpuddle, near Dorchester, who in 1834 were transported to Australia for forming a trade union. After a nationwide agitation they were pardoned two years later□

Tolstoy Alexei Nikolaievich 1882–1945. Russian novelist and dramatist, a soldier of the White Army who later came under the patronage of Stalin. His works include the trilogy of novels *The Road to Calvary* 1921–41 and the historical *Peter the Great* 1929–34; and the play *Ivan the Terrible*□

Tolstoy Leo Nikolaievich 1828–1910. Russian novelist. Born of noble family at Yasnaya Polyana, near Tula, he fought in the Crimean War, and made his name with *Tales from Sebastopol*. His masterpieces are *War and Peace* 1866, dealing with the Napoleonic wars, and *Anna Karenina* 1877. He later preached his own version of Christianity which resulted in his excommunication by the church and disruption of life with his family because of his desire to give up his property and live as a peasant. His didactic later books *What is Religion?* and *The Kreutzer Sonata* and his novel *Resurrection* 1900 reflect these interests, and influenced Gandhi◊. He finally fled his home and died of pneumonia at the railway station at Astapovo□

Toltecs American Indian people who ruled much of Mayan (see Maya◊) central Mexico 10th–12th centuries, with their capital at Tula (destroyed by the Aztecs◊). They had a remarkable religious centre at Teotihuacán, where there are massive remains of their temples of the sun and moon, and one (a stepped pyramid) to Quetzalcoatl◊□

toluene colourless, inflammable liquid, $C_6H_5CH_3$, derived from petroleum. It is used as a solvent, in aircraft fuels, in preparing ***phenol*** (carbolic acid, C_6H_5OH, used in making resins (see adhesive◊), pharmaceuticals, etc., and as a disinfectant) and the powerful high explosive ***TNT*** (trinitrotoluene, $C_6H_2(NO_2)_3CH_3$), which is a yellow, crystalline solid□

Tomasi Giuseppe, Prince of Lampedusa 1896–1957. Sicilian author of a single posthumously published historical novel *The Leopard* 1958, dealing with Garibaldi◊'s victory and the birth of modern Italy□

tomato annual S American plant *Lycopersicon esculentum*, family Solanaceae◊; the many-seeded red fruit is used in salads and cooking□

Tombstone former silver-mining town in the desert of SE Arizona; population 2000. The gun battle between Wyatt Earp and his brothers and the 'villainous' Clanton gang took place near the OK Corral 26 Oct 1881; modern research suggests it was a battle of political rivals, i.e. newcomer Reublicans and old-established Southern Democrats□

tommy-gun informal name for Thompson sub-machine gun; see under small arms◊□

tomography obtaining plane section photographs (which show a 'slice' through any object) by various methods; crystal detectors and amplifiers can be used which have a sensitivity a hundred times greater than X-ray◊ film, and in conjunction with a digital data-processing system can detect the difference between a brain tumour and healthy brain tissue. See Godfrey Hounsfield◊□

Tomsk industrial city (synthetic textiles, plastics, distilling, electric motors, sawmilling) in Siberia, USSR; population 467 000□

Tom Thumb a mini-hero of English folk tale, whose name has often been given to those of small stature, including ***Charles Sherwood Stratton*** 1838–83, nicknamed General Tom Thumb□

ton either the former imperial measure of weight, the long ton of 2240 lb; or the American short ton of 2000 lb. The metric ***tonne*** is 1000 kg/2204.6 lb□

Tone Theobald Wolfe 1763–98. Irish nationalist, a leader of the revolutionary society of the United Irishmen. In 1798 he accompanied the French invasion of Ireland, and when captured and condemned to death, cut his own throat□

Tonga or ***Friendly Islands***

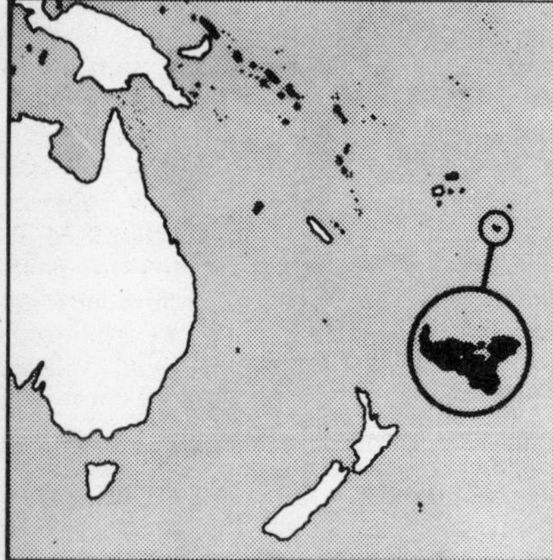

area 748 sq km/289 sq mi
capital Nuku'alofa on Tongatpu
features comprises three groups of islands in the SW Pacific, mostly coral formations, but the western are actively volcanic
exports copra and bananas
currency Tongan dollar or pa'anga
population 106 000
language Tongan and English
religion Wesleyan 47%, Roman Catholic 14%, Free Church of Tonga 14%, Mormon 9%, Church of Tonga 9%
government constitutional monarch Taufa-'ahau Tupou IV (born 1918) who in 1965 succeeded his mother, Queen Salote, remembered the UK for her 1952 visit for the coronation of Elizabeth II; and legislative assembly (Prime Minister Prince Tu'pelehake, younger brother of the king)
recent history Tasman visited the islands 1643, and in 1889 they came under British protection, attaining independence within the Commonwealth 1970□

tongue muscular organ in the floor of the mouth. It has a thick root attached to a U-shaped bone (hyoid) behind and a thin fold of mucous membrane connects its lower middle line with the floor of the mouth. It is covered with mucous membrane containing many nerves and also the 'taste buds', which distinguish the qualities called salt, sweet, sour and bitter. It aids the mastication of food, and the swallowing of both solids and liquids, and, by modifying the voice, forms articulate speech□

tonka S American tree *Coumarovana odorata*, family Leguminosae; its fruit, a dry, fibrous pod, encloses a black aromatic seed used in flavouring, perfumery, and the manufacture of snuff and tobacco□

Tonkin part of N Vietnam, a French protectorate 1884–1949□

Tonkin Gulf part of the S China Sea (Chinese Beibu Gulf), with oil resources: China and Vietnam disagree over their territorial limits here□

Tonkin Gulf Incident after a minor engagement on 2 Aug 1964, two US destroyers reported a night attack on 4 Aug by N Vietnamese torpedo boats (possibly radar and sonar effects were misinterpreted). A retaliatory air attack was made on N Vietnam which led to the eventual despatch of over 1 000 000 US troops to battle in S Vietnam□

Tonle Sap lake in W Kampuchea, with rich fisheries, both fed and drained by the Mekong◊; area 2600 sq km/1000 sq mi to 6500 sq km/2500 sq mi at the height of the monsoon□

tonnage and poundage duties granted (1371–1787) by Parliament to the Crown on imports and exports of wine and other goods. They were controversially levied by Charles I in 1626 without Parliamentary consent□

tonsillitis an inflamation of the tonsils◊□

tonsils pair of small bodies, composed of lymphoid tissue, between the two arches (fauces) of the soft palate at the back of the mouth. They assist in defending this entrance to the body against infection, and may become inflamed (tonsillitis), or form an abscess (quinsy). Owing to their protective role, they are now seldom removed, and antibiotics are usually effective□

tonsure the shaving of the hair of the head as a symbol of the clerical state. Until 1973 in the Roman Catholic Church, the crown was shaved (leaving a surrounding fringe to resemble Christ's crown of thorns); in the Eastern Orthodox Church the hair is merely shorn close□

Tony Awards annual awards by the League of New York Theatres to actors, authors, etc. in Broadway◊ plays. Named after Antoinette Perry□

Tooke John Horne 1736–1812. British Radical politician, who established a Constitutional Society for parliamentary reform in 1771. He was elected an MP in 1801□

tooth cross-section of a premolar

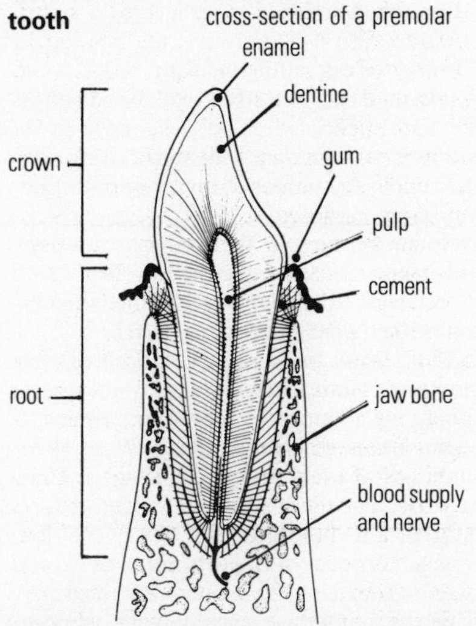

tooth a bonelike structure in the jaws of most vertebrates, for biting and chewing food. Humans have 20 'milk-teeth', which are replaced by a permanent dentition of 32 from the 6th year: two incisors, one canine (eye or dog tooth), two premolars, and three molars on each side of the jaw; ***wisdom teeth*** (third molars) may not appear till age 30. Made of the bony substance, dentine, a tooth comprises a root/roots set in a socket; a gum-covered neck; and a crown of hard white enamel. With normal teeth, the chief problem is caries (tooth decay); fluoridation (see fluorides◊) is effective in preventing this□

Toowoomba industrial and commercial centre (engineering, clothing) in SE Queensland, Australia; population 75 000□

topaz mineral (a fluosilicate of aluminium) which crystallizes in the rhombic system and has a perfect basal cleavage. It is usually yellow, or pink if it has been heated, and is used in jewellery□

tope a type of shark◊□

tope type of tumulus found in India and SE Asia, and usually built over a relic of Buddha or his disciples□

Topeka industrial city (engineering, textiles) and capital of Kansas, USA; population 115 270□

topiary the ornamental clipping of trees and shrubs originated by the Romans in the 1st century and revived in the 16th–17th centuries in formal gardens□

topography the surface features of a region as described, surveyed, or mapped□

topology the branch of geometry which deals with those properties of a figure which remain unchanged even when the figure is bent, stretched, etc., e.g. when a square painted on a rubber sheet is deformed by distorting the sheet. A famous topological problem is to provide a proof that only three colours are needed in producing a map, to give adjoining countries different colours. Topology has scientific applications, e.g. in the study of turbulence in flowing fluids□

Torah the first five books of the Old Testament; see under Judaism◊□

Torbay a resort in Devon, SW England; see under Torquay◊□

Torgau town in Leipzig district, E Germany. Frederick the Great defeated the Austrians nearby in 1760, and in World War II the US and Russian forces first made contact here□

Torino Italian name for the city of Turin◊□

tornado a severe cyclone◊ in which winds rotate downwards in a funnel shape. Tornadoes are small in area but highly destructive to property; they occur particularly in central USA and in Australia. See also meterology◊□

torong musical instrument of the aboriginal Tay people of central Vietnam (Nguyen) and now popular throughout Vietnam. Differing lengths of hanging bamboo are struck with a stick□

Toronto capital of Ontario, Canada, also a busy port on Lake Ontario; population

tornado

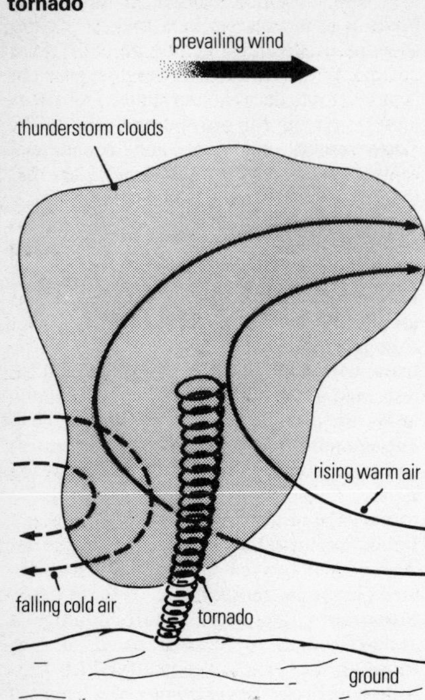

3 029 000. With cheap power from Niagara Falls, it is industrially important (shipbuilding, farm machinery, cars, meat packing and other food processing), and a great commercial, banking, and publishing centre. A French fort was established here 1749, and the site was chosen for the provincial capital (then named 'York') in 1793; it was renamed Toronto (Indian 'place of meeting') 1834, when incorporated as a city. Central Toronto now has underground shopping streets linking the giant complex, of which Toronto-Dominion Center and New City Hall form part. It is a major cultural focus, theatres include the O'Keefe Center, Massey Hall and Royal Alexander Theater; films are made and the city is the national television centre, and mounts an annual Canadian National Exhibition; the university dates from 1827. The CN Tower (built 1975 for radio, television and business communication) is the world's tallest free-standing structure at 553 m/1815 ft□

torpedo self-propelled underwater missile, invented by Robert Whitehead◊. Modern weapons are homing missiles; some resemble mines in that they lie on the seabed until activated by the acoustic signal of a passing ship. A television camera enables them to be remotely controlled, and in the final stage of attack they lock on to the radar or sonar signals of the target ship□

torpedo fish see under ray◊□

Torquay seaside resort in S Devon, England, from 1968 forming part of the district of Torbay which also includes the resort of Paignton and Brixham◊; total population 113 100. Parts of Regency and Victorian Torquay survive, but under threat; it also includes the medieval village of Cockington□

Torquemada Tomás de 1420–98. Spanish Dominican friar, confessor to Queen Isabella. In 1483 he revived the Inquisition on her behalf, and at least 2000 'heretics' were burned; Torquemada also expelled the Jews from Spain with a resultant decline of the economy□

Torrens salt lake 8 m/25 ft below sea level in eastern South Australia; area 5775 sq km/ 2230 sq mi. It is reduced to a marsh in dry weather□

Torres-Garcia d. 1949. Uruguayan artist, born in Montevideo. In Paris from 1926, he was influenced by Mondrian◊ and others, and after going to Madrid in 1932 by Inca and Nazca pottery. His mature style rests on a grid pattern derived from the Golden◊ Section□

Torres Strait channel separating New Guinea from Australia, with scattered reefs; width 130 km/80 mi. First European discovery by Spanish navigator Luis Vaez de Torres 1606□

Torres Vedras see Peninsular◊ War□

Torricelli Evangelista 1608–47. Italian physicist and pupil of Galileo, who devised the mercury barometer, demonstrating the ability of air pressure to support a finite column of mercury□

tortoise reptile of the order Testudines, which also includes the ***turtles***. Both have clawed legs and a bony box-like shell of horny plates; the upper shell or carapace has the ribs and vertebrae fused to it, and both this and the softer underpart, or plastron, may be hinged for greater freedom of movement. In turtles the shell is streamlined to aid swimming, and the legs are paddle-shaped. Members of the order may be vegetarian or carnivorous, but have no teeth, the jaws having a horny covering which forms a biting edge. Vision is not very good, and hearing is largely a matter of sensitivity to vibration throughout the body. In some species the eggs are hard like those of birds, and in others soft and leathery. The females are larger than the males. They can defend themselves only by withdrawal as far as possible into their shells. They include:

land tortoises family Testudinidae, including the ***common tortoise*** *Testudo graeca* of N

Africa and Asia Minor, imported to the unsuitable British climate in large quantities; ***giant tortoise*** of the Galépagos, Seychelles, etc, of which there are differing species in the genus *Testudo* which may reach up to 1.5 m/4.5 ft long and weigh up to 270 kg/600 lb.

marine turtles including the ***leathery turtle*** or ***leatherback*** *Dermochelys coriacea* of tropic seas, family Dermochelidae, which reaches 2.5 m/8 ft long and may weigh a tonne; ***green turtle*** *Chelonia mydas*, family Chelonidae, source of turtle soup (it lays up to 200 eggs, which are also a delicacy, on sandy beaches at annual seasonal gatherings); and ***hawksbill turtle*** *Eretmochelys imbricata*, from whose shell tortoiseshell is made.

freshwater turtles or ***terrapins*** including the ***diamond-back terrapin*** *Malaclemys terrapin*, family Emydidae, a coastal species of N America valued for the table; the females are twice the size of the males□

Tortuga an island off the NW coast of Haiti◊□

torture infliction of bodily pain, especially to extort evidence or confession under many early judicial systems. Legally abolished in England c1640, it survived in Scotland till 1708 and till 1789 in France. In the 20th century it has enjoyed a major resurgence.

Medieval tortures were usually physical, e.g. the rack (to stretch the victim's joints to breaking point), the thumbscrew, the boot (which crushed the foot), heavy weights which crushed the whole body, the iron maiden (a man-shaped cage with interior spikes to spear the occupant), etc. Modern techniques include 'brain-washing' developed by KGB and other Communist interrogators from the 1950s. From the early 1960s a technique used in the West replaced isolation by severe sensory deprivation, e.g. IRA guerrillas were prevented from seeing by a hood, from feeling by being swathed in a loose-fitting garment, and from hearing by a continuous loud noise at c85 decibels, while being forced to maintain themselves in a 'search' position against a wall by their fingertips. The European Commission of Human Rights found Britain guilty of torture, although the European Court of Human Rights classed it only as 'inhuman and degrading treatment'□

Torun industrial town in N Poland; population 372 000. It was founded by the Teutonic◊ Knights 1230, and was the birthplace of Copernicus◊□

Tory Party name applied c1680–1830 to the forerunner of the British Conservative◊ Party. The original Tories were Irish guerrillas who attacked the English, and the name was applied (at first insultingly) to royalists who opposed the Exclusion Bill (see under Duke of Monmouth◊). Although largely supporting the 1688 revolution, the Tories were suspected of Jacobite◊ sympathies, and were kept from power 1714–60, but then held office almost continuously until 1830. They were the party of the squire and parson, as opposed to the Whigs (supported by the trading classes and Nonconformists).

In the USA a Tory was an opponent of the break with Britain in the War of American Independence 1775–1883□

Toscanini Arturo 1867–1957. Italian conductor, long associated with La Scala, Milan. Rejecting Fascism in 1936, he worked in the USA, where the NBC Symphony Orchestra was formed for him 1937□

totalizator a system of betting on horse races; see under betting◊□

totemism Algonquin Indian 'my guardian spirit'. A belief in individual or clan 'kinship' with an animal, plant, or object, which is sacred to those concerned and which they are forbidden to eat or desecrate; marriage within such a clan is usually forbidden. ***Totem poles*** are used on the Pacific coast of N America, and incorporate totem objects (carved and painted) as a symbol of the people, or to commemorate the dead. A similar belief occurs among Australian aborigines, and was formerly prevalent in Europe and Asia□

Tottenham see under Haringey◊□

toucan a type of bird; see under woodpecker◊□

Toulon port, naval base, and industrial city (oil refining, chemicals, textiles) in SE France; population 378 500. It was taken by the British 1793, and Napoleon first attracted attention by retaking it by siege; in World War II the French fleet was scuttled here to avoid its passing to German control□

Toulouse industrial city (aerospace, e.g. Concorde, and textiles), capital of Midi-Pyrenées region, France; population 383 200. There is a 12th–13th century cathedral, and a university founded c1230. See under Peninsular◊ War 1814□

Toulouse-Lautrec Henri Raymonde de 1864–1901. French artist of noble descent, born at Albi, where there is a museum of his work. He lived and worked in Mountmarte, where he made studies of popular entertainers, circus acrobats, and prostitutes in posters and paintings□

Touquet-Paris-Plage Le. Resort in N France, fashionable in the 1920s–30s; population 4500□

touraco African birds in the family Musophagidae, order Cuculiformes (see cuckoo◊), e.g. the ***white-cheeked touraco*** *Tauraco leucotis* rather like a crested, multi-coloured magpie□

Touraine former province of NW France, capital Tours□

Tourcoing a town in NE France; see under Lille◊□

Tour de France the world's most famous bicycle race; see under bicycle◊□

tourmaline a complex of various metal borosilicates found in granite; it has piezoelectric properties. Common varieties are opaque ranging from black to pink; transparent gemstones include the Brazilian sapphire and emerald□

Tournai industrial (carpets, leather, cement) town (Flemish Doornik) in W Belgium; population 67 300□

tournament or ***tourney***. A sporting competition, originally a form of medieval war-training, which included mounted combat and mock fights with sword, spear, or dagger. Introduced to Britain from France in the 11th century, tournaments flourished until the 16th century, and have modern revivals□

Tourneur Cyril c1575–1626. English dramatist. His *Revenger's Tragedy* 1607 and *Atheist's Tragedy* 1611 are among the most powerful of Stuart dramas□

Tours industrial city (chemicals, textiles, machinery) in W France; population 245 650. An ancient city, see Charles◊ Martel, it was once the capital of Touraine◊, and in World War II was for four days the capital of France in 1940. The novelist Balzac◊ was born here□

Toussaint L'Ouverture Pierre Dominique c1746–1803. Haitian revolutionary leader, born a slave. He was made governor by the revolutionary French government and expelled the Spanish and British, but when Napoleon reimposed slavery, he revolted, was captured and died in prison in France. In 1983 his remains were returned to Haiti□

Tower Hamlets borough of E Greater London

features Tower of London and World Trade Centre in former St Katharine's Dock; ***Isle of Dogs*** bounded on three sides by the Thames, including the former India and Millwall Docks. Redevelopment includes Billingsgate fish market removed here in 1982, a proposed 'Wall Street on the Water', and a new light railway (with tube extension) planned to link the isle to the City. ***Limehouse district***, formerly known for its Chinese colony, still has the chapel hall in Fulbourne Street, venue of the Russian Social Democratic Congress 1907 (attended by Lenin, Stalin, and Trotsky); and also the home of David Owen (hence the *Limehouse Declaration* founding the Social Democratic Party in 1981). ***Spitalfields district*** was once home to Huguenot silk weavers, and some of their workshop houses are preserved; ***Bethnal Green*** has a Museum of Childhood; and Mile End Green (later Stepney Green) was where Richard◊ II met the rebels of 1381.

population 143 000, 15% Asian (from Pakistan and Bangladesh)□

Tower of London a fortress in the City of London; see under London◊□

town planning see under architecture◊□

Townsend Sue 1946– . British playwright (*The Great Celestial Cow* 1984) and novelist (*The Secret Diary of Adrian Mole, aged 13¾* 1982). Born in Leicester, she became writer-in-residence at the Phoenix Theatre there□

Townshend Charles 1725–67. British politician, Chancellor of the Exchequer from 1766. The ***Townshend Acts*** taxing such imports into Britain's N American colonies as tea, glass, and paper precipitated the War of Independence□

Townsville port (exports canned and chilled meat, wool, sugar, and minerals) in N Queensland, Australia; population 99 560. Founded 1868, it was attacked by Japanese aircraft 1942□

Townswomen's Guilds National Union of. See under Women's◊ Institutes□

toxaemia in general terms the presence of 'poisons' in the blood, especially those taken up from an infection at some point in the body. In late pregnancy a condition marked by high blood pressure, an unusual increase in weight, and convulsions (eclampsia); its causes are not precisely known□

toxocariasis infection of humans by a canine intestinal worm which results in a swollen liver and sometimes eye damage□

Toynbee Arnold 1852–83. British economist and social reformer, after whom the social and educational centre ***Toynbee Hall***, founded 1885 in Whitechapel, was named□

Toynbee Arnold J(oseph) 1889–1975. British historian, whose *A Study of History* 1934–61 was an attempt to discover the laws governing the rise and fall of civilizations. He was the nephew of Arnold Toynbee◊□

Trabzon port (formerly Trebizond) in NE Turkey; population 108 400. The University of the Black Sea was established 1963□

trace element chemical necessary for the health of both plants and animals, but in a minute quantity, e.g. magnesium which occurs in chlorophyll, essential to photosynthesis; and iodine in the thyroid gland□

trachoma contagious viral disease of the eye; see under conjunctivitis◊□

tracking agent chemical compound (most usually NPPD, nitrophenyl pentadien) used in espionage (applied to cars, and hands of agents, diplomats, and others on the enemy side, to trace their movements and contacts)□

Tractarianism another name for the Oxford◊ Movement□

tractor in agriculture, a multi-purpose vehicle with built-in facilities for all aspects of cultivation from ploughing to reaping; in military usage, a ***combat tractor*** is a 'work-horse' capable of crossing rivers, operating in nuclear radiation, clearing minefields by discharging an 'explosive hosepipe', and concealing a large tank in a matter of minutes by excavating two tonnes of soil in a single action□

trade mark a name or 'mark', legally registered by its proprietor, which is distinctive of a marketed product□

Tradescant John c1570–1638. English plant collector and gardener to Charles I. He and his son, ***John Tradescant, the Younger*** 1608–62, introduced the lilac, acacia, occidental plane; see Lambeth, tradescantia◊□

tradescantia genus of American plants (named after the elder Tradescant◊), family Commelinaceae; ***creeping spiderwort*** *T virginiana* is a common houseplant□

Trades Union Congress (TUC). Voluntary trade union organization in Britain, established in 1868. Delegates of affiliated unions meet annually in conference.□

trade(s) union organization of workers for collective bargaining, essentially the product of the Industrial Revolution. Illegal in the UK under the Combination Acts◊, they spread widely among craftsmen from 1824 (see Trades◊ Union Congress) and in the 1890s to unskilled labourers. The restrictive Trade Disputes and Trade Union Act 1927, which followed the General Strike◊, was repealed under the Attlee government in 1946, and the post-war period was marked by increased unionism among white-collar workers. Union power became so great that the Wilson government was forced to abandon an attempt at legislative reform in 1969. The Heath government's Industrial Relations Act 1971 was immediately repealed by the succeeding Wilson government of 1974, voluntary restraint being attempted under a Social◊ Contract. This completely broke down under Callaghan in the industrial disputes of the 'winter of discontent' 1978–9, and the Thatcher government, in the Employment Acts of 1980 and 1982, restricted the 'closed◊ shop', picketing, secondary action against anyone other than the employer in dispute, immunity of trade unions in respect of unlawful acts by their officials, and the definition of a trade dispute, which must be between workers and employers, not between workers.

In 1973 a European Trade Union Confederation (ETUC) was established, membership 29 000 000, and there is an International Labour Organization, established 1919 and affiliated to the United Nations from 1945, which formulates standards for labour and social conditions. See also American◊ Federation of Labor□

Trafalgar Cape. Low headland in SW Spain, near the W entrance to the Straits of Gibraltar, off which Nelson defeated a Franco-Spanish fleet 21 Oct 1805, and was mortally wounded□

Traherne Thomas c1637–74. English mystic, vicar of Teddington 1667 –74. His moving lyric poetry and his prose *Centuries of Meditations* written in the 1660s, were unpublished until 1903□

Trail mining centre (lead, zinc, copper smelting) in British Columbia, Canada; population 10 000□

Trajan (Marcus Ulpius Trajanus) c52–117AD. Roman emperor from 98, adopted heir of Nerva◊. Born in Seville, he was a just and conscientious ruler, corresponded with Pliny about the Christians, and conquered Dacia (approximately modern Romania) 101–7 and much of Parthia◊. ***Trajan's Column***, Rome, commemorates his victories□

tramway system whereby wheeled vehicles run along parallel rails, which originated in collieries in the 18th century. The earliest passenger system was in 1832, in New York, and by the 1860s horse-drawn trams plied in London and Liverpool. They are now powered either by electric conductor rails below ground or conductor arms connected to overhead wires, but their use on public roads is very limited because of their lack of manoeuvrability. Greater flexibility is achieved with the ***trolleybus***, similarly powered by conductor arms overhead, but without tracks, and in the 1980s these were in some areas being revived. Both vehicles have the advantage of being non-pollutant□

trance mental state in which the subject loses the ordinary perceptions of time and space, and even of his or her own body. In this highly aroused state, often induced by rhythmic music, 'speaking in tongues' may occur (see Pentecostal◊ Movement), which usually consists of the rhythmic repetition of apparently meaningless syllables, with a euphoric return to consciousness. It is also practised by Bushman healers, Afro-Brazilian spirit mediums, and Siberian shamans□

tranquillizer a calming drug; see sedatives◊□
Transcaucasia the part of the USSR south of the Caucasus. It includes Armenia, Azerbaijan and Georgia◊ which in 1922 formed the ***Transcaucasian Republic*** broken up in 1936 when each became a separate republic of the USSR□
transcendentalism philosophic concept chiefly associated with Kant, and 'concerned not with objects, but with our mode of knowing objects'. Introduced to England, it influenced Coleridge and Carlyle, and developed in New England c1840–60 into a mystical doctrine (Thoreau and Emerson) which saw God as immanent in nature and the human soul□
transducer device for converting such physical variables as acceleration, displacement, pressure, and temperature into electrical signals or vice versa. They may then be used for control and other purposes□
transfer orbit the orbit followed by a planetary probe in order to save fuel by moving for most of the journey in free fall. A probe aimed at Venus has to be 'slowed down' relative to the earth, so that it enters an elliptical transfer orbit with its perigee (point of closest approach to the sun) at the same distance as the orbit of Venus; with Mars, the vehicle has to be 'speeded up' relative to the earth, so that it reaches its apogee (furthest point from the sun) at the same distance as the orbit of Mars□
transformer device consisting in its simplest form of two coils of wire, a ***primary*** and ***secondary*** wound on a common iron core. An alternating voltage applied to the primary produces (by electromagnetic induction) a stepped-up or stepped-down voltage from the secondary, according to the ratio of numbers of turns in the coils. Transformers are widely used, especially in power transmission to domestic and other users and in domestic appliances□
transistor a semiconductor◊ device capable of amplifying an electrical signal, invented by Bardeen◊, Brattain◊, and Shockley in the Bell Telephone Laboratories, USA in 1948. Modern transistors are of two main types: ***bipolar*** and ***field effect*** (FET). They are an essential element in the circuitry of almost all silicon chips, whether for digital use (as in computers) or analog (as in radios and televisions).
In an non bipolar transistor, specially chosen impurities are introduced into a small piece of silicon to create three regions within it–a thin base region of p-type material sandwiched between regions of n-type, the emitter

transistor

npn transistor (schematic)

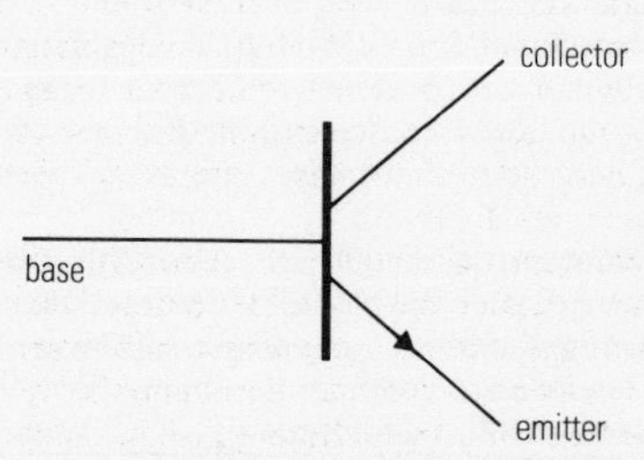

and the collector. (In p-type material free electrical charge carriers, called holes, which have a positive charge, predominate, while in n-type material the majority carriers are electrons◊, whose charge is negative.) A voltage of less than 1 volt applied between the emitter and the base so as to make the base positive will attract into it electrons from the emitter. However, the base is very thin and many more electrons will overshoot into the collector than actually leave the transistor through the base, provided that the collector is made positive enough – typically about 10V. This is the basis of the transistor's ability to amplify, for if a varying signal voltage is superimposed on the emitter voltage the resultant variations in the number of electrons leaving via the collector is much greater than in the number leaving via the base itself; thus amplification of currents has been achieved□
transition metals those with variable valency, e.g. cobalt, copper, iron, molybdenum. They are excellent conductors of electricity and generally form highly coloured compounds□
Transjordan name 1923–49 of the Hashemite kingdom of Jordan◊□
Transkei Bantustan in South Africa; the largest of South Africa's Bantu Homelands; self-governing 1963

area 43 800 sq km/16 910 sq mi
capital Umtata
towns port Mnganzana
features one of the two homelands of the Xhosa people, see Ciskei◊
exports livestock
population 2 517 000, including small white and coloured minorities
language Xhosa
government president (paramount chief Kaiser Matanzima from 1979, until his retirement 1986), and single chamber national assembly□

transmigration to pass from one body into another at death; see under incarnation◊□

transplant transfer of an organ from one part of the body to another or from one person to another; see under surgery◊□

Transport and General Workers Union was founded 1921 by amalgamating a number of dockers' and road transport workers' unions to form Britain's largest union. Bevin◊ was once its general secretary□

transportation from the late 17th century (in Britain until 1864), before the full development of a prison system, the sending of convicted criminals to a country's overseas possessions. See Botany◊ Bay and Tolpuddle◊ Martyrs□

transsexualism an unusually strong desire to change sex. Transsexuals think and feel emotionally in a way typically appropriate of members of the opposite sex, and may prefer the clothing of that sex (***transvestism***), or undergo surgery to modify sexual characteristics□

Trans-Siberian Railway see under Siberia◊□

transubstantiation doctrine that the whole substance of the bread and wine changes into the substance of the body and blood of Christ when consecrated in the Eucharist◊□

transuranic elements those chemical elements◊ with a greater number of protons in the nucleus than uranium. Apart from neptunium and plutonium none of these have been found in nature; they have been created in nuclear reactions□

Transvaal northern province of the Republic of S Africa
area 286 064 sq km/110 450 sq mi
capital Pretoria
towns Johannesburg, Benoni, Brakpan, Germiston, Springs
features rivers Vaal and Limpopo; Swaziland forms an enclave on the Natal border
products maize, fruit, tobacco; cattle and sheep; gold, diamonds, coal, iron, copper, lead, tin, manganese
population 8 350 500, including 5 644 700 Black, 2 362 000 White, 115 560 Asians, 228 200 Coloured
recent history settled by Voortrekkers who left Cape Colony in the Great Trek from 1831, Transvaal was recognized by Britain as independent until the settlers' difficulties with the conquered Zulus of the area led to British annexation in 1877. In 1880 the Transvaal rebelled, and defeated the British at Majuba Hill 1881, but republican rule was restored only under British suzerainty. After the S African War 1899–1902, the Transvaal was annexed by Britain until it entered the Union as a province in 1910□

Transylvania mountainous area of Romania, bounded to the S by the Transylvanian Alps (an extension of the Carpathians◊), formerly a province, with its capital at Cluj. It was part of Hungary from c1000 until its people voted to unite with Romania 1918. The Vienna Award 1940 (by Ribbentrop and Ciano◊) gave most of it back to Hungary, but this was reversed in 1947. The two countries still have wars of words over it, as in 1982□

Trapani port in NW Sicily, Italy; population 85 000□

Trappists members of a branch of the Cistercian◊ order of Christian monks□

Trasimeno lake in central Italy, west of Perugia, where Hannibal defeated the Romans 217BC□

travelator see under escalator◊

travel sickness nausea and vomiting caused by travel in ships, trains, buses, cars, aeroplanes, and space vehicles. Constant vibration and movement may stimulate changes in the semicircular canals forming the labyrinth of the middle ear, to which the individual fails to adapt, and to which are added visual and psychological factors. In space normal body movements result in unexpected and unfamiliar signals to the brain. Some proprietary cures contain anti-histamine drugs, and astronauts achieve some control of symptoms when weightless by wedging themselves in their bunks□

Traven Ben. Pseudonym of anarchist novelist ***Herman Feige*** 1882–1969, born in eastern Germany. He wrote *The Death Ship* 1926, and (as Hal Croves) the script of the film *The Treasure of Sierra Madre* 1948, which starred Humphrey Bogart◊□

Travers Ben(jamin) 1886–1980. British dramatist. He wrote (for Tom Walls, Ralph Lynn and Robertson Hare) the 'Aldwych farces', so-called from the theatre in which they were played. They include *A Cuckoo in the Nest* 1925 and *Rookery Nook* 1926□

treacle a viscous syrup obtained during the refining of sugar◊□

treadmill treadwheels used to raise water from a well (often by a donkey), turn a joint on a spit (by a dog), and so on, were ancient devices. In 1818 Sir William Cubitt 1785–1861, on the same principle, devised a large cylinder to be operated by convicts treading on steps on its periphery. Such treadmills went out of use early in the 20th century□

treason an act of treachery against the sovereign or state to which the perpetrator owes allegiance. In Britain it still carries the death penalty, and in the 20th century those hanged, either for treason or treachery, have included Roger Casement and William Joyce◊□

treasure trove in England, gold or silver, plate, or bullion of unknown ownership, either found concealed (when it belongs to the Crown) or lost or intentionally abandoned (when it belongs to the first finder). If buried without intention of recovery, as with an object in a burial mound, the treasure belongs to the owner of the ground□

treasury in Britain the government department established 1612 to collect and manage the public revenue. Technically, the Prime Minister is generally the First Lord of the Treasury, but the Chancellor of the Exchequer is the acting financial head□

Trebizond a variant spelling of Trabzon◊□

tree woody perennial plants with a distinct trunk; see oak, ash, pine, lime◊ etc. Tree worship (see Druid◊) survived in Europe till the 14th century, and the modern Christmas tree represents a distorted form (a substitute for Odin's sacred oak). See also dryad◊

In 1983 there was evidence that trees by releasing chemicals (pheromone◊) into the air signal to nearby members of the same species that insect attack is taking place. This results in defensive chemical changes in the foliage to render it less appetizing and more indigestible□

Tree Sir Herbert Beerbohm 1853–1917. British actor-manager, half brother of Max Beerbohm◊. Noted for his Shakespeare productions, he was founder of the Royal◊ Academy of Dramatic Art□

treecreeper small songbirds of genus *Certhia*, family Certhiidae, found in Eurasia and N America. The ***European treecreeper*** *C familiaris* creeps spirally up trees in search of insects which it catches in its curved beak□

tree kangaroo see under marsupial◊□

Trefusis Violet 1894–1972. British hostess and writer. Daughter of Mrs Keppel, who was later the mistress of Edward VII, she had a disastrous marriage to cavalry officer Denys Trefusis and a passionate elopement with Vita Sackville-West◊ recorded in Nigel Nicolson's *Portrait of a Marriage*□

trematode a class of worm; see under worm◊□

Trenchard Hugh Montague, 1st Viscount Trenchard 1873–1956. British airman, nicknamed 'Boom' because of his loud voice. He commanded the Royal Flying Corps in World War I 1915–17, and 1918–29 organized the Royal Air Force, becoming first Marshal of the RAF 1927. As Commissioner of the Metropolitan Police, he established the Police College at Hendon□

Trengganu a state of Malaysia; population 542 300. Capital Kuala Trengganu□

Trent third longest river in England, flowing from the S Pennines to the Humber; length 275 km/170 mi□

Trent Council of, 1545–1563. Held by the Roman Catholic Church at Trento, N Italy; see Counter-Reformation under Reformation◊□

Trentino-Alto Adige special autonomous region of N Italy: capital Trento for the Italian-speaking southern area, and Bolzano-Bozen for the northern German-speaking area of S Tirol (the whole region was long part of Austria until ceded to Italy in 1919); population 874 535. See Tirol◊□

Trento industrial city (electrical goods, chemicals) and capital of S Trentino-Alto◊ region, Italy; population 95 000. The Council of Trent◊ was held here□

Trenton industrial city (metalworking, ceramics) capital of New Jersey, USA; population 92 125. Washington defeated the British here 1776□

trepang any of various large sea cucumbers of tropical oriental seas; see echinoderm◊□

trespass in general speech, going on to the land of another without authority. It is not a crime, but the landowner has the right to eject a trespasser by the use of reasonable force, and can sue for any damage caused. A trespasser injured on another's land cannot recover damages from the landowner unless the latter did him some positive injury□

Trevelyan George Macaulay 1876–1962. British historian, son of Sir George Trevelyan◊. Regius professor of history at Cambridge 1927–40, he pioneered the study of social history, as in his *English Social History* 1942□

Trevelyan Sir George Otto 1838–1928. British politician and historian, a nephew of the historian Lord Macaulay, whose biography he wrote. See G M Trevelyan◊□

Trèves the French name for the city of Trier◊□

Treviso industrial city (machinery, ceramics) in Veneto, Italy; population 89 000. The 11th-century cathedral has a Titian altarpiece□

Trevithick Richard 1771–1833. British engineer, constructor of a steam road locomotive 1801, and the first steam engine to run on rails 1804□

Triad world's largest secret◊ society. Founded in China as a Buddhist cult in 386AD, it became known as the Triad because the triangle played an important part in the initiation ceremony. Later it became political, aiming at the overthrow of the Manchus, and backed the Taiping Rebellion 1851 and Sun Yat-sen's establishment of a republic. Today it is noted for Mafia-type activities (drugs, gambling, prostitution) among overseas Chinese, headquarters Hong Kong□

Trianon châteaux at Versailles◊□

triathlon a sports event in which the competitors complete a three mile sea swim, a 112 mile cycle ride, and 26.2 mile run (marathon) one after the other□

tribunal a court of justice, but in English usage more especially a body appointed by the government to arbitrate in disputes (e.g. over siting new roads, nuclear power stations; compensation for industrial injury or unfair dismissal; deportation orders against illegal immigrants). Members are usually local and unpaid, the chairman being the only lawyer□

tribune Roman magistrate of plebeian◊ family, elected annually to defend the interests of the common people; only two were originally provided for in 494BC, but there were later ten. They could veto the decisions of any other magistrate□

triceratops any rhinoceros-like herbivorous dinosaur; see under dinosaur◊□

Trichinopoly another name for the city of Tiruchirapalli◊□

Trier industrial city (French *Trèves*) in Rhineland-Palatinate, W Germany; population 100 000. Founded by Augustus c15BC, it was the capital of an ecclesiastical principality 14th–18th centuries. Karl Marx was born here□

Trieste free port opposite Venice on the Adriatic, capital of Friuli-Venezia-Julia, Italy; population 252 500, including a large Slovene minority. It was under Austrian rule from 1382 (apart from Napoleonic occupation 1809–14) until transferred to Italy 1918, but after World War II Yugoslavia laid claim to it, and the city and surrounding territory were divided 1954 between Italy and Yugoslavia. The International Centre for Theoretical Physics 1964 and the United◊ World College of the Adriatic 1982 are here□

trigonometry branch of mathematics dealing with the solution of problems relating to plane and spherical triangles, founded by Hipparchus◊, and used in surveying, navigation, etc.□

trilobite extinct marine arthropod (subphylum Trilobita) of the Palaeozoic era, with flattened, oval, segmented body. Trilobites looked rather like large woodlice, the biggest being up to 0.5 m/1.5 ft long. Their worldwide distribution, many species, and the immense quantities of their remains make them useful in dating remains of other creatures□

Trincomalee port in NE Sri Lanka; population 45 000. It was an early Tamil settlement, and a British naval base until 1957□

Trinidad and Tobago W Indian republic of

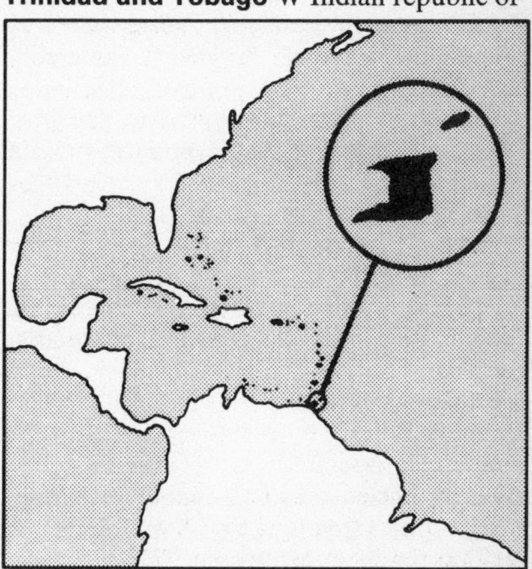

area Trinidad 4828 sq km/1864 sq mi and Tobago 300 sq km/116 sq mi
capital Port of Spain
towns San Fernando
features comprises the two main islands, and some smaller ones; Pitch Lake is a self-renewing source of asphalt and was used by Raleigh◊ when repairing his ships
exports angostura bitters, first blended from herbs as a stomach remedy in 1824, and now used to season food and fruit, and flavour 'pink' gin; asphalt, natural gas and oil
currency Trinidad and Tobago dollar
population 1 168 000 (equally divided between those of African and Indian descent)
language English (official), Hindi, French, Spanish
religion Roman Catholic 33%, Protestant 14%, Hinduism 25%, Islam 6%
government president, Ellis Clarke, from 1976, senate and house of representatives (Prime Minister George Chambers of the People's National Movement from 1981)
famous people V S Naipaul

recent history first European discovery by Columbus 1498. Trinidad was ceded to Britain by Spain 1802 after Britain had captured it in 1797, and amalgamated with Tobago 1888. The colony became independent 1962 and a republic 1976□

Trinity the threefold union of three persons in one godhead in the Christian faith, i.e. Father, Son, and Holy Ghost/Spirit. The precise meaning of the doctrine has been the cause of unending dispute, and was the chief cause of the split between the Eastern Orthodox and Roman Catholic churches. See also Unitarianism◊□

Tripoli capital and port (with light industries) of Libya; population 820 000. The magnificent ruins of the Roman city of Leptis Magna lie to the east□

Tripoli port in Lebanon, terminus of an oil-pipeline from Kirkuk; population 175 000□

Tripolitania former Libyan coastal province, between Tunisia and Cyrenaica; capital Tripoli□

Tripura state of north eastern India
area 10 477 sq km/4044 sq mi
capital Agartala
features agriculture on a shifting system in the jungle, now being superseded by modern methods
population 2 060 200
language Bengali
religion Hinduism□

trireme ancient Greek warship with three banks of oars (manned by 170 volunteers) as well as sails, 38 m/115 ft long. They were used at the battle of Salamis◊, and by the Romans until the 4th century AD□

Tristan hero of Celtic legend, who fell in love with Iseult, the bride he was sent to win for his uncle King Mark of Cornwall; the story became part of the Arthurian cycle. See Wagner◊□

Tristan da Cunha British island colony
area 105 sq km/40 sq mi
features comprises four islands: Tristan, Gough, Inaccessible, and Nightingale. Tristan consists of a single volcano 2060 m/6760 ft; it is an important meteorological and radio station.
exports crawfish
currency pound sterling
population 300
government administrator, plus Island Council, as a dependency of St◊ Helena
recent history first European discovery 1506 by the Portuguese admiral after whom they are named; they were annexed by Britain in 1816. Believed to be extinct, the Tristan volcano erupted in 1961, but in 1963 the evacuated population chose to return□

tritium unstable isotope of hydrogen◊ with two neutrons as well as one proton in its nucleus□

Triton in Greek mythology, a merman sea-god, the son of Poseidon◊ and the sea-goddess Amphitrite. He is shown blowing on a conch◊□

Triton the larger of the satellites of the planet Neptune◊□

triumvirs three magistrates sharing power in ancient Rome, as in the ***First Triumvirate*** 60BC Caesar, Pompey, Crassus◊; and ***Second Triumvirate*** 43BC Augustus, Antony and Lepidus◊□

Trivandrum industrial city (chemicals, textiles, rubber products), capital of Kerala, India; population 520 000. Once the capital of the princely state of Travancore, it has many palaces□

troglodytes Greek term for the cave-dwellers of the ancient world, especially the pastoral peoples of Egypt and Ethiopia□

trogon tropical birds of resplendent plumage of the Americas and Afro-Asia, order Trogoniformes. Most striking is the ***quetzal*** *Pharomachrus mocinno* of central America which has a crest and golden-green tail plumes 1 m/3 ft long, and body in red, green and blue. Sacred to the Aztecs and Mayas (see Quetzalcoatl◊), it is the emblem of Guatemala□

Trois Rivières industrial port (major world newsprint producer) port on the St Lawrence, Quebec, Canada; population 50 500. It was founded by Champlain 1634□

trolleybus electrically-driven public-transport vehicle; see under tramway◊□

Trollope Anthony 1815–82. British novelist. A Londoner, educated at Harrow, he became a post office clerk 1834, introduced the pillar box 1853, and achieved the responsible position of surveyor before retiring 1867. *The Warden* 1855 began the clerical series set in Barchester (a combination of Salisbury and Winchester), which includes *Barchester Towers* 1857, *Doctor Thorne* 1858, and *The Last Chronicle of Barset* 1867. He unsuccessfully tried to enter Parliament as a Liberal, and his political novels include *Can You Forgive Her?* 1864, *Phineas Finn* 1867–69, and *The Prime Minister* 1875–6, of which the hero is Plantagenet Palliser. His *Autobiography* 1883 was too practically frank for Victorian sensibilities□

Trollope Frances 1780–1863. British novelist (*The Vicar of Wrexhill* 1837) and travel writer (*Domestic Manners of the Americans* 1832) which infuriated its subjects. Anthony Trollope was her son□

trombone a musical instrument; see under brass◊□

Tromp Maarten Harpertszoon 1597–1653. Dutch admiral who disputed the British command of the seas in the 17th century. He was defeated by Blake in May 1652, but won a return battle in Nov. He fought a series of encounters Feb–Jun 1653 with the British commanders Blake, Monck, and Deane, and in Jul was finally killed in battle against Monck□

Tromsö fishing port in NW Norway, on Tromsö island; population 47 400. The battleship *Tirpitz* was sunk by British bombers 1944 in Tromsö fjord□

Trondheim fishing port in Norway with canneries, textile, margarine, and soap factories; population 134 200. It was the medieval capital of Norway and its kings are still crowned in the fine cathedral□

tropics the tropics of Cancer and Capricorn, defined by the parallels of latitude 23° 28′ N and S of the equator, are the limits of the area of earth's surface in which the sun can be directly overhead□

tropisms movements of plants in reaction to external stimulus, e.g. growth towards water (hydrotropism) and towards light (heliotropism). Sedentary animals show similar reactions□

troposphere the lowest layer of the atmosphere◊□

Trossachs a narrow wooded valley in central Scotland; see under Central◊□

Trotsky Leon Davidovitch. Assumed name of Russian revolutionary ***Lev D Bronstein*** 1879–1940. With Lenin, he organized the revolution of Nov 1917, and conducted the peace negotiations with Germany. He raised the Red Army which fought the Civil War 1918–20. However, he demanded world revolution, rather than concentrating on Russia alone, and this and other differences with the Communist Party led to his exile in 1929. He settled in Mexico, where he was assassinated, possibly at Stalin's instigation. His later works are critical of the Soviet regime, e.g. *The Revolution Betrayed.* His greatest work is his magisterial *History of the Russian Revolution*□

troubadours poets of Provence◊ 11th–13th centuries, often courtiers, who idealized the love of women and lauded the deeds of their patrons. Most famous was Bertran de Born 1140–c1215, referred to by Dante□

trout any of various game fish; see under salmon◊□

Trowbridge market town (with dairy produce and bacon and ham factories) in Wiltshire, England; population 20 200□

Troy ancient city (also called Ilium) of Asia Minor, which the poet Homer◊ described as besieged in the ten-year Trojan War (mid-13th century BC), and falling to the Greeks by the stratagem of leaving behind, in a feigned retreat, a wooden horse containing armed infiltrators to open the gates. Believing it to be a religious offering, the Trojans took it within the walls. Nine cities buried one beneath another on the site at Hissarlik, near the Dardanelles, were originally excavated by Schliemann◊. Recent research suggests that the 6th, sacked and burnt c1250BC, is probably the Homeric Troy, which was succeeded by a shanty town, sacked by the Sea◊ Peoples c780BC. It has been suggested that the Homeric war might have a basis in fact, e.g. a conflict arising from trade rivalry (Troy was on a tin trade route), which could have been triggered by such an incident as Paris running off with Helen◊. The wooden horse could have been a votive offering left behind by the Greeks after Poseidon (whose emblem was a horse) had opened breaches in the city walls for them by an earthquake. See Mycenae◊□

Troyes industrial town (textiles, food processing) in Champagne-Ardenne, NE France; population 75 500. The ***Treaty of Troyes*** 1420 granted the French crown to Henry V of England□

Trucial States a former name (until 1971) of the United◊ Arab Emirates□

Trudeau Pierre Elliott 1919– . Canadian Liberal statesman, Prime Minister 1968–79. Defeated by Joe Clark in the May 1979 elections, he won by a landslide in Feb 1980. In 1980 he defeated the Quebec independence movement in a referendum and gained control over the constitution 1982, but by 1984 had so lost support that he resigned□

Truffaut François 1932–84. French director, whose films include *Jules et Jim* 1961 and *Day for Night* 1973 (Oscar)□

truffle a type of fungus; see under Ascomycetes◊□

Trujillo industrial city (engineering, sugar milling, vehicle assembly) in Peru, with its port at Salaverry; population 355 000□

Trujillo Molina Rafael Leonidas 1891–1961. Dominican dictator, president 1930–8 and 1942–52, and the power behind his brother, when the latter assumed the presidency 1952. He transformed the island into a modern state, but his suppression of his opponents resulted in his assassination□

Truman Harry S. 1884–1972. Democrat president of the USA 1945–53. Born in Lamar, Missouri, he ran a clothing store that was bankrupted by the Great Depression. In Jan 1945 he became Democrat vice-president to Roosevelt, succeeding him in the presidency in Apr, and in 1948 was elected for a second term in a surprise victory over Thomas Dewey. He used the atom bomb against Japan to shorten World War II; launched the Marshall◊ Plan to restore W Europe's economy; nurtured the European Community, NATO (including the rearmament of W Germany), an independent Israel, and the lines of 'containment' in Europe and Asia (see Truman◊ Doctrine). In Korea, he intervened when the South was invaded (see Korean◊ War), but sacked General Macarthur◊ when the General's policy threatened to start World War III. Truman's decision not to enter Chinese territory, betrayed by Kim Philby◊, led to China's entry into the war. See Independence◊□

Truman Doctrine 1947. Harry S. Truman's doctrine that the USA would 'support free peoples who are resisting attempted subjugation by armed minorities or by outside pressures'□

trumpet a musical brass instrument; see under brass◊□

trumpeter a type of bird; see under crane◊□

Truong Sa one of the Spratly◊ Islands□

Truro city (administrative headquarters) in Cornwall, England; population 16 000. The cathedral dates from 1880–1910, and the museum and art gallery has works by Opie◊. Truro was the traditional meeting place of the Stannary (see under Cornwall◊); the nearby tin mines briefly flourished in the early 1980s□

trust an arrangement whereby a person or group of persons holds property for the benefit of others entitled to the beneficial interest. Types of trust include:

a ***legal arrangement*** under which A is empowered to administer property belonging to B for the benefit of C. A and B may be the same person; B and C may not

a ***business trust*** formed by linking several companies by transferring shares in them to trustees; or by the creation of a holding company, whose shares are exchanged for those of the separate companies. Competition is thus eliminated, and in the USA both types were outlawed by the Sherman Anti-Trust Act 1890 (first fully enforced by 'trust buster' Theodore Roosevelt◊, as in the break-up of the Standard Oil Company of New Jersey by the Supreme Court 1911)

a ***unit trust*** which holds and manages a number of marketable securities; by buying a 'unit' in such a trust, the purchaser has a proportionate interest in each of the securities so that his risk is spread

an ***investment trust*** which is not in modern times a trust, but a public company investing in marketable securities money subscribed by its shareholders who receive dividends from the income earned

a ***charitable trust*** such as the National◊ Trust, the Ford Foundation, etc.□

Trustee Public. In England an official empowered to act as executor and trustee, either alone or with others, of the estate of anyone who appoints him or her□

Trust Territory territory formerly held under the United Nations trusteeship system to be prepared for independence, i.e. former mandates◊, territories taken over by the Allies in World War II, or voluntarily placed under the United Nations by the administering state□

trypanosomiasis disease (nagana) transmitted by the tsetse fly in tropical Africa, which kills or debilitates cattle□

Ts'ao Chan another name for the Chinese novelist Cao◊ Chan□

Tsar the Russian imperial title, derived from Latin Caesar□

Tsaritsyn a former name (until 1925) of the city of Volgograd◊□

tsetse any of various African bloodsucking flies; see under fly◊□

Tsinan another name for the Chinese city of Jinan◊□

Tsingtao another name for the Chinese port of Qingdao◊□

Tsiolkovsky Konstantin 1857–1935. Russian scientist, who became permanently deaf at the age of ten. He published the first practical paper on astronautics in 1903, covering rocket space travel using liquid propellants, such as liquid oxygen. This method and his concept of space stations both proved sound□

Tsukuba the 'Academic City', 65 km/40 mi N of Tokyo, Japan; population 30 000. Founded 1968, it handles scientific research from space to agriculture□

tsunami a huge destructive wave, especially caused by an earthquake; given a Japanese name from their frequent occurrence there□

Tsushima small Japanese island between Korea and Japan in Tsushima Strait. The Russian fleet was destroyed by the Japanese here in 1905 (see Russo–Japanese◊ War)□

Tuamotu Islands a group of islands in French◊ Polynesia□

Tuareg nomadic people of the Sudan, see Hamite◊□

tuatara lizard-like single survivor of the reptilian order Rhynchocephalia, found in New Zealand. On the top of its head it has the so-called pineal organ or 'third eye', linked to the brain, and probably acting as a light meter. It lays eggs in burrows which it shares with seabirds, and has the longest incubation period of all reptiles (up to 15 months)□

tuba a brass musical instrument; see under brass◊□

tuberculosis disease caused by the tuberculus bacillus, most often affecting the lungs, and formerly known as ***consumption*** or ***phthisis***. Tuberculosis of the lymphatic glands in the neck was formerly known as ***scrofula*** or ***king's evil*** (because the royal touch was believed to cure it); Samuel Johnson◊ was a sufferer□

tuberose a Mexican flowering plant; see Amaryllidaceae◊□

Tubingen industrial city (textiles, surgical instruments) in Baden-Württemberg; population 70 000□

Tubuai Islands see French◊ Polynesia□

tufa a soft, porous rock, white in colour, consisting of calcium carbonate, $CaCO_3$, deposited from rivers□

Tu Fu another name for the Chinese poet Du Fu◊□

Tula capital city of the Toltecs◊□

Tula industrial city (engineering, metallurgy) in W central USSR; population 529 000. Leo Tolstoy◊'s estate was nearby□

tulip genus of bulbous plants *Tulipa*, family Liliaceae◊. Introduced from Turkey to Europe in the 16th century, they became a mania in Holland in the 17th century, bulbs being sold for enormous sums. They are commercially grown in the Netherlands and E Anglia. The ***tulip tree*** *Liriodendron tulipifera*, family Magnoliaceae, has large tulip-shaped leaves□

Tull Jethro 1674–1741. British agriculturalist in Berkshire, who c1701 invented a mechanical seed drill□

Tulsa industrial city (aviation, aerospace, oil refining) in Oklahoma, most inland seaport in the USA; population 360 000□

Tumbs The. Two islands in the Strait of Hormuz, annexed by Iran 1971 from other Gulf states; their return to their former owners was an Iraq war aim in the Gulf◊ War□

tuna a type of fish; see under perch◊□

tungsten element (also called ***wolfram***)
symbol W
atomic number 74
physical description greyish-white metal
features highest melting point of any metal
uses used in the steel industry, giving great strength and temperature resistance to the steel. The resultant steel is used in drill bits for oil prospecting; armour-piercing shells and armour plate, and lamp filaments; heat does not destroy the 'tempering' or resilient strength of tungsten steels□

tunicates a marine subphylum of the chordates◊, which includes the ***sea squirts*** class Ascidiacea. The adults are like little pockets (up to 3 cm/1 in long) sitting on anything solid, and drawing in food-carrying sea water through one siphon, and expelling it through another; however, the young are little 'tadpoles' adventurously free-swimming. The class Larvacea are minute, retain the tadpole form as adults, and when floating in swarms form patches of bright colour in the sea, and are luminous at night□

Tunis capital and industrial port (chemicals, textiles) of Tunisia; population 1 113 000. Carthage◊ is a modern suburb□

Tunisia Republic of

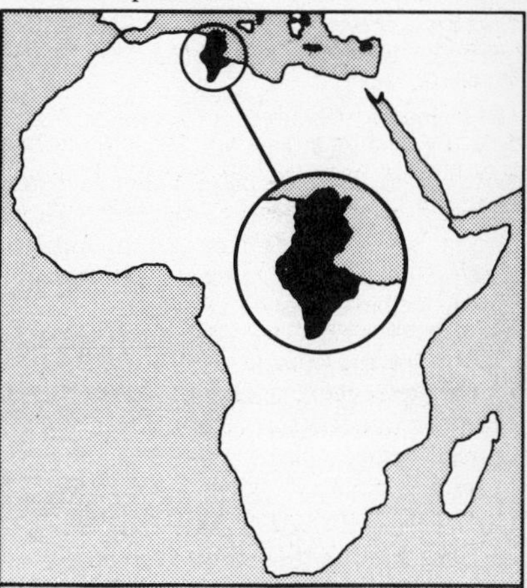

area 164 000 sq km/63 300 sq mi
capital and chief port Tunis
towns other ports Sfax, Sousse, Bizerta
features fertile island of Jerba, linked to the mainland by a causeway, and identified with the island of the lotus-eaters; Shott el Jerid salt lakes; holy city of Kairouan, ruins of Carthage
exports oil, phosphates, iron ore
currency dinar
population 7 202 000
language Arabic, official; French
religion Sunni Islam, with a politically active fundamentalist opposition to the government, Jewish and Christian minorities
government executive president (Habib Bourgiba◊ from 1957, for life from 1974), and national assembly, directly elected for five years
recent history for early history, see under Carthage◊; as part of the Ottoman◊ Empire from 16th century, and under subsequent independent rulers, it harboured the Barbary◊ pirates. A French protectorate 1881–1956, it then became independent and a republic in 1957□

tunnel an underground passageway; most famous include:
Channel Tunnel planned as a military measure by Napoleon 1802; excavations made from both shores 1882–3 (work halted by parliament as security hazard); in 1985 there were two schemes, 1 two rail tunnels of 7 m diameter and 2 a combined bridge and tunnel (road bridge linking two artificial islands to each coast, and a rail tunnel under the central section, through which cars would be transported by train for safety reasons). The former scheme was accepted by the French and UK governments in 1986.
Orange-Fish River 1975, longest irrigation tunnel 82 km/50 mi
Chesapeake Bay Bridge-Tunnel 1963, combined bridge and tunnel structure, 28 km/ 17.5 mi
St Gotthard 1980, longest road tunnel 16.3 km/10.1 mi
Seikan 1964–85, longest rail tunnel, Honshu–Hokkaido, under Tsugaru Strait, 53.85 km/33.5 mi, 23.3 km/14.4 mi undersea (it is a white elephant because a bullet train service can no longer be afforded)
Simplon 1906, longest rail tunnel on land 19.8 km/12.3 mi□

Tunnicliffe Charles Frederick 1901–79. British painter of birds, born in Macclesfield, who worked in Anglesey□

tunny a type of fish; see under perch◊□

Tupac Amaru 1743–81. Assumed name of Peruvian Indian leader José Gabriel Condorcanqui, executed for his revolt in 1780 against Spanish rule; he claimed to be descended from the last of the Incas◊. See Tupamaros under terrorism◊□

turbine

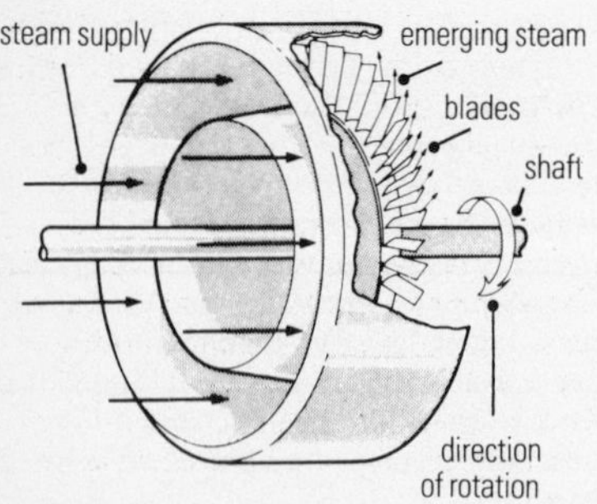

engine in which fast flowing water, steam, or gas is directed against angled vanes mounted on a shaft, which is thereby made to rotate. Thus a turbine is a fan in reverse. Steam turbines are used to drive electrical generators in power stations, the energy◊ to produce the high-pressure steam being converted from chemical energy in coal or oil, or from nuclear energy□

turbot a type of flatfish◊□

Turenne Henry de la Tour d'Auvergne, Vicomte de 1611–75. French marshal under Louis XIV, famous for siege technique□

Turgenev Ivan Sergeievich 1818–83. Russian writer, noted for his pessimism and characterization of women, as in the play *A Month in the Country* 1849, and the novels *A Nest of Gentlefolk* 1858, *Fathers and Sons* 1862, and *Virgin Soil* 1877. His series of *A Sportsman's Sketches* 1852 aided the abolition of serfdom. He lived abroad from 1856□

Turgot Anne Robert Jacques 1727–81. French finance minister 1774–6, whose reforming economies led to his dismissal□

Turin capital (Italian Torino) and industrial city (iron and steel, cars, silk and other textiles, fashion goods, chocolate, wine) of Piedmont, Italy; population 1 070 000. There is a university 1404, 15th-century cathedral, and Turin was the capital of the kingdom of Sardinia from 1720, and of united Italy 1861–4□

Turin Holy Shroud of. Ancient piece of linen bearing the imprint of a body with the traditional face of Christ, and claimed as that used to bury him after the Crucifixion□

Turing Alan Mathison 1912–54. British mathematician who worked at Bletchley Park (see Ultra◊) in World War II. He developed the modern computer◊, the concept of machine learning, and the use of mathematical models in biology, etc. His test for distinguishing between real (human) and simulated thought (computer) is known as the 'Chinese room': a human being is placed in one room, the machine in another, and an interrogator in yet another room asks any question that he wishes in order to distinguish between the two. When he can no longer do so, even if a distinction could potentially be made, the distinction no longer matters□

Turkana Lake. See Great◊ Lakes□

Turkestan geographical name for the area of central Asia divided among USSR (Kazakh, Kirghiz, Tadzhik, Turkmen and Uzbek SSRs), Afghanistan, and China (part of Xinjiang Uygur)□

Turkey Republic of
area 730 350 sq km/301 300 sq mi
capital Ankara
towns Istanbul and Izmir, also chief ports
features Bosporus and Dardanelles◊; Anatolian plateau, Taurus Mountains in SW (highest peak Kaldi Dağ 3734 m/12 251 ft); mountains on the Armenian/Iranian border including Mount Ararat◊; river Kizil Irmak (length 1150 km/715 mi), and the sources of

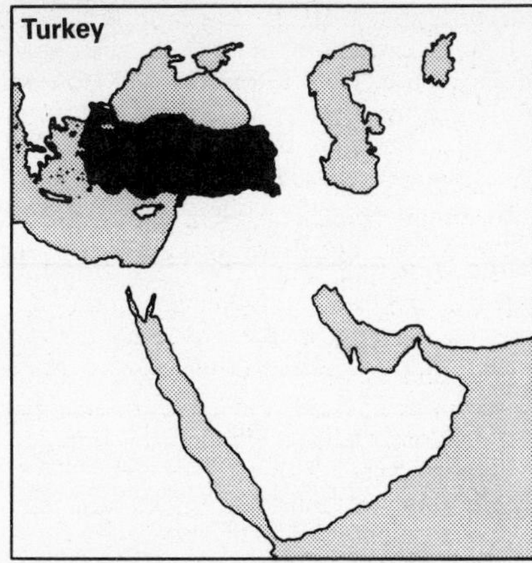

the Euphrates and Tigris. Archaeological sites include Catal Hüyük, Ephesus, and Troy◊; the still surviving rock villages of Cappadocia◊, and historic towns (Antioch, Iskenderun, Tarsus). See also whirling dervishes◊
exports cotton and yarn, hazelnuts, citrus, tobacco, dried fruit, chromium ores
currency Turkish lira
population 50 207 000 85%, Turkish, 12% Kurdish
language Turkish, official (it is related to Mongolian, but is written in the Western Latin script), Kurdish Arabic
famous people Santa Claus (St Nicholas◊ of Myra), Suleiman the Magnificent, Enver Pasha, Atatürk
religion Sunni Islam
government executive president (General Kenan Evren from 1980) reelected for seven years by the grand national assembly (elected 1983 with strictly 'vetted' candidates), with a civilian presidential council (the former military national security council). Prime Minister from 1983 Targut Özal
recent history for earlier Turkish history, see Seljuk and Ottoman empires◊. The modern republic was founded 1920, during the Turkish War of Independence 1919–22 by Atatürk◊, who became first president of the republic in 1923. He established a one-party dictatorship which endured till 1950; Islam ceased to be the state religion, and a policy of Westernization was pursued. The revival of Islam after World War II added to the instability which led to increasing military intervention from 1960. In 1974 Turkey invaded Cyprus◊. In 1980 the constitution was suspended following a military coup by General Kenan Evren 'to forestall a theocratic coup'. See Armenian◊ Question□

turkey a large gallinaceous bird; see under fowl◊□

Turkmenistan constituent republic (SSR) of the Soviet Union from 1924, part of Soviet Central Asia
area 488 100 sq km/187 000 sq mi
capital Ashkhabad
features Kara Kum 'Black Sands' desert, which occupies most of the republic, area c310 800 sq km/ 120 000 sq mi (on its edge is Altyn Depe, 'golden hill', site of a ruined city with a ziggurat excavated from 1967); river Amu◊ Darya
products silk, sheep; astrakhan fur, carpets; oil and chemical products
population 2 800 000, 66% Turkmenians
language west Turkic, closely related to Turkish◊
religion Sunni Islam
recent history the nomadic tribes of the area were subdued by Russia 1881–5□

Turks and Caicos Islands a British Crown Colony in the W Indies
area 430 sq km/166 sq mi
capital Cockburn Town on Grand Turk
features a group of 30 islands, seven are inhabited, of which the largest is Grand Caicos; they are an extension of the Bahamas, and since 1982 have developed as a tax haven
exports crayfish and conch, flesh and shell
currency US dollar
population 7 500, 90% of African descent
language English, French Creole
religion Christianity
government governor, with executive and legislative councils (chief minister from 1985 Nathaniel Francis, Progressive National Party)
recent history secured by Britain in 1766 against French and Spanish claims, they were a dependency of Jamaica 1873–1962, and in 1976 attained internal self-government. The chief minister, Norman Saunders, resigned 1985 after his arrest in Miami on drugs charges, on which he was convicted□

Turku port in SW Finland; population 242 400□

turmeric powdered rhizome of the tropical Asian plant *Curcuma longa*, family Zingiberaceae (including ginger and arrowroot◊), used as a condiment and yellow dye; see under herbs◊□

Turner Dame Eva 1899– . British soprano, excelling in *Aïda* and *Turandot*; Dame of the British Empire 1962□

Turner John Napier 1929– . Canadian Liberal statesman. He succeeded Trudeau as Prime Minister Jun 1984, but lost the September election to Brian Mulroney◊□

Turner Joseph Mallord William 1775–1851. British artist. Born in London, son of a barber, he studied at the Academy School and became professor of perspective in 1809. *Crossing the Brook* and his Venetian scenes reflect his travels in Italy, but in England he developed increasing freedom in capturing effects of light and weather, e.g. *Rain, Steam and Speed, Snow Storm,* etc. Not greatly appreciated in his lifetime, though championed by Ruskin◊, he is now recognized as probably the greatest of British artists. In 1984 the Clore Gallery extension to the Tate was under construction to house the collection of his works he left to the nation□

Turner Nat 1800–31. American Negro leader of a slave revolt in 1831 Southampton, Virginia; 54 whites were killed before he and 16 followers were hanged□

turnip plant *Brassica rapa*, family Cruciferae◊; the white/yellow fleshed root is a vegetable; closely allied is the ***swede*** (US ***rutabaga***) *B napobrassica*, with a firmer, more golden flesh, which also keeps longer and has greater food value□

turpentine solution of resins distilled from the sap of conifers, used in varnish and as a paint solvent, but largely replaced by white◊ spirit□

Turpin Dick 1706–39. English highwayman, hanged at York. His legendary ride from London to York on his mare Black Bess (described by Ainsworth◊) was originally attributed to an earlier thief, John Nevinson, in 1676□

turquoise hydrous phosphate of aluminium and copper. Opaque and blue-green, it is used as a gem: it is found in Iran, Turkestan and Mexico□

turtle an aquatic reptile; see under tortoise◊□

Tuscany region (Italian Toscana; Roman Etruria, see Etruscans◊) of NW Italy; capital Florence; population 3 581 745. Mainly agricultural, it has important mines (lignite, iron, etc) and marble quarries. Larderello has hot sulphur springs (220°C), used by the Romans for baths, and today for electricity generation. Tuscany is the home of the purest form of Italian, which was adopted as the literary standard□

Tussaud Madame 1760–1850. Swiss-born, French wax-modeller, born Anne Marie Grosholtz. She and her modeller uncle were forced during the French Revolution to take death masks of many of its victims and leaders. After separating from her husband, she settled in London 1802 and the updated exhibition of models of the famous and infamous (now in Marylebone Road) continues as a tourist attraction□

Tutankhamen king of Egypt of the 18th dynasty c1360–1350BC. A son of Ikhnaton◊ or of Amenhotep◊ III, he was probably about 11 at his accession. In 1922 his tomb was discovered by Lord Carnarvon and Howard Carter in the Valley of the Kings at Luxor, almost untouched by tomb robbers. The contents, which include many works of art and his solid gold coffin, captured the imagination of the world□

Tutu Desmond Mpilo 1931– . Anglican priest, Archbishop of Johannesburg, and general secretary of the S African Council of Churches, awarded Nobel peace prize 1984□

Tuva a republic of the USSR; area 170 500 sq km/65 180 sq mi; population 269 000. Chinese 1757–1912, it was annexed by Russia 1914. The capital is Kizyl□

Tuvalu SW Pacific state of

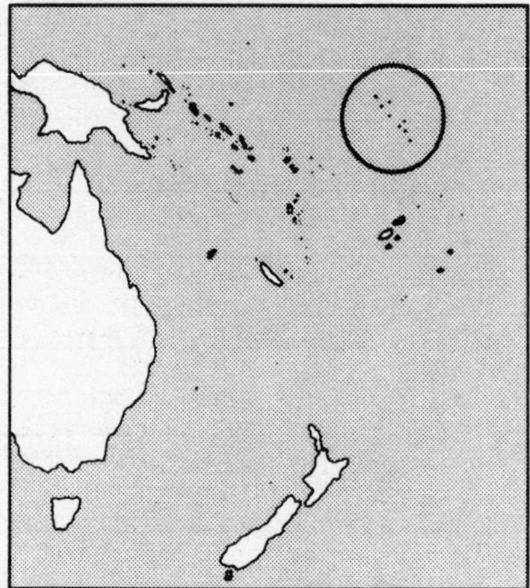

area 24.6 sq km/9.5 sq mi
capital on Funafuti
features the name means 'cluster of eight' islands (there are actually nine, but one is very small)
exports phosphates, copra, handicrafts, stamps
currency Australian dollar
population 8 000, mainly Polynesian
language Tuvaluan and English
religion Christianity, chiefly Protestant
government governor-general and parliament of 12 members, which elects a Prime Minister (Tomasi Puapua from 1981) and the majority of the Cabinet
recent history under the name Ellice Islands, they were part of the Gilbert and Ellice Islands colony 1915–75, when they became a separate British colony, and achieved independence 1978, as a member of the Commonwealth□

Tver the former name (until 1932) of the city of Kalinin◊□

Twain Mark. Pseudonym (a call used for depth sounding by Mississippi pilots) of the American humorous writer ***Samuel Langhorne Clemens*** 1835–1910. Born in Florida, Missouri, he established his reputation with his comic masterpiece *The Innocents Abroad* 1869 and the two children's books, *The Adventures of Tom Sawyer* 1876 and *The Adventures of Huckleberry Finn* 1885□

Tweed river in W Borders region, Scotland; length 156 km/97 mi□

tweed originally handwoven, unpatterned, largely weatherproof woollen cloth, especially as made on Harris in the Outer Hebrides◊□

Tweedsmuir Lord. Title of writer John Buchan◊□

Twelfth Day the twelfth and final day of the Christmas celebrations; see Epiphany◊□

Twickenham part of Richmond-upon-Thames◊; contains the English Rugby Football Union ground□

twins strictly speaking two individuals who are 'identical' twins, i.e. not merely produced at one birth, but the products of the division of a single fertilized ovum or egg cell (when they are always of the same sex). Non-identical twins may arise from eggs that are not fertilized at the same time, and may have different fathers□

Tyan-Shan mountain system (Chinese Tien-Shan) on the Soviet-Chinese border. Peaks include ***Kongur Shan*** in Xinjiang, China, 7719 m/25 325 ft (Chris Bonington◊ led an expedition which first conquered the summit 1981) and ***Pik Pobedy*** on the Kirgizia border 7439 m/24 406 ft□

Tyburn London stream (now underground) near which (at the junction of Oxford Street and Edgware Road) Tyburn gallows stood from 12th century to 1783□

Tyler John 1790–1862. President of the USA 1841–45. As a Virginia planter, he was a Confederate supporter; his government annexed Texas 1845□

Tyler Wat d. 1381. Leader of the Peasants' Revolt 1381, he was murdered by the 'Lord Mayor', Sir William Walworth, during a conference at Smithfield□

Tyndale William 1492–1536. English biblical translator. The printing of his New Testament (basis of the Authorized Version) was begun in 1525 in Cologne, and (after he had been forced to flee) completed in Worms. He was strangled and burnt as a heretic at Vilvorde in Belgium□

Tyne river in N England; length 72 km/45 mi. Kielder Water in the N Tyne Valley is Europe's largest man-made lake, 12 km/7.5 mi long and 0.8 km/0.5 mi wide□

Tyne and Wear former metropolitan county of NE England

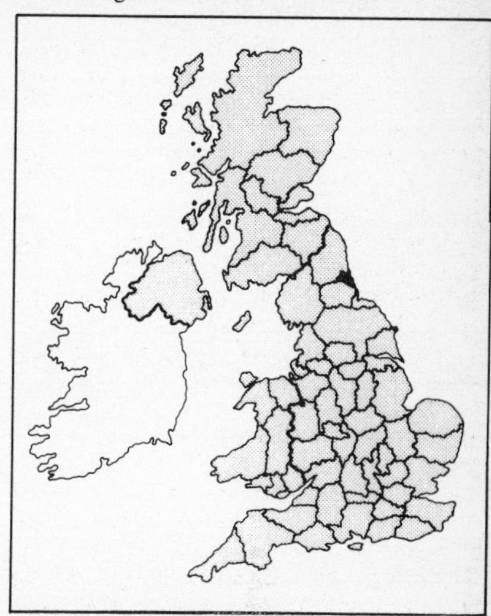

area 540 sq km/209 sq mi
towns administrative headquarters Newcastle upon Tyne; South Shields, Gateshead, Sunderland
features is bisected by the rivers Tyne and Wear; includes part of Hadrian◊'s Wall; Newcastle and Gateshead are linked with each other and with the coast on both sides by the Tyne and Wear Metro (a light railway using existing suburban lines, extending 54 km/34 mi beneath both cities)
products once a great centre of heavy industry, it is now being redeveloped and diversified
population 1 130 432
famous people Thomas Bewick, Robert Stephenson, Harry Patterson/'Jack Higgins'□

Tynemouth port and pleasure resort in Tyne and Wear, England; population 67 880□

Tynwald the parliament of Isle of Man◊□

typewriter hand-operated machine for producing characters on paper, resembling printing. The first practicable machine was built in USA by C L Sholes, C Glidden, and S W Soulé in 1867, and marketed from 1874 by Remington, the gunmakers. They are being superseded by word processors (see under microcomputer◊)□

typhoid fever infectious disease caused by the bacterium *Salmonella typhi* and usually contracted through infected water; there is a temporarily effective vaccine (treatment of the disease itself is by the antibiotic chloramphenicol). ***paratypoid fever*** caused by *S paratyphi* is a milder form. See also under food◊ poisoning□

typhoon another word for cyclone; see under meteorology◊□

typhus group of infectious diseases, of which epidemic typhus, the most severe, is transmitted by body lice infected by rickettsia parasites. It is often fatal□

Tyr in Norse mythology, the god of battles, whom the Anglo-Saxons called Týw, hence 'Tuesday'□

tyrannosaurus a class of dinosaur; see under dinosaur◊□

Tyre port in Lebanon (Arabic *Sur*), the chief port of the Phoenicians◊, which was sacked by Alexander 332BC, and by the Arabs who took it from the Crusaders in 1291, after which it never recovered. It was famous for the dye 'Tyrian purple'. In the 1970s it became a Palestinian guerrilla stronghold□

Tyrol a variant spelling of Tirol◊□

Tyrone county of Northern Ireland
area 3155 sq km/1218 sq mi
towns county town Omagh
features rivers Derg, Blackwater, and Foyle, famous for salmon and trout; Lough Neagh
products mainly agricultural
population 139 100□

Tyumen oldest town (founded 1586) in Siberia, central USSR; population 378 000. There are timber, tanning, and chemical industries□

Tzu-Hsi another spelling of Zi◊ Xi□

U

Ubangi-Shari see Central◊ African Republic□

U-boat German submarine (*Unterseeboot*), known by the letter U followed by a number, especially in both World Wars□

Uccello Paolo. Name by which Italian artist Paolo di Dono 1397–1475 was known. An apprentice of Ghiberti◊, he made decorative use of perspective, and his works included the *Nativity* fresco (Florence) and three battle pictures for the Palazzo Medici, one of which is in the National Gallery, London□

Udaipur industrial city (chemicals, asbestos) in Rajasthan, India; population 165 000. Formerly the capital of the princely state of Udaipur, it has notable palaces, especially a marble one on an island in a lake□

Udall Nicholas 1504–56. English schoolmaster and playwright, author of *Ralph Roister Doister* c1553, the first known English comedy□

Udine industrial city (chemicals, textiles, leather goods, paper) in Friuli-Venezia Giulia, Italy; population 101 180□

Udmurt a republic of central USSR conquered in the 15–16th centuries; area 42 100 sq km/16 250 sq mi; population 1 516 000. Capital Izhevsk□

Ufa industrial city (engineering, oil refining, petrochemicals, distilling, timber) and capital of the Republic of Bashkir, central USSR; population 1 048 000. It originated as a Russian fortress 1574□

Uffizi an art gallery in Florence◊□

Uganda Republic of

area 236 000 sq km/93 980 sq mi

capital Kampala

towns Jingar, M'Bale, Entebbe

features Ruwenzori◊ Range; national parks: Murchison Falls (chimps, some of Africa's largest crocodiles, and Nile perch to 72.5 kg/160 lb), Queen Elizabeth, Kidepo and Lake Mboro; Owen Falls, a cataract on the White Nile where it leaves Lake Victoria (a dam supplies hydroelectricity for Uganda and Kenya)

exports coffee, cotton, tea, and copper

currency Uganda shilling

population 14 268 000, comprising several ethnic groups: the largest are the Baganda (see Buganda◊), from whom the name of the country comes); others include the Langi and Acholi, and there are a few surviving pygmies

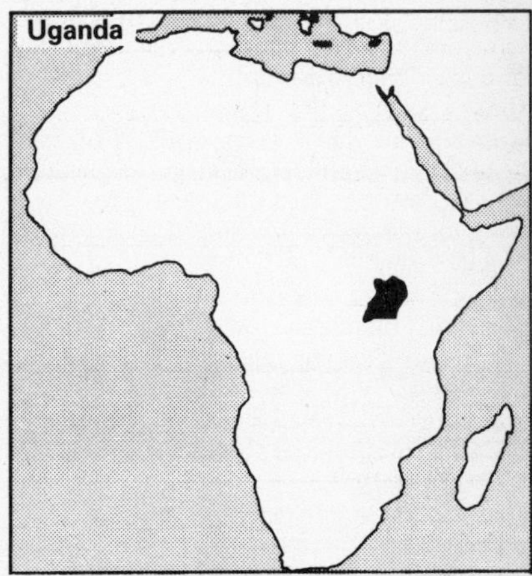

language English (official); Ki-Swahili is a lingua franca

religion 50% Christianity; 45% Animism, 5% Islam

government President Museveni of the National Resistance Movement (NRM) heads a new government in Kampala, with Dr Sampson Kisseka as Prime Minister. The NRM is gradually ousting from power General Okello and the former Ugandan army.

recent history under British protection from 1894, Uganda became independent in 1962, and a republic within the Commonwealth in 1967. The first president, Milton Obote◊ (Langi tribe), was deposed by Idi Amin◊ in 1971, who ruled as a tyrant, and expelled the Asians, on whom the economy depended. In 1979 he was in turn overthrown by combined Ugandan exile and Tanzanian invading forces, and Obote, leader of the Uganda People's Congress (UPC), returned to power until again overthrown (after the disappearance of some 300 000 of his people) by Major-General Tito Okello (Acholi people) in 1985. Yoweri Museveni led a revolt against Okello's brutal rule in 1985□

Uganda Martyrs twenty-two Africans of whom 12 were boy pages, who were put to

death 1885–7 by King Mwanga when they refused to renounce Christianity. They were canonized as the first African saints of the Roman Catholic Church in 1964□
Ugarit ancient trading city kingdom (modern Ras Shamra) on the Syrian coast, excavated by Claude Schaeffer from 1929. Finds ranged from c7000BC to 15–13th centuries BC, and include numerous cuneiform documents, as well as an early Ugaritic alphabet of 22 letters (the earliest alphabet known, and closely related to the Phoenician◊, from which our own is ultimately derived)□
Uist an island of the Hebrides◊□
Ujiji port on Lake Tanganyika, Tanzania, linked by rail with Dar es Salaam; population 25 000. Once an Arab trading post for slaves and ivory, it was here that Stanley◊ found Livingstone◊□
Ujung Padang port (formerly Macassar) on Sulawesi, Indonesia; population 709 000. There are fishing and food processing industries□
ukelele a type of small four-stringed guitar◊□
Ukraine constituent republic of the SE Soviet Union from 1923
area 603 700 sq km/233 000 sq mi
capital Kiev
towns Kharkov, Donetsk, Odessa, Dnepropetrovsk, Lvov, Zaporozhe, Krivoi Rog
features Russian plain, Carpathians and Crimean mountains; River Dnieper
products the granary of the USSR, it also has 60% of the Soviet coal reserves, as well as oil and other minerals
population 50 456 000; Ukrainian 75%, Russian 19%; Russian-speaking Jews 2%
language Ukrainian
religion traditionally Russian Orthodox
recent history divided between Russia and Austria in the 18th century, it was independent 1917–20□
Ulaan Baataar capital (formerly Ulan Bator, and until 1924, Urga) of the Mongolian Republic, linked with Ulan Ude by rail; population 400 000. There is a university, and trade in locally produced carpets, textiles, vodka□
Ulan Bator see Ulaan◊ Baataar□
Ulanova Galina 1910– . Russian dancer. Prima ballerina of the Bolshoi Theatre ballet 1944–61, she excelled as Juliet and Giselle, and created the title-role of *Cinderella*□
Ulan Ude industrial city (cars, glass, sawmills) and capital of the Republic of Buriat SE USSR, on the Trans-Siberian railway; population 329 000□
Ulbricht Walter 1893–1973. E German statesman. An exile in the USSR during the Nazi era, he was from 1950 First Secretary of the Socialist Unity Party, in E Germany, and (as Chairman of the Council of State 1960–73), built the Berlin Wall in 1961 and established E Germany's economy and recognition outside the Eastern European bloc□
ulcer sore of the surface skin or mucous membrane. ***Stomach ulcers*** occur in patients sensitive to gastric acids (possibly because of hormone deficiency), and are curable by a drug increasing protective prostaglandins□
Uleaborg see Oulu◊□
Ulm industrial city (vehicles, textiles, agricultural machinery, precision instruments) in Baden-Württemberg; population 94 000. The Gothic cathedral (1377) escaped the destruction of two-thirds of the city in World War II. Einstein was born here□
Ulster northernmost Irish province, of which six counties (Antrim, Armagh, Down, Fermanagh, Londonderry, and Tyrone) comprise Northern Ireland, and three (Cavan, Donegal and Monaghan) form part of the Republic; total area 21 585 sq km/8335 sq mi; population 1 578 420. The eldest son of the Duke of Gloucester, Alexander 1974– , bears the courtesy title, Earl of Ulster□
Ultra abbreviation of Ultra Secret, used by the British from spring 1940 in World War II to denote intelligence gained by deciphering German signals at the interception centre at Bletchley Park. See Battle of Anzio◊□
Ultramontanism 'beyond the mountains', i.e. the Alps: the tenets of the Italian party in the Roman Catholic Church who stress Papal authority, rather than nationalism in the church□
ultrasound physical vibrations in matter at frequencies above 20 000 hertz (above the limit of human hearing). The lower frequncies (20 000–80 000 hertz) are used in hospitals and industry for the cleaning of surfaces; higher frequencies are used in sonar◊, to detect flaws in metal, etc., and (when specially focused) high power ultrasound can destroy tissues deep in the body, which would be difficult to reach by surgery. Extremely high frequencies of over 1000 megahertz are used in ultrasonic microscopes◊. Ultrasound can also be used more cheaply, instead of heat, pressure, or light to start chemical reactions in industry.
In nature ultrasound is greatly used by animals in communication with each other, e.g. rats◊; and by humans to communicate with dogs by 'silent whistles'□
ultra-violet (U-V) radiation electromagnetic◊ radiation similar to light but of shorter wavelength than is detectable by the eye. Ultraviolet radiation is responsible for sunburn and helps the formation of vitamin D

in the body; the radiation is also germicidal. It reaches us from the sun, but may also be produced artificially from mercury vapour lamps. Many sunglasses fail to filter it out, and by encouraging the iris of the eye to open too widely in apparently dim light may cause damage to the retina□

Ulundi capital of KwaZulu◊□

Ulysses see Odysseus◊□

Umbelliferae family of dicotyledonous plants of northern temperate regions with about 180 genera, characterized by divided leaves and flowers borne in umbels, and including carrot, celery, and hemlock◊□

Umberto two kings of Italy:

Umberto I 1844–1900, king from 1878, he joined the Triple Alliance (see under World◊ War I), and his colonial ventures included the defeat at Aduwa◊. He was assassinated by an anarchist.

Umberto II 1904–83, last king, from the abdication of his father, Victor◊ Emmanuel III, 9 May–13 Jun 1946, when he also abdicated□

umbrella portable protection against the rain: when used against the sun, called a parasol or sunshade. In use in China more than a thousand years ago, they were also held over the rulers of ancient Egypt and Assyria as symbols of power, and had a similar significance for Aztec and African rulers, as well as in the Roman Catholic church. Women used them in England from the 17th century, but Jonas Hanway 1712–86 was the first to make it part of the Englishman's everyday 'uniform'□

Umbria mountainous central region of Italy; capital Perugia; population 810 225. It was the home of the Umbrian school of artists, e.g. Raphael◊□

Umm al Qaiwain see United Arab Emirates◊□

Umtali see Mutare◊□

Unamuno Miguel de 1864–1936. Spanish writer of Basque origin. He was exiled 1924–30 for criticism of the military directorate of Primo de Rivera◊. His works include the mystic poem on survival of death *The Velazquez Christ* 1920, and the philosophical prose study *The Tragic Sense of Life* 1913, concerned with the conflict of reason and belief in religion□

uncertainty (or **indeterminacy**) **principle of Heisenberg** an important prediction of quantum mechanics (see quantum◊ theory). It gives a theoretical limit to the precision with which a particle's momentum and position can be measured simultaneously: the more accurately the one is pinned down the more uncertainty there is in the other. The uncertainty arises because according to quantum mechanics it is meaningless to speak of a particle's position, momentum etc., except as results of measurements, but measuring involves an interaction (e.g. a photon of light bouncing off the particle under scrutiny), which must disturb the particle, though the disturbance is noticeable only at an atomic scale. The principle implies that one cannot, even in theory, predict the moment-to-moment behaviour of such a system□

Uncle Sam nickname for the USA. It originated during the war of 1812, probably from the initials US placed on government property□

underground the London underground, the world's first, was the concept of a solicitor to relieve traffic congestion. The first line Paddington-Farringdon Street, opened in 1863, was more of a roofed-in trench, but some lines now go very deep and also under the Thames. Most major cities have similar systems□

unemployment the involuntary lack of paid employment. Unemployment is generally subdivided into ***frictional*** unemployment (the inevitable temporary unemployment of those moving from one job to another); ***cyclical*** unemployment, caused by a downswing in the trade◊ cycle; ***seasonal*** unemployment, in an area where there is high demand only during holiday periods, for example; and ***structural*** unemployment, where changing technology or other long-term change in the economy results in large numbers without work, particularly in certain regions.

Most modern governments attempt to prevent some or all of the above forms of unemployment. The ideas of Keynes◊ were influential in the case of UK government unemployment policies during the fifties and sixties. The existence of a clear link between unemployment and inflation◊ (that high unemployment can only be dealt with by governments at the cost of higher inflation) is now disputed□

UNESCO *U*nited *N*ations *E*ducational, *S*cientific, and *C*ultural *O*rganization. See under United◊ Nations□

Union of Soviet Socialist Republics (USSR)

area 22 274 700 sq km/8 647 250 sq mi

capital Moscow

towns Kiev, Tashkent, Kharkov, Gorky, Novosibirsk, Minsk, Sverdlovsk, Kuibyshev, Chelyabinsk, Dnepropetrovsk, Tbilisi; ports Leningrad, Odessa, Baku, Archangelesk, Murmansk, Vladivostok, Vostochny, Rostov

features Ural and Caucasus mountains, and

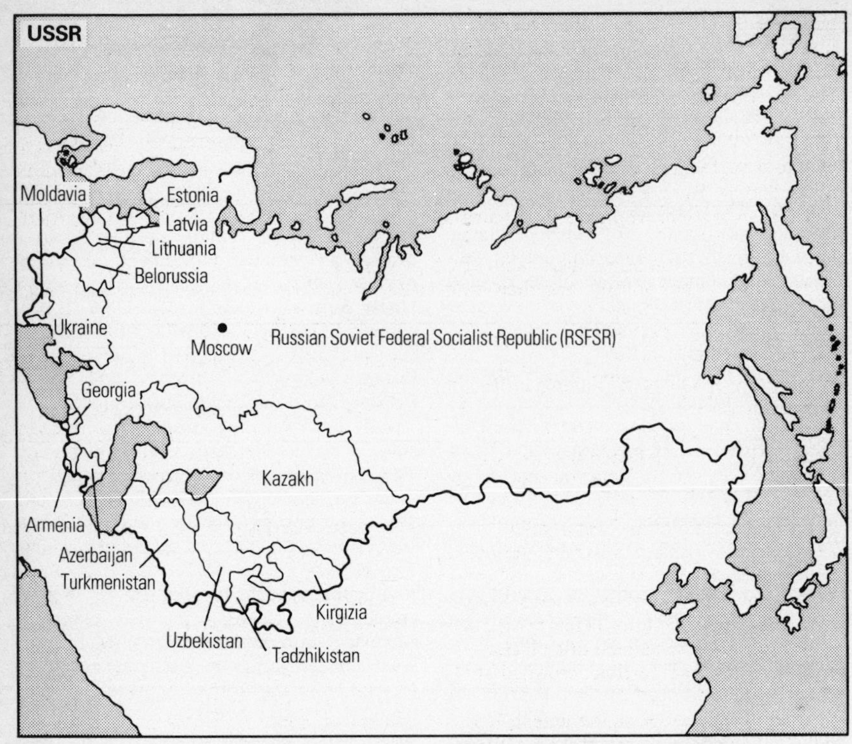

part of the Pamirs and Altai mountains; Karakum Desert; Black, Caspian and Aral Seas; rivers (in Europe) Don, Dnieper, Volga, Dvina, Pechora, Dneister, Neva, Kuban, and (in Asia) Ob, Yenisei, Lena, Amur, Amu Darya and Syr Darya; lakes Ladoga, Onega, Baikal, and Balkhash
exports cotton, timber; iron and steel, non-ferrous metals, electrical equipment, machinery, arms; oil and natural gas and their products; asbestos, gold, manganese. The USSR has 58% of world coal reserves; 59% of oil; 41% iron; 88% manganese; 54% potassium salts; 30% phosphates (55% of trade is with Communist countries)
currency rouble
population 272 500 000 (two-thirds living in towns, and of 125 different nationalities); 52% ethnic Russians; 17% Ukrainians
language Slavic (Russian, Ukranian, Byelorussian, Polish), Altaic (Turkish, etc.), other Indo-European, Uralian, Caucasian
religion 'freedom of conscience' is guaranteed under the constitution, but religious belief is discouraged and considered incompatible with party membership (17 500 000 members); the largest Christian denomination is the Orthodox Church◊ (30 000 000); but the largest religious sect is Sunni Islam (40 000 000), making the USSR the 5th largest Muslim nation; Jews 2 500 000
government under the constitution of 1977, the USSR comprises 15 republics, and (for smaller national groupings), autonomous republics, regions, and areas. The highest organ of government is the Supreme Soviet of two chambers elected for five years: the Soviet of the Union (one deputy for every 300 000 population) and of Nationalities (32 deputies from each constituent republic; 11 from each autonomous republic; five from each autonomous regions, and one from each national area). The Supreme Soviet elects the Council of Ministers, chaired by the prime minister, and also the presidium, chaired by the state president (Gromyko from 1985). No one can stand as candidate in any election without Communist Party approval. The inner cabinet of the party is the Politburo (General Secretary from 1985, Mikhail Gorbachev), which controls the entire system. Each constituent and autonomous republic also has its own Supreme Soviet, and local government is run by district, town, and village soviets□

Union of Soviet Socialist Republics: history

7th century BC–***7th century*** AD nomad

peoples displaced each other in turn as invaders of the steppes north of the Black Sea (see Scythians◊, Sarmatians◊, Goths◊, Huns◊, Avars◊)
7–11th century Khazar Empire (see Khazars◊)
c9th century Ukraine settled by the eastern Slavs, and the Russ, a conquering Varangian (see Viking◊) tribe, who gave their name to Russia
862 Varangians established their capital first under Rurik at Novgorod◊, and then under his descendants at Kiev◊
c988 Orthodox Christianity adopted by Prince Vladimir
12th century decline of the Varangian-Russian principality
1147 Moscow founded
1223 Gengis Khan defeated the Slav army
1237–40 country overrun by the Tatar◊ 'Golden Horde'
1240–1480 period of the 'Tatar yoke'
1326 Moscow (formerly Muscovy) the leading Russian principality
1380 Demetrius◊ Donskoi headed a coalition of Russian rulers in the first defeat of the Tatars
1480 Ivan◊ III first claimed title of Tsar
1547 Ivan◊ IV, the Terrible, crowned as first Tsar
1598–1605 Boris◊ Godunov extended Russia's boundaries, and established a Russian patriarchate; his reign was followed by anarchy
1613 Michael Romanov◊ elected Tsar
1649 system of peasant serfdom established
1689 Peter◊ the Great adopted a policy of westernization
1713 capital moved from Moscow to St Petersburg
1762–96 Russia the leading power of Europe under Catherine◊ II
1798–1801 and *1805–7* successive participations in the Napoleonic Wars
1807 Alexander◊ I forced to make peace with Napoleon at Tilsit◊
1812–14 invasion of Russia by Napoleon ended in retreat from Moscow and ***Patriotic War*** against him
1861 emancipation of the serfs by Alexander◊ II
1877–8 Russo-Turkish War in support of the Christians under Turkish rule, and to improve Russia's access to the sea through acquisitions in the Balkans
1878 Congress of Berlin◊ ended Russian expansion in the Balkans◊
1881 asassination of Alexander◊ II provoked highly repressive regime of Alexander◊ III
1905 abortive revolution broke out in St Petersburg and in Black Sea fleet (see 'Potemkin'◊)
1914 Russia defeated at Tannenberg◊ in World War I
1917 outbreak of revolution in Petrograd in Feb; abdication of Nicholas◊ II on 15 Mar; October Revolution, and the overthrow of Kerensky◊ government by the Bolsheviks (see Bolshevism◊ and Lenin◊)
1918 Treaty of Brest-Listovsk◊ took Russia out of World War I
1918–21 Civil War, in which British, French, Japanese, and US troops intervened on the side of the Whites◊
1922 USSR established
1924 Stalin◊ succeeded Lenin; dissension between Stalin and Trotsky◊
1930s series of political purges; see Stalin◊
1939 non-aggression pact with Hitler, following which Poland (in part); Estonia, Latvia, and Lithuania; part of Finland, etc., were annexed
1941–5 Great Patriotic War, following Hitler's invasion of Russia; see World War II◊
1949 Comecon◊ established
1953 triumvirate (Malenkov◊, Molotov◊, Beria◊) succeeded Stalin
1955 Warsaw◊ Pact
1956 Khrushchev◊ denounced Stalinism; temporary 'thaw' within the USSR and in overseas relations, but harsh suppression of the revolt in Hungary◊
1959 serious rift with China
1962 installation of missiles in Cuba resulted in crisis with USA; missiles withdrawn and Soviet naval programme accelerated
1964 Khrushchev ousted by Brezhnev◊
1968 Brezhnev Doctrine; invasion of Czechoslovakia
1979 invasion of Afghanistan◊
1980 troops massed on Polish border during 'Solidarity' unrest
1982 Andropov◊ succeeded Brezhnev
1984 Chernenko◊ succeeded Andropov
1985 Gorbachev◊ succeeded Chernenko; some détente with USA□

United Arab Emirates (UAE) federation of the emirates of Abu Dhabi, Ajman, Dubai, Fujairah, Sharjah, Umm al Qaiwain, Ras al Khaimah
total area 83 000 sq km/32 000 sq mi
towns chief town Abu Dhabi; chief port Dubai
features linked by their dependence on oil revenues
exports oil and natural gas
currency UAE dirham
population 1 523 000, 10% being nomadic
language Arabic (official)
religion 90% Moslem; Christian, Hindu
government the federation is headed by a supreme council of the seven rulers which

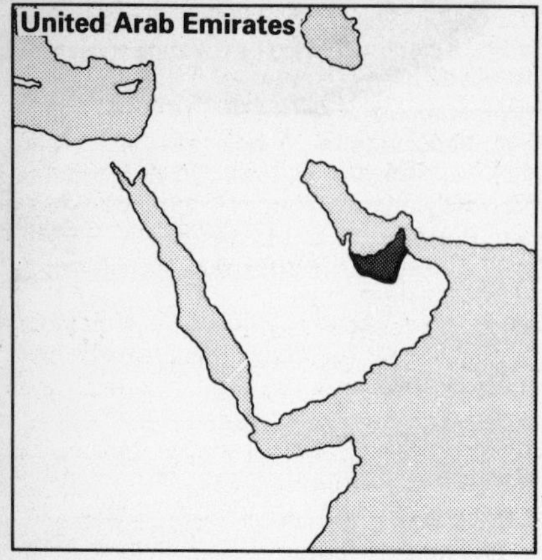

appoints a council of ministers, and there is an elected national council with no executive powers. The president is Sheikh Zaid (Abu Dhabi) and the vice-president is Sheikh Rashid (Dubai)
recent history the states – in treaty relations with Britain from 1820 (hence formerly known as Trucial States) – formed the federation in 1971, when the special relationship with Britain ended. There is dissension between those who want greater unity, and the minority who fear dominance by Abu Dhabi□

United Arab Republic union 1958–61 between Egypt◊ and Syria◊□

United Kingdom

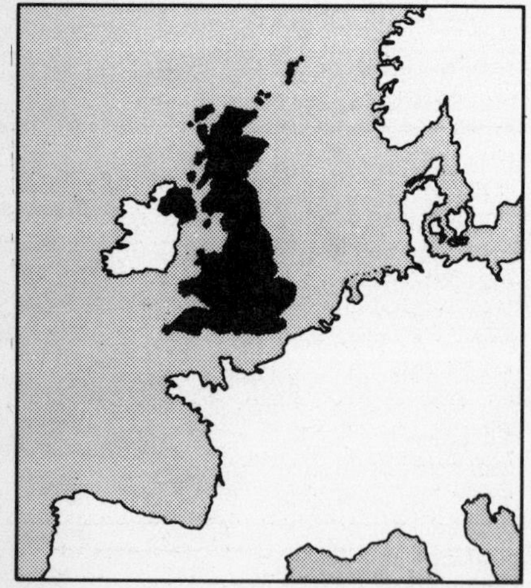

a kingdom in N Europe. It consists of England, Scotland, Wales and Northern Ireland. Historically, it was the name for England and Scotland together from the accession of James VI of Scotland as James I of England in 1603. The United Kingdom of Great Britain and Ireland was formed in 1801, becoming the United Kingdom of Great Britain and Northern Ireland after the formation of the Irish Free State in 1922□

United Nations (UN) association of states (successor to the League◊ of Nations) for international peace, security, and cooperation, with its headquarters in New York. Its charter was drawn up at the San Francisco Conference in 1945. There are six main organs:
General Assembly one member from each of 159 member states who meet annually; decisions on important questions require a two-thirds majority, on minor ones, a simple majority suffices
Security Council five permanent members (UK, USA, USSR, France, China, who exercise a veto in that their support is requisite for all decisions), plus six others elected for two years by the General Assembly
Economic and Social Council 18 members. It co-ordinates the activities of: ***Food and Agriculture Organization*** (FAO) established in 1945, headquarters in Rome; investment in agriculture, also emergency food supplies; ***General Agreement on Tariffs and Trade*** (GATT) established in 1948, headquarters in Geneva; reduction of trade barriers, anti-dumping code, assistance to trade of developing countries, etc.; ***International Atomic Energy Agency*** (IAEA) established in 1957, headquarters in Vienna; research centres in Austria and Monaco; International Centre for Theoretical Physics, Trieste; ***International Bank for Reconstruction and Development*** (IBRD) popularly known as the World◊ Bank; ***International Civil Aviation Organization*** (ICAO) established in 1947, headquarters in Montreal; safety and efficiency, international facilities and air law; ***International Development Association*** (IDA) administered by the World◊ Bank; ***International Finance Corporation*** (IFC) established in 1956; affiliated to World Bank; ***International Fund for Agricultural Development*** (IFAD) established in 1977, headquarters in Rome; additional funds for benefiting the poorest in developing countries; ***International Labour Organization*** (ILO) first established in 1919, headquarters in Geneva; ***International Maritime Organization*** (IMO) established in 1958, headquarters in London; ***International Monetary Fund*** (IMF) established in 1945, headquarters in Washington; promotes cooperation, international trade, exchange rate stability, and makes funds available to countries in difficulty subject to conditions; ***International Telecommunication Union*** (ITU) first established in 1934, head-

quarters in Geneva; allocation of radio frequencies; promotes low tariffs and life-saving measures; ***United Nations Educational, Scientific, and Cultural Organization*** (UNESCO) established in 1946, headquarters in Paris, from which the USA, contributor of 25% of its budget, withdrew in 1984 on grounds of its over-politicization, and Britain followed in 1985; ***Universal Postal Union*** (UPU) first established in 1875, headquarters in Berne; collaboration of postal services; ***World Health Organization*** (WHO) established in 1946, headquarters in Geneva; aims at health for all by 2000; ***World Intellectual Property Organization*** (WIPO) established in 1974, headquarters in Geneva; protection of copyright in the arts, science, and industry; ***World Meteorological Organization*** (WMO) established in 1951, headquarters in Geneva; ***Trusteeship Council*** members administer Trust◊ Territories.

International Court of Justice at The Hague, with 15 judges elected by the General Assembly and Security Council; United Nations members are pledged to accept decisions.

Secretariat headed by a Secretary General, Javier Pérez de Cuéllar (b. 1920) of Chile from 1982, who is elected for five years by the General Assembly. There are six official working languages: English, French, Russian, Spanish, Chinese, and Arabic□

United Nations Educational Scientific and Cultural Organization see under United◊ Nations

United States Central Command see under Rapid◊ Deployment Force□

United States of America (USA)

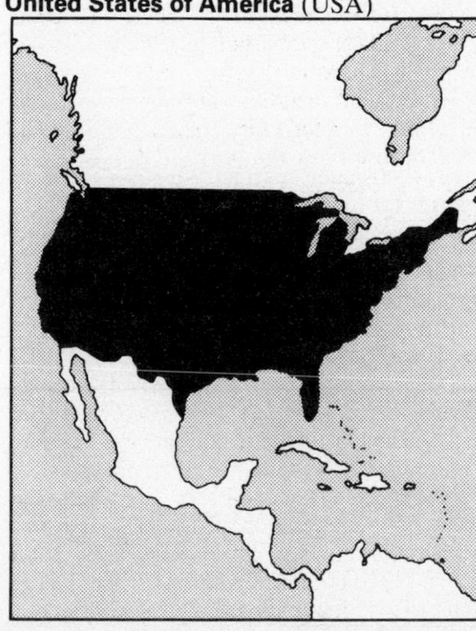

area 9 500 000 sq km/3 536 855 sq mi

capital Washington DC

towns largest cities, New York, Los Angeles, Chicago, Philadelphia, Detroit, San Francisco-Oakland, Washington, Dallas-Fort Worth, Houston, Boston, Nassau-Suffolk, St Louis, Pittsburgh, Baltimore, Minneapolis-St Paul, Atlanta, all metropolitan areas over two million population

currency US dollar

regions the 50 states and District of Columbia (seat of federal government) are usually divided into 10 regions by physical, historical, and economic criteria

Border States Arkansas, Kentucky, Maryland, Missouri, Tennessee, West Virginia ***area*** 622 sq km/240 172 sq mi ***economy*** called the Border States because they separate the traditional differing economic areas, and tend to a balance of agriculture and industry ***population*** 19 224 424.

Mid Atlantic States Delaware, New Jersey, Pennsylvania; ***area*** 143 035 sq km/55 226 sq mi; ***economy*** traditionally industrial with the vast coal, iron and steel area of Pittsburg, but with other industries and agriculture becoming important; ***population*** 19 826 000.

The Midwest Illinois, Indiana, Michigan, Ohio, Wisconsin; ***area*** 642 998 sq km/248 282 sq mi; ***economy*** agricultural, with Wisconsin the premier dairying state of the USA, but with important industries based on the iron ores of Michigan, especially the automobile industry of Chicago/Detroit; ***population*** 41 769 750.

Mountain States Arizona, Colorado, Idaho, Montana, Nevada, New Mexico, Utah, Wyoming; ***area*** 2 237 699 sq km/863 885 sq mi; ***economy*** traditionally based on ranching and mining, but irrigation has increased agricultural production, and Arizona is now the leading cotton state; vast mineral resources include coal (50% of US recoverable reserves); oil (larger reserves than Alaska); uranium (90% of US production); gold (70% US production); silver (50% US production); 50% of the land and 80% of its mineral resources are owned by the federal government; ***population*** 11 368 330.

New England Connecticut, Maine, Massachusetts, New Hampshire, Rhode Island, Vermont; ***area*** 172 516 sq km/66 608 sq mi; ***economy*** agriculture and forestry predominate; but industry and tourism are also important; ***population*** 12 350 000.

New York; area 128 400 sq km/49 576 sq mi; ***economy*** industrially the second most important state; ***population*** 17 557 300.

Pacific States Alaska, California, Hawaii, Oregon, Washington; ***area*** 251 180 sq km/96

981 sq mi; ***economy*** varied as the location of the states, from the tropical crops of Hawaii to the coal, oil, and natural gas of northern Alaska; Oregon is the leading US timber state, Washington also mainly rural, but diversifying; ***population*** 31 796 869, of which nearly 24 million are in California, the most populous US State.

Prairie States Iowa, Kansas, Minnesota, Nebraska, North Dakota, South Dakota; ***area*** 1 159 194 sq km/447 561 sq mi; ***economy*** agriculturally the most important area, Kansas being the premier US wheat state, and Iowa (95% under cultivation) being the wealthiest agricultural state, Nebraska also being very important; N Dakota now also has oil, S Dakota is the second largest US gold producer, and Minnesota mines 60% of US iron ore; ***population*** 12 266 600.

The South Alabama, Florida, Georgia, Louisiana, Mississippi, North Carolina, South Carolina, Virginia; ***area*** 1 009 790 sq km/389 869 sq mi; ***economy*** traditional agriculture is being overtaken by industrialization, Louisiana a leading oil state, Georgia producing kaolin and 30% of the world's phosphates; ***population*** 40 160 000.

The South West Oklahoma, Texas; ***area*** 873 495 sq km/337 258 sq mi; ***economy*** traditionally the realm of the cowboy, it has oil, with Texas supplying one third of US needs, and agriculture is being extended by dry farming; ***population*** 17 273 650.

Outlying Territories the Commonwealths of Puerto Rico, and Northern Marianas; the federated states of Micronesia; Guam, the US Virgin Islands, American Samoa, Wake Island, Midway Islands, Marshall Islands, Belau, and Johnston and Sand Islands.

population 226 505 000, the ethnic minorities include 26 500 000 black, and about 20 million Hispanic◊; one million American Indians (50% concentrated in Arizona, California, New Mexico, North Carolina, Oklahoma)

language English; largest minority language Spanish

religion 73 million Protestant; 50 million Roman Catholic; six million Jewish; four million Eastern orthodox

famous people see under individual states

government under the constitution of 1787, the states are self-governing, but general taxation, foreign affairs, and control of the armed forces are in the hands of the federal government.

Executive power is vested in the president, elected every four years by popularly elected electors for each state (equal to the number of senators and representatives it has in Congress); he or she is eligible for two terms only. The Cabinet, of heads of executive departments, is chosen by the president subject to Senate confirmation, but its members have far less power than their British equivalents, and may not be members of the legislature. Legislative power rests with the two Houses of Congress: the Senate comprises two members for each state, elected for six years, one third re-elected every two years; the House of Representatives comprises 435 members, states being represented in proportion to their population, elected every two years.

history see United States of America: history□

United States of America: history (for early history see North◊ America: history)

1565 first white settlements made (in what later became the USA) by Spain in Florida

1585–86 first English settlement made in Virginia◊ by settlers sent out by Raleigh

1607 first permanent English settlement at Jamestown, Virginia

1620 Pilgrim Fathers◊ landed at Plymouth

1664 New Amsterdam, founded by the Dutch, taken by the English and renamed New York

1775 the Thirteen◊ Colonies rose against the British home government: see American◊ Independence, War of

1776 Declaration of Independence

1783 Treaty of Paris: Britain recognized independence of the Thirteen Colonies

1787 US constitution drawn up

1789 Washington elected as first president

1803 Louisiana◊ Purchase

1812–14 War of 1812 with England, arising from commercial disputes caused by Britain's struggle with Napoleon

1819 Florida purchased from Spain

1823 Monroe◊ Doctrine

1835 Texas proclaimed independence from Mexico

1836 the Alamo◊

1841 first wagon-train left Missouri with emigrants for California

1842 Oregon◊ Trail opened up settlement of the state

1846–8 Mexican War resulted in cession to USA of Arizona, California, Colorado (part), Nevada, New Mexico, Texas, Utah

1846 Mormons, under Brigham Young◊, founded Salt Lake City

1848 California gold rush

1859 John Brown◊ seized US Armoury at Harpers Ferry

1860 Lincoln◊ elected president

1861–5 Civil◊ War

1865 slavery abolished

1865 assassination of Lincoln

1867 Alaska bought from Russia

United States

state	date of admission to union	area	population (1980)	capital
Alabama	1819	133,665	3,893,888	Montgomery
Alaska	1959	1,518,539	401,851	Juneau
Arizona	1912	295,023	2,718,215	Phoenix
Arkansas	1836	137,533	2,286,435	Little Rock
California	1850	411,013	23,667,902	Sacramento
Colorado	1876	270,240	2,889,964	Denver
Connecticut	1788	12,973	3,107,576	Hartford
Delaware	1787	5,328	594,338	Dover
Florida	1845	151,700	9,746,324	Tallahassee
Georgia	1788	152,500	5,463,105	Atlanta
Hawaii	1959	16,705	964,691	Honolulu
Idaho	1890	216,412	943,935	Boise
Illinois	1818	146,075	11,426,518	Springfield
Indiana	1816	93,994	5,490,224	Indianapolis
Iowa	1846	145,790	2,913,808	Des Moines
Kansas	1861	213,063	2,363,679	Topeka
Kentucky	1792	104,623	3,660,777	Frankfort
Louisiana	1812	125,675	4,205,900	Baton Rouge
Maine	1820	86,027	1,124,660	Augusta
Maryland	1788	27,394	4,216,975	Annapolis
Massachusetts	1788	21,385	5,737,037	Boston
Michigan	1837	150,777	9,262,078	Lansing
Minnesota	1858	217,735	4,075,970	St Paul
Mississippi	1817	123,584	2,520,638	Jackson
Missouri	1821	180,455	4,916,686	Jefferson City
Montana	1889	381,085	786,690	Helena
Nebraska	1867	200,036	1,569,825	Lincoln
Nevada	1864	286,300	800,493	Carson City
New Hampshire	1788	24,100	920,610	Concord
New Jersey	1787	20,295	7,364,823	Trenton
New Mexico	1912	315,113	1,302,894	Santa Fé
New York	1788	128,400	17,558,072	Albany
North Carolina	1789	136,523	5,881,766	Raleigh
North Dakota	1889	183,020	652,717	Bismark
Ohio	1803	106,714	10,797,630	Columbus
Oklahoma	1907	181,088	3,025,290	Oklahoma City
Oregon	1859	251,180	2,633,105	Salem
Pennsylvania	1787	117,412	11,863,895	Harrisburg
Rhode Island	1790	3,144	947,154	Providence
South Carolina	1788	80,432	3,121,820	Columbia
South Dakota	1889	199,550	690,768	Pierre
Tennessee	1796	109,412	4,591,120	Nashville
Texas	1845	692,407	14,229,191	Austin
Utah	1896	219,931	1,461,037	Salt Lake City
Vermont	1791	24,887	511,456	Montpelier
Virginia	1788	105,711	5,346,818	Richmond
Washington	1889	176,615	4,132,156	Olympia
West Virginia	1863	62,629	1,949,644	Charleston
Wisconsin	1848	145,438	4,705,767	Madison
Wyoming	1890	253,595	469,557	Cheyenne
District of Columbia	1791	179	638,333	
		9,363,404	226,545,805	

1872 first National Park (Yellowstone) established
1890 Battle of Wounded◊ Knee, the last major battle between American Indians and US troops
1898 war with Spain ended with the Spanish cession of Philippines, Puerto Rico, and Guam; also agreed that Cuba be independent
1898 Hawaii annexed
1903 Panama declared independent with US support and signed treaty for Panama◊ Canal
1917–18 USA entered World War I
1929 Wall◊ Street crash
1933 F D Roosevelt◊'s New Deal put into force
1941–5 Pearl◊ Harbor precipitated US entry into World War II
1946 Philippines granted independence
1947 Truman◊ Doctrine
1963 assassination of President Kennedy◊
1964–73 Vietnam◊ War – direct intervention by USA
1972 Richard Nixon◊ visited Peking and Moscow
1974 Nixon resigned as a consequence of Watergate◊
1979–80 Iran hostages crisis negotiations by Carter
1980 Carter◊ Doctrine
1980 Reagan◊ won landslide victory
1985 Geneva summit, Reagan-Gorbachev□

United States of America: Presidents

1. George Washington (*Federalist*) 1789
2. John Adams (*Federalist*) 1797
3. Thomas Jefferson (*Democrat Rep.*) 1801
4. James Madison (*Democrat Rep.*) 1809
5. James Monroe (*Democrat Rep.*) 1817
6. John Quincy Adams (*Democrat Rep.*) 1825
7. Andrew Jackson (*Democrat*) 1829
8. Martin Van Buren (*Democrat*) 1837
9. William Henry Harrison (*Whig*) 1841
10. John Tyler (*Whig*) 1841
11. James Knox Polk (*Democrat*) 1845
12. Zachary Taylor (*Whig*) 1849
13. Millard Fillmore (*Whig*) 1850
14. Franklin Pierce (*Democrat*) 1853
15. James Buchanan (*Democrat*) 1857
16. Abraham Lincoln (*Republican*) 1861
17. Andrew Johnson (*Democrat*) 1865
18. Ulysses Simpson Grant (*Republican*) 1869
19. Rutherford Birchard Hayes (*Republican*) 1877
20. James Abram Garfield (*Republican*) 1881
21. Chester Alan Arthure (*Republican*) 1881
22. Grover Cleveland (*Democrat*) 1885
23. Benjamin Harrison (*Republican*) 1889
24. Grover Cleveland (*Democrat*) 1893
25. William McKinley (*Republican*) 1897
26. Theodore Roosevelt (*Republican*) 1901
27. William Howard Taft (*Republican*) 1909
28. Woodrow Wilson (*Democrat*) 1913
29. Warren Gamaliel Harding (*Republican*) 1921
30. Calvin Coolidge (*Republican*) 1923
31. Herbert C. Hoover (*Republican*) 1929
32. Franklin Delano Roosevelt (*Democrat*) 1933
33. Harry S. Truman (*Democrat*) 1945
34. Dwight D. Eisenhower (*Republican*) 1953
35. John F. Kennedy (*Democrat*) 1961
36. Lyndon B. Johnson (*Democrat*) 1963
37. Richard M. Nixon (*Republican*) 1969
38. Gerald R. Ford (*Republican*) 1974
39. 'Jimmy' Carter (*Democrat*) 1977
40. Ronald Reagan (*Republican*) 1981

United World Colleges international educational movement open to all students aged 16–18 (under a scholarship system); it was the inspiration of Kurt Hahn◊. Its curriculum demands both academic achievement and service to the community. It consists of six colleges worldwide□

Universal Postal Union see under United◊ Nations□

universe the overall celestial system, containing thousands of millions of star-systems or galaxies: see under star◊. It is generally accepted that it originated in a 'big bang' some 20 thousand million years ago, and that it is either expanding indefinitely, or will collapse back into a fireball, perhaps to expand once more. The first stars would have originated soon after the 'big bang', when the universe consisted of dense gas□

unnilennium element
symbol Une
atomic number 109
features artificial transuranic◊ element, first synthesized 1974□

unnilhexium element
symbol Unh
atomic number 106
features artificial transuranic◊ element, first synthesized 1974□

unniloctium element
symbol Uno
atomic number 108
features artificial transuranic◊ element, first synthesized 1981□

unnilpentium element
symbol Unp
atomic number 105

features artificial transuranic◊ element. Credit for its discovery is disputed between USA (who named it ***hahnium***) and USSR (who named it ***nielsbohrium***)□

unnilquadium element
symbol Unq
atomic number 104
features artificial transuranic◊ element, also named *kurchatovium* and *rutherfordium* by teams in the USSR and USA who synthesized the element independently of each other in 1964□

unnilseptium element
symbol Uns
atomic number 107
features artificial transuranic◊ element, first synthesized 1976□

Upanishads an ancient collection of treatises, forming part of the Vedic writings. See Hinduism◊□

upas tree Asian tree *Antiaria toxicaria*, family Moraceae, with a poisonous latex used for poison arrows, and formerly reputed to kill all who fell asleep under it□

Updike John (Hoyer) 1932– . American author, born in Pennsylvania. He established his reputation with the novel *Couples* 1968, about married life in the contemporary USA. His work includes two series of novels and short stories about 'Rabbit' Angstrom (baseball player), and Bech (a Jewish-American novelist)□

Upper Volta former name of Burkina Faso□

Ur a city of the Sumerian civilization. See Iraq◊□

Urania in Greek mythology, the Muse◊ of astronomy□

uranium element
symbol U
atomic number 92
physical description blue-white metal
features radioactive; found in ***pitchblende***
uses to give pottery a yellow glaze, in glassmaking and as a mordant in dyeing; the radioisotope U-235 (the only naturally-occurring nuclear fission fuel) is used both in the atom bomb, and in controlled fission, in nuclear reactors. The USA, Australia, Brazil, etc., have large resources□

Uranus in Greek mythology, the sky-god, responsible both for the sun and rain, he was the son and husband of Gaia◊, by whom he fathered the Titans◊□

Uranus the seventh planet from the sun
mean distance from the sun 2 870 000 000 km/1 783 000 000 mi
diameter 50 800 km/ mi
rotation period 10 hr 49 min
year (sidereal period) 84 years
atmosphere greenish, thought to resemble that of Neptune, with cloud layers of methane and perhaps ammonia
surface temperature −213°C
surface no solid surface. Interior mainly hydrogen and helium
features low density
ring system about nine thin, ropelike, dark rings, composed of methane ice blackened by interaction with the radiation field
satellites 12 now known:
Miranda, Ariel, Umbriel, Titania and ***Oberon***, apparently all circular and forming a compact system, and seven others discovered by spacecraft *Voyager II* in 1985-6□

Urdu official language◊ of Pakistan, closely related to Hindi◊□

urinary system

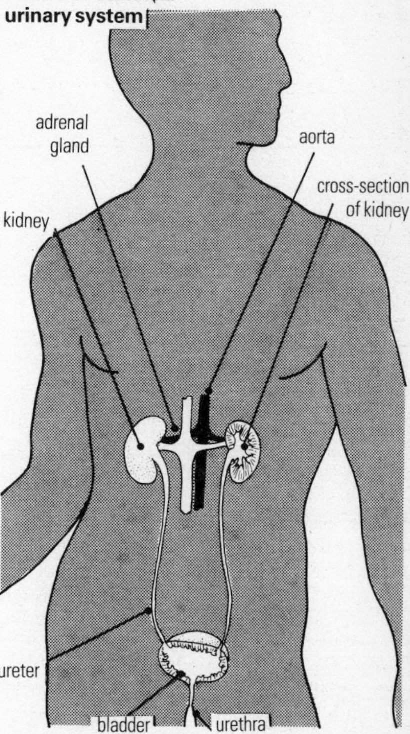

urinary system the organs of the human body concerned with the excretion of liquid waste matter. The body, to be healthy, must contain water and various salts in the right proportions. The blood is therefore filtered in the two kidneys, which remove such water and salts as are not needed. These, with a yellow pigment derived from bile, form the urine, which passes down through two fine tubes (ureters) into the bladder, a reservoir, from which the urine is emptied at intervals (micturition) through the uretha□

Uruguay Republic of

area 196 945 sq km/72 180 sq mi
capital Montevideo
features smallest of the S American republics; rivers Negro and Uruguay
exports meat and meat products; leather and wool; textiles
currency nuevo peso
population 2 960 000, mainly of Spanish and Italian descent, also Mestizo, Mulatto and Negro
language Spanish
religion Roman Catholicism 60%
government president (Julio María Sanguinetti Cairolo from 1985), senate and chamber of deputies
recent history formerly a province of Brazil, Uruguay declared independence in 1828, and maintained a democratic tradition until the growth of corruption after World War II led to the formation of a left-wing guerrilla movement, the Tupamaros (see terrorism◊). Following military intervention in 1973, civilian government was not restored until the elections of 1984 under a new constitution□

Urumchi see Ürümqi◊□

Ürümqi (formerly Urumchi) industrial city (textiles, cement, chemicals, steel) and capital of the autonomous region of Xinjiang, China; population 800 000□

Üsküdar see under Istanbul◊

Utah mountain state of the USA; Beehive State

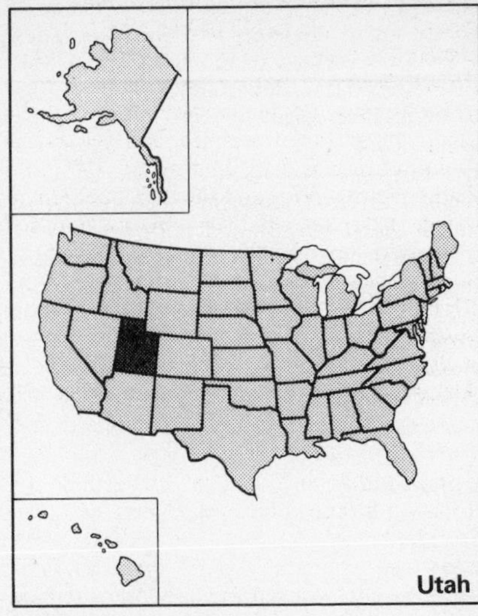

area 219 931 sq km/84 915 sq mi
capital Salt Lake City
features Great Salt Lake; Great American Desert; Colorado rivers system; Dinosaur National Monument; Rainbow Bridge
products wool; gold, silver, uranium, coal, salt; steel
population 1 461 037
famous people Brigham Young
history part of the area ceded by Mexico in 1848, it was developed by the Mormons, still the largest religious sect in the state. Organized as a territory in 1850, it was not admitted to statehood until 1896 because of Mormon reluctance to relinquish plural marriage□

Utamaro Kitagawa 1753–1806. Japanese print artist who produced naturalistic colour portraits of prostitutes, etc.□

UTC abbreviation for Co-ordinated Universal Time, the standard measurement of time◊□

Utica industrial city (textiles, firearms) in New York State, USA; population 75 500. The first Woolworth store was opened here 1879□

utilitarianism philosophy outlined by Bentham◊, and developed by James Mill◊ and J S Mill◊. In J S Mill's formulation, 'actions are right in proportion as they tend to promote happiness, wrong as they tend to produce the reverse of happiness'. Thus, we should aim for the greatest happiness of the greatest number. Its chief opponents were F H Bradley◊ and T H Green◊□

Utopia Sir Thomas More's ideal commonwealth in his *Utopia* 1516: other similar inventions include Plato's *Republic*; Bacon's *New Atlantis* 1626. Huxley's *Brave New World* is an example of the reverse (dystopia)□

Utrecht industrial city (metallurgy, textiles) in central Netherlands; population 234 550□

Utrecht Peace of. See War of the Spanish◊ Succession□

Uttar Pradesh state of northern India
area 294 413 sq km/113 643 sq mi
capital Lucknow
towns Varanasi
features most populous state, formerly the heart of the Mogul Empire, and generating point of the Indian Mutiny of 1857 and subsequent opposition to British rule; Himalayan peak, Nanda Devi 7817 m/25 645 ft
population 110 886 000
famous people Lal Bahadur Shastri, Indira Gandhi *music* Ravi Shankar
language Hindi
religion Hinduism 80%; Islam 15%□

Uzbekistan constituent republic of the SE Soviet Union from 1925, part of Soviet Central Asia
area 447 600 sq km/157 400 sq mi
capital Tashkent
towns Samarkand
features oases in the deserts, rivers Amu Darya, and Syr Darya, Fergana Valley
products rice, dried fruit, vines, grown by irrigation; cotton, silk
population 15 800 000; 65% Uzbek, 13% Russian
language Uzbek, related to Turkish
religion traditionally Sunni Islam
recent history part of Turkestan, it was conquered by Russia 1865-76□

V

Vaal see under Orange◊ river□

vaccine modified preparation of viruses, bacteria, etc., used to inoculate healthy persons, so as to induce the general reaction which produces immunity. Edward Jenner◊ in 1796 first successfully inoculated a child with cowpox virus to produce immunity to smallpox□

vaccinium genus of berried bushes of the northern hemisphere, family Ericaceae◊, especially commercially valuable in N America. It includes the bluish ***bilberry,*** or ***whortleberry*** *V myrtillus*; ***blueberry*** or ***huckleberry*** *V pennsylvanicum*; and the red ***cranberry*** *V oxycoccus*□

vacuum a region completely empty of matter, but, since this is very difficult to achieve, normally taken to mean any enclosure in which the gas pressure is considerably less than the atmosphere□

vacuum cleaner cleaning device invented in 1901 by Scotsman Hubert Cecil Booth 1871–1955. Having seen an ineffective dust-blowing machine, he reversed the process so that his machine (originally on wheels, and operated from the street by means of tubes running into the house) operated by suction□

vacuum flask originally known as a Dewar vessel (see James Dewar◊), it consists of a double-walled container, the space between being a vacuum, so that the contents are kept either hot or chilled. It was invented by James Dewar c1892 to store liquified gases□

Vadodara (formerly Baroda) industrial city and rail junction, Gujerat, India; population 744 000□

Vaduz capital of Liechtenstein; population 4650□

Valdai Hills small forested plateau between Leningrad and Moscow, where the Volga and W Dvina rivers rise. The Viking founders of the Russian state used it as a river route centre to reach the Baltic, Black, Caspian, and White Seas. From the 15th century it was dominated by Moscow□

Valdivia industrial port (foundries, furniture) and resort in Chile; population 115 700□

Valencia industrial city and agricultural centre in Venezuela; population 367 000□

Valencia industrial city in Valencia region, Spain; population 751 735. Ruled by El◊ Cid 1094–99, after he recaptured it from the Moors. There is a fine cathedral of the 13–15th centuries, and a university founded in 1500□

Valencia autonomous region of E Spain (including Alicante, Castellón, Valencia), formerly an independent kingdom; population 3 646 800. It is famous for the exploits of El◊ Cid, who reconquered it from the Moors□

valency the measure of an element's ability to combine with other elements, expressed as the number of atoms of hydrogen (or any other standard univalent element) capable of uniting with (or replacing) its atoms. Some elements have ***variable valency***, e.g. nitrogen and phosphorous, both 3 and 5□

Valentine St d. 270. According to tradition a bishop of Terni martyred at Rome, now omitted from the calendar of saints' days as probably non-existent. His festival was on 14 Feb, but the custom of sending 'valentines' to a loved one on that day seems to have arisen because the day accidentally coincided with the Roman mid-Feb festival of Lupercalia◊□

Valentino Rudolf 1895–1926. Italian film actor, the archetype romantic lover of the Hollywood silent films. His films include *The Four Horsemen of the Apocalypse* 1921, *The Sheik* 1922, and *Blood and Sand* 1922□

Valera see de◊ Valera□

valerian genus of perennial plants of the temperate north, family Valerianaceae; the roots of ***allheal*** *Valeriana officinalis* are the source of a sedative□

Valéry Paul 1871–1945. French mathematician, philosopher, and poet, with a high intellectual content in his verse, e.g. *La Jeune Parque* 1917, and the later *Le Cimetière marin* 1920 and *Charmes* 1922□

Valhalla in Norse mythology, the palace where Odin◊ feasts with the heroes of mortal battles□

Valkyries in Norse mythoogy, the female attendants of Odin◊□

Valladolid industrial town (food processing, textiles, engineering) in Castilla-León, Spain; population 330 245. The home of Cervantes◊ is preserved, and Columbus◊ died here□

Valle d'Aosta special autonomous region of NW Italy; capital Aosta; population 113 450, many of whom are French-speaking□

Valle-Inclén Ramón María del 1866–1936. Spanish novelist, e.g. his poetic prose *Sonatas* 1902–5 and, set in S America, *Tirano Banderas* 1926□

Valletta capital and port (with large repair yards) of Malta; population 14 050. Founded in 1566 by the Knights Hospitallers◊, it was named after their Grand Master Jean de la Valette 1494–1568, who fended off a Turkish siege May–Sept 1565. The 16th-century palace of the Grand Masters survives. Malta was formerly a British naval base, and was under heavy attack in World War II□

Valley Forge see War of American◊ Independence□

Valley of Ten Thousand Smokes see under Alaska◊□

Valley of the Kings see under Thebes◊□

Valmy Battle of. See under Revolutionary◊ Wars□

Valois branch of the Capetian dynasty (see Hugh Capet◊) in France, which began with Philip◊ VI and ended with Henry◊ III in 1589□

Valparaiso industrial port and commercial city in Chile; population 266 725. Founded in 1536, it was occupied by Drake◊ in 1578, and Hawkins◊ in 1595. It is prone to earthquakes□

vampire in Slav demonology, a corpse which returns to 'life' by sucking the blood of the living; see Dracula◊, and also under bat◊, finch◊, and porphyria◊□

vanadium element
symbol V
atomic number 23
physical description silvery-white metal
features a trace is found in the human body
uses in high-speed steels; compounds used in leather dyeing, the ceramic and glass industries, and the manufacture of sulphuric acid□

Van Allen James Alfred 1914– . US physicist. A pioneer of rocket research, he discovered in 1958 (from data supplied by two *Explorer* earth satellites) the ***Van Allen belts*** of particles from the sun trapped by earth's field. They form two zones of intense radiation between altitudes 2400 km/1500 mi and 20 000 km/12 000 mi. See atmosphere◊□

Vanbrugh Sir John 1664–1726. English architect and comic dramatist, whose works include Blenheim Palace and the plays *The Relapse* 1696 and *The Provok'd Wife* 1697□

Van Buren Martin 1782–1862. US Democrat President 1837–41□

Vance Cyrus 1917– . US Democrat Secretary of State 1977–80, when he resigned because unable to support Carter's abortive mission to rescue the US hostages in Iran□

Vancouver island off British Columbia, Canada; area 32 136 sq km/12 408 sq mi. The capital is Victoria; Esquimalt is a naval base. Its chief products are coal, timber and fish□

Vancouver industrial city (oil refining, engineering, shipbuilding) in mainland British Columbia; population 1 268 185. The terminus of the Canadian Pacific Railway, it has an international airport, and two universities. The site was claimed for Britain by George Vancouver◊ in 1792, and the city was founded by the Hudson's Bay Company in 1825□

Vancouver George c1758–98. British navigator, who served under Cook, and in his own Pacific voyage 1791–4 circumnavigated Vancouver Island, named after him□

Vandals Germanic people related to the Goths◊. In the 5th century AD they moved from N Germany to invade Roman Gaul and Spain, many settling in Andalusia (formerly Vandalitia) and others reaching N Africa in 429. They accepted Roman suzerainty in the 6th century□

Vane John 1923– . British pharmacologist. From 1973 in charge of the Wellcome◊ research centre, he discovered the wide role of prostaglandins in the human body, especially in response to illness and stress, sharing a Nobel prize in 1982□

Van Eyck Jan c1390–1441, who with his brother ***Hubert*** c1370–1426, was one of the earliest masters of Flemish oil painting. He served as court painter to Philip the Good, Duke of Burgundy. His portraits are marvels of delicate exactitude, e.g. *The Marriage of Giovanni Arnolfini* 1434□

vanilla flavouring derived from the dried fruits of the orchid *Vanilla planifolia*; also now produced synthetically□

Vanuatu Republic of
area 14 750 sq km/5700 sq mi
capital Vila on Efate
features comprises about 70 islands, the chief including Espiritu Santo, Malekala, and Efate; there are three active volcanoes
exports copra, fish, coffee; tourism is important
currency vatu
population 130 000, 90% Melanesian
language Bislama (Pidgin◊), English, French, all official
religion Anglican 14%; Presbyterian 40%; Roman Catholic 16%; Animist 15%
government there is a president, and representative assembly (Prime Minister Father

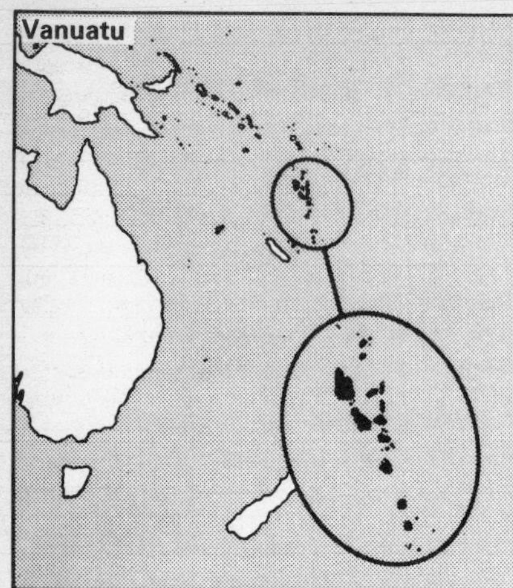

Walter Lini from 1980), and national council of chiefs
recent history formerly the New Hebrides, the islands were administered jointly by Britain and France 1906–80, when they became Vanuatu (the name means 'Our Land'). There was some secessionist activity, especially on Espiritu Santo□

Varah Chad. See under Samaritans◊□

Varanasi (Benares) holy city of the Hindus in Uttar Pradesh, India; population 794 000. There are 1500 golden shrines, and a 5 km/3 mi frontage to the Ganges with sacred stairways (ghats) for purification by bathing. At the burning ghats, the ashes of the dead are scattered on the river to ensure a favourable reincarnation□

Vatican City State

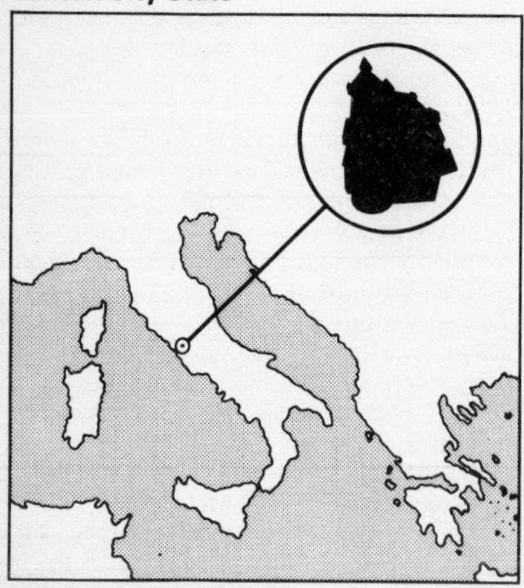

area 0.4 sq km/109 acres
features forms an enclave in the heart of Rome, including Vatican Palace, official residence of the Pope; the basilica and square of St Peter's; also includes a number of churches in and near Rome; the Pope's summer villa at Castel Gandolfo
currency issues its own coinage, which circulates together with that of Italy
population 1000
language Italian
government the Pope has absolute legislative, executive, and judicial powers, but delegates the government to a commission
recent history following the incorporation of the Papal States (see Papacy◊) into a united Italy in 1870, long-drawn negotiations ended in the creation in 1929 of the Vatican City State (see concordat◊)□

Vaughan Williams Ralph 1872–1958. British composer, born at Down Ampney, Gloucestershire. Works include choral arrangements of poems *Towards the Unknown Region* (Whitman) 1907; *On Wenlock Edge* (Housman) 1909; *A Sea Symphony* 1910; and the best-known setting of *Greensleeves*. Order of Merit in 1935.□

vector any physical quantity that has both magnitude and direction, such as the velocity or acceleration of a body, as distinct from a scalar◊ quantity (which has magnitude but no direction, e.g. speed, density, or mass)□

Veda see under Hinduism◊□

Veda one of four Sanskrit books, sacred in Hinduism◊□

Velázquez Don Diego de Silva y 1599–1660. Spanish painter, born in Seville. In 1623 he became court painter to Philip IV, the subject of some of Velázquez's greatest paintings. His work owes much to Titian◊, Rubens◊, and Tintoretto◊□

veld or ***veldt*** the open grassland plateau of S Africa□

Vence see Nice◊

Venda Black◊ National State from 1979, within South Africa
area 6500 sq km/25 100 sq mi
capital Thohoyandu
towns MaKearela
features homeland of the Vhavenda
exports coal, graphite, construction stone
population 400 000
language Luvenda, English
government executive president (paramount chief P R Mphephu) and national assembly□

Vendée War of the Peasant rising 1793–5 in the Western French Department of la Vendée against the Revolutionary government□

Vendôme Louis Joseph, Duc de Vendôme 1654–1712. Marshal of France, who lost his command after defeat by Marlborough◊ at Oudenarde◊ in 1708□

venereal disease (VD) any disease transmitted by sexual intercourse (from Latin *Venus* 'love'). See Aids◊, cancer◊, gonorrhoea◊, herpes◊, syphilis◊□

Veneto region of NE Italy; capital Venice, with industrial centres at Padua, Verona, and Vicenza; population 4 355 000. It includes part of the N Italian plain, as well as part of the Alps and Dolomites; products include cereals, fruit and vegetables, and wine□

Venezia see Venice◊□

Venezuela Republic of

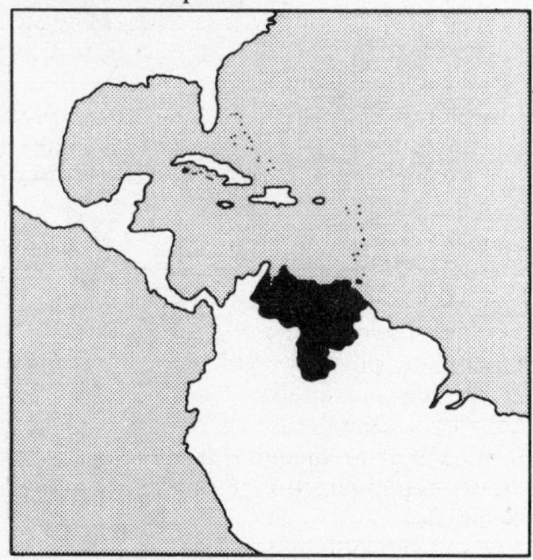

area 912 068 sq km/352 150 sq mi
capital Caracas
towns Barquisimeto, Valencia, and the port of Maracaibo
features Lake Maracaibo, River Orinoco, Angel Falls; unique flora and fauna; annual rainfall over 7600 mm/300 in
exports coffee, cocoa; timber; oil, aluminium, iron ore, petrochemicals
currency bolívar
population 16 000 000, 70% mestizos, but including 32 000 American Indians
religion Roman Catholicism
language Spanish (official), Indian languages 2%
famous people Simon Bolívar
government under the 1958 constitution there is an executive president (Jaime Lusinchi, Democratic Action, from 1984) and senate and chamber of deputies, all elected for five years
recent history independent from Spain, in a union with Colombia, it became a separate country in 1830. Exploited for its oil under Juan Vicente Gómez, in effect military dictator 1910–35, Venezuela developed a stable democracy through its new wealth. There are border disputes with Colombia and Guyana□

Venice (Italian *Venezia*) city, port, and naval base, capital of Veneto, on the Adriatic; population 346 000. The old city is built on piles in low-lying islands, and till recently suffered much flooding after the development of the industrial area (Mestre) and port (Porto Marghera) to the west of the Lagoon of Venice (on the marshy mainland) and the natural rise of the sea level. Traditional industries include glass, jewellery, textiles, lace, and book production. The Grand Canal divides the city and is crossed by the Rialto bridge; transport is by traditional gondola or modern motor boat. Features include St Mark's Square, on which stand the campanile, 11th-century Byzantine cathedral of St Mark, and the 14–15th-century Gothic Doge's Palace (linked to the state prison by the Bridge of Sighs). The nearby Lido is a holiday resort. The ***Venetian School*** of artists includes the Bellinis, Carpaccio, Giorgione, Titian, Tintoretto, and Veronese.
history founded in the 5th century by refugees from mainland cities sacked by the Huns, it became a wealthy independent trading republic (governed by an aristocratic oligarchy, the Council of Ten and the Senate, which appointed the Doge, or chief magistrate, 697–1797). It even crushed the Turks in the naval battle of Lepanto◊, but was overthrown by Napoleon in 1797. In 1815 Venice passed to Austria, but finally became part of the kingdom of Italy in 1866□

Venturi Robert 1925– . American Postmodernist architect. His works include Guild House 1963 in his native Philadelphia. In 1986 he was commissioned to design the extension to the National Gallery, London□

Venus the second planet from the sun
mean distance from the sun 108 000 000 km/67 000 000 mi
diameter 12 104km/7517 mi
rotation period 243.5 days
year (sidereal period) 224.7 days
atmosphere three times as much carbon dioxide and nitrogen as earth; three times as much krypton; 75 times as much argon, and 45 times as much neon; negligible water; and suspended in this very turbulent atmosphere are dense clouds of sulphuric acid droplets
surface temperature 480°C/900°F, high enough to melt lead
surface rolling upland plains rising to 2000 m/6560 ft; heavily cratered granitic crust (either impact or volcanic craters, which are eroded or lava-filled). There are two higher plateaux or 'continents': ***Aphrodite Terra***, half the size of Africa, and ***Ishtar Terra***, which includes the highest point, Maxwell Montes 10 600 m/35 000 ft. Any former oceans appear to have evaporated into space possibly through the 'greenhouse◊ effect', and their

disappearance would also have ended any life which may have existed on the planet. The surface seems to be similar to earth's volcanic rock.
features the nearest planet to earth (it may approach within 38 000 000 km/24 000 000 mi). Unlike other planets it is quite round, and rotates more slowly than any other, as well as in the opposite direction to all except Uranus. It radiates 15% more energy than it receives from the sun, and its volcanoes are still active, an eruption in 1978 having been more powerful than that of Krakatoa◊ in 1883. Lightning discharges are apparently formed in brilliantly coloured volcanic clouds of sulphuric acid droplets. The sky is bright orange.
ring system none
satellites none□

Venus in Roman mythology, the goddess of love□

Venus's fly trap see insectivorous◊ plants□

Veracruz city and port in Mexico, first founded on a nearby site by Cortés; population 305 460□

verbena mainly tropical family (Verbeuaceae) of flowering plants, with tubular flowers arranged in close spikes and ranging from white to purple□

Vercingetorix d. c45BC Gallic chieftain who led a revolt against Roman rule 52BC. He was displayed in Caesar's triumph 46BC, and later executed□

Verdi Giuseppe (Fortunino Francesco) 1813–1901. Italian composer, born at Busseto, near Parma. He wrote a symphony at 15, and in 1842 achieved success with his opera *Nabucco*, followed by *Ernani* 1844 and *Rigoletto* 1851, based on Hugo◊'s plays *Hernani* and *Le Roi s'amuse; Il Trovatore* and *La Traviata* both 1853; *Aida* 1871, and the masterpieces of his old age *Otello* 1887 and *Falstaff* 1893. His *Requiem* 1874 commemorates Alessandro Manzoni◊□

verdigris a basic copper acetate and irritant formerly used in wood preservatives, antifouling compositions and green paint□

Verlaine Paul 1844–96. French lyrical poet, born at Metz. At first influenced by Baudelaire◊, he wandered France, Belgium, and England with Rimbaud◊ 1871–3 until sentenced to two years in prison for attempting to shoot him. His volumes, *Poèmes saturniens* 1866, *Fêtes galantes* 1869 (inspired by Watteau◊) and *Romances sans paroles* 1874, gave a new music to French verse. After having touched bottom in alcoholism and dissipation, he regained his Roman Catholic faith in *Sagesse* 1888□

Vermeer Jan 1632–75. Dutch artist, born in Delft, of whose life little is known. He is highly regarded for his use of light and for an exquisite sense of balance and proportion in his depiction of domestic scenes. His works include *A View of Delft* (Mauritshuis, The Hague)□

Vermont New England state of the USA; Green Mountain State

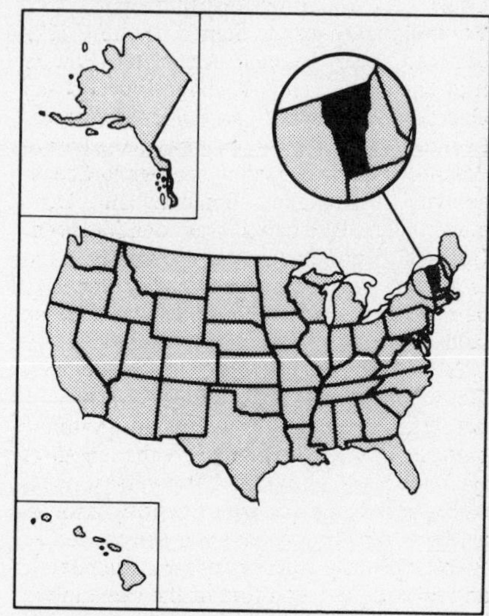

area 24 887 sq km/9608 sq mi
capital Montpelier
features noted for brilliant foliage in the autumn, and winter sports; Green mountains; Lake Champlain
products apples, maple syrup, dairy products; china clay, asbestos, granite, marble, slate; business machines, furniture, paper
population 511 456
famous people Alistair Cooke
history settled in 1724, it became a state in 1791. The Green Mountain Boys were irregulars (see Ethan Allen◊) who fought to keep Vermont from New York interference□

vermouth fortified wine flavoured with bitter herbs made especially in France and Italy□

Veronese Paolo 1528–88. Italian artist, born in Verona. A versatile draughtsman and master of colour, he excelled in banquets and pageantry, e.g. *The Family of Darius at the Feet of Alexander*, all in 16th-century dress□

Verrochia Andrea del 1435–88. Italian sculpture and goldsmith, born in Florence, who worked for the Medici◊. His sculptures include *Christ* and *St Thomas* in Or San Michele, Florence, and the equestrian statue of Bartolomeo Calleoni, Venice. Leonardo da Vinci and Perugino were his pupils□

Versailles city in N France; population 97 130. It grew up round the palace of Louis XV, where the German Empire was proclaimed 1871 after the France-Prussian◊ War, and (in revenge) the Treaty of Versailles was signed by a defeated Germany after World War I. Within the palace park are two small chateaux, Le Grand and Le Petit Trianon, built for Louis XIV (by Hardouin-Mansard) and Louis XV (by Gabriel) respectively□

Versailles Treaty of. Signed 28 June 1919 between the Allies and Associated Powers (the USA being an Associated Power), and Germany. The latter surrendered Alsace-Lorraine◊ to France. large areas in the east to Poland, and made smaller cessions to Czechozlovakia, Lithuania, Belgium, and Denmark. The Rhineland was demilitarized, German rearmament was restricted, and Germany accepted responsibility for war damage for which reparations were to be paid. The treaty was never ratified by the USA, a separate peace being made with Germany and Austria 1921□

verse arrangement of words in rhythmic pattern, which may depend on the length of syllables (as in Greek or Latin verse), or on stress, as in English. ***rhyme*** (identity of sound in the endings of words) was introduced to Western European verse in late Latin poetry, and ***alliteration*** (repitition of the same initial letter in successive words) was the dominant feature of Anglo-Saxon poetry. Both these elements helped to make verse easily remembered in the days when it was spoken rather than written. The pattern imposed by a rhyme scheme, such as the four-line ballad◊ metre abab; the Spenserian Stanza (so-called because Spenser◊ used it in *The Faerie Queen* which rhymes ababbcbcc; and the Shakespearean sonnet (first devised by Surrey◊) abab, cdcd, efef, gg, presents the poet with a challenge that stimulates creativity. ***blank verse*** as used by Marlowe◊, Shakespeare◊, and Milton, develops an inner cohesion which replaces the props provided by rhyme and stanza. ***free verse*** lacks rhyme, stanza form, and any obvious rhythmical basis, so that it needs either to be remarkably good or mercifully short□

vertebrate any animal with a backbone, i.e. mammals (including man), birds, reptiles, amphibians, fish; in all some 21 000 species□

Verulamium see St◊ Albans□

Verus Lucius Aurelius. Joint Roman emperor with Marcus◊ Aurelius 161–9AD□

Verwoerd Hendrik Frensch 1901–66. S African statesman. As Minister of Native Affairs 1950–8, he did much to improve black city housing, but was also the chief promoter of apartheid◊ legislation. Prime Minister from 1958, he made the country a republic in 1961. He was assassinated in the House of Assembly by a parliamentary messenger, Mozambique-born Dimitri Tsafendas□

Vespasian (*Titus Flavius Vespasianus*) 9–79AD. Roman emperor from 69, when he was so proclaimed by his troops while campaigning in Palestine. He began the construction of the Colosseum◊□

Vespers Sicilian. Massacre of the French rulers in Sicily in 1282, signalled by vesper bells on Easter Monday□

Vespucci Amerigo 1454–1512. Florentine navigator; the Americas are named after him because of the widespread circulation of his accounts of his explorations, of which the veracity is disputed□

Vesta in Roman mythology, the goddess of the hearth (Greek ***Hestia***). The sacred flame in her shrine in the Forum was kept constantly lit by the six ***Vestal Virgins***. See also under Athena◊□

Vesuvius active volcano south east of Naples; height 1277 m/4190 ft. In 79BC it destroyed Pompeii◊, Herculaneum◊, and Oplonti, which are still under excavation□

vetch several genera of trailing/climbing plants, family Leguminosae◊, with pinnate leaves and purple flowers, e.g. the fodder crop *Vicia sativa*. To the same genus belong the ***tares*** which are common weeds on cultivated land□

Veterans Day in the USA the name adopted for Armistice◊ Day in 1954, and from 1971 observed by most states on the 4th Monday in October; in Canada the 11th November is observed as Remembrance◊ Day□

veto exercise by a sovereign, branch of legislative, or other political power, of the right to prevent the enactment or operation of a law, or the taking of some course of action. In Britain the sovereign has a right to refuse assent to any measure passed by Parliament, but this has not been exercised since the 18th century; the House of Lords also has a suspensory veto on any except finance measures, but this is comparatively seldom exercised. At the United◊ Nations the members of the Security Council can exercise a veto on resolutions□

Viburnum genus of temperate and subtropical trees and shrubs, family Caprifoliaceae, e.g. ***wayfaring tree*** *V lantana* with white flowers, and oval red-black fruits; ***laurustinus*** *V tinus* with clusters of white flowers in winter, and ***guelder rose*** *V opulus*, with red translucent fruits□

vicar a church of England clergyman. See under rector◊□

Vicenza city in Veneto region, NE Italy; population 113 000. Textiles and musical instruments are made here, and it has a 13th-century cathedral and many buildings by Palladio◊, including the Teatro Olimpico finally completed in 1583□

Vichy health resort with thermal springs, known to the Romans, in Auvergne region, central France; population 33 000. It was the seat of Pétain◊'s government 1940–4, hence 'Vichy France', i.e. that part of France not occupied by German troops until Nov 1942□

Victor Emmanuel two kings of Italy:

Victor Emmanuel II 1820–78, first King of united Italy from 1861. King of Sardinia from 1849, he backed France and Britain in the Crimean War. In alliance with the French in 1859, he defeated the Austrians and annexed Lombardy, and brought the rest of the peninsula under his rule, making Rome his capital in 1870.

Victor Emmanuel III 1869–1947, King from the assassination of his father Umberto I in 1900, he acquiesced in the Fascist regime, and abdicated in 1946. See his son Umberto◊ II□

Victoria 1819–1901. Queen of the UK from 1837. Daughter of Edward, Duke of Kent, fourth son of George III, she succeeded her uncle William IV. In 1840 she married Albert◊, by whom she had four sons and five daughters (see Frederick◊ III), and after Albert's death in 1861 lived mainly in retirement. Nevertheless, she kept control of affairs, refusing the Prince of Wales (Edward VII) any active role, and her relations with her prime ministers ranged from the affectionate (Melbourne and Disraeli, the latter making her Empress of India in 1876) to the stormy (Peel, Palmerston, and Gladstone). Her favourite homes were Balmoral◊ and Osborne◊ House. Her golden jubilee in 1887 and diamond jubilee in 1897, marked a waning of republican sentiment which had developed with her withdrawal from public life. Her *Letters* and *Journal of Our Life in the Highlands* are of interest□

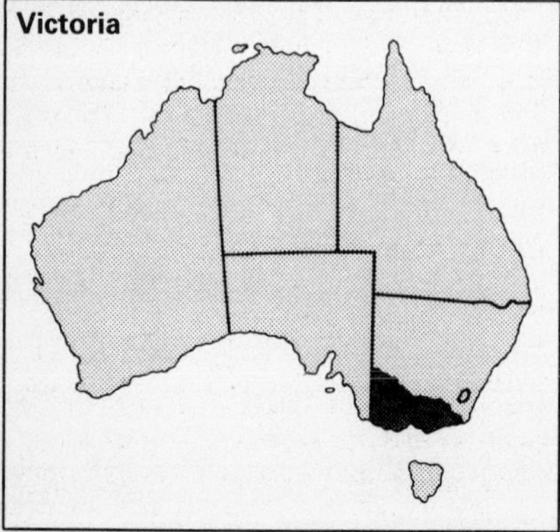

Victoria state of the Commonwealth of Australia

area 227 620 sq km/87 884 sq mi

capital Melbourne

towns Geelong, Ballarat, Bendigo

features part of Great Dividing Range runs east–west, and includes the larger part of the Australian Alps; Gippsland lakes, shallow lagoons on the coast. See also Mallee◊

products sheep, beef cattle, dairy products, wheat; vines for wine and dried fruit, orchard fruits, vegetables; gold, brown coal (Latrobe Valley), oil and natural gas in Bass Strait

population 3 948 555, 71% living in the Melbourne area

history reached by Europeans (Cook) in 1770, Victoria was settled in the 1830s. In 1851, after being part of New South Wales, it was created a separate colony and named after the Queen, and in 1901 became a state of the Commonwealth of Australia□

Victoria capital, port, and industrial centre (shipbuilding, chemicals, clothing, furniture) of British Columbia, Canada; population 240 400. Founded as Fort Victoria in 1843 by the Hudson's Bay Company, it has a university (1964)□

Victoria capital of Hong◊ Kong, but itself commonly referred to as Hong Kong□

Victoria Lake. See Great◊ Lakes□

Victoria Cross see under medals◊□

Victoria Falls see under Zambezi◊□

Victorian Order Royal. See under knighthood◊□

'Victory' Nelson◊'s flagship, now in permanent dock at Portsmouth◊□

vicuna an animal of the camel◊ family□

Vidal Gore 1925– . American novelist and essayist whose works include the novel *Myra Breckinridge* 1968, and screenplays, e.g. *Suddenly Last Summer*1958□

video camera movie camera in colour with an electronic viewfinder and zoom lens, producing an electrical output-signal corresponding to rapid line-by-line 'scanning' of the field of view. See videotape◊ recorder□

video disc disc (originating with Baird◊ in 1928, and commercially available from 1978) which is chiefly used to provide commercial films for personal viewing. The Philips system has a 30 cm/12 in rotating vinyl disc coated with a reflective material; laser scanning recovers information from the surface where it is recorded by means of a spiral of miniature pits□

videotape recorder (VTR) device for recording TV programmes for later viewing, or linked by cable with a video◊ camera; a ***cam-corder*** is a portable videotape recorder with a built-in camera□

videotext process (originally known as ***viewdata***) for delivering computerized information, by way of a two-way telephone connection, to an ordinary modified television set; ***teletext*** uses one-way broadcast signals rather than the telephone for the same purpose: ***teletex*** is a type of telex◊.
The world's prototype videotext service was Prestel, operated by British Telecom□

Vidocq François Eugène 1775–1857. French criminal who became in 1809 a spy for the Paris police, and rose to be chief of the detective department□

Vienna (German *Wien*) capital of the Austrian republic, on the River Danube at the foot of the Wienerwald ('Vienna Woods'); population 1 531 350. The near circular fortifications of the old city were replaced by the Ringstrasse in 1860. Notable buildings include the 13th-century cathedral of St Stephen; the Hofburg (former imperial palace, now the national library); Houses of Parliament (1883), the 17th-century royal palace of Schönbrunn; Rathaus (town hall) 1873–83; the university, founded in 1365; and the Burgtheater and Opera House. It was the capital of the Austro-Hungarian Empire 1278–1918, and after much destruction in World War II was divided into US, British, French, and Russian occupation zones 1945–55. The United Nations city founded in 1979 houses the United Nations Industrial Development Organization (UNIDO) and the International Atomic Energy Agency (IAEA). Vienna is associated with Haydn, Mozart, Beethoven, Schubert, Strauss waltzes and the development of atonal music, and movements including psychoanalysis◊ and Zionism◊ originated here□

Vienna Congress of. The international congress held 1814–15, which effected the settlement of Europe after the Napoleonic Wars (national representatives included Metternich, Alexander I of Russia, Castlereagh, Wellington, Talleyrand)□

Vientiane capital and chief port of Laos on the Mekong◊; population 120 000□

Vietnam The Socialist Republic of
area 336 000 sq km/129 000 sq mi
capital Hanoi
towns ports Ho Chi Minh City (formerly Saigon), Da Nang, and Haiphong
features Red river and Mekong deltas, where cultivation and population are concentrated; Vietnam ranks third among world Communist powers
products rice, rubber; coal, iron, apatite
currency dong
population 60 000 000; c750 000 refugees, the majority ethnic Chinese, left the country

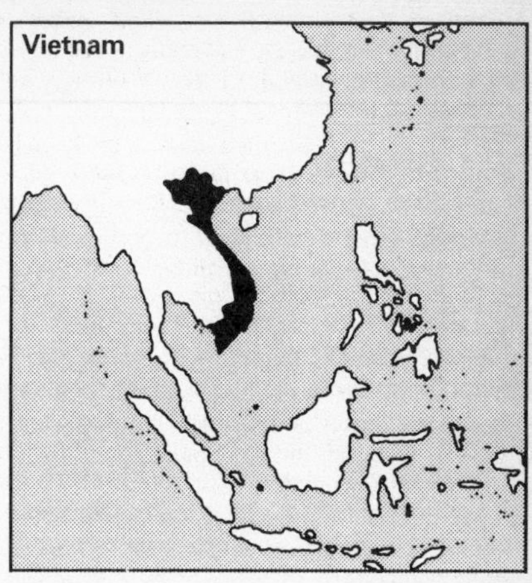

1975–9, some settling in SW China, others fleeing by sea (directly or via China), the 'boat people', to Hong Kong, and elsewhere
language Vietnamese, of uncertain origin, but tonal, in the same way as Chinese and Thai
religion traditionally Buddhism and Taoism
famous people Ho Chi Minh
government there is a Council of State (the country's collective presidency: chairman Truong Chinh from 1981) and a National Assembly (premier Pham Van Dong) elected for five years, but power rests with the Communist Party (First Secretary Truong Chinh from 1986)
recent history originally founded in 208 BC Vietnam was long under Chinese rule until the French conquest of 1858–84, when it became the colonies of Annam, Tonkin, and Cochin-China (merged with Cambodia in 1887 to form French Indochina). It was occupied by the Japanese 1940–45, when Ho◊ Chi Minh led the fight for independence first against the Japanese and then the French 1946–54, the French being finally defeated at Dien◊ Bien Phu. The Geneva Conference of 1954 divided the country at the 17th parallel into North Vietnam (capital Hanoi) and South Vietnam (capital Saigon). The Vietnam◊ War ensued, ending with reunification of the country in 1976. Vietnam invaded Kampuchea◊ 1977–8 to topple Pol◊ Pot (who was backed by China); there was a brief punitive invasion of Vietnam by China 17 Feb–16 Mar 1979, and border fighting in 1984: see Laos◊, Thailand◊. There was a partial withdrawal of troops from Kampuchea in 1983□

Vietnam War 1954–75 between N Vietnam (communist, then backed by China) and S Vietnam (democratic, backed by USA): see

Vietnam◊. Following the Tonkin◊ Gulf incident, America intervened directly in the war, but by 1968 President Johnson◊ offered to negotiate with N Vietnam (via Kissinger◊), and peace was concluded in Jan 1973. See Battle of Saigon◊. The North overran the South in Mar 1975, all US aid being withdrawn, and in 1976 Vietnam was reunited by the North. Unpopular with the left in the USA, the war was the first military defeat for the USA; 2 500 000 Americans went to Vietnam, 58 000 were killed or reported missing, 200 000 wounded, and 100 000 are alleged to have committed suicide; Vietnamese casualties are unknown□

viewdata see videotext◊□

Vigny Alfred, Comte de Vigny 1797–1863. French romantic writer, e.g. the historical novel *Cinq-Mars* 1826, the play *Chatterton* 1835, and poetry, e.g. *Les Destinées* 1864, stoically pessimistic□

Vigo industrial port (oil refining, distilling, paper, leather) and naval base in Galicia, NW Spain; population 259 000□

Vikings Scandinavian 'sea warriors' of the 8–11th centuries, sometimes called ***Norsemen*** who raided Europe in their narrow, shallow draught, highly manoeuvrable longships, penetrating far inland along rivers (see Valdai◊ Hills). With a thirst for warfare, gold, and land, they were dreaded, and growth of the feudal system was aided by the need for organized resistance to them. In England, where they were also known as 'Danes', they settled (e.g. in York◊) and greatly influenced the development of the language, and as 'Normans' (see Normandy◊) achieved a second conquest of the country. The Vikings had a gift for government (see Canute◊), and the Swedish Varangians were invited to settle differences among the Slav chieftains, establishing the first Russian state with its capital at Kiev. The Varangians also reached Constantinople, where they formed the imperial guard. In the west the Vikings reached Iceland, Greenland, and N America. See Eric◊ the Red, Leif◊ Ericsson□

vine climbing plant of Asia Minor *Vitis vinifera*, family Vitaceae, grown for its fruit (***grapes***) and probably introduced to England by the Romans. The dried fruits are ***raisins***, a name applied in particular to large, dark fruit; seedless white grapes form the golden ***sultanas***, and small seedless red grapes form ***currants***. See wine◊□

Villa-Lobas Heitor 1881–1959. Brazilian composer. His national style was based on folk tunes collected on his travels in the country e.g. *Bachianas Brasilieras* in which he treats them in the manner of Bach. He used orchestras of hundreds, choirs of thousands, and produced some 2000 works including 12 symphonies□

Villehardouin Geoffroy de c1160–1213. The first French historian whose work is in prose. He was a leader of the Fourth Crusade◊, of which his *Conquest of Constantinople* c1209 is a riveting account□

villeinage system of serfdom in medieval Europe where, in England, the villeins are recorded by the Domesday Book as the most numerous element in the population and continued so until a system of free tenure and labour developed by the 15th century; in France the system continued until the revolution of 1789□

Vilnius capital (Russian *Vilna*) of Lithuanian Republic, USSR; population 535 000. From a 10th century settlement, Vilnius became the Lithuanian capital 1323, then was Polish until the Russian annexation of 1795, and was again polish from 1921 until occupied by the USSR 1939□

Vimy town in N France. Nearby ***Vimy Ridge*** was taken by Canadian troops in an epic assault during the Battle of Arras◊, Apr 1917, which cost 11 285 lives□

Vincent de Paul St 1576–1660. French founder of the two charitable orders of Lazarists 1625 and Sisters of Charity 1634. Ordained in 1600, he was captured by Barbary pirates and was a slave in Tunis until he escaped in 1607; feast day 19 Jul□

vinegar a 4% solution of acetic acid produced by the oxidation of alcohol, used to flavour food and as a preservative in pickles; ***malt vinegar*** is brown and made from malted cereals; ***white vinegar*** is distilled from it. Other sources of vinegar include cider, inferior wine, and honey□

viol family bowed musical instruments of the 16th–18th centuries, similar to the violin◊ (which superceded them), but having six strings, instead of four, being tuned in fourths, and a flatter back. Members of the family include ***descant viol, viola da gamba*** or bass viol, and double-bass viol or ***violone***. Viols have been used increasingly in recent years for 'authentic' performances of early and baroque music□

violet genus of plants *Viola*, family Violaceae◊, with mauve/blue/white flowers, e.g. ***dog violet*** *V canina* and ***sweet violet*** *V odorata*.

pansies are very close relatives, and the Eurasian ***wild pansy*** or ***heart's-ease*** *V tricolor* with yellow and purple flowers, is one of the chief ancestors of garden varieties, which have been developed for size at the expense of scent□

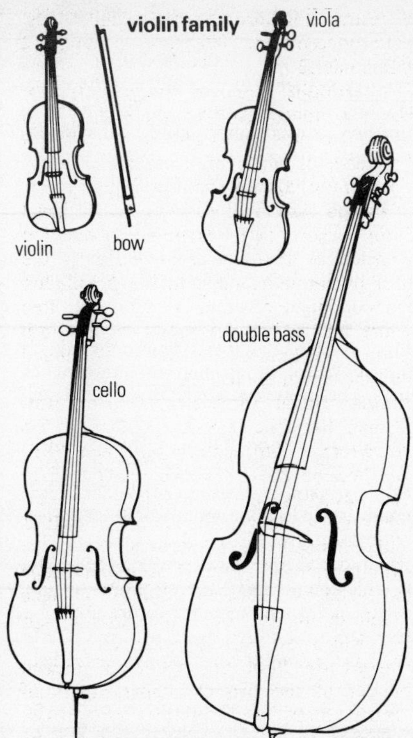

violin family musical instruments played with a bow drawn against a stretched string. Four members: ***violin, viola, violoncello*** or ***cello***, and ***double bass***. The violin superseded the viol from the 17th century; famous early makers were the Amati family in Cremona, Stradivari, and G A Guarnieri. Each of the instruments consists of a resonant hollow body, a neck with fingerboard attached, and four catgut strings, tuned in fifths, stretched over the body. The viola sounds a fifth below the violin; the cello is played seated, with the instrument between the knees, and the double bass is the largest of all□

Virgil (*Publius Vergilius Maro*) 70–19BC. Roman poet. Born near Mantua, he was of the small farmer class whose life he celebrated in his pastoral *Eclogues* 37BC, and *Georgics* or 'Art of Husbandry' 30BC. His epic poem, the *Aeneid*, glorified the dynasty of his patron Augustus◊. By the 3rd century his works were used for divination, and he was popularly thought a magician, but his apparent forecast of the birth of Christ in the fourth eclogue gave him Church approval□

virginals a small harpsochord. See under piano◊□

Virginia southern state of the USA; Old Dominion

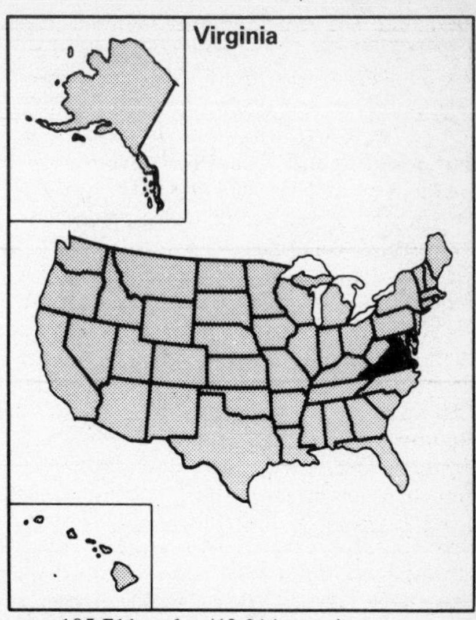

area 105 711 sq km/40 814 sq mi
capital Richmond
towns Norfolk, Newport News, Hampton, Portsmouth
features Blue Ridge mountains, which include the Shenandoah National Park, south of the Shenandoah river; Arlington National Cemetery; Mt Vernon, the village where Washington◊ lived 1752–99, and is buried on the family estate; Monticello (Jefferson◊'s home at Charlottesville); Stratford Hall (Robert E Lee◊'s birthplace in Lexington)
products sweet potatoes, corn, tobacco, apples, peanuts; coal; furniture, paper, chemicals, processed food, textiles, and cigarettes
population 5 346 279
famous people Richard E Byrd, Patrick Henry, Robert E Lee, Meriwether Lewis and William Clark, Edgar Allan Poe, Booker T Washington, George Washington
history named in honour of Elizabeth I. The first permanent English settlement in the New World was made here in Jamestown◊ in 1607. The state took a leading part in the revolutionary struggle against Britain, was one of the Thirteen◊ Colonies, and was a Confederate state in the Civil◊ War□

Virgin Islands island group, northernmost of the Leeward Islands in the Antilles, W Indies, strategically important on the approach to the Panama Canal. They lie in superb sailing waters and tourism is the chief industry.

American Virgin Islands St Thomas (with the capital, Charlotte Amalie), St John, and St Croix; area 347 sq km/134 sq mi; population 95 600. They were purchased from Denmark in 1917, and form an 'unincorporated territory'.

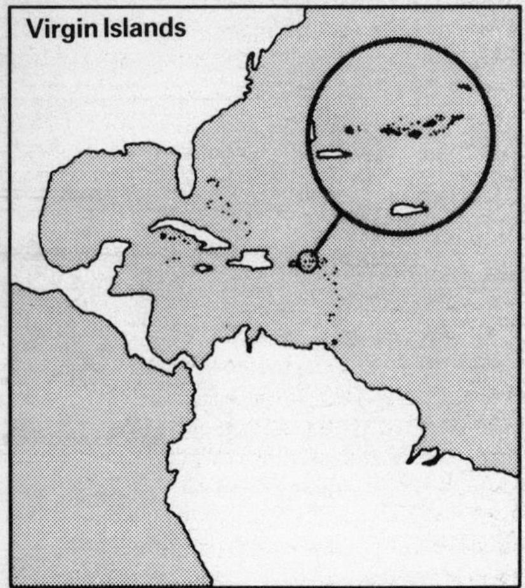

British Virgin Islands Tortola (with the capital, Road Town), Virgin Gorda, Anegada, Jost van Dykes; area 174 sq km/67 sq mi; population 12 000. They were taken over from the Dutch by British settlers in 1666, and have partial internal self-government□

virino alternative name for a prion◊, a submicroscopic organism between a virus and viroid□

viroid submicroscopic organism, smaller than a virus◊, and comprising a single strand of genes, which reproduces solely through the action of enzymes in the cell it infects. First isolated 1971, they cause stunting and malformation in plants, and some rare diseases in animals and man. See also virino◊□

virus submicroscopic organism, a 'core' of nucleic acids enclosed in a protein 'shell', which remains inert unless able to force its way into an animal or plant cell to function and reproduce. Viruses disorganize the host cell's DNA◊ and 'borrow' the use of its synthetic system to replicate themselves. A healthy human body reacts by producing an anti-viral protein, interferon◊, to prevent its spread and give rise to substances which destroy the virus. Viruses cause canine distemper, chickenpox, common cold, foot and mouth disease, hepatitis, herpes and shingles, influenza, measles, mumps, rabies, smallpox, typhus, yellow fever, and some forms of cancer. One virus infection of plants is tobacco mosaic disease, but the rice necrosis mosaic virus is advantageous to man in that it promotes growth and flower production, probably by stimulating growth-hormone production. See viroid◊, virino◊

anti-viral drugs are difficult to develop because viruses replicate by using the genetic machinery of host cells, so that drugs tend to affect the host cell as well as the virus. Acyclovir (used against the herpes group of diseases) is one of the few drugs so far developed that is successfully selective in its action□

viscose a substance used in synthetic textiles◊□

Vishnu in Hinduism◊ the supreme spirit□

Visigoths see under Goths◊□

Vitoria town in the Basque Country, Spain; population 192 775. In the Peninsular◊ War Wellington won a victory over the French here□

Vitruvius (Marcus Vitruvius Pollio) 1st century BC. Roman architect, whose ten-volume interpretation of Roman architectura *De architechtura* influenced Alberti, Palladio, etc.□

Vladimir I St Grand Duke of Kiev 956–1015. He married the sister of the Byzantine emperor, and established Orthodox Christianity as the Russian national faith; feast day, 15 Jul□

Vladivostok port (naval and commercial) in E USSR on the Pacific coast; population 565 000. It is the administrative centre of the Far East Science Centre (1969), with subsidiaries at Petropavlovsk, Khabarovsk, and Magadan□

void in astronomy, an area in space devoid of galaxies◊, e.g. in the constellation Bootes, there is one c350 million light years in diameter. They may occupy most of the volume of the universe◊□

Vojvodina see under Serbia◊

volcano a vent in the earth's crust, which is commonly cone-shaped, with a depression at the top called a 'crater', formed when its top is blasted off, sometimes changing shape in its successive eruptions. Mt Fujiyama◊, Japan, was formerly a more perfect cone. There are some 600 volcanoes on land and many more unseen beneath the sea, and they occur for the most part in a great chain which can be visualized as running up the west coast of the Americas from Cape Horn to Alaska (with a loop running out through the Caribbean area); it then goes down the east coast of Asia via Japan, where it splits. To the west it runs through central Asia and the Mediterranean to Gibraltar, and to the south continues until forking north of Australia to include Indonesia to the west and New Zealand to the east. The world's highest volcano is Guallatiri 6060 m/19 882 ft in the Central Andes, Chile. All the variety of material erupting from a volcano (molten rock or magma, clouds of ash and pumice, and vast quantities of gas) has been forced up from the molten regions which lie 60 km/35 mi to 100 km/60 mi beneath the earth's surface. It may find an easy escape route (see Mid◊-Atlantic Ridge), or it may fill a reservoir beneath a volcano. Here the mixture is thought to continue to 'cook', the lighter material gradually moving towards the top (the quiescent period of a volcano, which may last many years) until it reaches the critical point at which it 'boils over', and an eruption takes place. Changes in conditions under the earth at the site of a volcano may lead to its becoming 'extinct', and ceasing to erupt. See Erebus◊, Etna◊, Krakatoa◊, Mount St Helens◊, Stromboli◊□

Volcker Paul 1927– . American economist. As chairman of the American Federal Reserve Board from 1979, he controls the amount of money in circulation in the USA□

vole a small rodent◊□

Volgograd town in SW USSR, on the River Volga. Metal goods and machinery are manufactured, and there are saw mills, petroleum refineries, etc.; population (1979) 929 000.

volleyball

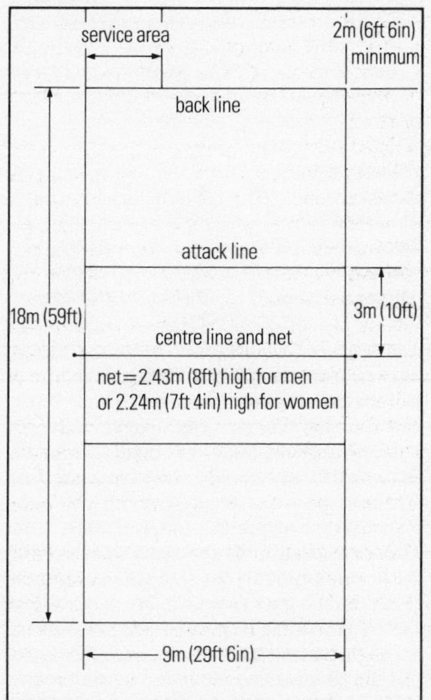

Volgograd was called Stalingrad 1925–61; its successful defence 1942–3, against the Germans was a turning point of World War II□

volleyball team game invented in the USA in 1895, played on a court 18m (59ft) long by 9m (29ft 6in), divided into two by a net 1m (3ft 3in) deep suspended 2.43m (8ft) above the court. The six players of each team rotate in position through the six sub-sections into which each half of the court is divided behind the attack line. The ball, slightly smaller than a basketball, is hit with palm or fist, the aim being to ground it in the opponents' court□

Voltaire pseudonym of French writer François-Marie Arouet (1694–1778). Born in Paris, son of a notary, he adopted his pseudonym in 1718. Between 1716 and 1726 he was twice imprisoned in the Bastille and three times exiled from the capital for libellous political verse. *Oedipe,* his first tragedy, was staged in 1718. He lived in England 1726–9; published the successful *Histoire de Charles XII* (1731). His *Lettres philosophiques sur les Anglais* (1733), a panegyric of English ways and political practice, led to his taking refuge with his mistress, the Marquise de Chatelet (d. 1749) at Cirey in Champagne where he wrote his best play *Mérope,* 1743, and much of *Le Siècle de Louis XIV*. In 1751–3 he was at the court of Frederick◊ the Great, but the association ended in deep enmity, and he spent the rest of his life at Ferney near Geneva. Other works include the satirical tale *Zadig; Candide* (1759), a parody on Leibneiz◊'s 'best of all possible worlds'; and the tragedy *Irene* (1778). In religion a Deist◊, Voltaire devoted himself to crushing the spirit of intolerance□

voodoo a set of magical beliefs and practices, especially in Haiti. See under witchcraft◊

Vorster Balthazar Johannes 1915–83. South African prime minister 1966–78, in succession to Verwoerd◊, and president 1978–9, when he resigned (the Department of Information had made unauthorized use of public funds during his premiership)□

Vulcan in Roman mythology, the god of fire and destruction, later identified with the Greek god Hephaestus◊□

vulture a large bird of prey. See under eagle◊□

W

wafer in microelectronics a 'super-chip' some 3–4 in in diameter, for which wafer-scale integration (WSI) is used to link together the equivalent of many individual silicon◊ chips, improving on reliability, speed, and cooling□

Wagner Richard (1813–83). German opera composer, born in Leipzig and educated at Dresden. His operas, all based on themes from German history and mythology, form one of the peaks of Romanticism◊. His masterpiece is *The Ring of the Nibelungen*, a sequence of four operas (1853–74): *The Rheingold, The Valkyrie, Siegfried,* and *The Twilight of the Gods*. The Ring cycle was first performed at Bayreuth, where Wagner had an opera house built to his instructions exclusively for the performance of his works. His other mature operas are *Tristan and Isolde* (1857–9); *The Mastersingers of Nuremberg* (1862–7), and *Parsifal* (1877–82). After the death of his first wife in 1866 he married Cosima, the daughter of Liszt◊□

wagtails and **pipits** insect-eating songbirds of family Motacillidae, order Passeriformes:
pipit genus of birds with longish beaks, long tails, and brown streaked and speckled plumage. They include the British ***meadow pipit*** *Anthus pratensis* and the ***rock pipit*** *A spinoletta.*
wagtail genus of slim, narrow-billed birds with characteristic flirtatious movement of the tail, which includes the ***pied wagtail*** *Motacilla alba yarrellii* with mingled black, grey, and white plumage; ***grey wagtail*** *M cinerea*, and the summer visitor ***yellow wagtail*** *M flava*□

Wahabi popular name for the purist Saudi Islamic sect founded by Mohammed ibn-Abd-al-Wahab 1703–92, which regards all others as heresies and their followers as liable to the death penalty□

Wales (Welsh *Cymru*), The Principality of
area 20 762 sq km/8030 sq mi
capital Cardiff
towns Swansea
features Snowdonia in the NW and in the SE the Black Mountain, Brecon Beacons, and Black Forest ranges; rivers Severn, Wye, Usk, and Dee; see Eisteddfod◊
exports traditional industries (coal and steel) have declined, but varied modern and high technology ventures are being developed: Wales has the largest concentration of Japanese-owned plant in the UK. It also has the highest density of sheep in the world and a dairy industry; tourism is important
currency pound◊ sterling
population 2 792 000
language English; Welsh-speaking 19% (1981)
religion nonconformist Protestant denominations; Roman Catholic minority
government returns 38 members to the British Parliament

Wales: Counties

	area in sq km	population (1982)	administrative headquarters
Clwyd	2,424	394,500	Mold
Dyfed	5,767	333,500	Carmathen
Mid Glamorgan	1,019	539,300	Cardiff
South Glamorgan	416	389,800	Cardiff
West Glamorgan	815	368,500	Caenarvon
Gwent	1,377	440,200	Cwmbran
Gwynedd	3,865	231,900	Caenarvon
Powys	5,079	110,500	Llandrindod Wells
	20,762	2,808,200	

recent history the Celts of Wales, like those of Britain, came under Roman rule, and c200AD had become Christian. The Saxon invasions of southern Britain c450–600 made Wales the chief Celtic stronghold to the west: see also Arthur◊ and St David◊. After the Norman Conquest there was continual pressure from across the English border (resisted notably by Llewelyn◊ I and II), but ending in acceptance of Edward◊ I as overlord in 1277. Welsh nationalist feeling continued (see Owen Glendower◊), but English rule became more harsh and the language continued to be suppressed or discouraged until the 19th century. Since World War II there has been a nationalist movement, and a revival of the language (there is a Welsh television channel)□

Walesa Lech 1943– . Polish leader of the trade union Solidarity◊; Nobel peace prize in 1983□

Walker William 1824–60. American adventurer who briefly established himself as president of a republic in NW Mexico, and in 1856 made himself president of Nicaragua, but was eventually executed. He is regarded as the symbol of American imperialism in Central America□

wallaby a type of marsupial◊□

Wallace Alfred Russel 1823–1913. British naturalist. Born in Usk, Gwent, he travelled in S America and Malaya, and his paper on the theory of evolution was read to the Linnean Society in 1858 on the same day as Darwin◊'s. Order of Merit in 1910◊□

Wallace George 1919– . US politician, governor of Alabama 1963–7, 1971–9, and 1983–6. In 1972, while campaigning for the Democratic presidential nomination, he was shot at a rally and became partly paralysed□

Wallace Lew(is) 1827–1905. US author, an officer in the Mexican and Civil Wars, whose novel *Ben-Hur* 1880 is set in Roman-ruled Judaea at the time of Christ□

Wallace Sir Richard 1818–90. British art connoisseur, whose collection, largely inherited from his father, the Marquis of Hertford, was left to the nation by his widow. The ***Wallace Collection*** in Hertford House, London, is particularly rich in paintings, furniture, and china from France□

Wallace Sir William c1272–1305. Scottish patriot, who led a revolt against English rule in 1297, won a victory at Stirling, and assumed the title 'governor of Scotland'. Edward I defeated him at Falkirk in 1298, and Wallace was captured and executed□

Wallace Line see under Lombok◊ Strait□

Wallachia independent medieval principality which was under Turkish rule 1387–1861, when it was united with Moldavia to form Romania◊□

Wallenstein Albrecht von 1583–1634. German commander of the imperial armies in the Thirty Years' War, who was dismissed in 1630 when the emperor feared his ambition. He was recalled in 1631 to face Gustavus◊ Adolphus, and plotted for a principality of his own. He was assassinated by his own officers. His life was dramatized by Schiller◊□

Waller Edmund 1606–87. English poet, who managed to eulogize both Cromwell◊ and Charles◊ II, but produced such lovely lyrics as 'Go, lovely rose'□

wallflower perennial plant *Cheiranthus cheiri*, family Cruciferae◊, with fragrant red or yellow flowers in spring□

Wallis and **Futuna** two island groups in the S Pacific. They became a French dependency in 1842, and an overseas territory from 1961; area 255 sq km/98 sq mi; population 13 000. Capital Mata Utu on Uvea□

Wallis Sir Barnes Neville 1887–1979. British aeronautical engineer, designer of the airship R 100; perfector of the 'bounce-bombs' used against the Möhne and Eder dams in 1943 by the Dambusters◊ Squadron; deviser of the geodetic construction of the Wellington bomber; sharer in the development of the Concorde supersonic airliner, and developer of the swing-wing aircraft. Knighted in 1968□

Walloon the people and language of SE Belgium◊□

Wall Street thoroughfare in New York, so called from a stockade erected in 1653. It is synonymous with the stock exchange, which is situated here□

walnut Eurasian tree *Juglans regia*, family Juglandaceae, grown for its nuts and timber, used (as is that of the American ***black walnut*** *J nigra*) for fine furniture□

Walpole Sir Horace, 4th Earl of Orford 1717–97. English author, youngest son of Sir Robert Walpole◊. A Whig MP 1741–67, he succeeded to the peerage in 1791. He converted his house at Strawberry Hill, Twickenham, to a Gothic castle (one of its rooms is preserved in the Victoria and Albert Museum) and his Gothic novel *The Castle of Otranto* 1765, set a fashion for 'tales of terror'□

Walpole Sir Robert, 1st Earl of Orford 1676–1745. British Whig statesman, the first 'prime◊ minister' as First Lord of the Treasury and Chancellor of the Exchequer 1715–17 and 1721–42. A byword for corruption, he was a capable manager of parliament, encouraged trade by his pacific foreign policy (until forced into the War of Jenkins◊'s Ear with Spain in 1739), and received an earldom when he eventually retired in 1742, redolent with wealth. See Horace Walpole◊□

Walpurgis St d. 779. English nun who preached Christianity in Germany. ***Walpurgis Night*** before 1 May, her feast day, was associated with witches' sabbaths, and particularly with that held on the Brocken◊□

walrus a large sea mammal. See under pinnipedia◊□

Walsall industrial town (castings and tubes, electrical equipment, leather goods) in West Midlands, England; population 265 300□

Walsingham see under Norfolk◊□

Walsingham Sir Francis c1530–90. English politician who, as Secretary of State from 1573, both advocated a strong anti-Spanish policy and ran the efficient government spy system which made it work□

Walter Hubert d. 1205. Archbishop of Canterbury 1193–1205. As justiciar (chief political and legal officer) 1193–8, he ruled England during Richard◊ I's absence and introduced the offices of coroner and justice of the peace□

Walter John 1739–1812. British newspaper editor, founder of *The Times* (originally the *Daily Universal Register*, 1785, but renamed in 1788)□

Walters Sir Alan 1926– . British monetarist economist. Professor of political economy at Johns Hopkins University, Maryland, from 1976, he became economic adviser to Margaret Thatcher in 1981□

Waltham Forest borough of Greater London

features includes Walthamstow, where William Morris◊ was born, and part of Epping Forest

population 215 000□

Walther von der Vogelweide c1170–c1230. German Minnesinger◊ at the Austrian ducal court, who became a wandering bard after his patron's death in 1198□

Walton Izaak 1593–1683. English author, a London ironmonger, best remembered for his *Compleat Angler* 1653□

Walton Sir William (Turner) 1902–83. British composer. Born at Oldham, he was educated at Christ Church, Oxford. His works include *Façade* 1923 (with Edith Sitwell); the oratorio *Belshazzar's Feast* 1931; *First Symphony* 1935; *Violin Concerto* 1939, for Heifetz◊; and film scores for Shakespeare's *Henry V* and *Richard III*. Order of Merit in 1967□

Walvis Bay chief port of SW Africa (Namibia); area 1124 sq km/434 sq m; population 17 000. Administered with SW Africa 1922–77, it was a detached part of Cape Province 1878–1922, and reincorporated in S Africa in 1977□

wampum beads made from sea shells and formerly used as currency/decoration by some N American Indians□

Wandering Jew legendary Jew (Ahasuerus) believed to have insulted Christ on his way to Calvary, and been condemned to wander the world until the second coming□

Wandsworth borough of S central Greater London

features Battersea Park, Battersea Dogs' Home; former power station being converted in 1984 as the centrepiece of a leisure park

population 253 000□

Wankie see Hwange◊□

wapiti a type of deer◊□

war see World◊ War I, II, etc.□

waratah Australian genus of shrubs/trees, family Proteaceae, especially the crimson-flowered *Teleopea speciosissima*, emblem of New South Wales□

Warbeck Perkin c1474–99. Flemish pretender to the English throne. Claiming to be Richard, brother of Edward◊ V, he led a rising against Henry VII in 1497, and was hanged after attempting to escape from the Tower of London□

warbler family of drab-coloured Old World songbirds, Muscicapidae, order Passeriformes. It includes the ***chiff chaff*** *Phylloscopus collybita* of European woodland, with greenish to fawn plumage, and a song resembling its name; ***blackcap*** *Sylvia atricapilla*; ***goldcrest*** *Regulus regulus* smallest of European birds (8 cm/3 in; weight 5 g/0.2 oz) which has a black-bordered yellow crest, and nests in conifers; ***willow-warbler*** *Phylloscopus trochilus* which builds spherical nests in woodland, has 2–3 broods and moults twice a year; and the tropical long-tailed ***tailor-bird*** *Orthotomus sutorius* which builds a nest inside two large leaves it sews together. The New World warblers, family Parulidae, are brighter and allied to the tanagers◊□

Warrington and **Runcorn** towns in Cheshire, England; population 140 200 (Runcorn 65 000). With some fine 18th-century architecture (see James Gibbs◊), they were designated a 'new town' in 1969; industries include engineering, chemicals, and vodka□

Warsaw capital of Poland on the River Vistula; population 2 342 000. Founded in the 13th century, it replaced Cracow as capital in 1595. It was taken by the Germans on 27 Sept 1939, in World War II, and there was a heroic but abortive rising against the German occupation on 1 Aug 1944. It was finally liberated on 17 Jan 1945□

Warsaw Pact a pact signed on 14 May 1955 by Albania (excluded in 1962), Bulgaria, Czechoslovakia, E Germany, Hungary,

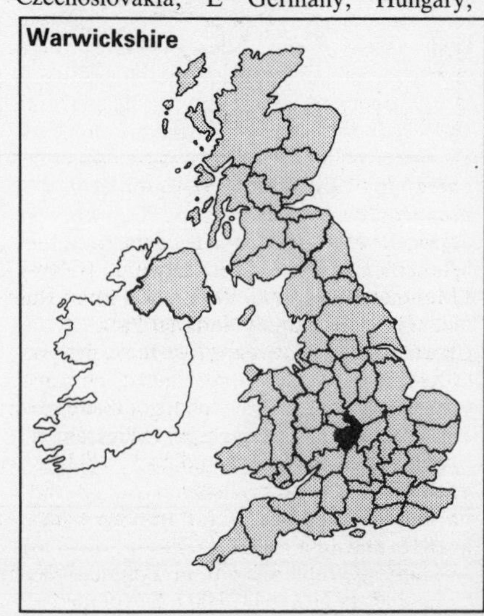
Warwickshire

Poland, Romania, and USSR; extended in 1985 for a further 20 years. It established an alliance on NATO lines — the Warsaw Treaty Organization□

Warwickshire Midland county of England
area 1981 sq km/765 sq mi
towns administrative headquarters Warwick; Leamington, Nuneaton, Rugby, Stratford-upon-Avon
features Kenilworth and Warwick Castles; remains of Shakespeare's Forest of Arden; site of the Battle of Edgehill
products mainly agricultural; formerly coalmining
population 480 100
famous people George Eliot, Shakespeare□

Wash The. Bay of the North Sea between Norfolk and Lincolnshire, England. King John◊ lost his baggage and treasure in crossing it in 1216□

Washington state of the USA; Evergreen State

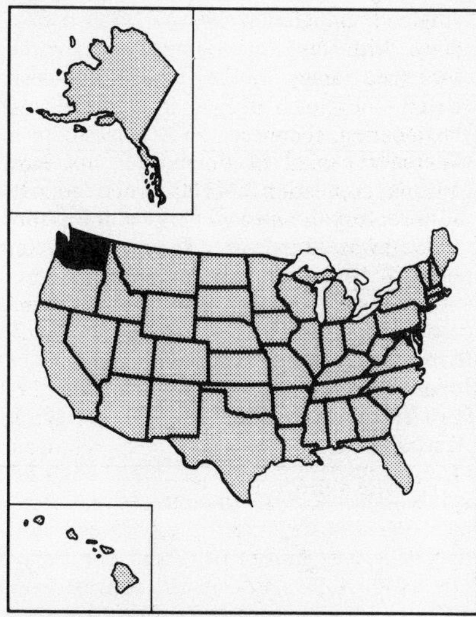

area 176 615 sq km/68 191 sq mi
capital Olympia
towns Seattle, Spokane, Tacoma
features Columbia river; Olympic (Olympic Mountains) National Park, and Mount Rainier (Cascade Range) National Park
products apples, cereals; livestock; processed food; timber, wood products; chemicals, cement, zinc, uranium, lead, gold, and silver; aircraft, ships, road transport vehicles
population 4 130 163, including 34 000 Indians
famous people Bing Crosby
history settled from 1811, it became a state in 1889□

Washington 'new town' in Tyne and Wear, England; population 55 000. Developed from the old village, the home of George Washington◊'s family□

Washington Booker T(aliaferro) 1856–1915. American black educationist, first principal of Tuskegee Institute, Alabama; author of *Up from Slavery* 1901□

Washington George 1732–99. 1st president of the USA 1789–97. Born in Virginia, he became a strong opponent of British government policy in the Continental Congresses of 1774 and 1775, was Commander-in-Chief from the outbreak of War (see American◊ Independence, War of), and became president of the Constitutional Convention in 1787. He refused to serve a third term (a precedent followed until Roosevelt in 1940) and was politically neutral. He was buried at his home, Mount Vernon, Virginia□

Washington DC (District of Columbia◊) national capital of the USA
features situated on the Potomac river, the city of Washington was designed by a French engineer, Pierre L'Enfant. Among buildings of architectural note are the Capitol, the Pentagon, the White House and the Lincoln Memorial
population 638 000□

wasp slender-bodied member of the order Hymenoptera, to which ants and bees also belong. About 25 000 species of wasps are grouped in the suborder Apocrita. The social species, e.g. common wasp *Vespula vulgaris*, form communities (with a caste system of queens, workers, and drones) which last only a single season, and live in nests made of a type of paper manufactured from scrapings of dead wood mixed with saliva. Many have stings painful to humans, and often have a bold black or brown and yellow 'warning' coloration. The ***hornet*** *Vespa crabro* is a large but unaggressive species living in dead trees. Solitary wasps (family Specidae) have less painful stings and are of value to humans in that they prey on insects damaging to agriculture. They usually nest in ground burrows, but may make nests of mud fixed to rocks or buildings. A third type, the parasitic wasps, live in the nests of other wasps or bees□

water colourless liquid, a compound of hydrogen and oxygen (H_2O). Natural water has small quantities of mineral salts dissolved in it which produce a taste. Pure water is tasteless. Water has a maximum density at 4°C/39°F□

water-boatman an insect of the order Hemiptera◊□

water bug an insect of the order Hemiptera◊□

watercress a plant of the genus *Nasturtium*◊□

waterfowl order of birds, Anseriformes, which includes the family Anatidae:
swan of which the common white ***mute swan*** *Cygnus olor*, has a wingspan of 2.5 m/7.5 ft, and weighs 20 kg/45 lb. The pair share the care of the young over a long period and often mate for life. The ***black swan*** *Cygnus atratus*, of Australia is acclimatized in Europe.
goose of which the species are among the most intelligent birds, with complex social relationships and varied calls. They include European ***greylag*** *Anser anser*, ancestor of the domesticated goose; Arctic ***snowgoose*** *Chen caerulescens*, with the brent goose the most northerly breeding birds; Hawaiian ***ne-ne*** *Branta sandvicensis*, near extinction; ***brent goose*** *Branta vernicla*; and the typical N American species, the ***Canada goose*** *Branta canadensis*.
duck more dependent on water than the swan or goose. The ancestor of domesticated ducks is the common European ***mallard*** *Anas platrhynchos*, the male having a burnished green head in the mating season. The genus also includes several species of small duck known as 'teal', closely related to the mallard, e.g. Eurasian ***common teal*** *Anas crecca* and the ***baikal teal*** *Anas formosa* with striking facial markings. Other handsome ducks are the ***shoveller*** *Anas clypeata*, with spoon-shaped bill, and ***wigeon*** *Anas penelope* with red-brown head, cream crown, and pink-grey breast, which winters in Britain. Attractive freshwater diving ducks are the ***tufted duck*** *Aythya fuligula* small, dark brown, with white sides and a tuft at the rear of the head; and European ***pochard*** *Aythya ferina* with a ruddy head and grey-black body. Marine diving ducks, genus *Mergus* include the British ***goosander*** *M merganser* the male combining dark-green, pink, white, and black in his handsome plumage. Particularly attractive species are the beautifully marked and coloured E Asian ***mandarin duck*** *Aix galericulata* now rare in the East, but acclimatized in Britain; the large marine ***eider duck*** *Somateria mollissima*, bred in Iceland and Norway for its soft down, used in 'eiderdowns'; and the ***common shelduck*** *Tadorna tadorna* red-billed, with black, white, green, and chestnut plumage□

water, heavy see heavy◊ water□

water lily aquatic flowering plants, family Nymphaeaceae, with fleshy roots, and round floating leaves, 'pads'. Native to Britain are the white-flowered *Nymphaea alba* and yellow *Nuphar luteum*; the Amazonian *Victoria regia* has leaves 2 m/6 ft in diameter. See lotus◊□

water melon a type of melon◊□

water table level of ground below which the earth and rocks are saturated with water. Thus, above a water table, water will drain downwards, but where a water table cuts the surface of the earth, a spring results. The water table tends to follow surface contours, and varies with rainfall□

water table

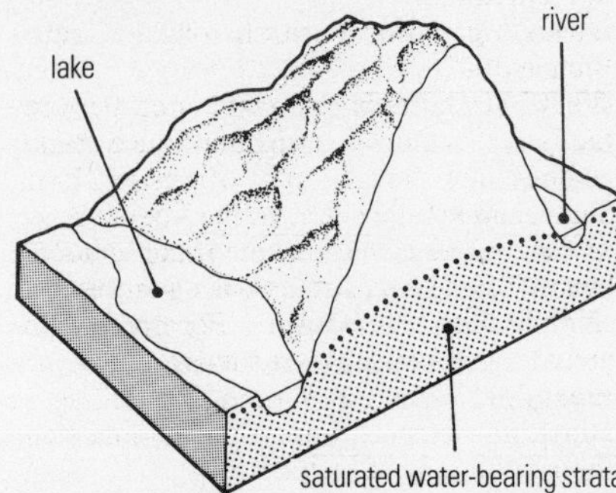

watt derived SI unit of power, named after James Watt; a rate of doing work, or of converting energy. 1 joule per second equals 1 watt□

Watt James 1736–1819. Scottish engineer who realized that Newcomen◊'s steam engine could be made vastly more efficient by cooling the used steam in a condenser separate from the main cylinder. Steam engines incorporating governors, sun-and-planet gears, and other devices of his invention were successfully built by him in partnership with Matthew Boulton, and were vital to the Industrial◊ Revolution□

wattle an Australian tree of the genus *Acacia*◊□

Waugh Evelyn Arthur St John 1903–66. British novelist. Oxford-educated, he made his name with social satire, e.g. *Decline and Fall* 1928, *Vile Bodies* 1930, and *The Loved One* 1948. A Roman Catholic convert from 1930, he developed a serious concern with such issues in *Brideshead Revisited* 1945. *The Ordeal of Gilbert Pinfold* 1957 is largely autobiographical□

wave in physics, a pulse or pattern of disturbances which travels through a medium by means of the forces between the particles of the medium. Waves transport energy and show the properties of reflection◊, refraction◊, diffraction◊, and interference. Sound waves are longitudinal, i.e. the particles of the medium (e.g. air) vibrate to and fro parallel to the direction in which the wave is travelling. Seismic waves in the earth's crust include both longitudinal and transverse components. Electromagnetic◊ waves (e.g. light) have many of the properties of an ordinary wave, but no medium is needed; the 'disturbance' takes the form of alternating electric and magnetic fields◻

wave ocean ridge or swell caused by wind, etc. Freak (episodic) deep ocean waves, formed under special weather conditions, are thought responsible for many sudden ship disappearances. They may reach 34 m/112 ft. See tsunami◊◻

wayfaring tree a shrub of the genus *Viburnum*◊◻

Weald (Old English 'forest') area between the N and S Downs◊, England, once thickly wooded, and forming part of Sussex, Kent, Surrey, and Hampshire. In the Middle Ages, its timber and iron ore made it the industrial heart of England, and its oaks were used in shipbuilding. Ashdown Forest (which includes much heath) is a survival◻

weapons tools for harming or killing in attack or defence. Important landmarks in their development include:

11th century gunpowder◊ in use by the Chinese

13th century gunpowder known in the West (described in 1242 by Roger Bacon◊)

c1300 guns invented by the Arabs, with bamboo muzzles reinforced with iron

1346 Battle of Crécy◊ in which gunpowder was probably used in battle for the first time

1376 Venice used explosive shells

17th century widespread and effective use of guns and cannon in the Thirty Years' War and English Civil War

1800 Henry Shrapnel◊ invented shrapnel for the British Army

1863 TNT◊ discovered by German chemist J Wilbrand

1867 dynamite◊ patented by Alfred Nobel◊

1915 poison gas (chlorine) used for the first time by the Germans in World War I◊

1916 tanks used for the first time by the British at Cambrai◊ (see Swinton◊)

1945 first test explosion of atom bomb (see Alamagordo◊, Bikini◊, Oppenheimer◊, Truman◊, Hiroshima◊)

1954–73 Vietnam◊ War, use of chemical◊ warfare (defoliants, etc.) by the USA

1973 rapid Egyptian initial advance made possible in the Fourth Arab-Israeli◊ War by electronically operated targeting devices

1982 Falklands◊ conflict, Argentines sank British destroyer with French Exocet missile fired from an aircraft

1983 'Star Wars' or 'Strategic Defence Initiative' to develop spatial laser and particle-beam weapons as a defence umbrella against ballistic missiles announced by USA◻

weasel family of carnivorous predatory mammals, Mustelidae, whose existence is often greatly threatened by man; in approximate upward range of size, it includes:

weasel the ***European weasel*** *Mustela nivalis* is short-legged, and brown above and white below; c25 cm/10 in long, including a 6 cm/2.5 in tail; it lives on rats, birds, etc. Very closely related are the ***stoat*** *M erminia* of Eurasia, also brown, but with black-tipped tail, and assuming a white coat (***ermine***) in winter in northern regions; and the semi-aquatic ***mink*** the N American *M vison* producing the best fur in the wild form, but it is also widely farmed, when special colour shades are produced. Mink 'escapes' outside the natural habitat are deadly to small wildlife.

polecat the Eurasian species *Mustela putorius*, larger than the weasel, and smells unpleasant; the domesticated albino form, the ***ferret*** is used for catching rabbits and rats.

marten the ***pine-marten*** *Martes martes* is found in Britain; 75 cm/2.5 ft long, including the tail, with handsome brown fur; the black ***fisher*** or ***pekan*** *M foina* of N America 125 cm/4 ft, is the largest of the group; and the ***sable*** *M zibellina* of E Siberia, provides one of the costliest furs and is difficult to farm.

skunk the American ***common skunk*** *Mephitis mephitis* has a rich black-brown fur, with white marking running down from the head on to the back, and, inclusive of a bushy tail, is 0.75 m/2.5 ft long. Its anal glands produce a liquid which can be spurted several metres at will, smells most offensively, and lingers long.

badger the Eurasian ***common badger*** *Meles meles* has distinctive black and white stripes on the head and greyish ground fur, and is c0.75 m/2.5 ft long, with a 20 cm/8 in tail. Nocturnal, it burrows maze-like 'sets', which are lived in for generations, and because of its great courage is used in the 'sport' of badger-baiting with dogs; this became illegal in 1850 in Britain, but continues secretly.

otter the Eurasian ***common otter*** *Lutra lutra*, has the typical broad head, short legs with webbed feet, elongated agile body with grey-brown fur, and is a remarkable swimmer. It is 0.75 m/2.5 ft long, with a 45 cm/1.5 ft tail, and lives on fish. The fur-bearing ***sea-otter*** *Latax lubris* of the N Pacific is commercially valuable, and the ferocious S American ***giant otter*** *Pteroneura brasiliensis* weighs 30 kg/70 lb, and is over 2 m/6 ft long◻

weather see meteorology◊◻

weather areas divisions of the sea areas around Great Britain for the purpose of weather forecasting for shipping, particularly to indicate where strong and gale-force winds are expected. See meteorology◊◻

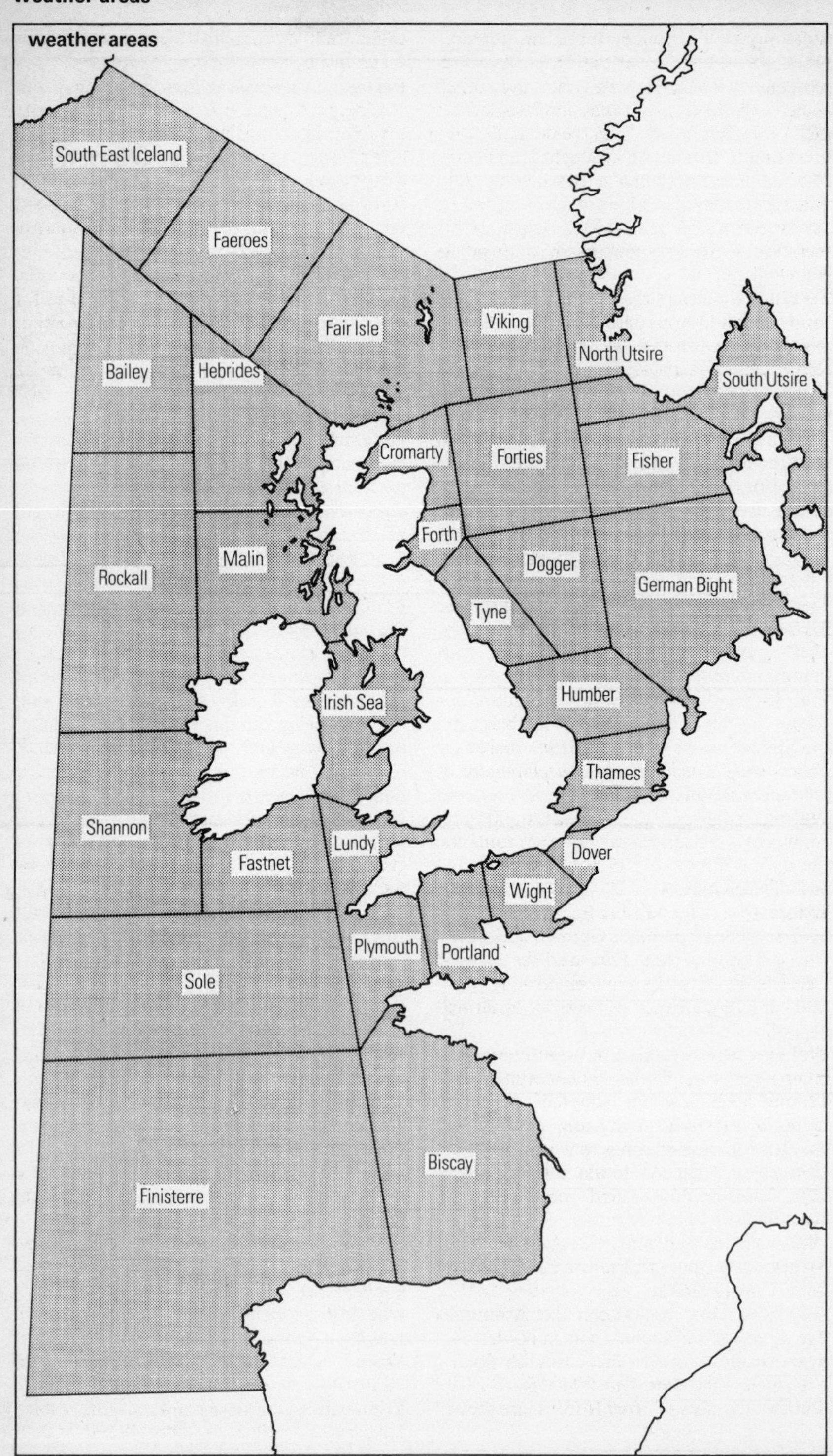
weather areas
South East Iceland
Faeroes
Fair Isle
Viking
North Utsire
South Utsire
Bailey
Hebrides
Cromarty
Forties
Fisher
Rockall
Malin
Forth
Dogger
German Bight
Tyne
Humber
Irish Sea
Thames
Shannon
Fastnet
Lundy
Dover
Wight
Plymouth
Portland
Sole
Biscay
Finisterre

weaving production of fabric on a loom, practised by hand from the Stone Age and perfected in Egypt, Assyria, and other ancient civilizations. It was mechanized by the power-loom in 1786, essentially the invention of Edmund Cartwright◊, and complex patterns were made possible by Jacquard◊. See textiles◊□

Webb Sir Aston 1849–1930. British architect. His works include the 'new' front to Buckingham Palace, Admiralty Arch, and the chief section of the Victoria and Albert Museum, all in London□

Webb Sidney, Baron Passfield 1859–1947. British socialist theorist, a founder of the Fabian◊ Societey 1884, and the London School of Economics 1895, and a believer in 'the inevitability of gradualness'. An MP from 1922, he was president of the Board of Trade 1924, Dominions Secretary 1929–30, and Colonial Secretary 1929–31; peerage 1929. He married 1892 ***Beatrice Potter*** 1858–1943, his collaborator in *History of Trade Unionism* 1894, *English Local Government* 1906, and *Soviet Communism* 1935, and sole author of *My Apprenticeship* 1926 and *Our Partnership* 1948□

Webber Andrew Lloyd 1948– . British composer of musicals which include *Jesus Christ Superstar* 1970, *Evita* 1978 (based on the life of Eva Perón◊), *Cats* 1981 (based on poems by T S Eliot◊), and *The Phantom of the Opera* 1986□

Weber Carl Maria von 1786–1826. German composer, the originator of the romantic opera: *Der Freischütz* 1820, *Euryanthe* 1823 and *Oberon* 1826□

Weber Ernst. See Gustav Fechner◊□

Weber Max 1864–1920. German sociologist whose *The Protestant Ethic and the Spirit of Capitalism* 1904–5 condemned the proliferating bureaucracy of both socialism and capitalism□

Webern Anton (von) 1883–1945. Austrian composer. A pupil of Schoenberg◊, whose 12-note technique he adopted, he wrote works of extreme brevity, e.g. the oratorio *Das Augenlicht* and songs to words by Stefan George◊ and Rilke◊. He was killed by a stray shot during the Allied occupation of Austria□

Webster Daniel 1782–1852. American orator and statesman, originally a Federalist and later a Whig. As Secretary of State 1841–3 and 1850–2, he negotiated the Ashburton Treaty fixing the Maine–Canada border□

Webster John c1580–1625. English dramatist whose tragedies *The White Devil* c1612 and *The Duchess of Malfi* 1613/14, are second only to Shakespeare□

Webster Noah 1758–1843. American lexicographer whose *American Dictionary of the English Language* 1828 standardized the spelling of American English□

Weddell Sea sea which cuts into Antarctica, SE of Cape Horn, and is largely covered with thick pack ice for most of the year; area 8 000 000 sq km/3 000 000 sq mi; the area is named after James Weddell, British Antartic explorer (1787–1834)□

Wedgwood Josiah 1730–95. British potter, most famous for his stoneware, made at his factory 'Etruria' in Burslem, Staffordshire, from 1769. See under pottery◊: history□

weever fish an edible fish. See under perch◊□

weevil a type of beetle◊□

Wegener Alfred 1880–1930. German meteorologist and geophysicist, responsible for the theory of continental◊ drift□

weightlessness condition in which no gravitational force acts upon a body, either having been cancelled out by equal and opposite acceleration, or failing to exert force because the body is beyond any gravitational field. Astronauts suffer muscular deterioration in such circumstances□

Weil Simone 1909–43. French author, a supporter of the Republican cause in Spain and briefly of de Gaulle in World War II. Her works, mainly posthumously published, advocate political quietism; they include *The Need for Roots* 1952 and *Waiting on God* 1951□

Weill Kurt 1900–50. German-born US composer, best known for his operas, in which he collaborated with Brecht◊, e.g. *The Threepenny Opera* 1928 (adapted from Gay◊'s *Beggars' Opera*) and *The Rise and Fall of the City of Mahagonny* 1930◊□

Weil's disease disease (caused by the organism leptospires) carried by rats, which pass it in their urine. The disease causes liver and kidney damage in human beings contracting it, but is treatable by drugs□

Weimar town in Erfurt district, E Germany, former capital of the grand-duchy of Saxe-Weimar (1815–1918); population 64 000. Goethe◊, Schiller◊, Herder◊, and Liszt◊ once lived here, and nearby is the former concentration camp of Buchenwald□

Weimar Republic German republican regime 1918–33, named from the democratic constitution drawn up by a constituent assembly there in Feb 1919; it was overthrown by Hitler◊□

Weinberg Steven 1933– . American physicist, originator of the theory explaining electromagnetic and weak forces, a theory independently arrived at by Abdus Salam◊. It involved the prediction of a new interaction, the neutral current (discovered in 1973). Both shared a Nobel prize with Sheldon Glashow◊ in 1979□

Weinberger Caspar ('Cap') Willard 1917– . American Republican statesman. He served under Presidents Nixon and Ford, and in 1981 became Reagan's Defence Secretary□

Weizmann Chaim 1874–1952. Russian chemist, discoverer in 1916 of a process for the manufacture of acetone◊, and who, as a Zionist, negotiated the Balfour◊ Declaration, becoming first president of Israel 1948–52□

Welland Ship Canal see St◊ Lawrence Seaway□

Welles Orson 1915–85. American actor-director. He started a panic fear of a Martian invasion in the USA in 1938 by a too realistic radio broadcast of H G Wells's *The War of the Worlds*. His film *Citizen Kane* 1940, based on the career of Hearst◊, which he wrote, produced, directed, and starred in, was a landmark in the history of film; he later played Harry Lime in the film *The Third Man* 1950□

Wellington capital, port, and industrial city (wollen textiles, footwear, bricks) of New Zealand in North Island on Cook Strait; population 342 500. Founded in 1840 by Edward Gibbon Wakefield, as the first settlement of the New Zealand Company, it has been the seat of government since 1865. A new assembly hall (designed by Basil Spence◊ and popularly called 'the beehive' because of its shape) was opened in 1977 alongside the original parliament building□

Wellington Arthur Wellesley, 1st Duke of Wellington 1769–1852. British soldier-statesman. Knighted for his army service in India, he was outstanding as commander in the Peninsular◊ War, finally expelling the French from Spain in 1814, and being raised to a dukedom. Following Napoleon's escape from Elba, he defeated him at Quatre-Bras and Waterloo in 1815, and, as a member of the Congress of Vienna, opposed the dismemberment of France and supported restoration of the Bourbons◊. As Tory Prime Minister 1828–30, he was forced to concede Roman Catholic emancipation and became unpopular for his opposition to parliamentary reform. He was Foreign Secretary 1834–5□

Wells cathedral city in Somerset, England; population 8700. The 12–13th-century cathedral has a unique west front rich in statues□

Wells H(erbert) G(eorge) 1866–1946. British author, born at Bromley, Kent. For some years a science teacher, he first made a name in science fiction with *The Time Machine* 1895, *The Invisible Man* 1897, and *The War of the Worlds* 1898. Later books included novels with an anti-establishment, anti-conventional humour, remarkable in its day, e.g. *Kipps* 1905, *Ann Veronica* 1909, and *The History of Mr Polly* 1910. His outline *History of the World* 1920 and *The Shape of Things to Come* 1933, which included several prophecies later fulfilled, provided a new ideology for a growing newly-literate class□

Welsh see under Celts◊ and Wales◊□

Welsh corgi a type of dog◊ originally bred for cattle herding, it has a short-legged, sturdy build and fox-like head; usually tan-coloured□

welwitschia African gymnosperm◊ desert plant *Welwitschia mirabilis* of the Gnetal order. It has a long water-absorbent taproot, and may live a hundred years□

Welwyn Garden City 'new town' (chemicals, electrical engineering, clothing, food processing) developed from 1946, from the foundation laid by Ebenezer Howard◊; population 47 000□

Wembley see under Brent◊□

Wenceslas St d. c929. Duke of Bohemia who attempted to christianize his people and was murdered by his brother. He is patron saint of Czechoslavakia and the 'good King Wenceslas' of the carol□

Wenchow see Wenzhou◊□

Wentworth William Charles 1790–1872. Australian statesman. He was a member of the 1813 expedition which first crossed the Blue Mountains, and in 1855 was in England to steer the New South Wales constitution through Parliament, and was a pioneer campaigner for Australian self-government□

werewolf folk belief that certain human beings are either turned by spell to wolves, or have the ability to assume either human or wolf form. See under porphyria◊□

Werner Alfred 1866–1919. Swiss chemist. He was awarded a Nobel prize in 1913 for his work on Valency◊ theory□

Wesker Arnold 1932– . British playwright born in Hackney, with a varied career including plumber's mate, and pastrycook. He made his name with the trilogy: *Chicken Soup with Barley, Roots, I'm Talking about Jerusalem* 1959–60; and established a catchphrase with *Chips with Everything* 1962□

Wesley Charles 1707–88. Methodist preacher and theologian, brother of John Wesley; his 6500 hymns include 'Jesus, lover of my soul'□

Wesley John 1703–91. British founder of Methodism◊, born in Epworth, Lincolnshire. He studied at Christ Church, Oxford, together with his brother Charles, their circle being nicknamed Methodists because of their religious observances. He was ordained in the

Church of England in 1728, but in 1738 was 'converted' to evangelicalism, and began taking the Gospel to the masses. The churches being closed to him, he toured the country on horseback, preaching in the open-air□

Wessex kingdom of the W Saxons (modern Berkshire, Devon, Dorset, Hampshire, Somerset, and Wiltshire) founded by Cerdic◊ c500AD; see also Egbert◊□

West, American. The Great Plains region of the US to the East of the Rocky Mountains from Canada to Texas

1775 Wilderness Road opened by Daniel Boone◊

1805 Zebulon Pike (see Pike'◊s Peak) explored the Mississippi

1819 Major Stephen Long explored the Great Plains

1822 Santa◊ Fe Trail established

1824 Jim Bridger◊ discovered the Great Salt Lake

1836 the Alamo◊

1840–60 Oregon◊ Trail in use

1846 Mormon trek to Utah under Brigham Young◊

1846–8 Mexican◊ War

1849–56 California◊ gold rush

1860 Pony Express (St Joseph, Missouri – San Francisco, California) 3 Apr–22 Oct, when superseded by the telegraph

1863 on 1 January the first homestead was filed; followed by the settlement of the Western Prairies and Great Plains

1865–90 period of the Indian Wars

1867–80s period of the 'cattle kingdom', and cowboy trails such as the Chisholm Trail from Texas to the railheads at Abilene, Wichita, Dodge City

1869 Canadian Pacific Railway, first transcontinental railroad, completed

1876 Battle of Little Big Horn; see Custer◊ and Plains◊ Indians

1890 Battle of Wounded◊ Knee; official census declaration that the West no longer had a frontier line

famous people Buffalo Bill, Billy the Kid, Christopher Carson, James Fenimore Cooper, Davy Crockett, Wyatt Earp (see Tombstone◊), 'Wild Bill Hickok', Jesse James, Calamity Jane, Annie Oakley; *artists* George Catlin, Paul Kane, Frederic Remington, Charles Russell; *writers* Owen Wister□

West Benjamin 1738–1820. American artist, born in Pennsylvania, who settled in London in 1792; he became president of the Royal Academy in 1792. Many early American artists studied under him, and his works include *The Death of Wolfe*□

West Mae 1892–1980. American vaudeville actress and film star (*She Done Him Wrong* 1933), famous for sayings, e.g. 'Come up and see me sometime', and an hour-glass figure□

West African Economic Community established in 1975; members in 1984 include: Burkina Faso, Ivory Coast, Mali, Mauritania, Niger, Senegal; observer status is held by Benin, Togo□

West Bromwich industrial town (metalworking, springs, tubes, etc.) in West Midlands, England; population 163 000□

Western Australia state of the Commonwealth of Australia

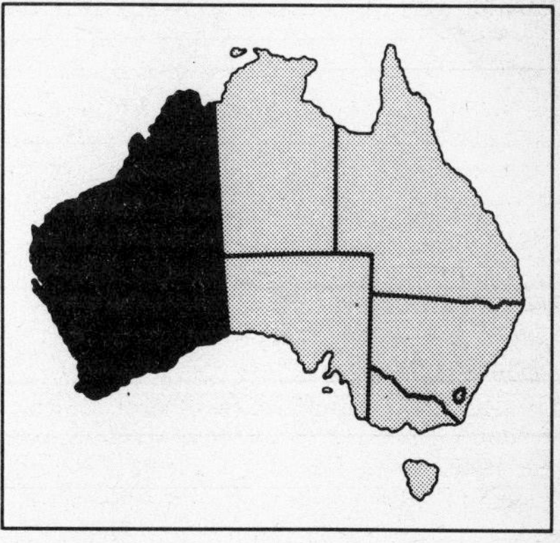

area 2 527 632 sq km/975 920 sq mi

capital Perth

towns the chief port Fremantle; Bunbury, Geraldton, Kalgoorlie-Boulder, Albany

features largest state of the Australian Commonwealth; Monte Bello Islands; rivers Fitzroy, Fortescue, Gascoyne, Murchison, and Swan; NW coast subject to hurricanes ('willy-willies'); see Lasseter◊'s Reef

exports wheat, fresh and dried fruit, meat and dairy products; natural gas (NW Shelf) and oil (Canning Basin); iron (The Pilbara); copper, nickel, uranium; gold and diamonds

population 1 299 100

history a convict settlement at King George Sound in 1826 was short-lived, and in 1829 Captain (later Sir) James Stirling founded the modern state at Perth. Responsible government was achieved in 1890, and in 1901 the state entered the Commonwealth□

Western Isles islands area of Scotland, comprising the Outer Hebrides (Lewis, Harris, N and S Uist, and Barra); unofficially used of the Hebrides generally

area 2901 sq km/1120 sq mi

towns administrative headquarters Stornoway on Lewis

features divided from the mainland by the Minch; Callanish monolithic circles of the Stone Age on Lewis

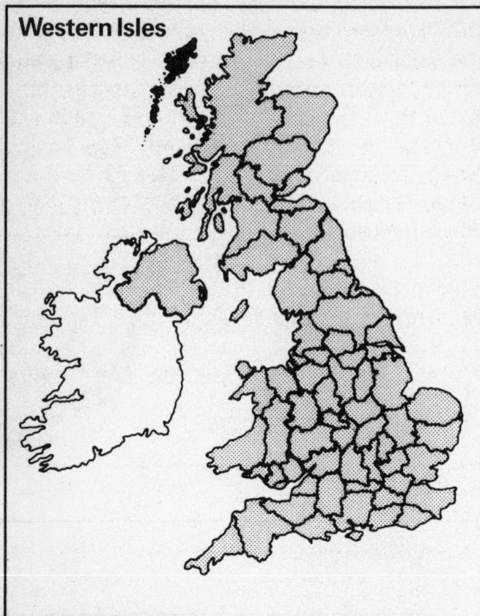

products Harris tweed
population 30 700□

Western Sahara

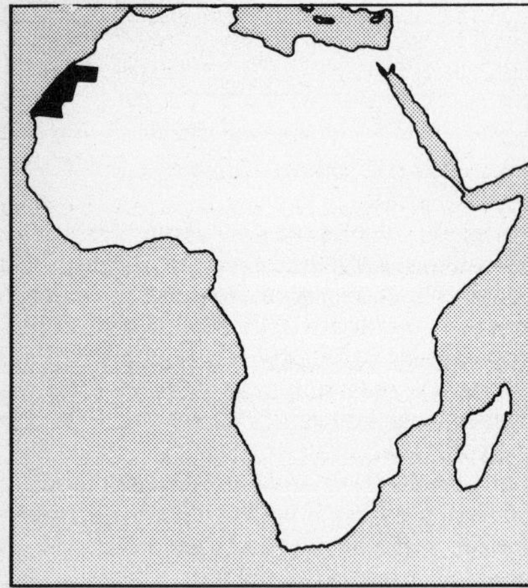

area 266 000 sq km/102 000 sq mi
capital La'Youn (Arabic *El Aaiún*)
towns phosphate mining town of Bou Craa
features defensive electrically-monitored fortified wall enclosing the phosphate area
exports phosphates
currency peseta
population c1 000 000 in the area occupied by Polisario; 400 000 in Algeria and Libya, and c73 000 in Morocco
language Arabic
religion Sunni Islam
government within the fortified wall Morocco rules, and outside, Polisario
recent history a Spanish possession until 1976, two thirds was taken over by Morocco, and one third by Mauritania (withdrew in 1979). The Popular Front for the Liberation of Saguia al Hamra and Rio de Oro (Polisario) proclaimed the Saharan Arab Democratic Republic in 1976, and is supported by Algeria and Libya; it currently controls the area formerly occupied by Mauritania□

Western Samoa

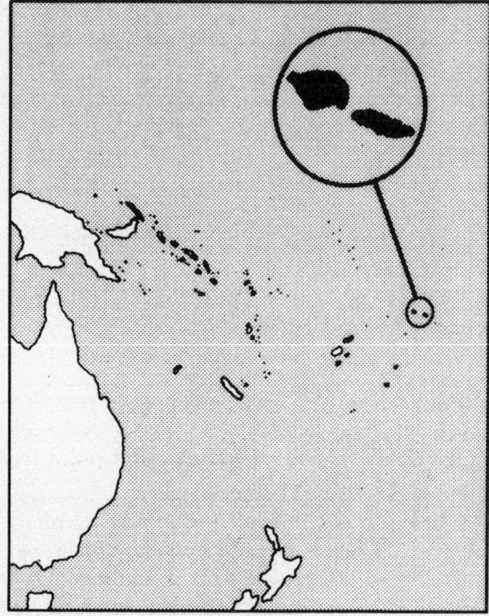

area 2842 sq km/1097 sq mi
capital Apia on Upolu
features comprises islands of Savai'i and Upolu, with two smaller islands and islets; mountain ranges on the main islands; huge lava flows on Savai'i which cut down the area available for agriculture
exports copra, bananas, cocoa; tourism is important
currency tala
population 162 000
language English and Samoan (official)
religion Christianity
government head of state, eventually to be elected for five years (Malietoa Tanumafili II, sole head for life from 1962); legislative assembly (Prime Minister Tofilan Eti Alesana from 1982)
recent history a German protectorate from 1900 until World War I, it was under New Zealand trusteeship 1920–61, and became independent within the Commonwealth 1962□

West Glamorgan county of S Wales
area 817 sq km/315 sq mi
towns administrative headquarters Swansea; Port Talbot, Neath
features Gower Peninsula, plants and wildlife
products tinplate, copper, steel
population 366 900

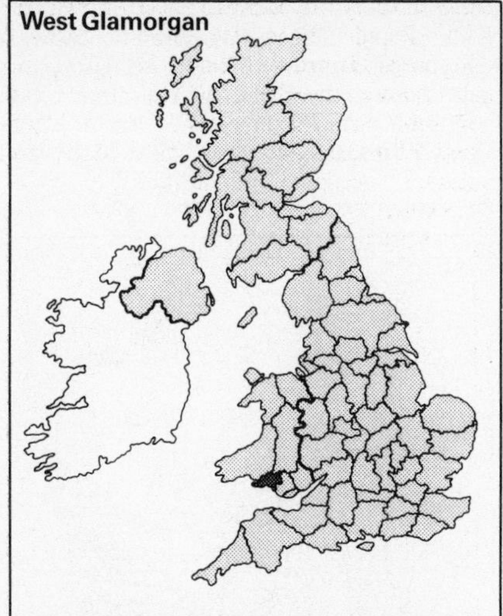
West Glamorgan

language English; Welsh-speaking 16%□

West Indies archipelago dividing the Atlantic from the Gulf of Mexico and the Caribbean. The islands comprise:
countries independent within the Commonwealth Bahamas, Barbados, Jamaica, Trinidad and Tobago, as well as (in the Leeward Islands) Anguilla, Antigua, Montserrat and St Kitts-Nevis, and (in the Windward Islands) Dominica, Grenada, St Lucia and St Vincent
French overseas departments Guadeloupe and Martinique;
Netherlands Antilles of which the largest is Curaçao
USA Puerto Rico
divided between UK and USA the Virgin Islands
independent Cuba, Haiti, Puerto and Dominican Republic◊□

West Indies, Federation of federal union comprising Antigua, Barbados, Dominica, Grenada, Jamaica, Montserrat, St Christopher with Nevis and Anguilla, St Lucia, St Vincent, and Trinidad and Tobago, which came into existence in 1958. This federation, of which the federal parliament was at Port-of-Spain, Trinidad, came to an end in 1962 when first Jamaica and then Trinidad and Tobago withdrew. Attempts at a new federation were abandoned in 1965□

Westland affair the events surrounding the takeover of the British Westland helicopter company in 1985–6. In financial difficulty, Westland was the subject of takeover bids from two sides, the American-Italian Sikorski-Fiat group, and a European consortium. Michael Heseltine◊, Minister of Defence, championed the European bid, and there was much political acrimony in the Cabinet and allegations of malpractice. The affair led to the resignation of two Cabinet ministers: Heseltine and Leon Brittan◊□

Westmeath county (county town Millingar) of the Republic of Ireland, province of Leinster◊□

West Midlands Midland county of England

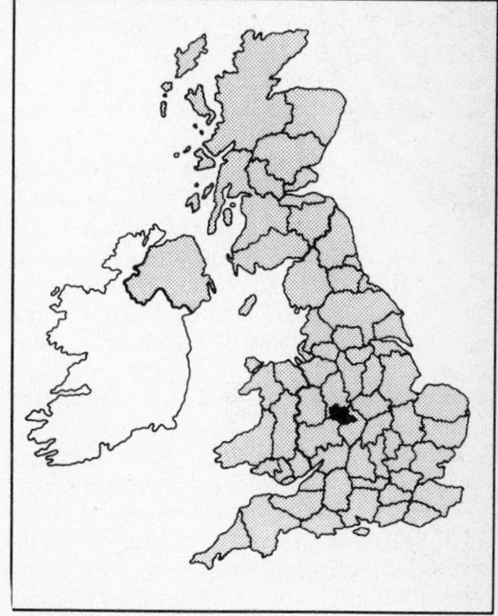

area 899 sq km/347 sq mi
towns administrative headquarters Birmingham
features created in 1974 from the area around and including Birmingham, and comprising Wolverhampton, Walsall, Dudley, West Bromwich, Smethwick, Coventry
products manufacturing industrial goods
population 2 686 700
famous people Philip Larkin□

Westminster City of. Borough of central Greater London
It includes the districts of ***Belgravia*** bounded to the N by Knightsbridge, which has magnificent squares laid out by Thomas Cubitt 1825–30; ***Bayswater*** to the N of Kensington Gardens residential area; ***Mayfair*** between Oxford Street and Piccadilly, which includes Park Lane and Grosvenor Square (with the American Embassy and Roosevelt Statue); ***Paddington*** which includes the picturesque 'little Venice' on the Grand Union Canal; ***Soho*** with many continental restaurants, a Chinese community, and strip clubs and sex shops; ***St John's Wood*** including Lord's Cricket Ground, and 11 Abbey Road (studios where the Beatles◊ recorded many of their songs); ***Westminster*** which includes Buckingham Palace, Green Park, St James's Park and St James's Palace, Marlborough House,

Westminister Abbey, Westminster Hall (1097–1401), Houses of Parliament and Big Ben, Whitehall (government offices), Downing Street (homes of the Prime Minister at No 10 and Chancellor of the Exchequer at No 11), New Scotland Yard, Tate Gallery (Turner collection, modern art), Hyde Park, where the Great Exhibition of 1851 was held, with the Albert Hall and Imperial College to the south; National Gallery, National Portrait Gallery, and Trafalgar Square
population 210 400□

Westminster Abbey built 1050–1745, includes Edward the Confessor's shrine, Henry VII's chapel, and the west towers by Hawksmoor◊; tombs of Henry III, Edward I, Henry VII, Elizabeth I, Mary Queen of Scots, Charles II, William III, Anne, and George II; Coronation Chair (including the Stone of Scone, on which Scottish Kings were crowned, brought here by Edward I in 1296); Poets' Corner□

Westmorland former English county, part of Cumbria from 1974□

Westphalia an independent medieval duchy, which became a province (capital Münster) of Prussia after the Napoleonic Wars, and since 1946 has been part of the region of North-Rhine◊ Westphalia□

Westphalia Treaty of. See under Thirty◊ Years' War□

West Point see under New◊ York state□

West Sussex southern county of England

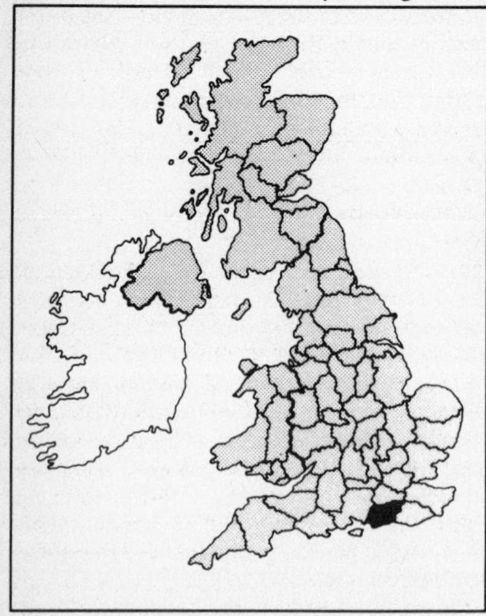

area 1989 sq km/768 sq mi
towns administrative headquarters Chichester; Arundel, Horley, Crawley, Horsham, Haywards Heath; resorts Worthing, Littlehampton, Bognor Regis; port Shoreham
features Weald, S Downs; rivers Arun, W Rother, Adur; Arundel and Bramber castles; Goodwood, Petworth House (see Turner◊), and Wakehurst Place, where Kew◊ has additional grounds

West Virginia State of the USA; Mountain State

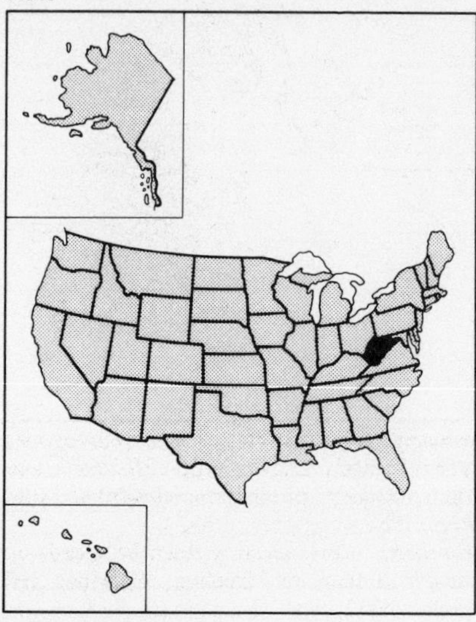

area 62 629 sq km/24 180 sq mi
capital Charleston
towns Huntington
features port of Harpers Ferry, restored as when John Brown◊ seized the US Armory in 1856
products fruit, poultry, dairy and meat products; timber; coal, natural gas, oil, chemicals, synthetic fibres, plastics, steel, glass and pottery
population 1 949 545
famous people Pearl Buck, Thomas 'Stonewall' Jackson
history on the secession of Virginia from the Union in 1862, West Virginians dissented, and formed an new state in 1863□

West Yorkshire
former metropolitan county of England (1976–86)
area 2039 sq km/787 sq mi
towns administrative headquarters Wakefield; Leeds, Bradford, Halifax, Huddersfield
features Ilkley Moor, Haworth Moor, Haworth Parsonage; part of the Peak District National Park. Ryedale is 'James Herriot◊' country
products coal, woollen textiles
population 2 018 000
famous people the Brontës, David Hockney, Henry Moore, J B Priestley, Joseph Priestley□

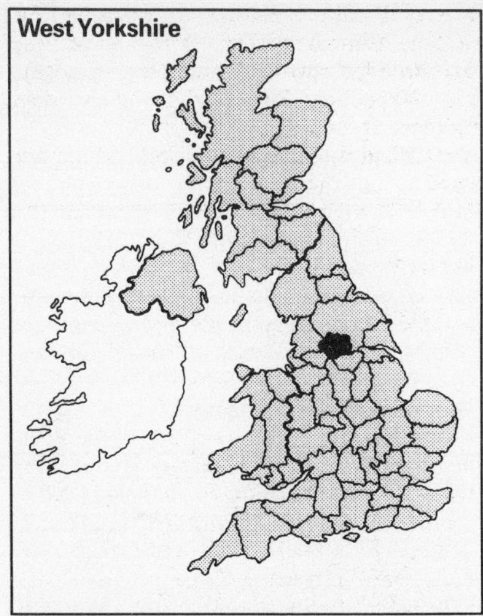
West Yorkshire

weta flightless insect *Deinacrida rugosa*, resembling a large grasshopper (8.5 cm/3.5 in long), found on offshore islands of New Zealand□

Wexford county (county town Wexford) of the Republic of Ireland, Province of Leinster◊□

Weyden Rogier van der c1399–1464. One of the greatest early Flemish painters, whose masterpiece, the *Deposition* (Prado, Madrid) shows his animated, emotive style at its best (and in great contrast to the dispassionate van◊ Eyck)□

whale large mammal adapted to marine life, order Cetacea◊. Being mammals they breathe air, and suckle their young; there are internal vestiges of hind limbs. When they surface to breathe, they eject exhausted air in a 'spout' through the blow-hole or nostril in the top of the head. The ***whalebone whales*** sub-order Mysticeti include the ***blue whale*** *Balaenoptera musculus* (30 m/90 ft long and weighing over 100 tonnes), the world's largest animal, but which feeds on plankton, strained through its whalebone 'plates'; the common ***rorqual*** *B physalas* is slate-coloured, and not quite so large. Largest of the ***toothed whales,*** sub-order Odontoceti, which feed on fish, etc., is the ***sperm whale*** *Physeter catodon* from whose head comes the glistening wax-like substance ***spermaceti***, c2.5 tonnes per animal, which was formerly much used in lubricants and cosmetics. The ***killer whale*** is a member of the dolphin◊ family.

Whales travel in herds, keeping in touch by 'songs', sung by the males. They probably navigate by following the earth's magnetic field, but in so doing seem not to take notice of danger signs. Mass strandings where herds of whales swim onto a beach occur occasionally for unknown reasons. Herd loyalty is strong, and the others follow their leader to disaster. The end of commercial whaling is planned for 1988□

Wharton Edith 1862–1937. American novelist, whose work was influenced by her friend Henry James◊, and includes *Ethan Frome* 1911, *The Age of Innocence* 1920, and *Old New York* 1924 (a series of four novelettes)□

wheat a type of grass. See grasses◊□

wheatear a small bird of the thrush◊ family□

Wheatstone Sir Charles 1802–75. British physicist, originally a musical instrument maker, and inventor of the concertina and harmonica. With W F Cooke◊, he patented the electric telegraph in 1837, and, developing an idea of Samuel Hunter Christie◊, devised the ***Wheatstone bridge*** an electrical network for measuring resistance□

Wheeler Sir Mortimer 1890–1976. British archaeologist, who as director-general of archaeology in India 1944–8 revealed the Indus◊ Valley Civilization□

whelk a shellfish of the gastropod◊ order□

Whig Party predecessor of the British Liberal Party. The name was first used of rebel Covenanters◊ and then for those who wished to exclude James II from the English succession (as a Roman Catholic). Thus, the Whigs strongly supported the 1688 Revolution and, led by a group of great landowners and, backed by the businessmen and Nonconformists, pressed for industrial and commercial development, a vigorous foreign policy, and religious toleration. During the French Revolution, the Whigs demanded parliamentary reform in Britain, and from the passing of the Reform Bill in 1832 became known as Liberals.

In the USA the Whig Party, during 1836–54, was one of the two major parties which opposed the radical policy of Andrew Jackson and defended commercial interests□

whip British Member of Parliament who (like the whipper-in of hounds at a foxhunt) ensures the presence of colleagues in the party when there is to be a vote in Parliament at the end of a debate. A three-line whip (three-times underlined) is the most urgent, meaning that the government is to some extent under threat□

whippet a small racing dog◊ like a greyhound□

whip-poor-will a N American nightjar◊□

Whipsnade see under Bedfordshire◊□

whisky distilled spirit (Gaelic *uisgebeatha* 'water of life') made from cereals: ***Scotch***

which is distilled from malt, the finest from Islay (see under Hebrides◊), though most of the distilleries are in Speyside, NW of Aberdeen; ***Irish whiskey*** (with an 'e') usually from barley, and American ***bourbon*** from Indian corn or rye□

whist predecessor of bridge◊, a card game for four, in which the partners try to win the balance of the 13 tricks (the highest card played being the winner)□

Whistler James Abbott McNeill 1834–1903. American Impressionist artist who settled in Chelsea, where he painted scenes using a limited, but evocative, palette, e.g. *Old Battersea Bridge*. His *Nocturnes* 1877 were attacked by Ruskin◊, and in the libel trial of 1878 Whistler won a farthing in damages□

Whitby fishing port in N Yorkshire, England; population 12 000. Captain Cook◊ served his apprenticeship here, and his ship, the *Resolution* was built here□

Whitby Synod of, 664. Summoned by King Oswy of Northumbria, it decided to adopt the Roman rather than the Celtic form of Christianity for Britain, so consolidating a link with the Continent□

White E(lwyn) B(rooks) 1899–1985. American writer, one of the makers of the *New Yorker* and an excellent satirist, e.g. *Is Sex Necessary?* 1929 (with Thurber◊), who also produced two children's classics, *Stuart Little* 1945 and *Charlotte's Web* 1952□

White Gilbert 1720–93. English cleric and naturalist, born at Selborne, Hampshire◊, and author of *Natural History and Antiquities of Selborne* 1789□

White Patrick 1912– . Australian novelist. Born in London, he settled in Australia in the 1940s. His novels (with allegorical overtones) include *The Aunt's Story* 1946, *Voss* (see Leichhardt◊) 1957, and *The Twyborn Affair* 1979. Nobel prize in 1973□

White T(erence) H(anbury) 1906–64. British writer, who retold the Arthurian legend in four volumes of *The Once and Future King* 1958□

whitebait the young of the herring◊□

Whitefield George 1714–70. British Methodist evangelist, who travelled Britain and America, greatly contributing to a religious revival. Whitefield's Tabernacle, Tottenham Court Road, London was founded in 1756 in his honour□

whitefish genus of silvery freshwater fish *Coregonus*, family Salmonidae, found in Eurasia and N America; most species are edible and also game fish□

Whitehall London street in which the Cenotaph◊ stands, and which is lined with government offices, so that the word has come to signify 'officialdom'□

Whitehaven port in Cumbria, England; population 26 300. Coal mines running beneath the sea have seen major disasters, and Britain's first nuclear power station was sited at Calder Hall to the SE, where there is also a plant for reprocessing spent nuclear fuel at Sellafield (formerly Windscale)□

Whitehead Alfred North 1861–1947. British philosopher-mathematician, who attempted a synthesis of metaphysics and science and collaborated with Bertrand Russell◊ in *Principia Mathematica* 1910–13□

White Horse see hillfigure◊□

White House official residence of the President of the USA, Washington, DC. Built to the designs of Hoban◊ 1792–9, it was fired by the British in 1814, but restored and painted white to hide the scars. It was rebuilt 1948-52□

Whitelaw William, Viscount Whitelaw 1918– . British Conservative politician. Leader of the House of Commons 1970–2, he was Secretary of State for N Ireland 1972–3 (when he introduced the concept of 'power-sharing'), for Employment 1973–4, and Home Secretary 1979–83, when he was created a peer□

White Russia see Belorussia◊□

Whites counter-revolutionary party during the French Revolution (the royalists used the royal white lily as their badge), and also in the Russian civil wars of 1917–21□

White Sea gulf of the Arctic◊ Ocean, on which Archangel stands and where there is a Soviet warship construction base, including nuclear submarines, at Severodvinsk. The N Dvina and Onega flow into it, and there are canal links with the Baltic, Black, and Caspian Seas□

white spirit colourless liquid derived from petrol, and used as a solvent, and in paints and varnishes□

whiting a fish of the cod◊ family□

Whitlam (Edward) Gough 1916– . Australian Labor statesman, leader of the party 1967–77 and Prime Minister 1972–5. He cultivated closer relations with Asia, and raised loans to increase national ownership of industry and resources. When the opposition blocked finance bills in the senate, following a crisis of confidence, he was dismissed by the Governor-General (Sir John Kerr), when he refused to call a general election. He was defeated in the general election eventually called by Fraser◊□

Whitman Walt(er) 1818–92. American poet. He worked as a printer, teacher, and journalist, and in 1855 published his influential

Leaves of Grass using unconventional free metres and scandalizing the public by his frank treatment of physical love. In the Civil War he was a war correspondent and worked nursing the wounded. His most famous poem is 'When Lilacs Last in the Dooryard Bloomed' (on Lincoln◊)□

Whit Sunday seventh Sunday after Easter, commemorating the descent of the Holy Spirit on the apostles; probably named from the white garments worn by baptismal candidates at the festival□

Whittier John Greenleaf 1807–92. American Quaker poet, the first to be widely popular, e.g. his nature-poem 'Snowbound' 1866; he was a powerful opponent of slavery□

Whittington Richard (Dick) d. 1423. English cloth merchant, who was mayor of London 1397–8, 1406–7, and 1419–20; according to legend, he came to London as a poor boy with his cat, and only the call of Bow Bells prevented his leaving before making his fortune□

Whittle Sir Frank 1907– . British engineer, designer of the first British jet, on which he worked from 1930; the Gloster E 28/39 aircraft flew with the Whittle engine in May 1941. Order of Merit in 1986□

whooping cough pertussis, an infectious fever marked by a long, crowing inspiration; it may continue months, and have complications. The vaccine used to give immunity to young children has been controversial because in rare cases it has side effects, including brain damage□

whortleberry a berried bush of the genus *Vaccinium*◊□

Whymper Edward 1840–1911. British mountaineer, first to climb the Matterhorn (see Alps◊), and wood engraver; he wrote *Scrambles amongst the Alps* 1871, etc.□

Wichita industrial city (oil refining, aircraft, motor vehicles) in Kansas, USA; population 279 835□

Wickham Sir Henry 1846–1928. British planter who broke Brazil's rubber monopoly by taking rubber seeds to found the industry in the Far East□

Wicklow county (county town Wicklow) of the Republic of Ireland, province of Leinster◊. It includes Wicklow Mountains, and the chief rivers are the Slane and Liffey. The village of Shillelagh gave its name to rough cudgels of oak or blackthorn made there□

Wien German name for Vienna◊□

Wigan industrial town (food processing, engineering, paper) in Greater Manchester, England; population 81 500. The ***Wigan Alps*** are a recreation area with ski slopes and water sports created from industrial dereliction including colliery spoil heaps. ***Wigan Pier*** 1 m/3 ft long on the canal, was immortalized by George Orwell in *The Road to Wigan Pier*□

wigeon a type of waterfowl◊□

Wight Isle of. S county of England
area 381 sq km/147 sq mi
towns administrative headquarters Newport; resorts Ryde, Sandown, Shanklin, Ventnor
features called *Vectis* ('separate division') by the Romans, it was conquered by Vespasian◊ in 43AD; the ***Needles*** a group of pointed chalk rocks up to 30 m/100 ft high in the sea to the W; the ***Solent*** the sea channel between Hampshire and the island (including the anchorage of ***Spithead*** opposite Portsmouth, used for naval reviews); the ruins of Carisbrooke castle, where Charles I was imprisoned 1647–8; Cowes, venue of Regatta Week and headquarters of the Royal Yacht Squadron; Osborne House, near Cowes, favourite home of Queen Victoria, for whom it was built in 1845; Farringford, home of Tennyson near Freshwater; Parkhurst prison
products agriculture; tourism is important
population 115 400□

Wilberforce Samuel 1805–73. British Anglican Bishop of Oxford 1845–69, and from 1869 of Winchester. He defended Anglican orthodoxy against the Tractarians◊□

Wilberforce William 1759–1833. British reformer whose bill for the abolition of the slave trade was passed in 1807; slavery was abolished through the British Empire by 1833□

Wilde Oscar. Adopted name of Fingal O'Flahertie Wills 1854–1900, Irish writer, born in Dublin. At Oxford he led the aesthetic circle burlesqued in Gilbert◊'s *Patience,* and astonished London society with *Poems* 1881, his only novel *The Picture of Dorian Gray* 1891, and the brilliantly witty comedies *Lady Windermere's Fan* 1892, *A Woman of no Importance* 1893, *An Ideal Husband* 1895, and *The Importance of Being Earnest* 1895. In 1895 he was imprisoned for homosexuality (see Lord Alfred Douglas◊ and Edward Carson◊) and wrote his *Ballad of Reading Gaol* 1898 and *De Profundis*, 1905 living on the continent after his release□

wildebeest see gnu◊□

Wilder Billy 1906– . Austrian-American film director whose work includes *Lost Weekend* 1945, *Sunset Boulevard* 1950, and *Some Like it Hot* 1959□

Wilder Thornton (Niven) 1897–1975. American novelist (e.g. *The Bridge of San Luis Rey* 1927) and playwright (e.g. *Our Town* 1938 and *The Skin of Our Teeth* 1942), who prepared the way for Arthur Miller◊ and Tennessee Williams◊□

Wilfrid St 634–709. Northumbrian-born Bishop of York from 665 who defended the cause of the Roman Church at the Synod of Whitby in 664 against that of Celtic Christianity; feast day, 12 Oct□

Wilkes John 1727–97. British Radical politician. Outlawed in 1764 for his attacks on Bute◊ in his paper *The North Briton*, he fled to France and on his return in 1768 was imprisoned. He was later four times elected MP for Middlesex without being able to take his seat, but was admitted to the House in 1774 and campaigned as an MP until 1790 for parliamentary reform, religious toleration, and American independence□

Wilkie Sir David 1785–1841. Scottish genre painter who made his reputation with such pictures as *Village Politicians* 1806 and *The Blind Fiddler*□

Wilkins Sir Hubert 1888–1958. Australian polar explorer, a pioneer in the use of surveys by both aircraft and submarine□

will legal document executed by person (being neither a minor nor a lunatic) to dispose of his/her property on death. Except for those on active service, a will must be written or printed, and signed by the testator in the presence of two witnesses who also sign and may not benefit under its provisions. Practice in the USA is similar□

William four kings of England:

William I the Conqueror c1027–87. King from 1066. The illegitimate child of Duke Robert the Devil, he succeeded his father as Duke of Normandy in 1035, and, claiming that his kinsman Edward◊ the Confessor had bequeathed him the English throne, invaded the country in 1066, defeating Harold◊ at Hastings◊, and was crowned (see Bayeux◊ Tapestry). He completed the establishment of feudalism in England (see Domesday◊ Book) and kept the barons firmly under control. He died at Rouen after a fall from his horse and is buried at Caen.

William II called Rufus, 'the Red' c1056–1100, king from 1087, he was the third son of William◊ I. For most of his reign he was trying to conquer Normandy from his brother Robert. His extortion of money from his barons led them to revolt and in the case of the church to confrontation with Anselm◊. He was killed while hunting in the New Forest.

William III called William of Orange 1650–1702. King of Great Britain and Ireland from 1688. The son of William II of Orange and Mary, daughter of Charles I, he was made *Stadtholder* in 1672 to resist the French invasion of his country. He forced Louis XIV to make peace in 1678 and henceforward concentrated on building up a European alliance against the French threat. In 1677 he married his cousin Mary, daughter of the future James II, and, when invited by the English opposition to James's rule, invaded England in 1688 and accepted the crown as joint sovereign with Mary in 1689. He spent much of his reign campaigning, first in Ireland, where in 1690 he defeated James II at the Boyne, and later against the French in Flanders.

William IV 1765–1837, King of United Kingdom from 1830, and 3rd son of George III. During the Reform◊ Bill crisis he secured its passage by agreeing to create new peers□

William (German *Wilhelm*) two emperors of Germany:

William I 1797–1888, King of Prussia from 1861 and declared emperor by Bismarck◊ in 1871, he pursued a policy largely dictated by Bismarck.

William II 1895–1941, emperor from 1888. In 1890 he forced Bismarck◊ to resign and his subsequent foreign policy was disastrous. In 1914 he first approved Austria's ultimatum to Serbia and then, when he realized war was becoming inevitable, tried in vain to prevent it. In 1918 he fled to Holland□

William three kings of the Netherlands:

William I 1772–1844, became king in 1814, after living in exile during the French occupation 1795–1813. The Austrian Netherlands was added to his kingdom in 1815 by the Allies, but secured its independence in 1830 (as Belgium), and by 1840 William was so unpopular with his own people that he abdicated.

William II 1792–1849, son of William I, who averted revolution by conceding a liberal constitution in 1848.

William III 1817–90, son of William II□

William the Lion 1143–1214. King of Scotland from 1165, he was captured by Henry II while invading England in 1174, and forced to do homage, but Richard I abandoned the English claim to suzerainty for a money payment in 1189□

William German Crown Prince. See Frederick◊ William□

William the Silent 1533–84. Prince of Orange from 1544, and appointed governor of Holland by Philip II of Spain in 1559. However, he joined the revolt of 1572 against Spain's oppressive rule, and, as a Protestant from 1573, became the national leader. He tried to unite the Catholic south and Protestant north provinces, but the former provinces submitted to Spain while the latter formed a federation in 1579 which repudiated Spanish suzerainty in 1581. He was assassinated by a Spanish agent. His nickname arose from his absolute discretion when necessary□

William of Malmesbury c1080–1143. English monk at Malmesbury Abbey, Wiltshire, whose works form a history of England to 1142□

William of Occam. See Occam◊□

William (of Wales) Prince 1982– . Prince of the United Kingdom. Born on 21 Jun 1982, eldest child of the Prince and Princess of Wales□

William of Wykeham c1323–1404. English churchman, Bishop of Winchester from 1367, Lord Chancellor 1367–72 and 1389–91, and founder of Winchester College in 1378 and New College, Oxford in 1379□

Williams (George) Emlyn 1905– . Welsh actor-playwright, born in Mostyn, Clwyd. His plays, in which he appeared, include *Night Must Fall* 1935 and *The Corn is Green* 1938□

Williams Sir George. See Young◊ Men's Christian Association□

Williams Roger c1604–84. English founder of Rhode Island colony in 1636, on a basis of democracy and complete religious freedom□

Williams Shirley 1930– . British Social◊ Democrat Party politician, the daughter of Vera Brittain◊, and married to Professor Bernard Williams 1955–74. Labour Minister for Prices and Consumer Protection 1974–6, and Education and Science 1976–9, she became a founder of the SDP in 1981, and its president in 1982. In 1983 she lost her parliamentary seat, the first time she had put her defection from the Labour Party to the public vote□

Williams Tennessee. Pseudonym of American playwright Thomas Lanier Williams 1911–83, born in Missouri. His women characters are especially affected by the frustrations of life in the Deep South, as in *The Glass Menagerie* 1945, *A Streetcar named Desire* 1947, and *The Night of the Iguana* 1961□

Williams William Carlos 1883–1963. American poet, noted for his spare images and language, and advanced verse forms in intellectual patterns□

Williamsburg city in Virginia, USA; population 10 000. Founded in 1632, and capital of the colony of Virginia 1699–1779, it has been restored to its 18th-century perfection with the aid of John D Rockefeller, Junior. The College of William and Mary (1693), is one of the oldest in the USA□

Williams-Ellis Sir Clough 1883–1978. British architect, designer of the Italianate fantasy resort of Portmeirion, Gwynedd◊□

Williamson Malcolm 1931– . British composer, born in Australia, who settled in Britain in 1953. His works include the opera *Our Man in Havana* 1963; he became Master of the Queen's Music in 1975□

Willis Ted, Baron Willis 1931– . British playwright, creator of the television police series *Dixon of Dock Green* 1953–63, and plays of working-class life, e.g. *Woman in a Dressing Gown* filmed 1958; life peer in 1963□

will-o'the-wisp light sometimes seen over marshy ground, believed to be burning gas from decaying organic matter. See under methane◊□

willow genus *Salix* of deciduous trees and shrubs of the cooler N hemisphere, family Salicaceae, with unisexual flowers borne in catkins, and tough, supple shoots used in basket-making, etc., e.g. ***white willow*** *S alba* (cricket bats are made from the variety *caerulea*); ***weeping willow*** *S babylonica*; ***pussy willow*** *S caprea*; and ***common osier*** *S viminalis*. Willows secrete salicin, an aspirin-like substance used to treat rheumatism and fever□

willowherb temperate plants, family Onagraceae, including the ***rosebay willowherb*** or ***fireweed*** *Chamaenerion angustifolium* with spikes of purple flowers. See evening◊ primrose, fuchsia◊□

willow warbler a bird of the warbler◊ family□

willy-willy Australian Aboriginal term for a cyclonic whirlwind□

Wilmington industrial port and city (chemicals, textiles, shipbuilding, iron and steel goods, headquarters of Du Pont enterprises) in Delaware, USA; population 70 200□

Wilson Sir Angus 1913– . British novelist, professor of English literature at East Anglia 1966–78. His acidly humorous books include *Anglo-Saxon Attitudes* 1956 and *The Old Men at the Zoo* 1961□

Wilson Charles Thomson Rees 1869–1959. British physicist, inventor in 1911 of the Wilson cloud chamber◊; shared Nobel prize in 1927□

Wilson Colin 1931– . British author of *The Outsider* 1956, which made the social misfit a hero, and of thrillers□

Wilson Edmund 1895–72. American critic, e.g. *Axel's Castle* (on the Symbolists) 1931, and *The Wound and the Bow* 1941, study of the link between art and neurosis□

Wilson Edward Osborne 1929– . American zoologist, specializing in social insects, whose *Sociobiology, the New Synthesis* 1975 originated the new study sociobiology◊□

Wilson (James) Harold, Baron Wilson 1916– . British Labour statesman. Born in Huddersfield, he was president of the Board of Trade 1947–51 (when he resigned because of social service cuts), and in 1963 succeeded Gaitskell◊ as Labour leader. He was Prime Minister 1964–70 (increasing his majority in 1966) and (following elections) formed a minority government in Feb 1974 and achieved a majority of three in Oct 1974. He resigned in 1976, to be succeeded by Callaghan◊. His premiership was dominated by the issue of UK admission to EEC◊ membership, the Social◊ Contract, and economic difficulties. He was knighted in 1976, and became a peer in 1983□

Wilson Henry Maitland 'Jumbo', 1st Baron Wilson 1881–1964. British field marshal. He was Commander-in-Chief in Egypt in 1939, led the unsuccessful Greek campaign of 1941, was Commander-in-Chief in the Middle East in 1943, and in 1944 was Supreme Allied Commander in the Mediterranean□

Wilson Richard 1714–82. Welsh pioneer landscape artist, depicting both Italian and native Welsh scenes□

Wilson Robert Woodrow 1936– . American astrophysicist. He discovered (with Arno Penzias◊) the cosmic microwave background radiation which confirmed the big◊ bang theory; shared Nobel prize in 1978□

Wilson (Thomas) Woodrow 1856–1924. 28th president of the USA 1913–21, born at Staunton, Virginia. A Democrat, he was forced to declare war on Germany by the U-boat campaign in 1917 (calling it the 'war to end war'), and in Jan 1918 issued 'Fourteen Points' as a basis for peace, his plan for a League of Nations being incorporated into the Treaty of Versailles, but he failed to get the Senate to accept the twin package. Campaigning in an appeal to the people, he had a stroke, never really recovering. His aim was 'open covenants, openly arrived at'□

Wiltshire SW county of England
area 3480 sq km/1344 sq mi
towns administrative headquarters Trowbridge; Salisbury, Swindon, Wilton
features Marlborough Downs, Savernake Forest; rivers Kennet, and Salisbury and Bristol Avons; Salisbury Plain, an area of open downland (775 sq km/300 sq mi) which includes Avebury◊, Silbury◊, and Stonehenge◊, and has been used as a military training area since Napoleonic times; Longleat House (Marquess of Bath), Wilton House (Earl of Pembroke), and Stourhead with 18th-century gardens
products wheat, cattle; carpets, rubber
population 527 700

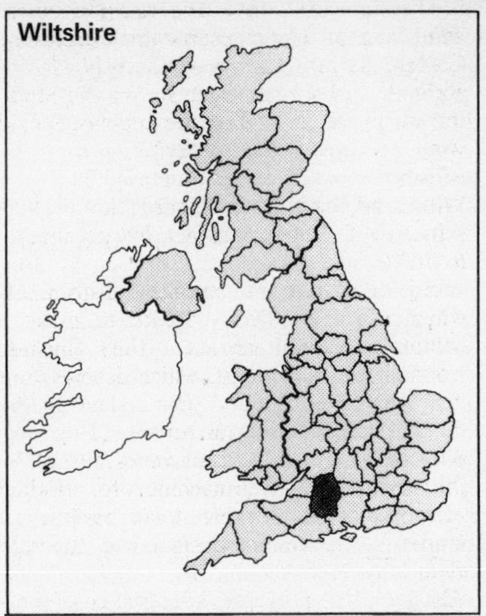

famous people George Crabbe, William Golding□

Wimbledon see Merton◊□

Winchester city and administrative headquarters of Hampshire on the River Itchen; population 92 500. The cathedral (1079–1528) is magnificent; William the Conqueror was crowned there, and those buried there include St Swithun◊, William◊ of Wykeham (founder of Winchester College), Izaac Walton◊, and Jane Austen◊. A medieval 'reconstruction' of Arthur's Round Table is preserved in the 13th-century hall (all that survives) of the castle. Winchester was the capital of Wessex◊□

wind a lateral movement of the earth's atmosphere. Though modified by features such as land and water, there is a basic system whereby a belt of low pressure (the ***doldrums***) lies along the equator. The ***trade winds*** blow towards this from the ***horse latitudes*** (high pressure areas c30°N and 30°S of the equator), blowing from the NE in the northern hemisphere, and from the SE in the southern. The ***westerlies*** (also from the horse latitudes) blow from the SW north of the equator and from the NW to the south. The ***monsoon*** (Arabic *mausim* 'season') is a seasonal wind of S Asia, blowing from the SW Apr–Oct to bring the rain on which crops depend, and from the NE in winter.

Famous or notorious warm winds include the ***chinook*** from the Pacific, after it has lost its moisture over the W Rocky Mountains; ***Föhn*** of Switzerland's alpine valleys; ***sirocco*** (Italy)/***khamsin*** (Egypt)/***sharav*** (Israel), etc., spring winds which bring warm air from the Sahara and Arabian deserts across the

Mediterranean; ***Santa Ana*** periodic warm wind from the inland deserts which strikes the California coast. The dry northerly ***bise*** (Switzerland) and ***mistral*** which strikes the Mediterranean area of France, are unpleasant cold winds. See also meteorology◊□

Windermere see under Cumbria◊□

Windhoek capital of Namibia/South West Africa, with hot springs nearby; population 61 260□

wind instruments musical instruments which use the player's breath to make a column of air vibrate. They include woodwind◊ instruments, which despite their name, may be of wood or metal, as in the flute. See also brass ◊ instruments□

windmill mill with sails or vanes, turned by the wind, which drives machinery for grinding corn, pumping water, etc. ***A wind turbine*** is a modern development designed to generate electricity□

Windsor lake port and industrial city (automobile engines, iron and steel goods, bricks) in Ontario, Canada; population 192 550□

Windsor Duke and Duchess of. See under Edward◊ VIII□

Windsor House of. Official name of the British royal family, adopted in place of 'Saxe-Coburg-Gotha' in 1917. Since 1960 those descendants of Elizabeth II not entitled to the prefix HRH have borne the surname Mountbatten-Windsor□

Windsor (born Wallis Warfield), Duchess of 1896–1986. She married Earl Winfield Spencer in 1916 (they divorced in 1927), Ernest Simpson in 1928 (they divorced in 1936) and the Duke of Windsor (formerly Edward◊ VIII) in 1937□

Windsor Castle royal residence in Windsor, Berkshire. Founded by William the Conqueror, it is on the site of an earlier fortress, and includes St George's Chapel (a fine example of Perpendicular architecture and the chapel of the Order of the Garter), Albert Memorial Chapel (beneath which George III, George IV, William IV, George V, and George VI are buried), and (beyond the Round Tower or Keep) the state apartments and the sovereign's private apartments. In the Home Park adjoining the castle is the Royal Mausoleum where Queen Victoria, the Prince Consort, and Edward VIII rest. Windsor Great Park, lies to the south□

windsurfing a type of surfing◊□

wind tunnel laboratory equipment to simulate conditions of flight for models of aircraft, etc., by blowing air past the stationary models. Used in the development of eventual full-scale planes□

wind turbine a type of windmill◊□

Windward Islands islands in the path of the prevailing wind, notably:
West Indies see under Antilles◊
Cape◊ Verde Islands (N group), see Netherlands◊ ***Antilles*** (St Maarten, St Eustatius, and Saba); ***French◊ Polynesia*** (Tahiti, Moorea, and Makatea)□

wine liquor of fermented grape pulp in which the sugar content has been converted to ethyl alcohol by the yeast◊ *Saccharomyces ellipsoideus* which lives on the skin of the grape. For ***dry wine*** the fermentation is allowed to go on longer than for ***sweet*** or ***medium***; ***red wine*** is the product of the grape with the skin, but ***white wine*** of the inner pulp only. Sparkling wines are bottled while still fermenting, but sparkling champagne is artificially carbonated. A ***vintage wine*** is that from a good year (as regards weather) in recognized vineyards of a particular area, i.e. in France, having a guarantee of origin, *appellation controlée*. The world's largest producers are Italy, France, Russia, and Spain; others include Germany, Australia, S Africa, California, and Chile; English-grown wines are small in quantity, but high in quality□

Wingate Orde Charles 1903–44. British soldier, whose Chindits◊ were guerrilla operators against Japan in Burma; he was killed in an air crash there□

winkle a shellfish of the gastropod◊ order□

Winnipeg capital of Manitoba, Canada, S of ***Lake Winnipeg*** (23 553 sq km/9094 sq mi); population 560 000. A financial centre, it has a grain market, sawmills, meatpacking, and other varied industries□

wintergreen an evergreen shrub. See under heath◊□

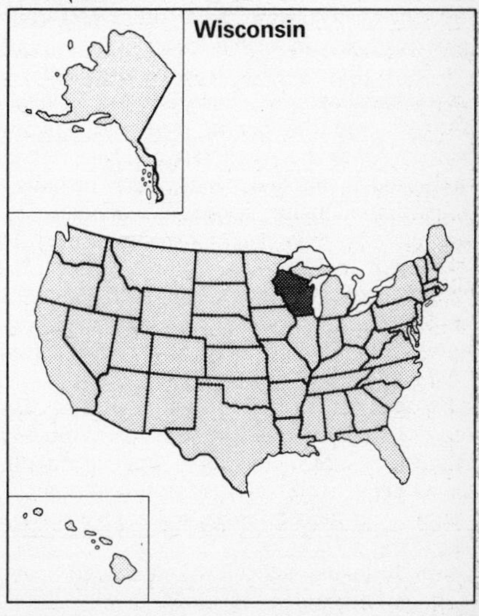

wireworm the larva of some types of beetle◊□

Wisconsin state of the USA; Badger State
area 145 438 sq km/56 153 sq mi
capital Madison
towns Milwaukee
features Great Lakes
products premier dairying state; cereals; coal, iron, zinc, lead; agricultural machinery, precision instruments, plumbing equipment
population 4 705 335
famous people Edna Ferber, Harry Houdini, Joseph McCarthy, Spencer Tracy, Orson Welles, Thornton Wilder, Frank Lloyd Wright
history originally settled by the French, it passed to Britain in 1763, became American in 1783, and in 1848 became a state□

Wiseman Nicholas Patrick Stephen 1802–65. British cardinal, first Roman Catholic Archbishop of Westminster from 1850; Newman◊ was his protégé□

Wishart George c1513–46. Scottish Protestant reformer burnt for heresy; he probably converted John Knox◊□

Wister Owen 1860–1938. American novelist, born Pennsylvania, famous for Western novel *The Virginian* 1902□

Wisteria genus of twining climbers, family Leguminosae◊, with scented mauve or white flowers in pendulous racemes□

witan council of the Anglo-Saxon kings, the forerunner of Parliament, but including only royal household officials, great landowners, and top churchmen□

witchcraft magical powers (***black magic*** if used with the aid of devils, and ***white*** if benign, as in the 'charming' of warts). Practitioners of witchcraft have often had considerable skill in herbal medicine, etc., and in 1976 the World Health Organization recommended the integration of witch doctors into the health teams of African states. ***obi*** is the witchcraft of black Africa imported to the West Indies, and including Christian elements; ***voodoo*** is a similar cult, similarly involving snake worship, especially prevalent in Haiti (see zombie◊). See also Joan◊ of Arc, Gilles de Rais◊, and Salem◊□

witch hazel shrub *Hamamelis virginiana* family Hamamelidaceae; the bark and leaves yield an astringent lotion□

witness person giving evidence in a case before court of law. The rules of admissible evidence are complex, but generally speaking it must be direct oral testimony as to relevant facts given by someone who was present□

Witt John de 1625–72. Dutch statesman, Grand Pensionary of Holland and virtual Prime Minister from 1653. His skilful diplomacy ended the Dutch◊ Wars of 1652–4 and 1665–7, and in 1668 he formed a triple alliance with England and Sweden against Louis XIV. He was murdered by a rioting mob□

Wittenberg town in Halle district, E Germany; population 53 870. Luther preached in the *Stadtkirche* (in which he is buried), nailed his 95 theses to the door of the *Schlosskirche* in 1517, and taught philosophy at the university (transferred to Halle in 1815) which was first established in 1502. The artists Lucas Granach◊, father and son, lived here□

Wittgenstein Ludwig (1889-1951). Viennese philosopher who taught at Cambridge in the 1930s and 40s and whose work on the foundations of mathematics, the philosophy of mind, and the nature and limits of language, has been very influential. In 1912 he went to study at Cambridge under Bertrand Russell◊ *Tractatus Logico-Philosophicus* 1922, written during World War I, was a detailed working out of a 'picture theory' of language: a sentence must be analysable into 'atomic propositions' whose elements stand for elements of the real world; otherwise, the sentence is not stating any fact. Wittgenstein's later philosophy (c1929–51) as presented, e.g., in *Philosophical Investigations* (published in 1954) developed a quite different, anthropological, view of language: words are used according to different rules in a variety of human activities — different 'language games' are played with them. The traditional philosophical problems arise through the assumption that words (like 'exists' in the sentence 'Physical objects do not really exist') carry a fixed meaning with them, independent of context□

Wittlesbach Bavarian dynasty ruling as dukes from 1180, electors from 1623, and kings 1806–1918. ***Prince Albrecht*** 1905– , grandson of Ludwig III and descendant of Elizabeth, daughter of James I of England, is technically a claimant to the British throne□

woad biennial plant *Isatis tinctoria*, family Cruciferae◊, with arrow-shaped leaves and clusters of yellow flowers; ancient Britons used its blue dye as a body paint in battle□

Wodehouse Sir P(elham) G(renville) 1881–1975. British humorist, a US citizen from 1955. His novels portray the aristocratic world of the socialite Bertie Wooster and his invaluable and impeccable man-servant Jeeves, with such subsidiary characters as Lord Emsworth of Blandings Castle and his pig, the Empress of Blandings. He also collaborated on the 'books' of musicals by Jerome Kern, Gershwin, and others. In 1941 he was in France, and was interned by the

Germans, making broadcasts from Berlin that were innocently meant rather than treasonable: he was later exonerated and knighted in 1975□

Woden see Odin◊□

Wöhler Friedrich 1800–82. German chemist who synthesized the first organic compound (urea) from an inorganic compound (ammonium cyanate): it had previously been thought impossible to convert an inorganic compound to an organic one. He also isolated the elements aluminium, beryllium, yttrium, and titanium□

wolf largest wild member of the dog family, Canidae: see Coyote◊, Dingo◊. The Euro-Asian common wolf *Canis lupus* has thick greyish fur; the North American ***timber wolf*** is a larger variety. Wolves have a highly organized social life with a fixed hierarchy and cooperate skilfully in hunting. Urban expansion has restricted their range and when they are near extermination because of shooting (as in Italy) their ecological niche is taken over by the feral dog, descendant of domestic 'escapes'□

Wolf Hugo 1860–1903. Austrian composer who became a Vienna music critic. His songs were among the greatest achievements of the Viennese *lieder* tradition□

Wolfe James 1727–59. British soldier. After service on the Continent, he served under Amherst in Canada in 1758, and in 1759, having been promoted major-general, commanded the victorious expedition against Quebec in which he lost his life□

Wolfe Thomas 1900–1938. American novelist, born in N Carolina. His belief in the unconscious as the source of good writing produced an enormous wordage which had to be cut and shaped by his publisher/editor Maxwell Perkins: *Look Homeward, Angel* 1929, *Of Time and the River* 1935, and the posthumous *The Web and the Rock* 1939 and *You Can't go Home Again* 1940□

Wolf-Ferrari Ermanno 1876–1948. Italo-German composer, whose operas include the comic *The Secret of Suzanne* 1909 and the realistic tragedy *The Jewels of the Madonna* 1911□

Wolfit Sir Donald 1902–68. British actor-manager, excelling in larger-than-life roles, e.g. Shakespeare's Shylock and Lear□

wolfram alternative name for tungsten◊□

Wolfsburg industrial town in Lower Saxony, W Germany, founded in 1938 as the headquarters of the Volkswagen car company; population 124 000□

Wolfson Sir Isaac 1897– . British store magnate, chairman of Great Universal Stores from 1946. He established the ***Wolfson Foundation*** in 1955 to promote health, education, and youth activities and in 1966 (with the Ford Foundation) endowed Wolfson College, Oxford□

Wollongong industrial town (coalmining, iron, and steel) in New South Wales, Australia, which includes Port Kembla; population 235 000□

Wollstonecraft Mary 1759–97. British feminist whose *Vindication of the Rights of Women* 1792 demanded equal educational opportunities for men and women. She married William Godwin and died in giving birth to a daughter, Mary, who married Shelley◊□

Wolseley Garnet Joseph, 1st Viscount Wolseley 1833–1913. British field marshal, who as Commander-in-Chief 1895–1900, began modernizing the British army□

Wolsey Thomas c1475–1530. English cardinal and statesman. Born at Ipswich, he was one of the 'new men' rapidly promoted by Henry VIII and was both raised to the cardinalate and became Lord Chancellor in 1515. For a decade he was one of the most powerful men in Europe. He began the dissolution of the monasteries with the smaller foundations, and in zeal for the 'new learning' established Cardinal (now Christ Church) College, Oxford. His reluctance to further Henry's divorce from Catherine of Aragon, partly because of his ambitions to be Pope, led to his downfall in 1529. He was charged with high treason in 1530 but died before being tried□

Wolverhampton industrial city (metal-working, chemicals, tyres, aircraft, commercial vehicles) in W Midlands, England; population 255 400□

wolverine an animal of the weasel◊ family□

wombat an animal of the family Marsupialia◊□

Women's Institutes national federation of local organizations in country districts for mutual fellowship, community welfare, and the practice of country crafts, they are non-class, non-sectarian, and non-party political. The first such institute was founded in 1897 at Stoney Creek, Ontario, under the presidency of Mrs Adelaide Hoodless; the National Federation of Women's Institutes in the UK was founded in 1915. The ***National Union of Townswomen's Guilds*** founded in 1929, is the city equivalent□

women's movement campaign for women's equality, of which early pioneers were Mary Wollstonecraft◊ and Emmeline Pankhurst◊, and which gained worldwide impetus after World War II with writers such as Simone de Beauvoir◊, the American Betty Friedan 1921– (*The Feminine Mystique*

1963), the German Eva Figes 1932– (*Patriarchal Attitudes* 1970), and the Australian Germaine Greer 1939– (*The Female Eunuch* 1970). Since 1975 discrimination against women in employment, education, housing, and provision of goods, facilities, and services to the public has been illegal in the UK, but a constitutional amendment prohibiting sex discrimination adopted by Congress in the USA in 1972 has never been ratified by the states□

Women's Services see under Armed Services◊□

wood hard, fibrous substance between the bark of the stem and branches of a shrub or tree: in the case of trees it forms the timber used in furniture and building construction, and supplies pulp for paper and the viscose fibre which has largely replaced cotton in textile manufacture. A super-hard wood is produced in wood plastic combinations (WPC), in which wood is impregnated with liquid plastic (monomer) and the whole is then bombarded with gamma-rays to polymerize the plastic□

Wood Mrs Henry 1814–87. British novelist. A pioneer of crime fiction, she is remembered for the melodramatic *East Lynne* 1861□

Wood Sir Henry 1869–1944. British conductor, founder of the Promenade◊ Concerts in 1895. He was the composer of a *Fantasia of Sea Songs*□

Wood John c1705–54. British architect, known as 'Wood of Bath' because of his many works in the city. As with many of his designs, Royal Crescent was executed by his son, also ***John Wood***, d. 1782□

wood carving an art form practised since prehistoric times, but surviving less often than sculpture in stone or metal because of the comparative fragility of the material, especially in tropical Africa where there is a fine tradition in West Africa, notably Nigeria. See also Veit Stoss◊ and Grinling Gibbons◊□

woodcock Eurasian game bird *Scolopax rusticola*, family Scolopacidae (see snipe◊), with mottled plumage, a long bill, short legs, and hardly any tail□

woodcut and ***wood engraving***. See print◊□

Woodforde James 1740–1803. British clergyman who held livings in Somerset and Norfolk, and whose diaries 1758–1802 form a record of rural England□

woodlouse arthropod of class Crustacea◊, order Isopoda, which lives on land, usually in damp, dark, cool habitats; has a segmented body and flattened underside; most common in Britain are the genera *Oniscus* and *Porcellio*. However, they adapt to less moisture and higher temperatures (e.g. central heating) and become prolific house pests (they live about five years, breed every six months, and have about 30 eggs at a time in the brood pouch)□

woodpecker order of birds, Piciformes, many drilling holes in tree trunks for nesting or to extract insects. They include:

woodpeckers e.g. the Eurasian ***great spotted woodpecker*** *Dendrocopos major* family Picidae, which substitute drumming with their beak on hollow wood for a mating song; European ***green woodpecker*** *Picus viridis* and the related Eurasian ***wrynecks*** *Jynginae* which habitually twist their heads and necks; they are not wood drillers

barbet small, brightly coloured African birds, family Capitonidae

toucans family Ramphistidae, of S America, which include the ***toco toucan*** *Ramphastos toco* 60 cm/2 ft long, with a hollow, almost banana-like beak 20 cm/8 in long and 8 cm/3 in thick at the head end□

Woodstock market town in Oxfordshire, England; population 2100. Blenheim◊ Palace is nearby. Woodstock Manor (destroyed after the Civil War) was a royal residence□

woodwind instruments musical instruments which use the player's breath to make a column of air vibrate. Woodwind instruments, despite their name, may be of wood or metal, as in the flute. They are distinguished from brass◊ instruments by not having a cupped metal mouthpiece. They fall into two categories: reed instruments, in which air vibration is set up by a reed, and those without a reed, where air is simply blown into or across a tube. In both cases, different notes are obtained by changing the length of the tube by covering holes along it. Reed instruments include:

clarinet invented by Joseph Denner (1655–1707); unusual in that it is played without any vibrato

oboe a double-reeded wooden tube with a bell and plaintive tone, derived from the earlier ***shawm*** and ***hautboy***

cor anglais (French 'English horn') a similar instrument to the oboe, but slightly longer, and with a deeper tone

bassoon the lowest woodwind instrument, consisting of a long tube bent back on itself; descended from the ***bass pommer***. It is equivalent to the cello in the violin◊ family; Woodwind instruments played without a reed include:

recorder blown through one end; they were most popular in the 17th and 18th centuries

flute a cylindrical metal tube, with an opening near one end across which the player blows. Capable of a greater volume and expressivity than the recorder, the flute largely replaced it in orchestral music by the end of the 18th century
piccolo a small type of flute which sounds an octave higher than the flute.
See also *saxophone*◊□

woodwind instruments

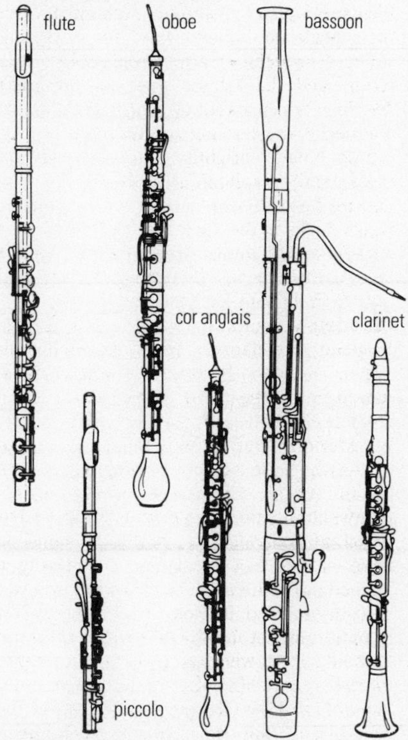

woodworm the larva of some types of beetle◊□

Wookey Hole see under Somerset◊□

wool the fibrous covering of the sheep, llama, angora goat, etc. Commercially most important is that of the domestic sheep◊, which varies from the soft, fine product of the merino to the coarse, hardwearing wool of Asiatic mountain breeds, used in carpets. The greatest producers are Australia, USSR, and New Zealand; lanolin◊ is a by-product□

Woolf Leonard Sidney 1880–1969. British literary critic who married Virginia Woolf in 1912 and in 1917 founded with her the Hogarth Press. He published a valuable autobiography 1960–9□

Woolf Virginia 1882–1941. British novelist and critic, the daughter of man-of-letters Sir Leslie Stephen 1832–1904, and wife of Leonard Woolf◊. Her novels include *Mrs Dalloway* 1925 (in which she perfected her 'stream of consciousness technique'), *To the Lighthouse* 1927 (in which her parents appear as Mr and Mrs Ramsay), *The Waves* 1931 (most advanced in its technique), and *The Years* 1937. Best known of her critical studies is *The Common Reader* 1925 and the essay *A Room of One's Own* 1929, a plea for the woman writer in a man's world. She drowned herself near her Sussex home□

woolsack the seat of the Lord High Chancellor in the House of Lords, still (as a reminder of the source of England's great wealth in the Middle Ages) a large square bag of wool□

Woolwich London district cut through by the Thames, the N section being in Newham◊ and the S in Greenwich◊. There is a famous ferry here and in 1984 a flood barrier, adjustable to allow river traffic to pass, was opened. The Royal Arsenal, an ordnance depot from 1518, was closed down in 1967□

Woolworth Frank Winfield 1852–1919. American who opened the first 'five and ten cent store' at Lancaster, Pennsylvania, in 1879□

Woomera (Aboriginal 'weapon-thrower') town in S Australia, site of a rocket range from 1946; population 4000□

Worcester cathedral city in Hereford and Worcester, England; population 47 900. Products include Worcester sauce, and the Royal Worcester Porcelain works (established in 1751). Elgar's birthplace at nearby Broadheath is a museum□

Worcester industrial port (engineering, printing, textiles) in Massachusetts, USA; population 372 940□

Worcester Battle of. See under Civil◊ War, English□

word processor see computer◊□

Wordsworth Dorothy 1771–1855. British writer, sister of William Wordsworth◊. She kept house for him until his marriage, and continued as a member of the household. After 1835 she was affected mentally by sclerosis. Her *Journals*, published 1896–1904, incorporate the basis of many of her brother's finest poems□

Wordsworth William 1770–1850. British poet. Born in Cockermouth, Cumbria, he was educated at Cambridge University. In 1791 he returned from a visit to France only just before the Terror◊, having fallen in love with Marie-Anne Vallon, who bore him an illegitimate daughter. In 1797 he settled with his sister Dorothy Wordsworth in Somerset to be near Coleridge◊, collaborating with him in

Lyrical Ballads 1798 (which included 'Tintern Abbey') and attempting to avoid poetic diction and 'give the charm of novelty to things of every day': see Romanticism◊. From 1799 he lived in the Lake District◊, and in 1802 married Mary Hutchinson. Outstanding among later works were the *poems* 1807 (including 'Intimations of Immortality'), and *The Prelude* (written by 1805, published 1850), which was written to form part of the great autobigraphical work *The Recluse*, never completed□

work in physics, work is done when a force's point of application moves through a distance in the same direction as that of the force. The quantity of work, measured in joules, is found by multiplying the force (in newtons) by the distance (in metres). Work is done when energy◊ is converted□

World Bank popular name for the ***International Bank for Reconstruction and Development*** (established in 1945, headquarters in Washington), an organ of the United◊ Nations which borrows in the commercial market and lends on commercial terms. The International Development Association (IDA, established in 1960) is part of it, and relies on donations from the developed world, which it relends to poorer countries at no interest, with repayment over 50 years□

World Council of Churches founded in 1948, headquarters in Geneva, it includes Anglican and other Protestant denominations, Orthodox and Old Catholics, and has increasing support from the Roman Catholic Church. Its financial support for liberation movements with terrorist associations has been controversial□

World Health Organization see under United◊ Nations□

World Intellectual Property Organization see under United◊ Nations□

World Meteorological Organization see under United◊ Nations□

World War I 1914–18. War between the Central European Powers (Germany, Austria-Hungary and allies), against the Triple Entente (Britain and the British Empire, France, and Russia), together with the USA, and their allies

outbreak on 28 Jun the heir to the Austrian throne was assassinated at Sarajevo; on 28 Jul Austria declared war on Serbia; as Russia mobilized, Germany declared war on Russia and France, taking a short-cut in the west by invading Belgium; on 4 Aug Britain declared war on Germany

1914 Western Front the German advance reached within a few miles of Paris, but an Allied counter-attack at Marne◊ drove them back to the River Aisne; the opposing lines then settled to trench warfare; ***Eastern Front*** Hindenburg halted the Russian advance at the Battle of Tannenberg◊; ***Africa*** on 16 Sept all Germany's African colonies were in Allied hands; ***Middle East*** on 1 Nov Turkey entered the war

1915 Western Front several offensives on both sides resulted in insignificant gains. Haig◊ became British Commander-in-Chief; ***Eastern Front*** Mackensen◊ and Hindenburg◊ drove back the Russians and took Poland; ***Middle East*** British attacks against Turkey in Mespotamia (Iraq), the Dardanelles◊, and at Gallipoli◊ were all unsuccessful; ***Italy*** declared war on Austria; Bulgaria joined the Central Powers; ***war at sea*** Germany declared all-out U-boat war, but the sinking of the liner *Lusitania* (with Americans among the 1198 lost) led to demands in the USA to enter the war

1916 Western Front German attack on the Verdun salient, countered by the Allies on the Somme and at Verdun; ***Eastern Front*** Romania joined the Allies but was soon overrun by Germany; ***Middle East*** Kut◊ was taken from the British by the Turks; ***war at sea*** the indecisive Battle of Jutland◊

1917 Western Front Germany withdrew N of the Somme to the fortified Hindenburg Line; the Allies captured Vimy Ridge but French losses provoked widespread mutinies; a British advance from Ypres to the coast (the Passchendaele offensive) failed; ***Italy*** the Italians were heavily defeated by the Germans and Austrians at Caporetto◊, and British and French troops had to be sent to Italy's aid; ***Eastern Front*** in Mar the Bolshevik◊ Revolution led to the overthrow of the Tsar (Nicholas II◊) and a halt to the fighting in Dec; ***Middle East*** Britain recaptured Kut and took Baghdad; Allenby◊ advanced from Egypt to capture Jerusalem; ***war at sea*** the German U-boat campaign reached its height, resulting in the British introduction of the convoy system, and on 6 Apr the entry of USA into the war

1918 Eastern Front on 3 Mar Russia signed the Treaty of Brest-Litovsk◊ with Germany; ***Western Front*** Germany began a final offensive. In Apr the Allies appointed Foch◊ supreme commander, but by Jun (when the first US troops went into battle) the Allies had lost all gains since 1915, and the Germans were on the Marne. The battle at Amiens◊ marked the launch of the Allied victorious offensive. ***Italy*** at Vittorio Veneto the British and Italians finally defeated the Austrians. German capitulation began with naval mutinies at Kiel, followed by uprisings in the major cities. Kaiser Wilhelm II abdicated, and on 11 Nov the armistice was signed

1919 18 June, Peace Treaty of Versailles◊□

World War II 1939–45. War between Germany, Italy, and Japan (the Axis powers), on one side, and Britain, the Commonwealth, France, the USA, USSR, and China on the other

1939 September German invasion of Poland; Britain and France declared war on Germany; USSR invaded Poland; fall of Warsaw (Poland divided between Germany and USSR); ***November*** USSR invaded Finland. On the Western front, the 'phoney war' with both sides entrenched behind defensive lines lasted until May 1940

1940 March Soviet peace treaty with Finland; ***April*** Germany invaded Denmark, Norway, Netherlands, Belgium, and Luxembourg. In Britain, a coalition government was formed under Churchill◊. ***May*** Germany outflanked the Maginot◊ defensive line; ***May-June*** British evacuation of Dunkirk◊; ***June*** Italy declared war on Britain and France; Germans entered Paris; Pétain◊ signed the armistice with Germany (see Vichy◊); ***July-October*** Battle of Britain◊ between British and German air forces; ***September*** Japanese invasion of French Indo-China; ***October*** abortive Italian invasion of Greece

1941 April Germany overran Greece and Yugoslavia; ***June*** Germany invaded USSR; Finland declared war on USSR; ***July*** Germans entered Smolensk; ***December*** Germans within 40 km/25 mi of Moscow, with Leningrad◊ under siege. First Soviet counter-offensive. Japan attacked Pearl◊ Harbor, and declared war on USA and Britain. Germany and Italy declared war on USA

1942 January Japanese conquest of Philippines; ***June*** naval battle of Midway◊, the turning point of the Pacific War; ***August*** German attack on Stalingrad; ***Oct-Nov*** Battle of Alamein◊, turn of the tide for the Western Allies; ***November*** Russian counter-offensive on Stalingrad

1943 January Casablanca◊ conference; German surrender at Stalingrad; ***March*** Russians drove Germans back to the River Donetz; ***May*** end of Axis resistance in N Africa; ***August*** beginning of campaign against Japanese in Burma; ***September*** Italy surrendered to Allies; Allied landings at Salerno◊; Russians retook Smolensk; ***October*** Italy declared war on Germany; ***November–December*** Tehran◊ conference

1944 January Allied landing at Anzio◊; ***March*** end of German U-boat campaign in the Atlantic; ***May*** fall of Monte Cassino; ***June*** D-Day: Allied landings in Normandy; ***July*** bomb plot against Hitler; ***August*** Romania joined Allies; ***September*** battle of Arnhem◊; Soviet armistice with Finland; ***October*** Tito◊ and Russians entered Belgrade; ***December*** German counter-offensive, Battle of the Bulge

1945 February Russians reached German border; Yalta conference; Allied bombing campaign over Germany (see Dresden◊); Americans landed on Iwo Jima; ***April*** Hitler committed suicide; ***May*** German surrender to the Allies; ***July*** Potsdam conference; ***August*** atom bombs dropped on Hiroshima◊ and Nagasaki◊; Japan surrendered

An estimated 55 million lives were lost, 20 million of them citizens of the USSR□

worm soft, elongated invertebrate, especially:

Annelida red-blooded worms, a phylum with long, many-segmented bodies and including (as representative of its three classes) the earthworm, the lugworm (bait of the sea angler), and the leech◊. The ***common earthworm*** *Lumbricus terrestris* is hermaphrodite, and feeds on organic matter in the soil. It turns and aerates the earth as it burrows, playing a major part in long-term landscape formation. The ***giant earthworm*** of Australia, *Megascolides australis*, may reach 3.6 m/12 ft. The ***tiger worm*** *Eisenia foetida* is one of those which lives in animal dung, and is being used to process farm waste for use as animal feed.

Nematoda unsegmented roundworms with a tough outer skin, including the ***hookworms***, family Ancylostomatidae, parasitic on men and animals, which bore through the skin to enter their hosts; the ***roundworm*** *Ascaris lumbricoides*, family Ascaridae, common to pigs and man, and one of man's largest parasites at 30 cm/1 ft long; the ***pinworm*** or ***threadworm*** *Enterobius vermicularis*, family Oxyuridae, an intestinal parasite, but of humans only; and agricultural pests such as the various genera of ***eelworm*** which attack plant roots, e.g. potatoes. They range in size from the microscopic species which lives on human eyelashes to the 8 m/26 ft species which infests the sperm whale. Worms are probably the most widespread of living animals and may be more numerous in species than insects.

Nemertea marine worms. The largest is the ***giant sea worm*** (discovered in 1979) 3 m/10 ft long, which lives at 2450 m/8000 ft in the hot water of the Mid-Pacific Rift.

Platyhelminthes flatworms, which include the fluke and tapeworm, animal parasites, e.g. the ***flukes*** of genus *schistosoma* cause schistosomiasis◊, and the ***pork tapeworm*** *Taenia* *solium* ingested by man from contaminated meat, reaches 3 m/9 ft in its human host□

Worms industrial town in Rhineland-Palatinate, W Germany; population 77 000. Luther◊ appeared before the ***Diet*** (Assembly) ***of Worms*** in 1521, and was outlawed by the emperor□

wormwood aromatic herb *Artemisia absinthium*, family Compositae◊, the leaves being used in absinthe◊□

Worthing holiday resort, in E Sussex, England; population 92 600□

Wotton Sir Henry 1568–1639. English poet-diplomat under James I, provost of Eton from 1624. *Reliquiae Wottonianae* 1651 include the lyric 'You meaner beauties of the night'□

Wounded Knee site of a massacre of Sioux Indians. See Plains◊ Indians□

Wouwerman Philip 1619–68. Dutch painter of landscape and battle scenes□

wrasse a warm-sea fish. See under perch◊□

wren genus of small brown birds of the mainly S American family Troglodytidae. Though Britain's commonest bird, the Eurasian species *Troglodytes troglodytes* is seldom seen; c10 cm/4 in long: it has a cocked-up tail□

Wren Sir Christopher 1632–1723. English architect. Professor of astronomy at Oxford from 1660, he was asked to plan the rebuilding of the city after the Great Fire of London of 1666 (see Monument◊). His plan was not adopted but his individual buildings include St Paul's Cathedral (1675–1910), and other City churches (St Michael's, Cornhill; St Bride's, Fleet Street; St Mary-le-Bow, Cheapside); the Sheldonian Theatre and Ashmolean Museum at Oxford, and part of Hampton Court Palace□

Wren P(ercival) C(hristopher) 1885–1941. British author of the novel of the Foreign Legion◊, *Beau Geste* 1924□

wrestling sport popular in ancient Egypt, Greece, and Rome, and included in the Olympics from 704BC. The two chief international styles are ***Graeco-Roman*** concentrating on above-waist holds, and ***freestyle***, which allows the legs to be used to hold or trip; in both the aim is to throw the opponent to the ground. In Britain there are three regional variants: Cumberland, West Country, and Lancashire. Japanese ***sumo*** is one of the martial◊ arts, and involves very overweight participants, who throw each other either to the ground or out of the ring□

Wrexham market town in Clwyd, Wales; population 40 000□

Wright Frank Lloyd 1869–1959. American architect whose freedom from convention and rule was influential world-wide, e.g. his own home Taliesin West, Wisconsin (1938); and the Guggenheim Museum, New York (1959)□

Wright Joseph 1734–97. British artist and portraitist, known as 'Wright of Derby' from his birthplace. He made remarkable use of light effects, e.g. *The Air Pump* 1768, Tate Gallery, London□

Wright Judith 1915– . Australian poet, author of *The Moving Image* 1946 and *Alive* 1972□

Wright Orville 1871–1948 and Wilbur 1867–1912. American pioneers of flight. In 1903 they built the first machine to make a powered, controlled, and sustained flight, on 17 Dec near Kitty Hawk, N Carolina□

Wright Richard 1908–60. American novelist, e.g. *Native Son* 1940 and the autobiographical *Black Boy* 1945□

writ document issued by the Lord Chancellor, or a judge, etc., commanding someone to do/not do some particular act; the first step in civil or criminal legal proceedings in the UK□

writer to the signet Scottish lawyer conducting cases in court, as does an English barrister/solicitor□

writing a written form of communication using one of various sets of symbols: see alphabet◊, cuneiform◊, hieroglyphic◊, both these last using ideographs (picture-writing) and phonetic word symbols side by side in the same way as modern Chinese. Syllabic writing, as in Japanese, develops from the continued use of a symbol to represent the sound of a short word. An advanced phonetic form of writing is shorthand◊□

Wroclaw industrial town in Poland (under the German name of *Breslau*, it was the capital of former German Silesia◊); population 608 000□

wryneck a type of woodpecker◊□

Wuchang see under Wuhan◊□

Wuhan river port and capital of Hubei prov, China, formed in 1950 as one of China's greatest industrial areas by the amalgamation of Hankou, Hanyang, and Wuchang; population 3 500 000. A centre of revolt in both the Taiping◊ Rebellion and the 1911 revolution, it saw a serious anti-Mao revolt in 1967 during the Cultural◊ Revolution□

Wuppertal industrial town of N Rhine-Westphalia, W Germany; population 392 000□

Württemberg former kingdom of SW Germany 1805–1918, which joined the German Reich in 1870, and is now part of Baden-Württemberg◊□

Würzburg industrial town (engineering, printing, brewing) in Bavaria, W Germany;

population 127 900. The bishop's palace was decorated by Tiepolo◊□

Wyatt Sir Thomas c1503–42. English poet and diplomat, who with Surrey◊ pioneered the use of the sonnet in England□

Wyatt Sir Thomas, the younger 1521–54. Son of the elder Sir Thomas, he was executed, as a leader of a revolt against Mary I's marriage with Philip of Spain□

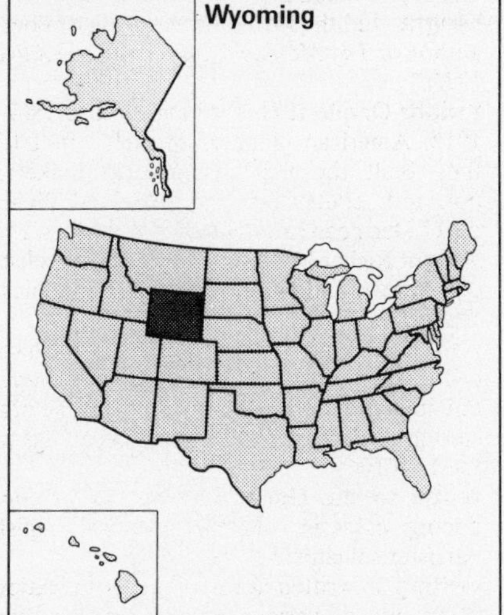

Wycherley William 1640–1710. English dramatist, best known for his licentious Restoration comedies *The Country Wife* 1675 and *The Plain Dealer* 1674□

Wycliffe John c1320–84. English religious reformer, condemned as a heretic for attacks on indulgences etc. He set his disciples to translate the Bible into English, and from 1374 was rector of Lutterworth, where he died□

Wyoming mountain state of the USA; Equality State
area 253 595 sq km/97 913 sq mi
capital Cheyenne
features Yellowstone (including the geyser Old Faithful) and Teton National Parks
products oil, natural gas, tin, sodium salts, coal, phosphates, sulphur, uranium; sheep and beef cattle
population 468 910
famous people Buffalo Bill Cody
history mainly part of the Louisiana◊ Purchase, Wyoming became a state in 1890, and in 1869 was the first to grant women the franchise□

Wyss Johann Rudolf 1781–1830. Swiss author of the children's classic *Swiss Family Robinson* 1813□

Xavier St Francis 1506–52. Born in Spain's Basque country, he was one of the first seven members of the Jesuit order in 1534, and in 1542 arrived in Goa as missionary to Portugal's Indian possessions. The mission he established in Japan 1549–51 lasted a hundred years. He died of fever in China□

xenon element
symbol Xe
atomic number 54
physical description colourless gas
features occurs in the atmosphere as 1 part in 20 million
uses in incandescent lamps, electronic flash lamps, lasers, and (in radioactive form) can be used in such techniques as measuring blood flow to the brain during acceleration on a centrifuge when testing the effect on human beings of supersonic flight speeds□

Xenophon c430–c354BC. Greek historian and soldier. Born in Athens, he was a disciple of Socrates (described in Xenophon's *Symposium*). In 401BC he joined a Greek mercenary army aiding the Persian prince Cyrus in a revolt against his brother, the king of Persia. He succeeded to the command on the death of Cyrus, and in his *Anabasis* described how he led the 10 000 Greeks in a 1000-mile march across enemy territory back to Greece□

xerography dry, non-chemical method of producing images, invented by Chester Carlson in 1938. An electrostatically charged photo-conductive plate is exposed in a camera to the item to be copied, the charge being allowed to remain only in the area corresponding to its image. The latent image on the plate is then developed by contact with powder, which adheres only to the image, and is then transferred to paper. The process is used in copying documents, preparing printing masters for offset litho, printing high-speed computer output, etc.□

Xerxes c519–465BC. King of Persia from 485, when he succeeded his father Darius◊, and, after several years' preparation, continued the Persian invasion of Greece. In 480BC he defeated the Greek fleet at Artemisium and, having stormed the pass of Thermopylae◊, captured and fired Athens. However, Themistocles◊ annihilated the Persian fleet at Salamis◊ and Xerxes was forced to retreat. He spent his later years in a grandiose extension of Persepolis◊ and was eventually murdered in a court intrigue□

Xhosa native people of S Africa, living mainly in the Cape Province. See under Transkei◊□

Xiamen port (formerly Amoy) in Fujian province, China; created a special export trade zone in 1979; population 250 000□

Xian industrial city and capital of Shaanxi province, China; population 2 600 000. Its name has often been changed; the Manchus called it Sian (Western Peace) now spelt Xian; it reverted to Changan (Long Peace) 1913–32; was Siking (western capital 1932–43), and again Sian from 1943. Its treasures include the 600-year old Ming wall; Qin (Chin) Army Vault Museum, built to house the pottery soldiers buried to protect the tomb of the first Qin emperor (see Shi◊ Huangdi); Big Wild Goose Pagoda, one of the oldest in China; and the Great Mosque 742AD□

Xian Incident The kidnapping of Chiang◊ Kai-shek 12 Dec 1936, by one of his own generals, to force his cooperation with the Communists against the Japanese invaders□

Xi Jiang river in S China; length 1900 km/1200 mi; Hong Kong island is at its mouth□

Xinhua official Chinese news agency□

Xining industrial city, capital of Qinghai province, China; population 500 000□

Xinjiang Uygur autonomous region (formerly Sinkiang Uighur) of NW China
area 1 646 800 sq km/613 665 sq mi
capital Urumqi
features largest of Chinese administrative areas; including Junggar Pendi (Dzungarian Basin) and Tarim Pendi (Tarim Basin, which includes Lop◊ Nur, China's nuclear testing ground) separated by the Tyan Shan mountains
products cereals, cotton, fruit in valleys and oases; uranium, coal, iron, copper, tin, and oil
population 12 560 000, including 50% Muslims
history the area was under Manchu rule from the 18th century, but large sections were

ceded to Tsarist Russia in 1864 and 1881, and the Chinese have raised the question of their return□

Xizang autonomous region of China. See Tibet◊□

Xochimilco see Mexico◊ City□

X-rays penetrating high frequency (short wavelength) electromagnetic◊ radiation in the electromagnetic spectrum next to ultra-violet rays (see Röntgen◊). Generally speaking, they are emitted when high-speed electrons suffer an abrupt loss of energy, and are invisible to the eye although detectable by photographic film, fluorescent screens, and the ionization they produce in gases. They penetrate materials opaque to ordinary light, e.g. a thin sheet of lead or several feet of wood, and in an X-ray photograph of the human body the bones of the skeleton and malignant growths show up because healthy cells are more resistant to X-rays than cancerous ones. This property enables X-rays to be used to attack and destroy cancer cells in radiotherapy, and they also have uses in industry.

Originating above earth's atmosphere, and penetrating it only to a limited extent ***cosmic X-rays*** were first studied from X-ray photographs taken by a captured German V-2 missile launched at White Sands, New Mexico, 1948. Besides a diffuse background radiation, a number of high-energy sources have been detected in the same area of the galaxy as the solar system. Some have been identified with objects visible through optical telescopes, e.g. in 1964 the Crab Nebula, which comprises the remains of a supernova recorded in 1054AD◊□

xylophone musical instrument comprising a number of wooden bars of varying lengths arranged in rows over resonators to produce sounds when struck with hammers□

Y

yacht light, small vessel used for pleasure cruising or racing, and sail or power driven. Oldest of yacht clubs is the Royal Yacht Squadron 1812, and the Yacht Racing Association (1875) regulates the sport in Britain. Famous races include the Admiral◊'s and America◊'s Cups, and the *Observer Singlehanded Transatlantic Race* 1960, held every four years□

yak wild black ox *Bos grunniens* of Tibet, related to the bison◊; c2 m/6 ft high, it has long shaggy hair on the underparts□

Yakut autonomous republic of the USSR from 1922, conquered in the 17th century; area 3 103 000 sq km/1 197 760 sq mi; population 883 000. Capital Yakutsk. It is one of the coldest inhabited places on earth, and produces sable, silver fox, etc., but its fabled mineral wealth of gold, diamonds, gas, coal, and tin is difficult to extract because of the climate□

Yakutsk capital of Yakut Republic, USSR; population 200 000. Coldest point of the Arctic, it has an institute for study of the permafrost (permanently frozen soil area)□

Yale University see under New◊ Haven□

Yalta holiday resort in Ukraine, USSR; population 63 000. The ***Yalta Conference*** 1945, during World War II, was held in the Livadia (summer palace built 1910–11 by Nicholas II). Churchill, Roosevelt, and Stalin completed plans for Germany's defeat, and the establishment of the United Nations□

Yalu River forms the northern boundary between N Korea and Jilin and Liaoning provinces (Manchuria) in China; length 790 km/491 mi. There was heavy fighting here in the Korean◊ War□

yam tuber of tropical plant, of genus *Dioscorea* family Dioscoreaceae, eaten as a vegetable. The ***Mexican yam D composita*** contains a chemical used to make the contraceptive pill□

Yamal Peninsula peninsula in NW Siberia, USSR. Gas reserves are estimated at six million million cubic metres, and supplies are piped to western Europe□

Yamoussoukro capital of Ivory coast from 1983; population 708 000□

Yamuna see under Ganges◊□

Yan'an industrial city (formerly Yenan) in Shaanxi province, China; population 220 000. The Long◊ March ended here Jan 1937, and it was the Communist headquarters 1936–47, the caves in which Mao lived being preserved□

Yangtze-Kiang see Chang Jiang and Jinsha Jiang◊ □

Yangzhou canal port, Jiangsu province, China; population 240 000. Famous for its gardens and pavilions□

Yankee usually disparaging term for an American, especially one from the New England states□

yard imperial measure of length, equal to 3 ft or 0.914 metres□

Yarkand walled, oasis city in Xinjiang Uygur, China; population 90 000. It is a centre of Islamic culture□

Yarmouth or ***Great Yarmouth*** holiday resort and port in Norfolk, England; population 50 000. Formerly a fishing town, it is now a leading base for North Sea oil and gas□

Yaroslavl industrial city (textiles, rubber, paint, commercial vehicles) in W central USSR; population 619 000□

yarrow plant ***milfoil*** of the northern hemisphere *Achillea millefolium* family Compositae◊, with flat-topped clusters of white or pink flowers□

yaws contagious tropical disease caused by bacteria and characterized by red, raspberry-like eruptions; it is treated by antibiotics□

Yazd or ***Yezd*** town of central Iran; population 136 000□

year the solar, tropical, or equinoctial year is the time taken by earth to revolve round the sun from equinox to equinox, i.e. 365 days 5 hr 48 min 46 sec; the ***sidereal year*** in which the observation is made on a star is 365 days 6 hr 9 min 9 sec□

yeast a type of fungus. See under Ascomycetes◊□

Yeats Jack Butler 1871–57. Irish artist, brother of the poet, who excelled in Irish scenes, e.g. *Back from the Races* in the Tate□

Yeats William Butler 1865–1939. Irish poet, born in Dublin, a leader of the Celtic revival, and a founder of the Abbey◊ Theatre. His early poetry was romantically lyrical, e.g.

'The Lake Isle of Innisfree', and plays *The Countess Cathleen* 1892 and *The Land of Heart's Desire* 1894. The end of his love for Maud Gonne, the actress and nationalist, when she married someone else, opened a more sinewy, astringent period, which also had a mystic aspect, reinforced by his marriage in 1917 with Georgie Hyde-Lees, a medium. His later books of poetry include *The Wild Swans at Coole* 1919 and *The Winding Stair* 1933. He was a senator of the Irish Free State 1922–8, Nobel prize 1923◊□

Yedo see Tokyo◊□

'Yellow Book' illustrated literary and artistic quarterly to which Beardsley, Max Beerbohm, and Henry James◊ contributed□

yellow fever tropical viral fever of which a symptom is a yellowish skin. It is carried by a mosquito (Aëdes), and the first vaccine was produced 1951□

Yellowknife capital of Northwest Territories, Canada; population 9750□

Yellow River see Huang◊ He□

Yellow Sea gulf (Chinese *Huang Hai*) of the Pacific into which the Huang◊ He flows□

Yellowstone National Park largest US national park, established 1872, mainly in Wyoming◊□

Yemen name of two countries (Yemen◊ Arab Republic, and People's Democratic Republic of Yemen◊), between whom union has been agreed since 1979, but not yet□

Yemen, North ***(Yemen Arab Republic)***

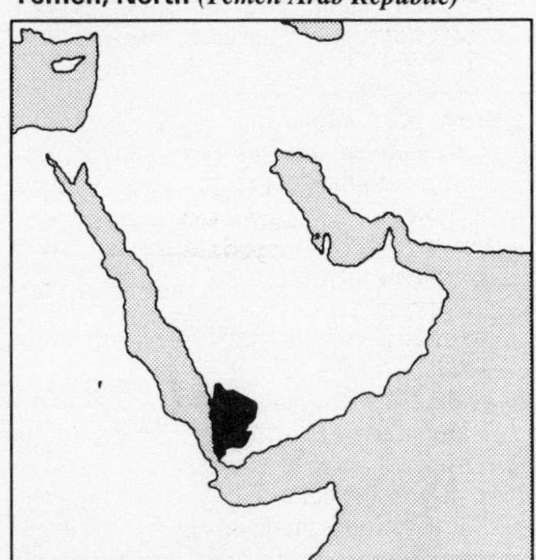

area 195 000 sq km/75 000 sq mi
capital San'a
towns Ta'iz, and chief port Hodeida
features hot moist coastal plan, rising to plateau (known in classical times as *Arabia felix* because of its fertility)
exports cotton, coffee, grapes
currency riyal
population 6 230 000
language Arabic
religion Sunni Islam 50%; Shiah Islam 50%
government executive president (Ali Abdullah Saleh) and assembly
recent history in the revolution of 1962 the king was killed and a republic established, but royalists (aided by Saudi Arabia) continued resistance to the republic (supported by Egypt) until a compromise peace 1970. Soviet aid replaced that of the USA in 1980□

Yemen, South ***(People's Democratic Republic of Yemen)***

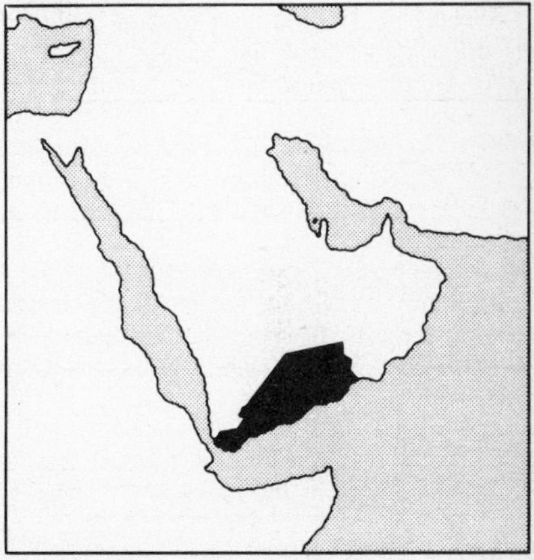

area 160 000 sq km/62 000 sq mi
capital Aden (used by the USSR as a naval base)
features less fertile than N Yemen; it includes the islands of Perim (in the strait of Bab-el-Mandeb, at the southern entrance to the Red Sea), Socotra◊, and Kamaran
exports cotton goods, coffee
currency Yemeni dinar
population 2 147 000
language Arabic
religion Sunni Islam 91%
government president and secretary general of the socialist party and supreme people's council, Ali Nasir Muhammad Husani, from 1980
recent history formerly the British colony of Aden, and protectorates of Eastern and Western Aden, it became independent (following terrorist activity from 1964 by the National Liberation Front, backed by USSR) in 1967. See also under Sheba◊. In 1986 dissension within the Marxist regime led to a revolt in which the more moderate president was replaced by the former prime minister Haider al Atlas□

Yenan see Yan'an◊□

Yenisei river of Asiatic Russia; length 3800 km/2360 mi□

Yeomen of the Guard military bodyguard of the English sovereign established by Henry VII in 1485, now purely ceremonial, e.g. Yeomen Warders at the Tower of London. Their fine physique led to the nickname 'Beefeaters'□

Yerevan capital of the Armenian Republic, USSR; population 1 050 000. Founded in the 7th century, it was alternately Turkish and Persian until ceded to Russia 1828□

Yesenin Sergei 1895–1925. Soviet peasant poet, founder of the imaginist group of poets in 1919. He was married to Isadora Duncan◊ 1922–3; he later became addicted to drugs and alcohol, and hanged himself□

yeti another name for the abominable◊ snowman□

Yevtushenko Yevgeny 1933– . Russian poet, whose anti-Stalinist verse, e.g. *Babi Yar* 1961, was published with the support of Khrushchev□

yew evergreen coniferous tree *Taxus baccata* family Taxaceae; the seeds and leaves are poisonous; the wood is hard and close-grained and was formerly used to make longbows□

Yezd see Yazd◊□

Yezidis heretical Christian-Islamic sect in Iraq which regards the Devil as God's agent and endeavours to keep in his favour□

Yezo see Hokkiado□

Yichang river port on the Chang Jiang, Hubei province, China; population 125 000□

Yiddish language (German *Jüdisch*, Jewish) formerly spoken by Polish and Russian Jews. It was based on German, but included many Hebrew, Russian, and Polish words, and in the 19th century developed an important literature, e.g. Isaac Bashevis Singer and Sholem Asch, both Nobel prizewinners. Since the foundation of Israel it has been replaced by Hebrew as a literary language□

yin Chinese 'bright' and **yang** Chinese 'dark'. The interdependent passive (thought of as feminine, negative, intuitive) and active (thought of as masculine, positive, intellectual) principles of nature. In Taoism◊ and Confucianism◊ they are represented by two interlocked curved shapes within a circle, one white, one black, but having a spot of the contrasting colour within the head of each□

yoga Hindu philosophic system (Sanskrit 'union') attributed to Patanjali who lived c150BC at Gonda, Uttar Pradesh. He preached mystical union with a personal deity by the practice of hypnosis and a rising above the senses by abstract meditation, adoption of special postures, and ascetic practices. Sira◊ was regarded as the Great Yogi. As practised in the West, yoga is more a system of induced relaxation□

Yogyakarta city (capital of Indonesia 1945–9) in Java, Indonesia; population 342 300. The Buddhist 'pyramid' shrine to the north west at Borobudur; 122 m/400 ft square, was built 750–850AD, restored 1983□

Yokohama port in Japan, south west of Tokyo; population 2 325 000. Commodore Perry◊ landed here 1854, and in 1859 it was the first Japanese port opened to foreign trade. It was almost destroyed by the 1923 earthquake, and was again rebuilt after World War II□

Yokosuka port and naval base south of Yokohama, Japan; population 427 000□

yoni in Hinduism, (an image of) the female genitals as an object of worship. See under lingam◊□

Yonkers industrial city on the Hudson, New York, USA, originally a Dutch settlement; population 195 350□

York city in N Yorkshire, England; population 104 750. It was a British city before becoming from 71AD the Roman fortress of Eboracum, and the first bishop of York (Paulinus) was consecrated in 627 in the wooden church which first preceded York Minster (1230–1474), famous for its medieval stained glass. In the 10th century it was a Viking settlement, and the Jorvik Viking Centre (1984) in Coppergate has a reconstructed section. Much of the 14th-century city walls survives, with four gates or 'bars', as well as the medieval shambles (slaughterhouse). Also notable are its 17–18th-century domestic architecture; the restored Theatre Royal; Castle Museum; National Railway Museum and the 19th-century railway station. Industries include railway rolling stock, scientific instruments, sugar, chocolate, and glass□

York English dynasty founded by Richard, Duke of York 1411–60, claimant to the throne (under Henry◊ VI of the rival House of Lancaster◊) through his descent from Lionel Duke of Clarence, third son of Edward III, whereas Henry VI was descended from the fourth son. The argument was fought out in the Wars of the Roses◊. York was killed at the Battle of Wakefield 1460, but next year his son became king as Edward◊ IV, in turn succeeded by his son Edward◊ V and then by his brother Richard◊ III, with whose death at Bosworth the line ended. The Lancastrian victor in that battle became king as Henry◊ VII, who consolidated his claim by marrying

Edward IV's eldest daughter, Elizabeth□

York Archbishop of. Metropolitan of the northern province of the Anglican church in England, and hence Primate of England□

York Duke of. Title often borne by younger sons of English sovereigns, e.g. George◊ V, George◊ VI, and Prince Andrew◊ on his marriage to Sarah◊ Ferguson□

York Frederick Augustus, Duke of 1763–1827. Second son of George III, he was a military incompetent who was British Commander-in-Chief 1798–1809. The nursery rhyme about the 'grand old Duke of York' who marched his troops up the hill and down again commemorates him, as does the Duke of York's column in Waterloo Place, London□

Young Brigham 1801–77. American Mormon◊ leader who led the migration to the Great Salt Lake in Utah 1846, founded Salt Lake City, and ruled the colony till his death□

Young David, Baron Young 1932– . British Conservative politician, head of the Manpower◊ Services Commission 1982–4. He was created a life peer in 1984□

Young Edward 1683–1765. British poet, whose *Night Thoughts on Life, Death and Immortality* were once very popular□

Young Men's Christian Association (YMCA) association for young men founded 1844 by London draper Sir George Williams 1821–1905. Without distinction of race or colour, it aims at self-improvement – spiritual, intellectual, and physical. From 1971 women were accepted as members□

Young Women's Christian Association (YWCA) association for women and girls established 1887 when two earlier organizations (founded by Emma Robarts and Lady Kinnaird in 1885) were merged□

Yourcenar Marguerite 1913– . French novelist, author of *Coup de Grâce* 1939, *Memoirs of Hadrian* 1954, *Fires* 1982, and *The Abyss* 1984; first woman member of the French Academy□

Ypres town (Flemish *Ieper*) in W Flanders, Belgium; population 21 000. The ***Menin Gate*** (on the road to the town of Menin) 1927, commemorates 54 896 British soldiers killed in the battles of Ypres in 1914–18□

Ypres 1st Earl of Ypres. See French◊, Sir John□

Ysselmeer alternative spelling of Ijsselmeer◊□

ytterbium element
symbol Yb
atomic number 70
physical description metal
features metal in the lanthanide◊ series; occurs in monazite
uses in steelmaking□

yttrium element
symbol Yt
atomic number 39
physical description silvery metal
features member of the lanthanide◊ series; occurs in monazite
uses to reduce steel corrosion□

Yucatán Central American peninsula including the three Mexican states, Campeche, Quintana Roo and Yucatán. It was a centre of Mayan◊ civilization from the pre-Christian era until the 18th century□

yucca genus of the plant family Agavaceae◊, native to Mexico and SW USA. They are stiff evergreens with sword-shaped leaves and may reach over 12 m/40 ft. The fragrant white flowers are borne on an erect panicle and last only one night. Each variety of yucca can only be pollinated by its own variety of yucca moth. The fruit, flowers, and twigs are all edible; the roots produce a natural soap; and the leaves are used for basket-making□

Yugoslavia Socialist Federal Republic of

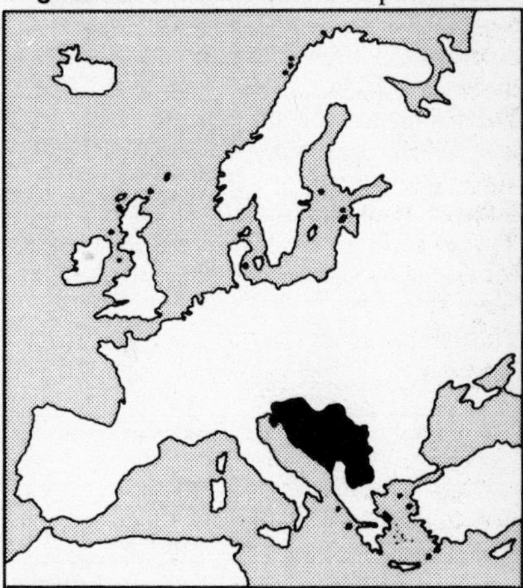

area 255 874 sq km/98 740 sq mi
capital Belgrade
towns Zagreb, Skopje, Ljubljana; ports Split and Rijeka
features see republics Bosnia-Hercegovina, Croatia, Macedonia, Montenegro, Serbia, Slovenia◊; River Danube; scenic Dalmatian coast and Dinaric Alps; Lake Shkodër
exports machinery, electrical goods, chemicals
currency dinar
population 22 997 000 including Serbs 35%; Croats 15%; Muslims 8%; Slovenes 7%; Albanians 7%; Macedonians 6%
language individual national languages have equality, but Serbo-Croat is the most widespread

religion Orthodox (Serbs); Roman Catholicism (Croats); Islam (50% in Bosnia)
government legislative assembly of two houses (federal chamber, and chamber of republics and provinces); direct election has been replaced by a complex delegational system. A collective state presidency of nine (representing the republics and provinces), has one of its members elected annually as head of state, from 1986 Sinan Hasani.
recent history the kingdom of Serbs, Croats and Slovenes (under Peter◊ I, King of Serbia) came into existence in 19Lßafter the collapse of the Austro-Hungarian Empire. His son Alexander, who succeeded in 1921, renamed the country Yugoslavia (country of the S Slavs) and established a military dictatorship in the face of Italian fascism; he was assassinated in Marseille in 1934. German invasion came in 1941, and Peter II fled to England. As the strongest of the guerrilla leaders, Tito◊ became head of a Communist republic in 1945, but took a line independent of the USSR which had aided him. In the 1970s violent national separatism, especially in Croatia, prompted a return to orthodoxy□

Yukon territory of NW Canada
area 536 327 sq km/207 076 sq mi
towns Whitehorse
features named after its chief river, the Yukon; includes the highest point in Canada Mt Logan 6050 m/19 850 ft

Yukon Territory

products oil and natural gas; gold, silver, coal; furs (trapped in the wild)
population 21 800
history settlement dates from the gold rush 1896–1910, when 30 000 people moved to the Klondike river valley (silver is now worked there). It was organized as a political unit from 1899 with Dawson as the original capital□

Yunnan province of SW China
area 436 200 sq km/168 370 sq mi
capital Kunming
features Chang Jiang, Salween and Mekong rivers; crossed by the Burma Road
products rice, tea; timber; tin, copper, lead
population 31 350 000, with minority ethnic groups, and including many Muslims□

Z

Zabrze industrial city (chemicals, coalmining, steel) in SW Poland, formerly German (Hindenburg); population 196 000□
Zadar port and resort in W Yugoslavia; population 116 174. Continually held and lost by the Venetian Republic from the 12th century until its seizure by Austria 1813, it was the capital of Dalmatia◊ 1815–1918, and Italian 1920–47, when it finally became part of Yugoslavia□
Zadkine Ossip 1860–1967. Russian-born French sculptor who represented the human form in abstract terms, e.g. his *Laocoon* and his variations on the theme of Orpheus□
Zagorsk town north east of Moscow, USSR; population 111 000. The restored walled monastery of St Sergius 1337 has some of the finest Russian medieval architecture and art. The Patriarch of Moscow still lives here□
Zagreb industrial city (heavy engineering, leather, carpets), capital of Croatia, Yugoslavia; population 1 174 500. It was a Roman city and has a fine Gothic cathedral□
Zaïre Republic of

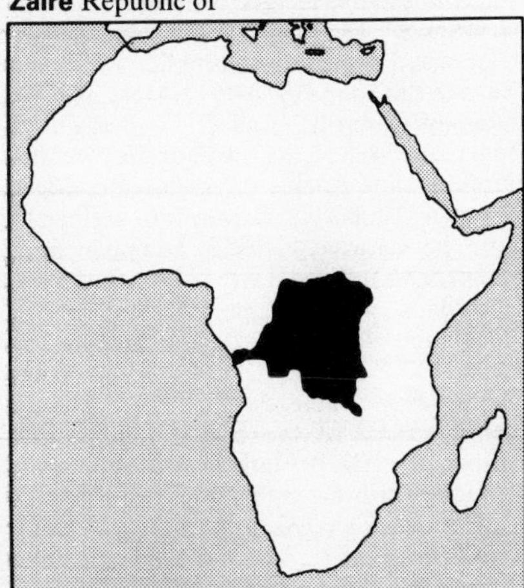

area 2 345 000 sq km/895 000 sq mi
capital Kinshasa
towns Kananga, Lubumbashi, Kisangani; ports, Matadi, Boma
features Zaïre river; lakes: Tanganyika, Mobutu Sese Seko, and Edward; Ruwenzori◊ mountains
exports palm oil, coffee, tea, rubber, timber; copper, cobalt (80% of world output), zinc, cadmium, industrial diamonds
currency zaïre
population 32 158 000
language French (official); Swahili, Lingala
religion 70% Christian; 10% Muslim
famous people Patrice Lumumba
government under the constitution of 1978, there is a directly elected president (Mobutu◊ from 1965) and unicameral legislature; only one party, the Popular Revolutionary Movement (MPR) is permitted
recent history following the dissolution of the Kingdom of Kongo◊, the Congo Free State was established (see Sir Henry Stanley◊) in 1885 under the personal rule of Leopold II of the Belgians. In 1908, following disclosure by Casement◊ and others of the atrocious treatment of native labour, it was annexed by the state as the Belgian Congo, and became independent as the Democratic Republic of Congo in 1960. The rich copper province of Katanga (now Shaba) attempted to break away, but this and other unrest was contained by a United Nations force 1960–64. Mobutu assumed power by a coup in 1965, and risings by Shaba insurgents in 1977 and 1978 (with Cuban and Angolan backing) failed. In 1971 the country was renamed Zaïre, as was the river, to avoid confusion with the People's

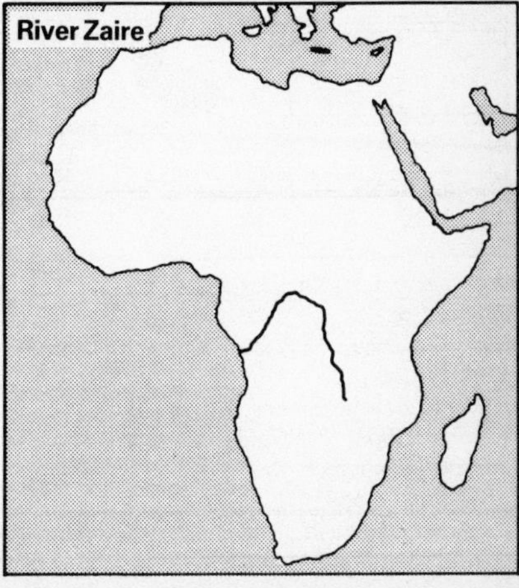

Republic of Congo◊. There is a boundary dispute with Zambia in the Kaputa/Lake Mweru area□

Zaïre second longest African river (formerly ***Congo***) 3475 km/2718 mi; second in volume only to the Amazon. The chief headstream is the Lualaba, and the chief tributary the Kasai, rising in Angola; length 2100 km/1300 mi; rich in alluvial diamonds. Navigation is interrupted by rapids, e.g. Boyoma (formerly Stanley) Falls, a series of seven cataracts. Pool Malebo (formerly Stanley Pool) is a widening of the river 560 km/350 mi from its mouth, on which Brazzaville and Kinshasa stand. Dams have made it an important source of electricity□

Zákinthos see Ionian◊ Islands□

Zama see Punic◊ Wars□

Zambezi river in central and SE Africa; length c2575 km/1600 mi via Zambia, Mozambique. It is interrupted by rapids, and includes the ***Victoria Falls*** (Mosi-oa-tunya) on the Zimbabwe/Zambia border, c1700 m/5580 ft wide, dropping 120 m/400 ft to flow through 30 m/100 ft wide gorge; and ***Kariba Dam*** on the Zambia-Zimbabwe border, which supplies power to both countries, and forms the reservoir of Lake Kariba with large fisheries. Major tributaries include the ***Kafue*** length 965 km/600 mi in Zambia□

Zambia Republic of

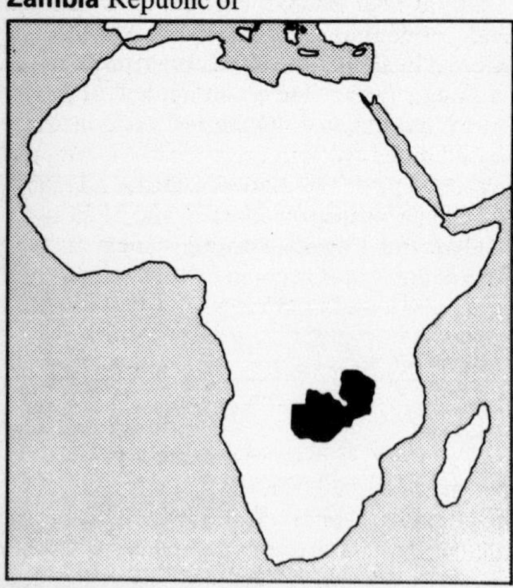

area 752 620 sq km/290 586 sq mi
capital Lusaka
towns Kitwe, Ndola, Kabwe, Chipata, Livingstone
features Zambezi river, Kariba Dam
exports copper, emeralds, tobacco
currency kwacha
population 6 554 000
language English, (official); the majority speak Bantu languages
religion mainly Animist, 21% Roman Catholic, also Protestant, Hindu and Moslem minorities
government from 1972 a one–party state (United National Independence Party: United Nations IP). There is an executive president (Kenneth Kaunda◊ from 1964), and the central committee of the party has precedence over the National Assembly. In 1982 Kaunda planned to adopt 'scientific socialism' as the country's political philosophy.
recent history formerly Northern Rhodesia, Zambia became the independent republic of Zambia, within the Commonwealth, in 1964. It includes the former African kingdom of Barotseland (now Western province), taken under British protection at the request of its ruler 1890□

Zamenhof Lazarus Ludovik 1859–1917. Polish◊ inventor of the international language Esperanto□

Zampieri Domenico see Domenichino◊□

Zannstad industrial town in W Netherlands which includes the port of ***Zaanstad*** where Peter the Great studied shipbuilding; population 128 415□

Zante Italian form of Zákinthos. See Ionian◊ Islands□

Zanzibar island, formerly a sultanate under British protection 1890–1963, when (together with the island of Pemba, some nearby islets, and a strip of mainland territory) it became a republic and was merged with Tanganyika as Tanzania◊. The chief town is Zanzibar. Cloves and copra are exported□

Zapata Emiliano c1877–1919. Mexican revolutionary guerrilla leader. A peasant of Indian blood, he led a revolt against dictator Profirio Díaz from 1911 under the slogan 'Land and Liberty'. Driven into retreat by 1915, he was assassinated by an opponent□

Zaporozhe industrial city (steel, chemicals, aluminium products) in Ukraine, USSR: population 844 000. The Dnieper Dam is sited here□

Zaragoza see Saragossa◊□

zebra animal of the horse◊ family, with stripes of black or dark brown on a white ground, which extend over all the body and legs. ***Burchell's zebra*** *Equus burchelli* roams the African plains, and has bold markings; ***Grevy's zebra*** *E grevyi* of NE Africa, is a larger species with finer markings; and the ***mountain zebra*** of SW Africa has shorter legs and longer ears.

The ***quagga*** *Equus quagga* reddish-brown with dark stripes on the head and forepart of the body, but with white underparts and legs, was hunted to extinction 1883. Examination of mitochondrial DNA taken from a preserved hide has shown that it was much more closely related to the zebra than, as was once thought, to the horse□

zebu a domesticated ox. See under cattle◊□

Zedekiah in Old Testament, last king of Judah 597–586BC. Placed on the throne by Nebuchadrezzar, he died a blinded captive in Babylon□

Zeebrugge small Belgian port, linked to Bruges by canal, which was blocked during World War I (when it was a submarine base) by a force under Admiral Keyes 23 Apr 1918□

Zeeland SW province of the Netherlands; capital Middelburg□

Zeffirelli Franco 1923– . Italian film director: *The Taming of the Shrew* 1966, *La Traviata* 1983 and many stylishly lavish drama and opera productions worldwide□

Zeiss Carl 1816–88. German manufacturer (with Ernst Abbe) of cameras, microscopes, field glasses, etc.□

Zelenograd see under Moscow◊□

Zen a variant of Buddhism◊□

Zendavesta the sacred scripture of Zoroastrianism◊□

zenith the upper pole of the celestial horizon, the point immediately above the observer; the ***nadir*** is the point diametrically opposite□

Zeno of Citium c335–262BC. Greek founder c300BC of Stoic philosophy. Pantheistic and materialist, it found happiness in acceptance of the laws of the universe, advocating the brotherhood of man and condemning slavery. Stoicism underlay Greek and Roman revolutionary movements 3rd–2nd centuries BC, but by the lst century had been adopted by the Roman ruling class. See Seneca◊, Epictetus◊, and Marcus◊ Aurelius□

Zeno of Elea born c490–c430BC. Greek philosopher, whose paradoxes raised 'modern' problems of space and time, e.g. Achilles can never overtake a tortoise in a race if space can be infinitely divided; whenever he reaches where the tortoise was the tortoise will have moved just ahead of him□

Zenobia queen of Palmyra 266–277AD. She assumed the crown as regent for her sons, after the death of her husband, and in 272 was defeated at Homs by Aurelian and taken captive to Rome□

zeolite any of the silica-rich (glassy) minerals formed naturally within lava flows, or synthetically, which are valuable for their microporosity, molecular sieving, and ion-exchange capacity. They can be used to make petrol, benzene, toluene, etc. from low-grade raw materials, e.g. coal, methanol, biomass□

Zeppelin Ferdinand, Count von Zeppelin 1838–1917. German pioneer of rigid airships (***zeppelins***) used to bomb Britain in World War I□

Zermatt resort and winter sports centre in S Switzerland at the foot of the Matterhorn; population 3 500□

Zeus in Greek mythology, chief of the gods (Roman Jupiter). He was the son of Cronus, whom he overthrew: his brothers and sisters included Demeter, Hades, Hera, and Poseidon◊. He ate his pregnant first wife Metis (goddess of wisdom), fearing their child (Athena◊) would be greater than himself. His second wife was Hera◊, but he had other relationships. The offspring, either gods and goddesses, or godlike humans, included: Apollo, Artemis, Castor and Polydeuces/Pollux, Dionysus, Hebe, Heracles, Hermes, Minos, Perseus, Persephone. His emblems are the thunderbolt and aegis (shield), representing the thunder-cloud□

Zhangjiakou trading centre (formerly Changchiakow, Mongolian name *Kalgan*) in Hebei province, China; population 300 000. Southern terminus of a road to Ulaanbaatar, it developed under the Manchus, and handled the Russia/China tea trade□

Zhao Ziyang 1919– . Chinese statesman. Disgraced in the Cultural Revolution 1967–71, he later achieved an economic miracle as ruler of Sichuan. Adopted as a protégé of Deng Xiaoping, he became prime minister in 1980, planning to use capitalist ideas within a Communist framework□

Zhdanov industrial port (steel) (formerly Mariupol) on the Sea of Azov, Ukraine, USSR; population 511 000□

Zhejiang province (formerly Chekiang) of SE China

area 101 800 sq km/32 295 sq mi

capital Hangzhou

features smallest of the Chinese provinces, it was the base of the Song dynasty 12–13th centuries

products rice, cotton, sugar; timber

population 37 920 000□

Zhengzhou capital (formerly Chengchow) of Henan province, China; population 1 100 000. Nearby is the Shaolin Temple where Kung-fu originated, and also the site of China's earliest city (1500BC) excavated in the 1970s□

Zhitomir industrial city (timber, furniture, food processing) in the Ukraine Republic, USSR; population 254 000□

Zhonghua Renmin Gonghe Guo see China◊□

Zhou En Lai 1898–1976. Chinese statesman (formerly Chou En-lai). Purged by Chiang

Kai-shek◊ in 1927, he went 'underground', but on the defeat of Chiang became prime minister 1949–76 (also Foreign Minister 1949–58). He restored orderly progress after the disruption of the Great Leap Forward and the Cultural Revolution, averted outright confrontation with the USSR by negotiation with Kosygin in 1969, and in 1972 received Nixon in Peking□

Zhu De 1886–1976. Chinese marshal (formerly Chu Teh), who led the army with Mao◊ Zedong on the Long March to Shaanxi 1934–5, and in the civil war 1946–9□

Zhukov Grigory Konstantinovich 1896–1974. Marshal of the Soviet Union. Chief of Staff from 1941, he defended Moscow 1941, counter-attacked at Stalingrad, organized the relief of Leningrad 1943, and led the offensive from the Ukraine in Mar 1944 which ended in the fall of Berlin□

Zian see Xian◊□

Zia-ul-Haq Mohammad 1924– . Pakistani general and statesman. Chief martial law administrationistrator in 1977 (president from 1978), following the overthrow of Bhutto◊, he had him executed, and introduced a fundamentalist Islamic regime□

Ziegler Karl 1898–1973. German organic chemist, who developed the technology of high polymers, e.g. polythene. Nobel prize 1963□

ziggurat a type of rectangular temple. See pyramid◊□

Zimbabwe Republic of

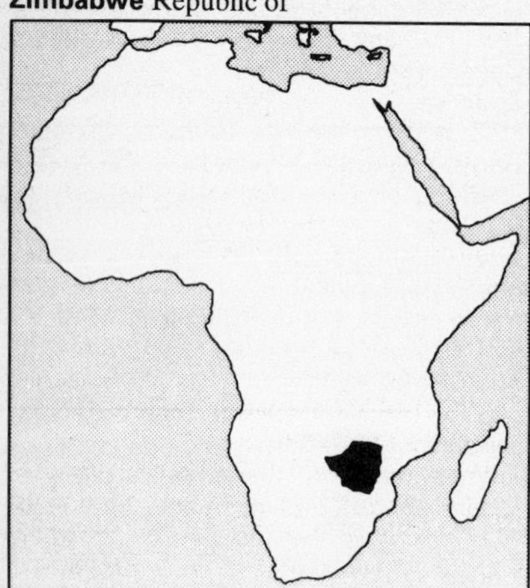

area 390 600 sq km/150 820 sq mi
capital Harare
towns Bulawayo, Gweru, Kwekwe, Mutare, Hwange
features Hwange National Park, part of Kalahari Desert
exports tobacco, citrus, tea, coffee; gold and silver
currency Zimbabwe dollar
population 8 325 000; Shona 80%; Ndbele (in Matabeleland, who are descendants of Zulus who in the early 19th century conquered the Shona) 20%; before independence there were c275 000 Europeans; in 1985 c100 000
language English, (official); Shona, Ndbele, Nyanja
religion Christianity
famous people Lobengula
government under the 1980 constitution there is a non-executive president, Senate and House of Representatives (prime minister from 1980 Robert Mugabe◊, ZANU (PF)), one fifth European
recent history in 1889 the area of modern Zambia and Zimbabwe (see Mashonaland◊, Matabeleland◊) was ceded to the British South Africa Company, and named Rhodesia. Southern Rhodesia became self-governing in 1923, and (after the creation of Zambia from N Rhodesia 1964) was popularly known simply as Rhodesia. Pressure mounted for independence under white rule, ending in a unilateral declaration of independence (UDI) in 1965 by Ian Smith◊. United Nations sanctions failed to force negotiations, and Rhodesia became a republic in 1970. An 'internal settlement' negotiated by Smith with moderates led to the established of ***Zimbabwe-Rhodesia***, with Bishop Abel Muzorewa as prime minister, Jan–Nov 1979. This was rejected by the United Nations, and guerrilla warfare under black leaders Robert Mugabe (Shona) and Joshua Nkomo (Ndbele)◊ intensified. In 1979 the London Conference (see Carrington◊) led to the recognition of Rhodesia's independence as Zimbabwe in 1980. Dissension ensued between Mugabe, of the ZANU (PF) party (Zimbabwe African National Union) and Nkomo of the ZAPU party (Zimbabwe African People's Union); violent government repression of Ndebele dissidents led to the flight of Nkomo from the country in 1983. A state of emergency has continued since 1965, and in 1985 a border wall and electrified fence was erected by South Africa on the joint border□

Zimbabwe Great. Massive granite-built ruins in Mashonaland, Zimbabwe, probably the work of the Shona people who occupied the site from before 1200AD□

Zimmerman Bernd Alois 1918–70. German composer, remembered for his multi-media, twelve-tone opera *Die Soldaten* (The Soldiers) 1965, which includes Gregorian chant, a rock band, film, and a split-level stage□

zinc element
symbol Zn

atomic number 30
physical description blue-white metal
features ore distributed widely especially in USA, Canada, Australia, and USSR; there is a trace of zinc in the human body
uses in producing brass and bronze, and galvanized iron; its compounds include zinc oxide, used as an ointment for skin diseases and cosmetics, as well as in the manufacture of paint, glass, and printing ink; zinc sulphide is used in TV screens and X-ray apparatus□

zinnia genus of annual plants from Mexico, family Compositae, but especially the cultivated hybrids of *Z elegans*, with brightly coloured, showy flowers□

Zinoviev Alexander 1922– . Russian philosopher, noted for his satire on the Soviet Union *The Yawning Heights* 1976, which led to his exile 1978, and *The Reality of communism* 1984, where he argued that Communism is the natural consequence of masses of people living under deprived conditions, and automatically bound to expand□

Zinoviev Grigory 1883–1936. Russian Bolshevik. His name was associated with a forged letter urging British Communists to rise, which helped topple the Labour government in 1924. He was shot for alleged complicity in the murder of Kirov◊□

Zion hill in Jerusalem on which David built the Temple, and so synonymous with Jerusalem and the 'city of God'□

Zionism movement from 1896 for a Jewish state in Palestine (see Zion◊): see Theodor Herzl◊. In World War I Weizmann◊ secured the Balfour Declaration◊, and in 1948 the state of Israel was established□

zirconium element
symbol Zr
atomic number 40
physical description a greyish white metal
features highly corrosion resistant, with low neutron absorption
uses as a deoxidizer in steel; it can be alloyed with niobium in superconductive magnets, and is also used as a coating in nuclear and chemical plants□

Zi Xi 1836–1908. Dowager empress of China (formerly Tzu-Hsi). Of humble birth, she was presented as a concubine to the emperor Hsien-Feng. On his death 1861, she became regent for her son, and when he died 1875, for her nephew Guang Xu. Her reactionary policies led to the establishment of the republic□

zodiac ancient Greek name for the zone of sky crossed by the paths of the sun, moon, and the five planets then known. Its stars were grouped into 12 constellations: Aries, Taurus, Gemini, Cancer, Leo, Virgo, Libra, Scorpio, Sagittarius, Capricorn, Aquarius, and Pisces. See astrology◊□

signs of the Zodiac

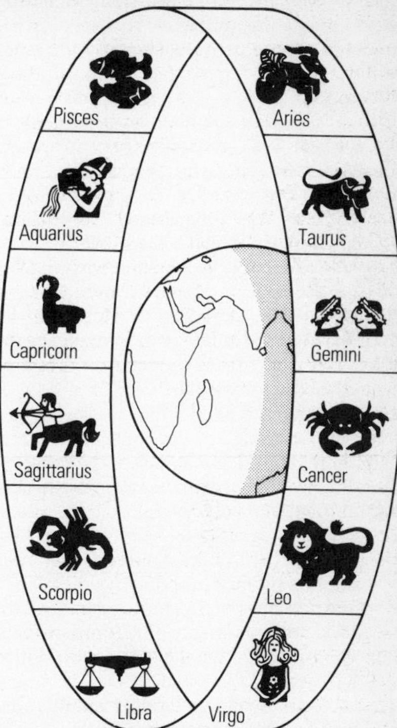

zodiacal light cone-shaped light (visible after sunset or before sunrise) sometimes seen extending from the sun along the ecliptic, and caused by thin-spread material in the central plane of the solar system□

Zoffany Johann 1733–1810. German artist, settled in England from 1758, noted for portraits□

Zog 1895–1961. King of Albania 1928–39, who had been prime minister 1922–25, and President of the Republic 1925–8. He was ejected by the Italians□

Zola Émile 1840–1902. French novelist. Born in Paris, where he became a journalist and clerk, he achieved fame with a study in remorse *Thérèse Raquin*, 1867 and embarked on a realistic series (*Les Rougon-Macquart* 1871–93) of 20 books dealing with a French family under the Second Empire. It includes *L'Assommoir* 1878, *Nana* 1880, *Germinal* 1885. In 1898 he publicly indicted the persecutors of Dreyfus in *J'Accuse*□

zombie corpse reanimated by a spirit, especially in Haiti. The idea possibly arose from voodoo priests using the nerve poison tetrodotoxin (from the puffer fish) to produce a semblance of death, from which the victim afterwards physically recovers, and is enslaved. Those eating incorrectly-prepared puffer◊ fish in Japan have been similarly affected□

zoo abbreviation for zoological gardens, a place where live animals are kept for show. Since ancient times wild animals have been kept in captivity as a 'show', e.g. the collection of Henry I at Woodstock, Oxfordshire, which was transferred to the Tower of London, and ultimately became the basis in 1831 of the Zoological Society's collection in Regent's Park, London. Zoos have an increasingly scientific and conservational role, especially in regenerating stocks of species close to extinction□

zoology study of animal life, concerned not only with existing species, but with animal evolution, as well as anatomy, physiology, embryology and morphology, geographical distribution, and ecology□

Zoroaster or ***Zarathustra*** c628–c551BC. Persian founder of Zoroastrianism◊, who was assassinated by rival prophets□

Zoroastrianism religion founded by Zoroaster◊, and still practised by the Parsees, who fled from Persia after the Arab conquest in the 8th century AD, and settled in India, especially in Bombay, forming an able and philanthropic business community.

The ***Zendavesta,*** the sacred scripture of the faith, comprises the *Avesta* liturgical books for the use of priests; *Gathas* the discourses and revelations of Zoroaster; and the *Zend* commentary upon them.

The theology is dualistic, ***Ahura Mazda*** or ***Ormuzd*** (the Good God) being in conflict with Ahriman (the Evil God), but the former is assured of victory. Worship is at altars on which the sacred fire burns, and the dead are exposed to vultures. It has links with Mithraism◊. See also Magi◊□

Zorrilla José 1817–93. Spanish poet and dramatist who took national legends as his theme□

Zouaves French infantry corps first recruited among the Kabyles, with dashing semi-Arab dress□

zucchini another name for courgette. See under marrow◊□

Zuider Zee see Ijsselmeer□

Zululand see KwaZulu◊□

Zurbarán Francisco de 1598–1664. Spanish Baroque painter, chiefly of religious subjects, e.g. a series on the life of St Bonaventura□

Zürich largest and economically most important city in Switzerland, on Lake Zürich; population 706 000. Its powerful financiers are sometimes referred to as the 'gnomes of Zürich'□

Zwickau coalmining and industrial town in Karlmarxstadt district, E Germany; population 122 600□

Zwingli Ulrich 1484–1531. Swiss Protestant reformer, killed in the war against the 'unconverted' cantons□

length

imperial/metric

1 inch (in)		= 2.54 cm
1 foot (ft)	= 12in	= 0.3048 m
1 yard (yd)	= 3ft	= 0.9144 m
1 mile	= 1760yd	= 1.6093 km

metric/imperial

1 millimetre (mm)		= 0.0394 in
1 centimetre (cm)	= 10mm	= 0.3937 in
1 metre (m)	= 100cm	= 1.0936 yd
1 kilometre (km)	= 1000m	= 0.6214 mile

area

imperial/metric

1 sq inch (in^2)		= 6.4516 cm^2
1 sq yard (yd^2)	= 9ft^2	= 0.8361 m^2
1 acre	= 4840yd^2	= 4046.9 m^2
1 sq mile ($mile^2$)	= 640 acres	= 2.59 km^2

metric/imperial

1 sq cm (cm^2)	= 100mm^2	= 0.1550 in^2
1 sq metre (m^2)	= 10,000cm^2	= 1.1960 yd^2
1 hectare (ha)	= 10,000m^2	= 2.4711 acres
1 sq km (km^2)	= 100ha	= 0.3861 $mile^2$

volume

imperial/metric

1 cu inch (in^3)		= 16.3877 cm^3
1 cu foot (ft^3)	= 1728in^3	= 0.0283 m^3
1 fluid ounce (fl oz)		= 28.413 ml
1 pint (pt)	= 20fl oz	= 0.5683 l
1 gallon (gal)	= 8pt	= 4.5461 l
1 US gallon	= 8 US pints	= 3.7854 l

metric/imperial

1 cu cm (cm^3)		= 0.0610 in^3
1 cu decimetre (dm^3)	= 1000cm^3	= 0.0353 ft^3
1 cu metre (m^3)	= 1000dm^3	= 1.3080 yd^3
1 litre (l)	= 1dm^3	= 1.76 pt
1 hectolitre (hl)	= 100l	= 21.997 gal